ATHLE

2002

THE INTERNATIONAL TRACK AND FIELD ANNUAL

ASSOCIATION OF TRACK & FIELD STATISTICIANS

EDITED BY PETER MATTHEWS

SPORTSBOOKS

Published by SportsBooks Ltd

SportsBooks Limited
PO Box 422
Worcester
WR1 1ZT
United Kingdom
Tel: 08700 713 965
Fax: 08700 750 888
e-mail randall@sportsbooks.ltd.uk
Website www.sportsbooks.ltd.uk

This publication incorporates the ATFS Annual.

Photographs supplied by Mark Shearman, 22 Grovelands Road, Purley, Surrey, CR8 4LA.
Tel: 0208-660-0156 Fax: 0208-660-3437

British Library Cataloguing in Publication Data

Athletics: the international track and
field annual – 2002
1. Athletics. Track & Field events –
Serials
1. International athletics annual (London)
796.4'2'05

ISBN 1899807 13 6

Printed for Compass Press Ltd

CONTENTS

INTRODUCTION

ALREADY THIS year, as I conclude my annual task of putting together this Annual, we have had much exciting athletics. The star of the indoor season was the young Russian Svetlana Feofanova, who won the European Indoor title with her fifth world indoor pole vault record at 4.75m, but even she was beaten for the honour of the top performance of that meeting. For this came in a truly great race, in which Jolanda Ceplak and Steffi Graf were both inside the previous world indoor record for 800 metres. Not the least satisfaction for us enthusiasts was that Ceplak front-ran her way to victory, was passed by Graf, and then fought back to take title and record. Earlier Marta Domínguez had similarly achieved a front-running victory and we also had a superb race in the men's 800m, where André Bucher was caught by Pawel Czapiewski. This was real racing, as opposed to the set-up world record attempts, so beloved by meeting promoters and which nearly always produce a publicity-destroying charge of failure.

We have also had some great road and cross-country racing and by the time this Annual appears, we will have seen whether exemplary form by the greatest men's and female distance stars of the day, Haile Gebrselassie and Paula Radcliffe, have led on to success on their marathon debuts in London.

All this competitive activity excites our passion for the season ahead. The European Championships and Commonwealth Games are the most significant championships, not to forget Asian Championships and Games, African Championships and the IAAF World Series events such as the World Junior Championships, World Cup and World Race Walking Cup. For some, such as the Americans, this is a gap year for championships, so that their attention will be on domestic competition and the Grand Prix season, headed by the Golden League events and the IAAF Grand Prix Final.

The format of this Annual remains substantially the same as in previous editions, with reviews, results, biographies, records and the deep ATFS lists, but I always try to squeeze in more where I can. An example is that in the all-time lists I have reintroduced ancillary marks (subsidiary marks in a field event series) where these would qualify for the 30 best performances. I have also given more space to the IAAF World Rankings; while many statisticians have reservations about the way such rankings can be compiled in a sport where competitors pick and choose their competitive challenges and in which there are varying measures of success, let alone the difficult task of comparing achievements at different events, these do provide an interesting way of highlighting the merits of top athletes and possibly attracting media coverage for our sport. With the retirement of several great athletes I have also increased, within the same number of pages, the number of athletes included in the biographies section to a record 732. These include 132 new entries, showing as ever the extent of change in the top personalities of our sport. There is now just one athlete – Heike Drechsler – who has featured in this section in all the 18 editions of his Annual that I have compiled.

There has been sadness with the deaths of some great champions, as reflected in the Obituaries section, and in one of the founding fathers of the ATFS, Don Potts, to whom Roberto Quercetani pays tribute. There was much concern also in some of the developments of our sport away from track action. For many British supporters the loss of the 2005 World Championships was not a complete surprise, but after the enthusiastic work by UK Athletics on plans for a new national stadium in the north of London, the actions of the British government in reneging on their promises of support for the project were an utter disgrace. One can but hope that the major British undertaking this year, the Common-wealth Games in Manchester, is staged successfully and in keeping with the traditions of this most attractive event, but can but note that the track will be removed immediately the Games are over as the stadium is handed over to Manchester City Football Club.

Athletics has to fight the domination of football in other countries as well as Britain, and must maintain favourable publicity in order to maintain major places in the hugely competitive sporting calendar. I have noted some possibly worrying signs of decline in athletics standards and I look at these in more detail in my Notes pages.

Finally, we are looking also, to you the reader, to help us expand our Hall of Fame next year as we stimulate debate by asking you to vote for the greatest athlete of all-time at each men's and women's event.

Peter Matthews
2 April 2002

Please send me information, results, corrections etc. to 10 Madgeways Close, Great Amwell, Ware, Herts SG12 9RU, England. Fax 44 1920-877392, Email: pmatthews@macunlimited.net

Information or requests re sales, distribution, publication etc. to our publisher, Randall Northam, SportsBooks Ltd, PO Box 422, Worcester, WR1 1ZT. Fax 08700 750888.
Email: randall@sportsbooks.ltd.uk

ABBREVIATIONS

Meeting Abbreviations

The following abbreviations have been used for meetings with, in parentheses, the first year that they were held.

AAA (GBR) Amateur Athletic Association Championships (1880)
AAU (USA) Amateur Athletic Union Championships (1888) (now TAC)
AfCh African Championships (1979)
AfG African Games (1965)
Af-J African Junior Championships
AmCp America's Cup (World Cup Trial)
APM Adriaan Paulen Memorial, Hengelo
AsiC Asian Championships (1973)
AsiG Asian Games (1951)
Asi-J Asian Junior Championships
ASV Weltklasse in Köln, ASV club meeting (1934)
Athl Athletissima, Lausanne (1976)
Balk Balkan Games (1929), C - Championships
Barr (Cuba) Barrientos Memorial (1950)
BGP Budapest Grand Prix (1978)
Bisl Bislett Games, Oslo (1965)
Bol Bolivar Games (1938)
BrGP British Grand Prix
CAC Central American and Caribbean Championships (1967)
CAG Central American and Caribbean Games (1926)
CalR California Relays (1942)
C.Asian Central Asian Championships
CAU Inter-counties, GBR (1934)
CISM International Military Championships (1946)
CG Commonwealth Games (1930)
DNG DN Galan, Stockholm (1966)
Drake Drake Relays (1910)
Drz Druzhba/Friendship Games
EAsG East Asian Games
EC European Championships (1934)
ECCp European Clubs Cup (1975)
EChall European Challenge (10,000m) (1997)
ECp European Cup - track & field (1965), multi-events (1973)
EI European Indoor Championships (1970, Games 1966-9)
EJ European Junior Championships (1970)
EU23 European Under-23 Championships (1997) and European Under-23 Cup (1992-4)
FBK Fanny Blankers-Koen Games, Hengelo (formerly APM)
FlaR Florida Relays (1939)
FOT (USA) Final Olympic Trials (1920)
Franc Francophone Games
Gaz Gaz de France meeting, Paris, Lille or Villeneuve d'Ascq (was BNP) (1968)
GGala Golden Gala, Roma (from 1980), Verona (1988), Pescara (1989), Bologna (1990)
GNR Great North Run – Newcastle to South Shields, GBR (1981)
GO Golden Oval, Dresden
GP Grand Prix
GPF IAAF Grand Prix Final (1985)
GS Golden Spike, Ostrava (1969)
Gugl Zipfer Gugl Grand Prix, Linz (1988)
GWG Goodwill Games (1986)
Herc Herculis, Monte Carlo, Monaco (1987)
IAAF International Amateur Athletic Federation
IAAFg IAAF Golden events (1978)
IAC IAC meeting (1968), formerly Coca-Cola meeting
IAU International Association of Ultrarunners
IbAm Ibero-American Championships (1983)
ISTAF Internationales Stadionfest, Berlin (1921)
Izv (URS) Izvestia Cup
Jen Bruce Jenner Classic, San Jose (1979)
Jerome Harry Jerome Track Classic (1984)
JUCO Junior Colleges Championships, USA
KansR Kansas Relays, Lawrence (1923)
King Martin Luther King Games (1969)
Kuso Janusz Kusocinski Memorial (1954)
Kuts Vladimir Kuts Memorial
LAT Los Angeles Times indoors (1960, from 1968 at Inglewood)
LHum L'Humanité, St-Denis (1984)
Macc Maccabiah Games, Israel
MAI Malmö AI Galan, Sweden (formerly Idag) (1958)
Mal Malinowski Memorial, Poland
McV McVitie's Challenge, Crystal Palace, London (1985-9), Sheffield (1990-1)
Mast Masters pole vault, Grenoble (1987)
McD McDonald's Games, Sheffield or London (1992)
MedG Mediterranean Games (1951)
Mill Millrose Games, New York indoors (1908)
ModR Modesto Relays
MSR Mt. San Antonio College Relays (1959)
NA Night of Athletics, Heusden (2000) formerly Hechtel
NC National Championships
NC-w National Winter Championships
NCAA National Collegiate Athletic Association Championships (1921)
NCp National Cup
NG National Games
Nik Nikaïa, Nice (1976)
NM Narodna Mladezhe, Sofia (1955)
N.Sch National Schools
Nurmi Paavo Nurmi Games (1957)
NYG New York Games (1989)
OD Olympischer Tag (Olympic Day)
OG Olympic Games (1896)
OT Olympic Trials
Owens Jesse Owens Memorial (1981)
PAm Pan American Games (1951)
PArab Pan Arab Championships (G- Games)
PennR Pennsylvania Relays (1895)
Pepsi Pepsi Cola Invitational
PG Peugeot (Talbot) Games (1980), Royal Mail Parcels Games 1989-90, Parcelforce Games 1991
Prav (URS) Pravda Cup

PTS	Pravda Televízia Slovnaft, Bratislava (1957) (now GPB)
Pre	Steve Prefontaine Memorial (1976)
RdVin	Route du Vin Half Marathon, Luxembourg
RomIC	Romanian International Championships (1948)
Ros	Evzen Rosicky Memorial, Praha (1947)
R-W	Rot-Weiss meeting, Koblenz
SACh	South American Championships (1919)
SEAG	South East Asia Games
SEC	Southeast Conference Championships
SGP	Softeland Grand Prix (walking)
Slovn	Slovnaft, Bratislava (formerly PTS) (1990)
Spark	Sparkassen Cup, Stuttgart (indoor) (1987)
Spart	(URS) Spartakiad (1956)
Stra	Stramilano Half marathon, Milan
TAC	(USA) The Athletics Congress Championships (1980-91)
TexR	Texas Relays (1925)
Toto	Toto International Super Meet, Tokyo
USOF	US Olympic Festival
VD	Ivo Van Damme Memorial, Brussels (1977)
Veniz	Venizelia, Haniá, Crete
WAAA	(GBR) Women's Amateur Athletic Association Championships (1922-91)
WAC	Western Athletic Conference Championships
WAfC	West African Championships
WCh	World Championships (1983)
WCp	World Cup - track & field (1977), marathon (1985)
	Walking – Lugano Trophy – men (1961), Eschborn Cup – women (1979)
WCT	World Championships Trial
WG	World Games, Helsinki (1961)
WI	World Indoor Championships (1987), World Indoor Games (1985)
WJ	World Junior Championships (1986)
WK	Weltklasse, Zürich (1962)
WmilG	World Military Games
WUG	World University Games (1923)
WY	World Youth Championships (1999)
Zat	Emil Zátopek Classic, Melbourne
Znam	Znamenskiy Brothers Memorial (1958)

-j, -y, -23 Junior, Youth or under-23

Dual and triangular matches are indicated by "v" (versus) followed by the name(s) of the opposition. Quadrangular and larger inter-nation matches are denoted by the number of nations and -N; viz 8-N designates an 8-nation meeting.

Events

CC	cross-country
Dec	decathlon
DT	discus
h	hurdles
Hep	heptathlon
HJ	high jump
HMar	half marathon
HT	hammer
JT	javelin
LJ	long jump
Mar	marathon
Pen	pentathlon
PV	pole vault
R	relay
SP	shot
St	steeplechase
TJ	triple jump
W	walk
Wt	weight

Miscellaneous abbreviations

+	Intermediate time in longer race
=	Tie (ex-aequo)
A	Made at an altitude of 1000m or higher
b	date of birth
D	Made in decathlon competition
dnf	did not finish
dnq	did not qualify
dns	did not start
exh	exhibition
h	heat
H	Made in heptathlon competition
hr	hour
i	indoors
kg	kilograms
km	kilometres
m	metres
M	mile
m/s	metres per second
mx	Made in mixed men's and women's race
O	Made in octathlon
P	Made in pentathlon
pb	personal best
Q	Made in qualifying round
qf	quarter final (or q in lists)
r	Race number in a series of races
sf	semi final (or s in lists)
w	wind assisted
WR	world record or best
WIR	world indoor record
y	yards
*	Converted time from yards to metres: For 200m: 220 yards less 0.11 second For 400m: 440 yards less 0.26 second For 110mh: 120yh plus 0.03 second

Countries

(IAAF membership reached 210 in 1999)

After the 2000 Olympic Games, the IAAF determined to align their abbreviations with those of the IOC, so we have switched also. Former IAAF abbreviations are shown in brackets in this list.

AFG	Afghanistan
AHO	Netherlands Antilles
AIA	Anguilla (ANG)
ALB	Albania
ALG	Algeria
AND	Andorra
ANG	Angola (ANO)
ANT	Antigua & Barbuda
ARG	Argentina
ARM	Armenia
ARU	Aruba
ASA	American Samoa (AMS)
AUS	Australia
AUT	Austria
AZE	Azerbaijan
BAH	Bahamas
BAN	Bangladash
BAR	Barbados
BDI	Burundi (BUR)
BEL	Belgium

BEN	Benin
BER	Bermuda
BHU	Bhutan
BIH	Bosnia Herzegovina (BSH)
BIZ	Belize
BLR	Belarus
BOL	Bolivia
BOT	Botswana
BRA	Brazil
BRK	Burkina Faso
BRN	Bahrain (BHR)
BRU	Brunei
BUL	Bulgaria
BUR	Burkina Faso (BKF)
CAF	Central African Republic
CAM	Cambodia
CAN	Canada
CAY	Cayman Islands
CGO	Congo
CHA	Chad
CHI	Chile
CHN	People's Republic of China
CIV	Côte d'Ivoire (Ivory Coast)
CMR	Cameroon
COD	Democratic Republic of Congo (ex ZAI Zaïre)
COK	Cook Islands (CKI)
COL	Colombia
COM	Comoros
CPD	Cape Verde Islands (CVD)
CRC	Costa Rica
CRO	Croatia
CUB	Cuba
CYP	Cyprus
CZE	Czech Republic
DEN	Denmark
DJI	Djibouti
DMA	Dominica (DMN)
DOM	Dominican Republic
ECU	Ecuador
EGY	Egypt
ENG	England
ERI	Eritrea
ESA	El Salvador
ESP	Spain
EST	Estonia
ETH	Ethiopia
FIJ	Fiji
FIN	Finland
FRA	France
FRG	Federal Republic of Germany (1948-90)
FSM	Micronesia
GAB	Gabon
GAM	The Gambia
GBR	United Kingdom of Great Britain & Northern Ireland
GBS	Guinea-Bissau
GDR	German Democratic Republic (1948-90)
GEO	Georgia
GEQ	Equatorial Guinea
GER	Germany (pre 1948 and from 1991)
GHA	Ghana
GIB	Gibraltar
GRE	Greece
GRN	Grenada
GUA	Guatemala
GUI	Guinea
GUM	Guam
GUY	Guyana
HAI	Haiti
HKG	Hong Kong, China
HON	Honduras
HUN	Hungary
INA	Indonesia
IND	India
IRI	Iran (IRN)
IRL	Ireland
IRQ	Iraq
ISL	Iceland
ISR	Israel
ISV	US Virgin Islands
ITA	Italy
IVB	British Virgin Islands (BVI)
JAM	Jamaica
JOR	Jordan
JPN	Japan
KAZ	Kazakhstan (KZK)
KEN	Kenya
KGZ	Kirgizstan
KIR	Kiribati
KOR	Korea
KSA	Saudi Arabia (from SAU)
KUW	Kuwait
LAO	Laos
LAT	Latvia
LBA	Libya
LBR	Liberia
LCA	St Lucia (STL)
LES	Lesotho
LIB	Lebanon
LIE	Liechtenstein
LTU	Lithuania (LIT)
LUX	Luxembourg
MAC	Macao
MAD	Madagascar
MAR	Morocco
MAS	Malaysia
MAW	Malawi
MDA	Moldova
MDV	Maldives (MLD)
MEX	Mexico
MGL	Mongolia
MKD	Former Yugoslav Republic of Macedonia
MLI	Mali
MLT	Malta
MNT	Montserrat
MON	Monaco
MOZ	Mozambique
MRI	Mauritius
MSH	Marshall Islands
MTN	Mauritania
MYA	Myanmar (formerly BIR Burma)
NAM	Namibia
NCA	Nicaragua
NED	Netherlands (changed from HOL)
NEP	Nepal
NFI	Norfolk Islands
NGR	Nigeria
NGU	Papua New Guinea (PNG)
NI	Northern Ireland
NIG	Niger
NMA	Northern Marianas Isl.
NOR	Norway
NRU	Nauru (NAU)
NZL	New Zealand
OMN	Oman
PAK	Pakistan
PAN	Panama
PAR	Paraguay
PER	Peru
PHI	Philippines
PLE	Palestine (PAL)
PLW	Palau
PNG	Papua New Guinea
POL	Poland
POR	Portugal
PRK	North Korea (DPR Korea)
PUR	Puerto Rico
QAT	Qatar
ROM	Romania
RSA	South Africa
RUS	Russia
RWA	Rwanda
SAM	Western Samoa
SCO	Scotland
SEN	Sénégal
SEY	Seychelles
SIN	Singapore
SKN	St Kitts & Nevis (STK)
SLE	Sierra Leone
SLO	Slovenia
SMR	San Marino
SOL	Solomon Islands
SOM	Somalia
SRI	Sri Lanka
STP	São Tomé & Principé
SUD	Sudan
SUI	Switzerland
SUR	Surinam
SVK	Slovakia
SWE	Sweden
SWZ	Swaziland
SYR	Syria
TAH	Tahiti
TAN	Tanzania
TCH	Czechoslovakia (to 1991)
TGA	Tonga (TON)
THA	Thailand
TJK	Tadjikistan
TKM	Turkmenistan
TKS	Turks & Caicos Islands
TOG	Togo
TPE	Taiwan (Chinese Taipeh)
TRI	Trinidad & Tobago
TUN	Tunisia
TUR	Turkey
UAE	United Arab Emirates
UGA	Uganda
UKR	Ukraine
URS	Soviet Union (to 1991)
URU	Uruguay
USA	United States
UZB	Uzbekistan
VAN	Vanuatu
VEN	Venezuela
VIE	Vietnam
VIN	St Vincent & the Grenadines (STV)
WAL	Wales
YEM	Republic of Yemen
YUG	Yugoslavia
ZAM	Zambia
ZIM	Zimbabwe

ACKNOWLEDGEMENTS

I AM once again most grateful to everybody who has helped to make this the supreme collection of information on our sport. Athletics statisticians strive for comprehensiveness and accuracy, and in a sport which has a limitless range of competitions it is not possible to get absolutely everything together. Nonetheless, we can take great pride in this and other ATFS publications, which benefit from the energies of many dedicated enthusiasts.

My thanks therefore to Jirí Havlín, Richard Hymans and Mirko Jalava, whose lists formed the basis from which I started my work on the world lists. Also to Marco Buccellato, Silvio Garavaglia, Winfried Kramer and Carlos Fernández who checked many of our lists so very thoroughly. Throughout the year I work with Mel Watman on *Athletics International*, and his help is thus invaluable.

Then the area specialists, whose work is so vital include: *Africa*: Yves Pinaud, *Asia*: Heinrich Hubbeling, *Central and South America*: Eduardo Biscayart and Luis Vinker, *Europe*: Nejat Kök.

Further information on specific areas was provided by:

Records Martin Rix, *Juniors* Milan Skocovsky, *Marathon* Dr. David E Martin, *Ultrarunning* Andy Milroy, *Indoor marks* Ed Gordon, *Walks and Relays* Emmerich Götze, *Men's middle and long distance* Ian Smith, *Multi events:* Hans van Kuijen, Enrique Tré, Enn Endjärv and Vaclav Klvana.

The following specialists supplied information for their respective areas and countries and in many cases provided details beyond their boundaries:

Albania: Luigi Mengoni; *Australia*: Paul Jenes and David Tarbotton; *Austria*: Dr Karl Graf; *Azerbaijan*: Oktay Morzaev; *Belgium*: André de Hooghe and Alain Monet; *Bulgaria*: Grigor Khristov and Alexander Vangelov; *Caribbean*: Bernard Linley; *Canada*: Cecil Smith; *China*: Mirko Jalava; *Cuba*: Roberto Ávila and Néstor Calixto; *Czech Republic*: Milan Skocovsky, Jirí Havlín and Milan Urban; *Denmark*: Erik Laursen; *Estonia*: Erlend Teemägi; *Finland*: Juhani Jalava, Mirko Jalava and Matti Hannus; *France*: Alain Bouillé, Jean Gilbert, Yves Pinaud and Pierre-Jean Vazel; *Germany*: Eberhard Vollmer; *Greece*: Thomas Konstas and Nikos Kriezis; *Hungary*: György Csiki; *Iceland*: Fridrik Oskarsson; *India*: Ranjit Bhatia and R Murali Krishnan; *Ireland*: Liam Hennessy and Sean Naughton; *Israel*: David Eiger; *Italy*: Raul Leoni; *Japan*: Yoshimasa Noguchi, Tatsuya Yamada, Isao Sugawara and Ken Nakamura; *Kenya*: Phil Minshull; *Latvia*: Andris Stagis; *Lithuania*: Stepas Misunas; *Luxembourg*: Georges Klepper; *Mexico*: Luis Pineda Rodríguez; *Netherlands*: Wilmar Kortleever; *New Zealand*: Tony Hunt; *Norway*: Tore Johansen and Børre Lilloe; *Poland*: Zbigniew Jonik, Janusz Rozum and Tadeusz Wolejko; *Portugal:* Manuel Arons Carvalho; *Puerto Rico*: Dr Pedro Anibal Diaz; *Romania*: Alexandru Boriga; *Russia*: Sergey Tikhonov; *San Marino:* Dr Giorgio Rizzoli; *Slovakia*: Alfons Juck; *Slovenia*: Zdravko Peternelj; *South Africa:* Gert le Roux, Hans Prinsloo and Riël Haumann; *Spain*: José Luis Hernández, Carles Baronet and the AEEA team; *Sweden*: A. Lennart Julin, Owe Fröberg and Birger Fält; *Switzerland*: Alberto Bordoli and Antonin Hejda; *Syria and Arab world*: Fouad Habbash; *Turkey* Nejat Kök; *Ukraine*: Leonid Epshteyn; *UK*: Peter Matthews and Ian Hodge; *USA*: Hal Bateman, Scott Davis, Jack Shepard and Track Newsletter; *Yugoslavia*: Ozren Karamata. Also various national federation lists and to those who post results or ranking lists to various web sites.

Also to: Mark Butler, Ottavio Castellini, Eric Cowe, Arild Gjerde, Stan Greenberg, Garry Hill, Ove Karlsson, Pino Mappa, Rooney Magnusson and Lionel Peters. And, as ever, for computer expertise and advice: Rob Whittingham.

My apologies to anybody whose name I may have missed or who have corresponded with other key ATFS personnel.

Keep the results flowing

During the year we publish all marks that we know about to ATFS standards in *Athletics International*, of which there are 30 issues per year. This serves as a base from which the lists in this book can be compiled, together with the major magazines that are published around the world, such as *Track & Field News* (USA) with its results spin-off *Track Newsletter*, and *Leichtathletik* (Germany).

Then there are the newsletters with particular spheres of interest such as Yves Pinaud's *Lettre de l'Athlétisme, Atletismo en España* by Francisco J Ascorbe and José Luis Hernández, Luis Vinker's *South America Bulletin*, and the Finnish newsletter *Tulossivut*.

Many of the national contributors to *Athletics International* are included in the list above. In order to ensure that the record of 2002 is as complete as possible I urge results contribution worldwide to *AI*, and then in turn our lists in *Athletics 2003* will be as comprehensive as we can make them.

ATFS MEMBERS

Executive Committee

President
Paul Jenes AUS
Secretary General
Scott Davis USA
Treasurer
Rob Whittingham GBR
Past Presidents
Rooney Magnusson SWE
Dr Roberto Quercetani ITA
Bob Sparks GBR
Committee
Jiří Havlín CZE
A.Lennart Julin SWE
Nejat Kök TUR
Gert le Roux RSA
Bernard Linley TRI
Peter J Matthews GBR
Yves Pinaud FRA
Tatsumi Senda JPN
Luis R Vinker ARG

Members
As at 1 January 2002

Argentina
Rubén Aguilera
Eduardo Biscayart
Edgardo Fontana
Luis R.Vinker

Australia
Luke Adams
Ron Casey
Paul Jenes
Stephen Lock
Fletcher McEwen
Roy McFadden
Michael J McLaughlin
Luciano Paolini
David Tarbotton

Austria
Dr Karl Graf
Dr Georg Werthner

Azerbaijan
Oktay Mirzoyev

Belgium
André de Hooghe
Alain Monet

Bermuda
Robert Oliver

Brazil
Ulf Lagerstrom

British Virgin Islands
Reynold O'Neal

Bulgaria
Georgi Kaburov
Grigor Khristov
Aleksander Vangelov

Canada
Gerard Dumas
Paul F Houde
Bill McNulty
Jonas Mureika
Ted Radcliffe
Cecil Smith

China
Gao Dianmin

Croatia
Mladen Delic

Cuba
Roberto Avila
Basilio Fuentes
Severo Nieto

Czech Republic
Milos Alter
Vladimír Braun
Svatopluk Dubský
Ludek Follprecht
Pavel Formánek
Jiří Havlín
Jiří Hetfleiš
Stanislav Hrnčíř
Dr Vladimír Jorda
Václav Klvaňa
Otto Kudelka
František Macák
Miroslav Malý
Karel Míšek
Miroslav Ondruška
Josef Potuček
Stanislav Sanda
Milan Skočovský
Štěpan Škorpil
Dr Lubomír Slavíček
Vladimír Tkačov
Milan Urban
Vladimír Višek
Jiří Vycichlo

Denmark
Erik Laursen

Estonia
Leo Heinla
Jaan Otsason
Eugen Piisang
Ants Teder
Erlend Teemägi

Finland
Matti Hannus
Juhani Jalava
Mirko Jalava
Erkki Kiilunen
Asko Koski
Esa Laitinen
Matti Pesola
Esko Saarinen
Arvo Siltanen
Björn-Johan Weckman (HM)

France
Jean-Louis Absin de Cassière
André Alberty
Patrice Bertignon
Alain Bouillé
Jacques Carmelli
Vincenzo Guglielmelli
André Halphen
Guy Kerfant
Gérard Leconte
Robert Parienté (HM)
Yves Pinaud
Daniel Urien

Georgia
Yevgeniy Gagua

Germany
Dr Hans-Peter Car
Werner Gessner
Heiner Göttke
Emmerich Götze
Hubert Hamacher
Max Heilrath
Raymund Herdt
Manfred Holzhausen
Heinrich Hubbeling
Andreas Janssen
Heinz Klatt
Winfried Kramer
Jakob Kusters
Sven Kuus
Ekkehard zur Megede (HM)
Axel Schäfer
Fritz Steinmetz (HM)
Otto Verhoeven

Greece
Angelos Kokkonis
Thomas Konstas
Nikos Kriezis
Karolos Sargologos
Leandros J Slavis
Mihalis Syngros
Haralambos Zannias

Hungary
György Csiki
Endre Kahlich
György Lévai
Gabriel Szabó

India
Ranjit Bhatia
Rameshchandra G Kharkar
R Murali Krishnan

Iran
Fred Sahebjam

Ireland
Fionnbar Callanan
Brian Cullen
Liam Hennessy
Pierce O'Callaghan
Tony O'Donoghue

Israel
David Eiger
Moshe Genuth
Prof. Uri Goldbourt

Italy
Maurizio Boer
Giancarlo Brunetti
Roberto Camano
Prof. Paulo De Bartolomeis
Gianni Galeotti
Silvio Garavaglia
Michelangelo Granata
Raul Leoni
Fabio Majocchi
Giorgio Malisani
Gabriele Manfredini
Giuseppe Mappa
Michele Marescalchi
Salvatore Massara
Luigi Mengoni (HM)
Gianni Menicatti
Pietro Nava
Gustavo Pallicca
Matteo Piombo
Dr Roberto Quercetani (HM)
Enzo Rivis
Dr Giorgio Rizzoli
Mauro Rossi
Pier Paulo Temeroli

Jamaica
Richard G Ashenheim
Hubert Lawrence

Japan
Atsushi Hoshino
Naoshi Ito
Wakaki Maeda
Yoshimasa Noguchi
Tatsumi Senda
Isao Sugawara
Seiichi Tanabe

Latvia
Andris Stagis

Malaysia
Balwant Singh Kler

Netherlands
Anton de Groot
Hans van Kuijen
Frieda Michiels

New Zealand
Barry Hunt
Tony Hunt

Nigeria
Samuel Fatunla

Norway
Arild Gjerde
Tore Johansen
Børre Lilloe
Jan Jørgen Moe
Einar Otto Øren
Ole Petter Sandvig
Bernt A Solaas

Papua New Guinea
Bob Snow

Poland
Marek Drzewowski
Wojciech Gaczkowski
Zygmunt Gluszek
Daniel Grinberg
Zbigniew Jonik
Henryk Kurzynski
Zbigniew Lojewski
Leszek Luftman
Adam Parczewski
Henryk Paskal
Maciej Petruczenko
Stefan J K Pietkiewicz
Józef Pliszkiewicz
Janusz Rozum
Maciej Rychwalski
Leslaw Skinder
Tadeusz Smolarski
Wlodzimierz Szymanski
Janusz Wasko
Tadeusz Wolejko

Portugal
M Arons Carvalho
Vitor Gomes da Silva
Luis Leite

Puerto Rico
Pedro Anibal Díaz

Romania
Alexandru Boriga
Adrian Ionescu
Nicolae Marasescu

Russia
Vladimir Andreyev
Nikolay Ivanov
Rostislav V Orlov
Vladimir A Otkalenko (HM)
Vladimir Spychkov
Sergey Tikhonov

Singapore
T C Ong

Slovakia
Gabriel Bogdanyi
Alfons Juck
Ladislav Krnáč
Marián Malek

Slovenia
Zdravko Peternelj
Marko Racič

South Africa
Naomi Beinart
Riël Haumann
Gert J J le Roux
Hans Prinsloo
Johan van Wyk
Frik Vermaak

Spain
Andrés de Acuña
Ignacio de Alava
Francisco Ascorbe
Carles Baronet
Félix Capilla
José Javier Etayo
Carlos Fernández
José María García
José Luis Hernández
Ignacio Mansilla
Ignacio Romo
Alberto Sánchez
Enrique Tré
Gabriel Velasco
Manuel Villuendas

Sweden
Mats Åkerlind
Mats Åkesson
Owe Fröberg
Jöran Hedberg
Bengt Holmberg
A.Lennart Julin
Ove Karlsson
Peter Larsson
Rooney Magnusson (HM)
Anders Melkersson
Stig Lennart Nilsson (HM)
Ture Widlund

Switzerland
Alberto Bordoli
Antonin Hejda

Syria
Fouad Habbash

Trinidad & Tobago
Bernard A Linley

Turkey
Turhan Göker
Nejat Kök
Cüneyt E Koryürek
I Süreyya Yigit

Ukraine
Leonid Epshteyn

UK
Ian Buchanan
Mark Butler
Eric L Cowe
Leslie J Crouch
Dr David P Dallman
Stan Greenberg
Roger W H Gynn
Ian M M Hodge
Andrew Huxtable (HM)
Richard Hymans
Tony Isaacs
Alan Lindop
Peter H Lovesey
Tim Lynch-Staunton
Norris D McWhirter (HM)
Peter V Martin
Peter J Matthews
Stuart Mazdon
Lionel Peters
Martin Rix
Michael Sheridan
Ian R Smith
Bob Sparks (HM)
Ian Tempest
M David Terry
Chris Turner
Mel Watman
Rob Whittingham

USA
Bill Allen
Jon W Alquist
David A Batchelor
Hal Bateman
John Blackburn
Norman Brand
Jed Brickner
Dave Carey
Tom Casacky
Pete Cava
Gene Cherry
Al Crepinsek
Scott S Davis
David Donley
James O Dunaway
Tom Feuer
Edward C Gordon
George Grenier
Dr Marc Grosso
Robert Hersh
Basil Honikman
Mike Hubbard
David Johnson
Michael Kennedy
Dr Clifford E Larrabee
Dan Lilot
Frank Litsky
Roar Lund
Dr Bill Mallon
Dr David E Martin
Alan Mazursky
K Ken Nakamura
Cordner B Nelson (HM)
Rich Perelman
Jack Pfeifer
Martin A Post
Shawn Price
Stan Saplin
Kevin Saylors
Alan Sigmon
James I Spier
Carol R Swenson
Michael Takaha
Frank Zarnowski

Yugoslavia
Olga Aćič
Ljubiša Gajić
Ozren Karamata
Ivan Popović

Died in 2001
José C Gonçalves BRA
Dr Donald H Potts (HM) USA
Louis Weisscher NED

Died in 2000
Edward Wiecek POL

The ATFS
The Association of Track and Field Statisticians) was founded in Brussels by 11 'track nuts' on 26 August 1950. Dr Roberto Quercetani was elected as the first President.

ATFS Membership is open to keen statisticians. For details please apply to the secretary:
Scott Davis, 4432 Snowbird Circle, Cerritos, California 90703, USA.
EMail address ssd@aol.com

METRIC – IMPERIAL CONVERSION TABLES

THROUGHOUT THIS book measurements are given in the metric system. For those readers who are more familiar with imperial units we give a basic conversion table which specifically covers those distances achieved by top class athletes in the field events.

1.70m	5ft 7in	17.50m	57ft 5in	6.00	19ft 8 ¼in	70.00	229ft 8in
1.75	5ft 8¾in	18.00	59ft 0%in	6.25	20ft 6 ¼in	72.00	236ft 3in
1.80	5ft 10 ¾in	18.50	60ft 8 ½in	6.50	21ft 4in	74.00	242ft 9in
1.85	6ft 0 ¾in	19.00	62ft 4in	6.75	22ft 1 ¾in	76.00	249ft 4in
1.90	6ft 2 ¾in	19.50	63ft 11 ¾in	7.00	22ft 11 ¾in	78.00	255ft 11in
1.95	6ft 4 ¾in	20.00	65ft 7 ½in	7.25	23ft 9 ½in	80.00	262ft 5in
2.00	6ft 6 ¾in	20.50	67ft 3 1/4in	7.50	24ft 7 ¼in	82.00	269ft 0in
2.05	6ft 8 ¾in	21.00	68ft 10 ¾in	7.75	25ft 5 ¼in	84.00	275ft 7in
2.10	6ft 10 ¾in	21.50	70ft 6 ½in	8.00	26ft 3in	86.00	282ft 2in
2.15	7ft 0 ½in	22.00	72ft 2 ¼in	8.25	27ft 0 ¾in	88.00	288ft 8in
2.20	7ft 2 ½in	22.50	73ft 10in	8.50	27ft 10 ¾in	90.00	295ft 3in
2.25	7ft 4 ½in	23.00	75ft 5 ½in	8.75	28ft 8 ½in	92.00	301ft 10in
2.30	7ft 6 ½in	50.00	164ft 0in	9.00	29ft 6 ½in	94.00	308ft 5in
2.35	7ft 8 ½in	52.00	170ft 7in	15.00	49ft 2 ½in	96.00	314ft 11in
2.40	7ft 10 ½in	54.00	177ft 2in	15.50	50ft 10 ¼in	98.00	321ft 6in
4.60	15ft 1in	56.00	183ft 9in	16.00	52ft 6in	100.00	328ft 1in
4.80	15ft 9in	58.00	190ft 3in	16.50	54ft 1 ¾in	102.00	334ft 8in
5.00	16ft 4 ¾in	60.00	196ft 10in	17.00	55ft 9 ¼in	104.00	341ft 2in
5.20	17ft 0 ¾in	62.00	203ft 5in				
5.40	17ft 8 ¾in	64.00	210ft 0in				
5.60	18ft 4 ¾in	66.00	216ft 6in				
5.80	18ft 0 ¾in	68.00	223ft 1in				

Yards	*Metres*	*Miles*	*Yards*	*Metres*
50	45.72	1m		1609.34
54.68	50	1m	427.23	2000
60	54.86	1m	1520.84	3000
65.62	60	2m		3218.69
100	91.44	3m		4828.03
109.36	100	3m	188.07	5000
218.72	200	6m		9656.06
220	201.17	6m	376.13	10000
437.44	400	10m		16093.44
440	402.34	12m	752.27	20000
874.89	800	18m	1128.40	30000
880	804.67	26m	385	42194.99(mar)
1000	914.40	31m	120.66	50,000
1093.61	1000			

IN THE biographies section, athletes' weights are given in kilograms, the following guide will help those who are more familiar with weights in pounds:

kg	*lbs*
50	110
60	132
70	154
80	176
90	198
100	220
110	243
120	265
130	287
140	309

DIARY OF 2001
by Peter Matthews

A chronological survey of highlights in major events in the world of track and field athletics during the year.

January

7 **Amorebieta**, Spain. Kenyans Paul Kosgei and Naomi Mugo were the winners of the IAAF Permit cross-country races.

19 **New York**, USA. Alan Webb, with 3:59.86, became the first American high school runner to break four minutes indoors.

21 **Elgoibar**, Spain. Paul Tergat suffered a rare cross-country defeat, as he was second to Abraham Chebii.

27 **Karlsruhe**, Germany. Svetlana Feofanova pole vaulted 4.58 to add 2cm to the European indoor record and 19 year-old Yuriy Borzakovskiy, after being last in 52+ at halfway, raced away to 1:44.15, second to Wilson Kipketer on the world indoor all-time list for 800m.

27-28 **AAA Indoor Championships**, Birmingham, GBR. World leading marks by Allyn Condon (200m 20.60) and Daniel Caines (400m 45.75) provided the twin highlights.

28 **Osaka**, Japan. Yoko Shibui won the annual international women's marathon with a world debut "record" of 2:23:11. She led from halfway, which she reached in an unofficial 70:22.

28 **Tourcoing**, France. Victory for Paula Radcliffe ensured her of success in the women's section of the Energizer European CrossCup series.

February

1 **Samara**, Russia. Jonathan Edwards showed impressive form with 17.60 in the triple jump.

2 **Erfurt**, Germany. Top performances came from Yelena Zadorozhnaya, who won the 3000m in a Russian record 8:41.44 from Gete Wami's Ethiopian record 8:43.38, and Danny Ecker's 5.85 vault.

2 **Millrose Games**, New York, USA. After five men had broken the world pole vault record in previous editions of this famous meeting, now in its 94th edition, Stacy Dragila cleared 4.63 at the second attempt to add a centimetre to her world indoor record. The only other meet record came from Terrence Trammell, whose 7.47 for 60mh remained the world best for the season. The 15,125 spectators were treated to victories by two 40 year-olds: Johnny Gray (who had first won at the Millrose in 1986), 800m in 1:50.40, and the ever astonishing Merlene Ottey, 60m by a metre in 7.20.

3-4 **Tallinn**, Estonia. Roman Sebrle was again the winner of the Erki Nool heptathlon with 6267; Erki himself was sixth at 6026.

4 **Beppu-Oita**, Japan. Takayuki Nishida won the 50th running of this famous marathon in 2:08:45.

4 **Donetsk**, Ukraine. Sergey Bubka's retirement from the sport was honoured at a ceremony at the Pole Vault Stars, the competition he founded. The winner was Alex Averbukh with an Israeli indoor record 5.80.

4 **Sparkassen Cup, Stuttgart**, Germany. The top meeting of the indoor season to date featured several world leading marks, and of these the women's mile times, won by Gabriela Szabo in 4:23.19 from Kutre Dulecha 4:23.33 and Yelena Zadorozhnaya 4:24.11, remained the best of the season.

9 **Pocatello**, USA. Stacy Dragila raised her world indoor vault record from 4.63 to 4.65 at this high (1361m) altitude venue, guesting in the Idaho State – Montana State meeting.

11 **Dortmund**, Germany. Svetlana Feofanova vaulted 4.64 in the Sparkassen meeting, a mark that was later ratified as a world record because there were no drug testing procedures in Pocatello for Dragila's 4.65. Gete Wami ran 5000m in 14:49.36, just two seconds outside the world indoor record and Danny Ecker improved his German indoor vault record from 5.96 (at Chemnitz 9 Feb) to 6.00.

15 **Stockholm**, Sweden. There was a sell-out crowd of 10,382 in the Globe Arena for the first of the Energizer EuroSeries 2001. An emphatic 1.99 high jump victory by Kajsa Bergqvist thrilled the crowd as did further Swedish high jump success when both Staffan Strand and Stefan Holm cleared 2.34. Stephanie Graf beat Maria Mutola 1:57.68 to 1:58.05 in the first of their intense series of 800m races of 2001 and the fastest miles of the indoor season came from Rui Silva 3:52.18, Noah Ngeny 3:53.31 and Reyes Estévez 3:53.49.

16-18 **Russian Indoor Championships**, Moscow. Tatyana Lebedeva won the triple jump with 15.00, the one women's 15m jump of the indoor season, and Larisa Peleshenko set a season's best of 20.12 to win the women's shot. Lyudmila Galkina won the long jump at 7.00, the first women's 7m jump of the year.

17 **Pocatello**, USA. Stacy Dragila is assistant coach for Idaho State and on her hometown runway she raised her world indoor record twice, to 4.66 (first attempt) and 4.70 (third attempt).

18 **Birmingham**, GBR. Undefeated at the distance for six years, Gabriela Szabo finally became a world record holder at 3000m. Running in the Norwich Union Grand Prix, the second Energizer EuroSeries meeting, the 25 year-old Romanian won a $50,000 record bonus for her 8:32.88 (100m 2:50.5, 2000m 5:43.1). An excellent men's 2 miles produced four national records and the 2nd, 3rd, 4th and 6th fastest ever indoor times as Hailu Mekonnen won in 8:11.84 from Million Wolde 8:12.10, Girma Tola 8:12.80 and Paul Bitok 8:13.28. Katharine Merry ran a Commonwealth record of 50.53 for 400m (having run a British record 51.54 in her only previous indoor 400m, in Cardiff on 11 Feb).

21 **Pireás**, Greece. Svetlana Feofanova added a centimetre to her European indoor vault record with 4.65 before failing at the world record height of 4.71.

23 **Gent**, Belgium. Making his first indoor appearance in two years, Hicham El Guerrouj just missed the world record for 2 miles with 8:09.89 (passing 3000m in a world-leading 7:36.85).

24-25 **German Indoor Championships**, Dortmund. Although banned from all competition until 21 Jan 2002, Dieter Baumann obtained a Frankfurt court injunction authorising him to run in this event. He won the 3000m in 7:47.29, but spectators jeered him during the race and his action jeopardised the careers of his eight opponents under the IAAF's "contamination" rule 53.1(ii). The IAAF initially suspended them, but reinstated them from 15 March, and Baumann's suspension was confirmed. Twenty years after she won her first GDR title, Heike Drechsler won her 15th national indoor long jump title, with 6.56.

25 **Liévin**, France. The Gaz de France meeting, the last of the four-meeting Energizer EuroSeries, produced world-leading performances in five events. These included Gabriela Szabo's 1500m 4:03.42 from Natalya Gorelova 4:03.51, Stephanie Graf's Austrian 800m record of 1:57.53 for her third indoor win of the season over Maria Mutola, and Noah Ngeny's 4:56.40 for 2000m. Final standings in the Energizer EuroSeries (1st prize Euro 20,000; 2nd 10,000; 3rd 5000): 60m: 1. Deji Aliu 34pts, 2. Greg Saddler 30, 3. Coby Miller 28; Middle Distance (1000/1500/1M/2000): 1. Noah Ngeny 40, 2. John Mayock 28, 3. Rui Silva 16; 60mh: 1. Shaun Bownes 36, 2. Tony Dees 32, 3. Stanislavs Olijars 26; Women 800m: 1. Graf 40, 2. Mutola 32, 3. Helena Fuchsová 24.

25 **Yokohama**, Japan. The Russian team of Lyubov Kremlyova, Lyudmila Petrova, Yelena Zadorozhnaya, Tatyana Tomashova, Lidiya Grigoryeva and Olga Yegorova set a course record of 2:12:50 to win the women's Ekiden.

March

1 **Melbourne**, Australia. The first IAAF Grand Prix II meeting of the year.

2-3 **US Indoor Championships**, Atlanta. This was Maurice Greene's one meeting of the indoor season. After a 6.57 60m heat, he equalled his own world record with a 6.39 semi and – easing up – a narrow 6.51 victory in the final over Tim Harden 6.53. In the pole vault Lawrence Johnson cleared a US record 5.96 and took three shots at a world record 6.16, pushed hard by Tye Harvey (5.93), while both Stacy Dragila and Kellie Suttle went over 4.56 first time, the world record holder winning her sixth consecutive title only on countback and taking the Golden Spike US Tour prize. Terrence Trammell, winner of the 60mh in 7.49, took the men's award. Coby Miller ran the world's fastest 200m of the season (20.31), but suffered a broken left fibula in a fall at the finish, and Adam Nelson went to no 1 on the shot list with 21.40.

3-4 **Russian Winter Walk Championships**, Adler. Olimpiada Ivanova reduced the women's world best for 20km walk to 1:24:50. Her 5km splits were 21:26, 42:34, 1:03:50. The winning times in both men's races also remained the world best times for 2001. Dmitriy Yesipchuk won the 20km in 1:18:05 from Viktor Burayev, who recorded a world junior best 1:18:06, and Aleksey Voyevodin won the 35km in 2:28:46.

4 **Otsu**, Japan. Four men, headed by Antonio Peña 2:07:34 broke 2:08 in the 56th Lake Biwa Marathon.

9-10 **NCAA Indoor Championships**, Fayetteville, Arkansas. Louisiana State University beat Texas Christian University for the men's title 34-33 – after TCU dropped the baton in the 4x400m relay. UCLA were clear women's winners with 53.5 to South Carolina 40. Janus Robberts equalled his own African shot record of 21.36 on his 22nd birthday and Kim Collins (6.58/20.55) became the first man ever to win both 60m and 200m at this meeting.

9-11 **World Indoor Championships**, Lisbon, Portugal. There were just two championship bests – by Pavla Hamácková (PV 4.56), and Natalya Sazanovich (pentathlon 4850). Roman Sebrle's 6420 in the heptathlon was just 4 points off the European record and was another season's best mark as were long jumps from Dawn Burrell 7.03 and Iván Pedroso's 8.43 – for a record fifth title. Pedroso, with Maria Mutola (800m 1:59.74) and Tereza Marinova (TJ 14.91m), were the only three winners from twelve 2000 Olympic champions in action. There were surprising defeats for two women who had set world records this season: Stacy Dragila was 4th at PV 4.51, and Gabriela Szabo, second at 3000m in 8:39.65 as Olga Yegorova (8:37.48) unleashed an unmatchable last 200m in 28.13. The USA (7 gold, 8 silver, 2 bronze) and Russia (4 gold, 5 silver, 6 bronze) were easily the two most dominant teams. *For leading results see Athletics 2001 p.591.*

11 **Alphen aan Rijn**, Netherlands. Lornah Kiplagat took seven seconds off the women's world best for 20km with 63:54.

14 **Madrid**, Spain. Svetlana Feofanova beat Stacy Dragila 4.61 to 4.46 and Merlene Ottey, reduced her world age-40 60m best to 7.12.

16 **Roodepoort**, South Africa. Szymon Ziolkówski improved his Polish hammer record to 82.13.

17-18 Ist **EAA Winter Throws Challenge**, Nice, France. Olga Kuzenkova's 71.30 hammer throw was the top mark and Russia won both men's and women's team competitions. *See Championships section for leading results.*

18 **Glasgow**, GBR. Russia was the winning team in the Norwich Union International. Jonathan Edwards gained revenge, 17.19 to 16.62. for his triple jump defeat at the World Indoors by Paulo Camossi.

23 **Pretoria**, South Africa. Engen Grand Prix and IAAF GP II. Despite blustery and cold conditions, there were many top-class performances, headed by 67.52 in the discus by Virgilijus Alekna.

24-25 **World Cross-Country Championships,** Ostend, Belgium. East African supremacy was maintained as Kenya won both senior men's titles and the women's long course and junior men's, and Ethiopia took the women's short course and junior women's. Mohammed Mourhit retained his long-course title with newcomer Enock Koech taking the short-course, and Paula Radcliffe and Gete Wami shared the honours in the women's races. Radcliffe won her first senior title, after two seconds and a third, on the first day, holding off Wami by three seconds in the 7.7km race, and Wami came back to out-kick her rival and have just one second to spare over 4.1km next day. *For details see Athletics 2001 p.592.*

31 **Stellenbosch**, South Africa. Virgilijus Alekna and Frantz Kruger produced one of the greatest discus contests of all time at the third and final Engen Series meeting of the year. Although losing to Kruger (66.02 to 66.34) in the first meeting, Alekna was crowned as the athlete of the series. He opened with 70.59 and improved to 70.99, the third best winning mark of his career, and Kruger exceeded his own expectations by setting a new African and Commonwealth record of 69.96 with two more throws over 69m.

April

1 **Berlin**, Germany. Fabián Roncero became the tenth man in history to break the hour for a half marathon. On a flat course in almost perfect conditions he set a Spanish record of 59:52.

1 **Carlsbad**, USA. Sammy Kipketer tied his world road best for 5km with 13:00.

1 **Lisbon**, Portugal. The course for this half marathon dropped 69m between start and finish and thus over the 1/1000 deemed appropriate for record purposes. Nonetheless the overall standard was superb as Hendrick Ramaala 60:26 beat Paul Tergat 60:27 and six men beat 61 minutes. Susan Chepkemei surpassed all previous times with 65:44, with Lornah Kiplagat also inside the previous best with 66:34. Derartu Tulu was third in 67:03 and a record ten women broke 70 minutes. The run won Chepkemei a bonus of $150,000 from the race organisers for bettering Masako Chiba's 66:43.

4-7 **Texas Relays**, Austin, USA. Maurice Greene started his 2001 season with some impressive relay running. He teamed up with Jon Drummond, Bernard Williams and Curtis Johnson for the HSI team that ran 37.88 for 4x100m before a sell-out 22,000 crowd.

7 **European Challenge 10,000m**, Barakaldo, Spain. Very strong winds ruined Paula Radcliffe's plans to attack the European record, but she still ran a fast 30:55.80, well ahead of Irina Mikitenko who set a pb of 31:29.55. José Rios won the men's race in 27:49.35 and Spain won both men's and women's team prizes. *See Championships section for medallists.*

8 **Brunssum**, Netherlands. Sammy Kipketer set a world road best for 10km of 27:18.

8 **Paris Marathon**, France. Simon Biwott (2:09:40) had his third successive major marathon win, following Berlin (2:07:42) and Milan (2:09:00) in 2001. Despite heavy rain and cold weather Mohammed Ezzher (b. 26 Apr 1960) was fourth in a personal best of 2:10:32 and set a new veterans' world record.

13-15 **Chinese Walks Championships**, Dandong. The great depth of walking talent in China was shown in the women's 20km, won by Gao Hongmiao 1:28:45, as there were 13 women under 1:31 and 38 under 1:40. 16 men were under 4 hours at 50km and 19 under 1:23 in the 20km.

14-16 **Carifta Games**, Bridgetown, Barbados. Veronica Campbell's 11.32/22.93 double was a highlight of the 30th edition of the Caribbean Junior meeting.

16 **Boston Marathon**, USA. Lee Bong-ju (2:09:43) and Catherine Ndereba (2:23:52 and a second half in just 1:10:47) were the winners at the 105th running of this race.

20-22 **Mt SAC Relays**, Walnut, California, USA. Marion Jones contested a 300m race for the first time – and won in 35.68. Tyree Washington ran a sparkling 44.47 for a season's best at 400m despite breezy conditions.

22 **London Marathon**. In conditions that were too windy to be ideal, Abdelkader El Mouaziz ran his fastest ever time of 2:07:11 to run away from first-timer Paul Tergat 2:08:15 in the 21st edition of this race. António Pinto, three times winner, was third in 2:09:36. For the first time, five women broke 2:25 in the same race and the times for all positions from fourth (2:24:15) to twelfth (2:29:01) were the quickest ever recorded. Leading home this galaxy of talent was Derartu Tulu, a marathon winner at her fifth attempt, in 2:23:57 from Svetlana Zakharova 2:24:04, Joyce Chepchumba 2:24:12, Lidia Simon 2:24:15 and Elfenesh Alemu 2:24:29.

22 **Rotterdam Marathon**, Netherlands. Josephat Kiprono won in 2:06:50 to equal the course record (Belayneh Dinsamo's 1988 WR) and became the first man to clock under 2:07 for a second time. The 2000 winner, Kenneth Cheruiyot, improved his best time from 2:08:22 to 2:07:18 in second place, while fifth went to the winner's younger brother, Isaac Kiprono, in 2:09:59 – making them the fastest marathoning brothers in history with a combined best of 4:16:43. The women's winner was Susan Chepkemei in a pb 2:25:45, after halfway in 71:25.

22 **Hamburg Marathon**, Germany. In his first race following a two year drugs ban, Julio Rey was a narrow winner in a course record of 2:07:46, which will count as a personal best as the 2:07:37 he ran in Rotterdam in 1999 was annulled due to the doping test result. Francisco Javier Cortes was second in 2:07:48 and Sonja Oberem was the women's winner in a pb of 2:26:13.

25-28 92nd **Drake Relays**, Des Moines, USA. Apart from the great depth of relay competition, vaulters starred at the annual Drake Relays. Kellie Suttle (4.58) became the fourth woman to clear 15ft in taking the event for the fourth successive year and Jeff Hartwig (5.74) won the men's event for the seventh successive year.

26-28 107th **Penn Relays**, Philadelphia, USA. Michael Johnson made his final racing appearance on an American track, anchoring the USA team to a 2:58.60 4x400m victory over Jamaica (2:59.78) with a 44.2 split. The women's 4x400m was also fast as LaTasha Colander-Richardson (49.7) and Marion Jones (49.4) helped the USA clock 3:21.34. Other highlights, watched by a record three-day attendance of 108,638 (48,922 on the final day), included an American hammer record of 70.62 by Dawn Ellerbe.

27 **Pocatello**, USA. Stacy Dragila raised her world outdoor vault record to 4.65 and then 4.70, matching her indoor mark and the unofficial outdoor mark that she had achieved on a platform runway at Santa Barbara in June 2000. She also competed in the first four events of the heptathlon the previous day (100mh 14.27, HJ 1.65, SP 10.62, 200m 26.34w) and after her vaulting was 2nd at LJ 5.58 and 3rd in the 100mh 14.18w.

May

4 **Stanford (Palo Alto)**, USA. The former Eritrean, Meb Keflezighi broke Mark Nenow's 15 year-old US record for 10,000m with 27:13.98 in 4th place behind three Kenyans: Abraham Chebii 27:04.20, Benjamin Maiyo 27:07.55 and Luke Kipkosgei 27:12.37. Most surprisingly these times remained the four best of 2001.

5 **USC v UCLA**, Los Angeles, USA. USC beat UCLA 82-81 in this most celebrated of all college dual meets in the USA to end a 22- year winning streak by UCLA, who won the women's contest for the ninth successive year 85-78.

6 **Rio de Janeiro**, Brazil. Highlight of the opening IAAF Grand Prix I meeting of the year was a 44.71 400m by Michael McDonald

12 60th **Modesto Relays**, USA. The 37-year-old Mike Powell, who last competed in the 1996 Olympics, returned to win the long jump with 8.06.

12 **Osaka** GP, Japan. Maurice Greene took his first 100 of the season by a clear two metres in 9.96 in virtually windless conditions and world indoor champion Shawn Crawford clocked 20.20 for 200m. Koji Murofushi produced a brilliant series in the hammer to defeat Olympic champion Szymon Ziolkówski 82.59 to 80.86, while Stacy Dragila was only 4th at 4.20 as Tatiana Grigorieva won the pole vault after a jump-off with Gao Shuying (Asian record) at 4.40. Revelation of the meeting was world junior 400m hurdles champion Marek Plawgo, who improved from 49.23 to a Polish record of 48.16.

18 **Doha**, Qatar. Top marks at the IAAF GP meeting included Olga Kuzenkova, HT 71.57, and a 3000m steeplechase win for Bernard Barmasai over Reuben Kosgei, 8:08.59 to 8:08.83.

18-20 **South American Championships**, Manaus, Brazil. The host nation was by far the most successful with 69 medals (31 gold, 24 silver, 14 bronze). Maureen Maggi won the long jump with 6.69 and set a South American record of 12.71 for 100m hurdles, but the 1.97 high jump by Solange Witteveen was disallowed when she failed a drugs test. A women's 3000m steeplechase was held for the first time in a major international championship. *See Championships section for medallists.*

19 **European Cup of Race Walking**, Dudince, Slovakia. Russians won four of the five

races and were first in all five team competitions. In all 280 walkers from 31 nations competed. Three athletes repeated their wins from 2000 (Tatyana Kozlova, junior women 10km 46:08, Olimpiada Ivanova, women 20km 1:26:48, and Jesús Angel García, 50km 3:44:26) and García now has three wins and one second place in this meeting. The junior Viktor Burayev won the senior men's 20k with 1:19:30. *See Championships section for details.*

23-26 3rd **East Asian Games**, Osaka, Japan. China with 47 medals (25 gold) and Japan with 41 (11 gold) dominated. Teams from Australia and Kazakhstan competed as guests. *See Championships section for winners.*

24-25 **European 24 Hours Challenge**, Apeldoorn, Netherlands. *See Championships section for medallists.*

26-27 **European Champion Clubs Cup**, Madrid, Spain. Sports Club Luch of Moscow, USSR had very easy wins in both men's and women's A events. Best individual performances came from Kostas Gatsioúdis, javelin 91.27 and Manuel Martínez, a Spanish shot record of 21.29. *See Championships section for details.*

26-27 **Götzis**, Austria. Roman Sebrle added 32 points to his compatriot Tomas Dvorák's world record and improved his own personal best by 269 points with 9026, the first score over 9000 with the current decathlon tables. His 8.11 long jump was a world decathlon best and he also set pbs at 100m, discus, javelin and 1500m. Erki Nool was second at 8604 and Dvorák third at 8527. Eunice Barber won the women's heptathlon with 6736 from Yelena Prokhorova 6576 and Natalya Roshchupkina 6551.

27 **Prefontaine Classic**, Eugene, USA. Hicham El Guerrouj opened his outdoor campaign with an unpressured 3:49.92 mile, covering the last 440y in 54.2. Alan Webb (18), who received massive publicity when he became the first US high school student to break four minutes for the mile indoors, excelled by clocking 3:53.43 in fifth place, breaking Jim Ryun's 36 year-old high school record of 3:55.3 (his 1500m time of 3:38.26 bettered Ryun's 3:39.0). Marion Jones had almost five metres to spare over world indoor champion Juliet Campbell with 22.26w for 200. Patrick Jarrett won the 100m in 9.89w 100m, but he had such a blatant flier that the electronic starting reaction time was registered at -0.042 sec, and thus this performance should be disregarded, as should the fourth place time of 9.95 by Bernard Williams, whose reaction time was 0.012 as against the allowable 0.100. The absence of any recall gun certainly affected Bruny Surin, who aborted his run, but everyone else kept going, with Tim Montgomery holding off Maurice Greene (who hesitated at 15m and came from far back) in 9.92.

30-Jun 2 **NCAA Championships**, Eugene, USA. Tennessee won the men's competition with 50 points, just one ahead of Texas Christian, and the women's winners were USC 64 from UCLA 55. Janus Robberts equalled Geoff Capes' 21 year-old Commonwealth shot record of 21.68 in the fifth round and then completed his series with a throw of 21.97, a mark which remained the best in the world this 2001. Justin Gatlin, still a junior, scored a remarkable sprint double, clocking 10.08 for 100m (just 0.02 away from the world junior record) and taking the 200m in 20.11w after 19.86w in his heat. Avard Moncur won easily in 44.84 and was the first man to retain the 400m title for 20 years. Angela Williams won a third 100m title in 11.05w, Brianna Glenn won a unique 200m/LJ double and Elizabeth Jackson set an American steeplechase record of 9:49.73 for third place on the world all-time list. *See USA section for winners.*

June

2 **Kalamáta**, Greece. Venelina Veneva high jmped 2.04, for the world's best of the year.

3 **Gresham**, USA. In the Portland GP II meeting, the wretched IAAF experimental rules were used (4 throws, 2 misses in HJ/PV) – and only one male pole vaulter (Pat Manson 5.35) cleared a height! Stacy Dragila fared better in the women's event, reaching 4.51.

4 **Hengelo**, Netherlands. At the Fanny Blankers-Koen Games, another GP II meeting, the pole vaulters gave vent to their feelings about being allowed only two attempts at each height by staging a sit-down protest five minutes before the event was due to start. Four men broke 27:30 in a top-class men's 10,000m won by Assefa Mezgebu 27:22.30 from Charles Kamathi 27:22.58.

6 **Milano**, Italy. Jonathan Edwards triple jumped 17.56 and Ben Limo beat Sammy Kipketer, 13:05.78 to 13:06.28, at 5000m.

8 **Seville**, Spain (GP II). Virgilijus Alekna beat Róbert Fazekas 68.09 to 68.00 in the discus, and there was an even closer triple jump duel between Tereza Marinova (14.73) and Tatyana Lebedeva (14.72). There were world-leading marks from Delloreen Ennis-London, 12.57 for 100mh, Osleidys Menéndez, 65.76 javelin, and Bernard Lagat, 3:33.80 for 1500m.

9 **Dortmund**, Germany. Two stalwarts had encouraging victories: Colin Jackson in 13.32 for 110mh, and Lars Riedel, 64.36 in the discus after a delayed start to the season due to a knee operation.

9 **New York**, USA. Paula Radcliffe achieved possibly the finest ever 10km road performance when winning the "Mini Marathon" in 30:47 on a hilly course, second only to Liz McColgan's 30:39 on a flat course in Orlando in 1989. Radcliffe, who led practically

throughout, won by over a minute from Restituta Joseph.

9 **Stanford Grand Prix**, USA. Stacy Dragila raised her world pole vault record to 4.71 (first attempt) and to 4.81 (second attempt) before taking three respectable tries at 16 ft (4.88m). Marion Jones, who made headlines days earlier by revealing she had separated from C J Hunter and was seeking a divorce, won the 200m comfortably enough from Juliet Campbell but in a modest 22.70. The men's highlight was John Godina's 21.95 shot put with a series that included five throws over 70ft (21.33).

9 **Torino**, Italy. The world's longest jumps of the season were registered at the second Primo Nebiolo Memorial meeting in the home town of the late IAAF President, by James Beckford with a sixth-round 8.41 and Tatyana Kotova with a fifth-round personal best of 7.12.

11 **Athens**, Greece. World leading performances for early in the 2001 season were set by Maurice Greene (100m 9.91), Kostas Kedéris (200m 20.10), Ali Saïdi-Sief (1500m 3:30.78), Sammy Kipketer (5000m 12:59.34), Anier García (110mh 13.30), Zhanna Pintusevich (100m 10.93), Katharine Merry (400m 49.59), Tatyana Lebedeva (TJ 14.91) and Nicoleta Grasu (DT 68.31), and Svetlana Feofanova vaulted 4.57 for a European outdoor best.

12 **Bratislava**, Slovakia. Top performance at this GP II meeting came from Tatyana Lebedeva, 14.82 triple jump.

14 **Helsinki**, Finland. In strong wind, driving rain and cold temperatures, Jan Zelezny won the javelin with 86.84 from Kostas Gatsioúdis 84.14 and Aki Parviainen 81.66, and Osleidys Menéndez improved the women's yearly best to 66.74.

16 **Dublin, Ireland.** Nathan Deakes set a Commonwealth record of 1:18:14 for 20km walk.

16-17 **US Junior Championships**, Richmond VA. Justin Gatlin won a unique triple: 100m 10.36, 200m 20.43 and 110mh 14.01.

17 **Nürnberg**, Germany. Jonathan Edwards (TJ 17.20), Hailu Mekonnen (5000m 13:12.98) and Anier García (110mh 13.32) had impressive wins at the Live 2001 meeting. Olga Kuzenkova won the women's hammer with 70.45 but was pressed hard by Yipsi Moreno's CAC records 69.44 and 70.41.

17 **Villeneuve d'Ascq**, France. Performances in this IAAF Permit meeting were affected by the rainy conditions, but eight women broke 32 minutes in the 10,000m, won by Berhane Adere 31:32.70.

18 **Odlozil Memorial**, Prague, Czech Republic. New Moroccans Abderrahim Goumri 27:26.01 and Jaouad Gharib 27:29.51 were 1-2 at 10,000m.

19 **Strasbourg**, France. Ali Saïdi-Sief ran the second fastest ever 2000m. Passing halfway in 2:23.7 and 1500m in 3:35.5, he clocked 4:46.88 to break Noureddine Morceli's 1995 Algerian record of 4:47.88.

19 **Tartu**, Estonia. Osleidys Menéndez set a Central American & Caribbean record of 68.40, a distance that only Trine Hattestad (69.48 and 68.91 in 2000) has ever exceeded with the current model of women's javelin.

21-23 **Kenyan Championships**, Nairobi. There was some wonderful distance running. Charles Kamathi ran the fastest ever time at high altitude (Nairobi is at 1675m) to win the 10,000m in 27:47.33 from John Korir 27:49.34, Paul Kosgei 27:51.87 and William Kalya 27:52.64. Bernard Barmasai, 8:16.0 for 3000mSt, and Richard Limo, 13:17.2 for 5000m from Sammy Kipketer 13:17.6, were also hugely impressive. *See Kenya section for winners.*

21-23 **US Championships,** Eugene. World leading marks for the year were set by Maurice Greene in the 100m (9.90 in a heat), Allen Johnson in the 110mh (13.22 into a 3.2m wind) and Marion Jones in the 200m (22.23), but the most eye catching achievement was Regina Jacobs' attempt to win three titles. One day after outkicking Suzy Favor Hamilton with a 59.4 last lap in the 1500m (4:06.12) for her tenth American title at the distance since 1987, the 37 year-old defeated Hazel Clark in the 800m (2:00.43) ... barely an hour before lining up for the 5000m! In that, legally blind Marla Runyan front ran to victory in 15:08.03, but Jacobs finished a good second in 15:10.78. These were the World Championships trials for the US, but Greene was assured of a place as a defending champion and needed only to make an appearance here, so he withdrew from further rounds of the 100m and the title went to Tim Montgomery 9.95w. Mike Powell, in the second meeting of his comeback, came a creditable fourth in the long jump with 8.10, but was unable to make the World team. Kip Janvrin, just a few days short of his 36th birthday, won his first national title with his 33rd win in 76 career decathlons. *See USA section for winners.*

22-24 **European Cup Second Leagues**. Held at Riga, Latvia and Nicosia, Cyprus. *See Championships section for details.*

23-24 **European Cup Super League**, Bremen, Germany. Poland, whose previous highest placing was third in 1965 and 1975 and who had only won promotion back into the Super League this year, won a great victory in the men's match, finishing 10 points ahead of France. Less surprisingly, Russia won the women's trophy for the fifth year running and provided the three outstanding results of the match: a European pole vault record of 4.60 by Svetlana Feofanova, a national and Cup 5000m record of 14:40.47 by Yelena Zadorozhnaya in her first ever race at the distance, and a world-leading 400mh 53.84 by Yuliya Nosova. *See Championships section for details.*

23-24 **European Cup First Leagues**. Held at Vaasa, Finland and Budapest, Hungary. *See Championships section for details.*

29 **Golden Gala, Rome**, Italy. Superlative distance running – with seven world leading marks for 2001 – and world record attempts by Stacy Dragila (after winning the vault at 4.72) provided the highlights of the first Golden League meeting of the year. Eleven women bettered the previous world best outdoor time of 2001 for 3000m, in which Olga Yegorova won in 8:23.96 with a last 200m in 28.1 from Yelena Zadorozhnaya 8:25.40 and Tatyana Tomashova 8:25.56. Gabriela Szabo, in her first race of the outdoor season, was 4th in 8:26.44 and in fifth Paula Radcliffe broke the British and Commonwealth record with 8.26.97. The times in depth have only ever been bettered by the amazing Chinese National Games race of 1993, and the three Russians moved to 3rd, 5th and 6th on the European all-time list and Radcliffe to 8th. Hicham El Guerrouj ran the sixth (and his fourth) fastest ever mile, 3:44.95, and a record six men broke 3:50. There was a great race at 800m, in which André Bucher just hung on by 0.01 from Yuriy Borzakovskiy's Russian record time of 1:44.02, Hailu Mekonnen 12:58.57 led 13 men under 13:10 and three under 13:00 in the 5000m, and Violeta Szekely won the women's 1500m in 4:00.92.

29-1 Jul **German Championships**, Stuttgart. Grit Breuer moved into second place on the world year list when winning the 400m title in 49.78, her fastest for three years. Heike Drechsler (6.65) won her 16th national outdoor long jump title, Lars Riedel his ninth discus title with 67.28 and Oliver-Sven Buder his eighth successive shot title with 19.96. 39 year-old Peter Blank won the javelin with a pb of 88.70 and there was a German women's pole vault record of 4.55 by Annika Becker. *See Germany section for winners*

29-1 Jul **Polish Championships**, Bydgoszcz. Monika Pyrek set a European outdoor pole vault best of 4.61. *See Poland section for winners*

30- 1 Jul **European Cup for Combined Events**. France (decathlon) and Russia (heptathlon) retained their Super League titles at Arles, France. The First League was held at Ried, Austria and the Second League at Kaunas, Lithuania. *See Championships section for details.*

July

1 **European Mountain Running Trophy**, Cerklje, Slovakia. *See Championships section for medallists.*

1 **GBR v USA v Russia**, Glasgow, UK. The US won with 135 to 131 for GBR and 111 for RUS. Phillips Idowu laid down a challenge with a second-round triple jump of 17.38w, but Jonathan Edwards responded immediately by leaping to 17.66, the world's best of 2001. Olga Yegorova stepped down to 1500m and ran a 59 sec last lap to win in 4:02.76 from Yelena Zadorozhnaya 4:04.64 and Paula Radcliffe 4:05.37.

1 **Réthimno**, Greece. Osleidys Menéndez set a world javelin record of 71.54. This came in the second round just as Stacy Dragila was trying for a world record 4.82 in the pole vault; she failed, but as in Rome cleared 4.72, a height only she has bettered.

1-4 **World Military Championships**, Beirut, Lebanon.

2 **Zagreb**, Croatia. GP II meeting. Mohamed Khaldi won the 1500m in 3:33.03 from Hudson de Souza, who set a South American record 3:33.99.

4 **Athletissima, Lausanne**, Switzerland. Highlight of a great evening's athletics for the local fans was André Bucher's characteristic front running victory in the 800m in 1:43.58. Ali Saïdi-Sief left Olympic champion Noah Ngeny trailing nearly 30m behind in third place as he clocked 3:29.51 for 1500m. Other world-leading marks came at 100m, where Maurice Greene tied his 2001 best with 9.90 from Ato Boldon 9.99, Dwain Chambers 10.00 and Tim Montgomery 10.01; 200m Ramon Clay's lifetime best 20.05; 3000m Paul Bitok 7:32.61; the 400m hurdles in which Angelo Taylor (47.95) overtook Stéphane Diagana (48.08, his best for three years) on the run-in; and the pole vault in which Jeff Hartwig equalled the year's outdoor best of 5.90. Marion Jones came perilously close to losing at 100m for the first time since 1997, just inching past Chandra Sturrup in the last stride or two to win by 0.01 sec in 11.04.

6 **Saint-Denis**, France. More than 50,000 spectators enjoyed a great night of athletics in the superb Stade de France stadium for the second Golden League meeting of 2001. Marion Jones had a clear 10.84 win at 100m, one of six world-leading performances and Maurice Greene won the men's race by a metre in 10.01. André Bucher won again at 800m with 1:43.34 and Yuriy Borzakovskiy improved his Russian record to 1:43.76. Hicham El Guerrouj was smoothly supreme at 1500m (3:28.38) and Allen Johnson had a significant win over the Olympic gold and silver medallists in the 110m hurdles and was rewarded with a year's best of 13.15. Olga Yegorova won the 3000m in 8:23.75 and Yelena Zadorozhnaya, Tatyana Tomashova and Gabriela Szabo were also under 8:30 followed by national records in 5th, 6th and 7th places.

7 **Madrid**, Spain. Avard Moncur ran an Bahamas record 44.45 to win the 400m and there

was an upset in the women's javelin where Sonia Bisset beat her compatriot Osleidys Menéndez, 66.54 to 66.38.

7-8 **Balkan Championships**, Tríkala, Greece. *See Championships section for winners.*

9 **Nikaïa**, Nice, France. Cristina Iloc-Casandra's world record for the women's 3000m steeplechase of 9:40.20 was smashed when, for the first time, the event was staged at an IAAF Grand Prix meeting. Despite windy conditions Justyna Bak went through 1000m in 3:14.46 and 2000m in 6:21.36 before moving well clear on the penultimate lap and winning in a stunning 9:25.31, her final kilometre taking just 3:03.95. Irene Limika – in her debut at the full distance – was also inside the old world figures for this young event with an African and Commonwealth record of 9:39.51, while Liz Jackson smashed her North American record with 9:43.36. Iloc-Casandra was fifth in 9:55.74. Stacy Dragila cleared 4.67 to win the pole vault from Svetlana Feofanova, who regained the European outdoor pole vault best with 4.62. Wilson Boit Kipketer ran a world-leading 8:05.78 to beat Bernard Barmasai 8:06.12 in the men's steeplechase.

12-15 **European Under-23 Championships**, Amsterdam, Netherlands. Highlight of the Championships in Amsterdam's renovated 1928 Olympic Stadium was a great hammer duel won by Nicolas Figère with a European under-23 record of 80.88 from Olli-Pekka Karjalainen 80.54, one centimetre below his best. Christian Olsson consolidated his position as a top triple jumper with 17.24 into a headwind. *See Championships section for medallists.*

12-15 **Russian Championships**, Tula. Svetlana Feofanova starred with a European pole vault record of 4.70. Larisa Peleshenko's 20.79 shot put improved the world best mark of 2001 by 50cm and the three fastest times of the year came in the women's 800m, won by Svetlana Cherkasova in 1:57.59. Olga Kuzenkova won her eighth Russian title with a 73.40 hammer throw and Tatyana Kotova retained her current status as the world's top woman long jumper with 7.09. *See Russia section for winners.*

12-15 **World Youth Championships**, Debrecen, Hungary. The sensation of the second edition of these Championships (for athletes born in 1984 or later) was Kenya's Isaac Songok. After winning his heat by almost 13 sec in 3:38.34, he set a fierce pace in the final (run in 38°C heat) with splits of 54.99, 1:55.82 and 2:55.58 for a time of 3:36.78. A striking aspect was the showing of athletes from Qatar, who won three golds and two silvers. *See Championships section for medallists.*

13 **Bislett Games**, Oslo, Norway. Aided by a wind exactly on the limit of 2m/s, Tim Montgomery ran a startling 9.84 for 100m, a time that that only Maurice Greene has ever bettered with a legal wind, followed by Ato Boldon 9.88 and Bernard Williams 9.99. Greene had withdrawn from the meeting when the organisers refused his demand of a $100,000 appearance fee, and one can but speculate whether he might have got the world record in this race. The name of Ali Saïdi-Sief was added to the list of winners of the Dream Mile; he won in 3:48.23 from Bernard Lagat 3:48.57 and Noah Ngeny 3:50.29. Paul Bitok had a splendid win at 5000m over ten men who had better pbs, but his 13:00.10 pb left him agonisingly short of breaking 13 minutes. Stephanie Graf again improved the year's best time for 800m, to 1:58.20, and again beat Maria Mutola.

13-15 **AAA Championships**, Birmingham. Dwain Chambers emphasised his high level consistency when clocking 10.01 in cool conditions to retain his 100m title. As usual in Britain Jonathan Edwards jumped just twice, but produced a championship record of 17.59 in round two. *See UK section for winners.*

14 **Heusden-Zolder**, Belgium. Shaun Bownes set an African record for 110mh at 13.26. but the best depth of performance came in the distance races.

17 **DN Galan**, Stockholm, Sweden. Stacy Dragila triumphed in a great pole vault contest with 4.72 – a height only she has ever exceeded – for a stadium record which earned her a special prize of a one carat diamond worth $10,000. Svetlana Feofanova was second with 4.62 and Monika Pyrek third at 4.57. Jonathan Edwards needed four rounds to produce a triple jump of 17.40 and hold off the challenge of Christian Olsson 17.28.

18 **Cottbus**, Germany. The 1996 Olympic hammer champion Balázs Kiss produced his best throw since 1998 with 81.36.

18-22 **Central American and Caribbean Championships**, Guatemala City. Kim Collins won the 100m.200m double in 10.04 and 20.55 at this high altitude (1402m) venue. *See Championships section for winners.*

19-22 **Asian Junior Championships**, B S Begawan, Brunei. *See Championships section for winners.*

19-22 **European Junior Championships**, Grosseto, Italy. Mark Lewis-Francis (the silver medallist in 1999) won the 100m in 10.09w and he anchored the British 4x100m team to a win in 39.24, one of just two men's championship records, the other being Aleksandr Ivanov, javelin 80.18. There were also three by women: Elvan Abeylegesse, Ethiopian born and running for Turkey, won the 5000m in 15:21.12 (and also took gold at 3000m), Yelena Isinbayeva vaulted 4.40 and Anastasiya Ilyina triple jumped 14.12. *See Championships section for medallists.*

19-23 4th **Francophone Games**, Ottawa,

Canada. Top performances included Stéphane Buckland's sprint double in 10.13 and 20.33, Nezha Bidouane's 400mh 53.92 , Ami Mbacké Thiam 400m 50.92 and Cristina Nicolau TJ 14.62. Canadian fans were cheered by Shane Niemi's 44.86 national record for 400m, 2.31 high jumps by Mark Boswell and Kwaku Boateng and by discus success for Jason Tunks, who beat Virgilijus Alekna, 65.10 to 64.35.. *See Championships section for medallists.*

20 **Herculis Zepter GP**, Monaco. The top race of the evening came in the men's 800m, where eight of the nine runners set seasonal bests, headed by André Bucher, who improved his Swiss record by 0.02 and again improved the world's best of the year – to 1:42.90; Yuriy Borzakovskiy made his usual late charge and smashed his Russian record with 1:43.17 and six men broke 1:44. The first sub-4 minute women's 1500m times of 2001 came here, with Violeta Szekely charging towards the Golden Jackpot as she took her fourth win of the series in 3:59.36 from Natalya Gorelova 3:59.70. Suzy Favor Hamilton 4:00.38 and Carla Sacramento 4:01.26 completed the world list 1-2-3-4. More world-leading marks came from Wilson Boit Kipketer, 3000m steeple 8:01.73, Paul Bitok, 3000m 7:32.11, and Maria Mutola, 1:57.11. A close second was Fabiane dos Santos, who smashed her Brazilian record and took 1.67 secs off her previous best with 1:57.16, but it was later revealed that she had failed a drugs test back in May, for which she received a two-year ban. In the pole vault, Dmitriy Markov cleared 5.95 to tie his Australian record and set a world best outdoor mark of the year, but there was a horrifying accident as Maksim Tarasov, apparently back to top form, suffered a dislocated ankle and shattered a bone in his leg at his first attempt at 5.85 – and was carried off to hospital for an emergency operation.

21-22 **Portuguese Championships**, Lisbon. Susana Feitor improved the world track record for the women's 20,000m walk to 1:29:36.4. *See Portugal section for winners.*

22 **Norwich Union British Grand Prix**, London (CP), UK. Steve Backley threw the javelin 90.81m, for his best throw since 1992. Although without quite the depth of performance of the Golden League, the capacity 17,000 crowd was thrilled by a superbly constructed meeting. Paula Radcliffe missed her British record by just 0.67 with a 5000m win in 14:44.21 and three British triple jumpers over 17m was also great for the home crowd. Hicham El Guerrouj was untroubled by Noah Ngeny (3:51.19) in the Emsley Carr Mile, seemingly almost trotting to victory in 3:49.41, and Felix Sanchez tied the world leading time of 47.95 in the 400m hurdles, easily beating Angelo Taylor 48.36. Stacy Dragila again cleared 4.72 before failing at 4.82.

23-26 **European Youth Olympic Festival**, Murcia, Spain. *See Championships section for winners.*

30 **Calgary**, Canada. The best mark from a series of pre-World Championships meetings came from Bronwyn Eagles with a hammer throw of 70.19. This will not count as an Australian and Commonwealth record as the field not officially surveyed, but it was reportedly slightly uphill.

August

3-8 8th **World Championships,** Edmonton, Canada. *See World Championships section for extensive details.*

16-19 **African Junior Championships**, Réduit, Mauritius. *See Championships section for winners.*

17 **Weltklasse, Zürich**, Switzerland. There were world-leading marks at men's 800m, 5000m, steeplechase, 400m hurdles and women's 800m and 3000m. Brahim Boulami made up for a disappointing World Championships by running away from the steeplechase field to record the third fastest ever time of 7:58.51, a 4.39 sec. improvement on his Moroccan record. Reuben Kosgei came in a well-beaten second, yet improved his best to 8:03.22 for fifth on the world all-time list. Gail Devers trimmed her season's best to 12.53 as she won the 100m hurdles and then came the women's 3000m, in which the controversial Olga Yegorova duly produced her trademark finishing kick with 240m to go and won in 8:23.26 from Gaby Szabo 8:24.19, 0.12 off her Romanian record, and Berhane Adere, an African record 8:25.62. The increasingly impressive Felix Sanchez moved up to 8= on the world all-time list with 47.38. Maria Mutola won the women's 800m easily in 1:56.95 and the end of year men's world lists showed 2nd to 6th all at this meeting, where André Bucher won with a Swiss record 1:42.55. Behind him Jean-Patrick Nduwimana 1:42.81, Wilfred Bungei 1:42.96, William Yiampoy 1:43.00 and Pawel Czapiewski 1:43.22 all took more than a second off their personal bests, followed by the best ever times for 6-9: Yuriy Borzakovskiy 1:43.30, Mbulaeni 1:44.01, Nils Schumann 1:44.32 and Hezekiél Sepeng 1:44.77. Richard Limo improved his 5000m best to 12:56.72, with only Mark Bett, 12:58.72, challenging. The Golden League Jackpot goes to those who win five of the seven races in the series and Violeta Szekely became the first to claim her share, with her fifth successive win at 1500m (3:59.94). Marion Jones bounced back to win the women's 100m in 10.94 as her Edmonton conqueror Zhanna Pintusevich was fourth in 11.16.

18 **San Sebastián**, Spain. Manuel Martínez set his sixth outdoor Spanish shot record of the year with 21.35.

18-19 **Rüdlingen**, Switzerland. Top marks at the annual throws carnival in this tiny village included a 21.53 shot mark by Adam Nelson, which he combined with 12.34 with his left hand to win a two hand competition. Szymon Ziolkówski won the hammer with 82.44 and Virgilijus Alekna beat Frantz Kruger 67.73 and Lars Reidel 67.25 with a 69.42 discus throw.

19 **Eberstadt**, Germany. Winner of the annual high jump competition was Vyacheslav Voronin at 2.37.

19 **Gateshead**, UK. Felix Sanchez improved his national record for 400m flat from 45.23 to 44.90 and beat Angelo Taylor 45.09 and Avard Moncur 45.15. Alex Averbukh improved his Israeli vault record to 5.91.

20 **Linz**, Austria. Three of the four world champions competing in this IAAF Grand Prix II meeting met with defeat. Despite hitting the first hurdle hard, Allen Johnson led most of the way in a rain-lashed 110m hurdles only to be pipped by Anier García, 13.17 to 13.20, Tatyana Lebedeva was beaten in the triple jump by Tereza Marinova, 14.48 to 14.70, and shot putter Yanina Korolchik failed to reach even 18m in fourth place. However, Nezha Bidouane kept on the winning path in a slow (55.48) 400m hurdles.

22 **Thessaloniki**, Greece. Tatyana Kotova beat Fiona May in the long jump, 7.00 to 6.92.

24 **Van Damme Memorial, Brussels**, Belgium. The 25th edition of this meeting proved to be the top Grand Prix meeting of the year, outshining even the Weltklasse. In hot weather with virtually no wind, the King Baudouin stadium was full to its capacity of 46,500 and there were five world-leading marks. Brahim Boulami set the first world record at a standard men's running event since Michael Johnson at Seville in 1999, when he ran beautifully to take the world record for the steeplechase, the first by a non-Kenyan since Anders Gärderud of Sweden ran 8:08.02 at the Montreal Olympics in 1976. The pace was set by Josephat Kapkory 2:39.66 and John Langat 5:19.45, before Boulami pulled clear to win in 7:55.28 from Reuben Kosgei, pb 7:57.29, and Stephen Cherono, world junior record 7:58.66. Another world junior record came from Kenenisa Bekele, 2nd in 7:30.67 to Hailu Mekonnen 7:30.53 in the 3000m and afterwards the top seven places on the 2001 world list were filled from this race. Hicham El Guerrouj reached 1200m in the fastest ever time (2:46.10) but missed his world record for 1500m by just 0.12 with his 3:26.12 and needed to run this fast (with a 53.5 last lap) as he was pushed hard by Bernard Lagat, whose Commonwealth record 3:26.34 was the third fastest time ever run. Joshua (JJ) Johnson, running in lane nine of the 200m, came from being a metre or so behind Francis Obikwelu in lane eight turning into the home straight to come through the field to run the only legal sub-20 time of the year as he improved his personal best from 20.48 to 19.88! Violeta Szekely won her sixth Golden League race of the year with 3:59.75 for 1500m, and Marion Jones joined her in taking a share of the Jackpot, by leading four women under 11 seconds in the 100m. André Bucher was, however, beaten for the first time outdoors in 2001 as Yuriy Borzakovskiy ran his usual even-paced race (51.0 and 51.5) to make up 15m on Bucher on the last lap and stride impressively past to set his third Russian record of the year in GL races with 1:42.47 from Bucher's 1:42.47.

26 **IAU World 100km Challenge**. Cléder, France. Yasufumi Mikami won in 6:33:28 and Elvira Kolpakova was women's winner in 7:31:12 with France and Russia taking the team titles. *See Championships section for medallists.*

26 **Leverkusen**, Germany. Nils Schumann won the 800m in 1:44.86 in his first race in Germany for 13 months.

27- Sep 1 **World University Games**, Beijing, China. Perhaps the top men's mark came at 400m hurdles, in which unheralded Alwyn Myburgh improved is best from 48.90A to 48.09. This was the one new Games record for men but there were three in women's events: Gao Shuying, Asian pole vault record 4.52, Tatyana Lebedeva, 14.81 TJ, and Osleidys Martínez, 69.92 JT. *See Championships section for medallists.*

31 **ISTAF, Berlin**, Germany. Olga Yegorova set a European 5000m record of 14:29.32, taking 13.59 sec off her personal best with the second fastest time ever run by a woman. Yet she had dropped some 25m behind the leaders, Paula Radcliffe and Gete Wami, after Edith Masai had finished her pace-setting role to 3400m. By 4000m Radcliffe (11:39.07) and Wami were ahead of world record pace but over the last two laps Yegorova reeled them in and went by with 250m to go. Wami ran 14:31.69 and Radcliffe a Commonwealth record 14:32.44. That win brought Yegorova a share of the Golden League Jackpot for 2001, with five wins in seven races, a feat matched here by André Bucher (800m), Allen Johnson (110mh in 13.04, the world best for 2001, from Anier García 13.07 and Larry Wade 13.12) and Hicham El Guerrouj (2000m), to join Marion Jones, who did not compete in Berlin, and Violeta Szekely, who must have wished that the Jackpot of 50 kilos of gold still went to those who won at all seven of the meetings (first here in 4:00.80). Michael Johnson ended his career in Europe in a 4x200m relay race. Given a clear lead he ran a 19.6 last leg to hold off the Ingo Schultz and received the acclaim of the 41,000 crowd in the Olympic Stadium. An even greater roar greeted the final discus throw of Jürgen Schult as the 41 year-old world record holder ended his competitive

career with 4th at 62.05, just 3cm below his best mark of the season. His successor as the world number one, Lars Riedel, won at 65.86. *See Championships section for all Golden League event winners.*

September

1-2 **Sweden v Finland**, Göteborg, Sweden. Sweden won the men's match 218-185 and the women's 213-197.

2 **London (Hyde Park)**. Paula Radcliffe tied the women's world road best (Liz McColgan GBR in Chicago 1991) for 5km with 14:57, although she had run much faster on the track in Berlin three days earlier.

3 **Rieti**, Italy. GP II meeting. Hicham El Guerrouj maintained his form to win at 1500m in 3:29.08.

4-7 **Goodwill Games,** Brisbane, Australia. Held before crowds averaging some 30,000, the four days of athletics competition staged in cool weather attracted high quality fields in every event, many of which were practically re-runs of World Championship finals and 14 world champions won again. Prize money ran from $20,000 for 1st to $1000 for 8th. Olimpiada Ivanova received a $100,000 bonus for smashing the world 20,000m track walk record with 1:26:52.3 made up of 5000m segments of 21:43.5, 21:40.9, 21:36.2 and 21:51.7. In the men's walk, Nathan Deakes beat the two Edmonton walks champions and set a Commonwealth 20,000m record of 1:19:48.1. Melissa Rollison ran away from the women's steeplechase field (five women under 9:47) to produce a remarkable world junior and Commonwealth record of 9:30.70. Marion Jones made a cautious getaway after being penalised for a false start, but overhauled her Edmonton conqueror Zhanna Pintusevich-Block (2nd in 11.01) to win the 100m in 10.84, equalling her best time for the year. Michael Johnson made his final appearance in a USA vest and anchored his 4x400 team to victory with a 45.06 leg, earning a standing ovation. *See Championships section for medallists.*

9 **IAAF Grand Prix Final,** Melbourne, Australia. André Bucher and Violeta Szekely won at 800m and 1500m respectively to take the $50,000 for individual event Grand Prix titles and the $100,000 for the overall winners. Allen Johnson took $60,000 for second overall, and would have won the title if he had won his event (110mh), but he was beaten 13.22 to 13.28 by Anier García. Hicham El Guerrouj had a routine win at 1500m in 3:31.25 and took the third overall prize of $30,000 in addition to his $50,000. The women's 2nd and 3rd overall were Maria Mutola (won 800m in 1:59.78) and Tatyana Tereshchuk (beaten 54.58 to 54.78 by Tonja Buford-Bailey in the 400mh. Kamila Skolimowska, still only 18, continued her successes in Australia; after Olympic and Goodwill gold, she threw a world junior record of 71.71 on her final attempt. Olga Yegorova was surprisingly only third to Tatyana Tomashova and Leah Malot in a very slow women's 3000m. *See Championships section for details.*

12-15 **Mediterranean Games,** Tunis, Tunisia. The top mark came in the women's 10,000m as Asmae Laghzaoui powered home to win in 31:15.94, the world's second fastest time of 2001. Bulgarian-born Nora Güner, representing Turkey, gained a splendid 100m/200m double and ran a startling wind-aided 10.98 in her 100m heat. *See Championships section for winners.*

12-16 XXI **South East Asia Games,** Kuala Lumpur, Malaysia. *See Championships section for medallists.*

15 **Yokohama**, Japan. Michael Johnson wound up his farewell tour by anchoring a hastily assembled American/Namibian team to victory in the Super Track & Field Meet in a 1000m medley relay, running his 400m leg in 45.4. The squad's 1:47.93 is the fastest ever time for a "Swedish Relay". There was a great hammer win for Koji Murofushi as his 82.08 headed Szymon Ziolkówski' s 81.82.

15-16 **Talence**, France. Aleksandr Yurkov was a clear winner in the decathlon with 8324 points and Shelia Burrell won the women's heptathlon with 6454, but Yelena Prokhorova's 6354 for second place was enough to ensure her victory in the IAAF Combined Events Challenge.

15-16 **World Mountain Running Trophy,** Arta Terme, Italy. Marco De Gaspari won the men's title for the third time. *See Championships section for medallists*

16 **Great North Run,** Newcastle to South Shields, GBR. Paul Tergat won by over a minute in 60:30, slowed by windy conditions. Susan Chepkemei was the women's winner in 68:40, five seconds ahead of Joyce Chepchumba.

23 **IAU 24 Hours World Challenge**. San Giovanni Lupatoto, Verona, Italy. Yiannis Kouros maintained his supremacy by covering 275,828km and Edith Bérces was women's winner with 235,029km. *See Championships section for medallists.*

26 **Berlin Marathon**, Germany. Naoko Takahashi became the first woman to break 2:20 for the marathon with 2:19:46 (69:50 + 69:56) after running the race on her own with no rival ever near to her. Her 5km splits (with Loroupe's corresponding 1999 times in brackets): 5k - 16:46 (16:20), 10k - 33:10 (32:32), 15k - 49:37 (49:12), 20k: 1:06:11 (1:06:04), half - 1:09:50 (1:09:49), 25k - 1:22:31 (1:23:15), 30k - 1:39:02 (1:40:38), 35k - 1:55:29 (1:57:07), 40k - 2:12:11 (2:13:33). Cheered on by a big crowd, there was a great atmosphere and the weather was ideal (c.15°C at the start, a little light rain and a slight wind). Tegla Loroupe, who had run the previ-

ous world best of 2:20:43 in Berlin two years earlier, finished more than a mile and a half behind, second in 2:28:03, with Berlin's Kathrin Wessel third in a pb of 2:28:27. Some 25,000 runners from 85 nations started the race. from an entry of 31,406. There was a surprise in the men's race, as pacemaker Joseph Ngolepus won in 2:08:47 after a halfway time of 64:13. Willy Cheruiyot was second in 2:09:08.

October

2-5 **XII Pan-Arab Championships**, Damascus, Syria. *See Championships section for winners.*
7 **Chicago Marathon**, USA. Just a week after Takahashi became the first woman to better the 2:20 barrier, Catherine Ndereba dramatically improved the world marathon record to 2:18:47. She also completed a unique feat of winning Boston and Chicago for two successive years. Her 5-mile splits were: 27:45, 54:18 (26:33), 1:20:03 (25:45), 1:46:12 (26:09), 2:12:21 (26:09). She pushed on after 10 miles and won by over six minutes as Elfenesh Alemu was second in 2:24:54. There was a Kenyan 1-2-3 in the men's race with Ben Kimondiu winning in 2:08:52 from Paul Tergat and Peter Githuka.
7 **World Half Marathon Championships**, Bristol, GBR. Haile Gebrselassie, who had made his half marathon debut by winning the Ethiopian title in August, won in 60:03 for the third fastest ever time. He, and second-placer Tesfaye Jifar 60:04, led Ethiopia to the team title. Paula Radcliffe also was a class apart, and she retained her title by the devastating margin of 49 seconds in a European record 66:47 with Kenya taking the women's team title. *See Championships section for details.*
14 **Beijing Marathon,** China. Gong Ke won in 2:10:11 and world junior records were set by Li Zhuhong, 7th in 2:10:46, and by the women's winner, Liu Min 2:23:27. Both winners came from Liaoning Province and are trained by Ma Junren.
18-20 **Pan-American Junior Championships**, Santa Fé, Argentina. *See Championships section for winners.*
21 **Amsterdam Marathon**, Netherlands. The Moroccan-born French Legionnaire Driss El Himer (who had run 2:27:08 in his only previous marathon in 1997) won in 2:07:02 to move to second on the European all-time list and take 53 seconds off the French record.
29 **Scanzorosciate**, Italy. Yelena Ginko smashed the women's world best for 50km walk with 4:34:16 (previously 4:41:47 by Kora Boufflért FRA in 1995). The winner of the men's 100km, Modris Liepins, achieved the second best ever time of 8:48:28.

November

4 **New York Marathon**, USA. There were course records for both men and women. Ideal weather conditions (13°C at the start) were a help, as was a modification of the course which eliminated one of the uphill stretches at 23 miles approaching the finish in Central Park, but there was no denying the quality of the runs by Tesfaye Jifar, whose 2:07:43 took 18 sec from Juma Ikangaa's record of 1989, and Margaret Okayo's pb of 2:24:21, 19 sec inside Lisa Ondieki's 1992 time. Jifar, who lost his right eye when gored by a bull when he was aged 11 or 12, finished well clear of Japhet Kosgei 2:09:19, and won an $80,000 first prize plus $50,000 for the course record and a Pontiac car.
11 **Nijmegen**, Netherlands. Felix Limo replaced fellow Kenyan Paul Tergat as the world's fastest ever road runner at 15 kilometres. Competing in the Zevenheuvenlenloop (Seven Hills Run), he was timed at 41:29 after covering the final 10km in an astonishing 27:15! Even Haile Gebrselassie, who smashed the previous best with 41:38, was left some 60m adrift.
17-23 9th **Chinese National Games**, Beijing. While there were many world-class performances, there were not the sort of marks that had amazed the world at the two previous editions of these Games, in 1993 and 1997. Ma Junren's current star athlete, Dong Yanmei, attempted an amazing triple and, in five races over six days, was 2nd at 1500m followed by wins at 5000m and 10,000m. There was an extraordinary series of performances by very young athletes, including a world junior record of 55.15 for women's 400mh by Huang Xiaoxiao, 2nd to the Asian record-equalling 53.96 by Song Yinglan. Perhaps the most notable win came with 13.36 for 110mh from 18 year-old Liu Xiang. *See China section for winners.*
18 **Tokyo**, Japan. Derartu Tulu won the annual international women's marathon in 2:25:08.
25 **Addis Ababa**, Ethiopia, Huge crowds watched their hero, Haile Gebrselassie, win a 10km road race in 30:30 from about 10,000 runners.
23 **Chiba**, Japan. The international Ekiden relay was won by South Africa in 2:01:56 and women's winners were Japan for the tenth successive year and in an event record 2:13:33 (Kayoko Fukushi 10k 31:37, Akiko Kawashima 5k 15:24, Yasuyo Iwamoto 10k 32:04, Yoko Shibui 5k 15:15, Haruko Okamoto 4.767k 15:21, Megumi Tanaka 7.428k 23:52).
29- Dec 1 **Central American Games**, Guatemala City. *See Championships section for winners.*

December

2 **Fukuoka**, Japan. Olympic and world champion Gezahegne Abera won the 55th annual marathon in 2:09:25.

9 **European Cross-country Championships**, Thun, Switzerland. Sergey Lebed won the men's title by 13 seconds from Kamiel Maase, and Yamna Belkacem won a closely-contested women's race. The widest margin of victory came in the shortest race, the junior women's event, where European junior 3000/5000m gold medallist Elvan Abeylegesse was in a class of her own, winning by 18 seconds, as she had been in the track championships in Grosseto in July. Team titles went to Spain (senior men), Portugal (senior women), Britain (junior men) and Russia (junior women). *See Cross-country section for details.*

Married in 2001

Jan 22 Dean Starkey and Jill Wittenwyler (USA)
Sep 15 Lee Newman and Shelley Drew (GBR)
Sep 16 Adam Goucher and Kara Grgas-Wheeler (USA)

Transfers of allegiance

Aleksey Kurdenko – from Belarus to Russia
El Hassan Lahssini – from Morocco to France
Ismaïl Sghir (Sghyr)– from Morocco to France.

IAAF Rule Changes

THE 43rd IAAF Congress, meeting in Edmonton, passed several new initiatives, including the removal of the world 'Amateur' from its title. After 89 years as the International Amateur Athletics Federation, the IAAF is now the International Association of Athletics Federations.

In total, Congress delegates considered 178 proposals for technical rule changes, some highly controversial,, with only 5 either withdrawn or rejected. Among the proposals agreed was one permitting athletes to communicate with their coaches within the competition area. It was also agreed that hands on medical examination of athletes, by medical officers and physiotherapists approved by the organisers, would now be permitted during events.

The suggested change for a 'no false start' rule, massively opposed by the world's best sprinters, was, at the last minute (and thus without due opportunity for consideration) changed to allow only one false start per race in events up to and including the 400m. Any athlete subsequently false starting will be disqualified immediately. A total of 81 delegates voted for this compared to 74 against (including, it is believed, most of the major nations). It was also agreed that this rule would not be introduced until 1 Jan 2003, to allow for a significant period of adaptation by competitors.

The IAAF made significant rule changes relating to race walking, in an effort to ensure the continued credibility of the discipline after a number of unfortunate incidents at the Sydney Olympics. Supported by the IAAF Council, the IAAF's Race Walking Committee proposed a number of improvements in the judging of race walking, which were all accepted by Congress. Furthermore, it was agreed that the new walking rules be made valid immediately; thus they were in force for the events in Edmonton. The main decision was to give the Chief Walking Judge extra powers so as to enable him to disqualify any walker he judges to have infringed the rules, regardless of whether the competitor has previous warnings, in the last part of the race: i.e. between the circuit and the stadium, and on the track right up to the finish. When an event takes place exclusively on road, or track, the Chief Judge will have this extraordinary power only in the final 100m of the race. There will also now be a Deputy Chief Judge on the circuit, and he will also be able to disqualify athletes if they have received three warnings. As of now, the warnings will be given on yellow rather than white cards.

In other rule changes, Congress agreed that, in response to a number of recent accidents, some of them fatal, landing sectors in the discus and hammer would be reduced from 40° to 34.920°, which would significantly improve safety. This rule will not come into effect until 1 Jan 2003.

It was also agreed that the current rule that gives organisers the possibility to reduce the number of attempts in field events if they so desire in international matches and cups, will be extended to include one day meetings, club competitions and continental cups. However, it is important to stress that this possibility remains at the discretion of organisers, and does not apply to major competitions like Continental Championships, World Championships and Olympic Games.

A controversial aspect of the pole vault was addressed, regarding athletes who replace the bar with their hand during a vault. Congress agreed that the previous wording of rule which states that "a competitor fails, if during the vault he replaces deliberately with his hands or fingers a bar which is about to fall off the supports" was open to misinterpretation and placed undue pressure on the judge and agreed this text will be replaced with: "a competitor fails, if during the vault he steadies or replaces the bar with his hand." Also vaulters will have just a minute to take their jumps once the bar is in place in the early stages of the competition, 30 seconds less than before. At the start of the first round in which three or fewer competitors are left, high jumpers will have 1:30 (down from 2 mins) and vaulters 2:00 (from 2:30), and once a single competitor is left he or she will get up to three minutes in the high jump (from 5 mins) and five minutes in the vault (from six).

A proposal to reduce attempts in the vertical jumps from three to two was withdrawn without coming to a vote.

Lamine Diack, acting President of the IAAF since the death of Primo Nebiolo in November 1999, was elected President, with a total of 168 Congress delegates voting for and just one against. Professor Helmut Digel (GER) also received significant support (151-11) in the election for Vice-President. There were no other candidates for either position. There were three new Council members: Sergey Bubka (UKR), Colonel Gianni Gola (ITA) and Asian AAA President Suresh Kalmadi (IND).

Congress approved a Council proposal that all athletics disputes be referred to the Court of Arbitration for Sport. CAS is already recognised as an independent final arbitral body for sporting disputes worldwide. This move is intended to bring athletics in line with other major Olympic sports. All disputes will be referred to CAS, which is based in Lausanne, within sixty days of the date upon which the disputed decision was made.

Another significant Congress decision was a change to Rule 4 to state that no athlete shall be eligible for international competition unless that athlete has signed an agreement with the IAAF by which he or she agrees to be bound by IAAF Rules and Procedural Guidelines and to submit, if necessary, to disputes he may have with the IAAF or a Member to arbitration in accordance with IAAF Rules. This new proposal is aimed to establish clear jurisdiction of the IAAF over its athletes and will allow them to enforce decisions more easily.

Yegorova Suspension Lifted

The IAAF announced on August 4, five days before the heats of the 5000m in Edmonton, that it had lifted the suspension of Olga Yegorova after receiving further information regarding the validation of the testing system which led to the athlete's positive finding for EPO at the Paris Golden League meeting on July 6. Testing for EPO was first conducted at a major Championship at the 2000 Olympics where athletes were asked to provide samples of both blood and urine. The Sydney protocol involved a screening of the blood sample to provide an indication of whether EPO was present in the athlete's body, and this was then confirmed by a follow up urine analysis. At this time, it remains the only means of testing for EPO that has been scientifically validated. Since Sydney, further extensive scientific research has been undertaken to finalise a single urine only test. The research is believed to be complete, but the IAAF was informed that the test still awaited final validation. The IAAF believed that, in the circumstances, the test conducted by the French authorities on Yegorova in Paris should not have been carried out. She was tested in Edmonton as part of the IAAF's own EPO testing programme, using the Sydney protocol of taking both blood and urine samples. The test proved negative.

The new IOC President, Jacques Rogge, has revealed that the IAAF received approximately $17.6 million from the **Sydney Olympics**, more than double the amount that was received by the governing body after the Atlanta Games in 1996.

The IAAF entered into an agreement with **Dentsu Inc**. (head office: Tokyo) to be the exclusive worldwide partner responsible for the commercial exploitation of marketing. Under the agreement, IAAF granted Dentsu, for the IAAF World Athletics Series 2001-2009, the worldwide rights for sponsorship, media including the Internet (except for EBU territory), and licensing. Dentsu and the IAAF will develop an innovative marketing programme for further expansion of the sport around the world.

The IAAF Council, meeting on November 27, agreed to make the **IAAF Grand Prix Final** a two day meeting (with a full programme of track and field events) from 2003 and also agreed that the competition should be hosted by Monaco for three consecutive years, to ensure the event has a stronger sense of identity, and to allow the possibility of hosting the World Athletics Gala on the same weekend in early September to further promote the sport. Monaco was selected, following a vote, in a direct contest with Stuttgart, because the third candidate, Madrid, withdrew.

It was agreed that qualifying rounds would be reintroduced for the field events at future editions of the **World Indoor Championships**, and that a World Indoor Combined Events Championships would be introduced at one of the existing major Indoor Combined Events meetings. Council also agreed to reduce the IAAF Golden League to five meetings starting in 2003.

European AA Decisions

The 17th Congress of the European AA determined:
1. That the Mountain Running Championships should be added to its programme. Seven editions have been organised (by the WMRA) of the European Mountain Racing Trophy and the first Championship will be in Camara de Lobos, Madeira, Portugal.
2. The European U23 Championships and Indoor Cup to be held in 2003 will not be in Athens, as due to changes in the construction planning for the Olympic Games, the city is not in a position to stage these events. Subject to evaluation, Bydgoszcz, Poland may hold the U23 Championships and Leipzig has expressed an interest in the new Indoor Cup.
3. To introduce European U23 Indoor records (by a margin of just 18-17).

Veterans: The WAVA changed its name in 2001 to World Masters Athletics (WMA).

ATHLETES OF 2001

By Peter Matthews

IF POSSIBLE one looks for perfection in any selection of Athlete of the Year. With very few athletes achieving a perfect record in 2001, it was thus not surprising that Hicham El Guerrouj headed most of the leading polls. For he went through the year undefeated – starting with three indoor races, one each at 1500m, 3000m and 2 miles, and then won all ten of his outdoor races. He put the disappointment of the Olympic year behind him and gained world titles both indoors (at 3000m) and outdoors (taking his third successive 1500m crown) and missed his own world record for 1500m by just 0.12 secs at Brussels. He also earned the right to a share of the Golden League Jackpot for a record third time, having previously done so in 1998 and 2000.

While he has yet to win Olympic gold, El Guerrouj has an extraordinary record, having won 61 of 64 races at 1500m or 1 mile and all five races at longer distances in the six years 1996-2001. Some have criticised the fact that Moroccan compatriots have set a pace for him in recent championship races, arguing that he is thus spared the uncertainty of knowing what the race tactics will be – and the race becomes too similar to the over-used Grand Prix style where meeting promoters, greedy for a world record, always ensure that pacemakers are employed to cut out whatever the master wants for a chance at one. On the other hand, that pace is there for all and El G has been left to take up the running himself for nearly two laps, thus being exposed to anyone good enough to challenge him. When at his best I believe that he is well capable of winning no matter how the race is run, because who could match his finish off a slow pace, or his ability to run fast all the way?

The only other top male athlete to go through 2001 undefeated was Maurice Greene at 100m, although that is only if you discard the race at Eugene on 27 May when Greene ran 9.92w for 100m, but the winner Patrick Jarrett (9.89w) got way to a blatant flyer.

Other men who came close to perfection included several world champions: André Bucher who was beaten just twice at 800m or 1000m, John Godina who lost two of 17 shot competitions and Jonathan Edwards, who won 5 of 7 triple jump competitions indoors and 15 of 17 outdoors. Jan Zelezny also only lost twice, and his competitive effort in coming from behind Aki Parviainen's championship record 91.31 in the World Championships, showed once again the true class of one of the greatest competitors on the history of sport.

In 2000 one noted that no world record fell at a standard men's event, but two were beaten in 2001. Amazingly, through injury, both the men who did so came only tenth at the World Championships. Roman Sebrle became the first to pass 9000 points on the current tables in the decathlon, when he amassed 9026 at Götzis in May, but he was held back by a groin injury to 8174 in Edmonton. There Brahim Boulami was not fully fit when he ran 8:21.95 for 3000m steeplechase, but he came down to 7:58.50 in his next race just nine days later in Zürich before taking 0.44 sec off the world record with 7:55.28 in Brussels.

Hicham El Guerrouj in 2001
Undefeated in 13 races

Date	Meeting	Venue	Event	Time
23 Feb		Gent (i)	2M	8:09.89 NR
			(3000m	7:36.85 NR)
25 Feb		Liévin (i)	1500m	3:37.20
11 Mar	WI	Lisboa (i)	3000m	7:37.74
		(1h1 8:05.50 on 9 Mar)		
27 May	Pre	Eugene	1M	3:49.92
29 Jun	GGala	Roma	1M	3:44.95
6 Jul	GL	Saint-Denis	1500m	3:28.28
22 Jul	BrGP	London (CP)	1M	3:49.41
12 Aug	WCh	Edmonton	1500m	3:30.68
		(1h1 3:36.97 on 9.8, 1s2 3:39.54 on 12/8)		
17 Aug	WK	Zürich	1500m	3:29.06
24 Aug	VD	Bruxelles	1500m	3:26.12
31 Aug	ISTAF	Berlin	2000m	4:51.17
2 Sep	GP	Rieti	1500m	3:29.08
9 Sep	GPF	Melbourne	1500m	3:31.25

NR = National Record

Male Athlete of the Year

MY SELECTION of the top 10 athletes of 2001 together with the list compiled by international experts polled by *Track & Field News* and those of *Athletics International* readers (who only voted for 1-2-3) is as follows:

	PJM	T&FN	AI
Hicham El Guerrouj	1	1	1
Maurice Greene	2	2	4
André Bucher	3	4	3
Jan Zelezny	4	3	2
Jonathan Edwards	5	5	5
Brahim Boulami	6	9	10
Tomás Dvorák	7	7	7
Felix Sanchez	8	8	9
John Godina	9	6	-
Iván Pedroso	10	13	-
Roman Sebrle	-	-	6
Koji Murofushi	-	10	-

The IAF included Allen Johnson, Lars Riedel and Roman Sebrle in their top ten (in place of Dvorák, Godina and Pedroso) of PJM's list. El Guerrouj was their Athlete of the Year.

For the third year, the European AA conducted an online poll on their website inviting votes from the public; 2217 people took part. Winners of their Waterford Crystal Trophy were André Bucher (from Jan Zelezny and Virgiljus Alekna) and Stephanie Graf (from Zhanna Pintusevich and Gabriela Szabo).

Runners World's runners of the year were Hicham El Guerrouj and Catherine Ndereba.

100 Metres

MAURICE GREENE was top ranked for the fourth successive year. He had problems with his left knee and suffered a series of injuries even as he won the world title at 100m. Despite that he still ran the third fastest ever 'legal' time of 9.82 in Edmonton. The wind was -0.2 m/s and if he can stay healthy he must surely smash the world record one day. He ran only the heat at the US Champs, assured of World selection with a wild card entry as defending champion, and including this was unbeaten at the event at eight meetings, apart from his third place at Eugene when Patrick Jarrett (9.89w) got away to a flier, and was never slower than 10.01 in a final.

Just ahead of him in Eugene, both running 9.92w, was Tim Montgomery, who went on to win the US title and to run a startling 9.84 in Oslo. With 9.85 for silver, Montgomery pushed Greene hard in Edmonton, and also had big wins in Zürich and Brussels. Bernard Williams was the US runner-up and World bronze medallist and shades Ato Boldon (4th Worlds), with whom he was 3-3 on win-loss. Dwain Chambers, who ended the year with a clear win over Montgomery (and Boldon 5th) at the Goodwill Games, was the fifth man under 10.00 in the World final and beat Williams 3-1 but was 2-3 against Boldon. Mark Lewis-Francis also broke 10 seconds in Edmonton, with 9.97 in his quarter-final but lost a possible world junior record due to malfunction of the wind gauge – opinions differ as to whether these races should or should not be adjudged as wind-aided.

Lewis-Francis won the European Junior title and at the European Cup, but was 5th in his semi in Edmonton and did not quite do enough to be ranked. The only other man to run a legal sub-10 in 2001 was Francis Obikwelu, who did not run at the Worlds; he beat Abdul Aziz Zakari (8th Worlds) 3-1. Perhaps just ahead of those two is the CAC champion and Worlds 6th placer, Kim Collins, although he did not meet Obikwelu and was 1-2 down to Zakari. Curtis Johnson and Jon Drummond were 3rd and 6th at the US Champs, with the former running infrequently and the latter coming, as usual, into good form in Europe.

Most 'legal' times under 10.00/10.10 (ignoring Edmonton qfs): Greene 7/9, Montgomery 4/9, Boldon 4/8, Williams 3/9, Chambers 1/6, Obikwelu 1/2, Zakari 0/4, Collins 0/3

1. Greene, 2. Montgomery, 3. B Williams, 4. Boldon, 5. Chambers, 6. Collins, 7. Obikwelu, 8. Zakari, 9. C Johnson, 10. Drummond

200 Metres

KONSTADÍNOS KEDÉRIS followed his surprising Olympic title with a clear win in Edmonton. He had earlier won at the Athens GP and at the European Cup, but lost his only other race: third behind Bernard Williams and Christian Malcolm in Zürich. There was an intense battle for the other medals in Edmonton, with Christopher Williams taking silver and Shawn Crawford and Kim Collins sharing the bronze, but with Malcolm 5th, Stéphane Buckland 6th and Kevin Little 7th, just 0.05 secs separated these six men. Crawford, Malcolm and C Williams had been the World Indoor 1-2-4. Outdoors Crawford won the US title and after 4th in Zürich finished strongly with wins in Linz, Goodwill Games and GP Final. He thus had a stronger overall season than B Williams, who headed him 2-1 and who beat C Williams 3-0, but who did not start the final of the US 200m and had just five other races (three wins and two seconds).

Chris Williams and Malcolm were 2-2 outdoors, and ranking next is Ramon Clay who pulled up lame in his World quarter-final after a good season, including US 2nd place. The most amazing run of the year came from J J Johnson at Brussels, where, running in the outside lane 9, he won in 19.88 (2. B Williams 20.01, 3. Malcolm 20.09). That took 0.60 off his previous best and was the only sub-20 time of the year, apart from Justin Gatlin's windy 19.86 at the NCAAs (he won the final in 20.11). Johnson could not build on that as he was 3rd at the Goodwill Games behind Crawford and C Williams in 20.54. Obikwelu beat Buckland 1-0 and Little 2-1 and Zakari beat Buckland 2-0.

Ato Boldon ran only two 200m races with a best of 20.24 for 4th in Brussels. Only Kedéris and Malcolm were in the top ten in both 2000 and 2001.

1. Kedéris, 2. Crawford, 3. B Williams, 4. C Williams, 5. Malcolm, 6. Clay, 7. Collins, 8. J Johnson, 9. Obikwelu, 10. Zakari.

400 Metres

IN HIS final season Michael Johnson competed only in relay races, and he left a void. The world's fastest time of 2001 was 44.28 run in May by Tyree Washington; this was his fifth successive win and fourth sub-45 time, but he was then third behind Michael McDonald and Antonio Pettigrew in Portland, and struggled in sixth in his semi-final at the US Championships with a season-ending hamstring injury. Arvad Moncur was unbeaten as he won the NCAA, Bahamas and World titles, and is the clear choice for world number one although he was then third at Gateshead behind Felix Sanchez and Angelo Taylor and was also runner-up to Greg Haughton at the Goodwill Games.

Haughton, world bronze medallist beat Pettigrew, US champion and World 4th, 3-0, but he was beaten at the Jamaican Championship by McDonald, who failed to finish in his semi at the Worlds but who beat Pettigrew 2-0. Ingo Schultz is difficult to rank; he came to Edmonton as an outsider, having a season's best of 45.27 and been 4th in the European Cup and 2nd in the German Championships, but he ran a startling 44.66 in his semi-final and followed with 44.87 to take the silver medal. He did not run again. Sanchez ran national records when winning both his 400m races (45.23 and 44.90) and Taylor ran only three flat 400m races, but won twice before Gateshead; so these hurdlers have seasons of high quality but which are too thin to rank highly. Taylor had a good win over McDonald, with Pettigrew only 7th at Princeton. Eric Milazar was 5th and Hamdan Al-Bishi 6th at the Worlds and Milazar was 2-2 against the US runner-up Leonard Byrd, who went out in the semis at the Worlds. Overall standards were well down and even Moncur's winning time in Edmonton of 44.64 would have been enough for only 7th in a semi at Seville two years earlier.

Most sub-45 second times: Moncur 10, McDonald 6, Haughton & Washington 4, Milazar 3.

1. Moncur, 2. Haughton, 3. McDonald, 4. Schultz, 5. Pettigrew, 6. Milazar, 7. Byrd, 8. Washington, 9. Taylor, 10. Al-Bishi

800 Metres

ANDRÉ BUCHER had a wonderful year. At 800m he won nine of this ten outdoor competitions, seven of them GP races including the final, and three of four indoors, and was a thoroughly deserving winner of the IAAF overall Grand Prix Final. He also won his two races at 1000m (in the two fastest times of the year). Typically he won his races with a drive for home from some 250-270m out, as he did in the World Championships. His only outdoor loss was to Yuriy Borzakovskiy at Brussels, when the brilliant 20 year-old ran the world's fastest time of the year in 1:42.47 to Bucher's 1:42.75. Bucher had run the previous best of 1:42.55 at Zürich a week earlier, when Borzakovskiy was 6th in 1:43.30. Borzakovskiy, as in 2000, showed hugely exciting potential as he ran his races off an even pace, often last at the bell before eating up the field in the closing stages, but he passed the opportunity of running in Edmonton, his advisers not wanting to push him too much. He had run three earlier Russian records, all in 2nd place to Bucher: 1:44.06 in Rome, 1:43.76 Paris and 1:43.17 Monaco, having run a record 1:44.15 indoors before taking the World Indoor title in 1:44.49 by nearly two seconds from Johan Botha and Bucher.

The world lists for the year are dominated by that Zürich race, as 1st to 5th ran their best times to rank 2nd to 6th. Between the big two came: Jean-Patrick Nduwimana, Wilfred Bungei, William Yiampoy and Pawel Czapiewski, and 7th and 8th were Mbulaeni Mulaudzi and Nils Schumann, all under 1:44.4. The consistent Kenyans Bungei and Yiampoy were 2nd and 4th at the Worlds and went 6-6 in head-to-head clashes. They were separated in Edmonton by Czapiewski, who improved from 1:46.07 to 1:43.22 during the year; he won at the European Cup, but 8th in Brussels, 7th in Berlin and 4th at the Goodwill Games (behind Yiampoy, Nduwimana and Bungei) lowers his ranking. The two Burundi runners, Nduwimana, and Arthémon Hatungimana went out in the semis at the Worlds, but had a good series of runs in the big races. Nduwimana was 4-3 v Yiampoy, 3-0 v Czapiewski and 2-1 against Joseph Mutua, who was only 4th at the Kenyan Championships, but had positive win-loss records against many top names. Hatungimana beat Mutua 3-2 and Nils Schumann (World 5th) 3-1. Mulaudzi (World 6th) beat his compatriot Hezekiel Sepeng (World 8th) 4-0.

Most times sub-1:45: Bucher 9, Bungei 8, Mutua & Yiampoy 7, Borzakovskiy 6+2i, Hatungimana & Sepeng 5, Glody Dube, Nduwimana & Schumann 4, Czapiewski 3

1. Bucher, 2. Borzakovskiy, 3. Bungei, 4. Yiampoy, 5. Nduwimana, 6. Hatungimana, 7. Mutua, 8. Czapiewski, 9. Schumann, 10. Mulaudzi

1500 Metres

HICHAM EL GUERROUJ was once again the king at 1500m and 1 mile (top for the fifth successive year), winning all nine races (plus one at 2000m and indoor races at 3000m and 2 miles). While there was again criticism for the use of a teammate to set a fast pace in the championship race, there was no doubting the Moroccan's pedigree. He ran four of the five fastest times of the year at 1500m and missed his world record by just 0.12 in a great race in Brussels, when he ran 3:26.12 but was pushed hard by Bernard Lagat 3:26.34. William Chirchir was well back at 3:29.29, but that still put him third on the world list for 2001. El Guerrouj and Lagat also ran the year's fastest miles, at Rome, but El G was well ahead, 3:44.95 to 3:47.28. Lagat won only 3 of his 16 outdoor races and 2 of 3 indoors, but he was 2nd to El G six times, including at the Worlds and GP final. Driss Maazouzi took World bronze, but was beaten 3-1 by Chirchir (World 4th) and 3-0 by Noah Ngeny.

The Olympic champion was dropped from the Kenyan team for refusing to return to a Kenyan training camp due to a previous racing commitment, but he was only 3rd at the Kenyan Championships and 4th at the GP Final; Chirchir beat him 3-1, but he beat Laban Rotich 6-3. Rotich was 2nd to Chirchir in the Kenyan Champs, and although he went out in the semis in Edmonton, he had his usual solid season on the GP circuit and beat Maazouzi 3-1. Reyes Estévez and José Redolat were 5th and 6th at the Worlds, but Estévez had poor form otherwise outdoors, where Redolat and Andrés Díaz were the top two Spaniards. Rui Silva, 7th at the Worlds, had a great win in Monaco in 3:30.36 from Benjamin Kipkurui and Lagat, but that was his only sub-3:35 time, whereas Kipkurui had five. Silva won a very slow World Indoor 1500m from Estévez, Ngeny and Rotich. Kipkurui beat Robert Rono 2-0 and Rono beat Enock Koech 3-0.

Ali Saïdi-Sief won his four races, and would have ranked third but for his positive drugs test.

Most times sub-3:34 or 3:51M: Lagat 10, El Guerrouj 9, Díaz & Vyacheslav Shabunin 5, Chirchir, Kipkurui, Maazouzi, Rotich & Saïdi-Sief 4; Estévez, Koech, Ngeny & Rono 3

1. El Guerrouj, 2. Lagat, 3. W Chirchir,
4. Ngeny, 5. Rotich, 6. Maazouzi,
7. Redolat, 8. Díaz, 9. Kipkurui (10),
10. Estévez (-). Including indoors: 9. Silva

3000 Metres/2 Miles

THE 3000m at Brussels provided the first seven places on the world list, followed by 2nd to 5th at Monaco. Mekonnen won 2/3 indoors but was third at Hengelo and Berlin and only 8th in the Grand Prix Final in his other 3000m races. The last was won by that consummate racer Paul Bitok, who had five races indoors and seven outdoors at 3000m or 2 miles. Bitok also won at Nice, Lausanne, Monaco and Berlin and was third in Brussels and 2nd in London. Kenenisa Bekele set a world junior record at 7:30.67 for 2nd in Brussels and was also 2nd at Hengelo and Helsinki (both to Abiyote Abate) and at the GP Final, and was 4th in Berlin. 4th to 7th in Brussels were John Kibowen (9 GPF), Richard Limo (5), Abderahim Goumri (10) and Abate (7). In Monaco, Bitok was followed by Luke Kipkosgei (1 London, 3 GPF), Benjamin Limo (3/4), Salah El Ghazi and Mark Carroll. Another fast face came at Lausanne, where the order behind Bitok was Kibowen, Sammy Kipketer, R Limo, Kipkosgei and Carroll. Hicham El Guerrouj set a world indoor record at 2 miles and won the Worl Indoor 3000m title.

1. Bitok, 2. Mekonnen, 3. Bekele,
4. Kibowen, 5. R Limo, 6. Kipkosgei,
7. Kipketer, 8. Abate, 9. B Limo, 10. Goumri.
Including indoors El Guerrouj at No. 7.

5000 Metres

NO ONE athlete dominated this event and indeed the season's fastest time of 12:56.72 is the slowest since 1994. The man who did that time, however, Richard Limo at Zürich, also won the World and Kenyan titles and is the obvious man to rank first, although he did lose twice – 4th in Rome and 6th at the Goodwill Games. Thereafter, however, there is no clear picture. Sammy Kipketer and Benjamin Limo were the two men to run twice under 13 minutes and with 6 and 5 respectively they also had the most sub-13:10 times (followed by John Kibowen and Daniel Komen with four each). Paul Bitok ran most often at 3000m, but his three 5000m races ensured him of a high ranking. He won at Oslo in a personal best time of 13:00.10, but sadly missed a first sub-13 time, as he also did when he was 4th at Zürich in 13:00.98.

He then won an appallingly slow Goodwill Games race in 15:26.10. Despite highish altitude the times in Edmonton were quick, with Richard Limo taking the World title from Ali Saïdi-Sief (who tested positive for drugs), Million Wolde, Kibowen, Alberto García, Ismaïl Sghir, Kipketer (who tried to run away from the field in the middle stages), Abiyote Abate and Hailu Mekonnen. Rome (13 under 13:10) and Zürich (11 under 13:08) produced the greatest depth of times; and those who were in both included Mekonnen 1st/3rd, B Limo 2nd/12th, Kipketer 3rd/8th, R Limo 4th/1st, Abate 5th/5th, Sghir 6th/9th, Wolde 7th/6th, Komen 12th/15th. The first three beat 13 minutes in Rome and first two in Zürich. Mark Bett was second there, but ran won one other 5000m, 4th at Heusden. The first five at Oslo were under 13:04: Bitok, B Limo, Kibowen, Luke Kipkosgei and Kipketer

1. R Limo, 2. Bitok, 3. Wolde, 4. Kibowen,

5. Mekonnen, 6. S Kipketer, 7. B Limo,
8. Abate, 9. García, 10. Sghir

10,000 Metres

THE WORLD'S fastest four times of 2001 were run at Palo Alto in May by Abraham Chebii, Benjamin Maiyo, Luke Kipkosgei and Mebrahtom Keflezighi, but only one of those, Maiyo 10th, makes my top ten merit rankings! Chebii, whose world leading mark was the slowest since 1992, ran just one more race at the distance, when he was 7th in the Kenyan Championships. That race was indeed intrinsically the quickest, as Charles Kamathi won in 27:47.33, the fastest time ever at high altitude, and he was followed by John Korir, Paul Kosgei and William Kalya, all under 27:53 with times worth perhaps a minute faster at sea-level. Kamathi had been second to Assefa Mezgebu at Hengelo and then reversed that order at the Worlds.

Kamathi was expected to break 27 minutes in Brussels, but faded badly in the closing stages and was beaten by Mark Bett (his only 10,000m of the year) and Robert Kipchumba (who had another fast time when third in Prague). Mezgebu won at the Goodwill Games from Maiyo (6th Kenyan Champs, 15th Brussels). The great Haile Gebrselassie took the World bronze; while at first sight it might appear amazing that he was beaten for the only time at 10,000m since his 3rd in the 1993 African Championships, he had not raced since his Achilles operation. Completing an Ethiopian 2-3-4 at the Worlds was a new man, Yibeltal Admassu, who was 2nd to Mekonnen in the Ethiopian Champs and had more solid runs: 5th Hengelo, 9th Brussels, 4th Goodwill. José Rios and Fabián Roncero were 1st and 2nd in the Spanish Championships, and while the order was reversed for 5th and 6th in Edmonton, Rios also won the European Challenge and was 10th in Brussels. Kosgei and Korir were 7th and 8th in Edmonton.

1. Kamathi, 2. Mezgebu, 3. Gebrselassie, 4. Bett, 5. Admassu, 6, Kipchumba, 7. Rios, 8, Roncero, 9. P Kosgei, 10. Korir

Half Marathon

HAILE GEBRSELASSIE made his debut at the half marathon when he won the Ethiopian title from Tesfaye Jifar and Tesfaye Tola. His time was slow, 64:34 at the high altitude of Addis Ababa, but he then came to Bristol where he won the World title in 60:03, with Jifar 2nd and Tola 5th. Fabián Roncero was the only man to run faster than Geb in 2001, with his 59:52 at Berlin, but he ran no more half marathons. John Yuda, after wins in the USA and Tanzania, took the World bronze, and Hendrick Ramaala was 4th. Interestingly Ramaala's time of 60:15 compared to the 60:26 with which he won on the slightly downhill course in Lisbon, and the World 6th placer Evans Rutto ran 60:43 in Bristol after 60:30 for 3rd in Lisbon. Paul Tergat had been second in Lisbon in 60:27, and went on to win the Great North Run in 60:30. Completing the top ten on fastest times were Titus Munji, 2nd in Berlin in 60:27, William Kiplagat, 4th Lisbon 60:38, and Patrick Ivuti, winner of the Stramilano in 60:42, but while these men had no other half marathon races, Christopher Cheboiboch backed up his 5th place in Lisbon with 8th in the Worlds.

1. Gebrselassie, 2. T Jifar, 3. Yuda,
4, Ramaala, 5, T Tola, 6. Rutto, 7. Roncero,
8, Tergat, 9, Cheboiboch, 10. Munji

Marathon

THE FASTEST marathon time of 2001 was run by Josephat Kiprono, 2:06:50 in Rotterdam. He did not finish in the World Championships, but came back for 2nd in Amsterdam in 2:07:06. There he was beaten by Driss El Himer's 2:07.02 in his first serious marathon. The London marathon was won, as in 1999, by Abdelkader El Mouaziz, but he was 6th at the Worlds in 2:15:41, an indication of how times were slowed by the hot conditions in Edmonton. There Gezahegne Abera added to his 2000 Olympic success by winning a fascinating race by just one second from Simon Biwott, with Stefano Baldini 3rd, Tesfaye Tola 4th and Shigeru Aburaya 5th. Abera had previously been only 16th in Boston in 2:17:04, Biwott won in Paris in 2:09:40, Baldini was 2nd in Turin and won in Madrid, Tola was 5th in Tokyo and Aburaya the third of four men under 2:08 in the Lake Biwa race.

Abera went on to win the Fuluoka race in December, but then Biwitt was only 8th. Antonio Peña was 1st and Giacomo Leone 2nd at Lake Biwa, but they were only 24th and 11th respectively at the Worlds. It soon becomes apparent that there was a confused picture at the event, and as most of the top men ran at the Worlds I have given that priority in my rankings. Running two or more good races, however, also matters and Tesfaye Jifar justifies a high ranking with an excellent record in four marathons: 2nd Tokyo, 4th London, 7th Worlds, 1st New York 2:07:43. Paul Tergat made a keenly anticipated debut at the marathon, but had to settle for 2:08 times in 2nd place – at London and Chicago (behind Ben Kimondiu.

1. Abera, 2. Kiprono, 3, Biwott, 4. Baldini,
5. El Mouaziz, 6. T Jifar, 7. T Tola,
8. Aburaya, 9. El Himer, 10. Tergat

3000 Metres Steeplechase

BRAHIM BOULAMI was troubled by a foot injury in the first part of the season and after two third places, including a season's best 8:07.28 at Monaco, a fourth and a dnf, he was 10th at the World Championships. He then shook off his problem and become the first non-Kenyan to break 8 minutes with 7:58.50 at

Zürich and then the first non-Kenyan to set a world record since Anders Gärderud in 1976, with his 7:55.28 at Brussels. He sealed his top ranking with wins in slowish races at the Goodwill Games and Grand Prix Final. Second to him in all those four races was Reuben Kosgei, who earlier had added World gold to his Olympic title. He had been second to Bernard Barmasai in Doha and the Kenyan Championships (but beat him 4-2 overall) and lost to Wilson Boit Kipketer at Saint-Denis, but won at Hengelo and Rome. Ali Ezzine maintained his good championship record with the World silver, but otherwise had three fourth places and two 8ths in GP races, and Barmasai took the bronze. 4th to 6th at the Worlds were Luis M Martín, Bob Tahri and Antonio Jiménez, but several Kenyans had better records. Stephen Cherono beat Kipkirui Misoi 3-1 and these men were 3rd and 4th in the GP Final, and Raymond Yator, 3rd in the Kenyan Champs, was unfortunate to fall in the Worlds final but disappointed in the year's final races.

Most times under 8:15: Misoi 7, Boit Kipketer 6, Yator 5 (+1 dq), R Kosgei 5, Barmasai, Ezzine, Elarbi Khattabi & Tahri 4, Boulami, Jiménez, John Kosgei, L Martín & Julius Nyamu 3

1. Boulami, 2. R Kosgei, 3. Barmasai,
4. Boit Kipketer, 5. Cherono. 6. Misoi,
7. Ezzine, 8. L Martín, 9. Tahri, 10. Yator

110 Metres Hurdles

ALLEN JOHNSON started the season slowly so that he came to the US Championships with a best of 13.46, but was ready when it mattered as he won that title in 13.22 and went on to regain the World title in the year's fastest time of 13.04. Anier García was 2nd in 13.07 and he and Johnson so dominated that of the 12 legal times at 13.21 or better in 2001 they ran 18 of them (García 10 and Johnson 8). Johnson had the edge overall, 6-5 against García. Dudley Dorival took the world bronze medal and had positive win-loss records against all the other top men, except Colin Jackson who beat him 4-3 and Larry Wade who beat him 6-2.

Jackson opted out of the championships, and was some way from his best, but still ran consistently and was 5-3 v Terrence Trammell, 4-3 v Dominique Arnold. However Larry Wade beat Jackson 6-2, and was also 5-5 v Trammell. Trammell was 2nd with Dawayne Wallace 3rd and Arnold 4th at the US Champs, with Wade only 7th. This group were closely matched and with no clear pattern of hierarchy. To take examples of major races: at Zürich the order behind Johnson was Trammell, Wade, Jackson, Mark Crear and Arnold, Then in Brussels García won from Wade, Johnson, Crear, Jackson, Dorival and Trammell with Arnold 9th.

At the Goodwill Games, Johnson, García and Wade took the medals, from Trammell, Jackson, Crear, Dorival and Wallace and at the GP Final it was García, from Johnson, Arnold, Dorival, Jackson, Wallace, Trammell and Wade. Crear had a lighter racing season than the others, but was 3-1 v Wallace and 5-1 v Arnold,. At the Worlds, 4th to 8th were: Yoel Hernández, Robert Kronberg, Yevgeniy Pechonkin, Wallace and Shane Bownes. Stanislav Olijars missed Edmonton, but beat Wallace 5-0, Trammell 2-1 and Hernández, who only contested six meetings, 1-0. Bownes, who beat Kronberg 4-1 and Pechonkin 4-1, just misses a ranking

Most times under 13.30: Garcia 14+1w, Johnson 12, Arnold 5, Trammell & Wade 3

1. Johnson, 2. García, 3. Wade, 4. Dorival,
5. Jackson, 6. Trammell, 7. Olijars, 8. Crear,
9. Wallace, 10. Arnold

400 Metres Hurdles

FELIX SANCHEZ just missed a ranking in 2000, but came through in 2001 to take the national record of the Dominican Republic, the land of his parents, from 48.33 to 47.95 at London, 47.49 at the Worlds and 47.38 in Zürich. He was beaten in his first four races and then went unbeaten in eight further meetings to take a clear top ranking. Fabrizio Mori took silver and Dai Tamesue (with two Japanese records) bronze at the World Championships and were followed by Hadi Al-Somaily, Chris Rawlinson and Pawel Januszewski, with Boris Gorban disqualified after finishing 6th, and I kept that ranking order, except to move up Januszewski as he beat Rawlinson on the other two occasions that they met.

Angelo Taylor went out in the semis at Edmonton, but was otherwise beaten only twice by Sanchez, and came back for 2nd at Zürich ahead of Mori and Tamesue. James Carter was another American to disappoint in Edmonton, but did well enough to justify a place in the rankings. There was continued disappointment for Stéphane Diagana, who had to end his season through injury after running 48.08 for 2nd in Lausanne and 48.13 for 2nd at Saint-Denis. Llewellyn Herbert also missed much of the season after running four sub-49 times in South Africa.

He ran in Edmonton as his first race back but could manage only 50.28 in his heat; he showed at the end of the year that he was coming back in to form as he was 2nd at the Goodwill Games to Sanchez and ahead of Al-Somaily, Gorban and Januszewski. Seventh and 8th fastest men were Alwyn Myburgh, who won the World Universities title in 48.09, and Marek Plawgo, who was inconsistent. Samuel Matete (best of 49.82) dropped out after 11 successive years ranked in the top ten.

Most times under 49.00: Mori, Sanchez & Tamesue 10, Al-Somaily 8, Gorban, Herbert,

Rawlinson & Taylor 5, Carter, Januszewski. Myburgh & Plawgo 4, Diagana & Ian Weakley 3.

1. Sanchez, 2. Mori, 3. Taylor, 4. Tamesue, 5. Al-Somaily, 6. Diagana, 7. Januszewski, 8. Rawlinson, 9. Gorban, 10. Carter

High Jump

JAVIER SOTOMAYOR was 5= in the World Indoors and 4th in the Worlds at Edmonton; he then announced his retirement at the end of the year, but a sad postscript came with the news that he had tested positive for nandrolene in July. He would have ranked 4th. Standards remained far below those in his heighday. Going into Edmonton a case could be made for a dozen men to win. One thought that someone would burst out of the pack to jump 2.35/2.36 and win, and so it proved as that man was Martin Buss, who otherwise had a best of only 2.30 in 2001. The Russians Yaroslav Rybakov and Vyacheslav Voronin tied for the silver medal in Edmonton and were probably the best overall on outdoor form with Rybakov winning 4-2 outdoors and 4-1 indoors. Stefan Holm was 5= outdoors with Sergey Klyugin as six men jumped 2.30 or more in Edmonton, and Holm won the World Indoor title and also the Goodwill Games at 2.33 from Voronin, Rybakov and Mark Boswell all of whom jumped 2.31, for the year's second best competition, with Sotomayor 5th at 2.28.

There were five men over 2.30 at Eberstadt, where Voronin jumped a season' best of 2.37 from Boswell 2.33 and with Wolfgang Kreissig, Rybakov and Sotomayor tied at 2.30 (Klyugin 6th, Holm 7th, Buss 9th, Strand 12th). Managing only 2.25 in the final in Edmonton were Boswell and Steffan Strand at 7=, while US champion Nathan Leeper went out with that in qualifying and the yearly leader at 2.35i and 2.34, Andrey Sokolovskiy could clear only 2.15. Boswell was 4-2 over Klyugin outdoors, but 0-3 indoors. Sokolovskiy and Strand took silver and bronze at the World Indoors. NCAA champion indoors and out, Charles Clinger, jumped 2.35A but had poor marks in Europe; he just shades Sergey Dymchenko, who was 8th and 15th at the worlds.

Most competitions over 2.30m (outdoors/ in): Rybakov 8/3, Holm 6/4, Voronin 4/1, Boswell 4, Martin Buss 3/1, Leeper 3, Strand 2/1

1. Rybakov, 2. Voronin, 3. Holm, 4. Buss, 5. Boswell (6), 6. Klyugin (7), 7. Strand (5), 8. Sokolovskiy, 9. Leeper, 10. Clinger. In brackets are changes including indoor form.

Pole Vault

DMITRIY MARKOV came into his own at Edmonton, where he won the competition at 5.90 and went on to 5.95 and 6.05 to take second equal place on the world all-time list and the highest ever cleared at a major championship. Markov was beaten 4-2 by Jeff Hartwig, who had the misfortune to fail to clear a height at the US Championships, but had the best depth of performances. Aleksandr Averbukh and Nick Hysong took the other medals at the Worlds, where the 4th and 5th placers, Michael Stolle and Romain Mesnil matched them in clearing 5.85. Indoors Lawrence Johnson had taken World gold with 5.95 from Tye Harvey, Mesnil and Averbukh, and won the US title indoors with 5.96. After winning the US title from Tim Mack and Hysong, Johnson's season was cut short by injury in July, but he beat Hysong 4-1. Danny Ecker, indoors, was the only other man to clear 6 metres in 2001, and was beaten only by Hartwig in number of 5.80+ competitions, but was only 11th in Edmonton.

Stolle, the European Cup winner, beat Ecker 6-5 outdoors and was 1-3 down indoors. Averbukh, who also won the World Universities title, was beaten 4-1 by Hartwig, but had the advantage over Ecker 3-2 (4-2 inc. indoors) and Hysong 4-3. Mack and Viktor Chistiakov, 9th and 10th at the Worlds, were 2-2 and Mack won at the Goodwill Games, where both he and Averbukh cleared 5.80, with Markov third at 5.75.

Most competitions over 5.80m (outdoors/ in, exhibitions = ex): Hartwig 11/1, Ecker 7+1ex/5, Averbukh 7/3, Stolle 5+1ex/2, Johnson 4/6, Mack 4/1, Chistiakov & Hysong 3, Harvey 1/4, Mesnil 1/2

1. Markov, 2. Hartwig (3), 3. Averbukh (4), 4. Johnson (2), 5. Hysong (6), 6. Stolle (9), 7. Ecker (5), 8. Mesnil (7), 9. Chistiakov (10), 10. Mack (-). – Harvey (8)

Long Jump

IVÁN PEDROSO won his fifth indoor and fourth outdoor World title in 2001. His is a truly wonderful record, but he did not need to produce the sort of distances that he achieved earlier in his career, and standards have slipped considerably from the days of Carl Lewis, Mike Powell and Larry Myricks. Powell himself returned, at the age of 37 and after five years out of competition, to jump 8.06 in May and then take 4th in the US Champs at 8.10w.

After winning all his six indoor competitions, Pedroso was troubled by a right leg injury so that his outdoor season's record was 10/17. His 8.43 indoors was the year's best followed by an outdoor best of 8.41 by James Beckford, who slipped to 7th in Edmonton. Savante Stringfellow won the US title with 8.47w and, while he had some poor competitions, showed improved consistency, was 4-5 v Pedroso (and one loss indoors), and took the World silver.

Miguel Pate and Dwight Phillips were the other US qualifiers for the Worlds, where they came 4th and 8th, but Kevin Dilworth, only 6th at the US Champs, had a fine season in Europe with

Golden League victories at Rome, Oslo and Zürich, although he slipped at the end with 4th at Goodwill Games and 7th Grand Prix Final compared to 2nd and 4th by Beckford, with whom he was 4-4 on win-loss. Pate added the World Universities title, but was only 5th at the NCAAs. Kareem Streete-Thompson and Aleksey Lukashevich were 5th and 6th in Edmonton, with Lukashevich having a decisive 6-2 advantage including 3rd to 5th at the GP Final, and they had better depth of performances than Carlos Calado, the surprise World bronze medallist.

Younès Moudrik started well but slumped in mid-season and missed the Worlds, before surprising to win the GP Final; he was also 2nd at the Mediterranean Games. Hussein Al-Sabee was 10th at the Worlds and just gets a ranking spot, helped by his 8.31 win at Doha; he beat Phillips 3-1, although the latter's case is improved with his US indoor title.

Most competitions over 8.15m (outdoors/in): Stringfellow 8+3w/1, Pedroso 6/4, Dilworth 6+1w, Beckford 5+1w, Calado 2/1, Pate 1+4w

1. Pedroso, 2. Stringfellow, 3. Dilworth, 4. Beckford, 5. Pate, 6. Lukashevich (7), 7. Streete-Thompson (8), 8. Calado (6), 9. Moudrik, 10. Al-Sabee. – Phillips (10).

Triple Jump

JONATHAN EDWARDS regained the World title that he had won in 1995, and had another fine season with 15 wins in 17 competitions outdoors and 5 in 7 indoors, where he was beaten for the world title by Paolo Camossi. Camossi was only 11th in Edmonton, where the silver medal was taken by a rising star, Christian Olsson, who improved from 16.97 in 2000 to 17.49, 2nd on the year lists to Edwards, who had four competitions over 17.50. Olsson was also the only man to beat Edwards outdoors (in his first and last outdoor competitions, at Helsinki and Yokohama).

Olsson won the European U23 title from Igor Spasovkhodskiy, who went on to World 3rd, World Universities 4th and Goodwill Games 6th. The standard in Edmonton was agreeably high as Yoel García was 4th at 17.40. Then followed the NCAA champion (and US 3rd) Walter Davis, CAC champion Brian Wellman, Larry Achike, Rostislav Dimitrov and Phillips Idowu. Dimitrov had only one other outdoor competition and Wellman also had several poor performances. LaMark Carter was 14th in Edmonton, but was unbeaten outdoors in the USA where he won national titles indoors and out, and he was also third behind Edwards and Olsson at the Goodwill Games. Michael Calvo beat García to take the Cuban title with 17.30, but did not compete after June. Also close to ranking spots are the World University Games 1st and 2nd: Kenta Bell, US 4th, and Marian Oprea, European Junior champion. Andre Murphy took the World Indoor bronze with 17.20, but did not beat 17m outdoors after March and was 17th in Edmonton.

Most competitions over 17m (outdoors/in): Edwards 15+1w/6, Olsson 11, Camossi 3/2, Davis 3+1w/1, García & Idowu 3+1w, Achike 3.

1. Edwards, 2. Olsson, 3. Spasovkhodskiy, 4. García, 5. Davis, 6. Achike, 7. Idowu (8), 8. Carter (9), 9. Camossi (6), 10. Calvo (-). –. Murphy (10).

Shot

JOHN GODINA returned to the top ranking he held in 1998, with world titles indoors and out and just two losses in 4 indoor and 13 outdoor competitions. Adam Nelson beat him easily, 21.40 to 20.57 at the US indoors, and again at the Goodwill Games, 20.91 to 20.76, but otherwise it was Godina supreme, with 7 of the top 10 performances of the year. He did not top the world list, however, as the young South African Janus Robberts produced 21.97 (to Godina's best of 21.95) to win the NCAA title. Roberts, who had twice set national records at 21.36 indoors, had just five outdoor competitions, three in the US in the spring including a previous record at 21.60, and then none after the NCAAs until Edmonton. There he led the qualifiers for the final with 21.26 but came last (12th) in the final with 20.18.

Nelson lost only to Godina except for once to Miguel Martínez indoors, and he and Martínez, who set seven Spanish records in 2001, were 2nd and 3rd indoors and 2nd and 4th outdoors at the Worlds. Arsi Harju was only fourth at the Finnish Championships, but came through to take the bronze medal in Edmonton.

He was closely matched by other Finns, as Ville Tiisanoja (World 9th) beat him 5-3 and he beat Conny Karlsson (World 7th) 5-3; Tiisanoja had a 6-4 advantage over Karlsson. Yuriy Belonog and Dragan Peric were 5th and 6th at the Worlds, but Peric is difficult to rate as he did not otherwise compete outside the Balkans apart from 4th at the European Clubs. The Canadian champion, Brad Snyder, was 8th at the Worlds ahead of Andrey Mihknevich and Paulo Dal Soglio, who had better top marks. Dal Soglio was 5th to Snyder's 11th at the World Indoors.

Most competitions over 21.00/20.50 (indoors and out): Godina 10/17, Martínez 6/22, Robberts 6/8, Nelson 5/15, Dal Soglio & Snyder 0/6, Belonog & Harju 0/5, Pavel Chumachenko & Tiisanoja 0/3

1. Godina, 2. Nelson, 3. Martínez, 4. Harju, 5. Belonog, 6. Robberts, 7. Tiisanoja, 8. Karlsson, 9. Peric, 10. Snyder (-). Including indoor form: 10. Dal Soglio.

Discus

VIRGILIJUS ALEKNA produced a championship record in the third round in Edmonton, only for Lars Riedel to exceed that twice, with 69.50 and 69.72 – a superb competition between two great athletes. Riedel thus won his fifth world title (to go with the bronze that he won in 1999 when suffering from a hip muscle injury) and had a season's record of 10 wins in 12 competitions to Alekna's 10 wins and 5 second places. In head-to-head clashes Alekna beat Riedel 2-1, as he won at Zürich with 69.95 to Riedel's 5th-placed 66.14 and at Rüdlingen 69.42 to 3rd at 67.25. Alekna also had the best set of marks, with the world's leading throw of 70.99 and 7 of the 13 performances over 68m to 2 by Riedel; he also had six GP wins to 1 by Riedel. These two men were a class above the rest.

Frantz Kruger probably did enough to retain his third ranking, as although he was only 8th at the Worlds, he had such good results as 3rd at Zürich, 1st and 2nd at Rüdlingen, 1st Goodwill Games and 3rd GP Final. Michael Möllenbeck won the World bronze, but did not have as good a record elsewhere as those following him in 4th to 6th places: Dmitriy Shevchenko, Adam Setliff and Vasiliy Kaptyukh.

There is not much in it, however, as win-loss records show conflicting evidence: Shevchenko was 4-2 against Setliff who was 3-1 v Möllenbeck, who was 2-1 v Shevchenko! Jason Tunks, 9th at the Worlds, was 5-3 v Kaptyukh, who was 2-1 v Möllenbeck. Róbert Fazekas fared disastrously in Edmonton, but beat his compatriot Roland Varga, who was 7th there, 4-2. Aleksander Tammert was only 16th in Edmonton, but after 8th in Zürich won the World Universities title and then was 2nd at the GP Final to Alekna and ahead of Kruger, Setliff, Tunks, Fazekas, Shevchenko and Kaptyukh. However, he lost 3-1 to John Godina, although 3-2 v Fazekas.

Most competitions over 65m: Alekna 14, Kruger & Riedel 11, Fazekas 10, Shevchenko & Tunks 7, Kaptyukh, Möllenbeck & Setliff 6, Godina 5, Zoltán Kövágó & Tammert 4

1. Alekna, 2. Riedel, 3. Kruger,
4. Shevchenko, 5. Setliff, 6. Tunks,
7. Kaptyukh, 8. Möllenbeck, 9. Fazekas,
10. Godina

Hammer

THERE WAS a super battle in Edmonton between Szymon Ziolkówski and Koji Murofushi, with the Pole coming through with a fifth round championship record of 83.38 to take gold ahead of Murofushi's 82.92 (and five throws at 81.43 or better). This was the fourth national record of the year for Ziolkówski and Murofushi set five to the year's top mark of 83.47. Murofushi takes top ranking because he was otherwise unbeaten, winning 12/13, including 4-1 against Ziolkówski, who won 15 times, was 2nd three times and 3rd once, when Nicola Vizzoni was 2nd in Rome.

Vizzoni also won World Military, Italian and World Universities titles and was 4th at the Worlds, a place behind Ilya Konovalov, whom he beat 3-2. At the Goodwill Games the order was Murofushi, Ziolkówski, Balázs Kiss (World 6th), Vizzoni, Konovalov, Igor Astapkovich (World 7th). Tibor Gécsek was the third most prolific thrower over 80m; he was 8th at the Worlds, but beat Kiss 3-2 and the 5th placer Andrey Skvaruk 2-1; Kiss was 4-1 v Konovalov and 3-2 v Skvaruk.

Adrián Annus produced the year's second longest throw of 83.39, but was 9th at the Worlds and 3rd at the World Universities, and Nicolas Figère won the French and European U23 titles (ahead of Olli-Pekka Karjalainen) and was 12th at Edmonton. Three men just beat 80m at the Russian Championships, Konovalov was 2nd, but 1st and 3rd, Sergey Kirmasov and Vasiliy Sidorenko did not otherwise better 76m.

Most competitions over 80m: Ziolkówski 16, Murofushi 9, Gécsek 6, Vizzoni 4.

1. Murofushi, 2. Ziolkówski, 3. Vizzoni,
4. Gécsek, 5. Kiss, 6. Konovalov,
7. Skvaruk, 8. Annus, 9. Astapkovich,
10. Figère

Javelin

THE MARVELLOUS Jan Zelezny won his third World title to go with his three Olympic golds, and, as ever, responded to the need of the moment. For his 92.80 in the second round in Edmonton came after Aki Parviainen had improved the championship record (90.76 by Zelezny in qualifying) to 91.31 in the first round and Kostas Gatsioúdis had thrown 88.39, a mark he later improved to 89.95 for the bronze medal. The javelin was a GP and Golden League event, so there was plenty of top-class competition. Zelezny won 9/11 in 2001, his only losses being to Parviainen at Vantaa and to Raymond Hecht in Zürich. Gatsioúdis had a 2-1 advantage over Parviainen, better depth of marks and he won 11/13, his only other loss being to Zelezny in Helsinki.

Steve Backley struggled with technical problems all year, and was most disappointed by missing the World final in 14th place, but just before then had joined the big three in exceeding 90m in 2001 with 90.81 at the British Grand Prix, his best throw for nine years. He had advantage on win-loss over the men who came 4th to 6th in Edmonton: 6-3 v Breaux Greer, 4-3 v Raymond Hecht and Boris Henry and was 2-2 with the 7th placer, Sergey Makarov. Hecht just edged his German rival Henry 10-9. Eriks Rags, 8th in the

Worlds, ended well with 3rd at the Goodwill Games (behind Zelezny and Greer) and 2nd at the GP Final, won by Zelezny with Henry 3rd. Backley, 3-3 v Rags overall, was 4th in both those events. Rags was 6-5 v Greer, 4-3 v Henry and 5-2 v Hecht, but 1-3 v Makarov. The German champion Peter Blank, takes the final rankings spot.

Two or more competitions over 85m: Gatsioúdis 12, Zelezny 11, Henry 7, Hecht & Parviainen 6, Greer 5, Backley & Makarov 4

1. Zelezny, 2. Gatsioúdis, 3. Parviainen, 4. Backley, 5. Greer, 6. Rags, 7. Hecht, 8. Henry, 9. Makarov, 10. Blank

Decathlon

AFTER SIX successive wins in major decathlons 1999-2000, Tomás Dvorák was held back by injury at the Olympic Games. But he returned to his best in great style to take the World title with 8902 points and followed that with a win at the Goodwill Games.

He was, however beaten to the target of being the first to score over 9000 points with the current scoring tables, as his compatriot Roman Sebrle added 32 points to Dvorák's world record by winning at Götzis with 9026 with Dvorák way behind, third at 8527. Sebrle, unfortunately struggled through the World Championships with a groin injury to come tenth at 8174. Erki Nool had the third and fourth best scores of the year and was second in each of the three top events: Götzis, World and Goodwill, and Dean Macey, in his only decathlon of the year, took the World bronze despite all sorts of injury problems.

Attila Zsivoczky and Lev Lobodin were 4th and 5th in Edmonton and 5th and 4th respectively at Götzis, while Aleksandr Yurkov, although 9th in the Worlds had three big wins: Arles, European Cup (2. Zsivoczky, 3. Laurent Hernu) and Talence. In the letter he was followed by Hernu (8th Worlds), Benjamin Jensen (10 Götzis, 14 Worlds) and Stefan Schmid (7th Worlds). Schmid also had an important win at Ratingen, where Nool and Lobodin failed to finish. Tom Pappas did not finish at the US trials, but was third in the Goodwill Games, in which Lobodin was 4th and Jirí Ryba (6th Worlds and 5th Talence) was 6th.

1. Dvorák, 2. Nool, 3. Sebrle, 4. Macey, 5. Lobodin, 6. Yurkov, 7. Zsivoczky, 8. Schmid, 9, Hernu, 10. Ryba

20 Kilometres Walk

RUSSIA TOOK a clean sweep of the medals at the World Championships with Roman Rasskazov, Ilya Markov and Viktor Burayev. Another Russian, Dmitriy Yesipchuk recorded the fastest time of the year, 1:18:05 in winning the Russian winter title by a second from the 18 year-old Buryayev, whose time was a world junior road best. Burayev then won at the European Cup (Yesipchuk only 11th), Rasskazov won the Russian Championship and Markov won at Calella. These three were then 3. Razzkazov, 4. Buryayev, 5. Markov at the Goodwill Games track event, won by Nathan Deakes from Robert Korzeniowski. Deakes was 4th at the Worlds, won the Australian title and improved the Commonwealth best to 1:18:14 when he won at Dublin, and Korzeniowski won his other two 20km races: L'Hospitalet and Polish Champs.

The World 5th placer, David Márquez, won at La Coruña but was only 20th in the European Cup and 10th at Calella, and 6th placer Joel Sánchez was third in the Mexican Champs in his only other race. Yevgeniy Misyulya and Andreas Erm did not complete the Worlds race, but were 2nd and 3rd at the European Cup, and won their other races: Erm the German title and at Eisenhüttenstadt and Misyulya at Hildesheim. And two others who did not finish in Edmonton, but had good seasons were: Francisco Fernández and Aigars Fadejevs, 2nd and 3rd at Calella and 4th and 8th at the European Cup. Fernández also won the Spanish title and was 2nd at L'Hospitalet, and Fadejevs was 2nd at Hildesheim.

1. Rasskazov, 2. Burayev, 3. Markov, 4. Deakes, 5. Korzeniowski, 6. Misyulya, 7. Erm, 8. Fernández, 9. Fadejevs, 10. Márquez.

50 Kilometres Walk

KORZENIOWSKI CONTINUED to seal his place as an all-time great as he regained the world title that he had won in 1997 to add to his European and Olympic titles. His 3:42:08 in Edmonton, his only 50k of the year, was the fastest time of 2001 and silver medallist Jesús Angel García's 3:43:07 was the next best. Nathan Deakes was the next quickest, 3:43.43 at Naumberg, but was disqualified in Mexico and Edmonton, and García had another fast time, 3:44:26 when winning the European Cup.

The other men bettering 3:45 were Aleksey Voyevodin and Germán Sánchez at Cheboksary; Voyevodin was 6th in the European Cup but did not finish at the Worlds, and Sánchez did not finish at Mexico City and was 3rd in the Pan-Am Cup. Placing 3-9 at the Worlds with their further races in brackets were: 3. Edgar Hernández (3 Mexico, 1 Pan-Am Cup), 4. Aigars Fadejevs, 5. Vladimir Potemin (3 Eur Cup), 6. Valentí Massana, 7. Curt Clausen, 8. Marco Giungi (1 Italy), 9. Tomasz Lipiec (2 Naumburg). Nikolay Matyukhin was 2nd in the European Cup, but disqualified in Edmonton, where the Spanish champion Mikel Odriozola was 17th.

1. Korzeniowski, 2. García, 3. Hernández, 4. Potemin, 5. Fadejevs, 6. Massana, 7. Deakes, 8. Matyukhin, 9. Lipiec, 10. Odriozola

WOMEN ATHLETES OF 2001

STACY DRAGILA was as clear a choice for Female Athlete of the Year as was Hicham El Guerrouj among the men. Dragila's season was not perfect, and indeed that is very hard to achieve in an event like the pole vault, and she slightly blotted her copybook with fourth place at the World Indoor Championships, but overall her record was wonderful. She set no less than eight world records – four indoors (4.63, 4.65, 4.66 and 4.70) and four outdoors (4,.65, 4.70, 4.71, 4.81), three times setting two in one meeting. Indoors she won eight of ten competitions and outdoors 14 of 15, her only defeat coming early on when she was 4th in Osaka at 4.20. She attacked the world record time after time and of course was pushed hard by Svetlana Feofanova, most notably in Edmonton when both cleared 4.75 and Dragila won the world title on count-back.

The tough, attractive, charming Dragila has a great competitive ability and is determined to raise women's standards at this new event, so much appreciated by the public, to new heights. 16 feet (4.87m), first achieved by a man early in the fibreglass era in 1962, is her first target and perhaps 5 metres.

One woman who went through the year undefeated may tend to get overlooked because she is a walker and her branch of the sport is not fully appreciated by all track fans, but a look at the season of Olimpiada Ivanova shows it to be truly exceptional. She won her one indoor race (44:38.8 at 10,000m) and then had five wins at 20km. These started with a world road best of 1:24:50 in Adler, followed by wins at the European Cup, La Coruña and World Championships and ending with a world record on the track, 1:26:52.3 at the Goodwill Games. While the walks events are perhaps not contested so widely as many mainstream track and field events, not the least of Ivanova's achievements is that with her 1:24:50 she became the first woman ever to achieve an ATFS MEN'S standard.

Other women who had unbeaten years at their events had only limited competition: Marion Jones won four times at 200m, including the world title, Katharine Merry won twice indoors and four times outdoors at 400m but lost the rest of the season through injury and illness, and Olga Yegorova won all four times at 5000m, although she lost at 3000m in the Grand Prix final after six wins at that distance.

Naoko Takahashi broke the 2:20 barrier for the women's marathon, but her 2:19:46 at Berlin was her only marathon of 2001; she also won a 30km race but had losses at shorter road distances. Catherine Ndereba bettered Takahashi's mark just one week later, with 2:18:47 at Chicago and had a better overall record as she won her other marathon, Boston, and won both her races at half marathon; she too, however, had losses at lesser distances.

The other event at which the world record was broken was the women's javelin, as Osleidys Menéndez became the first to throw the new (from 1999) specification javelin over 70m with 71.54 at Rethímno on 1 July. Her season, which included World and World University Games titles, was near perfection with just two losses in 13 competitions. Tatyana Lebedeva had six losses but had a sequence of ten wins including the world triple jump title at the peak of the season.

Female Athlete of the Year

MY SELECTION of the top 10 athletes of 2001 together with the list compiled by international experts polled by *Track & Field News* and those of *Athletics International* readers (who only voted for 1-2-3) is as follows:

	PJM	T&FN	AI
1 Dragila	1	1	1
2 Menéndez	2	4	2
3 Yegorova	3	3	7
4 Jones	4	2	3
5 Lebedeva	5	5	-
6 Szekely	6	6	6
7 O Ivanova	7	9	-
8 Mutola	8	8	4
9 Ndereba	9	7	5
10 Tulu	10	10	-
Naoko Takahashi	-	-	8
Paula Radcliffe	-	-	9
Zhanna Pintusevich-Block	-	-	10

The IAF included Zhanna Pintusevich-Block and Paula Radcliffe in their top ten (in place of Ivanova and Tulu of PJM's list). Dragila was their Athlete of the Year.

100 Metres

SHE IS top for the fifth sucessive year, but Marion Jones was not quite as good as in previous years, and her fallibility was shown when she was surprisingly beaten by Zhanna Pintusevich-Block for the World title. She was, however, still easily the best overall with four of the five fastest times of the year (10.84 to 10.86) and 10 wins in 11 competitions. Pintusevich-Block beat Ekateríni Thánou, the World bronze medallist, on the first two occasions that they met – in Athens and Edmonton, although Thánou came out ahead in three post-Edmonton meetings. Thánou was fourth in Athens, where the 2nd and 3rd, Myriam Mani and Kelli White, ran 10.98 and 10.99 respectively. Chandra Sturrup was fourth at the Worlds and 2-2 v Thánou, including 2nd places at Zürich and Brussels, in each of which races Jones was 1st, Thánou 3rd, Pintusevich 4th and Chryste Gaines 5th (as she was at the Worlds). Debbie Ferguson, White and Mercy Nku were 6th to 8th in Edmonton and I have kept the same top eight in the world rankings, but Nku beat White 3-1, so comes in at 7th. Endurance Ojokolu and Mani were 5th and 6th in semis at the Worlds, but LaTasha Jenkins takes the final ranking as she beat Mani 2-0. Ojokolu beat Mani 4-1.

Most times under 11.00/11.10: Jones 10/12, Pintusevich 5/9, Thánou 3/7, Sturrup 3/6, Gaines 1+1w/5+1w, White 2+2w.

1. Jones, 2. Pintusevich, 3. Thánou, 4. Sturrup, 5. Gaines, 6. Ferguson, 7. Nku, 8. White, 9. Ojokolu, 10. Jenkins

200 Metres

WITH THE 100m the Grand Prix event, the 200m was relegated in importance and standards declined to the lowest levels for a quarter of a century. Marion Jones ran the event at just four meetings, but she won them all, including the year's fastest, 22.23 at Eugene, and 22.39 to take the World title by 0.13 from Debbie Ferguson, who won 9/12 at this event. The World 3rd to 6th, Kelli White, LaTasha Jenkins, Cydonie Mothersill and Juliet Campbell maintain those places in the rankings. White and Jenkins were 2-2, but White added good 2nd places at the Goodwill Games and Grand Prix Final. Myriam Mani, 8th at the Worlds, won the GP Final and beat the World 7th placer Alenka Bikar 4-3. Bev McDonald went out in the semis at the Worlds, but beat Bikar 7-1 and was 1-2 down to Mani. Mercy Nku did not contest the Worlds, but was 6-1 against Bikar.

Indoors, Campbell won the World title from Jenkins and Natalya Safronnikova,

Most times under 22.80: Ferguson 8, Jenkins 7, Jones & Mothersill 6+1w, White 6, McDonald & Nku 4, Mani 3, Campbell 1+1w+1i

1. Jones, 2. Ferguson, 3. White, 4. Jenkins, 5. Mothersill (6), 6. Campbell (5), 7. Mani, 8. McDonald, 9. Nku, 10. Bikar. In brackets rankings including indoors.

400 Metres

THIS IS one of the most difficult events to determine top ranking. Katharine Merry ran the year's fastest time of 49.59 in Athens in June and looked to be heading for world success with an unbeaten record in two indoor races and four outdoors, but she succumbed to illness and injury and did not race after July. Grit Breuer was next fastest with 49.78 to win the German title; she won at the European Cup and six of her seven races overall. That loss, however, came with 4th at the Worlds where she faded to 50.49 while the three medallists all broke 50 seconds.

The surprising winner was Amy Mbacké Thiam, who improved her national record from 50.77 to 50.21 in the semi and then 49.86 in the final at Edmonton. Lorraine Fenton added the World silver to her 2000 Olympic silver and Ana Guevara took the bronze medal. These three also took the medals at the Goodwill Games, where the order was Guevara, Fenton, Thiam, and that perhaps most accurately reflects the season. Guevara won 10/13, Fenton 2/5 and Thiam 4/13. But even when not fully race-fit Merry had won the British Grand Prix in her last race of the season in 50.67 with Guevara 3rd at 51.43.

There was a gap after the top five and then little between those in the next group. Nadjina Kaltouma and Olesya Zykina were 5th and 6th at the Worlds while Falilat Ogunkoya did not finish that race, and two semi-finalists, Heide Seyerling and Sandie Richards come strongly into contention through depth of performance. Seyerling beat Kaltouma and Richards 2-1. Olympic champion Cathy Freeman sat out the season.

Richards won the World Indoor title from Olga Kotlyarova, Zykina and Kaltouma.

Most times under 51.00: Guevara 10, Breuer 7, Fenton & Zykina 5, Kaltouma, Richards & Seyerling 4, Merry 3+1i, Kotlyarova 1+2i

1. Guevara, 2. Fenton, 3. Thiam, 4. Merry, 5. Breuer, 6. Kaltouma, 7. Seyerling, 8. Richards, 9. Zykina, 10. Ogunkoya

800 Metres

THE CLASHES between Maria Mutola and Stephanie Graf continued to provide many thrilling races (see table), but after Graf had established an early advantage, Mutola came through to take the world title by just 0.03 secs and then go on to win the last three big races of the year, with Graf third in each. The big two were challenged by Fabienne dos Santos, who made a huge improvement from 2:01.70 in 2000 to a best of 1:57.16 in seven sub 2-minute races in Europe in June and July, culminating in a win in the British Grand Prix over Graf and Kelly Holmes.

But then came news that dos Santos had failed a drugs test at Rio back in May. Holmes returned from further injury problems to take 6th place in Edmonton and to end the year in fine style with 2nd places in Zürich, Brussels, Goodwill Games and GP Final. Natalya Tsyganova (1-7 down to Holmes) went out in the heats in Edmonton, but overall beat the bronze medallist Letitia Vriesde 7-3, while Vriesde was 4-3 over world 4th placer Faith Macharia, the Kenyan champion. Diane Cummins delighted her home crowd with 5th place in Edmonton and went on to an excellent record in European races, including 2nd place in Berlin, but the 7th placer, Mayte Martínez, did not have enough form otherwise to support a top ranking. Ivonne Teichmann was the World 8th and beat the Russian champion Svetlana Cherkasova 2-0 and was 3-1 v Zulia Calatayud, who was 4th at both Goodwill Games and GP Final, and who was 3-2 v Tsyganova, 4-3 v Vriesde, 1-1 v Cummins and 3-3 v Macharia. Jolanda Ceplak beat Cherkasova 4-1 outdoors and 2-0 indoors to take the final rankings place.

1. Mutola, 2. Graf, 3. Holmes, 4. Tsyganova, 5. Vriesde, 6. Macharia, 7. Cummins, 8. Teichmann, 9. Calatayud, 10. Ceplak.

1500 Metres

GABRIELA SZABO had a perfect year at the event, winning her three indoor races and her only outdoor competition. That was at the World Championships when her powerful sprint took her to victory in 4:00.57 over her compatriot Violeta Szekely. But her lack of races means that she is ranked below the three women who head the world list. Szekely was silver medallist in Edmonton and also took the World Indoor silver behind Hasna Benhassi (who did not run outdoors). But Szekely was the star of the event in 2001, winning all her other 12 races at 1500m or 1 Mile, including all seven Golden League races and the Goodwill Games and GP Final.

That last win sealed her success in taking the overall GP title and $150,000 to go with her share of the Golden League jackpot. Natalya Gorelova was 2nd in four of those Golden League races and third twice, adding third places in the Worlds and GP Final, and Carla Sacramento had two seconds, two thirds and a fourth in the Golden League, 4th in the Worlds, 3rd Goodwill and 2nd GPF. Gorelova and Sacramento were also 3rd and 4th at the World Indoors. Similar consistency was shown by Lidia Chojecka, 4th or 5th in most of the big races, and Lyudmila Vasilyeva, 5th, a place behind Chojecka at both GWG and GPF. It is, however, difficult to determine rankings 6-10. The Russian Champs 1-2, Tatyana Tomashova and Yelena Zadorozhnaya had only three races each at this event, but all of high quality and Tomashova was 2nd at the Goodwill Games. They had finished in the reverse order at Tula, where 3rd was Olga Yegorova, who went on to 2nd in the European Cup to Szekely and to a win in Glasgow over Zadorozhnaya. Suzy Favor Hamilton dropped out in her World semi and again at Brussels, but had earlier run fast times for 2nd in Oslo and 3rd in Rome, Paris and Monaco; she was beaten by Regina Jacobs for the US title. Kutre Dulecha did not run again after an African indoor record mile of 4:23.33 behind Szabo's 4:23.19 at Stuttgart in February.

Most times under 4:05 (outdoors/in): Szekely 9/1, Gorelova 7/1, Sacramento 7/2, Favor Hamilton 4, Zadorozhnaya 3, Szabo 1/2 (and 4:23.19Mi)

1. Szekely, 2. Gorelova, 3. Sacramento, 4. Szabo, 5. Chojecka, 6. Tomashova, 7. Zadorozhnaya, 8. Favor Hamilton, 9. Yegorova, 10. Vasilyeva.

3000 Metres

OLGA YEGOROVA swept through the Golden League races, recording the year's three fastest times – 8:23s at Zürich, Paris and Rome, with a further win at Brussels. But, in a very slow race, she was surprising-

Maria Mutola v Stephanie Graf at 800m

		Mutola	*Graf*
2001			
15 Feb	Stockholm	2-1:58.05	1-1:57.68
18 Feb	Birmingham	2-1:59.88	dq-(1:58.67)
23 Feb	Gent	2-1:58.85	1-1:58.82
25 Feb	Liévin	2-1:58.02	1-1:57.53
11 Mar	Lisbon – WI	1-1:59.74	2-1:59.78
6 Jul	Saint-Denis	2-2:00.13	1-2:00.00
13 Jul	Oslo	2-1:58.70	1-1:58.20
12 Aug	Edmonton – WCh	1-1:57.17	2-1:57.20
17 Aug	Zürich	1-1:56.85	3-1:57.98
24 Aug	Bruxelles	3-1:57.95	1-1:57.46
31 Aug	Berlin	1-1:59.19	3-1:59.42
5 Sep	Brisbane – GWG	1-1:58.76	3-2:00.93
9 Sep	Melbourne – GPF	1-1:59.78	3-2:00.40
2000			
11 Feb	Gent	2-1:59.23	1-1:59.13
1 Aug	Stockholm	1-1:56.98	2-1:57.32
11 Aug	Zürich	1-1:56.90	2-1:57.34
25 Sep	Sydney – OG	1-1:56.15	2-1:56.64
1999			
14 Feb	Birmingham	1-1:58.25	3-1:59.17
21 Feb	Liévin	1-1:57.06	2-1:59.27
7 Mar	Maebashi – WI	2-1:57.17	6-2:04.39
30 Jun	Oslo	2-1:58.17	3-1:58.72
7 Jul	Roma	4-1:58.57	3-1:58.31
21 Jul	Paris	1-1:58.25	2-1:58.73
11 Aug	Zürich	1-1:56.04	5-1:57.07
24 Aug	Sevilla – WCh	2-1:56.72	7-1:57.92
3 Sep	Bruxelles	2-1:57.67	4-1:58.19
11 Sep	München – GPF	1-1:59.10	5-2:00.47

1998: Mutola won 4-0

ly beaten at the Grand Prix Final by Tatyana Tomashova and Leah Malot. Yelena Zadorozhnaya was 2nd in Rome and Paris and Tomashova 3rd in both those races and 2nd in Brussels, although down to 7th in Zürich. There Gabriela Szabo, Berhane Adere, Gete Wami and Paula Radcliffe followed, all under 8:30. Szabo, not quite at her best in 2001, was 4th in Rome and Paris and 5th in Brussels and Adere was 4th in Brussels and 4th at the GP Final. Wami was 3rd in Brussels and 5th at the GP Final and Paula Radcliffe was 5th in Rome and 6th in Brussels. Edith Masai was the winner in Monaco (2. Ebru Kavaklioglu, 3. Alesya Turova), 6th Zürich and 7th GP Final. Indoors, Szabo had set a world record of 8:32.88 and at the World Indoors the order was Yegorova, Szabo, Zadorozhnaya, Marta Domínguez and Dong Yanmei. Outdoors Domínguez was 12th in Rome and 8th in Brussels.

1. Yegorova, 2. Zadorozhnaya,
3. Tomashova, 4. Szabo, 5. Adere, 6. Wami,
7. Radcliffe, 8. Masai, 9. Kavaklioglu,
10. Turova

5000 Metres

YEGOROVA was the centre of a media storm when she was reported to have tested positive for EPO on the eve of the World Championships. That was not proven satisfactorily and her ability to maintain her composure in such circumstances must be admired, even if the doubts remain. She won the world title in her first competition of the year at the distance, showing the devastating finish that she had displayed so well at shorter distances earlier in the year, and followed with a European record 14:29.32 at Berlin and end of season wins at Goodwill Games and in Yokohama.

In Berlin, Yegorova overcame the big lead that Gete Wami and Paula Radcliffe had opened up on her, but these two recorded easily the next fastest times of the year (14:31.69 and 14:32.44) and probably deserve to rank higher than the world silver and bronze medallists Marta Domínguez (season's best 14:58.12) and Ayelech Worku (14:54.00), although Worku was 3rd and Wami 5th (her only other 5000m of 2001) at Hengelo in a race won by Berhane Adere with Irina Mikitenko 2nd.

Mikitenko was also 2nd to Radcliffe in London and 5th in Edmonton. Yelena Zadorozhnaya was 6th and Edith Masai 7th in Edmonton, but the former beat Radcliffe to win the European Cup in devastating fashion in 14:40.47, and Masai won her other three races: Kenyan Champs, Oslo and Stockholm (2. Domínguez). Tatyana Tomashova was 10th in the Worlds but 4th at Berlin in 14:39.22, while Worku was only 10th in the race. Adere was 8th in Berlin and 2nd at the Goodwill Games. Dong Yanmei was 4th in the Worlds, won two titles, East Asian Games and World Universities, in slow times and then won the Chinese National Games in 14:51.58 and just takes 10th ranking ahead of Gabriela Szabo, who was 2nd in Oslo but slipped to 8th at the Worlds.

1. Yegorova, 2. Radcliffe, 3. Wami,
4. Zadorozhnaya, 5. Masai, 6. Domínguez,
7. Tomashova, 8. Worku, 9. Dong,
10. Mikitenko

10,000 Metres

DERARTU TULU added World gold to her two Olympic golds as she sprinted to victory over her teammates Berhane Adere and Gete Wami at Edmonton. Fourth was Paula Radcliffe, who once again ran admirably, but she left her drive for home too late to have much chance of shaking off her pursuers. The altitude there is not conducive to fast distance times, and Tulu's winning time was 31:48.81; she ranks as only 15th fastest of the year with her 31:48.19 win at the Goodwill Games, but is the obvious choice for top ranking. Adere won her other 10,000m race, 31:32.70 at the Lille meeting, but Wami did not run another. Radcliffe's 30:55.80 to win the European Challenge (from Irina Mikitenko 31:29.55) was much the year's fastest time, followed by Asmae Leghzaoui's 31:16.94 at the Mediterranean Games.

The Romanian champion Mihaela Botezan was 5th, Lyudmila Petrova 6th, and Leghzaoui 7th in Edmonton, and 10th placer Lyudmila Biktasheva also gets in the top ten as she had two other good runs – 31:30.6 to beat Petrova by 40 seconds at the Russian Championships, and 4th at the Goodwill Games, where Ayelech Worku was 2nd, as she was also at Lille, and Susie Power 3rd. Restituta Joseph was 3rd and Leah Malot 4th at Lille, but Joseph had no other races while Malot also won at Mito ahead of World 8th placer Yamna Belkacem. Power ran the year's fourth fastest time to win the Zátopek race in December. Dong Yanmei won the Chinese National Games in 31:43.59 and and also won the East Asian and World Universities titles.

1. Tulu, 2. Adere, 3. Wami, 4. Radcliffe,
5. Leghzaoui, 6. Worku, 7. Botezan,
8. Power, 9. Biktasheva, 10. Malot

Half Marathon

PAULA RADCLIFFE retained her world title and improved her European record to 66:47. That was the fastest time of the year, apart from those run by the first two in the slightly downhill Lisbon race in April, when Susan Chepkemei ran the fastest ever time (in any conditions) of 65:44 and Lornah Kiplagat was 2nd in 66:34. Chepkemei also won at Egmond and in the Great North Run, but was 49 seconds behind

Radcliffe in taking the world silver medal. Berhane Adere was only 18th at Lisbon but took the World bronze ahead of Mizuki Noguchi, who also won at Yamaguchi and Nagoya and in the East Asian Champs and was second to Lidia Simon at Sapporo, and Jelena Prokopcuka.

Derartu Tulu was third in both Lisbon and Great North Run, and Tegla Loroupe was 4th and Edith Masai 5th in Lisbon. Masai went on to win at Nice in 67:03. Catherine Ndereba won both her half marathons – at The Hague (where she was the sixth woman to break 68 in 2001) and Philadelphia – and Elana Meyer had a consistent season, with two wins in Japan, 7th at Lisbon and 6th in the Worlds.

1. Radcliffe, 2. Chepkemei, 3. Noguchi,
4. Kiplagat, 5. Tulu, 6. Masai, 7. Ndereba,
8. Adere, 9. Meyer, 10. Prokopcuka

Marathon

KEENLY ANTICIPATED for several years, the age of sub-2:20 women's marathon running arrived when Naoko Takahashi broke through to run 2:19:46 in Berlin. Just a week later Catherine Ndereba ran 2:18:47 in Chicago; as she also won in Boston (2:22:35) and Takahashi had no other marathons, Ndereba takes top ranking, reversing the positions of 2000. The London marathon had the greatest depth of times, with a record 12 women under 2:30 and the top five: Derartu Tulu (2:23:57), Svetlana Zakharova, Joyce Chepchumba, Lidia Simon and Elfenesh Alemu under 2:25. Simon went on to win the World title from Reiko Tosa, Zakharova, Yoko Shibui (winner in Osaka) and Sonja Oberem. Tulu ran no more marathons in 2001, and thus the opportunity for a higher ranking, but Zakharova and Chepchumba were 3rd and 4th in New York behind Margaret Okayo and Susan Chepkemei, who had respectively won at San Diego and Rotterdam. Alemu did not finish in Edmonton but came back for 2nd in Chicago. The Beijing Marathon, won by Liu Min 2:23:37, almost matched London with five under 2:25 and 11 under 2:30, but the top women did not run other major races.

1. Takahashi, 2. Ndereba, 3. Tulu. 4. Okayo,
5. Simon, 6. Chepkemei, 7. Zakharova,
8. Shibui, 9. Tosa, 10. Alemu

3000 Metres Steeplechase

NOT YET a Championship event, the world record for this new women's event was improved by nearly 15 seconds when Justyna Bak ran 9:25.31 in Nice and national and area records similarly tumbled. The event has, however, not become as rapidly popular as the other new women's events of recent years, pole vault, triple jump and hammer. The three fastest of the year all had only two races at the event. Bak also won at Poznan, Melissa Rollison set a world junior record of 9:30.70 to win at the Goodwill Games at Brisbane, and Irene Limika was second at both Nice and Brisbane.

These two races provided the top seven times of the year. Elizabeth Jackson was 3rd and 4th and the former world record holder Cristina Iloc-Casandra 5th in both. Russian champion Yekaterina Volkova was 3rd in Brisbane and had been 2nd to Bak in Poznan and third in the UK-US-Russia match behind Jackson and Tara Krzywicki. Laurence Duquénoy and Elodie Olivarès were 4th and 6th respectively in Nice and 1st and 2nd in the French Champs, but Olivarès easily reversed the positions at the Mediterranean Games.The ninth runner under 9:50 was Lisa Nye, who beat Jackson for the US title and was 6th in Brisbane

1. Bak, 2. Rollison, 3. Limika, 4. Jackson,
5. Iloc-Casandra, 6. Volkova, 7. Olivarès,
8. Duquénoy, 9. Nye, 10. Krzywicki

100 Metres Hurdles

ANJANETTE KIRKLAND became the world champion indoors and out – and yet on both occasions she started in an outside lane, as she was but fifth fastest in the semis of the World Indoor 60mh and seventh fastest in the World outdoor 100mh. In the latter she made a dramatic improvement of her pb from 12.63 to 12.42. This was, amazingly her only victory of the outdoor season. She was third to Gail Devers and Jenny Adams at the US Championships, only making the Worlds team by 0.01 over Donica Merriman, but had good runs in 2nd place at Stockholm, Monaco and Zürich and was third at the Goodwill Games to Devers and Adams. Devers beat her 4-1 and is top for the third successive year.

Olga Shishigina took the bronze medal in Edmonton from European Cup winner Svetla Dimitrova, Adams, Dianne Rose-Henley and Linda Ferga. Of these athletes, Adams had the best record on the GP circuit, with five successive wins prior to the Worlds, but she lost 1-2 to Shishigina. Delloreen Ennis-London won six successive races before 2nd to Adams at Lausanne, but was then suffered an injury in Paris, which ended her season; she beat Devers 2-0 and Dimitrova 1-0.

Glory Alozie changed nationality from Nigeria to Spain and was ineligible for the Worlds, but beat Shishigina 2-0 although 0-2 against Ennis-London and 0-4 against Adams. There was little between those contesting the final places in the rankings, but Rose-Henley beat Ferga 2-0, who in turn was 3-1 v Svetlana Laukhova, who was 3-1 v Bridgette Foster. The European under-23 champion Susanna Kallur improved during the year from 13.02 to 12.74 (in the heats in Edmonton).

Most times under 12.80: Adams 6+2w, Devers & Shishigina 6, Ennis-London 5, Foster 4+1w, Kirkland 4, Dimitrova 3+1w, Alozie & Perdita Felicien 3.

1. Devers, 2. Kirkland, 3. Adams,
4. Shishigina, 5. Ennis-London,
6. Dimitrova, 7. Alozie, 8. Rose-Henley,
9. Ferga, 10. Laukhova

400 Metres Hurdles

STANDARDS IN this event have fallen in recent years. Nezha Bidouane, however, ran much the fastest of the year, 53.34, in regaining her world title. She fell back to only 5th at the Goodwill Games and GP Final, but otherwise won 8 of her 9 finals, her only other loss being to Tatyana Tereshchuk at Oslo. Unfortunately Tereshchuk did not compete at Edmonton, but apart from losing 3-4 to Bidouane had positive records against all others, including 5-2, 7-1 and 6-3 against the World 2-3-4, Yuliya Nosova, Daimí Pernía and Tonja Buford-Bailey respectively.

Tereshchuk and Buford-Bailey went 1-2 and 2-1 at the Goodwill Games and GP Final, where Nosova and Sandra Glover (World 8th) each took a third and an eighth place. Debbie-Ann Parris (World 5th) was 4th at each and beat Deon Hemmings (World 7th) at the Jamaican Champs; she was also 5-3 v Nosova. Ionela Tîrlea was 6th at the Worlds and beat Hemmings 2-0 and Glover 6-2. Surita Febbraio completes the rankings with much better times than others, although, after good form in South Africa and the early European season, she fell back at the end of the year. Song Yinlan tied the Asian record of 53.96 at the Chinese National Games, but did not have good enough other results to back that up.

Most times under 55.0: Parris 12, Tereshchuk 11, Bidouane, Buford-Bailey & Nosova 10, Pernía 5, Tîrlea 4, Febbraio 3. Glover ran just one such time compared to 12 times in 2000.

1. Bidouane, 2. Tereshchuk, 3. Buford-Bailey,
4. Nosova, 5. Parris, 6. Pernía, 7. Tîrlea,
8. Hemmings, 9. Glover, 10. Febbraio

High Jump

WHILE NOT jumping as high as in 1999, Hestrie Cloete put behind her the disappointment of failing to make the World final that year by taking the gold medal this time. Although she lost in her first six meetings in Europe, she ended the season in style, with further wins in London, Zürich, Goodwill Games and GP Final. Inga Babakova and Kajsa Bergqvist took the World silver and bronze medals with Bergqvist ahead 6-5 outdoors and Babakova 3-2 indoors; Bergqvist took the World Indoor gold from Babakova, both clearing 2.00. For the rankings I swapped the order of the World 4th and 5th placers as Venelina Veneva (also World Indoor bronze) lost 2-7 to Vita Palamar (and 1-2 indoors).

Amy Acuff was 4th in the World Indoors and although slipping to 10= in Edmonton was, for instance, 6-1 against the junior Blanka Vlasic, who was the World 6th placer. Vlasic, however, beat Dora Györffy, World 7= with Monica Iagar, 5-2. Veneva led the world lists with 2.04 (4 competitions over 2.00) from Babakova 2.03 (5 + 1 indoors), Cloete 2.01 (3), Bergqvist (1+1i) and Györffy 2.00 (1). On outdoor form Olga Kaliturina beat Iagar 4-1 and Russian champion Yekaterina Aleksandrova 2-1, but was beaten in the European Cup by Susan Jones. There was little between this last group and Yelena Gulyayeva.

Most competitions over 1.95m (outdoors/in): Bergqvist 14/5, Babakova 14/4, Cloete & Palamar 10/1, Veneva 9/3, Acuff 6/2, Aleksandrova 4/-, Györffy 3/1

1. Cloete, 2. Babakova, 3. Bergqvist,
4. Palamar, 5. Veneva, 6. Acuff, 7. Vlasic,
8. Györffy, 9. Kaliturina (10), 10. Iagar (9 inc. indoors).

Pole Vault

STACY DRAGILA advanced the world record indoors to 4.70 and outdoors to 4.81. She was only 4th in the World Indoors but won a great contest outdoors against Svetlana Feofanova as both cleared 4.75 in Edmonton, well clear of the 4.55 with which Monika Pyrek and Tatiana Grigorieva were 3rd and 4th. Dragila won 14/15 outdoors and 8/10 indoors and Feofanova, who set European records indoors at 4.64 and 4.65 and outdoors at 4.57, 4.60, 4.62, 4.70 and 4.75, won 9/10 indoors and 6/14, placing 2nd to Dragila seven times. The big two were 1st and 2nd at both Goodwill Games and GP Final, with Pyrek 4th on each occasion (and Grigorieva and Kellie Suttle taking the third places). Indoors Pavla Hamácková won the world title and Feofanova and Suttle shared silver.

Pyrek won the European U23 title and beat Grigorieva 2-1. Gao Shuying was 5th in Edmonton and won the World Universities title and Suttle was clearly the second best American despite missing Edmonton after 8= at the US Champs; she beat the US third-placer Mary Sauer 7-2 outdoors and was 8-4 against another top American, Mel Mueller. Anzhela Balakhonova had a disappointing season, not clearing a height at the World Indoors or making the final of the Worlds outdoors. Yvonne Buschbaum was 6th and 7th in the World Championships and had a better sequence of marks than the World 6th placer, Thórey Elisdóttir. Hamácková, 8th in Edmonton, was 3-3 (and 2-1 indoors) with the European Junior champion Yelena Isinbayeva, and also 3-2 indoors and 1-3 against Buschbaum. Others to get close to the top ten were the World 9th and 10th placers, Janine Whitlock and Carolin

Hingst, and Annika Becker, who was German champion and European U23 silver medallist, but a non-qualifier at Edmonton.

Most competitions over 4.40m (outdoors/in, exhibitions = ex): Dragila 15/10, Feofanova 13/10, Pyrek 9+1ex, Suttle 8/4, Hamácková 7/5, Buschbaum 7/3, Grigorieva 7/-, Sauer 6/-, Isinbayeva 4/2, Balakhonova 3/3, Yelena Belyakova 2/4, Mueller 3+1ex, Elisdóttir 1/3.

1. Dragila, 2. Feofanova, 3. Pyrek,
4. Grigorieva, 5, Gao (6), 6. Suttle (5),
7. Buschbaum (8), 8. Isinabyeva (9),
9. Sauer (-), 10. Elisdóttir (10),
10. Hamácková (7 inc. indoors).

Long Jump

FOR MUCH of the year Fiona May was below her usual standard, and indeed only once exceeded 6.80 (at Thessaloniki when she jumped 6.92 behind Tatyana Kotova's 7.00). But May was superb at the World Championships, as she had five jumps in the final over 6.80, headed by 7.02w and two jumps at 6.97. She thus regained the title she had won in 1995, after 3rd in 1997 and 2nd in 1999. Overall May won 10 of her 17 outdoor competitions and she was also 4th at the World Indoors with 6.86, behind Dawn Burrell, Kotova and Niurka Montalvo. Kotova, only a centimetre behind May in Edmonton, was the only other 7m jumper in 2001 – and she had four competitions at that level, headed by 7.12 in Turin (May 3rd at 6.75). and beat May 3-2 overall.

But that might not be quite enough to take top ranking, especially as she was 3rd behind Eunice Barber and May in Zürich and was 3rd also at the Goodwill Games. Barber, who did not compete in the individual event in Edmonton, won 4/5 at long jump and apart from that big win in Zürich (6.97) was 2nd to Heike Drechsler in the European Cup. Drechsler was injured at the Worlds, where places 3-8 went to Montalvo, Tünde Vaszi, Valentina Gotovska, Niki Xánthou, Maggi and Lyudmila Galkina.

Elva Goulbourne was 10th, her only loss of the year, in which she won Jamaican and CAC titles. Olga Rublyova did not qualify for the final, but had been 2nd at the Russian Championships to Kotova, ahead of Galkina. Maggi won the World Universities and Goodwill Games titles and beat both Vaszi and Gotovska 3-2. Galkina was much better indoors than out. Burrell, after winning 4/5 indoors, was unable to compete outdoors through injury, and Erica Johansson was able to compete only three times. Marion Jones did not compete at the long jump in 2001.

Most competitions over 6.75m (outdoors/in): Kotova 8/3, May 7/1, Maggi 6, Montalvo 3+4w/3, Rublyova 3+1w, Drechsler 2/1, Gotovska, Goulbourne & Vaszi 2+1w

1. May, 2. Kotova, 3. Barber (4), 4. Montalvo (3), 5. Maggi, 6. Vaszi (8), 7. Gotovska (9), 8. Galkina (6), 9. Goulbourne (-),
10. Rublyova(-). Burrell (7), Drechsler (10). In brackets are changes including indoor form.

Triple Jump

TATYANA LEBEDEVA had a great year, including the only 15m plus jumps of the year – 15.00 to win the Russian indoor title and 15.11 and 15.25 in Edmonton where she won the World title by the massive margin of 65cm from Françoise Mbango. Lebedeva won 4/7 indoors and 13/16 outdoors. Although she slipped to third at Edmonton, Tereza Marinova was clearly second best; she beat Lebedeva for the World Indoor title and won 2/4 indoors and 9/13 outdoors. The former Cuban now competing for Italy, Magdelin Martínez, beat Mbango 3-2, but was 4th in Edmonton and also 4th to Mbango's 3rd at the GP Final (1. Marinova, 2. Lebedeva).

Although she was only 12th in Edmonton, Natalya Safronova ranks next; she was 2nd to Lebedeva in the European Cup and World Universities Games and was 4-0 against Yelena Oleynikova, who was 2nd in the Russian Champs, 3rd at the World Universities and 5th in both Goodwill Games and GP Final, although 14th at the Worlds. Oleynikova was 4-3 v Yelena Govorova. The women who were 5th to 8th in Edmonton (Heli Koivula, Cristina Nicolau, Ashia Hansen, Trecia Smith) had weaker overall seasons. Hansen beat Koivula 3-1. Fifth on the world list outdoors at 14.60 was Nadezhda Bazhenova, 6th in the Russian Champs. Indoors, Yelena Lebedenko jumped 14.83 and beat Lebedeva 2-1, but outdoors her best was 14.17. Huang Qiuyan set an Asian record of 14.72 at the Chinese National Games, but her next best competition was 13.99.

Most competitions over 14.40m (outdoors/in): Lebedeva 16+1w/6, Marinova 9+2w/3, Martínez 8+1w, Mbango 5, Oleynikova 3+1w, Safronova 2+1w/2, Nicolau 1+1w/1

1. Lebedeva, 2. Marinova, 3. Mbango,
4. Martínez, 5. Safronova, 6. Oleynikova,
7. Govorova (9), 8. Bazhenova (10),
9. Nicolau (7), 10. Hansen. – Rogova (8 inc. indoors).

Shot

YANINA KOROLCHIK maintained her record as a formidable big meeting competitor as she won the World title with a pb 20.61. As she had four of the top seven performances of the outdoor season, her top ranking is assured, although she ended with four competitions below 18m, including 5th places at Goodwill Games and GP Final. The Germans Astrid Kumbernuss and Nadine Kleinert-Schmitt, had the best depth of performances, but Larisa Peleshenko headed the world lists indoors (20.12) and outdoors (20.79). Kleinert-Schmitt and Vita Pavlysh took silver and bronze in Edmonton, and behind them in 4th to 9th came: Peleshenko, Irina Korzhanenko, Kumbernuss, Nadezhda Ostapchuk, Yumileidi Cumbá and Svetlana Krivelyova.

Pavlysh returned from her drugs ban and also won the EAAA Throws meet in Nice from Peleshenko, but otherwise had just two competitions at home in Ukraine. Peleshenko won at the Goodwill Games from Cumbá, Krystyana Zabawska and Kumbernuss, and Kumbernuss won the Grand Prix Final from Ostapchuk and Krivelyova. Lyudmila Sechko, 4th in the Russian Champs behind Peleshenko, Krivelyova and Korzhanenko, beat both Cumbá and the World 10th placer, Zabawska, 2-0. Sechko was also 3rd in Nice and 2nd at Rüdlingen (behind Ostapchuk and ahead of Korolchik and Korzhanenko).

Adding indoor competition, then picture changes and Peleshenko's record takes her past the others for top ranking. She won 3/3 and took the World Indoor title from Ostapchuk, Krivelyova, Kleinert-Schmitt and Cumbá, with Korolchik only 9th.

Most competitions over 20m/19m (indoors and out): Peleshenko 3/6, Korolchik 3/5, Krivelyova 1/7, Kleinert-Schmitt and Kumbernuss 0/10, Korzhanenko, Ostapchuk and Sechko 0/5, Pavlysh 0/4, Cumbá 0/2.

1. Korolchik (2), 2. Kleinert-Schmitt (3),
3. Pavlysh (4), 4. Peleshenko (1),
5. Kumbernuss, 6. Ostapchuk,
7. Krivelyova, 8. Korzhanenko, 9. Sechko,
10. Cumbá. In brackets are changes including indoor form.

Discus

THE TOP three discus throwers were closely matched. Nicoleta Grasu had the best depth of marks (8 of top 20), but she took the bronze medal behind Natalya Sadova and Ellina Zvereva at the Worlds. Zvereva only had one other competition that we know of – but that was the Goodwill Games where Sadova and Franka Dietzsch took the other medals. Sadova (world leader at 68.57) won 7/11 overall and Grasu 13/18. Dietzsch was 4th at Edmonton and also won at the European Cup from Sadova and Grasu. Anastasiá Kelesídou was 5th in Edmonton, and also won the Balkan Champs and at Patrá, but that was her whole season. Another to compete too rarely was Irina Yatchenko; she was fourth on the world list but was 10th in Edmonton. 6th to 9th in the Worlds – Seilala Sua, Vera Pospisilová, Kris Kuehl and Anja Möllenbeck – all had solid enough seasons for top ten rankings, with the final spot disputed by Ekateríni Vóggoli, Suzy Powell, Valentina Ivanova and Vladimira Racková.

Most competitions over 64m: Grasu 13, Sadova 10, Dietzsch 4.

1. Sadova, 2. Zvereva, 3. Grasu,
4. Dietzsch, 5. Kelesídou, 6. Sua, 7. Kuehl,
8. Möllenbeck, 9. Pospisilová, 10. Vóggoli.

Hammer

IT IS becoming a habit – Olga Kuzenkova comes into the major championship as the favourite and ends up with the silver medal. So it was again in 2001 when she won the silver medal at the World Championships to add to those she had won in 1997 World Universities, 1998 Europeans, 1999 Worlds and 2000 Olympics. Yet she remains clearly top of the rankings, with six of the top seven performances of the year and 11 of the 20 over 70m and 11 wins in 16 competitions. Her conqueror at Edmonton was Yipsi Moreno, whose 70.65 was her third CAC record of the year. The bronze medal was taken by Bronwyn Eagles and 4th was the Olympic champion and still a junior Kamila Skolimowska, who ended the year in great style with a 70.31 win at the Goodwill Games and 71.71 world junior record to win the Grand Prix Final, but was 1-2 down to Moreno overall and 2-2 with Eagles. In those two big end of season events Kuzenkova was 2nd and 3rd. Manuela Montebrun (World 5th) was 3rd in the Goodwill Games, with Moreno, Eagles, Gubkina and Dawn Ellerbe 4th to 7th.

At the Grand Prix Final, Eagles was 2nd, and 4th to 6th were: Ellerbe, Gubkina and Olga Tsander (World 10th). Montebrun won at the World University Games from Moreno, Gubkina, and Tsander, and was 3-1 against Lorraine Shaw, the world sixth placer. Ellerbe won her sixth US title, but narrowly missed qualifying for the final at the Worlds, and Gubkina was another to miss the cut. Florence Ezeh, Ivana Brkljacic (European Junior champion), Kirsten Münchow and Tsander were 7th to 10th at the Worlds. Tsander beat Münchow 3-2 and these two were 1-2 at the European Cup, with Shaw and Montebrun 3rd and 4th.

Ezeh won NCAA and Mediterranean Games titles, but was 7th at the World Universities. Katalin Divós would have ranked 7th but failed a drugs test; she was 2-4 down to Shaw in her competitions to early July.

Most competitions over 68m: Kuzenkova 16, Eagles 9, Montebrun 7, Moreno & Skolimowska 5, Ellerbe 3, (Divós 6)

1. Kuzenkova, 2. Moreno, 3. Skolimowska,
4. Eagles, 5. Montebrun, 6. Shaw,
7. Ellerbe, 8. Tsander, 9. Münchow, 10. Ezeh

Javelin

OSLEIDYS MENÉNDEZ had a brilliant season and at Rethimnó on 1 July became the first woman to throw the new specification javelin over 70m (with 71.54). She started with 63.48 (her worst winning throw of the year) and won 11 of her 13 competitions, including World, World Universities, Goodwill Games and Cuban titles. She lost once in March to Xiomara Rivero (World 7th) and once in June to Sonia Bisset (World 3rd), who were 2nd and 3rd to her in the Cuban Championships. As usual Mirela Tzelíli competed sparingly, winning three times in Greece and competing elsewhere just twice – but then she won at the European Cup 1A and took the World silver medal. Nikola Tomecková was 4th at the Worlds and then came second at both World Universities and Goodwill Games. Mikaela Ingberg and Tatyana Shikolenko were 3rd and 4th in the latter event, having been 6th and 9th at the Worlds.

Tomecková also won at the European Cup Super League from German champion Steffi Nerius (World 5th), Italian champion Claudia Coslovich (World 11th) and Russian champion Shikolenko (World 9th). The final ranking position was between Yekaterina Ivakina and Nikolett Szabó (2-2 on win-loss) and the World 8th placer Aggelíki Tsiolakoúdi. Overall there was a dearth of top-class competition, as the javelin was not a GP event this year.

Most competitions over 62m: Menéndez 14, Tomecková 8, Bisset 7, Shikolenko 6, Coslovich 5, Nerius 4, Tzelíli 3, (drugs dq – Ana Mirela Termure 7)

1. Menéndez, 2. Tzelíli, 3. Bisset,
4. Tomecková, 5. Nerius, 6. Ingberg,
7. Shikolenko, 8. Rivero, 9. Coslovich,
10. Szabó

Heptathlon

THE TWO best heptathletes in the world had mixed fortune in 2001. Olympic champion Denise Lewis did not feel fit enough to take on the event, and Eunice Barber made the gross error of having three no throws in the shot in Edmonton.

She had started very well in the first two events and looked on the way to take the gold medal by a big margin; earlier in the year she won at Götzis with the top score of the year, 6736. Yelena Prokhorova did not quite match that, as her 6694 won the World title, but her overall record earns her top ranking.

She contested three other heptathlons, and was second in each: to Barber at Götzis, to Natalya Roshchupkina in the Goodwill Games and to Shelia Burrell at Talence. Natalya Sazanovich (5th Götzis, 2nd Worlds and 3rd GWG) was 2-1 over Roshchupkina (3rd Götzis, 4th Worlds), and Burrell (3rd Worlds) beat Roshchupkina 2-0. Irina Belova, 4th at Götzis, was the only other woman to score more than Karin Ertl's 6365 but was 3rd Ratingen, 8th Worlds and 5th Talence while Ertl, 6th at Götzis was 2nd Ratingen 5th Worlds, 1st German Champs. DeDee Nathan beat Burrell to take the US title, but was 7th at the Worlds and 4th GWG. Liga Klavina, Svetlana Sokolova and Austra Skujyté won the European U23 medals, but whereas Klavina did not contest any other heptathlons, Sokolova won at the European Cup and Skujyté won 6th in the Worlds and 2nd to Jane Jamieson at the World University Games.

1. Prokhorova, 2. Barber, 3. Sazanovich,
4. Burrell, 5. Roshchupkina, 6. Ertl,
7. Belova, 8. Nathan, 9. Sokolova,
10. Klavina.

20 Kilometres Walk

OLIMPIADA IVANOVA had an outstanding season as she won all her five 20km races, with world records on the road, 1:24:50 for the Russian winter title at Adler, and track, 1:26:52.3 at the Goodwill Games. In between these races she won at the European Cup, La Coruña and World Championships. The 2nd, 3rd and 4th fastest in the world lists came from the Chinese National Games when Wang Yan, Wang Liping and Liu Hongyu took the medals. And 5th-6th-7th fastest came at the European Cup race from Natalya Fedoskina, Elisabetta Perrone and Erica Alfridi. The two Italians were 3rd and 4th at the Worlds but Fedoskina was disqualified there.

The world silver medallist, Valentina Tsybulskaya, however, fared less well elsewhere as she was 8th in the European Cup and 4th at the Goodwill Games, where Yelena Nikolayeva (5 Eur Cup, 1 Russian, dq Worlds) took the silver and Eva Pérez the bronze. Perrone also beat Alfridi to take the Italian title but the order was reversed at the Mediterranean Games. Tatyana Sibileva was 2nd and Fedoskina 3rd in Adler.

Susana Feitor had three sub 1:30 times, but was disqualified in both her major races, at the European Cup and Worlds, and Kjersti Plätzer, the winner at Leamington and Eisenhüttenstadt (where Melanie Seeger, Worlds 7th, was 2nd), also failed in those races. However, Maria Vasco was 7th and 5th and Norica Címpean, 6th in both European Cup and Worlds.

M Guadeloupe Sánchez won in Mexico City in April with Jane Saville (dq Worlds) 2nd, Alfridi 3rd, Perrone 4th, Cîmpean 5th and Vasco 7th, but was 9th in the Worlds. Gao Hongmiao and Wang Liping set 1:28 times in 1st and 2nd at the Chinese Championships, but did not compete in Edmonton, while the third placer Liu Hongyu win the East Asian title and was disqualified in Edmonton. Gao was only 12th at the National Games.

1. Ivanova, 2, Perrone, 3. Alfridi,
4. Nikolayeva, 5. Tsybulskaya, 6. Fedoskina,
7. Wang Yan, 8. Wang Liping, 9. Liu Hongyu, 10. Vasco

IAAF WORLD RANKINGS

AFTER A trial year in 2000, the IAAF World Rankings are now updated and issued every week, with the intention of giving statisticians, journalists and fans an image of how the leading athletes of our sport are performing.
Full rankings can be viewed at www.iaaf.org

Overall Ranking List – as at 31 December 2001

Event shown is main one, but athletes have often won points at other events as well. e.g. Decathletes also at indoor heptathlon, 5000m runners at 3000m etc.

Rank	*Name*	*Nat/Points*		*Event*
Men				
1	Hicham El Guerrouj	MAR	1466	1500m
2	Maurice Greene	USA	1449	100m
3	Tim Montgomery	USA	1443	100m
4	Allen Johnson	USA	1431	110mh
5	Anier García	CUB	1425	110mh
6	André Bucher	SUI	1421	800m
7	Reuben Kosgei	KEN	1416	3000mSt
8=	Bernard Lagat	KEN	1415	1500m
8=	Brahim Boulami	MAR	1415	3000mSt
10	Tomás Dvorák	CZE	1412	Dec
11	Felix Sánchez	DOM	1408	400mh
12	Jan Zeležny	CZE	1405	JT
13	Virgilijus Alekna	LTU	1395	DT
14=	Erki Nool	EST	1393	Dec
14=	Yuriy Borzakovskiy	RUS	1393	800m
14=	Iván Pedroso	CUB	1393	LJ
17	Ato Boldon	TRI	1392	100m
18	Wilson Boit Kipketer	KEN	1391	3000mSt
19	Richard Limo	KEN	1388	5000m
20=	John Godina	USA	1387	SP,DT
20=	Bernard Williams	USA	1387	100/200m
22	Jonathan Edwards	GBR	1381	TJ
23	Bernard Barmasai	KEN	1380	3000mSt
24=	William Chirchir	KEN	1375	1500m
24=	Paul Bitok	KEN	1375	5000m
26	Shawn Crawford	USA	1374	200m
27	Koji Murofushi	JPN	1373	HT
28	Angelo Taylor	USA	1370	400mh
29	Dmitriy Markov	AUS	1366	PV
29	Hailu Mekonnen	ETH	1366	5000m
31	John Kibowen	KEN	1364	5000m
32=	Kipkurui Misoi	KEN	1362	3000mSt
32=	Sammy Kipketer	KEN	1362	5000m
32=	Million Wolde	ETH	1362	5000m
32=	Terrence Trammell	USA	1362	110mh
36=	Ali Ezzine	MAR	1360	3000mSt
36=	Wilfred Bungei	KEN	1360	800m
38	Benjamin Limo	KEN	1359	5000m
39	Adam Nelson	USA	1358	SP
40=	Kostadínos Gatsioúdis	GRE	1356	JT
40=	Fabrizio Mori	ITA	1356	400mh
42	Christian Malcolm	GBR	1355	100/200m
43	Jeff Hartwig	USA	1354	PV
44	Konstadínos Kedéris	GRE	1353	100/200m
45	Luke Kipkosgei	KEN	1352	5000m
46=	Driss Maazouzi	FRA	1351	1500m
46=	Raymond Yator	KEN	1351	3000mSt
48=	Dwain Chambers	GBR	1348	100m
48=	Szymon Ziólkowski	POL	1348	HT
50	Noah Ngeny	KEN	1347	1500m
Women				
1	Stacy Dragila	USA	1462	PV
2	Marion Jones	USA	1445	100/200m
3	Olga Yegorova	RUS	1427	5000m
4	Maria Lurdes Mutola	MOZ	1411	800m
5	Gabriela Szabo	ROM	1410	1500/5000m
6=	Osleidys Menéndez	CUB	1399	JT
6=	Tatyana Lebedeva	RUS	1399	TJ
8	Violeta Szekely	ROM	1398	1500m
9	Svetlana Feofanova	RUS	1396	PV
10	Hestrie Cloete	RSA	1393	HJ
11=	Gete Wami	ETH	1390	5/10,000m
11=	Nezha Bidouane	MAR	1390	400mh
13	Anjanette Kirkland	USA	1388	100mh
14	Inga Babakova	UKR	1387	HJ
15	Gail Devers	USA	1386	100mh
16=	Stephanie Graf	AUT	1382	800m
16=	Yelena Prokhorova	RUS	1382	Hep
18	Zhanna Pintusevich	UKR	1381	100m
19=	Paula Radcliffe	GBR	1373	5/10,000m
19=	Kajsa Bergqvist	SWE	1373	HJ
21	Chandra Sturrup	BAH	1371	100m
22	Tereza Marinova	BUL	1368	TJ
23=	Olga Shishigina	KAZ	1362	100mh
23=	Natalya Gorelova	RUS	1362	1500m
25	Natalya Sazanovich	BLR	1360	Hep
26	Tatyana Kotova	RUS	1359	LJ
27	Yelena Zadorozhnaya	RUS	1354	5000m
28=	Debbie Ferguson	BAH	1353	100/200m
28=	Carla Sacramento	POR	1353	1500m
30	Ana Guevara	MEX	1351	400m
31	Edith Masai	KEN	1350	5000m
32	Tatyana Tereshchuk	UKR	1349	400mh
33	Ekateríni Thánou	GRE	1348	100m
34=	Jenny Adams	USA	1347	100mh
34=	Kellie White	USA	1347	100/200m
36	Chryste Gaines	USA	1346	100m
37	Fiona May	ITA	1345	LJ
38	Yuliya Nosova	RUS	1342	400mh
39	Tonja Buford-Bailey	USA	1340	400mh
40	Berhane Adere	ETH	1339	5/10,000m
41	Daimí Pernía	CUB	1338	400mh
42	Debbie-Ann Parris	JAM	1337	400mh
43=	Vita Palamar	UKR	1335	HJ
43=	Venelina Veneva	BUL	1335	HJ
45	Tatyana Tomashova	RUS	1334	1500/5000m
46	Juliet Campbell	JAM	1327	200m
47	Kelly Holmes	GBR	1325	800m
48	Irina Mikitenko	GER	1322	5000m
49	Marta Domínguez	ESP	1321	5000m
50=	Lorraine Graham-Fenton	JAM	1320	400m
50=	Monika Pyrek	POL	1320	PV
50=	Glory Alozie	ESP	1320	100mh

Event Ranking Lists

100m (50m - 55m - 60m)

1 Maurice Greene USA 1448
2 Tim Montgomery USA 1443
3 Ato BoldonTRI 1388
4 Bernard Williams USA 1363
5 Dwain Chambers GBR 1348
6= Francis Obikwelu POR 1322
6= Abdul Aziz Zakari GHA 1322
8 Kim Collins SKN 1303
9 Jon Drummond USA 1289
10 Deji Aliu NGR 1285
11 Freddy Mayola CUB 1272
12 Brian Lewis USA 1270
13 Mark Lewis-Francis GBR 1269
14 Tim Harden USA 1260
15=Christian Malcolm GBR 1258
15=Curtis Johnson USA 1258
17 Matt Shirvington AUS 1256
18 Dennis Mitchell USA 1245
19 Nobuharu Asahara JPN 1244
20 Chris Williams JAM 1242

200m

1 Shawn Crawford USA 1374
2 Kostas Kedéris GRE 1352
3 Christian Malcolm GBR 1347
4 Bernard Williams USA 1344
5 Chris Williams JAM 1322
6 Ramon Clay USA 1296
7 Kevin Little USA 1293
8 Stéphane Buckland MRI 1284
9 Francis Obikwelu POR 1282
10 Kim Collins SKN 1266
11 Abdul Aziz Zakari GHA 1265
12 Joshua Johnson USA 1262
13 André D da Silva BRA 1255
14 Patrick van Balkom NED 1253
15 Marlon Devonish GBR 1252
16 Shingo Suetsugu JPN 1216
17 Radek Zachoval CZE 1215
18 Joseph Batangdon CMR 1210
19 Marcin Urbas POL 1208
20 Oumar Loum SEN 1207

400m (300m - 500m Indoor)

1 Greg Haughton JAM 1325
2 Avard Moncur BAH 1318
3 Antonio Pettigrew USA 1275
4 Sanderlei Parrela BRA 1264
5 Michael McDonald JAM 1262
6 Daniel Caines GBR 1261
7 Eric Milazar MRI 1257
8 Hend. Mokganyetsi RSA 1255
9 Ingo Schultz GER 1246
10 Hamdan Al-Bishi KSA 1244
11 Leonard Byrd USA 1239
12 Danny Mcfarlane JAM 1228
13 Tyree Washington USA 1227
14= Milton Campbell USA 1224
14= Davian Clarke JAM 1224
16 David Canal ESP 1223
17 Andrew Pierce USA 1218
18 Jerome Young USA 1217
19 Robert Mackowiak POL 1216
20 Shane Niemi CAN 1206

800m (1000m)

1 André Bucher SUI 1421
2 Yuriy Borzakovskiy RUS 1393
3 Wilfred Bungei KEN 1360
4 William Yiampoy KEN 1339
5 Jean-P Nduwimana BDI 1332
6 Hezekiél Sepeng RSA 1315
7 Joseph Mutua KEN 1308
8 Mbuireni Mulaudzi RSA 1302
9= Glody Dube BOT 1299
9= Nils Schumann GER 1299
11= David Lelei KEN 1283
11= Pawel Czapiewski POL 1283
13= Arth. Hatungimana BDI 1274
13= Noah Ngeny KEN 1274
15 William Chirchir KEN 1260
16 Bram Som NED 1257
17 Kennedy Kimwetich KEN 1253
18 Japheth Kimutai KEN 1250
19 David Kiptoo KEN 1242
20 Johan Botha RSA 1240

1500m (Mile - 2000m)

1 Hicham El Guerrouj MAR 1465
2 Bernard Lagat KEN 1415
3 William Chirchir KEN 1375
4 Driss Maazouzi FRA 1351
5 Noah Ngeny KEN 1347
6 Laban Rotich KEN 1323
7 Benjamin Kipkurui KEN 1321
8 Andrés Díaz ESP 1314
9 Mehdi Baala FRA 1311
10= José A Redolat ESP 1307
10= Rui Silva POR 1307
12 Enock Koech KEN 1305
13 Reyes Estévez ESP 1299
14 Vyach.Shabunin RUS 1295
15 Kevin Sullivan CAN 1291
16 Youssef Baba MAR 1262
17 John Mayock GBR 1256
18 Hudson de Souza BRA 1250
19 Mohamed Khaldi ALG 1249
20 Gert-Jan Liefers NED 1243

5000 – 10,000m (also 3000m, 2M,CC)

1 Richard Limo KEN 1388
2 Paul Bitok KEN 1375
3 Hailu Mekonnen ETH 1366
4 John Kibowen KEN 1364
5= Sammy Kipketer KEN 1362
5= Million Wolde ETH 1362
7 Benjamin Limo KEN 1359
8 Luke Kipkosgei KEN 1352
9 Alberto García ESP 1343
10 Assefa Mezegebu ETH 1338
11 Charles Kamathi KEN 1334
12 Abiyote Abate ETH 1323
13 Mark Bett KEN 1317
14 Kenenisa Bekele ETH 1312
15= Daniel Komen KEN 1310
15= Ismaïl Sghyr FRA 1310
17 Abderrahim Goumri MAR 1293
18 Paul Kosgei KEN 1285
19 Tom Nyariki KEN 1281
20 Benjamin Maiyo KEN 1280

110mh (50mh - 55mh - 60mh)

1 Allen Johnson USA 1431
2 Anier García CUB 1425
3 Terrence Trammell USA 1362
4 Dudley Dorival HAI 1338
5 Larry Wade USA 1337
6 Dominique Arnold USA 1327
7= Yoel Hernández CUB 1325
7= Colin Jackson GBR 1325
9 Stanislavs Olijars LAT 1321
10 Mark Crear USA 1311
11 Dawane Wallace USA 1310
12= Shaun Bownes RSA 1309
12= Robert Kronberg SWE 1309
14 Yevgeniy Pechonkin RUS 1278
15 Chris Phillips USA 1266
16 Elmar Lichtenegger AUT 1264
17= Anthony Jarrett GBR 1246
17= Yunier Hernández CUB 1246
19= Zhivko Videnov BUL 1242
19= Florian Schwarthoff GER 1242

400mh

1 Felix Sánchez DOM 1408
2 Angelo Taylor USA 1370
3 Fabrizio Mori ITA 1356
4 Hadi Al-Somaily KSA 1344
5 Dai Tamesue JPN 1335
6 Pawel Januszewski POL 1316
7 Christ Rawlinson GBR 1303
8 James Carter USA 1295
9 Llewellyn Herbert RSA 1292
10 Eric Thomas USA 1287
11 Stéphane Diagana FRA 1286
12 Marek Plawgo POL 1285
13 Jirí Muéik CZE 1281
14 Boris Gorban RUS 1269
15 Ian Weakley JAM 1246
16 Calvin Davis USA 1239
17 Alwyn Myburgh RSA 1236
18 Neil Gardner JAM 1228
19 Rus. Mashchenko RUS 1226
20 Du'aine T-Ladejo GBR 1219

3000m Steeple (2000mSt)

1 Reuben Kosgei KEN 1416
2 Brahim Boulami MAR 1415
3 Wilson Boit Kipketer KEN 1391
4 Bernard Barmasai KEN 1380
5 Kipkurui Misoi KEN 1362
6 Ali Ezzine MAR 1360
7 Raymond Yator KEN 1351
8 Luis M Martín ESP 1342
9 Stephen Cherono KEN 1341
10= Bouabdallah Tahri FRA 1317
10= Julius Nyamu KEN 1317
12 Antonio Jiménez ESP 1313
13 John Kosgei KEN 1309
14 Elarbi Khattabi MAR 1299
15= John Lagat KEN 1250
15= Khamis S Abdullah QAT 1250
15= Tim Broe USA 1250
18 Abraham Cherono KEN 1238
19 Gaël Pencréach FRA 1231
20 Anthony Famiglietti USA 1230

High Jump
1 Stefan Holm SWE 1323
2 Vyacheslav Voronin RUS 1311
3 Yaroslav Rybakov RUS 1293
4 Staffan Strand SWE 1290
5 Javier Sotomayor CUB 1284
6 Mark Boswell CAN 1279
7= Sergey Klyugin RUS 1267
7= Martin Buss GER 1267
9 Andriy Sokolovskiy UKR 1252
10 Nathan Leeper USA 1247
11 Sergiy Dymchenko UKR 1220
12 Charles Austin USA 1218
13 Abd. Hammad ALG 1204
14 Charles Clinger USA 1200
15 Jan Jankú CZE 1184
16= Aleksandr Kravtsov RUS 1180
16= Kwaku Boateng CAN 1180
18 Oskari Frösén FIN 1179
19 Wolfgang Kreissig GER 1175
20= Grzegorz Sposòb POL 1165
20= Gennadiy Moroz BLR 1165

Pole Vault
1 Dmitriy Markov AUS 1366
2 Jeff Hartwig USA 1354
3= Nick Hysong USA 1341
3= Aleksandr Averbukh ISR 1341
5 Daniel Ecker GER 1330
6 Lawrence Johnson USA 1316
7 Michael Stolle GER 1314
8 Romain Mesnil FRA 1305
9 Viktor Chistyakov AUS 1283
10 Tim Lobinger GER 1279
11 Tye Harvey USA 1278
12 Timothy Mack USA 1261
13 Rich. Spiegelburg GER 1248
14 Adam Kolasa POL 1245
15 Chris Tamminga NED 1240
16 Maxim Tarasov RUS 1235
17 Patrik Kristiansson SWE 1234
18 Stépán Janácek CZE 1229
19 Lars Börgeling GER 1213
20 Okkert Brits RSA 1210

Long Jump
1 Iván Pedroso CUB 1393
2 Sav. Stringfellow USA 1345
3 Kevin Dilworth USA 1314
4 James Beckford JAM 1291
5 Oleks. Lukashevich UKR 1286
6 K Streete-Thompson CAY 1285
7 Hussein Al-Sabee KSA 1279
8 Younès Moudrik MAR 1265
9 Carlos Calado POR 1254
10 Miguel Pate USA 1245
11 Dwight Phillips USA 1243
12 Danila Burkenya RUS 1235
13 Vitaliy Shkurlatov RUS 1229
14 Peter Burge AUS 1228
15 Luis Meliz CUB 1220
16 Melvin Lister USA 1216
17 Cheikh Touré FRA 1201
18 Vladimir Malyavin RUS 1196
19 Gregor Cankar SLO 1193
20 Bogdan Tarus ROM 1190

Triple Jump
1 Jonathan Edwards GBR 1381
2 Christian Olsson SWE 1296
3 Paolo Camossi ITA 1257
4 Larry Achike GBR 1255
5 Charles Friedek GER 1234
6 I Spasovkhodskiy RUS 1232
7 Yoel García CUB 1229
8 Rostislav Dimitrov BUL 1228
9 Andrew Murphy AUS 1227
10 Phillips Idowu GBR 1219
11 Walter Davis USA 1207
12= LaMark Carter USA 1202
12= Fabrizio Donato ITA 1202
14 Michel Calvo CUB 1201
15 Brian Wellman BER 1200
16= Aleks. Glovatskiy BLR 1192
16= Marian Oprea ROM 1192
18 Jadel Gregorio BRA 1188
19 Karl Taillepierre FRA 1178
20 Robert Howard USA 1169

Shot
1 John Godina USA 1384
2 Adam Nelson USA 1358
3 Manuel Martínez ESP 1306
4 Yuriy Belonog UKR 1270
5 Arsi Harju FIN 1260
6 Brad Snyder CAN 1248
7 Janus Robberts RSA 1238
8 Dragan Peric YUG 1230
9= Paolo Dal Soglio ITA 1220
9= Milan Haborák SVK 1220
11 P Chumachenko RUS 1217
12 Conny Karlsson FIN 1216
13 Andy Bloom USA 1214
14 Gheorge Guset ROM 1196
15 Mikulás Konopka SVK 1193
16 John Davis USA 1189
17 Ville Tiisanoja FIN 1188
18 Joachim Olsen DEN 1178
19 Oliver-Sven Buder GER 1173
20 Tepa Reinikainen FIN 1169

Discus
1 Virgilijus Alekna LTU 1395
2 Lars Riedel GER 1337
3 Frantz Kruger RSA 1317
4 Dmitriy Shevchenko RUS 1296
5 Róbert Fazekas HUN 1292
6 Vasiliy Kaptyukh BLR 1289
7 Jason Tunks CAN 1283
8 Adam Setliff USA 1280
9 Michael Möllenbeck GER 1270
10 Aleksandr Tammert EST 1246
11 Zoltán Kövágó HUN 1241
12 John Godina USA 1226
13 Roland Varga HUN 1214
14 Libor Malina CZE 1209
15 Mario Pestano ESP 1197
16 Andy Bloom USA 1194
17 Timo Tompuri FIN 1186
18 Vlad. Dubrovshchik BLR 1172
19 Gábor Máté HUN 1153
20= Doug Reynolds USA 1152
20= Leonid Cherevko BLR 1152
20= Aleks. Borichevskiy RUS 1152

Hammer
1 Koji Murofushi JPN 1373
2 Szymon Ziólkowski POL 1348
3 Nicola Vizzoni ITA 1297
4 Andriy Skvaruk UKR 1277
5= Balázs Kiss HUN 1273
5= Tibor Gécsek HUN 1273
7 Ilya Konovalov RUS 1252
8 Igor Astapkovich BLR 1234
9 Adrián Annus HUN 1231
10 Olli-P Karjalainen FIN 1225
11 Vladislav Piskunov UKR 1213
12 Nicolas Figère FRA 1207
13 David Chaussinaud FRA 1205
14 Oleksiy Krykun UKR 1201
15= Vladimír Maäka CZE 1198
15= Aléx. Papadimitriou GRE 1198
17 Stuart Rendell AUS 1195
18 Aleksey Zagorniy RUS 1189
19= Hrístos Polihroníou GRE 1187
19= Karsten Kobs GER 1187

Javelin
1 Jan Zelezny CZE 1405
2 Kostas Gatsioúdis GRE 1356
3 Aki Parviainen FIN 1338
4 Steve Backley GBR 1301
5 Raymond Hecht GER 1290
6 Boris Henry GER 1289
7 Sergey Makarov RUS 1282
8 Breaux Greer USA 1276
9 Eriks Rags LAT 1271
10 Peter Blank GER 1255
11 Darius Trafas POL 1220
12 Harri Haatainen FIN 1213
13 Björn Lange GER 1186
14 Emeterio González CUB 1168
15 Aleksandr Ivanov RUS 1153
16 Pål Arne Fagernes NOR 1147
17 Andrew Currey AUS 1143
18 Nicholas Nieland GBR 1142
19= Sergey Voynov UZB 1141
19= Gregor Högler AUT 1141

Decathlon (Heptathlon Ind.)
1 Tomás Dvorák CZE 1412
2 Erki Nool EST 1393
3 Roman Sebrle CZE 1331
4 Lev Lobodin RUS 1317
5 Attila Zsivoczky HUN 1296
6 Oleksandr Yurkov UKR 1273
7 Stefan Schmid GER 1255
8 Laurent Hernu FRA 1251
9 Jirí Ryba CZE 1230
10 Mario Aníbal POR 1190
11 Kip Janvrin USA 1176
12 Chiel Warners NED 1175
13 Zsolt Körtösi HUN 1171
14 Phil McMullen USA 1169
15 Mike Maczey GER 1161
16 Klaus Ambrosch AUT 1158
17 Benjamin Jensen NOR 1155
18 Indrek Kaseorg EST 1152
19 Stefan Drews GER 1145
20 Oscar González ESP 1140

Women

100m (50m - 55m - 60m)

1 Marion Jones USA 1416
2 Zhanna Pintusevich UKR 1380
3 Chandra Sturrup BAH 1371
4 Ekateríni Thánou GRE 1348
5 Chryste Gaines USA 1346
6 Debbie Ferguson BAH 1312
7 Mercy Nku NGR 1310
8 Kellie White USA 1296
9 Myriam Mani CMR 1282
10 Sevatheda Fynes BAH 1281
11 Endurance Ojokolo NGR 1276
12 Angela Williams USA 1263
13 Marina Kislova RUS 1254
14 Anzh. Kravchenko UKR 1250
15 Petya Pendareva BUL 1247
16 Susant. Jayasinghe SRI 1240
17 Mary Onyali NGR 1233
18 Nat. Safronnikova BLR 1229
18 Glory Alozie ESP 1229
20= Latasha Jenkins USA 1226
20= Manuela Levorato ITA 1226

200m

1 Marion Jones USA 1335
2= Kellie White USA 1332
2= Debbie Ferguson BAH 1332
4 Juliet Campbell JAM 1327
5 Latasha Jenkins USA 1308
6 Myriam Mani CMR 1292
7 Beverly Mcdonald JAM 1276
8 Susant. Jayasinghe SRI 1273
9 Cydonie Mothersill CAY 1254
10 Mercy Nku NGR 1248
11 Alenka Bikar SLO 1247
12 Nat. Safronnikova BLR 1238
13 Ionela Tîrlea ROM 1228
14 Gabi Rockmeier GER 1219
15 Muriel Hurtis FRA 1218
16 Birgit Rockmeier GER 1217
17 Mary Onyali NGR 1210
18 Nora Güner TUR 1208
19 Aida Diop SEN 1206
20 Lauren Hewitt AUS 1203

400m (300m - 500m Indoor)

1 Ana Guevara MEX 1351
2 Lorraine Fenton JAM 1320
3 Katharine Merry GBR 1314
4= Amy Mbacké Thiam SEN 1308
4= Sandie Richards JAM 1308
4= Grit Breuer GER 1308
7 Nadjina Kaltouma CHA 1295
8 Olesya Zykina RUS 1294
9 Olga Kotlyarova RUS 1281
10 Monique Hennagan USA 1259
11 Michelle Collins USA 1252
12 Heide Seyerling RSA 1250
13 Failat Ogunkoya NGR 1246
14 Suziann Reid USA 1244
15 Mireille Nguingo CMR 1237
16 Olabisi Afolabi NGR 1228
17 Jearl Miles-Clark USA 1222
18 Latasha Colander-Richardson USA 1215

19 Shanta Ghosh GER 1212
20 Catherine Murphy GBR 1206

800m (1000m)

1 Maria Mutola MOZ 1411
2 Stephanie Graf AUT 1382
3 Kelly Holmes GBR 1325
4 Faith Macharia KEN 1311
5 Laetitia Vriesde SUR 1307
6 Natalya Tsyganova RUS 1300
7 Irina Mistyukevich RUS 1294
8 Diane Cummins CAN 1288
9 Olga Raspopova RUS 1283
10 Zulia Calatayud CUB 1282
11 Jolanda Ceplak SLO 1273
12 Helena Fuchsová CZE 1266
13= Ivonne Teichmann GER 1262
13= Svetl. Cherkasova RUS 1262
15 Yelena Afanasyeva RUS 1251
16= Luciana Mendes BRA 1247
16= Natalya Gorelova RUS 1247
18 Argentina Paulino MOZ 1242
19 Lisa John TAN 1232
20 Brigita Langerholc SLO 1228

1500m (Mile - 2000m)

1 Violeta Szekely ROM 1398
2 Natalya Gorelova RUS 1362
3 Carla Sacramento POR 1353
4 Gabriela Szabo ROM 1324
5 S Favor Hamilton USA 1319
6 Lidia Chojecka POL 1311
7 Lyudmila Vasilyeva RUS 1263
8 Hayley Tullett GBR 1260
9 Yuliya Kosenkova RUS 1259
10 Regina Jacobs USA 1257
11 Olga Nelyubova RUS 1252
12 Sarah Schwald USA 1249
13= Daniela Yordanova BUL 1247
13= Yel. Zadorozhnaya RUS 1247
15 Alesya Turova BLR 1240
16 Jacinta Muraguri KEN 1239
17 Abebech Negussie ETH 1236
18 Olga Yegorova RUS 1233
19 Kathleen Friedrich GER 1229
20 N Mérah-Benida ALG 1223

5000 –10,000m (3000m, CC)

1 Olga Yegorova RUS 1427
2 Gete Wami ETH 1390
3 Paula Radcliffe GBR 1373
4 Gabriela Szabo ROM 1365
5 Yel. Zadorozhnaya RUS 1354
6 Edith Masai KEN 1350
7 Berhane Adere ETH 1339
8 Irina Mikitenko GER 1322
9 Marta Domínguez ESP 1317
10 Tatyana Tomashova RUS 1316
11 Asmae Leghzaoui MAR 1307
12 Ayelech Worku ETH 1300
13= Dong Yanmei CHN 1279
13= Leah Malot KEN 1279
15 Ebru Kavaklioglu TUR 1271
16 Rose Cheruiyot KEN 1270
17 Benita Willis AUS 1266
18= Pam. Chepchumba KEN 1261
18= Yamna Belkacem FRA 1261

20 Tegla Loroupe KEN 1249

100mh (50mh - 55mh - 60mh)

1 Anjanette Kirkland USA 1388
2 Gail Devers USA 1385
3 Olga Shishigina KAZ 1362
4 Jenny Adams USA 1347
5 Glory Alozie ESP 1320
6 Del. Ennis-London JAM 1312
7 Linda Ferga FRA 1310
8 Svetlana Laukhova RUS 1301
9 Michelle Freeman JAM 1299
10 N Ramalalanirina FRA 1290
11 Dionne Rose-Henry JAM 1273
12 Vonette Dixon JAM 1266
13 Melissa Morrison USA 1265
14 Svetla Dimitrova BUL 1264
15 Aliuska López CUB 1261
16= Patricia Girard FRA 1236
16= Lacena Golding JAM 1236
18 Bridgette Foster JAM 1233
19 Olena Krasovska UKR 1232
20 Donica Merriman USA 1230

400mh

1 Nezha Bidouane MAR 1390
2 Tetyana Tereshchuk UKR 1349
3 Yuliya Nosova RUS 1342
4 Tonja Buford-Bailey USA 1340
5 Debbie-Ann Parris JAM 1337
6 Daimí Pernía CUB 1336
7 Sandra Glover USA 1307
8 Ionela Tîrlea ROM 1306
9 Deon Hemmings JAM 1290
10 Natalya Torshina KAZ 1246
11 Surita Febbraio RSA 1243
12 Natasha Danvers GBR 1240
13 Andrea Blackett BAR 1230
14 Sylviane Morandais FRA 1212
15 Malgorzata Pskit POL 1208
16 Heike Meissner GER 1203
17 Sonia Brito AUS 1200
18 Anna Olichwierczuk POL 1197
19 Yvonne Harrison PUR 1196
20 Brenda Taylor USA 1193

High Jump

1 Hestrie Cloete RSA 1393
2 Inga Babakova UKR 1387
3 Kajsa Bergqvist SWE 1373
4= Vita Palamar UKR 1335
4= Venelina Veneva BUL 1335
6 Amy Acuff USA 1311
7 Monica Iagar ROM 1258
8 Dóra Györffy HUN 1254
9 Blanka Vlaäic CRO 1240
10 Olga Kaliturina RUS 1213
11 Miki Imai JPN 1197
12 Yek. Aleksandrova RUS 1193
13 Yelena Gulyayeva RUS 1185
14 Susan Jones GBR 1181
15 Nicole Forrester CAN 1177
16 Irina Mikhalchenko UKR 1176
17 Svetlana Zalevskaya KAZ 1170
18 Yuliya Lyakhova RUS 1165
18 Karol Damon USA 1165
20 Tatyana Babashkina RUS 1164

Pole Vault

1 Stacy Dragila USA 1462
2 Svetlana Feofanova RUS 1396
3 Monika Pyrek POL 1320
4 Tatyana Grigoryeva AUS 1306
5 Kellie Suttle USA 1301
6 Pavla Hamácková CZE 1289
7 Gao Shuying CHN 1271
8 Anzh. Balakhonova UKR 1265
9 Yelena Isinbayeva RUS 1264
10 Yelena Belyakova RUS 1260
11 Yvonne Buschbaum GER 1257
12 Mary Sauer USA 1242
13 Melissa Mueller USA 1241
14 Thórey Elisdóttir ISL 1235
15 Tanya Koleva BUL 1220
16 Doris Auer AUT 1214
17 Nicole Humbert GER 1203
18 Janine Whitlock GBR 1201
19 Annika Becker GER 1191
20 Alica Warlick USA 1184

Long Junp

1 Tatyana Kotova RUS 1359
2 Fiona May ITA 1345
3 Niurka Montalvo ESP 1293
4 Maurren Maggi BRA 1280
5 Heike Drechsler GER 1265
6 Eunice Barber FRA 1245
7 Lyudmila Galkina RUS 1242
8 Tünde Vaszi HUN 1241
9 Olga Rublyova RUS 1232
10 Valentina Gotovska LAT 1226
11 Niki Xánthou GRE 1193
12 Elva Goulbourne JAM 1192
13 Guan Yingnan CHN 1188
14 Jacqueline Edwards BAH 1175
15 Bronwyn Thompson AUS 1166
16 Ol. Shekhovtsova UKR 1151
17 Jade Johnson GBR 1144
18 Aurélie Félix FRA 1143
19 Eva Miklos ROM 1142
20= Jenny Adams USA 1141
20= Trecia-Kaye Smith JAM 1141
20= Irina Melnikova RUS 1141
20= Chantal Brunner NZL 1141

Triple Jump

1 Tatyana Lebedeva RUS 1399
2 Tereza Marinova BUL 1368
3 Magdelin Martínez ITA 1299
4 Françoise Mbango CMR 1290
5 Cristina Nicolau ROM 1267
6 Olena Hovorova UKR 1254
7 Yelena Oleynikova RUS 1231
8 Heli Koivula FIN 1227
9 Natalya Safronova BLR 1223
10 Oksana Rogova RUS 1212
11 Trecia-Kaye Smith JAM 1201
12 Ashia Hansen GBR 1199
13 Tiombé Hurd USA 1198
14 Nad. Bazhenova RUS 1188
15 Anastasya Ilyina RUS 1180
16 Anja Valant SLO 1177
17 Olga Bolshova MDA 1175
18 Yelena Lebedyenko RUS 1173
19 Adelina Gavrila ROM 1172
20 Maria Dimitrova BUL 1168

Shot

1 Larisa Peleshenko RUS 1304
2 Yanina Korolchik BLR 1289
3 Nad. Ostapchuk BLR 1265
4 Astrid Kumbernuss GER 1263
5 N Kleinert-Schmitt GER 1250
6 Svetlana Krivelyova RUS 1243
7 Yumileidi Cumbá CUB 1203
8 Irina Korzhanenko RUS 1202
9 Vita Pavlysh UKR 1191
10 Lyudmila Sechko RUS 1178
11 Krystyna Zabawska POL 1161
12 Lieja Koeman NED 1146
13 Teri Tunks USA 1144
14 Connie Price-Smith USA 1142
15 Katarzyna Zakowicz POL 1134
16 Cheng Xioyan CHN 1130
17 Elisângela Adriano BRA 1119
18 Lee Myong-sun KOR 1099
19 Irina Khudoroshkina RUS 1095
20 Elena Hila ROM 1083

Discus

1 Natalya Sadova RUS 1304
2 Nicoleta Grasu ROM 1279
3 Ellina Zvereva BLR 1257
4 Franka Dietzsch GER 1253
5 Anastasia Kelesídou GRE 1190
6 Seilala Sua USA 1185
7 Kristin Kuehl USA 1178
8 Suzy Powell USA 1150
9 Ekateríni Vóggoli GRE 1144
10 Olena Antonova UKR 1137
11 Anja Möllenbeck GER 1131
12 Valentina Ivanova RUS 1127
13 Aretí Abatzí GRE 1125
14 Joanna Wisniewska POL 1123
15 Irina Yatchenko BLR 1121
16 Vladimíra Racková CZE 1120
17 Mel. Robert-Michon FRA 1118
18 Teresa Machado POR 1117
19 Vera Pospísilová CZE 1116
20 Marzena Wysocka POL 1106

Hammer

1 Olga Kuzenkova RUS 1307
2 Kamila Skolimowska POL 1288
3 Bronwyn Eagles AUS 1262
4 Manuela Montebrun FRA 1256
5 Yipsi Moreno CUB 1254
6 Dawn Ellerbe USA 1209
7 Olga Tsander BLR 1201
8 Lorraine Shaw GBR 1179
9 Kirsten Münchow GER 1170
10 Lyudmila Gubkina BLR 1169
11 Florence Ezeh FRA 1157
12 Ivana Brkljacic CRO 1151
13 Ester Balassini ITA 1150
14 Lisa Misipeka ASA 1144
15 Agn. Pogroszewska POL 1133
16 Anna Norgren USA 1118
17 Mia Strömmer FIN 1116
18 Tasha Williams NZL 1110
19 Martina Danisova SVK 1106
20 Irina Sekachova UKR 1100

Javelin

1 Osleidys Menéndez CUB 1399
2 Nikola Tomecková CZE 1269
3 Sonia Bisset CUB 1261
4 Mirela Tzelíli GRE 1260
5 Tatyana Shikolenko RUS 1232
6 Steffi Nerius GER 1220
7 Mikaela Ingberg FIN 1199
8 Xiomara Rivero CUB 1193
9 Claudia Coslovich ITA 1187
10 Yekaterina Ivakina RUS 1176
11 Nikolett Szabó HUN 1153
12= Aggeliki Tsiolakoúdi GRE 1143
12= Felicia Tilea ROM 1143
14 Wei Jianhua CHN 1114
15 Taina Kolkkala FIN 1111
16 Laverne Eve BAH 1110
17 Paula Huhtaniemi FIN 1106
18 Kristina Georgieva BUL 1095
19 Dörthe Friedrich GER 1091
20= Nadine Auzeil FRA 1076
20= Takako Miyake JPN 1076

Heptathlon (Pentathlon Ind.)

1 Yelena Prokhorova RUS 1382
2 Natalya Sazanovich BLR 1360
3 Nat. Roshchupkina RUS 1309
4 Sheila Burrell USA 1301
5 Karin -Ertl GER 1289
6 Irina Belova RUS 1236
7 Dedee Nathan USA 1230
8 Austra Skujyté LTU 1190
9 Svetlana Sokolova RUS 1182
10 Svetlana Kazanina KAZ 1165
11= Larisa Netse poruk EST 1162
11= Tatyana Gordeyeva RUS 1162
13 Urszula Wlodarczyk POL 1157
14 S Kesselschläger GER 1147
15 Alena Vindyuk RUS 1143
16 Jane Jamieson AUS 1141
17 Sabine Krieger GER 1136
18 Gertrud Bacher ITA 1134
19 Katja Keller GER 1128
20 Michaela Hejnová CZE 1127

Fastest Debut Marathons

Men

2:06:54	Ondoro Osoro KEN	Chicago	11 Oct 98
2:06:57	Tesfaye Tola ETH	Amsterdam	17 Oct 99
2:07:10	Khalid Khannouchi MAR	Chicago	19 Apr 97
2:07:54	Alejandro Gómez ESP	Rotterdam	20 Apr 97

Women

2:23:11	Yoko Shibui JPN	Osaka	27 Jan 01
2:23:37	Liu Min CHN	Beijing	14 Oct 01
2:23:44	Catherina McKiernan IRL	Berlin	28 Sep 97
2:24:07	Wang Junxia CHN	Tianjin	4 Apr 93

MICHAEL JOHNSON

Michael Johnson – the greatest 200m/400m runner of all-time – undertook a farewell tour in 2001, when he ran just relay events. We summarised his achievements when introducing him to our Hall of Fame in ATHLETICS 2001, Now we give as complete a career record for the great man as can be compiled. Personal bests are underlined.
He was at Baylor University 1987-90 and from then was affiliated to Nike.

100 Metres

Date	Meeting	Venue	Place	Time
7 May 88	Tex Inv	Austin	1	10.19w
14 May 88	SWC	Austin	4h1	10.26w
15 Apr 89		College Station	1	10.29
20 May 89	SWC	Waco	dnf	
		(3h2 10.13w 19 May)		
14 Aug 89	Gugl	Linz	8h	13.49
2 Jul 90	DNG	Stockholm	4	10.23w
11 Sep 91		Koblenz	3	10.23
1 May 93	UTA	Arlington	1	10.12
		(1h6 10.16)		
12 Mar 94	AUS Ch	Sydney	2	10.51
21 May 94		São Paulo	5	10.29
12 Jun 94		Duisburg	7	10.38
16 Jun 94		Knoxville	dns	
		(2h3 10.09, 3s2 10.30)		
8 Jul 94		Villeneuve d'Ascq	3B	10.45

150 Metres

Date	Meeting	Venue	Place	Time
1 Jun 97		Toronto	dnf	–

200 Metres

Johnson won 32 successive finals, including two indoors, from second place on 19 May 90 when he ran 19.91w behind Leroy Burrell 19.61w until his defeat at Rome on 9 Jun 1992 by Frankie Fredericks 20.23 to 20.25. He had another win streak of 21 successive finals in 1994-6.

Date	Meeting	Venue	Place	Time
86				21.30
86				21.0
21 Mar 87		Austin	1	20.67w
28 Mar 87		College Station	2	20.49
		(2h1 20.5)		
17 Apr 87		Waco	1	20.41
17 May 87	SWC	Lubbock	dnc	–
30 Jan 88		Baton Rouge	1	21.27i
13 Feb 88		Oklahoma City	1	21.27i
		(1h15 21.29)		
20 Feb 88	SWC	Fort Worth	2	21.30i
11 Mar 88	NCAA	Oklahoma City	dq h2	–
26 Mar 88		Austin	1	20.30
2 Apr 88		Hot Springs	1	20.4
16 Apr 88		College Station	1	20.09
30 Apr 88	DrakeR	Des Moines	1	20.46
15 May 88	SWC	Austin	2	20.07
		(1h2 20.27)		
21 May 88		Houston	1	20.58
3 Jun 88	NCAA	Eugene	dnf	–
		(3h2 20.33w)		
11 Feb 89		Oklahoma City	1	20.89i
		(1h2 20.96)		
18 Feb 89	SWC	Fort Worth	1	21.07i
		(1h1 21.44)		
11 Mar 89	NCAA	Indianapolis	1	AR 20.59i
		(1h1 20.73)		
25 Mar 89		Austin	1	20.06w
21 Apr 89		Waco	1	21.13
		(1h1 20.47)		
19 May 89	SWC	Waco (dnc final)	1h1	20.34w
31 May 89	NCAA	Provo	5h2	22.03A
3 Jun 89		Houston	6h2	20.94
8 Aug 89	BGP	Budapest	5	21.07
16 Aug 89	WK	Zürich	dnf	–
10 Feb 90		Oklahoma City	1	20.94i
		(1h7 21.01i)		
17 Feb 90	SWC	Fort Worth	1	20.96i
		(1h1 21.27i)		
11 Mar 90	NCAA	Indianapolis	1	20.72i
		(1h2 20.92i)		
18 Mar 90		Cosford	2	21.19i
19 May 90	SWC	College Station	2	19.91w
		(1h2 20.18w)		
2 Jun 90	NCAA	Durham	1	20.31
		(1h4 20.36, 1s2 20.18)		
16 Jun 90	NC	Norwalk	1	19.90
		(1h2 20.32, 1s2 20.16)		
29 Jun 90	BNP	Villeneuve d'Ascq	1	20.01
4 Jul 90	OD	Berlin	1	20.37
6 Jul 90	IAC	Edinburgh	1	19.85
16 Jul 90		Barcelona	1	20.06
24 Jul 90	GWG	Seattle	1	20.54
5 Aug 90	BGP	Budapest	1	20.30
8 Aug 90		Sestriere	1	19.88A
10 Aug 90	VD	Bruxelles	1	20.21
13 Aug 90		Grosseto	1	20.29
15 Aug 90	WK	Zürich	1	20.07
17 Aug 90	Pearl	Gateshead	1	20.21w
7 Sep 90	GPF	Athína	1	20.10
26 Jan 91		Liévin	1	20.55i
17 Feb 91		Cosford	1	20.74i
6 May 91		Shizuoka	1	20.22
19 May 91	GP	São Paulo	1	20.02
30 May 91	EXPO	Sevilla	1	20.29
15 Jun 91	NC	New York	1	20.31
		(1h1 20.23, 1s1 20.19)		
4 Jul 91		Udine	1	20.16
31 Jul 91		Sestriere	1	20.50A
3 Aug 91	Herc	Monaco	1	20.05
7 Aug 91	WK	Zürich	1	20.08
27 Aug 91	WCh	Tokyo	1	20.01
		(1h2 20.52, 1q3 20.05, 1s2 20.06)		
4 Sep 91		Rieti	1	19.98
13 Sep 91	VD	Bruxelles	1	19.89
15 Sep 91	McV	Sheffield	1	19.94
20 Sep 91	GPF	Barcelona	1	19.88
7 Mar 92		Yokohama	1	20.58i
25 Apr 92	DrakeR	Des Moines	1	19.9w
22 May 92		Houston	1	19.98
9 Jun 92	GGala	Roma	2	20.25
28 Jun 92	OT	New Orleans	1	19.79
		(1h2 20.44, 1q1 20.49, 2s2 20.29)		
8 Jul 92	Athl	Lausanne	1	20.10
13 Jul 92		Salamanca	1	19.91
5 Aug 92	OG	Barcelona	6s2	20.78
		(1h2 20.80, 2q1 20.55)		
24 Apr 93	Drake R	Des Moines	1	20.39
1 May 93	UTA	Arlington	1h1	20.15
		(did not compete in final, strained hamstring)		
5 Jun 93	Pre	Eugene	1	20.56
9 Jun 93	GGala	Roma	2	20.33
25 Jun 93		Indianapolis	1	20.16
5 Jul 93	DNG	Stockholm	2	20.25

7 Jul 93	Athl	Lausanne	2	20.06
10 Sep 93	GPF	London (CP)	3	20.41
13 Sep 93		New Delhi	1	20.38
18 Sep 93		Fukuoka	1	20.19
13 Feb 94		Maebashi	1	20.81i
5 Apr 94		Cape Town	1	20.47
21 May 94		São Paulo	1	20.18
10 Jun 94	GP II	Saint-Denis	2	20.49
12 Jun 94		Duisberg	1	20.08w
6 Jul 94	Athl	Lausanne	4	20.26
28 Jul 94	GWG	Sankt-Peterburg	1	20.10
2 Aug 94	Herc	Monaco	1	19.94
17 Aug 94	WK	Zürich	1	20.33
19 Aug 94	VD	Bruxelles	1	20.02
28 Aug 94		København	1	20.21
15 Sep 94	Super	Tokyo	1	20.09
14 May 95	GP	São Paulo	1	20.22
27 May 95	Jenner	San José	1	19.99w
4 Jun 95	Pre	Eugene	1	20.15
18 Jun 95	NC	Sacramento	1	19.83w
		(1h2 20.21w, 1s2 20.04)		
3 Jul 95	Gaz	Paris	1	19.92w
5 Jul 95	Athl	Lausanne	1	19.96w
10 Jul 95	DNG	Stockholm	1	20.15
11 Aug 95	WCh	Göteborg	1	19.79
		(1h2 20.57, 1q1 20.35,1s1 20.01)		
5 Sep 95	GP II	Rieti	1	20.09
9 Sep 95	GPF	Monaco	1	19.93
15 Sep 95	Super	Tokyo	1	20.06
4 May 96	GP	Rio de Janiero	1	20.27
18 May 96	GP	Atlanta	1	19.83
3 Jun 96	GP II	Saint-Denis	1	20.23
23 Jun 96	OT	Atlanta	1	WR 19.66
		(1h3 20.61, 1q2 20.23, 1s1 19.70w)		
5 Jul 96	Bisl	Oslo	2	19.85
8 Jul 96	DNG	Stockholm	1	19.77
1 Aug 96	OG	Atlanta	1	WR 19.32
		(1h4 20.55, 1q2 20.37, 1s1 20.27)		
30 Aug 96	ISTAF	Berlin	2	20.02
27 Apr 97	DrakeR	Des Moines	1	20.05
4 May 97	GP	Rio de Janeiro	1	20.29
25 May 97	Pre	Eugene	1	20.17
17 Aug 97		London (CP)	5	20.87
20 Aug 97		Malmö	4	20.85
2 May 98		Arlington	1	20.31
31 May 98	Pre	Eugene	3	20.28w
19 Mar 99		Roodepoort	1	20.10A
26 Mar 99		Cape Town	1	20.41
8 May 99		Fort-de-France	1	20.07
7 Jul 99	GGala	Roma	1	19.93
26 Jul 99	Gugl	Linz	1	20.11
3 Sep 99	VD	Bruxelles	1	19.93
18 Mar 00		Pietersburg	1	19.71A
9 Jun 00		Sevilla	1	19.91
23 Jul 00	OT	Sacramento	dnf	–
		(1h4 19.89, 2s1 20.14)		

300 Metres

9 Aug 91		Gateshead	1	31.95
30 Jul 93		Gateshead	1	31.72
22 Jul 94		Salamanca	1	31.56
24 Mar 00		Pretoria	1	WB 30.85A

400 Metres

Johnson won 57 successive finals from second in 47.22 to Antonio McKay 47.03 in TAC at New York in Feb 1989 to 5th in 45.74 behind: 1. Antonio Pettigrew 44.86, 2. Davis Kamoga 45.19, 3, Tyree Washington 45.26, 4. Chris Jones 45.61 in Paris on 25 Jun 1997.

11 Apr 87		Lafayette	1	46.29
26 Feb 88	NC	New York	2h4	48.83i
88				46.65i
22 Apr 88		Waco	1	45.23
16 Jul 88	OT	Indianapolis	7h3	49.48
21 Jan 89		Oklahoma City	1	46.6i
	(1h4 47.35i)			
28 Jan 89		Baton Rouge	1	46.60i
24 Feb 89	NC	New York	2	47.22i
		(3h1 47.33i)		
1 Apr 89		College Station	1	46.49
20 Jan 90		Oklahoma City	1h1	47.18i
27 Jan 90		Baton Rouge	1	47.26i
3 Feb 90		Norman	1	46.39i
23 Feb 90	NC	New York	1	47.43i
		(1h3 47.05i)		
14 Apr 90		College Station	1	45.54
20 Apr 90		Waco	1	45.36
23 Jun 90		Blaine	1	44.58
12 Jul 90	Athl	Lausanne	1	44.27
19 Aug 90	ASV	Köln	1	44.25
9 Sep 90		Rieti	1	44.21
3 Feb 91	Mobil 1	Fairfax	1	46.23i
19 Feb 91	DNG	Stockholm	1	46.29i
22 Feb 91	NC	New York	1	46.70i
		(1h2 46.90i)		
28 Feb 91		Sevilla	1	45.46i
27 Apr 91	Drake	Des Moines	1	44.73
21 Jun 91		Neubrandenburg	1	44.97
1 Jul 91	BNP	Villeneuve d'Ascq	1	45.09
10 Jul 91	Athl	Lausanne	1	44.17
12 Jul 91	PG	London (CP)	1	44.86
8 Sep 91	ASV	Köln	1	44.22
11 Apr 92		Norman	1	44.23
1 Jun 92		Bratislava	1	44.36
10 Jul 92	TSB	London (CP)	1	43.98
30 Jan 93		Glasgow	1	46.43i
7 Feb 93		Stuttgart	1	45.75i
20 Feb 93	TSB	Birmingham	1	45.14i
2 Mar 93		San Sebastián	1	45.68i
21 May 93		Houston	1	44.38
19 Jun 93	NC	Eugene	1	43.74
		(1h1 45.62, 2s1 45.05)		
10 Jul 93	Bisl	Oslo	1	44.89
4 Aug 93	WK	Zürich	1	44.22
17 Aug 93	WCh	Stuttgart	1	43.65
		(1h1 45.60, 1q3 44.72, 2s2 44.39)		
27 Aug 93	ISTAF	Berlin	1	43.94
29 Aug 93	McD	Sheffield	1	45.51
3 Sep 93	VD	Bruxelles	1	44.45
6 Feb 94	Mobil 1	Fairfax	1	45.81i
26 Feb 94	TSB	Birmingham	1	45.17i
13 Aug 94	US v Afr	Durham	1	44.32
30 Aug 94	ISTAF	Berlin	1	44.04
6 Sep 94		Madrid	1	43.90
10 Feb 95		Reno	1	WIR 44.97Ai
25 Feb 95		Fairfax	1	45.55i
14 Mar 95	NC	Atlanta	1	WIR 44.63i
		(1h5 46.66i)		
6 May 95	1st ht	Arlington	1	44.25
16 Jun 95	NC	Sacramento	1	43.66
		(1h3 45.47, 1s1 45.16)		
21 Jul 95	Bisl	Oslo	1	43.86
8 Aug 95	WCh	Göteborg	1	43.39
		(1h4 45.49, 1q4 45.15, 1s1 44.91)		
16 Aug 95	WK	Zürich	1	43.88
25 Aug 95	VD	Bruxelles	1	44.63
1 Sep 95	ISTAF	Berlin	1	44.56
24 Feb 96	Mobil	Fairfax	1	45.32i
2 Mar 96	NC	Atlanta	1	44.66i
		(1h4 46.37i)		
27 Apr 96	DrakeR	Des Moines	1	44.41
19 Jun 96	NC	Atlanta	1	43.44
		(2h2 44.80, 2q1 45.11, 2s1 44.81)		
3 Jul 96	Athl	Lausanne	1	43.66
29 Jul 96	OG	Atlanta	1	43.49
		(2h5 45.80, 1q3 44.62, 1s2 44.59)		
23 Aug 96	VD	Bruxelles	1	44.29

7 Sep 96	GPF	Milano	1	44.53
19 Apr 97		Waco	1	43.75
25 Jun 97	GP	Paris	5	45.76
18 Jul 97		Houston	1	45.03
5 Aug 97	WCh	Athína	1	44.12
		(1h5 45.66, 4q2 45.39, 1s2 44.37)		
13 Aug 97	WK	Zürich	1	44.31
18 Apr 98		Waco	1	45.04
9 Jul 98	Bisl	Oslo	3	44.58
14 Jul 98	GGala	Rome	1	44.40
21 Jul 98	GWG	Uniondale	1	43.76
8 Aug 98	Herc	Monaco	1	43.96
12 Aug 98	WK	Zürich	1	43.68
25 Aug 98	Athl	Lausanne	1	44.28
28 Aug 98	WK	Bruxelles	1	44.06
1 Sep 98	ISTAF	Berlin	1	44.62
17 Apr 99		Waco	1	44.51
30 May 99	Pre	Eugene	1	44.51
2 Jul 99	Athl	Lausanne	1	43.92
30 Jul 99	DNG	Stockholm	dnf	–
26 Aug 99	WCh	Sevilla	1	43.18
		(2h2 45.35, 1q2 45.10, 1s1 43.95)		
31 Mar 00		Cape Town	1	43.9
24 Jun 00	Pre	Eugene	1	43.92
16 Jul 00	OT	Sacramento	1	43.68
		(1h5 45.16, 1s1 44.63)		
25 Aug 00	VD	Bruxelles	1	44.07
1 Sep 00	ISTAF	Berlin	1	45.00
3 Sep 00	GP II	Rieti	1	44.46
25 Sep 00	OG	Sydney	1	43.84
	(1h7 45.25, 1q1 45.31, 2s1 44.65)			

4 x 100 Metres (y – 4x110 Yards)

For Baylor University, leg run shown in brackets

28 Mar 87		College Station	1	39.47y (1)
4 Apr 87	TexR	Austin	3	39.88 (1)
17 Apr 87		Waco	1	39.47y
3 Jun 87	NCAA	Baron Rouge	5h2	39.88 (1)
26 Mar 88		Austin	2	40.21
2 Apr 88		Hot Springs	1	40.0y
9 Apr 88	TexR	Austin	3	40.28
16 Apr 88		College Station	2	39.6
22 Apr 88		Waco	2	39.62
7 May 88	Tex Inv	Austin	2	39.97
15 May 88	SWC	Austin	4	39.73
21 May 88		Houston	1	39.64
2 Jun 88	NCAA	Eugene	3h1	39.63 (3)
20 May 89	SWC	Waco	2	39.39 (3)
1 Jun 90	NCAA	Durham	3	38.98 (3)
		(2h1 39.28)		

For Miscellaneous Teams

19 Aug 90		Köln	2	38.70 (2)
30 Apr 94	PennR	Philadelphia	1	39.05 (3)
30 Aug 96	ISTAF	Berlin	1	38.87 (2)

4 x 200 Metres

For Baylor University

24 Apr 87		Des Moines	1	1:21.24 (1)
6 Apr 90	TexR	Austin	1	1:21.77 (4) 18.5
28 Apr 90	DrakeR	Des Moines	1	1:22.58 (4)

For USA

30 Jan 93		Glasgow	3	1:27.73 (1)

For Miscellaneous Teams

21 Apr 91	MSR	Walnut	1	1:21.50 (4) 19.2
30 Apr 94	PennR	Philadelphia	1	1:20.60 (4)
29 Apr 95	PennR	Philadelphia	1	1:21.54 (4)
25 Apr 98	PennR	Philadelphia	1	1:21.54 (2)
24 Apr 99	PennR	Philadelphia	1	1:19.47 (4)
14 Jul 01		Gdansk	1	1:20.98 (4)
31 Aug 01	ISTAF	Berlin	1	1:21.45 (4) 19.6

4 x 400 Metres (y– 4x440 Yards)

For Baylor University

21 Feb 87	SWC	Fort Worth	1	3:13.80yi (2)
28 Feb 87		Lubbock	4	3:07.98y
14 Mar 87	NCAA	Oklahoma City	4	3:08.57i (3) 47.4
21 Mar 87		Austin	1	3:06.66
3 Apr 87	Tex R	Austin	1h2	3:05.04 (1) 44.9
4 Apr 87	Tex R	Austin	1	3:04.28 (3) 45.5
17 Apr 87		Waco	1	3:04.66y (3) 44.9
25 Apr 87	DrakeR	Des Moines	2	3:01.26 (3) 44.7
2 May 87	Tex Inv	Austin	1	3:02.14 (4)
4 Jun 87	NCAA	Baton Rouge	2h2	3:02.89 (3) 45.4
6 Jun 87	NCAA	Baton Rouge	3	3:00.83 (3) 45.2
13 Feb 88		Oklahoma City	1	3:12.82i
20 Feb 88	SWC	Fort Worth	1	3:11.60i (1) 46.9
11 Mar 88	NCAA	Oklahoma City	1r1	3:10.03i (1) 46.7
2 Apr 88		Hot Springs	1	3:07.0y
8 Apr 88	TexR	Austin	1h3	3:04.65 (3) 44.7
9 Apr 88	TexR	Austin	2	3:04.06 (1) 45.9
16 Apr 88		College Station	1	3:05.83 (1) 44.0
29 Apr 88	DrakeR	Des Moines	1h	3:05.12 (1) 44.4
30 Apr 88	DrakeR	Des Moines	2	3:03.26 (4) 43.5
15 May 88	SWC	Austin	1	3:02.51 (3)
21 May 88		Houston	2	3:06.29
21 Jan 89		Oklahoma City	1	3:12.23i
28 Jan 89		Baton Rouge	1	3:13.96i (2) 46.3
18 Feb 89	SWC	Fort Worth	1	3:09.42i (1) 46.5
11 Mar 89	NCAA	Indianapolis	2	3:07.33i (1) 45.65
25 Mar 89		Austin	1	3:05.95 (4) 44.6
1 Apr 89		College Station	1	3:08.54
7 Apr 89	TexR	Austin	1h2	3:04.34 (4) 44.0
8 Apr 89	TexR	Austin	1	3:04.46 (4) 45.3
29 Apr 89	DrakeR	Des Moines	1	3:04.30 (4) 45.5
6 May 89		Kingston	1	3:00.66 (4) 43.8
27 Jan 90		Baton Rouge	1	3:11.81i
10 Feb 90		Oklahoma City	1	3:12.47i
17 Feb 90	SWC	Fort Worth	1	3:09.08i (1) 46.3
9 Mar 90	NCAA	Indianapolis	1h2	3:07.24i (4) 45.7
10 Mar 90	NCAA	Indianapolis	1h2	3:06.49i (4) 45.1
31 Mar 90		Dallas	1	3:05.74
7 Apr 90	TexR	Austin	1	3:03.09 (4) 44.5
14 Apr 90		College Station	1	3:09.70
20 Apr 90		Waco	1	3:07.89
27 Apr 90	DrakeR	Des Moines	1h2	3:05.8
28 Apr 90	DrakeR	Des Moines	1	3:03.52 (4) 44.9
5 May 90		Kingston	1	3:01.59 (4) 43.9
19 May 90	SWC	College Station	1	3:05.77 (4) 45.6
31 May 90	NCAA	Baylor	1h2	3:01.46 (4) 43.5
2 Jun 90	NCAA	Baylor	1	3:01.86 (4) 43.7

For USA

29 Aug 89	WUG	Duisburg	1h1	3:03.31 (3)
30 Aug 89	WUG	Duisburg	2	3:02.75 (3)
7 Aug 92	OG	Barcelona	2h2	2:59.14 (2) 44.7
8 Aug 92	OG	Barcelona WR	1	2:55.74 (3) 44.7
21 Aug 93	WCh	Stuttgart	1h2	2:58.72 (4) 44.96
22 Aug 93	WCh	Stuttgart WR	1	2:54.29 (4) 42.94
29 Jul 94	GWG	St-Peterburg	1	2:59.42 (4) 45.3
13 Aug 95	WCh	Göteborg WR	1	2:57.32 (4) 44.11
22 Jul 98	GWG	Uniondale	1	2:54/20 (4) 43.2
29 Aug 99	WCh	Sevilla	1	2:56.45 (4) 43.49
30 Sep 00	OG	Sydney	1	2:56.35 (4) 44.29
7 Sep 01	GWG	Brisbane	1	3:00.52 (4) 45.06

For Miscellaneous Teams

21 Apr 91	MSR	Walnut	4	3:04.86 (3) 44.6
18 Apr 92	MSR	Walnut	1	3:00.48 (4) 44.0
29 Apr 00	PennR	Philadelphia	1	2:56.60 (4) 43.7
28 Apr 01	PennR	Philadelphia	1	2:58.60 (4) 44.2

Swedish Relay (100m, 200m, 300m, 400m)

For Miscellaneous Teams

17 Jul 01	DNG	Stockholm	1	1:49.09 (4) 46.54
15 Sep 01		Yokohama	1	1:47.93 (4) 45.4

CROSS-COUNTRY – NATIONAL CHAMPIONS 2001

	MEN (longer distance)	WOMEN (longer distance)
Argentina	Ricardo Ariel Franzon	Valeria Rodríguez
Australia (Trials)	Craig Mottram	Kerryn McCann
Austria	Günther Weidlinger	Sandra Baumann
Belgium	Tom Van Hooste	Anja Smolders
Canada (Dec)	Sean Kaley	Sarah Dupré
Croatia	Slavko Petrovic	Ivancica Cvitkovic
Czech Republic	Zdenek Dubravcik	Jana Klimesova
Denmark	Dennis Jensen	Jytte Pedersen
England	Michael Openshaw	Liz Yelling
Estonia	Heiki Sarapuu	Maile Mangusson
Ethiopia	Dejene Burhanu	Gete Wami
Finland	Jussi Utriainen	Annemari Sandell
France	Driss El Himer	Rakiya Quétier-Maraoui
Germany	André Green	Luminita Zaituc
Greece	Panayiótis Haramís	María Protóppa
Hungary	Miklós Zatykó	Beáta Rakonczai
Ireland	Seamus Power	Rosemary Ryan
Israel	Haile Satain	Mara Fissiha
Italy	Michele Gamba	Agata Balsamo
Japan Trials	Satoshi Irifune	Yoshiko Fujinaga
Kenya Trials	John Korir	Lydia Cheromei
Latvia	Janis Ozolins	Jelena Prokopcuka
Luxembourg	Romain Possing	Pascale Schmoetten
Netherlands	Kamiel Maase	Irma Heeren
New Zealand	Alan Bunce	Melissa Moon
Norway	Knut Erik Rame	Bynhild Synstnes
Poland	Piotr Drwal	Justyna Bak
Portugal	Paulo Guerra	Carla Sacramento
Romania	Adrian Maghiar	Elena Fidatov
Scotland	Chris Robison	Ellen Leggate
Slovakia	Marcel Matanin	Dana Janecková
Slovenia	Romeo Zivko	Sonja Roman
South Africa	Enoch Skosana	Sibongile Ngcongwana
Spain	Fabián Roncero	Jacqueline Martín
Sweden	Mattias Persson	Marie Söderström-Lundberg
Switzerland	Bruno Heuberger	Maja Neuenschwander
UK	Glynn Tromans	Liz Yelling
USA	Meb Keflezighi	Deena Drossin
Wales	Christian Stephenson	Catherine Dugdale
Yugoslavia	Sreten Ninkovic	Sonja Stolic
Asian	Jafar Babakhani IRN	Yasuyo Iwamoto JPN
European Clubs Teams	Olympique Marseille FRA	Maratona de Maia POR
NCAA	Boaz Cheboiwo KEN	Tara Chaplin USA
S.American	Adílson Ribeiro BRA	Ana de Souza BRA
Scandinavia	Jari Matinlauri FIN	Gunhild Halle-Haugen NOR

	Men (short distance)	**Women (short distance)**
Argentina	Julián Peralta	Maria Peralta
Austria	Günther Weidlinger	
Belgium	Jurgen Vandewiele	Véronique Collard
Czech Republic	Tomás Krutsky	–
Denmark	Dennis Jensen	Dorte Vibjerg
Ethiopia	Kenenisa Bekele	Worknesh Kidane
Finland	Samuli Vasala	
France	Laïd Bessou	Fatima Yvelain
Germany	Jens Borrmann	Luminita Zaituc
Hungary	Zsolt Benedek	–

Italy	Lorenzo Perrone	Sara Palmas
Kenya Trials	Enock Koech	
Lithuania	Mindaugas Pukstas	Rasa Drazdauskaite
Netherlands	Gert-Jan Liefers	Yvonne van der Kolk
New Zealand	Jonathan Wyatt	Melissa Moon
Poland	Rafal Wójcik	
Portugal	Rui Silva	Anália Rosa
Slovakia	Vladislav Lipovsky	
South Africa	Enos Matelane	Lauren Brentano
Sweden	Claes Nyberg	Hanna Karlsson
Switzerland	Christian Belz	Anita Weyermann
UK	Spencer Barden	Helen Pattinson
USA	Tim Broe	Regina Jacobs
S.American & CAC	Daniel Ferreira BRA	Fatima da Silva BRA

European Cross-Country Championships 2001

At Malmö, Sweden 10 December

Senior Men (9705m)
1. Paulo Guerra POR 29.29
2. Sergey Lebed UKR 29:39
3. Driss El Himer FRA 29:45
4. Lyes Ramoul FRA 29:47
5. Mustapha El Ahmadi FRA 29:47
6. Carlos Adan ESP 29:48
7. Kamiel Maase NED 29:49
8. Tom Van Hooste BEL 29:51
9. José M. Martínez ESP 29:52
10. Peter Matthews IRL 29:53
11. Yann Millon FRA 29:54
12. Jose Ramos POR 29:55
13. Alberto Maravilha POR 29:56
14. Seamus Power IRL 29:58
15. Claes Nyberg SWE 30:01

83 finished

Teams: 1. FRA 23, 2. ESP 51, 3. IRL 72, 4. POR 74, 5. BEL 98, 6. GBR 103, 7. ITA 144, 8. RUS 156, 9. UKR 166, 10. GER 168, 11, DEN 189, 12. SWE 189, 13, POL 257, 14. TUR 281.

Senior Women (4945m)
1. Katalin Szentgyörgyi HUN 16.34
2. Analidia Torre POR 16.35
3. Olivera Jevtic YUG 16.39
4. Zahia Dahmani FRA 16:49
5. Kathy Butler GBR 16:51
6. Monica Rosa POR 16:55
7. Anja Smolders BEL 16:55
8. Liz Yelling GBR 16:55
9. Anne Keenan-Buckley IRL 16:56
10. Analia Rosa POR 16:57
11. Gunhild Halle-Haugen NOR 16:57
12. Jacqueline Martin ESP 17:00
13. Michaela Möller GER 17:02
14. Rakiya Quetier-Maraoui FRA 17:02
15. Rosemary Ryan IRL 17:03

67 finished.

Teams: 1. POR 18, 2. GBR 33, 3. GER 54, 4. BEL 55, 5. ROM 60, 6. IRL 60, 7. FRA 60, 8. ESP 73, 9. ITA 106, 10. SWE 140, 11. POL 147.

Junior Men (6135m)
1. Wolfram Müller GER 18:58
2. Chris Thompson GBR 19:00
3. Martin Pröll AUT 19:05
4. Rui Pedro Silva POR 19:10
5. Mickael André FRA 19:11
6. Bruno Silva POR 19:11
7. Mohamed Farah GBR 19:12
8. Aleksandr Sekletov RUS 19:16
9. Henrik Ahnström SWE 19:17
10. Benoit Charpantier FRA 19:26

93 finished.

Teams: 1. POL 21, 2. GBR 25, 3. FRA 30, 4. ESP 48, 5. GER 62. 6. ITA 74, 7, SWE 85, 8. RUS 86, 9. NED 121, 10. BLR 126, 11. BEL 129, 12. UKR 142, 13. TUR 143, 14. AUT 144, 15. IRL 178, 16. SUI 194, 17. CZE 213, 18. HUN 214, 19. SLO 247.

Junior Women (3755m)
1. Jessica Augusto POR 12:55
2. Nicola Spirig SUI 12:56
3. Elvan Can TUR 12:56
4. Tatyana Chulakh RUS 12:56
5. Juliet Potter GBR 13:02
6. Olga Krivyak UKR 13:14
7. Jane Potter GBR 13:14
8. Olesya Dubovik UKR 13:15
9. Collette Fagan GBR 13:15
10. Türkan Erismis TUR 13:17

85 finished.

Teams: 1. GBR 21, 2. TUR 40, 3. SWE 49, 4. POR 55, 5. FIN 60, 6. UKR 69, 7. RUS 71, 8. ROM 83, 9. ESP 84, 10. BEL 102, 11. FRA 108, 12. BLR 115, 13. HUN 124, 14. SUI 126, 15. GER 140, 16. ITA 148, 17. YUG 161, 18. IRL 200, 19. NED 204, 20. CZE 224.

See Athletics 2001, page 592, for the results of the 2001 IAAF World Championships, and the end of this Annual for results from the 2002 IAAF World Championships

WORLD MARATHON REVIEW 2001

By David E Martin

KENYA AND Japan had the most top male marathoners in 2001, with 64 and 27 respectively of the top 200 in the world lists. Then followed Ethiopia and Italy 12 each and South Africa 10. Japan headed the women's lists with 43 from Russia 24, China 17, Kenya 16, and DPR Korea 11. The top 200 men cane from 34 countries and the top women from 33. In the accompanying summary of winners of major world marathons, the global dominance of the Kenyan men and Russian women is also clearly visible.

The 2:20 time barrier for women was broken twice and, while the men's record was not threatened, an unprecedented 301 sub-2:20:00 performances were delivered by Kenyan men – 30% of the total for the world – by 190 different athletes!

There were excellent results in the Japanese marathons during the cool weather of the first three months. At the 20th anniversary of the Osaka International Ladies Marathon, Yoko Shibui lowered the world debut record to 2:23:11, replacing Catherina McKiernan's 2:23:44 at Berlin in 1997. Shibui prepared by training at altitude in China, but although an injury early in January caused her to miss five days of training, it was a blessing in disguise that gave her full recovery and a hunger to race. Restituta Joseph led the field at a very fast early pace, and paid dearly later, but Shibui maintained contact, and took the lead at 20k, taking advantage of excellent weather (8.5ºC, cloudy, 52% humidity). By 23k her rivals were behind her, and she went clear despite a second-half slowdown (see Table of intermediate splits).

Takayuki Nishida became the first runner coached by Toshihiko Seko to win a major marathon in the 50th anniversary men's Oita-Beppu race; he defeated Brazil's Vanderlei de Lima by 73 seconds in 2:08:45. Two weeks later, in Tokyo, the Sydney Olympic silver and bronze medallists Eric Wainaina and Tesfaye Tola were joined by another sub-2:07 Ethiopian, Tesfaye Jifar – blind in his right eye after being gored by a bull as an early teenager. But Ken-ichi Takahashi had similar credentials, and although intense competition in the early stages slowed the finish, his dash over the final 100m on the track gave him a 16-second win over Jifar.

The 56th Lake Biwa marathon at Otsu in March was the national championships, and four runners broke 2:08 on Japanese soil for the first time. All set personal bests: Antonio Peña (2:07:34, a course record, thanks in part to excellent weather conditions – 8.5ºC and 72% humidity), Giacomo Leone (2:07:52), Shigeru Aburaya (2:07:52), and Yoshiteru Morishita (2:07:59). One week later the 19th Nagoya marathon for women also enjoyed good racing weather (8ºC, 46% humidity), and 12 athletes finished in less than 2:30. Kazumi Matsuo's 2:26:01 was her third victory in as many starts, but her three-second margin over Takami Ominami was the smallest in race history; both scored personal bests.

April has much marathon activity in Europe. This started with a fast race in Torino where Simretu Alemayehu ran negative splits of 64:08 and 63:36 for the fastest time on Italian soil.

Simon Biwott and David Kirui duelled to a sprint finish on a cold rainy day in Paris in 2:09:40 – just three seconds ahead of Fred Kiprop, with Biwott the winner. It was his third major victory, coming after Berlin (2:07:42) the previous September and Milano (2:09:00) in December. Amazingly, in fourth place was France's Mohammed Ezzher, whose 2:10:33 was a veteran's world best on a loop course – improving by 2:01 the time of Kjell-Erik Ståhl in Stockholm 1986.

A $1000 foreign-entrant fee included race accommodation, with a limit of 200 such participants at Pyongyang; where, as an example of free-market economy in a controlled country, event sponsor Fila became the first advertiser permitted at a sporting event in DPR Korea. Kim Jung-won won by 35 seconds in 2:11:48. His wife, Jong Song-ok, the 1999 Seville World Champion, and now retired, still managed to place tenth in a respectable 2:36:39 in the women's race.

On the same weekend at the 105th Boston marathon, Gezahegne Abera tried to capture the elusive Olympic/Boston double, but managed only 16th as a ten-year Kenyan domination on the podium was ended by the 1996 Olympic silver medallist Lee Bong-ju (2:09:43). Running negative splits, the 30-year-old defeated Silvio Guerra by 24 seconds after an epic duel over the final two miles. The women's race was just as amazing, as Catherine Ndereba trounced an outstanding field; her 2:23:52 was 2:19 faster than her 2000 Boston victory and her second half (1:10:48) was a course record – even faster than the 1:10:53 by Uta Pippig in 1994 with a tailwind. Malgorzata Sobanska was a distant second in 2:26:42.

London and Rotterdam were both on 22 April. In the former, Paul Tergat made his event debut at the age of 31 and his two chief challengers, Abdelkader El Mouaziz and Antonio Pinto, had collectively eight previous outings and three victories in London. Despite breezy weather, the 11ºC temperature permitted fast racing. Tergat was second in 2:08:15 as he was surprised by the repeated surging of El Mouaziz, who won in 2:07:11 and became the first to win New York and London in sequence. Pinto had to settle for third (2:09:36), but Tesfaye Jifar improved upon his Tokyo time by 1:22 for a personal best of 2:09:45.

In the London women's race Derartu Tulu, 29, scored her first marathon victory in five attempts. She skipped the World Cross Country Championships – which she had won three times – to focus properly. It paid off, literally, as the winners earned $55,000. Running 71:22 and 72:35 for the two halves of the race (2:23:57), the field she beat was so outstanding that an unprecedented seven women broke 2:26:00. Runner-up Svetlana Zakharova set a pb by 3:04 and third was Joyce Chepchumba, whose 2:24:12 was her seventh successive sub-2:26; this was her sixth year in the top three. Rounding out the top seven were Lidia Simon (2:24:15), Elfenesh Alemu (2:24:29), Nuta Olaru (2:25:18), and Alina Ivanova (2:25:34). Unlike most major mixed races, in London the women start at least 15 minutes earlier than the men, so that both races are show-cased. With 23,259 men and 6807 women finishers, London was the largest marathon of the year.

At Rotterdam, Josephat Kiprono ran an evenly-paced race (10k splits of 29:40, 30:13, 30:19, 30:02 plus a final 6:36 to match the then world best 2:06:50 run there by Belayneh Dinsamo in 1988. Kiprono is the first to run sub-2:07 twice, and his time remained the fastest of the year. Fifth place went to Josephat's brother Isaac, whose 2:09:59 combined to make them the fastest same-race brothers. Kenneth Cheruiyot (2:07:18) was runner-up, as in 2000. In the women's race, Susan Chepkemei showed that her half-marathon world best at Lisboa three weeks earlier was a good indication of her fitness and her 2:25:45 was too quick for runner-up Masako Koide's 2:28:28, but both ran personal bests. Koide's coach is her father, Yoshio, known better as the celebrated coach of Naoko Takahashi. After visiting both Berlin and Chicago, coach Koide declared that Takahashi would indeed focus her attention on breaking the 2:20:00 barrier at Berlin in September, opting out of the World Championships.

Most of the "commercial" marathons featuring elite competitors are scheduled for the cooler months to permit fast racing through adequate heat dissipation and most top marathoners opt to run one marathon in spring and one in the autumn. But the major championship marathons are held in the summer months, so that those who can best manage the heat capture the medals, with others falling victim to a devastating race of attrition. While not as hot as at Seville and Athens, Edmonton provided its own blend of challenging conditions. The men's race was choreographed into the Opening Ceremonies on 4 August, starting at 6:45pm on what developed as Edmonton's warmest day of its summer to that point (28ºC in the shade plus 5ºC added by solar radiation). The northern latitude kept the sun shining until nearly 8pm. Add to this the 630m (2100 feet) altitude, and the unique environmental mix proved difficult. The list of those not finishing included many great runners such as world record-holder Khalid Khannouchi, Josiah Thugwane and Lee Bong-ju. The winner was Gezahegne Abera, only 23 years old, showing again his ability to handle brutal conditions – recall how he conquered the hills and wind of Sydney. In the final stages it became a battle between him and Simon Biwott. The two entered the stadium side-by-side, dashing over the final 300m in an estimated 44 seconds, with Abera (2:12:41) one second ahead of Biwott. Abel Antón had previously won two IAAF World Championship titles, and Bikila and Cierpinski had previously won two Olympic titles. Abera's one of each – and only a year apart – is a unique achievement.

The women raced at Edmonton in the early morning in an atypically warm 21ºC and high humidity, in contrast to the several preceding cool, crisp mornings. Although several top stars were either not selected (Loroupe) or opted for autumn marathons (Ndereba, Takahashi), the quality of entrants was outstanding, with ten teams of at least three athletes vying for the prestigious Marathon World Cup trophy with its associated attractive team prize money. Constantina Tomescu led the pack out onto the streets at a pace six minutes faster than her personal best and her lead approached two minutes by 15km, but then the pack slowly reeled her in, catching her at 1:52:06, near the 33km mark. Reiko Tosa and Lidia Simon appeared the strongest, always pushing the pace, with Svetlana Zakharova close behind. This was Simon's day in the sun as she surged on the stadium road and increased her 5m lead as she happily dashed around the track; her 2:26:01 was excellent given the conditions. Her gold came after seven silver and bronze medals from previous Olympics and World Championships. Unfortunately her husband Liviu didn't see her win; he crashed on his bicycle while riding back to the stadium after having watched the action out on the course, broke his arm, and got the news of her win via cell phone as he lay on the pavement. Tosa headed the Japanese contingent (2:26:06) that captured the World Cup trophy over Russia.

At Berlin on 30 September, for the second time in as many years a designated pacemaker for the men's race was fit enough, after covering his assigned distance, to stay in the race and win. This year it was Joseph Ngolepus, 26, one of Tegla Loroupe's training partners in the stable of elite runners managed by Germany's Volker Wagner and based in Detmold. With a personal best 2:08:47 by two seconds, he led a Kenyan sweep of the medals, together with Willy Cheruiyot (2:09:08) and William Kiplagat (2:09:55).

It was the Berlin women's race, however, that

brought hundreds of journalists, especially from Japan, to watch the battle unfold between Tegla Loroupe – the reigning queen of speed in the event – and Naoko Takahashi – the Sydney Olympic champion – who wanted to break Loroupe's record where it was set, and with Loroupe in the race. So often in the marathon, much-hyped plans announced months in advance do not materialize, but this time coach Koide's plan was carried out magnificently. It had to be so – the women's race was televised live back to Japan as a prime-time sports spectacular, watched by 55% of the population – to not race well would have been a calamity! A headwind slowed Takahashi's first 5k (16:46), but then she changed direction, and her pace quickened. The use of computer chip technology permitted the media to track her progress in real time when each of the 5k split times were announced. Careful planning by organizers also ensured the presence of official timers at the appropriate points so that record performances could be processed and indeed Takahashi was quick enough at 25k (1:22:31) and 30k (1:39:02), and so was her finish time of 2:19:46, 31 seconds faster than the 1999 worl best of Loroupe, who was runner-up with a fine 2:28:03, but being 8:20 behind, she missed seeing the new record-holder crowned. Takahashi placed 36th overall, in this third largest marathon of the year (21,699 men, 4123 women finishers).

Catherine Ndereba had begun to taper her training for Chicago the next weekend when she received news of Takahashi's breakthrough. It had been her goal to be the first to race under 2:20. Now it was simply a matter of how much under the barrier she could run. It was chilly in Chicago at 7ºC, but women manage the cold better then men. All started together, and Ndereba was unable to determine her pace until 5k; by then she was running more slowly than planned, and she was even behind Takahashi's time. Attempting methodically to catch up but not enter into oxygen debt, by 30k Ndereba finally got within two seconds of Takahashi's Berlin time (see the accompanying table). By 40k she was 26 seconds ahead, and her final 2.195k was covered at a quick 5:09 per mile pace (3:12.3/km), compared to her average race pace of 5:17.5 (3:17.3). Her history-making effort was worth $175,000 in prize money and bonuses, plus a new car. In contrast to Shibui's debut and the world records by Loroupe and Takahashi, Ndereba ran negative splits. Amazingly, her 68:32 second half was only two seconds slower than her half- marathon course-record performance at Philadelphia three weeks earlier!

At the men's race in Chicago, Paul Tergat, hoping to improve upon his London runner-up status, hired a pacemaker, Ben Kimondiu, who had performed well at the Rock n' Roll (San Diego) and Country Music (Nashville) marathons. Kimondiu was as well-prepared as Ndereba, and essentially led from start to finish, switching from pacer to racer near the end and achieving an excellent personal best 2:08:52, 6:21 faster than his 2:15:13 runner-up at Los Angeles in March. It had been his plan to use Chicago as a tune-up run in preparation for racing at New York, doing only the pacing chores partway. To his delight, his plans suddenly changed, giving him a $90,000 payday and no real need to go to New York.

The Chicago marathon thus became the third marathon to simultaneously hold the men's and women's world best performances. Rotterdam had both from April to September 1998 (Densimo and Loroupe), and Berlin both from September to October 1999 (Costa and Loroupe). It was the year's largest American marathon (17,379 men and 11,451 women finishers), second globally to London (23,259 men, 6,807 women).

Following this history-making double-week-

Intermediate Times For World Best Women Marathon Performances

Split	Debut Best Yoko Shibui 28 Jan 2001		World best Tegla Loroupe 26 Sep 1999		World best Naoko Takahashi 30 Sep 2001		World best Catherine Ndereba 7 Oct 2001	
5k	16:40	16:40	16:20	16:20	16:46	16:46	17:41	17:41
10k	16:35	33:15	16:12	32:32	16:24	33:10	16:28	34:09
15k	16:41	49:56	16:40	49:12	16:27	49:37	16:30	50:39
20k	16:45	1:06:41	16:52	1:06:04	16:40	1:06:11	16:06	1:06:45
HMar		1:10:22		1:09:49		1:09:50		1:10:15
25k	16:49	1:23:30	17:11	1:23:15	16:20	1:22:31	16:04	1:22:49
30k	16:38	1:40:08	17:23	1:40:38	16:32	1:39:02	16:15	1:39:04
35k	16:57	1:57:05	16:29	1:57:07	16:27	1:55:29	16:17	1:55:21
40k	17:57	2:15:02	16:26	2:13:33	16:42	2:12:11	16:24	2:11:45
2.195k	8:09	2:23:11	7:10	2:20:43	7:35	2:19:46	7:02	2:18:47
2nd half		1:12:49		1:10:54		1:09:56		1:08:32
Min/km		3:23.6		3:20.1		3:18.7		3:17.3
Min/mi		5:27.6		5:22.0		5:19.8		5:17.5
Weather	8.5ºC, 52%		14ºC, 72%		13ºC, 82%		7ºC, 56%	

end of activity, records continued to fall, this time at Beijing as Chinese juniors – Li Zhuhong (2:10:46) and Liu Min (2:23:37), both only 17 – established world-best performances at their National Games in Beijing. Equalling London, there were seven women finishers under 2:26:00.

At the Amsterdam marathon, France's Driss El Himer set a French record of 2:07:02, the year's second fastest time. Runner-up was Josephat Kiprono, whose 2:07:06 gave him the first and third fastest times of the year, and he was joined by his two brothers, Lukas Kibet (3rd 2:10:18), who uses the other of his two Kenyan family names, and Isaac Kiprono (13th 2:18:55). Their combined time of 6:36:19 very nearly improved upon their previous combined best of 6:35:43 at the Rome Millennium marathon of 2000, which set the standard for a three-brother single-race performance.

Despite the terrorist events in New York on 11 September, little doubt existed among city and marathon officials that "the show must go on". Splendid weather (13ºC, cloudy, light breezes) plus a slightly modified course, eliminating one small rise at 23 miles, combined on 4 November to help an extraordinary field of both men and women finish with the fastest times ever recorded there. With 23,631 finishers (16,790 men, 6841 women), a reduction of 5742 from 2000, it was still the USA's second largest marathon, behind Chicago, and globally the fourth largest.

By half-way (63:51), most would have bet that a Kenyan would win, as there were nine at the front, plus Ecuador's Silvio Guerra. But lurking nearby was 25-year-old Tesfaye Jifar. Soon it was down to two, with Jifar proving superior in Central Park, racing alone to a record 2:07:43, 1:36 ahead of Japhet Kosgei. His was the first Ethiopian victory at New York, and he was no longer the fastest runner never to have won a marathon – that is now Moses Tanui.

In the women's race, Kenyan Margaret Okayo, also 25 years old – small but powerful and quick – added to her Rock n' Roll marathon win in May with a stunning demonstration of front running and surging. Her 2:24:21 victory by 51 seconds eclipsed Lisa Ondieki's 1992 event record by 19 seconds. Although she was racing at essentially 5:30 per mile pace, her 15th mile was a quick 5:13, and she never relinquished her resulting lead.

If Ndereba and Takahashi are ranked 1 & 2 for the year, a good candidate for the 3rd position would be London winner Derartu Tulu, who added the Tokyo marathon (2:25:08) to her victory list. She was the first Ethiopian to win in the race's 23-year history, only the second African, and verified that she could compete at the very highest level on turf, track and roads. Then, at Fukuoka an anticipated showdown between the Edmonton 1-2 Abera and Biwott didn't materialise, as Abera captured his second victory there (2:09:25) in three years, having to use his sprinting abilities once again to win by just three seconds over Japan's Koji Shimizu, but Biwott fell back to ninth.

Leading Marathons 2001

Date	Venue	Men	Time	Women	Time
5 Jan	Tiberias	Paul Tangus KEN	2:17:06	Nili Avramski ISR	2:44:57
12 Jan	Dubai	Wilson Kibet KEN	2:13:36	Ramilya Burangulova RUS	2:37:07
14 Jan	Hamilton, BER	Fyodor Ryzhov RUS	2:21:19	Lyudmila Korchagina RUS	2:43:18
14 Jan	Houston	Christopher Ciamarra USA	2:29:27	Stacie Alboucrek USA	2:43:42
21 Jan	Carlsbad	Andrey Kuznetsov RUS	2:17:39	Alena Vinitskaya BLR	2:49:20
28 Jan	Osaka	Women only		Yoko Shibui JPN	2:23:11
28 Jan	Port of Spain	Pamenos Ballentyne VIN	2:16:57	Tammy Slusser USA	2:52:45
28 Jan	Siracusa	Salvatore Bettiol ITA	2:19:55	Ginevra Benedetti ITA	3:01:26
4 Feb	Ageo	Minoru Isono JPN	2:15:49	Eri Kurotaki JPN	2:33:57
4 Feb	Beppu-Oita	Takayushi Nishida JPN	2:08:45	Men only	
4 Feb	Hong Kong	Dube Jillo ETH	2:23:21	Irina Bogacheva KGZ	2:33:43
4 Feb	Las Vegas	Michael Dudley USA	2:18:13	Irina Kazakova FRA	2:41:56
4 Feb	Valencia	John Njoroge Miaka KEN	2:13:47	Maria Luisa Larraga ESP	2:30:11
11 Feb	Genova	Emanuele Zenucchi ITA	2:17:00	Elena Riva ITA	2:55:26
11 Feb	Guadalajara	Simon Sawe KEN	2:16:25	Albina Galliamova RUS	2:46:22
18 Feb	Austin	Mukhamet Nazhipov RUS	2:11:14	Yelena Paramonova RUS	2:32:55
18 Feb	Tokyo	Kenichi Takahashi JPN	2:10:51	Men only	
25 Feb	Nobeoka	Yoshihisa Okamoto JPN	2:13:11	Men only	
25 Feb	Salsomaggiore	Giorgio Calcaterra ITA	2:16:49	Katiuscia Merati ITA	2:37:50
25 Feb	Sevilla	José Ramon Rey ESP	2:10:49	Faustina Maria ESP	2:34:41
4 Mar	Durban	Ian Syster RSA	2:13:30	Elisabeth Mongudhi NAM	2:49:20
4 Mar	Los Angeles	Stephen Ndungu KEN	2:13:13	Yelena Paramonova RUS	2:36:58
4 Mar	Otsu	Antonio Peña ESP	2:07:34	Men only	
4 Mar	Piacenza	Angelo Carosi ITA	2:13:41	Guliya Tazetdinova RUS	2:47:44
4 Mar	Torreón	Andrés Espinosa MEX	2:10:57	Adriana Fernández MEX	2:30:30
11 Mar	Nagoya	Women only		Kazumi Matsuo JPN	2:26:01

11 Mar	Vigarano Mainarda	Francis Kipketer KEN	2:15:22	Isabelle Ledroit CAN	2:38:59
18 Mar	Barcelona	Benedict Ako TAN	2:13:53	Leone Justino da Silva BRA	2:40:32
18 Mar	Napoli	Giovanni Ruggiero ITA	2:09:53	Lyudmila Korchagina RUS	2:35:39
18 Mar	Seoul	Josiah Bembe RSA	2:11:49	Yun Sun-sook KOR	2:32:09
25 Mar	Roma	Henry Cherono KEN	2:11:33	Maria Guida ITA	2:30:42
1 Apr	Torino	Simretu Alemayehu ETH	2:07:45	Tiziana Alagia ITA	2:27:54
7 Apr	Jinan	Chai Jiahua CHN	2:16:56	Zheng Guixia CHN	2:30:11
8 Apr	Bolzano Egna	Gideon Kiplagat KEN	2:14:09	Karina Szymanska POL	2:35:59
8 Apr	Canberra	Rachid Khaleed Jamal QAT	2:16:23	Susan Michelsson AUS	2:41:59
8 Apr	Debno	Miroslaw Plawgo POL	2:12:27	Elzbieta Jarosz POL	2:37:02
8 Apr	Paris	Simon Biwott KEN	2:09:40	Florence Barsosio KEN	2:27:53
15 Apr	Kunsan	Samson Kandie KEN	2:10:23	Oh Mi-ja KOR	2:35:48
15 Apr	Nagano	Maxwell Musambi KEN	2:12:20	Akiyo Onishi JPN	2:31:20
15 Apr	Pyongyang	Kim Jong-won PRK	2:11:48	Jong Yong-ok PRK	2:28:32
16 Apr	Boston	Lee Bong-ju KOR	2:09:43	Catherine Ndereba KEN	2:23:53
21 Apr	Beograd	Mluleki Nobanda RSA	2:15:11	Cristina Pomacu ROM	2:29:44
22 Apr	Hamburg	Julio Rey ESP	2:07:46	Sonja Oberem GER	2:26:13
22 Apr	London	Abdelkader El Mouaziz MAR	2:07:11	Derartu Tulu ETH	2:23:57
22 Apr	Rotterdam	Josephat Kiprono KEN	2:06:50	Susan Chepkemei KEN	2:25:45
22 Apr	Wroclaw	Bogdan Dziuba POL	2:19:24	Wioletta Uryga POL	2:41:15
25 Apr	Pisa	Philemon Kipkering KEN	2:15:29	Galina Zhulyayeva UKR	2:42:58
28 Apr	Nashville	Christopher Cheboiboch KEN	2:13:28	Aurica Buia ROM	2:34:40
29 Apr	Cleveland	Edilson da Silva BRA	2:12:43	Elvira Kolpakova RUS	2:42:06
29 Apr	Leipzig	Stephan Freigang GER	2:15:58	Tanya Semyonova UKR	2:53:45
29 Apr	Madrid	José Ramon Rey ESP	2:19:12	Mariela González CUB	2:44:18
29 Apr	Padova	Gideon Chirchir KEN	2:11:52	Rosaria Console ITA	2:30:55
29 Apr	Ravenna	Willy Kering KEN	2:22:07	Maria Cocchetti ITA	2:39:28
29 Apr	St.-Sylvain-D'Anjou	Philippe Remond FRA	2:21:45	Chantal Dällenbach FRA	2:34:19
5 May	Moskva	Mikhail Romanov RUS	2:16:08	Firiya Zhdanova RUS	2:34:58
6 May	Hannover	Andrey Gordeyev BLR	2:11:44	Anja Carlsohn GER	2:37:29
6 May	Mainz	Francis Mbiu KEN	2:17:36	Larisa Timkina MDA	2:34:06
6 May	Pittsburgh	Elly Rono KEN	2:17:15	Wioletta Kryza POL	2:34:16
6 May	Trieste	Roberto Barbi ITA	2:11:19	Franca Fiacconi ITA	2:29:58
6 May	Vancouver	Ulrich Steidl GER	2:18:56	Leteyesus Berhe ETH	2:45:51
13 May	Ottawa	Joseph Ndiritu KEN	2:15:51	Danuta Bartoszek CAN	2:37:59
20 May	Porto Alegre	Genilson da Silva BRA	2:15:55	Marizete D Rezende BRA	2:37:29
20 May	Praha	Andrew Sambu TAN	2:10:14	Maura Viceconte ITA	2:26:33
20 May	Wien	Luis Novo POR	2:10:28	Jane Salumäe EST	2:29:47
27 May	Enschede	Mustapha Riad MAR	2:12:20	Franca Fiacconi ITA	2:31:40
27 May	Regensburg	Dmitriy Kapitonov RUS	2:12:18	Valentina Delion MDA	2:43:35
3 Jun	Campinas	Alphonce Muindi KEN	2:14:52	Marizete D Rezende BRA	2:44:27
3 Jun	San Diego	John Kagwe KEN	2:10:07	Margaret Okayo KEN	2:25:05
9 Jun	Stockholm	Anders Szalkai SWE	2:18:17	Esther Kiplagat KEN	2:29:55
10 Jun	Caen	Emmanuel Kosgei KEN	2:16:26	Karina Szymanska POL	2:38:22
16 Jun	Duluth	Benjamin Matolo KEN	2:14:25	Lyubov Denisova RUS	2:35:13
17 Jun	Mont St. Michel	Julius Sugut KEN	2:12:37	Valentina Lunegova RUS	2:40:19
24 Jun	Gold Coast	Philip Costley NZL	2:13:36	Yuko Arimori JPN	2:35:40
24 Jun	Green Bay	Moges Taye ETH	2:18:44	Tatyana Titova RUS	2:38:13
1 Jul	Beirut	Kamal Saaidou MAR	2:20:18	Men only	
8 Jul	São Paolo	Stephen Rugut KEN	2:14:30	Marizete D Rezende BRA	2:38:57
4 Aug	Omsk	Eduard Tukbatoulin RUS	2:20:43	Irina Safarova RUS	2:33:08
5 Aug	Arusha	Joseph Rily KEN	2:14:18	Rukia Mkanda TAN	2:43:30
18 Aug	Helsinki	Daniel Komen Kipcheru KEN	2:18:43	Tatyana Zolotaryova RUS	2:45:56
26 Aug	Sapporo	Tsutomu Sassa JPN	2:13:45	Masako Chiba JPN	2:30:39
2 Sep	Cape Town	Keith Court RSA	2:16:23	Elana Meyer RSA	2:44:01
9 Sep	Moskva	Sergey Perminov RUS	2:22:09	Olga Bylinkina RUS	2:39:38
16 Sep	Krems	Joseph Kanda KEN	2:15:36	Karina Szymanska POL	2:42:34
23 Sep	Lyon	Rachid Ziar ALG	2:11:50	Zhanna Malkova RUS	2:34:44
23 Sep	Otterndorf	Marek Dryja POL	2:17:43	Wioletta Uryga POL	2:40:00
30 Sep	Berlin	Joseph Ngolepus KEN	2:08:47	Naoko Takahashi JPN	2:19:46
30 Sep	Budapest	Gebre Tolosa ETH	2:18:45	Judit Nagy HUN	2:39:04

30 Sep	Ciudad México (A)	Alejandro Villanueva MEX	2:17:19	Patricia Jardón MEX	2:39:41
6 Oct	Le Havre	Patrick Tambwe ZIM	2:16:25	Olga Loginova RUS	2:39:49
7 Oct	Chicago	Ben Kimondiu KEN	2:08:52	Catherine Ndereba KEN	2:18:47
7 Oct	Köln	Simon Lopuyet KEN	2:11:57	Judy Kiplimo KEN	2:31:08
7 Oct	Kosice	David Kariuki KEN	2:13:27	Galina Zhulyayeva UKR	2:36:55
7 Oct	St. Paul	Joshua Kipkemboi KEN	2:14:07	Zinaida Semyonova RUS	2:26:51
8 Oct	Providence	Elly Rono KEN	2:17:50	Tatyana Pozdnyakova UKR	2:30:28
13 Oct	Hartford	Reuben Chesang KEN	2:19:01	Lyudmila Korchagina RUS	2:39:35
14 Oct	Beijing	Gong Ke CHN	2:10:11	Liu Min CHN	2:23:37
14 Oct	Carpi	Joseph Maqala RSA	2:12:04	Patrizia Ritondo ITA	2:33:38
14 Oct	Eindhoven	Samuel Tangus KEN	2:12:47	Valentina Poltavskaya RUS	2:54:40
14 Oct	Graz	Mikola Antonenko UKR	2:15:28	Esther Barmasai KEN	2:51:49
14 Oct	Melbourne	Todd Ingraham AUS	2:23:58	Samantha Hughes AUS	2:39:44
14 Oct	München	Andrey Naumov UKR	2:13:57	Valentina Delion MDA	2:43:41
14 Oct	Odense	Vitaliy Meltsayev UKR	2:18:13	Gitte Karlshøj DEN	2:32:40
14 Oct	Poznan	Waldemar Glinka POL	2:15:38	Aniela Nikiel POL	2:43:59
21 Oct	Amsterdam	Driss El Himer FRA	2:07:02	Shitaye Gemeche ETH	2:28:40
21 Oct	Chunchon	Ji Young-joon KOR	2:15:32	Kwon Eun-joo KOR	2:31:33
21 Oct	Columbus	Kefa Keraro KEN	2:20:07	Tatyana Titova RUS	2:32:51
21 Oct	Dresden	Francis Mbui KEN	2:20:34	Dorota Ustianowska POL	2:38:00
21 Oct	Lausanne	Tesfaye Eticha ETH	2:12:39	Valentina Enaki MDA	2:39:43
21 Oct	Pompeii	Joseph Cheromei KEN	2:17:47	Giustina Menna ITA	2:39:44
21 Oct	Reims	Robert Cheruiyot KEN	2:13:17	Zhanna Malkova RUS	2:35:56
28 Oct	Dalian	Zhan Donglin CHN	2:18:58	Tian Mei CHN	2:39:15
28 Oct	Frankfurt	Pavel Loskutov EST	2:11:09	Luminita Zaituc GER	2:26:01
28 Oct	Madrid	Stefano Baldini ITA	2:09:59	Fatuma Roba ETH	2:28:33
28 Oct	Sydney	Damon Harris NZL	2:25:49	Krishna Stanton AUS	2:38:11
28 Oct	Venezia	Moges Taye ETH	2:10:08	Zahia Dahmani FRA	2:33:32
29 Oct	Dublin	Zachariah Mpolokeng RSA	2:14:03	Debbie Robinson GBR	2:35:40
4 Nov	Athína	Noah Bor KEN	2:19:26	Sonja Oberem GER	2:36:15
4 Nov	Florianapolis	Joseph Chebet KEN	2:18:30	Marizete D Rezende BRA	2:45:00
4 Nov	New York	Tesfaye Jifar ETH	2:07:43	Margaret Okayo KEN	2:24:21
4 Nov	Soweto	Mluleki Nobanda RSA	2:19:17	Gwen van Lingen RSA	2:45:37
4 Nov	Taipei	Vladimir Kotov BLR	2:21:37	Larisa Zyusko RUS	2:46:07
10 Nov	Richmond	Reuben Chesang KEN	2:17:49	Dorota Gruca POL	2:36:16
11 Nov	Istanbul	Bedasso Turube ETH	2:18:21	Lyudmila Pushkina UKR	2:38:21
11 Nov	Livorno	Philimon Kipkering KEN	2:22:48	Galina Zhulyayeva UKR	2:44:58
11 Nov	Long Beach	Joseph Kamau KEN	2:18:52	Lyubov Denisova RUS	2:34:13
18 Nov	Curitiba	João Assumpcão BRA	2:17:59	Marizete D Rezende BRA	2:42:21
18 Nov	Habana	Ignacio Alberto Cuba CUB	2:18:20	Emperatriz Wilson CUB	2:43:40
18 Nov	Philadelphia	Gennadiy Temnikov RUS	2:21:07	Olena Plastinina UKR	2:41:05
18 Nov	Tokyo	Women only		Derartu Tulu ETH	2:25:08
25 Nov	Bangkok	Vladimir Kotov BLR	2:26:55	Wioletta Kryza POL	2:48:30
25 Nov	Benidorm	Abdeslam Haimad MAR	2:18:57	Sandra Ruales ECU	2:42:11
25 Nov	Firenze	Daniel Kirwa Too KEN	2:10:38	Florinda Andreucci ITA	2:32:26
25 Nov	La Rochelle	John Ngeny KEN	2:16:19	Valentina Enaki MDA	2:35:42
25 Nov	Monaco	Wilson Kibet KEN	2:13:54	Judit Nagy HUN	2:38:23
25 Nov	San Sebastián	Samson Kandie KEN	2:10:21	Anne Kosgei KEN	2:31:19
2 Dec	Fukuoka	Gezahegne Abera ETH	2:09:25	Men only	
2 Dec	Lisboa	Stephan Freigang GER	2:14:27	Claudia Dreher GER	2:31:01
2 Dec	Macau	Benjamin Matolo KEN	2:18:58	Ren Xiujuan CHN	2:42:11
2 Dec	Mazatlan	Francisco Bautista MEX	2:15:06	Elana Meyer RSA	2:32:53
2 Dec	Milano	John Nada Saya TAN	2:08:57	Alice Chelangat KEN	2:26:36
2 Dec	Naha	Tetsuya Tanikubo JPN	2:25:19	Yoshiko Ichikawa JPN	2:35:52
2 Dec	Port Elizabeth	Simon Mpholo RSA	2:13:13	Maureen Dladla RSA	2:56:07
2 Dec	Sacramento	Bruce Deaton CAN	2:22:12	Irina Safarova RUS	2:36:49
2 Dec	Singapore	Tadesse Hailemariam ETH	2:23:02	Worknesh Tola ETH	2:53:29
8 Dec	Huntsville	Gennadiy Temnikov RUS	2:20:21	Alevtina Naumova RUS	2:39:38
8 Dec	Kisumu (A)	John Rono KEN	2:16:23	Grace Chebet KEN	2:51:35
8 Dec	Negril	Pamenos Ballentyne VIN	2:21:05	Ramilya Burangulova RUS	2:42:25
8 Dec	Palermo	Julius Bitok KEN	2:16:34	Agnes Jakab HUN	2:47:51

8 Dec	Shanghai	Li Guoliang CHN	2:21:25	Zhang Shujing CHN	2:31:54
9 Dec	Addis Ababa (A)	Tadesse Becho ETH	2:29:54	Deribe Hunde ETH	2:55:50
9 Dec	Calvia	Mulugeta Serbessa ETH	2:22:43	Janina Malska POL	2:43:49
9 Dec	Honolulu	Mbarak Hussein KEN	2:15:09	Lyubov Morgunova RUS	2:29:54
9 Dec	Latina	Philemon Kipkering KEN	2:15:10	Giovanna Ricotta ITA	2:37:50
16 Dec	Hofu	Hailu Neguse ETH	2:10:32	Men only	
16 Dec	Reggio Emilia	Farid Marrraffe MAR	2:18:34	Ida Kovács HUN	2:38:26

A =altitude over 1000 m

See also Championships section for marathons in those events

WORLD ROAD RACE REVIEW 2001

By David E Martin

THE USA's Road Running Information Center (RRIC), together with the American Sports Data Corporation, keeps detailed statistical information regarding trends in participation in running events. The 7,447,000 results submitted for 2000 showed that the worldwide road racing industry was growing. There was an 8% increase in participants in the average marathon and a 5% increase in half marathon entries as well as shorter-distance events. Similar trends were seen in Europe and in Southeast Asia, as well as in the larger cities of South America.

Although the greatest concentration of road races is in Europe and North America, it is the Kenyan men, and, increasingly, women, who achieve huge worldwide success and, much to the delight of their agents, they capture most of the available prize money. As an example, at the 24th Utica Boilermaker 15k, 22 of the top 28 men and 8 of the top 12 women were Kenyans. There were similarly figures at the Falmouth 7.1M with 14 of 17 and 8 of 15 women and at the Clarksburg 10k with 15 of 17 and 8 of 9. While European race directors prefer greater diversity, the Kenyan numbers are dominant there as well.

There was an interesting innovation at the Amsterdam-to-Zaandam 10M in September as the men started their race 6.47 minutes after the women; the time representing the difference in previous top finish times between men and women. Thus, both men and women were showcased; but the World 10k champion Charles Kamathi could not catch Susan Chepkemei (over 2 minutes ahead) or Isabella Ochichi (23 seconds).

Some races mix tourism with competition. A good example of latter is the so-called World's Best 10k, out and back over the 2.5k Teodoro Moscoso bridge in San Juan, Puerto Rico in February. The heat, humidity, and wind are always oppressive in that part of the Caribbean, but a friendly organizing committee and a huge bankroll ($400,000 in prize money in 2001) ensures that the best athletes come, do some warm-weather training, relax, and have the potential for a big payday. Paul Tergat took $20,000 as he won from the defending champion Khalid Khannouchi, as did Lornah Kiplagat, who won from Elana Mayer, with Tegla Loroupe and Catherine Nederba also running.

An annual series gaining in stature is the (third) Avon Running Global Championships – the culmination of women-only 10k and 5k walk/runs for every age and fitness level. The winners of races held in a dozen nations worldwide were flown to Budapest for the finale on 14 October – a week after the IAAF World Half Marathon and the Chicago marathon. Invitations were also extended to top women, and the turnout was indeed remarkable. Amazingly, Catherine Ndereba flew from Chicago to Budapest and after less than a week's recovery from her marathon world best, dominated her rivals as her 31:02 was the second fastest certified road 10k ever run in Europe – 11 seconds ahead of Meyer's national record 31:13. In third Olivera Jevtic set a Yugoslav national record. These and other athletes shared in the richest women's-only 10k prize purse ever offered ($53,000).

Total USA-athlete prize money for the USA Running Circuit, in its seventh year for the men and eighth year for the women in 2001 exceeded $330,000, divided for each event among the top ten runners for each event, who also earned points, which allowed an additional Grand Prix purse of $6,000, $4,000, and $2,500 to be awarded to the top three men and women scorers. California's Milena Glusac won the women's circuit, and Colorado's Dan Browne the men's.

Women's participation was especially increased globally in quality and quantity, due primarily to more women's-only events and woman-centered "events for a cause," such as the Revlon Run for Women and the Race for the Cure. The Stockholm all-women's 10k Tjemilen on 8 August had 20,381 finishers.

Irina Safarova and Irina Timofeyeva were 1-2 (50:53/51:15) at the European Inter-club championships for women in Salo, Italy, over 15k, helping Russia to a narrow team victory over Italy.

Catherine Ndereba on the Roads in 2001

Date	*Venue*	*Dist*	*Pl*	*Time*	*Event*
18 Feb	San Juan	10km	5	32:30	World's Best 10K
24 Mar	Den Haag	HMar	1	67:54 PB	City-Pier-City
7 Apr	Charleston	10km	1	32:33	Cooper River Bridge
16 Apr	Boston	Mar	1	2:23:53	Boston Marathon,
8 Jul	Utica	15km	1	48:06* PB	Utica Boilermarker
14 Jul	Farmingdale	5km	1	15:35	Vytra Women's 5K
21 Jul	Davenport	7M	1	37:05	Quad City Times Bix-7
28 Jul	Clarksburg	10km	1	33:15	Greater Clarksburg 10K
4 Aug	Cape Elizabeth	10km	1	31:34*	Beach to Beacon 10K
12 Aug	Falmouth	7.1M	2	36:34	Falmouth Road Race
18 Aug	Philadelphia	10km	1	33:33	Unity 10K
25 Aug	Flint	10M	1	52:36	Bobby Crim 10-mile
3 Sep	Marietta	10km	1	33:34	U.S. 10K Classic
16 Sep	Philadelphia	HMar	1	68:30*	Philadelphia Half Mar
7 Oct	Chicago	Mar	1	2:18:47* WB	LaSalle Bank Chicago
14 Oct	Budapest	10km	1	31:02* PB	Avon Global Champs.
23 Nov	Chiba	10km	1	31:35	Chiba Ekiden 1st leg

* = course record, # = world best performance, PB = personal best

Across the Atlantic, some 3700 finishers crossed the line in New York's Central Park in June for the all-women's 10k known as the Mini Marathon. Paula Radcliffe won by 66 seconds and ran the second fastest time in history for the distance (30:47). She continued her winning ways, as, just 35 hours after setting a Commonwealth track record over 5000m in Berlin (14:32.44), she ran a world road best 14:57 against 20,000 women at the Flora Light Challenge For Women over 5k in London's Hyde Park, 25 seconds ahead of Tegla Loroupe. Later she successfully defended her title at the IAAF World Half Marathon Championships in Bristol, showing superiority over a superb field with 66:47, both a championship record and European record, and just three seconds off Elana Meyer's world best on an unaided course. Runner-up Susan Chepkemei was 49 seconds behind and personal bests were set by the top seven finishers.

It was Chepkemei's third major race in four weekends, including a victory at the BUPA Great North Run from Newcastle to South Shields, England. This was one of Europe's largest road races, with more than 37,000 completing the half marathon. Chepkemei had an epic duel with Joyce Chepchumba after four miles when Derartu Tulu could no longer could no longer maintain the quick pace. Only in the final 600m did Chepkemei take the lead. Whereas she was preparing for the New York City marathon by using the shorter-distance races to improve speed, Paul Tergat (later to race the Chicago marathon) was similarly attempting to break the hour barrier. Winds slowed him to 60:30, but he was victorious nonetheless.

Haile Gebrselassie, who plans his marathon debut in 2002, won his national half-marathon championship in Addis Ababa and a 10k in Praha before taking on a superb field in Bristol, winning by one second (60:03) in a sprint finish over countryman Tesfaye Jifar – with Ethiopia winning the team trophy as well. Later in the year, Gebrselassie helped to create and support Africa's running event outside South Africa – the Great Ethiopian Run. With British ex-marathoner Richard Nerurkar serving as race director, nearly 10,000 runners toed the line in Addis Ababa (at 2440 m altitude) to race 10k through the city streets. Gebrselassie was again victorious in 30:15 over countryman Assefa Mezgebu (31:08).

Road racing for African women was given a boost by Lornah Kiplagat, who followed Gebrselassie's concept with the first international women's 10k road race in Africa at her High Altitude Training Centre at Iten (2400 m).. The race was an out-and-back trip from there into the city; 28 women finished, led by Jane Ekimat (32:15) and Ruth Chebeii (34:59).

James Koskei is a contender as male road racer of the year based solely on non-marathon road events, with his eight victories on the North American circuit (Charleston, New Orleans, Vancouver, Cleveland, San Francisco, Green Bay, Clarksburg, and Boulder). John Korir, however, while winning only five road races (Atlanta, Utica, Davenport, Falmouth, and Washington) faced more challenging fields.

Selection of a female road racer of the year was simple: 29-year old Catherine Ndereba. Even without considering her two marathon victories at Boston and Chicago, her excellence through the year was remarkable: in 15 road races, she won 13, losing twice to Lornah Kiplagat. She set personal bests at four distances, and ended her year with the fastest recorded lead-off leg (10k) at the Chiba Ekiden in Japan. The diversity of her year's activities in road racing are shown in the accompanying table, and serves as a useful glimpse into the extraordinary diversity that comprises today's road-racing scene.

2001 Road Races

1 Jan	Paris 10km	Sammy Kipketer KEN 28:31	Rakiya Quétier FRA 33:59
5 Jan	Maldonado 10km	Paul Tergat KEN 28:46	Lydia Cheromei KEN 33:13
6 Jan	Miyazaki HMar	Women only	Elana Meyer RSA 69:42
7 Jan	Ratingen 10km	Luka Keitany KEN 28:30	Leah Malot KEN 32:20
7 Jan	Seixal HMar	Dmitriy Maksimov RUS 63:27	Fernanda Ribeiro POR 72:56
12 Jan	Dubai 10km	Phalia Kimani KEN 30:30	Tezata Nuray Sürekli TUR 33:54
13 Jan	Cape Town 30km	Luketz Swartbooi NAM 1:37:22	Renee Scott RSA 2:05:02
13 Jan	Hamilton, BER 10km	Mohamed Amyn MAR 30:09	Courtney Babcock CAN 34:23
14 Jan	Egmond aan Zee HMar	Kamiel Maase NED 63:42	Susan Chepkemei KEN 70:36*
14 Jan	San Bartolomeo HMar	Salaho Ngadi TAN 63:24	Giglioli Borghini ITA 79:41
16 Jan	Jaen 8.4km	Alberto García ESP 24:15	Leah Malot KEN 27:43
21 Jan	Modena 12.25km	Alberico Di Cecco ITA 36:40	Maria Guida ITA 40:56
21 Jan	Carlsbad HMar	Janko Bensa YUG 63:55	Valentina Yegorova RUS 73:48
28 Jan	Best HMar	Enock Keter Kiptoo KEN 64:01*	Vivian Ruitjers NED 75:23*
28 Jan	Naples HMar	Elly Rono KEN 64:56	Ramilya Burangulova RUS 74:54
28 Jan	Redondo Beach 10km	Mebrahtom Keflezighi USA 29:53	Sylvia Mosqueda USA 32:21
28 Jan	Viana do Castelo HMar	Dmitriy Maksimov RUS 64:22	Fatima Silva POR 74:55
31 Jan	Modena 13.2km	David Makori KEN 37:15	Rita Jeptoo KEN 45:07
3 Feb	Bellville 10km	Warren Peterson RSA 29:43	Elana Meyer RSA 31:56
3 Feb	Catania 12km	Paul Tergat KEN 33:10	Men only
3 Feb	Pretoria HMar short	Simon Mphulanyane RSA 61:46	Sarah Mahlangu RSA 77:52
4 Feb	Austin HMar	Eddy Hellebuyck USA 64:13	Albina Gallyamova RUS 74:18
4 Feb	Coamo HMar	Christopher Cheboiboch KEN 64:21	Ramilya Burangulova RUS 76:06
4 Feb	Eldoret (A) HMar	Ben Kimondiu KEN 62:21	Men only
4 Feb	Hampton HMar	Shaun Creighton AUS 64:39	Yelena Paramonova RUS 74:13
4 Feb	Las Vegas HMar	Weldon Johnson USA 65:35	Rosa Gutierrez USA 73:17
4 Feb	Marugame HMar	Hidenori Noguchi JPN 62:28	Ikumi Nagayama JPN 69:28
10 Feb	Ein Gedi HMar	Gilbert Koech KEN 63:35*	Nili Avramski ISR 77:48
11 Feb	Karatsu 10M	Yuko Matsumiya JPN 46:35	Men only
18 Feb	Barcelona HMar	Michael Sarwath KEN 63:50	Eva Sanz ESP 72:52
18 Feb	Ferrara HMar	Aziz Laraichi MAR 62:41	Maria Cocchetti ITA 74:40
18 Feb	Ohme 30km	Makoto Ogura JPN 1:31:37	Naoko Takahashi JPN 1:41:57 WB
18 Feb	San Juan 10km	Paul Tergat KEN 28:25*	Lornah Kiplagat KEN 31:37*
25 Feb	Inuyama HMar	Hironori Arai JPN 63:47	Mio Kiuchi JPN 73:00
25 Feb	Kwangyang HMar	Lee Eui-soo KOR 63:59	Chung Bok-eun KOR 75:25
25 Feb	Osaka HMar	Hiroshi Miki JPN 62:54	Kazue Ogoshi JPN 70:24
25 Feb	Ostia HMar	Giuliano Battocletti ITA 62:24	Tiziana Alagia ITA 71:29
3 Mar	Frankfurt HMar	Julius Maritim KEN 65:37	Marleen Renders BEL 76:19
4 Mar	Paris HMar	Elijah Nyabuti KEN 62:26	Florence Barsosio KEN 71:22
4 Mar	Ravenna HMar	Daniele Caimmi ITA 62:32	Rita Jeptoo KEN 74:56
10 Mar	Jacksonville 15km	Mebrahtom Keflezighi USA 43:16	Deena Drossin USA 49:09
11 Mar	Alphen aan den Rijn 20km	Richard Mutai KEN 58:15	Lornah Kiplagat KEN 63:54WB
11 Mar	Kyoto HMar	Koichiro Nagata JPN 61:09	Fatuma Roba ETH 69:19
11 Mar	Pieve di Cento HMar	Moses Masai KEN 64:12	Sara Ferrari ITA 73:34
11 Mar	San José 10km	Simon Sawe KEN 29:14	Lyudmila Vasilyeva RUS 33:35
11 Mar	Sendai HMar	Kenichi Takahashi JPN 63:35	Elana Meyer RSA 70:12
11 Mar	Torino HMar	Haron Toroitich KEN 60:53	Ruth Kutol KEN 70:51
11 Mar	Yamaguchi HMar	Yuki Mori JPN 61:27*	Mizuki Noguchi JPN 68:45*
17 Mar	Kerzers 15km	Daniel Kirui KEN 45:07	Fatima Yvelain FRA 53:33
17 Mar	Virginia Beach 8km	John Thuo Itati KEN 22:38	Teresa Wanjiku KEN 26:00
18 Mar	Hastings HMar	Stephen Ariga KEN 64:11	Andrea Green GBR 77:08
24 Mar	Den Haag HMar	Rodgers Rop KEN 62:12	Catherine Ndereba KEN 67:54
24 Mar	Praha HMar	Anthony Korir KEN 62:09	Florence Barsosio KEN 72:51
25 Mar	Hamilton CAN 30km	Joseph Ndiritu KEN 1:36:40	Elisabeth Ruel CAN 1:54:21
25 Mar	Mobile 10km	Abraham Chebii KEN 27:26*	Gladys Asiba KEN 32:42
30 Mar	Doha HMar	Kamal Saaidou MAR 63:54	Men only
31 Mar	Milano HMar	Patrick Ivuti ITA 60:42	Men only
1 Apr	Azpeitia HMar	Simon Kasimili KEN 62:24	Eva Sanz ESP 71:57
1 Apr	Berkane 10km	Peter Chebet KEN 28:01	Men only

1 Apr	Berlin HMar	Fabián Roncero ESP 59:52*	Joyce Chepchumba KEN 69:37
1 Apr	Carlsbad 5km	Sammy Kipketer KEN 13:00*=WB	Sally Barsosio KEN 15:20
1 Apr	Chicago 8km	Shaun Creighton AUS 22:51*	Kathy Butler GBR 25:25*
1 Apr	La Courneuve 10km	Albert Chepkurui KEN 27:31	Asmae Leghzaoui MAR 31:23
1 Apr	Lisboa HMar	Hendrick Ramaala RSA 60:26	Susan Chepkemei KEN 65:44*WB
1 Apr	Madrid HMar	Abel Chimukoko KEN 63:22	Jane Salumäe EST 73:20
1 Apr	Wrzesnia HMar	Dariusz Kruczkowski POL 63:45	Malgorzata Sobanska POL 72:06
7 Apr	Charleston 10km	James Koskei KEN 28:45	Catherine Ndereba KEN 32:33
7 Apr	Toronto 8km	Benson Ogato KEN 23:44	Jackline Torori KEN 26:44
8 Apr	Barcelona 10km	David Tuwei KEN 28:24	Tausi Juma Ngaa TAN 32:33
8 Apr	Brunssum 10km	Sammy Kipketer KEN 27:18*WB	Pamela Chepchumba KEN 31:51*
8 Apr	Fieso D'Artico HMar	Anthony Korir KEN 63:22	Rosaria Console ITA 72:32
8 Apr	Marseille 10km	Mustapha Riad MAR 29:20	Isabella Ochichi KEN 31:29
8 Apr	Oostduinkerke 15km	Isaac Chemobwo KEN 47:24	Angelina Kanana KEN 55:38
8 Apr	Washington 10M	John Korir KEN 46:12	Elena Meyer RSA 52:16
14 Apr	Balmoral 5M	Mohammed Mourhit BEL 22:40	Gete Wami ETH 25:14
14 Apr	New Orleans 10km	James Koskei KEN 28:31	Elana Meyer RSA 32:07
15 Apr	Paderborn 10km	Richard Mutai KEN 28:34	Pamela Chepchumba KEN 31:27
15 Apr	Paderborn HMar	Christopher Kandie KEN 62:23	Petra Drajzajtlová CZE 72:49
16 Apr	Brugnera HMar	Jonah Koech KEN 63:22	Norah Maraga KEN 73:36
16 Apr	Dongio 10/5km	Paul Kosgei KEN 28:14	Isabella Ochichi KEN 15:42
16 Apr	Gualtieri 10km	Stephen Rerimoi KEN 28:09	Margaret Okayo KEN 32:38
16 Apr	Prato HMar	Philip Manyim KEN 62:54	Silvia Sommaggio ITA 73:52
22 Apr	Nice HMar	Peter Chebet KEN 61:32	Edith Masai KEN 67:53
22 Apr	Mt. Vernon 15km	Joseph Ndiritu KEN 44:42	Silviya Skvortsova RUS 55:01
22 Apr	Poznan 10km	John Yuda TAN 28:26	Margaret Ngotho KEN 32:52
22 Apr	Vitry-sur-Seine HMar	Laban Kipkemboi KEN 61:16	Maura Viceconte ITA 69:19
22 Apr	Vancouver 10km	James Koskei KEN 28:06	Sally Barsosio KEN 33:04
25 Apr	Leca da Palmeira 10km	David Kipruto KEN 28:43	Fernanda Ribeiro POR 32:45
28 Apr	Luzern 8.565/4.190km	Sammy Kipruto KEN 24:38	Tegla Loroupe KEN 13:04
29 Apr	Cleveland 10km	James Koskei KEN 28:08	Sally Barsosio KEN 31:43*
29 Apr	Dedham 10km	Stephen Kiogora KEN 28:45	Martha Komu KEN 32:54
29 Apr	Heillecourt 8.7/4.7km	Paul Kosgei KEN 24:03	Edith Masai KEN 14:15
29 Apr	Kansas City 4M	John Kariuki KEN 17:50	Elva Dryer USA 19:41*
29 Apr	Washington 10km	Joseph Ndiritu KEN 28:39	Yelena Paramonova RUS 33:48
29 Apr	Wurzburg 10km	John Yuda TAN 28:27	Linah Cheruiyot KEN 32:33
1 May	Marseille 10km	Driss El Himer FRA 28:13	Asmae Leghzaoui MAR 31:03
4 May	Indianapolis HMar	Simon Rono KEN 62:36	Yelena Paramonova RUS 71:36
5 May	Göteborg HMar	Pavel Loskutov EST 63:00	Stine Larsen NOR 71:07
5 May	Moskva HMar	Yuriy Chizhov RUS 64:29	Lyubov Morgunova RUS 71:14
6 May	Berlin 25km	Rodgers Rop KEN 1:13:44WB	Magdaline Chemjor KEN 1:25:11
6 May	Breda 10km	Hilaire N'Tirampeba BDI 43:09*	Caroline Kwambai KEN 49:18
6 May	Philadelphia 10M	Ronald Mogaka KEN 46:48*	Misti Demko USA 55:14
6 May	Setúbal HMar	Kibet Kigen KEN 62:03	Maura Viceconte ITA 71:25
6 May	Spokane 12km	Dominic Kirui KEN 34:29	Elana Meyer RSA 39:23
6 May	Toronto HMar	Benson Ogato KEN 28:23	Edna Kiplagat KEN 32:14
12 May	Bern 10M	Kenneth Cheruiyot KEN 48:26	Lornah Kiplagat KEN 55:31
12 May	Grand Rapids 25km	John Kagwe KEN 1:14:07	Svetlana Zakharova RUS 1:24:39*
13 May	Fiesole 15km	Ronald Munyao KEN 45:11	Gloria Marconi ITA 54:18
13 May	Ottawa 10km	Joseph Ndiritu KEN 28:29	Uta Pippig GER 32:32
13 May	Santos 10km	João N'Tyamba ANG 28:24	Leah Kiprono KEN 33:20
19 May	Cape Town 8km	Makhosonke Fika RSA 24:14	Elana Meyer RSA 26:29
19 May	Flemington 10km	Craig Mottram AUS 28:51	Susie Power AUS 32:37
20 May	Almeria HMar	Samuel Kimaiyo KEN 64:08	Dolores Pulido ESP 73:03
20 May	Coban HMar	Jackson Koech KEN 64:49	Lucia Subano KEN 76:56
20 May	Fafe 10km	Kibet Kigen KEN 28:40	Elizabeth Chemweno KEN 32:37
20 May	Far Hills 15km	Stephen Ondieki KEN 45:15	Zhanna Malkova RUS 54:37
20 May	Glasgow 10km	Women only	Lornah Kiplagat KEN 31:53
20 May	Lisboa 12km	Martin Hhaway Sulle TAN 34:32	Helena Sampaio POR 39:25
20 May	San Francisco 12km	James Koskei KEN 34:19	Jane Ngotho KEN 40:35
26 May	Wheeling 20km	John Yuda TAN 60:41	Teresa Wanjiku KEN 71:07

27 May	Bruxelles 20km	Joseph Sitienei KEN 61:23	Marleen Renders BEL 70:48
27 May	Den Haag 10km	Paul Kipkemoi Biwott KEN 27:58	Judy Kiplimo KEN 32:00
28 May	Boulder 10km (A)	James Koskei KEN 29:00	Deena Drossin USA 33:25
1 Jun	Logroño HMar	John Nada Saya TAN 63:38	Laura Pinula ESP 76:40
3 Jun	Tilburg 10 mi/10km	Rodgers Rop KEN 45:56*	Susan Chepkemei KEN 31:52
9 Jun	Bern 5km	Women only	Leah Malot KEN 15:27
9 Jun	Green Bay 10km	James Koskei KEN 28:01	Elana Meyer RSA 32:31
9 Jun	Neuss 10km	Tendai Chimusasa ZIM 28:29	Simona Staicu HUN 32:37
9 Jun	New York 10km	Women only	Paula Radcliffe GBR 30:47*
9 Jun	Peoria 4M	Shadrack Hoff RSA 17:45	Lornah Kiplagat KEN 19:33
10 Jun	Middletown 10km	John Yuda TAN 28:49	Teresa Wanjiku KEN 34:18
10 Jun	Mondsee HMar	Boniface Usisivu KEN 62:10	Mary Ptikany KEN 75:17
10 Jun	Saltillo HMar	Peter Chebet KEN 62:25*	Milkah Chepkieny KEN 73:28
17 Jun	Porto 15km	Samson Ramadhani KEN 44:03	Florence Barsosio KEN 49:28
23 Jun	Lelystad 10M	Moses Kemboi KEN 46:53	Stine Larsen NOR 54:06
24 Jun	Ballycotton 10M	Noel Berkeley IRL 49:54	Sonia O'Sullivan IRL 55:37
24 Jun	Fairfield HMar	John Yuda TAN 62:39*	Teresa Wanjiku KEN 76:02
24 Jun	Gold Coast HMar	Jonathan Wyatt NZL 63:14	Takako Kotorida JPN 72:11
26 Jun	Darmstadt 7.6/4.9km	Laban Chege KEN 21:11	Restituta Joseph TAN 15:12
1 Jul	Arona HMar	Antonio Peña ESP 64:51	Maria Abel ESP 73:00
1 Jul	Sapporo HMar	James Wainaina KEN 61:52	Lidia Simon ROM 69:46
4 Jul	Atlanta 10km	John Korir KEN 28:19	Lornah Kiplagat KEN 30:58
8 Jul	Oos Londen HMar	Abner Chipu RSA 61:50	Charne Rademeyer RSA 77:22
8 Jul	Utica 15km	John Korir KEN 42:57	Catherine Ndereba KEN 48:06*
14 Jul	Kingsport 8km	Alene Emere ETH 22:04	Irene Kwambai KEN 25:47
15 Jul	Recanati 10km	Yusuf Songoka KEN 28:08	Men only
21 Jul	Davenport 7M	John Korir KEN 32:24	Catherine Ndereba KEN 37:05
22 Jul	Lozere 22.4km	Elijah Nyabuti KEN 73:02	Ines Chenonge KEN 83:28
25 Jul	Voorthuizen 10km	Germán Silva MEX 29:08	Lornah Kiplagat KEN 31:19*
26 Jul	Castelbuono 11.026/5.5km	Benson Barus KEN 33:01	Daniela Rodica Moroianu FRA 18:11
28 Jul	Clarksburg 10km	James Koskei KEN 28:30*	Catherine Ndereba KEN 33:15
28 Jul	Namakgale HMar	Abner Chipu RSA 62:56	Elana Meyer RSA 72:25
4 Aug	Cape Elizabeth 10km	Evans Rutto KEN 28:30	Catherine Ndereba KEN 31:34*
11 Aug	Stockholm 10km	John Rotich KEN 28:57	Bente Landøy NOR 33:58
12 Aug	Falmouth 7.1M	John Korir KEN 32:26	Lornah Kiplagat KEN 36:26
12 Aug	Sydney 14km	John Yuda TAN 40:24	Susie Power AUS 45:08*
18 Aug	Arco 10km	Peter Chebet KEN 28:18	Men only
18 Aug	Parkersburg HMar	Dan Browne USA 63:55	Milena Glusac USA 72:13
18 Aug	Philadelphia 10km	Gilbert Okari KEN 28:24	Catherine Ndereba KEN 33:33
19 Aug	Amatrice 8.5km	Benson Barus KEN 24:17	Maura Viceconte ITA 27:30
19 Aug	Glasgow HMar	Abner Chipu RSA 63:23	Joyce Chepchumba KEN 69:15
19 Aug	San Diego HMar	Wilson Onsare KEN 62:45	Margaret Okayo KEN 70:38*
25 Aug	Flint 10M	Laban Kipkemboi KEN 46:41	Catherine Ndereba KEN 52:36
26 Aug	Rio de Janeiro HMar	João N'Tyamba ANG 63:31	Selma Reis BRA 75:02
26 Aug	Stockholm 10km	Women only	Lena Gavelin SWE 33:35
1 Sep	Lille HMar	Driss El Himer FRA 62:08	Hafida Gadi FRA 73:16
2 Sep	Altotting HMar	Tesfaye Eticha ETH 63:24	Judy Kiplimo KEN 70:18
2 Sep	Ciudad México 26.2km (A)	Paul Atodonyang KEN 1:21:53*	Pamela Chepchumba KEN 1:37:41*
2 Sep	Deurne HMar	Salim Kipsang KEN 62:09	Petra Drajzatjlová CZE 73:25
3 Sep	Düsseldorf 10km	Tendai Chimusasa ZIM 28:49	Linah Cheruiyot KEN 32:37
3 Sep	London 5km	Women only	Paula Radcliffe GBR 14:57 WB
3 Sep	Marietta 10km	Sammy Ngeno KEN 29:14	Catherine Ndereba KEN 33:34
3 Sep	New Haven 20km	Dan Browne USA 60:10	Milena Glusac USA 67:49
3 Sep	Park Forest 10M	Patrick Nthiwa KEN 47:20	Naomi Wangui KEN 55:02
3 Sep	Virginia Beach HMar	Shadrack Hoff RSA 62:19*	Deena Drossin USA 70:08*
9 Sep	Buenos Aires HMar	Angus Cheptot KEN 64:42	Ramilya Burangulova RUS 72:59
9 Sep	Cheltenham 10km	Julius Kibet KEN 28:36	Daniela Rodica Moroianu FRA 32:40
9 Sep	Pila HMar	John Rotich KEN 62:46*	Dorota Gruca POL 73:39
9 Sep	Salo 15km	Women only	Irina Safarova RUS 50:53
9 Sep	Vanderbijlpark 10km	Hendrick Ramaala RSA 28:50	Elana Meyer RSA 33:43
15 Sep	Gouda 10km	Paul Kiprotich KEN 28:37	Wilma van Onna NED 33:49

15 Sep	Novosibirsk HMar	Aleksandr Korobov RUS 63:51	Silviya Skvortsova RUS 69:37
16 Sep	Arezzo HMar	Stefano Baldini ITA 63:03	Maura Viceconte ITA 72:55
16 Sep	Philadelphia HMar	Ronald Mogaka KEN 61:25	Catherine Ndereba KEN 68:30*
16 Sep	Pietramurata HMar	Nicholas Kemboi KEN 61:41	Winfrida Kwamboka KEN 72:53
16 Sep	Providence 5km	Gilbert Okari KEN 13:30	Uta Pippig GER 15:30
16 Sep	South Shields HMar	Paul Tergat KEN 60:30	Susan Chepkemei KEN 68:40
23 Sep	Arusha HMar (A)	Zebedayo Bayo TAN 64:25	Martha Komu KEN 72:10
23 Sep	Den Bosch 10km	John Kipchumba KEN 28:25	Jane Kiptoo KEN 32:24*
23 Sep	Montbéliard HMar	Abdelgani Lahlali FRA 62:40	Zahia Dahmani FRA 73:32
23 Sep	Praha 10/5km	Haile Gebrselassie ETH 28:07*	Beáta Rakonczai HUN 15:58
23 Sep	St. Denis HMar	Eduardo Henriques POR 62:53	Beatrice Omwanza KEN 74:35
23 Sep	Torino HMar	Barnabas Rutto KEN 62:04	Anastasia Ndereba KEN 72:36
23 Sep	Toronto HMar	Joseph Ndiritu KEN 63:23	Jackline Torori KEN 72:19
23 Sep	Uster HMar	Christopher Kandie KEN 63:00	Judy Kiplimo KEN 69:46
23 Sep	Zaandam 10M	Charles Kamathi KEN 46:05	Susan Chepkemei KEN 51:23
30 Sep	Attleboro 5M	David Chelule KEN 22:32	Jane Ngotho KEN 25:56
30 Sep	Haarlem HMar	John Kipchumba KEN 62:51	Wilma van Onna NED 74:33
30 Sep	Lisboa HMar	David Makori KEN 62:18	Fatuma Roba ETH 70:29
30 Sep	Pittsburgh 10km 122m drop	Gilbert Koech KEN 27:32	Gladys Asiba KEN 32:10
30 Sep	Remich HMar	Paul Biwott KEN 63:05	Luminita Zaituc GER 71:04
30 Sep	Udine HMar	Japhet Kosgei KEN 61:23	Margaret Okayo KEN 68:51*
30 Sep	Versailles 16.3km	Francis Komu KEN 48:33	Isabella Ochichi KEN 54:13
7 Oct	Breda HMar	Wilson Kigen KEN 62:04	Linah Cheruiyot KEN 72:46
7 Oct	Youngstown 10km	Moses Macharia KEN 28:33	Jackline Torori KEN 34:20
8 Oct	Boston 10km	Women only	Colleen de Reuck USA 32:11
14 Oct	Budapest 10km Avon	Women only	Catherine Ndereba KEN 31:02*
14 Oct	Burnie 10km	Steve Moneghetti AUS 28:55	Susie Power AUS 32:11
14 Oct	Chula Vista 10km	Shadrack Hoff RSA 28:22	Colleen de Reuck USA 32:35
14 Oct	Portsmouth 10M	Khalid Skah MAR 46:17	Restituta Joseph TAN 52:36
21 Oct	Toronto 10km	Gilbert Koech KEN 28:37	Jackline Torori KEN 33:38
28 Oct	Cassis 20.3km	David Makori KEN 61:11	Magdalena Chemjor KEN 69:52
28 Oct	Palermo HMar	Philip Rugut KEN 61:28*	Carol Galea MLT 78:31
28 Oct	Sydney 10km	Ben DuBois AUS 29:53	Susie Power AUS 32:15
3 Nov	Mobile 10km	Nicholas Rogers USA 28:18	Elva Dryer USA 32:43
11 Nov	Barcelona 9.533/6.45km	Robert Mudogo KEN 28:16	Chantal Dällenbach FRA 21:25
11 Nov	Nijmegen 15km	Felix Limo KEN 41:29 WB	Rose Cheruiyot KEN 48:40
11 Nov	Phoenix 10km	John Thuo Itati KEN 29:45	Teresa Wanjiku KEN 33:25
16 Nov	Iten 10km (A)	Women only	Jane Ekimat KEN 32:15
22 Nov	Jacksonville HMar	Gabriel Muchiri KEN 63:15	Ramilya Burangulova RUS 72:56
22 Nov	Manchester 4.748M	Leonard Mucheru KEN 21:40	Svetlana Zakharova RUS 24:22
23 Nov	Nagoya HMar	James Wainaina KEN 61:04	Mizuki Noguchi JPN 68:28
25 Nov	Addis Ababa (A)	Haile Gebrselassie ETH 30:30	Berhane Adere ETH 35:07
25 Nov	Bilbao 15km	Philip Kipkoech KEN 43:39	Hawa Hussein TAN 50:40
1 Dec	Genève 7.25/4.78km	Thomas Nyariki KEN 20:22	Lornah Kiplagat KEN 15:03
1 Dec	Mazatlan 10km	Simson Limareng KEN 28:23	Pamela Chepchumba KEN 32:19*
1 Dec	Rota da Luz HMar	Augustine Togorn KEN 62:01	Ines Chenonge KEN 70:35
2 Dec	Mazatlan HMar	Gabino Apolonio MEX 63:19*	Colleen de Reuck USA 76:19*
2 Dec	Okayama 10km	Women only	Miwako Yamanaka JPN 32:10
2 Dec	Paris 20km	Philippe Rémond FRA 62:17	Chantal Dallenbach FRA 70:50
9 Dec	Heerenberg 15km	Kenenisa Bekele ETH 42:42	Sandra Van den Haesevelde BEL 52:15
9 Dec	Kosa 10M	Simon Maina KEN 45:29*	Men only
16 Dec	Arusha 10km (A)	Zebedayo Bayo TAN 28:32	Zakia Mrisho TAN 32:56
16 Dec	Kobe HMar	Women only	Miwako Yamanaka JPN 68:54
16 Dec	Los Palacios HMar	David Kimei KEN 62:29	Faustine Maria ESP 84:49
16 Dec	Zürich ~10/7km	Michael Tanui KEN 29:45	Berhane Adere ETH 22:18
30 Dec	Paris 10km	Benjamin Limo KEN 28:38	Ines Monteiro POR 32:41
31 Dec	Bolzano 10.05/5.05km	Sergey Lebed UKR 28:42	Susan Chepkemei KEN 16:27
31 Dec	Madrid 10km	Isaac Viciosa ESP 28:32	Maria Abel ESP 32:53
31 Dec	São Paolo 15km	Tesfaye Jifar ETH 44:15	Maria Zeferina Baldaia BRA 52:12

(A) = altitude over 1000 m

See also Championships section for road races in those events

ULTRA SUMMARY 2001

by Andy Milroy

2001 was far from being a vintage year at ultra-running's flagship distance, the 100km. For the first time in at least twenty years no male runner broke 6:30. (Before that time courses were often not accurate, so the reliability of the earlier sub 6:30 marks may be doubtful).

Japanese runners continued their rise but Yasufumi Mikami's 6:33:28 was the slowest winning time for the World Challenge since 1991. The exciting potential of newcomers Vladimir Netreba and Aleksey Belosludtsev, who ran the year's best two times in the Russian championships in May, was not fulfilled later, although Netreba did take the European title.

There was a South African winner at last in the Comrades and Andrew Kelehe's winning time was close to Bruce Fordyce's course record. Like most of the top male finishers in this 89k race, he ran only that one race during the year.

Yiannis Kouros, now approaching his third decade of world-class performances, ran his best 24 Hour mark since 1998 to win a very competitive event at Verona, with Lubomir Hrmo becoming the 6th best 24 Hour track performer of all-time right behind him. with 270.337 km.

Alain Prual was third with 259.778 km ahead of fellow Frenchman Loic Lebon's 257.064 km. The European title was won by Paul Beckers of Belgium with 260.559 km from Jens Lukas of Germany with 258.907 km.

Men's Rankings

1. Yasufumi Mikami JPN – top because he set two of the fastest times in the most competitive ultra event, the 100km, 1st in the World 100km (6:33:28); 1st at Lake Saroma (6:38:50).

2. Andrew Kelehe RSA – winner of the 89km Comrades Marathon (5:25:51), the world's largest and most competitive ultramarathon. His time was the best since Fordyce in 1986. The course distance changes slightly almost every year, so exact time comparisons have to be made carefully (Fordyce ran 5:24:07 for 88.7 km; Kelehe 5:25:51 for over 89.0 km; Vladimir Kotov had run 5:25:33 for 87.3km in 2000).

3. Yiannis Kouros AUS – winner at Verona (275.828km), the best 24 hour mark of the year in the top race.

4. Gregoriy Murzin RUS – 6th at Comrades 5:32:59 and 1st at the De Bezana 100km in Spain (6:35:19).

5. Vladimir Netreba RUS – winner of the Russian 100km Championship (6:30:07), the fastest 100km of the year; also won the European 100km Championship (6:45:45).

6. Leonid Shvetsov RUS – 2nd at Comrades (5:26:28) in his ultramarathon debut

7. Vladimir Kotov BLR – 3rd at Comrades (5:27:21).

8. Lubomir Hrmo SLO – 2nd at Verona (270.337 km), the second best 24 Hour mark of the year and 6th best all-time track mark

9. Rimas Jakelaitis LIT – 901 miles/1450km in 10 days and 600 miles/965.606km in 6 days, the best since 1990 and second best ever on a certified road course

10. Aleksey Belosludtsev RUS – 2nd in the Russian 100km Championships (6:31:40), the second best 100km mark of the year.

Women

Still over-shadowed by Tomoe Abe's amazing 6:33:11 100km the previous year, the year 2001 was not a particularly strong one for the women either. Birgit Lennartz of Germany had previously run three faster times than her 7:28:21, which was the year's fastest. However she did not contest the major international races. The feat of Russian Elvira Kolpakova, winning both Comrades and the World 100km title in the same year is unique, and clearly earns her the distinction of the year's No. 1 ranking. The consistency of her countrywoman Marina Bychkova is also remarkable.

Hungarian Edit Bérces was unable to produce the form of 2000, when she won the world title, but she successfully moved up to depose Russian Irina Reutovich from the No.1 spot at 24 hours.

American Deb Mattheus (formerly Deb Bollig, now married to South African Charl Mattheus) had a huge breakthrough in her pair of South African ultras. Ricarda Botzon's even more remarkable breakthrough (her previous best was 7:54:13 set in the World Challenge in 1995) to take the European 100km was unexpected.

Russian Irina Koval's consistency at the 24 hour event takes her above the 3rd and 4th placers in the 100km World Challenge, Monica Casiraghi of Italy and Tanja Schäfer of Germany.

Women's Rankings

1. Elvira Kolpakova RUS – winner of the World 100km (7:31:12) and Comrades (6:13:53).

2. Marina Bychkova RUS – 2nd in the World 100km (7:37:02) and at the Europeans (7:38:21), and third at Comrades (6:24:20).

3. Edit Bérces HUN – winner at Verona (235.029km), the most competitive 24 hour of the year, defeating Reutovich, who has dominated the event for several years. She ran poorly in the 100km World Challenge, but still finished 11th.

4. Irina Reutovich RUS – 2nd at Verona (226.781km); winner of the European 24 hour Challenge (226.634 km); winner of the Brno 48 hours overall (361,069 km

5. Birgit Lennartz GER – German champion (7:28:21). the fastest 100km mark of the year

6. Deb Mattheus USA – surprise runnerup at Comrades (6:23:04); 4th at Two Oceans 56km (3:51:56).

7. Ricarda Botzon GER – winner of the European Championship 100km (7:31:55).

8. Irina Koval RUS –2nd at Verona 24 Hour (222.445 km); 2nd in the European Challenge 24 hour (222.650 km).

9. Monica Casiraghi ITA – 3rd at the World 100km (7:39:42); winner of the Faenza 100km (8:11:43).

10. Tanja Schäfer GER – 4th in the World 100km (7:43:40); 2nd in the German 100km (7.46.28)

Longer Distances

The best 48 hour mark was set by Achim Heukemes of Germany in the Surgères 48 hours with 376.987km, and he also won the Köln 48 with 364.8km The best women's mark was by Irina Reutovich in winning outright the Brno indoor 48 with 361.069 km.

At 6 days, the best distance was, in fact run in a 10 day race! Lithuanian Rimas Jakelaitis emerged as the current best multi-day performer in the world, making a near-successful attempt to become the fastest ever 1000 mile performer in a 10 day race. He ran 1450km in 10 days; covering 965.606km in 6 days – the best mark since 1990, and the second best ever on a certified road course. Catherine Dipali Cunningham GBR/AUS ran the best female 6 day mark of the year, 820.7km.

An interesting development in the 6 day event is the growth of interest in South Africa, where, on a one kilometre course, Johannes Gawaxamab of Namibia set a new African 48 hour best of 332 km and Eric Wright a new African best of 815 km for 6 days.

The fastest 1000 mile marks of the year were run by Rimas Jakelaitis in 13 days 3:35:07 and Paula Mairer of Austria in 13 days17:49:52. The Baltic monopoly of the extreme ultra events was confirmed when the Finn, Asprihanal Aalto covered 5000km in 48 days 13:08:16 in New York to win the longest race on a certified course.

There were some interesting developments in the classic races. There was the first win by an Eastern European in the London to Brighton, when Ukrainian Andriy Kotsybka won the 51st edition in 6:42:13 in very difficult conditions, from Chris Finill's 6:45:03 and Brian Hennessey's 6:54:58 for the 88.5km journey. The first woman was British runner Liz Neville in 8:42:03 from Kim Masson in 8:59:22 with American Admas Belilgne running 9:40:49 for third.

The Spartathlon was won by the 1991 winner of the World 100km Challenge, Valmir Nunes of Brazil in 23:18:05. Jens Lukas of Germany was second in 24:46:51 and third was Ryoichi Sekiya of Japan in 25:27:30. Six of the first eleven runners in the men's race were Japanese, so their strength in the 24 hour event is growing steadily. Another former 100km specialist made a breakthrough in the women's race as Alzira Portela-Lario of Portugal won in 30:31:41, from Kimie Funada of Japan, 33:49:17, and the German Heike Pawzik, 34:41:10. The conditions and time limits of this race are tough, and of the 192 starters only 82 finished. There were thirty-five Japanese finishers, but just three Greeks.

Multi-day stage races had a revival in 2001 The Vienna to Budapest race was won by Attila Vozar of Hungary in 24:31:52 from the Russians Anatoliy Kruglikov 24:58:50 and Anatoliy Korepanov 25:18:26. Maria Bak of Germany took the women's race in 30:05:31 from Marina Bytchkova, who yet again finished second in 31:34:52, and Anke Drescher, third in 33:47:16.

A much tougher stage race took place earlier in the year. The 4355km Trans-Australia race was run in sixty-three stages. The winner was Anatoliy Kruglikov who had averaged 15km an hour. His winning elapsed time of 305:18:45 placed him well clear of his fellow countryman Andrei Derxen's 323:24:47. Slovenian Dusan Mravlje, a former winner of the Sydney to Melbourne, took third place in 360:50:25.

A race across France, La Trans Gaule went from Roscoff in Brittany on the English Channel to Nabonne Plage on the Mediterranean. The 1145km distance was broken into 18 daily stages. France's Maurice Mondon dominated the race in an elapsed time of 96:15:46 from Dominique Provost's 107:33:26 and Luc Dumont-Saint-Priest's 114:43:45.

There was a major blow to the sport at the end of 2001 when it was announced that Athletics South Africa would no longer be sending a team to the World 100km Challenge. This immediately removed the major African ultra nation from contention, and will obviously lessen the impact that Africa has on the sport.

OBITUARY 2001

See ATHLETICS 2001 for Colin ANDREWS, Igor CAGIGAS, József CSERMÁK, Adhemar Ferreira da SILVA, Marty GLICKMAN, Bret HYDE, Sam JEFFERSON, Sándor NOSZÁLY, Keith PARDOM, Papa Gallo THIAM.

Carlo ARRIGHI (Italy) (b. 24 Sep 1947 Carrara) on 24 September of cancer. He represented Italy in 38 internationals 1968-79 and won five national titles including the outdoor long jump in 1969. 4th in the 1978 European Indoors, pb 7.87 (1972).

Lennart ATTERWALL (Sweden) (b. 26 Mar 1911 Perstorp, formerly Ohlsson) on 23 April. At the javelin he was 4th at the 1936 Olympics and, after 6th in 1938, won the European title in 1946. He set Swedish records in 1936 and 1937 (74.77, as 75.10 was not ratified due to wind assistance). In 14 international matches he won 9 times and in 1935 he won the AAA title. He was national champion in 1934, 1937-41 and 1946. He also won at pentathlon with a NR 3492 (6.70, 66.60, 23.8, 40.71, 4:55.4) in 1937, and at decathlon (6268) in 1940.

Progression at Javelin (position on world list): 1931- 56.47, 1932- 58.12, 1933- 60.29, 1934- 68.14 (8), 1935- 68.56 (7), 1936- 71.72 (6), 1937- 75.10 (2), 1938- 73.73 (4), 1939- 72.36 (6), 1940- 70.54 (8), 1941- 67.64 (12), 1942- 67.36 (10), 1943- 66.91 (10), 1944- 66.21 (12), 1945- 67.47 (13), 1946- 68.74 (8), 1947- 68.93 (13), 1948- 65.18 (33), 1949- 59.95, 1950- 59.28, 1951- 59.44, 1952- 60.46, 1953- 63.11, 1954- 54.71. pb LJ 7.11 (1937).

Two brothers won bronze medals at the javelin at Swedish championships, Sture (1927 and 1928), Ivan (1938).

Karl-Heinz BECKER (Germany) (b. 19 Jun 1912 Hamburg) in Hamburg on 19 July. He ran for Germany in the 1936 Olympic 5000m and had pbs of: 1500m 3:57.2 (1936), 3000m 8:46.6 (1936), 5000m 15:06.2 (1936).

Ingvar BENGTSSON (Sweden) (b. 10 Apr 1922 Holmsund) on 6 April. After winning the Swedish junior 1500m title in 1942 he ran in the Swedish 800m each year 1943-50 finishing 3-2-4-2-2-1-1-1, and he was 5th in the 1948 Olympics and 4th in the 1950 Europeans. He represented Sweden in 12 international matches and was a member of the Nordic Team against USA in 1949. In 1947 he ran the 2nd leg in the Swedish 4x880y team that with 7:29.0 was 5.5 under the world record and equalled the 4x800m WR (the time was not approved since at the time team member Hans Liljekvist was barred from international competition). With his club Gefle IF he established 4 WR – 4x1500m: 15:34.6 (1947), 15:30.2 (1949); 4x1M: 16:55.8 (1948), 16:42.8 (1949). pbs: 400m 49.2 (1948); 800m 1:49.4 (1948); 1000m 2:22.2 (1948); 1500m 3:48.6 (1949); 1 mile 4:11.2 (1949).

Rich BILDER (USA) (b. 8 Oct 1951) on 27 November. He competed in three Olympic Trials as a shot putter; pb 19.89 (1980). He later became a coach at the University of Texas at El Paso.

Jacques BOXBERGER (France) (b. 16 Apr 1949) was trampled him to death by a lone bull elephant, which he was trying to film in a Kenyan nature reserve on 9 August. The 1972 European indoor 1500 champion, who later became French marathon record holder, was an astonishingly versatile runner. pbs 800m 1:49.2 (1972), 1000m 2:21.0 (1968), 1500m 3:36.8 (1973), 1M 3:57.6 (1971), 2000m 5:13.2 (1976), 10000m 28:30.6 (1977) and 3000mSt 8:49.6 (1977) as well as French records at: 3000m 7:43.76 (1976), 5000m 13:26.6 (1976) and 13:23.59 (1977), 20000m 59:07.8 & 1 Hour 20,340m (1980), Marathon 2:11:59 (1984) and 2:10:49 (1985). He competed in four Olympics: 6th 1500m 1968, sf 1500m 1972, ht 5000m 1976, 42nd Mar 1984, and was 5th in the 1971 European 5000m and 9th in the 1976 World CC. French champion at 1500m 1974, 5000m 1977 and 1982, 10000m 1977 and CC 1976 and 1983.

Amy BREMER (Australia) in November. Australia's first national champion at women's 220y, 26.1 in 1933; she was also 3rd in 1935-6, and set two national records at 220y, 25.3 in 1935 and 25.1 in 1936, and one at 100y, 11.0 (1937).

Simon Cyril BROOKS (UK) (b. 17 Dec 1929) at Ampleforth Abbey in September. He set a British record for 220y hurdles with 24.2 for Oxford/Cambridge v AAAs in June 1950 and ran 24.0 for a measured 219.5y in Cambridge in February 1951 on a track that may have been downhill.

Roberto CABREJAS (Spain) (28 Dec 1952) on 4 July when a car crashed into the motorbike that he was riding. He set a Spanish high jump record of 2.26 in 1983 and was five times Spanish champion outdoors and four times indoors. He coached in Barcelona and his notable athletes included Concepción Paredes, Carlos Sala, Antonio Corgos and Gustavo A. Becker.

Elta CARTWRIGHT Stromberg Henricksen (USA) (b. 21 Dec 1907 California) on 29 November. As a 20 year-old student at Humboldt State in 1928, the then Elta Cartwright easily won the 100m at the US Olympic Trials (also WAAU Champs) in 12.4. She became sick during the five-day voyage to Amsterdam for the Olympic Games and was fourth in her semi-final, while teammate Elizabeth Robinson, the runner-up at the Olympic Trials, won the gold medal. She was also AAU champion at 50y 1925-8 and 100y 1927 (2nd 1925) and set a US 100y record of 11.4 in 1927. pbs: 50y 6.1 (1925), LJ 5.43 (1926).

Richard CHELIMO (Kenya) (b. 21 Apr 1972 Chesubet) of a brain tumour in Eldoret on 15 August. His running career was brief but brilliant. He was second in the World Junior Cross-country and won the World Junior 10,000m in 1990 (with his younger brother Ismael Kirui second) and in 1991 placed a close second in the World Championships to Moses Tanui, 27:38.74 to 27:39.41, after heading the world list that year with a world junior record (which still stands) of 27:11.18 at Hengelo. He also set three world junior records at 5000m in 1991. Chelimo and Khalid Skah (third in the 1991 Worlds) clashed again in the 1992 Barcelona Olympics, when the Moroccan, controversially aided by his lapped compatriot Hammou Boutayeb, won with a 26.0 final 200m to win, 27:46.70 to 27:47.72.

For a few hours, after Skah was disqualified, Chelimo was hailed as Olympic champion but next day Skah was reinstated in time for the medal ceremony. Chelimo was 4th in 1991 and 5th in 1992 in the World Cross-country, and Kenyan 10,000m champion in 1992. In 1993 he briefly became world record holder at 10,000 (the youngest ever at 21), breaking Arturo Barrios' 27:08.23 with an evenly paced 27:07.91 in Stockholm, but then was a distant third to Haile Gebrselassie and Moses Tanui in the World Champs in Stuttgart ... and that effectively was the end. He contracted malaria in 1994 and then had a serious road accident in August 1995 and never rediscovered his old form.

Progression at 5000m, 10000m (position on world list): 1987- 14:31.4, 1989- 14:16.2, 1990- 13:59.49, 28:18.57 (58); 1991- 13:11.76 (5), 27:11.18 (1); 1992- 13:10.46 (9), 27:15.53 (2); 1993- 13:05.14 (5), 27:07.91 (2). pbs: 3000m 7:41.63 (1993), 2M 8:26.29 (1991).

Ruth CHRISTMAS (GBR) (b. 12 Nov 1904) in April. One of the pioneers of women's middle distance running and member of London Olympiades, she set her first British record in 1929, 2:23.8 for 800m close behind Marie Dollinger in Germany and the following year she was second in an estimated 2:21.8 to Gladys Lunn's world record 2:18.2 in the WAAA 880y. In 1932 she set a highly unofficial world best for the mile of 5:27.5 from scratch in a handicap race in London, timed by coaches and journalists. She won the WAAA 800m title in 1933, and, after marrying a Frenchman, as Ruth Christmas-Paysant won French titles at 800 in 1935 and cross country in 1936 and represented France against Italy. pb 440y 63.0 (1931). Her sister Esther ran 1 mile in 5:34.0 in 1935. She was the aunt of novelist Simon Raven.

Clifford **Clyde COFFMAN** (USA) (b. 2 Jun 1911) on 4 March. He was 7th in the 1932 Olympic decathlon after taking third place in the US Trials. Four years later he was 4th in the US Trials and thus just missed a second Olympic appearance, but he set a pb of 7175 (6702 on current tables). He also won the AAU pentathlon in 1935. Other pbs: 100m 10.8 (1931), 10.5w (1934); PV 4.16 (1934, 14= on world list that year), LJ 7.39 (1936).

John Frederick **'Jerry' CORNES** (GBR) (b. 23 Mar 1910 Darjeeling, India) on 19 June. The son of a judge in the Indian Civil Service, he first made his mark when third in the 1930 Empire Games mile, a placing he duplicated in 1934 when he ran his pb of 4:13.6e. He ran the third leg for the British team that set a world 4x1500m record of 15:55.6 in Cologne in 1931 and the following year, in Los Angeles, took the Olympic silver medal at 1500m in a British record 3:52.6. In Berlin 1936 he finished sixth in his fastest ever time, 3:51.4, another UK record. He was AAA mile champion in 1932. He worked for many years in the Colonial Service and later ran a preparatory school in England.

Danila COSTA (Italy) (b. 14 Jan 1941) on 18 March. Italian champion at 400m 1959-60 (pb and NR 56.6 in 1960); he competed at the European Champs in 1958.

Szilvia CSOCSÁNSZKY (Hungary) (b. 4 Nov 1975) on 12 January. She was 8th in the 1994 World Junior 800m in a pb 2:05.63.

Paul CUMMINGS (USA)(b. 5 Sep 1953) drowned in a fishing accident when his canoe tipped over in choppy conditions at Strawberry Reservoir, Utah on 17 September. He ran his fastest mile of 3:56.4 in 1974, and that year won the NCAA 1 mile for Brigham Young University. He won the US indoor mile in 1975 and 1976 and set a US indoor 1500m record of 3:37.6 in 1979, before moving up in distance, with 13:19.62 for 5000m in 1982 and 27:43.7 for 10000m in 1984, the year he ran in the Los Angeles Olympic 10,000 where an untimely recurrence of an allergy which affected his breathing caused him to be eliminated in his heat. In 1983 he set an American half marathon best of 61:32 and in 1986 he won the Houston Marathon in a career best 2:11:32. US champion at half marathon 1987. Other pbs: 2M 8:25.2i (1979), 3000mSt 8:52.5 (1979), 15km road 42:42 (US record, 1983).

S. J. **'Fanie' DU PLESSIS** (b. 23 Feb 1930) of cancer after a long illness in Pretoria on 13 August. He won gold medals in the discus at the Commonwealth Games in 1954 and 1958 and a bronze in the shot in 1954. At the Olympic Games he was 13th in 1956 and did not make the final in 1960. He won the South African discus title eleven times 1951-60 and 1967 and the shot four times, 1952, 1954-5, 1957. He held the Commonwealth record and set seven national records from 45.92 in 1952 to 56.33 in 1959, for 7th on the world list that year. Shot pb 15.69 (1954).

Werner ECKERT (Germany) (b. 29 Mar 1922 Lorrach) on 8 August. In 1954 he won the shot at the first German Indoor Championships and he was second in the outdoor championships in both 1953 and 1954. pb 15.18 (1954).

Harri ELJANKO (Finland) (b. 6 Nov 1900 Helsinki; né Ekqvist) in Helsinki on July 13. The last surviving competitor of the first-ever dual match between Finland and Sweden in 1925, he won the Finnish 800m title in 1927 and had pbs of 100m 11.3, 200m 23.3, 400m 50.3, 800m 1:56.7, 1000m 2:34.5, 1500m 4:09.8 and 400mh 58.3. He became one of the most respected sportswriters in Finland, authoring several books on the history of athletics and Olympic Games, and contributed to *Suomen Urheilulehti* and many newspapers until the early 1990s – a writing career of some 75 years! He was the first Finnish sportswriter and first international athlete to reach the age of 100.

Gun ENSTRÖM (Sweden) (b. 25 Mar 1911) on 31 October. As Gunvor Brundin she was 2nd in the Swedish 800m in 1929, 1931-2 and 1936. She ran for Sweden in the Pentangular International in Blackpool in 1936. For several years she worked at the office of the Swedish AA. pb 2:29.7 (1936).

Sebastian FREDRICH (Germany) (b. 3 Jan 1980) of leukaemia in December. He was fifth in the 1999 European Junior 10,000m in a pb 30:04.78. pb 5000m 14:15.26 (1999).

Sture FRÖBERG (Sweden) (b. 7 Sep 1943 Vimmerby) on 17 January. He represented Sweden in 12 internationals and 2nd at 110mh in the Swedish Champs 1967-8, pb 14.3 (1968).

Petar GALIC (Yugoslavia) (b. 3 Aug 1939) in July in Banja Luka. He was Yugoslav javelin champion 1962 and 1964-6 and was 11th at the 1962 European Championships 1962. He competed 16 times for the Yugoslav national team and had a best of 76.38 (1962).

Diego GARCIA (Spain) (b. 12 Oct 1961 Azkoitia) of a heart attack while coaching Alejandro Gómez in Azkoitia on 31 March. He made his marathon debut in 1989 and placed 9th in the 1992 Olympics, 2nd at the 1994 Europeans, and 6th in the 1995 World Champs. He set a Spanish record of 2:10:30 when 3rd at Fukuoka, where two years later he ran his fastest time of 2:09:51 in 4th place His one win in 29 marathons was Seville 1995.

Progression at Marathon: 1989- 2:12:48 sh, 1990- 2:13:48, 1991- 2:12:54, 1992- 2:10:30, 1993- 2:10:58, 1994- 2:10:46, 1995- 2:09:51, 1996- 2:11:31, 1997- 2:11:26, 1998- 2:10:35, 1999- 2:12:34, 2000- 2:11:48. pbs: 10000m 28:42.66 (1997), HMar 63:14 (1996).

Aurelio GENGHINI (Italy) (b. 1 Oct 1907) on 11 September. At the marathon he won a surprise bronze medal at the 1934 European Championships and he also ran at the 1936 Olympics, but did not finish. He ran a personal best time of 2:38:40 to win the Italian title in 1933 and he was champion again in 1937: He set an Italian record of 1:07:25 for 15 miles in 1933.

Dieter GIESEN (Germany) (b. 24 May 1918 Berlin) on 9 September. He was German champion at 800m in 1942 after being 3rd in 1939 and 2nd in 1941, when the winner was the great Rudolf Harbig, and made eight international appearances 1939-41. pbs: 400m 48.9 (1941), 800m 1:51.1 (1941, 10th in the world that year), 1000m 2:24.0 (1941), 1500m 3:55.6 (1940).

Herman GOFFBERG (USA) (b. 25 Jun 1921) on 17 August in State College, Pennsylvania. Having attended Eastern Michigan and Pennsylvania State Universities, he was 3rd at 10,000m at the 1942 AAUs. After serving in the US Navy he was again 3rd in the AAU 10,000m in 1948 in a pb 33:10.0, and qualified for the Olympic Games, where he dropped out on the 18th lap after being lapped by Emil Zátopek.

José Clemente GONÇALVES (Portugal/Brazil) (b. 22 Aug 1932 Lisbon, Portugal) on 6 September. An ATFS member for many years, he had devoted much time to the history of Brazilian athletics – a work expected to be published by the Brazilian Confederation, for whom he was the official statistician. He was a national junior high jump champion in Portugal and later won this event in Brazilian veterans competitions. An engineer, with a degree in PE as well, he worked for nine years for Shell in Angola before having to leave due to the civil war. He settled in Brazil in 1974, first in São Paulo and then in Santa Catarina State, but retained his Portuguese citizenship. He was married to Elizabeth Clara (née Müller) who won South American titles at 200m 1945, shot 1945 and 1954, high jump 1949 and 1952 and 4x100m 1949.

Ronald **GOODMAN** (UK) on 6 July at the age of 89. A member of Herne Hill Harriers, he was a leading official in Britain for many years and was president of the AAA 1984-7.

Helmut GUDE (Germany) (b. 23 Nov 1925 Düren) on 3 February in Philadelphia, USA. He placed 8th in the 1952 Olympic final and set German records when winning national titles in 1951 (9:02.4) and in 1952, when his 8:50.0 was, at the time, the second fastest of all time behind Vladimir Kazantsev's 8:48.6. Other pbs: 1500m 3:53.4 (1952), 3000m 8:13.6 (1952).

Václav HAUSENBLAS (Czech Republic) (b. 23 Sep 1920) on 6 May. He set a national high jump record of 1.98 (1940) that lasted for 12 years, was CS champion in 1940 and 1947 and 13th in the 1946 European Championships. From 1950 he lived in the USA and in 1997 he founded a foundation for the support of young Czech athletes.

Rositha HELLMANN (née Potreck; b. 11 Mar 1959 Ludwigslust) in May. She was javelin bronze medallist at the 1977 European Junior Champs and produced her longest ever throw of 66.08 when winning the GDR title in 1981 for sixth place on that year's world list.

John JEWELL (UK) on 18 August at the age of 89. A founder member of the Road Runners Club and former president of South London Harriers, he was editor of the RRC's informative newsletter from 1952 to 1992 and he was a pioneer of accurate course measurement for road races. He introduced the use of the calibrated bike into the measurement of road courses. This resulted from a detailed scientific study in which he, with others, examined all the methods of course measurement. That, he used to say, was the easy part. Persuading the federations and the IAAF to use the method was much harder.

Henry KÄLARNE (Sweden) (b. 12 May 1912) on 9 March. Kälarne, whose name until 1940 was Jonsson, set world records with 5:18.4 for 2000m in 1937 and 8:09.0 for 3000m in 1940 (a race in which his successor as world record holder, Gunder Hägg, was second in 8:11.8), while the following year he ran on his club Brandkårens IK WR relay runs at 4 x 1500m and 4 x 1 mile. He had earlier set three Swedish records at 3000m from 8:16.2 in 1936 to 8:15.2 in 1939, three at 5000m 1936-9 and at 1 mile, 4:08.8 (1937), 2M 8:57.8 (1936) and two at 3M to 14:03.4 (1938). At the 1936 Olympics he won the bronze medal in 14:29.0 behind the Finns, Gunnar Höckert and Lauri Lehtinen, and at the 1938 European Champs he was second to another Finn, Taisto Mäki, in 14:27.4. Although injury had already caused him to retire, he – along with Hägg and Arne Andersson – was banned for life in 1946 for accepting payments contrary to the amateur rules then in force. Other pbs: 1500m 3:48.7 (1940, beating Hägg by a tenth), 5000m 14:18.8 (1939), 10000m 32:15.7 (1934, his only race at the distance, in his first international). Swedish champion 1500m 1936, 1940; 5000m 1935, 1937-9, 8km cross 1935-9.

Progression at 1500m, 5000m (position on world list): 1933- 15:21.8, 1934- 4:04.8, 14:48.8 (11); 1935- 3:58.0 (31=), 14:44.6 (8); 1936- 3:57.0 (37=), 14:29.0 (3), 1937- 3:51.4 (4), 14:37.2 (9); 1938- 3:52.2 (7=), 14:27.4 (2=); 1939- 3:53.4 (14=), 14:18.8 (3); 1940- 3:48.8 (3=), 14:38.4 (14); 1941- 3:49.2 (3).

Jack KELLNER (USA) (b. 1916) on 26 June. He tied for seventh on the world list with his best for 120y hurdles of 14.3 in 1937. While at the University of Wisconsin he was 6th in the 1936 NCAA.

Leamon KING (USA) (b. 13 Feb 1936 Tulare, CA.) on 22 May in Delano, California. King had a short but meteoric career as a sprinter. After 9.6 for 100y in high school at Fresno in 1954, he ran 9.4 in 1955 and then tied the world record with 9.3 at Fresno in his first race of the 1956 season showing what Cordner Nelson in *Track & Field News* described as an 'astonishing explosion… as beautiful an exhibition of sheer speed as most people have ever seen". Seemingly tense in competition he was a disappointing 4th in the US Trials at 100m after 4th at the NCAAs and 2nd at the AAUs, but came into top form in pre-Olympic competition in California in October, when he twice tied the world record for 100m at 10.1, and he ran a superb second leg on the US team that won the 4x100m gold medal in Melbourne in a world record 39.5 (39.60 auto). Four days later he led off the US team that set a world record for 4x220y in Sydney. In 1957 he won the AAU 100y and was 3rd at 100y and 2nd at 220y for the University of California at the NCAAs. Pbs: 200m 21.0 (1957), 220ySt 20.5 (1953).

George KNOTT (Australia) (b. 1922) in January. He was 7th in his heat of the 10,000m walk at the 1948 Olympic Games and Australian champion at 1 mile walk 1947 and 2 mile walk 1948. pb 10000m walk 42:51.6dt (1948).

Charles **'Charlie' KOEN** (South Africa) (b. 10 Dec 1931 Knysna) on 7 October in Port Elizabeth. He competed at the 1958 Commonwealth Games and was South African hammer champion 1959-65. He set five national records from 57.12 to 61.72 (1962). His son Charlie Jnr won the SA hammer title nine times between 1981 and 1992.

Ray KRING (USA) (b. 26 Dec 1924 Empire, CA) on 16 February. He ranked in the world top ten at pole vault in 1945 (5th 4.16m), 1946 (9th 4.19), 1947 (10th= 4.26) and in 1953 (9th at a pb 4.31) and began a 38-year career as a coach in 1951.

Luise KRÜGER (Germany) (b. 11 Jan 1915 Dresden-Cotta) in Dresden on 13 June. The 1936 Olympic javelin silver medallist and bronze medallist at the 1938 European Champs had a pb of 46.27, which topped the world list in 1939. She was a fine all-rounder, winning the German pentathlon title in 1941 and 1942 and twice finishing third at 80m hurdles (pb 11.9 in 1941).

Vasiliy KUZNETSOV (USSR/Russia) (b. 7 Feb 1932 Kalikino) on 6 August in Moscow. The only man to have won the European decathlon title three times: 1954, 1958 and 1962; he was also bronze medallist at the Olympics in 1956 and 1960, with 7th in 1964, and won ten USSR titles, 1954-60 and 1962-3. He set seven European records at the decathlon from 1954 to 1959 and was the first man to better 8000 points on the 1950 scoring tables with 8014 (7653 on 1985 tables) at Krasnodar in May 1958; he set a second world record with 8357 (7839) at Moscow in May 1959. pbs: 100m 10.5 (1959), 200m 21.9 (1958), 400m 48.6 (1958), 1500m 4:33.2 (1963), 110mh 14.4 (1956), HJ 1.93, PV 4.47/4.50? (1964), LJ 7.49 (1958), SP 15.51 (1960), DT 52.00 (1959), JT 72.78 (1959). He also set three world bests at pentathlon: on current tables 3913 (1956), 4010 (1958), 4051 (1959).

Annual progression (position on world list): on 1934 tables: 1951- 5651, 1952- 5840, 1953- 7205 (6696 on 1985 tables) (3); on 1952 tables/1985 tables: 1954- 7292/7227 (2), 1955- 7645/7427 (2), 1956- 7733/7468 (3), 1957- 7379/7269 (1), 1958-8042/7658 (2), 1959- 8357/7839 (1), 1960- 7845/7559 (4), 1961- 7918/7603 (3), 1962- 8026/7653 (2), 1963- 7854/7609 (5), 1964- 7842/7488 (13).

Aubrey LEWIS (USA) (b. 1 Jan 1935) on 10 December in New York. At 400m hurdles he was the sixth fastest in the world in 1956 at 50.9 (when he fell in his semi-final at the US Olympic Trials) and the third fastest in 1957 at 50.5. While at Notre Dame he was NCAA champion in 1956 at 400mh and third at 220yh in 1957. He was also second in the 1954 AAU decathlon. Other pbs: 100m 10.7 (1956), 220y straight 20.9 (1953), 440y 48.1 (1957), 220yh straight 22.7 (1957), Dec 6600 (1956, current tables). He was a top footballer in high school and college and joined the Chicago Bears after graduation, but an injury cut short his career.

Jacob LINDAHL (Sweden) (b. 14 Aug 1907 Karlskrona) on 18 April. Swedish 400m hurdles champion in 1932. pb 55.4 (1931); he was 2nd in 55.8 behind Glenn Hardin's world record 50.6 in 1934. He was on the Board of the Swedish AA 1951-70 as Secretary and Vice President and was one of the main organizers of the 1958 European Championships. He was a member of the IAAF Council 1960-76 and a member of the European Committee of the IAAF before the founding of the EAA. He was a member of the jury of appeal at the Olympic Games 1964-76 as well as at European Championships.

Carol LINDROOS (Finland) (b. 29 May 1930 Pohja) in Helsinki on 9 December. He was one of the first Finnish athletes to go to an American University (Arizona State). In 1954, he beat Kalevi Kotkas´s 17 year-old national record for the discus with 51.58, and improved it four times to 55.31 against France in Helsinki in 1958, with a later pb of 55.79 (1960). Finnish champion in 1953-5, 1957-8 and 1961, with five other medals, he won 16 times in 36 internationals, including 4 of 10 against Sweden. An Olympic competitor in 1960, he was 7th in the 1958 European Championships in Stockholm. A strikingly tall and handsome figure, he was the flag-bearer of the national team in various opening ceremonies for many years.

Pat LITTLE (USA) on 16 July in Indianapolis at the age of 96. He was a finalist in the steeplechase at the 1928 Olympic Trials while at Indiana University.

Kim McDONALD (GBR) (b. 27 Sep 1956) from a suspected heart attack on 7 November while on holiday in Brisbane, Australia. Founder and chief executive of Kim McDonald International Management (KIM). pbs: 1M 4:02.1 (1983), 3000m 7:56.01 (1979), 5000m 13:49.1 (1979), 10,000m 28:58.1 (1982), marathon 2:19:34 (1981).

He was one of the first people to recognise and act on the realisation that athletes would need serious representation in the new professional world of the sport in the mid-1980s, and even earlier, on trips to East Africa in the 1970s, he had seen the potential for Kenyan athletic development, in which he would later play a huge role. He was soon representing a group of the world's leading athletes – Steve Ovett, John Walker, Peter Elliott, Liz McColgan, Sonia O'Sullivan, and many of the top Kenyans, led by Moses Kiptanui, and most recently, the young British sprinter, Mark Lewis-Francis. He was also a notable coach, with his skills helping athletes such as Peter Elliott and Noah Ngeny.

Paul MAGEE (Australia) (b. 21 Sep 1915) on 21 May in Sydney. At 440y hurdles he was Australian champion in 1937 and sixth in the Empire Games in 1938. He set Australian records in 1937 for the 440yh 53.5 (held record for 11 years) and 220yh 25.0 (for 10 years). His grandson Paul Greene was a top sprinter in the 1990s.

Bill MARLOW (GBR) at the age of 82. A former AAA National Coach for the Midlands, his most successful protégé was Peter Radford, who he coached from a schoolboy of 16 to a world record at 200m/220y and Olympic 100m bronze medal in 1960.

Piero MASSAI (Italy) on 31 August at the age of 78. He was head coach of the Italian athletics team in 1974-6. He was an athlete and then trainer of the historic club of Florence "Assi Giglio Rosso" and also a basketball international referee.

Marie MATESOVÁ (Czech Republic) (b. 10 Nov 1921 Rakovník) in June. She set three Czech 800m records: 2:22.4 (1947) and 2:20.6 and 2:20.5 (1949) and was 6th at 80mh in the 1946 European Championships. CS champion 200m 1941, 800m 1946-7, 1949; 80mh 1945-7. Other pbs: 400m 61.6 (1954), 800m 2:18.8 (1953), 80mh 12.4 (1946).

Helmut MEYER (Germany) (b. 26 Oct 1926 Herford) in Darmstadt on 13 May. The climax of a long career as a leading administrator came when he was director of the Bundesuasschusses Leistungssport (BAL) 1970-89 and president of the DLV 1989-93.

Matthews MOTHSWARATEU (South Africa) (b. 2 Nov 1958) in Baragwanath Hospital on 2 November (his 43rd birthday) after being shot four times in Soweto when he was robbed of his wallet containing only R30. Known as 'Loop and Val" due to his unusual running style, he won national titles at 5000m (1978-9) and 10,000m (1991) and also the inaugural SA half marathon in 1981. He went to the University of Texas at El Paso and for them won the NCAA cross-country in 1981 (after 2nd in 1980). On South Africa's return to world athletics in 1992 he competed at the World Half Marathon and the African Championships (2nd 10000m). He set national records at 5000m (13:29.6 in 1978) and 10000m (27:48.2 in 1979) at Stellenbosch. Other pbs: 3000m 7:51.8 (1979), 1 Hour 20,052m (1978); Road: 15km 43:06 (1992), HMar 61:21 (1989). At one stage of his career he moved to Botswana to try and compete internationally and was selected for them once but then returned to his native South Africa where he continued his running career until the early nineties.

Knut MOUM (Norway) (b. 30 Nov 1921) on 12 December. Competed at 200m and 4x100m at the 1946 Europeans. pbs (1950): 100m 10.8, 200m 22.3.

NAM Sung-Yong (Korea) (b. 23 Nov 1912) on 20 February. Competing for Japan in the era of their Korean occupation as **Shoryu NAN**, he took the bronze medal in the 1936 Olympic marathon won by his compatriot Sohn Kee-chung (Kitei Son). Nam's 2:31:42 was his personal best. pb 10000m 32:17.0 (1934).

Tei-ichi NISHI (Japan) (b. 31 Aug 1907) on 3 February. He anchored the 4x400m relay team that finished fifth at the 1932 Olympic Games, when he was a quarter-finalist at 200m. He won the Japanese 400m in 1931 and 1933 and was second in the Far-Eastern Games 400m in 1930. In 1933 he set the Japanese record (21.2) for straight 200m. After retiring, he established Nishi Sports, which produced athletic equipment.

Liv Olaug PAULSEN (Norway) (b. 29 Nov 1925) on 3 November. She competed at 100m and shot at the 1948 Olympic Games and 1946 Europeans (8th SP) and set Norwegian records for 100m at 12.5 and 12.4 (1947) and at shot: 10.36 (1946), 10.98 (1947) and 11.16 (1948) with a later SP pb 11.44 (1948). Norwegian champion SP 1947, 50m 1950. pb JT 32.57 (1949).

Brendan O'REILLY (Ireland) (b. 14 May 1930 Granard, Co. Longford) on 1 April. He set an Irish record at 1.97 in 1954 and improved to 2.01 while at the University of Michigan in the USA in 1956, He competed at the 1954 European Championships and 1956 Olympic Games and won the 1954 AAA title. A man of many talents, he became a well-known television presenter in Ireland.

Francis **'Frank' O'REILLY** (Ireland) (b. 7 Apr 1924) on 20 March. He set a world best of 16:54:15 for the 100 miles road walk in 1960 and won five successive road 100s in 1959 -63. He was the first race walker to represent Ireland in the Olympics, 20th at 50km in 1960.

Micheline OSTERMEYER (France) (b. 23 Dec 1922 Berck-sur-Mer, Pas-de-Calais) on 17 October at Rouen. She took gold medals for shot and discus and bronze at the high jump at the 1948 Olympics. Up against stiffer competition in the European Championships, with the USSR athletes also competing, she was 2nd in the shot in 1946, and third at 80m hurdles and shot in 1950. She would have benefited from multi-event competition, but the pentathlon was not added to the Olympic programme until years later. She started her athletics career with Orientale Tunis, competing for them 1942-5 and 1947-9, moving to Stade Français 1950-2. She won 12 French titles, six at the shot (1945-8 and 1950-1), two at pentathlon and one each at 60m, 80m hurdles, high jump and discus. Her 18 French records included her bests for high jump 1.61 (1946), shot 13.79 (1948), and discus 44.40 (1950).

The great-niece of the writer Victor Hugo, she was a distinguished concert pianist; she gave her first public concert in 1936, aged 13, and won first prize at the Paris Conservatory in 1946. She married René Ghazarian (d. 1965) in 1952.

Ruth OWENS (USA) the widow of Jesse Owens, in Chicago on 27 June, aged 86. Married to the Olympic legend for 45 years before he died in 1980.

Renato PANCIERA (Italy) (b. 8 Apr 1935) on 15 August. Italian 400m champion 1956 and 1959. He ran on the 4x400m team at the 1958 Europeans (4th) and 1960 Olympics (3:07.83 Italian record in semi). pbs: 100m 10.5 (1960), 200m 21.6 (1958), 400m 47.45 (1959).

Ernest POMFRET (GBR) (b. 18 Apr 1941 Haswell, Co Durham) of cancer on 1 May. A member of Houghton Harriers and a police constable at the time, he set his pb of 8:37.0 for 3000m steeplechase when 2nd in the 1967 AAAs (for the fifth successive year after 3rd in 1962), ranking him as the third fastest ever Briton at that time. He was 10th in the 1964 Olympics, 6th in the 1966 Commonwealth Games and 12th in the 1966 Europeans and had 19 internationals 1963-7. He set a British 2000m steeplechase best of 5:33.6 in 1967. Flat pbs: 3000m 8:10.4 (1967), 2M 8:48.8 (1967), 5000m 14:05.4 (1970).

Dr **Don**ald H **POTTS** (USA) (b. 15 Dec 1921 Seattle) on 1 November in Santa Barbara, California. President of the ATFS 1972-6, having been a founder member in 1950. With Roberto Quercetani he compiled *A Handbook on Olympic Games Track and Field Athletics*, first published in 1948 and in 1955 he produced *The All Time US List*. Such publications were immensely important pioneering stats books. He was a co-founder of the US statistics group, FAST, in 1983. After completing a BS in physics at Cal Tech in 1943, he obtained his PhD in mathematics there in 1947. He taught at Northwestern, Long Beach State, California Berkeley and finally at Cal State Northridge. *See appreciation by Roberto Quercetani.*

Hans RAMPF (Germany) (b. 2 Feb 1931) in Murnau on 6 May. He had a 100m pb of 10.8 (1955) but was best known as an ice hockey player, playing in 101 internationals for Germany 1945-64, including playing on the teams that were 6th at the 1956 and 1960 Olympic Games and 2nd at the 1953 World Championships.

Oto REBULA (Yugoslavia) (b. 14 Aug 1921) in Belgrade on 11 July. Yugoslav decathlon champion 1951-4, he took part at the 1950 European Championships (13th) and 1952 Olympic Games (15th) and set national records in pentathlon 1948 and decathlon 1952. He was later a well-known coach of many Yugoslav athletes.

Jens REIMERS (Germany) (b 15 Aug 1941 Salzwedel) in December. He set eight FRG discus records from 56.68 in 1961 to 59.28 in 1966, and was German champion in 1961-3 and 1965. His pb was 61.38 (1967) and he had a shot best of 17.62 (1969). One of the biggest of all discus throwers at 2.03 tall and weighing 125kg, he was a non-qualifier at the 1966 Europeans and 1968 Olympics and made 33 international appearances 1961-8.

Irvin 'Bo' ROBERSON (USA) (23 Jul 1935) on 19 April. Roberson took the lead in the second round of the 1960 Olympic long jump when he jumped 8.04 (from a previous pb of 7.92). That was passed by Ralph Boston's 8.12 in the third, but Roberson got so close with 8.11 in the last round for the silver medal. He was Pan-American champion 1959 and won the AAU indoors in 1960 and was third outdoors in 1959 and 1961. Cornell University. Other pbs: 100y 9.5 (1961), 220y 21.4 (1961).

Progression at long jump (position on world list): 1958- 7.58 (25=), 1959- 7.92 (4), 1960- 8.11 (2), 1961- 7.98 (3).

Bill ROBERTS (GBR) (b. 5 April 1912 Salford) on 5 December. He won an Olympic gold medal (contributing a 46.4 leg) at 4x400m in 1936 after running a personal best 46.8 (46.87 on automatic timing, just 0.03 behind the bronze medallist Jimmy Lu Valle USA) in the individual 400m. He competed at a second Olympics in 1948, when he was the British team captain; at 36 he remains Britain's oldest ever 400m international. His international career began at the 1934 Empire Games, when he was runner-up to Godfrey Rampling at 440y.

He did not run in the relay then, but took a silver in 1938 when he was the 440y champion and 6th at 220y (pb 21.5 in heat). He missed the 1938 Europeans but returned after War service in the RAF to earn a relay silver in 1946. He was AAA champion at 440y in 1935 and 1937, 2nd in 1946 and 3rd in 1948. He won six of his eight individual races in international matches 1935-46 and in the other two was second to his great rival Godfrey Brown. He retired to concentrate on his work with the family furniture business. A book of his life 'The Iron In His Soul' by Bob Phillips is to be published in May 2002.

Progression at 400m (* 440y less 0.3) (position on world list): 1934- 48.3* (23=), 1935- 47.7 (10=), 1936- 46.8/46.87 (6=), 1937- 47.5 (12=), 1938- 47.6* (19=), 1946- 48.3* (14=), 1947- 48.9 (c.80), 1948- 48.5 (c.80).

Katherine ROGAN (USA) (née Mearls) on 8 October at the age of 93. She was US indoor champion at 40y in 1928 and standing long jump each year 1927-31 and at this event had a best of 2.55m at the New England Championships in 1931. Other pbs: 100y 11.2 (1929), 80mh 12.2 dt 91930), HJ 1.524 (1930), LJ 5.33 (1929).

Augusto de Oliveira SANTOS (Brazil) (b. 13 Oct 1972) in his hometown of Aracaju on 28 November after a training session. He won the bronze medal at 200m at the 2001 South American Championships. pbs: 100m 10.36 (2000), 200m 20.80 (2000).

Jirí SANTRUCEK (Czech Republic) (b. 22 Sep 1925) on 21 December. In 1954 at 10000m he was Czechoslovak champion and 18th in the European Championships. He represented Czechoslovakia nine times in 1954-5 (with Emil Zátopek). pbs: 5000m 14:29.8 (1954), 10000m 30:01.4 (1955), Marathon 2:24:43 (1956).

Debra SAPENTER (later Speight) (USA) (b. 22 Feb 1952) on 5 March. At the 1976 Olympic Games she was 8th in the 400m and led off the US silver-medal winning 4x400m team and at the 1975 Pan-American Games she won silver medals at both event. AAU 400m champion in 1974 and 1975. pbs: 100m 11.8 (1974), 200m 23.52 (1976), 400m 51.23 (1976).

Ruhi **SARIALP** (Turkey) (b. 15 Dec 1924) in Istanbul on 5 March. His nation's one Olympic athletics medallist: 3rd at triple jump in 1948 (15.025). He was also 3rd in the 1950 Europeans and won the CISM (World Military) titles in 1951 and 1952. He set his best TJ mark of 15.07 for seventh in the world list for 1948.

Louise SCHRAMM (GBR) (b. 18 Dec 1971) in a car accident on 20 February. An international pole vaulter (pb 3.75 in 1998), she was a doctor.

Art SKIPPER (USA) (b. 31 Jul 1970) on 16 October in a plane crash south-east of Portland, Oregon, where he had recently become a firefighter. He set the still-standing US high school javelin record at 79.20 with the 700g javelin in 1988 and had a best with the senior javelin of 76.72 in 1992. That year, his last at the University of Oregon, he won the NCAA title and was 5th in the US Olympic Trials. In 1993 he was 2nd at the US Championships and competed at the World Championships.

Folke SKOOG (Sweden, naturalized US citizen in 1935) (b. 15 Jul 1908 Fjärås) on 15 February at Madison, Wisconsin. He ran for Sweden in the 1500m at the 1932 Olympics while a student at California Institute of Technology. He had an impressive career as a plant physiologist and he was Professor of Botany at University of Wisconsin 1947-69. His work has had a profound impact on agricultural and horticultural practices around the world and in 1991 he was awarded the National Medal of Science. pb 1500m 4:03.4 (1932).

Zdenek SOBOTKA (Czech Republic) (b. 17 Jan 1917) on 20 January. He set his high jump best of 1.90 in winning the 1936 CS title and competed that year at the 1936 Olympic Games.

Karen SONNECK (Germany) (b. 2 Oct 1928 Kiel, née Uthke) on 26 July in Merzen. German champion at shot in 1949 and at discus in 1949 and 1950, and 8th at discus at the 1954 European Championships. pbs: SP 13.72 (1955), DT 46.84 (1957), JT 38.74 (1954).

Erna STEINBERG (Germany) (née Boeck; b. 20 Jun 1911 Berlin) in Berlin on 21 April. In 1928 she won the German 100m and was fourth in the first ever Olympic women's 100m in 12.4 (her pb). Other pbs: 200m 26.4 and LJ 5.53 (both 1933).

Alfréd STRZÍNEK (Czech Republic) (b. 21 May 1929) on 21 November. He ran on the ÚDA Praha team that set a world record of 7:28.0 for 4x800m in 1953. Czech champion at 800m 1953, 1500m 1955. pbs: 800m 1:51.0 (1956), 1500m 3:46.0 (1955).

Jack STUBBS (GBR) (b. 19 Dec 1904) on 27 November. Well-known as a chief timekeeper for many years as major meetings, he had been a notable cross-country and road runner in a long career for South London Harriers 1926-48. He was 5th at 5000m at the World Student Games at Darmstadt in 1930, when he finished 115m behind the winner, Karl-Gustav Dahlström SWE who was timed at 15:24.3.

Susumu TAKAHASHI (Japan) (b. 17 Nov 1920 Hiroshima) on 13 May. He was Asian Games steeplechase champion in 1951 and 1954 and competed at the 1952 Olympics. Japanese champion each year 1947-55, he set seven national records to 9:01.8 (1953). He became a successful coach (with Kenji Kimihara taking Olympic silver in 1968) and was a prolific writer.

Guy TEXEREAU (France) (b. 14 May 1935) of cancer on 28 April at Saint-Astier. He made 52 international appearances for France 1959-71, won eight French steeplechase titles, 1960 and 1962-8, and set eight French records from 8:53.2 in 1962 to 1966. The diminutive (1.68/52kg) runner clocked his best ever time of 8:30.0 when 4th in the 1966 Europeans (he was 7th in 1962). He competed in three Olympics, finishing 6th in 1964. Flat pbs: 1500m 3:48.6, 3000m 7:57.6 (1967), 5000m 13:48.6 (1965), 10,000m 29:26.4 (1966).

Jaakko TUOMINEN (Finland) (b. 4 May 1944 Orimattila) from a heart attack on 27 October at Astoria, Oregon, USA, where – after working for many years for Nike – he had just opened an inn with his wife. He played handball for the Finnish national team and won athletics junior titles in six different events, including cross country and heptathlon – an unsurpassed feat to this day. At 400mh, he set five Finnish records: 50.5 and 50.4 in 1964 (which remains the fastest ever by a 20 year-old Finn) and three times at three different venues in the span of four days in 1968. He was 5th in the 1966 Europeans and was a semi-finalist at the 1964 and 1968 Olympics and the 1971 Europeans. Captain of the national team for many years and a massive point-collector against Sweden, he won five individual Finnish titles (400m 1968, 400mh 1964, 1966, 1968-9) and eight relay titles for his club Helsingin Kisa-Veikot.

After graduating at Brigham Young University in Utah (physical education), he returned to Finland, working as a World Games promoter in Helsinki. Other pbs: 100m 11.0, 200m 21.5, 400m 46.9 (1968), 800m 1:48.4 (1966), 1000m 2:34.0 (at age 17), 1500m 4:04.0 (at 18), 110mh 15.0, 200mh 23.8 (1964), LJ 6.96, JT 60.62.

Gilbert VALLAEYS (France) (b. 13 Mar 1944) of a heart condition on 15 May. He equalled the French high jump record with 2.10 and a month later improved the mark to 2.11 in 1965. 10 internationals 1962-6.

Kaare VEFLING (Norway) (b. 19 May 1920) on 6 September. Ran in the 1946 Europeans and 1948 Olympics at 1500m and was Norwegian champion 1947-8 and record holder for 1500m (3:53.0 in 1947). Other pbs: 800m 1:57.0 (1947), 1M 4:11.7 (1950), 3000m 8:34.8 (1950).

Lubos VOMÁCKA (Czech Republic) (b. 1 Jul 1923) on 8 September. He was CS champion at 1500m in 1947 and 8th in the 1946 European Championships. pbs (1947): 800m 1:54.2, 1000m 2:30.4, 1500m 3:55.0, 5000m 15:25.4.

Cornelius Anthony 'Dutch' **WARMERDAM**. (USA) (b. 22 Jun 1915 Long Beach, California) on 13 November in Clovis, California. The first 15ft pole vaulter dominated his contemporaries more than any other man in history, at least until Sergey Bubka. His career best of 4.79m indoors, with a bamboo pole, was not bettered until Robert Gutowski cleared 4.82 at Austin on 15 Jun 1957, 14 years 87 days later. Warmerdam first cleared 15ft *4.57m* at Berkeley on 13 Apr 1940, adding three centimetres to the world record, and he cleared 15ft or higher in 33 competitions between 1940 and 1944 when he cleared exactly that height in his final competition to win the AAU title. No other vaulter cleared 15ft until Bob Richards succeeded at 15ft 1in *4.59* indoors in New York on 27 Jan 1951. Warmerdam made seven improvements to the world record outdoors to 4.77 in 1942 and six indoors from 4.42 in 1939 to 4.79 (15 ft 8 1/2 ins) at Chicago in 1943. AAU champion outdoors 1938 and 1940-4 (2nd 1937, 1939), and indoors in 1939 and 1943. He won the Sullivan Award for 1942.

He was the third son of a Dutch immigrant to the USA and left high school at the age of 17; he tied for third in the 1932 California high school meet. He went to Fresno State University in 1934, after a travelling salesman who had seen him practising in a spinach patch had recommended him to them! An ankle injury kept him out of the US Olympic Trials in 1936, but after a fine collegiate season he won at the Pan-American Games meeting in 1937. He coached at Stanford 1946-7 and then at Fresno State until 1980.

Progression at PV (position on world list): 1929- 2.74, 1930- 3.05, 1931- 3.64, 1932- 3.73, 1934- 4.11 (19=), 1935- 4.29 (5=), 1936- 4.31 (7), 1937- 4.46 (3=), 1938- 4.42 (2=), 1939- 4.42i/4.40 (2), 1940- 4.60 (1), 1941- 4.71 (1), 1942- 4.77 (1), 1943- 4.79i/4.67 (1), 1944- 4.57 (1), 1947- 4.37 exh.

Stanley WEST (GBR) (b. 13 Feb 1913) on 13 August. He represented Britain seven times at high jump 1933-45, including at the 1936 Olympic Games, and was AAA champion indoors and out (in a pb of 1.90) in 1935.

Bruno WISCHMANN (Germany) (b. 26 Dec 1910 Tondern) on 25 September. Coach, later chief coach of FRG/German national teams 1938-74, Direktor for the newly founded Institut für Leibesübungen in Mainz from 1954, Professor at the Gutenberg-Universität in 1966. pb: PV 3.70 (1934).

Corissa YASEN (USA) (b. 5 Dec 1973) on 12 May in Coeur d'Alene, Idaho. While at Purdue University she won the NCAA heptathlon in 1996 and that year set a pb of 5912 when 8th at the US Olympic Trials. She was also 9= at the Trials high jump, with a best of 1.92 at Walnut. In high school, she was state champion at 400m and high jump and was the No. 1 runner on her cross country team. She won the national high school meet in the high jump, defeating Amy Acuff. She also played pro basketball in the WNBA.

Luigi ZARCONE (Italy) (b. 18 Jun 1950) on 9 June. Mediterranean Games 5000m champion 1979 and Italian 1500m 1974, 10,000m 1977 and 1979, CC 1979; he competed at the 1974 Europeans. pbs: 1500m 3:37.7 (1974), 3000m 7:47.54 (1977), 5000m 13:23.7 (1977), 10,000m 28:02.30 (1977). He became a successful coach.

Viktor ZSUFFKA (Hungary) (b. 9 Jul 1910) in San Francisco on 20 June, having lived in the USA from 1945. He was the first Hungarian pole vaulter to clear 4 metres with five national records from 1931 (3.92) to 1940 (4.10). Hungarian champion 1934-7 and 1939-42, he was equal sixth in the 1936 Olympics (4.00) and fourth in the 1934 European Champs.

Died in 2000

Martin BÍLEK (Czech Republic) (b. 7 Jan 1973) committed suicide on 1 August. The Twin of discus thrower Marek Bílek, he had a shot best of 19.48 (1997), and had been 10th in the 1991 European Juniors and 8th in the 1992 World Juniors.

Stig HÅKANSSON (Sweden) (b. 19 Oct 1918 Karlstad) on 7 August. He won a gold medal at 4x100m at the 1946 European Championship and was also 5th at 100m and long jump. Swedish champion 100m 1944, 1946; long jump: 1939, 1944-5, 6 internationals. pbs: 100m 10.6 (1940), 10.5w (1943), 200m 21.9 (1944), LJ 7.50 (1944).

Dr **Alphonse JUILLAND** (USA, born in Bucharest and raised in Switzerland) on 30 June at the age of 77. He was the William H. Bonsall Professor Emeritus of French in the Department of French and Italian, which he chaired in the 1980s, at Stanford University. He was an ATFS member and took up competitive sprinting late in life and set three world records for over-50s.

Otto KOPPENHÖFER (Germany) (b. 13 Nov 1928 Künzelsau) on 16 February. He was 15th in the European Championships and had a personal best of 52.02 in the discus in 1958.

Elijah KORIR (Kenya) (b. 15 Apr 1978 Kericho) in September of throat cancer. He was the 1997 World Junior cross country champion and had best times of 3000m 7:43.59 (1999), 5000m 13:18.00 (1998) and 10000m 27:27.87 (1997, while still a junior). He won the World Military Games 10000m title in 1999.

Evert NYBERG (Sweden) (b. 28 Feb 1925 Göteborg) on 17 August. He won his first Swedish title at 4x1500m in 1943 and was Swedish 3000m junior champion 1944-5; his national juniors record 8:21.2 (1945) stood for 20 years. In 1946 at 21 he won the European 5000m bronze medal, but he did not finish in the 1948 Olympic 5000m final. Swedish champion at 5000m 1946 and 1956, 10000m 1955, cross-country 8km 1950 and 4km 1955 and 1957, and with 10 road titles: 25 km (1955-7, 1960), 30 km (1961-2) and marathon (1955, 1957, 1962-3). At the marathon, he won the 1955 Kosice race in 2:25:40, was 8th (1956) and 58th (1960) in the Olympics, 18th in the 1962 Europeans, and 2nd in the 1961 Nordic Games. pbs: 1500m 3:55.4 (1945), 2000m 5:19.2 (1946), 3000m 8.15.6 (1947), 5000m 14:23.2 (1946), 10000m 29:33.4 (1955), 20000m: 1:03:40.0 (1955, NR), 1 hour 18812 m (1955, NR), Marathon: 2:25:08 (1957), 2:18:44 (1961) short course.

Arthur SAGER (USA) (b. 4 Jul 1904) on 17 January. Tenth in the javelin at the 1928 Olympic games; pb 63.87 (1928).

Alfréd STRZÍNEK (Czech Republic) (b. 21 May 1929 Cisovice) on 21 November. He ran the second leg (in 1:53.0) on the ÚDA Praha team that set a world record of 7:28.0 for 4x800m in 1953 and in all set six national records in relays. CS champion at 800m 1953, 1500m 1955. pbs: 400m 49.3 (1952), 800m 1:51.0 (1956), 1000m 2:25.6 (1956), 1500m 3:46.0 (1955).

Béla SZEKERES (Hungary) (b. 11 Jan 1938) on 24 February. Competed in the 5000m at the 1960 Olympics and 1962 Europeans. pbs: 1500m 3:43.2 (1959), 5000m 13:54.0 (1963).

Melvin WALKER (USA) (b. 27 Apr 1914) on 1 November. He was fourth equal at the 1936 US Olympic Trials, but came into his own in 1937 when he broke the world record for the high jump with 2.09 at Malmö on 12 August. Six days earlier he had jumped 2.08 at Stockholm, 1 cm above the previous record; this mark was accepted by the AAU but not by the IAAF, as the bar fell down some minutes after the jump. He had also set a world best off a dirt surface indoors at Indianapolis with 2.076 in March 1937. From 1936-9 he was successively 2nd, 2nd,

1st and 3rd in the AAU Championships and shared the 1936 NCAA title with Dave Albritton – both competing for Ohio State. Indoors he tied for the AAU title in 1938 and won it in 1939 and 1941. He used the 'Western Roll'.
Annual progression at HJ (position on world list): 1933- 1.925 (37), 1935- 1.956 (20=), 1936- 2.032 (7), 1937- 2.09 (1), 1938- 2.05 (1=), 1939- 2.032i/2.007 (2), 1940- 2.007 (8=), 1941- 2.019i (9), 1942- 1.937i (39=)

Edward WIECEK (Poland) (b. 19 May 1946) on 30 January at Kutno. ATFS Member.

Add to Obituaries in ATHLETICS 2001

Serge AVEDISSIAN (France) died 11 April 2000

Rod BONELLA (b. 19 Jun 1937) died April 2000.

Died in 1999

Ravilya AGLETDINOVA (Belarus) (b. 10 Feb 1960 Kurgan-Tyube, Tajikistan, lived in Belarus from 1980) in a car accident on 25 June near Zhlobino. Her married name was Kotovich. At 1500m she was the European champion in 1986 and ran her personal best 3:58.70 to win the European Cup in 1985. Also at 1500m she was 10th in the European Juniors in 1977 and 4th in 1983 and 15th in 1991 at the World Championships and was 2nd in the 1985 World Cup. In 1982 she ran her pb for 800m of 1:56.1 before coming 4th in the European 800m. She won the USSR 800m and 1500m in 1985 and the 3000m in 1990.

Progression at 800m, 1500m (position on world list): 1974- 2:24.8; 1975- 2:10.8, 4:39.6; 1976- 2:06.01, 4:21.5; 1977- 2:04.0, 4:14.42; 1978- 2:03.6, 4:16.1; 1979- 2:04.2, 4:11.5 (65=); 1980- 2:02.0 (85), 4:06.6 (45); 1981- 1:58.65 (14), 4:04.40 (23); 1982- 1:56.1 (4), 4:07.41 (47); 1983- 1:57.0 (7), 3:59.31 (2); 1984- 1:58.08 (18=), 3:58.70 (8); 1985- 1:56.24 (3), 3:58.40 (3); 1986- 1:59.37 (25), 3:59.84 (4); 1990- 4:04.12 (8); 1991- 2:01.81 (69), 4:05.53 (14); 1992- 2:02.8 (99=), 4:08.3 (47); 1993- 4:08.95 (46), 1994- 4:14.62i. Other pbs: 1000m 2:37.18i (1984), 2:38.67 (1993); 1M 4:37.05 (1989), 3000m 8:46.86 (1990).

Alan **PATERSON** (GBR) (b. 11 Jun 1928) on 8 May 1999 in Canada. With a high jump of 6 ft 5 in (1.95m) in 1946 Paterson became and remains, at 17 years 338 days, the youngest male British athletics record holder. He improved this record to 1.97 and 2.00 that year and to 2.02 at the Rangers' Sports in 1947, having set his first Scottish record at 1.87 a month after his 17th birthday. He was the youngest male medallist at the European Championships with his silver in 1946 and he went on to win in 1950. He was 7th equal at the 1948 Olympics and 2nd equal in the 1950 Empire Games and was ranked best in the world in 1949 although 8th on the world list at 2.007. A member of Victoria Park AAC and 2.00m tall, he was Scottish champion 1946 and 1948-51 and AAA champion 1946 and 1949-50.

He emigrated to Canada to pursue his accountancy career, although he returned to compete at the 1952 Olympics.

OBITUARY 2002

Bengt ANDERHOLM (Sweden) (b. 24 Jan 1937 Ängelholm) on 3 January. In 1953 he won the Swedish Schools 80m in a record 9.2 and in 1955 he ran a pb 10.7 for 100m (joint top of national rankings) and was 3rd in the Swedish 100m.

Kevin DARE (USA) (b. 16 Apr 1982) on 23 February. The winner of the 2001 US Junior pole vault title with 5.05, died after landing on his head during the Big Ten Indoor Champs in Minneapolis. In attempting a vault of 4.75, he tumbled backwards, headfirst, onto the metal box. He was at Penn State University.

Erna LOW (Austria/GBR) (b. Erni Löw 7 Jul 1909 Vienna) on 12 February. The renowned tour operator was a passionate skier and led skiing tours from Britain to the Alps pre WWII, in which she monitored German broadcasts for British intelligence, and pioneered package holidays afterwards. She was Austrian javelin champion in 1930, in which year came to Britain to research a PhD thesis and she was 2nd in the WAAAs in 1932 and 3rd in 1933 with 33.35. She became a British citizen in 1940. She sold her Erna Low Travel service in 1972 but bought it back three years later before selling for a second time in 1979, and she continued to be active in the travel business into her eighties.

John McNAMARA (Australia) (b. 8 Apr 1961) on 21 January in Melbourne. He was 10th in the World University Games shot in 1987, 2nd in the Australian Champs 1987, 1993 and 1995 and had a personal best of 18.39 (1986).

George Dimitri **VAROFF** (USA) (b. 25 Mar 1914) on 10 January in San Antonio, Texas. He added 4cm to the world record for the pole vault when he cleared 14' 6" (4.43m) to win the AAU title at Princeton on 4 Jul 1936. A week 14ft (4.26m) at the US Final Olympic Trials was good for only 4th behind three Californians Bill Graber, Bill Sefton and Earle Meadows who all cleared three inches higher, and Varoff missed an Olympic place. The latter two took his world record in April-May 1937, before Varoff improved his best to 4.46 in 4th at the 1937 AAUs, behind Sefton, Cornelius Warmerdam and Meadows, who all also cleared 4.46. Varoff was 2nd in 1938 and 1st in 1939 at the AAU. A captain in the US Army Air Forces during the Second World War, his bomber was shot down over Japanese-occupied China and he was for a while listed as missing in action, but he survived and returned to his home town of San Francisco in April 1945.

Annual progression at PV (position on world list): 1933- 4.05 (26=), 1934- 3.96, 1935- 3.81, 1936- 4.43 (1), 1937- 4.46 (3=), 1938- 4.38 (1), 1939- 4.37 (5=).

THE END OF A BEAUTIFUL RACE

A tribute to Don Potts – by Roberto L. Quercetani

SOONER OR later, the day inevitably comes when one cannot refuse to pass into history. That was one of Donald Harry Potts' favourite sayings. As destiny would have it, the doyen of modern track statisticians passed away at Santa Barbara on November 1, just a few weeks before his 80th birthday (he was born in Seattle on 15 December 1921). In his own country, the leading power of the sport, he was certainly the first to cultivate in a systematic way the hobby of keeping close tabs on track happenings from coast to coast. (No matter if low-key statistical compilations had occasionally appeared in AAU Annuals since the earliest days of the 20th century).

As a high school boy in Seattle, Don was a moderately fast sprinter, but he soon found he had a better aptitude for following the sport as a statistician and analyst. He used to put it this way: "I couldn't beat (Samuel) Johnson, so I settled for (James) Boswell." As a teen-ager he began to keep scrapbooks with cuttings from any newspaper he could lay his hands on. As a would-be mathematics professor – he was to take his PhD degree at the California Institute of Technology in Pasadena in 1947 – he liked to analyse track happenings from various angles. True to his origin, however, he had a marked preference for the sprints. As Bert Nelson, one of the founders of *Track & Field News* once put it "If it was up to him, the good doctor would turn everything into a dash."

In the early Forties there was no magazine in the USA which specialised in track and field. However, the monthly *Amateur Athlete*, official organ of the multi-sports AAU, had its share of track news, including a 10-deep US Year List during the summer months, alas confined to mark and surname of each athlete. (The same pattern then prevailed even in Europe, e.g. in Hans Borowik's famous Weltrangliste published in *Der Leichtathlet*, a German weekly). Be it as it may, the *Amateur Athlete* served as a good vehicle for Potts in opening the way to his first international contact. This happened early in 1946 when I dared to send to the Editor of the magazine, Dan Ferris, a 30-deep list of the best American quarter-milers of all time. In publishing it in his March issue, he was wise to append the following note: "There may be a number of American track fans who can add to this list. We'll be interested in hearing from you". As it turned out, there was at least one. A letter from Pasadena, signed Don Potts, reached me late in April. I lost no time in reacting. We thought "a mutual exchange of notes on the subject of track stats should prove interesting for both of us."

Neither could then imagine that such an "exchange" would go on for 55 years, cemented by what was to become a strong friendship, eventually involving our respective families. Our first joint venture, *A Handbook on Olympic Games Track & Field Athletics*, published in Evanston, Illinois, appeared early in 1948 (Don had by then moved to the shores of Lake Michigan to take up a teaching job at Northwestern University). Among other things it contained a 100-deep World All-time List for men as at the end of 1947 – to our knowledge the first detailed work of this kind ever to appear in book form. By that time the Nelson brothers, Cordner and Bert, had been bold enough to launch a new magazine – *Track and Field News*. Don and I were among the very first contributors and our main engagement concerned "World Ranking," an idea which had been mapped out by Cordner in the magazine's inaugural issue. We intended to rank the ten best athletes of the year in every Olympic event on the following criteria: 1) honours won, 2) win-loss record, and 3) sequence of marks. Don, as a mathematician, hoped this would help us avoid, at least in part, the vagaries of subjective reasoning. This game, started with the 1948 Olympic season, was to go on for over half a century. Don, true to his ethics as a man of science, was virtually impermeable to chauvinism. We did our best to treat all candidates evenly. I can recall only one major case in which we could not agree on the choice of no. 1 for a given event – he favoured an Italian and I favoured an American! A third party to whom we decided to resort helped us avoid a tie, which would have been against our 'regulations.'

At that time, neither Don nor I could afford to attend major meets held far from our respective homes, yet we remedied at least in part by taking sides for this or that athlete – just to feel closer to the atmosphere of the battles that lay ahead. For example: in 1948 we were interested in the Dillard v Porter feud in the high hurdles, chiefly in the perspective of the London Olympics. Don rooted for the latter, then one of his pupils at Northwestern in Evanston, whereas I rooted for 'Bones,' whom I had known and seen in action in Tuscany back in 1946, when I worked as an interpreter for the 5th US Army. The decision in Don's – pardon, Bill's – favour was made at the US Olympic Tryouts, ominously held at Evanston , when 'Bones,' then holder of the world's 120 yd. hurdles record (13.6), clipped several hurdles and failed to finish, while Porter won handily.

Don and I met for the first time at San Francisco in November 1956, more than ten years after the start of our epistolary venture. This was when we joined the *Track & Field News* group on their way to the Melbourne Olympics. Among eyewitnesses at our encounter was Norris McWhirter, who used his well-known humour to liken this to the first meeting between explorers Livingstone and Stanley in Africa in 1871!

Prior to that Don, always attentive to technical details, had made a discovery for the benefit of many track nuts while attending the Pan-American Games at Mexico City in March 1955. The meet was featured by 'surprising' world records in the 400 metres (45.4 by Lou Jones of USA) and the triple jump (16.56 by Adhemar Ferreira da Silva of Brazil). The reaction of most observers was of the kind: "When was the last time they measured this track?" or "What kind of wind gauge did they use?" But Don was quick to point to altitude as a 'benefactor' of anaerobic events – a theory that was to receive ample confirmation 13 years later, after what happened at the Mexico Olympics.

From 1956 onwards, over a period of nearly 40 years, Don and I visited each other on many occasions. In 1960 he spent about a month in Italy, before and during the Rome Olympics. One day he came to my home early in the morning and showed me with deep emotion an announcement in *La Gazzetta dello Sport* informing us that Ralph Boston had just broken Jesse Owens' 25-year world record for the long jump. Apart from our favourite sport, we often happened to talk of "cabbages and kings." An American of Swiss origin, he was deeply interested in Renaissance art. And he was for years an avid collector of stamps dating from the days of the Grand Duchy of Tuscany. In light-hearted conversation with close friends he could exhibit a nice collection of Polish jokes, seemingly acquired when he lived in the Middle West.

When the ATFS was founded in 1950, Don was the only non-European among the 11 founder members. He served as president from 1972 to 1976. At ATFS meetings, one of his favourite interlocutors was Hon. President Harold Abrahams. Even though they happened to be 'astrological twins' (both born on 15 December), their views on track matters would often differ. Harold was a staunch upholder of amateur sport, while Don supported open track – "athletes should compete as individuals, without regard to their nationality or amateur status" was one of Don's favourite refrains.

Throughout his long association with the world of athletics, Don Potts authored or co-authored many statistical works for the benefit of both the ATFS and FAST, the latter being the family of American statisticians, of which he was a co-founder in 1983 with his long-time friends Scott Davis and Stan Eales. As a mathematics professor he had a 45-year career at various US institutions.

After his retirement he intended to become "a full time historian" of the sport he loved so well. In 1993 he authored what may well be the richest biography ever devoted to one of the pioneers of modern athletics – *Lon*, a book on the career of his countryman Lon Myers, whom he regarded as the greatest talent of the 19th century. By the same time he acted as one of the General Editors for the ATFS historical series, of which four volumes have so far appeared. With the onset of Parkinson's Disease early in 2001, he was forced to put a definitive halt to his tireless activity. Surely he can be said to have run a most beautiful race.

Combined Events World Records

The IAAF have changed the rules regarding wind assistance in world records for combined events. Instead of a record being disallowed if the wind speed was in excess of 4m/s in any of the relevant events, now if the wind exceeds 4m/s in any event the record can be accepted if the average of all wind speeds in the relevant events does not exceed 2m/s. For example in the European Cup decathlon 2001, Aleksandr Yurkov had wind speeds of 0.9 for 100m, -2.3 for LJ and 6.1 for 110mh; under the old rules the 6.1 would have meant his 8380 mark being regarded as wa, now, as the average wind was 1.6, the mark is OK.

DRUGS BANS

The IAAF has a longstanding history in the fight against doping and continues to take a lead in the world of sport, conducting far more tests than any other international federation. The IAAF is the first international sport federation to test for EPO and related substances out of competition, all year round, and on an unannounced basis. Starting in May 2002, the IAAF will organise a new procedure, based on the system accepted by the IOC of joint blood and urine testing. Testing will also take place at all future World Athletic Series competitions, having started at the World Cross Country Championships in Dublin in April 2002. According to the most recent IOC statistics [from 2000], in that year 14,872 anti-doping tests were made in athletics followed by13,568 tests in football, 12,216 in cycling and 5750 in swimming.

The following cases were reported of athletes failing drug tests in 2001

Suspension: Life - life ban, 4y/2y = 4/2 years, 3m = 3 months, W = warning and disqualification, P = pending hearing

Leading athletes

Men	*Date*	
Falk Balzer GER	19 Jan	2y
Roberto Barbi ITA	30 Jul	4y
Ato Boldon TRI	22 Apr	W
Christophe Cheval FRA	24 May	2y
Tony Dees USA	18 Feb	Life
Alene Emere ETH	22 Jan	2y
Robert Howard USA	3 Mar	W
Patrick Jarrett JAM	22 Jun	2y
Olivier Jean-Théodore FRA	4 Sep	3m
Jake Jensen USA	20 Aug	2y
Rajmund Kólko POL	30 Jun	
Marcin Krzywanski POL	29 Jun	W
Burger Lambrechts RSA	23 Feb	2y
Jeff Laynes USA	18 Jul	2y
Andrea Longo ITA	9 Jun	2y
Miroslav Menc CZE	26 Apr	Life
Gregoriy Murzin RUS	6 Oct	W
Ali Saïdi-Sief ALG	10 Aug	2y
John Skeete GBR	27 Jan	2y
Dragutin Topic YUG	2 Feb	2y
Kofi Yekapor CAN	Jun	P
Women		
Hazel Clark USA	3 Mar	W
Venolyn Clarke CAN	31 Jul	4y
Katalin Divós	1 Jun	2y
Fabiane dos Santos BRA	6 May	
Svetlana Kanatova RUS	22 Jul	2y
Svetlana Laukhova RUS	10 Aug	W
Yekaterina Leshchova RUS	8 Aug	2y
Li Ji CHN	17 Jul	2y
Liu Jing CHN	10 Aug	2y
Zhanna Malkova RUS	21 Oct	2y
Natalya Sologub BLR	5 Aug	2y
Constanta Stucan ROM	15 Jul	3m
Ana Mirela Termure ROM	4 Aug	2y
Silvana Trampuz AUS	8 Apr	2y
Solange Witteveen ARG	19 May	2y

Others: Life: Milijenko Vukovic CRO (10 Jun), Rian Ingrim USA (9 Jul), 2y: Abdelrahmane Djemadi FRA (21 Jan), Ksenia Kokulina RUS (9 Feb), Abdel Djahara ALG (31 Mar), Silverio Manso POR (20 May), Dolores Pulido ESP (20 May), Ville Vakkuri FIN (18 Apr), Jörg Deerberg GER (2 May), Vuk Stojanovic YUG (26 May), Marina Haida GRE (26 May), Branislav Stojanovic YUG (7 Jul), Przemyslaw Rogowski POL (13 Jul), Edwin Cuesta VEN (16 Jul), Blerim Polisi DEN (21 Jul), Wansawang Sawatdee THA (14 Sep), Tedsak Boonchnsri THA (15 Sep), Wang Xiaoting CHN (15 Sep), Marc Tommeleyn BEL (2 Dec); 3m: Frank Vicet CUB (4 Jul), Adoración García ESP (22 Jul); Warning: Zina Wilsnach RSA (20 Jan), Laurence Perrin FRA (10 Mar), Minori Hayakari JPN (22 Apr), Joëlle Chorin FRA (22 Apr), Walid Abderazek EGY (2 Jun), Bobby Smith USA (17 Jun), Yves Denes FRA (14 Jul), Matsui Noriyuki (30 Sep). Yang Xuewei CHN, Qiu Xuexiong CHN – Sep

Add to list of athletes failing tests in 2000

Men		
Liu Yunfeng CHN	13 Jul	2y
Robert Naali TAN	1 Oct	W
Women		
Marina Anisimova RUS	5 Mar	2y
Seema Antil IND	19 Oct	W
Tonya Carter USA	15 Jul	W
Cui Danfeng CHN	16 Aug	2y
Rimma Dubovik UKR	26 Nov	3m
Assunta Legnante ITA	6 Sep	W
Rodica Mateescu ROM	24 Apr	2y
Mihaela Melinte ROM	7 Jun	2y
Iva Prandzheva BUL	5 Aug	Life
Carolin Soboll GER	23 Jun	2y
Song Liqing CHN	12 Jul	2y

Others: 2y: Blanca López MEX (13 Feb), Yang Chunlei CHN (27 Apr), Jan Erik Christiansen NOR (16 Sep) Antonio Gracía ESP (22 Oct); 8m: Fernando Cipollini ITA (3 Jun); 3m: Arthur Miklos ROM (26 Nov); W: Nathalie Chabran FRA (17 Sep)

And in 1999 – Men

Troy Douglas NED	26 Jun	2y
Gennadiy Skurygin RUS	25 Aug	2y
Women		
Inger Miller USA	7 Mar	W*
Liu Shixiang CHN		2y

* Miller tested positive for caffeine at the World Indoor Championships and thus lost her 60m bronze medal, which went to Philomenah Mensah CAN.

WORLD CHAMPIONSHIPS

Edmonton, Alberta, Canada, August 3-12

WHILE THERE were no world records set at these, the 8th IAAF World Championships, they were a great success in terms of exciting competition, great performances and enthusiastic crowds. The weather was superb (except for the long distance athletes) for the entire period and – despite criticism from some quarters that the stadium was packed only for the days of the opening and closing ceremonies, the total attendance figure was 400,886 – ranging from under 29,000 on Saturday, Aug 4 to a high of 54,920 on Day 10, the Closing Ceremony. This represented a daily average of 40,000, which was excellent for a non-Olympic athletics occasion held on North American soil. "It's the best ever," said IAAF general secretary István Gyulai. "We don't need better organisation. This was very perfect, very professional."

The ever-changing nature of world athletics was shown by the fact that only 8 of the 22 men's individual winners in Sydney repeated their successes and just 4 of the 20 women's. Championships records were set at eight events, and two Czechs were prominent in this list: Jan Zelezny, who demonstrated yet again why he is acknowledged as the greatest ever javelin thrower, and Tomás Dvorák, who produced the third highest decathlon score of all time. Top women's marks included championship records from Tatyana Lebedeva, 15.25 triple jump into a slight wind for the fourth longest ever, Osleidys Menéndez, 69.53 javelin, and the 4.75 pole vaults by Stacy Dragila and Svetlana Feofanova. Their superb battle for supremacy was typical of this meeting, which produced exciting races and field event competitions in so many events. Maurice Greene's 9.82 100m was the fastest ever time with a negative wind reading, and, with the benefit of the 652m altitude in Edmonton, the world record would surely have gone if the wind had been following. Dmitriy Markov's 6.05 vault equalled the best ever non-Bubka mark and Jonathan Edwards regained his triple jump title with 17.92, easily the world's best mark of the year. Lars Riedel won his fifth world discus title with the longest throw ever recorded in championship competition and Zelezny and Iván Pedroso won their fourth World Championships gold medals. Zhanna Pintusevich-Block had a dramatic 100m victory over Marion Jones, but Jones came back to take her World Championships gold total to five with wins at 200m and 4x100m.

Olga Yegorova was undoubtedly the most controversial athlete of the championships. Her appearance in the 5000m elicited more boos than cheers and Paula Radcliffe and some of her British team colleagues were sufficiently incensed to display a banner proclaiming "EPO Cheats Out". Because of irregular procedure with her EPO test in Paris, Yegorova had her suspension overturned by the IAAF and was allowed to run, but while many were unhappy with her victory, her tenacity in the face of this opprobrium must be admired. Four athletes (Ali Saïdi-Sief, who thus lost his silver medal at 5000m, subject to confirmation, Roberto Barbi, Natalya Sologub and Ana Mirela Termure) tested positive in Edmonton and the Canadian sprinter Verolyn Clarke was found to have failed a random test in Calgary on 31 July.

The trend of more and more countries sharing the honours continued. At the inaugural World Champs in 1983, just 14 countries provided all the winners; in Seville two years ago the figure was 21, while in Edmonton the champions were drawn from 23 nations, including the Dominican Republic and Senegal for the first time. Other medallists came for the first time from Cameroon, St Kitts & Nevis, Estonia and Haiti. Another trend is the continuing decline in USA and European domination. In 1983 they collected 38 of the 41 gold medals on offer; in 1999 the total was 35 out of 46 and this time it was 29 from 46. The US headed the points table, but fared poorly by their standards outside the sprint events.

100 Metres (h, qf 4th, sf, F 5th/–0.2)

GREENE EQUALLED Carl Lewis's tally of three world titles at 100m. Five men inside 10 sec, despite being run into an 0.2m breeze, made the final one of the greatest ever mass 100m races. Greene's 9.82 was the third quickest ever legal time behind his 1999 times of 9.79 (0.1) in Athens and 9.80 (0.2) in Seville – and yet he was running injured!

"I felt something in my quad, then I took another step and I felt something in my hamstring in the last 10 to 15m of the race." He managed to hold off Montgomery's closing rush before hobbling over the line and said that he could have run about 9.77 without the injuries. As in 1983 and 1991 at this event, the USA swept the medals, with Williams passing Boldon in the closing stages. The fourth American, Curtis Johnson withdrew with a hamstring twinge in warming-up.

Most regrettably the wind gauge went berserk in the quarter-finals, when conditions were ideal, and readings of –2.3, -5.1, –2.9, -2.8 and –1.1 were given for the races, won by Montgomery 9.92, Greene 9.88 and Mark Lewis-Francis GBR 9.97, Chambers 9.97 and Williams 9.95. An official statement was issued: "A malfunction of the wind gauge resulted in some unusual readings during the five quarter-final heats of the men's 100m, and also during three heats of the women's heptathlon 200m. After reviewing the device, and the accompanying data, Brian Roe (IAAF Technical Officer) has discovered that this was a temporary malfunction. It has since been corrected. The times recorded during these events will, therefore, be accompanied by the designation "No Wind Information"... any and all records achieved in these races will not stand."

Many initially felt that the wind at the time of the 100m races was below 2m in the athletes' favour, but the balance of opinion from statisticians who were close to the track (and Brian Roe) later came down in favour of the likelihood of following winds of 2-3 m/s in these races. Lewis-Francis (later 5th in his semi) lost the chance of a world junior record. There were headwinds in the semis (Greene fastest at 10.01/-1.2) and final the next day, so we never saw how fast the speedsters could go in potentially ideal conditions. The 1995 champion, Donovan Bailey was 6th in his semi and took a retirement lap of honour.

1. Maurice Greene USA	9.82
2. Tim Montgomery USA	9.85
3. Bernard Williams USA	9.94
4. Ato Boldon TRI	9.98
5. Dwain Chambers GBR	9.99
6. Kim Collins SKN	10.07
7. Christian Malcolm GBR	10.11
8. Abdul Aziz Zakari GHA	10.24

200 Metres (h, qf 7th, sf 8th, F 9th/+0.1)

THE SURPRISE Olympic champion, Kedéris, seemed to have something in hand as he took his semi in a world-leading Greek record of 20.03 and was a clear winner in the final, producing a great surge (9.7 for second 100m) from 7th entering the straight to a near-2m winning margin. Behind him just 0.047 separated 2nd to 7th with 1/100th sec times of 20.032 for the winner, 20.195 for Williams and 20.198 for the bronze medallists. Malcolm, who had set impressive Welsh records of 20.13 and 20.08 in quarter-final and semi despite easing up, tightened up under the strain and slipped to fifth. For him (and for Collins) it was their eighth race of the championships as they had both made the 100m final. Williams was fastest in the first round with 20.25.

A hamstring problem caused the world's fastest of the year (20.05), Ramon Clay USA, to trail in last in his quarter-final. Maurice Greene decided not to defend his title, and Ato Boldon, the 1997 champion, withdrew because of a back injury.

1. Konstadínos Kedéris GRE	20.04
2. Christopher Williams JAM	20.20
3= Shawn Crawford USA	20.20
3= Kim Collins SKN	20.20
5. Christian Malcolm GBR	20.22
6. Stéphane Buckland MRI	20.24
7. Kevin Little USA	20.25
8. Marlon Devonish GBR	20.38

400 Metres (h 4th, sf 5th, F 6th)

MONCUR CAME to Edmonton unbeaten in 2001 and with the world's quickest time of 44.45. He ran the fastest heat time of 44.88 and won his semi in 44.89, but three others ran faster in the other races: Haughton won in 44.83 and the massive (2.01/96) Schultz – who had set a pb of 45.11 in his heat – took the other in a startling 44.66 ahead of Mackowiak (pb of 44.84). There was a shock at the start of the final when Mackowiak simply walked out of his blocks and took no part in the race. Moncur ran with fine judgment, pulling away in the final straight for victory in 44.64, 2m clear of a fast finishing Schultz who overhauled Haughton for silver with Pettigrew a close 4th. The USA thus failed to medal in this event for the first time in a global 400m championship (apart from the boycott year of 1980) since the 1920 Olympics! The winning time was the slowest since the 1983 Worlds.

1. Avard Moncur BAH	44.64
2. Ingo Schultz GER	44.87
3. Greg Haughton JAM	44.98
4. Antonio Pettigrew USA	44.99
5. Eric Milazar MRI	45.13
6. Hamdam Al-Bishi KSA	45.23
7. Alleyne Francique GRN	46.23
dnf. Robert Mackowiak POL	–

800 Metres (h 4th, sf 5th, F 7th)

BUNGEI WAS fastest in the heats with 1:44.73 (the best ever in a meeting with three rounds) and Bucher in the semis with 1:44.47. Bungei set a swift pace (24.73, 50.41) in the final before Bucher moved ahead along the back straight. At 600m (76.39) he was 5m clear of the young Kenyan and by the finish he was even further ahead. The big surprise was Czapiewski, who had reduced his pb to 1:44.89 when 4th in his semi. The Pole was last when Bucher made his move and was still only 6th entering the finishing straight but he produced an inspired burst to snatch bronze with another pb. His 13.5 last 100m compared to Bucher's 14.7. Olympic champion Schumann in his first competition, due to injury, for two months, was too far behind for a high placing, but moved from 8th to 5th in the straight with 13.7 for the last 100m.

1. André Bucher SUI 1:43.70
2. Wilfred Bungei KEN 1:44.55
3. Pawel Czapiewski POL 1:44.63
4. William Yiampoy KEN 1:44.96
5. Nils Schumann GER 1:45.00
6. Mbulaeni Mulaudzi RSA 1:45.01
7. Khalid Tighazouine MAR 1:45.58
8. Hezekiél Sepeng RSA 1:46.68

1500 Metres (h 9th, sf 10th, F 12th)

EL GUERROUJ took his third world title. In the final he had the benefit of some brisk pacemaking by his compatriot Kaouch (55.41, 1:53.69) and went ahead soon after 800m, followed by Lagat, Chirchir and Estévez, and hit the bell in 2:35.93. By 1200 in 2:49.35 (55.66 for the lap) he held an unassailable lead and, blowing kisses to the crowd, eased his way to a 3m victory over Olympic bronze medallist Lagat, the final 300 taking 41.33. Moroccan-born Maazouzi won his first major medal at 31, producing a strong finish to overtake Chirchir for bronze with Estévez not far behind and a long way ahead of colleague Redolat, who had run the fastest time in the first round with 3:36.24. Lagat was quickest in the semis at 3:35.82.

1. Hicham El Guerrouj MAR 3:30.68
2. Bernard Lagat KEN 3:31.10
3. Driss Maazouzi FRA 3:31.54
4. William Chirchir KEN 3:31.91
5. Reyes Estévez ESP 3:32.34
6. José Antonio Redolat ESP 3:34.29
7. Rui Silva POR 3:35.74
8. Abdelkader Hachlaf MAR 3:36.54
9. Gert-Jan Liefers NED 3:36.99
10. Paul McMullen USA 3:39.35
11. Adil Kaouch MAR 3:48.45
12. Mehdi Baala FRA 3:55.36

5000 Metres (h 6th, F 10th)

THIS WAS a remarkably fast final, considering the altitude. Richard Limo ran the first lap in 59.07 and Kipketer reached 1000m in 2:32.51 – c.12:40 pace. Kipketer had opened up a 15m lead by 2000m (5:09.48) and was still 10m clear at 3000m (7:51.18) although the pack caught him soon afterwards. Saïdi-Sief moved ahead after 3200m, passed 4000m in 10:34.65 and then ran a 61.32 lap with Wolde and Limo on his heels. They were a stride apart at the bell (12:05.41) and with 200 to go (12:33.62; 57.65 for that lap) Saïdi-Sief was still 2m up on Limo. The 20 year-old Kenyan sprinted past around the last turn and pulled away with a last lap of 55.3 and last 100m of 13.5 to 15.2 by Saïdi-Sief. Limo said: "I wanted to show the world the Kenyans are back. We sat down and planned how the race could be won. We have to make the speed go higher and higher so this guy [Saïdi-Sief] gets tired." Making his major championship debut for France, Sghir was at first disqualified and then reinstated in sixth.

Later came the news that the Algerian Federation had suspended Saïdi-Sief due to a positive test for nandrolene.

1. Richard Limo KEN 13:00.77
2. Million Wolde ETH 13:03.47
3. John Kibowen KEN 13:05.20
4. Alberto García ESP 13:05.60
5. Ismaïl Sghir FRA 13:07.71
6. Sammy Kipketer KEN 13:08.46
7. Abiyote Abate ETH 13:14.07
8. Hailu Mekonnen ETH 13:20.24
9. Marius Bakken NOR 13:22.07
10. Adam Goucher USA 13:24.00
11. Driss El Himer FRA 13:28.14
12. Mohammed Amine MAR 13:28.90
13. Mohamed S El-Wardi MAR 13:43.40
14. Isaac Viciosa ESP 14:01.32
2 dq. Ali Saïdi-Sief ALG 13:02.16

10,000 Metres (8th)

THE GREAT Haile Gebrselassie had to settle for third, thus ending an eight-year win streak at 10,000m, but he was racing for the first time since an Achilles tendon operation late in 2000. There was a fascinating struggle for supremacy amongst the East Africans. Three Ethiopians placed in the top four but the title went to a Kenyan. The first half was a cagey affair, covered in 14:15.11 (2:50.25, 2:47.45, 2:56.03, 2:48.58, 2:52.80), and the lead continued to change hands with bewildering frequency as the pace gradually quickened. The next four kilometres were run in 2:46.93, 2:46.91, 2:45.21 and 2:43.08.

With a kilometre to go there were still nine men in the lead pack: four Ethiopians, three Kenyans and two Spaniards. With two laps remaining (25:51.49) Kamathi and Geb were at the front but Kosgei led at the bell (26:57.28). In the final lap, Geb struck for home but, understandably, lacked his usual potent finish. Mezgebu and Kamathi shadowed him and at the start of the finishing straight Kamathi produced a devastating kick, while Mezgebu overtook Geb for second. Kamathi covered the last lap in 55.9, the final kilometre taking 2:36.01 and the second half 13:38.14.

1. Charles Kamathi KEN 27:53.25
2. Assefa Mezgebu ETH 27:53.97
3. Haile Gebrselassie ETH 27:54.41
4. Yibeltal Admassu ETH 27:55.24
5. Fabián Roncero ESP 27:56.07
6. José Rios ESP 27:56.68
7. Paul Kosgei KEN 27:57.56
8. John Cheruiyot Korir KEN 27:58.06
9. Habte Jifar ETH 28:02.71
10. Kamiel Maase NED 28:05.41
11. Jaouad Gharib MAR 28:05.45
12. José M Martínez ESP 28:06.33
13. Jeff Schiebler CAN 28:07.06
14. Marco Mazza ITA 28:08.00
15. Toshinari Takaoka JPN 28:13.99

Marathon (3rd)

RUN IN conjunction with the opening ceremony for the first time, the marathon provided a memorable start to the Championships. Unfortunately race day proved to be Edmonton's hottest of the year so far, the race starting at 6.45 pm in 28°C heat. Add the humidity, the altitude and some testing inclines and the winning time of 2:12:42 was quite remarkable. Several world-class runners either ran outside 2:20 or failed to finish.

World record holder Khannouchi dropped out at around 26k with blisters on both feet. Halfway was reached in a cautious 66:59 and the first serious move came from El Mouaziz after 25k. He looked impressive when he held a 9 sec lead at 30k over Abera, Biwott and Baldini, with Tola and Aburaya close behind, but he was caught during the 31st kilometre and had dropped off the pace by 34k, leaving five men in contention. After 2 hours of running the race was between Abera and Biwott.

Biwott was marginally ahead into the stadium but after a thrilling sprint (44.7 last 300m) it was Abera who prevailed by just one second in one of the greatest of all marathon finishes. Baldini was a delighted third. Olympic champion Abera joins Abebe Bikila, Waldemar Cierpinski and Abel Antón as the only men to win two global marathon titles, the first in consecutive years. He also led Ethiopia to World Cup victory over Japan and Italy, based on aggregate times of their best three men. Only three of top 15 from 1999 repeated. 73 finished from 97 starters.

1. Gezahegne Abera ETH 2:12:42
2. Simon Biwott KEN 2:12:43
3. Stefano Baldini ITA 2:13:18
4. Tesfaye Tola ETH 2:13:58
5. Shigeru Aburaya JPN 2:14:07
6. Abdelkader El Mouaziz MAR 2:15:41
7. Tesfaye Jifar ETH 2:16:52
8. Yoshiteru Morishita JPN 2:17:05
9. Takayuki Nishida JPN 2:17:24
10. Simretu Alemayehu ETH 2:17:35
11. Giacomo Leone ITA 2:17:54
12. Atsushi Fujita JPN 2:18:23
13. Benoit Zwierzchlewski FRA 2:18:29
14. Ian Syster RSA 2:19:38
15. Oscar Fernández ESP 2:19:45

World Cup: 1. ETH 6:43:32. 2. JPN 6:48:36. 3. ITA 6:51:56, 4. FRA 7:05:57, 5. ESP 7:08:57, 6. MEX 7:15:09, 7. UKR 7:19:12, 8. AUS 7:19:42, 9. USA 7:25:38, 10. CAN 7:39:37, 11. GUA 7:44:52, 12. ECU 7:48:56

3000 Metres Steeplechase (h 6th, F 8th)

KOSGEI, fastest in the heats at 8:21.96, became the first steeplechaser to win Olympic and World titles. Held in windy conditions, the race started slowly (2:48.72 at 1000), speeded up a little in the middle stages (2:45.09), and finished at a frantic pace (2:41.35) as six men were closely packed at the bell. At the start of the back straight it was a Kenyan first three, but Yator fell at the final water jump when a close fourth. Kosgei led from Barmasai entering the final straight and sprinted away for a clear victory, while Ezzine sneaked past Barmasai in the final 30m to end a run of nine successive Kenyan 1-2s at Worlds and Olympics.

1. Reuben Kosgei KEN 8:15.16
2. Ali Ezzine MAR 8:16.21
3. Bernard Barmasai KEN 8:16.59
4. Luis Miguel Martín ESP 8:18.87
5. Bouabdallah Tahri FRA 8:19.56
6. Antonio Jiménez ESP 8:19.82
7. Khamis S Abdullah QAT 8:20.01
8. Raymond Yator KEN 8:20.87
9. Ralf Assmus GER 8:21.73
10. Brahim Boulami MAR 8:21.95
11. Tim Broe USA 8:23.07
12. Eliseo Martín ESP 8:27.78
13. Christian Belz SUI 8:31.43
14. Joël Bourgeois CAN 8:36.38
15. Gaël Pencréach FRA 8:41.51

110 Metres Hurdles (h 7th, sf 8th, F 9th)

JOHNSON, winner in 1995 (13.00) and 1997 (12.93), regained his title. He got out ahead of Olympic champion García (fastest in the heats 13.21 and semis 13.19) and although Johnson clobbered hurdles 2, 4, 6, 8 and 10, the Cuban never quite managed to get back on level terms. Johnson outdipped him, 13.04 to 13.07, the quickest times in the world in 2001. The bronze in a pb of 13.25 went to Dorival, who thus won Haiti's first global medal since Silvio Cator finished 2nd in the 1928 Olympic long jump. Terrence Trammell was unlucky in his semi; he was going well until he stumbled in mid-race and although he recovered well he failed by 1/100th (13.44) to catch Dorival and missed a place in the final. Anthony Jarrett GBR, medallist in 1991, 1993 and 1995, was disqualified for two false starts in his semi.

1. Allen Johnson USA 13.04
2. Anier García CUB 13.07
3. Dudley Dorival HAI 13.25
4. Yoel Hernández CUB 13.30
5. Robert Kronberg SWE 13.51
6. Yevgeniy Pechonkin RUS 13.52
7. Dawane Wallace USA 13.76
8. Shaun Bownes RSA 13.84

400 Metres Hurdles (h 7th, sf 8th, F 10th/-0.3)

SANCHEZ, fastest in the heats (48.64) and semis (48.07), ran the race of his life for victory in 47.49, for the 10th fastest in history and the Dominican Republic's first ever World Champs medal; his previous best was 47.95. There was little between Al-Somaily, Tamesue (who had set a Japanese record 48.10 in his semi), defending champion Mori and Sanchez as they headed into the final straight, but Sanchez and Mori possessed the strongest finishes. Mori finished a close second in an Italian record of 47.54 while Tamesue – at 1.70m – became easily the shortest man ever to break 48. Olympic champion Angelo Taylor went out in his semi (4th 49.23) after landing badly off the last hurdle and for the first time ever (except for the boycott year of 1980), the USA failed to provide a finalist in this event at a global championship.

1. Felix Sanchez DOM 47.49
2. Fabrizio Mori ITA 47.54
3. Dai Tamesue JPN 47.89
4. Hadi S Al-Somaily KSA 47.99
5. Chris Rawlinson GBR 48.54
6. Pawel Januszewski POL 48.57
7. Jirí Muzík CZE 49.07
dq. Boris Gorban RUS (48.27)

High Jump (Q 5th, F 8th)

IN ANTICIPATION this event looked wide-open, but even so the winner was a surprise, as Buss, the 1999 bronze medallist, had not cleared higher than 2.30 outdoors for two years. He had first time clearances at 2.20, 2.25 and 2.30 but lost a share of the lead when he failed his first attempt at 2.33, a height cleared first time by Sotomayor, the defending champion Voronin and Rybakov. Buss prudently saved his remaining attempts for the next height of 2.36 and he alone cleared, making what was a pb for him at his final try. Rybakov and Voronin tied for silver as they had a clean sheet previously whereas Sotomayor, who twice went very close to clearing 2.36, had one costly failure at 2.30.

1. Martin Buss GER 2.36
2= Yaroslav Rybakov RUS 2.33
2= Vyacheslav Voronin RUS 2.33
4. Javier Sotomayor CUB 2.33
5= Stefan Holm SWE 2.30
5= Sergey Klyugin RUS 2.30
7= Mark Boswell CAN 2.25
7= Staffan Strand SWE 2.25
9. Kwaku Boateng CAN 2.25
10= Charles Austin USA 2.20
10= Abderahmane Hammad ALG 2.20
12. Gilmar Mayo COL 2.20

Pole Vault (Q 7th, F 9th)

A record 13 men cleared 5.70m in qualifying and a record 10 cleared 5.75 in the final. Markov only cleared this, his opening height, on his third attempt and gambled by being the only man to pass at 5.85, a height cleared first time by Averbukh, at the second try by Hysong and Stolle and at the third by Mesnil. Markov had to clear the next height of 5.90 as failure would leave him 10th; he did and the 26 year-old Seville silver medallist was world champion.

He continued with the greatest ever display of vaulting in a major championship, clearing 5.95 at the first attempt and 6.05 at the second to share second place on the world all-time list with Tarasov and set new Commonwealth and Oceania records. The previous World Champs record was Tarasov's 6.02; the Olympic record stands at 5.92. Siberian-born Averbukh produced Israel's highest ever World Champs placing in any event with his silver medal, while Olympic champion Hysong took bronze on countback.

1. Dmitriy Markov AUS 6.05*
2. Aleksandr Averbukh ISR 5.85
3. Nick Hysong USA 5.85
4. Michael Stolle GER 5.85
5. Romain Mesnil FRA 5.85
6= Richard Spiegelburg GER 5.75
6= Christian Tamminga NED 5.75
8. Adam Kolasa POL 5.75
9. Tim Mack USA 5.75
10. Viktor Chistiakov AUS 5.75
11. Danny Ecker GER 5.65
12. Martin Eriksson SWE 5.50
nh. Rens Blom NED –

Long Jump (Q 9th, F 11th)

THERE ARE few greater big-time competitors than Pedroso, who took his fourth world title to add to his five indoors. The 28 year-old Cuban had not been jumping well in 2001, and he achieved only 8.00 in qualifying where Stringfellow 8.33/-0.1 and Beckford 8.19/-0.2 led the way. In the final Calado produced the first decent jump of 8.21 in round 2, only to be shaded by Pedroso's 8.23/-0.9, a lead he extended to 8.35/0.5 in round 3. Stringfellow opened with two fouls but then saved the day with 8.22/1.2 for second place, a distance he improved to 8.24 in round 4.

In round 5 Pate jumped 8.21w and moved into third on the basis of a better second jump (8.09 to Calado's 7.92) ... but his elation was short lived as Calado responded with 8.18 to snatch the bronze. Later in round 5 Pedroso sealed his victory with another season's best of 8.40, although that was the shortest winning mark at World Champs/Olympic level since 1976. Stringfellow had a massive final jump (8.60+) that was a no-jump by about 6cm.

1. Iván Pedroso CUB 8.40/1.2
2. Savante Stringfellow USA 8.24/1.6
3. Carlos Calado POR 8.21/1.1
4. Miguel Pate USA 8.21w/2.7
5. Kareem Streete-Thompson CAY 8.10/0.7
6. Aleksey Lukashevich UKR 8.10/0.8
7. James Beckford JAM 8.08/-0.4
8. Dwight Phillips USA 7.92/0.8
9. Grzegorz Marciniszyn POL 7.92/1.4
10. Hussein Al-Sabee KSA 7.90/0.0
11. Abdulrahman Al-Nubi QAT 7.63/0.7
12. Viktor Shkurlatov RUS 7.61/0.9

Triple Jump (Q 4th, F 6th)

EDWARDS WAS in deep trouble in qualifying after wasting his first jump and reaching only 16.51 on his second for 16th overall. One last try ... the Edwards magic returned and he bounced out to 17.46/-0.2 to lead the qualifiers from Davis 17.22/0.7 and Achike 17.15/0.7. In the final he opened with a modest 16.84 and after a tantalising second attempt (landing c.18m from the most miniscule of fouls) he was 4th behind Olsson (17.47), García (17.40) and Davis (17.20).

His third was an Edwards special of 17.92, his and the world's longest for three years and a distance only he, Kenny Harrison and Willie Banks have ever surpassed with legal wind. He had 7.8cm to spare on the board and at 35 was world champion again. The European U23 1-2 took silver and bronze. Olsson, competing with an injured heel, jumped within 2cm of his best and Spasovkhodskiy, whose previous pb was 17.08, produced a 5th round 17.44. Edwards did not register another mark; he had calf muscle cramps on his 4th and 6th attempts and passed his 5th.

1. Jonathan Edwards GBR 17.92/0.7
2. Christian Olsson SWE 17.47/1.2
3. Igor Spasovkhodskiy RUS 17.44/0.9
4. Yoel García CUB 17.40/1.2
5. Walter Davis USA 17.20/0.3
6. Brian Wellman BER 16.81/0.3
7. Larry Achike GBR 16.79/0.8
8. Rostislav Dimitrov BUL 16.72w/2.2
9. Phillips Idowu GBR 16.60/0.3
10. Johan Meriluoto FIN 16.54/1.1
11. Paulo Camossi ITA 16.18/-1.7
12. Konstadínos Zalaggítis GRE 16.13/1.6

Shot (Q & F 4th)

GODINA strengthened his claim to be considered among the greatest of championship shot putters. Winner of the world title in 1995 and 1997, he collected his third gold medal in some style. His campaign didn't start well as he needed all three tries to ensure qualification with 20.52 while world leader Robberts produced 21.26 at the first attempt, but the final was a different story. Robberts finished last of 12 whereas Godina opened up with 21.87 and 21.80 to crush the opposition before four no throws.

At the midway point Peric was 2nd at 20.91 and Nelson 3rd at 20.86, but in an eventful round 4 Olympic champion Harju shot from 8th at 20.59 to 2nd with a season's best of 20.93, while Martínez also overtook Peric at 20.91 on the basis of a superior second best. Moments later, Nelson – who had only just made the final as 12th qualifier at 20.13 – clicked with 21.24 for silver. There were the best ever marks for places 7-12 and Paulo Dal Soglio's 19.80 was the best-ever non-qualifying mark.

1. John Godina USA 21.87
2. Adam Nelson USA 21.24
3. Arsi Harju FIN 20.93
4. Manuel Martínez ESP 20.91
5. Dragan Peric YUG 20.91
6. Yuriy Belonog UKR 20.83
7. Conny Karlsson FIN 20.78
8. Brad Snyder CAN 20.63
9. Ville Tiisanoja FIN 20.45
10. Andrey Mikhenevich BLR 20.42
11. Joachim Olsen DEN 20.38
12. Janus Robberts RSA 20.18

Discus (Q 6th, F 8th)

RIEDEL WILL not threaten Al Oerter's four Olympic wins (the 34 year-old German has one gold, one silver) but now he can point to five world titles (plus a bronze in 1999 when suffering from a hip muscle injury), a single event tally which has been surpassed only by Bubka's six pole vault titles. Following knee surgery, Riedel made a late start to the season, in June, and timed his peak beautifully. He went to Edmonton with a season's best of 67.28 (only 8th among the competitors) but served notice of what was to come by leading the qualifying round with 68.26.

In the final, the first round leaders were Möllenbeck with a timely pb of 67.61, succeeded minutes later by Olympic champion Alekna (67.65), who in round 3 unleashed a championship record of 69.40. At that Riedel was third at 67.10, and fourth after Shevchenko threw 67.16 in round 4. But then Riedel took the lead with 69.50 and in the 5th round improved again to 69.72, the longest ever distance in a major championship. After that Shevchenko threw a pb of 67.57 in round 5 to come within 4cm of the bronze medal. There were best ever marks for places 6-7-8.

1. Lars Riedel GER	69.72*
2. Virgilijus Alekna LTU	69.40
3. Michael Möllenbeck GER	67.61
4. Dmitriy Shevchenko RUS	67.57
5. Adam Setliff USA	66.55
6. Vasiliy Kaptyukh BLR	66.25
7. Roland Varga HUN	65.86
8. Frantz Kruger RSA	65.27
9. Jason Tunks CAN	63.79
10. Tomo Tompuri FIN	62.82
11. Igor Primc SLO	62.36
12. Einar Tveitå NOR	59.11

Hammer (Q 4th, F 5th)

THERE WAS a marvellously exciting hammer contest on a hot afternoon between Olympic champion Ziolkówski and yearly leader at 83.47, Murofushi. The Pole opened with 81.88 but Murofushi, after 79.91 took over with 82.46, backed up by 81.95 and 81.43. In round 5, Ziolkówski came up with the longest throw of his life – a Polish record of 83.38 that also broke Sergey Litvinov's 1987 championship record of 83.06. Murofushi, next into the circle, went close with 82.92. Ziolkówski closed with 80.39 and while Murofushi's final throw was good, at 82.61 it fell short of what was required. He took Japan's first World Championship medal other than seven at marathon (two men and five women) and one at women's 10,000m before 2001. Konovalov, whose 80.27 opener was threatened by Vizzoni's fifth round 80.13, was a delighted bronze medallist. There were best ever marks for places 8-11.

1. Szymon Ziolkówski POL	83.38*
2. Koji Murofushi JPN	82.92
3. Ilya Konovalov RUS	80.27
4. Nicola Vizzoni ITA	80.13
5. Andrey Skvaruk UKR	79.93
6. Balázs Kiss HUN	79.75
7. Igor Astapkovich BLR	79.72
8. Tibor Gécsek HUN	79.34
9. Adrián Annus HUN	78.10
10. Olli-Pekka Karjalainen FIN	76.76
11. Maciej Palyszko POL	75.94
12. Nicolas Figère FRA	75.36

Javelin (Q 10th, F 12th)

THERE WAS compelling drama in the qualifying round, where in Group A Gatsioúdis threw 87.81 but Närhi injured his right arm and failed to register a throw and Backley could do no better than 81.50 when ended as 14th best, so missing a major final for the first time in a decade. Group B featured a championship record 90.76 by Zelezny. Contesting his 7th World Champs (equalling the record), as was Zeležny, Hill was an automatic qualifier with 84.88 but defending champion Parviainen only scraped in as 11th best with 81.82.

In the final, Parviainen opened with a championship record 91.31. Such a throw was calculated to destroy the hopes of anyone ... except for Zelezny, who thrives on such challenges. His second round response was 92.80, a distance only he (at five meetings between 1993 & 1997) and Parviainen himself (once in 1999) have ever surpassed. Parviainen fouled thereafter and had to settle for silver with the longest ever non-winning distance, an unwanted "record" he previously held with 90.97 behind Gatsioúdis in Kuortane in 2000. Hampered by a knee injury, Gatsioúdis, who reached 88.39 in round 2 and 89.95 in round 4, took bronze with a third place record distance. Greer raised his pb to 87.00 in 4th, close to the US record of 87.12.

"You can see that I am only getting better with age," said 35-year-old Zelezny, "and I think that is because I am understanding the javelin throw better as I get older. I am continuing to improve." Parviainen estimated the strong tailwind added "a couple of metres" to the distances.

1. Jan Zelezny CZE	92.80*
2. Aki Parviainen FIN	91.31
3. Kostas Gatsioúdis GRE	89.95
4. Breaux Greer USA	87.00
5. Raymond Hecht GER	86.46
6. Boris Henry GER	85.52
7. Sergey Makarov RUS	83.64
8. Eriks Rags LAT	82.62
9. Li Rongxiang CHN	81.80
10. Aleksandr Ivanov RUS	80.56
11. Voldemars Lusis LAT	79.70
12. Mick Hill GBR	77.81

Decathlon (6-7th)

THE WORLD record holder Sebrle was carrying a groin injury although he battled through to the end and Macey was also being hampered by a similar injury. Yet astonishingly, despite physical problems that intensified as the competition wore on, the Briton was the overnight leader with 4638 after pbs in the HJ (2.15) and 400m (a scintillating 46.21 after a great battle with Nool 46.23). Just one point behind was Dvorák, who set a pb LJ of 8.07, with Nool 3rd 4531 and Sebrle a distant 4th 4377. Dvorák ran a fine 13.80 to open up a 68 pt lead over Macey, who miraculously set a pb of 14.34 with his left thigh strapped and clearly in pain.

Macey picked up a few points over Dvorák in the discus and Nool came into his own by vaulting 5.40 to move into 2nd with 7224 to 7324 by Dvorák, who tied his outdoor best of 5.00, and 7195 for Macey, who was reduced to just 54.61 javelin by an arm injury. The 1500m did not affect anything and Dvorák totalled the third highest ever, bettering Daley Thompson's 1984 Olympic mark of 8847 as the highest ever in a championship. It was the Czech's third world title. Nool raised his Estonian record to 8815, for 5th on the world all-time list and the highest ever non-winning score, and Macey held his body and spirit together for his best score of 8603.

1. Tomás Dvorák CZE	8902*
2. Erki Nool EST	8815
3. Dean Macey GBR	8603
4. Attila Zsivoczky HUN	8371
5. Lev Lobodin RUS	8352
6. Jirí Ryba CZE	8332
7. Stefan Schmid GER	8307
8. Laurent Hernu FRA	8280
9. Aleksandr Yurkov UKR	8264
10. Román Sebrle CZE	8174
11. Michael Nolan CAN	8169
12. Mario Aníbal POR	8155
13. Zsolt Kürtösi HUN	8097
14. Benjamin Jensen NOR	8090
15. Phil McMullen USA	8079

20 Kilometres Walk (4th)

FOR THE first time in a world championship in this event all the medals went to one nation – Russia. As is often the case, the pace simply got faster as the race progressed. The first 5k took 20:40 (Markov leading), the second 20:25 (a fourth Russian, Andreyev, ahead but he was later disqualified), the third in 20:12 (Markov in front again) and the final 5k in just 19:14 as the Russians fought it out after Deakes slipped back in the closing stages. Rasskazov's 2 sec margin over Markov, who overtook 18 year-old Burayev early on the stadium lap, was the narrowest in a global 20km championship since the 1968 Olympics. Burayev was the only junior to win an individual medal in these championships, and at 18 years 264 days is the youngest ever men's walk medallist. Nearly a quarter of the field (9 from 37 starters) were disqualified.

1. Roman Rasskazov RUS	1:20:31
2. Ilya Markov RUS	1:20:33
3. Viktor Burayev RUS	1:20:36
4. Nathan Deakes AUS	1:20:55
5. David Márquez ESP	1:21:09
6. Joel Sánchez MEX	1:22:05
7. Satoshi Yanagisawa JPN	1:22:11
8. Jefferson Pérez ECU	1:22:20
9. Jirí Malysa CZE	1:22:42
10. Hatem Ghoula TUN	1:23:14
11. Alejandro López MEX	1:23:20
12. Alessandro Gandellini ITA	1:24:05
13. Li Zewen CHN	1:24:29
14. Robert Heffernan IRL	1:25:02
15. Ivan Trotskiy BLR	1:25:02

50 Kilometres Walk (11th)

AFTER 45:58 for the leaders at 10k, Lipiec (1:08:18, 1:30:24 1:52:28) built up a 24 sec lead over Korzeniowski, Clausen, Fadejevs, Potemin and Barrett with García and Hernández among those a further 2 sec behind. By 30k Lipiec was 6th (2:14:41) behind Fadejevs (2:14:26), Korzeniowski & Potemin (2:14:27), Matyukhin & García (2:14:38) with Hernández 11th (2:15:29). After that Korzeniowski started to pull away; he was 9 sec up on Fadejevs at 35k (2:36:05) and 47 sec clear of García at 40k (2:57:47) with Fadejevs a close third. Korzeniowski regained his world title as he completed his final 10k in 44:21 for the world's fastest time of the year. García closed in 44:23 and Hernández, moving from 6th to 3rd, in 45:00, took 10:24 from his previous best.

1. Robert Korzeniowski POL	3:42:08
2. Jesús Angel García ESP	3:43:07
3. Edgar Hernández MEX	3:46:12
4. Aigars Fadejevs LAT	3:46:20
5. Vladimir Potemin RUS	3:46:53
6. Valentí Massana ESP	3:48:28
7. Curt Clausen USA	3:50:46
8. Marco Giungi ITA	3:51:09
9. Tomasz Lipiec POL	3:53:06
10. Mike Trautmann GER	3:53:25
11. Denis Langlois FRA	3:53:42
12. David Boulanger FRA	3:53:52
13. Francesco Galdenzi ITA	3:54:42
14. Phillip Dunn USA	3:56:33
15. Mikel Odriozola ESP	3:57:17

4 x 100 Metres Relay (h 11th, sf & F 12th)

THE USA were the fastest heat winners in 38.35 but initially were disqualified as lead-off Drummond ran outside his lane. He suffered cramp in the right quadriceps muscle after about 40m and his leg buckled. By straying into the lane outside his he gained no advantage and impeded nobody, and the Jury of Appeal reinstated the team.

Germany were not so fortunate (dq in 38.82 after passing well outside the zone on the last change), while Britain – tipped as silver medallists at worst – and Cuba failed to transfer the baton on the last change. In the final the Americans won in 37.96 by some 5m, equalling the widest margin in World Champs history (USA 1983) – and that without Drummomd or Greene, who took no further part after his 100m victory. The South Africans ran above themselves; 4th in their semi in 38.63, they grabbed 2nd from the outside lane in 38.47 with Trinidad 3rd in 38.58, national records for both. Brazil was fastest at 38.23 in the semis but failed to finish in the final.

1. USA	37.92 (Grimes, Williams, Mitchell, Montgomery; alsogold: Drummond, J Johnson)
2. RSA	38.47 (Nagel, du Plessis, Newton, Quinn
3. TRI	38.58 (Burns, Boldon, Harper, Brown)

4. AUS	38.83	7. POL	39.71
5. JPN	38.96	dnf. BRA	–
6. CIV	39.18		

4 x 400 Metres Relay (h 11th, F 12th)

THEIRS WAS not a vintage team but the Americans were still strong enough to win their eighth consecutive world or Olympic title. The US team was fastest in the heats at 3:00.07. Individual 400 champion Moncur gave the Bahamas a big initial advantage in the final and at 800m they still held the Americans at bay with Jamaica 3rd. Brew opened a small lead for the USA against McIntosh (BAH) and Haughton (JAM) on the third leg with Poland (sorely missing Mackowiak) an isolated 4th, and Angelo Taylor (as in Seville) atoned for his 400mh demise by running a fine leg, anchoring in 43.71 for the race's fastest split. Despite missing McDonald, injured earlier in the meeting, Jamaica would have expected to finish 2nd but the Bahamian anchor, Munnings, crept past McFarlane to snatch silver in a national record 2:58.19.

1. USA 2:57.54 (Byrd, Pettigrew, Brew, Taylor 43.71; also gold: Young, Pierce)
2. BAH 2:58.19 (Moncur, C Brown, McIntosh, Munnings; also silver: Oliver)
3. JAM 2:58.39 (Simpson, C Williams, Haughton, McFarlane; also bronze: Blackwood, Mario Watts)

4. POL	2:59.71	7. ESP	3:02.24
5. BRA	3:01.09	8. GER	3:03.52
6. GBR	3:01.26		

Women

100 Metres (h, qf 5th; sf, F 6th/-0.3)

JONES WAS beaten over 100m, ending a 42 finals-win streak (if a false start disqualification in 1999 is overlooked) that had started in Feb 1998 after Merlene Ottey defeated her in Tokyo in Sep 1997. The initial loss was only a semi-final – Pintusevich-Block beat her, 10.94 to 10.95 into a 2.3m wind, but 100 minutes later the Ukrainian got away (as she had in the semis) to a rocket start, her reaction time being 0.023 faster than Jones'. Clearly ahead at halfway she was determination personified as she grimly held out against Jones' closing rush to win in her fastest ever time of 10.82 to the American's 10.85, into a slight wind, with Thánou gaining on both of them after a poor start for bronze. Pintusevich thus made up for Athens 1997, when, in a tight finish she was convinced she had beaten Jones for the world 100m title and excitedly set off on a victory lap, only to sink to her knees in disappointment and embarrassment when she heard the official result that Jones had won 10.83 to 10.86. Jones was the one runner under 11 secs in the first round at 10.93 and both she and Thánou won their quarter-finals in 10.97.

1. Zhanna Pintusevich-Block UKR	10.82
2. Marion Jones USA	10.85
3. Ekateríni Thánou GRE	10.91
4. Chandra Sturrup BAH	11.02
5. Chryste Gaines USA	11.06
6. Debbie Ferguson BAH	11.13
7. Kelli White USA	11.15
8. Mercy Nku NGR	11.17

200 Metres (h 8th, sf 9th, F 10th/-0.8)

JONES WON the 200m title that had eluded her in Seville and maintained her record of not having lost a final at the distance since 1995. But it was close; instead of pulling further away as the finish approached, her stride shortened and her winning margin over Ferguson was not much more than a metre, with White a close third. The time of 22.39 was the slowest yet to win a world title. Defending champion Miller was but a shadow of her former self, failing to reach the final (4s3 22.82), and Pintusevich-Block did not compete. Mothersill set a national record of 22.54 for fastest in the first round, and Ferguson 22.39 and Jones 22.40 won the quickest semis.

1. Marion Jones USA	22.39
2. Debbie Ferguson BAH	22.52
3. Kelli White USA	22.56
4. LaTasha Jenkins USA	22.85
5. Cydonie Mothersill CAY	22.88
6. Juliet Campbell JAM	22.99
7. Alenka Bikar SLO	23.00
8. Myriam Mani CMR	23.15

400 Metres (h 5th, sf 6th, F 7th)

BREUER AT 50.71 was fastest in the first round and Thiam's Senegalese record of 50.21 was the fastest of the semis. In the final, Guevara showed just ahead entering the finishing straight, but she faded and the race developed into a duel between Thiam and Fenton, who had only just recovered from a hamstring injury. Just 0.02 separated them as Thiam won on the dip in another national record to become the first woman from her country to win a medal – or even reach a final. However, the winning time of 49.86 was some way behind the absent Katharine Merry's best for the year (49.59) and was the slowest ever for a world title. One has to go back to 1972 for a slower winning time at Olympic level.

1. Amy Mbacké Thiam SEN 49.86
2. Lorraine Fenton JAM 49.88
3. Ana Guevara MEX 49.97
4. Grit Breuer GER 50.49
5. Nadjina Kaltouma CHA 50.80
6. Olesya Zykina RUS 50.93
7. Mireille Nguimbo CMR 51.97
dnf. Falilat Ogunkoya NGR –

800 Metres (h 9th, sf 10th, F 12th)

THE 36-year-old Vriesde was 6m clear of Graf at 200m (28.07) and reached 400m in 59.08 and 600m in 88.63, that surge of pace in the third 200 destroying everyone but Graf and Mutola. She was overtaken by Graf with just 60m to go but continued to fight hard. Graf could sense victory within her grasp, only for Mutola ("That is probably the most difficult race I have ever run") to inch ahead in the last couple of strides, with Vriesde still only a metre or so behind. Holmes faded from 4th at 600m to 6th behind Macharia and Cummins, the former South African who set a pb and became Canada's most successful athlete of the championships. Only Vriesde (1:59.51 and 1:59.58) and Mutola (1:59.96 and 1:59.58) bettered 2 minutes in the preliminary rounds.

1. Maria Lourdes Mutola MOZ 1:57.17
2. Stephanie Graf AUT 1:57.20
3. Letitia Vriesde SUR 1:57.35
4. Faith Macharia KEN 1:58.98
5. Diane Cummins CAN 1:59.49
6. Kelly Holmes GBR 1:59.76
7. Mayte Martínez ESP 2:00.09
8. Ivonne Teichmann GER 2:04.33

1500 Metres (h 4th, sf 5th, F 7th))

SZABO and Szekely are not best friends, with Szekely taking legal action against her rival for defamation. Nonetheless, they took a joint lap of honour (seemingly at Szabo's insistence) after their convincing one-two. The final lacked Jacobs (dropped out of her heat with a foot injury), out-of-form Olympic champion Mérah-Benida (non-starter in semi) and Favor Hamilton and Yordanova, both fallers in the semis.

In the final, Ayhan (fastest at 4:07.97 in the first round) set a swift pace (63.78 400) with Gorelova ahead at 800 (2:08.95), the bell (2:58.09) and 1200 (3:14.45). Szabo (4:10.77 heat and 4:07.04 in her semi) overtook Szekely for second with 200 to go and went past Gorelova just before the start of the finishing straight. Contesting her first outdoor 1500 of the year, she pulled away to win in 4:00.57 with Szekely getting the better of Gorelova. This was Szabo's first major outdoor title at 1500m and Szekely sixth second in global championships from 1991.

1. Gabriela Szabo ROM 4:00.57
2. Violeta Szekely ROM 4:01.70
3. Natalya Gorelova RUS 4:02.40
4. Carla Sacramento POR 4:03.96
5. Lidia Chojecka POL 4:06.70
6. Natalia Rodríguez ESP 4:07.10
7. Alesya Turova BLR 4:07.25
8. Süreyya Ayhan TUR 4:08.17
9. Yuliya Kosenkova RUS 4:08.84
10. Mardrea Hyman JAM 4:12.48
11. Leah Pells CAN 4:15.34
12. Nuria Fernández ESP 4:17.86

5000 Metres (h 9th, F 11th)

THE FINAL was a slow race, playing into the hands of such a renowned kicker as Yegorova. The first four kilometres took 3:10.06 (Recio), 3:03.47 (Mikitenko), 3:03.72 (Dong) and 3:04.43 (Dong). Former world record holder Dong, fastest in the heats at 15:09.44, made a move with just over a kilometre remaining. Szabo, not in top shape despite gold at 1500m, fell back two laps out, leaving five in the lead group.

With Zadorozhnaya in close attendance, the Chinese covered the next lap in 68.24, followed by a 32.98 200 to the bell (14:02.90), with Yegorova and Domínguez just behind and Worku next. Yegorova struck with 240m to go and completed the last lap in 60.49 (29.04 final 200) to win by some 20m from a joyful Domínguez, while Worku – who qualified only as a fastest loser – pipped Dong for bronze. The final kilometre took just 2:41.71. Zadorozhnaya (6th) collapsed at the finish. Yegorova, who had not previously raced at 5000m in 2001, and allowed to run after the faulty procedures in her EPO test, ran straight off the track at the finish.

1. Olga Yegorova RUS 15:03.39
2. Marta Domínguez ESP 15:06.59
3. Ayelech Worku ETH 15:10.17
4. Dong Yanmei CHN 15:10.73
5. Irina Mikitenko GER 15:13.93
6. Yelena Zadorozhnaya RUS 15:16.15
7. Edith Masai KEN 15:17.67
8. Gabriela Szabo ROM 15:19.55
9. Rose Cheruiyot KEN 15:23.18
10. Tatyana Tomashova RUS 15:23.83
11. Joanne Pavey GBR 15:28.41
12. Benita Willis AUS 15:36.75
13. Merima Denboba ETH 15:41.09
14. Fatima Yvelain FRA 15:53.52
15. Teresa Recio ESP 15:57.32

10,000 Metres (7th)

RADCLIFFE changed her strategy as she attempted to defeat the Ethiopians for a global track title, but the result remained the same. Second to Wami in the 1999 Worlds and 4th in the Olympics won by Tulu after leading most of the way, she decided this time to leave her bid until much later in the race. Belkacem led for much of the race at a sedate tempo with kilometres of 3:22.44, 3:16.15, 3:16.56, 3:18.44, 3:16.30 (16:29.89 at 5000) and 3:12.24. Adere cov-ered the next in 3:12.06 and Belkacem was ahead again as the big pack passed 8k in 26:03.72 (3:09.53). Radcliffe held back, striking with three and a half laps remaining, and the pace in-creased from 73/74s to 70.93, followed by 68.77. With the three Ethiopians in ominously close attendance, Radcliffe covered the ninth km in 2:58.80. But on the penultimate lap (68.69) she was back to 4th and a 63.36 last lap carried Tulu to a narrow victory over the much taller Adere, while Wami just held off the Briton for bronze. The second half took 15:18.92, the final 3000 8:54.62 and last 1000 2:46.29. It was Ethiopia's first ever clean sweep in the World Champs or Olympics.

1. Derartu Tulu ETH 31:48.81
2. Berhane Adere ETH 31:48.85
3. Gete Wami ETH 31:49.98
4. Paula Radcliffe GBR 31:50.06
5. Mihaela Botezan ROM 32:03.46
6. Lyudmila Petrova RUS 32:04.94
7. Asmae Leghzaoui MAR 32:06.35
8. Yamna Belkacem FRA 32:09.21
9. Haruko Okamoto JPN 32:14.56
10. Lyudmila Biktasheva RUS 32:18.64
11. Deena Drossin USA 32:18.65
12. Olivera Jevtic YUG 32:19.44
13. Mizuki Noguchi JPN 32:19.94
14. Aster Bacha ETH 32:25.81
15. Teresa Recio ESP 32:30.56

Marathon (12th)

DITA BLASTED away from the start, leading by 52 sec at 5k, 1:20 at 10k and 1:51 at halfway (1:12:17), followed by a group which included all the women who would fill the top nine places. By 30k Dita's lead was down to 40 sec and she was caught after 32k. Tosa forced the pace with only Simon, Shibui and Zakharova able to keep up. At 40k Tosa (2:18:48) and Simon (2:18:49) had drawn clear of the other two (2:19:02) and it was not until just outside the stadium that Simon went ahead. She ran the second half in an outstanding 1:11:53 for a well-deserved victory after bronze in 1997 and 1999 and the 2000 Olympic silver. Tosa was third and Zakharova outgunned world leader Shibui, who was running only her second marathon, for 3rd. Oberem maintained a remarkable sequence after 8th, 7th and 6th in the three previous World Championships. 52 of the 57 starters finished.

1. Lidia Simon ROM 2:26:01
2. Reiko Tosa JPN 2:26:06
3. Svetlana Zakharova RUS 2:26:18
4. Yoko Shibui JPN 2:26:33
5. Sonja Oberem GER 2:28:17
6. Florence Barsosio KEN 2:28:36
7. Shitaye Gemeche ETH 2:28:40
8. Lyubov Morgunova RUS 2:28:54
9. Kazumi Matsuo JPN 2:29:57
10. Constantina Dita ROM 2:30:38
11. Irina Timofeyeva RUS 2:30:48
12. Firiya Zhdanova RUS 2:30:58
13. Fatuma Roba ETH 2:31:10
14. Ornella Ferrera ITA 2:32:45
15. Nuta Olaru ROM 2:33:05

World Cup: 1. JPN 7:22.36, 2. RUS 7:26.00, 3. ROM 7:29.44, 4. ETH 7:33:33, 5. ITA 7:40:09, 6. ESP 7:48:38, 7. CAN 8:04:10, 8. USA 8:14:48, 9. GUA 9:29:53.

100 Metres Hurdles (h 9th, sf 10th, F 11th/2.0)

SIX ATHLETES succeeded in winning world indoor and outdoor titles this year: El Guerrouj, Pedroso, Godina, Mutola, Yegorova... and Kirkland. She began well by clocking the quickest heat time of 12.69 but ended up only 7th fastest of the eight semi-finalists (Devers fastest at 12.56). That led to Kirkland being drawn in lane 1 in the final with Olympic champion Shishigina out in lane 8. Devers (lane 6) recovered from a moderate start but hit the 8th hurdle hard and from then on had her hands full staving off Shishigina and Dimitrova (lane 3) and may have been unaware that on the inside Kirkland was running a flawless race to clock a startling 12.42, good for 8th on the all-time list, from a previous best of 12.63. Shishigina, in pain from an Achilles tendon injury, won the lunge against Dimitrova for bronze. Fast-starting Adams trimmed her pb to 12.63 despite hitting a hurdle.

1. Anjanette Kirkland USA 12.42
2. Gail Devers USA 12.54
3. Olga Shishigina KZK 12.58
4. Svetla Dimitrova BUL 12.58
5. Jenny Adams USA 12.63
6. Dianne Rose-Henley JAM 12.79
7. Linda Ferga FRA 12.80
8. Vonette Dixon JAM 13.02

400 Metres Hurdles (h 4th, sf 6th, F 8th)

NOSOVA WAS the fastest in the first round at 54.43, and with Pernía 53.81, Bidouane 53.85 and Parris pb 53.88 all inside 54 sec in the first semi and Nosova taking the second in 54.03, a closely fought final looked in prospect. It was no such thing as Bidouane (champion in 1997 and 2nd to Pernía by 0.01 in 1999) destroyed the field. She entered the finishing straight roughly level with Nosova and Pernía and seized her opportunity when the Cuban hesitated at the ninth hurdle and made a mess of the final barrier.

The 31 year-old Moroccan rocketed away to win by nearly a full second from Nosova, while Buford-Bailey nearly deprived Pernía of bronze. Bidouane's 53.34 was easily the fastest in the world in 2001, and her winning margin was the largest ever at World Champs/Olympic level.

1. Nezha Bidouane MAR 53.34
2. Yuliya Nosova RUS 54.27
3. Daimí Pernía CUB 54.51
4. Tonja Buford-Bailey USA 54.55
5. Debbie-Ann Parris JAM 54.68
6. Ionela Tîrlea ROM 55.36
7. Deon Hemmings JAM 55.83
8. Sandra Glover USA 57.42

High Jump (Q 10th, F 12th)

SIX WOMEN were left in at 1.97, the height at which medals would be won or lost. Bergqvist and Cloete cleared first time to share the lead; Babakova (3rd on countback) and Veneva made it on the second attempt while Palamar and world junior champion Vlasic fell by the wayside. At 2.00 Bergqvist and Veneva were eliminated, the Swede (who missed very narrowly) taking bronze. Babakova cleared at the 2nd attempt to go ahead but a few minutes later Cloete followed suit and the gold medal was hers when both she and Babakova failed at 2.02. Cloete with her distinctive arm flailing style became the first South African to win a senior global high jump title since Esther Brand in the 1952 Olympics and the first South African woman to win any World Champs medal. Babakova won her fifth Worlds medal. Olympic champion Yelesina failed to reach the final (1.88 for 13=).

1. Hestrie Cloete RSA 2.00
2. Inga Babakova UKR 2.00
3. Kajsa Bergqvist SWE 1.97
4. Venelina Veneva BUL 1.97
5. Vita Palamar UKR 1.94
6. Blanka Vlasic CRO 1.94
7= Monica Iagar ROM 1.90
7= Dóra Györffy HUN 1.90
9. Oana Pantelimon ROM 1.90
10= Amy Acuff USA 1.90
10= Yelena Gulyayeva RUS 1.90
12. Antonietta Di Martino ITA 1.85

Pole Vault (Q 4th, F 6th)

THIS WAS the greatest contest yet in the history of women's vaulting as eight cleared 4.45 and Gao found an Asian record of 4.50 sufficed only for 5th and a 4.55 by Grigorieva, equalling the pb she set for Olympic silver, for 4th. The Australian cleared at her second attempt, Pyrek (despite carrying a hamstring injury) at the first to claim bronze. Both Pyrek and Grigorieva failed at 4.60, a championship record equalling height which Dragila and Feofanova made first time. At 4.65, crucially as it would turn out, Dragila went over at the second attempt and Feofanova at the third. With the bar at 4.70 both slipped over faultlessly, equalling the European record in the Russian's case.

But still it wasn't over: at 4.75 Dragila, vaulting first and still in the lead, cleared at the first try ... and so did Feofanova. By mutual consent the two vaulters went for a world record 4.82 which carried a $100,000 bonus as well as the $60,000 first prize, but neither succeeded, Dragila coming the closer, and the pair took a joint lap of honour. Twelve women qualified for the final by clearing 4.35 with another nine at 4.25, and in the final there were the best ever marks for places 2, 4-9 and 12.

1. Stacy Dragila USA 4.75*
2. Svetlana Feofanova RUS 4.75*
3. Monika Pyrek POL 4.55
4. Tatiana Grigorieva AUS 4.55
5. Gao Shuying CHN 4.50
6. Thórey Elisdóttir ISL 4.45
7. Yvonne Buschbaum GER 4.45
8. Pavla Hamacková CZE 4.45
9. Janine Whitlock GBR 4.35
10. Caroline Hingst GER 4.25
11. Doris Auer AUT 4.25
12. Mary Sauer USA 4.25

Long Jump (Q 5th, F 7th)

MAY LED the qualifiers with 6.80/1.0, her season's best, and regained the title she won in 1995 (3rd 1997, 2nd 1999) with a splendid series. A 6.86w/3.7 opener put her into the lead and she reached 6.97/1.2 in the 2nd round (a new device informing us that she took off 10.3cm from the edge of the board, thus 7.07 from take off to landing) and 7.02w in the third (7.16 from take off). Her closest rivals at halfway were Vaszi with a Hungarian record of 6.86 (6.95 from take off) and Gotovska. In Round 4, Kotova, the favourite, improved from 6.82 to 7.01w (7.12 from take off) and Montalvo moved into 3rd with 6.88w. Nothing changed after that although May produced 6.97/1.3 (7.09 from take off) in round 5. There was the best ever mark for 9th place. Heike Drechsler was injured and had a token 4.45 in qualifying. Only three reached the automatic qualifying standard of 6.70 and 6.48 sufficed for the final. Only one qualifier made the IAAF B standard for the Championships of 6.75, an indication of how unreasonably high the IAAF entry standards were in field events.

1. Fiona May ITA 7.02w/2.6
2. Tatyana Kotova RUS 7.01w/3.6
3. Niurka Montalvo ESP 6.88w/2.1
4. Tünde Vaszi HUN 6.86/1.3
5. Valentina Gotovska LAT 6.84w/3.5
6. Níki Xánthou GRE 6.76w/3.1
7. Maurren Maggi BRA 6.73/-0.6
8. Lyudmila Galkina RUS 6.70/0.1
9. Guan Yingnan CHN 6.69w/3.5
10. Eva Goulbourne JAM 6.62/1.2
11. Kumiko Ikeda JPN 6.44/1.2
nj. Jenny Adams USA –

Triple Jump (Q 8th, F 10th)

LEBEDEVA'S initial jump was enough to win; taking off with 11.5cm to spare, she touched down at 15.11/-1.1 for the longest jump in the world so far in 2001 and jumped 14.93/1.4 in the 2nd round. At the end of three rounds Marinova was 2nd with 14.58 and Martínez, the former Cuban, 3rd at 14.52. Nothing changed until the final round, when Mbango moved into silver medal position with 14.60, Marinova fell just short with 14.57 (14.68 measured from take off) and Lebedeva – whose multi-coloured hairstyle was as spectacular as her jumping – brought the contest to a climactic finish with a leap of 15.25, her toe being just 1cm from the edge of the board, a distance which has only ever been bettered by Kravets and Lebedeva (15.32) herself. The three phases measured 5.52, 4.21 and 5.52. Marinova 14.89w/3.0, Mbango 14.64/0.1 and Martinez 14.59/1.9 all jumped farther in the qualifying contest, in which Hansen 14.51/1.1 produced her best mark for two years.

1. Tatyana Lebedeva RUS	15.25/-0.8
2. Françoise Mbango CMR	14.60/-0.6
3. Tereza Marinova BUL	14.58/-1.3
4. Magdelín Martínez ITA	14.52/0.9
5. Heli Koivula FIN	14.28/-0.2
6. Cristina Nicolau ROM	14.17/-1.1
7. Ashia Hansen GBR	14.10/-0.6
8. Trecia Smith JAM	13.92/-1.3
9. Olga Bolshova MDA	13.86/-0.5
10. Yelena Govorova UKR	13.85/-1.5
11. Camilla Johansson SWE	13.84/-0.2
12. Natalya Safronova BLR	13.82/-1.5

Shot (Q & F 5th)

KOROLCHIK'S 19.87 in qualifying was well ahead of the next best, Kleinert-Schmitt 19.35 and Korzhanenko 18.95, and it wasn't long before she dominated the final. After a first round foul, she threw 19.87 in the second round and a Belarus record 20.61 in the third. Kleinert-Schmitt led the opening round at 19.54 and stretched her pb to 19.86 in the final round. Pavlysh moved into 3rd with her second round 19.41, while indoor champion Peleshenko had three throws over 19.30 but good only for fourth place. Bidding for a fourth world title, Kumbernuss wound up sixth.

1. Yanina Korolchik BLR	20.61
2. Nadine Kleinert-Schmitt GER	19.86
3. Vita Pavlysh UKR	19.41
4. Larisa Peleshenko RUS	19.37
5. Irina Korzhanenko RUS	19.35
6. Astrid Kumbernuss GER	19.25
7. Nadezhda Ostapchuk BLR	18.98
8. Yumileidi Cumbá CUB	18.73
9. Svetlana Krivelyova RUS	18.70
10. Krystyna Zabawska POL	18.50
11. Elisângela Adriano BRA	18.06
12. Lieja Koemen NED	17.89

Discus (Q 9th, F 11th)

COMPETING FOR the first time since she became the oldest ever woman to win an Olympic title, suffering in the meantime from calf and groin injuries and now aged 40, Zvereva led the qualifiers with 65.78. In round 2 of the final, having opened with a foul, she overtook Sadova (66.87) to take the lead with a throw of 67.10. Sadova's next effort landed at 66.36 but in the 4th round the 29 year-old Russian un-leashed a world-leading throw of 68.57. Zvereva, who became the oldest ever World medallist, had no reply to that and Sadova finally landed a major title 11 years after winning at the World Juniors. Grasu moved past Kelesídou in round 5 with 66.24 to take bronze, with defending champion Dietzsch 5th.

1. Natalya Sadova RUS	68.57
2. Ellina Zvereva BLR	67.10
3. Nicoleta Grasu ROM	66.24
4. Anastasia Kelesídou GRE	65.50
5. Franka Dietzsch GER	65.38
6. Seilala Sua USA	63.74
7. Vera Pospísilová CZE	61.47
8. Kristin Kuehl USA	61.04
9. Anja Möllenbeck GER	60.49
10. Irina Yatchenko BLR	59.45
11. Li Qiumei CHN	57.81
12. Vladimíra Racková CZE	56.43

Hammer (Q 6th, F 7th)

KUZENKOVA WAS the inaugural world record holder, the first woman over 70m and some 3m ahead of everyone else in 2001, but once again she came second in a major championships. She was 2m clear of the field in qualifying with 70.43 (the shock elimination being Dawn Ellerbe (13th 64.34, the best ever non-qualifying mark), but in the final – despite a 70.61 opener – she was overhauled, albeit narrowly, by the CAC record of 70.65 in round 3 by Moreno, who had started with 69.55 and 69.34. In response Kuzenkova fouled twice and completed her series with a 69.78. Eagles was an immensely delighted third with her 68.87 from round 2, leaving heavily strapped Olympic champion Skolimowska – one of three juniors in the final – in 4th place. There was the best ever mark for 9th place.

1. Yipsi Moreno CUB	70.65
2. Olga Kuzenkova RUS	70.61
3. Bronwyn Eagles AUS	68.87
4. Kamila Skolimowska POL	68.05
5. Manuela Montebrun FRA	67.78
6. Lorraine Shaw GBR	65.89
7. Florence Ezeh FRA	65.88
8. Ivana Brkljacic CRO	65.43
9. Kirsten Münchow GER	64.39
10. Olga Tsander BLR	64.10
11. Zhang Wenxiu CHN	61.61
12. Melissa Price USA	61.57

Javelin (Q 4th, F 6th)

MENÉNDEZ, who smashed the world record with 71.54 in July, was never threatened from the moment she launched her first throw of 66.56, overtaking defending champion Tzelíli's competition opener of 64.69. In round 2 the Cuban improved to 69.42 to smash Tzelíli's championship record, and with her next throw she extended it to 69.53, a distance only she has ever bettered. She ended with x, 65.63 and 66.70. Tzelíli progressed to 65.78 in round 5 to consolidate her silver medal and Bisset, third from the opening round (63.14), also reached her best of 64.69 in the penultimate round. Fourth-placed Tomecková was not able to duplicate her qualification-leading throw of 65.71.

1. Osleidys Menéndez CUB 69.53*
2. Mirela Tzelíli GRE 65.78
3. Sonia Bisset CUB 64.69
4. Nikola Tomecková CZE 63.11
5. Steffi Nerius GER 62.08
6. Mikaela Ingberg FIN 61.94
7. Xiomara Rivero CUB 61.60
8. Aggelikí Tsiolakoúdi GRE 61.01
9. Tatyana Shikolenko RUS 60.91
10. Wei Jianhua CHN 58.45
11. Claudia Coslovich ITA 57.27
12. Taina Kolkkala FIN 57.21

Heptathlon (4th/5th)

BARBER, the reigning world champion, made a dream start, with a world class pb of 12.78 in the hurdles, chased by Burrell whose 13.05 was also a lifetime best, and high jumping 1.88, as did Prokhorova for a 5cm improvement on her best. But then came disaster, as Barber fouled three times in the shot when a safety standing put of around 10m would have kept her in contention. At the end of day one Sazanovich, aided by 15.90 in the shot, led at 3923 from Prokhorova 3835, Roshchupkina 3808 and Burrell, whose superb 200 pb of 22.92 lifted her from 10th to 4th (3741).

Burrell improved to 3rd overall (4732) after the long jump with a near pb of 6.45 as Sazanovich (4930) lost some of her advantage over Prokhorova (4878) thanks to the latter's 6.61. Sazanovich set a javelin best of 46.72, but Prokhorova set three pbs to 50.73 for a 5752-5727 lead with Burrell a safe third (5568). Prokhorova was able to tackle the 800m in a relaxed mood and she won overall by a commanding 155 points. Burrell scored a pb for the bronze. Olympic champion Denise Lewis withdrew on the eve of the competition with stomach problems.

1. Yelena Prokhorova 6694
2. Natalya Sazanovich BLR 6539
3. Shelia Burrell USA 6472
4. Natalya Roshchupkina RUS 6294
5. Karin Ertl GER 6283
6. Austra Skujyté LTU 6112
7. DeDee Nathan USA 6073
8. Irina Belova RUS 6061
9. Gertrud Bacher ITA 6010
10. Tiia Hautala FIN 6002
11. Maria Collonvillé FRA 5887
12. Nicole Haynes CAN 5786
13. Margaret Simpson GHA 5748
14. Tia Hellebaut BEL 5680
15. G Pramila Ganapathy IND 5492

20 Kilometres Walk (9th)

IVANOVA LED out of the stadium and was never headed. At 5k (22:18) she was only 1 sec ahead of Feitor and at 10k (43:50) her margin was the same from Nikolayeva, followed by Feitor and Tsybulskaya. With a decisive third 5k in 21:36 she reached 15k in 1:05:26 far ahead of Tsybulskaya 1:06:11, Perrone 1:06:29 and Plätzer 1:06:45. A closing 5k in 22:22 brought her to the finish over a minute clear in 1:27:48, the first eight breaking the inaugural championship record.

Tsybulskaya was a safe 2nd but then it took the photo finish to determine third place, Perrone taking the decision over Plätzer (who was then disqualified). Of 41 starters, 14 were disqualified, including also defending champion Liu Hongyu, 1996 Olympic champion Nikolayeva and Saville of Sydney Olympic fame.

1. Olimpiada Ivanova RUS 1:27:48*
2. Valentina Tsybulskaya BLR 1:28:49
3. Elisabetta Perrone ITA 1:28:56
4. Erica Alfridi ITA 1:29:48
5. María Vasco ESP 1:30:19
6. Norica Cîmpean ROM 1:30:39
7. Melanie Seeger GER 1:30:41
8. Annarita Sidoti ITA 1:31:40
9. M Guadeloupe Sánchez MEX 1:32:27
10. Victoria Palacios MEX 1:33:52
11. Athiná Papayiánni GRE 1:34:56
12. Nevena Mineva BUL 1:35:18
13. Olive Loughnane IRL 1:35:24
14. Kim Mi-jung KOR 1:35:30
15. Vera Zozulya UKR 1:35:32

4 x 100 Metres Relay (ht & F 11th)

THE US team streaked to a time of 41.71, fastest in the world for four years, and a winning margin of more than 6m over Germany, with France (fastest in the heats at 42.49) shading Jamaica for the bronze medals. Despite the presence of Sturrup and Fynes, the Bahamas chose not to defend their title. Thus, Marion Jones, who increased the US lead by 3m on the anchor leg, finished with two golds and a silver to bring her total of World Champs medals to eight, the same as Torrence, Miles-Clark and Devers, and surpassed among women only by Ottey's 14.

1. USA 41.71 (White, Gaines, Miller, Jones; also gold: A Williams, Edwards)

2. GER 42.32 (Pashcke, G Rockmeier, B Rockmeier, Wagner)
3. FRA 42.39 (S Félix, Bangué, Hurtis, Sidibé)
4. JAM 42.40   7. GRE 43.25
5. NGR 42.52   8. RUS 43.58
6. GBR 42.60

4 x 400 Metres Relay (h 11th, F 12th)

THE USA, who had run 3:21.97 in the heats, had a 12m lead at the final change thanks to the combined efforts of Miles-Clark 50.2, Hennagan 49.7 and Collins 49.96, but Suziann Reid quite unnecessarily attempted to transfer the baton from her left hand to the right. The ensuing juggling act ended in the stick falling to the track and by the time she ran back to retrieve it the other medal contenders were 40m or more ahead and fourth place was all that was possible.

The Americans' loss was Jamaica's gain and they won by over 10m from an equally elated German team in 3:20.65, a Commonwealth and CAC record which only five nations have ever bettered. Parris 49.70 was fastest for Jamaica with 49.70 as Fenton eased home in 49.95 and Breuer ran 49.65 for Germany on the anchor leg.

1. JAM 3:20.65 (Richards, Scott, Parris, Fenton; also gold: Burgher, Hemmings)
2. GER 3:21.97 (Ekpo-Umoh, Ghosh, Marx, Breuer
3. RUS 3:24.92 (Rosikhina, Nosova, Kapachinskaya, Zykina; also bronze: Shevtsova)
4. USA 3:26.88   7. POL 3:27.78
5. GBR 3:26.94   8. CAN 3:27.93
6. FRA 3:27.54

WORLD CHAMPIONSHIPS PLACING TABLE

Nation	*1st*	*2nd*	*3rd*	*4th*	*5th*	*6th*	*7th*	*8th*	*Points*	*1999*
USA	9	5	5*	6	4	1	5	3	198.5	209
RUS	6	7**	6	3	4	4	1	4	181	132
GER	2	4	1	2	7	3*	3	2	104.5	148.5
KEN	3	3	2	3	-	2	2	2	84	65
ETH	2	3	3	2	-	-	3	1	72	62
ESP	-	2	1	3	4	5	2	-	70	51
CUB	3	1	2	3	-	-	1	1	61	57
JAM	1	2	2	1	1	2	2	2	55	51.5
GBR	1	-	1	1	4	4	3	1	54	66
POL	2	-	2	2	1	1	2	1	50	29
ROM	2	1	1	-	1	3	1*	1	44.5	38
ITA	1	1	2	3	-	-	-	2	44	53
BLR	1	3	-	-	-	1	3	-	38	11
GRE	1	1	2	1	-	1	1	1	38	46
FRA	-	-	2	-	4	1	2	2	37	42
UKR	1	1	1	-	2	2	-	-	35	48
JPN	-	2	1	1	2	-	1	1	31	28
BAH	1	2	-	1	-	1	-	-	30	16
MAR	2	1	-	-	-	1	2	1	29	42
CZE	2	-	-	1	-	1	2	1	29	40
AUS	1	-	1	3	-	-	-	-	29	58
SWE	-	1	1	-	2	-	1	-	23	16
FIN	-	1	1	-	1	1	1	-	22	13
RSA	1	1	-	-	-	1	-	3	21	14
HUN	-	-	-	2	-	1	2*	1	17.5	23
BUL	-	-	1	2	-	-	-	1	17	15
MEX	-	-	2	-	-	1	-	-	15	12
POR	-	-	1	1	-	-	1	-	13	20
TRI	-	-	1	1	-	-	-	-	11	0
CMR	-	1	-	-	-	-	1	1	10	0
LTU	-	1	-	-	-	1	-	-	10	10
LAT	-	-	-	1	1	-	-	1	10	0
CHN	-	-	-	1	1	-	-	-	9	29

SKN (1B) 9; CAN, CAY, DOM (1G), KSA, MOZ (1G), SEN (1G), SUI (1G) 8; AUT (1S), BRA, EST (1S), ISR (1S), MRI 7; HAI (1S), KAZ (1S), SUR (1S); NGR 5; CHA, CRO, YUG 4; BER, ISL 3; NED 2.5; GRN, QAT, SLO 2; ECU, GHA. TUR 1

23 nations won gold medals, 41 medals of any colour, and 63 nations placed athletes in the top eight (compared to 21, 42 and 57 in 1999). * ties

Note: adjusted after removing Saïdi-Sief ALG from 5000m 2nd place.

2001 CHAMPIONSHIPS

IAAF World Half Marathon Championships

At Bristol, GBR, October 7

Men

1	Haile Gebrselassie ETH	60:03
2	Tesfaye Jifar ETH	60:04
3	John Yuda TAN	60:12
4	Hendrick Ramaala RSA	60:15
5	Tesfaye Tola ETH	60:24
6	Evans Rutto KEN	60:43
7	Peter Chebet KEN	60:56
8	Christopher Cheboiboch KEN	61:14
9	Jaouad Gharib MAR	61:41
10	Khalid Skah MAR	61:41
11	Salah Hissou MAR	61:56
12	Faustin Baha TAN	62:15
13	John Gwako KEN	62:15
14	Abner Chipu RSA	62:18
15	Mostafa Errebbah ITA	62:19
16	Haron Toroitich KEN	62:27
17	Takeshi Hamano JPN	62:28
18	Abdelhadi Habassa MAR	62:30
19	Rachid Ziar ALG	62:32
20	Tiyapo Maso BOT	62:33

117 of 125 finished.

Team: 1. ETH 3:00m:31, 2. KEN 3:02:53, 3. TAN 3:05:08, 4. MAR 3:05:18, 5. RSA 3:05:30, 6. JPN 3:08:42, 7. ALG 3:09:35, 8. ITA 3:09:35, 9. POR 3:10:12, 10. BOT 3:10:48, 11. GBR 3:11:03, 12. FRA 3:11:34, 13. USA 3:12:28, 14. UGA 3:12:31, 15. ESP 3:12:38, 16. BRA 3:13:56, 17. BEL 3:14:23, 18. ZAM 3:14:26, 19. MEX 3:15:39, 20. BLR 3:16:28, 21. CHL 3:21:50, 22. ANG 3:24:08, 23. UZB 3:33:36, 24. TKM 3:47:38.

Women

1	Paula Radcliffe GBR	66:47*
2	Susan Chepkemei KEN	67:36
3	Berhane Adere ETH	68:17
4	Mizuki Noguchi JPN	68:23
5	Jelena Prokopcuka LAT	68:43
6	Elana Meyer RSA	68:56
7	Olivera Jevtic YUG	69:51
8	Isabellah Ochichi KEN	70:01
9	Yasuyo Iwamoto JPN	70:06
10	Mihaela Botezan ROM	70:11
11	Nuta Olaru ROM	70:27
12	Caroline Kwambai KEN	70:27
13	Lyudmila Biktasheva RUS	70:31
14	Aurica Buia ROM	70:40
15	Restituta Joseph TAN	70:43
16	Viktoriya Klimina RUS	70:46
17	Meseret Kotu ETH	70:48
18	Joyce Chepchumba KEN	71:03
19	Lyubov Morgunova RUS	71:06
20	Teyeba Erkesso ETH	71:15

71 of 75 finished

Team: 1. KEN 3:28:04, 2. JPN 3:30:08, 3. ETH 3:30:20, 4. GBR 3:31:16, 5. ROM 3:31:18, 6. RUS 3:32:23, 7. HUN 3:38:17, 8. USA 3:40:18, 9. RSA 3:41:14, 10. BRA 3:41:45, 11. TAN 3:41:50, 12. ITA 3:42:25, 13. BEL 3:46:49, 14. BLR 3:57:45, 15. UZB 4:19:02.

2nd IAAF World Youth (U18) Championships

At Debrecen, Hungary, July 12-15

Men

100m	1. Darrel Brown TRI 10.31*
(-0.2)	2. Willie Hordge USA 10.41
	3. Jonathan Wade USA 10.53
200m	1. Jonathan Wade USA 20.95
(-1.1)	2. Michael Grant USA 21.30
	3. Dion Rodriguez TRI 21.36
400m	1. Karol Grzegorczyk POL 46.90*
	2. Piotr Kedzia POL 47.12
	3. Jermaine Gonzales JAM 47.51
800m	1. Salem Amer Al-Badri QAT 1:50.15*
	2. Cosmas Rono KEN 1:50.35
	3. Liao Fu-Pin TPE 1:51.35
1500m	1. Isaac Songok KEN 3:36.78*
	2. Sameuel Dadi ETH 3:39.78
	3. Abdul Rahman Suleiman QAT 3:42.03
3000m	1. Markos Geneti ETH 7:55.82*
	2. David Kilel KEN 7:56.95
	3. James Kwalia KEN 7:57.71
2000mSt	1. David Kirwa KEN 5:33.40
	2. Brimin Kipruto KEN 5:36.81
	3. Abrham Kebeto ETH 5:37.76
110mh	1. Nassim Messjian QAT 13.27
(0.2)	2. Marthinus van der Vyver RSA 13.35
(91.4cm)	3. Eddy Delepine FRA 13.39
400mh	1. Amine Alozen SYR 50.25
(84cm)	2. Jonathan Walker USA 51.32
	3. Kenji Narisako JPN 52.09
HJ	1. Aleksey Dmitrik RUS 2.23*
	2. James Watson AUS 2.21
	3. Aleksandr Plisko BLR 2.19
PV	1. Artyom Kuptsov RUS 5.15
	2. Vincent Favretta FRA 5.15
	3. Kishita Go JPN 5.00
LJ	1. Thiago Carahyba Dias BRA 7.72/0.1
	2. Abdulla Al-Walid QAT 7.62/1.1
	3. Andrew Howe-Besozzi ITA 7.61/0.5
TJ	1. Jonathan Moore GBR 16.36*/0.0
	2. David Girat CUB 16.33/-0.7
	3. Osniel Tosca CUB 15.67/-0.1

IAAF Combined Events Challenge 2001

Events included: Multistars (Desenzano del Garda, ITA), Hypo-Meeting (Götzis, AUT), Ruhrgas DLV Mehrkampf (Ratingen, GER), US Trials (Eugene, USA), European Cup (several venues), Francophone Games (Ottawa, CAN), World Championships (Edmonton, CAN), Universiade (Beijing, CHN), Goodwill Games (Brisbane, AUS), Talence, FRA.

Men Decathlon

1	Tomás Dvorák	CZE	25943	8527 Götzis	8902 WCh	8514 GWG
2	Erki Nool	EST	25839	8604 Götzis	8815 WCh	8420 GWG
3	Lev Lobodin	RUS	25044	8465 Götzis	8352 WCh	8227 GWG
4	Aleksandr Yurkov	UKR	24968	8380 ECp S	8264 WCh	8324 Talence
5	Attila Zsivoczky	HUN	24762	8173 Götzis	8218 ECp S	8371 WCh
6	Stefan Schmid	GER	24675	8287 Ratingen	8307 WCh	8081 Talence
7	Laurent Hernu	FRA	24605	8112 ECp S	8280 WCh	8213 Talence
8	Jirí Ryba	CZE	24249	7949 ECp 1	8332 WCh	7968 Talence
9	Benjamin Jensen	NOR	24247	8004 Götzis	8090 WCh	8153 Talence
10	Zsolt Kürtösi	HUN	24222	8099 Götzis	8026 ECp S	8097 WCh
11	Chiel Warners	NED	24207	8085 Götzis	8206 ECp 1	7916 WCh
12	Phil McMullen	USA	24155	8220 US Ch	8079 WCh	7856 GWG
13	Klaus Ambrosch	AUT	23862	8122 Götzis	7962 ECp 1	7778 Talence
14	Thomas Tebbich	AUT	23174	7632 Götzis	7964 ECp 1	7578 WUG
15	Kip Janvrin	USA	22677	8241 US Ch	7905 WCh	6531 GWG

Women Heptathlon

1	Yelena Prokhorova	RUS	19624	6576 Götzis	6694 WCh	6354 Talence
2	Natalya Roshchupkina	RUS	19357	6551 Götzis	6433 Ratingen	6373 GWG
3	Natalya Sazanovich	BLR	19264	6402 Götzis	6539 WCh	6323 GWG
4	Shelia Burrell	USA	18977	6051 US Ch	6472 WCh	6454 Talence
5	Irina Belova	RUS	18904	6528 Götzis	6315 Ratingen	6061 WCh
6	Karin Ertl	GER	18784	6136 Götzis	6365 Ratingen	6283 WCh
7	DeDee Nathan	USA	18522	6174 US Ch	6073 WCh	6275 GWG
8	Larisa Netseporuk	EST	18216	6172 ECp 2	5984 GWG	6060 Talence
9	Gertrud Bacher	ITA	18102	6030 Götzis	6062 ECp S	6010 WCh
10	Sonja Kesselschläger	GER	18090	6053 Götzis	6064 ECp S	5973 WUG
11	Svetlana Kazanina	KAZ	17831	6159 Desenzano	5835 Ratingen	5837 Talence
12	Michaela Hejnová	CZE	17784	5917 Desenzano	6026 ECp S	5841 WUG
13	Marie Collonvillé	FRA	17561	5798 ECp S	5887 WCh	5876 Talence
14	Katerina Nekolná	CZE	17092	5781 Ratingen	5746 ECp S	5565 WUG

SP (5kg) 1. Georgi Ivanov BUL 19.73
2. Yasser Ibrahim EGY 19.58
3. Lee Min-won KOR 19.57

DT (1.5kg) 1. Khalid Habash Al-Suwaidi QAT 62.67
2. Robert Harting GER 62.04
3. Omar Ahmed El Ghafaly EGY 61.06

HT (5kg) 1. József Horváth HUN 80.11*
2. Werner Smit RSA 79.48
3. Kirill Ikonnikov RUS 77.75

JT: (700g) 1. Teemu Wirkkala FIN 76.18
2. Hamad Khalifa QAT 73.56
3. Tero Järvenpää FIN 68.85

Octathlon 1. Rene Oruman EST 6219*
2. Essa Mufarrah KSA 6024
3. Jason Dudley AUS 5997

10,000W 1. Vladimir Kanaykin RUS 42:55.75
2. Mikolai Seredovich BLR 43:44.32
3. Francisco Flores MEX 43:53.13

Medley R 1. POL (Kaska, Zrada, Kedzia, Grzegorczyk) 1:50.46*
2. USA 1:50.90
3. RSA 1:51.35

Women

100m (0.5) 1. Allyson Felix USA 11.57
2. Kerron Stewart JAM 11.72
3. Zuzana Kosová CZE 11.83

200m (0.0) 1. Angela Perkins USA 23.07*
2. Amy Spencer GBR 23.45
3. Zuzana Kosová CZE 23.98

400m 1. Stephanie Smith USA 52.19*
2. Jerrika Chapple USA 52.80
3. Anneisha McLaughlin JAM 53.35

800m 1. Cherotich Ruto KEN 2:05.50*
2. Veronika Plesarová CZE 2:06.01
3. Carlene Robinson JAM 2:06.18

1500m 1. Georgie Clarke AUS 4:14.08*
2. Florence Kyala KEN 4:15.71
3. Sentayehu Ejigu ETH 4:17.51

3000m 1. Sally Chepyego KEN 9:09.95
2. Mestewat Tufa ETH 9:11.60
3. Fridah Domongole KEN 9:12.70

100mh (0.4) (84cm) 1. Kathrin Geissler GER 13.49
2= Ashley Lodree USA 13.75
2= Carla Fick RSA 13.75

400mh 1. Camille Robinson JAM 58.72
2. Kimberly Crow AUS 59.28
3. Olga Nikolayeva RUS 59.41

HJ 1. Aileen Wilson GBR 1.87
2. Petrina Price AUS 1.81
3. Lavern Spencer LCA 1.81

PV 1. Silke Spiegelburg GER 4.00

	2. Aleksandra Kiryashova RUS 4.00
	3. Anna Olko POL 3.95
LJ	1. Shermin Oksuz AUS 6.41*/0.9
	2. Elena Anghelescu ROM 6.32/1.5
	3. Angela Dies GER 6.03/0.1
TJ	1. Alina Popescu ROM 13.76/1.8
	2. Svetlana Bolshakova RUS 13.32/0.5
	3. Michelle Sanford USA 13.22/1.0
SP	1. Valerie Adams NZL 16.87*
	2. Michelle Carter USA 15.23
	3. Yuliya Leantsyuk BLR 15.08
DT	1. Ma Xuejun CHN 54.93*
	2. Darya Pishcholnikova RUS 49.37
	3. Amarachi Ukabam USA 46.13
HT	1. Andrea Kéri HUN 59.86
	2. Berta Castells ESP 59.65
	3. Maria Smaliachkova BLR 59.16
JT	1. Kimberly Mickle AUS 51.83
	2. Justine Robbeson RSA 51.54
	3. Andrea Kvetová CZE 51.49
Hep	1. Annett Wichmann GER 5470*
	2. Christine Schulz GER 5346
	3. Amandine Constantin FRA 5296
5000W	1. Jiang Kun CHN 22:49.21
	2. Ksenia Ishcheykina RUS 22:58.43
	3. Snezhana Yurchenka BLR 23:28.51
Medley R	1. USA (Lodree, Felix, Perkins, Smith) 2:03.83*
	2. JAM 2:07.45
	3. ROM 2:09.70

Georgie Clarke (1500m) retained her title.

Medal and Points (8-7-6-5-4-3-2-1) Table

Nation	G	S	B	Total	Points
USA	5	7	3	15	199
GER	3	2	1	6	107
RUS	3	4	2	9	92
KEN	4	4	2	10	82
RSA	-	3	2	5	68
AUS	3	3	2	7	67
JAM	1	2	3	6	57
JPN	-	-	2	2	56
QAT	3	2	1	6	55
GBR	2	1	-	3	47
POL	2	1	1	4	45
UKR	-	-	-	-	44
BLR	-	1	4	5	41
ETH	1	2	2	5	34
CHN	2	-	-	2	32
ROM	1	1	1	3	31
ESP	-	1	-	1	29
HUN	2	-	-	2	28
CZE	-	1	3	4	26

26 nations won medals (20 gold).

World University Games 2001

At Beijing, China, August 27 – September 1

Men

100m (-0.9)	1. Marcus Brunson USA 10.15
	2. Gennadiy Chernovol KAZ 10.29
	3. Chris Lambert GBR 10.38
200m (-0.8)	1. Marcin Urbas POL 20.56
	2. Gennadiy Chernovol KAZ 20.57
	3. Corné du Plessis RSA 20.58
400m	1. Andrew Pierce USA 45.34
	2. Clinton Hill AUS 45.63
	3. Andrey Tverdostup UKR 45.78
800m	1. Khalid Tighazouine MAR 1:45.27
	2. Derrick Peterson USA 1:45.49
	3. Otukile Lekote BOT 1:45.63
1500m	1. Pedro A Esteso ESP 3:43.98
	2. Gareth Turnbull IRL 3:44.48
	3. Aléxis Abraham FRA 3:44.48
5000m	1. Sergey Lebed UKR 13:44.24
	2. Mikhayil Yeginov RUS 13:46.63
	3. Christian Belz SUI 13:48.21
10,000m	1. John Kanyi KEN 28:27.42
	2. Ignacio Caceres ESP 28:43.63
	3. Kazuyoshi Tokumoto 28:47.34
HMar	1. Masakazu Fujiwara JPN 64:12
	2. Wodage Zvadya ISR 64:30
	3. Ryohji Matsushita JPN 64:53.
3000mSt	1. Anthony Famiglietti USA 8:21.97
	2. Jakub Czaja POL 8:23.00
	3. Christian Belz SUI 8:24.46
110mh (1.6)	1. Liu Xiang CHN 13.33
	2. Elmar Lichtenegger AUT 13.36
	3. Robert Kronberg SWE 13.40
400mh	1. Alwyn Myburgh RSA 48.09*
	2. Yevgeniy Meleshenko KAZ 48.46
	3. Chen Tien-Wen TPE 48.63
HJ	1. Aleksey Kravtsov RUS 2.28
	2. Gennadiy Moroz BLR 2.28
	3. Tora Harris USA 2.26
PV	1. Alex Averbukh ISR 5.80
	2. Stepan Janácek CZE 5.70
	3. Laurens Looije NED 5.60
LJ	1. Miguel Pate USA 8.07/0.0
	2. Stepan Louw NAM 8.04/-0.5
	3. Gable Garenomotse BOT 7.99/0.3
TJ	1. Kenta Bell USA 17.22/1.6
	2. Marian Oprea ROM 17.11/1.4
	3. Jadel Gregorio BRA 16.92/1.2
SP	1. Manuel Martínez ESP 20.9
	2. Yuriy Belonog UKR 20.16
	3. Milan Haborák SVK 19.90
DT	1. Aleksander Tammert EST 65.19
	2. Leonid Cherevko BLR 63.15
	3. Aleksandr Malashevich BLR 62.81
HT	1. Nicola Vizzoni ITA 78.41
	2. Vladislav Piskunov UKR 77.99
	3. Adrián Annus HUN 77.73
JT	1. Eriks Rags LAT 82.72
	2. Isbel Luaces CUB 81.68
	3. Gergely Horváth HUN 80.03
Dec	1. Raúl Duany CUB 8069
	2. Vladimir Mikhaylenko UKR 8019
	3. Qi Haifeng CHN 8019
20kW	1. Lorenzo Civallero ITA 1:24:42
	2. Juan Manuel Molina ESP 1:25:07
	3. He Xiaodong CHN 1:25:17
4x100m	1. JPN (Kawabata,Nara, Omae, Okusako) 38.77
	2. US (Conwright, G Williams, Brunson, Norman) 39.14

	3. ITA (Rabino, Verdecchia, Colombo, Donati) 39.35
4x400m	1. USA (G White, Gerding, Couts, Pierce) 3:02.83
	2. UKR (Kaydash, Zyukov, Tverdostud, Rybalka) 3:02.87
	3. JPN (M Sato, Yoshizawa, Muraki, Okusako) 3:03.63

Women

100m (-1.1)	1. Abiodun Oyepitan GBR 11.42
	2. Zeng Xiujun CHN 11.58
	3. Mireille Donders SUI 11.59
200m (0.5)	1. Li Xuemei CHN 22.86
	2. Kim Gevaert BEL 22.94
	3. Natalya Safronnikova BLR 23.16
400m	1. Demetria Washington USA 51.22
	2. Otilia Ruicu ROM 51.82
	3. Mikele Barber USA 51.92
800m	1. Brigita Langerholc SLO 2:00.96
	2. Nedia Semedo POR 2:01.64
	3. Tatyana Rodionova RUS 2:01.68
1500m	1. Süreyya Ayhan TUR 4:06.91
	2. Cristina Grosu ROM 4:08.84
	3. Sabine Fischer SUI 4:08.93
5000m	1. Dong Yanmei CHN 15:30.28
	2. Tatyana Khmeleva RUS 15:43.18
	3. Yoshiko Fujinaga JPN 15:43.94
10,000m	1. Dong Yanmei CHN 32:45.14
	2. Yoshiko Fujinaga JPN 32:53.55
	3. Yukiko Akaba JPN 32:57.35
HMar:	1. Ham Pong-sil PRK 75:24
	2. Miki Oyama JPN 75:31
	3. Kim Chang-ok PRK 75:36
100mh (-0.1)	1. Su Yiping CHN 12.95
	2. Maurren Maggi BRA 13.13
	3. Jacquie Munro AUS 13.17
400mh	1. Natasha Danvers GBR 54.94
	2. Malgorzata Pskit POL 55.27
	3. Sonia Brito AUS 55.72
HJ	1. Vita Palamar UKR 1.96
	2. Nicole Forrester CAN 1.94
	3. Nevena Lendjel CRO 1.91
PV	1. Gao Shuying CHN 4.52*
	2. Sabine Schulte GER 4.35
	3. Sárka Mládková CZE 4.20
LJ	1. Maurren Maggi BRA 6.83/1.6
	2. Guan Yingnan CHN 6.56/0.0
	3. Kumiko Ikeda JPN 6.52/0.9
TJ	1. Tatyana Lebedeva RUS 14.81*/1.4
	2. Natalya Safronova BLR 14.57/1.5
	3. Yelena Oleynikova RUS 14.39w/2.6
SP:	1. Yumileidi Cumbá CUB 18.90
	2. Lee Myung-sun KOR 18.79
	3. Katarzyna Zakowicz POL 18.31
DT	1. Li Qiumei CHN 61.66
	2. Li Yanfeng CHN 60.50
	3. Melina Robert-Michon FRA 58.04
HT	1. Manuela Montebrun FRA 69.78
	2. Yipsi Moreno CUB 68.39
	3. Lyudmila Gubkina BLR 67.97
JT	1. Osleidis Menéndez CUB 69.82*
	2. Nikola Tomecková CZE 62.20
	3. Wei Jianhua CHN 57.84
Hep	1. Jane Jamieson AUS 6041
	2. Svetlana Sokolova RUS 5985
	3. Sonja Kesselschläger GER 5973
10kW	1. Gao Hongmiao CHN 43:20*
	2. Susana Feitor POR 43:40
	3. Wang Liping CHN 44:01
4x100m	1. CHN (Chen Yueqin, Yan Jiankui, Li Xuemei, Zeng Xiujun) 43.72
	2. BRA (Machado, Moura, Maggi, Neto) 44.13
	3. FRA (Morandais, Okori, Benth, Thélamon) 44.24
4x400m	1. USA (Mel. Barber, Washington, C Jackson, Mik. Barber) 3:28.04
	2. GBR (Danvers, Duncan, Meadows, McConnell) 3:30.40
	3. BLR (Safronnikova, Usovich, Kozak, Khlyustova) 3:30.65

4th Francophone Games

At Ottawa, Canada, July 19-23

Men

100m (0.7)	1. Stéphane Buckland MRI 10.13
	2. Bruny Surin CAN 10.18
	3. Eric Pacôme N'dri CIV 10.24
200m (0.5)	1. Stéphane Buckland MRI 20.33
	2. Oumar Loum SEN 20.59
	3. Joseph Batangdon CMR 20.75
400m	1. Shane Niemi CAN 44.86*
	2. Eric Milazar MRI 44.96
	3. Sofiane Labidi TUN 45.45
800m	1. Khalid Tighazouine MAR 1:46.53*
	2. Mohcine Chéhibi MAR 1:46.63
	3. Zach Whitmarsh CAN 1:46.90
1500m	1. Pawel Czapiewski POL 3:45.08
	2. Abdelkader Hachlaf MAR 3:45.41
	3. Adil Kaouch MAR 3:45.64
5000m	1. Mohamed Amine MAR 13:37.14
	2. Abderrahim Goumri MAR 13:38.06
	3. Mohamed Saïd El Wardi MAR 13:43.12
10,000m	1. Ahmed Baday MAR 28:13.54
	2. Abdelhadi Habassa MAR 28:16.28
	3. Aloÿs Nizigama BDI 28:37.17
Mar	1. Mohamed El Hattab MAR 2:18:16
	2. El Mustafa Damaoui MAR 2:18:31
	3. Jean-Pierre Monciaux FRA 2:20:38
3000mSt	1. Elarbi Khattabi MAR 8:16.63*
	2. Lyès Ramoul FRA 8:25.12
	3. Zouhir El Ouardi MAR 8:28.72
110mh (-0.1)	1. Dudley Dorival HAI 13.60 (13.52* h)
	2. Vincent Clarico FRA 13.71
	3. Artur Kohutek POL 13.73
400mh	1. Pawel Januszewski POL 49.24
	2. J. Berlioz Rakotoarimiadry MAD 49.23
	3. Mustapha Sdad MAR 49.89
HJ	1. Mark Boswell CAN 2.31*
	2. Kwaku Boateng CAM 2.31*
	3. Jan Jankú CZE 2.21
PV	1. Adam Kolasa POL 5.60
	2. Stepan Janácek CZE 5.55
	3. Khalid Lachheb FRA 5.40
LJ	1. Jonathan Chimier MRI 7.89/0.5
	2. Arnaud Casquette MRI 7.88w/2.4
	3. Mickaél Loria FRA 7.86/2.0
TJ	1. Arius Filet FRA 17.15*/1.6
	2. Jérôme Romain FRA 16.29/1.4

	3. Djeke Mambo BEL 16.02/1.2
SP	1. Brad Snyder CAN 19.64
	2. Yves Niaré FRA 18.94
	3. Dylan Armstrong CAN 17.57
DT	1. Jason Tunks CAN 65.10*
	2. Virgilijus Alekna LTU 64.35
	3. Ionel Oprea ROM 63.64
HT	1. Szymon Ziolkówski POL 79.89*
	2. Maciej Palyszko POL 75.35
	3. Raphaël Piolanti FRA 72.71
Dec	1. Pierre-Alexandre Vial FRA 7890
	2. Hambi Dhouibi TUN 7548
	3. Stéphane Bamboux FRA 7320
20kW	1. Hatem Ghoula TUN 1:22:56*
	2. Denis Langlois FRA 1:23:21
	3. Gintaras Andriuškevicius LTU 1:23:35
4x100m	1. MRI 39.04
	2. CIV 39.33
	3. BEN 40.22
4x400m	1. POL 3:04.91
	2. FRA 3:06.27
	3. MAR 3:06.86

Women

100m	1. Makaridja Sanganoko CIV 11.27
(0.5)	2. Venolyn Clarke CAN 11.29 (drugs dq?)
	3. Hanitrinaiina Rakotondrabé MAD 11.40
200m	1. Nadjina Kaltouma CHA 23.07
(0.5)	2. Ionela Tîrlea ROM 23.11
	3. Aïda Diop SEN 23.20
400m	1. Amy Mbacké Thiam SEN 50.92*
	2. Nadjina Kaltouma CHA 51.03
	3. Mireille Nguimgo CMR 51.47
800m	1. Diane Cummins CAN 2:00.77*
	2. Irina Krakoviak LTU 2:01.27
	3. Peggy Babin FRA 2:01.66
1500m	1. Elena Iagar ROM 4:17.03
	2. Fatma Lanouar TUN 4:17.95
	3. Lidia Chojecka POL 4:18.16
5000m	1. Tina Connelly CAN 16:05.59*
	2. Zhor El Kamch MAR 16:15.56
	3. Inga Juodeskiene LTU 16:19.34
10,000m	1. Zhor El Kamch MAR 34:07.52
	2. Lisa Harvey CAN 34:23.70
	3. Diane Nukuri BUR 34:30.66
Mar	1. Michèle Laservoisier FRA 2:44:00*
	2. Clarisse Rasoarizay MAD 2:46:29
	3. Lesley Carson CAN 2:50:02
100mh	1. Perdita Felicien CAN 12.92*
(-0.5)	2. Patricia Buval FRA 13.02
	3. Nadine Faustin HAI 13.05
400mh	1. Nezha Bidouane MAR 54.91*
	2. Karlene Haughton CAN 56.19
	3. Malgorzata Pskit POL 56.25
HJ	1. Wanita May CAN 1.91*
	2. Nicole Forrester CAN 1.89
	3. Oana Pantelimon ROM 1.84
PV	1. Monica Pyrek POL 4.30*
	2. Pavla Hamácková CZE 4.20
	3. Julie Vigourt FRA 4.10
LJ	1. Alice Falaiye CAN 6.38/1.0
	2. Françoise Mbango CMR 6.37/1.0
	3. Krysma Bayley CAN 6.27/0.9
TJ	1. Cristina Nicolau ROM 14.62*/1.3
	2. Françoise Mbango CMR 14.56/1.7
	3. Adelina Gavrila ROM 13.91w/2.5
SP	1. Krystyna Zabawska POL 18.25*
	2. Elena Hila ROM 17.07
	3. Laurence Manfrédi FRA 16.82
DT	1. Nicoleta Grasu ROM 64.53*
	2. Joanna Wisniewska POL 56.94
	3. Mélina Robert-Michon FRA 56.81
HT	1. Kamila Skolimowska POL 67.95*
	2. Agnieszka Pogroszewska POL 65.44
	3. Florence Ezeh FRA 64.53
JT	1. Sarah Walter FRA 57.34*
	2. Ana Mirela Termure ROM 57.25
	3. Felicea Tilea ROM 56.58
Hep	1. Marie Collonvillé FRA 5719*
	2. Kim Vanderhoek CAN 5502
	3. Sophie Marrot FRA 5414
10kW	1. Norica Cîmpean ROM 44:32*
	2. Sonata Milusauskaite LTU 46:10
	3. Tatiana Boulanger FRA 47:11
4x100m	1. CAN 43.73
	2. CIV 43.89
	3. MAD 44.12
4x400m	1. POL 3:28.97*
	2. FRA 3:30.04
	3. CAN 3:31.08

Medal Table

Nation	G	S	B	Total
FRA	6	8	12	26
CAN	10	5	5	20
(plus 2 silvers for Québec)				
MAR	7	6	5	18
POL	9	3	3	15
ROM	4	3	4	11
MRI	4	2	-	6
LTU	-	4	2	6

19 nations won medals (11 gold).

Goodwill Games

At Brisbane, Australia, September 4-7

Men

100m	1. Dwain Chambers GBR 10.11
(-0.3)	2. Tim Montgomery USA 10.27
	3. Matt Shirvington AUS 10.30
200m	1. Shawn Crawford USA 20.17
(-0.2)	2. Christopher Williams JAM 20.38
	3. J J Johnson 20.54
400m	1. Greg Haughton JAM 45.02
	2. Arvard Moncur BAH 45.31
	3. Leonard Byrd USA 45.56
800m	1. William Yiampoy KEN 1:46.49
	2. Jean-Patrick Nduwimana BDI 1:46.79
	3. Wilfred Bungei KEN 1:47.15
1 Mile	1. Noah Ngeny KEN 3:56.64
	2. Kevin Sullivan CAN 3:56.81
	3. Laban Rotich KEN 3:56.88
5000m	1. Paul Bitok KEN 15:26.10
	2. Luke Kipkosgei KEN 15:26.61
	3. John Kibowen KEN 15:26.63
10,000m	1. Assefa Mezgebu ETH 28:06.48
	2. Benjamin Maiyo KEN 28:06.80
	3. Albert Chepkurui KEN 28:06.86
3000mSt	1. Brahim Boulami MAR 8:17.73
	2. Reuben Kosgei KEN 8:18.63
	3. Stephen Cherono KEN 8:19.98
110mh	1. Allen Johnson USA 13.16

(-0.4)	2. Anier García CUB 13.20
	3. Larry Wade USA 13.46
400mh	1. Felix Sanchez DOM 48.47
	2. Llewellyn Herbert RSA 48.93
	3. Hadi Al-Somaily KSA 48.94
HJ	1. Stefan Holm SWE 2.33
	2. Vyacheslav Voronin RUS 2.31
	3. Yaroslav Rybakov RUS 2.31
PV	1. Tim Mack USA 5.80
	2. Alex Averbukh ISR 5.80
	3. Dmitriy Markov AUS 5.75
LJ	1. Iván Pedroso CUB 8.16/0.5
	2. James Beckford JAM 8.07/0.4
	3. Hussein Al-Sabee KSA 7.97/0.4
TJ	1. Jonathan Edwards GBR 17.26/1.1
	2. Christian Olsson SWE 16.85/-0.5
	3. LaMark Carter USA 16.83/-0.5
SP	1. Adam Nelson USA 20.91
	2. John Godina USA 20.76
	3. Manuel Martínez ESP 20.44
DT	1. Frantz Kruger RSA 67.84*
	2. Virgilijus Alekna LTU 66.07
	3. Dmitriy Shevchenko RUS 63.53
HT	1. Koji Murofushi JPN 82.94
	2. Szymon Ziolkówski POL 80.71
	3. Balázs Kiss HUN 79.51
JT	1. Jan Zelezny CZE 87.52*
	2. Breaux Greer USA 85.86
	3. Eriks Rags LAT 84.68
Dec	1. Tomás Dvorák CZE 8514
	2. Erki Nool EST 8420
	3. Tom Pappas USA 8323
20kW	1. Nathan Deakes AUS 1:19:48.1*
	2. Robert Korzeniowski POL 1:19:52.0
	3. Roman Rasskazov RUS 1:21:09.0
4x100m	1. GBR (Barbour, Malcolm, Devonish, Chambers) 38.71
	2. JAM 38.92
	3. AUS 39.12
4x400m	1. USA (Byrd, Brew, Pettigrew, M Johnson) 3:00.52
	2. JAM 3:01.57
	3. BAH 3:01.67

Women

100m	1.Marion Jones USA 10.84*
(1.1)	2. Zhanna Pintusevich-Block UKR 11.01
	3. Chandra Sturrup BAH 11.13
200m	1. Debbie Ferguson 22.80
(-1.8)	2. Kelli White USA 23.05
	3. Juliet Campbell JAM 23.17
400m	1. Ana Guevara MEX 50.32
	2. Lorraine Fenton JAM 50.76
	3. Amy Mbacké Thiam SEN 51.25
800m	1. Maria Lourdes Mutola MOZ 1:58.76
	2. Kelly Holmes GBR 1:59.27
	3. Stephanie Graf AUT 2:00.93
1 Mile	1. Violeta Szekely ROM 4:38.03
	2. Tatyana Tomashova RUS 4:38.13
	3. Carla Sacramento POR 4:39.18
5000m	1. Olga Yegorova RUS 15:12.22
	2. Berhane Adere ETH 15:12.97
	3. Kathy Butler GBR 15:17.96
10,000m	1. Derartu Tulu ETH 31:48.19*
	2. Ayelech Worku ETH 31:48.57
	3. Susie Power 31:50.36
3000mSt	1. Melissa Rollison AUS 9:30.70*
	2. Irene Limika KEN 9:39.65
	3. Yekaterina Volkova RUS 9:41.54
100mh	1. Gail Devers USA 12.61
(0.3)	2. Jenny Adams USA 12.87
	3. Anjanette Kirkland USA 12.92
400mh	1. Tatyana Tereshchuk UKR 54.47
	2. Tonja Buford-Bailey USA 54.75
	3. Yuliya Nosova RUS 55.27
HJ	1. Hestrie Cloete RSA 2.00
	2. Kajsa Bergqvist SWE 1.97
	3= Vita Palamar UKR 1.93
	3= Amy Acuff USA 1.93
PV	1. Stacy Dragila USA 4.55
	2. Svetlana Feofanova RUS 4.45
	3. Tatiana Grigorieva AUS 4.45
LJ	1. Maurren Maggi BRA 6.94/1.7
	2. Bronwyn Thompson AUS 6.88/2.0
	3. Tatyana Kotova RUS 6.84/1.2
TJ	1. Tatyana Lebedeva RUS 14.58/0.0
	2. Tereza Marinova BUL 14.37/-0.2
	3. Yelena Govorova UKR 14.25/0.0
SP	1. Larisa Peleshenko RUS 18.65
	2. Yumiliedi Cumbá CUB 18.41
	3. Krysztyna Zabawska POL 18.23
DT	1. Ellina Zvereva BLR 66.36
	2. Natalya Sadova RUS 64.11
	3. Franka Dietzsch GER 62.59
HT	1. Kamila Skolimowska POL 70.31
	2. Olga Kuzenkova RUS 69.98
	3. Manuela Montebrun FRA 69.80
JT	1. Osleidys Menéndez CUB 66.14
	2. Nikola Tomecková CZE 64.70
	3. Mihaela Ingberg FIN 60.69
Hep	1. Natalya Roshchupkina RUS 6373
	2. Yelena Prokhorova RUS 6352
	3. Natalya Sazanovich BLR 6323
20kW	1. Olympiada Ivanova RUS 1:26:52.3*
	2. Yelena Nikolayeva RUS 1:27:49.3
	3. Eva Pérez ESP 1:32:22.4
4x100m	1. World All Stars (Alozie, Nku, Mani, Pintusevich-Block) 42.95
	2. USA 42.98
	3. JAM 43.13
4x400m	1. USA (Miles-Clark, Hennagan, Collins, Reid) 3:24.63
	2. JAM 3:24.87
	3. World All Stars 3:28.07

European U23 Championships

At Amsterdam, Netherlands, July 12-15

100m	1. Jonathan Barbour GBR 10.26w
(2.2)	2. Fabrice Calligny FRA 10.40
	3. Przemyslaw Rogowski POL 10.45
200m	1. Marcin Jedrusinski POL 20.94
(0.1)	2. Lukasz Chyla POL 20.99
	3. Mark Howard IRL 21.00
400m	1. Yuriy Borzakovskiy RUS 46.06
	2. Marc-Alexander Scheer GER 46.43
	3. Rafal Wieruszewski POL 46.57
800m	1. Antonio Reina ESP 1:47.74
	2. Joeri Jansen BEL 1:47.80

	3. Nicolas Aissat FRA 1:47.81
1500m	1. Wolfram Müller GER 3:38.94*
	2. Ivan Geshko UKR 3:39.37
	3. Sergio Gallardo ESP 3:39.50
5000m	1. Yusef El Nasri ESP 14:02.97
	2. Dmitriy Baranovskiy UKR 14:03.67
	3. Balázs Csillag HUN 14:04.84
10,000m	1. Dmitriy Baranovskiy UKR 29:13.36
	2. Koen Raymaekers NED 29:15.24
	3. Mattia Maccagnan ITA 29:15.32
3000mSt	1. Pavel Potapovich RUS 8:35.85
	2. Vadim Slobodenyuk UKR 8:37.09
	3. Henrik Skoog SWE 8:38.27
110mh (0.4)	1. Artur Budzillo POL 13.76
	2. Felipe Vivancos ESP 13.79
	3. Chris Baillie GBR 13.85
400mh	1. Matt Elias GBR 49.57
	2. Periklis Iakovakis GRE 49.63
	3. Mikael Jakobsson SWE 50.86
HJ	1. Rozle Prezelj SLO 2.21
	2. Aleksandr Veryutin BLR 2.18
	3. Fabrice Saint Jean FRA 2.18
PV	1. Lars Börgeling GER 5.60
	2. Mikko Latvala FIN 5.50
	3. Giuseppe Gibilisco ITA 5.50
LJ	1. Yann Domenech FRA 8.00/0.1
	2. Vladimir Zyuskov UKR 7.90/-0.2
	3. Shahriar Bigdeli GER 7.81/0.8
TJ	1. Christian Olsson SWE 17.24*/-0.8
	2. Igor Spasovkhodskiy RUS 17.08/0.2
	3. Ionut Punga ROM 16.81/-0.2
SP	1. Mikulas Konopka SVK 19.79*
	2. Yuriy Belov BLR 19.38
	3. Leszek Sliwa POL 19.08
DT	1. Zoltán Kövágó HUN 63.85*
	2. Heinrich Seitz GER 59.50
	3. Gabor Máté HUN 59.45
HT	1. Nicolas Figère FRA 80.88*
	2. Olli-Pekka Karjalainen FIN 80.54
	3. Miloslav Konopka SVK 76.28
JT	1. Björn Lange GER 80.85
	2. Aleksandr Baranovskiy RUS 76.74
	3. Janis Liepa LAT 74.26
Dec	1. Andre Niklaus GER 8042
	2. Jaakko Ojaniemi FIN 7907
	3. William Frullani ITA 7871
20kW	1. Juan Manuel Molina ESP 1:23:03
	2. Stepan Yudin RUS 1:23:10
	3. José Dominguez ESP 1:23:16
4x100m	1. POL (Kondratowicz, Chyla, Placheta, Rogowski) 39.41
	2. GBR (Oparka, Barbour, Chinn, Lewis) 39.45
	3. SLO (Sustersic, Osovnikar, Fridrih, Orel) 39.95
4x400m	1. GBR (Naismith, Potter, Chatt, Elias) 3:05.24
	2. GER (Kirch, Holz, Feller, Scheer) 3:05.39
	3. RUS (Mishukov, Babarykin, Bogdanov, Levedev) 3:06.41

Women

100m (-1.2)	1. Sina Schielke GER 11.52
	2. Abi Oyepitan GBR 11.58
	3. Johanna Manninen FIN 11.61
200m (-0.3)	1. Johanna Manninen FIN 23.30
	2. Sina Schielke GER 23.45
	3. Ciara Sheehy IRL 23.54
400m	1. Antonina Yefremova UKR 52.29
	2. Helen Thieme GBR 52.75
	3. Aneta Lemiesz POL 53.25
800m	1. Anna Zagorska POL 2:07.27
	2. Irina Somesan ROM 2:07.27
	3. Tatyana Rodionova RUS 2:07.60
1500m	1. Alesya Turova BLR 4:09.71
	2. Natalia Rodríguez ESP 4:11.20
	3. Kelly Caffel GBR 4:12.30
5000m	1. Katalin Szentgyörgyi HUN 15:40.55
	2. Anastasiya Zubova RUS 15:40.78
	3. Tatyana Khmelyova RUS 15:51.88
10,000m	1. Olga Romanova RUS 33:36.03
	2. Sonja Stolic YUG 33:37.02
	3. Sabrina Mockenhaupt GER 33:38.38
3000mSt	1. Melanie Schulz GER 10:03.34*
	2. Lívia Tóth HUN 10:04.99
	3. Sigrid Vanden Bempt BEL 10:08.46
100mh (1.2)	1. Susanna Kallur SWE 12.96 (12.95* ht)
	2. Jenny Kallur SWE 13.19
	3. Tessy Prediger GER 13.31
400mh	1. Sylvanie Morandais FRA 56.30
	2. Aleksandra Pieluzek POL 56.51
	3. Irena Zauna LAT 57.03
HJ	1. Ruth Beitia ESP 1.87
	2= Candeger Kilincer TUR 1.87
	2= Marina Kuptsova RUS 1.87
PV	1. Monika Pyrek POL 4.40*
	2. Annika Becker GER 4.40*
	3. Carolin Hingst GER 4.30
LJ	1. Jade Johnson GBR 6.52/1.0
	2. Concepción Montaner ESP 6.46/-0.5
	3. Aurélie Félix FRA 6.41/0.9
TJ	1. Irina Vasilyeva RUS 13.80/1.3
	2. Marija Martinovic YUG 13.72/0.0
	3. Amy Zongo FRA 13.68/1.2
SP	1. Nadezhda Ostapchuk BLR 19.73*
	2. Lucica Ciobanu ROM 17.59
	3. Kathleen Kluge GER 17.06
DT	1. Melina Robert-Michon FRA 58.52*
	2. Ileana Brindusoiu ROM 58.25
	3. Olga Goncharenko BLR 57.71
HT	1. Manuela Montebrun FRA 66.73
	2. Sini Pöyry FIN 64.71
	3. Cecilia Nilsson SWE 64.06
JT	1. Nikolett Szabó HUN 60.69*
	2. Mercedes Chilla ESP 57.78
	3. Moonika Aava EST 56.12
Hep	1. Liga Klavina LAT 6279*
	2. Svetlana Sokolova RUS 6179
	3. Austra Skujyté LTU 6087
20kW	1. Elisa Rigaudo ITA 1:29:54*
	2. Rita Turava BLR 1:30:15
	3. Larissa Safronova RUS 1:32:06
4x100m	1. GBR (Burnside, Roscoe, Scott, Oyepitan) 44.31
	2. BLR (Bartsevich, Drahun, Neumerzhytsk, Likhuta) 44.64
	3. FIN (Lax, Hannula, Manninen, Salivaara) 44.76
4x400m	1. GBR (Gear, Meadows, Duncan, Thieme) 3:31.74

2. POL (Pieluzek, Lemiesz, Bejnar, Karolkiewicz) 3:32.38
3. UKR (Zhuralyova, Sydorenko, Gurtovenko, Yefremova) 3:34.16

Medal and Points Table

Nation	G	S	B	Total	Points 1-8
GER	6	5	5	16	177
RUS	4	6	4	14	159.5
POL	5	3	4	12	128
GBR	6	3	2	11	127.5
FRA	5	1	4	10	127
ESP	4	4	2	10	113
FIN	1	4	2	7	87
BLR	2	4	1	7	76.5
UKR	2	4	1	7	67
ITA	1	-	3	4	64
SWE	2	1	3	6	62
HUN	3	1	2	6	51
ROM	-	3	1	4	45.5
GRE	-	1	-	1	43.5

24 nations won medals (15 gold)

European Junior (U20) Championships

At Grosseto, Italy, July 19-22

100m (2.4)
1. Mark Lewis-Francis GBR 10.09w
2. Tim Goebel GER 10.18
3. Igor Blazevic CRO 10.31

200m (0.8)
1. Ronald Pognon FRA 20.80
2. Kevin Rans BEL 20.89
3. Dwayne Grant GBR 20.92

400m
1. Tim Benjamin GBR 46.43
2. Johan Wissman SWE 46.81
3. Bastian Swillims GER 46.88

800m
1. René Herms GER 1:46.98
2. Arnoud Okken NED 1:48.02
3. Ricky Soos GBR 1:48.43

1500m
1. Cosimo Caliandro ITA 3:48.49
2. Tomasz Babiskiewicz POL 3:48.66
3. Arturo Casado ESP 3:48.76

5000m
1. Mohamed Farah GBR 14:09.91
2. Bruno Saramago POR 14:11.65
3. Noel Cutillas ESP 14:12.43

10,000m
1. Vasiliy Matvichuk UKR 30:43.19
2. Aleksandr Nikalayuk BLR 30:46.37
3. Abdulrahman Kara TUR 31:00.36

3000mSt
1. Radoslaw Poplawski POL 8:46.36
2. Mircea Bogdan ROM 8:49.76
3. Hristoforos Meroussis GRE 8:51.87

110mh (1.2)
1. Philip Nossmy SWE 13.81
2. Sebastian Siebert GER 13.83
3. Dominic Girdler GBR 14.16

400mh
1. Christian Duma GER 50.26
2. Henning Hackelbusch GER 50.76
3. Mikhail Lipskiy RUS 51.00

HJ
1. Andrey Chubsa BLR 2.23
2. Jiri Krehula CZE 2.21
3. Mickael Hanany FRA 2.19

PV
1. Dmitriy Kuptsov RUS 5.55
2. Kevin Rans BEL 5.50
3. Stavros Kouroupakis GRE 5.35

LJ
1. Louis Tsatoumas GRE 7.98w/2.5
2. Jan Zumer SLO 7.72w/2.7
3. Dmitriy Sapinski RUS 7.72/1.3

TJ
1. Marian Oprea ROM 16.65
2. Jonathan Moore GBR 16.43/1.0
3. Viktor Yastrebov UKR 16.43

SP
1. Michal Hodun POL 18.23
2. Robert Häggblom FIN 17.96
3. Marco Fortes POR 17.86

DT
1. Michal Hodun POL 57.95
2. Arnost Holovsky CZE 54.46
3. Dmitry Sivakov BLR 54.23

HT
1. Krisztián Pars HUN 69.42
2. Aleksey Yeliseyev RUS 68.32
3. Esref Apak TUR 67.56

JT
1. Aleksandr Ivanov RUS 80.18*
2. Andreas Thorkildsen NOR 76.98
3. Saku Kuusisto FIN 76.98

Dec
1. Ladji Doucouré FRA 7747
2. Lars Albert GER 7683
3. Atis Vaisjuns LAT 7497

10kW
1. Yevgeniy Demkov RUS 43:34.12
2. Sergey Lystov RUS 43:39.46
3. Beniamin Kucinski POL 43:44.87

4x100m
1. GBR (T Edgar, D Grant, Benjamin, Lewis-Francis) 39.24*
2. FRA (Bonvard, Pognon, Guillaume, Doucouré) 39.76
3. POL (Latkowski, Swierczynski, Koczon, Ptak) 39.96

4x400m
1. POL (Marciniszyn, Matyjaszczyk, Kedzia, Grzegorczyk) 3:06.12
2. GBR (Tobin, Nicholls, Ellis, Benjamin) 3:06.21
3. ESP (Melo, Ruiz, Vera, Artal) 3:07.47

Women

100m (2.1)
1. Katchi Habel GER 11.24w
2. Gwladys Bélliard FRA 11.50
3. Amelie Huyghes FRA 11.59

200m (1.4)
1. Vernicha James GBR 22.93
2. Katchi Habel GER 23.38
3. Maja Nose SLO 23.60

400m
1. Tatyana Firova RUS 52.94
2. Lisa Miller GBR 53.29
3. Kim Wall GBR 53.52

800m
1. Lucia Klocová SVK 2:03.76
2. Kerstin Werner GER 2:03.99
3. Tatyana Petlyuk UKR 2:04.15

1500m
1. Ljiljana Culibrk CRO 4:13.13
2. Emma Ward GBR 4:13.51
3. Riina Tolonen FIN 4:14.48

3000m
1. Elvan Abeylegesse TUR 8:53.42
2. Tatyana Chulak RUS 9:02.65
3. Ulla Tuimala FIN 9:07.35

5000m
1. Elvan Abeylegesse TUR 15:21.12*
2. Elina Lindgren FIN 16:11.55
3. Collette Fagan GBR 16:16.39

2000mSt
1. Catalina Oprea ROM 6:34.89*
2. Gwendoline Despres FRA 6:36.06
3. Antje Hoffmann GER 6:36.67

100mh (2.1)
1. Gergana Stoyanova BUL 13.04w (13.00w/3.5 ht, windy champ best)
2. Adrianna Lamalle FRA 13.08
3. Lucie Skrobáková CZE 13.30

400mh
1. Zofia Malachowska POL 57.78
2. Patricia Lopes POR 57.93
3. Mariya Menshikova RUS 58.83

HJ 1. Ramona Pop ROM 1.92
2. Anna Chicherova RUS 1.90
3. Anna Ksok POL 1.90

PV 1. Yelena Isinbayeva RUS 4.40*
2. Natalya Kusch UKR 4.15
3. Vanessa Boslak FRA 4.15

LJ 1. Anastasiya Ilyina RUS 6.38/0.0
2. Alina Militaru ROM 6.32
3. Katarzyna Klisowska POL 6.26

TJ 1. Anastasiya Ilyina RUS 14.12*/0.8
2. Athanassia Perra GRE 13.73w/3.0
3. Viktoriya Gurova RUS 13.68/1.1

SP 1. Natalya Kharaneka BLR 16.92
2. Kristin Marten GER 16.02
3. Claudia Villeneuve FRA 15.82

DT 1. Natalya Fokina UKR 56.69
2. Vera Begic CRO 55.02
3. Olga Chernogorova BLR 54.49

HT 1. Ivana Brkljacic CRO 64.18
2. Martina Danisová SVK 61.97
3. Berta Castells ESP 61.04

JT 1. Galina Kakhova BLR 55.40
2. Goldie Sayers GBR 55.40
3. Marion Bonaudo FRA 53.71

Hep 1. Carolina Klüft SWE 6022
2. Maren Freisen GER 5956
3. Olga Karas RUS 5745

10KW 1. Tatyana Kozlova RUS 46:22.67
2. Athanassia Tzoumeleka GRE 46:29.20
3. Beatriz Pascual ESP 46:49.81

4x100m 1. GER (Hentschke, Kaufmann, Grotzinger, Habel) 44.16
2. FRA (Huyghes, Sellier, Belliard, Lamalle) 44.37
3. GBR (Norville, Caney, Spencer, James) 44.66

4x400m 1. GBR (Wall, Hines, James, Miller) 3:34.63
2. GER (Müller, Hoffmann, Balkow, Kettenis) 3:36.20
3. ROM (Koroszi, Barbulescu, Manafu, Rus) 3:41.12

Medal and Points Table

Nation	G	S	B	Total	Points 1-8
GER	4	9	2	15	175
RUS	8	4	5	17	156
GBR	6	5	6	17	148
POL	5	1	4	10	127
FRA	2	5	5	12	124.5
BLR	3	1	2	6	85
ROM	3	2	1	6	66
UKR	2	1	2	5	57
ESP	-	-	5	5	55
CRO	2	1	1	4	51
FIN	-	2	3	5	51
ITA	1	-	-	1	43.3
GRE	1	2	2	5	39
SWE	2	1	-	3	38.3
HUN	1	-	-	1	36
TUR	2	-	2	4	35
SVK	1	1	-	2	32

25 nations won medals (16 gold)

European Cup 2001

Super-League at Bremen, GER, June 23-24

Men: 1. POL 107, 2. FRA 97, 3. RUS 95, 4. ITA 93, 5. GBR 91, 6. GER 91, 7. ESP 76, 8. GRE 66.

100m (1.4) 1. Mark Lewis-Francis GBR 10.13
2. Konstadínos Kedéris GRE 10.15
3. Frédéric Krantz FRA 10.27

200m (-0.7) 1. Konstadínos Kedéris GRE 20.31
2. Marlon Devonish GBR 20.59
3. Marcin Urbas POL 20.69

400m 1. Marc Raquil FRA 44.95
2. Robert Mackowiak POL 45.48
3. David Canal ESP 45.52

800m 1. Pawel Czapiewski POL 1:48.28
2. Andrea Longo ITA 1:48.54
3. Simon Lees GBR 1:48.80

1500m 1. José Redolat ESP 3:45.81
2. Mehdi Baala FRA 3:46.29
3. Leszek Zblewski POL 3:47.06

3000m 1. Driss Maazouzi FRA 7:52.26
2. Andrés Díaz ESP 7:52.59
3. John Mayock GBR 7:56.06

5000m 1. Ismaïl Sghir FRA 13:50.47
2. Alberto García ESP 13:50.96
3. Marco Mazza ITA 13:55.85

3000mSt 1. Bouabdallah Tahri FRA 8:38.02
2. Antonio Jiménez ESP 8:38.09
3. Ralf Assmus GER 8:39.34

110mh (1.3) 1. Yevgeniy Pechonkin RUS 13.38
2. Florian Schwarthoff GER 13.57
3. Anthony Jarrett GBR 13.58

400mh 1. Fabrizio Mori ITA 48.39
2. Marek Plawgo POL 48.98
3. Stéphane Diagana FRA 49.07

HJ 1. Yuriy Rybakov RUS 2.28
2. Grzegorz Sposób POL 2.23
3. Martin Buss GER 2.19

PV 1. Michael Stolle GER 5.75
2. Adam Kolasa POL 5.68
3. Vasiliy Gorshkov RUS 5.68

LJ 1. Danila Burkenya RUS 7.89/-1.8
2. Chris Tomlinson GBR 7.67/1.1
3. Grzegorz Marciniszyn POL 7.64/0.0

TJ 1. Jonathan Edwards GBR 17.26/-0.1
2. Hrístos Melétoglou GRE 17.19/1.7
3. Paulo Camossi ITA 16.97/0.0

SP 1. Manuel Martínez ESP 21.03
2. Pavel Chumachenko RUS 20.54
3. Paulo Dal Soglio ITA 20.02

DT 1. Lars Riedel GER 66.63
2. Mario Pestano ESP 65.60
3. Dmitriy Shevchenko RUS 65.26

HT 1. Szymon Ziolkówski POL 80.87
2. Nicola Vizzoni ITA 80.13
3. Hrístos Polyhroníou GRE 78.34

JT 1. Konstadínos Gatsioúdis GRE 88.33
2. Sergey Makarov RUS 83.24
3. Raymond Hecht GER 83.05

4x100m 1. ITA (Scuderi, Cavallaro, Checcucci, Colombo) 38.89
2. GBR 38.99
3. POL 39.00

4x400m 1. POL (Rysiukiewicz, Haczek, Dlugosielski, Mackowiak) 3:01.79

2. RUS 3:02.09
3. GER 3:02.71

Women: 1. RUS 126.5, 2. GER 117, 3. FRA 86, 4. GBR 82, 5. ROM 78, 6. ITA 72.5, 7. BLR 70, 8. CZE 47.

100m (2.8)	1. Marina Kislova RUS 11.23w
	2. Natalya Safronnikova BLR 11.26
	3. Katia Benth FRA 11.38
200m (0.3)	1. Natalya Safronnikova BLR 22.68
	2. Ionela Tîrlea ROM 22.85
	3. Svetlana Goncharenko RUS 22.87
400m	1. Grit Breuer GER 50.49
	2. Francine Landre FRA 51.21
	3. Natalya Antyukh RUS 51.37
800m	1. Irina Mistyukevich RUS 1:59.09
	2. Ivonne Teichmann GER 1:59.39
	3. Natalya Dukhnova BLR 1:59.95
1500m	1. Violeta Szekely ROM 4:06.43
	2. Olga Yegorova RUS 4:06.59
	3. Hayley Tullett GBR 4:07.83
3000m	1. Kathy Butler GBR 9:03.71
	2. Cristina Grosu ROM 9:04.91
	3. Fatima Yvelain FRA 9:05.30
5000m	1. Yelena Zadorozhnaya RUS 14:40.47*
	2. Paula Radcliffe GBR 14:49.84
	3. Mihaela Botezan ROM 15:08.78
100mh (0.6)	1. Irina Korotya RUS 13.06
	2. Linda Ferga FRA 13.10
	3. Kirsten Bolm GER 13.15
400mh	1. Yuliya Nosova RUS 53.84
	2. Ionela Tîrlea ROM 55.08
	3. Heike Meissner GER 55.33
HJ	1. Susan Jones GBR 1.95
	2. Alina Astafei GER 1.89
	3= Olga Kaliturina RUS
	3= Antonietta Di Martino ITA 1.89
PV	1. Svetlana Feofanova RUS 4.60*
	2. Janine Whitlock GBR 4.34
	3. Pavla Hamácková CZE 4.34
LJ	1. Heike Drechsler GER 6.79/-1.0
	2. Eunice Barber FRA 6.71/1.2
	3. Fiona May ITA 6.57/0.5
TJ	1. Natalya Lebedeva RUS 14.89/-1.2
	2. Natalya Safronova BLR 14.10w/2.5
	3. Cristina Nicolau ROM 13.83/0.0
SP	1. Nadine Kleinert-Schmitt GER 19.30
	2. Irina Korzhanenko RUS 19.27
	3. Assunta Legnante ITA 17.51
DT	1. Franka Dietzsch GER 64.04
	2. Natalya Sadova RUS 63.77
	3. Nicoleta Grasu ROM 62.33
HT	1. Olga Tsander BLR 68.40
	2. Kirsten Münchow GER 68.09
	3. Lorraine Shaw GBR 67.98
JT	1. Nikola Tomecková CZE 64.77
	2. Steffi Nerius GER 63.12
	3. Claudia Coslovich ITA 63.07
4x100m	1. GER (Paschke, Schielke, B Rockmeier, Wagner) 43.02
	2. RUS 43.15
	3. FRA 43.45
4x400m	1. GER (Marx, Ghosh, Ekpo-Umoh, Breuer) 3:23.81
	2. RUS 3:24.58
	3. FRA 3:26.23

First League Group A *at Vaasa FIN, June 23-24*

Men: 1. FIN 110, 2. SWE 106, 3. CZE 101, 4. NOR 94.5, 5. SUI 87.5, 6. POR 82.5, 7. BLR 77, 8. IRL 60.5. *Winners*: **100m/200m**: Tommi Hartonen FIN 10.21/20.94, **400m**: Jimisola Laursen SWE 45.82, **800m**: André Bucher SUI 1:46.72, **1500m/3000m**: Rui Silva POR 3:43.25/7:55.52, **5000m**: José Ramos POR 14:02.71, **3000mSt**: Jim Svenøy NOR 8:35.55, **110mh**: Robert Kronberg SWE 13.40, **400mh**: Jirí Muzík CZE 49.39, **HJ**: Stefan Holm SWE 2.28, **PV**: Patrik Kristiansson SWE 5.83, **LJ**: Peter Häggström SWE 7.75, **TJ**: Christian Olsson 17.00, **SP**: Dmitriy Goncharuk BLR 20.12, **DT**: Libor Malina CZE 63.34, **HT**: Ola-Pekka Karjalainen FIN 75.94, **JT**: Aki Parviainen FIN 92.41*, **4x100m**: NOR 39.93, **4x400m**: CZE 3:04.66.

Women: 1. POL 122, 2. ESP 106, 3. GRE 101, 4. SWE 95, 5. POR 76, 6. FIN 70, 7. BEL 63, 8. LTU 51. *Winners*: **100m**: (0.0) Ekateríni Thánou GRE 11.29, **200m**: Kim Gevaert 23.10, **400m**: Aneta Lemiesz POL 52.96, **800m**: Mayte Martínez ESP 2:03.61, **1500m**: Nuria Fernández ESP 4:35.21, **3000m**: Lidia Chojecka 9:02.45, **5000m**: Marta Dominguez ESP 15:42.84, **100mh**: Susanna Kallur SWE 12.92, **400mh**: Malgorzata Pskit POL 57.09, **HJ**: Kajsa Bergqvist SWE 1.92, **PV**: Monika Pyrek POL 4.50, **LJ**: Niurka Montalvo ESP 6.59, **TJ**: Heli Koivula FIN 14.13, **SP**: Krystyna Zabawska POL 18.76, **DT**: Joanna Wisniewska POL 63.20, **HT**: Kamila Skolimowska POL 64.47, **JT**: Miréla Tzelíli GRE 65.05, **4x100m**: GRE 43.42, **4x400m**: POL 3:32.66.

First League Group B *at Budapest HUN, June 23-24*

Men: 1. UKR 131, 2. ROM 104, 3. NED 97.5, 4. HUN 93.5, 5. SLO 86, 6. SVK 73 7. YUG 71, 8. BUL 60. **100m**: Konstantin Rurak UKR 10.39, **200m**: Patrick van Balkom NED 20.57, **400m**: Marcel Lopuchovsky SVK 46.02, **800m**: Bram Som NED 1:50.06, **1500m**: Ivan Geshko UKR 4:03.27, **3000m**: Kamiel Maase NED 8:58.09, **5000m**: Miroslav Vanko SVK 13:54.28, 3000SC: Simon Vroemen NED 8:37.11, **110mh**: Zhivko Videnov BUL 13.58, **400mh**: Gennadiy Gorbenko UKR 49.93, **HJ**: Andrey Sokolovskiy UKR 2.30, **PV**: Rens Blom NED 5.65, **LJ**: Bogdan Tarus ROM 8.15, **TJ**: Marian Oprea ROM J 17.13w, **SP**: Gheorghe Guset ROM 19.89, **DT**: Zoltán Kovágó HUN 65.97, **HT**: Adrián Annus HUN 78.77, **JT**: Gergely Horváth HUN 78.33, **4x100m**: UKR 39.44, **4x400m**: UKR 3:03.92

Women: 1. UKR 119, 2. BUL 109, 3. NED 92, 4. HUN 88, 5. SLO 83, 6. TUR 72.5, 7. AUT 62, 8. YUG 56.5. **100m/200m**: Alenka Bikar SLO 11.27/22.82, **400m**: Alice Kun 52.24, **800m**: Tsvetelina Kirilova BUL 2:02.92, **1500m**: Irina Lishchinskaya UKR 4:20.58, **3000m**: Daniela Yordanova BUL 8:57.77, **5000m**: Natalya Berkut UKR 15:21.95, **100mh**: Svetla Dimitrova BUL 12.61w, **400mh**: Tatyana Debelaya UKR 58.05, **HJ**: Venelina Veneva BUL 1.92, **PV**: Tanya Koleva BUL 4.20, **LJ**: Tünde Vaszi HUN 6.82w, **TJ**: Maria Dimitrova BUL 14.24w, **SP**: Lieja Koeman NED 18.16, **DT**: Viktoriya Boyko UKR 61.97, **HT**: Katalin Divós HUN 63.92, **JT**: Nikolett Szabó HUN 61.72, **4x100m**: BUL 44.48, **4x400m**: UKR 3:33.06

Second League Group A *at Riga LAT 22-23 June*
Men: 1. DEN 141, 2. LTU 126, 3. LAT 125, 4. EST 120, 5. TUR 115, 6. MOL 76, 7. GEO 64, 8. LUX 60, 9. ARM 51
Women: 1. NOR 136.5, 2. LAT 131, 3. IRL 129, 4. EST 116.5, 5. DEN 115, 6. MOL 97, 7. GEO 44, 8. LUX 43, 9. ARM 32

Second League Group B *at Nicosia CYP 23-24 June*
Men: 1. BEL 143, 2. AUT 118, 3. CRO 105, 4. ISR 93, 5. CYP 92, 6. ISL 71, 7. Small States 47, 8. BIH 45.
Women: 1. SUI 131, 2. SVK 109, 3. CRO 98, 4. ISR 93, 5. CYP 86, 6. ISL 78, 7. ALB 48, 8. Small States 32.

2002 Matches – all on June 22-23
SPAR European Cup *at Annecy FRA*
Men: FIN, FRA, GER, GBR, ITA, POL, RUS, UKR
Women: FRA, GER, GBR, ITA, POL, ROM, RUS, UKR
First League Group A at Banská Bystrica SVK
Men: BEL, CZE, GRE, HUN, LTU, NOR, ROM, SVK
Women: BUL, CZE, FIN, GRE, HUN, NOR, SVK, TUR
First League Group B at Sevilla ESP
Men: AUT, DEN, NED, POR, SLO, ESP, SWE, SUI
Women: BLR, LAT, NED, POR, SLO, ESP, SWE, SUI
Second League Group A at Tallinn EST
Men: BLR, CYP, EST, GEO, ISL, IRL, LAT, LUX
Women: CYP, DEN, EST, GEO, ISL, IRL, LTU, LUX
Second League Group B at Beograd YUG
Men: AASSE, ARM, BIH, BUL, CRO, ISR, MKD, MOL, TUR, YUG
Women: AASSE, ALB, ARM, AUT, BEL, BIH, CRO, ISR, MKD, MOL, YUG
AASSE = Athletic Assn of the Small States of Europe

European Cup for Combined Events 2001

Super League at Arles FRA 30 Jun - 1 Jul
Men Dec: 1. FRA 23,933, 2. UKR 23,779, 3. FIN 23,648, 4. GER 23,592, 5. HUN 23,406, 6. RUS 22,478, 7. SUI 22,018, 8. GRE 20,680. Ind: 1. Aleksandr Yurkov UKR 8380w, 2.Attila Zsivoczky HUN 8218w, 3. Laurent Hernu FRA 8112w.
Women Hep: 1. RUS 18,350, 2. GER 18,009, 3. ITA 17,473, 4. BLR 17,416, 5. CZE 17,403, 6. POL 17,199, 7. FIN 16,902, 8. FRA 16,847. Ind: 1. Svetlana Sokolova RUS 6270w, 2. Sonja Kesselschläger GER 6064w, 3. Tatyana Gordeyeva RUS 6064w
First League at Ried AUT 30 Jun - 1 Jul
Men Dec: 1. AUT 23,564, 2. NED 23,125, 3. ESP 22,782, 4. LAT 22,580, 5. ITA 22,574, 6. CZE 22,347, 7. EST 22,092, 8. SWE 21,727.
Ind: Chiel Warners NED 8206
Women Hep: 1. UKR 16,670, 2. GBR 17,404, 3. SWE 16,981, 4. GRE 16,870, 5. NED 16,635, 6. SUI 16,336, 7. HUN 15,740, 8. LTU 14,784.
Ind: 1. Yuliya Akulenko UKR 6001.
Second League at Kaunas LTU 30 Jun - 1 Jul
Men Dec: 1. POL 22,596, 2. BLR 21,820, 3. GBR 21,538, 4. BEL 20,140, 5. DEN 19,914, 6. LTU 19,492. Ind: Mário Aníbal POR 8213.
Women Hep: 1. EST 16,399, 2. BEL 16,038, 3. ESP 15,984, 4. AUT 15,209, 5. LAT 13,347.
Ind: Larisa Netseporuk EST 6172.

2002 Matches – all on 29-30 June
Super League at Bydgoszcz POL
Men: AUT, FIN, FRA, GER, HUN, NED, RUS, UKR
Women: BLR, CZE, GER, GBR, ITA, POL, RUS, UKR
First League at Riga LAT
Men: BLR, CZE, GRE, ITA, LAT, POL, ESP, SUI
Women: BEL, EST, FIN, FRA, GRE, NED, SWE, SUI
Second League at Maribor SLO
Men: DEN, EST, GBR, LTU, NOR, POR, SLO, SWE
individuals from BEL, CYP, GEO, ISL, ISR, MOL, ROM, SVK, TUR, YUG
Women: AUT, BEL, DEN, HUN, ISR, LAT, LTU, ROM, SLO, ESP
individuals from ALB, GEO, ISL, NOR, POR, SVK, TUR, YUG.

European Cup of Race Walking 2001

At Dudince, SVK, 19 May
Men 20km: 1. Viktor Burayev RUS J 1:19:30, 2. Yevgeniy Misyulya BLR 1:19:45, 3. Andreas Erm GER 1:19:51, 4. Francisco Fernández ESP 1:20:02, 5. Vladimir Andreyev RUS 1:20:14, 6. Jirí Malysa CZE 1:20:21, 7. Denis Nizhegorodov RUS 1:20:42, 8. Aigars Fadejevs LAT 1:20:51, 9. Ivan Trotskiy BLR 1:21:43, 10. Juan M Molina ESP 1:21:51, 65 finishers
Team: 1. RUS 13, 2. ESP 34, 3. ITA 55, 4. LAT 56, 5. FRA 80, 6. ROM 84, 7. CZE 85, 8. SVK 90, 9. GER 91, 10. POL 100, 11. FIN 141, 12. HUN 143, 13. UKR 161
Men 50km: 1. Jesús Angel García ESP 3:44:26, 2. Nikolay Matyukhin RUS 3:45:48, 3. Vladimir Potemin RUS 3:46:12, 4. Santiago Pérez ESP 3:46:52, 5. Denis Langlois FRA 3:48:06, 6. Aleksey Voyevodin RUS 3:48:51, 7. Viktor Ginko BLR 3:50:59, 8. David Boulanger FRA 3:51:36, 9. Stefan Malík SVK 3:51:58, 10. Denis Trautmann GER 3:52:16,, 40 finishers
Team: 1. RUS 11, 2. ESP 21, 3. FRA 24, 4. ITA 48, 5. GER 57, 6. POR 70, 7. SVK 81, 8. HUN 83.
Junior Men 10km: 1. Yevgeniy Demkov RUS 41:16, 2. Sergey Lystsov RUS 41:18, 3. Mikolai Seredovich BLR 41:30
Team: 1. RUS 3, 2. BLR 8, 3. POL 21, 4. GRE 23, 5. ITA 26, 6. UKR 30, 7. ESP 35, 8. CZE 39, 9. HUN 41, 10. ROM 54.
Women 20 km: 1. Olimpiada Ivanova RUS 1:26:48, 2. Natalya Fedoskina RUS 1:26:50, 3. Elisabetta Perrone ITA 1:27:09, 4. Erika Alfridi ITA 1:27:29, 5. Yelena Nikolayeva RUS 1:28:20, 6. Norica Cîmpean ROM 1:29:25, 7. María Vasco ESP 1:30:11, 8. Valentina Tsybulskaya BLR 1:30:37, 9. Gillian O'Sullivan IRL 1:31:13, 10. Natalya Misyulya BLR 1:31:21, 55 finishers
Team: 1. RUS 8, 2. ITA 18, 3. BLR 35, 4. ESP 48, 5. UKR 51, 6. ROM 57, 7. POR 84, 8. FRA 89, 9. FIN 114, 10. HUN 124, 11. SVK 143.
Junior Women 10km: 1. Tatyana Kozlova RUS 46:08, 2. Marina Tikhonava BLR 46:31, 3. Yekaterina Izmaylova RUS 46:42

Team: 1. RUS 4, 2. BLR 9, 3. GRE 12, 4. ESP 21, 5. HUN 35, 6. FRA 35, 7. POR 37, 8. POL 42, 9. SVK 44, 10. ROM 46.

1st European Winter Throws Challenge 2001

At Nice, France, March 17-18

Men: RUS 8386, ITA 8352, FRA 8144, GER 8089, FIN 8057, UKR 7981, ESP 7900, SWE 7369. **SP:** 1. Manuel Martínez ESP 20.27, 2. Paulo Dal Soglio ITA 19.96, 3. Gheorghe Guset ROM 19.50; **DT:** 1. Timo Tompuri FIN 61.79, 2. Andrzej Krawczyk POL 61.60, 3. Aleksandr Borichevskiy RUS 61.22; **HT:** 1. David Chaussinand 76.54, 2. Vladislav Piskunov UKR 76.41, 3. Alexandros Papadimitríou GRE 76.36; **JT:** 1. Peter Blank GER 82.10, 2. Gregor Högler AUT 8081, 3. Björn Lange GER 78.60. **Women**: RUS 8426. UKR 8066. FRA 7743. GER 7677. ITA 7504. SWE 6649. **SP:** 1. Viktoriya Pavlysh UKR 19.47, 2. Larisa Peleshenko RUS 18.77, 3. Lyudmila Sechko RUS 18.54; **DT:** 1. Nicoleta Grasu ROM 65.54, 2. Yelena Antonova UKR 61.88, 3. Melina Robert-Michon 61.67; **HT:** 1. Olga Kuzenkova RUS 71.30, 2. Manuela Montebrun 69.72, 3. Lorraine Shaw GBR 68.15; **JT:** 1. Tatyana Shikolenko RUS 63.96, 2. Ana Mirela Termure ROM 62.49, 3. Claudia Coslovich ITA 57.89.

European 10,000m Challenge 2001

At Barakaldo, Spain, April 7

Men: 1. José Rios ESP 27:49.35, 2. Helder Ornelas POR 28:01.94, 3. Kamiel Maase NED 28:02.37, Team: 1. ESP, 2. POR, 3. GBR. **Women**: 1. Paula Radcliffe 30:55.80, 2. Irina Mikitenko GER 31:29.55, 3. Monica Rosa POR 32:22.25, Team: 1. ESP, 2. GBR, 3. POR.

European Champion Clubs Cup 2001

Men Group A: *At Madrid, May 26-27*: 1. Sports Club Luch RUS 137, 2. Fiamme Gialle ITA 98, 3. Sporting Lisbon POR 95, 4. Airtel (previously Larios) ESP 93, 5. Belgrave Harriers GBR 88, 6. Dukla Prague CZE 87, 7. Panellinios GRE 77, 8. Partizan YUG 62. Competition records: **100m**: 10.12 Dwain Chambers GBR (Belgrave), **200m**: 20.37 Francis Obikwelu NGR (SC Lisboa. POR), **SP**: 21.29 Manuel Martínez (Airtel. ESP), **JT**: 91.97 Kostas Gatsioúdis (Panellínos. GRE), **Men Group B:** At Madrid 26-27 May: 1. Maccabi Tel Aviv ISR 112, 2. CA Montreuil FRA 111, 3. Sparta Copenhagen DEN 93, 4. AAC Amsterdam NED 76.5, 5. Slavia Stu. Bratislava SVK 61, 6. Olympia Limassol CYP 49.5, 7. RFC Liège Athlétisme BEL 45.

Women Group A: At Madrid 26-27 May: 1. Sports Club Luch RUS 131, 2. Valencia ESP 102.5, 3. Metanopoli ITA 86, 4. Panellinios GRE 85, 5. Sporting Lisbon POR 83.5, 6. Olimpia Praga CZE 83, 7. Sale Harriers GBR 49, 8. Partizan YUG 46. **Women JT**: 64.54 Yekaterina Ivakina (SC Luch. RUS), **4x100m**: 43.84 Valencia ESP.

Women Group B: At Gent 26 May: 1. CA Montreuil FRA 107, 2. Sp. København DEN 103, 3. L Tel Aviv ISR 84, 4. AC Amsterdam 74, 5. Banská Bystrica SVK 65, 6. KAA Gent BEL 63, 7. CA Dudelange LUX 26

South American Championships 2001

At Manaus, Brazil, May 18-20

Men

100m	1. Raphael de Oliveira BRA 10.36
(0.2)	2. Cláudio Sousa BRA 10.37
	3. Heber Viera URU 10.38
200m	1. André D da Silva BRA 20.52
(0.0)	2. Heber Viera URU 20.68
	3. Augusto Santos BRA 21.02
400m	1. Sanderlei Parrela BRA 45.11*
	2. Valdinei da Silva BRA 46.50
	3. Jonathan Palma VEN 46.78
800m	1. Hudson de Souza BRA 1:47.20
	2. Flávio Godoy BRA 1:47.65
	3. Simoncito Silvera VEN 1:48.54
1500m	1. Hudson de Souza BRA 3:36.47*
	2. Edgar de Oliveira BRA 3:43.56
	3. Sebastián González Cabot ARG 3:45.35
5000m	1. Elenilson da Silva BRA 14:10.94
	2. José Frazão Jr BRA 14:25.35
	3. Alejandro Semprún VEN 14:32.90
10,000m	1. Néstor García URU 30:17.09
	2. Alejandro Semprún VEN 30:24.56
	3. Oscar Cortinez ARG 31:12.45
110mh	1. Márcio de Souza BRA 13.64*
(0.0)	2. Redelen dos Santos BRA 13.87
	3. Paulo Villar COL 13.88
400mh	1. Anderson dos Santos BRA 50.48
	2. Carlos Zbinden CHI 50.99
	3. João dos Santos BRA 51.04
3000mSt	1. Celso Ficagna BRA 8:44.83
	2. Emigdio Delgado VEN 8:47.55
	3. Adelar Schuler BRA 8:51.70
HJ	1. Jessé de Lima BRA 2.20
	2. Alfredo Deza Jr PER 2.20
	3. Felipe Apablaza CHI 2.15
PV	1. Javier Benítez ARG 5.40*
	2. Ricardo Diez VEN 5.35
	3. Gustavo Rehder BRA 5.15
LJ	1. Nelson Ferreira Jr. BRA 7.67/1.6
	2. Lewis Asprilla COL 7.48w/2.2
	3. Esteban Copland VEN 7.31/1.7
TJ	1. Jadel Gregório BRA 16.98/1.4
	2. Messias Baptista BRA 16.23/1.5
	3. Freddy Nieves ECU 16.14/1.4
SP	1. Marco Antonio Verni CHI 18.57
	2. Yoger Medina VEN 18.49
	3. Edson Miguel BRA 17.00
DT	1. Marcelo Pugliese ARG 56.30
	2. João dos Santos BRA 54.40
	3. Julián Piñero ARG 54.10
HT	1. Juan Ignacio Cerra ARG 73.95*
	2. Adrián Marzo ARG 69.69
	3. Eduardo Acuña PER 63.53
JT	1. Luiz F da Silva BRA 74.50

2. Nery Kennedy PAR 74.41
3. Manuel Fuenmayor VEN 71.44

Dec 1. Edson L. Bindilati BRA 7564*
2. Eric Kerwitz ARG 7305
3. Enrique Aguirre ARG 7226

20kW 1. José Baggio BRA 1:31:42,84
2. Mario dos Santos Jr BRA 1:32:45.90
3. Xavier Moreno ECU 1:35:42.11

4x100m 1. BRA (Raphael de Oliveira, Claudio Sousa, Vicente de Lima, André D da Silva) 38.67
2. VEN 40.02
3. URU 40.34

4x400m 1. VEN (Jonathan Palma, Luis Luna, Simoncito Silvera, William Hernández) 3:06.31
2. BRA 3:06.64
3. ARG 3:13.88

Women

100m (0.6) 1. Lucimar de Moura BRA 11.55
2. María Isabel Coloma CHI 11.79
3. Rosemar Neto BRA 11.79

200m (0.0) 1. Felipe Palacios COL 23.36
2. Rosemar Neto BRA 23.52
3. Lucimar de Moura BRA 23.68

400m 1. Luciana Mendes BRA 52.76
2. Maria L Almirão BRA 53.14
3. Norma González COL 53.29

800m 1. Luciana Mendes BRA 2:00.94
2. Letitia Vriesde SUR 2:00.93
3. Marlene da Silva BRA 2:05.82

1500m 1. Letitia Vriesde SUR 4:19.97
2. Celia dos Santos BRA 4:23.91
3. Andrea Coelho BRA 4:28.01

5000m 1. Maria Rodrigues BRA 16:35.1
2. Selma dos Reis BRA 16:40.0
3. María Paredes ECU 16:53.5

10,000m 1. Maria Rodrigues BRA 35:25.70
2. Rosa Apaza BOL 35:30.04
3. Adriana de Souza BRA 35:30.06

100mh (0.1) 1. Maurren Maggi BRA 12.71*
2. Maila Machado BRA 13.18
3 .Sandrine Legenort VEN 13.88

400mh 1. Isabel Rocha Silva BRA 57.47
2. Princesa Oliveros COL 58.76
3. Luciana Franca BRA 58.87

3000mSt 1. Michelle da Costa BRA 10:31.30*
2. Claudia Camargo ARG 10:58.81
3. Magda Azevedo BRA 11:03.95

HJ 1. drugs dq. Solange Witteveen ARG 1.97*
2=. Luciana Dambacher BRA 1.83
2=. Thais de Andrade BRA 1.83

PV 1. Alejandra García ARG 4.00
2. Alina Alló ARG 3.90
3= María Paz Ausin CHI 3.70
3= Karem da Silva BRA 3.70

LJ 1. Maurren Maggi BRA 6.69/0.0
2. Luciana dos Santos BRA 6.10/0.0
3. Helena Guerrero COL 6.04/0.0

TJ 1. Keila Costa BRA 13.61/0.0
2. Luciana dos Santos BRA 13.48/0.8
3. Mónica Falcioni URU 13.43/1.6

SP 1. Elisãngela Adriano BRA 17.93
2. Andrea Pereira BRA 15.64
3. Marianne Berndt CHI 15.21

DT 1. Elisãngela Adriano BRA 58.40
2. Katiuscia de Jesús BRA 49.52
3. María Eugenia Giggi ARG 48.30

HT 1. Karina Moya ARG 60.83*
2. Josiane Soares BRA 58.81
3. Erika Melián ARG 55.70

JT 1. Carla Bispo BRA 51.98
2. Alessandra Resende BRA 50.83
3 Romina Maggi ARG 48.90

Hep 1. Elisete da Silva BRA 5338
2. Valeria Steffens CHI 5157
3. Mõnica Marques BRA 5125

20kW 1. Geovanna Irusta BOL 1:42:42.33
2. Gianetti Bonfim BRA 1:46:02.8
3. Cristina Bohorquez COL 1:48:18.75

4x100m 1. BRA (Lucimar de Moura, Rosemar Neto, Katia Santos, Thatiana Ignacio) 44.32
2. COL 45.43
3. VEN 47.22

4x400m 1. BRA (Maria Almirão, Maria Figueiredo, Lucimar Teodoro, Luciana Mendes) 3:32.43*
2. COL 3:40.27
3. VEN 3:44.74

Medal and Points Table

Nation	G	S	B	Total	Points 1-8
BRA	31	24	14	69	599
ARG	6^	4	8	18	175
VEN	1	5	8	14	163
CHI	1	3	3	7	99.5
COL	1	4	4	9	77
ECU	-	1	2	3	63
URU	1	1	3	5	40
BOL	1	1	-	2	19
PER	-	1	1	2	18.5
SUR	1	1	-	2	16
GUY	-	-	-	-	8
PAR	-	1	-	1	6
PAN	-	-	-	-	2

^ including Witteveen's drugs disqualification.

African Junior Championships 2001

August 16-19, Réduit, Mauritius.

Men: 100m: Enrico Louis MRI 10.79, **200m:** Omanansingh Kowlessur MRI 21.66, **400m:** Mandia Nkosi RSA 47.13, **800m/1500m:** Cornelius Chirchir KEN 1:49.02/3:41.16, **5000m:** Boniface Toroitich UGA 13:48.6, **10,000m:** Solomon Busiendigh KEN 28:40.36, **3000mSt:** Ezekiel Kemboi KEN 8:39.80, **110mh:** Janko Kotze RSA 14.38w, **400mh:** Pieter de Villiers RSA 50.76*, **HJ:** Idrissa Ndoye SEN 2.10, **PV:** Hamdi Dhouibi TUN 4.60, **LJ:** Jonathan Chimier MRI 7.48, **TJ:** Abdou Demba Lam SEN 15.11, **SP:** Yasser Ibrahim Farag EGY 15.44, **DT:** Ihab Ahmed Ali EGY 50.07, **HT:** Nicholas Li Yun Fong MRI 59.44, **JT:** Willie Human RSA 77.45*, **10kW:** Abderahmane Rahma ALG 47:29.9, **4x100m:** MRI 41.50, **4x400m:** RSA 3:14.14. **Women: 100m/LJ:** Ifiburo Tobin-West 11.86/5.93, **200m:** Taissir Amal MAR 24.22, **400m/Hep:** Glory Nwosu NGR 54.10/5111, **800m: 1500m:** Zanelle Grobler RSA 4:23.33, **5000m:** Vivian

Cheruiyot KEN 16:19.54, **10,000m**: Caroline Chepwony KEN 35:04.96, **100mh**: *not held*, **400mh**: Catherine Obilor NGR 60.14, **HJ**: Marizca Gertenbach RSA 1.77, **PV**: Maha Abdel Malek EGY 3.35, **TJ**: Mahaliona Ramanitra MAD 12.07, **SP**: Helda Marie SEY 13.58, **DT**: Amina Moudden MAR 45.44, **HT**: Raoudh Abdel Hussein EGY 48.79*, **JT**: Hana Ramadan EGY 45.30, **5000mW**: Nicolene Cronje RSA 24:48.89, **4x100m**: MRI 49.15, **4x400m**: NGR 3:50.53.

XII Pan-Arab Championships 2001

October 2-5, Damascus, Syria

Men: **100m**: Salem Al-Yami KSA 10.2, **200m**: Hammoud Al-Dalhami OMN 20.7, **400m**: Salaheddine Bakar Safi QAT 45.9, **800m**: Abou Ibrahim Youssef QAT 1:47.3, **1500m**: Jamal Noor Youssef QAT 3:52.72, **5000m/10,000m**: Mohamed Yagoub SUD 14:45.89/29:30.2, **HMar**: Ali M Zaïdi LBA 61:40 short?, **3000mSt**: Khamis Seif Abdullah QAT 8:14.38, 110H: Mubarak Ata Mubarak KSA 13.6, 400H: Mubarak Al-Nubi QAT 50.07, **HJ**: Jean-Claude Rabbath LIB 2.07, **PV**: Fahid Al-Mershad KUW 4.90, **LJ**: Saïd Mansour QAT 7.94, **TJ**: Mohammed Hamdi Awadh QAT 16.51, **SP**: Bilal Saad Mubarak QAT 18.90, **DT**: Rashid Al-Dosari QAT 62.43, **HT**: Nasser Al-Jarallah KUW 70.19, **JT**: Walid Abderrazak EGY 77.55, **Dec**: Ahmad H Moussa QAT 7372, 20kmW: Yasser Aboud SYR 1:36:11, **4x100m**: KSA 39.69, **4x400m**: KUW 3:07.88. **Women**: **100m/200m**: Awatef Hamrouni TUN 12.1/24.98, **400m/400mh**: Awatef Benhassine TUN 54.7/64.4, **800m/1500m**: Abir Nakhli TUN 2:08.4/4:36.66, **5000m/10,000m**: Soulef Bouguerra TUN 17:04.1/35:32.48, **100mh/HJ**: Alaa Abdulhadi JOR 15.2/1.63, **PV**: Nesrine Himam EGY 3.20, **LJ**: Mona Sabri Mahmoud EGY 5.78, **TJ**: Ghada Ismail Mustafa EGY 12/40, **SP**: Amel Benkhaled TUN 15.80, **DT**: Hiba Zaghari EGY 48.76, **HT**: Marwa A Hussein EGY 61.48, **JT**: Aïda Sellam TUN 52.00, **10kW:** Najoua Ibrahim Ali EGY 51:21.2, **4x100m/4x400m**: EGY 49.10/3:55.69.

Asian Junior Championships 2001

July 19-22, B S Begawan, Brunei.

Men: **100m/200m**: Salem Moh. Al-Yami KSA 10.49/ 20.81w, **400m/400mh**: Hamed Hamadan Al-Bishi KSA 46.16/50.94, **800m**: Salam Amer Al-Badri QAT 1:51.15, **1500m**: Jamal Noor Youssef QAT 3:47.68, **5000m**: Abdulaziz Al-Ameri QAT 14:20.72, **10,000m**: Hamid Moh. Ahmad Adam QAT 30:56.38, **3000mSt**: Yoshiyuki Musha JPN 9:07.89, **110mh**: Shi Dongpeng CHN 14.05, **HJ**: Park Jun-hwan KOR 2.15, **PV**: Sompong Sambankruay THA 4.60, **LJ**: Chao Chih-Chien TPE 7.66, **TJ**: Wang Yinglei CHN 15.99, **SP**: Amit Tyagi IND 17.66, **DT**: Tao CHN 60.14, **HT**: Dilshod Nazarov TJK 68.08, **JT**: Chen Qi CHN 77.22, **Dec**: Pavel Dubitskiy KAZ 705, **10kW**: Zhu Hongjun CHN 43:16.67, **4x100m**: THA 40.11, **4x400m**: JPN 3:12.22. **Women**: **100m/200m**: Ni Xiaoli CHN 11.74/23.91w, **400m**: Zhai Lin CHN/83 53.91, **800m/1500m**: Yang Wei CHN 2:08.77/4:28.36, **5000m/10,000m**: Zhang Yuhong CHN 16:17.80/35:28.24, **100mh**: Yelena Nikitenko KAZ 13.91, **400mh**: Chiu Hsiao-Chuan TPE 62.81, **HJ**: Marina Korzhova KAZ 1.85, **PV**: Sun Yufei CHN 4.11, **LJ**: Zhou Yangxia CHN 6.21, **TJ**: Tatyana Bocharova KAZ 13.24, **SP**: Zhang Xiaoyu CHN 18.04, **DT**: Xu Shaoyang CHN 58.03, **HT**: Yang Meiping CHN 65.21, **JT**: Yi Chunmei CHN 56.43, **Hep**: Anna Karpova KAZ 4992, **5000mW**: Sachiko Konishi JPN 48:12.05, **4x100m**: JPN 46.11, **4x400m**: CHN 3:41.65. **Medal Table Leaders**: CHN 19G-10B-3S, KAZ 5-0-0, JPN 4-8-12, QAT 4-5-2, KSA 4-0-0, TPE 2-3-9, THA 2-1-2, IND 1-6-3, KOR 1-3-2; 21 nations won medals.

56th Balkan Championships 2001

July 7-8, Tríkala, GRE. Marathons at Istanbul, TUR Nov 11, Walks at Parálio Ástros, GRE April 21

Men: 100m: Aléxandros Kóntzos GRE 10.58, **200m**: Panayiótis Sarris GRE 21.02, **400m**: Alexandru Mardan ROM 46.32, **800m**: Stelian Tufaru ROM 1:50.56, **1500m**: Panayotis Stroubakos GRE 3:42.03, **3000m**: Clement Hagima ROM 8:19.45, **5000m**: Dragoslav Prpa YUG 14:05.11, **Mar**: Sreten Ninkovic YUG 2:18:22, **3000mSt**: Iaroslav Musinschi MDA 8:49.61, **110mh**: Ioánnis Marakákis GRE 14.28, **400mh**: Ilya Dzhivondov BUL 50.98, **HJ**: Angel Kararadev BUL 2.23, **PV**: Spass Buchalov BUL 5.35, **LJ**: Mesut Yavas TUR 7.85, **TJ**: Marian Oprea ROM 16.78, **SP**: Gheorghe Guset ROM 20.38, **DT**: Sávvas Panávoglou 60.43, **HT**: Aléxandros Papadimitríou GRE 77.59, **JT**: Elefthérios Karasmanákis GRE 73.24, **4x100m**: ROM 40.12, **4x400m**: GRE 3:06.76, 20km: Costica Balan ROM 1:22:44.
Team: 1. GRE 132, 2, YUG 111.5, 3, ROM 110.5, 4, BUL 99, 5, TUR 53, 6, MKD 45, 7, ALB 42, 8, MDA 25.
Women: 100m: Ioánna Kafetzí GRE 11.71, **200m**: Monika Gachevska BUL 23.92, **400m**: Monica Bumbescu ROM 53.45, **800m**: Tsvetelina Kirilova BUL 2:02.33, **1500m**: Karolína Skoúrti 4:15.04, **3000m**: Hrisostomía Iakóvou 9:00.90, **5000m**: Luminita Gogîrlea ROM 16:28.18, **Mar**: Mehtap Sizmaz TUR 2:39:13, **100mh**: Hristiána Tabáki GRE 13.55, **400mh**: Eléni Kaloyírou GRE 58.44, **HJ**: Eleonora Milusheva BUL 1.90, **PV**: Tanya Koleva BUL 4.25, **LJ**: Antonia Yordanova BUL 6.42, **TJ**: Adelina Gavrila ROM 14.18, **SP**: Elena Hila ROM 17.57, **DT**: Aretí Abatzí 60.75, **HT**: Evdokía Tsámoglou GRE 65.05, **JT**: Hristina Georgieva BUL 56.09, **4x100m**: GRE 44.40, **4x400m**: BUL 3:35.91, 20km: Ana-Maria Groza ROM 1:32:12.
Team: 1. GRE 129.5, 2. ROM 107, 3. YUG 101, 4. BUL 96, 5. MKD 46, 6. ALB 40, 7. TUR 28.5, 8. MDA 7.

XVIII Central American and Caribbean Championships 2001

July 18-22, Guatemala City, Guatemala (altitude 1487m)

Men: 100m/200m: Kim Collins SKN 10.04*/20.55, **400m**: Danny McFarlane JAM 45.20, **800m**: Norberto

Téllez CUB 1:46.51, **1500m/3000mSt**: Salvador Miranda MEX 3:46.78/8:50.36, **5000m**: Teodoro Vega MEX 14:00.46, **10,000m**: Isaac Gómez MEX 30:40.96, **HMar**: Procopio Franco MEX 66:33, **110mh**: Maurice Wignall JAM 13.76, **400mh**: Mario Watts JAM 49.31, **HJ**: Henderson Dottin BAR 2.20, **PV**: Dominic Johnson LCA 5.20, **LJ**: Kareem Streete-Thompson CAY 7.97, **TJ**: Brian Wellman BER 17.24, **SP**: Yoger Medina VEN 18.86, **DT**: Michel Hemmings CUB 57.69, **HT**: Yosmel Monte CUB 69.24, **JT**: Manuel Fuenmayor VEN 68.73, **Dec**: Maurice Smith JAM 7755*, **4x100m**: BAH 39.27, **4x400m**: JAM 3:00.83*, **20kW**: Luis García GUA 1:25:44. **Women**: **100m**: Liliana Allen MEX 11.32, **200m**: Cydonie Mothersill CAY 22.54, **400m**: Michelle Burgher JAM 53.04, **800m/1500m**: Yanelis Lara CUB 2:01.86/4:32.37, **5000m/10,000m**: América Mateos MEX 16:27.59/34:42.91, **HMar**: Mariela González CUB 78:33, **100mh**: Dainelky Pérez CUB 13.31, **400mh**: Yvonne Harrison PUR 55.86, **HJ**: Lavern Spencer LCA 1.80, **PV**: Katiuska Pérez CUB 3.85*, **LJ**: Elva Goulbourne JAM 6.77, **TJ**: Trecia-Kaye Smith 14.12, **SP**: Misleidi González CUB 17.20, **DT**: Yania Ferrales CUB 56.34, **HT**: Yunaika Crawford CUB 58.68*, **JT**: Laverne Eve BAH 59.30, **4x100m/4x400m**: JAM 43.83*/3:33.96, **10kW**: Rosario Sánchez MEX 45:47*. **Medal Table Leaders**: CUB 11G-6B-4S, JAM 10-10-0, MEX 9-13-8, VEN 2-7-4, PUR 2-4-6, BAH 2-1-2, CAY, LCU & SKN 2-0-0, BAR & GUA 1-1-6. 18 nations won medals.

VII Central American Games 2001

Nov 29- Dec 1, Guatemala City (A).

Men 100m: Bob Colville CRC 10.54*, **200m**: Rolando Blanco GUA 21.17*, **400m**: Álvaro James CRC 46.83*, **800m**: César Arias ESA 1:56.82, **1500m**: Jefry Pérez CRC 3:59.68, **5000m**: José Amada García GUA 14:28.91, **10,000m/3000mSt**: Francisco Gómez CRC 30:30.91/9:12.83, Mar: Rafael Yax GUA 2:29:17, **110mh**: Yefry Pacheco GUA 14.55*, **400mh**: Roberto Cortez ESA 52.51*, **HJ**: Alton Berry BIZ 1.95, **PV**: N.Jorge Solórzano GUA 4.60*, **LJ**: Angelo Iannuzzelli ESA 7.17, **TJ**: Álvaro Paiz GUA 14.94, **SP**: Edson Monzón GUA 15.79, **DT**: Herbert Rodríguez ESA 48.06*, **HT**: Raúl Rivera GUA 61.83, **JT**: Rigoberto Calderón NCA 68.69, **20kW**: Luis F García GUA 1:27:52, **4x100m**: CRC 40.57, **4x400m**: ESA 3:15.71*. **Women**: **100m/200m**: Gabriela Petterson CRC 11.92*/24.21, **400m/100mh/400mh** Verónica Quijano ESA 54.72*/14.64w/59.20, **800m**: Ana Gabriela Quezada ESA 2:09.68*, **1500m/5000m/10,000m**: Elsa Monterroso GUA 4:34.55*/17:19.10/36:06.26*, Mar: Kriscia Lorena García ESA 3:02.25, **HJ**: Ana Regina Quiñones GUA 1.70, **PV**: Michelle Rivera ESA 3.40*, **LJ/TJ**: María José Paiz GUA 5.66/12.12*, **SP**: Eva María Dimas ESA 13.28*, **DT**: Ana Lucía Espinoza GUA 48.25*, **HT**: Nancy Guillén ESA 55.99*, **JT**: Dalila Rugama NCA 44.16*, **20kW**: Teresita Collado GUA 1:40:29*, **4x100m/4x400m**: ESA 46.93*/3:49.71*.

East Asian Games 2001

May 23-26, Osaka, Japan.

Men: 100m: Gennadiy Chernovol KAZ 10.28, **200m**: Shingo Suetsugu 20.34*, **400m**: Xu Zizhou CHN 45.25, **800m/1500m**: Mikhail Kolganov KAZ 1:49.00/3:46.43*, **5000m**: Toshinari Takaoka 13:56.23, **10,000m**: Katsuhiko Hanada 28:42.19*, **HMar**: Kazuo Ietani 64:49*, **3000mSt**:: Yasunori Uchitomi 8:33.98, **110mh**: Liu Xiang CHN 13.42*, **400mh**: Chen Tien-Wen TPE 49.18*, **HJ**: Lee Jin-taek KOR 2.23, **PV**: Manabu Yokoyama 5.60, **LJ**: Wang Cheng CHN 8.07, **TJ**: Gu Junjie CHN 16.56, **SP**: Liu Hao CHN 18.70, **DT**: Li Shaojie CHN 60.08, **HT**: Koji Murofushi 79.68*, **JT**: Li Rongxiang CHN 81.55*, **Dec**: Dmitriy Karpov 7567; **20kW**: Li Zewen CHN 1:24:10, **4x100m**: JPN (Kawabata, Yasui, Suetsugu, Ishizuka) 38.93*, **4x400m**: JPN (Sato, Osakada, Tamesue, Muraki) 3:03.74*. **Women** – **100m**: Zeng Xiujun CHN 11.48, **200m**: Liu Xiaomei CHN 22.87, **400m**: Bo Fanfang CHN 52.31, **800m**: Wang Yuanping CHN 2:03.21, **1500m**: Li Jingnan CHN 4:12.13, **5000m/10,000m**: Dong Yanmei CHN 15:32.71*/32:30.35, HMar: Mizuki Noguchi 71:18*, **100mh**: Feng Yun CHN 13.12*, **400mh**: Li Yulian CHN 56.43, **HJ**: Miki Imai 1.92*, **PV**: Gao Shuying CHN 4.20, **LJ**: Guan Yingnan CHN 6.61, **TJ**: Ren Ruiping CHN 13.80, **SP**: Cheng Xiaoyan CHN 18.47, **DT**: Li Qiumei CHN 60.99, **HT**: Zhao Wei CHN 63.98, **JT**: Wei Jianhui CHN 61.10, **Hep**: Svetlana Kazanina KAZ 6078*, **20kW**: Liu Hongyu CHN 1:32:06, **4x100m**: CHN (Zeng Xiujun, Liu Xiaomei, Qin Wangping, Li Xuemei) 44.08*, **4x400m**: CHN (Yan Jiankui, Li Yulian, Chen Yuxiang, Bo Fanfang) 3:30.51*.

6th European Youth Olympics Festival 2001

July 23-26, Murcia, Spain

Men: 100m/200m: Ivor Tit Jurisic CRO 10.70/21.61, **400m**: Piotr Zrada POL 47.03, **800m**: David Fiegen LUX 1:54.18, **1500m**: Olle Walleraeng SWE 3:57.59, **3000m**: Mark Shankey GBR 8:35.65, **2000mSt**: Milos Vuckovic YUG 5:48.43, **110mh** (91.4cm): Markus Tuomela FIN 13.46*, **400mh**: Rhys Williams GBR 53.42, **HJ**: Aleksey Dmitrik RUS 2.14, **PV**: Vladislav Revenko UKR 5.10*, **LJ**: Nelson Evora POR 7.49, **SP** (5kg): Georgi Ivanov BUL 19.63, **DT** (1.5kg): Andriy Semenov UKR 60.72, **4x100m**: FRA 41.92. **Women: 100m**: Jade Lucas-Read GBR 11.82w, **200m**: Jenny Ljunggren SWE 24.26, **400m**: Marita Driakhlova RUS 54.88, **800m**: Kitty Cziraki HUN 2:09.39, **1500m**: Katrina Wootton GBR 4:32.62, **3000m**: Snezana Kostic YUG 9:48.26, **100mh** (76.2cm): Sabrina Altermatt SUI 13.40*, **400mh**: Olga Nikolayeva RUS 59.33*, **HJ**: Emma Green SWE 1.82, **PV**: Aleksandra Kiryashova RUS 4.00*, **LJ**: Margerethe Renstrøm NOR 6.15, **SP**: Yuliya Leantsyuk BLR 14.47, **DT**: Darya Pishchalnikov RUS 53.93*, **JT**: Ilze Gribule LAT 49.27, **4x100m**: RUS 46.45.

XIV Mediterranean Games 2001

September 11-14, Tunis, Tunisia

Men: 100m: Aristotélis Gavélas GRE 10.14w, **200m**:

Anninos Marcoullides 20.60, **400m**: Malik Louahala ALG 45.56, **800m**: Adem Hecini ALG 1:49.21, **1500m**: Abdelkader Hachlaf MAR 3:46.45, **5000m**: Mohamed Khaldi 14:06.30, **10,000m**: Jaouad Gharib MAR 28:58.97, **Mar**: Sergio Chiesa ITA 2:21:07, **3000mSt**: Antonio Jiménez ESP 8:31.31, **110mh**: Vincent Clarico FRA 13.62, **400mh**: Periklís Iakovákis GRE 50.21, **HJ**: Abderrahmane Hammad ALG 2.25, **PV**: Andrea Giannini ITA 5.45, **LJ**: Sinisa Ergotic CRO 8.08, **TJ**: Fabrizio Donato ITA 17.05, **SP**: Manuel Martínez ESP 21.03*, **DT**: Diego Fortuna ITA 64.40, **HT**: David Chaussinand FRA 79.71, **JT**: Laurent Dorique FRA 80.88, **Dec**: Pródromos Korkízoglou GRE 7773w, **4x100m**: ITA 39.14, **4x400m**: GRE 3:07.28, **20kW**: Hatem Ghoula TUN 1:26:43. **Women: 100m/200m**: Nora Güner TUR 11.25/22.86w, **400m**: Marie-Louise Bévis FRA 52.90, **800m**: Seltana Aït Hammou MAR 2:04.28, **1500m**: Fatma Lanouar TUN 4:10.33, **5000m**: Ebru Kavaklioglu 15:26.33, **10,000m**: Asmae Leghzaoui 31:16.94*, **Mar**: Mehtap Sizmaz TUR 2:40:49, **3000mSt**: Elodie Olivarès FRA 9:44.68*, **100mh**: Patricia Girard FRA 12.82, **400mh**: Sylvanie Morandais FRA 57.02, **HJ**: Blanka Vlasic CRO 1.90, **PV**: Dana Cervantes ESP 4.10, **LJ**: Concepción Montaner ESP 6.48, **TJ**: Baya Rahouli ALG 14.30w, **SP**: Assunta Legnante ITA 17.23, **DT**: Aretí Abatzí GRE 61.42, **HT**: Florence Ezeh FRA 64.59, **JT**: Claudia Coslovich ITA 62.02, **Hep**: Anzhela Atroshchenko TUR 5833, **4x100m/4x400m** FRA 44.40/3:34.26, **20kW**: Erica Alfridi ITA 1:36:47

Pan-American Junior Championships 2001

October 18-20, Santa Fé, Argentina

Men: **100m**: Marc Burns TRI 10.28, **200m**: Alianny Echeverría CUB 21.16, **400m**: Damian Barry TRI 46.40, **800m**: Simoncito Silvera VEN 1:50.95, **1500m**: Fabiano Peçanha BRA 3:50.38, **5000m**: Fernando Fernandes BRA 14:34.15, **10,000m**: Franck de Almeida BRA 30:28.73, **3000mSt**: Mariano Mastromarino ARG 9:04.54, **110mh**: Thiago Dias BRA 14.24, **400mh**: José Ferrín ECU 53.05, **HJ**: Lysvanni Pérez CUB 2.18, **PV**: Jorge Naranjo CHI 5.30, **LJ**: Cleavon Dillon TRI 7.77, **TJ**: Yoandri Betanzos CUB 16.47, **SP**: Jeffrey Chakouian USA 19.92*, **DT**: Héctor Hurtado VEN 52.90, **HT**: Fabián Di Paolo ARG 65.04, **JT**: Trevor Snyder CAN 74.06*, **Dec**: Iván S C da Silva BRA 7107, **10kW**: Horacio Nava MEX 43:33.92, **4x100m/4x400m**: BRA 40.33/3:10.98. **Women**: **100m**: Thatiana Ignâcio BRA 11.54, **200m/400m**: Norma González COL 23.88w/53.38, **800m**: Janiel Williams ANT 2:13.36, **1500m**: Adriana Muñoz CUB 4:36.73, **3000m**: Inés Melchor PER 10:11.50, **5000m**: Janil Williams ANT 17:22.13, **100mh**: Ashley Purnell CAN 14.29, **400mh**: Perla R dos Santos BRA 56.52*, **HJ**: Kristen Matthews CAN 1.77, **PV**: Lacy Janson USA 3.85, **LJ**: Fernanda Gonçalves BRA 6.10, **TJ**: Mabel Gay CUB 13.63*, **SP**: Jillian Camarena USA 15.90, **DT**: Melisa Bickett USA 49.36, **HT**: Yunaika Crawford CUB 63.20*, **JT**: Ana Gutiérrez MEX 49.23, **Hep**: Valeria Steffens CHI 4956, **10kW**: Cristina López ESA 51:41.9*, **4x100m/4x400m**: BRA 45.36/3:45.84. **Medal Table Leaders**: BRA 12G-11S-7B, CUB 6-0-2, USA 4-1-2, CAN 3-5-3, TRI 3-1-3, VEN 2-5-4, MEX 2-4-5, ARG 2-4-3, COL 2-3-4, CHI 2-2-1, ANT 2-0-0, ECU 1-1-2. 18 nations won medals (14 gold).

33rd 2001 South American Junior Championships

October 12-13, Santa Fe, Argentina.
The medalists of 10000m, 10000m W, and both combined events were obtained from the classification of those events at the Pan American Junior Championships, that took place a week later on the same track.

Men: 100m: Bruno Campos BRA 10.62, **200m**: Bruno Pacheco BRA 21.26, **400m/800m**: Simoncito Silvera VEN 46.54/1:48.53*, **1500m**: Fabiano Peçanha BRA 3:52.21, **5000m**: Fernando Fernandes BRA 14:30.56, **10,000m**: Franck de Almeida BRA 30:28.73, **3000mSt**: Mariano Mastromarino ARG 8:54.51*, **110mh/LJ**: Thiago Dias BRA 14.39/7.43w, **400mh**: Denis de Santana BRA 52.34, **HJ**: Santiago Guerci ARG 2.09, **PV**: José Francisco Nava CHI 4.90, **TJ**: Jefferson Sabino BRA 15.56, **SP**: Gustavo de Mendonça BRA 16.81*, **DT**: Germán Lauro ARG 51.68, **HT**: Fabián Di Paolo ARG 63.97, **JT**: Alexon Maximiano BRA 71.31*, **Dec**: Ivan S da Silva 7107, **4x100m/4x400m**: BRA 40.17*/3:08.45*, **10kW**: Andrés Chocho ECU 43:58.89

Women: 100m: Thatiana Ignâcio BRA 11.64, **200m/400m**: Norma González COL 23.67*/54.06*, **800m/1500m**: Juliana de Azevedo BRA 2:08.84/4:42.84, **3000m**: Eliane Cardozo BRA 10:12.75, **5000m**: Inés Melchor PER 17:14.49, **3000mSt**: Giovanna Costa BRA 11:04.12, **100mh**: Janaína Sestrem BRA 14.60, **400mh**: Perla R dos Santos BRA 58.96*, **HJ**: Katherine Ibargüen COL 1.77, **PV**: Alina Alló ARG 3.80*, **LJ/TJ**: Keila da Silva BRA 6.20/13.66*, **SP**: Yanira Hurtado VEN 14.10, **DT**: Yesenia Gauna VEN 44.60, **HT**: Jennifer Dahlgren ARG 57.50*, **JT**: Leryn Franco PAR 47.01, **Hep**: Valeria Steffens CHI 4956, **4x100m/4x400m**: BRA 45.09*/3:41.04, **10kW**: Alessandra Picagevicz BRA 52:03.9. **Medal Table Leaders**: BRA 26G-13S-15B, ARG 6-7-10, VEN 4-10-4, COL 3-7-5, CHI 2-3-5, ECU 1-1-1, PER 1-0-2, PAR 1-0-0. 10 nations won medals.

XXI South East Asia Games 2001

September 12-16, Kuala Lumpur, Malaysia

Men: **100m**: Reanchai Srihawong THA 10.29/20.95, **400m**: Ernie Candelario PHI 46.59, **800m**: John Lozada PHI 1:49.39, **1500m**: Arumugam Munusamy MAS 3:50.53, **5000m/3000mSt**: Eduardo Buenavista PHI 14:15.13/8:40.77*, **10,000m**: Aung Thuya MYA 30:51.41, **Mar**: Roy Vence PHI 2:23:51, **110mh**: Nur Herman Majid MAS 14.02*, **400mh**: Jirachai Linglom THA 50.63, **HJ**: Loo Kum Zee MAS 2.18, **PV**: Teh Weng Chang MAS 4.90, **LJ/TJ**: Nattaporn Nomkanha

THA 7.73/16.37*, **SP**: Chatchawal Polyemg THA 17.26*, **DT**: James Wong Tuck Yim SIN 56.98, **HT**: Wong Tee Kue MAS 57.07, **JT**: Therdsak Boonchansri THA 72.89*, **Dec**: Fidel Gallenero PHI 6958, **20kW**: Teoh Boon Lim MAS 1:32:46, **50kW**: Govindasamy Saravanan MAS 4:34:04*, **4x100m/4x400m**: THA 39.66/3:07.81. **Women**: **100m/200m**: Supavadee Khawpeag THA 11.33/23.30*, **400m**: Wassana Winatho THA 53.46, **800m/1500m**: Pham Dinh Khanh Doan VIE 2:10.02/4:21.87, **5000m/10,000m**: Supriati Sutono INA 16:08.93*/33:50.06*, **Mar**: Cristabel Martes PHI 2:52:43, **100mh**: Trecia Roberts THA 13.21, **400mh**: Wassana Winatho THA 57.09, **HJ**: Netnapa Thaiking THA 1.80, **PV**: Ni Putu Desy Margawati INA 3.90*, **LJ**: Pham Thi Thu Lan VIE 6.46, **TJ**: Wacharee Ritthiwat THA 13.46, **SP/DT**: Juttaporn Krasaeyan THA 17.24/48.08, **HT**: Benchamas Ounkaew THA 49.84*, **JT**: Buaban Phamang THA 54.80*, **Hep**: Elma Muros Posadas PHI 5059, **20kW**: Yuan Yufang MAS 1:42:55*, **4x100m/4x400m**: THA 44.58/3:38.70.
Medal Table: THA 22-8-11, PHI 8-11-4, MAS 8-5-9, INA 3-13-6, VIE 3-4-10, MYA 1-3-5, SIN 1-2-1.

IAU 100km World Championships 2001

Aug 26, Cléder, France
Men: 1. Yasufumi Mikami JPN 6:33:28, 2. Rich Hanna USA 6:43:9, 3. Pascal Fétizon FRA 6:44:48, 4. Thierry Guichard FRA 6:45:47, 5. Jean-Marie Gehin FRA 6:46:36, 6. Pascal Piveteau FRA 6:47:23
Team: 1. FRA 20:17:11, 2. BEL 21:03:42, 3. GER 21:07:28
Women: 1. Elvira Kolpakova RUS 7:31:12, 2. Marina Bychkova RUS 7:38:21, 3. Monica Casiraghi ITA 7:39:42, 4. Tanja Schäfer GER 7:43:40, 5. Akiko Sekiya JPN 7:50:58, 6. Karine Herry FRA 7:54:27
Team: 1. RUS 23:31:12, 2. FRA 24:10:21, 3. GER..

IAU 24 Hours World Challenge 2001

Sep 23, San Giovanni Lupatoto. Verona. Italy
Men: 1. Yiannis Kouros GRE 275,828k, 2. Lubomir Hrmo SVK 270,337, 3. Alain Prual FRA 259,778, 4. Loic Lebon FRA 257,064, 5. Jaroslav Kocourek CZE 256,398, 6. Kenji Okiyama JPN 254,856
Women: 1. Edith Bercés HUN 235,029, 2. Irina Reutovich RUS 226,781, 3. Irina Koval RUS 222,445, 4. Hiroko Okiyama JPN 221,911, 5. Véronique Jeannot FRA 221,071, 6. Rimma Paltseva RUS 218,321

24 Hours European Challenge 2001

May 24-25, Apeldoorn, Netherlands
Men: 1. Paul Beckers BEL 260.559k, 2. Jens Lukas GER 258.907, 3. Vladimir Kurbatov RUS 252.801;
Women: 1. Irina Reutovich RUS 226.634k, 2. Irina Koval RUS 222.650, 3. Helga Backhaus GER 212.692.

European Mountain Racing Trophy 2001

July 1, Cerklje. Slovakia
Men: **9k**: 1. Antonio Molinari ITA 49:47, 2. Martin Bajcicak 50:01, 3. Raymond Fontaine FRA 50:14, **Team**: 1. ITA 16, 2. FRA 19, 3. AUT 31
Women: 1. Svetlana Demidenko RUS 56:30, 2. Angela Mudge SCO 57:08, 3. Catherine Lallemand BEL 57:28, **Team**: 1. FRA 30, 2. ENG 37, 3. ITA 45

World Mountain Racing Trophy 2001

Sep 15-16, Atra Terme. Italy
Men (12965m, 949m uphill): 1. Marco De Gaspari ITA 61:05, 2. Emanuele Manzi ITA 61:08, 3. Billy Burns GBR 61:21, 4. Alexis Gex-Fabry SUI 61:54, 5. Lucio Fregona ITA 62:04, **Team**: 1. ITA 19, 2. FRA 39, 3, ENG 104
Junior Men (8533m, 590m uphill): Stefano Scaini ITA 34:21, **Team**: ITA
Women (8533m, 590m uphill): 1. Melissa Moon NZL 38:02, 2. Anna Pichrtová CZE 38:17, 3. Izabela Zatorska POL 38:50, 4. Svetlana Demidenko RUS 38:57, 5. Angela Mudge SCO 39:28, **Team**: 1. ITA 38, 2. POL 41, 3. AUT 50
Junior Women (5416m, 325m uphill): Lea Vetsch SUI 27:25, **Team**: POL
** = Championships record throughout this section*

Winter Olympics 2002

MANY ATHLETES have successfully compted at bobsleigh in recent years, proving especially well-suited to the power needed to ensure fast starts for the bob. The two-woman event was introduced for the first time at the Winter Games in Salt Lake City 2002 and the US team of Jill Bakken and Vonetta Flowers won the gold medal. Flowers (née Jeffrey) (b. 29 Oct 1973), the first African-American to win a Winter Olympic medal, had pbs of 100m 11.32/ 11.31w (1995), 200m 23.05 (1995) and long jump 6.62 (1994). She is an assistant coach at the University of Alabama/Birmingham.

Winning silver medals with the US 4-man bob were Roddy Jones (100m 10.38), Garrett Hines (200m 20.97 '92) and Bill Schuffenhauer (8108 decathlon in 1997). Dan Steele (8130 decathlon in 1999, when he was 2nd at the Pan-Ams and 8th Worlds) won a bronze medal.

Other competitors included Torsten Voss, European 4-man gold medallist in 2001. He set the still-standing world junior record for the decathlon worth 8397 points in 1982 and won the World title in 1987 with 8680 and the Olympic silver in 1988.

IAAF GRAND PRIX

INTRODUCED IN 1985, the Grand Prix links the world's leading invitational meetings, so that athletes earn points over the season, with a final contested by the leaders in the points tables. Half the standard events are held each year. There is an Individual Event Grand Prix for each event and an Overall Grand Prix for men and women. There is now a three-tier Grand Prix structure. From 1998 the top GP meetings constitute the IAAF Golden League, and below them are Grand Prix I and Grand Prix II meetings.

Qualified athletes for the Grand Prix are those who, in the current or preceding year have achieved a performance equal to or better than the 50th best in the world in the past year.

Scoring

- Golden League meetings: 12 points for 1st, then 10-9-8-7-6-5-4 for 2nd to 8th
- GP I meetings: 8 points for 1st, then 7-6-5-4-3-2-1 for 2nd to 8th
- GP II meetings: 5 points for 1st, then 4-3-2-1 for 2nd to 5th
- Long throws events in GP II events score as GP I.
- Additional points are awarded in GP events prior to the GP Final: 6 for breaking a world record, 3 for equalling a world record.
- Athletes qualify for the Grand Prix Final on their total points over the season from a maximum of eight meetings for each designated event.
- IAAF GP Final: 24 points for 1st, then 21-18-15-12-9-6-3 for 2nd to 8th

Award structure

Men's and women's overall Grand Prix awards (all events): first $200,000, second $100,000, third $50,000, fourth $20,000, fifth $15,000, sixth $13,000, seventh $12,000, eight $10,000.
World record (broken not equalled) $100,000

Prize Money Structure

The standard prize money structure for GP meetings is as follows (in Euros) – 1st column for IAAF Golden League Premium Events, 2nd column for Golden League Classic Events, 3rd column for individual events at the IAAF Grand Prix Final.

Place	GL -P	GL -C	GP Final
1st	15,000	7500	$50,000
2nd	10,000	6000	30,000
3rd	6000	4000	20,000
4th	4000	2500	10,000
5th	3000	2000	8000
6th	2000	1000	7000
7th	1500	1000	6000
8th	1000	750	5000

In addition a Golden League Jackpot of 50 kilograms of gold is divided equally among all athletes who won the same discipline at each GL meeting and the Final.
A bonus of 50,000 Euros is available for a world record set in any of the designated Golden League disciplines in a GL meeting.
For the women's javelin, where the record with the new implement was established from 1 January 2000, the same rule applies as in the IAAF World Championships – the record bonus would be reduced by 50% in the first year and by 25% in the second year following the adoption of the new standard.

IAAF Golden League

The Golden League was initiated in 1998, bringing together the six leading Grand Prix meetings – Oslo, Zürich, Brussels, Berlin, Monte Carlo and Rome. In 1999 a seventh, Paris, was added. In 1998 and 1999 a jackpot of $1 million was divided among any athletes winning all of his or her Golden League events (provided that they also competed at the Grand Prix Final). A special bonus of $50,000 was paid to anyone breaking a world record in one of the Golden League events.

The IAAF Council decided that, in the interest of the athletes during an Olympic year, the Golden League Jackpot would be made easier to win in 2000. The IAAF Golden League Jackpot (50kg of gold bars) was to be shared among those competitors who win five Golden League events in total, as against the seven victories which were required in 1999. All Golden League meetings would therefore contain all the Golden League events, so that competitors had a choice of which meetings in which to participate. Jackpot contenders had to also compete (but not necessarily win) in the IAAF Grand Prix Final.

The seven Golden League meets had a revised format in 2001 in a move that organizers hoped would draw larger crowds and TV audiences. The 14 events in each meet were divided into premium events and classic events. The winners of premium events collected 15,000 Euro, with 7500 Euro going to classic event winners. There was no change, however, in the Golden League jackpot payout. Any athlete winning five of the seven meets – in a premium or classic event – collected a share of the end-of-season 50 kilograms of gold.
The men's premium events in 2001 were: 100m, 800m, 1500m or mile, and 3000m or 5000m. For women: 100m, 800m and 3000m or 5000m.

The classic events for men in 2001 were: 110m hurdles, 3000m steeplechase, javelin and long jump. For women: 1500m or mile, 400m hurdles and high jump.

The IAAF decided in December 2000 to maintain its current seven-meet format and venues through to 2002. The only change in 2002 will be moving the Oslo, Norway, meet from July 19 to June 27 to start the series. The IAAF Council has however deceided to reduce the Golden League to five meetings from 2003.

Golden League Jackpot winners:

1998: Marion Jones (women's 100m), Hicham El Guerrouj (1500m), Haile Gebrselassie (3000m/5000m).

1999: Gabriela Szabo (W 3000m/5000m), Wilson Kipketer (800m).

2000: Gail Devers (W 100mh), Trine Hattestad (W JT), Tatyana Kotova (W LJ).

Maurice Greene (100m) and Hicham El Guerrouj (1500m/1M) lost their share as they did not compete in the GP Final.

2001: Marion Jones (W 100m), Violeta Szekely (W 1500m), Olga Yegorova (W 3000/5000m), André Bucher (800m), Hicham El Guerrouj (1500m), Allen Johnson (110mh)

Winners of IAAF Golden League Events 2001

Event	*Roma 29.6*	*Paris 6/7*	*Oslo 13/7*	*Monaco 20.7*	*Zürich 17/8*	*Brussels 24/8*	*Berlin 31/8*
Men							
100m	M Greene	M Greene	T Montgomery	B Williams	T Montgomery	T Montgomery	F Obikwelu
800m	A Bucher	A Bucher	W Bungei	A Bucher	A Bucher	Y Borzakovskiy	A Bucher
1500m	H El Guerrouj	H El Guerrouj	A Saïdi-Sief	R Silva	H El Guerrouj	H El Guerrouj	H El Guerrouj
3/5000m	H Mekonnen	L Kipkosgei	P Bitok	P Bitok	R Limo	H Mekonnen	P Bitok
3000mSt	R Kosgei	W Kipketer B	W Kipketer B	W Kipketer B	B Boulami	B Boulami	S Cherono
110mh	C Jackson	A Johnson	A Johnson	A Johnson	A Johnson	A García	A Johnson
LJ	K Dilworth	I Pedroso	K Dilworth	D Burkenya	K Dilworth	S Stringfellow	I Pedroso
JT	K Gatsioúdis	K Gatsioúdis	P Blank	P Fagernes	R Hecht	J Zelezny	J Zelezny
Women							
100m	M Jones	M Jones	M Jones	C Gaines	M Jones	M Jones	M Mani
800m	S Graf	S Graf	S Graf	M Mutola	M Mutola	S Graf	M Mutola
1500m	V Szekely	V Szekely	V Szekely	V Szekely	V Szekely	V Szekely	V Szekely
3/5000m	O Yegorova	O Yegorova	E Masai	E Masai	O Yegorova	O Yegorova	O Yegorova
400mh	N Bidouane	T Tereshchuk	T Tereshchuk	D Pernía	N Bidouane	N Bidouane	Y Nosova
HJ	K Bergqvist	V Veneva	I Babakova	K Bergqvist	H Cloete	V Palamar	K Bergqvist

GOLDEN LEAGUE 2002

The IAAF have determined that the Golden League for 2002 will follow a similar format to that of 2001. Individual events will be:

Men: Classic events: 100m, 1500m, 3000 or 5000m, 400mH; Premium events: PV, TJ

Women: Classic events: 100m, 1500m; Premium events: 400m, 3000m or 5000m, 100mH, JT

Meetings will be held:

Jun 28 – Oslo, Jul 5 – Paris Saint-Denis, Jul 12 – Rome, Jul 19 – Monaco, Aug 16 – Zürich, Aug 30 – Brussels, Sep 6 – Berlin.

Grand Prix meetings 2001

Golden League

Jun 29 Golden Gala, Rome, ITA
Jul 6 Gaz de France Paris Saint-Denis, FRA
Jul 13 Exxon Mobil Bislett Games, Oslo, NOR
Jul 20 Herculis Zepter, Monaco, MON
Aug 17 Weltklasse, Zürich, SUI
Aug 24 Memorial Ivo van Damme, Brussels, BEL
Aug 31 ISTAF, Berlin, GER
Sep 9 Grand Prix Final: Melbourne, AUS

Grand Prix I meetings

May 6 Grand Prix Brasil de Atletismo, Rio de Janeiro, BRA
May 12 Japan Grand Prix, Osaka, JPN
May 18 Qatar Athletic Grand Prix, Doha, QAT
May 27 Prefontaine Classic, Eugene, Oregon, USA
Jun 9 US Open, Stanford GP, Palo Alto, California, USA
Jun 11 Athens Grand Prix, GRE
Jul 4 Athletissima, Lausanne, SUI
Jul 9 Nikaïa, Nice, FRA
Jul 17 DN Galan, Stockholm, SWE
Jul 22 Norwich Union British Grand Prix London (CP), GBR

Grand Prix II meetings – staging up to six Grand Prix events with points 5-4-3-2-1 adding to the main GP points:

Mar 1 Melbourne Track Classic, AUS
Mar 23 Engen Grand Prix, Pretoria, RSA
Jun 3 Adidas Oregon Track Classic, (Portland) Gresham OR, USA
Jun 4 Fanny Blankers-Koen Games, Hengelo, NED
Jun 8 Gran Premio, Sevilla, ESP
Jun 12 Cena Slovenska, Bratislava, SVK
Jun 14 Ericsson GP, Helsinki, FIN
Jul 2 Zagreb Grand Prix, CRO
Aug 19 Norwich Union Classic, Gateshead
Aug 20 Gugl Grand Prix, Linz, AUT
Sep 2 Rieti

IAAF Permit meetings 2001

Sydney 16/2, Cape Town (Engen GP Final) 30/3, Fort-de-France 28/4, Milano 6/6, Tula (Znamenskiy Memorial) 8-9/6, Torino 9/6, Villeneuve d'Ascq (Lille) 17/6, Nürnberg 17/6, Budapest 1/7, Thessaloniki 22/8, Yokohama 15/9

IAAF GRAND PRIX FINAL 2001

At Melbourne, Australia 9 September
Results with scores (and positions in brackets) prior to the final, and leading scorers who did not compete in Melbourne.

Men

200 Metres (1.0)
1. Shawn Crawford USA 20.37 34 (4=)
2. Bernard Williams USA 20.39 35 (2=)
3. Francis Obikwelu NGR 20.52 25 (7)
4. Christian Malcolm GBR 20.55 35 (2=)
5. Christopher Williams JAM 20.59 38 (1)
6. Abdul Aziz Zakari GHA 20.63 30 (6)
7. Kevin Little USA 20.95 34 (4=)
8. André D da Silva BRA 21.26 23 (8=)

Other GP leaders prior to final: Ramon Clay USA 23, Stéphane Buckland MRI 22

800 Metres
1. André Bucher SUI 1:46.71 78 (1)
2. Yuriy Borzakovskiy RUS 1:46.78 56 (4)
3. Jean-Patrick Nduwimana BDI 1:46.88 59 (2)
4. William Yiampoy KEN 1:46.99 58 (3)
5. Joseph Mwengi Mutua KEN 1:47.09 32 (9)
6. Glody Dube BOT 1:47.15 36 (7)
7. Wilfred Bungei KEN 1:47.79 51 (5)
8. Hezekiél Sepeng RSA 1:48.81 44 (6)

Other GP leaders prior to final: Mbulaeni Mulaudzi RSA 33, William Chirchir KEN 19

1500 Metres
1. Hicham El Guerrouj MAR 3:31.25 76 (1)
2. Bernard Lagat KEN 3:32.10 73 (2)
3. William Chirchir KEN 3:34.06 33 (8=)
4. Noah Ngeny KEN 3:34.76 37 (5)
5. Laban Rotich KEN 3:35.13 43 (3)
6. Craig Mottram AUS 3:35.40 12 (20=)
7. Kevin Sullivan CAN 3:35.50 26 (11)
8. Driss Maazouzi FRA 3:35.99 33 (8=)
9. Vyacheslav Shabunin RUS 3:39.43 39 (4)
10. Enock Koech KEN 3:41.35 36 (6=)
11. Benjamin Kipkurui KEN 3:48.53 32 (10)

Other GP leaders prior to final: Ali Saïdi-Sief ALG 36, Andrés DiazESP 20

3000 Metres
1. Paul Bitok KEN 7:53.85 76 (1)
2. Kenenisa Bekele ETH 7:54.39 36 (8)
3. Luke Kipkosgei KEN 7:54.39 58 (2)
4. Benjamin Limo KEN 7:54.46 57 (3)
5. Richard Limo KEN 7:54.82 34 (9)
6. Sammy Kipketer KEN 7:54.98 42 (5=)
7. Abiyote Abate ETH 7:54.98 39 (7)
8. Hailu Mekonnen ETH 7:55.15 48 (4)
9. John Kibowen KEN 7:55.37 42 (5=)
10. Abderrahim Goumri MAR 7:56.43 27 (10=)

Other GP leaders prior to final: Daniel Komen KEN 27, Tom Nyariki KEN 26, Mark Bett KEN 25

3000 Metres Steeplechase
1. Brahim Boulami MAR 8:16.14 50 (3)
2. Reuben Kosgei KEN 8:17.64 49 (4)
3. Stephen Cherono KEN 8:18.85 32 (8=)
4. Kipkirui Misoi KEN 8:19.01 61 (1)
5. John Kosgei KEN 8:19.29 34 (7)
6. Luis Miguel Martín ESP 8:22.04 31 (10)
7. Julius Nyamu KEN 8:22.85 35 (6)
8. Raymond Yator KEN 8:31.21 36 (5)

dns. Wilson Boit Kipketer KEN 55 (2)

Other GP leaders prior to final: Bernard Barmasai KEN 32, Ali Ezzine MAR 29, Antonio Jiménez ESP 23

110 Metres Hurdles (-1.7)
1. Anier García CUB 13.22 71 (2)
2. Allen Johnson USA 13.28 80 (1)
3. Dominique Arnold USA 13.43 51 (6)
4. Dudley Dorival HAI 13.56 53 (5)
5. Colin Jackson GBR 13.68 48.5 (7)
6. Dawane Wallace USA 13.72 47 (8)
7. Terrence Trammell USA 14.17 65 (3)
8. Larry Wade USA 14.22 57 (4)

Other GP leaders prior to final: Shaun Bownes RSA 36, Mark Crear USA 32, Stanislavs Olijars LAT 30, Terry Reese USA 23

Long Jump
1. Younés Moudrik MAR 8.23/1.0 40 (7)
2. Savanté Stringfellow USA 8.19/1.4 49 (3)
3. Aleksey Lukashevich UKR 7.93/1.3 46 (5)
4. James Beckford JAM 7.92/1.9 38 (8)
5. Kareem Streete-Thompson CAY 7.87/0.8 43 (6)
6. Iván Pedroso CUB 7.83/1.0 48 (4)
7. Kevin Dilworth USA 7.81/1.6 78 (1)
8. Hussein Al-Sabee KSA 7.72/0.1 64 (2)

Other GP leaders prior to final: Vitaliy Shkurlatov RUS 36. Dwight Phillips USA 28, Melvin Lister USA 20

Discus
1. Virgilijus Alekna LTU 64.42 51 (1)
2. Aleksander Tammert EST 63.87 28 (7)
3. Frantz Kruger RSA 63.61 38 (3)
4. Adam Setliff USA 63.59 35 (4)
5. Jason Tunks CAN 62.78 47 (2)
6. Róbert Fazekas HUN 62.61 32 (5)
7. Dmitriy Shevchenko RUS 62.34 25 (8)
8. Vasiliy Kaptyukh BLR 61.60 29 (6)

Other GP leaders prior to final: Zoltán Kövágó HUN 22, Michael Möllenbeck GER 20

Javelin

1. Jan Zelezny CZE 88.98 50 (7)
2. Eriks Rags LAT 85.75 55 (4)
3. Boris Henry GER 85.43 66 (1)
4. Steve Backley GBR 85.38 52 (6)
5. Breaux Greer USA 82.63 49 (8)
6. Raymond Hecht GER 81.28 60 (2)
7. Dariusz Trafas POL 80.06 58 (3)
8. Peter Blank GER 73.82 53 (5)

Other GP leaders prior to final: Konstadínos Gatsioúdis GRE 39, Aki Parviainen FIN 36, Sergey Makarov RS 33, Harri Haatainen FIN & Gregor Högler AUT 23

Overall Final Standings

1. André Bucher SUI 102 78 (2=)
2. Allen Johnson USA 101 80 (1)
3. Hicham El Guerrouj MAR 100 76 (4=)
4. Paul Bitok KEN 100 76 (4=)
5. Anier García CUB 95 71 (7)
6. Bernard Lagat KEN 94 73 (6)
7. Boris Henry GER 84 66 (8)
8. Kevin Dilworth USA 84 78 (2=)
9. Yuriy Borzakovskiy RUS 77 56 (19)
10. Jean-Patrick Nduwimana BDI 77 59 (13)

Other GP leaders prior to final: 19. Terrence Trammell USA 71 65 (9)
27. Hussein Al-Sabee KSA 67 64 (10)

Women

200 Metres (-2.6)

1. Myriam Mani CMR 22.93 23 (5)
2. Kelli White USA 22.98 27 (4)
3. Debbie Ferguson BAH 23.00 30 (1)
4. Juliet Campbell JAM 23.15 28 (2=)
5. Beverly McDonald JAM 23.29 28 (2=)
6. Mercy Nku NGR 23.40 22 (6)
7. Lauren Hewitt AUS 23.88 0
8. Alenka Bikar SLO 24.04 14.5 (9)

Other GP leaders prior to final: LaTasha Jenkins USA 19, Marion Jones USA 16

800 Metres

1. Maria Lourdes Mutola MOZ 1:59.78 81 (1)
2. Kelly Holmes GBR 2:00.02 47 (5)
3. Stephanie Graf AUT 2:00.40 74 (2)
4. Zulia Calatayud CUB 2:00.89 39 (8)
5. Natalya Tsyganova RUS 2:01.04 57.5 (3)
6. Jolanda Ceplak SLO 2:01.07 46 (6=)
7. Faith Macharia KEN 2:01.33 46 (6=)
8. Letitia Vriesde SUR 2:16.92 49 (4)

Other GP leaders prior to final: Irina Mistyukevich RUS 38, Olga Raspopova RUS 33.5, Ivonne Teichmann GER 27

1500 Metres

1. Violeta Szekely ROM 4:03.46 92 (1)
2. Carla Sacramento POR 4:04.41 46 (3)
3. Natalya Gorelova RUS 4:06.48 64 (2)
4. Lidia Chojecka POL 4:09.67 35 (5)
5. Lyudmila Vasilyeva RUS 4:10.21 24 (7)
6. Yuliya Kosenkova RUS 4:11.12 23 (8)
7. Sarah Schwald USA 4:11.14 26 (6)
8. Georgie Clarke AUS 4:15.10 0
9. Suzy Walsham AUS 4:15.51 0
10. Mardrea Hyman JAM 4:22.70 18 (10=)

Other GP leaders prior to final: Suzy Favor Hamilton USA 45, Regina Jacobs USA 19, Jacinta Muragiri KEN & Olga Nelyubova RUS 18

3000 Metres

1. Tatyana Tomashova RUS 9:30.39 36 (6)
2. Leah Malot KEN 9:31.41 26 (9)
3. Olga Yegorova RUS 9:31.82 60 (1)
4. Berhane Adere ETH 9:32.27 38 (4)
5. Gete Wami ETH 9:32.29 32 (7)
6. Alesya Turova BLR 9:32.45 19 (13)
7. Edith Masai KEN 9:33.30 45 (2)
8. Benita Willis AUS 9:33.31 10 (24)

Other GP leaders prior to final: Gabriela Szabo ROM 43, Paula Radcliffe GBR 37, Asmae Leghzaoui MAR 29, Rose Cheruiyot KEN 21

400 Metres Hurdles

1. Tonja Buford-Bailey USA 54.58 61 (3)
2. Tatyana Tereshchuk UKR 54.78 75 (1)
3. Sandra Glover USA 55.01 52 (6)
4. Debbie-Ann Parris JAM 55.04 71 (2)
5. Nezha Bidouane MAR 55.05 54 (5)
6. Ionela Tirlea ROM 55.52 55 (4)
7. Daimí Pernía CUB 55.81 47 (7=)
8. Yuliya Nosova RUS 56.55 47 (7=)

Other GP leaders prior to final: Natalya Torshina KAZ 29, Surita Febbraio RSA 25

High Jump

1. Hestrie Cloete RSA 1.98 69.5 (2)
2= Amy Acuff USA 1.96 62 (4)
2= Inga Babakova UKR 1.96 66 (3)
4. Kajsa Bergqvist SWE 1.94 77.5 (1)
5. Vita Palamar UKR 1.90 55.5 (6)
6= Monica Iagar ROM 1.85 33 (8)
6= Venelina Veneva BUL 1.85 56.5 (5)
8. Dóra Györffy HUN 1.80 35.7 (7)

Other GP leaders prior to final: Olga Kaliturina RUS 23.5, Blanka Vlasic CRO 19

Pole Vault

1. Stacy Dragila USA 4.50 68 (1)
2. Svetlana Feofanova RUS 4.45 46 (2)
3. Kellie Suttle USA 4.45 36.5 (3)
4. Monika Pyrek POL 4.20 30 (6)
5. Melissa Mueller USA 4.20 35.5 (4)
6. Yelena Isinbayeva RUS 4.00 26 (8)
nh. Tatiana Grigorieva AUS 31.5 (5)
nh. Mary Sauer USA 28.5 (7)

Other GP leaders prior to final: Doris Auer AUT 24, Anzhela Balakhonova UKR & Pavla Hamácková CZE 22

Triple Jump

1. Tereza Marinova BUL 14.77/0.3 27 (3)
2. Tatyana Lebedeva RUS 14.61/0.9 45 (1)
3. Françoise Mbango CMR 14.47/0.4 21 (4=)
4. Magdelín Martínez ITA 14.35/1.1 32 (2)
5. Yelena Oleynikova RUS 14.16/0.0 21 (4=)
6. Yelena Govorova UKR 14.10/-0.2 20 (7)
7. Heli Koivula FIN 14.00/2.7 16 (8)

8. Cristina Nicolau ROM 13.97/0.8 21 (4=)
Other GP leaders prior to final: Oksana Rogova RUS 14, Tiombé Hurd USA 11

Shot
1. Astrid Kumbernuss GER 18.94 22 (3=)
2. Nadezhda Ostapchuk BLR 18.82 26 (1)
3. Svetlana Krivelyova RUS 18.21 19 (6)
4. Lieja Koeman NED 17.86 22 (3=)
5. Yanina Korolchik BLR 17.77 20 (5)
6. Connie Price-Smith USA 17.15 24 (2)
7. Valentina Fedyushina AUT 17.01 13 (8)
Other GP leaders prior to final: Lyudmila Sechko RUS 15, Terri Tunks USA 12, Assunta Legnante ITA 10

Hammer
1. Kamila Skolimowska POL 71.71 31 (3)
2. Bronwyn Eagles AUS 68.38 29 (5)
3. Olga Kuzenkova RUS 68.27 38 (1)
4. Dawn Ellerbe USA 65.92 30 (4)
5. Lyudmila Gubkina BLR 65.85 15 (9=)
6. Olga Tsander BLR 63.12 28 (6)
7. Karyne DiMarco AUS 60.42 16 (8)
8. Tatyana Konstantinova RUS 60.33 13 (11=)
Other GP leaders prior to final: Katalin Divós HUN 36, Manuela Montebrun FRA 21, Lisa Misapeka AMS 15

Overall Final Standings

1. Violeta Szekely ROM	116	92 (1)
2. Maria Lourdes Mutola MOZ	105	81 (2)
3. Tatyana Tereshchuk UKR	96	75 (4)
4. Hestrie Cloete RSA	93.5	69.5 (8)
5. Kajsa Bergqvist SWE	92.5	77.5 (3)
6. Stacy Dragila USA	92	68 (9)
7. Stephanie Graf AUT	92	74 (5)
8. Natalya Gorelova RUS	82	70 (7)
9. Debbie-Ann Parris JAM	86	71 (6)
10. Inga Babakova UKR	85.5	66 (10)
11. Tonja Buford-Bailey USA	85	61 (12)
12. Amy Acuff USA	81.5	62 (11)
13. Olga Yegorova RUS	78	60 (13)

IAAF/MOBIL Overall Grand Prix winners

Year	*Men*	*Women*
1985	Doug Padilla USA	Mary Slaney USA
1986	Saïd Aouita MAR	Yordanka Donkova BUL
1987	Tonie Campbell USA	Merlene Ottey JAM
1988	Saïd Aouita MAR	Paula Ivan ROM
1989	Saïd Aouita MAR	Paula Ivan ROM
1990	Leroy Burrell USA	Merlene Ottey JAM
1991	Sergey Bubka URS	Heike Henkel GER
1992	Kevin Young USA	Heike Drechsler GER
1993	Sergey Bubka UKR	Sandra Farmer-Patrick USA
1994	Noureddine Morceli ALG	Jackie Joyner-Kersee USA
1995	Moses Kiptanui KEN	Maria Mutola MOZ
1996	Daniel Komen KEN	Ludmila Engquist SWE
1997	Wilson Kipketer DEN	Astrid Kumbernuss GER
1998	Hicham El Guerrouj MAR	Marion Jones USA
1999	Bernard Barmasai KEN	Gabriela Szabo ROM
2000	Angelo Taylor USA	Trine Hattestad NOR
2001	André Bucher SUI	Violeta Szekely ROM

Ivanova's Amazing Feat

In achieving a time of 1:24:50 for 20 kilometres walk in 2001, the Russian Olimpiada Ivanova became the first women athlete at any event ever to have bettered the MEN's qualifying standard for the deep ATFS lists published in this Annual.
The standard for 20km walk is 1:25:00, and Ivanova's time was bettered by 11 men in 2001.
Of course, it may be argued that the depth of performace levels in walking is not as good as for many other events – but no woman is remotely close to other men's standards which range from 10.35 for 100m to 2:14:00 for marathon, or 2.20, 5.35, 7.80 and 16.25 in the jumps.

MAJOR INTERNATIONAL EVENTS 2002-2006

2002

European 10000m Challenge – Camaiore, Italy (6 April)
South American Junior Championships – Bogatá, Colombia (10-12 April)
IAAF World Half Marathon Championships – Kortrijk, Belgium (5 May)
Ibero-American Championships – La Pedrera, Guatemala (11-12 May)
IAU 100km World Challenge – Torhout, Belgium (21 June)
European Cup – (Super League – Annecy, France) (21-22 June)
European Combined Events Cup (29-30 June)
European Mountain Running Championships – Camara de Lobos, Madeira, POR (7 July)
IAAF World Junior Championships – Kingston, Jamaica (16-21 July)
Commonwealth Games – Manchester, GBR (26-30 July)
African Championships, Tunis, Tunisia (6-10 Aug)
European Championships – Munich, Germany (6-11 Aug)
Asian Championships – Colombo, Sri Lanka (7-12 Aug)
European Veterans Championships – Potsdam, Germany (15-25 Aug)
World Mountain Racing Trophy, Innsbruck, Austria (13-14 Sep)
IAAF Grand Prix Final – Paris (Charléty), France (14 Sep)
IAAF World Cup – Madrid, Spain (20-21 Sep)
World Masters Games – Melbourne, Australia (5-13 Oct)
Asian Games – Pusan, Korea (7-14 Oct)
IAAF World Race Walking Cup – Torino, Italy (12-13 Oct)
Asian Junior Championships – Bangkok, Thailand (28-31 Oct)
CAC Games – San Salvador, El Salvador (2-8 Dec)
European Cross-country Championships – Pula, Croatia (8 Dec)

2003

European Indoor Cup – Leipzig (15 Feb)
IAAF World Indoor Championships – Birmingham, GBR (14-16 Mar)
IAAF World Cross-country Championships – Lausanne, Switzerland (29-30 Mar)
European Cup of Race Walking – (18 May)
European Cup – Super League – Firenze, Italy (21-22 June)
IAAF World Youth Championships – Sherbrooke, Canada (10-13 July)
European Under 23 Championships – Bydgoszcz, Poland (17-20 July)
European Junior Championships – Tampere, Finland (24-27 July)
Pan-American Games – Santo Domingo, Dominican Republic (24 Jul – 2 Aug)
World University Games – Daegu, Korea (21-31 Aug?)
IAAF World Championships – Paris, France (23-31 Aug)
IAAF Grand Prix Final – Monaco (12-13 Sep?)
IAAF World Half Marathon Championships – Vilamoura, Portugal (4 Oct?)
WMA World Masters Championships – Puerto Rico
All-Africa Games, Abuja, Nigeria
European Cross-country Championships – Edinburgh, GBR (14 Dec)

2004

IAAF World Indoor Championships – Budapest, Hungary (Mar)
IAAF World Cross-country Championships – Brussels, Belgium
IAAF World Race Walking Cup – Naumburg, Germany
IAAF World Junior Championships
Olympic Games – Athens, Greece (13-29 Aug)
European Cross-country Championships – Heringsdorf, Germany (12 Dec)

2005

European Indoor Championships – Madrid, Spain
IAAF World Cross-country Championships – Le Mans, France
IAAF World Championships –
World University Games – Izmir, Turkey (July)
Francophone Games – Niamey, Niger (7-17 Dec)
WMA World Masters Championships – San Sebastián, Spain

2006

IAAF World Indoor Championships
Commonwealth Games – Melbourne, Australia (15-26 Mar)
European Championships – Göteborg, Sweden (Aug)
Asian Games – Doha, Qatar

COMMONWEALTH GAMES 2002

The 17th Commonwealth Games will be staged in Manchester, England from 25 July to 4 Aug 2002, the first English venue since the second edition of the Games in 1934. A total of 72 countries are expected be represented. The athletics events will be held in the newly built City of Manchester Stadium (38,000 seats), which will become home to Manchester City Football Club from the 2003/4 season (with the track removed).

These multi-sport competitions are held every four years, and contested by athletes representing the nations of the British Commonwealth. They were first staged as the British Empire Games at Hamilton, Canada in 1930. The Games became the British Empire and Commonwealth Games in 1954, and simply the British Commonwealth Games in 1970, in which year the Games went metric, rather than the yards and miles Imperial distances raced hitherto.

Games best performances after 1998

Men

Event	Mark	Athlete	Year
100m	9.88	Ato Boldon TRI	1998
200m	19.97	Frank Fredericks NAM	1994
400m	44.52	Iwan Thomas WAL	1998
800m	1:43.22	Steve Cram ENG	1986
1500m	3:32.16	Filbert Bayi TAN	1974
5000m	13:14.4	Ben Jipcho KEN	1974
10000m	27:46.4	Richard Tayler NZL	1974
Mar	2:09:12	Ian Thompson ENG	1974
3000mSt	8:14.72	Johnstone Kipkoech KEN	1994
110mh	13.08	Colin Jackson WAL 1990 & 1994	
400mh	48.28	Dinsdale Morgan JAM	1998
HJ	2.36	Nick Saunders BAH	1990
PV	5.60	Riaan Botha RSA	1998
LJ	8.39w	Yusuf Alli NGR	1990
	8.22	Obinna Eregbu NGR (q)	1994
	8.22	Peter Burge AUS	1998
	8.22	Jai Taurima AUS	1998
TJ	17.81w	Keith Connor ENG	1982
	17.10	Larry Achike ENG	1998
SP	20.74	Geoff Capes ENG	1978
DT	64.42	Frantz Kruger RSA	1998
HT	75.66	Sean Carlin AUS	1990
JT	88.75	Marius Corbett RSA	1998
(old)	89.48	Michael O'Rourke NZL	1982
Dec	8663	Daley Thompson ENG	1986
4x100mR	38.20	England	1998
4x400mR	2:59.03	Jamaica	1998
20kmW	1:24:59	Nick A'Hern AUS	1998
30kmW	2:07:47	Simon Baker AUS	1986
50kmW	4:10:05	Govindaswamy Saravanan MAS	1998

Women

Event	Mark	Athlete	Year
100m	10.92w	Angella Taylor CAN	1982
	11.00	Angella Taylor CAN in sf 1982	
200m	22.19w	Merlene Ottey JAM	1982
	22.25	Cathy Freeman AUS	1994
400m	50.17	Sandie Richards JAM	1998
800m	1:57.60	Maria Mutola MOZ	1998
1500m	4:05.27	Jackline Maranga KEN	1998
3000m	8:32.17	Angela Chalmers CAN	1994
5000m	15:52.74	Katie Anderson AUS	1998
10000m	31:41.42	Liz McColgan SCO	1986
Mar	2:25:28	Lisa Martin AUS	1990
100mh	12.70	Gillian Russell JAM	1998
400mh	53.91	Deon Hemmings JAM	1998
HJ	1.94	Alison Inverarity AUS	1994
	1.94	Charmaine Weavers RSA	1994
PV	4.20	Emma George AUS	1998
LJ	6.91w	Shonel Ferguson BAH	1982
	6.78	Jane Flemming AUS	1990
TJ	14.32	Ashia Hansen ENG	1998
SP	19.00	Gael Martin AUS	1986
DT	65.92	Beatrice Faumuiná NZL	1998
HT	66.56	Debbie Sosimenko NZL	1998
JT	69.80	Tessa Sanderson ENG	1986
Hep	6695	Jane Flemming AUS	1990
4x100mR	42.99	Nigeria	1994
4x400mR	3:27.06	England	1994
10kmW	43:57	Jane Saville AUS	1998

Most gold medals - all events

Men

6 Don Quarrie JAM 100m 1970-74-78, 200m 1970-74, 4x100mR 1970

Women

7 Marjorie Jackson AUS 100y 1950-54, 220y 1950-54, 4x110yR 1954, 440yR and 660yR 1950

7 Raelene Boyle AUS 100m 1970-74, 200m 1970-74, 400m 1982, 4x100mR 1970-74

6 Pam Kilborn/Ryan AUS 80mh 1962-66-70, LJ 1962, 4x100mR 1966-70

5 Decima Norman AUS 100y, 220y, LJ, 440yR, 660yR 1938

5 Valerie Sloper/Young NZL SP 1962-66-70, DT 1962-66

5 Sally Gunnell ENG 100mh 1986, 400mh 1990-94, 4x400mR 1990-94

Most medals - all events

Men

6 Don Quarrie 1970-78

6 Harry Hart 1930-34

6 Allan Wells 1978-82

Women

9 Raelene Boyle 1970-82
8 Denise Robertson/Boyd AUS 1974-82
7 Marjorie Jackson 1950-54
7 Valerie Young 1958-72
7 Kathy Cook ENG 1978-86
7 Angella Issajenko CAN 1982-86
7 Debbie Flintoff AUS 1982-90
6 Pam Ryan 1962-70
6 Gael Martin AUS 1978-86
6 Sally Gunnell ENG 1986-94
6 Judy Oakes ENG 1978-98 (uniquely at one event)

Most medals at one Games

Men 4 Keith Gardner 1958 2G, 1S, 1B
Women 5 Decima Norman 1938 5G;
5 Shirley Strickland 1950 3G, 2S

Most Games contested

6 Robin Tait NZL 1962-82, successively 4-3-6-1-4-8 at discus
6 Judy Oakes ENG 1978-98, successively 3-1-2-2-1-1 at women's shot

Oldests (y years, d days)

Men

Winner	42y 335d	Jack Holden ENG marathon 1950
Medallist	42y 335d	Jack Holden

Women

Winner	40y 216d	Judy Oakes ENG SP 1998
Medallist	40y 252d	Rosemary Payne SCO 2nd DT 1974

Youngests

Men

Winner	16y 263d	Sam Richardson CAN LJ 1934
Medallist	16y 260d	Sam Richardson CAN 2nd TJ 1934

Women

Winner	17y 137d	Debbie Brill CAN HJ 1970
Medallist	c15y	Sabine Chebichi KEN 3rd 800m 1974

Commonwealth Games Timetable 2002

July 26: (pm) Hep 100H (W), HT (W) qual, 100 (M) hts, Hep HJ (W), 400 (M) hts, 100 (W) hts, DT (M) qual; (evening) Hep SP (W), TJ (M) qual, 3000SC (M) hts, 100 (M) qf, HT (W) F, 400 (M) qf, 400 (W) hts, Hep 200 (W), 5000 (W) hts, 10,000 (M) F
July 27: (am) Dec 100 (M), HT (M) qual, Hep LJ (W), SP (W) qual, 400H (W) hts, Dec LJ (M), 400H (M) hts; (pm) 800 (M) hts, 800 (W) hts; (evening) Dec SP (M), PV (W) qual, Hep JT (W), 100 (W) sf, 100 (M) sf, Dec HJ (M), 3000SC (M) F, DT (M) F, 400 (W) sf, 400 (M) sf, Hep 800 (W) FEVENT; 100 (W) F, 100 (M) F, Dec 400 (M)
July 28: (am) Marathon (M & W), JT (W) qual, HJ (M) qual, Dec 110H (M), LJ (M) qual; (pm) Dec DT (M), 400H (M) sf, 200 (W) hts, 200 (M) hts, HT (M) F, Dec PV (M); (evening) 800 (W) sf, TJ (M) F, 800 (M) sf, 200 (W) sf, SP (W) F, 200 (M) qf, 400H (W) F, Dec JT (M), 5000 (M) hts; 400 (W) F, 400 (M) F, Dec 1500 (M) F EVENT, 5000 (W) F
July 29: (am) HJ (W) qual, 110H (M) hts, PV (M) qual, DT (W) qual, 100H (W) hts, LJ (M) qual; (evening) LJ (W) F, HJ (M) F, 200 (M) sf, PV (W) F, 110H (M) sf, JT (W) F, 800 (M) F, 800 (W) F, 200 (W) F, 200 (M) F, 400H (M) F
July 30: (am) 20k Walk (W; at Wythenshawe Park), 100H (W) sf, JT (M) qual, TJ (W) qual, SP (M) qual, 4x100 (W) hts; (pm) 4x100 (M) hts, 20k Walk (M; at Wythenshawe Park); (evening) PV (M) F, DT (W) F, 1500 (W) hts, HJ (W) F, 1500 (M) hts, LJ (M) F, 110H (M) F, 4x400 (W) hts, 4x400 (M) hts, 10,000 (W) F
July 31: (evening) 100H (W) F, JT (M) F, TJ (W) F, SP (M) F, 5000 (M) F, 1500 (W) F, 4x100 (W) F, 4x100 (M) F, 1500 (M) F, 4x400 (W) F, 4x400 (M) F
August 1: (am) 50k Walk (M; at Wythenshawe Park).
[schedule subject to change]

Feofanova's World Records

Svetlana Feofanova improved the world indoor record for the pole vault five times within a month in the 2002 indoor season: 4.71 Stuttgart 3 Feb, 4.72 Stockholm 6 Feb, 4.73 Gent 10 Feb, 4.74 :Liévin 24 Feb, 4.75 Wien 2 Mar.
This feat is unprecedented for official world records, but in the early days of women's pole vaulting Sun Caiyun (China) set five indoor 'records' in Germany in 1995: 4.10 on 27 Jan, 4.11 on 3 Feb, 4.12 on 10 Feb, 4.13 on 12 Feb and 4.15 on 15 Feb. Sergey Bubka set four world indoor records and absolute world bests (6.08-6.12) in six weeks in 1981.
At different distances Gunder Hägg had nine world record races in 1942: four in July and five within a month, 23 August to 20 September.
Including unratified marks, Gisela Mauermayer (Germany) improved the world best for the women's discus six times at four meetings in June 1935, from 44.34 to 46.97.

EUROPEAN CHAMPIONSHIPS 2002

THE FIRST European Championships were staged at the Stadio Comunale, Torino, Italy in 1934 for men only. Women's championships were held separately in 1938, but men's and women's events were combined at one venue from 1946. The championships are held at four-yearly intervals, although there was a break in that pattern when they were held in 1969 and 1971. The 18th Championships will be held in Munich, Germany 6-11 August, 2002, based at the Olympic Stadum built for the Games in 1972.

Championship bests

Men

100m	10.04	Darren Campbell GBR	1998
	10.00w	Linford Christie GBR	1990
200m	20.11	John Regis GBR	1990
400m	44.52	Iwan Thomas GBR	1998
800m	1:43.84	Olaf Beyer GDR	1978
1500m	3:35.27	Fermín Cacho ESP	1994
5000m	13:10.15	Jack Buckner GBR	1986
10000m	27:30.99	Martti Vainio FIN	1978
Mar	2:10:31	Martín Fiz ESP	1994
3000mSt	8:12.66	Francesco Panetta ITA	1990
110mh	13.02	Colin Jackson GBR (sf and F)	1998
400mh	47.48	Harald Schmid FRG	1982
HJ	2.35	Steinar Hoen NOR	1994
PV	6.00	Rodion Gataullin URS	1994
LJ	8.41	Robert Emmiyan URS	1986
	8.41w	Lutz Dombrowski GDR	1982
TJ	17.99	Jonathan Edwards GBR	1998
SP	22.22	Werner Günthör SUI	1986
DT	67.20	Wolfgang Schmidt GDR (q)	1978
HT	86.74	Yuriy Sedykh URS	1986
JT	89.72	Steve Backley GBR	1998
Dec	8811	Daley Thompson GBR	1986
4x100mR	37.79	France	1990
4x400mR	2:58.22	United Kingdom	1990
20 kmW	1:18:45	Mikhail Shchennikov RUS	1994
50 kmW	3:40:55	Hartwig Gauder GDR	1986

Women

100m	10.73	Christine Arron FRA	1998
200m	21.71	Heike Drechsler GDR	1986
400m	48.15	Marita Koch GDR	1982
800m	1:55.41	Olga Minayeva URS	1982
1500m	3:57.80	Olga Dvirna URS	1982
3000m	8:30.28	Svetlana Ulmasova URS	1982
5000m	15:06.50	Sonia O'Sullivan IRL	1998
10000m	30:23.25	Ingrid Kristiansen NOR	1986
Mar	2:27:10	Manuela Machado POR	1998
100mh	12.38	Yordanka Donkova BUL	1986
400mh	53.32	Marina Styepanova URS	1986
HJ	2.02	Ulrike Meyfarth FRG	1982
PV	4.31	Anzhela Balakhonova UKR	1998
	4.31	Nicole Humbert GER	1998
	4.31	Yvonne Buschbaum GER	1998
LJ	7.30	Heike Drechsler GDR	1990
TJ	14.89	Anna Biryukova RUS	1994
SP	21.69	Viktoriya Pavlysh UKR	1998
DT	71.36	Diane Sachse GDR	1986
HT	71.17	Mihaela Melinte ROM	1998
JT	77.44	Fatima Whitbread GBR (q)	1986
Hep	6717	Anke Behmer GDR	1986
4x100mR	41.68	GDR	1990
4x400mR	3:16.87	GDR	1986
10kmW	42:37	Sari Essayah FIN	1994

Medals by Nation for European Championships 1934-98

Nation	*Men*			*Women*			*Total*
	G	*S*	*B*	*G*	*S*	*B*	*Medals*
USSR	65	69	60	54	41	43	332
GDR	39	37	32	51	45	33	237
United Kingdom	66	40	40	12	18	22	198
FR Germany	27	24	36	9	20	18	134
France	26	30	21	8	6	11	102
Poland	20	24	19	14	7	18	102
Italy	27	30	21	4	6	12	100
Finland	25	25	30	4	1	4	89
Sweden	19	30	30	1	3	2	85
Germany *	18	13	13	14	11	11	80

26 other nations have won medals

* Germany - 1934 and 1938 Championships. The Federal Republic took part from 1954 and the GDR from 1958. Germany again from 1994.

The European nations from the ex-USSR, Czech Republic and Slovakia from Czechoslovakia and the ex-constituent nations of Yugoslavia competed from 1994.

Most gold medals at all events:

Men
5 Harald Schmid FRG 1978-86
5 Roger Black GBR 1986-94
Women
6 Marita Koch GDR 1978-86
5 Fanny Blankers-Koen HOL 1946-50
5 Irena Szewinska POL 1966-74
5 Marlies Göhr GDR 1978-86
5 Heike Drechsler GDR/GER 1986-98
Most medals (gold/silver/bronze)
Men
6 Harald Schmid FRG 5/1/0 1978-86
6 Pietro Mennea ITA 3/2/1 1971-74
6 Roger Black GBR 5/1/0 1986-94
Women
10 Irena Szewinska POL 5/1/4 1966-78
8 Fanny Blankers-Koen HOL 5/1/2 1938-50
8 Renate Stecher GDR 4/4/0 1969-74
7 Marlies Göhr GDR 5/1/1 1978-86
6 Yevgeniya Sechenova URS 2/2/2 1946-50
6 Marita Koch GDR 6/0/0 1978-86
6 Heike Drechsler GDR/GER 5/1/0 1986-98
6 Irina Privalova RUS 3/2/1 1994-8
Most medals at one event:
5 Igor Ter-Ovanesyan URS long jump 3/2/0 1958-71

Most medals at one Championships:

Men
4 John Regis GBR 2/1/1 1990
Women
4 Fanny Blankers-Koen HOL 3/1/0 1950
4 Irena Kirszenstein/Szewinska POL 3/1/0 1966
4 Stanislawa Walasiewicz POL 2/2/0 1938
Most championships contested
6 Ludvik Danek TCH 1962-78
6 Abdon Pamich ITA 1954-71
6 Nenad Stekic YUG 1971-90

European Championships Timetable

Tuesday, Aug 6: 09.00 – DT (W) qual A; 09.30 – 400mh (W) hts; 10.10 – SP (M) qual A & B, 400m (W) hts; 10.40 – TJ (M) qual A & B; 10.45 – 400m (M) hts, DT (W) qual B; 11.20 – 100m (M) hts; 12.05 – 100m (W) hts; 12.40 – HT (M) qual A; 14.25 – HT (M) qual B
Opening Ceremony 18.00 – HJ (M) qual A & B, JT (W) qual A; 18.05 – 20k Walk (M) start; 18.15 – 1500m (M) hts; 18.20 – LJ (W) qual A & B; 18.45 – 800m (W) hts; c.19.23 – 20k Walk (M) Finish; 19.45 – JT (W) qual B; 19.55 – 100m (W) 2nd Rd; 20.00 – SP (M) F; 20.25 – 100m (M) 2nd Rd; 21.00 – 10,000m (W) F.
Wednesday, Aug 7: 09.00 – JT (M) qual A, PV (W) qual A & B; 09.15 – Dec 100m (M); 09.50 – 20k Walk (W) start; 10.15 – 400mh (M) hts; 10.30 – JT (M) qual B, Dec LJ (M); 11.15 – 20k Walk (W) Finish; 12.00 – HT (W) qual A; 12.30 – Dec SP (M); 13.45 – HT (W) qual B
16.20 – HT (M) F; 17.00 – Dec HJ (M); 17.55 – 400mh (W) semis; 18.15 – 400m (W) semis; 18.35 – 100m (W) semis; 18.45 – 100m (M) semis, LJ (W) F; 19.05 – 3000SC (M) hts; 19.35 – 400m (M) semis; 19.55 – 100m (W) F; 20.00 – DT (W) F; 20.10 – 800m (W) semis; 20.30 – 100m (M) F; 20.45 – Dec 400m (M); 21.10 – 10,000m (M) F.
Thursday, Aug 8: 09.05 – 50k Walk (M) start; 09.20 – Dec 110H; 09.30 – PV (M) qual A & B; 10.00 – 100mh (W) hts; 10.20 – TJ (W) qual A & B; 10.30 – Dec DT A (M); 11.00 – 200m (W) hts; 11.40 – 200m (M) hts; 12.05 – Dec DT B (M); c.12.48 – 50k Walk (M) Finish.
15.30 – Dec PV (M); 18.00 – Dec JT A (M); 18.30 – 400mh (M) semis, HJ (M) F; 18.55 – 200m (W) 2nd Rd; 19.20 – 200m (M) 2nd Rd; Dec JT B (M); 19.50 – 1500m (M) F; 20.05 – TJ (M) F; 20.20 – 400mh (W) F; 20.35 – 400m (M) F; 20.50 – 800m (W) F, JT (W) F; 21.10 – 400m (W) F; 21.30 – Dec 1500m (M); 22.00 – 5000m (W) hts.
Friday, Aug 9: 09.30 – SP (W) qual A & B; 10.00 – Hep 100mh (W); 10.30 – DT (M) qual A; 10.35 – 1500m (W) hts; 11.05 – 800m (M) hts; 11.15 – Hep HJ (W); 11.45 – 110H (M) hts; 12.15 – DT (M) qual B.
15.20 – HT (W) F; 16.00 – Hep SP (W); 17.45 – HJ (W) qual; 18.00 – 200m (W) semis, PV (W) F; 18.20 – 200m (M) semis; 18.40 – 100mh (W) semis; 19.30 – Hep 200m (W); 19.45 – JT (M) F; 19.55 – 400mh (M) F; 20.10 – 200m (W) F; 20.25 – 200m (M) F; 20.40 – 100mh (W) F; 21.00 – 5000m (M) hts.
Saturday, Aug 10: 09.15 – Marathon (W) start; 09.30 – LJ (M) qual A & B; 11.00 – Hep LJ (W); c.11.43 – Marathon (W) Finish
15.00 – PV (M) F; 15.05 – Hep JT A (W); 15.10 – 110H (M) semis, TJ (W) F; 15.30 – 4x100m (W) hts; 15.50 – 4x100m (M) hts; 16.10 – 800m (M) semis; 16.25 – Hep JT B (W); 16.30 – 3000SC (M) F; 17.00 – 110H (M) F, SP (W) F; 17.15 – 5000m (W) F; 17.40 – 4x400m (M) hts; 18.05 – Hep 800m (W); 18.25 – 4x400m (W) hts.
Sunday, Aug 11: 09.00 – Marathon (M) start; 11.08 – Marathon (M) Finish;
15.20 – HJ (W) F; 16.00 – DT (M) F, 4x100m (W) F; 16.20 – 800m (M) F; 16.25 – LJ (M) F; 16.40 – 4x100m (M) F; 17.00 – 1500m (W) F; 17.20 – 4x400m (W) F; 17.40 – 5000m (M) F; 18.00 – 4x400m (M) F.

Entry Standards

These entry standards must be achieved in a bona fide competition (indoors or outdoors) between 1 Jan 2001 and 26 Jul 2002. There are no entry standards for the marathons, relays and women's 20k walk.
Men: 100 – 10.50, 200 – 21.10, 400 – 46.70, 800 – 1:47.20, 1500 – 3:41.00, 5000 – 13:40.00, 10,000 – 28:35.00, 3000SC – 8:35.00, 110H – 13.90; 400H – 50.60, HJ – 2.25, PV – 5.55, LJ – 7.95, TJ – 16.50, SP – 18.90, DT – 62.00, HT – 75.00, JT – 78.00, Dec – 7850, 20kW – 1:28:00, 50kW – 4:20:00.
Women: 100 – 11.60, 200 – 23.60, 400 – 53.30, 800 – 2:02.50, 1500 – 4:13.00, 5000 – 15:44.00, 10,000 – 33:20.00, 100H – 13.50, 400H – 57.75, HJ – 1.90, PV – 4.00, LJ – 6.45, TJ – 13.70, SP – 16.80, DT – 57.00, HT – 58.00, JT – 56.00, Hep – 5750.

NOTES FROM THE EDITOR

Declining Standards?

OVER THE half-century of ATFS Annuals we have become accustomed to ever-rising standards in world athletics. This can best be shown by the fact, as I indicated in the introduction to the 2001 Annual, that only seven men's marks made in any event in 1950 would have qualified for current year lists in 2000, even though we now list up to 200 deep per event! These are the seven: 100m 10.1 Lloyd LaBeach PAN, 200m 20.6w Herb McKenley JAM, 400m: 45.8 George Rhoden JAM, 46.0 Herb McKenley JAM; 110mh: 13.5 Dick Attlesey USA, LJ: 7.85 James Holland USA, 7.81 Jerome Biffle USA. Women's lists were not given in 1950 but no women's mark made then meets our current standards.

However, the pace of record breaking has slowed considerably from that of the mid-1950s through the 1960s and 1970s. In 2000 there was no world record at any standard men's event – the first time that this had happened since 1907 – and none at any women's event, apart from the 'new' ones. That changed a little in 2001 as men's records were set at steeplechase and decathlon and women's at the marathon as well as further progress in the 'new' events of steeplechase, pole vault, new specification javelin and 20km walk.

I was struck, in putting together the deep 2001 lists for this Annual, by a sharp decline in so many events (particularly running, except marathon) in the numbers meeting our standards compared to those of 2000. Now this might just be the effect of a post-Olympic season, but it also reflects some long-standing trends, and in particular the decline in the developed world. That is shown by a very considerable drop in distance running standards over the past 20 years in the countries of Northern Europe, USA, Australia etc., with the numbers being filled by athletes from Africa etc., and by a fascinating decline in the high jump, for both men and women.

Number of athletes achieving base level standards for world lists:

Men		2001	2000	1999	1998	1997
100m	10.34	195	212	206	197	188
200m	20.85	163	194	203	173	174
400m	46.29	158	209	188	173	167
800m	1:47.99	168	212	197	204	178
1500m	3:41.4	163	202	185	194	205
5000m	13:42.0	165	205	170	157	146
10000m	28:42.0	178	220	197	169	183
HMar	62:50	174	205	169	159	154
Mar	2:13:30	214	188	198	176	164
3000mSt	8:40.0	137	163	148	137	138
110mh	13.99	202	204	203	176	194
400mh	50.85	194	201	202	190	165
HJ	2.20	167	193	184	179	190?
PV	5.35	156	199	179	197	201
LJ	7.80	154	172	161	157	169
TJ	16.30	132	135	127	139	137
SP	18.25	184	198	174	164	161
DT	57.80	139	166	155	153	147
HT	68.00	152	161	150	151	151
JT	74.00	147	148	142	158	150
Dec	7400	147	156	154	156	174
20kmW	1:25:00	122	116	112	127	133
50kmW	4:10:00	119	123	132	117	124
Women						
100m	11.54	185	217	183	162	174
200m	23.55	166	193	194	200	175
400m	53.29	184	207	198	207	172
800m	2:04.5	175	200	184	179	184
1500m	4:15.5	176	188	166	150	165
5000m	15:48.0	167	205	170	143	140
10000m	33:15.0	140	203	124	107	119
HMar	72:59	193	170	137	122	156
Mar	2:37:00	197	194	190	167	171
100mh	13.54	183	193	170	172	165
400mh	58.44	162	168	169	141	145
HJ	1.85	120	148	138	135	141
PV	3.90	211	199	141	109	66
LJ	6.33	159	200	192	189	176
SP	15.85	150	156	162	146	145
DT	53.65	144	151	154	149	149
HT	57.00	204	184	155	114	63
JT	53.00	138	157	135	old spec	
Hep	5450	168	180	150	155	151
20kmW	1:40:00	157	171	155	(66)	

See also the Trends in 10th and 100th bests.

Another possibly disturbing trend, noticed just as I go to press, is that of the number of runners in the World Cross-country championships. In in 2001 the numbers were down in every race compared to those of 2000, when the number of finishers was less than that in 1999 in five of the six races. This may be just a temporary aberration, but it should also be pointed out that most nations do not enter this great event.

The Fight for Audiences

SPORTS ENTHUSIASTS have a massive and ever-growing number of events to follow and to watch – and among these events there is huge competition to attract public interest and, most particularly, television coverage. The top events can command very large audiences, but the public demands quality and events not reaching the highest standards can be left behind.

Athletics is a universally popular sport – but it is not the major one in most of the world's largest nations and indeed comes some way down the list in many, being especially lowly regarded in the USA. To generalise, it can attract a wide audience who like watching athletics, but who are not passionate about it in the way that fans follow their favourite team at football, baseball, basketball etc. Perhaps this is the inevitable consequence of a focus on individual achievement, but while the diversity of athletics provides rich enjoyment for us enthusiasts, its complexity can also be a major problem.

In fighting for its position in world sport, the IAAF have successfully introduced many major events over the past 25 years as the sport has developed from semi-amateur to fully-professional. I remain, however, concerned that in the fight for popularity some promoters and indeed governing bodies pander excessively for what they see to be the interests of television – and that can be to the detriment of spectators and athletes without being of any benefit to TV audiences either. Reducing the number of field events (or jumps and throws) will not mean that what is left will be any better covered; it merely means that incompetent television directors will miss less. If television authorities believe that their audiences are only capable of absorbing short-attention-span events and need the sort of pap generated by US companies for Olympic coverage, then no amount of simplifying a meeting will help. What we have to do is to try to ensure that the top meetings are organised and presented so as to fulfill the needs of the athletes for top competition and of the spectators for exciting sport based on intensive competition.

EPO and the Yegorova Case

THE MAJOR controvery of the year was surely the story of OlgaYegorova's drugs disqualification and reinstatement, followed by World Championships victory at 5000m. Yegorova had shown superb form in the major meetings leading up to the Championships, with her trademark being an unmatchable finishing sprint. On the eve of competition in Edmonton came media reports that she had failed a test for EPO (erythropoietin) at the Paris Golden League meeting. But an apparent ban was overturned and she was allowed to run.

Arne Ljungqvist, chairman of the IAAF Anti-Doping Commission, explained that she had taken not only the standard IAAF drugs testing, which she had apparently passed, but also a urine test for EPO, and it was this which gave rise to the reports of her test failure. However, while the French-developed test had been approved along with a blood sample at the Sydney Olympics, Ljungqvist was quoted as saying that an IOC expert panel was "very critical and... found that the sole validated, scientifically acceptable method for EPO detection would be a blood analysis to find out changes in the blood parametres together with a confirmation of the presence of erythropoietin in urine."

No blood test was carried out on Yegorova in Paris and the urine analysis alone was insufficient evidence; accordingly she was allowed to compete – and despite the pressure of such attention, took the gold medal – and presumably passed all tests in Edmonton Fair-minded athletes will continue to push for rigorous testing procedures, so that all can benefit from a "level playing-field" and their case was led in Edmonton by Paula Radcliffe who with some British team colleagues displayed a banner proclaiming "EPO cheats out".

The IAAF and many, though not all, national federations are to be commended for the lead they are taking in combating the evils of illegal drug taking. But it continues to be a tough battle against what one hopes is a minority of athletes who are prepared to cheat, the scientific developments which produce performance-enhancing products, and the costly legal procedures brought in by those accused, We all rush to defend someone who might be innocently accused and face a career-threatening suspension, but it must be right that all sport takes a tough line and insists that the athletes have the ultimate responsibilty for their bodies. Without that line it is all too easy for anyone to find an excuse and escape any penalty.

With regard to EPO, marathon expert David Martin writes: "Interestingly, at the 13th World Congress of the Association of International Marathons (AIMS) held in conjunction with the World Championships, there was considerable discussion regarding the announcement in March by five major marathons (Berlin, Boston, Chicago, London, and New York) that they supported blood testing at major races in an attempt to discourage the use of such substances as erythropoietin (EPO), the kidney hormone that increases blood haemoglobin concentration by increasing red blood cell production. The resulting elevated oxygen transport capabilities of the blood significantly quickens the sustainable marathon race pace. As a result of the Congress, an additional 21 AIMS events subsequently endorsed the recommendation. Relevant anti-doping agencies are still undecided as to the best strategy for implementing urine testing (which detects synthetic EPO itself) and/or blood testing (which only identifies the effects of clandestine EPO use, such as high haemoglobin, high red cell count, etc.). EPO use among top-level athletes remains unquantified, but suspected, causing mixed reaction when fast performances are achieved."

IAAF Rule Changes

THERE WAS a huge raft of rule changes approved by the IAAF Congress in Edmonton, 2001. Some of these have, however, have caused great concern. Extraordinarily, the weight of implements used for top-level junior competition have been lessened, depite that fact that the senior implements have posed no problems at this level of competition over many years. Now the junior shot and hammer are 6kg and discus 1.75kg.

Most particularly, the IAAF proposals for changing the Hammer, particularly in that the handle should change from a curved handle to a 115mm equilateral triangle, have horrified experts at the event. The Hammer Circle in the UK put forward a detailed petition:

1. That the hammer handle reverts to its specification pre the Edmonton 2001 conference, and that manufacturers must ensure that their handles will not stretch or they are banned, because: a. Many throwers cannot get their hands into the new specification, b. A straight handle will present a greater chance of injury as most of the pressure will be on the index and little fingers, c. All hammer wires would have to be changed as the recommended handle is now 10.4mm shorter than before the Edmonton Conference, d. The weight of all the existing hammer heads would need to be changed to accommodate a heavier handle.
2. That the 5kg hammer reverts to its specification pre the Edmonton 2001 conference, because by reducing the overall length by 1.5cm, and increasing the size of the hammer head, everyone has now to buy new competition hammers and all the records are invalidated.
3. That the inclusion of the ruling of a 6kg hammer for Under 20 men in Major Domestic and International competitions be removed for safety reasons, and the rules revert to the specification pre the Edmonton 2001 conference. Because reducing the junior men's hammer by almost 17.5%, down to 6kg, and using this weight for the major international U20 comps is a real concern for the safety of the event. It should be noted that the top juniors in the world last year were throwing over 70m with the 7.26kg hammer.
4. That the sector reverts to it's specification pre the Edmonton 2001 conference of 40°. because narrowing the sector to 34.29° in the interests of safety does not unfortunately make hammer throwing safer; it has the opposite effect and could easily lull people into a false sense of security. With the sector at 80m now only 48.00m (cut down from 54.72m). This ruling has therefore made the event potentially dangerous. Almost all long throws are down the left-hand hand sector.
5. That hammer cages are correctly sighted in all existing stadia before a safety certificate is issued, and that future stadia be standardised.

Participation

The IAAF announced that 14 member nations competed in all of the 2001 IAAF World Athletic Series events: Belarus, Brazil, Ethiopia, France, Great Britain, Italy, Kenya Morocco, Portugal, Romania, Russia, South Africa Spain and the United States.

Carried forward from Page 524:

Women 100th Bests

	1984	1988	1992	1995	1996	1997	1998	1999	2000	2001
100m	11.51	11.43	11.45	11.47	11.44	11.40	11.39	11.41	**11.36**	11.43
200m	23.39	23.32	23.36	23.36	23.32	23.25	23.24	23.22	**23.21**	23.27
400m	52.63	52.50	52.60	52.59	52.29	52.66	52.40	52.46	**52.26**	52.49
800m	**2:01.50**	2:01.66	2:02.80	2:03.23	2:02.96	2:02.56	2:02.6	2:02.53	2:02..50	2:03.02
1500m	**4:10.22**	4:11.70	4:11.80	4:13.97	4:11.87	4:11.97	4:12.68	4:11.79	4:11.18	4:12.13
3000m	9:01.50	9:01.60	9:01.83	9:07.95*	- -					
5000m				15:39.12	15:35.62	15:39.95	15:40.74	15:37.76	**15:29.36**	15:34.49
10000m	34:26.36	33:11.31	33:05.80	33:00.33	32:56.63	32:59.33	33:11.36	32:59.05	**32:32.47**	32:35.90
Marathon	2:37:29	2:35:29	2:36:14	2:34:25	2:33:24	2:33:38	2:33:45	2:33:05	2:32:25	**2:31:05**
100mh	13.48	13.39	13.35	13.37	13.31	13.35	13.33	13.32	**13.22**	13.31
400mh	58.07	57.50	57.60	57.91	57.63	57.64	57.74	57.59	**57.48**	57.50
HJ	1.87	**1.88**	**1.88**	1.87	1.87	1.86	1.86	1.86	1.87	1.86
PV				-	3.60	3.77	3.90	4.00	**4.10**	4.08
LJ	6.48	**6.53**	6.45	6.46	6.50	6.48	6.48	6.48	6.49	6.45
TJ			13.16	13.36	13.45	13.53	13.51	13.64	**13.68**	13.60
SP	17.18	17.02	16.40	16.33	16.34	16.70	16.58	16.53	16.44	16.57
DT	**58.50**	57.40	56.20	55.84	56.86	56.04	56.28	56.02	56.22	55.54
HT				-	53.84	55.72	57.66	59.08	60.66	**61.46**
JT	57.74	**58.14**	56.36	56.04	56.16	55.48	54.80	54.54*	55.55*	54.56*
Heptathlon		**5741**	5661	5609	5649	5620	5604	5596	5647	5640
10kmW	50:17	?	45:59	46:06	**45:48**	46:01	46:05			
20kmW								1:36:59	**1:34:44**	1:35:15

All-time record levels indicated in bold. * Note new javelin from 1999.

Other peaks: 3000m 9:00.65 (1993), HJ 1.88 (also 1986, 1987, 1993), SP 17.19 (1987)

HALL OF FAME

OUR Hall of Fame was introduced in ATHLETICS 2002. Every year we will select five athletes – to be a mix of former greats and athletes with notable achievements during the past year to add to career brilliance over at least ten years. The initial five were: Sergey Bubka, Heike Drechsler, Michael Johnson, Emil Zátopek and Jan Zelezny. Here are this year's selections:

Fanny Blankers-Koen was voted by the IAAF as its Woman Athlete of the 20th Century. She was the heroine of the 1948 Olympic Games when she won four gold medals, at 100m, 200m, 80m hurdles and sprint relay. At the European Championships she won the same individual events in 1950, but took silver in the relay; having won gold at hurdles and relay in 1946 and bronze at 100m and 200m in 1938.

She first competed at the Olympic Games in 1936 at the age of 18 and, having set her first Dutch record for 800m in 1935, her exceptional versatility is shown by the fact that she set 16 world records at eight different events, 100y, 100m, 200m, 80m hurdles, high jump, long jump and pentathlon as well as at 4x110y relay.

Jonathan Edwards took triple jumping to new levels in 1995, when he set world records of 18.16 and 18.29 with his first two jumps in the final at the World Championships in Göteborg. Earlier that year, at the European Cup, he jumped 18.43w and 18.39w. He was disappointed to take silver at the 1996 Olympics and 1997 Worlds and bronze at the 1999 Worlds, but bounced back to win the Olympic gold in 2000 and regain his World title in 2001. The latter was his fifth successive World medal. He was European Champion indoors and out in 1998, and in 2002 will be hoping to improve on the silver medal that he won at the Commonwealth Games in both 1994 and 1998.

Jackie Joyner-Kersee has a prime claim as the world's greatest all-round woman athlete. She won both long jump and heptathlon by huge margins at the 1987 World Championships and went on to do the same Olympic double in 1988. She added a second Olympic heptathlon title in 1992 with bronze medals at long jump in 1992 and in 1996, having previously taken silver at heptathlon in 1984 when she was fifth at long jump. She set four world records at heptathlon, from 7148 in 1986 to 7291 in 1988. Her final mark, set when winning Olympic gold in Seoul, still stands. She also set a world long jump record at 7.45 in 1987 and twice ran a world indoor best of 7.37 for 55m hurdles in 1989.

Carl Lewis has the greatest collection of gold medals, with nine at the Olympic Games and eight at World Championships. At full stride in sprinting and long jumping he brought a sublime combination of speed, power, grace and technique to the world of sport, maintaining his form at the top for well over a decade.

At his first Olympic Games in Los Angeles 1984 he emulated Jesse Owens by winning four gold medals, at 100m, 200m, long jump and sprint relay. He went on to win the long jump at four successive Games (matching Al Oerter's record for any event) and also won gold at 100m in 1988, and sprint relay in 1992. At the World Championships of 1983 and 1987 Lewis won at 100m, long jump and relay, and almost repeated this in 1991, when, after becoming the first man to exceed the 23-year-old world record of Bob Beamon by jumping 8.91m (with wind assistance), he was passed by Mike Powell's 8.95m. Lewis won the 100 metres in a world record 9.86 and added another world record when he anchored the US sprint relay team to victory.

Cornelius Warmerdam was indisputably the world's greatest ever pole vaulter – until Sergey Bubka came along. Denied the chance of two Olympic gold medals by World War II, he became the first 15ft vaulter and established a dominance well over that height a decade before any other vaulter could do so. *See the Obituaries section for details of his career*.

Expansion of Hall of Fame

In order to give us a more solid foundation for our Hall of Fame, with an ongoing five selections a year, we are going to give a major boost to the numbers in ATHLETICS 2003. To do this we invite all discerning enthusiasts to vote for the greatest athlete of all time at each standard event, and the winners will be included.

Some are there already, for it is surely inconceivable to deny such a title to Sergey Bubka for pole vault, Michael Johnson for 200m and 400m, or Jackie Joyner-Kersee for women's multi-events, or Carl Lewis and Jan Zelezny?

Please take great care with your voting, making due consideration of the achievements of athletes throughout the history of our sport.

One qualification – athletes still competing must have at least ten years in international competition. So such as Haile Gebrselassie, Edwards and Zelezny will qualify, but Maurice Greene and Marion Jones will not (yet!).

Please vote for one athlete at each standard event – and also select an additional five over the full spread of events. Votes to SportsBooks Limited, PO Box 422, Worcester, WR1 1ZT, UK (or email: randall@sportsbooks.ltd.uk)

Jackie Joyner-Kersee – the world's greatest all-round woman athlete won six Olympic medals including three gold and four World Championships gold medals at heptathlon and long jump.

In 2001 Jonathan Edwards won his fifth World triple jump medal and regained the title that he had won in 1995 with the world record of 18.29m.He also has Olympic gold and silver.

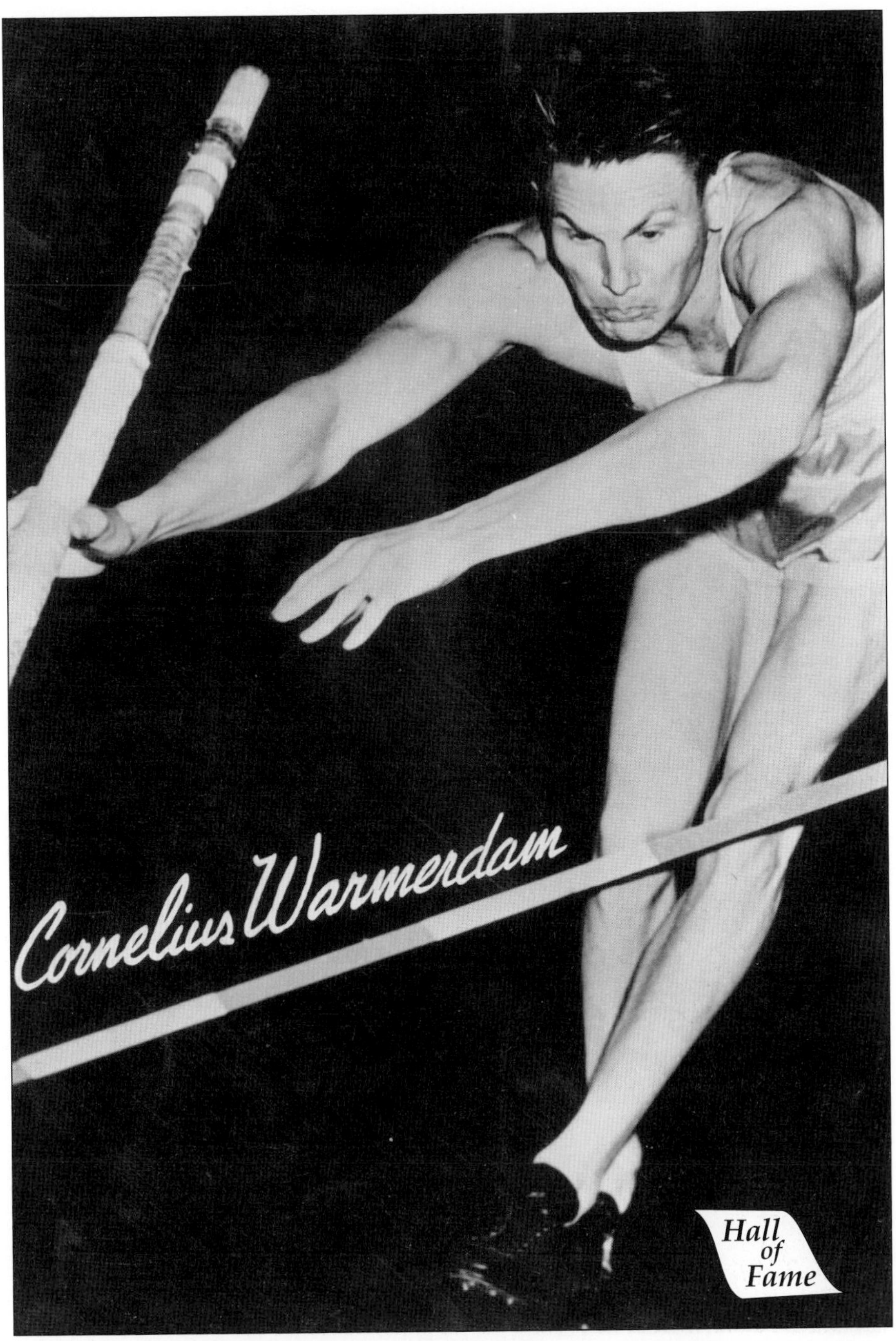

Cornelius 'Dutch' Warmerdam set 13 world records at the pole vault, seven outdoors and six indoors. His best of 4.79m indoors in 1943 was not bettered until 1957. (See Obituary).

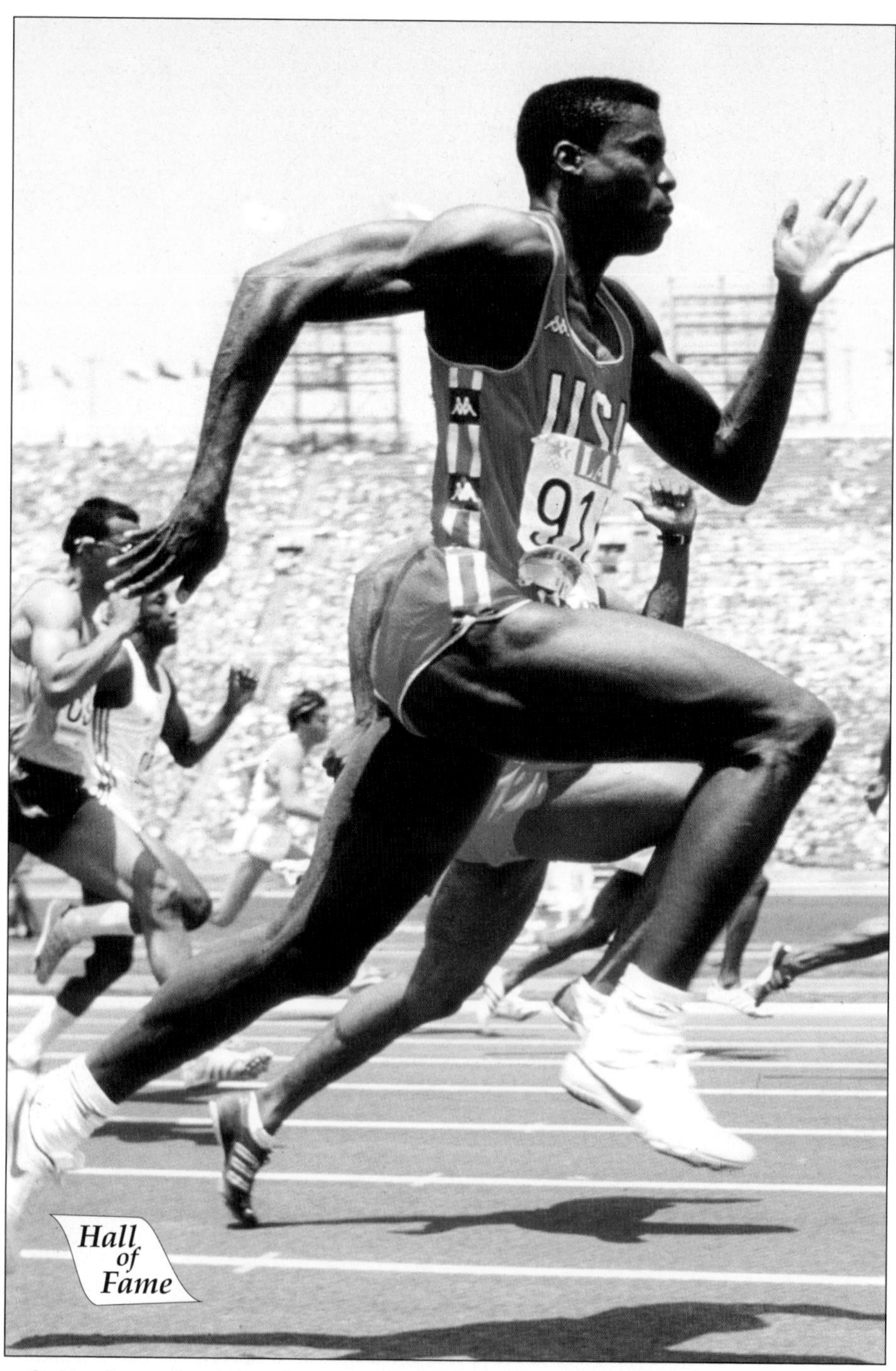

Carl Lewis was the choice of many as the Greatest Athlete of the 20th Century. He won nine Olympic gold medals, including four successive at long jump, and eight at the worlds.

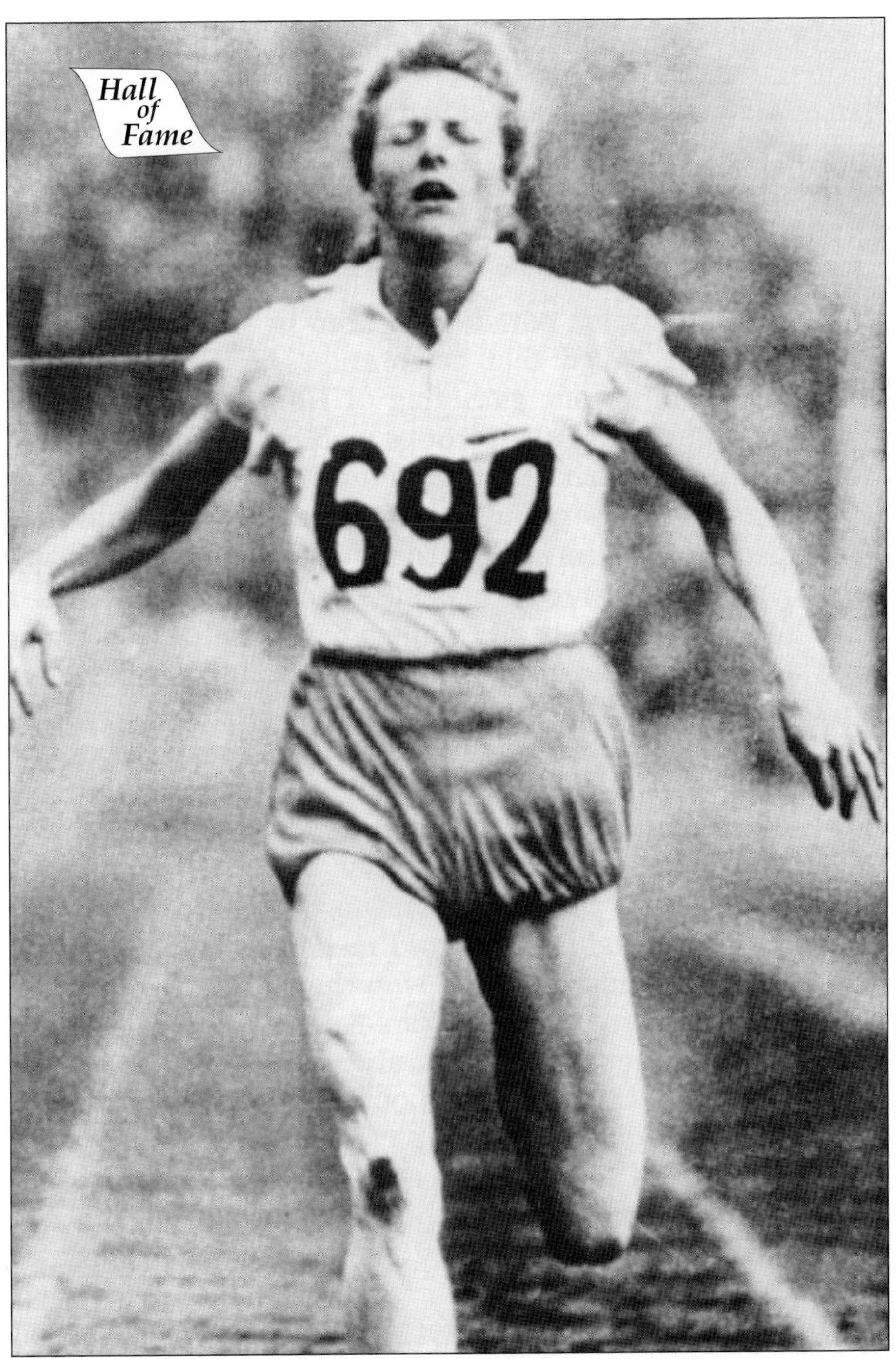

Fanny Blankers-Koen, the IAAF's female Athlete of the Century, won four gold medals at the 1948 Olympics and in all set 16 world records at eight different events.

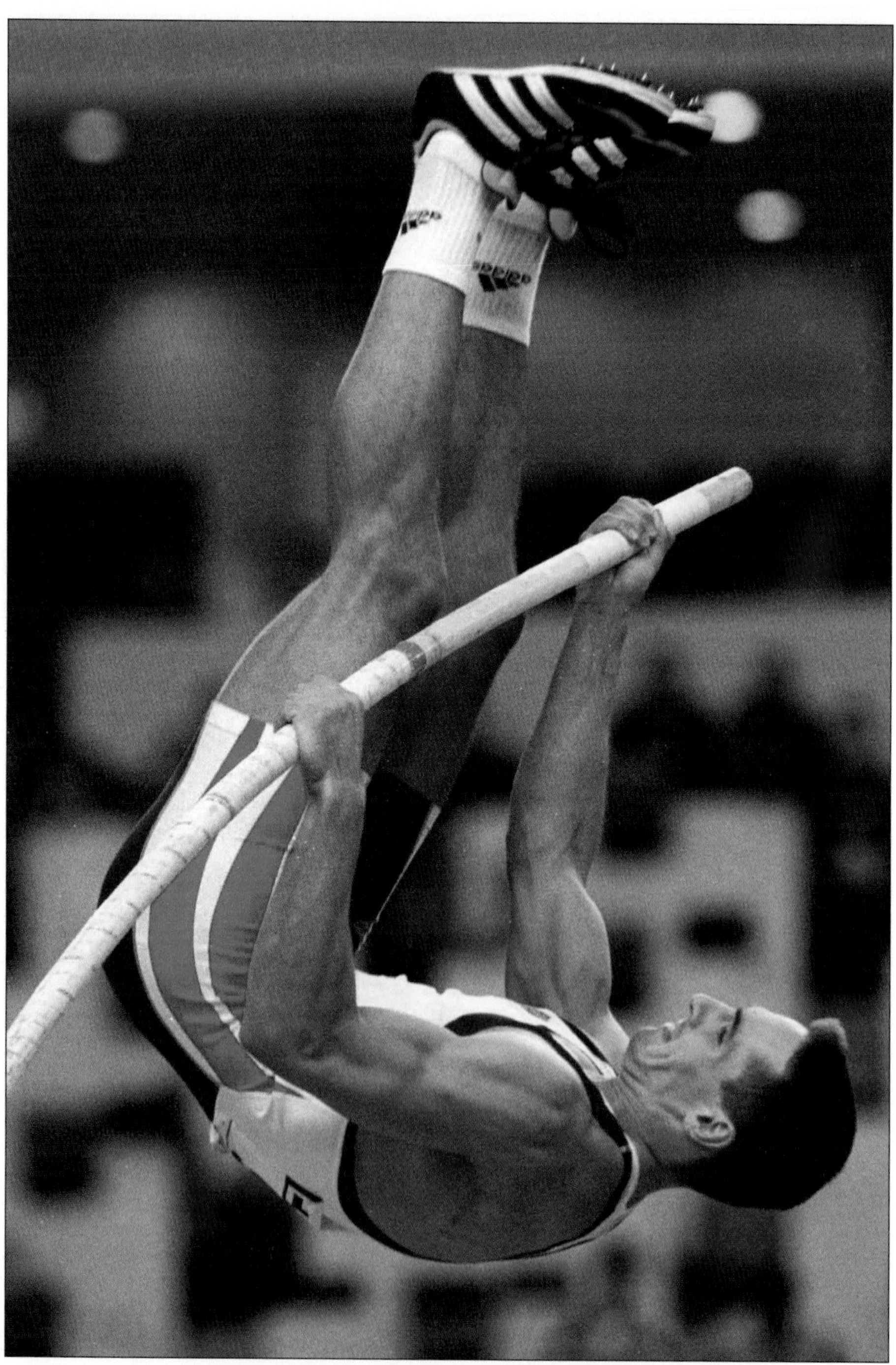

Roman Sebrle, of the Czech Republic, could manage only 10th in Edmonton due to injury but he set a new world record earlier in the year.

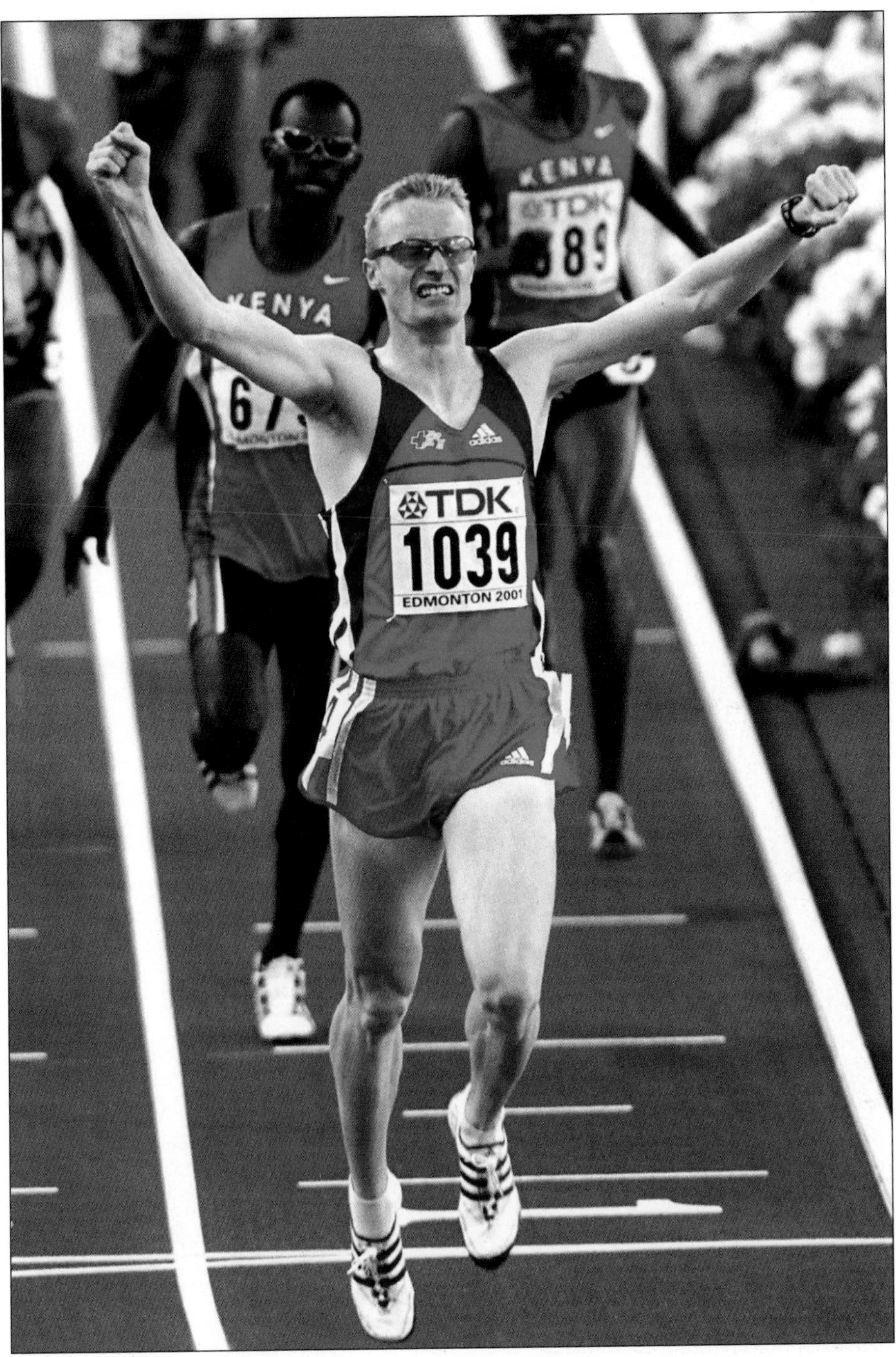

Andreas Bucher, of Switzerland, wins the world title in a season during which he was beaten only once

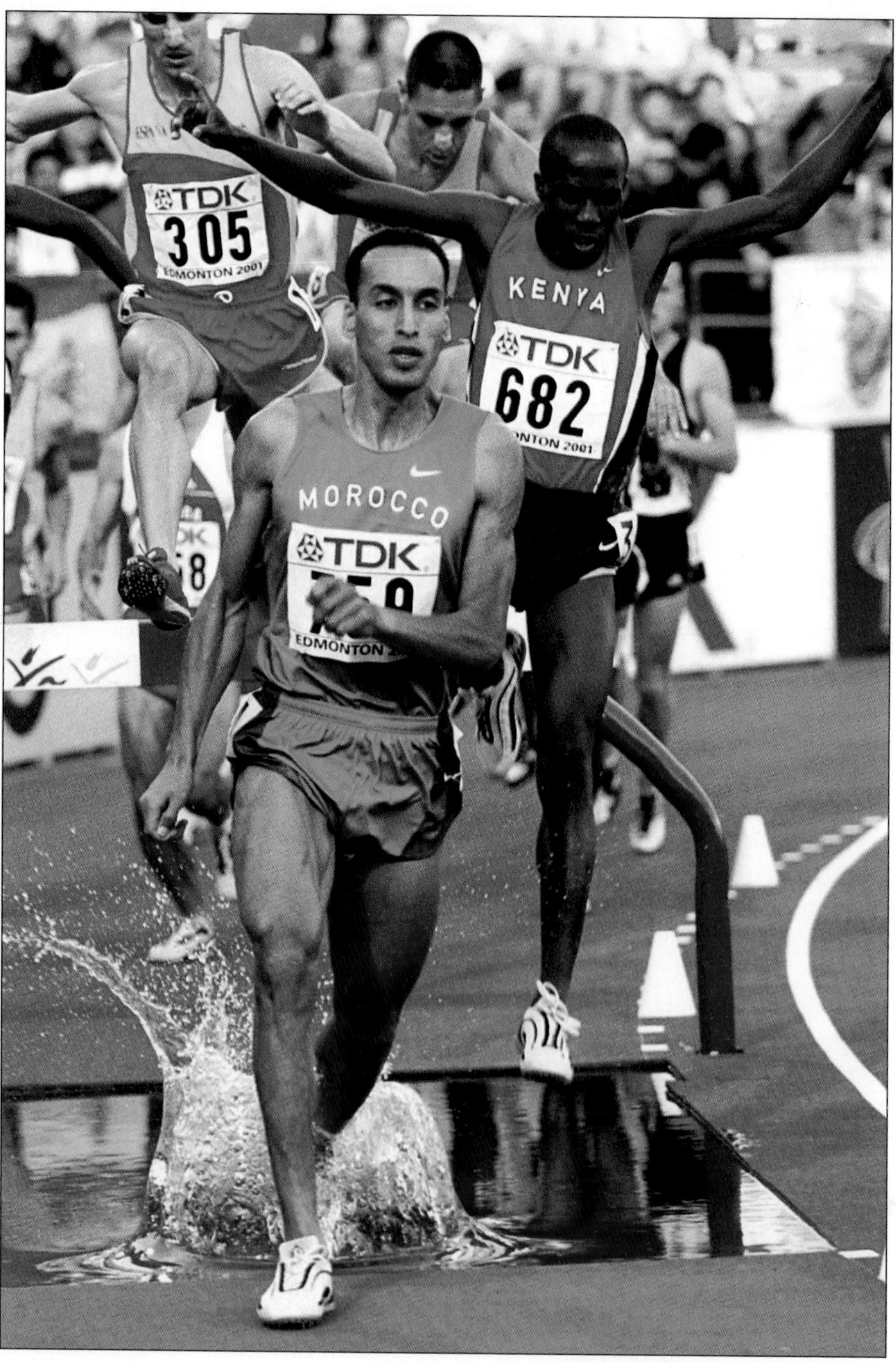

Brahim Boulami, of Morocco, did not distinguish himself in Edmonton but went on to break the world steeplechase record in Brussels.

ATHLETICS REFERENCE BOOKS 2001/2002

Reviewed by Peter Matthews

Running Through The Ages by Edward S. Sears. 280x160mm. A5 330 pages. A splendid evocation of running from pre-historic times to 1999, this book deals extensively with the earliest days of running as a necessity and as a sport, and half the book is for the pre-1900 period. So the story takes us through running in Ancient Egypt, Greece and Rome, to the ages of pedestrianism and the amateurs to the modern worldwide professional sport, although the modern chapters have a slant towards the US. At $55 ($59 postpaid in US), the book is very expensive but is an important addition to the literature of our sport. Published by McFarland & Company, Inc., Box 611, Jefferson, North Carolina 28640, USA. Order line 1-800-253-2187. www.mcfarlandpub.com.

Fields of Green, Lanes of Gold, The Story of Athletics in Australia by Paul Jenes. This 304 page hard cover book with over 200 black and white and colour photographs not only covers the history of the parent body – Athletics Australia – but also the formation of State Associations, clubs and how athletics developed in Australia from the early 1800s to just after the Sydney Olympics. Available for A$60 plus postage from Athletics Australia, Suite 22, 431 St Kilda Road, Melbourne, Victoria, Australia 3004. E-mail: www.athletics.org.au; Fax: 61-3-9820 3544.

History of Athletics – Central American & Caribbean Championships. A5 302 pages. Basilio Fuentes, the ATFS member from Cuba, has provided the complete results of the 17 editions of the CAC Championships from 1967 to 1999. The book is available for £15 or $20 to Basilio's daughter: Marianela Collishaw, 17 Coniston Road, Beeston, Nottingham NG9 3AD, UK.

The History of Welsh Athletics by John Collins, Alan & Brenda Currie, Mike Walters and Clive Williams. Two books (sold together) 362 and 248 (statistics only) pp, 253x178mm. This massive work presents enthusiastically the story of athletics in Wales over the past 200 years. Interwoven with the evolution of the sport there are 40 pen pictures of the most influential athletes and officials, and there is a chapter on the link between rugby and athletics. The statistics volume is hugely comprehensive, with progressive records, all-time lists and lists of Welsh championships winners and medallists including summaries of all major championships and details of Welsh athletes competing for Britain. £28 plus p &p (£5 UK, £10 Europe, £20 elsewhere). UK orders to 'The Sports Bookshop', 26 Royal Arcade, Cardiff CF10 1AE. Non-UK orders (cheques drawn on a UK bank payable to Dragon Sports Books Ltd) to A.Currie, 3 Henfaes Terrace, Tonna, Neath, W.Glam SA11 3EQ, UK.

Zá-to-pek! Zá-to-pek! Zá-to-pek! The Life and Times of the World's Greatest Distance Runner. By Bob Phillips. 140pp A5 Hardback. This slim volume is an evocative and fitting memorial to the Emil Zátopek, who was a wonderful runner and a great man. The author draws upon Fratisek Kozík's biography published in 1954, from reports of his races in contemporary magazines, from his own memories and with tributes from Roberto Quercetani, Mel Watman, Colin Young and Neil Allen. There is a detailed statistical summary by Milan Skocovsky and Stanislav Hrcir, including all Zátopek's races at 3000m, 5000m and 10,000m. Published by The Parrs Wood Press, St Wilfrid's Enterprise Centre, Royce Road, Manchester M15 5BJ, UK. £14.95 post-free in the UK.
See www.parrswoodpress.com

Men's All-Time World List (2001 edition). A5. The fourth edition of this major work by Roberto Quercetani and Giuseppe Mappa. 1000 best performances in each of the men's Olympic events as at 1 January 2001 and an index of athletes. $24 from the publishers, the International Athletic Foundation, Stade Louis II, Avenue du Prince Héréditaire Albert, MC 98000, Monaco.

Weltrekorde und Weltrekordler Kugelstoßen, Diskuswarf. A4 128 pages. Manfred Holzhausen continues his series of splendidly detailed surveys (in German) of world records and world record holders in the IAAF-era (i.e. from 1912). There are profiles (and illustrations) of all world-record-holders, with detailed surveys of their careers and a table of yearly world bests for each year 1900-2001. This book covered the men's shot and discus, and previous works have been for: 100m/200m/220y, 800m/1000m, 1500m/1M, HJ/LJ, HT/JT. Details from Manfred Holzhausen, Dresdener Str. 4, 41516 Grevenbroich, Germany, Tel: +49 211813049, FAX: +49 211811849 (m.holzhausen@planet- interkom.de).

TAFWA All-Time Indoor List 2002. A5 204pp. Ed Gordon's excellent annual compilation which contains world all-time indoor lists of performers (c.200 deep) and performances (c. 100 deep) for all events, men and women has been updated to include the 2001 season. Contact EdGordon007@compuserve.com.

World Youth Athletics Handbook 2001. A5, 60pp. By Lionel Peters. Published to coincide with this year's IAAF World Youth Champs, contents are: world and area bests for athletes under 18 in the year of competition, top tens for 2000 and all-time, age bests for 14, 15, 16 & 17, progressive world bests and results from the inaugural World Youth Champs in 1999 and other events. Price £5 (Europe) or £6 outside Europe if paid by cheque payable at a UK bank or by international postal/money order or in currency notes; add 5% for payment by Visa/Mastercard. Send to World Junior Athletics News, 40 Berkeley Road, London NW9 9DG.

European Junior Athletics Handbook 2001. Also edited by Lionel Peters and published as two separate 60-page A5 booklets (Part 1: Men; Part 2: Women). Total price £10 (Europe) or £12 elsewhere, details as above. Contents include all previous European & World Junior medallists, all-time lists, age bests (12-19) national records and progressive European Junior records.

World Junior Athletics Annual 2000-2001. By Lionel Peters. A5, 84pp. World, Area and Regional results for track and field and cross-country in 2000. The World Junior best performers lists by Milan Skocovsky are 50 deep and include the 10 best performances. Also **World Junior Cross-Country Annual 2001-02** (36pp). Each (including postage) £5 (UK & Europe), £6 (outside Europe). £8 for payment by non-UK cheque or 5% by credit card. Pounds, US Dollars, Euros accepted, from Lionel Peters as above.

Listas Mundiais de Sempre (World All-Time Lists). 232 pp A4. 300 deep for men and 200 deep for women. Luís Leite has updated and extended his lists to the end of 2001. One pre-war athlete still makes the list: Jesse Owens with his 8.13 long jump, ranked 254th equal. Available from Luis at: Av. Alm. Gago Coutinho 154, 1700-033 Lisboa, Portugal for 18 Euro within Europe, $20 US elsewhere.

Asian Athletics All-time Rankings. A5 212 pages. DM 40/Euro 20 in Europe, US $20 outside Europe in cash or Eurocheque (in DM only) or by International Money Order from the author, Heinrich Hubbeling, Haydnstrasse 8, 48691 Vreden, Germany. Included are Asian all-time top 100 performers for all events, with additional performers for countries outside the dominant nations of China and Japan and all national records.

Welsh Women's Athletics 1919-1959 by John Brant. In two A4 folders. This work details a large number of results in the period before the sport became widely recognised for women in Wales. The second part ends with Commonwealth record progressions 1891-1959. £20, including postage, from John Brant, 40 The Quadrant, Cottingham Road, Hull HU6 8NX, UK.

An Athletics Compendium – A Guide to the UK Literature of Track and Field. By Tom McNab, Peter Lovesey and Andrew Huxtable. Tom McNab provides an extensive review of athletics literature in his own idiosyncratic style, and this is followed by individual entries for books on athletics published in the UK and Ireland (from 1531 to 2000), with informed annotation and extensive indexes. This is an invaluable work, although unfortunately flawed by inadequate and inaccurate details of modern statistical works, including this series of Annuals (!). This is the third of a series of sports bibliographies (Rugby 1998, Football 1999) published by the British Library, Boston Spa, Wetherby, West Yorkshire LS23 7BQ (www.bl.uk). Price £30 from: Turpin Distribution, Blackhorse Road, Letchworth, Herts SG6 1HN, UK.

The College Sports – University College and Queen's College, Cork – 1869-1914 by Catherine and Colm Murphy. A5 96pp. Each of the Annual Sports in Cork is given a double page spread, with results faced by contemporary newspaper reports and a round-up of significant happenings. This gives a fascinating insight into a past age and of an event that featured all the great Irish athletes of the period. Price £10 plus £1 postage. A companion volume of c.200 pages tracing the history of the Cork University Athletic Club will be ready very soon – £15 plus £1 postage.

Sports Comparisons ... You *Can* Compare Apples to Oranges. By Dale Harder. A4, 130 pages. $14.95 + $3 in USA, or $5 surface mail to rest of world, or $9.75 airmail to rest of world. Payment in US dollars or international money order from the author at Education Plus, 18584 Carlwyn Drive, Castro Valley, CA 94546-2032, USA. The author attempts to compare achievements in athletics and a wide range of other sports – much fascinating material, although one can argue with the results.

ANNUALS

For most Annuals below referring to 2000, there will be new issues covering 2001.

Combined Events Annual 2001 by Hans van Kuijen. A5, 216pp. The 9th edition of this attractively produced annual includes top 200 men's and women's lists for 2001, including all decathlons over 7500 points and heptathlons over 5600, and all-time world lists for the multis. There are also results of major events, profiles and complete career details for 100 of the world's top multi-eventers, records etc. and a special feature on the European Cup for Combined Events. 25 euro by international money order or cash (add 7.5 euro for bank charges for cheques or payments to ABN-AMRO bank account); or £20 sterling, US $25 (cash) in Europe; US $30 cash or $35 cheques elsewhere from Hans van Kuijen, de Bergen 66, 5706 RZ Helmond, Netherlands. email: hvankuijen@wxs.nl

L'Athlétisme Africain/African Athletics 2001. A5, 152p. By Yves Pinaud. 100 deep men's and women's lists for Africa for 2000, with all-time lists, national championships and major meetings results. FF 130 (or US $20) from Polymédias, 103 rue de Paris, 94220 Charenton le Pont, France. (Previous annuals 1979-2000 available at various prices). Also available at £12 from Tony Isaacs, 11 Manton Close, Trowbridge, Wiltshire BA14 0RZ, England.

Atletismo 2001 – Argentina. A5, 212pp. By Luis Vinker, Edgardo Fontana, Rubén Aguilera and Salvador Fontana for the Confederación Argentina de Atletismo, 21 de Noviembre No. 207, 3260 Concepción del Uruguay, Entre Ríos, Argentina. Comprehensive results, records and ranking lists for 2000 for Argentina.

Asian Athletics 2000 rankings. A5 88 pages. DM 30/US $15 in Europe, DM 40/US $20 outside Europe in cash or Eurocheque (in DM only) or by International Money Order from the author, Heinrich Hubbeling, Haydnstrasse 8, 48691 Vreden, Germany (or for £10 from Tony Isaacs, 11 Manton Close, Trowbridge, Wiltshire BA14 0RZ, England.). Top 30s for 2000 for athletes from Asian nations, together with continuation lists for countries other than China and Japan and all new national records set during the year. Also included are Asian records. Copies also available for Asia 1993, 1995, 1997 and 1998.

Athletics Australia 2001 Season Guide. A5 424p. 45th year of issue. The usual comprehensive annual lists (for 2000), records, results and 30-deep all-time lists compiled by Paul Jenes are combined with Athletics Australia's guide to the season and profiles of about 150 top Australian athletes. From the publishers Athletics Australia. www.athletics.org.au

Jaarboek 2000 (Belgian Athletics Annual). 368 A4 pages include deep 2000 lists for all age groups plus all-time lists, championship results etc. 600 Belgian francs plus postage from Michel Jordens, Koning Boudewijnstadion 119C, 1020 Brussel, Belgium.

Caribbean Athletics Annual 2000 A5, 152pp. £10 or US $16 ($20 outside Europe) by Bernard Linley. Results are given of major meetings and championships in the Caribbean in 2000, with 20-deep CAC lists for 2000 and c.40-deep all-time lists. This year's major feature is the compilation of all medallists at the CAC Championships 1967-99; and there are also 30 deep Trinidad and Tobago all-time lists. Price £10 from Tony Isaacs, 11 Menton Close, Trowbridge, Wiltshire BA14 0RZ, England.

Atletické Vykony 2000. A5 234pp. Edited by Ludek Follprecht and Milan Urban. Deep ranking lists for all age groups in 2000 for the Czech Republic and detailed results of championships. A special feature gives top ten lists for 1946. Published by Ceská Atletiky svaz, Mezi stadiony – PS 40, 160 17 Praha 6, Czech Republic.

DAF 2000 I tal. A5 278p. The Danish athletics annual, edited by Erik Laursen, provides, as ever, most comprehensive records with 2000 and all-time lists. Price 125 DKr from the Dansk Athletic Federation, Idrattens Hus, 2605 Brondby, Denmark or on-line at www.dansk-atletik.dk.

Laursens's lille lommebog 2001. A6. 84pp. Danish ranking lists for 2001, and all-time indoor lists for all events, with men's 1500m lists 1950-9. 60 DKr (plus DKr 24 in Europe, 38 DKr elsewhere) from Erik Laursen, Sandbakken 95, 8270 Høbjerg, Denmark. Tel/fax 86 27 96 34 (Giro 1 46 5333).

Eesti Kergejõustiku Aastraamat 2001. 264pp. Edited by Ants Teder and Erlend Teemägi. Estonian ranking lists for 2000, with results and records and 8 pages of colour photographs. From Eesti Kergejõustikuliit, Regati pst. 1, 11911 Tallinn, Estonia.

European Athletics Yearbook 2001-02. A5 458pp. The official yearbook of the European Athletic Association. 20 Euro in Europe (25 overseas), cash or Eurocheque to the publishers Ph. Reinheimer Druckerei GmbH & Co. KG, Alsfeder Straße 27, 64289 Darmstadt, Germany. Contents include deep European lists for 2001 (seniors, under-23 and juniors) and all-time compiled by Nejat Kök, results of major 2001 European events, records and useful addresses.

Yleisurheilu 2001. A5 638pp. The Finnish annual, published in December 2001 includes very deep Finnish lists for all age groups – down to 9! – with results of championships and international matches. It also contains indoor and outdoor world lists for 2001 with information received by Mirko Jalava as at mid-November. 20 euro or equivalent from Tilastopaja Oy,

Raskinpolku 9 E 88, 20360 Turku, Finland. Can be ordered by email from juhani@tilastopaja.fi – there is also a credit card facility.

Athlerama 2000. The French Annual, edited by Jean Gilbert. A5, 588pp. Packed with information on French athletics – deep year lists for 2000, profiles, results, all-time lists. 150 FF including postage from the FFA, 33 avenue Pierre de Coubertin, 75640 Paris CEDEX 13, France.

Deutsche Bestenliste 2000 A5 198 pp. 30 DM or US $20. Edited by Klaus Amrhein for the Deutschen Gesellschaft für Leichtathletik-Dokumentation (DGLD). Deep performance and performer year lists for Germany for 2000 (although unfortunately no indoor marks are listed). See DGLD details at the end of this review.

DLV-Jahrbuch 2001/2002. A5 392pp. The official yearbook of the German Federation. Articles and review, with articles on top athletes, detailed results of 2001 meetings, records and top tens, with illustrations in colour. Euro 17.90 plus postage, from Deutsche Leichtathletik Marketing GmbH, Postfach 10 04 63, 64219 Darmstadt, Germany.

DLV-Bestenliste 2001. A5 432pp. The DLV's ranking lists for 2001 for all events compiled by Eberhard Vollmer, generally 50-deep for seniors and Jugend-A, 30-deep for other age groups.

Israeli Amateur Athletic Association 2001 Annual compiled by David and Arik Cooks. 44pp 235 x 168mm. $6 US, 7 Euro or equivalent from David Eiger, 10 Ezra Hozsofer Str, Herzliya 46 371, Israel. Records, championship results, 2001 top ten and all-time lists, and profiles of leading Israeli athletes.

Japan Athletics Annual 2001. A5 264pp. Japan AAF. Annual and all-time list with championship results. Also articles on top athletes in English. Available from Yoshimasa Noguchi, Track & Field Magazine, BBM Co. Ltd., 3-10-10 Misaki-cho, Chiyoda-ku, Tokyo 101-8381, Japan.

Latvijas Vieglatletikas Gadagramata 2002. A5 312 pp. Most comprehensive coverage of Latvian athletics, including 2001 and all-time lists, results and biographies, compiled by Andris Stagis. From the Latvian Athletic Association, Augsiela 1, Riga LV-1009, Latvia.

Annuare FLA 2001. A4 96p. The Luxembourg Annual, edited by Georges Klepper has every possible detail for this nation. Details from FLA, BP 503, L-2015 Luxembourg.

Scottish Athletics Yearbook 2001. A5 272p. Edited by Arnold Black for the SATS, this is the usual very comprehensive review of Scottish athletics. There are deep Scottish lists for all age groups, records, event reviews and championship results for the year 2000. As ever, remarkable value at £6 including postage in the UK, £7 Europe, £8 elsewhere, cheques payable to S.A.T.S. From Arnold Black, 19 Millbrae Crescent, Langside, Glasgow G42 9UW, UK.

2000 SA Athletics Annual. A5 80p. The annual publication of the South African Athletics Statisticians (SAAS) edited by Hans Prinsloo had to be greatly reduced this year due to unexpected financial difficulties. Nonetheless all the essential features – records, 2000 and all-time lists – are incorporated. Rand 35 by surface mail or R70 airmail from SA Athletics Annual, PO Box 35209, Menlo Park, 0102 South Africa.

El Atletismo Sudamericano 2001. A5, 184pp. By Luis Vinker and Edgardo Fontana for Confederación Sudamericana de Atletismo. South American ranking lists for 2000 with records, results and articles.

Anuario Atlético Español 2000/2001. A5, 742pp. Edited by José Luis Hernández and Ignacio Mansilla. This hugely comprehensive Annual includes deep Spanish year lists for all age groups, all-time lists and biographies with index of best Spanish athletes, as well as detailed results from the Spanish season in 2001. Details from Federación Española de Atletismo, Avda, Valladolid 81 – 1°, 28.008 Madrid, Spain.

Sverige Bästa 2000. A5 240p. Edited by A Lennart Julin. Detailed Swedish lists. Published by the Svenska Friidrottsförbundet, Box 11, 171 18 Solna, Sweden.

Friidrott 2000. A5 382pp. The eighth edition of this attractive annual by Göran Lenz covering world and Scandinavian athletics. Detailed championships results with narrative and world outdoor top 50 year and all-time lists, top 25 Scandinavian year and all-time lists plus indoor top tens. $49 Europe, $52 rest of the world. 395 kr. Details from Gordons Förlag, Bärnstensvägen 2, 226 51 Lund, Sweden. email: goran.lenz@swipnet.se

Schweizer Leichtathletik-Jahrbuch 2000. A5 320p. Published by the Swiss Federation (SLV/FSA). Comprehensive compilation of Swiss records, results, year lists and all-time top tens. From the Schweizerischer Leichtathletik Verband (SLV), Postfach 8222, CH 3001, Bern.

British Athletics 2001. The NUTS Annual, edited by Rob Whittingham and Peter Matthews. 416 pages including 16 of colour photographs. Contents include deep UK ranking lists for all age groups in 2000, top 12 merit rankings, all-time lists, results etc. £15 UK, £17 rest of Europe,

£18 outside Europe; from Umbra Software Ltd, Unit 1, Bredbury Business Park, Bredbury Park Way, Stockport, SK6 2SN, England.

Note that Rob Whittingham plans to produce a book on **Commonwealth Games** athletics results in the summer of 2002.

2001 USA Track & Field Media Guide & FAST Annual (general editors: Jill M Geer & Scott S Davis). A5 542pp. The 23rd edition of the FAST Annual is again combined with the USATF Media Guide (first 160 pages of this edition). Packed with US statistics and extensive index material including annual progressions etc for all top American athletes. Amazingly, however, the US lists for 2000 take just 38 pages and are given only 25 deep per event, although there are deeper all-time lists. Price $20 ($24 sea-mail, $32 airmail to Europe) from Scott Davis, 4432 Snowbird Circle, Cerritos, CA 90703, USA.

Pacific Statistics - Athletics in Melanesia, Polynesia & Micronesia. Issue no.21 reviewed performances in 2000 in the Melanesian area covering Fiji, New Caledonia, Papua New Guinea, West New Guinea (i.e. Indonesian Papua), the Solomon Islands and Vanuatu, with detailed results at international and national championships; top 20s for 2000 and national records plus a Pacific-wide feature on the men's javelin in 2000. Price £5 (Europe) or £6 (airmail outside Europe) from the compiler, Tony Isaacs, 11 Manton Close, Trowbridge, Wiltshire, BA14 0RZ, England. Payment with order. tony.isaacs@tinyworld.co.uk

Statistical bulletins

The **DGLD – German** statistical group, the Deutschen Gesellschaft für Leichtathletik-Dokumentation, was founded in 1990. Its members produce annual national ranking lists (see **Deutsche Bestenliste**) for Germany and most impressive quarterly bulletins of up to 268 pages, packed with historical articles and statistical compilations. A major feature in each issue is detailed statistical profiles of athletes born in that quarter 70 years ago, 75, 80, 85, 90 etc. In 2001 bulletins no. 30-32 were published (each DM 30 or US $20). Membership, with free Deutsche Bestenliste costs Euro 45 per year. Details from Hans Waynberg, Grefrather Weg 100, 41464 Neuss/Rh, Germany. Website: www.ladgld.de

New books included

Das große Lexikon der DDR-Sportler by Volker Kluge. 24x17 cm. 448pp. Biographies of 1000 top names of the amazing era of GDR sport. DM39.80 from AGON-Sportverlag, Frankfurter Straße 92a, 34121 Kassel, Germany.

Alle Deutschen bei **Olympischen Spielen Welt – und Europameisterschaften 1896-2000** by Fritz Steinmetz. All German performances in international championships. DM37 from Fritz Steinmetz, Teichstraße 35, 34130 Kassel, Germany.

100 Jahre Leichtathletik in Deutschland. Band 4 – 800m-Lauf Männer. 254pp. Euro 10, and **Band 14 – Gehen Männer**. 368pp. Euro 17.5. By Jürgen Kollosche, covering the men's walks. The latest in the DGLD's detailed series giving comprehensive results, ranking lists and profiles by event.

TRACK STATS

The NUTS quarterly bulletin, edited by Bob Phillips, includes a wealth of fascinating statistics and articles. A5 size, 64-80 pages. Annual subscription (4 issues) is £17 (UK), £21 (rest of Europe) or £26 (elsewhere); contact Liz Sissons, 9 Fairoak Lane, Chessington, Surrey KT9 2NS, UK.

March 2001 contained features on F. R. (Dick) Webster, Micheline Ostermeyer and Taisto Mäki, detailed results of the 1938 British Empire Games.

June 2001 had a 400m flavour with articles on Britain's John Mark (the 1948 Olympic torch bearer), Canada's Bill Fritz, the USA's Ollie Matson and Trinidad's Wendell Mottley. There was also a compilation of the fastest 4x1500m relay times, and a career record of more than 800 races for Linford Christie.

September 2001 included features on Freddie Green, Frank Sando, Ed Moses and Elias Katz, plus statistics galore, including the UK indoor lists for 2001.

December 2001 –"Canada's Finest" featured four top athletes from that nation. Many other articles included: the first heroines of one-lap racing, the Polish women discus stars of the 1920s and 1930s, Mark Pharaoh and a detailed analysis of Paavo Nurmi's barnstorming tour of the USA in 1925.

March 2002 included career details for Denise Lewis, Scottish athletes at the Olympic Games, more details on Emil Zátopek's racing career to those in Bob Phillips' book, features on Doug Harris, C E W Mackintosh and others, and the second part of Ulf Lagerström's history of the 400m hurdles (started in the Dec 2001 issue).

Track Stats Historical Series: 1500 metres (Men) by Peter Matthews and **Triple Jump** (men and women) by Ian Tempest

The fourth and fifth in the NUTS series of event reviews for British athletics were published in February 2002. Each A5 booklet contained 80 pages packed with statistics and profiles. Contents include: progressive UK records, senior and U20, indoors and out, age bests and deep UK performer and performance all-time lists, best performances for each decade from the

1850s, results of all British internationals, national and area champions, and biographies.

Price for each including postage: £5 in UK $7 or 10 Euro) in cash in sterling or Money Orders from outside Britain from Dave Terry, 34 Windmill Hill, Ruislip, Middlesex HA4 8PX, UK. (Email mdterry@dial.pipex.com).

Due for publication by the NUTS in the summer of 2002: **AAC/AAA Championships Results 1866-1939** by Ian Buchanan and **Track Stats Specials on the Commonwealth Games**.

The **Spanish group**, the **AEEA** reaches new standards with their splendid publications, with four A5 bulletins each year packed with statistical items. AEEA secretary is Ignacio Mansilla – imansilla2000@hotmail.com.

AEEA bulletin 59 March 2000 (324 pp) was a very special issue, marking the end of the XXth Century. It included biographies (deep statistical profiles) of the male and female world athletes of the century Carl Lewis and Fanny Blankers-Koen and the two top Spaniards – Fermín Cacho and Carmen Valero. The complete contents of Atletismo en España 2000 took 166 pages. This Bulletin was dedicated to José María García, president of the AEEA from its inception.

No. 60 Jun 2001 (148pp) was a Spanish Athletics Annual for the years 1939-41 with championship results, provincial records and year lists.

No. 61 Nov 2001 (228p) included the first third of a major project – 1000 profiles of the all-time greats of athletics by Enric Pla. 122 pages of this issue ranged from Abascal to Gutterson; in Spanish, but easily accessible with lots of figures. Also included were 30-deep all-time Spanish U18 lists.

No. 62 Dec 2001 (210p) included the second part of all-time greats – from Haase to Owens. There followed world indoor lists for 2000/01, 50 deep performances and performers.

An annual subscription is 55 euros, £32 or $45 in Europe (or 61 euros, £35, $50 for the rest of the world) payable in cash or international money order to Asociación Española de Estadisticos de Atletismo. Orders and enquiries to: José Luis Hernández, C/Carril 21 – 28530 Morata de Tajuña. Madrid, Spain.

World Junior Athletics News. Lionel Peters has, for health reasons, discontinued publishing his magazine. But he has set up a web site (http://www.wjan.org) to include the following items: 1 International Junior Results, 2 World Junior Best Performance Lists, 3 Other Statistics.

From January 2002 a new monthly magazine, **British Runner**, a stablemate of "Athletics Weekly" has been published by Descartes Publishing Ltd. Edited by Richard Lewis, this is devoted to the road running scene. Subscription £30 per year from British Runner Subscriptions, Warners Group Holdings, West Street, Bourne, Lincs PE10 9PH, UK.

Polymédias, 103 rue de Paris, 94220 Charenton le Pont, France will handle subscriptions for the major athletics Magazines. Their own **la letter de l'athlétisme** (42 euro outside France), and also for **Leichtathletik**, (German), **Track and Field News** (USA), and **Athletics International** (UK). www.polymedias.fr.

IAAF Handbooks

These and a long list of other productions from the IAAF, 17 rue Princesse Florestine, BP 359, MC 98007, Monaco. All prices (by Visa, Master Card or Eurocard) include postage by airmail.

IAAF Magazine/Newsletter. The quarterly magazine is a top-quality colour production (A4, 60 plus pages) with reports and results of major competitions and articles by leading authorities. The regular newsletters are generally 16 pages. $75 subscription for text in English and French. The special edition **The Magic of Athletics – A Century of Great Moments** was $20.

IAAF Handbook 2002-2003. 169 x114mm. 212pp. Rules and regulations in English, French or Spanish. Each $10.

IAAF Directory and Calendar 2002. A5, 226 pages. Contact details for officials, organisations and national federations, with calendar and lists of champions. $16.

8th IAAF World Championships in Athletics – Statistics Handbook Edmonton 2001. A5 660pp. Edited by Mark Butler. The superb quality of this series was maintained with the usual very comprehensive results of previous World Championships with medallists from other World Athletic Series events, Olympic Games and continental championships, world, continental and national records, world and area all-time lists, and who's who in world athletics. Also complete results of the IAAF World Indoors and Cross-country Championships. $20.

8th IAAF World Indoor Championships– Statistics Handbook Lisbon 2001. A5 294pp. Edited by Mark Butler. Similar contents to the above – with all the indoor details.

IAAF World Rankings Handbook. A5 424pp. This new handbook includes comprehensive details of the rankings, with 100 deep lists and season's records for leading athletes.

Note that the IAAF also sells videos of highlights of its World Series meetings, including all World Championships from 1991.

NATIONAL CHAMPIONS 2001 and BIOGRAPHIES OF LEADING ATHLETES

By Peter Matthews

THIS SECTION incorporates biographies of 731 of the world's top athletes, 404 men and 327 women, listed by nation. There are also national champions at standard events in 2001 for the leading countries prominent in athletics.

Those profiled have, as usual, changed quite considerably from the previous year, not only that all entries have been updated, but also that many newcomers have been included to replace those who have retired or faded a little from the spotlight. The choice of who to include is always invidious, but I have concentrated on those who are currently in the world's top 10-15 per event, those who have the best championship records and some up-and-coming athletes who I consider may make notable impact during the coming year.

Since this section was introduced in the 1985 Annual, biographies have been given for a total of 2828 athletes (1660 men and 1168 women).

The high turnover is relected in the fact that there are 132 newcomers (76 men, 56 women), with 13 (4 men, 9 women) reinstated from previous Annuals. This has been quite a watershed year, with the retirement of several of the biggest names in our sport. Every year I review the list of athletes who have been featured in all editions of this Annual since I introduced the biographies in 1985. With the retirement of the two men, Jürgen Schult and Javier Sotomayor who had been ever-present, and with Merlene Ottey dropping out of the world top ten with just two races in 2001, there is now just one athlete left with the distinction of having ranked each year of this series – Heike Drechsler.

As ever, no doubt some of those dropped from this compilation will also again make their presence felt; the keen reader can look up their credentials in previous Annuals, and, of course, basic details may be in the athletes' index at the end of this book. Athletes included in these biographies are identified in the index by * for those in this Annual and by ^ for these included in previous Annuals,

The biographical information includes:

a) Name; date and place of birth; height (in metres); weight (in kilograms).
b) Previous name(s) for married women; club or university; occupation.
c) Major championships record – all placings in such events as the Olympic Games, World Championships, European Championships, Commonwealth Games, World Cup and European Cup Super League; leading placings in finals of the World Indoor Championships, European or World Junior Championships, and other Continental Championships; and first three to six in European Indoors or World University Games. IAAF Grand Prix first three at each event or overall.
d) National titles won or successes in other major events.
e) Records set: world, continental and national; indoor world records/bests (WIR/WIB).
f) Progression of best marks over the years at major event(s).
g) Personal best performances at other events.
h) Other comments.

See Introduction to this Annual for lists of abbreviations used for events and championships. Note that for comparison purposes decathlons and heptathlons made before the introduction of the current tables have been rescored using the 1984 IAAF Tables, except those marked *, for which event breakdowns were unavailable. Women's pentathlons (p) have not been rescored.

Information given is as known at 30 March 2002 (to include performances at the European Indoor Championships and the World Cross-country Championships as well as some early outdoor events).

I am most grateful to various ATFS members who have helped check these details. Additional information or corrections would be welcomed for next year's Annual.**Peter Matthews**

ALBANIA

Governing body: Federata Shqiptare e Atletikes, Rruga Dervish Hima n 31, Tirana.

National Championships first held in 1945 (women 1946). **2001 Champions**: **Men**: 100m: Arben Maka 10.4, 200m: Enos Mirushi 22.6, 400m/800m: Albert Marashi 50.9/2:00.5, 1500m/5000m: Genci Lugja 4:13.9/16:08.7, 10000m: Z Kryeziu 33:15.1, 3000mSt: Bledar Mesi 9:50.3, 110mh: Leka Fresku 15.5, 400mh: Ardian Zhuri 58.2, HJ: Elton Kodra 1.95, PV: Neritan Tançica 4.30, LJ: Bendis Spaho 6.95, TJ: G Gujashi 13.55, SP: Dhimitraq Cepa 15.08, DT: Admir Dizdari 40.65, HT: Dorian Collaku 69.70, JT: Vladimir Sokoli 63.35. **Women**: 100m/LJ: Ina Çeliku 12.0/5.80, 200m/400m: Klodiana Shala 24.5/57.7, 800m: A Hasanaj 2:19.2, 1500m: Eriola Xeka 5:22.5, 5000m/10000m: Miranda Greca 17:43.0/39:39.3, 100mh: Anila Meta 14.7, 400mh: Donika Smaçi 62.4, HJ/Hep: Laura Derhemi 1.70/4993, TJ: A Zajmi 10.29, SP: Valbona Laukaj 12.95, DT: E Gashi 28.15, HT: Emiliana Ciko 55.57, JT: Zhuje Bajka 44.20.

ALGERIA

Governing body: Fédération Algerienne d'Athlétisme, BP n°61, Dely-Ibrahim, Alger. Founded 1963.

Abderahmane HAMMAD b. 27 May 1977 1.89m 70kg.
At HJ: OG: '00- 3; WCh: '99- 10=, '01- 10=; WJ: '96- dnq 22=; AfG: '99- 2; AfCh: '98- 1, '00- 1, Af-J: '95- 1; won MedG 2001.
Three African high jump records 1999-2000.
Progression at HJ: 1993- 2.00, 1994- 2.10, 1995- 2.12, 1996- 2.16, 1997- 2.24, 1998- 2.21, 1999- 2.32, 2000- 2.34, 2001- 2.29.

Djabir SAÏD-GUERNI b. 29 Mar 1977 Algers 1.87m 70kg. Army sergeant.
At 800m: OG: '00- 3; WCh: '99- 3; WJ: '94- h; AfCh: '00- 1/1R; WUG: '99- 4.
Two Algerian 800m records 1999.
Progression at 800m: 1997- 1:46.84, 1998- 1:45.72, 1999- 1:43.09, 2000- 1:43.25, 2001- 1:44.55. pbs: 400m 46.15 '00; 1000m 2:14.52 '99.
Made huge breakthrough at 1999 World Champs, when he reduced his pb of 1:45.72 to 1:45.65, 1:45.17 and 1:44.18 in successive rounds, taking the bronze medal with the last. Then 3rd in Brussels in 1:43.09. In 2001 he married Wassila Rédoune, African champion who competed for ALG at the 2000 Olympic Games at fencing. His older brother Chakib ran on the team that was 2nd at 4x100m in the 1994 African Junior Champs.

Ali SAÏDI SIEF b. 15 Mar 1978 Constantine 1.80m 68kg.
At 1500m: WCh: '97- h, '99- sf; WJ: '96- 7; AfCh: '98- 3. At 3000m: WI: '99- 9; 2nd GP 2000. At 5000m: OG: '00- 2; WCh: '01- dq 2; AfCh: '00- 1. World CC: '97- 17J, '00- 16 (4k).
World junior 2000m record 1997. Algerian records 3000m and 5000m 2000, 2000m 2001.
Progression at 1500m, 5000m: 1996- 3:41.6, 1997- 3:37.47, 1998- 3:35.87, 1999- 3:30.91, 13:39.5; 2000- 3:30.82, 12:50.86; 2001- 3:29.51, 13:02.16. pbs: 1M 3:48.23 '01, 2000m 4:46.88 '01, 3000m 7:25.02 '00.
Tested positive for Nandrolene after taking second place in World 5000m 2001.

Women

Nouria MÉRAH-BENIDA b. 19 Oct 1970 1.62m 52kg. née Mérah.
At (800m)/1500m: OG: '00- 1; WCh: '97- sf/h, '99- h, '01- sf; AfG: '95- 6, '99- 2/2; AfCh: '98- 4/4; '00- 2/1; won Med G 1500m 1997. 3rd GP 1500m 2000.
Progression at 800m, 1500m: 1994- 2:09.14, 1995- 2:02.8, 1996- 2:01.43, 4:10.67; 1997- 2:00.46, 4:07.69; 1998- 2:00.77, 4:14.22; 1999- 1:59.49, 4:05.44; 2000- 1:59.68, 3:59.12; 2001- 2:01.6, 4:08.16. pbs: 100m 11.7 '94, 200m 23.8 '94, 400m 54.1 '95, 1000m 2:34.60 '99, 1M 4:28.90i '00, 2000m 5:46.67i '00, 3000m 9:01.20 '00.
Expecting a baby in April 2002.

AMERICAN SAMOA

Governing body: American Samoa Track & Field Association, PO Box 855, Pago Pago, American Samoa 96799. Founded 1976.

Lisa MISIPEKA b. 3 Jan 1975 1.70m 84kg. Was at University of South Carolina.
At HT: OG: '00- dnq 14; WCh: '99- 3, '01- dnq 20; won NCAA 1998. At SP: OG: '96- dnq 25; WCh: '95- dnq 22. Samoan records at SP, DT, HT.
Progression at HT: 1994- 48.70, 1995- 53.20, 1996- 60.94dq/54.86, 1997- 63.24, 1998- 65.00, 1999- 67.00, 2000- 67.55, 2001- 67.46. pbs: SP 16.67 '95, DT 51.76 '97.
At Seville 1999, won the first ever international medal for American Samoa. Three months drugs ban 1996.

ARGENTINA

Governing body: Confederación Argentina de Atletismo, 21 de Noviembre No. 207. 3260 Concepción del Uruguay, Entre Ríos.

National Championships first held in 1920 (men), 1939 (women). **2001 Champions: Men**: 100m: Gabriel Simón 10.39, 200m: Matías Fayos 21.56, 400m: Gustavo Aguirre 48.40, 800m/1500m: Sebastián González Cabot 1:52.17/3:56.76, 5000m: Julián Peralta 14:27.61, 10000m: Oscar Amaya 29:26.10, HMar: Antonio Silio 66:27, Mar: Oscar Alarcón 2:21:25, 3000mSt: Mariano Tarilo 9:12.97, 110mh: Oscar Ratto 14.47w, 400mh: Gabriel Heredia 52.66, HJ: Erasmo Jara 2.06, PV: Javier Benítez 5.00, LJ: Diego Suárez 7.11, TJ: Leandro Simes 15.44, SP: Andrés Calvo 16.82, DT:

Marcelo Pugliese 59.40, HT: Adrián Marzo 67.89, JT: Pablo Pietrobelli 65.56, Dec: Eric Kerwitz 7182, 20000mW: Jorge Loréfice 1:37:24.8. **Women**: 100m/200m: Vanesa Wohlgemuth 11.77/24.23, 400m/400mh: Cristina Ferrarini 58.82/63.17, 800m: Laura Garciarena 2:16.15, 1500m/5000m: Valeria Rodríguez 4:40.57/16:36.52, 10000m: Estela Martínez 36:45.25, HMar: Elisa Cobanea 74:48, Mar: Mónica Cervera 2:48:10, 3000mSt: Claudia Camargo 10:41.04, 100mh: Verónica Depaoli 14.30, HJ: Solange Witteveen 1.85, PV: Alejandra García 3.70, LJ/TJ: Andrea Ávila 6.43w/13.00, SP: Paola Cheppi 13.63, DT: María Eugenia Giggi 47.81, HT: Karina Moya 59.52, JT: Romina Maggi 45.35, Hep: María Cecilia Marcobecchio 4351, 20000mW: Gladys Gibert 1:55:47.9.

AUSTRALIA

Governing body: Athletics Australia, Suite 22, Fawkner Tower, 431 St.Kilda Rd, Melbourne, Victoria 3004. Founded 1897.

National Championships first held in 1893 (men) (Australasian until 1927), 1930 (women). **2001 Champions**: **Men**: 100m: Matt Shirvington 10.19, 200m: Patrick Johnson 20.59, 400m: Paul Pearce 45.87, 800m: Kris McCarthy 1:47.08, 1500m: Clinton Mackevicius 3:41.74, 5000m: Michael Power 13:30.50, 10000m: Craig Mottram 28:19.26, HMar: Darren Wilson 63:12, Mar: Damon Harris NZL 2:25:49, 3000mSt: Peter Nowill 8:46.52, 110mh: Kyle Vander-Kuyp 13.55, 400mh: Blair Young 49.89, HJ: Nick Moroney 2.22, PV: Dmitriy Markov 5.65, LJ: Peter Burge 7.97, TJ: Andrew Murphy 16.96, SP: Justin Anlezark 18.48, DT: Aaron Neighbour 55.71, HT: Stuart Rendell 77.76, JT: William Hamlyn-Harris 74.76, Dec: Matt McEwen 7825, 20kmW: Nathan Deakes 1:21:02, 30kmW: Troy Sundstrom 2:17:17, 50kmW: Liam Murphy 3:54:37. **Women**: 100m/200m: Lauren Hewitt 11.31/22.90, 400m: Nova Peris 52.49, 800m: Tamsyn Lewis 2:02.95, 1500m: Suzy Walsham 4:14.61, 5000m: Elizabeth Miller 15:52.66, 10000m: Susie Power 31:26.34, HMar: Samantha Hughes 75:12, Mar: Krishna Stanton 2:38:11, 3000mSt: Rachel Penney NZL 10:30.04, 100mh: Jacquie Munro 13.15, 400mh: Jana Pittman 57.19, HJ: Carmen Hunter 1.82, PV: Tatiana Grigorieva 4.25, LJ: Shermin Oksuz 6.65w, TJ: Nicole Mladenis 13.74, SP: Michelle Haage 15.68, DT: Alison Lever 59.74, HT: Bronwyn Eagles 66.58, JT: Rosie Hooper 53.88, Hep: Jane Jamieson 6070, 10kmW: Lyn Ventris 48:11, 20kmW: Kerry Saxby-Junna 1:34:58.

Viktor CHISTIAKOV b. 9 Feb 1975 Moskva, Russia 2.02m 92kg. SASI.

At PV: OG: '96- dnq 17, '00- 5=; WCh: '01- 10; EI: '96- 3; WJ: '94- 1; EJ: '93- 3; E23Cp: '94- 2. AUS champion 1999.

Progression at PV: 1988- 3.00, 1989- 3.70, 1990- 4.30, 1991- 4.60, 1992- 5.10, 1993- 5.35, 1994- 5.70, 1995- 5.85, 1996- 5.81i/5.80, 1997- 5.80, 1998- 5.72, 1999- 5.90/5.95exh, 2000- 5.80, 2001- 5.80.

Ex Russian, AUS from 1999, married to pole vaulter Tatiana Grigorieva (qv). His mother Natalya Burda/Pechenkina/Chistyakova was 3rd in the 1968 Olympic 400m in her pb 52.25 and in the 1971 European 4x400m. His sister Nadezhda was world's 3rd best junior at 100mh (13.22) 1988.

Nathan DEAKES b. 17 Aug 1977 Geelong 1.83m 66kg. Bellarine, AIS. Sports administrator.

At 20kmW(/50kmW): OG: '00- 8/6; WCh: '99- 7, '01- 4/dq; CG: '98- 3. At 10000mW: WJ: '96- 3. Won GWG 20000mW 2001, AUS 20kmW 2000-01, 50kmW 1999 (t).

Commonwealth walk records at 20km, 20,000m track (1:19:48.1) 2001.

Progression at 20kmW, 50kmW: 1997- 1:23:58, 1998- 1:23:25, 1999- 1:20:15, 3:52:53; 2000- 1:21:03, 3:47:29; 2001- 1:18:14, 3:43:43. pbs: 3000mW 11:17.0 '98, 5000mW 19:27.4 '97, 10000m 38:44.87 '02, 30kmW 2:11:10 '98, 35kmW 2:35:05 '00.

Dmitriy MARKOV b. 14 Mar 1975 Vitebsk, Belarus 1.82m 85kg. WAIS.

At PV: OG: '96- 6, '00- 5=; WCh: '97- nh, '99- 2, '01- 1; EI: '96- 1; WJ: '94- 2; EJ: '93- 6. 3rd GP 1999. AUS champion 1998, 2001.

Commonwealth pole vault record 2001, four BLR records 1996-8, four AUS 1999-2001.

Progression at PV: 1991- 4.80, 1992- 5.10, 1993- 5.42, 1994- 5.50, 1995- 5.65, 1996- 5.86, 1997- 5.95, 1998- 6.00, 1999- 5.95, 2000- 5.85, 2001- 6.05.

Became an Australian citizen in May 1999, a month after his wife Valentina, who was granted citizenship as a result of spending two consecutive years in Australia after becoming a permanent resident in April 1997.

Craig MOTTRAM b. 18 Jun 1980 Frankston, Victoria 1.88m 73kg. MTC & Deakin AC. Degree from Deakin Iniversity

At 1500m: WCh: '01- sf. At 3000m: WI: '01- 8. At 5000m: OG: '00- h. World CC: '99- 18J, 4k: '01-02: 8/5. Won AUS 5000m 2002, 10000m 2001.

Australian 5000m record 2002.

Progression at 5000m: 1999- 13:40.48, 2000- 13:26.20, 2001- 13:23.94, 2002- 13:12.04. pbs: 1500m: 3:35.40 '01, 1M 3:53.06 '01, 2000m 5:06.97 '01, 3000m 7:41.35 '01, 10000m 28:19.26 '01.

Andrew MURPHY b. 18 Dec 1969 Melbourne 1.85m 82kg. Sydney University.

At TJ: OG: '96- dnq 34, '00- 10; WCh: '95- dnq 22, '99- 4, '01- dnq 17; CG: '90- 6, '94- 10; WJ: '88- 10; WI: '97 –5. '01- 3; WCp: '92- 7, '94- 8, '98- 6. Won AUS TJ 1990, 1994-2001.

Progression at TJ: 1986- 14.96/15.56w, 1987- 15.60, 1988- 15.84/16.33w, 1989- 17.18, 1990- 16.57, 1991- 16.64, 1992- 16.30, 1993- 16.29, 1994- 16.76, 1995- 16.79, 1996- 17.07/17.28w, 1997- 17.18,

1998- 16.89A/16.59, 1999- 17.32, 2000- 17.12, 2001- 17.20i/ 17.07/17.28w. pbs: 100m 10.46/ 10.35w '96, LJ 7.88 '91.
Set an Australian junior record in 1989 with 17.18, but did not better that with legal wind until the 1999 World Championships in Seville, when he excelled with 17.32 for 4th.

Jai TAURIMA b. 26 Jun 1972 Southport, Queensland 1.88m 79kg. AIS.
At LJ: OG: '00- 2; WCh: '99- 4; CG: '94- 6, '98- 2; WCp: '98 -2. AUS champion 1994, 1996.
Four Oceania long jump records 1998-2000.
Progression at LJ: 1990- 7.17, 1991- 7.65, 1992- 7.88, 1993- 7.84, 1994- 7.98/8.10Aw, 1995- 7.89, 1996- 8.05, 1997- 7.88/8.00w, 1998- 8.32A/8.22/ 8.26w, 1999- 8.35, 2000- 8.49, 2001- 7.93. pb 110mh 13.95 '92.

Women

Bronwyn EAGLES b. 23 Aug 1980 Camden, New South Wales1.78m 100kg. Campbelltown Collegians.
At HT: WCh: '01- 3; WJ: '98- 8. AUS champion 2000-01. Four AUS hammer records (68.83 & 68.87) 2001, (69.38, 69.65) 2002.
Progression at HT: 1996- 52.08, 1997- 54.88, 1998- 59.79, 1999- 62.02, 2000- 66.55, 2001- 70.19, 2002- 69.65. pb SP 12.07 '01.

Cathy FREEMAN b. 16 Feb 1973 Mackay, Qld 1.64m 56kg. Ringwood. Married Alexander Bodecker (USA) in September 1999.
At 400m/4x100mR (200m): OG: '92- qf, '96- 2 (sf), '00- 7 (1); WCh: '93- (sf); '95- 4 (sf, 3 4x400R), '97- 1, '99- 1; CG: '90- 1R, '94- 1/2R (1); WJ: '90- (5, sf 100m), '92- (2); WI: '99- 2 4x400mR; WCp: '94- 3R (3). Won GP 400m 1996, 2nd 1994. Won AUS 100m 1994, 1996; 200m 1990-1, 1994, 1996, 2000; 400m 1995, 1997-2000; AAA 200m 1993, 400m 1992.
AUS records: 200m (2), 400m (5) 1994-6.
Progression at 200m, 400m: 1988- 24.50, 55.53; 1989- 23.86, 1990- 23.36, 1991- 23.50, 54.24; 1992- 23.09, 51.14; 1993- 22.37, 51.34; 1994- 22.25, 50.04; 1995- 22.50, 50.21; 1996- 22.55/22.53w, 48.63; 1997- 22.68/22.50w, 49.39; 1998- 22.55, 50.02; 1999- 22.81, 49.67; 2000- 22.53, 49.11. pbs: 100y 10.62 '93, 100m 11.24/11.15w '94, 300m 35.97 '99.
Lit the flame at the Opening Ceremony for the 2000 Olympic Games in Sydney before going on to gold at 400m. First Aboriginal to represent AUS at Olympics and first world champion. At the 1994 Commonwealth Games she won both 200m and 400m, took silver at 4 x 100m, and crossed the line first in the 4x400, only to be disqualified for baulking Yusuf NGR on the final turn. Set four AUS 400m records in 1996, improving by 0.96 to take the Olympic silver medal. Unbeaten for 21 finals at 400m from 1996 to Oslo 1998, when season cut short by injury (bruised foot), then unbeaten again in 11 finals in 1999 and in 10 in 2000. Took a year off competition in 2001.

Emma GEORGE b. 1 Nov 1974 Beechworth, Victoria 1.72m 60kg. WA. Studied arts and commerce at Deakin University, Melbourne.
At PV: OG: '00- dnq 15=; WCh: '99- 14=; CG: '98- 1; WI: '97- 2, '99- 6; WUG: '97- 1. Won AUS 1995, 1997-8, 2000.
12 world and 18 Australian PV records 1995-9, including first 15ft vault by a woman (4.57 '98). Two world indoor records 1996 (4.30 and 4.40).
Progression at PV: 1994- 3.05, 1995- 4.28, 1996- 4.45, 1997- 4.55, 1998- 4.59, 1999- 4.60, 2000- 4.50. pbs: 100m 12.0, HJ 1.60, LJ 5.66w '91, TJ 11.15.
As a schoolgirl she was a trapeze artist in the Flying Fruit Flies Circus for four years. Just a year and two weeks after clearing 2.55m in her first competition (12 Nov 1994) she became the fourth Australian to set a world record in a field event with 4.25m. Had surgery on her feet for three stress fractures at end of 2000.

Tatyana GRIGORIEVA b. 8 Oct 1975 St Petersburg, Russia 1.72m 60kg. SASI.
At PV: OG: '00- 2; WCh: '99- 3, '01- 4; WI: '99- 9=. Won AUS 1999, 2001.
Progression at PV: 1997- 3.90, 1998- 4.35, 1999- 4.50/4.55ex, 2000- 4.55, 2001- 4.56. pb 400mh 58.54 '96.
She moved with her husband Viktor Chistiakov to Australia.

Lauren HEWITT b. 25 Nov 1978 Warracknabeal, Victoria 1.70m 60kg. Ringwood. Student.
At 200m/4x100m (100m): OG: '96- 7R, '00- sf; WCh: '97- qf (qf), '99- 7, '01- sf; CG: '98- 3/1R (4); WJ: '96- 2 (8); WCp: '98- 6R (7). Won AUS 100m & 200m 1999, 2001.
Progression at 200m: 1993- 23.99, 1994- 23.91, 1995- 23.83, 1996- 23.24/23.2w, 1997- 23.09/ 22.66w, 1998- 22.62, 1999- 22.53, 2000- 22.52, 2001- 22.90. pbs: 100m 11.28 '99, 11.18w '00.

Jana PITTMAN b. 9 Nov 1982 Sydney 1.82m 68kg. Baulkham Hills, AIS. Student.
At 400mh(/400m): OG: '00- h; WJ: '00- 1/1; WY: '99- 1/7. AUS champion 2001.
Equalled world junior record 400mh 2000.
Progression at 400mh: 1998- 59.75, 1999- 56.23, 2000- 55.20A, 2001- 55.93, 2002- 55.53. pbs: 100m 11.94 '01, 200m 23.60 '99, 400m 51.74 '01, 100mh 13.92 '00.

Susie POWER b. 26 Mar 1975 Ferntree Gully, Victoria 1.75m 53kg. Glenhuntly
At 3000m: CG: '94- 5; WJ: '92- 8, '94- 2; WCp: '94- 5. World CC: '92-3-4: 12J-5J-12J. Won AUS 1500m 1993.
Progression at 5000m, 10000m: 1996- 33:00.09, 1999- 15:23.18, 2000- 15:27.07, 2001- 15:23.87, 31:26.34. pbs: 1000m 2:39.4 '93, 1500m 4:12.02 '95, 1M 4:32.73 '92, 2000m 5:50.47 '94, 3000m 8:56.93 '94.
Set Australian junior records at 1000m, 1M and

2000m 1992-4 and made great breakthrough in late 2001 after the birth of her son Jai in December 2000. Her brother **Michael** (b. 9 May 1976) AUS 5000m in 2000 (pb 13:27.07 '00).

Melissa ROLLISON b. 13 Apr 1983 Adelaide 1.66m 50kg. Victory Sports. Student.
At 3000mSt: Won GWG 2001, AUS champion 1999-2000. At 1500m: WJ: '00- 8
Three world junior records 3000mSt 1999-2001.
Progression at 3000mSt: 1999- 10.15.73, 2000- 10:10.73, 2001- 9:30.70. pbs: 800m 2:06.10 '01, 1500m 4:12.83 '02, 3000m 9:03.64 '01, 2000mSt 6:32.23 '01.

Jane SAVILLE b. 5 Nov 1974 Sydney 1.64m 53kg. Randwick Botany H.
At 20kmW: OG: '00- dq: WCh: '99- 7, '01- dq. At 10kmW: OG: '96- 26; WCh: '97- h; CG: '94- 8, '98- 1. At 5000mW: WJ: '92- 2. Won AUS 5000mW 1997, 10kmW 1991-2, 1997-8, 20kmW 2000.
Commonwealth 20km walk record 2000.
Progression at 10kmW, 20kmW: 1990- 52:24, 1991- 47:10, 1992- 46:02, 1993- 47:29.1, 1994- 46:04, 1995- 45:10, 1996- 45:22, 1997- 42:59, 1998- 43:38, 1:37:53; 1999- 42:15, 1:31:58; 2000- 44:06, 1:28:56; 2001- 44:40, 1:31:20. pbs: 3000mW 12:27.74 '93, 5000mW 21:32.26 '97.
Disqualified when leading just outside stadium at Sydney Olympics. Her sister **Natalie** (b. 7 Sep 1978) has represented AUS at WJ and WCp, pbs: 10kmW 45:10 '97, 20kmW 1:36:32 '99.

Debbie SOSIMENKO b. 5 Apr 1974 Sydney 1.70m 90kg. Bankstown Sports. Teacher.
At HT: OG: '00- 5; WCh: '99- 5; CG: '98- 1; WUG: '97- 3. AUS champion 1993-5, 1998-9.
14 Commonwealth, 15 AUS hammer records 1993-2000. World junior hammer record 1993.
Progression at HT: 1989- 32.30, 1990- 44.30, 1991- 47.14, 1992- 51.48, 1993- 58.90, 1994- 62.38, 1995- 65.24, 1996- 62.86, 1997- 66.60, 1998- 67.16, 1999- 66.78/67.40dh, 2000- 67.95. pb DT 45.00 '91.

AUSTRIA

Governing body: Österreichischer Leichtathletik Verband, 1040 Vienna, Prinz Eugenstrasse 12. Founded 1900.
National Championships first held in 1911 (men), 1918 (women). **2001 Champions: Men**: 100m: Michael Kummer 11.02, 200m: Hans-Peter Welz 21.23, 400: Andreas Rechbauer 47.01, 800m: Sebastian Resch 1:51.72, 1500m: Roland Waldner 3:57.45, 5000m/10000m: Harald Steindorfer 14:39.83/31:01.75, HMar/Mar: Roman Weger 66:11/2:22:06, 3000mSt: Georg Mlynek 9:35.15, 110mh: Elmar Lichtenegger 13.50, 400mh: Karl Lang 52.42, HJ: Günther Gasper 2.01, PV: Martin Tischler 5.05, LJ: Martin Löbel 7.83, TJ: Boris Bjanov 16.02, SP: Andreas Vlasny 17.90, DT: Gerhard Mayer 57.20, HT: Walter Edletisch 65.22, JT: Gregor Högler 78.44, Dec: Markus Walser 7443, 20kmW/50kmW: Stephan Wögerbauer 1:42:11/4:49:36. **Women**: 100m: Bettina Müller 11.83, 200m/LJ: Bianca Dürr 24.55/6.30w, 400m: Bettina Germann 54.66, 800m: Brigitte Mühlbacher 2:10.40, 1500m: Martina Winter 4:38.01, 5000m/10000m: Susanne Pumper 16:51.29/ 35:21.19 , HMar: Dagmar Rabensteiner 75:37, Mar: Ulrike Puchner 2:45.35, 3000mSt: Andrea Mayr 10:54.17, 100mh: Daniela Wöckinger 13.49, 400mh: Sabine Gasselseder 60.73, HJ: Katrin Schöftner 1.77, PV: Michaela Kohlbauer 3.96, TJ: Olivia Wöckinger 12.97, SP: Valentina Fedyushina 15.58, DT: Sonja Spendelhofer 50.59, HT: Claudia Stern 52.41, JT/Hep: Ulrika Kalss 44.44/ 5278, 10kmW: Viera Toporek 54:33.

Elmar LICHTENEGGER b. 25 May 1974 Klagenfurt 1.87m 83kg. VST Laas. Soldier.
At 110mh: OG: '96- h, '00- sf; WCh: '97- qf, '99/01- sf; EC: '98- h; WUG: '97- 5, '01- 2. Won Austrian 100m 1998, 110mh 1997-2001. At 60mh: WI: '99- 7, '01- 6; EI: '02- 2..
Progression at 110mh: 1993- 14.86, 1995- 13.84, 1996- 13.63, 1997- 13.70, 1998- 13.73, 1999- 13.33, 2000- 13.34, 2001- 13.36. pbs: 100m 10.68 '01, 50mh 6.54i '01, 60mh 7.44i '02.

Günther WEIDLINGER b. 5 Apr 1978 Braunau 1.69m 54kg. SU Igla Harmonie Natternbach.
At 3000mSt: OG: '00- 8; WCh: '99- 9; EC: '98- h; WJ: '96- 6; EU23: '99- 1; EJ: '95- 8, '97- 1. Eur CC: '97- 2J, '98- 4. Won World Univs CC 2000. Won AUT 1500m 1999-2000, 3000mSt 1998-9.
Three Austrian 3000mSt records 1999.
Progression at 3000mSt, 1995- 9:02.15, 1996- 8:38.97, 1997- 8:31.43, 1998- 8:23.13, 1999- 8:10.83, 2000- 8:11.51, 2001- 8:23.62. pbs: 1500m 3:34.69 '00, 3000m 7:47.79i '00, 5000m 14:32.58 '97, 10000m 29:23.28 '97.

Women

Doris AUER b. 10 May 1971 Wien 1.68m 55kg. LCC Wien. Teacher.
At PV: OG: '00- 9; EC: '98- dnq 17=; WUG: '97- 3. Austrian champion 1996-7, 1999-2000.
19 Austrian pole vault records 1996-2001.
Progression at PV: 1996- 3.60, 1997- 4.10, 1998- 4.12, 1999- 4.33, 2000- 4.40, 2001- 4.40.

Stephanie GRAF b. 26 Apr 1973 Klagenfurt 1.70m 60kg. Klagenfurter LC.
At 800m: OG: '00- 2; WCh: '97- h, '99- 7, '01- 2; EC: '98- 3; WI: '99- 6, '01- 2; EI: '00- 1. '02- 1; 3rd GP 2001. Won AUT 400m 1997-2000, 800m 1994-7, 1500m 1993-4.
Five Austrian 800m records 1998-2000.
Progression at 800m: 1989- 2:12.72, 1990- 2:10.72, 1991- 2:12.80, 1992- 2:09.20, 1993- 2:06.22, 1994- 2:05.36, 1995- 2:05.06, 1996- 2:01.54, 1997- 2:00.27, 1998- 1:57.97, 1999- 1:57.07, 2000- 1:56.64, 2001- 1:57.20, 2002- 1:55.85i. pbs: 200m 25.42 '96, 400m 52.69 '99, 1000m 2:34.47 '98, 1500m 4:13.58 '96.
Broke WIR 800m by 0.55 at European Indoors 2002, but beaten by Jolanda Ceplak. Her mother

Rita Graf (née Merva) was Austrian 800m champion in 1974, pb 2:09.4 '71.

AZERBAIJAN

Governing body: Azerbaijan Athletic Federation, 5 Olympic Street, 370072 Baku. Founded 1955.

National Champioships first held 1922. **2001 Champions: Men**: 100m: Dmitri Kolesnikov 10.97, 200m: Teymur Gasumov 21.60, 400m/800m: Valentin Bulichov 49.90/1:55.01, 1500m: Sergey Anohin 4:00.09, 3000m Nizami Mamedov 9:28.62, LJ: Ziya Jabbarov 7.18, TJ: Oleg Panyutin 15.02, SP: Soltan Babaev 10.82, DT: Oktay Shahtahtinski 36.90, JT Bahtiyar Zeinalov 47.62. **Women**: 100m/200m: Yuliya Tishkova 12.78/25.60, 400m: Olesya Kulichkina 59.03: 800m: Yuliya Belkova 2:20.42, 1500m: Nailya Novruzova 4:55.01, LJ: Anna Ribkina 5.13, TJ: Juliya Kolesnikova 12.95, SP: H.Yusubova 8.59, DT S. Ismailova 21.08.

BAHAMAS

Governing body: Bahamas Amateur Athletic Association, P.O.Box SS 5517, Nassau. F'd 1952.

National Champions 2001: **Men**: 100m/200m: Dominic Demeritte 10.4/20.80, 400m: Avard Moncur 44.61, LJ/TJ: Leevan Sands 7.65/15.78, **Women**: 100m/200m: Debbie Ferguson 11.31/23.13, 400m: Christine Amertil 52.70, LJ: Jackie Edwards 6.55, JT: Lavern Eve 56.89.

Avard MONCUR b. 2 Nov 1978 Nassau 1.96m 82kg. Was at University of Auburn.
At 400m/4x400mR: OG: '00- sf; WCh: '01- 1/2R; WJ: '96- sf; PAm: '99- 7; PAmJ: '97- 2; won NCAA 400m 2000-01, BAH 1999-2001.
Three Bahamas 400m records 2000-01.
Progression at 400m: 1995- 47.40, 1996- 47.09, 1997- 46.46, 1998- 46.45, 1999- 45.09, 2000- 44.72, 2001- 44.45.

Women

Debbie FERGUSON b. 16 Jan 1976 1.70m 57kg. Student at University of Georgia.
At 100m/4x100mR (/200m): OG: '96- sf/res (2)R, '00- 8/5/1R; WCh: '95- 4R (h), '97- sf, '99- sf/5/1R, '01- 6/2; CG: 94- (sf); WJ: '92- qf/sf, '94- 5/4; PAm: '99- (1); won CAC 100m 1997, 200m 1995, NCAA 100m & 200m 1998, PAm-J 100m & 200m 1995, CAC-J 100m 1994, GWG 200m 2001. 3rd GP 200m 2001
Bahamas 200m record 1999.
Progression at 100m, 200m: 1991- 11.75, 24.26; 1992- 11.79, 23.97w; 1993- 23.82/23.32w, 1994- 11.48/11.1, 23.32/23.1; 1995- 11.19/10.9w, 22.86/22.7; 1996- 11.26/11.07Aw, 22.92; 1997- 11.20, 1998- 10.97/10.94w, 22.53; 1999- 10.98/10.91w, 22.19; 2000- 10.96, 22.37; 2001- 11.04, 22.39. pbs: 55m 6.71i '99, 60m 7.24i '99, 400m 54.68 '92.

Savatheda FYNES b. 17 Oct 1974 Abaco 1.65m 58kg. Was at Michigan State University, USA.
At 100m/4x100mR: OG: '96- 2R (qf), '00- 7/1R; WCh: '95- qf (h), '97- 3, '99- sf/1R; PAm-J: '91- 3, '93- 2 (2, 3 4x400); won NCAA 100m 1997, 200m 1995, 1997. Won GP 200m 1999, 100m: 2nd 1998, 3rd 2000. At 60m: WI: '99- 4, '01- 4.
Bahamas 100m record 1999.
Progression at 100m, 200m: 1991- 11.58, 24.49; 1992- 11.52w, 23.49w; 1993- 11.55, 23.43A; 1994- 11.42/11.2w, 23.38/23.10w; 1995- 11.12/10.7w, 22.63; 1996- 11.24, 23.01; 1997- 11.03/11.00w, 22.60/22.51w; 1998- 11.02, 1999- 10.91, 22.32; 2000- 11.03, 22.87; 2001- 11.17, 23.02. pbs: 50m 6.05i '00, 55m 6.65i '97, 60m 7.01i '99, 400m 53.40 '95.

Chandra STURRUP b. 12 Sep 1971 1.63m 55kg. Was at Norfolk State University, USA.
At 100m(/200m/4x100mR): OG: '96- 4/6/2R, '00- 6/qf/1R; WCh: '99- 7/sf/1R, '01- 4; CG: '98- 1; PAm: '99- 1; CAG: '93- 3/5, '98- 1; WJ: '88- sf/sf, '90- sf/6; WCp: '98- 2/2R. At 60m: WI: '97- 2, '01- 1.
BAH records 100m (3) 1996-2000, 200m 1996.
Progression at 100m, 200m: 1987- 11.75, 1988- 11.93/11.70w, 23.96w; 1989- ?, 1990- 11.62, 23.77; 1992- 11.54, 23.55; 1993- 11.20, 22.85; 1994- 11.75, 1995- 11.39/11.35w/11.1w, 23.31/23.14w; 1996- 11.00, 22.33; 1997- 11.26, 22.77; 1998- 10.95, 23.52/22.64w; 1999- 10.96/10.94w, 22.75; 2000- 10.86, 22.57; 2001- 10.95, 22.99. pbs: 50m 6.11+ '99, 55m 6.73i '96, 60m 7.05i '01, 300m 37.95 '01, 400m 54.77 '00, LJ 6.70 '00, 6.80w '95.

BARBADOS

Governing body: Amateur Athletic Association of Barbados, P.O.Box 46, Bridgetown. F'd 1947.

National Champions 2001: **Men**: 100m: Everton Evelyn 10.5, 200m: Gabriel Burnett 21.36, 400m: Wilan Louis 46.03, 800m/1500m: Dale Jones ANT 1:56.02/4:08.16, 110mh: Stephen Jones 13.68, 400mh: Ryan Smith 51.36, HJ: Henderson Dottin 2.10, LJ: Kevin Bartlett 7.21, TJ: Gregory Hughes 15.29, SP: Charles Walcott 14.85, DT: Dave Taylor 49.52, JT: Justin Cummins 63.99. **Women**: 100m: Genna Williams 11.86, 200m/100mh: Keitha Moseley 24.08/14.10, 400m: Letitia Gilkes 55.54, 800m: Lydia Brathwaite 2:16.92, 400mh: Andrea Blackett 58.99, LJ: Ayesha Maycock 6.01, SP/DT: Shernelle Nicholls 13.82/40.11, JT: Nikkisha Maynard 38.25.

Obadele THOMPSON b. 30 Mar 1976 St Michael 1.75m 67kg. Studied business at University of Texas, El Paso, USA.
At 100m (/200m): OG: '96- sf /4, '00- 3/4; WCh: '95- qf/sf, '97- sf/6, '99- 4/4, '01- sf; CG: '94- sf, '98- 3; CAG: '98- 1; WJ: '94- 4/sf; WI: '99- (2); WUG: '95- 2; WCp: '98- 1. 2nd GP 100m 1998, 200m 1997. Won CAC 100m 1993, 1995, 1999; 200m 1995; NCAA 100m & 200m 1997, CAC-J 100m & 200m 1994.
World junior 100m record 1994. BAR records:

100m (6) 1994-8, 200m (4) 1996-7. World indoor best 55m 1997.
Progression at 100m, 200m: 1991- 10.81/10.5w, 22.26; 1992- 10.59w, 21.61; 1993- 10.71/10.30w, 21.18; 1994- 10.08A/10.0, 20.71; 1995- 10.18, 20.49A/20.57; 1996- 10.07A/9.69wA, 20.14; 1997- 10.09, 20.03; 1998- 9.87A/10.00, 20.38/ 20.17w; 1999- 9.96, 20.09; 2000- 9.97, 19.97; 2001- 10.03?w/10.25. pbs: 50m 5.63+ '99, 55m 5.99Ai '97, 60m 6.50+ '99, 400m 45.38A '96.
Ran the fastest ever 100m at high altitude in El Paso 1996. His father won the British Universities 100y in 1966, while at the University of London.

Women

Andrea BLACKETT b. 24 Jan 1976 London, GBR 1.60m 54kg. Was at Rice University, USA.
At 400mh/4x400mR: OG: '00- sf; WCh: '97- 8, '99- 4, '01- h; CG: '98- 1; PAm: '99- 2/3R; CAG: '98- 2/3R; WJ: '94- h; WCp: '98- 2R; 2nd GP 1999; won CAC 1997 (3rd 100mh), 1999; 2nd 1998.
Barbadian 400mh records 1994-8, 100mh 1997-8.
Progression at 400mh: 1994- 58.75, 1995- 58.59, 1996- 57.35A, 1997- 54.74, 1998- 53.74, 1999- 53.36, 2000- 54.41, 2001- 55.68. pbs: 55mh 7.65i '97, 200m 23.73 '00, 800m 2:10.47 '99, 100mh 13.2, 13.42, 13.41w '98.

BELARUS

Governing body: Belarus Athletic Federation, 2 Surganov Street, Minsk 220012. Founded 1991.
National Champions 2001: *Partial*. **Men**: 100m/200m: Aleksandr Slunkov 10.51/21.37, 400m: Sergey Kozlov 46.46, 1500m Mark Romanchuk 3:47.54, 400mh: Leonid Vershinin 50.06, HJ: Aleksey Lesnichy 2.25, PV: Dmitriy Smirnov 5.10, TJ: Aleksandr Glavatskiy 16.85, DT: Alekdansr Malashkevich 61.63, HT: Ivan Tikhon 78.73, JT: Pavel Stasuk 76.92, Dec: Aleksandr Parkhomenko 7424. **Women**: 100m: Oksana Dragun 11.54, 400m: Anna Kozak 51.50, 800m: Natalya Vasko 2:04.25, 100mh: Yevgeniya Likhuta 13.76, 400mh: Tatyana Kurochkina 56.18, HJ: Tatyana Gulevich 1.92, TJ: Natalya Safronova 14.41, SP: Natalya Khoroneko 16.84, DT: Lyudmila Starovoytova 61.68, HT: Tatyana Gromada 65.00, JT: Oksana Velichko 58.68, Hep: Tania Dobrivitskaya 5912.

Igor ASTAPKOVICH b. 4 Jan 1963 Minsk 1.91m 118kg. Minsk. Sports instructor.
At HT: OG: '92- 2, '96- 7, '00- 3; WCh: '91- 2, '93- 2, '95- 2, '97- 5, '99- 9, '01- 7; EC: '90- 1, '94- 2, '98- 7; WUG: '87- 1, '89- 1; ECp: '89- 2, '91- 1. Won GWG 1990. USSR champion 1989-90, CIS 1992, BLR 2000. Won GP 1992, 2nd 1988, 1994, 1996.
BLR hammer record 1992.
Progression at HT: 1981- 66.56, 1982- 68.08, 1983- 75.02, 1984- 79.98, 1985- 80.16, 1986- 80.68, 1987- 82.96, 1988- 83.44, 1989- 82.52, 1990- 84.14, 1991- 84.26, 1992- 84.62, 1993- 82.28, 1994- 83.14, 1995- 82.60, 1996- 81.76, 1997- 82.44, 1998- 83.62, 1999- 80.12, 2000- 82.58, 2001- 82.76.
World number one in 1990, when he lost just once, and won the Goodwill Games (84.12) and European titles with pbs. Since then he has won five major silver medals. Married to Irina Yatchenko (qv). Brother **Konstantin** (b. 23 Oct 1970) has a best of 79.08 '99 and was BLR champion 1995 and 1998-9.

Vladimir DUBROVSHCHIK b. 7 Jan 1972 Grodno 1.91m 115kg. Grodno. PE student.
At DT: OG: '96- 2, '00- 7; WCh: '95- 2, '97- 4, '99- 7, '01- dnq 13; EC: '94- 1, '98- 6; EJ: '91- 1; WUG: '97- 1; WCp: '94- 1. BLR champion 1993-6, 1999. 3rd GP 1995.
Progression at DT: 1989- 53.04, 1990- 56.76, 1991- 61.40, 1992- 61.80, 1993- 63.26, 1994- 65.80, 1995- 66.60, 1996- 67.90, 1997- 66.40, 1998- 65.78, 1999- 67.80, 2000- 69.28, 2001- 64.41. pb SP 17.47i '99, 16.57 '94.
Won the first European gold medal for Belarus.

Viktor GINKO b. 7 Dec 1965 Sharkovshchina 1.86m 77kg. Sports instructor.
At 50kmW: OG: '96- 5, '00- dq; WCh: '93- 11, '95- dq, '97/9- dnf; WCp: '95- 6, '97- 12, '99- 7; EC: '94 & '98- dq; ECp: '98- 8, '01- 7. BLR champion 50kmW 1993, 20kmW 1995-6.
Progression at 50kmW: 1988- 4:09:16, 1990- 3:50:45, 1991- 3:51:35, 1992- 3:48:42/3:40:46sh, 1993- 3:53:41, 1994- 3:45:34, 1995- 3:42:20, 1996- 3:42:52, 1997- 3:44:45, 1998- 3:48:27, 1999- 3:43:15, 2000- 3:47:53, 2001- 3:50:28. pb 20kmW 1:20:03sh '93, 1:20:31 '98; 30kmW 2:05:36 '93, 35kmW 2:31:58 '93, 100kmW 8:43:30 '00 (world best).

Aleksandr GLAVATSKIY b. 2 May 1970 Soligarsk 1.85m 72kg.
At LJ (TJ): OG: '96- 7; WCh: '93- 7, '95- dnq 22, '97- 6, '01- (dnq 16); EC: '94- 10, '98- dnq 13 (4); WI: '97- 9, '01- 8; EI: '02- (3); WUG: '95- 5. Won BLR LJ 1998, TJ 1998, 2001.
Progression at LJ, TJ: 1988- 7.57, 1989- 7.55, 1990- 8.10, 1991- 7.97, 1992- 7.88/7.97w, 16.28i; 1993- 8.05, 1994- 8.21, 17.12i/16.94; 1995- 8.22, 1996- 8.33A/8.30, 1997- 8.20/8.29w, 16.46; 1998- 8.26, 17.53; 2000- 16.68, 2001- 7.61i/7.43, 17.06i/17.00.

Vasiliy KAPTYUKH b. 27 Jun 1967 Molodechno 1.97m 120kg. Minsk TR. Sports instructor.
At DT: OG: '96- 3, '00- 4; WCh: '91- dns, '93- 7, '95- 3, '97- 11, '01- 6; EC: '90- 4; WJ: '86- 3; EJ: '85- 3.
Progression at DT: 1985- 57.18, 1986- 60.24, 1988- 61.60, 1989- 62.92, 1990- 63.72, 1991- 62.88, 1992- 63.34, 1993- 66.18, 1994- 58.86, 1995- 66.30, 1996- 66.92, 1997- 65.52, 2000- 67.59, 2001- 67.48. pb SP 17.26 '00.
Father Boris (1950s) and aunt Vera Kaptyukh (1960s, Pen) were prominent athletes.

Ivan TIKHON b. 24 Jul 1976 Slonim 1.88m 105kg.
At HT: OG: '00- 4; WCh: 97- nt (12), '01- dnq 22; EC: '98- dnq 30; EU23: 97- 1; EJ: '95- 9. BLR champion 2001.

Progression at HT: 1994- 62.66, 1995- 66.84, 1996- 75.32, 1997- 77.46, 1998- 78.03, 1999- 70.37, 2000- 79.85, 2001- 78.73.

Women

Lyudmila GUBKINA b. 13 Aug 1973 Novopolotsk 1.74m 76kg. Novopolotsk TU.
At HT: OG: '00- 6; WCh: '99- 6, '01- dnq 19; EC: '98- 6; WUG: '97- 4, '99- 2, '01- 3; ECp: '97- 3. Won BLR 1996, 2000.
Three BLR hammer records 1997-9.
Progression at HT: 1992- 55.90, 1993- 59.62, 1994- 57.58, 1995- 60.78, 1996- 65.02, 1997- 68.24, 1998- 67.83, 1999- 68.27, 2000- 69.92, 2001- 67.97.

Yanina KOROLCHIK b. 26 Dec 1976 1.86m 87kg.
At SP: OG: '00- 1; WCh: '97- dnq 18; '99- 4, '01- 1; EC: '98- 3; EU23: '97- 3 (3 DT); EJ: '95- 2; WI: '01- 9. BLR champion 2000.
Progression at SP: 1994- 16.00, 1995- 17.07, 1996- 17.48, 1997- 18.67, 1998- 19.23, 1999- 19.58, 2000- 20.56, 2001- 20.61. pb DT 59.90 '97.

Nadezhda OSTAPCHUK b. 12 Oct 1980 1.80m 78kg.
At SP: WCh: '99- dnq 17, '01- 7; WJ: '98- 1; EJ: '99- 1; EU23: '01- 1; WI: '01- 2, EI: '00- 6; 2nd GP 2001. BLR champion 1999-2000.
Progression at SP: 1997- 14.23, 1998- 18.23, 1999- 18.73, 2000- 19.13i/18.83, 2001- 19.73.

Natalya SAFRONOVA b. 11 Apr 1974 1.76m 60kg. née Klimovets.
At TJ: OG: '00- dnq 15; WCh: '99- dnq 18, '01- 12; EC: '98- 7; WUG: '99- 5, '01- 2; ECp: '01- 2 (8 LJ). BLR champion LJ 2000, TJ 1994, 1998, 2000-01. BLR triple jump record 2000.
Progression at TJ: 1991- 12.38, 1992- 13.25, 1993- 13.65, 1994- 13.74, 1995- 14.01/14.08w, 1997- 13.69, 1998- 14.26, 1999- 14.12i/13.93/14.21w, 2000- 14.65, 2001- 14.57. pb LJ 6.62 '00.

Natalya SAZANOVICH b. 15 Aug 1973 Baranovich 1.79m 65kg. Gomel. Sports instructor.
At Hep: OG: '96- 2, '00- 3; WCh: '97- 5, '01- 2; EC: '98- 3; ECp: '95- 7, '96- 1, '00- 1B; WJ: '92- 1; EJ: '91- 1. At Pen: WI: '01- 1. Won BLR LJ 1996.
Progression at Hep: 1989- 5431, 1990- 5725, 1991- 5896, 1992- 6036, 1995- 6020, 1996- 6563, 1997- 6442, 1998- 6410, 2000- 6527, 2001- 6539. pbs: 200m 23.62 '96, 800m 2:16.41 '00, 60mh 8.24i '96, 100mh 13.28 '01, HJ 1.84 '95, LJ 6.86 '96, SP 16.58 '01, JT 46.72 '01, Pen 4850i '96.

Olga TSANDER b. 18 May 1976 1.74m 83kg.
At HT: OG: '00- dnq; WCh: '01- 10; ECp: '01- 1. At DT: WJ: '94- 5; EJ: '95- 2.
Progression at HT: 1998- 58,88, 1999- 64.56, 2000- 69.81, 2001- 68.94. pb DT 59.82 '97.

Valentina TSYBULSKAYA b. 19 Feb 1968 Rostov-na-Donu, RUS 1.63m 54kg.
At 20kmW: OG: '00- 28; WCh: '01- 2; ECp: '00- 8; At 10kmW: OG: '96- 8; WCh: '95- 12, '97- 3; EC: '94- 12, '98- 15; WCp: '95- 13, '97- 11, '99- 25; ECp: '96- 6. Won BLR 10000mW 1999.
BLR record 20,000m track walk (1:38:25.5) 2001.
Progression at 10kmW, 20kmW: 1987- 46:07, 1988- 46:15, 1989- 45:15, 1991- 46:26, 1992- 45:13, 1993- 43:50, 1994- 43:16, 1995- 42:35, 1996- 43:05, 1997- 42:21, 1998- 43:47, 1:32:25; 1999- 42:06, 1:29:20; 2000- 43:35, 1:30:19; 2001- 43:51, 1:28:49. pb 5000mW: 21:33.22i '95, 20:33R '01.

Alesya TUROVA b. 6 Dec 1979 1.80m 64kg.
At 1500m: WCh: '01- 7; WJ: '98- h; EU23: '99- 5, '01- 1; EJ: '97- 11; WI: '01- 6; EI: '02- 3; ECp: '01- 4. BLR records: 2000m & 3000m (2) 2001, 5000m 2001.
Progression at 1500m, 5000m: 1997- 4:24.64, 1998- 4:21.53, 1999- 4:12.8, 2000- 4:05.99, 15:23.84; 2001- 4:07.25, 15:30.63; 2002- 4:07.69i. pbs: 800m 2:04.52 '99, 1M 4:33.88i '02, 2000m 5:42.55 '01, 3000m 8:32.89 '01.

Irina YATCHENKO b. 31 Oct 1965 Gomel 1.87m 96kg. Grodno. Sports instructor.
At DT: OG: '92- 7, '96- 12, '00- 3; WCh: '91- 7, '95- 9, '97- 5, '99- 9, '01- 10; EC: '90- 5, '98- 8; ECp: '95- 3, '96- 3. 2nd GP 1992. BLR champion 1997.
Progression at DT: 1982- 50.72, 1983- 57.04, 1984- 59.54, 1985- 60.56, 1986- 57.58, 1987- 63.00, 1988- 67.44, 1989- 62.38, 1990- 68.60, 1991- 64.92, 1992- 68.94, 1993- 58.74, 1995- 66.14, 1996- 65.80, 1997- 68.32, 1998- 64.00, 1999- 66.18, 2000- 66.51, 2001- 66.65. Married to Igor Astapkovich (qv).

Ellina ZVEREVA b. 16 Nov 1960 Dolgoprudny 1.86m 96kg. formerly Kisheyeva. Minsk Dyn. Sports instructor.
At DT: OG: '88- 5, '96- 3, '00- 1; WCh: '91- 9, '95- 1, '97- 2, '99- 10, '01- 2; EC: '90- 6, '94- 2, '98- 4; WCp: '94- 2; ECp: '93- 1B, '94- 3. 2nd GP 1996, 2000; 3rd 1994. USSR champion 1986, BLR 1993, 2000; GWG 2001.
Progression at DT: 1979- 44.06, 1980- 51.38, 1981- 59.88, 1982- 62.52, 1983- 65.18, 1984- 68.56, 1985- 66.64, 1986- 68.96, 1987- 60.84, 1988- 71.58, 1990- 66.20, 1991- 63.80, 1992- 66.26/68.82dq, 1993- 66.32, 1994- 67.44, 1995- 68.84, 1996- 68.60, 1997- 65.94, 1998- 67.46, 1999- 67.60, 2000- 68.40, 2001- 67.10. BLR discus record 1988.
Drugs ban reported after positive steroids test when first at CIS Trials 1992, but back in 1993. At 39y 315d in 2000 she became the oldest ever women's Olympic champion at athletics and at 40y 268y in 2001 the oldest ever World Championships medalist.

BELGIUM

Governing bodies: Ligue Royale Belge d'Athlétisme, Stade Roi Baudouin, avenue du Marathon 199B, 1020 Bruxelles (KBAB/LRBA). Vlaamse Atletiekliga (VAL); Ligue Belge Francophone d'Athlétisme (LBFA). Original governing body founded 1889.
National Championships first held in 1889 (women 1921). **2001 Champions**: **Men**: 100m: Bongelemba Bongelo 10.21w, 200m: Erik Wij-

meersch 20.60, 400m: Cedric Van Branteghem 46.35, 800m: Joeri Jansen 1:47.17, 1500m: Jurgen Vandewiele 4:00.37, 5000m: Tom Compernolle 14:09.59, 10000m: Stefan Van Den Broek 29:21.66, HMar: Koen Allaert 65:29, Mar: Chris Verbeeck 2:23:16, 3000mSt: Maarten Vergote 8:55.69, 110mh: Jonathan Nsenga 13.90, 400mh: Stijn Verleyen 50.51, HJ: Stijn Stroobants 2.14, PV: Kevin Rans 5.35, LJ: David Branle 7.77, TJ: Djeke Mambo 16.29, SP: Wim Blondeel 17.47, DT: Kris Coene 54.77, HT: Jelle Degraeuwe 63.35, JT: Marc Van Mensel 72.61, Dec: Serge De Smedt 6815, 10kmW/ 20000mW: Benjamin Leroy 46:59/1:36:04. **Women**: 100m/200m: Kim Gevaert 11.26/23.06, 400m: Sandra Stals 53.69, 800m: Mieke Geens 2:07.79, 1500m: Veerle Dejaeghere 4:16.11, 5000m: Stefanija Statkuviene 16:41.90, 10000m: Mounia Aboulahcen 35:42.09, HMar: Ann Parmentier 79:14. Mar: Katja Merlin 2:48:31, 3000mSt: Sigrid Vanden Bempt 10:13.24, 100mh: Nadine Grouwels 13.51, 400mh: Ann Mercken 56.34, HJ: Sabrina De Leeuw 1.83, PV: Caroline Goetghebuer 3.95, LJ/TJ: Sandra Swennen 5.99/13.14, SP/DT: Veerle Blondeel 15.59/55.12, HT: Sarah Luyimi-Mbala 48.80, JT: Heidi Marien 49.60, Hep: Joke Vissers 5066, 5000mW: Liesbet Desmet 29:32.5.

Mohammed MOURHIT b. 10 Oct 1970 Khouribga, Morocco 1.64m 55kg.
At 5000m: WCh: '99- 3. At 10000m: OG: '00- dnf; WCh: '97- dns, '01- dnf. At 3000m: WI: '01- 2; EI: '00- 4. World CC: '97-8-9-00-01: 5/8/7/1/1; HMar: '97- 5; Eur CC: '98- 2. 3rd GP 3000m 1999. Won MAR 1500m 1992, 1995; 5000m 1993; BEL 1500m 1999, CC 1997-9.
Records: European 10000m 1999, 3000m & 5000m 2000; Belgian 3000m (2), 5000m (5), 10,000m (2), HMar 1997-9.
Progression at 5000m, 10000m: 1988- 13:57.91, 29:17.3; 1989- 14:05.59, 29:37.55; 1990- 14:08.52, 1991- 13:29.20, 1993- 13:47.7, 1996- 13:46.94, 1997- 13:05.49, 27:17.09; 1998- 13:06.20, 1999- 12:58.45, 26:52.30; 2000- 12:49.71, 27:45.75; 2001- 13:09.63. pbs: 800m 1:48.23 '93, 1500m 3:36.14 '00, 1M 3:56.41 '91, 2000m 4:58.8 '00, 3000m 7:26.62 '00, 2M 8:14.88 '97, HMar 60:18 '97.
Ex-Moroccan with Belgian wife. BEL citizenship confirmed July 1997. Brother **Hassan** (b. 2 Jan 1982) ran 2 miles indoors in 8:31.77 in 2001.

Women

Marleen RENDERS b. 24 Dec 1968 1.66m 47kg.
At Mar: OG: '96- 25, '00- dnf; WCh: '01- 18; EC: '98- 5. At 10000m: WCh: '87- 12, '95- 17, '97- dnf, '99- 9; EC: '94- 10; WJ: '86- 3. World HMar: '94- 7, '95- 13. Won BEL 3000m 1987, 5000m 1995-6, 10000m 1988, 1994, 1998-2000; HMar 1994-5, 1998. World junior 10000m record 1987. Belgian records: 10000m 2000, marathon (4) 1997-2000.
Progression at 10000m, Mar: 1986- 33:41.13, 1987- 32:12.51, 1988- 32:11.49, 1991- 32:04.2mx, 1994- 32:11.18, 1995- 32:33.38, 2:28:57; 1996- 32:02.55, 2:27:42; 1997- 31:57.87, 2:25:56; 1998- 32:01.80, 2:25:22; 1999- 31:51.21, 2:23:58; 2000- 31:03.60, 2:23:43; 2001- 2:28:31. pbs: 1500m 4:18.07 '87, 3000m 9:03.64 '97, 5000m 15:19.20 '89, HMar 69:29 '94.
Won Antwerp marathon 1995, Paris 2000; 2nd Rotterdam 1997, Amsterdam 2001. Berlin: 3rd 1997, 1st 1998, 2nd 1999.

BERMUDA

Governing body: Bermuda T & F Association, P.O.Box DV 397, Devonshire. Founded 1946.

Brian WELLMAN b. 8 Sep 1967 1.75m 72kg. Was at University of Arkansas, USA.
At TJ: OG: '88- dnq, '92- 5, '96- 6, '00- dnq 20; WCh: '91- 6, '93- 8, '95- 2, '97- 5, '99- dnq 24, '01- 6; WJ: '86- 8; WI: '93- 3, '95- 1; CG: '90- 11, '94- 3; PAm: '91-99: 5/4; WUG: '91- 1. 2 PAm Jnr 1986; Won NCAA 1991, CAC 1999, 2001. 3rd GP 1992. BER TJ records 1986-95, Commonwealth 1995.
Progression at TJ: 1986- 16.18, 1988- 16.38, 1989- 16.44w, 1990- 16.23, 1991- 17.07/17.41w, 1992- 17.24/17.30w, 1993- 17.27i/17.14, 1994- 17.41A, 1995- 17.72i/17.62A/17.75w, 1996- 17.51A/17.15/ 17.56Aw, 1997- 17.22, 1998- 16.98A/16.97/17.15Aw, 1999- 17.18, 2000- 17.05Ai/16.50/17.09Aw, 2001- 17.24A/16.81. pb LJ 7.61 '94.
Advanced to third in 1993 World Indoors after drugs disqualification of Nikolay Raev.

BRAZIL

Governing body: Confederação Brasileira de Atletismo (CBAT), Avenida Sete de Setembro 874, 4to. andar, Manaus, Amazonas 69005-140. Founded 1914 (Confederação 1977).
2001 National Champions: Men: 100m: Raphael de Oliveira 10.35, 200m: André D da Silva 20.72, 400m: Flávio Godoy 45.56, 800m: Valdinei da Silva 1:46.81, 1500m: Hudson de Souza 3:39.06, 5000m/10000m: Elenilson da Silva 14:10.14/ 28:59.85, 3000mSt: Celso Ficagna 8:45.72, 110mh: Walmes de Souza 13.75, 400mh: Eronilde de Araújo 49.87, HJ: Fabrício Romero 2.22, PV: Henrique Martins 5.05, LJ: Nelson Ferreira Jr 7.86, TJ: Jadel Gregório 16.83w, SP: Adílson Oliveira 17.69, DT: Mateus Monari 52.75, HT: Mário Leme 62.68, JT: Luiz F da Silva 66.64, Dec: Édson Bindilatti 7631, 20000mW: Sérgio Galdino 1:27:51.4. **Women:** 100m/200m: Lucimar de Moura 11.33/23.19, 400m: Maria Laura Almirão 52.64, 800m: Luciana Mendes 2:04.62, 1500m/ 5000m: Fabiana C da Silva 4:17.18/ 16:10.80, 10000m: Lucélia Peres 34:05.5, 3000mSt: Maria Vieira 10:56.63, 100mh: Maíla Machado 13.46, 400mh: Isabel R Silva 57.02, HJ: Luciane Dambacher 1.88, PV: Fabiana Murer 3.90, LJ: Maurren Maggi 6.70, TJ: Luciana dos Santos 13.55, SP/DT: Elisângela Adriano 18.48/56.94, HT: Josiane Soares 58.37, JT: Alessandra Rezende 52.80, Hep: Elizete da Silva 5590, 20000mW:

Gianetti Bonfim 1:42:36.8.

Sanderlei Claro **PARRELA** b. 7 Oct 1974 Santos, São Paulo 1.94m 77kg. São Raimundo.
At 400m/4x400mR: OG: '96- qf, '00- 4; WCh: '95- h, '97- sf, '99- 2; PAm: '99- 4/2R; SACh: '95- 1/1R, '97- 1/1R, '01- 1. Won SA-J 1991, 1993; Ib-Am 1996, 2000; BRA 1996-7, 1999. 2nd GP 2000.
Six BRA and South American 400m records 1997-9
Progression at 400m: 1990- 50.3, 1991- 47.74, 1992- 46.98, 1993- 47.86, 1994- 46.84/46.7, 1995- 45.74, 1996- 45.17, 1997- 44.96, 1998- 45.27, 1999- 44.29, 2000- 44.65, 2001- 45.11. pbs: 100m 10.61 '00, 200m 20.60A '00, 20.83 '97; 300m 32.10+ '99, 800m 1:46.34 '98.
Failed a drugs test on 14 May 2000, but there were apparently discrepancies between his A and B samples and he was reinstated by his national federation in time to compete at Olympic Games.

Claudinei Quirino **da SILVA** b. 19 Nov 1970 Lençóis Paulista, São Paulo 1.86m 86kg. Ulbra/Prudente.
At 200m (100m/4x100mR): OG: '96- qf, '00- 6/2R; WCh: '95- 5, '97- 3, '99- 2/4R; '01- sf (qf); PAm: 99- 1 (3, 1R/2R); SACh: '95- 2, '97- 1/1R. Won GP 200m 1999, Ib-Am 200m 2000, BRA 100m 1998-9, 200m 1996, 1998-2000.
South American 200m record 1999.
Progression at 100m, 200m: 1992- 10.59, 1993- 10.60, 1994- 10.41/10.26dt, 21.19/20.6; 1995- 10.41/10.27w/10.1w, 20.28; 1996- 10.28/10.08dt/ 10.2/10.0w, 20.51/20.0w; 1997- 10.28, 20.27/ 20.26w; 1998- 10.21, 20.46/20.28w; 1999- 10.12, 19.89; 2000- 10.16, 20.23; 2001- 10.35, 20.58. pb 400m 46.14 '00.
Ran 44.6 leg on Pan-Am 4x400m relay. Ran successive pbs of 20.22, 20.13 and 20.00 at 1999 Worlds, and then South American record 19.89 to beat Maurice Greene for GP title.

Women

Maurren Higa **MAGGI** b. 25 Jun 1976 São Carlos, São Paulo 1.78m 66kg. Funilense.
At LJ (/100mh): OG: '00- dnq 25; WCh: '99- 8/qf, '01- 7/h; PAm: '99- 1/2; SACh: '97- 2/1, 99- 1/1, '01- 1/1; WUG: '99- 3, '01- 1/2/2R. Won GWG 2001, IbAm 2000, SA-J 100mh 1994, BRA 100mh 1997-2000, LJ 1999-2000.
Three BRA and one South American long jump records 1999, 6 BRA & 4 SA 100mh records 1999-2001, S.Am TJ record 2002.
Progression at 100mh, LJ: 1994- 14.13. 5.86; 1995- 14.46/14.3w, 5.75/6.02w; 1996- 13.99, 6.47; 1997- 13.67/13.53w, 6.54; 1998- 13.60, 6.42; 1999- 12.86, 7.26A/6.79/6.81w, 2000- 6.93, 2001- 12.71, 6.94/6.98w; 2002- 7.01. pbs: 60mh 8.12i '00 (S.Am rec), TJ 14.21 '02.
Formerly a gymnast, made huge breakthrough in 1999 with her 7.26 LJ at the high altitude of Bogotá from a previous best of 6.79.

BULGARIA

Governing body: Bulgarian Athletic Federation, 75 bl. Vassil Levski, Sofia 1000. F'd 1924.
National Championships first held in 1926 (men), 1938 (women). **2001 Champions**: **Men**: 100m/200m: Petko Yankov 10.59/20.95, 400m/ 400mh: Ilia Dzhivondov 46.45/50.65, 800m/ 1500m: Vancho Stoyanov MKD 1:51.66/3:56.93, 5000m: Petko Stefanov 14:57.60, 10000m: , Mar: Petko Stefanov 2:21:18, 3000mSt: Stefan Stefanov 9:12.66, 110mh: Nikolay Koikov 14.17, HJ: Angel Kararadev 2.21, PV: Spas Bukhalov 5.40, LJ: Nikolay Atanasov 8.07, TJ: Vasil Gergov 16.26, SP: Krasimir Aleksandrov 17.54, DT: Ivan Stanev 49.65, HT: Rosen Zhelev 67.54, JT: Kolyo Neshev 63.17, Dec: Miroslav Shishkov 5821, 10000mW/ 20kmW: Ivaylo Minkov 49:19.31/1:44:01. **Women**: 100m/200m: Monika Gachevska 11.58/23.30, 400m: Nedyalka Nedkova 54.63, 800m: Tsvetanka Kirilova 2:00.56, 1500m: Yoanna Parusheva 4:27.41, 5000m/Mar: Milka Mikhailova 16:50.43/ 2:40:54, 10000m: Rumyana Pasnovska 35:05.76:, 100mh: Yana Kasova 13.70, 400mh: Venya Stambolova 61.77, HJ: Eleonora Milusheva 1.89, PV: Vyara Chavdarova 4.00, LJ: Antonia Yordanova 6.41, TJ: Maria Dimitrova 14.02, SP/HT: Anelia Yordanova 13.54/50.59, DT: Tsvetanka Khristova 47.70, JT: Kristina Georgieva 56.72, Hep: Maria Nikolva 4783, 5000mW/20kmW: Nevena Mineva 21:11.46/1:32:11.

Petar DACHEV b. 15 Jun 1979 Troyan 1.81m 77kg. CSKA Sofia.
At LJ: OG: '00- 11; EC: '98- 3; WJ: '98- 1; EI: '00- 1, '02- 3. BUL champion 2000, Balkan 2000.
Progression at LJ: 1997- 7.41, 1998- 8.14, 1999- 7.76, 2000- 8.30, 2001- 8.02i/7.75, 2002- 8.27i. pb 100m 10.54 '99, 10.5 '01.

Rostislav DIMITROV b. 26 Dec 1974 Ruse 1.82m 80kg. Chendini.
At TJ: OG: '00- 9; WCh: '97- dnq 18, '99- 2, '01- 8; EC: '98- 3; EJ: '93- 2; WI: '99- dq (2), '01- 5; EI: '00-02: 2/5. 2nd GP 2000. Won Balkan 1997, 1999.
Progression at TJ: 1990- 14.70, 1991- 15.49, 1992- 15.98, 1993- 16.35, 1994- 16.11, 1995- 16.18, 1996- 16.48, 1997- 16.88, 1998- 17.07/17.26w, 1999- 17.49, 2000- 17.30, 2001- 16.91i/16.90. pb LJ 7.48 '97.
Positive test for ephedrine cost him the silver medal from the 1999 World Indoor Champs.

Women

Svetla DIMITROVA b. 27 Jan 1970 Burgas 1.70m 65kg. Married name Pishtikova. Spirala.
At 100mh: OG: '96- sf, '00- sf; WCh: '97- 2, '99- 5, '01- 4; EC: '94- 1/3R, '98- 1; WCp: '94- 2. At Hep: OG: '88- 12, '92- 5; WCh: '93- 4; WJ: '86- 1, '88- 1; ECp: '89- 3dq. Won GP 100mh and 2nd overall 1994. Won BUL Hep 1989, 100mh 1992-3, 1998.
Progression at 100mh, Hep: 1986- 6041; 1988- 12.9w, 6343; 1989- 6534 dq/6428; 1992- 13.22,

6658; 1993- 12.71, 6594; 1994- 12.53/12.50w, 1996- 12.57, 1997- 12.58/12.4, 1998- 12.56, 1999- 12.72/12.64w, 2000- 12.78, 2001- 12.58. pbs: 200m 23.06w '92, 23.10 '93; 800m 2:07.90 '92, 60mh 7.94i '00, 400mh 59.35 '01, HJ 1.88 '86, LJ 6.64 '92, SP 15.50 '93, JT 48.18 '93.
Suspended for a positive drugs test when third in the 1989 European Cup heptathlon in what would have been a world junior record. Won Götzis heptathlon 1993, but has since concentrated on hurdling and was clearly the world's best in 1994. In November 1994 she left her husband and coach Ilian Pishtikov to seek Austrian citizenship, but returned in 1995. Her son Kristian was born on 30 Dec 1995.

Tereza MARINOVA b. 5 Sep 1977 Pleven 1.73m 56kg. Chendini.
At TJ: OG: '00- 1; WCh: '97- 6, '01- 3; EC: '98- 3; WJ: '94- dnq 15, '96- 1; EJ: '95- 1; WI: '97-9=01: 8/4/1; EI: '02- 1; E23: '94- 6; won GP 2001. Balkan champion 1996, 2000; BUL 1998.
Two world junior triple jump records (one unofficial) 1996. Bulgarian TJ record 2000.
Progression at TJ: 1993- 12.18, 1994- 13.23/13.51w, 1995- 13.90, 1996- 14.62, 1997- 14.34/14.53w, 1998- 14.67, 1999- 14.76i/14.64, 2000- 15.20, 2001- 14.91i/14.77, 2002- 14.81i. pb LJ 6.46 '00, 6.63w '01.
Smashed personal bests when winning European (1995) and World (1996) Junior gold medals and again to win 2000 Olympic title. Her father Moncho Marinov set a Bulgarian 800m record of 1:47.7 in 1974 and brother Tsvetomir (b. 10 Jul 1976) was 3rd in the 1995 European Junior 400m.

Venelina VENEVA b. 13 Jun 1974 Ruse 1.79m 61kg. 'Champion' Sofia.
At HJ: OG: '96- dnq 29=, '00- 9=; WCh: '91- dnq, '95- dnq 14, '99- dnq 14=, '01- 4; EC: '98- 5; EJ: '91- 2; WI: '01- 3; EI: '00- 4. BUL champion 1995.
Progression at HJ: 1988- 1.80, 1989- 1.86, 1990- 1.93i/1.90, 1991- 1.91, 1992- 1.91, 1993- 1.89i/1.85, 1994- 1.90, 1995- 1.94, 1996- 1.94i/1.88, 1998- 2.03, 1999- 1.90, 2000- 2.01, 2001- 2.04. pb TJ 12.51 '95.
Daughter Neapola born in 1997. World age-15 best of 1.93i in 1990.

BURUNDI

Governing body: Fédération d'Athlétisme du Burundi, BP 1095, Bujumbura. Founded 1960.

Arthémon HATUNGIMANA b. 21 Jan 1974 Muhweza 1.80m 64kg. Paris UC. Tutsi. Studied commerce at Créteil University, France.
At 800m: OG: '96- sf, '00- h; WCh: '95- 2, '97- qf, '99- h, '01- sf; AfG: '95- 1; AfCh: '93- 3, '98- 6. Won French 800m 1994-5, 2001.
Burundi records: 800m (3), 1000m 1995-2000.
Progression at 800m: 1993- 1:46.42, 1994- 1:45.02, 1995- 1:43.56, 1996- 1:43.46, 1997- 1:43.56, 1998- 1:45.56, 1999- 1:46.23, 2000- 1:45.12, 2001- 1:43.38. pbs: 400m 46.78 '95, 1000m 2:15.48 '95, 1500m 3:44.98 '96.
Lived in France since 1993.

Jean-Patrick NDUWIMANA b. 9 May 1978 1.78m 61kg. Studied business management at University of Arizona.
At 800m: OG: '00- sf; WCh: '99- h, '01- sf; WJ: '96- sf. NCAA champion 2000.
Burundi 800m record 2001.
Progression at 800m: 1996- 1:47.68, 1997- 1:48.11, 1998- 1:46.31, 1999- 1:46.03, 2000- 1:44.06, 2001- 1:42.81. pbs: 400m 46.32 '99, 1000m 2:16.98 '00.

CAMEROON

Governing body: Fédération Camerounaise d'Athlétisme, BP 353, Yaoundé. Founded 1957.

Léonie **Myriam MANI** b. 21 May 1977 1.64m 60kg.
At 100m(/200m): OG: '96- h, '00- sf/sf; WCh: '97- h, '99 – h/qf, '01- sf/8; CG: '98- 8, AfG: '95- (7), '99- 2/2; AfCh: '96- 3/3, '00-1/1. 1st GP 200m 2001.
CMR records 100m, 200m from 1998.
Progression at 100m, 200m: 1991- 24.2; 1992- 12.0, 24.5; 1993- 24.0, 1994- 23.6, 1995- 24.40A, 1996- 11.71/11.4, 23.33; 1997- 11.62/11.54w, 23.68; 1998- 11.35/11.1w, 23.01; 1999- 11.24A/11.22w, 22.66A; 2000- 11.01, 22.41; 2001- 10.98, 22.54. pbs: 60m 7.18i '00, 400m 53.0 '98.

Françoise MBANGO b. 14 Apr 1976 1.72m 63kg.
At TJ(/LJ): OG: '00- 10; WCh: '99- dnq 13, '01- 2; CG: '98- 2/10, AfG: '99- 1/2; AfCh: '96-8-00: 3/2/1. French champion 1999, 2001.
Four African triple jump records 1999, CMR records LJ from 1993, TJ from 1997.
Progression at TJ: 1994- 12.18, 1995- 11.92, 1996- 12.59, 1997- 13.75A, 1998- 14.02, 1999- 14.70A/14.65, 2000- 14.18, 2001- 14.65. pbs: 100m 12.18/11.5w '00, LJ 6.55A/6.43 '99.
First athlete from CMR to win a World medal.

CANADA

Governing body: Athletics Canada, Suite 606, 1185 Eglinton Avenue East, Toronto, Ontario, L3X 1T6. Formed as Canadian AAU in 1884.
National Championships first held in 1884 (men), 1925 (women). **2001 champions: Men**: 100m: Donovan Bailey 10.24, 200m/ 400m: Shane Niemi 20.61/45.98, 800m: Achraf Tadili 1:45.48, 1500m: Graham Hood 3:51.65, 5000m: Jeremy Deere 14:08.32, 10000m: Jeff Schiebler 28:48.95, 3000mSt: Joël Bourgeois 8:44.93, Mar: Bruce Deacon 2:18:54, 110mh: Andrew Woodley 13.77w, 400mh: Monte Raymond 49.78, HJ: Mark Boswell 2.23, PV: Rob Pike 5.35, LJ: Richard Duncan 7.88, TJ: Evgeniy Timofeev 16.12, SP: Brad Snyder 20.57, DT: Jason Tunks 64.84, HT: Dylan Armstrong 65.18, JT: Scott Russell 80.17, Dec: Mike Nolan 7784, 20kmW: Tim Berrett

1:23:46. **Women**: 100m: Venolyn Clarke 11.49, 200m: Ladonna Antoine-Watkins 23.13, 400m: Foy Williams 52.12, 800m: Diane Cummins 2:04.56, 1500m: Leah Pells 4:14.75, 5000m: Courtney Babcock 16:07.29, 10000m: Tina Connelly 32:46.48, Mar: Danuta Bartoszek 2:37:59, 3000mSt: Karen Harvey 10:30.64, 100mh: Angela Whyte 13.10, 400mh: Karlene Haughton 56.96, HJ: Wanita May 1.90, PV: Stephanie McCann 4.15, LJ: Alice Falaiye 6.40, TJ: Michelle Hastick 13.77, SP: Georgette Reed 15.23, DT: Nicole Chimko 52.62, HT: Caroline Wittrin 62.03, JT: Dominique Bilodeau 50.32, Hep: Jessica Zelinka 5356, 20kmW: Karen Foan 1:41:08.

Kwaku BOATENG b. 30 Jun 1974 Eastmont, Ghana 1.93m 84kg. St Laurent Select. Graphic artist, studied psychology at Concordia University.
At HJ: OG: '00- 12; WCh: '99- 6=, '01- 9; CG: '94- dnq; PAm: '99- 1=. Canadian champion 1997-9.
Progression at HJ: 1993- 2.13, 1994- 2.15, 1996- 2.24, 1997- 2.27i, 1998- 2.20, 1999- 2.29, 2000- 2.34, 2001- 2.31.
Competed for Ghana at 1994 CG.

Mark BOSWELL b. 28 Jul 1977 Mandeville, Jamaica 1.89m 77kg. Lightning T&F. Student at University of Texas.
At HJ: OG: '00- 6=; WCh: '99- 2, '01- 7=; WJ: '96: 1; PAm: '99- 1=; WUG: '99- 2; Won NCAA 1999-2000, Canadian 1997, 2000-01.
Four Canadian high jump records 1999-2000.
Progression at HJ: 1994- 2.10, 1995- 2.00, 1996- 2.24, 1997- 2.28, 1998- 2.29, 1999- 2.35, 2000- 2.35, 2001- 2.33. Moved to Canada in 1988.

Brad SNYDER b. 8 Jan 1976 Windsor, Ontario 1.96m 128kg. Windsor Legion. Studied criminal justice at University of South Carolina, USA.
At SP: OG: '96- dnq 30, '00- dnq 13; WCh: '97- dnq 21, '01- 8; WJ: '94- dnq 14; PAm: '99- 3; WUG: '99- 4. Won Pan-Am J 1995, NCAA 1998, Canadian 1996, 1998-9, 2001.
Progression at SP: 1994- 16.73, 1995- 17.34, 1996- 19.70, 1997- 19.68i/19.51, 1998- 20.40, 1999- 20.51, 2000- 20.24, 2001- 20.79. pb DT 58.65 '99.
Younger brother Trevor has JT pb 74.59 '01.

Kevin SULLIVAN b. 20 Mar 1974 Brantford, Ontario 1.80m 68kg. Windsor. Civil engineering graduate of University of Michigan, USA.
At 1500m: OG: '00- 5; WCh: '95- 5, '97- sf, '99- h, '01- sf; WJ: '92- 3; CG: '94- 2; 3rd GP 2000. At 800m: WJ: '90- h. World CC: '93- 13J. Won CAN 1500m 1992-5, 2000; PAmJ 800m 1993, NCAA 1500m 1995.
CAN records 1M 1995 & 2000, 1500m 1997 & 2000.
Progression at 1500m: 1991- 3:46.52, 1992- 3:39.11, 1993- 3:39.43, 1994- 3:36.78, 1995- 3:35.77, 1996- 3:42.2, 1997- 3:35.19, 1998- 3:34.80, 1999- 3:34.61, 2000- 3:31.71, 2001- 3:33.91. pbs: 800m 1:47.06 '95, 1000m 2:17.59 '00, 1M 3:50.26 '00, 3000m 7:51.65i '98, 2M 8:23.67i '01.
Married Karen Harvey on 8 Aug 1998.

Bruny SURIN b. 12 Jul 1967 Cap-Haïtien, Haiti 1.80m 81kg. Vidéotron, Montreal.
At 100m/4x100m: OG: '92- 4, '96- sf/1R, '00- sf; WCh: '91- 8, '93- 5/3R, '95- 2/1R, '97- 7/1R, '99- 2, '01- sf; CG: '90- 3 (7 LJ), '94- sf/1R. At LJ: OG: '88- dnq 15; PAm: '87- dnq 15. At TJ: WJ: '86- 11. At 60m: WI: '91- 8, '93- 1, '95- 1, '97- 5, '99- 8. Won Canadian 100m 1989-92, 1998-2000.
Six Canadian 100m records 1989-99. Commonwealth 100m record 1999.
Progression at 100m, LJ: 1986- 10.95, 7.66, 1987- 10.62, 8.03; 1988- 10.71, 8.02/8.19w; 1989- 10.14/10.1, 8.00; 1990- 10.24/10.12w, 7.85w; 1991- 10.07/10.01w, 1992- 10.05/9.9, 1993- 10.02, 1994- 10.08, 1995- 9.97/9.92w, 1996- 10.03, 1997- 10.06, 1998- 9.89, 1999- 9.84, 2000- 10.08/10.05w, 2001- 10.11. pbs: 50m 5.53+ '99, 55m 6.15i '96, 60m 6.38+ '99, 200m 20.21 '99, TJ 15.96 '86.
Moved to Canada in 1975. Set four Canadian records 1989-92 and reached peak form in 1999, when in a record fifth successive World 100m final, he took the silver medal, equalling Donovan Bailey's Canadian (and former world) record of 9.84.

Jason TUNKS b. 7 May 1975 London, Ontario 1.97m 120kg. London Western. Was at Southern Methodist University, USA.
At DT (SP): OG: '96- dnq 33, '00- 6; WCh: '97- 9, '99- dnq 20, '01- 9; WJ: '94- 8 (10); CG: '98- 3; PAm: '99- 3 (5). Won NCAA 1997; Canadian SP 1997, DT 1995, 1997-2001.
Two CAN (one Commonwealth) DT records 1998.
Progression at DT: 1992- 48.38, 1993- 51.52, 1994- 58.76, 1995- 58.66, 1996- 63.86, 1997- 65.20, 1998- 67.88, 1999- 65.54, 2000- 66.28, 2001- 67.70. pb SP 19.06 '97.
Was married to Teri Steer (USA) pb SP 19.21 '01, 3 WI '99, 3 PAm 99, 9 WCh 99, pb DT 56.60 '98.

Women

Diane CUMMINS b. 19 Jan 1974 Durban, South Africa 1.65m 50kg. Pacific Sport.
At 800m/4x400m: WCh: '01- 5; CG: '98- sf/3R; PAm: '99- 5; won CAN 800m 1998, 2000-01.
Canadian 800m record 2001.
Progression at 800m: 1997- 2:08.65, 1998- 2:03.45, 1999- 2:02.14, 2000- 2:01.95, 2001- 1:58.39. pbs: 400m 53.89 '01, 1500m 4:05.02 '01, 1M 4:42.42i '02.. Came to Canada from South Africa in November 1994.

CAYMAN ISLANDS

Governing Body: Cayman Islands Amateur Athletic Association, PO Box 527, George Town, Grand Cayman. Founded 1980.

Kareem **STREETE-THOMPSON** b. 30 Mar 1973 Ithaca, New York 1.83m 84kg. Nike. Degree in political science from Rice University, USA.

At LJ (100m): OG: '92- dnq (h), '00- dnq 13; WCh: '91- dnq, '95- 14, '99- dnq 24 (8), '01- 5; WI: '01- 2; CG: '90- 11 (qf); WJ: '88- dnq; '90- 3; PAm: '99- 2; WUG: '93- 1. Won CAC Jnr 1990 and 1992, NCAA 1995, CAC 2001. 2nd GP 1995.
Cayman Islands records 100m 1991-9, 200m 1991-2, LJ 1990-2000.
Progression at 100m, LJ: 1988- 6.84, 1989- 10.88, 7.83; 1990- 7.95, 1991- 10.59/10.50w, 8.09/8.40w; 1992- 10.57, 8.12/8.39w; 1993- 10.30/10.19Aw, 8.36A; 1994- 10.21A/10.29, 8.63/8.64w; 1995- 10.16, 8.56; 1996- 10.23, 8.34; 1997- 9.96, 8.08A/8.30Aw; 1998- 10.07, 8.17; 1999- 10.14, 8.15/8.22Aw; 2000- 10.22Aw, 8.31; 2001- 8.20. pbs: 50m 5.76i '97, 55m 6.16i '94, 60m 6.53i '98, 200m 20.3 '97, 21.34 '93.
Until 1992 he represented the Cayman Islands, where he lived for the first 18 years of his life, apart from his first month as he was born in the USA of Jamaican parents while his mother was visiting friends. He became a US citizen in 1994, but in 1999 reverted to the Cayman Islands.

Women

Cydonie MOTHERSILL b. 19 Mar 1978 Kingston, Jamaica 1.70m 54kg. Was at Clemson University, USA.
At 200m(/100m): OG: '96- (h), '00- qf/qf; WCh: '97- (h), '01- 5; WJ: '96- sf/6; PAm: '99- 5; PAmJ: '97- 3/3; won CAC 2001.
Cayman Islands records 100m & 200m 1994-01, 400m 1998-9.
Progression at 200m: 1994- 24.31, 1995- 23.83, 1996- 23.65, 1997- 23.80, 1998- 23.48, 1999- 22.81, 2000- 22.66, 2001- 22.54. pbs: 100m 11.34 '01, 11.21w '00; 300m 35.82 '00, 400m 53.13 '99.

CHAD

Governing Body: Fédération Tchadienne d'Athlétisme, BP 373, N'Djamena. F'd 1963

Nadjina KALTOUMA b. 16 Nov 1976 1.71m 60kg.
At 400m (200m): OG: '00- qf; WCh: 97- h (h), 99- qf, '01- 5; WI: '01- 4/1R; AfG: '95- (6), '99- 8 (7); AfCh: '00- 3.
Chad records 200m & 400m from 1994.
Progression at 400m: 1994- 56.08, 1995- 55.10A, 1996- 54.5/54.61, 1997- 53.19, 1998- 53.89, 1999- 51.90, 2000- 52.27, 2001- 50.38. pbs: 200m 22.97 ' 01, 300m 36.10 '01. Now lives in Canada.

CHILE

Governing body: Federación Atlética de Chile, Calle Santo Toribio No 660, Ñuñoa, Santiago de Chile. Founded 1917.
2001 National Champions: **Men**: 100m/200m: Rodrigo Roach 10.72/21.41, 400m: Sebastián Cantuarias 48.25, 800m: Pablo de la Cámara 1:51.92, 1500m: Sebastián Pino 3:52.11, 5000m: Jonathan Monje 14:30.60, 10000m: Carlos Jaramillo 29:33.22, 3000mSt: Raúl Mora 8:57.11, 110mh: Carlos Vega 14.92, 400mh: Carlos Zbinden 51.92, HJ: Felipe Apablaza 2.16, PV: Cristian Castillo 4.80, LJ: Claudio Bossay 7.33, TJ: Francisco Castro 13.89, SP/DT: Marco Antonio Verni 18.32/50.51, HT: Patricio Palma 66.76, JT: Diego Moraga 69.62, 10000mW: Cristián Bascuñán 44:48.59, 20kmW: Cristian Muñoz 1:27:33.0. **Women**: 100m/200m: Daniela Pavez 12.36/25.28, 400m: Roxana González 56.46, 800m: Verónica Bravo 2:18.89, 1500m: Johana Osorio 4:41.66, 5000m: Silvia González 17:44.09, 10000m: Flor Venegas 36:40.60, 100mh: Francisca Guzmán 14.51, 400mh: Minerva Navarrete 62.22, HJ: Ana Kerstin Weiss 1.65, PV: María Paz Ausin 3.60, LJ: Mónica Castro 5.69, TJ: Rocío Gorigoytia 11.34, SP: Valeria Steffens 12.72, DT: Ximena Araneda 40.27, HT: Odette Palma 50.25, JT: Catalina Toro 38.99, 20kmW: Mabel Vásquez 2:07:53.

CHINA

Governing body: Athletic Association of the People's Republic of China, 9 Tiyuguan Road, Beijing 100763.
National Championships first held in 1910 (men), 1959 (women). **2001 Champions**. **Men**: 100m: Chen Haijian 10.25, 200m: Han Chaoming 21.15, 400m: Jiang Bo 46.53, 800m: Li Huiquan 1:50.80, 1500m: Dou Zhaobo 3:44.72, 5000m/10000m: Zhang Yunshan 13:56.41/30:36.24, Mar: Zhu Ronghua 2:16:56, 3000mSt: Sun Jiawei 8:47.71, 110mh: Chen Yanhao 13.48, 400mh: Tan Chunhua 50.23, HJ: Zhou Zhongge 2.24, PV: Wu Jun 5.30, LJ: Li Dalong 8.22, TJ: Lao Jianfeng 16.64, SP: Wen Jili 19.00, DT: Wu Tao 58.74, HT: Ye Kuigang 70.56, JT: Li Rongxiang 80.46, Dec: Qi Haifeng 7694, 20kmW: Li Zewen 1:21:10, 50kmW: Wang Yinhang 3:50:20. **Women**: 100m: Chen Yueqin 11.38, 200m: Huang Mei 23.04, 400m: Chen Yuxiang 52.17, 800m: Feng Lei 2:03.40, 1500m/5000m: Wang Chunmei 4:20.17/15:52.21, 10000m: Dai Yanyan 34:26.33, Mar: Zheng Guixia 2:30:11, 100mh: Feng Yun 12.96, 400mh: Song Yinglan 56.69, HJ: Jing Xuezhu 1.86, PV: Gao Shuying 4.30, LJ: Zhong Mei 6.69, TJ: Wu Lingmei 14.10, SP: Cheng Xiaoyan 18.67, DT: Song Aimin 61.27, HT: Zhao Wei 65.12, JT: Ha Xiaoyan 59.76, Hep: Wang Hailan 5917, 10kmW: Li Hong 44:29, 20kmW: Gao Hongmiao 1:28:45.

LI Zewen b. 5 Dec 1973 Qujing, Yunnan Prov. 1.72m 55kg. Sports psychology student.
At 20kmW: OG: '96- 28, WCh: '95- 5, '97- 5, '99- 4, '01- 13; WCp: '95- 1, '97- 4, '99- 18; AsiG: '98- 3; AsiC: '98- 1. Won E.Asian 2001, CHN 2001, CHN National Games 1997, 2001.
Progression at 20kmW: 1992- 1:23:36.9, 1993- 1:22:30, 1995- 1:19:44, 1996- 1:19:41, 1997- 1:18:32, 1998- 1:22:53, 1999- 1:24:03, 2000- 1:21:12, 2001- 1:20:49.

LIU Xiang b. 15 Jul 1983. 1.86m 74kg.

At 110mh: WCh: '01- sf; WJ: '00- 4; WUG: '01- 1. Won E.Asian 2001. World Junior records indoors 50mh (2) & 60mh (2) 2002.
Progression at 110mh: 1999- 14.19, 2000- 13.75, 2001- 13.32. pbs: 50mh 6.52i '02, 60mh 7.55i '02.

Women

CHENG Xiaoyan b. 30 Nov 1975 Shandong Prov. 1.74m 100kg.
At SP: OG: '00- 11; WCh: '99- 5, '01- dnq 15; WI: '01- 7; WJ: '94- 1; WUG: '95- 2; AsiG: '98- 2. Won E.Asian 2001, CHN 1999, 2001.
Progression at SP: 1993- 18.00, 1994- 20.02, 1995- 18.29, 1996- 18.40, 1997- 18.28, 1998- 18.55, 1999- 18.91, 2000- 19.31, 2001- 18.67.

DONG Yanmei b. 16 Dec 1979 or 16 Feb 1977? Xuengdong, Liaoning Prov. 1.66m 51kg.
At 5000 (/10000m): WCh: '01- 4; WUG: '01- 1/1; At 3000m: WI: '01- 5. Won E.Asian 5000m & 10000m 2001, CHN National Games 10000m 1997, 2001; 5000m 2001.
World record 5000m 1997.
Progression at 1500m, 5000m, 10000m, Mar: 1993- 17:23.0, 1994- 16:09.37, 1995- 15:11.80, 32:04.42, 2:38:57; 1996- 4:18.41, 15:58.55, 33:24.19, 2:34:52; 1997- 3:55.07, 14:29.82, 30:38.09, 2:28:09; 1998- 32:59.85, 2000- 15:03.99, 32:23.21; 2001- 4:07.72, 14:51.58, 31:43.59. pb 3000m 8:33.07 '00.

GAO Hongmiao b. 17 Mar 1974 Liaoning 1.62m 51kg. Computing student.
At 20kmW: WCh: '99- 15; WCp: '99- 7. At 10kmW: OG: '96- dq; WCh: '95- dq; WCp: '95- 1; WUG: '01- 1; AsiG: '94- 1; AsiC: '93- 1. At 5000mW: WJ: '92- 1. Won CHN 10kmW 1994, 1996; 20kmW 2001.
World junior 10,000m walk records track 1992, road 1993. Asian 10 km walk record 1994.
Progression at 10kmW, 20kmW: 1991- 42:56.09, 1992- 42:49.7, 1993- 41:57, 1994- 41:38, 1995- 42:19, 1996- 42:16, 1999- 43:37, 1:30:03; 2000- 44:36.0t, 1:33:01; 2001- 43:20, 1:28:45. pb 5000mW 21:20.03 '92.
Disqualified outside the stadium when leading World 10km 1995. Date of birth originally shown as 8 Jul 1974, then as 1972. However, the Chinese federation confirmed in 1995 that her date of birth was as above.

GAO Shuying b. 28 Oct 1979 1.80m 63kg.
At PV: OG: '00- 10; WCh: '01- 5; WJ: '98- 8; WUG: '01- 1. CHN champion 2000-01, E.Asian 2001, CHN NG 2001.
Seven Asian pole vault records 2000-01.
Progression at PV: 1996- 3.30, 1997- 3.70, 1998- 3.90, 1999- 4.10, 2000- 4.35, 2001- 4.52.

GUAN Yingnan b. 25 Apr 1977 Shanghai 1.77m 60kg.
At LJ: OG: '00- dnq 19; WCh: '99- dnq 17, '01- 9; WJ: '96- 1; AsiG: '98- 1; AsiC: '98- 1; WI: '99- 6, '01- 7; WUG: '01- 2; WCp: '98- 3. Won Asi-J 1996, CHN 1998-2000, E.Asian 2001.
Progression at LJ: 1994- 6.11, 1995- 6.48, 1996- 6.68, 1997- 6.86, 1998- 6.91, 1999- 6.80, 2000- 6.95, 2001- 6.77. pbs: 100mh 14.53 '95, HJ 1.80 '94, JT 39.64 '95, Hep 5637 '95.

LAN Lixin b. 14 Feb 1979 Liaoning Prov. 1.66m 50kg.
At 1500m (3000m): WCh: '01- sf; WJ: '98- 1 (4). Won Asian Junior 3000m 1997.
World Junior 1500m record 1997.
Progression at 1500m, 5000m, 10000m: 1997- 3:53.97, 14:45.33, 30:39.41; 1998- 4:10.05, 15:56.84; 1999- 4:11.62, 15:29.25, 33:26.51; 2000- 4:03.95, 15:31.05; 2001- 4:11.09. pb 3000m 8:39.67 '00.

LIU Hongyu b. 11 Jan 1975 Liaoning Prov. 1.64m 51kg.
At 20kmW: WCh: '99- 1, '01- dq; WCp: '99- 1; won E.Asian 2001. At 10kmW: WCh: '95- 8, '97- 4; WCp: '93- 18, '95- 3, '97- 12; AsiG: '98- 1. At 5000mW: WJ: '94- 8.
World best 20km walk 1995.
Progression at 10kmW, 20kmW: 1993- 43:49.5, 1994- 42:47, 1995- 42:38.24t, 1:27:30; 1996- 42:55, 1997- 42:57, 1:33:31; 1998- 43:57.28t, 1999- 41:45, 1:27:32; 2000- 44:08, 1:27:55; 2001- 1:26:35. pbs: 5kmW: 21:15 '95.

WANG Liping b. 8 Jul 1976 Liaoning Prov. 1.65m 48kg.
At 20kmW: OG: '00- 1. CHN champion 2000. At 10kmW: WCp: '97- 10; WUG: '01- 3.
Progression at 10kmW, 20kmW: 1994- 1:35:09, 1995- 46:19.83t, 1:29:26; 1997- 42:53, 1:36:22; 1998- 45:12, 2000- 44:55, 1:28:33; 2001- 44:01, 1:26:23.

WANG Yan b. 3 May 1971 Liaoning 1.68m 50kg. Student.
At 20kmW: WCh: '99- 2; WCp: '99- 5. At 10kmW: OG: '96- 3; WCh: '93- dq, '97- 12; AsiC: '98- 5; WCp: '93- 1, '95- 14. Chinese champion 1993, 1998, National Games 2001.
World walk records in 1986: 3000m: 12:39.1, 5000m: 21:33.8, with the latter at 14 years 310 days the youngest ever to set a world record. World junior 10kmW record 1986, Asian 10km walks records 1993 and 1999.
Progression at 10kmW: 1984- 49:01, 1985- 46:09, 1986- 44:59.3t, 1987- 45:22.24t, 1992- 42:50, 1993- 42:26, 1995- 44:25, 1:28:54; 1996- 42:19, 1997- 42:42, 1998- 45:03, 1999- 41:16, 1:29:15; 2000- 43:11, 1:28:27; 2001- 1:26:22. pbs: 5kmW 21:10 '97.

COLOMBIA

Governing body: Federación Colombiana de Atletismo, Calle 28 No. 25-18, Apartado Aéreo 6024, Santafé de Bogotá. Founded 1937.
National Games 2001: Men: 100m/200m: John Córdoba 10.44/21.21, 400m: Jacner Palacios 47.50, 800m: José Bermúdez 1:52.72, 1500m: José Perea 3:53.62, 5000m: William Naranjo 14:46.08, 10000m:

William Roldán 31:07.86, 3000mSt: Richard Rosero 9:46.53, 110mh: Paulo Villar 13.77, 400mh: José Carvajal 52.31, HJ: Gilmar Mayo 2.24, PV: Jackson Angulo 4.40, LJ: Lewis Asprilla 7.29, TJ: Alvin Rentería 16.24w, SP: Johnny Rodríguez 18.03, DT: Orlando Ibarra 50.42, HT: Fabián Vera 53.68, JT: Noraldo Palacios 68.54, Dec: Jackson Angulo 6173, 20000mW: Luis Fernando López 1:26:31. **Women:** 100m: Mirtha Brock 11.65, 200m: Miriam Caicedo 24.49, 400m: Norma González 53.01, 800m: Rosibel García 2:13.72, 1500m/5000m/3000mSt: Bertha Sánchez 4:37.50/ 17:25.98/11:34.05, 10000m: Iglandini González 37:08.73, 100mh: Brigith Merlano 14.59, 400mh: Rosibel García 61.10, HJ: Katerina Ibarguen 1.76, PV: Milena Agudelo 3.40, LJ: Helena Guerrero 6.29w, TJ: Yvonne Patarroyo 12.35, SP/DT: Luz Dary Castro 15.79/54.17, HT: María Eugenia Villamizar 57.40, JT: Zuleima Araméndiz 54.18, Hep: Zorobabelia Córdoba 5213, 20kmW: Cristina Bohorquez 1:46:48.

CROATIA

Governing body: Hrvatski Atletski Savez, Tg Sportova 11, 10000 Zagreb. Founded 1912.

Champions 2001: **Men**: 100m: Dejan Vojnovic 10.60, 200m: Elvis Persic 21.36, 400m: Branimir Peitel 46.68, 800m: Tomislav Capuder 1:53.65, 1500m: Slavko Petrovic 3:54.09, 3000m/5000m/ 10000m: Perica Brkic 8:33.97/15:01.43/31:16.5, HMar/Mar: Drago Paripovic 66:14/2:35:52; 3000mSt: Dario Nemec 9:44.96, 110mh: Jurica Grabusic 14.36, 400mh: Nenad Miksec 53.22, HJ: Luka Brkljacic 2.05, PV: Bosko Trisovic 4.70, LJ: Luka Aracic 7.57, TJ: Edi Stipic 14.77 (drugs dq, Miljenko Vukovic 15.65), SP: Stevimir Ercegovac 19.14, DT: Dragan Mustapic 57.68, HT: Sasa Novoselec 61.19, JT: Edi Ponos 73.94, 20kmW: Zeljko Konosic 1:47:58. **Women**: 100m: Rahela Markt 12.19, 200m: Katarina Perosevic 24.95, 400m: Danijela Cvetkovic 55.44, 800m: Petra Pticek 2:11.92, 1500m: Irena Topalovic 4:41.81, 3000m: Liljana Culibrk 9:24.21, 10000m: Ivancica Cvitkovic 38:53.1, HMar: Slavica Brcic 85:39; Mar: Marija Paulus 3:15:24, 100mh: Martina Makos 14.19, 400mh: Sanja Hap 61.85, HJ: Blanka Vlasic 1.95, PV: Ivona Jerkovic 3.40, LJ/TJ: Sanela Mitrovic 5.99/12.29, SP: Martina Lulic 14.21, DT: Vera Begic 54.94, HT: Ivana Brkljacic 63.56, JT: Ivana Bizaca 49.74.

Women

Ivana BRKLJACIC b. 25 Jan 1983 Vinningen-Schweningen, Germany 1.70m 65kg. Mladost Zagreb.
At HT: OG: '00- 11; WCh: '01- 8; WJ: '98- dnq 15, '00- 1; WY: '99- 3; EJ: '99- 5, '01- 1. CRO champion 1999, 2001. CRO hammer record from 1998.
Progression at HT: 1998- 56.84, 1999- 58.51, 2000- 68.18, 2001- 66.49.

Blanka VLASIC b 8 Nov 1983 Split 1.89m 65kg.
At HJ: OG: '00- dnq 17; WCh: '01- 6; WJ: '00- 1; WY: '99- 9; EJ: '01- 7. Won MedG, CRO 2001.
Progression at HJ: 1998- 1.68, 1999- 1.80, 2000- 1.93, 2001- 1.95.
Her father Josko set the Croatian decathlon record with 7659 (1983).

CUBA

Governing body: Federación Cubana de Atletismo, 13 y C Vedado 601, Zone Postal 4, La Habana 10400. Founded 1922.

National Champions 2001: **Men**: 100m: Freddy Mayola 10.08w, 200m: Alianni Echevarría 21.21, 400m: Edel Hevia 46.45, 800m: Norberto Téllez 1:50.37, 1500m: Ereisis Torres 3:48.63, 5000m/ 10000m: Aguelmis Rojas 14:21.01/29:43.84, 3000mSt: Bismark Ramirez 8:50.20, 110mh: Emilio Valle 13.62w, 400mh: Yacnier Luis 50.05, HJ: Javier Sotomayor 2.24, PV: Amaury Fernández 5.10, LJ: Yoelmis Pacheco 7.57, TJ: Michael Calvo 17.30, SP: Jhony Rodríguez 17.91, DT: Alexis Elizalde 62.82, HT: Yosmel Monte 71.68, JT: Emeterio González 82.77, Dec: Yonelvis Aguila 7585, 20kmW: Francisco Gutierrez 1:28:01. **Women**: 100m: Virgen Benavides 11.33w, 200m: Ana W López 23.51, 400m: Yudalis Díaz 52.52, 800m: Zulia Calatayud 2:02.21, 1500m: Yanelis Lara 4:27.73 4:31.37, 5000m/10000m: Yudelkis Martínez 16:49.89/35:22.81, 100mh: Dainelky Pérez 13.02w; 400mh: Daimí Pernía 55.87, HJ: Ioamnet Quintero 1.83, PV: Mariana McCarthy 3.70, LJ: Lissette Cuza 6.39, TJ: Yusmay Bicet 13.71, SP: Yumileidi Cumbá 18.28, DT: Yania Ferrales 56.69, HT: Yipsi Moreno 68.32, JT: Osleidys Menéndez 64.09, Hep: Orisis Pedroso 5335, 20kmW: Oslaidis Cruz 1:37:38.

Anier Octavio **GARCÍA** b. 9 Mar 1976 Santiago de Cuba 1.89m 85kg.
At 110mh: OG: '96- qf, '00- 1; WCh: '97- sf, '99- 2, '01- 2; WJ: '94- 5; PAm: '99- 1; CAG: '98- 1; WCp: '98- 3. Won GP 2001, PAm-J 1995, IbAm 1996, Cuban 1997-2000. At 60mh: WI: '97-9-01: 1/6/2. Five CAC & Cuban 110mh records 1997-2000. CAC indoor records at 50mh & 60mh 2000.
Progression at 110mh: 1993- 14.61, 1994- 13.91, 1995- 13.63/13.6, 1996- 13.39A/13.43, 1997- 13.11, 1998- 13.14A/13.24, 1999- 13.07, 2000- 13.00, 2001- 13.07. pb 50mh 6.36i '00, 60mh 7.37i '00.
Ricoh Tour 60mh winner 2000. Withdrew from 1997 World 110mh semis due to a leg injury.

Yoel GARCÍA b. 25 Nov 1973 Nueva Gerona, Isla de la Juventud 1.82m 83kg. Adidas.
At TJ: OG: '96- dnq 20, '00- 2; WCh: '95- 5, '97- dnq 15, '99- dnq 21, '01- 4; WI: '97- 1; PAm: '95- 3. Cuban champion 1999.
Progression at TJ: 1990- 14.98, 1991- 15.36, 1993- 16.39, 1994- 16.62, 1995- 17.47, 1996- 17.36, 1997- 17.62i/17.37, 1998- 17.04, 1999- 17.07, 2000- 17.47, 2001- 17.40. pb LJ 7.58 '95.

Emeterio GONZÁLEZ b. 11 Apr 1973 San Juan

y Martínez, Pinar del Río 1.84m 105kg.
At JT: OG: '96- dnq 18, '00- 8; WCh: '95- dnq 17, '97- 7, '99- 7, '01- dnq 18; WJ: '92- 6; : '94- 7; PAm: '95- 1, '99- 1; CAG: '93- 3, '98- 1; WUG: '97- 2, '99- 4; WCp: '98- 5. Won CUB 1996-2002, CAC 1997, Ib-Am 2000.
Nine CAC & Cuban javelin records 1995-2000.
Progression at JT: 1989- 60.36, 1990- 67.40, 1991- 65.78, 1992- 73.56, 1993- 74.14, 1994- 78.18, 1995- 82.64, 1996- 82.10, 1997- 83.56, 1998- 84.20, 1999- 84.32, 2000- 87.12, 2001- 82.77.

Yoel HERNÁNDEZ b. 12 Dec 1977 Manacas, Villa Clara 1.84m 77kg
At 110mh: OG: '00- sf; WCh: '99- 6, '01- 4; WJ: '94- sf, '96- 1; PAm: '99- 2. At 60mh: WI: '01- 5.
Progression at 110mh: 1994- 14.20, 1995- 13.81, 1996- 13.81/13.72w, 1997- 13.70, 1998- 13.45, 1999- 13.24, 2000- 13.24/13.20w, 2001- 13.30, 2002- 13.30. pbs: 100m 10.69 '99, 200m 21.18 '99, 50mh 6.42i '00, 60mh 7.40i '00.

Luis Felipe **MELIZ** b. 11 Aug 1979 Villa Clara 1.77m 76kg
At LJ: OG: '00- 7; WCh: '99/01- dnq 18/17; WI: '01- 9; WJ: '98 - 3; PAm: '99- 3; WUG: '99- 2.
Progression at LJ: 1997- 7.65, 1998- 8.05, 1999- 8.14/8.23 irreg, 2000- 8.43, 2001- 8.11i/8.10.

Iván Lázaro **PEDROSO** b. 17 Dec 1972 La Habana 1.76m 70kg. Adidas.
At LJ: OG: '92- 4, '96- 12, '00- 1; WCh: '93- nj, '95- 1, '97- 1, '99- 1, '01- 1; WI: '93/95/97/99/01- 1; WJ: '90- 4; WUG: '97- 1; PAm: '91-5-8: 3/1/1; CAG: '98- 1; WCp: '92- 1, '98- 1. Won GP 1995, 1997, 1999; GWG 1998, 2001; PAm J 1991, IbAm 1992, CAC 1997, Cuban 1992-3, 1995, 1997-8, 2000.
Three CAC & Cuban long jump records 1992-5.
Progression at LJ: 1988- 7.43, 1989- 7.43, 1990- 8.06, 1991- 8.22, 1992- 8.53/8.79w, 1993- 8.49, 1994- 8.26i/8.16, 1995- 8.71/8.96Aw, 1996- 8.46i/8.32, 1997- 8.63, 1998- 8.54, 1999- 8.62i/8.60, 2000- 8.65, 2001- 8.43i/8.40. pb TJ 16.05 '91.
Won fifth successive World Indoor title and fourth successive outdoor title in 2001. Clearly the world top long jumper in 1995, when he had a narrow foul at 9.03 at the Pan-American Games and jumped 8.96 at Sestriere. This was shown to have a wind of just 1.2 m/s, but allegations were made of interference by an official standing in front of the gauge and the mark was not recognised. Unbeaten in 26 LJ competitions 1995 to Jan 1996. Hamstring surgery in 1996 meant that he was not fully fit at the Olympics, but he was back at the top in 1997, and has won 84/99 competitions in 1997-2001. Cousin of Aliuska López (Pedroso).

Yoelbi Luis **QUESADA** b. 4 Aug 1973 Trinidad, Sancti Spíritus 1.81m 71kg. Adidas.
At TJ: OG: '92- 6, '96- 3, '00- 4; WCh: '91- 7, '93- 12, '95- 4, '97- 1, '99- 10; WI: '93- 5, '95- 2, '99- 4; WJ: '90- 2, '92- 1; WUG: '97- 1, '99- 1; WCp: '94- 1, '98- 3; PAm: '91- 1, '95- 1, '99- 1; CAG: '93- 1, '98- 1. Won CAC-J 1990, PAmJ 1991, IbAm 1992, Cuban 1991-5, 1997-8. 2nd GP 1996.
Cuban triple jump record 1997.
Progression at TJ: 1989- 16.11, 1990- 16.68, 1991- 17.13, 1992- 17.23, 1993- 17.68, 1994- 17.61, 1995- 17.67/17.97w, 1996- 17.75, 1997- 17.85, 1998- 17.43i/17.27, 1999- 17.40, 2000- 17.37, 2001- 16.55. pb LJ 7.88 '94.
Set world age bests for each age from 15 to 19 in 1989-93.

Norberto TÉLLEZ b. 22 Jan 1972 Rodas, Cienfuegos 1.86m 78kg. Adidas.
At 800m: OG: '96- 4; WCh: '97- 2, '99- 4; WJ: '90- 3; PAm: '99- 2; CAG: '98- 1/1R; WUG: '97- 1, '99- 1; WCp: '98- 3. At 400m/4x400mR: OG: '92- 2R; WCh: '93- sf, '95- sf; PAm: '95- 1/1R; CAG: '93- 1/1R. Won Cuban 400m 1994-7, 1999-2000; 800m 1995, 1997-8; CAC 800m 1997, 2001.
Cuban 800m record 1996.
Progression at 400m, 800m: 1989- 48.98, 1:50.83; 1990- 46.83, 1:47.33; 1991- 46.69, 1:51.76; 1992- 45.70, 1993- 45.51, 1994- 45.27, 1995- 45.38, 1:47.85; 1996- 45.48, 1:42.85; 1997- 45.66, 1:44.00; 1998- 45.71, 1:44.51; 1999- 46.52, 1:44.05; 2000- 45.72, 1:45.39; 2001- 1:45.01. pb 200m 21.10 '94.
Ran first sub-1:44 time with 1:43.79 in 1996 Olympic semi, improving to 1:42.85 in the final, to beat the national record set by Alberto Juantorena at 1:43.44 in 1977. Former baseball player, centerfield position.

Women

Sonia BISSET b. 1 Apr 1971 Palma Soriano, Santiago de Cuba 1.71m 69kg.
At JT: OG: '00- 5; WCh: '97- 6, '99- 6, '01- 3; CAG: '98- 1; WUG: '97- 2; WCp: '98- 2. CAC champion 1995, IbAm 1996, Cuban 1998, GP 2000.
Progression at JT: 1987- 50.40, 1988- 58.28, 1989- 55.94, 1990- 55.20, 1991- 57.64, 1992- 58.38, 1993- 59.52, 1994- 61.42, 1995- 62.52, 1996- 64.54, 1997- 68.24, 1998- 67.59; new: 1999- 63.52, 2000- 65.87, 2001- 66.54.

Zulia Inés **CALATAYUD** b. 9 Nov 1979 Ciudad Habana 1.69m 59kg.
At 800m: OG:'00- 6; WCh: '99- h, '01- sf; PAm:'99- 2. At 400m: WJ: '98- sf. Won Cuban 400m 1999, 800m 1999-2001.
Progression at 800m: 1995- 2:18.9, 1996- 2:13.80, 1997- 2:12.7, 1999- 2:00.67, 2000- 1:58.66, 2001- 1:58.60. pbs: 200m 24.33/24.2 '98, 400m 50.87 '01.

Yumileidi CUMBÁ b. 11 Feb 1975 Guantánamo 1.85m 85kg. PE student.
At SP: OG: '96- dnq 13, '00- 6; WCh: '99- 6, '01- 8; PAm: '95- 3, '99- 2; CAG: '93- 2, '98- 1; WJ: '92- 4, '94- 2; WI: '99- 6, '01- 5; WUG: '99- 1, '01- 1; WCp: '98- 4. Won Cuban 1994-5, 1998, 2000-02.
Progression at SP: 1990- 14.53, 1991- 15.84, 1992- 17.44, 1993- 17.70, 1994- 18.78, 1995- 19.11, 1996- 18.57, 1998- 19.20, 1999- 19.29, 2000- 19.48, 2001- 19.10i/19.00. pb DT 42.84 '93.

Osleidys MENÉNDEZ b. 14 Nov 1979 Martí, Matanzas 1.78m 80kg.
At JT: OG: '00- 3; WCh: '97- 7, '99- 4, '01- 1; WJ: '96- 1, '98- 1; WUG: '01- 1; PAm: '99- 1; CAG: '98- 2. Won GWG 2001, PAm-J 1995, 1997; Cuban 1997, 1999-2002; CAC 1997. 3rd GP 2000. Word javelin record 2001, Eight CAC bests and one world (66.45 '99) new javelin 1999-2001.
Progression at JT: 1994- 53.98, 1995- 54.30, 1996- 62.54, 1997- 66.92, 1998- 68.17, 1999- 67.59; new 1999- 66.49, 2000- 67.83, 2001- 71.54.
On 1 July 2001 she became the first Cuban woman to set a world record in athletics.

Yipsi MORENO b. 19 Nov 1980 Camagüey 1.68m 70kg.
At HT: OG: '00- 4; WCh: '99- 18, '01- 1; WJ: '98- 4; PAm: '99- 2; WUG: '01- 2. Won PAm-J 1997, Cuban 2000-02. World junior hammer record 1999, 14 CAC records 1999-2002.
Progression at HT: 1996- 53.94, 1997- 61.96, 1998- 61.00, 1999- 66.34, 2000- 69.36, 2001- 70.65, 2002- 71.07.

Daimí PERNÍA b. 27 Dec 1976 La Palma, Pinar del Rio 1.73m 59kg. PE student.
At 400mh/4x400mR: OG: '00- 4; WCh: '99- 1, '01- 3; PAm: '99- 1/1R; WUG: '97- 3/2R, '99- 1. Won Cuban 400mh 1997, 1999, 2001.
Seven Cuban 400mh records 1997-9.
Progression at 400mh: 1996- 59.2, 1997- 55.51, 1998- 57.40, 1999- 52.89, 2000- 53.68, 2001- 53.81. pbs: 200m 23.43 '99, 400m 51.10 '01.
Formerly a basketball player.

Xiomara RIVERO b. 22 Dec 1968 Guane, Pinar del Río 1.77m 74kg. Adidas.
At JT: OG: '96- 5, '00- 6; WCh: '95- dnq 16, '99- dnq 19, '01- 7; PAm: '95- 1, '99- 2; WJ: '86- 1; CAG: '93- 2. Cuban champion 1994, Ib-Am 2000.
Progression at JT: 1983- 38.90, 1984- 48.36, 1985- 56.26, 1986- 64.56, 1987- 57.36, 1990- 55.56, 1991- 55.52, 1992- 60.10, 1993- 59.60, 1994- 62.44, 1995- 67.06, 1996- 66.14, 1997- 61.26, 1998- 65.07, 1999- 64.00; new: 1999- 62.46, 2000- 62.92, 2001- 65.29.
Having been world junior champion in 1986 at the age of 17, she did not improve until 1995.

CZECH REPUBLIC

Governing body: Cesky atleticky svaz, Diskarská100, 169 00 Praha 6 -Strahov, PO Box 40. AAU of Bohemia founded in 1897.
National Championships first held in 1907 (Bohemia), 1919 (Czechoslovakia), 1993 CZE.
2001 Champions: **Men**: 100m: Vít Havlícek 10.52, 200m: Jirí Vojtík 21.28, 400m: Karel Bláha 46.28, 800m: Stanislav Tábor 1:49.04, 1500m: Michal Sneberger 3:46.74, 5000m: Tomás Krutsky 14:09.36, 10000m: Pavel Faschingbauer 29:28.37, HMar/Mar: Jan Bláha 68:41/2:15:52, 3000mSt: Michael Nejedly 8:54.88, 110mh: Tomás Dvorák 14.05, 400mh: Jirí Muzík 49.32, HJ: Jan Janku 2.25, PV: Stepán Janácek 5.60, LJ: Milan Kovár 7.55, TJ: Tomás Cholensky 15.68, SP: Petr Stehlík 18.71, DT: Libor Malina 67.13, HT: Vladimír Maska 77.24, JT: Miroslav Guzdek 77.80, Dec: Pavel Havlícek 7253, 20kmW: Jirí Malysa 1:20:47, 50kmW: Frantisek Kmenta 4:08:22. **Women**: 100m: Erika Suchovská 11.75, 200m: Lenka Ficková 23.60, 400m: Tereza Zízalová 53.97, 800m: Petra Sedláková 2:03.15, 1500m: Renata Hoppová 4:27.06, 5000m: Jana Klimesová 16:46.06, 10000m: Marie Volná 34:22.43, HMar: Petra Drajzajtlová 76:07, Mar: Alena Peterková 2:37:07, 100mh: Lucie Skrobáková 13.52, 400mh: Alena Rücklová 57.74, HJ: Barbora Laláková 1.83, PV: Katerina Badurová 4.20, LJ: Lucie Komrsková 6.44, TJ: Dagmar Urbánková 13.30, SP: Vera Pospísilová 16.92, DT: Vladimíra Racková 60.27, HT: Lucie Vrbenská 63.99, JT: Nikola Tomecková 61.71, Hep: Katerina Nekolná 5689, 20kmW: Barbora Dibelková 1:42:32.

Tomás DVORÁK b. 11 May 1972 Gottwaldov (now Zlín) 1.86m 88kg. TJ Dukla Praha. Soldier.
At Dec: OG: '96- 3 (h 110mh), '00- 6; WCh: '93- 10, '95- 5, '97- 1, '99- 1, '01- 1; EC: '94- 7, '98- 5; ECp: '94- 3, '95- 1, '99- 1; WJ: '90- 17; EJ: '91- 2; won GWG 2001. At Hep: WI: '95- 2, '99- 4; EI: '94-6-8-00-02: 4/2/4/1/2. Won Czech 110mh 1994-6, 1998-2001.
World decathlon record 1999, three Czech 1996-9. European indoor heptathlon record 2000.
Progression at Dec: 1989- 6911, 1990- 7251w/7138, 1991- 7748, 1992- 7392, 1993- 8054, 1994- 8313, 1995- 8347, 1996- 8664, 1997- 8837, 1998- 8592, 1999- 8994, 2000- 8900, 2001- 8902. pbs: 60m 6.90i '97. 100m 10.54 '99, 200m 21.39 '98, 400m 47.56 '97, 1500m 4:29.69 '94, 50mh 6.59i '96, 60mh 7.78i '97, 110mh 13.61/13.6 '97, HJ 2.09 '00, PV 5.00 '97, LJ 8.07 '01, SP 16.88 '00, DT 50.28 '00, JT 72.32 '99, Hep 6309i '99.
Set four pbs en route to Olympic bronze in 1996 and six pbs when he won World gold in 1997. In 1999 he won all his four decathlons and added 103 points to Dan O'Briens' world record, missing 9000 by just six points and setting five pbs in this supreme effort. After 2nd 1996-8, won at Götzis 1999 and 2000 and Talence 2000 before injury held him back to sixth in Sydney. Won the IAAF Combined Events Challenge in 1999 and 2001. Married Gabriela Vánová (pb LJ 6.28/6.30w '93, daughter of his coach).

Jirí RYBA b. 15 Jun 1976 Chrudim 1.92m 89kg. T&F Pardubice.
At Dec: OG: '00- 14; WCh: '01- 6; WJ: '94- dnf; EU23: '97- dnf; EJ: '95- 3; ECp: '99- 8, '01- 5.
Progression at Dec: 1994- 6946, 1995- 7511, 1996- 8061, 1997- 8088w/8068, 1998- 7885, 1999- 8015, 2000- 8339, 2001- 8332. pbs: 100m 11.02 '96, 10.97w '00; 400m 47.93 '97, 1500m 4:12.14 '00, 60mh 8.16i '98, 110mh 14.33 '01, HJ 2.12i '99, 2.09 '01; PV 5.20 '00, LJ 7.44/7.52w '97, SP 14.99 '96, DT 47.40 '01, JT 61.55 '00, Hep 5913i '99.

Roman SEBRLE b. 26 Nov 1974 Lanskroun 1.86m 88kg. TJ Dukla Praha. Soldier.
At Dec: OG: '00- 2; WCh: '97- 9, '99- dnf, '01- 10; EC: '98- 6; WUG: '97- 1; ECp: '97-8-9: 1/2/2. At Hep: WI: '99- 3, '01- 1; EI: '00- 2, '02- 1. At 110mh: ECp: '99- 6. Won Czech Dec 1996, LJ 1998.
Progression at Dec: 1992- 6541, 1993- 7066, 1994- 7153, 1995- 7642, 1996- 8210, 1997- 8380, 1998- 8589, 1999- 8527, 2000- 8757, 2001- 9026. pbs: 60m 6.91i '99, 100m 10.64 '00, 200m 21.83 '00, 400m 47.76 '99, 1000m 2:37.86i '01, 1500m 4:21.98 '01, 60mh 7.86i '01, 110mh 13.79 '99, 13.68w '01; HJ 2.15 '00, PV 5.00 '99, LJ 8.11 '01, SP 15.96 '02, DT 48.01 '01, JT 70.16 '01, Hep 6420i '01.
Married Eva Kasalová (b. 4 Dec 1976, pb 800m 2:02.79 '98), on 14 Oct 2000. At Götzis in 2001 he became the first decathlete to exceed 9000 points with the current scoring tables, setting five personal bests. Unfortunately he then sustained a groin injury which held him back at the Worlds.

Jan ZELEZNY b. 16 Jun 1966 Mladá Boleslav 1.86m 88kg. Dukla Praha.
At JT: OG: '88- 2, '92- 1, '96- 1, '00- 1; WCh: '87- 3, '91- dnq 18, '93- 1, '95- 1, '97- 9, '99- 3, '01- 1; EC: '86- dnq 18, '90- dnq 13, '94- 3; EJ: '83- 6, '85- 4; WCp: '92- 1; ECp: '87-89-91-3: 3/2/1/1. Won GP JT 1991, 1993, 1995, 1997 (2nd overall first 3 years), 2001; 2nd 1999. Won CS 1986, 1990, CZE 1994, 1996.; GWG 2001.
Five world javelin records 1987-96, eight CS records 1986-93, five CZE records 1992-6.
Progression at JT: 1979- 44.44, 1982- 57.22, 1983- 74.34, 1984- 80.32, 1985- 84.68, new: 1986- 82.48, 1987- 87.66, 1988- 86.88, 1989- 84.74, 1990- 89.66, 1991- 90.72, 1992- 94.74, 1993- 95.66, 1994- 91.82, 1995- 92.28, 1996- 98.48, 1997- 94.02, 1999- 89.06, 2000- 90.59A, 2001- 92.80.
His third successive Olympic gold in 2000 surely sealed Zelezny's place as the greatest ever javelin thrower. He won 109 of 136 competitions 1991-2001. In his career with the new javelin 1986-2001 his competition bests average 85.47, with 142 throws in all over 88m. To 2001 his 100 best throws average 90.69m, 200 best 89.20 and 300 best 88.00. His 94.74 throw in 1992 was made with a new 'Németh' javelin, later ruled illegal by the IAAF. In 1993 he added 4.08m to Backley's world record with 95.54 at Pietersburg, South Africa in April, and threw 95.56 at Sheffield in August. Entered hospital at the end of the 1989 season due to a fractured vertebra, but recovered to regain the world record in 1990. In 1991 he was most unlucky not to qualify for the World final, when he fell, perhaps over the line, on a long throw. Serious injury cost him the 1998 season amid fears that he might never compete again, but he was back in full training by the end of the year. In December 1999 he was amongst the first group of ten active participants to be elected a member of the IOC, having already been a member of its athletes' commission, but he resigned in December 2001.
His father, Jaroslav, threw the javelin 68.46m in 1969 and his mother Jana 43.23 in 1959.

Women

Ludmila FORMANOVÁ b. 2 Jan 1974 Cáslav 1.68m 60kg. AC Cáslav.
At 800m/4x400mR (400m): OG: '96- sf, '00- h; WCh: '93- 7R, '95- h (h), '97- 5/5R, '99- 1/4R; EC: '94- h, '98- sf/5R; WI: '95- sf/2R, '97- sf/4R, '99- 1; WJ: '92- h; EJ: '91- (6)/4R, '93- 1; WI: '99- 1; EI: '96- 4, '98- 1; ECp: '98- 3/2R. 2nd GP 1999. At 400m: E23Cp: '94- 3. Won Czech 800m 1994-5, 1997, 1999-2000.
Progression at 800m: 1990- 2:15.5, 1991- 2:11.85, 1992- 2:05.29, 1993- 2:03.78, 1994- 2:02.54, 1995- 2:01.09, 1996- 1:59.28, 1997- 1:58.54, 1998- 1:59.44, 1999- 1:56.56, 2000- 1:57.53. pbs: 200m 24.30 '95, 400m 51.84 '95, 600m 1:26.0i '99, 1000m 2:35.06 '99
Ran second fastest of all-time to win 1999 World Indoors – and later completed double with World outdoor title. Out of action following an ankle operation on an injury which caused her to drop out of her heat at the Sydney Olympics. Coached by Jarmila Kratochvílová.

Helena FUCHSOVÁ b. 3 Jun 1965 Tábor 1.70m 68kg. née Dziurová. PSK Olymp Praha.
At 400m: OG: '96- qf; WCh: '93- 7R, '95- h, '97- 6, '99- sf/4R; EC: '98- 2; WI: '95- 2R, '97- 3; EI: '98- 3, '00- 3; WCp: '98- 4; ECp: '98- 1/2R. At 800m: OG: '00- 5; WI: '01- 3; ECp: '99- 2. Won Czech 200m 2000, 400m 1992, 1996-7, 1999; 800m 1992.
Progression at 400m, 800m: 1980- 61.0, 1981- 59.0, 1982- 58.00, 1985- 55.83, 1986- 54.79, 1987- 53.59, 2:06.14; 1988- 53.15, 2:06.6; 1989- 54.19, 2:04.81i; 1990- 54.35, 2:04.08; 1991- 54.58, 2:03.92i; 1992- 52.91, 2:03.50; 1993- 53.67, 2:09.75; 1994- 53.54, 2:08.19; 1995- 51.96, 2:04.53; 1996- 51.70, 2:08.34; 1997- 50.36, 1998- 50.21, 2:02.19i; 1999- 50.84, 1:58.81; 2000- 50.71, 1:58.56; 2001- 51.99i, 1:58.37i/1:59.88. pbs: 100m 11.97 '96, 200m 23.29 '97, 300m 36.44 '99, 1500m 4:34.05 '91, 400mh 62.0 '94.

Pavla HAMÁCKOVÁ b. 20 May 1978 Chomutov 1.70m 68kg. TJ Dukla Praha.
At PV: OG: '00- dnq 22=; WCh: '99- 6=, '01- 8; EC: '98- 12=; EJ: '97- 5; EU23: '99- 7; WUG: '99- 1; WI: '99- 7, '01- 1; EI: '00- 1, '02- 6; ECp: '99- 3, '01- 3. Czech champion 1999.
Progression at PV: 1993- 2.40i, 1994- 3.20, 1995- 3.21i/3.28i exh, 1997- 3.95, 1998- 4.15, 1999- 4.40, 2000- 4.45, 2001- 4.56i/4.47, 2002- 4.56i.

Zuzana HLAVONOVÁ b. 16 Apr 1973 Sala, SVK 1.78m 60kg. née Kovácikova. USK Mogul NOCC Praha.
At HJ: OG: '96- 12, '00- 11=; WCh: '95- dnq 24=, '97- dnq 21, '99- 4=; EC: '94- 11, '98- 11; WJ: '92- 12; EJ: '91- 11; WI: '99- 2; EI: '00- 2; ECp: '98- 1, '99- 3; E23Cp: '94- 1. 2= GP 1999; Czech champion 1994-7, 1999-2000.

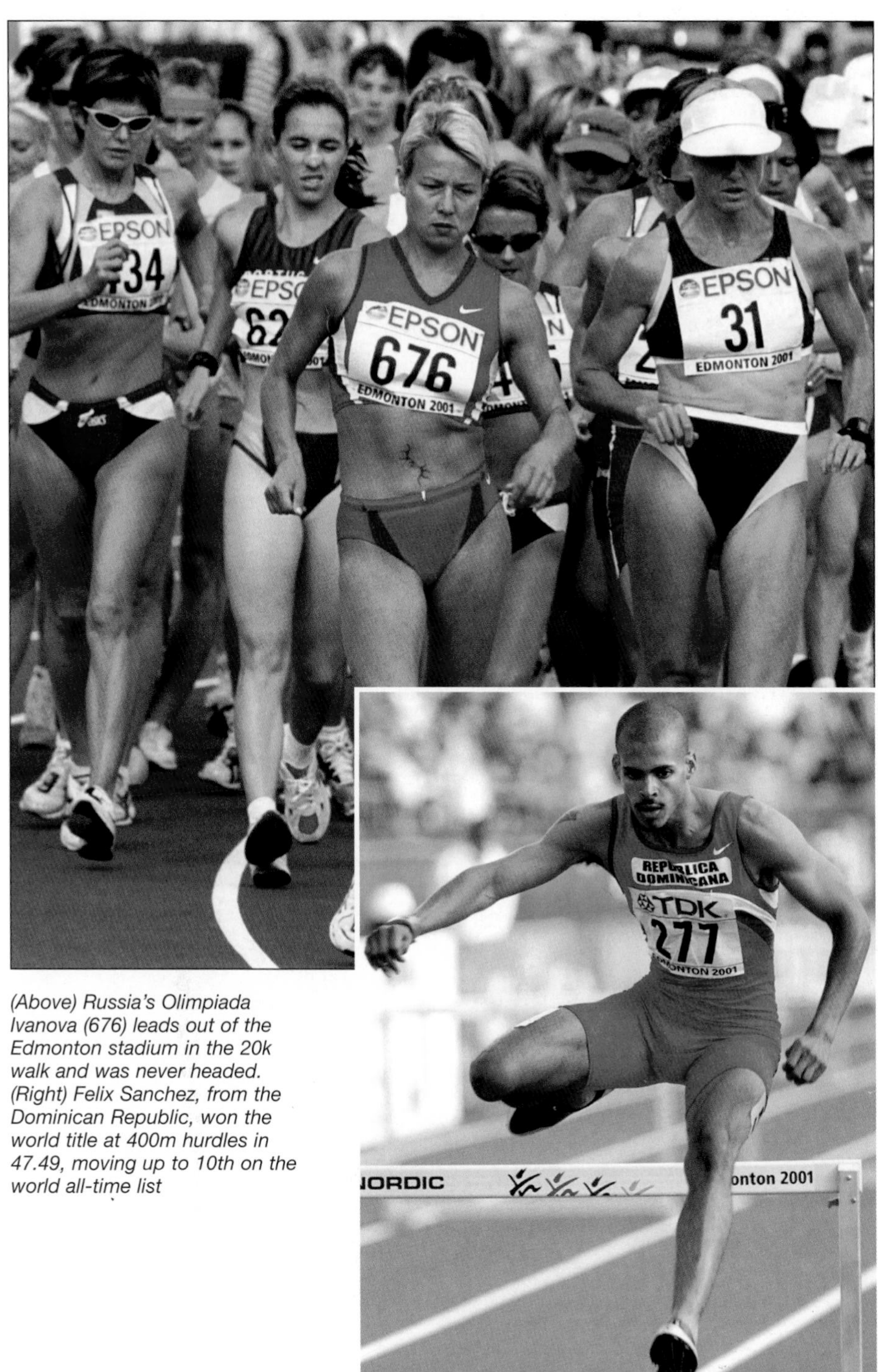

(Above) Russia's Olimpiada Ivanova (676) leads out of the Edmonton stadium in the 20k walk and was never headed. (Right) Felix Sanchez, from the Dominican Republic, won the world title at 400m hurdles in 47.49, moving up to 10th on the world all-time list

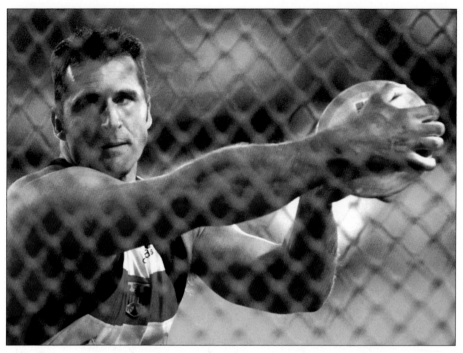

Lars Reidel, of Germany, took his fifth World discus title in Edmonton

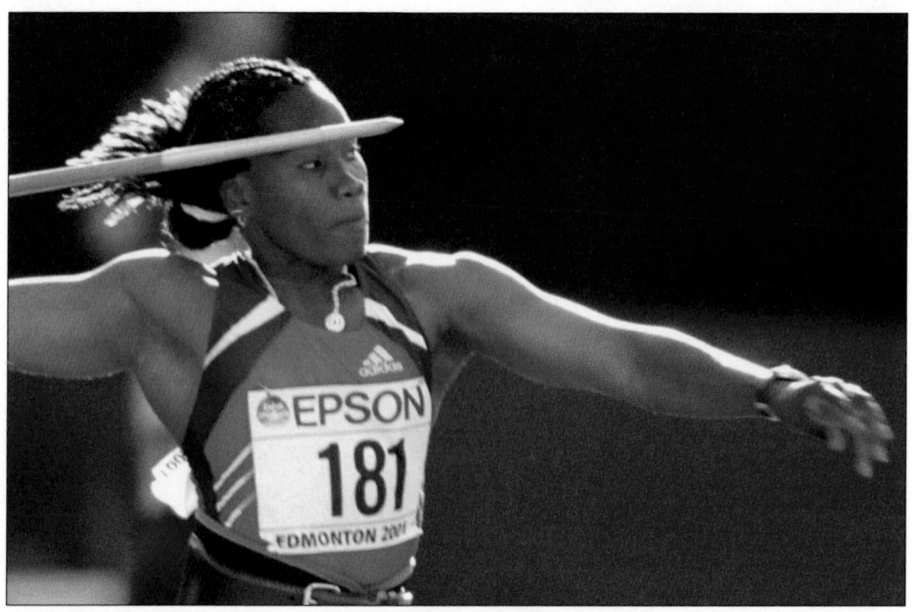

Cuban Osleidys Menéndez led from the start in Edmonton to add a world title and championship best to the world record she set earlier in the season

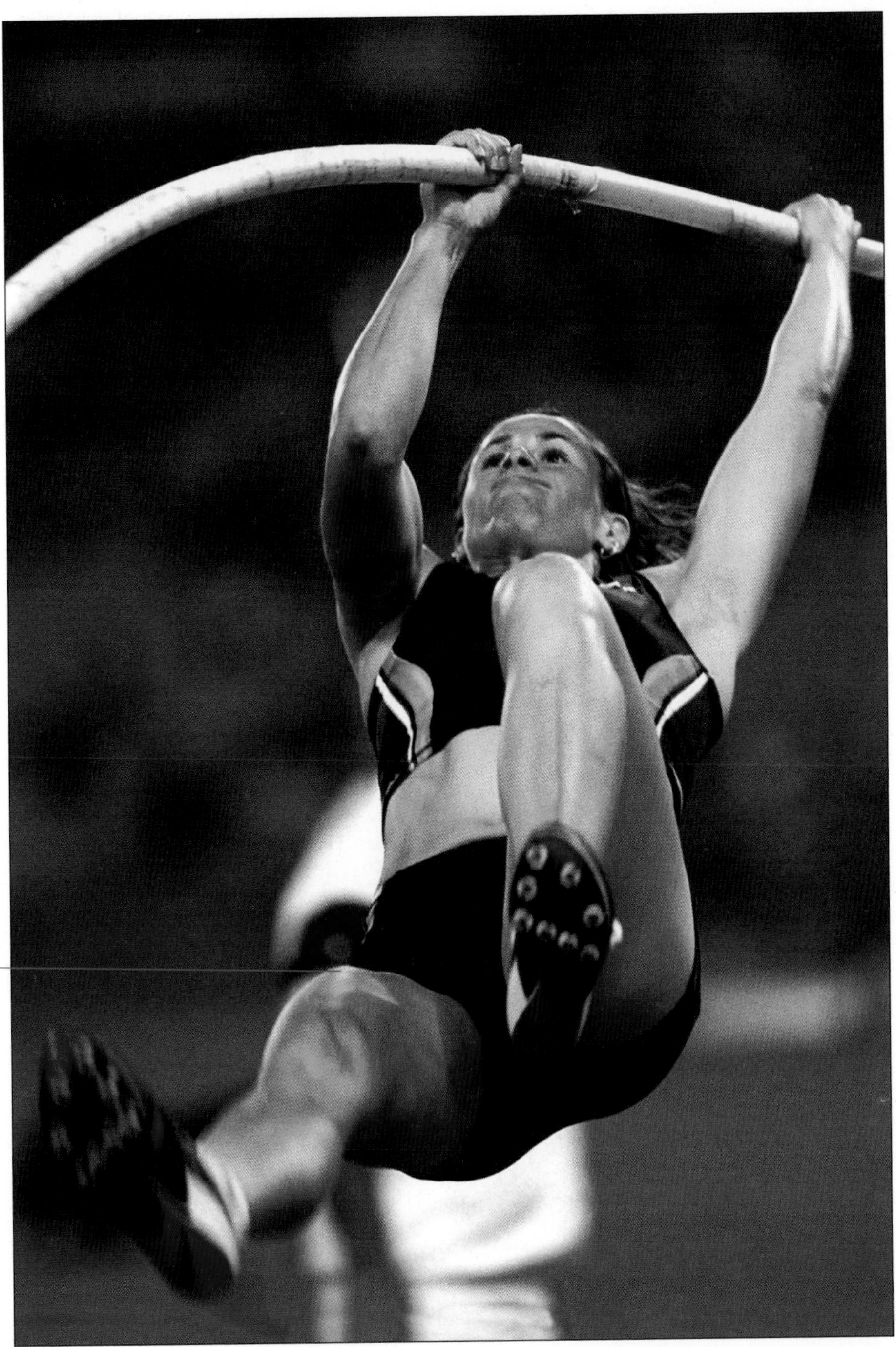

Stacy Dragila, of the USA, vaulted to the narrowest of victories in the greatest of competitions in the Edmonton championships. She set world records in 2002.

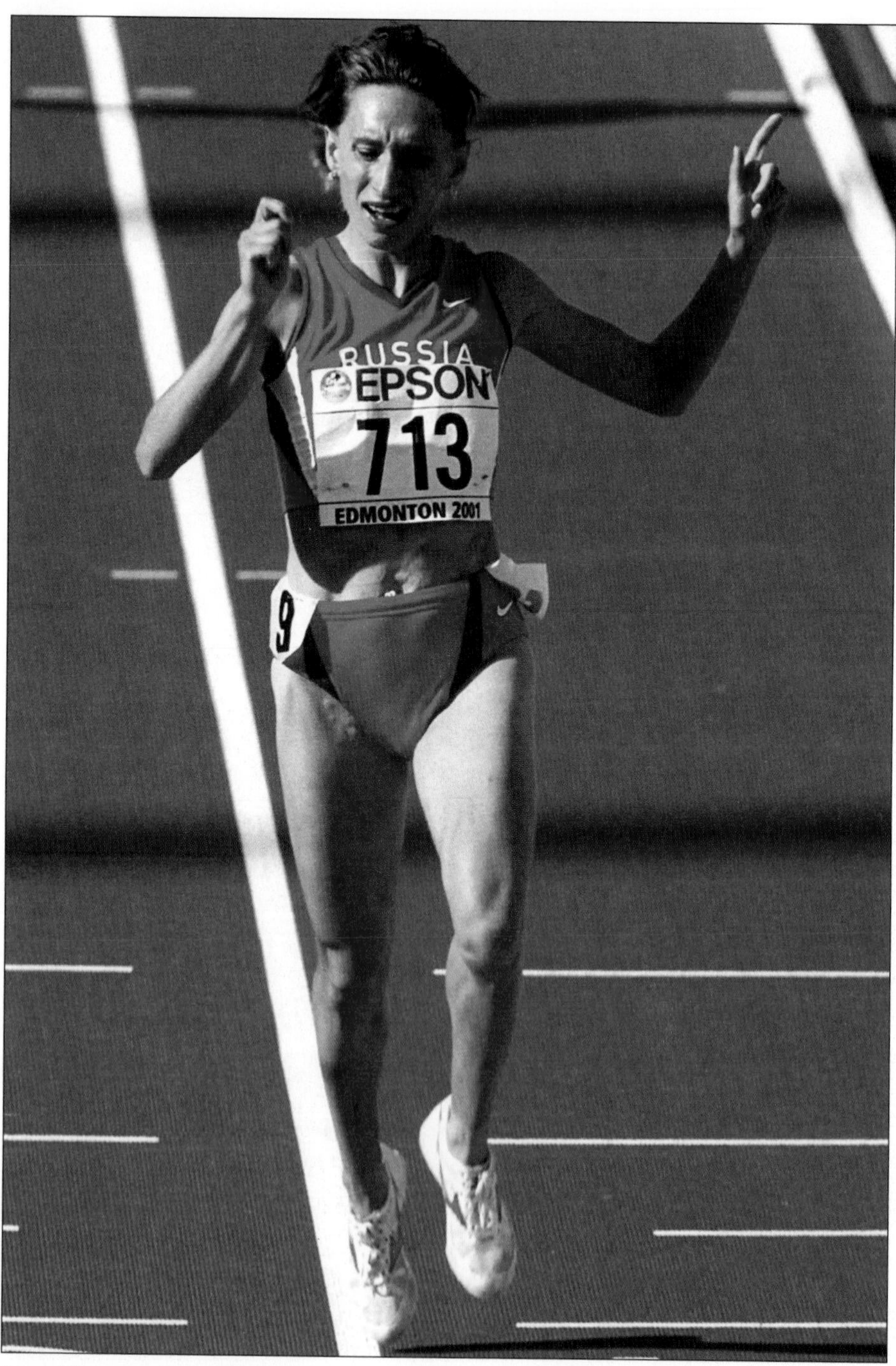

One of the more controversial victories of the year to put it mildly! Olga Yegerova, of Russia, wins the 5000m world title after being cleared of a doping offence on a technicality

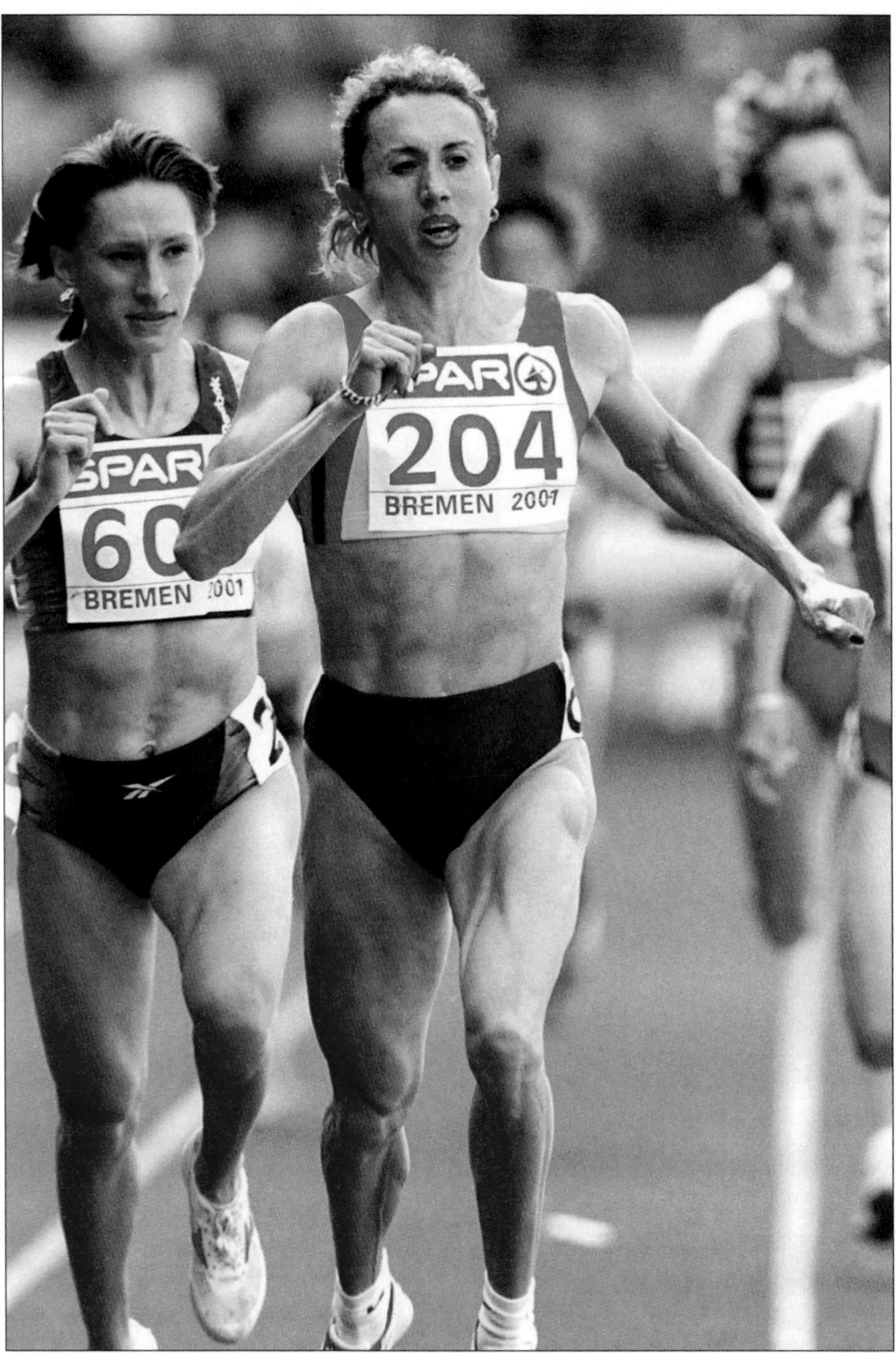

Romanian Violeta Szekely won the IAAF Grand Prix 1500m and overall standing and here wins at the European Cup final from Olga Yegerova (60).

(Above) The USA's Tim Montgomery (9) wins the Oslo 100m from Ato Bolden (2), of Trinidad and Tobago, in the second fastest legal time ever run.
(Right) Route 66. Bahamian Avard Moncur (66) takes the world 400m title from Germany's Ingo Schultz (470) and Jamaica's Greg Haughton

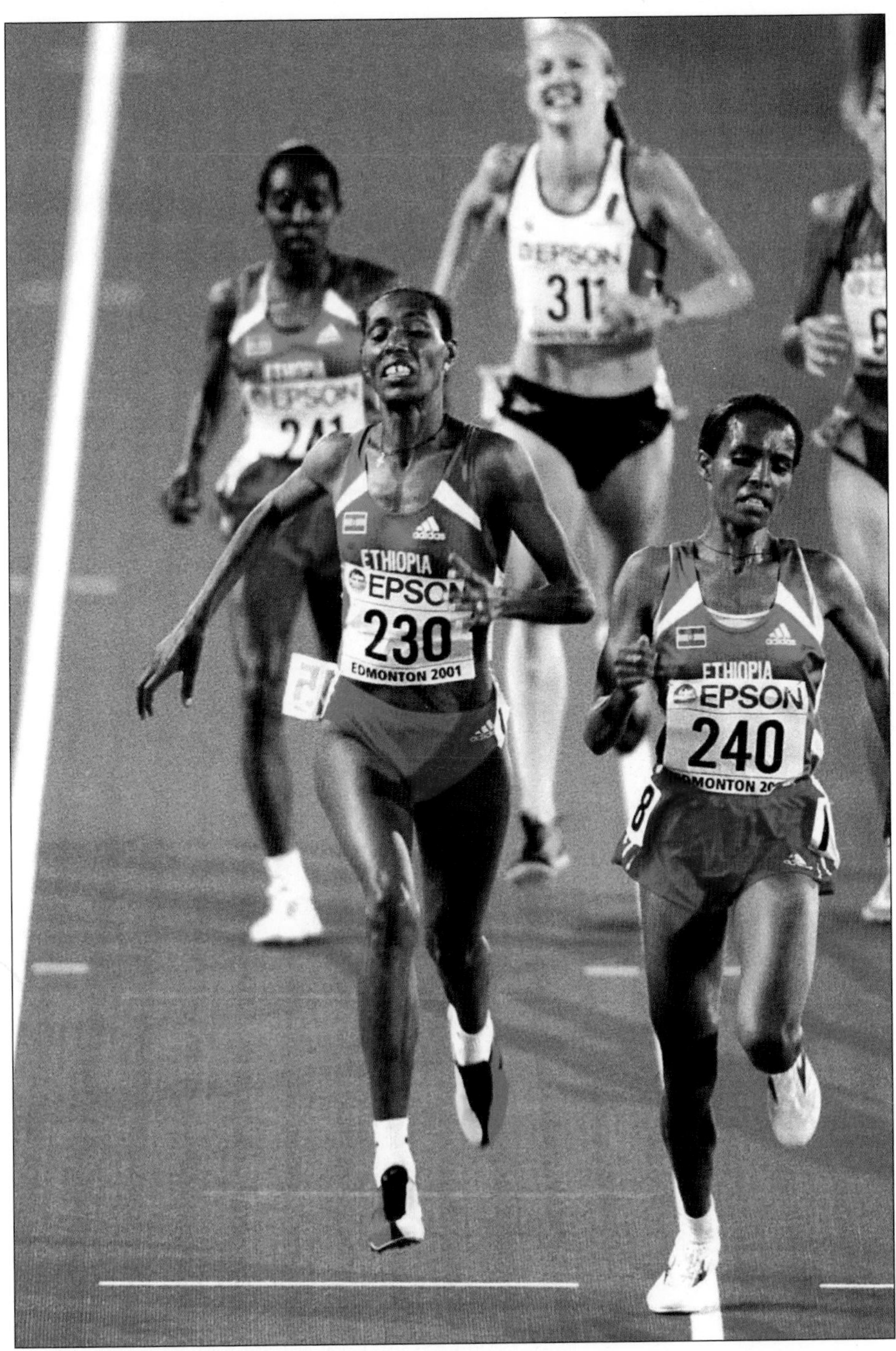

One of the great 10,000m races. Deratu Tulu (240) wins from fellow Ethiopians Berhane Adere (230) and Gete Wami (241) with Great Britain's Paula Radcliffe (311) fourth.

Roman Rasskazov led home a clean sweep of Russians in the World Championship 20k walk

Four Czech high jump records 1997-2000.
Progression at HJ: 1986- 1.57, 1987- 1.63, 1988- 1.71, 1989- 1.73, 1990- 1.77, 1991- 1.83, 1992- 1.88, 1993- 1.89, 1994- 1.94, 1995- 1.92, 1996- 1.94, 1997- 1.96, 1998- 1.98, 1999- 1.99, 2000- 2.00.
Gave birth to son Ondrej on 28 August 2001.

Sárka KASPÁRKOVÁ b. 20 May 1971 Karviná 1.87m 68kg. USK Mogul NOCC Praha. Was at Masaryks University. Sports instructor.
At TJ: OG: '96- 3, '00- nj (12); WCh: '93- 7, '95- dnq 13, '97- 1, '99- 6; EC: '94- 6, '98- 2; WI: '93- 7, '95- 4, '97- 3, '99- 3; EI: '92- 4, '94- 4, '96- 2, '98- 2; WUG: '93- 2, '95- 1; ECp: '98- 2; E23Cp: '92- 1; 2nd GP 1997. At HJ: OG: '92- dnq; WJ: '88- 6; EJ: '89- 3. Won CS HJ 1988, CZE TJ 1993-4, 1996-8, 2000.
Ten Czech triple jump records 1992-7.
Progression at HJ, TJ: 1983- 1.42, 1984- 1.59, 1985- 1.71, 1986- 1.77, 1987- 1.80, 1988- 1.89, 1989- 1.91, 1990- 1.81, 1991- 1.78, 1992- 1.92, 14.00; 1993- 1.95i/1.84, 14.16; 1994- 1.82, 14.46i/14.14/14.20w; 1995- 1.82, 14.38; 1996- 1.80i/1.79, 14.98; 1997- 15.20, 1998- 1.81, 14.98; 1999- 14.87i/14.54, 2000- 14.34. pbs: 100mh 14.72 '94, LJ 6.56 '98.
Daughter Terezka born on 7 June 2001.

Nikola TOMECKOVÁ b. 25 Jun 1974 Gottwaldov (now Zlín) 1.80m 77kg. PSK Olymp Praha. Sports instructor.
At JT: OG: '96- dnq 25, '00- 8; WCh: '93- dnq 22, '95- dnq 17, '97- dnq 26, '99- dnq 21, '01- 4; EC: '98- dnq 13; WJ: '92- 11; EJ: '91- 2, '93- 5; WUG: '01- 2; ECp: '98-9-01: 2/5/2; E23Cp: '94- 5. Czech champion 1993-2001.
Nine Czech new javelin records 1999-2001.
Progression at JT: 1987- 32.22, 1988- 39.80, 1989- 42.24, 1990- 49.22, 1991- 55.80, 1992- 59.78, 1993- 57.48, 1994- 56.68, 1995- 63.80, 1996- 64.50, 1997- 62.96, 1998- 64.18; new: 1999- 60.92A, 2000- 64.19, 2001- 65.71.

DENMARK

Governing body: Dansk Athletik Forbund, Idraettens Hus, Brøndby Stadion 20, DK-2605 Brøndby.
National Championships first held in 1894.
2001 Champions: **Men**: 100m: Morten Jensen 10.74, 200m/400m: Christian Birk 21.44/46.97, 800m: Jeppe A Thomsen 1:51.73, 1500m: Paw Nielsen 3:48.76, 5000m: Dennis Jensen 13:45.57, 10000m: Ismail Abdi 30:08.05, HMar: Carsten Jørgensen 66:48, Mar: Torben Juul Nielsen 2:20:03, 3000mSt: Morten Tjalve 9:12.7, 110mh: Anders Sækmose 14.36, 400mh: Søren Bank 52.58, HJ/TJ: Anders Møller 2.02/15.60, PV/LJ: Piotr Buciarski 5.21/7.71, SP/DT: Joachim B Olsen 20.41/58.80, HT: Jan Bielecki 73.13, JT: Richard A Knudsen 66.93, Dec: Niels Uth 6693, 20kmW: Jacob Sørensen 1:27:14, 50kmW: *no finishers*. **Women**: 100m: Sille Søndergard 11.92, 200m: Sofie Abildtrup 25.05, 400m: Rikke Rønholt 55.06, 800m/1500m: Heidi Jensen 2:04.96/4:13.80, 5000m/Mar: Gitte Karlshøj 16:21.17/2:32:41, 10000m: Annemette Jensen 34:10.40, HMar: Tina H Jensen 77:27, 100mh: Anna K Andersen 14.35, 400mh: Rikke Sørensen 60.52, HJ: Kathrine Nielsen 1.72, PV: Marie B Rasmussen 4.01, LJ: Lotte Thiesen 5.73, TJ: Lisbeth Bertelsen 12.57, SP: Henrietta Lykke 12.96, DT/JT: Ane Nørgaard 39.31/49.08, HT: Vanessa Mortensen 54.15, Hep: no entries, 10/20kmW: *not held*..

Wilson KIPKETER b. 12 Dec 1970 Kenya 1.72m 62kg. Sparta. Student of electronic engineering.
At 800m: OG: '00- 2; WCh: '95- 1, '97- 1, '99- 1; EC: '98- 8; WI: '97- 1, '99- 2; WJ: '88- dq, '90- 4. Won GP 1997 (and overall), 1999 (3rd overall), 2nd 1995. Danish champion 1993-4.
Three world 800m records 1997. WIR: 800m (2) 1997, 1000m (2) 2000 (2:15.25 & 2:14.96). 12 Danish 800m records 1995-7.
Progression at 800m: 1985- 1:49.6, 1986- 1:50.3, 1987- c.1:52, 1988- 1:47.0, 1989- 1:47.2, 1990- 1:45.7, 1991- 1:46.19, 1992- 1:45.62, 1993- 1:45.46, 1994- 1:43.29, 1995- 1:42.87, 1996- 1:41.83, 1997- 1:41.11, 1998- 1:43.18, 1999- 1:42.27, 2000- 1:43.35. pbs: 400m 46.85 '94, 1000m 2:14.96i '00, 2:16.29 '95; 1500m 3:42.80 '93, 1M 3:59.57 '93.
Went to live in Denmark in 1990. Competed for Kenya in World Juniors with year of birth 1972, but back in 1985 he was shown as second fastest African junior at 1:49.6 and born 1968! World no.1 at 800m in 1994 and allowed by the IAAF to compete for Denmark although not yet a citizen in 1995, when he was seemingly a class apart from the rest of the world at 800m. In 1996 his Olympic entry was blocked by the Kenyan Federation, but he was again the world no. 1, with five successive 1:42 times followed by a 1:43.43 and then just missing the world record with 1:41.83. Took the world indoor record from 1:44.84 to 1:43.96 in his heat and 1:42.67 in the final of the 1997 World Indoors. In 1997 he tied Seb Coe's WR for 800m at 1:41.73 in Stockholm and after retaining his world title, improved it to 1:41.24 in Zürich and 1:41.11 in Köln. Unbeaten in 27 800m races in 1996 and 1997. 1998 season restricted due to malaria in January and later pneumonia, but in 1999 won third world title and a half share of the $1m Golden League jackpot. Missed 2001 season with a foot injury.

Joachim B **OLSEN** b. 31 May 1977 1.84m 120kg. History student at University of Idaho, USA. Århus 1900.
At SP: OG: '00- dnq 17; WCh: '99- dnq 22, 01- 11; EU23: '99- 2; EI: '02- 2. At DT: WJ: '96- dnq. Won DEN SP 1997-2001, DT 1999-01, NCAA SP 2000. Three Danish shot records 2000 (and 13 indoor 1999-2002).
Progression at DT: 1994- 13.27, 1995- 14.54, 1996- 14.89, 1997- 17.11, 1998- 18.40, 1999- 19.75, 2000- 20.88, 2001- 20.43, 2002- 21.48i. pb DT 60.20 '01.

DOMINICAN REPUBLIC

Governing body: Federación Dominicana de Atletismo. Santo Domingo. Founded 1953.

Felix SANCHEZ b. 30 Aug 1977 New York, USA 1.78m 73kg. Was at University of Southern California.
At 400mh: OG: '00- sf; WCh: '99- ht; PAm: '99- 4. Won NCAA 2000, GWG 2001.
DOM records: 400mh (9) 1997-2001, 400m (2) 2001; CAC 400mh record 2001.
Progression at 400mh: 1995- 51.33, 1996- 51.19, 1997- 50.01, 1999- 48.60, 2000- 48.33, 2001- 47.38. pbs: 200m 20.87 '01, 400m 44.90 '01.
Born in New York and raised in California, he first competed for the Dominican Republic, where his parents were born, in 1999 after placing 6th in US championships at 400mh.

ECUADOR

Governing body: Federación Ecuatoriana de Atletismo, Casilla 01-01-736, Cuenca. F'd 1925.

Jefferson PÉREZ b. 1 Jul 1974 Cuenca 1.74m 59kg. Graduate of business management from University of Azuay.
At 20kmW: OG: '92- dnf, '96- 1, '00- 4; WCh: '95- 32, '97- 14, '99- 2, '01- 8; WCp: '97- 1; PAm: '95- 1; SAmCh: '93- 1. Won SAm Cup 1994-5, 1997-8. At 10kmW: WJ: '90- 3, '92- 1; won SAm-J 1989-93, PAm-J 1993. At 50km: WCp: '99- dnf.
South American 20km walk record 1997, 8 Ecuador records 1992-7.
Progression at 20kmW: 1992- 1:25:50.5, 1993- 1:24:03, 1994- 1:23:27, 1995- 1:22:53, 1996- 1:20:07/ 1:20:55.4t, 1997- 1:18:24, 1998- 1:19:19, 1999- 1:20:46, 2000- 1:20:18, 2001- 1:22:20. pbs: 5000mW 19:49.54i '90, 10,000mW 39:50.73 '93.
In 1996 he became the youngest ever Olympic walking champion and Ecuador's first Olympic medallist at any sport. He then walked 459km from Quito, along the Pan-American Freeway at an altitude of between 2500 and 4800m, to his home-town of Cuenca, as a religious promise. The Ecuador postal authorities issued a stamp with his picture.

ESTONIA

Governing body: Eesti Kergejôustikuliit, Regati pst. 1, Tallinn 11911. Founded 1920.
National Championships first held in 1917. **2001 Champions: Men**: 100m: Garol Pärn 10.86, 200m: Martin Vihmann 21.67, 400m/800m: Urmet Uusorg 48.06/1:51.46, 1500m: Rainis Mitt 4:09.50, 5000m: Risto Ütsmüts 15:16.43, 10000m/HMar: Pavel Loskutov30:45.58/64:29, Mar: Kaupo Sabre 2:40:51, 3000mSt: Kaupo Tiislär 9:08.06, 110mh: Rene Oruman 14.40, 400mh: Andrei Oll 53.03, HJ: Ramon Kaju 2.15, PV: Eigo Siimu 4.60, LJ: Risko Nuuma 7.60, TJ: Ilja Tumorin 16.65, SP: Margus Tammaru 17.67, DT: Aleksander Tammert 63.54, HT: Martti Merila 58.88, JT: Heiko Väät 71.65, Dec: Ingrek Kaseorg 7943, 20000mW: Margus Luik 1:45:46.0, 50kmW: Lauri Lelumees 4:52:30. **Women**: 100m/200m: Katrin Käärt 11.92/24.58, 400m/400mh: Julia Krasnova 56.27/60.29, 800m/1500m: Maile Mangusson 2:06.53/4:29.10, 5000m: Kadri Kelve 17:48.72, HMar: Külli Kaljus 74:24, Mar: Sirje Velba 3:18:12, 100mh: Mirjam Liimask 13.92, HJ: Tiina Mägi 1.83, PV: Margit Randver 3.60, LJ/TJ: Diana Nikitina 6.05/13.18, SP/DT: Eha Rünne 14.50/52.00, HT: Terje Matsik 51.96, JT: Moonika Aava 53.01, 10000mW: Jekaterina Jutkina 55:29, 20kmW: Kerly Lillemets 1:51:49.

Erki NOOL b. 25 Jun 1970 Vôru 1.84m 84kg. Tallinna West-Sport.
At Dec: OG: '92- dnf, '96- 6, '00- 1; WCh: '95- 4, '97- 6, '99- 14, '01- 2; EC: '94- 10, '98- 1; ECp: '94-6-7-8: 1C/1B/2/1. At Hep: WI: '95/7/9/01-7/2/2/5; EI: '94-6-00-02: 5/1/3/3. Won EST 100m 1999, 110mh 1998-9, PV 1989, 1994, 1996-7; Dec 1990, 1992.
Estonian records: 200m and LJ 1995, Decathlon (4) 1995-2001.
Progression at Dec: 1988- 6662, 1989- 7351, 1990- 7771, 1992- 8001, 1993- 7425, 1994- 8093, 1995 - 8575, 1996- 8543, 1997- 8534, 1998- 8672, 1999- 8664, 2000- 8742, 2001- 8815. pbs: 60m 6.72i '96, 100m 10.43 '95, 10.34w '97; 200m 21.03A '95, 400m 46.23 '01, 1500m 4:29.48 '00, 60mh 8.02i '01, 110mh 14.37 '00, HJ 2.05i '91, 2.03 '98; PV 5.60 '98, LJ 8.10 '95, 8.22w '96; SP 15.11 '00, DT 44.47 '99, JT 71.91 '98, Hep 6374i '99.
Won Götzis decathlon 1995 and 1998, IAAF Combined Events Challenge 1998 and 2000. Failed opening height (5.10) in 1999 World Champs; with 5.30 or higher he would have come 2nd. Became Estonia's first-ever Olympic athletics champion at Sydney, although very fortunate to avoid three no throws in the discus.

Aleksander TAMMERT b. 2 Feb 1973 Tartu 1.96m 117kg. Was at Southern Methodist University, USA.
At DT: OG: '96- dnq 25, '00- 9; WCh: '95- dnq 23, '97- 12, '99- 10, '01- dnq 16; EC: '98- dnq 20; WUG: '97- 5, '99- 4, '01- 1. EST champion 1993-5, 1997-2001.
Three Estonian discus records 1998-2000.
Progression at DT: 1990- 42.06, 1991- 48.24, 1992- 51.12, 1993- 54.54, 1994- 55.50, 1995- 60.24, 1996- 64.80, 1997- 64.78, 1998- 65.35, 1999- 66.95, 2000- 67.41, 2001- 67.10. pb SP 18.41 '01.
Father (also Aleksander) was 1966 European Junior shot champion, pb 19.41 '76.

ETHIOPIA

Governing body: Ethiopian Athletic Federation, Addis Ababa Stadium, PO Box 3241, Addis Ababa. Founded 1961.

Abiyote ABATE b. 20 Nov 1980 1.74m 56kg.
At 5000m: WCh: '01- 8. World CC: '99- 4J, 4k: '00-02: 11/15. Won ETH 5000m 2001, 4k CC 1998.
Progression at 5000m: 1999- 13:23.41, 2000- 13:10.7, 2001- 13:00.36. pbs: 3000m 7:32.38 '01.

Gezahegne ABERA b. 23 Apr 1978 1.68m 57kg.
At Mar: WCh: '99- 11, '01- 1; OG: '00- 1. World 4k CC: '00- 14.
Progression at Mar: 1999- 2:07:54, 2000- 2:09:47, 2001- 2:09:25. pbs: HMar 60:30 '00.
Won Fukuoka 1999 (his third marathon starting with 4th at LA 1999 in 2:13:59). He was 2nd in Boston 2000, before becoming the first man to win both Olympic and World marathons and later in 2001 he won again at Fukuoka.

Yibeltal ADMASSU b. 1980. 1.65m 52kg.
At 10000m: WCh: '01- 4. World CC: '97-8-9-01: 10J/4J/10J/14.
Progression at 10000m: 2001- 27:55.24. pbs: 3000m 7:52.49i '02, 5000m 13:44.92 '01.

Dagne ALEMU b. 15 Oct 1980 1.71m 58kg.
At 5000m: OG: '00- 6; AfG: '99- 4. World CC 4k: '00-01- 14/13.
Progression at 5000m: 1997- 14:04.42, 1998- 13:21.60, 1999- 13:18.39, 2000- 13:07.73. pbs: 3000m 7:47.52 '00.

Kenenisa BEKELE b. 13 Jun 1982 1.60m 54kg.
At 5000m: WJ: '00- 2. At 3000m: WY: '99- 2. World CC: '99- 9J, 4k: '01- 1J/2 4k, '02- 1/1.
World junior record 3000m 2001.
Progression at 5000m: 2000- 13:20.57, 2001- 13:13.33. pbs: 3000m 7:30.67 '01, 10km Rd 27:40 '01.
Had record winning margin off 33 seconds for the World Junior CC title in 2001, a day after coming second in senior 4km.

Haile GEBRSELASSIE b. 18 Apr 1973 Arssi 1.64m 53kg.
At 10000m (5000m): OG: '96- 1, '00- 1; WCh: '93- 1 (2), '95- 1, '97- 1, '99- 1, '01- 3; WJ: '92- 1 (1); AfG: '93- 3 (2). At 3000m: WI: '97- 1, '99- 1 (1 1500m). Won GP 3000m 1995, 1998. World CC: '91-2-3-4-5-6: 8J/2J/7/3/4/5; HMar: '00- 1; Rd Rly team: '94- 2.
World records 5000m (4) 1994-8, 10000m (3) 1995-8. World best 2M 1995 (8:07.46) & 1997. World indoor records 2000m 1998, 3000m (7:30.72 '96, 7:26.14 '98), 5000m (13:10.98 '96, 12:59.04 '97, 12:50.38 '99). ETH records 1993-8: 1500m (2), 3000m (6), 5000m (5), 10000m (3).
Progression at 5000m, 10000m: 1992- 13:36.06, 28:03.99; 1993- 13:03.17, 27:30.17; 1994- 12:56.96, 27:15.00; 1995- 12:44.39, 26:43.53; 1996- 12:52.70, 27:07.34; 1997- 12:41.86, 26:31.32; 1998- 12:39.36, 26:22.75; 1999- 12:49.64, 27:57.27; 2000- 12:57.95, 27:18.20; 2001- 27:54.41. pbs: 800m 1:49.35i '97, 1000m 2:20.3+i '98, 1500m 3:31.76i '98, 3:33.73 '99; 1M 3:52.39 '99, 2000m 4:52.86i '98, 4:56.1 '97; 3000m 7:25.09 '98, 2M 8:01.08 '97; Road: 15km 41:38 '01, HMar 59:41 '02, Mar c.2:48 '88.
A beautifully smooth runner, whose right to be named as the greatest ever grows steadily. After finishing a place behind Ismael Kirui at two successive World Junior CC championships, he outkicked his rival for a brilliant double at the 1992 World Juniors. He set the first of his 15 world records in Hengelo in 1994 at 5000m and in 1995 he took 8.7 secs off the 10,000m WR and regained the 5000m record by taking 10.91 secs off Kiptanui's mark. Between these feats he won the World 10,000m, running the last 200m in 25.1!. He ran the second 5000m in c.13:11.6 to win the 1996 Olympic 10,000m and in 1997 took 6.76 secs off the world 10,000m record in Oslo. In 1998 he regained both the 5000m and 10000m world records. Has 12 wins in 14 competitions at 10,000m (his only losses 3rd in the 1993 African Champs and in the 2001 Worlds), with 21 wins at 3000m/2M from 2nd to Noureddine Morceli at Monaco in 1994 to 2000, and 16 wins at 5000m from 2nd to Daniel Komen in Zürich 1996 to 2000. In 1997 and 1998 he lost just indoors once at 1500m in 1997 and once each at 800m in 1997 and 1998. In 1999 he won all 15 finals from 1500m to 10,000m and he was unbeaten in five races in 2000.
Based during the summer in the Netherlands. His brother Tekeye was 13th in the 1991 London Marathon (World Cup) in 2:12:05, with pb 2:11:45 '94.

Habte JIFAR b. 29 Jan 1976 1.76m 53kg.
At 10000m (5000m): WCh: '97- 7, '99- 6, '01- 9; WJ: '94- 4 (2); AfG: '95- 2 (2), '99- 3; Af-J: '94- 1 (2). World CC: '93- 6J, '96-7-8-9-02: 17/11/13/9/21. Won ETH 5000m 1994, 10000m 1995, CC 1996.
Progression at 5000m, 10000m: 1994- 13:43.92, 29:04.57; 1995- 13:45.11A, 28:26.3A; 1996- 13:25.30, 1997- 13:12.88, 27:30.26; 1998- 13:10.74, 27:29.97; 1999- 13:21.01, 27:06.45; 2001- 27:57.23. pb 3000m 7:54.54 '99, 15km Rd 43:28 '01.

Tesfaye JIFAR b. 23 Apr 1976 1.68m 55kg.
At Mar: WCh: '01- 7. World HMar: '99- 3, '00- 3, '01- 2.
Ethiopian marathon record 1999.
Progression at Mar: 1998- 2:22:13, 1999- 2:06:49, 2000- 2:15:59, 2001- 2:07:43. pbs: HMar 60:04 '01.
At Amsterdam in 1999 he took a second off Belayneh Dinsamo's Ethiopian marathon record, placing 2nd in 2:06:49, the fifth fastest of all-time. Missed 2000 Olympics through illness, from which he returned for 15th in Chicago Marathon and then third in the World Half marathon. Won New York in fourth marathon of 2001.

Hailu MEKONNEN b. 4 Apr 1980 1.72m 61kg.
At 5000m: WCh: '99- 7, '01- 9; WJ: '98- 6; AfCh: '98- 2 (4 3000m). At 1500m: OG: '00- sf; WI: '01- 7; AfG: '99- 1. World CC J & 4k: '97- 12J, '98-3J, '99- 1J/3, '00-01-02: 6/10/3.
WIR 2 miles 2000. World junior record 3000m 1999. ETH 1500m record 2000.
Progression at 1500m, 5000m: 1998- 13:36.61, 1999- 3:35.63, 13:10.98; 2000- 3:33.14, 2001- 3:38.41i,

12:58.57. pbs: 1M 3:53.40 '00, 2000m 5:02.06 '98, 3000m 7:33.00 '99, 2M 8:09.66i '00.
Placed third in the 4km race at the 1999 World CC Championships and returned the next day to win the junior race. Was unbeaten indoors in 2000 at distances from 1500m to 2 miles.

Assefa MEZGEBU b. 19 Jun 1978 1.75m 55kg.
At 10000m (5000m): OG: '96- (sf), '00- 3; WCh: '95/7/9/01- 14/5/3/2; WJ: '96- 1 (1); AfG: '95- 8, '99- 1 (5). World CC: '95-6-7-8-9-00-02: 1J/2J/13/3/11/2/12. Won GWG 10000m 2001.
Progression at 5000m, 10000m: 1995- 13:33.82, 27:56.06, 1996- 13:17.68, 28:27.78; 1997- 13:05.48, 27:25.01; 1998- 12:53.84, 1999- 13:13.77, 27:18.28; 2000- 13:06.13, 27:19.75; 2001- 13:00.86, 27:22.30. pbs: 1500m 3:35.58i '00, 1M 3:54.78i '00, 3000m 7:28.45 '98, 2M 8:09.96i '00.
Began running in 1994, and in 1995 won the World Junior CC at the age of 16. His brother **Ayele** (b. 6 Jan 1973) was 2nd at the 1992 World Junior 3000mSt and in the 1998 World Road relay team; pbs: 5000m 13:21.21 '94, 10000m 28:22.06 '97, 3000mSt 8:32.43 '92.

Girma TOLA b. 13 Oct 1975 1.74m 57kg.
At 10000m: OG: '00- 11; WCh: '99- 4; AfG: '99- 6. World CC: '99- 17.
Progression at 5000m, 10000m: 1997- 28:55.67, 1998- 13:15.72, 27:32.02; 1999- 27:13.48, 2000- 13:21.04, 27:20.03; 2001- 27:22.84. pbs: 2000m 5:02.01 '98, 3000m 7:38.68i '00, 7:42.98 '99; 2M 8:12.80i '01.

Tesfaye TOLA b. 19 Oct 1974 1.67m 60kg.
At Mar: OG: '00- 3; WCh: '99- 4, '01- 4. World HMar: '97- 18, '99- 8, '01- 5. Won ETH CC 1999-2000. Ethiopian Half marathon record 2000.
Progression at Mar: 1997- 28:55.67, 1998- 13:15.72, 27:32.02; 1999- 2:06:57, 2000- 2:11:10, 2001- 2:12:05. pbs: 10000m 28:12.32 '99; road: 10M: 46:01 '99, 15km 43:13 '01, HMar 59:51w '00.
2:06:57 on marathon debut for 4th at Amsterdam 1999.

Million WOLDE b. 17 Mar 1979 1.75m 59kg
At 5000m: OG: '00- 1; WCh: '99- 8, '01- 3; WJ: '98- 1. At 3000m: WI: '99- 3, '01- 5. At 3000mSt: WJ: '96- 6. World CC: '96-7-8: 8J/2J/1J, 4k: '99-00-02: 4/15; 2nd Rd Rly team '98.
Progression at 5000m: 1996- 13:28.86, 1997- 13:32.02, 1998- 12:59.39, 1999- 13:19.41, 2000- 13:02.94, 2001- 13:02.17. pbs: 1500m 3:39.15 '98, 1M 3:58.21 '99, 2000m 5:01.6+ '00, 3000m 7:32.36 '00, 2M 8:12.10i '01, 8:24.53 '99; 3000mSt 8:29.21 '97.

Women

Birhane ADERE b. 21 Jul 1973 1.70m 48kg. Married to Lemme Hirpassie.
At 10000m: OG: '96- 18, '00- 12; WCh: '95-h, '97- 4, '99- 7, '01- 2; AfCh: '93- 1 (5 3000m). At 5000m: AfCh: '98- 1; WCp: '98- 3. World CC: '96-7-00: 10/14/14/16; HMar: '01- 3. Won Rd Rly team '96, ETH 3000m & 10000m 1993.
World indoor 3000m (8:29.15) record 2002. Ethiopian 3000m records 1997 and 2001.
Progression at 5000m, 10000m: 1992- 34:13.3, 1993- 32:48.52, 1995- 15:44.46, 32:02.94; 1996- 14:59.17, 32:21.09; 1997- 15:08.22, 31:48.95; 1998- 15:22.34, 32:06.42; 1999- 14:54.88, 31:32.51; 2000- 14:52.61, 30:51.30; 2001- 14:51.67, 31:32.70. pbs: 1500m 4:05.54i 02, 2000m 5:39.47i '02, 5:39.7 '01; 3000m 8:25.62 '01; road: 15km 48:11 '01, 10M 53:16 '98, HMar 68:17 '01.

Elfenesh ALEMU b. 10 Jun 1975 1.71m 57kg.
At Mar: OG: '00- 6; WCh: '99- 5, '01- dnf; WCp: '95- 18; AfG: '95- 3.
Progression at Mar: 1993- 2:57:32A, 1994- 3:08:05, 1995- 2:40:04, 1996- 2:36:29, 1997- 2:37:37, 1998- 2:30:19; 1999- 2:28:52, 2000- 2:24:47, 2001- 2:24:29. pb HMar 69:46 '00.
2nd in Nagoya marathon 1998. Broke 2:25 twice in 2000: 4th Osaka and 1st Nagano before 2:26:45 at Olympics, and again in 2001: 5th London and 2nd Chicago.

Merima DENBOBA b. 21 Aug 1974 1.68m 48kg.
At 5000m: OG: '96- h; WCh: '97- 10, '01- 13; AfG: '95- 5, '99- 4; AfCh: '98- 3, '00- 3. At 10000m: WJ: '92- 5. World CC: '91-2-3-4-5: 18/20/19/4/7, '97-8-9-00-01-02: 6/4/2/8/8 & 4 4k/6; Rd Rly team: '98- 1. Won ETH 10000m 1995, CC 1995, 1998 and 1997/8 World CC challenge.
Progression at 5000m, 10000m: 1992- 33:57.21, 1993- 35:15.5A, 1994- 15:47.86, 32:16.50; 1995- 15:47.12, 34:20.6A; 1996- 15:19.86, 1997- 15:11.71, 32:10.36; 1998- 15:30.06, 32:04.89; 1999- 15:08.52, 31:32.63; 2000- 15:15.17, 31:43.2; 2001- 15:06.08, 31:57.10. pbs: 1500m 4:14.60 '94, 3000m 8:44.21 '99.

Kutre DULECHA b. 22 Aug 1978 1.68m 48kg.
At 1500m (800m): OG: '96- sf (h), '00- 4; WCh: '97- 9, '99- 3; WI: '97- 9, '99- 8; WJ: '94- 5 (3), '96- 1; AfG: '95- 1 (3), '99- 1; Af-J: '94- 2 (2); 2nd GP 1998, 2000. World CC: '96- 1J, 4k: '98-9-00: 3/12/1. Ethiopian records: 1500m (5) 1997-8, 800m 1999. World junior record indoor 1500m 1997.
Progression at 1500m: 1994- 4:15.59, 1995- 4:08.70, 1996- 4:07.69, 1997- 4:05.67, 1998- 3:58.38, 1999- 4:00.96, 2000- 3:59.02, 2001- 4:05.75i. pbs: 800m 1:59.17i/1:59.37 '99, 1000m 2:37.82 '99, 1M 4:23.33i '01, 4:39.04 '97.

Merima HASHIM b. 1981 1.62m 42kg.
At 10000m: WCh: '99- 6; AfG: '99- 2. Won Afr-J 1997. World CC: '97-8-00- 23J/8J/5J.
Progression at 10000m: 1997- 34:48.68, 1998- 35:40.1A, 1999- 31:32.06, 2000- 30:59.92. pbs: 3000m 9:07.71 '99, 5000m 15:14.42 '00.

Werknesh KIDANE b. 21 Nov 1981 1.58m 42kg.
At 5000m: OG: '00- 7; WCh: '01- h; WJ: '98- 6; AfG: '99- 4. At 3000m: WI: '01- 9. World CC: '97-8-9-00: 13J/3J/1J/9J; 4k: '01-02: 5/2.
Progression at 5000m, 10000m: 1998- 15:50.10, 1999- 15:24.56, 2000- 14:47.40, 33:48.7A; 2001- 15:29.96, 31:43.41. pb 3000m 8:44.14 '00.c

Fatuma ROBA b. 18 Dec 1973 1.60m 49kg.
At Mar: OG: '96- 1, '00- 9; WCh: '95- 19, '97- dnf, '99- 4, '01- 13. At 10000m: AfCh: '90- 4 (4 3000m), '93- 3. World CC: '91- 12; HMar: '92- 6, '94- 11.
Progression at Mar: 1993- 2:44:20A, 1994- 2:35:25, 1995- 2:39:27sh, 1996- 2:26:05, 1997- 2:26:23, 1998- 2:23:21, 1999- 2:23:25, 2000- 2:26:27, 2001- 2:27:20, 2002- 2:29:31. pbs: 10000m 32:55.32 '93, Rd 10km 32:39 '95, HMar 69:01 '01.
Six wins in 18 Marathons: set national records in three wins in 1996: 2:30:50 Marrakech, 2:29:05 Rome, 2:26:05 Olympics and again when won Boston in 1998. Also won Boston 1997 and 1999.

Derartu TULU b. 21 Mar 1972 Bejoki, Arusi province 1.55m 45kg. Employed by the prison police in Addis Ababa.
At 10000m (3000m): OG: '92- 1, '96- 4, '00- 1; WCh: '91- 8, '95- 2, '97- h, '01- 1; WJ: '90- 1; AfG: '91- 1; AfCh: '90- 1 (1), '92- 1 (1); WCp: '92- 1 (1). World CC: '89- 23, '90-1-5-6-7-00: 15/2/1/4/1/1; HMar: '99- 14. Won GWG 10000m 2001.
Three African 10000m records 1992-2000. World junior 10000m record 1991 (32:08.74), Ethiopian records 1500m, 5000m (4), 10000m (5) 1991-2000, HMar 1995 & 2000.
Progression at 5000m, 10000m, Mar: 1990- 16:56.7, 32:56.26; 1991- 15:21.29, 31:45.95; 1992- 15:36.5, 31:06.02; 1994- 15:40.29, 31:48.93; 1995- 14:57.65, 31:08.10; 1996- 14:50.88, 31:10.46; 1997- 33:25.99, 2:30:28; 1999- 2:40:55, 2000- 14:44.57, 30:17.49, 2:26:09; 2001- 31:48.19, 2:23:47. pbs: 1500m 4:12.08 '92, 3000m 8:46.32 '00, HMar 67:03 '01.
Daughter born 1998. Returned to road racing in 1999 and to a third world CC title and second Olympic title in 2000. 5th Boston on marathon debut 1997; 6th London and 3rd Tokyo in 2000, won London and Tokyo marathons 2001.

Getenesh WAMI b. 11 Dec 1974 Debre Birhan 1.54m 45kg. Married Geteneh Tessema in Nov. 1999.
At 10000m (5000m): OG: '96- 3, '00- 2 (3); WCh: '95- 18, '97- dnf, '99- 1, '01- 3; WJ: '92- 2; AfG: '95- 3, '99- 1; AfCh: '92- 4. Won GP 3000m 1998, 2nd 5000m 1996. World CC: '91-2: 5J/9J, '95-6-7-8-9-00-01: 5/1/3/3/1/2/2 &1 4k; Rd Rly team: '96/8- 1/1.
African records 5000m 2000, 10000m 1999. Ethiopian records: 3000m 1998, 5000m (4) 1996-8.
Progression at 5000m, 10000m: 1992- 32:34.68, 1994- 36:15.0A, 1995- 15:28.65, 32:17.41; 1996- 14:46.45, 31:06.65; 1997- 14:54.05, 32:05.73; 1998- 14:36.08, 34:23.4A; 1999- 15:25.5, 30:24.56; 2000- 14:30.88, 30:22.48; 2001- 14:31.69, 31:49.98. pbs: 1500m 4:01.47 '98, 2000m 5:39.9 '01, 3000m 8:27.62 '01.

Ayelech WORKU b. 12 Jun 1979 1.65m 47kg.
At 5000m: OG: '96- 12, '00- 4; WCh: '97- 12, '99- 3, '01- 3; WJ: '96- 1 (3000m 4); AfG: '95- 2, '99- 1. World CC: '95-6-7-8-9-00-01-02: 11J/11J/3J/9/4/9/18/13. Rd Rly team: '98- 1. Won ETH 5000m 1995.
Progression at 5000m: 1995- 15:48.3A, 1996- 15:16.74, 1997- 15:18.19, 1998- 15:12.43, 1999- 14:44.22; 2000- 14:41.23, 2001- 14:54.00, 31:38.08. pbs: 1500m: 4:15.93 '98, 3000m 8:39.51 '99, 10000m 37:09.1A '94.

FINLAND

Governing body: Suomen Urheiluliitto, Radiokatu 20, SF-00240 Helsinki. Founded 1906.
National Championships first held in 1907 (men), 1913 (women). **2001 Champions**: **Men**: 100m: Kari Louramo 10.64, 200m: Tommi Hartonen 21.04, 400m: Mikko Karppi 47.53, 800m/1500m: Juha Kukkamo 1:50.38/3:50.62, 5000m: Samuli Vasala 13:57.01, 10000m: Janne Holmen 29:58.04; HMar: Pasi Mattila 66:11, Mar: Jaako Kero 2:26:23, 3000mSt: Kim Bergdahl 8:45.99, 110mh: Jarno Jokihaara 14.12, 400mh: Kimmo Haapasalo 51.16, HJ: Mika Polku 2.15, PV: Vesa Rantanen 5.50, LJ: Tommi Evilä 8.01, TJ: Johan Meriluoto 17.04w, SP: Conny Karlsson 20.49, DT: Timo Tompuri 63.62, HT: Olli-Pekka Karjalainen 76.00, JT: Aki Parviainen 83.51, Dec: Jaakko Ojaniemi 7716, 20kmW: Jani Lehtinen 1:34:35, 50kmW: Seppo-Juhani Savolainen 4:38:19. **Women**: 100m/200m: Johanna Manninen 11.55/23.66, 400m/800m: Suvi Myllymäki 54.78/2:04.94, 1500m: Minna Nummela 4:14.63, 5000m: Elina Lindgren 16:47.84, 10000m: Kirsi Valasti 35:20.81,HMar: Maria Söderström 76:42, Mar: Maija Kukkohovi 2:49:09, 3000mSt: Johanna Risku 10:33.76, 100mh: Susanna Rajamäki 13.78, 400mh: Ilona Ranta 60.53, HJ: Hanna Mikkonen 1.87, PV: Teija Saari 4.00, LJ: Johanna Halkoaho 6.41, TJ: Heli Koivula 14.14, SP: Anna Rauhala 15.31, DT: Tiina Kankaanpää 55.27, HT: Mia Strömmer 66.89, JT: Paula Huhtaniemi 57.52, Hep: Sanna Saarman 5575, 10kmW: Heidi Lindewall 49:07, 20kmW: Outi Sillanpää 1:38:37.

Timo AALTONEN b. 11 Apr 1969 Vehmaa 1.89m 129kg. Turun Urhelluliitto.
At SP: OG: '00- 12; EC: '98- 12; WI: '01- 4; EI: 00- 1.
Progression at SP: 1992- 14.97, 1993- 16.39, 1994- 16.79, 1995- 17.86, 1996- 18.50, 1997- 19.05, 1998- 20.12, 1999- 20.48, 2000- 20.70, 2001- 20.27i/19.47.
Won national U16 title and then gave up shot putting until 1992, becoming a construction worker.

Harri HAATAINEN b. 5 Jan 1978 Lapua 1.86m 85kg. Lapuan Virkiä.
At JT: OG:'00- dnq 19; WCh: '99- 11, '01- dnq 15; WJ: '96- 2; EU23: '99- 1; EJ: '95- 2.
World junior javelin record 1996.
Progression at JT: 1993- 62.74, 1994- 72.02, 1995- 77.50, 1996- 82.52, 1997- 80.16, 1998- 79.07, 1999- 83.02, 2000- 86.10, 2001- 86.63.

Harri HAKKARAINEN b. 16 Oct 1969 Kaavi 1.94m 110kg. Kuopion Sisu-Veikot.
At JT: OG: '96- dnq 14, '00- dnq; WCh: '95- 12;

EC: '94- dnq 13; ECp: '96- 3.
Progression at JT: 1986- 60.38, 1987- 63.88, 1988- 65.78, 1989- 70.06, 1990- 71.52, 1991- 83.16, 1992- 83.46, 1993- 84.36, 1994- 85.46, 1995- 87.82, 1996- 87.44, 1997- 86.48, 1998- 85.34, 1999- 85.00, 2000- 85.65, 2001- 83.67.

Mika HALVARI b. 13 Feb 1970 Kemi 1.91m 135kg. Kemin Kunto.
At SP: OG: '96- dnq 14; WCh: '95- 2, '97- 5, '99- dnq 15; WI: '95- 1, '97- 6; EC: '94- 4, '98- 6; EI: '98- 2; WJ: '88- 7; EJ: '89- 5; ECp: '98- 1. Finnish champion 1994-5, 1997.
Progression at SP: 1986- 14.64, 1987- 16.06, 1988- 17.62, 1989- 17.96, 1990- 18.65, 1991- 18.71, 1992- 18.60i/18.45, 1993- 20.08, 1994- 19.93i/19.87, 1995- 21.50, 1996- 20.81i/20.42, 1997- 21.11, 1998- 20.79, 1999- 21.00, 2000- 22.09i/21.04, 2001- 19.89. pbs: DT 47.72 '88, HT 42.16 '89.
A 'spinner', he ruptured his Achilles tendon in February 1996, which meant that he was below par in Atlanta. He produced a startling 22.09 indoors in February 2000, but suffered another Achilles rupture in August 2000.

Eduard HÄMÄLÄINEN (ex-BLR) b. 21 Jan 1969 Karaganda, Kazakhstan 1.94m 93kg. Kuortaneen Kunto.
At Dec: OG: '92- dnf, '96- 5, '00- 24; WCh: '91- 7, '93- 2, '95- 2, '97- 2, '01- dnf; EC: '94- dnf, '98- 2; WJ: '88- 3; ECp: '01- 4. CIS champion 1992, Finnish 2000. At Hep: WI inv: '93- 3.
BLR decathlon records 1993-4, two Finnish 1997.
Progression at Dec: 1987- 7369, 1988- 7596, 1989- 7891, 1990- 7845, 1991- 8233, 1992- 8483w, 1993- 8724, 1994- 8735, 1995- 8489, 1996- 8613, 1997- 8730, 1998- 8587, 2000- 8224, 2001- 8071w/8028. pbs: 100m 10.69/10.50w '94, 400m 46.71 '97, 1500m 4:22.5 '87, 60mh 7.93i '93, 110mh 13.57 '93, HJ 2.15i '95, 2.11 '94; PV 5.30 '93, LJ 7.56 '97, 7.67w '93; SP 16.74 '96, DT 52.20 '94, JT 61.88 '93, Hep 6096i '92.
Won Götzis decathlon 1993 and 1994, Talence 1995. In 1993 he set world decathlon records for 100mh at 13.65 and 13.57 in the World Champs. However, he fell in the 110mh when leading the 1994 Europeans. His grandfather was deported from Finland to the USSR in 1917, and hometown was Grodno, Belarus, but has lived in Kuortane, Finland since 1996 and became eligible to compete for Finland in 1997. Missed 1999 season after an Achilles tendon operation.

Arsi HARJU b. 18 Mar 1974 Kurikka 1.83m 125kg. Perhon Kiri.
At SP: OG: '96- dnq, '00- 1; WCh: '95- dnq 17, '97- dnq 15, '99- nt (12), '01- 3; EC: '98- 9; WI: '97- 8, '99- 5; EI: '98- 3; WJ: '92- 11; EJ: '93- 3. Finnish champion 1998, 2000.
Progression at SP: 1989- 11.82, 1990- 15.65, 1991- 16.27, 1992- 17.60, 1993- 18.40, 1994- 18.74, 1995- 19.58, 1996- 19.84, 1997- 20.66, 1998- 21.04, 1999- 20.60, 2000- 21.39, 2001- 20.98.
A 'spinner' since 1996, he improved his pb by 35cm in the 2000 Olympic qualifying to 21.39, and threw 21.29 to win the gold medal in the final.

Olli-Pekka KARJALAINEN b. 7 Mar 1980 Töysä 1.94m 108kg. Töysän Veto.
At HT: OG: '00- dnq 34; WCh: '99- 11, '01- 10; WJ: '98- 1; EJ: '97- 3, '99- 1; EU23: '01- 2. Finnish champion 1998-2001.
World junior hammer record 2000.
Progression at HT: 1995- 48.26, 1996- 58.80, 1997- 69.84, 1998- 75.08, 1999- 78.33, 2000- 80.55, 2001- 80.54.

Conny KARLSSON b. 30 Dec 1975 Dragsfjärd 1.95m 120kg. Pargas IF.
At SP: WCh: '01- 7; EU23: '97- 1; WJ: '94- 6. Finnish champion 2001.
Progression at SP: 1993- 15.62, 1994- 17.08, 1995- 17.94, 1996- 18.59, 1997- 19.48, 1998- 19.21i/18.76, 1999- 19.31, 2000- 19.46, 2001- 20.78. pb DT 52.30 '97. Raised pb from 20.49 to 20.72 (q) and 20.78 at 2001 Worlds.

Juha LAUKKANEN b. 6 Jan 1969 Pielavesi 1.86m 90kg. Laukkalan Luja. Marketing student.
At JT: OG: '92- 6; WCh: '01- dnq 19; EC: '94- dnq 18, '98- 5; WJ: '88- 10; EJ: '87- 6. Finnish champion 1992, 1994.
World junior javelin record 1987.
Progression at JT: 1986- 74.40, 1987- 79.46, 1988- 77.08, 1989- 78.68, 1990- 83.36, 1991- 87.06, 1992- 88.22, 1993- 84.58, 1994- 85.54, 1995- 82.54, 1996- 87.12, 1997- 87.10, 1998- 86.96, 1999- 85.53, 2000- 82.35, 2001- 85.40. pb DT 42.50.

Matti NÄRHI b. 17 Aug 1975 Viitasaari 1.88m 100kg. Viitasaaren Viesti. Was at UTEP, USA
At JT: WCh: '99- 12, '01- dnq; EC: '98- 8; E23: '97- 2; WJ: '94- 2; EJ: '93- 2. NCAA champion 1999.
World indoor javelin best 85.78 in 1996.
Progression at JT: 1992- 70.24, 1993- 73.18, 1994- 76.14, 1995- 83.14, 1996- 85.78i/84.42, 1997- 88.24, 1998- 84.38, 1999- 87.88, 2000- 82.74, 2001- 84.21. pb PV 3.90 '93.
Suffered a ruptured Achilles tendon at the 1999 World Championships.

Aki PARVIAINEN b. 26 Oct 1974 Helsinki 1.91m 96kg. Joensuun Kataja.
At JT: OG: '00- 5; WCh: '95- 9, '97- 8, '99- 1, '01- 2; EC: '98- 9; WJ: '92- 1; EJ: '91- 3; ECp: '98- 3. Finnish champion 1999-2001.
Finnish javelin records 1998 and 1999.
Progression at JT: 1990- 63.50, 1991- 79.96, 1992- 80.94, 1993- 78.18i/69.94, 1994- 78.76, 1995- 85.60, 1996- 84.96, 1997- 87.48, 1998- 90.88, 1999- 93.09, 2000- 90.97, 2001- 92.41. pbs: SP 12.26 '96, DT 36.78 '96.
Set world age records at 14-16-17. The first Finn to win world titles at junior and senior level. Missed most of 1993-4 seasons through an arm injury. Older brother Mika threw 80.26 in 1992.

Ville TIISANOJA b. 24 Dec 1975 Vantaa 1.92m 119kg. Kenttäurheilijat-58 (Vantaa).
At SP: OG: '00- dnq 15; WCh: '99- 8, '01- 9; EU23: '97- 4; WJ: '94- 3 (10 DT); EJ: '93- 7; EI: '02- 5. Finnish champion 1999.
Progression at SP: 1992- 16.41, 1993- 17.35, 1994- 17.90, 1995- 19.10, 1996- 18.29, 1997- 19.40, 1998- 19.13, 1999- 20.49, 2000- 20.76, 2001- 20.78. pbs: DT 54.10 '94, HT 51.36 '94.

Women

Mikaela INGBERG b. 29 Jul 1974 Vaasa 1.74m 75kg. Vasa Idrottssällskap.
At JT: OG: '96- 7, '00- 9; WCh: '95- 3, '97- 4, '99- 9, '01- 6; EC: '94- dnq 16, '98- 3; EJ: '91- 15, '93- 1; WCp: '98- 3. Finnish champion 1994, 1999-2000. Finnish record new javelin 2000
Progression at JT: 1987- 33.70, 1988- 41.78, 1989- 43.92, 1990- 51.96, 1991- 52.30, 1992- 54.00, 1993- 58.26, 1994- 58.70, 1995- 65.16, 1996- 65.66, 1997- 67.32, 1998- 66.43; new 1999- 61.50, 2000- 64.03, 2001- 63.13. pbs: HJ 1.57 '88, SP 12.67 '99, DT 39.56 '95.

Heli KOIVULA b. 27 Jun 1975 Kauhajoki 1.74m 60kg. Kauhajoen Karhu.
At TJ (LJ): OG: '96- dnq 24 (dnq); WCh: '95- (dnq), '97- dnq 19 (dnq 13); 99- dnq 23, '01- 5; EC: '98- dnq 21 (dnq 23); WJ: '92- (4), '94- (2); EU23: '97- 3 (4); EJ: '91- (7). Won FIN LJ 1995-6, 1998, TJ 1996, 1998, 2000-01.
Five Finnish triple jump records 1996-9.
Progression at TJ: 1994- 13.20 1995- 13.47/13.79w, 1996- 13.74/13.89w, 1997- 13.92, 1998- 14.04, 1999- 14.34, 2000- 13.68, 2001- 14.28. pbs: 100m 11.72 '95, 200m 25.20 '93, 100mh 15.16 '93, HJ 1.56 '90, LJ 6.59 '98, 6.64w '94.

Taina KOLKKALA b. 24 Oct 1976 Pori 1.73m 74kg. née Uppa. Porin Tarmo.
At JT: OG: '96- dnq 19, '00- dnq 20; WCh: '95- dnq 24, '97- dnq 20, '99- 10, '01- 12; EC: '94- 10, '98=- dnq 14; EU23: '94- 4Cp, '97- 1; WJ: '94- 1; EJ: '95- 1.
Finnish record new javelin 2000.
Progression at JT: 1990- 39.58, 1991- 49.78, 1992- 54.78, 1993- 52.08, 1994- 61.78, 1995- 66.00, 1996- 63.78, 1997- 61.00, 1998- 62.31; new 1999- 63.63, 2000- 64.06, 2001- 60.55.

FRANCE

Governing body: Fédération Française d'Athlétisme, 33 avenue Pierre de Coubertin, 75640 Paris cedex 13. Founded 1920.
National Championships first held in 1888 (men), 1918 (women). **2001 Champions: Men**: 100m: Frédéric Krantz 10.17, 200m: Joseph Batangdon CMR 20.48, 400m: Stéphane Diagana 45.57, 800m: Arthémon Hatungimana BDI 1:49.35, 1500m: Driss Maazouzi 3:40.47, 5000m: Rachid Chékhémani 13:29.56, 10000m: Mustapha El Ahmadi 28:41.31, HMar: Abdelgani Lahlali 62:40, Mar: Philippe Rémond 2:21:45, 3000mSt: Frédéric Denis 8:23.84, 110mh: J-Berlioz Randriamihaja MAD 13.69, 400mh: Yvon Rakotoarimiandry MAD 49.68, HJ: Grégory Gabella 2.21, PV: Romain Mesnil 5.75, LJ: Kader Klouchi 8.24w, TJ: Karl Taillepierre 16.85, SP: Yves Niaré 19.28, DT: Jean-Claude Retel 59.20, HT: Nicolas Figère 79.48, JT: Laurent Dorique 80.40, Dec: Ladji Doucouré 7794, 20kmW/50kmW: Denis Langlois 1:26:07/4:07:41. **Women**: 100m: Frédérique Bangué 11.27, 200m: Fabé Dia 23.18, 400m: Mireille Nguingo CMR 51.60, 800m: Virginie Fouquet 2:03.15, 1500m: Hanane Sabri-Baala 4:17.20, 5000m: Fatima Yvelain 15:42.38, 10000m: Yamna Belkacem 32:05.98, HMar: Zahia Dahmani 73:32, Mar: Chantal Dällenbach 2:34:19, 3000mSt: Laurence Duquénoy 9:58.31, 100mh: Patricia Girard 12.81w, 400mh: Sylvanie Morandais 55.79, HJ: Lucie Finez 1.83, PV: Vanessa Boslak 4.25, LJ: Aurélie Félix 6.57, TJ: Françoise Mbango CMR 14.65, SP: Natalya Lisovskaya 17.33, DT: Mélina Robert-Michon 62.92, HT: Manuela Montebrun 68.66, JT: Nadine Auzeil 57.32, Hep: Marie Collonvillé 5678, 10kmW: Fatiha Ouali 46:20, 20kmW: Christine Guinaudeau 1:39:50.

Mehdi BAALA b. 17 Aug 1978 Strasbourg 1.83m 66kg. ASPTT Strasbourg.
At 1500m (800m): OG: '00- 4; WCh: '01- 12; WJ: '96- h; EU23: '99- 3; EJ: '97- 7; EI: '00- 3; ECp: '00- 1 (1), '01- 2.
Progression at 1500m: 1994- 4:08.1, 1995- 3:48.74, 1996- 3:43.50, 1997- 3:45.34, 1998- 3:41.86, 1999- 3:34.83, 2000- 3:32.05, 2001- 3:31.97. pbs: 800m 1:46.24 '00, 1000m 2:15.45 '00, 3000m 8:08.06i '98, 8:23.69 '98.
Married Hanane Sabri (ht WC 1500m '01, FRA champion 2001) in September 2000.

Stéphane DIAGANA b. 23 Jul 1969 Saint-Affrique, Aveyron 1.84m 75kg. EA Franconville. Biology student.
At 400mh/4x400mR: OG: '92- 4; WCh: '93- 4, '95- 3, '97- 1, '99- 2; EC: '90- 5, '94- 3/2R, '98- sf; EI: '02- 2R; WCp: '92- 3, '94- 3R; ECp: '93-4-9-01: 1/3/6/3 (3R 93-4). Won GP 1998 (3rd 1994). Won French 400m 1992-5, 1997, 2001; 400mh 1990. European 400mh record 1995, eight French 1990-5.
Progression at 400mh: 1987- 54.1, 1989- 51.60, 1990- 48.92, 1992- 48.13, 1993- 47.64, 1994- 48.22, 1995- 47.37, 1997- 47.70, 1998- 48.04, 1999- 48.12, 2000- 48.70, 2001- 48.08. pbs: 100m 10.94 '88, 200m 20.81i '92, 20.95 '93; 300m 33.25 '99, 400m 45.18 '92, 60mh 8.10i '88, 110mh 14.56 '87, 200mh 22.94 '94, 22.9 '99.
Big advance in 1990, when he ran 50.11 to win the French title, then 49.26 and 48.92 at the Europeans in Split. In 1992 he ran 48.55 and then French records in each round at Olympics. In 1995 he took the European record, which had stood at 47.48 to Harald Schmid since 1982. Missed most of 1996 season through injury (stress fracture in foot) and was restricted by injury to just one

hurdles race in 2000. Elected president of the French athletes' association in October 1996. In 1999 he completed a set of World Champs 1-2-3-4.

Driss EL HIMER b. 4 Apr 1974 Rabat, Morocco 1.78m 58kg. RE Puyloubier.
At 5000m: WCh: '01- 12; EC: '98- 7. World CC: '99- 13 4k, '01- 6 12k; Eur CC: '98- 3, '00- 3. Won French 5000m 1998, 2000; 10000m 2000, CC 1999
French records: 3000m 1998, marathon 2001.
Progression at 5000m, 10000m, Mar: 1997- 2:27:08, 1998- 13:15.67, 1999- 13:20.94, 2000- 13:10.99, 28:11.26; 2001- 13:15.10, 2:07:02. pbs: 1500m 3:37.01 '99, 3000m 7:34.46 '98, 2M 8:23.53 '99, HMar 62:08 '01.
Gained French citizenship by joining the French Foreign Legion.

Nicolas FIGÈRE b19 May 1979 Moulins 1.77m 91kg. ES Viry NSE.
At HT: WCh: '01- 12; WJ: '98- 6; EJ: '97- dnq 14; EU23: '01- 1. French champion 2001.
Progression at HT: 1995- 51.36, 1996- 58.70, 1997- 62.16, 1998- 68.48, 1999- 75.13, 2000- 79.01, 2001- 80.88. pbs: HJ 1.86 '94, PV 3.30 '94, SP 13.34 '00, DT 42.45 '00.

Jean GALFIONE b. 9 Jun 1971 Paris 1.84m 82kg. Stade Français (Paris).
At PV: OG: '92- dnq 13, '96- 1, '00- dnq 16=; WCh: '91- 10, '93- 8, '95- 3, '97/9- nh; EC: '94- 3, '98- 3; WJ: '90- 1; EJ: 89- 9; WI: '93- 3, '99- 1; EI: '92- 4, '94- 2; WUG: '93- 3; WCp: '94- 2; ECp: '93-4-6-7-8: 4/1/5=/2/5=; 2nd GP 1998. French champion 1993-8.
Five French pole vault records 1993-9.
Progression at PV: 1987- 4.15, 1988- 5.16, 1989- 5.50, 1990- 5.60i/5.45, 1991- 5.80, 1992- 5.90, 1993- 5.93, 1994- 5.94, 1995- 5.86, 1996- 5.92, 1997- 5.80/ 6.00exh, 1998- 5.97, 1999- 6.00i/5.98, 2000- 5.81i/ 5.80, 2001- 5.55. pbs: 100m 10.7 '92, 10.90 '94; 400m 48.96 '96, 1500m 4:51.48 '95, 110mh 14.75, 200mh 25.50 '98, HJ 2.01 '92, LJ 7.21 '95, TJ 14.00 '87, SP 11.90, DT 35.84 '95, JT 49.88 '95, Dec 7415 '95.
Set (then) world decathlon PV best of 5.75 in 7206 decathlon at Talence 1996. Had an operation on a collapsed lung in May 2000. Nephew of 1968 Olympic fencing gold medallist (team foil) Jean-Claude Magnan. and his father, Serge, won a European team fencing gold medal in 1963.

Laurent HERNU b. 22 Aug 1976 Creil 1.90m 87kg. St. Nogent-sur-Oise.
At Dec: OG: '00- 19; WCh: '01- 8; ECp: '00-01: 2/3. French champion 2000
Progression at Dec: 1996- 6277, 1997- 5975, 1998- 7566w/7390, 1999- 7937, 2000- 8178, 2001- 8280. pbs: 100m 10.97 '01, 400m 49.31 '01, 1500m 4:27.49 '00, 60mh 7.96i '00, 110mh 14.01/13.94w '01, HJ 2.10 '00, PV 5.15 '01, LJ 7.48 '98, 7.49w '00; SP 14.80 '01, DT 46.76 '01, JT 60.14 '01, Hep 6069i '00.

Driss MAAZOUZI b. 15 Oct 1969 Meknès, Morocco 1.80m 65kg. Coquelicots St-Etienne.
At 1500m: OG: '96- 10, '00- 11; WCh: '97- sf, '99- 8, '01- 3. At 3000m: ECp: '99-00-01: 3/1/1. World 4k CC: '02- 10. Won FRA 1500m 1997-2001, 4k CC 1998-9; MedG 1500m 1997.
French records 1000 (2), 1500m (2) 1998-9, 2000m 2001.
Progression at 1500m: 1990- 3:45.8, 1991- 3:42.12, 1993- 3:43.3, 1994- 3:37.04, 1995- 3:35.45, 1996- 3:34.08, 1997- 3:35.26, 1998- 3:31.59, 1999- 3:31.51, 2000- 3:32.01, 2001- 3:31.54. pbs: 800m 1:46.3 '96, 1000m 2:15.26 '99, 1M 3:51.79 '00, 2000m 4:55.55 '01, 3000m 7:36.21 '98, 5000m 13:50.12 '94, 10km Rd 29:58 '94, HMar 64:44 '95, 3000mSt 9:08.6 '91.
Competed for Morocco to 1997, then switched allegiance (naturalised for France 23/7/96), but unable to compete for France until clearance granted by Morocco for 1999.

Romain MESNIL b. 13 Jul 1977 Plessis Bouchard 1.88m 79kg. ECLA Albi. Engineering student.
At PV: OG: '00- dnq 31; WCh: '99- nh, '01- 5; EU23: '99-1; WJ: '96- dnq 13=; WI: '99- 6=, '01- 3; ECp: '00- 5. French champion 2000-01.
Progression at PV: 1993- 4.30, 1994- 4.65, 1995- 5.15, 1996- 5.30, 1997- 5.40, 1998- 5.80, 1999- 5.93, 2000- 5.75, 2001- 5.86i/5.85. pb Dec 5724 '98.
Former gymnast.

Ismaïl SGHYR b. 16 Mar 1972 Douar Aïn Chaib Ould Teima, Morocco 1.68m 50kg. Stade Bordelais. Bordeaux University.
At 5000m: OG: '96- 11; WCh: '95- 4, '97- 4, '01- 5; ECp: '01- 1. At 10000m: WCh: '99- 15. At 3000m: WI: '97- 3. World CC: '96-7-02: 8/8/13. Won MedG 10000m 1997.
French 5000m record 2000.
Progression at 5000m, 10000m: 1993- 14:05.03, 28:42.76; 1994- 13:13.47, 1995- 13:04.19, 1996- 12:58.99, 1997- 13:00.62, 28:05.74; 1999- 13:03.69, 27:12.39; 2000- 12:58.83, 27:33.20; 2001- 13:01.64. pbs: 1500m 3:36.20 '95, 1M 3:54.2 '95, 2000m 4:52.88 '95, 3000m 7:30.09 '95, 2M 8:11.73 '96, HMar 63:55 '95, 3000mSt 8:42.49 '01.
Switched nationality from Morocco in 2000.

Bouabdellah TAHRI b. 20 Dec 1978 Metz 1.90m 65kg. ASPTT Metz.
At 3000mSt: OG: '00- h; WCh: '99- 12, '01- 5; EC: '98- 10; WJ: '96- 7; ECp: '00/01- 1. At 5000m: EJ: '97- 1. Won FRA 3000mSt 1998.
Progression at 3000mSt: 1996- 8:44.65, 1998- 8:19.75, 1999- 8:12.24, 2000- 8:16.14, 2001- 8:09.23. pbs: 800m 1:48.96 '01, 1000m 2:23.26 '97, 1500m 3:36.34i '02, 3:36.5 '01, 3:36.53 '99; 2000m 4:57.72 '01, 3000m 7:41.41i '02, 7:48.98 '97; 5000m 13:24.08 '99, 10km Rd 30:32 '96, 2000mSt 5:19.33 '01.

Women

Christine ARRON b. 13 Sep 1973 Abymes, Guadeloupe 1.78m 64kg. Avia, Issy-Les-Moulineaux.
At 100m/4x100m (200m): OG: '00- sf/4R; WCh: '97- 4/3R, '99- 6/2R; EC: '98- 1/1R, ECp: '97- (1)/2R, '98- 2/3R, '99- 1/1R, '00- 2/1R; WJ: '92-

sf. Won French 100m 2000, 200m 1997. MedG 200m 1997.
European and four French 100m records 1998.
Progression at 100m, 200m: 1988- 12.04, 1989- 11.64/11.6, 25.43; 1990- 12.41/12.3/12.0w, 1991- 11.97, 24.4; 1992- 11.51, 23.75; 1993- 11.93/11.92w, 1994- 24.18, 1995- 23.92, 1996- 23.26, 1997- 11.03, 22.62/22.57w, 1998- 10.73, 22.95i; 1999- 10.97, 22.26; 2000- 10.99/10.89w, 2001- 11.15, 23.42/ 23.14w. pbs: 50m 6.05+ '99, 60m 7.00+ '99, 400m 53.76 '95.
The superstar of the 1998 European Championships followed a majestic 100m victory in a European record 10.73 with an awesome final sprint relay leg to take France to gold. She first set French age records at 14 in 1988 (for 80m and 150m). Made great breakthrough in 1997, setting a French indoor 200m record (23.13), stepping in for Marie-José Pérec to win European Cup 200m and placing 4th in World 100m. Missed most of 2001 season,

Eunice BARBER b. 17 Nov 1974 Freetown, Sierra Leone 1.75m 68kg. EFS Reims.
At Hep (100mh): OG: '92- 26 (h), '96- 5 (dnq LJ), '00- dnf; WCh: '93- dnf, '95- 4, '97- dnf, '99- 1 (qf), '01- dnf; WJ: '92- 14. At Pen: WI: '97- 6. At LJ: AfG: '95- 1; ECp: '99- 1, '01- 2.
French long jump and heptathlon records 1999. African heptathlon record 1996. SLE records 100mh, HJ, LJ, SP, JT, Hep 1992-8.
Progression at LJ, Hep: 1990- 5.47, 1991- 5.66, 1992- 6.02, 5048; 1993- 5.94, 5308; 1994- 5.93, 5378; 1995- 6.57/6.70Aw, 6340; 1996- 6.59/6.66w, 6416; 1997- 6.70, 1998- 6.86i/6.75/6.90w, 1999- 7.01, 6861; 2000- 6.85, 6842; 2001- 6.97, 6736. pbs: 60m 7.36i '00, 100m 11.90 '99, 200m 23.53 '99, 800m 2:10.55 '01, 60mh 8.11i '00, 100mh 12.78 '01, 200mh 27.47 '99, HJ 1.93 '99, SP 13.40 '01, JT 52.44 '95, new: 51.91 '00; Pen 4558i '97.
Became a French citizen in February 1999, having previously represented Sierra Leone, but living in Reims from 1992. After concentrating on the long jump for a couple of years and taking the French record to 7.01, she returned in 1999 to the heptathlon where she had wins at 6461 (Arles) and 6505 (European Cup) before adding 356 points to her pb with a superlative display in Seville to take the world title. Another win at Talence (6514) secured her the IAAF Combined Events Challenge award. Won at Götzis with world's best score of 2000, but then held back by injuries; returned for Olympics but unable to continue beyond long jump in heptathlon. In 2001 she won again at Götzis, and started the World Championships heptathlon in great form with a clear lead after two events, but then made the terrible of error of having three no throws in the shot and withdrew.

Yamna BELKACEM b. 20 Feb 1974 Hagou, Morocco 1.64m 52kg. née Oubouhou. CS Meaux.
At 10000m: WCh: '01- 8. At 5000m: OG: '00- h; WCh: '99- 8; ECp: '00- 3, '01- 4. At 3000m: WI: '99- 4. World 4k CC: '99-00-01: 2/11/7; Eur CC: '96-7-8-01: 7/7/6/1. Won French 1500m 1999-2000, 10000m 2001.
French records: 3000m 1999, 5000m (5) 1999-2000.
Progression at 3000m, 5000m, 10000m: 1991- 9:51.0, 1993- 9:53.29, 1995- 9:46.94, 1996- 9:22.85, 16:03.90; 1997- 9:22.15, 15:50.92; 1999- 8:38.13, 15:02.34; 2000- 8:41.54, 14:47.79; 2001- 8:44.00, 15:17.95, 32:05.98. pbs: 800m 2:10.8 '94, 1000m 2:52.9 '94, 1500m 4:08.60 '99, 2000m 5:39.44 '99, Rd 10km 32:00 '01.
Married to Henri Belkacem (b. 16 Mar 1964) 3000mSt pb 8:23.47 '99, French champion 1999.

Florence EZEH b. 29 Dec 1977 Lomé, Togo 1.73m 96kg. Racing Club de France. Student at Southern Methodist University, USA.
At HT: WCh: '99- 16, '01- 7; EC: '98- dnq 14; EU23: '99-1; ECp: '99- 3. NCAA champion 1999-2001, MedG 2001.
Four French hammer records 1999.
Progression at HT: 1994- 43.82, 1995- 56.52, 1996- 58.28, 1997- 55.68, 1998- 61.14, 1999- 66.12, 2000- 64.74, 2001- 66.85. pb 20lbWt: 22.24i '01 (European record).

Linda FERGA b. 24 Dec 1976 Paris 1.69m 51kg. Ile de France.
At 100mh (/LJ): OG: '00- 7/4R; WCh: '97- (dnq), '01- 7; EC: '98- 8/7; EJ: '95- 3/1; EU23: '99- 1R; EI: '98- (3); ECp: '97- (5), '98- (3), '00- 1/1R, '01- 2. At 60mh: WI: '99- 5, '01- 6; EI: '00- 1, '02- 2. Won FRA LJ 1997.
Progression at 100mh: 1992- 14.13, 1994- 14.12, 1995- 13.61, 1996- 13.32/13.2, 1997- 13.34/13.02w, 1998- 12.95, 1999- 12.98/12.84w, 2000- 12.81/ 12.77w, 2001- 12.67. pbs: 60m 7.23i '97, 100m 11.35 '98, 50mh 6.82i '00, 60mh 7.88i '00, LJ 6.80 '97, 6.82w '98.

Patricia GIRARD b. 8 Apr 1968 Pointe-à-Pitre, Guadeloupe 1.62m 48kg. Neuilly Plaisance Sports.
At 100mh/4x100m (100m): OG: '88- 7R (h), '92- 4R (sf), '96- 3/6R, '00- qf; WCh: '93- sf/4R, '95- sf/5R, '97- dq/3R, '99- 8/2R, '01- sf; EC: '94- (sf), '98- 5; ECp: '93- 2R, '95- 3R, '97- 2/2R, '98- 2/3R, '99- 1/1R; Won FRA 1993, 1995, 1997, 1999, 2001; MedG 1997, 2001. At 60m: WI: '93- 8, '97- 3=; EI: '90- 4, '94- 3. At 60mh: WI: '93- 3, '95- dnf; EI: '94-6-8-00-02: 6/1/1/2/4.
Progression at 100mh: 1985- 14.4, 1986- 14.54/ 13.82w, 1987- 13.45, 1988- 13.42, 1989- 13.53, 1992- 12.91, 1993- 12.91, 1994- 12.93, 1995- 12.87, 1996- 12.59, 1997- 12.67, 1998- 12.80, 1999- 12.73, 2000- 12.88, 2001- 12.82/12.77w/12.62 irreg. pbs: 50m 6.27i '95, 60m 7.16i '94, 100m 11.11 '94, 10.9w '96; 200m 23.40 '95, 400m 56.55 '93, 50mh 6.76i '00, 60mh 7.84i '95, 200mh 25.82 '99, 25.6 '01 (both world bests); 400mh 63.86 '85. LJ 5.72 '93, JT 37.94 '85.
Two year drugs ban from 17 Mar 1990. Formerly married (1995) to European kick-boxing champion Eddy Léno.

Muriel HURTIS b. 25 Mar 1979 Bondy 1.80m 68kg. Ile de France.
At 200m/4x100m: OG: '00- sf/4R; WCh: '99- sf/2R; WJ: '98- 1/2R; EJ: '97- 2; EU23: '99- 2/1R; WI: '01- 5; EI: '00- 1. '02- 1; ECp: '00- 1/1R. Won French 200m 2000.
Progression at 200m: 1995- 23.91, 1996- 23.92, 1997- 23.79, 1998- 22.76/22.72w, 1999- 22.31, 2000- 22.70; 2001- 23.06i/23.35/23.14w, 2002- 22.51i. pbs: 50m 6.31i '01, 60m 7.32i '01, 100m 11.33/11.3 '99, 11.28w '00; 400m 54.44 '98, LJ 6.04i '97, 5.86 '95.

Manuela MONTEBRUN b. 13 Nov 1979 Laval 1.75m 92kg. Stade Laval. Student.
At HT: OG: '00- dnq 24; WCh: '99- 12, '01- 5; EC: '98- dnq 26; WJ: '98- 5; EU23: '99- 4, '01- 1; WUG: '99- 3, '01- 1; ECp: '00- 3, '01- 4. French champion 2000-01.
Five French hammer records 1999-2000.
Progression at HT: 1996- 47.34, 1997- 52.58, 1998- 62.79, 1999- 68.11, 2000- 71.18, 2001- 70.28. pb SP 13.99 '99.

Marie-José PÉREC b. 9 May 1968 Basse Terre, Guadeloupe 1.80m 60kg. Stade Français.
At 400m/4x100m (4x400m): OG: '92- 1 (4 4x100mR), '96- 1 (1 200m); WCh: '91- 1/5R, '95- 1; EC: '90- 3, '94- 1 (1R); WCp: '89- dq, '94- (4R); ECp: '91- 1 (won B 1989). At 200m: OG: '88- qf; WCh: '93- 4/4R, '97- sf; EI: '89- 1; WI: '89- 6; WCp: '92- 1/2R; ECp: '93- 2/2R (2 100m), '96- 1/3R. At 400mh: ECp: '95- 1. Won GP 400m 1994, French 100m 1991, 200m 1992, 1995; 400m 1988, 400mh 1989.
French records: 100m 1991, three 200m 1991-3, eight 400m 1988-96, four 400mh 1995.
Progression at 200m, 400m: 1984- 25.44/25.0; 1985- 24.14; 1986- 24.33/24.00w; 1987- 24.52; 1988- 22.72, 51.35; 1989- 22.36, 51.05; 1990- 22.92, 50.84; 1991- 22.26, 49.13; 1992- 22.20, 48.83; 1993- 21.99; 1994- 22.61, 49.77; 1995- 22.79, 49.28; 1996- 22.07, 48.25; 1997- 22.67, 1999- 23.25, 2000- 22.71, 50.32. At 400mh: 1989- 55.76, 1995- 53.21. pbs: 60m 7.29i '92, 100m 10.96 '91, 300m 36.81 '88.
Preceded Michael Johnson to win 1996 Olympic double at 200m and 400m. Disqualified for breaking lane when winning the 1989 World Cup 400m in 50.30. Ran French records of 50.53 and 49.32 in her first two races at 400m in 1991, then 49.76 to win in Nice and then improved to 49.13 to win the world title. Did not compete in 1998 due to the effects of a virus illness but returned in 1999. Had one race at 200m and one at 400m (3rd in Nice, her first at 400m for three years) and went to Sydney but fled from there when confronted with the pressure of the much-hyped intended clash with Cathy Freeman at 400m.

Nicole RAMALALANIRINA b. 5 Mar 1972 Soavinandriana, Madagascar 1.64m 57kg. Married name Válerie. Neuilly Plaisance Sports.
At 100mh: OG: '92- h, '96- sf, '00- 6; WCh: '93/95/99/01- sf, '97- ht; EC: '98- 4; AfG: '91- 3/3R, '95- 4; AfC: '90- 6, '92- 4/3R, '93- 1/2R; WCp: '94- 4, '98- dnf; WSG: '93- 3, '95- 1. At 60mh: WI: '01- 3; EI: '02- 5. Won FRA 100mh 1998, 2000.
African record 60mh indoors 1996.
Progression at 100mh: 1990- 13.91, 1991- 13.69, 1992- 13.40, 1993- 13.11/12.92w, 1994- 13.11, 1995- 12.92, 1996- 12.90, 1997- 13.02, 1998- 12.85/12.76w, 1999- 12.84, 2000- 12.76, 2001- 12.91/12.84w/12.87 irreg. pbs: 50m 6.53i '96, 60m 7.40i '94, 100m 11.56 '96, 11.53w '95; 200m 24.3A '91, 24.34w '00; 400m 56.42 '91, 50mh 6.87i '02, 60mh 7.89i '96, 200mh 26.70 '98, 400mh 59.88 '94. LJ 5.54 '94.
Changed citizenship from Madagascar (for whom she was also a basketball international) to France in February 1998.

GERMANY

Governing body: Deutscher Leichtathletik Verband (DLV), Alsfelder Str. 27, 64289 Darmstadt. Founded 1898.
National Championships first held in 1891.
2001 Champions: **Men**: 100m: Tim Goebel 10.21, 200m: Alexander Kosenkow 20.64, 400m: Lars Figura 45.93, 800m: Rene Herms 1:46.81, 1500m: Wolfram Müller 3:37.61, 5000m: Jan Fitschen 13:41.75, 10000m: Thomas Greger 28:41.16, HMar: Carsten Eich 63:50, Mar: Michael Fietz 2:16:23, 3000mSt: Ralf Assmus 8:28.33, 110mh: Mike Fenner 13.49, 400mh: Jan Schneider 49.63, HJ: Martin Buss 2.30, PV: Richard Spiegelburg 5.85, LJ: Schahriar Bigdeli 8.05, TJ: Thomas Moede 16.90, SP: Oliver-Sven Buder 19.97, DT: Lars Riedel 67.28, HT: Karsten Kobs 75.61, JT: Peter Blank 88.70, Dec: Jörg Goedicke 7801, 10000mW/20kmW: Andreas Erm 40:42.00/1:19:32, 50kmW: Denis Franke 4:00:00. **Women**: 100m/200m: Gabi Rockmeier 11.17/22.68, 400m: Grit Breuer 49.78, 800m: Ivonne Teichmann 2:01.78, 1500m: Kathleen Friedrich 4:15.17, 5000m: Sabrina Mockenhaupt 16:04.27, 10000m/Mar: Luminita Zaituc 32:35.90/2:26:01, HMar: Petra Wassiluk 70:36, 100mh: Kirsten Bolm 12.98, 400mh: Heike Meissner 55.03, HJ: Alina Astafei 1.84, PV: Annika Becker 4.55, LJ: Heike Drechsler 6.65, TJ: Nicole Herschmann 13.54, SP: Nadine Kleinert-Schmitt 18.69, DT: Franka Dietzsch 63.31, HT: Kirsten Münchow 66.72, JT: Steffi Nerius 61.26, Hep: Karin Ertl 6152, 5000mW/20kmW: Melanie Seeger 21:20.76/1:30:52.
In championships won below, note FRG and GDR to 1990, GER from 1991.

Dieter BAUMANN b. 9 Feb 1965 Blaustein 1.78m 64kg. LAV Tübingen.
At 5000m: OG: '88- 2, '92- 1, '96- 4; WCh: '91- 4, '95- 9, '97- 5; EC: '86- h, '94- 1, '98- 13 (2 10000m); WCp: '98- 3; ECp: '94- 1. At 3000m: WI: '89- 3; EI: '87- 2, '89- 1; WCp: '98- 1; ECp: '96-7-8-9: 1/1/1/4. At 1500m: WCh: '87- sf; WI: '87- 7; ECp: '87- 5, '89- dq. Won FRG/GER 1500m 1987-9, 1995-6, 1998; 5000m 1986, 1988, 1991-2, 1995-1999; 10000m 1994, 1998; CC 1995-7, 2002.

European records: 5000m 1997, indoor 3000m (7:37.51) 1995. German records 3000m (4) 1991-8; 5000m (3) 1992-7, 10000m 1997.
Progression at 1500m, 5000m, 10000m: 1982- 4:03.75, 15:42.96; 1983- 3:52.99, 14:40.4; 1984- 3:50.37, 14:21.59; 1985- 3:40.48, 13:48.0; 1986- 3:36.40, 13:35.04; 1987- 3:33.54, 13:30.85; 1988- 3:34.82, 13:15.52; 1989- 3:34.25, 13:18.58, 29:03.33; 1990- 3:40.38; 1991- 3:34.93, 13:24.58; 1992- 3:33.91, 13:09.03; 1994- 3:38.49, 13:12.47, 28:20.66; 1995- 3:34.48, 13:01.72; 1996- 3:36.77, 13:08.81; 1997- 3:33.51, 12:54.70, 27:21.53; 1998- 3:38.28i/ 3:42.00, 13:04.10, 27:32.31; 1999- 3:37.22, 13:02.63; 2000- 3:37.18dq, 13:13.84dq. pbs: 800m: 1:48.40 '90, 1000m 2:18.79i '89, 2:22.4 '86, 1M 3:51.12 '92, 2000m 4:59.88 '87, 3000m 7:30.50 '98.
Undefeated in 5000m finals in 1992 and 1994. Beat 13-min for 5000m with a European record 12:54.70 for 5th in Zürich 1997. Married to his coach Isabell (née Hozang) who was 11th in the 1981 European Junior 1500m for Austria.
Two year ban after positive tests for Nandrolene in October/November 1999. He competed, without IAAF authorisation but after a German court ruling, in the GER indoor 3000m 2001 (and won).

Peter BLANK b. 10 Apr 1962 Frankfurt-am-Main 1.95m 103kg. Eintracht Frankfurt.
At JT: OG: '96- 9; WCh: '91- 11, '93/9/01- dnq 29/13/17; EC: '90- dnq, '94- dnq 20, '98- 7; ECp: '91- 3. FRG champion 1988, 1990; GER 2001.
Progression at JT: 1978- 58.42, 1979- 64.92, 1980- 65.76, 1981- 72.84, 1982- 76.04, 1983- 78.22, 1984- 81.98, 1985- 82.34, new: 1986- 71.02, 1987- 77.94, 1988- 80.84, 1989- 79.60, 1990- 82.82R, 1991- 82.62, 1992- 81.12, 1993- 80.76, 1994- 82.56, 1995- 83.18, 1996- 88.12, 1997- 86.84, 1998- 86.99, 1999- 87.11, 2000- 85.45, 2001- 88.70. pbs: HJ 2.23 '83, LJ 7.41 '88, Dec 7651 '90.
Set a world decathlon javelin best 79.80 in 1992.

Lars BÖRGELING b. 16 Apr 1979 Neuss 1.87m 84kg. Bayer Leverkusen.
At PV: WJ: '96- 8=, '98- 2; EU23: '99- 2, '01- 1; EJ: '97- 1; EI: '02- 3.
Progression at PV: 1993- 3.83, 1994- 4.30, 1995- 4.60, 1996- 5.20, 1997- 5.50, 1998- 5.62, 1999- 5.80, 2000- 5.75ex/5.70, 2001- 5.80. pbs: Dec 6478 '99.

Oliver-**Sven BUDER** b. 23 Jun 1966 Erlabrunn 2.00m 140kg. LAZ Leipzig. Clerk.
At SP: OG: '96- 5, '00- 8; WCh: '91- 4, '93- 7, '95- 6, '97- 2, '99- 2, '01- dnq 21; EC: '90- 2, '94- dnq 16, '98- 2; EJ: '85- 1; WCp: '94- 4, '98- 3; ECp: '93-4-5-6-7-8-9: 4/4/2/2/1/2/1; WI: '91- 7, '93- 8, '97- 4; EI: '90- 3, '96- 3, '98- 1. Won GER 1991, 1993-2001.
Progression at SP: 1984- 16.58, 1985- 19.34, 1986- 19.29, 1987- 20.14, 1988- 19.05, 1989- 20.22, 1990- 21.06, 1991- 20.20, 1992- 19.76i/19.70, 1993- 20.15, 1994- 20.44, 1995- 20.84, 1996- 20.67, 1997- 21.24, 1998- 21.47i/20.98, 1999- 21.42, 2000- 20.71i/20.41, 2001- 20.32. pb DT 54.14 '91.
Improved 7 year-old personal best to take 1997 world silver medal.

Frank BUSEMANN b. 26 Feb 1975 Recklinghausen 1.92m 87kg. Bayer Leverkusen.
At Dec: OG: '96- 2, '00- 7; WCh: '97- 3, '99- dnf; ECp: '96- 1. At 110mh: WJ: '94- 1; EJ: '93- 3; EU23: '97- 1.
World junior 60mh best 7.67i '94.
Progression at Dec: 1994- 7938, 1995- 7879, 1996- 8706, 1997- 8652, 1998- 8231, 1999- 8414, 2000- 8531, 2001- 8192. pbs: 100m 10.59 '93, 200m 21.61 '96, 400m 48.32 '97, 1500m 4:23.04 '98, 60mh 7.52i '97, 110mh 13.45 '96, HJ 2.10i '02, 2.09 '97; PV 5.10 '99, LJ 8.07 '96, SP 15.24 '99, DT 46.70 '97, JT 66.96 '97, Hep 6291i '02 (GER rec).
Five personal bests and a decathlon world best 13.47 for 110mh at the 1996 Olympics. Suffered from lower back injury 1998. His mother won a German U21 shot title and his brother Lars Achim Busemann (b. 31 Jan 1978) has a pole vault pb of 5.30 '01.

Martin BUSS b. 7 Apr 1976 Berlin 1.95m 82kg. Bayer Leverkusen.
At HJ: WCh: '97- 9, '99- 3, '01- 1; EC: '98- 4; EJ: '95- 2; EU23: '97- 2; WI: '99- 4, '01- 5=; EI: '00- 2; WCp: '98- 4; ECp: '97-8-9-01: 3/4=/1/3. Won GER 1997-9, 2001.
Progression at HJ: 1993- 1.85, 1994- 2.04, 1995- 2.19, 1996- 2.27, 1997- 2.31, 1998- 2.33, 1999- 2.35, 2000- 2.34i, 2001- 2.36. pb LJ 7.75 '99.

Danny ECKER b. 21 Jul 1977 Leverkusen 1.92m 78kg. Bayer Leverkusen.
At PV: OG: '00- 8; WCh: '99- 4=, '01- 11; EC: '98- 4; WI: '99- 3; EI: '98- 3; WJ: '96- 3; ECp: '98- 4.
Progression at PV: 1990- 2.90, 1991- 3.30, 1992- 3.80, 1993- 4.40, 1994- 4.70, 1995- 5.12, 1996- 5.61, 1997- 5.72i/5.71, 1998- 5.93, 1999- 5.90, 2000- 5.90, 2001- 6.00i/5.85. pbs: HJ 2.00 '99. LJ 6.83 99.
Son of Heide Rosendahl, 1972 Olympic LJ champion (and 2nd Pen) (WR 6.84 '70), and US basketball player John Ecker.

Andreas ERM b. 12 Mar 1976 Berlin 1.84m 70kg. TV Friesen Naumburg. Soldier.
At 20kmW: OG: '96- 24, '00- 5; WCh: '97- dq, '99/01- dnf; EC: '98- 4; EU23: '97- 5; ECp: '98-00-01 4/2/3. At 10000mW: WJ: '94- 9; EJ: '95- 1. Won GER 20kmW 1998-2001, 10000mW 2000-01. German 20km walk record 2000, world best indoor 3000m walk 2001.
Progression at 20kmW: 1994- 1:26:41, 1995- 1:23:20, 1996- 1:22:16, 1997- 1:21:05, 1998- 1:20:57, 1999- 1:19:24, 2000- 1:18:42, 2001- 1:19:32. pbs: 3000mW 10:31.42i '01, 11:10.20 '01; 5000mW 18:22.25i '01, 10000mW 39:54.23 '00.

Charles-Michael **FRIEDEK** b. 26 Aug 1971 Giessen 1.84m 80kg. TSV Beyer Leverkusen. Law student.
At TJ: OG: '00- nj (12); WCh: '97- 11, '99- 1; EC: '98- 6; WJ: '90- 12; EJ: '89- dnq; WI: '97- 4, '99- 1, '01- 4; EI: '98- 2, '00- 1; WUG: '97- 5, '99- 2; WCp:

'98- 1; ECp: '96-7-8-01: 4/3/3/8. Won GP 1998, GER 1996-2000.
Progression at TJ: 1987- 13.67, 1988- 15.13, 1989- 15.85, 1990- 16.34, 1991- 15.77, 1992- 16.10, 1993- 16.32i/16.26/16.51w, 1994- 16.31, 1995- 16.34/ 16.60w, 1996- 17.10, 1997- 17.59, 1998- 17.42A/ 17.38, 1999- 17.59, 2000- 17.41, 2001- 17.13i/16.90. pbs: 100m 11.01 '92, 200m 22.23 '89, LJ 7.66 '97.

Raymond HECHT b. 11 Nov 1968 Gardelegen 1.91m 95kg. SG Magdeburg. Mechanical engineer.
At JT: OG: '96- 4, '00- 4; WCh: '91- 12, '93- dnq 23, '95- 4, '97- dnq 13, '99- 5, '01- 5; EC: '90- 10, '94- 5, '98- 3; WCp: '94- 2, '98- 3; ECp: '93-4-5-6-9-01: 4/2/1/1/3; EJ: '87- 3. GER champion 1993-4, 1996, 1999. 2nd GP 1993, 1995.
Five German javelin records 1991-5.
Progression at JT: 1984- 66.20, 1985- 69.32; new: 1986- 71.08 (71.14 old), 1987- 75.90, 1990- 83.24, 1991- 90.84R, 1992- 79.58, 1993- 88.90, 1994- 90.06, 1995- 92.60, 1996- 92.28, 1997- 87.32, 1998- 88.08, 1999- 88.67, 2000- 87.76, 2001- 88.88.
As a junior was ranked fourth in the world in 1987. Injured 1988-9.

Boris HENRY b. 14 Dec 1973 Völklingen 1.93m 108kg. SV Saar 05 Saarbrücken. Army staff sergeant.
At JT: OG: '96- 5, '00- 7; WCh: '93- dnq, '95- 3, '97- 6, '99- 6, '01- 6; EC: '94- 11; WJ: '92- 2; EJ: '91- 4; ECp: '97-8-00: 3/1/3. 2nd/3rd GP 1997/99. GER champion 1995, 1997-8, 2000.
Progression at JT: 1989- 58.20, 1990- 65.86, 1991- 74.78, 1992- 76.92, 1993- 84.12, 1994- 82.02, 1995- 88.46, 1996- 88.00, 1997- 90.44, 1998- 89.21. 1999- 88.62, 2000- 86.65, 2001- 86.53. pbs: SP 14.37 '94, DT 46.24 '94, Pen 3503 '93.
For several years wore a red baseball cap given to him as an 18th birthday present, now sports a white one.

Damian KALLABIS b. 10 Jun 1973 Gleiwitz (Gliwice), Poland 1.77m 64kg. VfB Stuttgart. Was at the University of Texas, El Paso, USA.
At 3000mSt: OG: '00- 15; WCh: '99- 4; EC: '98- 1; WCp: '98- 1; ECp: '99-00: 2/2. German champion 1998, 2000.
German 3000m steeplechase record 1999.
Progression at 3000mSt: 1991- 9:24.6, 1992- 8:49.99, 1993- 8:43.92, 1994- 8:40.40, 1995- 8:38.39, 1996- 8:42.13, 1997- 8:37.35, 1998- 8:13.10, 1999- 8:09.48, 2000- 8:14.53, 2001- 8:36.20. pbs: 1500m 3:43.77 '98, 3000m 7:49.38 '99, 5000m 14:29.87 '97.
Made a superb breakthrough in 1998, running away with the European title and later upsetting Bernard Barmasai to win at the World Cup. Coached by Stéphane Franke. At 14 he was regional champion at 80mh and HJ (1.73m).

Karsten KOBS b. 16 Sep 1971 Dortmund 1.96m 125kg. TSV Bayer Leverkusen.
At HT: OG: '96- dnq 18, '00- dnq 31; WCh: '93- dnq 16, '95- dnq 16, '97- 9, '99- 1; EC: '94- 10, '98- 3; WJ: '90- 4; EJ: '89- 10; ECp: '93-5-6-9-00-01: 7/3/1/3/3/5; E23Cp: '92- 2. German champion 1996, 1999-2001. 3rd GP 2000.
Progression at HT: 1988- 59.80, 1989- 65.02, 1990- 70.02, 1991- 71.82, 1992- 74.36, 1993- 75.94, 1994- 76.30, 1995- 76.80, 1996- 78.92, 1997- 79.08, 1998- 81.21, 1999- 82.78, 2000- 80.21, 2001- 79.15. pb SP 15.53 '98.
Has improved every year of his career to reach the world number one ranking in 1999. His father, Reiner, had HT pb of 58.90 (1974).

Tim LOBINGER b. 3 Sep 1972 Rheinbach 1.93m 83kg. LG Eintracht Frankfurt.
At PV: OG: '96- 7, '00- 13; WCh: '93- dnq, '95- 11, '97- 4, '99- 6; EC: '94- dnq 21=, '98- 2; WI: '97- 5; EI: '98- 1, '02- 1; WJ: '90- dnq; EJ: '91- 3; WCp: '98- 2; ECp: '93-4-5-6-7-00: 5/3/nh/2/3/2; E23Cp: '92- 1, '94- 4. Won GP 2000, 3rd 1997, German champion 1993-4, 1997-2000.
Three German pole vault records 1997-9.
Progression at PV: 1986- 3.46, 1987- 3.90, 1988- 4.60, 1989- 4.85, 1990- 5.32, 1991- 5.35, 1992- 5.50, 1993- 5.55, 1994- 5.60, 1995- 5.70, 1996- 5.91, 1997- 6.00, 1998- 5.92, 1999- 6.00, 2000- 5.95i/5.85, 2001- 5.80. pbs: 110mh 14.78 '99, HJ 1.97 '99, DT 42.76 '99, Dec 7346 '99.
Set (then) world decathlon PV best of 5.75 in 7346 decathlon at Leverkusen 1999. His wife **Petra** (b. 24 Jan 1967 Siegen-Weidenau, née Laux) set four German indoor TJ records from 14.15 '96 to 14.36 '97 (5 WI), outdoor pb 14.31/ 14.35w '97; German champion 1992, 1996-7, 10 WCh '97; they have one child.

Michael MÖLLENBECK b. 12 Dec 1969 Wesel 2.00m 120kg. TV Wattenscheid. Businessman.
At DT: OG: '96- dnq, '00- 10; WCh: '95- dnq 16, '99- 6, '01- 3; WJ: '88- 9; EJ: '87- 6.
Progression at DT: 1988- 53.00, 1989- 59.26, 1990- 60.16, 1991- 58.86, 1992- 62.12, 1993- 62.82, 1994- 58.26, 1995- 65.78, 1996- 67.44, 1997- 66.66, 1998- 67.18, 1999- 67.00, 2000- 65.49, 2001- 67.61. pb SP 16.78 '95.
Threw pb in first round of 2001 World discus final. Married discus thrower Anja Gündler (qv) in 1996.

Lars RIEDEL b. 28 Jun 1967 Zwickau 1.99m 110kg. LAC Chemnitz. Computer salesman.
At DT: OG: '92- dnq 14, '96- 1, '00- 2; WCh: '91- 1, '93- 1, '95- 1, '97- 1, '99- 3, '01- 1; EC: '90- dnq 15, '94- dns, '98- 1; WJ: '86- 4; WUG: '93- 1; WCp: '98- 2; ECp: '93-5-7-00-01: 1/1/1/1/1. GER champion 1992-8, 2000-01. Won GP 1993, 1995, 1997 (2nd overall), 1999; 2nd 1991.
Progression at DT: 1985- 52.02, 1986- 58.66, 1988- 62.26, 1989- 60.84, 1990- 64.86, 1991- 67.78, 1992- 68.66, 1993- 68.42, 1994- 66.08, 1995- 69.08, 1996- 71.06, 1997- 71.50, 1998- 68.21, 1999- 69.18, 2000- 69.72, 2001- 69.72. pbs: SP 15.93 '91, JT 61.14 '93, Dec 6087 '93.
The top discus thrower of the 1990s with four world titles (and a fifth in 2001) and the 1996

Olympic gold. In 1992 improved to 67.90, but failed at the Olympics before making a fine comeback with four throws over 68m at the ISTAF meeting. In 1994 a bad back caused his withdrawal from European final. He exceeded 70m for the first time in Zürich in 1995.

Stefan SCHMID b. 6 May 1970 Würzburg 1.87m 85kg. LG Karlstadt.
At Dec: OG: '00- 9; WCh: '97- 7, '01- 7; EC: '94- 5, '98- 14; ECp: '93- 6; WUG: '91- 4. Won GER 1992.
Progression at Dec: 1990- 7532, 1991- 7866, 1992- 8012, 1993- 8061, 1994- 8309, 1996- 8478dq, 1997- 8360, 1998- 8011, 1999- 7981, 2000- 8485, 2001- 8307. pbs: 100m 10.69 '00, 10.67w '90; 200m 21.68 '91, 400m 47.86 '01, 1500m 4:26.51 '94, 60mh 7.98i '97, 110mh 13.93dq '96, 14.16 '01; HJ 2.01 '00, 2.06dq '96; PV 5.10 '01, LJ 7.83 '94, SP 14.73 '98, DT 45.16 '98, JT 71.68 '94, Hep 6058i '97.
After a season in which he broke into the world's top ten he had a cartilege operation at the end of 1994. Returned for his best decathlon in two years to win German title late in 1996 with four pbs; but a drugs test on this occasion found him to have taken a banned stimulant, although one that had been prescribed by a doctor for shoulder pains earlier in the year.

Ingo SCHULTZ b. 26 Jul 1975 Lingen 2.01m 96kg. Studying for PhD in electrical engineering. LG Olympia Dortmund.
At 400m/4x400mR: WCh: '01- 2; EI: '00- 2R; ECp: '01- 4/2R.
Progression at 400m: 1999- 45.99, 2000- 45.79, 2001- 44.66. pbs: 100m 10.57 '01, 200m 20.71 '01.
While in the army in 1997 he ran the Hamburg Marathon in 3:37, and started track racing after that. He ran 52.45 for his first 400m in May 1998.

Nils SCHUMANN b. 20 May 1978 Bad Frankenhausen 1.92m 77kg. SV Creaton Grossengottern.
At 800m: OG: '00- 1; WCh: '99- 8, '01- 5; EC: '98- 1; WJ: '96- 5; EJ: '97- 1; EU23: '99- 1; EI: '98- 1, '00- 2; WCp: '98- 1; ECp: '00- 2. German champion 1999-2000.
Progression at 800m: 1988- 2:26.5, 1989- 2:21.0, 1990- 2:18.3, 1991- 2:14.0, 1994- 2:03.6, 1995- 1:53.0, 1996- 1:48.35, 1997- 1:46.61, 1998- 1:44.89, 1999- 1:44.47, 2000- 1:44.22, 2001- 1:44.32. pbs: 400m 46.62 '99, 1000m 2:17.44 '99, 1500m 3:40.36 '00.
Burst to the fore with an astonishing sequence of championship victories.

Florian SCHWARTHOFF b. 7 May 1968 Dortmund 2.01m 83kg. OSC Berlin. Studied architecture.
At 110mh: OG: '88- qf, '92- 5. '96- 3, '00- 6; WCh: '87- sf, '91- 7, '93- 5, '95- sf (fell), '97- 4, '99- 7, '01- sf; EC: '90- sf, '94- 2, '98- 4; WCp: '94- 4; ECp: '89-91-9-4-5-6-7: 3/2/2/1/1/1/1 (5 200m '91); EJ: '87- 2; WUG: '89- 3. 3rd GP 1995, 2nd 1997. FRG/GER champion 1987-8, 1990-2, 1994-7, 1999-2000. At 60mh: WI: '93- 4; EI: '90- 3, '02- 5.
Four FRG 110mh records 1988-92 and three at 60mh indoors in 1990; GER 110mh record 1995.
Progression at 110mh: 1986- 14.13, 1987- 13.69, 1988- 13.50, 1989- 13.37, 1990- 13.37, 1991- 13.38, 1992- 13.13, 1993- 13.27. 1994- 13.16, 1995- 13.05, 1996- 13.11, 1997- 13.11, 1998- 13.19, 1999- 13.19, 2000- 13.23, 2001- 13.53. pbs: 100m 10.57 '96, 10.46w '90; 200m 20.86 '91, 60mh 7.52i '90, LJ 7.69 '86.
Perhaps the tallest ever top-class high hurdler.

Andreas SEELIG b. 6 Jul 1970 Berlin 2.00m 120kg. USC Mainz.
At DT: WCh: '97- 6, '99- dnq 14; EC: '94- 10, '98- 7; WJ: '88- 1; EJ: '89- 1.
Progression at DT: 1986- 45.06, 1987- 54.24, 1988- 61.84, 1989- 59.72, 1990- 59.36, 1991- 58.88, 1992- 60.82, 1993- 61.90, 1994- 62.22, 1995- 62.90, 1996- 63.62, 1997- 66.00, 1998- 65.47, 1999- 65.83, 2000- 64.51, 2001- 64.57.

Michael STOLLE b. 17 Dec 1974 Buxtehude 1.92m 85kg. Bayer Leverkusen.
At PV: OG: '96- 9=, '00- 4; WCh: '99- 7=, '01- 4; WI: '97- 8=, '01- 9=; EI: '98- 2; WJ: '90- dnq; EJ: '91- dnq; ECp: '99- 1, '01- 1. German champion 1996.
Progression at PV: 1989- 3.70, 1990- 4.20, 1991- 4.75, 1992- 5.05, 1993- 5.10i/5.05, 1994- 5.41, 1995- 5.50, 1996- 5.71i/5.70, 1997- 5.70i/5.60, 1998- 5.83, 1999- 5.91, 2000- 5.95, 2001- 5.85. pb Dec 5817 '99.

Women

Christine ADAMS b. 28 Feb 1974 Georgsmarienhütte 1.82m 72kg. Beyer Leverkusen.
At PV: EI: '96-00-02: 2/2=/5; WUG: '99- 4, ECp: '01- 4. German champion 1995-6.
Two German pole vault records 1995, and one indoors 1996.
Progression at HJ: 1991- 3.20, 1992- 3.70, 1993- 3.80, 1994- 3.90, 1995- 4.02, 1996- 4.15, 1997- 4.06Ai/3.95, 1998- 3.95i/3.85, 1999- 4.21/4.23exh, 2000- 4.40i/4.30, 2001- 4.35, 2002- 4.66i. pbs: LJ 5.85 '91, SP 12.02 '94, DT 53.44 '93.

Annika BECKER b. 12 Nov 1981 Rotenburg/ Fulda 1.70m 63kg. Alheimer Rotenberg/Bebra.
At PV: WCh: '01- dnq 14; WJ: '00- 2; EU23: '01- 2; EJ: '97- 1, '99- 2; EI: '02- 4. Won German 2001.
German pole vault record 2001.
Progression at PV: 1996- 3.40, 1997- 4.01, 1998- 4.15, 1999- 4.30, 2000- 4.22, 2001- 4.55, 2002- 4.62i.

Kirsten BOLM b. 4 Mar 1975 Köln 1.81m 69kg. LT DHSS Köln. Was at Brigham Young University, USA.
At 100mh: WCh: '99- qf, '01- h; WJ: '92- 5, '94- 1 (5 LJ); WUG: '99- 5/3R; ECp: '99-01- 6/3; Won German 2000-01. At 60mh: EI: '02- 3.
Progression at 100mh: 1991- 13.49, 1992- 13.42, 1993- 13.52, 1994- 13.26, 1995- 13.60, 1996- 13.57, 1998- 13.75, 1999- 13.04/12.86Aw, 2000- 12.92, 2001- 12.98, pbs: 100m 11.92 '94, 50mh 7.12i '01, 60mh 7.89i '02, HJ 1.75 '91, LJ 6.55 '94.

Grit BREUER b. 16 Feb 1972 Röbel 1.66m 60kg. SC Magdeburg.
At 400m/4x400mR: OG: '88- res (3)R, '96- 8/3R; WCh: '91- 2/3R (3 4x100mR), '97- 4/1R, '99- 7/3R, '01- 4/2R; EC: '90- 1/1R, '98- 1/1R; WJ: '88- 1 (1R & 1 4x100mR); WI: '91- 1R (3 200m), '97- 6/3R, '99- 1; EI: '96- 1, '98- 1; WCp: '89- 2/2R, '98- 2/1R; ECp: '89-91-6-7-01: 1/2/1/1/1 (1R/2R/1R/-/1R). Won GDR 400m 1989-90, GER 200m 1997, 400m 1996-7, 1999-2001.
World junior records 400m 1990 and 1991, 4x100m and 4x400m 1988, indoor 200m 1991. WIR 4x400m 1991.
Progression at 200m, 400m: 1985- 56.21, 1986- 55.7/55.5i, 1987- 24.03, 52.59; 1988- 23.04, 51.14; 1989- 22.82, 50.48; 1990- 22.49, 49.50; 1991- 22.45, 49.42; 1992- 22.71i, 1995- 23.63, 51.68; 1996- 50.22, 1997- 22.73, 49.98; 1998- 22.95i, 49.51; 1999- 23.02, 50.16; 2000- 23.46, 51.06; 2001- 22.79, 49.78. pbs: 100m 11.13 '90, 300m 36.51+ '99.
Set world age records for 400m at 16-17-18-19. Olympic bronze medal at age 16 as she ran in heats of 4x400m relay. Although a junior until 1991, she did not contest the 1989 or 1991 European or 1990 World Juniors, but concentrated with great success on senior competition. Drugs ban in 1992, first for allegedly tampering with sample. That ban was lifted by the DLV, but then caught again for use of Clenbuterol. She returned to competition when her three-year ban ended in August 1995. Ran a brilliant final leg of 48.69 to come from behind and take the gold medal for Germany in the 1997 World 4x400m. She withdrew from the 2000 Olympic team and underwent surgery for back and knee problems, but made a fine comeback in 2001.

Yvonne BUSCHBAUM b. 14 Jul 1980 Ulm 1.70m 55kg. LG Stuttgart.
At PV: OG: '00- 6; WCh: '99- 14=, '01- 7; EC: '98- 3; WJ: '98- 4; WI: '01- 6; EI: '02- 2; ECp: '99-00: 1/2. German champion 1999-2000.
Four world junior pole vault records 1999, German record 1999. Three German indoor records 2002.
Progression at PV: 1994- 2.81, 1995- 3.30, 1996- 3.55, 1997- 4.00, 1998- 4.31, 1999- 4.42/4.45ex, 2000- 4.45, 2001- 4.46, 2002- 4.65i. pbs: 100mh 14.54 '98, HJ 1.75 '98, LJ 5.81 '98.

Tanja DAMASKE b. 16 Nov 1971 Berlin 1.77m 69kg. OSC Berlin. Psychology student.
At JT: WCh: '95- 6, '97- 3; EC: '94- 6, '98- 1; WJ: '90- 1; WUG: '93- 2; WCp: '98- 5; ECp: '96-7-8-9: 3/3/1/1. Won GP 1996, 1998. GER champion 1995, 1997-2000.
Two world bests new javelin 1999.
Progression at JT: 1986- 44.38, 1987- 48.04, 1988- 52.50, 1989- 51.20, 1990- 61.06, 1991- 59.84, 1992- 55.86, 1993- 60.96, 1994- 64.24, 1995- 65.94, 1996- 66.62, 1997- 69.36, 1998- 70.10; new: 1999- 66.91, 2000- 66.73. pb SP 15.49i '97.
Set pb in last round for World bronze medal 1997 and had a splendid season in 1998 including the first 70m plus throw for three years when she threw 70.10 to win the German title in her hometown of Berlin. Warmed up but unable to compete at 1999 Worlds through injury, and also missed the 2000 Olympics.

Franka DIETZSCH b. 22 Jan 1968 Wolgast 1.83m 92kg. SC Neubrandenburg. Bank employee.
At DT: OG: '92- 12, '96- 4, '00- 6; WCh: '91- dnq 13, '93- 8, '95- 7, '97- dnq, '99- 1, '01- 5; EC: '94- 9, '98- 1; WJ: '86- 2; WUG: '89- 4; WCp: '98- 1; ECp: '97-9-01: 2/3/1; Won GP 2000, 2nd 1998. GER champion 1997-2001.
Progression at DT: 1981- 27.70, 1982- 43.80, 1983- 50.04, 1984- 51.16, 1985- 56.94, 1986- 64.34, 1987- 66.34, 1988- 65.56, 1989- 68.26, 1990- 67.42, 1991- 61.22, 1992- 64.64, 1993- 62.06, 1994- 62.76, 1995- 62.26, 1996- 66.66, 1997- 67.66, 1998- 68.91, 1999- 69.51, 2000- 68.06, 2001- 65.87A. pb SP 15.02 '85.

Heike DRECHSLER b. 16 Dec 1964 Gera 1.81m 68kg. née Daute. LG Karlsruhe.
At LJ/R- 4x100mR: OG: '88- 2 (3 100m & 200m), '92- 1, '00- 1; WCh: '83- 1, '87- 3 (2 100m), '91- 2/3R, '93- 1, '95- 9 (dnf Hep), '97-4, '01- dnq; EC: '82- 4, '86- 1 (1 200m), '90- 1 (2 200m), '94- 1, '98- 1; WI: '87- 1 (1 200m), '91- 2, '97- 7, '01- 5; EI: '83- 3, '85- 3, '86- 1, '87- 1, '88- 1, '94- 1, '00- 2; EJ: '81- 1; WCp: '85- 1, '92- 1, '98- 1; ECp: '83- 1, '85- 2, '87- 1/1R (2 4x400mR), '91- 1/2R, '93-4-5-2001: 1/1/1/1. Won GDR LJ 1981, 1983-8, 1990; 200m 1986, 1988; GER LJ 1991-2, 1994-5, 1998-2001; 100m 1992; GWG LJ 1994. Won GP LJ 1990, 1992, 2000 (2nd 1996, 3rd 1994); won overall 1992 (2nd 1990).
World records: three LJ 1985-6, two 200m 1986. WIB: LJ (6): 6.88 '83, 6.99 '84 & '85, 7.25 & 7.29 '86, 7.37 '88; 100y: 10.24 '86, 10.24 & 10.15 '87; 200m: 22.27 '87. World junior LJ records 1981 and 1982, heptathlon 1981. 8 GDR LJ records 1983-8, GER record 1992.
Progression at 100m, 200m, LJ, Hep: 1977- 13.1, 4.40; 1978- 5.69, 1979- 12.3, 6.07; 1980- 6.64/6.70w, 5780; 1981- 11.75, 24.16, 6.91/7.01w, 5812; 1982- 6.98, 1983- 7.14/7.27w, 1984- 7.40, 1985- 23.19, 7.44; 1986- 10.91/10.80w, 21.71, 7.45; 1987- 10.95, 22.18, 7.40; 1988- 10.91/10.85w, 21.84, 7.48; 1990- 11.14, 22.19, 7.30; 1991- 11.09, 22.58/22.4, 7.37/7.39w; 1992- 11.24, 7.48/7.63Aw; 1993- 11.36, 23.16, 7.21; 1994- 11.38, 22.84, 7.29/7.39Aw, 6741; 1995- 23.02i/23.04, 7.09i/7.07, 6375; 1996- 23.17i, 6.96i/ 6.75/6.87w; 1997- 11.70, 6.95i/6.89/7.02w; 1998- 11.82w, 7.16; 1999- 6.91, 2000- 6.99/7.07w, 2001- 6.79. pbs: 800m 2:11.53 '94, 100mh 13.34 '94, HJ 1.88i '92, TJ 13.94i '97, 13.35 '93; SP 13.88 '95, JT 40.64 '94.
World age records for long jump each age 15-19. The youngest gold medallist of the 1983 world championships, at LJ she had 27 successive wins until injured at the 1987 World

Champs and from 1982 to 2000 won 240 of 330 competitions. She has had more than 409 jumps and 159 competitions over 7m (her 100th came at the 1992 Olympics). Her 7.63w at the high altitude of Sestriere in 1992 was the first 25 ft long jump by a woman; the wind just over the legal limit at +2.1. Missed 1996 Olympics and 1999 Worlds through injury, but came back in triumph in 2000 to regain her Olympic title. In all she has won 32 GDR/GER LJ titles – 16 indoors (1981, 1983-4, 1986-8, 1991-5, 1997, 1999-2002) 16 out. She made a sensational breakthrough in 1986 into a great sprinter, winning the GDR indoor 100y title in 10.24, and equalling Marita Koch's world 200m record and she showed further versatility with a 50.0 400m relay leg in the 1987 European Cup. In her first heptathlon since her world junior record in 1981, she scored a marvellous 6741 points to win at Talence in 1994.
Son, Toni Drechsler, born 1 Nov 1989. Her partner and coach is French decathlete Alain Blondel.

Karin ERTL b. 23 Jun 1974 Immenstadt 1.77m 65kg. née Specht. LAC Quelle Fürth/München.
At Hep: OG: '00- 7; WCh: '99- 6, '01- 5; EC: '98- 7; EJ: '93- 2; ECp: '97- 6. German champion 1999, 2001. At Pen: WI: '01- 3; EI: '98- 3, '00- 1.
Progression at Hep: 1993- 5591, 1994- 5779, 1995- 5871, 1996- 6047, 1997- 6128, 1998- 6366, 1999- 6332, 2000- 6396, 2001- 6365. pbs: 100m 12.10 '97, 200m 23.92 '98, 800m 2:16.08 '99, 60mh 8.26i 98, 100mh 13.24 '98, HJ 1.87 '96, LJ 6.47 '98, SP 14.79i/14.34 '01, JT 45.89 '01, Pen 4678i '01.

Claudia GESELL b. 18 Dec 1977 Tirschenreuth 1.70m 58kg. Bayer Leverkusen.
At 800m: OG: '00- sf; WCh: '99- sf; WJ: '96- 1 (1R); EU23: '97- 4, '99- 1. Won GER 1998-2000.
Progression at 800m: 1993- 2:12.16, 1994- 2:18.61, 1995- 2:07.20, 1996- 2:02.67, 1997- 2:02.52, 1998- 2:01.28, 1999- 1:59.87, 2000- 1:58.34. pbs: 400m 54.37 '96, 1000m 2:37.86 '99.
Won a German Universities title at triathlon.

Nadine KLEINERT-SCHMITT b. 20 Oct 1975 Magdeburg 1.90m 90kg. née Kleinert. SC Magdeburg.
At SP: OG: '00- 8; WCh: '97- 7, '99- 2, '01- 2; EC: '98- 6; WJ: '92- 12, '94- 6; EU23: '94- 3Cp, '97- 1; EJ: '93- 2; WI: '99- 5, '01- 4; EI: '00- 2; ECp: '99- 2, '01- 1. Won GP 1999. German champion 1998, 2000-01.
Progression at SP: 1990- 13.85, 1991- 15.08, 1992- 16.32, 1993- 17.07, 1994- 17.44, 1995- 17.13, 1996- 18.37, 1997- 18.91, 1998- 19.22, 1999- 19.61, 2000- 19.81, 2001- 19.86. pb DT 50.99 '01.

Astrid KUMBERNUSS b. 5 Feb 1970 Grevesmühlen 1.86m 89kg. SC Neubrandenburg.
At SP (DT): OG: '96- 1, '00- 3; WCh: '93- 6, '95- 1, '97- 1, '99- 1, '01- 6; EC: '90- 1, '94- 2; WI: '97- 2; EI: '92- 3, '94- 1, '96- 1, '00- 3; WJ: '88- (2); EJ: '87- (2), '89- 1 (1); WCp: '94- 3; ECp: '91-4-5-6-7-00: 2/1/1/1/1/1. Won GP 1995, 1997 (and Overall), 2001; 2nd 1993, 1999; 3rd 1991. Won GER SP 1995-7, 1999.
World junior shot record 1989.
Progression at SP, DT: 1983- 11.16, 33.48; 1984- 13.44/14.01i, 44.00; 1985- 14.23, 46.96; 1986- 15.39, 53.92; 1987- 18.20, 63.88; 1988- 18.73, 66.60; 1989- 20.54, 64.74; 1990- 20.77, 65.42; 1991- 19.67, 60.88; 1992- 20.03i/19.69, 1993- 19.92, 59.64; 1994- 20.06, 1995- 21.22, 59.90; 1996- 20.97, 1997- 21.22, 1999- 19.85, 2000- 20.23, 2001- 19.87.
Unbeaten in 51 competitions 1995-6. In 1995 she had eight GP wins prior to the final, and won the world title by 1.18m, the largest ever margin of victory at World/Olympic level. She had knee surgery in November 1997 and missed the 1998 season; her son Philipp was born on 7 July 1998. Returned to take third world title in 1999.

Irina MIKITENKO b. 23 Aug 1972 Bakankas, Kazahstan 1.58m 49kg. née Volynskaya. LG Eintracht Frankfurt.
At 5000m: OG: '96- h, '00- 5; WCh: '99- 4, '01- 5; ECp: '99-00: 2/2. At 10000m: EC: '98- 8; WCp: '98- 5. 3rd GP 3000m 1999. World 4k CC: '00- 19. Won Central Asian 1500m 1995; German 10000m 1998, 5000m 1999-2000.
German records 3000m 2000, 5000m (3) 1999.
Progression at 5000m, 10000m: 1995- 15:47.85, 1996- 15:49.59, 1997- 15:48.29, 1998- 15:18.86, 32:10.61; 1999- 14:42.03, 31:38.68; 2000- 14:43.59; 2001- 14:53.00, 31:29.55. pbs: 800m 2:09.97 '98, 1500m 4:06.08 '01, 2000m 5:40.6 '01, 3000m 8:30.39 '00
German parents; changed nationality from Kazakhstan to Germany in March 1998. Son Alexander.

Anja MÖLLENBECK b. 18 Mar 1972 Frankenberg 1.84m 86kg. née Gündler. TV Wattenscheid. Detective.
At DT: OG: '96- 11; WCh: '93- 5, '99- 12, '01- 9; EC: '98- 10; WJ: '90- 3; EJ: '91- 1 (SP- 1); WUG: '93- 3, '95- 2; ECp: '98- 2; E23Cp: '92- 2, '94- 3. German champion 1993.
Progression at DT: 1986- 40.04, 1987- 48.68, 1988- 53.96, 1989- 55.42, 1990- 59.52, 1991- 60.66, 1992- 60.34, 1993- 62.92, 1994- 61.20, 1995- 60.78, 1996- 63.80, 1997- 61.00, 1998- 64.63, 1999- 63.63, 2000- 62.63, 2001- 63.42. pb SP 17.44 '90.
Married Michael Möllenbeck (qv) in 1996.

Kirsten MÜNCHOW b. 21 Jan 1977 Auetal-Rehren 1.72m 75kg. LG Eintracht München. Designer.
At HT: OG: '00- 3; WCh: '99- 8, '01-9; EC: '98- 3; EU23: '97- 5, '99- 2; ECp: '98-9-00-01: 2/5/2/2. German champion 2000-01.
Four German hammer records 1998-2000.
Progression at HT: 1992- 42.48, 1994- 50.96, 1995- 57.62, 1996- 59.40, 1997- 63.06, 1998- 66.82, 1999- 66.08, 2000- 69.28, 2001- 68.09. pbs: SP 12.65 '98, DT 37.88 '96.

Steffi NERIUS b. 1 Jul 1972 Bergen/Rügen 1.78m 72kg. Bayer Leverkusen. PE teacher.
At JT: OG: '96- 9, '00- 4; WCh: '93- 9, '95- 11, '99- dnq 16, '01- 5; EC: '98- 6; EJ: '91- 3; WUG: '97- 5; WCp: '92- 6; ECp: '95- 1, '01- 2. 2nd GP 1996. German champion 2001.
Progression at JT: 1985- 30.12, 1987- 45.16, 1988- 48.00, 1989- 56.88, 1990- 56.14, 1991- 60.02, 1992- 59.46, 1993- 63.88, 1995- 68.42, 1996- 69.42, 1997- 64.58, 1998- 67.33; new: 1999- 61.56. 2000- 65.76, 2001- 63.72.

Sonja OBEREM b. 24 Feb 1973 Rheydt 1.71m 49kg. née Krolik. Beyer Leverkusen.
At Mar: OG: '96- 8, '00- 24; WCh: '95- 8, '97- 7, '99- 6, '01- 5; EC: '98- 12. Won GER 10000m 1997, HMar 1998.
Progression at Mar: 1993- 2:38:02, 1994- 2:31:35, 1995- 2:32:17sh, 1996- 2:29:24, 1997- 2:28:02, 1998- 2:29:30, 1999- 2:28:55, 2000- 2:27:25, 2001- 2:26:13. pbs: 5000m 16:08.37 '95, 10000m 32:39.50 '97, HMar 70:13 '96.
At triathlon was World Junior champion 1990 and 1992 and European champion at Olympic (short) distance 1992 and 1994. Her first marathon wins came in 2001 in her 16th and 18th races at the distance: Hamburg and Athens. In between she completed a remarkable sequence of 8-7-6-5 in World Champs marathons. 4th Boston 1996, London 1997; 2nd Amsterdam 1998.

GHANA

Governing body: Ghana Amateur Athletic Association, National Sports Council, PO Box 1272, Accra. Founded 1944.

Abdul **Aziz ZAKARI** b. 2 Sep 1976 1.78m 73kg.
At 100m(/200m): OG: '00- dnf; WCh: '97- qf, '01- 8; CG: '98- sf/sf; AfCh: '98- (4), '00-1/1/1R.
Progression at 100m, 200m: 1995- 10.4, 21.36/21.0; 1996- 10.30, 20.90; 1997- 10.26, 20.88; 1998- 10.29, 20.62; 1999- 10.35/10.08w, 20.84; 2000- 10.06, 20.23; 2001- 10.04, 20.27.

GREECE

Governing body: Hellenic Amateur Athletic Association (SEGAS), 137 Siggroú Avenue, 171 21 Nea Smirni, Athens. Founded 1897.
National Championships first held in 1896 (men), 1930 (women). **2001 Champions**: **Men**: 100m: Konstadínos Kedéris 10.21, 200m: Prodromos Katsantonis CYP 20.82, 400m: Anastásios Goúsis 46.59, 800m: Panayiótis Stroubákos 1:50.11, 1500m: Pávlos Faroúggias 3:46.32, 5000m: Anastásios Frággos 14:04.39, 10000m:Hrístos Zarkádas 29:54.6, Mar: Nikólaos Poliás 2:23:58, 3000mSt: Yeógyios-Vasílios Koboyiánnis 8:50.87, 110mh: Dimítrios Piétris 13.92, 400mh: Periklís Iakovákis 49.76, HJ: Dimítrios Sirrákos 2.21, PV: Mários Evaggélou 5.30, LJ: Konstadínos Koukodímos 7.74, TJ: Hrístos Melétoglou 16.71, SP: Váios Tíggas 18.74, DT: Sávvas Panávoglou 60.54, HT: Hrístos Polihroníou 77.69, JT: Konstadínos Gatsioúdis 88.61, Dec: Pávlos Kouromihalákis 7410, 20kmW: Theódoros Stamatópoulos 1:25:10, 50kmW: Spirídon Kastánis 3:59:43. **Women**: 100m: Ekateríni Thánou 11.09, 200m: Olga Kaidantzí 23.36, 400m: Hristiána Panágou 53.34, 800m: Anastasía Miloná 2:09.47, 1500m: Karolína Skoúrti 4:15.55, 5000m: Hrisistomía Iakóvou 15:33.03, 10000m: Spiridoúla Soúma 34:17.88, Mar: Yeorgía Abatzídou 2:48:37, 3000mSt: Konstadína Efedáki 10:34.69, 100mh: Flóra Redoúmi 13.26, 400mh: Eléni Kaloyírou 57.58, HJ: Agni Charalambous CYP 1.84, PV: Yeoryía Tsiliggíri 4.36, LJ: Stilianí Pilátou 6.46, TJ: Ioánna Kafetzí 13.65, SP: Kalliópi Ouzoúni 17.38, DT: Ekateríni Vóggoli 63.47, HT: Alexeandra Papayeoryíou 61.80, JT: Miréla Tzelíli 66.70, Hep: Asimína Vanakára 5643, 20kmW: Athiná Papayiánni 1:34:30.

Konstadínos **'Kostas' GATSIOUDIS** b. 17 Dec 1973 Didimótiho 1.89m 95kg. Panellínios GS (Athens). Officer of the Fire Brigade.
At JT: OG: '96- 10, '00- 6; WCh: '93- dnq 17, '97- 3, '99- 2, '01- 3; EC: '94- dnq 14; WJ: '90- 6, '92- 3; EJ: '91- 9; ECp: '97-9-00-01: 2/3/2/1; E23Cp: '94- 1. Won GP 1999 (2nd overall), Greek champion 1992-4, 1999-2001; Balkan 1992, MedG 1997.
Eleven Greek javelin records 1992-2000. World junior record 1992.
Progression at JT: 1990- 70.20, 1991- 72.58, 1992- 80.30, 1993- 78.44, 1994- 83.82, 1995- 82.70, 1996- 87.12, 1997- 89.22, 1998- 88.13, 1999- 89.84, 2000- 91.69, 2001- 91.27.
Threw Greek record 87.12 in qualifying at 1996 Olympics, but only 81.46 in the final. Over 84m in all 49 competitions in 1999-2001.

Konstadínos **'Kostas' KEDÉRIS** b. 11 Jun 1973 Mitilíni 1.80m 78kg. Olympiakós SF Piraeus. Air Force officer. PE Graduate of Thessaloníki University.
At 200m: OG: '00- 1; WCh: '99- qf, '01- 1; WJ: '92- 6; EI: '00- 5; ECp: '00- 3, '01- 1 (2 100m). At 400m: EC: '98- sf; EJ: '91- 4; ECp: '99- 3. Won MedG 400m 1993, Greek champion 100m 2001, 200m 1999, 400m 1991-3, 1998.
Greek records 200m (4) 2000-01, 400m 1993, 1998.
Progression at 200m: 1991- 21.63, 1992- 21.05, 1993- 20.76, 1994- 20.93i, 1995- 20.89, 1996- 21.17, 1997- 20.83/20.64w, 1999- 20.50, 2000- 20.09, 2001- 20.03. pbs: 100m 10.15 '01, 300m 32,99i '99, 400m 45.60 '98.
Started 2000 by running a Greek record of 20.25 for 200m and became the most surprising gold medallist of the Olympic Games in Sydney, where he improved to 20.14 and 20.09. From early on he was considered a rare talent with big potential in both 200m/400m. However a series of injuries from the 1994 indoor season held him back. In March 2000 he decided to leave Thessaloníki due to its poor training facilities, relocate to Athens and concentrate on 200m.

Aléxandros PAPADIMITRÍOU b. 18 Jun 1973

Lárisa 1.83m 123kg, G.S. Iraklís Thessaloníki. MSc in kinesiology at UTEP, Texas, USA.
At HT: OG: '96- dnq 16; '00- 12; WCh: '97-9-01- dnq 19/27/16 ; WJ: '92- 6; EC: '98- dnq 27; EJ: '91- 7; ECp: '97-00: 3/2; E23Cp: '94- 2. Greek champion 1994-7, 2000; Balkan 1997, 2000-01.
Three Greek hammer records 1996-2000.
Progression at HT: 1990- 61.72, 1991- 65.82, 1992- 69.48, 1993- 70.74, 1994- 73.74, 1995- 74.80, 1996- 77.84, 1997- 76.72, 1998- 77.60, 1999- 78.88, 2000- 80.45, 2001- 79.52.

Hrístos POLÍHRONÍOU b. 31 Mar 1972 Athína 1.86m 107kg. Olympiakós SF Piraeus. Harbour guard officer. Studied PE at Athens University.
At HT: OG: '96- dnq, '00- dnq 24; WCh: '95/97- dnq, '99- 6, '01- dnq 26; EC: '98- 6; WJ: '90- 9; EJ: '91- 5; WUG: '99- 2; ECp: '99- 1, '01- 3. Greek champion 1998-9, 2001.
Five Greek hammer records 1995-9.
Progression at HT: 1989- 60.00, 1990- 63.52, 1991- 67.74, 1992- 67.50, 1993- 73.16, 1994- 73.04, 1995- 76.68, 1996- 77.36, 1997- 75.58, 1998- 78.92, 1999- 79.83, 2000- 79.57, 2001- 78.34.

Women

Anastasía KELESÍDOU b. 28 Nov 1972 Hamburg, Germany 1.92m 91kg. GS Iraklís Thessaloníki. Navy Officer. PE graduate of Thessaloniki University.
At DT: OG: '96- dnq 18, '00- 2; WCh: '95- 11, '97- dnq 15, '99- 2, '01- 4; EC: '94- dnq 22, '98- 7; EU23: '94- 2; EJ: '91- 11; ECp: '00- 3. Won MedG 1997, Balkan 2001, Greek 1991, 1993-7, 1999-2000.
Eight Greek discus records 1994-9.
Progression at DT: 1987- 41.82, 1988- 45.00, 1989- 48.36/49.74u, 1990- 47.90, 1991- 50.90, 1992- 54.34, 1993- 57.44, 1994- 60.50, 1995- 60.92, 1996- 62.76, 1997- 66.18, 1998- 66.18, 1999- 67.70, 2000- 67.12, 2001- 65.52. pb SP 12.68 '92.

Miréla MANJANI (formelry **TZELILI**) b. 21 Dec 1976 Dirráhio (Durrás), Albania 1.65m 65kg, Olympiakós SF Piraeus. Navy Officer.
At JT: OG: '96- dnq 24, '00- 2; WCh: '95- 12, '97- 11, '99- 1, '01- 2; EC: '94- dnq 22, 98- 9; WJ: '94- 8; EJ: '95- 2; ECp: '00- 3. Greek champion 1999, 2001; Balkan 1994, 1997.
Two World records (64.99 and 67.09) new javelin 1999. Six Greek records 1999-2000.
Progression at JT: 1993- 54.86, 1994- 57.20, 1995- 62.40, 1996- 62.46, 1997- 63.50, 1998- 65.14, 1999- 67.09, 2000- 67.51, 2001- 66.70.
Switched from Albania to become Greek citizen in 1997. Married to weightlifter Yeóryios Tzelílis (4th 1996 Olympics 64kg, 2nd 1999 Worlds 69kg) from November 1996 until late 2001.

Ekateríni **'Katerina' THÁNOU** b. 1 Feb 1975 Athína 1.65m 61kg. Olympiakós SF Piraeus. Air Force Officer. Was at University of Athens.
At 100m: OG: '96- qf, '00- 2; WCh: '95- sf, '97- sf, '99- 3, '01- 3; EC: '94- qf, '98- 3; WJ: '94- 4; WUG: '95- 2, '97- 1. At 60m: WI: '99- 1; EI: '96- 1, '98- 4, '00- 1. Won GRE 100m 1995, 2000-01; MedG 100m 1997.
Seven Greek 100m records 1995-9.
Progression at 100m: 1993- 12.09/12.07w, 1994- 11.43, 1995- 11.09, 1996- 11.28, 1997- 11.13, 1998- 10.87/10.8w, 1999- 10.83/10.77w, 2000- 10.91/ 10.84w, 2001- 10.91. pbs: 50m 6.01+ '99, 60m 6.96i/6.96+ '99, 200m 24.46/23.93w '94.
Brilliant run to win 1999 World Indoor 60m; Greek records in semi and final 1998 Europeans and in quarter and semi at 1999 Worlds.

Paraskeví TSIAMÍTA b. 10 Mar 1972 Vólos 1.71m 60kg. Panellínios GS (Athens). Air Force officer. PE graduate of Athens University.
At TJ: WCh: '99- 1; EC: '98- 9; WI: '99- 5; EU23: '94- 3. 2nd GP 1999. At LJ: EJ: '87- dnq. Won Greek LJ 1998, TJ 1999.
Three Greek triple jump records 1999.
Progression at TJ: 1994- 13.17, 1995- 13.27, 1998- 14.23, 1999- 15.07, 2001- 14.06. pb LJ 6.93 '99.
Jumped 5.34 LJ at age 12 in 1984 and 6.00/6.07w in 1987 at 15. Out of action 1992-3 and 1996-7 due to injuries, studies and lack of motivation, but remained fit by working as aerobics teacher. Triple jumped 13.07i in her comeback competition in 1998, adding 2m with her world-leading mark of 1999. Suffered from a stress fracture in 2000.

Stilianí **'Stella' TSIKOÚNA** b. 19 Oct 1972 Halkída 1.71m 88kg. ASE Doúka (Athens). Navy officer. Was at University of Texas, El Paso, USA. PE student at Athens University.
At DT: OG: '96- dnq 31, '00- 5; WCh: '95- dnq 29, '97- 7, '99- 8, '01- dnq 13; EC: '98- 12. Greek champion 1992, Balkan 2000.
Two Greek records 1992.
Progression at DT: 1987- 41.84, 1988- 44.18, 1989- 43.90, 1990- 45.38, 1991- 52.10, 1992- 56.48, 1993- 55.48, 1994- 56.98, 1995- 61.02, 1996- 61.30A, 1997- 63.30, 1998- 65.00, 1999- 64.16, 2000- 65.13, 2001- 63.18. pb SP 14.78i '95, 14.66 '01.

Ólga-Anastasia VASDÉKI b. 26 Sep 1973 Vólos 1.74m 59kg. Panellínios GS (Athens). Harbour guard officer. PE graduate of Athens University
At TJ: OG: '96- 5, '00- 7; WCh: '97- 4, '99- 3; EC: '98- 1; EI: '96- 3, '98- 4; WCp: '98- 1. Won GRE 1993, 1995-6, 1998; MedG 1997.
Eleven Greek triple jump records 1993-8.
Progression at TJ: 1992- 12.77, 1993- 13.37, 1994- 13.25i, 1995- 13.45/13.73w, 1996- 14.48/14.51w, 1997- 14.62, 1998- 14.64A/14.59, 1999- 14.67, 2000- 14.26. pb LJ 6.60 '98, 6.66w '99.
Huge improvement in 1996. Her brother Spirídon Vasdékis (b. 23 Jan 1970) had LJ best of 8.19 '95 and 8.29Aw '96, 3 EI '96, 8 WI '97, 16 OG '92, 14 OG '96.

Ekateríni **'Katerina' VÓGGOLI** b. 30 Oct 1970 Lárisa 1.75m 87kg. Olympiakós SF Piraeus. PE graduate of Thessaloniki University.
At DT: OG: '96- dnq 22, '00- 9; WCh: '99- 11, '01- dnq 14; EC: '98- 5; WJ: '88- 10. Greek champion

1989-90, 1998, 2001; Balkan 1994.
Four Greek discus records 1992-4.
Progression at DT: 1985- 39.84, 1986- 46.10, 1987- 46.74, 1988- 51.18, 1989- 51.96, 1990- 51.94, 1991- 53.24, 1992- 57.86, 1993- 59.70, 1994- 62.32, 1996- 60.34, 1997- 61.24, 1998- 64.78, 1999- 64.82, 2000- 64.35, 2001- 63.47. pb SP 13.53 '00.

Níki XÁNTHOU b. 11 Oct 1973 Rhodos 1.74m 56kg. Olympiakós SF Piraeus. Harbour guard officer.
At LJ: OG: '96- 4, '00- dnq 18; WCh: '95- dnq 15, '97- 2, '99- dnq 26, '01- 6; EC: '94- 10; WJ: '92- 8, WI: '95- 9, '97- 5, '99- 4; EI: '98-00-02- 5/8/1; EU23: '94- 1. Greek champion 1992, 1995, 1997, 1999; MedG 1997.
Nine Greek long jump records 1994-7.
Progression at LJ: 1987- 5.32, 1988- 5.42, 1989- 5.60/5.73w, 1990- 5.96, 1991- 5.90/5.99w, 1992- 6.60, 1993- 6.09, 1994- 6.74, 1995- 6.94/7.12Aw, 1996- 7.01, 1997- 7.03, 1998- 6.83/6.84w, 1999- 6.98/7.01w, 2000- 6.81, 2001- 6.80.
Married to her coach Dimítrios Hatzópoulos (pb LJ 8.07 '94, 8.08w '89).

HAITI

Governing body: Fédération Haitienne d'Athlétisme Amateur, BP 2405, Port-au-Prince. Founded 1969.

Dudley DORIVAL b. 1 Sep 1975 Elizabeth, New Jersey, USA 1.85m 77kg. Sales consultant, studied sociology at University of Connecticut,
At 110mh: OG: '00- 7; WCh: '99- sf, '01- 3; WJ: '94- 2; WUG: '97- 3. At 60mh: WI: '01- 7.
Six Haitian 110mh records from three at 13.42 in 1999 to 2001.
Progression at 110mh: 1994- 13.79/13.65w, 1995- 13.53A, 1996- 13.60/13.59w, 1997- 13.48, 1998- 13.30, 1999- 13.38/13.29w, 2000- 13.33, 2001- 13.25. pbs: 200m 20.64w '98, 50mh 6.50i '01, 55mh 7.16i '96, 60mh 7.55i '01.
Switched from USA to take up Haitian nationality (his parents are from Haiti) from July 1999. At the 2001 Worlds he won Haiti's first global medal since Silvio Cator won the Olympic long jump in 1928.

HUNGARY

Governing body: Magyar Atlétikai Szövetség, 1143 Budapest, Dózsa György utca 1-3. Founded 1897.
National Championships first held in 1896 (men), 1932 (women). **2001 Champions**. **Men**: 100m: Viktor Kovács 10.64, 200m/400m: Zsolt Szeglet 21.13/46.08, 800m: István Kerékjártó 1:52.22, 1500m/5000m: Balázs Csillag 3:47.12/ 14:07.42, 10000m: Miklós Zatykó 29:27.76, HMar: Zsolt Benedek 62:28sh, Mar: Antal Szücs 2:20:16, 3000mSt: Máté Németh 9:05.61, 110mh: Levente Csillag 13.86, 400mh: Dusán Kovács 50.07, HJ: Román Fehér 2.13, PV: Deszö Szabó 4.90, LJ: Tamás Margl 7.54, TJ: Péter Tölgyesi 15.51, SP: Szilárd Kiss 19.37, DT: Zoltán Kövágó 64.84, HT: Tibor Gécsek 81.68, JT: Gergely Horváth 80.80, Dec Tamás Polonyi 7349, 20kmW/50kmW: Sándor Urbanik 1:22:35/3:48:41. **Women**: 100m: Krisztina Lórincz 11.95, 200m: Barbara Petráhn 23.73, 400m: Alice Kun 53.04, 800m: Judit Varga 2:08.50, 1500m: Lívia Tóth 4:27.65, 5000m/ 10000m/HMar: Simona Staicu 15:54.68/32:36.88/ 68:36sh, Mar: Judit Földing-Nagy 2:39:04, 100mh: Edit Vári 14.06, 400mh: Orsolya Dóczi 59.52 HJ: Dóra Györffy 2.00, PV: Krisztina Molnár 4.20, LJ: Tünde Vaszi 6.65, TJ/Hep: Zita Ajkler 13.26/5323, SP/DT: Eva Kürti 15.24/54.74, HT: Barbara Sugár 59.94, JT: Nikolett Szabó 57.82, 10kmW/20kmW: Mária Urbanik 46:37/1:37:56.

Adrián ANNUS b. 28 Jun 1973 Szeged 1.94m 102kg. Haladás VSE.
At HT: OG: '96- dnq 28, '00- dnq 17; WCh: '01- 9; EC: '98- 8; WJ: '92- 11; WUG: '01- 3. Hungarian champion 1996.
Progression at HT: 1990- 50.80, 1991- 57.42, 1992- 68.50, 1993- 69.26, 1994- 72.56, 1995- 74.68, 1996- 76.48, 1997- 76.62, 1998- 81.22, 1999- 81.73, 2000- 78.15, 2001- 83.39. pbs: SP 16.87 '99, DT 50.16 '95.

Róbert FAZEKAS b. 18 Aug 1975 Szombathely 1.93m 105kg. Haladás VSE.
At DT: OG: '00- dnq 16; WCh: '99- 11, '01- dnq 26; EC: '98- 4; EU23: '97- 6; WJ: '94- 6 (dnq 18 HT). HUN champion 1998, 2000.
Progression at DT: 1992- 40.08, 1993- 53.48, 1994- 58.00, 1995- 60.34, 1996- 55.08, 1997- 59.32, 1998- 66.61, 1999- 64.92, 2000- 66.11, 2001- 68.09. pb HT 75.33 '98.

Tibor GÉCSEK b. 22 Sep 1964 Szentgotthárd 1.85m 107kg. Dobó SE. Entrepreneur, formerly diesel engine mechanic.
At HT: OG: '88- 6, '92- 4, '00- 7; WCh: '87- 7, '91- 4, '93- 3, '95- 3, '99- 4, '01- 8; EC: '90- 2, '94- 5, '98- 1; EJ: '83- 6; WCp: 92- 1, '98- 1; ECp: '91- 2. Won HUN 1986-94, 1999, 2001. Won GP 1988, 1998 (2nd 1990).
Six Hungarian hammer records 1987-98.
Progression at HT: 1980- 34.26, 1981- 50.62, 1982- 60.60, 1983- 67.90, 1984- 73.66, 1985- 77.62, 1986- 77.66, 1987- 79.14, 1988- 81.68, 1989- 77.30, 1990- 80.92, 1991- 80.72, 1992- 81.02, 1993- 81.00, 1994- 80.22, 1995- 80.98, 1996- 74.18dq, 1997- 77.00, 1998- 83.68, 1999- 82.57, 2000- 81.92, 2001- 81.76. pbs: SP 14.65 '85, DT 48.72 '85.
Positive drugs test at Berlin on 30 Aug 1995 was originally overturned by the Hungarian federation, but confirmed as four-year ban in 1996. He returned, however, to competition in September 1997 with the reduction by the IAAF of such suspensions to two years. In 1998 he smashed his 10-year-old pb to win the European title, went on to win the Grand Prix Final and World Cup and add two national records to the four he had set in 1987-8.

Balázs KISS b. 21 Mar 1972 Veszprém 1.92m 115kg. VEDAC. Was at University of Southern California, USA.
At HT: OG: '96- 1; WCh: '95- 4, '97- 4, '99- dnq 20, '01- 6; EC: '94- 12, '98- 2; WUG: '93- 2, '95- 1, '97- 1; EJ: '91- 3. 2nd GP 1998, HUN champion 1995, 1998, 2000; NCAA 1993-6 (5th 4-time winner). Five Hungarian hammer records 1995-8.
Progression at HT: 1988- 56.24, 1989- 61.24, 1990- 62.82, 1991- 70.66, 1993- 77.18, 1994- 77.74, 1995- 82.56, 1996- 81.76, 1997- 82.90, 1998- 83.00, 1999- 80.87, 2000- 79.22, 2001- 81.36. pb DT 39.72 '91.

Zoltán KÖVAGÓ b. 10 Apr 1979 Szolnok 2.04m 127kg. Debreceni AK.
At DT: OG: '00- dnq; WCh: '01- dnq 20; WJ: '96- 4, '98- 1; EJ: '97- 3; EU23: '99- 6, '01- 1. HUN champion 2001.
Progression at DT: 1995- 49.78, 1996- 59.70, 1997- 62.16, 1998- 60.27, 1999- 63.23, 2000- 66.76, 2001- 66.93. pb SP 15.93 '01.

Zsolt NÉMETH b.9 Nov 1971 Szombathely 1.90m 110kg. Dobó SE.
At HT: OG: '96- dnq 22, '00- dnq 25; WCh: '97- dnq 26, '99- 2; WJ: '90- 6; WUG: '99- 1. HUN champion 1997.
Progression at HT: 1986- 41.00, 1987- 51.02, 1988- 56.60, 1989- 61.60, 1990- 67.66, 1991- 68.32, 1992- 71.14, 1993- 68.88, 1994- 73.14, 1995- 75.22, 1996- 77.48, 1997- 76.04, 1998- 80.19, 1999- 81.56, 2000- 80.02, 2001- 77.87. pbs: SP 18.51 '00, DT 54.33 '98.

Roland VARGA b. 22 Oct 1977 1.97m 102kg. Újpesti TE.
At DT: WCh: '01- 7; WJ: '96- 2; EU23: '99- 2; WUG: '01- 4.
Progression at DT: 1993- 43.60, 1994- 48.18, 1995- 52.88, 1996- 55.20, 1997- 58.70, 1998- 60.33, 1999- 62.78, 2000- 65.39, 2001- 65.86. pb SP 16.23 '01.

Attila ZSIVOCZKY b. 29 Apr 1977 Budapest 1.93m 82kg. Debreceni AK. Was at Kansas State University, USA.
At Dec: OG: '00- 8; WCh: '99- 10, '01- 4; EC: '98- 16; WJ: '96- 1; EU23: '97- 4, '99- 1; ECp: '98-9-01: 5/5/2. At Hep: EI: '00- 4, '02- 5.
Progression at Dec: 1995- 7242, 1996- 7582, 1997- 7804, 1998- 8103, 1999- 8379, 2000- 8554, 2001- 8371. pbs: 60m 7.11i '00, 100m 10.97 '01, 10.64w '00; 400m 47.93 '00, 1500m 4:20.94 '99, 60mh 8.49i '00, 110mh 14.86 '01, 14.81w '01; HJ 2.23i '98, 2.22 '94; PV 4.91i '02, 4.90 '01; LJ 7.31 '99, SP 15.72 '00, DT 47.43 '00, JT 65.87 '00, Hep 6033i '00.

Women

Dóra GYÖRFFY b. 23 Feb 1978 Budapest 1.76m 58kg. BEAC. Student at Harvard University, USA.
At HJ: OG: '00- 18=; WCh: '01- 7=; EC: '98- dnq 19; WJ: '94- 7=, '96- 2; EJ: '95- 5=, '97- 5; EU23: '99- 5; WI: '01- 5=; EI: '02- 2=. HUN champion 1998-2001.
Two Hungarian high jump records 2001.
Progression at HJ: 1991- 1.69, 1992- 1.76, 1993- 1.71, 1994- 1.84, 1995- 1.87, 1996- 1.92, 1997- 1.93, 1998- 1.92, 1999- 1.94, 2000- 1.97i/1.95, 2001- 2.00. pbs: LJ 5.88 '95, TJ 13.05 '01.

Nikolett SZABÓ b. 3 Mar 1980 Budapest 1.68m 65kg. FTC.
At JT: OG: '00- dnq 14; WCh: '97- dnq 19, '01- dnq 14; EC: '98- 8; WJ; '96- 2, '98- 4; EU23: '01- 1; EJ: '95- 7, '97- 1, '99- 1. HUN champion 1997-2001. Three Hungarian records new javelin 1999-2001.
Progression at JT: 1993- 45.28, 1994- 49.78, 1995- 55.32, 1996- 58.88, 1997- 61.76, 1998- 65.10; new: 1999- 61.79, 2000- 61.23, 2001- 64.62. pbs: SP 12.92 '95, DT 36.43 '98.

Katalin SZENTGYÖRGYI b. 1 Jan 1979 Szeged 1.66m 48kg Szeged Nyíregyházi VSC
At 5000m (3000m): WCh: '99- 14; WJ: '96- 13 (dnq); EJ: '95- (8), '97- 1; EU23: '99- 1, '01- 1. Eur CC: '98- 1J, '00- 1. Won Hungarian 5000m 1999. Hungarian records: 3000m 2001, 5000m 1999.
Progression at 5000m, 10000m: 1996- 16:35.32, 35:56.92; 1997- 16:10.15, 1999- 15:18.80, 2001- 15:40.55, 32:27.69. pbs: 800m 2:10.26 '94, 1500m 4:11.18 '99, 3000m 8:32.70 '01.
Missed 2000 outdoor season due to stress fracture of the right foot.

Tünde VASZI b. 18 Apr 1972 Piskolt, Romania 1.70m 60kg. Honvéd-Steffl.
At LJ: OG: '96- 8, '00- 8; WCh: '95/97/99- dnq, '01- 4; EC: '98- 4; WI: '97- 9, '99- 5; EI: '00- 5; WCp: '98- 5. Won HUN 100m 1999, LJ 1996-9, 2001; TJ 1995.
Hungarian long jump record 2001.
Progression at LJ: 1990- 5.80, 1991- 6.05, 1992- 6.22, 1993- 5.81/6.04w, 1994- 6.43/6.46w, 1995- 6.58, 1996- 6.73/6.82Aw, 1997- 6.76/6.78w, 1998- 6.77/6.82w, 1999- 6.82i/6.66, 2000- 6.70, 2001- 6.86. pbs: 100m 11.50 '96, 200m 24.11 '96, 100mh 13.84 95, HJ 1.63 '96, PV 4.30i '02, 4.15 '99; TJ 13.39i '97, 13.38 '95.

ICELAND

Governing body: Frjálsíthróttasamband Islands, Sport Centre Laugardalur, Engjavegur 6, 104 Reykjavik. Founded 1947. **National Championships** first held in 1927. **2001 Champions: Men**: 100m: Sveinn Þórainsson 11.53, 200m/HJ: Bjarni Þór Traustason 22.16/1.90, 400m: Björgvin Víkingsson 49.83, 800m: Björn Margeirsson 1:54.14, 1500m/5000m/3000mSt: Sveinn Margeirsson 4:07.59/14:58.94/9:25.65, 110mh/PV/LJ/SP: Jón Arnar Magnússon 15.06/4.60/6.90/15.08, 400mh: Unnstein Grétarsson 52.40, TJ: Sigtryggur Adalbjörnsson 14.37, DT: Eggert Bogason 51.24, HT: Gudmundur Karlsson 60.05, JT: Jón Ásgrímsson 62.21. **Women**: 100m/200m/400m: Silja Úlfarsdóttir 12.84/24.47/57.97, 800m/1500m: Birna Björnsdóttir 2:15.54/4:46.63, 3000m: Rakel Ingólfsdóttir 10:54.54, 100mh: Sólveig Hildur Björnsdóttir 14.83, 400mh: Ylfa Jónsdóttir 66.82,

HJ: Ágústa Tryggvadóttir 1.60, PV: Thórey Elísdóttir 4.00, LJ: Sigurbjörg Ólafsdóttir 5.42, TJ: Sigrídur Anna Gudjónsdóttir 11.90, SP: Audur Adalbjarnardóttir 12.82, DT: Halla Heimisdóttir 42.50, HT: Gudleif Hardardóttir 45.81, JT: Vigdís Gudjónsdóttir 49.50.

Jón Arnar MAGNUSSON b. 28 Jul 1969 Selfoss 1.83m 87kg. Teacher.
At Dec: OG: '96- 12, '00- dnf; WCh: '95/97/99/01- dnf; EC: '98- 4; WJ: '87- dnf. At Hep: WI: '97- 3, '99- 5, '01- 2; EI: '96-8-02: 3/5/4. Won ISL 100m 1994-5, 2000; 200m 1998-2000, 110mh 1994, 1998-2001; PV 1998-9, 2001; LJ 1995, 1999-2001; SP 2001, Dec 1992.
Icelandic records: 100m 1997, 110mh 1994-7, LJ 1994, decathlon 1994-8.
Progression at Dec: 1987- 6232, 1988- 6975, 1989- 7351, 1992- 7570, 1994- 7896, 1995- 8248, 1996- 8274, 1997- 8470, 1998- 8583w/8573, 1999- 6813, 2000- 8206, 2001- 7938. pbs: 60m 6.85i/6.6i '97, 100m 10.56 '97, 10.2w '95; 200m 21.17 '96, 300m 33.86 '94, 400m 46.49 '98, 1500m 4:32.23 '98, 50mh 6.76i '00, 60mh 7.98i '00, 7.8 '97; 110mh 13.91 '97, HJ 2.07 '98, PV 5.20 '98, LJ 8.00 '94, 8.01w '00; SP 16.61 '98, DT 51.30 '96, HT 40.02 '97, JT 64.16 '98, Hep 6293i '99.
Missed 1993 season due to a broken leg.

Women

Thórey Edda ELISDOTTIR b. 30 Jun 1977 1.81m 64kg. Was at University of Georgia, USA.
At PV: OG: '00- dnq 22=; WCh: '99- 13, '01- 6; EC: '98- dnq 22; EU23: '97- 9, '99- 5. ISL champion 2001.
Progression at PV: 1997- 3,80, 1998- 4.21, 1999- 4.37i/4.22, 2000- 4.30, 2001- 4.51i/4.45.

Vala FLOSADOTTIR b. 16 Feb 1978 Reykjavik 1.80m 67kg. Reykjavik and Malmö, Sweden.
At PV: OG: '00- 3; WCh: '99- 12, '01- dnq 22; EC: '98- 9; WI: '97- 8, '99- 2; EI: '96- 1, '98- 3, '00- 4; EJ: '97- 2. ISL champion 1998-2000.
Two world and three European indoor pole vault records 1998, five world junior indoor records 1995-7, European junior record 1996.
Progression at PV: 1994- 3.40, 1995- 3.81, 1996- 4.17, 1997- 4.20i/4.10, 1998- 4.44i/4.36, 1999- 4.45i/4.30, 2000- 4.50, 2001- 4.22. pbs: HJ 1.82 '96, Hep 4911 '96. Has lived in Malmö, Sweden since 1992.

INDIA

Governing body: Amateur Athletic Federation of India, Room No.1148, Gate No 28, East Block, Jawaharlal Nehru Stadium, Lodi Complex, New Delhi 110003. Founded 1946.
National Championships first held as Indian Games in 1924. **2001 National (Inter-State) Champions: Men**: 100m/200m: Anil Kumar 10.37/21.20, 400m: K J Manoj Lal 46.46, 800m: K M Binu 1:47.80, 1500m: T M Sanjeev 3:51.73, 5000m/10000m: Krishnan Shankar 14:22.4/30:43.8, 3000mSt: T Arun D´Souza 9:03.82, 110mh/400mh: Gurpreet Singh 14.18/51.8, HJ: M Lorans 2.15, PV: Ramdhari Singh 4.75, LJ/TJ: Sanjay Kumar Rai 8.02w/16.23, SP: Bahadur Singh 19.29, DT: Anil Kumar 53.51, HT: Pramod Kumar Tiwari 70.05, JT: Jagdish Singh Bishnoi 76.74, Dec: Kulwinder Singh 6792, 20kmW: Gurdev Singh 1:35:32.4. **Women:** 100m/200m: Kavita Pandya 11.90/24.28, 400m: K Mathews Beenamol 53.04, 800m: C Latha 2:06.37, 1500m: Sunitha Kumari 4:30.67, 5000m/10000m: Madhuri Gurnule 17:03.75/36:24.5, 100mh: Anuradha Biswal 13.95, 400mh: Sahebani Oraon 59.12, HJ: Sangeetha Jr 1.75, PV: Karamjeet Kaur 3.00, LJ: G Pramila Ganapathy 6.43, TJ: Lekha Roy 12.63, SP: N Latha 15.31, DT: Neelam J Singh 58.80, HT: Hardeep Kaur 58.31, JT: Manisha Mondal 47.25, Hep: Soma Biswas 5739, 20kmW: Jasmin Kaur 1:51:14.2.
Inter-State Champions: Men: 100m/200m: Anil Kumar 10.50/21.24, 400m: Purukottam Ramachandran 46.78, 800m: S P Primesh 1:50.34, 1500m: T M Sanjeev 3:50.64, 5000m: Krishnan Shankar 14:29.22, 10000m: Gojen Singh 31:19.37, 3000mSt: Rajesh Kumar 9:14.50, 110mh: Gurpreet Singh 14.07, 400mh: Shebin Joseph 53.05, HJ: Omveer Singh 2.05, PV: Shamsher Singh 4.70, LJ: Sanjay Kumar Rai 7.92, TJ: Pritpal Singh 15.57, SP: Bahadur Singh 19.55, DT: Krishnakumar Sharma 51.96, HT: Pramod Kumar Tiwari 68.98, JT: Sunil Kumar Goswami 72.16, Dec: Dharam Pal Singh 6612, 20kmW: Gurdev Singh 1:32:26. **Women:** 100m: Saraswati Dey 11.71, 200m: Kavita Pandya 24.05, 400m: Sunita Dahiya 53.31, 800m: C Latha 2:05.83, 1500m: Geeta Manral 4:23.09, 5000m: H Sagini Devi 17:31.04, 10000m: Pushpa Devi 37:29.72, 100mh: Soma Biswas 14.10, 400mh: Sapinder Kaur 59.10, HJ: Harshini Kumari 1.63, PV: Karamjeet Kaur 3.17, LJ: Jetty C Joseph 6.27, TJ: Manisha Dey 13.12, SP: N Latha 15.50, DT: Harwant Kaur 53.50, HT: Phool Pati Jakkar 52.07, JT: Manisha Mondal 52.24, Hep: Uday Laxmi 4878, 20kmW: Jasmin Kaur 1:52:41.

IRELAND

Governing Body: The Athletic Association of Ireland (AAI), 11 Prospect Road, Glasnevin, Dublin 9. Founded in 1967. Original Irish AAA founded in 1885.
National Championships first held in 1873. **2001 champions**: **Men**: 100m: John McAdorey 10.55, 200m: Mark Howard 21.56, 400m: Tomas Coman 45.99; 800m: Daniel Caulfield 1:48.28, 1500m: James Nolan 3:44.41, 5000m: Mark Carroll 13:48.26, 10000m: Peter Matthews 29:19.08, HMar: Vinny Mulvey 67:50, Mar: Pauric McKinney 2:25:42, 3000mSt: Cormac Smyth 9:00.55, 110mh: Peter Coghlan 13.73, 400mh: Stephen McDonnell 51.97, HJ: Mark Crowley GBR 2.05, PV: Leigh Walker GBR 4.40, LJ/TJ: Sean Lonergan 7.25w/15.41w, SP: Iain

McMullen GBR 15.95, DT: John Menton 55.59, HT: Roman Linscheid 69.53, JT: Terry McHugh (18th consecutive) 77.20, Dec: Cathal McGinley 6149, 10000mW/20kmW: Robert Heffernan 38:58.83/1:23:41. **Women**: 100m/200m: Sarah Reilly 11.90/23.78, 400m: Karen Shinkins 52.17, 800m: Aoife Byrne 2:03.71, 1500m: Una English 4:14.93, 5000m: Brid Dennehy-Willis 15:31.92, HMar: Anne Lennon 78:55, Mar: Susan Waterstone 3:04:50, 100mh: Derval O'Rourke 13.96, 400mh: Michelle Carey 59.99, HJ/TJ/Hep: Sharon Foley 1.72/12.44w/4832, PV: Zoe Brown GBR 3.30, LJ: Antoinette Furlong 6.07, SP/DT: Eva Massey GBR 15.00/47.23, HT: Eileen O'Keefe 56.15, JT: Jennifer O'Sullivan 44.19, 5000mW/20kmW: Gillian O'Sullivan 20:50.13/1:36:38.

Mark CARROLL b. 15 Jan 1972 Cork 1.77m 66kg. Leevale. Was at Providence University, USA.
At 5000m: OG: '00- h; WCh: '95- 12, '97- h, '99- 14, '01- h; EC: '98- 3; EJ: '91- 1. At 3000m: WI: '01- 7; EI: '00- 1. World CC: '90 19J. Won Irish 1500m 1995, 1999; 5000m 1999-2001.
Irish records 3000m (2) 1998-9, 5000m 1998, 10000m 2000.
Progression at 1500m, 5000m: 1990- 14:32.1, 1991- 3:43.36, 14:09.52; 1992- 4:00.81Mi, 1993- 3:39.67, 1994- 3:56.44Mi, 1995- 3:36.52, 13:13.94; 1996- 3:38.31, 1997- 3:37.50, 13:14.08; 1998- 3:38.12, 13:03.93; 1999- 3:35.00, 13:31.31; 2000- 3:34.91, 13:09.64; 2001- 3:35.09, 13:08.32. pbs: 800m 1:48.21i '00, 1:48.93 '01; 1000m 2:20.63i '94, 1M 3:50.62 '00, 3000m 7:30.36 '99, 10000m 27:46.82 '00.

Women

Sonia O'SULLIVAN b. 28 Nov 1969 Cobh 1.73m 53kg. Ballymore Cobh/Reebok RC. Studied accountancy at Villanova University, USA.
At 5000m (1500m): OG: '96- dnf (h), '00- 2 (6 10000m); WCh: '95- 1, '97- h (8); EC: '98- 1 (1 10000m); WCp: '98- 1. At 3000m (/1500m): OG: '92- 4/sf; WCh: '93- 4/2; WI: '97- 2, '01- 7/9; EC: '90- 11, '94- 1; WJ: '88- h; WUG: '91- 2/1; WCp: '94- (5). World CC (4k): '92-7-8-00-02: 7/9/1 (1)/7 (15)/(7). Won overall GP 1993 (3rd 1994), 3000m 1993, 1995, 2000; 5000m 1992, 1994; NCAA 3000m 1990-1, CC 1990; Irish CC 1987, 800m 1992, 1500m 1987, 1990, 1995-6, 2000; 5000m 1990, 1998.
Records: WIR 5000m 15:17.28 '91, World 2000m & European 3000m 1994, World best 2 miles 1998. Irish 1990-2000: 800m, 1000m, 1500m (6), 1M (2), 2000m (3), 3000m (6), 5000m (4), 10000m.
Progression at 1500m, 3000m, 5000m, 10000m: 1986- 10:02.7, 1987- 9:01.52, 1988- 9:13.6, 1989- 9:10.62, 1990- 4:08.49, 8:52.65, 15:26.9; 1991- 4:05.81, 8:54.16, 15:17.28i; 1992- 4:01.23, 8:39.67, 14:59.11; 1993- 3:59.60, 8:28.74, 14:45.92; 1994- 3:59.10, 8:21.64, 15:06.18; 1995- 3:58.85, 8:27.57, 14:41.40; 1996- 3:59.91, 8:35.32, 14:48.36; 1997- 4:05.31, 8:46.19i/8:53.53, 15:10.98; 1998- 4:01.05, 8:28.82, 14:51.61, 31:29.33; 2000- 4:01.70, 8:27.58, 14:41.02, 30:53.37; 2001- 4:06.34, 8:43.51. pbs: 800m 2:00.69 '94, 1000m 2:34.66 '93, 1M 4:17.25 '94, 2000m 5:25.36 '94, 2M 9:19.56 '98, HMar 70:05 '99, Mar 2:35:40 '00.
In 1992 she set six Irish records from 1500m to 5000m, including five in eleven days in August, and improved further in 1993. Records tumbled in 1994, when she also won the first ever European title for an Irish woman. In 1998 she took both World CC titles and then won a 5000m/10,000m double at the Europeans, the latter in her track debut at 10k. She also won the Great North Run in her first half marathon. She gave birth to daughter Ciara on 10 July 1999, and was soon back in action, setting a world road best for 5 miles with 24:27 on 16 October. In 2000 she set her first Irish records for five years – both 5000m and 10000m (taking 36 secs off her previous best) at the Olympics. Later she won the Dublin Marathon at her debut at the distance. Her second daughter Sophie was born in December 2001.

ISRAEL

Governing body: Israeli Athletic Association, PO Box 24190, Tel Aviv 61241. Founded as Federation for Amateur Sport in Palestine 1931.
National Championships first held in 1935.
2001 Champions: 100m/200m: Gidon Jablonka 10.43/21.20, 400m: Naor Greene 47.09, 800m: Gabriel Tiggebo 1:53.73, 1500m: Doran Gyat 3:57.39, 5000m: Haile Satain 14:21.69, 10000m/HMar: Vodage Zvadia 30:18.21/65:16, Mar: Asaf Bimro 2:18:46, 3000mSt: Michael Majler 9:25.20, 110mh: Ophir Shmueli 14.70, 400mh: David Nakhimovski 54.42, HJ: Yoav Shuster 2.21, PV: Aleksandr Averbukh 5.50, LJ: Mark Malisov 7.33, TJ: Avi Tayari 16.42, SP: Shai Shalev 17.10, DT: Lior Peretz 52.41, HT: Shlomi Ben-Shoshan 59.27, JT: Vadim Bavikin 78.08. **Women**: 100m/200m/100mh: Irina Lenskiy 11.77/24.23/13.25, 400m/400mh: Olga Dor 56.47/60.09, 800m/1500m: Noah Beitler 2:06.33/4:32.27, 5000m/10000m/HMar/Mar: Nili Avramski 16:52.71/36:16.42/74:25/2:44:57 (now 31 national titles), HJ/SP: Olga Kurakulin 1.79/12.88, PV: Vicki Argoss 3.55, LJ: Keren Sarri 6.10, TJ: Lior Gertner 12.91, DT: Yael Dror 40.71, HT: Galit Sehada 33.83, JT: Dorit Naor 43.35.

Alex AVERBUKH b. 1 Oct 1974 1.78m 76kg. Maccabi Tel-Aviv.
At PV: OG: '00- 10=; WCh: '99- 3, '01- 2; WI: '01- 4; EI: '00- 1; EJ: '93- dnq; WUG: '01- 1. EI Hep: '98- 6. Won ISR PV 2000-01, RUS Dec 1997.
Five ISR pole vault records 1999-2001 (from 5.80).
Progression at PV, Dec: 1993- 5.30, 1994- 5.20, 1995- 5.50, 7598w; 1996- 5.40, 7716; 1997- 5.60, 8084; 1998- 5.70, 7658; 1999- 5.81, 2000- 5.85, 2001- 5.91. pbs: 60m 6.89i '98, 6.6i '97; 100m 10.64 '00, 400m 48.74 '98, 1500m 4:33.79 '97, 60mh 8.36i '98, 8.2i '97; 110mh 14.14 '97, HJ 2.06 '95, LJ 7.53i/7.50

'97, SP 15.12 '98, DT 41.51 '00, JT 53.26 '97, Hep 6144i '98.
Emigrated from Russia to Israel, and became a citizen on 3 August 1999, just in time to compete at World Championships.

ITALY

Governing Body: Federazione Italiana di Atletica Leggera (FIDAL), Via Flaminia Nuova 830, 00191 Roma. Constituted 1926. First governing body formed 1896.
National Championships first held in 1906 (men), 1927 (women). **2001 champions**: **Men**: 100m: Francesco Scuderi 10.32, 200m: Marco Torrieri 20.64, 400m: Andrea Barberi 46.42, 800m: Andrea Giocondi 1:48.53, 1500m: Lorenzo Lazzari 3:42.40, 5000m: Salvatore Vincenti 13:55.64, 10000m/HMar: Stefano Baldini 28:21.38/63:03, Mar: Angelo Carosi 2:12:46, 3000mSt: Giuseppe Maffei 8:43.04, 110mh: Emiliano Pizzoli 13.78, 400mh: Laurent Ottoz 49.47, HJ: Giulio Ciotti 2.25, PV: Ruben Scotti 5.40, LJ: Nicola Trentin 7.88, TJ: Paolo Camossi 17.11, SP: Paolo Dal Soglio 20.09, DT: Diego Fortuna 61.72, HT: Nicola Vizzoni 78.81, JT: Alberto Desiderio 78.01, Dec: William Frullani 7509, 10000mW: Michele Didoni 41:17.48, 20kmW: Giovanni De Benedictis 1:26:18, 50kmW: Marco Giungi 3:54:16. **Women**: 100m/200m: Manuela Levorato 11.30/22.98, 400m: Daniela Graglia 53.36, 800m: Elisabetta Artuso 2:05.45, 1500m: Sara Palmas 4:14.92, 5000m: Elisa Rea 16:04.98, 10,000: Maria Guida 33:39.33, HMar: Maura Viceconte 72:55, Mar: Patrizia Ritondo 2:33:38, 3000mSt: P.Angela Baronchelli 10:19.52, 100mh: Margaret Macchiut 13.17, 400mh: Monika Niederstätter 56.21, HJ: Antonietta Di Martino 1.98, PV: M.Carla Bresciani 4.15, LJ: Laura Gatto 6.27, TJ: Silvia Biondini 14.15, SP: Assunta Legnante 17.48, DT: Agnese Maffeis 58.63, HT: Ester Balassini 67.00, JT: Claudia Coslovich 63.82, Hep: Gertrud Bacher 5663, 5000W: Cristiana Pellino 21:35.5, 20kmW: Elisabetta Perrone 1:33:38.

Stefano BALDINI b. 25 May 1971 Castelnovo di Sotto, Reggio Emilia 1.76m 58kg. Works for Corradini Excelsior Rubiera.
At Mar: OG: '00- dnf; WCh: '01- 3; EC: '98- 1. At 10,000m (5000m): OG: '96- 18 (sf); WCh: '95- 18, '97- 9; EC: '94- 20; WJ: '90- (6); EJ: '89- (9); ECp: '95- 1. World HMar: '96- 1, '97- 9. Eur CC: '99- 10. Won ITA 10,000m 1993-6, 2001; HMar 1995, 1998, 2001.
Italian records: half marathon 1997 & 2000, marathon 1997.
Progression at 10,000m, Mar: 1990- 29:48.5, 1992- 28:50.16, 1993- 28:25.98, 1994- 27:57.86, 1995- 27:50.17, 2:11:01sh; 1996- 27:43.98; 1997- 28:07.81, 2:07:57; 1998- 27:55.92, 2:09:33; 2000- 2:09:45, 2001- 28:21.38, 2:08:51. pbs: 1500m 3:45.7 '91, 3000m 7:43.14 '96, 5000m 13:23.43 '96, HMar 60:50w '00.
Won Rome and EC marathons 1998, Madrid 2001; 2nd London and 3rd New York 1997. On 9 Oct 1999 married **Virna De Angeli** (b. 27 Feb 1976) (2 WJ 400mh 1994, Italian record 400m 51.31 '97). Older brother Marco (b. 14 May 1968) has marathon best of 2:16:32 sh '95.

Paolo CAMOSSI b. 6 Jan 1974 Gorizia 1.76m 68kg. Fiamme Azzure Roma.
At TJ (LJ): OG: '00- 8; WCh: '97- dnq, '99- 5, '01- 11; EC: '98- dnq 19 (5); EJ: '91- 11, '93- 1; WI: '01- 1; EI: '00- 3; ECp: '01- 3. Won MedG 1997, ITA 1996-9, 2001.
Progression at TJ: 1990- 14.36, 1991- 15.68, 1992- 15.43i/15.39, 1993- 16.41, 1994- 15.70i/15.46, 1995- 16.25, 1996- 16.49/16.68w, 1997- 16.82/16.96w, 1998- 17.20, 1999- 17.29, 2000- 17.45, 2001- 17.34. pb LJ: 8.16 '98, 8.21ex '99.
Improved from 15.73 to 16.41 NJR to win the 1993 European Junior TJ, and in 1999 bettered the oldest Italian record (Gentile ex-WR 17.22 at the 1968 OG). In 1998 he married Giada Gallina (ex ITA 100m record 11.23 '97, 2nd EJ 200m 1991).

Paulo DAL SOGLIO b. 29 Jul 1970 Schio, Vicenza 1.89m 115kg. Carabinieri Bologna.
At SP: OG: 96- 4, '00- dnq 19; WCh: '93- dnq, '95- 9, '97- 9, '99/01- dnq 16/13; EC: '94- 8, '98- 5; WJ: '88- dnq; EJ: '89- 6; WUG: '93- 2, '97- 2; WI: '93/5/7/9/01- 5/7/6/5; EI: '96- 1; ECp: '93-4-5-6-9-00-01: 2/1/2/1/2/1/3; E23Cp: '92- 5. 3rd GP 1996. Won ITA 1994-6, 1998-2001; MedG 1993.
Progression at SP: 1988- 17.69, 1989- 18.23, 1990- 18.48, 1991- 18.60, 1992- 19.76, 1993- 20.43/ 20.65i, 1994- 20.68, 1995- 20.57, 1996- 21.23, 1997- 21.03i/20.69, 1998- 20.65, 1999- 20.46i/20.39, 2000- 20.75, 2001- 20.86. pb DT 53.80 '89.

Fabrizio DONATO b. 14 Aug 1976 Latina 1.90m 83kg. Fiamme Galle.
At TJ: OG: '00- dnq 25; EJ: '95- 5; WI: '01- 6; EI: '02- 4; ECp: '00- 2. Won MedG 2001, Italian 2000. Italian triple jump record 2000.
Progression at TJ: 1993- 14.36, 1994- 15.27, 1995- 15.81, 1996- 16.35, 1997- 16.40A, 1998- 16.73, 1999- 16.66i/16.53w, 2000- 17.60, 2001- 17.05. pb LJ 7.79i '01, 7.74/7.88w '00.

Alessandro GANDELLINI b. 30 Apr 1973 Monza 1.79m 68kg. Fiamme Oro Padova. Policeman.
At 20kmW: OG: '00- 9; WCh: '97- 12, '99- 5, '01- 12; EC: '98- 12; WCp: '97- 17, '99- 8.
Progression at 20kmW: 1993- 1:28:55, 1994- 1:28:35, 1995- 1:25:22, 1996- 1:25:35, 1997- 1:20:31, 1998- 1:22:01, 1999- 1:21:01, 2000- 1:20:28, 2001- 1:21:42. pbs: 3000mW 11:46.14i '98, 5000mW 18:27.15i '00, 10000mW 39:27.5 '98, 15000mW 1:00:01.2 '00, 30kmW 2:08:09 '01.

Giacomo LEONE b. 10 Apr 1971 Francavilla Fontana, Brindisi 1.71m 56kg. Fiamme Oro Padova. Policeman.
At Mar: OG: '00- 5; WCh: '97- 7, '01- 11; EC: '98-

dnf. World HMar: '95- 15, '96- 9. At 20kmRd: WJ: '90- 5; EJ: '89- 3.
Italian marathon record 2001.
Progression at Mar: 1991- 2:27:31, 1992- 2:14:49, 1995- 2:09:34sh, 1996- 2:09:54, 1997- 2:09:07, 1998- 2:09:46, 1999- 2:09:36, 2000- 2:08:41, 2001- 2:07:52. pbs: 3000m 8:04.87 '95, 5000m 13:47.90 '95, 10000m 28:47.93 '99, HMar 61:10 '97.
Was 15th at WUG in his first marathon in 1991, 2nd Venice 1995. New York 1996 is his one win in 13 marathons; 6th London and 4th New York 1999. 2nd Rome's Milennium Marathon 1 Jan 2000 and at Lake Biwa 2000.

Fabrizio MORI b. 28 Jun 1969 Livorno 1.75m 68kg. Fiamme Gialle Ostia.
At 400mh: OG: '92- h, '96- 6, '00- 7; WCh: '91- sf, '93- sf, '95- sf, '97- 4, '99- 1, '01- 2; EC: '94- sf, '98- 3; ECp: '89-91-4-6-7-8-9-00-01: 8/3/4/1/1/2/1/3/1 (2R 95 & 98). Won ITA 400mh 1989, 1991, 1996.
Seven Italian 400mh records 1996-2001.
Progression at 400mh: 1987- 52.55, 1988- 51.46, 1989- 49.86, 1990- 52.00, 1991- 48.92, 1992- 49.16, 1993- 49.23, 1994- 49.24, 1995- 49.27, 1996- 48.33, 1997- 47.79, 1998- 48.36, 1999- 47.72, 2000- 48.40, 2001- 47.54. pbs: 100m 10.6, 200m 21.8, 400m 46.19 '96, 300mh 35.7 '96.
Survived an initial disqualification in the semis to win the World title in Seville.

Nicola VIZZONI b. 4 Nov 1973 Pietrasanta, Lucca 1.94m 126kg. Fiamme Gialle Ostia.
At HT: OG: '00- 2; WCh: '97- dnq 22, '99- 7, '01- 4; EC: '98- dnq 17; WJ: '92- 5; EJ: '91- 8; WUG: '97- 5, '99- 5, '01- 1; ECp: '99- 4, '01- 2; E23Cp: '92- 5. Won ITA 1998, 2000-01.
Progression at HT: 1991- 66.62, 1992- 69.32, 1993- 70.76, 1994- 71.78, 1995- 74.48, 1996- 75.30, 1997- 77.10, 1998- 77.89, 1999- 79.59, 2000- 79.64, 2001- 80.50. Left-handed thrower.

Women

Erika ALFRIDI b. 22 Feb 1968 Tregnago, Verona 1.68m 53kg. Metanopoli.
At 20kmW: OG: '00- 4; WCh: '99- 6, '01- 4; ECp: '00- 4, '01- 4. At 10kmW: WCh: '97- 5; WCp: '97- 4; EC: '98- 2; ECp: '96- 7, '98- 9. Won ITA 5000mW 1998, 10kmW 1988, 1997; 20kmW 1996-7, 1999.
European 20km walk record 1997.
Progression at 10kmW, 20kmW: 1985- 55:30, 1987- 53:36, 1988- 46:57.5t, 1989- 44:34, 1993- 46:11.7t, 1995- 43:54, 1996- 43:27, 1:32:53; 1997- 42:15, 1:28:13; 1998- 42:54, 1999- 43:19.8, 1:31:52; 2000- 43:09, 1:28:06; 2001- 43:23, 1:27:29. pbs: 3000mW 11:58.06 '00, 5000mW 20:54.04 '98, 10000mW 43:19.8 '99.

Franca FIACCONI b. 4 Oct 1965 Roma 1.73m 56kg.
At Mar: WCh: '97- 13; EC: '98- 4; WUG: '93- 2; WCp: '93- 30. Italian champion 1996, 1998.
Progression at Mar: 1989- 2:44:02, 1990- 2:41:27, 1991- 2:41:04, 1992- 2:39:26, 1993- 2:38:43, 1994- 2:37:43, 1995- 2:30:10, 1996- 2:28:22, 1997- 2:28:51, 1998- 2:25:17, 1999- 2:28:33, 2000- 2:26:03, 2001- 2:26:49. pbs: 5000m 17:22.1, 10000m 33:17.85 '99, HMar 72:37 '98.
Has won 14 of her 37 marathons: Cinzia Taroni 1989, Bologna 1990, Livorno 1993, Enschede 1994 & 2001, Merano 1994, Cesano Boscone 1995, Turin 1996 & 1998, Carpi 1996, Rome and New York 1998, Prague 1999, Padua 2000, Trieste 2001. 2nd New York 1996 & 2000, 3rd 1997; 2nd Osaka 2001. Ran three sub-2:30s in 1996 and in 1998 (with a fourth at 2:30:21). Unable to run in 1999 World Champs due to a broken arm, but returned for 4th in New York. Married to Luciano Milani.

Magdelin MARTINEZ b. 10 Feb 1976 Cuba 1.74m 63kg. CS San Rocchino Brescia.
At TJ: WCh: '01- 4; PAm: '99- 3.
Progression at TJ: 1992- 12.82, 1993- 13.07, 1994- 13.60, 1995- 13.74, 1996- 14.13/14.17w, 1997- 13.78/14.96w, 1998- 14.26, 1999- 14.14/14.18w, 2000- 14.40, 2001- 14.59.
Changed nationality from Cuba to Italy.

Fiona MAY b. 12 Dec 1969 Slough, GBR 1.81m 60kg. Metanopoli. Economics graduate of Leeds University. Married to Gianni Iapichino (PV 5.70 ITA rec '94).
At LJ: OG: '88- 6, '92- dnq, '96- 2, '00- 2; WCh: '91- dnq 19, '93- dnq 14, '95- 1, '97- 3, '99- 2, '01- 1; EC: '90- 7, '94- 3, '98- 2; CG: '90- 3; WJ: '86- 8, '88- 1; EJ: '87- 1; WI: '97- 1, '01- 4; EI: '98- 1; WUG: '91- 2; ECp: '89-91-3-5-7-8-9-00-01: 3/3/3/2/1/1/1/3/3 (TJ '98-9: 1/3). 3rd GP 1996, 1998. Won UK 1989, 1991, 1993; AAA 1989-92, Italian 1994, 1996.
Italian records: eight LJ 1994-8, three TJ 1998.
Progression at LJ, TJ: 1982- 5.34, 1983- 5.91, 1984- 6.30, 1985- 6.22/6.23w, 1986- 6.27/6.47w, 1987- 6.53/6.64w, 1988- 6.82/6.88w, 1989- 6.98w/6.80, 1990- 6.88, 1991- 6.77/6.91w, 1992- 6.73/6.76w, 1993- 6.86, 1994- 6.95A/6.90/7.00wA, 1995- 6.96/7.23Aw, 1996- 7.02/7.12w, 1997- 6.97/6.98w, 1998- 7.11, 14.65; 1999- 7.04, 14.39; 2000- 7.09, 2001- 6.97/7.02w. pbs: 60m 7.7i '92, 100m 11.94 '97, 11.88w '89; 200m 25.4 '89, HJ 1.72 '83.
Competed for Britain to 1993, Italy from 1994; now lives in Firenze. In her first ever triple jump competition in 1998, she smashed the Italian indoor record with 14.56, ninth on the world all-time list indoors. Expecting a baby in 2002.

Elisabetta PERRONE b. 9 Jul 1968 Camburzano, Vercelli 1.68m 60kg. Forestale.
At 20kmW: OG: '00- dq; WCh: '99- 21, '01- 3; WCp: '99- 20; ECp: '00- 2, '01- 3. At 10kmW: OG: '92- 19, '96- 2; WCh: '93- 4, '95- 2, '97- 10; EC: '94- 7, '98- 11; WCp: '93- 10, '95- 6, 97- 25; ECp: '96- 5. Won ITA 5000mW 1994, 1996-7; 10kmW 1994-5, 20kmW 2001; MedG 10kmW 1997.
Italian records 20km walk 2000 & 2001.
Progression at 10kmW, 20kmW: 1988- 53:08, 1989- 51:18, 1990- 48:23, 1991- 46:19, 1992- 44:19,

1993- 43:26/41:56sh/44:01.6t, 1:33:37; 1994- 42:15/43:27.6t, 1995- 42:16, 1996- 42:09, 1997- 42:39, 1998- 44:04, 1:34:32; 1999- 42:45, 1:32:21; 2000- 43:15, 1:27:42; 2001- 43:07, 1:27:09. pbs: 3000mW 11:56.40 '93, 2MW 13:03.87 '96, 5000mW 20:33.42 '95.

Annarita SIDOTI b. 25 Jul 1969 Gioiosa Marea, Messina 1.50m 42kg. Sai Assicura Roma. Sports town councilor in Gioiosa Marea.
At 20kmW: OG: '00- dnf; WCh: '99- dnq, '01- 8; ECp: '00- 5; At 10kmW OG: '92- 7, '96- 11; WCh: '91- 9, '93- 9, '95- 13, '97- 1; EC: '90- 1, '94- 2, '98- 1; WCp: '89- 8, '91- 9, '93- 7, '95- 8, 97- 6; ECp: '96- 1; WUG: '91- 3, '95- 1, '97- 3. At 5000mW: WJ: '88- 4; EJ: '87- 7. At 3000mW: WI: '93- 6; EI: '90- 3, '92- 4, '94- 1. Won Italian 5000mW 1995, 10kmW 1991, 20kmW 1992, 1995, 2000.
European 5000m walk record 1995.
Progression at 10kmW, 20kmW: 1986- 53:23, 1987- 49:37, 1988- 47:57.9t, 1989- 44:59, 1990- 44:00, 1991- 43:37, 1992- 43:03, 1:36:54; 1993- 42:41, 1994- 41:46, 1995- 42:04, 1996- 43:04, 1997- 42:20, 1:30:57; 1998- 42:49, 1999- 43:38.2, 1:34:00; 2000- 43:35, 1:28:38; 2001- 43:48, 1:31:40. Track pbs: 1MW 6:46.53 '90, 3000mW 11:54.32i '94, 12:09.3 '95; 5000mW 20:21.69 '95, 10000mW 42:55.49 '97.
Perhaps the smallest ever major champion when she won the 1990 European title. Took 1997 world title after coming in as a last-minute replacement for Rossella Giordano.

Maura VICECONTE b. 3 Oct 1967 Susa, Torino 1.66m 51kg. Maratona Torino Asics.
At Mar: OG: '96- dnf, '00- 12; EC: '98- 3; WCp: '95- 15. At 5000m: ECp: '00- 4. Won ITA HMar 2000-01, Mar 1995.
Italian records 10000m and marathon 2000.
Progression at Mar: 1994- 2:35:15, 1995- 2:29:11sh/ 2:38:22, 1997- 2:28:16, 1998- 2:28:31, 1999- 2:29:36, 2000- 2:23:47, 2001- 2:26:33. pbs: 5000m 15:18.80 '00, 10000m 31:05.57 '00, HMar 69:19 '01.
Seven wins in 13 marathons: Cesano Boscone 1994, Venice 1995, Monaco 1997, Carpi 1998, Rome 1999, Vienna 2000, Prague 2001.

JAMAICA

Governing body: Jamaica Amateur Athletic Association, PO Box 272, Kingston 5. Founded 1932. **2001 Champions**: **Men**: 100m/200m: Christopher Williams 10.07/20.27, 400m: Michael McDonald 44.89, 800m: Marvin Watts 1:48.66, 1500m: Courtney Chambers 3:55.01, 5000m: Michael Tomblin 14:44.58, 10000m: Kevin Webb 34:59.26, 110mh: Maurice Wignall 13.70, 400mh: Ian Weakley 49.03, HJ: Claston Bernard 2.13, PV: Jabari Ennis 5.00, LJ: Antholow Dawkins 7.43, TJ: Noel Comrie 16.24, SP/DT: Maurice Smith 14.40/48.85. JT: Kevin Bennett 55.72. **Women**: 100m/200m: Aleen Bailey 11.14/22.96, 400m: Lorraine Fenton 50.69, 800m: Charmaine Howell 2:01.02, 1500m: Mardrea Hyman 4:12.01, 100mh: Delloreen Ennis-London 12.62, 400mh: Debbie-Ann Parris 54.91, HJ: Maresa Cadienhead 1.84, PV: Sande Swaby 2.90, LJ: Elva Goulbourne 6.66w, TJ: Trecia-Kaye Smith 14.11, DT: Angella Mitchell 40.63. JT: Brenda-Grace Hunt 43.19.

James BECKFORD b. 9 Jan 1975 St Mary 1.83m 73kg. Was a PE student at Blinn JC, USA.
At LJ (TJ): OG: '96- 2, '00- dnq 14; WCh: '95- 2 (6/4R), '97- 4, '01- 7; WI: '97- 5, '99- 5; CAG: '98- 1. 2nd GP LJ 1997, 1999 (3rd 1995). Won JAM LJ 1995-8, 2000; TJ 1995.
Commonwealth records: LJ 1995 & 1997, TJ 1995, Jamaican records: LJ (5), TJ (4) 1994-7.
Progression at LJ, TJ: 1993- 7.53, 15.70; 1994- 8.13/8.29w, 17.29; 1995- 8.45/8.68w, 17.92; 1996- 8.52, 16.43i; 1997- 8.62, 1998- 8.60/8.61w, 16.09; 1999- 8.50, 2000- 8.42, 2001- 8.41.
An outstanding long/triple jumper, now concentrating on the long jump. After positive test for ephedrine on 25 June 1997 was re-admitted to competition with the IAAF new warning procedure and thus competed at the World Champs. Did not compete at 1999 Worlds as he had not attended the Jamaican Champs.

Gregory HAUGHTON b. 10 Nov 1973 St Mary 1.85m 79kg. Was at George Mason University, USA.
At 400m/4x400mR: OG: '96- 3R, '00- 3/3R; WCh: '93- 6, '95- 3/2R, '97- 3R, '99- 7/3R, '01- 3/3R; CG: '98- 6/1R; PAm: '99- 1/1R; CAG: '98- 2R; WI: '97- 2R, '01- 4R; WJ: '92- sf/2R. Won GWG 2001, CAC 400m 1993, 1999; Jamaican 1994-5, 1999-2000; NCAA 1995.
Progression at 400m: 1991- 47.30, 1992- 46.88, 1993- 44.78, 1994- 44.93, 1995- 44.56, 1996- 45.07, 1997- 45.18, 1998- 45.24, 1999- 44.59, 2000- 44.70, 2001- 44.58. pbs: 200m 20.64 '96, 300m 32.25+ '99.

Michael McDONALD b. 17 Mar 1975 St Mary 1.83m 85kg.
At 400m/4x400mR: OG: '96- sf/3R; WCh: '95- 2R, '97- sf/3R, '99- qf/3R, '01- sf; CG: '98- 1R; PAm: '95- 8, '99- 1R; CAG: '98- 2R; WJ: '94- 1/2R; WI: '97- 2R; WCp: '98- 3R. Won JAM 400m 1996, 2001; CAC 1999, CAC-J 1994.
Progression at 400m: 1993- 46.86/46.7, 1994- 45.83/45.6, 1995- 45.46, 1996- 44.64A/44.75, 1997- 44.65, 1998- 44.92, 1999- 45.13, 2000- 45.24, 2001- 44.71. pb 200m 21.08 '96.
Younger brother of Beverley (qv).

Danny McFARLANE b. 14 Jun 1972 1.85m 81kg. Was at University of Oklahoma, USA.
At 400m/4x400mR: OG: '00- 8/3R; WCh: '95- sf/2R, '97- 3R, '99- sf/3R, '01- 1R; WI: '01- 3; PAm: '99- 1R. Won CAC 1997, 2001.
Progression at 400m: 1993- 45.82, 1994- 45.74, 1995- 44.90, 1996- 46.18i/46.23, 1997- 45.47, 1998- 45.61, 1999- 45.37, 2000- 45.26, 2001- 45.20A/ 45.59. pb 200m 21.17 '95.

Christopher WILLIAMS b. 15 Mar 1972 Manchester 1.78m 68kg. Went to Riverside CC, USA.

At 200m/4x400mR (100m): OG: '00- sf/3R (qf, 4 4x100m); WCh: '99- sf, '01- 2/3R; PAm: '99- 7 (3 4x100m); WI: '01- 4. Won CAC 1999, JAM 100m 2001, 200m 1999-2001.
Progression at 200m: 1996- 20.69, 1997- 20.95, 1999- 20.48/20.40w, 2000- 20.02, 2001- 20.11. pbs: 60m 6.61i '01, 100m 10.05/10.04w '00.

Women

Juliet CAMPBELL b. 17 Mar 1970 St Thomas 1.78m 62kg. Was at Auburn University, USA (business education).
At 200m/4x100mR: OG: '00- qf; WCh: '97- sf, '99- 8, '01- 6; CG: '98- 2/2R, CAG: '98- 2; WI: '99- 5, '01- 1/2R. At 400m/4x400mR: OG: '92- qf, '96- sf/4R; WCh: '93- 7/4R (3 4x100m). Won NCAA 400m 1993, JAM 400m 1993, 1996.
Jamaican 400m record 1993.
Progression at 200m, 400m: 1987- 23.71w, 1988- 24.25, 1989- 24.20/23.7, 53.1; 1990- 23.52, 53.01; 1991- 53.59, 1992- 23.06, 51.11; 1993- 22.80/22.66w, 50.11; 1994- 23.69, 51.65; 1995- 22.77, 51.4/52.00; 1996- 22.71/22.55w, 50.11; 1997- 22.61, 52.30; 1998- 22.69/22.63w, 51.09; 1999- 22.50, 52.77; 2000- 22.70i/22.86, 2001- 22.64i/22.68. pbs: 60y 6.72i '90, 60m 7.23i '01, 100m 11.15w '93, 11.32/11.0 '95; 300m 36.59 '92. Lives in Auburn, USA.

Veronica CAMPBELL b. 15 May 1982 Trelawny 1.63m 61kg. Student at Barton CC, USA.
At 100m/4x100mR (200m): OG: '00- 2R; WJ: '98- qf, '00- 1/2R (1); WY: '99- 1/1R. Won CAC-J 100m 2000.
Progression at 100m, 200m: 1999- 11.49, 23.73; 2000- 11.12/11.1, 22.87; 2001- 11.13/22.92. pb 60m 7.17i '02.
In 2000 became the first woman to become World Junior champion at both 100m and 200m.

Voentte DIXON b. 26 Nov 1975 1.70m 62kg. Was at Auburn University, USA.
At 100mh: WCh: '01- 8.
Progression at 100mh: 1996- 13.52/13.30w, 1997- 13.26, 1998- 13.52, 1999- 13.40, 2000- 12.90, 2001- 12.83. pbs: 100m 11.47/11.40w '00, 200m 23.57/ 23.48w '00, 50mh 6.85i '02, 55mh 7.55i '00, 60mh 7.92i '02.

Delloreen ENNIS-LONDON b. 5 Mar 1975 St Catherine 1.78m 67kg. née Ennis. Business management graduate of Abilene Christian University, USA.
At 100mh: OG: '00- 4; WCh: '99- 7; WJ: '92- sf. 3rd GP 2000. Jamaican champion 1999-2001.
CAC 100mh record 2000.
Progression at 100mh: 1992- 13.81, 1996- 13.53/ 13.30w, 1997- 13.60/13.51w, 1998- 13.27/13.1w, 1999- 12.71/12.60w, 2000- 12.52, 2001- 12.57. pbs: 100m 11.50 '99, 11.43w '00; 55mh 7.56i '99.

Lorraine FENTON b. 8 Sep 1973 Mandeville 1.74m 59kg. née Graham. Graduated in criminal justice from Lincoln University, USA.
At 400m/4x400mR: OG: '00- 2/2R; WCh: '97- sf/3R, '99- 3, '01- 2/1R. Won JAM 400m 1997, 1999-2001. Won GP 2000.
Progression at 400m: 1994- 53.31, 1995- 53.63, 1996- 51.85, 1997- 50.69, 1998- 50.23, 1999- 49.92, 2000- 49.58, 2001- 49.88. pbs: 100m 11.73 '99, 200m 22.63 '01, 300m 36.00+ '00.

Bridgette FOSTER b. 7 Nov 1974 St Elizabeth 1.70m 62kg. Was at South West Texas State University, USA.
At 100mh: OG: '00- 8; WCh: '01- sf; CG: '98- 5/2R; WJ: '92- sf. Jamaican champion 1999-2000. CAC 100mh record 2000.
Progression at 100mh: 1993- 14.22, 1996- 13.34, 1998- 13.19/13.13w/12.9w, 1999- 13.35, 2000- 12.70, 2001- 12.70. pbs: 100m 11.54 '00, 11.38w '98; 200m 23.51/23.35w '98, 60mh 8.09i '01, 400mh 64.62 '93.

Merlene FRAZER b. 27 Dec 1973 Trelawny 1.74m 62kg. Was at University of Texas, USA.
At 200m/4x100mR (100): OG: '00- res 2R; WCh: '91- res 1R, 97- sf/2R, '99- 3=/3R, '01- 4R; CG: '94- 7; WI: '97- 4; WJ: '90- 1R (5), '92- 3/1R (3); PAm: '91- 3/1R. Won PAm-J 1991 (1R, 100m 2), NCAA 1994, JAM 1994. At 400m: OG: '96- sf (4 4x400m); WCh: '95- h.
Progression at 200m: 1990- 23.89, 1991- 23.48, 1992- 23.19, 1993- 22.91, 1994- 22.65/22.49w, 1995- 22.77, 1996- 23.10/22.63w, 1997- 22.66, 1998- 22.63, 1999- 22.18, 2000- 23.05, 2001- 22.99. pbs: 60m 7.20i '97, 100m 11.20 '95, 300m 37.47 '96, 400m 51.18 '96.
She is, at 17 yr 248 days, the youngest ever World Championships gold medallist as she ran in the heats of the 1991 4x100m relay and Jamaica went on to win the final.

Michelle FREEMAN b. 5 May 1969 St Catherine 1.70m 63kg. Was at University of Florida, now assistant coach at University of Texas.
At 100mh/4x100mR: OG: '92- qf, '96- 6/R, '00- qf; WCh: '91- sf, '93- 7/3R, '95- sf/res R (2), '97- 3; CG: '94- 1; WJ: '88- h (sf 100m); PAm: '91- 5. At 100m: CG: '90- h. At 60mh: WI: '93/5/7/01- dnf/7/1/2. Won JAM 100mh 1991-4, 1997; NCAA 1992. Won GP 100mh 1998 (3rd 1992), 3rd overall 1996.
WIR 55mh 1992. Eight JAM 100mh records 1990-8, inc. five Commonwealth 1992-8 and four CAC 1996-8.
Progression at 100mh: 1988- 13.70, 1989- 13.61/ 13.4, 1990- 13.18/13.09w, 1991- 12.98, 1992- 12.75, 1993- 12.77, 1994- 12.93/12.74w, 1995- 12.98, 1996- 12.57, 1997- 12.52/12.40w, 1998- 12.52, 2000- 12.57, 2001- 12.89. pbs: 55m 6.66i '93, 60m 7.12i '98, 100m 11.16 '93, 11.13w '92; 200m 22.87 '92, 50mh 6.75i '96, 55mh 7.34i '92, 60mh 7.74i '98.
Had to withdraw from 1988 Olympic team through injury.

Elva GOULBOURNE b. 21 Jan 1980 St Ann 1.70m 50kg. Student at Central Arizona State

University, USA.
At LJ: OG: '00- 10; WCh: '01- 10; PAm: '99- 3. Won P-Am Jnr 1997/99, CAC-J 1998, CAC 2001, JAM 2000-01.
Commonwealth indoor LJ record 2002.
Progression at LJ: 1997- 6.10, 1998- 6.47, 1999- 6.49, 2000- 6.74/6.79w, 2001- 6.86/6.90w, 2002- 6.91i. pbs:100m 11.30 '00, 200m 23.60/23.51w '01.

Deon HEMMINGS b. 9 Oct 1968 St Ann 1.76m 63kg. Studied business administration at Central State University, Ohio, USA.
At 400mh/4x400mR: OG: '92- 7, '96- 1, '00- 2/2R; WCh: '91- h, '93- 6, '95- 3, '97- 2/3R, '99- 3, '01- 7/res (1)R; CG: '94- 2/2R; PAm: '91- 2; CAG: '98- 1; WCp: '98- 2/2R; 3rd GP 1995, 2nd 1997 (2nd overall). At 400m: WI: '93- 1R, '95- 4, '99- 6. Won CAC 400mh 1991; JAM 400m 1995, 400mh 1992-2000.
Five CAC & Jamaican 400mh records 1993-6.
Progression at 400mh: 1990- 61.72, 1991- 56.5, 1992- 54.70, 1993- 54.12, 1994- 54.48, 1995- 53.48, 1996- 52.82, 1997- 52.98, 1998- 53.03A/53.27, 1999- 53.16, 2000- 53.45, 2001- 54.47. pbs: 100m 11.58/11.29w '97, 200m 22.64 '98, 22.6w '95, 300m 37.71 '93, 400m 50.63 '95.
Jamaica's first female Olympic champion.

Beverley McDONALD b. 15 Feb 1970 St Mary 1.69m 59kg. Was at Texas Christian University, USA.
At 100m/4x100mR (200m): OG: '00- sf/2R (4); WCh: '91- sf/1R, '93- sf, '95-sf/2R (sf), '97- qf/2R, '99- (2)/3R, '01- (sf); PAm: '91- 3/1R; CAG: '98- 2 (2); WJ: '88- 7; WCp: '98- 2R (4). At 60m: WI: '95- 5. 3rd GP 200m 1999. Won JAM 100m 1998, 200m 1998-2000.
Progression at 100m, 200m: 1987- 11.2, 23.40/23.3; 1988- 11.61, 24.15/23.7; 1990- 11.52/11.27w, 23.20w; 1991- 11.37/11.29w/11.2w, 23.48/23.31w; 1992- 11.43/11.19w, 23.31; 1993- 11.22/11.05w, 22.67; 1994- 11.47, 23.02w; 1995- 11.20/11.17w, 22.56; 1996- 11.16, 23.04; 1997- 11.13A/11.11w, 22.62; 1998- 10.99, 22.24; 1999- 11.10, 22.22; 2000- 11.11, 22.35; 2001- 11.27/11.1, 22.57. pb 60m 7.16i '95. Brother Michael (qv) is a top 400m runner.

Debbie Ann **PARRIS** b. 24 Mar 1973 Trelawny 1.62m 52kg. Was at Louisiana State University, USA.
At 400mh/4x400mR: OG: '96- 4; WCh: '93- sf, '95- h, '97- 5, '99- 8, '01- 5/2R; CG: '94- 3; CAG: '98- 3; WJ: '92- 8/2R; WUG: '93- 2. NCAA champion 1993-4, CAC 1993, JAM 2001.
Progression at 400mh: 1992- 57.34, 1993- 55.80, 1994- 55.17, 1995- 54.29, 1996- 53.97, 1997- 54.19, 1998- 54.49, 1999- 54.55, 2000- 55.90, 2001- 53.88. pbs: 200m 23.50 '98, 400m 51.42 '01, 800m 2:13.35 '99, 100mh 13.51 '93.

Sandie RICHARDS b. 6 Nov 1968 Clarendon 1.75m 67kg. Was at University of Texas, USA (sociology).
At 400m/4x400mR: OG: '88- qf/5R, '92- 7/5R, '96- 7/4R, '00- sf/2R; WCh: '87- sf/6R, '93- 3/4R, '95- 8, '97- 2/3R, '01- sf/1R; CG: '94- 3/2R, '98- 1; WI: '93- 1/2R, '95- 2, '97- 2, '99- 5, '01- 1/2R; WJ: '86- 3; WUG: '87- 3; PAm: '87- 8/3R, '91- 6/3R; CAG: '98- 1; WCp: '94- 3R, '98- 3/2R. Won JAM 400m 1991-2, 1994, 1998; PAm Jnr 1986, GP 1992.
Jamaican 400m record 1987.
Progression at 400m: 1986- 52.18, 1987- 50.92, 1988- 51.62, 1989- 51.46, 1990- 51.94, 1991- 51.06, 1992- 50.19, 1993- 50.44, 1994- 50.69, 1995- 50.53, 1996- 50.45, 1997- 49.79, 1998- 50.03, 1999- 51.54i/51.66, 2000- 50.42, 2001- 50.71. pbs: 200m 23.38A '98, 23.66 '86, 23.15w '87; 300m 36.15 '93, 800m 2:04.60 '96.

Dionne ROSE-HENLEY b. 7 Nov 1969 Kingston 1.69m 57kg. Was at Universities of Florida and Middle Tennessee State, USA.
At 100mh (LJ): OG: '92- sf (dnq 25), '96- 5; WCh: '93- sf (dnq 25), '95- 7 (dnq 31), '97- 5, '99- 6, '01- 6; CG: '94- 4 (7); PAm: '90- dnf (7); CAG: '98- 1; WCp: '98- 4. At 60mh: WI: '99- 7. Won JAM LJ 1993, 1995; 100mh 1996, 1998.
Jamaican 100mh record 1995.
Progression at 100mh: 1988- 15.18/14.9, 1989- 14.42/14.1w, 1990- 14.44/13.49w, 1991- 13.39/13.29w, 1992- 13.03, 1993- 13.03, 1994- 13.13/13.06w, 1995- 12.86/12.85w, 1996- 12.64, 1997- 12.75, 1998- 12.64, 1999- 12.79, 2000- 13.15/12.93Aw, 2001- 12.77. pbs: 100m 11.54 '98, 11.38w '95, 11.4 '97; 50mh 6.84i '99, 60mh 7.96i '97, LJ 6.72 '95, TJ 12.73w '90.
Ran three personal bests in qualifying at 1996 Olympic Games.

JAPAN

Governing body: Nippon Rikujo-Kyogi Renmei, 1-1-1 Jinnan, Shibuya-Ku, Tokyo 150-8050. Founded 1911.

National Championships first held in 1914 (men), 1925 (women). **2001 Champions**: **Men**: 100m: Nobuharu Asahara 10.45, 200m: Shingo Suetsugu 20.48, 400m: Jun Osakada 45.26, 800m: Masaharu Nakano 1:51.60, 1500m: Fumikazu Kobayashi 3:44.46, 5000m/10000m: Alene Emere ETH 13:26.33/27:29.53, Mar: Shigeru Aburaya 2:07:52, 3000mSt: Yoshitaka Iwamizu 8:26.77, 110mh: Masato Naito 13.65 13.72, 400mh: Dai Tamesue 48.66, HJ: Takahiro Kimino 2.22, PV: Manabu Yokoyama 5.50, LJ: Daisuke Watanabe 8.03, TJ: Takanori Sugibayashi 16.46, SP: Yasutada Noguchi 17.99, DT: Shigeo Hatakeyama 54.19, HT: Koji Murofushi 78.83, JT: Yukifumi Murakami 77.22, Dec: Takuro Hirata 7527, 20kmW: Satoshi Yanagisawa 1:21:20, 50kmW: Fumio Imamura 3:54:44. **Women**: 100m/200m: Motoka Arai 11.31w/23.67, 400m: Kazue Kakinuma 53.62, 800m: Tomoko Matsushima 2:03.21, 1500m: Ikuko Tamura 4:16.80, 5000m/10000m: Haruko Okamoto 15:32.33/31:50.39, Mar: Kazumi Matsuo 2:26:01, 100mh: Kumiko Ikeda 13.38, 400mh: Makiko Yoshida 57.40, HJ: Miki Imai

1.92, PV: Takayo Kondo 4.00, LJ/TJ: Maho Hanaoka 6.82/13.59, SP: Chinatsu Mori 16.84, DT: Miyoko Nakanishi 54.09, HT: Masumi Aya 62.13, JT: Takako Miyake 60.12, Hep: Sayoko Sato 5713, 20kmW: Kaori Nikaido 1:33:29.

Shigeru ABURAYA b. 6 Feb 1977 Yamaguchi pref. 1.63m 52kg. Chuguko Electric.
At Mar: WCh: '01- 5; JPN champion 2001. At HMar: WCh: '99- 23.
Progression at Mar: 2000- 2:10:48, 2001- 2:07:52. pbs: 5000m 13:40.87 '99, 10000m 28:13.76 '00, HMar 62:05 '98.

Atsushi FUJITA b. 6 Nov 1976 Fukushima pref. 1.66m 52kg. Fujitsu. Graduate of Komazawa University.
At Mar: WCh: '99- 6, '01- 12. Japanese chanpion 2000. At HMar: WCh: '98- 30.
Asian marathon record 2000.
Progression at Mar: 1999- 2:10:07, 2000- 2:06:51, 2001- 2:18:23, 2002- 2:11:32. pbs: 5000m 14:02.58 '00, 10000m 28:19.94 '00, HMar 62:19 '00.
Second in debut marathon at Lake Biwa in March 1999. Won at Fukuoka in third marathon December 2000 and at Seoul 2002.

Takayuki INUBUSHI b. 11 Aug 1972 Tokushima pref. 1.70m 58kg. Otsuka Pharmaceuticals.
At Mar: OG: '00- dnf.
Asian marathon record 1999.
Progression at Mar: 1995- 2:25:16, 1998- 2:13:15, 1999- 2:06:57, 2000- 2:08:16, 2001- 2:11:42. pbs: 800m 1:53.9 '92, 1500m 3:48.86 '92, 3000m 8:12.8 '96, 5000m 13:46.74 '95, 10000m 28:26.98 '00; road: 10M 46:42 '93, HMar 62:47 '98, 30km 1:30:29 '94.
Shot to prominence with his second place in the 1999 Berlin marathon, when he took 5:27 off his previous pb.

Koji MUROFUSHI b. 8 Oct 1974 Shizuoka 1.87m 97kg. Was at Chukyo Univ. Mizuno.
At HT: OG: '00- 9; WCh: '95- dnq, '97- 10, '99- dnq 14, '01- 2; WJ: '92- 8; AsiG: '94- 2, '98- 1; AsiC: '93- 2, '95- 2, '98- 2. Won GWG 2001, 2nd GP 2000. Won E.Asian 1997, 2001. Japanese champion 1995-2001.
17 Japanese hammer records 1998-2001.
Progression at HT: 1991- 61.76, 1992- 66.30, 1993- 68.00, 1994- 69.54, 1995- 72.32, 1996- 73.82, 1997- 75.72, 1998- 78.57, 1999- 79.17, 2000- 81.08, 2001- 83.47.
His father Shigenobu Murofushi won a record five Asian Games gold medals 1970-86 and held the Japanese hammer record with 75.96 (Los Angeles 1984) until Koji broke it for the first time on 26 Apr 1998. His mother was a Romanian javelin thrower. His sister Yuka (b. 11 Feb 77) was Japanese discus champion and record setter (56.84) 1999 and 6th World Juniors 1996.

Dai TAMESUE b. 3 Mar 1978 Hiroshima pref. 1.70m 67kg. Student at Hosei University.
At 400mh: OG: '00- h; WCh: '01- 3; WJ: '96- 4/2R. Japanese champion 2001.
Two Japanese records 2001.
Progression at 400mh: 1996- 49.09, 1998- 49.19, 1999- 49.12, 2000- 48.47, 2001- 47.89. pbs: 200m 21.23 '96, 400m 45.94 '96.
One of the shortest top-class 400m hurdlers.

Women

Tomoe ABE b. 13 Aug 1971 Oita pref. 1.50m 38kg. Asahi Kasei Chemical.
At Mar: WCh: '93- 3, '97- 29. Japanese champion 1994. At 10,000m: WJ: '90- 11.
Japanese marathon record 1994.
Progression at Mar: 1993- 2:26:27, 1994- 2:26:09, 1996- 2:28:00, 1997- 2:45:19, 1998- 2:31:12, 1999- 2:27:05, 2000- 2:28:01, 2001- 2:27:02, 2002- 2:29:16. pbs: 3000m 9:22.15 '89, 5000m 15:53.46 '93, 10000m 32:55.78 '93, 20km Rd 67:39 '93, HMar 72:00 '99, 100km 6:33:11 '00.
Second in 2:26:27 on marathon début at Osaka 1993, and won there in a national record in 1994, returning for 5th in 1996 and 2002, 6th in 1999 and 2000. Won Sapporo 1996. Ran a sensational women's world best for 100km at Lake Saroma in 2000, improving the previous best by 27 minutes 37 seconds!

Kayoko FUKUSHI b. 25 Mar 1982 1.61m 45kg. Wacoal.
At 5000m: WJ: '00- 4. World CC: '02- 15.
Progression at 5000m, 10,000m: 1998 - 16:56.35, 1999 - 16:38.69, 35:37.54; 2000- 15:29.70, 2001- 15:10.23, 31:42.05. pb 3000m 8:52.3 '01.
Set Japanese junior records at 3000m, 5000m and 10000m in 2001.

Harumi HIROYAMA b. 2 Sep 1968 Tokushima pref. 1.60m 47kg. née Suzuki. Graduate of Kokushikan University. Shiseido.
At 10000m: OG: '00- 20; WCh: '99- 4. At 5000m: OG: '96- h; WCh: '97- 8. At 3000m: WCh: '93- h (h 1500m); AsiG: '94- 2. Won E.Asian 5000m 1997, JPN 1500m & 3000m 1992, 10000m 1997, 1999, Mar 2000.
Japanese records: 1500m 1992 and 1994, 3000m (2) 1994, 5000m 1997 and 1998.
Progression at 5000m, 10000m, Mar: 1990- 17:18.21, 1991- 16:55.0, 1993- 15:30.78, 1994- 15:33.53, 1995- 15:28.17, 32:03.35; 1996- 15:09.69, 31:43.99; 1997- 15:07.75, 31:22.72; 1998- 15:03.67, 2:28:12; 1999- 15:21.04, 31:26.84; 2000- 15:20.36, 31:59.60, 2:22:56; 2001- 15:29.73, 31:39.80, 2:29:01; 2002- 2:24:34. pbs: 800m 2:06.19 '94, 1500m 4:11.10 '94, 3000m 8:50.40 '94, HMar 69:41 '01.
Third at Nagoya on marathon debut 1998, and 2nd at Osaka in 2000 and 2001. Married to marathon runner Tsutomu Hiroyama (b. 22 Oct 1966, pb 2:11:37 '90).

Yuko KAWAKAMI b. 1 Aug 1975 Kobe 1.52m 45kg. Miyazaki Oki electric company.
At 10000m: OG: '96- 7, '00- 10; WCh: '99- 12;

AsiG: '98- 1. At 5000m: WCh: '97- 15. Won JPN 10000m 1998.
Japanese 10000m record 2000.
Progression at 5000m, 10000m: 1991- 16:39.9, 1993- 16:13.4, 1994- 15:49.42, 1995- 15:45.83, 1996- 15:27.77, 31:20.19; 1997- 15:17.34, 31:26.67; 1998- 15:24.16, 31:39.35; 1999- 15:25.01, 31:43.01; 2000- 15:23.59, 31:09.46. pbs: 3000m 8:55.8 '98, 2M 9:35.04 '98, HMar 69:38 '02, Mar 2:34:09 '99.

Kazumi MATSUO b. 18 Apr 1974 Hyogo pref. 1.65m 47kg. Tenmaya, graduate of Tokyo University of Agriculture.
At Mar: WCh: '01- 9; JPN champion 2001. At HMar: WCh: '98- 22.
Progression at Mar: 1999- 2:32:14, 2000- 2:26:15, 2001- 2:26:01. pbs: 1500m 4:21.52 '97, 3000m 9:08.69 '97, 5000m 15:40.75 '00, 10000m 32:39.66 '00, HMar 70:29 '01.
Three successive marathon wins: Sapporo 1999, Berlin 2000, Nagoya 2001 prior to 2001 Worlds.

Mizuki NOGUCHI b. 3 Jul 1978 Mie pref. 1.50m 40kg. Globary.
At HMar: WCh: '99- 2, '00- 4, '01- 4. At 10000m: WCh: '01- 13. Won Asian CC 1999, E.Asian HMar 2001.
Progression at 10000m: 1999- 33:09.98, 2000- 32:05.23, 2001- 31:51.13. pbs: 5000m 15:34.36 '99, Rd: 15km 48:11 '01, HMar 68:22 '02, Mar 2:25:35 '02. Won Nagoya Marathon on debut 2002.

Yoko SHIBUI b. 14 Mar 1979 Kuroiso, Tochigi pref.1.65m 50kg. Mitsui.
At Mar: WCh: '01- 4.
Progression at 10000m, Mar: 1997- 33:53.20, 1999- 32:43.02, 2000- 31:48.89, 2001- 31:48.73, 2:23:11. pbs: 5000m 15:35.79 '00, HMar 69:31 '00.
Ran the fastest ever debut marathon by a woman with 2:23:11 to win at Osaka in January 2001. Her breakthrough came with a 31:59 eki-den road relay leg in January 2000 and she had shown brilliant form with 10km legs of 31:09 and 31:11 in November 2000.

Naoko TAKAHASHI b. 6 May 1972 Gifu 1.63m 50kg. Sekisui Chemical. Graduate of Osaka Gakuin University.
At Mar: OG: '00- 1; AsiG: '98- 1. At 5000m: WCh: '97- 13. Won JPN marathon 1998.
World marathon record 2001, Asian and two Japanese records 1998.
Progression at 10000m, Mar: 1994- 34:02.02, 1996- 31:48.23, 1997- 32:34.50, 2:31:32; 1998- 31:55.95, 2:21:47; 2000- 2:22:19, 2001- 2:19:46. pbs: 1500m 4:22.89 '94, 3000m 9:13.00 '94, 5000m 15:21.15 '98, HMar 68:55 '00.
She made her marathon debut with 7th at Osaka in 1997. After graduating from University she joined the Recruit team coached by Yoshio Koide and later followed him to the Sekisui team. In 1998 she set national records, 2:25:48 at Nagoya in March, and then a superb 2:21:47, on her own all the way and despite slowing in intense heat and humidity, to win the Asian Games gold medal in December. Withdrew, injured, from 1999 World Champs on the eve of the race, but returned with a superb 2:22:19 (69:39 second half) to win at Nagoya in March 2000 and later took the Olympic gold in great style. In her sixth marathon, at Berlin in 2001, she became the first women to break 2:20.

Reiko TOSA b. 11 Jun 1976 Ehime pref.1.66m 51kg.Mitsui. Graduate of Matsuyama University.
At Mar: WCh: '01- 2. At HMar: WCh: '99- 6.
Progression at Mar: 1998- 2:54:57, 2000- 2:24:36, 2001- 2:26:06. pbs: 10000m 32:15.63 '00, HMar 69:36 '99. 2nd Nagoya (2:24:36) and Tokyo (2:24:47) marathons 2000.

Eri YAMAGUCHI b. 14 Jan 1973 Takino, Hyogo pref. 1.63m 47kg. Tenmaya, Okayama.
At Mar: OG: '00- 7. Japanese champion 1999.
Progression at Mar: 1995- 2:32:47, 1996- 2:31:43, 1997- 2:39:46, 1998- 2:27:36, 1999- 2:22:12, 2000- 2:27:03. pbs: 3000m0 9:26.86 '98, 5000m 15:42.3 '98, 10000m 32:07.25 '00. HMar 70:04 (69:31+) '99.
Made amazing breakthrough to win 1999 Tokyo women's marathon in 2:22:12, the fastest ever time in a women's only marathon on an out-and-back course. This was her second win in eight marathons; she had also won at Sapporo in 1998.

KAZAKHSTAN

Governing body: Athletic Federation of the Republic of Kazakhstan, Abai Street 48, 480072 Almaty. Founded 1959.

2001 National Champions: Men: 100m: Denis Kondratyev 10.73, 200m/400m: Denis Rypakov 21.80/47.15, 800m: Yevgeniy Shelestov 1:51.35, 1500m: Dmitriy Tarasenko 3:59.96, 5000m: Yevgeniy Medvednik 15:00.64, 3000mSt: Andrey Konyushak 10:09.8, 110mh: Andrey Sklyarenko 14.49, 400mh: Aleksandr Pogorelov KGZ 54.4, HJ: Maksim Sidorov 2.00, PV: Aleksandr Akhmedov 4.60, LJ: Andrey Pakhomov 7.63, TJ: Meyram Beispekov 16.09, SP: Sergey Rubtsov 17.30, DT: Yevgeniy Buchatskiy 51.30; HT: Ruslan Gazimov 43.94, JT: Dmitriy Shnaider KGZ 62.50, 10000m/20kmW: Sergey Korepanov 41:46.07/1:26:05. **Women**: 100m/200m: Natalya Vorobyeva 11.87/24.47, 400m: Tatyana Roslanova 54.00, 800m: Gulmira Tasiybekova 2:07.09, 1500m: Svetlana Lukashova 4:30.06, 5000m: Garifa Kuku 17:25.24, HMar: Yekaterina Shatnaya 78:33, 100mh: Olga Lapina 14.67w, 400mh: Tatyana Asarova 63.0, HJ: Svetlana Stavskaya 1.82, PV: Yelena Reznik 4.00, LJ: Yelena Parfenova 6.10, TJ: Olga Lapina 13.50, SP: Svetlana Kazanina 13.66, DT: Yekaterina Mitina 44.10, HT: Natalya Kozylenkova 34.22, JT: Natalya Molchkova 36.57, 10000mW/20kmW: Maya Sazonova 47:48.8/1:29:36.

Sergey KOREPANOV b. 9 May 1964 Almaty 1.70m 61kg. State Unversity, Izhevsk.
At 50kmW: OG: '96- 8, '00- 15; WCh: '93- 10, '95- 9,

'97- 12, '99- dnf, '01- 20; WCp: '95- 9, '99- 1; AsiG: '94- 1, '98- 2. At 20kmW: AsiC: '93- 3.
Asian 50km record 1999. KZK 50km walk records 1993-9.
Progression at 50kmW: 1989- 3:58:13, 1990- 3:56:33, 1991- 3:55:47, 1992- 4:08:02sh, 1993- 3:52:50, 1994- 3:54:37, 1995- 3:48:06, 1996- 3:48:42, 1997- 3:42:16, 1998- 3:45:15, 1999- 3:39:22, 2000- 3:53:05, 2001- 3:59:57. pbs: 5000mW 19:14.00i '95, 20kmW 1:20:34 '95.
His World Cup win at 50km walk in 1999 was the first world medal for Kazakhstan.

Women

Olga SHISHIGINA b. 23 Dec 1968 1.62m 57kg.
At 100mh: OG: '00- 1; WCh: '95- 2, '99- 4, '01- 3; AsiG '94- 1, '98- 1; AsiC: '98- 1; WCp: '98- dnf; won Central Asian 1995, 1999 (and 100m). At 60mh: WI: '95/9/01- 2/1/4
Asian 100mh record 1995, Asian records indoors: 60mh (6) 1995-9 (two in 1996 lost due to positive drugs test), 50mh (3) 1995-9. KZK 100m record 2000.
Progression at 100mh: 1990- 14.04, 1991- 13.47, 1993- 13.29, 1994- 12.78, 1995- 12.44/12.41w, 1998- 12.63, 1999- 12.47, 2000- 12.65, 2001- 12.58. pbs: 100m 11.13 '00, 200m 23.6 '94, 50mh 6.70i '99, 60mh 7.82i '99, 7.78i drugs dq '96.
Son Vitaliy born 1988. Served two years drugs ban for positive test on 7 Feb 1996 at Gent. Became Kazakhstan's first individual Olympic champion in athletics in 2000.

Svetlana ZALEVSKAYA b. 14 Jun 1973 1.88m 65kg.
At HJ: OG: '96- 13, '00- 6; WCh: '93- 11=, '95- dnq 15, '99- 8, '01- dnq 20; WJ: '92- 2=; EJ: '91- 5; WUG: '95- 2; WCp: '94- 5; AsiG: '94- 2; AsiC: '93- 1, '95- 1. Won C.Asian 1999.
Asian high jump record 1996.
Progression at HJ: 1990- 1.83, 1991- 1.89, 1992- 1.89, 1993- 1.94, 1994- 1.89, 1995- 1.96, 1996- 1.98i/1.97, 1997- 1.96dq/1.95i/1.93, 1999- 1.93, 2000- 1.97, 2001- 1.91i/1.90.
Drugs disqualification 1997.

KENYA

Governing body: Kenya Amateur Athletic Association, PO Box 46722, 00100 Nairobi. Founded 1951.
2001 National Champions: **Men**: 100m: Gilbert Opiyo 10.3, 400m: Ezra Sambu 44.47, 800m: William Yiampoy 1:44.24, 1500m: William Chirchir 3:40.15, 5000m: Richard Limo 13:17.2, 10000m: Charles Kamathi 27:47.33, 3000mSt: Bernard Barmasai 8:16.0, 400mh: Hilary Maritim 50.93, TJ: Paul Koech 16.31, 20kmW: David Kimutai 1:22:42. **Women**: 800m: Faith Macharia 2:03.91, 1500m: Jacinta Muraguri 4:13.3, 5000m: Edith Masai 15:24.4, 10000m: Susan Chepkemei 33:23.3, 2000mSt: Irene Limika 6:30.62, LJ: Hellen Chemutai 5.99.

Bernard BARMASAI b. 6 May 1974 Keiyo 1.73m 55kg. Keiyo.
At 3000mSt: OG: '00- 4; WCh: '97- 3, '99- 5, '01- 3; CG: '98- 1; AfG: '95- 1; AfCh: '98- 1; WCp: '98- 2. Won GWG 1998, GP (and overall) 1999 (3rd 1997). Kenyan champion 1998-9, 2001. World CC: '97- 6.
World 3000m steeplechase record 1997.
Progression at 3000mSt: 1994- 8:14.18, 1995- 8:08.56, 1996- 8:10.84, 1997- 7:55.72, 1998- 8:00.67, 1999- 7:58.98, 2000- 8:02.76, 2001- 8:05.00. pbs: 1500m 3:37.24 '00, 3000m 7:36.40 '97, 2000mSt 5:28.31 '95, 10km road 28:08 '97.
After setting a world record in 1997, Barmasai was ranked world number one at the steeplechase in 1998 and 1999. Won six of seven Golden League steeplechases in 1999, just losing to Ali Ezzine in the last, at Berlin. However, he had lost his chance of sharing the Jackpot when the IAAF determined that he had brought the sport into disrepute by apparently telling Christopher Kosgei not to beat him in Zürich.

Mark BETT b. 22 Dec 1976 1.80m 64kg.
World CC: '95- 8J.
Progression at 5000m, 10000m: 1997- 13:15.97, 27:41.14; 1998- 13:22.36, 27:18.66; 1999- 13:14.27, 27:38.64; 2000- 12:55.63, 28:15.98; 2001- 12:58.72, 27:24.68. pb 3000m 7:36.66 '01.

Paul BITOK b. 26 Jun 1970 Kilibwoni 1.73m 58kg. Nandi. Airman (SPTE).
At 5000m: OG: '92- 2, '96- 2; WCh: '93- 8, '97- 13; WJ: '88- 9; AfG: '93- 4. At 3000m: WI: '97- 2, '99- 2. Won GP 5000m 1992, 3000m 2001 (2nd 1999); GWG 5000m 2001. World Rd Rly team: '92- 1.
Progression at 5000m: 1988- 14:08.8, 1992- 13:08.89, 1993- 13:08.68, 1994- 13:07.30, 1995- 13:16.39, 1996- 13:04.48, 1997- 13:04.74, 1998- 13:14.26, 1999- 13:15.22i/13:31.01; 2000- 13:04.15, 2001- 13:00.10. pbs: 1500m 3:31.96 '01, 1M 3:56.39i '00, 3:59.6 '96; 2000m 4:54.36 '99, 3000m 7:28.41 '96, 2M 8:13.28i '01, 8:16.44 '99; 10000m 28:51.6 '95, Rd 10km 28:31 '93.
Still yet to break 13 minutes for 5000m, but has a great racing record. Won the Paavo Nurmi Challenge 1997 with 1500m in 3:36.87 followed by 5000m in 13:26.25.

Simon BIWOTT b. 3 Mar 1970.
At Mar: WCh: '99- 9, 01- 2..
Progression at Mar: 1998- 2:12:14, 1999- 2:07:41, 2000- 2:07:42, 2001- 2:09:40. road pbs: 10km 28:33A '99, HMar 61:27 '99.
5 wins in 11 marathons from 5th in Rome 1998 on debut: Mexico City and Cancun 1998, Berlin (when he was a pacemaker but kept on to win in 2:07:42) and Milan 2000, Paris 2001. Best 2:07:41 when 4th at Rotterdam 1999.

Wilson BOIT KIPKETER b. 6 Oct 1973 1.67m 52kg. Keiyo.
At 3000mSt: OG: '00- 2; WCh: '97- 1, '99- 2; AfG:

'99- 2. 2nd GP 1999. World CC: '98- 5.
World 3000m steeplechase record 1997.
Progression at 3000mSt: 1993- 8:39.0A, 1994- 8:27.90A, 1995- 8:33.6A, 1996- 8:11.29, 1997- 7:59.08, 1998- 8:01.05, 1999- 8:07.10, 2000- 8:07.33, 2001- 8:01.73. pbs: 1500m 3:40.29 '00, 2000m 5:02.1e '97, 3000m 7:33.96 '97, 10000m 28:43.89A '97.

Wilfred Kipkemboi **BUNGEI** b. 24 Jul 1980 Kabirisang, near Kapsabet 1.72m 60kg. Nandi (Kalenjin).
At 800m: WCh: '01- 2; WJ: '98- 2.
Progression at 800m: 1998- 1:47.21, 1999- 1:45.14, 2000- 1:44.23, 2001- 1:42.96. pbs: 600m 1:14.94 '99.

Abrahim CHEBII b. 23 Dec 1979 Kapsowar 1.72m 63kg.
World 4k CC: '00- 5.
Progression at 5000m, 10000m: 1999- 13:30.41, 2000- 13:01.9, 2001- 13:12.53, 27:04.20. pbs: 1500m 3:39.76 '00, 1M 3:55.31 '00, 3000m 7:40.30 '01.

David CHELULE b. 7 Jul 1977 1.79m 63kg.
At 10000 m (5000m): OG: '00- (5); WCh: '99- 9; WJ: '94- (h), '96- 2 (2); AfG: '99- 2. World CC: '95- 3J, '96- 1J. Won Kenyan 10000m 1999.
Progression at 5000m, 10000m: 1994- 13:56.8, 1995- 13:32.53, 1996- 13:24.48, 27:32.18; 1997- 13:02.52, 28:49.2A; 1999- 12:57.79, 27:51.90; 2000- 13:13.72, 27:57.10A; 2001- 28:22.39. pbs: 2000m 5:01.7e '97, 3000m 7:37.36 '99, 3000mSt 8:55.2 '94, road 10km 27:19 '00.

Albert CHEPKURUI b. 4 Apr 1981 Keiyo 1.70m 54kg.
World CC: '99-01-02: 5J/6 4k/6.
Progression at 5000m, 10000m: 1998- 13:49.48, 1999- 13:25.18, 2000- 12:59.90, 2001- 13:18.71, 28:06.86. pbs: 1500m 3:42.42 '00, 3000m 7:43.01 '99, rd 10km 27:31 '01.

Stephen CHERONO b. 15 Oct 1982 Keiyo 1.77m 64kg.
At 2000mSt: WY: '99- 1. At 3000mSt: 3rd GP 2001. World junior record 3000m steeplechase 2001.
Progression at 3000mSt: 1997- 8:43.0A, 1999- 8:19.12, 2001- 7:58.66. pbs: 1500m 3:35.47 '01, 2000m 5:03.06 '01, 3000m 7:46.03 '01, 2M 8:18.80 '99.

William CHIRCHIR b. 6 Feb 1979 Bomet 1.77m 55kg. Kipsigis.
At 800m: WJ: '98- 1. At 1500m: OG: '00- h; WCh: '01- 4; 3rd GP 2001. Won Kenyan 1500m 2001.
Ratified world junior 1500m record 1998.
Progression at 800m, 1500m: 1997- 1:47.08, 3:35.44; 1998- 1:44.69, 3:33.24; 1999- 1:43.33, 3:36.22; 2000- 1:43.84, 3:31.02; 2001- 1:44.02, 3:29.29. pbs: 1000m 2:14.99 '99, 1M 3:47.94 '00, 3000m 7:55.78 '97, HJ 1.90 '97.
Won Kenyan Schools decathlon in 1997. His younger brother **Cornelius** (b. 7 Oct 1983) won the 1500m at the 1999 World Youth Champs and at the 2000 World Juniors; he set a world age-16 best of 3:35.16 in 2000, improving to 3:34.53 in 2001, when he also ran 1:44.98 for 800m.

Julius GITAHI b. 29 Apr 1978 Nyeri 1.68m 52kg. Based in Japan.
At 5000m: OG: '00- 9; AfG: '99- 1; Kenyan champion 2000. At 10000m: Won GWG 1998, JPN Ch 1997. 3rd GP 3000m 1998.
Progression at 5000m, 10000m: 1994- 13:51.11, 28:43.96; 1995-13:22.58, 28:00.12; 1996- 13:24.98, 27:28.60; 1997- 13:05.64, 27:44.49; 1998- 13:01.89, 27:11.17; 1999- 13:05.45, 27:17.66; 2000- 13:23.12; 2001- 13:11.66, 28:01.60. pbs: 3000m 7:31.13 '98. HMar 61:33 '98.
Started running when he went to Japan to study in 1994.

Patrick Mutuku **IVUTI** b. 30 Jun 1978 1.65m 52kg.
At 10000m: OG: '00- 4. World CC: '96-7-9-00-01: 9J/6J/2/4/7.
Progression at 5000m, 10000m: 1999- 28:48.0A, 2000- 13:02.68, 27:09.79; 2001- 13:24.48, 28:53.7A. pb HMar 59:31 '00.

William KALYA b. 4 Aug 1974 1.71m 62kg.
At 10000m: CG: '98- 2. At 5000m: AfCh: '98- 3.
Progression at 5000m, 10000m: 1990- 14:00.3, 1995- 13:03.08, 1997- 13:12.76, 1998- 13:20.85, 28:06.3A; 1999- 28:31.30, 2000- 13:32.25, 27:23.65; 2001- 13:17.00, 27:52.26. pbs: 1500m 3:37.95 '91, 2000m 5:01.6+ '95, 3000m 7:31.14 '97.

Charles KAMATHI b. 18 May 1978 1.65m 51kg. Police constable.
At 10,000m: WCh: '01- 1. World CC: '00-01-02: 7/3/5. Won KEN 10000m 2001.
Progression at 5000m, 10000m: 1999- 13:05.29, 26:51.49; 2000- 13:23.24; 2001- 13:05.16, 27:22.58. pbs: 1500m 3:41.6? '99, 3000m 7:43.50 '00.
Made a sensational debut in European competition when he won at 10000m in 26:51.49 in Brussels in September 1999. He had won in India in July at 3000m 7:56.56 and 5000m 13:45.91 in his only previous races outside Kenya, where he had been 2nd at 5000m and 10,000m in the Kenyan Police Championships (c. 14:01 and 28:57) and had a 5000m best of c.13:43.

John Kemboi **KIBOWEN** 21 Apr 1969 Changach 1.75m 64kg. Nandi.
At 5000m: WCh: '01- 4. At 1500m: WCh: '97- h; CG: '98- 4. World CC 4k: '98-00-01: 1/1/7; Rd Rly team: '98- 1. Won KEN 1500m 1998.
Commonwealth 2000m record 1998.
Progression at 1500m, 5000m: 1996- 3:38.6, 13:48.5; 1997- 3:30.44, 1998- 3:30.18, 2000- 3:33.04, 2001- 12:59.97. pbs: 1M 3:47.88 '97, 2000m 4:48.74 '98, 3000m 7:29.09 '98.
Trained as an aircraft technician 1992-5. before concentrating on running. Missed 1999 season through injury.

Japheth KIMUTAI Butia b. 20 Dec 78 Lelmokwo, Nandi 1.73m 55kg.
At 800m: OG: '00- sf; WCh: '99- 5; CG: '98- 1; AfG: '99- 1; AfCh: '98- 1; WJ: '94- 2, '96- 4; WCp: '98- 4; AfJ: '95- 1 (1 1500m). 3rd GP 1999. Kenyan champion 1999.
World junior 800m record 1997.
Progression at 800m: 1994- 1:47.6, 1995- 1:47.0, 1996- 1:45.4, 1997- 1:43.64, 1998- 1:42.76, 1999- 1:42.69, 2000- 1:43.87, 2001- 1:45.75. pbs: 1000m 2:14.28 '00, 1500m 3:34.14 '00.
A product of St Patrick's High School and the renowned coach Brother Colm O'Connell. After the disappointment of losing World Juniors in 1996, came back the following year to break Joaquim Cruz's 16 year-old 800m WJR. While still a teenager in 1998, ranked as world no.1 and in Zürich broke the three year unbeaten run of Wilson Kipketer. Trains in Iten, but based during the European summer in Tubingen, Germany.

Kenneth KIMWETICH (NGETICH) b. 1 Jan 1973 Eldoret 1.83m 73kg.
At 800m: WCh: '99- 7; CG: '98- 8; AfG: '99- 5. Kenyan champion 1998.
Progression at 800m: 1998- 1:43.03, 1999- 1:43.98, 2000- 1:44.20, 2001- 1:44.21. pb 1000m 2:13.56 '99. Did not race prior to 1998.

Robert KIPCHUMBA b. 24 Feb 1984 1.70m 62kg.
At 10000m: WJ: '00- 1. World CC: '00- 1J.
Progression at 5000m, 10000m: 2000- 13:46.03, 27:43.14; 2001- 13:19.76, 27:25.55. pb 3000m 7:44.36 '01.
Won 2000 World 10000m title at 16 years 235 days.

Sammy KIPKETER b. 29 Sep 1981 Keiyo 1.66m 52kg.
At 5000m: WCh: '01- 7. 3rd GP 3000m 2000. World CC: '99- 6J, 4k: '00-01: 2/4. Won KEN 4k CC 2002.
Official world junior record 3000m 1999.
Progression at 5000m: 1999- 12:58.10, 2000- 12:54.07, 2001- 12:59.34. pbs: 1500m 3:41.3A '00, 2000m 5:00.0e '99, 3000m 7:33.62 '01, 10km Rd 27:18 '01.
World age-17 bests at 3000m and 5000m 1999.

Luke KIPKOSGEI b. 27 Nov 1975 Iten 1.76m 57kg.
Won GWG 5000m 1998, GP 3000m 2000 (3rd 2001). World 4kCC: '02- 2.
Progression at 5000m, 10000m: 1996- 13:15.00, 27:26.12; 1997- 13:22.68, 27:29.44; 1998- 12:57.32, 27:22.54; 1999- 13:00.83, 2000- 12:56.50, 27:57.11; 2001- 13:02.25, 27:12.37. pbs: 1500m 3:35.48 '98, 1M 3:56.4+ '98, 2000m 4:52.82 '98. 3000m 7:27.59 '98, 2M 8:17.53 '98.
Ran 27:26.12 on track debut at 10000m in Melbourne, December 1996.

Benjamin KIPKURUI b. 28 Dec 1980 Molo 1.74m 57kg. Kipsigis.
At 1500m (/800m): WJ: '98- 2; AfG: '99- (4); AfJ: '97- 1/1.
World junior records 1000m and 1500m 1999.
Progression at 800m, 1500m: 1997- 1:49.3, 3:44.17; 1998- 1:44.71, 3:35.35, 1999- 1:44.56, 3:33.16; 2000- 1:46.30, 3:30.73; 2001- 1:44.80, 3:30.67. pbs: 1000m 2:15.00 '99, 1M 3:49.34 '00.
World age-17 bests at 800m and 1500m in 1998.

Josephat KIPRONO b. 12 Dec 1973 Eldoret 1.72m 52kg. FILA, Italy.
At Mar: WCh: '01- dnf. At HMar: WCh: '96- 2.
Kenyan marathon record to win at Berlin 1999.
Progression at Mar: 1998- 2:07:27, 1999- 2:06:44, 2000- 2:07:29, 2001- 2:06:50. pbs: 5000m 13:50.37 '95, 10000m 28:57.1 '93, Road: 10km 28:39 '96, 15km 43:46 '96, HMar 60:27 '98, 59:46sh '96; 3000mSt 8:42.2 '95.
Second in 1996 Stramilano half marathon, when course was short by 49m. Marathon debut with 4th at Rotterdam (2:09:11), then 2nd Berlin 1998. In 1999 he was 5th in London before winning at Berlin. He won the Milennium Marathon in Rome on 1 Jan 2000 and was second in Chicago 2000. He won at Rotterdam 2001 in 2:06:50 to become the first man to run two sub 2:07s and his 2nd at Amsterdam 2001 in 2:07:06 is the fastest third best. His half-brother **Isaac Kiprono** has a marathon pb of 2:09:59 '01 and another brother **Luke Kibet** 2:10:18 '01.

Fred KIPROP b. 3 Jun 1974. FILA.
Progression at Mar: 1997- 2:08:19, 1998- 2:11:15, 1999- 2:06:47, 2000- 2:08:23, 2001- 2:09:43, 2002- 2:09:08. pbs: road 10km 27:52 '99.
2nd in Chicago 1997, has three wins in his ten marathons: Gold Coast 1998 and 1999 before his fourth fastest of all-time at Amsterdam 1999.

Enock KOECH b. 4 Apr 1981 1.78m 64kg.
World 4k CC: '10- 1. Won KEN 4k CC 2001.
Progression at 1500m: 2000- 3:40.5A, 2001- 3:31.38. pbs: 1M 3:51.50 '01, 2000m 4:55.92 '01.
First ever race outside Kenya was World short-course CC win in 2001.

Daniel Kipngetich **KOMEN** b. 17 May 1976 Mwen 1.70m 60kg. Keiyo.
At 5000m (10000m): WCh: '97- 1, '99- 5; CG: '94- (9), '98- 1; AfCh: '98- 1; WJ: '94- 1 (1); WCp: '98- 1. Won overall & 5000m GP 1996. World CC: '94- 2J, '98- 2 4k. Won Kenyan 5000m 1997.
World record: 3000m 1996, 5000m 1997, world best 2 miles 1996 (8:03.54) and 1997. WIR 3000m 7:24.90 '98 and 5000m 12:51.48 '98. World junior records 1500m, 5000m 1995. Commonwealth & Kenyan records 2000m 1998, 3000m 1996, 5000m (4) 1996-7, Kenyan 1500m & 1M 1997.
Progression at 1500m, 5000m, 10000m: 1993- 13:58.30, 1994- 13:31.10, 28:29.74; 1995- 3:34.63, 12:56.15, 28:12.79; 1996- 3:34.17, 12:45.09; 1997- 3:29.46, 12:39.74; 1998- 3:30.49, 12:51.48i/12:54.82; 1999- 3:35.42, 12:55.16; 2000- 3:43.5A, 13:01.78; 2001- 13:01.98. pbs: 1M 3:46.38 '97, 2000m

4:51.30 '98, 3000m 7:20.67 '96, 2M 7:58.61 '97, 3000mSt 8:54.5 '94, Road 10km 27:46 '94.
Ran 57.42 first lap in 1994 Commonwealth Games 5000m. In August 1996 he missed world records by narrow margins: 3000m by 0.05 at Monaco 10th, 5000m by 0.70 at Zürich on 14th, 3000m by 0.76 in Brussels on 23rd; then, on 1 September, came his superb 3000m at Rieti, in which he took 4.44 sec off Noureddine Morceli's old record, running under 60 secs for each 400m. In 1997 he ran first sub-8 minute 2 miles at Hechtel and lopped 2.12 secs off Gebrselassie's 9-day old 5000m world record at Brussels. Former high jumper and soccer goalkeeper.

John Cheruiyot **KORIR** b. 13 Dec 1981 1.72m 57kg.
At 10000m: OG: '00- 5; WCh: '01- 8. Kenyan champion 2000.
Progression at 5000m,10000m: 1999- 13:24.22, 27:38.86; 2000- 13:09.58, 27:24.75; 2001- 13:19.58, 27:49.34A. pbs: 3000m 7:43.35 '00, 5000m 13:18.00 '98, HMar 61:00 '02. Ran fastest ever 10,000m at high altitude, 27:48,42, to win 2000 Kenyan title.

Japhet KOSGEI b. 20 Dec 1968. 1.65m 52kg. FILA, Milan.
Progression at Mar: 1998- 2:09:59, 1999- 2:07:09, 2000- 2:07:15. 2001- 2:09:19. pb HMar 60:01 '99.
Won first four marathons: Turin and Venice 1998, Rotterdam 1999, Tokyo 2000; then dnf London and 2nd New York 2000 & 2001, 5th London 2001. Also won 1999 Lisbon half marathon in 60:01.

John KOSGEI b. 13 Jul 1973 Elgayo Marakwet 1.84m 71kg.
At 3000mSt: CG: '98- 1; AfCh: '92- 7. World CC 4k: '98- 5, '99- 8; Rd Rly team: '98- 1. Won KEN 4k CC 1998.
Progression at 1500m, 3000mSt: 1990- 9:12.0A, 1991- 8:54.0A, 1992- 3:43.98, 8:32.03; 1994- 8:48.5A, 1995- 3:40.25, 1996- 3:34.50, 8:05.68; 1997- 3:34.09, 8:03.89; 1998- 3:41.55, 8:09.08; 1999- 3:43.2, 8:42.52; 2000- 3:37.74, 8:19.47; 2001- 8:12.11. pbs: 1M 3:54.7 '96, 2000m 4:53.7 '96, 3000m 7:37.39 '96, 5000m 13:28.62 '96, 2000mSt 5:25.17 '92, road 10km 28:56.
As pacemaker, took Daniel Komen to 2000m in his epic 3000m world record in Rieti in 1996. Six days later he made an extraordinary breakthrough at 3000m steeplechase at Milan, beating a top-class field in 8:05.68.

Paul KOSGEI Malakwen b. 22 Apr 1978 Marakwet 1.75m 57kg.
At 3000mSt: WCh: '99- 7. At 10000m: WCh: '01- 7. World CC: '97- 3J, 4k: '98-9-00: 3/2/3; 12k: '01- 5; Rd Rly team: '98- 1.
World junior record 3000m steeplechase 1997.
Progression at 5000m, 10000m, 3000mSt: 1997- 8:07.69, 1998- 8:07.86, 1999- 8:07.13, 2000- 13:05.44, 27:38.22, 8:29.57; 2001- 13:06.29, 27:51.87A. pbs: 1500m: 3:42.7A '00, 2000m 5:03.1+ '00, 3000m 7:39.15 '00, 2000mSt 5:19.78 '98.
Won his heat at 1999 World Champs in 8:10.34, the fastest ever time in a preliminary round. Ran world road best 10km 27:03 in 2000.

Reuben KOSGEI b. 2 Aug 1979 Kapsabet 1.70m 55kg.
At 3000mSt: OG: '00- 1; WCh: '01- 1; WJ: '98- 1; Afr-J: '97- 1. Kenyan champion 2000.
Progression at 3000mSt: 1998- 8:23.76, 1999- 8:12.33, 2000- 8:03.92, 2001- 7:57.29. pbs: 1500m 3:37.24 '00, 3000m 7:41.86i '00.
After his World Championship success in 2001, he improved his best ever time to 8:03.22 at Zürich, but was well beaten by Brahim Boulami as he was when Boulami set a world record a weerk later in Brussels, but Kosgei improved again to 7:57.29, to make him fourth fastest of all-time at the event.

Bernard LAGAT b. 12 Dec 1974 Kapsabet 1.75m 61kg. Studied business management at Washington State University, USA. Nandi.
At 1500m: OG: '00- 3; WCh: '01- 2; WUG: '99- 1; 2nd GP 1999-2000. At 3000m: WI: '01- 6. Won NCAA 5000m 1999 (and indoor 1M/3000m).
Commonwealth and KEN 1500m record 2001.
Progression at 1500m: 1996- 3:37.7A, 1997- 3:41.19, 1998- 3:34.48, 1999- 3:30.56, 2000- 3:28.51, 2001- 3:26.34. pbs: 800m 1:46.02 '98, 1000m 2:18.70 '00, 1M 3:47.28 '01, 2000m 4:55.49 '99, 3000m 7:33.51 '00, 5000m 13:23.46 '00.
After impressive results in GP races he gave up his final year of scholastic eligibility (as under NCAA rules no payments can be received) at his university in order to compete (for money) in the 1999 Grand Prix Final, in which he was 2nd. Had a great outdoor season in 2001, but only won 3 of 17 races at 1500m or 1 mile as he was 2nd to Hicham El Guerrouj seven times, including his 3:26.34 at Brussels for 2nd on the world all-time list.

Elijah LAGAT b. 19 Jun 1966 Saniak, Kapsabet district 58kg. Nandi.
At Mar: OG: '00- dnf.
Progression at Mar: 1993- 2:17:14, 1994- 2:18:07, 1995- 2:12:40, 1996- 2:11:54, 1997- 2:07:41, 1998- 2:08:52, 1999- 2:08:50, 2000- 2:09:47. pbs: 10000m 28:09.1A '98; HMar 60:24 '99.
Four wins in 13 marathons: Jerez 1994, Berlin 1997, Prague 1998, Boston 2000; 2nd Mombasa 1993, Frankfurt 1995, Turin 1997. Based in Italy with the FILA group of Dr Gabriele Rosa.

David LELEI b. 10 May 1971 Uasin Gishu 1.76m 60kg. Also known as David Kimeli.
At 1500m: WCh: '99- 7; AfG: '99- 2. At 800m: WI: '01- 4.
Progression at 800m, 1500m: 1996- 1:47.51A, 1997- 1:45.44, 3:33.83; 1998- 1:46.96, 3:31.53; 1999- 1:45.35, 3:32.84; 2000- 1:43.97, 3:36.38; 2001- 1:44.96. pbs: 1000m 2:17.74 '01, 1M 3:53.14 '99, 2000m 5:01.1 '98.

Benjamin LIMO b. 23 Aug 1974 Kaptagat 1.78m 65kg. Army engineer.
At 5000m: WCh: '99- 2. Won GP 3000m 1999. World 4k CC: '98-9-01- 4/1/3; Rd Rly team: '98- 1.
Progression at 5000m: 1998- 13:07.38, 1999- 12:55.86, 2000- 12:55.82, 2001- 12:59.53. pbs: 1500m 3:37.59 '99, 2000m 4:59.2e '99, 3000m 7:28.67 '99.
Only began running seriously in November 1997. Has great finishing speed.

Felix LIMO b. 22 Aug 1980 Nandi. 1.74m 58kg. World best for 15km road with 41:29 at Nijmegen 2001. pb HMar 61:15 '02.
Progression at 5000m, 10000m: 1998- 28:48A, 1999- 13:23.43, 28:23.30; 2000- 13:33.90, 27:04.54; 2001- 13:16.42, 27:26.86. pbs: 3000m 7:40.67 '01.

Richard Kipkemei **LIMO** b. 18 Nov 1980 Cheptigit 1.67m 53kg. Kalenjin.
At 5000m: OG: '00- 10; WCh: '01- 1; CG: '98- 3; AfG: '99- 6. At 3000mSt: AfCh: '98- 2. World CC: '98-9-02: 2J/ 2J/4. Won KEN 5000m 2001, CC 2002.
World junior records 3000m 1998, 2M 1999.
Progression at 5000m, 10000m: 1998- 13:21.59, 1999- 12:58.15, 2000- 12:58.70, 2001- 12:56.72, 27:25.27. pbs: 2000m 5:00.6 '99, 3000m 7:32.23 '01, 2M 8:13.47 '99, 3000mSt 8:20.67 '98; Road 10km 27:12 '00.

Simon MAINA Munyi b. 18 Mar 1978 Nyeri 1.77m 52kg. Kikuyu. Lives in Japan.
At 10000m: CG: '98- 1; AfG: '99- 4. Won JPN 5000m 1997-8, KEN 10000m 1998.
Progression at 5000m, 10000m: 1997- 13:33.1, 27:36.5; 1998- 13:10.71, 27:21.14; 1999- 13:15.88, 27:18.74; 2000- 13:19.60, 27:18.95; 2001- 13:15.92, 27:56.82. Rd pbs: 10M 45:29 '01; HMar 60:48 '00.

Benjamin MAIYO b. 6 Oct 1978 Trans Nzoia 1.75m 58kg.
At 10000m: WCh: '99- 7; AfG: '99- 5.
Progression at 5000m, 10000m: 1998- 13:18.98, 27:34.38; 1999- 13:02.38, 28:01.8A; 2000- 13:02.28, 28:28.7A; 2001- 13:05.43, 27:07.55. pbs: 1500m 3:42.30 '99, 2000m 5:01.9+ '00; 3000m 7:32.36 '00.

Kipkirui MISOI b. 23 Dec 1978 Bomet 1.77m 59kg.
At 3000mSt: CG: '98- 3; WJ: '96- 2; AfG: '99- 1. World CC: '98- 8 4k.
World junior record 3000m steeplechase 1998.
Progression at 3000mSt: 1995- 8:56.0A, 1996- 8:33.31, 1997- 8:16.76, 1998- 8:09.46, 1999- 8:08.62, 2000- 8:07.21, 2001- 8:01.69. pbs: 1500m 3:39.17 '98, 1M 4:01.12 '01, 3000m 7:40.93 '00, 5000m 13:26.83 '98.

Jospeh Mwengi MUTUA b. 10 Dec 1978 1.70m 58kg.
At 800m: OG: '00- h; WJ: '96- 1.
Progression at 800m: 1995- 1:48.3A, 1996- 1:46.3A, 1997- 1:48.0A, 1998- 1:47.81, 1999- 1:48.8A, 2000- 1:45.49A, 2001- 1:43.63. pb 1500m 3:43.17 '99.

Noah Kiprono **NGENY** b. 2 Nov 1978 Kabenas 1.82m 68kg.
At 1500m: OG: '00- 1; WCh: '99- 2; WI: '01- 3; WJ: '96- 8 (tripped on final lap). Won GP 1999-2000, KEN 1500m 1999-2000, GWG 1M 2001.
Records: World and two records 1000m 1999, Commonwealth: 1500m (3), 1M 1999-2000.
Progression at 1500m: 1996- 3:42.44, 1997- 3:32.91, 1998- 3:30.34, 1999- 3:28.73/3:28.6+u, 2000- 3:28.12, 2001- 3:31.94. pbs: 800m 1:44.49 '00, 1000m 2:11.96 '99, 1M 3:43.40 '99, 2000m 4:50.08 '99, 3000m 7:35.46 '00.
Tripped on the first lap in the final of the 1996 World Juniors, sprinted to the front and led for three laps before being tripped again with 200m to go and losing his rhythm. Came through in 1997 to run world junior records. Although beaten three times by Hicham El Guerrouj, he had a wonderful season in 1999, following his World silver medal at 1500m, with the world record for 1000m (beating Seb Coe's 1981 mark) and a win in the Grand Prix Final 1500m. Then he ended El Guerrouj's winning run with Olympic gold in 2000. Brother of **Philip Kibitok** (b. 23 Mar 1971) pb 800m 1:43.55 '96.

Thomas NYARIKI 27 Sep 1971 Nyamira 1.70m 62kg.
At 5000m: OG: '96- 5; WCh: '97- 3; CG: '98- 2; AfG: '99- 3. 2nd GP 1997. Kenyan champion 1996, 1998. At 3000m: AfCh: '98- 1; WCp: '98- 3. World CC: '97- 3, '98- 4; Rd Rly team: '98- 1.
Progression at 5000m: 1996- 12:59.19, 1997- 12:55.94, 1998- 13:00.04, 1999- 13:04.07, 2001- 13:03.60. pbs: 1500m 3:42.8 '95, 1M 3:59.6 '96, 2000m 4:55.79 '97, 3000m 7:27.75 '96, road 10km 27:30 '01.
Ex sprinter. Married to Jackline Maranga (qv).

Laban ROTICH 20 Jan 1969 Mosoriot 1.63m 45kg. Fireman in Kenyan Air Force. Nandi.
At 1500m: OG: '96- 4; WCh: '97- 11, '99- 6, '01- sf; CG: '98- 1; AfCh: '98- 1; WI: '99- 2, '01- 4; WCp: '98- 1. 3rd GP 1996 & 1999. Won Kenyan 1500m 1997. Kenyan records 1500m (3) 1996-7, 1000m & 1M 1997.
Progression at 800m, 1500m: 1995- 3:39.85, 1996- 1:45.8A, 3:31.06; 1997- 1:44.47, 3:30.13; 1998- 1:43.65, 3:29.91; 1999- 3:31.60, 2000- 1:48.14, 3:32.93; 2001- 3:31.38. pbs: 1000m 2:14.43 '97, 1M 3:47.65 '97, 2000m 4:56.09i '99, 4:57.63 '96.
World high altitude best 1500m 3:33.1 '98.

Evans RUTTO b. 8 Apr 1978 Marakwet 1.68m 56kg.
World CC: 1999- 5; HMar: '01- 6.
Progression at 5000m, 10000m: 1999- 13:24.84, 28:06.60; 2000- 13:02.71, 27:21.32; 2001- 13:28.25. pbs: 2000m 5:02.3+ '99; 3000m 7:36.38 '00; Road: 15km 43:15 '01; 10M 46:26 '01, HMar 60:30 '01.

Wilberforce Kapkeny TALEL b. 10 Jan 1980.
World CC: '00-02: 5/3.

Progression at 5000m, 10000m: 1999- 29:33.4A, 2000- 13:13.15, 27:36.48; 2001- 13:25.59, 28:02.30.

Paul TERGAT b. 17 Jun 1969 Kabarnet, Barango 1.82m 62kg. Air Force sergeant (SPTE). Tugen.
At 10000m: OG: '96- 2, '00- 2; WCh: '95- 3, '97- 2, '99- 2. World HMar: '92-4-9-00: 5/11/1/1. World CC: '93-4-5-6-7-8-9-00: 10/4/1/1/1/1/1/3. Won Kenyan CC 1992, 1995-6.
World 10,000m record 1997. World road best 15km 1994 (42:13). World best half marathon 59:17 '98 and 59:06 '00 (40m dh at Lisbon) 58:51 at Milano 1996 was on course 49m short.
Progression at 5000m, 10000m, Mar: 1991- 29:46.8A, 1992- 13:48.64, 1993- 13:20.16, 27:18.43; 1994- 13:15.07, 27:23.89; 1995- 13:07.49, 27:14.08; 1996- 12:54.72, 26:54.41; 1997- 12:49.87, 26:27.85; 1998- 12:58.74, 26:44.44; 1999- 12:55.37, 27:10.08; 2000- 12:55.18, 27:03.87, 2:08:15. pbs: 1500m 3:42.3 '96, 1M 3:58.4 '96, 2000m 4:57.4 '96, 3000m 7:28.70 '96, HMar 59:06 '00, 58:51sh '96.
A former basketball player, he made a sensational impact when he emerged to win the Kenyan CC title in 1992; he had however to miss his first run outside Kenya at the World CC Champs through injury. Now has a record five successive World Cross-country titles. Won the Stramilano half marathon each year 1994-9 and unbeaten at that distance 1995-2000. On the track he has won four silver medals and a bronze behind the great Haile Gebrselassie in global 10,000m races. In 2001 he was second in London (2:08:15) and Chicago (2:08:56) in his first marathons.

Eric WAINAINA b. 19 Dec 1973 Nyahururu 1.75m 58kg. Lives in Japan.
At Mar: OG: '96- 3, '00- 2; WCh: '95- 18.
Progression at Mar: 1994- 2:15:03, 1995- 2:10:31, 1996- 2:10:37, 1997- 2:13:35, 2000- 2:10:17, 2001- 2:13:38. pbs: 10000m 28:52.6 '96, HMar 62:49 '95.
Marathon wins at Sapporo 1994, Tokyo 1995, Hokkaido 1997, Nagano 2000.

Raymond YATOR b. 7 Apr 1981 1.72m 55kg.
At 3000mSt: WCh: '01- 8; WJ: '00- 1; Af-J: '99-1.
World junior record 3000m steeplechase 2000.
Progression at 3000mSt: 1999- 8:15.31, 2000- 8:03.74, 2001- 8:09.20. pbs: 1500m 3:38.62 '01, 1M 3:55.12 '01, 5000m 13:30.02 '01, 10km Rd: 28:36 '00.

William Oloonkishu **YIAMPOY** b. 17 May 1974 Emarti, near Kilgoris 1.83m 70kg. Masai.
At 800m: OG: '00- sf; WCh: '01- 4. Kenyan & GWG champion 2001.
Progression at 800m: 1999- 1:44.38, 2000- 1:44.23, 2001- 1:43.00. pbs: 1000m 2:14.41 '99, 1500m 3:34.12 '01. Joined Kenya Police in 1990, began running in 1996.

Women

Selina (Sally) BARSOSIO b. 21 Mar 1978 Keiyo 1.65m 46kg. Schoolgirl. Elgeyo Marakwet.
At 10000m (5000m): OG: '96- 10, '00- 17; WCh: '93- 3, '95- (11), '97- 1; WJ: '92- 3; AfG: '95- 1; AfCh: '92- 5 (5), '98- (2). Won GP 5000m 1997 (3rd 3000m 2000), Kenyan 5000m 1998, 10000m 1993, 1997; CC 1996-7, African Junior 1500m & 3000m 1994. World CC: '93-4-5-6-7-8-00-01: 3J/1J/3/11/5/10/8 (4k)/18; Rd Rly team: '98- 2.
World Junior records: 10000m 1993 (not ratified as no drugs test) and 1997, 3000m 1997; Kenyan records 10000m 1993, 5000m 1996, 3000m 1997.
Progression at 5000m, 10000m: 1992- 32:41.76, 1993- 31:15.38, 1994- 15:42.45; 1995- 15:05.75, 32:22.26, 1996- 14:47.81, 31:36.00; 1997- 14:46.71, 31:32.92; 1998- 15:27.22, 32:50.16; 1999- 15:42.79, 32:26.28; 2000- 14:53.61, 31:57.41. pbs: 1500m 4:13.11 '00, 2000m 5:39.4 '97, 3000m 8:35.89 '97.
A prodigious talent at 15 (18 according to some sources, including her mother!), but remarkably fortunate to be reinstated after disqualification in the 1993 World 10,000m to become the youngest ever World Championship medallist. She had caused havoc during the race by continually baulking Elana Meyer and running across several other runners. Four years later she became Kenya's first senior woman track world champion. Missed 1999 season through injury.
Her elder sister Jepkemboi (**Florence**) Barsosio (b. 11 Aug 1976) was 6th in World marathon and won Paris marathon 2001, pb 2:27:00 '00; Kenyan champion and 13th World 5000m 1995, World CC: '96- 16, '97- 13. Niece of Paul Koech.

Joyce CHEPCHUMBA Koech b. 6 Nov 1970 Kericho 1.60m 52kg. Kenyan postal service.
At Mar: OG: '96- dnf, '00- 3. World HMar: '97-8-9-01: 4/6/5/18; CC: '94- 18.
Kenyan marathon record 1997.
Progression at Mar: 1995- 2:33:51, 1996- 2:29:38, 1997- 2:26:51, 1998- 2:23:57, 1999- 2:23:22, 2000- 2:24:02, 2001- 2:24:12. pbs: 800m 2:11.2 '94, 1500m 4:36.3A '91, 3000m 9:23.26 '95, 5000m 15:26.19 '00, 10000m 32:07.50 '99, road 5km 15:52 '94, 10km 32:19 '96, 15km 49:21 '97, 10M 54:27 '95, HMar 68:18 '00.
Five major wins in 15 marathons: London 1997 and 1999 (when she won the biggest ever prize of $230,000) (also 2nd 1996, 3rd 1998, 2000-01), Chicago 1998 and 1999, Tokyo 2000 (2nd 1997). New York: 4th (on marathon debut) 1995, 3rd 1996, 4th 2001. Won Great North Run 1999. Has a training base in Dettmond, Germany. Son born in 1991.

Susan CHEPKEMEI b. 25 Jun 1975 1.64m 48kg.
World HMar: '00- 2, '01- 2; CC: '98-9-00-01: 12/5/3/3; Rd Rly team: '98- 2. Won Kenyan 10,000m 2001.
Progression at Mar: 1998- 2:28:19, 1999- 2:26:38, 2001- 2:25:12. pbs: 3000m 8:43.95 '01, 5000m 14:55.27 '01, 10000m 33:01.2A '99; Road: 10km 31:52 '01, 15km 47:54 '01, 10M 51:23 '01, HMar 65:44 '01.

Second in her first two marathons: Berlin 1998 and Rotterdam 1999; then won Rotterdam and 2nd New York 2001. World best for half marathon on the slightly downhill Lisbon course in 2001; also won Great North Run 2001. Made big improvement on the track in 2001.

Lydia CHEROMEI b. 11 May 1977 1.62m 47kg. Married Hosea Kogo (5000m 13:24.22 '97) in December 1996.
At 5000m: OG: '96- h, '00- 6; WCh: '97- 5; AfG: '95- 3; 2nd GP 1997 At 10000m: OG: '92- h; WJ: '90- 3, '92- 4; AfG: '91- 2; AfCh: '92- 2, '93- 2 (8 3000m). World CC: '91-2: 1J/3J, '97-00-01: 11/4/3. Won Kenyan 10000m 1991-2, 5000m 1997, 2000.
Records: World junior 5000m 1995, African junior 3000m 1992, Kenyan 5000m 1995, 3000m 1997 and 2000.
Progression at 5000m, 10000m: 1990- 16:56.7, 33:20.83; 1991- 33:07.7, 1992- 15:17.31, 31:41.09; 1993- 32:54.55, 1994- 36:29.0, 1995- 14:53.44, 1996- 15:18.34, 1997- 14:46.72, 2000- 14:47.35. pbs: 1500m 4:09.32 '97, 2000m 5:38.9 '97, 3000m 8:29.14 '00.
At 13 in 1991, she is the youngest ever world junior cross-country champion. World age bests for 3000m, 5000m and 10000m at 13, 5000m at 15.

Rose CHERUIYOT b. 21 Jul 1976 Sabor, Keiyo county 1.63m 48kg. Elgeyo Marakwat.
At 5000m: OG: '00- 11; WCh: '95- 7, '01- 9; AfG: '95- 1. At 3000m: CG: '94- 6; Af-J: '94- 2 (1500m 3). At 1500m: WJ: '94- 4. World CC: '94-5-6-02: 2J/8/2/8, 4k: '00-01: 12/8. Won Kenyan CC 1995. Kenyan 5000m record 1996. Two world junior 5000m records 1995. World road bests at 5km (15:05) and 10M 1995.
Progression at 3000m, 5000m: 1993- 9:13.46, 1994- 9:00.89, 15:44.05; 1995- 8:47.35, 14:57.29; 1996- 8:39.34, 14:46.41; 2000- 8:39.88, 14:55.88; 2001- 8:41.74, 14:48.97. pbs: 1500m 4:16.41 '94, road 10km 31:43 '95, 15km 48:40 '01, 10M 51:40 '95.
Second World CC challenge 1994/5. Married Ismael Kirui (qv) on 16 Nov 1996.

Lornah KIPLAGAT b. 20 Mar 1974. 1.61m 47kg.
Progression at Mar: 1997- 2:33:50, 1998- 2:34:03, 1999- 2:25:29, 2000- 2:22:36, 2001- 2:27:56, 2002- 2:23:55. pbs: 3000m 8:52.82 '00, 5000m 15:06.40 '99, Road: 5M 25:09 '97 (former world best), 10km 30:52 '00, 15km 49:08 '99, 10M 53:30 '99, HMar 66:34 '01.
Marathon wins: Los Angeles 1997 and 1998, Rotterdam 1999, Osaka 2001. Capped a brilliant series of road runs with second in Chicago marathon 2000. Fourth Boston 2001.

Tegla LOROUPE Chepkite b. 9 May 1973 Kapsoit, West Pokot 1.56m 40kg. Pokot. Kenyan Post & Telecommunication Corporation.
At 10000m (Mar): OG: '92- 17, '96- 6, '00- 5 (13); WCh: '93- 4, '95- 3, '97- 6, '99- 3. World HMar: '93-7-8-9: 3/1/1/1; CC: '89- 28J, '90- 16J. Won GWG 10000m 1994, 1998; KEN 10000m 1995, 2000.
World records: marathon 1998 and 1999, 1 hour 1998, 20,000m 2000; three African marathon records 1997-9, KEN records: 3000m 1999, 5000m 2000, 10000m 1993 & 1999, Marathon (3) 1994-8.
Progression at 5000m, 10000m, Mar: 1989- 34:36.1A, 1990- 35:06.0A, 1991- 35:02.8A, 1992- 31:34.30mx/32:34.07, 1993- 15:08.03, 31:21.20; 1994- 15:22.54, 31:52.39, 2:27:37; 1995- 15:08.86, 31:17.66, 2:28:06; 1996- 15:08.79, 31:23.22, 2:28:37; 1997- 15:19.78, 31:20.53, 2:22:07; 1998- 14:47.77, 32:15.44, 2:20:47; 1999- 14:49.12, 30:32.03, 2:20:43; 2000- 14:45.95, 30:37.26, 2:24:33; 2001- 15:09.31, 31:50.97, 2:26:10. pbs: 1500m 4:29.39 '90, 3000m 8:30.95 '00, 1Hr 18340m '98, 20000m 1:05:26.6 '00; road 15km 48:52 '95, HMar 67:12 '96.
Eight wins in 19 marathons to 2nd Berlin 2001. She made a brilliant début to win in New York in 1994 and won again there in 1995; 2nd Boston 1996 and won at Rotterdam in 1997 in the second fastest ever by a woman. Faded to 7th in New York marathon 1996 and 1997, but recovered from what was at first thought a severe injury to place 7th in Osaka in January and then win in Rotterdam in a new world best time in April 1998. There was controversy, however, concerning this race as she was paced throughout by men. She was also illegally paced by a lapped runner in a 1 hour race at Borgholzhausen in August 1998 but this was ratified by the IAAF as a world record. 2nd Osaka and 1st in Rotterdam 1999. On the track in 1999 she won a World bronze at 10,000m and showed her speed by improving her pre-season 3000m pb of 9:01.62 to 8:33.36. Then she had an amazing 22 days in September-October, in which she ran on successive weekends: won HMar 69:20, world marathon record 2:20:43 in Berlin, won World HMar 68:48, 2nd Great North Run 69:35. Won London Marathon 2000, but ill for Olympic marathon.

Faith MACHARIA b. 9 Feb 1976 Nyeri 1.65m 55kg.
At 800m: WCh: '01- 4; won KEN 800m 2001. Kenyan 1000m record 2001.
Progression at 800m, 1500m: 1996- 2:05.51, 1997- 2:03.01, 4:18.96; 1998- 2:04.4, 1999- 2:01.33, 4:08.04; 2000- 2:01.09, 4:09.57; 2001- 1:58.34. pb 1000m 2:35.39 '01.

Leah MALOT b. 7 Jun 1972 1.68m 46kg.
At 10000m: WCh: '87- h, 99- dnf; AfG: '87- 1, '99- 3. World CC: '98-9-00-01-02: 8/9/6/6/11; HMar: '98- 10; Rd Rly team: '98- 2. 2nd GP 3000m 2000. Kenyan records: 3000m 1999, 5000m 2000.
Progression at 5000m, 10000m: 1987- 33:58.15, 1988- 38:09.8A, 1989- 36:40.4A, 1994- 35:53.2A, 1996- 16:20.91A, 1997- 15:10.12, 32:09.37, 1998- 15:09.75, 32:04.64; 1999- 15:03.75, 31:31.73; 2000- 14:39.83, 30:57.70; 2001- 14:56.95, 31:41.74. pbs:

800m 2:04.07 '00, 1000m 2:42.77 '99, 1500m 4:10.17 '99, 3000m 8:35.74 '99; Rd: 15km 49:06 '99, 10M 53:11 '98, HMar 69:43 '01.
Won African 10,000m title at age 15 in 1987. Ran for Kenyan World CC team in 1987 and 1994 before emerging in world class in 1997.

Edith MASAI b. 4 Apr 1967 1.68m 55kg.
At 5000m: WCh: '01- 7; Kenyan champion 2001. World 4km CC: '01- 3, '02- 1.
Progression at 5000m: 2001- 14:45.86. pbs: 2000m 5:40.3 '01, 3000m 8:31.76 '01; Road: 10km 31:27 '01, 15km 48:37 '01, HMar 67:53 '01.
Made an astonishing breakthough into world class at the age of 34 in 2001.

Naomi Wanjiku **MUGO** b. 2 Jan 1977 Nyahururu 1.63m 50kg.
At 1500m: OG: '96- dns, '00- h; CG: '98- 4; AfCh: '96- 1 (1 800m). Won Kenyan 1500m 1996-7. World CC: '94-6-7-8: 6J/3/8/11, 4k: '01- 11; Rd Rly team: '98- 2.
Kenyan 1500m record 1996 (also African Junior). Progression at 1500m: 1993- 9:29.6, 1995- 4:19.0A, 1996- 4:04.29, 1997- 4:10.07, 1998- 3:58.12, 1999- 4:10.59, 2000- 4:01.64, 2001- 4:05.10. pbs: 800m 2:02.13 '96, 1M 4:24.43 '98, 2000m 5:42.66 '01, 3000m 8:43.55 '00, 5000m 15:25.13 '00.

Catherine NDEREBA b. 21 Jul 1972.
At HMar: WCh: '99- 3.
Progression at Mar: 1999- 2:27:34, 2000- 2:21:33, 2001- 2:18:47. pbs: 1500m 4:27.6A '94, 3000m 9:25.10 '99, 5000m 15:27.84 '00, 10000m 32:17.58 '00; Road 5km 15:07 '98, 10km 31:02 '01, 15km 48:06 '01, 10M 52:25 '98. HMar 67:54 '01.
World marathon record 2001.
Marrried to Anthony Maina. Has had great success on the US road running circuit, where she was top ranked in 1996 and 1998, having had a baby, Jane, in 1997. Made marathon debut with 6th in Boston, followed by second in New York 1999 and wins in Boston and Chicago in both 2000 and 2001.

Isabellah OCHICHI b. 1979.
World 4k CC: '02: 3; HMar: '01- 8.
Road pbs: 10km 31:29 '01, 15km 47:54 '01, 10M 51:46 '01, HMar 68:38 '01.

Margaret OKAYO b. 30 May 1976.
At HMar: WCh: '99- 4.
Progression at Mar: 1999- 2:26:00, 2000- 2:26:36, 2001- 2:24:21. pb: 5000m 15:30.0A '01, Road: 10km 32:32 '99, 15km 49:09 '99, HMar 68:49 '02.
Made a brilliant marathon debut with 2:26:00 for 2nd at Chicago 1999, and won at San Diego 2000 and 2001 and New York 2001 (3rd 2000).

Esther WANJIRU b. 27 Mar 1977 1.62m 42kg. Based in Japan.
At 10000m: CG: '98- 1. At Mar: OG: '00- 4; WCh: '99- 11. Won Kenyan 10000m 1998.
World road 20km best (64:01) 2000, Kenyan Half Marathon record 1999.
Progression at 10000m, Mar: 1992- 34:38.05, 1994- 32:23.25, 1995- 32:04.27, 1996- 31:58.86, 1997- 31:52.44, 1998- 31:52.98, 1999- 32:07.05, 2:25:40; 2000- 2:23:31. pbs: 800m 2:09.43 '93, 1500m 4:19.97 '93, 3000m 9:11.71 '93, 5000m 15:16.42 '99, HMar 66:49 '99.
Brilliant marathon debut for 3rd in Osaka January 1999 and 3rd again in 2000.

KOREA

Governing body: Korea Amateur Athletic Federation, 10 Chamshil Dong, Songpa-Gu, Seoul. Founded 1945. **National Champions 2001**: **Men:** 100m: Shin Jung-ki 10.53, 200m: Park Sung-jin 21.81, 400m: Kim Jae-da 47.28, 800m: Lee Jae-hoon 1:48.32, 1500m: Lee Du-haeng 3:43.97, 5000m/10000m: Lee Dong-kil 14:23.23/30:02.62, 3000mSt: Huh In-gu 9:00.44, 110mh: Lee Jung-ho 14.31, 400mh: Shon Jung-ho 51.48, HJ: Park Jung-chul 2.15, PV: Kim Se-in 5.20, LJ: Park Hyung-min 7.41, TJ: Kim Young-mo 15.77, SP: Kim Jae-il 17.88, DT: Kim Young-chul 50.91, HT: Lee Jung-geam 59.48, JT: Park Jae-myong 72.13, Dec: Kim Kun-woo 7247, 20kmW: Kang Won-mo 1:44:51. **Women**: 100m/200m: Huh Soon-bok 11.98/24.52, 400m: Kim Dong-hyun 55.76, 800m/1500m: Noh Ryu-yeon 2:10.25/4:23.76, 5000m: Kim Ok-bin 16:38.88, 10000m: Chang Jin-suk 34:49.01, 100mh: Lee Yeon-kyong 13.87, 400mh: Lee Yun-kyong 60.91, HJ: Kim Young-ja 1.70, PV: Kim Mi-jung 3.20, LJ: Kim Su-yeon 6.10, TJ: Lee Kyong-sun 13.13, SP: Lee Myung-sun 18.32, DT: Won Soon-mi 47.48, HT: Chang Bok-shim 53.00, JT: Chang Jung-yeon 55.48, Hep: P Shin Myong-hee 4725, 20kmW: Kim Dan-oh 1:55:07.
Winners at **82nd National Games 2001: Men:** 100m: Kim Sang-do 10.58, 200m: Sun Min-suk 21.62, 400m: Kim Chung-hoon 48.34, 800m/1500m: Kim Soon-hyung 1:48.50/3:46.41, 5000m: Shon Mun-kyu 14:12.25, 10000m: Baek Seung-do 29:07.70, Mar: Lee Eui-soo 2:19:37, 3000mSt: Yun Sun-hoon 9:09.74, 110mh: Park Tae-kyong 14.07, 400mh: Lee Doo-yeon 50.08, HJ: Lee Jin-taek 2.24, PV/LJ: Kim Se-in 5.20/7.69, TJ: Kim Hyuk 16.07, SP: Kim Jae-il 17.95, DT: Kim Young-chul 51.41, HT: Mun Jun-heum 59.83, JT: Chu Ki-young 77.56, Dec: Kim Kun-woo 7304, 20kmW: Kim Dong-young 1:23:28. **Women**: 100m/200m: Huh Soon-bok 11.97/24.54, 400m: Lee Yun-kyong 56.38, 800m: Ryu Su-hee 2:10.59, 1500m: Han Jung-yeon 4:23.96, 5000m: Bae Hae-jin 16:21.25, 10000m: Oh Mi-ja 33:42.38, 20kmRd: Bae Hae-jin 71:05, 100mh: Shim Mi-ra 13.97, 400mh: Choi Hae-nam 59.94, HJ: Kim Mi-ok 1.76, LJ: Yu Soon-chun 6.34, TJ: Lee Kyong-Sun 13.43, SP: Lee Myung-sun 17.89, DT: Won Soon-mi 49.97, JT: Chang Jung-yeon 56.30, Hep: Kim Ju-mi 4725, 20kmW: Kim Mi-jung 1:38:49.

LEE Bong-ju b. 11 Oct 1970 1.68m 56kg. Samsung Ekectronics.

At Mar: OG: '96- 2, '00- 24; WCh: '95- 22, '01- dnf; AsiG: '98- 1. Korean champion 1992-3.
Korean marathon records 1998 and 2000.
Progression at Mar: 1992- 2:13:32, 1993- 2:13:16, 1994- 2:09:57, 1995- 2:10:58, 1996- 2:08:26, 1997- 2:10:33, 1998- 2:07:44, 1999- 2:12:11, 2000- 2:07:20, 2001- 2:09:11.
Won Kwangju and Honolulu marathons 1993, Gyeongju 1995, Fukuoka 1996, Boston 2001. 2nd Rotterdam 1998, Tokyo and Fukuoka 2000.

LATVIA

Governing body: Latvian Athletic Association, 1 Augsiela Str, Riga LV-1009. Founded 1921.
National Championships first held in 1920 (men), 1922 (women). **2001 Champions**: **Men**: 100m: Sergejs Insakovs 10.65, 200m: Inguns Sviklins 21.77, 400m: Dmitrijs Milkevics 46.66, 800m: Aivars Zacs 1:52.83, 1500m: Vitalijs Bulatnijs 3:54.09, 5000m/3000mSt: Dmitrijs Slesarjonoks 15:00.43/9:11.63, 10000m: Viktors Slesarjonoks 31:23.28, HMar: Rolands Kaimins 72:25, Mar: Ziedonis Zalkalns 2:27:25, 110mh/LJ: Janis Karlivans 14.73/7.18, 400mh: Egils Tebelis 52.04, HJ: Maris Prikulis 2.03, PV: Janis Patasnieks 4.20, TJ: Raitis Freimanis 15.72, SP: Maris Petrasko 16.82, DT: Maris Urtans 50.98, HT: Igors Sokolovs 61.26, JT: Eriks Rags 80.13, Dec: Normunds Jakusonoks 6713, 20kmW: Modris Liepins 1:26:35, 50kmW: Ugis Bruvelis 4:07:57. **Women**: 100m: Margarita Bondarenko 12.33, 200m/400m: Irena Zauna 24.95/54.25, 800m: Ieva Zunda 2:07.90, 1500m/3000m: Inna Poluskina 4:40.01/9:29.50, 5000m/HMar: Inara Luse 18:04.16/88:18, Mar: Laila Ceika 3:11:45, 2000mSt: Irina Stula 7:20.58, 100mh: Liga Klavina 14.29, 400mh: Liga Svirkste 67.11, HJ/Hep: Iveta Grunte 1.77/4471, PV: Elina Ringa 3.20, LJ: Esenija Volzankina 5.82, TJ: Ineta Radevica 12.84, SP: Irina Vasiljeva 10.70, DT: Dace Ruskule 54.68, HT: Vineta Verse 36.14, JT: Ilze Gribule 49.02, 10kmW/20kmW: Yolanta Dukure 46:46/1:31:47.

Aigars FADEJEVS b. 27 Dec 1975 Valmiera 1.75m 59kg. ASK.
At 20kmW (50kmW): OG: '96- 6, '00- 14 (2); WCh: '97- dnf, '99- dnf (dq), '01- dnf (4); EC: '94- 17, '98- 2; EU23: '97- 1; WCp: '97- 15, '99- (9); ECp: '98-00-01: 3/6/8. At 10kmW: EJ: '93- 11; WJ: '94- dq. Won LAT 50kmW 1998.
Latvian records 20kmW 1996, 50kmW 1998.
Progression at 20kmW, 50kmW: 1993- 1:36:19, 1994- 1:23:41, 4:02:18; 1995- 1:22:56, 1996- 1:20:40, 1997- 1:19:36, 1998- 1:19:44, 3:43:18; 1999- 1:20:31, 3:46:36; 2000- 1:20:18, 3:43:40; 2001- 1:19:53, 3:46:20. pbs: 5000mW 18:48.30 '98, 10000mW 39:17.8 '98, Mar (run) 2:27:20 '01.

Stanislav OLIJAR b. 22 Mar 1979 Chelyabinsk, Russia 1.90m 80kg. ASK.
At 110mh: OG: '00- sf; WCh: '97- qf, '99- sf; EC: '98- sf; WJ: '96- h (dnq LJ), '98- 1; EJ: '97- 2; EU23: '99- 2. At 60mh: WI: '01- 8; EI: '00- 2, '02- 4. Won LAT 100m 1999.
Latvian 110mh record 2000.
Progression at 110mh: 1996- 14.52, 1997- 13.62, 1998- 13.49, 1999- 13.28, 2000- 13.25, 2001- 13.29. pbs: 60m 6.70i '98, 6.6i '01; 100m 10.45 '98, 200m 20.97 '00, 400m 46.66 '00, 50mh 7.56i '01, 60mh 7.50i '00, LJ 7.94i '00, 7.57A '97.
His mother (and coach) Ludmila Olijar (b. 5 Feb 1958) was the Latvian record holder for 100mh 12.90 (1989).

Eriks RAGS b. 1 Jun 1980 Ventspils 1.83m 93kg. Ventspils.
At JT: OG: '00- dnq 26; WCh: '97- dnq 22, '99- 10, '01- 8; EC: '98- dnq 21; WJ: '94- dnq 28; EU23: '97- 4; WUG: '99- 1, '01- 1. 2nd GP 2001. Latvian champion 1997, 1999-2001.
Five Latvian javelin records 1999-2001.
Progression at JT: 1991- 63.50, 1992- 60.90, 1993- 65.22, 1994- 68.42, 1995- 75.32, 1996- 76.92, 1997- 79.04, 1998- 80.50, 1999- 83.78, 2000- 83.61, 2001- 86.47.

Women

Valentina GOTOVSKA b. 3 Sep 1965 Kraslava 1.76m 62kg. née Tolstik. Arkadija. Hairdresser.
At HJ: OG: '92- 13=; WCh: '93- 8; EC: '90- 7, '94- dnq 26. At LJ: OG: '96- dnq 28, '00- dnq 20; WCh: '95- dnq 26, '97 dnq 29, '99- dnq 15, '01- 5; EC: '98- dnq 15. Won Latvian HJ 1982, 1989-96, 100m 1995, LJ 1995-9, Hep 1994, 1996.
LAT records: high jump 1990, long jump (3) 2000.
Progression at HJ, LJ: 1980- 1.50, 4.53; 1981- 1.65, 4.94; 1982- 1.82i/1.78, 5.41; 1988- 1.90, 1989- 1.95, 1990- 1.97, 1991- 1.92, 1992- 1.92, 1993- 1.95, 1994- 1.94, 6.18; 1995- 1.88, 6.66; 1996- 1.86i/1.84, 6.41/6.67w; 1997- 1.90, 6.67; 1998- 1.85, 6.70; 1999- 6.73, 2000- 6.91, 2001- 6.88. pbs: 100m 11.76 '95, 200m 24.77 '97, 24.75w '96; 100mh 14.54w '96, 14.81 '98; TJ 12.11i '98, Hep 5786w/5575 '96.
Married to Yuriy Gotovskis (HJ 2.29). Son born June 1986.

Liga KLAVINA b. 27 Jan 1980 Tukums 1.80m 69kg. Tukums/LU.
At Hep: EU23: '01- 1. At HJ: OG: '00- dnq; WCh: '01- dnq 22; EJ: '99- 11. At Pen: WI: '01- 7. Won LAT Hep 1998, HJ 2000, 100mh 2001.
Latvian heptathlon record 2001.
Progression at HJ. Hep: 1993- 1.57, 1995- 1.76, 1996- 1.81, 5020; 1997- 1.77i/1.75, 5251; 1998- 1.82, 5305; 1999- 1.85, 2000- 1.94, 2001- 1.93, 6279. pbs: 100m 12.27 '00, 200m 24.45 '01, 800m 2:26.22 '01, 60mh 8.52i '01, 100mh 13.96 '01, LJ 6.50 '01, SP 14.82 '01, JT 41.87 '01, pen 4452i '01.

Jelena PROKOPCUKA b. 21 Sep 1976 Riga 1.68m 51kg. née Celnova. Arkadija.
At 5000m (/10000m): OG: '96- h, '00- 9/19; WCh: '97- h; EC: '98- 16; EU23: '97- 5/6. At 3000m (/10000m): WJ: '94: h/13; EJ: '95- 5/4; EI: '98- 4, '00- 4. W HMar: '00- 5. Won LAT 1500m

1994, 1997-8, 3000m 1992-3, 1998-9, 5000m 1995-7, HMar 1995, 1999.
Latvian records 5000m (4) 1997-2000, 10000m 2000, HMar 2001.
Progression at 5000m, 10000m: 1994- 35:22.44, 1995- 16:20.7, 34:21.84; 1996- 15:59.00, 33:59.9; 1997- 15:40.68, 33:41.51; 1998- 15:30.76, 33:29.04; 1999- 16:09.22, 2000- 14:47.71, 31:27.86; 2001- 15:14.73, 32:02.96. pbs: 400m 60.46 '98, 800m 2:05.82 '00, 1500m 4:12.36 '00, 3000m 8:44.66i/ 8:46.97 '00, 15km 48:47 '01, HMar 68:43 '01.
Took over two minutes off her 10000m pb when winning European Challenge B race in 2000. Married to Aleksandrs Prokopchuks (Latvian marathon record 2:15:56 '95).

LITHUANIA

Governing body: Athletic Federation of Lithuania, Zemaites 6, Vilnius LT 2009. Founded 1921.

2001 National Champions: **Men**: 100m: Sigitas Kavaliauskas 10.96, 200m: Vytautas Kancleris 21.56, 400m: Raimundas Turla 48.15, 800m/ 1500m: Evaldas Martinka 1:50.26/3:49.39, 5000m: Dainius Saucikovas 14:54.01, 10000m/3000mSt: Mindaugas Pukstas 29:47.98/8:43.40, 110mh: Vytautas Kancleris 14.33, 400mh: Tomas Alisauskas 55.53, HJ: Aurelijus Eirosius 2.17, PV: Regimantas Kicas 4.30, LJ: Arinijus Veiknys 7.75, TJ: Audrius Raizgys 16.08, SP: Saulius Kleiza 18.67, DT: Virgilijus Alekna 68.20, HT: Edgaras Brinkis 60.47, JT: Tomas Intas 78.12, Dec: Jonas Spudis 6760, 20kmW: Gintaras Andriuskevicius 1:22:10, 50kmW: Anatolijus Launikonis 4:19:34. **Women**: 100m: Audra Dagelyté 11.67, 200m/ 400m: Zana Minina 24.08/53.94, 800m/1500m: Irina Krakoviak 2:04.33/4:12.56, 5000m: Inga Juodeskiené 15:57.93, 10000m: Diana Maciusonyté 35:06.78, 2000mSt: Ieva Bièkuté 7:22.54, 100mh: Diana Radaviciené 14.55, 400mh: Inesa Kliukoityte 61.71, HJ: Nelé Zilinskiené 1.92, PV: Rita Snarskaité 3.10, LJ: Zivilé Siksnelyté 6.11, TJ: Zivilé Zebarauskaité 13.31, SP: Austra Skujytë 16.03, DT: Raminta Sakalauskaité 47.91, HT: Lina Skladaityté 45.42, JT: Rita Ramanauskaité 57.07, Hep: Ernesta Paulauskaité 5383, 10000mW/ 20kmW: Sonata Milusauskaité 46:49.0/1:34:08.

Virgilijus ALEKNA b. 13 Feb 1972 Terpeikiai, Kupiskis 2.00m 130kg. PE student and (from 1995) guard of the Lithuanian president.
At DT: OG: '96- 5, '00- 1; WCh: '95- dnq 19, '97- 2, '99- 4, '01- 2; EC: '98- 3; WCp: '98- 1. Won GP 2001 (2nd 1999). LIT champion 2000-01.
Four Lithuanian discus records 2000.
Progression at DT: 1990- 52.84, 1991- 57.16, 1992- 60.86, 1993- 62.84, 1994- 64.20, 1995- 62.78, 1996- 67.82, 1997- 67.70, 1998- 69.66A, 1999- 68.25, 2000- 73.88, 2001- 70.99. pb SP: 19.99 '97.
His 69.66 discus throw at the 1998 World Cup is the longest ever in a major event, and he threw 69.30 to win 2000 Olympic gold. His 72.35 and 73.88 at the 2000 LTU Championships were the second and third longest ever. On 4 Mar 2000 he married Kristina Sablovskyte (pb LJ 6.14 '96, TJ 12.90 '97, sister of Remigija Nazaroviene).

LUXEMBOURG

Governing body: Fédération Luxembourgeoise d'Athlétisme, Boite Postale 503, 2015 Luxembourg. Founded 1928.

2001 National Champions: **Men**: 100m: Christian Kemp 11.12, 200m/400m: Marc Reuter 22.25/ 50.68, 800m: Christian Thielen 1:55.18, 1500m/ 5000m/HMar: Vincent Nothum 4:01.89/15:19.94/ 71:07, 10000m: Romain Possing 31:43.10, Mar: Luc Dahmen 2:28:46, 3000mSt: Marc Freimann 11:03.47, 110mh/400mh: Claude Godart 14.68/ 53.06, HJ: Marc Thieffels 1.90, PV: Fabian Mores 4.73, LJ: Richard Czerwonka 6.92, TJ/Dec: Frank Krier 14.25/6387, SP: Fernand Heintz 14.94, DT: Marcel Weber 43.42, HT: Charles De Ridder 65.28, JT: Antoine Collette 65.18. **Women**: 100m: Chantal Hayen 12.72, 200m: Sandra Frisch 25.98, 400m: Martine Nobili 58.42, 800m/1500m: Monique Bausch 2:22.20/4:55.02, 3000m/10000m/ HMar: Pascale Schmoetten 10:06.62/36:33.20/ 83:50, Mar: Martine Schroeder 3:16:55, 100mh: Linda Rippinger 16.43, 400mh: Anouk Jacoby 70.36, HJ: Laurence Baum 1.65, PV/JT: Nora Mores 3.00/33.81, LJ/TJ: Laurence Kipgen 5.52/ 10.98, SP: Sandra Felten 11.25, DT: Vanessa Bignoli 35.17, HT: Tessy Biver 41.94, Hep: Sandy Debra 3209.

MAURITIUS

Governing body: Mauritius Amateur Athletic Association, Nebiolo House, Maryse Justin Stadium, Réduit. Founded 1952.

Stéphane BUCKLAND b. 20 Jan 77 Floréal 1.87m 73kg.
At 100m/(200m): OG: '00- qf/sf; WCh: '99- qf, '01- -/6; AfG: '99- 8; AfCh: '00- 2.
MRI records: 100m from 1997, 200m from 1996.
Progression at 100m, 200m: 1994- 10.5, 1995- 10.61/10.4, 1996- 10.49/10.4, 21.14/21.0; 1997- 10.47, 1998- 10.47, 1999- 10.22/10.0A, 2000- 10.16, 20.31; 2001- 10.13, 20.15.

Éric MILAZAR b. 1 Jun 1975 Rodriguez I 1.92m 80kg.
At 400m: OG: '00- qf; WCh: '01- 5; AfG: '98- 7; AfCh: '00- 1. At 200m: CG: '98- qf.
MRI records: 200m 1998, 400m from 1998.
Progression at 400m: 1994- 47.25, 1995- 46.53A, 1996- 46.54, 1997- 46.43, 1998- 45.31, 1999- 45.53A/45.54/45.5, 2000- 44.87, 2001- 44.69. pbs: 200m 20.72, 20.2w '98.

MEXICO

Governing body: Federación Mexicana de Atletismo, Anillo Periférico y Av. del

Conscripto, 11200 México D.F. Founded 1933.
2001 National Champions: Men: 100m: Luis Cardoz 10.90, 200m: Juan Pedro Toledo 20.80, 400: Alejandro Cárdenas 46.02, 800m: Juan Luis Barrios 1:51.82, 1500m: Alejandro Suárez 3:44.49, 5000m: Jonathan Morales 14:29.13, 10000m: Isaac García 30:02.68, 3000m St: Salvador Miranda 8:50.40, 110mh: Roberto Carvajal 14.28, 400mh: Oscar Juanz 50.49, HJ: Gerardo Martínez 2.12, PV: Jorge Tienda 5.20, LJ: Sergio Sauceda 7.44, TJ: Gerardo Carrasco 16.12, SP: Paulino Ríos 15.44, DT: Mauricio Serna 50.64, HT: Guillermo Guzmán 64.89, JT: Juan Gerardo de la Garza 62.90, Dec: José Francisco Herrera 6967, 20kmW: Noé Hernández 1:23:03. **Women:** 100m/200m: Liliana Allen 11.28/23.14, 400m/400mh: Mayra González 54.22/59.86, 800m: Alhelí Tapia 2:10.75, 1500m: Margarita Tapia 4:29.75, 5000m/10000m: América Mateos 16:30.51/34:37.05, 100mh: Lucilia Contreras 13.90, HJ: Lizette Castillo 1.65, PV: Lorena Espinoza 3.60, LJ: Romary Rifka 5.91, TJ: Mónica Martínez 12.64, SP: Tamara Lechuga 12.58, DT: Flor Acosta 44.03, HT: Violeta Guzmán 54.53, JT: Lorena Rivera 46.02, Hep: Beatriz Pompa 4590, 20kmW: Guadalupe Sánchez 1:34:03

Manuel **Alejandro CÁRDENAS** Robles b. 4 Oct 74. Hermosillo, Sonora 1.86m 73kg.
At 400m/4x400mR: OG: '96/00- qf; WCh: '97- qf, '99- 3, '01- hR; WI: '99- 3; PAm: '99- 3; CAG: '98- 3; CAC: '95- 2R, '01- 3/2R; IbAm: '94- 2, '98- 1R (1 4x100m). At 100m: WJ: '92- h. At Dec/ 4x100m: PAm: '95- 3/3R; IbAm: '96- 2/1R.
Mexican records 200m 1998, 400m 1996-9, decathlon 1995-6.
Progression at 400m: 1994- 48.52, 1995- 46.68A, 1996- 45.05A/45.33, 1997- 46.26, 1998- 44.92, 1999- 44.31, 2000- 44.92, 2001- 45.85A. pbs: 100m 10.2A '96/10.56W '94, 200m 20.63A '98, 20.71 '00; 300m 32.11+ '99, LJ: 7.72A '96, Dec 7614A '96.
Having set a Mexican record of 44.92 for the Pan-American bronze, he improved substantially to 44.37 in the semi-final and 44.31 in the World final in 1999.

Edgar HERNÁNDEZ b. 6 Aug 1977 Ciudad de México 1.74m 57kg..
At 50kmW: WCh: '01- 3. Won MEX 20kmW 2000, PAmCup 20kmW 2001.
Progression at 50kmW: 2000- 3:56:36, 2001- 3:46:12. pbs: 10000mW 19:33.37 '01, 20kmW 1:21:30 '00.
Improved pb by over ten minutes to take World bronze in 2001.

Noé HERNÁNDEZ b. 15 Mar 1978 Chimalhuacán, Estado de México 1.75m 64kg.
At 20kmW: OG: '00- 2; WCh: '01- dq. Won CAC 1999, IbAm 2000, 2nd PAm Cup 2000, MEX 2001.
Progression at 20kmW: 1998- 1:26:17, 1999- 1:20:12, 2000- 1:19:03, 2001- 1:23:03.

Miguel Ángel **RODRÍGUEZ** Gallegos b. 15 Jan 1967 Chihuahua 1.74m 62kg. Chihuahua. Trained as an engineer.
At 50kmW: OG: '92- 8 (dq 20k), '00- 7; WCh: '93- dq, '95- 4, '97- 3, '01- 24; WCp: '89-91-3-5-7-9: 17/7/4/5/6/19; PAm: '91- 2, '95- 2, '99- 2; CAmG: '93- 4. Won PAm Cup 2000, Aztec Cup 1997, 2nd America's Cup 1992 & 1994.
Progression at 50kmW: 1989- 3:58:41, 1990- 4:08:30, 1991- 3:54:36, 1992- 3:50:55, 1993- 3:54:22, 1994- 3:52:06, 1995- 3:44:07, 1996- 4:00:11, 1997- 3:42:45, 1998- 3:43:15, 1999- 3:49:53, 2000- 3:43:52, 2001- 3:55:44A. pb 20kmW 1:20:59 '93.

Joel SÁNCHEZ b. 15 Sep 1966 Ciudad de México 1.75m 53kg.
At 50kmW (20kmW): OG: 00- 3; WCh: '97- dq (16), '99- dnf, '01- (6); PAm: '99- 1; WCp: '97 (13). 2nd PAm Cup 20kmW 1990.
Progression at 20kmW, 50kmW: 1988- 1:22:00, 1989- 1:24:53, 1990- 1:22:09. 1991- 1:21:17, 1992- 1:21:07.8t, 1993- 1:22:55, 4:01:06; 1996- 1:23:54.4t, 4:22:17; 1997- 1:20:05, 1998- 1:19:45, 4:01:16; 1999- 1:19:00, 3:49:51A; 2000- 1:20:53, 3:44:3; 2001- 1:22:05.

Bernardo SEGURA Rivera b. 11 Feb 1970 San Mateo Atenco 1.75m 62kg. Estado de México.
At 20kmW: OG: '96- 3, '00- dq; WCh: '93- dq, '95- dnf, '99- dnf; WCp: '95- 3, '99- 1; PAm: '95- dq, '99- 1; CAG: '98- 2; WUG: '93- 3. Won America's Cup 1992, PAmCp 1994, 2000; GWG 1994.
World record 20,000m track walk 1994.
Progression at 20kmW: 1991- 1:22:01, 1992- 1:24:09, 1993- 1:19:39, 1994- 1:17:25.6t, 1995- 1:19:09, 1996- 1:19:05, 1997- 1:23:19, 1998- 1:19:46, 1999- 1:20:17, 2000- 1:22:47. pbs: 10,000mW 38:24 '94, 1HrW: 15,577.3m '94, 50kmW 4:03:51 '94.
Disqualified after 'winning' the Olympic 20km walk in 2000 and taking his lap of honour. Director of the National Sports Institute. He has named his son Jefferson Daniel Segura after the last two 20kmW Olympic gold medallists. His brother **Jorge** (b. 23 Apr 1975) won the world junior 10,000m walk title in 1994 and at 20km was CAC champion 1995, pb 1:22:50 '95.

Women

Adriana FERNÁNDEZ b. 4 Apr 1971 Ciudad de México 1.63m 59kg.
At Mar: OG: '96- 51, '00- 16. At 5000m (10000m): WCh: '95- h, '97: h (h), '99- h; PAm: '95- 1, '99- 1; CAG: '98- (1). At 1500m/3000m: CAC: '93- 2/2, '95- 2/1.
Records: CAC 10000m 1996 & 2000, marathon 1998 and 1999. MEX 5000m 1995-7, 3000m 2000.
Progression at 5000m, 10000m, Mar: 1995- 15:46.32, 33:06.66; 1996- 31:53.36, 2:31:59; 1997- 15:23.8, 33:09.22; 1998- 34:06.16, 2:26:33; 1999- 15:14.33, 32:39.05, 2:24:06; 2000- 15:16.45, 31:10.12, 2:25:42; 2001- 15:43.73, 2:26:22. pbs: 1500m: 4:18.02 '00, 3000m 8:53.53 '00, HMar 71:20+ '01.
Completed five years of study for a law degree

before taking up running seriously. Three major marathon 2nd places: Houston 1996 (debut), New York 1998, London 1999, followed by win in New York 1999. Coached by Rodolfo Gómez (2:09:12 marathon in 1983).

Ana Gabriela **GUEVARA** b. 4 Mar 77 Nogales, Sonora. 1.73m 61kg.
At 400m/4x400m (800m): OG: '00- 5; WCh: '99- sf, '01- 3; WI: '99- 4. WJ: '96- sf; PAm: '99- 1; CAG: '98- 2 (2); WUG: '97- (6). Won GWG 2001, IbAm 1998.
MEX records 400m (4) 1998-2000, 800m (2) 1998.
Progression at 400m, 800m: 1996- 54.75A, 2:09.80; 1997- 52.46A, 2:02.90; 1998- 50.65, 2:01.12; 1999- 50.70, 2:03.69, 2000- 49.70A/49.96, 2:02.88; 2001- 49.97. pb 200m: 23.78A '98.
She became the first Mexican woman to win a medal at any IAAF World Championship in track when 3rd in Edmonton 400m.

Guadalupe SÁNCHEZ b. 3 Jan 1971 Ciudad de México 1.69m 53kg.
At 20kmW: OG: '00- 5; WCh: '99- 25, '01- 9; WCp: '99- 34. Won PAm Cup 2000.
Progression at 10kmW, 20kmW: 1994- 50:12.2, 1997- 47:24, 1998- 46:21, 1:34:50; 1999- 43:27, 1:35:33; 2000- 44:34, 1:30:49; 2001- 45:00, 1:32:27.

MOROCCO

Governing Body: Fédération Royale Marocaine d'Athlétisme, Complex Sportif Prince Moulay Abdellah, PO Box 1778 R/P, Rabat. Founded 1957.

Saïd BÉRIOUI b. 3 Jun 1975? 1.78m 65kg.
At 10000m: OG: '00- 6; WCh: '97- 17, '99- 16; WJ: '98- dnf (birthdate then given as 3.4.79). At 5000m: AfCh: '00- 2.
Progession at 5000m, 10000m: 1996- 13:39.2, 1997- 13:20.93, 27:35.34; 1998- 13:21.92, 27:31.00; 1999- 13:15.10, 2000- 13:23.38, 27:37.83; 2001- 13:24.16. pbs: 3000m 7:42.39 '98.

Brahim BOULAMI b. 20 Apr 1972 Safi 1.80m 64kg.
At 3000mSt: OG: '96- 7, 00- 7; WCh: '97- 10, '01- 10; AfCh: '98- 3; won MedG 1997, GWG & GPF 2001. World CC: '97- 22, 4k: '98-01: 6/7. Won Moroccan CC 1997.
Two World 3000m steeplechase records 2001, four Moroccan 2000-01.
At 3000mSt: 1995- 8:20.64, 1996- 8:18.49, 1997- 8:10.84, 1998- 8:11.30, 2000- 8:02.90, 2001- 7:55.28. pbs: 3000m 7:42.99 '98, 5000m 13:28.06 '98.
Younger brother of Khalid Boulami (b. 7 Aug 1969, 5000m: 3 OG 1996, 2 WCh 1995 & 1997, pb 12:53.41 '97). Succeeded Ali Ezzine as fastest ever non-Kenyan steeplechaser in 2000 and in 2001 became the first non-Kenyan to set a world record for the event for 25 years.

Hicham EL GUERROUJ b. 14 Sep 1974 Berkane 1.76m 58kg.
At 1500m: OG: '96- 12, '00- 2; WCh: '95- 2, '97- 1, '99- 1, '01- 1; WI: '95- 1, '97- 1. At 3000m: WI: '01- 1; At 5000m: WJ: '92- 3. World Rd Rly team: '94- 1. World CC: '92- 14J. Won GP 1500m 1996, 1998 and 2001 (2nd 1M 1997).
World records: 1500m 1998, 1M and 2000m 1999. World indoor records 1500m (3:31.18) and 1M (3:48.45) 1997. Moroccan records: 1500m & 1M 1997 and 1998, 2000m 1998.
Progression at 1500m, 1M: 1994- 3:33.61, 3:53.71; 1995- 3:31.16, 3:48.69; 1996- 3:29.05, 1997- 3:28.91, 3:44.90; 1998- 3:26.00, 3:44.60; 1999- 3:27.65, 3:43.13; 2000- 3:27.21, 3:45.96; 2001- 3:26.12, 3:44.95. pbs: 1000m 2:16.85 '95, 2000m 4:44.79 '99, 3000m 7:23.09 '99, 2M 8:09.89i '01, 5000m 13:46.79 '92.
He won 61 of 64 races at 1500m or 1M 1996-2001. His only losses being when he fell just before the bell in the 1996 Olympic 1500m final, a loss in his last race of 1997 to Robert Andersen at 1M in the GP Final, and second to Noah Ngeny in the 2000 Olympics. In 1998 he took 1.37 secs off Morceli's 1500m WR with a majestic run at Rome on 14 July, and a year later added world records at 1M and 2000m and a superb World Championships win at 1500m. His unbeaten record in 1999 also included the second best ever 3000m time of 7:23.09 at Brussels in 1999, from a previous best of 7:49.84 (1994) and a time-trial 7:39.74 in February 1996. Made a great breakthrough in 1994 to run 3:33.61 for 1500m at Nice with no known form at this event before, although he had taken the 5000m bronze medal at the 1992 World Juniors. At Stuttgart on 2 Feb 1997 he took 2.98 secs off Morceli's world indoor 1500m record.

Abdelkader EL MOUAZIZ b. 1 Jan 1969 Settat. 1.72m 58kg.
At Mar: OG: '96- 44, '00- 7; WCh: '97- dnf, '01- 6.
Progression at Mar: 1994- 2:15:45, 1995- 2:14:45, 1996- 2:09:50, 1997- 2:09:50, 1998- 2:08:07, 1999- 2:07:57, 2000- 2:07:33, 2001- 2:07:11. pb HMar 61:49 '96.
Eight wins in 19 marathons. He had won at Marrakech in 1996 and 1997 in the same time of 2:09:50 and again in 1999 in 2:08:15. Won London 1999 and 2001, 2nd 1998 and 2000; won New York 2000. Spent four years 1990-4 in Granada, Spain. Younger brother **Hamid** (b. 17 Feb 1979) has 1500m pb 3:38.04 '01.

Ali EZZINE b. 3 Sep 1978 1.75m 57kg.
At 3000mSt: OG: '00- 3; WCh: '99- 3, '01- 2; WJ: '96- 3. World CC: '97- 11J; 4k: '98- 12, '00- 13.
Three MAR 3000m steeple records 1999-2000.
Progression at 3000mSt: 1996- 8:34.2, 1997- 8:23.18, 1998- 8:15.85, 1999- 8:06.70, 2000- 8:03.57, 2001- 8:10.23. pbs: 1500m 3:43.8 '98, 2000m 5:00.84 '98, 3000m 7:51.6/7:48.62i '98, 5000m 13:32.56 '97.
Became the fastest ever non-Kenyan steeplechaser in 1999 with 8:07.31 in Paris and 8:06.70

in Berlin when he ended Bernard Barmasai's hopes of winning at all seven Golden League meetings; improving to 8:03.57 in 2000.

Abderrahim GOUMRI b. 21 May 1976 1.67m 60kg.
At 10000m: WCh: '01- 16. World CC: '96-02: 25J/7.
Progression at 5000m, 10000m: 1999- 13:20.70, 2001- 13:03.60, 27:26.01. pbs: 3000m 7:32.36 '01, HMar 61:19 '01.

Salah HISSOU b. 16 Jan 1972 Kasba Tadla 1.76m 62kg.
At 5000m: WCh: '99- 1; WJ: '90: dnf h. At 10000m: OG: '96- 3; WCh: '95- 4, '97- 3. 2nd GP 5000m 1996. Won Pan-Arab 10000m & CC, 2nd 5000m 1992, Moroccan 5000m 1991. World CC: '90- 12J, '91- 14J, '94- 11, '95- 3, '96- 2, '97- 2; HMar: '94- 18, '01- 11; Rd Rly team: '94- 1.
World 10000m record 1996, Moroccan records: 5000m 1996, 10000m 1995-6, 3000m 1999.
Progession at 5000m, 10000m: 1989- 14:15.0, 1990- 14:05.9, 1991- 13:37.40, 1992- 13:41.55, 28:31.62; 1993- 13:49.5, 1994- 13:04.93, 27:21.75; 1995- 13:02.25, 27:09.30; 1996- 12:50.80, 26:38.08; 1997- 12:52.39, 27:09.07; 1998- 12:57.73; 1999- 12:52.53, 2000- 13:00.06. pbs: 1500m 3:33.95 '96, 1M 3:52.54 '99, 2000m 4:58.4 '99, 3000m 7:28.93 '99; Road: 20km 58:20 '94 (world best), HMar 61:56 '01.

Elarbi KHATTABI b. 16 May 1967 Casablanca 1.74m 61kg.
At 3000mSt: OG: '92- 10, '00- h; WCh: '93- 7, '95- sf, '97- 11, '99- h, '01- h. Won Moroccan 1997. World CC: '94- 14, '95- 11, '97- 16, '98- 11; Rd Rly team: '94- 1.
Progression at 3000mSt: 1986- 9:28.1, 1987- 9:00.2, 1988- 8:52.55, 1989- 8:30.87, 1990- 8:40.0, 1991- 8:42.39, 1992- 8:23.82, 1993- 8:16.60, 1994- 8:16.18, 1995- 8:12.02, 1996- 8:17.29, 1997- 8:11.50, 1998- 8:10.67, 1999- 8:09.03, 2000- 8:10.15, 2001- 8:09.49. pbs: 1500m 3:44.0 '94, 3000m 7:43.06 '98, 5000m 13:18.92 '95, HMar 62:43 '93.

Brahim LAHLAFI b. 15 Apr 1968 1.72m 62kg. Stade Sotteville CC, France.
At 5000m: OG: '96- 8, '00- 3; WCh: '95- 5, '99- 4; WCp: '94- 1. At 3000m: AfCh: '98- 2. World CC: '93- 11, '95- 5, '98- 17.
Moroccan records 3000m 1998, 5000m 2000.
Progession at 5000m: 1988- 14:02.2, 1989- 14:13.0, 1990- 13:21.11, 1991- 13:23.79, 1993- 13:15.85, 1994- 13:03.36, 1995- 13:18.46, 1996- 13:08.05, 1998- 13:00.56, 1999- 12:59.09, 2000- 12:49.28. pbs: 1500m 3:43.2 '97, 2000m 4:58.6 '00, 3000m 7:28.94 '99, 2M 8:16.11 '94, 10000m 27:43.05 '95; Road: 15km 42:40 97, HMar 61:39 '94.

Younès MOUDRIK b. 1 Oct 1977 1.84m 72kg.
At LJ: OG: '00- dnq 17; WCh: '97- dnq 24, '99- 8; WJ: '94- dnq 24, '96- 8; AfCh: '00- 1; Af-J: '94- 3 (1 HJ). Won GP 2001, Arab & MAR champion 1997.
Moroccan long jump records 1997 & 1999.
Progression at LJ: 1994: 7.55, 1995- 7.76, 1996- 7.80/ 8.04w, 1997- 8.11, 1998- 8.10/8.12w, 1999- 8.20, 2000- 8.34, 2001- 8.23. pbs: 100m 10.4 '95, 10.30w '00; HJ 2.12 '94.

Khalid SKAH b. 29 Jan 1967 Midelt 1.70m 58kg. Based in the summer in Norway. IL i BUL, Oslo.
At 10000m (5000m): OG: '92- 1, '96- 7; WCh: '91- 3 (6), '93- (5), '95- 2, '99- 10; WCp: '94- 1; AfCh: '89- (5). Won GP 5000m 1990, 1994. World CC: '90- 1, '91- 1, '92- 4, '93- 6, '94- 5, '96- 7. World HMar: '94- 1, '98- 3, '01- 10; Rd Rly team: '94- 1. Won MedG 10000m 1993, NOR 5000m 1997-8, 2000. World 2 miles best 1993. Moroccan 10000m record 1993.
Progression at 5000m, 10000m: 1986- 14:28.4, 1987- 14:26.11, 1988- 13:56.1, 1989- 13:17.30, 1990- 13:09.55, 27:29.27; 1991- 13:17.72, 27:23.29; 1992- 13:09.10, 27:46.70; 1993- 13:06.82, 27:17.74; 1994- 13:00.54, 27:38.74; 1995- 13:04.20, 27:14.53; 1996- 13:15.32, 27:46.98; 1997- 13:23.71, 27:44.33; 1998- 13:32.41, 27:31.87; 1999- 13:19.94, 28:25.10; 2000- 27:37.44, 2001- 27:51.87. pbs: 1000m 2:26.0 '90, 1500m 3:38.10 '92, 2000m 5:03.9 '90, 3000m 7:36.76 '94, 2M 8:12.17 '93, 3000mSt 8:19.30 '94, HMar 60:24 '98.
2nd Arab junior CC and 68th World Junior CC in 1986. After winning the World CC he ran 27:29.27 in his 10000m track début in Brussels 1990. At first disqualified after Olympic 10000m in 1992 due to the alleged help rendered by lapped compatriot Hammou Boutayeb, he was reinstated and awarded gold medal. His wife is Norwegian and he was granted NOR citizenship on 18 Sep 1995, but has continued to compete for Morocco.

Women

Hasna BENHASSI b. 1 Jun 1978 1.66m 47kg.
At 800m: OG: '00- 8; WCh: '97- sf; AfCh: '98- 2, '00- 1; WJ: '96- sf; WI: '99- 5; won MedG 1997, Moroccan 1996. At 1500m: WI: '01- 1.
MAR records 800m (3), 1000m, 1500m (2) 1998-9.
Progression at 800m, 1500m: 1995- 2:11.0, 1996- 2:04.6, 4:31.4; 1997- 2:00.48, 4:27.1; 1998- 1:58.47, 4:05.15; 1999- 1:57.45, 4:05.29; 2000- 1:58.47, 4:14.28; 2001- 1:59.86i, 4:04.48i. pbs: 400m 54.04 '00, 1000m 2:33.15 '99, 1M 4:32.99 '98.

Nezha BIDOUANE b. 18 Sep 1969 1.74m 65kg.
At 400mh: OG: '92- sf, '00- 3; WCh: '91- sf, '93- h, '95- h, '97- 1, '99- 2, '01- 1; AfCh: '90- 1 (2 100mh), '98- 1; WCp: '92- 6, '94- 5, '98- 1; won MedG 1991, 1993, 1997. Arab champion 100m, 200m, 100mh & 400mh 1992 & 1995, 400m 1992; MAR 100m 1991, 200m 1988-90, 1992-3; 400m 1994, 100mh 1989-91, 1995; 400mh 1988-91, 1995.
Five African and Moroccan 400mh records 1997-9. Moroccan records: 200m 1998 400m (3) 1996-8.
Progression at 400mh: 1987- 65.2, 1988- 59.88, 1989- 59.45, 1990- 56.69/56.3, 1991- 55.13, 1992- 55.08, 1993- 56.09, 1994- 55.19, 1995- 55.85, 1996- 55.31, 1997- 52.97, 1998- 52.96A/53.23, 1999- 52.90, 2000- 53.53, 2001- 53.34. pbs: 100m 11.73

'95, 11.5 '94; 200m 23.29 '98, 23.0 '00; 400m 51.67 '98, 800m 2:09.8 '96, 100mh 13.55 '90.
After not finishing in her heat in 1993 and being disqualified in heat in 1995, she became Morocco's first female world champion in 1997. Married to Abdelaziz Sahere (b. 18 Sep 1967), African champion at 3000mSt 1990, six MAR 3000mSt record to 8:09.02 '95.

Asmae LEGHZAOUI b. 30 Aug 1976 1.55m 40kg.
At 10,000m (/5000m): OG: '00- 18; WCh: '99- h, '01- 7; AfCh: '00- (1). At 3000m: WI: '01- 10. World 4km CC: '99- 7, '01- 9. Won MedG 10000m 2001, Arab 1999.
Three Moroccan 10000m records 1999-01.
Progression at 5000m, 10000m: 1996- 37:33.1, 1999- 32:18.1, 2000- 14:48.31, 31:59.21; 2001- 14:49.32, 31:16.94. pbs: 2000m 5:41.3 '01, 3000m 8:33.85 '00, Rd: 10km 31:03 '01, 15km 48:56 '01, HMar 68:34 '99.

MOZAMBIQUE

Governing body: Federaçao Moçambicana de Atletismo,Parque dos Continuardores, CP 1094, Maputo. Founded 1978.

Maria de Lurdes **MUTOLA** b. 27 Oct 1972 Maputo 1.62m 61kg.
At 800m (1500m): OG: '88- h, '92- 5 (9), '96- 3, '00- 1; WCh: '91- 4, '93- 1, '95 dq sf, '97- 3, '99- 2, '01- 1; WI: '93/5/7/9/01- 1/1/1/2/1; CG: '98- 1; AfCh: '88- 2, '90- 1 (1), '93- 1, '98- 1; AfG: '91- 1, '95- 1, '99- 1; WCp: '92- 1/3R, '94- 1, '98- 1. Won GWG 1994, 2001; GP 1993, 1995 (won overall), 1999 (2nd overall), 2001; 2nd 1997.
Records: World 1000m 1995, two WIR 1000m (2:32.08 '96 and 2:30.94 '99). African: 800m (8) 1991-4, 1000m (4) 1993-5; Commonwealth 800m 1997. African junior 800m (3) and 1500m 1991. MOZ 200m to 3000m.
Progression at 800m, 1500m: 1988- 2:04.36, 1989- 2:05.7, 4:31.5; 1990- 2:13.54, 4:25.27; 1991- 1:57.63, 4:12.72; 1992- 1:57.49, 4:02.60; 1993- 1:55.43, 4:04.97; 1994- 1:55.19, 4:13.93; 1995- 1:55.72, 4:01.6mx; 1996- 1:57.07, 4:01.63; 1997- 1:55.29, 4:09.1mx; 1998- 1:56.11, 1999- 1:56.04, 2000- 1:56.15, 4:02.39; 2001- 1:56.85. pbs: 200m 23.86 '94, 300m 37.16mx '94, 400m 51.37 '94, 600m 1:25.8i '99, 1000m 2:29.34 '95, 1M 4:36.09 '91, 2000m 6:03.84 '92, 3000m 9:27.37 '91, 5000m 18:15.1 '90; Rd 1M 4:32.4 '95.
Star soccer player at school in Maputo; enabled to attend school in Eugene, Oregon, USA by a grant from the Olympic Solidarity Committee. 50 successive wins in 800m finals 1992-6, excluding her disqualification for stepping out of her lane after finishing first in her World Championship semi-final, ending with her Olympic bronze in 1996. Her 1:56.36 for 800m in 1998 was disallowed as a world indoor record as she ran inside the lane. She became Mozambique's first ever CG champion in 1998, following her country's admittance to the Commonwealth.

NAMIBIA

Governing body: Namibia AAU, PO Box 195, Swakopmund. Founded 1990.

Frank FREDERICKS b. 2 Oct 1967 Windhoek 1.80m 73kg. Graduate of Brigham Young University, USA.
At 100m/200m: OG: '92- 2/2, '96- 2/2; WCh: '91- 5/2, '93- 6/1, '95- 4/2, '97- 4/2, '99- sf, dns; CG: '94- 3/1, '98- 2/-; AfG: '91- 1/1, '99- 3/; AfCh: '98- 2/1. At 200m: WI: '99- 1; WCp: '94- 1, '98- 1/3R. At 60m: WI: '93- 2. Won NCAA 100m & 200m 1991, South African 200m 1987. Won GP 100m 1998, 200m 1993, 1997 (2nd 1991, 1995).
WIR 100m (10.05), 200m (19.92) 1996. African records: 100m 1991 & 1996 (2), 200m (9) 1989-96.
Progression at 100m, 200m: 1985- 10.73, 21.68; 1986- 10.1, 20.6A; 1987- 10.36A, 20.58/20.41Aw; 1988- 10.32A, 20.57; 1989- 10.02A, 20.31A/20.09Aw; 1990- 10.16A/10.14Aw, 20.32/20.20Aw; 1991- 9.95/9.89w; 20.08/20.0/19.90w; 1992- 10.02/9.91w, 19.97; 1993- 10.03, 19.85; 1994- 10.04/10.00w, 19.97; 1995- 10.03A, 19.93A; 1996- 9.86, 19.68; 1997- 9.90, 19.81; 1998- 9.93, 19.97A/19.99; 1999- 9.94, 19.87; 2000- 20.79, 2001- 10.06, 20.64. pbs: 50m 5.59+ '97, 55m 6.13i '93, 60m 6.45+ '97, 400m 46.28 '89, LJ 7.57i '91, 7.46A '90.
Fredericks has won all four Namibian Olympic medals and was the first to win a world title for his country. A former soccer player, he was sent to the USA by the Rossing Uranium Mine, for whom he now works, to study computer science. He became the first non-US sprinter to win the NCAA double. Able to compete internationally once Namibia gained independence in 1990 and IAAF affiliation 1991. At Oslo in 1996 he ended Michael Johnson's 2-year undefeated run at 200m. He ran a season's record nine sub-20 sec 200m times in 1996, and at 100m had a record nine legal sub-10.00 times in 1997 with a career record 26 in all to end 1999. Withdrew injured from semi of 100m and then from final of 200m at 1999 World Championships and restricted by injury to just one race in 2000.

NETHERLANDS

Governing body: Koninklijke Nederlandse Atletiek Unie (KNAU), Postbus 230, 3400 AE Ijsselstein. Founded 1901.

National Championships first held in 1910 (men), 1921 (women). **2001 Champions**: **Men**: 100m: Troy Douglas 10.27, 200m: Caimin Douglas AHO 20.48, 400m: Bob Keus 46.62, 800m: Bram Som 1:47.99; 1500m: Wouter Timmer 3.53.52, 5000m: Kamiel Maase 13:42.52, 10000m: Marcel Versteeg 28:33.60, HMar: Marco Gielen 62:55, Mar: Peter van Egdom 2:19:24, 3000mSt:

Simon Vroemen 8:41.67, 110mh: Marcel van der Westen 13.80, 400mh: Thomas Kortbeek 52.00, HJ: Wilbert Pennings 2.15, PV: Rens Blom 5.55, LJ: Jurgen Cools 7.71w, TJ: Martijn Delissen 15.40, SP: Erik van Vreumingen 18.60, DT: Pieter van der Kruk 56.86, HT: Frank van der Dool 67.87, JT: Oscar Schermer 74.64, Dec: Rick Wassenaar 7537, 50kmW: Pedro Hintjens 4:56:03. **Women**: 100m/200m: Jacqueline Poelman 11.54/ 23.38, 400m: Judith Baarssen 56.01, 800m: Stella Jongmans 2.07.23, 1500m: Anjolie Wisse 4.27.41, 5000m/10000m: Vivian Ruijters 16.26.31/33:39.44; HMar/Mar: Nadezhda Wijenberg 74:38/2:30:25, 100mh: Judith Vis 13.45, 400mh: Marjolein de Jong 56.87, HJ: Marloes Lammerts 1.79, PV: Monique van der Wilt 3.95, LJ/TJ: Karin Ruckstuhl 6.01/12.41, SP: Lieja Koeman 18.56, DT: Ilona Rutjes 55.25, HT: Debby van der Schilt 57.90, JT: Kitty van Haperen 52.84, Hep: Frenke Bolt 5397.

Robin KORVING b. 29 Jul 1974 Heerhugowaard 1.88m 87kg. AAC Amsterdam. Construction engineering student.
At 110mh: WCh: '97/99- sf; EC: '98- 3; WJ: '92- 4; EJ: '93- 1; WCp: '99- 4; WUG: '97- 4. Dutch champion 1993-2000.
Eleven Dutch 110mh records 1993-9.
Progression at 110mh: 1992- 14.04, 1993- 13.85, 1994- 13.83, 1995- 13.83/13.65w, 1996- 13.58, 1997- 13.34, 1998- 13.20, 1999- 13.15, 2000- 13.25, 2001- 13.83. pbs: 100m 10.90 '93, 200m 21.78 '95, 400m 47.79 '97, 60mh 7.60i '99, 200mh 23.67 '97.
Kknee operation in Sydney after injury at 2000 Olympics; returned to competition at end of 2001.

Kamiel MAASE b. 20 Oct 1971 Nijmegen 1.91m 71kg. Graduate of Universities of Texas and Leiden. Leiden.
At 10000m: WCh: '97- 11, '99- 8, '01- 10; EC: '98- 8; WUG: '97- 1. At Mar: OG: '00- 13. World HMar: '99- 13. Eur CC '96-00-01: 20/7/2. Won NED 5000m 1995-7, 1999-2001; CC 1997-8, 2001.
Diutch 10,000m record 1999, 4000m 2000.
Progression at 5000m, 10000m: 1992- 14:44.90, 1993- 13:48.85; 1994- 13:45.38; 1995- 28:52.99; 1996- 13:39.33, 28:01.4; 1997- 13:30.38, 27:35.72; 1998- 13:29.20, 27:51.42; 1999- 13:25.17, 27:34.02; 2000- 13:14.13, 27:56.94; 2001- 13:19.86, 28:02.37. pbs: 1500m 3:42.84 '01, 3000m 7:45.44 '99, HMar 62:08 '00, Mar 2:10:08 '99.

NEW ZEALAND

Governing body: Athletics New Zealand, PO Box 741, Wellington.
National Championships first held in 1887 (men), 1926 (women). **2001 Champions: Men**: 100m/200m: Matthew Coad 10.23w/20.82w, 400m/800m: Mark Rodgers 47.30/1:50.84, 1500m: Hamish Christensen 3:49.59, 3000m: Alan Bunce 8:01.55, 5000m: Jonathan Wyatt 13:56.72, 10000m: John Henwood 27:57.5, Mar: Alastair Snowdon 2:22:12, 3000mSt: Phil Costley 8:55.84, 110mh: Tony Pownall 14.30, 400mh: Nic O'Brien 51.04, HJ: Glenn Howard 2.10, PV: Paul Gibbons 4.80, LJ: Aaron Langdon 7.55w, TJ: Scott Clements 14.51w, SP/DT: Ian Winchester 16.57/61.84, HT: Phil Jensen 62.80, JT: Andrew Harrison 68.94, Dec: David Hansen 6850, 3000mW/20kmW/ 50kmW: Craig Barrett 12:08.04/1:31:17/3:59:30 **Women**: 100m/LJ: Chantal Brunner 11.40w/ 6.63w, 200m: Caro Hunt 23.36w, 400m: Jane Arnott 53.01, 800m: Michelle Prowse 2:10.26, 1500m/3000m: Nina Rillstone 4:23.76/9:25.69, 5000m/10000m: Melissa Moon 16:26.62/33:46.91, Mar: Anne Clarke 2:47:55, 3000mSt: Rachel Penney 10:31.84, 100mh/400mh/Hep: Nicola Kidd 13.98w/59.37/4716, HJ: Karen Brown 1.80, PV: Jenni Dryburgh 4.16, TJ: Kelera Nacewa 13.01w, SP: Valerie Adams 16.11, DT: Adrienne Lynn 48.24, HT: Tasha Williams 65.91, JT: Hayley Wilson 46.24, 3000mW: Carma Watson 14:05.12, 20kmW: Gabrielle Gorst 1:46:41.

Women

Beatrice FAUMUINA b. 23 Oct 1974 Auckland 1.85m 125kg. Student.
At DT (SP): OG: '96- dnq 23, '00- 12; WCh: '95- dnq 28, '97- 1, '99- 5; CG: '94- 2 (9), '98- 1 (4); WJ: '92- 5; WCp: '98- 4. 3rd GP 2000. Won NZ DT 1993-2000, 2002; SP 1994, 1997-9; AUS SP 1998, DT 1997-8.
Eleven NZ discus records 1993-7.
Progression at DT: 1990- 45.06, 1991- 46.04, 1992- 53.02, 1993- 55.20, 1994- 57.94, 1995- 60.28, 1996- 64.04, 1997- 68.52, 1998- 67.58, 1999- 64.62, 2000- 65.41A, 2001- 61.54, 2002- 64.25. pbs: SP 16.96 '98, HT 44.24 '95.
Had 37 successive wins at discus Jan 1997 - June 1998. Parents came from Western Samoa. Her first important success was winning the discus at the Pacific Schools Games in 1992.

NIGERIA

Governing body: The Athletic Federation of Nigeria, P.O.Box 211, Marina, Lagos. F'd 1944.
2001 National Champions: **Men**: 100m: Chinedu Orialla 10.25, 200m: Uchenna Emedolu 20.55, 400m: Sunday Bada 46.00. **Women**: 100m: Endurance Ojokolo 11.13, 200m: Mary Onyali 22.86, 400m: Falilat Ogunkoya 51.17, 800m: Alice Nwosu 2:02.79, 400mh: Omolade Akinremi 55.98, LJ: Chioma Ajunwa 6.65, SP: Viv. Peters 17.83.

Deji ALIU b. 22 Nov 1975 1.87m 75kg.
At 100m/4x100m (200m): OG: '96- qf, '00- sf; WCh: '95- qf, '97- (sf), '99- qf; CG: '94- qf; WJ: '92- 3R, '94- 1 (2); AfG: '99- 4/1R; WUG: '95- 4; Af-J: '94- 1 (1). At 60m: WI: '99- 5, '01- dq.
Two African indoor 60m records 1999.
Progression at 100m: 1993- 10.64, 1994- 10.17/10.0, 1995- 10.02, 1996- 10.12/10.11w/9.9, 1997- 10.15/ 10.09w, 1998- 10.20/10.08w, 1999- 10.11A/10.15/ 10.07w, 2000- 10.15/10.10w, 2001- 10.07. p

50m 5.61i '99, 60m 6.48i '99, 200m 20.43A '98, 20.43 '99.

Women

Olabisi AFOLABI b. 31 Oct 1975 1.71m 62kg.
At 400m/4x400mR: OG: '96- sf/2R, '00- qf/4R; WCh: '95- h, '97/99- sf; WJ: '94- 1; CG: '94- 7; AfG: '95- 3, '99- 2/1R; WUG: '95- 1; Af-J: '94- 1. Nigerian champion 1995-6.
Two African 4x400m records 1996.
Progression at 400m: 1993- 53.42, 1994- 51.97, 1995- 50.50, 1996- 50.49/50.4, 1997- 50.41A/50.58, 1998- 50.85, 1999- 50.34A/50.40, 2000- 50.45A, 2001- 51.52. pbs: 100m 11.68 '96, 200m 23.37 '96, 600m 1:27.99 '95, 800m 2:06.92 '96.

Chioma AJUNWA b. 25 Dec 1970 Umuihiokwu Ogbe 1.61m 62kg.
At LJ/4x100mR (100m): OG: '96- 1 (sf); WCh: '97- 12 (sf), '01- dnq 15; WI: '97- 2 (4 60m); CG: '90- 4/3R; WCp: '98- 7; AfG: '91- 1/1R; AfCh: '89- 1, '90- 1/1R, '91- (2), '98- 1. Won NGR 100m 1990, LJ 1989-90, 1996, 1999, 2001; TJ 1991.
African records 100m 1992, long jump 1992 and 1996, indoor 60m 1997.
Progression at 100m, LJ: 1988- 12.05, 5.87; 1989- 11.41, 6.53; 1990- 11.41, 6.50; 1991- 11.32, 6.67; 1992- 10.84, 6.90/7.06dq; 1996- 11.14/10.9/11.12w, 7.12; 1997- 11.14, 7.01; 1998- 11.20/11.08w, 6.82; 1999- 6.83, 2001- 6.65. pbs: 60m 7.05i '97, 200m 22.93 '92, TJ 12.51 '91.
Played football for Nigeria at the 1991 Women's World Championships. Four-year drugs ban from 11 June 1992. After leading the qualifiers she was injured and could only manage one jump in the final of the 1997 World long jump.

Mercy NKU b. 17 Jul 1976 1.70m 67kg.
At 100m/(200m): OG: '96- sf, '00- sf/sf; WCh: '99- 8/qf, '01- 8; AfG: '99- 1/1R; AfCh: '96- h/sf; Af-J: '94- 3/4/1R, '95- 1/1. At 60m: WI: '01- 5.
Progression at 100m. 200m: 1992- 12.36, 1993- 12.20, 1994- 11.35, 24.11; 1995- 11.38/11.3, 23.63; 1996- 11.38/11.3, 24.15; 1997- 11.19/11.1, 23.35; 1998- 11.52/11.4, 23.9; 1999- 11.03A/11.08/10.98w, 22.53; 2000- 11.20, 22.95; 2001- 11.06, 22.66. pbs: 50m 6.13i '01, 60m 7.11i '01.
World's fastest junior at 100m in 1994.

Falilat OGUNKOYA b. 12 May 1968 1.72m 66kg. LIAZ Jablonec. Was at Mississippi State University, USA. Married to former 800m runner Tony Osheku.
At 400m/4x400mR: OG: '96- 3/2R, '00- 7/4R; WCh: '95- 6, '97- 5, '99- 4, '01- dnf; WI: '99- 2; WCp: '89- 3, '98- 2; AfG: '95- 2/1R, '99- 1/1R; AfCh: '89- 1/1R, '98- 1; won GWG 1998, GP 1998 (2nd 1996, 2000). At 200m/4x100m: OG: '88- qf; WCh: '87- sf; WJ: '86- 1/3R; WUG: '87- 3R; WCp: '98- 1; AfG: '87- 2/1R (2 100m, 1 4x400mR); AfCh: '88- 1 (2 100m), '89- 2, '98- 1.
African records: 400m 1996, 4x100m 1987, 4x400m (3) 1987-96; Nigerian 800m 1997.
Progression at 200m, 400m: 1984- 24.3, 1985- 23.5, 1986- 23.11, 1987- 22.95A/22.87w, 52.2A; 1988- 22.88, 1989- 22.82A, 51.22; 1990- 23.53, 52.26; 1994- 24.05, 53.54; 1995- 22.99, 50.31A/50.72; 1996- 22.97/22.58w, 49.10; 1997- 22.94, 49.48; 1998- 22.22, 49.52A/49.60; 1999- 22.77, 49.62; 2000- 23.18, 22.93Aw, 50.04; 2001- 50.50. pbs: 100m 11.19 '88, 300m 35.95+ '99, 800m 2:04.57 '97.
The former world junior champion, who has one child, made a great return to top-class action in 1995 after five years out. Son, Tony, born in 1993.

NORWAY

Governing body: Norges Fri-Idrettsforbund, Serviceboks 1, Ullevaal Stadium, 0840 Oslo. Founded 1896.
National Championships first held in 1897 (men), 1947 (women). **2001 Champions**: **Men**: 100m/200m: John Ertzgaard 10.31w/21.01, 400m: Quincy Douglas 47.05, 800m: Kjetil Hodnekvam 1:51.41, 1500m: Marius Bakken 3:40.41, 5000m: Knut Erik Rame 14:22.80, 10000m: Johan Rasmussen 29:55.77, HMar: Bjarte Vik 65:52, Mar: Tor Erik Nyqvist 2:25:11, 3000mSt: Jim Svenøy 8:43.02, 110mh: Kenneth Halhjem 14.19w, 400mh: Ragnar Bergheim 51.95, HJ: Jan Olav Husbyn 2.17, PV: Ketil Rønneberg 5.30, LJ: Arjan Bos 7.47, TJ: Ketill Hanstveit 15.97, SP: Gjøran Sørli 19.59, DT: Einar Kr. Tveitå 60.15, HT: Anders Halvorsen 62.03, JT: Andreas Thorkildsen 79.98, Dec: Vegard Sellæg 6823, 5000mW/10000mW/20kmW: Erik Tysse 20:37.48/42:22.06/1:25:41. **Women**: 100m: Inger E. Tørre 11.67w, 200m: Ann Helen Rinden 23.83, 400m: Christina Page Fagerland 55.18, 800m: Kristin Roset 2:03.64, 1500m: Ragnhild Kvarberg 4:17.46, 5000m: Gunhild Halle Haugen 15:36.68, 10000m: Brit-Helen Langeland 36.39.03, HMar/Mar: Brynhild Syntsnes 75:13/2:38:22, 3000mSt: Susanne Wigene 10:18.73, 100mh: Anne Beth Hoven 13.90, 400mh: Ma Heidi Trollsås 58.62, HJ: Anne Gerd Eieland 1.81, PV: Christine Gulbrandsen Kurth 3.55, LJ: Cecilie Rise 6.00, TJ: Lene Espegren 13.86w, SP: Katar a Longe 14.34, DT: Grete Etholm 49.86, HT: Eva Danielsen 56.11, JT: Line Svarstad 50.60, Hep: Rannveig Kvalvik 5457, 3000mW/5000mW/10kmW: Kjersti Plätzer 12:04.42/20:37.83/42:23, 20km: Elin Ceselie Loftesnes 1:41:05.

Marius BAKKEN b. 27 Mar 1978 Sandefjord 1.82m 63kg. IL Runar.
At 5000m: OG: '00- h, WCh: '99- h, '01- 10; EU23: '99- 2. Won NOR 1500m 2001.
Norwegian records 3000m (2), 5000m (2) 2000-01
Progression at 5000m: 1999- 13:22.58, 2000- 13:11.30, 2001- 13:09.19. pbs: 800m 1:51.19 '97, 1500m 3:40.41 '01, 2000m 5:04.66 '01, 3000m 7:40.77 '01, 10000m 28:26.36 '00.

Women

Kjersti TYSSE PLÄTZER b. 18 Jan 1972 Os, Bergen 1.74m 54kg. née Tysse. IL Norna-Salhus, Bergen.
At 20kmW: OG: '00- 2; WCh: '99- 9, '01- dq; EC: '94- 16, '98- 9; ECp: '00- 3. At 5000mW: WJ: '86- 5. Won NOR 5000mW 1985-7, 1992, 1994-6, 1998-2001, 10kmW 1994-5, 1998, 200-01; 20kmW 1998-9.
World bests 1M and 3000m walk 2001. NOR walks records: 3000m (3), 5000m (4), 10km (5), 10000m, 20km (4) 1996-2001.
Progression at 10kmW, 20kmW: 1986- 48:01, 1987- 45:45, 1994- 46:10, 1995- 45:12, 1996- 44:40, 1:39:36; 1998- 42:44, 1:32:55; 1999- 41:54, 1:28:35; 2000- 43:21.10t, 1:27:53; 2001- 42:23, 1:29:55. pbs: 1MW 6:16.45 '01, 3000mW 11:53.1 '01, 5000mW 20:37.83 '01; running: 3000m 10:43.19 '01, 5000m 17:57.55 '01.
Married to Stephan Plätzer GER (b. 12 Sep 66), pbs 800m 1:46.53 '89, 1500m 3:40.26 '89.

PAKISTAN

Governing body: Pakistan Amateur Athletic Federation. Islamabad, Founded 1947.
28th National Games 2001: Men: 100m: Asif Hameed 10.3, 200m: Maqsood Ahmad 20.8, 400m: Basit Munir 48.0, 800m/1500m: Sher Ahmad 1:52.0/3:55.1, 5000m: Atta Miran 15:04.2, 10000m: Abdul Latif 31:31.3, Mar: Muhammad Javed 2:24:57, 3000mSt: Allah Ditta II 9:19.1, 110mh: Mumtaz Ahmad 14.0, 400mh: Allah Ditta 51.9, HJ: Ahmed Bilal 2.04, PV: Muhammad Ayub 4.75, LJ/TJ: Asif Gulzar 7.60?/14.55, SP: Ghufrain Hussain 17.60, DT: Imran Mirza 50.92, HT: G. Shabir Hussain 60.50, JT: Zahid Ali Mahmood 78.25, Dec: Ghulam Abbas 6747. **Women**: 100m: Shazia Youssef Khan 12.2, 10000m: Shazia Hadayat 43:24.6, 100mh: Farah Naz 14.9, 400mh: Bashiran Bibi 64.3 , PV: Rabia Malik 2.15, SP/HT: Zeenat Parveen 12.70/35.49, JT: Shabana Kausar 37.20.

POLAND

Governing body: Polski Zwiazek Lekkiej Atletyki (PZLA), 01-809 Warszawa, ul. Ceglowska 68/70. Founded 1919.
National Championships first held in 1920 (men), 1922 (women). **2001 Champions**: **Men**: 100m: Piotr Balcerzak 10.30, 200m: Marcin Urbas 20.71, 400m: Robert Mackowiak 45.20, 800m: Pawel Czapiewski 1:46.44, 1500m: Leszek Zblewski 3:47.91, 5000m: Leszek Biegala 14:11.36, 10000m: Dariusz Kruczkowski 28:41.06, HMar: Adam Dobrzynski 63:18, Mar: Miroslaw Plawgo 2:12:27, 3000mSt: Kan Zakrzewski 8:34.64, 110mh: Artur Kohutek 13.63, 400mh: Marek Plawgo 48.94, HJ: Grzegorz Sposób 2.22, PV: Adam Kolasa 5.60, LJ: Grzegorz Marciniszyn 8.00, TJ: Jacek Kazimierowski 16.17, SP: Leszek Sliwa 19.32, DT: Olgierd Stanski 60.41, HT: Szymon Ziólkowski 81.34, JT: Dariusz Trafas 81.89, Dec: Michal Modelski 7460, 20kmW: Robert Korzeniowski 1:20:31. **Women**: 100m: Agnieszka Rysiukiewicz 11.62, 200m: Zuzanna Nielacna 23.77, 400m: Grazyna Prokopek 52.48, 800m: Anna Zagórska 2:04.70, 1500m/5000m: Justyna Bak 4:15.37/16:05.84, 10000m/HMar: Doruta Gruca-Giezek 34:05.97/73:39, Mar: Elzbieta Jarosz 2:37:02, 3000mSt: Patrycja Wlodarczyk 10:21.22, 100mh: Aneta Sosnowska 13.12, 400mh: Malgorzata Pskit 55.04, HJ: Anna Ksok 1.88, PV: Monika Pyrek 4.61, LJ/TJ: Liliana Zagacka 6.51/13.95, SP: Krystyna Zabawska 18.85, DT: Marzena Wysocka 62.09, HT: Kamila Skolimowska 68.12, JT: Monika Mrówka 58.24, Hep: Izabella Oblekowska 5873, 10mW/20kmW: Joanna Baj 46:24/1:36:56.

Pawel CZAPIEWSKI b. 30 Mar 1978 Stargard Szczecinski 1.78m 57kg. LKS Lubusz Slubice.
At 800m: WCh: '01- 3; EC: '98- h; WI: '01- 6; WJ: '96- h; EU23: '99- 3; EJ: '97- 8; EI: '02- 1; ECp: '01- 1. Won POL 1998, 2001.
Polish 800m record 2001.
Progression at 800m: 1995- 1:52.93, 1996- 1:49.66, 1997- 1:48.28, 1998- 1:46.57, 1999- 1:46.71, 2000- 1:46.07, 2001- 1:43.22, 2002- 1:44.78i. pbs: 1000m 2:19.00i/2:21.66 '01, 1500m 3:38.96i '02, 3:43.80 '01.

Pawel JANUSZEWSKI b. 2 Jan 1972 Pyrzyce 1.78m 68kg. Skra Waszawa.
At 400mh (4x400mR): OG: 96- h, '00- 6; WCh: '95- h, '97- sf, '99- 5, '01- 6; EC: '94- sf, '98- 1; EJ: '91- 2R; WUG: '99- 1; WCp: '98- 4; ECp: '95- 7, '99- 3. Polish champion 1995, 1997, 1999-2000.
Three Polish 400mh records 1997-8.
Progression at 400mh: 1991- 52.96, 1992- 51.71, 1993- 51.88, 1994- 49.95, 1995- 49.43, 1996- 49.63, 1997- 48.94, 1998- 48.17, 1999- 48.19, 2000- 48.42, 2001- 48.40. pbs: 200m 21.64 '96, 400m 46.79 '96.
Survived a serious car crash in September 1997 (at first reported dead).

Robert KORZENIOWSKI b. 30 Jul 1968 Lubaczów 1.68m 60kg. US Tourcoing, France & Wawel Kraków TC. PE teacher.
At 20kmW (50kmW): OG: '92- dnf (dq), '96- 8 (1), '00- 1 (1); WCh: '91- 10 (dnf), '93- (dq), '95- (3), '97- (1), '99- (dq), '01- (1); EC: '90- 4, '94- dq (5), '98- (1); WCp: '89- 40, '91- 7, '93- 4, '95- 9, '99- 4; ECp: '96- 1, '98- 2, '00- 1; WUG: '91- 1, '93- 1. At 10kmW: EJ: '87- dq. At 5000mW: WI: '93- 2. Won Polish 20kmW 1990-2001, 50kmW 1993.
World bests: 5km road walk (18:21 '90), track 1997. Polish records 1990-2001: 5000mW (5), 10kmW (4), 20kmW (5), 50kmW (3).
Progression at 20kmW, 50kmW: 1986- 1:32:33, 1987- 1:29:48, 1988- 1:26:04, 1989- 1:23:19, 1990- 1:19.32, 1991- 1:21:19, 1992- 1:19:14, 3:46:42; 1993- 1:20:55, 3:44:24; 1994- 1:20:55, 3:45:57; 1995- 1:20:52, 3:45:57; 1996- 1:20:51, 3:42:40; 1997- 1:19:43, 3:44:46; 1998- 1:19:36, 3:43:51; 1999- 1:18:40, 2000- 1:18:22, 3:41:50; 2001- 1:19:52, 3:42:08. pbs: 3000mW 11:05.20 '97, 5000mW

18:17.22 '92, 10000mW 38:44.74 '01, 1 Hr 14,794m '92; road 35kmW 2:28:30 (world best) '93.
Disqualified in 2nd place in the stadium just before finish of the 1992 Olympic 50km walk, but won this event in 1996. In 2000 won a unique Olympics walks double and became the first man ever to retain the 50km title. His sister Silwia was Polish 20km walk champion in 2000m and5th in the European U23 Champs in a p[b 1:32:47 in 2001.

Tomasz LIPIEC b. 10 May 1971 Warszawa 1.85m 72kg. Polonia Warszawa.
At 50kmW (20kmW): OG: '00- dnf; WCh: '97- 5, '99- dq, '01- 9; EC: '98- 5; WCp: '93- 13, '97- 5, '99- 2; ECp: '98- 1, '00- (7). At 10kmW: EJ: 89- 10. Won POL 50kmW 1992, 1996, 1999.
Polish 50km walk records 1997 and 1999.
Progression at 50kmW: 1992- 4:01:13, 1993- 4:03:09, 1996- 3:49:30, 1997- 3:41:58, 1998- 3:42:57, 1999- 3:40:08, 2001- 3:48:51. pbs: 5000mW 19:27.64 '00, 10000mW 39:56.00 '00, 20kmW 1:20:48 '00, 35kmW 2:34:00 '97.

Robert MACKOWIAK b. 13 May 1970 Rawicz 1.81m 76kg. Slask Wroclaw. Soldier.
At 400m/4x400mR: OG: '00- 5; WCh: '97- sf/4R, '99- qf/2R, '01- dnf; EC: '94- 6R, 98- 2/2R; WI: '97- 4, '99- 2R, '01- 1R; EI: '98- 3;, '02- 1R ECp: '99- 4/2R, '01- 2/1R. At 200m/4x100mR: OG: '96- qf; WCh: '91- hR, 95- h; EJ: '89- 1R; EI: '02- 3. Won POL 200m 1995-7, 400m 1998, 2000-01.
Three Polish 400m records 1997-8.
Progression at 400m: 1991- 47.43, 1994- 46.50, 1995- 46.05, 1996- 45.91, 1997- 45.26, 1998- 45.04, 1999- 45.17, 2000- 45.01, 2001- 44.84. pbs: 100m 10.45 '90, 10.44w '93; 200m 20.61 '96.

Marek PLAWGO b. 25 Feb 1981 Ruda Slaska 1.81m 72kg. Warszawianka.
At 400mh: WCh: '01- sf; WJ: '00- 1/3R; EJ: '99- 4; ECp: '01- 2. Won POL 2001. At 400m/4x400m: EJ: '02- 1/1R
Polish 400mh record 2001.
Progression at 400mh: 1999- 51.97, 2000- 49.23, 2001- 48.16. pbs: 100m 10.60 '01, 200m 21.13 '01, 400m 45.49i '02, 46.40 '01.
Making rapid progress. Ran flat 400m pb of 46.01 in Feb 2002, then Polish indoor records 45.49 and 45.29 at European Indoors.

Darius TRAFAS b. 16 May 1972 Kolobrzeg 1.88m 94kg. AZS-AZW Gorzów Wielkopolski. Studied finance at University of Florida, USA.
At JT OG: '00- 10; WCh: '99- dnq 18, '01- dnq 16; EC: '98- 11; WJ: '90- 2; EJ: '91- 6. Polish champion 1996, 1998-9, 2001.
Four Polish javelin records 1999-2000 (87.21 unratifed, so official mark 85.78 in 2001).
Progression at JT: 1988- 60.08, 1989- 69,12, 1990- 75.00, 1991- 73.84, 1992- 76.38, 1993- 77.38, 1994- 78.66, 1995- 76.60, 1996- 78.06, 1997- 77.46, 1998- 81.90, 1999- 83.23, 2000- 87.17, 2001- 85.78.
He lost the forefinger of his throwing hand in a sawmill accident in 1990. Coached by Uwe Hohn (104.80m WR with 'old' javelin 1984).

Marcin URBAS b. 17 Sep 1976 Kraków 1.80m 77kg. AZS-AWF Kraków. Typography technician.
At 200m/4x100mR: OG: '00- qf; WCh: '99- 5, '01- sf; EC: '98- h; EI: '02- 1; WUG: '01- 1; ECp: '99- 1, '01- 3/3R. Won POL 1998-2001.
Polish 200m record 1999.
Progression at 200m: 1992- 23.07, 1993- 22.43, 1994- 22.01, 1995- 21.60, 1996- 21.45, 1997- 20.83, 1998- 20.64, 1999- 19.98, 2000- 20.43, 2001- 20.41/20.39w. pbs: 60m 6.70i '02, 100m 10.30 '99.
Improved from 20.64 in 1998 to 20.62, 20.34 (to win European Cup), 20.32 and, becoming the third European under 20-seconds, 19.98 (World Championships) in 1999. Sings with the group 'Sceptic'.

Szymon ZIÓLKOWSKI b. 1 Jul 1976 Poznan 1.88m 104kg. AZS Poznan.
At HT: OG: '96- 10, '00- 1; WCh: '95- dnq 22, '99- dnq 23, '01- 1; EC: '98- 5; WJ: '94- 1; EJ: '93= 7, '95- 1; EU23: '97- 2; ECp: '95/6/2001- 6/2/1. Polish champion 1996-7, 1999-2001.
Six Polish hammer records 2000-01.
Progression at HT: 1991- 55.96, 1992- 63.84, 1993- 67.34, 1994- 72.48, 1995- 75.42, 1996- 79.52, 1997- 79.14, 1998- 79.58, 1999- 79.01, 2000- 81.42, 2001- 83.38.
His sister Michalina (b. 1983) was second in the 2000 Polish U18 Championships, pb 52.94 '00. Married javelin thrower (50.90 '98) Joanna Domagala in December 2000.

Women

Justyna BAK b. 1 Aug 1974 Bilgoraj 1.64m 48kg. née Mlynarska. Skra Warszawa.
Eur CC: '99-01- 14/3. Won Polish 1500m 2001, 5000m 1997, 2000-01, 10000m 2000, CC 1997, 1999-2001.
World 3000m steeple record 2001 and four Polish records 1997-2001.
Progression at 3000mSt: 1999- 9:58.77, 2000- 9:57.03, 2001- 9:25.31. pbs: 800m 2:08.65 '97, 1500m 4:12.09 '99, 3000m 8:59.83 '97, 5000m 15:41.18 '00, 10000m 32:58.97 '00.
Her 9:25.31 for 3000m steeplechase at Nice in 2001 took 14.89 seconds off the world record for this new event. This was her fourth steeplechase, each won in a Polish record time. Coached by her husband Stanislav Bak.

Lidia CHOJECKA b. 25 Jan 1977 Siedlce 1.63m 47kg. WLKS Siedlce.
At 150 0m (3000m): OG: '00- 5; WCh: '99- 9, '01- 5; EC: '98- 6; WJ: '94- 7, '96- 5; EJ: '95- 1; EU23: '97- 2, '99- 1; WUG: '97- 3; WI: '97- 4, '99- 3; EI: '98- 2, '00- (2); ECp: '99 (3). Won POL 800m 1996, 1500m 1999-2000.
POL records: 1500m 2000, 3000m (3) 1999-2000.
Progression at 1500m: 1993- 4:40.84, 1994- 4:18.70, 1995- 4:15.27, 1996- 4:11.36, 1997-

4:05.74, 1998- 4:03.32, 1999- 4:01.36, 2000- 3:59.22, 2001- 4:03.51. pbs: 800m 1:59.97 '99, 1000m 2:40.49 '98, 1M 4:24.44i '00, 4:25.18 '98; 3000m 8:33.35 '00, 5000m 16:29.87 '99.

Monika PYREK b. 11 Aug 1980 Gdynia 1.74m 52kg. KS Lechia Gdansk.
At PV: OG: '00- 7; WCh: '01- 3; EC: '98- 7; WJ: '98- 2=; EU23: '01- 1; EJ: '97- 10, '99- 4; EI: '02- 3. Polish champion 1999-2001.
21 (+) Polish pole vault records 1997-2001, European (outdoor) record 2001.
Progression at PV: 1995- 2.30, 1996- 3.60, 1997- 3.83, 1998- 4.15, 1999- 4.21i/4.16, 2000- 4.40, 2001- 4.61, 2002- 4.60i. pb HJ 1.70.

Kamila SKOLIMOWSKA b. 4 Nov 1982 Warszawa 1.80m 88kg. Warszawianka.
At HT: OG: '00- 1; WCh: '99- 21, '01- 4; WJ: '98 & '00- dnq; WY: '99- 1; EC: '98- 7; EJ: '97- 1, ECp: '99- 4; Won GPF & GWG 2001. Polish champion 1996-7, 1999, 2001.
Five World junior hammer records 1999-2001, nine Polish hammer records 1997-2001.
Progression at HT: 1996- 47.66, 1997- 63.48, 1998- 62.72, 1999- 66.62, 2000- 71.16, 2001- 71.71.
Youngest ever Polish champion and record holder (at 13y 229d), won European Junior title at 14y 264 and became the youngest Olympic champion in Sydney 2000 at 17 years 331 days. Father, Robert, was junior world champion at weightlifting in 1976 and 7th at super-heavyweight at the 1980 Olympics (his weight 155kg).

Malgorzata SOBANSKA b. 25 Apr 1969 Poznan 1.65m 50kg. AZS-AWF Wroclaw.
At Mar: OG: '96- 11; WCh: '95- 4. Won Polish HMar 1999.
Progression at Mar: 1991- 2:35:50, 1992- 2:34:54, 1993- 2:29:21, 1994- 2:29:06, 1995- 2:27:43, 1996- 2:30:17, 1997- 2:32:02, 1998- 2:29:39, 1999- 2:27:30, 2000- 2:27:52, 2001- 2:26:08. pbs: 800m 2:10.22 '88, 1500m 4:20.74 '89, 3000m 9:14.01 '95, 5000m 16:02.22 '94, 10000m 33:17.83 '95, HMar 72:06 '94.
Won at London 1995 in her sixth marathon. Won Köln Marathon 1998 and 2000. 2nd Boston 2001, 3rd Berlin 1993 and 1994, London 1996; 4th Berlin 1999 and Chicago 2001.

Krystyna ZABAWSKA b. 14 Jan 1968 Dabrowa Bialostocka 1.83m 92kg. née Danilczyk. Podlasie Bialystok. Storekeeper.
At SP: OG: '92- 10, '00- 5; WCh: '91- 12, '93 dnq 17, '97- 8, '99- 8, '01- 10; EC: '94- 9, 98- '11; WI: '99- 2. '01- 8; EI: '98- 4, '00- 5; ECp: '91-3-9: 5/5/1. Polish champion 1991-4, 1997-2001.
Progression at SP: 1985- 10.98, 1986- 12.20, 1987- 14.48, 1988- 15.70, 1990- 18.21, 1991- 19.03, 1992- 19.42, 1993- 18.31, 1994- 19.23, 1995- 16.38, 1996- 18.62, 1997- 19.06, 1998- 19.24, 1999- 19.26i/19.23, 2000- 19.18, 2001- 19.10.
Married to Przemyslaw Zabawski, Polish shot champion 1997 & 2000, pb 18.76 '00.

PORTUGAL

Governing body: Federação Portuguesa de Atletismo, Largo da Lagoa, 15-B, 2795 Linda-a-Velha. Founded 1921.
National Championships first held in 1910 (men), 1937 (women). **2001 Champions**: **Men**: 100m/200m: Ricardo Alves 10.50/21.29, 400m: Paulo Ferreira 47.15, 800m: Luís Feiteira 1:50.10, 1500m: Rui Silva 3:40.05, 5000m: José Ramos 13:53.31, Mar: Carlos Valente 2:22:24, 3000mSt: Mário Teixeira 8:36.32, 110mh: Luis Sá 14.26, 400mh: Carlos Silva 50.35, HJ: Rafael Gonçalves 2.17, PV: João André 5.45, LJ: Carlos Calado 8.10w, TJ: Américo Castelbranco 15.63, SP: Herédio Costa 16.97, DT: Paulo Bernardo 53.68, HT: Vítor Costa 74.44, JT: Filipe Ventura 69.58, Dec: Mário Aníbal 7990, 20000mW: João Vieira 1:24:08.8, 50kmW: Pedro Martins 3:55:54. **Women**: 100m/200m: Severina Cravid 11.62/23.98w, 400m: Céu Nunes 56.16, 800m: Nédia Semedo 2:03.90, 1500m: Carla Sacramento 4:15.98, 5000m: Ana Dias 15:26.41, Mar: Fátima Silva 2:35:16, 100mh: Isabel Abrantes 13.39, 400mh: Carmo Tavares 57.80, HJ: Sónia Carvalho 1.80, PV: Elisabete Tavares 3.88, LJ: Marta Godinho 6.31, TJ: Sandra Cruz 12.81, SP/DT: Teresa Machado 16.42/61.15, HT: Vânia Silva 60.83, JT: Sílvia Cruz 49.09, Hep: Enezenaide Gomes 5606w, 10000mW/20kmW: Susana Feitor 44:38.87/1:32:40.

Carlos CALADO b. 5 Oct 1975 Alcanena 1.86m 80kg. Sporting Club de Portugal.
At LJ(/TJ): OG: '96- dnq 24/dnq 19, '00- 10; WCh: '97 dnq 15 (qf 100m), '99- dnq 25 (qf 100m), '01- 3; WJ: '94- 8/6. '01- 8; EU23: '97- 1 (2 100m); WI: '01- 3; EI: '98- 2; Won POR 100m 1996, 1999, 200m 1996-7, LJ 1994, 2001, TJ 1994-5.
Portuguese records 100m (3), LJ (6), TJ (2) 1996-9.
Progression at LJ: 1991- 5.64, 1992- 6.92, 1993- 7.30, 1994- 7.51/7.78w, 1995- 7.52, 1996- 8.25, 1997- 8.36, 1998- 8.11i/8.05, 1999- 8.34, 2000- 8.13/8.15w, 2001- 8.21. pbs: 60m 6.60i '99, 100m 10.11 '99, 10.07w '97; 200m 20.90 '97, HJ 2.01i '97, TJ: 17.09i '99, 17.08 '96.

Paulo GUERRA b. 21 Aug 1970 Barrancos 1.74m 64kg. Maratona CP.
At 10000m: OG: '96- h; WCh: '95- 8; EC: '94- 5, '98- 14. At 3000mSt: EJ: '89- 8. World CC: '93-4-5-6-7-8-9-2000-01: 21/13/6/dnf/12/3/25/4. Eur CC '94-5-6-8-9-00-01: 1/1/2/11/1/1/10. Won POR 10000m 1994-5, CC 1995-7, 1999, 2001.
Progression at 5000m, 10000m: 1990- 14:00.90, 1991- 14:12.02, 1992- 14:07.11, 1993- 13:42.35, 28:11.14; 1994- 13:25.13, 27:52.44; 1995- 13:18.59, 27:52.55; 1996- 13:18.60, 28:09.56; 1998- 13:59.87, 27:50.17; 1999- 27:55.43. pbs: 1500m 3:45.21 '95, 1M 4:09.7 '91, 3000m 7:49.94 '96, 3000mSt 8:43.86 '91, HMar 61:53 '96, Mar 2:11:02 '98.
In a breakthrough 1994 season he was the top European placer in the World cross-country, won the Iberian 10,000m and was 5th in the

Europeans, and then ran away with the inaugural European cross-country, a title he has now won four times. 2nd World Cross Challenge 1994/5. He is the only European senior man to earn a World Cross medal in the 1990s.

Francis Obiorah **OBIKWELU** b. 22 Nov 1978 Nigeria 1.95m 74kg. Sporting Clube de Portugal.
At 200m (/100m): OG: '96- sf, '00- sf; WCh: '97- 2R (sf), '99- 3; WI: '97- 3, '99- 4; WJ: '96- 1/1; AfG: '99- 1/2/1R. 3rd GP 200m 1999, 2001. At 400m: WJ: '94- sf;Af-J: '94- 2. Won NGR 100m 1999-200m, 200m 1997, 1999.
Two Nigerian 200m records 1999
Progression at 100m, 200m: 1994- 21.16, 1995- 10.31, 21.22; 1996- 10.12, 20.24; 1997- 10.10, 20.53/20.27Aw; 1998- 10.01, 20.17; 1999- 10.01A/ 10.13/10.11w, 19.84; 2000- 9.97, 20.01; 2001- 9.98, 20.33. pb 400m 46.79 '94.
An Ibo, and thus in an ethnic minority group in Nigeria, his family emigrated to Portugal in 1994 and he became a Portuguese citizen on 26 October 2001.

António PINTO b. 22 Mar 1966 Amarante 1.71m 61kg. Maratona CP
At 10000m: OG: '88- 13, WCh: '95- 19, '99- 5; EC: '90- 14, '98- 1. At Mar: OG: '92- dnf, '96- 14, '00- 11; WCh: '97- dnf; EC: '94- 9. Eur CC: '94- 8. Won POR CC 1992, 5000m 1994, 1999.
World best half marathon 1998, European records: 10000m 1999, Marathon 2000; POR 5000m 1998.
Progression at 10000m, Mar: 1986- 31:13.3, 1987- 28:28.73, 1988- 28:01.00, 1989- 28:30.11, 1990- 28:14.32; 1991- 28:30.3, 2:12:39; 1992- 28:59.02, 2:10:02; 1994- 27:48.1, 2:08:31; 1995- 28:06.18, 2:08:48; 1996- 2:08:38, 1997- 2:07:55, 1998- 27:15.76, 2:08:13; 1999- 27:12.47, 2:09:00; 2000- 2:06:36, 2001- 2:09.36. pbs: 1500m 3:39.25 '98, 3000m 7:41.33 '99, 5000m 13:02.86 '98, HMar 59:43 '98.
Previously a cyclist, started running in 1986. He has a great record in the London marathon with wins in 1992, 1997 and 2000, 2nd 1999 and 3rd 1995, 1998 and 2001. He has run 18 marathons from 7th at Carpi 1991 on his début and won Berlin 1994; 2nd Paris 1994, Tokyo 1996; 3rd Berlin. Had four in succession under 2:09 in 1994-6 and after the Olympics ran 2:07:55, to win his second London marathon. Had a poor record in championships until his European 10,000m title during a sensational season in 1998, when his times ranged from 3:39.25 for 1500m to 2:08:13 for marathon.

Rui SILVA b. 3 Aug 1977 1.74m 62kg. Sporting Club de Portugal.
At 1500m:OG: '00- h; WCh: '99- sf (fell), '01- 7; EC: '98- 2; WJ: '96- 6; EJ: '95- 8; EU23: '99- 1; WI: '99- 5. '01- 1; EI: '98- 1, '02- 1; WCp: '98- 2. At 3000m: EI: '00- 2. Won POR 1500m 1999, 2001; CC sh 2001.
Portuguese records: 1500m (5) 1998-2001, 1000m, 1M, 2000m 1999.
Progression at 1500m: 1994- 3:50.9, 1995- 3:44.8, 1996- 3:40.09, 1997- 3:44.6, 1998- 3:34.00, 1999- 3:30.88, 2000- 3:32.60, 2001- 3:30.36. pbs: 800m 1:45.29 '00, 1000m 2:16.30 '99, 1M 3:50.91 '99, 2000m 4:54.66 '99, 3000m 7:39.44i '00, 7:53.87 '99; 5000m 13:36.56 '01.

Women

Susana FEITOR b. 28 Jan 1975 Alcobertas 1.60m 52kg. C Natação Rio Maior.
At 20kmW: OG: '00- 14; WCh: '99- 4, '01- dq; WCp: '99- 9. At 10kmW: OG: '92- dq, '96- 13; WCh: '93- 11, '95- 17, '97- h; EC: '94- 8, '98- 3; EU23: '97- 3; WUG: '95- 4, '97- 4, '01- 2; WCp: '93- 8, '95- 15; ECp: '96- 3. At 5000mW: WJ: '90- 1, '92- dq, 94- 2; EJ: '89- 6, '91- 2, '93- 1. Won POR 10kmW 1992, 1994-2000, 20kmW 1998-9, 2001-02.
POR walks records 1989-2001: 3000m (10), 5000m (9), 10km (9), 20km (3), 20,000m track (1:29:36.4 WR '01). World junior 5000m best (21:01.8) 1993.
Progression at 10kmW, 20kmW: 1991- 45:37, 1992- 45:24, 1993- 43:44, 1994- 43:30, 1995- 44:05, 1996- 43:37, 1997- 44:26, 1998- 42:55, 1:31:03, 1999- 44:36, 1:30:13; 2000: 43:55, 1:28:19; 2001- 42:39, 1:27:55. Track pbs: 3000mW 12:08.30 '01, 5000mW 20:40.24 '01, 10000mW 44:36.79 '00.
Had a hugely successful junior career to her world silver medal in front of her home crowd in 1994, four years after she had won this title.

Fernanda RIBEIRO b. 23 Jun 1969 Penafiel 1.61m 48kg. FC Porto,
At 10000m (5000m): OG: '96- 1, '00- 3; WCh: '93- 10, '95- 1 (2), '97- 2 (3), '99- dnf; EC: '90- dnf, '94- 1, '98- 2; WCp: '94- 2; won E.Chall '98. At 3000m: OG: '88- h, '92- h; WCh: '87- h, '91- h; WI: '97- 3; EC: '86- h, '90- h; EI: '94- 1, '96- 1, '98- 2; WJ: '86- 4, '88- 2; EJ: '83- 11, '85- 4, '87- 1. World CC: '94- 10, '96- 6, '00- 10 (4k); Rd Rly team: '92- 1. Eur CC: '94- 6, '98- 4. Won IbAm 5000m 2000, POR 1500m 1989-90, 1995, 1998-9; 3000m 1985, 1993; 5000m 2000, 10000m 1992, 1996; CC 1996-9.
World 5000m record 1995. Portuguese records: 3000m (3), 5000m (3), 10000m (4) 1994-2000.
Progression at 3000m, 5000m, 10000m: 1982- 9:53.7, 1983- 9:21.71, 1984- 9:11.62, 1985- 9:14.19, 1986- 9:09.39, 1987- 8:56.33, 1988- 9:00.38, 1989- 9:04.33, 32:38.07; 1990- 9:03.35, 32:39.34; 1991- 8:57.64, 33:45.45; 1992- 8:56.10, 32:22.70; 1993- 8:51.91, 31:50.51; 1994- 8:42.13, 15:06.91, 31:04.25; 1995- 8:41.99, 14:36.45, 31:04.99; 1996- 8:39.49i/ 8:45.56, 14:41.07, 31:01.63; 1997- 8:37.14, 14:53.25, 31:39.15; 1998- 8:42.95, 15:22.8, 30:48.06; 1999- 8:30.66, 14:52.59; 2000- 8:34.99, 15:01.49, 30:22.88; 2001- 8:53.41i. pbs: 800m 2:05.83 '94, 1500m 4:05.97 '97, 1M 4:32.66 '99, HMar 68:23 '00.
At 11 was second in a half marathon in 1:24:02, just 4 secs behind Rosa Mota. Made international debut at 13 and set national age records each

age 13-22 at 3000m and 14-18 and 20 at 1500m. She fulfilled her long-time promise in 1994 with brilliant performances to win European titles indoors and out, and has added World and Olympic titles in the following years.

Carla SACRAMENTO b. 10 Dec 1971 Lisboa 1.73m 58kg. Maratona CP.
At 1500m (800m): OG: '92- sf (sf), '96- 6, '00- 10; WCh: '93- 11 (h), '95- 3, '97- 1, '99- 5, '01- 4; EC: '94- 6 (6), '98- 2; WI: '93/5/7/01- 7/2/5/4; EI: '92- (4), '94- (3), '96- 1; EJ: '89- (4); WUG: '97- 2; WCp: '98- 3. At 3000m: EI: '02- 2. World 4k CC: '98-00-01: 19/7/7; Eur CC: '94- 11. Won GP 1M 1997 (1500m 3rd 1998, 2nd 2001), Ib-Am 1500m 1998, Portuguese 800m 1986-7, 1993-5; 1500m 1991, 2001; CC 2000-2.
Portuguese records 1989-99: 800m (7), 1500m (9), 1M (4), 1000m (2), 2000m and 3000m (1)
Progression at 800m, 1500m: 1985- 2:15.15/ 2:13.56dq, 1986- 2:10.48, 1987- 2:09.3, 4:35.96; 1988- 2:04.27, 4:29.41; 1989- 2:03.89, 4:21.92; 1990- 2:04.83, 4:15.06; 1991- 2:04.94, 4:20.43; 1992- 2:00.57, 4:04.10; 1993- 1:59.42, 4:06.33; 1994- 1:59.39, 4:06.05; 1995- 1:59.78, 4:03.79; 1996- 2:00.24, 4:02.64; 1997- 1:58.94, 4:01.86; 1998- 2:02.3, 3:57.71; 1999- 1:59.54, 4:01.29; 2000- 2:00.22, 4:00.35; 2001- 4:00.32. pbs: 200m 25.49 '92, 400m 55.21 '89, 500m 1:10.83 '96, 1000m 2:34.85 '95, 1M 4:23.00i '02, 4:23.41 '98; 2000m 5:40.25 '96, 3000m 8:30.22 '99, 5000m 15:52.54 '00.
Ran three 3000m races in range 8:30.22 to 8:34.70 in 1999 after previous best of 9:32.7 (1990).

QATAR

Governing body: Qatar Amateur Athletic Federation, PO Box 8139, Doha. Founded 1963.

Khamis Seif ABDULLAH b. 1 Dec 1976 1.81m 64kg.
At 3000mSt: OG: '00- 10; WCh: '99- h, '01- 7; AsiC: '00- 1; WUG: '99- 2. Won Arab 2001.
Four Qatar records 1999-2001.
Progression at 3000mSt: 1999- 8:18.58, 2000- 8:17.56, 2001- 8:14.38. pbs: 1500m 3:41.2 '00, 5000m 13:36.93 '99.

ROMANIA

Governing body: Federatia Romana de Atletism, Str. Dr Primo Nebiolo nr.2, Bucuresti 71331. Founded 1912.

National Championships first held in 1914 (men), 1925 (women). **2001 Champions**: **Men**: 100m: Adrian Stefan 10.72, 200m: Adrian Guianu 21.34, 400m: Ioan Vieru 46.68, 800m: Stelian Tufaru 1.49.44, 1500m: Daniel Oniciuc 3:44.67, 5000m: Clement Hagima 14.20.02, 10000m: Gabriel Andreescu 30:13.60, HMar: Ion Veliciu 65.49, Mar: Arthur Mikos 2.22.47, 3000mSt: Florin Ionescu 8:38.12, 110mh: Mihai Marghescu 13.96, 400mh: Mugur Mateescu 51.58, HJ: Stefan Vasilache 2.18, PV: Tiberiu Agoston 5.00, LJ: Bogdan Tarus 8.13, TJ: Marian Oprea 16.86, SP: Gheorghe Guset 19.81, DT: Ionel Oprea 61.72, HT: Cosmin Sorescu 72.79, JT: Dorel Greta 69.44, Dec: Nicolae Istrate 6725, 20kmW: Silviu Casandra 1.25.04, 50kmW: Daniel Andrei 4:23:10. **Women**: 100m: Ionela Tîrlea 11.32, 200m: Monica Bumbescu 23.64, 400m: Otilia Ruicu 51.89, 800m: Elena Iagar 2:04.03, 1500m/5000m: Cristina Grosu 4:10.76/16:06.28, 10000m: Mihaela Botezan 31:45.06, HMar: Iulia Olteanu 71:31, Mar: Rodica Chirita 2.47.52, 3000mSt: Cristina Iloc-Casandra 9:51.88, 100mh: Carmen Zamfir 13.82, 400mh: Mariana Florea 59.46, HJ: Oana Pantelimon 1.93, PV: Silvia Ristea 3.50, LJ: Eva Miklos 6.65, TJ: Cristina Nicolau 14.11, SP: Elena Hila 17.91, DT: Nicoleta Grasu 64.33, HT: Cristina Buzau 61.55, JT: Ana-Mirela Termure 65.08, Hep: Mihaela Gîndila 5737, 10kmW/20kmW: Norica Cîmpean 45:19/1:33:43.

Marian OPREA b. 27 Sep 1972 1.90m 77kg.
At TJ: WCh: '01- dnq 13; WJ: '00- 1, WY: '99- 4; EJ: '99- 3, '01- 1; EI: '02- 2; WUG: '00- 2. ROM and Balkan champion 2001.
Progression at TJ: 1997- 14.78, 1999- 15.98, 2000- 16.49, 2001- 17.11, 2002- 17.29i. pb LJ 7.41i '01.

Women

Mihaela BOTEZAN b. 21 Nov 1976 Ocna Mure 1.60m 46kg. CSU Cluj-Napolca & Telecom Petrom Ploseti. Sports tecaher.
At 10000m: WCh: '01- 5; Romanian champion 2001. At 5000m: ECp: '01- 3. World HMar: '01- 10. Eur CC: 2001- 11.
Progression at 5000m, 10000m: 1995- 16.29.14, 1996- 16.34.72, 1997- 17.05.6, 34.58.83; 1998- 17.16.6, 35.26.45; 1999- 15:54.86, 34.33.01; 2000- 34.00.27; 2001-15.08.78, 31.45.06. pbs: 3000mSt 10:08.46 '99; Rd: 15km 49:35 '01, HMar 70:07 '00.

Norica CÎMPEAN b. 22 Mar 1972 Teius 1.64m 58kg. CSM Unirea Alba Iulia. Civil servant.
At 20kmW: OG: '00- 6; WCh: '99- dnf, '01- 6; WCp: '99- 3; ECp: '00- 6, '01- 6. At 10kmW: OG: '96- 29; WCh: '95- 20; EC: '98- dq; WCp: '97- 17; ECp: '98- 12. Won ROM 10kmW 1993-7, 1999-2000; 20kmW 1995-8, 2000-01; Balkan 1994, 1999.
ROM walks records: 10km (4), 20km (2) 1995-9.
Progression at 10kmW, 20kmW: 1990- 53:45, 1991- 51:51, 1992- 46:05, 1993- 45:42, 1994- 45:10.4, 1995- 43:48, 1:37:14; 1996- 42:55, 1997- 43:21, 1:35:20; 1998- 42:57, 1:35:44, 1999- 42:16, 1:27:46; 2000- 43:51, 1:28:59; 2001- 43:39, 1:29:25. pb 5000mW 21:34.20/21:05R '98.

Nicoleta GRASU b. 11 Sep 1971 Secuieni 1.76m 88kg. née Gradinaru. Administration officer. Dinamo Bucuresti.
At DT: OG: '92- dnq 13, '96- 7, '00- dnq 19; WCh: '93- 7, '95- dnq 18, '97- 10, '99- 3, '01- 3; EC: '94- 4, '98- 3; WJ: '90- 6; WUG: '97- 3, '99- 1; WCp: '98- 2; ECp: '97-9-00-01: 4/2/1/3; E23Cp: '92- 1. Won Balkan 1992, 1997, 1999; ROM 1992-3, 1995-7, 1999-2001. 3rd GP 1996.

Progression at DT: 1985- 36.02, 1986- 43.56, 1987- 50.82, 1988- 51.06, 1989- 52.54, 1990- 56.02, 1991- 59.90, 1992- 65.66, 1993- 65.16, 1994- 64.40, 1995- 64.62, 1996- 65.26, 1997- 64.68, 1998- 67.80, 1999- 68.80, 2000- 68.70, 2001- 68.31. pb SP 15.00i '92, 14.56 '91.
Married her coach Costel Grasu (b. 5 Jul 1967) DT pb 67.08 '92; 4 OG 1992.

Elena IAGAR b. 16 Jan 1975 Brasov 1.73m 54kg. nee Buhaianu. ASTRA Brasov, Civil servant.
At 1500m (800m): OG: '00- sf; WCh: '99- 6, '01- h, EC: '98- 10 (h); EI: '02- 2; WUG: '99- 1 (3); ECp: '99- (4), '00- 6, '01- (8). Won ROM 800m 1998, 2000-01; 1500m 1998-2000, CC 1997, Balkan 1500m 1999.
Progression at 800m, 1500m: 1992- 2:15.16i, 4:37.51; 1993- 2:07.08, 4:30.74; 1994- 2:07.96, 4:27.71i; 1995- 2:08.89, 4:20.46; 1996- 2:05.69, 1997- 2:04.32, 4:16.67; 1998- 2:01.44, 4:08.11; 1999- 2:00.26, 4:04.27; 2000- 2:01.29, 4:06.57; 2001- 2:04.03, 4:09.25. pbs: 1M 4:30.62 '99, 3000m 8:59.99i '01.

Monica IAGAR b. 2 Apr 1973 Sighetul Marmatiei 1.86m 68kg. Dinamo Bucuresti. Sports teacher. Married name Dinescu.
At HJ: OG: '00- 9=; WCh: '95- dnq 17=, '97- 13, '99- 10=, '01- 7=; EC: '94- dnq, '98- 1; WI: '97/9/01- 9=/4/8; EI: '96- 5, '98- 1; WUG: '97- 2, '99- 1; WCp: '98- 1; ECp: '94-7-9-00: 2/5/2/1; E23Cp: '94- 4; 3rd GP 1997, ROM champion 1995-8, 2000; Balkan 1997.
Four Romanian high jump records 1997-2000.
Progression at HJ: 1987- 1.70, 1988- 1.78, 1989- 1.64, 1990- 1.78, 1992- 1.78, 1993- 1.87i/1.84, 1994- 1.91, 1995- 1.97i/1.92, 1996- 1.96i/1.95dq/1.93, 1997- 2.00, 1998- 2.02, 1999- 2.03i/2.01, 2000- 2.02, 2001- 1.97i/1.92.
World number one high jumper of 1998. Six months drugs suspension 1996.

Cristina NICOLAU b. 9 Aug 1977 Bucuresti 1.84m 66kg. Steaua Bucuresti. Civil Servant.
At TJ (LJ): OG: '00- 6; WCh: '97- dnq 34, '99- 8, '01- 6; WJ: '94- (9), '96- 2 (2); EJ: '95- (2); EU23: '97- 1 (2), '99- 1 (4); WI: '01- 6; EI: '00- 2, '02- 5; WUG: '97- 5 (3); ECp: '99- 1, '01- 3 At LJ: WJ: '96- 2; EJ: '93- 3, '95- 2; E23Cp: '94- 3. Won ROM LJ 1996, 1999; TJ 1999, 2001.
Progression at TJ: 1996- 13.89, 1997- 14.22/14.23i, 1998- 14.20, 1999- 14.70, 2000- 14.94i/14.19/14.22w, 2001- 14.62. pbs: HJ 1.82 '95, LJ 6.61i '00, 6.58 '96, 6.69w '99.
Set European age-14 LJ best (6.19 '91). Her father Mihai Nicolau won the ROM decathlon in 1975 and 1977, pb 7465 '75.

Oana PANTELIMON b. 27 Sep 1972 Tecuci 1.78m 61kg. née Musunoi.
At HJ: OG: '00- 3=; WCh: '01- 9; WJ: '90- dnq, ECp: '01- 5; E23Cp: '92- 3. Romanian champion 1999, 2001; Balkan 2000.
Progression at HJ: 1987- 1.78, 1988- 1.86, 1989- 1.90, 1990- 1.85, 1991- 1.87i/1.86, 1992- 1.94, 1993- 1.91i/1.87, 1994- 1.88, 1995- 1.92, 1996- 1.92, 1997- 1.93, 1999- 1.80+, 2000- 1.99, 2001- 1.93.
Her bronze medal at the 2000 Olympics was a startling accomplishment, as this was her first major championship and after matching her pb of 1.94 to qualify she raised it with 1.96 and 1.99 in the final.

Lidia SIMON b. 4 Sep 1973 Târgu Cârbunesti 1.57m 44kg. née Slavuteanu. Dinamo Bucuresti.
At Mar: OG: '96- 6, '00- 2; WCh: '95- 10, '97- 3, '99- 3, '01- 1; EC: '94- 10; WCp: '95- 2; won Balkan 1994. At 10000m: EC: '98- 3. World HMar: '96-7-8-00: 2/3/3/3.
Romanian marathon records 1997 and 1999, half marathon 2000.
Progression at 10000m, Mar: 1990- 2:58:18, 1991- 34:23.52, 2:52:20; 1993- 2:56:10, 1994- 2:32:38, 1995- 2:31:46, 1996- 2:30:13, 1997- 2:27:04, 1998- 31:32.64, 2:28:31; 1999- 2:23:24, 2000- 2:22:54, 2001- 2:24:15. pbs: 1500m 4:22.57 '91, 3000m 9:25.84 '91, HMar 68:34 '00.
Won marathons at Kastoria and Lyon 1994. Took over 3 minutes off her pb for 3rd in Osaka (2:27:04), almost matched that when 3rd in London (2:27:11) and had third 3rd of 1997 at the Worlds. Won Osaka 1998, 1999 (in a brilliant ROM record 2:23:24, the then fastest ever in a women's only race on an out and back course), and in 2000, when she moved to eighth on world all-time list with 2:22:54. 2nd London 2000 and 4th 2001. Married to her coach Liviu Simon.

Gabriela SZABO b. 14 Nov 1975 Bistrita 1.58m 43kg. Sports teacher. Rapid Bucuresti.
At 5000m (1500m): OG: '96- h (2), '00- 1 (3); WCh: '95- 4, '97- 1, '99- 1, '01- 8 (1); EC: '98- 2; WUG: '95- 1 (1), '97- (1); ECp: '95- 1B, '97- 1 (2), '99 (1 1500 & 3000). At 3000m: EC: '94- 3; WJ: '92- 2, '94- 1; EJ: '91- 1, '93-1; WI: '95- 1, '97- 1, '99- 1 (1), '01- 2; EI: '98- 1, '00- 1; WCp: '94- 3, '98- 1; E23Cp: '92- 2, '94- 1. Won GP 3000m (and overall) 1999. World CC: '94- 4J, '95- 10, '96- 9. Won ROM 3000m 1993.
Records: World indoor 2000m 1998, 5000m (14:47.35) 1999, 3000m (8:32.88) 2001; European 5000m 1998, European junior 3000m 1994. ROM 3000m 1998 and 2001, 5000m (4) 1995-8.
Progression at 1500m, 3000m, 5000m: 1991- 4:17.07, 9:19.28; 1992- 4:12.57, 8:48.28; 1993- 4:10.32, 8:50.97; 1994- 4:14.43, 8:40.08; 1995- 4:11.73, 8:30.03, 14:53.91; 1996- 4:01.54, 8:36.07, 14:41.12; 1997- 4:06.14i/4:06.25, 8:27.78, 14:42.43; 1998- 3:56.97, 8:24.31, 14:31.48; 1999- 4:03.23i/ 4:13.61, 8:25.03, 14:40.59; 2000- 4:00.73, 8:26.35, 14:40.61; 2001- 4:00.57, 8:24.19, 14:46.92. pbs: 1000m 2:36.74 '89, 1M 4:19.30 '98, 2000m 5:30.53i '98, 5:36.88+ '97.
Had a marvellous season in 1997 when she won World titles indoors and out and lost just once, to Kelly Holmes at 1500m. In 1998 she was the world's fastest at 1500m, 1M, 2000m, 3000m and

5000m, the only woman to beat Svetlana Masterkova at 1500m, and after the disappointment of a European silver, ran a European record at 5000m in Berlin. In 1999 she won a brilliant double at 1500m and 3000m at the World Indoors and went on outdoors to annex the World title at 5000m, a half-share of the $1 million jackpot for her seven wins at 3000m/5000m in Golden League meetings and to become the overall IAAF Grand Prix champion. She also won a 1500m/3000m double for Romania in the European Cup and had 15 successive wins from 2nd to Kutre Dulecha in an indoor 1500m on 7 Feb 1999. She has not raced in Romania since 1994. Married her coach Zsolt Gyöngyössy on 2 October 1999.

Violeta SZEKELY b. 26 Mar 1965 Dolhestii Mari 1.69m 52kg. née Beclea. Technician. Rapid Bucuresti.
At 1500m (800m): OG: '92- sf, '00- 2; WCh: '91- 10, '93- 9, '99- 4, '01- 2; EC: '94- h, '98- 5 (4); WI: '89- (4), '91- (2), '93- 2, '95 dq, '99- 2 (5 3000m), '01- 2; EI: '90- (3), '98- 3, '00- 1; ECp: '93- 2, '94- 3 (5), '01- 1. Won ROM 800m 1993-4, 1500m 1990-1, 1993-4. Won GP 1500m 1999-2001 (3rd 1M 1993), won overall 2001.
Progression at 800m, 1500m: 1982- 2:05.07, 4:23.85, 1983- 2:03.63, 1985- 2:00.75, 4:11.01; 1986- 1:58.7, 4:04.56; 1987- 1:59.53, 4:07.56; 1988- 1:59.35, 4:07.94; 1989- 1:58.94, 4:07.24; 1990- 2:01.05, 4:03.14; 1991- 2:00.19, 4:02.21; 1992- 4:03.29; 1993- 1:59.13, 3:59.35; 1994- 1:59.30i/2:00.47, 4:03.76; 1998- 1:58.57, 3:59.67; 1999- 3:59.31, 2000- 2:00.81i, 3:58.29; 2001- 3:59.35. pbs: 1000m 2:34.89i '95, 2:36.74 '89; 1M 4:21.69 '93, 2000m 5:39.36i '00, 3000m 8:46.39i '01, 8:47.3 '98.
Three year drugs ban from 15 Feb 1995, which cost her the World Indoor 1500m 4th place. She had a wonderful season in 2001, when won the IAAF overall Grand Prix for women and also won at all seven of the Golden League meetings to share the Jackpot. She lost just two races but both were World Championships – indoors to Hasna Benhassi and outdoors to Gabriela Szabo. Her husband and coach Adrian Szekely won three ROM judo titles 1989-91. Daughter Aleksandra born June 1996.

Felicia TILEA b. 29 Sep 1967 Mâgura Ilvei 1.69m 70kg. Married name **Moldovan**. Teacher. Rapid Bucuresti. Sports teacher.
At JT: OG: '96- 10, '00- dnq 15; WCh: '93- 8, '95- 2, '97- 5, '99- 11, '01- dnq 16; EC: '90- dq (9), '94- 3, '98- 10; WUG: '95- 1; ECp: '93-4-6-7: 1/3/1B/2. ROM champion 1990, 1994, 1996-8.
Romanian javelin record 1996, new spec (2) 2000.
Progression at JT: 1981- 36.62, 1982- 44.00, 1983- 48.40, 1984- 46.80, 1985- 47.74, 1986- 51.42, 1987- 51.44, 1988- 47.42, 1989- 59.54, 1990- 64.02, 1993- 65.62, 1994- 66.40, 1995- 65.22, 1996- 69.26, 1997- 65.76, 1998- 65.10, 1999- 65.27; new: 60.97, 2000- 63.12, 2001- 62.27.
Two-year drugs ban after positive test for steroids when 9th at 1990 European Champs.

Ionela TÎRLEA b. 9 Feb 1976 Horezu 1.69m 54kg. Atletismul Arâdean Arad. Sports teacher.
At 400mh/4x400mR (200m): OG: '96- 7, '00- 6; WCh: '95- 7, '01- 6; EC: '94- 7, '98- 1/4R; WJ: '94- 1/3R; EJ: '93- 1, '95- 1; WUG: '95- 2; WCp: '98- 4; ECp: '93- (7), '94- 7 (8), '97- 8, '99- 3R (4, 1-400, 4-100), '01- 2 (2); WI: '99 (1); E23Cp: '94- 1 (2). At 400m: WUG: '99- 1; WJ: '92- 3/1R; WI: '97- 4; EI: '94- 4, '96- 4, '98- 2; E23Cp: '92- 2 (4). Won ROM 100m 1998, 2001; 200m 1998-9, 400m 1996, 1999; 400mh 1994-6.
Romanian records: 100m (2) 1998-9, 200m (3) 1998-9, 400m (2) 1998-9, 400mh (6) 1996-9. European Junior 400mh record 1995.
Progression at 200m, 400m, 400mh: 1991- 24.51, 1992- 23.84, 52.13; 1993- 23.49, 56.30H; 1994- 23.60, 56.25H; 1995- 23.54, 55.26H; 1996- 54.40, 1997- 23.07, 52.06i, 55.04; 1998- 22.65/22.5A, 50.32, 53.37; 1999- 22.35, 49.88, 53.25; 2000- 51.84, 54.35; 2001- 22.77, 52.64i, 54.65. pb 100m 11.30 '99.

RUSSIA

Governing body: All-Russia Athletic Federation, Luzhnetskaya Nab. 8, Moscow 119992. Founded 1911.

National Championships first held 1908, USSR women's from 1922. **2001 Champions**: **Men**: 100m: Sergey Bychkov 10.40, 200m: Oleg Sergeyev 20.82, 400m: Dmitriy Golovastov 45.81, 800m: Boris Kaveshnikov 1:45.82, 1500m: Andrey Zadorozhniy 3:45.02, 5000m: Mikhayil Yeginov 13:37.98, 10000m: Dmitriy Semyonov 29:07.3, HMar: Dmitriy Maksimov 63:35, Mar: Mikhayil Romanov 2:16:08, 3000mSt: Roman Usov 8:35.89, 110mh: Andrey Kislykh 13.88, 400mh: Boris Gorban 48.54, HJ: Sergey Klyugin 2.31, PV: Vasiliy Gorshkov 5.75, LJ: Danila Burkenya 8.31, TJ: Viktor Gushchinskiy 16.91, SP: Pavel Chumachenko 19.73, DT: Dmitriy Shevchenko 65.44, HT: Sergey Kirmasov 80.07, JT: Sergey Makarov 84.08, Dec: Nikolay Afanasyev 7812, 20kmW: Roman Rasskazov 1:20:35, 50kmW: Aleksey Voyevodin 3:44:32. **Women**: 100m/200m: Yekaterina Leshchova 11.25/22.70, 400m: Olesya Zykina 50.15, 800m: Svetlana Cherkasova 1:57.59, 1500m: Tatyana Tomashova 4:03.96, 5000m: Olga Rosseyeva 15:35.83, 10000m: Lyudmila Biktasheva 31:30.6, Mar: Firiya Sultanova 2:34:58, 3000mSt: Yekaterina Volkova 9:54.46, 100mh: Svetlana Laukhova 12.72, 400mh: Yuliya Nosova 55.67, HJ: Yekaterina Aleksandrova 1.95, PV: Svetlana Feofanova 4.70, LJ: Tatyana Kotova 7.09, TJ: Tatyana Lebedeva 14.84, SP: Larisa Peleshenko 20.79, DT: Natalya Sadova 62.23, HT: Olga Kuzenkova 73.40, JT: Tatyana Shikolenko 62.81, Hep: Alena Vindyuk 6146, 20kmW: Yelena Nikolayeva 1:28:11.

Note: Clubs abbreviations: Dyn – Dynamo, MS – Moskva City sports club, TU – Trade Union sports society, VS – Army, YR – Yunest Rossii.

Vladimir ANDREYEV b. 7 Sep 1966 Yamanchurino, Chuvashiya 1.80m 68kg. Cheboksary VS. Electrician.
At 20kmW: OG: '92- 13, '00- 3; WCh: '93- 19, '97- dnf, '99/01- dq; WCp: '93- 11, '97- 10, '99- 3; ECp: '01- 5. USSR champion 1989, CIS 1992, Russian 1993-4.
Progression at 20kmW: 1989- 1:20:08, 1990- 1:19:21, 1991- 1:19:17, 1992- 1:19:53, 1993- 1:19:43, 1994- 1:21:53, 1995- 1:18:32, 1996- 1:19:11, 1997- 1:18:39, 1998- 1:18:40, 1999- 1:19:57, 2000- 1:18:16, 2001- 1:20:14, 2002- 1:19:18. pbs: 5000mW 18:31.63i '92, 10000mW 39:27.0i '95, 1HrW 14,735m '92, 30kmW 2:09:07 '01, 35kmW 2:29:31 '01.
Won the Russian winter 20km title 1995-8.

Aleksandr BORICHEVSKIY b. 25 Jun 1970 Zhukovskiy 1.95m 120kg. St.Petersburg VS.
At DT: OG: '96- dnq 31, '00- dnq 15; WCh: '97- dnq 28; '99- 8; EC: '98- dq; WCp: '97- 2; ECp: '99- 2. Russian champion 1997-8.
Progression at DT: 1990- 52.64, 1991- 59.12, 1992- 58.48, 1993- 60.78, 1994- 62.46, 1995- 63.00, 1996- 64.32, 1997- 62.32, 1998- 64.05, 1999- 65.08, 2000- 64.38A, 2001- 64.66.

Yuriy BORZAKOVSKIY b. 12 Apr 1981 Kratovo, Moskva reg. 1.81m 70kg. Zhukovskiy Dyn. Student.
At 800m: OG: '00- 6; EJ: '99- 1; WI: '01- 1; EI: '00- 1; ECp: '99- 1; 2nd GP 2001. At 400m: EU23: '01- 1. Records: Two world junior indoor 800m 2000, European Junior 800m (2) & 1000m 2000; Four Russian 800m 2001.
Progression at 800m: 1997- 1:52.8i/1:53.69, 1998- 1:47.71, 1999- 1:46.13, 2000- 1:44.33, 2001- 1:42.47. pbs: 200m 22.56 '99, 400m 45.84 '00, 1000m 2:17.40 '00, 1500m 3:47.1 '98.
He won at the World Youth Games in 1998, and at the age of 18 had a startling victory when he sprinted to victory in the European Cup 800m. In January 2000 he set Russian senior and world junior indoor records of 1:45.91 to win in Sindelfingen and a hugely impressive 1:44.38 in Dortmund. He impressed outdoors also, but typically leaves himself a tremendous amount to do on the second lap of his 800m races.

Viktor BURAYEV b. 23 Aug 1982 1.76m 58kg.
At 20kmW: '01- 3; ECp: '01- 1. At 10kmW: WJ: '00- 3; EJ: '91- 1.
World junior walks records 10000m 2000, 20km 2001.
Progression at 20kmW: 2001- 1:18:06. pb 10000mW 38:46.4 '00.
At 18 years 264 days he became the youngest ever men's walk medallist at the World Championships – and he was the only junior to win a medal in 2001.

Pavel GERASIMOV b. 29 May 1979 Aleksin, Tula reg. 1.93m 84kg. Moskva TU.
At PV: OG: '00- dnq 26=; WJ: '98- 1; EJ: '97- 2; WI: '01- 5, EI: '02- 6.
Progression at PV: 1995- 4.40, 1996- 5.10i/5.00, 1997- 5.30, 1998- 5.55, 1999- 5.65/5.70ex, 2000- 5.90, 2001- 5.81i/5.50.

Boris GORBAN b. 26 Sep 1978 Dushanbe, Tadjikistan 1.92m 74kg. Luch Moskva.
At 400mh/4x400mR: OG: '00- sf; WCh: '01- dq; EC: '98- h; WJ: '96- sf; EJ: '97- 1; EU23: '99- 2; WI: '01- 3R; ECp: '01- 2R. Russian champion 2001.
Progression at 400mh: 1995- 53.39, 1996- 51.61, 1997- 50.95, 1998- 49.87, 1999- 49.94, 2000- 49.09, 2001-48.50. pbs: 300m 32.8i '01, 400m 46.33i '01.
Finished fifth in 48.27 the 2001 World final, but was disqualified for a trailing leg.

Denis KAPUSTIN b. 5 Oct 1970 Kazan 1.90m 86kg. KazanVS. Teacher.
At TJ: OG: '00- 3; WCh: '93- 6, '95- dnq 23, '97- 4, '99- 9; EC: '94- 1, '98- 2; EI: '94- 2; EJ: '89- 1; WUG: '91- 4; WCp: '98- 2; ECp: '94-7-9: 1/2/1. 2nd GP 1998. Russian champion 2000.
Progression at TJ: 1989- 16.37/16.63w, 1990- 16.68, 1991- 17.34, 1992- 17.48, 1993- 17.54, 1994- 17.62/17.86w, 1995- 17.42, 1996- 17.06, 1997- 17.59, 1998- 17.65, 1999- 17.40/17.65w, 2000- 17.46, 2001- 16.73i/16.42. pb LJ: 7.68i '91.

Vadim KHERSONTSEV b. 8 Jul 1974 Kursk region 1.92m 106kg. St Petersburg TU.
At HT: OG: '96- dnq 15; WCh: '97- 7, '99- 8; EJ: '93- 3; WUG: '97- 4; ECp: '97- 2. Russian champion 1996.
Progression at HT: 1992- 68.58, 1993- 72.72, 1994- 76.78, 1995- 76.94, 1996- 80.68, 1997- 78.58, 1998- 79.10, 1999- 78.82, 2000- 78.16, 2001- 81.26.

Sergey KIRMASOV b. 25 Mar 1970 Mcensk Oryol region 1.80m 115kg. Mcensk VS. Soldier.
At HT: WCh: '01- dnq 15; EC: '98- dnq 18; EJ: '89- 1; ECp: '99- 7, '00- 5. Russian champion 1992, 1998, 2001.
Progression at HT: 1988- 71.20, 1989- 75.52, 1990- 77.66, 1991- 81.14, 1992- 79.92, 1993- 82.54, 1994- 79.20dq, 1998- 82.62, 1999- 79.55, 2000- 78.44, 2001- 80.07.
Four year drugs ban 1994.

Sergey KLYUGIN b. 24 Mar 1974 Kineshma, Ivanova region 1.92m 82kg. Moskva TU. Teacher.
At HJ: OG: '00- 1; WCh: '97- 11, '99- dnq 24, '01- 5=; EC: '98- 3; WJ: '92- 5=, EJ: '91- 2; EU23Cp: '94- 2; ECp: '97-8-00: 2/1/3=. Russian champion 2000-01.
Progression at HJ: 1986- 1.55, 1987- 1.65, 1988- 1.80, 1989- 1.98, 1990- 2.16, 1991- 2.27, 1992- 2.28i/2.24, 1993- 2.26i/2.24, 1994- 2.28i/2.26, 1995- 2.26, 1996- 2.28, 1997- 2.31i/2.30, 1998- 2.36, 1999- 2.33, 2000- 2.35, 2001- 2.31.

Ilya KONOVALOV b. 4 Mar 1971 Kursk region 1.92m 109kg. Kursk Dyn. Soldier.

At HT: OG: '96- 6, '00- 5; WCh: '95- 7, '97- 6, '99- 10, '01- 3; EC: '98- 9; WUG: '97- 3; ECp: '95- 1, '98- 2. Russian champion 1995, 1999.
Progression at HT: 1988- 63.10, 1989- 71.30, 1990- 74.66, 1991- 76.26, 1992- 77.04, 1993- 77.44, 1994- 78.30, 1995- 79.66, 1996- 79.46, 1997- 78.92, 1998- 79.82, 1999- 80.51, 2000- 81.93, 2001- 80.27.

Lev LOBODIN b. 1 Apr 1969 Voronezh 1.88m 93kg. Luch Moskva. Teacher.
At Dec: OG: '96- dnf, '00- 13; WCh: '95- 7, '97- dnf, '99- 5, '01- 5; EC: '94- 3, '98- 3; ECp: '94- 2, '95- 6. UKR champion 1991. At Hep: WI: '93- 4, '99- 6, '01- 3; EI: '92- 6, '98- 3.
Progression at Dec: 1988- 7091h, 1991- 8018, 1992- 7998, 1993- 8156, 1994- 8201, 1995- 8286, 1996- 8315, 1997- 8184, 1998- 8571, 1999- 8494, 2000- 8071, 2001- 8465. pbs: 60m 6.83i '98, 100m 10.66 '01, 10.65w '94; 400m 48.39 '96, 1500m 4:29.95 '91, 60mh 7.79i '98, 110mh 13.94 '99, HJ 2.10 '91, PV 5.25i '99, 5.20 '98; LJ 7.56/7.68i?/7.74w '99, SP 16.39i '01, 16.19 '00; DT 50.72 '99, JT 59.00 '95, Hep 6226i '98.
Changed nationality UKR to RUS after 1996.

Sergey MAKAROV b. 19 Mar 1973 Lyubertsy 1.92m 100kg. Moskva Dyn.
At JT: OG: '96- 6, '00- 3; WCh: '97- 5, '99- 9, '01- 7; EC: '98- 4; WCp: '98- 2; ECp: '96-7-8-9-00-01: 2/4/2/2/2/2; E23Cp: '94- 2. Won GWG 1998, RUS 1996-7, 2000-01.
Three Russian records 1996-9.
Progression at JT: 1991- 73.48, 1992- 76.08, 1993- 75.78, 1994- 82.54, 1995- 84.42, 1996- 88.86, 1997- 88.54, 1998- 86.96, 1999- 89.93, 2000- 89.92, 2001- 88.42.
His father Aleksandr Makarov (b. 11 Feb 1951) was 2nd in the 1980 Olympic JT with a pb 89.64 (old javelin). Married to Oksana Ovchinnikova (b. 21 Jul 1971, Russian 'old' javelin record 68.72 '96. 2 WJ 1990).

Ilya MARKOV b. 19 Jun 1972 Asbest, Sverdlovsk reg. 1.76m 64kg. Asbest VS. Soldier.
At 20kmW: OG: '96- 2, '00- 15; WCh: '95- 4, '97- dq, '99- 1, '01- 2; EC: '94- 18, '98- 1; WUG: '97- 1; WCp: '95- 30, '97- 3, '99- 7; Won RUS 1995, GWG 1998. At 10kmW: WJ: '90- 1; EJ: '91- 1.
Progression at 20kmW: 1991- 1:33:46, 1992- 1:23:27, 1993- 1:20:19, 1994- 1:24:07, 1995- 1:18:53, 1996- 1:18:48, 1997- 1:18:30, 1998- 1:19:46, 1999- 1:18:50, 2000- 1:20:53, 2001- 1:19:36. pbs: 3000mW 11:08.2i '92, 5000mW 18:36.71i '99, 18:46.96 '01; 10000mW 39:15.6 '98.

Ruslan MASHCHENKO b. 11 Nov 1971 Voronezh 1.93m 89kg. Moskva Dyn.
At 400mh/4x400mR: OG: '96- h, '00- sf; WCh: '95- 4, '97- 6, '01- sf; EC: '94- sf, '98- 2; WUG: '97- 2; ECp: '94-5-6-7-8-9-00-01: 7/2/5/3/1/4//4 (2R '94/01). At 400m: WI: '01- 3R; EI: '98- 1. Won RUS 400mh 1995-6, 400m 1997.
Russian 400mh record 1995.
Progression at 400mh: 1986- 59.7, 1987- 57.9, 1988- 55.7, 1989- 53.5, 1990- 52.12, 1991- 51.87, 1993- 51.11, 1994- 49.13, 1995- 48.47, 1996- 49.16, 1997- 48.51, 1998- 48.06, 1999- 49.39, 2000- 48.76, 2001- 48.88. pb 400m 45.89 '97.
Sister Lyudmila (b. 19 Apr 1974) was 3rd in 1993 European Junior heptathlon.

Nikolay MATYUKHIN b. 13 Dec 1968 Zhukovskiy, Moskva region 1.79m 68kg. Moskva Dyn.
At 50kmW: OG: '96- 25, '00- 5; WCh: '95- 10, '97- 15, '99- 2, '01- dq; EC: '98- 16; WCp: '95- 17, '97- 4, '99- 3; ECp: '01- 2. Russian champion 1995.
Progression at 20kmW, 50kmW: 1990- 1:23:52, 4:10.04; 1991- 1:22:36, 1992- 1:21:16, 1993- 1:19:43, 1994- 3:45:34, 1995- 3:51:13, 1996- 1:22:18, 3:42:30; 1997- 1:24:51, 3:41:36; 1998- 1:20:12, 3:45:29; 1999- 3:40:13, 2000- 3:42:02, 2001- 1:22:13, 3:45:48. pbs: 10000mW 41:46.30t '94, 30kmW 2:06:36 '97, 35kmW 2:27:29 '97.

Yevgeniy PECHONKIN b. 9 Oct 1973 Krasnodar 1.90m 90kg. Novosibirsk VS.
At 110mh: OG: '96- h, '00- sf; WCh: '93- h; '01- 6; WJ: '92- 1 (5 LJ); EJ: '91- 2; ECp: '96-9-00-01: 3/8/dq/1. Russian champion 1996, 2000. At 60mh: EI: '02- 3.
Progression at 110mh: 1988- 15.4, 1989- 15.08, 1990- 14.69, 1991- 14.05, 1992- 13.77, 1993- 13.60, 1994- 13.95/13.81w, 1995- 13.57/13.4, 1996- 13.38, 1999- 13.90, 2000- 13.39/13.37w, 2001- 13.38. pbs: 50mh 6.48i '01, 60mh 7.46i '02, LJ 7.90 '93.
Broke leg in June 1998. His father Gennadiy was formely married to Natalya Burda/Pechonkina (3rd OG 400m 1968).

Andrey PLOTNIKOV b. 12 Aug 1967 Vladimir 1.86m 77kg. Vladimir VS. Soldier.
At 50kmW: OG: '96- dnf; EC: '90- dq, '94- 8, '98- 3; WCp: '97- 10. Russian champion 1996, 1998.
Progression at 50kmW: 1986- 4:08:40, 1987- 3:58:21, 1988- 3:53:42, 1989- 3:46:14, 1990- 3:40:07, 1991- 3:48:43, 1992- 3:37:05sh, 1993- 4:14:45, 1994- 3:47:53, 1995- 4:02:09, 1996- 3:40:58, 1997- 3:44:00, 1998- 3:41:14, 2000- 3:44:30, 2001- 3:50:32. pbs: 20kmW 1:21:36 '91, 30kmW 2:05:53 '93, 35kmW 2:28:22 '97.

Vladimir POTEMIN b. 15 Jan 1980 Insar, Morodoviya 1.70m 67kg. Saransk VS.
At 50kmW: WCh: '01- 5; ECp: '01- 3. At 20kmW: OG: '00- 26. 10000mW: EJ: '99- 2.
World U23 best 50km walk 2000.
Progression at 50kmW: 2000- 3:39:21, 2001- 3:46.12. pbs: 10000mW 40:28.26 '99, 30kmW 2:08:05 '01, 35kmW 2:29:03 '01.

Roman RASSKAZOV b. 28 Apr 1979 Mordoviya 1.86m 64kg. Saransk VS. Student.
At 20kmW: OG: '00- 6; WCh: '99- dnf, 01- 1. RUS champion 1999-2001. At 10000mW: WJ: '98- 1.
World best and two RUS records 20km walk 2000.
Progression at 20kmW: 1997- 1:31:24, 1999-

1:19:36, 2000- 1:17:46, 2001- 1:20:31. pbs: 5000mW 19:02.1i '00, 10kmW 37:11 (world best) '00.

Yaroslav RYBAKOV b. 22 Nov 1980 Mogilyev, Belarus 1.98m 84kg.
At HJ: WCh: '01- 2=; WJ: '98- 5; EJ: '99- 3; EI: '02- 3; ECp: '01- 1; WI: '01- 7.
Progression at HJ: 1997- 2.10i/2.09, 1998- 2.20, 1999- 2.19i/2.18, 2000- 2.28, 2001- 2.33.

Vyacheslav SHABUNIN b. 27 Sep 1969 Kamyshlov, Sverdlovsk region 1.71m 56kg. Luch Moskva. Teacher.
At 1500m: OG: '96/00- h; WCh: '95- sf, '97/99- h; EC: '94- 5, '98- 9; WI: '95- 5; EI: '00- 5; ECp: '94-5-7-8-00: 6/2/3/7 (5 5000)/3. At 5000m: WCp: '92- 8. At 3000m: ECp: '99- 2. Won RUS 1500m 1992, 1994-6.
Russian records 1500m (3) 1997-2000, 1M (4) 1994-2001, 2000m, 3000m 1994-5.
Progression at 1500m/1M: 1988- 4:12.7, 1990-3;54.6, 1991- 3:44.68, 1992- 3:40.49, 1993- 3:36.59, 1994- 3:38.61/3:53.54M, 1995- 3:34.79/3:51.02M, 1996- 3:34.50, 1997- 3:33.47, 1998- 3:33.30/3:53.30M, 1999- 3:34.01/3:52.23M, 2000- 3:32.28/3:50.54M, 2001- 3:33.01/3:49.83M. pbs: 800m 1:47.00 '96, 2000m 4:57.18 '97, 3000m 7:39.24 '95, 5000m 13:43.39 '94, HMar 61:29 '96.

Dmitriy SHEVCHENKO b. 13 May 1968 Taganrog, Rostov-na-Donu 2.00m 140kg. Krasnodar Dyn. Teacher.
At DT: OG: '92- 8, '00- 11; WCh: '91- 7, '93- 2, '95-8, '99- dnq 19, '01- 4; EC: '94- 2, '98- dnq; ECp '93-4-8-01: 2/1/1/3; won GP 1995. USSR champion 1991, CIS 1992, Russian 1992-3, 1999-2001; GWG 1994.
Progression at DT: 1986- 57.30, 1987- 60.34, 1988-59.68, 1989- 59.38/61.62?, 1990- 64.10, 1991- 63.70, 1992- 67.30, 1993- 66.90, 1994- 64.74, 1995-68.04dq/66.74, 1998- 65.14, 1999- 65.68, 2000-66.66, 2001- 67.57. pb SP 17.94 '99.
Four year drugs ban for positive test at Cologne 18 Aug 1995, so disqualified from his GP Final win three weeks later; reinstated 1998.

Vitaliy SHKURLATOV b. 25 May 1979 Volgograd 1.82m 76kg. Volgograd VS.
At LJ: WCh: '01- 12; WJ: '98- 8; EU23: '99- 2; EJ: '97- 4; WI: '01- 8; EI: '00- 3, '02- 7; ECp: '00- 1.
Progression at LJ: 1995- 6.84, 1996- 7.64, 1997-7.92, 1998- 7.79i, 1999- 8.06, 2000- 8.38i/8.22, 2001- 8.18. pb 60m 6.4/6.78i '02.

Vasiliy SIDORENKO b. 1 May 1961 Volgograd 1.87m 110kg. Volgograd Dyn. Welder.
At HT: OG: '96- 12, '00- dnq 21; WCh: '93- 5, '95-dnq, '97- 3, '99- dnq 17, '01- dnq 21; EC: '94- 1, '98- dnq 13; WCp: '94- 4; ECp: '94- 1. 3rd GP 1994. Won GWG 1998, Russian 1992, 1997, 2000. World M40 record 2001.
Progression at HT: 1979- 59.98, 1980- 68.78, 1981- 69.30, 1983- 74.10, 1984- 76.80, 1985- 80.40, 1986- 80.70, 1987- 80.02, 1988- 80.52, 1989- 82.30, 1990- 80.98, 1991- 79.76, 1992- 82.54, 1993- 80.04, 1994- 82.02, 1995- 81.46, 1996- 78.82, 1997- 80.76, 1998- 80.89, 1999- 79.95, 2000- 81.75, 2001- 80.03.

Yevgeniy SMIRYAGIN b. 17 May 1976 Leningrad 1.84m 79kg. St-Peterburg TU.
At PV: OG: '00- 10=, WCh: '97- 8; WJ: '94- 11; EJ: '95- 1; EU23: '97- 1; ECp: '98- 1, '00- 1.
Progression at PV: 1992- 4.80, 1993- 5.20, 1994-5.40, 1995- 5.55, 1996- 5.65i/5.60, 1997- 5.85, 1998- 5.85, 1999- 5.65, 2000- 5.85, 2001- 5.71i/5.70.

Kirill SOSUNOV b. 1 Nov 1975 Ryazan 1.90m 85kg. Ryazan TU. Student.
At LJ: OG: '00- dnq 16; WCh: '97- 3; EC: '98- 1; WUG: '95- 1; WJ: '94- dnq; EU23: '97- 2; WI: '97- 2; EI: '02- 5; WCp: '98- 4; ECp: '96-7-8-9: 4/1/1/7.
Progression at LJ: 1990- 6.70, 1991- 6.85, 1992-7.11, 1993- 7.66, 1994- 7.96, 1995- 8.28/8.48w, 1996- 8.27i/8.17, 1997- 8.41i/8.30, 1998- 8.38, 1999- 7.98, 2000- 8.34, 2001- 7.82. pb 60m 6.5i '98.
Married to Olga Kaliturina (qv).

Igor SPASOVKHODSKIY b. 1 Aug 1979 Moskva 1.91m 91kg. Moskva TU.
At TJ: OG: '00- dnq 32; WCh: '01- 3; EU23: '01- 2; EI: '02- 7; WUG: '01- 4.
Progression at TJ: 1997- 14.42, 1998- 15.30, 1999-16.32, 2000- 16.86, 2001- 17.44.

Maksim TARASOV b. 2 Dec 1970 Yaroslavl 1.94m 80kg. Yaroslavl TU. Student.
At PV: OG: '92- 1, '00- 3; WCh: '91- 3, '93- 3=, '95- 2, '97- 2, '99- 1; EC: '98- 1; WJ: '88- 2; EJ: '89- 1; WI: '95- 7=, '97- 3; WCp: '98- 1. Won GP 1996, 1998, 1999 (2nd 1997, 3rd 1993/95), CIS PV 1992. Three world junior records 1989.
Progression at PV: 1982- 2.90, 1983- 3.30, 1984-3.80, 1985- 4.50, 1986- 5.00, 1987- 5.40, 1988- 5.60, 1989- 5.80, 1990- 5.85, 1991- 5.85/5.90ex, 1992-5.90, 1993- 5.90, 1994- 5.90, 1995- 5.91, 1996- 5.90, 1997- 6.00, 1998- 5.95, 1999- 6.05, 2000- 5.90, 2001- 5.75. pbs: 100m 10.8 '89, HJ 1.95, LJ 7.40.
All world age bests from 16 to 19, 1987-90. Very consistent vaulter, world number one of 1998 and 1999. Has lived in Budapest since 1992.

Vyacheslav VORONIN b. 5 Apr 1974 Vladikavkaz 1.90m 78kg. Vladikavkaz Dyn.
At HJ: OG: '00- 10; WCh: '99- 1, '01- 2=; EJ: '93- 2; WI: '99- 2, '01- 9; EI: '98- 2, '00- 1; ECp: '99- 2. Won GP 2000, Russian champion 1999.
Russian high jump record 2000.
Progression at HJ: 1992- 2.15, 1993- 2.18, 1995-2.18, 1996- 2.29, 1997- 2.26/2.30sq, 1998- 2.32i/2.28, 1999- 2.37, 2000- 2.40, 2001- 2.37.

Aleksey ZAGORNYY b. 31 May 1978 Yaroslavl 1.99m 128kg. Moskva TU.
At TJ: OG: '00- dnq 22; EJ: '97- 5; EU23: '99- 7; WUG: '01- 4.
Progression at HT: 1994- 59.90, 1995- 71.00, 1996- 71.94, 1997- 71.30, 1998- 77.03, 1999- 77.20, 2000- 79.68, 2001- 80.80, 2002- 83.43.

Women

Yelena AFANASYEVA b. 1 Mar 1967 Kulebyaki Gorkiy reg. 1.64m 56kg. née Vlasova. Moskva reg. Dyn. Teacher.
At 800m: OG: '96- 5; WCh: '93- h, '95- sf, '97- 2; EC: '98- 1; WI: '93- 4, '95- 2; EI: '92- 3; WCp: '92- 3, '98- 2; ECp: '94-5-7: 7/1/1. Won RUS 800m 1995, 1998. WIR 4 x 800m relay 1994.
Progression at 1500m: 1985- 2:07.83, 1986- 2:00.90, 1988- 1:57.77, 1991- 1:59.85, 1992- 1:59.12, 1993- 1:58.88, 1994- 2:00.52, 1995- 1:59.20, 1996- 1:57.77, 1997- 1:56.61, 1998- 1:56.63, 1999- 2:00.37, 2000- 2:03.83, 2001- 1:58.73i/2:00.81. pbs: 400m 52.78 '97, 1000m 2:34.60 '98, 1500m 4:07.8 '88.

Natalya ANTYUKH b. 26 Jun 1981 Leningrad 1.81m 68kg.
At 400m/4x400mR: EI: '02- 1; ECp: '01- 3/1R.
Progression at 400m: 2000- 54.79, 2001- 51.19, 2002- 51.17i. pbs: 200m 23.58i '02, 400mh 58.30 '00.

Nadezhda BAZHENOVA b. 22 Sep 1978 Vladimir 1.76m 63kg.
At TJ: EI: '02- 4.
Progression at TJ 1997- 13.21, 1998- 13.04, 1999- 14.25, 2000- 14.13, 2001- 14.60, 2002- 14.65i. pb LJ 6.58 '01.

Irina BELOVA b. 27 Mar 1968 Angarsk 1.75m 63kg. née Ilyichova. Irkutsk TU.
At Hep: OG: '92- 2; WCh: '91- 3, '99- dnf, '01- 8; EC: '90- 4, '98- 5; ECp: '91- 8, '99- 2. Won CIS Hep 1992. At Pen: WI: '93inv- 1, '99- 2; EI: '98- 2. WIR pentathlon: 4720 and 4991 '92.
Progression at Hep: 1985- 5377, 1986- 5596, 1987- 5710, 1988- 6056, 1989- 6274, 1990- 6521, 1991- 6448, 1992- 6845, 1997- 5876, 1998- 6466, 1999- 6467, 2001- 6528. pbs: 200m 23.34 '92, 400m 52.87 '91, 800m 2:02.06 '01, 60mh 8.20 '93, 100mh 13.25 '92, 400mh 57.6 '87, HJ 1.93i/1.88 '92, LJ 6.82 '92, SP 14.12 '01, JT 44.64 '99.
Set personal bests at five events plus an outdoor high jump best when taking the 1992 Olympic heptathlon silver medal. Won non-championship heptathlon at World Indoors 1993, but was then caught for a positive drugs test. Won Götzis heptathlon 1998.

Yelena BELYAKOVA b. 7 Apr 1976 Dolgoprudniy, Moskva reg. 1.78m 55kg. Luch Moskva. Teacher.
At PV: OG: '00- dnq; WCh: '99- 8; EC: '98- nh; EI: '00- 2, '02- 8; ECp: '98- nh, '99- 4; Won GWG 1998, RUS 1998-9.
Three Russian pole vault records 1998-2000.
Progression at PV: 1995- 3.40, 1996- 3.90, 1997- 4.15, 1998- 4.38, 1999- 4.46, 2000- 4.50, 2001- 4.55i/4.42, 2002- 4.50i.

Madina BIKTAGIROVA b. 20 Sep 1964 Osh, Kirgizstan 1.58m 50kg. Moskva Dyn.
At Mar: OG: '92- dq (4), '96- dnf, '00- 5; WCh: '93- 5; EC: '98- 2. USSR champion 1991.
BLR marathon record 1992.
Progression at Mar: 1987- 2:38:18sh, 1988- 2:38:00, 1989- 2:38:56, 1990- 2:36:02, 1991- 2:32:02, 1992- 2:26:23, 1993- 2:31:32, 1994- 2:30:00, 1995- 2:29:00, 1996- 2:31:38, 1997- 2:24:46, 1998- 2:27:19, 2000- 2:26:33, 2001- 2:27:12. pb HMar 71:30 '95.
Won Los Angeles marathon 1992, Nagoya 1997; 2nd New York 1994, Berlin 1997, Nagoya 1998; 3rd Boston 1995. Lost Olympic 4th place in 1992 due to a positive test for stimulants, for which she received a three-month ban. Transferred nationality to Russia in 1997. Baby born 1999.

Alla DAVYDOVA b. 21 May 1966 Frunze, KGZ 1.67m 86kg. née Fyodorova. Luch Moskva. Teacher
At HT: OG: '00- dnq 18; EC: '98- 8; ECp: '01- 6. Russian champion 1996.
Two world hammer records 1991.
Progression at HT: 1989- 58.30, 1990- 59.66, 1991- 64.44, 1992- 60.80, 1994- 61.84, 1995- 63.20, 1996- 67.48, 1998- 64.61, 1999- 66.06, 2000- 68.47, 2001- 65.81.

Natalya FEDOSKINA b. 25 Jun 1980 Saransk 1.67m 52m. Saransk.
At 20kmW: WCh: '99/01- dq; WCp: '99- 2; ECp: '01- 2.
Two world junior 20km walk records 1999.
Progression at 10kmW, 20kmW: 1998- 44:59, 1999- 43:58, 1:27:35; 2000- 43:56, 1:28:52; 2001- 43:44, 1:26:50; 2002- 1:27:45. pb 3000mW 12:18.29 '00.

Svetlana FEOFANOVA b. 16 Jul 1980 Moskva 1.63m 52kg. Luch Moskva.
At PV: OG: '00- dnq; WCh: '01- 2; WI: '01- 2; EI: '00- 5, '02- 1, ECp: '00- 1; 2nd GP 2001. Russian champion 2001.
Six European pole vault records 2001, 8 Russian 2000-01, 5 world indoor 2002, 9 European indoor 2001-02.
Progression at PV: 1998- 3.90, 1999- 4.10, 2000- 4.50, 2001- 4.75, 2002- 4.75i.

Lyudmila GALKINA b. 20 Jan 1972 Saratov 1.72m 59kg. Saratov TU.
At LJ (TJ): OG: '96- dnq, '00- 9; WCh: '93- 5, '95- dnq 17, '97- 1, '99- 4, '01- 8; EC: '94- dnq 16, '98- 3; WJ: '90- (7); EJ: '89- 3, '91- 2 (1); WI: '95- 1, '01- 6; EI: '02- 3; WUG: '95- 3; WCp: '98- 4; ECp: '98-99- 2/3; E23Cp: '94- 1. Won RUS LJ 1997.
Progression at LJ: 1985- 5.52, 1986- 5.85, 1987- 6.14, 1988- 6.34, 1989- 6.52/6.62w, 1990- 6.63, 1991- 6.62, 1992- 6.60, 1993- 6.75, 1994- 6.78, 1995- 6.95i/6.71/6.85w, 1996- 6.88, 1997- 7.05, 1998- 6.99/7.06w, 1999- 6.95/7.08w, 2000- 6.89, 2001- 7.00i/6.70. pb TJ 13.67 '91.
Set personal best to win 1995 World Indoor title and 1997 World outdoor win was her first time over 7m.

Svetlana GONCHARENKO b. 28 May 1971 Rostov na Donu 1.76m 61kg. née Doronina. Stavropol VS.
At 400m/4x400mR: OG: '96- sf, '00- 3R; WCh:

'95- 2R, '99- sf/1R; EC: '94- 2/2R; EI: '94- 1, WUG: '97- 1R; WCp: '98- 3R; ECp: '94- 1/3R. At 200m: EC: '98- sf/2R; EJ: '87- 5 (2 4x100mR); WI: '95- 1R; '97- 3/1R, '99- 2/1R; EI: '98- 1; ECp: '99- 1/2R, '01- 3. Won RUS 200m 1998, 400m 1996.
World indoor 4x400m world record 1999.
Progression at 200m, 400m: 1987- 23,93, 1988- 23.5, 54.22; 1989- 23.61, 1990- 24.11, 1991- 24.02, 1992- 23.62, 53.69; 1993- 23.40, 54.00; 1994- 22.6/23.58, 51.00; 1995- 22.89, 51.47; 1996- 23.01, 50.84; 1997- 22.84i, 53.06i; 1998- 22.46/21.9/22.43i; 1999- 22.59/22.4/22.52w, 50.75; 2000- 23.24i/23.42, 50.23; 2001- 22.86. pbs: 60m 7.21i '99, 100m 11.13/10.7 '98, 300m 35.48i '98.

Natalya GORELOVA b. 18 Apr 1973 Moskva 1.73m 56m. née Zaytseva. Luch Moskva. Teacher.
At 800m: WCh: '99- 6. At 1500m: OG: '00- h; WCh: '01- 3; WI: '01- 3; 3rd GP 2001. Won Russian 800m 1999.
Progression at 800m, 1500m: 1997- 2:02.44, 1998- 2:02.21, 4:13.43; 1999- 1:57.90, 4:05:12; 2000- 2:00.24, 4:01.50; 2001- 1:58.7, 3:59.70. pb 1000m 2:34.25 '01.

Tatyana GUDKOVA b. 23 Jan 1978 Magnitogorsk 1.70m 60kg. Magnitogorsk TU. Teacher
At 20kmW: OG: '00- 8. Russian champion 2000. World best 20km walk 2000.
Progression at 10kmW, 20kmW: 1998- 44:42, 1999- 42:51, 1:33:05; 2000- 42:42, 1:25:18; 2001- 43:17, 1:30:12.

Yelena GULYAYEVA b. 14 Aug 1967 Moskva 1.82m 64kg. née Rodina. Luch Moskva. Teacher.
At HJ: OG: '96- 4; WCh: '93- 4=, '99- 12, '01- 10=; EC: '94- 2, '98- 6; ECp: '91-4-8-9: dq (1)/3/3/1; WI: '91- 6=, '95- 5; EI: '98- 4; WCp: '98- 4; 3rd GP 1995. USSR champion 1988, 1991.
Progression at HJ: 1981- 1.70, 1982- 1.70, 1983- 1.80, 1984- 1.84, 1985- 1.80, 1987- 1.80, 1988- 1.94, 1989- 1.89i/1.88, 1990- 1.92i/1.91, 1991- 1.99, 1993- 1.98, 1994- 2.00i/1.98, 1995- 1.99, 1996- 2.00, 1998- 2.01, 1999- 1.99, 2000- 1.95, 2001- 1.95.
Two years suspension for positive drugs test at the 1991 European Cup ('won' HJ).

Yelena ISINBAYEVA b. 3 Jun 1982 Volgograd 1.74m 65kg. Volgograd SA.
At PV: OG: '00- dnq; WI: '01- 7; WJ: '98- 9, '00- 1, WY: '99 – 1; EJ: '99- 5, '01- 1.
World junior indoor pole vault records 2000 and 2001.
Progression at PV: 1997- 3.30, 1998- 4.00, 1999- 4.20, 2000- 4.45i/4.40, 2001- 4.47i/4.46, 2002- 4.55i.

Olimpiada IVANOVA b. 5 May 1970 Munsyuty Chuvashiya 1.68m 54kg. Cheboksary Dyn.
At 20kmW: ECp: '00- 1. At 10kmW: WCh: '97- drugs dq (2); WCp: '93- 12, '97- 2; won GWG 1994. At 5000mW: EJ: '85- 9.
World best 20km walk 2001.
Progression at 10kmW, 20kmW: 1987- 45:15, 1992- 45:18, 1993- 42:24, 1994- 42:30.31t, 1995- 41:30, 1996- 41:46, 1:30:58; 1997- 41:24, 1999- 43:31, 1:28:21; 2000- 42:43, 1:26:08; 2001- 42:34, 1:24:50. pbs: 3000mW 12:02.2 '95, 5000mW 20:50.6i '97, 20:56.10 '94, 20:51R '97.
Lost her 1997 World silver medal when she tested positive for Stanozolol, receiving a two-year ban. World best 20km walk time when she won Russian winter championship in March 2001.

Olga KALITURINA b. 9 Mar 1976 Moskva 1.80m 57kg. Ryazan VS. Married to Kirill Sosunov (qv).
At HJ: WCh: '97- 2=; WJ: '94- 1; EI: '00- 3; ECp: '01- 3=. Russian champion 1997.
Progression at HJ: 1991- 1.77, 1992- 1.85, 1993- 1.86, 1994- 1.89, 1995- 1.95i/1.92, 1996- 1.85, 1997- 1.96, 1999- 1.90, 2000- 1.96i/1.94, 2001- 1.96, 2002- 1.97i.

Tatyana KONSTANTINOVA b. 18 Nov 1970 Smolensk 1.79m 95lg. Smolensk Dyn
At HT: OG: '00- dnq 15; WCh: '99- 11; EC: '98- dnq 16.
Progression at HT: 1990- 57.42, 1991- 56.72, 1992- 55.58, 1993- 56.00, 1994- 59.50, 1995- 62.16, 1996- 60.64, 1997- 58.68, 1998- 65.77, 1999- 72.09, 2000- 69.73, 2001- 64.32.

Irina KORZHANENKO b. 16 May 1974 Azov, Rostov/Don reg. 1.78m 85kg. Rostov/Don VS.
At SP: OG: '96- 8; WCh: '95- 12, '97- dnq 16, '01- 5; EC: '98- 2; EJ: '93- 7; WI: '97- 3, '99- dq (2); EI: '98- 1; WUG: '97- 1; WCp: '98- 2; ECp: '95-8-01: 2/2/2; E23Cp: '94- 1. 3rd GP 1997. Russian champion 1995.
Progression at SP: 1991- 15.58, 1992- 15.92, 1993- 17.92i/17.02, 1994- 18.36, 1995- 20.06, 1996- 19.46, 1997- 19.69, 1998- 20.82, 1999- 21.15i dq, 2001- 19.37.
After Vita Pavlysh was given a drugs disqualification, she stepped up to take gold at the 1999 World Indoors – but lost that when she also was disqualified.

Olga KOTLYAROVA b. 12 Apr 1976 Sverdlovsk 1.80m 65kg. Student. Yekaterinburg TU.
At 400m/4x400mR: OG: '96- qf/5R, '00- 8/3R; WCh: '97- sf, '99- 8/1R; EC: '98- 3/2R; WJ: '94- 4R; EJ: '95- 1/2R; EU23: '97- 2R; WI: '97- 1R, '99- 1R, '01- 2/1R; EI: '96- 2; WUG: '97- 2/1R; WCp: '98- 3R; ECp: '96- 4/3R, '97- 3/1R, '99- 2/1R. Russian champion 1998.
World indoor 4x400m record 1997 & 1999.
Progression at 400m: 1994- 53.67, 1995- 52.03/51.8, 1996- 51.17, 1997- 50.63, 1998- 50.38, 1999- 50.32, 2000- 49.95, 2001- 50.42i/50.81A. pbs: 200m 23.35A '98, 300m 36.91+ '99, 800m 2:05.17 '00.

Tatyana KOTOVA b. 11 Dec 1976 Kokand, Uzbekistan 1.82m 59kg. Moskva TU.
At LJ: OG: '00- 4; WCh: '99- dnq 13, '01- 2; WI: '99- 1, '01- 2; EU23: '97- 1. Russian champion 1999-2001.
Progression at LJ: 1994- 6.32, 1995- 6.32, 1996-

6.65, 1997- 6.76, 1998- 6.82/6.97w, 1999- 6.99/7.01w, 2000- 7.04 (7.05iu), 2001- 7.12. pbs: HJ 1.75i '02, TJ 13.69i/13.64 '98.
Born in Uzbekistan, she moved to Taboshari (Tajikistan) and now lives in Central Siberia. Her father came from Cherkassy in the Ukraine.

Svetlana KRIVELYOVA b. 13 Jun 1969 Bryansk 1.83m 95kg. Moskva Dyn. Teacher.
At SP: OG: '92- 1, '96- dnq 15, '00- 4; WCh: '91- 3, '93- 2, '97- 10, '99- 3, '01- 9; EC: '98- 4; WJ: '88- 4; WI: '91/3/9/01- 8/1/1/3; EI: '00- 4; WUG: '91- 1; ECp: '96- 3, '99- 3; 3rd GP 2001. USSR champion 1991, Russian 1992, 1998-2000. Won GP 1993.
Progression at SP: 1985- 15.18, 1986- 16.76, 1987- 17.51, 1988- 18.35, 1989- 18.36, 1990- 19.70, 1991- 20.36, 1992- 21.06, 1993- 20.84, 1996- 18.97, 1997- 19.32i/19.18, 1998- 20.53, 1999- 20.69i/20.26, 2000- 20.72, 2001- 20.17.
Took World Student Games gold in 1991 and World Indoor gold in 1999 after disqualifications.

Marina KUPTSOVA b. 22 Dec 1981 Moskva 1.85m 68kg. Moskva TU.
At HJ: OG: '00- dnq 26=; WJ: '98- 1, '00- 2; EJ: '97- 2, '99- 3; WI: '01- 7; EI: '02- 1. Russian champion 2000.
Progression at PV: 1995- 1.78i, 1996- 1.89, 1997- 1.90, 1998- 1.95i/1.90, 1999- 1.94, 2000- 1.96, 2001- 1.91i/1.90, 2002- 2.03i.

Olga KUZENKOVA b. 4 Oct 1970 Smolensk 1.76m 76kg. Smolensk Dyn. Army Officer, has a diploma in physical education.
At HT: OG: '00- 2; WCh: '99- 2, '01- 2; EC: '98- 2; WUG: '97- 2; ECp: '97-8-9-00: 1/1/2/1; 3rd GP 2001. RUS champion 1992-4, 1997-2001; CIS 1992.
Eleven world hammer records 1992-8 (six officially ratified), inc. unratified 69.46 '96 and 73.80 '98 due to no drugs testing procedures; 66.84 in 1994 was the first record for the event accepted by the IAAF. 14 Russian records 1993-2000.
Progression at HT: 1990- 59.50, 1991- 61.52, 1992- 65.40, 1993- 64.64, 1994- 66.84, 1995- 68.16, 1996- 69.46, 1997- 73.10, 1998- 73.80, 1999- 74.30, 2000- 75.68, 2001- 73.62.
Became the first 70-m hammer thrower in 1997.

Yelena LEBEDENKO b. 16 Jan 1971 Moskva 1.77m 63kg. Moskva VS. Teacher.
At Hep: OG: '96- 17; WCh: '95- 18. At Pen: EI: '96- 1. At TJ: EC: '98- 10; WI: '99- 6; EI: '98- 3; ECp: '99- 4.
Progression at Hep: 1989- 5308, 1990- 5703, 1994- 5963, 1995- 6342, 1996- 6143. At TJ: 1998- 14.57i/14.41, 1999- 14.74i/14.37, 2000- 14.66i, 2001- 14.83i/14.17, 2001- 14.83i/14.17, 2002- 14.60i. pbs: 200m 24.67 '96, 800m 2:18.50 '95, 60mh 8.23i '96, 100mh 13.37 '96, HJ 1.85i '96, 1.83 '95; LJ 6.75 '96, SP 14.71 '95, JT 45.02 '96, Pen 4735i 96.
Former football and rugby player. Made triple jump debut with 14.33 indoors in January 1998, improving to 14.57 to win Russian indoor title.

Tatyana LEBEDEVA b. 21 Jul 1976 Sterlitamak, Bashkortostan 1.71m 60kg. Volgograd VS.
At TJ (LJ): OG: '00- 2; WCh: '99- 4, '01- 1; EC: '98- 5; WJ: '94- 3 (10); EJ: '95- 2 (6); WI: '01- 2; EI: '00- 1; WUG: '01- 1; WCp: '98- 2; ECp: '00- 1, '01- 1. GP: 3rd 1999, 2nd 2001. Won GWG 2001, Russian 1998-2001.
Two Russian triple jump records 2000.
Progression at TJ: 1991- 12.91, 1992- 13.03, 1993- 13.13i/12.94, 1994- 13.69, 1995- 13.88, 1996- 13.62, 1997- 13.89i/13.56, 1998- 14.45/14.58w, 1999- 14.89, 2000- 15.32, 2001- 15.25. pb LJ 6.71i '01, 6.65 '94.
Won 2001 World gold by massive margin of 65cm

Yuliya LYAKHOVA b. 8 Jul 1977 Moskva 1.85m 60kg. Luch Moskva.
At HJ: OG: '96- dnq 19=; WCh: '97- 4; EC: '98- 12; WJ: '96- 1; EJ: '95- 3; EU23: '97- 1; WI: '99- 6; ECp: '00- 2. 2nd GP 1997.
Progression at HJ: 1993- 1.75, 1994- 1.90, 1995- 1.92i/1.90, 1996- 1.94, 1997- 1.99, 1998- 1.96i/1.95, 1999- 2.00i, 2000- 1.96, 2001- 1.96i/1.92.
Sister of **Sergey Lyakhov** (b. 1 Mar 1968) pbs: SP 20.03 '00, DT 66.78 '95.

Irina MISTYUKEVICH b. 17 Jun 1977 Kurgan region 1.82m 69kg. Kurgan VS. Teacher.
At 800m: OG: '00- sf; WCh: '01- h; EU23: '99- 7; EJ: '95- 2R; ECp: 00- 1, '01- 1.
Progression at 800m: 1995- 2:06.40, 1996- 2:03.8, 1997- 2:03.85, 1998- 2:01.93, 1999- 1:58.33, 2000- 1:57.49, 2001- 1:58.02. pbs: 400m 51.87 '00, 1000m 2:34.52 '01.

Yelena NIKOLAYEVA b. 1 Feb 1966 Akshiki Chuvashia 1.68m 58kg. née Kuznetsova. Cheboksary Dyn.
At 10kmW: OG: '92- 2, '96- 1; WCh: '87- 5, '93- 7, '95- 3, '97- 9; EC: '94- 3; WCp: '87- 5, '93- 3, '95- 2. Won GWG 1998, USSR champion 1987-8, CIS 1992, RUS 1996. At 20kmW: WCh: '99- 12, '01- dq; WCp: '99- 4; ECp: '01- 5; Won RUS 2001. At 3000mW: WI: '91- 5, '93- 1; EI: '94- 4.
Three world 10km track walk records 1986-8, road best 1996, European records 3000m 1992, 5000m: 21:32.4 '87, 21:08.65 '88.
Progression at 10kmW, 20kmW: 1984- 48:29.1, 1985- 46:37, 1986- 44:32.50t, 1987- 43:57, 1988- 43:36.41t, 1991- 43:25, 1992- 42:40, 1993- 43:11, 1994- 42:43, 1995- 42:20, 1996- 41:04, 1997- 41:41, 1998- 43:51.97t, 1999- 42:04, 1:28:01; 2000- 45:55, 2001- 42:55, 1:27:49.3t. pbs: 3000mW 11:49.73i '93, 12:01.53 '98; 5000mW 21:00.80 '91, 20:48R '94.

Yelena OLEYNIKOVA 9 Dec 1976 Zernograd, Rostov-na-Donu reg. 1.76m 56kg.
At TJ: WCh: '01- dnq 14; WI: '02- 3; WUG: '01- 3.
Progression at TJ: 1995- 12.79, 1996- 13.22, 1997- 13.38, 1998- 13.58, 1999- 13.85, 2000- 14.25, 2001- 14.59, 2002- 14.60i.

Yuliya PECHONKINA b. 21 Apr 1978 Krasnoyarsk 1.80m 65kg. née Nosova. Krasnoyarsk VS.
At 400mh/4x400mR: OG: '00- sf; WCh: '01-

2/3R; EC: '98- h; WJ: '96- h; EJ: '97- 6; WI: '01- 1R; ECp: '01- 1/2R. RUS champion 1999, 2001.
Progression at 400mh: 1993- 63.47, 1994- 60.86, 1995- 60.30, 1996- 57.04, 1997- 57.53, 1998- 56.13, 1999- 53.98, 2000- 54.31, 2001- 53.84. pb 400m 52.25i/53.22 '01. At 400m: EI: '02- 5.

Larisa PELESHENKO b. 29 Feb 1964 Slantsy, Leningrad region 1.87m 95kg. née Agapova. St Petersburg VS. Teacher.
At SP: OG: '00- 2; WCh: '93- 9, '01- 4; EC: '94- 5; WI: '95- 1, '01- 1; EI: '88- 2, '94- 2, '00- 1; WUG: '87- 3, '89- 4; ECp: '89- 3, '94- 3. Won GWG 2001, Russian champion 2001.
Progression at SP: 1981- 14.60, 1982- 15.95, 1983- 18.23, 1984- 19.30, 1985- 18.78i, 1986- 19.26, 1987- 20.99, 1988- 20.89, 1989- 19.68, 1990- 19.56, 1992- 19.65, 1993- 19.90i/19.23, 1994- 20.00i/19.81, 1995- 19.89i/19.93i dq, 1999- 19.18, 2000- 21.46, 2001- 20.79.
4 year drugs ban 20 Feb 95. Has a son, Grigoriy.

Lyudmila PETROVA b. 7 Oct 1968 Novocheboksary 1.60m 44kg.
At 10000m: OG: '96- 14; WCh: '01- 6. At Mar: EC: '98- 9. World HMar: '97- 7. Won RUS 10000m 1996.
Progression at 10000m, Mar: 1996- 31:58.84, 1997- 32:14.39, 2:39:26; 1998- 2:30:26, 1999- 2:29:13, 2000- 31:52.75, 2:25:45; 2001- 32:04.94, 2:26:18. pbs: 3000m 8:59.15i/9:00.2 '96, 5000m 15:20.44 '96, Rd 10km 31:41 '01, 15km 48:31 '98, HMar 69:26 '00.
Won New York Marathon 2001, Moscow 1998. Did not run between 1987 and 1994, when her two children were born.

Olga POLYAKOVA b. 23 Sep 1980 Penza reg. 1.71m 49kg. Saransk VS, Student.
At 20kmW: OG: '00- dnf.
World road best 5km walk 2000.
Progression at 20kmW: 1999- 1:29:09, 2000- 1:25:20, 2001- 1:32:45.7t. pbs: 5kmW 20:05 '00, 10kmW 42:43 '00.

Irina PRIVALOVA b. 22 Nov 1968 Malakhovka, Moskva region 1.75m 66kg. Married name was Sergeyeva. Moskva TU. Degree in journalism from Moscow State University.
At 100m (/200m, 4x100mR): OG: '92- 3/4/2R; '96- sf/sf/4R; WCh: '91- 4/4/2R, '93- 4/3/1R (2 4x400mR), '95- 3/2, '97- qf; EC: '90- 6, '94- 1/1/2R, '98- 2/1/3R; WJ: '86- sf/5R; EJ: '85- h; WCp: '94- 1/2 (1 400m), '98- 5/5; ECp: '89- 3/5; '91- 1/1/1R, '93- 1/1/1R, '98- 1/1R. At 60m/200m: WI: '91- 1/2, '93- 2/1, '97- 6/-. At 400m: WI: '95- 1. At 400mh/4x400m: OG: '00- 1/3R. Won USSR 100m 1989-90, CIS 100m/200m 1992, RUS 100m 1999, 200m 1993, 1996; 400mh 2000. GP 100m: 2nd 1993, 3rd 1994.
Records: European 100m 1994. Two USSR/CIS 100m 1991-2, three 200m 1992, Russian 200m (2) 1993-5, 100m 1994; WIR: 50m 6.05 and 6.00 (not ratified due to inaccurate camera alignment) '93, 6.03 '94, 5.96 '95; 60m 6.92 '93 & '95, 300m 1993. European IR 60m 6.97 '92, 200m 22.26 '92, 22.10 '95.
Progression at 100m, 200m, 400m: 1982- 11.9, 1983- 11.7, 1984- 11.79; 1985- 11.59, 24.54; 1986- 11.3i/11.52/11.37w, 24.10; 1987- 11.44/11.2, 23.3; 1989- 11.26, 23.00; 1990- 11.21, 23.01; 1991- 10.98, 22.21; 1992- 10.82/10.81w, 21.93; 1993- 10.94, 21.88, 49.89; 1994- 10.77, 22.02/21.82w, 50.62; 1995- 10.90, 21.87, 50.23i; 1996- 11.03/11.00w, 22.27; 1997- 22.52i; 1998- 10.83, 22.61A/22.62; 1999- 11.05, 23.09i; 2000- 11.37, 51.63. At 400mh: 2000- 53.02. pbs 300m 35.45i '93, 60mh 8.16i '00, 100mh 13.56 '00, 13.4 '87; HJ 1.72 '82, LJ 6.48i '85, 6.45 '84, TJ 13.72i '89.
Son Aleksey born 1988 and, now married to her coach Vladimir Paraschuk (pb 100m 10.3), she gave birth to a daughter, Mariya, on 25 Dec 2001. Formerly a speed skater. Long jumped 6.45 at 15 in 1984. Won CIS 100m in 1992 with 10.81 to equal European record, but time later adjusted to 10.82. On successive days at the 1994 World Cup she won the 100m, was 2nd at 200m and then won the 400m in just her second ever race at the distance (ran 49.89 on debut July 1993). In 2000 she ran at 60mh indoors and outdoors made her 400mh debut with 54.49 – improving to 54.21 and 54.06 then 54.02 and 53.02 at the Olympics, taking the gold medal in just her eighth race at the event. Suffered a serious knee injury in training for the 2001 season.

Yelena PROKHOROVA b. 16 Apr 1978 Kemerovo 1.71m 59kg. Kemerovo TU. Student.
At Hep: OG: '00- 2; WCh: '01- 1; EU23: '99- 2; ECp: '99- 6. At Pen: WI: '01- 2; EI: '00- 5, '02- 1. Won RUS Hep 2000.
Progression at Hep: 1994- 4919, 1995- 4621, 1996- 5152, 1997- 5600, 1998- 5776, 1999- 6132, 2000- 6765, 2001- 6694. pbs: 200m 23.37 '00, 800m 2:04.27 '00, 60mh 8.46i '01, 100mh 13.54 '00, HJ 1.88 '01, LJ 6.72 '00, SP 14.30 '00, JT 50.73 '01, Hep 4711i '01.
Won IAAF Combined Events Challenge in 2001.

Yekaterina PUZANOVA b. 1 Jan 1999 Vyksa, Gorkiy reg. 1.68m 57kg.
At 1500m: EI: '02- 1.
Progression at 800m, 1500m: 1997- 2:08.89, 1998- 2:07.62, 1999- 2:05.44, 2000- 2:01.86, 2001- 2:01.29, 4:11.28; 2002- 2:01.42i, 4:05.53i.

Olga RASPOPOVA b. 27 Dec 1978 Barabinsk, Novosibirsk reg 1.76m 62kg. Novosibirsk Dyn. Student.
At 800m: OG: '00- h.
Progression at 800m: 1997- 2:12.0, 1999- 2:03.88, 2000- 1:56.85, 2001- 1:58.77. pb 1000m 2:34.77 '01.

Oksana ROGOVA b. 7 Oct 1978 Tambov 1.80m 60kg. Tambov Sp. Student, Tambov University.
At TJ: OG: '00- 8; WCh: '99- 9; WJ: '96- 4; EU23:

'99- 2; WI: '01- 5; EI: '00- 5.
Progression at TJ: 1993- 11.52, 1994- 12.48, 1995- 13.14, 1996- 13.49, 1997- 13.31, 1998- 14.14, 1999- 14.59/14.65w, 2000- 14.28i/14.27, 2001- 14.37i/ 14.20/14.23w; 2002- 14.70i.

Natalya ROSHCHUPKINA b. 13 Jan1978 Lipetsk 1.82m 70kg. Lipetsk Dyn. Teacher.
At Hep: OG: '00- 6; WCh: '99- 10, '01- 4; EC: '98- 9; WJ: '96- 5; EU23: '99- 1; ECp: '98- 2, '00- 1; won GWG 2001. At Pen: WI: '99- 7, '01- 4.
Progression at Hep: 1993- 4772, 1994- 5191, 1995- 5383, 1996- 5767, 1997- 5920, 1998- 6370h, 1999- 6219, 2000- 6633, 2001- 6551. pbs: 200m 23.27/22.84w '01, 800m 2:06.67 '01, 60mh 8.60i '01, 100mh 13.70 '00, HJ 1.91 '00, LJ 6.45 '00, SP 14.96 '01, JT 45.65 '01, Pen 4664i '01.

Olga RUBLYOVA b. 28 Oct 1974 Volgograd 1.76m 65kg. Volgograd VS.
At LJ: OG: '96- dnq 19, '00- 5; WCh: '95- 4, '99- 11, '01- dnq 19; EC: '94- 11; WJ: '92- 17; EJ: '93- 2; EI: '00- 4, '02- 2; ECp: '94-4-00-01: 2/4/1/4 (8 TJ '91). Russian champion 1995-6, 1998.
Progression at LJ: 1988- 5.77, 1989- 6.10, 1990- 6.29, 1991- 6.17, 1992- 6.46, 1993- 6.74, 1994- 6.76, 1995- 6.90/7.01w, 1996- 6.87, 1998- 6.88, 1999- 6.82, 2000- 6.90i/6.89, 2001- 6.86. pb TJ 14.45i/ 14.21 '00.
Married to Viktor Sotnikov (b. 12 Sep 1974) TJ 17.11 '96, 9th OG 1996.

Nadezhda RYASHKINA b. 22 Jan 1967 Sokol 1.60m 47kg. Chelyabinsk Sp.
At 10kmW: EC: '90- dq, '98- 7; WCp: '91- 8; ECp: '98- 1. Won GWG 1990; USSR champion 1990, Russian 1997. 3000mW: WI: '89- 4.
World 10km track walk records 1989 and 1990, equalled world best for 20km road walk 1999.
Progression at 10kmW, 20kmW: 1988- 44:07.97t, 1:32:33; 1989- 43:08.4t, 1990- 41:56.23t, 1991- 44:29, 1:33:13; 1992- 44:30, 1994- 44:15.76t, 1997- 44:29, 1998- 42:25, 1999- 42:45, 1:27:30; 2000- 42:42, 1:28:06; 2002- 1:29:23. pbs: 3000mW 12:12.98i '89, 5000mW 20:49.4 '90.
Previously a runner, took up walking in 1987.

Natalya SADOVA b. 15 Jun 1972 Gorkiy 1.80m 100kg. née Koptyukh. Nizhniy Novgorod VS. Teacher.
At DT: OG: '96- 2, '00- 4; WCh: '95- 5, '97- 3, '99- 4, '01- 1; EC: '94- 11, '98- 2; WJ: '90- 1; EJ: '89- 5; WUG: '95- 1, '97- 1; WCp: '98- 3; ECp: '95-7-8-9-01: 1/1/1/1/2; E23Cp: '94- 1. Won GP 1998, Russian champion 1995-6, 1999-2001.
Progression at DT: 1988- 53.02, 1989- 55.34, 1990- 61.44, 1991- 59.10, 1992- 57.82, 1993- 58.14, 1994- 62.12, 1995- 66.86, 1996- 67.22, 1997- 67.72, 1998- 68.50, 1999- 70.02, 2000- 67.33, 2001- 68.57. pb SP 14.21 '99.
Has a daughter Viktoriya.

Lyudmila SECHKO b. 27 Nov 1974 Leningrad 1.80m 80kg. St-Peterburg VS.
At SP: EI: '00- 8, '02- 5; ECp: 00- 8.
Progression at SP: 1992- 14.53, 1993- 15.27i, 1994- 16.66, 1995- 18.18, 1996- 18.04, 1997- 18.67, 1998- 18.04, 1999- 18.51, 2000- 19.51, 2001- 19.34, 2002- 19.29i.

Tatyana SHIKOLENKO b. 10 May 1968 Gelenjik, Krasnodar reg.1.75m 79kg. Gelenjik Krasnodar TU.
At JT: OG: '00- 7; WCh: '93- 4, '97- 8, '99- 2, '01- 9; EC: '98- 2; WJ: '86- 4; EJ: '85- 5; WUG: '91- 1; WCp: '98- 4; ECp: '00-01- 2/4; 2nd GP 1998, Russian champion 1997-2001.
Russian javelin record 2000
Progression at JT: 1984- 59.40, 1985- 59.90, 1986- 55.70, 1987- 59.74, 1988- 64.70, 1989- 60.74, 1990- 64.98, 1991- 63.56, 1992- 62.20, 1993- 65.18, 1994- 64.94, 1996- 60.94, 1997- 67.34, 1998- 67.84; new: 1999- 66.37, 2000- 67.20, 2001- 66.09.
Belarus prior to 1996. Younger sister of Natalya (1 WCh '95, 2 OG '92, pb 71.40 '94).

Irina STANKINA b. 25 Mar 1977 Saransk 1.67m 50kg. Saransk VS. Student.
At 20kmW: OG: '00- dnf; WCh: '99- 17. At 10kmW: OG: '96- dq; WCh: '95- 1, '97- dq; WCp: '97- 1. At 5000mW: WJ: '94- 1, '96- 1; EJ: '93- 3, '95- 1. Won RUS 20kmW 1999.
World junior road best 10km walk 1995, world junior record 5000m walk 1996.
Progression at 10kmW, 20kmW: 1995- 41:55, 1996- 42:01. 1997- 41:17, 1999- 1:29:00, 2000- 42:44, 1:25:29. pb 5000mW 20:31.4 '96.
At 18 years 135 days she became the youngest ever world champion in 1995. Twin sister Inna and older brother **Vladimir** (b. 2 Jan 1974, pb 1:19:14 '01) are also race walkers. She has a daughter, Yekaterina.

Tatyana TOMASHOVA b. 1 Jul 1975 Perm 1.68m 58kg. Samara VS.
At 5000m: OG: '00- 13; WCh: '01- 10; ECp: '00- 1. Won GP 3000m 2001, RUS 1500m 2001, 5000m 2000.
Progression at 1500m, 5000m: 1996- 4:17.97, 1997- 4:16.39, 1998- 4:13.50, 1999- 4:08.5?, 15:26.67; 2000- 4:04.80, 14:53.00; 2001- 4:03.31, 14:39.22. pbs: 800m 2:01.6 '99, 1M 4:38.13 '01, 2000m 5:43.3 '01, 3000m 8:25.56 '01, road 10km 32:48 '99.

Natalya TSYGANOVA b. 7 Feb 1971 Frunze, Kirgizstan 1.62m 52kg. Moskva Dyn. ex Ukraine. Teacher.
At 800m: OG: '00- h; WCh: '99- 5, '01- h; EC: '98- sf; WI: '99- 3; EI: '00- 2; ECp: '99- 1. Won RUS 800m 2000.
Progression at 800m: 1992- 2:04.97, 1993- 2:02.7, 1994- 2:04.26, 1995- 2:02.30, 1998- 1:58.92, 1999- 1:57.15, 2000- 1:56.60, 2001- 1:57.97. pbs: 400m 52.02 '98, 600m 1:25.9+i '99, 1000m 2:32.77 '99, 1500m 4:08.07 '99.

Olga YEGOROVA b. 28 Mar 1972 Novocheboksarsk, Chuvashiya 1.60m 48kg. Cheboksary

SA. Economist.
At 5000m: OG: '00- 8; WCh: '99- h, '01- 1; EC: '98- 11; won RUS 1999, GWG 2001. At 3000m: WI: '97/9/01- 6/6/1; EI: '00- 6; ECp: '98- 1, '99- 3. At 1500m: WJ: '90- 9; EJ: '91- 3.
European 5000m record 2001, 2 Russian records 2000-01.
Progression at 3000m, 5000m: 1996- 16:00.07, 1997- 15:42.47, 1998- 15:32.74, 1999- 8:33.02, 15:22.80; 2000- 8:49.18i/8:53.76, 14:42.91; 2001- 8:23.26, 14:29.32. pbs: 1500m 4:02.76 '01, 1M 4:25.54i '00, 2000m 5:39.9 '01.
Daughter Yevgeniya bron June 1994.

Yelena YELESINA b. 4 Apr 1970 Chelyabinsk 1.83m 64kg. Moskva VS.
At HJ: OG: '00- 1; WCh: '91- 2, '99- 2, '01- dnq 13=; EC: '90- 3; WJ: '88- 2; EJ: '87- 3=, '89- 1; WUG: '91- 4; EI: '92- 3, '98- 3. Won GWG & USSR 1990, Russian 1999.
Progression at HJ: 1983- 1.55, 1984- 1.65, 1985- 1.70, 1986- 1.83, 1987- 1.89, 1988- 1.98, 1989- 1.95, 1990- 2.02, 1991- 1.98, 1992- 1.94i/1.93, 1993- 1.91, 1994- 1.95, 1997- 1.95, 1998- 1.98i/1.94, 1999- 2.01, 2000- 2.01, 2001- 1.95.
She has a son, Boris. Lives in Melbourne with her husband, Agvan Grigoryan ARM who plans to represent Australia at wrestling from 2002.

Yelena ZADOROZHNAYA b. 3 Dec 1977 Ust-Kut, Irkutsk reg. 1.57m 42kg. Irkutsk VS.
At 5000m: WCh: '01- 6; ECp: '01- 1. At 3000m: WI: '01- 3; EI: '02- 3. At 1500m: EU23: '99- 2; ECp: '00- 2.
Russian 5000m record 2001.
Progression at 1500m, 5000m: 1998- 4:12.70, 1999- 4:09.3, 2000- 4:03.32, 2001- 4:02.16, 14;40.47. pbs: 800m 2:01.74 '98, 1M 4:24.11i '01, 2000m 5:41.61i '02, 5:43.4 '01; 3000m 8:25.40 '01.

Svetlana ZAKHAROVA b. 15 Sep 1970. née Vasilyeva.
At Mar: OG: '00- 3. World HMar: '98-9- 10/13
Progression at Mar: 1996- 2:35:36, 1997- 2:33:14, 1999- 2:27:08, 2000- 2:28:11, 2001- 2:24:04. pbs: 10000m 32:49.01 '97, HMar 70:29 '97.
Won Honolulu Marathon 1997 (2nd 1998-2000), 2nd Los Angeles 1999, London 2001; 3rd New York 2001.

Olesya ZYKINA b. 7 Oct 1980 Kaluga 1.70m 60kg. Tula TU.
At 400m/4x400m: OG: '00- res (3)R; WCh: '01- 6/3R; WJ: '98- 2R (8 100m); EJ: '99- 1/1R; WI: '01- 3/1R; ECp: '00- 1R. Russian champion 2001.
Progression at 400m: 1999- 51.31, 2000- 50.36, 2001- 50.15. pbs: 100m 11.84 '98, 200m 22.78 '00, 22.3 '99; 300m 36.70 '00.

SAINT KITTS & NEVIS

Governing body: Saint Kitts Amateur Athletic Association, Church Street, PO Box 932, Basseterre, St Kitts. Founded 1961.

Kim COLLINS b. 5 Apr 1976 1.75m 64kg. Texas Christian University, USA.
At 100m (/200m): OG: '96- fq, 00- 7/sf; WCh: '97- h, 99- h/h, '01- 6/3=; CAC: '99- 2, '01- 1/1. Won NCAA indoor 60m & 200m 2001.
Progression at 100m, 200m: 1995- 10.63, 1996- 10.27, 1998- 10.18/10.16w, 20.88/20.78w; 1999- 10.21, 20.43, 2000- 10.13A/10.15/10.02w, 20.31A/ 20.18w; 2001- 10.04A/10.00?/9.99w, 20.20/ 20.08w. pbs: 60m 6.53i '00.
In 2000/2001 he became the first athlete from his country to make Olympic and World finals.

SAUDI ARABIA

Governing body: Saudi Arabian Amateur Athletic Federation, PO Box 5802, Riyadh 11432. Founded 1963.

Hamdan Odha **AL-BISHI** b. 5 May 1981 1.80m 70kg.
At 400mh: OG: '00- sf; WCh: '01- 6; WJ: '98- sf, '00- 1; AsiC: '00- 2; AsiJ: '97/99- 2.
Four Asian junior 400m records 2000. Six KSA 400m records 1998-2000.
Progression at 400m: 1996- 47.74, 1997- 46.51A, 1998- 46.2, 1999- 45.98, 2000- 44.66, 2001- 45.00. pbs: 200m 21.1 '00, 300m 33.42 '00.

Hadi Soua'an AL-SOMAILY b. 30 Dec 1976 Taïf 1.91m 72kg. Teacher.
At 400mh: OG: '96- h, '00- 2; WCh: '95/99- h, '01- 4; AsiG: '94- 6; AsiC: '00- 1. Pan-Arab champion 1995, 1999. 2nd GP 2000.
Two Asian 400mh records 2000. Six KSA records 1994-2000.
Progression at 400mh: 1993- 52.28, 1994- 50.58, 1995- 49.30, 1996- 49.48, 1998- 51.1, 1999- 49.14/ 49.1A, 2000- 47.53, 2001- 47.99. pb 400m 47.10 '95.
Lives in the mountainous area of Saudi Arabia. Coached by John Smith in Los Angeles.

SENEGAL

Governing body: Fédération Sénégalaise d'Athlétisme, BP 1737, Stade Iba Mar DIOP, Dakar. Founded 1960.

Amy Mbacké THIAM b. 10 Nov 1976 1.83m 70kg. Racing Club de France.
At 400m: OG: '00- sf; WCh: '99- sf, '01- 1; Af G: '99- 3; AfCh: '98- 4. French cham[ion 1998-2000.
Eight SEN 400m records 1999-2001.
Progression at 400m: 1996- 54.40, 1997- 53.25, 1998- 51.60, 1999- 50.77, 2000- 50.88, 2001- 49.86. pbs: 100m, 100m 11.84 '98, 200m 23.20, 23.0A '99; 300m 36.37 '00.

SLOVAKIA

Governing body: Slovak Athletic Federation, Junácka 6, 832 80 Bratislava. Founded 1939.
National Championships first held in 1939.
2001 Champions: Men: 100m/200m: Martin Brinarsky 10.77/20.98, 400m/400mh: Marcel

Lopuchovsky 48.19/51.47, 800m: Stefan Javorka 1:53.55, 1500m: Dusan Hlubocky 3:54.52, 5000m/10000m/HMar: Marcel Matanin 15:07.31/30:30.46/66:15, Mar: Vladislav Lipovsky 2:18:33, 3000mSt: Jozef Dubasák 9:40.08, 110mh: Ivan Doros 14.56, HJ: Peter Horák 2.14, PV: Rudolf Haraksim 4.85, LJ: Andrej Benda 7.53w, TJ: Martin Malovec 15.87, SP: Milan Haborák 20.58, DT: Jaroslav Zitnansky 55.36, HT: Miloslav Konopka 78.38, JT: Mikulás Vyrostek 64.04, Dec: Branislav Puvak 6686, 20kmW: Martin Pupis 1:23:46, 50kmW: Matej Spisiak 3:54:24. **Women**: 100m: Margaréta Trnková 12.74, 200m/400mh: Miriam Hrdlicková 23.70/59.49, 400m: Lucia Klocová 54.48, 800m: Anikó Mezöová 2:14.14, 1500m: Alena Jatiová 4:50.33, 5000m: Helena Sluková 17:15.53, 10000m/HMar/Mar: Dana Janecková 35:37.85/79:17/2:47:19, 100mh: Miriam Bobková 13.92, HJ: Renata Medgyesová 1.81, PV: Slavomíra Slúková 3.75, LJ: Jana Veldáková 6.27w, TJ: Irina Beskrovnaja 13.67w, SP: Lucia Korceková 15.27, DT: Ivona Tomanová 49.88, HT: Martina Danisová 64.47, JT: Silvia Strasíková 46.58, Hep: Dana Veldáková 5191, 20kmW: Mária Gáliková 1:43:08.

Mikulás KONOPKA b. 23 Jan 1979 Rimavska Sobota 1.92m 105kg. Slavia UK Bratislava.
At LJ: '00- dnq 24; WCh: '01- dnq 22; EC: '98- dnq; EU23: '99- 1, '01- 1; WJ: '96- 5, '98- 1; EJ: '97- 2; EI: '02- 3. SVK champion 2000.
Three Slovakian shot records 2001.
Progression at SP: 1995- 15.42, 1996- 17.35, 1997- 18.60, 1998- 19.68, 1999- 19.71, 2000- 19.94, 2001- 20.66, 2002- 20.87i. pb DT 51.42 '99.
His twin brother **Miloslav** set SVK hammer record 78.58 '01, 3 EU23 '01.

SLOVENIA

Governing body: Atletska Zveza Slovenije, Aljazeva ul.32, 1000 Ljubljana. Current organisation founded 1945.
2001 National Champions: **Men**: 100m/200m: Matic Osovnikar 10.39/21.00, 400m: Matija Sestak 46.62, 800m: Borut Veber 1:55.40, 1500m: Bostjan Buc 3:51.19, 5000m: Romeo Zivko 15:03.15, 10000m: Joze Petkovsek 31:20.95, HMar/Mar: Roman Kejzar 67:11/2:22:57, 3000mSt: Pavel Pori 9:31.74, 110mh/400mh: Damjan Zlatnar 13.72/50.72, HJ: Rozle Prezelj 2.24, PV: Jurij Rovan 5.10, LJ: Gregor Cankar 8.12, TJ: Bostjan Simunic 16.44, SP: Miran Vodovnik 17.98, DT: Igor Primc 62.74, HT: Primoz Kozmus 67.62, JT: Robi Tersek 72.82, Dec: Uros Kogal 7262. **Women**: 100m: Alenka Bikar 11.21, 200m: Maja Nose 24.24, 400m: Brigita Langerholc 53.25, 800m: Sonja Roman 2:06.35, 1500m: Marija Zajfrid 4:39.70, 3000m: Helena Javornik 9:22.57, 10000m: Veronika Zupanc 37:28.30, Hmar: Lidija Perse 88:33, Mar: Nada Rotovnik Kozjek 3:09:47, 2000mSt: Lidija Tamse 7:20.72, 100mh: Urska Beti 13.55, 400mh: Meta Macus 56.93, HJ: Lea Cimperman 1.84, PV: Teja Melink 4.00, LJ: Tina Carman 6.16, TJ: Andreja Ribac 13.75, SP/DT: Mojca Crnigoj 14.84/44.04, HT: Simona Kozmus 58.12, JT: Elizabeta Randjelovic 47.13, Hep: *not held*.

Gregor CANKAR b. 25 Jan 1975 Celje 1.80m 68kg. Kladivar Cetis, Celje. Sports student.
At LJ: OG: '96- 6, '00- dnq 15; WCh: '95/97/01- dnq, '99- 3; EC: '94- dnq 23, '98- 6; WJ: '94- 1; WUG: '95- 3, '97- 3; WI: '97- 7, '99- 4; EI: '96- 4, '00- 5. Won SLO LJ 1995-7, 1998, 2000-01; TJ 1995, MedG LJ 1997.
Two Slovenian long jump records 1996-7.
Progression at LJ: 1989- 6.00, 1990- 6.70, 1991- 7.35, 1992- 7.51, 1993- 7.60/7.65w, 1994- 7.92/8.04w, 1995- 8.04/8.28sq/8.18w, 1996- 8.30, 1997- 8.40, 1998- 8.07, 1999- 8.36, 2000- 8.15/8.23w, 2001- 8.12/8.19w. pbs: 100m 10.61 '95, HJ 2.13 '94, TJ 16.51 '99.
First Slovenian to win a World Junior title.

Women

Alenka BIKAR b. 7 Jan 1974 Ljubljana 1.61m 54kg. Ministry of Foreign Affairs.
At 200m (100m): OG: '96- sf, '00- qf 17; WCh: '97/99- qf, '01- 7 (qf); EC: '98- sf; WI: '01- 6; EI: '96- 4, '00- 2. At 60m: EI: '96- 5, '00- 5. Won SLO 100m 1998, 2000-01; 200m 1994-7.
Slovenian records: 100m (3) 1998- 2001, 200m (7) 1996- 2001.
Progression at 100m, 200m: 1993- 12.12, 25.15; 1994- 11.90, 23.98; 1995- 11.82, 23.98; 1996- 11.50/11.37w, 22.82; 1997- 11.44/11.36w, 22.81; 1998- 11.30, 22.88; 1999- 11.35, 22.79; 2000- 11.35, 22.90; 2001- 11.21/11.16w, 22.76. pbs: 60m 7.20i '00, 300m 37.48 '01.

Jolanda CEPLAK b. 12 Sep 1976 1.68m 55kg. Née Steblovnik.
At 800m: WCh: 97- h, '01- sf; WI: '01- 6; EI: '00- 4, '02- 1; ECp: '98- 8. At 1500m: EJ: '95- 3. Won SLO 800m 2000, 1500m 1996, 1999; 3000m 1996.
WIR 800m 2002, Slovenian 800m record 1997.
Progression at 800m: 1993- 2:07.91, 1994- 2:06.53, 1995- 2:06.43, 1996- 2:04.76, 1997- 2:00.94, 1998- 2:02.71, 1999- 2:02.53, 2000- 2:00.80, 2001- 1:58.71, 2002- 1:55.82i. pbs: 400m 54.67 '00, 600m 1:26.68i '02, 1500m 4:05.44i '02, 4:13.19 '01.
Broke WIR 800m by 0.58 at European Indoors 2002, front-running to 600m and reclaiming lead from Steffi Graf in a superb race.

Brigita LANGERHOLC b. 23 Jul 1976 Kranj 1.70m 56kg. University of South California, USA. Marketing and finance manager.
At 800m: OG: '00- 4; WCh: '99- sf, '01- h; WUG: '99- 2, '01- 1; won NCAA 2001. At 400m: EJ: '95- 5; EU23: '97- 5; ECp: '98- 8. Won SLO 400m 1996-8, 2001; 800m 1996, 1998.
SLO records: 400m 2000m, 800m (3) 1999-2000.
Progression at 800m: 1996- 2:06.57, 1998- 2:04.16, 1999- 1:59.87, 2000- 1:58.51, 2001- 1:59.86. pb 400m 52.02 '00.

SOUTH AFRICA

Governing body: Athletics South Africa, PO Box 2712, Houghton 2041. Original body founded 1894.

National Championships first held in 1894 (men), 1929 (women). **2001 Champions**: **Men**: 100m: Bradley Agnew 10.29, 200m: Marcus la Grange 20.45w, 400m: Hendrik Mokganyetsi 45.11, 800m: Mbulaeni Mulaudzi 1:45.70, 1500m: Hezekiel Sepeng 3:42.69, 5000m: Shadrack Hoff 13:54.88, 10000m: Hendrick Ramaala 28:13.89, HMar: Abner Chipu 61:50, Mar: Ian Syster 2:13:30, 3000mSt: Petrus Sithole 8:33.90, 110mh: Bruce Bickell 14.34, 400mh: Llewellyn Herbert 48.77, HJ: Jacques Freitag 2.20, PV: Fanie Jacobs 5.20, LJ: Felix Coetzee 7.76, TJ: Nathan van Wyk 15.56w, SP: Karel Potgieter 19.03, DT: Frantz Kruger 62.70, HT: Chris Harmse 76.72, JT: Marius Corbett 80.12, Dec: Jannie Botha 6542, 20kmW: Tapelo Mangole 1:36:01. **Women**: 100m: Dikeledi Moropane 11.70, 200m/400m: Heide Seyerling 22.63/51.01, 800m: Zanelle Grobler 2:04.97, 1500m/5000m: Rene Kalmer 4:08.94/16:13.98, 10000m: Elana Meyer 32:56.29, HMar: Charne Rademeyer 77:22, Mar: Gwen van Lingen 2:51:59, 3000mSt: Promise Mathonsi 10:42.31, 100mh/400mh: Surita Febbraio 13.10/55.34, HJ: Hestrie Cloete 1.90, PV: Elmarie Gerryts 4.20, LJ: Charlene Lawrence 6.31, TJ: Ramona Gabriels 12.38, SP: Veronica Abrahamse 17.29, DT: Elizna Naude 55.00, HT: Elmarie Knoetzen 55.48, JT: Marna Dippenaar 51.14, Hep: *not held*, 20kmW: Daleen Enslin 1:46:48.

Jacques FREITAG b. 11 Jun 1982 Warrenton 2.04m 83kg.
At HJ: WCh: '01- dnq 24; WJ: '00- 1; WY: '99- 1. RSA champion 2000.
Two African and seven South African high jump records 2000-02 (three African Junior 2000-01).
Progression at HJ: 1998- 2.08, 1999- 2.25A; 2000- 2.30A, 2001- 2.31, 2002- 2.37.
Mother was South African high jump champion in 1973.

Shaun BOWNES b. 24 Oct 1970 Johannesburg 1,94m 90kg. Computer operator. Liberty-Nike, Potchefstroom.
At 110mh: OG: '00- sf; WCh: '99- qf, '01- 8; CG: '98- 3; AfG: '99- 5; AfCh: '98- 1; Won SA 1994, 1998, 2000, 2002. At 60mh: WI: '01- 3.
Records: African 110mh (7) 1998-2001, 60mh indoors (3) 2000-01. Nine SA 110mh 1998-2001.
Progression at 110mh: 1989- 14.5A, 1990- 15.00A, 1991- 14.43A, 1992- 13.97A, 1993- 14.19A, 1994- 13.98A, 1995- 14.21A/14.19Aw, 1997- 13.97A/ 13.5A, 1998- 13.53/13.2A, 1999- 13.39, 2000- 13.41/ 13.38w, 2001- 13.26. pbs: 200m 21.35A '00, 50mh 6.48i '01, 60mh 7.52 '01.
Received four-year drugs ban for steroid use in 1995, commuted to two years.

Okkert BRITS b. 22 Aug 1973 Uitenhage 1.98m 84kg. Mr Price-Stellenbosch.
At PV: OG: '96- dnq, '00- 7; WCh: '93- dnq 16=, 95- 4, '97- dnq, '99- 10; CG: '94- nh; WJ: '92- 3; WI: '95- 3=, '97- 6, '01- 7; AfCh: '92- 1, '93- 1; AfG: '95- 1, '99- 1; AfCh: '98- 1; WCp: '92- 3, '94- 1. Won GP 1995, 3rd 2000. SA champion 1993-5, 1998, 2000, 2002.
23 SA (1992-5), 19 African (1993-5) and 9 Commonwealth (1994-5) pole vault records.
Progression at PV: 1989- 4.50, 1990- 4.80, 1991- 5.25, 1992- 5.46, 1993- 5.71, 1994- 5.90, 1995- 6.03, 1996- 6.01, 1997- 5.92, 1998- 5.90, 1999- 5.75A, 2000- 5.85/5.90ex, 2001- 5.70i/5.60A. pb 100m 10.96 '96.
Younger brother Pieter (b. 14 Oct 1975) has PV best of 5.50 '97.

Llewellyn HERBERT b. 21 Jul 1977 Bethal 1.85m 80kg. Rentmeester-Tuks, Pretoria.
At 400mh: OG: '96- h, '00- 3; WCh: '97- 2, '01- h; WJ: '96- 2; WUG: '97- 1. Won SA 110mh 1996-7, 400mh 1996-2002.
Seven SA 400mh records 1997-2001.
Progression at 400mh: 1995- 51.25, 1996- 48.76A, 1997- 47.86, 1998- 48.43A/48.76, 1999- 47.83A/ 48.28, 2000- 47.81, 2001- 48.52A/48.77. pbs: 100m 10.30A/10.20Aw '99; 200m 20.50wA/21.06 '99, 400m 46.16A '98, 110mh 13.91A '98, 13.7A '97.
Customarily faces away from direction of running before taking his marks. Season cut short by injury in 1998, 1999 and 2001.

Frantz KRUGER b. 22 May 1975 Kempton Park 2.03m 118kg. Medical student at Free State University, Bloemfontein, Liberty-Nike.
At DT: OG: '00- 3; WCh: '99- dnq 17, '01- 8; CG: '98- 2; WJ: '94- 1; AfG: '99- 1; AfCh: '98- 1; WUG: '97- 6, '99- 1; WCp: '98- 3. Won GWG 2001, SA DT 1996, 1999-2001; Af-J SP & DT 1994.
African and Commonwealth discus records 2000 and 2001.
Progression at DT: 1993- 58.28, 1994- 58.52, 1995- 60.06, 1996- 60.66, 1997- 61.64, 1998- 65.73, 1999- 67.38, 2000- 69.75A, 2001- 69.96.

Hendrik MOKGANYETSI b. 7 Sep 1975 1.90m 76kg. Rentmeester-Tuks.
At 400m: OG: '96- qf, '00- 6; WCh: '01- sf; CG: '98- qf; At 800m: WCh: '97- qf. Won SA 400m 2000-01. SA 400m record 2000.
Progression at 400m, 800m: 1995- 47.25, 1996- 45.39A, 1:46.93; 1997- 45.52A, 1:44.62; 1998- 45.30A, 1:45.62A; 1999- 45.92A, 1:46.60; 2000- 44.59, 1:47.60; 2001- 44.70. pbs: 200m 21.79A '96, 600m 1:15.57 '97.

Mbulaeni MULAUDZI b. 8 Sep 1980 1.71m 62kg. Vaal Technikon.
At 800m: WCh: '01- 6; AfCh: '00- qf; Won AfrJ 1999, RSA 2001-02.
Progression at 800m: 1998- 1:50.33A, 1999- 1:48.33A; 2000- 1:45.55, 2001- 1:44.01. pbs: 400m 47.20A '99, 1000m 2:19.77 '01, 1500m 3:41.15 '02.

Morne NAGEL b. 23 Feb 1978 Vereeniging 1.82m 71kg.
At 100m/4x100m: WCh: '99- 7R, '01- qf/2R
Progression at 100m: 1998- 10.55/10.47Aw, 1999- 10.36A/10.22Aw, 2000- 10.40, 2001- 10.15A/ 10.20w?/10.33, 2002- 10.16A. pbs: 50m 5.62i '02, 60m 6.48i '02, 200m 20.54i '02, 20.59A/20.5w '01, 110mh 14.90 '98. Won RSA 100m 2002.

Hendrick RAMAALA b. 2 Feb 1972 GaMalepo, Pietersburg 1.72m 58kg. Law graduate of Wits University. Mr Price AC.
At 10000m: OG: '96- h; WCh: '95- 17, '97- 14, '99- 11; AfG: '99- 7. At Mar: OG: '00- 12. World HMar: '97-8-9-01: 4/2/2/4. Won SA 5000m 1995, 1999; 10000m 1995, 1999-2001; HMar 1997.
SA records 10000m (3) 1997-9, HMar 1997, 2000.
Progression at 10000m: 1995- 27:54.59, 1996- 27:57.8, 1997- 27:36.30, 1998- 27:30.57, 1999- 27:29.94, 2000- 27:46.38, 2001- 27:38.36. pbs: 3000m 8:10.38 '95, 5000m 13:24.43 '98, HMar 59:20 '00, Mar 2:09:43 '00.
Won Great North Run half marathon 1997.

Janus ROBBERTS b. 10 Mar 1979 Louis Trichardt 1.97m 117kg. Rentmeester AC. Southern Methodist University, USA.
At SP (DT): OG: '00- 7; WCh: '99- dnq 20, '01- 12; CG: '98- 5; WJ: '98- 2 (7); AfG: '99- 2. Won NCAA SP 1999, Afr-J SP/DT 1997.
Two African shot records 2001. Official world junior record 1998, African indoor (twice) 2001.
Progression at SP: 1997- 18.61, 1998- 20.39, 1999- 20.10, 2000- 20.34, 2001- 21.97. pb DT 61.18 '99.
Led the qualifying at the 2001 Worlds with 21.26, but 20.18 for 12th in the final.

Hezekiél SEPENG b. 30 Jun 1974 Potchefstroom 1.82m 70kg. Was at Rand Afrikaans University. Mr Price AC, Johannesburg.
At 800m: OG: '96- 2, '00- 4; WCh: '93- 5, '95- sf, '97- sf, '99- 2, '01- 8; CG: '94- 2, '98- 2; WJ: '92- 5; AfG: '95- 6, '99- 3; AfCh: '93- 4; WUG: '95- 1, '97- 2. 2nd GP 1999. Won SA 800m 1993-4, 1997-8; 1500m 2001. Three SA 800m records 1996-9.
Progression at 800m: 1992- 1:47.51, 1993- 1:45.46, 1994- 1:45.32, 1995- 1:45.36, 1996- 1:42.74, 1997- 1:43.19, 1998- 1:44.44, 1999- 1:42.69, 2000- 1:43.98, 2001- 1:43.57. pbs: 400m 46.62A '01, 1000m 2:16.47 '00, 1500m 3:38.24 '96, 1M 3:57.33 '96, 3000m 8:21.58A '01.
Lost to Wilson Kipketer by just 0.02 in 1999 World Champs.

Gert THYS b. 12 Nov 1971 Prieska 1.67m 55kg. Security officer, Johannesburg City Council.
At Mar: OG: '96- 33; WCh: '93- dnf, '99- 15, '01- dnf. World HMar: '97- 6, '98- 5.
African & Commonwealth marathon record 1999.
Progression at Mar: 19909- 2:19:05, 1992- 2:17:16, 1993- 2:09:31, 1995- 2:13:28, 1996- 2:08:30, 1997- 2:11:55, 1998- 2:07:45, 1999- 2:06:33, 2000- 2:11:32, 2001- 2:12:02. pbs: 5000m 13:55.30 '91, 10000m 28:26.71 '01; Road: 10km 27:58 '96, 15km 43:04 '92, HMar 60:23 '97.
Won three of 16 marathons: on his debut in 1990 and then Beppu 1996 and Tokyo in February 1999, when he ran the second fastest ever time and became the first man to have run three sub-2:08 times, having been the first ever to run two sub-2:08s in one year with 3rd at Boston and Chicago 1998. 2nd Fukuoka 1993.

Women

Hestrie CLOETE b. 26 Aug 1978 Germiston 1.85m 68kg. née Storbeck. Mr Price AC.
At HJ: OG: '00- 2; WCh: '97- 10=, '99- dnq 14=, '01- 1; WJ: '96- 6=; AfG: '95- 1, '99- 1; AfCh: '98- 1; WCp: '98- 2. Won GP 1999, 2001; GWG 2001, RSA 1996-2002, African Jnr 1997.
12 African high jump records 1998-9, 4 Commonwealth and 2 RSA 1999, African Junior 1996.
Progression at HJ: 1993- 1.75, 1994- 1.79, 1995- 1.91, 1996- 1.92, 1997- 1.94, 1998- 1.96, 1999- 2.04, 2000- 2.01, 2001- 2.01. pbs: 400m 56.0A '94, 800m 2:11.9 '95, LJ 5.75A '95.
Top world ranked in 1999, but had a lapse of concentration in failing to qualify for world final. Top junior in the world in 1997.

Elana MEYER b. 10 Oct 1966 Albertinia 1.58m 55kg. née van Zyl. Mr Price Maties AC. Graduate of Stellenbosch University.
At 10000m: OG: '92- 2, '00- 8; WCh: '93- dnf, '95- 5, '97- 17; CG: '94- 2; WCp: '94- 1. At 5000m: AfG: '99- 2. At 1500m: AfCh: '92- 1, '93- 1. At Mar: OG: '96- dnf. World CC: '93-4: 6/6; HMar '94-8-9-01: 1/2/7/6. Won SA 1500m 1992; 3000m 1987-9, 1992-3; 10000m 1991, 1999-2001; HMar 1990-1, 1999.
World road bests Half Marathon 1991, 1998 & 1999; 15km 1991. African marathon & 10000m records 1994, 5000m 1993 and 1995. Commonwealth records: 10000m 1994, 5000m 1995, Half Marathon 1999.
SA records 2000m 1987, 3000m 1991, 5000m (3) 1991-5, 10000m (5) 1989-94, Mar 1994.
Progression at 3000m, 5000m, 10000m, Mar: 1981- 10:00.2, 1982- 9:24.9, 1983- 9:09.32, 1984- 9:12.20, 1985- 8:58.73; 1986- 9:17.16, 1987- 8:52.39, 1988- 8:54.84, 1989- 8:55.78, 15:35.07, 32:28.9; 1990- 8:54.83, 1991- 8:32.00, 14:49.35, 31:33.46; 1992- 8:38.45, 14:44.15, 31:11.75; 1993- 8:32.81, 14:46.41, 32:28.02; 1994- 9:02.43, 15:25.59, 30:52.51, 2:25:15; 1995- 8:44.70, 14:44.05, 31:23.96, 2:26:51; 1996- 15:19.56, 32:23.53; 1997- 33:05.82, 2:27:09; 1998- 2:27:20, 1999- 15:42.76, 32:15.25, 2:27:17; 2000- 14:57.48, 31:14.70, 2:31:59; 2001- 32:02.37, 2:31:43. pbs: 800m 2:06.23 '85, 1000m 2:43.63 '87, 1500m 4:02.15 '92, 1M 4:30.21 '89, 2000m 5:40.7 '92. Road (all RSA records): 10km 31:13 '01, 15km 46:57 '91, 10M 52:16 '01, HMar 66:44 '99.
Gave up in World 10000m final in 1993 after being repeatedly baulked by Sally Barsosio. Her first win in 12 marathons came in Mexico in

December 2001 in 2:32:53. She has six sub-2:28 times: Boston: 3rd 1994 (début), 2nd 1995 & 1997; 3rd Chicago 1998 & 1999, 5th London 1999. Her husband Michael ran 1500m in 3:47.47 at age of 19 in 1986.

Heide SEYERLING b. 19 Aug 1976 Port Elizabeth 1.68m 55kg. Rentmeester AC, Durban.
At 400m: OG: '00- 6; AfG: '99- 7. At 200m: WCh: '95- h, '99- h, '01- sf; CG: '98- 5; WJ: '94- 1; AfCh: '98- 3, Af-J: '94- 1 (100m 2). Won SA 100m 1998-9, 200m 1995, 1998-2001, 400m 2000-01.
SA 400m record 2000.
Progression at 200m, 400m: 1991- 24.4, 1992- 23.8, 1993- 24.08A/23.94Aw, 1994- 23.22A/22.80w, 1995- 23.36, 1996- 23.28, 1997- 24.19A, 1998- 22.89, 53.8; 1999- 22.88A, 51.33A; 2000- 22.87A/ 22.59Aw, 50.05; 2001- 22.63, 50.36. pbs: 100m 11.35 '99, 11.33Aw '01, 11.1w '97; 300m 37.02 '00.

SPAIN

Governing body: Real Federación Española de Atletismo, Avda. Valladolid, 81 - 1°, 28008 Madrid, Spain. Founded 1918.
National Championships first held in 1917 (men), 1931 (women). **2001 Champions**: **Men**: 100m: Diego M Santos 10.49, 200m: Adrián Fernández 20.98w, 400m: David Canal 45.54, 800m: Antonio M Reina 1:49.85, 1500m: José Antonio Redolat 3:39.05, 5000m: Alberto García 13:23.83, 10000m: José Rios 27:38.57, HMar: Antonio Peña 64:51, Mar: Benito Ojeda 2:20:36, 3000mSt: Antonio Jiménez 8:24.17, 110mh: Felipe Vivancos 13.76w, 400mh: Iván Rodríguez 49.46, HJ: Javier Villalobos 2.21, PV: Javier Gazol 5.45, LJ: Antonio Adsuar 7.94, TJ: Raúl Chapado 16.34w, SP: Manuel Martínez 20.61, DT: Mario Pestano 67.92, HT: Moises Campeny 70.70, JT: Eduardo Veranes 72.31, Dec: Oscar González 7944, 20kmW: Francisco Fernández 1:22:27, 50kmW: Mikel Odriozola 3:45:22, **Women**: 100m: Carme Blay 11.68, 200m: Isabel Vert 24.26, 400m: Julia Alba 52.87, 800m: Mayte Martínez 2:01.84, 1500m: Natalia Rodríguez 4:23.88, 5000m: Marta Domínguez 15:40.49, 10000m: M. Luisa Larraga 32:24.17, HMar: Maria Abel 73:30, Mar: Maria Jesus Zorraquin 2:51:22, 100mh: Glory Alozie 12.93, 400mh: Eva Paniagua 58.18, HJ: Marta Mendía 1.88, PV: Mar Sánchez 4.31, LJ: Niurka Montalvo 6.73w, TJ: Carlota Castrejana 13.70, SP: Martina de la Puente 17.42, DT: Alice Matejková 59.07, HT: Dolores Pedrares 58.95, JT: Marta Míguez 59.43, Hep: María Peinado 5607, 10000W/ 20kmW: Maria Vasco 43:02.04/1:33:12.

Fermín CACHO b. 16 Feb 1969 Agreda, Soria 1.75m 65kg. Reebok.
At 1500m: OG: '92- 1, '96- 2; WCh: '91- 5, '93- 2, '95- 8, '97- 2, '99- 4; EC: '90- 11, '94- 1, '98- 3; WJ: '88- 3; EJ: '87- 12; WCp: '89- 6, '92- 4; ECp: '93-5-6-7: 2/3/1/1; WI: '91- 2, '95- 6; EI: '90- 2. Won Spanish 1500m 1989-93, 1995-6.
European records: 1500m 1997, indoor 3000m 1996, Spanish records 1000m 1993, 1500m 1997.
Progression at 1500m: 1986- 3:58.17, 1987- 3:45.9, 1988- 3:42.56, 1989- 3:36.23, 1990- 3:37.04, 1991- 3:32.03, 1992- 3:32.69, 1993- 3:32.01, 1994- 3:35.27, 1995- 3:34.25, 1996- 3:32.58, 1997- 3:28.95, 1998- 3:32.62, 1999- 3:31.34, 2000- 3:42.56. pbs: 800m 1:45.37 '91, 1000m 2:16.13 '93, 1M 3:49.56 '96, 2000m 5:02.68 '97, 3000m 7:36.61i '96, 7:37.02 '99.
Good footballer at school, concentrated on athletics from age 17. Having compiled a great championships record, at last ran a very fast time, with 3:28.95 to take Steve Cram's European record at 1500m in Zürich 1997. Completed five successive World Champs top eight placings at 1500m in 1999.

Andrés Manuel **DÍAZ** b. 12 Jul 1969 La Coruña 1.87m 71kg. Marineda At.
At 1500m: OG: '00- 7; WCh: '99- 5, '01- h; EC: '98- 11; WI: '97- 5, '99- 3; EI: '98- 4. At 800m: OG: '96- h; WCh: '95- h; EC: '94- h; WUG: '95- 2, EI: '96- 4. At 3000m: EI: '00- 5; ECp: '01- 2. Won Spanish 1500m 1999.
European indoor 1500m record 1999.
Progression at 1500m: 1988- 3:47.7, 1989- 3:42.27, 1990- 3:41.85, 1991- 3:41.32, 1992- 3:47.1, 1993- 3:43.04, 1994- 3:48.32i, 1996- 3:42.32, 1997- 3:34.52, 1998- 3:32.17, 1999- 3:31.83, 2000- 3:31.48, 2001- 3:32.66. pbs: 800m 1:45.89 '96, 1000m 2:19.2 '92, 1M 3:48.38 '01, 2000m 4:56.87i '99, 5:05.66 '00; 3000m 7:46.15i '99, 7:52.59 '01.

Réyes ESTÉVEZ b. 2 Aug 1976 Barcelona 1.87m 70kg. Adidas.
At 1500m: OG: '96- sf; WCh: '97- 3, '99- 3, '01- 5; EC: '98- 1; WJ: '94- 4; EJ: '93- 1, '95- 1; EU23: '97- 1; WI: '01- 2; ECp: '98- 2. World CC: '94- 8J. Won Spanish 1500m 1997-8.
European Junior 1500m record 1995.
Progression at 1500m: 1992- 3:54.7, 1993- 3:42.36, 1994- 3:39.28, 1995- 3:35.51, 1996- 3:34.86, 1997- 3:33.40, 1998- 3:30.87, 1999- 3:30.57, 2000- 3:40.64, 2001- 3:32.34. pbs: 800m 1:46.90 '96, 1000m 2:17.45 '00, 1M 3:52.61 '97, 2000m 5:10.64 '00, 3000m 7:44.87 '99, 5000m 14:08.8 '96.
Has won four European titles U20 to senior.

Francisco Javier **FERNÁNDEZ** b. 5 Mar 1977 Guadix, Granada 1.72m 65kg. Sevilla Abierta.
At 20kmW: OG: '00- 7; WCh: '99- 15, '01- dnf; WCp: '97- 47, '99- 12; EC: '98- 3; EU23: '97- 2; ECp: '9800-01: 1/3/4. Spanish champion 1998-2001. At 10kmW: WJ: '96- 1; EJ: '95- 2.
Spanish walks records 10000m 1999, 10km 2001, 20km 2000.
Progression at 20kmW: 1997- 1:21:59, 1998- 1:20:31, 1999- 1:21:55, 2000- 1:18:56, 2001- 1:19:47. pb 5000mW 18:54.4 '99, 10000mW 38:42.38 '99, 10kmRd 38:02 '01.

Alberto GARCÍA b. 22 Feb 1971 Madrid 1.63m 45kg. Airtel AAM.
At 5000m: OG: '00- h; WCh: '99- h, '01- 5; EC:

'98- 10; ECp: '98- 1, '01- 2; Won MedG 1997, Spanish 2001. At 3000m: WI: '01- 3; EI: '98- 3, '02- 1. World CC: '01- 16, '02- 17 4k.
Spanish 5000m record 1998 & 2001.
Progression at 5000m, 10000m: 1990- 14:43.14, 1992- 14:25.23, 1993- 14:05.73, 1994- 14:09.70, 1995- 13:50.78, 1996- 13:31.19, 1997- 13:20.44, 1998- 13:04.64, 1999- 13:08.13, 27:46.12; 2000- 13:09.50, 28:01.11; 2001- 13:02.54. pbs: 1500m 3:35.69 '01, 1M 3:58.81 '98, 2000m 4:56.08 '97, 3000m 7:36.53 '01.
Won 1999 European Challenge on 10,000m debut.

Jesús Ángel GARCÍA b. 17 Oct 1969 Madrid 1.71m 62kg. Canal de Isabel II.
At 50kmW: OG: '92- 10, '96- dnf, '00- 12; WCh: '93- 1, '95- 5, '97- 2, '99- dnf, '01- 2; EC: '94- 4, '98- dq; WCp: '93- 2, '95- 2, '97- 1, '99- 4; ECp: '96-8-00-01: 1/2/1/1. At 20kmW: WUG: '91- 5. Won SPA 50kmW 1997, 2000.
Progression at 50kmW: 1991- 4:05:10, 1992- 3:48:24, 1993- 3:41:41, 1994- 3:41:28, 1995- 3:41:54, 1996- 3:46:59, 1997- 3:39.54, 1998- 3:43:17, 1999- 3:40:40, 2000- 3:42:51, 2001- 3:43:07. pbs: 5000mW 19:33.3 '01, 10000mW 41:31.8 '01, road: 10kmW 40:38 '91, 20kmW 1:23:34 '01, 30kmW 2:08:47 '01.
In 1997 he married Carmen Acedo, who won a rhythmic gymnastics world title in 1993.

Antonio David **JIMENEZ** b. 18 Feb 1977 Sevilla 1.78m 61kg. Sevilla Abierta
At 3000mSt: WCh: '01- 6, ECp: '01- 2, EU23: '99- 3; Won MedG '01, ESP 1999, 2001. At 3000m: EI: '02- 2. World 4k CC: '02- 7. Eur CC: '01- 3. Won Spanish 4k CC 2002.
Progression at 3000mSt: 1995- 9:24.74; 1996- 9:17.93; 1997- 9:19.3; 1998- 8:54.90; 1999- 8:37:29; 2000- 8:20:34; 2001- 8:11.52. pbs: 1500m 3:43.78 '00, 3000m 7:50.30 '00, 2000mSt 5:20.07 '01 (Spanish record).

Yago LAMELA b. 24 Jul 1977 Avilés, Asturias 1.78m 68kg. Computer engineering student at University of Oviedo. Areia.
At LJ (TJ): OG: '00- dnq 19; WCh: '99- 2; EC: '98- 8; WJ: '94- (dnq 14), '96- 4; EU23: '99- 1; EJ: '95 (12); WI: '99- 2; EI: '02- 2; ECp: '98- 7, '01- 8. Won IbAm LJ 1998, Spanish LJ 1998-2000.
Five Spanish long jump records 1999.
Progression at LJ: 1991- 5.91, 1992- 6.62, 1993- 6.89, 1994- 7.27, 1995- 7.66, 1996- 7.80/8.04w, 1997- 7.87/7.97w, 1998- 8.14/8.20w, 1999- 8.56, 2000- 8.22, 2001- 8.07. pb TJ 16.72 '98.
In 1999, after setting Spanish indoor records at 8.20 and 8.22, had a superb World Indoors, with successive records of 8.29, 8.42 and 8.56, when second to Iván Pedroso, as he was also at the outdoor World Champs.

David MÁRQUEZ b. 13 Oct 1977 Barcelona 1.83m 60kg. Integra2 L'H C.N.B.
At 20kmW: OG: '00- 20; WCh: '01- 5; EU23: '99- 1. At 10000mW: WJ: '96- 2.
Spanish 30km walk record 2001.
Progression at 20kmW: 1997- 1:25:14, 1998- 1:24:07, 1999- 1:23:42, 2000- 1:21:44, 2001- 1:21:09. pbs: 5000mW 19:30.4 '00, 10000mW 41:08.33 '99, 30kmW 2:06:45 '01, 10kmRd 40:47 '98.

Eliseo MARTÍN b. 5 Nov 1973 Monzón, Huesca 1.73m 62kg. Transbaso Monzón Polidux.
At 3000mSt: OG: '00- 6; WCh: '99- 6, '01- 12; EC: '98- 7. At 10000m: WJ: '92- 7. Won Spanish 3000mSt 1999.
Progression at 3000mSt: 1992- 9:02.55, 1993- 8:45.77, 1994- 8:32.89, 1995- 8:31.27, 1996- 8:31.99, 1997- 8:30.50, 1998- 8:25.92, 1999- 8:13.59, 2000- 8:13.63, 2001- 8:19.20. pbs: 1500m 3:40.96 '00, 3000m 7:58.60 '00, 5000m 13:47.77 '01, 10000m 28:39.11 '99, 2000mSt 5:22.93 '01.

Luis Miguel MARTÍN b. 11 Jan 1972 Madrid 1.80m 69kg. Nike.
At 3000mSt: OG: '00- 5; WCh: '99- h, '01- 4; EC: '98- 4; won IbAm 1998, Spanish 2000. At 1500m: WJ: '90- h; EJ: '91- h.
Three Spanish records 3000mSt 1999-2001.
Progression at 3000mSt: 1998- 8:20.54, 1999- 8:11.18, 2000- 8:09.77, 2001- 8:08.74. pbs: 1500m 3:39.07 '96, 3000m 7:50.27 '00, 5000m 14:13.37 '01.

Manuel MARTÍNEZ b. 7 Dec 1974 León 1.85m 140kg. Airtel A.A.M.
At SP: OG: '96- dnq 15, '00- 6; WCh: '93- 11, '95- dnq 21, '97- dnq 13, '01- 4; EC: '94- dnq 14, '98- 7; WI: '95/7/9/01- 4/5/4/3; EI: '94-00-02: 4/2/1; WJ: '92- 2; EJ: '93- 1; WUG: '01- 1; ECp: '93/5/6/7/8/01- 7/4/4/3//1; E23Cp: '94- 1. Won Spanish 1993-8, 2000-01; IbAm 1998, 2000; MedG 2001.
15 Spanish shot records 1993-2001.
Progression at SP: 1991- 15.57, 1992- 18.14, 1993- 19.53, 1994- 20.16, 1995- 19.97i/19.69, 1996- 20.12, 1997- 20.37i/20.27, 1998- 20.50i/20.08; 1999- 20.79i/20.04, 2000- 20.55, 2001- 21.35. pb DT 41.38 '01.

Valentí MASSANA b. 5 Jul 1970 Barcelona 1.65m 51kg. Integra 2 L'H C.N.B.
At 20kmW (50kmW): OG: '92- dq, '96- 20 (3), '00- (4); WCh: '91- 5, '93- 1, '95- 2, '99- (4), '01- (6); EC: '90- 5, '94- 3, '98- 9; WCp: '91- 10, '93- 2, '97- 19, '99- (8); ECp: '96- 6, '98- 10. At 10kmW: WJ: '88- 2; EJ: '87- 2, '89- 1. At 5000mW: WI: '91- 5. Won Spanish 20kmW 1991-5, 1997; 50kmW 1993-6.
Spanish walks records 20km 1992, 50km 1994, 10,000m track 1997.
Progression at 20kmW, 50kmW: 1987- 1:31:50, 1990- 1:22:33, 1991- 1:20:29, 1992- 1:19:25, 1993- 1:20:50, 3:46:11; 1994- 1:20:33, 3:38:43; 1995- 1:20:23, 3:42:13; 1996- 1:22:23, 3:44:19; 1997- 1:20:39, 1998- 1:21:21, 1999- 1:26:33, 3:45:29; 2000- 1:26:19, 3:46:01; 2001- 1:28:26, 3:48:28. pbs: 5000mW 18:59.60i '91, 19:36.5 '89; 10000mW 39:31.81 '97, 1HrW 14,367m '90; road 10kmW 39:27 '92, 30kmW 2:07:58 '93.

Antonio PEÑA b. 26 Aug 1970 Felanitx, Mallorca 1.75m 60kg. Nike.

At Mar: WCh: '99- dnf, '01- 24; EC: '94- 32, '98- 6. Won Spanish Mar 1997, HMar 2000-01. World HMar: '92- 13.
Progression at Mar: 1992- 2:11:35, 1993- 2:13:06, 1994- 2:17:19, 1995- 2:13:39, 1997- 2:10:49dh, 1998- 2:13:53, 2000- 2:07:47, 2001- 2:07:34. pbs: 5000m 13:52.70 '92, 10000m 28:02.1 '00, HMar 61:48 '92.
Won at Lake Biwa 2001 for his fourth win in 14 marathons; 5th Rotterdam and 2nd Berlin 2000.

José Antonio REDOLAT b. 17 Feb 1976 Valencia 1.81m 66kg. Terra I Mar.
At 1500m: OG: '00- sf; WCh: '01- 6; EJ: '95- 2; EI: '00- 1; ECp: '98- 8, '01- 1. Spanish champion 2001. At 800m: EC: '98- h; WJ: '98- 7.
Progression at 1500m: 1993- 3:55.66, 1994- 3:46.5, 1995- 3:42.76, 1996- 3:42.01, 1997- 3:42.91, 1998- 3:35.90, 1999- 3:35.65, 2000- 3:31.48, 2001- 3:31.21. pbs: 800m 1:45.39 '00, 1M 3:49.60 '01, 2000m 5:04.27 '00, 3000m 7:53.67 '00, 5000m 13:48.34 '98.

José RIOS b. 15 Mar 1974 Barcelona 1.70m 50kg. Adidas.
At 10,000m: OG: '00- 18; WCh: '01- 6. Spanish champion 2000-01, EChall 2001.
Progression at 5000m, 10000m: 1991- 15:04.82, 31:15.89; 1992- 14:26.50, 31:24.50; 1993- 14:25.76, 29:48.44, 1994- 14:23.37, 29:35.2; 1995- 14:03.30, 29:03.6; 1996- 13:49.44, 29:00.34; 1997- 13:51.32, 28:37.52; 1998- 14:11.52, 28:56.51; 1999- 13:41.03, 28:30.53; 2000- 13:07.59, 27:22.20; 2001- 13:09.83, 27:38.57. pbs: 1500m 3:51.11 '01, 3000m 7:42.51 '00. Was a butcher, major breakthrough in 2000.

Fabián RONCERO b. 19 Oct 1970 Madrid 1.71m 58kg. Nike.
At 10000m: WCh: '01- 5. At Mar: WCh: '97- 6, '99- dnf. World CC: '98- 10. Won Spanish HMar 1995, CC 2001.
Spanish records 10000m 1998, Mar 1998 & 1999.
Progression at 10000m, Mar: 1991- 30:35.40, 1992- 29:59.55, 1993- 29:26.10, 1995- 28:38.2, 2:14:36; 1996- 28:47.87, 2:09:43; 1997- 28:21.38, 2:16:53; 1998- 27:14.44, 2:07:26; 1999- 27:58.02, 2:07:23; 2001- 27:45.17, 2:10:08. pbs: 3000m 7:41.48 '00, 5000m 13:22.46 '01, HMar 59:52 '01.
Two wins in six marathons: Carpi 1996 and Rotterdam 1998, the latter in a Spanish record just two weeks after taking over a minute off his best with a Spanish record to win the European Challenge 10,000m. He improved his marathon record by 3 secs when 2nd in Rotterdam 1999.

Women

Glory ALOZIE b. 30 Dec 1977 1.55m 51kg. Valencia Terra i Mar.
At 100mh: OG: '00- 2; WCh: '99- 2; WJ: '96- 2; AfG: '99- 1/1R; AfCh: '96- 1, '98- 1, '00- 1; Af-J: '95- 2; WCp: '98- 1. 2nd GP 2000, 3rd 1998. At 60mh: WI: '99- 2; EI: '02- 1. Won NGR 100mh 1999-2000, ESP 100mh 2001.
Records: African: 100m 1999, 100mh (5) 1998-9; two Commonwealth 100mh 1999, two Spanish 2001 (12.87 & 12.78).
Progression at 100mh: 1993- 14.99, 1994- 14.25, 1995- 13.86, 1996- 13.30, 1997- 12.96, 1998- 12.44/12.4w, 1999- 12.44, 2000- 12.54, 2001- 12.69. pbs: 60m 7.20i '99, 100m 10.90 '99; 200m 23.09 '01, 22.91w '98; 50mh 6.86i '01, 60mh 7.82i '99.
Based in Spain since January 1997, she became a Spanish citizen on 7 July 2001. Won 17 of 19 finals in 1998 at 100mh. Her fiancée Hyginus Anugo was killed in a road accident in Sydney just prior to the 2000 Games.

Marta DOMÍNGUEZ b. 3 Nov 1975 Palencia 1.63m 52kg. Nike International.
At 5000m: OG: '00- h; WCh: '99- 9, '01- 2; EC: '98- 3; EU23: '97- 3 (1500m 5). At 3000m: WI: '95- 6, '97- 5; WI: '01- 4; EI: '96-8-00-02: 3/3/3/1; ECp: '96- 3. At 1500m: OG: '96- h; WCh: '95- sf; WJ: '94- 2; EJ: '93- 1. World 4k CC: '00- 14. Won Spanish 1500m 1996, 5000m 1998-2001.
Spanish record 3000m 2000.
Progression at 3000m, 5000m: 1990- 10:15.0, 1991- 9:47.03, 1993- 9:35.16, 1994- 9:24.10, 1995- 9:01.79i, 1996- 8:53.34i/9:06.27, 1997- 8:52.74i/9:01.96, 15:41.91; 1998- 8:44.10, 14:59.49; 1999- 8:46.14, 15:16.93; 2000- 8:28.80, 15:26.00; 2001- 8:36.33, 14:58.12. pbs: 800m 2:06.1 '95, 1000m 2:50.1 '91, 1500m 4:06.08 '00, 2000m 5:49.55i '98.

Niurka MONTALVO b. 4 Jun 1968 La Habana, Cuba 1.72m 57kg. Valencia Terra i Mar.
At TJ (LJ): OG: '96- (dnq 18); WCh: '93- 4, '95- dnq (2), '99- (1), '01- (3); WI: '91- (5), '95- 6, '01- (3); PAm: '91- (10), '95- 2 (1); WUG: '93- 1; WCp: '94- 5 (2); CAG: '93- 1 (1). At LJ: ECp: '01- 1; 3rd GP 2000. Won CAC LJ 1987, 1990, 1993; TJ 1993, Cuban LJ 1988, 1990, 1993-5, TJ 1993-4; Spanish LJ 1999-2001, TJ 1999.
Cuban records: LJ (3) 1990-3, TJ (6, also CAC) 1992-4; Spanish LJ (4) 1999.
Progression at LJ, TJ: 1984- 5.83, 1985- 6.18, 1986- 6.29, 1987- 6.32/6.52w, 1988- 6.62, 1989- 6.53, 1990- 6.87, 1991- 6.69, 12.51; 1992- 6.88, 13.92; 1993- 6.64/6.75w, 14.51; 1994- 6.71/6.78w, 14.60; 1995- 6.89, 14.31; 1996- 6.62, 13.68; 1997- 6.72/6.73w, 13.96; 1998- 6.93, 1999- 7.06, 13.93/14.17w; 2000- 6.87/6.95w, 13.20/13.86w; 2001- 6.91, 14.02i/13.57. pb 100mh 13.57 '90.
Married a Spaniard on 26 Jan 1998, and became a Spanish citizen on 5 May 1999. Just over three months later she won the first gold medal for Spain at the 1999 World Champs in Seville, coming from 2nd at 6.88 to a Spanish record 7.06 to win in the final round. The Cuban Federation did not recognise would-be records 6.92 and 6.93 in 1998, due to her defection, and did not allow her to compete for Spain at the 2000 Olympics.

Natalia RODRIGUEZ b. 2 Jun 1979 Tarragona 1.64m 49kg. Adidas.
At 1500m: WCh: '01- 6, EU23: '99- 4, '01- 2, WJ:

'98- 6, EJ: '97- 5. Won Spanish 1500m 2000-01.
Progression at 800, 1500m: 1995- 2:05.97, 1996- 2:03.76, 4:17.35; 1997- 2:03.97, 4:27.06; 1998- 2:02.21, 4:14.05; 1999- 2:01.76, 4:07.46; 2000- 2:05.76, 4:04.24; 2001- 2:01.35, 4:06.32. pbs: 400m 55.79 '99, 3000m 9:13.84i '01.

María VASCO b. 26 Dec 1975 Barcelona 1.56m 47kg. Integra 2 L'H C.N.B..
At 20kmW: OG: '00- 3; WCh: '99- 10, '01- 5; WCp: '99- 23; ECp: '01- 7. At 10kmW: OG: '96- 28; WCh: '95- 26; EC: '98- 5; EU23: '97- 2; WCp '95- 26, '97- 22. At 5000mW: WJ: '90- 15, '92- 6, '94- 4; EJ: '93- 4. Won Spanish 10kmW 1996, 10000mW (t) 1997-9, 2001; 20kmW (3) 1998-2001.
Spanish records 5000m 1997, 10,000m track (3) 1997-2001, 10km 1998, 20km (4) 1998-2002.
Progression at 10kmW, 20kmW: 1993- 47:11, 1994- 47:05, 1995- 44:53, 1996- 44:51.60t, 1997- 43:54, 1998- 43:02, 1:34:11; 1999- 43:35, 1:32:38; 2000- 43:33.92t, 1:30:20; 2001- 43:02.04t, 1:30:09;, 2002- 1:28:47. pb 3000mW 12:42.72 '97, 5000mW 21:36.22 '97, 21:26R '98; HMar 81:00 '91.

SRI LANKA

Governing body: Amateur Athletic Association of Sri Lanka, n°33 Torrington Avenue, Colombo 7. Founded 1922. **National Champions 2001**: **Men:** 100m/200m: Ravindra Kumara 10.70/21.10, 400m/PV: Rohan Pradeep Kumara 46.36/4.70, 800m: S A M R Bandara 1:51.04, 1500m: Indika Chaminda Wijekoon 3:48.41, 5000m: K Chandradasa 14:31.65, 10000m: A K C Wasantha 31:17.32, Mar: Ajith Bandara 2:24:28, 110mh: Inndika Kumara 14.56, 400mh: Harijan Ratnayake 50.86, HJ: W M S B Weerasinghe 2.02, LJ: Duminda De Silva 7.47w, TJ: Sampath Weerasinghe 15.52, SP/DT: Talavou F Alaileema 14.89/48.91, JT: Pradeep Nishantha 68.94, Dec: H R Priyantha 6318, 20kmW (actually c.23.5k): M D Nimal 2:07:58. **Women**: 100m: Pradeepa Herath 12.17, 200m: Jani Chaturangani 25.27, 400m/800m: Mangala Priyadharshani 55.79/2:09.64, 1500m: Udeni Kanchanamala 4:27.36, 5000m/10000m/ Mar: Dalugoda A Inoka 17:35.55/37:04.55/ 2:56:16, 100mh: Sriyani Kulawansa 13.39, 400mh: K K C Priyahharshani 62.58, HJ: Janitha Chaturi Kodikara 1.66, LJ: Nayanthi K Chandrasena 6.45w, TJ: Anusha E Kariyawasam 12.94, SP: Nadeeka Muthunayake 11.79, DT: Padma Wijesundara 42.40, JT: Anne Maheshi De Silva 49.81, Hep: G S M De Silva 2859, 10kmW: D L R Priyadharshani 56:41.

SURINAM

Governing body: Surinaamse Athletiek Bond, PO Box 1758, Paramaribo. Founded 1955.

Letitia Alma **VRIESDE** b. 5 Oct 1964 Paramaribo 1.59m 55kg. AVR, Netherlands.
At 800m (/1500m): OG: '88- sf/h, '92- sf/sf, '96- sf, '00- h; WCh: '91- 5/9, '95- 2, '97- 4, '99- sf, '01- 3; WI: '95- 3, '97- 4; PAm: '91- 4/2, '95- 3/4, '99- 1; SAm: '01- 2; CAG '90- 2/1, '93- 1/1, '98- 1; WCp: '98- 3. 3rd GP 1997.
South American records 1990-5: 800m (6), 1000m (3) 1500m (2); indoors 1992-5: 800m (3), 1000m, 1500m, 3000m. SUR records 400m 1990-7, 3000m 1990-1.
Progression at 800m, 1500m: 1981- 5:25.41, 1982- 2:41.6, 5:24.0; 1983- 2:25.4, 5:11.3; 1984- 2:22.2, 5:19.1; 1986- 2:14.6, 4:34.01; 1987- 2:08.37, 4:36.86; 1988- 2:01.83, 4:16.29; 1989- 2:03.44, 4:24.64; 1990- 1:59.79, 4:11.88; 1991- 1:58.25, 4:05.67; 1992- 1:57.96, 4:08.82; 1993- 2:00.30, 1994- 2:01.53i/ 2:02.94, 1995- 1:56.68, 1996- 1:57.09, 1997- 1:57.86, 1998- 1:58.16, 1999- 1:58.99, 4:18.84; 2000- 1:58.62, 2001- 1:57.35, 4:17.46. pbs: 200m 24.41w '95, 400m 52.01 '97, 1000m 2:32.25 '91, 1M 4:30.45 '92, 3000m 9:07.08i '93, 9:15.64 '91.
The military administration in Surinam rejected her nomination for the 1984 Olympic Games, and did not grant funds to enable her to participate. She felt humiliated by that and went to the Netherlands, returning to athletics two years later. In 1995 she became the first South American female athlete to win medals in the indoor and outdoor World Championships.

SWEDEN

Governing body: Svenska Friidrottsförbundet, Box 11, 171 18 Solna. Founded 1895.
National Championships first held in 1896 (men), 1927 (women). **2001 Champions**: **Men**: 100m: Mikael Ahl 10.49, 200m: Johan Wissman 20.81, 400m: Jimisola Laursen 46.63, 800m/1500m: Rickard Pell 1:47.49/3:47.48, 5000m/ 3000mSt: Henrik Skoog 14:16.47/8:39.35, 10000m: Claes Nyberg 29:03.94, Mar: Alfred Shemweta 64:29, Mar: Anders Szalkai 2:18:17, 110mh: Robert Kronberg 13.45, 400mh: Mikael Jakobsson 49.94, HJ: Stefan Holm 2.29, PV: Patrik Kristiansson 5.64, LJ: Mattias Sunneborn 7.75, TJ: Christian Olsson 17.10, SP: Jimmy Nordin 19.33, DT: Kristian Pettersson 56.16, HT: Bengt Johansson 71.34, JT: Daniel Ragnvaldsson 77.34, Dec: Patrik Melin 7137, 10kmW/20kmW: Bengt Bengtsson 41:51/1:28:36, 50kmW: Fredrik Svensson 3:59:12. **Women**: 100m/200m: Annika Amundin 11.54/ 23.68, 400m: Nadja Petersen 54.20, 800m: Camilla Nyquist 2:05.92, 1500m: Lena Nilsson 4:24.63, 5000m: Malin Öhrn 16:29.69, 10000m/Mar: Marie Söderström-Lundberg 34:19.07/2:31:28, HMar: Lena Gavelin 73:09, 3000mSt: Isabell Ahlström 10:34.49, 100mh: Anna Pettersson 13.66, 400mh: Erica Mårtensson 57.54, HJ: Kajsa Bergqvist 1.96, PV: Kirsten Belin 4.22, LJ/Hep: Carolina Klüft 6.30w/5521, TJ: Camilla Johansson 13.77, SP: Linda-Marie Mårtensson 16.52, DT: Anna Söderberg 59.06, HT: Cecilia Nilsson 62.56, JT: Annika Petersson 55.23, 5kmW/ 10kmW: Monica Svensson 24:10/51:48, 20kmW: Ann-Christine Bengtsson 2:43:31.

Stefan HOLM b. 25 May 1976 Forshaga 1.81m 69kg. Kils AIK.
At HJ: OG: '00- 4; WCh: '99- 10=, '01- 5=; EC: '98- 7; WJ: '94- 7=; EJ: '93- 11, '95- 6; WI: '97- 8=, 99- 6=, '01- 1; EI: '00- 4, '02- 2; WUG: '99- 4; ECp: '00- 1. Won GWG 2001, Swedish 1998-2001.
Progression at HJ: 1987- 1.40, 1988- 1.51, 1989- 1.61, 1990- 1.83, 1991- 1.94, 1992- 2.09i/2.06, 1993- 2.14, 1994- 2.18, 1995- 2.21, 1996- 2.26, 1997- 2.30i/2.22, 1998- 2.33, 1999- 2.32, 2000- 2.34, 2001- 2.34i/2.33. pbs: 100m 11.42 '99, 110mh 16.23 '99, LJ 7.18 '99; TJ 12.35i '91.
One of the smallest top high jumpers. Maintains on his web site (www.scholm.com) a complete record of his clashes with Staffan Strand – from 1989 to 2001, score is 49-41 to Holm with 1 tie.

Robert KRONBERG b. 15 Aug 1976 Göteborg 1.82m 80kg. IF Kville.
At 110mh: OG: '00- 8; WCh: '97/99- qf, '01- 5; WJ: '94- sf; EJ: '95- 2; WUG: '01- 3; ECp: '00- 3. At 60mh: WI: '01- 4; EI: '00-02: 6/6. Won Swedish 110mh 1997-2001.
Three Swedish 110mh records 2001.
Progression at 110mh: 1993- 15.09, 1994- 14.21, 1995- 14.06, 1996- 13.97, 1997- 13.63, 1998- 13.61, 1999- 13.58, 2000- 13.36, 2001- 13.35. pbs: 100m 10.73 '98, 200m 22.31 '98, 50mh 6.46i '01, 60mh 7.54i '01, HJ 1.90 '95, LJ 7.52 '97, TJ 14.23 '94.

Christian OLSSON b. 25 Jan 1980 Göteborg 1.92m 73kg. Örgryte IS.
At TJ (/HJ): OG: '00- dnq 17; WCh: '01- 2; EU23: '01- 1; EJ: '99- 2/1; EI: '02- 1; ECp: '00- 4. Won Swedish TJ 2000-01.
Swedish triple jump record 2000-01. E.Ind 2002.
Progression at TJ: 1995- 12.20w, 1996- 12.44, 1998- 14.48, 1999- 16.30/16.59w, 2000- 16.97, 2001- 17.49, 2002- 17.80i. pbs: 110mh 16.21 '98, HJ 2.28i '02, 2.22 '99; PV 4.04 '99, LJ 6.98 '99.
Considered himself a high jumper, but took his TJ best from 14.48 to 16.27w in his first competition of 1999 and had a superb season at his new event in 2001 when he was the only man to defeat Jonathan Edwards (and did so twice).

Staffan STRAND b. 18 Apr 1976 Upplands-Väsby 1.88m 74kg. Hässelby SK. Was at University of Minnesota, USA.
At HJ: OG: '00- 6=; WCh: '97- dnq, '99- 5, '01- 7=; EC: '98- 8; EU23: '97- 1; EJ: '95- 5; WI: '99- 5, '01- 3; EI: '02- 1. Won Swedish 1995-7.
Progression at HJ: 1987- 1.45i, 1988- 1.60i, 1989- 1.65i, 1990- 1.70, 1991- 1.71, 1992- 1.80, 1993- 1.91i/1.88, 1994- 2.11, 1995- 2.22, 1996- 2.27, 1997- 2.28, 1998- 2.31, 1999- 2.30, 2000- 2.32, 2001- 2.34i/2.31, 2002- 2.35i. pbs: PV 3.40 '95, LJ 6.90 '96, TJ 15.16 '96, 15.23w '00; Dec 5022 '95.

Women

Kajsa BERGQVIST b. 12 Oct 1976 Sollentuna 1.75m 59kg. Turebergs FK. Was at Southern Methodist University, USA.
At HJ: OG: '96- dnq 14, '00- 3=; WCh: '95- dnq 17=, 97- 5=, '99- 4=, '01- 3; EC: '98- dnq 14; WJ: '94- 2; EU23: '97- 2; EJ: '93- 8, '95- 2; WI: '97- 8, '01- 1; EI: '00- 1, '02- 2=. Swedish champion 1997-2001, NCAA 1997, 1999.
Six Swedish high jump records 1997-2000.
Progression at HJ: 1988- 1.38, 1989- 1.56, 1990- 1.61i/1.56, 1991- 1.61, 1992- 1.77, 1993- 1.84, 1994- 1.90, 1995- 1.92i/1.90, 1996- 1.93, 1997- 1.95, 1998- 1.93, 1999- 1.98A, 2000- 2.01, 2001- 2.00. pbs: 100mh 14.98/14.8w '94, LJ 5.73 '95, TJ 11.74 '98, SP 11.95 '96, JT 36.60 '99, Hep 4952 '94.
Father Gunnar had a 110mh best of 15.0 (1972).

Erica JOHANSSON b. 5 Feb 1974 Mölndal 1.78m 69kg. Mölndals AIK.
At LJ: OG: '00- dnq 17; WCh: '97- 8, '99- 10; EC: '94- dnq 22, '98- 5; WJ: '90-2; '92- 1; EJ: '89- 2, '91- 4, '93- 1; WI: '93- 6, '99- 9; EI: '00- 1. Won SWE LJ 1990-3, 1996-9; 100mh 1999.
Eleven Swedish records 1989-2000.
Progression at LJ: 1988- 5.71, 1989- 6.50, 1990- 6.56i/6.53, 1991- 6.55i/6.52, 1992- 6.72, 1993- 6.78i/6.56, 1994- 6.17/6.39w, 1995- 6.21/6.50w, 1996- 6.71, 1997- 6.64/6.66w, 1998- 6.85, 1999- 6.92/6.95w, 2000- 6.99/7.07Aw, 2001- 6.87. pbs: 60m 7.63i '99, 100m 11.82 '99, 200m 23.75 '97, 800m 2:21.95 '89, 60mh 8.93i '97, 100mh 13.63 '98, HJ 1.78 '89, TJ 13.95/14.32w '99.
Foot injury caused her to miss much of the 1993 season, yet she still won the European Junior title after eight weeks out of competition. At the 1989 European Juniors, aged 15, she improved from 6.25 to 6.50 to take the silver medal and equal the Swedish senior record. On her competitive debut at triple jump – in the match against Finland in 1999 – she won at 14.32w, and also set a national record 13.95. Expecting a baby in April 2002.

Susanna KALLUR b. 16 Feb 1981 Huntington, New York, USA 1.70m 62kg. Falu IK. Student at University of Illinois, USA.
At 100mh: WCh: '01- sf; WJ: '98- 3, '00- 1/3R; EU23: '01- 1; EJ: '99- 5. Won Swedish 1998, 2000.
Progression at 100mh: 1997- 14.11, 1998- 13.48, 1999- 13.41, 2000- 13.02, 2001- 12.74. pbs: 50m 6.56i '00, 60m 7.51i '00, 100m 11.56 '01, 200m 24.11 '01, 50mh 7.01i '00, 60mh 8.10i '00, HJ 1.72 '98, PV 3.00i '98, LJ 6.11 '01, TJ 11.22 '98, Hep 5282 '98.
Twin sister **Jenny** was 2nd in European U23s 2001, 6th WJ 2000, pb 13.15/13.11w '01. Their father Anders played for the New York Islanders at ice hockey, winning Stanley Cup four times.

SWITZERLAND

Governing body: Schweizerischer Leichtathletikverband (SLV), 43/Postfach 45, 3250 Lyss. Formed 1905 as Athletischer Ausschuss des Schweizerischen Fussball-Verbandes.
National Championships first held in 1906

(men), 1934 (women). **2001 Champions**: **Men**: 100m: Daniel Dubois 10.30, 200m: Marc Schneeberger 20.86, 400m: Nicolas Baeriswyl 47.79, 800m Ramon Waechter 1:49.59, 1500m: Nicolas Berset 3:49.97, 5000m:, 10000m/HMar: Stéphane Schweickhardt 30:08.57/66:07, Mar: Éticha Tesfaye ETH 2:12:38, 3000mSt: Markus Hagmann 8:57.49, 110mh: Thomas Keller 13.82, 400mh: Alain Rohr 49.58, HJ: Martin Stauffer 2.23, PV: Patrick Schuetz 5.10, LJ: Andrei Plattner 7.58, TJ: Ruben Kiefer 15.43, SP: Marc Sandmeier 18.40, DT: Peter Müller 50.74, HT: Samuele Dazio 73.89, JT: Felix Loretz 71.58, Dec: Adrian Krebs 7993, 20kmW: Nicolas Perrier 1:36:36; 50kmW:. **Women**: 100m/200m: Mireille Donders 11.34/ 23.24, 400m: Anita Brägger 53.26, 800m: Sabine Fischer 2:09.61, 1500m: Anita Weyermann 4:32.46, 5000m:, 10000m:, HMar: Chantal Dällenbach 74:13, 100mh: Monica Pelegrinelli 13.41, 400mh: Nathalie Zamboni 57.14, HJ: Corinne Müller 1.82, PV: Petra Pechstein 4.00, LJ: Laura Imberti 5.96, TJ: Dejana Cachot 13.14, SP: Katharina Roth 13.46, DT: Carmela Flury 42.93. HT: Laurence Locatelli, JT: Catherine Manigley 44.47, Hep: Simone Oberer 5701, 20kmW: Marie Polli 1:45:02.

André BUCHER b. 19 Oct 1976 Neudorf 1.85m 75kg. LR Beromünster. History graduate of Bern University. Teacher.
At 800m: OG: '96- sf, '00- 5; WCh: '97- sf, '99- sf, '01- 1; EC: '98- 2; EU23: '97- 2; EJ: '95- 2; WI: '01- 3; EI: '02- 2; WUG: '99- 2; won GP 2001. At 1500m: WJ: '94- 2. Won Swiss 800m 1995, 1997-9, 1500m 1994, 1996.
Swiss records 800m (5), 1000m (2) 1998-2001.
Progression at 800m: 1993- 1:56.40, 1994- 1:48.32, 1995- 1:45.71, 1996- 1:46.41, 1997- 1:45.33, 1998- 1:44.96, 1999- 1:42.92, 2000- 1:43.12, 2001- 1:42.55. pbs: 200m 22.18w '01. 400m 46.32 '00, 600m 1:14.72 (European best) '99, 1000m 2:15.63 '01, 1500m 3:38.44 '96, 3000m 8:16.9 '98, 5000m 14:06.77 '98, 10000m 30:40.5 '95, 3000mSt 9:09.73 '95.
He had a glorious year in 2001, when he became world champion, shared the Golden League jackpot, and won the overall Grand Prix title; he won 12 of 14 races at 800m and two at 1000m.

Women

Anita WEYERMANN b. 8 Dec 1977 1.62m 50kg. GG Bern. Student.
At 5000m: OG: '96- 14. At 1500m: OG: '00- sf; WCh: '97- 3, '99- 12; EC: '98- 3; WJ: '94- 1, '96- 7. At 3000m: WJ: '96- 1; EJ: '95- 2. World CC 4k: '98- 4; Eur CC: '99- 1. 2nd GP 1500m 1999. Won Swiss 1500m 1996, 2001; CC 1995-8, 2000; 4k CC 1999-2000.
European junior records 1500m and 5000m 1996. Swiss records: 1500m & 1M 1998, 3000m 1997 & 1999, 5000m 1996, 3000mSt 2001.
Progression at 1500m, 3000m, 5000m: 1993- 4:28.37, 10:08.62; 1994- 4:13.97, 9:19.25; 1995- 4:15.53, 9:10.89, 16:01.72; 1996- 4:03.45, 8:50.73, 14:59.28; 1997- 4:04.70, 8:37.69, 15:06.97; 1998- 3:58.20, 8:54.97, 15:26.41; 1999- 3:59.82, 8:35.83, 15:41.91; 2000- 4:05.38, 2001- 4:18.05, 9:42.01. pbs: 400m 58.50 '93, 800m 2:02.73 '98, 1000m 2:39.44 '00, 1M 4:23.92 '98, 3000mSt 9:57.06 '01, 400mh 67.30 '01.
Skis downhill and slalom for regional team.

TANZANIA

Governing body: Tanzania Amateur Athletic Association, PO Box 2172, Dar es Salaam. Founded 1954.

Faustin BAHA Sulle b. 30 May 1982.
At World HMar: '99-00-01: 15/2/12; CC: '00- 6J. World Junior and Tanzanian half marathon record 2000.
pbs: road: 10km 27:43 '00, HMar 59:38 '00.

John YUDA b. 9 Jun 1979 Dodoma.
At World HMar: 01- 3; CC: '01- 14 (4k), '02- 2. TAN HMar champion 2001.
pbs: road: 10km 28:26 '01, HMar 60:12 '01.

TRINIDAD & TOBAGO

Governing body: National Amateur Athletic Association of Trinidad & Tobago, PO Box 605, Port of Spain, Trinidad. Founded 1945, reformed 1971.
2001 National Champions: **Men**: 100m: Darrel Brown 10.28, 200m: Dion Rodriguez 21.50, 400m: Damion Barry 46.41, 800m: Sheridan Kirk 1:51.34, 1500m: Jules LaRode 4:02.72, 5000m: Wayne Gernes 17:57.04, 110mh: Nsatakki Dasent 15.75, 400mh: Daniel Greaves 54.37, PV: Kenneth Goodridge 3.40, LJ: Mickey Ruben 6.96, TJ: Anton Quashie 13.69, SP: Dave Stoute 17.27, DT: Keefdon Thomas 42.88, Dec: Alan Mitchell 6111. **Women**: 100m/200m: Fana Ashby 11.60/ 23.96w, 400m: Romona Modeste 56.05, 800m/ 1500m: Janil Williams ANT 2:06.80/4:44.46, 100mh: Alicia Cave 14.53, HJ: Danille Prime 1.70, LJ: Charisse Bacchus 5.47, TJ: Sheron Mark 11.03, SP/JT: Rachel Hercules 12.27/36.64.

Ato BOLDON b. 30 Dec 1973 Port of Spain 1.76m 75kg. Studied engineering at San José City College and at UCLA, USA.
At 100m/200m: OG: '92- h/h, '96- 3/3, '00- 2/3; WCh: '93- qf/-, '95- 3/qf, '97- 5/1, '01- 4/3R; WI: '97- dnf 200m; CG: '94- 4/sf, '98- 1/-; WJ: '92- 1/1. Won GWG 200m 1998, NCAA 200m 1995, 100m 1996; TRI 100m 1993-4, 200m 1992.
CAC records: 100m (9), 200m (3) 1996-9; TRI records: 100m (13) 1995-9, 200m (3) 1996-7.
Progression at 100m, 200m: 1990- 10.8, 21.3; 1991- 10.54/10.44w, 21.07; 1992- 10.22, 20.63/20.6; 1993- 10.23/10.0, 20.59; 1994- 10.07, 20.53; 1995- 10.03/10.01w, 20.08; 1996- 9.90, 19.80; 1997- 9.87, 19.77; 1998- 9.86, 19.88; 1999- 9.86, 19.86; 2000- 9.95, 19.97; 2001- 9.88, 20.24. pbs: 50m 5.58+ '97, 55m 6.04Ai '97, 60m 6.45+ '97.

Moved with mother and young brother to USA at age 14, living in New York and Los Angeles, until resettling in Trinidad late 2001. Best ever one-day sprint double, 9.90 and 19.77 in Stuttgart 1997. Missed 1999 World Championships through injury, but made a big hit with his knowledgeable interviewing.

TURKEY

Governing body: Türkiye Amator Atletizm Federasyonu, Ulus Ishani A Blok Kat 3, Ankara. Founded 1922. **National Champions 2001**: **Men**: 100m/200m: Resat Oguz 10.92/21.16, 400m: Ercan Sunu 47.60, 800m: Cevat Kücük 1:51.31, 1500m: Alibey Sükürov 3:51.46, 3000m: Metin Sazak 8:19.66, 5000m: Abdülkadir Türk 14:32.89, 10000m: Satilmis Atmaca 29:23.20 (lap short), 3000mSt: Mustafa Yoldar 9:16.73, 110mh: Sedat Özer 15.02, 400mh: Cetin Maral 53.79, HJ: Metin Durmusoglu 2.16, PV: Bülent Erkaya 4.85, LJ: Murat Ayaydin 7.64w, TJ: Berk Tuna 16.03, SP/DT: Ercüment Olgundeniz 17.31/58.47, HT: Esref Apak 67.71, JT: Gürbüz Cam 68.32, 20kmW: Abdülkadir Öz 1:31:44. **Women**: 100m/100mh: Esen Kizildag 12.18/13.68, 200m: Züleyha Tokay 25.91, 400m: Öznur Dursun 54.88, 800m: Yaprak Kalemoglu 2:10.94, 1500m: Kilinc 4:35.43, 3000m/5000m: Serap Aktas 9:45.21/16:58.52, 10000m: Gülsen Asikoglu 37:36.08, 400mh: Arzu Uyar 61.08, HJ: Candeger Kilincer 1.83, PV: Songül Kilic 3.40, LJ: Asli Uzunoglu 5.62w, TJ: Efhanim Temizsoy 12.31, SP: Sevda Sener 14.70, DT: Suzan Balkesen 47.57, HT: Zübeyde Yildiz 57.10, JT: Aysenur Yazicioglu 47.76, Hep: Serpil Kocak 4228, 10000mW: Yeliz Ay 48:33.5.

Süreyya AYHAN b. 6 Sep 1978 1.63m 52kg.
At 1500m: OG: '00- sf; WCh: '01- 8; EJ: '97- 8; WUG: '01- 1.
TUR records: 800m 2000, 1500m (4) 1999-2000.
Progression at 1500m: 1998- 4:22.81, 1999- 4:14.8, 2000- 4:03.02, 2001- 4:06.91. pbs: 800m 2:00.64 '00.

Ebru KAVAKLIOGLU b. 14 Mar 1970 1.67m 58kg. Was Yelena Kopytova RUS.
At 5000m: OG: '00- h; WCh:'99- 5; EC: '98- h; won Russian 1997, Med G 2001. At 3000m: OG: '92- 6; WCh: '93- 11. Road relay gold 1994. TUR records 1500m, 3000m (4), 5000m (2) 1999-2001.
Progression at 3000m, 5000m: 1991- 9:05.44, 1992- 8:47.21, 1993- 8:50.49, 1995- 15:39.59, 1997- 9:11.36, 15:37.19; 1998- 15:34.06, 1999- 8:38.98, 14:51.69; 2000- 8:56.13i, 15:49.15; 2001- 8:35.26, 15:02.62. pbs: 1500m 4:08.45 '99, 1M 4:34.40 '00, 2000m 5:45.73 '99.
Ran for Russia prior to 1998. In November 1998 she married her coach Anatoliy Bychkov, who had moved to Turkey in 1997.

UKRAINE

Governing body: Ukrainian Athletic Federation, Esplanadnaya Str. 42, Kiev 23. Founded 1991.

National Champions 2001: **Men**: 100m/200m: Anatoliy Dovgal 10.30/21.33, 400mYevgeniy Zyukov 45.99, 800m: Vladimir Kovalik 1:48.47, 1500m: Ivan Geshko 3:39.15, 5000m: Sergey Lebed 13:37.17, 10000m: Nikolay Rudik 29:42.76, 3000mSt: Sergey Redko 8:34.74, 110mh: Sergey Smolenskiy 14.20, 400mh: Gennadiy Gorbenko 49.46, HJ: Andrey Sokolovskiy 2.34, PV: Ruslan Yeremenko 5.70, LJ: Vladimir Zyuskov 8.13, TJ: Sergey Izmailov 16.28, SP/DT: Yuriy Belonog 20.77/62.23, HT: Andrey Skvaruk 82.34, JT: Oleg Statsenko 69.94, Dec: Sergey Blonskiy 7890, 20kmW: Aleksey Shelest 1:25:35/ 1:27:07. **Women**: 100m: Anzhela Kravchenko 11.32, 200m: Tatyana Tkalich 23.65, 400m: Olga Mishchenko 52.11, 800m: Galina Misiruk 1:59.83, 1500m: Irina Lishchinskaya 4:05.38, 5000m: Tatyana Belovol 15:39.96, 10000m: Natalya Berkut 31:22.76, 3000mSt: Anzhelika Averkova 10:13.53, 100mh: Yelena Krasovskaya 12.99, 400mh: Tatyana Tereshchuk 55.30, HJ: Vita Palamar 1.96, PV: Anzhela Balakhonova 4.30, LJ: Yelena Shekhovtsova 6.45, TJ: Yelena Govorova 14.06, SP: Vita Pavlysh 19.62, DT: Yelena Antonova 63.12, HT: Irina Sekachova 65.67, JT: Tatyana Lyakhovich 55.89, Hep: Marina Bryukhach 5828, 20kmW: Valentina Savchuk 1:30:36 & Vita Zozulya 1:32:25.

Yuriy BELONOG (Bilonog) b. 9 Mar 1974 2.00m 125kg. Odessa Dyn.
At SP: OG: '00- 5; WCh: '97- 4, '99- 5, '01- 6; EC: '98- 3; WI: '95/7/9/01- 5/1/3/8; WJ: '92- 1; WUG: '95- 1, '97- 1, '01- 2; ECp: '96- 3. 2nd GP 1998, 2nd overall 2000. Won UKR SP & DT 2001. UKR shot record 2000.
Progression at SP: 1990- 15.60, 1991- 17.91, 1992- 19.02, 1993- 18.39, 1994- 18.72, 1995- 20.05, 1996- 21.20i/20.05, 1997- 21.02i/20.75, 1998- 20.92, 1999- 20.89i/20.65, 2000- 21.64, 2001- 20.98. pb DT 65.32 '99.
Mother-in-law Valentina Korsak: DT 63.92 '84.

Sergey LEBED b. 15 Jul 1975 1.80m 65kg.
At 5000m: OG: '00- 7; WCh: '99/01- h; EC: '98- 13; WUG: '99- 1, '01- 1; EU23: '97- 7 (10000m 2). At 3000m: EI: '98- 5. World CC: '00- 8 (10 4k), '01- 2; Eur CC: '95-7-8-9-00-01: 11/3/1/7/2/1. Won UKR 1500m 1998, 5000m 1995-6, 1999-2001. UKR 5000m record 2001.
Progression at 5000m: 1993- 14:23.54, 1994- 14:11.27, 1995- 13:52.39, 1996- 13:39.31, 1997- 13:50.51, 1998- 13:30.23, 1999- 13:18.18, 2000- 13:27.53, 2001- 13:14.51. pbs: 1500m 3:39.95 '98, 3000m 7:37.76 '99, 10000m 28:39.71 '97, 10km Rd 28:23 '99. HMar 62:09 '01.

Olexiy (Aleksey) **LUKASHEVICH** b. 11 Jan 1977 Dnepropetrovsk 1.75m 70kg.
At LJ: OG: '00- 4; WCh: '97- dnq 16, '99- dnq 22, '01- 6; EC: '98- dnq 20; WJ: '96- 1; EU23: '97- 3; EI: '98-00-02: 1/4/4; WUG: '99- 1. 3rd GP 2001. UKR champion 2000.

Progression at LJ: 1994- 7.68, 1995- 7.57, 1996- 7.91/8.10w, 1997- 7.95/8.09w, 1998- 8.06i/8.03, 1999- 8.16/8.17w, 2000- 8.27, 2001- 8.20.

Vladislav PISKUNOV b. 7 Jun 1978 Novaya Kavhokva 1.83m 106kg.
At HT: OG: '00- dnq 14; WCh: '99- 3, '01- dnq 14; EC: '98- 10; WJ: '94- dq; EU23: '99- 1; WUG: '99- 3, '01- 2. UKR champion 1998-2000.
Progression at HT: 1993- 68.96, 1994- 73.66, 1998- 78.66, 1999- 80.00, 2000- 81.56, 2001- 79.60.
Used five turns when gaining 1999 World bronze medal. Threw the hammer 73.64 in June 1994 at 16 years 4 days, but disqualified for drugs use after winning (71.66) at the World Junior Championships a month later. Returned to competition in 1998 after four-year ban.
His brother Eduard had a hammer best of 75.64 '88 and threw 75.10 as a junior in 1986.

Roman SHCHURENKO b. 14 Sep 1976 Nikipol 1.88m 82kg. University of PE, Kiev
At LJ: OG: '00- 3; WCh: '99- dnq 15, '01- dnq 15; EJ: '95- 1; WUG: '99- 4. UKR champion 1998-9.
UKR Long jump record 2000.
Progression at LJ: 1993- 7.47, 1995- 7.85, 1996- 7.85, 1997- 7.98, 1998- 8.02, 1999- 8.30, 2000- 8.35, 2001- 7.97i/7.80/8.00w, 2002- 8.33i.

Andrey SKVARUK b. 9 Mar 1967 Brodivski 1.86m 106kg. Rovno ZS.
At HT: OG: '96- 4, '00- 10; WCh: '93- nt, '97- 2, '99- 5, '01- 5; EC: '94- 1, '98- dnq 14; ECp: '93-4-00: 3/2/10. Won GP 2000. UKR champion 1992, 1994-6, 2001.
Progression at HT: 1985- 65.42, 1986- 72.54, 1989- 73.60, 1990- 77.24, 1991- 71.60, 1992- 80.22, 1993- 80.80, 1994- 81.72, 1995- 78.00, 1996- 80.52, 1997- 81.46, 1998- 78.96, 1999- 80.75, 2000- 81.43, 2001- 82.34.

Andriy (Andrey) **SOKOLOVSKIY** b. 16 Jul 1978 Moskva, Russia 1.96m 80kg. Sports instructor.
At HJ: OG: '00- dnq 16=; WCh: '99/01- dnq 27=/22=; WI: '99- 6=, '01- 2; EU23: '99- 2; EI: '02- 5. UKR champion 2000-01.
Progression at HJ: 1997- 2.10, 1998- 2.22, 1999- 2.32, 2000- 2.28, 2001- 2.35i/2.34.

Roman VIRASTYUK b. 20 Apr 1968 Ivano Frankovsk 1.89m 135kg. Ivano Frankovsk ZS.
At SP: OG: '96- 6, '00- dnq 20; WCh: '95- 7, '97- 6, '99- dnq 13; ECh: '94- 3; EI: '98- 5, '00- 5; ECp: '94- 2. UKR champion 2000.
Progression at SP: 1986- 16.69, 1987- 18.53, 1988- 18.47i/18.25, 1989- 19.62, 1990- 20.03, 1991- 20.04i, 1993- 19.48, 1994- 20.00, 1995- 20.71, 1996- 21.23, 1997- 20.66, 1998- 20.63i/20.37, 1999- 20.59, 2000- 21.34, 2001- 20.08.
Two-year drugs ban 1991. Brother **Vasiliy** (b. 22 Apr 1974) has pb 19.75 '00 (EC: '98- dnq 13).

Aleksandr YURKOV b. 21 Jul 1975 Prosyanaya 1.83m 84kg. Dnepropetrovsk Dyn. Sports instructor.
At Dec: OG: '00- 16; WCh: '01- 9; WJ: '94- dnf; EU23: '97-2, ECp: '00-01: 1/1. At Hep: WI: '01- 6.
Progression at Dec: 1994- 7161, 1995- 7617, 1996- 7676, 1997- 7888, 1998- 8034, 1999- 8215, 2000- 8574, 2001- 8408. pbs: 60m 6.94i '01, 100m 10.69 '00, 400m 48.66 '00, 1500m 4:32.49 '00, 60mh 8.13i '00, 110mh 14.41 '01, HJ 2.06 '99, PV 5.40i/5.30 '01, LJ 7.93 '00, SP 15.39 '01, DT 50.44 '99, JT 60.06 '01, Hep 6160i '01.
Won at Talence 2001.

Women

Olena (Yelena) **ANTONOVA** b. 16 Jun 1972 Nikipol 1.82m 95kg. Elektrometallurg Nikipol.
At DT: OG: '96- dnq 29, '00- dnq 13; WCh: '97- dnq 13, '99- 7, '01- dnq 16; EC: '98- 11; EJ: '91- 3; WUG: '97- 4; ECp: '97-8-00: 3/3/6. UKR champion 1995-7, 1999-2001.
Progression at HJ: 1989- 55.84, 1990- 57.30, 1991- 57.12, 1992- 61.94, 1993- 58.34, 1994- 59.80, 1995- 61.54, 1996- 63.60, 1997- 61.62, 1998- 65.44, 1999- 64.32, 2000- 66.67, 2001- 64.20. pb HT 54.82 '95.

Inha (Inga) **BABAKOVA** b. 27 Jun 1967 Ashkabad, Turkmenistan 1.80m 60kg. née Butkus.
At HJ: OG: '96- 3, '00- 5; WCh: '91/5/7/9/01- 3/3/2/1/2; EC: '94- 4; WI: '93/7/01- 3/2/2; ECp: '93- 4=. Won GP 1995, 1997; 2= 1999, 3rd 1991. UKR champion 1991-2.
Three UKR high jump records 1995.
Progression at HJ: 1987- 1.89, 1988- 1.92, 1989- 1.89i, 1991- 2.02, 1992- 2.00, 1993- 2.00i/1.96, 1994- 2.00, 1995- 2.05, 1996- 2.03, 1997- 2.02, 1999- 2.01, 2000- 2.00, 2001- 2.03.
Born in Turkmenistan, Lithuanian by family and lives in Ukraine. Improved 10cm in 1991, with no previous international experience. After four World/Olympic silver and bronze medals, won gold at the 1999 Worlds. 13 competitions at 2.00 or higher in 1995 and 10 in 1996. Coached by her husband Sergey Babakov, their first son Georgiy was born in June 1990 and a second son was born prior to her World success in 1999.

Anzhela BALAKHONOVA b. 18 Dec 1972 1.62m 55kg. Kiev Dyn.
At PV: OG: '00- nh (12=); WCh: '99- 2, '01- dnq 13; EC: '98- 1; WI: '97- 9; EI: '98- 1; WUG: '97- 4=. UKR champion 1996-7, 1999-2001.
PV Records: WIR and two European indoor 1998, 8 European 1997-2000, 17 UKR 1996-9.
Progression at PV: 1996- 3.98/4.05sq, 1997- 4.36/ 4.45ex, 1998- 4.45i/4.40, 1999- 4.55, 2000- 4.56, 2001- 4.52. pbs: 100m 11.60/11.2 '95, 200m 23.63 '94, 23.4 '95; LJ 6.40 '96.
Started as a sprinter and rhythmic gymnast.

Olena (Yelena) GOVOROVA b. 18 Sep 1973 Izmail 1.75m 63kg. Odessa ZS.
At TJ: OG: '96- 9, '00- 3; WCh: '95- 10, '97- 3, '99- 7, '01- 10; EC: '98- 6; WJ: '92- 3; WI: '95- 7, '97- 7; EI: '00- 4; WUG: '97- 1, '99- 1; ECp: '96-8-00: 2/3/2. UKR champion 1997-2001.

Progression at TJ: 1990- 12.70, 1991- 13.19i/13.10, 1992- 13.43, 1993- 13.14i, 1994- 14.22, 1995- 14.08i/ 14.07, 1996- 14.60/14.75w, 1997- 14.67, 1998- 14.51/14.70w, 1999- 14.66/14.99w, 2000- 14.96, 2001- 14.33/14.48w. pb LJ 6.36 '98.

Viktoriya PALAMAR b. 12 Oct 1977 1.87m 64kg. At HJ: OG: '00- 7; WCh: '01- 5; WJ: '96- 6=; WI: ' 01- 5=; EI: '00- 5; WUG: '01- 1. Won UKR 2001.
Progression at HJ: 1992-, 1993- 1.83, 1994- 1.91, 1995- 1.88, 1996- 1.89, 1997- 1.88, 1998- 1.89, 1999- 1.93, 2000- 1.98, 2001- 1.99.

Viktoriya PAVLYSH b. 15 Jan 1969 Kharkov 1.74m 85kg. Kharkov Dyn.
At SP: OG: '92- 8, '96- 4; WCh: '93- dnq, '95- 11, '97- 2, '01- 3; WI: '97- 1, '99- dq; EC: '94- 1, '98- 1; EI: '98- 2, '02- 1; EJ: '87- 6; WCp: '94- 4, '98- 1. 2nd GP 1997, 3rd 1993. UKR champion 1993, 1995-6, 2001. Ukrainian shot record 1998.
Progression at SP: 1986- 15.73, 1987- 16.48, 1988- 16.28, 1989- 17.28, 1990- 17.86, 1991- 18.76, 1992- 19.66, 1993- 19.22, 1994- 19.61, 1995- 19.30, 1996- 19.79, 1997- 20.73, 1998- 21.69, 1999- 21.43idq, 2001- 19.62, 2002- 20.34i.
Married Aristotle Mavridis on 22 Jul 1995. Her 21.69 to win the 1998 European title was the longest SP in the world for ten years, although she said afterwards that she had thrown 21.73 in a practice session in Kharkov. Disqualified and two-year drugs ban after 'winning' at 1999 World Indoors with 21.43. Returned to win European Throws Challenge SP in March 2001.

Zhanna PINTUSEVICH-BLOCK b. 6 Jul 1972 Nezhin, nr Chernigov 1.64m 62kg. née Tarnopolskaya. Kiev Dyn.
At 100m (/200m): OG: '96- 8/qf, '00- 5/8; WCh: '93- sf, '95- 5/h, '97- 2/1, '99- 4/qf, '01- 1; EC: '94- 2/2/4R, '98- 4/2; EJ: '91- 1/1/4R; WCp: '98- 4/3; ECp: '93- 3/4, '94- 1/1R. At 60m: WI: '93- 3; EI: '92- 1. Won UKR 100m 1994-5.
WIR 50m at 6.09 for a few minutes in 1993. UKR records: 100m (5) 1994-2001, 200m 1997.
Progression at 100m, 200m: 1987- 11.8, 1988- 11.75/11.5, 23.75; 1989- 11.64/11.5, 24.03; 1990- 11.99, 1991- 11.29/11.0, 23.56; 1992- 11.17, 1993- 11.08, 22.79; 1994- 10.99, 22.66; 1995- 11.01, 22.71/ 22.64w; 1996- 11.07, 23.15; 1997- 10.85/10.6, 22.17A/22.32; 1998- 10.92/10.9A, 22.35A/22.46; 1999- 10.94, 22.42; 2000- 10.93, 22.66; 2001- 10.82, 22.74. pbs: 50m 6.03+ '97, 60m 6.97+ '97.
She won the 1997 World title at 200m in 22.32, five days after she thought that she had won the 100m, only for the photo-finish to show that Marion Jones had held on to beat her 10.83 to 10.85. Four years later it was the other way round, as she beat Jones 10.82 to 10.85. Married athletics agent Mark Block in 1999. Formerly married to Igor Pintsuvich (3rd WJ 110mh 1992).

Tetyana TERESHCHUK b. 11 Oct 1969 1.85m 63kg. Lugansk Dyn.
At 400mh: OG: '96- sf, '00- 5; WCh: '95- 5, '97- 4, '99- 7; EC: '94- 6, '98- 2; WUG: '97- 1; ECp: '94-5-6-8-00: 2/3/4/1/1. Won GWG 2001, 3rd/2nd GP 1997/2000. UKR champ 1994, 1996, 1999, 2001. Four UKR 400mh records 1997.
Progression at 400mh: 1989- 57.58, 1990- 57.98, 1991- 57.19, 1993- 58.20/57.9, 1994- 54.96, 1995- 54.88, 1996- 54.68, 1997- 53.64, 1998- 53.40, 1999- 53.46, 2000- 53.98, 2001- 53.89A/54.01. pbs: 200m 24.03 '97, 100mh 12.8 '95, 13.12A '98, 13.14 '97.
Set UKR 400mh records in four successive races in 12 days in 1997: World semi and final, then Zürich and Monaco. Missed 2001 Worlds through injury.

UNITED KINGDOM

Governing body: UK Athletics, Athletics House, 10 Harborne Road, Edgbaston, Birmingham B15 3AA. Founded 1999 (replacing British Athletics, founded 1991, which succeeded BAAB, founded 1932). The Amateur Athletic Association was founded in 1880 and the Women's Amateur Athletic Association in 1922.
National Championships (first were English Championships 1863-79). **AAA Championships** first held in 1880 (women 1922). **2001 Champions**: 100m: Dwaian Chambers 10.01, 200m: Marlon Devonish 20.52, 400m: Mark Richardson 45.79, 800m: Neil Speaight 1:49.63, 1500m: John Mayock 3:44.05, 5000m: Jon Wild 13:52.72, 10000m: Glynn Tromans 28:31.33, Mar: Mark Steinle 2:10:46, 3000mSt: Ben Whitby 8:32.68, 110mh: Anthony Jarrett 13.66, 400mh: Chris Rawlinson 48.68, HJ: Ben Challenger 2.17, PV: Paul Williamson 5.30, LJ: Nathan Morgan 7.80, TJ: Jonathan Edwards 17.59, SP: Mark Proctor 18.38, DT: Glen Smith 59.99, HT: Michael Jones 74.40, JT: Mark Roberson 80.80, Dec: John Heanley 7129, 5000mW: Lloyd Finch 20:47.23. **Women**: 100m: Sarah Wilhelmy 11.41w, 200m: Sarah Reilly IRL 23.42, 400m: Lesley Owusu 52.27, 800m: Kelly Holmes 2:02.61, 1500m: Helen Pattinson 4:14.49, 5000m: Jo Pavey 15:15.98, 10000m: Penny Thackray 33:25.74, Mar: Bev Hartigan 2:37:45, 100mh: Diane Allahgreen 13.11, 400mh: Sinead Dudgeon 56.37, HJ: Susan Jones 1.91, PV: Janine Whitlock 4.40, LJ: Ann Danson 6.15, TJ: Ashia Hansen 14.09, SP: Joanne Duncan 16.84, DT: Shelley Drew 57.22, HT: Lorraine Shaw 66.97, JT: Karen Martin 54.82, Hep: Laura Redmond 5068, 5000mW: Niobe Menendez 23:46.30. **UK Champions**: HMar: Kasse Tadesse 64:04, 20kmW: Matthew Hales 1:28:40, Women 3000mSt: Tara Krzywicki 9:55.01, HMar: Liz Yelling 72:54. **National Road Walk Champions**: **Men**: 20kmW: Andy Penn 1:31:56, 50kmW: Michael Smith 4:33.17. **Women**: 10km: Olive Lougnane IRL 46:35, 20km: Shula Bull 2:18:53.

Onochie **'Larry' ACHIKE** b. 31 Jan 1975 Islington, London 1.88m 75kg. Shaftesbury Barnet.
At TJ: OG: '00- 5; WCh: '99- 11, '01- 7; EC: '98- dnq 21; CG: '98- 1; WJ: '92- 11, '94- 1; EJ: '93- 3;

ECp: '00- 1. 3rd GP 2000.
Progression at TJ: 1989- 13.71, 1990- 14.18, 1991- 15.28, 1992- 15.97, 1993- 16.49, 1994- 16.53/16.67w, 1995- 15.91/15.94w, 1996- 16.36, 1997- 15.77, 1998- 17.10, 1999- 16.96, 2000- 17.30/17.31w, 2001- 17.21. pbs: 100m 10.95 '94, 200m 21.68 '97, 21.6 '96; LJ 7.46 '93.
Over 17m for the first time in June 1998 with 17.07, improving to 17.10 for Commonwealth title. Lifetime best 17.31w to win the European Cup in 2000, and maintained that form with 17.30 (q) and 17.29 for fifth at the Olympics.

Stephen BACKLEY b. 12 Feb 1969 Sidcup 1.96m 100kg. Cambridge H.
At JT: OG: '92- 3, '96- 2, '00- 2; WCh: '91- dnq 15, '93- 4, '95- 2, '97- 2, '99- 8, '01- dnq 14; EC: '90- 1, '94- 1, '98- 1; CG: '90- 1, '94- 1, '98- 2; WJ: '88- 2; EJ: '87- 1; WCp: '89- 1, '94- 1, '98- 1; ECp: '89-95-97: 1/3/1; WUG: '89- 1, '91- 1. Won GP 1989 (3rd overall), 3rd 1995, UK 1988-90, 1997; AAA 1989, 1992, 1998-2000.
Javelin records: Three world 1990-2, world junior 1988. Eight UK and Commonwealth 1989-92.
Progression at JT (old): 1985- 64.34, new: 1986- 64.98 (69.74), 1987- 78.16, 1988- 79.50, 1989- 85.90, 1990- 90.98, 1991- 91.36, 1992- 91.46, 1993- 85.10, 1994- 85.20, 1995- 88.54, 1996- 87.44, 1997- 89.02, 1998- 89.89, 1999- 87.59, 2000- 89.85, 2001- 90.81.
The first British male thrower to set a world record: 89.58 in Stockholm with a Sandvik javelin, and 90.98 at Crystal Palace on his second throw with a Németh model, both 1990. When these were banned at the end of 1991 his 89.58 was reinstated as the world record and in New Zealand in 1992 he achieved the first 90m throw with the revised javelin specification. Won third successive European title in 1998. In 2000 he became the first Briton in any athletics event to win an Olympic medal in three Games.

Jon BROWN b. 27 Feb 1971 Bridgend 1.75m 57kg. Sheffield. Studied journalism at Iowa State University, USA.
At Mar: OG: '00- 4. At 10000m: OG: '96- 10; WCh: '99- dnf; EC: '98- 4. At 5000m: WCh: '93- h; CG: '94- 4; WJ: '90- 13; WSG: '91- 4; EU23Cp: '92- 3. World CC: '96- 12, '97- 14; Eur CC: '95- 6, '96- 1, '99- 3. Won UK and AAA 5000m 1993.
Progression at 5000m, 10000m, Mar: 1988- 14:24.82, 1989- 14:23.38, 1990- 14:03.09, 29:21.9; 1991- 13:35.62, 28:38.36; 1992- 13:24.84, 28:19.6; 1993- 13:19.78, 1994- 13:23.96, 1995- 13:37.83, 28:08.31; 1996- 13:20.10, 27:59.72; 1997- 13:44.9, 27:27.47, 2:10:13; 1998- 13:19.03, 27:18.14, 2:11:10; 1999- 13:23.35, 2:09:44; 2000- 2:11:17, 2001- 2:11:24. pbs: 800m 1:54.9 '93, 1500m 3:40.53 '92, 1M 4:06.2 '89, 3000m 7:45.41 '98. Road 15km 42:39 '94, HMar 61:47 '97.
Lived in Germany for 15 months before moving to Vancouver, Canada in 1996, in which year he won the Gasparilla 15km in a UK best, then was first non-African in the World CC, and at the end of the year won the European CC. He was the first non-African in the 2000 Olympic marathon.

Daniel CAINES b. 15 May 1979 Solihull 1.80m 72kg. Birchfield H. Law graduate of Swansea University.
At 400m/4x400mR: OG: '00- sf/6R; WJ: '98- 5R; WI: '01- 1; EI: '00-6. At 200m: EI: '02- 4.
Progression at 400m: 1998- 47.13, 1999- 47.29i, 2000- 45.37, 2001- 45.58. pbs: 60m 6.99i '98, 200m 20.62i '02, 21.05 '01; 300m 32.7i '02.
His mother, Blondelle Thompson, set a British record at 13.0 for 100mh in 1974 and his father Joe Caines was a British junior international in 1970-1 with a 400m best of 48.2 at age 19 in 1971.

Darren CAMPBELL b. 12 Sep 1973 Manchester 1.85m 86kg. Belgrave H.
At 100m/4x100mR (200m): OG: '96- ht R, '00- 6 (2); WCh: '97- sf/3R, '99- sf/2R; EC: '98- 1/1R; CG: '98- 5/1R; WJ: '92- 2/1R (2); EJ: '91- 1/2R (1); ECp: '96-8-9-00: 3R/1R/1R/1&1R; Won AAA 100m 1998, 200m 2000; GP 100m 2000.
Progression at 100m, 200m: 1988- 11.39, 23.2; 1989- 10.78w/11.0, 21.8/21.72w; 1990- 10.81, 21.51; 1991- 10.37/10.28w, 20.89/20.61w; 1992- 10.37, 20.87/20.68w; 1993- 10.39/10.29w, 20.86/20.69w; 1994- 10.54, 21.23i; 1995- 10.34, 1996- 10.17, 20.98; 1997- 10.13, 20.84; 1998- 10.04, 20.48; 1999- 10.12/10.11w, 21.05/20.51w; 2000- 10.06, 20.13; 2001- 10.16, 20.41. pbs: 50m 5.77i '99, 60m 6.60i '99, LJ 6.63w? '89.
After junior successes played football for two years 1993-5. Missed the 2001 World Championships through injury.

Dwain CHAMBERS b. 5 Apr 1978 London 1.80m 83kg. Belgrave H.
At 100m/4x100mR: OG: '00- 4; WCh: '97- resR, '99- 3/2R, '01- 5 (qf 200m); EC: '98- 2/resR; CG: '98- sf/1R; WJ: '96- 5; EJ: '95- 1/1R, '97- 1/1R; WCp: '98- 3/1R; ECp: '99- 1. Won AAA 2000-1, GWG 2001.
World junior 100m record 1997.
Progression at 100m: 1994- 10.75/10.56w, 1995- 10.41, 1996- 10.42, 1997- 10.06, 1998- 10.03rA/10.10, 1999- 9.97, 2000- 10.08, 2001- 9.99/9.97?. pbs: 50m 5.57+ '99, 60m 6.41+ '99, 200m 20.31 '01.
Older sister Christine Chambers (b. 4 Mar 1969) was 8th at 100m at 1987 European Juniors. pbs: 60m 7.46i '92, 100m 11.84 '87, 11.68w '92.

Jonathan EDWARDS b. 10 May 1966 London 1.82m 73kg. Gateshead. Physics graduate from Durham University.
At TJ: OG: '88- dnq 23, '92- dnq 35, '96- 2, '00- 1; WCh: '93- 3, '95- 1, '97- 2, '99- 3, '01- 1; EC: '94- 6, '98- 1; CG: '90- 2, '94- 2; WI: '93- 6, '01- 2; EI: '98- 1; WCp: '89- 3, '92- 1; ECp: '93-4-5-6-7-8-9-01: 2/4/1/1/1/1/2/1. Won GP 1996 (2nd overall), 2000; GWG 2001; UK 1989, 1992; AAA 1989, 1994, 1998, 2001.
3 world and 7 British triple jump records 1995.

Progression at TJ: 1983- 13.84, 1984- 14.87/15.01w, 1985- 15.09, 1986- 16.05, 1987- 16.35, 1988- 16.74, 1989- 17.28, 1990- 16.51/16.93w, 1991- 17.43, 1992- 17.34, 1993- 17.44/17.70w, 1994- 17.39, 1995- 18.29/18.43w, 1996- 17.88, 1997- 17.74, 1998- 18.01, 1999- 17.52/17.71w, 2000- 17.71, 2001- 17.92. pbs: 60m 6.73i '98, 100m 10.48 '96, 200m 22.2 '89, LJ 7.41/7.45w '92.
A committed Christian who previously refused to compete on Sundays, thus passing the 1991 World Championships, until 1993. He hit wondrous form in 1995, taking triple jumping into a new era, sailing well beyond 18m at the European Cup, with a wind just over the limit. His best of 18.43w was comprised: 6.50 hop, 5.60 step, 6.33 jump. After taking the world record with 17.98 at Salamanca, he achieved the unprecedented feat of world records on his first two jumps in the World final in Göteborg – 18.16 and 18.29, thus the first 18m and 60ft jumps with legal wind. His run of 22 successive victories 1995-6 was ended by Kenny Harrison at the 1996 Olympic Games. Had keyhole surgery on his left ankle at the end of the 1998 season, causing him to miss the Commonwealth Games. Although ranked number one in the world , he had to settle for silver and bronze at World Championships in 1997 and 1999, but returned to top the podium at the 2000 Olympics and the 2001 Worlds (for his fifth successive medal at this event).

Jason GARDENER b. 18 Sep 1975 Bath 1.75m 70kg. Bath & Wessex.
At 100m/4x100mR: OG: '00- qf; WCh: '95- sf R, '99- 7/2R; CG: '98- res (1)R; WJ: '94- 2/1R; ECp: '95-7-9: 1R/3R/1R. At 60m: WI: '99- 3; EI: '98-00-02: 2/1/1. Won AAA 100m 1997, 1999.
Progression at 100m: 1992- 11.0, 1993- 10.62/10.46w, 1994- 10.25, 1995- 10.33, 1996- 10.5/10.41w, 1997- 10.31/10.17w, 1998- 10.30/10.17w/10.0w, 1999- 9.98, 2000- 10.09/10.04w, 2001- 10.23. pbs: 50m 5.61i '00 (= European record), 60m 6.46i '99, 200m 20.65 '99.
Broke Linford Christie's European record for 60m with 6.46 for 3rd in World Indoors 1999, and outdoors became the third European to break 10 seconds for 100m. Back from injury.

Michael '**Mick**' **HILL** b. 22 Oct 1964 Leeds 1.90m 95kg. Leeds City. Athletics development officer for Leeds.
At JT: OG: '88- dnq 20, '92- 11, '96- 12, 00- 11; WCh: '87- 7, '91- 5, '93- 3, '95- 6, '97- 4, '99- dnq 14, '01- 12; EC: '86- 8, '90- 4, '94- 6, '98- 2; CG: '86- 2, '90- 2, '94- 2, '98- 3; EJ: '83- 11; WCp: '92- 5; ECp: '87-91-3-4-8-9: 4/5/2/3/4/4. Won UK 1985-7, 1992-3; AAA 1987, 1990-1, 1994-5. 2nd GP 1987, 3rd 1993.
UK and Commonwealth javelin record 1987.
Progression at JT: 1980- 56.32, 1981- 59.14, 1982- 64.72, 1983- 74.36, 1984- 71.08, 1985- 82.30, 1986- 82.04; new: 1986- 78.56, 1987- 85.24, 1988- 81.30, 1989- 82.56, 1990- 85.88, 1991- 86.32, 1992- 85.32, 1993- 86.94, 1994- 86.36, 1995- 84.14, 1996- 81.42, 1997- 86.54, 1998- 86.92, 1999- 84.94, 2000- 83.71, 2001- 84.88.
Earned World bronze 1993 after disqualification of Dmitriy Polyunin. Operations on left knee in 1989 and March 1990. Missed only two finals in 19 major championships 1986-2001. A seven handicap golfer.

Phillips IDOWU b. 30 Dec 1978 Hackney, London 1.92m 87kg. Belgrave H.
At TJ: OG: '00- 6; WCh: '01- 9; EU23: '99-5; EJ: '97- 4. Won AAA 2000.
Progression at TJ: 1995- 13.90, 1996- 15.12/15.53w, 1997- 15.86/16.34w, 1998- 16.35, 1999- 16.41, 2000- 17.12, 2001- 17.33/17.38w. pbs: 100m 10.81 '01, LJ 7.83 '00.

Colin JACKSON b. 18 Feb 1967 Cardiff 1.82m 73kg. Brecon.
At 110mh: OG: '88- 2, '92- 7, '96- 4, '00- 5; WCh: '87- 3, '91- sf, '93- 1/2 4x100mR, '97- 2, '99- 1; EC: '90- 1, '94- 1, '98- 1; CG: '86- 2, '90- 1, '94- 1; WJ: '86- 1; EJ: '85- 2; WCp: '89- 2, '92- 1; ECp: '87-9-91-3-6-7-8: 2/1/1/1/2/2/1 (3 100m). Won UK 1986, 1989-90, 1992; AAA 1986, 1988-90, 1992-3, 1996, 1998-2000; GWG 1994. Won GP 1993, 3rd 1989. At 60mh: WI: '87-9-93-7-9: 4/2/2/2/1; EI: '87-9-94-02: 2/1/1/1 (1 60m '94).
Records: World 110mh 1993, 60mh indoors 1994; 7 European 8 Commonwealth and 9 UK 110mh 1988-93; 9 UK, 4 Commonwealth & European 60mh to WIRs 7.36 & 7.30 '94. European indoor 50mh 1999. European junior 110mh 1986. World best 200mh 1991.
Progression at 110mh: 1984- 13.92, 1985- 13.69, 1986- 13.44/13.42w, 1987- 13.37, 1988- 13.11, 1989- 13.11/12.95w, 1990- 13.08/12.8w, 1991- 13.09, 1992- 13.04, 1993- 12.91, 1994- 12.98/ 12.94Aw, 1995- 13.17, 1996- 13.13, 1997- 13.05, 1998- 13.02, 1999- 13.04, 2000- 13.10, 2001- 13.32. pbs: 60m 6.49i '94, 100m 10.29 '90, 200m 21.19/21.0 '88, 21.18w '89; 50mh 6.40i '99, 200mh 22.63 '91, HJ 1.81 '82, LJ 7.96w '86, 7.56 '85; JT 52.86 '84.
Ranked in the world top ten at 110mh each year 1986-2001, and top 1992-4. He had a record 15 sub-13.20 times in 1992 although an injury held him back to 7th in the Olympics, and he had 13 sub-13.20 in 1993, when he set the world record to win his first World title, and in 1994, when he was undefeated. 44 successive hurdles victories 29 Aug 1993 to 9 Feb 1995 when Allen Johnson beat him at Madrid at 60mh, both running 7.42. Injury cost him the chance of medal at the 1986 Europeans, and he had operations on right knee 1990 and on left in 1991, after he had to withdraw from World semis following a warm-up accident. Unique double with European Indoor 60m/60mh 1994. After three silvers at last won World Indoor 60mh in 1999 and completed a double by regaining the world title at 110mh.

Mark LEWIS-FRANCIS b. 4 Sep 1982 1.83m 88kg. Birchfield H.
At 100m/4x100mR: WJ: '00- 1/1R; WY: '99- 1; EJ: '99- 2, '01- 1/1R; ECp: '01- 1/2R. At 60m: WI: '01- 3; EI: '02- 2.
World junior record 60m indoors 2001.
Progression at 100m: 1996- 11.37/11.31w, 1997- 10.93, 1998- 10.49/10.36w, 1999- 10.31/10.26w, 2000- 10.10, 2001- 10.12/9.97w?. pbs: 50m 5.73i '02, 60m 6.51i '01, 200m 21.82 '99, 21.8 '98.
Improved his pb of 6.65 to successive British junior records of 6.61, 6.56 and 6.51 in 2001 World Indoor 60m. After wins at the European Cup and European Juniors, he ran a scintiallating 9.97 in the quarter-finals at the World Championship, but was denied a possible World Junior record as the wind gauge did not function.

Dean MACEY b. 12 Dec 1977 Rochford, Essex 1.96m 92kg. Harrow.
At Dec: OG: '00- 4; WCh: '99- 2, '01- 3; WJ: '96- 2; EU23: '97/99- dnf.
Progression at Dec: 1994- 5648, 1995- 6662, 1996- 7480, 1999- 8556, 2000- 8567, 2001- 8603. pbs: 100m 10.69/10.65w '99, 400m 46.21 '01, 1500m 4:23.45 '00, 110mh 14.34 '01, HJ 2.15 '01, PV 4.80 '00, LJ 7.77 '00, TJ 14.26/14.53w '94, SP 15.77 '01, DT 47.77 '99, JT 64.03 '99.
Macey has amazed with both his World Championships medals. In 1999 he set six individual event personal bests in his score of 8556 on his senior international debut for Britain. Earlier he had won at Arles with 8347, a huge improvement on his pb from his last completed decathlon, 7480 for 2nd at the 1996 World Juniors. He was heading for a similar score and a gold or silver medal when he fell in the 110mh at the European Under-23 championships after a first-day score of 4358 and 'legal' pbs at 100m and long jump. Despite only one competition (at which he did three events) pre-Sydney in 2000, he excelled to take fourth at the Olympics, setting pbs at LJ, 400m, PV and 1500m but held back in the throws by elbow problems. And in 2001 he improved his best again for bronze at the Worlds, despite a groin injury which meant that he very nearly withdrew before both 400m and 110mh, in both of which he set personal bests!

Christian MALCOLM b. 3 Jun 1979 Cardiff 1.74m 67kg. Cardiff AAC.
At 200m/4x100mR (100m): OG: '00- 5; WCh: '01- 5 (7); CG: '98- 2 (4 4x100m); WJ: '96- sf, '98- 1 (1); EJ: '97- 1/1R (2); EU23: '99- 2/1R (2=); WI: '01- 2; EI: '00- 1, '02- 2; ECp: '00- 1/1R, '01- 2R.
European Junior 200m record 1998.
Progression at 100m, 200m: 1993- 11.74, 1994- 10.88, 22.36/22.2; 1995- 10.85, 21.58/21.41w; 1996- 10.60/10.5, 21.27; 1997- 10.24, 20.83/20.48w; 1998- 10.12, 20.29; 1999- 10.22/10.20w, 20.47; 2000- 10.29, 20.19; 2001- 10.11/10.09w?, 20.08. pb 50m 5.81i '02, 60m 6.64i '01, 6.65 '00.

John MAYOCK b. 26 Oct 1970 Barnsley 1.77m 66kg. Barnsley. Sports development officer.
At 1500m: OG: '96- 11, '00- 9; WCh: '95/99/01- sf, '97- 9; EC: '98- 5; CG: '94- 3, '98- 2; ECp: '97-8-9: 4/3/4. At 3000m: WI: '93-5-7-01: 6/5/6/4; EI: '92-8-00-02: 2/1/3/3=. At 5000m: EJ: '89- 2; WUG: '91- 1; WCp: '92- 7; ECp: '94- 4. World CC: '89- 29J; Rd Rly team: '92- 3. Won AAA 1500m 1995-6, 1998-2001; UK 1997.
Progression at 1500m: 1987- 4:00.02, 1988- 3:48.46, 1989- 3:45.9, 1990- 3:48.05, 1991- 3:41.68, 1992- 3:37.76, 1993- 3:36.45, 1994- 3:37.20, 1995- 3:34.05, 1996- 3:33.38, 1997- 3:31.86, 1998- 3:32.82, 1999- 3:33.97, 2000- 3:34.69, 2001- 3:34.43. pbs: 800m 1:47.8 '98, 1000m 2:18.48 '96, 1M 3:50.32 '96, 2000m 4:56.75 '99, 3000m 7:41.09i '02, 7:47.28 '95; 2M 8:17.06i '02, 8:32.54 '91; 5000m 13:26.97 '92.
Competed at 5000m at the 1991 World Student Games as a late replacement; took 5.39 off his pb in the heat and a further 22.16 secs off to win the gold medal. Showed similar ability to improve his 3000m pb from 8:01.54 to 7:53.11 in his heat and 7:48.47 in the final to take the silver medal at the 1992 European Indoors.

Carl MYERSCOUGH b. 21 Oct 1979 2.09m 149kg. BLackpool & Fylde. Student at University of Nebraska, USA.
At SP(/DT): WJ: '06- dnq 22, '98- 3/6; EJ: '97- dnq/6; EU23: '99- 8/9. Won AAA 1999.
Progression at SP: 1995- 13.20, 1996- 17.30, 1997- 17.66, 1998- 19.46, 1999- 18.97, 2002- 21.26i. pb DT 62.17 '02.
Made a sensational return in his first competition after serving a two-year drugs ban, as at Lincoln, Nebraska on 23 Feb 2002 he won the shot with 21.08, to take Geoff Capes's 26-year old British indoor record. Two weeks later he improved that to 21.26 to win the NCAA Indoor title.

Chris RAWLINSON b. 19 May 1972 Rotherham 1.85m 82kg. Belgrave H, Loughborough Univ.
At 400mh/4x400mR: OG: '00- sf; WCh: '97- h, '01- 5; EC: '98- h; WUG: '97- (res 3R), '99- 5/2R; ECp: '97-0-00: 5/5/1&2R. Won AAA 1999-2001, UK 1997.
Progression at 400mh: 1992- 54.6, 1993- 52.9/53.62, 1994- 52.0/52.32, 1995- 50.90, 1996- 50.36, 1997- 49.69, 1998- 49.81, 1999- 48.14, 2000- 48.22, 2001- 48.27. pbs: 100m 10.9 '00, 200m 21.53 '00, 400m 47.18 '99, 60mh 8.17i '97, 110mh 14.2/14.25w '97, 300mh 34.59 '00, PV 4.40 '92, Dec 6291 '95 (6562u).
Fractured right ankle in 1999 and missed World Championships.

Mark RICHARDSON b. 26 Jul 1972 Slough 1.80m 74kg. Windsor, Slough & Eton AC. Sports science degree from Loughborough University.
At 400m/4x400mR: OG: '92- resR, '96- 2R; WCh: '91- resR, '95- 5/4R, '97- 4/2R, '99- 6, '01- sf; EC: '98- 3/1R; CG: '98- 2/2R; WJ: '88-4, '90- 3/2R; EJ: '89- h, '91- 2/1R (2 4x100mR); WCp: '92-

2/3R; ECp: '95-6-7-8-9: 1&1R/1R/1R/1&1R/1 &1R. Won GP 1998, 2000; AAA 1995, 2000-01.
Progression at 400m: 1987- 50.8, 1988- 46.43, 1989- 47.13, 1990- 46.33, 1991- 45.53, 1992- 45.09, 1993- 45.94i/46.46, 1994- 46.11i, 1995- 44.81, 1996- 44.74, 1997- 44.47, 1998- 44.37, 1999- 44.47, 2000- 44.72, 2001- 45.14. pbs: 100m 10.35 '98, 200m 20.62 '97, 20.6w '96; 300m 31.87 '98, 800m 1:55.9 '97.
Set a UK age-15 best for 400m of 47.57 in 1988, improving to 47.32 on his junior international debut, and then age-16 bests of 46.63 and 46.43 in the heats and semis of the World Juniors. Injuries cost him most of 1989, 1993-4 seasons. After gold and silver at the European Juniors he won relay medals as a reserve, running heats not finals: World gold 1991 and Olympic bronze 1992. At the 1996 Olympics his 43.62 for the 3rd leg in the final was the fastest split at the Games and the fastest ever run by a British runner. Tested marginally positive for nandrolene in February 2000; he vehemently denied knowingly taking any banned substance, and was cleared to compete but case pending with IAAF.

Iwan THOMAS b. 5 Jan 1974 Huntington, Cambridge 1.88m 80kg. Newham & Essex Beagles.
At 400m/4x400mR: OG: '96- 5/2R, '00- 6R; WCh: '97- 6/2R, '01- sf; EC: '98- 1/1R; CG: '94- sf/7R (qf 200m), '98- 1/3R; WJ: '92- 5R; WCp: '98- 1/2R; ECp: '95-7-8-01: 1R/1R/1R/4; EU23: '94- 3R. 3rd GP 1998. Won AAA 1998.
Two British 400m records 1997.
Progression at 400m: 1992- 47.37, 1993- 47.94i/48.04, 1994- 45.98, 1995- 45.58, 1996- 44.66A/44.69, 1997- 44.36, 1998- 44.38, 2000- 45.82, 2001- 45.77. pbs: 200m 20.87 '97, 300m 32.08+ '97.
Started athletics in 1992 after being ranked fourth in Europe at BMX cycle racing. Powered to three major titles in 1998. Missed 1999 season and underwent minor telescopic surgery to repair damage to his ankle after a stress fracture.

Women

Natasha DANVERS b. 19 Sep 1977 London 1.75m 61kg. Shaftesbury Barnet, was at University of Southern California, USA.
At 400mh/4x400mR: OG: '00- 8; WCh: '99/01- h; EC: '98: h/3R res; CG: '98- 5; EU23: '99- 1; ECp: '00-01: 3R/8; WUG: '99- 5/3R, '01- 1/2R; AAA 1998, NCAA 2000. At 100mh: WJ: '96- 6; EJ: '95- 2.
Progression at 400mh: 1993- 66.9, 1997- 56.84, 1998- 55.69, 1999- 55.75, 2000- 54.95, 2001- 54.94. pbs: 200m 24.99 '00, 300m 37.80 '00, 400m 53.26 '98, 60mh 8.32i '86, 100mh 13.20 '98, 13.19w '00, 12.8w '99; HJ 1.82 '98.

Donna FRASER b. 7 Nov 1972 Shirley, Surrey 1.81m 70kg. Croydon H.
At 400m/4x400mR (200m): OG: '96- qf, '00- 4/6R; WCh: '97- 6R, '99- qf, '01- sf; EC: '98: 6/3R; CG: '98- 3/2R (3 4x100R); WJ: '90- 2 4x100R; EJ: '91- 1/5R (2 4x100R); EU23: '94- 5/5R; EI: '98- (5); ECp: '96-7-8-9-00: 7/2&3R/3R/7/2&3R (6). Won UK 1997, AAA 2000.
Progression at 400m: 1988- 55.03; 1989- 55.3, 1991- 52.54, 1992- 56.54, 1994- 53.44, 1995- 52.04, 1996- 51.58, 1997- 50.87, 1998- 50.85, 1999- 51.80, 2000- 49.79, 2001- 51.77. pbs: 60m 7.46i '98, 100m 11.57 '00, 11.32w '97, 11.2wA '98; 200m 22.96i/22.90w '97, 23.08 '00; 300m 35.71 '00, 800m 2:09.44 '01.
Confirmed a leap forward into top world class at the Sydney Olympics, where she reduced her personal best from 50.85 to 50.77 in the quarter-final, 50.21 in the semi and 49.79 in the final of the 400m. Injured for much of 2001

Ashia HANSEN b. 5 Dec 1971 Evansville, Indiana, USA 1.70m 63kg. Shaftesbury Barnet.
At TJ: OG: '96- 4, '00- 11; WCh: '95- dnq 21, '97- 5, '99- 12, '01- 7; EC: '94- dnq 15; CG: '98- 1; WI: '97- 2, '99- 1; EI: '98- 1, '02- 1; ECp: '95-6-7-9: 1/1/3/2. Won GP 1997, 1999; AAA 1996, 2001; UK 1997.
Records: 10 UK & Commonwealth triple jump 1994-7 and 1 unratified (no wind gauge) 1994. WIR 1998, 9 UK & Commonwealth indoor 1994-8.
Progression at TJ: 1990- 10.84, 1991- 12.68, 1992- 13.31, 1993- 13.48i/13.25/13.55w, 1994- 14.22, 1995- 14.66, 1996- 14.78, 1997- 15.15, 1998- 15.16i/14.32, 1999- 15.02i/14.96, 2000- 14.29, 2001- 14.51. 2002- 14.71i. pbs: 60m 7.51i '98, 100m 11.7 '95, 11.95 '96, 11.81w '94; 200m 24.57i '95, 25.1 '92; LJ 6.47A '96.
Born in the USA, original name Ashia Nana Koramdina, she was adopted at three months by an English woman and her Ghanaian husband, They lived in Ghana for six years before settling in London.

Kelly HOLMES b. 19 Apr 1970 Pembury, Kent 1.64m 55kg. Middlesex Ladies.
At 1500m (800m): OG: '96- 11 (4), '00- 7 (3); WCh: '93- (sf), '95- 2 (3), '97- h, '99- (sf), '01- (6); EC: '94- 2; CG: '94- 1, '98- 2; WCp: '94- 3; ECp: '94- 2, '95- 1, '96- (2), '97- 1. 2nd GP 800m 1995 and 2001. Won UK 800m 1993, 1995, 1997; AAA 800m 1993, 1995-6, 1999-2001; 1500m 1994, 1996. Commonwealth 1500m record 1997. UK records 800m (2) 1995, 1000m 1995 & 1997.
Progression at 800m, 1500m: 1984- 2:15.1, 4:35.3; 1985- 2:13.1, 4:41.4; 1986- 2:11.0, 4:26.9; 1987- 2:09.45, 4:26.10; 1989- 2:12.1, 1991- 2:11.8, 1992- 2:03.94, 4:27.7; 1993- 1:58.64, 4:17.3; 1994- 1:59.43, 4:01.41; 1995- 1:56.21, 4:03.04; 1996- 1:57.84, 4:01.13; 1997- 1:57.14, 3:58.07; 1998- 4:06.10; 1999- 1:58.24, 4:04.58; 2000- 1:56.80, 4:05.35; 2001- 1:57.88. pbs: 200m 25.29 '95, 400m 53.8 '96, 1000m 2:32.55 '97, 1M 4:28.04 '98, 3000m 9:08.7 '95, 10km Rd 34:54 '96.
The winner of the English Schools Junior 1500m in 1983, she hardly competed for four years after being a Junior International in 1987, and joining the Army at 18. Ran with a stress fracture of her left leg at the 1996 Olympics and was injured again at the 1997 Worlds. Returned to gain 1998 Commonwealth silver and again in

2000 where she ran wondrously well at the Olympics after a very limited racing programme of just four competitions at 800m during the year. In 1997 she left the Army, for whom she had played at volleyball and been judo champion..

Denise LEWIS b. 27 Aug 1972 West Bromwich 1.73m 64kg. Birchfield H.
At Hep (LJ): OG: '96- 3 (dnq 24), '00- 1; WCh: '95- 7, '97- 2, '99- 2; EC: '94- (dnq 19), '98- 1; CG: '94- 1 (8), '98- 1; EJ: '91- 5; ECp: '94- 12 (5), '95- 1 (8), '96- (4), '97- (4). Won AAA LJ 1996, 1998.
Three UK and two Commonwealth heptathlon records 1996-2000.
Progression at Hep: 1989- 5277, 1990- 5193, 1991- 5484, 1992- 5812, 1993- 5774, 1994- 6325, 1995- 6299, 1996- 6645, 1997- 6736, 1998- 6559, 1999- 6724, 2000- 6831. pbs: 200m 24.10 '97, 24.01w '00; 800m 2:12.20 '00, 60mh 8.30i/8.2i '96, 100mh 13.13 '00, HJ 1.87 '99, LJ 6.69 '00, 6.77w '97; SP 16.12 '99, JT 56.50 '96, new 51.13 '00.
A 5.1m improvement to her javelin pb followed by 2 seconds off her best for 800m gave her a narrow victory at the 1994 Commonwealth Games. Despite missing crucial weeks through injury, won double gold in 1998, and, again with an injury-shortened season, took World silver in 1999 with pbs at HJ and SP, ending just 12 points short of her record score. Despite the recurrence of an Achilles injury, she held on to take the Olympic gold in Sydney, having earlier set five pbs when she added 95 points to her Commonwealth heptathlon record at Talence. In 2001 she was unable to contest the World Championships (or any heptathlon) through injury. She and partner Patrick Stevens (Belgian sprinter) are expecting their first child in April 2002.

Katharine MERRY b. 21 Sep 1974 Dunchurch 1.70m 61kg Birchfield H.
At 400m: OG: '00- 3; WCh: '99- 5. At 200m/4x100mR (100m): OG: '96- qf/8R; WCh: '93- qf; EC: '94- sf/5R; WJ: '90- (8)/2R; '92- 5/4R (6); EJ: '89- 5 (7 100m), '91- 3/2R, '93- 1/1R (2); ECp: '93-4-6-9-01: 6-2-3-8-6, 2 100m & 2R '94. Won UK 200m 1993 & 1997, AAA 100m & 200m 1994, 200m 1998, 400m 1999.
Progression at 200m, 400m: 1987- 25.4, 1988- 24.9, 1989- 23.94/23.54w/23.9, 1990- 23.65, 1991- 23.50/23.41w, 1992- 23.38, 1993- 23.20, 1994- 22.85, 54.0; 1995- 1996- 22.88, 1997- 22.77, 1998- 22.93, 51.01; 1999- 22.83i/22.90, 50.21; 2000- 22.76, 49.72; 2001- 23.12, 49.59. pbs: 60m 7.34i '94, 100m: 11.34/11.27w '94, 300m 36.00 '00, HJ 1.74 '88, LJ 5.55 '87, 6.05w '88.
Has overcome injuries to make a big impression at 400m, but was unable to compete at the 2001 Worlds because of injury. Ran numerous UK age records and still holds the British best at under-13 for 70 and 75m hurdles, high jump and pentathlon and at under-15 for 100m, 200m and pentathlon. In 1989 she won the AAA girls (U15) indoor 60m with a stunning 7.35. Six years as a British junior international, with 11 national age-group titles. Engaged to Olivier-Jean Théodore FRA, who has a 400mh best of 49.21 (2001).

Joanne PAVEY b. 20 Sep 1973 Honiton 1.62m 51kg. née Davis. Bristol.
At 5000m: OG: '00- 12. At 1500m: WCh: '97- sf. Won UK 1500m 1997, AAA 5000m 2001.
Progression at 3000m, 5000m: 1993- 9:56.1, 1996- 9:37.6, 1997- 9:05.87, 1998- 8:58.2, 2000- 8:36.70, 14:58.27; 2001- 8:36.58, 15:00.56. pbs: 800m 2:09.68 '90, 1500m 4:07.28 '97, 1M 4:30.77 '97, 2000m 5:44.0e '00.
Set a British under-15 record at 1500m with 4:27.9 in 1988 and won four national titles at U15/U17 level, but did not compete much in the early 1990s. Missed two years through injury 1998-2000. Married to middle-distance runner Gavin Pavey.

Paula RADCLIFFE b. 17 Dec 1973 Northwich 1.73m 54kg. Bedford & County. Degree in European languages from Loughborough University.
At 10000m: OG: '00- 4; WCh: '99- 2, '01- 4; EC: '98- 5; At 5000m: OG: '96- 5; WCh: '95- 5, '97- 4; ECp: '98-9-01: 1-1-2 (2 1500m '98); 3rd GP 1997. At 3000m: WCh: '93- 7; WJ: '92- 4; EJ: '91- 4; ECp: '97- 3. World HMar: '00- 1, '01- 1; CC: '91- 15J, '92- 1J, '93-5-6-7-8-9-00-01-02: 18/18/19/2/2/3/5 (4 4k)/1 (2 4k)/1. Eur CC: '98- 1. Won AAA 5000m 1996, 2000; UK 1997.
Records: Commonwealth & UK 1998-2001: 3000m (2), 5000m (2), 10000m (4); UK 5000m (4) 1996-2001. European half marathon 2000 & 2001.
Progression at 1500m, 3000m, 5000m, 10000m: 1988- 4:41.0, 1989- 4:34.9, 1990- 4:31.3, 9:41.4; 1991- 4:23.68, 9:23.29; 1992- 4:16.82, 8:51.78, 16:16.77i; 1993- 4:11.6, 8:40.40; 1994- 4:23.84, 1995- 4:06.84, 8:40.82, 14:49.27; 1996- 4:08.42, 8:37.07, 14:46.76; 1997- 4:06.93, 8:35.28, 14:45.51; 1998- 4:05.81, 8:38.84, 14:51.27, 30:48.58; 1999- 4:06.71, 8:27.40, 14:43.54, 30:27.13; 2000- 4:11.45, 8:28.85, 14:44.36, 30:26.97; 2001- 4:05.37, 8:26.96, 14:32.44, 30:55.80. pbs: 400m 58.9 '92, 800m 2:05.22 '95, 1000m 2:47.17 '93, 1M 4:24.94 '96, 2000m 5:39.20 '93, 2M 9:27.5e (1998), 9:32.07 (1999); Road: 15km 47:44 '01, HMar 66:47 '01.
Fastest ever track debut for 10,000m when 2nd in 1998 European Challenge, 30:48.58. She improved this Commonwealth record to 30:40.70 to win this race in 1999 and in Seville to 30:27.13. There, forcing the pace throughout, despite searing heat; she was passed on the last lap by Gete Wami, but won a glorious silver medal. She set an even faster pace at the 2000 Olympics, but was outkicked and finished fourth. Followed that with brilliant form on the roads, including European half marathon record to win Great North Run and then the World Half marathon title by a margin of 33 seconds. Won 5th Avenue Mile 1996 & 1997.
Her great aunt Charlotte Radcliffe won an

Olympic swimming silver medal at 4x100m freestyle relay in 1920. Married 3:34.76 1500 man Gary Lough on 15 April 2000 but continues to race under her maiden name.

Lorraine SHAW b. 2 Apr 1968 Gloucester 1.70m 87kg. Sale H Manchester.
At HT: OG: '00- 9; WCh: '01- 6; EC: '98- 11; CG: '98- 2; ECp: '98-9-00-01: 5/6/4/3. Won UK 1993, AAA 1994, 1998, 2000-01. At DT: CG: '94- 10. Won Irish DT 1990-2, HT 1992.
15 British hammer records 1994-2001, Commonwealth records 1995 and 2000.
Progression at HT: 1991- 35.52, 1992- 44.40/ 45.24lt, 1993- 56.56, 1994- 59.94, 1995- 64.90, 1996- 61.34, 1998- 63.30, 1999- 67.10, 2000- 67.44, 2001- 68.15. pbs: SP 14.21 '94, DT 55.04 '94.
Having competed for Ireland at discus in 1992, opted for British nationality in 1993. Had a disc removed from her back and missed nearly two years of competition before return in April 1998.

USA

Governing body: USA Track and Field, P.O. Box 120, Indianapolis, Indiana 46206-0120. Founded 1979, when it replaced the AAU (founded 1888) as the governing body.
National Championships first held in 1876 (men), 1923 (women). **2001 Champions**: **Men**: 100m: Tim Montgomery 9.95w, 200m: Shawn Crawford 20.54, 400m: Antonio Pettigrew 45.08, 800m: David Krummenacker 1:47.40, 1500m: Andy Downin 3:37.63, 5000m: Bob Kennedy 13:28.72, 10000m: Abdi Abdirahman 28:23.82, HMar: Dan Browne 63:55, Mar: Scott Larsen 2:15:26, 3000mSt: Thomas Chorny 8:22.16, 110mh: Allen Johnson 13.22, 400mh: Angelo Taylor 48.53, HJ: Nathan Leeper 2.30, PV: Lawrence Johnson 5.85, LJ: Savante Stringfellow 8.47w, TJ: LaMark Carter 17.17, SP: John Godina 21.60, DT: Adam Setliff 66.85, HT: Kevin McMahon 76.52, JT: Breaux Greer 85.23, Dec: Kip Janvrin 8241, 20kmW: Curt Clausen 1:24:50, 50kmW: Philip Dunn 3:57:18. **Women**: 100m: Chryste Gaines 10.89w, 200m: Marion Jones 22.52, 400m: LaTasha Colander-Richardson 50.79, 800m/1500m: Regina Jacobs 2:00.43/4:06.12, 5000m: Marla Runyan 15:08.03, 10000m/Mar: Deena Drossin 32:05.14/ 2:26:58, HMar: Milena Glusac 72:13, 3000mSt: Lisa Nye 9:49.41, 100mh: Gail Devers 12.91, 400mh: Sandra Glover 55.08, HJ: Amy Acuff 1.88, PV: Stacy Dragila 4.62, LJ: Jenny Adams 6.71w, TJ: Tiombé Hurd 14.04, SP/DT: Seilala Sua 17.97/63.35, HT: Dawn Ellerbe 69.08, JT: Kim Kreiner 55.76, Hep: DeDee Nathan 6174w, 10kmW: Debbie Lawrence 46:48, 20kmW: Michelle Rohl 1:32:49.
NCAA Championships first held in 1921 (men), 1982 (women). **2001 champions**: **Men**: 100m/ 200m: Justin Gatlin 10.08/20.11w, 400m: Avard Moncur BAH 44.84, 800m: Otukile Lekote BOT 1:46.68, 1500m: Bryan Berryhill 3:37.05, 5000m: Jonathon Riley 13:42.51, 10000m: Ryan Shay 29:05.44, 3000mSt: Daniel Lincoln 8:42.31, 110mh: Ron Bramlett 13.54w, 400mh: Bayano Kamani 48.99, HJ: Charles Clinger 2.30, PV: Denis Kholev ISR 5.65, LJ: Savante Stringfellow 8.27, TJ: Walter Davis 16.56w, SP: Janus Robberts RSA 21.97, DT: Tolga Köseoglu GER 62.43, HT: Andras Haklits CRO 75.50, JT: John Stiegeler 77.07, Dec: Santiago Lorenzo ARG 7889. **Women**: 100m: Angela Williams 11.05w, 200m/LJ: Brianna Glenn 22.92w/6.56w, 400m: Allison Beckford JAM, 800m: Brigita Langerholc SLO 2:01.61, 1500m: Mary Jayne Harrelson 4:14.30, 5000m: Lauren Fleshman 15:52.21, 10000m: Amy Yoder-Begley 33:59.96, 3000mSt: Elizabeth Jackson 9:49.73, 100mh: Donica Merriman 12.73w, 400mh: Brenda Taylor 55.88, HJ: Dóra Györffy HUN 1.90, PV: Andrea Dutoit 4.20, TJ: Shelly-Ann Gallimore JAM 13.29, SP: Christina Tolson 17.39, DT: Katja Schreiber GER 60.32, HT: Florence Ezeh FRA 66.85, JT: AInga Stasiulionyté LTU 52.52, Hep: Austra Skujyte LTU 5857.

Dominique ARNOLD b. 14 Sep 1973 Long Beach, California 1.85m 76kg. Nike. Was at Washington State University.
At 110mh: PAm: '99- 4. 3rd GP 2001. Won NCAA 1996.
Progression at 110mh: 1992- 14.55, 1993- 14.17, 1995- 14.00, 1996- 13.46/13.32w, 1998- 13.54/13.5/ 13.48w, 1999- 13.21/13.2, 2000- 13.11, 2001- 13.14. pbs: 55mh 7.15i '98, 60mh 7.51i '00.

Charles AUSTIN b. 19 Dec 1967 Bay City, Texas 1.84m 77kg. Was at Southwest Texas State University.
At HJ: OG: '92- 8=, '96- 1, '00- dnq 20; WCh: '91- 1, '95- dnq 13=, '97- dnq 13, '99- 8=, '01- 10=; WI: '91- 6=, '97- 1, '99- 3; WCp: '98- 1. Won NCAA 1990, US 1995-2000. US high jump record 1991.
Progression at HJ: 1986- 2.11, 1987- 2.16, 1988- 2.19, 1989- 2.27, 1990- 2.35, 1991- 2.40, 1992- 2.33i/2.32, 1993- 2.35i, 1994- 2.32, 1995- 2.34i/ 2.33, 1996- 2.39, 1997- 2.35i/2.32, 1998- 2.33, 1999- 2.33i/2.32, 2000- 2.32, 2001- 2.31i/2.30. pb TJ 14.91i '90.
Decline after 1991 world title due to right knee injury, which was operated on in July 1993. Made slow recovery, climaxed by Olympic victory in Atlanta with his best jump for five years. His older brother Russell ran on 4x100m team that set a world Masters record in 1992.

Andy BLOOM b. 11 Aug 1973 Stamford, Ct. 1.85m 125kg. Nike. Was at Wake Forest University.
At SP (/DT): OG: '00- 4; WCh: '97- (dnq 16), '99- 4/nt, '01- (dnq 23); WJ: '92- 9/6; WI: '99- 9; WUG: '97- (2), '99- 1/2. Won GP SP 2000, NCAA SP & DT 1996.
Progression at SP, DT: 1991- 16.44, 48.66; 1992- 17.52, 53.50; 1993- 18.21, 55.34; 1994- 18.31, 54.28; 1995- 18.56, 63.48; 1996- 19.82, 64.86; 1997- 20.19i/ 19.96, 65.30; 1998- 20.45, 66.42; 1999- 21.27, 67.46;

2000- 21.82, 68.46; 2001- 20.94, 66.17.
Second best ever SP/DT combination thrower (after John Godina).

Ron BRAMLETT b. 22 Oct 1979 1.81m 68kg. University of Alabama, formerly Middle Tennessee State.
At 110mh: WUG: '01-4; NCAA champion 2001.
Progression at 110mh: 1998- 14.01/13.93w, 1999- 13.72, 2000- 13.47, 2001- 14.43/13.38w. pbs: 55mh 7.03i '02, 60mh 7.52i '02.

Leonard BYRD b. 17 Mar 1975 Fort Rocker, Alabama 1.78m 64kg. Nike. Was at University of Texas – San Antonio.
At 400m/400mR: WCh: '01- sf/1R; WI: '01- 2R; WUG: '95- 1R.
Progression at 400m: 1993- 46.75, 1994- 45.46A/ 45.70, 1995- 45.24, 1996- 44.88, 1997- 45.63, 1998- 45.62, 1999- 45.33, 2000- 45.00, 2001- 44.83.

Milton CAMPBELL b. 15 May 1976 Atlanta 1.78m 75kg. Adidas. Was at University of North Carolina.
At 400m: WI: '99- 2/1R, '01- 2/2R; WJ: '94- 1R.
Progression at 400m: 1993- 47.17, 1994- 46.09, 1995- 45.84, 1996- 45.29, 1997- 44.67, 1998- 45.04, 1999- 45.02, 2000- 45.37, 2001- 45.3/45.39. pb 200m 20.56i/20.66 '98.

James CARTER b. 7 May 1978 Baltimore 1.85m 77kg. Nike. Was at Hampton College.
At 400mh: OG: 00- 4; WCh: '01- sf.
Progression at 400mh: 1998- 50.17, 1999- 49.45, 2000- 48.04, 2001- 48.44. pbs: 400m 46.21 '01, LJ 7.25 '99.

LaMark CARTER b. 23 Aug 1970 Shreveport, Louisiana 1.80m 75kg. Nike. Graduate (now assistant track coach) of Northwestern Louisiana University.
At TJ: OG: '00- dnq 19; WCh: '95- dnq 18, '99- 6, '01- dnq 14; PAm: '95- 4, '99- 2; WI: '95- 6, '99- 2; WUG: '95- 3; WCp: '98- 5. US champion 1998-9, 2001.
Progression at TJ: 1987- 13.91, 1988- 15.06, 1989- 15.58, 1991- 15.98/16.07w, 1992- 16.68, 1993- 16.78/16.83w, 1994- 16.94, 1995- 16.92i/16.77, 1996- 17.12i/17.06, 1997- 17.06i/16.76/17.15w, 1998- 17.44, 1999- 17.10/17.15w, 2000- 16.96/ 16.97w, 2001- 17.17. pb LJ 7.98 '96.

Curt CLAUSEN b. 9 Oct 1967 Trenton, New Jersey 1.86m 71kg. NYAC. Graduate of Duke University.
At 50kmW: OG: '00- 22; WCh: '99- 3, '01- 7; WCp: '99- 11. At 20kmW: OG: '96- 50; WCh: '97- 34; PAm: '99- 6. At 10000mW: WJ: '86- 28. Won US 20kmW 1996-7, 1999, 2001; 50kmW 1999- 2000, 2002.
US records 50km walk (2) 1999, 20000m (1:23:55.8) 30000m & 2 hours track 2000.
Progression at 50kmW: 1988- 4:27:25, 1990- 4:28:27, 1998- 3:57:24, 1999- 3:48:04, 2000- 3:56:16, 2001- 3:50:46. pbs: 3000mW 11:22.55i '99, 5000mW 19:35.20 '99, 20kmW 1:23:34 '99, 30000mW 2:11:00.4 '00, 2HrW 27,360m '00.
Having tried the distance ten years earlier, Clausen did not return to the 50km walk until 1998, and swiftly evolved from a fringe international contender to world class. He finished fourth at the 1999 World Championships, but two years later the winner German Skurygin (Rus) received a two-year ban from a positive drugs test in Seville, and Clausen took bronze.

Ramon CLAY b. 29 Jun 1975 Memphis 1.86m 77kg. Asics, Was at Norfolk State University.
At 200m: WCh: '01- qf. 400m/4x400mR: WJ: '94- 2/1R.
Progression at 200m, 400m: 1993- 21.30/21.0w, 1994- 21.48/21.1, 45.82; 1995- 20.81/20.36w, 45.48; 1996- 20.08/19.99w, 1997- 20.49, 1998- 20.06/20.0A, 1999- 20.26, 2000- 20.30, 2001- 20.05. pbs: 60m 6.20i '97, 100m 10.25 '01, 400m 45.48 '95.
Suffered hamstring injury at 2001 Worlds.

Charles CLINGER b. 28 Dec 1976 Jackson Hole, Wyoming 2.06m 100kg. Weber State University, Previously Bosie State.
At HJ: WCh: '99- dnq 27=; PAm: '99- 3; NCAA champion 2001.
Progression at HJ: 1995- 2.13, 1996- 2.16i, 1999- 2.29A, 2000- 2.31A, 2001- 2.35A. pbs: LJ 7.62i '01, 7.58 '00; TJ 16.24i '01, 16.10 '00.
Went on church mission to Australia 1997-8.

Shawn CRAWFORD b. 14 Jan 1978 Van Wyck, SC 1.81m 75kg. Mizuno. Was at Clemson Univ.
At 200m: WCh: '01- 3=; WI: '01- 1; Won US, GWG & GP 2001, NCAA 2000.
Progression at 100m, 200m: 1996- 10.62, 1997- 10.51w, 20.83; 1998- 10.34/10.15w, 20.44A/20.12w; 1999- 20.39, 2000- 10.16, 20.09; 2001- 10.09, 20.17. pbs: 60m 6.49i '02, 100m 10.16 '00, 10.15w '98.
US indoor record 20.26 to win NCAA indoor 200m 2000.

Mark CREAR b. 2 Oct 1968 San Francisco 1.86m 79kg. Godwin. Sociology degree from University of Southern California.
At 110mh: OG: '96- 2, '00- 3; WCh: '93- sf, '97- 7, '99- qf. Won GP 110mh 1995, 1997, 1999; 3rd overall 1995, 1997; NCAA champion 1992, US 1994, 1999; GWG 1998.
Progression at 110mh: 1990- 13.65/13.51w, 1992- 13.33, 1993- 13.26/13.22w/12.9w, 1994- 13.07, 1995- 13.02, 1996- 13.05, 1997- 13.03, 1998- 13.00, 1999- 12.98, 2000- 13.11/13.10w, 2001- 13.26. pbs: 50mh 6.41Ai '95, 55mh 7.18i '94, 60mh 7.38i '98.
Ordained as a minister after finishing his Masters degree in theology. World's top high hurdler of 1995, but he went out in the semi-finals of the US Champs. Disqualified for two false starts in his quarter-final at the Worlds, but ranked no.1 in the world on his overall record in 1999. Formerly married to Keisha Marvin (2nd 1994 NCAA 400mh in pb 56.62).

Calvin DAVIS b. 2 Apr 1972 Eutan, Alabama 1.83m 79kg. Adidas. Was at Univ. of Arkansas.
At 400mh: OG: '96- 3; WCh: '01- sf. At 400m/4x400m: WI: '95- 6/1R.
Progression at 400m: 1989- 47.51, 1992- 45.85, 1993- 45.04, 1994- 45.20, 1995- 45.94, 1996- 45.06, 1997- 46.14i, 1998- 46.31i/46.68, 2001- 46.62. At 400mh: 1996- 47.91, 1997- 48.75, 1998- 48.57, 1999- 48.33, 2000- 48.92, 2001- 48.75.
Made his debut at 400mh in 1996 and was 3rd in the US Trials in his 7th race at the event – progressing to Olympic bronze.

Walter DAVIS b. 2 Jul 1979 LaFayette, Louisiana 1.88m 83kg. Student at Louisiana State Univ..
At TJ: OG: '00- 11; WCh: '01- 5. Won NCAA 2001.
Progression at LJ, TJ: 1997- 15.67, 1998- 15.29w, 1999- 7.88i/7.70, 16.38/16.47w; 2000- 8.16, 17.07/17.08w, 2001- 8.14i/8.13/8.19w, 17.22. pb 200m 20.98 '96, 20.87w '95, 20.6w '94.
Formerly a basketball player.

Kevin DILWORTH b. 14 Feb 1974 Jacksonville, Texas 1.80m 76kg. Adidas, Was at Abilene Christian University.
At LJ: WCh: '97- 8, '99- 8; WI: '01- 6. US champion 1999.
Progression at LJ: 1992- 7.52/7.73w, 1993- 7.66/7.87w, 1994- 7.73; 1995- 7.83/7.90w; 1996- 8.47, 1997- 8.29, 1998- 8.30, 1999- 8.09/8.12w, 2000- 8.28, 2001- 8.30. pb 200m 20.98 '96, 20.87w '95, 20.6w '94.

Jon DRUMMOND b. 9 Sep 1968 Philadelphia 1.75m 75kg. Nike. Was at Texas Christian University.
At 200m/4x100mR (100m): OG: '96- 2R (sf), '00- 1R (5); WCh: '93- 1R, '95- hR, '97- 7, '99- 1R. '01- 1R (res); WUG: '91- 1/1R. Won US 200m 1997. 3rd GP 100m 1994, 200m 1997. At 60m: WI: '93- 4. World record 4x100m relay 1993.
Progression at 100m, 200m: 1986- 10.5; 1987- 10.28/10.23w, 20.64; 1988- 10.25/10.0w, 20.79i; 1989- 10.21, 20.82; 1990- 10.10, 1991- 10.19/10.03w, 20.58; 1992- 10.12, 20.37; 1993- 10.03/9.92w, 21.05i; 1994- 9.99; 1995- 10.10/10.08w, 20.49/20.10w; 1996- 9.98, 20.05; 1997- 9.92, 20.03; 1998- 9.94, 20.15; 1999- 10.04, 20.29/20.24w; 2000- 9.96, 20.17; 2001- 10.09/10.04w, 20.44. pbs: 50m 5.63i '99, 55m 6.14i '90, 60m 6.46i '98, 100y 9.33 '94, 400m 45.55 '00.
Self-styled 'Crown Prince of Track'. Sings with the gospel group 'Kirk Franklin & The Family'; their first album reached No.1 on the *Billboard* gospel chart in 1993. Returned from viral meningitis to run 5th at 100m and 6th at 200m at US Champs in 1999, qualifying for World team where he ran first leg on gold medal-winning sprint relay team.

Justin GATLIN b. 10 Feb 1982 1.85m 79kg. Student at University of Tennessee.
Won NCAA 100m & 200m 2001 (60m/200m i '02)
Progression at 100m, 200m: 2000- 10.36, 2001- 10.08, 20.09/19.86w. pbs: 60m 6.54i '02, 110mh 13.78/13.74w '01.
Top hurdler in high school (110mh 13.66 and 300mh 36.74 on junior hurdles), now concentrating on sprints. He became the first man ever to win three events at the US Junior Championships wiuh 100m/200m/110mh in 2001.

John GODINA b. 31 May 1972 Fort Sill, Oklahoma 1.93m 129kg. Adidas. Studied biology at UCLA.
At SP/DT: OG: '96- 2/dnq 14, '00- 3/dnq 17; WCh: '95- 1/10, '97- 1/5, '99- 7/dnq 16, '01- 1/dnq 21; WI: '97- 3, '99- 2, '01- 1; WCp: '98- 1/4. Won GP SP 1996 (3rd 2000), 3rd DT 1997. Won US SP 1998-9, 2001; DT 1997-8, NCAA SP 1995, DT 1994-5, PAm-J SP & DT 1991; GWG SP 1998.
Progression at SP, DT: 1990- 53.58, 1991- 17.75, 58.60; 1992- 19.68, 61.52; 1993- 20.03, 60.48; 1994- 20.03, 62.24; 1995- 22.00, 64.92; 1996- 21.25, 64.58; 1997- 21.75, 67.40; 1998- 21.78, 69.91; 1999- 22.02, 69.05; 2000- 21.51, 68.32; 2001- 21.95, 67.66.
Undefeated in 24 shot competitions July 1997 to February 1999. Only 4th in the US trials shot in 1997, but gained World Championships place with a 'wild card' entry for a defending champion; came second but took gold after the disqualification of Aleksandr Bagach. He achieved the best ever one day SP-DT doubles with 21.78 and 66.47 at Mt SAC and 21.58 and 69.91 at Salinas in 1998. He stepped into the US Olympic shot team after the withdrawal of CJ Hunter in 2000 and took bronze.

Maurice GREENE b. 23 Jul 1974 Kansas City, Kansas 1.76m 75kg. Nike.
At 100m(/200m)/4x100mR: OG: '00- 1/1R; WCh: '95- qf, '97- 1, '99- 1/1/1R, '01- 1; Won US 100m 1997, 1999-2000; 200m 1999; GWG 100m 1998. 2nd GP 200m 1999. At 60m: WI: '95- 4, '99- 1. World 100m record 1999; three world indoor 60m records 1998-2001.
Progression at 100m, 200m: 1993- 10.43, 21.00; 1995- 10.19/9.88w, 1996- 10.08, 1997- 9.86, 19.86; 1998- 9.90/9.79w, 20.03/19.88w; 1999- 9.79, 19.90; 2000- 9.86, 20.02/19.93w, 2001- 9.82. pbs: 50m 5.55+ '97, 55m 6.15i '96, 60m 6.39i/6.39+ '98.
Moved from Kansas to train with John Smith in Los Angeles in September 1996. In 1997 ran 100m in 9.90 to win US Champs and twice in Athens before 9.86 to win World 100m title. Took 0.05 off world record for 100m at Athens in June 1999, and went on the confirm his place as world's fastest man with World Champs treble (the first man to win 100m and 200m at World Champs). Despite hobbling at the finish, he ran 9.82 to win the 2001 world title at 100m with a wind of –0.2. His elder brother Ernest was a former US junior college champion at 200m (20.60 '92).

Breaux GREER b. 19 Oct 1976 Houston 1.88m 102kg. New York AC. Was at Northeast

Louisiana University.
At JT: OG: '00- 12; WCh: '01- 4. Won US 2000-01.
Progression at JT: 1995- 70.92, 1996- 79.98, 1997- 78.12, 1998- 79.68, 2000- 82.63, 2001- 87.00.
Set five pbs in 2001, including to win US title (85.23) and in first round of World final.

Tim HARDEN b. 27 Jan 1974 Kansas City, Missouri 1.78m 77kg. Nike. Was at Univ. of Kentucky.
At 100m/4x100mR: OG: '96- 1R; WCh: '99- 5; PAm: '99- 4; WCp: '98- 4/2R. 2nd PAm-J 1993. Won US 100m 1998, NCAA 1995 (2nd 1994, 1996). At 60m: WI: '99- 2, '01- 1.
Progression at 100m: 1992- 10.3/10.2w, 1993- 10.32, 1994- 10.14/10.03w, 1995- 10.05, 1996- 10.02/9.94w, 1997- 10.26, 1998- 10.03A/10.09/ 9.88w, 1999- 9.92, 2000- 10.20, 2001- 10.14. pbs: 50m 5.60+ '99, 55m 6.06i '95, 60m 6.43i '99, 200m 20.54/20.38w '94.
Won US indoor 60m 1998 but then stripped of title and given public warning for doping violation (ephedrine). He won this title in 1999 in a pb 6.44 ahead of Maurice Greene and improved to third fastest of all-time at 60m when 2nd to Greene in Maebashi.

Alvin HARRISON b. 20 Jan 1974 Orlando, Florida 1.88m 80kg. Nike.
At 400m/4x400mR: OG: '96- 4/1R, '00- 2/1R; PAm: '99- 3R; PAm-J: '93- 3/1R.
Progression at 400m: 1993- 46.25, 1996- 44.09, 1997- 45.37, 1998- 44.19, 1999- 45.17, 2000- 44.18, 2002- 44.75. pbs: 100m 10.52 '99, 200m 20.41 '96, 300m 32.00 '96.
The twins Alvin and Calvin, who both ran at the Pam Juniors in 1993, were homeless in 1995 and sleeping in an old Ford Mustang. Returning to the sport in 1996 Alvin made a huge breakthrough when he ran sub-45 seconds for the first time at the 1996 US Trials – running successively 44.93, 44.66, 44.43 and 44.09 in the four rounds.

Calvin HARRISON b. 20 Jan 1974 Orlando, Florida 1.86m 75kg. Nike.
At 400m/4x400mR: OG: '00- 1R; PAm-J: '93- 1/1R.
Progression at 400m: 1993- 45.25/45.07dq, 1994- 46.26, 1996- 44.70, 1997- 45.59, 1998- 44.68A/45.13, 2000- 44.64, 2001- 44.97. pb 200m 20.57 '93.
Tested positive for pseudoephedrine at 1993 US Junior Championships in 45.07. Dropped out of school, Hartnell Junior College, Salinas, in 1994 and returned to Florida. Came back to California and to the sport in 1996.

Jeff HARTWIG b. 25 Sep 1967 St Louis 1.90m 82kg. Nike. Was at Arkansas State University.
At PV: OG: '96- 11=; WCh: '99- dnq 14=; WI: '99- 2; WCp: '98- 3. Won GWG 1998, US 1998-9. 2nd GP 1999. Four US pole vault records 1998-2000.
Progression at PV: 1983- 3.35, 1984- 3.81, 1985- 4.42, 1986- 4.57, 1987- 4.90, 1988- 5.10, 1989- 5.34, 1990- 5.40i/5.35, 1991- 5.35, 1992- 5.60i/5.50, 1993- 5,35, 1994- 5.63, 1995- 5.72, 1996- 5.80, 1997- 5.85, 1998- 6.01, 1999- 6.02, 2000- 6.03, 2001- 5.90, 2002- 6.02i.
The first 6m-vaulter from the USA, Hartwig is also a snake rancher, with a herd of pythons and boa constrictors. Clearly headed world rankings in 2000, but failed to clear his opening height in the qualifying round of the US Trials, when he had problems with his eyes.

Tye HARVEY b. 25 Sep 1974 1.86m 73kg. New Balance. Was at University of Minnesota.
At PV: WI: '01- 2
Progression at PV: 1992- 4.87, 1993- 5.21, 1994- 5.10, 1995- 5.35, 1996- 5.20, 1997- 5.55i/5.52, 1998- 5.47, 1999- 5.67, 2000- 5.80, 2001- 5.93i/5.80.

Ja'Warren HOOKER b. 24 Sep 1978 1.83m 77kg. Student at University of Washington.
Won 100m & 4x100m PAm-J 1997.
Progression at 200m, 400m: 1996- 47.77, 1997- 21.02, 46.23; 1998- 20.54, 46.42; 1999- 20.48A, 2000- 20.23A/20.33, 44.78; 2001- 20.56i/20.57/20.33w, 45.79. pbs: 55m 6.09A '98, 6.12i '01; 60m 6.51A/6.57i '01, 100m 10.18 '98.

Nick HYSONG b. 9 Dec 1971 Winslow, Arizona 1.83m 77kg. Nike. Marketing degree from Arizona State University.
At PV: OG: '00- 1; WCh: '99- 4=, '01- 3; WJ: '90- 6; WI: '95- 5=, '99- 8. Won NCAA 1994. 2nd GP 2000.
Progression at PV: 1989- 4.87, 1990- 5.30, 1991- 5.45, 1992- 5.52, 1993- 5.57i/5.50, 1994- 5.70, 1995- 5.85i/5.70, 1996- 5.71A, 1997- 5.67A, 1998- 5.70, 1999- 5.85i/5.80, 2000- 5.90, 2001- 5.85.

Allen JOHNSON b. 1 Mar 1971 Washington DC 1.78m 70kg. Nike. Was at University of North Carolina.
At 110mh: OG: '96- 1, '00- 4; WCh: '95- 1, '97- 1, '99- sf, '01- 1; WCp: '94- 2, '98- 2R; 2nd GP 1995 & 2001. Won GWG 2001, US 1996-7, 2000-01. At 60mh: WI: '95- 1.
US 110mh record 1996.
Progression at 110mh: 1991- 14.11, 1992- 13.63, 1993- 13.47/13.34w, 1994- 13.25/13.23Aw, 1995- 12.98, 1996- 12.92, 1997- 12.93, 1998- 12.98, 1999- 13.01, 2000- 12.97, 2001- 13.04. pbs: 60m 6.62i '98, 100m 10.41/10.10w '99, 200m 20.26 '97, 400m 48.27 '96, 50mh 6.47i '95, 55mh 7.03i '94, 60mh 7.38i '95, 400mh 52.00 '91, HJ 2.11 '89, LJ 8.14i/7.91w '93, 7.85 '91; TJ 14.83 '89.
Having leapt into world class in 1994, on 8 Feb 1995 in Madrid he ended Colin Jackson's string of 44 sprint hurdles victories. He went on to win world titles indoors and out, adding Olympic gold in 1996, when he missed the world record by just 0.01 at the US Trials, and another world gold in 1997. Had to withdraw from the 1999 World semis through injury, but came back to take his third title in 2001.

Curtis JOHNSON b. 24 Dec 1973 1.80m 80kg. Nike.
At 100m: OG: '00- sf; WJ: '90- sf, '92- sf/2R.

Progression at 100m: 1988- 10.64, 1989- 10.55, 1990- 10.27/10.25w, 1991- 10.24, 1992- 10.40/ 10.36w, 1993- 10.38, 1994- 10.59, 1995- 10.53/ 10.40w, 1997- 10.42/10.32w, 1998- 10.37, 1999- 10.09, 2000- 10.07, 2001- 10.10/10.00w. pbs: 55m 6.14i '00, 200m 20.78 '95.
Withdrew from 2001 World 100m when he felt a hamstring twinge in warming up..

Joshua J JOHNSON b. 10 May 1976 1.91m 91kg. Pioneer TC.
At 4x100mR: OG: '00- res (1)R.
Progression at 100m, 200m: 2000- 10.24/10.19w, 20.60; 2001- 10.22/10.11w, 19.88. pb 60m 6.55i '02.
Played basketball at Oklahoma Panhandle State University and after failing to make professional leagues joined IBM. He approached coach Nicholson Scott of the Pioneer Track Club in Arlington, Texas and said he wanted to become a professional sprinter. He trained with Scott for the next year and in 2000 was 7th in US 100m and ran in heats of World Champs. Made a sensational improvement from 20.48 to 19.88 at Brussels.

Lawrence JOHNSON b. 7 May 1974 Norfolk, Virginia 1.85m 86kg. Adidas. Was at University of Tennessee. Pianist and composer.
At PV: OG: '96- 8, '00- 2; WCh: '97- dnq; WI: '97- 2, '01- 1; WUG: '95- 2. US champion 1996-7, 2000-01; NCAA 1995-6. PAm-J 1993.
US pole vault record 1996.
Progression at PV: 1991- 4.87, 1992- 5.33, 1993- 5.71, 1994- 5.83i/5.80, 1995- 5.70, 1996- 5.98, 1997- 5.90, 1998- 5.80, 1999- 5.85, 2000- 5.90, 2000- 5.96i/ 5.90. pbs: 400m 49.55 '93, 110mh 14.60 '93, HJ 1.99 '93, Dec 7576 '93.
Broke an ankle in a motorcycle accident in 1999. Had to withdraw from 2001 Worlds team due to tress fracture of the right fibula.

Bob KENNEDY b. 18 Aug 1970 Bloomington, Indiana 1.83m 66kg. Nike. Was at Indiana University.
At 5000m: OG: '92- 12, '96- 6; WCh: '91- 12, '93- h, '95- 7, '97- 6, '99- 9. At 3000m: WI: '93- 4. World CC: '95-98-01: 14/16/12. Won US 5000m 1995-7, 2001; CC 1992, PAm-J 1500m 1989, NCAA CC 1988, 1992; 1500m 1990.
US records 3000m (4) 1994-8, 2M 1997, 5000m (2) 1996.
Progression at 5000m: 1989- 14:21.40, 1990- 13:42.80, 1991- 13:22.17, 1992- 13:28.18, 1993- 13:14.91, 1994- 13:02.93, 1995- 13:03.37, 1996- 12:58.21, 1997- 13:06.62, 1998- 13:03.57, 1999- 13:05.54, 2000- 13:42.15, 2001- 13:17.51. pbs: 800m 1:53.44 '89, 1500m 3:38.32 '91, 1M 3:56.21 '94, 2000m 4:59.9 '96, 3000m 7:30.84 '98, 2M 8:11.59 '97, 10000m 27:38.37 '99.
Injured in a car accident in May 2000.

Khalid KHANNOUCHI b. 22 Dec 1971 Meknès, Morocc 1.65m 57kg. New Balance.
At Mar: WCh: '01- dnf. At 5000m: WUG: '93- 1. World best for the marathon 1999. World best road 20km 1998 (57:37). Moroccan records HMar and Mar 1997, US marathon record 2000.
Progression at Mar: 1997- 2:07:10, 1998- 2:07:19, 1999- 2:05:42, 2000- 2:07:01. pbs: 3000m 8:01.89i '96, 5000m 13:41.6 '95, 10000m 29:00.8 sh '89; Rd: 5km 13:24 '97, 10km 27:47 '98, 15km 42:57 '98, HMar 60:27 '97.
Won the WUG 5000m in Buffalo, New York, USA. Having felt that he was not appreciated in his home country, he returned to Buffalo a few months later and eventually settled in Brooklyn, becoming a US citizen in 2000. He is coached and managed by his wife Sandra Natal, who originally came from the Dominican Republic. He showed great form at shorter distances on the roads in 1997 before running the fastest ever debut marathon to win at Chicago in 1997, just 20 seconds off the world record. A year later he was second in Chicago and in 1999 returned there to earn $165,000 for his win in a new world best time of 2:05:42. After 3rd in London, won again in Chicago 2000.

Nathan LEEPER b. 13 Jun 1977 Greensburg, Kansas 1.88m 82kg. Nike. Was at Kansas State University.
At HJ: OG: '00- 11; WCh: '00- dnq 14; WI: '01- 4. Won US 2001, NCAA 1998. 2nd GP 2000.
Progression at HJ: 1995- 2.16, 1996- 2.14, 1997- 2.23i/2.21, 1998- 2.30, 2000- 2.35, 2001- 2.33i/2.30, 2002- 2.32i.

Brian LEWIS b. 5 Dec 1974 Sacramento 1.72m 72kg. Was at Norfolk State University.
At 100m/4x100mR: OG: '00- 1R; WCh: '97- hR, 99- sf/1R. US champion 1999.
Progression at 100m, 200m: 1992- 10.59, 21.36; 1993- 10.37w, 21.38/21.13w; 1994- 10.27, 20.70; 1995- 10.24/10.03w, 20.75/20.61w; 1996- 10.03, 20.54, 1997- 10.00, 1998- 10.03/9.98w, 20.40A/ 20.52; 1999- 10.02/10.00w, 20.34; 2000- 10.02/ 9.96w, 20.06r/20.26; 2001- 10.10, 20.42. pbs: 50m 5.66i '02, 60m 6.54i '98.
Led off, but failed to transfer baton to Tim Montgomery in 1997 World Champs relay heat.

Melvin LISTER b. 29 Aug 1977 New York 1.83m 77kg. HSI. University of Arkansas.
At LJ: OG: '00- dnq 25; WI: '01- 5; WJ: '96- 11. Won NCAA LJ 1999, TJ 2000.
Progression at LJ, TJ: 1996- 7.70, 15.65; 1997- 7.86, 1998- 8.05i/7.98w, 16.37i/15.48; 1999- 8.18, 17.02; 2000- 8.49, 16.96; 2001- 8.10i/7.92/8.08w. pbs: 200m 20.51 '00, 400m 45.67 '98.

Kevin LITTLE b. 3 Apr 1968 Des Moines 1.83m 73kg. Nike. Degree in marketing from Drake University.
At 200m: WCh: '95- qf, '97- sf, '99- 6, '01- 7; WI: '89- 3, '93- 3, '97- 1, '99- 3, '01- dns; PAm: '91- 2; WUG: '89- 6
Progression at 200m: 1984- 22.62, 1985- 22.30,

1986- 21.5, 1987- 21.04/20.80w, 1988- 20.55, 1989- 20.37A/20.39, 1990- 20.37, 1991- 20.63/ 20.48w; 1992- 20.33, 1993- 20.56, 1995- 20.60/ 19.94w, 1996- 20.29/20.09w, 1997- 20.24, 1998- 20.49, 1999- 20.10/20.08w, 2000- 20.30, 2001- 20.13. pbs: 55m 6.14Ai '98, 60m 6.64Ai '01, 100m 10.13/10.12w '98, 10.11Aw '92, 400m 44.77 '96.
Severed left Achilles tendon in 1993. Has made nine US World Championship teams at 200m.

Tim MACK b. 15 Sep 1972 Cleveland 1.88m 78kg. Nike. University of Tennessee.
At PV: WCh: '01- 9. Won GWG 2001.
Progression at PV: 1993- 5.31, 1994- 5.52, 1995- 5.60, 1996- 5.65, 1998- 5.70, 1999- 5.70i/5.43, 2000- 5.81, 2001- 5.81, 2002- 5.85i.

Coby MILLER b. 19 Oct 1976 Ackermann, Miss. 1.68m 68kg. Nike. Studied criminal justice at Auburn University.
At 200m/4x100m: OG: '00- 7; WUG: '99- 1/1R.
Progression at 100m, 200m: 1997- 10.24/10.19w, 20.73; 1998- 10.32/10.23w, 20.64; 1999- 10.03, 20.04; 2000- 9.98/9.88w, 19.96; 2001- 20.31i. pbs: 50m 5.70i '01, 55m 6.11i '99, 60m 6.50A/6.52i '99.
Was All-American at both football and track in high school and played football for a year in junior college before concentrating on sprinting.

Tim MONTGOMERY b. 28 Jan 1975 Gaffney, SC 1.78m 69kg. Asics. Was at Norfolk State Univ.
At 100m/4x100m: OG: '96- res (2)R, '00- res (1)R; WCh: '97- 3, '99- 6/1R, '01- 2/1R; US champion 2001, 2nd GP 2000. At 60m: WI: '01- 2.
Progression at 100m: 1992- 10.45w, 1993- 10.61/ 10.3, 1994- 10.11/9.96 irreg, 1995- 10.27/9.95w, 1996- 10.08, 1997- 9.92, 1998- 10.00/9.99w, 1999- 10.01/10.00w, 2000- 10.01/9.96w, 2001- 9.84. pbs: 50m 5.57+ '97, 60m 6.43+ '97, 200m 20.52 '99, 20.44w '97.
Ran 100m in 9.96 to win the Junior Colleges title in 1994; but the wind gauge (+1.7) illegally placed on the outside of the track prevented ratification as world junior record; the track was also reported to have measured 99.96m. Ran in heat and semi on US 4x100m team at 1996 Olympics and in heat in 2000.

Adam NELSON b. 7 Jul 1975 Atlanta 1.81m 115kg. Nike. Was at Dartmouth University. Training as a financial consultant.
At SP: OG: '00- 2; WCh: '01- 2; WI: '01- 2; WJ: '94- 1; WUG: '99- 2. 2nd GP 2000 (3rd overall). Won PAm-J 1993, GWG 2001, NCAA 1997, US 2000.
Progression at SP: 1993- 16.56, 1994- 18.34, 1995- 18.27, 1996- 19.14, 1997- 19.62, 1998- 20.61, 1999- 20.64, 2000- 22.12, 2001- 21.53. pb DT 54.38 '97.
Had a great season in 2000, when he improved his best from 20.64 to 21.70 and then the wortd's longest throw for four years, 22.12 (to take the US title) in July. Small for a shot putter, but very fast and dynamic in the circle. Played American Football at high school and college.

Tom PAPPAS b. 6 Sep 1976 Azalea, Oregon 1.93m 93kg. Adidas. Was at Univ. of Tennessee.
At Dec: OG: '00- 5; WCh: '99- dnf. Won Pam-J 1995, NCAA 1999, US 2000.
Progression at Dec: 1995- 7198, 1996- 7499, 1997- 7677, 1999- 8463, 2000- 8467, 2001- 8323. pbs: 60m 6.93i '02, 100m 10.70 '00, 400m 48.34 '99, 1500m 4:45.10 '00, 60mh 7.94i '02, 110mh 14.00 '99, 13.95w '01; HJ 2.21 '00, PV 5.10 '00, LJ 7.52 '99, SP 15.71i/15.38 '99, DT 48.66 '99, JT 66.12 '00, Hep 6113i '02.
Grandfather was a professional wrestler, father (Nick) set a world motor speed record.

Miguel PATE b. 13 Jun 1979 St Francisville, Louisiana 1.88m 84kg. Studying criminal justice at University of Alabama.
At LJ: WCh: '01- 4; WUG: '01- 1. Won US 2001, NCAA 2000-01.
Progression at LJ: 1998- 7.68/7.73w, 2000- 8.26, 2001- 8.20/8.48w, 2002- 8.59i. pbs: HJ 2.18i '00, TJ 16.48 '01. Won 2002 US indoor title with 8.59.

Antonio PETTIGREW b. 3 Nov 1967 Macon, Georgia 1.83m 76kg. Adidas. Was at St Augustine's College.
At 400m/4x400m relay: OG: '00- 7/1R; WCh: '91- 1/2R, '93- res (1)R, '97- 7/1R, '99- 5/1R, '01- 4/1R; WCp: '89- 5/2R, '92- 4R, '94- 1, '98- 1R. 2nd GP 1994, 3rd 2000. US champion 1989, 1991, 1994, 1997, 2001. World record 4x400m 1998.
Progression at 400m: 1986- 47.19, 1987- 46.31, 1988- 45.36, 1989- 44.27, 1990- 45.26, 1991- 44.36, 1992- 44.71, 1993- 44.45, 1994- 44.43, 1995- 45.74, 1996- 45.19, 1997- 44.23, 1998- 44.40, 1999- 44.21, 2000- 44.57, 2001- 44.99. pbs: 100m 10.42 '94, 200m 20.38 '94, 300m 32.15+ '99.
Ran a 43.1 relay (2nd) leg at 1997 Worlds.

Dwight PHILLIPS b. 1 Oct 1977 Decatur, Georgia 1.81m 82kg. Nike. was at Arizona State University.
At LJ: OG: '00- 8; WCh: '01- 8; PAm: '99- 7. 2nd US and NCAA 2000.
Progression at LJ: 1999- 8.18, 2000- 8.21/8.30w, 2001- 8.13/8.23w. pbs: 60m 6.61Ai '02, 100m 10.28/10.11w '00, 200m 20.68 '02, 400m 47.50 '96, TJ 16.41 '99.

Tom PUKSTYS b. 28 May 1968 Glen Ellyn, Illinois 1.88m 98kg. Adidas. Degree in public relations from University of Florida.
At JT: OG: '92- 10, '96- 8; WCh: '91- dnq 26, '93- 9, '95-7-01 dnq 19/14/20; WCp: '92- 4. US champion 1992-3, 1995, 1997-9.
Six US javelin records 1993-7.
Progression at JT: 1987- 71.34, 1988- 75.72, 1989- 74.82, 1990- 83.30, 1991- 81.68, 1992- 83.20, 1993- 85.70, 1994- 82.32, 1995- 84.50, 1996- 86.82, 1997- 87.12, 1998- 85.06, 1999- 84.11, 2000- 84.25, 2001- 79.48. Of Lithuanian descent, races motorcycles.

Gred SADDLER b. 29 Jun 1974 Sacramento 1.72m 72kg. Nike. Was at Univ. of Mississippi.

At 100m: 3rd GP 2000.
Progression at 100m: 1992- 10.51, 1993- 10.38/10.25w, 1994- 10.20/10.11w, 1997- 10.26, 1998- 10.20/10.10w, 1999- 10.11, 2000- 10.08, 2001- 10.29. pbs: 50m 5.66i '00, 55m 6.11i '94, 60m 6.51i '00, 200m 20.56 '99, 20.46w '98.

Adam SETLIFF b. 15 Dec 1969 El Dorado, Arizona 1.93m 125kg. Nike. Was at University of Washington.
At DT: OG: '96- 12, '00- 5; WCh: '97- 7, '01- 5. 2nd GP 1997. US champion 2000-01.
Progression at DT: 1990- 55.46, 1991- 59.40, 1992- 61.54, 1993- 64.08, 1994- 62.08, 1995- 64.96, 1996- 66.86, 1997- 66.14, 1998- 68.45, 2000- 68.51, 2001- 69.44.
Portrayed Mac Wilkins in Steve Prefontaine movie 1998. Missed 1999 season due to a hernia.

Savanté STRINGFELLOW b. 6 Nov 1978 Jackson, Miss. 1.91m 84kg. New York AC. University of Mississippi.
At LJ: OG: '00- dnq 22; WCh: '99- dnq 39, '01- 2; PAm: '99- 8. 2nd GP 2001. Won US 2001, NCAA 2000-01.
Progression at LJ: 1999- 8.12, 2000- 8.30, 2001- 8.38/8.47w. pbs: 100m 10.43w '01, 200m 20.66 '01, HJ 2.14 '01, 2.18i '98?.

Angelo TAYLOR b. 29 Dec 1978 Albany, Georgia 1.88m 77kg. Nike. Was at Georgia Tech University, plane to enrol at Morris Brown College.
At 400mh/4x400mR: OG: '00- 1/res (1)R; WCh: '99- h/1R, '01- sf/1R; WJ: '96- 3; won GP 2000 (and overall), PAm-J 1997, NCAA 1998, US 1999-2001.
Progression at 400m, 400mh: 1995- -, 52.76, 1996- 46.7, 50.18; 1997- 46.19i/46.81, 48.72; 1998- 45.14, 47.90; 1999- 45.50i, 48.15; 2000- 44.89, 47.50; 2001- 44.68, 47.95. pb 200m 20.67 '97.
Had a brilliant year in 1998, when he ran the fastest ever time by a 19 year-old and lost just twice, on both occasions to Bryan Bronson, at 400mh. Went out in his heat (misjudging the finish) when favourite for the 400mh title at the 1999 Worlds, but made amends with relay gold, and after winning Olympic gold in 2000, met with similar fortune in 2001, when he stumbled off the last hurdle in his 400mh semi. Won US indoor 400m 1999.

Eric THOMAS b. 1 Dec 1973 Carthage, Texas 1.90m 88kg. Nike. Was at Abilene Christian University.
At 400mh: OG: '00- sf; PAm: '99- 2.
Progression at 400mh: 1993- 49.83, 1994- 49.29, 1995- 49.14, 1996- 48.20, 1997- 48.57, 1998- 48.45, 1999- 48.40, 2000- 47.94, 2001- 48.53. pb 400m 46.33 '97.

Kevin TOTH b. 29 Dec 1967 Cleveland 1.93m 134kg. ZMA. Was at McNeese State University. General manager of engineering company.
At SP: WCh: '93- 9, '97- 7, '99- nt (11).
Progression at SP: 1990- 18.06, 1991- 18.78, 1992- 20.99, 1993- 21.29, 1994- 21.25i/21.07, 1995- 21.17i/20.71, 1996- 21.15, 1997- 21.78, 1998- 21.10i/20.95, 1999- 21.59, 2000- 21.46, 2001- 20.43.

Terrrence TRAMMELL b. 23 Nov 1978 Atlanta 1.88m 84kg. Mizuno. Was at University of South Carolina.
At 110mh/4x100m: OG: '00- 2; WCh: '01- sf; WUG: '99- 1/1R; Won NCAA 1999-2000. At 60mh: WI: '01- 1.
Progression at 110mh: 1997- 13.87, 1998- 13.32, 1999- 13.28, 2000- 13.16, 2001- 13.23. pbs: 55m 6.12i '99, 60m 6.45Ai/6.51i '00, 100m 10.04 '00, 200m 20.74 '98, 20.45w '99; 55mh 6.94i '99, 60mh 7.47i '01.

Larry WADE b. 22 Nov 1974 Giddings, Texas 1.87m 83kg. Nike. Was at Texas A&M University.
At 110mh: Won NCAA 1998, 3rd GP 1999.
Progression at 110mh: 1994- 14.06/13.74w, 1995- 13.41, 1997- 13.38, 1998- 13.37, 1999- 13.01, 2000- 13.26, 2001- 13.12. pbs: 50mh 6.51i '99, 55mh 7.08A '98, 60mh 7.47i '02, 400mh 50.82 '95.
Fine year in 1999, but only 7th (cramp) at US Trials. Moved from Elgin, Texas to Los Angeles in October 1998 to train with John Smith.

Dawain WALLACE b. 30 Dec 1976 1.90m 79kg. Adidas. Was at University of Tennessee.
At 110mh: WCh: '01- 7; WUG: '99- 3.
Progression at 110mh: 1996- 14.04w, 1997- 13.88/13.73w, 1998- 13.79/13.65w, 1999- 13.57/13.34w, 2000- 13.22, 2001- 13.22. pbs: 50mh 6.50i '02, 55mh 7.13i '00, 60mh 7.58i '02, LJ 7.19 '95.

Tyree WASHINGTON b. 28 Aug 1976 1.85m 84kg. Reebok, San Bernardino Valley TC, CA.
At 400m/4x400mR: WCh: '97- 3/1R.
World record 4x400m 1998.
Progression at 200m, 400m: 1995- 46.34, 1996- 20.88w, 46.00; 1997- 20.10, 44.38; 1998- 20.29, 44.29; 1999- 20.09, 45.50; 2000- 44.72, 2001- 44.28. pb 500y 55.6i '98.
Made substantial breakthrough in 1997. Started as sprinter and won 1994 California prep LJ title. Ran world's fastest time for 400m but suffered hamstring injury at US Championships.

Bernard WILLIAMS b. 19 Jan 1978 Baltimore 1.83m 81kg. HIS. Was at University of Florida, moving to UCLA.
At 100m/4x100mR: OG: '00- 1R; WCh: '01- 3/1R; PAm: '99- 1/4R. NCAA champion 2000. 2nd GP 200m 2001.
Progression at 100m, 200m: 1997- 10.45, 21.13; 1998- 10.03, 20.46w; 1999- 10.08, 20.69Ai/20.71; 2000- 9.99, 20.03; 2001- 9.94, 20.01. pbs: 55m 6.08A '98, 60m 6.56iA '99, 6.59i '01.

Joey WOODY b. 22 May 1973 Iowa City 1.88m 78kg. Reebok. Degree in public relations from Northern Iowa University.
At 400mh/4x400mR: WCh: '97- sf, '99- 6/ res (1)R; WUG: '97- 5; WCp: '98- 5/1R. NCAA

champion 1997. WIR 4x800m 2000.
Progression at 400mh: 1993- 50.76, 1994- 50.42, 1995- 49.97, 1996- 48.62, 1997- 48.18, 1998- 47.97, 1999- 48.22, 2000- 48.72, 2001- 49.03. pbs: 400m 46.04 '99, 800m 1:47.75i '96, 1:48.41 '94; 110mh 13.98/13.63w '97.

Jerome YOUNG b. 14 Aug 1976 Jamaica 1.81m 79kg. Adidas. Was at Wallace State CC.
At 400m/4x400mR: OG: '00- res (1)R; WCh: '97- 5/1R, '99- 4, '01- sf/res (1)R; WI: '01- 2R; WCp: '98- 2/1R; PAm-J: '95- 2/1R (2 4x100R). US champion 1998-9. World record 4x400m 1998.
Progression at 400m: 1993- 47.25, 1994- 46.31, 1995- 45.01, 1996- 44.96, 1997- 44.50, 1998- 44.09, 1999- 44.24, 2000- 44.70, 2001- 45.32. pbs: 200m 20.41 '98, 20.31w '00; 300m 31.95+ '99.
Ex-Jamaican, raised in Hartford, Connecticut, became US citizen in May 1995.

Women

Amy ACUFF b. 14 Jul 1975 Port Arthur, Texas 1.88m 66kg. Asics. Biology graduate of UCLA. Part-time model.
At HJ: OG: '96- dnq 24=, '00- dnq 31; WCh: '95- 8=, '97- dnq 14, '99- 9, '01- 10=; WI: '01- 4; WJ: '92- 9, '94-3=; WUG: '97- 1. 3rd GP 2001. Won PAm-J 1993, NCAA 1995-6, US 1995, 1997, 2001.
Progression at HJ: 1988- 1.73, 1990- 1.83, 1991- 1.89, 1992- 1.90, 1993- 1.93, 1994- 1.89, 1995- 1.98, 1996- 1.94, 1997- 2.00, 1998- 1.94, 1999- 1.95, 2000- 1.91, 2001- 1.98.

Jenny ADAMS b. 8 Jul 1978 Tomball, Texas 1.65m 55kg. Nike. Was at Univ. of Houston.
At 100mh: WCh: '01- 5 (nj LJ). Won US LJ 2001, NCAA LJ 2000.
Progression at 100mh: 1995- 14.45w, 1996- 13.98/13.93w, 1997- 13.47, 1998- 13.25/13.22w, 1999- 12.98/12.86w, 2000- 12.86, 2001- 12.63/ 12.61w. pbs: 200m 23.59 '00, 60mh 8.12i '00, LJ: 6.68i/6.75w '01, 6.64 '00.
Won five successive Grand Prix races at 100mh in 2001.

Kim BATTEN b. 29 Mar 1969 McRae, Georgia 1.70m 57kg. Reebok RC. Was at Florida State University.
At 400mh: OG: '96- 2, '00- sf; WCh: '91- 5, '93- 4, '95- 1, '97- 3/2R; PAm: '95- 1; WCp: '98- 3; won GP 1995, 1997 (3rd overall), 3rd 1993. At 400m: WI: '93 -6. Won US 400mh 1991, 1994-8.
World record 400mh 1995.
Progression at 400mh: 1986- 61.1, 1987- 60.94, 1988- 58.31, 1989- 58.60, 1990- 55.45, 1991- 53.98, 1992- 54.35, 1993- 53.84, 1994- 53.72, 1995- 52.61, 1996- 53.08, 1997- 52.97, 1998- 52.74, 1999- 53.99, 2000- 54.70, 2001- 55.49mx/55.80. pbs: 55m 6.85i '96, 200m 23.52 '90, 400m 50.61 '98, 800m 2:10.35 '97, 50mh 7.01i '92, 55mh 7.55i '92, 100mh 13.14/ 13.06w '91, 13.0 '90; LJ 6.21i '91, 6.15/6.34w '90; TJ 12.95i '91, 12.92 '90.
Set collegiate 400m hurdles record in 1991, and remained at similar level until she improved her best by 1.11 secs to take the world record and world title at Göteborg 1995.

Tonja BUFORD-BAILEY b. 13 Dec 1970 Dayton, Ohio 1.76m 61kg. Nike. née Buford. Was at University of Illinois.
At 400mh: OG: '92- sf, '96- 3, '00- h; WCh: '93- 5, '95- 2, '97- 6, '01- 4; PAmG: '91- 3. Won GP 2001 (2nd 1995), NCAA 1992.
Progression at 400mh: 1987- 62.5, 1988- 61.86, 1989- 60.93, 1990- 59.46, 1991- 56.45, 1992- 54.75, 1993- 54.38, 1994- 55.26, 1995- 52.62, 1996- 53.22, 1997- 54.05, 1999- 58.29, 2000- 54.80, 2001- 54.15. pbs: 100m 11.50 '92, 200m 23.25 '96, 400m 52.61i '96, 53.10 '94; 55mh 7.60i '93, 100mh 13.07/ 12.94w '92.
Inside old world record, but 0.01 behind Kim Batten in 1995 Worlds. Married Kansas City Chiefs football player Victor Bailey 28 Oct 1995, son, Victor Jr., born 28 Sep 1998.

Dawn BURRELL b. 1 Nov 1973 1.75m 58kg. Nike. Was at University of Houston.
At LJ: OG: '00- 11; WCh: '99- 6; WI: '01- 1; PAm: '95- 5; WI: '99- 8; 2nd GP 2000. US champion 1999, indoors 1997-8. At 100mh: WJ: '92- 7.
Progression at LJ: 1989- 5.62, 1990- 6.09, 1991- 6.16i/6.08, 1992- 5.87, 1993- 6.01/6.02w, 1994- 6.46/6.55w, 1995- 6.22/6.38w, 1996- 6.46, 1997- 6.57/6.78w, 1998- 6.92i/6.90, 1999- 6.96, 2000- 6.98/6.99w, 2001- 7.03i. pbs: 100m 11.56/11.37w '99, 100mh 13.21 '99, TJ 12.34 '93.
She missed the 2001 outdoor season after tearing a cruciate ligament in her right leg in April. Her brother Leroy (b. 21 Feb 1967) ran world records for 100m 9.88 '91 and 9.85 '94 (OG 92 5/1R, WCh 91- 2/1R, 93- 1R).

Shelia BURRELL b. 15 Jan 1972 Albuquerque 1.73m 64kg. Nike. Was at UCLA.
At Hep: OG: '00- 26 (nh HJ); WCh: '99- 11, '01- 3; PAm: '99- 2. US champion 1999.
Progression at Hep: 1995- 5735, 1996- 5601, 1998- 6294w/6270, 1999- 6261, 2000- 6422, 2001- 6472. pbs: 100m 11.63 '95, 200m 22.92?w/23.25 '01, 400m 56.1 '90, 800m 2:10.29 '00, 100mh 13.05 '01, HJ 1.76 '99, LJ 6.46 '00, SP 13.76 '00, JT 50.31 '00. Won Talence heptathlon 2001.

Hazel CLARK b. 3 Oct 1977 Livingston, NJ 1.78m 55kg. Nike. Was at University of Florida.
At 800m: OG: '00- 7; WCh: '01- sf. Won NCAA 1998.
Progression at 800m: 1994- 2:10.24, 1995- 2:05.50, 1996- 2:05.08i/2:06.66, 1997- 2:01.42, 1998- 2:00.23, 1999- 2:01.77i/2:02.01, 2000- 1:58.75, 2001- 1:59.95. pbs: 400m 53.69 '98, 1000m 2:36.47 '01, 1500m 4:16.04 '00, 1M 4:40.82 '00.
Sister of **Joetta** (b. 1 Aug 1962) who competed at four Olympics 1988-2000 (7th 1992) and five World Champs (7th 1997) and has ranked in US top ten at 800m for 22 successive years 1979-

2000; pb 1:57.84 (1998). Their brother (and coach) J J Clark married Jearl Miles-Clark and their father is the celebrated school principal, Joe Clark, portrayed in the movie *Lean On Me*.

LaTasha COLANDER-RICHARDSON b. 23 Aug 1976 Portsmouth, Va 1.68m 52kg. Nike. Was at University of North Carolina.
At 400m/4x400mR: OG: '00- qf/1R. At 100mh: WJ: '94- 2. Won US 400m 2000-01.
Progression at 200m, 400m: 1993- 23.99, 1994- 23.56/23.3w, 1995- 23.80/23.60w, 1996- 23.26w, 1997- 23.21, 1998- 23.50i, 2000- 22.49, 49.87; 2001- 22.63, 50.79. pbs: 100m 11.64/11.60w '95, 300m 36.00 '00, 100mh 13.07 '96, 12.99w '97; 400mh 56.88 '99.
Having first made her name as a 100m hurdler, she won the US title in her first season at 400m in 2000. Unable to compete at 2001 World Champs. Married Roderick Richardson in February 2000.

Michelle COLLINS b. 12 Feb 1971 Canal Zone, Panama 1.77m 62kg. Nike. Graduate of University of Houston.
At 400m/4x400mR: OG: '00- h; WCh: '93- sf/res (1)R, '97- res (2)R, '99- sf/2R, '01- sf; WI: '99- 3R; PAm: '99- 2/2R; WCp: '94- 5R; WUG: '91- (200m 3), '93- 1/1R.
Progression at 400m: 1993- 51.59, 1994- 51.19, 1995- 50.84A, 1996- 51.84, 1997- 50.77, 1998- 51.17, 1999- 50.67, 2000- 50.11, 2001- 50.66. pbs: 100m 11.19 '00, 200m 22.57 '00.
Limited by a right hip stress fracture at the 2000 Olympics.

Sharon COUCH-JEWELL b. 13 Sep 1967 Richmond, Virginia 1.72m 63kg. Reebok. Was at University of North Carolina. Business development manager. Married to Maurice Jewell.
At LJ: OG: '92- 6; WCh: '93/5/7- dnq 24/28/25=; WJ: '88- 11; WCp: '92- 4. At 100mh: OG: '00- sf.
Progression at 100mh, LJ: 1987- 13.82A/13.96w, 5.86A; 1988- 13.74, 6.32; 1989- 13.74w, 6.29; 1990- 13.65/13.40w, 6.23i/6.44w; 1991- 13.38, 6.54; 1992- 6.68; 1993- 6.51/6.62w, 1994- 13.24, 6.54/6.57w; 1995- 13.38/13.34w, 6.90; 1996- 6.70, 1997- 13.06, 6.77/7.07wA; 1998- 6.57/6.72w, 1999- 12.73/12.65w, 2000- 12.68, 2001- 13.16. pbs: 100m 11.66/11.64w '93, 200m 24.23 '93, 55mh 7.63i 91, 60mh 7.94i '00, TJ 12.62i '90.

Gail DEVERS b. 19 Nov 1966 Seattle 1.60m 55kg. Nike International. Studied sociology at UCLA. Married to Ron Roberts 1988-92; now partner of Kenny Harrison.
At 100mh/4x100mR (100m): OG: '88- sf; '92- 5 (1), '96-4/1R (1), '00- sf; WCh: '91- 2, '93- 1/2R (1), '95- 1, '97- 1R, '99- 1 (5), '01- 2; PAm: '87- (1)/1R. At 60m: WI: '93- 1, '99- 2. Won NCAA 100m 1988, US 100m 1993-4, 100mh 1991-2, 1995-6, 1999-2001. Won GWG 100mh 2001; GP 100mh 2000 (2nd 1992), 2nd 100m 1996. 3rd overall 2000.
US records 100mh (6) 1988-2000, indoor 60m 1993.
Progression at 100m, 100mh: 1983- 11.69; 1984- 11.51/11.34w, 14.32; 1985- 11.19, 13.16/13.15w; 1986- 11.12/10.96w, 13.08; 1987- 10.98/10.85w, 13.28/13.1w; 1988- 10.97/10.86w, 12.61; 1991- 11.29, 12.48; 1992- 10.82, 12.55; 1993- 10.82, 12.46; 1994- 11.12/10.77w; 1995- 11.04/10.8w, 12.61; 1996- 10.83, 12.62; 1997- 10.88; 1999- 10.94, 12.37; 2000- 10.99, 12.33; 2001- 12.53. pbs: 50m 6.00+ '99, 60m 6.95i '93, 200m 22.71/22.55w '87, 400m 52.66 '87, 800m 2:11.07 '82, 55mh 7.58i '92, 60mh 7.85i '94, 400mh 59.26 '85, LJ 6.77 '88, TJ 12.97/13.31w '86.
The fastest ever woman sprinter-hurdler. A serious thyroid disorder (Graves's Disease) caused her to miss competition in 1989-90, but after being close to having to have a foot amputated she made an astonishingly speedy return to the top to win the TAC 100mh in 1991, and on to world silver and the US record in Berlin. In 1992 she was a surprise winner of the Olympic 100m but tripped over the last hurdle when well clear of the field in the 100mh. Won 16 successive 100mh finals from 18 Jun 93 to Olympic 4th 1996, after she had become only the second woman to retain Olympic 100m title. Missed 1998 outdoor season, but was back in prime form indoors in 1999 and won the World outdoor title at 100mh, with her first US record for six years. Having been a class apart during the season, she was a clear favourite to take the 2000 Olympic gold at 100mh (at last), but, feeling a hamstring problem, pulled up after four hurdles in her semi final. She was also unable to run in the sprint relay in Sydney, but, needing to compete to ensure her share of the Golden League jackpot, she ran in the GP Final 100mh a week later, and, although heavily strapped, did more than just start but won to ensure a huge payday, including third in the overall Grand Prix.

Stacy DRAGILA b. 25 Mar 1971 Auburn, California 1.72m 62kg. née Mikaelson. Reebok. Graduate of Idaho State University.
At PV: OG: '00- 1; WCh: '99- 1, '01- 1; WI: '97- 1, '99- 8, '01- 4. Won GWG 2001, GP 2001, US 1996-7, 1999-2001.
Seven world pole vault records 1999-2001, nine WIR 1997-2001. 17 US records 1996-2001 (and 18 indoors 1996-2001).
Progression at PV: 1995- 3.70, 1996- 4.20, 1997- 4.45, 1998- 4.48i/4.42A, 1999- 4.60, 2000- 4.70b/4.63. 2001- 4.81. pbs: 100mh 13.88A '98, HJ 1.70 '97, LJ 5.81A '98, 5.97w '01; JT 44.28A '98, Hep 5488A '98.
Won first women's world vault titles both indoors (1997) and outdoors (1999), and both in world records, and also won inaugural Olympic title.

Deena DROSSIN b. 14 Feb 1973 Waltham, Mass. 1.63m 48kg.Asics. Graduate of University of Arkansas.

At 10000m: OG: '00- h; WCh: '99- 11, '01- 11; WUG: '97- 1. World CC: '99-00-01-02: 10/12/12/2; Won US 10000m 2000-01, CC 1997, 1999-2001.
Progression at 5000m, 10000m: 1992- 16:21.47, 1993- 15:52.80i/16:07.73, 1994- 16:45.17, 34:10.89; 1996- 16:29.17, 34:13.75; 1997- 15:43.63, 32:47.44; 1998- 15:07.83, 1999- 14:56.84, 32:00.72; 2000- 14:51.62, 31:51.05; 2001- 15:08.02, 32:05.14. pbs: 1500m: 4:07.82 '00, 2000m 5:42.76 '01, 3000m 8:42.59 '00; Road: 15km 48:12 '02, HMar 70:08 01, Mar 2:26:58 01.

Dawn ELLERBE b. 3 Apr 1974 Brooklyn, New York 1.86m 111kg. New York AC. Graduate of University of South Carolina.
At HT: OG: '00- 7; WCh: '99- 10, '01- dnq 13; PAm: '99- 1; WUG: '97- 6. US champion 1995-7, 1999-2001, NCAA 1996-7.
Nine US hammer records 1996-2001. Eight WIB 20lb weight from 21.86 to 23.60 '00.
Progression at HT: 1994- 51.72, 1995- 58.00, 1996- 63.76, 1997- 64.22, 1998- 63.56, 1999- 70.16, 2000- 70.46, 2001- 70.62. pbs: SP 16.83i '98, 16.70 '97; DT 59.56 '00.

Suzy FAVOR HAMILTON b. 8 Aug 1968 Stevens Point, Wisconsin 1.60m 50kg. née Favor. Nike. Graphic design graduate of University of Wisconsin.
At 1500m (800m): OG: '92- h, '96- (h), '00- 12; WCh: '91- h, '95/97/99- sf; WUG: '89- 2; WJ: '86- 9; WCp: '98- 4. Won PAm-J 1984 & 1986. US champion 1990-1, 1998, and record nine NCAA titles: 800m 1990, 1500m 1987-90, indoor 1M 1987, 1989-90; 3000m 1990. World 4k CC: '02- 5.
US 1000m record 1995.
Progression at 1500m: 1983- 4:55.23 1M, 1984- 4:19.46, 1985- 4:19.43, 1986- 4:18.62, 1987- 4:09.20, 1988- 4:13.91, 1989- 4:09.7, 1990- 4:08.00, 1991- 4:06.13, 1992- 4:04.53, 1993- 4:10.69, 1994- 4:04.57, 1995- 4:05.14, 1996- 4:08.18, 1997- 4:03.50, 1998- 3:58.43, 1999- 4:13.96i, 2000- 3:57.40, 2001- 4:00.38. pbs: 800m 1:58.10 '00, 1000m 2:33.93 '95, 1M 4:22.93 '98, 2000m 5:42.86 '94, 3000m 8:46.16 '00, 5000m 15:06.48 '00.
Won 21 individual and two relay Big 10 conference titles. Married Mark Hamilton, former baseball player, in 1991. Broke 4 minutes for 1500m for the first time on her 30th birthday.

Chryste GAINES b. 14 Sep 1970 Lawton, Oklahoma 1.70m 57kg. Adidas. Psychology degree from Stanford University.
At 100m/4x100mR: OG: '96- 1R, '00- sf/3R; WCh: '95- 1R, '97- 8/1R, '01- 5/1R; PAm: '91-1 2/3R, '95- 1/1R; WUG: '91- 1/1R, '93- 5/1R; PAm-J: '89- 2/1R; 2nd GP 2000. At 200m: WCp: '94- 8, '98- 1R. At 60m: WI: '95- 7, '01- 3. Won US 100m 2001, NCAA 100m 1992.
Progression at 100m, 200m: 1985- 24.11/23.7, 1986- 11.76/11.4w, 23.68y; 1987- 11.50, 23.56/23.3; 1988- 11.50, 23.30y; 1989- 11.44, 24.24; 1990- 11.31, 23.71; 1991- 11.27/11.09w, 23.21/22.96w; 1992- 11.16/10.90w, 23.00; 1993- 11.25, 22.81; 1994- 11.32/11.2/10.99w, 23.32; 1995- 11.02, 22.92; 1996- 10.96, 22.82; 1997- 11.06, 22.91/22.53w; 1998- 10.89/10.8A, 23.08; 1999- 11.56A, 2000- 10.97, 23.04/22.83w, 2001- 10.98/10.89w, 23.50/23.01w. pbs: 50m 6.16i '99, 55m 6.68i '92, 60m 7.12i '01, LJ 5.84w '86.
1992 Olympic relay reserve, but did not compete. Won first-ever US titles in 2001 – at 60m indoors and 100m outdoors. Married to Darnell Miller.

Sandra GLOVER b. 30 Dec 1968 Palestine, Texas 1.72m 57kg. née Cummings. Nike. Teacher, graduate of University of Houston.
At 400mh: OG: '00- sf; WCh: '99- 5, '01- 8; US champion 1999-2001. 3rd GP 1999, 2001.
Progression at 400mh: 1988- 61.08, 1989- 59.99, 1990- 57.68, 1991- 56.97, 1992- 55.77, 1993- 56.76, 1994- 56.66, 1995- 57.39, 1996- 56.31mx/56.92, 1997- 55.63, 1998- 55.11, 1999- 53.65, 2000- 53.33, 2001- 54.30. pbs: 200m 23.73 '00, 100mh 13.79/13.62w '91.
Made huge improvement in 1999 at the age of 30. Coached by her husband, Don Glover.

Monique HENNAGAN b. 26 May 1976 Columbia, SC 1.73m 57kg. Adidas. Degree in psychology from University of North Carolina.
At 400m/4x400mR: OG: '00- qf/1R; WCh: '01- sf; WI: '99- 3R, '01- 5/4R; WJ: '92- sf/4R, '94- 2/1R; PAm-J: '93- 2/2R. Won NCAA 800m 1996.
Progression at 400m: 1992- 53.58, 1993- 52.30, 1994- 52.19, 1995- 52.32, 1996- 51.44, 1997- 52.00, 1998- 51.11, 1999- 51.05, 2000- 50.82, 2001- 50.98. pbs: 100m 11.86 '92, 11.3 '93, 11.69w '94; 200m 23.23 '01, 300m 36.52 '01, 800m 2:02.5 '96.

Regina JACOBS b. 28 Aug 1963 Los Angeles 1.68m 51kg. Nike. Graduate of Stanford University. Married her coach Tom Craig in December 1995.
At 1500m: OG: '88- h, '92- sf, '96- 10; WCh: '87- h, '97- 2, '99- 2, '01- h; WI: '95- 1; WCp: '89- 9. At 3000m (5000m): WI: '99- 3; WCp: '98- 3 (2). Won US 800m 2001, 1500m 1987, 1989, 1992, 1994-7, 1999-2001; 5000m 1998-2000.
US records 5000m 1998 and 2000, 1000m 1999. World best 2 miles (with illegal pacing) 1999, world indoor best 2M (9:23.38) 2002..
Progression at 1500m, 5000m: 1980- 4:32.6, 1981- 4:25.0, 1983- 4:13.09, 1984- 4:11.33, 1985- 4:15.41, 1986- 4:02.6, 1987- 4:03.70, 1988- 4:00.46, 1989- 4:10.91, 1992- 4:03.72, 1993- 4:15.71, 1994- 4:02.15, 1995- 4:05.18, 1996- 4:01.77, 1997- 4:03.42, 14:58.79; 1998- 4:02.29, 14:52.49; 1999- 4:00.35, 15:24.80; 2000- 4:01.01, 14:45.35; 2001- 4:04.85, 15:10.78. pbs: 400m 56.79 '99 (54.49 '86?), 800m 1:58.08 '00, 1000m 2:31.80 '99, 1M 4:20.93 '98, 2000m 5:38.42 '94, 3000m 8:39.14i '99, 8:39.56 '98, 2M 9:11.97mx '99.
Had a fine year in 1999, when she reduced her pb at 800m after 12 years and at 1500m after 11 years, and won a fine double at the 2000 US

Trials, taking seven seconds off her US record for 5000m. Won both 800m and 1500m and was 2nd at 5000m at 2001 US Champs. Withdrew from 1995 Worlds and 2000 Olympics through injury and viral infection respectively. Cousin of Wayne Collett (1972 Olympic silver at 400m).

LaTasha JENKINS b. 19 Dec 1977 Calumet Park, Illinois 1.70m 56kg. Nike. Was at Ball State University.
At 200m: WCh: '01- 4; WI: '01- 2; Won NCAA 1999.
Progression at 100m, 200m: 1996- 11.79/11.70w, 24.00/23.63w; 1997- 11.93/11.47w, 23.13/23.09w; 1998- 11.62/11.24w, 22.93; 1999- 11.08, 22.29/ 22.22w; 2000- 11.14, 22.86/22.54w; 2001- 11.02, 22.39.
Withdrew due to a collapsed lung from 1999 WUG and Worlds after 2nd in US 200m.

Marion JONES b. 12 Oct 1975 Los Angeles 1.78m 68kg. Nike. Studied journalism at University of North Carolina at Chapel Hill.
At 100m/4x100m (200m): OG: 1/3R (1, 3 LJ, 1 4x400); WCh: '97- 1/1R (10 LJ), '99- 1 (sf, 3 LJ); '01- 2/1R (2); WJ: '92- 5/2R (7); WCp: '98- 1 (1, 2 LJ). Won GP 100m 1998, 2000; 200m 1997; won overall 1998. 2nd 2000. Won US 100m 1997-8, 200m 1998-9, 2001; LJ 1997-8; GWG 100m/200m 1998, 100m 2001.
Progression at 100m, 200m, 400m, LJ: 1988- 13.0, c.59.0; 1989- 12.01, 24.46/24.06w/23.8w, 56.73; 1990- 11.62, 23.70, 54.21; 1991- 11.17, 22.76, 52.91; 1992- 11.14, 22.58, 54.44; 1993- 11.28/11.2, 23.01/ 22.79w, 6.71/6.75w; 1994- 11.40, 23.32, 6.75; 1995- 11.68, 23.96w, 6.64; 1997- 10.76, 21.76, 6.93; 1998- 10.65A/10.71, 21.62A/21.80, 50.36, 7.31; 1999- 10.70, 21.81, 50.79, 7.01; 2000- 10.75/10.68w, 21.84, 49.59, 7.02; 2001- 10.84, 22.23. pbs: 50m 5.93+ '97, 60m 6.85+ '99, 300m 35.68 '01.
The woman athlete of 1998, when she won 34 individual events until her 2nd to Heike Drechsler in World Cup LJ. Had another brilliant season in 1999, with 5 wins at 100m to World gold and 10 at 200m until pulled up with back spasms in her semi at the Worlds. In 2000 she won a record five medals at the Olympic Games, including three golds and in 2001 she won two golds and a silver at the Worlds, suffering her one loss of the year at any event in the 100m.
Had dual nationality as mother was born in Belize, but opted for the USA. US junior champion at 100m & 200m 1991-2. 5th at 100m and 4th at 200m in 1992 US Olympic Trials, but declined Olympic relay reserve place. World 100m age bests for age 14-15-16 and 200m 15-16. She played point guard on the North Carolina basketball team that won the NCAA Division 1 title 1994, but broke her left foot in August and December 1995. Her return to a track career in 1997 was stunning. Married shot putter C J Hunter (1999 World champ) on 3 Oct 1998, but separated in 2001.

Anjanette KIRKLAND b. 24 Feb 1974 Pineville, Louisiana 1.72m 66kg. Nike. Was at Texas A & M University.
At 100mh: WCh: '97- sf, '01- 1. At 60mh: WI: '01- 1.
Progression at 100mh: 1992- 13.99, 1993- 13.49/ 13.47w, 1994- 13.22, 1995- 13.09/12.89w, 1996- 13.24, 1997- 12.74/12.70w, 1998- 12.83, 1999- 12.91/12.68w, 2000- 12.63, 2001- 12.42. pbs: 50mh 6.83i '01, 55mh 7.61i '96, 60mh 7.85i '01, 400mh 57.75 '97.

Kristin KUEHL b. 30 Jul 1970 Windam, Minneapolis 1.83m 91kg. M-F Athletics. Was at Concordia Minnesota University.
At DT: OG: '00- dnq 19; WCh: '93- dnq 24, '99- dnq 30, '01- 8; PAm: '95- 3, '99- 3.
Progression at DT: 1989- c.45.42, 1990- 50.10, 1991- 51.04, 1992- 55.02, 1993- 60.16, 1994- 59.54, 1995- 61.86, 1996- 60.52, 1997- 61.46, 1998- 63.26, 1999- 62.82, 2000- 65.34, 2001- 65.27. pb SP 16.57 '94.

Jearl MILES CLARK b. 4 Sep 1966 Gainesville 1.70m 60kg. New Balance. Was at Alabama A&M University.
At 400m (800m): OG: '92- sf/2R, '96- 5/1R, '00- 1R (sf); WCh: '91- 5/2R, '93- 1/1R, '95- 3/1R, '97- 3/2R, '99 (4)/2R, '01- 4R; WI: '93- 3, '95- 5, '97- 1/2R, '99- 3; PAm: '91- 3; WUG: '89- 2/1R; WCp: '92- 1, '94- 3, '98- (4). Won US 400m 1993, 1995, 1997; 800m 1998-9; GWG 400m 1994.
Three US 800m records 1997-9. WIR 500y 60.61 '00.
Progression at 400m, 800m: 1986- 52.41, 1987- 52.36, 1988- 51.28, 1989- 51.52, 1990- 51.76, 1991- 50.19, 1992- 50.30, 2:04.78; 1993- 49.82, 1994- 50.11, 1995- 50.00, 2:00.86; 1996- 49.55, 1:58.91; 1997- 49.40, 1:56.78; 1998- 50.11, 1:56.43; 1999- 49.98, 1:56.40; 2000- 50.04, 1:59.12; 2001- 50.80, 2:00.96i. pbs: 100m 11.78/11.50w '93, 200m 23.03 '97, 300m 36.0 '95, 36.07 '00; LJ 6.45 '86, 6.47w '88.
Married long-time coach J J Clark, who had a 1500m pb of 3:41.5 (1988) and is brother of Joetta and Hazel Clark, on 30 Nov 1996.

Inger MILLER b. 12 Jun 1972 Los Angeles 1.63m 55kg. Nike. Degree in biological sciences from University of Southern California.
At 200m/4x100m (100m): OG: '96- 4/1R; WCh: '97- 5/1R (5), '99- 1 (2), '01- sf/1R; WUG: '95- 1R; WCp: '98- 1R. Won US 100m 1999, 200m 1997. At 60m: WI: '99- 3dq.
Progression at 100m, 200m: 1988- 11.64/11.43w, 23.69; 1989- 11.53/11.38w, 23.62; 1990- 11.48, 23.57; 1991- 11.64/11.52w, 1992- 11.16/10.9w, 23.19/22.8/22.43w; 1993- 11.11, 22.33; 1994- 11.32/10.99w, 22.73/22.47w; 1995- 11.47; 1996- 10.96, 22.25; 1997- 11.04, 22.37/22.27w; 1998- 11.01/10.84w, 22.20; 1999- 10.79, 21.77; 2000- 10.91, 22.09; 2001- 11.34/11.09w, 22.82. pbs: 50m 6.00+ '99, 60m 6.94+ '99, 400m 52.76 '94.
Her father Lennox Miller (Jam) won Olympic silver in 1968 and bronze in 1972 at 100m; they are the first ever father-daughter Olympic medallists

at individual events in athletics – following the 4x100m silvers of Friedrich Hendrix (1932) and Brunhilde Hendrix (1960) for Germany. At the 1999 World Champs Miller improved her pb at 100m of 10.96 to 10.86, 10.81 and 10.79 (2nd) and at 200m from 22.10 to 21.77 when winning in great style. Withdrew from 2000 Olympic team through injury and also missed much of 2001, but ran on a wild card in World 200m and won a gold medal at the 4x100m. In October 2001 USATF announced that she was disqualified from her bronze medal at the 1999 World Indoor 60m for a positive test for caffeine.

Melissa **MORRISON** b. 9 Jul 1971 Mooresville, NC 1.64m 56kg. Adidas. Was at Appalachian State University .
At 100mh: OG: '00- 3; WCh: '97- h; US champion 1997. At 60mh: WI: '97- 5, '99- 6.
Progression at 100mh: 1988- 14.37, 1989- 14.09, 1991- 13.63w, 1992- 13.24, 1993- 13.24, 1994- 13.24, 1995- 13.05A, 1996- 12.92/12.81w, 1997- 12.61, 1998- 12.53, 1999- 12.67/12.55w, 2000- 12.57, 2001- 13.00/12.82w. pbs: 100m 11.45A '93, 200m 24.07 '93, 50mh 6.81i '99, 60mh 7.85i '99, LJ 6.23 '93, TJ 12.55 '93.

Melissa **MUELLER** b. 16 Nov 1972 Waukesha WI 1.78m 68kg. Nike. Was at Wisconsin State University/Oshkosh. Married to Michael Clark.
At PV: OG: '00- dnq 14; WI: '99- 5.
Progression at PV: 1996- 3.53, 1997- 3.95, 1998- 4.22, 1999- 4.50i/4.38, 2000- 4.50b/4.45, 2001- 4.47/4.62ex, 2002- 4.60Ai. pbs: 100mh 14.22, HJ 1.77 '93.
Started out as a hurdler and later a high jumper, before starting vaulting in 1995. She made a great breakthrough in the 1999 indoor season, improving from 4.22 to US records 4.49 and 4.50.

LeShundra **'DeDee' NATHAN** b. 20 Apr 1968 Fort Wayne 1.80m 75kg. Indiana Invaders. Was at Indiana University.
At Hep: OG: '00- 9; WCh: '93- 17, '95- 8, '97- 7, '01- 7; PAm: '91- 1, '95- 3; US champion 2000-01. At Pen: WI: '97- 7, '99- 1.
Progression at Hep: 1990- 5855, 1991- 5998, 1992- 6162, 1993- 6038, 1994- 6189, 1995- 6283, 1996- 6327, 1997- 6317, 1998- 6479, 1999- 6577, 2000- 6343, 2001- 6275. pbs: 200m 24.11 '98, 800m 2:13.82 '96, 60mh 8.26i '99, 100mh 13.10 '96, 400mh 57.39A '89, 57.78 '88; HJ 1.86i '99, 1.83 '96; LJ 6.59/6.65w '98, SP 16.06 '01, JT 50.08 '99, Pen 4743i '99.
Added 230 points to pb when taking the 1999 World Indoor heptathlon gold. Won at Götzis but then missed Worlds after no height in the high jump in US heptathlon.

Nanceen PERRY b. 19 Aug 1977 Fairfield, Texas 1.75m 69kg. Adidas. Was at University of Texas.
At 200m/4x100mR: OG: '00- sf/3R; WCh: '99- qf/4R; WJ: '96- 6/1R; WUG: '99- 3/1R.
Progression at 200m: 1993- 23.57, 1994- 23.98/ 23.66w, 1995- 23.49, 1996- 23.17/22.88w, 1997- 22.73, 1998- 23.05/22.98w, 1999- 22.55/22.49w, 2000- 22.38/22.16w, 2001- 23.23. pbs: 60m 7.13i '00, 100m 11.15 '99, 11.10w '00; LJ 5.93/6.03w '94, TJ 12.36 '94.

Mary SAUER b. 31 Oct 1975 Green Bay, Wisconsin 1.64m 59kg. Asics. Was at Azusa Pacific University.
At PV: WCh: '01- 12.
Progression at PV: 1998- 3.81, 1999- 4.15A, 2000- 4.47, 2001- 4.61, 2002- 4.61Ai. pbs: HJ 1.65 '97, TJ 12.36w '97.
Began pole vaulting after graduating in 1997.

Seilala SUA b. 25 Feb 1978 1.87m 109kg. Studied sociology at UCLA.
At DT/(SP): OG: '00- 10; WCh:'99- 6, '01- 6/dnq 17; WJ: '96- 2/8; PAm-J: '95- 2/1, '97- 1/1. Won US DT 1998-2001, SP 2001; NCAA SP 1999-2000, DT 1997-2000.
Progression at DT: 1994- 44.22, 1995- 53.84, 1996- 56.78, 1997- 63.44, 1998- 64.67, 1999- 64.89, 2000- 65.90, 2001- 65.64. pbs: SP 17.97 '01, HT 60.60 '00, JT 49.12 '99, 20lb Wt 20.52i '99.
With the discus 1997-2000, Sua is only the second woman ever to win four successive NCAA titles at the same event (after Suzy Hamilton 1500m 1987-90). Her 107 points at shot, discus and weight indoors (38) and out (69) is a new NCAA record for any athlete.

Kellie SUTTLE b. 9 May 1973 St Peters, Missouri 1.70m 59kg. Nike. Was at Arkansas State University.
At PV: OG: '00- 11; WCh: '99- 9; WI: '01- 2=; PAm: '99- 2. Won US 1998.
Progression at PV: 1995- 3.71i/3.67, 1996- 3.85i/ 3.66, 1997- 3.90, 1998- 4.27, 1999- 4.46i/4.35, 2000- 4.53, 2001- 4.60. pb LJ 5.86 '93.
Started pole vaulting in 1994 while working as a gymnastics instructor.

Tisha WALLER b. 1 Dec 1970 South Boston, Virginia 1.83m 61kg. Was at University of North Carolina. Kindergarten teacher.
At HJ: OG: '96- 9=; WCh: '91- dnq 20, '93- dnq 17=, '99- 4=; WUG: '91- 3; WI: '99- 3; WCp: '98- 3. Won GWG 1998, US 1996, 1998-9.
Progression at HJ: 1986- 1.65, 1987- 1.65, 1988- 1.78, 1989- 1.78, 1990- 1.83, 1991- 1.93i/1.92, 1992- 1.92, 1993- 1.94, 1994- 1.96, 1995- 1.98, 1996- 1.99i/1.98, 1997- 1.84, 1998- 2.01i/1.98, 1999- 2.00, 2000- 1.96i/1.94, 2002- 1.95i. pb LJ 5.61 '88, TJ 12.74 '92. Set US indoor record when winning the US indoor title in 1998.

Kelli WHITE b. 1 Aor 1977 Oakland, California 1.63m 52kg. Nike. Was at Univ. of Tennessss.
At 100m/200m/4x100mR: WCh: '01- 7/3/1R; PAm-J: '95-/2/1R. 2nd GP 200m 2001.
Progression 100m, 200m: 1993- 11.81w, 24.09w; 1994- 11/87/11.68w, 23.80; 1995- 11.55/11.43w, 23.49/23.33w; 1996- 11.60/11.45w, 23.85i/23.60w;

1997- 11.42/11.39w, 23.30/23.28w; 1998- 11.27/ 11.21w, 22.58; 1999- 11.20/10.96w, 22.65/22.49w; 2000- 11.19, 23.08/22.94w; 2001- 10.99/10.93w, 22.38. pbs: 55m 6.76i '99, 60m 7.14i '02, 300m 36.61 '01, 400m 53.94A '95.
Her father Willie White was a top sprinter with pbs 100y 9.4 '57 and 100m 10.3 '58, and her mother Debbie Byfield ran for Jamaica at 4x100m at the 1972 Olympics. pb 100y 10.7 '73.

Angela WILLIAMS b. 30 Jan 1980 Bellflower, California 1.56m 52kg. Student at University of Southern California.
At 100m/4x100mR: WCh: '01- sf/res (1)R; WJ: '98- 2/1R; PAm: '99- 2/2R; WUG: '99- 1/1R; PAm-J: '95- 2, '97- 1/1R; Won NCAA 1999-2001. At 60m: WI: '01- 2.
Progression at 100m: 1990- 12.85, 1992- 12.10, 1993- 11.79, 1994- 11.78, 1995- 11.24, 1996- 11.73/ 11.4w, 1997- 11.14/10.98w, 1998- 11.11/11.10w, 1999- 11.04/10.96w, 2000- 11.12/11.1/11.01w, 2001- 11.18/11.01w. pbs: 50m 6.17i '01, 60m 7.09i '01, 200m 23.02 '98, 22.78w '00; 400m 53.40 '95, 800m 2:16.78 '92, LJ: 5.83/6.00w '97.

VENEZUELA

Governing body: Federación Venezolana de Atletismo, Apartado Postal 29059, Caracas. Founded 1948.
National Champions 2001: **Men**: 100m: Juan Morillo 10.48w, 200m: José Manuel Carabalì 21.57w, 400m: Luis Luna 48.75, 800m: Simoncito Silvera 1:51.19, 1500m: Emigdio Delgado 3:54.73, 5000m: Freddy González 14:03.04, 10000m: Alejandro Semprún 30:36.65, 3000mSt: Néstor Nieves 8:54.75, 110mh: Marleán Reina 14.18w, 400mh: José Turbay 52.09, HJ: León Beltrán 2.11, PV: Johnny Romero 4.95, LJ: José Reyes 7.48w, TJ: Julio Solarte 15.21, SP: Ronny Jimenez 17.96, DT: Jesús Parejo 51.67, HT: Aldo Bello 63.94, JT: Manuel Fuenmayor 72.74, Dec: Rubén Arcia 6387, 20000mW: Carlos Ramones 1:44:20.4. **Women**: 100m: Wilmary Álvarez 11.76w, 200m: Osmary Sequea 24.50w, 400m/400mh: Yusmelys Garcìa 55.79/60.31, 800m: Yenny Mejías 2:14.52, 1500m: Yoli Mendoza 4:46.56, 5000m/10000m: Norelis Lugo 17:02.04/36:10.26, 2000mSt: Yoli Mendoza 7:18.86, 100mh: Tamara Chourio 14.46w, HJ: Jetzalida Péez 1.70, PV: Jetzalida Pérez 1.70, PV: Norelis Díaz 3.20, LJ/TJ: Jennifer Arveláez 5.68w/13.09, SP/DT: Neolanis Suárez 14.69/ 52.02, HT: Dubraska Rodríguez 56.06, JT: María González 49.10, Hep: Thaimara Rivas 4650, 20000mW: Carolina Flores 1:59:16.5.

YUGOSLAVIA

Governing body: Atletski Savez Jugoslavije, Strahinjica Bana 73a, 11000 Beograd. Founded in 1921.
National Championships first held in 1920 (men) and 1923 (women). **2001 champions**: **Men**: 100m/400m: Marko Jankovic 10.68/47.66, 200m: Slobodan Spasic 21.54, 800m: Darko Radomirovic 1:50.84, 1500m: Dejan Pajkic 3:45.86, 5000m/ 10000m/HMar/Mar: Sreten Ninkovic 14:54.99/ 29:50.39/66:34/2:16:11, 3000mSt: Dejan Bogicevic 9:16.22, 110mh: Miroslav Novakovic 14.11, 400mh: Slavoljub Nikolic 54.23, HJ: Marko Niketic 2.20, PV: Fedja Kamasi 4.90, LJ: Danial Jahic 7.62, TJ: Zoran Rankovic 15.26, SP: Dragan Peric 20.35, DT: Veljko Cegar 55.40, HT: Zoran Loncar 54.90, JT: Slavisa Radosavljev 62.46, Dec/20kmW: *not held*, 10000mW: Aleksandar Rakovic 40:41.72. **Women**: 100m/200m: Vukosava Djapic 11.58/ 23.75, 400m: Jovana Miljkovic 53.97, 800m: Ivana Popadic 2:11.00, 1500m: Tanja Radonjic 4:28.83, 5000m: Zorana Adzic 16:31.29, 10000m: Mira Preradovic 35:48.5, HMar/Mar: Vesna Stevanovic 84:41/2:44:23, 100mh/400mh: Olivera Stojanovic 14.38/59.95, HJ: Marija Plazinic 1.68, PV: Slavica Semenjuk 3.50, LJ/TJ: Marija Martinovic 6.20/ 13.89, SP: Snezana Milinkovic 14.31, DT: Dragana Tomasevic 48.88, HT: Danijela Jankovic 50.13, JT: Ivana Scekic 45.30, Hep: Biljana Bogunovic 4715, 5000mW: Ankica Barzut 23:35.4.

Dragan PERIC b. 8 May 1964 Zivinice 1.86m 115kg. Crvena Zvezda, Beograd.
At SP: OG: '92- 7, '96- 8, '00- dnq 16; WCh: '91- 7, '93- 5, '97- dnq 19, '99- 6, '01- 5; EC: '90- 13, '94- 6, '98- 4; WI: '95- 3; EI: '94- 2, '98- 4. Won YUG champion SP 1990-4, 1996-2001; DT 1992-4, 1997; Balkan SP 1996, 1998.
Yugoslav records: shot (3) 1993-8, discus 1991.
Progression at SP: 1980- 11.35, 1981- 12.23, 1982- 14.88, 1983- 17.24, 1985- 16.89, 1986- 17.70, 1987- 18.86, 1988- 19.92, 1989- 20.42, 1990- 20.06, 1991- 20.47, 1992- 20.91, 1993- 21.26, 1994- 20.64i/20.57, 1995- 20.36i/20.14, 1996- 20.90, 1997- 20.78, 1998- 21.77, 1999- 20.74, 2000- 19.88, 2001- 20.91/ 21.27lt. pb DT 61.94 '91.

Women

Olivera JEVTIC b. 24 Jul 1977 Titovo Uzice 1.74m 52kg. Mladost-Niskogradnja, Uzice.
At 10000m (/5000m): OG: '00- 11/dnf; WCh: '97- h/h, '99- 10, '01- 12/h; EC: '98- 4/4; EU23: '97- 1, '99- 1/3; WJ: '94- (3000m 10), 96- -/2 (3000m 5); EJ: '95- 2 (3000m 3). World HMar: '98-99-01: 4/21/7; CC: '95- 17J, '00-01: 15/9; Eur CC: '96-7-8-9-00-01: 13/3/3/3/3/4. Won YUG 1500m 1996, 5000m 1996, HMar 1998-9, CC 1994-7, 1999; Balkan 5000m 1998, CC 2002.
Yugoslav records: 5000m (7) 1995-2000, 10000m (2) 1998-2000, HMar (3) 1998-2001.
Progression at 5000m, 10000m: 1995- 16:03.34, 33:48.61; 1996- 15:40.59, 32:38.0; 1997- 15:34.65, 32:43.42; 1998- 15:16.61, 31:34.26; 1999- 15:19.08, 31:57.67; 2000- 15:11.25, 31:29.65; 2001- 15:26.84, 31:33.08. pbs: 8000m 2:12.41 '93, 1500m 4:16.16 '98, 3000m 8:59.21 '98, Rd: 10km 31:31 '01, 15km 49:06 '01, HMar 69.34 '01.

INTRODUCTION TO WORLD LISTS AND INDEX

Records

World, World U20 and U18, Olympic, Continental and Area records are listed for standard events. In running events up to and including 400 metres, only fully automatic times are shown. Marks listed are those which are considered statistically acceptable by the ATFS, and thus may differ from official records where, for instance the performance was set indoors.

World All-time and Year Lists

These lists are presented in the following format: Mark, Wind reading (where appropriate), Name, Nationality (abbreviated), Date of birth, Position in competition, Meeting name (if significant), Venue, Date of performance.

In standard events the best 30 or so performances are listed followed by the best marks for other athletes. Position, meet and venue details have been omitted for reasons of space beyond 100th in year lists.

In the all-time lists performances which have been world records (or world bests, thus including some unratified marks) are shown with WR against them – outdoor records only.

Indexes

These lists contain the names of all athletes ranked with full details in the world year lists for standard events (and others such as half marathon). The format of the index is as follows:

Family name, First name, Nationality, Birthdate, Height (cm) and Weight (kg), 2001 best mark, Lifetime best (with year) as at the end of 2000.

* before the name indicates an athlete who is profiled in the Biographies section, and a ^ symbol one who has been profiled in previous editions.

General Notes

Altitude aid

Marks set at an altitude of 1000m or higher have been suffixed by the letter "A".

Although there are not as yet separate world records for altitude assisted events, it is understood by experts that in all events up to 400m in length (with the possible exclusion of the 110m hurdles), and in the horizontal jumps, altitude gives a material benefit to performances. For events beyond 800m, however, the thinner air of high altitude has a detrimental effect.

Supplementary lists are included in relevant events for athletes with seasonal bests at altitude who have low altitude marks qualifying for the main list.

Some leading venues over 1000m

Addis Ababa ETH	2365m
Air Force Academy USA	2194
Albuquerque USA	1555
Ambato ECU	2544
Antananarivo MAD	1350
Arusha TAN	c.1400
Avila ESP	1128
Bloemfontein RSA	1392
Bogotá COL	2644
Boulder USA	1655
Calgary CAN	1045
Cali COL	1046
Ciudad de Guatemala	1402
Ciudad de México MEX	2247
Cochabamba BOL	2558
Colorado Springs USA	1823
Cuenca ECU	2561
Denver USA	1609
Echo Summit USA	2250
El Paso USA	1187
Flagstaff USA	2105
Font-Romeu FRA	1850
Fort Collins USA	1521
Germiston RSA	1661
Guadalajara MEX	1567
Harare ZIM	1473
Johannesburg RSA	1748
Krugersdorp RSA	1740
Gyumri (Leninaken) ARM	1556
Medellín COL	1541
Monachil ESP	2320
Nairobi KEN	1675
Pietersberg RSA	1230
Pocatello USA	1361
Potchefstroom RSA	1351
Pretoria RSA	1400
Provo USA	1380
Reno USA	1369
Roodepoort RSA	1720
Rustenburg RSA	1157
Secunda RSA	1628
Segovia ESP	1000
Sestriere ITA	2050
Soría ESP	1056
South Lake Tahoe USA	1909
Toluca MEX	2700
Tsakhkadzor ARM	1980
Tunja COL	c.2500
Windhoek NAM	1725

Some others over 500m

Almaty KZK	847
Ankara TUR	902
Bern SUI	555
Boise USA	818
Canberra AUS	581
La Chaux de Fonds SUI	997
Caracas VEN	922
Edmonton CAN	652
Las Vegas USA	619
Lubbock USA	988
Madrid ESP	640
Malles ITA	980
Moscow, Idaho USA	787

München GER	520
Salamanca ESP	806
Santiago de Chile CHI	520
(Apoquindo)	950
São Paulo BRA	725
Sofia BUL	564
Spokane USA	576
Taiyuan	780
Tucson USA	728

300m-500m

Annecy FRA	448
Atlanta USA	302
Banská Bystrica SVK	362
Genève SUI	385
Götzis AUS	448
Johnson City USA	499
Lausanne SUI	375
Rieti ITA	402
Sindelfingen GER	440
Tashkent UZB	477
Zürich SUI	410

Automatic timing

In the main lists for sprints and hurdles, only times recorded by fully automatic timing devices are included.

Hand timing

In the sprints and hurdles supplementary lists are included for races which are hand timed. Any athlete with a hand timed best 0.01 seconds or more better than his or her automatically timed best has been included, but hand timed lists have been terminated close to the differential levels considered by the IAAF to be equivalent to automatic times, i.e. 0.24 sec. for 100m, 200m, 100mh, 110mh, and 0.14 sec. for 400m and 400mh. It should be noted that this effectively recognises bad hand timekeeping, for there should be no material difference between hand and auto times, but what often happens is that badly trained timekeepers anticipate the finish, as opposed to reacting to the flash at the start.

In events beyond 400m, automatically timed marks are integrated with hand timed marks, the latter identifiable by times being shown to tenths. All-time lists also include some auto times in tenths of a second, where the 1/100th time is not known, but these are identified with the symbol '.

Indoor marks

Indoor marks are included in the main lists for field events and straightway track events, but not for other track events. This is because track sizes vary in circumference (200m is the international standard) and banking, while outdoor tracks are standardised at 400m. Outdoor marks for athletes whose seasonal bests were set indoors are shown in a supplemental list.

Mixed races

For record purposes athletes may not, except in road races, compete in mixed sex races. Statistically there would not appear to be any particular logic in this, and women's marks set in such races are shown in our lists - annotated with mx. In such cases the athlete's best mark in single sex competition is appended.

Field event series

I have tried to include field event series for marks in the top 30 performances list for 2000. Sadly such information is missing from some meetings, and I hope that correspondents will help provide such more details in future.

Tracks

As with climatic conditions, the type and composition of tracks and runways will affect standards of performance.

Wind assistance

In the lists for sprints, long jump and triple jump, anemometer readings have been shown where available. The readings are given in metres per second to one decimal place. Where the figure was given originally to two decimal places, it has been rounded to the next tenth upwards, e.g. a wind reading of +2.01 m/s, beyond the IAAF legal limit of 2.0, is rounded to +2.1; or -1.22 m/s is rounded up to -1.2.
For multi-events a wind-assisted mark in one in which any of these events is aided by a wind over 4.0 m/s; such assisted marks are shown with a capital W.

Drugs bans

The IAAF have determined that the IAAF Executive Council may decertify an athlete's records, titles and results if he or she later admits to having used a banned substance before those performances. We have not removed any such athletes from all-time lists, but for information have shown ¶ after the name of any athlete who has at any stage in his or her career undergone a drugs suspension of a year or more (thus not including athletes receiving 3 month bans (now warnings) for stimulants etc., which for that year only are indicated with a #). This should not be taken as implying that the athlete was using drugs at that time. Nor have those athletes who have subsequently unofficially admitted to using banned substances been indicated; the ¶ is used only for those who have been caught.

Venues

From time to time place names are changed. Our policy is to use names in force at the time that the performance was set. Thus Leningrad prior to 1991, St Petersburg from its re-naming.

Amendments

Keen observers may spot errors in the lists. They are invited to send corrections to the editor, who will also welcome news and results for 2002.

Peter Matthews, 10 Madgeways Close, Great Amwell, Ware, Herts SG12 9RU, England
Fax 44 1920 877392
Email peter@matthews.in2home.co.uk

Amendments to ATHLETICS 2001

World rankings 2000
p.41 – Women 5000: 2. Wami, 3. O'Sullivan
Road Races: p.62: 15 Apr Turku: Maria Söderström FIN 79:26 (not Lundberg)
p.64: 16 Jun Forssa: Maria Söderström FIN 77:21 (not Lundberg)
Obituary
Helmut **JANZ:** 1966- 51.7 (64=), 1967- 54.1, 1968- 53.2, 1969- 54.7, 1970- 58.0, 1975- 56.9, pb 200mh 23.9 (1960).
Championships
p.101 World Juniors: Women DT: Seema Antil – drugs public warning and disqualificatioon
p.110 World Mountain Running Trophy at Bergen, GER
p.117 World Championships: Oldest champion: 36 yr 308 days Antón; Youngest medallist: not Mitchell but 17yr 248d Merlene Frazer JAM 4x100m (ran heat) 1991
National Champs 2000
France: 110mh: Sébastian Denis 13.85
UK: AAA W Mar: Lodge 2:40:51

World Lists 2000
Men
100m: 10.23 Sean Ogunkoya NGR 28.12.77 NC Lagos 22 Jul (& 10.0 hand 1 Enugu 24 Mar); 202 men to 10.33; wa: 10.27w Abdenabi Abid & 10.30w Younès Moudrik MAR 1.10.77 27 May; hand: 10.0 Chinedu Oriala NGR Kano 2 Jun (from 10.1)
200m: 31/14 so all (10s) wrong 100th 20.66. 20.84 Ezenwa; Hand: 20.4 Udo-Obong J 1 Lagos 1 Jul (from 20.5); Suspended: Effiong – his 20.58w was prior to drugs dq
400m: 45.68 Udo-Obong NGR-J NC Lagos 21 Jul (from 45.75), 45.88 Udeme Ekpeyong NGR 28.3.73 22 Jul, 45.97 Fidelis Gadzama (from 46.05) 21 Jul, 46.05 Abderahim Elhaouzy MAR .75 30 Aug (see 46.0); 46.16A Lebo 22 Jul (from 46.19); 46.25 Hyginus Anugho NGR 29.11.77 22 Jul; Hand: 46.2A Abednigo Matilu KEN 21.11.68 26 May
800m: 1:44.21 Korir 15.7.77, 1:47.4A Maina (from 1:47.1); 1:47.5A Nicholas Kemboi KEN 24 Jun, 1:47.8A Alfred Kemei KEN 8 Jul; Jnrs: 1:48.94 Amine Laalou MAR .82 Casablanca 27 Jul
1500m: 3:35.66 James Koskei (not Kimutai) (& 7:36.33, 13:04.3), 3:35.78 Amyn 25.5.76, 3:39.28 Hachlaf 3.7.78, 3:40.3A Samuel Kereng KEN 24 Jun, 3:41.3A Sammy Kipketer KEN-J 29.9.81 Nairobi 26 May; Jnrs: 3:42.42 Albert Chepkirui KEN-J 4.4.81 5 Palo Alto 17 Jun
1M: 20th is 3:54.90
3000m: 7:46.8+ Driss El Himer FRA Bruxelles 25 Aug (from 7:50.96), 7:46.95 Bekele 13.6.82 (& 5000m 13:20.57), 7:51.37 Getanda 5.7.72 (& 5000m 13:31.02), 7:52.87 Kimutai Kosgei .71 5 Jul, 7:52.94 Abdelhak El Gourch MAR 20.7.74 11 Jun
5000m: 13:37.3A Isaac Songok 25.4.84, 13:41.5A Nicholas Kemboi .83; Juniors: 13:46.33 Mutanya 10.8.81, 13:46.53 Gilbert Koech KEN .81 8 Formia 8 Jun
10000m: 28:32.5A Michael Kite KEN .73 20 Jul, 28:38.9 Bara .70
HMar: 59:51 William Kiplagat 21.6.72 (& Mar 2:09:06), 62:28 Willy Kipkering, 62:41 Kennedy Kiragu KEN 10 Jun
3000mSt: 8:27.04 Ramoul ALG/FRA
110mh: 13.60 0.6 Knight 2h2 Sondershausen 25 Aug, 13.60/13.5 Yuniel Hernández, 13.87 Devis Favaro
400mh: Jnrs: 50.72 Mikheyko 3rd
HJ: 2.20 De Paepe 25.2.76; Jnrs: 2.18 Damon Thompson BAR at Bridgetown 22 Mar
LJ: 8.08 Mattias Sunneborn, 8.00 Noúsios 25.2.79, 7.81w 2.2 Kummle
TJ: 16.47 Awadh 4.12.81, 16.40 Dominic Ukwume NGR 12 May
SP: 21.39 Q and 21.29 1 Harju at OG; 20.11 Reinikainen, 19.79 Hoffa 4; 19.19 Sack 4, 18.99 Vial 22 Jul, 18.27 1 Liu Yu CHN 15.2.78 1 Sep
DT: 69.72 Riedel – 4th throw in series 69.72
HT: Jnrs: 64.27 Saber Souad EGY .81 Alger 8 Jun
JT: Gatsioúdis 88.74 (also 1st throw of series), 76.97 Maher Ridane 1 Tunis 20 Feb (80.18 with irregular implement); 75.56 irreg? Walid Mohamed 4.4.72 – 74.26 1 Sep
Dec: 8209h Razbeyko at Novosibirsk, delete 7702 Kovalenko and unconfirmed 7627 Gans. 100th best 7633.
4x100m: 40.3 TOG and 40.37 BEN 20 May
4x400m: 2:59.02 BAH (2. McIntosh 45.04)
10000mW: 13/12 not 12/11; 40:12.10 Ivan Azaronok BLR 17.7.79 1 Minsk 21 May
30kmW: 2:13:09A David Kimutai KEN 19.8.69 29 Apr
50kmW: short course at Yverdon was 49060m
100kmW: 9:53:46 Regy

Women
00m: wa: 11.37 Fatma Zohra Dkouk MAR .77 27 May; Hand timed: 11.1 Emen Emen NGR-J 15.10.83 Calabar 13 May, 11.3 Wafae Tayssir MAR 26 Mar, 11.3 Nwogwugwu Oluchi NGR 13 May, 11.3 Beatrice Utondu NGR 23.11.69 20 Jul
200m: 23.29 0.9 Neto, 23.42 Calista Onyejiaka NGR-J 3.4.83 NC Lagos 22 Jul, 23.49 Beatrice Utondu NGR 23.11.69 22 Jul
400m: 50.45A Afolabi 2 Ciudad de México 1 Jul (50.30 was wrong, but what was her time on 22 Jul?), 51.84 Rosemary Okafor NGR-J 22.5.81 NC Lagos 21 Jul, 51.95 Bu 10.2.78, 51.95 Doris Jacob NGR .78 (16.12.81?) NC Lagos 22 Jul; 100th best 52.25, 52.67 Omatayo Akinremi NGR 13.9.74 22 Jul, 52.67 Kudirat Akhigbe NGR-J 29.12.81 (add to jnrs) 1 Lisboa 18 Jun; 52.85 Saidat Onanuga NGR 18.6.74 22 Jul; hand timed: 52.8 Hajarat Yusuf NGR-J 8.3.82 3 Jun, 52.8 Mabel Madojemu NGR-J 26.6.82 Lagos 1 Jul (and add Jnrs), 53.0 Omobolanle Aikhena NGR 1 Jul
800m: 1:58.77 Anisimova to drugs dq; 2:01.09 Macharia 9.2.76 (& 1500m 4:09.57), 2:03.60 Saadia Saadi MAR .73 27 May, 2:04.32 Dupe Osime NGR 22 Apr; 100th best 2:02.51
1000m: 2:39.8 Kathleen Friedrich GER 13.7.77 24 May
1500m: 4:12.9A Florence Kyalo KEN-J 12.2.86 Nairobi 22 Sep; Jnrs: 4:17.0A Rose Kosgei KEN 22.8.81 Nairobi 22 Sep, 4:18.00 Malika Assahssah MAR 24.9.82 Rabat 20 May
5000m: 15:08.36 Defar 19.11.83 (& 1500m 4:15.19, 3000m 8:59.90)
10000m: 32.17.7 Chaabi 19.5.79
10km Rd: 32:30 Susie Power 26.3.75 1 Melbourne 2 Apr, 33:02 Iris Biba-Pöschl GER 27.5.64 21 Oct
HMar: 72:36 Jevtic 22 Apr course OK
2000mSt: 6:34.47A Panistine Chepkorir KEN 1 NC Nairobi 21 Jul, 6:36:73A Esther Chebor KEN 2 NC Nairobi 21 Jul
3000mSt: 9:52.40 Volkova 16.2.78, 10:11.86 Cherepanova 9.3.67
100mh: 13.26/13.24w Cherry 13.11.77
400mh: 56.03 Price 17.7.72, 58.24 Esther Erharuyi NGR 22 Jul (& 57.7 hand timed 1 Jul); hand timed: 57.8 Catherine Obilor NGR 13 May, 58.1 Laraba Nasiru and 58.2 Glory Nwosu NGR-J 24.12.84 Kano 3 Jun
HJ: 2.02 Dinescu b. 2.4.73
PV: 4.30i Schulte 1 Potsdam 4 Mar
LJ: 6.71 Yermolayeva 14.10.79; wa: 6.36 Fatma Zohra Dkouk MAR .77 27 May

TJ: 13.45 Grace Efago NGR 13 May, 13.44 Gurova 22.5.82, 13.40 (not A) Ouaba BUR, 13.36 Cachot YUG/SUI, 13.35 Nkechinyere Mbaoma NGR 3 Jun, 13.29 Wewe Kilani NGR 21 Jul

SP: 17.84 Legnante dq (public warning) next best 17.31 3 Padova 27 Aug, 16.50 Hanaa Salah El Melegi 1 Cairo 29 Jun (from 16.01); 100th best 16.46, Jnrs: 15.72 Adams.

DT: 60.50 Kankaanpää, Juniors: Antil # 55.27 at WJ was disqualified.

HT: Kuzenkova 70.20 1st, 67.44 Shaw 4th, 60.66 dh Pilsner-Steinke – and 60.16 6 Jul; 57.67 Papayeoryíou 17.12.80

JT: 64.03 Mikaela Ingberg, 53.48 Ihefo Sorochukwu NGR 21 Jul; Old model?: 53.68 Lindy Leveau SEY 14.11.78 Victoria 24 Jun

Hep: 6422 Shelia Burrell, 6187 Parfyonova 14.7.73, 5771 Peltosaari on 14 May, 5739 Vindyuk 31.7.79

4x100m: Hand: note 43.4A was in mixed race; Best LA: 44.25 RSA (Febbraio, Hartman, Holtshausen, Seyerling)

4x400m: 3:26.31 BLR (4. Kozak 51.09), 3:28.02 SEN (2 M T Diouf 52.70), 3:42.41 GHA-J 1 WAf-J Kumasi 9 Jun

20kmW: 1:35:22 Stevenson USA 15.10.79 (& 3k 12:39.62, 5k 22:00.88, 10k 46:40+); best track times: 1:35:23.67 Saltanovic.

World Indoor Lists 2001

Men: 60m: 6.57A Spies 9.9.78; **200m**: 20.46dq Malcolm – replace by 20.58 1 Euro Birmingham 18 Feb, 20.78 Evans; **400m**: 46.22A o/s Michael Campbell JAM 11.9.78; **800m**: 1:47.72 Joseph 27.12.81; **50mh/60mh**: 6.44/7.52 Tony Dees ¶ drugs dq; drugs dq confirmed for Falk Balzer ¶; **HJ**: 2.31 Chubsa at Vitebsk, 2.31 Topic ¶ drugs dq, best before 2.27 1 Piréas 27 Jan; **PV**: 5.61 Tiberiu Agoston ROM 25.12.76 4 Mar; **LJ**: 7.96 Krause; **SP**: 19.52 Cichocki was exhibition.

Women: 50/60m: Savatheda Fynes; **200m**: 23.31 Mikhaylovskaya 20.11.75; **800m**: 2:01.43 drugs dq Clark # - and 2:02.89 10 Feb; **1M**: 4:24.11 Zadorozhnaya; **60mh**: 6.87+ Linda Ferga FRA 24.12.76 18 Feb, 6.88+ Nicole Ramalalanirina FRA 5.2.72 18 Feb; **PV**: 4.35 Poissonnier 25 Mar, 4.24 Sánchez 4 Mar, 4.20 Agnès Livebardon FRA 31.5.80 25 Mar; **SP**: 17.87 Zhang 16.3.83; **Hep**: 4251 Yepimashko BLR

World Lists in Previous Annuals

2000 Indoors

Women Hep: 4464 (8.99, 1.85, 13.74, 5.99, 2:15.35) Svetlana Kazanina KAZ 1 and 4417 Irina Naumenko (8.85, 1.85, 12.59, 6.13, 2:18..453) KAZ 2 both Karaganda 11/12 Feb

1999

5000m: 13:40.01 Kimutei Kosgei KEN 71 25 Jul

Women HMar: 69:26 Pana – drugs disqualification (also remove from result on page 87); TJ Jnr: 13.38 Meng Jiao CHN .81 2x Jul

1998

100m: 10.32 Yang Xiaodong 18 Apr; 5000m: 13:41.55 Kimutei Kosgei KEN 71 2 Aug

400mh: Bryan Bronson drugs dq on 14 Jul, so following marks need to be moved to footnote: 47.15. 47.70, 47.76, 47.93, 48.03, 48.22, 48.25

Women 400mh: 53.17A Batten 3rd 11 Sep

1997 – 1M: 3:58.8 Howard GBR not CAN; 5000m: 13:36.88 Kimutei Kosgei KEN 71 20 Aug

1995 – Taiyuan, venue of Chinese championships, is at 780m and thus performances should not be marked A.

1993

Women LJ: 6.46 Peng Fengmei CHN-J 27.7.7, DT: 61.16 Li Qiumei CHN-J, JT: Li Lei CHN-J 4.5.74 – all 1 NSch at Qingdao – Aug

1992 – 4x400m: 3:08.81 TCH 13 Jun

1986 – Women 3000mW: 12:43.56 Wang Yan 1 NSch Anshan c.1 Aug

1978

SP: 18.88 Matt Byrnes USA 4.12.52 1 Napperville 28 Apr

1999 World Championships

After a two-year investigation by the Russian Federation, German Skurygin was given a two-year ban for a positive test for human chorionic gonadotropin after winning the 50km title in Seville. The result thus changes (see ATHLETICS 2000) and gold went to Ivano Brugnetti ITA, silver to Nikolay Matyukhin RUS and bronze to Curt Clauson USA.

Women's Name Changes – For women in all-time and 2001 lists

From	*To*
Anders	Gummelt
Andersen	Waitz
Beclea	Szekely
Buhaianu, E	Iagar
Burova	Chernyavskaya
Celnova	Prokopcuka
Clayton	Boswell
Cummings	Glover
Danilczyk	Zabawska
Daute	Drechsler
Davis, P	Davis-Thompson
Decker	Slaney
Dita	Tomescu
Drew	Newman
Dulgheru	Renda
Dziurová	Fuchsová
Goddard, C	Kenah
Graham, L	Fenton
Gündler	Möllenbeck
Halle	Haugen
Iagar, M	Dinescu
Iloc	Casandra
Ilyina	Wijenberg
Ivanova, N	Güner
Johnson, L	Hickman
Junkerman	Clifton
Kinet	Atroshchenko
Klimovets	Safronova
Kopytova	Kavakloioglu
Kovácíková	Hamácková
Krolik	Oberem
Kuzina	Kilpeläinen
Lenskaya	Lenskiy
McPaul	Currey
Makolova	Nacharkina
Manjani	Tzelíli
Martin, L	Ondieki
Mertínez, Y	Pérez
Miller, G	Tjirose
Motkova	Babashkina
Musunoi	Pantelimon
Nagel	Moroainu
Narozhilenko	Engquist
Neary	Dutoit
Negura	Olteanu
Nicholson	Hartigan
Nikolayeva T	Shchrenko
Nosova	Pechonkina
Onyali	Omagbemi
Oubouhou	Belkacem
Parry, H	Tullett
Perkins, K	DiMarco
Peters, V	Chukwuemaka
Pomoshchnikova	Voronova
Rainbird	McIvor
Rieger, N	Humbert
Rodina	Gulyayeva
Rosza	Urbanik
Sabri	Baala
Savitskaya	Grin
Slavuteanu	Simon
Sprecht	Ertl
Steblovnik	Ceplak
Storbeck	Cloete
Stoyanova, A	Yordanova
Sultanova, F	Zhdanova
Talbot, E	Yelling
Tarnopolskaya	Pintusevich(-Block)
Taylor, A	Issajenko
Tecuta	Gherasim
Tilea	Moldovan
Tysse	Plätzer
Ullrich, K	Wessel
Uppa	Kolkkala
Vasilyeva, S	Zakharova
Wittenwyler	Starkey
Zaykova	Köstem - Polnova
Zheleznyak	Barak

Not included are women who have added their husband's name to their own, as in Jearl Miles-Clark or Nadine Kleinert-Schmitt

WORLD & CONTINENTAL RECORDS

As at end of 2001. **Key:** W = World, Afr = Africa, Asi = Asia, CAC = Central America & Caribbean, Eur = Europe, NAm = North America, Oce = Oceania, SAm = South America, Com = Commonwealth, W20 = World Junior (U20), W18 = World Youth (U18, noy officially ratified by IAAF).
Successive columns show: World or Continent, performance, name, nationality, venue, date.
A altitude over 1000m, + timing by photo-electric-cell, * awaiting ratification, § not officially ratified

100 METRES

W, NAm	9.79	Maurice GREENE	USA	Athína	16 Jun 1999
Com	9.84	Donovan BAILEY	CAN	Atlanta	27 Jul 1996
	9.84	Bruny SURIN	CAN	Sevilla	22 Aug 1999
Afr	9.86	Frank FREDERICKS	NAM	Atlanta	27 Jul 1996
CAC	9.86	Ato BOLDON	TRI	Walnut	19 Apr 1998
	9.86	BOLDON also at Athína 17 Jun 1998, Athína 16 Jun 1999 and Lausanne			2 Jul 1999
Eur	9.87	Linford CHRISTIE	GBR	Stuttgart	15 Aug 1993
SAm	10.00A	Róbson da SILVA	BRA	Ciudad de México	22 Jul 1988
Asi	10.00	Koji ITO	JPN	Bangkok	13 Dec 1998
Oce	10.03	Matt SHIRVINGTON	AUS	Kuala Lumpur	17 Sep 1998
W20	10.05 §	Davidson EZINWA	NGR	Bauchi	3 Jan 1990
	10.06	Dwain CHAMBERS	GBR	Ljubljana	25 Jul 1997
W18	10.24	Darrel BROWN	TRI	Bridgetown	14 Apr 2001

200 METRES

W, NAm	19.32	Michael JOHNSON	USA	Atlanta	1 Aug 1996
Afr	19.68	Frank FREDERICKS	NAM	Atlanta	1 Aug 1996
Eur	19.72A	Pietro MENNEA	ITA	Ciudad de México	12 Sep 1979
CAC	19.77	Ato BOLDON	TRI	Stuttgart	13 Jul 1997
Com	19.68	Frank FREDERICKS	NAM	Atlanta	1 Aug 1996
SAm	19.89	Claudinei da SILVA	BRA	München	11 Sep 1999
Oce	20.06A	Peter NORMAN	AUS	Ciudad de México	16 Oct 1968
Asi	20.16	Koji ITO	JPN	Kumamoto	2 Oct 1998
W20	20.07 §	Lorenzo DANIEL	USA	Starkville	18 May 1985
	20.13	Roy MARTIN	USA	Indianapolis	16 Jun 1985
W18	20.39	Clinton DAVIS	USA	Barquisimeto	1 Aug 1982

400 METRES

W, NAm	43.18	Michael JOHNSON	USA	Sevilla	26 Aug 1999
CAC	44.14	Roberto HERNÁNDEZ	CUB	Sevilla	30 May 1990
Afr, Com	44.17	Innocent EGBUNIKE	NGR	Zürich	19 Aug 1987
SAm	44.29	Sanderlei PARRELA	BRA	Sevilla	26 Aug 1999
Eur	44.33	Thomas SCHÖNLEBE	GER	Roma	3 Sep 1987
Oce	44.38	Darren CLARK	AUS	Seoul	26 Sep 1988
Asi	44.56	Mohamed AL-MALKY	OMN	Budapest	12 Aug 1988
W20	43.87	Steve LEWIS	USA	Seoul	28 Sep 1988
W18	45.14	Obea MOORE	USA	Santiago de Chile	2 Sep 1995

800 METRES

W, Eur	1:41.11	Wilson KIPKETER	DEN	Köln	24 Aug 1997
Com	1:41.73	Sebastian COE	GBR	Firenze	10 Jun 1981
SAm	1:41.77	Joaquim CRUZ	BRA	Koln	26 Aug 1984
Afr	1:42.28	Sammy KOSKEI	KEN	Koln	26 Aug 1984
NAm	1:42.60	Johnny GRAY	USA	Koblenz	28 Aug 1985
CAC	1:42.85	Norberto TELLEZ	CUB	Atlanta	31 Jul 1996
Asi	1:44.14	LEE Jin-il	KOR	Seoul	17 Jun 1994
Oce	1:44.3 m	Peter SNELL	NZL	Christchurch	3 Feb 1962
W20	1:43.64	Japheth KIMUTAI	KEN	Zürich	13 Aug 1997
W18	1:46.9A	Jonah BIRIR	KEN	Nairobi	17 Jun 1988

1000 METRES

W, Afr, Com	2:11.96	Noah NGENY	KEN	Rieti	5 Sep 1999
Eur	2:12.18	Sebastian COE	GBR	Oslo	11 Jul 1981
NAm	2:13.9	Rick WOHLHUTER	USA	Oslo	30 Jul 1974
SAm	2:14.09	Joaquim CRUZ	BRA	Nice	20 Aug 1984
Oce	2:16.57	John WALKER	NZL	Oslo	1 Jul 1980
CAC	2:17.0	Byron DYCE	JAM	København	15 Aug 1973
Asi	2:18.91	Mohamed SULEIMAN	QAT	Lindau	28 Jul 1995
W20	2:15.00	Benjamim KIPKURUI	KEN	Nice	17 Jul 1999
W18	2:17.59	Japheth KIMUTAI	KEN	København	23 Aug 1995

1500 METRES

W, Afr	3:26.00	Hicham EL GUERROUJ	MAR	Roma	14 Jul 1998
Com	3:26.34	Bernard LAGAT	KEN	Bruxelles	24 Aug 2001
Eur	3:28.95	Fermin CACHO	ESP	Zürich	13 Aug 1997
NAm	3:29.77	Sydney MAREE	USA	Köln	25 Aug 1985
Oce	3:31.96	Simon DOYLE	AUS	Stockholm	3 Jul 1991
Asi	3:32.10	Mohammed SULEIMAN	QAT	Zürich	13 Aug 1997
SAm	3:33.99	Hudson de SOUZA	BRA	Zagreb	2 Jul 2001
CAC	3:36.60	Stephen AGAR (now CAN)	DMN	Abbotsford	2 Jun 1996
W20	3:32.91 §	Noah NGENY (no doping control)	KEN	Monaco	16 Aug 1997
	3:33.16	Benjamin KIPKIRUI	KEN	Zürich	11 Aug 1999
W18	3:35.16	Cornelius CHIRCHIR	KEN	Rieti	3 Sep 2000

1 MILE

W, Afr	3:43.13	Hicham El GUERROUJ	MAR	Roma	7 Jul 1999
Com	3:43.40	Noah NGENY	KEN	Roma	7 Jul 1999
Eur	3:46.32	Steve CRAM	GBR	Oslo	27 Jul 1985
NAm	3:47.69	Steve SCOTT	USA	Oslo	7 Jul 1982
Oce	3:49.08	John WALKER	NZL	Oslo	7 Jul 1982
Asi	3:51.12	Mohammed SULEIMAN	QAT	Zürich	16 Aug 1995
SAm	3:53.00	Joaquim CRUZ	BRA	Los Angeles	13 May 1984
CAC	3:57.34	Byron DYCE	JAM	Stockholm	1 Jul 1974
W20	3:50.41	Noah NGENY	KEN	Nice	16 Jul 1997
W18	3:54.56	Isaac SONGOK	KEN	Linz	20 Aug 2001

2000 METRES

W, Afr	4:44.79	Hicham EL GUERROUJ	MAR	Berlin	7 Sep 1999
Com	4:48.74	John KIBOWEN	KEN	Hechtel	1 Aug 1998
Eur	4:51.39	Steve CRAM	GBR	Budapest	4 Aug 1985
Oce	4:51.52	John WALKER	NZL	Oslo	30 Jun 1976
NAm	4:52.44	Jim SPIVEY	USA	Lausanne	15 Sep 1987
Asi	4:55.57	Mohammed SULEIMAN	QAT	Roma	8 Jun 1995
W20	4:59.14	Ali SAÏDI-SIEF	ALG	Villeneuve d'Ascq	29 Jun 1997
CAC	5:03.4	Arturo BARRIOS	MEX	Nice	10 Jul 1989
SAm	5:03.58	Hudson Santos de SOUZA	BRA	Hechtel	1 Aug 1998

3000 METRES

W, Afr, Com	7:20.67	Daniel KOMEN	KEN	Rieti	1 Sep 1996
Eur	7:26.62	Mohammed MOURHIT	BEL	Monaco	18 Aug 2000
NAm	7:30.84	Bob KENNEDY	USA	Monte Carlo	8 Aug 1998
CAC	7:35.71	Arturo BARRIOS	MEX	Nice	10 Jul 1989
Oce	7:37.49	John WALKER	NZL	London	17 Jul 1982
Asi	7:38.20	Mohammed SULEIMAN	QAT	Berlin	27 Aug 1993
SAm	7:42.55	Hudson de SOUZA	BRA	Nice	9 Jul 2001
W20	7:30.67	Kenenisa BEKELE	ETH	Bruxelles	24 Aug 2001
W18	7:44.36	Robert KIPCHUMBA	KEN	Lausanne	4 Jul 2001

5000 METRES

W, Afr	12:39.36	Haile GEBRSELASSIE	ETH	Helsinki	13 Jun 1998
Com	12:39.74	Daniel KOMEN	KEN	Bruxelles	22 Aug 1997
Eur	12:49.71	Mohammed MOURHIT	BEL	Bruxelles	25 Aug 2000
NAm	12:58.21	Bob KENNEDY	USA	Zürich	14 Aug 1996
CAC	13:07.79	Arturo BARRIOS	MEX	London	14 Jul 1989
Oce	13:12.87	Dick QUAX	NZL	Stockholm	5 Jul 1977
Asi	13:13.40	Toshinari TAKAOKA	JPN	Hechtel	1 Aug 1998
SAm	13:19.64	Antonio SILIO	ARG	Roma	17 Jul 1991
W20	12:53.72	Philip MOSIMA	KEN	Roma	5 Jun 1996
W18	13:15.67	Ismael KIRUI	KEN	London (CP)	10 Jul 1992

10,000 METRES

W, Afr	26:22.75	Haile GEBRSELASSIE	ETH	Hengelo	1 Jun 1998
Com	26:27.85	Paul TERGAT	KEN	Bruxelles	22 Aug 1997
Eur	26:52.30	Mohammed MOURHIT	BEL	Bruxelles	3 Sep 1999
CAC	27:08.23	Arturo BARRIOS	MEX	Berlin	18 Aug 1989
NAm	27:13.98	Mebrahtom KEFLEZIGHI	USA	Palo Alto	4 May 2001
Oce	27:31.92	Shaun CREIGHTON	AUS	Melbourne	25 Nov 1996
Asi	27:35.09	Toshinari TAKAOKA	JPN	Palo Alto	4 May 2001
SAm	27:38.72	Antonio SILIO	ARG	Bruxelles	3 Sep 1993
W20	27:11.18	Richard CHELIMO	KEN	Hengelo	25 Jun 1991
W18	27:25.55	Robert KIPCHUMBA	KEN	Bruxelles	24 Aug 2001

MARATHON

W, Afr	2:05:42	Khalid KHANNOUCHI	MAR	Chicago	24 Oct 1999
SAm	2:06:05	Ronaldo da COSTA	BRA	Berlin	20 Sep 1998
Com	2:06:16	Moses TANUI	KEN	Chicago	24 Oct 1999
Eur	2:06:36	António PINTO	POR	London	16 Apr 2000
Asi	2:06:51	Atsushi FUJITA	JPN	Fukuoka	3 Dec 2000
NAm	2:07:01	Khalid KHANNOUCHI (ex MAR)	USA	Chicago	22 Oct 2000
CAC	2:07:19	Andrés ESPINOSA	MEX	Boston	18 Apr 1994
Oce	2:07:51	Rob DE CASTELLA	AUS	Boston	21 Apr 1986
W20	2:10:46	LI Zhuhong	CHN	Beijing	14 Oct 2001

Boston course has an overall net drop of 139m (0.33%), and in 1994 there was a strong following wind.

3000 METRES STEEPLECHASE

W, Afr	7:55.28	Brahim BOULAMI	MAR	Bruxelles	24 Aug 2001
Com	7:55.72	Bernard BARMASAI	KEN	Köln	24 Aug 1997
Eur	8:07.62	Joseph MAHMOUD	FRA	Bruxelles	24 Aug 1984
Asi	8:08.26	Saad AL-ASMARI	SAU	Stockholm	7 Jul 1997
NAm	8:09.17	Henry MARSH	USA	Koblenz	28 Aug 1985
Oce	8:14.05	Peter RENNER	NZL	Koblenz	29 Aug 1984
SAm	8:14.41	Wander MOURA	BRA	Mar del Plata	22 Mar 1995
CAC	8:25.69	Salvador MIRANDA	MEX	Barakaldo	9 Jul 2000
W20	7:58.66	Stephen CHERONO	KEN	Bruxelles	24 Aug 2001
W18	8:19.12	Stephen CHERONO	KEN	Zürich	11 Aug 1999

110 METRES HURDLES

W, Eur, Com	12.91	Colin JACKSON	GBR	Stuttgart	20 Aug 1993
NAm	12.92	Roger KINGDOM	USA	Zürich	16 Aug 1989
	12.92	Allen JOHNSON	USA	Atlanta	23 Jun 1996
	12.92	Allen JOHNSON	USA	Bruxelles	23 Aug 1996
CAC	13.00	Anier GARCIA	CUB	Sydney	25 Sep 2000
Asi	13.25	LI Tong	CHN	Linz	4 Jul 1994
Afr	13.26	Shaun BOWNES	RSA	Heusden	14 Jul 2001
Oce	13.29	Kyle VANDER-KUYP	AUS	Göteborg	11 Aug 1995
SAm	13.38	Márcio de SOUZA	BRA	Rio de Janeiro	3 Jun 1999
W20	13.23	Renaldo NEHEMIAH	USA	Zürich	16 Aug 1978
W18	13.43	SHI Dongpeng	CHN	Shanghai	5 May 2001

400 METRES HURDLES

W, NAm	46.78	Kevin YOUNG	USA	Barcelona	6 Aug 1992
Afr, Com	47.10	Samuel MATETE	ZAM	Zürich	7 Aug 1991
Eur	47.37	Stéphane DIAGANA	FRA	Lausanne	5 Jul 1995
Asi	47.53	Hadi Sou'an AL-SOMAILY	KSA	Sydney	27 Sep 2000
CAC	47.38	Felix SÁNCHEZ	DOM	Zürich	17 Aug 2001
SAm	48.04	Eronilde de ARAUJO	BRA	Nice	12 Jul 1995
Oce	48.28	Rohan ROBINSON	AUS	Atlanta	31 Jul 1996
W20	48.02	Danny HARRIS	USA	Los Angeles	17 Jun 1984
W18	50.03	Hiroshi KAKIMORI	JPN	Ise	31 Aug 1985

HIGH JUMP

W, CAC	2.45	Javier SOTOMAYOR	CUB	Salamanca	27 Jul 1993
Eur	2.42	Patrik SJÖBERG	SWE	Stockholm	30 Jun 1987
	2.42 i§	Carlos THRÄNHARDT	GER	Berlin	26 Feb 1988
NAm	2.40 i§	Hollis CONWAY	USA	Sevilla	10 Mar 1991
		Charles AUSTIN	USA	Zürich	7 Aug 1991
Asi	2.39	ZHU Jianhua	CHN	Eberstadt	10 Jun 1984
Com	2.38i	Steve SMITH	GBR	Wuppertal	4 Feb 1994
	2.38	Troy KEMP	BAH	Nice	12 Jul 1995
Oce	2.36	Tim FORSYTH	AUS	Melbourne	2 Mar 1997
Afr	2.34	Abderrahmane HAMMAD	ALG	Alger	14 Jul 2000
SAm	2.33	Gilmar MAYO	COL	Pereira	17 Oct 1994
W20	2.37	Dragutin TOPIC	YUG	Plovdiv	12 Aug 1990
		Steve SMITH	GBR	Seoul	20 Sep 1992
W18	2.33	Javier SOTOMAYOR	CUB	La Habana	19 May 1984

POLE VAULT

W, Eur	6.15 i§	Sergey BUBKA	UKR	Donetsk	21 Feb 1993
	6.14 A	Sergey BUBKA	UKR	Sestriere	31 Jul 1994
Afr, Com	6.03	Okkert BRITS	RSA	Köln	18 Aug 1995
NAm	6.03	Jeff HARTWIG	USA	Jonesboro	14 Jun 2000
Oce	6.05	Dmitriy MARKOV	AUS	Edmonton	9 Aug 2001

Asi	5.92i	Igor POTAPOVICH	KAZ	Stockholm	19 Feb 1998
	5.90	Grigoriy YEGOROV	KAZ	Stuttgart 19 Aug 1993 & London	10 Sep 1993
	5.90	Igor POTAPOVICH	KAZ	Nice	10 Jul 1996
SAm	5.76	Tom HINTNAUS	BRA	Zürich	21 Aug 1985
CAC	5.70A	Dominic JOHNSON	LCA	El Paso	26 Aug 2000
	5.72 §	Paul BENAVIDES	MEX	El Paso	18 Jun 1994
W20	5.80	Maksim TARASOV	RUS	Bryansk	14 Jul 1989
W18	5.50	István BAGYULA	HUN	Milano	19 Jun 1986

LONG JUMP

W, NAm	8.95	Mike POWELL	USA	Tokyo	30 Aug 1991
Eur	8.86 A	Robert EMMIYAN	ARM	Tsakhkadzor	22 May 1987
CAC	8.71	Iván PEDROSO	CUB	Salamanca	18 Jul 1995
Com	8.62	James BECKFORD	JAM	Orlando	5 Apr 1997
Oce	8.49	Jai TAURIMA	AUS	Sydney	28 Sep 2000
Afr	8.46	Cheikh TOURÉ	SEN	Bad Langensalza	15 Jun 1997
SAm	8.40	Douglas de SOUZA	BRA	São Paulo	15 Feb 1995
Asi	8.40	LAO Jianfeng	CHN	Zhaoqing	28 May 1997
W20	8.34	Randy WILLIAMS	USA	München	8 Sep 1972
W18	8.25	Luis Alberto BUENO	CUB	La Habana	28 Sep 1986

TRIPLE JUMP

W, Eur, Com	18.29	Jonathan EDWARDS	GBR	Göteborg	7 Aug 1995
NAm	18.09	Kenny HARRISON	USA	Atlanta	27 Jul 1996
CAC	17.92	James BECKFORD	JAM	Odessa, Texas	20 May 1995
SAm	17.89 A	João Carlos de OLIVEIRA	BRA	Ciudad de México	15 Oct 1975
Oce	17.46	Ken LORRAWAY	AUS	London	7 Aug 1982
Asi	17.35	Oleg SAKIRKIN	KAZ	Moskva	5 Jun 1994
Afr	17.34	Ndabezinhle MDHLONGWA	ZIM	Lafayette	28 Mar 1998
W20	17.50	Volker MAI	GER	Erfurt	23 Jun 1985
W18	16.89	GU Junjie	CHN	Dalian	5 May 1985

SHOT

W, NAm	23.12	Randy BARNES	USA	Westwood	20 May 1990
Eur	23.06	Ulf TIMMERMANN	GER	Hania	22 May 1988
Afr, Com	21.97	Janus ROBBERTS	RSA	Eugene	2 Jun 2001
SAm	20.90	Gert WEIL	CHL	Wirges	17 Aug 1986
CAC	20.78	Alexis PAUMIER	CUB	La Habana	29 Jul 2000
Asi	20.60	Shakti SINGH	IND	Bangalore	5 Jul 2000
Oce	20.35	Justin ANLEZARK	AUS	Gold Coast (RB)	10 Sep 2000
W20	21.05 i§	Terry ALBRITTON	USA	New York	22 Feb 1974
	20.65 §	Mike CARTER	USA	Boston	4 Jul 1979
	20.39	Janus ROBBERTS	RSA	Germiston	7 Mar 1998
W18	18.73	Karsten STOLZ	GER	Essen	2 Sep 1981

DISCUS

W, Eur	74.08	Jürgen SCHULT	GER	Neubrandenburg	6 Jun 1986
NAm	72.34 ¶	Ben PLUCKNETT	USA	Stockholm	7 Jul 1981
	71.32 §	Ben PLUCKNETT	USA	Eugene	4 Jun 1983
CAC	71.06	Luis DELIS	CUB	La Habana	21 May 1983
Afr, Com	69.96	Frantz KRUGER	RSA	Stellenbosch	30 Mar 2001
Oce	65.62 §	Werner REITERER	AUS	Melbourne	15 Dec 1987
	65.06	Wayne MARTIN	AUS	Newcastle	3 Jan 1979
Asi	65.16	LI Shaojie	CHN	Nanjing	7 May 1996
SAm	64.30	Ramón JIMÉNEZ-GAONA	PAR	Eugene	23 May 1992
W20	65.62 §	Werner REITERER	AUS	Melbourne	15 Dec 1987
	63.64	Werner HARTMANN	GER	Strasbourg	25 Jun 1978
W18	62.36	NU Ermaimaiti	CHN	Guangzhou	21 Nov 2001

¶ Disallowed by the IAAF following retrospective disqualification for drug abuse, but ratified by the AAU/TAC

HAMMER

W, Eur	86.74	Yuriy SEDYKH	UKR/RUS	Stuttgart	30 Aug 1986
Asi	83.47	Koji MUROFUSHI	JPN	Toyota	14 Jul 2001
NAm	82.52	Lance DEAL	USA	Milano	7 Sep 1996
Afr, Com	79.40	Chris HARMSE	RSA	Pretoria	7 Nov 2001
CAC	77.78	Alberto SANCHEZ	CUB	La Habana	15 May 1998
Oce	78.93	Stuart RENDELL	AUS	Szombathely	15 Jul 2001
	78.99 §	Stuart RENDELL (unsurveyed field)	AUS	Calgary	30 Jul 2001
SAm	76.42	Juan CERRA	ARG	Trieste	25 Jul 2001
W20	78.33	Olli-Pekka KARJALAINEN	FIN	Seinäjoki	5 Aug 1999
W18	73.66	Vladislav PISKUNOV	UKR	Live	11 Jun 1994

JAVELIN

W, Eur	98.48	Jan ZELEZNY	CZE	Jena	25 May 1996
Com	91.46	Steve BACKLEY	GBR	Auckland (NS)	25 Jan 1992
NAm	89.16 §	Tom PETRANOFF	USA	Potchefstroom	1 Mar 1991
	87.12	Tom PUKSTYS	USA	Jena	25 May 1997
Afr	88.75	Marius CORBETT	RSA	Kuala Lumpur	21 Sep 1998
Oce	88.20	Gavin LOVEGROVE	NZL	Oslo	5 Jul 1996
Asi	87.60	Kazuhiro MIZOGUCHI	JPN	San José	27 May 1989
CAC	87.12	Emeterio GONZALEZ	CUB	Jena	3 Jun 2000
SAm	84.70	Edgar BAUMANN	PAR	San Marcos	17 Oct 1999
W20	83.87	Andreas THORKILDSEN	NOR	Fana	7 Jun 2001
W18	79.96	Aki PARVIAINEN	FIN	Pyhäselkä	12 Sep 1991

DECATHLON

W,Eur	9026	Roman SEBRLE	CZE	Götzis	27 May 2001
NAm	8891	Dan O'BRIEN	USA	Talence	5 Sep 1992
Com	8847	Daley THOMPSON	GBR	Los Angeles	9 Aug 1984
Oce	8490	Jagan HAMES	AUS	Kuala Lumpur	18 Sep 1998
Asi	8445	Ramil GANIYEV	UZB	Athína	6 Aug 1997
CAC	8252	Ra'l DUANY	CUB	La Habana	24 Jul 2000
SAm	8291 m	Tito STEINER	ARG	Provo	23 Jun 1983
	8266	Pedro da SILVA	BRA	Walnut	24 Apr 1987
Afr	7934 h	Ahmed MAHOUR BACHA	ALG	El Djezair (Alger)	9 Jul 1985
	7642	Anis RIAHI	TUN	Talence	31 Jul 2000
W20	8397	Torsten VOSS	GER	Erfurt	7 Jul 1982
W18	8104h	Valter KÜLVET	EST	Viimsi	23 Aug 1981
	7829	Valter KÜLVET	EST	Stockholm	13 Sep 1981

20 KILOMETRES WALK

CAC	1:17:25.6 t	Bernardo SEGURA	MEX	Fana	7 May 1994
W, Eur	1:17:46	Roman RASSKAZOV	RUS	Moskva	19 May 2000
Asi	1:18:04	BO Lingtang	CHN	Beijing	7 Apr 1994
Oce, Com	1:18:14	Nathan DEAKES	AUS	Dublin	16 Jun 2001
SAm	1:18:24	Jefferson PEREZ	ECU	Podebrady	19 Apr 1997
Afr	1:19:02	Hatem GHOULA	TUN	Eisenhüttenstadt	10 May 1997
NAm	1:21:03	Arturo HUERTA	CAN	Etobicoke	7 Jul 2000
W20	1:18:06 §	Viktor BURAYEV	RUS	Adler	4 Mar 2001

20,000 METRES TRACK WALK

W, CAC	1:17:25.6	Bernardo SEGURA	MEX	Fana	7 May 1994
Eur	1:18:35.2	Stefan JOHANSSON	SWE	Fana	15 May 1992
Oce, Com	1:19:48.1	Nathan DEAKES	AUS	Brisbane	4 Sep 2001
Asi	1:20:24.4	LI Mingcai	CHN	Jinan	15 Mar 1992
SAm	1:20:55.4	Jefferson PEREZ	ECU	Fana	4 May 1996
NAm	1:22:27.0	Tim BERRETT	CAN	Edmonds, WA	9 Jun 1996
Afr	1:22:51.84	Hatem GHOULA	TUN	Leutkirch	8 Sep 1994
W20	1:21:29.2	Viktor BURAYEV	RUS	Brisbane	4 Sep 2001
W18	1:24:28.3	ZHU Hongjun	CHN	Xian	15 Sep 1999

50 KILOMETRES WALK

W, Eur	3:37:26	Valeriy SPITSYN	RUS	Moskva	21 May 2000
Asi	3:39:22	Sergey KOREPANOV	KAZ	Mézidon-Canon	2 May 1999
CAC	3:41:20	Raúl GONZALEZ	MEX	Praha-Podebrady	11 Jun 1978
Oce, Com	3:43:13	Simon BAKER	AUS	L'Hospitalet	28 May 1989
NAm	3:47:48	Marcel JOBIN	CAN	Québec	20 Jun 1981
SAm	3:52:16	Héctor MORENO	COL	Naumberg	25 May 1997
Afr	4:07:30	Johan MOERDYK	RSA	Durban	14 Sep 1996
W20	3:43:41	ZHANG Huiqiang	CHN	Zhuhai	12 Mar 1996
W18	3:45:46	YU Guoping	CHN	Guangzhou	23 Nov 2001

50,000 METRES TRACK WALK

W, Eur	3:40:57.9	Thierry TOUTAIN	FRA	Héricourt	29 Sep 1996
CAC	3:41:38.4	Raúl GONZALEZ	MEX	Fana	25 May 1979
Oce, Com	3:43:50.0	Simon BAKER	AUS	Melbourne	9 Sep 1990
Asi	3:48:13.7	ZHAO Yongshen	CHN	Fana	7 May 1994
NAm	3:56:13.0	Tim BERRETT	CAN	Saskatoon	21 Jul 1991
SAm	4:14:28.5	Jorge LOREFICE	ARG	Buenos Aires	9 May 1993
	4:14:28.5	Benjamin LOREFICE	ARG	Buenos Aires	9 May 1993
Afr	4:21:44.5	Abdelwahab FERGUÈNE	ALG	Toulouse	25 Mar 1984

4 X 100 METRES RELAY

W, NAm	37.40	USA (Marsh, Burrell, Mitchell, C.Lewis)	Barcelona	8 Aug 1992
	37.40	USA (Drummond, Cason, Mitchell, Burrell)	Stuttgart	21 Aug 1993
Com	37.69	CAN (Esmie, Gilbert, Surin, Bailey)	Atlanta	3 Aug 1996
Eur	37.73	GBR (Gardener, Campbell, Devonish, Chambers)	Sevilla	29 Aug 1999
SAm	37.90	BRA (V Lima, Ribeiro, A da Silva, Cl da Silva)	Sydney	30 Sep 2000
Afr	37.91	NGR (Asonze, Obikwelu, Effiong, Aliu)	Sevilla	29 Aug 1999
CAC	38.00	CUB (Simón, Lamela, Isasi, Aguilera)	Barcelona	8 Aug 1992
Oce	38.17	AUS (Henderson, Jackson, Brimacombe, Marsh)	Göteborg	12 Aug 1995
Asi	38.31	JPN (Inoue, K Ito, Tsuchie, Asahara)	Athína	9 Aug 1997
	38.31	JPN (Kawabata, K ito, Suetsugu, Asahara)	Sydney	29 Sep 2000
W20	39.00A	USA (Jessie, Franklin, Blalock, Mitchell)	USAF Academy	18 Jul 1983
W18	40.03	JAM (W Smith, M Frater, Spence, O Brown)	Bydgoszcz	18 Jul 1999

4 X 400 METRES RELAY

W, NAm	2:54.20	USA (Young, Pettigrew, Washington, Johnson)	Uniondale, NY	22 Jul 1998
Eur	2:56.60	GBR (Thomas, Baulch, Richardson, Black)	Atlanta	3 Aug 1996
CAC, Com	2:56.75	JAM (McDonald, Haughton, McFarlane, Clarke)	Athína	10 Aug 1997
SAm	2:58.56	BRA (C da Silva, A J dosSantos, de Araújo, Parrela)	Winnipeg	30 Jul 1999
Afr	2:58.68	NGR (Chukwu, Monye, Nada, Udo-Obong)	Sydney	30 Sep 2000
Oce	2:59.70	AUS (Frayne, Clark, Minihan, Mitchell)	Los Angeles	11 Aug 1984
Asi	3:00.76	JPN (Karube, K Ito, Osakada, Omori)	Atlanta	3 Aug 1996
W20	3:01.90	USA (Campbell, Rish, Waddle, Reed)	Athína	20 Jul 1986
W18	3:13.48	USA (Los Angeles Jets)	Baton Rouge	27 Jul 1997

World Records at other men's events recognised by the IAAF

20km	56:55.6	Arturo BARRIOS (now USA)	MEX	La Flèche	30 Mar 1991
1 Hour	21,101 m	Arturo BARRIOS (now USA)	MEX	La Flèche	30 Mar 1991
25km	1:13:55.8	Toshihiko SEKO	JPN	Christchurch	22 Mar 1981
30km	1:29:18.8	Toshihiko SEKO	JPN	Christchurch	22 Mar 1981
4 x 200m	1:18.68	Santa Monica Track Club (Michael Marsh, Leroy Burrell, Floyd Heard, Carl Lewis)	USA	Walnut	17 Apr 1994
4 x 800m	7:03.89	United Kingdom Team (Peter Elliott, Garry Cook, Steve Cram, Sebastian Coe)	GBR	London	30 Aug 1982
4 x l500m	14:38.8 m	F.R.Germany Team (Thomas Wessinghage, Harald Hudak, Michael Lederer, Karl Fleschen)	GER	Köln	17 Aug 1977
Track Walking					
2 Hours	29,572m	Maurizio DAMILANO	ITA	Cuneo	4 Oct 1992
30km	2:01:44.1	Maurizio DAMILANO	ITA	Cuneo	4 Oct 1992

WOMEN

100 METRES

W, NAm	10.49	Florence GRIFFITH JOYNER	USA	Indianapolis	16 Jul 1988
Eur	10.73	Christine ARRON	FRA	Budapest	19 Aug 1998
CAC, Com	10.74	Merlene OTTEY	JAM	Milano	7 Sep 1996
Asi	10.79	LI Xuemei	CHN	Shanghai	18 Oct 1997
Afr	10.90	Glory ALOZIE	NGR	La Laguna	5 Jun 1999
	10.84 §	Chioma AJUNWA	NGR	Lagos	11 Apr 1992
Oce	11.12A	Melinda GAINSFORD/TAYLOR	AUS	Sestriere	31 Jul 1994
SAm	11.17A	Lucimar de MOURA	BRA	Bogotá (sf)	25 Jun 1999
	11.17A	Lucimar de MOURA	BRA	Bogotá	25 Jun 1999
W20	10.88	Marlies OELSNER/GÖHR	GER	Dresden	1 Jul 1977
W18	11.13	Chandra CHEESEBOROUGH	USA	Eugene	21 Jun 1976

200 METRES

W, NAm	21.34	Florence GRIFFITH JOYNER	USA	Seoul	29 Sep 1988
CAC, Com	21.64	Merlene OTTEY	JAM	Bruxelles	13 Sep 1991
Eur	21.71	Marita KOCH	GER	Chemnitz	10 Jun 1979
	21.71 §	Marita KOCH	GER	Potsdam	21 Jul 1984
	21.71	Heike DRECHSLER	GER	Jena	29 Jun 1986
	21.71 §	Heike DRECHSLER	GER	Stuttgart	29 Aug 1986
Asi	22.01	LI Xuemei	CHN	Shanghai	22 Oct 1997
Afr	22.06 A§	Evette DE KLERK	RSA	Pietersburg	8 Apr 1989
	22.07	Mary ONYALI	NGR	Zürich	14 Aug 1996
Oce	22.23	Melinda GAINSFORD-TAYLOR	AUS	Stuttgart	13 Jul 1997
SAm	22.60A	Lucimar de MOURA	BRA	Bogotá	26 Jun 1999
W20	22.19	Natalya BOCHINA	RUS	Moskva	30 Jul 1980
W18	22.58	Marion JONES	USA	New Orleans	28 Jun 1992

400 METRES

W, Eur	47.60	Marita KOCH	GER	Canberra	6 Oct 1985
Oce, Com	48.63	Cathy FREEMAN	AUS	Atlanta	29 Jul 1996
NAm	48.83	Valerie BRISCO	USA	Los Angeles	6 Aug 1984
Afr	49.10	Falilat OGUNKOYA	NGR	Atlanta	29 Jul 1996
CAC	49.28	Pauline DAVIS	BAH	Atlanta	29 Jul 1996
	49.2 mA	Ana Fidelia QUIROT	CUB	Bogotá	13 Aug 1989
SAm	49.64	Ximena RESTREPO	COL	Barcelona	5 Aug 1992
Asi	49.81	MA Yuqin	CHN	Beijing	11 Sep 1993
W20	49.42	Grit BREUER	GER	Tokyo	27 Aug 1991
W18	50.01	LI Jing	CHN	Shanghai	18 Oct 1997

800 METRES

W, Eur	1:53.28	Jarmila KRATOCHVÍLOVÁ	CZE	München	26 Jul 1983
CAC	1:54.44	Ana Fidelia QUIROT	CUB	Barcelona	9 Sep 1989
Afr	1:55.19	Maria Lurdes MUTOLA	MOZ	Zürich	17 Aug 1994
Com	1:55.29	Maria Lurdes MUTOLA	MOZ	Köln	24 Aug 1997
Asi	1:55.54	LIU Dong	CHN	Beijing	9 Sep 1993
NAm	1:56.40	Jearl MILES-CLARK	USA	Zürich	11 Aug 1999
SAm	1:56.68	Letitia VRIESDE	SUR	Göteborg	13 Aug 1995
Oce	1:58.25	Toni HODGKINSON	NZL	Atlanta	27 Jul 1996
W20, W18	1:57.18	WANG Yuan	CHN	Beijing	8 Sep 1993

1000 METRES

W, Eur	2:28.98	Svetlana MASTERKOVA	RUS	Bruxelles	23 Aug 1996
Afr	2:29.34	Maria Lurdes MUTOLA	MOZ	Bruxelles	25 Aug 1995
Com	2:29.66	Maria Lurdes MUTOLA	MOZ	Bruxelles	23 Aug 1996
NAm	2:31.80	Regina JACOBS	USA	Brunswick	3 Jul 1999
SAm	2:32.25	Letitia VRIESDE	SUR	Berlin	10 Sep 1991
CAC	2:33.21	Ana Fidelia QUIROT	CUB	Jerez de la Frontera	13 Sep 1989
Asi	2:33.6 §	Svetlana ULMASOVA	UZB	Podolsk	5 Aug 1979
Oce	2:38.54	Alison WRIGHT	NZL	Berlin	17 Aug 1979
W20	2:35.4a	Irina NIKITINA	RUS	Podolsk	5 Aug 1979
	2:35.4	Katrin WÜHN	GDR	Potsdam	12 Jul 1984
W18					

1500 METRES

W, Asi	3:50.46	QU Yunxia	CHN	Beijing	11 Sep 1993
Eur	3:52.47	Tatyana KAZANKINA	RUS	Zürich	13 Aug 1980
Afr	3:55.30	Hassiba BOULMERKA	ALG	Barcelona	8 Aug 1992
NAm	3:57.12	Mary DECKER/SLANEY	USA	Stockholm	26 Jul 1983
Com	3:57.41	Jackline MARANGA	KEN	Monaco	8 Aug 1998
Oce	4:01.34	Margaret CROWLEY	AUS	Oslo	5 Jul 1996
CAC	4:01.84	Yvonne GRAHAM	JAM	Monaco	25 Jul 1995
SAm	4:05.67	Letitia VRIESDE	SUR	Tokyo	31 Aug 1991
W20	3:51.34	LANG Yinglai	CHN	Shanghai	18 Oct 1997
W18	3:54.52	ZHANG Ling	CHN	Shanghai	18 Oct 1997

1 MILE

W, Eur	4:12.56	Svetlana MASTERKOVA	RUS	Zürich	14 Aug 1996
NAm	4:16.71	Mary SLANEY	USA	Zürich	21 Aug 1985
Com	4:17.57	Zola BUDD	GBR	Zürich	21 Aug 1985
Afr	4:20.79	Hassiba BOULMERKA	ALG	Oslo	6 Jul 1991
CAC	4:24.64	Yvonne GRAHAM	JAM	Zürich	17 Aug 1994
Oce	4:25.84	Margaret CROWLEY	AUS	Monaco	10 Aug 1996
SAm	4:30.05	Soraya TELLES	BRA	Praha	9 Jun 1988
Asi	4:35.34	WANG Qingfen	CHN	Linz	5 Jul 1998
W20	4:17.57	Zola BUDD	GBR	Zürich	21 Aug 1985
W18	4:32.73	Susie POWER	AUS	Melbourne	17 Dec 1992

2000 METRES

W, Eur	5:25.36	Sonia O'SULLIVAN	IRL	Edinburgh	8 Jul 1994
Com	5:26.93	Yvonne MURRAY	GBR	Edinburgh	8 Jul 1994
Asi	5:29.43 §	WANG Junxia	CHN	Beijing	12 Sep 1993
NAm	5:32.7	Mary SLANEY	USA	Eugene	3 Aug 1984
Afr	5:37.6 §	Zahra OUAZIZ	MAR	Bruxelles	3 Sep 1999
Oce	5:44.67	Anne HARE	NZL	London (CP)	11 Jul 1986
W20	5:33.15	Zola BUDD	GBR	London (CP)	13 Jul 1984
W18	5:46.5+	Sally BARSOSIO	KEN	Zürich	16 Aug 1995

3000 METRES

W, Asi	8:06.11	WANG Junxia	CHN	Beijing	13 Sep 1993
Eur	8:21.64	Sonia O'SULLIVAN	IRL	London	15 Jul 1994
Afr	8:25.62	Berhane ADERE	ETH	Zürich	17 Aug 2001
NAm	8:25.83	Mary SLANEY	USA	Roma	7 Sep 1985
Com	8:26.97	Paula RADCLIFFE	Eng	Roma	29 Jun 2001
CAC	8:37.07	Yvonne GRAHAM	JAM	Zürich	16 Aug 1995
Oce	8:42.95	Benita WILLIS	AUS	Roma	29 Jun 2001
SAm	9:02.37	Delirde BERNARDI	BRA	Linz	4 Jul 1994
W20	8:28.83	Zola BUDD	GBR	Roma	7 Sep 1985
W18	8:36.45	MA Ningning	CHN	Jinan	6 Jun 1993

5000 METRES

W, Asi	14:28.09	JIANG Bo	CHN	Shanghai	23 Oct 1997
Eur	14:29.32	Olga YEGOROVA	RUS	Berlin	31 Aug 2001
Afr	14:30.88	Getenesh WAMI	ETH	Heusden	5 Aug 2000
Com	14:32.44	Paula RADCLIFFE	Eng	Berlin	31 Aug 2001
NAm	14:45.35	Regina JACOBS	USA	Sacramento	21 Jul 2000
CAC	15:06.54	Nora ROCHA	MEX	Berlin	1 Sep 1998
Oce	15:08.69	Kerryn McCANN	AUS	Brisbane	3 Sep 2000
SAm	15:22.01	Carmen de OLIVEIRA	BRA	Hechtel	31 Jul 1993
W20	14:39.96 §	YIN Lili (no doping control)	CHN	Shanghai	22 Oct 1997
	14:45.90	JIANG Bo	CHN	Nanjing	24 Oct 1995
W18	14:45.71	SONG Liqing	CHN	Shanghai	21 Oct 1997

10,000 METRES

W, Asi	29:31.78	WANG Junxia	CHN	Beijing	8 Sep 1993
Eur	30:13.74	Ingrid KRISTIANSEN	NOR	Oslo	5 Jul 1986
Afr	30:17.49	Derertu TULU	ETH	Sydney	30 Sep 2000
Com	30:26.97	Paula RADCLIFFE	GBR	Sydney	30 Sep 2000
CAC	31:10.12	Adriana FERNANDEZ	MEX	Brunswick	1 Jul 2000
Oce	31:11.72	Lisa ONDIEKI	AUS	Helsinki	30 Jun 1992
NAm	31:19.89	Lynn JENNINGS	USA	Barcelona	7 Aug 1992
SAm	31:47.76	Carmen de OLIVEIRA	BRA	Stuttgart	21 Aug 1993
W20	30:39.41	LAN Lixin	CHN	Shanghai	19 Oct 1997
W18	31:11.26	SONG Liqing	CHN	Shanghai	19 Oct 1997

MARATHON

W, Afr, Com	2:18:47	Catherine NDEREBA	KEN	Chicago	7 Oct 2001
Asi	2:19:46	Naoko TAKAHASHI	JPN	Berlin	30 Sep 2001
Eur	2:21:06	Ingrid KRISTIANSEN	NOR	London	21 Apr 1985
NAm	2:21:21	Joan BENOIT/SAMUELSON	USA	Chicago	20 Oct 1985
Oce	2:23:51	Lisa MARTIN/ONDIEKI	AUS	Osaka	31 Jan 1988
CAC	2:24:06	Adriana FERNANDEZ	MEX	London	18 Apr 1999
SAm	2:27:41	Carmen de OLIVEIRA	BRA	Boston	18 Apr 1994

Boston course has an overall net drop of 139m (0.33%), and in 1994 there was a strong following wind.

W20	2:23:37	LIU Min	CHN	Beijing	14 Oct 2001

3000 METRES STEEPLECHASE

W, Eur	9:25.31	Justyna BAK	POL	Nice	9 Jul 2001
W20,Oce,Com	9:30.70	Melissa ROLLISON	AUS	Brisbane	4 Sep 2001
NAm	9:41.94	Elizabeth JACKSON	USA	Brisbane	4 Sep 2001
Afr	10:23.55	Sonia AGOUN	TUN	Bucuresti	7 Aug 2000
SAm	10:26.00	Michelle Barreto DA COSTA	BRA	Rio de Janeiro	5 Aug 2000
W18	10:10.73	Melissa ROLLISON	AUS	Sydney	25 Feb 2000

100 METRES HURDLES

W, Eur	12.21	Yordanka DONKOVA	BUL	Stara Zagora	20 Aug 1988
NAm	12.33	Gail DEVERS	USA	Sacramento	23 Jul 2000
Asi	12.44	Olga SHISHIGINA	KAZ	Luzern	27 Jun 1995
Afr, Com	12.44	Glory ALOZIE	NGR	Monaco	8 Aug 1998
	12.44	Glory ALOZIE	NGR	Bruxelles	28 Aug 1998
	12.44	Glory ALOZIE	NGR	Sevilla	28 Aug 1999
CAC	12.52	Michelle FREEMAN	JAM	Athína	10 Aug 1997
	12.52	Michelle FREEMAN	JAM	Zürich	12 Aug 1998
	12.52	Delloreen ENNIS-LONDON	JAM	Kingston	22 Jul 2000
SAm	12.71	Maurren MAGGI	BRA	Manaus	19 May 2001
Oce	12.93	Pam RYAN	AUS	München	4 Sep 1972
W20	12.84	Aliuska LÓPEZ	CUB	Zagreb	16 Jul 1987
W18	12.95	Candy YOUNG	USA	Walnut	16 Jun 1979

400 METRES HURDLES

W, NAm	52.61	Kim BATTEN	USA	Göteborg	11 Aug 1995
Eur, Com	52.74	Sally GUNNELL	GBR	Stuttgart	19 Aug 1993
CAC	52.82	Deon HEMMINGS	JAM	Atlanta	31 Jul 1996
Afr	52.90	Nezha BIDOUANE	MAR	Sevilla	25 Aug 1999
Oce	53.17	Debbie FLINTOFF-KING	AUS	Seoul	28 Sep 1988
Asi	53.96	HAN Qing	CHN	Beijing	9 Sep 1993
	53.96	SONG Yinglan	CHN	Guangzhou	22 Nov 2001
SAm	56.05	Ximena RESTREPO	ECU	Valencia, VEN	26 Nov 1994
W20	55.15	HUANG Xiaoxiao	CHN	Guangzhou	22 Nov 2001
	54.93 §	LI Rui (no doping control)	CHN	Shanghai	22 Oct 1997
W18	55.15	HUANG Xiaoxiao	CHN	Guangzhou	22 Nov 2001

HIGH JUMP

W, Eur	2.09	Stefka KOSTADINOVA	BUL	Roma	30 Aug 1987
CAC	2.04	Silvia COSTA	CUB	Barcelona	9 Sep 1989
Afr, Com	2.04	Hestrie CLOETE	RSA	Monaco	4 Aug 1999
NAm	2.03	Louise RITTER	USA	Austin	8 Jul 1988
		Louise RITTER	USA	Seoul	30 Sep 1988
Oce	1 98	Vanessa WARD	AUS	Perth	12 Feb 1989
	1.98	Alison INVERARITY	AUS	Ingolstadt	17 Jul 1994
Asi	1.97	JIN Ling	CHN	Hamamatsu	7 May 1989
	1.97*	Svetlana ZALEVSKAYA	KAZ	Pierre-Benité	14 Jun 1996
	1.97	Svetlana ZALEVSKAYA	KAZ	Lausanne	5 Jul 2000
SAm	1.96	Solange WITTEVEEN	ARG	Oristano	8 Sep 1997
W20	2.01	Olga TURCHAK	KAZ	Moskva	7 Jul 1986
	2.01	Heike BALCK	GER	Chemnitz	18 Jun 1989
W18	1.96A	Charmaine GALE	RSA	Bloemfontein	4 Apr 1981
	1.96	Olga TURCHAK	KAZ	Donetsk	7 Sep 1984

POLE VAULT

W, NAm	4.81	Stacy DRAGILA	USA	Palo Alto	9 Jun 2001
Eur	4.75	Svetlana FEOFANOVA	RUS	Edmonton	6 Aug 2001
Oce, Com	4.60	Emma GEORGE	AUS	Sydney	20 Feb 1999
Asi	4.52	GAO Shuying	CHN	Beijing	29 Aug 2001
SAm	4.42	Alejandra GARCIA	ARG	Sydney	20 Feb 2000
Afr	4.42	Elmarie GERRYTS	RSA	Wesel	12 Jun 2000
CAC	4.05	Katiuska PÉREZ	CUB	La Habana	31 May 2001
W20	4.46 §	Yelena ISINBAYEVA	RUS	Berlin	31 Aug 2001
	4.47i	Yelena ISINBAYEVA	RUS	Budapest (OH)	10 Feb 2001
W18	4.31	Monika GÖTZ	GER	Troisdorf	9 May 1998

LONG JUMP

W, Eur	7.52	Galina CHISTYAKOVA	RUS	Sankt-Peterburg	11 Jun 1988
NAm	7.49	Jackie JOYNER-KERSEE	USA	New York	22 May 1994
	7.49A*	Jackie JOYNER-KERSEE	USA	Sestriere	31 Jul 1994
SAm	7.26A	Maurren MAGGI	BRA	Bogotá	26 Jun 1999
Afr	7.12	Chioma AJUNWA	NGR	Atlanta	1 Aug 1996
Asi	7.01	YAO Weili	CHN	Jinan	5 Jun 1993
CAC	6.99	Lissette CUZA	CUB	Jena	3 Jun 2000
Com	6.90	Beverly KINCH	GBR	Helsinki	14 Aug 1983
Oce	6.88	Bronwyn THOMPSON	AUS	Brisbane	7 Sep 2001
W20	7.14	Heike DAUTE/Drechsler	GER	Bratislava	4 Jun 1983
W18	6.91	Heike DAUTE/Drechsler	GDR	Jena	9 Aug 1981

TRIPLE JUMP

W, Eur	15.50	Inessa KRAVETS	UKR	Göteborg	10 Aug 1995
Com	15.16i	Ashia HANSEN	GBR	Valencia	26 Feb 1998
	15.16	Ashia HANSEN	GBR	Fukuoka	13 Sep 1997
CAC	14.77	Yamilé ALDAMA	CUB	Winnipeg	28 Jul 1999
Asi	14.72	HUANG Qiuyan	CHN	Guangzhou	22 Nov 2001
Afr	14.70A	Françoise MBANGO	CMR	Johannesburg	18 Sep 1999
NAm	14.41	Sheila HUDSON	USA	Stockholm	8 Jul 1996
SAm	14.01	Luciana dos SANTOS	BRA	São Paulo	18 Jun 2000
Oce	13.82	Nicole MLADENIS	AUS	Perth	9 Dec 2000
W20	14.62	Tereza MARINOVA	BUL	Sydney	25 Aug 1996
W18	14.57	HUANG Qiuyan	CHN	Shanghai	19 Oct 1997

SHOT

W, Eur	22.63	Natalya LISOVSKAYA	RUS	Moskva	7 Jun 1987

Asi	21.76	LI Meisu	CHN	Shijiazhuang	23 Apr 1988
CAC	20.96	Belsy LAZA	CUB	Ciudad de México	2 May 1992
NAm	20.18	Ramona PAGEL	USA	San Diego	25 Jun 1988
Oce, Com	19.74	Gael MARTIN	AUS	Berkeley	14 Jul 1984
SAm	19.30	Elisângela ADRIANO	BRA	Tunja	14 Jul 2001
Afr	17.93	Vivian PETERS	NGR	Dortmund	8 Jul 2000
W20	20.54	Astrid KUMBERNUSS	GER	Orimattila	1 Jul 1989
W18	19.08	Ilke WYLUDDA	GDR	Chemnitz	9 Aug 1986

DISCUS

W, Eur	76.80	Gabriele REINSCH	GER	Neubrandenburg	9 Jul 1988
Asi	71.68	XIAO Yanling	CHN	Beijing	14 Mar 1992
CAC	70.88	Hilda RAMOS	CUB	La Habana	8 May 1992
Oce, Com	68.72	Daniela COSTIAN	AUS	Auckland	22 Jan 1994
NAm	66.10	Carol CADY	USA	San José	31 May 1986
SAm	62.23	Elisângela ADRIANO	BRA	Palma de Mallorca	12 Jul 1999
Afr	61.74	Monia KARI	TUN	Tunis	1 May 1996
W20	74.40	Ilke WYLUDDA	GER	Berlin	13 Sep 1988
W18	65.86	Ilke WYLUDDA	GDR	Neubrandenburg	1 Aug 1986

HAMMER

W, Eur	76.07	Mihaela MELINTE	ROM	Rüdlingen	29 Aug 1999
CAC	70.65	Yipsi MORENO	CUB	Edmonton	7 Aug 2001
NAm	70.62	Dawn ELLERBE	USA	Philadelphia	28 Apr 2001
Oce, Com	68.87	Bronwyn EAGLES	AUS	Edmonton	7 Aug 2001
	70.19 #	Bronwyn EAGLES (unsurveyed field)	AUS	Calgary	30 Jul 2001
Asi	66.97	GU Yuan	CHN	Guangzhou	22 Nov 2001
Afr	63.28	Morwa Ahmed HUSSEIN	EGY	El Qâhira	2 Sep 2001
SAm	62.16	Carina MOYA	ARG	Santa Fé	9 Jun 2001
W20	71.71	Kamila SKOLIMOWSKA	POL	Melbourne	9 Sep 2001
W18	68.18	Ivana BRKLJACIC	CRO	Pula	28 Apr 2000

JAVELIN (NEW)

W, CAC	71.54	Osleidys MENÉNDEZ	CUB	Réthymno	1 Jul 2001
Eur	69.48	Trine HATTESTAD	NOR	Oslo	28 Jul 2000
Oce, Com	66.80	Louise CURREY	AUS	Gold Coast	5 Aug 2000
Asi	63.92	WEI Jianhua	CHN	Beijing	18 Aug 2000
SAm	61.98A	Sueli dos SANTOS	BRA	Bogotá	6 May 2000
NAm	58.61	Lynda BLUTREICH	USA	New Haven	1 Jul 2000
Afr	56.20	Aïda SELLAM	TUN	Tunis	3 Jun 2001
W20	61.99	WANG Yaning	CHN	Huizhou	14 Oct 1999
W18	60.90	LIANG Lili	CHN	Shenyang	18 Jun 1999

HEPTATHLON

W, NAm	7291	Jackie JOYNER-KERSEE	USA	Seoul	24 Sep 1988
Eur	7007	Larisa NIKITINA	RUS	Bryansk	11 Jun 1989
Asi	6942	Ghada SHOUAA	SYR	Götzis	26 May 1996
Com	6831	Denise LEWIS	GBR	Talence	30 Jul 2000
Oce	6695	Jane FLEMMING	AUS	Auckland	28 Jan 1990
CAC	6527	Diane GUTHRIE-GRESHAM	JAM	Knoxville	3 Jun 1995
Afr	6416	Eunice BARBER	SLE	Talence	15 Sep 1996
SAm	6017	Conceição GEREMIAS	BRA	Caracas	25 Aug 1983
W20	6465	Sibylle THIELE	GER	Schwechat	28 Aug 1983
W18	6185	SHEN Shengfei	CHN	Shanghai	18 Oct 1997

10 KILOMETRES WALK

W, Eur	41:04	Yelena NIKOLAYEVA	RUS	Sochi	20 Apr 1996
Asi	41:16	WANG Yan	CHN	Eisenhüttenstadt	8 May 1999
Oce, Com	41:30	Kerry SAXBY-JUNNA	AUS	Canberra	27 Aug 1988
CAC	42:42	Graciella MENDOZA	MEX	Naumburg	25 May 1997
NAm	44:17	Michelle ROHL	USA	Göteborg	7 Aug 1995
SAm	45:03	Geovana IRUSTA	BOL	Podebrady	19 Apr 1997
Afr	45:06A	Susan VERMEULEN	RSA	Bloemfontein	17 Apr 1999
W20	41:55	Irina STANKINA	RUS	Adler	11 Feb 1995

10,000 METRES TRACK WALK

W, Eur	41:56.23	Nadyezhda RYASHKINA	RUS	Seattle	24 Jul 1990
Oce	41:57.22	Kerry SAXBY-JUNNA	AUS	Seattle	24 Jul 1990
Asi	42:30.13	GAO Hongmiao	CHN	Nanjing	24 Oct 1995
NAm	44:30.1 m	Alison BAKER	CAN	Fana	15 May 1992
	44:06 no kerb	Michelle ROHL	USA	Kenosha	2 Jun 1996

CAC	44:51.81	Graciela MENDOZA	MEX	Athína	4 Aug 1997
SAm	45:59.95	Geovana IRUSTA	BOL	Rio de Janeiro	20 May 2000
Afr	51:11.2 m	Sabeha MANSOURI	ALG	Cairo	26 Aug 1995
W20	42:49.7 §	GAO Hongmiao	CHN	Jinan	15 Mar 1992
	43:35.2	Lyudmila YEFIMKINA	RUS	Msokva	20 May 2000
W18	42:56.09t	GAO Hongmiao	CHN	Tangshan	27 Sep 1991

20,000 METRES TRACK WALK

W, Eur	1:26:52.3	Olimpiada IVANOVA	RUS	Brisbane	6 Sep 2001
Oce,Com	1:33:40.2	Kerry SAXBY-JUNNA	AUS	Brisbane	6 Sep 2001
CAC	1:34:56.7	Maria del Rosario SÁNCHEZ	MEX	Xalapa	16 Jul 2000
NAm	1:35:45.7	CHEN Yueling	USA	San Diego	23 Jan 2000
Asi	1:36:18.2	LI Yuxin	CHN	Qufu	27 Sep 1999
SAm	1:39:27.0	Miriam RAMÓN	ECU	Bogotá	27 Jun 1999
W20, W18	1:37:33.9	GAO Kelian	CHN	Xian	18 Sep 1999

20 KILOMETRES WALK

W, Eur	1:24:50	Olimpiada IVANOVA	RUS	Adler	4 Mar 2001
Asi	1:26:22	WANG Yan	CHN	Guangzhou	19 Nov 2001
Oce, Com	1:28:56	Jane SAVILLE	AUS	Vallansbæk	6 May 2000
CAC	1:30:03	Graciela MENDOZA	MEX	Mézidon-Canon	2 May 1999
NAm	1:31:51	Michelle ROHL	USA	Kenosha	13 May 2000
SAm	1:34:37	Geovana IRUSTA	BOL	Naumburg	30 Apr 2000
Afr	1:36:18	Susan VERMEULEN	RSA	Mézidon-Canon	2 May 1999
W20	1:27:35	Natalya FEDOSKINA	RUS	Mézidon-Canon	2 May 1999
W18	1:30:52	JIANG Kun	CHN	Dandong	13 Apr 2001

4 X 100 METRES RELAY

W, Eur	41.37	GDR (Gladisch, Rieger, Auerswald, Göhr)	Canberra	6 Oct 1985
NAm	41.47	USA (Gaines, Jones, Miller, Devers)	Athína	9 Aug 1997
CAC, Com	41.92	BAH (Fynes, Sturrup, Davis-Thompson, Ferguson)	Sevilla	29 Aug 1999
Asi	42.23	Sichuan CHN (Xiao Lin, Li Yali, Liu Xiaomei, Li Xuemei)	Shanghai	23 Oct 1997
Afr	42.39	NGR (Utondu, Idehen, Opara-Thompson, Onyali)	Barcelona	7 Aug 1992
Oce	42.99A	AUS (Massey, Broadrick, Lambert, Gainsford-Taylor)	Pietersburg	18 Mar 2000
SAm	43.42	COL (Mera, Palacios, Rodríguez, Brock)	Göteborg	12 Aug 1995
W20	43.33 §	GDR (Breuer, Krabbe, Dietz, Henke)	Berlin	20 Jul 1988
	43.38	USA (A Joyce, Aleah Williams, Robinson, Buchanan)	Tampa	11 Jul 1999
W18	44.05	GDR (Koppetsch, Oelsner, Sinzel, Brehmer)	Athína	24 Aug 1975

4 X 400 METRES RELAY

W, Eur	3:15.17	URS (Ledovskaya, Nazarova, Pinigina, Bryzgina)	Seoul	1 Oct 1988
NAm	3:15.51	USA (D.Howard, Dixon, Brisco, Griffith Joyner)	Seoul	1 Oct 1988
Afr	3:21.04	NGR (Bisi Afolabi, Yusuf, Opara, Ogunkoya)	Atlanta	3 Aug 1996
Com	3:21.21	CAN (Crooks, Richardson, Killingbeck, Payne)	Los Angeles	11 Aug 1984
CAC	3:21.30	JAM (Turner, L Graham, Hemmings, Richards)	Athína	10 Aug 1997
Oce	3:23.81	AUS (Peris, Lewis, Gainsford-Taylor, Freeman)	Sydney	30 Sep 2000
Asi	3:24.28	CHN / Hebei (An, Bai, Cao, Ma)	Beijing	13 Sep 1993
SAm	3:29.22A	BRA (Montalvão, R de Oliveira, Telles, Figueiredo)	Ciudad de México	24 Jul 1988
W20	3:28.39	GDR (Derr, Fabert, Wöhlk, Breuer)	Sudbury	31 Jul 1988
W18	3:36.98	GBR (Ravenscroft, E McMeekin, Kennedy, Pettett)	Duisburg	26 Aug 1973

World Records at other events recognised by the IAAF

1 Hour	18,340 m	Tegla LOROUPE	KEN	Borgholzhausen	7 Aug 1998
20km	1:05:26.6	Tegla LOROUPE	KEN	Borgholzhausen	3 Sep 2000
25km	1:29:29.2	Karolina SZABÓ	HUN	Budapest	22 Apr 1988
30km	1:47:05.6	Karolina SZABÓ	HUN	Budapest	22 Apr 1988
4x200m	1:28.15	GDR (Göhr, R Müller, Wöckel, Koch)		Jena	9 Aug 1980
4x800m	7:50.17	USSR (Olizarenko, Gurina, Borisova, Podyalovskaya)		Moskva	5 Aug 1984

WORLD BESTS AT NON-STANDARD EVENTS

50m	5.53	Bruny Surin	CAN	Sevilla (in 100m)	22 Aug 1999
	6.53	Ben Johnson ¶	CAN	Rome (in 100m)	30 Aug 1987
	drugs dq 6.52	Ben Johnson		Seoul (in 100m)	24 Sep 1988
60m	6.38	Bruny Surin	CAN	Sevilla (in 100m)	22 Aug 1999
	6.38	Ben Johnson ¶	CAN	Roma (in 100m)	30 Aug 1987
drugs dq	6.37	Ben Johnson	CAN	Seoul (in 100m)	24 Sep 1988
150m	14.8	Pietro Mennea	ITA	Cassino	22 May 1983
	14.93	John Regis	GBR	Stuttgart (in 200m)	20 Aug 1993
300m	30.85A	Michael Johnson	USA	Pretoria	24 Mar 2000
	31.48	Danny Everett	USA	Jerez de la Frontera	3 Sep 1990
	31.48	Roberto Hernández	CUB	Jerez de la Frontera	3 Sep 1990

500m	1:00.08	Donato Sabia	ITA	Busto Arsizio	26 May 1984
600m	1:12.81	Johnny Gray	USA	Santa Monica	24 May 1986
2 miles	7:58.61	Daniel Komen	KEN	Hechtel	19 Jul 1997
2000m Steeple	5:14.43	Julius Kariuki	KEN	Rovereto	21 Aug 1990
200mh	22.55	Laurent Ottoz	ITA	Milano	31 May 1995
(hand time)	22.5	Martin Lauer	FRG	Zürich	7 Jul 1959
220yh straight	21.9	Don Styron	USA	Baton Rouge	2 Apr 1960
300mh	34.59	Chris Rawlinson	GBR	Loughboroigh	30 Jul 2000
35lb weight	25.41	Lance Deal	USA	Azusa	20 Feb 1993
Pentathlon (1985 tables)	4282 points	Bill Toomey (7.58, 66.18, 21.3, 44.52, 4:20.3)	USA	London (CP)	16 Aug 1969
Double decathlon	14274 pts	Indrek Kaseorg	EST	Punkalaidun	12/13 Sep 1992

11.75, 7.00, 200mh 25.01, 12.13, 5k 17:36.07, 2:04.84, 1.99, 400m 50.72, HT 32.26, 3kSt 10:50.14
15.11, DT 37.04, 200m 23.30, 4.30, 10:18.50, 400mh 54.00, 57.78, 4:47.36, TJ 14.05, 10k 45:35.95

5 km road walk	18:21	Robert Korzeniowski	POL	Hildesheim	16 Sep 1990
10 km road walk	37:11	Roman Rasskazov	RUS	Saransk	28 May 2000
100 km road walk	8:43:30	Viktor Ginko	BLR	Scanzorosciate	29 Oct 2000

Women

60m	5.93	Marion Jones	USA	Sevilla (in 100m)	22 Aug 1999
60m	6.85	Marion Jones	USA	Sevilla (in 100m)	22 Aug 1999
150m	16.10	Florence Griffith-Joyner	USA	Seoul (in 200m)	29 Sep 1988
300m	34.1	Marita Koch	GDR	Canberra (in 400m)	6 Oct 1985
500m	1:05.9	Tatána Kocembová	CZE	Ostrava	2 Aug 1984
600m	1:22.63A	Ana Fidelia Quirot	CUB	Guadalajara	25 Jul 1997
2 miles	9:11.97 mx	Regina Jacobs	USA	Los Gatos	12 Aug 1999
2000m Steeple	6:11.84	Marina Pluzhnikova	RUS	Sankt Peterburg	25 Jul 1994
200mh	25.6	Patricia Girard	FRA	Nantes	23 Aug 2001
	25.82	Patricia Girard	FRA	Nantes	22 Sep 1999
Double heptathlon	10824 pts	Irina Stasenko	RUS	Punkalaidun	12/13 Sep 1992

100mh 14.95, HJ 1.57, 1500m 4:44.41, 400mh 61.82, SP 12.71, 200m 25.58, 100m 12.86
LJ 5.56, 400m 59.09, JT 37.52, 800m 2:17.88, 200mh 28.98, DT 30.32, 3000m 10:46.93

Decathlon	7731	Marie Collonvillé	FRA	Lage	9/10 Sep 2000

12.61, 6.03, 11.55, 1.75, 56.48, 14.28, 31.91, 3.40, 43.94, 5:13.70

5000m walk	20:03.0	Kerry Saxby-Junna	AUS	Sydney	11 Feb 1996
50 km road walk	4:34:16	Yelena Ginko	BLR	Scanzorosciate	29 Oct 2001
100 km road walk	10:13:56	Kora Boufflert	FRA	Roubaix	9 Oct 1994

LONG DISTANCE WORLD BESTS – MEN TRACK

	hr:min:sec	*Name*	*Nat*	*Venue*	*Date*
15 km	0:42:34.0	Arturo Barrios	MEX	La Flèche	30 Mar 1991
10 miles	0:45:57.6	Jos Hermens	NED	Papendal	14 Sep 1975
15 miles	1:11:43.1	Bill Rodgers	USA	Saratoga, Cal.	21 Feb 1979
20 miles	1:39:14.4	Jack Foster	NZL	Hamilton, NZ	15 Aug 1971
30 miles	2:42:00	Jeff Norman	GBR	Timperley, Cheshire	7 Jun 1980
50 km	2:48:06	Jeff Norman	GBR	Timperley, Cheshire	7 Jun 1980
40 miles	3:48:35	Don Ritchie	GBR	London (Hendon)	16 Oct 1982
50 miles	4:51:49	Don Ritchie	GBR	London (Hendon)	12 Mar 1983
100 km	6:10:20	Don Ritchie	GBR	London (CP)	28 Oct 1978
150 km	10:36:42	Don Ritchie	GBR	London (CP)	15 Oct 1977
100 miles	11:30:51	Don Ritchie	GBR	London (CP)	15 Oct 1977
200 km	15:10:27	Yiannis Kouros	AUS	Adelaide	4-5 Oct 1997
200 miles	27:48:35	Yiannis Kouros	GRE	Montauban	15-16 Mar 1985
500 km	60:23.00	Yiannis Kouros	GRE	Colac, Aus	26-29 Nov 1984
500 miles	105:42:09	Yiannis Kouros	GRE	Colac, Aus	26-30 Nov 1984
1000 km	136:17:00	Yiannis Kouros	GRE	Colac, Aus	26-31 Nov 1984
1500 km	10d 17:28:26	Petrus Silkinas	LTU	Nanango, Qld	11-21 Mar 1998
1000 mile	11d 13:54:58	Petrus Silkinas	LTU	Nanango, Qld	11-22 Mar 1998
2 hrs	37.994 km	Jim Alder	GBR	Walton-on-Thames	17 Oct 1964
12 hrs	162.400 km	Yiannis Kouros	GRE	Montauban	15 Mar 1985
24 hrs	303.506 km *	Yiannis Kouros	AUS	Adelaide	4-5 Oct 1997
48 hrs	473.797 km	Yiannis Kouros	AUS	Surgères	3-5 May 1996
6 days	1030.000 indoor	Jean-Gilles Bousiquet	FRA	La Rochelle	16-23 Nov 1992
Outdoors	1023.200 km *	Yiannis Kouros	GRE	Colac, Aus	26 Nov-1 Dec 1984
	1022.068 km	Yiannis Kouros	GRE	New York	2-8 Jul 1984

 # Running watch time, no stopped times known.

LONG DISTANCE ROAD BESTS – MEN

Where superior to track bests and run on properly measured road courses.

	hr:min:sec	Name	Nat	Venue	Date
10 km	0:27:11	Sammy Kipketer	KEN	New Orleans	30 Mar 2002
15 km	0:41:29	Felix Limo	KEN	Nijmegen	11 Nov 2001
10 miles	0:44:45	Paul Koech	KEN	Amsterdam-Zaandam	21 Sep 1997
20 km	0:56:18+	Paul Tergat	KEN	Milano	4 Apr 1998
Half mar	0:59:17	Paul Tergat	KEN	Milano	4 Apr 1998
	0:59:06	Paul Tergat	KEN	Lisboa (downhill 40m)	26 Mar 2000
30 km	1:28:40+	Steve Jones	GBR	Chicago	10 Oct 1985
20 miles	1:35:22+	Steve Jones	GBR	Chicago	10 Oct 1985
30 miles	2:37:31+	Thompson Magawana	RSA	Claremont-Kirstenbosch	12 Apr 1988
50km	2:43:38	Thompson Magawana	RSA	Claremont-Kirstenbosch	12 Apr 1988
40 miles	3:45:39	Andy Jones	CAN	Houston	23 Feb 1991
50 miles	4:50:21	Bruce Fordyce	RSA	London-Brighton	25 Sep 1983
1000 miles	10d:10:30:35	Yiannis Kouros	GRE	New York	21-30 May 1988
Ekiden (6)	1:57:56		MAR	Litóhoro, GRE	17 Apr 1994
12 hrs	162.543 km	Yiannis Kouros	GRE	Queen's, New York	7 Nov 1984
6 days	1028.370 km	Yiannis Kouros	GRE	New York	21-26 May 1988

LONG DISTANCE WORLD BESTS – WOMEN TRACK

	hr:min:sec	Name	Nat	Venue	Date
15 km	0:49:44.0	Silvana Cruciata	ITA	Roma	4 May 1981
10 miles	0:54:21.8	Lorraine Moller	NZL	Auckland	9 Jan 1993
20 miles	1:59:09 !	Chantal Langlacé	FRA	Amiens	3 Sep 1983
30 miles	3:12:25	Carolyn Hunter-Rowe	GBR	Barry, Wales	3 Mar 1996
50 km	3:18:52	Carolyn Hunter-Rowe	GBR	Barry, Wales	3 Mar 1996
40 miles	4:26:43	Carolyn Hunter-Rowe	GBR	Barry, Wales	7 Mar 1993
50 miles	5:55:41	Valentina Lyakhova	RUS	Nantes	28 Sep 1996
100 km	7:23:28	Valentina Lyakhova	RUS	Nantes	28 Sep 1996
150 km	13:45:54	Hilary Walker	GBR	Blackpool	5-6 Nov 1988
100 miles	14:29:44	Ann Trason	USA	Santa Rosa, Cal.	18-19 Mar 1989
200 km	19:28:48 *	Eleanor Adams	GBR	Melbourne	19-20 Aug 1989
	19:49:36	Irina Reutovich	RUS	Verona	25-26 Sep 1999
200 miles	39:09:03	Hilary Walker	GBR	Blackpool	5-7 Nov 1988
500 km	77:53:46	Eleanor Adams	GBR	Colac, Aus.	13-16 Nov 1989
500 miles	130:59:58	Sandra Barwick	NZL	Campbelltown, AUS	18-23 Nov 1990
1000 km	8d 00:27:06	Eleanor Robinson	GBR	Nanango, Qld	11-19 Mar 1998
1500 km	12d 06:52:12	Eleanor Robinson	GBR	Nanango, Qld	11-23 Mar 1998
1000 miles	13d 02:16:49	Eleanor Robinson	GBR	Nanango, Qld	11-24 Mar 1998
2 hrs	32.652 km	Chantal Langlacé	FRA	Amiens	3 Sep 1983
12 hrs	147.600 km	Ann Trason	USA	Hayward, Cal	3-4 Aug 1991
24 hrs	242.624 km *	Irina Reutovich	RUS	Moskva	9-10 May 1998
	240.169 km	Eleanor Adams/Robinson	GBR	Melbourne	19-20 Aug 1989
48 hrs	377.892 km	Sue Ellen Trapp	USA	Surgères	2-4 May 1997
6 days	883.631 km	Sandra Barwick	NZL	Campbelltown, AUS	18-24 Nov 1990
Indoors where superior to track best					
200 km	19:00:31	Eleanor Adams	GBR	Milton Keynes	3/4 Feb 1990
24 hrs	248.901 km	Yelena Siderenkova	RUS	Podolsk	10-11 Feb 1996

! Timed on one running watch only, * lap recorded by computer

LONG DISTANCE ROAD BESTS - WOMEN

	hr:min:sec	Name	Nat	Venue	Date
10 km	0:30:39	Liz McColgan	GBR	Orlando	11 Mar 1989
15 km	0:46:57	Elana Meyer	RSA	Cape Town	2 Nov 1991
10 miles	0:51:16	Colleen de Reuck	RSA	Washington, DC	5 Apr 1998
	0:50:31 u	Ingrid Kristiansen	NOR	Amsterdam	11 Oct 1989
20 km	1:03:54	Lornah Kiplagat	KEN	Alphen aan Rijn	11 Mar 2001
Half mar	1:06:40 ?	Ingrid Kristiansen	NOR	Sandnes	5 Apr 1987
	1:06:44	Elana Meyer	RSA	Tokyo	15 Jan 1999
25 km	1:21:21+	Ingrid Kristiansen	NOR	London	10 May 1987
30 km	1:38:27+	Ingrid Kristiansen	NOR	London	10 May 1987
20 miles	1:46:04+	Ingrid Kristiansen	NOR	London	10 May 1987
30 miles	3:01:16+	Frith van der Merwe	RSA	Claremont-Kirstenbosch	25 Mar 1989
50 km	3:08:39	Frith van der Merwe	RSA	Claremont-Kirstenbosch	25 Mar 1989
40 miles	4:26:13+	Ann Trason	USA	Houston	23 Feb 1991
50 miles	5:40:18	Ann Trason	USA	Houston	23 Feb 1991
100 km	6:33:11	Tomoe Abe	JPN	Yubetsu	25 Jun 2000
100 miles	13:47:41	Ann Trason	USA	Queen's, New York	4 May 1991
200 km	19:00:31	Eleanor Adams	GBR	Milton Keynes (indoor)	3-4 Feb 1990
1000 km	7d 01:11:00	Sandra Barwick	NZL	New York	16-23 Sep 1991
1000 miles	12d 14:38:40	Sandra Barwick	NZL	New York	16-29 Sep 1991

Ekiden (6)	2:11:41		CHN	Beijing	28 Feb 1998
12 hours	144.840 km	Ann Trason	USA	Queen's, New York	4 May 1991
24 hours	243.657 km	Sigrid Lomsky	GER	Basel	1-2 May 1993

100 KILOMETRES CONTINENTAL RECORDS

W, Asi	6:13:33	Takahiro SUNADA	JPN	Yubetsu	21 Jun 1998
Eur	6:16:41	Jean-Paul PRAET	BEL	Torhout	24 Jun 1989
SAm	6:18:09	Valmir NUNES	BRA	Winschoten	16 Sep 1995
Afr	6:25:07	Bruce FORDYCE	RSA	Stellenbosch	4 Feb 1989
Oce	6:29:23	Tim SLOAN	AUS	Ross-Richmond	23 Apr 1995
NAm	6:30:11	Tom JOHNSON	USA	Winschoten	16 Sep 1995
WOMEN					
W, Asi	6:33:11	Tomoe ABE	JPN	Yubetsu	25 Jun 2000
NAm	7:00:48	Ann TRASON	USA	Winschoten	16 Sep 1995
Eur	7:18:57	Birgit LENNARTZ	GER	Hanau	28 Apr 1990
SAm	7:20:22	Maria VENANCIO	BRA	Cubatão	8 Aug 1998
Afr	7:31:47	Helena JOUBERT	RSA	Winschoten	16 Sep 1995
Oce	7:40:58	Linda MEADOWS	AUS	North Otago	18 Nov 1995

WORLD INDOOR RECORDS

Men					to March 2002
50 metres	5.56A	Donovan Bailey	CAN	Reno	9 Feb 1996
	5.56r	Maurice Greene	USA	Los Angeles	13 Feb 1999
	5.55 §	Ben Johnson ¶	CAN	Ottawa	31 Jan 1987
60 metres	6.39	Maurice Greene	USA	Madrid	3 Feb 1998
	6.39	Maurice Greene	USA	Atlanta	3 Mar 2001
200 metres	19.92	Frank Fredericks	NAM	Liévin	18 Feb 1996
400 metres	44.63	Michael Johnson	USA	Atlanta	4 Mar 1995
800 metres	1:42.67	Wilson Kipketer	KEN	Paris (Bercy)	9 Mar 1997
1000 metres	2:14.96	Wilson Kipketer	KEN	Birmingham	20 Feb 2000
1500 metres	3:31.18	Hicham El Guerrouj	MAR	Stuttgart	2 Feb 1997
1 mile	3:48.45	Hicham El Guerrouj	MAR	Gent	12 Feb 1997
2000 metres #	4:52.86	Haile Gebrselassie	ETH	Birmingham	16 Feb 1998
3000 metres	7:24.90	Daniel Komen	KEN	Budapest	6 Feb 1998
2 miles #	8:09.66	Hailu Mekonnen	ETH	Birmingham	20 Feb 2000
5000 metres	12:50.38	Haile Gebrselassie	ETH	Birmingham	14 Feb 1999
50 m hurdles	6.25	Mark McKoy	CAN	Kobe	5 Mar 1986
60 m hurdles	7.30	Colin Jackson	GBR	Sindelfingen	6 Mar 1994
High jump	2.43	Javier Sotomayor	CUB	Budapest	4 Mar 1989
Pole vault	6.15	Sergey Bubka	UKR	Donetsk	21 Feb 1993
Long jump	8.79	Carl Lewis	USA	New York	27 Jan 1984
Triple jump	17.83	Aliecer Urrutia	CUB	Sindelfingen	1 Mar 1997
Shot	22.66	Randy Barnes	USA	Los Angeles	20 Jan 1989
Javelin #	85.78	Matti Närhi	FIN	Kajaani	3 Mar 1996
35 lb weight #	25.86	Lance Deal	USA	Atlanta	4 Mar 1995
5000m walk	18:07.78	Mikhail Shchennikov	RUS	Moskva	14 Feb 1995
4 x 200m	1:22.11	United Kingdom		Glasgow	3 Mar 1991
		(Linford Christie, Darren Braithwaite, Ade Mafe, John Regis)			
4 x 400m	3:02.83	USA		Maebashi	7 Mar 1999
		(Andre Morris, Desmond Johnson, Deon Minor, Milton Campbell))			
4 x 800m	7:13.94	USA/Global Athletics & Marketing		Roxbury	6 Feb 2000
		(Joey Woody, Karl Paranya, Rich Kenah, David Krummenacker)			
Heptathlon	6476 points	Dan O'Brien	USA	Toronto	13/14 Mar 1993
	(6.67 60m, 7.84 LJ, 16.02 SP, 2.13 HJ, 7.85 60mh, 5.20 PV, 2:57.96 1000m)				
Women					
50 metres	5.96	Irina Privalova	RUS	Madrid	9 Feb 1995
60 metres	6.92	Irina Privalova	RUS	Madrid 11 Feb 1993 &	11 Feb 1993
200 metres	21.87	Merlene Ottey	JAM	Liévin	13 Feb 1993
400 metres	49.59	Jarmila Kratochvílová	CZE	Milano	7 Mar 1982
800 metres	1:55.82	Jolanda Ceplak	SLO	Wien	3 Mar 2002
1000 metres	2:30.94	Maria Lurdes Mutola	MOZ	Stockholm	25 Feb 1999
1500 metres	4:00.27 +	Doina Melinte	ROM	East Rutherford	9 Feb 1990
1 mile	4:17.14	Doina Melinte	ROM	East Rutherford	9 Feb 1990
2000 metres #	5:30.53	Gabriela Szabo	ROM	Sindelfingen	8 Mar 1998
3000 metres	8:29.15	Berhane Adere	ETH	Stuttgart	3 Feb 2002
2 miles #	9:23.38	Regina Jacobs	USA	Boston (Roxbury)	27 Jan 2002
5000 metres	14:47.35	Gabriela Szabo	ROM	Dortmund	13 Feb 1999
50 m hurdles	6.58	Cornelia Oschkenat	GDR	Berlin	20 Feb 1988
60 m hurdles	7.69	Lyudmila Narozhilenko	RUS	Chelyabinsk	4 Feb 1990

High jump	2.07	Heike Henkel	GER	Karlsruhe	9 Feb 1992
Pole vault	4.75	Svetlana Feofanova	RUS	Wien	3 Mar 2002
Long jump	7.37	Heike Drechsler	GDR	Wien	13 Feb 1988
Triple jump	15.16	Ashia Hansen	GBR	Valencia	28 Feb 1998
Shot	22.50	Helena Fibingerová	CZE	Jablonec	19 Feb 1977
Javelin #	60.83	Mikaela Ingberg	FIN	Mustasaari	28 Feb 1999
20 lb weight #	23.11	Dawn Ellerbe	USA	New York	4 Feb 2000
3000m walk	11:40.33	Claudia Iovan	ROM	Bucuresti	30 Jan 1999
5000m walk #	20:42.33	Yelena Gruzinova	RUS	Samara	1 Mar 1997
4 x 200m	1:32.55	SC Eintracht Hamm	FRG	Dortmund	20 Feb 1988
		(Helga Arendt, Silke-Beate Knoll, Mechthild Kluth, Gisela Kinzel)			
	1:32.55	LG Olympia Dortmund	GER	Karlsruhe	21 Feb 1999
		(Esther Möller, Gabi Rockmeier, Birgit Rockmeier, Andrea Philipp)			
4 x 400m	3:24.25	Russia		Maebashi	7 Mar 1999
		(Tatyana Chebykina, Svetlana Goncharenko, Olga Kotlyarova, Natalya Nazarova)			
4 x 800m	8:18.71	Russia		Moskva	4 Feb 1994
		(Olga Kuznetsova, Yelena Afanasyeva, Yelena Zaytseva, Yekaterina Podkopayeva)			
Pentathlon	4991 points	Irina Belova	RUS	Berlin	14/15 Feb 1992
		(8.22 60mh, 1.93 HJ, 13.25 SP, 6.67 LJ, 2:10.26 800m)			

 # events not official recognised by the IAAF

¶ The IAAF stripped Johnson of his records in January 1990, after he had admitted long-term steroid use.

WORLD VETERANS/MASTERS RECORDS

MEN - Aged 40 or over at time of performances

100 metres	10.84	Erik Oostweegel (29.4.60)	NED		10 Jun 2000
	10.6	Eddie Hart (24.4.49)	USA	Berkeley	16 Sep 1989
200 metres	21.86	Bill Collins (20.11.50)	USA	Spokane	15 Aug 1992
400 metres	47.87	Manuel Ulacio	VEN	Santiago de Chile	14 Nov 1981
	47.5u	Lee Evans (25.2.47)	USA		Apr 1989
800 metres	1:50.69	Colin Rothery (.60)	IRL	Stretford	5 Sep 2000
	1:48.81i	Johnny Gray (19.6.60)	USA	Atlanta	3 Mar 2001
1500 metres	3:44.89	Luiz José Gonçalves (4.12.58)	BRA	Rio de Janeiro	4 Jun 1999
1 mile	4:02.53	David Moorcroft (10.4.53)	GBR	Belfast	19 Jun 1993
	3:58.15i	Eamonn Coghlan (21.11.52)	IRL	Boston	20 Feb 1994
3000 metres	8:05.08	Martti Vainio (30.12.50)	FIN	Mikkeli	12 Jun 1991
5000 metres	13:43.15	Mohamed Ezzher (26.4.60)	FRA	Sotteville	3 Jul 2000
10000 metres	28:30.88	Martti Vainio (30.12.50)	FIN	Hengelo	25 Jun 1991
Marathon	2:10:32	Mohammed Ezzher (26.4.60)	FRA	Paris	8 Apr 2001
3000m steeple	8:41.5	Gaston Roelants (5.2.37)	BEL	Oslo	6 Jul 1977
110m hurdles	14.16	Carlos Sala (20.3.60)	ESP	Castellón	16 Aug 2000
400m hurdles	52.62	Antônio Eusébio Dias Ferreira (2.3.60)	BRA	Rio de Janeiro	23 Jul 2000
High jump	2.15	Glen Conley (9.1.57)	USA	Troy, New York	2 Aug 1997
Pole vault	5.50A	Larry Jessee (31.3.52)	USA	El Paso	24 Aug 1996
Long jump	7.57	Hans Schicker (3.10.47)	FRG	Kitzingen	16 Jul 1989
Triple jump	16.58	Ray Kimble (19.4.53)	USA	Edinburgh	2 Jul 1993
Shot	21.41	Brian Oldfield (1.6.45)	USA	Innsbruck	22 Aug 1985
Discus	69.46	Al Oerter (19.9.36)	USA	Wichita	31 May 1980
Hammer	80.03	Vasiliy Sidorenko (1.5.61)	RUS	Tula	14 Jul 2001
Javelin	78.84	Jorma Markus (28.11.52)	FIN	Kempele	21 Jun 1994
Pentathlon	3510 pts	Werner Schallau (8.9.38)	FRG	Gelsenkirchen	24 Sep 1978
		6.74, 59.20, 23.0, 43.76, 5:05.7			
Decathlon	6642 pts	Greg Richards (25.4.56)	GBR	Enfield	4 Aug 1996
		12.02, 6.81, 13.71, 1.86, 54.51, 15.63, 44.86, 4.00, 50.84, 5:18.14			
20 km walk	1:21:36	Willi Sawall (7.11.41)	AUS	Melbourne	4 Jul 1982
50 km walk	3:49:06	José Marín (21.1.50)	ESP	Badalona	22 Mar 1992
4x100m	42.79	Austin, Collins, Mitchell, Hartfield	USA		5 Feb 1992
4x400m	3:20.83	S Allah, K Morning, E Gonera, R Blackwell	USA	Philadelphia	27 Apr 2001

WOMEN – aged 35 or more

100 metres	10.74	Merlene Ottey (10.5.60)	JAM	Milano	7 Sep 1996
200 metres	21.93	Merlene Ottey (10.5.60)	JAM	Bruxelles	25 Aug 1995
400 metres	50.56	Aurelia Penton (18.2.43)	CUB	Medellin	16 Jul 1978
800 metres	1:56.53	Lyubov Gurina (6.8.57)	RUS	Hechtel	30 Jul 1994
1000 metres	2:31.5	Maricica Puica (29.7.50)	ROM	Poiana Brasov	1 Jun 1986
1500 metres	3:57.73	Maricica Puica (29.7.50)	ROM	Bruxelles	30 Aug 1985
1 mile	4:17.33	Maricica Puica (29.7.50)	ROM	Zürich	21 Aug 1985
2000 metres	5:28.69	Maricica Puica (29.7.50)	ROM	London	11 Jul 1986
3000 metres	8:27.83	Maricica Puica (29.7.50)	ROM	Roma	7 Sep 1985
5000 metres	14:45.35	Regina Jacobs (28.8.63)	USA	Sacramento	21 Jul 2000
10000 metres	31:20.28	Ingrid Kristiansen (21.3.56)	NOR	Hechtel	10 Aug 1991

3000m steeple	10:06.8	Marina Pluzhnikova (25.2.63)	RUS	Moskva	5 Jun 1999
Marathon	2:24:35	Katrin Dörre-Heinig (6.10.61)	GER	Hamburg	25 Apr 1999
100m hurdles	12.47	Ludmila Engqvist (21.4.64)	SWE	Sevilla	28 Aug 1999
400m hurdles	52.94	Marina Styepanova (1.5.50)	RUS	Tashkent	17 Sep 1986
High jump	1.94i	Yelena Panikarovskikh (4.12.59)	RUS	Banská Bystrica	8 Feb 1995
	1.92	Yelena Panikarovskikh		St Peterburg	4 Jul 1996
Pole vault	4.22	Gabriela Mihalcea (27.1.64)	ROM	Dreux	11 Jun 1999
	4.25i	Gabriela Mihalcea (27.1.64)	ROM	Pireas	13 Feb 1999
Long jump	6.99	Heike Drechsler (16.12.64)	GER	Sydney	29 Sep 2000
Triple jump	14.02	Galina Cistjakova (26.7.62)	SVK	Athína	2 Aug 1997
Shot	21.46	Larisa Peleshenko (29.2.64)	RUS	Moskva	26 Aug 2000
	21.47i	Helena Fibingerová (13.7.49)	CZE	Jablonec	9 Feb 1985
Discus	69.60	Faina Melnik (9.7.45)	RUS	Donetsk	9 Sep 1980
Hammer	65.02	Alla Davydova (21.5.66)	RUS	Tula	9 Jun 2001
Javelin	64.89	Yekaterina Ivakina (4.12.64)	RUS	Oslo	28 Jul 2000
Heptathlon	6533 pts	Jane Frederick (7.4.52)	USA	Talence	27 Sep 1987
		13.60, 1.82, 15.50, 24.73; 6.29, 49.70, 2:14.88			
5000m walk	21:20.61	Maya Sazonova (28.5.65)	KAZ	Almaty	28 My 2000
	21:00.0i	Tamara Kovalenko (5.6.64)	RUS	Moskva	23 Jan 2000
10km walk	42:42+	Tamara Kovalenko (5.6.64)	RUS	Moskva	19 May 2000
20km walk	1:25:59	Tamara Kovalenko (5.6.64)	RUS	Moskva	19 May 2000
4x100m	48.63	Desmier, Sulter, Andreas, Apavou	FRA	Eugene	8 Jun 1989
4x400m	3:50.80	Mitchell, Mathews, Beadnall, Gabriel	GBR	Gateshead	8 Aug 1999

WOMEN – aged 40 or more

100 metres	10.99	Merlene Ottey (10.5.60)	JAM	Thessaloniki	30 Aug 2000
200 metres	24.66A	Sara Montecinos (8.3.54)	CHI	Cali	18 Mar 1994
	24.70	Zdenka Musinská (14.4.1957)	CZE	Bilina	14 Sep 1997
400 metres	53.68A	Sara Montecinos (8.3.54)	CHI	Cali	19 Mar 1994
	53.73	Sara Montecinos (8.3.54)	CHI	Santiago de Chile	12 Nov 1994
800 metres	1:59.25	Yekaterina Podkopayeva (11.6.52)	RUS	Luxembourg	30 Jun 1994
1000 metres	2:36.16	Yekaterina Podkopayeva (11.6.52)	RUS	Nancy	14 Sep 1994
	2:36.08i	Yekaterina Podkopayeva (11.6.52	RUS	Liévin	13 Feb 1993
1500 metres	3:59.78	Yekaterina Podkopayeva (11.6.52)	RUS	Nice	18 Jul 1994
1 mile	4:23.78	Yekaterina Podkopayeva (11.6.52)	RUS	Roma	9 Jun 1993
3000 metres	9:11.2	Joyce Smith (26.10.37)	GBR	London	30 Apr1978
5000 metres	15:20.59	Elena Fidatov (24.7.60)	ROM	Bucuresti	7 Aug 2000
10000 metres	32:12.07	Nicole Lévêque (27.1.51)	FRA	Helsinki	13 Aug 1994
Marathon	2:26:51	Priscilla Welch (22.11.44)	GBR	London	10 May 1987
3000m steeple	10:38.98	Soraya Telles (15.9.58)	BRA	Rio de Janeiro	5 Jun 1999
100 m hurdles	13.55	Clova Court (10.2.60)	GBR	Bedford	19 Aug 2000
400 m hurdles	58.3	Gowry Hodge (21.6.60))	BRA	Hoo	3 Sep 2000
High jump	1.76	Debbie Brill (10.3.53) #	CAN	Gateshead	6 Aug 1999
Pole vault	3.45	Dawn Hartigan (13.11.56)	AUS	Melbourne	20 Nov 1999
Long jump	6.41	Vera Olenchenko (21.3.59)	RUS	Rostov-na-Donu	26 Jun 2000
Triple jump	12.31	Conceição Geremias (23.7.56)	BRA	São Paulo	24 May 1997
Shot	19.05	Antonina Ivanova (25.12.32)	RUS	Oryol	28 Aug 1973
	19.16i	Antonina Ivanova	RUS	Moskva	24 Feb 1974
Discus	67.10	Ellina Zvereva (16.11.60)	BLR	Edmonton	11 Aug 2001
Hammer	51.12	Margrith Duss-Müller (5.12.58)	SUI	Olten	15 Jul 2000
Javelin (old)	64.06	Tessa Sanderson (14.3.56)	GBR	London (CP)	12 Jul 1996
Heptathlon	4359 pts	Conceição Geremias (23.7.56)	BRA	São Caetano do Sul	7 Sep 1997
		15.61, 1.57, 12.14, 28.26, 5.49, 32.08, 2:56.10			
5000m walk	22:49.06	Suzanne Griesbach (22.4.45)	FRA	Annecy	9 Aug 1987
10km walk	45:09+	Kerry Saxby-Junna (2.6.61)	AUS	Edmonton	9 Aug 2001
20km walk	1:33:40.2t	Kerry Saxby-Junna (2.6.61)	AUS	Brisbane	6 Sep 2001
4x100m	50.07	Horwedel, Fritsche, Grissmer, Stopka	GER	Gateshead	8 Aug 1999
4x400m	3:58.70	Foreman, Thompson, Board, Libal	GBR	Eugene	24 Aug 1996

 # W45 record

WORLD AND CONTINENTAL RECORDS SET IN 2001

OUTDOORS - MEN

100m	W20	9.97 w? §	Mark LEWIS-FRANCIS	GBR	Edmonton	4 Aug 2001
1500m	SAm	3:33.99	Hudson de SOUZA	BRA	Zagreb	2 Jul 2001
	Com	3:26.34	Bernard LAGAT	KEN	Bruxelles	24 Aug 2001
3000m	SAm	7:42.55	Hudson de SOUZA	BRA	Nice	9 Jul 2001
	W20	7:30.67	Kenenisa BEKELE	ETH	Bruxelles	24 Aug 2001
10000m	NAm	27:13.98	Mebrahtom KEFLEZIGHI	USA	Palo Alto	4 May 2001
	Asi	27:35.09	Toshinari TAKAOKA	JPN	Palo Alto	4 May 2001
Mar	W20	2:10:46	LI Zhuhong	CHN	Beijing	14 Oct 2001
300mSt	W,Afr	7:55.28	Brahim BOULAMI	MAR	Bruxelles	24 Aug 2001

Event	Record	Mark	Athlete	Nat	Venue	Date
	W20	7:58.66	Stephen CHERONO	KEN	Bruxelles	24 Aug 2001
110mh	Afr	13.34A	Shaun BOWNES	RSA	Pretoria	23 Mar 2001
	Afr	13.26	Shaun BOWNES	RSA	Heusden	14 Jul 2001
400mh	CAC	47.38	Felix SÁNCHEZ	DOM	Zürich	17 Aug 2001
Pole vault	Oce,Com	6.05	Dmitriy MARKOV	AUS	Edmonton	9 Aug 2001
Shot	Afr	21.22 §	Janus ROBBERTS	RSA	Des Moines	28 Apr 2001
	Afr	21.60	Janus ROBBERTS	RSA	Fresno	19 May 2001
	Afr,Com	21.68, 21.97	Janus ROBBERTS	RSA	Eugene	2 Jun 2001
Discus	Afr,Com	69.96	Frantz KRUGER	RSA	Stellenbosch	30 Mar 2001
Hammer	Oce	78.40	Stuart RENDELL	AUS	Canberra	3 Mar 2001
	SAm	75.04	Juan CERRA	ARG	Santa Fe	2 Jun 2001
	Oce, Com	78.90	Stuart RENDELL	AUS	Szombathely	3 Jul 2001
	Asi	83.47	Koji MUROFUSHI	JPN	Toyota	14 Jul 2001
	Oce,Com	78.93	Stuart RENDELL	AUS	Szombathely	15 Jul 2001
	SAm	76.42	Juan CERRA	ARG	Trieste	25 Jul 2001
	Oce,Com	78.99 §	Stuart RENDELL	AUS	Calgary	30 Jul 2001
	Afr	78.88	Chris HARMSE	RSA	Pretoria	7 Nov 2001
	Afr,Com	79.40	Chris HARMSE	RSA	Pretoria	7 Nov 2001
Javelin	W20	83.87	Andreas THORKILDSEN	NOR	Fana	7 Jun 2001
Decathlon	W,Eur	9026	Roman SEBRLE	CZE	Götzis	27 May 2001
20km t walk	Oce,Com	1:19:48.1	Nathan DEAKES	AUS	Brisbane	4 Sep 2001
	W20	1:21:29.2§	Viktor BURAYEV	RUS	Brisbane	4 Sep 2001
20km r walk	W20	1:18:06	Viktor BURAYEV	RUS	Adler	4 Mar 2001
	Oce,Com	1:18:14	Nathan DEAKES	AUS	Dublin	16 Jun 2001

OUTDOORS - WOMEN

Event	Record	Mark	Athlete	Nat	Venue	Date
3000m	Com	8:26.97	Paula RADCLIFFE	Eng	Roma	29 Jun 2001
	Oce	8:42.95	Benita WILLIS	AUS	Roma	29 Jun 2001
	Afr	8:25.62	Berhane ADERE	ETH	Zürich	17 Aug 2001
5000m	Eur	14:29.32	Olga YEGOROVA	RUS	Berlin	31 Aug 2001
	Com	14:32.44	Paula RADCLIFFE	Eng	Berlin	31 Aug 2001
Half Mar	W,Afr,Com	1:05:44 §	Susan CHEPKEMEI	KEN	Lisboa	1 Apr 2001
	Eur	1:06:47	Paula RADCLIFFE	GBR	Bristol	7 Oct 2001
Mar	W,Asi	2:19:46	Naoko TAKAHASHI	JPN	Berlin	30 Sep 2001
	W,Afr,Com	2:18:47	Catherine NDEREBA	KEN	Chicago	7 Oct 2001
	W20	2:23:37	LIU Min	CHN	Beijing	14 Oct 2001
3000mSt	NAm	9:55.63	Elizabeth JACKSON	USA	San Diego	18 May 2001
	NAm	9:49.73	Elizabeth JACKSON	USA	Eugene	1 Jun 2001
	Afr	10:18.50	Hana CHAOUACH	TUN	Tunis	3 Jun 2001
	NAm	9:49.41	Lisa NYE	USA	Eugene	23 Jun 2001
	NAm	9:48.72	Elizabeth JACKSON	USA	Glasgow (S)	1 Jul 2001
	Com	9:52.71	Tara KRZYWICKI	Eng	Glasgow (S)	1 Jul 2001
	Afr	10:05.15	Margaret KERUBO	KEN	Reims	5 Jul 2001
	W,Eur	9:25.31	Justyna BAK	POL	Nice	9 Jul 2001
	Afr,Com	9:39.51	Irene LIMIKA	KEN	Nice	9 Jul 2001
	NAm	9:43.36	Elizabeth JACKSON	USA	Nice	9 Jul 2001
	W20	10:04.99	Ulla TUIMALA	FIN	Göteborg	2 Sep 2001
	W20,Oce,Com	9:30.70	Melissa ROLLISON	AUS	Brisbane	4 Sep 2001
	NAm	9:41.94	Elizabeth JACKSON	USA	Brisbane	4 Sep 2001
100mh	SAm	12.71	Maurren MAGGI	BRA	Manaus	19 May 2001
400mh	Asi=	53.96	SONG Yinglan	CHN	Guangzhou	22 Nov 2001
	W20	55.15	HUANG Xiaoxiao	CHN	Guangzhou	22 Nov 2001
High jump	SAm	1.97 Drugs dq	Solange WITTEVEEN	ARG	Manaus	19 May 2001
Pole vault	Asi	4.40	GAO Shuying	CHN	Ningbo	27 Apr 2001
	W,NAm	4.65A, 4.70A §	Stacy DRAGILA	USA	Pocatello	27 Apr 2001
	Asi=	4.40	GAO Shuying	CHN	Osaka	12 May 2001
	CAC	4.05	Katiuska PÉREZ	CUB	La Habana	31 May 2001
	W,NAm	4.71	Stacy DRAGILA	USA	Palo Alto	9 Jun 2001
	W,NAm	4.81	Stacy DRAGILA	USA	Palo Alto	9 Jun 2001
	Eur	4.57 §	Svetlana FEOFANOVA	RUS	Athína	11 Jun 2001
	Eur	4.60 §	Svetlana FEOFANOVA	RUS	Bremen	23 Jun 2001
	W20	4.42 §	Yelena ISINBAYEVA	RUS	Roma	29 Jun 2001
	Eur	4.61 §	Monika PYREK	POL	Bydgoszcz	1 Jul 2001
	Eur	4.62 §	Svetlana FEOFANOVA	RUS	Nice	9 Jul 2001
	Eur	4.65, 4.70	Svetlana FEOFANOVA	RUS	Tula	14 Jul 2001
	Asi	4.42	GAO Shuying	CHN	Stockholm	17 Jul 2001
	Asi	4.45, 4.50	GAO Shuying	CHN	Edmonton	6 Aug 2001
	Eur	4.70, 4.75	Svetlana FEOFANOVA	RUS	Edmonton	6 Aug 2001
	Asi	4.52	GAO Shuying	CHN	Beijing	29 Aug 2001
	W20	4.46 §	Yelena ISINBAYEVA	RUS	Berlin	31 Aug 2001
Long jump	Oce	6.88	Bronwyn THOMPSON	AUS	Brisbane	7 Sep 2001

Event	Record	Mark	Athlete	Nat	Venue	Date
Triple jump	Asi	14.72	HUANG Qiuyan	CHN	Guangzhou	22 Nov 2001
Shot	Sam	19.30	Elisângela ADRIANO	BRA	Tunja	14 Jul 2001
Hammer	Oce,Com	68.73	Bronwyn EAGLES	AUS	Canberra	18 Feb 2001
	Oce,Com	68.83	Bronwyn EAGLES	AUS	Hobart	11 Mar 2001
	NAm	70.62	Dawn ELLERBE	USA	Philadelphia	28 Apr 2001
	Asi	66.30	ZHANG Wenxiu	CHN	Jinan	12 May 2001
	SAm	62.16	Karina MOYA	ARG	Santa Fe	9 Jun 2001
	CAC	69.44, 70.41	Yipsi MORENO	CUB	Nürnberg	17 Jun 2001
	Oce,Com	69.24 §	Bronwyn EAGLES	AUS	Calgary	26 Jul 2001
	Oce,Com	70.19 §	Bronwyn EAGLES	AUS	Calgary	30 Jul 2001
	Oce,Com	68.87	Bronwyn EAGLES	AUS	Edmonton	7 Aug 2001
	CAC	70.65	Yipsi MORENO	CUB	Edmonton	7 Aug 2001
	Afr	63.28	Morwa Ahmed HUSSEIN	EGY	El Qâhira (Cairo)	2 Sep 2001
	W20	71.71	Kamila SKOLIMOWSKA	POL	Melbourne	9 Sep 2001
	Asi	66.97	GU Yuan	CHN	Guangzhou	22 Nov 2001
Javelin	Afr	56.20	Aïda SELLAM	TUN	Tunis	3 Jun 2001
	CAC	68.40	Osleidys MENÉNDEZ	CUB	Tartu	19 Jun 2001
	W,CAC	71.54	Osleidys MENÉNDEZ	CUB	Réthimno	1 Jul 2001
4x400m	CAC,Com	3:20.65	JAM (Richards,Scott,Parris,Fenton)		Edmonton	12 Aug 2001
20km t walk	W,Eur	1:29:36.4	Susana FEITOR	POR	Lisboa	21 Jul 2001
	W,Eur	1:26:52.3	Olimpiada IVANOVA	RUS	Brisbane	6 Sep 2001
	Oce,Com	1:33:40.2	Kerry SAXBY-JUNNA	AUS	Brisbane	6 Sep 2001
20km r walk	W,Eur	1:24:50	Olimpiada IVANOVA	RUS	Adler	4 Mar 2001
	Asi	1:26:22	WANG Yan	CHN	Guangzhou	19 Nov 2001

INDOORS - MEN

Event	Record	Mark	Athlete	Nat	Venue	Date
60m	W=,NAm=	6.39	Maurice GREENE	USA	Atlanta	3 Mar 2001
	W20	6.51	Mark LEWIS-FRANCIS	GBR	Lisboa	11 Mar 2001
1M	SAm	3:56.26	Hudson DE SOUZA	BRA	Fayetteville	10 Feb 2001
3000m	Oce	7:50.21	Craig MOTTRAM	AUS	Lisboa	9 Mar 2001
	Oce	7:48.34	Craig MOTTRAM	AUS	Lisboa	11 Mar 2001
5000m	Oce	13:44.27	Michael AISH	NZL	Boston (Roxbury)	10 Mar 2001
50mh	Afr	6.48+	Shaun BOWNES	RSA	Liévin	25 Feb 2001
60mh	Afr	7.57	Shaun BOWNES	RSA	Wien	12 Feb 2001
	Afr	7.52	Shaun BOWNES	RSA	Gent	23 Feb 2001
PV	NAm	5.96	Lawrence JOHNSON	USA	Atlanta	3 Mar 2001
LJ	Oce=	8.11	Peter BURGE	AUS	Sindelfingen	4 Mar 2001
	Oce=	8.11	Peter BURGE	AUS	Lisboa	11 Mar 2001
TJ	Oce	17.15, 17.20	Andrew MURPHY	AUS	Lisboa	9 Mar 2001
SP	Afr	20.56	Janus ROBBERTS	RSA	Fayetteville	26 Jan 2001
	Afr,Com	21.36	Janus ROBBERTS	RSA	Reno	24 Feb 2001
	Afr=,Com=	21.36	Janus ROBBERTS	RSA	Fayetteville	10 Mar 2001
4x400m	Afr	3:09.76	NGR (Monye,Gadzama,Bada,Udo-Obong)		Lisboa	10 Mar 2001
3000mW	W	10:31.42 §	Andreas ERM	GER	Halle	4 Feb 2001

INDOORS - WOMEN

Event	Record	Mark	Athlete	Nat	Venue	Date
50m	Asi	6.31+	Susanthika JAYASINGHE	SRI	Liévin	25 Feb 2001
200m	Asi	23.23	Susanthika JAYASINGHE	SRI	Birmingham	18 Feb 2001
	Asi	22.99	Susanthika JAYASINGHE	SRI	Lisboa	9 Mar 2001
400m	Com	50.53	Katharine MERRY	Eng	Birmingham	18 Feb 2001
1500m	Afr	4:04.48	Hasna BENHASSI	MAR	Dortmund	11 Feb 2001
	Oce	4:13.21	Georgie CLARKE	AUS	Lisboa	10 Mar 2001
	Asi	4:14.64	LAN Lixin	CHN	Lisboa	10 Mar 2001
	Com	4:06.75	Hayley TULLETT	Wal	Glasgow	18 Mar 2001
1M	Afr	4:23.33	Kutre DULECHA	ETH	Stuttgart	4 Feb 2001
3000m	W,Eur	8:32.88	Gabriela SZABO	ROM	Birmingham	18 Feb 2001
	Asi	8:41.34	DONG Yanmei	CHN	Lisboa	10 Mar 2001
	Oce	8:42.75	Benita WILLIS	AUS	Lisboa	10 Mar 2001
5000m	Afr	14:49.36	Gete WAMI	ETH	Dortmund	11 Feb 2001
	NAm	15:07.33	Marla RUNYAN	USA	New York (A)	18 Feb 2001
50mh	Afr	6.76+	Glory ALOZIE	NGR	Liévin	25 Feb 2001
High jump	Afr	1.87, 1.91	Hestrie CLOETE	RSA	Stockholm	15 Feb 2001
	Afr	1.91, 1.94, 1.97	Hestrie CLOETE	RSA	Birmingham	18 Feb 2001
Pole vault	Eur	4.58	Svetlana FEOFANOVA	RUS	Karlsruhe	27 Jan 2001
	W,NAm	4.63	Stacy DRAGILA	USA	New York	2 Feb 2001
	W,NAm	4.66A	Stacy DRAGILA	USA	Pocatello	9 Feb 2001
	W20	4.47	Yelena ISINBAYEVA	RUS	Budapest (OH)	10 Feb 2001
	Eur	4.64	Svetlana FEOFANOVA	RUS	Dortmund	11 Feb 2001
	W,NAm	4.66A, 4.70A	Stacy DRAGILA	USA	Pocatello	17 Feb 2001
	Eur	4.65	Svetlana FEOFANOVA	RUS	Pireás	21 Feb 2001
Triple jump	Afr	13.72	Baya RAHOULI	ALG	Eaubonne	7 Feb 2001

WORLD MEN'S ALL-TIME LISTS

100 METRES

Mark	Wind	Name		Nat	Born	Pos	Meet	Venue	Date
9.79 WR	0.1	Maurice	Greene	USA	23.7.74	1rA	GP II	Athína	16 Jun 99
9.80	0.2		Greene			1	WCh	Sevilla	22 Aug 99
9.82	-0.2		Greene			1	WCh	Edmonton	5 Aug 01
9.84 WR	0.7	Donovan	Bailey	CAN	16.12.67	1	OG	Atlanta	27 Jul 96
9.84	0.2	Bruny	Surin	CAN	12.7.67	2	WCh	Sevilla	22 Aug 99
9.84	2.0	Tim	Montgomery	USA	28.1.75	1	Bisl	Oslo	13 Jul 01
9.85 WR	1.2	Leroy	Burrell	USA	21.2.67	1rA	Athl	Lausanne	6 Jul 94
9.85	0.8		Greene			1	GGala	Roma	7 Jul 99
9.85	-0.2		Montgomery			2	WCh	Edmonton	5 Aug 01
9.86 WR	1.2	Carl	Lewis	USA	1.7.61	1	WCh	Tokyo	25 Aug 91
9.86	-0.4	Frank	Fredericks	NAM	2.10.67	1rA	Athl	Lausanne	3 Jul 96
9.86	0.2		Greene			1	WCh	Athína	3 Aug 97
9.86	1.8	Ato	Boldon	TRI	30.12.73	1rA	MSR	Walnut	19 Apr 98
9.86	-0.4		Boldon			1		Athína	17 Jun 98
9.86	0.1		Boldon			2rA	GP II	Athína	16 Jun 99
9.86	0.4		Boldon			1rA	Athl	Lausanne	2 Jul 99
9.86	-0.2		Greene			1	ISTAF	Berlin	1 Sep 00
9.87	0.3	Linford	Christie	GBR	2.4.60	1	WCh	Stuttgart	15 Aug 93
9.87	1.9		Fredericks			1	WG	Helsinki	25 Jun 96
9.87	1.3		Boldon			1q1	WCh	Athína	2 Aug 97
9.87A	-0.2	Obadele	Thompson	BAR	30.3.76	1	WCp	Johannesburg	11 Sep 98
9.87	0.6		Greene			1	DNG	Stockholm	30 Jul 99
9.87	-0.3		Greene			1	OG	Sydney	23 Sep 00
9.88	1.2		Burrell			2	WCh	Tokyo	25 Aug 91
9.88	-0.1		Boldon			1	CG	Kuala Lumpur	17 Sep 98
9.88	2.0		Boldon			2	Bisl	Oslo	13 Jul 01
9.89	0.7		Fredericks			2	OG	Atlanta	27 Jul 96
9.89	0.8		Boldon			1r2	ModR	Modesto	10 May 97
9.89	1.5		Surin			1	NC	Montreal	1 Aug 98
9.90		12 performances: 7 by Greene, 2 by Boldon, 1 each Burrell, Fredericks, Montgomery							
		(41 performances by 10 athletes)							
9.91	1.2	Dennis	Mitchell ¶	USA	20.2.66	3	WCh	Tokyo	25 Aug 91
9.92	0.3	Andre	Cason	USA	20.1.69	2	WCh	Stuttgart	15 Aug 93
9.92	0.8	Jon	Drummond	USA	9.9.68	1h3	NC	Indianapolis	12 Jun 97
9.92A	-0.2	Seun	Ogunkoya	NGR	28.12.77	2	WCp	Johannesburg	11 Sep 98
9.92	1.0	Tim	Harden	USA	27.1.74	1		Luzern	5 Jul 99
9.93A WR	1.4	Calvin	Smith	USA	8.1.61	1	USOF	USAF Academy	3 Jul 83
9.93	-0.6	Michael	Marsh	USA	4.8.67	1	MSR	Walnut	18 Apr 92
9.94	0.2	Davidson	Ezinwa	NGR	22.11.71	1	Gugl	Linz	4 Jul 94
9.94	-0.2	Bernard	Williams	USA	19.1.78	3	WCh	Edmonton	5 Aug 01
9.95A WR	0.3	Jim	Hines	USA	10.9.46	1	OG	Ciudad de México	14 Oct 68
		(20)							
9.95A	1.9	Olapade	Adeniken	NGR	19.8.69	1A		El Paso	16 Apr 94
9.95	0.8	Vincent	Henderson	USA	20.10.72	1		Leverkusen	9 Aug 98
9.96	0.1	Mel	Lattany	USA	10.8.59	1r1		Athens, Ga.	5 May 84
9.96	1.2	Ray	Stewart	JAM	18.3.65	6	WCh	Tokyo	25 Aug 91
9.96	0.8	Kareem	Streete-Thompson	CAY/USA	30.3.73	2h3	NC	Indianapolis	12 Jun 97
9.97	0.2	Dwain	Chambers	GBR	5.4.78	3	WCh	Sevilla	22 Aug 99
9.97	1.0	Francis	Obikwelu	NGR	22.11.78	2	Athl	Lausanne	5 Jul 00
9.98A	0.6	Silvio	Leonard	CUB	20.9.55	1	WPT	Guadalajara	11 Aug 77
9.98	0.3	Daniel	Effiong ¶	NGR	17.6.72	2s1	WCh	Stuttgart	15 Aug 93
9.98	1.4	Percy	Spencer	JAM	24.2.75	1	NC	Kingston	20 Jun 97
		(30)							
9.98	1.6	Leonard	Myles-Mills	GHA	9.5.73	1	NCAA	Boise	5 Jun 99
9.98	0.4	Jason	Gardener	GBR	18.9.75	3rA	Athl	Lausanne	2 Jul 99
9.98	0.4	Coby	Miller	USA	19.10.76	1s1	NCAA	Durham	2 Jun 00
10.00	2.0	Marian	Woronin	POL	13.8.56	1	Kuso	Warszawa	9 Jun 84
10.00	1.0	Chidi	Imo ¶	NGR	27.8.63	1	ISTAF	Berlin	15 Aug 86
10.00#A	1.6	Robson	da Silva	BRA	4.9.64	1h3	IbAm	Ciudad de México	22 Jul 88
		May not have been with auto-timing. Next best: 10.02 1.8 1 IbAm						La Habana	27 Sep 86
10.00	0.9	Brian	Lewis	USA	5.12.74	1h2	NC	Indianapolis	12 Jun 97
10.00	1.9	Koji	Ito	JPN	29.1.70	1s2	AsiG	Bangkok	13 Dec 98
10.00	1.1	Eric	Nkansah	GHA	12.12.74	3		Nürnberg	13 Jun 99
10.01A	0.9	Pietro	Mennea	ITA	28.6.52	1		Ciudad de México	4 Sep 79
		(40)							

Mark	Wind	Name		Nat	Born	Pos	Meet	Venue	Date
10.01A	1.9	Bode	Osagiobare	NGR	1.12.70	2A		El Paso	16 Apr 94
10.01	0.6	Jeff	Laynes ¶	USA	3.10.70	1		Tempe	6 Apr 96
10.02AWR	2.0	Charles	Greene	USA	21.3.45	1q4	OG	Ciudad de México	13 Oct 68
10.02	1.0	James	Sanford	USA	27.12.57	1	Pepsi	Westwood	11 May 80
10.02	0.7	Daniel	Sangouma	FRA	7.2.65	2	BNP	Villeneuve d'Ascq	29 Jun 90

Some observers felt that this was run with the benefit of a flying start, but it was ratified as a French record

Mark	Wind	Name		Nat	Born	Pos	Meet	Venue	Date
10.02	-0.1	Deji	Aliu	NGR	22.11.75	1		Bauchi	18 Mar 95
10.02@	0.9	Vladislav	Dologodin	UKR	23.2.72	1		Kiyev	17 May 96
10.02	0.3	Jeff	Williams	USA	31.12.65	1h2	NC	Atlanta	14 Jun 96
10.02	1.7	Michael	Green	JAM	7.11.70	1		Knoxville	11 Apr 97
10.02	2.0	Nobuharu	Asahara	JPN	21.6.72	4	Bisl	Oslo	13 Jul 01
		(50)	100th man 10.08, 200th man 10.14						

Faulty wind gauge – possibly wind assisted

Mark	Wind	Name		Nat	Born	Pos	Meet	Venue	Date
9.88			Greene			1q2	WCh	Edmonton	4 Aug 01
9.97		Mark	Lewis-Francis	GBR	4.9.82	1q3	WCh	Edmonton	4 Aug 01
10.00		Kim	Collins	SKN	5.4.76	2q1	WCh	Edmonton	4 Aug 01

Doubtful wind reading

Mark	Wind	Name		Nat	Born	Pos	Meet	Venue	Date
9.91	-2.3	Davidson	Ezinwa	NGR	22.11.71	1		Azusa	11 Apr 92

Low altitude marks for athletes with lifetime bests at high altitude

Mark	Wind	Name	Pos	Meet	Venue	Date	Mark	Wind	Name	Pos	Meet	Venue	Date
9.94	0.1	Ogunkoya	1	AfCh	Dakar	19 Aug 98	9.97	1.6	C Smith	1	WK	Zürich	24 Aug 83
9.96	0.6	O Thompson	2	DNG	Stockholm	30 Jul 99	9.97	1.2	Adeniken	1	TexR	Austin	4 Apr 92

Wind-assisted – 14 performances to 9.86, performers listed to 9.96

Mark	Wind	Name		Nat	Born	Pos	Meet	Venue	Date
9.69A	5+	Obadele	Thompson	BAR	30.3.76	1		El Paso	13 Apr 96
9.78	5.2	Carl	Lewis	USA	1.7.61	1	OT	Indianapolis	16 Jul 88
9.79	5.3	Andre	Cason	USA	20.1.69	1h4	NC	Eugene	16 Jun 93
9.79	4.5		Cason			1s1	NC	Eugene	16 Jun 93
9.79	2.9	Maurice	Greene	USA	23.7.74	1	Pre	Eugene	31 May 98
9.80	4.3		Lewis			1q2	WCh	Tokyo	24 Aug 91
9.83	7.1	Leonard	Scott	USA	19.1.80	1r1	Sea Ray	Knoxville	9 Apr 99
9.84	3.3		Greene			1h2	NC	New Orleans	19 Jun 98
9.84	3.5		Greene			1	Pre	Eugene	30 May 99
9.85	5.3		Burrell			2h4	NC	Eugene	16 Jun 93
9.85	4.8		Cason			1	NC	Eugene	17 Jun 93
9.85	4.8	Dennis	Mitchell ¶	USA	20.2.66	2	NC	Eugene	17 Jun 93
9.86	5.2		Mitchell			2	OT	Indianapolis	16 Jul 88
9.86	2.5		Burrell			1rA	TexR	Austin	9 Apr 94
9.87	11.2	William	Snoddy	USA	6.12.57	1		Dallas	1 Apr 78
9.87	4.9	Calvin	Smith	USA	8.1.61	1s2	OT	Indianapolis	16 Jul 88
9.87	2.4	Michael	Marsh	USA	4.8.67	1rA	MSR	Walnut	20 Apr 97
9.88	2.3	James	Sanford	USA	27.12.57	1		Westwood	3 May 80
9.88	5.2	Albert	Robinson	USA	28.11.64	4	OT	Indianapolis	16 Jul 88
9.88	4.9	Tim	Harden	USA	27.1.74	1	NC	New Orleans	20 Jun 98
9.88	4.5	Coby	Miller	USA	19.10.76	1		Auburn	1 Apr 00
9.89	4.2	Ray	Stewart	JAM	18.3.65	1s1	PAm	Indianapolis	9 Aug 87
9.90	5.2	Joe	DeLoach	USA	5.6.67	5	OT	Indianapolis	16 Jul 88
9.90	7.1	Kenny	Brokenburr	USA	29.10.68	2r1	Sea Ray	Knoxville	9 Apr 99
9.91	5.3	Bob	Hayes	USA	20.12.42	1s1	OG	Tokyo	15 Oct 64
9.91	4.2	Mark	Witherspoon	USA	3.9.63	2s1	PAm	Indianapolis	9 Aug 87
9.92A	4.4	Chidi	Imo ¶	NGR	27.8.63	1s1	AfG	Nairobi	8 Aug 87
9.92A	2.8	Olapade	Adeniken	NGR	19.8.69	1rA		Sestriere	29 Jul 95
9.93	7.5	Pablo	Montes	CUB	23.11.47	1s1	CAC	Panama City	1 Mar 70
9.94	2.7	Vitaliy	Savin	KZK	23.1.66	1	CIS Ch	Moskva	22 Jun 92
9.94	2.5	Daniel	Effiong ¶	NGR	17.6.72	2	TexR	Austin	9 Apr 94
9.94	7.0	Ousmane	Diarra	MLI	30.9.66	1		La Laguna	13 Jul 96
9.94	5.2	Osmond	Ezinwa	NGR	22.11.71	1		Pula	4 Sep 96
9.94	3.9	Vincent	Henderson	USA	20.10.72	1s1	WUG	Catania	29 Aug 97
9.94	2.8	Bryan	Howard	USA	7.10.76	2r7	MSR	Walnut	16 Apr 00
9.95	8.9	Willie	Gault	USA	5.9.60	1		Knoxville	2 Apr 83
9.95	2.4	Mel	Lattany	USA	10.8.59	1		Athens, Ga	7 May 83
9.95	7.1	Anthony	Jones	USA	12.12.71	3r1	Sea Ray	Knoxville	9 Apr 99
9.96	8.5	Anthony	Barnes	USA	23.12.65	1		Fresno	1 Apr 95
9.96	3.2	Percy	Spencer	JAM	24.2.75	1		Arlington	2 May 98
9.96	3.4	Brian	Lewis	USA	5.12.74	1h1	Conseil	Fort-de-France	29 Apr 00

Disqualified for drug abuse

Mark	Wind	Name		Nat	Born	Pos	Meet	Venue	Date
9.79	1.1	Ben	Johnson ¶	CAN	30.12.61	-	OG	Seoul	24 Sep 88
9.83	1.0		Johnson			(1)	WCh	Roma	30 Aug 87
10.02	1.9	Horace	Dove-Edwin ¶	SLE	10.2.67	(2)	CG	Victoria	23 Aug 94

Rolling start

Mark	Wind	Name		Nat	Born	Pos	Meet	Venue	Date
9.89w	3.7	Patrick	Jarrett ¶	JAM	2.10.77	1	Pre	Eugene	27 May 01

Mark	Wind	Name		Nat	Born	Pos	Meet	Venue	Date
Hand timing									
9.7	1.9	Donovan	Powell ¶	JAM	31.10.71	1rA		Houston	19 May 95
9.7	1.9	Carl	Lewis	USA	1.7.61	2rA		Houston	19 May 95
9.7	1.9	Olapade	Adeniken	NGR	19.8.69	3rA		Houston	19 May 95
9.7w	3.8	Osvaldo	Lara	CUB	13.7.55	1		Santiago de Cuba	24 Feb 82
9.7w	6.6	Rod	Mapstone	AUS	19.11.69	1r1		Perth	21 Dec 96
9.7w	8.1	Sayon	Cooper	LBR	24.4.74	1		Abilene	28 Mar 98
Drugs dq:	9.7w 3.5		Ben Johnson ¶	CAN	30.12.61	1		Perth	24 Jan 87

200 METRES

Mark	Wind	Name		Nat	Born	Pos	Meet	Venue	Date
19.32 WR	0.4	Michael	Johnson	USA	13.9.67	1	OG	Atlanta	1 Aug 96
19.66 WR	1.7		Johnson			1	NC	Atlanta	23 Jun 96
19.68	0.4	Frank	Fredericks	NAM	2.10.67	2	OG	Atlanta	1 Aug 96
19.71A	1.8		Johnson			1rA		Pietersburg	18 Mar 00
19.72A WR	1.8	Pietro	Mennea	ITA	28.6.52	1	WUG	Ciudad de México	12 Sep 79
19.73	-0.2	Michael	Marsh	USA	4.8.67	1s1	OG	Barcelona	5 Aug 92
19.75	1.5	Carl	Lewis	USA	1.7.61	1	TAC	Indianapolis	19 Jun 83
19.75	1.7	Joe	DeLoach	USA	5.6.67	1	OG	Seoul	28 Sep 88
19.77	0.6		Johnson			1	DNG	Stockholm	8 Jul 96
19.77	0.7	Ato	Boldon	TRI	30.12.73	1rA		Stuttgart	13 Jul 97
19.79	1.7		Lewis			2	OG	Seoul	28 Sep 88
19.79	1.0		Johnson			1	OT	New Orleans	28 Jun 92
19.79	0.5		Johnson			1	WCh	Göteborg	11 Aug 95
19.80	-0.9		Lewis			1	OG	Los Angeles	8 Aug 84
19.80	0.4		Boldon			3	OG	Atlanta	1 Aug 96
19.81	0.3		Fredericks			1	GPF	Fukuoka	13 Sep 97
19.82A	2.0		Lewis			1		Sestriere	11 Aug 88
19.82	1.1		Fredericks			1	Bisl	Oslo	5 Jul 96
19.82	1.6		Boldon			1rA	DNG	Stockholm	7 Jul 97
19.83A WR	0.9	Tommie	Smith	USA	12.6.44	1	OG	Ciudad de México	16 Oct 68
19.83	1.7		Johnson			1	GP I	Atlanta	18 May 96
19.84	0.2		Lewis			1q3	OT	Los Angeles	19 Jun 84
19.84	1.7	Francis	Obikwelu	NGR	22.11.78	1s2	WCh	Sevilla	25 Aug 99
19.85	0.4		Johnson			1	IAC	Edinburgh	6 Jul 90
19.85	0.3		Fredericks			1	WCh	Stuttgart	20 Aug 93
19.85	-0.9		Boldon			1	Athl	Lausanne	3 Jul 96
19.85	1.1		Johnson			2	Bisl	Oslo	5 Jul 96
19.85	-0.3	John	Capel (10)	USA	27.10.78	1	NC	Sacramento	23 Jul 00
19.86A	1.0	Don	Quarrie	JAM	25.2.51	1	PAm	Cali	3 Aug 71
19.86	-0.2		Lewis			1	OT	Los Angeles	21 Jun 84
19.86	1.0		Marsh			2	OT	New Orleans	28 Jun 92
19.86	1.6	Maurice	Greene	USA	23.7.74	2rA	DNG	Stockholm	7 Jul 97
19.86	0.4		Boldon			1rA	GP II	Athína	16 Jun 99
		(33/12)							
19.87	0.8	Lorenzo	Daniel	USA	23.3.66	1	NCAA	Eugene	3 Jun 88
19.87A	1.8	John	Regis	GBR	13.10.66	1		Sestriere	31 Jul 94
19.87	1.2	Jeff	Williams	USA	31.12.65	1		Fresno	13 Apr 96
19.88	-0.3	Floyd	Heard	USA	24.3.66	2	NC	Sacramento	23 Jul 00
19.88	0.1	Joshua 'J.J'	Johnson	USA	10.5.76	1	VD	Bruxelles	24 Aug 01
19.89	-0.8	Claudinei	da Silva	BRA	19.11.70	1	GPF	München	11 Sep 99
19.92A WR	1.9	John	Carlos	USA	5.6.45	1	FOT	Echo Summit	12 Sep 68
19.96	-0.9	Kirk	Baptiste	USA	20.6.63	2	OG	Los Angeles	8 Aug 84
		(20)							
19.96	0.4	Robson	da Silva	BRA	4.9.64	1	VD	Bruxelles	25 Aug 89
19.96	-0.3	Coby	Miller	USA	19.10.76	3	NC	Sacramento	23 Jul 00
19.97	-0.9	Obadele	Thompson	BAR	30.3.76	1	Super	Yokohama	9 Sep 00
19.98	1.7	Marcin	Urbas	POL	17.9.76	2s2	WCh	Sevilla	25 Aug 99
19.99	0.6	Calvin	Smith	USA	8.1.61	1	WK	Zürich	24 Aug 83
20.00	0.0	Valeriy	Borzov	UKR	20.10.49	1	OG	München	4 Sep 72
20.01	-1.0	Michael	Bates	USA	19.12.69	3rA	WK	Zürich	19 Aug 92
20.01	0.1	Bernard	Williams	USA	19.1.78	2	VD	Bruxelles	24 Aug 01
20.02	1.7	Christopher	Williams	JAM	15.3.72	1r5	MSR	Walnut	16 Apr 00
20.03	1.6	Clancy	Edwards	USA	9.8.55	1		Westwood	29 Apr 78
		(30)							
20.03	1.5	Larry	Myricks	USA	10.3.56	2	TAC	Indianapolis	19 Jun 83
20.03	1.2	Jon	Drummond	USA	9.9.68	1	VD	Bruxelles	22 Aug 97
20.03	0.7	Konstadínos	Kedéris	GRE	11.6.73	1s2	WCh	Edmonton	8 Aug 01
20.04	1.7	Kenny	Brokenburr	USA	29.10.68	2r5	MSR	Walnut	16 Apr 00

Mark	Wind	Name		Nat	Born	Pos	Meet	Venue	Date
20.05	1.0	Roy	Martin	USA	25.12.66	3	OT	Indianapolis	20 Jul 88
20.05	1.0	Albert	Robinson	USA	28.11.64	4	OT	Indianapolis	20 Jul 88
20.05	-0.1	Ramon	Clay	USA	29.6.75	1	Athl	Lausanne	4 Jul 01
20.06A	0.9	Peter	Norman	AUS	15.6.42	2	OG	Ciudad de México	16 Oct 68
20.06	1.7	Silvio	Leonard	CUB	20.9.55	1	Kuso	Warszawa	19 Jun 78
20.07		James (40)	Mallard	USA	29.11.57	1		Tuscaloosa	20 Apr 79
20.08	0.9	LaMonte	King	USA	18.12.59	1	TAC	Walnut	15 Jun 80
20.08A	1.6	Dwayne	Evans	USA	13.10.58	1		Albuquerque	13 Jun 87
20.08	0.3	Danny	Everett	USA	1.11.66	2	TAC	Norwalk	16 Jun 90
20.08	1.7	Aaron	Armstrong	USA	14.10.77	1		Norman	10 Apr 99
20.08	1.0	Christian	Malcolm	GBR	3.6.79	1s1	WCh	Edmonton	8 Aug 01
20.09	1.7	Linford	Christie	GBR	2.4.60	4	OG	Seoul	28 Sep 88
20.09A	1.9	Dennis	Mitchell ¶	USA	20.2.66	1	NCAA	Provo	2 Jun 89
20.09	2.0	Tyree	Washington	USA	28.8.76	1	GP	Edwardsville	22 May 99
20.09	1.0	Shawn	Crawford	USA	14.1.78	1	NCAA	Durham	3 Jun 00
20.10	1.7	Millard	Hampton	USA	8.7.56	1	OT	Eugene	22 Jun 76
20.10	-0.2	Daniel	Effiong ¶	NGR	17.6.72	1	Jen	San José	28 May 94
20.10	1.7	Kevin (52)	Little	USA	3.4.68	3s2	WCh	Sevilla	25 Aug 99
			100th man 20.21, 200th man 20.37						

Wind-assisted 5 performances to 19.83, performers listed to 20.05

Mark	Wind	Name		Nat	Born	Pos	Meet	Venue	Date
19.61	>4.0	Leroy	Burrell	USA	21.2.67	1	SWC	College Station	19 May 90
19.70	2.7		Johnson			1s1	NC	Atlanta	22 Jun 96
19.79A	4.0		Marsh			1		Sestriere	21 Jul 92
19.83	3.5		Johnson			1	NC	Sacramento	18 Jun 95
19.83	9.2	Bobby	Cruse	USA	20.3.78	1r2	Sea Ray	Knoxville	9 Apr 99
19.86	4.6	Roy	Martin	USA	25.12.66	1	SWC	Houston	18 May 86
19.86	4.0	Justin	Gatlin	USA	10.2.82	1h2	NCAA	Eugene	30 May 01
19.91		James	Jett	USA	28.12.70	1		Morgantown	18 Apr 92
19.93	2.4	Sebastián	Keitel	CHI	14.2.73	1		São Leopoldo	26 Apr 98
19.94	4.0	James	Sanford	USA	27.12.57	1s1	NCAA	Austin	7 Jun 80
19.94	3.7	Chris	Nelloms	USA	14.8.71	1	Big 10	Minneapolis	23 May 92
19.94	2.3	Kevin	Little	USA	3.4.68	1s3	NC	Sacramento	17 Jun 95
19.95	3.4	Mike	Roberson	USA	25.3.56	1h3	NCAA	Austin	5 Jun 80
19.96	2.2	Rohsaan	Griffin	USA	21.2.74	1s1	NC	Eugene	26 Jun 99
19.99	2.7	Ramon	Clay	USA	29.6.75	2s1	NC	Atlanta	22 Jun 96
20.00A	3.4	Olapade	Adeniken	NGR	19.8.69	1		USAF Academy	23 May 92
20.01	2.5	Derald	Harris	USA	5.4.58	1		San José	9 Apr 77
20.03	6.5	Alvis	Whitted	USA	4.9.74	1		College Park	20 Apr 96
20.05A	3.8	Cyprean	Enweani	CAN	19.3.64	1		Calgary	3 Jul 88

Low altitude marks for athletes with lifetime bests at high altitude

19.94 0.3 Regis 2 WCh Stuttgart 20 Aug 93 | 20.06 0.4 Quarrie 1 WK Zürich 16 Aug 74
19.96 0.0 Mennea 1 Barletta 17 Aug 80 |

Hand timing

Mark	Wind	Name		Nat	Born	Pos	Meet	Venue	Date
19.7A		James	Sanford	USA	27.12.57	1		El Paso	19 Apr 80
19.7A	0.2	Robson C.	da Silva	BRA	4.9.64	1	AmCp	Bogotá	13 Aug 89
19.8"	WR1.3	Don	Quarrie	JAM	25.2.51	1	Pre	Eugene	7 Jun 75
19.8*	WR1.3	Steve	Williams	USA	13.11.53	2	Pre	Eugene	7 Jun 75
19.8	1.6	James	Mallard	USA	29.11.57	1	SEC	Tuscaloosa	13 May 79
19.8*w		Carl	Lawson	JAM	27.10.47	1		Moscow	19 May 73
19.8*w	3.4	James	Gilkes	GUY	21.9.52	1	NCAA	Austin	8 Jun 74
19.8w	4.4	Desmond	Ross	USA	30.12.61	1	Big8	Manhattan	11 May 85

*" during 220 yards race, * 220 yards less 0.1 seconds*

300 METRES

In 300m races only, not including intermediate times in 400m races

Mark	Name		Nat	Born	Pos	Meet	Venue	Date
30.85A	Michael	Johnson	USA	13.9.67	1		Pretoria	24 Mar 00
31.48	Danny	Everett	USA	1.11.66	1		Jerez de la Frontera	3 Sep 90
31.48	Roberto	Hernández	CUB	6.3.67	2		Jerez de la Frontera	3 Sep 90
31.56		Johnson			1		Salamanca	22 Jul 94
31.56	Doug	Walker ¶	GBR	28.7.73	1		Gateshead	19 Jul 98
31.61	Anthuan	Maybank	USA	30.12.69	1		Durham	13 Jul 96
31.67	John	Regis	GBR	13.10.66	1	Vaux	Gateshead	17 Jul 92
31.70	Kirk	Baptiste	USA	20.6.63	1	Nike	London (CP)	18 Aug 84
31.73	Thomas	Jefferson	USA	8.6.62	1	DCG	London (CP)	22 Aug 87
31.74	Gabriel	Tiacoh	CIV	10.9.63	1		La Coruña	6 Aug 86
31.82	Steve	Lewis (10)	USA	16.5.69	2	Vaux	Gateshead	17 Jul 92
31.87	Mark	Richardson	GBR	26.7.72	2		Gateshead	19 Jul 98
31.88	Darren	Clark	AUS	6.9.65	1	UlstG	Belfast	30 Jun 86
31.96	Marc	Foucan	FRA	14.10.71	1r1		Strasbourg	29 Jun 99
31.97	Innocent	Egbunike	NGR	30.11.61	1	IAC	London (CP)	8 Aug 86

400 METRES

Mark	Wind	Name		Nat	Born	Pos	Meet	Venue	Date
43.18	WR	Michael	Johnson	USA	13.9.67	1	WCh	Sevilla	26 Aug 99
43.29	WR	Butch	Reynolds ¶	USA	8.6.64	1	WK	Zürich	17 Aug 88
43.39			Johnson			1	WCh	Göteborg	9 Aug 95
43.44			Johnson			1	NC	Atlanta	19 Jun 96
43.49			Johnson			1	OG	Atlanta	29 Jul 96
43.50		Quincy	Watts	USA	19.6.70	1	OG	Barcelona	5 Aug 92
43.65			Johnson			1	WCh	Stuttgart	17 Aug 93
43.66			Johnson			1	NC	Sacramento	16 Jun 95
43.66			Johnson			1rA	Athl	Lausanne	3 Jul 96
43.68			Johnson			1	WK	Zürich	12 Aug 98
43.68			Johnson			1	NC	Sacramento	16 Jul 00
43.71			Watts			1s2	OG	Barcelona	3 Aug 92
43.74			Johnson			1	NC	Eugene	19 Jun 93
43.75			Johnson			1		Waco	19 Apr 97
43.76			Johnson			1	GWG	Uniondale, NY	22 Jul 98
43.81		Danny	Everett	USA	1.11.66	1	OT	New Orleans	26 Jun 92
43.83			Watts			1	WK	Zürich	19 Aug 92
43.84			Johnson			1	OG	Sydney	25 Sep 00
43.86A	WR	Lee	Evans	USA	25.2.47	1	OG	Ciudad de México	18 Oct 68
43.86			Johnson			1	Bisl	Oslo	21 Jul 95
43.87		Steve	Lewis	USA	16.5.69	1	OG	Seoul	28 Sep 88
43.88			Johnson			1	WK	Zürich	16 Aug 95
43.90			Johnson			1		Madrid	6 Sep 94
43.91			Reynolds			2	NC	Atlanta	19 Jun 96
43.92			Johnson			1	Athl	Lausanne	2 Jul 99
43.92			Johnson			1	Pre	Eugene	24 Jun 00
43.93			Reynolds			1	OT	Indianapolis	20 Jul 88
43.93			Reynolds			2	OG	Seoul	28 Sep 88
43.94			Johnson			1	ISTAF	Berlin	27 Aug 93
43.95			Johnson			1s1	WCh	Sevilla	24 Aug 99
		(30/6)							
43.97A		Larry	James	USA	6.11.47	2	OG	Ciudad de México	18 Oct 68
44.09		Alvin	Harrison	USA	20.1.74	3	NC	Atlanta	19 Jun 96
44.09		Jerome	Young	USA	14.8.76	1	NC	New Orleans	21 Jun 98
44.13		Derek	Mills	USA	9.7.72	1	Pre	Eugene	4 Jun 95
		(10)							
44.14		Roberto	Hernández	CUB	6.3.67	2		Sevilla	30 May 90
44.15		Anthuan	Maybank	USA	30.12.69	1rB	Athl	Lausanne	3 Jul 96
44.17		Innocent	Egbunike	NGR	30.11.61	1rA	WK	Zürich	19 Aug 87
44.18		Samson	Kitur	KEN	25.2.66	2s2	OG	Barcelona	3 Aug 92
44.20A		Charles	Gitonga	KEN	5.10.71	1	NC	Nairobi	29 Jun 96
44.21		Ian	Morris	TRI	30.11.61	3s2	OG	Barcelona	3 Aug 92
44.21		Antonio	Pettigrew	USA	3.11.67	1		Nassau	26 May 99
44.26		Alberto	Juantorena	CUB	3.12.50	1	OG	Montreal	29 Jul 76
44.27		Alonzo	Babers	USA	31.10.61	1	OG	Los Angeles	8 Aug 84
44.28		Andrew	Valmon	USA	1.1.65	4	NC	Eugene	19 Jun 93
		(20)							
44.28		Tyree	Washington	USA	28.8.76	1		Eagle Rock	12 May 01
44.29		Derrick	Brew	USA	28.12.77	1	SEC	Athens, Ga	16 May 99
44.29		Sanderlei	Parrela	BRA	7.10.74	2	WCh	Sevilla	26 Aug 99
44.30		Gabriel	Tiacoh	CIV	10.9.63	1	NCAA	Indianapolis	7 Jun 86
44.30		Lamont	Smith	USA	11.12.72	4	NC	Atlanta	19 Jun 96
44.31		Alejandro	Cárdenas	MEX	4.10.74	3	WCh	Sevilla	26 Aug 99
44.33		Thomas	Schönlebe	GDR	6.8.65	1	WCh	Roma	3 Sep 87
44.34		Darnell	Hall	USA	26.9.71	1	Athl	Lausanne	5 Jul 95
44.36		Iwan	Thomas	GBR	5.1.74	1	NC	Birmingham	13 Jul 97
44.37		Roger	Black	GBR	31.3.66	2rA	Athl	Lausanne	3 Jul 96
		(30)							
44.37		Davis	Kamoga	UGA	17.7.68	2	WCh	Athína	5 Aug 97
44.37		Mark	Richardson	GBR	26.7.72	1	Bisl	Oslo	9 Jul 98
44.38		Darren	Clark	AUS	6.9.65	3s1	OG	Seoul	26 Sep 88
44.40		Fred	Newhouse	USA	8.11.48	2	OG	Montreal	29 Jul 76
44.41A		Ron	Freeman	USA	12.6.47	3	OG	Ciudad de México	18 Oct 68
44.45A		Ronnie	Ray	USA	2.1.54	1	PAm	Ciudad de México	18 Oct 75
44.45		Darrell	Robinson	USA	23.12.63	2	Pepsi	Westwood	17 May 86
44.45		Avard	Moncur	BAH	2.11.78	1		Madrid	7 Jul 01
44.47		Michael	Franks	USA	23.9.63	1	WCp	Canberra	5 Oct 85

MEN All-time

Mark	Wind	Name		Nat	Born	Pos	Meet	Venue	Date
44.47		David	Grindley	GBR	29.10.72	4s2	OG	Barcelona	3 Aug 92
		(40)							
44.47A		Ezra	Sambu	KEN	4.9.78	1	NC	Nairobi	23 Jun 01
44.48		Roddie	Haley	USA	6.12.65	1	SWC	Houston	18 May 86
44.49		Roxbert	Martin	JAM	5.11.69	1	NC	Kingston	21 Jun 97
44.50		Erwin	Skamrahl	FRG	8.3.58	1r1		München	26 Jul 83
44.50		Derek	Redmond	GBR	3.9.65	1s2	WCh	Roma	1 Sep 87
44.50		Bert	Cameron	JAM	16.11.59	4s1	OG	Seoul	26 Sep 88
44.51		Jerome	Davis	USA	20.8.77	5s1	WCh	Sevilla	24 Aug 99
44.56		Mohamed	Al Malky	OMN	1.12.62	1	BGP	Budapest	12 Aug 88
44.56		Greg	Haughton	JAM	10.11.73	3	WCh	Göteborg	9 Aug 95
44.57		Jamie	Baulch	GBR	3.5.73	3rB	Athl	Lausanne	3 Jul 96
		(50)	100th man 44.77, 200th man 45.12						
Hand timing									
44.1		Wayne	Collett	USA	20.10.49	1	OT	Eugene	9 Jul 72
44.2*		John	Smith	USA	5.8.50	1	AAU	Eugene	26 Jun 71
44.2		Fred	Newhouse	USA	8.11.48	1s1	OT	Eugene	7 Jul 72
44.4A	WR	Vince	Matthews	USA	16.12.47	1		Echo Summit	31 Aug 68

600 METRES

Mark	Wind	Name		Nat	Born	Pos	Meet	Venue	Date
1:12.81		Johnny	Gray	USA	19.6.60	1		Santa Monica	24 May 86
1:13.2 + ?		John	Kipkurgat	KEN	16.3.44	1		Pointe-à-Pierre	23 Mar 74
1:13.80		Earl	Jones	USA	17.7.64	2		Santa Monica	24 May 86
1:14.15		David	Mack	USA	30.5.61	3		Santa Monica	24 May 86
1:14.3 A		Lee	Evans	USA	25.2.47	1		Echo Summit	31 Aug 68
1:14.41		Andrea	Longo	ITA	26.6.75	1		Rovereto	30 Aug 00
1:14.48		Trinity	Gray	USA	3.4.78	2		Rovereto	30 Aug 00
1:14.6 A		Larry	James	USA	6.11.47	2		Echo Summit	31 Aug 68

800 METRES

Mark	Wind	Name		Nat	Born	Pos	Meet	Venue	Date
1:41.11	WR	Wilson	Kipketer	DEN	12.12.70	1	ASV	Köln	24 Aug 97
1:41.24	WR		Kipketer			1rA	WK	Zürich	13 Aug 97
1:41.73!	WR	Sebastian	Coe	GBR	29.9.56	1		Firenze	10 Jun 81
1:41.73			Kipketer			1rA	DNG	Stockholm	7 Jul 97
1:41.77		Joaquim	Cruz	BRA	12.3.63	1	ASV	Köln	26 Aug 84
1:41.83			Kipketer			1	GP II	Rieti	1 Sep 96
1:42.17			Kipketer			1	TOTO	Tokyo	16 Sep 96
1:42.20			Kipketer			1	VD	Bruxelles	22 Aug 97
1:42.27			Kipketer			1	VD	Bruxelles	3 Sep 99
1:42.28		Sammy	Koskei	KEN	14.5.61	2	ASV	Köln	26 Aug 84
1:42.33	WR		Coe			1	Bisl	Oslo	5 Jul 79
1:42.34			Cruz			1r1	WK	Zürich	22 Aug 84
1:42.41			Cruz			1	VD	Bruxelles	24 Aug 84
1:42.47		Yuriy	Borzakovskiy	RUS	12.4.81	1	VD	Bruxelles	24 Aug 01
1:42.49			Cruz			1		Koblenz	28 Aug 85
1:42.51			Kipketer			1	Nik	Nice	10 Jul 96
1:42.54			Cruz			1	ASV	Köln	25 Aug 85
1:42.55		André	Bucher	SUI	19.10.76	1rA	WK	Zürich	17 Aug 01
1:42.57			Kipketer			1	Herc	Monaco	4 Aug 99
1:42.58		Vebjørn	Rodal	NOR	16.9.72	1	OG	Atlanta	31 Jul 96
1:42.59			Kipketer			1	Herc	Monaco	10 Aug 96
1:42.60		Johnny	Gray	USA	19.6.60	2r1		Koblenz	28 Aug 85
1:42.61			Kipketer			1rA	WK	Zürich	14 Aug 96
1:42.61			Kipketer			1rA	Athl	Lausanne	2 Jul 97
1:42.62		Patrick	Ndururi	KEN	12.1.69	2rA	WK	Zürich	13 Aug 97
1:42.65			Gray			1	WK	Zürich	17 Aug 88
1:42.69		Hezekiél	Sepeng	RSA	30.6.74	2	VD	Bruxelles	3 Sep 99
1:42.69		Japheth	Kimutai	KEN	20.12.78	3	VD	Bruxelles	3 Sep 99
1:42.74			Sepeng			2	OG	Atlanta	31 Jul 96
1:42.75			Bucher			2	VD	Bruxelles	24 Aug 01
		(30/11)							
1:42.79		Fred	Onyancha	KEN	25.12.69	3	OG	Atlanta	31 Jul 96
1:42.81		Jean-Patrick	Nduwimana	BDI	9.5.78	2rA	WK	Zürich	17 Aug 01
1:42.85		Norberto	Téllez	CUB	22.1.72	4	OG	Atlanta	31 Jul 96
1:42.88		Steve	Cram	GBR	14.10.60	1rA	WK	Zürich	21 Aug 85
1:42.96		Wilfred	Bungei	KEN	24.7.80	3rA	WK	Zürich	17 Aug 01
1:42.97		Peter	Elliott	GBR	9.10.62	1		Sevilla	30 May 90
1:42.98		Patrick	Konchellah	KEN	20.4.68	2	ASV	Köln	24 Aug 97
1:43.00		William	Yiampoy	KEN	17.5.74	4rA	WK	Zürich	17 Aug 01

Mark	Wind	Name		Nat	Born	Pos	Meet	Venue	Date
1:43.03		Kennedy	Kimwetich	KEN	1.1.73	2		Stuttgart	19 Jul 98
		(20)							
1:43.06		Billy	Konchellah	KEN	20.10.62	1	WCh	Roma	1 Sep 87
1:43.08		José Luiz	Barbosa	BRA	27.5.61	1		Rieti	6 Sep 91
1:43.09		Djabir	Saïd Guerni	ALG	29.3.77	5	VD	Bruxelles	3 Sep 99
1:43.16		Paul	Ereng	KEN	22.8.67	1	WK	Zürich	16 Aug 89
1:43.17		Benson	Koech	KEN	10.11.74	1		Rieti	28 Aug 94
1:43.20		Mark	Everett	USA	2.9.68	1rA	Gugl	Linz	9 Jul 97
1:43.22		Pawel	Czapiewski	POL	30.3.78	5rA	WK	Zürich	17 Aug 01
1:43.26		Sammy	Langat (Kibet)	KEN	24.1.70	1rB	WK	Zürich	14 Aug 96
1:43.30		William	Tanui	KEN	22.2.64	2		Rieti	6 Sep 91
1:43.31		Nixon	Kiprotich	KEN	4.12.62	1		Rieti	6 Sep 92
		(30)							
1:43.33		Robert	Chirchir	KEN	26.11.72	3		Stuttgart	19 Jul 98
1:43.33		William	Chirchir	KEN	6.2.79	6	VD	Bruxelles	3 Sep 99
1:43.35		David	Mack	USA	30.5.61	3r1		Koblenz	28 Aug 85
1:43.38		David (Singoei)	Kiptoo	KEN	26.6.65	2	Herc	Monaco	10 Aug 96
1:43.38		Rich	Kenah	USA	4.8.70	3rA	WK	Zürich	13 Aug 97
1:43.38		Arthémon	Hatungimana	BDI	21.1.74	3	VD	Bruxelles	24 Aug 01
1:43.44	WR	Alberto	Juantorena	CUB	3.12.50	1	WUG	Sofiya	21 Aug 77
1:43.50		Mahjoub	Haïda	MAR	1.7.70	2	GGala	Roma	14 Jul 98
1:43.5*	WR	Rick	Wohlhuter	USA	23.12.48	1		Eugene	8 Jun 74
1:43.54		William	Wuyke	VEN	21.5.58	2		Rieti	7 Sep 86
		(40)							
1:43.55		Philip	Kibitok	KEN	23.3.71	3	GP II	Rieti	1 Sep 96
1:43.56		Rob	Druppers	NED	29.4.62	4	ASV	Köln	25 Aug 85
1:43.57		Mike	Boit	KEN	6.1.49	1	ISTAF	Berlin	20 Aug 76
1:43.57		Joseph	Tengelei	KEN	8.12.72	3rB	WK	Zürich	16 Aug 95
1:43.60		Abdi	Bile	SOM	28.12.62	3	WK	Zürich	16 Aug 89
1:43.62		Earl	Jones	USA	17.7.64	2r1	WK	Zürich	13 Aug 86
1:43.63		Agberto	Guimarães	BRA	18.8.57	3		Koblenz	29 Aug 84
1:43.63		Joseph Mwengi	Mutua	KEN	10.12.78	4	Herc	Monaco	20 Jul 01
1:43.65		Willi	Wülbeck	FRG	18.12.54	1	WCh	Helsinki	9 Aug 83
1:43.65		Laban	Rotich	KEN	20.1.69	4		Stuttgart	19 Jul 98
		(50)	100th man 1:44.3, 200th man 1:45.13						
			! photo-electric cell time						
Indoors									
1:42.67			Kipketer			1	WI	Paris (B)	9 Mar 97

1000 METRES

Mark	Wind	Name		Nat	Born	Pos	Meet	Venue	Date
2:11.96	WR	Noah	Ngeny	KEN	2.11.78	1	GP II	Rieti	5 Sep 99
2:12.18	WR	Sebastian	Coe	GBR	29.9.56	1	OsloG	Oslo	11 Jul 81
2:12.66			Ngeny			1	Nik	Nice	17 Jul 99
2:12.88		Steve	Cram	GBR	14.10.60	1		Gateshead	9 Aug 85
2:13.40	WR		Coe			1	Bisl	Oslo	1 Jul 80
2:13.56		Kenneth	Kimwetich	KEN	1.1.73	2	Nik	Nice	17 Jul 99
2:13.73		Noureddine	Morceli	ALG	28.2.70	1	BNP	Villeneuve d'Ascq	2 Jul 93
2:13.9	WR	Rick	Wohlhuter	USA	23.12.48	1	King	Oslo	30 Jul 74
2:14.09		Joaquim	Cruz	BRA	12.3.63	1	Nik	Nice	20 Aug 84
2:14.28		Japheth	Kimutai	KEN	20.12.78	1	DNG	Stockholm	1 Aug 00
2:14.41		William	Yampoy	KEN	19.5.74	2	GP II	Rieti	5 Sep 99
2:14.43		Laban	Rotich (10)	KEN	20.1.69	1	Nik	Nice	16 Jul 97
2:14.50		Abdi	Bile	SOM	28.12.62	1		Jerez de la Frontera	13 Sep 89
2:14.52		Djabir Saïd	Guerni	ALG	29.3.77	3	GP II	Rieti	5 Sep 99
2:14.53		Willi	Wülbeck	FRG	18.12.54	2	Bisl	Oslo	1 Jul 80

1500 METRES

Mark	Wind	Name		Nat	Born	Pos	Meet	Venue	Date
3:26.00	WR	Hicham	El Guerrouj	MAR	14.9.74	1	GGala	Roma	14 Jul 98
3:26.12		Hicham	El Guerrouj	MAR	14.9.74	1	VD	Bruxelles	24 Aug 01
3:26.34		Bernard	Lagat	KEN	12.12.74	2	VD	Bruxelles	24 Aug 01
3:26.45			El Guerrouj			1 rA	WK	Zürich	12 Aug 98
3:27.21			El Guerrouj			1	WK	Zürich	11 Aug 00
3:27.37	WR	Noureddine	Morceli	ALG	28.2.70	1	Nik	Nice	12 Jul 95
3.27.52			Morceli			1	Herc	Monaco	25 Jul 95
3:27.65			El Guerrouj			1	WCh	Sevilla	24 Aug 99
3:28.12		Noah	Ngeny	KEN	2.11.78	2	WK	Zürich	11 Aug 00
3:28.21+			El Guerrouj			1	in 1M	Roma	7 Jul 99
3.28.37			Morceli			1	GPF	Monaco	9 Sep 95
3:28.37			El Guerrouj			1	Herc	Monaco	8 Aug 98
3:28.38			El Guerrouj			1	GP	Saint-Denis	6 Jul 01

MEN All-time

Mark	Wind	Name		Nat	Born	Pos	Meet	Venue	Date
3:28.51			Lagat			3	WK	Zürich	11 Aug 00
3:28.57			El Guerrouj			1rA	WK	Zürich	11 Aug 99
3:28.6+			Ngeny			2	in 1M	Roma	7 Jul 99
3:28.73			Ngeny			2	WCh	Sevilla	24 Aug 99
3:28.84			Ngeny			1	GP	Paris (C)	21 Jul 99
3:28.86	WR		Morceli			1		Rieti	6 Sep 92
3:28.91			El Guerrouj			1rA	WK	Zürich	13 Aug 97
3:28.92			El Guerrouj			1	VD	Bruxelles	22 Aug 97
3:28.93			Ngeny			1	GPF	München	11 Sep 99
3:28.95		Fermín	Cacho	ESP	16.2.69	2rA	WK	Zürich	13 Aug 97
3:29.05			El Guerrouj			1	VD	Bruxelles	23 Aug 96
3:29.06			El Guerrouj			1rA	WK	Zürich	17 Aug 01
3:29.08			El Guerrouj			1	GP II	Rieti	2 Sep 01
3:29.12			El Guerrouj			1	Bisl	Oslo	9 Jul 98
3:29.18		Vénuste	Niyongabo	BUR	9.12.73	2	VD	Bruxelles	22 Aug 97
3:29.19			Ngeny			1	VD	Bruxelles	3 Sep 99
3:29.20			Morceli			1	MedG	Narbonne	20 Jun 93
3:29.29		William	Chirchir	KEN	6.2.79	3	VD	Bruxelles	24 Aug 01
3:29.30			El Guerrouj			1rA	DNG	Stockholm	7 Jul 97
3:29.43			Niyongabo			3rA	WK	Zürich	13 Aug 97
3:29.46	WR	Saïd	Aouita	MAR	2.11.59	1	ISTAF	Berlin	23 Aug 85
3:29.46		Daniel	Komen	KEN	17.5.76	1	Herc	Monaco	16 Aug 97
		(35/10)							
3:29.51		Ali	Saïdi Sief ¶	ALG	15.3.78	1	Athl	Lausanne	4 Jul 01
3:29.67	WR	Steve	Cram	GBR	14.10.60	1	Nik	Nice	16 Jul 85
3:29.77		Sydney	Maree	USA	9.9.56	1	ASV	Köln	25 Aug 85
3:29.77		Sebastian	Coe	GBR	29.9.56	1		Rieti	7 Sep 86
3:29.91		Laban	Rotich	KEN	20.1.69	2rA	WK	Zürich	12 Aug 98
3:30.18		John	Kibowen	KEN	21.4.69	3rA	WK	Zürich	12 Aug 98
3:30.36		Rui	Silva	POR	3.8.77	1	Herc	Monaco	20 Jul 01
3:30.55		Abdi	Bile	SOM	28.12.62	1		Rieti	3 Sep 89
3:30.57		Reyes	Estévez	ESP	2.8.76	3	WCh	Sevilla	24 Aug 99
3:30.58		William	Tanui	KEN	22.2.64	3	Herc	Monaco	16 Aug 97
		(20)							
3:30.67		Benjamin	Kipkurui	KEN	28.12.80	2	Herc	Monaco	20 Jul 01
3:30.77	WR	Steve	Ovett	GBR	9.10.55	1		Rieti	4 Sep 83
3:30.92		José Luis	González	ESP	8.12.57	3	Nik	Nice	16 Jul 85
3:30.94		Isaac	Viciosa	ESP	26.12.69	5	Herc	Monaco	8 Aug 98
3:31.01		Jim	Spivey	USA	7.3.60	1	R-W	Koblenz	28 Aug 88
3:31.13		José Manuel	Abascal	ESP	17.3.58	1		Barcelona	16 Aug 86
3:31.17		Robert K.	Andersen	DEN	12.12.72	5rA	WK	Zürich	13 Aug 97
3:31.21		José Antonio	Redolat	ESP	17.2.76	1	DNG	Stockholm	17 Jul 01
3:31.28		Enock	Koech	KEN	4.4.81	3rA	WK	Zürich	17 Aug 01
3:31.40		William	Kemei	KEN	22.2.69	2	Nik	Nice	12 Jul 95
		(30)							
3:31.48		Azzedine	Sediki	MAR	21.5.70	3rA	ASV	Köln	18 Aug 95
3:31.48		Andrés	Díaz	ESP	12.7.69	2	Herc	Monaco	18 Aug 00
3:31.49		Robert	Rono	KEN	11.10.74	4	Herc	Monaco	20 Jul 01
3:31.51		Driss	Maazouzi	FRA	15.10.69	3	GP	Paris (C)	21 Jul 99
3:31.52		Steve	Holman	USA	2.3.70	6	VD	Bruxelles	22 Aug 97
3:31.53		David	Lelei	KEN	10.5.71	3		Stuttgart	19 Jul 98
3:31.58		Thomas	Wessinghage	FRG	22.2.52	2		Koblenz	27 Aug 80
3:31.70		Ali	Hakimi	TUN	24.4.76	7	VD	Bruxelles	22 Aug 97
3:31.71		Kevin	Sullivan	CAN	20.3.74	4	GGala	Roma	30 Jun 00
3:31.75		Pierre	Délèze	SUI	25.9.58	1	WK	Zürich	21 Aug 85
		(40)							
3:31.76		Steve	Scott	USA	5.5.56	4	Nik	Nice	16 Jul 85
3:31.86		John	Mayock	GBR	26.10.70	8	VD	Bruxelles	22 Aug 97
3:31.87		Stephen	Kipkorir	KEN	24.10.70	2	Athl	Lausanne	3 Jul 96
3:31.89		Sammy	Rono	KEN	74	4		Stuttgart	19 Jul 98
3:31.96		Harald	Hudak	FRG	28.1.57	3		Koblenz	27 Aug 80
3:31.96		Simon	Doyle	AUS	9.11.66	2	DNG	Stockholm	3 Jul 91
3:31.96		Paul	Bitok	KEN	26.6.70	3	DNG	Stockholm	17 Jul 01
3:31.97		Mehdi	Baala	FRA	17.8.78	5	Herc	Monaco	20 Jul 01
3:32.06		Nadir	Bosch	FRA	16.5.73	4	GP	Paris (C)	21 Jul 99
3:32.07		Elijah Kipruto	Maru	KEN	12.6.76	4	GP II	Rieti	1 Sep 96
		(50)	100th man 3:33.79, 200th man 3:35.48						
Indoors									
3:31.76		Haile	Gebrselassie	ETH	18.4.73	1		Stuttgart	1 Feb 98

Mark Wind	Name		Nat	Born	Pos	Meet	Venue	Date
								1 MILE
3:43.13 WR	Hicham	El Guerrouj	MAR	14.9.74	1	GGala	Roma	7 Jul 99
3:43.40	Noah	Ngeny	KEN	2.11.78	2	GGala	Roma	7 Jul 99
3:44.39 WR	Noureddine	Morceli	ALG	28.2.70	1		Rieti	5 Sep 93
3:44.60		El Guerrouj			1	Nik	Nice	16 Jul 98
3:44.90		El Guerrouj			1	Bisl	Oslo	4 Jul 97
3:44.95		El Guerrouj			1	GGala	Roma	29 Jun 01
3:45.19		Morceli			1	WK	Zürich	16 Aug 95
3:45.64		El Guerrouj			1	ISTAF	Berlin	26 Aug 97
3:45.96		El Guerrouj			1	BrGP	London (CP)	5 Aug 00
3:46.24		El Guerrouj			1	Bisl	Oslo	28 Jul 00
3:46.32 WR	Steve	Cram	GBR	14.10.60	1	Bisl	Oslo	27 Jul 85
3:46.38	Daniel	Komen	KEN	17.5.76	2	ISTAF	Berlin	26 Aug 97
3:46.70	Vénuste	Niyongabo	BUR	9.12.73	3	ISTAF	Berlin	26 Aug 97
3:46.76	Saïd	Aouita	MAR	2.11.59	1	WG	Helsinki	2 Jul 87
3:46.78		Morceli			1	ISTAF	Berlin	27 Aug 93
3:46.92		Aouita			1	WK	Zürich	21 Aug 85
3:47.10		El Guerrouj			1	BrGP	London (CP)	7 Aug 99
3:47.28	Bernard	Lagat	KEN	12.12.74	2	GGala	Roma	29 Jun 01
3:47.30		Morceli			1	VD	Bruxelles	3 Sep 93
3:47.33 WR	Sebastian	Coe	GBR	29.9.56	1	VD	Bruxelles	28 Aug 81
3:47.65	Laban	Rotich	KEN	20.1.69	2	Bisl	Oslo	4 Jul 97
	(21/10)							
3:47.69	Steve	Scott	USA	5.5.56	1	OsloG	Oslo	7 Jul 82
3:47.79	José Luis	González	ESP	8.12.57	2	Bisl	Oslo	27 Jul 85
3:47.88	John	Kibowen	KEN	21.4.69	3	Bisl	Oslo	4 Jul 97
3:47.94	William	Chirchir	KEN	6.2.79	2	Bisl	Oslo	28 Jul 00
3:48.23	Ali	Saïdi-Sief ¶	ALG	15.3.78	1	Bisl	Oslo	13 Jul 01
3:48.38	Andrés	Díaz	ESP	12.7.69	3	GGala	Roma	29 Jun 01
3:48.40 WR	Steve	Ovett	GBR	9.10.55	1	R-W	Koblenz	26 Aug 81
3:48.80	William	Kemei	KEN	22.2.69	1	ISTAF	Berlin	21 Aug 92
3:48.83	Sydney	Maree	USA	9.9.56	1		Rieti	9 Sep 81
3:49.08	John	Walker	NZL	12.1.52	2	OsloG	Oslo	7 Jul 82
	(20)							
3:49.20	Peter	Elliott	GBR	9.10.62	2	Bisl	Oslo	2 Jul 88
3:49.22	Jens-Peter	Herold	GDR	2.6.65	3	Bisl	Oslo	2 Jul 88
3:49.31	Joe	Falcon	USA	23.6.66	1	Bisl	Oslo	14 Jul 90
3:49.34	David	Moorcroft	GBR	10.4.53	3	Bisl	Oslo	26 Jun 82
3:49.34	Benjamin	Kipkurui	KEN	28.12.80	3	VD	Bruxelles	25 Aug 00
3:49.40	Abdi	Bile	SOM	28.12.62	4	Bisl	Oslo	2 Jul 88
3:49.45	Mike	Boit	KEN	6.1.49	2	VD	Bruxelles	28 Aug 81
3:49.56	Fermín	Cacho	ESP	16.2.69	2	Bisl	Oslo	5 Jul 96
3:49.60	José Antonio	Redolat	ESP	17.2.76	4	GGala	Roma	29 Jun 01
3:49.75	Leonard	Mucheru	KEN	13.6.78	5	GGala	Roma	29 Jun 01
	(30)							
3:49.77	Ray	Flynn	IRL	22.1.57	3	OsloG	Oslo	7 Jul 82
3:49.77	Wilfred	Kirochi	KEN	12.12.69	2	Bisl	Oslo	6 Jul 91
3:49.80	Jim	Spivey	USA	7.3.60	3	Bisl	Oslo	5 Jul 86
3:49.83	Vyacheslav	Shabunin	RUS	27.9.69	6	GGala	Roma	29 Jun 01
3:49.91	Simon	Doyle	AUS	9.11.66	4	Bisl	Oslo	6 Jul 91
3:49.98	Thomas	Wessinghage	FRG	22.2.52	3	ISTAF	Berlin	17 Aug 83
3:50.26	Kevin	Sullivan	CAN	20.3.74	4	Bisl	Oslo	28 Jul 00
3:50.32	John	Mayock	GBR	26.10.70	3	Bisl	Oslo	5 Jul 96
3:50.33	Eric	Dubus	FRA	28.2.66	3	WK	Zürich	16 Aug 95
3:50.34	Todd	Harbour	USA	24.3.59	5	OsloG	Oslo	11 Jul 81
	(40)							
3:50.38	Pierre	Délèze	SUI	25.9.58	4	R-W	Koblenz	25 Aug 82
3:50.40	Steve	Holman	USA	2.3.70	5	Bisl	Oslo	4 Jul 97
3:50.52	Hauke	Fuhlbrügge	GER	21.3.66	6	Bisl	Oslo	6 Jul 91
3:50.54	José Manuel	Abascal	ESP	17.3.58	2	GP-GG	Roma	10 Sep 86
3:50.57	William	Tanui	KEN	22.2.64	5	ISTAF	Berlin	26 Aug 97
3:50.57	Ali	Hakimi	TUN	24.4.76	6	ISTAF	Berlin	26 Aug 97
3:50.60	Sammy	Mutai	KEN	20.12.74	7	GGala	Roma	29 Jun 01
3:50.62	Mark	Carroll	IRL	15.1.72	7	Bisl	Oslo	28 Jul 00
3:50.64	Graham	Williamson	GBR	15.6.60	4		Cork	13 Jul 82
3:50.73	Wilson	Waigwa	KEN	15.2.49	2	R-W	Koblenz	31 Aug 83
	(50)	100th man 3:52.64, 200th man 3:54.96						
Indoors								
3:49.78	Eamonn	Coghlan	IRL	24.11.52	1		East Rutherford	27 Feb 83

Mark Wind	Name		Nat	Born	Pos	Meet	Venue	Date

2000 METRES

Mark Wind	Name		Nat	Born	Pos	Meet	Venue	Date
4:44.79 WR	Hicham	El Guerrouj	MAR	14.9.74	1	ISTAF	Berlin	7 Sep 99
4:46.88	Ali	Saïdi-Sief ¶	ALG	15.3.78	1		Strasbourg	19 Jun 01
4:47.88 WR	Noureddine	Morceli	ALG	28.2.70	1		Paris	3 Jul 95
4:48.36		El Guerrouj			1		Gateshead	19 Jul 98
4:48.69	Vénuste	Niyongabo	BUR	9.12.73	1	Nik	Nice	12 Jul 95
4:48.74	John	Kibowen	KEN	21.4.69	1		Hechtel	1 Aug 98
4:49.00		Niyongabo			1		Rieti	3 Sep 97
4:49.55		Morceli			1	Nik	Nice	10 Jul 96
4:50.08	Noah	Ngeny	KEN	2.11.78	1	DNG	Stockholm	30 Jul 99
4:50.81 WR	Saïd	Aouita	MAR	2.11.59	1	BNP	Paris	16 Jul 87
4:51.17		El Guerrouj			1	ISTAF	Berlin	31 Aug 01
4:51.30	Daniel	Komen	KEN	17.5.76	1		Milano	5 Jun 98
4:51.39 WR	Steve	Cram	GBR	14.10.60	1	BGP	Budapest	4 Aug 85
4:51.52 WR	John	Walker	NZL	12.1.52	1	Bisl	Oslo	30 Jun 76
	(14/10)							
4:52.20	Thomas	Wessinghage	FRG	22.2.52	1		Ingelheim	31 Aug 82
4:52.40	José Manuel	Abascal	ESP	17.3.58	1		Santander	7 Sep 86
4:52.44	Jim	Spivey	USA	7.3.60	1	Athl	Lausanne	15 Sep 87
4:52.53	Moses	Kiptanui	KEN	1.10.70	1	ISTAF	Berlin	21 Aug 92
4:52.82	Peter	Elliott	GBR	9.10.62	2	Athl	Lausanne	15 Sep 87
4:52.82	Luke	Kipkosgei	KEN	27.11.75	2	Slovn	Bratislava	9 Jun 98
4:52.88	Ismaïl	Sghyr	MAR/FRA	16.3.72	2	Nik	Nice	12 Jul 95
4:53.06	Jack	Buckner	GBR	22.9.61	3	Athl	Lausanne	15 Sep 87
4:53.69	Gary	Staines	GBR	3.7.63	4	Athl	Lausanne	15 Sep 87
4:53.7+	John	Kosgei (20)	KEN	13.7.73	2	in 3k	Rieti	1 Sep 96
Indoors								
4:52.86	Haile	Gebrselassie	ETH	18.4.73	1	BUPA	Birmingham	15 Feb 98

3000 METRES

Mark Wind	Name		Nat	Born	Pos	Meet	Venue	Date
7:20.67 WR	Daniel	Komen	KEN	17.5.76	1		Rieti	1 Sep 96
7:23.09	Hicham	El Guerrouj	MAR	14.9.74	1	VD	Bruxelles	3 Sep 99
7:25.02	Ali	Saïdi-Sief	ALG	15.3.78	1	Herc	Monaco	18 Aug 00
7:25.09	Haile	Gebrselassie	ETH	18.4.73	1	VD	Bruxelles	28 Aug 98
7:25.11 WR	Noureddine	Morceli	ALG	28.2.70	1	Herc	Monaco	2 Aug 94
7:25.16		Komen			1	Herc	Monaco	10 Aug 96
7:25.54		Gebrselassie			1	Herc	Monaco	8 Aug 98
7:25.87		Komen			1	VD	Bruxelles	23 Aug 96
7:26.02		Gebrselassie			1	VD	Bruxelles	22 Aug 97
7:26.03		Gebrselassie			1	GP II	Helsinki	10 Jun 99
7:26.5 e		Komen			1	in 2M	Sydney	28 Feb 98
7:26.62	Mohammed	Mourhit	BEL	10.10.70	2	Herc	Monaco	18 Aug 00
7:27.18	Moses	Kiptanui	KEN	1.10.70	1	Herc	Monaco	25 Jul 95
7:27.3+		Komen			1	in 2M	Hechtel	19 Jul 97
7:27.42		Gebrselassie			1	Bisl	Oslo	9 Jul 98
7:27.50		Morceli			1	VD	Bruxelles	25 Aug 95
7:27.59	Luke	Kipkosgei	KEN	27.11.75	2	Herc	Monaco	8 Aug 98
7:27.67		Saïdi-Sief			1	Gaz	Saint-Denis	23 Jun 00
7:27.75	Tom	Nyariki	KEN	27.9.71	2	Herc	Monaco	10 Aug 96
7.28.04		Kiptanui			1	ASV	Köln	18 Aug 95
7:28.28		Kipkosgei			2	Bisl	Oslo	9 Jul 98
7:28.41	Paul	Bitok (10)	KEN	26.6.70	3	Herc	Monaco	10 Aug 96
7:28.45	Assefa	Mezegebu	ETH	19.6.78	3	Herc	Monaco	8 Aug 98
7:28.67	Benjamin	Limo	KEN	23.8.74	1	Herc	Monaco	4 Aug 99
7:28.70	Paul	Tergat	KEN	17.6.69	4	Herc	Monaco	10 Aug 96
7:28.92		Komen			3	Herc	Monaco	18 Aug 00
7:28.93	Salah	Hissou	MAR	16.1.72	2	Herc	Monaco	4 Aug 99
7:28.94	Brahim	Lahlafi	MAR	15.4.68	3	Herc	Monaco	4 Aug 99
7:28.96 WR		Kiptanui			1	ASV	Köln	16 Aug 92
7:29.09	John	Kibowen	KEN	21.4.69	3	Bisl	Oslo	9 Jul 98
	(30/16)							
7:29.34	Isaac	Viciosa	ESP	26.12.69	4	Bisl	Oslo	9 Jul 98
7:29.45 WR	Saïd	Aouita	MAR	2.11.59	1	ASV	Köln	20 Aug 89
7:30.09	Ismaïl	Sghyr	MAR/FRA	16.3.72	2	Herc	Monaco	25 Jul 95
7:30.36	Mark	Carroll	IRL	15.1.72	5	Herc	Monaco	4 Aug 99
	(20)							
7:30.50	Dieter	Baumann ¶	GER	9.2.65	6	Herc	Monaco	8 Aug 98
7:30.53	El Hassan	Lahssini	MAR	1.1.74	6	Herc	Monaco	10 Aug 96

Mark Wind	Name		Nat	Born	Pos	Meet	Venue	Date
7:30.53	Hailu	Mekonnen	ETH	4.4.80	1	VD	Bruxelles	24 Aug 01
7:30.67	Kenenisa	Bekele	ETH	13.6.82	2	VD	Bruxelles	24 Aug 01
7:30.78	Mustapha	Essaïd	FRA	20.1.70	7	Herc	Monaco	8 Aug 98
7:30.84	Bob	Kennedy	USA	18.8.70	8	Herc	Monaco	8 Aug 98
7:30.99	Khalid	Boulami	MAR	7.8.69	1	Nik	Nice	16 Jul 97
7:31.13	Julius	Gitahi	KEN	29.4.78	6	Bisl	Oslo	9 Jul 98
7:31.14	William	Kalya	KEN	4.8.74	3	Herc	Monaco	16 Aug 97
7:31.59	Manuel	Pancorbo	ESP	7.7.66	7	Bisl	Oslo	9 Jul 98
	(30)							
7:32.1 WR	Henry	Rono	KEN	12.2.52	1	Bisl	Oslo	27 Jun 78
7:32.23	Richard	Limo	KEN	18.11.80	5	VD	Bruxelles	24 Aug 01
7:32.32	Enrique	Molina	ESP	25.2.68	5	Bisl	Oslo	4 Jul 97
7:32.36	Million	Wolde	ETH	17.3.79	3	Gaz	Saint-Denis	23 Jun 00
7:32.36	Benjamin	Maiyo	KEN	6.10.78	2	GPII	Athína	28 Jun 00
7:32.36	Abderrahim	Goumri	MAR	21.5.76	6	VD	Bruxelles	24 Aug 01
7:32.38	Abiyote	Abate	ETH	20.11.80	7	VD	Bruxelles	24 Aug 01
7:32.79	David	Moorcroft	GBR	10.4.53	1		London (CP)	17 Jul 82
7:33.13	Shem	Kororia	KEN	25.9.72	7	Herc	Monaco	10 Aug 96
7:33.37	Sydney	Maree	USA	9.9.56	2		London (CP)	17 Jul 82
	(40)							
7:33.42	Salah	El Ghazi	MAR	2.11.75	4	Herc	Monaco	20 Jul 01
7:33.51	Bernard	Lagat	KEN	12.12.74	5	Herc	Monaco	18 Aug 00
7:33.62	Sammy	Kipketer	KEN	29.9.81	3	Athl	Lausanne	4 Jul 01
7:33.79	Paul	Koech	KEN	25.6.69	5	Herc	Monaco	16 Aug 97
7:33.96	Wilson	Kipketer (Boit)	KEN	6.10.73	7	Nik	Nice	16 Jul 97
7:34.03	Vénuste	Niyongabo	BUR	9.12.73	3	ASV	Köln	16 Aug 96
7:34.18	Yobes	Ondieki	KEN	21.2.61	3	ASV	Köln	16 Aug 92
7:34.46	Driss	El Himer	FRA	4.4.74	5	GP	Paris	29 Jul 98
7:34.67	Mohamed Saïd	El Wardi	MAR	19.4.72	4	Gaz	Saint-Denis	23 Jun 00
7:34.96	Adam	Goucher	USA	18.2.75	6	Herc	Monaco	20 Jul 01
	(50)	100th man 7:39.15, 200th man 7:43.05						
Indoors								
7:24.90		Komen			1		Budapest	6 Feb 98
7:26.15		Gebrselassie			1		Karlsruhe	25 Jan 98
7:26.80		Gebrselassie			1		Karlsruhe	24 Jan 99

2 MILES

Mark Wind	Name		Nat	Born	Pos	Meet	Venue	Date
7:58.61 WR	Daniel	Komen	KEN	17.5.76	1		Hechtel	19 Jul 97
7:58.91		Komen			1		Sydney	28 Feb 98
8:01.08 WR	Haile	Gebrselassie	ETH	18.4.73	1	APM	Hengelo	31 May 97
8:01.72		Gebrselassie			1	BrGP	London (CP)	7 Aug 99
8:01.86		Gebrselassie			1	APM	Hengelo	30 May 99
8:03.54 WR		Komen			1		Lappeenranta	14 Jul 96
8:07.46 WR		Gebrselassie			1		Kerkrade	28 May 95
8:09.01 WR	Moses	Kiptanui	KEN	10.10.70	1		Hechtel	30 Jul 94
8:10.98	Khalid	Boulami	MAR	7.8.69	1		Hechtel	6 Jul 96
8:11.59	Bob	Kennedy	USA	18.8.70	2		Hechtel	19 Jul 97
8:11.73	Ismaïl	Sghyr	MAR/FRA	16.3.72	2		Hechtel	6 Jul 96
ndoors								
8:09.66	Hailu	Mekonnen	ETH	4.4.80	1		Birmingham	20 Feb 00
8:09.89	Hicham	El Guerrouj	MAR	14.9.74	1	Euro	Gent	23 Feb 01

5000 METRES

Mark Wind	Name		Nat	Born	Pos	Meet	Venue	Date
12:39.36 WR	Haile	Gebrselassie	ETH	18.4.73	1	GP II	Helsinki	13 Jun 98
12:39.74 WR	Daniel	Komen	KEN	17.5.76	1	VD	Bruxelles	22 Aug 97
12:41.86 WR		Gebrselassie			1	WK	Zürich	13 Aug 97
12:44.39 WR		Gebrselassie			1	WK	Zürich	16 Aug 95
12:44.90		Komen			2	WK	Zürich	13 Aug 97
12:45.09		Komen			1	WK	Zürich	14 Aug 96
12:48.98		Komen			1	GGala	Roma	5 Jun 97
12:49.28	Brahim	Lahlafi	MAR	15.4.68	1	VD	Bruxelles	25 Aug 00
12:49.64		Gebrselassie			1	WK	Zürich	11 Aug 99
12:49.71	Mohammed	Mourhit	BEL	10.10.70	2	VD	Bruxelles	25 Aug 00
12:49.87	Paul	Tergat	KEN	17.6.69	3	WK	Zürich	13 Aug 97
12:50.80	Salah	Hissou	MAR	16.1.72	1	GGala	Roma	5 Jun 96
12:50.86	Ali	Saïdi Sief	ALG	15.3.78	1	GGala	Roma	30 Jun 00
12:51.60		Komen			1	DNG	Stockholm	8 Jul 96
12:52.38		Komen			1	GPF	Milano	7 Sep 96
12:52.39		Hissou			2	GGala	Roma	5 Jun 97

Mark Wind		Name	Nat	Born	Pos	Meet	Venue	Date
12:52.53		Hissou			1		Milano	9 Jun 99
12.52.70		Gebrselassie			2	WK	Zürich	14 Aug 96
12.53.19		Gebrselassie			1	ISTAF	Berlin	1 Sep 95
12:53.41	Khalid	Boulami	MAR	7.8.69	4	WK	Zürich	13 Aug 97
12:53.45		Hissou			2	WK	Zürich	11 Aug 99
12:53.72	Philip	Mosima	KEN	2.1.77	2	GGala	Roma	5 Jun 96
12:53.84	Assefa	Mezegebu (10)	ETH	19.6.78	1	VD	Bruxelles	28 Aug 98
12:53.92		Gebrselassie			1	Bisl	Oslo	30 Jun 99
12:54.07	Sammy	Kipketer	KEN-J	29.9.81	2	GGala	Roma	30 Jun 00
12:54.08		Gebrselassie			1	WK	Zürich	12 Aug 98
12:54.60		Gebrselassie			1		Nürnberg	13 Jun 97
12:54.70	Dieter	Baumann	GER	9.2.65	5	WK	Zürich	13 Aug 97
12:54.72		Tergat			3	WK	Zürich	14 Aug 96
12:54.82		Komen			2	VD	Bruxelles	28 Aug 98
	(30/12)							
12:54.85	Moses	Kiptanui	KEN	1.10.70	3	GGala	Roma	5 Jun 96
12:55.63	Mark	Bett	KEN	22.12.76	2	Bisl	Oslo	28 Jul 00
12:55.82	Benjamin	Limo	KEN	23.8.74	3	Bisl	Oslo	28 Jul 00
12:55.94	Tom	Nyariki	KEN	27.9.71	1	DNG	Stockholm	7 Jul 97
12:56.29	Paul	Koech	KEN	25.6.69	6	WK	Zürich	13 Aug 97
12:56.50	Luke	Kipkosgei	KEN	27.11.75	5	Bisl	Oslo	28 Jul 00
12:56.72	Richard	Limo	KEN	18.11.80	1	WK	Zürich	17 Aug 01
12:57.23	Worku	Bikila	ETH	6.5.68	3	GGala	Roma	8 Jun 95
	(20)							
12:57.79	David	Chelule	KEN	7.7.77	5	GGala	Roma	7 Jul 99
12:58.21	Bob	Kennedy	USA	18.8.70	5	WK	Zürich	14 Aug 96
12:58.39WR	Saïd	Aouita	MAR	2.11.59	1	GGala	Roma	22 Jul 87
12:58.57	Hailu	Mekonnen	ETH	4.4.80	1	GGala	Roma	29 Jun 01
12:58.99	Ismaïl	Sghyr	MAR/FRA	16.3.72	6	WK	Zürich	14 Aug 96
12:59.39	Million	Wolde	ETH	17.3.79	5	WK	Zürich	12 Aug 98
12:59.90	Albert	Chepkirui	KEN	4.4.81	8	Bisl	Oslo	28 Jul 00
12:59.97	John	Kibowen	KEN	21.4.69	3	GP	Athína	11 Jun 01
13:00.10	Paul	Bitok	KEN	26.6.70	1	Bisl	Oslo	13 Jul 01
13:00.36	Abiyote	Abate	ETH	20.11.80	5	GGala	Roma	29 Jun 01
	(30)							
13:00.41WR	David	Moorcroft	GBR	10.4.53	1	OsloG	Oslo	7 Jul 82
13:00.54	Khalid	Skah	MAR	29.1.67	1	BNP	Villeneuve d'Ascq	8 Jul 94
13:01.15	Sydney	Maree	USA	9.9.56	2	Bisl	Oslo	27 Jul 85
13:01.41	Brahim	Jabbour	MAR	2.10.70	1	GP II	Saint-Denis	3 Jul 99
13:01.82	Yobes	Ondieki	KEN	21.2.61	1	WK	Zürich	7 Aug 91
13:01.89	Julius	Gitahi	KEN	29.4.78	5	DNG	Stockholm	5 Aug 98
13:01.9	Abraham	Chebii	KEN	23.12.79	2		Milano	7 Jun 00
13:02.15	Mustapha	Essaïd	FRA	20.1.70	4	VD	Bruxelles	28 Aug 98
13:02.28	Benjamin	Maiyo	KEN	6.10.78	2	Athl	Lausanne	5 Jul 00
13:02.54	Alberto	García	ESP	22.2.71	8	GGala	Roma	29 Jun 01
	(40)							
13:02.68	Patrick	Ivuti	KEN	30.6.78	7	WK	Zürich	11 Aug 00
13:02.71	Evans	Rutto	KEN	8.4.78	2	Live	Nürnberg	25 Jun 00
13:02.75	Ismael	Kirui	KEN	20.2.75	1	WCh	Stuttgart	16 Aug 93
13:02.80	Shem	Kororia	KEN	25.9.72	1	DNG	Stockholm	10 Jul 95
13:02.86	António	Pinto	POR	22.3.66	9	WK	Zürich	12 Aug 98
13:03.08	William	Kalya	KEN	4.8.74	2	DNG	Stockholm	10 Jul 95
13:03.29	Vénuste	Niyongabo	BUR	9.12.73	1		Saint-Denis	3 Jun 96
13:03.60	Abderrahim	Goumri	MAR	21.5.76	3	GP	Saint-Denis	6 Jul 01
13:03.76	Stéphane	Franke	GER	12.2.64	5	WK	Zürich	16 Aug 95
13:03.85	Noureddine	Morceli	ALG	28.2.70	1	WK	Zürich	17 Aug 94
	(50)	100th man 13:11.25, 200th man 13:17.9						
Indoors								
12:50.38		Gebrselassie			1	BUPA	Birmingham	14 Feb 99
12:51.48		Komen			1		Stockholm	19 Feb 98

10,000 METRES

Mark Wind		Name	Nat	Born	Pos	Meet	Venue	Date
26:22.75WR	Haile	Gebrselassie	ETH	18.4.73	1	APM	Hengelo	1 Jun 98
26:27.85WR	Paul	Tergat	KEN	17.6.69	1	VD	Bruxelles	22 Aug 97
26:31.32WR		Gebrselassie			1	Bisl	Oslo	4 Jul 97
26:36.26	Paul	Koech	KEN	25.6.69	2	VD	Bruxelles	22 Aug 97
26:38.08WR	Salah	Hissou	MAR	16.1.72	1	VD	Bruxelles	23 Aug 96
26:43.53WR		Gebrselassie			1	APM	Hengelo	5 Jun 95
26:46.44		Tergat			1	VD	Bruxelles	28 Aug 98
26:47.89		Koech			2	VD	Bruxelles	28 Aug 98

Mark	Wind	Name		Nat	Born	Pos	Meet	Venue	Date
26:51.49		Charles	Kamathi	KEN	18.5.78	1	VD	Bruxelles	3 Sep 99
26:52.23	WR	William	Sigei	KEN	11.10.69	1	Bisl	Oslo	22 Jul 94
26:52.30		Mohammed	Mourhit	BEL	10.10.70	2	VD	Bruxelles	3 Sep 99
26:54.41			Tergat			2	VD	Bruxelles	23 Aug 96
26:56.78			Koech			3	VD	Bruxelles	23 Aug 96
26:58.38	WR	Yobes	Ondieki	KEN	21.2.61	1	Bisl	Oslo	10 Jul 93
27:03.87			Tergat			1	VD	Bruxelles	25 Aug 00
27:04.20		Abraham	Chebii	KEN	23.12.79	1		Palo Alto	4 May 01
27:04.54		Felix	Limo (10)	KEN	22.8.80	2	VD	Bruxelles	25 Aug 00
27:06.44		Worku	Bikila	ETH	6.5.68	1	VD	Bruxelles	25 Aug 95
27:06.45		Habte	Jifar	ETH	29.1.76	1	APM	Hengelo	30 May 99
27:06.59		Ismael	Kirui	KEN	20.2.75	2	VD	Bruxelles	25 Aug 95
27:07.34			Gebrselassie			1	OG	Atlanta	29 Jul 96
27:07.55		Benjamin	Maiyo	KEN	6.10.78	2		Palo Alto	4 May 01
27:07.91	WR	Richard	Chelimo	KEN	21.4.72	1	DNG	Stockholm	5 Jul 93
27:08.17			Tergat			2	OG	Atlanta	29 Jul 96
27:08.23	WR	Arturo	Barrios	MEX	12.12.63	1	ISTAF	Berlin	18 Aug 89
27:09.07			Hissou			3	VD	Bruxelles	22 Aug 97
27:09.30			Hissou			3	VD	Bruxelles	25 Aug 95
27:09.79		Patrick	Ivuti	KEN	30.6.78	3	VD	Bruxelles	25 Aug 00
27:10.08			Tergat			1	DNG	Stockholm	30 Jul 99
27:10.34		Josphat	Machuka	KEN	12.12.73	4	VD	Bruxelles	25 Aug 95
27:10.38			Koech			3	VD	Bruxelles	3 Sep 99
27:11.17		Julius	Gitahi	KEN	29.4.78	1		Kobe	26 Apr 98
27:11.18			Chelimo			1	APM	Hengelo	25 Jun 91
27:11.62		John	Ngugi ¶	KEN	10.5.62	1	VD	Bruxelles	13 Sep 91
		(34/20)							
27:12.37		Luke	Kipkosgei	KEN	27.11.75	3		Palo Alto	4 May 01
27:12.39		Ismaïl	Sghyr	MAR/FRA	16.3.72	2	DNG	Stockholm	30 Jul 99
27:12.47		António	Pinto	POR	22.3.66	3	DNG	Stockholm	30 Jul 99
27:13.38		Girma	Tola	ETH	13.10.75	2	APM	Hengelo	30 May 99
27:13.81	WR	Fernando	Mamede	POR	1.11.51	1	DNG	Stockholm	2 Jul 84
27:13.98		Mebrahtom	Keflezighi	USA	5.5.75	4		Palo Alto	4 May 01
27:14.26		Fita	Bayissa	ETH	15.12.72	1	Bisl	Oslo	4 Jul 92
27:14.44		Fabián	Roncero	ESP	19.10.70	1rA	EChall	Lisboa	4 Apr 98
27:14.53		Khalid	Skah	MAR	29.1.67	2	WCh	Göteborg	8 Aug 95
27:16.50		Salvatore	Antibo	ITA	7.2.62	1	WG	Helsinki	29 Jun 89
		(30)							
27:17.20		William	Kiptum	KEN	30.3.71	2	Bisl	Oslo	22 Jul 94
27:17.48		Carlos	Lopes	POR	18.2.47	2	DNG	Stockholm	2 Jul 84
27:17.82		Addis	Abebe	ETH	5.9.70	2	WG	Helsinki	29 Jun 89
27:18.02		Shem	Kororia	KEN	25.9.72	6	VD	Bruxelles	25 Aug 95
27:18.14		Jon	Brown	GBR	27.2.71	4	VD	Bruxelles	28 Aug 98
27:18.28		Assefa	Mezgebu	ETH	19.6.78	4	APM	Hengelo	30 May 99
27:18.32		Moses	Tanui	KEN	20.8.65	2	VD	Bruxelles	3 Sep 93
27:18.59		Armando	Quintanilla	MEX	19.4.68	3	Bisl	Oslo	22 Jul 94
27:18.66		Mark	Bett	KEN	22.12.76	5	VD	Bruxelles	28 Aug 98
27:18.74		Simon	Maina Munyi	KEN	18.3.78	5	APM	Hengelo	30 May 99
		(40)							
27:20.38		Aloÿs	Nizigama	BUR	18.6.66	1		London (CP)	7 Jul 95
27:20.56		Mark	Nenow	USA	16.11.57	1	VD	Bruxelles	5 Sep 86
27:21.29		Luka	Keitany	KEN	.79	7	APM	Hengelo	30 May 99
27:21.32		Evans	Rutto	KEN	8.4.78	3		Villeneuve d'Ascq	17 Jun 00
27:21.46		M Brahim	Boutayeb	MAR	15.8.67	1	OG	Seoul	26 Sep 88
27:21.53		Dieter	Baumann	GER	9.2.65	1	EChall	Barakaldo	5 Apr 97
27:22.20		José	Rios	ESP	15.3.74	1	NC	Gijón	12 Aug 00
27:22.47!	WR	Henry	Rono	KEN	12.2.52	1		Wien	11 Jun 78
27:22.78		Antonio	Martins	FRA	23.8.63	3	Bisl	Oslo	4 Jul 92
27:23.06		Eamonn	Martin	GBR	9.10.58	1	Bisl	Oslo	2 Jul 88
		(50)	100th man 27:34.58, 200th man 27:46.52						

20,000m 1 HOUR

Mark	Distance	Name		Nat	Born	Pos	Venue	Date
56:55.6+	21 101m	Arturo	Barrios	MEX	12.12.63	1	La Flèche	30 Mar 91
57:24.19+	20 944	Jos	Hermens	NED	8.1.50	1	Papendal	1 May 76
57:18.4+	20 943	Dionísio	Castro	POR	22.11.63	1	La Flèche	31 Mar 90
57:28.7+	20 855	Carl	Thackery	GBR	14.10.62	2	La Flèche	31 Mar 90
57:44.4+	20 784	Gaston	Roelants	BEL	5.2.37	1	Bruxelles	20 Sep 72
57:48.7		Toshihiko	Seko	JPN	15.7.56	1	Odawara	11 May 85

HALF MARATHON

Included in these lists are the slightly downhill courses: Newcastle to South Shields 30.5m, Tokyo 33m. Lisboa 40m

Mark	Wind	Name		Nat	Born	Pos	Meet	Venue	Date
59:06		Paul	Tergat	KEN	17.6.69	1		Lisboa	26 Mar 00
59:17			Tergat			1		Milano	4 Apr 98
59:20		Hendrick	Ramaala	RSA	2.2.72	2		Lisboa	26 Mar 00
59:22			Tergat			1	Stra	Milano	17 Apr 99
59:31		Patrick	Ivuti	KEN	30.6.78	3		Lisboa	26 Mar 00
59:38		Faustin	Baha	TAN	30.5.82	4		Lisboa	26 Mar 00
59:43		António	Pinto	POR	22.3.66	1		Lisboa	15 Mar 98
59:47		Moses	Tanui	KEN	20.8.65	1		Milano	3 Apr 93
59:51		William	Kiplagat	KEN	21.6.72	5		Lisboa	26 Mar 00
59:51	w	Tesfaye	Tola	ETH	19.10.74	1		Malmö	12 Jun 00
59:52		Fabián	Roncero	ESP	19.10.70	1		Berlin	1 Apr 01
59:56			Tergat			1		Milano	1 Apr 95
59:56		Shem	Kororia (10)	KEN	25.9.72	1	WCh	Kosice	4 Oct 97
59:58			Tanui			2	WCh	Kosice	4 Oct 97
60:00		Kenneth	Cheruiyot	KEN	2.8.74	3	WCh	Kosice	4 Oct 97
60:00	w	Philip	Rugut	KEN	18.5.77	2		Malmö	12 Jun 00
60:01		Paul	Koech	KEN	25.6.69	1	WCh	Uster	27 Sep 98
60:01		Japhet	Kosgei	KEN	68	1		Lisboa	21 Mar 99
60:02		Benson	Masya	KEN	14.5.70	1	GNR	South Shields	18 Sep 94
60:02		Darren	Wilson	AUS	9.8.68	1		Tokyo	19 Jan 97
60:03			Tanui			2	GNR	South Shields	18 Sep 94
60:03		Haile	Gebrselassie	ETH	18.4.73	1	WCh	Bristol	7 Oct 01
60:04		Joseph	Kimani	KEN	21.9.72	2		Lisboa	15 Mar 98
60:04		Tesfaye	Jifar	ETH	23.4.76	2	WCh	Bristol	7 Oct 01
60:05			Rugut			1		Trieste	2 May 99
60:05	w		Baha			3		Malmö	12 Jun 00
60:06		Steve	Moneghetti	AUS	26.9.62	1		Tokyo	24 Jan 93
60:07			Ramaala			4	WCh	Kosice	4 Oct 97
60:09	Sh?	Paul	Evans	GBR	13.4.61	1		Marrakesh	15 Jan 95
60:11		Matthews	Temane	RSA	14.12.60	1	NC	East London	25 Jul 87
60:11		Zithulele	Sinqe	RSA	9.6.63	2	NC	East London	25 Jul 87
60:11		Todd	Williams	USA	7.3.69	2		Tokyo	24 Jan 93
		(32/24)							
60:12	Sh?	Laban	Chege	KEN	70	2		Marrakesh	15 Jan 95
60:12		John	Yuda	TAN	9.6.79	3	WCh	Bristol	7 Oct 01
60:14		Armando	Quintanilla	MEX	19.4.68	1		Tokyo	21 Jan 96
60:15		Sammy	Korir	KEN	12.12.71	1	RdVin	Grevenmacher	27 Sep 98
60:17		Dionicio	Cerón	MEX	9.10.65	3		Tokyo	24 Jan 93
60:18		Mohamed	Mourhit	BEL	10.10.70	5	WCh	Kosice	4 Oct 97
		(30)							
60:23		Vincent	Rousseau	BEL	29.7.62	1		Tokyo	23 Jan 94
60:23		Gert	Thys	RSA	12.11.71	6	WCh	Kosice	4 Oct 97
60:24		Philip	Tarus	KEN	11.9.74	2		Milano	4 Apr 98
60:24		Khalid	Skah	MAR	29.1.67	3	WCh	Uster	27 Sep 98
60:24		Elijah	Lagat	KEN	72	1		Grevenmacher	26 Sep 99
60:26		Simon	Lopuyet	KEN	24.12.72	1		Lisboa	12 Mar 95
60:26		Tendai	Chimusasa	ZIM	28.1.71	1		Grevenmacher	24 Sep 95
60:26		Zebedayo	Bayo	TAN	20.5.76	3		Lisboa	15 Mar 98
60:27		Joseph	Kibor	KEN	22.12.72	2		Gualtieri	31 Mar 97
60:27		Khalid	Khannouchi	MAR/USA	22.12.71	1		Philadelphia	28 Sep 97
		(40)							
60:27		Josephat	Kiprono	KEN	12.12.73	4		Lisboa	15 Mar 98
60:27		Titus	Munji	KEN	79	2		Berlin	1 Apr 01
60:28		Germán	Silva	MEX	9.1.68	2	WCh	Oslo	24 Sep 94
60:29	w	Róbert	Stefko	SVK	28.5.68	4		Malmö	12 Jun 00
60:30		Eduardo do	Nascimento	BRA	2.8.72	5		Lisboa	15 Mar 98
60:30		Ken-ichi	Takahashi	JPN	16.1.73	1		Tokyo	10 Jan 00
60:30		Gezahegne	Abera	ETH	23.4.78	5		Malmö	12 Jun 00
60:30		Evans	Rutto	KEN	8.4.78	3		Lisboa	1 Apr 01
60:31		Julius	Korir	KEN	12.5.58	1		Grevenmacher	22 Sep 91
60:31		Ibrahim	Seïd	ETH	65	4	WCh	Uster	27 Sep 98
		(50)	100th man 61:00, 200th man 61:26						

Short courses

Mark	Wind	Name		Nat	Born	Pos	Meet	Venue	Date
58:51		Paul	Tergat	KEN	17.6.69	1	Stra	Milano 49m sh	30 Mar 96
59:24		Sammy	Lelei	KEN	14.8.64	1		Lisboa 97m	13 Mar 93
59:46		Josephat	Kiprono	KEN	12.12.73	2	Stra	Milano 49m	30 Mar 96

MARATHON

Note Boston marathon is downhill overall (139m) and, as a point-to-point course, in some years, such as 1994, has been strongly wind-aided - next bests are shown if to standard as a supplement.
In second column: L = loop course or start and finish within 30%, P = point-to-point or start and finish more than 30% apart, D = point-to-point and downhil over 1/1000

Mark	Wind	Name		Nat	Born	Pos	Meet	Venue	Date
2:05:42	L WR	Khalid	Khannouchi	MAR/USA	22.12.71	1		Chicago	24 Oct 99
2:06:05	L WR	Ronaldo da	Costa	BRA	7.6.70	1		Berlin	20 Sep 98
2:06:16	L	Moses	Tanui	KEN	20.8.65	2		Chicago	24 Oct 99
2:06:33	L	Gert	Thys	RSA	12.11.71	1		Tokyo	14 Feb 99
2:06:36	L	António	Pinto	POR	22.3.66	1		London	16 Apr 00
2:06:44	L	Josephat	Kiprono	KEN	12.12.73	1		Berlin	26 Sep 99
2:06:47	L	Fred	Kiprop	KEN	3.6.74	1		Amsterdam	17 Oct 99
2:06:49	L	Tesfaye	Jifar	ETH	23.4.76	2		Amsterdam	17 Oct 99
2:06:50	L WR	Belayneh	Dinsamo	ETH	28.6.65	1		Rotterdam	17 Apr 88
2:06:50	L	William	Kiplagat	KEN	21.6.72	3		Amsterdam	17 Oct 99
		(10)							
2:06:50	L		Kiprono			1		Rotterdam	22 Apr 01
2:06:51	L	Atsushi	Fujita	JPN	6.11.76	1		Fukuoka	3 Dec 00
2:06:54	L	Ondoro	Osoro	KEN	3.12.67	1		Chicago	11 Oct 98
2:06:57	L	Takayuki	Inuhishi	JPN	11.8.72	2		Berlin	26 Sep 99
2:06:57	L	Tesfaye	Tolla	ETH	19.10.74	4		Amsterdam	17 Oct 99
2:07:01	L		Khannouchi			1		Chicago	22 Oct 00
2:07:02	L	Sammy	Lelei	KEN	14.8.64	1		Berlin	24 Sep 95
2:07:02	L	Driss	El Himer	FRA	4.4.74	1		Amsterdam	21 Oct 01
2:07:06	L		Kiprono			2		Amsterdam	21 Oct 01
2:07:07	L	Ahmed	Salah	DJI	31.12.56	2		Rotterdam	17 Apr 88
2:07:09	L	Japheth	Kosgei	KEN	28.12.68	1		Rotterdam	18 Apr 99
2:07:10	L		Khannouchi			1		Chicago	19 Oct 97
2:07:11	L	Abdelkader	El Mouaziz	MAR	1.1.69	1		London	22 Apr 01
2:07:12	L WR	Carlos	Lopes (20)	POR	18.2.47	1		Rotterdam	20 Apr 85
2:07:13	L	Steve	Jones	GBR	4.8.55	1		Chicago	20 Oct 85
2:07:15	D	Cosmas	Ndeti	KEN	24.11.71	1		Boston	18 Apr 94
2:07:15	L		Japheth Kosgei			1		Tokyo	13 Feb 00
2:07:18	L	Kenneth	Cheruiyot	KEN	2.8.74	2		Rotterdam	22 Apr 01
2:07:19	D	Andrés	Espinosa	MEX	4.2.63	2		Boston	18 Apr 94
2:07:19	L		Khannouchi			2		Chicago	11 Oct 98
		(30/24)							
2:07:20	L	Vincent	Rousseau	BEL	29.7.62	2		Berlin	24 Sep 95
2:07:20	L		Lee Bong-ju	KOR	11.10.70	2		Tokyo	13 Feb 00
2:07:23	L	Fabián	Roncero	ESP	19.10.70	2		Rotterdam	18 Apr 99
2:07:28	L	Josiah	Thugwane	RSA	15.4.71	1		Fukuoka	7 Dec 97
2:07:34	L	Antonio	Peña	ESP	26.8.70	1	L.Biwa	Otsu	4 Mar 01
2:07:35	L	Taisuke	Kodama	JPN	26.7.58	1		Beijing	19 Oct 86
		(30)							
2:07:35	L	Abebe	Mekonnen	ETH	9.1.64	1		Beijing	16 Oct 88
2:07:37	D	Joseph	Chebet	KEN	23.8.70	2		Boston	20 Apr 98
2:07:40	L	Hiromi	Taniguchi	JPN	5.4.60	2		Beijing	16 Oct 88
2:07:41	L	Elijah	Lagat	KEN	19.6.66	1		Berlin	28 Sep 97
2:07:41	L	Simon	Biwott	KEN	3.3.70	4		Rotterdam	18 Apr 99
2:07:43	L	Erick	Kimaiyo	KEN	8.7.69	2		Berlin	28 Sep 97
2:07:45	L	Simeretu	Alemayehu	ETH	18.10.70	1		Torino	1 Apr 01
2:07:46	L	Julio	Rey ¶	ESP	13.1.72	1		Hamburg	22 Apr 01
2:07:48	L	Francisco Javier	Cortés	ESP	25.10.71	2		Hamburg	22 Apr 01
2:07:49	L		Kim Yi-yong	KOR	20.9.73	4		Rotterdam	18 Apr 99
		(40)							
2:07:51	D	Robert	de Castella	AUS	27.2.57	1		Boston	21 Apr 86
2:07:51	L	Domingos	Castro	POR	22.11.63	1		Rotterdam	20 Apr 97
2:07:52	L	Giacomo	Leone	ITA	10.4.71	2	L.Biwa	Otsu	4 Mar 01
2:07:52	L	Shigeru	Aburaya	JPN	6.2.77	3	L.Biwa	Otsu	4 Mar 01
2:07:54	L	Alejandro	Gómez	ESP	11.4.67	2		Rotterdam	20 Apr 97
2:07:54	L	Gezahegne	Abera	ETH	23.4.78	1		Fukuoka	5 Dec 99
2:07:55	L	Mohamed	Ouaadi	FRA	1.1.69	2		Fukuoka	5 Dec 99
2:07:57	L	Kunimitsu	Ito	JPN	6.1.55	2		Beijing	19 Oct 86
2:07:57	L	Stefano	Baldini	ITA	25.5.71	2		London	13 Apr 97
2:07:57	L	Abel	Antón	ESP	24.10.62	1		London	26 Apr 98
		(50)	100th man 2:08:47, 200th 2:09:45, 300th 2:10:28, 400th 2:10:54						

Drugs Disqualification

Mark	Wind	Name		Nat	Born	Pos	Meet	Venue	Date
2:07:37		Julio	Rey ¶	ESP	13.1.72	(3)		Rotterdam	18 Apr 99

2000 METRES STEEPLECHASE

Mark	Wind	Name		Nat	Born	Pos	Meet	Venue	Date
5:14.43		Julius	Kariuki	KEN	12.6.61	1		Rovereto	21 Aug 90
5:16.22		Phillip	Barkutwo	KEN	6.10.66	2		Rovereto	21 Aug 90
5:16.85		Eliud	Barngetuny	KEN	20.5.73	1		Parma	13 Jun 95
5:18.28		Richard	Kosgei	KEN	29.12.70	2		Parma	13 Jun 95
5:18.36		Alessandro	Lambruschini	ITA	7.1.65	1		Verona	12 Sep 89
5:18.38		Azzedine	Brahmi	ALG	13.9.66	1		Verona	17 Jun 92
5:18.51		John	Langat	KEN	27.11.74	1		Rovereto	29 Aug 01
5:18.60		Stanley	Kibiwott	KEN	8.8.69	2		Rovereto	29 Aug 01
5:19.21		Joseph	Keter	KEN	13.6.69	3		Rovereto	23 Aug 95
5:19.33		Bouabdellah	Tahri	FRA	20.12.78	1		Tomblaine	2 Sep 01

3000 METRES STEEPLECHASE

Mark	Wind	Name		Nat	Born	Pos	Meet	Venue	Date
7:55.28	WR	Brahim	Boulami	MAR	20.4.72	1	VD	Bruxelles	24 Aug 01
7:55.72	WR	Bernard	Barmasai	KEN	6.5.74	1	ASV	Köln	24 Aug 97
7:56.16		Moses	Kiptanui	KEN	1.10.70	2	ASV	Köln	24 Aug 97
7:57.29		Reuben	Kosgei	KEN	2.8.79	2	VD	Bruxelles	24 Aug 01
7:58.50			Boulami			1	WK	Zürich	17 Aug 01
7:58.66		Stephen	Cherono	KEN	15.10.82	3	VD	Bruxelles	24 Aug 01
7:58.98			Barmasai			1	Herc	Monaco	4 Aug 99
7:59.08	WR	Wilson	Boit Kipketer	KEN	6.10.73	1	WK	Zürich	13 Aug 97
7:59.18	WR		Kiptanui			1	WK	Zürich	16 Aug 95
7.59.52			Kiptanui			1	VD	Bruxelles	25 Aug 95
8:00.35			Barmasai			2	WK	Zürich	13 Aug 97
8:00.54			Kiptanui			1		Rieti	3 Sep 97
8:00.67			Barmasai			1	Herc	Monaco	8 Aug 98
8:00.78			Kiptanui			3	WK	Zürich	13 Aug 97
8:01.05			Boit Kipketer			1		Stuttgart	19 Jul 98
8:01.53			Barmasai			1	Nik	Nice	16 Jul 98
8:01.69		Kipkirui	Misoi	KEN	23.12.78	4	VD	Bruxelles	24 Aug 01
8:01.73			Boit Kipketer			1	Herc	Monaco	20 Jul 01
8:01.80			Kiptanui			1	DNG	Stockholm	7 Jul 97
8:01.98			Barmasai			1	WK	Zürich	12 Aug 98
8:02.08	WR		Kiptanui			1	WK	Zürich	19 Aug 92
8:02.45			Kiptanui			1	GPF	Monaco	9 Sep 95
8:02.76			Barmasai			1	Herc	Monaco	18 Aug 00
8:02.77			Kipketer			2	DNG	Stockholm	7 Jul 97
8:02.81			Barmasai			1		Paris	29 Jul 98
8:02.85			Kiptanui			1	Herc	Monaco	16 Aug 97
8:02.90			Boulami			2	Herc	Monaco	18 Aug 00
8:02.94			Barmasai			2	Herc	Monaco	16 Aug 97
8:03.08			Barmasai			1	VD	Bruxelles	3 Sep 99
8:03.22			Reu. Kosgei			2	WK	Zürich	17 Aug 01
		(30/7)							
8:03.41		Patrick	Sang	KEN	11.4.64	3	ASV	Köln	24 Aug 97
8:03.57		Ali	Ezzine	MAR	3.9.78	1	Gaz	Saint-Denis	23 Jun 00
8:03.74		Raymond	Yator	KEN	7.4.81	3	Herc	Monaco	18 Aug 00
		(10)							
8:03.89		John	Kosgei	KEN	13.7.73	3	Herc	Monaco	16 Aug 97
8:05.01		Eliud	Barngetuny	KEN	20.5.73	1	Herc	Monaco	25 Jul 95
8:05.35	WR	Peter	Koech	KEN	18.2.58	1	DNG	Stockholm	3 Jul 89
8:05.37		Philip	Barkutwo	KEN	6.10.66	2		Rieti	6 Sep 92
8:05.4	WR	Henry	Rono	KEN	12.2.52	1		Seattle	13 May 78
8:05.43		Christopher	Kosgei	KEN	14.8.74	2	WK	Zürich	11 Aug 99
8:05.51		Julius	Kariuki	KEN	12.6.61	1	OG	Seoul	30 Sep 88
8:05.99		Joseph	Keter	KEN	13.6.69	1	Herc	Monaco	10 Aug 96
8:06.77		Gideon	Chirchir	KEN	24.2.66	2	WK	Zürich	16 Aug 95
8:06.88		Richard	Kosgei	KEN	29.12.70	2	GPF	Monaco	9 Sep 95
		(20)							
8:07.13		Paul	Kosgei	KEN	22.4.78	2	GP II	Saint-Denis	3 Jul 99
8:07.59		Julius	Nyamu	KEN	1.12.77	5	VD	Bruxelles	24 Aug 01
8:07.62		Joseph	Mahmoud	FRA	13.12.55	1	VD	Bruxelles	24 Aug 84
8:07.96		Mark	Rowland	GBR	7.3.63	3	OG	Seoul	30 Sep 88
8:08.02	WR	Anders	Gärderud	SWE	28.8.46	1	OG	Montreal	28 Jul 76
8:08.12		Matthew	Birir	KEN	5.7.72	3	GGala	Roma	8 Jun 95
8:08.26		Saad Shaddad	Al-Asmari	KSA	24.9.68	6	DNG	Stockholm	7 Jul 97
8:08.57		Francesco	Panetta	ITA	10.1.63	1	WCh	Roma	5 Sep 87
8:08.74		Luis Miguel	Martín	ESP	11.1.72	6	VD	Bruxelles	24 Aug 01

Mark	Wind	Name		Nat	Born	Pos	Meet	Venue	Date
8:08.78		Alessandro	Lambruschini	ITA	7.1.65	3	WCh	Stuttgart	21 Aug 93
		(30)							
8:09.02		Abdelaziz	Sahere	MAR	18.9.67	5	GGala	Roma	8 Jun 95
8:09.03		Elarbi	Khattabi	MAR	16.5.67	3	GGala	Roma	7 Jul 99
8:09.11		Bronislaw	Malinowski	POL	4.6.51	2	OG	Montreal	28 Jul 76
8:09.17		Henry	Marsh	USA	15.3.54	1	R-W	Koblenz	28 Aug 85
8:09.18		Boguslaw	Maminski	POL	18.12.55	2	VD	Bruxelles	24 Aug 84
8:09.23		Bouabdellah	Tahri	FRA	20.12.78	7	VD	Bruxelles	24 Aug 01
8:09.48		Damian	Kallabis	GER	10.6.73	4	WK	Zürich	11 Aug 99
8:09.54		Johnstone	Kipkoech	KEN	20.12.68	2	VD	Bruxelles	25 Aug 95
8:09.76		Mark	Croghan	USA	8.1.68	5	WCh	Stuttgart	21 Aug 93
8:09.77		Luis Miguel	Martín	ESP	11.1.72	5	Herc	Monaco	18 Aug 00
		(40)							
8:10.01		William	van Dijck	BEL	24.1.61	1	VD	Bruxelles	5 Sep 86
8:10.10		Hicham	Bouaouiche	MAR	16.6.74	3	Nik	Nice	16 Jul 98
8:10.23		Laïd	Bessou	ALG	5.2.76	8	Herc	Monaco	18 Aug 00
8:10.32		Hagen	Melzer	GDR	16.6.59	2	WCh	Roma	5 Sep 87
8:10.36		Frank	Baumgartl	GDR	29.5.55	3	OG	Montreal	28 Jul 76
8:10.41		Julius	Chelule	KEN	25.12.78	6	VD	Bruxelles	3 Sep 99
8:10.46			Sun Ripeng	CHN	25.1.74	1	NG	Shanghai	19 Oct 97
8:10.74		William	Mutwol	KEN	10.10.67	3	OG	Barcelona	7 Aug 92
8:10.83		Günther	Weidlinger	AUT	5.4.78	4h1	WCh	Sevilla	21 Aug 99
8:11.04		Krzysztof	Wesolowski	POL	9.12.56	1	VD	Bruxelles	30 Aug 85
		(50)	100th man 8:16.10, 200th man 8:22.49						

110 METRES HURDLES

Mark	Wind	Name		Nat	Born	Pos	Meet	Venue	Date
12.91 WR	0.5	Colin	Jackson	GBR	18.2.67	1	WCh	Stuttgart	20 Aug 93
12.92 WR	-0.1	Roger	Kingdom	USA	26.8.62	1	WK	Zürich	16 Aug 89
12.92	0.9	Allen	Johnson	USA	1.3.71	1	NC	Atlanta	23 Jun 96
12.92	0.2		Johnson			1	VD	Bruxelles	23 Aug 96
12.93 WR	-0.2	Renaldo	Nehemiah	USA	24.3.59	1	WK	Zürich	19 Aug 81
12.93	0.0		Johnson			1	WCh	Athína	7 Aug 97
12.94	1.6	Jack	Pierce	USA	23.9.62	1s2	NC	Atlanta	22 Jun 96
12.95	0.6		Johnson			1	OG	Atlanta	29 Jul 96
12.97A	2.0		Kingdom			1		Sestriere	11 Aug 88
12.97A	-1.6		Jackson			1A		Sestriere	28 Jul 93
12.97	-0.5		Johnson			1		Stuttgart	13 Jul 97
12.97	1.5		Johnson			1	NC	Sacramento	23 Jul 00
12.98	1.5		Kingdom			1	OG	Seoul	26 Sep 88
12.98	0.2		Jackson			1	TOTO	Tokyo	15 Sep 94
12.98	0.2		Johnson			1	ASV	Köln	18 Aug 95
12.98	-0.3		Johnson			1rA	WK	Zürich	12 Aug 98
12.98	0.6	Mark	Crear	USA	2.10.68	1		Zagreb	5 Jul 99
12.99	1.2		Jackson			1	VD	Bruxelles	3 Sep 93
12.99	-0.3		Jackson			1		Madrid	6 Sep 94
13.00 WR	0.9		Nehemiah			1	Pepsi	Westwood	6 May 79
13.00	0.5	Anthony	Jarrett	GBR	13.8.68	2	WCh	Stuttgart	20 Aug 93
13.00	-0.1		Johnson			1	WCh	Göteborg	12 Aug 95
13.00	-0.3		Crear			2rA	WK	Zürich	12 Aug 98
13.00	0.6	Anier	García	CUB	9.3.76	1	OG	Sydney	25 Sep 00
13.01	0.3	Larry	Wade	USA	22.11.74	1rA	Athl	Lausanne	2 Jul 99
13.01	0.8		Johnson			1	GGala	Roma	7 Jul 99
13.02	0.6		Kingdom			1	ISTAF	Berlin	18 Aug 89
13.02	0.9		Jackson			1A	ISTAF	Berlin	30 Aug 94
13.02	1.5		Crear			1		Luzern	27 Jun 95
13.02	1.9		Jackson			1s1	EC	Budapest	22 Aug 98
13.02	1.5		Jackson			1	EC	Budapest	22 Aug 98
		(31/9)							
13.03	-0.2	Greg	Foster (10)	USA	4.8.58	2	WK	Zürich	19 Aug 81
13.03	1.0	Reggie	Torian	USA	22.4.75	1	NC	New Orleans	21 Jun 98
13.05	1.4	Tony	Dees	USA	6.8.63	1		Vigo	23 Jul 91
13.05	-0.8	Florian	Schwarthoff	GER	7.5.68	1	NC	Bremen	2 Jul 95
13.08	1.2	Mark	McKoy	CAN	10.12.61	1	BNP	Villeneuve d'Ascq	2 Jul 93
13.11	1.4	Dominique	Arnold	USA	14.9.73	2		Leverkusen	20 Aug 00
13.12	1.5	Falk	Balzer	GER	14.12.73	2	EC	Budapest	22 Aug 98
13.12	1.0	Duane	Ross	USA	5.12.72	3	WCh	Sevilla	25 Aug 99
13.13	1.6	Igor	Kovác	SVK	12.5.69	1	DNG	Stockholm	7 Jul 97
13.15	0.3	Robin	Korving	NED	29.7.74	5rA	Athl	Lausanne	2 Jul 99
13.16	0.6	Terrence	Trammell	USA	23.11.78	2	OG	Sydney	25 Sep 00
		(20)							

Mark	Wind	Name		Nat	Born	Pos	Meet	Venue	Date
13.17	-0.4	Sam	Turner	USA	17.6.57	2	Pepsi	Westwood	15 May 83
13.17	0.0	Tonie	Campbell	USA	14.6.60	3	WK	Zürich	17 Aug 88
13.17	0.5	Courtney	Hawkins	USA	11.7.67	1		Ingolstadt	26 Jul 98
13.17	0.4	Mike	Fenner	GER	24.4.71	1		Leverkusen	9 Aug 98
13.18	0.5	Emilio	Valle	CUB	21.4.67	3s1	OG	Atlanta	29 Jul 96
13.19	1.9	Steve	Brown	USA/TRI	6.1.69	1h4	NC	Atlanta	21 Jun 96
13.20	2.0	Stéphane	Caristan	FRA	31.5.64	1	EC	Stuttgart	30 Aug 86
13.20	1.8	Aleksandr	Markin ¶	RUS	8.9.62	1	Znam	Leningrad	11 Jun 88
13.20	1.7	Larry	Harrington	USA	24.11.70	2s1	NC	Atlanta	22 Jun 96
13.21	WR 0.6	Alejandro	Casañas	CUB	29.1.54	1	WUG	Sofiya	21 Aug 77
		(30)							
13.21	1.8	Vladimir	Shishkin	RUS	12.1.64	2	Znam	Leningrad	11 Jun 88
13.21	0.9	Eugene	Swift	USA	14.9.64	3	NC	Atlanta	23 Jun 96
13.22	-0.2	Terry	Reese	USA	20.6.67	2	ASV	Köln	24 Aug 97
13.22	1.5	Dawane	Wallace	USA	30.12.76	4	NC	Sacramento	23 Jul 00
13.24	WR 0.3	Rod	Milburn	USA	18.5.50	1	OG	München	7 Sep 72
13.24	2.0	Arthur	Blake	USA	19.8.66	2	Athl	Lausanne	24 Jun 88
13.24	1.1	Yoel	Hernández	CUB	12.12.77	2	PAm	Winnipeg	30 Jul 99
13.25	0.1	Andre	Phillips	USA	5.9.59	1	USOF	Baton Rouge	28 Jul 85
13.25	-0.1		Li Tong	CHN	6.5.67	2rA	Gugl	Linz	4 Jul 94
13.25	1.9	Jonathan	N'senga	BEL	21.4.73	3s1	EC	Budapest	22 Aug 98
		(40)							
13.25	0.2	Stanislav	Olijar	LAT	22.3.79	2	Herc	Monaco	18 Aug 00
13.25	-0.3	Dudley	Dorival	HAI	1.9.75	3	WCh	Edmonton	9 Aug 01
13.26	1.6	Willie	Gault	USA	5.9.60	1	USOF	Indianapolis	25 Jul 82
13.26	0.0	Igor	Kazanov	LAT	24.9.63	2s1	WCh	Stuttgart	19 Aug 93
13.26	1.7	Erik	Batte	CUB	10.12.74	4s2	OG	Atlanta	29 Jul 96
13.26	0.0	Dan	Philibert	FRA	6.8.70	5	WCh	Athína	7 Aug 97
13.26	0.6	Yuniel	Hernández	CUB	28.3.81	1		Salamanca	13 Jul 01
13.26	1.4	Shaun	Bownes	RSA	24.10.70	1	NA	Heusden	14 Jul 01
13.27	1.8	Sergey	Usov	BLR	16.1.64	3	Znam	Leningrad	11 Jun 88
13.27	1.2	Artur	Kohutek	POL	1.5.71	2q2	WCh	Athína	5 Aug 97
13.27	1.6	Chris	Phillips	USA	24.7.72	3		Palo Alto	1 Jul 00
		(51)	100th man 13.42, 200th man 13.54						
Rolling start but accepted by race officials									
13.10A	2.0	Falk	Balzer	GER	14.12.73	1	WCp	Johannesburg	13 Sep 98
Doubtful timing									
13.06	1.3	Mike	Fenner	GER	24.4.71	1		Scheessel	4 Jun 95
13.08	1.3	Eric	Kaiser	GER	7.3.71	2		Scheessel	4 Jun 95
Wind-assisted marks to 13.26									
12.87	2.6	Roger	Kingdom	USA	26.8.62	1	WCp	Barcelona	10 Sep 89
12.91	3.5	Renaldo	Nehemiah	USA	24.3.59	1	NCAA	Champaign	1 Jun 79
12.94A	2.8		Jackson			1rA		Sestriere	31 Jul 94
12.95	2.6		Jackson			2	WCp	Barcelona	10 Sep 89
12.99	2.7		Jackson			1	v3N	Birmingham	23 Jun 89
13.00	3.5		Nehemiah			1	USOF	Syracuse	26 Jul 81
13.00	2.7		Kingdom			1		Sacramento	21 Jul 84
13.00	3.8		Johnson			1s1	NC	Sacramento	17 Jun 95
13.06	2.1	Mark	McKoy	CAN	10.12.61	1	Gugl	Linz	13 Aug 92
13.14	2.9	Igor	Kazanov	LAT	24.9.63	1r1	Znam	Leningrad	8 Jun 86
13.15	2.1	Courtney	Hawkins	USA	11.7.67	1		Salamanca	10 Jul 98
13.18	4.7	Robert	Reading	USA	9.6.67	1		Azusa	23 Apr 94
13.20	2.4	Arthur	Blake	USA	19.8.66	2	IAC	Edinburgh	6 Jul 90
13.20	3.1	Yoel	Hernández	CUB	12.12.77	2		Camagüey	10 Mar 00
13.21A	2.5	Eric	Cannon	USA	2.3.67	2	NCAA	Provo	3 Jun 89
13.24	2.4	Glenn	Terry	USA	10.2.71	1s2	WUG	Buffalo	18 Jul 93
13.25	2.7	Tomasz	Scigaczewski	POL	18.11.78	1		Grudziadz	20 Jun 98
13.26A	2.6	Antti	Haapakoski	FIN	6.2.71	1rB		Sestriere	31 Jul 94
13.26	7.8		Chen Yanhao	CHN	7.2.72	1		Maebashi	27 Apr 96
Hand timing									
12.8	1.0	Renaldo	Nehemiah	USA	24.3.59	1		Kingston	11 May 79
13.0	WR 1.8	Guy	Drut	FRA	6.12.50	1	ISTAF	Berlin	22 Aug 75
13.0	1.0	Greg	Foster	USA	4.8.58	2		Kingston	11 May 79
13.0	0.8	Mark	McKoy	CAN	10.12.61	1	Nik	Nice	16 Jul 85
13.0		Stéphane	Caristan	FRA	25.1.64	1		Creteil	3 May 86
13.0		Vladimir	Shishkin	RUS	12.1.64	1		Stayki	7 May 88
13.0*	WR 2.0	Rod	Milburn	USA	18.5.50	1s1	AAU	Eugene	25 Jun 71
13.0	0.4	Tomasz	Scigaczewski	POL	18.11.78	1	NC	Wroclaw	28 Jun 98

Mark	Wind	Name		Nat	Born	Pos	Meet	Venue	Date
Wind-assisted									
12.8	2.4	Colin	Jackson	GBR	18.2.67	1		Sydney	10 Jan 90
12.9	4.1	Mark	Crear	USA	2.10.68	1rA	S&W	Modesto	8 May 93
13.0		Alejandro	Casañas	CUB	29.1.54	1	Barr	La Habana	22 May 77
13.0		Tonie	Campbell	USA	14.6.60	1		Los Angeles	16 Jul 86
13.0		Keith	Talley	USA	28.1.64	1		Tuscaloosa	26 Mar 88
13.0	4.1		Li Tong	CHN	6.5.67	2rA	S&W	Modesto	8 May 93

200 METRES HURDLES

Mark	Wind	Name		Nat	Born	Pos	Meet	Venue	Date
22.55		Laurent	Ottoz	ITA	10.4.70	1		Milano	31 May 95
22.59	0.2	Darryl	Wohlsen	AUS	6.3.73	1		Brisbane	14 Mar 96
22.63	-0.3	Colin	Jackson	GBR	18.2.67	1		Cardiff	1 Jun 91
22.68		Stefano	Cellario	ITA	16.3.72	1		Modena	17 Sep 97
22.69 WR	0.0	Glenn	Davis	USA	12.9.34	1		Bern	20 Aug 60

400 METRES HURDLES

Mark	Name		Nat	Born	Pos	Meet	Venue	Date
46.78 WR	Kevin	Young	USA	16.9.66	1	OG	Barcelona	6 Aug 92
47.02 WR	Edwin	Moses	USA	31.8.55	1		Koblenz	31 Aug 83
47.03	Bryan	Bronson	USA	9.9.72	1	NC	New Orleans	21 Jun 98
47.10	Samuel	Matete	ZAM	27.7.68	1rA	WK	Zürich	7 Aug 91
47.13 WR		Moses			1		Milano	3 Jul 80
47.14		Moses			1	Athl	Lausanne	14 Jul 81
47.17		Moses			1	ISTAF	Berlin	8 Aug 80
47.18		Young			1	WCh	Stuttgart	19 Aug 93
47.19	Andre	Phillips	USA	5.9.59	1	OG	Seoul	25 Sep 88
47.23	Amadou	Dia Bâ	SEN	22.9.58	2	OG	Seoul	25 Sep 88
47.27		Moses			1	ISTAF	Berlin	21 Aug 81
47.32		Moses			1		Koblenz	29 Aug 84
47.37		Moses			1	WCp	Roma	4 Sep 81
47.37		Moses			1	WK	Zürich	24 Aug 83
47.37		Moses			1	OT	Indianapolis	17 Jul 88
47.37		Young			1	Athl	Lausanne	7 Jul 93
47.37	Stéphane	Diagana	FRA	23.7.69	1	Athl	Lausanne	5 Jul 95
47.38		Moses			1	Athl	Lausanne	2 Sep 86
47.38	Danny	Harris	USA	7.9.65	1	Athl	Lausanne	10 Jul 91
47.38	Felix	Sánchez	DOM	30.8.77	1rA	WK	Zürich	17 Aug 01
47.40		Young			1	WK	Zürich	19 Aug 92
47.42		Young			1	ASV	Köln	16 Aug 92
47.43		Moses			1	ASV	Köln	28 Aug 83
47.45 WR		Moses			1	AAU	Westwood	11 Jun 77
47.46		Moses			1	WCh	Roma	1 Sep 87
47.48	Harald	Schmid	FRG	29.9.57	1	EC	Athína	8 Sep 82
47.48		Harris			2	WCh	Roma	1 Sep 87
47.48		Schmid			3	WCh	Roma	1 Sep 87
47.49		Harris			1	Athl	Lausanne	12 Jul 90
47.49		Sánchez			1	WCh	Edmonton	10 Aug 01
	(30/10)							
47.50	Angelo	Taylor	USA	29.12.78	1	OG	Sydney	27 Sep 00
47.53	Hadi Soua'an	Al-Somaily	KSA	30.12.76	2	OG	Sydney	27 Sep 00
47.54	Derrick	Adkins	USA	2.7.70	2	Athl	Lausanne	5 Jul 95
47.54	Fabrizio	Mori	ITA	28.6.69	2	WCh	Edmonton	10 Aug 01
47.60	Winthrop	Graham	JAM	17.11.65	1	WK	Zürich	4 Aug 93
47.75	David	Patrick	USA	12.6.60	4	OT	Indianapolis	17 Jul 88
47.81	Llewellyn	Herbert	RSA	21.7.77	3	OG	Sydney	27 Sep 00
47.82 WR	John	Akii-Bua	UGA	3.12.49	1	OG	München	2 Sep 72
47.82	Kriss	Akabusi	GBR	28.11.58	3	OG	Barcelona	6 Aug 92
47.89	Dai	Tamesue	JPN	3.5.78	3	WCh	Edmonton	10 Aug 01
	(20)							
47.91	Calvin	Davis	USA	2.4.72	1s2	OG	Atlanta	31 Jul 96
47.92	Aleksandr	Vasilyev	BLR	26.7.61	2	ECp	Moskva	17 Aug 85
47.94	Eric	Thomas	USA	1.12.73	1	GGala	Roma	30 Jun 00
47.97	Maurice	Mitchell	USA	14.5.71	2rA	WK	Zürich	14 Aug 96
47.97	Joey	Woody	USA	22.5.73	3	NC	New Orleans	21 Jun 98
47.98	Sven	Nylander	SWE	1.1.62	4	OG	Atlanta	1 Aug 96
48.04	Eronilde	de Araújo	BRA	31.12.70	2	Nik	Nice	12 Jul 95
48.04	James	Carter	USA	7.5.78	4	OG	Sydney	27 Sep 00
48.05	Ken	Harnden	ZIM	31.3.73	1	GP	Paris	29 Jul 98
48.06	Oleg	Tverdokhleb	UKR	3.11.69	1	EC	Helsinki	10 Aug 94
	(30)							

Mark	Wind	Name		Nat	Born	Pos	Meet	Venue	Date
48.06		Ruslan	Mashchenko	RUS	11.11.71	1	GP II	Helsinki	13 Jun 98
48.09		Alwyn	Myburgh	RSA	13.10.80	1	WUG	Beijing	31 Aug 01
48.12A	WR	David	Hemery	GBR	18.7.44	1	OG	Ciudad de México	15 Oct 68
48.13		Dinsdale	Morgan	JAM	19.11.72	2	GGala	Roma	14 Jul 98
48.13		Marcel	Schelbert	SUI	26.2.76	3	WCh	Sevilla	27 Aug 99
48.14		Chris	Rawlinson	GBR	19.5.72	1rB	WK	Zürich	11 Aug 99
48.16		Tony	Rambo	USA	30.5.60	3s1	OT	Los Angeles	17 Jun 84
48.16		Marek	Plawgo	POL	25.2.81	1	GP	Osaka	12 May 01
48.17		Pawel	Januszewski	POL	2.1.72	1	EC	Budapest	20 Aug 98
48.17A		Mubarak	Al-Nubi	QAT	30.12.77	2	WCp	Johannesburg	11 Sep 98
		(40)							
48.18		Torrance	Zellner	USA	6.1.70	4rA	WK	Zürich	14 Aug 96
48.24		Erick	Keter	KEN	22.7.66	2s2	WCh	Stuttgart	17 Aug 93
48.26		Kazuhiko	Yamazaki	JPN	10.5.71	3	GP	Osaka	8 May 99
48.27		Jirí	Muzík	CZE	1.9.76	3s3	WCh	Athína	3 Aug 97
48.28		Tranel	Hawkins	USA	17.9.62	3	OT	Los Angeles	18 Jun 84
48.28		Everson	Teixeira	BRA	23.11.74	2s2	OG	Atlanta	31 Jul 96
48.28		Rohan	Robinson	AUS	15.11.71	4s2	OG	Atlanta	31 Jul 96
48.30		Neil	Gardner	JAM	8.12.74	5s2	OG	Atlanta	31 Jul 96
48.30A		Ibou	Faye	SEN	13.12.69	1	AfG	Johannesburg	17 Sep 99
48.34		Vasiliy	Arkhipenko	UKR	28.1.57	2	ECp	Torino	4 Aug 79
48.34		McClinton	Neal	USA	11.7.68	4rA	Athl	Lausanne	8 Jul 92
48.34		Shunji	Karube	JPN	8.5.69	1	NC	Tokyo	5 Oct 97
		(52)	100th man 48.78, 200th man 49.30						
48.1	**Hand**	Jim	Bolding	USA	24.3.49	1		Milano	2 Jul 74
Drugs Disqualification		47.15	Bronson			1	GWG	Uniondale, NY	19 Jul 98

HIGH JUMP

Mark	Wind	Name		Nat	Born	Pos	Meet	Venue	Date
2.45	WR	Javier	Sotomayor	CUB	13.10.67	1		Salamanca	27 Jul 93
2.44	WR		Sotomayor			1	CAC	San Juan	29 Jul 89
2.43	WR		Sotomayor			1		Salamanca	8 Sep 88
2.43i			Sotomayor			1	WI	Budapest	4 Mar 89
2.42	WR	Patrik	Sjöberg	SWE	5.1.65	1	DNG	Stockholm	30 Jun 87
2.42i	WR	Carlo	Thränhardt	FRG	5.7.57	1		Berlin	26 Feb 88
2.42			Sotomayor			1		Sevilla	5 Jun 94
2.41	WR	Igor	Paklin	KGZ	15.6.63	1	WUG	Kobe	4 Sep 85
2.41i			Sjöberg			1		Pireás	1 Feb 87
2.41i			Sotomayor			1	WI	Toronto	14 Mar 93
2.41			Sotomayor			1	NC	La Habana	25 Jun 94
2.41			Sotomayor			1	TSB	London (CP)	15 Jul 94
2.40	WR	Rudolf	Povarnitsyn	UKR	13.6.62	1		Donetsk	11 Aug 85
2.40i			Thränhardt			1		Simmerath	16 Jan 87
2.40i			Sjöberg			1		Berlin	27 Feb 87
2.40			Sotomayor			1	NC	La Habana	12 Mar 89
2.40			Sjöberg			1	ECp-B	Bruxelles	5 Aug 89
2.40			Sotomayor			1	AmCp	Bogota	13 Aug 89
2.40		Sorin	Matei	ROM	6.7.63	1	PTS	Bratislava	20 Jun 90
2.40i		Hollis	Conway	USA	8.1.67	1	WI	Sevilla	10 Mar 91
2.40			Sotomayor			1		Saint Denis	19 Jul 91
2.40		Charles	Austin	USA	19.12.67	1	WK	Zürich	7 Aug 91
2.40			Sotomayor			1	Barr	La Habana	22 May 93
2.40			Sotomayor			1	TSB	London (CP)	23 Jul 93
2.40			Sotomayor			1	WCh	Stuttgart	22 Aug 93
2.40i			Sotomayor			1		Wuppertal	4 Feb 94
2.40i			Sotomayor			1	TSB	Birmingham	26 Feb 94
2.40			Sotomayor			1		Eberstadt	10 Jul 94
2.40			Sotomayor			1	Nik	Nice	18 Jul 94
2.40			Sotomayor			1	GWG	Sankt-Peterburg	29 Jul 94
2.40			Sotomayor			1	WCp	London (CP)	11 Sep 94
2.40			Sotomayor			1	PAm	Mar del Plata	25 Mar 95
2.40		Vyacheslav	Voronin	RUS	5.4.74	1	BrGP	London (CP)	5 Aug 00
		(33/9)							
2.39	WR		Zhu Jianhua	CHN	29.5.63	1		Eberstadt	10 Jun 84
2.39i		Dietmar	Mögenburg	FRG	15.8.61	1		Köln	24 Feb 85
2.39i		Ralf	Sonn	GER	17.1.67	1		Berlin	1 Mar 91
2.38i		Gennadiy	Avdeyenko	UKR	4.11.63	2	WI	Indianapolis	7 Mar 87
2.38		Sergey	Malchenko	RUS	2.11.63	1		Banská Bystrica	4 Sep 88
2.38		Dragutin	Topic	YUG	12.3.71	1		Beograd	1 Aug 93

Mark	Wind	Name		Nat	Born	Pos	Meet	Venue	Date
2.38i		Steve	Smith	GBR	29.3.73	2		Wuppertal	4 Feb 94
2.38i		Wolf-Hendrik	Beyer	GER	14.2.72	1		Weinheim	18 Mar 94
2.38		Troy	Kemp	BAH	18.6.66	1	Nik	Nice	12 Jul 95
2.38		Artur	Partyka	POL	25.7.69	1		Eberstadt	18 Aug 96
2.38i		Matt	Hemingway	USA	24.10.72	1	NC	Atlanta	4 Mar 00
		(20)							
2.37		Valeriy	Sereda	RUS	30.6.59	1		Rieti	2 Sep 84
2.37		Tom	McCants	USA	27.11.62	1	Owens	Columbus	8 May 88
2.37		Jerome	Carter	USA	25.3.63	2	Owens	Columbus	8 May 88
2.37		Sergey	Dymchenko	UKR	23.8.67	1		Kiyev	16 Sep 90
2.37i		Dalton	Grant	GBR	8.4.66	1	EI	Paris	13 Mar 94
2.36	WR	Gerd	Wessig	GDR	16.7.59	1	OG	Moskva	1 Aug 80
2.36		Sergey	Zasimovich	KZK	6.9.62	1		Tashkent	5 May 84
2.36		Eddy	Annys	BEL	15.12.58	1		Ghent	26 May 85
2.36i		Jim	Howard	USA	11.9.59	1		Albuquerque	25 Jan 86
2.36i		Jan	Zvara	CZE	12.2.63	1	vGDR	Jablonec	14 Feb 87
		(30)							
2.36i		Gerd	Nagel	FRG	22.10.57	1		Sulingen	17 Mar 89
2.36		Nick	Saunders	BER	14.9.63	1	CG	Auckland	1 Feb 90
2.36		Doug	Nordquist	USA	20.12.58	2	TAC	Norwalk	15 Jun 90
2.36		Georgi	Dakov	BUL	21.10.67	2	VD	Bruxelles	10 Aug 90
2.36		Lábros	Papakóstas	GRE	20.10.69	1	NC	Athína	21 Jun 92
2.36i		Steinar	Hoen	NOR	8.2.71	1		Balingen	12 Feb 94
2.36		Tim	Forsyth	AUS	17.8.73	1	NC	Melbourne	2 Mar 97
2.36		Sergey	Klyugin	RUS	24.3.74	1	WK	Zürich	12 Aug 98
2.36		Konstantin	Matusevich	ISR	25.2.71	1		Perth	5 Feb 00
2.36		Martin	Buss	GER	7.4.76	1	WCh	Edmonton	8 Aug 01
		(40)							
2.35i		Vladimir	Yashchenko	UKR	12.1.59	1	EI	Milano	12 Mar 78
2.35	WR	Jacek	Wszola	POL	30.12.56	1		Eberstadt	25 May 80
2.35i		Aleksandr	Kotovich	UKR	6.11.61	1		Vilnius	13 Jan 85
2.35i		Brent	Harken	USA	1.12.61	1		Moscow	15 Feb 91
2.35		Darrin	Plab	USA	26.9.70	2	NC	New Orleans	28 Jun 92
2.35i		Jean-Charles	Gicquel	FRA	24.2.67	2	EI	Paris	13 Feb 94
2.35		Mark	Boswell	CAN	28.7.77	2	WCh	Sevilla	23 Aug 99
2.35		Nathan	Leeper	USA	13.6.77	1		Sacramento	21 May 00
2.35i		Andrey	Sokolovskiy	UKR	16.7.78	1		Arnstadt	17 Feb 01
2.35A		Charles	Clinger	USA	28.12.76	1		Pocatello	19 May 01
			(50)	18 men at 2.34, 100th man 2.32, 200th man 2.30					

Best outdoor marks for athletes with indoor bests

Mark	Name	Pos	Meet	Venue	Date	Mark	Name	Pos	Meet	Venue	Date
2.39	Conway	1	USOF	Norman	30 Jul 89	2.36	Howard	1		Rehlingen	8 Jun 87
2.38	Avdeyenko	2=	WCh	Roma	6 Sep 87	2.36	Zvara	1		Praha	23 Aug 87
2.37	Thranhärdt	2		Rieti	2 Sep 84	2.36	Grant	4	WCh	Tokyo	1 Sep 91
2.37	Smith	1	WJ	Seoul	20 Sep 92	2.36	Hoen	1		Oslo	1 Jul 97
2.36	Mögenburg	3		Eberstadt	10 Jun 84	2.35	Nagel	1		Forbach	7 Aug 88

Ancillary jumps – en route to final marks

Mark	Name	Date	Mark	Name	Date	Mark	Name	Date
2.40	Sotomayor	8 Sep 88	2.40	Sotomayor	29 Jul 89	2.40	Sotomayor	5 Jun 94

POLE VAULT

Mark	Wind	Name		Nat	Born	Pos	Meet	Venue	Date
6.15i		Sergey	Bubka	UKR	4.12.63	1		Donetsk	21 Feb 93
6.14i			Bubka			1		Liévin	13 Feb 93
6.14A	WR		Bubka			1		Sestriere	31 Jul 94
6.13i			Bubka			1		Berlin	21 Feb 92
6.13	WR		Bubka			1	TOTO	Tokyo	19 Sep 92
6.12i			Bubka			1	Mast	Grenoble	23 Mar 91
6.12	WR		Bubka			1		Padova	30 Aug 92
6.11i			Bubka			1		Donetsk	19 Mar 91
6.11	WR		Bubka			1		Dijon	13 Jun 92
6.10i			Bubka			1		San Sebastián	15 Mar 91
6.10	WR		Bubka			1	MAI	Malmö	5 Aug 91
6.09	WR		Bubka			1		Formia	8 Jul 91
6.08i			Bubka			1	NC	Volgograd	9 Feb 91
6.08	WR		Bubka			1	Znam	Moskva	9 Jun 91
6.07	WR		Bubka			1	Super	Shizuoka	6 May 91
6.06	WR		Bubka			1	Nik	Nice	10 Jul 88
6.05	WR		Bubka			1	PTS	Bratislava	9 Jun 88
6.05i			Bubka			1		Donetsk	17 Mar 90
6.05i			Bubka			1		Berlin	5 Mar 93
6.05			Bubka			1	GPF	London (CP)	10 Sep 93

MEN All-time

Mark	Wind	Name		Nat	Born	Pos	Meet	Venue	Date
6.05i			Bubka			1	Mast	Grenoble	6 Feb 94
6.05			Bubka			1	ISTAF	Berlin	30 Aug 94
6.05			Bubka			1	GPF	Fukuoka	13 Sep 97
6.05		Maksim	Tarasov	RUS	2.12.70	1	GP II	Athína	16 Jun 99
6.05		Dmitriy	Markov (ex BLR)	AUS	14.3.75	1	WCh	Edmonton	9 Aug 01
6.03	WR		Bubka			1	Ros	Praha	23 Jun 87
6.03i			Bubka			1		Osaka	11 Feb 89
6.03		Okkert	Brits	RSA	22.8.73	1	ASV	Köln	18 Aug 95
6.03		Jeff	Hartwig	USA	25.9.67	1		Jonesboro	14 Jun 00
6.02i		Rodion	Gataullin	RUS	23.11.65	1	NC	Gomel	4 Feb 89
6.02			Bubka			1	GP	Atlanta	18 May 96
6.02			Hartwig			1	NC	Eugene	27 Jun 99
6.02			Tarasov			1	WCh	Sevilla	26 Aug 99
		(33/6)							
6.01		Igor	Trandenkov	RUS	17.8.66	1	NC	Sankt Peterburg	4 Jul 96
6.00		Tim	Lobinger	GER	3.9.72	1	ASV	Köln	24 Aug 97
6.00i		Jean	Galfione	FRA	9.6.71	1	WI	Maebashi	6 Mar 99
6.00i		Danny	Ecker	GER	21.7.77	1		Dortmund	11 Feb 01
		(10)							
5.98		Lawrence	Johnson	USA	7.5.74	1		Knoxville	25 May 96
5.97		Scott	Huffman	USA	30.11.64	1	NC	Knoxville	18 Jun 94
5.96		Joe	Dial	USA	26.10.62	1		Norman	18 Jun 87
5.95		Andrei	Tivontchik	GER	13.7.70	1	ASV	Köln	16 Aug 96
5.95		Michael	Stolle	GER	17.12.74	1	Herc	Monaco	18 Aug 00
5.94i		Philippe	Collet	FRA	13.12.63	1	Mast	Grenoble	10 Mar 90
5.93i		Billy	Olson	USA	19.7.58	1		East Rutherford	8 Feb 86
5.93		Romain	Mesnil	FRA	13.7.77	1	EU23	Göteborg	1 Aug 99
5.93i		Tye	Harvey	USA	25.9.74	2	NC	Atlanta	3 Mar 01
5.92		István	Bagyula	HUN	2.1.69	1	Gugl	Linz	5 Jul 91
		(20)							
5.92		Igor	Potapovich	KZK	6.9.67	2		Dijon	13 Jun 92
5.92		Dean	Starkey	USA	27.3.67	1	Banes	São Paulo	21 May 94
5.91	WR	Thierry	Vigneron	FRA	9.3.60	2	GGala	Roma	31 Aug 84
5.91i		Viktor	Ryzhenkov	UZB	25.8.66	2		San Sebastián	15 Mar 91
5.91A		Riaan	Botha	RSA	8.11.70	1		Pretoria	2 Apr 97
5.91		Alex	Averbukh	ISR	1.10.74	1	GP II	Gateshead	19 Aug 01
5.90		Pierre	Quinon	FRA	20.2.62	2	Nik	Nice	16 Jul 85
5.90i		Ferenc	Salbert	FRA	5.8.60	1	Mast	Grenoble	14 Mar 87
5.90		Miroslaw	Chmara	POL	9.5.64	1	BNP	Villeneuve d'Ascq	27 Jun 88
5.90i		Grigoriy	Yegorov	KZK	12.1.67	1		Yokohama	11 Mar 90
		(30)							
5.90		Denis	Petushinskiy	RUS	29.1.67	1	Znam	Moskva	13 Jun 93
5.90i		Pyotr	Bochkaryov	RUS	3.11.67	1	EI	Paris	12 Mar 94
5.90		Jacob	Davis	USA	29.4.78	1	Tex R	Austin	4 Apr 98
5.90		Viktor	Chistiakov	RUS/AUS	9.2.75	1		Salamanca	15 Jul 99
5.90		Pavel	Gerasimov	RUS	29.5.79	1		Rüdlingen	12 Aug 00
5.90		Nick	Hysong	USA	9.12.71	1	OG	Sydney	29 Sep 00
5.89		Kory	Tarpenning	USA	27.2.62	1	OT	Indianopolis	21 Jul 88
5.87		Earl	Bell	USA	25.8.55	1		Jonesboro	14 May 88
5.86		Vasiliy	Bubka	UKR	26.11.60	1		Chelyabinsk	16 Jul 88
5.86		Bill	Payne	USA	21.12.67	1	SWC	Houston	19 May 91
		(40)							
5.86		Valeri	Bukrejev	EST	15.6.64	1		Somero	3 Jul 94
5.86A		Pavel	Burlachenko	RUS	7.4.76	1		Pretoria	23 Mar 01
5.85		Konstantin	Volkov	RUS	28.2.60	1	Izv	Kiyev	22 Jun 84
5.85		Pat	Manson	USA	29.11.67	2	TOTO	Tokyo	15 Sep 94
5.85		Alain	Andji	FRA	20.11.74	1		Bonneuil-sur-Marne	18 May 97
5.85		Yevgeniy	Smiryagin	RUS	17.5.76	1	Nurmi	Turku	12 Jun 97
5.85		Vadim	Strogalyov	RUS	9.2.75	2		Hania	27 May 98
5.85		Richard	Spiegelburg	GER	12.8.77	1	NC	Stuttgart	30 Jun 01
5.84		Mike	Tully	USA	21.10.56	1		Irvine	1 May 88
5.83i		Jani	Lehtonen	FIN	11.8.68	1	DNG	Stockholm	8 Mar 94
		(50)	100th man 5.75, 200th man 5.65						
5.83		Patrik	Kristiansson	SWE	3.6.77	1	ECp-1A	Vaasa	24 Jun 01

Best outdoor marks for athletes with lifetime bests indoors

6.00	Gataullin	1	Tokyo	16 Sep 89	5.90	Yegorov	2	WChStuttgart	19 Aug 93
5.98	Galfione	1	Amiens	23 Jul 99	5.86	Bochkaryov	5	OGAtlanta	2 Aug 96
5.93	Ecker	1	Ingolstadt	26 Jul 98	5.85	Collet	2	Paris	22 Jul 86

Ancillary jump: 6.05i Bubka 13 Feb 93

Mark	Wind	Name		Nat	Born	Pos	Meet	Venue	Date
Outdoors on built-up runway									
5.90		Pyotr	Bochkaryov	RUS	3.11.67	1		Karlskrona	28 Jun 96
5.86		Denis	Petushinskiy	RUS	28.6.67	1		Karlskrona	23 Jul 94
Exhibition or Market Square competitions									
6.00		Jean	Galfione	FRA	9.6.71	1		Besançon	23 May 97
5.95		Viktor	Chistyakov	AUS	9.2.75	1		Chiari	8 Sep 99
5.86		Gennadiy	Sukharev	BLR	3.2.65	1		Bisceglie	23 Jul 91
5.86i		Larry	Jessee	USA	31.3.52	1		Newcastle	16 Oct 85

LONG JUMP

Mark	Wind	Name		Nat	Born	Pos	Meet	Venue	Date
8.95 WR	0.3	Mike	Powell	USA	10.11.63	1	WCh	Tokyo	30 Aug 91
8.90A WR	2.0	Bob	Beamon	USA	29.8.46	1	OG	Ciudad de México	18 Oct 68
8.87	-0.2	Carl	Lewis	USA	1.7.61	*	WCh	Tokyo	30 Aug 91
8.86A	1.9	Robert	Emmiyan	ARM	16.2.65	1		Tsakhkadzor	22 May 87
8.79	1.9		Lewis			1	TAC	Indianapolis	19 Jun 83
8.79i	-		Lewis			1		New York	27 Jan 84
8.76	1.0		Lewis			1	USOF	Indianapolis	24 Jul 82
8.76	0.8		Lewis			1	OT	Indianapolis	18 Jul 88
8.75	1.7		Lewis			1	PAm	Indianapolis	16 Aug 87
8.74	1.4	Larry	Myricks	USA	10.3.56	2	OT	Indianapolis	18 Jul 88
8.74A	2.0	Erick	Walder	USA	5.11.71	1		El Paso	2 Apr 94
8.72	-0.2		Lewis			1	OG	Seoul	26 Sep 88
8.71	-0.4		Lewis			1	Pepsi	Westwood	13 May 84
8.71	0.1		Lewis			1	OT	Los Angeles	19 Jun 84
8.71	1.9	Iván	Pedroso	CUB	17.12.72	1		Salamanca	18 Jul 95
8.70	0.8		Myricks			1	TAC	Houston	17 Jun 89
8.70	0.7		Powell			1		Salamanca	27 Jul 93
8.70	1.6		Pedroso			1	WCh	Göteborg	12 Aug 95
8.68	1.0		Lewis			Q	OG	Barcelona	5 Aug 92
8.68	1.6		Pedroso			1		Lisboa	17 Jun 96
8.67	0.4		Lewis			1	WCh	Roma	5 Sep 87
8.67	-0.7		Lewis			1	OG	Barcelona	6 Aug 92
8.66	0.8		Lewis			*	MSR	Walnut	26 Apr 87
8.66	1.0		Myricks			1		Tokyo	23 Sep 87
8.66	0.9		Powell			1	BNP	Villeneuve d'Ascq	29 Jun 90
8.66A	1.4		Lewis			*		Sestriere	31 Jul 94
8.66	0.3		Pedroso			1		Linz	22 Aug 95
8.65	0.2		Lewis			1	VD	Bruxelles	24 Aug 84
8.65	0.7		Lewis			1	TAC	San José	26 Jun 87
8.65	1.5		Pedroso			1	OD	Jena	3 Jun 00
		(30/7)							

Most 'legal' competitions over 8.50m: 39 Lewis, 30 Pedroso, 17 Myricks, 16 Powell, 4 Beckford

Mark	Wind	Name		Nat	Born	Pos	Meet	Venue	Date
8.63	0.5	Kareem	Streete-Thompson	CAY/USA	30.3.73	1	GP II	Linz	4 Jul 94
8.62	0.7	James	Beckford	JAM	9.1.75	1		Orlando	5 Apr 97
8.56i	-	Yago	Lamela	ESP	24.7.77	2	WI	Maebashi	7 Mar 99
		(10)							
8.54	0.9	Lutz	Dombrowski	GDR	25.6.59	1	OG	Moskva	28 Jul 80
8.53	1.2	Jaime	Jefferson	CUB	17.1.62	1	Barr	La Habana	12 May 90
8.51	1.7	Roland	McGhee	USA	15.10.71	2		São Paulo	14 May 95
8.50	0.2	Llewellyn	Starks	USA	10.2.67	2		Rhede	7 Jul 91
8.49	2.0	Melvin	Lister	USA	29.8.77	1	SEC	Baton Rouge	13 May 00
8.49	0.6	Jai	Taurima	AUS	26.6.72	2	OG	Sydney	28 Sep 00
8.48	0.8	Joe	Greene	USA	17.2.67	3		São Paulo	14 May 95
8.47	1.9	Kevin	Dilworth	USA	14.2.74	1		Abilene	9 May 96
8.46	1.2	Leonid	Voloshin	RUS	30.3.66	1	NC	Tallinn	5 Jul 88
8.46	1.6	Mike	Conley	USA	5.10.62	2		Springfield	4 May 96
		(20)							
8.46	1.8	Cheikh Tidiane	Touré	SEN	25.1.70	1		Bad Langensalza	15 Jun 97
8.45	2.0	Nenad	Stekic	YUG	7.3.51	1	PO	Montreal	25 Jul 75
8.44	1.7	Eric	Metcalf	USA	23.1.68	1	TAC	Tampa	17 Jun 88
8.43	0.8	Jason	Grimes	USA	10.9.59	-	TAC	Indianapolis	16 Jun 85
8.43	1.8	Giovanni	Evangelisti	ITA	11.9.61	1		San Giovanni Valdarno	16 May 87
8.43i	-	Stanislav	Tarasenko	RUS	23.7.66	1		Moskva	26 Jan 94
8.43	0.1	Luis	Meliz	CUB	11.8.79	2	OD	Jena	3 Jun 00
8.41	1.5	Craig	Hepburn	BAH	10.12.69	1	NC	Nassau	17 Jun 93
8.41i	-	Kirill	Sosunov	RUS	1.11.75	2	WI	Paris (B)	8 Mar 97
8.40	1.4	Douglas de	Souza	BRA	6.8.72	1		São Paulo	15 Feb 95
		(30)							

Mark	Wind	Name		Nat	Born	Pos	Meet	Venue	Date
8.40	0.4	Robert	Howard	USA	26.11.75	1	SEC	Auburn	17 May 97
8.40	2.0	Gregor	Cankar	SLO	25.1.75	1		Celje	18 May 97
8.40	0.0		Lao Jianfeng	CHN	24.5.75	1	NC	Zhaoqing	28 May 97
8.39	0.8	Dion	Bentley	USA	26.8.71	2	NCAA	New Orleans	3 Jun 93
8.38	0.4	Konstantin	Semykin	RUS	26.5.60	1	Drz	Moskva	17 Aug 84
8.38	1.1		Huang Geng	CHN	10.7.70	1	NC	Taiyuan	18 May 95
8.38i	–	Vitaliy	Shkurlatov	RUS	25.5.79	1		Samara	30 Jan 00
8.38	0.6	Savanté	Stringfellow	USA	6.11.78	1		Lake Buena Vista	22 Jul 01
8.37A	0.4	Leroy	Burrell	USA	21.2.67	2	NCAA	Provo	2 Jun 89
8.37	1.5	Bogdan	Tudor	ROM	1.2.70	2		Bad Cannstatt	9 Jul 95
		(40)							
8.36	1.0	João Carlos	de Oliveira	BRA	28.5.54	1		Rieti	21 Jul 79
8.36	1.6	Frank	Paschek	GDR	25.6.56	1	OD	Berlin	28 May 80
8.36	1.5		Chen Zunrong	CHN	20.10.62	*		Shizuoka	5 May 92
8.36	1.6	Konstadinos	Koukodímos	GRE	14.9.69	1		Hania	5 Jun 94
8.36A	0.8	Nelson	Ferreira Jr	BRA	1.1.73	*	IbAm	Medellín	10 May 96
8.36	1.2	Carlos	Calado	POR	5.10.75	1		Lisboa	20 Jun 97
8.35 WR	0.0	Ralph	Boston	USA	9.5.39	1	CalR	Modesto	29 May 65
8.35AWR	0.0	Igor	Ter-Ovanesyan	RUS	19.5.38	1	PreO	Ciudad de México	19 Oct 67
8.35	0.8	Josef	Schwarz	FRG	20.5.41	1	vUSA	Stuttgart	15 Jul 70
8.35	-0.6	Arnie	Robinson	USA	7.4.48	1	OG	Montreal	29 Jul 76
8.35	2.0	Henry	Lauterbach	GDR	22.10.57	1		Erfurt	2 Aug 81
8.35	2.0	Sergey	Layevskiy	UKR	3.3.59	1		Dnepropetrovsk	16 Jul 88
8.35	1.4	Dmitriy	Bagryanov	RUS	18.12.67	1		Granada	30 May 92
8.35	0.7	Roman	Shchurenko	UKR	14.9.76	1		Kiev	25 Jul 00
		(54)	100th man 8.27, 200th man 8.17						

Sand layer insufficient: 8.37i Sean Robbins USA 9.10.72 1 Bowling Green 10 Feb 96

Irregular conditions: 8.39 1.2 Joan Lino Martínez CUB 17.1.78 1 La Habana 5 Feb 99

Wind-assisted marks performances to 8.70, performers to 8.39

Mark	Wind	Name		Nat	Born	Pos	Meet	Venue	Date
8.99A	4.4	Mike	Powell	USA	10.11.63	1		Sestriere	21 Jul 92
8.96A	1.2+	Iván	Pedroso	CUB	17.12.72	1		Sestriere	29 Jul 95
8.95A	3.9		Powell			1		Sestriere	31 Jul 94
8.91	2.9	Carl	Lewis	USA	1.7.61	2	WCh	Tokyo	30 Aug 91
8.90	3.7		Powell			1	S&W	Modesto	16 May 92
8.79	3.0		Pedroso			1	Barr	La Habana	21 May 92
8.77	3.9		Lewis			1	Pepsi	Westwood	18 May 85
8.77	3.4		Lewis			1	MSR	Walnut	26 Apr 87
8.73	4.6		Lewis			Q	TAC	Sacramento	19 Jun 81
8.73	3.2		Lewis			Q	TAC	Indianapolis	17 Jun 83
8.73A	2.6		Powell			1		Sestriere	31 Jul 91
8.73	4.8		Pedroso			1		Madrid	20 Jun 95
8.72	2.2		Lewis			1	NYG	New York	24 May 92
8.72A	3.9		Lewis			2		Sestriere	31 Jul 94
8.70	2.5		Pedroso			1		Padova	16 Jul 95
8.68	4.9	James	Beckford	JAM	9.1.75	1	JUCO	Odessa, Tx	19 May 95
8.66A	4.0	Joe	Greene	USA	17.2.67	2		Sestriere	21 Jul 92
8.64	3.5	Kareem	Streete-Thompson	CAY/USA	30.3.73	2	NC	Knoxville	18 Jun 94
8.63	3.9	Mike	Conley	USA	5.10.62	2	TAC	Eugene	20 Jun 86
8.57	5.2	Jason	Grimes	USA	10.9.59	1	vFRG,AFR	Durham	27 Jun 82
8.49	2.6	Ralph	Boston	USA	9.5.39	1	FOT	Los Angeles	12 Sep 64
8.49	4.5	Stanislav	Tarasenko	RUS	23.7.66	2		Madrid	20 Jun 95
8.48	2.8	Kirill	Sosunov	RUS	1.11.75	1		Oristano	18 Sep 95
8.48	3.4	Peter	Burge	AUS	3.7.74	1		Gold Coast (RB)	10 Sep 00
8.48	5.6	Miguel	Pate	USA	13.6.79	1		Fort Worth	21 Apr 01
8.47	2.5	Savanté	Stringfellow	USA	6.11.78	1	NC	Eugene	22 Jun 01
8.46	3.4	Randy	Williams	USA	23.8.53	1		Eugene	18 May 73
8.46		Vernon	George	USA	6.10.64	1		Houston	21 May 89
8.44		Keith	Talley	USA	28.1.64	Q		Odessa, Tx	16 May 85
8.42		Anthony	Bailous	USA	6.4.65	Q		Odessa, Tx	16 May 85
8.42A	4.5	Milan	Gombala	CZE	29.1.68	3		Sestriere	21 Jul 92
8.41	4.3	Shamil	Abbyasov	KGZ	16.4.57	2	vUSA	Indianapolis	3 Jul 82
8.41	3.3	Andre	Ester	USA	27.4.65	1	TexR	Austin	4 Apr 87
8.41A	3.2	Nelson	Ferreira Jr	BRA	1.1.73	1	IbAm	Medellín	10 May 96
8.40	4.3	Henry	Hines	USA	12.2.49	1	CalR	Modesto	27 May 72
8.40	2.1	Anthuan	Maybank	USA	30.12.69	1	DrakeR	Des Moines	24 Apr 93
8.40	3.4	Konstadínos	Koukodímos	GRE	14.9.69	1	ECp I	Valencia	11 Jun 94
8.39	6.2	Gary	Honey	AUS	26.7.59	2		Sacramento	21 Jul 84
8.39	3.5	Edrick	Floreal	CAN	5.10.66	1		Fayetteville	22 Apr 89
8.39	5.7	Yusuf	Alli	NGR	28.7.60	1	CG	Auckland	1 Feb 90

Mark	Wind		Name	Nat	Born	Pos	Meet	Venue	Date
8.39	2.4		Chen Zunrong	CHN	20.10.62	1		Shizuoka	5 May 92
Exhibition: 8.46		Yuriy	Naumkin	RUS	4.11.68	1		Iglesias	6 Sep 96

Best outdoors

8.56 1.3 Lamela 1 Torino 24 Jun 99 | 8.38 1.1 Sosunov 1 ECp Sankt-Peterburg 27 Jun 98

Ancillary marks – other marks during series (to 8.66/8.71w)

8.84	1.7	Lewis	30 Aug 91	8.66		Lewis	26 Apr 87	8.75w	2.1	Lewis	16 Aug 87
8.71	0.6	Lewis	19 Jun 83	8.84Aw	3.8	Powell	21 Jul 92	8.75A	3.4	Powell	21 Jul 92
8.68	0.3	Lewis	18 Jul 88	8.83w	2.3	Lewis	30 Aug 91	8.73w	2.4	Lewis	18 May 85
8.68	0.0	Lewis	30 Aug 91	8.80Aw	4.0	Powell	21 Jul 92	8.73w		Powell	16 May 92
8.67	-0.2	Lewis	5 Sep 87	8.78Aw		Powell	21 Jul 92	8.71Aw		Powell	31 Jul 91

TRIPLE JUMP

Mark	Wind		Name	Nat	Born	Pos	Meet	Venue	Date
18.29	WR 1.3	Jonathan	Edwards	GBR	10.5.66	1	WCh	Göteborg	7 Aug 95
18.09	-0.4	Kenny	Harrison	USA	13.2.65	1	OG	Atlanta	27 Jul 96
18.01	0.4		Edwards			1	Bisl	Oslo	9 Jul 98
18.00	1.3		Edwards			1	McD	London (CP)	27 Aug 95
17.99	0.5		Edwards			1	EC	Budapest	23 Aug 98
17.98	WR 1.8		Edwards			1		Salamanca	18 Jul 95
17.97	WR 1.5	Willie	Banks	USA	11.3.56	1	TAC	Indianapolis	16 Jun 85
17.93	1.6		Harrison			1	DNG	Stockholm	2 Jul 90
17.92	1.6	Khristo	Markov	BUL	27.1.65	1	WCh	Roma	31 Aug 87
17.92	1.9	James	Beckford	JAM	9.1.75	1	JUCO	Odessa, Tex	20 May 95
17.92	0.7		Edwards			1	WCh	Edmonton	6 Aug 01
17.90	1.0	Vladimir	Inozemtsev	UKR	25.5.64	1	GPB	Bratislava	20 Jun 90
17.89A	WR 0.0	João Carlos	de Oliveira	BRA	28.5.54	1	PAm	Ciudad de México	15 Oct 75
17.88	0.9		Edwards			2	OG	Atlanta	27 Jul 96
17.87	1.7	Mike	Conley	USA	5.10.62	1	TAC	San José	27 Jun 87
17.86	1.3	Charles	Simpkins	USA	19.10.63	1	WUG	Kobe	2 Sep 85
17.86	0.3		Conley			1	WCh	Stuttgart	16 Aug 93
17.85	0.9	Yoelbi	Quesada (10)	CUB	4.8.73	1	WCh	Athína	8 Aug 97
17.84	0.7		Conley			1		Bad Cannstatt	4 Jul 93
17.83i	-	Aliecer	Urrutia	CUB	22.9.74	1		Sindelfingen	1 Mar 97
17.82	1.6		Edwards			1	WG	Helsinki	25 Jun 96
17.81	2.0		Markov			1	Nar	Sofia	31 May 87
17.80	0.6		Markov			1	BGP	Budapest	11 Aug 86
17.79	-0.8		Harrison			1	OD	Berlin	4 Jul 90
17.79	-0.7		Edwards			1	WK	Zürich	14 Aug 96
17.78	1.0	Nikolay	Musiyenko	UKR	16.12.59	1	Znam	Leningrad	7 Jun 86
17.78	0.6	Lázaro	Betancourt ¶	CUB	18.3.63	1	Barr	La Habana	15 Jun 86
17.78	-0.8		Harrison			1	WCh	Tokyo	26 Aug 91
17.77	1.9		Markov			1	ECp-B	Budapest	11 Aug 85
17.77	1.0	Aleksandr	Kovalenko	RUS	8.5.63	1	NC	Bryansk	18 Jul 87
17.77	1.4		Markov			1	NC	Sofia	3 Sep 88
17.77i	-	Leonid	Voloshin	RUS	30.3.66	1		Grenoble	6 Feb 94
		(32/15)							
17.75	0.3	Oleg	Protsenko	RUS	11.8.63	1	Znam	Moskva	10 Jun 90
17.72i		Brian	Wellman	BER	8.9.67	1	WI	Barcelona	12 Mar 95
17.69	1.5	Igor	Lapshin	BLR	8.8.63	1		Stayki	31 Jul 88
17.66	1.7	Ralf	Jaros	GER	13.12.65	1	ECp	Frankfurt-am-Main	30 Jun 91
17.65	1.0	Aleksandr	Yakovlev	UKR	8.9.57	1	Znam	Moskva	6 Jun 87
		(20)							
17.65	0.8	Denis	Kapustin	RUS	5.10.70	2	Bisl	Oslo	9 Jul 98
17.62i	-	Yoel	García	CUB	25.11.73	2		Sindelfingen	1 Mar 97
17.60	0.6	Vladimir	Plekhanov	RUS	11.4.58	2	NC	Leningrad	4 Aug 85
17.60	1.9	Fabrizio	Donato	ITA	14.8.76	1		Milano	7 Jun 00
17.59i	-	Pierre	Camara	FRA	10.9.65	1	WI	Toronto	13 Mar 93
17.59	0.3	Vasiliy	Sokov	RUS	7.4.68	1	NC	Moskva	19 Jun 93
17.59	0.8	Charles	Friedek	GER	26.8.71	1		Hamburg	23 Jul 97
17.58	1.5	Oleg	Sakirkin	KZK	23.1.66	2	NC	Gorkiy	23 Jul 89
17.57A	0.0	Keith	Connor	GBR	16.9.57	1	NCAA	Provo	5 Jun 82
17.56	1.9	Maris	Bruziks	LAT	25.8.62	1		Riga	3 Sep 88
		(30)							
17.55	0.3	Vasiliy	Grishchenkov	RUS	23.1.58	1	Spart	Moskva	19 Jun 83
17.55	0.9	Serge	Hélan	FRA	24.2.64	2	EC	Helsinki	13 Aug 94
17.53	1.0	Aleksandr	Beskrovniy	RUS	5.4.60	2	Spart	Moskva	19 Jun 83
17.53	1.6	Zdzislaw	Hoffmann	POL	27.8.59	1		Madrid	4 Jun 85
17.53	1.0	Gennadiy	Valyukevich	BLR	1.6.58	1		Erfurt	1 Jun 86
17.53	1.6	Al	Joyner	USA	19.1.60	Q	TAC	San José	26 Jun 87

Mark	Wind	Name		Nat	Born	Pos	Meet	Venue	Date
17.53	0.9	Milán	Mikulás	CZE	1.4.63	1	NC	Praha	17 Jul 88
17.53	1.9	Oleg	Denishchik	BLR	10.11.69	2	NC	Kiyev	12 Jul 91
17.53	0.5	Aleksandr	Glavatskiy	BLR	2.5.70	2	WK	Zürich	12 Aug 98
17.50	0.4	Volker	Mai	GDR	3.5.66	1	vURS	Erfurt	23 Jun 85
		(40)							
17.49	1.4	Rostislav	Dimitrov	BUL	29.12.74	2	WCh	Sevilla	25 Aug 99
17.49	1.6	Christian	Olsson	SWE	25.1.80	1		Réthimno	1 Jul 01
17.48	1.9	Jorge	Reyna	CUB	10.1.63	1		Santiago de Cuba	27 Feb 87
17.48	1.6	Jerome	Romain	DMN	12.6.71	Q	WCh	Göteborg	5 Aug 95
17.46	1.7	Ken	Lorraway	AUS	6.2.56	1		London (CP)	7 Aug 82
17.45	1.9	Aleksandr	Leonov ¶	BLR	7.2.62	1		Sochi	24 May 87
17.45	1.5	Paolo	Camossi	ITA	6.1.74	2		Milano	7 Jun 00
17.44 WR	-0.?	Viktor	Saneyev	GEO	3.10.45	1		Sukhumi	17 Oct 72
17.44	2.0	Dirk	Gamlin	GDR	26.10.63	1		Dresden	7 Jul 85
17.44	0.4	Andrey	Kurennoy	RUS	12.5.72	1	NC	Tula	9 Jul 97
17.44	1.7	LaMark	Carter	USA	23.8.70	1	NC	New Orleans	20 Jun 98
17.44	0.9	Igor	Spasovkhodskiy	RUS	1.8.79	3	WCh	Edmonton	6 Aug 01
		(52)	100th man 17.24, 200th man 17.03						
Wind-assisted marks – performances to 17.80									
18.43	2.4	Jonathan	Edwards	GBR	10.5.66	1	ECp	Villeneuve d'Ascq	25 Jun 95
18.20	5.2	Willie	Banks	USA	11.3.56	1	OT	Indianapolis	16 Jul 88
18.17	2.1	Mike	Conley	USA	5.10.62	1	OG	Barcelona	3 Aug 92
18.08	2.5		Edwards			1	BUPA	Sheffield	23 Jul 95
18.03	2.9		Edwards			1	GhG	Gateshead	2 Jul 95
18.01	3.7		Harrison			1	NC	Atlanta	15 Jun 96
17.97	7.5	Yoelbi	Quesada	CUB	4.8.73	1		Madrid	20 Jun 95
17.93	5.2	Charles	Simpkins	USA	19.10.63	2	OT	Indianapolis	16 Jul 88
17.91	3.2		Simpkins			1	TAC	Eugene	21 Jun 86
17.86	3.9		Simpkins			1	OT	New Orleans	21 Jun 92
17.86	5.7	Denis	Kapustin	RUS	5.10.70	1		Sevilla	5 Jun 94
17.84	2.3		Conley			2	TAC	Eugene	21 Jun 86
17.82	3.6		Banks			1	Jen	San José	31 May 86
17.81	4.6	Keith	Connor	GBR	16.9.57	1	CG	Brisbane	9 Oct 82
17.75		Gennadiy	Valyukevich	BLR	1.6.58	1		Uzhgorod	27 Apr 86
17.75	7.1	Brian	Wellman	BER	8.9.67	2		Madrid	20 Jun 95
17.73	4.1	Vasiliy	Sokov	RUS	7.4.68	1		Riga	3 Jun 89
17.63	4.3	Robert	Cannon	USA	9.7.58	3	OT	Indianapolis	16 Jul 88
17.59	2.1	Jerome	Romain	DMN	12.6.71	3	WCh	Göteborg	7 Aug 95
17.58	5.2	Al	Joyner	USA	19.1.60	5	OT	Indianapolis	16 Jul 88
17.56	3.7	Ron	Livers	USA	20.7.55	1	AAU	Walnut	17 Jun 79
17.55	3.6	Zdzislaw	Hoffmann	POL	27.8.59	1	Kuso	Warszawa	9 Jun 84
17.54	3.2	Ken	Lorraway	AUS	6.2.56	2	CG	Brisbane	9 Oct 82
17.53	4.8	Ray	Kimble	USA	19.4.53	7	OT	Indianapolis	16 Jul 88
17.51	3.0		Chen Yanping	CHN	17.1.66	1	AsiG	Beijing	3 Oct 90
17.49	4.5	Vladimir	Melikhov	RUS	30.3.69	2		Sevilla	5 Jun 94
17.48	2.9	Georges	Sainte-Rose	FRA	3.9.69	1		Montgeron	23 Jun 91
17.47	3.7	Joseph	Taiwo	NGR	24.8.59	1	GP	São Paulo	17 May 92

Best outdoor marks for athletes with lifetime bests indoors

17.75 1.0 Voloshin 2 WCh Tokyo 26 Aug 91 | 17.62A Wellman 1 El Paso 15 Apr 95
17.70 1.7 Urrutia 1 GP II Sevilla 6 Jun 96 | 17.47 1.8 García 1 Bad Cannstatt 9 Jul 95

Ancillary marks – other marks during series (to 17.78/17.84w)

18.16 WR 1.3 Edwards 7 Aug 95 | 18.39 3.7 Edwards 25 Jun 95 | 17.90 2.5 Edwards 25 Jun 95
17.99 0.1 Harrison 27 Jul 96 | 18.06 4.9 Banks 16 Jul 88 | 17.84 2.1 Edwards 23 Aug 98

SHOT

Mark	Name		Nat	Born	Pos	Meet	Venue	Date
23.12 WR	Randy	Barnes ¶	USA	16.6.66	1		Westwood	20 May 90
23.10		Barnes			1	Jen	San José	26 May 90
23.06 WR	Ulf	Timmermann	GDR	1.11.62	1		Hania	22 May 88
22.91 WR	Alessandro	Andrei	ITA	3.1.59	1		Viareggio	12 Aug 87
22.86	Brian	Oldfield	USA	1.6.45	1	ITA	El Paso	10 May 75
22.75	Werner	Günthör	SUI	1.6.61	1		Bern	23 Aug 88
22.66i		Barnes			1	Sunkist	Los Angeles	20 Jan 89
22.64 WR	Udo	Beyer	GDR	9.8.55	1		Berlin	20 Aug 86
22.62 WR		Timmermann			1		Berlin	22 Sep 85
22.61		Timmermann			1		Potsdam	8 Sep 88
22.60		Timmermann			1	vURS	Tallinn	21 Jun 86
22.56		Timmermann			1		Berlin	13 Sep 88
22.55i		Timmermann			1	NC	Senftenberg	11 Feb 89
22.52	John	Brenner	USA	4.1.61	1	MSR	Walnut	26 Apr 87

Mark	Wind	Name		Nat	Born	Pos	Meet	Venue	Date
22.51			Timmermann			1		Erfurt	1 Jun 86
22.47			Timmermann			1		Dresden	17 Aug 86
22.47			Günthör			1	WG	Helsinki	2 Jul 87
22.47			Timmermann			1	OG	Seoul	23 Sep 88
22.45			Oldfield			1	ITA	El Paso	22 May 76
22.43			Günthör			1	v3-N	Lüdenscheid	18 Jun 87
22.42			Barnes			1	WK	Zürich	17 Aug 88
22.40			Barnes			1		Rüdlingen	13 Jul 96
22.39			Barnes			2	OG	Seoul	23 Sep 88
22.36	@		Timmermann			1		Athína	16 May 88
22.31			Beyer			1	NC	Potsdam	20 Aug 87
22.28			Oldfield			1	ITA	Edinburgh	18 Jun 75
22.28			Barnes			1	MSR	Walnut	22 Apr 90
22.26i			Günthör			1	NC	Magglingen	8 Feb 87
22.26			Brenner			1		Westwood	18 Apr 87
22.25			Günthör			1	WK	Zürich	19 Aug 87
22.24		Sergey	Smirnov	RUS	17.9.60	2	vGDR	Tallinn	21 Jun 86
22.24i			Timmermann			1	WCh	Indianapolis	7 Mar 87
		(32/8)							
22.12		Adam	Nelson	USA	7.7.75	1	NC	Sacramento	15 Jul 00
22.10		Sergey	Gavryushin	RUS	27.6.59	1		Tbilisi	31 Aug 86
		(10)							
22.09		Sergey	Kasnauskas	BLR	20.4.61	1		Stayki	23 Aug 84
22.09i		Mika	Halvari	FIN	13.2.70	1		Tampere	7 Feb 00
22.02i		George	Woods	USA	11.2.43	1	LAT	Inglewood	8 Feb 74
22.02		Dave	Laut	USA	21.12.56	1		Koblenz	25 Aug 82
22.02		John	Godina	USA	31.5.72	1	NC	Eugene	27 Jun 99
22.00	WR	Aleksandr	Baryshnikov	RUS	11.11.48	1	vFRA	Colombes	10 Jul 76
21.98		Gregg	Tafralis ¶	USA	9.4.58	1		Los Gatos	13 Jun 92
21.97		Janus	Robberts	RSA	10.3.79	1	NCAA	Eugene	2 Jun 01
21.96		Mikhail	Kostin	RUS	10.5.59	1		Vitebsk	20 Jul 86
21.93		Remigius	Machura ¶	CZE	3.7.60	1		Praha	23 Aug 87
		(20)							
21.87		C.J.	Hunter ¶	USA	14.12.68	2	NC	Sacramento	15 Jul 00
21.85	WR	Terry	Albritton	USA	14.1.55	1		Honolulu	21 Feb 76
21.83i		Aleksandr	Bagach ¶	UKR	21.11.66	1		Brovary	21 Feb 99
21.82	WR	Al	Feuerbach	USA	14.1.48	1		San José	5 May 73
21.82		Andy	Bloom	USA	11.8.73	1	GPF	Doha	5 Oct 00
21.78	WR	Randy	Matson	USA	5.3.45	1		College Station	22 Apr 67
21.78		Kevin	Toth	USA	29.12.67	2	NC	Indianapolis	12 Jun 97
21.77i		Mike	Stulce ¶	USA	21.7.69	1	v GBR	Birmingham	13 Feb 93
21.77		Dragan	Peric	YUG	8.5.64	1		Bar	25 Apr 98
21.76		Mike	Carter	USA	29.10.60	2	NCAA	Eugene	2 Jun 84
		(30)							
21.74		Janis	Bojars	LAT	12.5.56	1		Riga	14 Jul 84
21.73		Augie	Wolf ¶	USA	3.9.61	1		Leverkusen	12 Apr 84
21.69		Reijo	Ståhlberg	FIN	21.9.52	1	WCR	Fresno	5 May 79
21.68		Geoff	Capes	GBR	23.8.49	1	4-N	Cwmbrân	18 May 80
21.68		Edward	Sarul	POL	16.11.58	1		Sopot	31 Jul 83
21.67		Hartmut	Briesenick	GDR	17.3.49	1		Potsdam	1 Sep 73
21.64		Yuriy	Belonog	UKR	9.3.74	1		Koncha-Zaspa	28 Apr 00
21.61		Kevin	Akins	USA	27.1.60	1	S&W	Modesto	14 May 83
21.60		Jim	Doehring ¶	USA	27.1.62	2		Los Gatos	13 Jun 92
21.58		Vladimir	Kiselyov	UKR	1.1.57	3	Drz	Moskva	17 Aug 84
		(40)							
21.53		Yevgeniy	Mironov ¶	RUS	1.11.49	1	NC	Kiyev	24 Jun 76
21.51		Ralf	Reichenbach	FRG	31.7.50	1	ISTAF	Berlin	8 Aug 80
21.47		Brent	Noon ¶	USA	29.8.71	1	SEC	Tuscaloosa	21 May 95
21.47i		Oliver-Sven	Buder	GER	23.6.66	1	EI	Valencia	28 Feb 98
21.44		Mikhail	Domorosov	BLR	5.3.55	2		Stayki	23 Aug 84
21.43		Mike	Lehmann	USA	11.3.60	2	Jen	San José	28 May 83
21.42i		Fred	DeBernardi	USA	2.3.49	1	ITA	Portland	20 Apr 74
21.42		Sergey	Donskikh	RUS	25.1.56	1		Leningrad	25 Aug 84
21.39		Arsi	Harju	FIN	18.3.74	1	OG	Sydney	22 Sep 00
21.35		Ron	Semkiw	USA	28.3.54	1		Mesa	5 Mar 74
21.35		Sergey	Nikolayev	RUS	12.11.66	1		Voronezh	5 Aug 89
21.35		Manuel	Martínez	ESP	7.12.74	1		San Sebastián	18 Aug 01

(52) 100th man 20.91, 200th 20.37 @ competitive meeting but unsanctioned by GDR federation

Mark	Wind	Name		Nat	Born	Pos	Meet	Venue	Date
Not recognised by GDR authorities									
22.11		Rolf	Oesterreich	GDR	24.8.49	1		Zschopau	12 Sep 76
Drugs disqualification									
22.84			Barnes			1		Malmö	7 Aug 90
21.82		Mike	Stulce ¶	USA	21.7.69	1		Brenham	9 May 90

Best outdoor marks for athletes with lifetime bests indoors

Mark	Name	Pos	Meet	Venue	Date	Mark	Name	Pos	Meet	Venue	Date
21.70	Stulce ¶	1	OG	Barcelona	31 Jul 92	21.47	Bagach ¶	1	Veniz	Haniá	31 May 97
21.63	Woods	2	CalR	Modesto	22 May 76	21.42	Buder	2	WCh	Sevilla	21 Aug 99
21.50	Halvari	1		Hämeenkyrö	9 Jul 95	21.41	DeBernardi	1	ITA	El Paso	27 Apr 74

Ancillary marks – other marks during series (to 22.42)

Mark	Name	Date	Mark	Name	Date	Mark	Name	Date
22.84 WR	Andrei	12 Aug 87	22.72 WR	Andrei	12 Aug 87	22.55	Barnes	20 May 90
22.76	Barnes	20 May 90	22.70	Günthör	23 Aug 88	22.45	Timmermann	22 May 88
22.74	Andrei	12 Aug 87	22.58	Beyer	20 Aug 86	22.44	Barnes	20 May 90

DISCUS

Mark	Wind	Name		Nat	Born	Pos	Meet	Venue	Date
74.08	WR	Jürgen	Schult	GDR	11.5.60	1		Neubrandenburg	6 Jun 86
73.88		Virgilijus	Alekna	LTU	13.2.72	1	NC	Kaunas	3 Aug 00
71.86	WR	Yuriy	Dumchev	RUS	5.8.58	1		Moskva	29 May 83
71.50		Lars	Riedel	GER	28.6.67	1		Wiesbaden	3 May 97
71.32		Ben	Plucknett ¶	USA	13.4.54	1	Pre	Eugene	4 Jun 83
71.26		John	Powell	USA	25.6.47	1	TAC	San José	9 Jun 84
71.26		Rickard	Bruch	SWE	2.7.46	1		Malmö	15 Nov 84
71.26		Imrich	Bugár	CZE	14.4.55	1	Jen	San José	25 May 85
71.18		Art	Burns	USA	19.7.54	1		San José	19 Jul 83
71.16	WR	Wolfgang	Schmidt	GDR	16.1.54	1		Berlin	9 Aug 78
		(10/10)							
71.14			Plucknett			1		Berkeley	12 Jun 83
71.14		Anthony	Washington	USA	16.1.66	1eA		Salinas	22 May 96
71.12			Alekna			1	WK	Zürich	11 Aug 00
71.06		Luis M.	Delís ¶	CUB	6.12.57	1	Barr	La Habana	21 May 83
71.06			Riedel			1	WK	Zürich	14 Aug 96
71.00			Bruch			1		Malmö	14 Oct 84
70.99			Alekna			1		Stellenbosch	30 Mar 01
70.98		Mac	Wilkins	USA	15.11.50	1	WG	Helsinki	9 Jul 80
70.98			Burns			1	Pre	Eugene	21 Jul 84
70.92			Schmidt	FRG		1		Norden	9 Sep 89
70.86	WR		Wilkins			1		San José	1 May 76
70.82			Plucknett			1		Salinas	1 Jun 83
70.72			Bugár			1	vHUN,AUT	Schwechat	18 Jun 83
70.66			Wilkins			1	AAU	Walnut	16 Jun 79
70.60			Riedel			1	ISTAF	Berlin	30 Aug 96
70.58			Delís			1		Salinas	19 May 82
70.48			Wilkins			1		San José	29 Apr 78
70.48			Wilkins			1	Pre	Eugene	31 May 78
70.48			Bruch			1		Malmö	12 Sep 84
70.46			Schult			1		Berlin	13 Sep 88
		(30/13)	47 performances over 70m						
70.38	WRu	Jay	Silvester	USA	27.8.37	1		Lancaster	16 May 71
70.06		Romas	Ubartas ¶	LIT	26.5.60	1		Smolininkay	8 May 88
70.00		Juan	Martínez ¶	CUB	17.5.58	2	Barr	La Habana	21 May 83
69.96		Frantz	Kruger	RSA	22.5.75	2		Stellenbosch	30 Mar 01
69.91		John	Godina	USA	31.5.72	1		Salinas	19 May 98
69.70		Géjza	Valent	CZE	3.10.53	2		Nitra	26 Aug 84
69.62		Knut	Hjeltnes ¶	NOR	8.12.51	2	Jen	San José	25 May 85
		(20)							
69.62		Timo	Tompuri	FIN	9.6.69	1		Helsingborg	8 Jul 01
69.46		Al	Oerter	USA	19.9.36	1	TFA	Wichita	31 May 80
69.44		Georgiy	Kolnootchenko	BLR	7.5.59	1	vUSA	Indianapolis	3 Jul 82
69.44		Adam	Setliff	USA	15.12.69	1		La Jolla	21 Jul 01
69.40		Art	Swarts ¶	USA	14.2.45	1		Scotch Plains	8 Dec 79
69.36		Mike	Buncic	USA	25.7.62	1		Fresno	6 Apr 91
69.28		Vladimir	Dubrovshchik	BLR	7.1.72	1	NC-w	Stayki	3 Jun 00
69.26		Ken	Stadel	USA	19.2.52	2	AAU	Walnut	16 Jun 79
68.88		Vladimir	Zinchenko	UKR	25.7.59	1		Dnepropetrovsk	16 Jul 88
68.64		Dmitriy	Kovtsun ¶	UKR	29.9.55	1		Riga	6 Jul 84
		(30)							
68.58		Attila	Horváth	HUN	28.7.67	1		Budapest	24 Jun 94
68.52		Igor	Duginyets	UKR	20.5.56	1	NC	Kiyev	21 Aug 82
68.50		Armin	Lemme	GDR	28.10.55	1	vUSA	Karl-Marx-Stadt	10 Jul 82

Mark Wind	Name		Nat	Born	Pos	Meet	Venue	Date
68.48 WR	John	van Reenen	RSA	26.3.47	1		Stellenbosch	14 Mar 75
68.46	Andy	Bloom	USA	11.8.73	2cA		La Jolla	25 Mar 00
68.44	Vaclovas	Kidykas	LIT	17.10.61	1		Sochi	1 Jun 88
68.30	Stefan	Fernholm	SWE	2.7.59	1		Västerås	15 Jul 87
68.12	Markku	Tuokko ¶	FIN	24.6.51	1	WCR	Fresno	5 May 79
68.12	Iosif	Nagy	ROM	20.11.46	2		Zaragoza	22 May 83
68.12	Erik	de Bruin ¶	NED	25.5.63	1		Sneek	1 Apr 91
	(40)							
68.09	Róbert	Fazekas	HUN	18.8.75	1	GP II	Sevilla	8 Jun 01
68.08	Hein-Direck	Neu ¶	FRG	13.2.44	1		Bremerhaven	27 May 77
68.00	Svein Inge	Valvik	NOR	20.9.56	1		Juarez	31 May 82
67.92	Mario	Pestano	ESP	8.4.78	1	NC	Valencia	22 Jul 01
67.90	Vitaliy	Sidorov	UKR	23.3.70	1		Kiev	3 May 98
67.89	Nick	Sweeney	IRL	26.3.68	1		Helsingborg	4 Sep 98
67.88	Jason	Tunks	CAN	7.5.75	1		Abilene	14 May 98
67.82	Velko	Velev ¶	BUL	4.1.48	1		Riga	13 Aug 78
67.80	Alwin	Wagner	FRG	11.8.50	1		Melsungen	1 Jul 87
67.80	Adewale	Olukoju	NGR	27.7.68	1	S&W	Modesto	11 May 91
	(50)	100th man 66.16, 200th man 64.40						
Subsequent to or at drugs disqualification			! recognised as US record					
72.34!	Ben	Plucknett ¶	USA	13.4.54	1	DNG	Stockholm	7 Jul 81
71.20		Plucknett			1	CalR	Modesto	16 May 81
70.84	Kamy	Keshmiri ¶	USA	23.1.69	1		Salinas	27 May 92
68.04	Dmitriy	Shevchenko ¶	RUS	13.5.68	(1)	ASV	Köln	18 Aug 95
Sloping ground								
72.08	John	Powell	USA	25.6.47	1		Klagshamn	11 Sep 87
69.80	Stefan	Fernholm	SWE	2.7.59	1		Klagshamn	13 Aug 87

Ancillary marks – other marks during series (to 70.50)

72.35	Alekna	3 Aug 00	70.84	Riedel	3 May 97	70.59	Alekna	30 Mar 01
71.08	Plucknett	4 Jun 83	70.60	Alekna	11 Aug 00			

HAMMER

Mark Wind	Name		Nat	Born	Pos	Meet	Venue	Date
86.74 WR	Yuriy	Sedykh	RUS	11.6.55	1	EC	Stuttgart	30 Aug 86
86.66 WR		Sedykh			1	vGDR	Tallinn	22 Jun 86
86.34 WR		Sedykh			1		Cork	3 Jul 84
86.04	Sergey	Litvinov	RUS	23.1.58	1	OD	Dresden	3 Jul 86
85.74		Litvinov			2	EC	Stuttgart	30 Aug 86
85.68		Sedykh			1	BGP	Budapest	11 Aug 86
85.60		Sedykh			1	PTG	London (CP)	13 Jul 84
85.60		Sedykh			1	Drz	Moskva	17 Aug 84
85.20		Litvinov			2		Cork	3 Jul 84
85.14		Litvinov			1	PTG	London	11 Jul 86
85.14		Sedykh			1	Kuts	Moskva	4 Sep 88
85.02		Sedykh			1	BGP	Budapest	20 Aug 84
84.92		Sedykh			2	OD	Dresden	3 Jul 86
84.88		Litvinov			1	GP-GG	Roma	10 Sep 86
84.80		Litvinov			1	OG	Seoul	26 Sep 88
84.72		Sedykh			1	GWG	Moskva	9 Jul 86
84.64		Litvinov			2	GWG	Moskva	9 Jul 86
84.62	Igor	Astapkovich	BLR	4.1.63	1	Expo	Sevilla	6 Jun 92
84.60		Sedykh			1	8-N	Tokyo	14 Sep 84
84.58		Sedykh			1	Znam	Leningrad	8 Jun 86
84.48	Igor	Nikulin	RUS	14.8.60	1	Athl	Lausanne	12 Jul 90
84.46		Sedykh			1		Vladivostok	14 Sep 88
84.40	Jüri	Tamm	EST	5.2.57	1		Banská Bystrica	9 Sep 84
84.36		Litvinov			2	vGDR	Tallinn	22 Jun 86
84.26		Sedykh			1	Nik	Nice	15 Jul 86
84.26		Astapkovich			1		Reims	3 Jul 91
84.16		Tamm			1		Kharkov	19 Jun 88
84.14 WR		Litvinov			1	Spart	Moskva	21 Jun 83
84.14		Sedykh			1	WG	Helsinki	7 Jul 86
84.14		Astapkovich			1	EC	Split	31 Aug 90
	(30/5)							
83.68	Tibor	Gécsek ¶	HUN	22.9.64	1		Zalaegerszeg	19 Sep 98
83.47	Koji	Murofushi	JPN	8.10.74	1		Toyota	14 Jul 01
83.46	Andrey	Abduvaliyev	TJK/ UZB	30.6.66	1		Adler	26 May 90
83.40 @	Ralf	Haber	GDR	18.8.62	1		Athína	16 May 88
	82.54				1		Potsdam	9 Sep 88

@ competitive meeting but unsanctioned by GDR federation

Mark Wind	Name		Nat	Born	Pos	Meet	Venue	Date
83.39	Adrián	Annus	HUN	28.6.73	1		Zalaegerszeg	9 Jun 01
	(10)							
83.38	Szymon	Ziólkowski	POL	1.7.76	1	WCh	Edmonton	5 Aug 01
83.04	Heinz	Weis	GER	14.7.63	1	NC	Frankfurt	29 Jun 97
83.00	Balázs	Kiss	HUN	21.3.72	1	GP II	Saint-Denis	4 Jun 98
82.78	Karsten	Kobs	GER	16.9.71	1		Dortmund	26 Jun 99
82.64	Günther	Rodehau	GDR	6.7.59	1		Dresden	3 Aug 85
82.62	Sergey	Kirmasov ¶	RUS	25.3.70	1		Bryansk	30 May 98
82.54	Vasiliy	Sidorenko	RUS	1.5.61	1		Krasnodar	13 May 92
82.52	Lance	Deal	USA	21.8.61	1	GPF	Milano	7 Sep 96
82.40	Plamen	Minev	BUL	28.4.65	1	NM	Plovdiv	1 Jun 91
82.38	Gilles	Dupray	FRA	2.1.70	1		Chelles	21 Jun 00
	(20)							
82.34	Andrey	Skvaruk	UKR	9.3.67	1	NC	Kiev	2 Jul 01
82.24	Benjaminas	Viluckis	LIT	20.3.61	1		Klaipeda	24 Aug 86
82.24	Vyacheslav	Korovin	RUS	8.9.62	1		Chelyabinsk	20 Jun 87
82.22	Holger	Klose	GER	5.12.72	1		Dortmund	2 May 98
2.16	Vitaliy	Alisevich	BLR	15.6.67	1		Parnu	13 Jul 88
82.08	Ivan	Tanev	BUL	1.5.57	1	NC	Sofia	3 Sep 88
82.00	Sergey	Alay	BLR	11.6.65	1		Stayki	12 May 92
81.93	Ilya	Konovalov	RUS	14.3.71	1		Rostov-na-Donu	28 Jun 00
81.88	Jud	Logan ¶	USA	19.7.59	1		University Park	22 Apr 88
81.79	Christophe	Épalle	FRA	23.1.69	1		Clermont-Ferrand	30 Jun 00
	(30)							
81.78	Christoph	Sahner	FRG	23.9.63	1		Wemmetsweiler	11 Sep 88
81.70	Aleksandr	Seleznyov	RUS	25.1.63	2		Sochi	22 May 93
81.64	Enrico	Sgrulletti	ITA	24.4.65	1		Ostia	9 Mar 97
81.56	Sergey	Gavrilov	RUS	22.5.70	1	Army	Rostov	16 Jun 96
81.56	Zsolt	Németh	HUN	9.11.71	1		Veszprém	14 Aug 99
81.56	Vladislav	Piskunov	UKR	7.6.78	1		Yalta	25 Mar 00
81.52	Juha	Tiainen	FIN	5.12.55	1		Tampere	11 Jun 84
81.44	Yuriy	Tarasyuk	BLR	11.4.57	1		Minsk	10 Aug 84
81.36	Vadim	Devyatovskiy ¶	BLR	20.3.77	1	NC	Brest	1 Aug 00
81.32	Klaus	Ploghaus	FRG	31.1.56	1		Paderborn	25 May 86
	(40)							
81.28	Vladimir	Maska	CZE	6.2.73	1		Pacov	25 Sep 99
81.20	Igor	Grigorash	RUS	18.8.59	1		Kiyev	23 Aug 84
81.18	Albert	Sinka	HUN	22.11.62	1		Székesfehérvár	7 Aug 88
81.10	Sergey	Ivanov	RUS	3.1.62	1		Chelyabinsk	27 Jun 87
81.08	Koji	Murofushi	JPN	8.10.74	1	Super	Yokohama	9 Sep 00
80.99	David	Chaussinand	FRA	19.4.73	2		Rüdlingen	19 Aug 01
80.98	Loris	Paoluzzi	ITA	14.5.74	1	NC	Pescara	4 Jul 99
80.92	Matthias	Moder	GDR	17.6.63	1		Halle	11 Jun 85
80.90	Yaroslav	Chmyr	UKR	29.11.66	1		Chernigov	2 Jun 90
80.88	Nicolas	Figère	FRA	19.5.79	1	EU23	Amsterdam	15 Jul 01
	(50)	100th man 78.78, 200th man 76.25						
Extra trial: 81.04	Mariusz	Tomaszewski	POL	23.4.56	-		Zabrze	1 Jul 84
Over-long Chain: 81.12	Grigoriy	Shevtsov	RUS	16.8.58	1		Sochi	12 May 83

Ancillary marks – other marks during series (to 84.85)

Mark	Name	Date	Mark	Name	Date	Mark	Name	Date
86.68	Sedykh	30 Aug 86	85.52	Sedykh	13 Jul 84	85.26	Sedykh	11 Aug 86
86.62	Sedykh	30 Aug 86	85.46	Sedykh	30 Aug 86	85.24	Sedykh	11 Aug 86
86.00	Sedykh	3 Jul 84	85.42	Sedykh	11 Aug 86	85.20	Sedykh	3 Jul 84
86.00	Sedykh	22 Jun 86	85.42	Litvinov	3 Jul 86	85.04	Sedykh	13 Jul 84
85.82	Sedykh	22 Jun 86	85.28	Sedykh	30 Aug 86	84.98	Sedykh	4 Sep 88
						84.92	Litvinov	3 Jul 86

JAVELIN

Mark Wind	Name		Nat	Born	Pos	Meet	Venue	Date
98.48 WR	Jan	Zelezny	CZE	16.6.66	1		Jena	25 May 96
95.66 WR		Zelezny			1	McD	Sheffield	29 Aug 93
95.54A WR		Zelezny			1		Pietersburg	6 Apr 93
94.64		Zelezny			1	GS	Ostrava	31 May 96
94.02		Zelezny			1		Stellenbosch	26 Mar 97
93.09	Aki	Parviainen	FIN	26.10.74	1		Kuortane	26 Jun 99
92.80		Zelezny			1	WCh	Edmonton	12 Aug 01
92.60	Raymond	Hecht	GER	11.11.68	1	Bisl	Oslo	21 Jul 95
92.42		Zelezny			1	GS	Ostrava	28 May 97
92.41		Parviainen			1	ECp-1A	Vaasa	24 Jun 01
92.28		Zelezny			1	GPF	Monaco	9 Sep 95
92.28		Hecht			1	WK	Zürich	14 Aug 96
92.12		Zelezny			1	McD	London (CP)	27 Aug 95

Mark	Wind	Name		Nat	Born	Pos	Meet	Venue	Date
92.12			Zelezny			1	TOTO	Tokyo	15 Sep 95
91.82			Zelezny			1	McD	Sheffield	4 Sep 94
91.69		Kostadínos	Gatsioúdis	GRE	17.12.73	1		Kuortane	24 Jun 00
91.68			Zelezny			1	GP	Gateshead	1 Jul 94
91.50			Zelezny			1	Kuso	Lublin	4 Jun 94
91.50A			Zelezny			1		Pretoria	8 Apr 96
91.50			Hecht			1		Gengenbach	1 Sep 96
91.46	WR	Steve	Backley	GBR	12.2.69	1		Auckland	25 Jan 92
91.40			Zelezny			1	BNP	Villeneuve d'Ascq	2 Jul 93
91.34			Zelezny			1		Cape Town	8 Apr 97
91.31			Parviainen			2	WCh	Edmonton	12 Aug 01
91.30			Zelezny			1	ISTAF	Berlin	1 Sep 95
91.28			Zelezny			1	BNP	Villeneuve d'Ascq	8 Jul 94
91.27			Gatsioúdis			1	ECCp	Madrid	26 May 01
91.23			Zelezny			1		Poznan	8 Jun 01
91.04			Zelezny			1		Kuortane	22 Jun 96
90.97			Parviainen			2		Kuortane	24 Jun 00
		(30/5)	54 performances over 90m, further 14 by Zelezny, 4 Parviainen, 3 Hecht, 1 Backley						
90.60		Seppo	Räty	FIN	27.4.62	1		Nurmijärvi	20 Jul 92
90.44		Boris	Henry	GER	14.12.73	1	Gugl	Linz	9 Jul 97
89.93		Sergey	Makarov	RUS	19.3.73	1	GP II	Athína	16 Jun 99
89.16A		Tom	Petranoff	USA	8.4.58	1		Potchefstroom	1 Mar 91
89.10	WR	Patrik	Bodén	SWE	30.6.67	1		Austin	24 Mar 90
		(10)							
88.75		Marius	Corbett	RSA	26.9.75	1	CG	Kuala Lumpur	21 Sep 98
88.70		Peter	Blank	GER	10.4.62	1	NC	Stuttgart	30 Jun 01
88.24		Matti	Närhi	FIN	17.8.75	1		Soini	27 Jul 97
88.22		Juha	Laukkanen	FIN	6.1.69	1		Kuortane	20 Jun 92
88.20		Gavin	Lovegrove	NZL	21.10.67	1	Bisl	Oslo	5 Jul 96
88.00		Vladimir	Ovchinnikov	RUS	2.8.70	1		Tolyatti	14 May 95
87.82		Harri	Hakkarainen	FIN	16.10.69	1		Kuortane	24 Jun 95
87.60		Kazuhiro	Mizoguchi	JPN	18.3.62	1	Jen	San José	27 May 89
87.40		Vladimir	Sasimovich	BLR	14.9.68	2		Kuortane	24 Jun 95
87.34		Andrey	Moruyev	RUS	6.5.70	1	ECp	Birmingham	25 Jun 94
		(20)							
87.20		Viktor	Zaytsev	UZB	6.6.66	1	OT	Moskva	23 Jun 92
87.17		Dariusz	Trafas	POL	16.5.72	1		Gold Coast (RB)	17 Sep 00
87.12		Tom	Pukstys	USA	28.5.68	2	OD	Jena	25 May 97
87.12		Emeterio	González	CUB	11.4.73	1	OD	Jena	3 Jun 00
87.00		Breaux	Greer	USA	19.10.76	4	WCh	Edmonton	12 Aug 01
86.98		Yuriy	Rybin	RUS	5.3.63	1		Nitra	26 Aug 95
86.94		Mick	Hill	GBR	22.10.64	1	NC	London (CP)	13 Jun 93
86.80		Einar	Vihljálmsson	ISL	1.6.60	1		Reykjavik	29 Aug 92
86.74		Pål Arne	Fagernes	NOR	8.6.74	q	OG	Sydney	22 Sep 00
86.67		Andrew	Currey	AUS	7.2.71	1		Wollongong	22 Jul 01
		(30)							
86.64		Klaus	Tafelmeier	FRG	12.4.58	1	NC	Gelsenkirchen	12 Jul 87
86.63		Harri	Haatainen	FIN	5.1.78	2	GP II	Gateshead	19 Aug 01
86.50		Tapio	Korjus	FIN	10.2.61	1		Lahti	25 Aug 88
86.47		Eriks	Rags	LAT	1.6.75	2	BrGP	London	22 Jul 01
85.96		Kimmo	Kinnunen	FIN	31.3.68	3	NC	Seinäjoki	8 Aug 99
85.74		Dmitriy	Polyunin ¶	UZB	6.4.69	2	OT	Moskva	23 Jun 92
85.70		Andrey	Shevchuk	RUS	8.3.70	2	Slovn	Bratislava	1 Jun 93
85.67		Mark	Roberson	GBR	13.3.67	2		Gateshead	19 Jul 98
85.60		Peter	Esenwein	GER	7.12.67	1		Riederich	25 May 97
85.42		Andreas	Linden	GER	20.2.65	2		Mülheim-Kärlich	17 Sep 95
		(40)							
85.28		Donald-Aik	Sild	EST	3.10.68	2		St Denis	10 Jun 94
85.21		Björn	Lange	GER	15.6.79	4	GP II	Gateshead	19 Aug 01
85.18		Ari	Pakarinen	FIN	14.5.69	Q		Lapua	22 Jul 95
85.16		Viktor	Yevsyukov	KZK	6.10.56	1	vGDR	Karl-Marx-Stadt	21 Jun 87
85.09		Nick	Nieland	GBR	31.1.72	2	NC	Birmingham	13 Aug 00
85.02		Dag	Wennlund	SWE	9.10.63	1		Alvesta	28 May 95
84.95		Rajmund	Kólko ¶	POL	1.3.71	1	Kuso	Warszawa	17 Jun 01
84.84		Volker	Hadwich	GDR	23.9.64	1	vITA,TCH	Macerata	5 Sep 89
84.80		Pascal	Lefévre	FRA	25.1.65	2	Nik	Nice	10 Jul 90
84.80		Sergey	Voynov	UZB	26.2.77	1		Villeneuve d'Ascq	17 Jun 00
		(50)	100th man 82.06, 200th man 79.56						

Mark	Wind	Name		Nat	Born	Pos	Meet	Venue	Date

Ancillary marks – other marks during series (to 91.40)

Mark	Name	Date	Mark	Name	Date	Mark	Name	Date
95.34	Zelezny	29 Aug 93	92.26	Zelezny	26 Mar 97	91.44	Zelezny	25 May 96
92.88	Zelezny	25 May 96	91.88	Zelezny	27 Aug 95	91.44	Zelezny	26 Mar 97
92.30	Zelezny	26 Mar 97	91.48	Zelezny	15 Sep 95			

Javelins with roughened tails, now banned by the IAAF

Mark	Wind	Name		Nat	Born	Pos	Meet	Venue	Date
96.96	WR	Seppo	Räty	FIN	27.4.62	1		Punkalaidun	2 Jun 91
94.74	Irreg		Zelezny			1	Bisl	Oslo	4 Jul 92
91.98	WR		Räty			1	Super	Shizuoka	6 May 91
91.36			Backley			1	McV	Sheffield	15 Sep 91
90.98	WR		Backley			1	PG	London (CP)	20 Jul 90
90.82		Kimmo	Kinnunen	FIN	31.3.68	1	WCh	Tokyo	26 Aug 91
87.00		Peter	Borglund	SWE	29.1.64	1		Stockholm	13 Aug 91
85.52		Dag	Wennlund	SWE	9.10.63	1	NC	Helsingborg	27 Jul 91
85.08		Radoman	Scekic	YUG	1.10.67	1		Zagreb	12 Jun 91
84.94		Sigurdur	Einarsson	ISL	28.9.62	2	Super	Shizuoka	6 May 91

DECATHLON

Mark	Wind	Name		Nat	Born	Pos	Meet	Venue	Date
9026	WR	Roman	Sebrle	CZE	26.11.74	1		Götzis	27 May 01
10.64/0.0	8.11/1.9	15.33	2.12	47.79	13.92/-0.2	47.92	4.80	70.16	4:21.98
8994	WR	Tomás	Dvorák	CZE	11.5.72	1	ECp	Praha	4 Jul 99
10.54/-0.1	7.90/1.1	16.78	2.04	48.08	13.73/0.0	48.33	4.90	72.32	4:37.20
8902			Dvorák			1	WCh	Edmonton	7 Aug 01
10.62/1.5	8.07/0.9	16.57	2.00	47.74	13.80/-0.4	45.51	5.00	68.53	4:35.13
8900			Dvorák			1		Götzis	4 Jun 00
10.54/1.3	8.03/0.0	16.68	2.09	48.36	13.89/-1.0	47.89	4.85	67.21	4:42.33
8891	WR	Dan	O'Brien	USA	18.7.66	1		Talence	5 Sep 92
10.43w/2.1	8.08/1.8	16.69	2.07	48.51	13.98/-0.5	48.56	5.00	62.58	4:42.10
8847	WR	Daley	Thompson	GBR	30.7.58	1	OG	Los Angeles	9 Aug 84
10.44/-1.0	8.01/0.4	15.72	2.03	46.97	14.33/-1.1	46.56	5.00	65.24	4:35.00
8844w			O'Brien			1	TAC	New York	13 Jun 91
10.23	7.96	16.06	2.08	47.70	13.95W/4.2	48.08	5.10	57.40	4:45.54
8837			Dvorák			1	WCh	Athína	6 Aug 97
10.60/0.8	7.64/-0.7	16.32	2.00	47.56	13.61/0.8	45.16	5.00	70.34	4:35.40
8832	WR	Jürgen	Hingsen	FRG	25.1.58	1	OT	Mannheim	9 Jun 84
10.70w/2.9	7.76/	16.42	2.07	48.05	14.07/0.2	49.36	4.90	59.86	4:19.75
8825	WR		Hingsen			1		Bernhausen	5 Jun 83
10.92/0.0	7.74	15.94	2.15	47.89	14.10	46.80	4.70	67.26	4:19.74
8824			O'Brien			1	OG	Atlanta	1 Aug 96
10.50/0.7	7.57/1.4	15.66	2.07	46.82	13.87/0.3	48.78	5.00	66.90	4:45.89
8817			O'Brien			1	WCh	Stuttgart	20 Aug 93
10.57/0.9	7.99/0.4	15.41	2.03	47.46	14.08/0.0	47.92	5.20	62.56	4:40.08
8815		Erki	Nool	EST	25.6.70	2	WCh	Edmonton	7 Aug 01
10.60/1.5	7.63/2.0	14.90	2.03	46.23	14.40/0.0	43.40	5.40	67.01	4:29.58
8812			O'Brien			1	WCh	Tokyo	30 Aug 91
10.41/-1.6	7.90/0.8	16.24	1.91	46.53	13.94/-1.2	47.20	5.20	60.66	4:37.50
8811			Thompson			1	EC	Stuttgart	28 Aug 86
10.26/2.0	7.72/1.0	15.73	2.00	47.02	14.04/-0.3	43.38	5.10	62.78	4:26.16
8792		Uwe	Freimuth	GDR	10.9.61	1	OD	Potsdam	21 Jul 84
11.06/	7.79/	16.30	2.03	48.43	14.66/	46.58	5.15	72.42	4:25.19
8774	WR		Thompson			1	EC	Athína	8 Sep 82
10.51/0.3	7.80/0.8	15.44	2.03	47.11	14.39/0.9	45.48	5.00	63.56	4:23.71
8762		Siegfried	Wentz	FRG	7.3.60	2		Bernhausen	5 Jun 83
10.89	7.49/	15.35	2.09	47.38	14.00	46.90	4.80	70.68	4:24.90
8757			Sebrle			2		Götzis	4 Jun 00
10.64/1.3	7.88/1.6	15.19	2.15	49.05	13.99/-1.0	47.21	4.75	67.23	4:35.06
8755			O'Brien			1	GWG	Uniondale, NY	20 Jul 98
10.71/-2.3	7.78w/2.2	15.67	2.11	48.04	13.67/0.4	48.87	5.20	66.31	5:08.77
8744			Dvorák			1	WCh	Sevilla	25 Aug 99
10.60/0.1	7.98/0.1	16.49	2.00	48.42	13.75/0.7	46.26	4.60	70.11	4:39.87
8742			Nool			3		Götzis	4 Jun 00
10.69/1.3	7.78/1.8	14.14	1.97	47.18	14.37/-0.1	44.16	5.55	69.10	4:35.59
8741	WR		Hingsen			1	NC	Ulm	15 Aug 82
10.74w	7.85	16.00	2.15	47.65	14.64	44.92	4.60	63.10	4:15.13
8738			Dvorák			1		Götzis	30 May 99
10.71/-1.2	7.77/-0.9	16.43	2.00	48.21	13.85/-0.9	46.54	4.80	68.66	4:33.99
8735		Eduard	Hämäläinen	FIN/BLR	21.1.69	1		Götzis	29 May 94
10.50w/2.1	7.26/1.0	16.05	2.11	47.63	13.82/-3.0	49.70	4.90	60.32	4:35.09
8733			Dvorák			1	Deca	Talence	30 Jul 00
10.75/-1.2	7.58/2.0	16.14	1.95	48.07	13.93/0.8	49.22	4.90	69.37	4:30.83

Mark Wind	Name		Nat	Born	Pos	Meet	Venue		Date
8730 WR		Thompson			1		Götzis		23 May 82
10.50w/2.3	7.95/1.8	15.31	2.08	46.86	14.31/-0.8	44.34	4.90	60.52	4:30.55
8730		Hingsen			2	EC	Stuttgart		28 Aug 86
10.87w/2.5	7.89w/2.8	16.46	2.12	48.79	14.52/-0.3	48.42	4.60	64.38	4:21.61
8730		Hämäläinen			2	WCh	Athína		6 Aug 97
10.81/0.8	7.56/0.9	15.71	1.97	46.71	13.74/0.8	50.50	5.20	59.82	4:37.10
8727w/8705	Dave	Johnson	USA	7.4.63	1		Azusa		24 Apr 92
10.96/0.4	7.52W/4.5 (7.43)	14.61	2.04	48.19	14.17/0.3	49.88	5.28	66.96	4:29.38
(30/10)									
8709	Aleksandr	Apaychev	UKR	6.5.61	1	vGDR	Neubrandenburg		3 Jun 84
10.96/	7.57/	16.00	1.97	48.72	13.93/	48.00	4.90	72.24	4:26.51
8706	Frank	Busemann	GER	26.2.75	2	OG	Atlanta		1 Aug 96
10.60/0.7	8.07/0.8	13.60	2.04	48.34	13.47/0.3	45.04	4.80	66.86	4:31.41
8698	Grigoriy	Degtyaryov	RUS	16.8.58	1	NC	Kiyev		22 Jun 84
10.87/0.7	7.42/0.1	16.03	2.10	49.75	14.53/0.3	51.20	4.90	67.08	4:23.09
8694	Chris	Huffins	USA	15.4.70	1	NC	New Orleans		20 Jun 98
10.31w/3.5	7.76w/2.5	15.43	2.18	49.02	14.02/1.0	53.22	4.60	61.59	4:59.43
8680	Torsten	Voss	GDR	24.3.63	1	WCh	Roma		4 Sep 87
10.69/-0.3	7.88/1.2	14.98	2.10	47.96	14.13/0.1	43.96	5.10	58.02	4:25.93
8667 WR	Guido	Kratschmer	FRG	10.1.53	1		Bernhausen		14 Jun 80
10.58w/2.4	7.80/	15.47	2.00	48.04	13.92/	45.52	4.60	66.50	4:24.15
8644	Steve	Fritz	USA	1.11.67	4	OG	Atlanta		1 Aug 96
10.90/0.8	7.77/0.9	15.31	2.04	50.13	13.97/0.3	49.84	5.10	65.70	4:38.26
8634 WR	Bruce	Jenner	USA	28.10.49	1	OG	Montreal		30 Jul 76
10.94/0.0	7.22/0.0	15.35	2.03	47.51	14.84/0.0	50.04	4.80	68.52	4:12.61
8627	Robert	Zmelík	CZE	18.4.69	1		Götzis		31 May 92
10.62w/2.1	8.02/0.2	13.93	2.05	48.73	13.84/1.2	44.44	4.90	61.26	4:24.83
8626	Michael	Smith	CAN	16.9.67	1		Götzis		26 May 96
11.23/-0.6	7.72/0.6	16.94	1.97	48.69	14.77/-2.4	52.90	4.90	71.22	4:41.95
(20)									
8603	Dean	Macey	GBR	12.12.77	3	WCh	Edmonton		7 Aug 01
10.72/-0.7	7.59/0.4	15.41	2.15	46.21	14.34/0.0	46.96	4.70	54.61	4:29.05
8583w	Jón Arnar	Magnússon	ISL	28.7.69	1	ECp-2	Reykjavik		5 Jul 98
10.68/2.0	7.63/2.0	15.57	2.07	47.78	14.33W/5.2	44.53	5.00	64.16	4:41.60
8574	Christian	Plaziat	FRA	28.10.63	1	EC	Split		29 Aug 90
10.72/-0.6	7.77/1.1	14.19	2.10	47.10	13.98/0.7	44.36	5.00	54.72	4:27.83
8574	Aleksandr	Yurkov	UKR	21.7.75	4		Götzis		4 Jun 00
10.69/0.9	7.93/1.8	15.26	2.03	49.74	14.56/-0.9	47.85	5.15	58.92	4:32.49
8571	Lev	Lobodin	RUS	1.4.69	3	EC	Budapest		20 Aug 98
10.66w/2.2	7.42/0.2	15.67	2.03	48.65	13.97/0.9	46.55	5.20	56.55	4:30.27
8566	Sebastian	Chmara	POL	21.11.71	1		Alhama de Murcia		17 May 98
10.97w/2.9	7.56/1.2	16.03	2.10	48.27	14.32/1.8	44.39	5.20	57.25	4:29.66
8554	Attila	Zsivoczky	HUN	29.4.77	5		Götzis		4 Jun 00
10.64w/2.1	7.24/-1.0	15.72	2.18	48.13	14.87/-0.9	45.64	4.65	63.57	4:23.13
8548	Paul	Meier	GER	27.7.71	3	WCh	Stuttgart		20 Aug 93
10.57/0.9	7.57/1.1	15.45	2.15	47.73	14.63/0.0	45.72	4.60	61.22	4:32.05
8547	Igor	Sobolevskiy	UKR	4.5.62	2	NC	Kiyev		22 Jun 84
10.64/0.7	7.71/0.2	15.93	2.01	48.24	14.82/0.3	50.54	4.40	67.40	4:32.84
8534	Siegfried	Stark	GDR	12.6.55	1		Halle		4 May 80
11.10w	7.64	15.81	2.03	49.53	14.86w	47.20	5.00	68.70	4:27.7
(30)									
8534w/8478	Antonio	Peñalver	ESP	1.12.68	1		Alhama		24 May 92
10.76w/3.9	7.42W/6.2 (7.19w/4.0)	16.50	2.12	49.50	14.32/0.8	47.38	5.00	59.32	4:39.94
8526	Francisco Javier	Benet	ESP	25.3.68	2		Alhama de Murcia		17 May 98
10.72w/2.9	7.45/-1.2	14.57	1.92	48.10	13.83/1.8	46.12	5.00	65.37	4:26.81
8524	Sébastien	Levicq	FRA	25.6.71	4	WCh	Sevilla		25 Aug 99
11.05/0.2	7.52/-0.4	14.22	2.00	50.13	14.48/0.6	44.65	5.50	69.01	4:26.81
8519	Yuriy	Kutsenko	RUS	5.3.52	3	NC	Kiyev		22 Jun 84
11.07/0.5	7.54/-0.1	15.11	2.13	49.07	14.94/0.3	50.38	4.60	61.70	4:12.68
8506	Valter	Külvet	EST	19.2.64	1		Stayki		3 Jul 88
11.05/-1.4	7.35/0.4	15.78	2.00	48.08	14.55/-0.8	52.04	4.60	61.72	4:15.93
8500	Christian	Schenk	GER	9.2.65	4	WCh	Stuttgart		20 Aug 93
11.22/-0.9	7.63/0.0	15.72	2.15	48.78	15.29/0.0	46.94	4.80	65.32	4:24.44
8491	Aleksandr	Nevskiy	UKR	21.2.58	2		Götzis		20 May 84
10.97/-1.6	7.24/1.2	15.04	2.08	48.44	14.67/1.0	46.06	4.70	69.56	4:19.62
8490	Jagan	Hames	AUS	31.10.75	1	CG	Kuala Lumpur		18 Sep 98
10.77/0.0	7.64/0.8	14.73	2.19	49.67	14.07/0.4	46.40	5.00	64.67	5:02.68
8485	Konstantin	Akhapkin	RUS	19.1.56	1	NC	Moskva		2 Aug 82
11.10/0.2	7.72/0.2	15.25	2.02	49.14	14.38/1.8	45.68	4.90	62.42	4:19.60

Mark Wind	Name		Nat	Born	Pos	Meet	Venue		Date
8485	Stefan	Schmid	GER	6.5.70	1	OT	Ratingen		23 Jul 00
10.82/0.0	7.59/-0.6	14.14	2.01	48.99	14.20/-1.6	44.24	5.06	67.63	4:31.76
(40)									
8467	Tom	Pappas	USA	6.9.76	1	NC	Sacramento		21 Jul 00
10.70/1.1	7.41/-1.4	15.32	2.14	48.91	14.27/-0.4	45.81	5.10	63.45	4:59.74
8466 WR	Nikolay	Avilov	UKR	6.8.48	1	OG	München		8 Sep 72
11.00/	7.68/	14.36	2.12	48.45	14.31/	46.98	4.55	61.66	4:22.82
8462w	Kip	Janvrin	USA	8.7.65	1	vGER	Edwardsville		18 Jul 96
10.61W/4.1	7.34w/3.1	14.64	1.96	48.20	14.48W/5.7	45.84	5.00	61.82	4:20.12
8461	Mike	Maczey	GER	28.9.72	7		Götzis		4 Jun 00
10.99/0.9	7.59/0.3	14.75	2.06	49.83	14.16/-1.0	44.56	5.15	62.27	4:29.93
8453	Alain	Blondel	FRA	7.12.62	1	EC	Helsinki		13 Aug 94
11.12/0.6	7.50w/3.2	13.78	1.99	48.91	14.18/0.9	45.08	5.40	60.64	4:20.48
8447	Robert	de Wit	NED	7.8.62	1	NC	Eindhoven		22 May 88
11.07/0.5	6.98/0.2	15.88	2.04	48.80	14.32/0.7	46.20	5.00	63.94	4:20.98
8445	Ramil	Ganiyev	UZB	23.9.68	5	WCh	Athína		6 Aug 97
10.94/0.2	7.58/0.7	14.76	2.06	48.34	14.34/-0.1	46.04	5.30	55.14	4:36.78
8437	Richardas	Malakhovskis	LIT	28.4.65	2		Stayki		3 Jul 88
10.93/0.6	7.04/0.6	14.94	2.09	47.77	14.34/-0.9	44.04	4.90	59.58	4:13.67
8436	Dezsö	Szabó	HUN	4.9.67	2	EC	Split		29 Aug 90
11.06/-0.2	7.49/1.1	13.65	1.98	47.17	14.67/0.0	40.78	5.30	61.94	4:11.07
8417	Sergey	Zhelanov	RUS	14.6.57	4	NC	Kiyev		22 Jun 84
11.04/0.5	7.50/-0.0	14.31	2.13	48.94	14.40/-0.1	43.44	5.00	65.90	4:37.24
(50)	100th man 8250, 200th man 8079								

4 x 100 METRES RELAY

Mark	Nat	Team	Pos	Meet	Venue	Date
37.40 WR	USA	Marsh, Burrell, Mitchell, C Lewis	1	OG	Barcelona	8 Aug 92
37.40 WR	USA	Drummond, Cason, D Mitchell, L Burrell	1s1	WCh	Stuttgart	21 Aug 93
37.48	USA	Drummond, Cason, D Mitchell, L Burrell	1	WCh	Stuttgart	22 Aug 93
37.50 WR	USA	Cason, Burrell, Mitchell, C Lewis	1	WCh	Tokyo	1 Sep 91
37.59	USA	Drummond, Montgomery, B Lewis, Greene	1	WCh	Sevilla	29 Aug 99
37.61	USA	Drummond, Williams, B Lewis, Greene	1	OG	Sydney	30 Sep 00
37.65	USA	Drummond, Williams, C Johnson, Greene	1	ISTAF	Berlin	1 Sep 00
37.67 WR	USA	Marsh, Burrell, Mitchell, C Lewis	1	WK	Zürich	7 Aug 91
37.69	CAN	Esmie 10.47, Gilbert 9.02, Surin 9.25, Bailey 8.95	1	OG	Atlanta	3 Aug 96
37.73	GBR	Gardener, Campbell, Devonish, Chambers	2	WCh	Sevilla	29 Aug 99
37.75	USA	Cason, Burrell, Mitchell, Marsh	1h2	WCh	Tokyo	31 Aug 91
37.77	GBR	Jackson, Jarrett, Regis, Christie	2	WCh	Stuttgart	22 Aug 93
37.79 WR	FRA	Morinière, Sangouma, Trouabal, Marie-Rose	1	EC	Split	1 Sep 90
37.79 WR	Santa Monica TC/USA	Marsh, Burrell, Heard, C Lewis	1	Herc	Monaco	3 Aug 91
37.79	USA - Santa Monica TC	Marsh, Burrell, Heard, C Lewis	1	MSR	Walnut	17 Apr 94
37.82	USA	Drummond, Williams, B.Lewis, Greene	1s1	OG	Sydney	29 Sep 00
37.83 WR	USA	Graddy, R Brown, C Smith, C Lewis	1	OG	Los Angeles	11 Aug 84
37.83	CAN	Esmie, Gilbert, Surin, Mahorn	3	WCh	Stuttgart	22 Aug 93
37.86 WR	USA	E King, Gault, C Smith, C Lewis	1	WCh	Helsinki	10 Aug 83
37.86	CAN	Esmie, Gilbert, Surin, Bailey	1	WCh	Athína	10 Aug 97
37.87	FRA	Morinière, Sangouma, Trouabal, Marie-Rose	2	WCh	Tokyo	1 Sep 91
37.88	USA (HSI)	Drummond, B Williams, C.Johnson, Greene	1	TexR	Austin	7 Apr 01
37.89	Santa Monica TC (USA)	Marsh, Burrell, Heard, C Lewis	1	TexR	Austin	9 Apr 94
37.90	USA	McRae, L McNeill, Glance, C Lewis	1	WCh	Roma	6 Sep 87
37.90	USA	Drummond, Harden, Mitchell, Greene	1	GWG	Uniondale, NY.	22 Jul 98
37.90	BRA	de Lima, Ribeiro, A da Silva, Cl da Silva	2	OG	Sydney	30 Sep 00
37.91	NGR	Asonze, Obikwelu, Effiong, Aliu	3	WCh	Sevilla	29 Aug 99
37.93	Santa Monica TC/USA	Witherspoon, Burrell, Heard, C Lewis	1		Barcelona	16 Jul 90
37.94	NGR	O Ezinwa, Adeniken, Obikwelu, D Ezinwa	1s2	WCh	Athína	9 Aug 97
37.95	USA	Drummond, Williams, A Johnson, Greene	1	GP II	Gateshead	28 Aug 00
	(30 by 6 nations)	Further bests by nations:				
38.00	CUB	Simón, Lamela, Isasi, Aguilera	3	OG	Barcelona	8 Aug 92
38.02	URS	Yevgenyev, Bryzgin, Muravyov, Krylov	2	WCh	Roma	6 Sep 87
38.12	GHA	Duah, Nkansah, Zakari, Tuffour	1s1	WCh	Athína	9 Aug 97
38.17	AUS	Henderson, Jackson, Brimacombe, Marsh	1s2	WCh	Göteborg	12 Aug 95
	(10)					
38.20	JAM	L Frater, D Thomas, C Williams, Bredwood	4	OG	Sydney	30 Sep 00
38.29	GDR	Schröder, Kübeck, Prenzler, Emmelmann	2	vUSA	Karl-Marx-Stadt	9 Jul 82
38.31	JPN	Inoue, K Ito, Tsuchie, Asahara	5s2	WCh	Athína	9 Aug 97
38.33	POL	Zwolinski, Licznerski, Dunecki, Woronin	2	OG	Moskva	1 Aug 80
38.37	ITA	Tilli, Simionato, Pavoni, Mennea	2	WCh	Helsinki	10 Aug 83
38.46	URS/RUS	Zharov, Krylov, Fatun, Goremykin	4	EC	Split	1 Sep 90

Mark	Wind	Name	Nat	Born	Pos	Meet	Venue	Date
38.47		RSA Nagel, du Plessis, Newton, Quinn			2	WCh	Edmonton	12 Aug 01
38.53		UKR Rurak, Osovich, Kramarenko, Dologodin			1	ECp	Madrid	1 Jun 96
38.54		FRG Heer, Haas, Klein, Schweisfurth			1	R-W	Koblenz	28 Aug 88
38.58		TRI Burns, Boldon, Harper, Brown			3	WCh	Edmonton	12 Aug 01
38.60		ESP Feo, José, Mayoral, Berlanga			3s1	WCh	Athína	9 Aug 97
		(20, with RUS and UKR for USSR)						
38.60		CIV Meité, Douhou, Sonan, N'Dri			3s1	WCh	Edmonton	12 Aug 01
38.61		GRE Séggos, Alexópoulos, Panayiotópoulos, Hoídis			2	ECp	Paris (C)	19 Jun 99
38.63		SWE Karlsson, Mårtensson, Hedner, Strenius			3s2	OG	Atlanta	2 Aug 96
38.67		HUN Karaffa, Nagy, Tatár, Kovács			1	BGP	Budapest	11 Aug 86
38.80		THA Natenee, Sophanich, Janthana, Suwonprateep			1	AsiC	Jakarta	31 Aug 00
38.81		CHN Li Xiaoping, Lin Wei, Huang Danwei, Chen Wenzhong			2h3	WCh	Göteborg	12 Aug 95
38.81		ISR Jaar, Jablonka, Kafri, Porkhomovskiy			3h2	WCh	Sevilla	28 Aug 99
38.82		TCH/CZE Matousek, Demec, Kynos, Bohman			4	OG	München	10 Sep 72
38.91		SLE Lisk, Ganda, Jos. Thomas, Turay			5s1	OG	Atlanta	2 Aug 96
38.96		NOR Ramirez, Ertzgaard, Sivle, Moen			2	ECp	München	21 Jun 97
Multi-nation teams								
37.82		Drummond/USA, Jarrett/GBR, Regis/GBR, Mitchell/USA			2	MSR	Walnut	17 Apr 94
37.93		HSI (USA) Drummond, B Williams, Bolden TRI, Greene			1	BrGP	London (CP)	22 Jul 01

4 x 200 METRES RELAY

Mark		Team	Pos	Meet	Venue	Date
1:18.68	WR	USA - Santa Monica TC Marsh, Burrell, Heard, Lewis	1	MSR	Walnut	17 Apr 94
1:19.10		World All-Stars Drummond/USA, Mitchell/USA, Bridgewater/USA, Regis/GBR	2	MSR	Walnut	17 Apr 94
1:19.11	WR	Santa Monica TC/USA M.Marsh, L Burrell, Heard, C Lewis	1	Penn	Philadelphia	25 Apr 92
1:19.38	WR	Santa Monica TC/USA Everett, Burrell, Heard, C Lewis	1	R-W	Koblenz	23 Aug 89
1:19.39		USA Blue Drummond, Crawford, B Williams, Greene	1	PennR	Philadelphia	28 Apr 01
1:19.45		Santa Monica TC/USA DeLoach, Burrell, C.Lewis, Heard	1	Penn	Philadelphia	27 Apr 91
1:19.47		Nike Int./USA Brokenburr, A Harrison, Greene, M Johnson	1	Penn	Philadelphia	24 Apr 99
Best non-US nations						
1:20.79		Central Arizona DC/Jamaica Bucknor, Campbell, O'Conner, Davis)	1		Walnut	24 Apr 88
1:21.10		ITA Tilli, Simionato, Bongiorno, Mennea	1		Cagliari	29 Sep 83
1:21.22		POL Tulin, Balcerzak, Pilarczyk, Urbas	2		Gdansk	14 Jul 01
1:21.29		GBR Adam, Mafe, Christie, Regis	1		Birmingham	23 Jun 89
1:21.32		UKR Vanyaykin, Tverdokhleb, Streltsov, Dolgodin	1	EurR	Portsmouth	5 Jun 93

4 x 400 METRES RELAY

Mark		Team	Pos	Meet	Venue	Date
2:54.20	WR	USA Young 44.3, Pettigrew 43.2, Washington 43.5, M Johnson 43.2	1	GWG	Uniondale, NY	22 Jul 98
2:54.29	WR	USA Valmon 44.43, Watts 43.59, Reynolds 43.23, Johnson 42.94	1	WCh	Stuttgart	22 Aug 93
2:55.74	WR	USA Valmon 44.6, Watts 43.00, M.Johnson 44.73, S Lewis 43.41	1	OG	Barcelona	8 Aug 92
2:55.99		USA L Smith 44.62, A Harrison 43.84, Mills 43.66, Maybank 43.87	1	OG	Atlanta	3 Aug 96
2:56.16A	WR	USA Matthews 45.0, Freeman 43.2, James 43.9, Evans 44.1	1	OG	Ciu. México	20 Oct 68
2:56.16	WR	USA Everett 44.0, S Lewis 43.6, Robinzine 44.74, Reynolds 43.94	1	OG	Seoul	1 Oct 88
2:56.35		USA A Harrison 44.36, Pettigrew 44.17, C Harrison 43.53, Johnson 44.29	1	OG	Sydney	30 Sep 00
2:56.45		USA J Davis 45.2, Pettigrew 43.9, Taylor 43.92, M Johnson 43.49	1	WCh	Sevilla	29 Aug 99
2:56.47		USA Young 44.6, Pettigrew 43.1, Jones 44.80, Washington 44.80	1	WCh	Athína	10 Aug 97
2:56.60		GBR I Thomas 44.92, Baulch 44.19, Richardson 43.62, Black 43.87	2	OG	Atlanta	3 Aug 96
2:56.60		USA Red Taylor 45.0, Pettigrew 44.2, Washington 43.7, Johnson 43.7	1	PennR	Philadelphia	29 Apr 00
2:56.65		GBR Thomas 44.8, Black 44.2, Baulch 44.08, Richardson 43.57	2	WCh	Athína	10 Aug 97
2:56.75		JAM McDonald 44.5, Haughton 44.4, McFarlane 44.37, Clarke 43.51	3	WCh	Athína	10 Aug 97
2:57.29		USA Everett 45.1, Haley 44.0, McKay 44.20, Reynolds 44.00	1	WCh	Roma	6 Sep 87
2:57.32		USA Ramsey 44.9, Mills 44.6, Reynolds 43.74, Johnson 44.11	1	WCh	Göteborg	13 Aug 95
2:57.53		GBR Black 44.7, Redmond 44.0, Regis 44.22, Akabusi 44.59	1	WCh	Tokyo	1 Sep 91
2:57.54		USA Byrd 45.9, Pettigrew 43.9, Brew 44.03, Taylor 43.71	1	WCh	Edmonton	12 Aug 01
2:57.57		USA Valmon 44.9, Watts 43.4, D.Everett 44.31, Pettigrew 44.93	2	WCh	Tokyo	1 Sep 91
2:57.87		USA L Smith 44.59, Rouser 44.33, Mills 44.32, Maybank 44.63	1s2	OG	Atlanta	2 Aug 96
2:57.91		USA Nix 45.59, Armstead 43.97, Babers 43.75, McKay 44.60	1	OG	Los Angeles	11 Aug 84
2:57.97		JAM McDonald , Haughton , McFarlane, D Clarke	1	PAm	Winnipeg	30 Jul 99
2:58.00		POL Rysiukiewicz 45.6, Czubak 44.2, Haczek 44.0, Mackowiak 44.2	2	GWG	Uniondale, NY	22 Jul 98
2:58.19		BAH Moncur 45.1, C Brown 44.5, McIntosh 44.42, Munnings 44.13	2	WCh	Edmonton	12 Aug 01
2:58.22		GBR Sanders 45.85, Akabusi 44.48, Regis 43.93, Black 43.96	1	EC	Split	1 Sep 90
2:58.23		USA Ramsey 44.6, Mills 44.0, Lyles 44.41, Hall 45.22	1h1	WCh	Göteborg	12 Aug 95
2:58.29		JAM McDonald 45.1, D Clarke 43.8, Blake 44.80, McFarlane 44.60	2h1	WCh	Göteborg	12 Aug 95
2:58.33		JAM Haughton, M McDonald, Blackwood, D Clarke	3	GWG	Uniondale, NY	22 Jul 98
2:58.39		JAM Simpson 45.71, C Williams 44.50, Haughton 43.88, McFarlane 44.30	3	WCh	Edmonton	12 Aug 01
2:58.42		JAM McDonald 44.54, Blake 44.75, Haughton 44.60, Martin 44.53	2s2	OG	Atlanta	2 Aug 96

Mark	Wind	Name	Nat	Born	Pos	Meet	Venue	Date
2:58.56	BRA	Parrela, da Silva, dos Santos, de Araújo			2	PAm	Winnipeg	30 Jul 99
	(30/6)	Further bests by nations:						
2:58.68	NGR	Chukwu 45.18, Monye 44.49, Bada 44.70, Udo-Obong 44.31			2	OG	Sydney	30 Sep 00
2:59.13	CUB	Martínez 45.6, Herrera 44.38, Tellez 44.81, Hernández 44.34			1h2	OG	Barcelona	7 Aug 92
2:59.63	KEN	D Kitur 45.4, S Kitur 45.13, Kipkemboi 44.76, Kemboi 44.34			3h2	OG	Barcelona	7 Aug 92
2:59.70	AUS	Frayne 45.38, Clark 43.86, Minihan 45.07, Mitchell 45.39			4	OG	Los Angeles	11 Aug 84
	(10)							
2:59.86	GDR	Möller 45.8, Schersing 44.8, Carlowitz 45.3, Schönlebe 44.1			1	vURS	Erfurt	23 Jun 85
2:59.95	YUG	Jovkovic, Djurovic, Macev, Brankovic 44.3			2h3	WCh	Tokyo	31 Aug 91
2:59.96	FRG	Dobeleit 45.7, Henrich 44.3, Itt 45.12, Schmid 44.93			4	WCh	Roma	6 Sep 87
3:00.09	FRA	Rapnouil 45.5, Hilaire 45.5, Farraudière 44.86, Diagana 44.19			4	WCh	Stuttgart	22 Aug 93
3:00.16	URS	Lovachov, Lomtyev, Kurochkin, Markin 43.9			1	Drz	Moskva	18 Aug 84
3:00.20	RSA	van Oudtshoorn 46.5, Mokganyetsi 44.5, A Botha 45.43, Malherbe 43.78			4	WCh	Sevilla	29 Aug 99
3:00.44	RUS	Kliger 45.72, Kosov 45.09, Vdovin 44.73, Golovastov 44.90			5	WCh	Stuttgart	22 Aug 93
3:00.64	SEN	Diarra 46.53, Dia 44.94, Ndiaye 44.70, Faye 44.47			4	OG	Atlanta	3 Aug 96
3:00.76	JPN	Karube 45.88, Ito 44.86, Osakada 45.08, Omori 44.94			5	OG	Atlanta	3 Aug 96
3:00.79	ZIM	Chiwira 46.2, Mukomana 44.6, Ngidhi 45.79, Harnden 44.20			2h3	WCh	Athína	9 Aug 97
3:01.05	TRI	Delice, A Daniel, De Silva, Morris			1h1	OG	Barcelona	7 Aug 92
	(20 inc. RUS/URS)							
3:01.12	FIN	Lönnqvist 46.7, Salin 45.1, Karttunen 44.8, Kukkoaho 44.5			6	OG	München	10 Sep 72
3:01.37	ITA	Bongiorni 46.2, Zuliani 45.0, Petrella 45.3, Ribaud 44.9			4	EC	Stuttgart	31 Aug 86
3:01.42	ESP	I Rodríguez 46.0, Canal 44.1, Andrés 45.88, Reina 45.48			4h1	WCh	Edmonton	11 Aug 01
3:01.60	BAR	Louis 46.67, Peltier 44.97, Edwards 45.04, Forde 44.92			6	OG	Los Angeles	11 Aug 84
3:01.61	BUL	Georgiev 45.9, Stankulov 46.0, Raykov 45.07, Ivanov 44.66			2h1	WCh	Stuttgart	21 Aug 93
3:02.09	UGA	Govile 46.72, Kyeswa 44.60, Rwamu 46.40, Okot 44.37			7	OG	Los Angeles	11 Aug 84
3:02.11	MAR	Kasbane, Dahane, Belcaid, Lahlou 44.5			1h2	WCh	Tokyo	31 Aug 91
3:02.35	UKR	Kaybash 46.8, Tverdostup 44.8, Rybalka 45.73, Zyukov 45.01			4h3	WCh	Edmonton	11 Aug 01
3:02.46	SUI	Clerc 46.55, Rusterholz 45.28, Rohr 45.72, Schelbert 44.91			5h3	WCh	Sevilla	28 Aug 99
3:02.57	SWE	Carlgren 46.0, Faager 45.5, Öhman 45.3, Rönner 45.8			7	OG	München	10 Sep 72
Multi-nation team								
2:58.52	Adidas	McDonaldJAM, Pettigrew, Campbell, Young			1	PennR	Philadelphia	24 Apr 99

4 x 800 METRES RELAY

Mark	Team	Name	Pos	Meet	Venue	Date
7:03.89 WR	GBR	Elliott 1:49.14, Cook 1:46.20, Cram 1:44.54, Coe 1:44.01	1		London (CP)	30 Aug 82
7:04.70	RSA	G van Oudtshoorn 1:46.9, Sepeng 1:45.2, J Kotze 1:48.3, J, Botha 1:44.3	1		Stuttgart	6 Jun 99
7:04.89	KEN/ex-St Patrick's School	D Kiptoo 1:46.4, Tengelei 1:48.2, W Chirchir 1:45.7, Kimutai 1:44.6	2		Stuttgart	6 Jun 99
7:06.5	Santa Monica TC/USA)	J Robinson 1:49.8, Mack 1:46.7, E Jones 1:45.2, Gray 1:44.8	1	MSR	Walnut	26 Apr 86
7:07.40	URS	Masunov, Kostetskiy, Matvetev, Kalinkin	1		Moskva	5 Aug 84

4 x 1500 METRES RELAY

Mark	Team	Name	Pos	Meet	Venue	Date
14:38.8 WR	FRG	Wessinghage 3:38.8, Hudak 3:40.2, Lederer 3:42.6, Fleschen 3:37.3	1		Köln	16 Aug 77
14:40.4 WR	NZL	Polhill 3:42.9, Walker 3:40.4, Dixon 3:41.2, Quax 3:35.9	1		Oslo	22 Aug 73
14:45.63	URS	Kalutskiy, Yakovlev, Legeda, Lotarev	1		Leningrad	4 Aug 85
14:46.16	Larios, ESP	Jiménez 3:40.9, Pancorbo 3:41.2, A García 3:43.9, Viciosa 3:40.2	1		Madrid	5 Sep 97
14:46.3	USA	Aldridge, Clifford, Harbour, Duits	1	Int	Bourges	23 Jun 79
14:48.2	FRA	Begouin, Lequement, Philippe, Dien	2	Int	Bourges	23 Jun 79

4 x 1 MILE RELAY

Mark	Team	Name	Pos	Venue	Date
15:49.08	IRL	Coghlan 4:00.2, O'Sullivan 3:55.3, O'Mara 3:56.6, Flynn 3:56.98	1	Dublin	17 Aug 85

10,000 METRES TRACK WALK

Mark	First name	Name	Nat	Born	Pos	Meet	Venue	Date
38:02.60	Jozef	Pribilinec	SVK	6.7.60	1		Banská Bystrica	30 Aug 85
38:06.6	David	Smith	AUS	24.7.55	1		Sydney	25 Sep 86
38:12.13	Ronald	Weigel	GDR	8.8.59	1		Potsdam	10 May 86
38:18.0+	Valdas	Kazlauskas	LTU	23.2.58	1		Moskva	18 Sep 83
38:24 0+	Bernardo	Segura	MEX	11.2.70	1	SGP	Fana	7 May 94
38:24.31	Hatem	Ghoula	TUN	7.6.73	1		Tunis	30 May 98
38:26.4	Daniel	García	MEX	28.10.71	1		Sdr Omme	17 May 97
38:37.6+	Jefferson	Pérez	ECU	1.7.74	1	in 20k	Fana	9 May 98
38:38.0	Walter	Arena	ITA	30.5.64	1		Catania	13 Apr 90
38:40.18	Giovanni	De Benedictis	ITA	8.1.68	1	NC	Cesenatico	1 Jul 95
Indoors								
38:31.4	Werner	Heyer	GDR	14.11.56	1		Berlin	12 Jan 80

20 KILOMETRES WALK

Mark Wind	Name		Nat	Born	Pos	Meet	Venue	Date
1:17:25.6t	Bernardo	Segura	MEX	11.2.70	1	SGP	Fana	7 May 94
1:17:46	Roman	Rasskazov	RUS	28.4.79	1	NC	Moskva	19 May 00
1:17:46	Julio	Martínez	GUA	27.9.73	1		Eisenhüttenstadt	8 May 99
1:17:56	Alejandro	López	MEX	9.2.75	2		Eisenhüttenstadt	8 May 99
1:18:04 WR		Bo Lingtang	CHN	12.8.70	1	NC	Beijing	7 Apr 94
1:18:05	Dmitriy	Yesipchuk	RUS	17.11.74	1	NC-w	Adler	4 Mar 01
1:18:06	Viktor	Burayev	RUS	23.2.82	2	NC-w	Adler	4 Mar 01
1:18:07		Rasskazov			1	NC-w	Adler	20 Feb 00
1:18:12	Artur	Meleshkevich	BLR	11.4.75	1		Brest	10 Mar 01
1:18:13 WR	Pavol	Blazek	SVK	9.7.58	1		Hildesheim	16 Sep 90
1:18:14	Mikhail	Khmelnitskiy (10)	BLR	24.7.69	1	NC	Soligorsk	13 May 00
1:18:14	Nathan	Deakes	AUS	17.8.77	1		Dublin	16 Jun 01
1:18:16	Vladimir	Andreyev	RUS	7.9.66	2	NC	Moskva	19 May 00
1:18:18	Yevgeniy	Misyulya	BLR	13.3.64	1		Eisenhüttenstadt	11 May 96
1:18:20 WR	Andrey	Perlov	RUS	12.12.61	1	NC	Moskva	26 May 90
1:18:20	Denis	Nizhegorodov	RUS	26.7.80	3	NC-w	Adler	4 Mar 01
1:18:22	Robert	Korzeniowski	POL	30.7.68	1		Hildesheim	9 Jul 00
1:18:23	Andrey	Makarov	BLR	2.1.71	2	NC	Soligorsk	13 May 00
1:18:24	Jefferson	Pérez	ECU	1.7.74	1	WCp	Podebrady	19 Apr 97
1:18:27	Daniel	García	MEX	28.10.71	2	WCp	Podebrady	19 Apr 97
1:18:29		Korzeniowski			1	ECp	Eisenhüttenstadt	17 Jun 00
1:18:30	Ilya	Markov (20)	RUS	19.6.72	3	WCp	Podebrady	19 Apr 97
1:18:32		Andreyev			1	NC-w	Adler	11 Feb 95
1:18:32		Li Zewen	CHN	5.12.73	4	WCp	Podebrady	19 Apr 97
1:18:35.2t	Stefan	Johansson	SWE	11.4.67	1	SGP	Fana	15 May 92
1:18:36	Mikhail	Shchennikov	RUS	24.12.67	1	NC	Sochi	20 Apr 96
1:18:37	Aleksandr	Pershin	RUS	4.9.68	2	NC	Moskva	26 May 90
1:18:37	Ruslan	Shafikov	RUS	27.6.75	1	NC-w23	Adler	11 Feb 95
1:18:37		Shchennikov			1		Eisenhüttenstadt	14 May 95
1:18:37		Shchennikov			2		Eisenhüttenstadt	11 May 96
	(30/25)							
1:18:40.0t WR	Ernesto	Canto	MEX	18.10.59	1	SGP	Fana	5 May 84
1:18:41	Igor	Kollár	SVK	26.6.65	3		Eisenhüttenstadt	11 May 96
1:18:42	Andreas	Erm	GER	12.3.76	2	ECp	Eisenhüttenstadt	17 Jun 00
1:18:46		Tan Mingjun	CHN	17.7.70	2	NC	Beijing	7 Apr 94
1:18:48	Rishat	Shafikov	RUS	23.1.70	2		Cheboksary	30 Aug 98
	(30)							
1:18:49 WR?	Daniel	Bautista	MEX	4.8.52	1	LT	Eschborn	29 Sep 79
1:18:51	Frants	Kostyukevich	BLR	4.4.63	3	NC	Moskva	26 May 90
1:18:54	Maurizio	Damilano	ITA	6.4.57	1	7N	La Coruña	6 Jun 92
1:18:56	Grigoriy	Kornev	RUS	14.3.61	4	NC	Moskva	26 May 90
1:18:56	Francisco	Fernández	ESP	5.3.77	3	ECp	Eisenhüttenstadt	17 Jun 00
1:19:00	Joel	Sánchez	MEX	15.9.66	3		Eisenhüttenstadt	8 May 99
1:19:02	Hatem	Ghoula	TUN	7.6.73	2		Eisenhüttenstadt	10 May 97
1:19:03	Noe	Hernández	MEX	15.3.78	2	OG	Sydney	22 Sep 00
1:19:12	Axel	Noack	GDR	23.9.61	1	vURS	Karl-Marx-Stadt	21 Jun 87
1:19:14	Vladimir	Stankin	RUS	2.1.74	4	NC-w	Adler	4 Mar 01
	(40)							
1:19:16		Chen Shaoguo	CHN	20.1.71	3	NC	Beijing	7 Apr 94
1:19:18	Jirí	Malysa	CZE	14.8.66	4	ECp	Eisenhüttenstadt	17 Jun 00
1:19:18.3t	Ronald	Weigel	GDR	8.8.59	1	SGP	Fana	26 May 90
1:19:19	Mikhail	Orlov	RUS	25.6.67	4	NC-w	Adler	11 Feb 95
1:19:22	David	Smith	AUS	24.7.55	1		Hobart	19 Jul 87
1:19:22.5t	Aleksey	Pershin	RUS	23.9.62	1	SGP	Fana	7 May 88
1:19:24	Carlos	Mercenário	MEX	3.5.67	1	LT	New York	3 May 87
1:19:24.1t	Walter	Arena	ITA	30.5.64	2	SGP	Fana	26 May 90
1:19:25	Valentí	Massana	ESP	5.7.70	2	7N	La Coruña	6 Jun 92
1:19:28	Ruslan	Alukayev	RUS	8.9.78	3		Cheboksary	30 Aug 98
	(50)	100th man 1:20:29, 200th man 1:21:48						

Probable short course:							
1:18:33	Mikhail Shchennikov	RUS	24.12.67	1	4-N	Livorno	10 Jul 93
1:19:08	Yuriy Kuko	BLR	23.1.68	2	4-N	Livorno	10 Jul 93

50 KILOMETRES WALK

Mark	Name		Nat	Born	Pos	Meet	Venue	Date
3:37:26 WR	Valeriy	Spitsyn	RUS	5.12.65	1	NC	Moskva	21 May 00
3:37:41 WR	Andrey	Perlov	RUS	12.12.61	1	NC	Leningrad	5 Aug 89
3:38:17 WR	Ronald	Weigel	GDR	8.8.59	1	IM	Potsdam	25 May 86
3:38:29	Vyacheslav	Ivanenko	RUS	3.3.61	1	OG	Seoul	30 Sep 88

Mark	Wind	Name		Nat	Born	Pos	Meet	Venue	Date
3:38:31	WR		Weigel			1		Berlin	20 Jul 84
3:38:43		Valentin	Massana	ESP	5.7.70	1	NC	Orense	20 Mar 94
3:38:56			Weigel			2	OG	Seoul	30 Sep 88
3:39:21		Vladimir	Potemin	RUS	15.1.80	2	NC	Moskva	21 May 00
3:39:22		Sergey	Korepanov	KAZ	9.5.64	1	WCp	Mézidon-Canon	2 May 99
3:39:34		Valentin	Kononen	FIN	7.3.69	1		Dudince	25 Mar 00
3:39:45		Hartwig	Gauder	GDR	10.11.54	3	OG	Seoul	30 Sep 88
3:39:47			Perlov			1		Leningrad	3 Aug 85
3:39:54		Jesús Angel	García (10)	ESP	17.10.69	1	WCp	Podebrady	20 Apr 97
3:40:02		Aleksandr	Potashov	BLR	12.3.62	1	NC	Moskva	27 May 90
3:40:07			Perlov			1		Kharkov	5 Sep 87
3:40:07		Andrey	Plotnikov	RUS	12.8.67	2	NC	Moskva	27 May 90
3:40:08		Tomasz	Lipiec	POL	10.5.71	2	WCp	Mézidon-Canon	2 May 99
3:40:12		Oleg	Ishutkin	RUS	22.7.75	2	WCp	Podebrady	20 Apr 97
3:40:13		Nikolay	Matyukhin	RUS	13.12.68	3	WCp	Mézidon-Canon	2 May 99
3:40:40			J A García			4	WCp	Mézidon-Canon	2 May 99
3:40:46	WR	José	Marin	ESP	21.1.50	1		Valencia	13 Mar 83
3:40:53			Gauder			1	WCh	Roma	5 Sep 87
3:40:54		German	Skurygin	RUS	15.9.63	5	WCp	Mézidon-Canon	2 May 99
3:40:55			Gauder			1	EC	Stuttgart	31 Aug 86
3:40:57.9t		Thierry	Toutain	FRA	14.2.62	1		Héricourt	29 Sep 96
3:40:58			Plotnikov			1	NC	Sochi	21 Apr 96
3:41:00			Potashov			4	OG	Seoul	30 Sep 88
3:41:07			Spitsyn			1	EC	Helsinki	13 Aug 94
3:41:09			Kononen			3	WCp	Podebrady	20 Apr 97
3:41:14			Plotnikov			1	NC	Izhevsk	16 May 98
3:41:20	WR	Raul	González	MEX	29.2.52	1		Podebrady	11 Jun 78
3:41:20			Zhao Yongsheng	CHN	16.4.70	1	WCp	Beijing	30 Apr 95
		(32/20)							
3:41:28.2t		René	Piller	FRA	23.4.65	1	SGP	Fana	7 May 94
3:41:33		Aleksey	Voyevodin	RUS	9.8.70	1		Naumburg	25 May 97
3:41:50		Robert	Korzeniowski	POL	30.7.68	1	NC	Ponte de Sôr	5 Mar 00
3:41:51		Venyamin	Nikolayev	RUS	7.10.58	2		Leningrad	3 Aug 85
3:41:56		Yevgeniy	Shmalyuk	RUS	14.1.76	6	WCp	Mézidon-Canon	2 May 99
3:42:00		Stanislav	Vezhel	BLR	11.10.58	3	NC	Moskva	27 May 90
3:42:03		Carlos	Mercenario	MEX	3.5.67	1	WCp	San José	2 Jun 91
3:42:04		Yevgeniy	Yevsyukov	RUS	2.1.50	3		Leningrad	3 Aug 85
3:42:20		Pavel	Szikora	SVK	26.3.52	1		Dudince	4 Apr 87
3:42:20		Viktor	Ginko	BLR	7.12.65	2		Palma	5 Mar 95
		(30)							
3:42:36		Reima	Salonen	FIN	19.11.55	1	NC	Vantaa	24 May 86
3:42:37		Valeriy	Suntsov	RUS	10.7.55	4		Leningrad	3 Aug 85
3:42:45		Miguel Angel	Rodríguez	MEX	15.1.67	6	WCp	Podebrady	20 Apr 97
3:43:13		Simon	Baker	AUS	6.2.58	1	LT	L'Hospitalet	28 May 89
3:43:14		Dietmar	Meisch	GDR	10.2.59	3	LT	New York	2 May 87
3:43:16			Zhou Yongshen	CHN	15.10.72	1	NC	Beijing	10 Apr 94
3:43:18		Aigars	Fadejevs	LAT	27.12.75	1	NC	Ogre	6 Jun 98
3:43:36		Martín	Bermúdez	MEX	19.7.58	1	LT	Eschborn	30 Sep 79
3:43:41			Zhang Huiqiang	CHN	14.10.77	2	NC	Zhuhai	12 Mar 96
3:43:43		Nathan	Deakes	AUS	17.8.77	1		Naumburg	8 Apr 01
		(40)							
3:43:46		Mikhail	Shchennikov	RUS	24.12.67	2	OG	Atlanta	2 Aug 96
3:43:50		Axel	Noack	GER	23.9.61	4	WCh	Stuttgart	21 Aug 93
3:43:55		Giovanni	Perricelli	ITA	25.8.67	3	EC	Helsinki	13 Aug 94
3:43:57		Vitaliy	Matsko	RUS	8.6.60	2	NC	Leningrad	5 Aug 89
3:43:57		Vitaliy	Popovich	UKR	22.10.62	3	NC	Leningrad	5 Aug 89
3:43:59		Enrique	Vera-Ybánez	MEX	31.5.54	2	LT	Eschborn	30 Sep 79
3:44:08		Viktor	Dorovskikh	RUS	19.10.50	5		Leningrad	3 Aug 85
3:44.12		Anatoliy	Grigoryev	RUS	24.12.60	1		Yevpatoriya	1 Oct 89
3:44:24		Erling	Andersen	NOR	22.9.60	2	WCp-s	Borås	15 Jun 85
3:44:24		Daniel	Plaza	ESP	3.7.66	3	NC	Palma	5 Mar 95
		(50)	100th man 3:48:12						

100 KILOMETRES WALK

Mark	First name	Name	Nat	Born	Pos	Venue	Date
8:43:30	Viktor	Ginko	BLR	7.12.65	1	Scanzorosciate	29 Oct 00
8:48:28	Modris	Liepins	LAT	3.8.66	1	Scanzorosciate	28 Oct 01
8:54:35	Aleksey	Rodionov	RUS	5.3.57	1	Scanzorosciate	15 Nov 98
8:55:12	Pascal	Kieffer	FRA	6.5.61	1	Besançon	18 Oct 92
8:55:40	Vitaliy	Popovich	UKR	22.10.62	1	Scanzorosciate	31 Oct 99

JUNIOR MEN'S ALL-TIME LISTS

100 METRES

Mark	Wind	Name		Nat	Born	Pos	Meet	Venue	Date
10.05		Davidson	Ezinwa	NGR	22.11.71	1		Bauchi	4 Jan 90
10.06	2.0	Dwain	Chambers	GBR	5.4.78	1	EJ	Ljubljana	25 Jul 97
10.07	2.0	Stanley	Floyd	USA	23.6.61	1		Austin	24 May 80
10.08	0.0	Andre	Cason	USA	13.1.69	1	TAC-j	Tallahassee	24 Jun 88
10.08	0.0	Justin	Gatlin	USA	10.2.82	1	NCAA	Eugene	2 Jun 01
10.08A	1.9	Obadele	Thompson	BAR	30.3.76	3		El Paso	16 Apr 94
10.09A	1.8	Mel	Lattany	USA	10.8.59	2r2	USOF	USAF Academy	30 Jul 78
10.10	1.9	Stanley	Kerr	USA	19.6.67	1	TAC-j	Towson	28 Jun 86
10.10	1.2	Francis	Obikwelu	NGR	22.11.78	1		Lisboa	20 Jun 97
10.10	1.9	Mark	Lewis-Francis	GBR	4.9.82	1B	BrGP	London (CP)	5 Aug 00
Wind assisted									
9.83	7.1	Leonard	Scott	USA	19.1.80	1		Knoxville	9 Apr 99
9.97	??	Mark	Lewis-Francis	GBR	4.9.82	1q3	WCh	Edmonton	4 Aug 01
10.07	2.9	Lee	McRae	USA	23.1.66	2h5	NCAA	Austin	30 May 85
10.08	4.0	Johnny	Jones	USA	4.4.58	1		Austin	20 May 77
10.08	2.2	Billy	Fobbs	USA	29.2.76	1r3		Houston	19 May 95
10.09	4.1	Stanley	Blalock	USA	18.3.64	1		Athens, Ga	19 Mar 83
10.09	3.1	Innocent	Asunze	NGR	30.12.72	1r1		Lagos	10 Jun 90

200 METRES

Mark	Wind	Name		Nat	Born	Pos	Meet	Venue	Date
20.07	1.5	Lorenzo	Daniel	USA	23.3.66	1	SEC	Starkville	18 May 85
20.13	1.7	Roy	Martin	USA	25.12.66	1		Austin	11 May 85
20.16A	-0.2	Riaan	Dempers	RSA	4.3.77	1	NC-j	Germiston	7 Apr 95
20.22	1.7	Dwayne	Evans	USA	13.10.58	2	OT	Eugene	22 Jun 76
20.23	0.5	Michael	Timpson	USA	6.6.67	1		University Park	16 May 86
20.24	0.2	Joe	DeLoach	USA	5.6.67	3		Los Angeles	8 Jun 85
20.24	0.2	Francis	Obikwelu	NGR	22.11.78	2rB		Granada	29 May 96
20.29	1.5	Clinton	Davis	USA	17.8.65	1	TAC-j	University Park	26 Jun 83
20.29	-0.2	Christian	Malcolm	GBR	3.6.79	2	CG	Kuala Lumpur	19 Sep 98
20.29	0.6	Justin	Gatlin	USA	10.2.82	1	SEC	Columbia, SC	11 May 01
20.29	0.6	Yusuke	Omae	JPN	6.4.82	1	NC-j	Matsumoto	30 Jun 01
Wind assisted									
19.86	4.0	Justin	Gatlin	USA	10.2.82	1h2	NCAA	Eugene	30 May 01
20.01	2.5	Derald	Harris	USA	5.4.58	1		San José	9 Apr 77
20.08	9.2	Leonard	Scott	USA	19.1.80	2r2		Knoxville	9 Apr 99
20.10	4.6	Stanley	Kerr	USA	19.6.67	2r2	SWC	Houston	18 May 86
Hand timing									
19.9		Davidson	Ezinwa	NGR	22.11.71	1		Bauchi	18 Mar 89

400 METRES

Mark	Name		Nat	Born	Pos	Meet	Venue	Date
43.87	Steve	Lewis	USA	16.5.69	1	OG	Seoul	28 Sep 88
44.66	Hamdam	Al-Bishi	KSA	5.5.81	1	WJ	Santiago de Chile	20 Oct 00
44.69	Darrell	Robinson	USA	23.12.63	2	USOF	Indianapolis	24 Jul 82
44.73A	James	Rolle	USA	2.2.64	1	USOF	USAF Academy	2 Jul 83
44.75	Darren	Clark	AUS	6.9.65	4	OG	Los Angeles	8 Aug 84
44.75	Deon	Minor	USA	22.1.73	1s1	NCAA	Austin	5 Jun 92
45.01	Thomas	Schönlebe	GDR	6.8.65	1		Berlin	15 Jul 84
45.01	Jerome	Young	USA	14.8.76	1	NC-j	Walnut	24 Jun 95
45.04A	Wayne	Collett	USA	20.10.49	1q2	OT	Echo Summit	13 Sep 68
45.04	Brandon	Couts	USA	17.2.79	1	DrakeR	Des Moines	25 Apr 98
45.05	Roberto	Hernández	CUB	6.3.67	2		Santiago de Cuba	21 Feb86
44.9+A	Steve	Williams	USA	13.11.53	1	WAC	El Paso	13 May 72

800 METRES

Mark	Name		Nat	Born	Pos	Meet	Venue	Date
1:43.64	Japheth	Kimutai	KEN	20.12.78	3rB	WK	Zürich	13 Aug 97
1:44.3*	Jim	Ryun	USA	29.4.47	1	USTFF	Terre Haute	10 Jun 66
1:44.3	Joaquim	Cruz	BRA	12.3.63	1		Rio de Janeiro	27 Jun 81
1:44.33	Yuriy	Borzakovskiy	RUS	12.4.81	2s2	OG	Sydney	25 Sep 00
1:44.46	Nicholas	Wachira	KEN	19.11.82	5	GP II	Rieti	2 Sep 01
1:44.56	Benjamin	Kipkurui	KEN	28.12.80	2		Rehlingen	24 May 99
1:44.69	William	Chirchir	KEN	6.2.79	6	Herc	Monaco	8 Aug 98
1:44.77	Benson	Koech	KEN	10.11.74	1	WJ	Seoul	19 Sep 92
1:44.98	Cornelius	Chirchir	KEN	7.10.83	4		Rovereto	29 Aug 01
1:45.14	Wilfred	Bungei	KEN	24.7.80	3		Pátra	1 Aug 99
1:45.3A	Emmanuel	Kemboi	KEN	.81	1		Kakamega	9 Apr 00

Mark	Wind	Name		Nat	Born	Pos	Meet	Venue	Date

1000 METRES

Mark	Wind	Name		Nat	Born	Pos	Meet	Venue	Date
2:15.00		Benjamin	Kipkurui	KEN	28.12.80	5	Nik	Nice	17 Jul 99
2:16.84		Ali	Hakimi	TUN	24.4.76	1		Lindau	28 Jul 95
2:16.86		Japheth	Kimutai	KEN	20.12.78	1	VD	Bruxelles	22 Aug 97
2:17.10		Julius	Achon	UGA	12.12.76	1		Rhede	30 Jul 95

1500 METRES

Mark	Wind	Name		Nat	Born	Pos	Meet	Venue	Date
3:32.91		Noah	Ngeny	KEN	2.11.78	9	Herc	Monaco	16 Aug 97
3:33.16		Benjamin	Kipkurui	KEN	28.12.80	1rB	WK	Zürich	11 Aug 99
3:33.24		William	Chirchir	KEN	6.2.79	8rA	WK	Zürich	12 Aug 98
3:34.53		Cornelius	Chirchir	KEN	7.10.83	3	GP II	Rieti	2 Sep 01
3:34.63		Daniel	Komen	KEN	17.5.76	2	Znam	Moskva	5 Jun 95
3:34.92		Kipkoech	Cheruiyot	KEN	2.12.64	1		München	26 Jul 83
3:35.47		Stephen	Cherono	KEN	15.10.82	5	GP II	Zagreb	2 Jul 01
3:35.51		Reyes	Estévez	ESP	2.8.76	2	WK	Zürich	16 Aug 95
3:35.55		Isaac	Songok	KEN	25.4.84	1		Leverkusen	26 Aug 01
3:35.63		Hailu	Mekonnen	ETH	4.4.80	3		Arnhem	10 Jul 99

1 MILE

Mark	Wind	Name		Nat	Born	Pos	Meet	Venue	Date
3:50.41		Noah	Ngeny	KEN	2.11.78	2	Nik	Nice	16 Jul 97
3:51.3		Jim	Ryun	USA	29.4.47	1		Berkeley	17 Jul 66
3:53.15		Graham	Williamson	GBR	15.6.60	3	OsloG	Oslo	17 Jul 79
3:53.43		Alan	Webb	USA	13.1.83	5	Pre	Eugene	27 May 01

2000 METRES

Mark	Wind	Name		Nat	Born	Pos	Meet	Venue	Date
4:56.86		Isaac	Songok	KEN	25.4.84	6	ISTAF	Berlin	31 Aug 01
4:59.14		Ali	Saïdi-Sief	ALG	15.3.78	9	Gaz	Villeneuve d'Ascq	29 Jun 97
5:00.0+		Sammy	Kipketer	KEN	29.9.81	8	in3k	Monaco	4 Aug 99
5:00.6+		Richard	Limo	KEN	18.11.80	2	APM	Hengelo	30 May 99

3000 METRES

Mark	Wind	Name		Nat	Born	Pos	Meet	Venue	Date
7:30.67		Kenenisa	Bekele	ETH	13.6.82	2	VD	Bruxelles	24 Aug 01
7:33.00		Hailu	Mekonnen	ETH	4.4.80	2		Stuttgart	6 Jun 99
7:34.32		Richard	Limo	KEN	18.11.80	4	VD	Bruxelles	3 Sep 99
7:34.58		Sammy	Kipketer	KEN	29.9.81	5	VD	Bruxelles	3 Sep 99
7:35.52		Philip	Mosima	KEN	2.1.77	1	GP	London (CP)	12 Jul 96
7:38.09		Daniel	Komen	KEN	17.5.76	7	GPF	Monaco	9 Sep 95
7:39.82		Ismael	Kirui	KEN	20.2.75	3	ISTAF	Berlin	27 Aug 93
7:40.69		James	Getanda	KEN	5.7.82	4	BrGP	London (CP)	22 Jul 01
7:42.93		Andrew	Sambu	TAN	5.10.72	1		Grossetto	11 Aug 91
7:43.01		Albert	Chepkirui	KEN	4.4.81	2		Caorle	10 Jul 99

5000 METRES

Mark	Wind	Name		Nat	Born	Pos	Meet	Venue	Date
12:53.72		Philip	Mosima	KEN	2.1.77	2	GGala	Roma	5 Jun 96
12:54.07		Sammy	Kipketer	KEN	29.9.81	2	GGala	Roma	30 Jun 00
12:56.15		Daniel	Komen	KEN	17.5.76	2	GG	Roma	8 Jun 95
12:58.15		Richard	Limo	KEN	18.11.80	6	GGala	Roma	7 Jul 99
12:59.39		Million	Wolde	ETH	17.3.79	5	WK	Zürich	12 Aug 98
12:59.90		Albert	Chepkirui	KEN	4.4.81	8	Bisl	Oslo	28 Jul 00
13:02.75		Ismael	Kirui	KEN	20.2.75	1	WCh	Stuttgart	16 Aug 93
13:05.48		Assefa	Mezegebu	ETH	19.6.78	4	GGala	Roma	5 Jun 97
13:05.64		Julius	Gitahi	KEN	29.4.78	2	GP	Osaka	10 May 97
13:09.58		John Cheruiyot	Korir	KEN	13.12.81	11	WK	Zürich	11 Aug 00
13:10.98		Hailu	Mekonnen	ETH	4.4.80	12	GGala	Roma	7 Jul 99

10,000 METRES

Mark	Wind	Name		Nat	Born	Pos	Meet	Venue	Date
27:11.18		Richard	Chelimo	KEN	21.4.72	1	APM	Hengelo	25 Jun 91
27:17.82		Addis	Abebe	ETH	5.9.70	2	WG	Helsinki	29 Jun 89
27:24.75		John Cheruiyot	Korir	KEN	13.12.81	5	OG	Sydney	25 Sep 00
27:25.01		Assefa	Mezegebu	ETH	19.6.78	1	APM	Hengelo	31 May 97
27:25.55		Robert	Kipchumba	KEN	24.2.84	2	VD	Bruxelles	24 Aug 01
27:27.87		Elijah H.	Korir	KEN	15.4.78	5	VD	Bruxelles	22 Aug 97
27:28.60		Julius	Gitahi	KEN	29.4.78	1		Konosu	5 Oct 96
27:32.18		David	Chelule	KEN	7.7.77	2	Slovn	Bratislava	29 May 96
27:36.5		Simon	Maina Munyi	KEN	18.3.78	1		Hachioji	30 Nov 97
27:42.75		Salim	Kipsang	KEN	22.12.79	10	VD	Bruxelles	28 Aug 98
27:48.34		Alene	Emere ¶	ETH	5.3.82	3	Odlozil	Praha	5 Jun 00
		Drugs disqualification: 27:29.53				1	JPN Ch	Tokyo	9 Jun 01

Mark	Wind	Name		Nat	Born	Pos	Meet	Venue	Date

3000 METRES STEEPLECHASE

Mark	Wind	Name		Nat	Born	Pos	Meet	Venue	Date
7:58.66		Stephen	Cherono	KEN	15.10.82	3	VD	Bruxelles	24 Aug 01
8:03.74		Raymond	Yator	KEN	7.4.81	3	Herc	Monaco	18 Aug 00
8:07.69		Paul	Kosgei	KEN	22.4.78	5	DNG	Stockholm	7 Jul 97
8:16.76		Kipkirui	Misoi	KEN	23.10.78	2		Dortmund	8 Jun 97
8:18.71		Julius	Chelule	KEN	25.12.78	4	Slovn	Bratislava	10 Jun 97
8:19.21		Daniel	Njenga	KEN	7.5.76	1	JPN Ch	Tokyo	12 Jun 94
8:20.07		Christopher	Soget	KEN	15.5.80	2	Afr-J	Tunis	23 Jul 99
8:20.67		Richard	Limo	KEN	18.11.80	2	AfrC	Dakar	20 Aug 98
8:20.73		Paul	Chemase	KEN	24.8.76	10	Herc	Monaco	25 Jul 95
8:22.96		Abraham	Cherono	KEN	21.7.80	2		Linz	26 Jul 99
8:23.18		Ali	Ezzine	MAR	3.9.78	14	WK	Zürich	13 Aug 97

110 METRES HURDLES

Mark	Wind	Name		Nat	Born	Pos	Meet	Venue	Date
13.23	0.0	Renaldo	Nehemiah	USA	24.3.59	1r2	WK	Zürich	16 Aug 78
13.32	1.9		Liu Xiang	CHN	13.7.83	1		Shanghai	6 May 01
13.43	1.9		Shi Dongpeng	CHN	6.1.84	3		Shanghai	6 May 01
13.44	-0.8	Colin	Jackson	GBR	18.2.67	1	WJ	Athína	19 Jul 86
13.46	1.8	Jon	Ridgeon	GBR	14.2.67	1	EJ	Cottbus	23 Aug 85
13.47	1.9	Holger	Pohland	GDR	5.4.63	2	vUSA	Karl-Marx-Stadt	10 Jul 82
13.49	0.6	Stanislavs	Olijars	LAT	22.3.79	1		Valmiera	11 Jul 98
13.51!	1.2	Tomasz	Scigaczewski	POL	18.11.78	1		Lodz	7 Sep 97
13.52	2.0	Alejandro	Casañas	CUB	29.1.54	1		Warszawa	28 Jun 72
13.52	0.6	Ubeja	Anderson	USA	30.3.74	1		Knoxville	16 May 93
Wind assisted									
13.42	4.5	Colin	Jackson	GBR	18.2.67	2	CG	Edinburgh	27 Jul 86
13.47	2.1	Frank	Busemann	GER	26.2.75	1	WJ	Lisboa	22 Jul 94

400 METRES HURDLES

Mark	Wind	Name		Nat	Born	Pos	Meet	Venue	Date
48.02		Danny	Harris	USA	7.9.65	2s1	OT	Los Angeles	17 Jun 84
48.68		Bayano	Kamani	USA	17.4.80	1	NCAA	Boise	4 Jun 99
48.72		Angelo	Taylor	USA	29.12.78	2	NCAA	Bloomington	6 Jun 97
48.74		Vladimir	Budko	BLR	4.2.65	2	DRZ	Moskva	18 Aug 84
48.76A		Llewellyn	Herbert	RSA	21.7.77	1		Pretoria	7 Apr 96
		49.15				2	WJ	Sydney	23 Aug 96
49.07		Mubarak	Al-Nubi	QAT	30.12.77	1	WJ	Sydney	23 Aug 96
49.09		Dai	Tamesue	JPN	3.5.78	1		Hiroshima	14 Oct 96
49.10		Yoshihiko	Saito	JPN	12.2.72	1		Kanazawa	17 Oct 91
49.23		Marek	Plawgo	POL	25.2.81	1	WJ	Santiago de Chile	21 Oct 00
49.30		Hadi Soua'an	Al-Somaily	KSA	30.12.76	1	PArab	Cairo	27 Aug 95

HIGH JUMP

Mark	Wind	Name		Nat	Born	Pos	Meet	Venue	Date
2.37		Dragutin	Topic	YUG	12.3.71	1	WJ	Plovdiv	12 Aug 90
2.37		Steve	Smith	GBR	29.3.73	1	WJ	Seoul	20 Sep 92
2.36		Javier	Sotomayor	CUB	13.10.67	1		Santiago de Cuba	23 Feb 86
2.35i		Vladimir	Yashchenko	UKR	12.1.59	1	EI	Milano	12 Mar 78
		2.34				1	Prv	Tbilisi	16 Jun 78
2.35		Dietmar	Mögenburg	FRG	15.8.61	1		Rehlingen	26 May 80
2.34		Tim	Forsyth	AUS	17.8.73	1	Bisl	Oslo	4 Jul 92
2.33			Zhu Jianhua	CHN	29.5.63	1	AsiG	New Delhi	1 Dec 82
2.33		Patrik	Sjöberg	SWE	5.1.65	1	OsloG	Oslo	9 Jul 83
2.31		Jörg	Freimuth	GDR	10.9.61	3	OG	Moskva	1 Aug 80
2.31		Lochsley	Thomson	AUS	20.8.73	3	NC	Adelaide	8 Mar 92
2.31i		Andrey	Chubsa	BLR	29.11.82	1		Vitebsk	12 Jan 01
2.31		Jacques	Freitag	RSA	11.6.82	1		Rehlingen	4 Jun 01

POLE VAULT

Mark	Wind	Name		Nat	Born	Pos	Meet	Venue	Date
5.80		Maksim	Tarasov	RUS	2.12.70	1	vGDR-j	Bryansk	14 Jul 89
5.71		Lawrence	Johnson	USA	7.5.74	1		Knoxville	12 Jun 93
5.70		Viktor	Chistyakov	RUS	9.2.75	1		Leppävirta	7 Jun 94
5.65		Radion	Gataullin	UZB	23.11.65	2	NC	Donetsk	8 Sep 84
5.65		István	Bagyula	HUN	2.1.69	1	WJ	Sudbury	28 Jul 88
5.65i		Jacob	Davis	USA	29.4.78	1	Big 12	Lincoln	21 Feb 97
		5.62				2		Austin	5 Apr 97
5.62		Gérald	Baudouin	FRA	15.11.72	1	NC-j	Dreux	7 Jul 91
5.62		Lars	Börgeling	GER	16.4.79	1		Mannheim	13 Jun 98
5.61		Thierry	Vigneron	FRA	9.3.60	1		Longwy	30 Sep 79
5.61i		Grigoriy	Yegorov	KZK	12.1.67	1	vGDR-j	Moskva	16 Feb 86
5.61		Danny	Ecker	GER	21.7.77	1		Ljubljana	28 Sep 96

Jnr MEN All-time

Mark	Wind	Name		Nat	Born	Pos	Meet	Venue	Date
LONG JUMP									
8.34	0.0	Randy	Williams	USA	23.8.53	Q	OG	München	8 Sep 72
8.28	0.8	Luis A	Bueno	CUB	22.5.69	1		La Habana	16 Jul 88
8.24	0.2	Eric	Metcalf	USA	23.1.68	1	NCAA	Indianapolis	6 Jun 86
8.24	1.8	Vladimir	Ochkan	UKR	13.1.68	1	vGDR-j	Leningrad	21 Jun 87
8.22		Larry	Doubley	USA	15.3.58	1	NCAA	Champaign	3 Jun 77
8.22		Ivan	Pedroso	CUB	17.12.72	1		Santiago de Cuba	3 May 91
8.21A	2.0	Vance	Johnson	USA	13.3.63	1	NCAA	Provo	4 Jun 82
8.20	1.5	James	Stallworth	USA	29.4.71	Q	WJ	Plovdiv	9 Aug 90
8.18		LaMonte	King	USA	18.12.59	2	CalR	Modesto	20 May 78
8.16	1.1	Dion	Bentley	USA	26.8.71	1	PAm-j	Santa Fé	23 Jun 89
8.16	1.8		Wang Cheng	CHN	4.11.80	1		Chengdu	19 Apr 98
Wind assisted									
8.40	3.2	Kareem	Streete-Thompson	CAY	30.3.73	1		Houston	5 May 91
8.35	2.2	Carl	Lewis	USA	1.7.61	1	NCAA	Austin	6 Jun 80
8.29	2.3	James	Beckford	JAM	9.1.75	1		Tempe	2 Apr 94
8.23	4.4	Peller	Phillips	USA	23.6.70	1		Sacramento	11 Jun 88
8.21	2.8	Masaki	Morinaga	JPN	27.3.72	1		Hamamatsu	7 Sep 91
TRIPLE JUMP									
17.50	0.4	Volker	Mai	GDR	3.5.66	1	vURS	Erfurt	23 Jun 85
17.42	1.3	Khristo	Markov	BUL	27.1.65	1	Nar	Sofiya	19 May 84
17.40A	0.4	Pedro	Pérez	CUB	23.2.52	1	PAm	Cali	5 Aug 71
17.29	1.3	James	Beckford	JAM	9.1.75	1		Tempe	2 Apr 94
17.27		Aliecer	Urrutia	CUB	22.9.74	1		Artemisa	23 Apr 93
17.23	0.2	Yoelbi	Quesada	CUB	4.8.73	1	NC	La Habana	13 May 92
17.11	1.4	Marian	Oprea	ROM	6.6.82	2	WUG	Beijing	31 Aug 01
17.03	0.6	Osiris	Mora	CUB	3.10.73	2	WJ	Seoul	19 Sep 92
17.00		Gustavo	Plá	CUB	29.7.54	1		La Habana	5 May 73
17.00		Yevgeniy	Timofeyev	RUS	22.2.74	1		Krasnodar	26 May 93
17.13w	4.1	Marian	Oprea	ROM	6.6.82	1	ECp-1B	Budapest	24 Jun 01
SHOT									
21.05i		Terry	Albritton	USA	14.1.55	1	AAU	New York	22 Feb 74
		20.38				2	MSR	Walnut	27 Apr 74
20.65		Mike	Carter	USA	29.10.60	1	vSU-j	Boston	4 Jul 79
20.39		Janus	Robberts	RSA	10.3.79	1	NC	Germiston	7 Mar 98
20.20		Randy	Matson	USA	5.3.45	2	OG	Tokyo	17 Oct 64
20.20		Udo	Beyer	GDR	9.8.55	2	NC	Leipzig	6 Jul 74
20.13		Jeff	Chakouian	USA	20.4.82	2		Atlanta	18 May 01
19.99		Karl	Salb	USA	19.5.49	4	OT	Echo Summit	10 Sep 68
19.74		Andreas	Horn	GDR	31.1.62	2	vSU-j	Cottbus	24 Jun 81
19.71		Vladimir	Kiselyov -1	UKR	1.1.57	1		Yalta	15 May 76
19.69		Mikulás	Konopka	SVK	23.1.79	2	NC	Nitra	11 Jul 98
DISCUS									
65.62		Werner	Reiterer	AUS	27.1.68	1		Melbourne	15 Dec 87
63.64		Werner	Hartmann	FRG	20.4.59	1	vFRA	Strasbourg	25 Jun 78
63.26		Sergey	Pachin	UKR	24.5.68	2		Moskva	25 Jul 87
63.22		Brian	Milne	USA	7.1.73	1		University Park	28 Mar 92
62.52		John	Nichols	USA	23.8.69	1		Baton Rouge	23 Apr 88
62.36			Nu Ermaimaiti	CHN	8.3.84	2	NG	Guangzhou	21 Nov 01
62.16		Zoltán	Kövágó	HUN	10.4.79	1		Budapest	9 May 97
62.04		Kenth	Gardenkrans	SWE	2.10.55	2		Helsingborg	11 Aug 74
61.84		Attila	Horváth	HUN	28.7.67	2		Budapest	18 May 85
61.84		Andreas	Seelig	GDR	6.7.70	1		Halle	15 May 88
HAMMER									
78.33		Olli-Pekka	Karjalainen	FIN	7.3.80	1	NC	Seinäjoki	5 Aug 99
78.14		Roland	Steuk	GDR	5.3.59	1	NC	Leipzig	30 Jun 78
78.00		Sergey	Dorozhon	UKR	17.2.64	1		Moskva	7 Aug 83
76.54		Valeriy	Gubkin	BLR	3.9.67	2		Minsk	27 Jun 86
76.42		Ruslan	Dikiy	TJK	18.1.72	1		Togliatti	7 Sep 91
75.52		Sergey	Kirmasov	RUS	25.3.70	1		Kharkov	4 Jun 89
75.42		Szymon	Ziolkowski	POL	1.7.76	1	EJ	Nyíregyhazá	30 Jul 95
75.24		Christoph	Sahner	FRG	23.9.63	1	vPOL-j	Göttingen	26 Jun 82
75.22		Yaroslav	Chmyr	UKR	29.11.66	1		Kiyev	9 Sep 85
75.20		Igor	Nikulin	RUS	14.8.60	2		Leselidze	1 Jun 79

JAVELIN

Mark	Wind	Name		Nat	Born	Pos	Meet	Venue	Date
83.87		Andreas	Thorkildsen	NOR	1.4.82	1		Fana	7 Jun 01
83.55		Aleksandr	Ivanov	RUS	25.5.82	2	NC	Tula	14 Jul 01
82.52		Harri	Haatainen	FIN	5.1.78	4		Leppävirta	25 May 96
81.80		Sergey	Voynov	UZB	26.2.77	1		Tashkent	6 Jun 96
80.94		Aki	Parviainen	FIN	26.10.74	4	NC	Jyväskylä	5 Jul 92
80.30		Konstadínos	Gatsioúdis	GRE	17.12.73	1	NC	Athína	20 Jun 92
80.26		Vladimir	Ovchinnikov	RUS	2.8.70	Q	OG	Seoul	24 Sep 88
79.58		Gavin	Lovegrove	NZL	21.10.67	2		Nouméa	26 Oct 86
79.50		Steve	Backley	GBR	12.12.69	1	NC	Derby	5 Jun 88
79.46		Juha	Laukkanen	FIN	6.1.69	1		Joutsa	19 Jul 87

DECATHLON

Mark	Name		Nat	Born	Pos	Meet	Venue	Date
8397	Torsten	Voss	GDR	24.3.63	1	NC	Erfurt	7 Jul 82
	10.76 7.66 14.41 2.09 48.37 14.37 41.76 4.80 62.90 4:34.04							
8114	Michael	Kohnle	FRG	3.5.70	1	EJ	Varazdin	26 Aug 89
	10.95 7.09/0.1 15.27 2.02 49.91 14.40 45.82 4.90 60.82 4:49.43							
8104	Valter	Külvet	EST	19.2.64	1		Viimsi	23 Aug 81
	10.7 7.26 13.86 2.09 48.5 14.8 47.92 4.50 60.34 4:37.8							
8082	Daley	Thompson	GBR	30.7.58	1	ECp/s	Sittard	31 Jul 77
	10.70/0.8 7.54/0.7 13.84 2.01 47.31 15.26/2.0 41.70 4.70 54.48 4:30.4							
8036	Christian	Schenk	GDR	9.2.65	5		Potsdam	21 Jul 84
	11.54 7.18 14.26 2.16 49.23 15.06 44.74 4.20 65.98 4:24.11							
8021		Qi Haifeng	CHN	7.8.83	1	NG	Guangzhou	22 Nov 01
	11.13/0.6 7.38/-0.3 13.29 1.96 49.52 14.67/0.5 47.63 4.70 59.16 4:30.75							
7938	Frank	Busemann	GER	26.2.75	1		Zeven	2 Oct 94
	10.68/1.6 7.37/1.1 13.08 2.03 50.41 14.34/-1.1 39.84 4.40 63.00 4:37.31)							
7913	Raul	Duany	CUB	4.1.75	2		La Habana	26 May 94
	11.50 7.13 13.99 2.10 49.70 14.77 37.76 4.50 65.58 4:24.03							
7906	Mikhail	Romanyuk	UKR	6.2.62	1	EJ	Utrecht	21 Aug 81
	11.26/1.8 7.11w/3.7 13.50 1.98 49.98 14.72w/4.0 42.94 4.90 59.74 4:30.63							
7897	Dennis	Leyckes	GER	20.4.82	1	WJ	Santiago de Chile	19 Oct 00
	10.98/1.6 7.22/0.4 13.46 1.95 47.59 14.61/-0.1 39.52 4.80 54.76 4:33.10							

10,000 METRES WALK

Mark	Name		Nat	Born	Pos	Meet	Venue	Date
38:46.4	Viktor	Burayev	RUS	23.8.82	1	NC-j	Moskva	20 May 00
38:54.75	Ralf	Kowalsky	GDR	22.3.62	1		Cottbus	24 Jun 81
39:44.71	Giovanni	De Benedictis	ITA	8.1.68	1	EJ	Birmingham	7 Aug 87
39:49.22		Pei Chuang	CHN	5.12.81	2	NSG	Chengdu	8 Sep 00
39:50.73	Jefferson	Pérez	ECU	1.7.74	1	PAmJ	Winnipeg	15 Jul 93
39:55.52	Ilya	Markov	RUS	19.6.72	1	WJ	Plovdiv	10 Aug 90
39:56.49	Alberto	Cruz	MEX	6.6.72	2	WJ	Plovdiv	10 Aug 90
39:59.58	Sergey	Tyulenyev	RUS	14.3.71	1		Kharkov	4 Jun 90
40:05.62	Michele	Didoni	ITA	7.3.74	1	EJ	San Sebastián	30 Jul 93
40:13.11	Yevgeniy	Shmalyuk	RUS	14.1.76	1		Sankt-Peterburg	28 May 94

4 x 100 METRES RELAY

Mark	Nat	Team	Pos	Meet	Venue	Date
39.00A	USA	Jessie, Franklin, Blalock, Mitchell	1		Colorado Springs	18 Jul 83
39.13	USA	Nelloms, Bridges, Harris, Stallworth	1	WJ	Plovdiv	12 Aug 90
39.05	GBR	Edgar, Grant, Benjamin, Lewis-Francis	1	WJ	Santiago de Chile	22 Oct 00
39.25	FRG	Dobeleit, Klameth, Evers, Lübke	1	EJ	Schwechat	28 Aug 83
39.33	FRA	Pognon, Calligny, Doucoure, Djhone	2	WJ	Santiago de Chile	22 Oct 00
39.47	JPN	Mogi, Kitamura, Omaer, Miyazaki	3	WJ	Santiago de Chile	22 Oct 00
39.51	CIV	Y.Sonan, Ahmed Douhou, A.Byo, Ibrahim Meité	1	Afr-J	Bouaké	22 Jul 95
39.53	URS	Inshakov, Gromadskiy, Semyonov, Goremykin	1h3	WJ	Plovdiv	11 Aug 90
39.54	NGR	Tetengi, D Ezinwa, Nwankwo, Adeniken	1h2	WJ	Sudbury	30 Jul 88

4 x 400 METRES RELAY

Mark	Nat	Team	Pos	Meet	Venue	Date
3:01.90	USA	Campbell, Rish, Waddle, Reed	1	WJ	Athína	20 Jul 86
3:03.80	GBR	Grindley, Patrick, Winrow, Richardson	2	WJ	Plovdiv	12 Aug 90
3:04.12	JAM	R McDonald, D Clarke, Watts, M McDonald	2	WJ	Lisboa	24 Jul 94
3:04.22	CUB	Cadogan, Mordoche, González, Hernández	2	WJ	Athína	20 Jul 86
3:04.58	GDR	Preusche, Löper, Trylus, Carlowitz	1	EJ	Utrecht	23 Aug 81
3:04.74	AUS	McFarlane, Batman, Thom, Vincent	1	WJ	Annecy	2 Aug 98
3:05.60	URS	Angelov, Oleynikov, Belikov, Golovastov	4	WJ	Plovdiv	12 Aug 90
3:05.77	FRG	Grüber, Seybold, Mikisch, Just	2	EJ	Schwechat	28 Aug 83
3:06.01	JPN	Takahashi, Tamesue, Okusako, Morita	2	WJ	Sydney	25 Aug 96
3:06.12	POL	Marciniszyn, Matyjaszczyk, Kedzia, Grzegorczyk	1	EJ	Grosseto	22 Jul 01

WOMEN'S ALL-TIME WORLD LISTS

100 METRES

Mark	Wind	Name		Nat	Born	Pos	Meet	Venue	Date
10.49WR	0.0	Florence	Griffith-Joyner	USA	21.12.59	1q1	OT	Indianapolis	16 Jul 88
		@ Probably strongly wind-assisted, but recognised as a US and world record							
10.61	1.2		Griffith-Joyner			1	OT	Indianapolis	17 Jul 88
10.62	1.0		Griffith-Joyner			1q3	OG	Seoul	24 Sep 88
10.65A	1.1	Marion	Jones	USA	12.10.75	1	WCp	Johannesburg	12 Sep 98
10.70	1.6		Griffith-Joyner			1s1	OT	Indianapolis	17 Jul 88
10.70	-0.1		Jones			1	WCh	Sevilla	22 Aug 99
10.71	0.1		Jones			1		Chengdu	12 May 98
10.71	2.0		Jones			1s2	NC	New Orleans	19 Jun 98
10.72	2.0		Jones			1	NC	New Orleans	20 Jun 98
10.72	0.0		Jones			1	Herc	Monaco	8 Aug 98
10.72	0.0		Jones			1	Athl	Lausanne	25 Aug 98
10.73	2.0	Christine	Arron	FRA	13.9.73	1	EC	Budapest	19 Aug 98
10.74	1.3	Merlene	Ottey	JAM	10.5.60	1	GPF	Milano	7 Sep 96
10.75	0.6		Jones			1	GGala	Roma	14 Jul 98
10.75	-0.4		Jones			1	OG	Sydney	23 Sep 00
10.76WR	1.7	Evelyn	Ashford	USA	15.4.57	1	WK	Zürich	22 Aug 84
10.76	0.9		Jones			1	VD	Bruxelles	22 Aug 97
10.76	0.3		Jones			1q4	WCh	Sevilla	21 Aug 99
10.77	0.9	Irina	Privalova	RUS	22.11.68	1rA	Athl	Lausanne	6 Jul 94
10.77	-0.9		Jones			1rA	WK	Zürich	12 Aug 98
10.78A	1.0	Dawn	Sowell	USA	27.3.66	1	NCAA	Provo	3 Jun 89
10.78	1.7		Ottey			1	Expo	Sevilla	30 May 90
10.78	0.4		Ottey			1	GPF	Paris	3 Sep 94
10.78	1.1		Jones			1	BrGP	London (CP)	5 Aug 00
10.78	0.1		Jones			1	ISTAF	Berlin	1 Sep 00
10.79AWR	0.6		Ashford			1	USOF	USAF Academy	3 Jul 83
10.79	1.7		Ottey			1		Vigo	23 Jul 91
10.79	0.0		Li Xuemei	CHN	5.1.77	1	NG	Shanghai	18 Oct 97
10.79	-0.6		Jones			1		Osaka	9 May 98
10.79	-0.1	Inger	Miller	USA	12.6.72	2	WCh	Sevilla	22 Aug 99
		(30 performances by 9 athletes)							
10.81WR	1.7	Marlies	Göhr' (10)	GDR	21.3.58	1	OD	Berlin	8 Jun 83
10.82	-1.0	Gail	Devers	USA	19.11.66	1	OG	Barcelona	1 Aug 92
10.82	0.4	Gwen	Torrence	USA	12.6.65	2	GPF	Paris	3 Sep 94
10.82	-0.3	Zhanna	Pintusevich-Block	UKR	6.7.72	1	WCh	Edmonton	6 Aug 01
10.83	1.7	Marita	Koch	GDR	18.2.57	2	OD	Berlin	8 Jun 83
10.83	0.0	Sheila	Echols	USA	2.10.64	1q2	OT	Indianapolis	16 Jul 88
10.83	-1.0	Juliet	Cuthbert	JAM	9.4.64	2	OG	Barcelona	1 Aug 92
10.83	0.1	Ekateríni	Thánou	GRE	1.2.75	2s1	WCh	Sevilla	22 Aug 99
10.84	1.3	Chioma	Ajunwa ¶	NGR	25.12.70	1		Lagos	11 Apr 92
10.85	2.0	Anelia	Nuneva	BUL	30.6.62	1h1	NC	Sofiya	2 Sep 88
10.85	0.4	Zhanna	Pintusevich	UKR	6.7.72	2	WCh	Athína	3 Aug 97
		(20)							
10.86	0.6	Silke	Gladisch/Möller	GDR	20.6.64	1	NC	Potsdam	20 Aug 87
10.86@	0.0	Diane	Williams	USA	14.12.60	2q1	OT	Indianapolis	16 Jul 88
		10.94A	0.6			2	USOF	USAF Academy	3 Jul 83
10.86	0.1	Chandra	Sturrup	BAH	12.9.71	1	NC	Nassau	21 Jul 00
10.89	1.8	Katrin	Krabbe ¶	GDR	22.11.69	1		Berlin	20 Jul 88
10.89	0.0		Liu Xiaomei	CHN	11.1.72	2	NG	Shanghai	18 Oct 97
10.89	2.0	Chryste	Gaines	USA	14.9.70	2	NC	New Orleans	20 Jun 98
10.90	1.4	Glory	Alozie	NGR/ESP	30.12.77	1		La Laguna	5 Jun 99
10.91	0.2	Heike	Drechsler'	GDR	16.12.64	2	GWG	Moskva	6 Jul 86
10.91	1.1	Savatheda	Fynes	BAH	17.10.74	2	Athl	Lausanne	2 Jul 99
10.92	0.0	Alice	Brown	USA	20.9.60	2q2	OT	Indianapolis	16 Jul 88
10.92	1.1	D'Andre	Hill	USA	19.4.73	3	NC	Atlanta	15 Jun 96
		(30)							
10.93	1.8	Ewa	Kasprzyk	POL	7.9.57	1	NC	Grudziadz	27 Jun 86
10.94	1.0	Carlette	Guidry	USA	4.9.68	1	TAC	New York	14 Jun 91
10.95	1.0	Bärbel	Wöckel'	GDR	21.3.55	2	NC	Dresden	1 Jul 82
10.96	1.2	Marie-José	Pérec	FRA	9.5.68	1	NC	Dijon	27 Jul 91
10.96	2.0	Galina	Malchugina	RUS	17.12.62	2	CIS Ch	Moskva	22 Jun 92
10.96	1.0	Eldece	Clarke-Lewis	BAH	13.2.65	1	Conseil	Fort-de-France	29 Apr 00
10.96	0.1	Debbie	Ferguson	BAH	16.1.76	2	NC	Nassau	21 Jul 00
10.97	0.0	Angella	Issajenko' ¶	CAN	28.9.58	3	ASV	Köln	16 Aug 87
10.97	0.2	Mary	Onyali	NGR	3.2.68	1q2	WCh	Stuttgart	15 Aug 93

Mark	Wind	Name		Nat	Born	Pos	Meet	Venue	Date
10.97	0.1	Pauline	Davis-Thompson	BAH	9.7.66	3	NC	Nassau	21 Jul 00
		(40)							
10.98	0.1	Marina	Zhirova	RUS	6.6.63	2	ECp	Moskva	17 Aug 85
10.98	0.8	Angela	Bailey	CAN	28.2.62	2	BGP	Budapest	6 Jul 87
10.98	1.6	Natalya	Pomoshchnikova'	RUS	9.7.65	2q2	OG	Seoul	24 Sep 88
10.98	0.6	Léonie Myriam	Mani	CMR	21.5.77	2rA	GP	Athína	11 Jun 01
10.99	1.3	Valerie	Brisco-Hooks	USA	6.7.60	1	Pepsi	Westwood	17 May 86
10.99	0.7	Beverly	McDonald	JAM	15.2.70	1	GP II	Doha	7 May 98
10.99	0.6	Kelli	White	USA	1.4.77	3rA	GP	Athína	11 Jun 01
11.01WR	0.6	Annegret	Richter	FRG	13.10.50	1s1	OG	Montreal	25 Jul 76
11.01	0.8	Pam	Marshall	USA	16.8.60	2	Athl	Lausanne	15 Sep 87
11.02	2.0	Romy	Müller'	GDR	26.7.58	3	OT	Dresden	24 May 80
11.02	-0.2	Lyudmila	Kondratyeva	RUS	11.4.58	2	Drz	Praha	16 Aug 84
11.02	-0.1	LaTasha	Jenkins	USA	19.12.77	1		Athens, GA	5 May 01
		(52)	100th women 11.11, 200th women 11.22						
Probably semi-automatic timing									
10.87	1.9	Lyudmila	Kondratyeva	RUS	11.4.58	1		Leningrad	3 Jun 80
10.99	1.9	Natalya	Bochina	RUS	4.1.62	2		Leningrad	3 Jun 80
Low altitude best: 10.91	1.6		Sowell			1	TAC	Houston	16 Jun 89
Wind-assisted to 10.78 performances and 10.96 performers									
10.54	3.0		Griffith-Joyner			1	OG	Seoul	25 Sep 88
10.60	3.2		Griffith-Joyner			1h1	OT	Indianapolis	16 Jul 88
10.68	2.2		Jones			1	DNG	Stockholm	1 Aug 00
10.70	2.6		Griffith-Joyner			1s2	OG	Seoul	25 Sep 88
10.75	4.1		Jones			1h3	NC	New Orleans	19 Jun 98
10.77	2.3	Gail	Devers	USA	19.11.66	1	Jen	San José	28 May 94
10.77	2.1		Jones			1	Pre	Eugene	31 May 98
10.77	2.3	Ekateríni	Thánou	GRE	1.2.75	1		Rethymno	28 May 99
10.78	3.1		Ashford			1		Modesto	12 May 84
10.78	5.0	Gwen	Torrence	USA	12.6.65	1q3	OT	Indianapolis	16 Jul 88
10.78	2.3		Ottey			1s2	WCh	Tokyo	27 Aug 91
10.79	3.3	Marlies	Göhr'	GDR	21.3.58	1	NC	Cottbus	16 Jul 80
10.80	2.9	Pam	Marshall	USA	16.8.60	1	TAC	Eugene	20 Jun 86
10.80	2.8	Heike	Drechsler'	GDR	16.12.64	1	Bisl	Oslo	5 Jul 86
10.82	2.2	Silke	Gladisch/Möller	GDR	20.6.64	1s1	WCh	Roma	30 Aug 87
10.84	2.9	Alice	Brown	USA	20.9.60	2	TAC	Eugene	20 Jun 86
10.89	3.1	Kerstin	Behrendt	GDR	2.9.67	2		Berlin	13 Sep 88
10.91	4.6	Carlette	Guidry	USA	4.9.68	1s1	NCAA	Eugene	31 May 91
10.91	2.5	Debbie	Ferguson	BAH	16.1.76	1	NC	Nassau	18 Jun 99
10.92	3.3	Bärbel	Wöckel'	GDR	21.3.55	2	NC	Cottbus	16 Jul 80
10.92	3.4	Angella	Taylor' ¶	CAN	28.9.58	1s2	CG	Brisbane	4 Oct 82
10.92	3.4	Torri	Edwards	USA	31.1.77	1	MAI	Malmö	7 Aug 00
10.93	3.8	Sonia	Lannaman	GBR	24.3.56	1	ECp/sf	Dublin	17 Jul 77
10.93	3.3	Ingrid	Auerswald'	GDR	2.9.57	3	NC	Cottbus	16 Jul 80
10.93	4.2	Holli	Hyche	USA	6.9.71	2h2	NC	Eugene	16 Jun 93
10.93	3.5	Kelli	White	USA	1.4.77	2	NC	Eugene	22 Jun 01
10.94	3.9	Jackie	Washington	USA	17.7.62	1		Houston	18 May 86
10.94A	3.0	Evette	de Klerk'	RSA	21.8.65	1h	NC	Germiston	20 Apr 90
10.96	2.9	Brenda	Morehead	USA	5.10.57	1s2	AAU	Walnut	16 Jun 79
10.96	4.2	Olga	Naumkina'	RUS	20.5.64	1	Znam	Volgograd	11 Jun 89
10.96A	2.5	Michelle	Finn	USA	8.5.65	1		Sestriere	8 Aug 90
10.96	3.7	Angela	Williams	USA	30.1.80	1		Las Vegas	3 Apr 99
Hand timing									
10.6	0.1	Zhanna	Pintusevich	UKR	6.7.72	1		Kiev	12 Jun 97
10.7		Merlene	Ottey	JAM	10.5.60	1h		Kingston	15 Jul 88
10.7	1.1	Juliet	Cuthbert	JAM	9.4.64	1	NC	Kingston	4 Jul 92
10.7		Mary	Onyali	NGR	3.2.68	1	NC	Lagos	22 Jun 96
10.7	-0.2	Svetlana	Goncharenko	RUS	28.5.71	1		Rostov	30 May 98
10.7w	2.6	Savatheda	Fynes	BAH	17.10.74	1		Nassau	22 Jun 95

200 METRES

Mark	Wind	Name		Nat	Born	Pos	Meet	Venue	Date
21.34WR	1.3	Florence	Griffith-Joyner	USA	21.12.59	1	OG	Seoul	29 Sep 88
21.56WR	1.7		Griffith-Joyner			1s1	OG	Seoul	29 Sep 88
21.62A	-0.6	Marion	Jones	USA	12.10.75	1	WCp	Johannesburg	11 Sep 98
21.64	0.8	Merlene	Ottey	JAM	10.5.60	1	VD	Bruxelles	13 Sep 91
21.66	-1.0		Ottey			1	WK	Zürich	15 Aug 90
21.71WR	0.7	Marita	Koch	GDR	18.2.57	1	v Can	Karl-Marx-Stadt	10 Jun 79
21.71WR	0.3		Koch			1	OD	Potsdam	21 Jul 84
21.71WR	1.2	Heike	Drechsler'	GDR	16.12.64	1	NC	Jena	29 Jun 86
21.71WR	-0.8		Drechsler			1	EC	Stuttgart	29 Aug 86

Mark	Wind	Name		Nat	Born	Pos	Meet	Venue	Date
21.72	1.3	Grace	Jackson	JAM	14.6.61	2	OG	Seoul	29 Sep 88
21.72	-0.1	Gwen	Torrence	USA	12.6.65	1s2	OG	Barcelona	5 Aug 92
21.74	0.4	Marlies	Göhr'	GDR	21.3.58	1	NC	Erfurt	3 Jun 84
21.74	1.2	Silke	Gladisch'	GDR	20.6.64	1	WCh	Roma	3 Sep 87
21.75	-0.1	Juliet	Cuthbert (10)	JAM	9.4.64	2s2	OG	Barcelona	5 Aug 92
21.76	0.3		Koch			1	NC	Dresden	3 Jul 82
21.76	0.7		Griffith-Joyner			1q1	OG	Seoul	28 Sep 88
21.76	-0.8		Jones			1	WK	Zürich	13 Aug 97
21.77	-0.1		Griffith-Joyner			1q2	OT	Indianapolis	22 Jul 88
21.77	1.0		Ottey			1	Herc	Monaco	7 Aug 93
21.77	-0.3		Torrence			1	ASV	Köln	18 Aug 95
21.77	0.6	Inger	Miller	USA	12.6.72	1	WCh	Sevilla	27 Aug 99
21.78	-1.3		Koch			1	NC	Leipzig	11 Aug 85
21.79	1.7		Gladisch			1	NC	Potsdam	22 Aug 87
21.80	-1.1		Ottey			1	Nik	Nice	10 Jul 90
21.80	0.4		Jones			1	GWG	Uniondale, NY	20 Jul 98
21.81	-0.1	Valerie	Brisco	USA	6.7.60	1	OG	Los Angeles	9 Aug 84
21.81	0.4		Ottey			1	ASV	Köln	19 Aug 90
21.81	-0.6		Torrence			1	OG	Barcelona	6 Aug 92
21.81	0.0		Torrence			1	Herc	Monaco	25 Jul 95
21.81	1.6		Jones			1	Pre	Eugene	30 May 99
		(30/12)							
21.83	-0.2	Evelyn	Ashford	USA	15.4.57	1	WCp	Montreal	24 Aug 79
21.85	0.3	Bärbel	Wöckel'	GDR	21.3.55	2	OD	Potsdam	21 Jul 84
21.87	0.0	Irina	Privalova	RUS	22.11.68	2	Herc	Monaco	25 Jul 95
21.93	1.3	Pam	Marshall	USA	16.8.60	2	OT	Indianapolis	23 Jul 88
21.95	0.3	Katrin	Krabbe ¶	GDR	22.11.69	1	EC	Split	30 Aug 90
21.97	1.9	Jarmila	Kratochvílová	CZE	26.1.51	1	PTS	Bratislava	6 Jun 81
21.99	0.9	Chandra	Cheeseborough	USA	10.1.59	2	TAC	Indianapolis	19 Jun 83
21.99	1.1	Marie-José	Pérec	FRA	9.5.68	1	BNP	Villeneuve d'Ascq	2 Jul 93
		(20)							
22.01	-0.5	Anelia	Nuneva'	BUL	30.6.62	1	NC	Sofiya	16 Aug 87
22.01	0.0		Li Xuemei	CHN	5.1.77	1	NG	Shanghai	22 Oct 97
22.04A	0.7	Dawn	Sowell	USA	27.3.66	1	NCAA	Provo	2 Jun 89
22.06A	0.7	Evette	de Klerk'	RSA	21.8.65	1		Pietersburg	8 Apr 89
22.07	-0.1	Mary	Onyali	NGR	3.2.68	1	WK	Zürich	14 Aug 96
22.10	-0.1	Kathy	Cook'	GBR	3.5.60	4	OG	Los Angeles	9 Aug 84
22.13	1.2	Ewa	Kasprzyk	POL	7.9.57	2	GWG	Moskva	8 Jul 86
22.14	-0.6	Carlette	Guidry	USA	4.9.68	1	NC	Atlanta	23 Jun 96
22.17A	-2.3	Zhanna	Pintusevich	UKR	6.7.72	1		Monachil	9 Jul 97
22.18	-0.6	Dannette	Young-Stone	USA	6.10.64	2	NC	Atlanta	23 Jun 96
		(30)							
22.18	0.9	Galina	Malchugina	RUS	17.12.62	1s2	NC	Sankt Peterburg	4 Jul 96
22.18	0.5	Merlene	Frazer	JAM	27.12.73	1s2	WCh	Sevilla	25 Aug 99
22.19	1.5	Natalya	Bochina	RUS	4.1.62	2	OG	Moskva	30 Jul 80
22.19	0.0	Debbie	Ferguson	BAH	16.1.76	1	GP II	Saint-Denis	3 Jul 99
22.22	0.6	Beverly	McDonald	JAM	15.2.70	2	WCh	Sevilla	27 Aug 99
22.21 WR	1.9	Irena	Szewinska'	POL	24.5.46	1		Potsdam	13 Jun 74
22.22	-0.9	Falilat	Ogunkoya	NGR	12.5.68	1	AfCh	Dakar	22 Aug 98
22.23	0.8	Melinda	Gainsford-Taylor	AUS	1.10.71	1		Stuttgart	13 Jul 97
22.24	0.3	Gesine	Walther	GDR	6.10.62	2	NC	Dresden	3 Jul 82
22.24	0.1	Maya	Azarashvili	GEO	6.4.64	1		Kiyev	16 Aug 88
		(40)							
22.25A	0.8	Angella	Taylor'	CAN	28.9.58	1		Colorado Springs	20 Jul 82
22.25	1.3	Cathy	Freeman	AUS	16.2.73	1	CG	Victoria	26 Aug 94
22.25	1.8	Andrea	Philipp	GER	29.7.71	2s1	WCh	Sevilla	25 Aug 99
22.26	0.0	Christine	Arron	FRA	13.9.73	2	GP II	Saint-Denis	3 Jul 99
22.27	1.2	Elvira	Barbashina'	UZB	25.2.63	3	GWG	Moskva	8 Jul 86
22.27	0.7	Pauline	Davis-Thompson	BAH	9.7.66	2	OG	Sydney	28 Sep 00
22.28	1.1	Fatima	Yusuf	NGR	2.5.71	2q2	WCh	Sevilla	24 Aug 99
22.28	0.7	Susanthika	Jayasinghe	SRI	17.12.75	3	OG	Sydney	28 Sep 00
22.29	0.7	Silke-Beate	Knoll	GER	21.2.67	1		Ingolstadt	19 Jul 92
22.29	0.6	LaTasha	Jenkins	USA	19.12.77	1	NCAA	Boise	5 Jun 99
		(50)	100th woman 22.51, 200th woman 22.80						

Wind-assisted

Mark	Wind	Name		Nat	Born	Pos	Meet	Venue	Date
21.82	3.1	Irina	Privalova	RUS	22.11.68	1	Athl	Lausanne	6 Jul 94
22.16	3.1	Dannette	Young-Stone	USA	6.10.64	2	Athl	Lausanne	6 Jul 94
22.16	3.2	Nanceen	Perry	USA	19.4.77	1		Austin	6 May 00
22.18A	2.8	Melinda	Gainsford-Taylor	AUS	1.10.71	1		Pietersburg	18 Mar 00

Mark	Wind	Name		Nat	Born	Pos	Meet	Venue	Date
22.19A	3.1	Angella	Taylor'	CAN	28.9.58	1		Colorado Springs	21 Jul 82
22.22	2.7	LaTasha	Jenkins	USA	19.12.77	1s1	NCAA	Boise	4 Jun 99
22.25	3.8	Peta-Gaye	Dowdie	JAM	18.1.77	1		Baton Rouge	17 Apr 99
Hand timing									
21.9	-0.1	Svetlana	Goncharenko	RUS	28.5.71	1		Rostov-na-Donu	31 May 98
22.0	-0.6	Marina	Molokova	RUS	24.8.62	1	Ros	Praha	23 Jun 87
21.6w	2.5	Pam	Marshall	USA	16.8.60	1	TAC	San José	26 Jun 87

300 METRES

Times in 300m races

Mark	Wind	Name		Nat	Born	Pos	Meet	Venue	Date
35.46		Kathy	Cook'	GBR	3.5.60	1	Nike	London (CP)	18 Aug 84
35.46		Chandra	Cheeseborough	USA	10.1.59	2	Nike	London (CP)	18 Aug 84
35.68		Marion	Jones	USA	12.10.75	1	MSR	Walnut	22 Apr 01
35.70		Irena	Szewinska'	POL	24.5.46	1		London (CP)	4 Jul 75
35.71		Donna	Fraser	GBR	7.11.72	1		Gateshead	28 Aug 00
35.82		Cydonie	Mothersill	CAY	19.3.78	1r3		Sydney	14 Sep 00
Indoors									
35.45		Irina	Privalova	RUS	22.11.68	1		Moskva	17 Jan 93
35.48	#	Svetlana	Goncharenko	RUS	28.5.71	1		Tampere	4 Feb 98

400 METRES

Mark	Wind	Name		Nat	Born	Pos	Meet	Venue	Date
47.60 WR		Marita	Koch	GDR	18.2.57	1	WCp	Canberra	6 Oct 85
47.99 WR		Jarmila	Kratochvílová	CZE	26.1.51	1	WCh	Helsinki	10 Aug 83
48.16 WR			Koch			1	EC	Athína	8 Sep 82
48.16			Koch			1	Drz	Praha	16 Aug 84
48.22			Koch			1	EC	Stuttgart	28 Aug 86
48.25		Marie-José	Pérec	FRA	9.5.68	1	OG	Atlanta	29 Jul 96
48.26			Koch			1	GO	Dresden	27 Jul 84
48.27		Olga	Vladykina'	UKR	30.6.63	2	WCp	Canberra	6 Oct 85
48.45			Kratochvílová			1	NC	Praha	23 Jul 83
48.59		Tatána	Kocembová'	CZE	2.5.62	2	WCh	Helsinki	10 Aug 83
48.60 WR			Koch			1	ECp	Torino	4 Aug 79
48.60			Vladykina			1	ECp	Moskva	17 Aug 85
48.61			Kratochvílová			1	WCp	Roma	6 Sep 81
48.63		Cathy	Freeman	AUS	16.2.73	2	OG	Atlanta	29 Jul 96
48.65			Bryzgina'			1	OG	Seoul	26 Sep 88
48.73			Kocembová			2	Drz	Praha	16 Aug 84
48.77			Koch			1	v USA	Karl-Marx-Stadt	9 Jul 82
48.82			Kratochvílová			1	Ros	Praha	23 Jun 83
48.83		Valerie	Brisco	USA	6.7.60	1	OG	Los Angeles	6 Aug 84
48.83			Pérec			1	OG	Barcelona	5 Aug 92
48.85			Kratochvílová			2	EC	Athína	8 Sep 82
48.86			Kratochvílová			1	WK	Zürich	18 Aug 82
48.86			Koch			1	NC	Erfurt	2 Jun 84
48.87			Koch			1	VD	Bruxelles	27 Aug 82
48.88			Koch			1	OG	Moskva	28 Jul 80
48.89 WR			Koch			1		Potsdam	29 Jul 79
48.89			Koch			1		Berlin	15 Jul 84
48.94 WR			Koch			1	EC	Praha	31 Aug 78
48.96			Vladykina			1	NC	Leningrad	3 Aug 85
48.97			Koch			1	WCp	Montreal	26 Aug 79
48.97			Koch			1		Berlin	22 Sep 85
		(31/7)							
49.05		Chandra	Cheeseborough	USA	10.1.59	2	OG	Los Angeles	6 Aug 84
49.10		Falilat	Ogunkoya	NGR	12.5.68	3	OG	Atlanta	29 Jul 96
49.11		Olga	Nazarova ¶	RUS	1.6.65	1s1	OG	Seoul	25 Sep 88
			(10)						
49.19		Mariya	Pinigina'	UKR	9.2.58	3	WCh	Helsinki	10 Aug 83
49.24		Sabine	Busch	GDR	21.11.62	2	NC	Erfurt	2 Jun 84
49.28 WR		Irena	Szewinska'	POL	24.5.46	1	OG	Montreal	29 Jul 76
49.28		Pauline	Davis	BAH	9.7.66	4	OG	Atlanta	29 Jul 96
49.29		Charity	Opara ¶	NGR	20.5.72	1	GGala	Roma	14 Jul 98
49.30		Petra	Müller'	GDR	18.7.65	1		Jena	3 Jun 88
49.40		Jearl	Miles-Clark	USA	4.9.66	1	NC	Indianapolis	14 Jun 97
49.42		Grit	Breuer ¶	GER	16.2.72	2	WCh	Tokyo	27 Aug 91
49.43		Kathy	Cook'	GBR	3.5.60	3	OG	Los Angeles	6 Aug 84
49.43A		Fatima	Yusuf	NGR	2.5.71	1		Harare	15 Sep 95
		(20)							
49.47		Aelita	Yurchenko	UKR	1.1.65	2	Kuts	Moskva	4 Sep 88
49.56		Bärbel	Wöckel'	GDR	21.3.55	1		Erfurt	30 May 82

WOMEN All-time

Mark Wind	Name		Nat	Born	Pos	Meet	Venue	Date
49.57	Grace	Jackson	JAM	14.6.61	1	Nik	Nice	10 Jul 88
49.58	Dagmar	Rübsam'	GDR	3.6.62	3	NC	Erfurt	2 Jun 84
49.58	Lorraine	Graham/Fenton	JAM	8.9.73	2	OG	Sydney	25 Sep 00
49.59	Marion	Jones	USA	12.10.75	1r6	MSR	Walnut	16 Apr 00
49.59	Katharine	Merry	GBR	21.9.74	1	GP	Athína	11 Jun 01
49.61	Ana Fidelia	Quirot	CUB	23.3.63	1	PAm	Habana	5 Aug 91
49.64	Gwen	Torrence	USA	12.6.65	2	Nik	Nice	15 Jul 92
49.64	Ximena	Restrepo	COL	10.3.69	3	OG	Barcelona	5 Aug 92
49.59	Katharine	Merry	GBR	21.9.74	1	GP	Athína	11 Jun 01
49.66	Christina	Lathan'	GDR	28.2.58	3	OG	Moskva	28 Jul 80
	(30)							
49.66	Lillie	Leatherwood	USA	6.7.64	1	TAC	New York	15 Jun 91
49.67	Sandra	Myers	ESP	9.1.61	1	Bisl	Oslo	6 Jul 91
49.70A	Ana	Guevara	MEX	4.3.77	1	IMSS	Ciudad de México	1 Jul 00
49.74	Anja	Rücker	GER	20.12.72	2	WCh	Sevilla	26 Aug 99
49.75	Gaby	Bussmann	FRG	8.10.59	4	WCh	Helsinki	10 Aug 83
49.79	Sandie	Richards	JAM	6.11.68	2	WCh	Athína	4 Aug 97
49.79	Donna	Fraser	GBR	7.11.72	4	OG	Sydney	25 Sep 00
49.81		Ma Yuqin	CHN	11.9.72	1	NG	Beijing	11 Sep 93
49.84	Diane	Dixon	USA	23.9.64	3s1	OG	Seoul	25 Sep 88
	(40)							
49.86	Ami Mbacké	Thiam	SEN	10.11.76	1	WCh	Edmonton	7 Aug 01
49.87	Denean	Howard/Hill	USA	5.10.64	4s1	OG	Seoul	25 Sep 88
49.87	LaTasha	Colander-Richardson	USA	23.8.76	1	NC	Sacramento	16 Jul 00
49.88	Ionela	Tîrlea	ROM	9.2.76	1	WUG	Palma de Mallorca	12 Jul 99
49.89	Irina	Privalova	RUS	22.11.68	1	Kuts	Moskva	30 Jul 93
49.91	Marita	Payne'	CAN	7.10.60	4	OG	Los Angeles	6 Aug 84
49.91	Jillian	Richardson	CAN	10.3.65	5s1	OG	Seoul	25 Sep 88
49.95	Olga	Kotlyarova	RUS	12.4.76	1	Super	Yokohama	9 Sep 00
49.98	Tatyana	Alekseyeva	RUS	7.10.63	1	NC	Tula	8 Jul 97
49.99	Pam	Marshall	USA	16.8.60	1	Pepsi	Westwood	17 May 86
	(50)	100th woman 50.62, 200th woman 51.16						
Low altitude best: 49.77		Yusuf			6	OG	Atlanta	29 Jul 96
Hand timing								
48.9	Olga	Nazarova ¶	RUS	1.6.65	1	NP	Vladivostok	13 Sep 88
49.2A	Ana Fidelia	Quirot	CUB	23.3.63	1	AmCp	Bogotá	13 Aug 89

600 METRES

Mark	Name		Nat	Born	Pos	Meet	Venue	Date
1:22.63	Ana Fidelia	Quirot	CUB	23.3.63	1		Guadalajara	25 Jul 97
1:23.5	Doina	Melinte	ROM	27.12.56	1		Poiana Brasov	27 Jul 86
1:24.4	Patrizia	Spuri	ITA	18.2.73	1		Rieti	29 Sep 99
1:24.48+	Sigrun	Wodars	GDR	7.11.65	1	WCp	Barcelona	7 Sep 89
1:24.56	Martina	Steuk'	GDR	11.11.59	1		Erfurt	1 Aug 81

800 METRES

Mark	Name		Nat	Born	Pos	Meet	Venue	Date
1:53.28 WR	Jarmila	Kratochvílová	CZE	26.1.51	1		München	26 Jul 83
1:53.43 WR	Nadezhda	Olizarenko'	UKR	28.11.53	1	OG	Moskva	27 Jul 80
1:54.44	Ana Fidelia	Quirot	CUB	23.3.63	1	WCp	Barcelona	9 Sep 89
1:54.68		Kratochvílová			1	WCh	Helsinki	9 Aug 83
1:54.81	Olga	Mineyeva	RUS	1.9.52	2	OG	Moskva	27 Jul 80
1:54.82		Quirot			1	ASV	Köln	24 Aug 97
1:54.85 WR		Olizarenko			1	Prav	Moskva	12 Jun 80
1:54.94 WR	Tatyana	Kazankina ¶	RUS	17.12.51	1	OG	Montreal	26 Jul 76
1:55.04		Kratochvílová			1	OsloG	Oslo	23 Aug 83
1:55.05	Doina	Melinte	ROM	27.12.56	1	NC	Bucuresti	1 Aug 82
1:55.1 '		Mineyeva			1	Znam	Moskva	6 Jul 80
1:55.19	Maria Lurdes	Mutola	MOZ	27.10.72	1	WK	Zürich	17 Aug 94
1:55.26	Sigrun	Wodars/Grau	GDR	7.11.65	1	WCh	Roma	31 Aug 87
1:55.29		Mutola			2	ASV	Köln	24 Aug 97
1:55.32	Christine	Wachtel	GDR	6.1.65	2	WCh	Roma	31 Aug 87
1:55.41		Mineyeva			1	EC	Athína	8 Sep 82
1:55.42	Nikolina	Shtereva (10)	BUL	25.1.55	2	OG	Montreal	26 Jul 76
1:55.43		Mutola			1	WCh	Stuttgart	17 Aug 93
1:55.46	Tatyana	Providokhina	RUS	26.3.53	3	OG	Moskva	27 Jul 80
1:55.5		Mineyeva			1	Kuts	Podolsk	21 Aug 82
1:55.54	Ellen	van Langen	NED	9.2.66	1	OG	Barcelona	3 Aug 92
1:55.54		Liu Dong	CHN	24.12.73	1	NG	Beijing	9 Sep 93
1:55.56	Lyubov	Gurina	RUS	6.8.57	3	WCh	Roma	31 Aug 87
1:55.60	Elfi	Zinn	GDR	24.8.53	3	OG	Montreal	26 Jul 76

Mark Wind	Name		Nat	Born	Pos	Meet	Venue	Date
1:55.62		Mutola			1A	WK	Zürich	4 Aug 93
1:55.68	Ella	Kovacs	ROM	11.12.64	1	RomIC	Bucuresti	2 Jun 85
1:55.69	Irina	Podyalovskaya	RUS	19.10.59	1	Izv	Kiyev	22 Jun 84
1:55.70		Wodars			2	WCp	Barcelona	9 Sep 89
1:55.72		Mutola			1	GPF	Monaco	9 Sep 95
1:55.74	Anita	Weiss'	GDR	16.7.55	4	OG	Montreal	26 Jul 76
	(30/18)							
1:55.87	Svetlana	Masterkova	RUS	17.1.68	1	Kuts	Moskva	18 Jun 99
1:55.96	Lyudmila	Veselkova	RUS	25.10.50	2	EC	Athína	8 Sep 82
	(20)							
1:55.96	Yekaterina	Podkopayeva'	RUS	11.6.52	1		Leningrad	27 Jul 83
1:55.99	Lilia	Nurutdinova ¶	RUS	15.12.63	2	OG	Barcelona	3 Aug 92
1:56.0 WR	Valentina	Gerasimova	KZK	15.5.48	1	NC	Kiyev	12 Jun 76
1:56.0	Inna	Yevseyeva	UKR	14.8.64	1		Kiyev	25 Jun 88
1:56.1	Ravilya	Agletdinova'	BLR	10.2.60	2	Kuts	Podolsk	21 Aug 82
1:56.2 '	Totka	Petrova ¶	BUL	17.12.56	1		Paris	6 Jul 79
1:56.2	Tatyana	Mishkel	UKR	10.6.52	3	Kuts	Podolsk	21 Aug 82
1:56.21	Martina	Kämpfert'	GDR	11.11.59	4	OG	Moskva	27 Jul 80
1:56.21	Zamira	Zaytseva	UZB	16.2.53	2		Leningrad	27 Jul 83
1:56.21	Kelly	Holmes	GBR	19.4.70	2	GPF	Monaco	9 Sep 95
	(30)							
1:56.24		Qu Yunxia	CHN	25.12.72	2	NG	Beijing	9 Sep 93
1:56.40	Jearl	Miles-Clark	USA	4.9.66	3	WK	Zürich	11 Aug 99
1:56.42	Paula	Ivan	ROM	20.7.63	1	Balk	Ankara	16 Jul 88
1:56.44	Svetlana	Styrkina	RUS	1.1.49	5	OG	Montreal	26 Jul 76
1:56.51	Slobodanka	Colovic	YUG	10.1.65	1		Beograd	17 Jun 87
1:56.53	Patricia	Djaté	FRA	3.1.71	3	GPF	Mpnaco	9 Sep 95
1:56.56	Ludmila	Formanová	CZE	2.1.74	4	WK	Zürich	11 Aug 99
1:56.57	Zoya	Rigel	RUS	15.10.52	3	EC	Praha	31 Aug 78
1:56.60	Natalya	Tsyganova	RUS	7.2.71	1	NC	Tula	25 Jul 00
1:56.6	Tamara	Sorokina'	RUS	15.8.50	5	Kuts	Podolsk	21 Aug 82
	(40)							
1:56.61	Yelena	Afanasyeva	RUS	1.3.67	3	WK	Zürich	13 Aug 97
1:56.62	Tina	Paulino	MOZ	7.7.73	2	NYG	New York	22 May 93
1:56.64	Nadezhda	Loboyko	KAZ	30.6.61	1	NC	Kiyev	7 Jul 90
1:56.64	Stephanie	Graf	AUT	26.4.73	2	OG	Sydney	25 Sep 00
1:56.67	Fita	Lovin'	ROM	14.1.51	2	Prav	Moskva	12 Jun 80
1:56.68	Letitia	Vriesde	SUR	5.10.64	2	WCh	Göteborg	13 Aug 95
1:56.7	Dalia	Matuseviciene	LIT	12.11.62	2		Kiyev	25 Jun 88
1:56.78	Lyudmila	Borisova	RUS	30.7.59	3	Izv	Kiyev	22 Jun 84
1:56.82	Lyudmila	Rogachova	RUS	10.10.66	1		Parnu	13 Jul 88
1:56.84	Nina	Ruchayeva	RUS	17.4.56	2r1	NP/s	Moskva	19 Jul 84
	(50)	100th woman 1:57.9, 200th woman 1:59.17						

1000 METRES

Mark Wind	Name		Nat	Born	Pos	Meet	Venue	Date
2:28.98 WR	Svetlana	Masterkova	RUS	17.1.68	1	VD	Bruxelles	23 Aug 96
2:29.34 WR	Maria Lurdes	Mutola	MOZ	27.10.72	1	VD	Bruxelles	25 Aug 95
2:29.66		Mutola			2	VD	Bruxelles	23 Aug 96
2:30.6 WR	Tatyana	Providokhina	RUS	26.3.53	1		Podolsk	20 Aug 78
2:30.67 WR	Christine	Wachtel	GDR	6.1.65	1	ISTAF	Berlin	17 Aug 90
2:30.85	Martina	Kämpfert'	GDR	11.11.59	1		Berlin	9 Jul 80
2:31.50	Natalya	Artyomova ¶	RUS	5.1.63	1	ISTAF	Berlin	10 Sep 91
2:31.5	Maricica	Puica	ROM	29.7.50	1		Poiana Brasov	1 Jun 86
2:31.51	Sandra	Gasser ¶	SUI	27.7.62	1		Jerez de la Frontera	13 Sep 89
2:31.6 '	Beate	Liebich	GDR	21.2.58	2		Berlin	9 Jul 80
2:31.65	Olga	Dvirna	RUS	11.2.53	1		Athína	1 Sep 82

1500 METRES

Mark Wind	Name		Nat	Born	Pos	Meet	Venue	Date
3:50.46 WR		Qu Yunxia	CHN	25.12.72	1	NG	Beijing	11 Sep 93
3:50.98		Jiang Bo	CHN	13.3.77	1	NG	Shanghai	18 Oct 97
3:51.34		Lang Yinglai	CHN	22.8.79	2	NG	Shanghai	18 Oct 97
3:51.92		Wang Junxia	CHN	9.1.73	2	NG	Beijing	11 Sep 93
3:52.47 WR	Tatyana	Kazankina ¶	RUS	17.12.51	1	WK	Zürich	13 Aug 80
3:53.91		Yin Lili	CHN	11.11.79	3	NG	Shanghai	18 Oct 97
3:53.96	Paula	Ivan'	ROM	20.7.63	1	OG	Seoul	1 Oct 88
3:53.97		Lan Lixin	CHN	14.2.79	4	NG	Shanghai	18 Oct 97
3:54.23	Olga	Dvirna	RUS	11.2.53	1	NC	Kiyev	27 Jul 82
3:54.52		Zhang Ling (10)	CHN	13.4.80	5	NG	Shanghai	18 Oct 97
3:55.0 ' WR		Kazankina ¶			1	Znam	Moskva	6 Jul 80
3:55.01		Lan Lixin			1h2	NG	Shanghai	17 Oct 97

Mark Wind		Name	Nat	Born	Pos	Meet	Venue	Date
3:55.07		Dong Yanmei	CHN	16.2.77	6	NG	Shanghai	18 Oct 97
3:55.30	Hassiba	Boulmerka	ALG	10.7.68	1	OG	Barcelona	8 Aug 92
3:55.38		Qu Yunxia			2h2	NG	Shanghai	17 Oct 97
3:55.47		Zhang Ling			3h2	NG	Shanghai	17 Oct 97
3:55.82		Dong Yanmei			4h2	NG	Shanghai	17 Oct 97
3:56.0 WR		Kazankina ¶			1		Podolsk	28 Jun 76
3:56.14	Zamira	Zaytseva	UZB	16.2.53	2	NC	Kiyev	27 Jul 82
3:56.22		Ivan			1	WK	Zürich	17 Aug 88
3:56.31		Liu Dong	CHN	24.12.73	5h2	NG	Shanghai	17 Oct 97
3:56.50	Tatyana	Pozdnyakova	RUS	4.3.56	3	NC	Kiyev	27 Jul 82
3:56.56		Kazankina ¶			1	OG	Moskva	1 Aug 80
3:56.63	Nadezhda	Ralldugina	UKR	15.11.57	1	Drz	Praha	18 Aug 84
3:56.65	Yekaterina	Podkopayeva'	RUS	11.6.52	1		Rieti	2 Sep 84
3:56.7 '	Lyubov	Smolka	UKR	29.11.52	2	Znam	Moskva	6 Jul 80
3:56.7	Doina	Melinte	ROM	27.12.56	1		Bucuresti	12 Jul 86
3:56.77+	Svetlana	Masterkova (20)	RUS	17.1.68	1	WK	Zürich	14 Aug 96
3:56.8 '	Nadezhda	Olizarenko'	UKR	28.11.53	3	Znam	Moskva	6 Jul 80
3:56.9 '		Zaytseva			4	Znam	Moskva	6 Jul 80
	(30/21)							
3:56.91	Lyudmila	Rogachova	RUS	10.10.66	2	OG	Barcelona	8 Aug 92
3:56.97	Gabriela	Szabo	ROM	14.11.75	1	Herc	Monaco	8 Aug 98
3:57.03		Liu Jing	CHN	.2.71	6h2	NG	Shanghai	17 Oct 97
3:57.05	Svetlana	Guskova	MDA	19.8.59	4	NC	Kiyev	27 Jul 82
3:57.12	Mary	Decker/Slaney	USA	4.8.58	1	vNord	Stockholm	26 Jul 83
3:57.22	Maricica	Puica	ROM	29.7.50	1		Bucuresti	1 Jul 84
3:57.40	Suzy	Favor Hamilton	USA	8.8.68	1	Bisl	Oslo	28 Jul 00
3:57.4 '	Totka	Petrova ¶	BUL	17.12.56	1	Balk	Athína	11 Aug 79
3:57.41	Jackline	Maranga	KEN	16.12.77	3	Herc	Monaco	8 Aug 98
	(30)							
3:57.46		Zhang Linli	CHN	6.3.73	3	NG	Beijing	11 Sep 93
3:57.71	Christiane	Wartenberg'	GDR	27.10.56	2	OG	Moskva	1 Aug 80
3:57.71	Carla	Sacramento	POR	10.12.71	4	Herc	Monaco	8 Aug 98
3:57.72	Galina	Zakharova	RUS	7.9.56	1	NP	Baku	14 Sep 84
3:57.92	Tatyana	Dorovskikh ¶	UKR	12.8.61	4	OG	Barcelona	8 Aug 92
3:58.07	Kelly	Holmes	GBR	19.4.70	1		Sheffield	29 Jun 97
3:58.12	Naomi	Mugo	KEN	2.1.77	5	Herc	Monaco	8 Aug 98
3:58.20	Anita	Weyermann	SUI	8.12.77	6	Herc	Monaco	8 Aug 98
3:58.2 '	Natalia	Marasescu' ¶	ROM	3.10.52	1	NC	Bucuresti	13 Jul 79
3:58.29	Violeta	Szekely' ¶	ROM	26.3.65	1	Herc	Monaco	18 Aug 00
	(40)							
3:58.37	Tatyana	Providokhina	RUS	26.3.53	1	Kuts	Podolsk	22 Aug 82
3:58.38	Kutre	Dulecha	ETH	22.8.78	7	Herc	Monaco	8 Aug 98
3:58.40	Ravilya	Agletdinova'	BLR	10.2.60	1	ECp	Moskva	18 Aug 85
3:58.5 '	Ileana	Silai ¶	ROM	14.10.41	2	NC	Bucuresti	13 Jul 79
3:58.64		Wang Renmei	CHN	5.7.70	4	NG	Beijing	11 Sep 93
3:58.65	Gabriella	Dorio	ITA	26.6.57	2		Tirrenia	25 Aug 82
3:58.67	Hildegard	Körner'	GDR	20.12.59	2	WCh	Roma	5 Sep 87
3:58.71	Lyubov	Kremlyova ¶	RUS	21.12.61	1	WK	Zürich	19 Aug 92
3:58.74		Yan Wei	CHN	12.10.71	4h1	NG	Shanghai	17 Oct 97
3:58.76	Svetlana	Ulmasova	UZB	4.2.53	2	Kuts	Podolsk	22 Aug 82
	(50)	100th woman 4:01.38, 200th woman 4:04.72						

1 MILE

Mark Wind		Name	Nat	Born	Pos	Meet	Venue	Date
4:12.56 WR	Svetlana	Masterkova	RUS	17.1.68	1	WK	Zürich	14 Aug 96
4:15.61 WR	Paula	Ivan'	ROM	20.7.63	1	Nik	Nice	10 Jul 89
4:15.8	Natalya	Artyomova ¶	RUS	5.1.63	1		Leningrad	5 Aug 84
4:16.71 WR	Mary	Slaney (Decker)	USA	4.8.58	1	WK	Zürich	21 Aug 85
4:17.25	Sonia	O'Sullivan	IRL	28.11.69	1	Bisl	Oslo	22 Jul 94
4:17.33	Maricica	Puica	ROM	29.7.50	2	WK	Zürich	21 Aug 85
4:17.57	Zola	Budd'	GBR	26.5.66	3	WK	Zürich	21 Aug 85
4:18.13	Doina	Melinte	ROM	27.12.56	1	Bisl	Oslo	14 Jul 90
4:19.30	Gabriela	Szabo	ROM	14.11.75	1		Bellinzona	1 Jul 98
4:19.41	Kirsty	McDermott/Wade	GBR	6.8.62	2	Bisl	Oslo	27 Jul 85
Indoors								
4:17.14	Doina	Melinte	ROM	27.12.56	1		East Rutherford	9 Feb 90

2000 METRES

Mark Wind		Name	Nat	Born	Pos	Meet	Venue	Date
5:25.36 WR	Sonia	O'Sullivan	IRL	28.11.69	1	TSB	Edinburgh	8 Jul 94
5:26.93	Yvonne	Murray	GBR	4.10.64	2	TSB	Edinburgh	8 Jul 94
5:28.69 WR	Maricica	Puica	ROM	29.7.50	1	PTG	London (CP)	11 Jul 86

Mark Wind	Name		Nat	Born	Pos	Meet	Venue	Date
5:28.72 WR	Tatyana	Kazankina ¶	RUS	17.12.51	1		Moskva	4 Aug 84
5:29.43+		Wang Junxia	CHN	9.1.73	1h2	NG	Beijing	12 Sep 93
5:29.64	Tatyana	Pozdnyakova	UKR	4.3.56	2		Moskva	4 Aug 84
5:30.19	Zola	Budd'	GBR	26.5.66	3	PTG	London (CP)	11 Jul 86
5:30.92	Galina	Zakharova	RUS	7.9.56	3		Moskva	4 Aug 84
5:32.7 ' WR	Mary	Decker/Slaney	USA	4.8.58	1		Eugene	3 Aug 84
5:32.83	Roberta	Brunet (10)	ITA	20.5.65	1		Torino	14 Sep 96
Indoors								
5:30.53	Gabriela	Szabo	ROM	14.11.75	1		Sindelfingen	8 Mar 98

3000 METRES

Mark Wind	Name		Nat	Born	Pos	Meet	Venue	Date
8:06.11 WR		Wang Junxia	CHN	9.1.73	1	NG	Beijing	13 Sep 93
8:12.18		Qu Yunxia	CHN	25.12.72	2	NG	Beijing	13 Sep 93
8:12.19 WR		Wang Junxia			1h2	NG	Beijing	12 Sep 93
8:12.27		Qu Yunxia			2h2	NG	Beijing	12 Sep 93
8:16.50		Zhang Linli	CHN	6.3.73	3	NG	Beijing	13 Sep 93
8:19.78		Ma Liyan	CHN	6.9.68	3h2	NG	Beijing	12 Sep 93
8:21.26		Ma Liyan			4	NG	Beijing	13 Sep 93
8:21.64	Sonia	O'Sullivan	IRL	28.11.69	1	TSB	London (CP)	15 Jul 94
8:21.84		Zhang Lirong	CHN	3.3.73	5	NG	Beijing	13 Sep 93
8:22.06 WR		Zhang Linli			1h1	NG	Beijing	12 Sep 93
8:22.44		Zhang Lirong			2h1	NG	Beijing	12 Sep 93
8:22.62 WR	Tatyana	Kazankina ¶	RUS	17.12.51	1		Leningrad	26 Aug 84
8:23.26	Olga	Yegorova	RUS	28.3.72	1	WK	Zürich	17 Aug 01
8:23.75		Yegorova			1	GP	Saint-Denis	6 Jul 01
8:23.96		Yegorova			1	GGala	Roma	29 Jun 01
8:24.19	Gabriela	Szabo	ROM	14.11.75	2	WK	Zürich	17 Aug 01
8:24.31		Szabo			1	GP	Paris	29 Jul 98
8:25.03		Szabo			1	WK	Zürich	11 Aug 99
8:25.40	Yelena	Zadorozhnaya (10)	RUS	3.12.77	2	GGala	Roma	29 Jun 01
8:25.56	Tatyana	Tomashova	RUS	1.7.75	3	GGala	Roma	29 Jun 01
8:25.59		Szabo			1	GP	Paris (C)	21 Jul 99
8:25.62	Berhane	Adere	ETH	21.7.73	3	WK	Zürich	17 Aug 01
8:25.82		Szabo			1	VD	Bruxelles	3 Sep 99
8:25.83	Mary	Slaney	USA	4.8.58	1	GGALA	Roma	7 Sep 85
8:26.35		Szabo			1	WK	Zürich	11 Aug 00
8:26.44		Szabo			4	GGala	Roma	29 Jun 01
8:26.48	Zahra	Ouaziz	MAR	20.12.69	2	WK	Zürich	11 Aug 99
8:26.53	Tatyana	Samolenko' ¶	UKR	12.8.61	1	OG	Seoul	25 Sep 88
8:26.64		Ouaziz			2	GP	Paris (C)	21 Jul 99
8:26.78 WR	Svetlana	Ulmasova	UZB	4.2.53	1	NC	Kiyev	25 Jul 82
	(30/16)							
8:26.97	Paula	Radcliffe	GBR	17.12.73	5	GGala	Roma	29 Jun 01
8:27.12 WR	Lyudmila	Bragina	RUS	24.7.43	1	v USA	College Park	7 Aug 76
8:27.15	Paula	Ivan'	ROM	20.7.63	2	OG	Seoul	25 Sep 88
8:27.62	Gete	Wami	ETH	11.12.74	4	WK	Zürich	17 Aug 01
	(20)							
8:27.83	Maricica	Puica	ROM	29.7.50	2	GGALA	Roma	7 Sep 85
8:28.80	Marta	Domínguez	ESP	3.11.75	3	WK	Zürich	11 Aug 00
8:28.83	Zola	Budd'	GBR	26.5.66	3	GGALA	Roma	7 Sep 85
8:29.02	Yvonne	Murray	GBR	4.10.64	3	OG	Seoul	25 Sep 88
8:29.14	Lydia	Cheromei	KEN	11.5.77	5	WK	Zürich	11 Aug 00
8:29.36	Svetlana	Guskova	MDA	19.8.59	2	NC	Kiyev	25 Jul 82
8:30.18	Mariya	Pantyukhova	RUS	14.8.74	4	WK	Zürich	11 Aug 99
8:30.22	Carla	Sacramento	POR	10.12.71	2	Herc	Monaco	4 Aug 99
8:30.39	Irina	Mikitenko	GER	23.8.72	6	WK	Zürich	11 Aug 00
8:30.45	Yelena	Romanova	RUS	20.3.63	4	OG	Seoul	25 Sep 88
	(30)							
8:30.59	Daniela	Yordanova	BUL	8.3.76	5	GP	Saint-Denis	6 Jul 01
8:30.66	Fernanda	Ribeiro	POR	23.6.69	3	Herc	Monaco	4 Aug 99
8:30.95	Tegla	Loroupe	KEN	9.5.73	2	Herc	Monaco	18 Aug 00
8:31.67	Natalya	Artyomova ¶	RUS	5.1.63	5	OG	Seoul	25 Sep 88
8:31.75	Grete	Waitz'	NOR	1.10.53	1	OsloG	Oslo	17 Jul 79
8:31.76	Edith	Masai	KEN	4.4.67	6	WK	Zürich	17 Aug 01
8:32.00	Elana	Meyer'	RSA	10.10.66	1		Durban	29 Apr 91
8:32.0	Tatyana	Pozdnyakova	UKR	4.3.56	1		Ryazan	11 Aug 84
8:32.17	Angela	Chalmers	CAN	6.9.63	1	CG	Victoria	23 Aug 94
8:32.70	Katalin	Szentgyörgyi	HUN	1.1.79	6	GP	Saint-Denis	6 Jul 01
	(40)							

Mark	Wind	Name		Nat	Born	Pos	Meet	Venue	Date
8:32.89		Alesya	Turova	BLR	6.12.79	7	GP	Saint-Denis	6 Jul 01
8:33.07			Dong Yanmei	CHN	16.2.77	1	GP	Athína	28 Jun 00
8:33.35		Lidia	Chojecka	POL	25.1.77	1	Gaz	Saint-Denis	23 Jun 00
8:33.40		Galina	Zakharova	RUS	7.9.56	3	NC	Kiyev	25 Jul 82
8:33.53		Natalia	Marasescu' ¶	ROM	3.10.52	2	EC	Praha	29 Aug 78
8:33.53		Yelena	Sipatova	RUS	7.6.55	1		Moskva	12 Jul 80
8:33.85		Asmae	Leghzaoui	MAR	30.8.76	3	Herc	Monaco	18 Aug 00
8:33.9 '		Tatyana	Sychova	RUS	29.11.57	2		Moskva	12 Jul 80
8:33.97		Elly	van Hulst	NED	9.6.59	1	WK	Zürich	17 Aug 88
8:33.99		Olga	Bondarenko'	RUS	2.6.60	1	EC	Stuttgart	28 Aug 86
		(50)	100th woman 8:40.97, 200th 8:47.7						
Indoors: 8:33.82		Elly	van Hulst	NED	9.6.59	1	WI	Budapest	4 Mar 89

2 MILES

Mark	Wind	Name		Nat	Born	Pos	Meet	Venue	Date
9:11.97mx		Regina	Jacobs	USA	28.8.63	1		Los Gatos	12 Aug 99
9:19.56		Sonia	O'Sullivan	IRL	28.11.69	1		Cork	27 Jun 98

5000 METRES

Mark	Wind	Name		Nat	Born	Pos	Meet	Venue	Date
14:28.09	WR		Jiang Bo	CHN	13.3.77	1	NG	Shanghai	23 Oct 97
14:29.32		Olga	Yegorova	RUS	28.3.72	1	ISTAF	Berlin	31 Aug 01
14:29.82			Dong Yanmei	CHN	16.2.77	2	NG	Shanghai	23 Oct 97
14:30.88		Gete	Wami	ETH	11.12.74	1	NA	Heusden	5 Aug 00
14:31.27	WR		Dong Yanmei			1h1	NG	Shanghai	21 Oct 97
14:31.30			Jiang Bo			2h1	NG	Shanghai	21 Oct 97
14:31.48		Gabriela	Szabo	ROM	14.11.75	1	ISTAF	Berlin	1 Sep 98
14:31.69			Wami			2	ISTAF	Berlin	31 Aug 01
14:32.08		Zahra	Ouaziz	MAR	20.12.69	2	ISTAF	Berlin	1 Sep 98
14:32.33			Liu Shixiang ¶	CHN	13.1.71	3h1	NG	Shanghai	21 Oct 97
14:32.44		Paula	Radcliffe	GBR	17.12.73	3	ISTAF	Berlin	31 Aug 01
14:36.08			Wami		4	3	ISTAF	Berlin	1 Sep 98
14:36.45	WR	Fernanda	Ribeiro	POR	23.6.69	1		Hechtel	22 Jul 95
14:37.33	WR	Ingrid	Kristiansen' (10)	NOR	21.3.56	1		Stockholm	5 Aug 86
14:38.14			Liu Shixiang			3	NG	Shanghai	23 Oct 97
14:39.22		Tatyana	Tomashova	RUS	1.7.75	4	ISTAF	Berlin	31 Aug 01
14:39.83		Leah	Malot	KEN	7.6.72	1	ISTAF	Berlin	1 Sep 00
14:39.96			Yin Lili	CHN	11.11.79	4	NG	Shanghai	23 Oct 97
14:40.19			Ouaziz			1	DNG	Stockholm	5 Aug 98
14:40.47		Yelena	Zadorozhnaya	RUS	3.12.77	1	ECp-S	Bremen	24 Jun 01
14:40.59			Szabo			1	ISTAF	Berlin	7 Sep 99
14:40.61			Szabo			2	ISTAF	Berlin	1 Sep 00
14:40.79			Szabo			1	OG	Sydney	25 Sep 00
14:41.02		Sonia	O'Sullivan	IRL	28.11.69	2	OG	Sydney	25 Sep 00
14:41.07			Ribeiro			1	Bisl	Oslo	5 Jul 96
14:41.12			Szabo			2	Bisl	Oslo	5 Jul 96
14:41.23		Ayelech	Worku	ETH	12.6.79	1	BrGP	London (CP)	5 Aug 00
14:41.34			Ouaziz			2	ISTAF	Berlin	7 Sep 99
14:41.40			O'Sullivan			1	ISTAF	Berlin	1 Sep 95
14:41.47			Yin Lili			1h2	NG	Shanghai	21 Oct 97
		(30/16)							
14:42.03		Irina	Mikitenko	GER	23.8.72	3	ISTAF	Berlin	7 Sep 99
14:44.05		Elana	Meyer	RSA	10.10.66	2		Hechtel	22 Jul 95
14:44.50		Roberta	Brunet	ITA	20.5.65	2	ASV	Köln	16 Aug 96
14:44.57		Derartu	Tulu	ETH	21.3.72	3	DNG	Stockholm	1 Aug 00
		(20)							
14:44.95		Julia	Vaquero	ESP	18.9.70	3	Bisl	Oslo	5 Jul 96
14:45.33			Lan Lixin	CHN	14.2.79	2h2	NG	Shanghai	21 Oct 97
14:45.35		Regina	Jacobs	USA	28.8.63	1	NC	Sacramento	21 Jul 00
14:45.71			Song Liqing	CHN	.1.80	3h2	NG	Shanghai	21 Oct 97
14:45.86		Edith	Masai	KEN	4.4.67	1	DNG	Stockholm	17 Jul 01
14:45.95		Tegla	Loroupe	KEN	9.5.73	3	BrGP	London (CP)	5 Aug 00
14:46.41		Rose	Cheruiyot	KEN	21.7.76	3	ASV	Köln	16 Aug 96
14:46.71		Sally	Barsosio	KEN	21.3.78	3	VD	Bruxelles	22 Aug 97
14:46.72		Lydia	Cheromei	KEN	11.5.77	2	ISTAF	Berlin	26 Aug 97
14:47.20			Dong Zhaoxia	CHN	13.11.74	5	NG	Shanghai	23 Oct 97
		(30)							
14:47.40		Worknesh	Kidane	ETH	21.11.81	7	OG	Sydney	25 Sep 00
14:47.51		Pauline	Konga	KEN	10.4.70	6	ASV	Köln	16 Aug 96
14:47.71		Jelena	Prokopcuka	LAT	21.9.76	5	DNG	Stockholm	1 Aug 00
14:47.79		Yamna	Belkacem	FRA	20.2.74	6	DNG	Stockholm	1 Aug 00

Mark Wind	Name		Nat	Born	Pos	Meet	Venue	Date
14:48.07 WR	Zola	Budd'	GBR	26.5.66	1	McV	London (CP)	26 Aug 85
14:48.31	Asmae	Leghzaoui	MAR	30.8.76	4	ISTAF	Berlin	1 Sep 00
14:48.45		Wang Dongmei	CHN	3.12.72	6	NG	Shanghai	23 Oct 97
14:49.40	Catherina	McKiernan	IRL	30.11.69	7	ASV	Köln	16 Aug 96
14:51.62	Deena	Drossin	USA	14.2.73	9	DNG	Stockholm	1 Aug 00
14:51.67	Berhane	Adere	ETH	21.7.73	1	FBK	Hengelo	4 Jun 01
	(40)							
14:51.69	Ebru	Kavaklioglou	TUR	14.3.70	5	WCh	Sevilla	27 Aug 99
	(ex Yelena	Kopytova	RUS)					
14:51.87		Wang Junxia	CHN	9.1.73	1	NC	Nanjing	5 May 96
14:54.08	Natalya	Artyomova ¶	RUS	5.1.63	1		Podolsk	9 Sep 85
14:55.27	Susan	Chepkemei	KEN	25.6.75	5	Bisl	Oslo	13 Jul 01
14:55.76	Olga	Bondarenko'	RUS	2.6.60	2		Podolsk	9 Sep 85
14:55.82	Viktoriya	Nenasheva	RUS	26.6.70	1	DNG	Stockholm	8 Jul 96
14:56.04	Amy	Rudolph	USA	18.9.73	2	DNG	Stockholm	8 Jul 96
14:56.07	Annette	Peters	USA	31.5.65	2	ISTAF	Berlin	27 Aug 93
14:56.15		Xing Huina	CHN	25.2.84	2	NG	Guangzhou	23 Nov 01
14:56.22	Annemari	Sandell	FIN	2.1.77	4	DNG	Stockholm	8 Jul 96
	(50)	100th woman 15:08.05, 200th woman 15:20.36						

10,000 METRES

Mark Wind	Name		Nat	Born	Pos	Meet	Venue	Date
29:31.78 WR		Wang Junxia	CHN	9.1.73	1	NG	Beijing	8 Sep 93
30:13.37		Zhong Huandi	CHN	28.6.67	2	NG	Beijing	8 Sep 93
30:13.74 WR	Ingrid	Kristiansen'	NOR	21.3.56	1	Bisl	Oslo	5 Jul 86
30:17.49	Derartu	Tulu	ETH	21.3.72	1	OG	Sydney	30 Sep 00
30:22.48	Gete	Wami	ETH	11.12.74	2	OG	Sydney	30 Sep 00
30:22.88	Fernanda	Ribeiro	POR	23.6.69	3	OG	Sydney	30 Sep 00
30:23.25		Kristiansen			1	EC	Stuttgart	30 Aug 86
30:24.56		Wami			1	WCh	Sevilla	26 Aug 99
30:26.97	Paula	Radcliffe	GBR	17.12.73	4	OG	Sydney	30 Sep 00
30:27.13		Radcliffe			2	WCh	Sevilla	26 Aug 99
30:32.03	Tegla	Loroupe	KEN	9.5.73	3	WCh	Sevilla	26 Aug 99
30:37.26		Loroupe			5	OG	Sydney	30 Sep 00
30:38.09		Dong Yanmei	CHN	16.2.77	1	NG	Shanghai	19 Oct 97
30:39.41		Lan Lixin (10)	CHN	14.2.79	2	NG	Shanghai	19 Oct 97
30:39.98		Yin Lili	CHN	11.11.79	3	NG	Shanghai	19 Oct 97
30:40.70		Radcliffe			1rA	EChall	Barakaldo	10 Apr 99
30:47.22		Dong Zhaoxia	CHN	13.11.74	4	NG	Shanghai	19 Oct 97
30:47.72		Wang Dongmei	CHN	3.12.72	5	NG	Shanghai	19 Oct 97
30:48.06		Ribeiro			1	EChall	Lisboa	4 Apr 98
30:48.51		Kristiansen			1	Bisl	Oslo	1 Jul 89
30:48.58		Radcliffe			2	EChall	Lisboa	4 Apr 98
30:49.30		Wang Junxia			1	WCh	Stuttgart	21 Aug 93
30:50.34		Wang Junxia			1	AsiG	Hiroshima	15 Oct 94
30:51.30	Berhane	Adere	ETH	21.7.73	1	NA	Heusden	5 Aug 00
30:52.51	Elana	Meyer	RSA	10.10.66	1	WCp	London (CP)	10 Sep 94
30:53.37	Sonia	O'Sullivan	IRL	28.11.69	6	OG	Sydney	30 Sep 00
30:55.80		Radcliffe			1	E Chall	Barakaldo	7 Apr 01
30:55.83		Liu Shixiang ¶	CHN	13.1.71	6	NG	Shanghai	19 Oct 97
30:56.4		Tulu			1		Gijón	12 Aug 00
30:57.07	Liz	McColgan	GBR	24.5.64	1	APM	Hengelo	25 Jun 91
30:57.21	Olga	Bondarenko'	RUS	2.6.60	2	EC	Stuttgart	30 Aug 86
30:57.70	Leah	Malot	KEN	7.6.72	2	NA	Heusden	5 Aug 00
	(32/20)							
30:59.92	Merima	Hashim	ETH	.81	3	NA	Heusden	5 Aug 00
31:03.60	Marleen	Renders	BEL	24.12.68	4	NA	Heusden	5 Aug 00
31:03.62	Kathrin	Ullrich'	GER	14.8.67	1	ECp	Frankfurt-am-Main	30 Jun 91
31:05.57	Maura	Viceconte	ITA	3.10.67	5	NA	Heusden	5 Aug 00
31:06.94		Li Ji ¶	CHN	19.9.79	7	OG	Sydney	30 Sep 00
31:07.88	Jill	Hunter	GBR	14.10.66	2	ECp	Frankfurt-am-Main	30 Jun 91
31:08.41	Catherina	McKiernan	IRL	30.11.69	1		Villeneuve d'Ascq	17 Jun 95
31:09.25		Zhang Lirong	CHN	3.3.73	3	NG	Beijing	8 Sep 93
31:09.40	Yelena	Zhupiyova'	UKR	18.4.60	2	WCh	Roma	4 Sep 87
31:09.46	Yuko	Kawakami	JPN	1.8.75	2		Brunswick	1 Jul 00
	(30)							
31:10.12	Adriana	Fernández	MEX	4.4.71	3		Brunswick	1 Jul 00
31:10.46		Ma Liyan	CHN	6.9.68	4	NG	Beijing	8 Sep 93
31:11.26		Song Liqing	CHN	.1.80	7	NG	Shanghai	19 Oct 97
31:11.72	Lisa	Ondieki'	AUS	12.5.60	1	WG	Helsinki	30 Jun 92

Mark	Wind		Name	Nat	Born	Pos	Meet	Venue	Date
31:12.58			Wang Mingxia	CHN	6.6.71	8	NG	Shanghai	19 Oct 97
31:13.21			Ren Xiujuan	CHN	14.9.74	2	NT	Nanjing	8 May 96
31:14.51		Julia	Vaquero	ESP	18.9.70	1	EChall	Barakaldo	5 Apr 97
31:15.00		Galina	Zakharova	RUS	7.9.56	2	Izv	Kiyev	24 Jun 84
31:15.38		Sally	Barsosio	KEN	21.3.78	3	WCh	Stuttgart	21 Aug 93
31:16.28			Zhang Linli	CHN	6.3.73	5	NG	Beijing	8 Sep 93
		(40)							
31:16.39			Yang Siju	CHN	19.4.73	9	NG	Shanghai	19 Oct 97
31:16.42		M Conceição	Ferreira	POR	13.3.62	2	WG	Helsinki	30 Jun 92
31:16.94		Asmae	Leghzaoui	MAR	30.8.76	1	MedG	Tunis	12 Sep 01
31:18.18		Viorica	Ghican	ROM	9.6.65	1	WG	Helsinki	27 Jun 90
31:19.40		Hiromi	Suzuki	JPN	6.12.68	1	NC	Osaka	9 Jun 96
31:19.76		Ulrike	Bruns'	GDR	17.11.53	3	EC	Stuttgart	30 Aug 86
31:19.89		Lynn	Jennings	USA	10.7.60	3	OG	Barcelona	7 Aug 92
31:20.46		Masako	Chiba	JPN	18.7.76	3	NC	Osaka	9 Jun 96
31:21.27		Lidiya	Grigoryeva	RUS	21.1.74	9	OG	Sydney	30 Sep 00
31:21.36		Uta	Pippig	GER	7.9.65	2	OD	Jena	28 May 92
		(50)	100th woman 31:42.02, 200th woman 32:00.11						

1 HOUR

Mark		Name	Nat	Born	Pos	Venue	Date
18,340 WR	Tegla	Loroupe	KEN	9.5.73	1	Borgholzhausen	7 Aug 98
18,084 WR	Silvana	Cruciata	ITA	15.2.53	1	Roma	2 May 81
18,027	Rosa	Mota	POR	29.6.58	1	Lisbon	14 May 83

20,000 METRES

Mark		Name	Nat	Born	Pos	Venue	Date
1:05:26.6 WR	Tegla	Loroupe	KEN	9.5.73	1	Borgholzhausen	3 Sep 00
1:06:48.8 WR	Izumi	Maki	JPN	10.12.68	1	Amagasaki	19 Sep 93
1:06:55.5 WR	Rosa	Mota	POR	29.6.58	1	Lisboa	14 May 83

HALF MARATHON

Included are the slightly downhill courses: Newcastle to South Shields 30.5m, Tokyo 33m (to 1998), Lisboa 40m

Mark	Wind		Name	Nat	Born	Pos	Meet	Venue	Date
65:44		Susan	Chepkemei	KEN	25.6.75	1		Lisboa (60m dh)	1 Apr 01
66:34		Lornah	Kiplagat	KEN	20.3.74	2		Lisboa	1 Apr 01
66:40*		Ingrid	Kristiansen	NOR	21.3.56	1	NC	Sandnes	5 Apr 87
66:43		Masako	Chiba	JPN	18.7.76	1		Tokyo	19 Jan 97
66:44		Elana	Meyer	RSA	10.10.66	1		Tokyo	15 Jan 99
66:47		Paula	Radcliffe	GBR	17.12.73	1	WCh	Bristol	7 Oct 01
66:49		Esther	Wanjiru	KEN	27.3.77	2		Tokyo	15 Jan 99
66:56			L Kiplagat			1	City-Pier	Den Haag	25 Mar 00
67:03		Derartu	Tulu	ETH	21.3.72	3		Lisboa	1 Apr 01
67:07			Radcliffe			1	GNR	South Shields	22 Oct 00
67:11		Liz	McColgan	GBR	24.5.64	1		Tokyo	26 Jan 92
67:12		Tegla	Loroupe (10)	KEN	9.5.73	1		Lisboa	10 Mar 96
67:22			Meyer			1		Tokyo	24 Jan 93
67:24			Loroupe			1		Lisboa	26 Mar 00
67:29			Meyer			1		Kyoto	8 Mar 98
67:32			Loroupe			1		Den Haag	28 Mar 98
67:33			Meyer			1		Tokyo	10 Jan 00
67:36			Meyer			1		Kyoto	9 Mar 97
67:36			Chepkemei			2	WCh	Bristol	7 Oct 01
67:37 L			Kiplagat			1		Zaandam	17 Sep 00
67:41			Wanjiru			2		Tokyo	10 Jan 00
67:43			Loroupe			2		Tokyo	19 Jan 97
67:48		Kerryn	McCann	AUS	2.5.67	3		Tokyo	10 Jan 00
67:50		Catherina	McKiernan	IRL	30.11.69	1		Lisboa	15 Mar 98
67:52			Loroupe			1		Lisboa	21 Mar 99
67:53		Edith	Masai	KEN	4.4.67	1		Nice	22 Apr 01
67:54		Catherine	Ndereba	KEN	21.7.72	1		Den Haag	24 Mar 01
67:57			Meyer			1		Kyoto	14 Mar 99
67:58		Uta	Pippig	GER	7.9.65	1		Kyoto	19 Mar 95
67:59			Meyer			1	NC	East London	18 May 91
67:59			Pippig			1		Kyoto	20 Mar 94
67:59			Wanjiru			1		Sendai	14 Mar 99
67:59	w	Restituta	Joseph	TAN	30.7.71	1		Malmö	12 Jun 00
		(33/16)							
68:09		Cristina	Pomacu	ROM	15.9.73	2		Lisboa	15 Mar 98
68:17		Berhane	Adere	ETH	21.7.73	3	WCh	Bristol	7 Oct 01
68:18		Izumi	Maki	JPN	10.12.68	2		Tokyo	21 Jan 96
68:18		Yoshiko	Ichikawa	JPN	18.4.76	3		Tokyo	19 Jan 97
		(20)							

Mark	Wind	Name		Nat	Born	Pos	Meet	Venue	Date
68:18	w	Joyce	Chepchumba	KEN	6.11.70	2		Malmö	12 Jun 00
68:21		Albertina	Dias	POR	26.4.65	3		Lisboa	10 Mar 96
68:23		Fernanda	Ribeiro	POR	23.6.69	3		Lisboa	26 Mar 00
68:23		Mizuki	Noguchi	JPN	3.7.78	4	WCh	Bristol	7 Oct 01
68:30		Maria	Guida	ITA	23.1.66	4		Lisboa	10 Mar 96
68:33		Lisa	Ondieki	AUS	12.5.60	2		Tokyo	26 Jan 92
68:34		Joan	Benoit	USA	16.5.57	1		Philadelphia	16 Sep 84
68:34		Olga	Appell	MEX	2.8.63	2		Tokyo	24 Jan 93
68:34		Asmae	Leghzaoui	MAR	30.8.76	1		Marrakech	31 Jan 99
68:34		Lidia	Simon	ROM	4.9.73	4		Tokyo	10 Jan 00
		(30)							
68:38		Colleen	de Reuck	RSA	13.4.64	1	NC	Durban	23 Jul 89
68:38		Isabella	Ochichi	KEN	79	2		Nice	22 Apr 01
68:41		Junko	Kataoka	JPN	13.6.70	1		Tokyo	23 Jan 94
68:43		Jelena	Prokopcuka	LAT	21.9.76	5	WCh	Bristol	7 Oct 01
68:45	w	Lyubov	Morgunova	RUS	14.1.71	3		Malmö	12 Jun 00
68:48	w	Abeba	Tolla	ETH	3.6.77	4		Malmö	12 Jun 00
68:49		Grete	Waitz	NOR	1.10.53	1	GNR	South Shields	24 Jul 88
68:51		Margaret	Okayo	KEN	30.5.76	1		Udine	30 Sep 01
68:54		Miwako	Yamanaka	JPN	24.5.78	1		Kobe	16 Dec 01
68:55		Naoko	Takahashi	JPN	6.5.72	1		Chiba	23 Jan 00
		(40)							
68:55		Yasuko	Hashimoto	JPN	12.8.75	2		Kobe	16 Dec 01
68:56		Carla	Beurskens	NED	10.2.52	1		Grevenmacher	21 Sep 86
68:58		Nadezhda	Ilyina	RUS	2.4.64	1		Chelyabinsk	18 Jun 94
68:58			Zheng Guixia	CHN	24.6.73	2		Yamaguchi	11 Mar 01
69:01		Fatuma	Roba	ETH	18.12.73	3		Kobe	16 Dec 01
69:04		Takako	Kotorida	JPN	2.4.77	3		Yamaguchi	11 Mar 01
69:05		Delillah	Asiago	KEN	24.2.72	1	GWR	Exeter	5 May 91
69:08		Firaya	Sultanova	RUS	29.4.61	2		Chelyabinsk	18 Jun 94
69:10		Alina	Tecuta-Gherasim	ROM	10.11.71	3		Marrakech	31 Jan 99
69:12		Yukiko	Okamoto	JPN	29.11.74	1		Yamaguchi	12 Mar 00
		(50)	100th woman 69:46, 200th 70:48						

* uncertain course measurement

Downhill

Mark		Name		Nat	Born	Pos	Meet	Venue	Date
68:12		Claudia	Metzner	GER	5.5.66	1		Las Vegas (260m)	4 Feb 95
68:13		Petra	Wassiluk	GER	27.10.69	1		Las Vegas	9 Feb 97

Drugs disqualification: 68:50 Yasuko Kimura # JPN 6.1.76 (3) Tokyo 21 Jan 96

MARATHON

Note Boston times included in main list, but course is downhill overall (139m) and sometimes, as in 1994, strongly wind-aided - next bests are shown if to standard

In second column: first character: L = loop course or start and finish within 30%, P = point-to-point or start and finish more than 30% apart, D + point-to-point and downhil over 1/1000

Second character: M mixed marathon (men and women), W women only race or separated start by time

Mark		Name		Nat	Born	Pos	Meet	Venue	Date
2:18:47	LM	Catherine	Ndereba	KEN	21.7.72	1		Chicago	7 Oct 01
2:19:46	LM	Naoko	Takahashi	JPN	6.5.72	1		Berlin	30 Sep 01
2:20:43	LM	Tegla	Loroupe	KEN	9.5.73	1		Berlin	26 Sep 99
2:20:47	LM		Loroupe			1		Rotterdam	19 Apr 98
2:21:06	LM	Ingrid	Kristiansen	NOR	21.3.56	1		London	21 Apr 85
2:21:21	LM	Joan	Benoit'	USA	16.5.57	1		Chicago	20 Oct 85
2:21:33	LM		Ndereba			1		Chicago	22 Oct 00
2:21:45	DM	Uta	Pippig	GER	7.9.65	1		Boston	18 Apr 94
2:21:47	PW		N Takahashi			1	AsiG	Bangkok	6 Dec 98
2:22:07	LM		Loroupe			1		Rotterdam	20 Apr 97
2:22:12	LW	Eri	Yamaguchi	JPN	14.1.73	1		Tokyo	22 Nov 99
2:22:19	LW		N Takahashi			1		Nagoya	13 Mar 00
2:22:19	LW		N Takahashi			1		Nagoya	12 Mar 00
2:22:23	LM	Catherina	McKiernan	IRL	30.11.69	1		Amsterdam	1 Nov 98
2:22:36	LM	Lornah	Kiplagat	KEN	20.3.74	2		Chicago	22 Oct 00
2:22:43	DM		Benoit			1		Boston	18 Apr 83
2:22:48	LM		Kristiansen			1		London	10 May 87
2:22:48	LM		Loroupe			1		Rotterdam	18 Apr 99
2:22:54	LW	Lidia	Simon (10)	ROM	4.9.73	1		Osaka	30 Jan 00
2:22:56	LW	Harumi	Hiroyama	JPN	2.9.68	2		Osaka	30 Jan 00
2:23:05	LM		Kristiansen			2		Chicago	20 Oct 85
2:23:11	LW	Yoko	Shibui	JPN	14.3.79	1		Osaka	28 Jan 01
2:23:14	PW		N Takahashi			1	OG	Sydney	24 Sep 00
2:23:21	DM	Fatuma	Roba	ETH	18.12.73	1		Boston	20 Apr 98
2:23:22	LW	Joyce	Chepchumba	KEN	6.11.70	1		London	18 Apr 99

Mark	Wind		Name	Nat	Born	Pos	Meet	Venue	Date
2:23:22	PW		Simon			2	OG	Sydney	24 Sep 00
2:23:24	LW		Simon			1		Osaka	31 Jan 99
2:23:25	DM		Roba			1		Boston	19 Apr 99
2:23:29	LM	Rosa	Mota	POR	29.6.58	3		Chicago	20 Oct 85
2:23:31	LW	Esther	Wanjiru	KEN	27.3.77	3		Osaka	30 Jan 00
2:23:33	DM	Valentina	Yegorova	RUS	16.2.64	2		Boston	18 Apr 94
2:23:37	LM		Liu Min	CHN	29.11.83	1		Beijing	14 Oct 01
2:23:43	DM	Olga	Markova	RUS	6.8.68	1		Boston	20 Apr 92
2:23:43	LM	Marleen	Renders	BEL	24.12.68	1		Paris	9 Apr 00
		(34/20)							
2:23:47	LM	Maura	Viceconte	ITA	3.10.67	1		Wien	21 May 00
2:23:51	LW	Lisa	Martin/Ondieki	AUS	12.5.60	1		Osaka	31 Jan 88
2:23:57	LW	Derartu	Tulu	ETH	21.3.72	1		London	22 Apr 01
2:24:02	LM		Wei Yanan	CHN	6.12.81	2		Beijing	14 Oct 01
2:24:04	LW	Svetlana	Zakharova	RUS	15.9.70	2		London	22 Apr 01
2:24:06	LW	Adriana	Fernández	MEX	4.4.71	2		London	18 Apr 99
2:24:07	LW		Wang Junxia	CHN	9.1.73	1		Tianjin	4 Apr 93
2:24:18	DM	Wanda	Panfil	POL	26.1.59	1		Boston	15 Apr 91
2:24:21	PM	Margaret	Okayo	KEN	30.5.76	1		New York	4 Nov 01
2:24:22	LM		Ren Xiujuan	CHN	14.9.74	3		Beijing	14 Oct 01
		(30)							
2:24:29	LW	Elfenesh	Alemu	ETH	10.6.75	5		London	22 Apr 01
2:24:32	LW		Qu Yunxia	CHN	25.12.72	2		Tianjin	4 Apr 93
2:24:35	PM	Katrin	Dörre-Heinig	GER	6.10.61	1		Hamburg	25 Apr 99
2:24:36	LW	Reiko	Tosa	JPN	11.6.76	2		Nagoya	12 Mar 00
2:24:41	LM		Dai Yanyan	CHN	8.1.80	4		Beijing	14 Oct 01
2:24:42	LW		Zhang Linli	CHN	6.3.73	3		Tianjin	4 Apr 93
2:24:42	LM		Zhang Shujing	CHN	13.9.78	5		Beijing	14 Oct 01
2:24:46	LM	Madina	Biktagirova ¶	RUS	20.9.64	2		Berlin	28 Sep 97
2:24:52	LW		Zhang Lirong	CHN	3.3.73	4		Tianjin	4 Apr 93
2:24:54	LM	Grete	Waitz	NOR	1.10.53	1		London	20 Apr 86
		(40)							
2:25:09	LW	Manuela	Machado	POR	9.8.63	3		London	18 Apr 99
2:25:12	PM	Susan	Chepkemei	KEN	25.6.75	2		New York	4 Nov 01
2:25:14	LW	Kayoko	Obata	JPN	18.9.71	5		Osaka	30 Jan 00
2:25:15	DM	Elana	Meyer	RSA	10.10.66	3		Boston	18 Apr 94
2:25:17	PM	Franca	Fiacconi	ITA	4.10.65	1		New York	1 Nov 98
2:25:18	LW	Nuta	Olaru	ROM	28.8.70	6		London	22 Apr 01
2:25:19	LM	Alena	Peterková ¶	CZE	13.11.60	4		Boston	18 Apr 94
2:25:29	LW	Irina	Timofeyeva	RUS	5.4.70	2		Tokyo	18 Nov 01
2:25:34	LW	Alina	Ivanova	RUS	16.3.69	7		London	22 Apr 01
2:25:35	LW	Bruna	Genovese	ITA	24.9.76	3		Tokyo	18 Nov 01
		(50)	100th woman 2:27:25, 200th 2:28:53, 300th 2:30:41, 400th 2:32:14						

2000 METRES STEEPLECHASE

Mark		Name	Nat	Born	Pos	Meet	Venue	Date
6:11.84	Marina	Pluzhnikova	RUS	25.2.63	1	GWG	Sankt-Peterburg	25 Jul 94
6:14.52	Svetlana	Rogova	RUS	4.8.67	1	Znam	Moskva	11 Jun 92
6:16.49	Yelena	Motalova	RUS	28.1.71	1	NC	Moskva	2 Aug 98
6:17.80	Irina	Mozharova	RUS	19.7.58	1	NC	Gorkiy	23 Jul 89
6:18.2	Svetlana	Vinogradova	RUS	71	1	Army	Rostov	16 Jun 96
6:19.00	Irene	Limika	KEN	28.8.79	1		Loughborough	20 May 01

3000 METRES STEEPLECHASE

Mark			Name	Nat	Born	Pos	Meet	Venue	Date
9:25.31	WR	Justyna	Bak	POL	1.8.74	1	Nik	Nice	9 Jul 01
9:30.70		Melissa	Rollison	AUS	13.4.83	1	GWG	Brisbane	4 Sep 01
9:39.51		Irene	Limika	KEN	28.8.79	2	Nik	Nice	9 Jul 01
9:39.65			Limika			2	GWG	Brisbane	4 Sep 01
9:40.20	WR	Cristina	Iloc-Casandra	ROM	21.10.77	1		Reims	30 Aug 00
9:41.54		Yekaterina	Volkova	RUS	16.2.78	3	GWG	Brisbane	4 Sep 01
9:41.94		Elizabeth	Jackson	USA	27.10.77	4	GWG	Brisbane	4 Sep 01
9:43.36			Jackson			3	Nik	Nice	9 Jul 01
9:43.64	WR		Iloc-Casandra			1	NC	Bucuresti	7 Aug 00
9:44.36			Bak			1		Poznan	8 Jun 01
9:44.68		Elodie	Olivarès	FRA	22.5.76	1	MedG	Tunis	11 Sep 01
9:45.12			Iloc-Casandra			1	FBK	Hengelo	4 Jun 01
9:45.92			Casandra			1		Noisy-le-Grand	19 Jun 01
9:46.53			Olivarès			2		Noisy-le-Grand	19 Jun 01
9:46.56			Casandra			5	GWG	Brisbane	4 Sep 01
9:48.72			Jackson			1	v2N	Glasgow	1 Jul 01
9:48.88	WR	Yelena	Motalova	RUS	28.1.71	1	NC	Tula	31 Jul 99

Mark	Wind	Name		Nat	Born	Pos	Meet	Venue	Date
9:48.84		Laurence	Duquénoy	FRA	29.9.69	4	Nik	Nice	9 Jul 01
9:49.41		Lisa	Nye	USA	17.11.68	1	NC	Eugene	23 Jun 01
9:49.73			Jackson			1	NCAA	Eugene	1 Jun 01
		(20/10)							
9:52.71		Tara	Krzywicki	GBR	9.3.74	2	v2N	Glasgow	1 Jul 01
9:54.10		Anzhelika	Averkova	UKR	13.3.69	1	NC	Kiev	5 Aug 00
9:54.84		Rebecca	Bennion	USA	16.9.80	2	NCAA	Eugene	1 Jun 01
9:54.86		Daniela	Petrescu	ROM	13.4.68	2	NC	Bucuresti	7 Aug 00
9:54.99		Melanie	Schulz	GER	27.8.79	1		Malmö	20 Aug 01
9:55.07		Natalya	Cherepanova	RUS	9.3.67	1	Znam	Tula	8 Jun 01
9:55.49		Kelly	MacDonald	USA	27.9.78	3	NC	Eugene	23 Jun 01
9:56.99		Luminita	Gogîrlea	ROM	5.11.71	3	NC	Bucuresti	7 Aug 00
9:57.06		Anita	Weyermann	SUI	8.12.77	2	FBK	Hengelo	4 Jun 01
9:57.62		Svetlana	Rogova	RUS	4.8.67	1	GWG	Uniondale, NY	19 Jul 98
		(20)							
9:59.28		Courtney	Meldrum	USA	31.1.77	4	NCAA	Eugene	1 Jun 01
9:59.50		Nanette	Evans	USA	18.8.81	5	NCAA	Eugene	1 Jun 01
9:59.75		Ida	Nilsson	SWE	8.2.81	6	NCAA	Eugene	1 Jun 01

100 METRES HURDLES

Mark	Wind	Name		Nat	Born	Pos	Meet	Venue	Date
12.21 WR	0.7	Yordanka	Donkova	BUL	28.9.61	1		Stara Zagora	20 Aug 88
12.24	0.9		Donkova			1h		Stara Zagora	28 Aug 88
12.25 WR	1.4	Ginka	Zagorcheva	BUL	12.4.58	1	v TCH,GRE	Drama	8 Aug 87
12.26 WR	1.5		Donkova			1	Balk	Ljubljana	7 Sep 86
12.26	1.7	Lyudmila	Narozhilenko ¶	RUS	21.4.64	1rB		Sevilla	6 Jun 92
		(now Ludmila Engquist SWE)							
12.27	-1.2		Donkova			1		Stara Zagora	28 Aug 88
12.28	1.8		Narozhilenko			1	NC	Kiyev	11 Jul 91
12.28	0.9		Narozhilenko			1rA		Sevilla	6 Jun 92
12.29 WR	-0.4		Donkova			1	ASV	Köln	17 Aug 86
12.32	1.6		Narozhilenko			1		Saint-Denis	4 Jun 92
12.33	1.4		Donkova			1		Fürth	14 Jun 87
12.33	-0.3	Gail	Devers	USA	19.11.66	1	NC	Sacramento	23 Jul 00
12.34	-0.5		Zagorcheva			1	WCh	Roma	4 Sep 87
12.35 WR	0.1		Donkova			1h2	ASV	Köln	17 Aug 86
12.36 WR	1.9	Grazyna	Rabsztyn	POL	20.9.52	1	Kuso	Warszawa	13 Jun 80
12.36 WR	-0.6		Donkova			1	NC	Sofiya	13 Aug 86
12.36	1.1		Donkova			1		Schwechat	15 Jun 88
12.37	1.4		Donkova			1	ISTAF	Berlin	15 Aug 86
12.37	0.7		Devers			1	WCh	Sevilla	28 Aug 99
12.38	0.0		Donkova			1	BGP	Budapest	11 Aug 86
12.38	-0.7		Donkova			1	EC	Stuttgart	29 Aug 86
12.38	0.2		Donkova			1	OG	Seoul	30 Sep 88
12.39	1.5	Vera	Komisova'	RUS	11.6.53	1	GGala	Roma	5 Aug 80
12.39	1.5		Zagorcheva			2	Balk	Ljubljana	7 Sep 86
12.39	1.8	Natalya	Grigoryeva ¶	UKR	3.12.62	2	NC	Kiyev	11 Jul 91
12.39	-0.7		Devers			1	WK	Zürich	11 Aug 00
12.40	0.4		Donkova			1	GWG	Moskva	8 Jul 86
12.42	1.8	Bettine	Jahn	GDR	3.8.58	1	OD	Berlin	8 Jun 83
12.42	1.0		Zagorcheva			1		Sofiya	14 Aug 85
12.42	-0.2		Donkova			1	VD	Bruxelles	5 Sep 86
12.42	0.2		Narozhilenko			1	GGala	Roma	9 Jun 92
12.42	2.0	Anjanette	Kirkland	USA	24.2.74	1	WCh	Edmonton	11 Aug 01
12.43	-0.9	Lucyna	Kalek (Langer)	POL	9.1.56	1		Hannover	19 Aug 84
12.43	0.7		Zagorcheva			1	BGP	Budapest	6 Jul 87
		(34/10)							
12.44	-0.5	Gloria	Uibel (-Siebert)	GDR	13.1.64	2	WCh	Roma	4 Sep 87
12.44	-0.8	Olga	Shishigina	KZK	23.12.68	1		Luzern	27 Jun 95
12.44	0.4	Glory	Alozie	NGR/ESP	30.12.77	1	Herc	Monaco	8 Aug 98
12.45	1.3	Cornelia	Oschkenat'	GDR	29.10.61	1		Neubrandenburg	11 Jun 87
12.47	1.1	Marina	Azyabina	RUS	15.6.63	1s2	NC	Moskva	19 Jun 93
12.50	0.0	Vera	Akimova'	RUS	5.6.59	1		Sochi	19 May 84
12.52	-0.4	Michelle	Freeman	JAM	5.5.69	1s1	WCh	Athína	10 Aug 97
12.52	1.9	Delloreen	Ennis-London	JAM	5.3.75	1	NC	Kingston	22 Jul 00
12.53	0.2	Tatyana	Reshetnikova	RUS	14.10.66	1rA	GP II	Linz	4 Jul 94
12.53	-0.4	Svetla	Dimitrova ¶	BUL	27.1.70	1	Herc	Stara Zagora	16 Jul 94
		(20)							
12.53	1.0	Melissa	Morrison	USA	9.7.71	1	DNG	Stockholm	5 Aug 98
12.54	0.4	Kerstin	Knabe	GDR	7.7.59	3	EC	Athína	9 Sep 82
12.54	0.9	Sabine	Paetz/John'	GDR	16.10.57	1		Berlin	15 Jul 84

Mark	Wind	Name		Nat	Born	Pos	Meet	Venue	Date
12.56	1.2	Johanna	Klier'	GDR	13.9.52	1	NC	Cottbus	17 Jul 80
12.56	1.2	Monique	Ewanje-Epée	FRA	11.7.67	1	BNP	Villeneuve d'Ascq	29 Jun 90
12.59 WR	-0.6	Anneliese	Ehrhardt	GDR	18.6.50	1	OG	München	8 Sep 72
12.59	0.0	Natalya	Shekhodanova ¶	RUS	29.12.71	1	NC	Sankt Peterburg	3 Jul 96
12.59	1.0	Patricia	Girard	FRA	8.4.68	2s2	OG	Atlanta	31 Jul 96
12.59	0.2	Brigita	Bukovec	SLO	21.5.70	2	OG	Atlanta	31 Jul 96
12.61	0.3	Svetlana	Gusarova	KZK	29.5.59	2	NC	Leningrad	3 Aug 85
		(30)							
12.61	0.2	Jackie	Joyner-Kersee	USA	3.3.62	1	Jenn	San José	28 May 88
12.61	1.4	Katie	Anderson	CAN	9.1.68	1		Villeneuve d'Ascq	13 Jun 99
12.62	1.2	Mihaela	Pogacian'	ROM	27.1.58	2	BNP	Villeneuve d'Ascq	29 Jun 90
12.62	1.1	Yuliya	Graudyn	RUS	13.11.70	1A	ISTAF	Berlin	30 Aug 94
12.63	1.8	Zofia	Bielczyk	POL	22.9.58	1h1	Kuso	Warszawa	18 Jun 79
12.63	1.4	Heike	Terpe/Theele	GDR	4.10.64	2	NC	Jena	27 Jun 86
12.63	0.0	Angie	Vaughn	USA	4.11.76	1	GP	Edwardsville	25 Jul 98
12.63	2.0	Jenny	Adams	USA	8.7.78	5	WCh	Edmonton	11 Aug 01
12.64	0.4	Paraskeví	Patoulídou	GRE	29.3.65	1	OG	Barcelona	6 Aug 92
12.64	0.1		Zhang Yu	CHN	8.4.71	1	NG	Beijing	9 Sep 93
		(40)							
12.64	1.0	Dionne	Rose-Henley	JAM	7.11.69	4s2	OG	Atlanta	31 Jul 96
12.65A	0.0	Danuta	Perka	POL	22.6.56	1h3	WUG	Ciudad de México	9 Sep 79
12.65	0.0	Nadezhda	Korshunova'	UKR	18.5.61	2		Sochi	19 May 84
12.66	0.0	Yelena	Biserova	RUS	24.3.62	3		Sochi	19 May 84
12.66	0.7	Lidiya	Yurkova '	BLR	15.1.67	1s2	NC	Kiyev	5 Jul 90
12.66	2.0	Gillian	Russell	JAM	28.9.73	2	CAG	Maracaibo	16 Aug 98
12.67	0.6	Tatyana	Anisimova	RUS	19.10.49	2	EC	Praha	2 Sep 78
12.67	0.2	Lynda	Tolbert/Goode	USA	3.10.67	3	WCh	Stuttgart	20 Aug 93
12.67	1.4	Aliuska	López	CUB	29.8.69	2q2	OG	Atlanta	29 Jul 96
12.67	1.3	Joanna	Hayes	USA	23.12.76	2s1	NC	Sacramento	23 Jul 00
12.67	-0.3	Linda	Ferga	FRA	24.12.76	2s2	WCh	Edmonton	10 Aug 01
		(51)	100th woman 12.81, 200th woman 13.00						

Wind assisted performances to 12.39, performers to 12.66

Mark	Wind	Name		Nat	Born	Pos	Meet	Venue	Date
12.28	2.7	Cornelia	Oschkenat'	GDR	29.10.61	1		Berlin	25 Aug 87
12.29	3.5		Donkova			1	Athl	Lausanne	24 Jun 88
12.35	2.4	Bettine	Jahn	GDR	3.8.58	1	WCh	Helsinki	13 Aug 83
12.37	2.7	Gloria	Uibel/Siebert'	GDR	13.1.64	2		Berlin	25 Aug 87
12.39	2.8		Rabsztyn			1	4-N	Bremen	24 Jun 79
12.40	2.1	Michelle	Freeman	JAM	5.5.69	1	GPF	Fukuoka	13 Sep 97
12.41	2.2	Olga	Shishigina	KZK	23.12.68	1rA	Athl	Lausanne	5 Jul 95
12.42	2.4	Kerstin	Knabe	GDR	7.7.59	2	WCh	Helsinki	13 Aug 83
12.50	2.7	Svetla	Dimitrova ¶	BUL	27.1.70	1		Saint-Denis	10 Jun 94
12.51	3.2	Johanna	Klier'	GDR	13.9.52	1	NC	Cottbus	17 Jul 80
12.51	3.6	Sabine	Paetz/John'	GDR	16.10.57	1		Dresden	27 Jul 84
12.51A	3.3	Yuliya	Graudyn	RUS	13.11.70	1		Sestriere	31 Jul 94
12.53	2.2	Mihaela	Pogacian	ROM	27.1.58	1	IAC	Edinburgh	6 Jul 90
12.61	4.0	Jenny	Adams	USA	8.7.78	1h1	NC	Eugene	23 Jun 01
12.63	2.8	Eva	Sokolova	RUS	25.3.62	1s1	NC	Moskva	19 Jun 93
12.64	5.0	Anne	Piquereau	FRA	15.6.64	3		Dijon	12 Jun 94
12.65	3.2	Dawn	Bowles	USA	12.11.68	1q1	NC	Atlanta	22 Jun 96
12.65	2.6	Sharon	Couch-Jewell	USA	13.9.69	1		Hechtel	7 Aug 99
12.66	2.6	Yelena	Politika	UKR	24.8.64	3	NC	Tallinn	5 Jul 88
12.66	4.7	Lynda	Tolbert/Goode	USA	3.10.67	1	BNP	Villeneuve d'Ascq	6 Jul 92
12.66	2.7	Nadezhda	Bodrova	UKR	13.7.61	1	NC	Kiyev	8 Jun 96

Probably hand timed

Mark	Wind	Name		Nat	Born	Pos	Meet	Venue	Date
12.4	0.7	Svetla	Dimitrova	BUL	27.1.70	1		Stara Zagora	9 Jul 97

Officially 12.36, but subsequent investigations showed this unlikely to have been auto-timed

Mark	Wind	Name		Nat	Born	Pos	Meet	Venue	Date
12.63		Angela	Atede	NGR	8.2.72	1	NC	Lagos	28 Jun 97

Hand timed

Mark	Wind	Name		Nat	Born	Pos	Meet	Venue	Date
12.3 WR	1.5	Anneliese	Ehrhardt	GDR	18.6.50	1	NC	Dresden	22 Jul 73
12.3		Marina	Azyabina	RUS	15.6.63	1		Yekaterinburg	30 May 93
12.0w	2.1	Yordanka	Donkova	BUL	28.9.61	1		Sofiya	3 Aug 86
12.1w	2.1	Ginka	Zagorcheva	BUL	12.4.58	2		Sofiya	3Aug 86

400 METRES HURDLES

Mark	Name		Nat	Born	Pos	Meet	Venue	Date
52.61 WR	Kim	Batten	USA	29.3.69	1	WCh	Göteborg	11 Aug 95
52.62	Tonja	Buford-Bailey	USA	13.12.70	2	WCh	Göteborg	11 Aug 95
52.74 WR	Sally	Gunnell	GBR	29.7.66	1	WCh	Stuttgart	19 Aug 93
52.74		Batten			1	Herc	Monaco	8 Aug 98
52.79	Sandra	Farmer-Patrick	USA	18.8.62	2	WCh	Stuttgart	19 Aug 93
52.82	Deon	Hemmings	JAM	9.10.68	1	OG	Atlanta	31 Jul 96

Mark	Wind	Name		Nat	Born	Pos	Meet	Venue	Date
52.84			Batten			1	WK	Zürich	12 Aug 98
52.89		Daimí	Pernía	CUB	27.12.76	1	WCh	Sevilla	25 Aug 99
52.90			Buford			1	WK	Zürich	16 Aug 95
52.90		Nezha	Bidouane	MAR	18.9.69	2	WCh	Sevilla	25 Aug 99
52.94	WR	Marina	Styepanova'	RUS	1.5.50	1s	Spart	Tashkent	17 Sep 86
52.96A			Bidouane			1	WCp	Johannesburg	11 Sep 98
52.97			Batten			1	NC	Indianapolis	14 Jun 97
52.97			Bidouane			1	WCh	Athína	8 Aug 97
52.98			Hemmings			1rA	WK	Zürich	13 Aug 97
52.99			Hemmings			1s1	OG	Atlanta	29 Jul 96
53.02		Irina	Privalova	RUS	22.11.68	1	OG	Sydney	27 Sep 00
53.03A			Hemmings			2	WCp	Johannesburg	11 Sep 98
53.05			Bidouane			1	GGala	Roma	7 Jul 99
53.06			Batten			1	Herc	Monaco	16 Aug 97
53.06			Batten			1	Gaz	Paris	29 Jul 98
53.08			Batten			2	OG	Atlanta	31 Jul 96
53.08			Bidouane			1	Athl	Lausanne	2 Jul 99
53.09			Hemmings			2	WCh	Ath'na	8 Aug 97
53.11		Tatyana	Ledovskaya	BLR	21.5.66	1	WCh	Tokyo	29 Aug 91
53.16			Gunnell			2	WCh	Tokyo	29 Aug 91
53.16			Hemmings			3	WCh	Sevilla	25 Aug 99
53.17		Debbie	Flintoff-King	AUS	20.4.60	1	OG	Seoul	28 Sep 88
53.17			Batten			1	Nik	Nice	16 Jul 98
53.17A			Batten			1	WCp	Johannesburg	11 Sep 98
		(30/11)							
53.21		Marie-José	Pérec	FRA	9.5.68	2	WK	Zürich	16 Aug 95
53.24		Sabine	Busch	GDR	21.11.62	1	NC	Potsdam	21 Aug 87
53.25		Ionela	Tîrlea	ROM	9.2.76	2	GGala	Roma	7 Jul 99
53.33		Sandra	Glover	USA	30.12.68	1	NC	Sacramento	17 Jul 00
53.36		Andrea	Blackett	BAR	24.1.76	4	WCh	Sevilla	25 Aug 99
53.40		Tatyana	Tereshchuk	UKR	11.10.69	2		Villeneuve d'Ascq	11 Jul 98
53.47		Janeene	Vickers	USA	3.10.68	3	WCh	Tokyo	29 Aug 91
53.48		Margarita	Ponomaryova'	RUS	19.6.63	3	WCh	Stuttgart	19 Aug 93
53.58		Cornelia	Ullrich'	GDR	26.4.63	2	NC	Potsdam	21 Aug 87
		(20)							
53.63		Ellen	Fiedler'	GDR	26.11.58	3	OG	Seoul	28 Sep 88
53.65A		Myrtle	Bothma'	RSA	18.2.64	mx		Pretoria	12 Mar 90
		53.74A				1		Johannesburg	18 Apr 86
53.84		Yuliya	Nosova	RUS	21.4.78	1	ECp-S	Bremen	23 Jun 01
53.88		Debbie-Ann	Parris	JAM	24.3.73	3s1	WCh	Edmonton	6 Aug 01
53.96			Han Qing ¶	CHN	4.3.70	1	NG	Beijing	9 Sep 93
53.96			Song Yinglan	CHN	14.9.75	1	NG	Guangzhou	22 Nov 01
54.02	WR	Anna	Ambraziené'	LIT	14.4.55	1	Znam	Moskva	11 Jun 83
54.02A		Judit	Szekeres	HUN	18.11.66	1		Roodepoort	23 Jan 98
54.03		Heike	Meissner	GER	29.1.70	5	OG	Atlanta	31 Jul 96
54.04		Gudrun	Abt	FRG	3.8.62	6	OG	Seoul	28 Sep 88
		(30)							
54.10A		Surita	Febbraio	RSA	27.12.73	2		Roodepoort	16 Mar 01
54.11		Anna	Knoroz	RUS	30.7.70	3	Nik	Nice	18 Jul 94
54.14		Yekaterina	Fesenko/Grun	RUS	10.8.58	1	WCh	Helsinki	10 Aug 83
54.15		Ann-Louise	Skoglund	SWE	28.6.62	4	EC	Stuttgart	30 Aug 86
54.15		Michelle	Johnson	USA	12.4.74	5	WK	Zürich	11 Aug 99
54.17		Tonya	Williams	USA	5.10.74	3	Athl	Lausanne	3 Jul 96
54.21		Ryan	Tolbert	USA	16.6.76	3	NC	Indianapolis	14 Jun 97
54.22A		Silvia	Rieger	GER	14.11.70	5	WCp	Johannesburg	11 Sep 98
54.23		Judi	Brown King	USA	14.7.61	1	PAm	Indianapolis	12 Aug 87
54.24		Susanne	Losch	GDR	12.2.66	1	v FRG	Düsseldorf	19 Jun 88
		(40)							
54.25		Anita	Protti	SUI	4.8.64	6	WCh	Tokyo	29 Aug 91
54.27		Genowefa	Blaszak'	POL	22.8.57	1	DNG	Stockholm	2 Jul 85
54.28	WR	Karin	Rossley	GDR	5.4.57	1		Jena	17 May 80
54.31		Susan	Smith	IRL	14.9.71	7	WK	Zürich	12 Aug 98
54.34		Tatyana	Pavlova'	UZB	12.12.58	1h1	NC	Leningrad	2 Aug 85
54.35		Petra	Krug	GDR	9.11.63	1	vSU	Bryansk	14 Jul 89
54.36		LaTanya	Sheffield	USA	11.10.63	3s1	OG	Seoul	26 Sep 88
54.37		Vera	Ordina	RUS	4.6.68	2s1	OG	Barcelona	3 Aug 92
54.37		Gudrun	Arnardóttir	ISL	24.9.71	2	BrGP	London (CP)	5 Aug 00
54.39		Tatyana	Kurochkina'	BLR	15.9.67	7	OG	Seoul	28 Sep 88
54.39		Rosey	Edeh	CAN	13.8.66	6	OG	Atlanta	31 Jul 96
		(50)	100th woman 55.20, 200th woman 55.94						

WOMEN All-time

Mark Wind		Name	Nat	Born	Pos	Meet	Venue	Date

Low altitude bests

54.44 Bothma 1 NC Durban 22 Apr 89 | 54.27 Rieger 2s2 OG Atlanta 29 Jul 96

54.48 Febbraio 1 Stellenbosch 23 Mar 01

Drugs disqualification

Mark		Name	Nat	Born	Pos	Meet	Venue	Date
53.38		Jiang Limei ¶	CHN	.3.70	(1)	NG	Shanghai	22 Oct 97
54.47		Guo Yue ¶	CHN	23.1.69	(2)	NG	Beijing	9 Sep 93

HIGH JUMP

Mark		Name	Nat	Born	Pos	Meet	Venue	Date
2.09 WR	Stefka	Kostadinova	BUL	25.3.65	1	WCh	Roma	30 Aug 87
2.08 WR		Kostadinova			1	NM	Sofiya	31 May 86
2.07 WR	Lyudmila	Andonova ¶	BUL	6.5.60	1	OD	Berlin	20 Jul 84
2.07 WR		Kostadinova			1		Sofiya	25 May 86
2.07		Kostadinova			1		Cagliari	16 Sep 87
2.07		Kostadinova			1	NC	Sofiya	3 Sep 88
2.07i	Heike	Henkel'	GER	5.5.64	1	NC	Karlsruhe	8 Feb 92
2.06		Kostadinova			1	ECp	Moskva	18 Aug 85
2.06		Kostadinova			1		Fürth	15 Jun 86
2.06		Kostadinova			1		Cagliari	14 Sep 86
2.06		Kostadinova			1		Wörrstadt	6 Jun 87
2.06		Kostadinova			1		Rieti	8 Sep 87
2.06i		Kostadinova			1		Pireás	20 Feb 88
2.05 WR	Tamara	Bykova	RUS	21.12.58	1	Izv	Kiyev	22 Jun 84
2.05		Kostadinova			1		Wörrstadt	14 Jun 86
2.05		Kostadinova			1		Rieti	7 Sep 86
2.05i		Kostadinova			1	WI	Indianapolis	8 Mar 87
2.05		Kostadinova			1	Bisl	Oslo	4 Jul 87
2.05		Kostadinova			1		Padova	13 Sep 87
2.05		Kostadinova			1	BGP	Budapest	12 Aug 88
2.05		Henkel			1	WCh	Tokyo	31 Aug 91
2.05i		Kostadinova			1	NC	Sofiya	1 Feb 92
2.05		Kostadinova			1		San Marino	4 Jul 92
2.05		Kostadinova			1	Toto	Fukuoka	18 Sep 93
2.05	Inga	Babakova	UKR	27.6.67	1		Tokyo	15 Sep 95
2.05		Kostadinova			1	OG	Atlanta	3 Aug 96
	(26/5) 2.04 performances: 12 Kostadinova, 5 Henkel, 2 Bykova, 1Babakova and four with pb							
2.04	Silvia	Costa	CUB	4.5.64	1	WCp	Barcelona	9 Sep 89
2.04i	Alina	Astafei	GER	7.6.69	1		Berlin	3 Mar 95
2.04	Hestrie	Cloete	RSA	26.8.78	1	Herc	Monaco	4 Aug 99
2.04	Venelina	Veneva	BUL	13.6.74	1		Kalamáta	2 Jun 01
2.03 WR	Ulrike	Meyfarth	FRG	4.5.56	1	ECp	London (CP)	21 Aug 83
	(10)							
2.03	Louise	Ritter	USA	18.2.58	1		Austin	8 Jul 88
2.03	Tatyana	Motkova	RUS	23.11.68	2		Bratislava	30 May 95
2.03	Níki	Bakoyiánni	GRE	9.6.68	2	OG	Atlanta	3 Aug 96
2.03i	Monica	Iagar/Dinescu	ROM	2.4.73	1		Bucuresti	23 Jan 99
2.02i	Susanne	Beyer'	GDR	24.6.61	2	WI	Indianapolis	8 Mar 87
2.02	Yelena	Yelesina	RUS	5.4.70	1	GWG	Seattle	23 Jul 90
2.01 WR	Sara	Simeoni	ITA	19.4.53	1	v Pol	Brescia	4 Aug 78
2.01	Olga	Turchak	UKR	5.3.67	2	GWG	Moskva	7 Jul 86
2.01	Desiré	du Plessis	RSA	20.5.65	1		Johannesburg	16 Sep 86
2.01i	Gabriele	Günz	GDR	8.9.61	2		Stuttgart	31 Jan 88
	(20)							
2.01	Heike	Balck	GDR	19.8.70	1	vSU-j	Karl-Marx-Stadt	18 Jun 89
2.01i	Ioamnet	Quintero	CUB	8.9.72	1		Berlin	5 Mar 93
2.01	Hanne	Haugland	NOR	14.12.67	1	WK	Zürich	13 Aug 97
2.01i	Tisha	Waller	USA	1.12.70	1	NC	Atlanta	28 Feb 98
2.01	Yelena	Gulyayeva	RUS	14.8.67	2		Kalamata	23 May 98
2.01	Kajsa	Bergqvist	SWE	12.10.76	1	NC	Uppsala	19 Aug 00
2.00 WR	Rosemarie	Ackermann'	GDR	4.4.52	1	ISTAF	Berlin	26 Aug 77
2.00i	Coleen	Sommer'	USA	6.6.60	1		Ottawa	14 Feb 82
2.00	Charmaine	Gale/Weavers	RSA	27.2.64	1		Pretoria	25 Mar 85
2.00i	Emilia	Dragieva'	BUL	11.1.65	3	WI	Indianapolis	8 Mar 87
	(30)							
2.00	Lyudmila	Avdyeyenko'	UKR	14.12.63	1	NC	Bryansk	17 Jul 87
2.00	Svetlana	Isaeva/Leseva	BUL	18.3.67	2	v TCH,GRE	Drama	8 Aug 87
2.00i	Larisa	Kositsyna	RUS	14.12.63	2	NC	Volgograd	11 Feb 88
2.00	Jan	Wohlschlag'	USA	14.7.58	1	Bisl	Oslo	1 Jul 89
2.00	Yolanda	Henry	USA	2.12.64	1	Expo	Sevilla	30 May 90
2.00	Biljana	Petrovic ¶	YUG	28.2.61	1		St. Denis	22 Jun 90
2.00	Tatyana	Shevchik ¶	BLR	11.6.69	1		Gomel	14 May 93

Mark Wind	Name		Nat	Born	Pos	Meet	Venue	Date
2.00i	Britta	Bilac'	SLO	4.12.68	1		Frankfurt	9 Feb 94
2.00	Amy	Acuff	USA	14.7.75	2	VD	Bruxelles	22 Aug 97
2.00i	Yuliya	Lyakhova	RUS	8.7.77	1		Wuppertal	5 Feb 99
	(40)							
2.00	Zuzana	Hlavonová	CZE	16.4.73	1	Odlozil	Praha	5 Jun 00
2.00	Dóra	Győrffy	HUN	23.2.78	1	NC	Nyíregyháza	26 Jul 01
1.99i	Debbie	Brill	CAN	10.3.53	1		Edmonton	23 Jan 82
1.99i	Andrea	Bienias'	GDR	11.11.59	2	EI	Milano	7 Mar 82
1.99i	Katalin	Sterk	HUN	30.9.61	3	EI	Milano	7 Mar 82
1.99	Kerstin	Brandt'	GDR	9.12.61	3	ECp	London (CP)	21 Aug 83
1.99	Yelena	Topchina ¶	RUS	28.9.66	1		Rieti	5 Sep 93
1.99	Khristina	Kalcheva	BUL	29.5.77	1		Sofia	16 May 98
1.99	Svetlana	Lapina	RUS	12.4.78	3	WCh	Sevilla	29 Aug 99
1.99	Oana	Pantelimon	ROM	27.9.72	3=	OG	Sydney	30 Sep 00
1.99	Vita	Palamar	UKR	12.10.77	2	WK	Zürich	17 Aug 01
	(51)	100th woman 1.96, 200th woman 1.93						

Best outdoor marks

2.02	Iagar/Dinescu	1		Budapest	6 Jun 98
2.01	Astafei	2		Wörrstadt	27 May 95
2.00	Quintero	1	Herc	Monaco	7 Aug 93
2.00	Kositsyna	1		Chelyabinsk	16 Jul 88
2.00	Bilac	1	EC	Helsinki	14 Aug 94
2.00	Waller	1	MSR	Walnut	18 Apr 99
1.99	Beyer'	3	WCh	Roma	30 Aug 87
1.99	Lyakhova	2	GPF	Fukuoka	13 Sep 97

Ancillary jumps – en route to final marks

2.06 Kostadinova 30 Aug 87 2.05i Henkel 8 Feb 92

Drugs disqualification: 1.99 Antonella Bevilacqua # ITA 15.10.71 (4) OG Atlanta 3 Aug 96

POLE VAULT

Mark Wind	Name		Nat	Born	Pos	Meet	Venue	Date
4.81 WR	Stacy	Dragila	USA	25.3.71	1	GP	Palo Alto	9 Jun 01
4.75		Dragila			1	WCh	Edmonton	6 Aug 01
4.75	Svetlana	Feofanova	RUS	16.7.80	2	WCh	Edmonton	6 Aug 01
4.72		Dragila			1	GGala	Roma	29 Jun 01
4.72		Dragila			1		Rethimno	1 Jul 01
4.72		Dragila			1	DNG	Stockholm	17 Jul 01
4.72		Dragila			1	BrGP	London (CP)	22 Jul 01
4.70 b		Dragila			1		Santa Barbara	11 Jun 00
4.70Ai		Dragila			1		Pocatello	17 Feb 01
4.70A WR		Dragila			1		Pocatello	27 Apr 01
4.70		Feofanova			1	NC	Tula	14 Jul 01
4.67		Dragila			1	Nik	Nice	9 Jul 01
4.65Ai		Dragila			1		Pocatello	9 Feb 01
4.65i		Feofanova			1		Pireás	21 Feb 01
4.65		Feofanova			2	BrGP	London (CP)	22 Jul 01
4.64i		Feofanova			1		Dortmund	11 Feb 01
4.63 WR		Dragila			1	NC	Sacramento	23 Jul 00
4.63i		Dragila			1		New York	2 Feb 01
4.62i		Dragila			1	NC	Atlanta	3 Mar 00
4.62 WR		Dragila			1		Phoenix	26 May 00
4.62		Dragila			1	NC	Eugene	23 Jun 01
4.62		Feofanova			2	Nik	Nice	9 Jul 01
4.62		Feofanova			2	DNG	Stockholm	17 Jul 01
4.62		Feofanova			1		Thessaloníki	22 Aug 01
4.61Ai		Dragila			1		Pocatello	19 Feb 00
4.61i		Feofanova			1		Madrid	14 Mar 01
4.61		Dragila			1	Pre	Eugene	27 May 01
4.61	Mary	Sauer	USA	31.10.75	1		Irvine	16 Jun 01
4.61	Monika	Pyrek	POL	11.8.80	1	NC	Bydgoszcz	1 Jul 01
	(29/4)	6 marks at 4.60: 3 by Dragila, 1 each Feofanova, George, Suttle						
4.60 WR	Emma	George	AUS	1.11.74	1		Sydney	20 Feb 99
4.60	Kellie	Suttle	USA	9.5.73	1	Mod R	Modesto	12 May 01
4.56i	Nicole	Rieger/Humbert	GER	5.2.72	1		Stockholm	25 Feb 99
4.56	Anzhela	Balakhonova	UKR	18.12.72	1	Gugl	Linz	8 Aug 00
4.56i	Pavla	Hamácková	CZE	20.5.78	1	WI	Lisboa	9 Mar 01
4.56	Tatiana	Grigorieva	AUS	8.10.75	1		Yokohama	15 Sep 01
	(10)							
4.55i	Yelena	Belyakova	RUS	7.4.76	2		Pireás	21 Feb 01
4.55	Annika	Becker	GER	12.11.81	1	NC	Stuttgart	1 Jul 01
4.52		Gao Shuying	CHN	28.10.79	1	WUG	Beijing	29 Aug 01
4.51	Daniela	Bártová	CZE	6.5.74	1	Slovn	Bratislava	9 Jun 98
4.51i	Zsuzsanna	Szabó	HUN	6.5.73	1		Budapest	4 Feb 99
4.51i	Thórey Edda	Elísdottír	ISL	30.6.77	1	NCAA	Fayetteville	10 Mar 01

Mark	Wind	Name		Nat	Born	Pos	Meet	Venue	Date
4.50i		Melissa	Mueller	USA	16.11.72	1		Roxbury	7 Feb 99
4.50i		Nastja	Ryshich	GER	19.9.77	1	WI	Maebashi	5 Mar 99
4.50		Vala	Flosadóttir	ISL	16.2.78	3	OG	Sydney	25 Sep 00
4.50		Alicia	Warlick	USA	11.10.77	1		Houston	24 Mar 01
		(20)							
4.50		Carolin	Hingst	GER	18.9.80	2	NC	Stuttgart	1 Jul 01
4.47i		Yelena	Isinbayeva	RUS	3.6.82	1		Budapest	10 Feb 01
4.46		Yvonne	Buschbaum	GER	14.7.80	3	ISTAF	Berlin	31 Aug 01
4.45		Tracy	O'Hara	USA	20.7.80	1	USTCA	Austin	22 Apr 00
4.44i		Doris	Auer	AUT	10.5.71	2		Glasgow	18 Mar 01
4.43		Tania	Koleva	BUL	8.3.72	1		Athína	30 May 01
4.42		Alejandra	García	ARG	13.6.73	1		Sydney	20 Feb 00
4.42		Elmarie	Gerryts	RSA	25.8.72	1		Wesel	12 Jun 00
4.42		Martina	Strutz	GER	4.11.81	1		Schwerin	24 Jun 01
4.41		Krisztina	Molnár	HUN	8.4.76	1		Budapest	13 Jun 01
		(30)							
4.40i		Christine	Adams	GER	28.2.74	2		Chemnitz	18 Feb 00
4.40		Janine	Whitlock	GBR	11.8.73	1	NC	Birmingham	14 Jul 01
4.37		Lesa	Kubishta	USA	19.4.78	1		Irvine	7 May 00
4.37		Becky	Holliday	USA	12.3.80	1		Spokane	24 May 01
4.36		Melissa	Price	USA	20.9.77	1		Houston	23 May 98
4.36		Yeoryía	Tsiliggíri	GRE	21.6.72	1	NC	Athína	17 Jun 01
4.35i			Cai Weiyan	CHN	25.10.73	3	WI	Paris (B)	9 Mar 97
4.35		Marie	Poissonnier	FRA	4.5.79	1		Bron	7 May 00
4.35		Marie B	Rasmussen	DEN	1.11.72	8	OG	Sydney	25 Sep 00
4.35		Jenny	Dryburgh	NZL	30.8.78	1	Aus Ch	Brisbane	25 Mar 01
		(40)							
4.35		Monique	de Wilt	NED	21.3.76	1		Kassel	13 Jun 01
4.35		Sabine	Schulte	GER	29.1.76	2	WUG	Beijing	29 Aug 01
4.33i		Eszter	Szemerédi	HUN	12.2.76	2		Karlsruhe	25 Jan 98
4.32		Vanessa	Boslak	FRA	11.6.82	1		La Roche-sur-Yon	23 Sep 00
4.31		Monika	Götz	GER	15.6.81	1		Troisdorf	9 May 98
4.31i		Tatyana	Gubareva	RUS	4.12.73	1		Moskva	14 Feb 99
4.31		Amandine	Homo	FRA	24.12.80	3	GP II	Saint-Denis	3 Jul 99
4.31		Maria Mar	Sánchez	ESP	25.12.79	1	NC	Valencia	22 Jul 01

(48) and 8 women at 4.30 — 100th woman 4.17, 200th 4.00

Outdoor best

Mark	Name	Pos	Meet	Venue	Date
4.51	Humbert	1		Salamanca	13 Jul 01
4.50	Belyakova	3	GP	Athína	28 Jun 00
4.47	Hamácková	4	GP	Athína	11 Jun 01
4.47	Mueller	1	GP II	Zagreb	2 Jul 01
4.46	Isinbayeva	2	ISTAF	Berlin	31 Aug 01
4.45	Elísdottír	6	WCh	Edmonton	6 Aug 01
4.44	Ryshich	3	Nik	Nice	17 Jul 99
4.40	Szabó	4	WCh	Sevilla	21 Aug 99
4.40	Isinbayeva	2	NC	Tula	24 Jul 00
4.40	Auer	2		Gold Coast (RB)	17 Sep 00
4.35	Adams	1		Weissach	8 Jun 01
4.33	Cai Weiyan	1		Shenzhen	5 Oct 96
4.32	Boslak	1		La Roche-sur-Yon	23 Sep 00

Ancillary jumps – en route to final marks

Mark	Name	Date
4.70	Feofanova	6 Aug 01
4.66Ai	Dragila	17 Feb 01
4.65A	Dragila (WR)	27 Apr 01
4.65	Feofanova	14 Jul 01
4.65	Dragila	22 Jul 01
4.65	Dragila	6 Aug 01
4.65	Feofanova	6 Aug 01
4.62	Dragila	29 Jun 01
4.62	Dragila	1 Jul 01
4.62	Dragila	17 Jul 01

Street competition, raised runway, slightly uphill

Mark	Name		Nat	Born	Pos	Venue	Date
4.62	Melissa	Mueller	USA	16.11.72	1	Clovis	4 Aug 01

Exhibition or 'town square' meetings under questionable conditions

Mark	Name		Nat	Born	Pos	Venue	Date
4.40	Andrea	Müller	GER	29.6.74	1	Zweibrücken	8 Oct 95
4.31	Janet	Zach	GER	19.6.75	1	Recklinghausen	30 May 97

LONG JUMP

Mark	Wind	Name		Nat	Born	Pos	Meet	Venue	Date
7.52 WR	1.4	Galina	Chistyakova	RUS	26.7.62	1	Znam	Leningrad	11 Jun 88
7.49	1.3	Jackie	Joyner-Kersee	USA	3.3.62	1	NYG	New York	22 May 94
7.49A	1.7		Joyner-Kersee			1		Sestriere	31 Jul 94
7.48	1.2	Heike	Drechsler	GER	16.12.64	1	v ITA	Neubrandenburg	9 Jul 88
7.48	0.4		Drechsler			1	Athl	Lausanne	8 Jul 92
7.45 WR	0.9		Drechsler'			1	v URS	Tallinn	21 Jun 86
7.45 WR	1.1		Drechsler			1	OD	Dresden	3 Jul 86
7.45 WR	0.6		Joyner-Kersee			1	PAm	Indianapolis	13 Aug 87
7.45	1.6		Chistyakova			1	BGP	Budapest	12 Aug 88
7.44 WR	2.0		Drechsler			1		Berlin	22 Sep 85
7.43 WR	1.4	Anisoara	Cusmir/Stanciu	ROM	28.6.62	1	RomIC	Bucuresti	4 Jun 83
7.40	1.8		Daute' (Drechsler)			1		Dresden	26 Jul 84
7.40	0.7		Drechsler			1	NC	Potsdam	21 Aug 87
7.40	0.9		Joyner-Kersee			1	OG	Seoul	29 Sep 88
7.39	0.3		Drechsler			1	WK	Zürich	21 Aug 85

Mark	Wind		Name	Nat	Born	Pos	Meet	Venue	Date
7.39	0.5	Yelena	Byelevskaya'	BLR	11.10.63	1	NC	Bryansk	18 Jul 87
7.39			Joyner-Kersee			1		San Diego	25 Jun 88
7.37i	-		Drechsler			1	v2N	Wien	13 Feb 88
7.37A	1.8		Drechsler			1		Sestriere	31 Jul 91
7.37		Inessa	Kravets	UKR	5.10.66	1		Kiyev	13 Jun 92
7.36	0.4		Joyner			1	WCh	Roma	4 Sep 87
7.36	1.8		Byelevskaya			2	Znam	Leningrad	11 Jun 88
7.36	1.8		Drechsler			1		Jena	28 May 92
7.35	1.9		Chistyakova			1	GPB	Bratislava	20 Jun 90
7.34	1.6		Daute'			1		Dresden	19 May 84
7.34	1.4		Chistyakova			2	v GDR	Tallinn	21 Jun 86
7.34			Byelevskaya			1		Sukhumi	17 May 87
7.34	0.7		Drechsler			1	v URS	Karl-Marx-Stadt	20 Jun 87
7.33	0.4		Drechsler			1	v URS	Erfurt	22 Jun 85
7.33	2.0		Drechsler			1		Dresden	2 Aug 85
7.33	-0.3		Drechsler			1	Herc	Monaco	11 Aug 92
		(31/6)							
7.31	1.5	Yelena	Kokonova'	UKR	4.8.63	1	NP	Alma-Ata	12 Sep 85
7.31	1.9	Marion	Jones	USA	12.10.75	1	Pre	Eugene	31 May 98
7.26A	1.8	Maurren	Maggi	BRA	25.6.76	1	SACh	Bogotá	26 Jun 99
7.24	1.0	Larisa	Berezhnaya	UKR	28.2.61	1	Blanc	Granada	25 May 91
		(10)							
7.21	1.6	Helga	Radtke	GDR	16.5.62	2		Dresden	26 Jul 84
7.20 WR	-0.5	Valy	Ionescu	ROM	31.8.60	1	NC	Bucuresti	1 Aug 82
7.20	2.0	Irena	Ozhenko'	LIT	13.11.62	1		Budapest	12 Sep 86
7.20	0.8	Yelena	Sinchukova'	RUS	23.1.61	1	BGP	Budapest	20 Jun 91
7.20	0.7	Irina	Mushayilova	RUS	6.1.67	1	NC	Sankt-Peterburg	14 Jul 94
7.17	1.8	Irina	Valyukevich	BLR	19.11.59	2	NC	Bryansk	18 Jul 87
7.16		Iolanda	Chen	RUS	26.7.61	1		Moskva	30 Jul 88
7.14	1.8	Niole	Medvedyeva ¶	LIT	20.10.60	1		Riga	4 Jun 88
7.14	1.2	Mirela	Dulgheru	ROM	5.10.66	1	Balk G	Sofiya	5 Jul 92
7.12	1.6	Sabine	Paetz/John'	GDR	16.10.57	2		Dresden	19 May 84
		(20)							
7.12	0.9	Chioma	Ajunwa ¶	NGR	25.12.70	1	OG	Atlanta	2 Aug 96
7.12	0.5	Tatyana	Kotova	RUS	11.12.76	1		Torino	9 Jun 01
7.11	0.8	Fiona	May	ITA	12.12.69	2	EC	Budapest	22 Aug 98
7.09 WR	0.0	Vilma	Bardauskiene	LIT	15.6.53	Q	EC	Praha	29 Aug 78
7.09	1.5	Ljudmila	Ninova	AUT	25.6.60	1	GP II	Sevilla	5 Jun 94
7.08	0.5	Marieta	Ilcu	ROM	16.10.62	1	RumIC	Pitesti	25 Jun 89
7.07	0.0	Svetlana	Zorina	RUS	2.2.60	1		Krasnodar	15 Aug 87
7.06	0.4	Tatyana	Kolpakova	KGZ	18.10.59	1	OG	Moskva	31 Jul 80
7.06	-0.1	Niurka	Montalvo	CUB/ESP	4.6.68	1	WCh	Sevilla	23 Aug 99
7.05	0.6	Lyudmila	Galkina	RUS	20.1.72	1	WCh	Athína	9 Aug 97
		(30)							
7.04	0.5	Brigitte	Künzel/Wujak	GDR	6.3.55	2	OG	Moskva	31 Jul 80
7.04	0.9	Tatyana	Proskuryakova'	RUS	13.1.56	1		Kiyev	25 Aug 83
7.04	2.0	Yelena	Yatsuk	UKR	16.3.61	1	Znam	Moskva	8 Jun 85
7.04	0.3	Carol	Lewis	USA	8.8.63	5	WK	Zürich	21 Aug 85
7.03	0.6	Níki	Xánthou	GRE	11.10.73	1		Bellinzona	18 Aug 97
7.03i	-	Dawn	Burrell	USA	1.11.73	1	WI	Lisboa	10 Mar 01
7.01	-0.4	Tatyana	Skachko	UKR	18.8.54	3	OG	Moskva	31 Jul 80
7.01	-0.3	Eva	Murková	SVK	29.5.62	1	PTS	Bratislava	26 May 84
7.01	-1.0	Marina	Kibakina'	RUS	2.8.60	1		Krasnoyarsk	10 Aug 85
7.01	1.4		Yao Weili	CHN	6.5.68	1	NC	Jinan	5 Jun 93
		(40)							
7.01	1.1	Shana	Williams	USA	7.4.72	Q	NC	Atlanta	21 Jun 96
7.01	-0.4	Eunice	Barber	FRA	17.11.74	1	GP	Paris (C)	21 Jul 99
7.00	2.0	Jodi	Anderson	USA	10.11.57	1	OT	Eugene	28 Jun 80
7.00		Margarita	Butkiene	LIT	19.8.49	1		Vilnius	25 May 83
7.00	-0.2	Birgit	Grosshennig	GDR	21.2.65	2		Berlin	9 Jun 84
7.00	0.6	Silvia	Khristova'	BUL	22.8.65	1		Sofiya	3 Aug 86
7.00		Susen	Tiedtke ¶	GER	23.1.69	2		Seoul	18 Aug 91
6.99 WR	2.0	Sigrun	Thon/Siegl	GDR	29.10.54	1	OD	Dresden	19 May 76
6.99	0.4	Lissette	Cuza	CUB	26.2.75	1	OD	Jena	3 Jun 00
6.99	1.9	Erica	Johansson	SWE	5.2.74	*	Athl	Lausanne	5 Jul 00
		(50)	100th woman 6.86, 100th woman 6.75						
Drugs dq: 7.03	0.1		Xiong Qiying	CHN	14.10.67	Q	NG	Shanghai	21 Oct 97
Wind assisted									
7.63A	2.1	Heike	Drechsler	GER	16.12.64	1		Sestriere	21 Jul 92
7.45	2.6		Joyner-Kersee			1	OT	Indianapolis	23 Jul 88

Mark	Wind		Name	Nat	Born	Pos	Meet	Venue	Date
7.39	2.6		Drechsler			1		Padova	15 Sep 91
7.39	2.9		Drechsler			1	Expo	Sevilla	6 Jun 92
7.39A	3.3		Drechsler			2		Sestriere	31 Jul 94
7.36	2.2		Chistyakova			1	Znam	Volgograd	11 Jun 89
7.35	3.4		Drechsler			1	NC	Jena	29 Jun 86
7.23A	4.3	Fiona	May	ITA	12.12.69	1		Sestriere	29 Jul 95
7.19A	3.7	Susen	Tiedtke ¶	GER	23.1.69	1		Sestriere	28 Jul 93
7.17	3.6	Eva	Murková	SVK	29.5.62	1		Nitra	26 Aug 84
7.14A	4.5	Marieke	Veltman	USA	18.9.71	2		Sestriere	29 Jul 95
7.12A	5.8	Níki	Xánthou	GRE	11.10.73	3		Sestriere	29 Jul 95
7.12A	4.3	Nicole	Boegman	AUS	5.3.67	4		Sestriere	29 Jul 95
7.09	2.9	Renata	Nielsen	DEN	18.5.66	2		Sevilla	5 Jun 94
7.08	2.2	Lyudmila	Galkina	RUS	20.1.72	1		Thessaloniki	23 Jun 99
7.07A	5.6	Valentina	Uccheddu	ITA	26.10.66	5		Sestriere	29 Jul 95
7.07A	2.7	Sharon	Couch	USA	13.9.67	1		El Paso	12 Apr 97
7.07A	w	Erica	Johansson	SWE	5.2.74	1		Vygieskraal	15 Jan 00
7.06	3.4		Ma Miaolan	CHN	18.1.70	1	NG	Beijing	10 Sep 93
7.01	2.2	Olga	Rublyova	RUS	28.10.74	1	NC	Moskva	16 Jun 95
7.00	3.8	Ramona	Neubert'	GDR	26.7.58	1	v GBR	Dresden	14 Jun 81
7.00	4.2	Sue	Hearnshaw'	GBR	26.5.61	1	NC	Cwmbran	27 May 84

Best at low altitude: 7.12w 3.4 May 1 NC Bologna 25 May 96

Ancillary marks – other marks during series (to 7.34/7.36w)

7.45 1.0 Chistyakova 11 Jun 88 | 7.47Aw 3.1 Drechsler 31 Jul 94 | 7.38w 2.2 Chistyakova 11 Jun 88
7.37 Drechsler 9 Jul 88 | 7.39Aw 3.1 Drechsler 31 Jul 94 | 7.36w Joyner-Kersee 31 Jul 94

TRIPLE JUMP

Mark	Wind		Name	Nat	Born	Pos	Meet	Venue	Date
15.50 WR	0.9	Inessa	Kravets	UKR	5.10.66	1	WCh	Göteborg	10 Aug 95
15.33	-0.1		Kravets			1	OG	Atlanta	31 Jul 96
15.32	0.5	Tatyana	Lebedeva	RUS	21.7.76	1	Super	Yokohama	9 Sep 00
15.25	-0.8		Lebedeva			1	WCh	Edmonton	10 Aug 01
15.20	0.0	Sarka	Kaspárková	CZE	20.5.71	1	WCh	Athína	4 Aug 97
15.20	-0.3	Tereza	Marinova	BUL	5.9.77	1	OG	Sydney	24 Sep 00
15.18	0.3	Iva	Prandzheva ¶	BUL	15.2.72	2	WCh	Göteborg	10 Aug 95
15.16	0.1	Rodica	Mateescu	ROM	13.3.71	2	WCh	Athína	4 Aug 97
15.16i	-	Ashia	Hansen	GBR	5.12.71	1	EI	Valencia	28 Feb 98
15.15	1.7		Hansen			1	GPF	Fukuoka	13 Sep 97
15.14	-0.1		Mateescu			1	RomIC	Bucuresti	14 Jun 97
15.12	2.0		Prandzheva			1	TOTO	Tokyo	19 Sep 98
15.09 WR	0.5	Anna	Biryukova	RUS	27.9.67	1	WCh	Stuttgart	21 Aug 93
15.09	-0.5	Inna	Lasovskaya	RUS	17.12.69	1	ECCp-A	Valencia	31 May 97
15.08	1.4		Biryukova			3	WCh	Göteborg	10 Aug 95
15.08	0.7		Lasovskaya			1		Madrid	12 Jun 96
15.07	-0.6	Paraskeví	Tsiamíta (10)	GRE	10.3.72	Q	WCh	Sevilla	22 Aug 99
15.04	0.9		Prandzheva			1	NC	Sofia	17 Jun 00
15.03i		Iolanda	Chen	RUS	26.7.61	1	WI	Barcelona	11 Mar 95
15.03	0.0		Biryukova			1	WK	Zürich	16 Aug 95
15.02i	-		Hansen			1	WI	Maebashi	7 Mar 99
15.01i	-		Lasovskaya			1	WI	Paris (B)	8 Mar 97
15.01	1.9		Mateescu			1		Villeneuve d'Ascq	11 Jul 98
15.01	1.1		Lebedeva			1	Veniz	Haniá	14 Jun 00
15.00	1.3		Lebedeva			2	OG	Sydney	24 Sep 00
15.00i			Lebedeva			1	NC	Moskva	18 Feb 01
14.99	-0.2		Biryukova			1	GPF	Monaco	9 Sep 95
14.98	1.8	Sofiya	Bozhanova ¶	BUL	4.10.67	1		Stara Zagora	16 Jul 94
14.98	1.1		Lasovskaya			2	OG	Atlanta	31 Jul 96
14.98	-0.6		Kaspárková			3	OG	Atlanta	31 Jul 96
14.98	0.5		Kaspárková			1		Rovereto	26 Aug 98
14.98	0.9		Lebedeva			1	ECp-S	Gateshead	16 Jul 00
		(32/12)							
14.96	0.7	Yelena	Govorova	UKR	18.9.73	4	OG	Sydney	24 Sep 00
14.94i	–	Cristina	Nicolau	ROM	9.8.77	1	NC	Bucuresti	5 Feb 00
14.83i	-	Yelena	Lebedenko	RUS	16.1.71	1		Samara	1 Feb 01
14.79	1.7	Irina	Mushayilova	RUS	6.1.67	1	DNG	Stockholm	5 Jul 93
14.77	1.2	Yamilé	Aldama	CUB	14.8.72	1	PAm	Winnipeg	28 Jul 99
14.76	0.9	Galina	Chistyakova	RUS	26.7.62	1		Luzern	27 Jun 95
		later Cistjaková SVK							
14.76	1.1	Gundega	Sproge	LAT	12.12.72	3		Sheffield	29 Jun 97
14.72	1.8		Huang Qiuyan	CHN	25.1.80	1	NG	Guangzhou	22 Nov 01
		(20)							

Mark	Wind	Name		Nat	Born	Pos	Meet	Venue	Date
14.71	0.5	Adelina	Gavrila	ROM	26.11.78	1		Bucuresti	12 Jun 99
14.70A	0.5	Françoise	Mbango	CMR	14.4.76	1	AfG	Johannesburg	18 Sep 99
14.69	1.2	Anja	Valant	SLO	8.9.77	3		Kalamáta	4 Jun 00
14.67	1.2	Ólga	Vasdéki	GRE	26.9.73	1		Haniá	28 Jul 99
14.66	1.9		Ren Ruiping	CHN	1.2.76	1	Oda	Hiroshima	29 Apr 97
14.65	0.3	Fiona	May	ITA	12.12.69	1	ECp	Sankt-Peterburg	27 Jun 98
14.65	2.0	Natalya	Safronova	BLR	11.4.74	1	NCp	Stayki	3 Jun 00
14.64A	0.2	Baya	Rahouli	ALG	27.7.79	2	AfG	Johannesburg	18 Sep 99
14.60	0.7	Niurka	Montalvo	CUB/ESP	4.6.68	1	NC	La Habana	24 Jun 94
14.60		Nadezhda	Bazhenova	RUS	22.9.78	1		Moskva	23 Jun 01
		(30)							
14.59	1.1	Oksana	Rogova	RUS	7.10.78	*	EU23	Göteborg	1 Aug 99
14.59	0.3	Yelena	Oleynikova	RUS	9.12.76	2	NC	Tula	15 Jul 01
14.59	1.9	Magdelin	Martínez	CUB/ITA	10.2.76	Q	WCh	Edmonton	8 Aug 01
14.58	0.3	Yelena	Donkina	RUS	15.3.73	2	NC	Tula	10 Jul 97
14.57		Irina	Vasilyeva	RUS	9.4.79	2		Moskva	23 Jun 01
14.55	0.9		Li Huirong	CHN	14.4.65	1	Nambu	Sapporo	19 Jul 92
14.55	-0.3	Jelena	Blazevica	LAT	11.5.70	1	NC	Riga	8 Jun 96
14.54i	-	Mariya	Sokova	RUS	2.9.70	1	NC	Volgograd	24 Feb 95
14.52	0.6	Anastasiya	Ilyina	RUS	16.1.82	q	WJ	Santiago de Chile	20 Oct 00
14.51		Natalya	Kayukova	RUS	10.12.66	1		Vladivostok	29 May 99
		(40)							
14.50	-0.1	Betty	Lise	FRA	5.9.72	Q	WCh	Athína	2 Aug 97
14.47	1.8	Olga	Yershova	RUS	13.8.76	4	Veniz	Haniá	14 Jun 00
14.46	1.0	Helga	Radtke	GER	16.5.62	1	NC	Erfurt	3 Jul 94
14.46			Peng Fengmei	CHN	2.7.79	1		Chengdu	19 Apr 98
14.45		Yelena	Stakhova	BLR	4.1.69	1		Bialystok	17 Jun 96
14.45i	–	Olga	Rublyova	RUS	28.10.74	2		Moskva	27 Jan 00
14.43	1.1	Laiza	Carrillo	CUB	27.11.68	1		La Habana	23 Feb 95
14.43	0.7	Olga	Cepero	CUB	4.5.75	1		La Habana	6 Feb 98
14.41	1.1	Sheila	Hudson	USA	30.6.67	2	DNG	Stockholm	8 Jul 96
14.39	-0.5		Wu Lingmei	CHN	16.2.73	2		Beijing	6 Jun 98
		(51)	100th woman 14.08, 200th woman 13.77						

Wind assisted performances to 14.99, performers to 14.43

Mark	Wind	Name		Nat	Born	Pos	Meet	Venue	Date
15.07	2.5		Marinova			1		Réthimno	10 Jun 00
15.05	2.7		Lasovskaya			1		Sevilla	3 Jun 95
15.00	2.5		Lebedeva			2		Réthimno	10 Jun 00
14.99	6.8	Yelena	Govorova	UKR	18.9.73	1	WUG	Palma de Mallorca	11 Jul 99
14.88	3.8	Trecia	Smith	JAM	5.11.75	1	Kans R	Lawrence	21 Apr 01
14.84	4.1	Galina	Chistyakova	RUS	26.7.62	1		Innsbruck	28 Jun 95
14.83	8.3		Ren Ruiping	CHN	1.2.76	1	NC	Taiyuan	21 May 95
14.75	4.2	Jelena	Blazevica	LAT	11.5.70	1	v2N	Kaunas	23 Aug 97
14.66	3.2	Sheila	Hudson	USA	30.6.67	1	NC	Sacramento	17 Jun 95
14.65	2.6	Oksana	Rogova	RUS	7.10.78	2	EU23	Göteborg	1 Aug 99
14.55	5.5		Wu Lingmei	CHN	16.2.73	2	WUG	Palma de Mallorca	11 Jul 99
14.43	2.7	Yelena	Lysak ¶	RUS	15.3.75	1	EJ	Lisboa	21 Jul 94
14.43	2.3		Miao Chunqing	CHN	27.2.78	2	NG	Guangzhou	22 Nov 01

Best outdoor mark for athlete with all-time best indoors

14.97WR 0.9 Chen 1 NC Moskva 18 Jun 93 | 14.50 Sokova 2 Znam Moskva 5 Jun 99

14.70 1.3 Nicolau 1 EU23 Göteborg 1 Aug 99 | 14.41 -0.2 Lebedenko 1 ECCp-A Vilamoura 30 May 98

Best low altitude:

14.65 1.8 Mbango 1 La-Roche-sur-Yon 11 Jul 99 | 14.42w 2.6 Rahouli 1 Adelaide 8 Mar 00

Ancillary marks – other marks during series (to 14.99)

15.16 Lebedeva 9 Sep 00 | 15.15 Lebedeva 9 Sep 00 | 15.01 0.4 Kaspárková 4 Aug 97

15.15 Lebedeva 9 Sep 00 | 15.11 -1.1 Lebedeva 10 Aug 01

SHOT

Mark	Name		Nat	Born	Pos	Meet	Venue	Date
22.63 WR	Natalya	Lisovskaya	RUS	16.7.62	1	Znam	Moskva	7 Jun 87
22.55		Lisovskaya			1	NC	Tallinn	5 Jul 88
22.53 WR		Lisovskaya			1		Sochi	27 May 84
22.53		Lisovskaya			1		Kiyev	14 Aug 88
22.50i	Helena	Fibingerová	CZE	13.7.49	1		Jablonec	19 Feb 77
22.45 WR	Ilona	Slupianek' ¶	GDR	24.9.56	1		Potsdam	11 May 80
22.41		Slupianek			1	OG	Moskva	24 Jul 80
22.40		Slupianek			1		Berlin	3 Jun 83
22.38		Slupianek			1		Karl-Marx-Stadt	25 May 80
22.36 WR		Slupianek			1		Celje	2 May 80
22.34		Slupianek			1		Berlin	7 May 80
22.34		Slupianek			1	NC	Cottbus	18 Jul 80
22.32 WR		Fibingerová			1		Nitra	20 Aug 77

Mark	Wind	Name		Nat	Born	Pos	Meet	Venue	Date
22.24			Lisovskaya			1	OG	Seoul	1 Oct 88
22.22			Slupianek			1		Potsdam	13 Jul 80
22.19		Claudia	Losch	FRG	10.1.60	1		Hainfeld	23 Aug 87
22.14i			Lisovskaya			1	NC	Penza	7 Feb 87
22.13			Slupianek			1		Split	29 Apr 80
22.06			Slupianek			1		Berlin	15 Aug 78
22.06			Lisovskaya			1		Moskva	6 Aug 88
22.05			Slupianek			1	OD	Berlin	28 May 80
22.05			Slupianek			1		Potsdam	31 May 80
22.04			Slupianek			1		Potsdam	4 Jul 79
22.04			Slupianek			1		Potsdam	29 Jul 79
21.99	WR		Fibingerová			1		Opava	26 Sep 76
21.98			Slupianek			1		Berlin	17 Jul 79
21.96			Fibingerová			1	GS	Ostrava	8 Jun 77
21.96			Lisovskaya			1	Drz	Praha	16 Aug 84
21.96			Lisovskaya			1		Vilnius	28 Aug 88
21.95			Lisovskaya			1	IAC	Edinburgh	29 Jul 88
		(30/4)							
21.89	WR	Ivanka	Khristova	BUL	19.11.41	1		Belmeken	4 Jul 76
21.86		Marianne	Adam	GDR	19.9.51	1	v URS	Leipzig	23 Jun 79
21.76			Li Meisu	CHN	17.4.59	1		Shijiazhuang	23 Apr 88
21.73		Natalya	Akhrimenko	RUS	12.5.55	1		Leselidze	21 May 88
21.69		Viktoriya	Pavlysh ¶	UKR	15.1.69	1	EC	Budapest	20 Aug 98
21.66			Sui Xinmei ¶	CHN	29.1.65	1		Beijing	9 Jun 90
		(10)							
21.61		Verzhinia	Veselinova	BUL	18.11.57	1		Sofiya	21 Aug 82
21.60i		Valentina	Fedyushina	UKR	18.2.65	1		Simferopol	28 Dec 91
21.58		Margitta	Droese/Pufe	GDR	10.9.52	1		Erfurt	28 May 78
21.57	@	Ines	Müller'	GDR	2.1.59	1		Athína	16 May 88
		21.45				1		Schwerin	4 Jun 86
21.53		Nunu	Abashidze ¶	UKR	27.3.55	2	Izv	Kiyev	20 Jun 84
21.52			Huang Zhihong	CHN	7.5.65	1	NC	Beijing	27 Jun 90
21.46		Larisa	Peleshenko ¶	RUS	29.2.64	1	Kuts	Moskva	26 Aug 00
21.45	WR	Nadezhda	Chizhova	RUS	29.9.45	1		Varna	29 Sep 73
21.43		Eva	Wilms	FRG	28.7.52	2	HB	München	17 Jun 77
21.42		Svetlana	Krachevskaya'	RUS	23.11.44	2	OG	Moskva	24 Jul 80
		(20)	*@ competitive meeting, but unsanctioned by GDR federation*						
21.31	@	Heike	Hartwig'	GDR	30.12.62	2		Athína	16 May 88
		21.27				1		Haniá	22 May 88
21.27		Liane	Schmuhl	GDR	29.6.61	1		Cottbus	26 Jun 82
21.22		Astrid	Kumbernuss	GER	5.2.70	1	WCh	Göteborg	5 Aug 95
21.21		Kathrin	Neimke	GDR	18.7.66	2	WCh	Roma	5 Sep 87
21.19		Helma	Knorscheidt	GDR	31.12.56	1		Berlin	24 May 84
21.15i		Irina	Korzhanenko ¶	RUS	16.5.74	1	NC	Moskva	18 Feb 99
21.10		Heidi	Krieger	GDR	20.7.65	1	EC	Stuttgart	26 Aug 86
21.06		Svetlana	Krivelyova	RUS	13.6.69	1	OG	Barcelona	7 Aug 92
21.05		Zdenka	Silhavá' ¶	CZE	15.6.54	2	NC	Praha	23 Jul 83
21.01		Ivanka	Petrova-Stoycheva	BUL	3.2.51	1	NC	Sofiya	28 Jul 79
		(30)							
21.00		Mihaela	Loghin	ROM	1.6.52	1		Formia	30 Jun 84
21.00		Cordula	Schulze	GDR	11.9.59	4	OD	Potsdam	21 Jul 84
20.96		Belsy	Laza	CUB	5.6.67	1		Ciudad de México	2 May 92
20.95		Elena	Stoyanova ¶	BUL	23.1.52	2	Balk	Sofiya	14 Jun 80
20.91		Svetla	Mitkova	BUL	17.6.64	1		Sofiya	24 May 87
20.80		Sona	Vasícková	CZE	14.3.62	1		Praha	2 Jun 88
20.72		Grit	Haupt/Hammer	GDR	4.6.66	3		Neubrandenburg	11 Jun 87
20.61		María Elena	Sarría	CUB	14.9.54	1		Habana	22 Jul 82
20.61		Yanina	Korolchik	BLR	26.12.76	1	WCh	Edmonton	5 Aug 01
20.60		Marina	Antonyuk	RUS	12.5.62	1		Chelyabinsk	10 Aug 86
		(40)							
20.54			Zhang Liuhong	CHN	16.1.69	1	NC	Beijing	5 Jun 94
20.53		Iris	Plotzitzka	FRG	7.1.66	1	ASV	Köln	21 Aug 88
20.50i		Christa	Wiese	GDR	25.12.67	2	NC	Senftenberg	12 Feb 89
20.47		Nina	Isayeva	RUS	6.7.50	1		Bryansk	28 Aug 82
20.47			Cong Yuzhen	CHN	22.1.63	2	IntC	Tianjin	3 Sep 88
20.44		Tatyana	Orlova	BLR	19.7.55	1		Staiki	28 May 83
20.40			Zhou Tianhua ¶	CHN	10.4.66	1		Beijing	5 Sep 91
20.34		Stephanie	Storp	FRG	28.11.68	1		Wolfsburg	1 Jul 90
20.32		Irina	Khudorozhkina	RUS	13.10.68	1		Sochi	25 May 96
20.27		Danguole	Bimbaite'	LIT	10.12.62	2		Leselidze	13 May 87

Mark	Wind	Name		Nat	Born	Pos	Meet	Venue	Date
20.27		Lyudmila	Voyevudskaya	UKR	22.6.59	1		Nikolayev	7 Aug 87
		(51)	100th woman 19.43, 200th woman c.18.44						

Best outdoor marks

21.08 Fedyushina 1 Leselidze 15 May 88 | 20.82 Korzhanenko ¶ 1 Rostov na Donu 30 May 98

Ancillary marks – other marks during series (to 22.09)

22.60	Lisovskaya (WR)	7 Jun 87	22.20	Slupianek	13 Jul 80	22.12	Slupianek	13 Jul 80
22.40	Lisovskaya	14 Aug 88	22.19	Lisovskaya	5 Jul 88	22.11	Slupianek	7 May 80
22.34	Slupianek	11 May 80	22.14	Slupianek	25 May 80	22.10	Slupianek	25 May 80
22.33	Slupianek	2 May 80	22.14	Slupianek	13 Jul 80	22.09	Slupianek	7 May 80

DISCUS

Mark	Wind	Name		Nat	Born	Pos	Meet	Venue	Date
76.80	WR	Gabriele	Reinsch	GDR	23.9.63	1	v ITA	Neubrandenburg	9 Jul 88
74.56	WR	Zdenka	Silhavá' ¶	CZE	15.6.54	1		Nitra	26 Aug 84
74.56		Ilke	Wyludda	GDR	28.3.69	1	NC	Neubrandenburg	23 Jul 89
74.44			Reinsch			1		Berlin	13 Sep 88
74.40			Wyludda			2		Berlin	13 Sep 88
74.08		Diana	Gansky'	GDR	14.12.63	1	v URS	Karl-Marx-Stadt	20 Jun 87
73.90			Gansky			1	ECp	Praha	27 Jun 87
73.84		Daniela	Costian ¶	ROM	30.4.65	1		Bucuresti	30 Apr 88
73.78			Costian			1		Bucuresti	24 Apr 88
73.42			Reinsch			1		Karl-Marx-Stadt	12 Jun 88
73.36	WR	Irina	Meszynski	GDR	24.3.62	1	Drz	Praha	17 Aug 84
73.32			Gansky			1		Neubrandenburg	11 Jun 87
73.28		Galina	Savinkova'	RUS	15.7.53	1	NC	Donetsk	8 Sep 84
73.26	WR		Savinkova			1		Leselidze	21 May 83
73.26			Sachse/Gansky			1		Neubrandenburg	6 Jun 86
73.24			Gansky			1		Leipzig	29 May 87
73.22		Tsvetanka	Khristova ¶	BUL	14.3.62	1		Kazanlak	19 Apr 87
73.10		Gisela	Beyer	GDR	16.7.60	1	OD	Berlin	20 Jul 84
73.04			Gansky			1		Potsdam	6 Jun 87
73.04			Wyludda			1	ECp	Gateshead	5 Aug 89
72.96			Savinkova			1	v GDR	Erfurt	23 Jun 85
72.94			Gansky			2	v ITA	Neubrandenburg	9 Jul 88
72.92		Martina	Opitz/Hellmann	GDR	12.12.60	1	NC	Potsdam	20 Aug 87
72.90			Costian			1		Bucuresti	14 May 88
72.78			Hellmann			2		Neubrandenburg	11 Jun 87
72.78			Reinsch			1	OD	Berlin	29 Jun 88
72.72			Wyludda			1		Neubrandenburg	23 Jun 89
72.70			Wyludda			1	NC-j	Karl-Marx-Stadt	15 Jul 88
72.54			Gansky			1	NC	Rostock	25 Jun 88
72.52			Hellmann			1		Frohburg	15 Jun 86
72.52			Khristova			1	BGP	Budapest	11 Aug 86
		(31/10)							
72.14		Galina	Murashova	LIT	22.12.55	2	Drz	Praha	17 Aug 84
71.80	WR	Maria	Vergova/Petkova	BUL	3.11.50	1	NC	Sofiya	13 Jul 80
71.68			Xiao Yanling ¶	CHN	27.3.68	1		Beijing	14 Mar 92
71.58		Ellina	Zvereva' ¶	BLR	16.11.60	1	Znam	Leningrad	12 Jun 88
71.50	WR	Evelin	Schlaak/Jahl	GDR	28.3.56	1		Potsdam	10 May 80
71.30		Larisa	Korotkevich	RUS	3.1.67	1	RusCp	Sochi	29 May 92
71.22		Ria	Stalman	NED	11.12.51	1		Walnut	15 Jul 84
70.88		Hilda	Ramos	CUB	1.9.64	1		Habana	8 May 92
70.80		Larisa	Mikhalchenko	UKR	16.5.63	1		Kharkov	18 Jun 88
70.68		Maritza	Martén	CUB	16.8.63	1	Ib Am	Sevilla	18 Jul 92
		(20)							
70.50	WR	Faina	Melnik	RUS	9.6.45	1	Znam	Sochi	24 Apr 76
70.34	@	Silvia	Madetzky	GDR	24.6.62	3		Athína	16 May 88
		69.34				1		Halle	26 Jun 87
70.02		Natalya	Sadova	RUS	15.6.72	1		Thessaloniki	23 Jun 99
69.86		Valentina	Kharchenko	RUS	.49	1		Feodosiya	16 May 81
69.72		Svetla	Mitkova	BUL	17.6.64	2	NC	Sofiya	15 Aug 87
69.68		Mette	Bergmann	NOR	9.11.62	1		Florø	27 May 95
69.51		Franka	Dietzsch	GER	22.1.68	1		Wiesbaden	8 May 99
69.50		Florenta	Craciunescu'	ROM	7.5.55	1	Balk	Stara Zagora	2 Aug 85
69.08		Carmen	Romero	CUB	6.10.50	1	NC	Habana	17 Apr 76
69.08		Mariana	Ionescu/Lengyel	ROM	14.4.53	1		Constanta	19 Apr 86
		(30)							
68.94		Irina	Yatchenko	BLR	31.10.65	1	Nik	Nice	15 Jul 92
68.92		Sabine	Engel	GDR	21.4.54	1	v URS,POL	Karl-Marx-Stadt	25 Jun 77
68.80		Nicoleta	Grasu	ROM	11.9.71	1		Poiana Brasov	7 Aug 99
68.64		Margitta	Pufe'	GDR	10.9.52	1	ISTAF	Berlin	17 Aug 79

Mark	Wind		Name	Nat	Born	Pos	Meet	Venue	Date
68.62			Yu Hourun	CHN	9.7.64	1		Beijing	6 May 88
68.62			Hou Xuemei	CHN	27.2.62	1	IntC	Tianjin	4 Sep 88
68.60		Nadezhda	Kugayevskikh	RUS	19.4.60	1		Oryol	30 Aug 83
68.58		Lyubov	Zverkova	RUS	14.6.55	1	Izv	Kiyev	22 Jun 84
68.52		Beatrice	Faumuiná	NZL	23.10.74	1	Bisl	Oslo	4 Jul 97
68.38		Olga	Burova'	RUS	17.9.63	2	RusCp	Sochi	29 May 92
		(40)							
68.18		Tatyana	Lesovaya	KZK	24.4.56	1		Alma-Ata	23 Sep 82
68.18		Irina	Khval	RUS	17.5.62	1		Moskva	8 Jul 88
68.18		Barbara	Hechevarría	CUB	6.8.66	2		Habana	17 Feb 89
67.96		Argentina	Menis	ROM	19.7.48	1	RomIC	Bucuresti	15 May 76
67.90		Petra	Sziegaud	GDR	17.10.58	1		Berlin	19 May 82
67.82		Tatyana	Belova	RUS	12.2.62	1		Irkutsk	10 Aug 87
67.80		Stefenia	Simova ¶	BUL	5.6.63	1		Stara Zagora	27 Jun 92
67.70		Anastasía	Kelesídou	GRE	28.11.72	2		Réthimno	29 May 99
67.54		Svetlana	Petrova	BLR	19.12.51	1		Brest-Litovsk	20 Sep 78
67.50			Li Qiumei	CHN	20.4.74	1		Beijing	10 May 94
		(50)	100th woman 65.20, 200th woman c.62.84						

Unofficial meeting

Mark		Name	Nat	Born	Pos	Venue	Date
78.14	Martina	Hellmann	GDR	12.12.60	1	Berlin	6 Sep 88
75.36	Ilke	Wyludda	GDR	28.3.69	2	Berlin	6 Sep 88

Ancillary marks – other marks during series (to 72.92)

Mark	Name	Date	Mark	Name	Date	Mark	Name	Date
73.32	Reinsch	13 Sep 88	73.28	Gansky	27 Jun 87	73.10	Reinsch	9 Jul 88
73.28	Gansky	11 Jun 87	73.16	Wyludda	13 Sep 88	73.06	Gansky	27 Jun 87
						72.92	Hellmann	20 Aug 87

HAMMER

Mark	Wind		Name	Nat	Born	Pos	Meet	Venue	Date
76.07	WR	Mihaela	Melinte ¶	ROM	27.3.75	1		Rüdlingen	29 Aug 99
75.97	WR		Melinte			1		Clermont-Ferrand	13 May 99
75.68		Olga	Kuzenkova	RUS	4.10.70	1	NCp	Tula	4 Jun 00
75.21			Melinte			1c1		Rüdlingen	28 Aug 99
75.20			Melinte			1	WCh	Sevilla	24 Aug 99
74.90			Melinte			1		Bucuresti	4 Jul 99
74.77			Melinte			1		Nürnberg	13 Jun 99
74.48			Melinte			1	ECp	Paris (C)	20 Jun 99
74.30			Kuzenkova			1	Znam	Moskva	4 Jun 99
74.24			Melinte			1	WUG	Palma de Mallorca	9 Jul 99
74.22			Melinte			1		Bucuresti	29 May 99
74.20			Melinte			1		Poiana Brasov	7 Aug 99
74.00			Kuzenkova			1	Kuts	Moskva	26 Aug 00
73.85			Kuzenkova			1		Togliatti	14 May 00
73.80	UWR		Kuzenkova			1		Tolyatti	15 May 98
73.62			Kuzenkova			1	NC-w	Adler	24 Feb 01
73.60			Melinte			1		Bugeat	28 Jun 99
73.40			Kuzenkova			1	NC	Tula	13 Jul 01
73.14	WR		Melinte			1		Poiana Brasov	16 Jul 98
73.10	WR		Kuzenkova			1	ECp	München	22 Jun 97
72.81			Kuzenkova			1	Live	Nürnberg	25 Jun 00
72.74			Kuzenkova			1		Clermont-Ferrand	30 Jun 00
72.64			Melinte			1	GWG	Uniondale, NY	21 Jul 98
72.56			Kuzenkova			2	WCh	Sevilla	24 Aug 99
72.19			Melinte			1		Mersin	29 Mar 00
72.17			Kuzenkova			2c1		Rüdlingen	28 Aug 99
72.12			Melinte			1		Halle	15 May 99
72.10			Melinte			1		Onesti	20 May 00
72.09		Tatyana	Konstantinova	RUS	18.11.70	2	Znam	Moskva	4 Jun 99
71.92			Kuzenkova			1	NC	Tula	1 Aug 99
		(30/3)							
71.71		Kamila	Skolimowska	POL	4.11.82	1	GPF	Melbourne	9 Sep 01
71.18		Manuela	Montebrun	FRA	13.11.79	1		Vittel	2 Sep 00
70.79		Katalin	Divós ¶	HUN	11.5.74	2	GP	Doha	18 May 01
70.65		Yipsi	Moreno	CUB	19.11.80	1	WCh	Edmonton	7 Aug 01
70.62		Dawn	Ellerbe	USA	3.4.74	1	Penn R	Philadelphia	28 Apr 01
70.19		Bronwyn	Eagles	AUS	23.8.80	1		Calgary	30 Jul 01
69.92		Lyudmila	Gubkina	BLR	13.8.73	1		Staiki	19 Aug 00
		(10)							
69.81		Olga	Tsander	BLR	18.5.76	1		Sochi	26 Feb 00
69.63		Mia	Strömmer	FIN	26.2.74	1		Potchefstroom	24 Mar 01
69.53		Irina	Sekacheva	UKR	21.7.76	1		Kiev	16 Jun 00
69.28		Kirsten	Münchow	GER	21.1.77	3	OG	Sydney	29 Sep 00

Mark Wind	Name		Nat	Born	Pos	Meet	Venue	Date
68.50	Martina	Danisová	SVK	21.3.83	1		Kladno	16 Jun 01
68.50	Ester	Balassini	ITA	20.10.77	1		Ancona	15 Jul 01
68.47	Alla	Davydova	RUS	21.5.66	1	Mos Ch	Moskva	11 Jul 00
68.40	Bianca	Achilles	GER	17.4.81	1		Dortmund	25 Sep 99
68.28	Amy	Palmer	USA	20.4.75	2	PennR	Philadelphia	29 Apr 00
68.21	Svetlana	Sudak	BLR	20.3.71	1		Minsk	17 Jul 99
	(20)							
68.18	Ivana	Brkljacic	CRO	25.1.83	1		Pula	28 Apr 00
68.15	Lorraine	Shaw	GBR	2.4.68	3	EAA	Nice	17 Mar 01
68.07	Susanne	Keil	GER	18.5.78	1		Baunatal	23 Jun 01
67.98	Agnieszka	Pogroszewska	POL	20.2.77	2		Poznan	8 Jun 01
67.95	Debbie	Sosimenko	AUS	5.4.74	5	OG	Sydney	29 Sep 00
67.55	Lisa	Misipeka	ASA	3.1.75	4		Rüdlingen	12 Aug 00
67.13	Simone	Mathes	GER	13.5.75	3		Halle	15 May 99
66.97		Gu Yuan	CHN	9.5.82	1	NG	Guangzhou	22 Nov 01
66.88	Anna	Norgren	USA	19.12.74	1		Knoxville	13 Apr 01
66.85	Florence	Ezeh	FRA	29.12.77	1	NCAA	Eugene	2 Jun 01
	(30)							
66.58	Marina	Grin	BLR	23.1.76	1		Staiki	30 Jun 01
66.52	Jesseca	Cross	USA	10.5.75	3		Logan	1 Jul 00
66.40	Natalya	Kunitskaya	UKR	17.8.72	1		Kiev	17 May 01
66.31	Sini	Pöyry	FIN	3.2.80	1		Uppsala	12 Jun 01
66.30	Manuela	Priemer	GER	29.11.78	1		Mannheim	18 Jun 99
66.30		Zhang Wenxiu	CHN	11.2.83	1		Jinan	12 May 01
66.25	Melissa	Price	USA	5.9.79	3	NC	Eugene	22 Jun 01
66.20	Lucie	Vrbenská	CZE	12.5.77	1		Pardubice	22 Aug 01
66.16		Zhao Wei	CHN	27.1.79	1		Shanghai	7 May 01
66.15		Liu Yinghui	CHN	29.6.79	2	NG	Guangzhou	22 Nov 01
	(40)							
65.91	Tasha	Williams	NZL	31.7.73	1	NC	Hastings	24 Feb 01
65.91	Markéta	Hajdu	CZE	9.9.74	1		Praha	2 Jun 01
65.88	Yunaika	Crawford	CUB	2.11.82	1		Las Tunas	3 Mar 00
65.86	Marina	Rezanova'	UKR	28.8.74	1		Kiev	8 Jun 01
65.83	Evdokía	Tsámoglou	GRE	15.12.78	1		Thessaloníki	27 May 01
65.54	Christina	Tolson	USA	16.1.78	2	NCAA	Eugene	2 Jun 01
65.46	Yelena	Matoshko	BLR	23.6.82	2		Staiki	30 Jun 01
65.39	Cécile	Lignot	FRA	19.11.71	2		Castres	8 Aug 99
65.38	Karyne	Perkins-DiMarco	AUS	14.3.78	2		Brisbane (N)	6 Sep 00
65.35	Anelia	Yordanova	BUL	27.4.72	1		Sofia	10 Jun 00
	(50)	100th woman 62.69, 200th 59.08						

Ancillary marks – other marks during series (to 73.80)

76.05	Melinte	29 Aug 99	74.58	Melinte	29 Aug 99	74.10	Melinte	9 Jul 99
75.29	Melinte	13 May 99	74.47	Melinte	28 Aug 99	74.02	Melinte	29 Aug 99
75.16	Kuzenkova	4 Jun 00	74.21	Melinte	24 Aug 99	73.94	Melinte	7 Aug 99
74.65	Melinte	28 Aug 99	74.21	Melinte	28 Aug 99	73.92	Melinte	29 May 99
						73.87	Kuzenkova	26 Aug 00

Drugs disqualification

74.80	Melinte	1	Rüdlingen	12 Aug 00	73.74	Melinte	1	Noisy-le-Grand	20 Jun 00
74.32	Melinte	1	Nitra	26 Aug 00	72.54	Melinte	1	Milano	7 Jun 00
73.75	Melinte	1	NC Bucuresti	6 Aug 00	72.46	Melinte	2	Clermont-Ferrand	30 Jun 00

JAVELIN

Mark Wind	Name		Nat	Born	Pos	Meet	Venue	Date
71.54 WR	Osleidys	Menéndez	CUB	14.11.79	1		Réthimno	1 Jul 01
69.82		Menéndez			1	WUG	Beijing	29 Aug 01
69.53		Menéndez			1	WCh	Edmonton	7 Aug 01
69.48 WR	Trine	Hattestad	NOR	18.4.66	1	Bisl	Oslo	28 Jul 00
68.91		Hattestad			1	OG	Sydney	30 Sep 00
68.40		Menéndez			1		Tartu	19 Jun 01
68.32		Hattestad			1	ISTAF	Berlin	1 Sep 00
68.22 WR		Hattestad			1	GGala	Roma	30 Jun 00
68.19 WRu		Hattestad			1		Fana	28 Jul 99
67.92		Hattestad			1	DNG	Stockholm	1 Aug 00
67.83		Menéndez			2	ISTAF	Berlin	1 Sep 00
67.76		Hattestad			1	VD	Bruxelles	25 Aug 00
67.51 WR	Miréla	Manjani/Tzelíli	GRE	21.12.76	2	OG	Sydney	30 Sep 00
67.34		Menéndez			Q	OG	Sydney	29 Sep 00
67.20	Tatyana	Shikolenko	RUS	10.5.68	1	Herc	Monaco	18 Aug 00
67.09		Tzelíli			1	WCh	Sevilla	28 Aug 99
66.96		Hattestad			1	ECp1A	Nadderud	8 Jul 00
66.91	Tanja	Damaske	GER	16.11.71	1	NC	Erfurt	4 Jul 99

WOMEN All-time

Mark	Wind	Name		Nat	Born	Pos	Meet	Venue	Date
66.80		Louise	Currey	AUS	24.1.69	1		Gold Coast (RB)	5 Aug 00
66.74			Menéndez			1	GPII	Helsinki	14 Jun 01
66.73			Damaske			1	NC	Braunschweig	29 Jul 00
66.73			Hattestad			2	Herc	Monaco	18 Aug 00
66.70			Manjani			1	NC	Athína	16 Jun 01
66.55			Tzelíli			1	NC	Athína	7 Aug 99
66.54			Hattestad			1		Fana	27 Jun 00
66.54		Sonia	Bisset	CUB	1.4.71	1		Madrid	7 Jul 01
66.50			Hattestad			1	WK	Zürich	11 Aug 00
66.49			Menéndez			1		Leverkusen	5 Sep 99
66.45			Menéndez			1	Athl	Lausanne	2 Jul 99
66.44			Hattestad			1		Lapinlahti	16 Jul 00
		(30/7)							
65.76		Steffi	Nerius	GER	1.7.72	Q	OG	Sydney	29 Sep 00
65.71		Nikola	Tomecková	CZE	25.6.74	Q	WCh	Edmonton	4 Aug 01
65.30		Claudia	Coslovich	ITA	26.4.72	1		Ljubljana	10 Jun 00
		(10)							
65.29		Xiomara	Rivero	CUB	22.11.68	1		Santiago de Cuba	17 Mar 01
65.17		Karen	Forkel	GER	24.3.70	2	NC	Erfurt	4 Jul 99
65.08		Ana Mirela	Termure ¶	ROM	13.1.75	1	NC	Bucuresti	10 Jun 01
64.89		Yekaterina	Ivakina	RUS	4.12.64	4	Bisl	Oslo	28 Jul 00
64.62		Joanna	Stone	AUS	4.10.72	2		Gold Coast (RB)	5 Aug 00
64.62		Nikolett	Szabó	HUN	3.3.80	1		Pátra	22 Jul 01
64.61		Oksana	Makarova	RUS	21.7.71	2	ECp	Paris (C)	19 Jun 99
64.06		Taina	Uppa/Kolkkala	FIN	24.10.76	1		Pihtipudas	23 Jul 00
64.03		Mihaela	Ingberg	FIN	29.7.74	6	ISTAF	Berlin	1 Sep 00
63.92			Wei Jianhua	CHN	23.3.79	1		Beijing	18 Aug 00
		(20)							
63.73		Laverne	Eve	BAH	16.6.65	1		Nashville	22 Apr 00
63.69			Li Lei	CHN	4.5.74	1	OT	Jinzhou	8 Jun 00
63.32		Khristina	Georgieva	BUL	3.1.72	3	GP	Athína	28 Jun 00
63.12		Felicia	Tilea-Moldovan	ROM	29.9.67	1		Poiana Brasov	22 Jul 00
63.05		Paula	Huhtaniemi	FIN	17.2.73	1	v SWE	Göteborg	1 Sep 01

Ancillary marks – other marks during series (to 66.70)

69.42	Menéndez	7 Aug 01	67.51	Tzelíli	30 Sep 00	66.83	Menéndez	19 Jun 01
67.61	Hattestad	28 Jul 99	67.04	Hattestad	28 Jul 99	66.70	Menéndez	7 Aug 01

Specification changed from 1 May 1999. See ATHLETICS 2000 for Old specification all-time list. Top 10:

Mark	Wind	Name		Nat	Born	Pos	Meet	Venue	Date
80.00	WR	Petra	Felke	GDR	30.7.59	1		Potsdam	9 Sep 88
77.44	WR	Fatima	Whitbread	GBR	3.3.61	Q	EC	Stuttgart	28 Aug 86
74.76	WR	Tiina	Lillak	FIN	15.4.61	1		Tampere	13 Jun 83
74.20	WR	Sofía	Sakorafa	GRE	29.4.57	1	NC	Haniá	26 Sep 82
73.58		Tessa	Sanderson	GBR	14.3.56	1		Edinburgh	26 Jun 83
72.70		Anna	Veroúli ¶	GRE	13.11.56	1		Haniá	20 May 84
72.16		Antje	Kempe-Zöllkau	GDR	23.6.63	2		Celje	5 May 84
72.12		Trine	Hattestad'	NOR	18.4.66	1	Bisl	Oslo	10 Jul 93
71.88	WR	Antoaneta	Todorova'	BUL	8.6.63	1	ECp	Zagreb	15 Aug 81
71.82		Ivonne	Leal	CUB	27.2.66	1	WUG	Kobe	30 Aug 85

HEPTATHLON

Mark	Wind	Name		Nat	Born	Pos	Meet	Venue	Date
7291	WR	Jackie	Joyner-Kersee	USA	3.3.62	1	OG	Seoul	24 Sep 88
		12.69/0.5	1.86	15.80	22.56/1.6	7.27/0.7		45.66	2:08.51
7215	WR		Joyner-Kersee			1	OT	Indianapolis	16 Jul 88
		12.71/-0.9	1.93	15.65	22.30/ 0.0	7.00/-1.3		50.08	2:20.70
7158	WR		Joyner-Kersee			1	USOF	Houston	2 Aug 86
		13.18/-0.5	1.88	15.20	22.85/1.2	7.03/2.9		50.12	2:09.69
7148	WR		Joyner-Kersee			1	GWG	Moskva	7 Jul 86
		12.85/0.2	1.88	14.76	23.00/0.3	7.01/-0.5		49.86	2:10.02
7128			Joyner-Kersee			1	WCh	Roma	1 Sep 87
		12.91/0.2	1.90	16.00	22.95/1.2	7.14/0.9		45.68	2:16.29
7044			Joyner-Kersee			1	OG	Barcelona	2 Aug 92
		12.85/-0.9	1.91	14.13	23.12/0.7	7.10/1.3		44.98	2:11.78
7007		Larisa	Nikitina ¶	RUS	29.4.65	1	NC	Bryansk	11 Jun 89
		13.40/1.4	1.89	16.45	23.97/1.1	6.73/4.0		53.94	2:15.31
6985		Sabine	Braun	GER	19.6.65	1		Götzis	31 May 92
		13.11/-0.4	1.93	14.84	23.65/2.0	6.63/2.9		51.62	2:12.67
6979			Joyner-Kersee			1	TAC	San José	24 Jun 87
		12.90/2.0	1.85	15.17	23.02/0.4	7.25/2.3		40.24	2:13.07
6946	WR	Sabine	Paetz'	GDR	16.10.57	1	NC	Potsdam	6 May 84
		12.64/0.3	1.80	15.37	23.37/0.7	6.86/-0.2		44.62	2:08.93

Mark Wind		Name	Nat	Born	Pos	Meet	Venue	Date
6942	Ghada	Shouaa	SYR	10.9.72	1		Götzis	26 May 96
	13.78/0.3	1.87	15.64	23.78/0.6	6.77/0.6	54.74	2:13.61	
6935 WR	Ramona	Neubert	GDR	26.7.58	1	v URS	Moskva	19 Jun 83
	13.42/1.7	1.82	15.25	23.49/0.5	6.79/0.7	49.94	2:07.51	
6910		Joyner			1	MSR	Walnut	25 Apr 86
	12.9/0.0	1.86	14.75	23.24/2.8	6.85/2.1	48.30	2:14.11	
6897		John'			2	OG	Seoul	24 Sep 88
	12.85/0.5	1.80	16.23	23.65/1.6	6.71/ 0.0	42.56	2:06.14	
6878		Joyner-Kersee			1	TAC	New York	13 Jun 91
	12.77	1.89	15.62	23.42	6.97/0.4	43.28	2:22.12	
6875		Nikitina			1	ECp-A	Helmond	16 Jul 89
	13.55/-2.1	1.84	15.99	24.29/-2.1	6.75/-2.5	56.78	2:18.67	
6861	Eunice	Barber	FRA	17.11.74	1	WCh	Sevilla	22 Aug 99
	12.89/-0.5	1.93	12.37	23.57/0.5	6.86/-0.3	49.88	2:15.65	
6859	Natalya	Shubenkova	RUS	25.9.57	1	NC	Kiyev	21 Jun 84
	12.93/1.0	1.83	13.66	23.57/-0.3	6.73/0.4	46.26	2:04.60	
6858	Anke	Vater/Behmer	GDR	5.6.61	3	OG	Seoul	24 Sep 88
	13.20/0.5	1.83	14.20	23.10/1.6	6.68/0.1	44.54	2:04.20	
6847		Nikitina			1	WUG	Duisburg	29 Aug 89
	13.47	1.81	16.12	24.12	6.66	59.28	2:22.07	
6845 WR		Neubert			1	v URS	Halle	20 Jun 82
	13.58/1.8	1.83	15.10	23.14/1.4	6.84w/2.3	42.54	2:06.16	
6845	Irina	Belova ¶ (10)	RUS	27.3.68	2	OG	Barcelona	2 Aug 92
	13.25/-0.1	1.88	13.77	23.34/0.2	6.82/0.0	41.90	2:05.08	
6842		Barber			1		Götzis	4 Jun 00
	12.97/0.2	1.88	12.23	23.84/0.5	6.85/-0.1	51.91	2:11.55	
6841		Joyner			1		Götzis	25 May 86
	13.09/-1.3	1.87	14.34	23.63/-0.8	6.76/-0.3	48.88	2:14.58	
6837		Joyner-Kersee			1	WCh	Stuttgart	17 Aug 93
	12.89/0.1	1.81	14.38	23.19/0.0	7.04/1.4	43.76	2:14.49	
6831	Denise	Lewis	GBR	27.8.72	1		Talence	30 Jul 00
	13.13/1.0	1.84	15.07	24.01w/3.6	6.69/-0.4	49.42	2:12.20	
6813		Paetz			1	OD	Potsdam	21 Jul 84
	12.71/0.4	1.74	16.16	23.23w	6.58	41.94	2:07.03	
6805		Behmer			1		Götzis	19 Jun 88
	13.28/1.6	1.84	14.38	22.73/4.0	6.62/1.1	40.48	2:04.64	
6803	Jane	Frederick	USA	7.4.52	1		Talence	16 Sep 84
	13.27/1.2	1.87	15.49	24.15/1.6	6.43/0.2	51.74	2:13.55	
6797		Braun			2	WCh	Stuttgart	17 Aug 93
	13.25/0.1	1.90	14.62	24.12/0.0	6.54/1.0	53.44	2:17.82	
	(30/12)							
6765	Yelena	Prokhorova	RUS	16.4.78	1	NC	Tula	23 Jul 00
	13.54/-2.8	1.82	14.30	23.37/-0.2	6.72/1.0	43.40	2:04.27	
6750		Ma Miaolan	CHN	18.1.70	1	NG	Beijing	12 Sep 93
	13.28/1.5	1.89	14.98	23.86/	6.64/	45.82	2:15.33	
6741	Heike	Drechsler	GER	16.12.64	1		Talence	11 Sep 94
	13.34/-0.3	1.84	13.58	22.84/-1.1	6.95/1.0	40.64	2:11.53	
6703	Tatyana	Blokhina	RUS	12.3.70	1		Talence	11 Sep 93
	13.69/-0.6	1.91	14.94	23.95/-0.4	5.99/-0.3	52.16	2:09.65	
6702	Chantal	Beaugeant ¶	FRA	16.2.61	2		Götzis	19 Jun 88
	13.10/1.6	1.78	13.74	23.96/3.5	6.45/0.2	50.96	2:07.09	
6695	Jane	Flemming	AUS	14.4.65	1	CG	Auckland	28 Jan 90
	13.21/1.4	1.82	13.76	23.62/2.4	6.57/1.6	49.28	2:12.53	
6660	Ines	Schulz	GDR	10.7.65	3		Götzis	19 Jun 88
	13.56/0.4	1.84	13.95	23.93/2.8	6.70/0.7	42.82	2:06.31	
6658	Svetla	Dimitrova ¶	BUL	27.1.70	2		Götzis	31 May 92
	13.41/-0.7	1.75	14.72	23.06/2.4	6.64/1.9	43.84	2:09.60	
	(20)							
6646	Natalya	Grachova	UKR	21.2.52	1	NC	Moskva	2 Aug 82
	13.80	1.80	16.18	23.86	6.65/3.5	39.42	2:06.59	
6635	Sibylle	Thiele	GDR	6.3.65	2	GWG	Moskva	7 Jul 86
	13.14/0.6	1.76	16.00	24.18	6.62/1.0	45.74	2:15.30	
6635	Svetlana	Buraga	BLR	4.9.65	3	WCh	Stuttgart	17 Aug 93
	12.95/0.1	1.84	14.55	23.69/	6.58/-0.2	41.04	2:13.65	
6633	Natalya	Roshchupkina	RUS	13.1.78	2	NC	Tula	23 Jul 00
	14.05/-2.8	1.88	14.28	23.47/-0.2	6.45/0.4	44.34	2:07.93	
6623	Judy	Simpson'	GBR	14.11.60	3	EC	Stuttgart	30 Aug 86
	13.05/0.8	1.92	14.73	25.09/0.0	6.56/2.5	40.92	2:11.70	
6619	Liliana	Nastase	ROM	1.8.62	4	OG	Barcelona	2 Aug 92
	12.86/-0.9	1.82	14.34	23.70/0.2	6.49/-0.3	41.30	2:11.22	

Mark	Wind	Name		Nat	Born	Pos	Meet	Venue	Date	Splits
6616		Malgorzata	Nowak'	POL	9.2.59	1	WUG	Kobe	31 Aug 85	13.27/4.0 1.95 15.35 24.20/0.0 6.37/3.9 43.36 2:20.39
6604		Remigia	Nazaroviene'	LIT	2.6.67	2	URSCh	Bryansk	11 Jun 89	13.26/1.4 1.86 14.27 24.12/0.7 6.58/0.9 40.94 2:09.98
6604		Irina	Tyukhay	RUS	14.1.67	3		Götzis	28 May 95	13.20/-0.7 1.84 14.97 24.33/1.7 6.71/0.5 43.84 2:17.64
6598		Svetlana	Moskalets	RUS	1.11.69	1	NC	Vladimir	17 Jun 94	13.20/0.8 1.82 13.78 23.56/0.1 6.74/0.8 42.48 2:14.54
		(30)								
6577		DeDee	Nathan	USA	20.4.68	1		Götzis	30 May 99	13.28/-0.1 1.76 14.74 24.23/0.2 6.59/1.6 50.08 2:16.92
6573		Rita	Ináncsi	HUN	6.1.71	3		Götzis	29 May 94	13.66/2.0 1.84 13.94 24.20/2.5 6.78/1.4 46.28 2:16.02
6572		Heike	Tischler	GDR	4.2.64	2	EC	Split	31 Aug 90	14.08/-0.9 1.82 13.73 24.29/0.9 6.22/-0.7 53.24 2:05.50
6563		Natalya	Sazanovich	BLR	15.8.73	2	OG	Atlanta	28 Jul 96	13.56/-1.6 1.80 14.52 23.72/-0.3 6.70/1.1 46.00 2:17.92
6552		Nadezhda	Vinogradova'	RUS	1.5.58	2	NC	Kiyev	21 Jun 84	13.92/1.0 1.80 15.19 23.84/0.2 6.67/0.1 38.60 2:06.80
6551		Yelena	Martsenyuk	RUS	21.2.61	2		Staiki	2 Jul 88	13.54/-0.4 1.82 15.32 24.25/0.3 6.25/0.7 47.56 2:12.72
6546		Mona	Steigauf	GER	17.1.70	1	WUG	Catania	27 Aug 97	13.13/1.6 1.85 12.83 24.14/1.7 6.56/1.3 43.86 2:11.15
6542		Urszula	Wlodarczyk	POL	22.12.65	4	WCh	Athína	4 Aug 97	13.55/0.3 1.81 14.16 24.48/0.1 6.63/0.6 44.18 2:09.59
6541		Mila	Kolyadina	RUS	31.12.60	4	v GDR	Moskva	19 Jun 83	14.05 1.82 16.28 24.81 6.48/0.8 48.26 2:15.26
6539		Tatyana	Shpak	UKR	17.11.60	3		Staiki	2 Jul 88	13.57/-0.4 1.76 15.30 23.61/0.5 6.52/-0.6 39.28 2:07.25
		(40)								
6536		Yekaterina	Smirnova	RUS	22.10.56	3	v GDR	Moskva	19 Jun 83	13.41 1.82 14.82 24.84 6.56/1.1 45.66 2:13.38
6531		Peggy	Beer	GDR	15.9.69	3	EC	Split	31 Aug 90	13.27/-0.2 1.82 13.46 23.99/0.4 6.38/0.9 42.10 2:05.79
6527		Diane	Guthrie-Gresham	JAM	24.10.71	1	NCAA	Knoxville	3 Jun 95	13.86w/2.5 1.86 13.80 24.91/-1.3 6.92w/2.5 49.04 2:20.82
6523		Sabine	Everts	FRG	4.3.61	1	v URS	Mannheim	10 Jun 82	13.45 1.89 12.39 23.73 6.75 36.02 2:07.73
6500		Birgit	Clarius	GER	18.3.65	1	NC	Vaterstetten	20 Jun 93	13.61/1.3 1.81 15.22 24.69w/2.1 6.08/-0.6 50.20 2:11.29
6493		Svetlana	Filatyeva '	RUS	3.4.64	1		Kiyev	14 Aug 88	13.77 1.89 13.89 24.94 6.30 48.44 2:11.89
6487		Birgit	Dressel	FRG	4.5.60	4	EC	Stuttgart	30 Aug 86	13.56/-1.6 1.92 14.12 24.68/0.0 6.28/1.1 45.70 2:15.78
6474		Marianna	Maslennikova	RUS	17.5.61	2	NC	Kiyev	2 Aug 88	13.37/0.4 1.83 13.68 24.07/-0.0 6.28/0.2 40.42 2:05.60
6472		Shelia	Burrell	USA	15.1.72	3	WCh	Edmonton	5 Aug 01	13.05/0.5 1.67 12.87 22.92 6.45/0.4 48.74 2:14.24
6465		Kelly	Blair-LaBounty	USA	24.11.70	1	NC	Indianapolis	12 Jun 97	13.47w/2.5 1.74 13.28 24.13/1.0 6.52w/2.2 51.60 2:15.31
		(50)	100th woman 6300, 200th woman 6082							

DECATHLON

Mark	Name		Nat	Born	Pos	Venue	Date	Splits
7885	Mona	Steigauf	GER	17.1.70	1	Ahlen	21 Sep 97	12.15/1.2 5.93 12.49 1.73 55.34 13.75/0.2 34.68 3.10 42.24 5:07.95
7731	Marie	Collonvillé	FRA	23.11.73	1	Lage	10 Sep 00	12.61 6.03 11.55 1.75 56.48 14.28 31.91 3.40 43.94 5:13.70
7577	Tiffany	Lott-Hogan	USA	1.8.75	2	Lage	10 Sep 00	12.31 5.77 13.86 1.69 58.01 13.57 38.39 3.00 46.93 6:01.24

4 x 100 METRES RELAY

Mark		Nat	Team	Pos	Meet	Venue	Date
41.37	WR	GDR	Gladisch, Rieger, Auerswald, Göhr	1	WCp	Canberra	6 Oct 85
41.47		USA	Gaines, Jones, Miller, Devers	1	WCh	Athína	9 Aug 97
41.49		RUS	Bogoslovskaya, Malchugina, Voronova, Privalova	1	WCh	Stuttgart	22 Aug 93
41.49		USA	Finn, Torrence, Vereen, Devers	2	WCh	Stuttgart	22 Aug 93
41.52		USA	Gaines, Jones, Miller, Devers	1h1	WCh	Athína	8 Aug 97
41.53	WR	GDR	Gladisch, Koch, Auerswald, Göhr	1		Berlin	31 Jul 83
41.55		USA	Brown, Williams, Griffith, Marshall	1	ISTAF	Berlin	21 Aug 87
41.58		USA	Brown, Williams, Griffith, Marshall	1	WCh	Roma	6 Sep 87
41.60	WR	GDR	Müller, Wöckel, Auerswald, Göhr	1	OG	Moskva	1 Aug 80

Mark	Wind	Name	Nat	Born	Pos	Meet	Venue	Date
41.61A		USA Brown, Williams, Cheeseborough, Ashford			1	USOF	USAF Academy	3 Jul 83
41.63		USA Brown, Williams, Cheeseborough, Ashford			1	v GDR	Los Angeles	25 Jun 83
41.65		USA Brown, Bolden, Cheeseborough, Ashford			1	OG	Los Angeles	11 Aug 84
41.65		GDR Gladisch, Koch, Auerswald, Göhr			1	ECp	Moskva	17 Aug 85
41.68		GDR Möller, Krabbe, Behrendt, Günther			1	EC	Split	1 Sep 90
41.69		GDR Gladisch, Koch, Auerswald, Göhr			1	OD	Potsdam	21 Jul 84
41.71		USA White, Gaines, Miller, Jones			1	WCh	Edmonton	11 Aug 01
41.73		GDR Möller, Behrendt, Lange, Göhr			1		Berlin	13 Sep 88
41.76		GDR Gladisch, Koch, Auerswald, Göhr			1	WCh	Helsinki	10 Aug 83
41.79		GDR Gladisch, Drechsler, Auerswald, Göhr			1	v URS	Karl-Marx-Stadt	20 Jun 87
41.84		GDR Gladisch, Gunther, Auerswald, Göhr			1	EC	Stuttgart	31 Aug 86
		(20 performances by 3 nations) from here just best by nation						
41.92		BAH Fynes, Sturrup, Davis-Thompson, Ferguson			1	WCh	Sevilla	29 Aug 99
41.94		JAM Duhaney, Cuthbert, McDonald, Ottey			1	WCh	Tokyo	1 Sep 91
42.06		FRA Girard, Hurtis, Benth, Arron			2	WCh	Sevilla	29 Aug 99
42.08mx		BUL Pavlova, Nuneva, Georgieva, Ivanova			mx		Sofiya	8 Aug 84
		42.29 Pencheva, Nuneva, Georgieva, Donkova			1		Sofiya	26 Jun 88
42.23		CHN (Sichuan) Xiao Lin, Li Yali, Liu Xiaomei, Li Xuemei			1	NG	Shanghai	23 Oct 97
42.39		NGR Utondu, Idehen, Opara-Thompson, Onyali			2h2	OG	Barcelona	7 Aug 92
42.43		GBR Hunte, Smallwood, Goddard, Lannaman			3	OG	Moskva	1 Aug 80
		(10)						
42.59		FRG Possekel, Helten, Richter, Kroniger			2	OG	Montreal	31 Jul 76
42.71		POL Tomczak, Pakula, Pisiewicz, Kasprzyk			3	ECp	Moskva	17 Aug 85
42.77		CAN Bailey, Payne, Taylor, Gareau			2	OG	Los Angeles	11 Aug 84
42.89		CUB Ferrer, López, Duporty, Allen			6	WCh	Stuttgart	22 Aug 93
42.97		UKR Khristosenko, Kot, I Slyusar, German			1	SPART	Taskent	16 Sep 86
42.98		CZE/TCH Sokolová, Soborová, Kocembová, Kratochvilová			1	WK	Zürich	18 Aug 82
42.99A		AUS Massey, Broadrick, Lambert, Gainsford-Taylor			1		Pietersburg	18 Mar 00
43.07		GRE Tsóni, Kóffa, Vasarmídou, Thánou			2	MedG	Bari	18 Jun 97
43.19		GHA Akoto, Twum, Anim, Nsiah			5s1	OG	Sydney	29 Sep 00
43.25A		RSA Hartman, Moropane, Holtshausen, Seyerling			2		Pietersburg	18 Mar 00
		(20)						
43.35		KZK Aleksandrova, Kvast, Miljauskiene, Sevalnikova			2	SPART	Taskent	16 Sep 86
43.37		FIN Pirtimaa, Hanhijoki, Hernesniemi, Salmela			7	WCh	Stuttgart	22 Aug 93
43.42		COL Mera, Palacios, Rodriguez, Brock			4h2	WCh	Göteborg	12 Aug 95
43.44A	WR	NED van den Berg, Sterk, Hennipman, Bakker			4	OG	Ciudad de México	20 Oct 68
43.44		ITA Pistone, Graglia, Grillo, Levorato			1		Barletta	26 Jul 00
43.61		MAD Rahanitraniriana, Ratsimbazafy, Rakotozafy, Rakotondrabé			4h4	OG	Sydney	29 Sep 00
43.62		BLR Molchan, Safronnikova, Sologub, Grigorovska			5	ECp	Madrid	1 Jun 96
43.82		UZB Shmonina, Olenchenko, Barabashina, Vilisova			3	SPART	Moskva	20 Jun 83
43.89		BRA Gomes, K Santos, Amaral, Moura			7h1	WCh	Athína	8 Aug 97
43.89		CIV Gnahore, Allou, Sanganoko, Ayétoché			2	Franc	Ottawa	23 Jul 01
		320)						
43.89		SRI Jayasinghe, Sooriyaarachchi, De Soysa, Dharsha			5h1	WCh	Edmonton	11 Aug 01

Best at low altitude

Mark	Nat	Name	Pos	Meet	Venue	Date
43.18	AUS	Wilson, Wells, Robertson, Boyle	5	OG	Montreal	31 Jul 76
43.48	NED	Cooman, Tromp, Olyslager, Vader	5s1	OG	Seoul	1 Oct 88

4 x 200 METRES RELAY

Mark		Team	Name	Pos	Meet	Venue	Date
1:27.46	WR	USA Blue	Jenkins, Colander-Richardson, Perry, Jones	1	PennR	Philadelphia	29 Apr 00
1:28.15	WR	GDR	Göhr, R.Müller, Wöckel, Koch	1		Jena	9 Aug 80
1:29.24		Nike International USA	Roberts, Miller, Green, M Jones	1	Penn	Philadelphia	25 Apr 98
1:30.20		Nike International USA	Mondie-Milner, Green, Gaines, Miller	1	Penn	Philadelphia	26 Apr 97
1:30.23		JAM	McDonald, Frazier, V Campbell, A Walker	1	PennR	Philadelphia	28 Apr 01

4 x 400 METRES RELAY

Mark		Nat	Pos	Meet	Venue	Date
3:15.17	WR	URS	1	OG	Seoul	1 Oct 88
		Ledovskaya 50.12, O.Nazarova 47.82, Pinigina 49.43, Bryzgina 47.80				
3:15.51		USA	2	OG	Seoul	1 Oct 88
		D.Howard 49.82, Dixon 49.17, Brisco 48.44, Griffith-Joyner 48.08				
3:15.92	WR	GDR G.Walther 49.8, Busch 48.9, Rübsam 49.4, Koch 47.8	1	NC	Erfurt	3 Jun 84
3:16.71		USA	1	WCh	Stuttgart	22 Aug 93
		Torrence 49.0, Malone 49.4, Kaiser-Brown 49.48, Miles 48.78				
3:16.87		GDR Emmelmann 50.9, Busch 48.8, Müller 48.9, Koch 48.3	1	EC	Stuttgart	31 Aug 86
3:18.29		USA	1	OG	Los Angeles	11 Aug 84
		Leatherwood 50.50, S.Howard 48.83, Brisco-Hooks 49.23, Cheeseborough 49.73				
3:18.29		GDR Neubauer 50.58, Emmelmann 49.89, Busch 48.81, Müller 48.99	3	OG	Seoul	1 Oct 88
3:18.38		RUS	2	WCh	Stuttgart	22 Aug 93
		Ruzina 50.8, Alekseyeva 49.3, Ponomaryova 49.78, Privalova 48.47				

Mark	Wind	Name	Nat	Born	Pos	Meet	Venue	Date
3:18.43		URS Ledovskaya 51.7, Dzhigalova 49.2, Nazarova 48.87, Bryzgina 48.67			1	WCh	Tokyo	1 Sep 91
3:18.58		URS I.Nazarova, Olizarenko, Pinigina, Vladykina			1	ECp	Moskva	18 Aug 85
3:18.63		GDR Neubauer 51.4, Emmelmann 49.1, Müller 48.64, Busch 49.48			1	WCh	Roma	6 Sep 87
3:19.04	WR	GDR Siemon' 51.0, Busch 50.0, Rübsam 50.2, Koch 47.9			1	EC	Athína	11 Sep 82
3:19.12		URS Baskakova, I.Nazarova, Pinigina, Vladykina			1	Drz	Praha	18 Aug 84
3:19.23	WR	GDR Maletzki, Rohde, Streidt, Brehmer			1	OG	Montreal	31 Jul 76
3:19.49		GDR Emmelmann, Busch, Neubauer, Koch			1	WCp	Canberra	4 Oct 85
3:19.50		URS Yurchenko, O.Nazarova, Pinigina, Bryzgina			2	WCh	Roma	6 Sep 87
3:19.60		USA Leatherwood, S.Howard, Brisco-Hooks, Cheeseborough			1		Walnut	25 Jul 84
3:19.62		GDR Kotte, Brehmer, Köhn, Koch			1	ECp	Torino	5 Aug 79
3:19.66		GDR Busch, Emmelmann, Neubauer, Müller			1	v FRG	Düsseldorf	20 Jun 88
3:19.73		GDR K.Walther, Busch, Koch, Rübsam			1	WCh	Helsinki	14 Aug 83
(20/4 with USSR and Russia counted separately)								
3:20.32		CZE/TCH Kocembová, Matejkovicová, Moravcíková, Kratochvílová			2	WCh	Helsinki	14 Aug 83
3:20.65		JAM Richards 50.9, Scott 50.1, Parris 49.70, Fenton 49.95			1	WCh	Edmonton	12 Aug 01
3:21.04		NGR Afolabi 51.13, Yusuf 49.72, Opara 51.29, Ogunkoya 48.90			2	OG	Atlanta	3 Aug 96
3:21.21		CAN Crooks, Richardson, Killingbeck, Payne			2	OG	Los Angeles	11 Aug 84
3:21.94		UKR Dzhigalova, Olizarenko, Pinigina, Vladykina			1	URSCh	Kiyev	17 Jul 86
3:22.01		GBR Hanson, Smith, Gunnell, Keough			4	WCh	Tokyo	1 Sep 91
		(10)						
3:22.34		FRA Landre 51.3, Dorsile 51.1, Elien 50.54, Pérec 49.36			1	EC	Helsinki	14 Aug 94
3:22.49		FRG Thimm, Arendt, Thomas, Abt			4	OG	Seoul	1 Oct 88
3:23.81		AUS Peris-Kneebone, Lewis, Gainsford-Taylor, Freeman			5	OG	Sydney	30 Sep 00
3:24.23		CUB Bonne, Duporty, Morales, Quirot			2h2	OG	Atlanta	2 Aug 96
3:24.28		CHN (Hebei) An X, Bai X, Cao C, Ma Y			1	NG	Beijing	13 Sep 93
3:24.65		POL Kasprzyk, Wojdecka, Kapusta, Blaszak			3	EC	Stuttgart	31 Aug 86
3:25.68		ROM Ruicu, Rîpanu, Barbu, Tîrlea			2	ECp	Paris (C)	20 Jun 99
3:25.7a		FIN Eklund, Pursiainen, Wilmi, Salin			2	EC	Roma	8 Sep 74
3:25.81		BUL Ilieva, Stamenova, Penkova, Damyanova			1	v Hun,Pol	Sofiya	24 Jul 83
3:26.31		BLR Sologub, Budnik, Khlyustova, Kozak			3h1	OG	Sydney	29 Sep 00
		(20)						
3:26.69		ITA Perpoli, Spuri, Carbone, De Angeli			5	ECp	Paris (C)	20 Jun 99
3:27.54		LIT Navickaite, Valiuliene, Mendzoryte, Ambraziene			3	SPART	Moskva	22 Jun 83
3:27.57		ESP Merino, Lacambra, Myers, Ferrer			7	WCh	Tokyo	1 Sep 91
3:27.86		HUN Orosz, Forgács, Tóth, Pál			5	OG	Moskva	1 Aug 80
3:28.02		SEN Diop, M T Diouf, A Diouf, Thiam			4h3	OG	Sydney	29 Sep 00
3:28.11		IND Kuriakose, Philip, P Kaur, Beenamol			1	NC	Chennai	31 Jul 00
3:28.52		SUI Burkart, Zürcher/Scalabrin, Brillante, Lüthi			8	WCh	Stuttgart	22 Aug 93
3:28.94A		KEN Shitandayi, Wanjiru, Kavaya, Chepkurui			2	AfG	Nairobi	12 Aug 87
3:29.22A		BRA Montalvão, Oliveira, Telles, Figueiredo			1	IbAm	Cd de México	24 Jul 88
3:29.38		POR Moreira, Coelho, Amaral, Jardim			4h2	OG	Barcelona	7 Aug 92

5000 METRES WALK (TRACK)

Mark	Wind	Name		Nat	Born	Pos	Meet	Venue	Date
20:03.0	WR	Kerry	Saxby-Junna	AUS	2.6.61	1		Sydney	11 Feb 96
20:07.52	WR	Beate	Anders/Gummelt	GDR	4.2.68	1	vURS	Rostock	23 Jun 90
20:21.69		Annarita	Sidoti	ITA	25.7.69	1	NC	Cesenatico	1 Jul 95
20:27.59	WR	Ileana	Salvador	ITA	16.1.62	1		Trento	3 Jun 89
20:28.62		Sari	Essayah	FIN	21.2.67	1	NC	Tuusula	9 Jul 94
20:29.63		Claudia	Iovan	ROM	25.2.78	1		Istanbul	19 Jun 99
20:31.4		Irina	Stankina	RUS	25.3.77	1	NC-wj	Adler	10 Feb 96
20:33.42		Elisabetta	Perrone	ITA	9.7.68	2	NC	Cesenatico	1 Jul 95
20:37.7			Jin Bingjie	CHN	1.4.71	1	NC	Hefei	3 Mar 90
20:37.83		Kjersti	Plätzer (Tysse)	NOR	18.1.72	1	NC	Drammen	7 Jul 01

10 KILOMETRES WALK

Mark	Wind	Name		Nat	Born	Pos	Meet	Venue	Date
41:04	WR	Yelena	Nikolayeva	RUS	1.2.66	1	NC	Sochi	20 Apr 96
41:16			Wang Yan	CHN	3.5.71	1		Eisenhüttenstadt	8 May 99
41:17		Irina	Stankina	RUS	25.3.77	1	NC-w	Adler	9 Feb 97
41:24		Olimpiada	Ivanova ¶	RUS	5.5.70	2	NC-w	Adler	9 Feb 97
41:29	WR	Larisa	Ramazanova	RUS	23.9.71	1	NC	Izhevsk	4 Jun 95
41:30	WR	Kerry	Saxby-Junna	AUS	2.6.61	1	NC	Canberra	27 Aug 88
41:30			O Ivanova			2	NC	Izhevsk	4 Jun 95
41:31		Yelena	Gruzinova	RUS	24.12.67	2	NC	Sochi	20 Apr 96
41:38			Gao Hongmiao	CHN	17.3.74	1	NC	Beijing	7 Apr 94
41:38		Rossella	Giordano	ITA	1.12.72	1		Naumburg	25 May 97
41:41			Nikolayeva			2		Naumburg	25 May 97
41:45			Liu Hongyu (10)	CHN	11.1.75	2		Eisenhüttenstadt	8 May 99
41:46		Annarita	Sidoti	ITA	25.7.69	1		Livorno	12 Jun 94

Mark	Wind	Name		Nat	Born	Pos	Meet	Venue	Date
41:46			O Ivanova			1	NC/w	Adler	11 Feb 96
41:47			Saxby-Junna			1		Eisenhüttenstadt	11 May 96
41:48			Li Chunxiu	CHN	13.8.69	1	NG	Beijing	8 Sep 93
41:49			Ramazanova			3	NC	Sochi	20 Apr 96
41:49			Nikolayeva			1	OG	Atlanta	29 Jul 96
41:50		Yelena	Arshintseva	RUS	5.4.71	1	NC-w	Adler	11 Feb 95
41:51		Beate	Anders/Gummelt	GER	4.2.68	2		Eisenhüttenstadt	11 May 96
41:52			Stankina			1	WCp	Podebrady	19 Apr 97
41:54		Kjersti	Plätzer (Tysse)	NOR	18.1.72	3		Eisenhüttenstadt	8 May 99
41:55			Stankina			1	NC-wj	Adler	11 Feb 95
41:56		Yelena	Sayko	RUS	24.12.67	2	NC/w	Adler	11 Feb 96
41:56			Khmelnitskaya	(Ramazanova)		1		Eisenhüttenstadt	10 May 97
41:56.23t		Nadezhda	Ryashkina	RUS	22.1.67	1	GWG	Seattle	24 Jul 90
41:57			Gao Hongmiao			2	NG	Beijing	8 Sep 93
41:57.22t			Saxby-Junna			2	GWG	Seattle	24 Jul 90
41:58			Gruzinova			2	NC-w	Adler	11 Feb 95
41:59			O Ivanova			2	WCp	Podebrady	19 Apr 97
		(30/17)							
42:01		Tamara	Kovalenko	RUS	5.6.64	3	NC-w	Adler	11 Feb 95
42:01		Olga	Panfyorova	RUS	21.8.77	1	NC-23	Izhevsk	16 May 98
42:06		Valentina	Tsybulskaya	BLR	19.2.68	4		Eisenhüttenstadt	8 May 99
		(20)							
42:07		Ileana	Salvador	ITA	16.1.62	1		Sesto San Giovanni	1 May 92
42:09		Elisabetta	Perrone	ITA	9.7.68	4		Eisenhüttenstadt	11 May 96
42:11		Nina	Alyushenko	RUS	29.5.68	3	NC	Izhevsk	4 Jun 95
42:13		Natalya	Misyulya	BLR	16.4.66	5		Eisenhüttenstadt	8 May 99
42:13.7t		Madelein	Svensson	SWE	20.7.69	2	SGP	Fana	15 May 92
42:15			Gu Yan	CHN	17.3.74	3	WCp	Podebrady	19 Apr 97
42:15		Erica	Alfridi	ITA	22.2.68	5		Naumburg	25 May 97
42:15		Jane	Saville	AUS	5.11.74	6		Eisenhüttenstadt	8 May 99
42:16		Alina	Ivanova	RUS	16.3.69	1		Novopolotsk	27 May 89
42:16		Norica	Cîmpean	ROM	22.3.72	1		Calella	9 May 99
		(30)							
42:17		Katarzyna	Radtke	POL	31.8.69	5		Eisenhüttenstadt	11 May 96
42:20		Sari	Essayah	FIN	21.2.67	4	WCh	Göteborg	7 Aug 95
42:29		Olga	Kardopoltseva	BLR	11.9.66	4		Eisenhüttenstadt	10 May 97
42:31		Vera	Nacharkina'	RUS	17.2.66	1	NC	Izhevsk	16 May 98
42:32		Maya	Sazonova	KZK	28.5.68	4	Rus Ch	Sochi	20 Apr 96
42:34		Mária	Rosza/Urbaník	HUN	12.2.67	7	WCh	Göteborg	7 Aug 95
42:37		Claudia	Iovan	ROM	25.2.78	2		Calella	9 May 99
42:37		Olga	Lukyanchuk	UKR	7.12.76	1		Mukachevo	21 Oct 00
42:39		Susana	Feitor	POR	28.1.75	1		Lanciano	11 Mar 01
42:40		Yuliya	Odzilyayeva	RUS	17.10.71	5		Livorno	12 Jun 94
		(40)							
42:40.37t			Feng Haixia	CHN	23.2.75	3		Nanjing	24 Oct 95
42:42		Graciela	Mendoza	MEX	22.3.63	11		Naumburg	25 May 97
42:42+		Tatyana	Gudkova	RUS	23.1.78	1=	in 20k	Moskva	19 May 00
42:43+		Olga	Polyakova	RUS	23.9.80	4=	in 20k	Moskva	19 May 00
42:44		Irina	Strakhova	RUS	4.3.59	3		Sochi	17 Feb 91
42:44			Long Yuwen	CHN	1.8.75	3		Shenzhen	18 Feb 93
42:45			Li Yuxin	CHN	4.12.74	4		Shenzhen	18 Feb 93
42:46.7t			Cui Yingzi	CHN	26.1.71	1	NC	Jinan	15 Mar 92
42:46.7t			Chen Yueling	CHN	1.4.68	2	NC	Jinan	15 Mar 92
42:48		M del Rosario	Sánchez	MEX	26.10.73	8		Eisenhüttenstadt	8 May 99
		(50)	100th woman 43:47, 200th woman 44:51						

Probable short course

Mark	Wind	Name		Nat	Born	Pos	Meet	Venue	Date
41:30		Ileana	Salvador	ITA	16.1.62	1	4-N	Livorno	10 Jul 93
41:56		Elisabeta	Perrone	ITA	9.7.68	2	4-N	Livorno	10 Jul 93

Best track times

Mark	Wind	Name		Nat	Born	Pos	Meet	Venue	Date
41:57.22		Kerry	Saxby-Junna	AUS	2.6.61	2	GWG	Seattle	24 Jul 90
42:11.5		Beate	Anders/Gummelt	GER	4.2.68	1	SGP	Fana	15 May 92
42:23.7		Ileana	Salvador		16.1.62	2	SGP	Fana	8 May 93
42:30.13			Gao Hongmiao	CHN	17.3.74	1		Nanjing	24 Oct 95
42:30.31		Olimpiada	Ivanova ¶	RUS	5.5.70	1	GWG	Sankt-Peterburg	26 Jul 94
42:37.0		Sari	Essayah	FIN	21.2.67	3	SGP	Fana	8 May 93
42:38.24			Liu Hongyu	CHN	11.1.75	2		Nanjing	24 Oct 95
42:43.23		Yelena	Sayko	RUS	16.2.68	2	GWG	Sankt-Peterburg	26 Jul 94
42:45.0		Elisabetta	Perrone	ITA	9.7.68	1		Catania	30 May 99
42:47.4		Katarzyna	Radtke	POL	31.8.69	4	SGP	Fana	8 May 93

WOMEN All-time

20 KILOMETRES WALK

Mark Wind	Name		Nat	Born	Pos	Meet	Venue	Date
1:24:50 WR	Olimpiada	Ivanova	RUS	5.5.70	1	NC-w	Adler	4 Mar 01
1:25:18 WR	Tatyana	Gudkova	RUS	23.1.78	1	NC	Moskva	19 May 00
1:25:20	Olga	Polyakova	RUS	23.9.80	2	NC	Moskva	19 May 00
1:25:29	Irina	Stankina	RUS	25.3.77	3	NC	Moskva	19 May 00
1:25:59	Tamara	Kovalenko	RUS	5.6.64	4	NC	Moskva	19 May 00
1:26:08		Ivanova			5	NC	Moskva	19 May 00
1:26:22		Wang Yan	CHN	3.5.71	1	NG	Guangzhou	19 Nov 01
1:26:23		Wang Liping	CHN	8.7.76	2	NG	Guangzhou	19 Nov 01
1:26:35		Liu Hongyu	CHN	11.1.75	3	NG	Guangzhou	19 Nov 01
1:26:48		Ivanova			1	ECp	Eisenhüttenstadt	17 Jun 00
1:26:48		Ivanova			1	ECp	Dudince	19 May 01
1:26:50	Natalya	Fedoskina	RUS	25.6.80	2	ECp	Dudince	19 May 01
1:26:53.2 t		Ivanova			1	GWG	Brisbane	6 Sep 01
1:27:09	Elisabetta	Perrone (10)	ITA	9.7.68	3	ECp	Dudince	19 May 01
1:27:29	Erica	Alfridi	ITA	22.2.68	4	ECp	Dudince	19 May 01
1:27:30 WR		Liu Hongyu			1		Beijing	1 May 95
1:27:30 WR	Nadezhda	Ryashkina	RUS	22.1.67	1	NC-w	Adler	7 Feb 99
1:27:32		Liu Hongyu			1	WCp	Mézidon-Canon	2 May 99
1:27:33	Tatyana	Sibilyeva	RUS	17.5.80	2	NC-w	Adler	4 Mar 01
1:27:35		Fedoskina			2	WCp	Mézidon-Canon	2 May 99
1:27:35		Fedoskina			3	NC-w	Adler	4 Mar 01
1:27:42		Perrone			2	ECp	Eisenhüttenstadt	17 Jun 00
1:27:46	Norica	Cîmpean	ROM	22.3.72	1		Békéscsaba	28 Mar 99
1:27:48		Cîmpean			3	WCp	Mézidon-Canon	2 May 99
1:27:48		Ivanova			1	WCh	Edmonton	9 Aug 01
1:27:49.3 t	Yelena	Nikolayeva	RUS	1.2.66	2	GWG	Brisbane	6 Sep 01
1:27:53	Kjersti	Tysse Plätzer	NOR	18.1.72	3	ECp	Eisenhüttenstadt	17 Jun 00
1:27:54		Song Lijuan	CHN	9.2.75	2		Beijing	1 May 95
1:27:55		Liu Hongyu			1		Rio Maior	15 Apr 00
1:27:55	Susana	Feitor	POR	28.1.75	1		Rio Maior	7 Apr 01
	(30/18)							
1:28:18		Kong Yan	CHN	6.7.73	3		Beijing	1 May 95
1:28:24	Natalya	Misyulya (20)	BLR	16.4.66	1	NC	Soligorsk	13 May 00
1:28:38	Annarita	Sidoti	ITA	25.7.69	5	ECp	Eisenhüttenstadt	17 Jun 00
1:28:39		Gu Yan	CHN	17.3.74	4		Beijing	1 May 95
1:28:45		Gao Hongmiao	CHN	17.3.74	1	NC	Dandong	13 Apr 01
1:28:49	Valentina	Tsybulskaya	BLR	19.2.68	2	WCh	Edmonton	9 Aug 01
1:28:51	Olga	Kardopoltseva	BLR	11.9.66	2		Brest	4 Jun 99
1:28:56	Jane	Saville	AUS	5.11.74	1		København	6 May 00
1:28:56	Larisa	Khmelnitskaya	BLR	23.9.71	2	NC	Soligorsk	13 May 00
1:28:56	Valentina	Savchuk	UKR	19.1.75	4	RUS-w	Adler	4 Mar 01
1:29:08	Olga	Lukyanchuk	UKR	7.12.76	5	RUS-w	Adler	4 Mar 01
1:29:12	Rossella	Giordano	ITA	1.12.72	2	NC	Cassino	9 Mar 97
	(30)							
1:29:15		Feng Haixia	CHN	23.2.75	1	NC	Zhuhai	12 Mar 96
1:29:23	Lyudmila	Dolgopolova	BLR	11.8.69	3	NC	Soligorsk	13 May 00
1:29:31	Margarita	Turova	BLR	28.12.80			Brest	10 Mar 01
1:29:31		Jian Xingli	CHN	4.12.83	3	NG	Guangzhou	19 Nov 01
1:29:36	Kerry	Saxby-Junna	AUS	2.6.61	2		Naumburg	30 Apr 00
1:29:36	Maya	Sazonova	KAZ	28.5.65	1		Almaty	31 Mar 01
1:29:39	Claudia	Iovan ¶	ROM	25.2.78	6	WCp	Mézidon-Canon	2 May 99
1:29:39	Yuliya	Voyevodina	RUS	17.10.71	7	NC	Moskva	19 May 00
1:29:39		Gao Kelian	CHN	15.8.83	5	NG	Guangzhou	19 Nov 01
1:29:43		Li Hong	CHN	1.6.79	4	NC	Dandong	13 Apr 01
	(40)							
1:29:44		Wang Qingqing	CHN	7.2.83	6	NG	Guangzhou	19 Nov 01
1:29:45		Sun Chunfang	CHN	1.3.77	2	NC2	Lushun	3 Jun 00
1:29:47		Pan Hailian	CHN	21.11.77	7	NG	Guangzhou	19 Nov 01
1:29:54	Elisa	Rigaudo	ITA	17.6.80	1	EU23	Amsterdam	15 Jul 01
1:29:57	Gillian	O'Sullivan	IRL	21.8.76	1		Douglas	17 Feb 01
1:29:59	Ana Maria	Groza	ROM	1.6.76	2		Békéscsaba	9 Apr 00
1:30:00		Xu Aihui	CHN	25.4.78	6	NC	Dandong	13 Apr 01
1:30:03		Li Jingxue	CHN	10.2.70	7		Beijing	1 May 95
1:30:03	Graciela	Mendoza	MEX	23.3.63	8	WCp	Mézidon-Canon	2 May 99
1:30:09	María	Vasco	ESP	26.12.75	1		Prat de Llobregat	18 Feb 01
	(50)	100th best woman 1:32:05						

Uncertain distance

Mark Wind	Name		Nat	Born	Pos	Meet	Venue	Date
1:29:23	Svetlana	Tolstaya	KZK	9.8.71	1	NC	Almaty	27 Mar99

Mark	Wind	Name		Nat	Born	Pos	Meet	Venue	Date

JUNIOR WOMEN'S ALL-TIME LISTS

Based on the age regulations introduced for 1988, that is under 20 in year of competition.

100 METRES

Mark	Wind	Name		Nat	Born	Pos	Meet	Venue	Date
10.88	2.0	Marlies	Oelsner	GDR	21.3.58	1	NC	Dresden	1 Jul 77
10.89	1.8	Katrin	Krabbe	GDR	22.11.69	1rB		Berlin	20 Jul 88
11.03	1.7	Silke	Gladisch	GDR	20.6.64	3	OD	Berlin	8 Jun 83
11.04	1.4	Angela	Williams	USA	30.1.80	1	NCAA	Boise	5 Jun 99
11.08	2.0	Brenda	Morehead	USA	5.10.57	1	OT	Eugene	21 Jun 76
11.11	0.2	Shakedia	Jones	USA	15.3.79	1		Los Angeles (Ww)	2 May 98
11.11	1.1	Joan Uduak	Ekah	NGR	16.12.80	5	Athl	Lausanne	2 Jul 99
11.12	2.0	Veronica	Campbell	JAM	15.5.82	1	WJ	Santiago de Chile	18 Oct 00
11.13	2.0	Chandra	Cheeseborough	USA	10.1.59	2	OT	Eugene	21 Jun 76
11.13	-1.0	Grit	Breuer	GDR	16.2.72	1		Jena	6 Jun 90
Uncertain timing: 10.99	1.9	Natalya	Bochina	RUS	4.1.62	2		Leningrad	3 Jun 80
Wind assisted									
10.96	3.7	Angela	Williams	USA	30.1.80	1		Las Vegas	3 Apr 99
10.97	3.3	Gesine	Walther	GDR	6.10.62	4	NC	Cottbus	16 Jul 80
11.02	2.1	Nikole	Mitchell	JAM	5.6.74	1	Mutual	Kingston	1 May 93
11.06	2.2	Brenda	Morehead	USA	5.10.57	1s	OT	Eugene	21 Jun 76
11.09		Angela	Williams	TRI	15.5.65	1		Nashville	14 Apr 84
11.12	4.1	Marion	Jones	USA	12.10.75	1h		Cerritos	31 May 91

200 METRES

Mark	Wind	Name		Nat	Born	Pos	Meet	Venue	Date
22.19	1.5	Natalya	Bochina	RUS	4.1.62	2	OG	Moskva	30 Jul 80
22.37	1.3	Sabine	Rieger	GDR	6.11.63	2	vURS	Cottbus	26 Jun 82
22.42	0.4	Gesine	Walther	GDR	6.10.62	1		Potsdam	29 Aug 81
22.45	0.5	Grit	Breuer	GER	16.2.72	2	ASV	Köln	8 Sep 91
22.51	2.0	Katrin	Krabbe	GDR	22.11.69	3		Berlin	13 Sep 88
22.52	1.2	Mary	Onyali	NGR	3.2.68	6	WCh	Roma	3 Sep 87
22.58	0.8	Marion	Jones	USA	12.10.75	4	TAC	New Orleans	28 Jun 92
22.70		Marita	Koch	GDR	18.2.57	1		Halle	16 May 76
22.70A	1.9	Kathy	Smallwood	GBR	3.5.60	2	WUG	Ciudad de México	12 Sep 79
22.72	1.3	Silke	Gladisch	GDR	20.6.64	3	NC	Karl-Marx-Stadt	18 Jun 83
22.72	0.4	Nora	Ivanova	BUL	1.6.77	1		Zagreb	21 Jun 96
Wind assisted									
22.34	2.3	Kathrin	Krabbe	GDR	22.11.69	1	WJ	Sudbury	30 Jul 88
22.49	2.3	Brenda	Morehead	USA	5.10.57	1	OT	Eugene	24 Jun 76
22.53	2.5	Valerie	Brisco	USA	6.7.60	2	AAU	Walnut	17 Jun 79
22.64	2.3	Chandra	Cheeseborough	USA	16.1.59	2	OT	Eugene	24 Jun 76
22.65	3.5	Shakedia	Jones	USA	15.3.79	1	NC-j	Edwardsville IL	27 Jun 98
22.66	5.0	Lauren	Hewitt	AUS	25.11.78	3	NC	Melbourne	2 Mar 97
22.70	2.5	Kinshasa	Davis	USA	10.7.79	1		Long Beach	30 May 97

400 METRES

Mark	Name		Nat	Born	Pos	Meet	Venue	Date
49.42	Grit	Breuer	GER	16.2.72	2	WCh	Tokyo	27 Aug 91
49.77	Christina	Brehmer	GDR	28.2.58	1		Dresden	9 May 76
50.01		Li Jing	CHN	14.2.80	1	NG	Shanghai	18 Oct 97
50.19	Marita	Koch	GDR	18.2.57	3	OD	Berlin	10 Jul 76
50.59	Fatima	Yusuf	NGR	2.5.71	1	HGP	Budapest	5 Aug 90
	50.5 hand				1	NC	Lagos	25 Aug 90
50.74	Monique	Henderson	USA	18.2.83	1		Norwalk	3 Jun 00
50.86	Charity	Opara	NGR	20.5.72	2		Bologna	7 Sep 91
50.87	Denean	Howard	USA	5.10.64	1	TAC	Knoxville	20 Jun 82
50.87	Magdalena	Nedelcu	ROM	12.5.74	1	NC-j	Bucuresti	31 Jul 92
50.90	Sheila	Ingram	USA	23.3.57	3s1	OG	Montreal	28 Jul 76

800 METRES

Mark	Name		Nat	Born	Pos	Meet	Venue	Date
1:57.18		Wang Yuan	CHN	8.4.76	2h2	NG	Beijing	8 Sep 93
1:57.45	Hildegard	Ullrich	GDR	20.12.59	5	EC	Praha	31 Aug 78
1:57.62		Lang Yinglai	CHN	22.8.79	1	NG	Shanghai	22 Oct 97
1:57.63	Maria	Mutola	MOZ	27.10.72	4	WCh	Tokyo	26 Aug 91
1:57.77		Lu Yi	CHN	10.4.74	4	NG	Beijing	9 Sep 93
1:57.86	Katrin	Wühn	GDR	19.11.65	1		Celje	5 May 84
1:58.16		Lin Nuo	CHN	.1.80	3	NG	Shanghai	22 Oct 97
1:58.18	Marion	Hübner	GDR	29.9.62	2		Erfurt	2 Aug 81
1:58.24	Christine	Wachtel	GDR	6.1.65	3		Potsdam	25 May 84
1:58.37	Gabriela	Sedláková	SVK	2.3.68	4	ISTAF	Berlin	21 Aug 87

Mark	Wind	Name	Nat	Born	Pos	Meet	Venue	Date

1000 METRES

Mark	Wind	Name	Nat	Born	Pos	Meet	Venue	Date
2:35.4		Irina Nikitina	RUS	16.1.61	5	Kuts	Podolsk	5 Aug 79
2:35.4		Katrin Wühn	GDR	19.11.65	3		Potsdam	12 Jul 84

1500 METRES

Mark	Wind	Name	Nat	Born	Pos	Meet	Venue	Date
3:51.34		Lang Yinglai	CHN	22.8.79	2	NG	Shanghai	18 Oct 97
3:53.91		Yin Lili	CHN	11.11.79	3	NG	Shanghai	18 Oct 97
3:53.97		Lan Lixin	CHN	14.2.79	4	NG	Shanghai	18 Oct 97
3:54.52		Zhang Ling	CHN	13.4.80	5	NG	Shanghai	18 Oct 97
3:59.81		Wang Yuan	CHN	8.4.76	7	NG	Beijing	11 Sep 93
3:59.96		Zola Budd	GBR	26.5.66	3	VD	Bruxelles	30 Aug 85
4:00.05		Lu Yi	CHN	10.4.74	8	NG	Beijing	11 Sep 93
4:01.71		Li Ying	CHN	24.6.75	4h2	NG	Beijing	10 Sep 93
4:03.45		Anita Weyermann	SUI	8.12.77	1	Athl	Lausanne	3 Jul 96
4:03.5		Svetlana Guskova	MOL	19.8.59	3	Kuts	Podolsk	13 Aug 78

1 MILE: 4:17.57 Zola Budd GBR 26.5.66 3 WK Zürich 21 Aug 85

2000 METRES: 5:33.15 Zola Budd GBR 26.5.66 1 London 13 Jul 84

3000 METRES

Mark	Wind	Name	Nat	Born	Pos	Meet	Venue	Date
8:28.83		Zola Budd	GBR	26.5.66	3	GG	Roma	7 Sep 85
8:35.89		Sally Barsosio	KEN	21.3.78	2	Herc	Monaco	16 Aug 97
8:36.45		Ma Ningning	CHN	1.6.76	4	NC	Jinan	6 Jun 93
8:40.08		Gabriela Szabo	ROM	14.11.75	3	EC	Helsinki	12 Aug 94
8:42.39		Li Ying	CHN	24.6.75	8	NG	Beijing	13 Sep 93
8:44.1mx		Donna Gould	AUS	10.6.66	-		Eugene	13 Jul 84
8:44.14		Worknesh Kidane	ETH	21.11.81	6		Milano	7 Jun 00
8:44.57		Ayelech Worku	ETH	12.6.79	3	APM	Hengelo	1 Jun 98
8:45.07		Beatrice Chepchumba	KEN	25.11.83	11	GP	Saint-Denis	6 Jul 01
8:46.86		Zhang Linli	CHN	6.3.73	1	WJ	Seoul	20 Sep 92

5000 METRES

Mark	Wind	Name	Nat	Born	Pos	Meet	Venue	Date
14:39.96		Yin Lili	CHN	11.11.79	4	NG	Shanghai	23 Oct 97
14:45.33		Lan Lixin	CHN	14.2.79	2h2	NG	Shanghai	21 Oct 97
14:45.71		Song Liqing	CHN	20.1.80	3h2	NG	Shanghai	21 Oct 97
14:45.90		Jiang Bo	CHN	13.3.77	1		Nanjing	24 Oct 95
14:46.71		Sally Barsosio	KEN	21.3.78	3	VD	Bruxelles	22 Aug 97
14:47.40		Worknesh Kidane	ETH	21.11.81	7	OG	Sydney	25 Sep 00
14:48.07		Zola Budd	GBR	26.5.66	1	McV	London (CP)	26 Aug 85
14:53.44		Lydia Cheromei	KEN	11.5.77	3	ISTAF	Berlin	1 Sep 95
14:56.15		Xing Huina	CHN	25.2.84	2	NG	Guangzhou	23 Nov 01
14:56.22		Annemari Sandell	FIN	2.1.77	4	DNG	Stockholm	8 Jul 96

10,000 METRES

Mark	Wind	Name	Nat	Born	Pos	Meet	Venue	Date
30:39.41		Lan Lixin	CHN	14.2.79	2	NG	Shanghai	19 Oct 97
30:39.98		Yin Lili	CHN	11.11.79	3	NG	Shanghai	19 Oct 97
30:59.92		Merima Hashim	ETH	.81	3	NA	Heusden	5 Aug 00
31:11.26		Song Liqing	CHN	20.1.80	7	NG	Shanghai	19 Oct 97
31:15.38		Sally Barsosio	KEN	21.3.78	3	WCh	Stuttgart	21 Aug 93
31:32.15		Feng Wenhui	CHN	21.1.74	9	NG	Beijing	8 Sep 93
31:40.42		Annemari Sandell	FIN	2.1.77	6h2	OG	Atlanta	27 Jul 96
31:40.56		Delillah Asiago	KEN	24.2.72	1	JPN Ch	Tokyo	15 Jun 91
31:41.09		Lydia Cheromei	KEN	11.5.77	2	AfrCh	Belle Vue Mauricia	27 Jun 92
31:42.05		Kayoko Fukushi	JPN	25.3.82	1rA		Kanazawa	29 Sep 01

HALF MARATHON

Mark	Wind	Name	Nat	Born	Pos	Meet	Venue	Date
69:05		Delillah Asiago	KEN	24.2.72	1	GWR	Exeter	5 May 91
69:21		Ann Wamuchi	KEN	29.9.78	5		Tokyo	19 Jan 97
69:48		Yuka Hata	JPN	3.2.79	4		Lisboa	15 Mar 98
70:35		Iress Chenonge	KEN	1.2.82	1		Aveiro	1 Dec 01

MARATHON

Mark	Wind	Name	Nat	Born	Pos	Meet	Venue	Date
2:23:37		Liu Min	CHN	29.11.83	1		Beijing	14 Oct 01
2:25:48		Jin Li	CHN	29.5.83	6		Beijing	14 Oct 01
2:26:34		Wei Yanan	CHN	6.12.81	1		Beijing	15 Oct 00
2:27:30		Ai Dongmei	CHN	15.10.79	3	NG	Beijing	4 Oct 97
2:29:12		Chika Horie	JPN	15.2.81	4		Nagano	9 Apr 00
2:30:15		Gu Dongmei	CHN	5.11.74	9		Tianjin	4 Apr 93
2:30:30		Akemi Masuda	JPN	1.1.64	1		Eugene	11 Sep 83

Mark	Wind	Name		Nat	Born	Pos	Meet	Venue	Date

3000 METRES STEEPLECHASE

Mark	Wind	Name		Nat	Born	Pos	Meet	Venue	Date
9:30.70		Melissa	Rollison	AUS	13.4.83	1	GWG	Brisbane	4 Sep 01

100 METRES HURDLES

Mark	Wind	Name		Nat	Born	Pos	Meet	Venue	Date
12.84	1.5	Aliuska	López	CUB	29.8.69	2	WUG	Zagreb	16 Jul 87
12.88	1.5	Yelena	Ovcharova	UKR	17.6.76	2	ECp	Villeneuve d'Ascq	25 Jun 95
12.92	0.0		Sun Hongwei	CHN	24.11.79	6	NG	Shanghai	18 Oct 97
12.95	1.5	Candy	Young	USA	21.5.62	2	AAU	Walnut	16 Jun 79
12.95A	1.5	Cinnamon	Sheffield	USA	8.3.70	2	NCAA	Provo	3 Jun 89
13.00	0.7	Gloria	Kovarik	GDR	13.1.64	3h2	NC	Karl-Marx-Stadt	16 Jun 83
13.00	2.0	Lyudmila	Khristosenko	UKR	14.10.66	1	NC-j	Krasnodar	16 Jul 85
13.02	-1.7	Susanna	Kallur	SWE	16.2.81	1	WJ	Santiago de Chile	19 Oct 00
13.02	0.5	Gergana	Stoyanova	BUL	3.1.82	1h3	NC-j	Sofia	15 Jun 01
13.05	1.8	Heike	Terpe	GDR	4.10.64	4	OD	Berlin	8 Jun 83
Wind assisted to 13.02									
12.90	3.0	Adrianna	Lamalle	FRA-J	27.9.82	1		Fort-de-France	28 Apr 01
13.00	3.5	Gergana	Stoyanova	BUL	3.1.82	1h1	EJ	Grosseto	20 Jul 01
13.02	4.1	LaVonna	Martin	USA	18.11.66	5	NCAA	Austin	1 Jun 85

400 METRES HURDLES

Mark	Wind	Name		Nat	Born	Pos	Meet	Venue	Date
54.93			Li Rui	CHN	22.11.79	1	NG	Shanghai	22 Oct 97
55.15			Huang Xiaoxiao	CHN	15.2.85	2	NG	Guangzhou	22 Nov 01
55.20		Lesley	Maxie	USA	4.1.67	2	TAC	San Jose	9 Jun 84
55.20A		Jana	Pittman	AUS	9.11.82	1		Pietersburg	18 Mar 00
		55.63				1		Sydney	13 Feb 00
55.26		Ionela	Tîrlea	ROM	9.2.76	1	Nik	Nice	12 Jul 95
55.43			Li Shuju	CHN	20.7.81	1h2	NG	Shanghai	21 Oct 97
55.53		Radostina	Dimitrova	BUL	1.6.66	3	OD	Potsdam	21 Jul 84
55.62		Melanie	Walker	JAM	1.1.83	1		Bridgetown	19 May 01
55.65		Schowonda	Williams	USA	3.12.66	3	NCAA	Austin	31 May 85
55.72			Zheng Liyuan	CHN	1.4.74	5	NG	Beijing	9 Sep 93
55.72			Li Yulian	CHN	20.1.79	3h2	NG	Shanghai	21 Oct 97
Drugs disqualification: 54.54			Peng Yinghua ¶	CHN	21.2.79	(2)	NG	Shanghai	22 Oct 97

HIGH JUMP

Mark	Wind	Name		Nat	Born	Pos	Meet	Venue	Date
2.01		Olga	Turchak	KZK	5.3.67	2	GWG	Moskva	7 Jul 86
2.01		Heike	Balck	GDR	19.8.70	1	vURS-j	Karl-Marx-Stadt	18 Jun 89
2.00		Stefka	Kostadinova	BUL	25.3.65	1		Sofiya	25 Aug 84
2.00		Alina	Astafei	ROM	7.6.69	1	WJ	Sudbury	29 Jul 88
1.98		Silvia	Costa	CUB	4.5.64	2	WUG	Edmonton	11 Jul 83
1.98		Yelena	Yelesina	RUS	5.4.70	1	Druzh	Nyiregyháza	13 Aug 88
1.97		Svetlana	Isaeva	BUL	18.3.67	2		Sofiya	25 May 86
1.96A		Charmaine	Gale	RSA	27.2.64	1	NC-j	Bloemfontein	4 Apr 81
1.96i		Desislava	Aleksandrova	BUL	27.10.75	2	EI	Paris	12 Mar 94
1.96		Marina	Kuptsova	RUS	22.12.81	1	NC	Tula	26 Jul 00

POLE VAULT

Mark	Wind	Name		Nat	Born	Pos	Meet	Venue	Date
4.47i		Yelena	Isinbayeva	RUS	3.6.82	1		Budapest	10 Feb 01
		4.46				2	ISTAF	Berlin	31 Aug 01
4.42		Yvonne	Buschbaum	GER	14.7.80	1		Rheinau-Freistett	27 Jun 99
4.33i		Vanessa	Boslak	FRA-J	11.6.82	5		Liévin	25 Feb 01
		4.32				1		La Roche-sur-Yon	23 Sep 00
4.31		Monika	Götz	GER	15.6.81	1		Troisdorf	9 May 98
4.31		Amandine	Homo	FRA	24.12.80	3	GP-II	Saint-Denis	3 Jul 99
4.30		Annika	Becker	GER	12.11.81	2		Mannheim	18 Jun 99
4.30		Katerina	Badurová	CZE	18.12.82	3		Turnov	11 Jun 00
4.25		Bridgid	Isworth	AUS	15.10.81	4		Brisbane	11 Feb 00
4.21i		Monika	Pyrek	POL	11.8.80	1		Spala	13 Feb 99
4.21		Amy	Linnen	USA	15.7.82	1	NC-j	Richmond	17 Jun 01

LONG JUMP

Mark	Wind	Name		Nat	Born	Pos	Meet	Venue	Date
7.14	1.1	Heike	Daute	GDR	16.12.64	1	PTS	Bratislava	4 Jun 83
7.00	-0.2	Birgit	Grosshennig	GDR	21.2.65	2		Berlin	9 Jun 84
6.94	-0.5	Magdalena	Khristova	BUL	25.2.77	2		Kalamata	22 Jun 96
6.91	0.0	Anisoara	Cusmir	ROM	29.6.62	1		Bucuresti	23 May 81
6.90	1.4	Beverly	Kinch	GBR	14.1.64	*	WCh	Helsinki	14 Aug 83
6.88	0.6	Natalya	Shevchenko	RUS	28.12.66	2		Sochi	26 May 84
6.84		Larisa	Baluta	UKR	13.8.65	2		Krasnodar	6 Aug 83
6.82	1.8	Fiona	May	GBR	12.12.69	*	WJ	Sudbury	30 Jul 88

Jnr WOMEN All-time

Mark	Wind	Name		Nat	Born	Pos	Meet	Venue	Date
6.81	1.6	Carol	Lewis	USA	8.8.63	1	TAC	Knoxville	20 Jun 82
6.81	1.4	Yelena	Davydova	KZK	16.11.67	1	NC-j	Krasnodar	17 Jul 85
Wind assisted									
7.27	2.2	Heike	Daute	GDR	16.12.64	1	WCh	Helsinki	14 Aug 83
6.93	4.6	Beverly	Kinch	GBR	14.1.64	5	WCh	Helsinki	14 Aug 83
6.88	2.1	Fiona	May	GBR	12.12.69	1	WJ	Sudbury	30 Jul 88
6.84	2.8	Anu	Kaljurand	EST	16.4.69	2		Riga	4 Jun 88

TRIPLE JUMP

Mark	Wind	Name		Nat	Born	Pos	Meet	Venue	Date
14.62	1.0	Teresa	Marinova	BUL	5.9.77	1	WC	Sydney	25 Aug 96
14.57	0.2		Huang Qiuyan	CHN	25.1.80	1	NG	Shanghai	19 Oct 97
14.52	0.6	Anastasiya	Ilyina	RUS	16.1.82	q	WJ	Santiago de Chile	20 Oct 00
14.46	1.0		Peng Fengmei	CHN	2.7.79	1		Chengdu	18 Apr 98
14.37i	-		Ren Ruiping	CHN	1.2.76	3	WI	Barcelona	11 Mar 95
	14.36		0.0			1	NC	Beijing	1 Jun 94
14.32	-0.1	Yelena	Lysak ¶	RUS	19.10.75	1		Voronezh	18 Jun 94
14.23			Li Jiahui	CHN	8.8.79	1	Asi-J	Bangkok	6 Nov 97
14.19	2.0	Anna	Pyatkh	RUS	4.4.81	1		Lapinlahti	16 Jul 00
14.18i	-	Yevgeniya	Stavchanskaya	UKR	25.9.81	2		Lvov	7 Feb 99
14.10	1.4		Wang Zhuri	CHN	.9.80	Q	NG	Shanghai	17 Oct 97
Wind assisted									
14.83A	8.3		Ren Ruiping	CHN	1.2.76	1	NC	Taiyuan	21 May 95
14.43	2.7	Yelena	Lysak ¶	RUS	19.10.75	1	WJ	Lisboa	21 Jul 94
14.15w	2.2	Keila	Costa	BRA	6.2.83	1		São Caetano do Sul	22 Apr 01

SHOT

Mark	Name		Nat	Born	Pos	Meet	Venue	Date
20.54	Astrid	Kumbernuss	GDR	5.2.70	1	vFIN-j	Orimattila	1 Jul 89
20.51i	Heidi	Krieger	GDR	20.7.65	2		Budapest	8 Feb 84
	20.24				5		Spilt	30 Apr 84
20.23	Ilke	Wyludda	GDR	28.3.69	1	NC-j	Karl-Marx-Stadt	16 Jul 88
20.12	Ilona	Schoknecht	GDR	24.9.56	2	NC	Erfurt	23 Aug 75
20.02		Cheng Xiaoyan	CHN	30.11.75	3	NC	Beijing	5 Jun 94
19.90	Stephanie	Storp	FRG	28.11.68	1		Hamburg	16 Aug 87
19.63		Wang Yawen	CHN	23.8.73	1		Shijiazhuang	25 Apr 92
19.57	Grit	Haupt	GDR	4.6.66	1		Gera	7 Jul 84
19.48	Ines	Wittich	GDR	14.11.69	5		Leipzig	29 Jul 87
19.42	Simone	Michel	GDR	18.12.60	3	vSU	Leipzig	23 Jun 79

DISCUS

Mark	Name		Nat	Born	Pos	Meet	Venue	Date
74.40	Ilke	Wyludda	GDR	28.3.69	2		Berlin	13 Sep 88
67.38	Irina	Meszynski	GDR	24.3.62	1		Berlin	14 Aug 81
67.00	Jana	Günther	GDR	7.1.68	6	NC	Potsdam	20 Aug 87
66.80	Svetla	Mitkova	BUL	17.6.64	1		Sofiya	2 Aug 83
66.60	Astrid	Kumbernuss	GDR	5.2.70	1		Berlin	20 Jul 88
66.34	Franka	Dietzsch	GDR	22.1.68	2		St Denis	11 Jun 87
66.30	Jana	Lauren	GDR	28.6.70	1	vURS-j	Karl-Marx-Stadt	18 Jun 89
66.08		Cao Qi	CHN	15.1.74	1	NG	Beijing	12 Sep 93
65.96	Grit	Haupt	GDR	4.6.66	3		Leipzig	13 Jul 84
65.22	Daniela	Costian	ROM	30.4.65	3		Nitra	26 Aug 84

HAMMER

Mark	Name		Nat	Born	Pos	Meet	Venue	Date
71.71	Kamila	Skolimowska	POL	4.11.82	1	GPF	Melbourne	9 Sep 01
68.50	Martina	Danisová	SVK	21.3.83	1		Kladno	16 Jun 01
68.40	Bianca	Achilles	GER	17.4.81	1		Dortmund	25 Sep 99
68.18	Ivana	Brkljacic	CRO	25.1.83	1		Pula	28 Apr 00
66.97		Gu Yuan	CHN-J	9.5.82	1	NG	Guangzhou	22 Nov 01
66.34	Yipsi	Moreno	CUB	19.11.80	1		Ciudad de México	29 May 99
66.30		Zhang Wenxiu	CHN	11.2.83	1		Jinan	12 May 01
65.88	Yunaika	Crawford	CUB	2.11.82	1		Las Tunas	3 Mar 00
65.48	Mihaela	Melinte	ROM	27.3.75	1		Bucuresti	25 Feb 94
65.46	Yelena	Matoshko	BLR	23.6.82	2		Staiki	30 Jun 01

JAVELIN

Mark	Name		Nat	Born	Pos	Meet	Venue	Date
61.99		Wang Yaning	CHN	4.1.80	1	NC	Huizhou	14 Oct 99
61.79	Nikolett	Szabó	HUN	3.3.80	1		Schwechat	23 May 99
60.90		Liang Lili	CHN	16.11.83	2		Shenyang	18 Jun 99
Pre 1999 specification								
71.88	Antoaneta	Todorova	BUL	8.6.63	1	ECp	Zagreb	15 Aug 81
71.82	Ivonne	Leal	CUB	27.2.66	1	WUG	Kobe	30 Aug 85
70.12	Karen	Forkel	GDR	24.9.70	1	EJ	Varazdin	26 Aug 89

Mark	Wind	Name		Nat	Born	Pos	Meet	Venue	Date
68.94		Trine	Solberg	NOR	18.4.66	1	vURS	Oslo	16 Jul 85
68.38		Antje	Kempe	GDR	23.6.63	Q	EC	Athína	8 Sep 82
68.17		Osleidys	Menéndez	CUB	14.11.79	1	WJ	Annecy	29 Jul 98

HEPTATHLON

Mark	Wind	Name		Nat	Born	Pos	Meet	Venue	Date
6465		Sibylle	Thiele	GDR	6.3.65	1	EJ	Schwechat	28 Aug 83
		13.49 1.90 14.63 24.07 6.65 36.22 2:18.36							
6436		Sabine	Braun	FRG	19.6.65	1	vBUL	Mannheim	9 Jun 84
		13.68 1.78 13.09 23.88 6.03 52.14 2:09.41							
6428		Svetla	Dimitrova ¶	BUL	27.1.70	1	NC	Sofiya	18 Jun 89
		13.49/-0/7 1.77 13.98 23.59/-0.2 6.49/0.7 40.10 2:11.10							
6403		Emilia	Dimitrova	BUL	13.11.67	6	GWG	Moskva	7 Jul 86
		13.73 1.76 13.46 23.17 6.29 43.30 2:09.85							
6276		Larisa	Nikitina	RUS	29.4.65	8	URS Ch	Kiyev	21 Jun 84
		13.87/1.6 1.86 14.04 25.26/-0.7 6.31/0.1 48.62 2:22.76							
6218		Jana	Sobotka	GDR	3.10.65	6	OD	Potsdam	21 Jul 84
		14.40 1.74 13.28 24.19 6.27 43.64 2:06.83							
6198		Anke	Schmidt	GDR	5.2.68	7		Götzis	24 May 87
		13.80/0.9 1.72 13.32 23.82/0.3 6.63/2.0 35.78 2:12.44							
6194		Camelia	Cornateanu	ROM	23.1.67	2	NC	Pitesti	8 Aug 86
		14.35 1.86 14.70 24.97 6.15 38.94 2:11.93							
6187		Ionica	Domniteanu	ROM	8.1.69	1	Bal-j	Pitesti	26 Jul 87
		13.51 1.77 14.56 24.66 6.00 43.86 2:17.60							
6185			Shen Shengfei	CHN	21.1.81	2	NG	Shanghai	18 Oct 97
		14.23/1.6 1.83 14.37 24.13/0.0 5.93/-1.1 44.50 2:17.81							
Disqualified for positive drugs test									
6534		Svetla	Dimitrova	BUL	27.1.70	H	ECp	Helmond	16 Jul 89
		13.30/1.0 1.84 14.35 23.33/-2.2 6.47/-1.4 39.20 2:13.56							

10 KILOMETRES WALK

Mark	Wind	Name		Nat	Born	Pos	Meet	Venue	Date
41:55		Irina	Stankina	RUS	25.3.77	1	NCw-j	Adler	11 Feb 95
41:57			Gao Hongmiao	CHN	17.3.74	2	NG	Beijing	8 Sep 93
42:44			Long Yuwen	CHN	1.8.75	3	NC	Shenzen	18 Feb 93
42:45			Li Yuxin	CHN	4.12.74	4		Shenzhen	18 Feb 93
42:47			Liu Hongyu	CHN	1.12.75	5	NC	Shenzen	18 Feb 93
42:50			Gu Yan	CHN	17.3.74	4	NG	Beijing	8 Sep 93
42:53.9t			Tan Lihong	CHN	13.2.73	6	NC	Jinan	15 Mar 92
43:07			Song Lijuan	CHN	1.2.76	6	NG	Beijing	8 Sep 93
43:10.4			Zhang Qinghua	CHN	6.3.73	8	NC	Jinan	15 Mar 92
43:15			Li Hong	CHN	1.6.79	7	NC	Zhuhai	10 Mar 96

20 KILOMETRES WALK

Mark	Wind	Name		Nat	Born	Pos	Meet	Venue	Date
1:27:35		Natalya	Fedoskina	RUS	25.6.80	2	WCp	Mézidon-Canon	2 May 99
1:29:09		Olga	Polyakova	RUS	23.9.80	5	NC-w	Adler	7 Feb 99
1:29:26			Wang Liping	CHN	8.7.76	6		Beijing	1 May 95
1:29:31			Jian Xingli	CHN	4.12.83	3	NG	Guangzhou	19 Nov 01
1:29:39			Gao Kelian	CHN	15.8.83	5	NG	Guangzhou	19 Nov 01
1:29:53		Tatyana	Sibelyeva	RUS	17.5.80	1	NC	Cheboksary	29 Aug 98

4 X 100 METRES RELAY

Mark	Nat	Team	Pos	Meet	Venue	Date
43.38	USA	Joyce, A.Williams, Robinson, Buchanan	1	PAm-J	Tampa	11 Jul 99
43.44A	NGR	Utondu, Iheagwam, Onyali, Ogunkoya	1	AfrG	Nairobi	9 Aug 87
43.48	GDR	Breuer, Krabbe, Dietz, Henke	1	WJ	Sudbury	31 Jul 88
	Unsanctioned race 43.33	Breuer, Krabbe, Dietz, Henke	1		Berlin	20 Jul 88
43.69	JAM	Goulbourne, A Bailey, V Campbell, Sharpe	2	PAm-J	Tampa	11 Jul 99
43.87	URS	Lapshina, Doronina, Bulatova, Kovalyova	1	vGDR-j	Leningrad	20 Jun 87
44.04	CUB	Riquelme, Allen, López, Valdivia	2	WJ	Sudbury	31 Jul 88
44.07	FRA	Thélamon, Hurtis, Imalouan, Rapp	2	WJ	Annecy	2 Aug 98
44.16	GBR	Soper, DSmith, Fraser, Merry	2	WJ	Plovdiv	12 Aug 90
43.9 h	FRA	Ropars, Simioneck, Declerk, Sidibé	1		Thaon	12 Aug 89

4 X 400 METRES RELAY

Mark	Nat	Team	Pos	Meet	Venue	Date
3:28.39	GDR	Derr, Fabert, Wöhlk, Breuer	1	WJ	Sudbury	31 Jul 88
3:29.66	JAM	Stewart, Morgan, Walker, Hall	1	PennR	Philadelphia	28 Apr 01
3:30.38	AUS	Scamps, R Poetschka, Hanigan, Andrews	1	WJ	Plovdiv	12 Aug 90
3:30.45	USA	Harris, Pritchett, Downing, Vickers	1	WJ	Athína	20 Jul 86
3:30.72	BUL	Kireva, Angelova, Rashova, Dimitrova	3	v2N	Sofiya	24 Jul 83
3:31.41	URS	Zakharova, Kiryukhina, Ponomaryova, Zhdanova	2	EJ	Utrecht	23 Aug 81
3:31.57	ROM	Petrea, Florea, Tîrlea, Nedelcu	1	WJ	Seoul	20 Sep 92
3:31.81	CUB	Casanova, Duporty, Limonta, McLeon	3	WJ	Plovdiv	12 Aug 90

ALL-TIME INDOOR LISTS

60 METRES MEN

Mark	Name		Nat	Born	Pos	Meet	Venue	Date
6.39	Maurice	Greene	USA	23.7.74	1rA		Madrid	3 Feb 98
6.41	Andre	Cason	USA	20.1.69	1		Madrid	14 Feb 92
6.43	Tim	Harden	USA	27.1.74	2	WI	Maebashi	7 Mar 99
6.45	Bruny	Surin	CAN	12.7.67	1		Liévin	13 Feb 93
6.45A	Leonard	Myles-Mills	GHA	5.9.73	1	WAC	Air Force Academy	20 Feb 99
6.45A	Terrence	Trammell	USA	23.11.78	1		Pocatello	17 Feb 01
6.46	Jon	Drummond	USA	9.9.68	2rA	Spark	Stuttgart	1 Feb 98
6.46A	Marcus	Brunson	USA	24.4.78	1		Flagstaff	30 Jan 99
6.46	Jason	Gardener	GBR	17.9.75	3	WI	Maebashi	7 Mar 99
6.46	Tim	Montgomery	USA	28.1.75	2	WI	Lisboa	11 Mar 01
6.47	Linford	Christie	GBR	2.4.60	1		Liévin	19 Jan 95
6.48	Leroy	Burrell	USA	21.2.67	1		Madrid	13 Feb 91
6.48	Deji	Aliu	NGR	22.11.75	1		Liévin	21 Feb 99
6.48	Leonard	Scott	USA	19.1.80	1h1	SEC	Lexington	24 Feb 01
6.48	Morne	Nágel	RSA	23.3.78	2		Dortmund	27 Jan 02

60 METRES HURDLES MEN

Mark	Name		Nat	Born	Pos	Meet	Venue	Date
7.30	Colin	Jackson	GBR	18.2.67	1		Sindelfingen	6 Mar 94
7.36r?	Greg	Foster	USA	4.8.58	1	Sunk	Los Angeles	6 Jan 87
	7.42				1		San Sebastián	15 Mar 91
7.37	Roger	Kingdom	USA	26.8.62	1		Pireas	8 Mar 89
7.37	Anier	García	CUB	9.3.76	1		Pireás	9 Feb 00
7.37	Tony	Dees	USA	6.8.63	1		Chemnitz	18 Feb 00
7.38	Allen	Johnson	USA	1.3.71	1		Karlstruhe	12 Feb 96
7.38	Mark	Crear	USA	2.10.68	1		Sindelfingen	8 Mar 98
7.38	Reggie	Torian	USA	22.4.75	1	NC	Atlanta	27 Feb 99
7.41	Courtney	Hawkins	USA	11.7.67	2	WI	Barcelona	12 Mar 95
7.41	Falk	Balzer	GER	14.12.73	1h2		Chemnitz	29 Jan 99
7.42	Igor	Kazanov	LAT	24.9.63	1		Moskva	25 Feb 89
7.42	Anthony	Jarrett	GBR	13.8.68	2		Liévin	19 Feb 95
7.43	Duane	Ross	USA	5.12.72	1	NC	Atlanta	28 Feb 98
7.44	Mark	McKoy	CAN	10.10.61	1		Sindelfingen	3 Mar 91
7.44	Elmar	Lichtenegger	AUT	25.5.74	2	EI	Wien	2 Mar 02

60 METRES WOMEN

Mark	Name		Nat	Born	Pos	Meet	Venue	Date
6.92	Irina	Privalova	RUS	12.11.68	1		Madrid	11 Feb 93
6.95	Gail	Devers	USA	19.11.66	1	WI	Toronto	12 Mar 93
6.95	Marion	Jones	USA	12.10.75	1		Maebashi	7 Mar 98
6.96	Merlene	Ottey	JAM	10.5.60	1		Madrid	14 Feb 92
6.96	Ekateríni	Thánou	GRE	1.2.75	1	WI	Maebashi	7 Mar 99
7.00	Nelli	Cooman	NED	6.6.64	1	EI	Madrid	23 Feb 86
7.01	Savatheda	Fynes	BAH	17.10.74	2s1	WI	Maebashi	7 Mar 99
7.02	Gwen	Torrence	USA	12.6.65	1	Mill	New York	2 Feb 96
7.02	Christy	Opara-Thompson	NGR	2.5.70	2		Gent	12 Feb 97
7.02	Chioma	Ajunwa	NGR	25.12.70	1		Liévin	22 Feb 98
7.02	Philomenah	Mensah	CAN	11.5.75	1h2	WI	Maebashi	7 Mar 99
7.03	Anelia	Nuneva	BUL	30.6.62	2s1	EI	Liévin	22 Feb 87
7.04	Marita	Koch	GDR	18.2.57	1	NC	Senftenberg	16 Feb 85
7.04	Silke	Möller'	GDR	20.6.64	1s1	EI	Budapest	6 Mar 88
7.04	Carlette	Guidry	USA	4.9.68	2	NC	Atlanta	4 Mar 95
7.04	Petya	Pendareva	BUL	20.1.71	1s1	WI	Lisboa	11 Mar 01

60 METRES HURDLES WOMEN

Mark	Name		Nat	Born	Pos	Meet	Venue	Date
7.69	Lyudmila	Narozhilenko ¶	RUS	21.4.64	1	NC	Chelyabinsk	4 Feb 90
7.73	Cornelia	Oschkenat'	GDR	29.10.61	1		Wien	25 Feb 89
7.74	Yordanka	Donkova	BUL	28.9.61	1	NC	Sofia	14 Feb 87
7.74	Michelle	Freeman	JAM	5.5.69	1		Madrid	3 Feb 98
7.75	Bettine	Jahn	GDR	3.8.58	1	EI	Budapest	5 Mar 83
7.76	Gloria	Siebert'	GDR	13.1.64	1		Sindelfingen	5 Feb 88
7.77	Zofia	Bielczyk	POL	22.9.58	1	EI	Sindelfingen	1 Mar 80
7.78	Brigita	Bukovec	SLO	21.5.70	1		Stuttgart	7 Feb 99
7.81	Jackie	Joyner-Kersee	USA	3.3.62	1		Fairfax	5 Feb 89
7.82	Yelizaveta	Chernyshova	RUS	26.1.58	1	WI	Budapest	5 Mar 89
7.82	Monique	Ewanje-Epée	FRA	11.7.67	1	6N	Paris	23 Feb 91
7.82	Glory	Alozie	ESP	30.12.77	1h1		Madrid	16 Feb 99
7.82	Olga	Shishigina ¶	KZK	23.12.68	1		Liévin	21 Feb 99
7.83	Melissa	Morrison	USA	9.7.71	2		Liévin	23 Feb 98

MEN'S WORLD LISTS 2001

100 METRES

Mark	Wind	Name		Nat	Born	Pos	Meet	Venue	Date
9.82	-0.2	Maurice	Greene	USA	23.7.74	1	WCh	Edmonton	5 Aug
9.84	2.0	Tim	Montgomery	USA	28.1.75	1	Bisl	Oslo	13 Jul
9.85	-0.2		Montgomery			2	WCh	Edmonton	5 Aug
9.88	2.0	Ato	Boldon	TRI	30.12.73	2	Bisl	Oslo	13 Jul
9.90	0.3		Greene			1h4	NC	Eugene	21 Jun
9.90	1.1		Greene			1rA	Athl	Lausanne	4 Jul
9.90	0.2		Montgomery			1	WK	Zürich	17 Aug
9.91	-0.3		Greene			1	GP	Athína	11 Jun
9.94	-0.2	Bernard	Williams	USA	19.1.78	3	WCh	Edmonton	5 Aug
9.96	-0.1		Greene			1	GP	Osaka	12 May
9.96	0.3		B Williams			2h4	NC	Eugene	21 Jun
9.96	-0.4		Greene			1	GP	Saint-Denis	6 Jul
9.96	0.0		Montgomery			1	VD	Bruxelles	24 Aug
9.97	-0.3		Boldon			2	GP	Athína	11 Jun
9.98	-0.8		Greene			1	BrGP	London (CP)	22 Jul
9.98	-0.2		Boldon			4	WCh	Edmonton	5 Aug
9.98	0.6	Francis	Obikwelu	NGR	22.11.78	1	ISTAF	Berlin	31 Aug
9.99	1.1		Boldon			2rA	Athl	Lausanne	4 Jul
9.99	2.0		B Williams			3	Bisl	Oslo	13 Jul
9.99	-0.2	Dwain	Chambers	GBR	5.4.78	5	WCh	Edmonton	5 Aug
10.00	1.1		Chambers			3rA	Athl	Lausanne	4 Jul
10.01	0.6		Chambers			1	GP II	Sevilla	8 Jun
10.01	0.5		Greene			1	GGala	Roma	29 Jun
10.01	1.1		Montgomery			4rA	Athl	Lausanne	4 Jul
10.01	1.7		Chambers			1	NC	Birmingham	14 Jul
10.01	-1.2		Greene			1s1	WCh	Edmonton	5 Aug
10.02	1.1		Obikwelu			5rA	Athl	Lausanne	4 Jul
10.02	2.0	Nobuharu	Asahara	JPN	21.6.72	4	Bisl	Oslo	13 Jul
(28/8) and see below for 7 times to10.03 with uncertain wind in Edmonton qf 4 Aug									
10.04A	-0.2	Kim	Collins	SKN	5.4.76	1	CAC	C.de Guatemala	20 Jul
10.04	0.4	Abdul Aziz	Zakari	GHA	2.9.76	1	Gugl	Linz	20 Aug
10.05	1.4	Leonard	Scott (10)	USA	19.1.80	1h3	NCAA	Eugene	31 May
10.06	1.8	Frank	Fredericks	NAM	2.10.67	2	GP II	Rieti	2 Sep
10.07	0.4	Chris	Williams	JAM	15.3.72	1s1	NC	Kingston	22 Jun
10.07	0.1	Deji	Aliu	NGR	22.11.75	2rB	Athl	Lausanne	4 Jul
10.08	0.0	Justin	Gatlin	USA-J	10.2.82	1	NCAA	Eugene	2 Jun
10.09	1.1	Shawn	Crawford	USA	14.1.78	1h1	NC	Eugene	21 Jun
10.09	0.5	Jon	Drummond	USA	9.9.68	2	Herc	Monaco	20 Jul
10.10	1.6	Marcus	Brunson	USA	24.4.78	1h2	NCAA	Eugene	31 May
10.10	0.1	Brian	Lewis	USA	5.12.74	3rB	Athl	Lausanne	4 Jul
10.10	0.6	Curtis	Johnson	USA	24.12.73	2	DNG	Stockholm	17 Jul
10.11	1.9	Matt (20)	Shirvington	AUS	25.10.78	1		Perth	4 Mar
10.11	1.5	Lindel	Frater	JAM	13.11.77	1	WAC	Fresno	19 May
10.11	1.1	Dennis	Mitchell	USA	20.2.66	2h1	NC	Eugene	21 Jun
10.11	0.1	Bruny	Surin	CAN	12.7.67	4rB	Athl	Lausanne	4 Jul
10.11	-0.6	Freddy	Mayola	CUB	1.11.77	1		Getafe	10 Jul
10.11	-0.2	Christian	Malcolm	GBR	3.6.79	7	WCh	Edmonton	5 Aug
10.11	0.6	Uchenna	Emedolu	NGR	17.9.76	3	ISTAF	Berlin	31 Aug
10.12	-1.3	Mark	Lewis-Francis	GBR-J	4.9.82	1		Tallahassee	14 Apr
10.12	1.1	Patrick	Jarrett ¶	JAM	2.10.77	1	Penn R	Philadelphia	28 Apr
10.13	1.9	Kenny	Brokenburr	USA	29.10.68	2		Perth	4 Mar
10.13	0.4	Llewellyn (30)	Bredwood	JAM	30.4.76	2s1	NC	Kingston	22 Jun
10.13	0.7	Stéphane	Buckland	MRI	20.1.77	1	FraG	Ottawa	21 Jul
10.14	0.0	Tim	Harden	USA	27.1.74	1		Tempe	14 Apr
10.14	2.0	Aristotélis	Gavélas	GRE	10.11.78	1h2	MedG	Tunis	11 Sep
10.15A	0.4	Morné	Nagel	RSA	23.3.78	1	GP II	Pretoria	23 Mar
10.15	1.4	Konstadínos	Kedéris	GRE	11.6.73	2	ECp-S	Bremen	23 Jun
10.16	0.7	Gerald	Williams	USA	24.2.78	2rB	MSR	Walnut	22 Apr
10.16	1.3	Darren	Campbell	GBR	12.9.73	1		Austin	5 May
10.16	1.6	Darvis	Patton	USA	4.12.77	1	UTA	Arlington	5 May
10.17	1.5	Eric Pacôme	N'Dri	CIV	24.3.78	1rB	Tex R	Austin	7 Apr
10.17	2.0	Josh (40)	Norman	USA	26.7.80	1		Sacramento	19 May

MEN 2001

Mark	Wind	Name		Nat	Born	Pos	Meet	Venue	Date
10.17	1.4	Sean	Lambert	GRN-J	16.8.82	3h3	NCAA	Eugene	31 May
10.17	1.6	André Domingos	da Silva	BRA	26.11.72	1		Lisboa (U)	16 Jun
10.17	1.0	Frédéric	Krantz	FRA	13.9.78	1	NC	Saint-Etienne	30 Jun
10.18	1.2	Jeffery	Fourth	USA	9.9.79	1		Durham	7 Apr
10.18	0.7	Mickey	Grimes	USA	10.10.76	2h3	NC	Eugene	21 Jun
10.18	1.0	Antoine	Boussombo	GAB	18.5.68	2	FRA Ch	Saint-Etienne	30 Jun
10.19	1.7	Pierre	Browne	CAN	14.1.80	1rC	Tex R	Austin	7 Apr
10.19	0.7	Jeff	Laynes ¶	USA	3.10.70	3rB	MSR	Walnut	22 Apr
10.19	0.0	Dwight	Thomas	JAM	23.9.80	5	NC	Kingston	22 Jun
10.19	1.6	Oumar	Loum	SEN	31.12.73	1h1	FRA Ch	St Etienne	30 Jun
		(50)							
10.19	0.2	Troy	Douglas	NED	30.11.62	4	WK	Zürich	17 Aug
10.20	1.2	Gerald	Wright	USA		2		Durham	7 Apr
10.20	1.8	Cláudio Roberto	Sousa	BRA	14.10.73	1h1		São Caetano do Sul	21 Apr
10.20	0.7	Kaaron	Conwright	USA	8.8.76	4rB	MSR	Walnut	22 Apr
10.20	0.0	Donovan	Bailey	CAN	16.12.67	1		Ingolstadt	27 May
10.20	1.1	Nicolas	Macrozonaris	CAN	22.8.80	1		Sherbrooke	16 Jun
10.20	1.9		Chen Haijian	CHN	5.4.80	1		Almaty	23 Jun
10.20	0.7	Francesco	Scuderi	ITA	4.10.77	1h2		Nuoro	11 Jul
10.21	1.4	Jacey	Harper	TRI	20.5.80	4h3	NCAA	Eugene	31 May
10.21	0.0	Julien	Dunkley	JAM	20.12.75	6	NC	Kingston	22 Jun
		(60)							
10.21	0.5	Tommi	Hartonen	FIN	12.5.77	1	ECp-1A	Vaasa	23 Jun
10.21	1.2	Tim	Goebel	GER-J	4.3.82	1	NC	Stuttgart	30 Jun
10.21		Taiwo	Bamidele	NGR		1s	NC	Lagos	20 Jul
10.22	0.1	Terence	Newman	USA	4.9.78	3		Tempe	24 Mar
10.22A	2.0	Kenneth	Andam	GHA	8.1.76	1h2		Provo	4 May
10.22	1.6	Kenji	Nara	JPN	26.12.79	1		Kitakami	14 Jul
10.22	2.0	Joshua 'J.J'	Johnson	USA	10.5.76	3	NA	Heusden	14 Jul
10.22	1.7	Lukasz	Chyla	POL	31.3.81	1		Ottawa	28 Jul
10.23	1.8	Raphael R.	de Oliveira	BRA	5.2.79	2h1		São Caetano do Sul	21 Apr
10.23	1.6	Anninos	Marcoullides	CYP	8.2.71	1	GSSE	San Marino	30 May
		(70)							
10.23	1.6	Lewis	Turner	USA	77	2h2	NCAA	Eugene	31 May
10.23	0.9	Jason	Gardener	GBR	18.9.75	2h1	GP II	Sevilla	8 Jun
10.23	0.9	Ricardo	Williams	JAM	29.9.76	3s2	NC	Kingston	22 Jun
10.23	1.9	Gennadiy	Chernovol	KAZ	6.6.76	2		Almaty	23 Jun
10.23	1.6	Shingo	Kawabata	JPN	15.5.78	2		Kitakami	14 Jul
10.24	0.0	Darrel	Brown	TRI-J	11.10.84	1		Bridgetown	14 Apr
10.24	0.8	Jonathan	Carter	USA	10.5.72	3h2	NC	Eugene	21 Jun
10.24	1.1	Jamal	Al-Saffar	KSA	24.10.71	1		Västerås	3 Jul
10.24	1.6	Chris	Lambert	GBR	6.4.81	2s2	NC	Birmingham	14 Jul
10.25A	0.4	Kevin	Braunskill	USA	31.3.69	2		Pretoria	23 Mar
		(80)							
10.25	1.0	Patrick	Johnson	AUS	26.9.72	1s1	NC	Brisbane	24 Mar
10.25	-0.5	Obadele	Thompson	BAR	30.3.76	2		Bridgetown	19 May
10.25	1.5	Aaron	Egbele	USA	29.1.79	4	WAC	Fresno	19 May
10.25	0.8	Salem Mubarak	Al-Yami	KSA-J	9.2.82	1rB	GP II	Helsinki	14 Jun
10.25	1.6	Ibrahim	Meité	CIV	18.11.76	1		Reims	5 Jul
10.25	-1.1	Ramon	Clay	USA	29.6.75	1		Madrid	7 Jul
10.25	2.0	Corne	du Plessis	RSA	20.3.78	5	NA	Heusden	14 Jul
10.25	-0.3	Chinedu	Oriala	NGR	17.12.75	1	NC	Lagos	21 Jul
10.25	1.2	Jérôme	Éyana	FRA	5.7.77	1h4	WUG	Beijing	27 Aug
10.25	2.0	Dejan	Vojnovic	CRO	23.3.75	2h2	MedG	Tunis	11 Sep
		(90)							
10.25	0.5		Yin Hanzhao	CHN	18.2.76	1	NG	Guangzhou	18 Nov
10.25	0.5		Liu Yang	CHN	16.2.80	2	NG	Guangzhou	18 Nov
10.26	-0.8	Devon	Ward	USA	10.11.80	1		Los Angeles	24 Mar
10.26	1.0	Paul	Di Bella	AUS	12.2.77	2s1	NC	Brisbane	24 Mar
10.26	1.6	Michael	Frater	JAM-J	6.10.82	2	UTA	Arlington	5 May
10.26		Okedikwu Raymond	Ejiogu	NGR	76	1h3		Palafrugell	19 May
10.26	2.0	Jabari	Fields	USA	10.9.81	2		Sacramento	19 May
10.26	0.3	Marco	Torrieri	ITA	14.5.78	1		Bressanone	16 Jun
10.26	0.5	John	Ertzgaard	NOR	18.6.77	2	ECp-1A	Vaasa	23 Jun
10.26	1.5	Anthony	Ferro	BEL	12.12.80	1h3	NC	Bruxelles	30 Jun
		(100)							
10.26	1.0	Fabrice	Calligny	FRA	4.11.81	5	NC	Saint-Etienne	30 Jun
10.26	2.0	Aham	Okeke	NOR	19.8.69	6	Bisl	Oslo	13 Jul
10.26	1.1	Stefano	Tilli	ITA	22.8.62	1		Avezzano	19 Aug
10.26	1.3	Gabriel	Simón	ARG	25.10.74	1		Buenos Aires	3 Nov
10.26	1.3	Heber	Viera	URU	29.4.79	2		Buenos Aires	3 Nov

Mark	Wind	Name		Nat	Born	Date
10.27	-0.8	Darrell	Rideaux	USA	27.12.79	24 Mar
10.27	0.7	Ja'Warren	Hooker	USA	24.9.78	31 Mar
10.27	1.2	Andre	Totton	USA	17.7.80	7 Apr
10.27	0.9	Aaron	Armstrong	USA	14.10.77	21 Apr
10.27	1.3	Taiwo	Ajibade	NGR-J	17.6.82	28 Apr
10.27	1.8	Saidric	Williams	USA	16.12.81	5 May
10.27	-0.8	Josephus	Howard	USA	14.4.78	13 May
10.27	1.9	Sultan	McCullough	USA	12.2.80	19 May
10.27	0.7	Terrence	Trammell	USA	23.11.78	21 Jun
10.27	0.1	Abu	Duah	GHA	5.6.78	14 Jul
10.27	1.6	David	Patros	FRA	11.9.77	18 Jul
10.27	1.8	Maurizio	Checcucci	ITA	26.2.74	2 Sep
10.28	0.4	Dominic	Demeritte	BAH	22.2.78	21 Apr
10.28	1.9	Marlon	Barnaby	JAM	26.10.79	27 Apr
10.28	1.6	Christie	van Wyk	NAM	12.10.77	5 May
10.28		Tyson	Gay	USA-J	9.9.82	9 May
10.28	2.0	Anson	Henry	CAN	9.3.79	12 May
10.28	2.0	Anthony	Buchanan	USA	10.9.81	12 May
10.28	1.1	Floyd	Heard	USA	24.3.66	21 Jun
10.28	0.7	Bryan	Howard	USA	7.10.76	21 Jun
10.28		Matic	Sustercic	SLO	27.2.80	30 Jun
10.28	1.2	Alexander	Kosenkow	GER	14.3.77	30 Jun
10.28	0.0	Serge	Bengono	CMR	3.8.77	20 Jul
10.28	0.3	Jonathan	Barbour	GBR	3.11.80	22 Aug
10.28	0.7	Marc	Burns	TRI-J	7.1.83	18 Oct
10.28	0.5		Wang Peng	CHN	16.12.78	18 Nov
10.29	-0.1	Bradley	Agnew	RSA	21.2.79	2 Mar
10.29	0.3	Jermaine	Joseph	CAN	25.7.80	23 Jun
10.29	0.0	Luis	Pérez Rionda	CUB	16.8.69	30 Jun
10.29	1.2	Marc	Blume	GER	28.12.73	30 Jun
10.29	2.0	Greg	Saddler	USA	29.6.74	8 Jul
10.29	-0.5	Reanchai	Sriharwong	THA	24.3.76	12 Sep
10.30	1.5	DeMario	Wesley	USA	20.4.80	7 Apr
10.30	1.7	Devon	Davis	CAN	29.12.78	7 Apr
10.30	0.6	Douglas	Bignall	GBR	20.10.74	22 Apr
10.30	0.0	Ellis	Ollarves	VEN	17.7.81	4 May
10.30	1.7	DaBryan	Blanton	USA-J	83?	12 May
10.30	1.8	Donovan	Powell	JAM	31.10.71	19 May
10.30	0.6	Marlon	Devonish	GBR	1.6.76	8 Jun
10.30	-0.2	Hiroyasu	Tsuchie	JPN	14.6.74	9 Jun
10.30	1.1	Derwin	Davis	USA		21 Jun
10.30	1.5	Ian	Mackie	GBR	27.2.75	23 Jun
10.30	0.2	Piotr	Balcerzak	POL	25.6.75	29 Jun
10.30	1.4	Daniel	Dubois	SUI	24.12.71	30 Jun
10.30	0.0	Jose A.	Cesar	CUB	4.1.78	30 Jun
10.30	1.9	Alex	Porkhomovskiy	ISR	12.8.72	30 Jun
10.30	-0.4	Anatoliy	Dovgal	UKR	29.1.76	1 Jul
10.30	0.2	Harálabos	Papadiás	GRE	24.1.75	14 Jul
10.30	1.6	Peter	Häggstrom	SWE	27.1.76	28 Jul
10.31	-0.8	Miguel	Fletcher	USA	17.2.80	24 Mar
10.31	-1.2	Detrion	Woodson	USA	5.8.78	12 May
10.31	1.3	Shingo	Suetsugu	JPN	2.6.80	18 May
10.31	0.9	Konstantin	Rurak	UKR	9.4.74	25 May
10.31	1.5	Tadashi	Imori	JPN	11.4.77	9 Jun
10.31	1.2	Martijn	Ungerer	NED	6.6.78	7 Jul
10.32	0.4	Sherwin	Vries	NAM	22.3.80	23 Mar
10.32	0.0	Chris	Chandler	USA	27.10.78	14 Apr
10.32	0.0	Dwight	Phillips	USA	1.10.77	14 Apr
10.32	1.4	Robert	Foster	USA	15.5.81	12 May
10.32	1.7	Edorian	McCullough	USA-J	.83	12 May
10.32	-1.2	Chris	Johnson	USA-J	28.4.82	12 May
10.32	0.8	Lawrence	Armstrong	USA	19.3.78	19 May
10.32	0.8	Adam	Wooten	USA-J	18.3.82	19 May
10.32	2.0	Derrick	Burks	USA-J	82	19 May
10.32	0.9	Jake	Jensen ¶	USA	29.5.74	2 Jun
10.32	1.0	Marcin	Krzywanski	POL	29.8.75	2 Jun
10.32	1.1	Shomari	Wilson	USA	6.6.72	21 Jun
10.32	1.4	Patric	Clerc	SUI	14.6.76	30 Jun
10.32	0.0	Andrea	Rabino	ITA	23.4.78	11 Jul
10.32	1.7	Yuta	Kanno	JPN	13.12.80	14 Jul
10.32	-0.1	Marc	Kochan	GER	30.12.78	18 Aug
10.32	0.0	Patrik	Lövgren	SWE	12.10.75	20 Aug
10.32	0.0	Zbigniew	Tulin	POL	1.4.76	7 Sep
10.33	-0.9	Mardy	Scales	USA	10.9.81	12 May
10.33	2.0	Luis	Mello	USA		19 May
10.33	2.0	Frantz	Valbona	HAI	11.10.77	19 May
10.33	1.5	Takao	Kawabe	JPN	14.4.74	9 Jun
10.33	1.9	Cecilio	Maestra	ESP	28.12.80	16 Jun
10.33	1.6	Yusuke	Omae	JPN-J	6.4.82	1 Jul
10.33	1.3	Igor	Blazevic	CRO-J	17.2.83	2 Jul
10.33A	-0.2	Renward	Wells	BAH	23.2.70	20 Jul
10.33	-0.7	Juan	Pita	CUB	29.7.79	28 Aug
10.33	0.5		Liu Dapeng	CHN-J	1.8.83	18 Nov
10.34	-0.1	Lee-Roy	Newton	RSA	19.12.78	2 Mar
10.34	0.3	Venancio	José	ESP	19.4.76	21 Apr
10.34	1.6	Raymond	Stewart	JAM	18.3.65	5 May
10.34	1.1	Nikela	Ndebele	ZIM	80	6 May
10.34	0.0	Andrea	Colombo	ITA	14.2.74	27 May
10.34	1.7	Hisashi	Miyazaki	JPN	19.3.81	14 Jul
10.34	1.6	Shigeyuki	Kojima	JPN	25.9.79	14 Jul
			(195)			

Faulty wind gauge – possibly wind assisted all at WCh, Edmonton 4 Aug

Mark	Name		Nat	Born	Pos
9.88		Greene			1q2
9.92		Montgomery			1q1
9.95		B Williams			1q5
9.97	Mark	Lewis-Francis	GBR-J	4.9.82	1q3
9.97	Dwain	Chambers	GBR	5.4.78	1q4
10.00	Kim	Collins	SKN	5.4.76	2q1
10.03	Obadele	Thompson	BAR	30.3.76	2q3
10.06	Uchenna	Emedolu	NGR	17.9.76	3q1
10.09	Troy	Douglas	NED	30.11.62	4q1
10.09	Christian	Malcolm	GBR	3.6.79	2q5
10.11	Donovan	Bailey	CAN	16.12.67	3q2
10.15	Aham	Okeke	NOR	19.8.69	4q4
10.17	Jamal	Al-Saffar	KSA	24.10.71	5q4
10.21	Salem Mubarak	Al-Yami	KSA-J	9.2.82	5q3
10.22	Fabrice	Calligny	FRA	4.11.81	6q3
10.25	John	Ertzgaard	NOR	18.6.77	6q1
10.27	Serge	Bengono	CMR	3.8.77	5q2
10.28	Alex	Porkhomovskiy	ISR	12.8.72	8q1

Wind assisted

Mark	Wind	Name		Nat	Born	Pos	Meet	Venue	Date
9.92	3.7		Montgomery			2	Pre	Eugene	27 May
9.92	3.7		Greene			3	Pre	Eugene	27 May
9.95	3.1		Montgomery			1	NC	Eugene	22 Jun
9.96	2.7		Montgomery			1r2	ModR	Modesto	12 May
9.98	3.1		B Williams			2	NC	Eugene	22 Jun
9.99	2.1	Kim	Collins	SKN	5.4.76	1rA	Tex R	Austin	7 Apr
9.99	6.6	Christie	van Wyk	NAM	12.10.77	1		Abilene	10 May
10.00	2.9	Curtis	Johnson	USA	24.12.73	1rA	Mod R	Modesto	12 May
10.04	2.9	Jon	Drummond	USA	9.9.68	2rA	Mod R	Modesto	12 May
10.06	4.0	Marcus	Brunson	USA	24.4.78	1h3	Pac-10	Berkeley	19 May
10.07	3.1	Dennis	Mitchell	USA	20.2.66	4	NC	Eugene	22 Jun
10.08	3.2	Freddy	Mayola	CUB	1.11.77	1	NC	La Habana	25 May
10.09	6.2	DeMario	Wesley	USA	20.4.80	1h2	Tex R	Austin	6 Apr
10.09A	4.4	Andre	Totton	USA	17.7.80	1		El Paso	14 Apr
10.09	3.5	Maurizio	Checcucci	ITA	26.2.74	1h3	MedG	Tunis	11 Sep
10.10	2.3	Marlon	Barnaby	JAM	26.10.79	1		St Louis	7 Apr
10.10	2.1	Joshua 'J.J'	Johnson	USA	10.5.76	2rA	Tex R	Austin	7 Apr
10.10	2.7	André Domingos	da Silva	BRA	26.11.72	1		Americana	29 Apr

Mark	Wind	Name		Nat	Born	Pos	Meet	Venue	Date
10.11	5.0	Eric Pacôme	N'Dri	CIV	24.3.78	1h1	Tex R	Austin	6 Apr
10.11	6.6	Saidric	Williams	USA	16.12.81	2		Abilene	10 May
10.12A	3.2	Kenneth	Andam	GHA	8.1.76	1		Ogden	14 Apr
10.12	3.7	Lewis	Turner	USA	77	1		Houston	19 May
10.13	2.5	Patrick	Johnson	AUS	26.9.72	1		Canberra	18 Feb
10.13	2.4	Sean	Lambert	GRN-J	16.8.82	2		Knoxville	7 Apr
10.13	3.8	Jonathan	Barbour	GBR	3.11.80	1	NC-23	Bedford	30 Jun
10.14	2.1	Darvis	Patton	USA	4.12.77	3rA	Tex R	Austin	7 Apr
10.15	3.9	Lawrence	Armstrong	USA	19.3.78	1		College Station	10 May
10.16	2.8	Raphael R.	de Oliveira	BRA	5.2.79	2		São Caetano do Sul	21 Apr
10.17	3.6	Pierre	Browne	CAN	14.1.80	1h6	Tex R	Austin	6 Apr
10.17	4.3	Tyrone	Edgar	GBR-J	29.3.82	1	NC-j	Bedford	30 Jun
10.17	5.5	Kazuki	Ishikura	JPN	1.10.80	1h2		Tsuyama	18 Aug
10.18	3.2	José Ángel	César	CUB	4.1.78	2	NC	La Habana	25 May
10.18	2.4	Tim	Goebel	GER-J	4.3.82	2	EJ	Grosseto	20 Jul
10.18	2.4	Anninos	Marcoullides	CYP	8.2.71	1h1	MedG	Tunis	11 Sep
10.19	3.6	Devon	Davis	CAN	29.12.78	2h8	Tex R	Austin	6 Apr
10.19	3.9	Brian	Dzingai	ZIM	29.4.81	1h1		Joplin, Mo.	5 May
10.19	2.2	Ian	Mackie	GBR	27.2.75	3	v2N	Glasgow	1 Jul
10.21	6.8	Robert	Foster	USA	15.5.81	1h2	Tex R	Austin	6 Apr
10.21	3.9	Donovan	Powell	JAM	31.10.71	2		College Station	10 May
10.21	3.2	Juan	Pita	CUB	29.11.79	3	NC	La Habana	25 May
10.21	2.8	Nathan B.	Bongelo	BEL	2.12.73	1	NC	Bruxelles	30 Jun
10.21	3.7	Paul	Di Bella	AUS	12.2.77	1h3		Budapest	1 Jul
10.21	3.5	Matic	Osovnikar	SLO	19.1.80	2h3	MedG	Tunis	11 Sep
10.22A	2.9	Paul	Gorries	RSA	28.2.81	2		Bloemfontein	2 Feb
10.22	3.7	Detrion	Woodson	USA	5.8.78	3		Houston	19 May
10.22	3.2	Luis	Pérez Rionda	CUB	16.8.69	4	NC	La Habana	25 May
10.22	4.3	Dwayne	Grant	GBR-J	17.7.82	2	NC-j	Bedford	30 Jun
10.23	2.5	Kevin	Braunskill	USA	31.3.69	2		Canberra	18 Feb
10.23	3.6	Matthew	Coad	NZL	9.8.75	1		Hastings	24 Feb
10.23	4.6	Adam	Wooten	USA-J	18.3.82	1		College Station	14 Apr
10.23	2.1	LeShaunte	Edwards	USA	26.7.79	1		Akron	21 Apr
10.23	3.7	Niconnor	Alexander	TRI	4.2.77	2		Stephenville	21 Apr
10.23		Lancford	Davis	JAM	11.10.78	1h1	JUCO	Odessa, TX	11 May
10.23	2.6	Jonathan	Carter	USA	10.5.72	4s2	NC	Eugene	22 Jun
10.23	2.8	Erik	Wijmeersch	BEL	23.1.70	2	NC	Bruxelles	30 Jun
10.23	3.6	John	Ertzgaard	NOR	18.6.77	1		Drammen	24 Aug

Mark	Wind	Name		Nat	Born	Date
10.24	2.1	Bobby	Cruse	USA	20.3.78	21 Apr
10.24	2.5	David	Patros	FRA	11.9.77	17 Jul
10.25A	4.4	Taiwo	Ajibade	NGR-J	17.6.82	14 Apr
10.25A	4.4	Vitaliy	Medvedev	KAZ	6.1.77	14 Apr
10.25		Mardy	Scales	USA	10.9.81	21 Apr
10.25	2.1	Chad	Bullett	USA	20.12.78	21 Apr
10.25	2.5	Amar	Johnson	USA	27.9.79	5 May
10.25	2.9	Terry	Bowen	USA	15.9.71	12 May
10.25	4.0	Anthony	Buchanan	USA	10.9.81	19 May
10.25	3.2	Francisco	Cornelio	DOM	22.6.74	25 May
10.25	2.4	Terrence	Trammell	USA	23.11.78	22 Jun
10.26	2.5	Douglas	Turner	GBR	2.12.66	1 Jul
10.27A	2.9	Lee-Roy	Newton	RSA	19.12.78	2 Feb
10.27	4.0	Anson	Henry	CAN	9.3.79	19 May
10.27	2.9	Manabu	Esaki	JPN	31.7.74	10 Jun
10.28A	2.9	Bradley	Agnew	RSA	21.2.79	2 Feb
10.28	4.8	Dennis	Baker	USA	12.9.80	31 Mar
10.28	5.5	Ibrahim	Tanko Braimah	GHA	12.5.79	6 Apr
10.28A	4.4	Clint	Crenshaw	USA	11.9.79	14 Apr
10.28	3.1	Kingsley	Umeh	USA		13 May
10.28	3.7	Saad Faraj	Al Shahwani	QAT-J	83	1 Jul
10.29A	4.4	Ronald	Promesse	LCA	31.8.74	14 Apr
10.29	2.3	Kevin	Garrett	USA	29.7.80	18 May
10.29	2.6	Marlon	Devonish	GBR	1.6.76	27 May
10.29	3.8	Carlos	Calado	POR	5.10.75	17 Jun
10.29	2.2	Douglas	Bignall	GBR	20.10.74	13 Jul
10.29	2.6	Jake	Jensen ¶	USA	29.5.74	17 Aug
10.30	6.2	Roy	Bailey	JAM	17.5.79	6 Apr
10.30	8.5	Tim	Mason	USA		21 Apr
10.30	2.7	Jarmiene	Holloway	USA	6.3.77	28 Apr
10.30		Nikela	Ndebele	ZIM	80	12 May
10.30	3.5	Francois	Ngapout	CMR	79	14 May
10.30	3.3	Urban	Acman	SLO	28.3.76	3 Jun
10.30	2.2	Danny	Johnson	USA-J	11.5.83	6 Jun
10.30	3.5	Igor	Blazevic	CRO-J	17.2.83	11 Sep
10.31	2.5	Trey	Griffin	USA-J	20.4.82	11 May
10.31	5.8	Jason	Smoots	USA	13.7.80	26 May
10.31	3.1	Andrea	Rabino	ITA	23.4.78	10 Jun
10.31	4.3	Aidan	Syers	GBR-J	29.6.83	30 Jun
10.31	2.2	Geir	Moen	NOR	26.6.69	6 Jul
10.32	3.5	Lachie	McLellan	NZL	13.2.81	24 Feb
10.32	3.2	Jerome	Avery	USA	18.4.78	31 Mar
10.32		Tyree	Gailes	USA-J	.82?	28 Apr
10.32	2.1	Andrea	Colombo	ITA	14.2.74	9 Jun
10.32	2.6	Kenta	Fukui	JPN	26.3.81	30 Jun
10.33	2.5	Troy	Davies	AUS	23.10.79	18 Feb
10.33	2.2	Jason	Shelton	JAM	19.3.74	22 Apr
10.33		Nicholas	Johnson	USA	12.11.83	28 Apr
10.33	2.7	Pedro Pablo	Nolet	ESP	1.6.70	19 May
10.33	5.8	Marquis	Davis	USA	14.8.80	26 May
10.33	2.7	Daniel	Money	GBR	7.10.76	1 Jul
10.33	6.0	Mio	Torii	JPN	18.8.79	14 Oct
10.34A	2.4	Nnamdi	Anusim	NGR	11.7.72	27 Jan
10.34A	2.4	Radek	Zachoval	CZE	6.7.78	27 Jan
10.34	2.4	Drew	Smith	USA	12.6.78	7 Apr
10.34	2.9	Kevin	Mills	TRI	79	14 Apr
10.34	2.7	Vicente	Lenilson de Lima	BRA	4.6.77	29 Apr
10.34	2.5	Danieal	Manning	USA-J		11 May
10.34	5.8	Jordan	Vaden	USA		26 May
10.34	2.5	Leo	Settle	USA	19.10.75	7 Jul
10.34	3.5	Aléxandros	Kóntzos	GRE	12.10.80	11 Sep

Best at low altitude

10.06 0.1 Collins 1rB Athl Lausanne 4 Jul

10.31 0.9 Braunskill 2 Jun | 10.34w 4.8 Crenshaw 31 Mar | 10.33 -1.5 Nagel 30 Mar

10.20 w? 4 Aug

Rolling start- wind assisted

Mark	Wind	Name		Nat	Born	Pos	Meet	Venue	Date
9.89	3.7	Patrick	Jarrett ¶	JAM	2.10.77	1	Pre	Eugene	27 May
9.95	3.7		B Williams			4	Pre	Eugene	27 May

Mark	Wind	Name		Nat	Born	Pos	Meet	Venue	Date
Hand Timing									
10.0		Chinedu	Oriala	NGR	17.12.75	1		Bauchi	5 May

10.1 Darrel Brown TRI-J 11.10.84 7 Apr | 10.1 0.0 Anatoliy Dovgal UKR 29.1.76 15 Aug
10.1 1.8 Tan Kok Lim MAS 8.1.78 16 Jun | 10.1A 0.7 Morne Nagel RSA 23.3.78 3 Nov
| 10.1A 1.2 Nico Grimbeek RSA-J 11.2.82 3 Nov

Mark	Wind	Name		Nat	Born	Pos	Meet	Venue	Date
Wind assisted									
10.0	?	Tim	Walls	USA		1		Wake Forest	24 Mar
10.0	?	Titus	Haygood	USA	19.10.78	2		Wake Forest	24 Mar
10.0		Edorian	McCullough	USA-J	83	1		Garland	6 Apr

10.1 DaBryan Blanton USA-J .83? 19 Apr | 10.1 Ron Mitchell USA-J May

Mark	Wind	Name		Nat	Born	Pos	Meet	Venue	Date
Doubtful Timing									
10.0		Nabil	Jabir	MAR		1		Oujda	26 May

Germiston (A), 3 Nov, all RSA: 10.0w Lance Dickson 1.3.83, 10.0w Brenden Harmse 19.5.83, 10.1w Hannes Botha 1.3.81

Mark	Wind	Name		Nat	Born	Pos	Meet	Venue	Date
Drugs disqualifcation									
10.08dq	0.0	Patrick	Jarrett ¶	JAM	2.10.77	2	NC	Kingston	22 Jun
10.21	1.0	Christophe	Cheval ¶	FRA	25.2.71	3	NC	St Etienne	30 Jun
10.23	0.2	Marcin	Krzywanski #	POL	29.8.75	1	NC	Bydgoszcz	29 Jun

JUNIORS

See main list for top 7 juniors. 13 (and 1 wind?) performances by 4 men to 10.21. Additional marks and further juniors:

Gatlin 10.16 0.6 1s1 NCAA Eugene 1 Jun
Lewis-Francis 10.12 1.7 2 NC Birmingham 14 Jul | 10.18 1.8 1 Mannheim 16 Jun
10.13 1.1 2 PennR Philadelphia 28 Apr | 10.20 2.0 1h2 NC Birmingham 13 Jul
10.13 1.4 1 ECp-S Bremen 23 Jun | 10.20 0.0 6 VD Bruxelles 24 Aug
10.14 1.6 1s2 NC Birmingham 14 Jul | 10.21 0.7 1h8 WCh Edmonton 4 Aug

Mark	Wind	Name		Nat	Born	Pos	Meet	Venue	Date
10.27	1.3	Taiwo	Ajibade	NGR	17.6.82	1	Drake R	Des Moines	28 Apr
10.28		Tyson	Gay	USA	9.9.82	1		Lafayette	9 May
10.28	0.7	Marc	Burns	TRI	7.1.83	1		Santa Fé	18 Oct
10.30	1.7	DaBryan	Blanton	USA	83?	1r3		Austin	12 May
10.32	1.7	Edorian	McCullough	USA	.83	1		Austin	12 May
10.32	-1.2	Chris	Johnson	USA	28.4.82	2h1		New Orleans	12 May
10.32	0.8	Adam	Wooten	USA	18.3.82	3	Big 12	College Station	19 May
10.32	2.0	Derrick	Burks	USA	82	3		Sacramento	19 May
10.33	1.6	Yusuke	Omae	JPN	6.4.82	1	NC-j	Matsumoto	1 Jul
10.33	1.3	Igor	Blazevic	CRO	17.2.83	1rB	GP II	Zagreb	2 Jul
10.33	0.5		Liu Dapeng	CHN	1.8.83	4	NG	Guangzhou	18 Nov
10.38	1.7	Tyree	Gailes	USA		2r5		Austin	12 May
10.38	0.9	Omar	Brown	JAM	21.6.82	5s2	NC	Kingston	22 Jun
10.38		José Carlos	Peña	CUB	18.7.82	1	NC-j	Santiago de Cuba	4 Jul
10.38	1.8	Nathan	Taylor	CAN	30.1.83	1		London, ON	20 Aug

Wind assisted see main lists for five juniors – sixperformances to 10.20w adding
Gatlin 10.08w 2.2 1h1 NCAA Eugene 30 May | 10.12w 2.4 1 Knoxville 7 Apr
Lewis-Francis 10.09w 2.4 1 EJ Grosseto 20 Jul

Mark	Wind	Name		Nat	Born	Pos	Meet	Venue	Date
10.25A	4.4	Taiwo	Ajibade	NGR	17.6.82	2		El Paso	14 Apr
10.28	3.7	Saad Faraj	Al Shahwani	QAT	83	2h3		Budapest	1 Jul
10.30	2.2	Danny	Johnson	USA	11.5.83	1		Princeton	6 Jun
10.30	3.5	Igor	Blazevic	CRO	17.2.83	3h3	MedG	Tunis	11 Sep
10.31	2.5	Trey	Griffin	USA	20.4.82	1rB		Austin	11 May
10.31	4.3	Aidan	Syers	GBR	29.6.83	3	NC-j	Bedford	30 Jun
10.32		Tyree	Gailes	USA	.82?	1		Lubbock	28 Apr
10.34	2.5	Danieal	Manning	USA		2rB		Austin	11 May
10.36		Glenn	McFadden	USA	16.2.82	1		New Britain	5 Jun
10.36	5.9	Tim	Benjamin	GBR	2.5.82	4		Bangor	2 Jun

150 METRES

Mark	Wind	Name		Nat	Born	Pos	Meet	Venue	Date
15.07w	2.5	Frédéric	Krantz	FRA	13.9.78	1		Bordeaux	13 Jun

200 METRES

Mark	Wind	Name		Nat	Born	Pos	Meet	Venue	Date
19.88	0.1	Joshua 'J.J'	Johnson	USA	10.5.76	1	VD	Bruxelles	24 Aug
20.01	0.1	Bernard	Williams	USA	19.1.78	2	VD	Bruxelles	24 Aug
20.03	0.7	Konstadínos	Kedéris	GRE	11.6.73	1s2	WCh	Edmonton	8 Aug
20.04	0.1		Kedéris			1	WCh	Edmonton	9 Aug
20.05	-0.1	Ramon	Clay	USA	29.6.75	1	Athl	Lausanne	4 Jul
20.08	1.0	Christian	Malcolm	GBR	3.6.79	1s1	WCh	Edmonton	8 Aug
20.09	0.1		Malcolm			3	VD	Bruxelles	24 Aug
20.10	0.5		Kedéris			1	GP	Athína	11 Jun
20.11	0.7	Chris	Williams	JAM	15.3.72	2s2	WCh	Edmonton	8 Aug
20.13	1.2		Malcolm			1q1	WCh	Edmonton	7 Aug
20.13	1.0	Kevin	Little	USA	3.4.68	2s1	WCh	Edmonton	8 Aug
20.15	1.0	Stéphane	Buckland	MRI	20.1.77	3s1	WCh	Edmonton	8 Aug
20.17	-0.2	Shawn	Crawford	USA	14.1.78	1	GWG	Brisbane	6 Sep

Mark	Wind	Name		Nat	Born	Pos	Meet	Venue	Date
20.18	-1.3		B Williams			1	Pre	Eugene	27 May
20.18	0.3		C Williams			1		Thessaloníki	22 Aug
20.19	1.2		Crawford			2q1	WCh	Edmonton	7 Aug
20.19	-1.1		B Williams			1	WK	Z'ürich	17 Aug
20.19	0.8	Troy	Douglas	NED	30.11.62	1	GP II	Rieti	2 Sep
20.20	0.2		Crawford			1	GP	Osaka	12 May
20.20	-0.1		Clay			1s1	NC	Eugene	23 Jun
20.20	0.1		C Williams			2	WCh	Edmonton	9 Aug
20.20	0.1	Kim	Collins	SKN	5.4.76	3=	WCh	Edmonton	9 Aug
20.20	0.1		Crawford			3=	WCh	Edmonton	9 Aug
20.21	-0.1		Little			2s1	NC	Eugene	23 Jun
20.21	0.7		Crawford			3s2	WCh	Edmonton	8 Aug
20.22	0.1		Malcolm			5	WCh	Edmonton	9 Aug
20.23	1.2		Buckland			3q1	WCh	Edmonton	7 Aug
20.23	0.0		B Williams			1	GP II	Gateshead	19 Aug
20.24	-0.3		C Williams			1q3	WCh	Edmonton	7 Aug
20.24	0.1		Buckland			6	WCh	Edmonton	9 Aug
20.24	-1.1		Malcolm			2	WK	Z'ürich	17 Aug
20.24	0.1	Ato	Boldon	TRI	30.12.73	4	VD	Bruxelles	24 Aug
		(32/12)							
20.27	0.1	Abdul Aziz	Zakari	GHA	2.9.76	5	VD	Bruxelles	24 Aug
20.29	0.6	Justin	Gatlin	USA-J	10.2.82	1	SEC	Columbia, SC	11 May
20.29	0.6	Yusuke	Omae	JPN-J	6.4.82	1	NC-j	Matsumoto	30 Jun
20.29	0.7	Marlon	Devonish	GBR	1.6.76	4s2	WCh	Edmonton	8 Aug
20.30	0.3	Shingo	Suetsugu	JPN	2.6.80	1		Tokyo	30 Sep
20.31	1.0	Darvis	Patton	USA	4.12.77	1h2	NC	Eugene	23 Jun
20.31	-0.6	Dwain	Chambers	GBR	5.4.78	1	BrGP	London (CP)	22 Jul
20.31	1.2	Joseph	Batangdon	CMR	29.7.78	4q1	WCh	Edmonton	7 Aug
		(20)							
20.33	0.1	Francis	Obikwelu	NGR	22.11.78	6	VD	Bruxelles	24 Aug
20.34	1.3	Leonard	Scott	USA	19.1.80	1h3	SEC	Columbia, SC	11 May
20.34	0.8	Uchenna	Emedolu	NGR	17.9.76	2	GP II	Rieti	2 Sep
20.36A	0.4	Patrick	van Balkom	NED	14.9.74	1		Pretoria	23 Mar
20.36	-0.1	André Domingos	da Silva	BRA	26.11.72	3	Athl	Lausanne	4 Jul
20.37	1.3	Marcus	Brunson	USA	24.4.78	1rA	MSR	Walnut	22 Apr
20.37	1.6	DaBryan	Blanton	USA-J	83?	1rA		Austin	12 May
20.38	0.7	Marco	Torrieri	ITA	14.5.78	5s2	WCh	Edmonton	8 Aug
20.39A	0.4	Corne	du Plessis	RSA	20.3.78	2	GP II	Pretoria	23 Mar
20.39	1.4	Kevin	Braunskill	USA	31.3.69	1		Athens, GA	5 May
		(30)							
20.40	0.5	Floyd	Heard	USA	24.3.66	2rA	GP	Athína	11 Jun
20.41	1.7	Darren	Campbell	GBR	12.9.73	1r1		Austin	5 May
20.41		Darrel	Brown	TRI-J	11.10.84	1		Port of Spain	6 May
20.41	0.5	Marcin	Urbas	POL	17.9.76	3h7	WCh	Edmonton	7 Aug
20.42	1.6	Brian	Lewis	USA	5.12.74	1h3	NC	Eugene	23 Jun
20.43	1.2	Oumar	Loum	SEN	31.12.73	5q1	WCh	Edmonton	7 Aug
20.44	-0.1	Jon	Drummond	USA	9.9.68	4s1	NC	Eugene	23 Jun
20.45	0.4	Dennis	Mitchell	USA	20.2.66	1rB		Athína	11 Jun
20.46	0.1	Dominic	Demeritte	BAH	22.2.78	1		Auburn	21 Apr
20.46	-0.4	Bobby	Cruse	USA	20.3.78	1	Owens	Columbus	6 May
		(40)							
20.47	1.3	Llewelyn	Bredwood	JAM	30.4.76	2	NC	Kingston	23 Jun
20.47	1.5	Gennadiy	Chernovol	KAZ	6.6.76	1s2	WUG	Beijing	31 Aug
20.48	0.0	Caimin	Douglas	AHO	11.5.77	1	NED Ch	Tilburg	8 Jul
20.49	1.8	Frédéric	Krantz	FRA	13.9.78	2	NC	Saint-Etienne	1 Jul
20.50	1.5	Brian	Dzingai	ZIM	29.4.81	1		Joplin, Mo.	6 May
20.52	1.2	Patrick	Johnson	AUS	26.9.72	1h2	NC	Brisbane	25 Mar
20.54	1.3	Doug	Turner	GBR	2.12.66	1	Welsh	Cardiff	17 Jun
20.55	0.2	Deji	Aliu	NGR	22.11.75	4	GP	Osaka	12 May
20.55	0.2	Geno	White	USA	10.3.78	1		Atlanta	19 May
20.56	1.7	Brendan	Christian	USA-J	11.12.83	1rB		Austin	12 May
		(50)							
20.56	0.2	Ricardo	Williams	JAM	29.9.76	5	GP	Osaka	12 May
20.56	-0.4	Alessandro	Cavallaro	ITA	22.2.80	1		Bressanone	17 Jun
20.56	1.0	Toshiyuki	Fujimoto	JPN	25.6.79	6s1	WCh	Edmonton	8 Aug
20.57	0.9	Ja'Warren	Hooker	USA	24.9.78	1		Berkeley	17 Mar
20.57	1.5	Pierre	Browne	CAN	14.1.80	1		Waco	21 Apr
20.57	1.1	Tommi	Hartonen	FIN	12.5.77	2h6	WCh	Edmonton	7 Aug
20.58	0.0	Jake	Jensen ¶	USA	29.5.74	2		Bridgetown	19 May
20.58	-1.2	Aaron	Armstrong	USA	14.10.77	1		Nassau	9 Jun

Mark	Wind	Name		Nat	Born	Pos	Meet	Venue	Date
20.58	1.0	Josephus	Howard	USA	14.4.78	2h2	NC	Eugene	23 Jun
20.58	-1.4	Claudinei	da Silva	BRA	19.11.70	4q4	WCh	Edmonton	7 Aug
		(60)							
20.59A	0.4	Morné	Nagel	RSA	23.3.78	5	GP II	Pretoria	23 Mar
20.59	0.6	Leon	Settle	USA	19.10.75	1		Rhede	13 Jul
20.60	-1.0	Marcus	la Grange	RSA	12.12.77	1		Parow	12 Jan
20.60	0.5	Erik	Wijmeersch	BEL	23.1.70	1	NC	Bruxelles	1 Jul
20.60	1.4	Anninos	Marcoullides	CYP	8.2.71	1	MedG	Tunis	13 Sep
20.60	1.4	Andrea	Colombo	ITA	14.2.74	2	MedG	Tunis	13 Sep
20.60	-0.6		Xu Zizhou	CHN	8.1.81	1	NG	Guangzhou	22 Nov
20.61	1.0	Mickey	Grimes	USA	10.10.76	3h2	NC	Eugene	23 Jun
20.61	1.8	Shane	Niemi	CAN	2.6.78	1	NC	Edmonton	24 Jun
20.62	1.8	Marcel	Carter	USA	26.3.71	5h4	NC	Eugene	23 Jun
		(70)							
20.63A	0.4	Paul	Gorries	RSA	28.2.81	6	GP II	Pretoria	23 Mar
20.63	0.1	Alexander	Kosenkow	GER	14.3.77	3h4	WCh	Edmonton	7 Aug
20.64	0.6	Dwayne	Grant	GBR-J	17.7.82	1r2		Mannheim	16 Jun
20.64	-0.7	Frank	Fredericks	NAM	2.10.67	3		Madrid	7 Jul
20.65	1.2	Steve	Slowly	JAM	18.4.79	1		College Station	14 Apr
20.65	0.6	Jordan	Vaden	USA		1		Athens, GA	5 May
20.65	-0.6	Mardy	Scales	USA	10.9.81	1		New Orleans	13 May
20.66	1.1	Paul	Di Bella	AUS	12.2.77	2	NC	Brisbane	25 Mar
20.66A	0.0	Kenneth	Andam	GHA	8.1.76	1		Provo	5 May
20.66	1.9	Savanté	Stringfellow	USA	6.11.78	1h5	SEC	Columbia, SC	11 May
		(80)							
20.67A	-0.6	Radek	Zachoval	CZE	6.7.78	1		Rustenburg	22 Jan
20.67	1.3	Tim	Benjamin	GBR-J	2.5.82	2	Welsh	Cardiff	17 Jun
20.67	0.8	John	Ertzgaard	NOR	18.6.77	5	GP II	Rieti	2 Sep
20.68	1.4	Cláudio Roberto	Sousa	BRA	14.10.73	1h1		São Caetano do Sul	22 Apr
20.68	1.3	Ryo	Matsuda	JPN	26.12.79	1		Shizuoka	3 May
20.68	1.5	Michael	Mitchell	USA	16.5.81	1		Walnut	12 May
20.68	0.0	Heber	Viera	URU	29.4.79	2	SACh	Manaus	20 May
20.68	0.4	Tobias	Unger	GER	10.7.79	2		Mannheim	16 Jun
20.68	-0.3	Enefiok	Udo-Obong	NGR-J	22.5.82	1		Formia	14 Jul
20.69	0.0	Marcin	Jedrusinski	POL	28.9.81	2	Kuso	Warszawa	17 Jun
		(90)							
20.70	1.6	Robert	Foster	USA	15.5.81	1		Tampa	12 May
20.71	0.4	Christie	van Wyk	NAM	12.10.77	1		Abilene	24 Mar
20.71	-0.9	Jacey	Harper	TRI	20.5.80	1		Orlando	21 Apr
20.71	2.0	Contrell	Ash	USA	21.10.80	1	Big 10	Bloomington	20 May
20.71	-1.3	Kazuteru	Matsumoto	JPN-J	25.11.83	1		Kyoto	16 Jun
20.71	0.6	Ingo	Schultz	GER	26.7.75	3		Rhede	13 Jul
20.72	1.5	Haddow	Weatherborne	USA		2		Walnut	12 May
20.72	-0.4	Alessandro	Attene	ITA	10.9.77	2		Bressanone	17 Jun
20.72	1.4	Panayiótis	Sarrís	GRE	14.9.75	3	MedG	Tunis	13 Sep
20.74	1.7	Stanford	Routt	USA-J	.83	2		Austin	12 May
		(100)							
20.74	0.5	Anthony	Ferro	BEL	12.12.80	2	NC	Bruxelles	1 Jul

Mark	Wind	Name		Nat	Born	Date
20.75A	0.0	Josef	van der Linde	RSA	8.4.79	16 Mar
20.75A	0.4	Lee-Roy	Newton	RSA	19.12.78	23 Mar
20.75	1.1	Paul	Pearce	AUS	8.1.77	25 Mar
20.75	1.1	Darryl	Wohlsen	AUS	6.3.73	25 Mar
20.75	1.3	Ladji	Doucouré	FRA-J	28.3.83	5 May
20.75	0.0	Sean	Lambert	GRN-J	16.8.82	11 May
20.75	1.0	Kenny	Brokenburr	USA	29.10.68	23 Jun
20.75	1.8	Jermaine	Joseph	CAN	25.7.80	24 Jun
20.75	-0.8	Sherwin	Vries	NAM	22.3.80	31 Aug
20.76	-1.3	Brandon	Evans	USA	30.10.79	31 Mar
20.76	1.3	Tatsuya	Ito	JPN	21.12.76	3 May
20.76	1.1	Julian	Raeburn	TRI	18.9.78	5 May
20.76	1.4	Reggie	Hill	USA	2.1.79	5 May
20.76	-0.6	DeRico	Tilley	USA	10.2.77	13 May
20.76	0.8	Masayuki	Okusako	JPN	2.4.79	13 Oct
20.77	-0.4	Jonathan	Carter	USA	10.5.72	6 May
20.77	-0.6	Ibrahim	Tanko Braimah	GHA	12.5.79	13 May
20.77	1.8	Antoine	Boussombo	GAB	18.5.68	1 Jul
20.77	-0.7	Greg	Saddler	USA	29.6.74	7 Jul
20.77	0.5	Moustapha	Diarra	SEN	27.12.70	2 Sep
20.78	2.0	Robert	Parham	USA-J	2.6.82	14 Apr
20.78	1.2	Adam	Wooten	USA-J	18.3.82	18 May
20.78	-0.5	Hisashi	Miyazaki	JPN	19.3.81	20 May
20.78	2.0	Thomas	Gerding	USA	17.12.78	20 May
20.78		Eric Pacome	N'Dri	CIV	24.3.78	26 May
20.78	1.8	Jonathan	Barbour	GBR	3.11.80	25 Aug
20.79	-0.6	Glenn	McFadden	USA-J	16.2.82	9 Jun
20.79	-1.4	Petko	Yankov	BUL	6.10.77	10 Jun
20.79	1.0	Curtis	Perry	USA	26.10.74	23 Jun
20.79A	1.9	Renward	Wells	BAH	23.2.70	21 Jul
20.80	0.5	Ibrahim	Meité	CIV	18.11.76	24 Apr
20.80	0.8	Ronald	Pognon	FRA-J	16.11.82	21 Jul
20.80	-0.3	Juan Pedro	Toledo	MEX	17.6.78	7 Aug
20.80	1.2	Prodromos	Katsantonis	CYP	20.10.75	18 Aug
20.81	1.1	Bradley	Agnew	RSA	21.2.79	3 Mar
20.81	1.3	Kendrick	Triggs	USA-J	27.8.82	22 Apr
20.81	-0.1		Chang Po-chih	TPE	22.8.78	29 Apr
20.81	0.8	Babatunde	Ridley	USA	12.3.78	11 May
20.81	2.0	Andrew	Pierce	USA	8.6.79	20 May
20.81	1.8	Holger	Blume	GER	28.12.73	10 Jun
20.81	0.6	Steffen	Otto	GER	9.9.80	16 Jun
20.81	-0.8	Maurizio	Checcucci	ITA	26.2.74	17 Jun
20.81	0.9	Tatsuro	Yoshino	JPN-J	11.9.82	30 Jun
20.81	1.7	Jerome	Young	USA	14.8.76	3 Jun
20.81	1.1	Julian	Golding	GBR	17.2.75	14 Jul
20.81	0.2	Johan	Wissman	SWE-J	2.12.82	26 Aug
20.81	0.8	José Carlos	Peña	CUB-J	18.7.82	30 Aug
20.82?	1.6	Seth	Amoo	USA-J	20.3.83	19 May
20.82	-1.2	Troy	McIntosh	BAH	29.3.73	9 Jun
20.82	0.0	Lukasz	Chyla	POL	31.3.81	17 Jun

Mark	Wind	Name		Nat	Born	Pos	Meet	Venue	Date

Mark	Wind	Name		Nat	Born	Date
20.82	0.5	Kevin	Rans	BEL-J	19.8.82	1 Jul
20.82	-0.3	Oleg	Sergeyev	RUS	9.3.75	14 Jul
20.83	0.0	Chris	Chandler	USA	27.10.78	24 Mar
20.83	1.0	Lawrence	Armstrong	USA	19.3.78	18 May
20.83	-0.9	Raphael R	de Oliveira	BRA	5.2.79	3 Jun
20.84	1.4	Curtis	Coleman	USA		5 May
20.84	1.9	Jabari	Fields	USA	10.9.81	19 May
20.84	0.2	Kendrick	Campbell	USA	16.12.77	19 May
20.84	1.2	Sergey	Osovich	UKR	16.12.73	20 Aug
20.84	0.0	Chris	Lambert	GBR	6.4.81	30 Aug
20.85	1.5	Andre	Ammons	USA	12.11.78	10 Mar
20.85	1.4	Andre	Totton	USA	17.7.80	31 Mar
20.85	1.2	Ian	Mackie	GBR	27.2.75	24 Jun
		(163)				

Indoors

Mark	Wind	Name		Nat	Born	Pos	Meet	Venue	Date
20.31i		Coby	Miller	USA	19.10.76	1	NC	Atlanta	3 Mar
20.56i		Ja'Warren	Hooker	USA	24.9.78	2	NCAA	Fayetteville	9 Mar
20.60i		Allyn	Condon	GBR	24.8.74	1	NC	Birmingham	28 Jan
20.74i		Jimmie	Hackley	USA	11.9.75	1h4		Atlanta	2 Mar

Wind assisted

Mark	Wind	Name		Nat	Born	Pos	Meet	Venue	Date
19.86	4.0	Justin	Gatlin	USA-J	10.2.82	1h2	NCAA	Eugene	30 May
20.08	5.1	Kim	Collins	SKN	5.4.76	1h3	NCAA	Eugene	30 May
20.10A	2.8	Radek	Zachoval	CZE	6.7.78	1		Pietersburg	27 Jan
20.10	2.9	Leonard	Scott	USA	19.1.80	1h1	NCAA	Eugene	30 May
20.11	5.0		Gatlin			1	NCAA	Eugene	2 Jun
20.19	2.9	Caimin	Douglas	AHO	11.5.77	2h1	NCAA	Eugene	30 May
20.25	2.1		B Williams			1h1	NC	Eugene	23 Jun
20.33	4.1	Ja'Warren	Hooker	USA	24.9.78	1		Palo Alto	1 Apr
20.35	5.6	LeShaunte	Edwards	USA	26.7.79	1		Akron	21 Apr
20.36	5.6	Bobby	Cruse	USA	20.3.78	2		Akron	21 Apr
20.37	2.1	Aaron	Armstrong	USA	14.10.77	3h1	NC	Eugene	23 Jun
20.39	2.7		Xu Zizhou	CHN	8.1.81	1s1	WUG	Beijing	31 Aug
20.39	2.7	Marcin	Urbas	POL	17.9.76	2s1	WUG	Beijing	31 Aug
20.41	2.8	Frédéric	Krantz	FRA	13.9.78	1h2	NC	Saint-Etienne	1 Jul
20.45	3.4	Marcus	la Grange	RSA	12.12.77	1	NC	Durban	3 Mar
20.47	2.9	Josephus	Howard	USA	14.4.78	3h1	NCAA	Eugene	30 May
20.50	2.1	Geno	White	USA	10.3.78	1		Baton Rouge	17 Mar
20.51	3.4	Paul	Gorries	RSA	28.2.81	3	NC	Durban	3 Mar
20.51A	2.8	Andre	Totton	USA	17.7.80	3		El Paso	14 Apr
20.53	2.6	Rohsaan	Griffin	USA	21.2.74	1rB		Austin	5 May
20.53	2.7	Sherwin	Vries	NAM	22.3.80	3s1	WUG	Beijing	31 Aug
20.55	3.4	Lee-Roy	Newton	RSA	19.12.78	4	NC	Durban	3 Mar
20.58	2.5	Brandon	Couts	USA	17.2.79	2		College Station	10 May
20.59	2.4	Adam	Wooten	USA-J	18.3.82	1	Big 12	College Station	19 May
20.60		Lancford	Davis	JAM	11.10.78	1	JUCO	Odessa, TX	12 May
20.62	3.5	Sean	Lambert	GRN-J	16.8.82	1		Knoxville	7 Apr
20.62	2.4	Lawrence	Armstrong	USA	19.3.78	2	Big 12	College Station	19 May
20.62	4.0	Kendrick	Campbell	USA	16.12.77	3h2	NCAA	Eugene	30 May
20.64	2.8	Ryo	Matsuda	JPN	26.12.79	2h1		Shizuoka	3 May
20.67A	2.8	Jermaine	Joseph	CAN	25.7.80	4		El Paso	14 Apr
20.67	4.2	Christie	van Wyk	NAM	12.10.77	1		Stephenville	21 Apr
20.67	2.1	Heber	Viera	URU	29.4.79	3	GP	Rio de Janeiro	6 May

Mark	Wind	Name		Nat	Born	Date
20.70		Erick	Wilson	USA-J	.82?	4 May
20.71	3.4	Josef	van der Linde	RSA	8.4.79	3 Mar
20.71	3.2	Yukio	Morita	JPN-J	31.3.83	19 May
20.71	2.7	Kaaron	Conwright	USA	8.8.76	31 Aug
20.72	2.6	Takayuki	Kon	JPN	15.7.77	18 Aug
20.72	2.6	Hideki	Ishizuka	JPN	14.10.74	18 Aug
20.73	2.8	Antoine	Boussombo	GAB	18.5.68	1 Jul
20.74	3.4	Bradley	Agnew	RSA	21.2.79	3 Mar
20.74	2.6	Orville	Taylor	JAM	11.5.70	26 May
20.75	3.4	Jopie	van Oudsthoorn	RSA	5.2.76	3 Mar
20.75	5.6	Jamie	Johnson	USA		21 Apr
20.76	2.2	Bryan	Bridgewater	USA	7.9.70	12 May
20.78	2.5	Lewis	Turner	USA	77	10 May
20.78	4.7	Tatsuhiko	Watanabe	JPN	1.6.76	15 Jul
20.78	2.6	Manabu	Esaki	JPN	31.7.74	18 Aug
20.81	4.7	Takahiro	Mazuka	JPN	29.6.76	15 Jul
20.81	2.9	Salem Mubara	Al Yami	KSA-J	9.2.82	22 Jul
20.82	4.3	Matthew	Coad	NZL	9.8.75	25 Feb
20.83	2.3	Angelo	Taylor	USA	29.12.78	2 Jun
20.83	3.0	Graham	Beasley	GBR	24.10.77	18 Jul
20.83A	4.8	John Jairo	Córdoba	COL	12.5.77	22 Jul
20.85	5.7	Courtney	Charles	CAN	17.4.77	21 Apr
20.85	2.6	Lindel	Frater	JAM	13.11.77	21 Apr

Low altitude best

Mark	Wind	Name	Pos	Meet	Venue	Date
20.57	1.2	van Balkom	1	ECp-1B	Budapest	24 Jun
20.58		du Plessis	3	WUG	Beijing	31 Aug
20.69i	–	Zachoval	1		Wien	12 Feb
20.76	1.1	Gorries	2s1	NC	Durban	3 Mar

Hand Timed

Mark	Wind	Name		Nat	Born	Date
20.6		Jimmy	Pino	COL	12.8.78	5 May
20.6		Danny	Johnson	USA-J	11.5.83	12 May
20.6		Marko	Jankovic	YUG	29.2.76	14 May
20.6A		David	Kirui	KEN	15.12.74	26 May

Mark	Wind	Name		Nat	Born	Pos	Meet	Venue	Date
20.3w		Brendan	Christian	USA-J	11.12.83	1		Lockhart	19 Apr
20.4w	3.0	Carlos	Garcia	USA	20.9.76	1		Baton Rouge	18 May
20.4w	3.1	Ronald	Pognon	FRA-J	16.11.82	1		Le François	16 Jun
20.4w	3.7	Dwayne	Grant	GBR	17.7.82	1	NC-j	Bedford	1 Jul

Mark	Wind	Name		Nat	Born	Date
20.5w	3.1	Morné	Nagel	RSA	23.3.78	28 Dec
20.6w	3.7	Timothy	Benjamin	GBR-J	2.5.82	1 Jul

Drugs Disqualification

Mark	Wind	Name		Nat	Born	Pos	Meet	Venue	Date
20.58	0.7	Christophe	Cheval ¶	FRA	25.2.71	1		Villeneuve d'Ascq	17 Jun
		20.56w	2.2			1		Forbach	2 Jun
20.62	0.0	Jeff	Laynes ¶	USA	3.10.70	1		La Laguna	14 Jul

Mark	Wind	Name		Nat	Born	Pos	Meet	Venue	Date

JUNIORS

See main list for top 10 juniors. 10 performances by 5 men to 20.58. Additional marks and further juniors:

Gatlin 20.32 0.4 1 SEC Columbia SC 13 May; 20.52i# 1h4 SEC Lexington 24 Feb
20.43 2.0 1 NC-j Richmond 16 Jun; 20.58i# 2 SEC Lexington 25 Feb
20.55 -0.1 2 Knxoville 14 Apr

Mark	Wind	Name		Nat	Born	Pos	Meet	Venue	Date
20.75	1.3	Ladji	Doucouré	FRA	28.3.83	1		Créteil	5 May
20.75	0.0	Sean	Lambert	GRN	16.8.82	2h4	SEC	Columbia	11 May
20.78	2.0	Robert	Parham	USA	2.6.82	2		Baton Rouge	14 Apr
20.78	1.2	Adam	Wooten	USA	18.3.82	1h1	Big 12	College Station	18 May
20.79	-0.6	Glenn	McFadden	USA	16.2.82	1		Sacramento	9 Jun
20.80	0.8	Ronald	Pognon	FRA	16.11.82	1	EJ	Grosseto	21 Jul
20.81	1.3	Kendrick	Triggs	USA	27.8.82	3r3	MSR	Walnut	22 Apr
20.81	0.9	Tatsuro	Yoshino	JPN	11.9.82	1h2	NC-j	Matsumoto	30 Jun
20.81	0.2	Johan	Wissman	SWE	2.12.82	1	NC	Växjö	26 Aug
20.81	0.8	José Carlos	Peña	CUB	18.7.82	3q1	WUG	Beijing	30 Aug

Wind assisted see main lists for threemen – three performances by 2 men to 20.55w

Omae 20.55w 2.0 1h1 NC-j Matsumoto 1 Jul two marks (in main list) by Gatlin

Mark	Wind	Name		Nat	Born	Pos	Meet	Venue	Date
20.70		Erick	Wilson	USA	.82?	1		Miami	4 May
20.71	3.2	Yukio	Morita	JPN	31.3.83	1		Maebashi	19 May
20.81	2.9	Salem Mubara	Al Yami	KSA	9.2.82	1	Asi	B.S. Begawan	22 Jul

300 METRES

Mark	Wind	Name		Nat	Born	Pos	Meet	Venue	Date
32.37		Marcus	la Grange	RSA	12.12.77	1		Brasschaat	15 Aug
32.43		Shane	Niemi	CAN	2.6.78	1		Victoria	25 May
32.46		Marc	Raquil	FRA	2.4.77	1		Montauban	17 Jul
32.48		Alessandro	Cavallaro	ITA	22.2.80	1		Pliezhausen	13 May
32.53		Sofiane	Labidi	TUN	29.9.79	1		Namur	17 Aug
32.74A		Corné	du Plessis	RSA	20.3.78	1		Johannesburg	7 Feb
32.82		Milton	Campbell	USA	15.5.76	1		Loughborough	4 Jul
32.89A		Troy	McIntosh	BAH	29.3.73	1r1		Calgary	30 Jul
32.95A		Gary	Kikaya	COD	4.2.78	2		Johannesburg	7 Feb

Hand timed

Mark	Wind	Name		Nat	Born	Pos	Meet	Venue	Date
32.7		David	Canal	ESP	7.12.78	1		Sabadell	29 Apr

400 METRES

Mark	Wind	Name		Nat	Born	Pos	Meet	Venue	Date
44.28		Tyree	Washington	USA	28.8.76	1		Eagle Rock	12 May
44.45		Avard	Moncur	BAH	2.11.78	1		Madrid	7 Jul
44.47			Washington			1	MSR	Walnut	22 Apr
44.47A		Ezra	Sambu	KEN	4.9.78	1	NC	Nairobi	23 Jun
44.58		Greg	Haughton	JAM	10.11.73	1	GP II	Sevilla	8 Jun
44.61			Moncur			1	NC	Nassau	23 Jun
44.64			Moncur			1	WCh	Edmonton	6 Aug
44.66		Ingo	Schultz	GER	26.7.75	1s3	WCh	Edmonton	5 Aug
44.68		Angelo	Taylor	USA	29.12.78	1		Princeton	12 May
44.69		Éric	Milazar	MRI	1.6.75	2		Madrid	7 Jul
44.70		Hendrik	Mokganyetsi	RSA	7.9.75	2	GP II	Sevilla	8 Jun
44.70			Moncur			1		Thessaloníki	22 Aug
44.71		Michael	McDonald	JAM	17.3.75	1	GP	Rio de Janeiro	6 May
44.78			McDonald			2		Princeton	12 May
44.78			Moncur			1	SEC	Columbia SC	13 May
44.80		Derrick	Brew	USA	28.12.77	1rA		Indianapolis	28 Jul
44.83			Washington			1		Northridge	24 Mar
44.83		Leonard	Byrd	USA	17.3.75	1		Milano	6 Jun
44.83			Haughton			1s2	WCh	Edmonton	5 Aug
44.84			Moncur			1	NCAA	Eugene	2 Jun
44.84		Robert	Mackowiak	POL	13.5.70	2s3	WCh	Edmonton	5 Aug
44.85			Washington			1		Los Angeles (Ww)	14 Apr
44.85			McDonald			1	GP II	Gresham	3 Jun
44.85			Haughton			2		Milano	6 Jun
44.86		Shane	Niemi	CAN	2.6.78	1	Franc	Ottawa	21 Jul
44.87		Ato	Modibo	TRI	19.6.79	1		Orlando	21 Apr
44.87			Schultz			2	WCh	Edmonton	6 Aug
44.88			Moncur			1		Tempe	16 Apr
44.88			Moncur			1h1	WCh	Edmonton	4 Aug
44.89			McDonald			1	NC	Kingston	23 Jun
44.89			Moncur			1s1	WCh	Edmonton	5 Aug
		(31/14)							
44.90		Felix	Sánchez	DOM	30.8.77	1	GP II	Gateshead	19 Aug

400 METRES

Mark	Name		Nat	Born	Pos	Meet	Venue	Date
44.28	Tyree	Washington	USA	28.8.76	1		Eagle Rock	12 May
44.45	Avard	Moncur	BAH	2.11.78	1		Madrid	7 Jul
44.47		Washington			1	MSR	Walnut	22 Apr
44.47A	Ezra	Sambu	KEN	4.9.78	1	NC	Nairobi	23 Jun
44.58	Greg	Haughton	JAM	10.11.73	1	GP II	Sevilla	8 Jun
44.61		Moncur			1	NC	Nassau	23 Jun
44.64		Moncur			1	WCh	Edmonton	6 Aug
44.66	Ingo	Schultz	GER	26.7.75	1s3	WCh	Edmonton	5 Aug
44.68	Angelo	Taylor	USA	29.12.78	1		Princeton	12 May
44.69	Éric	Milazar	MRI	1.6.75	2		Madrid	7 Jul
44.70	Hendrik	Mokganyetsi	RSA	7.9.75	2	GP II	Sevilla	8 Jun
44.70		Moncur			1		Thessaloníki	22 Aug
44.71	Michael	McDonald	JAM	17.3.75	1	GP	Rio de Janeiro	6 May
44.78		McDonald			2		Princeton	12 May
44.78		Moncur			1	SEC	Columbia SC	13 May
44.80	Derrick	Brew (10)	USA	28.12.77	1rA		Indianapolis	28 Jul
44.83		Washington			1		Northridge	24 Mar
44.83	Leonard	Byrd	USA	17.3.75	1		Milano	6 Jun
44.83		Haughton			1s2	WCh	Edmonton	5 Aug
44.84		Moncur			1	NCAA	Eugene	2 Jun
44.84	Robert	Mackowiak	POL	13.5.70	2s3	WCh	Edmonton	5 Aug
44.85		Washington			1		Los Angeles (Ww)	14 Apr
44.85		McDonald			1	GP II	Gresham	3 Jun
44.85		Haughton			2		Milano	6 Jun
44.86	Shane	Niemi	CAN	2.6.78	1	Franc	Ottawa	21 Jul
44.87	Ato	Modibo	TRI	19.6.79	1		Orlando	21 Apr
44.87		Schultz			2	WCh	Edmonton	6 Aug
44.88		Moncur			1		Tempe	16 Apr
44.88		Moncur			1h1	WCh	Edmonton	4 Aug
44.89		McDonald			1	NC	Kingston	23 Jun
44.89		Moncur			1s1	WCh	Edmonton	5 Aug
	(31/14)							
44.90	Felix	Sánchez	DOM	30.8.77	1	GP II	Gateshead	19 Aug
44.94	Andrew	Pierce	USA	8.6.79	1	Big 10	Bloomington	20 May
44.95	Marc	Raquil	FRA	2.4.77	1	ECp-S	Bremen	23 Jun
44.97	Calvin	Harrison	USA	20.1.74	1h2	NC	Eugene	21 Jun
44.98	Davian	Clarke	JAM	30.4.76	2	OD	Jena	2 Jun
44.99	Alleyne	Francique	GRN	7.6.76	2	SEC	Columbia, SC	13 May
	(20)							
44.99	Antonio	Pettigrew	USA	3.11.67	4	WCh	Edmonton	6 Aug
45.00	Hamdam Odha	Al Bishi	KSA	5.5.81	1h3	WCh	Edmonton	4 Aug
45.04	David	Canal	ESP	7.12.78	3	GP II	Sevilla	8 Jun
45.08A	Marcus	la Grange	RSA	12.12.77	1rA		Roodepoort	16 Mar
45.11	Sanderlei	Parrela	BRA	7.10.74	1	SACh	Manaus	19 May
45.12A	Arnaud	Malherbe	RSA	20.11.72	2rA		Roodepoort	16 Mar
45.13	Malik	Louahla	ALG	19.12.77	1h7	WCh	Edmonton	4 Aug
45.14A	Adriaan	Botha	RSA	8.3.77	3rA		Roodepoort	16 Mar
45.14	Mark	Richardson	GBR	26.7.72	4s1	WCh	Edmonton	5 Aug
45.20A	Danny	McFarlane	JAM	14.2.72	1	CAC	C.de Guatemala	21 Jul
	(30)							
45.22	Rickey	Harris	USA	29.9.81	1		Atlanta	19 May
45.25		Xu Zizhou	CHN	8.1.81	1	EAsG	Osaka	24 May
45.26	Jun	Osakada	JPN	2.4.74	1	NC	Tokyo	10 Jun
45.29	Geno	White	USA	10.3.78	3	SEC	Columbia, SC	13 May
45.32	Jerome	Young	USA	14.8.76	3	NC	Eugene	23 Jun
45.33	Jerome	Davis	USA	20.8.77	2r2		Indianapolis	28 Jul
45.35	Godfrey	Herring	USA	18.5.78	2		Atlanta	19 May
45.38	Thomas	Gerding	USA	17.12.78	2	Big 10	Bloomington	20 May
45.39	Milton	Campbell	USA	15.5.76	4	GP II	Sevilla	8 Jun
45.40	Mitch	Potter	USA	16.9.80	1		Knoxville	13 Apr
	(40)							
45.40	Sofiane	Labidi	TUN	29.9.79	1		Beirut	2 Jul
45.41	Brandon	Couts	USA	17.2.79	2h2	NC	Eugene	21 Jun
45.41	Sugath	Thilakeratne	SRI	30.7.73	3h3	WCh	Edmonton	4 Aug
45.43	Mike	Kenyon	USA	26.8.79	1		Tempe	5 May
45.43	Zsolt	Szeglet	HUN	4.5.77	1	Big 12	College Station	19 May
45.43	Orville	Taylor	JAM	11.5.70	1		Nassau	9 Jun
45.45	Chris	Brown	BAH	14.10.79	2		Durham	7 Apr

Mark		Name	Nat	Born	Pos	Meet	Venue	Date
	C Brown	45.20 ?			2	NC	Nassau	23 Jun
45.46A	Julius	Chepkwony	KEN	6.6.69	2	NC	Nairobi	23 Jun
45.46A	Brandon	Simpson	JAM	6.9.81	2	CAC	C.de Guatemala	21 Jul
45.47A	Paul	Gorries	RSA	28.2.81	3		Potchefstroom	12 Feb
	(50)							
45.47	Anderson J.	dos Santos	BRA	23.4.72	4h1	WCh	Edmonton	4 Aug
45.48	Glauder	Garzón	CUB-J	13.2.82	1	NC-j	Santiago de Cuba	4 Jul
45.52	Troy	McIntosh	BAH	29.3.73	3	NC	Nassau	23 Jun
45.54	Clinton	Hill	AUS	19.4.80	3	EAsG	Osaka	24 May
45.54	Jude	Monye	NGR	16.11.73	7		Madrid	7 Jul
45.54	Jimisola	Laursen	SWE	13.7.77	4h6	WCh	Edmonton	4 Aug
45.55	Michael	Jennings	USA	80	2		Orlando	21 Apr
45.55	Piotr	Rysiukewicz	POL	14.7.74	2	NC	Bydgoszcz	30 Jun
45.55A	Jonathan	Palma	VEN	8.12.81	1	Bol G	Ambato	13 Sep
45.56	Flávio	Godoy	BRA	13.12.69	1	NC	Rio de Janeiro	20 Jul
	(60)							
45.57	Stéphane	Diagana	FRA	23.7.69	1	NC	Saint-Etienne	1 Jul
45.58A	Gary	Kikaya	COD	4.2.78	1rB		Roodepoort	16 Mar
45.58	Daniel	Caines	GBR	15.5.79	6	GP II	Sevilla	8 Jun
45.58	Sanjay	Ayre	JAM	19.6.80	3	NC	Kingston	23 Jun
45.58	Alianni	Hechavarría	CUB-J	10.10.82	2	NC-j	Santiago de Cuba	4 Jul
45.61	Tony	Berrian	USA	12.2.79	2		Tempe	5 May
45.61	Pat	Dwyer	AUS	3.11.77	2		Bron	21 Jul
45.62	Simon	Pierre	TRI	3.12.79	1		Port of Spain	6 May
45.62	Derek	Mills	USA	9.7.72	2		Bridgetown	19 May
45.65	Nduka	Awazie	NGR	4.4.81	4		Knoxville	13 Apr
	(70)							
45.65	Michael	Campbell	JAM	11.9.78	3		Tempe	5 May
45.66	Michael	Blackwood	JAM	29.8.76	3rA		Indianapolis	28 Jul
45.67A	Jopie	van Oudtshoorn	RSA	5.2.76	1		Bloemfontein	2 Feb
45.67	Yevgeniy	Zyukov	UKR	31.5.78	1		Kiev	17 May
45.67	Piotr	Dlugosielski	POL	4.4.77	3	NC	Bydgoszcz	30 Jun
45.70	Iwan	Thomas	GBR	5.1.74	1		Watford	25 Jul
45.72	Kenji	Tabata	JPN	24.9.74	2	NC	Tokyo	10 Jun
45.74	Benjamin	Youla	CGO	12.11.75	1		Fairfax	5 May
45.75	Damion	Barry	TRI-J	3.3.82	2		Port of Spain	6 May
45.76	Rafal	Wieruszewski	POL	24.2.81	4	NC	Bydgoszcz	30 Jun
	(80)							
45.76	Rohan Pradeep	Kumara	SRI	10.3.75	1		Colombo	1 Jul
45.77	David	Kirui	KEN	15.12.74	2		Beirut	2 Jul
45.78	Takahiko	Yamamura	JPN	13.8.79	3	NC	Tokyo	10 Jun
45.78	Andrey	Tverdostup	UKR	18.6.77	3	WUG	Beijing	29 Aug
45.79A	Otis	Harris	USA-J	30.6.82	1		El Paso	14 Apr
45.79	Oleg	Mishukov	RUS	31.8.81	1	NC-23	Cheboksary	14 Jun
45.79	Ja'Warren	Hooker	USA	24.9.78	1	NA	Heusden	14 Jul
45.81	Timothy	Munnings	BAH	22.6.66	4	NC	Nassau	23 Jun
45.81	Dmitriy	Golovastov	RUS	14.7.71	1	NC	Tula	13 Jul
45.82	Karel	Blaha	CZE	1.6.75	5h1	WCh	Edmonton	4 Aug
	(90)							
45.83	Sunday	Bada	NGR	21.6.69	1s	NC	Lagos	21 Jul
45.85A	Alejandro	Cárdenas	MEX	4.10.74	3	CAC	C.de Guatemala	21 Jul
45.87	Paul	Pearce	AUS	8.1.77	1	NC	Brisbane	24 Mar
45.87	Lancford	Davis	JAM	11.10.78	1		Overland Park	28 Apr
45.88	Ryuji	Muraki	JPN	29.12.79	1h2		Yokohama	18 May
45.89	Andre	Ammons	USA	12.11.78	2		Eagle Rock	12 May
45.89	Mike	Decker	USA	13.6.78	1	IC4A	Princeton	20 May
45.89	Valdinei	da Silva	BRA	29.3.72	3	NC	Rio de Janeiro	20 Jul
45.90	Robert	Wilson	USA	19.6.77	2		Atlanta	2 Jun
45.90	Tomas	Coman	IRL	10.11.79	6h1	WCh	Edmonton	4 Aug
	(100)							

Mark	First	Last	Nat	Born	Date
45.91	Wilan	Louis	BAR-J	1.3.83	19 May
45.92	Alessandro	Attene	ITA	10.9.77	23 Jun
45.93	Daniel	Batman	AUS	20.3.81	24 Mar
45.93	Lars	Figura	GER	25.3.76	30 Jun
45.95A	Mandla	Nkosi	RSA-J	15.1.82	20 Apr
45.97	Andrey	Semyonov	RUS	16.8.77	13 Jul
46.01A	Juan Pedro	Toledo	MEX	17.6.78	16 Mar
46.01A	Otukile	Lekote	BOT	19.10.78	14 Apr
46.02	Marcel	Lopuchovsky	SVK	2.5.77	23 Jun
46.02	Marc	Foucan	FRA	14.10.71	30 Jun
46.03	Casey	Vincent	AUS	17.3.79	6 May
46.03		Jiang Bo	CHN	18.2.81	17 Nov
46.04	Kelly	Willie	USA-J	28.8.82	9 Jun
46.04	Alexandr	Kaydash	UKR	30.5.76	1 Jul
46.05	Meshaal Saad	Al Harbi	KUW	29.1.75	1 Jul
46.06	Yuriy	Barzakovskiy	RUS	12.4.81	14 Jun
46.06	Masayuki	Okusako	JPN	2.4.79	28 Sep
46.07	Mark	Ormrod	AUS-J	1.12.82	24 May
46.07	Fidelis	Gadzama	NGR	20.10.79	8 Jun
46.07	Robert	Daly	IRL	26.1.78	21 Jul
46.08	Ibrahima	Wade	FRA	6.9.68	8 Jun
46.09	Mark	Hylton	GBR	24.9.76	22 Jul
46.10	Timothy	Benjamin	GBR-J	2.5.82	25 Aug
46.11	Terrence	McBryde	USA	6.1.80	28 Apr

Mark	Name		Nat	Born	Date	Mark	Name		Nat	Born	Date
46.11	Michael	Mitchell	USA	16.5.81	12 May	46.21	Peter	Coley	JAM	21.2.81	31 May
46.11	Piotr	Haczek	POL	26.1.77	30 Jun	46.21	Abderrahim	El Haouzy	MAR	.75	15 Jun
46.12A	François	Maasdorp	RSA	27.1.79	20 Apr	46.21	Jimmie	Hackley	USA	11.9.75	21 Jun
46.12	Darold	Williamson	USA-J	19.2.83	12 May	46.21	Quincy	Douglas	NOR	7.9.75	23 Jun
46.13	Edel	Hevia	CUB	22.2.77	25 May	46.21	Dean	Macey	GBR	12.12.77	6 Aug
46.13	Alexandru	Mardan	ROM	25.8.78	23 Jun	46.23	Enefiok	Udo-Obong	NGR-J	22.5.82	12 Jun
46.15	Yoshihiro	Horigome	JPN	2.1.81	18 May	46.23	Erki	Nool	EST	25.6.70	6 Aug
46.15	Jamie	Baulch	GBR	3.5.73	4 Aug	46.24	Vitaliy	Ignatov	RUS	73	13 Jul
46.16	Hamed Hamadan	Al Bishi	KSA-J	3.3.82	20 Jul	46.25	Marc-Alexander	Scheer	GER	16.5.79	30 Jun
46.17	Khaled Atiq	Al-Johar	KUW	29.1.75	28 Apr	46.26	Bruno	Wavelet	FRA	20.11.74	1 Jun
46.17	Takahito	Tanaka	JPN	11.9.79	18 May	46.27	Jebreh	Harris	USA	22.9.78	21 Apr
46.17	Kempa	Busby	USA	9.10.73	21 Jun	46.27	Iván	Rodríguez	ESP	7.4.78	10 Jul
46.18	Fawzi	Al Shammari	KUW	13.2.79	2 Jul	46.27	Amin	Badany Gomaa	EGY	9.12.79	29 Aug
46.19	Anton	Booth	AUS	7.3.70	18 Feb	46.28	Michael	Hazel	AUS	12.12.76	23 Mar
46.19		Liang Chao	CHN-J	21.6.83	17 Nov	46.29	Ashton	Collins	USA-J	84?	31 Mar
46.20A	Innis	Viviers	RSA	26.8.80	20 Apr	46.29A	Matt	Nielsen	USA	29.4.78	5 May
46.21	Kashus	Perona	USA	12.4.78	12 May	46.29	David	Spencer	JAM	20.11.78	19 May
							(158)				

Indoors

45.79	James	Davis	USA	19.3.76	1h1	NC	Atlanta	2 Mar
46.20	Bayano	Kamani	USA	17.4.80	1r1	NCAA	Fayetteville	10 Mar

Hand Timing

45.1	Sanderlei	Parrela	BRA	7.10.74	2		Torino	9 Jun
45.3	Milton	Campbell	USA	15.5.76	2		Nitra	25 Aug
45.4A	Mojafela	Mosili	LES	3.12.78	1		Harare	1 Jul
45.5	Robert	Parham	USA-J	2.6.82	2		Baton Rouge	18 May
45.5	Enefiok	Udo-Obong	NGR-J	22.5.82	3		Torino	9 Jun
45.6	Peter	Coley	JAM	21.2.81	3		Baton Rouge	18 May

45.8	Dedrick	Evans	USA	4.2.73	18 May	45.9	Salaheddin	Bakar El Safi	QAT-J	12.12.85?	3 Oct
45.9A	Calfornia	Molefe	BOT	2.5.80	1 Jul	46.1A	Lloyd	Zvasiya	ZIM		1 Jul

Low altitude best

45.20	la Grange	2h1WCh	Edmonton	4 Aug	45.59	McFarlane	3	NC	Kingston	23 Jun
45.30	Malherbe	2	Stellenbosch	30 Mar	45.68	Simpson	2s1	NC	Kingston	24 Jun
45.42	A Botha	5	Stellenbosch	30 Mar	45.68	van Oudtshoorn	6		Stellenbosch	30 Mar

45.92 Sambu 1 Jul 46.19 Harris 19 May 45.9h Palma 23 Jun

Unconfirmed

45.50	Leroy	Colquhoun	JAM	1.3.80	1		Houston	31 Mar

JUNIORS

See main list for top 4 juniors. 11 performances by 9 men to 46.10. Additional marks and further juniors:

Garzón 46.04A 1 Xalapa 10 Nov

Louis 46.03 1 NC Bridgetown 17 Jun

45.91	Wilan	Louis	BAR	1.3.83	4		Bridgetown	19 May
45.95A	Mandla	Nkosi	RSA	15.1.82	1		Pretoria	20 Apr
46.04	Kelly	Willie	USA	28.8.82	1		Sacramento	9 Jun
46.07	Mark	Ormrod	AUS	1.12.82	4	EAsG	Osaka	24 May
46.10	Timothy	Benjamin	GBR	2.5.82	1		Edinburgh	25 Aug
46.12	Darold	Williamson	USA	19.2.83	1rB		Austin	12 May
46.16	Hamed Hamadan	Al Bishi	KSA	3.3.82	1	Asi-J	B.S. Begawan	20 Jul
46.19		Liang Chao	CHN	21.6.83	1h3	NG	Guangzhou	17 Nov
46.23	Enefiok	Udo-Obong	NGR	22.5.82	3		Gdansk	12 Jun
46.29	Ashton	Collins	USA	84?	1		New Orleans	31 Mar
46.37	Robert	Parham	USA	2.6.82	1		Austin	21 Apr
46.37	Brandon	Matlock	USA	82	1	NC-j	Richmond	17 Jun
46.38	Dmitriy	Petrov	RUS	4.1.82	1		Krasnodar	22 May
46.40	Jason	Barton	USA	9.4.82	4	Pac10	Berkeley	20 May
46.40	Johan	Wissman	SWE	2.12.82	2	vFIN	Göteborg	1 Sep
46.41	Moh. Zaiful	Zainal Abidin	MAS	26.6.82	2	Asi-J	B S Begawan	20 Jul

600 METRES

1:15.1+	André	Bucher	SUI	19.10.76	1	in 800	Zürich	17 Aug
1:15.4+	Jean-Patrick	Nduwimana	BDI	9.5.78	2	in 800	Zürich	17 Aug
1:15.6+	Wilfred	Bungei	KEN	24.7.80	3	in 800	Zürich	17 Aug
1:15.6+	Nils	Schumann	GER	20.5.78	4	in 800	Zürich	17 Aug
1:16.2+	William	Yiampoy	KEN	17.5.74	5	in 800	Zürich	17 Aug
1:16.4+	Mbulaeni	Mulaudzi	RSA	8.9.80	6	in 800	Zürich	17 Aug
1:16.5+	Yuriy	Borzakovskiy	RUS	12.4.81	2	in 800	Bruxelles	24 Aug

Indoors

1:16.19i	Tom	Gerding	USA	17.12.78	1		University Park	25 Feb

Symbols/Abbreviations

+ intermediate time in longer race, A made at an altitude of 1000m or higher, D made in a decathlon, h made in a heat, qf quarter-final, sf semi-final, i indoors, Q qualifying round, r race number, -J juniors (born 1982 or later)

800 METRES

Mark	Name		Nat	Born	Pos	Meet	Venue	Date
1:42.47	Yuriy	Borzakovskiy	RUS	12.4.81	1	VD	Bruxelles	24 Aug
1:42.55	André	Bucher	SUI	19.10.76	1rA	WK	Zürich	17 Aug
1:42.75		Bucher			2	VD	Bruxelles	24 Aug
1:42.81	Jean-Patrick	Nduwimana	BDI	9.5.78	2rA	WK	Zürich	17 Aug
1:42.90		Bucher			1	Herc	Monaco	20 Jul
1:42.96	Wilfred	Bungei	KEN	24.7.80	3rA	WK	Zürich	17 Aug
1:43.00	William	Yiampoy	KEN	17.5.74	4rA	WK	Zürich	17 Aug
1:43.17		Borzakovskiy			2	Herc	Monaco	20 Jul
1:43.22	Pawel	Czapiewski	POL	30.3.78	5rA	WK	Zürich	17 Aug
1:43.30		Borzakovskiy			6rA	WK	Zürich	17 Aug
1:43.34		Bucher			1	GP	Saint-Denis	6 Jul
1:43.38	Arthémon	Hatungimana	BDI	21.1.74	3	VD	Bruxelles	24 Aug
1:43.57	Hezekiél	Sepeng	RSA	30.6.74	3	Herc	Monaco	20 Jul
1:43.58		Bucher			1	Athl	Lausanne	4 Jul
1:43.63	Joseph Mwengi	Mutua	KEN	10.12.78	4	Herc	Monaco	20 Jul
1:43.70		Bucher			1	WCh	Edmonton	7 Aug
1:43.76		Borzakovskiy			2	GP	Saint-Denis	6 Jul
1:43.78		Nduwimana			3	GP	Saint-Denis	6 Jul
1:43.82		Bucher			1	ISTAF	Berlin	31 Aug
1:43.89		Sepeng			2	Athl	Lausanne	4 Jul
1:43.91		Nduwimana			5	Herc	Monaco	20 Jul
1:43.98	Bram	Som (10)	NED	20.2.80	6	Herc	Monaco	20 Jul
1:43.98		Mutua			4	VD	Bruxelles	24 Aug
1:44.00		Mutua			1	GPII	Rieti	2 Sep
1:44.01		Bucher			1	GGala	Roma	29 Jun
1:44.01	Mbulaeni	Mulaudzi	RSA	8.9.80	7rA	WK	Zürich	17 Aug
1:44.01		Bungei			2	ISTAF	Berlin	31 Aug
1:44.02		Borzakovskiy			2	GGala	Roma	29 Jun
1:44.02	William	Chirchir	KEN	6.2.79	3	Athl	Lausanne	4 Jul
1:44.06		Yiampoy			4	GP	Saint-Denis	6 Jul
1:44.06		Yiampoy			3	ISTAF	Berlin	31 Aug
1:44.12		Hatungimana			4	ISTAF	Berlin	31 Aug
	(32/12)							
1:44.21	Kenneth	Kimwetich	KEN	1.1.73	7	Herc	Monaco	20 Jul
1:44.32	Nils	Schumann	GER	20.5.78	8rA	WK	Zürich	17 Aug
1:44.46	Nicholas	Wachira	KEN-J	19.11.82	5	GP II	Rieti	2 Sep
1:44.47	Otukile	Lekote	BOT	19.10.78	1		Montreal (McG)	10 Jul
1:44.52	Joeri	Jansen	BEL	28.5.79	6	VD	Bruxelles	24 Aug
1:44.54	Trinity	Gray	USA	3.4.78	2		Rovereto	29 Aug
1:44.55	Andrea	Longo ¶	ITA	26.6.75	1		Milano	6 Jun
1:44.55	Djabir Saïd	Guerni	ALG	29.3.77	2		Milano	6 Jun
	(20)							
1:44.59	Glody	Dube	BOT	2.7.78	6	GP	Saint-Denis	6 Jul
1:44.80	Benjamin	Kipkurui	KEN	28.12.80	2		Leverkusen	26 Aug
1:44.85	Noah	Ngeny	KEN	2.11.78	4		Milano	6 Jun
1:44.87	Adem	Hecini	ALG	13.12.75	6	GP II	Rieti	2 Sep
1:44.96	David	Lelei	KEN	10.5.71	8	Herc	Monaco	20 Jul
1:44.98	Nicolas	Aïssat	FRA	24.7.80	3		Rovereto	29 Aug
1:44.98	Cornelius	Chirchir	KEN-J	7.10.83	4		Rovereto	29 Aug
1:45.01	Norberto	Téllez	CUB	22.1.72	6	Athl	Lausanne	4 Jul
1:45.02	Paul	Korir	KEN	15.7.77	9	Herc	Monaco	20 Jul
1:45.14	Wolfram	Müller	GER	8.7.81	5		Leverkusen	26 Aug
	(30)							
1:45.15	Khadevis	Robinson	USA	19.7.76	3	Pre	Eugene	27 May
1:45.24	Michael	Rotich	KEN	78	1		Bydgoszcz	15 Jun
1:45.25	Henry	Rotich	KEN	5.12.81	6		Leverkusen	26 Aug
1:45.27	Fred	Onyancha	KEN	25.12.69	5		Milano	6 Jun
1:45.27	Khalid	Tighazouine	MAR	18.6.77	1	WUG	Beijing	1 Sep
1:45.29	Anthony	Kabara	KEN	9.3.75	2		Durham	7 Apr
1:45.39	Bernard	Kisilu	KEN	6.12.74	2		Lappeenranta	15 Jul
1:45.44	David	Krummenacker	USA	24.5.75	4rB	WK	Zürich	17 Aug
1:45.48	Achraf	Tadili	CAN	8.7.80	1	NC	Edmonton	23 Jun
1:45.49	Derrick	Peterson	USA	28.11.77	2	WUG	Beijing	1 Sep
	(40)							
1:45.64	Arnoud	Okken	NED-J	20.4.82	4	WUG	Beijing	1 Sep
1:45.71	Paul	McMullen	USA	19.2.72	8	ISTAF	Berlin	31 Aug
1:45.74	David	Kiptoo Singoei	KEN	26.6.65	5	Pre	Eugene	27 May
1:45.75	Japheth	Kimutai	KEN	20.12.78	7	Athl	Lausanne	4 Jul

Mark	Name		Nat	Born	Pos	Meet	Venue	Date
1:45.75	Grant	Cremer	AUS	9.6.78	6	DNG	Stockholm	17 Jul
1:45.81	Francis	Marwa	KEN	76	1		Madrid	7 Jul
1:45.82	Boris	Kaveshnikov	RUS	30.9.74	1	NC	Tula	15 Jul
1:45.93	Tom	Omey	BEL	24.4.75	4		Arnhem	4 Jul
1:45.97	Grzegorz	Krzosek	POL	10.1.76	3		Bydgoszcz	15 Jun
1:46.00	Antonio Manuel	Reina	ESP	13.6.81	1		San Sebastián	18 Aug
	(50)							
1:46.0A	Joel	Marwa	KEN	30.8.74	1		Nairobi	26 May
	1:46.05				3	GP	Doha	18 May
1:46.02	Dmitriy	Bogdanov	RUS	11.4.79	2		Lapinlahti	22 Jul
1:46.03	Bryan	Berryhill	USA	15.12.77	1		San Diego	19 May
1:46.03	Jess	Strutzel	USA	4.1.78	3	NA	Heusden	14 Jul
1:46.04	Osmar B.	dos Santos	BRA	20.10.68	1		Nuoro	11 Jul
1:46.12	Zach	Whitmarsh	CAN	5.4.77	1		Victoria	25 May
1:46.15	Kris	McCarthy	AUS	15.10.79	5	WUG	Beijing	1 Sep
1:46.16	Jimmy	Lomba	FRA	30.6.78	9	GP	Saint-Denis	6 Jul
1:46.22	Marko	Koers	NED	3.11.72	4	FBK	Hengelo	4 Jun
1:46.23	Assane	Diallo	SEN	10.2.75	1		Funchal	30 Jun
	(60)							
1:46.25	Sergey	Kozhevnikov	RUS	12.5.70	2	NC	Tula	15 Jul
1:46.27	Willy	Rotich	KEN	23.3.76	3		Lapinlahti	22 Jul
1:46.3A	Werner	Botha	RSA	31.1.78	1		Johannesburg	2 Nov
1:46.3A	Lucky	Hadebe	RSA	2.1.80	2		Johannesburg	2 Nov
1:46.34	João	Pires	POR	10.6.79	2		Lisboa (U)	16 Jun
1:46.38	Nico	Motchebon	GER	13.11.69	2		Kassel	13 Jun
1:46.43	Marvin	Watts	JAM	21.5.75	5h5	WCh	Edmonton	4 Aug
1:46.49	Shawn	Abrahams	RSA	4.7.70	4	NC	Durban	3 Mar
1:46.53	Artyom	Mastrov	RUS	12.11.76	3	NC	Tula	15 Jul
1:46.53	Franck	Barré	FRA	15.7.77	2		La Chaux-de-Fonds	19 Aug
	(70)							
1:46.54	Mouhsin	Chéhibi	MAR	28.1.78	2		Valencia	8 Jul
1:46.54	Wilson	Kirwa	FIN	28.12.74	5		Lapinlahti	22 Jul
1:46.58	Moise	Joseph	USA	27.12.81	2	SEC	Columbia, SC	13 May
1:46.60	Rui	Silva	POR	3.8.77	1		Lisboa (U)	20 May
1:46.60	Nathan	Brannen	CAN-J	8.9.82	2	NC	Edmonton	23 Jun
1:46.60	Bryce	Knight	USA	4.4.78	2		Montreal (McG)	10 Jul
1:46.61	Sylas	Kimutai	KEN-J	12.10.83	7	FBK	Hengelo	4 Jun
1:46.63	Franek	Haschke	GER	28.3.80	8		Leverkusen	26 Aug
1:46.65	Sergio	Gallardo	ESP	22.3.79	3		Madrid	7 Jul
1:46.65	Daryl	Fillion	CAN	10.2.73	3		Montreal (McG)	10 Jul
	(80)							
1:46.71	Stefan	Beumer	NED	28.4.81	3		Nijmegen	24 May
1:46.71	José Antonio	Redolat	ESP	17.2.76	4		Valencia	8 Jul
1:46.76	Andrea	Giocondi	ITA	17.1.69	7		Milano	6 Jun
1:46.80	Daniel	Caulfield	IRL	16.10.72	5	GP II	Gresham	3 Jun
1:46.80	Florent	Lacasse	FRA	21.1.81	3		La Chaux-de-Fonds	19 Aug
1:46.8A	Robert	Chirchir	KEN	26.11.72	5		Nairobi	12 May
1:46.81	René	Herms	GER-J	17.7.82	1	NC	Stuttgart	1 Jul
1:46.81	Valdinei	da Silva	BRA	29.3.72	1	NC	Rio de Janeiro	22 Jul
1:46.83	Gabe	Jennings	USA	25.1.79	1		Palo Alto	13 May
1:46.84	Juan Carlos	Higuero	ESP	3.8.78	1		Cáceres	20 Jun
	(90)							
1:46.85	Tarik	Bourrouag	GER	9.7.76	1		Dessau	30 May
1:46.86	Ivan	Komar	BLR	18.3.70	4		Bydgoszcz	15 Jun
1:46.86	Lubert	Lewis	USA	6.8.78	4		Montreal (McG)	10 Jul
1:46.9A	Philip	Kibitok	KEN	23.3.71	5		Nairobi	26 May
1:46.93A	Isaiah	Nkuna	RSA	5.3.77	1		Pretoria	23 Mar
1:46.93	Reyes	Estévez	ESP	2.8.76	5		Valencia	8 Jul
1:46.93	Ramil	Aritkulov	RUS	78	4	NC	Tula	15 Jul
1:46.94	Mehdi	Baala	FRA	17.8.78	2h1	NC	Saint-Etienne	30 Jun
1:46.99	Rachid	Khouya	MAR	9.11.79	3h2	FrG	Ottawa	20 Jul
1:47.00	Philemon	Kibet	KEN-J	20.11.82	9		Milano	6 Jun
	(100)							

Mark	Name		Nat	Born	Date
1:47.04	Mark	Rodgers	NZL	24.7.76	31 Aug
1:47.05	Johan	Botha	RSA	10.1.74	30 Mar
1:47.07	Ali	Hakimi	TUN	24.4.76	20 Jul
1:47.08	Vladimir	Bozhko	RUS	72	15 Jul
1:47.1A	Dedan	Maina	KEN		26 May
1:47.14	Fernando	Almeida	POR	22.6.81	30 Jun
1:47.16	Nicholas	Muchoki	KEN		19 May
1:47.16	Neil	Speaight	GBR	9.9.78	19 Jun
1:47.16	Pávlos	Faroúggias	GRE	6.6.77	22 Jul
1:47.17	Eliud	Njubi	KEN	27.7.79	31 Mar
1:47.17	Michael	Stember	USA	30.1.78	13 May
1:47.17	Massimo	De Meo	ITA	21.2.73	11 Jul
1:47.17	Vyacheslav	Shabunin	RUS	27.9.69	15 Jul
1:47.20	Flávio	Godoy	BRA	13.12.69	6 May
1:47.20	Ricardo	Etheridge	PUR	12.5.78	12 May
1:47.20	Hudson	de Souza	BRA	25.2.77	18 May
1:47.20	Dirk	Heinze	GER	2.7.76	19 May
1:47.21	Juan Carlos	Esteso	ESP	13.10.76	18 Aug

Mark	Name		Nat	Born	Date
1:47.28	Mao	Tjiroze	NAM	4.12.77	19 May
1:47.30	Jebreh	Harris	USA	22.9.78	13 May
1:47.3	David	Cheruiyot	KEN	1.9.72	26 May
1:47.3	Abdou Ibrahim	Yousef	QAT	27.9.80	3 Oct
	1:47.33				26 Aug
1:47.31	Sebastian	Miller	POL	24.7.76	15 Jun
1:47.31	Abdirizak	Dirshe	SWE	5.1.72	27 Jun
1:47.33	Paul	Mwangi	KEN	19.11.73	1 Sep
1:47.35	Simon	Lees	GBR	19.11.79	22 Jul
1:47.37	Floyd	Thompson	USA	22.11.78	4 May
1:47.38	Pavel	Pelepyagin	BLR	29.6.78	30 Jun
1:47.39	Enock	Koech	KEN	4.4.81	4 Jul
1:47.40	Kevin	Elliott	USA	7.11.78	12 May
1:47.40	Rickard	Pell	SWE	24.3.79	27 Jun
1:47.40	Panayiótis	Stroubákos	GRE	8.9.72	22 Aug
1:47.42	Amine	Laalou	MAR-J	.82	23 May
1:47.42	James	McIlroy	GBR	30.12.76	25 May
1:47.42	Wojciech	Kaldowski	POL	16.4.76	8 Jun
1:47.5	Jackson	Kiprotich	KEN		21 Jun
1:47.5	Réda	Abdenouz	ALG	25.9.68	19 Jul
1:47.5	Andrew	Graffin	GBR	20.12.77	29 Aug
1:47.57	Abdelkébir	Louraïbi	MAR	9.2.81	23 May
1:47.6	Stephen	Kiprotich	KEN		26 May
1:47.6	Adam	Abdou	QAT-J	85	3 Oct
1:47.60	Frazer	Dowling	AUS	4.12.79	24 Mar
1:47.67	Christian	Neunhäuserer	ITA	21.6.78	6 Jun
1:47.69	Adam	Davis	USA	1.12.81	13 May
1:47.70	Jeff	DeLong	USA	7.11.77	13 May
1:47.70	Robert	Mitchell	USA	17.5.77	13 May
1:47.70	Aleksandr	Trutko	BLR	31.10.78	15 Jun
1:47.7A	Charles	Makau	KEN	13.3.71	21 Jun
1:47.7	John	Kemboi	KEN	13.8.74	25 Jun
1:47.74	Alan	Webb	USA-J	13.1.83	2 Jun
1:47.78	Cosmas	Rono	KEN-J	12.12.84	27 May
1:47.80	K.M.	Binu	IND	20.12.80	21 Oct
1:47.82	Graham	Hood	CAN	2.4.72	25 May
1:47.83	Israel	Domínguez	ESP	16.10.77	30 Jun
1:47.84	Urmet	Uusorg	EST	27.9.76	22 Jul
1:47.86	Christian	Köhler	GER	14.10.80	30 Jun
1:47.86	Tim	Rogge	BEL	3.2.77	14 Jul
1:47.88	Jason	Van Swol	USA	10.1.80	20 May
1:47.88	Jason	Lunn	USA	19.9.74	25 Jul
1:47.9A	Crispen	Mutakanyi	ZIM	15.3.70	1 Jul
1:47.92	Simon	Kimata	KEN	22.11.76	4 May
1:47.93	Felix	Leiter	GER	18.12.75	1 Jul
1:47.94	Juha	Kukkamo	FIN	1.4.76	22 Jul
1:47.95	Peter	Biwott	KEN	22.8.76	12 Jul
1:47.96	Phillip	Malakwen	KEN	79	19 May
1:47.96	Davide	Cadoni	ITA	4.5.73	30 Jun
1:47.96	Jimmy	Jean-Joseph	FRA	15.10.72	30 Jun
1:47.97	Jason	Long	USA	23.10.78	19 May
	(168)				

Indoors

Mark	Name		Nat	Born	Pos	Meet	Venue	Date
1:45.80	Johan	Botha	RSA	10.1.74	3		Stockholm	15 Feb
1:45.95	Dirk	Heinze	GER	2.7.76	2	NCAA	Fayetteville	10 Mar
1:46.48	Roberto	Parra	ESP	6.4.76	4		Stockholm	15 Feb

Mark	Name		Nat	Born	Date
1:47.25	Elliott	Gaskins	USA	3.1.74	3 Mar
1:47.71	Roman	Oravec	CZE	5.4.78	10 Mar
1:47.80	Lukás	Vydra	CZE	23.8.73	4 Feb
1:47.86	James	Karanu	KEN	5.1.76	10 Feb
1:47.93#	James	Doaty	USA	17.10.81	25 Feb
1:47.97	Erkin	Isakov	UZB	25.11.74	1 Feb

JUNIORS

See main list for top 7 juniors. 10 performances by 3 men to 1:46.4. Additional marks and further juniors:

	Mark	Pos	Meet	Venue	Date	Mark	Pos	Meet	Venue	Date
Wachira	1:44.49	1		Rovereto	29 Aug	1:45.84	3		Formia	14 Jul
	1:45.36A	3	NC	Nairobi	23 Jun	1:45.97	4h5	WCh	Edmonton	4 Aug
	1:45.8A	2s2	NC	Nairobi	22 Jun	1:46.00	8	Athl	Lausanne	4 Jul
Okken	1:46.40	2s1	WUG	Beijing	31 Aug					

Mark	Name		Nat	Born	Pos	Meet	Venue	Date
1:47.42	Amine	Laalou	MAR-J	.82	2		Rabat	23 May
1:47.6	Adam	Abdou	QAT	85	2	PArab	Damescus	3 Oct
1:47.74	Alan	Webb	USA	13.1.83	1		Richmond	2 Jun
1:47.78	Cosmas	Rono	KEN	12.12.84	2		Ingostadt	27 May
1:48.0	Idriss Hilal	Al-Sharji	OMN	.84	3	PArab	Damascus	3 Oct
1:48.08	Vincent	Kemboi	KEN	29.5.82	3	Slovn	Bratislava	12 Jun
1:48.12A	Simoncito	Silvera	VEN	20.6.82	1	CAC	C. de Guatemala	22 Jul
1:48.2	Ahmad	Ismail	SUD	10.9.84	4	PArab	Damascus	3 Oct
1:48.2	Ibrahim	Sadiq	SUD		5	PArab	Damascus	3 Oct
1:48.21	Jonathan	Johnson	USA	5.3.82	1		Austin	12 May
1:48.29	Johan	Cronje	RSA	13.4.82	2		Rhede	13 Jul
1:48.42	Jesse	O'Connell	USA		2r2		Princeton	12 May
1:48.43	Ricky	Soos (20)	GBR	28.6.83	3	EJ	Grosseto	21 Jul
1:48.44	David	Freeman	USA	28.4.82	6		Columbia	13 May
1:48.51	Salem Amer	Al-Badri	QAT	12.12.85?	4		Kassel	13 Jun
1:48.54	David	Karonei	KEN	,83	1		Mannheim	16 Jun
1:48.54	Yuriy	Koldin	RUS	1.11.83	4	EJ	Grosseto	21 Jul

1000 METRES

Mark	Name		Nat	Born	Pos	Meet	Venue	Date
2:15.63	André	Bucher	SUI	19.10.76	1		Langenthal	24 May
2:16.42		Bucher			1		Willisau	12 May
2:16.53	William	Yiampoy	KEN	17.5.74	1	Nik	Nice	9 Jul
2:16.86	Nicolas	Aïssat	FRA	24.7.80	1		Strasbourg	19 Jun
2:16.93	Noah	Ngeny	KEN	2.11.78	2	Nik	Nice	9 Jul
	(5/4)							
2:17.10	Driss	Maazouzi	FRA	15.10.69	3	Nik	Nice	9 Jul
2:17.26	Hezekiél	Sepeng	RSA	30.6.74	4	Nik	Nice	9 Jul
2:17.34	Arthémon	Hatungimana	BDI	21.1.74	2		Strasbourg	19 Jun
2:17.34	Jean-Patrick	Nduwimana	BDI	9.5.78	5	Nik	Nice	9 Jul
2:17.35	Kenneth	Kimwetich	KEN	1.1.73	6	Nik	Nice	9 Jul
2:17.74	David	Lelei (10)	KEN	10.5.71	9	Nik	Nice	9 Jul
2:17.79	Seneca	Lassiter	USA	12.3.77	10	Nik	Nice	9 Jul
2:17.80	Mehdi	Baala	FRA	17.8.78	3		Strasbourg	19 Jun

Mark	Name		Nat	Born	Date
2:18.00	Aléxis	Abraham	FRA	14.2.76	19 Jun
2:18.13	Nicholas	Wachira	KEN-J	19.11.82	9 Jul
2:18.74	Francis	Marwa	KEN	76	9 Jul
2:19.04	Ivan	Geshko	UKR	19.8.79	16 Jun
2:19.29	Wolfram	Müller	GER	8.7.81	24 Aug
2:19.68	Franck	Barre	FRA	15.7.77	2 Sep

Indoors

Mark	Name		Nat	Born	Pos	Meet	Venue	Date
2:17.36	Mehdi	Baala	FRA	17.8.78	1	Euro	Gent	23 Feb
2:17.36	Rui	Silva	POR	3.8.77	3	Euro	Gent	23 Feb

Mark	Name		Nat	Born	Date
2:18.23	Bram	Som	NED	20.2.80	23 Feb
2:18.45	Marko	Koers	NED	3.11.72	23 Feb
2:18.61	Japheth	Kimutai	KEN	20.12.78	21 Feb
2:18.65	Joeri	Jansen	BEL	28.5.79	23 Feb
2:18.88	Johan	Botha	RSA	10.1.74	2 Feb
2:19.00	Pawel	Czapiewski	POL	30.3.78	2 Feb
2:19.22	Laban	Rotich	KEN	20.1.69	4 Feb
2:19.24	Benjamin	Kipkurui	KEN	28.12.80	16 Feb
2:19.39	Birhane	Alemu	ETH-J	16.7.82	2 Feb

JUNIORS

Mark	Name		Nat	Born	Pos	Meet	Venue	Date
2:18.13	Nicholas	Wachira	KEN	19.11.82	11	Nik	Nice	9 Jul
2:19.39i	Birhane	Alemu	ETH-J	16.7.82	4		Erfurt	2 Feb
2:20.6A	Johan	Cronje	RSA	13.4.82	1		Bloemfontein	26 Mar
	2:20.81				1		Hamburg	15 Jul

1500 METRES

Mark	Name		Nat	Born	Pos	Meet	Venue	Date
3:26.12	Hicham	El Guerrouj	MAR	14.9.74	1	VD	Bruxelles	24 Aug
3:26.34	Bernard	Lagat	KEN	12.12.74	2	VD	Bruxelles	24 Aug
3:28.38		El Guerrouj			1	GP	Saint-Denis	6 Jul
3:29.06		El Guerrouj			1rA	WK	Zürich	17 Aug
3:29.08		El Guerrouj			1	GP II	Rieti	2 Sep
3:29.29	William	Chirchir	KEN	6.2.79	3	VD	Bruxelles	24 Aug
3:29.51	Ali	Saïdi Sief ¶	ALG	15.3.78	1	Athl	Lausanne	4 Jul
3:29.85+		El Guerrouj			1	in 1M	Roma	29 Jun
3:30.36	Rui	Silva	POR	3.8.77	1	Herc	Monaco	20 Jul
3:30.61		Lagat			2rA	WK	Zürich	17 Aug
3:30.67	Benjamin	Kipkurui	KEN	28.12.80	2	Herc	Monaco	20 Jul
3:30.68		El Guerrouj			1	WCh	Edmonton	12 Aug
3:30.78		Saïdi-Sief			1	GP	Athína	11 Jun
3:30.83		Lagat			2	GP	Saint-Denis	6 Jul
3:31.01+		Lagat			2	in 1M	Roma	29 Jun
3:31.08		Lagat			3	Herc	Monaco	20 Jul
3:31.10		Lagat			2	WCh	Edmonton	12 Aug
3:31.16		Saïdi-Sief			1	Nik	Nice	9 Jul
3:31.20		Chirchir			3	GP	Saint-Denis	6 Jul
3:31.21	José Antonio	Redolat	ESP	17.2.76	1	DNG	Stockholm	17 Jul
3:31.25		El Guerrouj			1	GPF	Melbourne	9 Sep
3:31.28	Enock	Koech	KEN	4.4.81	3rA	WK	Zürich	17 Aug
3:31.38	Laban	Rotich	KEN	20.1.69	4rA	WK	Zürich	17 Aug
3:31.49	Robert	Rono (10)	KEN	11.10.74	4	Herc	Monaco	20 Jul
3:31.54	Driss	Maazouzi	FRA	15.10.69	3	WCh	Edmonton	12 Aug
3:31.57		Chirchir			5rA	WK	Zürich	17 Aug
3:31.64		Rotich			4	VD	Bruxelles	24 Aug
3:31.69		Lagat			2	DNG	Stockholm	17 Jul
3:31.91		Chirchir			4	WCh	Edmonton	12 Aug
3:31.94	Noah	Ngeny	KEN	2.11.78	2	GP	Athína	11 Jun
3:31.96	Paul	Bitok	KEN	26.6.70	3	DNG	Stockholm	17 Jul
3:31.97	Mehdi	Baala	FRA	17.8.78	5	Herc	Monaco	20 Jul
3:32.10		Lagat			2	GPF	Melbourne	9 Sep
3:32.15		Maazouzi			5	VD	Bruxelles	24 Aug
3:32.30	Juan Carlos	Higuero	ESP	3.8.78	6	VD	Bruxelles	24 Aug
3:32.34	Reyes	Estévez	ESP	2.8.76	5	WCh	Edmonton	12 Aug
3:32.37		Kipkirui			4	DNG	Stockholm	17 Jul
	(37/16)							
3:32.66+	Andrés	Díaz	ESP	12.7.69	3	in 1M	Roma	29 Jun
3:32.89	Gert-Jan	Liefers	NED	26.9.78	7	VD	Bruxelles	24 Aug
3:33.01	Vyacheslav	Shabunin	RUS	27.9.69	8	VD	Bruxelles	24 Aug
3:33.03	Mohamed	Khaldi	ALG	3.5.75	1	GP II	Zagreb	2 Jul
	(20)							
3:33.59	Abdelkader	Hachlaf	MAR	3.7.78	11	VD	Bruxelles	24 Aug
3:33.79+	Leonard	Mucheru	KEN	13.6.78	4	in 1M	Roma	29 Jun
3:33.89	Paul	McMullen	USA	19.2.72	8	Herc	Monaco	20 Jul
3:33.89	Fouad	Chouki	FRA	1.10.78	9	Herc	Monaco	20 Jul
3:33.91	Kevin	Sullivan	CAN	20.3.74	5	Athl	Lausanne	4 Jul
3:33.99	Hudson	de Souza	BRA	25.2.77	2	GP II	Zagreb	2 Jul
3:34.12	William	Yiampoy	KEN	17.5.74	6	Athl	Lausanne	4 Jul
3:34.12	Benson	Koech	KEN	10.11.74	2rB	WK	Zürich	17 Aug

Mark	Name		Nat	Born	Pos	Meet	Venue	Date
3:34.20	Luís	Feiteira	POR	21.4.73	10	Herc	Monaco	20 Jul
3:34.21	Youssef	Baba	MAR	7.8.79	7	Athl	Lausanne	4 Jul
	(30)							
3:34.26	Salah	El Ghazi	MAR	2.11.75	2		Padova	26 Aug
3:34.32	Seneca	Lassiter	USA	12.3.77	8	GP	Saint-Denis	6 Jul
3:34.35	Nadir	Bosch	FRA	16.5.73	3rB	WK	Zürich	17 Aug
3:34.43	John	Mayock	GBR	26.10.70	13	VD	Bruxelles	24 Aug
3:34.53	Cornelius	Chirchir	KEN-J	7.10.83	3	GP II	Rieti	2 Sep
3:34.81	Peter	Biwott	KEN	22.8.76	3	GP II	Zagreb	2 Jul
3:34.88+	Sammy	Mutai	KEN	20.12.74	8	in 1M	Roma	29 Jun
3:34.88	Anthony	Whiteman	GBR	13.11.71	4rB	WK	Zürich	17 Aug
3:34.93	Jürgen	Vandewiele	BEL	10.5.74	14	VD	Bruxelles	24 Aug
3:34.98	Graham	Hood	CAN	2.4.72	5	Nik	Nice	9 Jul
	(40)							
3:35.07	Richard	Geemi	KEN	23.8.73	2		Formia	14 Jul
3:35.09	Mark	Carroll	IRL	15.1.72	9	DNG	Stockholm	17 Jul
3:35.16	Shadrack	Korir	KEN	14.12.78	8	GP	Athína	11 Jun
3:35.31	Fred	Cheruiyot	KEN	20.9.70	4	GP II	Zagreb	2 Jul
3:35.40	Craig	Mottram	AUS	18.6.80	6	GPF	Melbourne	9 Sep
3:35.47	Stephen	Cherono	KEN-J	15.10.82	5	GP II	Zagreb	2 Jul
3:35.48	Bryan	Berryhill	USA	15.12.77	7rB	WK	Zürich	17 Aug
3:35.55	Isaac	Songok	KEN-J	25.4.84	1		Leverkusen	26 Aug
3:35.64	Saïd	Chébili	FRA	6.5.73	11	GP	Saint-Denis	6 Jul
3:35.69	Alberto	García	ESP	22.2.71	4		Madrid	7 Jul
	(50)							
3:35.88	Peter	Philipp	SUI	18.2.72	10	GP	Athína	11 Jun
3:35.95	Paul	Mwangi	KEN	19.11.73	2		Leverkusen	26 Aug
3:35.97	Andrew	Graffin	GBR	20.12.77	7	Nik	Nice	9 Jul
3:36.01	Adil	Kaouch	MAR	1.1.79	2s1	WCh	Edmonton	10 Aug
3:36.05	Aléxis	Abraham	FRA	14.2.76	8	Nik	Nice	9 Jul
3:36.22	Tarek	Boukensa	ALG	19.11.81	5	GP II	Rieti	2 Sep
3:36.50	James	Nolan	IRL	27.1.77	7	GP II	Zagreb	2 Jul
3:36.5	Bouabdellah	Tahri	FRA	20.12.78	6	NA	Heusden	14 Jul
3:36.5	Jason	Lunn	USA	19.9.74	7	NA	Heusden	14 Jul
3:36.64	Adam	Goucher	USA	18.2.75	12	DNG	Stockholm	17 Jul
	(60)							
3:36.70	Andy	Downin	USA	12.5.73	11	Athl	Lausanne	4 Jul
3:36.87	Musa	Kimeli	KEN	23.6.68	8	GP II	Zagreb	2 Jul
3:36.9	Michael	Stember	USA	30.1.78	8	NA	Heusden	14 Jul
3:37.08	Marko	Koers	NED	3.11.72	8	GP II	Sevilla	8 Jun
3:37.10	Ivan	Geshko	UKR	19.8.79	1		Kalamáta	2 Jun
3:37.11	Ismaïl	Sghyr	FRA	16.3.72	7	GP II	Rieti	2 Sep
3:37.3	Pedro A	Esteso	ESP	13.10.76	11	NA	Heusden	14 Jul
3:37.56	Gabe	Jennings	USA	25.1.79	2	NCAA	Eugene	2 Jun
3:37.60	Julius	Achon	UGA	12.12.76	1	GP	Rio de Janeiro	6 May
3:37.61	Wolfram	Müller	GER	8.7.81	1	NCAA	Stuttgart	1 Jul
	(70)							
3:37.66	Abdelhaq	Abdellah	MAR	13.8.68	3		Leverkusen	26 Aug
3:37.81	Youcef	Abdi	AUS	7.12.77	1		Nantes	23 Aug
3:37.83	Leszek	Zblewski	POL	25.12.73	3		Nürnberg	17 Jun
3:37.99	Daniel	Gachara	KEN	19.12.72	6		Madrid	7 Jul
3:38.04	Hamid	El Mouaziz	MAR	17.2.79	3		Dortmund	9 Jun
3:38.19	Ibrahim	Aden	USA	11.11.72	6		San Sebastián	18 Aug
3:38.2	Shadrack	Langat	KEN	22.7.78	12	NA	Heusden	14 Jul
3:38.25	Daniel	Zegeye	ETH	13.3.79	10rB	WK	Zürich	17 Aug
3:38.26+	Alan	Webb	USA-J	13.1.83	4	in 1M	Eugene	27 May
3:38.28	Gareth	Turnbull	IRL	14.5.79	2		Loughborough	20 May
	(80)							
3:38.3+	Tom	Mayo	GBR	2.5.77	5	in 1M	London (CP)	22 Jul
	3:38.34				5	GP II	Gateshead	19 Aug
3:38.39	Samuli	Vasala	FIN	29.11.76	6	GP II	Gateshead	19 Aug
3:38.40	Martin	Keino	KEN	20.6.72	16	DNG	Stockholm	17 Jul
3:38.40	Isaac	Viciosa	ESP	26.12.69	7		San Sebastián	18 Aug
3:38.46	Abdelkader	Chékhémani	FRA	18.7.71	13	GP	Saint-Denis	6 Jul
3:38.52	Lorenzo	Perrone	ITA	26.9.81	1		Milano	1 Jul
3:38.53	Clay	Schwabe	USA	3.7.79	6	NC	Eugene	23 Jun
3:38.56	Franek	Haschke	GER	28.3.80	2	NC	Stuttgart	1 Jul
3:38.62+	Raymond	Yator	KEN	7.4.81	6+	in 1M	Eugene	27 May
3:38.70	Darko	Radomirovic	YUG	5.8.77	1		Beograd	30 Aug
	(90)							

Mark	Name		Nat	Born	Pos	Meet	Venue	Date
3:38.74	David	Kimani	KEN	28.2.78	3	NCAA	Eugene	2 Jun
3:38.74	Ferdinando	Vicari	ITA	26.9.73	8	GP II	Rieti	2 Sep
3:38.78	Ralf	Assmus	GER	28.1.77	3		Kassel	13 Jun
3:38.8	Mohammed	Mourhit	BEL	10.10.70	14	NA	Heusden	14 Jul
3:38.83	Brian	Treacy	IRL	29.7.71	9		Madrid	7 Jul
3:38.84	Benoit	Nicolas	FRA	17.4.77	2		Nantes	23 Aug
3:38.86	Panayiótis	Stroubákos	GRE	8.9.72	11	GP	Athína	11 Jun
3:38.87	Rüdiger	Stenzel	GER	16.4.68	3	NC	Stuttgart	1 Jul
3:38.87	Paul	Koech	KEN	10.11.81	6		Leverkusen	26 Aug
3:38.94	Michael (100)	East	GBR	20.1.78	2		Arnhem	4 Jul

Mark	Name		Nat	Born	Date
3:39.06	Abdeslam	Kennouche	ALG	7.10.80	23 Aug
3:39.09	Michael	Too	KEN-J	3.8.83	24 May
3:39.12	Jeremy	Huffman	USA	13.2.76	21 Jul
3:39.2A	John	Kibowen	KEN	21.4.69	10 May
3:39.21	David	Galván	MEX	6.4.76	3 Jun
3:39.27	Donald	Sage	USA	5.10.81	2 Jun
3:39.39	Jamal Noor	Yousef	QAT-J	13.8.82	14 Jul
3:39.40	Joel	Atwater	USA	18.8.80	2 Jun
3:39.44	Gennaro	Di Napoli	ITA	5.3.68	26 Aug
3:39.46	Vasil	Tsikalo	UKR	2.3.80	2 Jul
3:39.49	Andrea	Longo ¶	ITA	26.6.75	18 May
3:39.50	Sergio	Gallardo	ESP	22.3.79	14 Jul
3:39.58	Christian	Obrist	ITA	20.11.80	14 Jul
3:39.60	Glody	Dube	BOT	2.7.78	24 May
3:39.60	Siakha	Bamba	CIV	24.5.75	23 Aug
3:39.64	Yusef	El Nasri	ESP	28.7.79	25 Jul
3:39.70	Hamish	Christensen	NZL	1.9.72	16 Feb
3:39.78	Samuel	Dadi	ETH-J	85	15 Jul
3:39.82	Edwin	Maranga	KEN	15.8.71	18 Feb
3:39.87	Philemon	Kibet	KEN-J	20.11.82	4 Jun
3:39.88	Angus	Maclean	GBR	20.9.80	9 Jun
3:40.02	Khalid	Elamri	MAR	79	14 Jul
3:40.06	Justin	Niedzialek	USA	11.6.77	9 Jun
3:40.22	Tim	Broe	USA	20.6.77	7 Jul
3:40.23	Mickaël	Damian	FRA	9.11.69	6 Jul
3:40.23	Ali Nabil	Maataoui	MAR	80	18 Jul
3:40.29	Johan	Cronje	RSA-J	13.4.82	21 Jul
3:40.3	John	Kosgei	KEN	13.7.73	12 May
3:40.31	Eliud	Njubi	KEN	27.7.79	2 Jun
3:40.36	Andrew	Walker	IRL	6.5.77	18 Feb
3:40.37	Manuel	Damião	POR	19.7.78	21 Jul
3:40.37	Henry	Rotich	KEN	5.12.81	17 Aug
3:40.41	Adrian	Blincoe	NZL	4.11.79	9 Jun
3:40.41	Marius	Bakken	NOR	27.3.78	7 Jul
3:40.50	Andrey	Zadorozhniy	RUS	3.9.73	17 Jun
3:40.55	Lorenzo	Lazzari	ITA	23.8.74	26 Aug
3:40.58	Pol	Guillén	ESP	1.10.77	25 Jul
3:40.68	Stephen	Kipkorir	KEN	24.10.70	14 Jul
3:40.72	Youcef	Allem	FRA	16.11.69	23 Aug
3:40.73	Christian	Hesch	USA		13 May
3:40.75	Benjamin	Hetzler	GER	17.4.78	4 Jul
3:40.75	Rubén	Villarroya	ESP	30.10.76	25 Jul
3:40.76	Michael	Power	AUS	9.5.76	18 Feb
3:40.76	Rafiei	Bouazza	MAR	21.10.78	13 Jun
3:40.79	Anthony	Famiglietti	USA	8.11.78	18 May
3:40.8A	Benjamin	Cheruiyot	KEN		26 May
3:40.86	Alexis	Sharangabo	RWA	9.11.78	30 Jun
3:40.87	Mattias	Norling	SWE	1.6.77	20 Aug
3:40.94	Jesús	España	ESP	21.8.78	26 Aug
3:40.95	Kipkirui	Misoi	KEN	23.12.78	27 May
3:40.97	Javier	Moro	ESP	16.4.75	7 Jul
3:40.98	Stefano	Alessandroni	ITA	30.3.81	26 Aug
3:41.0A	Boniface	Kiprotich	KEN		12 May
3:41.05	Kamal	Boulahfane	ALG	1.7.76	18 May
3:41.15	Redouane	Harroufi	MAR	30.7.81	7 Jul
3:41.21	Tom	Compernolle	BEL	13.11.75	21 Jul
3:41.22	Sébastien	Cosson	FRA	15.3.80	25 May
3:41.22	Philip	Mosima	KEN	2.1.77	27 May
3:41.27		Yang Weize	CHN-J	10.2.83	18 Nov
3:41.28	Markos	Geneti	ETH-J	.84	14 Jul
3:41.3A	Paul	Korir	KEN	15.7.77	21 Apr
3:41.30	Charlie	Gruber	USA	6.8.78	21 Jun
3:41.36	Samson	Kiplagat	KEN-J	10.11.86	4 Jul
3:41.47	David	Byrne	AUS	30.1.81	16 Feb
3:41.47	Japheth (165)	Kimutai	KEN	20.12.78	12 May

Indoors

Mark	Name		Nat	Born	Pos	Meet	Venue	Date
3:37.24	Japheth	Kimutai	KEN	20.12.78	2	Spark	Stuttgart	4 Feb
3:38.41	Hailu	Mekonnen	ETH	4.4.80	3h1	WI	Lisboa	9 Mar
3:38.61	Kamal	Boulahfane	ALG	1.7.76	5	Spark	Stuttgart	4 Feb
3:38.75	Birhane	Alemu	ETH-J	16.7.82	7	Euro	Birmingham	18 Feb
3:39.55	Branko	Zorko	CRO	1.7.67	5h3	WI	Lisboa	9 Mar

JUNIORS

See main list for top 4 juniors. 10 performances by 5 men to 3:39.0. Additional marks and further juniors:

Name	Mark	Pos	Meet	Venue	Date	Mark	Pos	Meet	Venue	Date
Cherono	3:37.27	2	GP II	Gateshead	19 Aug					
Songok	3:36.78	1	WY	Debrecen	15 Jul	3:38.34	1h1	WY	Debrecen	13 Jul
	3:38.00	1	U23	Zürich	17 Aug					
Webb	3:38.50	5	NC	Eugene	23 Jun					

Mark	Name		Nat	Born	Pos	Meet	Venue	Date
3:39.09	Michael	Too	KEN	3.8.83	1		Nijmegen	24 May
3:39.39	Jamal Noor	Yousef	QAT	13.8.82	1rB	NA	Heusden	14 Jul
3:39.78	Samuel	Dadi	ETH	85	2	WY	Debrecen	15 Jul
3:39.87	Philemon	Kibet	KEN	20.11.82	3	Veniz	Haniá	4 Jun
3:40.29	Johan	Cronje	RSA	13.4.82	4		Cuxhaven	21 Jul
3:41.27		Yang Weize	CHN	10.2.83	1	NG	Guangzhou	18 Nov
3:41.28	Markos	Geneti	ETH	.84	1	WY	Debrecen	14 Jul
3:41.36	Samson	Kiplagat	KEN	10.11.86	6		Arnhem	4 Jul
3:41.53	Ali Abubaker	Kamal	QAT	3.12.82	8		Kassel	13 Jun
3:41.80	Nathan	Brannen	CAN	8.9.82	2		Montreal	10 Jul
3:42.03	Abdul Rahman	Suleiman	QAT	.84	3	WY	Debrecen	15 Jul
3:42.21	James	Kwalia	KEN	12.6.84	2		Zanzibar	28 Oct
3:42.70	Ryan	Hall	USA	14.10.82	5		Palo Alto	9 Jun
3:42.72	Philemon	Tanui	KEN	20.11.83	2	Afr-J	Réduit	17 Aug
3:42.82	Kifletsion	Habtal	ERI		3	Afr-J	Réduit	17 Aug
3:43.11	Josh	Spiker (20)	USA	8.3.82	1		Madison	12 May
3:43.14	Ryan	Hayden II	CAN	27.1.82	3r5	MSR	Walnut	21 Apr
3:43.27		Dou Zhaobo	CHN	23.9.83	1		Jinan	12 May

1 MILE

Mark	Name		Nat	Born	Pos	Meet	Venue	Date
3:44.95	Hicham	El Guerrouj	MAR	14.9.74	1	GGala	Roma	29 Jun
3:47.28	Bernard	Lagat	KEN	12.12.74	2	GGala	Roma	29 Jun
3:48.23	Ali	Saïdi-Sief ¶	ALG	15.3.78	1	Bisl	Oslo	13 Jul
3:48.38	Andrés	Díaz	ESP	12.7.69	3	GGala	Roma	29 Jun
3:48.57		Lagat			2	Bisl	Oslo	13 Jul
3:49.41		El Guerrouj			1	BrGP	London (CP)	22 Jul
3:49.60	José Antonio	Redolat	ESP	17.2.76	4	GGala	Roma	29 Jun
3:49.75	Leonard	Mucheru	KEN	13.6.78	5	GGala	Roma	29 Jun
3:49.83	Vyacheslav	Shabunin	RUS	27.9.69	6	GGala	Roma	29 Jun
3:49.92		El Guerrouj			1	Pre	Eugene	27 May
3:50.29	Noah	Ngeny	KEN	2.11.78	3	Bisl	Oslo	13 Jul
3:50.60	Sammy	Mutai	KEN	20.12.74	7	GGala	Roma	29 Jun
3:51.19		Ngeny			2	BrGP	London (CP)	22 Jul
3:51.50	Enock	Koech (10)	KEN	4.4.81	8	GGala	Roma	29 Jun
3:51.82	Kevin	Sullivan	CAN	20.3.74	2	Pre	Eugene	27 May
	(15/11)							
3:52.19	Laban	Rotich	KEN	20.1.69	4	Bisl	Oslo	13 Jul
3:52.52	Benjamin	Kipkurui	KEN	28.12.80	11	GGala	Roma	29 Jun
3:52.68	Reyes	Estévez	ESP	2.8.76	5	Bisl	Oslo	13 Jul
3:52.86	William	Chirchir	KEN	6.2.79	1	GP	Palo Alto	9 Jun
3:53.06	Craig	Mottram	AUS	18.6.80	6	Bisl	Oslo	13 Jul
3:53.16	Peter	Biwott	KEN	22.8.76	12	GGala	Roma	29 Jun
3:53.40	Adil	Kaouch	MAR	1.1.79	4	Pre	Eugene	27 May
3:53.43	Alan	Webb	USA-J	13.1.83	5	Pre	Eugene	27 May
3:53.75	Hudson	de Souza	BRA	25.2.77	7	Bisl	Oslo	13 Jul
	(20)							
3:54.05	Robert	Rono	KEN	11.10.74	8	Bisl	Oslo	13 Jul
3:54.05	John	Mayock	GBR	26.10.70	4	BrGP	London (CP)	22 Jul
3:54.36	Seneca	Lassiter	USA	12.3.77	9	Bisl	Oslo	13 Jul
3:54.56	Isaac	Songok	KEN-J	25.4.84	1	Gugl	Linz	20 Aug
3:54.62	Graham	Hood	CAN	2.4.72	7	Pre	Eugene	27 May
3:54.79	Fred	Cheruiyot	KEN	20.9.70	6	BrGP	London (CP)	22 Jul
3:54.87	Bryan	Berryhill	USA	15.12.77	2	Gugl	Linz	20 Aug
3:54.94	Paul	McMullen	USA	19.2.72	7	BrGP	London (CP)	22 Jul
3:55.08	Paul	Mwangi	KEN	19.11.73	3	Gugl	Linz	20 Aug
3:55.10	Youssef	Baba	MAR	7.8.79	9	Pre	Eugene	27 May
	(30)							
3:55.12	Raymond	Yator	KEN	7.4.81	10	Pre	Eugene	27 May
3:55.16	Anthony	Whiteman	GBR	13.11.71	8	BrGP	London (CP)	22 Jul
3:55.42	Andrew	Graffin	GBR	20.12.77	5	Gugl	Linz	20 Aug
3:55.47	Adam	Goucher	USA	18.2.75	2	GP II	Gresham	3 Jun
3:55.57	Tom	Mayo	GBR	2.5.77	9	BrGP	London (CP)	22 Jul
3:55.72	Shadrack	Korir	KEN	14.12.78	10	BrGP	London (CP)	22 Jul
3:55.80	Edwin	Maranga	KEN	15.8.71	3	GP II	Gresham	3 Jun
3:56.25	Andy	Downin	USA	12.5.73	4	GP II	Gresham	3 Jun
3:56.60	David	Chemweno	KEN	18.12.81	3	GP II	Melbourne	1 Mar
3:56.67	Marko	Koers	NED	3.11.72	11	BrGP	London (CP)	22 Jul
	(40)							

Mark	Name		Nat	Born	Date
3:56.69	David	Kimani	KEN	28.2.78	22 Apr
3:56.72	James	Karanu	KEN	5.1.76	3 Jun
3:56.76	Hamid	El Mouaziz	MAR	17.2.79	15 Aug
3:56.77	Hamish	Christensen	NZL	1.9.72	6 Jan
3:56.84	Eliud	Njubi	KEN	27.7.79	28 Apr
3:56.87	Martin	Keino	KEN	20.6.72	27 May
3:56.95	Ibrahim	Aden	USA	11.11.72	3 Jun
3:57.13	Mike	Miller	USA	19.1.74	12 May
3:57.40	Daniel	Zegeye	ETH	13.3.79	3 Jun
3:58.36	John	Thuo Itati	KEN	26.12.73	11 Aug
3:58.47	Charlie	Gruber	USA	6.8.78	3 Jun
3:58.49	Daniel	Gachara	KEN	19.12.72	25 May
3:58.59	Benson	Koech	KEN	10.11.74	20 Aug
3:58.88	Michael	Power	AUS	9.5.76	1 Mar
3:58.91	Clay	Schwabe	USA	3.7.79	7 Jul
3:59.01	Jason	Lunn	USA	19.9.74	7 Jul
3:59.20	Michael	Stember	USA	30.1.78	9 Jun
3:59.49	Simon	Maunder	NZL	20.8.72	20 Jan
3:59.55	Bashir Omar	Ibrahim	ex-KUW	14.3.79	28 Apr
3:59.57	Youcef	Abdi	AUS	7.12.77	1 Mar
3:59.61	Michael	East	GBR	20.1.78	22 Jul
3:59.74	Christian	Obrist	ITA	20.11.80	29 Jun
3:59.85	Nathan	Brannen	CAN-J	8.9.82	8 Jul
	(63)				

Indoors

Mark	Name		Nat	Born	Pos	Meet	Venue	Date
3:52.18	Rui	Silva	POR	3.8.77	1		Stockholm	15 Feb
3:54.21	Seneca	Lassiter	USA	12.3.77	2	Tyson	Fayetteville	10 Feb
3:54.27	Clyde	Colenso	RSA	11.5.77	3	Tyson	Fayetteville	10 Feb
3:54.5	Mark	Carroll	IRL	15.1.72	1		Boston	18 Feb
3:55.45	Benson	Koech	KEN	10.11.74	5		Stockholm	15 Feb
3:56.33	Jason	Pyrah	USA	6.4.69	5	Tyson	Fayetteville	10 Feb
3:56.50	James	Nolan	IRL	27.1.77	6		Stockholm	15 Feb

Mark	Name		Nat	Born	Date
3:58.02	Javier	Moro	ESP	16.4.75	15 Feb
3:58.42	Jason	Lunn	USA	19.9.74	4 Feb
3:58.54	Gabriel	Jennings	USA	25.1.79	10 Mar
3:58.90	Michael	Stember	USA	30.1.78	4 Feb

Mark	Name		Nat	Born	Pos	Meet	Venue	Date
3:59.14	Dan	Wilson	USA	19.2.79				4 Feb
3:59.60	Sharif	Karie	USA	1.1.78				10 Feb
3:59.61	Christian	Goy	GER	9.9.76				10 Mar
3:59.74	Matt	Holthaus	USA	2.11.71				20 Jan
3:59.99	Jeremy	Tolman	USA	5.6.77				10 Mar

JUNIORS

Mark	Name		Nat	Born	Pos	Meet	Venue	Date
3:53.43	Alan	Webb	USA	13.1.83	5	Pre	Eugene	27 May
3:54.56	Isaac	Songok	KEN	25.4.84	1	Gugl	Linz	20 Aug
3:59.85	Nathan	Brannen	CAN	8.9.82	1		Halifax	8 Jul
4:01.32	Nick	Willis	NZL	25.4.83	4		Wangabui	20 Jan
4:01.47	Ryan	Hayden II	CAN	27.1.82	1		Villanova	14 May
	4:00.78i				7		Fayetteville	10 Feb
4:01.71	Philemon	Kibet	KEN	20.11.82	1		Avellino	13 Jun

2000 METRES

Mark	Name		Nat	Born	Pos	Meet	Venue	Date
4:46.88	Ali	Saïdi-Sief ¶	ALG	15.3.78	1		Strasbourg	19 Jun
4:51.17	Hicham	El Guerrouj	MAR	14.9.74	1	ISTAF	Berlin	31 Aug
4:55.55	Driss	Maazouzi	FRA	15.10.69	2	ISTAF	Berlin	31 Aug
4:55.92	Enock	Koech	KEN	4.4.81	3	ISTAF	Berlin	31 Aug
4:56.56	Gert-Jan	Liefers	NED	26.9.78	4	ISTAF	Berlin	31 Aug
4:56.62	Shadrack	Korir	KEN	14.12.78	5	ISTAF	Berlin	31 Aug
4:56.86	Isaac	Songok	KEN-J	25.4.84	6	ISTAF	Berlin	31 Aug
4:57.24	Vyacheslav	Shabunin	RUS	27.9.69	7	ISTAF	Berlin	31 Aug
4:57.44		Maazouzi			1		Villeneuve d'Ascq	17 Jun
4:57.72	Bouabdellah	Tahri	FRA	20.12.78	1		Marly	12 Jun
4:57.81		Shabunin			2		Villeneuve d'Ascq	17 Jun
4:57.97	Abdelkader	Hachlaf (10)	MAR	3.7.78	3		Villeneuve d'Ascq	17 Jun
4:58.06	Mohamed	Khaldi	ALG	3.5.75	4		Villeneuve d'Ascq	17 Jun
4:59.22	Hamid	El Mouaziz	MAR	17.2.79	8	ISTAF	Berlin	31 Aug
4:59.31	Saïd	Chébili	FRA	6.5.73	5		Villeneuve d'Ascq	17 Jun
5:00.7+	Martin	Keino	KEN	20.6.72	1	Nik	Nice	9 Jul
5:00.83	Abdelhaq	Abdellah	MAR	13.8.68	1		Viareggio	22 Aug
5:01.85	Michael	Power	AUS	9.5.76				17 Jun
5:02.20	Nadir	Bosch	FRA	16.5.73				17 Jun
5:02.26	Réda	Benzine	ALG	19.4.71				22 Aug
5:02.29	Moses	Kigen	KEN	22.4.73				24 May
5:02.45	Joseph	Kosgei	KEN	74				24 May
5:02.45	Josphat	Boit	KEN-J	83				24 May
5:03.06	Stephen	Cherono	KEN-J	15.10.82				17 Jun
5:03.25	Aléxis	Abraham	FRA	14.2.76				17 Jun
5:03.29	Gennaro	Di Napoli	ITA	5.3.68				22 Aug
5:03.3+	Mohammed	Mourhit	BEL	10.10.70				20 Jul
5:03.4+	Paul	Bitok	KEN	26.6.70				20 Jul
5:03.5+	Salah	El Ghazi	MAR	2.11.75				20 Jul
5:03.64	David	Tuwei	KEN	22.2.79				24 May
5:03.7+	Philip	Mosima	KEN	2.1.77				20 Jul
5:03.77	Ali Nabil	Maataoui	MAR	.80				19 Jun
5:03.81	Ferdinando	Vicari	ITA	26.9.73				22 Aug

Indoors

Mark	Name		Nat	Born	Pos	Meet	Venue	Date
4:56.40	Noah	Ngeny	KEN	2.11.78	1	Euro	Liévin	25 Feb
4:57.09	John	Mayock	GBR	26.10.70	2	Euro	Liévin	25 Feb
4:58.93	Youssef	Baba	MAR	7.8.79	3	Euro	Liévin	25 Feb
5:01.99	Kamel	Boulahfane	ALG	1.7.76				25 Feb
5:03.95	Rui	Silva	POR	3.8.77				25 Feb

JUNIORS

Mark	Name		Nat	Born	Pos	Meet	Venue	Date
5:02.45	Josphat	Boit	KEN	83	3		Florø	24 May
5:03.06	Stephen	Cherono	KEN	15.10.82	8		Villeneuve d'Ascq	17 Jun
5:04.08	Philemon	Kibet	KEN	20.11.82	4		Strasbourg	19 Jun
5:06.47	Pius	Muli	KEN	15.12.82	6		Viareggio	22 Aug

3000 METRES

Mark	Name		Nat	Born	Pos	Meet	Venue	Date
7:30.53	Hailu	Mekonnen	ETH	4.4.80	1	VD	Bruxelles	24 Aug
7:30.67	Kenenisa	Bekele	ETH-J	13.6.82	2	VD	Bruxelles	24 Aug
7:31.00	Paul	Bitok	KEN	26.6.70	3	VD	Bruxelles	24 Aug
7:31.58	John	Kibowen	KEN	21.4.69	4	VD	Bruxelles	24 Aug
7:32.11		Bitok			1	Herc	Monaco	20 Jul
7:32.23	Richard	Limo	KEN	18.11.80	5	VD	Bruxelles	24 Aug
7:32.36	Abderrahim	Goumri	MAR	21.5.76	6	VD	Bruxelles	24 Aug
7:32.38	Abiyote	Abate	ETH	20.11.80	7	VD	Bruxelles	24 Aug
7:32.61		Bitok			1	Athl	Lausanne	4 Jul
7:32.68	Luke	Kipkosgei	KEN	27.11.75	2	Herc	Monaco	20 Jul
7:33.10	Benjamin	Limo	KEN	23.8.74	3	Herc	Monaco	20 Jul
7:33.36		Kibowen			2	Athl	Lausanne	4 Jul
7:33.42	Salah	El Ghazi (10)	MAR	2.11.75	4	Herc	Monaco	20 Jul
7:33.52	Mark	Carroll	IRL	15.1.72	5	Herc	Monaco	20 Jul
7:33.62	Sammy	Kipketer	KEN	29.9.81	3	Athl	Lausanne	4 Jul
7:33.71		R Limo			4	Athl	Lausanne	4 Jul
7:34.74		Bitok			1	Nik	Nice	9 Jul
7:34.96	Adam	Goucher	USA	18.2.75	6	Herc	Monaco	20 Jul
7:35.35	Mohammed	Amine	MAR	25.5.76	2	Nik	Nice	9 Jul
7:35.35	Leonard	Mucheru	KEN	13.6.78	3	Nik	Nice	9 Jul

Mark	Name		Nat	Born	Pos	Meet	Venue	Date
7:35.98	Assefa	Mezgebu	ETH	19.6.78	8	VD	Bruxelles	24 Aug
7:36.22		B Limo			4	Nik	Nice	9 Jul
7:36.53	Alberto	García	ESP	22.2.71	9	VD	Bruxelles	24 Aug
7:36.66	Mark	Bett	KEN	22.12.76	1	GP II	Rieti	2 Sep
7:36.70		Goumri			5	Nik	Nice	9 Jul
7:36.74		Kipkosgei			5	Athl	Lausanne	4 Jul
7:37.38		García			2	GP II	Rieti	2 Sep
7:37.85		El Ghazi			3	GP II	Rieti	2 Sep
7:38.26		Kipkosgei			1	BrGP	London (CP)	22 Jul
7:38.30	Tom	Nyariki	KEN	27.9.71	7	Herc	Monaco	20 Jul
7:38.37	Ismaïl	Sghyr	FRA	16.3.72	6	Nik	Nice	9 Jul
	(31/20)							
7:38.57	Rachid	Chékhémani	FRA	1.10.73	8	Herc	Monaco	20 Jul
7:38.78	Mohamed	Khaldi	ALG	3.5.75	5	GP II	Rieti	2 Sep
7:38.83	Mustapha	Essaïd	FRA	20.1.70	9	Herc	Monaco	20 Jul
7:39.17	Philip	Mosima	KEN	2.1.77	10	Herc	Monaco	20 Jul
7:39.22	Jaouad	Gharib	MAR	22.5.72	7	Nik	Nice	9 Jul
7:39.45	Tim	Broe	USA	20.6.77	7	Athl	Lausanne	4 Jul
7:39.59	Million	Wolde	ETH	17.3.79	10	VD	Bruxelles	24 Aug
7:40.30	Abraham	Chebii	KEN	23.12.79	8	Athl	Lausanne	4 Jul
7:40.64	Bob	Kennedy	USA	18.8.70	3	GP	Palo Alto	9 Jun
7:40.67	Felix	Limo	KEN	22.8.80	6	GP II	Rieti	2 Sep
	(30)							
7:40.69	James	Getanda	KEN-J	5.7.82	4	BrGP	London (CP)	22 Jul
7:40.77	Marius	Bakken	NOR	27.3.78	13	VD	Bruxelles	24 Aug
7:41.03	Mohammed	Mourhit	BEL	10.10.70	14	VD	Bruxelles	24 Aug
7:41.35	Craig	Mottram	AUS	18.6.80	1		Sydney	16 Feb
7:41.83	Benjamin	Maiyo	KEN	6.10.78	4	GP	Palo Alto	9 Jun
7:41.97	Mohamed Saïd	El Wardi	MAR	19.4.72	9	Nik	Nice	9 Jul
7:42.14	Paul	Koech	KEN	10.11.81	8	GP II	Rieti	2 Sep
7:42.55	Hudson	de Souza	BRA	25.2.77	10	Nik	Nice	9 Jul
7:43.07	Sergey	Lebed	UKR	15.7.75	10	Athl	Lausanne	4 Jul
7:43.36	José	Ríos	ESP	15.3.74	11	Nik	Nice	9 Jul
	(40)							
7:43.76	Daniel	Komen	KEN	17.5.76	4	GP	Doha	18 May
7:43.82	David	Kimani	KEN	28.2.78	11	Athl	Lausanne	4 Jul
7:44.36	Robert	Kipchumba	KEN-J	24.2.84	12	Athl	Lausanne	4 Jul
7:44.56	Enrique	Molina	ESP	25.2.68	12	Nik	Nice	9 Jul
7:44.72	Réda	Benzine	ALG	19.4.71	13	Athl	Lausanne	4 Jul
7:44.94	Pius	Muli	KEN-J	15.12.82	1		Lignano	21 Jul
7:45.21+	Martin	Keino	KEN	20.6.72	1+	WK	Zürich	17 Aug
7:45.40	Daniel	Gachara	KEN	19.12.72	5	GP	Palo Alto	9 Jun
7:45.41	Wolfram	Müller	GER	8.7.81	6	ISTAF	Berlin	31 Aug
7:45.47	Samir	Moussaoui	MAR	15.5.75	9	GP II	Rieti	2 Sep
	(50)							
7:45.60	Gordon	Mugi	KEN	27.11.81	2		Lignano	21 Jul
7:46.03	Stephen	Cherono	KEN-J	15.10.82	2		Sydney	16 Feb
7:46.03	Richard	Geemi	KEN	23.8.73	3		Lignano	21 Jul
7:46.60	Girma	Tola	ETH	13.10.75	6	GP	Doha	18 May
7:46.79	Isaac	Viciosa	ESP	26.12.69	10	GP II	Rieti	2 Sep
7:47.0+	Charles	Kamathi	KEN	18.5.78	3	in 5km	Roma	29 Jun
7:47.14	Marco	Mazza	ITA	25.6.77	11	GP II	Rieti	2 Sep
7:47.30	Alan	Culpepper	USA	15.9.72	6	GP	Palo Alto	9 Jun
7:47.63	Abdi	Abdirahman	USA	1.1.77	7	GP	Palo Alto	9 Jun
7:47.84	Michael	Power	AUS	9.5.76	5	GP II	Helsinki	14 Jun
	(60)							
7:47.89	Jackson	Koech	KEN	79	1		Xalapa	11 Nov
7:48.02	Matt	Lane	USA	5.9.77	8	GP	Palo Alto	9 Jun
7:48.47	William	Kalya	KEN	4.8.74	5	FBK	Hengelo	4 Jun
7:48.65	Mohamed	Yagoub	SUD	2.9.77	8	GP	Doha	18 May
7:48.7	Abdelhaq	Abdellah	MAR	13.8.68	2		Barletta	6 Sep
7:48.74	Saïd	Bérioui	MAR	3.6.75	8	FBK	Hengelo	4 Jun
7:48.90	Albert	Chepkurui	KEN	4.4.81	9	GP	Palo Alto	9 Jun
7:49.02	Ricardo	Fernández	ESP	7.5.74	12	GP II	Rieti	2 Sep
7:49.2+	Evans	Rutto	KEN	8.4.78	8	in 5km	Athína	11 Jun
7:49+ ?e	Driss	El Himer	FRA	4.4.74		in 5km	Roma	29 Jun
	(70)							

Mark	Name		Nat	Born	Date
7:50.39	Simone	Zanon	ITA	30.5.75	2 Sep
7:50.41	Kipkirui	Misoi	KEN	23.10.78	30 May
7:50.75	Ralf	Assmus	GER	28.1.77	31 Aug
7:50.91	Stephen	Kipkorir	KEN	24.10.70	16 Jun
7:51.0	David	Galván	MEX	6.4.76	29 May
7:51.10	Joseph	Kosgei	KEN	74	31 May
7:51.34	Rudiger	Stenzel	GER	16.4.68	30 May
7:51.35	Lofti	Türki	TUN	6.3.75	16 Jun

Mark	Name		Nat	Born	Date
7:51.61	Tom	Van Hooste	BEL	23.9.72	4 Jun
7:51.75	Michael	Gottschalk	GER	22.6.72	30 May
7:51.93	Simon	Maunder	NZL	20.8.72	16 Feb
7:52.06	David	Tuwei	KEN	22.2.79	14 Jun
7:52.09	Dennis	Jensen	DEN	11.9.69	4 Jun
7:52.14	Moses	Kigen	KEN	22.4.73	3 Jul
7:52.21	Joshua	Killy	KEN	74	16 Jun
7:52.26	Driss	Maazouzi	FRA	15.10.69	24 Jun
7:52.33	Ivan	Geshko	UKR	19.8.79	8 Jun
7:52.47	Josphat	Boit	KEN-J	83	3 Jul
7:52.59	Andrés	Díaz	ESP	12.7.69	24 Jun
7:52.70	Mario	Kröckert	GER	2.3.78	30 May
7:53.29	Blair	Martin	NZL	25.4.75	16 Feb
7:53.45	Tom	Compernolle	BEL	13.11.75	4 Jun
7:53.52 ?	Paul	Koech	KEN	25.6.69	3 Jul
7:53.75	Tadesse	Kebede	ETH	81	3 Jun
7:54.10	Michael	Openshaw	GBR	8.4.72	20 May
7:54.19	Michael	May	GER	21.8.79	30 May
7:54.51	Gennaro	Di Napoli	ITA	5.3.68	8 Jun
7:54.76	Kamiel	Maase	NED	20.10.71	9 Sep
7:54.81	Samuli	Vasala	FIN	29.11.76	22 Aug
7:54.88	John	Henwood	NZL	30.8.72	17 Feb
7:54.90	Luís	Feiteira	POR	21.4.73	16 Jun
7:54.92	Stephen	Rerimoi	KEN	22.12.73	22 Jul
7:54.95	Michal	Bartoszak	POL	21.6.70	8 Jun
7:54.97	Cyrus	Kataron	KEN-J	16.5.82	4 Jun
	(104)				

Indoors

Mark	Name		Nat	Born	Pos	Meet	Venue	Date
7:36.85+	Hicham	El Guerrouj	MAR	14.9.74	1+	in 2M	Gent	23 Feb
7:37.74		El Guerrouj			1	WI	Lisboa	11 Mar
7:37.99	Million	Wolde	ETH	17.3.79	1	Spark	Stuttgart	4 Feb
7:38.48	Girma	Tola	ETH	13.10.75	2	Spark	Stuttgart	4 Feb
7:38.94	Mohammed	Mourhit	BEL	10.10.70	2	WI	Lisboa	11 Mar
7:39.52	Rui	Silva	POR	3.8.77	4	Spark	Stuttgart	4 Feb
7:42.68	Bouabdellah	Tahri	FRA	20.12.78	7	Spark	Stuttgart	4 Feb
7:43.1	Daniel	Komen	KEN	17.5.76	4+	Euro	Birmingham	18 Feb
7:43.59	Roberto	García	ESP	20.8.75	2		Sevilla	3 Feb
7:44.08	John	Mayock	GBR	26.10.70	4	WI	Lisboa	11 Mar
7:45.52	Bernard	Lagat	KEN	12.12.74	6	WI	Lisboa	11 Mar
7:47.86	Günther	Weidlinger	AUT	5.4.78	2		Wien	12 Feb
7:48.26	Yusef	El Nasri	ESP	28.7.79	3		Dortmund	11 Feb
7:48.46	Daniel	Zegeye	ETH	13.3.79	2		Boston (R)	4 Feb
7:48.66	Saïd	Bérioui	MAR	3.6.75	2+	Euro	Gent	23 Feb
7:48.76	Jan	Fitschen	GER	2.5.77	1		Erfurt	2 Feb
7:48.79	Jonathan	Riley	USA	29.12.78	4		Boston (R)	4 Feb

Mark	Name		Nat	Born	Date
7:50.11	Jesús	España	ESP	21.8.78	3 Feb
7:50.39	Kamal	Boulahfane	ALG	1.7.76	12 Feb
7:50.67	Antonio	Jiménez	ESP	18.2.77	3 Feb
7:50.7	Kevin	Sullivan	CAN	20.3.74	18 Feb
7:51.08	Anacleto	Jiménez	ESP	24.2.67	3 Feb
7:51.20	Brad	Hauser	USA	28.3.77	4 Feb
7:51.87	Yousef	Baba	MAR	7.8.79	27 Jan
7:52.73	Carsten	Schütz	GER	28.8.75	2 Feb
7:52.75	Vyacheslav	Shabunin	RUS	27.9.69	27 Jan
7:52.76	Adil	El Kaouch	MAR	1.1.79	27 Jan
7:53.13	Youcef	Allem	FRA	16.11.69	17 Feb
7:53.44	Eric	Dubus	FRA	28.2.66	17 Feb
7:53.98	Christian	Knoblich	GER	1.10.76	11 Feb
7:54.31	Carsten	Eich	GER	9.1.70	2 Feb
7:54.87	Fouad	Chouki	FRA	1.10.78	2 Feb
7:54.95	Brian	Baker	USA	8.6.70	10 Feb

Drugs disqualification

Mark	Name		Nat	Born	Pos	Meet	Venue	Date
7:47.29i	Dieter	Baumann ¶	GER	9.2.65	(1)	NC	Dortmund	25 Feb
7:52.5+e+	Ali	Saïdi Sief ¶	ALG	15.3.78	(2)	in 5km	Edmonton	10 Aug

JUNIORS

See main list for top 5 juniors. 10 performances by 5 men to 7:48.0. Additional marks and further juniors:

	Mark	Pos	Meet	Venue	Date	Mark	Pos	Venue	Date
Bekele	7:43.28	2	APM	Hengelo	4 Jun	7:46.71	2	Helsinki	14 Jun
	7:45.05	4	ISTAF	Berlin	31 Aug				
Getanda	7:46.86	2		Newcastle	3 Feb				
Cherono	7:46.23	1		Newcastle	3 Feb				

Mark	Name		Nat	Born	Pos	Meet	Venue	Date
7:52.47	Josphat	Boit	KEN	83	3		Västerås	3 Jul
7:54.97	Cyrus	Kataron	KEN	16.5.82	11	FBK	Hengelo	4 Jun
7:55.20	Muneria	Kiplimo	KEN	28.8.83	1		Pergine Valsugana	20 Jul
7:55.82	Markos	Geneti	ETH	.84	1	WY	Debrecen	14 Jul
7:56.95	David	Kilel	KEN	21.5.84	2	WY	Debrecen	14 Jul
7:57.11	Ezekiel	Kemboi	KEN	.82	2		Torino	9 Jun
7:57.71	James	Kwalia	KEN	12.6.84	3	WY	Debrecen	14 Jul
7:59.57	Ali Abdalla	Afringi	ERI	2.11.82	4		Torino	9 Jun
8:05.31	Yassine	Mandour	MAR	21.1.85	4	WY	Debrecen	14 Jul
8:08.12	Nicholas	Kemboi	KEN	25.11.83	1		Lisboa	26 May

2 MILES

Mark	Name		Nat	Born	Pos	Meet	Venue	Date
8:27.2+	Mebrahtom	Keflezighi	USA	5.5.75		in 5km	Eugene	27 May

Indoors

Mark	Name		Nat	Born	Pos	Meet	Venue	Date
8:09.89i	Hicham	El Guerrouj	MAR	14.9.74	1	Euro	Gent	23 Feb
8:11.85i	Hailu	Mekonnen	ETH	4.4.80	1	Euro	Birmingham	18 Feb
8:12.10i	Million	Wolde	ETH	17.3.79	2	Euro	Birmingham	18 Feb
8:12.80i	Girma	Tola	ETH	13.10.75	3	Euro	Birmingham	18 Feb
8:13.28i	Paul	Bitok	KEN	26.6.70	4	Euro	Birmingham	18 Feb
8:16.89i	Daniel	Komen	KEN	17.5.76	5	Euro	Birmingham	18 Feb
8:21.16	Saïd	Bérioui	MAR	3.6.75	3	Euro	Gent	23 Feb
8:21.33	Ismaïl	Sghyr	FRA	16.3.72	6	Euro	Birmingham	18 Feb
8:21.57	Sergey	Lebed	UKR	15.7.75	7	Euro	Birmingham	18 Feb
8:23.67	Kevin	Sullivan	CAN	20.3.74	8	Euro	Birmingham	18 Feb

Mark	Name		Nat	Born	Pos	Meet	Venue	Date
8:25.11	Mohamed Saïd	El Wardi	MAR	19.4.72	4	Euro	Gent	23 Feb
Drugs Disqualification								
8:28.5+	Ali	Saïdi Sief ¶	ALG	15.3.78	1	in 5km	Edmonton	10 Aug
		JUNIORS						
8:31.77i	Hassan	Mourhit	MAR	2.1.82	5	Euro	Gent	23 Feb

5000 METRES

Mark	Name		Nat	Born	Pos	Meet	Venue	Date
12:56.72	Richard	Limo	KEN	18.11.80	1	WK	Zürich	17 Aug
12:58.57	Hailu	Mekonnen	ETH	4.4.80	1	GGala	Roma	29 Jun
12:58.72	Mark	Bett	KEN	22.12.76	2	WK	Zürich	17 Aug
12:59.34	Sammy	Kipketer	KEN	29.9.81	1	GP	Athína	11 Jun
12:59.53	Benjamin	Limo	KEN	23.8.74	2	GGala	Roma	29 Jun
12:59.60		B Limo			2	GP	Athína	11 Jun
12:59.94		Kipketer			3	GGala	Roma	29 Jun
12:59.97	John	Kibowen	KEN	21.4.69	3	GP	Athína	11 Jun
13:00.10	Paul	Bitok	KEN	26.6.70	1	Bisl	Oslo	13 Jul
13:00.32		R Limo			4	GGala	Roma	29 Jun
13:00.36	Abiyote	Abate	ETH	20.11.80	5	GGala	Roma	29 Jun
13:00.69		Mekonnen			3	WK	Zürich	17 Aug
13:00.77		R Limo			1	WCh	Edmonton	10 Aug
13:00.86	Assefa	Mezgebu	ETH	19.6.78	4	GP	Athína	11 Jun
13:00.98		Bitok			4	WK	Zürich	17 Aug
13:01.08		Abate			5	WK	Zürich	17 Aug
13:01.64	Ismaïl	Sghyr (10)	FRA	16.3.72	6	GGala	Roma	29 Jun
13:01.88		B Limo			2	Bisl	Oslo	13 Jul
13:01.98	Daniel	Komen	KEN	17.5.76	5	GP	Athína	11 Jun
13:02.01		Mekonnen			6	GP	Athína	11 Jun
13:02.17	Million	Wolde	ETH	17.3.79	7	GGala	Roma	29 Jun
13:02.25	Luke	Kipkosgei	KEN	27.11.75	1	GP	Saint-Denis	6 Jul
13:02.26		Wolde			6	WK	Zürich	17 Aug
13:02.54	Alberto	García	ESP	22.2.71	8	GGala	Roma	29 Jun
13:02.88		Kibowen			3	Bisl	Oslo	13 Jul
13:02.97		Kibowen			7	WK	Zürich	17 Aug
13:03.47		Wolde			2	WCh	Edmonton	10 Aug
13:03.48		Kipkosgei			4	Bisl	Oslo	13 Jul
13:03.60	Tom	Nyariki	KEN	27.9.71	2	GP	Saint-Denis	6 Jul
13:03.60	Abderrahim	Goumri	MAR	21.5.76	3	GP	Saint-Denis	6 Jul
	(30/16)							
13:05.16	Charles	Kamathi	KEN	18.5.78	10	GGala	Roma	29 Jun
13:05.43	Benjamin	Maiyo	KEN	6.10.78	4	GP	Saint-Denis	6 Jul
13:05.44	Mohammed	Amine	MAR	25.5.76	11	GGala	Roma	29 Jun
13:06.29	Paul	Kosgei	KEN	22.4.78	2	DNG	Stockholm	17 Jul
	(20)							
13:08.32	Mark	Carroll	IRL	15.1.72	7	Bisl	Oslo	13 Jul
13:09.19	Marius	Bakken	NOR	27.3.78	8	Bisl	Oslo	13 Jul
13:09.31	Zakayo	Ngatho	KEN	18.3.78	1		Kanazawa	30 Sep
13:09.63	Mohammed	Mourhit	BEL	10.10.70	4	DNG	Stockhom	17 Jul
13:09.83	José	Ríos	ESP	15.3.74	13	GGala	Roma	29 Jun
13:10.29	David	Kimani	KEN	28.2.78	2	NA	Heusden	14 Jul
13:11.66	Julius	Gitahi	KEN	29.4.78	2	GP	Osaka	12 May
13:12.53	Abraham	Chebii	KEN	23.12.79	9	Bisl	Oslo	13 Jul
13:13.33	Kenenisa	Bekele	ETH-J	13.6.82	2	GP II	Sevilla	8 Jun
13:14.51	Sergey	Lebed	UKR	15.7.75	3		Nürnberg	17 Jun
	(30)							
13:14.94	Leonard	Mucheru	KEN	13.6.78	2	Pre	Eugene	27 May
13:15.10	Driss	El Himer	FRA	4.4.74	15	GGala	Roma	29 Jun
13:15.92	Simon	Maina Munyi	KEN	18.3.78	3	GP	Osaka	12 May
13:15.94	Isaac	Viciosa	ESP	26.12.69	11	Bisl	Oslo	13 Jul
13:16.42	Felix	Limo	KEN	22.8.80	7	DNG	Stockholm	17 Jul
13:16.78	Joseph	Kosgei	KEN	74	12	Bisl	Oslo	13 Jul
13:17.00	William	Kalya	KEN	4.8.74	5	GP II	Sevilla	8 Jun
13:17.06	James Kimutai	Koskei	KEN	23.11.68	3	NA	Heusden	14 Jul
13:17.12	Josphat	Boit	KEN-J	83	13	Bisl	Oslo	13 Jul
13:17.40	Gordon	Mugi	KEN	27.11.81	14	Bisl	Oslo	13 Jul
	(40)							
13:17.51	Bob	Kennedy	USA	18.8.70	16	Bisl	Oslo	13 Jul
13:18.20	Enrique	Molina	ESP	25.2.68	17	Bisl	Oslo	13 Jul
13:18.71	Albert	Chepkurui	KEN	4.4.81	13	WK	Zürich	17 Aug
13:19.58	John Cheruiyot	Korir	KEN	13.12.81	5	NA	Heusden	14 Jul

Mark	Name		Nat	Born	Pos	Meet	Venue	Date
13:19.69	Jaouad	Gharib	MAR	22.5.72	18	Bisl	Oslo	13 Jul
13:19.76	Robert	Kipchumba	KEN-J	24.2.84	2		San Sebastián	18 Aug
13:19.82	Abdi	Abdirahman	USA	1.1.77	6	NA	Heusden	14 Jul
13:19.86	Kamiel	Maase	NED	20.10.71	7	NA	Heusden	14 Jul
13:20.13	Tom	Compernolle	BEL	13.11.75	8	NA	Heusden	14 Jul
13:20.14	Rachid	Chékhémani	FRA	1.10.73	8	GP	Saint-Denis	6 Jul
	(50)							
13:20.32	Muneria	Kiplimo	KEN-J	28.8.83	9	NA	Heusden	14 Jul
13:20.71	Samir	Moussaoui	ALG	15.5.75	10	NA	Heusden	14 Jul
13:21.18	Ahmed Ibrahim	Warsama	QAT	4.2.66	3		San Sebastián	18 Aug
13:21.88	Mohamed Saïd	El Wardi	MAR	19.4.72	18	GGala	Roma	29 Jun
13:22.12	Satoshi	Irifune	JPN	14.12.75	11	NA	Heusden	14 Jul
13:22.29	Adam	Goucher	USA	18.2.75	14	WK	Zürich	17 Aug
13:22.32	Khoudir	Aggoune	ALG	5.1.81	1		Sotteville	12 Jul
13:22.46	Fabián	Roncero	ESP	19.10.70	4		San Sebastián	18 Aug
13:22.85	Francis	Kiprop	KEN		12	NA	Heusden	14 Jul
13:23.15	Hélder	Ornelas	POR	6.5.74	5		San Sebastián	18 Aug
	(60)							
13:23.16	Mebrahtom	Keflezighi	USA	5.5.75	5	Pre	Eugene	27 May
13:23.56	Michael	Power	AUS	9.5.76	4	GP	Osaka	12 May
13:23.59	James	Getanda	KEN-J	5.7.82	1	GP II	Melbourne	1 Mar
13:23.68	Mauricio	Díaz	CHI	7.8.68	13	NA	Heusden	14 Jul
13:23.94	Craig	Mottram	AUS	18.6.80	1		Solihull	23 Jun
13:24.13	Tim	Broe	USA	20.6.77	1		Palo Alto	4 May
13:24.16	Saïd	Bérioui	MAR	3.6.75	3		Milano	6 Jun
13:24.27	Pius	Muli	KEN-J	15.12.82	3		Rovereto	29 Aug
13:24.44	Mike	Openshaw	GBR	8.4.72	15	NA	Heusden	14 Jul
13:24.48	Patrick	Ivuti	KEN	30.6.78	4		Milano	6 Jun
	(70)							
13:24.63	Karl	Keska	GBR	7.5.72	16	NA	Heusden	14 Jul
13:25.05	Marco Antonio	Rufo	ESP	9.3.68	17	NA	Heusden	14 Jul
13:25.07	Yonas	Kifle	ERI	24.3.77	7		San Sebastián	18 Aug
13:25.25	Obed	Mutanya	ZAM	10.8.81	8		San Sebastián	18 Aug
13:25.38	Matt	Lane	USA	5.9.77	2		Palo Alto	4 May
13:25.59	Wilberforce Kapkeny	Talel	KEN	10.1.80	9		San Sebastián	18 Aug
13:26.17	Jackson	Koech	KEN	79	1		Victoria	25 May
13:26.26	Daniele	Caimmi	ITA	17.12.72	5		Milano	6 Jun
13:26.36	Nicholas	Kemboi	KEN-J	25.11.83	1		Maia	14 Jul
13:26.46	Daniel	Gachara	KEN	19.12.72	19	GGala	Roma	29 Jun
	(80)							
13:26.46	Dennis	Jensen	DEN	11.9.69	18	NA	Heusden	14 Jul
13:26.50	Philip	Mosima	KEN	2.1.77	8	DNG	Stockholm	17 Jul
13:26.68	Ricardo	Fernández	ESP	7.5.74	20	GGala	Roma	29 Jun
13:26.94	José Manuel	Martínez	ESP	22.10.71	10		San Sebastián	18 Aug
13:27.09	Mohamed	Yagoub	SUD	2.9.77	2		Solihull	23 Jun
13:27.38	Mustapha	Essaïd	FRA	20.1.70	10	DNG	Stockholm	17 Jul
13:27.44	Réda	Benzine	ALG	19.4.71	11	DNG	Stockholm	17 Jul
13:28.25	Evans	Rutto	KEN	8.4.78	8	GP	Athína	11 Jun
13:28.94	George	Okworo	KEN	12.5.79	2		Victoria	25 May
13:29.15	Jeff	Schiebler	CAN	1.6.73	2		Palo Alto	31 Mar
	(90)							
13:29.32	Shadrack	Hoff	RSA	19.5.73	1		Stellenbosch	30 Mar
13:29.66	Alan	Culpepper	USA	15.9.72	2	NC	Eugene	22 Jun
13:29.8+	Salim	Kipsang	KEN	22.12.79	6	in 10k	Bruxelles	24 Aug
13:29.86	Abdelhak	El Gorche	MAR	20.7.74	12	DNG	Stockholm	17 Jul
13:29.90	David	Tuwei	KEN	22.2.79	1	Sule	Tartu	19 Jun
13:30.02	Raymond	Yator	KEN	7.4.81	2		Melbourne	1 Mar
13:30.32	James	Ndungu	KEN	30.4.79	3		Shizuoka	3 May
13:30.35	Julius	Ndiritu	KEN	76	2		Stellenbosch	30 Mar
13:30.54	Bernard	Lagat	KEN	12.12.74	1		Walnut	20 Apr
13:30.56	Matthew	O'Dowd	GBR	15.4.76	3		Solihull	23 Jun
	(100)							

Mark	Name		Nat	Born	Date
13:30.59	John	Henwood	NZL	30.8.72	1 Mar
13:30.64	Patrick	Nthiwa	KEN-J	82	30 Mar
13:31.16	James	Wainaina	KEN	16.6.81	10 Jun
13:31.28	Eduardo	Vargas	ESP	13.11.76	17 Jun
13:31.88	Bolota	Asmerom	ERI	12.10.78	20 Apr
13:31.94	Boaz	Kipsang/Cheboiywo	KEN		25 May
13:32.02	Solomon	Khambule	RSA	11.6.76	30 Mar
13:32.61	Simone	Zanon	ITA	30.5.75	29 Jun
13:32.77	Solomon	Wachira	KEN	5.11.76	3 May
13:33.05	El Hassan	Lahssini	FRA	1.1.75	17 Jun
13:33.05	Benson	Barus	KEN	4.7.80	13 Jul
13:33.51	Loïc	Letellier	FRA	1.10.76	8 Jun
13:33.55	Brahim	Jabbour	MAR	2.10.70	6 Jun
13:33.64	Barnabas	Kipkoech	KEN		14 Jul
13:33.86	Jan	Fitschen	GER	2.5.77	6 Jun
13:34.12	Marco	Mazza	ITA	25.6.77	6 Jun
13:34.48	Teodoro	Vega	MEX	14.7.76	27 May
13:35.07	Mickaël	Thomas	FRA	23.3.71	8 Jun
13:35.62	Janne	Holmén	FIN	26.9.77	15 Jul
13:35.68	Nick	Rogers	USA	2.5.75	22 Jun

Mark	Name		Nat	Born	Date
13:35.80	Andrea	Arlati	ITA	7.5.70	6 Jun
13:36.30	Robert	Denmark	GBR	23.11.68	23 Jun
13:36.51	Nasser	Suleiman	QAT	20.12.79	14 Jul
13:36.56	Rui	Silva	POR	3.8.77	17 Jun
13:36.79	Ray	Hughes	USA	9.5.75	14 Jul
13:37.17	Glen	Stewart	GBR	7.12.70	23 Jun
13:37.24	Takashi	Maeda	JPN	3.10.77	14 Jul
13:37.56	Mario	Kröckert	GER	2.3.78	6 Jun
13:37.63	Jason	Hubbard	USA	20.1.75	20 Apr
13:37.63	Iván	Hierro	ESP	14.2.78	18 Aug
13:37.80	Yasunori	Uchitomi	JPN	24.10.72	14 Jul
13:37.98	Mikhail	Yeginov	RUS	9.8.76	14 Jul
13:38.16	Greg	Jimmerson	USA	1.2.75	14 Jul
13:38.39	Franklyn	Sanchez	USA-J	6.3.82	31 Mar
13:38.65	Alfred	Rugema	BDI	20.4.80	31 Mar
13:38.87	Toshinari	Takaoka	JPN	24.9.70	12 May
13:38.88	Sébastien	Boiton	FRA	14.11.76	8 Jun
13:38.97	Lee	Troop	AUS	22.3.73	1 Mar
13:39.07	Sander	Schutgens	NED	31.12.75	14 Jul
13:39.08	Alejandro	Suárez	MEX	30.11.80	25 May
13.39.2	Ahmed Ibrahim	Baday	MAR	12.1.79	5 May
13:39.27	Khalid	Elamri	MAR	79	17 Jun
13:39.28	Hosea	Kogo	KEN	11.8.72	17 Jun
13:39.77	David	Kariuki	KEN	23.5.80	3 May
13:40.05	Samuli	Vasala	FIN	29.11.76	22 Jul
13:40.07	Allen	Graffin	GBR	20.12.77	12 Jun
13:40.13	Jonathan	Riley	USA	29.12.78	22 Jun
13:40.16		Zheng Kai	CHN	27.2.80	23 Nov
13:40.41	Samuel	Kabil	KEN-J	6.6.83	18 Jan
13:40.44	Daisuke	Isomatsu	JPN	17.12.73	14 Jul
13:40.51	Pablo	Olmedo	MEX	8.5.75	27 May
13:40.54	Sean	Kaley	CAN	26.2.75	4 May
13:40.61	David	Bazzi	USA	29.10.77	20 Apr
13:40.64	Takayuki	Matsumiya	JPN	21.2.80	26 May
13:40.67	Matt	Downin	USA	10.2.77	14 Jul
13:40.78	Peter	Sherry	USA	22.8.68	22 Jun
13:40.82	Claes	Nyberg	SWE	3.3.71	14 Jul
13:40.95		Kang Yanwei	CHN	23.2.78	23 Nov
13:41.11	Kenji	Noguchi	JPN	23.2.75	14 Jul
13:41.17	Andre	Williams	USA	11.10.71	22 Jun
13:41.44		Li Zhuhong	CHN-J	22.10.83	23 Nov
13:41.6	Nobuya	Matsunaga	JPN	8.11.74	6 Oct
13:41.69	Brian	Baker	USA	8.6.70	22 Jun
13:41.76	Wolfram	Müller	GER	8.7.81	9 May
13:41.98	Chad	Johnson	USA	20.4.76	22 Jun
	(165)				

Drugs Disqualification

Mark	Name		Nat	Born	Pos	Meet	Venue	Date
13:02.16	Ali	Saïdi Sief ¶	ALG	15.3.78	(2)	WCh	Edmonton	10 Aug
13:26.33	Alene	Emere ¶	ETH-J	5.3.82	1	JPN Ch	Tokyo	10 Jun

JUNIORS

See main list for top 7 juniors. 12 performances by men to 13:28.0. Additional marks and further juniors:

Bekele 13:13.44 6 GP Saint-Denis 6 Jul; 13:15.39 16 GGala Roma 29 Jun
13:15.22 4 Nürnberg 17 Jun; 13:25.86 19 Bisl Oslo 13 Jul
Kipchumba 13:22.95 2 Sotteville 12 Jul
Drugs dq: Emere 13:26.33 and 13:27.40 1 Nobeoka 26 May

Mark	Name		Nat	Born	Pos	Meet	Venue	Date
13:30.64	Patrick	Nthiwa	KEN	82	3		Stellenbosch	30 Mar
13:38.39	Franklyn	Sanchez	USA	6.3.82	3		Palo Alto	31 Mar
13:40.41	Samuel	Kabil	KEN	6.6.83	1		Rifu	18 Jan
13:41.44		Li Zhuhong	CHN	22.10.83	3	NG	Guangzhou	23 Nov
13:42.48	Shadrack	Kosgei	KEN	.84	1		Brunswick	7 Jul
13:44.26	James	Kwalia	KEN	12.6.84	1		Zanzibar	28 Oct
13:44.70	Dathan	Ritzenheim	USA	30.12.82	11	NC	Eugene	22 Jun
13:47.05	Johnson	Muiruri	KEN	.83	6		Stellenbosch	30 Mar
13:47.1	Abdelaziz	Al-Ameeri	QAT	82	2		Meknès	9 Jun
	13:47.19				6		Villeneuve d'Ascq	17 Jun
13:48.6	Martin	Toroitich	UGA	10.8.83	1	Afr-J	Réduit	18 Aug
13:49.14		Dou Zhaobo	CHN	23.9.83	5	NG	Guangzhou	23 Nov
13:49.38	John	Kariuki	KEN	.86	1		Yokohama	2 Dec
13:49.64	Matt	Tegenkamp (20)	USA	19.1.82	12	NC	Eugene	22 Jun
13:49.9	Solomon	Busienei	KEN	10.1.84	2	Afr-J	Réduit	18 Aug

10,000 METRES

Mark	Name		Nat	Born	Pos	Meet	Venue	Date
27:04.20	Abraham	Chebii	KEN	23.12.79	1		Palo Alto	4 May
27:07.55	Benjamin	Maiyo	KEN	6.10.78	2		Palo Alto	4 May
27:12.37	Luke	Kipkosgei	KEN	27.11.75	3		Palo Alto	4 May
27:13.98	Mebrahtom	Keflezighi	USA	5.5.75	4		Palo Alto	4 May
27:22.30	Assefa	Mezgebu	ETH	19.6.78	1	FBK	Hengelo	4 Jun
27:22.58	Charles	Kamathi	KEN	18.5.78	2	FBK	Hengelo	4 Jun
27:22.84	Girma	Tola	ETH	13.10.75	3	FBK	Hengelo	4 Jun
27:24.68	Mark	Bett	KEN	22.12.76	1	VD	Bruxelles	24 Aug
27:25.27	Richard	Limo	KEN	18.11.80	4	FBK	Hengelo	4 Jun
27:25.55	Robert	Kipchumba (10)	KEN-J	24.2.84	2	VD	Bruxelles	24 Aug
27:26.01	Abderrahim	Goumri	MAR	21.5.76	1	Odlozil	Praha	18 Jun
27:26.55		Kamathi			3	VD	Bruxelles	24 Aug
27:26.86	Felix	Limo	KEN	22.8.80	4	VD	Bruxelles	24 Aug
27:29.09	Gordon	Mugi	KEN	27.11.81	5	VD	Bruxelles	24 Aug
27:29.51	Jaouad	Gharib	MAR	22.5.72	2	Odlozil	Praha	18 Jun
27:33.93	Alan	Culpepper	USA	15.9.72	5		Palo Alto	4 May
27:35.09	Toshinari	Takaoka	JPN	24.9.70	6		Palo Alto	4 May
27:36.01	Jeff	Schiebler	CAN	1.6.73	7		Palo Alto	4 May
27:37.87		Kipchumba			3	Odlozil	Praha	18 Jun
27:38.36	Hendrick	Ramaala	RSA	2.2.72	1		Port Elizabeth	16 Feb
27:38.57	José	Ríos	ESP	15.3.74	1	NC	Mataró	15 Jul
27:45.17	Fabián	Roncero (20)	ESP	19.10.70	2	NC	Mataró	15 Jul

Mark	Name		Nat	Born	Pos	Meet	Venue	Date
27:47.33A		Kamathi			1	NC	Nairobi	23 Jun
27:48.65	Shadrack	Hoff	RSA	19.5.73	2		Port Elizabeth	16 Feb
27:49.34A	John Cheruiyot	Korir	KEN	13.12.81	2	NC	Nairobi	23 Jun
27:49.35		Ríos			1	E Chall	Barakaldo	7 Apr
27:50.3		Gharib			1		Rabat	23 May
27:51.87A	Paul	Kosgei	KEN	22.4.78	3	NC	Nairobi	23 Jun
27:51.87	Khalid	Skah	MAR	29.1.67	6	VD	Bruxelles	24 Aug
27:52.26	William	Kalya	KEN	4.8.74	7	VD	Bruxelles	24 Aug
	(30/25)							
27:53.92	Satoshi	Irifune	JPN	14.12.75	8		Palo Alto	4 May
27:54.25	Marco	Mazza	ITA	25.6.77	3	ESP Ch	Mataró	15 Jul
27:54.41	Haile	Gebrselassie	ETH	18.4.73	3	WCh	Edmonton	8 Aug
27:54.81	José Manuel	Martínez	ESP	22.10.71	4	NC	Mataró	15 Jul
27:55.24	Yibeltal	Admassu	ETH	80	4	WCh	Edmonton	8 Aug
	(30)							
27:56.82	Simon	Maina Munyi	KEN	18.3.78	1A		Hachioji	28 Nov
27:57.23	Habte	Jifar	ETH	29.1.76	6	FBK	Hengelo	4 Jun
27:57.33	Solomon	Wachira	KEN	5.11.76	2A		Hachioji	28 Nov
27:57.5	John	Henwood	NZL	30.8.72	1		Inglewood	10 Mar
28:00.91	Teodoro	Vega	MEX	14.7.76	1	Jerome	Burnaby	3 Jun
28:01.02	Abdi	Abdirahman	USA	1.1.77	9		Palo Alto	4 May
28:01.11	Zakayo	Ngatho	KEN	18.3.78	1		Kobe	22 Apr
28:01.60	Julius	Gitahi	KEN	29.4.78	2		Kobe	22 Apr
28:01.94	Hélder	Ornelas	POR	6.5.74	2	E Chall	Barakaldo	7 Apr
28:02.30	Wilberforce Kapkeny	Talel	KEN	10.1.80	4	Odlozil	Praha	18 Jun
	(40)							
28:02.37	Kamiel	Maase	NED	20.10.71	3	E Chall	Barakaldo	7 Apr
28:03.41	James	Wainaina	KEN	16.6.81	1		Nobeoka	26 May
28:05.43	Daniel	Njenga	KEN	7.5.76	1		Yokohama	30 Apr
28:05.7	Abdelhadi	Habassa	MAR	13.1.76	1		Rabat	27 Jun
28:05.93	James	Ndungu	KEN	30.4.79	4A		Hachioji	28 Nov
28:05.95	Tomoo	Tsubota	JPN	16.6.77	5A		Hachioji	28 Nov
28:06.29	Karl	Keska	GBR	7.5.72	4	E Chall	Barakaldo	7 Apr
28:06.49	Salim	Kipsang	KEN	22.12.79	8	VD	Bruxelles	24 Aug
28:06.86	Albert	Chepkurui	KEN	4.4.81	3	GWG	Brisbane	7 Sep
28:08.92	Simon	Mpholo	RSA	17.8.75	3		Port Elizabeth	16 Feb
	(50)							
28:09.3	Mustapha	Bamouh	MAR	21.12.72	2		Rabat	27 Jun
28:09.3	Ahmed Ibrahim	Baday	MAR	12.1.79	3		Rabat	27 Jun
28:09.32A	Benson	Barus	KEN	4.7.80	5	NC	Nairobi	23 Jun
28:10.14	Weldon	Johnson	USA	24.7.73	1		Montreal (McG)	10 Jul
28:10.79	Teodoro	Cuñado	ESP	13.2.70	8	FBK	Hengelo	4 Jun
28:11.03	Enoch	Skosana	RSA	20.2.74	4		Port Elizabeth	16 Feb
28.12.6	Aïssa	Dghoughi	MAR		4		Rabat	27 Jun
28:12.64	Hiroyuki	Ikegaya	JPN	29.4.75	2rA		Kanazawa	29 Sep
28:13.18	Atsushi	Sato	JPN	8.5.78	3rA		Kanazawa	29 Sep
28:13.63	Takayuki	Matsumiya	JPN	21.2.80	6		Kobe	22 Apr
	(60)							
28:13.83	Kazuo	Ietani	JPN	25.8.75	4rA		Kanazawa	29 Sep
28:14.08	Tomohiro	Seto	JPN	19.10.76	5rA		Kanazawa	29 Sep
28:14.10	Muneria	Kiplimo	KEN-J	28.8.83	6	Odlozil	Praha	18 Jun
28:14.23	Richard	Mavuso	RSA	30.3.78	2	NC	Durban	2 Mar
28:14.45	Laban	Kagika	KEN	17.7.78	6rA		Kanazawa	29 Sep
28:16.17	Kazuhiro	Maeda	JPN	19.4.81	1C		Isahaya	2 Dec
28:17.12	El Hassan	Lahssini	FRA	1.1.75	12	VD	Bruxelles	24 Aug
28:17.36	Pablo	Olmedo	MEX	8.5.75	2	Jerome	Burnaby	3 Jun
28:17.50	Dennis	Jensen	DEN	11.9.69	5	E Chall	Barakaldo	7 Apr
28:17.65	Alejandro	Suárez	MEX	30.11.80	3	Jerome	Burnaby	3 Jun
	(70)							
28:18.19	Susumu	Ichinose	JPN	11.7.75	7rA		Kanazawa	29 Sep
28:18.38	Seamus	Power	IRL	28.11.70	1		Watford	9 Jun
28:19.26	Craig	Mottram	AUS	18.6.80	1	Zat	Melbourne	6 Dec
28:19.81	Hosea	Kogo	KEN	11.8.72	1		Mulhouse	13 Jun
28:20.05	Makoto	Otsu	JPN	3.7.80	2C		Isahaya	2 Dec
28:20.50	Miroslav	Vanko	SVK	14.2.73	9	FBK	Hengelo	4 Jun
28:20.89	Koen	Allaert	BEL	29.9.72	7	E Chall	Barakaldo	7 Apr
28:21.01	Samuel	Kabil	KEN-J	6.6.83	1		Konosu	29 Sep
28:21.38	Stefano	Baldini	ITA	25.5.71	1		Camaiore	27 May
28:21.4	Jonathan	Wyatt	NZL	20.12.72	2		Inglewood	10 Mar
	(80)							
28:22.39	David	Chelule	KEN	7.7.77	13	VD	Bruxelles	24 Aug

Mark	Name		Nat	Born	Pos	Meet	Venue	Date
28:22.54	José Carlos	Adán	ESP	22.7.67	8	E Chall	Barakaldo	7 Apr
28:22.83	David	Kariuki	KEN	23.5.80	9		Kobe	22 Apr
28:23.60	Motsehi	Moeketsane	RSA	2.1.70	5		Port Elizabeth	16 Feb
28:23.84	Janne	Holmén	FIN	26.9.77	14	VD	Bruxelles	24 Aug
28:24.15	Hiroyuki	Ogawa	JPN	17.6.78	2		Konosu	29 Sep
28:24.19	Toyoshi	Ishige	JPN	16.4.75	6A		Hachioji	28 Nov
28:24.31	Toshihiro	Iwasa	JPN	18.5.76	10		Palo Alto	4 May
28:25.18	Naoki	Mishiro	JPN	16.3.77	5	NC	Tokyo	9 Jun
28:25.56	Andrew	Letherby	AUS	19.9.73	11		Palo Alto	4 May
	(90)							
28:25.59	Kazuyoshi	Tokumoto	JPN	22.6.79	1		Yokohama	1 Dec
28:25.77	Rachid	Berradi	ITA	29.8.75	1		Conegliano Veneto	22 Jun
28:26.04	John	Kanyi	KEN	6.9.80	1		Tokyo	28 Sep
28:26.18	Yoshitaka	Iwamizu	JPN	20.6.79	2		Nobeoka	26 May
28:26.54	Takeshi	Hamano	JPN	30.7.74	11		Kobe	22 Apr
28:26.6	Abdellah	Bay	MAR	.75	1		Kokubu	13 Oct
28:26.71	Gert	Thys	RSA	12.11.71	4	NC	Durban	2 Mar
28:26.80	Alan	Bunce	NZL	23.8.67	12		Palo Alto	4 May
28:27.23	Blair	Martin	NZL	25.4.75	2	Zat	Melbourne	6 Dec
28:27.33	Takenori	Oda	JPN	5.12.80	2		Yokohama	1 Dec
	(100)							

Mark	Name		Nat	Born	Date
28:27.84	Toshinari	Suwa	JPN	29.1.77	28 Nov
28:28.05	Masayuki	Kobayashi	JPN	4.4.74	6 May
28:28.10	Samuel	Rongo	KEN	72	4 Jun
28:28.26	James	Kimani	KEN		29 Sep
28:28.29	Yuki	Mori	JPN	8.3.79	2 Dec
28:28.40	Marco	Bartoletti	ITA	7.11.78	22 Jun
28:28.89	Tetsuo	Nishikawa	JPN	14.7.77	28 Nov
28:28.92	John	Yuda	TAN	9.6.79	29 Oct
28:28.97	Matt	Lane	USA	5.9.77	31 Mar
28:29.14	Takashi	Maeda	JPN	3.10.77	1 Dec
28:29.55	Kenjiro	Jitsui	JPN	16.12.68	1 Dec
28:30.20	Yoshinari	Horikawa	JPN	19.6.75	12 May
28:30.27	Clint	Wells	USA	2.5.75	4 May
28:30.71	Naosato	Yoshimura	JPN	5.12.81	1 Dec
28:30.92	Takashi	Matsuyama	JPN	15.1.74	1 Dec
28:31.16	Samuli	Vasala	FIN	29.11.76	1 Sep
28:31.22	Kurao	Umeki	JPN	30.9.75	1 Dec
28:31.27	Tadayuki	Ojima	JPN	22.11.76	12 May
28:31.33	Glyn	Tromans	GBR	17.3.69	9 Jun
28:31.58	Yoji	Yamaguchi	JPN	12.6.75	4 May
28:31.73	Michitaka	Hosokawa	JPN	26.4.76	2 Dec
28:32.09	Hiroshi	Miki	JPN	10.6.75	12 May
28:32.25	Takashi	Horiguchi	JPN	.79	1 Dec
28:32.29	Obed	Mutanya	ZAM	10.8.81	18 May
28:32.44	Koichiro	Nagata	JPN	19.12.78	9 Jun
28:32.5	Lahcen	Benyoussef	MAR		27 Jun
28:32.55	Keith	Kelly	IRL	1.10.77	20 Apr
28:32.75	Masakazu	Fujiwara	JPN	6.3.81	22 Apr
28:33.55	Yuki	Nakamura	JPN	21.6.81	1 Dec
28:33.60	Marcel	Versteeg	NED	20.8.65	14 Apr
28:33.71	Jonathan	Riley	USA	29.12.78	31 Mar
28:34.15	Daisuke	Isomatsu	JPN	17.12.73	19 May
28:34.16	Masayoshi	Koide	JPN	6.11.72	1 Dec
28:34.54	David	Bazzi	USA	29.10.77	31 Mar
28:34.54	Tatsumi	Morimasa	JPN	3.4.76	28 Nov
28:34.6	Robbie	Johnston	NZL	21.8.67	10 Mar
28:34.95	Remco	Kortenoeven	NED	22.6.72	14 Apr
28:35.20	Haile	Mesfin	ETH	81	4 Jun
28:35.50	Toshihide	Kato	JPN	4.7.73	29 Sep
28:35.72	Terukazu	Omori	JPN	3.9.79	28 Nov
28:35.91	Aloys	Nizigama	BDI	18.6.66	7 Sep
28:35.97	Masatoshi	Ibata	JPN	20.8.72	1 Dec
28:36.35	Ryoji	Matsushita	JPN	7.11.80	1 Dec
28:36.89	Shinji	Matsumura	JPN	21.5.72	1 Dec
28:36.9	Abdelhak	El Gorche	MAR	20.7.74	23 May
28:37.27	Michael	Aish	NZL	24.7.76	4 May
28:37.3	Craig	Kirkwood	NZL	18.10.74	10 Mar
28:37.60	Daisuke	Chuma	JPN	23.8.75	13 Oct
28:37.68	Atsushi	Fujita	JPN	6.11.76	1 Dec
28:37.88	Masayoshi	Kuroda	JPN	22.11.81	1 Dec
28:38.74	Ken-ichiro	Setoguchi	JPN	12.12.80	20 Oct
28:38.77	Tsuyoshi	Ogata	JPN	11.5.73	6 May
28:38.78	Sisay	Bezabeh	AUS	9.9.77	6 Dec
28:38.80	Said	Bérioui	MAR	3.6.75	8 Aug
28:38.88	Claes	Nyberg	SWE	3.3.71	1 Sep
28:39.17	Brandon	Leslie	USA	20.4.76	20 Apr
28:39.18	Dmitriy	Maksimov	RUS	6.5.77	7 Apr
28:39.33	Jon	Wild	GBR	30.8.73	9 Jun
28:39.47	George	Mofokeng	RSA	19.2.79	2 Mar
28:39.48	Jeroen	van Damme	NED	29.9.72	14 Apr
28:39.65	Samuel	Mucheke	KEN	3.10.74	13 Oct
28:39.66	Francis	Mwihia	KEN	27.2.78	6 May
28:39.88	Shuichi	Fujii	JPN-J	14.2.82	18 May
28:40.03	Ryan	Shay	USA	4.5.79	31 Mar
28:40.14	Glen	Stewart	GBR	7.12.70	9 Jun
28:40.36	Solomon	Busienei	KEN-J	10.1.84	16 Aug
28:40.43	Tadakatsu	Mukae	JPN	17.10.76	22 Apr
28:40.48	Toshiaki	Tezuka	JPN	7.12.76	13 Oct
28:40.63	Ian	Hudspith	GBR	23.9.70	9 Jun
28:40.63	Gilbert	Okari	KEN	78	29 Oct
28:40.80	Kikuo	Ozawa	JPN	14.10.74	28 Nov
28:40.82	Jean-Philippe	Vindex	FRA	6.11.69	9 Jun
28:41.06	Dariusz	Kruczkowski	POL	4.5.75	29 Jun
28:41.11	Daisuke	Kojima	JPN	15.7.76	28 Nov
28:41.16	Thomas	Greger	GER	7.1.72	19 May
28:41.31	Mustapha	El Ahmadi	FRA	8.7.68	13 Jun
28:41.42	Kensuke	Takahashi	JPN	30.5.75	13 Oct
28:41.57	Yosuke	Osawa	JPN	1.9.67	28 Nov
	(178)				

Drugs Disqualification

Mark	Name		Nat	Born	Pos	Meet	Venue	Date
27:29.53	Alene	Emere ¶	ETH-J	5.3.82	1	JPN Ch	Tokyo	9 Jun

JUNIORS

See main list for top 3 juniors. 9 performances by 7 men to 28:50.0. Additional marks and further juniors:

Kabil	28:49.5	1r2	Hachioji	25 Nov	plus drugs dq:	
Emere ¶	28:07.24	1	Kumamoto	8 Apr	28:13.63 7 Kobe	22 Apr

Mark	Name		Nat	Born	Pos	Meet	Venue	Date
28:39.88	Shuichi	Fujii	JPN	14.2.82	2		Yokohama	18 May
28:40.36	Solomon	Busienei	KEN	10.1.84	1	Afr-J	Réduit	16 Aug
28:45.76	Martin	Toroitich	UGA	10.8.83	2	Afr-J	Réduit	16 Aug
28:46.38	Kei	Ide	JPN	22.2.83	8C		Isahaya	1 Dec
28:59.01	Terefe	Desalegn	ETH	20.11.82	2		Kandel	19 May
28:59.77	Ryuichi	Hashinokuchi	JPN	25.1.82	4		Yokohama	18 May
29:02.45	Valentine	Orare	KEN	82	1		Kisii	31 May
29:05.00	Keita	Tsuchihashi	JPN	30.4.84	3B		Isahaya	1 Dec

Mark	Name		Nat	Born	Pos	Meet	Venue	Date
29:05.29	Takashi	Otsu	JPN	15.7.83	4B		Isahaya	1 Dec
29:05.55	Takyuki	Ota	JPN	29.11.82	18		Yokohama	1 Dec
29:05.74	Koichi	Murakami	JPN	4.9.83	6B		Isahaya	1 Dec
29:06.30	Josphat Muchiri	Ndambiri	KEN	12.2.85	1		Naka	10 Jul
29:06.73	Hiroki	Tanaka	JPN	15.6.86	24		Yokohama	1 Dec
29:07.36	Josh	Rohatinsky	USA	7.3.82	11		Palo Alto	31 Mar
29:10.05	Satoru	Kasuya	JPN	8.7.83	8B		Isahaya	1 Dec
29:11.92	Yukihiro	Motoda	JPN	11.11.82	7		Nobeoka	20 Oct
29:13.57	Michinori	Takano (20)	JPN	30.1.82	3r5		Kobe	8 Dec
29:13.58	Abdul Hamed	Mohamed	QAT		3		Troisdorf	25 Aug

10 KILOMETRES ROAD

Mark	Name		Nat	Born	Pos	Meet	Venue	Date
27:18	Sammy	Kipketer	KEN	29.9.81	1		Brunssum	8 Apr
27:26	Abraham	Chebii	KEN	23.12.79	1		Mobile	24 Mar
27:30	Thomas	Nyariki	KEN	27.9.71	2		Mobile	24 Mar
27:31	Albert	Chepkurui	KEN	4.4.81	1		La Courneuve	1 Apr
27:37	Hailu	Mekonnen	ETH	4.4.80	1		Rennes	14 Oct
27:40	Kenenisa	Bekele	ETH	13.6.82	2		Rennes	14 Oct
27:43	Enoch	Mitei	KEN	26.11.80	2		La Courneuve	1 Apr
27:48	Nicholas	Kemboi	KEN	25.11.83	3		Rennes	14 Oct
27:53+	Haile	Gebrselassie	ETH	18.4.73	1	in 15k	Nijmegen	11 Nov
27:54+	Felix	Limo	KEN	22.8.80	2	in 15k	Nijmegen	11 Nov
27:58	Paul	Biwott	KEN	78	1		Den Haag	27 May
27:59+	Salim	Kipsang	KEN	22.12.79	3	in 15k	Nijmegen	11 Nov
Others where superior to 10,000m track bests:								
28:01	Rodgers	Rop	KEN	73	2		Den Haag	27 May
28:01	James	Koskei	KEN	23.11.68	1		Green Bay	9 Jun
28:02	Gebremehden	Gebremarian	ETH	80	3		Halluin	14 Oct
28:03	Wesley	Ochoro	KEN	78	1	29m dh	Taulé-Morlaix	28 Oct
28:04	Reuben	Cheruiyot	KEN	13.3.74	3		Mobile	24 Mar
28:04	Abdellah	Béhar	FRA	5.7.63	2		Berkane	31 Mar
28:07	Evans	Rutto	KEN	8.4.78	2		Vancouver	22 Apr
28:07	Joseph	Kimani	KEN	1.9.72	2		Green Bay	9 Jun
28:08	Yusuf	Songok	KEN	79	1		Recanati	15 Jul
28:09	Stephen	Rerimoi	KEN	22.12.73	1		Gualtieri	16 Apr
28:10	Jackson	Koech	KEN	79	3		Vancouver	22 Apr
28:10+	Paul	Tergat	KEN	17.6.69	1	inHM	South Shields	16 Sep
28:11	Yarba	Lakhal	MAR	12.2.75	4		Halluin	14 Oct
28:13	Kibet	Cherop	KEN	11.7.74	3		Mobile	24 Mar
28:13	John	Thuo Itati	KEN	26.12.73	3		Cleveland	29 Apr
28:13	Driss	El Himer	FRA	4.4.74	1		Marseille	1 May
28:14	David	Chelule	KEN	7.7.77	1		Arco	18 Aug
28:15	Dominic	Nyabuto	KEN		4		Cleveland	29 Apr
28:16		Dhougi ? Boughra	MAR		5		Halluin	14 Oct
28:18	Peter	Chebet	KEN	74	1		Berkane	31 Mar
28:18	Nick	Rogers	USA	2.5.75	1	NC	Mobile	3 Nov
28:19	Daniel	Gachara	KEN	19.12.72	5		Mobile	24 Mar
28:19	John	Korir	KEN	15.12.75	1	Peach	Atlanta	4 Jul
28:22	Francis	Komu	KEN	5.5.74	3		La Courneuve	1 Apr
28:23	David	Maina	KEN		4		La Courneuve	1 Apr
28:23	Benson	Ogato	KEN	80	1		Toronto	6 May
28:23	Gilbert	Koech	KEN	81	1		Toronto	6 May
28:23	Simson	Limareng	KEN	2.6.77	1		Mazatlan	1 Dec
28:24	David	Tuwei	KEN	22.2.79	1		Barcelona	8 Apr
28:24	João	Ntyamba	ANO	20.3.68	1		Santos	13 May
28:24	Gilbert	Okari	KEN	78	1		Philadelphia	18 Aug
28:24	Sergey	Lebed	UKR	15.7.75	2		Arco	18 Aug
28:25	Cyrus	Kataron	KEN-J	16.5.82	3		Den Haag	27 May
28:25	John	Kipchumba	KEN		1		's Hertogenbosch	23 Sep
28:26	Thomas	Omwenga	KEN	81	7		Mobile	24 Mar
28:26	John	Yuda	TAN	9.6.79	1		Poznan	22 Apr
28:26	Sergey	Drygin	RUS		6		Halluin	14 Oct
28:27	Abel	Chimukoko	KEN		2		Barcelona	8 Apr

Mark	Name		Nat	Born	Date
28:28	Khalid	Khannouchi	USA	22.12.71	18 Feb
28:29	Tendai	Chimusasa	ZIM	28.1.71	9 Jun
28:29	Richard	Mutai	KEN	74	9 Jun
28:29	Julius	Ndiritu	KEN	76	12 May
28:29 29mdh		Sochia	KEN		28 Oct
28:30	Luka	Keitany	KEN		7 Jan
28:31	Atsushi	Fujita	JPN	6.11.76	3 Nov
28:31	Ronald	Munyao	KEN	2.2.74	23 Sep
28:31	Dan	Browne	USA	24.6.75	3 Nov
28:32	Haron	Toroitich	KEN	78	16 Apr
28:32	Elenilson	da Silva	BRA	24.1.72	13 May
28:32	John	Kanda	KEN		14 Sep
28:32	Ronald	Mogaka	KEN	17.4.78	14 Oct
28:32	Zebedayio	Bayo	TAN	20.5.76	16 Dec
28:32	Isaac	Viciosa	ESP	26.12.69	31 Dec
28:33	Jan	Bialk	POL	4.9.69	22 Apr

Mark	Name		Nat	Born	Pos	Meet	Venue	Date
28:33	Lazarus	Nyakeraka	KEN	22.11.75				4 Jul
28:33	William	Cheseret	KEN	71				14 Sep
28:33	Moses	Macharia	KEN	75				7 Oct
28:33	Stephen	Rogath	TAN					16 Dec
28:33	Jesús	España	ESP	21.8.78				31 Dec
28:34	Stephen	Sego	KEN	78				8 Apr
28:34	Michal	Bartoszak	POL	21.6.70				22 Apr
28:34	Aloys	Nizigama	BDI	18.6.66				23 Sep
28:35	Zorislav	Gapeyenko	BLR	15.1.75				22 Apr
28:35	David Ngeny	Cheruiyot	KEN	.80				18 Aug
28:35	David	Ruto	KEN					1 Dec
28:35	Kamal	Saïdou	MAR	9.12.64				14 Sep
28:36	Ismail	Sghyr	FRA	16.3.72				18 Mar
28:36	Sammy	Rongo Alengur	KEN	74				8 Apr
28:36	Julius	Kibet	KEN					9 Sep
28:36 29mdh	Fabrice	Jaouen	FRA	27.7.75				28 Oct
28:37	Juan Carlos	de la Ossa	ESP	25.11.76				8 Apr
28:37	Daniel	Ferreira	BRA	2.2.67				13 May
28:37	Paul	Kiprotich	KEN					15 Sep
28:37	David	Kilel	KEN-J	25.5.84				11 Nov
28:38	Enock Kiptoo	Keter	KEN-J	83				7 Jan
28:38	Kipchirchir	Mitei	KEN	81				14 Apr
28:38	Laban	Chege	KEN	10.9.69				1 May
28:38	Benjamin	Itok	KEN	.72				9 Jun
28:38	Douglas	Rono	KEN	29.12.74				15 Sep
28:38	Joseph	Sitienei	KEN	75				14 Sep
28:39	Jean Bertrand	Ndayisenga	BDI					1 Apr
28:39	Alphonce	Muindi	KEN	28.4.72				13 May
28:39	Abdelaziz	Boughra	MAR	66				15 Sep
Doubtful distance								
28:01	Peter	Chebet	KEN	74	1		Berkane	31 Mar
28:01	Zsolt	Benedek	HUN	24.3.69	1		Pinkafeld	16 Apr
28:15	Dariusz	Kruczkowski	POL	4.5.75	1		Dresden	24 Mar
28:17	Daniel	Kirui	KEN	29.12.77	2		Dresden	24 Mar
28:18	Krzystow	Przybyla	POL	4.9.69	3		Dresden	24 Mar
28:25	Leszek	Beblo	POL	8.7.66	4		Dresden	24 Mar
28:26	Oscar	Cortínez	ARG	4.8.73	1		Montevideo	1 Dec
28:32	Wolfram	Müller	GER	8.7.81				24 Mar
28:38	Ben	Limo	KEN	23.8.74				30 Dec

Downhill: 23 Jul, Salt Lake City (A): 1. Wilson Kakanyang KEN 27:55, 2. Simon Sawe KEN 23.3.74 28:30, 3. Simon Kiprop KEN 28:33
30 Sep, Pittsburgh: 1. Gilbert Koech KEN 81 27:32, 2. Gilbert Okari KEN 78 27:34, 3. Lazarus Nyakeraka KEN 22.11.75 27:44; 4. Moses Macharia KEN 75 27:52, 5. Julius Ndiritu KEN 27:58. 6. Wilson Onsare KEN .76 28:06

15 KILOMETRES ROAD

Mark	Name		Nat	Born	Pos	Meet	Venue	Date
41:29	Felix	Limo	KEN	22.8.80	1		Nijmegen	11 Nov
41:38	Haile	Gebrselassie	ETH	18.4.73	2		Nijmegen	11 Nov
42:01	Salim	Kipsang	KEN	22.12.79	3		Nijmegen	11 Nov
42:22+	Paul	Tergat	KEN	17.6.69	1	in HM	South Shields	16 Sep
42:42	Kenenisa	Bekele	ETH	13.6.82	1		Heerenberg	9 Dec
42:43	Paul	Kosgei	KEN	22.4.78	1		Le Puy-en-Velay	1 May
42:51+	Titus	Munji	KEN	79	1=	in HM	Berlin	1 Apr
42:51+	Fabián	Roncero	ESP	19.10.70	1=	in HM	Berlin	1 Apr
42:51	Sileshi	Sihen	ETH		2		Heerenberg	9 Dec
42:57	John	Korir	KEN	15.12.75	1		Utica	8 Jul
42:58	Shadrack	Hoff	RSA	19.5.73	2		Utica	8 Jul
42:59	Alene	Emere ¶	ETH-J	5.3.82	3		Utica	8 Jul
42:59+	John	Yuda	TAN	9.6.79	1	in HM	Bristol	7 Oct
42:59+	Tesfaye	Jifar	ETH	23.4.76	2	in HM	Bristol	7 Oct
42:59+		Gebrselassie			3	in HM	Bristol	7 Oct
42:59+	Tesfaye	Tola	ETH	19.10.74	4	in HM	Bristol	7 Oct
42:59+	Evans	Rutto	KEN	8.4.78	5	in HM	Bristol	7 Oct
42:59+	Peter	Chebet	KEN	74	6	in HM	Bristol	7 Oct
42:59+	Hendrik	Ramaala	RSA	2.2.72	7	in HM	Bristol	7 Oct
43:00	Patrick	Ivuti	KEN	30.6.78	2		Le Puy-en-Velay	1 May
43:02	Gilbert	Okari	KEN	78	4		Utica	8 Jul
43:02+	Christopher	Cheboiboch	KEN	3.3.77	8	in HM	Bristol	7 Oct
43:03	Gilbert	Koech	KEN	81	5		Utica	8 Jul
43:06	David	Makori	KEN	6.11.73	6		Utica	8 Jul
43:08	Lazarus	Nyakeraka	KEN	22.11.75	7		Utica	8 Jul
43:08+	Jaouad	Gharib	MAR	22.5.72	9	in HM	Bristol	7 Oct
43:14	Mebrahtom	Keflezighi	USA	5.5.75	1	NC	Jacksonville	10 Mar
43:15	Solomon	Businei	KEN-J	10.1.84	5		Nijmegen	11 Nov
43:16+	Khalid	Skah	MAR	29.1.67	10	in HM	Bristol	7 Oct
43:17	Eliud	Lagat	KEN	19.6.66	9		Utica	8 Jul
43:18	Tadesse	Kebede	ETH	.81	10		Utica	8 Jul
43:24+	James	Wainaina	KEN	16.6.81	1	in HM	Sapporo	1 Jul
43:26	Gabriel	Muchiri	KEN	15.4.80	11		Utica	8 Jul
43:28	Habte	Jifar	ETH	29.1.76	6		Nijmegen	11 Nov
43:30+	Salah	Hissou	MAR	16.1.72	11	in HM	Bristol	7 Oct
43:33	Reuben	Cheruiyot	KEN	13.3.74	12		Utica	8 Jul
43:35	Alan	Culpepper	USA	15.9.72	2	NC	Jacksonville	10 Mar
43:35+	Faustin	Baya	TAN-J	30.5.82	13	in HM	Bristol	7 Oct
43:43+	John	Gwako	KEN	4.9.78				7 Oct
43:43+	Haron	Toroitich	KEN	78				7 Oct
43:45	Alberto	Maravilha	POR	27.12.65				1 May
43:46	Philip	Mosima	KEN	2.1.77				11 Nov
43:48	Luc	Krotwaar	NED	25.1.68				11 Nov
43:48+	Rachiz	Ziar	ALG	72				7 Oct

Uncertified course: Breda 6 May: 1. Hilaire N'Tirampeba BDI 1.7.70 43:09, 2. Daniel Andrew TAN 43:46.

10 MILES ROAD

Mark	Name		Nat	Born	Pos	Meet	Venue	Date
45:29	Simon	Maina Munyi	KEN	18.3.78	1		Kosa	9 Dec
45:52	James	Wainaina	KEN	16.6.81	2		Kosa	9 Dec
45:56	Rodgers	Rop	KEN	73	1		Tilburg	3 Jun
46:05	Charles	Kamathi	KEN	18.5.78	1		Zaandam	23 Sep
46:09	Peter	Chebet	KEN	74	2		Zaandam	23 Sep
46:12	John	Korir	KEN	15.12.75	1		Washington DC	8 Apr
46:12	Wilson Kipkemboi	Kigen	KEN	80	3		Zaandam	23 Sep
46:13	Reuben	Cheruiyot	KEN	13.3.74	2		Washington DC	8 Apr
46:13	Richard	Kiprono	KEN	74	2		Tilburg	3 Jun
46:15	Christopher	Cheboiboch	KEN	3.3.77	4		Zaandam	23 Sep
46:17	Khalid	Skah	MAR	29.1.67	1		Portsmouth	14 Oct
46:19	George	Okworo	KEN	12.5.79	2		Portsmouth	14 Oct
46:26	Evans	Rutto	KEN	8.4.78	3		Washington DC	8 Apr
46:27	Solomon	Wachira	KEN	5.11.76	3		Kosa	9 Dec
46:34	Philip	Mosima	KEN	2.1.77	5		Zaandam	23 Sep
46:35	Yuko	Matsumiya	JPN	21.2.80	1		Karatsu	11 Feb
46:35	Philip	Singoei	KEN	31.12.75	6		Zaandam	23 Sep
46:36	Paul	Koech	KEN	25.6.69	7		Zaandam	23 Sep
46:38	Hilary	Lelei	KEN		3		Portsmouth	14 Oct
46:39	Enoch	Mitei	KEN	26.11.80	4		Washington DC	8 Apr
46:41	Felix	Limo	KEN	22.8.80	5		Washington DC	8 Apr
46:41	Laban	Kipkemboi	KEN	30.12.77	1		Flint	25 Aug
46:42	James	Kimani	KEN		4		Kosa	9 Dec
46:43	Yoshitaka	Iwamizu	JPN	20.6.79	2		Karatsu	11 Feb
46:44	Makoto	Otsu	JPN	3.7.80	5		Kosa	9 Dec
46:46	Kenichiro	Setuguchi	JPN	12.12.80	3		Karatsu	11 Feb
46:46	Koichiro	Nagata	JPN	19.12.78	6		Kosa	9 Dec
46:47	Habte	Jifar	ETH	29.1.76	8		Zaandam	23 Sep
46:48	Ronald	Mogaka	KEN	17.4.78	1		Philadelphia	6 May
46:48	Faustin	Baha	TAN-J	30.5.82	4		Tilburg	3 Jun
46:48	Simon	Kiprop	KEN		5		Tilburg	3 Jun
46:48	Takeshi	Hamano	JPN	30.7.74	7		Kosa	9 Dec
46:49	Elarbi	Khattabi	MAR	16.5.67	6		Washington DC	8 Apr
46:49	John	Thuo Itati	KEN	26.12.73	2		Philadelphia	6 May
46:49	Tetsuo	Nishikawa	JPN	14.7.77	8		Kosa	9 Dec

Mark	Name		Nat	Born	Date	Mark	Name		Nat	Born	Date
46:52	Toyoshi	Ishige	JPN	16.4.75	9 Dec	46:54	Junji	Mishima	JPN	29.6.76	9 Dec
46:53	Fita	Bayissa	ETH	15,12.72	8 Apr	46:55	Hiroshi	Miki	JPN	10.6.75	11 Feb
46:53	Moses	Kemboi	KEN		23 Jun	46:56	Simon	Kasimili	KEN	12.12.80	25 Aug
46:54	Shadrack	Hoff	RSA	19.5.73	25 Aug	46:57	Larbi	Zéroual	FRA	10.1.71	23 Sep

20 KILOMETRES ROAD

Mark	Name		Nat	Born	Pos	Meet	Venue	Date
56:51+	Fabián	Roncero	ESP	19.10.70	1=	in HM	Berlin	1 Apr
57:16+	Paul	Tergat	KEN	17.6.69	1	in HM	South Shields	16 Sep
58:09	Michele	Gamba	ITA	2.10.72	1		Almeirim	21 Jan
58:10	Paulo	Catarino	POR	30.9.63	2		Almeirim	21 Jan
58:11	Alberto	Chaiça	POR	12.9.73	3		Almeirim	21 Jan
58:15	Richard	Mutai	KEN	74	1		Alphen aan Rijn	11 Mar
58:16	William	Kiplagat	KEN	72	2		Alphen aan Rijn	11 Mar
58:18	Salaho	Ngadhi	TAN	12.3.79	4		Almeirim	21 Jan
58:18	Benjamin Kosgei Kimutai		KEN		3		Alphen aan Rijn	11 Mar
58:23	Worku	Bikila	ETH	6.5.68	4		Alphen aan Rijn	11 Mar
58:28	Elicha	Birgem	TAN		5		Almeirim	21 Jan
58:36+	James	Wainaina	KEN	16.6.81	1	in HM	Sapporo	1 Jul

Mark	Name		Nat	Born	Date	Mark	Name		Nat	Born	Date
58:55	Peter	Musyoki	KEN	80	11 Mar	59:03	John	Kanyi	KEN	6.9.80	20 Oct
58:55	Moses	Saina	KEN		11 Mar	59:07	Domingos	Castro	POR	22.11.63	11 Mar
58:56	Benjamin	Itok	KEN	72	11 Mar						

HALF MARATHON

Mark	Name		Nat	Born	Pos	Meet	Venue	Date
59:52	Fabián	Roncero	ESP	19.10.70	1		Berlin	1 Apr
60:03	Haile	Gebrselassie	ETH	18.4.73	1	WCh	Bristol	7 Oct
60:04	Tesfaye	Jifar	ETH	23.4.76	2	WCh	Bristol	7 Oct
60:12	John	Yuda	TAN	9.6.79	3	WCh	Bristol	7 Oct
60:15	Hendrick	Ramaala	RSA	2.2.72	4	WCh	Bristol	7 Oct
60:24	Tesfaye	Tola	ETH	19.10.74	5	WCh	Bristol	7 Oct
60:26		Ramaala			1		Lisboa (dh 69m)	1 Apr
60:27	Titus	Munji	KEN	79	2		Berlin	1 Apr
60:27	Paul	Tergat	KEN	17.6.69	2		Lisboa	1 Apr
60:30	Evans	Rutto	KEN	8.4.78	3		Lisboa	1 Apr

Mark	Name		Nat	Born	Pos	Meet	Venue	Date
60:30		Tergat			1	GNR	South Shields	16 Sep
60:38	William	Kiplagat (10)	KEN	21.6.72	4		Lisboa	1 Apr
60:42	Patrick	Ivuti	KEN	30.6.78	1		Milano	31 Mar
60:43		Rutto			6	WCh	Bristol	7 Oct
60:45	Christopher	Cheboiboch	KEN	3.3.77	5		Lisboa	1 Apr
60:49	Haron	Toroitich	KEN	78	6		Lisboa	1 Apr
60:53		Toroitich			1		Torino	11 Mar
60:56	Peter	Chebet	KEN	74	7	WCh	Bristol	7 Oct
60:57	Rodgers	Rop	KEN	73	3		Berlin	1 Apr
61:04	James	Wainaina	KEN	16.6.81	1		Nagoya	23 Nov
61:05	Joshua	Chelanga	KEN	7.4.73	7		Lisboa	1 Apr
61:09	Koichiro	Nagata	JPN	19.12.78	1		Kyoto	11 Mar
61:14		Cheboiboch			8	WCh	Bristol	7 Oct
61:16	Yusuf	Songok	KEN	79	2		Torino	11 Mar
61:16	António	Pinto (20)	POR	22.3.66	8		Lisboa	1 Apr
61:16	Laban	Chege	KEN	10.9.69	1		Vitry-sur-Seine	22 Apr
	(26/21)							
61:18	Joseph	Waweru	KEN	22.6.77	2		Vitry-sur-Seine	22 Apr
61:19	Abderrahim	Goumri	MAR	21.5.76	1		Safi	29 Apr
61:23	Simon	Lopuyet	KEN	24.12.72	9		Lisboa	1 Apr
61:23	Japhet	Kosgei	KEN	20.12.68	1		Udine	30 Sep
61:25	Ronald	Mogaka	KEN	17.4.78	1		Philadelphia	16 Sep
61:27	Yuki	Mori	JPN	8.3.79	1		Yamaguchi	11 Mar
61:28	Luis	Jesus	POR	19.11.68	10		Lisboa	1 Apr
61:28	Philip	Rugut	KEN	18.5.77	1		Palermo	28 Oct
61:30	Kazuo	Ietani	JPN	25.8.75	2		Yamaguchi	11 Mar
	(30)							
61:30	Stefano	Baldini	ITA	25.5.71	3		Torino	11 Mar
61:31	Eliud	Kurgat	KEN	20.8.73	11		Lisboa	1 Apr
61:32	Naotaka	Takahashi	JPN	28.6.76	3		Yamaguchi	11 Mar
61:33	Tomoo	Tsubota	JPN	16.6.77	4		Yamaguchi	11 Mar
61:33	Nobuya	Matsunaga	JPN	8.11.74	5		Yamaguchi	11 Mar
61:34	Yukihiro	Yoshida	JPN	16.7.76	6		Yamaguchi	11 Mar
61:35	Satoshi	Watanabe	JPN	6.5.80	7		Yamaguchi	11 Mar
61:36	Jaouad	Gharib	MAR	22.5.72	2		Safi	29 Apr
61:36	Julius	Kimutai	KEN		2	GNR	South Shields	16 Sep
61:38	Tatsumi	Morimasa	JPN	3.4.76	8		Yamaguchi	11 Mar
	(40)							
61:39	David	Makori	KEN	6.11.73	12		Lisboa	1 Apr
61:40	Laban	Kipkemboi	KEN	30.12.77	3		Philadelphia	16 Sep
61:41	Moses	Kemboi	KEN		1		Pietramurata	16 Sep
61:41	Khalid	Skah	MAR	29.1.67	10	WCh	Bristol	7 Oct
61:42	Tetsuo	Nishikawa	JPN	14.7.77	9		Yamaguchi	11 Mar
61:44	Toyoshi	Ishige	JPN	16.4.75	10		Yamaguchi	11 Mar
61:45	Simon	Kasimili	KEN	12.12.80	2		Philadelphia	16 Sep
61:46	Daisuke	Kojima	JPN	15.7.76	11		Yamaguchi	11 Mar
61:46	Salaho	Ngadi	TAN	12.3.79	2		Udine	30 Sep
61:50	Abner	Chipu	RSA	2.1.72	1	NC	East London	8 Jul
	(50)							
61:51	Wilson	Onsare	KEN	15.6.76	4		Philadelphia	16 Sep
61:52	Kazushi	Hara	JPN	16.11.80	12		Yamaguchi	11 Mar
61:53	Faustin	Baha	TAN-J	30.5.82	2		Kyoto	11 Mar
61:55	Jackson	Koech	KEN	79	1		Monterrey	1 Apr
61:55	Philip	Tarus	KEN	11.9.74	3		Udine	30 Sep
61:56	Simon	Mpholo	RSA	17.8.74	2	NC	East London	8 Jul
61:56	Salah	Hissou	MAR	16.1.72	11	WCh	Bristol	7 Oct
61:57	Joseph	Kimani	KEN	1.9.72	14		Lisboa	1 Apr
61:58	Masaki	Kido	JPN	10.12.70	13		Yamaguchi	11 Mar
61:58	Makhosonke	Fika	RSA	20.1.72	3	NC	East London	8 Jul
	(60)							
61:58	John	Nada Saya	TAN	8.8.78	1		Seoul	4 Nov
61:59	Martin Hhaway	Sulle	TAN-J	28.12.82	2		Seoul	4 Nov
62:01	Zebedayio	Bayo	TAN	20.5.76	15		Lisboa	1 Apr
62:01	John	Kagwe	KEN	9.1.69	16		Lisboa	1 Apr
62:01	Augustine	Togom	KEN		1		Aveiro	1 Dec
62:02	Luke	Metto	KEN	76	3		Vitry-sur-Seine	22 Apr
62:03	Kibet	Kigen	KEN	23.2.75	1		Sétubal	6 May
62:04	Barnabas	Rutto	KEN	.77	1		Torino	23 Sep
62:04	Wilson Kipkemboi	Kigen	KEN	80	1		Breda	7 Oct
62:05	George	Mofokeng	RSA	19.2.79	4	NC	East London	8 Jul
	(70)							

Mark	Name		Nat	Born	Pos	Meet	Venue	Date
62:05	David	Kipruto	KEN	20.11.75	4		Udine	30 Sep
62:08	Tomokazu	Sakamoto	JPN	21.7.76	14		Yamaguchi	11 Mar
62:08	Driss	El Himer	FRA	4.4.74	1		Lille	1 Sep
62:08	Paul	Biwott	KEN	78	2		Breda	7 Oct
62:09	Takashi	Ota	JPN	27.4.76	15		Yamaguchi	11 Mar
62:09	Anthony	Korir	KEN	25.10.80	1		Praha	24 Mar
62:09	Sergey	Lebed	UKR	15.7.75	2		Milano	31 Mar
62:09	Paulo	Catarino	POR	30.9.63	3		Sétubal	6 May
62:09	Sammy	Mpror	KEN		2		Lille	1 Sep
62:09	Salim	Kipsang	KEN	22.12.79	1		Deurne	2 Sep
	(80)							
62:10	Boniface	Usivivu	KEN	5.9.74	1		Mondsee	10 Jun
62:11	Stephen	Tapala	KEN		2		Mondsee	10 Jun
62:12	Tsuyoshi	Nakano	JPN	12.3.73	16		Yamaguchi	11 Mar
62:12	Josephat	Kipchoge Rop	KEN	68	1		Den Haag	24 Mar
62:12	Richard	Mutai	KEN	74	2		Praha	24 Mar
62:12	William	Cheseret	KEN	71	1		Auray-Vannes	9 Sep
62:12	Jumanne	Tluway	TAN	5.7.80	2		Aveiro	1 Dec
62:13	Philip	Kemei	KEN	6.6.77	2		Torino	23 Sep
62:14	Tadakatsu	Mukae	JPN	17.10.76	17		Yamaguchi	11 Mar
62:14	Mathias	Ntawulikiura	RWA	14.7.64	5		Udine	30 Sep
	(90)							
62:14	Tomoaki	Kunichika	JPN	22.7.73	2		Nagoya	23 Nov
62:15	Daniel	Kirwa Too	KEN	21.11.76	2		Gargnano	30 Sep
62:15	John	Gwako	KEN	4.9.78	13	WCh	Bristol	7 Oct
62:16	Julius	Maritim	KEN	80	2		Den Haag	24 Mar
62:18	Daisuke	Nakahara	JPN	10.8.74	18		Yamaguchi	11 Mar
62:18	Germán	Silva	MEX	9.1.68	2		Monterrey	1 Apr
62:19	Kazutoshi	Takatsuka	JPN	8.8.76	19		Yamaguchi	11 Mar
62:19	Yukiyoshi	Kino	JPN	10.9.80	20		Yamaguchi	11 Mar
62:19	Shadrack	Hoff	RSA	19.5.73	1		Virginia Beach	2 Sep
62:19	Mostafa	Errebbah	ITA	1.8.71	15	WCh	Bristol	7 Oct
	(100)							

Mark	Name		Nat	Born	Date
62:20	Takashi	Ishijima	JPN	7.9.76	11 Mar
62:20	Róbert	Stefko	SVK	28.5.68	1 Apr
62:21	Benedict	Kimondiu	KEN	30.11.77	4 Feb
62:21	Noah	Bor	KEN	28.7.77	22 Apr
62:21	Alberto	Chaiça	POR	17.9.73	30 Sep
62:22	Rachid	Ziar	ALG	15.11.73	1 Sep
62:23	Christopher	Kandie	KEN	69	14 Apr
62:24	David	Rutto	KEN	80	4 Feb
62:24	Giuliano	Battocletti	ITA	1.8.75	25 Feb
62:24	Benjamin	Korir	KEN		6 May
62:25	Joseph	Ngolepus	KEN	75	14 Apr
62:25	Elijah	Nyabuti	KEN	10.10.79	22 Apr
62:26	Fekadu	Deguefu	ETH	72	4 Nov
62:27	Ottaviano	Andriani	ITA	4.1.74	25 Feb
62:27	Robert	Cheruiyot	KEN	20.12.74	24 Mar
62:27	Norman	Dlomo	RSA	18.4.75	8 Jul
62:28	Hidemori	Noguchi	JPN	22.2.80	4 Feb
62:28	Frans	Motsamai	RSA	11.8.72	8 Jul
62:28	Takeshi	Hamano	JPN	30.7.74	7 Oct
62:29	Ken-ichi	Takahashi	JPN	16.1.73	4 Feb
62:29	Yoshitaka	Iwamizu	JPN	20.6.79	11 Mar
62:29	Michael	Kite	KEN	73	23 Sep
62:29	Saïd	Bouhmandi	MAR	18.7.74	1 Dec
62:29	David	Kemei Kipruto	KEN	3.4.72	16 Dec
62:30	Mbarak	Hussein	KEN	4.4.65	1 Apr
62:30	Elicha	Birgem	TAN	28.2.80	1 Sep
62:30	Wilberforce	Kapkeny	KEN	10.1.80	2 Sep
62:30	Abdelhadi	Habassa	MAR	13.1.76	7 Oct
62:30	Toshiaki	Tezuka	JPN	7.12.76	23 Nov
62:32	Francesco	Ingargiola	ITA	15.2.73	25 Feb
62:32	Daniele	Caimmi	ITA	17.12.72	4 Mar
62:32	Francisco Javier	Cortés	ESP	25.10.71	1 Apr
62:33	Tiyapo	Maso	BOT	30.12.72	7 Oct
62:36	Simon	Rono	KEN	9.4.72	4 May
62:36	Timothy Cheren	Simatwa	KEN	82	16 Dec
62:37	Clement	Kipbor	KEN	81	23 Sep
62:38	Danilo	Goffi	ITA	3.12.72	31 Mar
62:38	Elijah	Yator	KEN-J	20.10.82	11 Nov
62:39	Abderrazak	Ghabbar	MAR		31 Mar
62:39	Daniel	Kirui	KEN	29.12.77	1 Apr
62:39	Francis	Komu	KEN	5.5.74	21 Oct
62:40	Roberto	Barbi ¶	ITA	25.3.65	25 Feb
62:40	Abdelghani	Lahlali	FRA	11.9.77	23 Sep
62:40	Matthew	O'Dowd	GBR	15.4.76	7 Oct
62:41	Aziz	Laraichi	MAR	72	18 Feb
62:41	Ibrahim	Mitei	KEN	15.8.78	18 Feb
62:41	Phil	Costley	NZL	16.3.70	3 Jun
62:41	Wesley	Ochoro	KEN	78	21 Oct
62:42	Paul	Ngeny	KEN		30 Sep
62:43	Wilson	Musto	KEN	18.2.76	4 May
62:43	Shinichiro	Okuda	JPN	4.1.80	14 Oct
62:43	Samuel	Mucheke	KEN	3.10.74	23 Nov
62:44	Giacomo	Leone	ITA	10.4.71	18 Feb
62:44	Ian	Syster	RSA	20.1.76	8 Jul
62:44	Gert	Thys	RSA	12.11.71	8 Jul
62:44	Mohamed	Serbouti	FRA	3.3.71	23 Sep
62:44	Eduardo	Henriques	POR	24.3.68	7 Oct
62:45	Yukiyasu	Nagao	JPN	25.4.74	11 Mar
62:45	João	Ntyamba	ANO	20.3.68	26 May
62:46	Motsehi	Moeketsana	RSA	2.1.70	8 Jul
62:46	John	Rotich	KEN	68	9 Sep
62:46	David	Ramard	FRA	3.2.78	23 Sep
62:46	George	Okworo	KEN	12.5.79	28 Oct
62:47	Meck	Mothuli	RSA	12.4.76	8 Jul
62:47	Gabriel	Muchiri	KEN	15.4.80	19 Aug
62:47	Viktor	Röthlin	SUI	14.10.74	9 Sep
62:47	Augusto	Gomes	FRA	5.3.74	23 Sep
62:48	Takamasa	Uchida	JPN	17.10.81	11 Mar
62:49	Takashi	Nabeshima	JPN	81	11 Mar
62:49	John	Mutai	KEN	26.5.66	16 Sep
62:49	Godfrey	Nyombi	UGA	10.10.78	16 Sep
62:49	Simon	Bor	KEN	13.2.69	30 Sep
62:49	Francis	Robert Naali	TAN	1.4.71	7 Oct
62:50	Yoshinori	Yokota	JPN	30.1.68	11 Mar
	(174)	203 under 63:00			

Over 500m short:12 Jul, Kibaha: 2. Benedict Ako TAN 5.8.68 61:33, 3. Faustion Baha TAN 30.5.82 61:51
Uncertain distance: 8 Apr, Arusha: 1. Martin Hhaway Sulle 28.12.82 61:53, 2. Jumanne Tluway 5.7.80 61:54,3. Hussein Ramadhani 62:05, 4, Egobert Robert Naali 72 62:14 (all TAN)

Mark		Name		Nat	Born	Pos	Meet	Venue	Date
		JUNIORS							
61:53		Faustin	Baha	TAN	30.5.82	2		Kyoto	11 Mar
61:59		Martin Hhaway	Sulle	TAN	28.12.82	2		Seoul	4 Nov
62:38		Elijah	Yator	KEN	20.10.82	1		Nazare	11 Nov
63:23		Francis	Yiga	UGA	4.2.82	35	WCh	Bristol	7 Oct
63:25		Takayuki	Kawano	JPN	7.3.82	1		Ageo	18 Nov
63:27		Paul	Wakou	UGA	17.10.83	36	WCh	Bristol	7 Oct
63:34		Ombeche	Mokamba	KEN	6.4.82	8		Sapporo	1 Jul
63:57		Enock Kiptoo	Keter	KEN	83	3		Egmond aan Zee	14 Jan
64:01		Hiyashi	Yotsuji	JPN	24.12.82	4		Ageo	18 Nov
64:08		Takashi	Koga	JPN	2.10.82	8		Ageo	18 Nov
64:14		Shuichi	Fujii	JPN	14.2.82	4		Tokyo	4 Mar
64:37		Nobue	Ide	JPN	1.3.82	29		Kyoto	11 Mar
64:40		Tomoyuki	Honda	JPN	20.1.83	12		Oita	4 Feb

MARATHON

D in second column = aided course due to possible net tailwind or downslope from point-to-point arrangement (>30% start/finish separation). L = loop or out-and-back course, P - Point-to-point

Mark		Name		Nat	Born	Pos	Meet	Venue	Date
2:06:50	L	Josephat	Kiprono	KEN	12.12.73	1		Rotterdam	22 Apr
2:07:02	L	Driss	El Himer	FRA	4.4.74	1		Amsterdam	21 Oct
2:07:06	L		Kiprono			2		Amsterdam	21 Oct
2:07:11	L	Abdelkader	El Mouaziz	MAR	1.1.69	1		London	22 Apr
2:07:18	L	Kenneth	Cheruiyot	KEN	2.8.74	2		Rotterdam	22 Apr
2:07:34	L	Antonio	Peña	ESP	26.8.70	1	L.Biwa	Otsu	4 Mar
2:07:43	P	Tesfaye	Jifar	ETH	23.4.76	1		New York	4 Nov
2:07:45	L	Simeretu	Alemayehu	ETH	18.10.70	1		Torino	1 Apr
2:07:46	L	Julio	Rey	ESP	13.1.72	1		Hamburg	22 Apr
2:07:48	L	Francisco Javier	Cortés	ESP	25.10.71	2		Hamburg	22 Apr
2:07:52	L	Giacomo	Leone	ITA	10.4.71	2	L.Biwa	Otsu	4 Mar
2:07:52	L	Shigeru	Aburaya	JPN	6.2.77	3	L.Biwa	Otsu	4 Mar
2:07:59	L	Yoshiteru	Morishita	JPN	26.5.71	4	L.Biwa	Otsu	4 Mar
2:08:14	L	Sammy	Korir	KEN	12.12.71	3		Rotterdam	22 Apr
2:08:15	L	Paul	Tergat	KEN	17.6.69	2		London	22 Apr
2:08:45	L	Takayuki	Nishida	JPN	26.4.77	1	Beppu	Oita	4 Feb
2:08:47	L	Joseph	Ngolepus	KEN	75	1		Berlin	30 Sep
2:08:51	L	Stefano	Baldini	ITA	25.5.71	2		Torino	1 Apr
2:08:52	L	Hideyuki	Obinata	JPN	2.12.76	5	L.Biwa	Otsu	4 Mar
2:08:52	L	Ben	Kimondiu	KEN	30.11.77	1		Chicago	7 Oct
2:08:56	L		Tergat			2		Chicago	7 Oct
2:08:57	L	John	Nada Saya	TAN	8.8.78	1		Milano	2 Dec
2:08:58	L	William	Cheruiyot	KEN	67	2		Milano	2 Dec
2:09:00	L	Peter	Githuka	KEN	14.2.69	3		Chicago	7 Oct
2:09:05	L	Abdellah	Béhar	FRA	5.7.63	4		Rotterdam	22 Apr
2:09:07	L	Ottaviano	Andriani	ITA	4.1.74	3		Milano	2 Dec
2:09:08	L		W Cheruiyot			2		Berlin	30 Sep
2:09:11	L		Lee Bong-ju	KOR	11.10.70	4		Milano	2 Dec
2:09:19	P	Japhet	Kosgei	KEN	28.12.68	2		New York	4 Nov
2:09:25	L	Gezahegne	Abera	ETH	23.4.78	1		Fukuoka	2 Dec
2:09:26	L	Mohamed	Ouaadi	FRA	1.1.69	4		Chicago	7 Oct
2:09:27	L	Simon	Bor	KEN	13.2.69	6	L.Biwa	Otsu	4 Mar
2:09:28	L	Koji	Shimizu	JPN	17.10.69	2		Fukuoka	2 Dec
		(33/30)							
2:09:35	L	Noriaki	Igarashi	JPN	28.10.72	5		Chicago	7 Oct
2:09:36	L	António	Pinto	POR	22.3.66	3		London	22 Apr
2:09:40	L	Simon	Biwott	KEN	3.3.70	1		Paris	8 Apr
2:09:40	L	David Kiptoo	Kirui	KEN	29.12.77	2		Paris	8 Apr
2:09:41	L	Toshinari	Takaoka	JPN	24.9.70	2		Fukuoka	2 Dec
2:09:43	L	Fred	Kiprop	KEN	3.6.74	3		Paris	8 Apr
2:09:51	P	Rodgers	Rop	KEN	73	3		New York	4 Nov
2:09:55	L	William	Kiplagat	KEN	21.6.72	3		Berlin	30 Sep
2:09:59	L	Isaac	Kiprono	KEN	5.9.76	5		Rotterdam	22 Apr
2:10:02	L	Vanderlei	de Lima	BRA	11.8.69	2	Beppu	Oita	4 Feb
		(40)							
2:10:04	L	Lee	Troop	AUS	22.3.73	6		Rotterdam	22 Apr
2:10:06	L	Tsuyoshi	Ogata	JPN	11.5.73	4		Berlin	30 Sep
2:10:07	D	Silvio	Guerra	ECU	18.9.68	2		Boston (139m dh)	16 Apr
2:10:07	L	John	Kagwe	KEN	9.1.69	1		San Diego (76m dh)	3 Jun
2:10:08	L	Fabián	Roncero	ESP	19.10.70	7		Rotterdam	22 Apr
2:10:08	P	Moges	Taye	ETH	12.11.73	1		Venezia	28 Oct

Mark		Name		Nat	Born	Pos	Meet	Venue	Date
2:10:10	P	Henry	Tarus	KEN	6.12.78	2		Venezia	28 Oct
2:10:11	L		Gong Ke	CHN	16.8.79	1	NG	Beijing	14 Oct
2:10:14	L	Andrew	Sambu	TAN	5.10.72	1		Praha	20 May
2:10:18	L	Lukas	Kibet	KEN	19.6.73	3		Amsterdam	21 Oct
		(50)							
2:10:19	L	David	Ngetich	KEN	12.5.72	2		Praha	20 May
2:10:21	L	Samson	Kandie	KEN	20.4.71	1		San Sebastián	25 Nov
2:10:24	L	Laban	Kagika	KEN	17.7.78	4		Fukuoka	2 Dec
2:10:25	L		Li Aiguo	CHN	12.6.79	2	NG	Beijing	14 Oct
2:10:26	L		Wang Yonghua	CHN	23.5.81	3	NG	Beijing	14 Oct
2:10:26	P	Daniele	Caimmi	ITA	17.12.72	3		Venezia	28 Oct
2:10:28	L	Luis	Novo	POR	29.5.70	1		Wien	20 May
2:10:29	D	Joshua	Chelanga	KEN	7.4.73	3		Boston	16 Apr
2:10:30	L	Sergio	Chiesa	ITA	7.9.72	5		Milano	2 Dec
2:10:32	L	Nobuyuki	Sato	JPN	8.8.72	4	NG	Beijing	14 Oct
		(60)							
2:10:32	L	Hailu	Negussie	ETH		1		Hofu	16 Dec
2:10:33	L	Mohamed	Ezzher	FRA	26.4.60	4		Paris	8 Apr
2:10:33	L	Tesfaye	Eticha	ETH	16.9.74	5		Paris	8 Apr
2:10:33	L	Oscar	Fernández	ESP	23.10.74	8		Rotterdam	22 Apr
2:10:35	L	Danilo	Goffi	ITA	3.12.72	5		Berlin	30 Sep
2:10:36	L	Shinji	Kawashima	JPN	4.6.66	3	Beppu	Oita	4 Feb
2:10:36	L	Kamal	Ziani	ESP	20.2.72	9		Rotterdam	22 Apr
2:10:36	L	Frederick	Chumba	KEN	24.7.74	6		Berlin	30 Sep
2:10:36	P	Salaho	Ngadi	TAN	12.3.79	4		Venezia	28 Oct
2:10:37	L	Ambesse	Tolossa	ETH	28.8.77	5	NG	Beijing	14 Oct
		(70)							
2:10:38	L		Zhan Donglin	CHN	15.7.70	6	NG	Beijing	14 Oct
2:10:38	L	Daniel	Kirwa Too	KEN	21.11.76	1		Firenze	25 Nov
2:10:41	L	Robert	Cheruiyot	KEN	20.12.74	10		Rotterdam	22 Apr
2:10:41	P	Mark	Sainah	KEN	10.11.70	5		Venezia	28 Oct
2:10:41	L	Francisco Javier	Caballero	ESP	24.3.72	6		Milano	2 Dec
2:10:44	L	James	Moiben	KEN	20.4.77	11		Rotterdam	22 Apr
2:10:45	L	Koen	Allaert	BEL	29.9.72	12		Rotterdam	22 Apr
2:10:45	L	Ashebir	Demissie	ETH	77	4		Amsterdam	21 Oct
2:10:46	L	Mark	Steinle	GBR	22.11.74	6	1 NC	London	22 Apr
2:10:46	L		Li Zhuhong	CHN-J	22.10.83	7	NG	Beijing	14 Oct
		(80)							
2:10:47	L	Makhosonke	Fika	RSA	20.1.72	7		Berlin	30 Sep
2:10:47	L	Joseph	Cherono	KEN		8	NG	Beijing	14 Oct
2:10:49	L	José Ramón	Rey	ESP	3.11.67	1		Sevilla	25 Feb
2:10:51	L	Ken-ichi	Takahashi	JPN	16.1.73	1		Tokyo	18 Feb
2:10:54	L	Viktor	Röthlin	SUI	14.10.74	8		Berlin	30 Sep
2:10:57	L	Andrés	Espinosa	MEX	4.2.63	1		Torreón	4 Mar
2:10:58	L	Benjamín	Paredes	MEX	7.8.61	2		Torreón	4 Mar
2:10:58	L	Nelson	Ndereva Njeru	KEN	14.7.67	9	NG	Beijing	14 Oct
2:11:01	L	Takayuki	Shimazaki	JPN	3.5.69	10	NG	Beijing	14 Oct
2:11:04	L	Simon	Lopuyet	KEN	24.12.72	3		Hamburg	22 Apr
		(90)							
2:11:04	P	Migidio	Bourifa	ITA	31.1.69	6		Venezia	28 Oct
2:11:06	L	Hakim	Bagy	FRA	31.3.68	7		Paris	8 Mar
2:11:06	L	Barnabas	Rutto	KEN	77	4		Praha	20 May
2:11:09	L	Dmitriy	Kapitonov	RUS	10.4.68	3		Tokyo	18 Feb
2:11:09	L	Pavel	Loskutov	EST	2.12.69	1		Frankfurt am Main	28 Oct
2:11:11	L	Eliud	Keiring	KEN	74	5		Praha	20 May
2:11:12	L	Zebedayio	Bayo	TAN	20.5.76	4		Tokyo	18 Feb
2:11:14	L	Shigekatsu	Kondo	JPN	17.10.74	4	Beppu	Oita	4 Feb
2:11:14	D	Mukhamet	Nazipov	RUS	10.9.64	1		Austin (137m dh)	18 Feb
2:11:18	P	Hendrick	Ramaala	RSA	2.2.72	5		New York	4 Nov
		(100)							

Mark		Name		Nat	Born	Date
2:11:19	L	Roberto	Barbi ¶	ITA	25.3.65	6 May
2:11:22	L	Francesco	Ingargiola	ITA	15.2.73	2 Dec
2:11:24	P	Jon	Brown	GBR	27.2.71	4 Nov
2:11:30	L	Elijah	Korir	KEN	13.3.66	28 Oct
2:11:33	L	Henry Kosgei	Cherono	KEN	17.7.78	25 Mar
2:11:40	L	João	Ntyamba	ANG	20.3.68	30 Sep
2:11:40	L	Rod	DeHaven	USA	21.9.66	7 Oct
2:11:40	P	Michael	Kite	KEN	73	28 Oct
2:11:40	L	Stephen	Rugut	KEN	7.4.76	25 Nov
2:11:42	D	Andrzej	Krzyoscin	POL	16.8.67	18 Feb
2:11:42	L	Takayuki	Inubushi	JPN	11.8.72	22 Apr
2:11:42	L	Jimmy	Muindi	KEN	14.8.73	30 Sep
2:11:43	L	Stephen	Ndungu	KEN	1.6.67	3 Jun
2:11:43	L		Li He	CHN-J	3.3.84	14 Oct
2:11:44	L	Andrey	Gordeyev	BLR	7.8.73	6 May
2:11:44	L	Ondoro	Osoro	KEN	3.12.67	7 Oct
2:11:45	L	Katsuhiko	Hanada	JPN	12.6.71	4 Mar
2:11:45	L	Masami	Soeta	JPN	29.3.77	14 Oct
2:11:45	L	Tadayuki	Ojima	JPN	22.11.76	2 Dec
2:11:46	L	Artur	Osman	POL	1.3.70	28 Oct
2:11:47	D	David Kiptum	Businei	KEN	22.12.74	16 Apr
2:11:47	L	André Luiz	Ramos	BRA	20.1.70	30 Sep
2:11:48	L	Worku	Bikila	ETH	6.5.68	8 Apr
2:11:48	L		Kim Jung-won	PRK	20.9.73	15 Apr

Mark		Name		Nat	Born	Pos	Meet	Venue	Date
2:11:48	L	Abraham	Limo	KEN	10.12.63				20 May
2:11:49	L	Josiah	Bembe	RSA	28.11.74				18 Mar
2:11:50	L	Rachid	Ziar	ALG	15.11.73				23 Sep
2:11:52	L	Josiah	Thugwane	RSA	15.4.71				18 Mar
2:11:52	L	Gideon	Chirchir	KEN	24.2.66				29 Apr
2:11:52	L	Masayoshi	Koide	JPN	6.11.72				14 Oct
2:11:52	L	Toshio	Mano	JPN	28.7.72				2 Dec
2:11:54	L	Shaun	Creighton	AUS	14.5.67				7 Oct
2:11:55	L	Hiroshi	Miki	JPN	10.6.75				18 Mar
2:11:57	L	Abel	Antón	ESP	24.10.62				22 Apr
2:12:01	D	Mbarak	Hussein	KEN	4.4.65				16 Apr
2:12:04	P	Joseph	Maqala	RSA	29.12.66				14 Oct
2:12:05	L	Tesfaye	Tola	ETH	19.10.74				18 Feb
2:12:09	L	Fekadu	Deguefu	ETH	72				18 Mar
2:12:10	L	Steven	Cheptoo	KEN					21 Oct
2:12:11	L	Gert	Thys	RSA	12.11.71				22 Apr
2:12:14	L	Elenilson	da Silva	BRA	24.1.72				30 Sep
2:12:15	L	Muneyuki	Ojima	JPN	25.9.75				2 Dec
2:12:17	D	Igor	Osmak	UKR	30.11.65				18 Feb
2:12:17	L	Joshua	Kimaiyo	KEN	11.11.73				18 Mar
2:12:19	L		Kim Yi-yong	KOR	20.9.73				18 Mar
2:12:20	L	Mustapha	Riad	MAR	5.8.75				27 May
2:12:20	P	Aleksandr	Kuzin	UKR	21.10.74				14 Oct
2:12:21	L	John	Moiben	KEN	12.4.68				1 Apr
2:12:23	L		Song Yong-ok	PRK	78				15 Apr
2:12:24	L	Rômulo	da Silva	BRA	26.5.77				30 Sep
2:12:25	L	Mitsunori	Hirayama	JPN	23.10.76				7 Oct
2:12:25	L	Elijah	Lagat	KEN	19.6.66				28 Oct
2:12:27	L	Patrick	Chumba	KEN	24.7.74				18 Mar
2:12:27	L	Miroslaw	Plawgo	POL	4.1.70				8 Apr
2:12:29	L	Benjamin Mutua	Matolo	KEN	12.4.71				27 May
2:12:29	L	Adam	Dobrzynski	POL	19.12.74				30 Sep
2:12:30	L		Hu Gangjun	CHN	4.12.70				14 Oct
2:12:31	L	Andrey	Naumov	UKR	21.12.73				20 May
2:12:35	L	Toshihiro	Iwasa	JPN	18.5.76				4 Feb
2:12:35	L	Isaac	García	MEX	5.4.68				4 Mar
2:12:36	L	Tendai	Chimusasa	ZIM	28.1.71				7 Oct
2:12:36	L	Pavel	Andreyev	RUS	20.4.70				14 Oct
2:12:37	L	Kazuo	Ietani	JPN	25.8.75				18 Feb
2:12:37	L	Julius	Sugut	KEN					17 Jun
2:12:40	L	Douglas	Rono	KEN	29.12.74				21 Oct
2:12:41	L	Raymond Kipkoech	Chemwolo	KEN	75				27 May
2:12:43	D	Anders	Szalkai	SWE	17.4.70				18 Feb
2:12:43	L	Alberico	Di Cecco	ITA	19.4.74				25 Mar
2:12:43	L	Edílson	Silva	BRA	1.11.73				29 Apr
2:12:44	D	Laban	Nkete	RSA	13.11.70				16 Apr
2:12:44	L	Simon	Mphulanyane	RSA	10.9.70				7 Oct
2:12:45	L		Lim Jin-soo	KOR	16.3.78				18 Mar
2:12:46	P	Angelo	Carosi	ITA	20.1.64				14 Oct
2:12:47	L	Samuel	Tangus	KEN	.64				14 Oct
2:12:47	L	Yoshifumi	Miyamoto	JPN	9.2.73				28 Oct
2:12:48	P	Ezekiel	Kibiwott	KEN	18.8.63				14 Oct
2:12:48	L	Daisuke	Isomatsu	JPN	17.12.73				2 Dec
2:12:50	L	Fidencio	Torres	MEX	16.8.73				4 Mar
2:12:50	L	Francis	Kipketer	KEN	17.4.76				30 Sep
2:12:50	L	Tomix	da Costa	BRA	9.12.62				7 Oct
2:12:51	L	Elias	Chelanga	KEN	69				8 Apr
2:12:54	L	Tadesse	Hailemariam	ETH	17.9.72				3 Jun
2:12:55	L	Frank	Pooe	RSA	2.12.74				14 Oct
2:12:56	L	Stephen	Lagat	KEN	62				22 Apr
2:12:56	L	Joseph	Kariuki	KEN	.70				2 Dec
2:12:57	L	Michael	Buchleitner	AUT	14.10.69				20 May
2:12:58	L	Josephat	Kipchoge Rop	KEN	68				21 Oct
2:12:59	L	Luis	Fonseca	VEN	3.6.77				29 Apr
2:12:59	P	Matteo	Palumbo	ITA	9.9.73				14 Oct
2:12:59	L	Michal	Bartoszak	POL	21.6.70				28 Oct
2:13:02	L	Eliud	Kurgat	KEN	20.8.73				28 Oct
2:13:03	L	Ronnie	Holassie	TRI	29.7.71				29 Apr
2:13:07	P	Joseph	Chebet	KEN	23.8.70				4 Nov
2:13:10	L	António	Sousa	POR	26.2.70				22 Apr
2:13:11	L	Yoshihisa	Okamoto	JPN	76				25 Feb
2:13:11	L	John	Lagat	KEN					8 Apr
2:13:11	P	Mathias	Ntawulikura	RWA	14.7.64				28 Oct
2:13:13	L	Mark	Hudspith	GBR	19.1.69				22 Apr
2:13:13	L	Simon	Mpholo	RSA	17.8.74				2 Dec
2:13:14	L	Daisuke	Tokunaga	JPN	28.11.65				4 Feb
2:13:15	L	Ryo	Murazato	JPN	21.6.78				4 Feb
		(201)	245 under 2:14:00						

Downhill

Mark		Name		Nat	Born	Pos	Meet	Venue	Date
2:12:20	D	Maxell	Musambi	KEN					15 Apr

Short Course

Mark		Name		Nat	Born	Pos	Meet	Venue	Date
2:09:53	L	Giovanni	Ruggiero	ITA	19.1.74	1		Napoli	18 Mar
2:11:23	L	Nicola	Ciavarella	ITA	27.9.68	2		Napoli	18 Mar

JUNIORS

Mark		Name		Nat	Born	Pos	Meet	Venue	Date
2:10:46	L		Li Zhuhong	CHN	22.10.83	7	NG	Beijing	14 Oct
2:11:43	L		Li He	CHN	3.3.84	11	NG	Beijing	14 Oct
2:14:45		Samson	Ramadhani	TAN	25.12.82	2		Arusha	5 Aug
2:14:55	L		Han Shouhui	CHN	11.6.84	18	NG	Beijing	14 Oct
2:15:37	L		Du Pengyuan	CHN	30.9.84	21	NG	Beijing	14 Oct

100 KILOMETRES

Mark	Name		Nat	Born	Pos	Meet	Venue	Date
6:30:07	Vladimir	Netreba	RUS	21.10.67	1		Moscow	22 Apr
6:31:40	Aleksey	Belosludtsev	RUS	29.7.73	2		Moscow	22 Apr
6:33:28	Yasafumi	Mikami	JPN	14.1.66	1	WC	Cléder	26 Aug
6:37:40	Jean Marie	Géhin	FRA	4.8.61	1		Chavagnes-en-Paillers	26 May
6:38:45	Rainer	Müller	GER	24.5.66	1	NC	Neuwittenbek	12 May
6:38:50		Mikami			1		Yufutsu	24 Jun
6:38:57	Piotr	Sekowski	POL	5.9.67	1	NC	Kalisz	7 Nov
6:40:57	Ildar	Akhmetsin	RUS	.70	3		Moscow	22 Apr
6:43:09	Rich	Hanna	USA	.64	2	WC	Cléder	26 Aug
6:43:53	Gino	Deleu	BEL	8.7.66	1		Torhout	22 Jun
6:44:27	Valmir	Nuñes	BRA	16.1.64	2		Torhout	22 Jun
6:44:48	Pascal	Fétizon	FRA	30.8.62	3	WC	Cléder	26 Aug
6:45:43		Netreba			1	EC	Winschoten	29 Sep
6:45:47	Thierry	Guichard	FRA	29.5.60	4	WC	Cléder	26 Aug
6:46:36		Gehin			5	WC	Cléder	26 Aug
6:46:55	Hideo	Nojo	JPN		2		Yubetsu	24 Jun
6:47:23	Pascal	Piveteau	FRA	7.10.61	6	WC	Cléder	26 Aug
6:47:27	Andrey	Shchalybin	RUS	.80	4		Moscow	22 Apr
6:47:57	Attila	Vozár	HUN	27.11.74	2	EC	Winschoten	29 Sep
6:48:21	Marcio	de Oliveira	BRA	14.10.68	7	WC	Cléder	26 Aug
6:48:45		Akhmetsin			3		Torhout	22 Jun
6:48:48	Valeriy	Sinyushkin	RUS	31.3.67	5		Moscow	22 Apr
6:49:19	Anatoliy	Korepanov	RUS	1.2.59	2		Santa Cruz de Bezana	6 Oct

Mark		Name		Nat	Born	Pos	Meet	Venue	Date
6:50:02		Bernard	Bretaud	FRA	17.8.67				26 May
6:50:47		Rik	Goethals	BEL	16.7.59				22 Jun
6:51:52		Jorge	Aubeso	ESP	5.12.66				11 Mar
6:52:24		Bruno	Heubi	FRA	14.3.60				26 May
6:52:47		Miroslav	Vindis	SLO					29 Sep
6:55:15		Bruno	Blanchard	FRA	17.6.63				26 Aug

Drugs Disqualification

Mark		Name		Nat	Born	Pos	Meet	Venue	Date
6:35:19		Grigoriy	Murzin	RUS	23.1.70	1		Santa Cruz de Bezana	6 Oct

24 HOURS

Mark		Name		Nat	Born	Pos	Meet	Venue	Date
275.828	t	Yiannis	Kouros	AUS/GRE	13.2.56	1		Verona	22-23 Sep
270.337	t	Lubomir	Hrmo	SVK	25.2.61	2		Verona	22-23 Sep
260.559		Paul	Beckers	BEL	22.8.62	1	EC	Apeldoorn	25-26 May
259.778	t	Alain	Prual	FRA	24.9.59	3		Verona	22-23 Sep
258.907		Jens	Lukas	GER	13.4.66	2	EC	Apeldoorn	25-26 May
257.064	t	Loic	Lebon	FRA	5.10.48	4		Verona	22-23 Sep
256.398	t	Jaroslav	Kocourek	TCH	17.06.49	5		Verona	22-23 Sep
254.856	t	Kenji	Okiyama	JPN	3.6.65	6		Verona	22-23 Sep
252.801		Vladimir	Kurbatov	RUS	.58	3	EC	Apeldoorn	25-26 May
249.414	t	Karl	Graf	GER	17.12.50	7		Verona	22-23 Sep
248.662		Yevgeniy	Anisimov	RUS	17.7.67	4	EC	Apeldoorn	25-26 May
246.000	t	Ryoichi	Sekiya	JPN	12.2.67	1		Taipei	3-4 Mar
244.340		Eduard	Khirov	RUS	.61	1	NC	Sankt-Peterburg	8-9 Sep
243.323	t	Ivan	Labutin	RUS	20.3.59	1	NC	Moscow	12-13 May
243.104		Rudy	Afanador	USA	23.8.58	1	NC	Sylvania	15-16 Sep
240.595		Mohamed	Magroun	FRA	15.7.59	2	NC	Fleurbaix	30 Jun-1 Jul
240.572	t	Dusan	Mravlje	SLO	13.2.53	8		Verona	22-23 Sep
240.428		Max	Granier	FRA	19.4.51	5	EC	Apeldoorn	25-26 May
240.421		Alexander	Satorato	BRA		6	EC	Apeldoorn	25-26 May
240.364		Timor	Abzalilov	RUS	27.7.58	2	NC	Sankt-Peterburg	8-9 Sep

2000 METRES STEEPLECHASE

Mark	Name		Nat	Born	Pos	Meet	Venue	Date
5:18.51	John	Langat	KEN	27.11.74	1		Rovereto	29 Aug
5:18.60	Stanley	Kibiwott	KEN	8.8.69	2		Rovereto	29 Aug
5:18.61		Langat			1		Padova	26 Aug
5:19.33	Bouabdellah	Tahri	FRA	20.12.78	1		Tomblaine	2 Sep
5:20.07	Antonio	Jiménez	ESP	18.2.77	1		Andújar	5 Sep
5:20.60		Kibiwott			2		Padova	26 Aug
5:21.26	Benson	Koech	KEN	10.11.74	3		Padova	26 Aug
5:22.93	Eliseo	Martín	ESP	5.11.73	2		Andújar	5 Sep
5:22.97	Tim	Broe	USA	20.6.77	4		Padova	26 Aug
5:24.43	José Luis	Blanco	ESP	3.6.75	3		Andújar	5 Sep
5:26.71	Philip	Tarus	KEN	11.9.74				29 Aug
5:27.89	Luciano	Di Pardo	ITA	3.2.75				29 Aug
5:28.22	Angelo	Iannelli	ITA	27.7.76				29 Aug
5:28.48	Laïd	Bessou	ALG	5.2.76				29 Aug
5:29.11	Stafano	Ciallelle	ITA	22.4.74				29 Aug
5:29.62	Robert	Gary	USA	5.4.73				26 Aug

JUNIORS

Mark	Name		Nat	Born	Pos	Meet	Venue	Date
5:33.40	David	Kirwa	KEN	1.8.85	1	WY	Debrecen	15 Jul
5:36.81	Brimin	Kipruto	KEN	31.7.85	2	WY	Debrecen	15 Jul
5:37.76	Abraham	Kebeto	ETH	86	3	WY	Debrecen	15 Jul

3000 METRES STEEPLECHASE

Mark	Name		Nat	Born	Pos	Meet	Venue	Date
7:55.28	Brahim	Boulami	MAR	20.4.72	1	VD	Bruxelles	24 Aug
7:57.29	Reuben	Kosgei	KEN	2.8.79	2	VD	Bruxelles	24 Aug
7:58.50		Boulami			1	WK	Zürich	17 Aug
7:58.66	Stephen	Cherono	KEN-J	15.10.82	3	VD	Bruxelles	24 Aug
8:01.69	Kipkirui	Misoi	KEN	23.12.78	4	VD	Bruxelles	24 Aug
8:01.73	Wilson	Boit Kipketer	KEN	6.10.73	1	Herc	Monaco	20 Jul
8:03.22		R Kosgei			2	WK	Zürich	17 Aug
8:04.47		Misoi			1	WK	Zürich	17 Aug
8:05.00	Bernard	Barmasai	KEN	6.5.74	4	WK	Zürich	17 Aug
8:05.78		Boit Kipketer			1	Nik	Nice	9 Jul
8:06.12		Barmasai			2	Nik	Nice	9 Jul
8:06.81		Misoi			2	Herc	Monaco	20 Jul
8:07.28		Boulami			3	Herc	Monaco	20 Jul
8:07.59	Julius	Nyamu	KEN	1.12.77	5	VD	Bruxelles	24 Aug
8:08.13		Boit Kipketer			1	GP	Saint-Denis	6 Jul
8:08.59		Barmasai			1	GP	Doha	18 May
8:08.74	Luis Miguel	Martín	ESP	11.1.72	6	VD	Bruxelles	24 Aug
8:08.83		R Kosgei			2	GP	Doha	18 May
8:08.90		Misoi			3	Nik	Nice	9 Jul
8:08.99		R Kosgei			2	GP	Saint-Denis	6 Jul
8:09.01		Boit Kipketer			1	GS	Ostrava	31 May

Mark	Name		Nat	Born	Pos	Meet	Venue	Date
8:09.12		R Kosgei			1	GGala	Roma	29 Jun
8:09.20	Raymond	Yator	KEN	7.4.81	2	GGala	Roma	29 Jun
8:09.23	Bouabdellah	Tahri (10)	FRA	20.12.78	7	VD	Bruxelles	24 Aug
8:09.49	Elarbi	Khattabi	MAR	16.5.67	1	GP II	Sevilla	8 Jun
8:09.59		S Cherono			1	ISTAF	Berlin	31 Aug
8:09.63		Yator			3	GP	Saint-Denis	6 Jul
8:09.78		Barmasai			3	GGala	Roma	29 Jun
8:09.94		Yator			5	WK	Zürich	17 Aug
8:10.23	Ali	Ezzine	MAR	3.9.78	4	Nik	Nice	9 Jul
8:10.53		L M Martín			4	Herc	Monaco	20 Jul
8:10.53		Ezzine			8	VD	Bruxelles	24 Aug
8:11.40		Ezzine			4	GP	Saint-Denis	6 Jul
8:11.47		Khattabi			1		Nürnberg	17 Jun
8:11.52	Antonio	Jiménez	ESP	18.2.77	2	GP II	Sevilla	8 Jun
8:11.76		Yator			1		Palo Alto	9 Jun
8:11.80		Misoi			5	GP	Saint-Denis	6 Jul
8:11.88		Jiménez			6	GP	Saint-Denis	6 Jul
8:12.11	John	Kosgei	KEN	13.7.73	6	WK	Zürich	17 Aug
	(39/14)							
8:14.38	Khamis Seif	Abdullah	QAT	1.12.76	1	PArab	Damascus	4 Oct
8:14.82	Tim	Broe	USA	20.6.77	7	GGala	Roma	29 Jun
8:15.01	Sa'ad Shaddad	Al-Asmari	KSA	24.9.68	2	PArab	Damascus	4 Oct
8:15.17	John	Langat	KEN	27.11.74	5	ISTAF	Berlin	31 Aug
8:15.36	José Luis	Blanco	ESP	3.6.75	3	GP II	Sevilla	8 Jun
8:15.92	Paul	Koech II	KEN	10.11.81	6	ISTAF	Berlin	31 Aug
	(20)							
8:16.00	Stéphane	Desaulty	FRA	8.1.72	4	GP II	Sevilla	8 Jun
8:16.28	David	Chepkisa	KEN	1.1.74	2		Milano	6 Jun
8:16.57	Abraham	Cherono	KEN	21.7.80	2	GP II	Athína	11 Jun
8:16.62	Stanley	Kibiwott	KEN	8.8.69	3	GP II	Athína	11 Jun
8:17.98	Gaël	Pencréach	FRA	5.8.77	2		Nürnberg	17 Jun
8:19.20	Eliseo	Martín	ESP	5.11.73	9	VD	Bruxelles	24 Aug
8:19.32	Ralf	Assmus	GER	28.1.77	10	WK	Zürich	17 Aug
8:19.87	Laïd	Bessou	ALG	5.2.76	7	GP	Saint-Denis	6 Jul
8:20.67	Simon	Vroemen	NED	11.5.69	7	Herc	Monaco	20 Jul
8:21.00	Anthony	Famiglietti	USA	8.11.78	4	DNG	Stockholm	17 Jul
	(30)							
8:21.66	Jim	Svenøy	NOR	22.4.72	4	FBK	Hengelo	4 Jun
8:21.78	Lotfi	Turki	TUN	6.3.75	4		Milano	6 Jun
8:22.03	Frédéric	Denis	FRA	3.3.75	6	Nik	Nice	9 Jul
8:22.06	Alberto	Álvarez	ESP	22.12.75	5	GP II	Sevilla	8 Jun
8:22.16	Thomas	Chorny	USA	23.11.76	1	NC	Eugene	24 Jun
8:22.24	Christian	Belz	SUI	11.9.74	5	FBK	Hengelo	4 Jun
8:22.49	Jan	Zakrzewski	POL	21.12.70	1		Bialogard	29 Sep
8:22.91	Francisco Javier	Munuera	ESP	7.7.72	1		Málaga	28 Jul
8:23.00	Jakub	Czaja	POL	12.9.80	2	WUG	Beijing	29 Aug
8:23.29	Irba	Lakhal	MAR	12.2.75	6	FBK	Hengelo	4 Jun
	(40)							
8:23.62	Günther	Weidlinger	AUT	5.4.78	3	GS	Ostrava	31 May
8:23.66	Ezekiel	Kemboi	KEN-J	25.5.82	1	Veniz	Haniá	4 Jun
8:23.94	Billy	Herman	USA	3.7.77	1		Cottbus	18 Jul
8:24.22	Badredin	Zioini	FRA	25.3.76	7	FBK	Hengelo	4 Jun
8:24.3	Zouhair	El Ouardi	MAR	15.2.72	1		Rabat	5 May
8:25.12	Lyès	Ramoul	FRA	17.4.76	2	Franc	Ottawa	19 Jul
8:25.25	Hicham	Guermoud	MAR	79	3		Strasbourg	19 Jun
8:25.29	Vladimir	Pronin	RUS	27.5.69	8	FBK	Hengelo	4 Jun
8:25.69	Aziz	Driouche	MAR	15.11.77	4	WUG	Beijing	29 Aug
8:25.73	Clint	Wells	USA	2.5.75	4	NC	Eugene	24 Jun
	(50)							
8:25.94	Ray	Hughes	USA	9.5.75	3h1	NC	Eugene	22 Jun
8:26.14	Mark	Croghan	USA	8.1.68	1		New Brunswick	7 Jul
8:26.45	Steve	Slattery	USA	14.8.80	4h1	NC	Eugene	22 Jun
8:26.52	José María	González	ESP	3.3.73	7	GP II	Sevilla	8 Jun
8:26.77	Yoshitaka	Iwamizu	JPN	20.6.79	1	NC	Tokyo	9 Jun
8:26.82	Hamid	Jaoane	FRA	3.4.72	4		Strasbourg	19 Jun
8:26.90	Merzak	Ould Bouchiba	ALG	27.4.75	5		San Sebastián	18 Aug
8:26.91	Dan	Lincoln	USA	20.10.80	5	NC	Eugene	24 Jun
8:26.92	Joël	Bourgeois	CAN	25.4.71	6h1	WCh	Edmonton	6 Aug
8:27.07	Rafal	Wójcik	POL	18.9.72	4		Bydgoszcz	15 Jun
	(60)							

Mark	Name		Nat	Born	Pos	Meet	Venue	Date
8:27.44	Ramiro	Morán	ESP	17.5.69	5		Nürnberg	17 Jun
8:27.51	Sergey	Redko	UKR	24.1.73	5		Bydgoszcz	15 Jun
8:27.54	Robert	Gary	USA	5.4.73	1		Minneapolis	14 Jul
8:27.92	Moses	Kigen	KEN	22.4.73	9	FBK	Hengelo	4 Jun
8:28.08	André	Green	GER	21.4.73	10	FBK	Hengelo	4 Jun
8:28.08	Martin	Pröll	AUT	21.3.81	6		Nürnberg	17 Jun
8:28.2A	Matthew	Birir	KEN	5.7.72	5	NC	Nairobi	23 Jun
8:28.85	Mourad	Benslimani	ALG	19.2.74	8		Strasbourg	19 Jun
8:28.90	Philip	Tarus	KEN	11.9.74	4	Mal M	Grudziadz	7 Sep
8:29.13	Angelo	Carosi	ITA	20.1.64	6		Milano	6 Jun
	(70)							
8:29.50	Angelo	Iannelli	ITA	27.7.76	7		Milano	6 Jun
8:29.63	Yasunori	Uchitomi	JPN	29.10.72	2	NC	Tokyo	9 Jun
8:30.12	David	Chemweno	KEN	18.12.81	1		Canberra	18 Feb
8:30.32	Henrik	Skoog	SWE	17.4.79	9	GS	Ostrava	31 May
8:30.37	Eliud	Kirui	KEN	15.8.75	6		Bydgoszcz	15 Jun
8:31.43	Filmon	Ghirmai	GER	25.1.79	7		Nürnberg	17 Jun
8:31.88	Greg	Jimmerson	USA	1.2.75	6h1	NC	Eugene	22 Jun
8:32.22	Manuel	Silva	POR	8.10.78	7		San Sebastián	18 Aug
8:32.3	Abdellatif	Chemlal	MAR- J	1.1.82	3		Rabat	5 May
8:32.5A	Michael	Kiptanui	KEN		4h3	NC	Nairobi	21 Jun
	(80)							
8:32.52	Dave	Cullum	USA	26.10.73	2		Palo Alto	4 May
8:32.68	Ben	Whitby	GBR	6.1.77	1	NC	Birmingham	15 Jul
8:32.82	Abderrahmane	Daas	ALG	8.12.73	8		San Sebastián	18 Aug
8:32.84	Luciano	Di Pardo	ITA	3.2.75	8		Milano	6 Jun
8:32.89	Sandu	Rebenciuc	USA	26.5.69	7h1	NC	Eugene	22 Jun
8:33.15	Stuart	Stokes	GBR	15.12.76	2	NC	Birmingham	15 Jul
8:33.48	Peter	Nowill	AUS	15.6.79	1	Zat	Melbourne	6 Dec
8:33.53	Mário	Teixeira	POR	20.9.74	1		Maia	14 Jul
8:33.71	Christian	Knoblich	GER	1.10.76	10		Milano	6 Jun
8:33.75	Carlos	Suárez	ESP	25.9.75	9	NC	Valencia	21 Jul
	(90)							
8:33.90	Petros	Sithole	RSA	29.3.76	1	NC	Durban	2 Mar
8:34.00	Michael	Nejedly	CZE	1.10.69	1		Rehlingen	4 Jun
8:34.01	Marcin	Grzegorzewski	POL	5.6.78	7		Bydgoszcz	15 Jun
8:34.08	Gianni	Crepaldi	ITA	19.10.68	11		Milano	6 Jun
8:34.12	Vincent	Le Dauphin	FRA	28.6.76	2		Vanves	25 May
8:34.66	Giuseppe	Maffei	ITA	28.1.74	6	Gugl	Linz	20 Aug
8.34.93	Taoufik	Faouzi	MAR	.73	1		Rabat	23 May
8:35.06	Kim	Bergdahl	FIN	5.3.78	1		Kuortane	17 Jun
8:35.08	Roman	Usov	RUS	4.6.78	6	WUG	Beijing	29 Aug
8:35.17	Julius	Chelule	KEN	25.12.78	4		Cottbus	18 Jul
	(100)							

Mark	Name		Nat	Born	Date
8:35.21	Salvador	Miranda	MEX	22.8.71	3 Jun
8:35.23	Markus	Hagmann	SUI	3.7.75	4 Jun
8:35.85	Pavel	Potapovich	RUS	1.1.79?	14 Jul
8:36.20	Damian	Kallabis	GER	10.6.73	20 Aug
8:36.22	Vadim	Slobodenyuk	UKR	17.3.81	2 Jul
8:36.23	Antonio	Martínez	ESP	20.12.78	28 Jul
8:36.25		Sun Wenli	CHN	9.2.78	19 Nov
8:36.33	Martin	Dent	AUS	8.2.79	6 Dec
8:36.45	Jared	Cordes	USA	22.7.72	4 May
8:36.48	Wataru	Izumi	JPN	22.9.72	24 May
8:36.59	Simon	Mayisela	RSA	9.5.72	3 Mar
8:36.61	César	Pérez	ESP	7.4.75	14 Jul
8:37.02	Tuomo	Lehtinen	FIN	2.2.79	17 Jun
8:37.57	Peter	Kipkassi	KEN		14 Jul
8:37.73	Florin	Ionescu	ROM	3.2.71	4 Jun
8:37.90	Marc	Ostendarp	GER	24.1.73	1 Jul
8:38.01	Andy	Tate	USA	27.11.77	20 Apr
8:38.03	Joel	Kgokong	RSA	13.10.75	3 Mar
8:38.1A	David	Kirwa	KEN-J	1.8.85	12 May
8:38.25	Michal	Kaczmarek	POL	19.9.77	29 Jun
8:38.46	Christian	Stephenson	GBR	22.7.74	23 May
8:38.56	Jaroslav	Muschinschi	MDA	8.8.76	9 Jun
8:38.62	Angelo	Giardiello	ITA	18.2.70	14 Jul
8:38.74	Raúl	Moya	ESP	18.1.79	11 Jun
8:38.91	Aleksey	Gurkin	RUS	.79	12 Jul
8:38.93	Dave	Smith	USA		11 Apr
8:38.95	Tony	Cosey	USA	5.10.74	3 Jun
8:39.02	Joan	Herrera	ESP	13.3.73	14 Jul
8:39.2	Donald	Naylor	GBR	5.9.71	23 Jun
8:39.21	Solomon	Kandie	KEN		31 Mar
8:39.25	Mikael	Talasjoki	FIN	27.3.79	26 Aug
8:39.39	Raphael	Schäfer	GER	6.3.81	18 Jul
8:39.6A	Philip	Maru	KEN		12 May
8:39.75	Elisardo	de la Torre	ESP	10.10.71	14 Jul
8:39.78	Hassan Ali	Al Asmari	KSA	76	4 Oct
8:39.83	Mickaël	Damian	FRA	9.11.69	20 May
8:39.88	Eliud	Barngetuny	KEN	20.5.73	20 May
	(137)				

Mark	Name	Nat	Born	Pos	Meet	Venue	Date
Disqualified: 8:10.51	Yator			1	GP II	Gresham	3 Jun
8:38.85	Sun Jiawei	CHN	3.1.78	19	Nov		

JUNIORS

See main list for top 3 juniors. 10 performances by men to 8:26.0. Additional marks and further juniors:

	Mark	Pos	Meet	Venue	Date	Mark	Pos	Meet	Venue	Date
Cherono 2+	8:18.85	3	GPF	Melbourne	9 Sep	8:22.98	2	GP II	Gresham	3 Jun
	8:19.43	3	GP II	Doha	18 May	8:24.58	8	Nik	Nice	9 Jul
	8:19.98	3	GWG	Brisbane	5 Sep	8:25.98	2		Palo Alto	9 Jun
	8:21.94	1		Hobart	11 Mar					

Mark	Name		Nat	Born	Pos	Meet	Venue	Date
8:38.1A	David	Kirwa	KEN	1.8.85	1		Nairobi	12 May
8:40.02		Nu Xueren	CHN	1.2.82	2	NG	Guangzhou	19 Nov
8:41.26	Michael	Kipyego	KEN	2.10.83	2	Afr-J	Réduit	19 Aug
8:41.53	Ali Abubaker	Kamal	QAT	3.12.82	1	Gulf-j	Muscat	15 Mar
8:41.9	Mimoun	Ouerani	MAR		1		Meknès	12 May
8.42.04	Mircea	Bogdan	ROM	6.5.82	9	WUG	Beijing	29 Aug
8:46.36	Radoslaw	Poplawski	POL	16.1.83	1	EJ	Grosseto	22 Jul
8:47.08	Erik	Emilsson	SWE	10.3.82	3	NC	Växjö	25 Aug
8:51.87	Hristoforos	Merousis	GRE	22.3.82	3	EJ	Grosseto	22 Jul
8:52.26	Cyrus	Njui	KEN	.86	1		Utsunomiya	18 Jun
8:52.37	Hidenobu	Koshikawa	JPN	16.12.82	5		Tokyo	29 Sep
8:52.41	Keita	Tsuchihashi	JPN	40.4.84	1	NG	Rifu	16 Oct
8:52.90	Yoshiyuki	Musha	JPN	2.9.83	3	NG	Rifu	16 Oct
8:53.84	Terefe	Dessaleng	ETH	20.11.82	3		Schweinfurt	29 Jul
8:53.90	Sergey	Berdnik	BLR	18.5.82	4	EJ	Grosseto	22 Jul
8:53.95	Grzegorz	Wojtczak	POL	7.2.83	5	EJ	Grosseto	22 Jul
8:54.51	Mariano	Mastromarino	ARG	15.9.82	1	SAm-J	Sabta fe	12 Oct

110 METRES HURDLES

Mark	Wind	Name		Nat	Born	Pos	Meet	Venue	Date
13.04	-0.3	Allen	Johnson	USA	1.3.71	1	WCh	Edmonton	9 Aug
13.04	1.0		Johnson			1	ISTAF	Berlin	31 Aug
13.07	-0.3	Anier	García	CUB	9.3.76	2	WCh	Edmonton	9 Aug
13.07	0.2		García			1	VD	Bruxelles	24 Aug
13.12	0.2	Larry	Wade	USA	22.11.74	2	VD	Bruxelles	24 Aug
13.14	2.0	Dominique	Arnold	USA	14.9.73	1		Königs Wusterhausen	28 Aug
13.15	0.1		Johnson			1	GP	Saint-Denis	6 Jul
13.15	1.0		García			2	ISTAF	Berlin	31 Aug
13.16	-0.4		Johnson			1	GWG	Brisbane	5 Sep
13.17	-0.2		García			1	Gugl	Linz	20 Aug
13.18	-0.7		Johnson			1	Herc	Monaco	20 Jul
13.18	0.0		Johnson			1rA	WK	Zürich	17 Aug
13.19	-0.7		García			2	Herc	Monaco	20 Jul
13.19	1.0		García			1s1	WCh	Edmonton	8 Aug
13.19	0.8		García			1		Yokohama	15 Sep
13.20	-0.2		Johnson			2	Gugl	Linz	20 Aug
13.20	-0.4		García			2	GWG	Brisbane	5 Sep
13.21	1.4		García			1		Rivas	27 Jun
13.21	0.9		Johnson			1	Bisl	Oslo	13 Jul
13.21	1.7		García			1h3	WCh	Edmonton	9 Aug
13.21	1.0		Arnold			3	ISTAF	Berlin	31 Aug
13.22	-3.2		Johnson			1	NC	Eugene	24 Jun
13.22	0.7	Dawane	Wallace	USA	30.12.76	1rB	WK	Zürich	17 Aug
13.22	-1.7		García			1	GPF	Melbourne	9 Sep
13.23	0.1		García			2	GP	Saint-Denis	6 Jul
13.23	0.0	Terrence	Trammell	USA	23.11.78	2rA	WK	Zürich	17 Aug
13.24	-0.4		García			1rA	Athl	Lausanne	4 Jul
13.24	0.1		Trammell			3	GP	Saint-Denis	6 Jul
13.24	0.9		Trammell			2	Bisl	Oslo	13 Jul
13.24	0.0		Wade			3rA	WK	Zürich	17 Aug
13.24	0.2		Johnson			3	VD	Bruxelles	24 Aug
		(31/6)							
13.25	-0.3	Dudley	Dorival	HAI	1.9.75	3	WCh	Edmonton	9 Aug
13.26	0.6	Yuniel	Hernández	CUB	28.3.81	1		Salamanca	13 Jul
13.26	1.4	Shaun	Bownes	RSA	24.10.70	1	NA	Heusden	14 Jul
13.26	0.2	Mark	Crear	USA	2.10.68	4	VD	Bruxelles	24 Aug
		(10)							
13.29	-0.4	Stanislav	Olijar	LAT	22.3.79	3rA	Athl	Lausanne	4 Jul
13.30	-0.3	Yoel	Hernández	CUB	12.12.77	4	WCh	Edmonton	9 Aug
13.32	1.9		Liu Xiang	CHN-J	13.7.83	1		Shanghai	6 May
13.32	0.0	Chris	Phillips	USA	24.7.72	1		Ingolstadt	27 May
13.32	0.8	Colin	Jackson	GBR	18.2.67	1		Dortmund	9 Jun
13.35	1.7	Robert	Kronberg	SWE	15.8.76	2rA	Athl	Lausanne	4 Jul
13.36	1.6	Elmar	Lichtenegger	AUT	25.5.74	2	WUG	Beijing	28 Aug
13.37	1.9		Chen Yanhao	CHN	2.1.72	2		Shanghai	6 May
13.37	0.1	Mike	Fenner	GER	24.4.71	1		Malles	14 Jul
13.38	1.3	Yevgeniy	Pechonkin	RUS	9.10.73	1	ECp-S	Bremen	24 Jun
		(20)							
13.42	1.2	Aubrey	Herring	USA	19.9.78	2		Knoxville	13 Apr
13.43	1.9		Shi Dongpeng	CHN-J	6.1.84	3		Shanghai	6 May

Mark	Wind	Name		Nat	Born	Pos	Meet	Venue	Date
13.43	1.5	Ron	Bramlett	USA	22.10.79	1h2	NCAA	Eugene	31 May
13.43	1.7	Zhivko	Videnov	BUL	23.5.77	4rB	Athl	Lausanne	4 Jul
13.44	0.8	Terry	Reese	USA	20.6.67	3	GP II	Zagreb	2 Jul
13.45	0.2	Anthony	Jarrett	GBR	13.8.68	2	GP II	Helsinki	14 Jun
13.47	0.0	Arend	Watkins	USA	23.5.79	1		Berkeley	17 Mar
13.47	1.4	Jeff	York	USA	3.9.71	3h3	NC	Eugene	23 Jun
13.47	0.1	Derek	Knight	USA	11.10.67	2		Malles	14 Jul
13.49	1.8	Thavius 'T.J'	Nelson	USA	7.12.77	1	Big 10	Bloomington	20 May
		(30)							
13.50	1.2	Márcio	de Souza	BRA	24.1.75	1		São Paulo	18 Mar
13.50	0.1	Masato	Naito	JPN	31.7.80	1		Rifu	17 Oct
13.51	0.0	Jerome	Crews	GER	20.2.77	1		Sondershausen	24 Aug
13.53	1.8	Peter	Coghlan	IRL	27.3.75	1		Fort-de-France	28 Apr
13.53	0.5	Florian	Schwarthoff	GER	7.5.68	5		Nürnberg	17 Jun
13.53	1.7	Artur	Kohutek	POL	1.5.71	1rB		Bydgoszcz	1 Jul
13.54	2.0	Duane	Ross	USA	5.12.72	2h2	NC	Eugene	23 Jun
13.54	1.1	Claude	Edorh	GER	27.2.72	3	NC	Stuttgart	1 Jul
13.55	1.8	Kyle	Vander-Kuyp	AUS	30.5.71	1	NC	Brisbane	25 Mar
13.55	0.0	Vincent	Clarico	FRA	8.1.66	1		La Chaux-de-Fonds	19 Aug
		(40)							
13.56	1.8	Guy	Rose	USA	6.2.80	2	Big 10	Bloomington	20 May
13.58	1.7	Ladji	Doucouré	FRA-J	28.3.83	1	NC	Sainte-Etienne	30 Jun
13.58	1.1	Ralf	Leberer	GER	26.10.73	4	NC	Stuttgart	1 Jul
13.58A	0.3	Paulo	Villar	COL	28.7.78	1	Bol G	Ambato	13 Sep
13.60		Todd	Matthews	USA	28.6.79	1		Clemson	24 Mar
13.60	1.5	Kris	Allen	USA	14.4.79	1rA	Tex R	Austin	7 Apr
13.60	1.6	Kimihiro	Asami	JPN	8.11.72	1		Kyoto	23 Jun
13.61	0.4	Eugene	Swift	USA	14.9.64	2	MSR	Walnut	22 Apr
13.61	-0.6	Joseph-Berlioz	Randriamihaja	MAD	30.11.75	4h2	WCh	Edmonton	7 Aug
13.62	0.4	Cédric	Lavanne	FRA	13.11.80	1		Obernai	29 Jul
		(50)							
13.63	1.4	Jonathan	Nsenga	BEL	21.4.73	3	NA	Heusden	14 Jul
13.63	1.4	Paul	Gray	GBR	25.5.69	1	BIG	Bedford	18 Jul
13.64	0.3	Chris	Pinnock	USA-J?	81/82	1	Kans R	Lawrence	21 Apr
13.64	1.5	Stephen	Jones	BAR	25.7.78	3h2	NCAA	Eugene	31 May
13.64	1.4	William	Erese	NGR	12.9.73	4	NA	Heusden	14 Jul
13.64A	0.3	Jackson	Quiñónez	ECU	12.6.80	2	Bol G	Ambato	13 Sep
13.65	2.0	Adrian	Woodley	CAN	25.11.75	5	GP	Palo Alto	9 Jun
13.65	1.7	Krzysztof	Mehlich	POL	2.8.74	2	NC	Bydgoszcz	1 Jul
13.65	0.0	Philip	Nossmy	SWE-J	6.12.82	2	NC	Växjö	24 Aug
13.66	1.1	Damjan	Zlatnar	SLO	16.12.77	1		Trieste	18 Jul
		(60)							
13.67	0.3	Wenston	Riley	USA	24.4.77	2h3	NCAA	Eugene	31 May
13.67	1.2	Jean Marc	Grava	FRA	2.12.71	1h3	NC	Sainte-Etienne	30 Jun
13.67	-0.4	Redelén	dos Santos	BRA	24.4.76	1		São Paulo	30 Jun
13.68	0.8	Damien	Greaves	GBR	9.9.77	2	NC	Birmingham	15 Jul
13.68	1.0	Emiliano	Pizzoli	ITA	29.6.74	4	GP II	Rieti	2 Sep
13.69	-1.5	Ryan	Wilson	USA	19.12.80	1		Los Angeles	24 Mar
13.69	1.8	Ken-ichi	Sakurai	JPN	26.12.76	1		Joetsu	22 Apr
13.69	1.2	Sultan	Tucker	LBR	24.10.78	1		Clemson	13 May
13.69	1.2	Gabriel	Burnett	BAR	20.9.75	1		Bridgetown	19 May
13.69	0.7	Walmes	de Souza	BRA	14.9.74	1h1		Americana	16 Jun
		(70)							
13.69	-0.4	Emerson	Perin	BRA	17.3.75	2		São Paulo	30 Jun
13.70	2.0	Jermaine	Cooper	USA	31.8.80	1rB	Tex R	Austin	7 Apr
13.70	1.8	Eddie	Jackson	USA	19.12.80	2r4	MSR	Walnut	22 Apr
13.70	0.7	Maurice	Wignall	JAM	17.4.76	1	NC	Kingston	23 Jun
13.70	1.2	Artur	Budzillo	POL	21.7.79	1	NC-23	Gdansk	18 Aug
13.70	0.4		Qi Zhen	CHN	4.8.76	4	NG	Guangzhou	19 Nov
13.71	1.1	Robert	Foster	JAM	12.7.70	1		Northridge	24 Mar
13.71	-0.5	Marcel	van de Westen	NED	1.8.76	2	ECp-1B	Budapest	24 Jun
13.72	0.3	Shinri	Yamada	JPN	17.6.79	2		Yokohama	20 May
13.72	1.0	Mubarak Ata	Mubarak	KSA	17.12.81	5h6	WCh	Edmonton	7 Aug
		(80)							
13.73	0.1	Garland	Martin	USA	1.3.81	1		Tuscaloosa	24 Mar
13.73	1.8	Stuart	Anderson	AUS	19.6.79	2	NC	Brisbane	25 Mar
13.73	0.0	Reggie	Harrell	USA	28.11.81	1	WAC	Fresno	19 May
13.73	1.5	Micah	Harris	USA	30.4.79	6h2	NCAA	Eugene	31 May
13.73	1.2	Satoru	Tanigawa	JPN	5.7.72	2	NC	Tokyo	9 Jun
13.73		Sergey	Khodanovich	BLR	11.6.78	1		Minsk	30 Jun
13.74	-0.8	Bashir	Ramzy	USA	4.5.79	1		College Station	17 Mar

Mark	Wind	Name		Nat	Born	Pos	Meet	Venue	Date
13.74	1.6	Yasunori	Yoshioka	JPN	19.5.75	2		Kyoto	23 Jun
13.74	0.4	Ivan	Bitzi	SUI	4.8.75	3	ECp-1A	Vaasa	24 Jun
13.74	0.3	Javier	Vega	ESP	10.12.75	1		Mataró	4 Jul
		(90)							
13.75	2.0	Derrick	James	USA	18.10.76	2rB	Tex R	Austin	7 Apr
13.75	0.3	Jasper	Demps	USA	22.10.79	4h3	NCAA	Eugene	31 May
13.75	1.1	Jarno	Jokihaara	FIN	2.9.73	1		Lappeenranta	15 Jul
13.76	1.7	Philippe	Lamine	FRA	4.10.76	1s1		Dijon	1 Jun
13.76	1.4	Hipólito	Montesinos	ESP	24.5.76	4		Rivas	27 Jun
13.77	-0.5	Levente	Csillag	HUN	22.3.73	3	ECp-1B	Budapest	24 Jun
13.77	0.1	Devis	Favaro	ITA	14.7.72	5		Malles	14 Jul
13.78	1.6	Justin	Gatlin	USA-J	10.2.82	1h1	SEC	Columbia, SC	12 May
13.78	0.4	Leonard	Hudec	AUT	13.6.73	1h2		Innsbruck	8 Jul
13.78	-0.3	Tasuku	Tanonaka	JPN	23.9.78	2	Nambu	Sapporo	8 Jul
		(100)							

Mark	Wind	Name		Nat	Born	Date
13.79	1.7	Thomas	Martin	FRA	19.2.80	1 Jun
13.79	-0.7	João Luiz	do Rosário	BRA	27.8.73	16 Jun
13.79	0.4	Felipe	Vivancos	ESP	16.6.80	15 Jul
13.80	2.0	Andy	Long	USA	30.11.78	7 Apr
13.80	1.1	Rod	Jett	USA	28.10.66	5 May
13.80	1.8	Corey	Taylor	USA	2.5.81	12 May
13.80	-0.4	Tomás	Dvorák	CZE	11.5.72	7 Aug
13.81i		Andrey	Kislykh	RUS	24.11.76	12 Feb
		13.85	-0.8			13 Jul
13.81	-0.3	Sébastien	Denis	FRA	4.5.71	1 Jun
13.81	1.5	Thomas	Keller	SUI	25.5.73	4 Jun
13.81	1.6		Cao Jing	CHN	31.1.78	15 Jun
13.81	1.2	Thomas	Blaschek	GER	5.4.81	1 Jul
13.81	-1.6	Robert	Howard	USA	26.11.75	10 Jul
13.81	1.5	Frikkie	van Zyl	RSA	30.7.81	13 Nov
13.82	1.2	Charles	Allen	GUY	29.3.77	13 May
13.82	0.8	Chris	Baillie	GBR	21.4.81	7 Jul
13.82	1.0	Andrea	Giaconi	ITA	11.4.74	2 Sep
13.83	1.8	E.J.	Martin	USA	.76	22 Apr
13.83	1.5	Jeremichael	Williams	USA	30.12.76	5 May
13.83	1.0	Roman	Sebrle	CZE	26.11.74	12 May
13.83	0.0	Rashad	Stafford	USA	26.1.78	19 May
13.83	1.1	Jens	Buchholz	GER	17.6.76	1 Jul
13.83	0.2	Robin	Korving	NED	29.7.74	8 Jul
13.83	0.8	Dominic	Bradley	GBR	22.12.76	14 Jul
13.83	1.2	Sebastian	Siebert	GER-J	23.6.82	21 Jul
13.84	1.9	Dimiírios	Piétris	GRE	24.10.79	19 May
13.84	0.2	Andrea	Putignani	ITA	31.12.70	14 Jul
13.84	0.1	Tsuyoshi	Tsutsumi	JPN	27.9.76	17 Oct
13.84	0.4		Zhang Feng	CHN	9.5.72	19 Nov
13.85	-1.5	Djéké	Mambo	BEL	4.3.77	24 Mar
13.85	1.8	Charles	Johnson	USA	6.11.68	28 Apr
13.85	-0.5	Yuriy	Volkov	RUS	77	8 Jun
13.85	-0.5	Emilio	Valle	CUB	21.4.67	21 Jul
13.86	1.1	Gergely	Palágyi	HUN	19.4.79	19 May
13.86	0.2	Sven	Ootjers	NED	24.6.73	8 Jul
13.86	0.8	Raphaël	Monachon	SUI	8.2.73	25 Aug
13.87	0.8	Neil	Owen	GBR	18.10.73	14 Jul
13.88	2.0	Joey	Scott	USA		21 Apr
13.88	1.8	Greg	Richardson	USA	27.12.76	28 Apr
13.88	1.8	Karl	Jennings	USA	14.5.79	12 May
13.88	0.7	Ricardo	Melbourne	JAM-J	26.2.82	23 Jun
13.88	0.8	Mensah	Elliott	GBR	29.8.76	14 Jul
13.89	-0.4	Lewis	Edmonson	USA		31 Mar
13.89	1.6	Michael	Thomas	USA	21.12.81	12 May
13.89	0.9	Shannon	Flowers	USA	17.9.71	20 Jul
13.90	-0.5	Chris	Stokes	USA	1.2.79	31 Mar
13.90	0.0	Tony	Galaviz	USA	23.9.78	14 Apr
13.90	1.8	Seam	Lightfoot	USA	8.6.79	22 Apr
13.90	1.7	Moussa	Sissoko	MLI/FRA	27.10.74	19 May
13.90	1.3	Jalilu	Mayo	USA	2.1.78	9 Jun
13.90	0.4	Kenneth	Halhjem	NOR	10.7.76	24 Jun
13.90	-0.6	Balázs	Kovács	HUN	14.6.77	25 Jul
13.90	0.0	Nenad	Loncar	YUG	6.3.81	12 Sep
13.91	2.0	Kevin	Walker	USA	26.2.78	6 May
13.91	0.0	Nicola	Comencini	ITA	7.5.78	2 Jun
13.91	1.1	Andrew	Lissade	CAN	4.1.76	27 Aug
13.91	0.5	Luiz André	Balcers	BRA	18.10.73	1 Sep
13.92	0.4	Dominique	DeGrammont	USA	13.3.79	22 Apr
13.92	0.0	Lee	Mays	USA	18.9.78	19 May
13.92	1.7	Jan	Schindzielorz	GER	8.8.78	1 Jun
13.92	0.0	Stefan	Drews	GER	12.2.79	3 Jun
13.92	2.0	Deworski	Odom	USA	11.4.77	9 Jun
13.92	1.2	Andrey	Sklyarenko	KAZ	10.1.76	24 Jun
13.93	1.8	Neil	Gardner	JAM	8.12.74	22 Apr
13.93	-0.6	Carlos	Patterson	CUB	20.2.78	25 May
13.93	1.0	Jared	McLeod	CAN	3.4.80	24 Jun
13.93	0.4	Rafal	Lis	POL	25.2.79	15 Jul
13.94	0.3	Igor	Kazanov	LAT	24.9.63	21 Apr
13.94	-1.7	Antonio	De Sanctis	ITA	18.10.72	27 May
13.94	1.2	Doudou	Felou Sow	SEN	76	1 Jun
13.94	0.4	Philipp	Unfried	AUT	30.7.78	10 Jun
13.94	1.5	Luca	Giovannelli	ITA	29.9.75	7 Jul
13.94	0.6	Erik	Batte	CUB	10.12.74	13 Jul
13.95	-0.4	Paolo	Della Santa	SUI	11.9.73	12 May
13.95	0.3	Mitsuru	Miyazawa	JPN	13.5.78	20 May
13.95	0.8	Zoran	Miljus	CRO	26.5.76	2 Jul
13.96	1.2	Ron	Andrews	USA	12.10.79	13 Apr
13.96	1.8		Galruise	USA		22 Apr
13.96	1.8	Robby	Hughes	USA	10.10.78	28 Apr
13.96	1.1	Antti	Haapakoski	FIN	6.2.71	3 Jun
13.96	-0.1	Mihai	Marghescu	ROM	26.9.76	9 Jun
13.96	0.0	Andrea	Alterio	ITA	11.6.73	19 Aug
13.96	0.5	Nobuto	Watanabe	JPN	20.10.76	30 Sep
13.97	0.5	Antoine	Johnson	USA	22.12.80	27 Apr
13.97	1.8	Sean	Lightfoot	USA	8.6.79	12 May
13.97	1.7	Jeff	Young	USA	9.3.81	19 May
13.97	0.0	Jurica	Grabusic	CRO-J	28.3.83	12 Sep
13.98	-1.1	Montrell	Person	USA	.81	7 Apr
13.98	1.3		Li Qiang	CHN	13.2.74	22 Apr
13.98	1.8		Galruise	USA		22 Apr
13.98	1.7	Twann	Atkins	USA	12.12.80	12 May
13.98	1.2	Tino	Ngoy	COD	1.3.80	1 Jun
13.98	1.6	Toru	Momoi	JPN	17.9.77	23 Jun
13.98	-0.1	Yuji	Ohashi	JPN-J	5.9.83	6 Aug
13.98	1.4	Thiago	Dias	BRA-J	2.3.84	25 Aug
13.99	1.5	De'Andre	Eiland	USA-J	4.6.82	31 Mar
13.99	1.0	Samuel	Glover	USA	22.1.80	12 May
13.99	1.9	Greg	Hines	JAM	16.9.75	19 May
13.99	1.2	Jorn	Lichtenhagen	GER	30.4.76	1 Jun
13.99	1.1	Marko	Ritola	FIN	29.1.79	3 Jun
13.99	0.0	Florian	Seibold	GER	27.6.79	29 Jul
		(202)				

Wind assisted

Mark	Wind	Name		Nat	Born	Pos	Meet	Venue	Date
13.36		Aubrey	Herring	USA	19.9.78	1		Charleston	7 Apr
13.39	2.2	Ron	Bramlett	USA	22.10.79	1h1	WUG	Beijing	27 Aug
13.49	2.8	Márcio	de Souza	BRA	24.1.75	1		Americana	29 Apr
13.49	2.1	Eugene	Swift	USA	14.9.64	3	Mod R	Modesto	12 May
13.52	3.6	Kris	Allen	USA	14.4.79	1	USTCA	Austin	21 Apr
13.52	3.6	Jermaine	Cooper	USA	31.8.80	2	USTCA	Austin	21 Apr
13.54		Chris	Pinnock	USA-J?	81/82	1	JUCO	Odessa, TX	12 May
13.58	2.8	Bashir	Ramzy	USA	4.5.79	2h1	NCAA	Eugene	31 May
13.59	2.7	Deworski	Odom	USA	11.4.77	3h4	NC	Eugene	23 Jun

Mark	Wind	Name		Nat	Born	Pos	Meet	Venue	Date
13.62	3.4	Emilio	Valle	CUB	21.4.67	1	NC	La Habana	25 May
13.62	2.5	Damjan	Zlatnar	SLO	16.12.77	1		Celje	9 Jun
13.67	4.4	Frikkie	van Zyl	RSA	30.7.81	2		Parow	28 Dec
13.68	2.8	Roman	Sebrle	CZE	26.11.74	1		Thum	20 May
13.69	2.8		Cao Jing	CHN	31.1.78	1		Jinan	13 May
13.70	3.8	Rich	Benoy	USA	14.7.68	1		Azusa	14 Apr
13.70	2.1	Chris	Baillie	GBR	21.4.81	6	v2N	Glasgow	1 Jul
13.70	4.5	Dimítrios	Piétris	GRE	24.10.79	1h2	MedG	Tunis	12 Sep
13.74	2.6	Justin	Gatlin	USA-J	10.2.82	1		Knoxville	7 Apr
13.75	2.8		Zhang Feng	CHN	9.5.72	2		Jinan	13 May
13.76	2.2	Felipe	Vivancos	ESP	16.6.80	1	NC	Valencia	21 Jul
13.77	2.1	Tasuku	Tanonaka	JPN	23.9.78	1h2		Kitakami	14 Jul
13.77	4.0	Erik	Batte	CUB	10.12.74	1		Montauban	17 Jul

Mark	Wind	Name		Nat	Born	Date
13.79	5.7	Stefan	Drews	GER	12.2.79	1 Jul
13.80	3.4	Carlos	Patterson	CUB	20.2.78	25 May
13.81	4.9	Eric	Moss	USA		26 May
13.83	2.5	Chris	Stokes	USA	1.2.79	31 Mar
13.83	4.3	Balázs	Kovács	HUN	14.6.77	1 Jul
13.84	2.5	Joey	Scott	USA		14 Apr
13.85	2.7	Rickey	Harris	USA	29.9.81	17 Mar
13.86	4.1	Rui	Palma	POR	4.1.78	14 Jul
13.87	2.5		Liu Jie	CHN	29.5.79	28 Apr
13.87	w?	Thierry	Herbé	FRA	27.1.71	20 May
13.87		Shannon	Flowers	USA	17.9.71	13 Jun
13.87	4.5	Juha	Sonck	FIN	15.4.81	12 Aug
13.88	2.4	Tony	Galaviz	USA	23.9.78	23 Jun
13.89	4.3	Jalilu	Mayo	USA	2.1.78	7 Apr
13.89	2.3	Moussa	Sissoko	MLI/FRA	27.10.74	13 Jun
13.89		Antoine	Johnson	USA	22.12.80	13 Jun
13.90	4.5	Marko	Ritola	FIN	29.1.79	12 Aug
13.91	3.2	Ron	Andrews	USA	12.10.79	14 Apr
13.92	3.8	Calvin	Williams	USA	23.1.79	7 Apr
13.92		Ricardo	Moody	USA	24.9.80	12 May
13.92	3.0	Luca	Giovannelli	ITA	29.9.75	20 Jul
13.93	3.1	Gus	Martin	USA	27.7.78	17 Mar
13.93	2.8		Gao Yang	CHN	21.3.76	13 May
13.94	w?	Nobuto	Watanabe	JPN	20.10.76	18 Mar
13.94	6.1	Laurent	Hernu	FRA	22.8.76	1 Jul
13.95	2.3	Tom	Pappas	USA	6.9.76	22 Jun
13.96	4.3	Brandon	Hon	USA	7.7.79	11 May
13.96	4.4	Nikolay	Koykov	BUL	12.10.81	19 May
13.96	2.6	Stephan	Zeyen	GER	11.9.78	20 May
13.96	4.9	Nicolas	Nestor	FRA	1.6.73	26 May
13.98	3.7	Mike	Mills	USA	29.7.81	10 May
13.98	4.9	Dustin	Brock	USA		26 May
13.99	2.7	Bryan	Clay	USA	3.1.80	20 Apr

Best at low altitude

Mark	Wind	Name		Nat	Born	Date
13.82	-0.6	Paulo	Villar	COL	28.7.78	7 Aug
13.89	1.6	Jackson	Quiñónez	ECU	12.6.80	10 Jun

Hand Timing

Mark	Wind	Name		Nat	Born	Pos	Meet	Venue	Date
13.5	1.7	Nikolay	Koykov	BUL	12.10.81	1		Sofia	12 May

Mark	Wind	Name		Nat	Born	Date
13.6		Todd	Matthews	USA	28.6.79	24 Mar
13.6		Mubarak	Atah Mubarak	KSA	17.12.81	3 Oct
13.7		Andrea	Giaconi	ITA	11.4.74	9 Sep
13.6w	2.3	Miroslav	Novakovic	YUG	14.9.76	13 May
13.6w	3.0	Wenston	Riley	USA	24.4.77	18 May
13.6w	3.0	Derrick	James	USA		18 May
13.7w	2.3	Nenad	Loncar	YUG	6.3.81	13 May

JUNIORS

See main list for top 6 juniors. 11 performances by 3 men to 13.61. Additional marks and further juniors:

Name	Mark	Wind	Pos	Meet	Venue	Date	Mark	Wind	Pos	Meet	Venue	Date
Liu Xiang	13.33	1.6	1	WUG	Beijing	28 Aug	13.51	0.2	4s3	WCh	Edmonton	8 Aug
	13.36	0.4	1	NG	Guangzhou	19 Nov	13.61	2.0	1h4	WUG	Beijing	27 Aug
	13.42	0.0	1	EAsG	Osaka	24 May	13.61	-1.3	1s1	WUG	Beijing	27 Aug
Shi Dongpeng	13.48	1.6	2	NC	Baoding	15 Jun	13.49	0.4	3	NG	Guangzhou	19 Nov

Mark	Wind	Name		Nat	Born	Pos	Meet	Venue	Date
13.83	1.2	Sebastian	Siebert	GER	23.6.82	2	EJ	Grosseto	21 Jul
13.88	0.7	Ricardo	Melbourne	JAM	26.2.82	2	NC	Kingston	23 Jun
13.97	0.0	Jurica	Grabusic	CRO	28.3.83	6	MedG	Tunis	12 Sep
13.98	-0.1	Yuji	Ohashi	JPN	5.9.83	1		Kumamoto	6 Aug
13.98	1.4	Thiago	Dias	BRA	2.3.84	1		São Paulo	25 Aug
13.99	1.5	De'Andre	Eiland	USA	4.6.82	1		Athens	31 Mar
14.05	0.6	André	Streese	GER	1.6.83	1B		Mannheim	16 Jun
14.06	1.7	Nathan	Palmer	GBR	16.6.82	2h1	EJ	Grosseto	20 Jul
14.09	0.4		Wu Jia	CHN	6.5.83	3h2	NG	Guangzhou	18 Nov
14.11		Andrey	Shalonko	BLR	20.3.83	3		Minsk	30 Jun
14.13	1.1	Nassim Meziane	Brahimi	QAT	84	2		Doha	28 Mar
14.15	-0.9	Stefanos	Ioannou	CYP	12.6.82	1		Nicosia	14 Jun
14.15A	-0.7	Janko	Kotze	RSA	7.7.82	1		Johannesburg	16 Jun
14.16	1.2	Dominic	Girdler (20)	GBR	6.3.82	3	EJ	Grosseto	21 Jul
14.16A	0.3	Marleán	Reyna	VEN	15.1.82	3	BolG	Ambato	13 Sep

Wind assisted see main lists for two men – three performances by 2 men to 13.60w

Name	Mark	Wind	Pos	Venue	Date	Mark	Wind	Pos	Meet	Venue	Date
Liu Xiang	13.45w	2.5	1	Ningbo	28 Apr	13.60w	2.1	3h4	WCh	Edmonton	7 Aug

Mark	Wind	Name		Nat	Born	Pos	Meet	Venue	Date
14.07	4.4	Dominic	Girdler	GBR	6.3.82	2h2	EJ	Grosseto	20 Jul

Hand Timed

Mark	Wind	Name		Nat	Born	Pos	Meet	Venue	Date
13.8	0.0	Marlián	Reyna	VEN	15.1.82	1		Caracas	28 Jul

200 METRES HURDLES

Mark	Wind	Name		Nat	Born	Pos	Venue	Date
22.86	0.9	Darryl	Wohlsen	AUS	6.3.73	1	Brisbane	26 Mar

300 METRES HURDLES

Mark	Name		Nat	Born	Pos	Venue	Date
34.7	Thomas	Goller	GER	28.10.77	1r2	Pliezhausen	13 May
35.0	Giorgio	Frinolli	ITA	12.7.70	2e1	Pliezhausen	13 May
35.88	Alain	Rohr	SUI	25.12.71	1	Langenthal	24 May

400 METRES HURDLES

Mark	Name		Nat	Born	Pos	Meet	Venue	Date
47.38	Felix	Sánchez	DOM	30.8.77	1rA	WK	Zürich	17 Aug
47.49		Sánchez			1	WCh	Edmonton	10 Aug
47.54	Fabrizio	Mori	ITA	28.6.69	2	WCh	Edmonton	10 Aug
47.89	Dai	Tamesue	JPN	3.5.78	3	WCh	Edmonton	10 Aug
47.95	Angelo	Taylor	USA	29.12.78	1rA	Athl	Lausanne	4 Jul
47.95		Sánchez			1	BrGP	London (CP)	22 Jul
47.99	Hadi Soua'an	Al-Somaily	KSA	30.12.76	4	WCh	Edmonton	10 Aug
48.07		Sánchez			1s3	WCh	Edmonton	8 Aug
48.08	Stéphane	Diagana	FRA	23.7.69	2rA	Athl	Lausanne	4 Jul
48.09	Alwyn	Myburgh	RSA	13.10.80	1	WUG	Beijing	31 Aug
48.10		Taylor			1	GP	Saint-Denis	6 Jul
48.10		Tamesue			2s3	WCh	Edmonton	8 Aug
48.13		Diagana			2	GP	Saint-Denis	6 Jul
48.16	Marek	Plawgo	POL	25.2.81	1	GP	Osaka	12 May
48.21		Taylor			2	WK	Zürich	17 Aug
48.27	Chris	Rawlinson	GBR	19.5.72	1s2	WCh	Edmonton	8 Aug
48.30		Mori			1		Torino	9 Jun
48.34		Al-Somaily			3	GP	Saint-Denis	6 Jul
48.36		Taylor			2	BrGP	London (CP)	22 Jul
48.38		Tamesue			3rA	Athl	Lausanne	4 Jul
48.39		Mori			1	ECp-S	Bremen	23 Jun
48.40	Pawel	Januszewski	(10) POL	2.1.72	3s3	WCh	Edmonton	8 Aug
48.42		Sánchez			1		Madrid	7 Jul
48.44	James	Carter	USA	7.5.78	4	GP	Saint-Denis	6 Jul
48.46		Sánchez			1	Herc	Monaco	20 Jul
48.46	Yevgeniy	Meleshenko	KAZ	19.1.81	2	WUG	Beijing	31 Aug
48.47		Sánchez			1	GWG	Brisbane	4 Sep
48.49		Mori			1s1	WCh	Edmonton	8 Aug
48.50	Boris	Gorban	RUS	26.9.78	2s2	WCh	Edmonton	8 Aug
48.51		Carter			1	GGala	Roma	29 Jun
	(30/13)							
48.52A	Llewellyn	Herbert	RSA	21.7.77	1		Pretoria	23 Mar
48.53	Eric	Thomas	USA	1.12.73	1	GP II	Sevilla	8 Jun
48.53	Jirí	Muzík	CZE	1.9.76	3s2	WCh	Edmonton	8 Aug
48.63		Chen Tien-Wen	TPE	1.6.78	3	WUG	Beijing	31 Aug
48.65	Yoshihiro	Chiba	JPN	29.4.79	1		Yokohama	20 May
48.71	Neil	Gardner	JAM	8.12.74	1h1	NC	Kingston	21 Jun
48.75	Calvin	Davis	USA	2.4.72	2	NC	Eugene	23 Jun
	(20)							
48.80	Ian	Weakley	JAM	24.2.74	2		Rovereto	29 Aug
48.87	Periklís	Iakovákis	GRE	24.3.79	4	WUG	Beijing	31 Aug
48.88	Ruslan	Mashchenko	RUS	11.11.71	2rA		Madrid	7 Jul
48.96	Mustapha	Sdad	MAR	11.4.70	2h2	WCh	Edmonton	7 Aug
48.96	Martin	Willemse	RSA	23.4.75	5	WUG	Beijing	31 Aug
48.99	Bayano	Kamani	USA	17.4.80	1	NCAA	Eugene	1 Jun
49.02	William	Porter	USA	15.4.73	1		Fort-de-France	28 Apr
49.03	Joey	Woody	USA	22.5.73	1rA		Indianapolis	28 Jul
49.04	Giorgio	Frinolli	ITA	12.7.70	3		Milano	6 Jun
49.05A	Willie	Smith	NAM	20.9.77	3		Roodepoort	16 Mar
	(30)							
49.07	Carlos	Silva	POR	8.6.74	6	WUG	Beijing	31 Aug
49.19	Alain	Rohr	SUI	25.12.71	8rA	Athl	Lausanne	4 Jul
49.21	Olivier	Jean-Théodore	FRA	13.11.74	1		La Chaux-de-Fonds	19 Aug
49.28	Torrance	Zellner	USA	6.1.70	1		Atlanta	7 Apr
49.29	Du'aine	Thorne-Ladejo	GBR	14.2.71	1	Znam	Tula	9 Jun
49.30	Dinsdale	Morgan	JAM	19.11.72	2		Bridgetown	19 May
49.30	Anthony	Borsumato	GBR	13.12.73	3		Rovereto	29 Aug
49.31A	Mario	Watts	JAM	21.5.75	1	CAC	C.de Guatemala	22 Jul
49.31	Regan	Nichols	USA	26.7.73	2rA		Indianapolis	28 Jul
49.34	Michael	Smith	USA	26.4.79	2	NCAA	Eugene	1 Jun
	(40)							
49.36	Mubarak	Al-Nubi	QAT	30.12.77	1		Doha	29 Mar
49.40	Hani	Mourhej	SYR	20.10.81	2	WMilG	Beirut	4 Jul
49.40A	Ockert	Cilliers	RSA	21.4.81	1		Potchefstroom	24 Oct
49.41	Laurent	Ottoz	ITA	10.4.70	7rB	WK	Zürich	17 Aug
49.42		Tan Chunhua	CHN	13.3.77	3	GP	Osaka	25 May
49.46	Gennadiy	Gorbenko	UKR	22.9.75	1	NC	Kiev	3 Jul
49.46	Iván	Rodríguez	ESP	7.4.78	1		Valencia	22 Jul

Mark	Name		Nat	Born	Pos	Meet	Venue	Date
49.49A	Stepán	Tesarík	CZE	6.7.78	1		Rustenberg	22 Jan
49.51	Louis	Sales	USA	29.11.71	5		Bridgetown	19 May
49.53	Hideaki	Kawamura	JPN	15.9.74	4	EAsG	Osaka	25 May
	(50)							
49.53	Yvon	Rakotoarimiandry	MAD	5.1.76	2	Franc	Ottawa	23 Jul
49.54	Eronilde	de Araújo	BRA	31.12.70	1		São Paulo	24 Jun
49.55	Ken	Yoshizawa	JPN	7.7.78	2		Kitakami	15 Jul
49.57A	Marthinus	Kritzinger	RSA-J	10.2.82	1	NC-23	Pretoria	20 Apr
49.57	Matthew	Elias	GBR	25.4.79	1	EU23	Amsterdam	14 Jul
49.60	Viktors	Lacis	LAT	28.11.77	3	NCAA	Eugene	1 Jun
49.60	Fred	Sharpe	USA	21.8.78	1rB		Indianapolis	28 Jul
49.62	Vadim	Zadoinov	MDA	24.5.69	1		Barcelona	25 Jul
49.63	Jan	Schneider	GER	24.1.76	1	NC	Stuttgart	30 Jun
49.63	Vladislav	Shiryayev	RUS	30.10.73	2	NC	Tula	14 Jul
	(60)							
49.64	Edivaldo	Monteiro	POR	28.4.76	1rB		Madrid	7 Jul
49.65A	Ter	de Villiers	RSA-J	13.7.82	2	NC-23	Pretoria	20 Apr
49.65	Rickey	Harris	USA	29.9.81	1	SEC	Columbia, SC	13 May
49.68	Matthew	Douglas	GBR	26.11.76	4		Réthimno	1 Jul
49.70	Naohiro	Kawakita	JPN	10.7.80	2		Yokohama	20 May
49.74	Dusán	Kovács	HUN	31.7.71	4		Padova	26 Aug
49.76	Ken	Garrett	USA	9.11.76	1		Athens, GA	5 May
49.77	Brian	Derby	USA	18.2.81	1	Big 10	Bloomington	20 May
49.77	Ibou	Faye	SEN	13.12.69	2		La Chaux-de-Fonds	19 Aug
49.78	Monte	Raymond	CAN	18.11.73	1	NC	Edmonton	24 Jun
	(70)							
49.80	Sylvester	Omodiale	NGR	5.9.77	2		Funchal	30 Jun
49.82	Samuel	Matete	ZAM	27.7.68	5	ECCp	Madrid	26 May
49.82	Aleksandr	Derevyagin	RUS	79	3	NC	Tula	14 Jul
49.87	Adam	Kunkel	CAN	24.2.81	2	NC	Edmonton	24 Jun
49.89	Blair	Young	AUS	5.4.71	1	NC	Brisbane	25 Mar
49.89	José María	Romera	ESP	2.9.80	2		San Sebastián	18 Aug
49.91A	Brett	Guymon	USA	9.1.77	1		Ogden	9 May
49.91	Sherman	Armstrong	USA	22.9.78	2	Big 10	Bloomington	20 May
49.92	Rohan	Robinson	AUS	15.11.71	1		Canberra	24 Feb
49.92	Jaime	Juan	ESP	28.8.77	5rA		Madrid	7 Jul
	(80)							
49.92	Marcel	Lopuchovsky	SVK	2.5.77	3		Pátra	22 Jul
49.94	Mikael	Jakobsson	SWE	9.1.81	1	NC	Växjö	26 Aug
49.95	Yuki	Omoto	JPN	29.10.78	5	GP	Osaka	12 May
49.95	Konstantinos	Pochanis	CYP	29.7.73	1		Veszprém	7 Jul
49.96	Leonid	Vershinin	BLR	23.6.77	1		Minsk	30 Jun
49.97	Masashi	Wakae	JPN	28.4.80	1		Hiroshima	15 Sep
50.00	Aaron	Lacy	USA	1.4.71	2rB		Indianapolis	28 Jul
50.03	Marcel	Schelbert	SUI	26.2.76	1h3	WUG	Beijing	30 Aug
50.05	Kurt	Duncan	JAM	3.6.78	2		Fairfax	5 May
50.05	Yacnier	Luis	CUB-J	24.1.82	2	NC	La Habana	27 May
	(90)							
50.05	Laurent	Claudel	FRA	12.3.78	1		Castres	18 Jul
50.05A	Jorge	Moreno	CUB	25.5.77	2	CAC	C. de Guatemala	22 Jul
50.06A	Francois	Coertze	RSA	23.2.79	2	NC-23	Pretoria	20 Apr
50.06	Hennie	Botha	RSA	20.2.75	3		Port Elizabeth	28 Apr
50.07	Stefan	Bönisch	GER	10.8.77	2	NC	Stuttgart	30 Jun
50.08	Karol	Radke	POL	13.1.76	1	Kuso	Warszawa	17 Jun
50.08		Lee Doo-yeon	KOR	9.4.75	1	NG	Chunan	12 Oct
50.09	Gianni	Carabelli	ITA	30.5.79	2		Bressanone	17 Jun
50.11A	Oscar	Juanz	MEX	17.9.73	3	CAC	Guatemala	22 Jul
50.12	Anderson C	dos Santos	BRA	15.6.75	1		São Caetano do Sul	22 Apr
	(100)							

Mark	Name		Nat	Born	Date
50.13	Adrian	Mann	USA	23.5.78	21 Apr
50.13	Ken	Harnden	ZIM	31.3.73	12 May
50.14	Orentheus	Hutcherson	USA		5 May
50.14	LaBoris	Bean	USA	24.10.78	30 May
50.16	Matt	Mason	USA-J	30.6.82	12 May
50.16	Kazuhiko	Yamazaki	JPN	10.5.71	8 Jul
50.16	Damjan	Zlatnar	SLO	16.12.77	11 Jul
50.18A	Henk	Meyer	RSA	26.3.81	20 Apr
50.18	Ian	Harnden	ZIM	23.9.76	5 May
50.21	David	Aaron	USA	9.12.78	19 May
50.22	Corrado	Agrillo	ITA	31.10.74	8 Jul
50.24	Charles	Robertson-Adams	GBR	5.12.77	4 Jul
50.24	Darko	Juricic	CRO	28.8.69	25 Jul
50.25		Meng Yan	CHN	30.9.80	28 Apr
50.26	Nick	Stewart	CAN	6.4.79	19 May
50.26	Jamaal	Jackson	USA		26 May
50.26	Cleverson O	da Silva	BRA	5.9.73	26 May
50.26	Christian	Duma	GER-J	5.2.82	21 Jul
50.27	Salah Eddy	Ghaïdi	FRA	12.5.79	13 Jul
50.28	Eric	Dudley	USA	18.4.80	1 Jun
50.28	Juan	Herrero	ESP	19.1.76	22 Jul
50.30	Iñigo	Monreal	ESP	26.9.74	22 Jul
50.30	Ari-Pekka	Lattu	FIN	22.6.78	26 Aug
50.31	Jan	Reinberg	GER	18.1.80	30 Jun
50.32	Samuel	Glover	USA	22.1.80	26 Apr
50.32	Tommaso	Galvanini	ITA	27.5.78	8 Jul

Mark	Name		Nat	Born	Date
50.32	Bader Aman	Abdulrahman	KUW	14.6.77	5 Oct
50.33		Zhang Shibao	CHN-J	12.3.84	22 Nov
50.37	Dwight	Ruff	USA-J	31.3.83	17 Jun
50.37	Jean-Laurent	Heusse	FRA	8.4.74	1 Jul
50.38	Omar	Brown	JAM	26.12.75	28 Apr
50.38	Koji	Hoshino	JPN	3.7.79	20 May
50.39	Naman	Keita	FRA	9.4.78	22 Jul
50.40	Tomasz	Rudnik	POL	6.3.79	30 Jun
50.40	Henning	Kuschewitz	GER	9.4.81	30 Jun
50.40	James	Hillier	GBR	3.4.78	1 Jul
50.41	Federico	Rubeca	ITA	10.6.81	1 Jul
50.41	Akihiro	Yoshioka	JPN	5.9.78	29 Sep
50.42	Derrick	Adkins	USA	2.7.70	13 Apr
50.42	Youssoupha	Sarr	SEN	16.10.78	19 May
50.42	John	Hall	USA	6.3.78	21 Jun
50.43	Michael	Brown	USA	9.1.79	21 Jun
50.44	João Carlos	dos Santos	BRA	28.4.75	24 Jun
50.44	Guilhem	Barthes	FRA	25.7.78	22 Jul
50.45	Samy	Barka	FRA	22.1.78	22 Jul
50.46	Gregory	Little	JAM-J	20.2.83	21 Jun
50.50	Russell	Peterson	USA	20.8.80	19 May
50.51	Carlos	Zbinden	CHI	2.12.76	10 Jun
50.51	Stijn	Verleyen	BEL	21.7.78	1 Jul
50.52	Mike	King	USA	21.2.79	19 May
50.52	Martin	Leiser	SUI	17.6.78	19 Aug
50.54	Kyle	Erickson	USA	11.1.81	14 Apr
50.54	Paul	Tucker	GUY	30.1.76	14 Jul
50.55	Justin	Davis	USA	6.2.76	9 Jun
50.57	Sebastian	Aryee	GER	21.6.77	30 Jun
50.59A	Barend	Kotze	RSA	14.3.77	23 Mar
50.59	Tibor	Bédi	HUN	22.3.74	18 Jun
50.59	Yevgeniy	Mikheyko	BLR	24.4.81	30 Jun
50.59	Janne	Mäkelä	FIN	2.2.79	22 Jul
50.60	Minoru	Kobayashi	JPN	24.5.78	25 Aug
50.61	Nate	Garcia	USA-J	82	13 Apr
50.61	Lukás	Soucek	CZE	10.7.75	20 May
50.62	Masato	Kishida	JPN	20.4.79	17 May
50.62	Jun	Iwasaki	JPN	3.6.78	8 Jun
50.63	Byron	Taylor	USA	21.3.80	14 Apr
50.63	Sergio	Hierrezuelo	CUB-J	15.3.82	26 May
50.63	Alberto	González	ESP	28.6.71	25 Jul
50.63	Jirachai	Linglom	THA	2.1.78	14 Sep
50.65	Iliya	Dzhivondov	BUL	6.3.78	10 Jun
50.66	Nick	O'Brien	NZL	3.1.80	1 Mar
50.66		Lu Xiaobing	CHN	13.1.79	17 Jun
50.67	Claudio	Citterio	ITA	1.8.79	8 Jul
50.68		Zhuang Zhenping	CHN	6.1.76	22 Apr
50.69A	Chris	Kemp	USA		5 May
50.69	Erkin	Isakov	UZB	25.11.74	14 Jul
50.70	Richard	McDonald	GBR	11.1.80	17 Aug
50.72	Calvin	Williams	USA	23.1.79	7 Apr
50.73		Li Jinsheng	CHN	13.3.77	22 Nov
50.74	Joey	Scott	USA		24 Mar
50.74		Li Zhijun	CHN	5.1.80	21 Nov
50.75	De'Jun	Spann	USA	11.11.80	13 May
50.76	Henning	Hackelbusch	GER-J	23.2.82	21 Jul
50.76	Kamel	Tabbal	TUN	13.2.78	11 Sep
50.80A	Jean-Dominiq	Dieme	SEN	18.9.69	12 Feb
50.80	Jaciel	Zamora	CUB	5.4.74	27 May
50.80	Makio	Haywood	USA	19.10.78	9 Jun
50.81A	Daniël	van Heerden	RSA	4.11.76	22 Jan
50.81	Matt	Woodhouse	AUS	2.3.74	25 Mar
50.81	Satoshi	Oshikawa	JPN	18.8.79	20 May
50.81	Gerko	Siemer	GER	21.4.78	2 Jun
50.81	Lyubomir	Lyubenov	BUL	23.3.77	10 Jun
50.82	Ryan	Wilson	USA	19.12.80	19 May
50.82	Kimmo	Haapasalo	FIN	23.7.77	26 Aug
50.85	Vitaliy	Balykin	RUS	6.6.77	25 May
	(194)				

Hand timing

48.8	Giorgio	Frinolli	ITA	12.7.70	1	Rieti	20 May

Low altitude best

48.77	Herbert	1	NC	Durban		3 Mar
49.61	Watts	3	NC	Kingston		22 Jun
49.87	Tesarík	6s1	WUG	Beijing		30 Aug
49.98	de Villiers	1		Maia		14 Jul

50.35 Kritzinger 28 Apr, 50.44 Guymon 28 May, 50.53 Cilliers 30 Mar, 50.59 Kotze 30 Mar

JUNIORS

See main list for top three juniors. 11 performances by 5 men to 50.30. Additional marks and further juniors:

Kritzinger	49.58A	5		Roodepoort	16 Mar	50.06A	5		Pretoria	23 Mar
De Villiers	49.98	1		Maia	14 Jul	50.19	2	Kuso	Warszawa	17 Jun
	50.02	4	NC	Durban	4 Mar	50.28	1		Braga	4 Jul

50.16	Matt	Mason	USA-J	30.6.82	3		Tallahassee	12 May
50.26	Christian	Duma	GER-J	5.2.82	1	EJ	Grosseto	21 Jul
50.33		Zhang Shibao	CHN-J	12.3.84	2	NG	Guangzhou	22 Nov
50.37	Dwight	Ruff	USA-J	31.3.83	1	NC-j	Richmond	17 Jun
50.46	Gregory	Little	JAM-J	20.2.83	1h2	NC	Kingston	21 Jun
50.61	Nate	Garcia	USA-J	82	1rC		Knoxville	13 Apr
50.63	Sergio	Hierrezuelo	CUB-J	15.3.82	2h1	NC	La Habana	26 May
50.76	Henning	Hackelbusch	GER-J	23.2.82	2	EJ	Grosseto	21 Jul
50.86	Bershawn	Jackson	USA	83	1		Sacramento	29 Jul
50.92	Masahiro	Yoshikata	JPN	23.8.82	1		Kurume	13 Oct
50.94	Hamed Hamadan	Al-Bishi	KSA	3.3.82	1	Asi-J	B S Begawan	22 Jul
51.00	Mikhayil	Lipskiy	RUS	6.3.82	3	EJ	Grosseto	21 Jul
51.14A	Louis	van Zyl	RSA	20.7.85	1	NC-j	Pretoria	20 Apr
51.23	Derrick	Williams	USA	25.3.82	1	NSch	Raleigh	17 Jun
51.29	Yuki	Arakawa	JPN	17.11.83	1		Kurume	13 Oct
51.33		Shon Jung-ho	KOR	9.6.82	1	NG	Chunan	12 Oct
51.33	Kenji	Narisako (20)	JPN	25.7.84	2		Rifu	15 Oct
Hand timed: 50.8A	Julius	Bungei	KEN	16.6.84	h	NC	Nairobi	22 Jun

HIGH JUMP

2.37		Vyacheslav	Voronin	RUS	5.4.74	1		Eberstadt	19 Aug
					2.27/1 2.33/1 2.37/2 2.41/xxx				
	2.33	2= WCh	Edmonton	8 Aug	2.25/1 2.30/1 2.33/1 2.36/xxx				
2.36		Martin	Buss	GER	7.4.76	1	WCh	Edmonton	8 Aug
				2.20/1	2.25/1 2.30/1 2.33/x 2.36/2				
2.35i		Andrey	Sokolovskiy	UKR	16.7.78	1		Arnstadt	17 Feb
	2.34	1 NC	Kiev	3 Jul	? ? 2.34/3				
	2.33i	1 NC	Brovary	10 Feb	?				
	2.32	1	Kalamatá	2 Jun	2.10,2.15,2.18/1 2.21,2.24/3 2.27/2 2.30,2.32/1, 2.34/xxx				

Mark	Name		Nat	Born	Pos	Meet	Venue	Date
2.35A	Charles	Clinger	USA	28.12.76	1		Pocatello	19 May
				2.11/1 2.17/2 2.26/1 2.32/1 2.35/2				
	2.32 1 Västerås		3 Jul	2.15/1 2.20/1 2.27/3 2.32/2 2.34/x 2.36/xx				
2.35	Javier	Sotomayor	CUB	13.10.67	1		Somoskö	26 Aug
				2.18/1 2.25/2 2.30/2 2.35/2 2.38/xxp				
	2.33 4 WCh Edmonton		8 Aug	2.25/1 2.30/2 2.33/1 2.36/xxx				
2.34i	Staffan	Strand	SWE	18.4.76	1		Stockholm	15 Feb
				2.20/1 2.28/1 2.31/1 2.34/2 2.40/x				
2.34i	Stefan	Holm	SWE	25.5.76	2		Stockholm	15 Feb
				2.20/1 2.24/1 2.28/2 2.31/1 2.34/3 2.36/xxx				
	2.33 1 GWG Brisbane		7 Sep	2.20/1 2.24/2 2.28/1 2.31/2 2.33/1 2.35/xxx				
	2.32i 1 WI Lisboa		11 Mar	2.20/1 2.25/1 2.29/1 2.32/1 2.36/xxx				
2.33i	Nathan	Leeper	USA	13.6.77	1		Manhattan, KS	19 Jan
2.33i	Yaroslav	Rybakov	RUS	22.11.80	1		Moskva	25 Feb
				2.18/1 2.22/1 2.25/1 2.28/1 2.31/1 2.33/1 2.35/xx				
	2.33 2= WCh Edmonton		8 Aug	2.20/1 2.25/1 2.30/1 2.33/1 2.36/xxx				
	2.32 1 Lapinlahti		22 Jul	2.19/1 2.24/1 2.29/2 2.32/3 2.35/xx				
2.33	Gennadiy	Moroz	BLR	27.5.78	1		Brest	21 Jul
2.33	Mark	Boswell	CAN	28.7.77	2		Eberstadt	19 Aug
				2.20/1 2.24/1 2.30/3 2.33/2 2.37/xxx				
2.32	Sergey	Dymchenko	UKR	23.8.67	2		Kalamáta	2 Jun
				2.18/1 2.21/1 2.24/2 2.30/1 2.32/2 2.34/xxx				
	(22/12) and 23 performances at 2.31							
2.31i	Andrey	Chubsa	BLR-J	29.11.82	1		Vitebsk	12 Jan
2.31i	Charles	Austin	USA	19.12.67	2		Arnstadt	17 Feb
2.31	Jacques	Freitag	RSA-J	11.6.82	1		Rehlingen	4 Jun
2.31	Sergey	Klyugin	RUS	24.3.74	1	NC	Tula	14 Jul
2.31	Aleksandr	Kravtsov	RUS	18.3.74	3	NC	Tula	14 Jul
2.31	Kwaku	Boateng	CAN	30.6.74	2	Franc	Ottawa	21 Jul
2.31	Wolfgang	Kreissig	GER	29.8.70	1		Bühl	27 Jul
2.30	Dave	Hoffman	USA	22.4.75	2	NCAA	Eugene	31 May
	(20)							
2.30	Oskari	Frösén	FIN	24.1.76	1		Kuortane	17 Jun
2.30	Grzegorz	Sposób	POL	12.2.76	1		Biala Podlaska	6 Jul
2.29	Abderahmane	Hammad	ALG	27.5.77	1	NC	Alger	19 Jul
2.29	Pyotr	Bryako	RUS	27.3.77	2		Bühl	27 Jul
2.28i	Einar Karl	Hjartarson	ISL	28.10.80	1		Reykjavik	18 Feb
2.28A	Gilmar	Mayo	COL	30.9.69	1		Medellin	21 Jul
2.28	Jan	Jankú	CZE	10.8.71	1	ECCp	Madrid	27 May
2.28	Aleksey	Krysin	RUS	25.11.76	5	NC	Tula	14 Jul
2.27i	Dragutin	Topic ¶	YUG	12.3.71	1		Pireás	27 Jan
2.27i	Henry	Patterson	USA	27.5.75	2	Millrose	New York	2 Feb
	(30)							
2.27	Tora	Harris	USA	21.9.78	1		Princeton	6 May
2.27	Elvir	Krehmic	BIH	27.4.73	1		Sarajevo	9 Jun
2.27	James	Nieto	USA	2.11.76	1		Long Beach	9 Jun
2.27	Steven	Smith	USA	11.1.71	1		Indianapolis	9 Jun
2.27	Giulio	Ciotti	ITA	5.10.76	3		Bühl	27 Jul
2.27	Nicola	Ciotti	ITA	5.10.76	4		Bühl	27 Jul
2.26i	Dalton	Grant	GBR	8.4.66	4		Banská Bystrica	14 Feb
2.26i	Djordje	Niketic	YUG	11.3.76	5		Banská Bystrica	14 Feb
2.26i	Shaun	Guice	USA	11.8.80	2	NCAA	Fayetteville	10 Mar
2.26i	Kenny	Evans	USA	6.4.79	3	NCAA	Fayetteville	10 Mar
	(40)							
2.26	Svatoslav	Ton	CZE	20.10.78	1		Olomouc	8 May
2.26	Dimítrios	Kokótis	GRE	12.4.72	1		Kós	20 May
2.26	Ben	Challenger	GBR	7.3.78	1	BIG	Bedford	21 Jul
2.26		Wang Zhouzhou	CHN	20.4.77	5	WUG	Beijing	29 Aug
2.26	Jirí	Krehula	CZE-J	17.7.82	1		Uhersky Brod	20 Sep
2.25i	Aleksey	Lyolin	BLR	27.11.78	2		Gomel	20 Jan
2.25i	David	Antona	ESP	18.11.78	1		Valencia	27 Jan
2.25i	Marko	Aleksejev	EST	14.2.79	1	NC-j	Tallinn	28 Jan
2.25i	Patrick	De Paepe	BEL	25.2.76	1		Gent	28 Jan
2.25i	Konstantin	Matusevich	ISR	25.1.71	7		Weinheim	4 Feb
	(50)							
2.25i A	Marc	Chenn	USA	6.3.76	1		Air Force Academy	17 Feb
2.25i	Mikhayil	Tsvetkov	RUS	4.5.80	3		Moskva	25 Feb
2.25	Shawn	Brown	USA	.79	1		Orlando	21 Apr
2.25	Adrian	Shears	USA	.78	1		Tallahassee	4 May
2.25	Matthew	Vincent	USA	6.3.81	2	SEC	Columbia, SC	13 May
2.25	Brandon	Campbell	USA	12.7.80	1		Long Beach	19 May

Mark	Name		Nat	Born	Pos	Meet	Venue	Date
2.25	Grégory	Gabella	FRA	22.6.80	1		Montreuil-sous-Bois	20 May
2.25	Mike	Ponikvar	CAN	26.12.79	1	Pac-10	Berkeley	20 May
2.25	Aleksandr	Veryutin	BLR	18.11.79			Brest	24 May
2.25	Tomás	Ort	CZE	9.9.76	1		Praha	2 Jun
	(60)							
2.25	Jessé	de Lima	BRA	17.2.81	1		São Paulo	3 Jun
2.25	Aleksey	Lesnichiy	BLR	3.2.78	1		Brest	9 Jun
2.25	Takahiro	Uchida	JPN	9.12.80	1		Hiroshima	1 Jul
2.25	Pavel	Fomenko	RUS	29.6.76	1	Kuts	Moskva	28 Jul
2.25	Robert	Mitchell	GBR	14.9.80	1		Bedford	28 Jul
2.25	Mika	Polku	FIN	19.7.75	3	vSWE	Göteborg	1 Sep
2.24i	Martin	Stauffer	SUI	7.7.75	1		Eaubonne	28 Jan
2.24i	Wilbert	Pennings	NED	12.2.75	2=		Wupertal	2 Feb
2.24i	Artur	Partyka	POL	25.7.69	4=		Spala	9 Feb
2.24i	Lavar	Miller	USA	16.2.77	1	Tyson	Fayetteville	10 Feb
	(70)							
2.24	Nick	Moroney	AUS	3.8.72	1		Auckland	31 Mar
2.24	Fabrice	Saint-Jean	FRA	21.11.80	1		Montgeron	26 May
2.24	Christian	Rhoden	GER	27.3.74	3		Rehlingen	4 Jun
2.24		Zhou Zhongge	CHN	15.2.67	1	NC	Baoding	15 Jun
2.24	Stefan	Vasilache	ROM	9.5.79	2	ECp-1B	Budapest	23 Jun
2.24	Rozle	Prezelj	SLO	26.9.79	1	NC	Maribor	8 Jul
2.24	Mustapha	Raifak	FRA	9.9.75	1		Nantes	23 Aug
2.24	Aleksey	Gordienko	UKR	9.5.79	1		Banská Bystrica	31 Aug
2.24		Lee Jin-taek	KOR	13.4.72	1	NG	Chunan	14 Oct
2.24		Bae Kyung-ho	KOR	16.3.76	2	NG	Chunan	14 Oct
	(80)							
2.24		Liang Tong	CHN	30.5.78	3	NG	Guangzhou	19 Nov
2.23i	Yoshiteru	Kaihoko	JPN	19.11.71	1		Yokohama	24 Feb
2.23i	Shaun	Kologinczak	USA	13.10.79	1	Big 12	Lincoln	24 Feb
2.23	Adam	Shunk	USA	29.8.79	1		Durham	7 Apr
2.23	Jimmy	Baxter	USA	17.11.81	1		Gainesville	21 Apr
2.23	Robert	Jordan	USA	22.6.80	1	JUCO	Odessa, TX	12 May
2.23	Alfred	Neale	USA	1.7.81	2	JUCO	Odessa, TX	12 May
2.23	Ruslan	Glivinskiy	UKR	7.2.75	1		Kiev	18 May
2.23	Frédéric	Schinz	SUI	25.6.77	2	NC	Genève	30 Jun
2.23	Angel	Kararadev	BUL	18.4.79	1	BalkC	Tríkala	7 Jul
	(90)							
2.23	Aleksey	Dimitrik	RUS-J	12.4.84	1	WY	Debrecen	14 Jul
2.22i	Bjørn	Olsson	NOR	10.8.75	1		Oslo	26 Jan
2.22	Raúl	Touset	CUB	14.7.78	1		La Habana	16 Feb
2.22	Lisvany	Pérez	CUB-J	24.1.82	2		La Habana	16 Feb
2.22i	Oleg	Prokopov	BLR	8.3.77	5		Moskva	25 Feb
2.22i	Aleksey	Belov	RUS	76	6		Moskva	25 Feb
2.22	Dawid	Jaworski	POL	31.1.78	1		Los Angeles	3 Mar
2.22	Dimítrios	Sirrákos	GRE	26.1.74	1		Thessaloníki	27 May
2.22	Toni	Huikuri	FIN	17.9.79	1		Espoo	31 May
2.22A	Felipe	Apablaza	CHI	19.4.77	1		Cochabamba	3 Jun
	(100)							
2.22	Jay	Meystedt	USA	15.10.77	1		Indianapolis	9 Jun
2.22	Takahiro	Kimino	JPN	19.2.73	1	NC	Tokyo	10 Jun
2.22	Fabrício	Romero	BRA	13.5.78	1		São Leopoldo	1 Jul
2.22	Pawel	Gulcz	POL	28.1.79	2	NC	Bydgoszcz	1 Jul
2.22	Marcin	Kaczocha	POL	22.9.77	2		Biala Podlaska	6 Jul
2.22	Alessandro	Talotti	ITA	7.10.80	2	NC	Catania	8 Jul
2.22i	Shane	Lavy	USA	15.2.76	1		Manhattan, KS	7 Dec

Mark	Name		Nat	Born	Date
2.21i		Bi Hongyong	CHN	16.11.74	27 Jan
2.21i	Dieudonne	Opota	COD/FRA	24.8.79	18 Feb
2.21i		Zhu Wannan	CHN-J	15.2.83	20 Feb
2.21	Ryan	Sheppard	USA	12.4.80	17 Mar
2.21	Sam	Hill	USA	1.9.72	12 May
2.21	Dave	Arundel	USA	28.4.80	20 May
2.21	Jason	Boness	USA	11.2.80	20 May
2.21	Daniel	Olson	USA-J	27.9.82	24 May
2.21	Ivan	Bernasconi	ITA	19.10.74	6 Jun
2.21	Andrea	Bettinelli	ITA	6.10.78	6 Jun
2.21	Steve	Parker	USA	4.7.72	12 Jun
2.21	Yeóryios	Mitrákos	GRE	2.10.76	17 Jun
2.21	Danny	Graham	GBR	3.8.79	19 Jun
2.21	David	Furman	USA	5.11.78	22 Jun
2.21	Arturo	Ortiz	ESP	18.9.66	23 Jun
2.21	Yoav	Schuster	ISR-J	2.3.82	9 Jul
2.21	James	Watson	AUS-J	23.1.85	14 Jul
2.21	Joan	Charmant	FRA	4.6.78	15 Jul
2.21	Javier	Villalobos	ESP	1.9.74	22 Jul
2.21	Christian	Olsson	SWE	25.1.80	25 Aug
2.21		Kim Tae-hoi	KOR	3.9.73	14 Oct
2.21		Liu Jianmin	CHN	27.10.78	19 Nov
2.21		Tao Rui	CHN	26.1.72	19 Nov
2.20	Ronald	Garlett	AUS	18.12.79	19 Jan
2.20A	Malcolm	Hendriks	RSA	27.4.77	27 Jan
2.20i	Igor	Savenkov	RUS	73	27 Jan
2.20i	Samson	Oni	NGR	25.6.81	28 Jan
2.20i	Tomasz	Smialek	POL	16.1.81	9 Feb
2.20i	Dejan	Vreljakovic	YUG	24.1.77	11 Feb
2.20i	Igor	Sukharev	RUS	1.1.72	17 Feb
2.20i	Marat	Rakipov	RUS	7.6.79	17 Feb
2.20i		Yin Xueli	CHN	23.1.79	21 Feb

Mark	Name		Nat	Born	Pos	Meet	Venue	Date
2.20i	Andrey	Karmelyuk	UKR	9.2.79				23 Feb
2.20i	Nick	Decker	USA	18.4.78				28 Feb
2.20	Malcolm	Reynolds	USA	30.1.81				31 Mar
2.20	Damon	Thompson	BAR-J	5.3.83				14 Apr
2.20		Xu Hao	CHN-J	19.5.83				28 Apr
2.20	Adam	Chubb	USA	5.7.81				6 May
2.20	Franco	Moy	PER	8.2.73				6 May
2.20	Collat	Johnson	USA	78				10 May
2.20	Matt	Zuber	USA	30.9.66				12 May
2.20		Loo Kum Zee	MAS	2.12.74				12 May
2.20	Erasmo	Jara	ARG	25.3.76				13 May
2.20	Alfredo	Deza	PER	24.8.79				18 May
2.20	Michal	Titinger	POL	23.9.77				19 May
2.20	Takahisa	Yoshida	JPN	17.2.70				26 May
2.20	Daniel	Turner	GBR	23.11.78				28 May
2.20	Jeff	Caton	CAN	3.11.75				24 Jun
2.20	Wágner	Principe	BRA	2.6.79				24 Jun
2.20A	Raúl	Lozano	ESP	25.2.78				4 Jul
2.20	Mauro	Tavella	ITA	20.10.71				10 Jul
2.20	Julio	Luciano	DOM	10.10.77				14 Jul
2.20	Aleksey	Cherkasov	RUS	73				14 Jul
2.20A	Henderson	Dottin	BAR	4.1.80				22 Jul
2.20	Metin	Durmusoglu	TUR	11.1.74				29 Jul
2.20	Luka	Brkljacic	CRO	20.7.78				25 Aug
2.20A	Jackson	Quiñónez	ECU	12.6.80				15 Sep
2.20	Lubos	Benko	SVK	27.2.74				20 Sep
2.20	Dalibor	Hon	CZE	2.8.78				20 Sep
2.20	Stanislav	Sajdok	CZE-J	22.7.83				29 Sep
	(167)							

Best outdoor marks for athletes with seasonal bests indoors

Mark	Name	Pos	Meet	Venue	Date
2.34	Sokolovskiy	1	NC	Kiev	3 Jul
2.33	Rybakov	2=	WCh	Edmonton	8 Aug
2.33	Holm	1	GWG	Brisbane	7 Sep
2.31	Strand	1		Båstad	1 Jul
	2.30	2	GP II	Sevilla	8 Jun
2.30	Leeper	1	GP II	Sevilla	8 Jun
2.30	Austin	2	NC	Eugene	22 Jun
2.27	Patterson	3	NC	Eugene	22 Jun
2.25	Evans	2	Tex R	Austin	7 Apr
2.25	Hjartarson	1		Serravalle	2 Jun
2.25	Chubsa	1		Viersen	17 Jun
2.23	Miller	2		Athens	31 Mar
2.23	Grant	1	CAU	Bedford	28 May
2.23	Antona	1		Alcalá de H	30 Jun
2.23	Stauffer	1	NC	Genève	30 Jun
2.22	Guice	3	Tex R	Austin	7 Apr
2.22A	Chenn	1		Provo	5 May
2.22	Niketic	3	ECCp	Madrid	27 May

Mark	Name	Date
2.21	De Paepe	27 May
2.21	Belov	8 Jun
2.21	Prokopov	30 Jun
2.20	Vreljakovic	1 May
2.20	Kaihoko	6 May
2.20	Kologinczak	11 May
2.20	Yin Xueli	12 May
2.20	Smialek	17 Jun
2.20	Savenkov	14 Jul
2.20	Rakipov	14 Jul
2.20	Aleksejev	29 Aug

Drugs Disqualiication

Mark	Name		Nat	Born	Pos	Meet	Venue	Date
2.31i	Dragutin	Topic ¶	YUG	12.3.71	1		Wuppertal	2 Feb

Low altitude best

Mark	Name		Nat	Born	Pos	Meet	Venue	Date
2.32	Charles	Clinger	USA	28.12.76	1		Västerås	3 Jul
2.25	Gilmar	Mayo	COL	30.9.69	Q	WCh	Edmonton	5 Aug

JUNIORS

See main list for top 5 juniors. 11 performances by 3 men to 2.25. Additional marks and further juniors:

Name	Mark	Pos	Meet	Venue	Date	Mark	Pos	Venue	Date
Chubsa 2+	2.28i	1	NC	Minsk	23 Feb	2.25i	1	Gersweiler	4 Feb
	2.25i	1		Minsk	21 Feb				
Freitag	2.26	1		Réduit	8 Apr	2.25i	1	Tampere	12 Feb
	2.26A	1	NC-23	Pretoria	20 Apr	2.25A	1	Pretoria	10 Mar

Mark	Name		Nat	Born	Pos	Meet	Venue	Date
2.21i		Zhu Wannan	CHN	15.2.83	2		Beijing	20 Feb
	2.18				Q	NC	Baoding	14 Jun
2.21	Daniel	Olson	USA	27.9.82	1		Albany	24 May
2.21	Yoav	Schuster	ISR	2.3.82	1	NC	Tel Aviv	9 Jul
2.21	James	Watson	AUS	23.1.85	2	WY	Debrecen	14 Jul
2.20	Damon	Thompson	BAR	5.3.83	1	Carifta	Bridgetown	14 Apr
2.20		Xu Hao	CHN	19.5.83	3		Ningbo	28 Apr
2.20	Stanislav	Sajdok	CZE-J	22.7.83	1		Praha	29 Sep
2.19	Yu	Inoue	JPN	22.12.83	1		Chiba	27 Apr
2.19	Aleksandr	Plisko	BLR	28.10.84	3	WY	Debrecen	14 Jul
2.19	Mickaël	Hanany	FRA	25.3.83	3	EJ	Grosseto	21 Jul
2.19	Michal	Bieniek	POL	17.5.84	1		Poznan	22 Sep
2.18	Chuka	Enih-Snell	GBR	2.3.84	1	MSR-j	Walnut	21 Apr
2.18		Wu Xinrong	CHN	28.1.84	2		Shanghai	7 May
2.18	Kurtiss	Dilley	USA		1		Sacramento	19 May
2.18	Jason	Hill	USA	82	1	GWest	Sacramento	9 Jun
2.18	Wojciech	Borysiewicz (20)	POL	18.10.82	1		Sopot	10 Jun
2.18		Zheng Ting	CHN	5.2.85	Q	NC	Baoding	14 Jun
2.18	Andrey	Tereshin	RUS	15.12.82	1	NC-j	Kazan	27 Jun
2.18	Pavel	Chetvertakov	RUS	83	2	NC-j	Kazan	27 Jun
2.18	Kevin	Moffatt	USA	14.10.83	2	PAm-J	Santa Fe	19 Oct
2.18	Beltrán	León	VEN	.82	1	NJG	Barquisimeto	c14 Dec

POLE VAULT

Mark	Name		Nat	Born	Pos	Meet	Venue	Date
6.05	Dmitriy	Markov	AUS	14.3.75	1	WCh	Edmonton	9 Aug
				5.75/3	5.90/1	5.95/1	6.05/2	6.10/xxx
	5.95 1 Herc	Monaco	20 Jul	.65/1	5.80/3	5/90/2	5..95/1	6.01/xxx
6.00i	Danny	Ecker	GER	21.7.77	1		Dortmund	11 Feb
				5.60/1	5.80/2	6.00/3		
	5.96i 1	Chemnitz	9 Feb	5.60/2	5.80/1	5.96/1	6.00/xxx	
	5.85i 1	Erfurt	2 Feb	5.50/1	5.70/2	5.85/3	5.96/xxx	
	5.85 2 NC	Stuttgart	30 Jun	5.50/1	5.70/1	5.80/x	5.85/1	6.01/xxx

Mark	Name		Nat	Born	Pos	Meet	Venue	Date
5.96i	Lawrence	Johnson	USA	7.5.74	1	NC	Atlanta	3 Mar
				5.70/1 5.80/1 5.90/2 5.96/2 6.16/xxx				
	5.95i 1 WI	Lisboa	10 Mar	5.70/1 5.85/1 5.95/3 6.01/xxx				
	5.90 1	Knoxville	7 Apr	.... 6.04/xxx				
	5.85 1	Princeton	12 May	5.75/1 5.85/1 6.04/xxx				
	5.85 1 NC	Eugene	24 Jun	5.65/2 5.75/1 5.85/1 6.05/xxx				
5.93i	Tye	Harvey	USA	25.9.74	2	NC	Atlanta	3 Mar
			5.55/15.65/2	5.75/2 5.80/1 5.85/2 5.90/2 5.93/1 5.96/x 5.99/xx				
	5.90i 2 WI	Lisboa	10 Mar	5.45/1 5.60/1 5.70/1 5.85/xx 5.90/1 5.95/xxx				
	5.85i 1	Potsdam	18 Feb	?				
5.91	Alex	Averbukh	ISR	1.10.74	1	GP II	Gateshead	19 Aug
				5.60/2 5.80/2 5.91/1 6.00/xxx				
	5.90 1	Tel Aviv	30 Jun	5.60/1 5.80/1 5.90/2 6.02/xxp				
	5.86i 1 Euro	Stockholm	15 Feb	5.55/2 5.73/2 5.86/1 6.01/xxx				
	5.85 2 Athl	Lausanne	4 Jul	5.60/1 5.75/1 5.85/1 5.95/xxx				
	5.85 2 WCh	Edmonton	9 Aug	5.65/2 5.75/1 5.85/1 5.90/x 5.95/xx				
5.90	Jeff	Hartwig	USA	25.9.67	1	Mod R	Modesto	12 May
				5.45/1 5.60/2 5.80/3 5.90/2 6.00/xxx				
	5.90 1	Dessau	30 May	5.50/1 5.70/3 5.80/1 5.90/3 6.00/xxx				
	5.90 1 Athl	Lausanne	4 Jul	5.50/1 5.70/1 5.80/1 5.90/1 6.00/xxx				
	5.90 1 VD	Bruxelles	24 Aug	5.50 5.70/1 5.80/1 5.90/2 6.00/xxx				
	5.85 1 WK	Zürich	17 Aug	5.50/2 5.70/1 5.80/1 5.85/2 5.96/xxx				
5.86i	Romain	Mesnil	FRA	13.7.77	1		Toulouse	4 Mar
				?... 6.01/xxx				
	5.85i 3 WI	Lisboa	10 Mar	5.45/1. 5.70/1 5.80/1 5.85/1 5.90/x 5.95/xx				
	5.85 5 WCh	Edmonton	9 Aug	5.65/3 5.75/1 5.85/3 5.90/xxx				
5.86A	Pavel	Burlachenko	RUS	7.4.76	1		Pretoria	23 Mar
			5.05/1	5.35/1 5.55/1 5.65/1 5.75/1 5.86/2 5.91/xx-				
5.85i	Michael	Stolle	GER	17.12.74	2		Potsdam	18 Feb
	5.85 4 WCh	Edmonton	9 Aug	5.50/3 5.65/1 5.75/1 5.85/2 5.90/xxx				
5.85	Richard	Spiegelburg	GER	12.8.77	1	NC	Stuttgart	30 Jun
			5.40/1	5.60/1 5.70/1 5.80/1 5.85/1 5.90/xxx				
5.85	Nick	Hysong	USA	9.12.71	3	WCh	Edmonton	9 Aug
				5.65/1 5.75/1 5.85/2 5.90/xxx				
	(32/11)							
5.83	Patrik	Kristiansson	SWE	3.6.77	1	ECp-1A	Vaasa	24 Jun
5.82	Derek	Miles	USA	28.9.72	1		Jonesboro	18 Jun
5.81i	Pavel	Gerasimov	RUS	29.5.79	2		Toulouse	4 Mar
5.81	Tim	Mack	USA	15.9.72	2	MSR	Walnut	22 Apr
5.81	Russ	Buller	USA	10.9.78	3	MSR	Walnut	22 Apr
5.80i	Lars	Börgeling	GER	16.4.79	1=		Sindelfingen	4 Mar
5.80	Tim	Lobinger	GER	3.9.72	5	NC	Stuttgart	30 Jun
5.80	Viktor	Chistiakov	AUS	9.2.75	1		Gdansk	14 Jul
5.75i	Stepán	Janácek	CZE	12.6.77	3		Sindelfingen	4 Mar
	(20)							
5.75A	Nick	Buckfield	GBR	5.6.73	1		El Paso	14 Apr
5.75	Kurt	Hanna	USA	23.4.75	1		Abilene	10 May
5.75	Maksim	Tarasov	RUS	2.12.70	3	Nik	Nice	9 Jul
5.75	Vasiliy	Gorshkov	RUS	5.2.77	1	NC	Tula	12 Jul
5.75	Chris	Tamminga	NED	30.4.74	1		Tel Aviv	21 Jul
5.75	Adam	Kolasa	POL	2.8.75	8	WCh	Edmonton	9 Aug
5.72i	Andrei	Tivontchik	GER	13.7.70	1		Clermont-Ferrand	16 Mar
5.72	Vesa	Rantanen	FIN	2.12.75	1		Hamburg	15 Jul
5.71	Paul	Burgess	AUS	14.8.79	1		Perth	20 Jan
5.71i	Yevgeniy	Smiryagin	RUS	17.5.76	3		Toulouse	4 Mar
	(30)							
5.70i	Montxu	Miranda	ESP	27.12.76	1		Sevilla	3 Feb
5.70i	Okkert	Brits	RSA	22.8.73	2		Donyetsk	4 Feb
5.70i	Denis	Yurchenko	UKR	27.1.78	3		Donyetsk	4 Feb
5.70i	Grigoriy	Yegorov	KAZ	12.1.67	4		Donyetsk	4 Feb
5.70i	Chad	Harting	USA	20.2.72	5	Tyson	Fayetteville	10 Feb
5.70i	Rodion	Gataullin	RUS	23.11.65	2	Euro	Gent	23 Feb
5.70	Ruslan	Yeremenko	UKR	31.7.78	1	NC	Kiev	2 Jul
5.70	Rens	Blom	NED	1.3.77	Q	WCh	Edmonton	7 Aug
5.70	Martin	Eriksson	SWE	15.6.71	Q	WCh	Edmonton	7 Aug
5.69	Brian	Hunter	USA	28.3.79	1	Penn R	Philadelphia	28 Apr
	(40)							
5.68i	Jacob	Pauli	USA	15.6.79	1	NCAA	Fayetteville	9 Mar
5.68i	Adam	Keul	USA	27.1.80	2	NCAA	Fayetteville	9 Mar
5.68	Khalid	Lachheb	FRA	16.1.75	4	ECp-S	Bremen	24 Jun
5.66	Mikko	Latvala	FIN	8.7.80	1		Somero	1 Jul

Mark	Name		Nat	Born	Pos	Meet	Venue	Date
5.65	Dennis	Kholev	ISR	21.10.75	1	NCAA	Eugene	30 May
5.62	Adam	Ptácek	CZE	8.10.80	1		Praha	6 Jul
5.62	Oscar	Janson	SWE	22.7.75	1		Uddevalla	28 Jul
5.61i	Tiberiu	Agoston	ROM/FRA	25.12.76	6		Toulouse	4 Mar
5.61	Piotr	Buciarski	DEN	22.11.75	1		Eugene	17 Mar
5.60i	Igor	Pavlov	RUS	18.7.79	1		Moskva	19 Jan
	(50)							
5.60i	Ilian	Efremov	BUL	2.8.70	1		Sofia	3 Feb
5.60i	Yuriy	Yeliseyev	RUS	27.5.75	2		Moskva	4 Feb
5.60i	Alain	Andji	FRA	20.11.74	7		Donyetsk	4 Feb
5.60i	Giuseppe	Gibilisco	ITA	5.1.79	8		Donyetsk	4 Feb
5.60i	Pyotr	Bochkaryov	RUS	3.11.67	3		Eaubonne	7 Feb
5.60	Jon	Nance	USA	28.8.77	2	USTCA	Austin	21 Apr
5.60	Taoufik	Lachheb	FRA	16.1.75	1		Clermont-Ferrand	20 May
5.60	Manabu	Yokoyama	JPN	20.7.74	1	EAsG	Osaka	23 May
5.60	Vadim	Strogalyov	RUS	9.2.75	2		Praha	18 Jun
5.60	Martin	Kysela	CZE	25.3.74	2	NC	Jablonec	1 Jul
	(60)							
5.60	Laurens	Looije	NED	12.1.73	1		Arnhem	4 Jul
5.60	Dominic	Johnson	LCA	31.10.75	1		Tel Aviv	9 Jul
5.60	Kevin	Rans	BEL-J	19.8.82	10=	VD	Bruxelles	24 Aug
5.56i		Xu Gang	CHN	4.2.79	1	v JPN	Beijing	21 Feb
5.56i	Paul	Terek	USA	20.10.79	1	Big 10	University Park	24 Feb
5.55i	Javier	García	ESP	22.7.66	2		Zaragoza	20 Jan
5.55Ai	Pat	Manson	USA	29.11.67	1		Colorado Springs	27 Jan
5.55	Jeff	Hansen	USA	13.10.76	2	NCAA	Eugene	30 May
5.55	Massimo	Allevi	ITA	23.11.69	1		Beirut	2 Jul
5.55	Jean	Galfione	FRA	9.6.71	10=	GP II	Saint-Denis	6 Jul
	(70)							
5.55	Dmitriy	Kuptsov	RUS-J	9.11.82	1	EJ	Grosseto	22 Jul
5.55i	Aleksandr	Korchmyd	UKR-J	22.1.82	1H		Brovary	19 Dec
5.52i	Javier	Gazol	ESP	27.10.80	1		Vilafranca	11 Feb
5.52i	Pierre-Charles	Peuf	FRA	27.4.79	6		Clermont-Ferrand	16 Mar
5.52	Daichi	Sawano	JPN	16.9.80	1		Gotenba	13 Oct
5.51i	João	André	POR	28.5.76	2		Valencia	25 Feb
5.51	Scott	Slover	USA	9.7.75	4	MSR	Walnut	22 Apr
5.51	Björn	Otto	GER	16.10.77	7		Kassel	13 Jun
5.50i	Yevgeniy	Mikhaylichenko	RUS	13.2.79	2		Moskva	19 Jan
5.50i	Ralf	Schmidt	GER	1.9.75	1		Ludwigshafen	20 Jan
	(80)							
5.50i ?	Aleksey	Khanafin	RUS	27.4.81	2		Erfurt	2 Feb
5.50i	Stefan	Drews	GER	12.2.79	1		Bad Segeberg	3 Feb
5.50i	Georgi	Wassilew	GER	16.2.80	4		Halle	16 Feb
5.50i	Nuno	Fernandes	POR	1.4.69	1	NC	Espinho	17 Feb
5.50i	François	Thénault	FRA	4.5.72	1		Sherbrooke	11 Mar
5.50	Mike	Westlund	USA	24.3.80	2		Abilene	10 May
5.50	Petr	Spacek	CZE	23.7.75	3		Ingolstadt	27 May
5.50	Gildas	Verbist	FRA	9.6.79	2		Miramas	13 Jun
5.50	Mathieu	Boisrond	FRA	8.1.77	2		Sotteville	12 Jul
5.50A	Rob	Pike	CAN	8.1.70	1		Calgary	30 Jul
	(90)							
5.49	Alhaji	Jeng	SWE	13.12.81	3	NC	Växjö	26 Aug
5.48i	Eric	Eshbach	USA	4.2.81	4	NCAA	Fayetteville	9 Mar
5.48i	Dino	Efthimiou	USA	23.7.79	5	NCAA	Fayetteville	9 Mar
5.48i	Brad	Walker	USA	21.6.81	7	NCAA	Fayetteville	9 Mar
5.47	Mark	Calvin	USA	17.11.74	1		Irvine	24 Mar
5.45i	Jurij	Rovan	SLO	23.1.75	1		Pireás	27 Jan
5.45i	Tom Erik	Olsen	NOR	20.10.74	1		Oslo	9 Feb
5.45i	Nicolas	Jolivet	FRA	24.3.77	3		Liévin	17 Feb
5.45	Matt	Phillips	USA	28.12.77	2		Eugene	17 Mar
5.45	Chad	Walters	USA	19.5.79	1	TexR	Austin	6 Apr
	(100)							
5.45	Bubba	McLean	USA	2.9.79	5	NCAA	Eugene	30 May
5.45	Nicolas	Durand	FRA	23.1.79	1		Aix-les-Bains	23 Jun
5.45	Trond	Barthel	NOR	11.9.70	2		Halmstad	15 Jul
5.45	Matti	Mononen	FIN-J	25.11.83	1		Lappeenranta	27 Aug
5.45	Andrea	Giannini	ITA	18.12.76	1	MedG	Tunis	14 Sep

Mark	Name		Nat	Born	Date
5.42i	Damien	Inocencio	FRA	29.7.77	16 Mar
5.42	Hendrik	Hübner	GER	11.6.76	26 Aug
5.42	Christof	Gross	GER	11.3.76	26 Aug
5.41i	Charles	DeWildt	USA	30.3.79	1 Mar
5.41i	Fumiaki	Kobayashi	JPN	10.12.74	20 Mar
5.41	David	Lemen	USA	13.11.79	13 Apr
5.41	Brent	Callaway	USA	16.8.79	14 Apr
5.41	Tobias	Ulrich	GER	6.4.79	27 May

Mark	Name		Nat	Born	Date
5.41	Ketil	Rønneberg	NOR	9.12.76	31 May
5.41	Rico	Tepper	GER-J	16.4.82	31 May
5.40i	Ruslan	Gataullin	RUS	1.12.79	19 Jan
5.40i	Christoph	Völker	GER	26.11.79	20 Jan
5.40i	Spas	Bukhalov	BUL	14.11.80	27 Jan
5.40i	Chris	Steddum	USA	21.5.80	9 Feb
5.40i	Tim	Thomas	GBR	18.11.73	11 Feb
5.40i	Radek	Honcl	CZE	12.11.76	17 Feb
5.40i	Satoru	Yasuda	JPN	27.7.75	18 Feb
5.40i	Aleksandr	Yurkov	UKR	21.7.75	20 Feb
5.40i	Wesley	Rombaut	BEL	12.11.77	23 Feb
5.40A	Fanie	Jacobs	RSA	21.4.76	16 Mar
5.40	Toby	Stevenson	USA	19.11.76	25 Mar
5.40	Brad	Tyler	USA	14.7.80	31 Mar
5.40	Javier	Benítez	ARG	30.6.76	7 Apr
5.40	Kevin	Brown	USA	15.8.71	21 Apr
5.40	Russell	Watson	USA		10 May
5.40	Kiyonobu	Kigoshi	JPN	7.5.76	18 May
5.40	Jim	Autenreith	USA	20.9.79	19 May
5.40A	Giovani	Linaro	MEX		16 Jun
5.40	Robert	Villa	ESP	13.1.81	23 Jun
5.40	Danny	Krasnov	ISR	27.5.70	23 Jun
5.40	Scott	Hennig	USA	17.4.69	24 Jun
5.40	Marvin	Osei-Tutu	GER	22.4.81	30 Jun
5.40	Christian	Schmitt	GER	12.7.78	30 Jun
5.40	Ruben	Scotti	ITA	20.8.76	7 Jul
5.40	Fabio	Pizzolato	ITA	16.3.75	7 Jul
5.40	Maurilio	Mariani	ITA	22.4.73	27 Jul
5.40	Erki	Nool	EST	25.6.70	7 Aug
5.38	Bobby	Most	USA-J	13.12.82	9 Jun
5.37i	Geoff	Fairbanks	USA	1.6.79	12 Jan
5.37i	Fabrice	Fortin	FRA	2.2.80	8 Dec
5.36i	Fílippos	Sgoúros	GRE	26.9.81	18 Feb
5.35i	Jukien	Costes	FRA	11.2.79	7 Jan
5.35i	Pascal	Couturier	FRA	24.2.79	25 Jan
5.35i	Jarno	Koivunen	FIN	3.1.75	18 Feb
5.35	Lon	Badeaux	USA	9.3.73	14 Apr
5.35A	Steve	Deming	USA		5 May
5.35	Takuya	Kanno	JPN	17.1.79	20 May
5.35	Ricardo	Diez	VEN	29.3.75	20 May
5.35	Tony	Moore	USA	27.1.78	26 May
5.35	Stávros	Kouroupákis	GRE-J	17.5.83	23 Jun
5.35	Santiago	Bañón	ESP	26.7.74	8 Jul
	(156)				

Best outdoor marks for athletes with seasonal bests indoors

Mark	Name	Pos	Meet	Venue	Date
5.90	L Johnson	1		Knoxville	7 Apr
5.85	Ecker	2	NC	Stuttgart	30 Jun
5.85	Stolle	4	WCh	Edmonton	9 Aug
5.85	Mesnil	5	WCh	Edmonton	9 Aug
5.80	Harvey	2	ModR	Modesto	12 May
5.80	Börgeling	3	NC	Stuttgart	30 Jun
5.75	Janácek	1		Praha	2 Jun
5.70	Smiryagin	2	NC	Tula	12 Jul
5.65	Pauli	1	TexR	Austin	7 Apr
5.65	Yurchenko	1		Villeneuve d'Ascq	17 Jun
5.65	Gataullin	3	NC	Tula	12 Jul
5.60A	Brits	1		Rustenberg	22 Jan
5.60	Miranda	1		Rivas	12 May
5.59	Keul	4	Drake	Des Moines	28 Apr
5.55	Manson	2		Phoenix	27 May
5.55	Yegorov	10=	GP II	Saint-Denis	6 Jul
5.50	García	2		Madrid	16 Jun
5.50	Tivontchik	6	NC	Stuttgart	30 Jun
5.50	Gerasimov	10	Nik	Nice	9 Jul
5.50	Bochkaryov	6	NC	Tula	12 Jul
5.50	Gibilisco	3	EU23	Amsterdam	15 Jul
5.50	Peuf	3	EU23	Amsterdam	15 Jul
5.50	Andji	2		La Roche-sur-Yon	22 Aug
5.47	Gazol	1		Mataró	4 Jul
5.45	Eshbach	4	TexR	Austin	7 Apr
5.45	André	1	NC	Lisboa (U)	22 Jul

Mark	Name	Date
5.42	Olsen	4 Jun
5.40	Terek	20 Apr
5.40	Xu Gang	22 Apr
5.40	Jolivet	20 May
5.40	Yeliseyev	22 May
5.40	Thénault	24 May
5.40	Bukhalov	26 May
5.40	T Thomas	30 May
5.40	Mikhaylichenko	9 Jun
5.40	Rovan	4 Jul
5.40	Inocencio	7 Jul
5.40	Yasuda	15 Jul
5.40	Inocencio	18 Jul
5.40	Kobayashi	20 Jul
5.36	Walker	22 Apr
5.35	Koivunen	22 Jun
5.35	Costes	23 Jun

Exhibition

Mark	Name		Nat	Born	Pos	Venue	Date
5.81	Vasiliy	Gorshkov	RUS	5.2.77	1	Chiari	12 Sep
5.71	Denis	Yurchenko	UKR	27.1.78	1	Lódz	24 Aug
5.63	Björn	Otto	GER	16.10.77	3	Recklinghausen	26 May
5.60i	Jean	Galfione	FRA	9.6.71	1	Champagnole	30 Mar
5.60	Andrei	Tivontchik	GER	13.7.70	3	Koln	5 Sep
5.50	Matteo	Rubbiani	ITA	31.8.78	1	Vicenza	30 Jun

Mark	Name		Nat	Born	Date
5.43	Alexey	Khanafin	RUS	27.4.81	26 May
5.40	Radek	Honcl	CZE	12.11.76	20 Jun

JUNIORS

See main list for top 4 juniors. 10 performances by 5 men to 5.41. Additional marks and further juniors:

Name	Mark	Pos	Meet	Venue	Date
Rans	5.56	1		Oordegem	2 Aug
	5.50	2	EJ	Grosseto	22 Ju;
	5.50	2	ECp-2B	Nicosia	24 Jun
	5.41	1		Sint Niklaas	24 May
Korchmyd	5.50i	2	NC	Brovary	10 Feb

Mark	Name			Nat	Born	Pos	Meet	Venue	Date
5.41	Rico	Tepper		GER	16.4.82	1		Cottbus	31 May
5.38	Bobby	Most		USA	13.12.82	1	GWest	Sacramento	9 Jun
5.35	Stávros	Kouroupákis		GRE	17.5.83	1		Kateríni	23 Jun
5.30i	Dennis	Leyckes		GER	20.4.82	1	NC-j	Neubrandenburg	17 Feb
5.30	Steven	Hooker		AUS	16.7.82	1	NC-j	Brisbane	25 Mar
5.30	Takehito	Ariki		JPN	15.1.82	1		Yokohama	20 Apr
5.30		Kim Yoo-suk		KOR	19.1.82	1c		Modesto	12 May
5.30	Vincent	Favretto		FRA	5.4.84	1		Antony	20 May
5.30	Igor	Alekseyev		RUS	7.4.83	2		Krasnodar	22 May
5.30	Sergey	Chemovskoy		RUS	83	3		Krasnodar	22 May
5.30	Vasiliy	Petrov		RUS	5.2.83	4		Krasnodar	22 May
5.30	Ivan	Bonchev		BUL	29.3.82	2	NC	Sofia	9 Jun
5.30	Damiel	Dossévi		FRA	3.2.83	1		Mannheim	16 Jun
5.30	Alexander	Streller		GER	27.2.82	3		Mannheim	16 Jun
5.30	Ruslan	Shturkhalyov		UKR	19.10.84	1		Bila Tserkva	29 Jun
5.30	Takuro	Mori	(20)	JPN	21.6.83	1	NC-j	Matsumoto	1 Jul
5.30	Przemyslaw	Czerwinski		POL	28.7.83	5		Gdansk	14 Jul
5.30	Toshiro	Imura		JPN	14.6.82	1		Tsukuba	9 Sep
5.30	Jorge	Naranjo		CHI	18.1.82	1	PAm-J	Santa Fe	18 Oct

LONG JUMP

Mark	Wind	Name		Nat	Born	Pos	Meet	Venue	Date	Series
8.43i	-	Iván	Pedroso	CUB	17.12.72	1	WI	Lisboa	11 Mar	7.95 x 8.43 x x p
8.40	1.2					1	WCh	Edmonton	11 Aug	x 8.23/-0.9 8.35/0.5 6.18 8.40 x
8.32i						1		Madrid	14 Mar	8.08 x 7.91 8.03 x 8.32
8.31i						1		Pireás	21 Feb	8.05 x x x x 8.31
8.30	-0.1					2	VD	Bruxelles	24 Aug	8.00 7.89 x x 8.30 8.27
8.29	1.5					1		Yokohama	15 Sep	x 8.01 8.04 8.29 p x
8.41	1.3	James	Beckford	JAM	9.1.75	1	Neb M	Torino	9 Jun	8.22 8.23 x x 8.11w 8.41
8.19	-0.2					Q	WCh	Edmonton	9 Aug	8.05 8.19 2 jumps
8.24w	2.2					1		Padova	26 Aug	x 7.91 7.88 x 8.24w 7.99
8.38	0.6	Savanté	Stringfellow	USA	6.11.78	1		Lake Buena Vista	22 Jul	?
8.33	-0.1					Q	WCh	Edmonton	9 Aug	8.33 only jump
8.31	0.0					1	VD	Bruxelles	24 Aug	x 8.24 8.31 x 8.19 x
8.28	0.2					1	Athl	Lausanne	4 Jul	8.28 8.09 7.95 p x x
8.27	0.1					1	NCAA	Eugene	31 May	8.26 p p 8.19 8.23 8.27
8.24	1.6					2	WCh	Edmonton	11 Aug	x x 8.22/1.2 8.24 x x
8.23i						1		Gainesville	3 Feb	?
8.19	1.4					2	GPF	Melbourne	9 Sep	8.01 x 81.4 7.79 8.19 8.07
8.31	0.6	Hussein	Al-Sabee	KSA	14.11.79	1	GP II	Doha	18 May	7.62 8.31 x x 8.25 8.10
8.31		Danila	Burkenya	RUS	20.7.78	1	NC	Tula	14 Jul	x 8.14 8.31 8.18 8.31 8.28
8.30	-0.2	Kevin	Dilworth	USA	14.2.74	3	VD	Bruxelles	24 Aug	7.83 8.09 8.22 x 8.30 x
8.25	-0.6					1	Veniz	Haniá	4 Jun	8.12 x 8.05 x 8.20/-0.1 8.25
8.20	-1.7					1		Lubbock	31 Mar	?
8.28	0.8	Grzegorz	Marciniszyn	POL	22.5.77	1		Malles	14 Jul	7.87 8.00 x 7.92 8.28 7/72
8.23	1.0	Younès	Moudrik	MAR	1.10.77	1	GPF	Melbourne	9 Sep	8.23 x x x 8.13 8.07
8.20	0.1					2		Doha	18 May	7.98 7.94 8.12 8.20 8.18 8.13
8.22	-0.9		Li Dalong	CHN	21.10.80	1	NC	Baoding	15 Jun	
8.22		Vladimir	Malyavin (10)	RUS	4.3.73	1	Kuts	Moskva	27 Jul	
8.21	1.1	Carlos	Calado	POR	5.10.75	3	WCh	Edmonton	11 Aug	x 8.21 x 7.92 8.18/1.7 8.01
8.20	0.3	Kareem	Streete-Thompson	CAY	30.3.73	1		Fort-de-France	28 Apr	7.83 7.85 7.89w 7.72w 7.92 8.20
8.20	1.9	Aleksey	Lukashevich	UKR	11.1.77	2	Neb M	Torino	9 Jun	x 8.01w 8.05 x 8.20
8.20	1.5	Miguel	Pate	USA	13.6.79	Q	WUG	Beijing	27 Aug	8.20 only jump
		(30/14)								
8.18	1.0	Vitaliy	Shkurlatov	RUS	25.5.79	3	GPF	Doha	18 May	
8.18	-1.8	Roland	McGhee	USA	15.10.71	2		Orlando	22 Jul	
8.15A	0.5	Stephan	Louw	NAM	26.2.75	1		Johannesburg	21 Feb	
8.15	1.9	Bogdan	Tarus	ROM	1.8.75	1	ECp-1B	Budapest	23 Jun	
8.15	0.5	Schahriar	Bigdeli	GER	26.3.80	1		Leverkusen	26 Aug	
8.14i	-	Walter	Davis	USA	2.7.79	1	SEC	Lexington	24 Feb	
		(20)								
8.13i	-	Kofi Amoah	Prah	GER	20.12.74	1		Erfurt	2 Feb	
8.13	0.9	Vladimir	Zyuskov	UKR	29.8.81	1	NC	Kiev	2 Jul	
8.13	1.1	Dwight	Phillips	USA	1.10.77	2	Athl	Lausanne	4 Jul	
8.13	1.9	Yann	Doménech	FRA	17.3.79	1		Bron	21 Jul	
8.12	0.1	Darvis	Patton	USA	4.12.77	1		Arlington	31 Mar	
8.12	1.8	Luka	Aracic	CRO	13.3.81	1	ECp-2B	Nicosia	23 Jun	
8.12	0.5	Gregor	Cankar	SLO	25.1.75	1	NC	Maribor	7 Jul	
8.12	1.5	Kader	Klouchi	FRA	1.6.69	*	NC	Saint-Etienne	30 Jun	
8.12		Yahya	Berrabah	MAR	13.10.81	1	NC	Casablanca	30 Jun	
8.11i		Yevgeniy	Tretyak	RUS	18.7.71	1	NC	Moskva	18 Feb	
		(30)								
8.11i		Luis	Meliz	CUB	11.8.79	2		Pireás	21 Feb	
8.11i	-	Peter	Burge	AUS	3.7.74	1		Sindelfingen	4 Mar	
8.11	1.9	Roman	Sebrle	CZE	26.11.74	1D		Götzis	26 May	
8.11	1.5	Vladimir	Yakushev	RUS	.79	1		Tula	29 May	
8.11	1.4	Raúl	Fernández	ESP	8.3.78	1		Getafe	10 Jul	
8.10i	-	Mickaël	Loria	FRA	9.6.73	1	NC	Liévin	17 Feb	
8.10i	-	Melvin	Lister	USA	29.8.77	5	WI	Lisboa	11 Mar	

Mark	Wind	Name		Nat	Born	Pos	Meet	Venue	Date
8.10	1.6	Daisuke	Watanabe	JPN	29.5.75	2		Shizuoka	3 May
8.10	0.8		Lao Jianfeng	CHN	24.5.75	2	NC	Baoding	15 Jun
8.08	0.3		Wang Cheng	CHN	4.11.80	1		Ningbo	28 Apr
		(40)							
8.08		Dmitriy	Mitrofanov	RUS	76	2	Kuts	Moskva	27 Jul
8.08	1.0	Joan Lino	Martínez	CUB	17.1.78	*		Padova	26 Aug
8.07	1.8	Nikolay	Atanasov	BUL	11.12.74	1		Sofia	10 Jun
8.07	0.9	Yago	Lamela	ESP	24.7.77	1		Guadalajara	13 Jun
8.07	0.9	Tomás	Dvorák	CZE	11.5.72	1D	WCh	Edmonton	6 Aug
8.06	-0.4	Masaki	Morinaga	JPN	27.3.72	2		Baton Rouge	14 Apr
8.06	0.0	Danijal	Jahic	YUG	1.7.79	1		Beograd	16 Jun
8.05i	-	Peter	Häggström	SWE	27.1.76	2		Sindelfingen	4 Mar
8.05	1.9	Mike	Powell	USA	10.11.63	1	Mod R	Modesto	12 May
8.05	0.6	Cheikh Tidiane	Touré	FRA	25.1.70	*	Neb M	Torino	9 Jun
		(50)							
8.04	1.5	Tommy	Evilä	FIN	6.4.80	1	NC-23	Eurajoki	11 Aug
8.04	0.4	Frank	Busemann	GER	26.2.75	1	ISTAF	Berlin	31 Aug
8.03	1.8	Mattias	Sunneborn	SWE	27.9.70	1		Visby	3 Jun
8.03	1.1	Antonio	Adsuar	ESP	4.7.78	1		Castellón	24 Jul
8.02i	-	Petar	Dachev	BUL	15.6.79	1		Sofia	20 Jan
8.02		Mark Anthony	Aere	GHA	16.7.71	1		Sondershausen	24 Aug
8.01	1.5	Brian	Johnson	USA	25.3.80	*	NCAA	Eugene	31 May
8.00	1.6	Allen	Simms	USA-J	26.7.82	1		Lynchburg	20 Apr
7.99	0.8	Shin-ichi	Terano	JPN	10.7.79	2	NC	Tokyo	9 Jun
7.99	0.3	Gable	Garenamotse	BOT	28.2.77	3	WUG	Beijing	29 Aug
		(60)							
7.98i	-	Dmitriy	Ruban	RUS	77	5	NC	Moskva	18 Feb
7.98i	-	Astérios	Noúsios	GRE	25.2.79	3		Pireás	21 Feb
7.98i	-	Konstadínos	Koukodímos	GRE	14.9.69	1	NC	Pireás	25 Feb
7.98	2.0	Jonathan	Moore	GBR-J	31.5.84	1	vFRA-j	Dôle	29 Jul
7.98	2.0	Sinisa	Ergotic ¶	CRO	14.9.68	*		Padova	26 Aug
7.97i	-	Roman	Shchurenko	UKR	14.9.76	5		Pireás	21 Feb
7.97	0.0	Martin	McClintock	RSA	30.6.75	1		Port Elizabeth	27 Apr
7.97	1.0	Nathan	Morgan	GBR	30.6.78	1		Loughborough	20 May
7.97	0.9	Konstantin	Krause	GER	8.10.67	2		Dortmund	9 Jun
7.96	1.9	Rémi	Robert	FRA	21.1.76	2		Pierrelatte	26 May
		(70)							
7.95	1.9	Cedric	Rogers	USA	18.2.79	1		Landover	5 Jun
7.95	0.8	Emmanuel	Bangué	FRA	21.7.71	1		Tomblaine	2 Sep
7.94	0.7	Tim	Parravacini	AUS	25.4.81	2	NC	Brisbane	24 Mar
7.94	1.7	Joe	Allen	USA	7.7.78	2		Clemson	7 Apr
7.94	0.6	Tyrone	Johnson	USA	5.2.81	1	IC4A	Princeton	19 May
7.94	1.0	Dimítrios	Filíndras	GRE	9.2.73	5	Veniz	Haniá	4 Jun
7.94	0.0	Said Mansour	Al-Bekheet	QAT		1	PArab	Damascus	2 Oct
7.93	2.0	Jai	Taurima	AUS	26.6.72	2		Sydney	16 Feb
7.93A	-0.8	Francois	Coetzee	RSA	30.7.75	1		Roodepoort	16 Mar
7.93	0.9	Leigh	Stuart	AUS	2.1.71	3	NC	Brisbane	24 Mar
		(80)							
7.93	1.8	Okoineme	Giwa-Agbomeirle	NGR	30.11.78	2		Landover	5 Jun
7.93	1.3	Loúis	Tsátoumas	GRE-J	12.2.82	1		Spárti	25 Jul
7.92	1.6	Chris	Hercules	USA	14.5.79	1	Big 12	College Station	18 May
7.92	-0.7	Sanjay Kumar	Rai	IND	1.5.79	1		Lucknow	19 Sep
7.92	0.0	Abdulrahman	Al-Nubi	QAT	17.10.79	2	PArab	Damascus	2 Oct
7.91		Khaled	Al-Bekheet	KUW	12.1.76	1		Al Kuwait	20 Feb
7.91		Yoelmis	Pacheco	CUB-J	9.6.82	1		La Habana	2 Mar
7.91	0.7	Richard	Duncan	CAN	25.12.73	4		Gosier	1 May
7.91	1.6		Fang Zetao	CHN	11.2.79	1		Tianjin	19 May
7.91	-0.2		Liu Zhiwen	CHN	17.1.75	Q	NC	Baoding	14 Jun
		(90)							
7.91	1.3	Giacomo	D'Apolito	ITA	23.10.71	2		Malles	14 Jul
7.91	0.6	Leslie	Djhone	FRA	18.3.81	*		Bron	21 Jul
7.90i	-	Lenton	Herring	USA	4.12.78	1		Madison	13 Jan
7.90	1.2	Kenta	Bell	USA	16.3.77	1		Baton Rouge	18 May
7.90	0.1	Esteban	Copland	VEN	12.10.79	1		Caracas	27 Jul
7.89i	-	Mesut	Yavas	TUR	14.4.78	1		Norman	3 Feb
7.89i	-	Alessio	Rimoldi	ITA	4.7.76	1	NC	Torino	25 Feb
7.89i	-	Tommy	Oleksy	USA	26.3.81	4	NCAA	Fayetteville	9 Mar
7.89A	1.3	Johan	Stroh	RSA	3.8.80	1		Germiston	24 Mar
7.89	0.0		Zhou Can	CHN	20.5.79	3		Zhongshan	21 Apr
		(100)							
7.89	0.5	Jonathan	Chimier	MRI-J	6.8.82	1	Franc	Ottawa	22 Jul

Mark	Wind	Name		Nat	Born	Date
7.88i		William	Montgomery	USA	23.6.80	2 Feb
7.88	1.0	Kazushige	Inadomi	JPN	14.5.78	15 Apr
7.88	-0.8	Zyrus	Hill	USA	14.1.75	21 Apr
7.88	1.8		Zhang Xin	CHN-J	24.4.83	19 May
7.88		Milan	Kovár	CZE	24.2.72	20 May
7.88	0.8	Nicola	Trentin	ITA	20.6.74	7 Jul
7.88	0.9	Simon	Sundsten	FIN	27.5.78	7 Jul
7.88	0.2	José Miguel	Martínez	ESP	5.5.76	21 Jul
7.88	0.6	Hrístos	Kirítsis	GRE	7.9.78	25 Jul
7.88	-0.8		Huang Le	CHN	25.9.77	18 Nov
7.87i		Rostislav	Mestechkin	UKR	13.1.76	10 Feb
7.87i		Ron	Nelson	USA	15.1.80	3 Mar
7.87		Aleksey	Mekerin	RUS	78	27 Jul
7.87	0.8	Chris	Tomlinson	GBR	15.9.81	18 Aug
7.86i		Denis	Savelyev	RUS	74	18 Feb
7.86	1.4	Andrew	Curtis	AUS	23.12.79	24 Mar
7.86		Arnaud	Casquette	MRI	16.4.78	21 Apr
7.86	-2.3	Deandre	Free	USA	15.1.81	28 Apr
7.86	-0.2	Marko	Milinkov	YUG	12.3.77	27 May
7.86	-0.8	Nelson	Ferreira Junior	BRA	1.1.73	19 Jul
7.85	1.5	Nabil	Adamou	ALG	8.4.75	24 Mar
7.85	0.0	Daniel	Kaczmarczyk	POL	28.6.81	6 Jul
7.85A	0.2	Leevan	Sands	BAH	16.8.81	21 Jul
7.84	1.3	Maurice	Lewis	USA	14.1.78	14 Apr
7.84	1.6	Steffen	Landgraf	GER	26.8.80	4 Jun
7.84	1.5	Nouzalte	Abreu	POR	8.4.80	30 Jun
7.84	-1.0	Imre	Lörincz	HUN-J	12.3.82	6 Jul
7.84	1.6	Milko	Campus	ITA	2.4.69	14 Jul
7.83i		Bogdan	Tudor	ROM	1.2.70	21 Jan
7.83i		Stefano	Dacastello	ITA	17.2.80	4 Feb
7.83i		Jean	Cummings	VIN	29.12.80	9 Mar
7.83	1.5	Sergey	Seliverstov	UKR	12.3.80	18 May
7.83	-1.1	Salim	Sdiri	FRA	26.10.78	2 Jun
7.83	-0.6	Shigeru	Tagawa	JPN	22.11.75	9 Jun
7.83		Sergey	Pavlov	RUS	6.5.79	27 Jun
7.83	2.0	Martin	Löbel	AUT	27.8.76	7 Jul
7.82i		Ladji	Doucouré	FRA-J	28.3.83	14 Feb
7.82	0.1		Cai Peng	CHN-J	28.3.83	28 Apr
7.82	0.0		Chen Daming	CHN-J	16.5.83	13 May
7.82	1.8	Bostjan	Fridrih	SLO	20.9.79	13 May
7.82	-0.5	Kirill	Sosunov	RUS	1.11.75	27 May
7.82	nwi	Fréderic	Miyoupu	CMR-J	20.11.82	3 Jul
7.81	0.5	Cameron	Howard	USA	15.10.78	12 May
7.81	0.6		Chen Jing	CHN	10.3.76	13 May
7.81			Liu Xing	CHN	3.2.83	19 Jun
7.81	1.7	David	Branle	BEL	13.10.73	23 Jun
7.81		Ruslan	Gataullin	RUS	1.12.79	27 Jul
7.81		Marijo	Bakovic	CRO-J	11.4.82	9 Sep
7.80	1.1		Tan Zhengze	CHN	10.1.74	19 May
7.80	1.8	Erki	Nool	EST	25.6.70	26 May
7.80	0.8	Krasimir	Argirov	BUL	13.4.80	27 May
7.80	1.8	Kryzsztof	Luczak	POL	13.1.75	2 Jun
7.80	-0.2	Michael	Hessek	GER	15.3.75	4 Jun
		(154)				

Wind assisted

Mark	Wind	Name		Nat	Born	Pos	Meet	Venue	Date
8.48	5.6	Miguel	Pate	USA	13.6.79	1		Fort Worth	21 Apr
8.35w	2.5					2	NC	Eugene	22 Jun
		8.14w/3.5 x 8.35w 8.11/0.8 p 7.57/1.1							
8.26w	3.2					1		Clemson	7 Apr
		?							
8.21w	2.7					4	WCh	Edmonton	11 Aug
		x 8.09/-0.4 7.83 7.89 8.21w 7.94							
8.47	2.5	Savanté	Stringfellow	USA	6.11.78	1	NC	Eugene	22 Jun
		8.44w/5.3 8.47w 8.31w/2.6 p 8.09/1.8 p							
8.40w	3.9					1	TexR	Austin	Apr
		8.40w 8.28w p p p x							
8.22w	3.1					1		Baton Rouge	14 Apr
		?							
8.26	4.9	Gable	Garenamotse	BOT	28.2.77	1		Ashford	11 Aug
		x 7.98w 7.91w 8.26w 7.94w 7.82w							
8.24	2.9	Kader	Klouchi	FRA	1.6.69	1	NC	Saint-Etienne	1 Jul
		7.94 8.24w 8.10w x 8.09w 8.12/1.5							
8.24	3.1	Yann	Doménech	FRA	17.3.79	2	NC	Saint-Etienne	1 Jul
		7.64 8.24w 7.92/1.9 p p p							
8.23	3.0	Dwight	Phillips	USA	1.10.77	3	NC	Eugene	22 Jun
		7.73 8.06w 8.03w 8.23w 8.13w x							
8.19	2.8	Walter	Davis	USA	2.7.79	2	NCAA	Eugene	31 May
		8.19w 8.18w x x x 8.13/0.8							
8.19	4.0	Gregor	Cankar	SLO	25.1.75	1		Celje	9 Jun
8.19	4.5	Chris	Tomlinson	GBR	15.9.81	2	vFRA	Ashford	11 Aug
8.18	2.3	Masaki	Morinaga	JPN	27.3.72	1		Shizuoka	3 May
8.18	4.1	Nicola	Trentin	ITA	20.6.74	1		Rieti	19 May
8.18A	3.1	Esteban	Copland	VEN	12.10.79	1	Bol G	Ambato	13 Sep
8.17	3.1	Cheikh Tidiane	Touré	FRA	25.1.70	3	vGBR	Ashford	11 Aug
8.15	2.7	Mattias	Sunneborn	SWE	27.9.70	1		Visby	19 Jul
8.13	2.9	Joan Lino	Martínez	CUB	17.1.78	2		Padova	26 Aug
8.12	5.8	Rémi	Robert	FRA	21.1.76	1		Arles	10 Jun
8.11	2.6	Tommy	Evilä	FIN	6.4.80	1		Lapinlahti	22 Jul
8.10	5.5	Robert	Howard	USA	26.11.75	1	Kans R	Lawrence	20 Apr
8.10	3.4	Mike	Powell	USA	10.11.63	4	NC	Eugene	22 Jun
8.09	3.0	Simon	Sundsten	FIN	27.5.78	2		Visby	19 Jul
8.09	2.2	Sinisa	Ergotic ¶	CRO	14.9.68	3		Padova	26 Aug
8.08	2.6	Nelson	Ferreira Junior	BRA	1.1.73	1		São Caetano do Sul	22 Apr
8.08	4.8	Yusuke	Maeda	JPN	16.3.78	1		Shizuoka	15 Jul
8.06	2.5	Brian	Johnson	USA	25.3.80	3	NCAA	Eugene	31 May
8.06	2.9	Leslie	Djhoné	FRA	18.3.81	2		Montauban	17 Jul
8.03	2.7	Jonathan	Chimier	MRI-J	6.8.82	3	FRA Ch	Saint-Etienne	30 Jun
8.02	2.2	Sanjay Kumar	Rai	IND	1.5.79	1	NC	Chennai	19 Oct
8.00	6.6	Leevan	Sands	BAH	16.1.81	1	JUCO	Odessa, TX	11 May
8.00	2.3	Roman	Shchurenko	UKR	14.9.76	1		Kalamáta	2 Jun
8.00	6.2	Remmy	Limo	KEN	25.8.71	2		Arles	10 Jun
8.00	2.4	Kenta	Bell	USA	16.3.77	9	NC	Eugene	22 Jun
7.99A	2.8	Francois	Coetzee	RSA	30.7.75	1		Bloemfontein	2 Feb
7.98	3.1	LeJuan	Simon	USA	7.2.81	3	Kans R	Lawrence	20 Apr
7.98	2.5	Loúis	Tsátoumas	GRE-J	12.2.82	1	EJ	Grosseto	20 Jul

Mark	Wind	Name		Nat	Born	Pos	Meet	Venue	Date
7.97	2.2	Shigeru	Tagawa	JPN	22.11.75	3	NC	Tokyo	9 Jun
7.95A	3.3	Brian	Veal	USA-J	4.1.82	2		El Paso	14 Apr
7.95	2.7	Iván	Román	ESP	22.3.78	4		Rivas	27 Jun
7.94	2.7	Mesut	Yavas	TUR	14.4.78	1		Istanbul	16 Jun
7.92	2.2		Cai Peng	CHN-J	28.3.83	2		Ningbo	28 Apr
7.92	5.0	John	Moffitt	USA	81	2		Baton Rouge	18 May
7.92	4.3	Bakri	Darouèche	FRA	22.8.74	4		Pierrelatte	26 May

Mark	Wind	Name		Nat	Born	Date
7.91	4.1	Daisuke	Arakawa	JPN	19.9.81	30 Jun
7.91	2.8	Salim	Sdiri	FRA	26.10.78	22 Sep
7.89	2.8	Daniel	Kaczmarczyk	POL	28.6.81	18 May
7.89	2.7	Hrístos	Kirítsis	GRE	7.9.78	25 Jul
7.88	3.3	Bashir	Ramzy	USA	4.5.79	14 Apr
7.88	4.8	Bostjan	Fridrih	SLO	20.9.79	9 Jun
7.88	2.4	Arnaud	Casquette	MRI	16.4.78	22 Jul
7.87	2.9	Brandon	Campbell	USA	12.7.80	18 May
7.86	3.0	Jadel	Gregório	BRA	16.9.80	22 Apr
7.86	4.1	Kenneth	Kastrén	FIN	8.11.75	19 Jul
7.86	3.4	Milko	Campus	ITA	2.4.69	22 Sep
7.85	3.1	Jón Arnar	Magnússon	ISL	28.7.69	13 Jul
7.85	2.1	Andrew	Owusu	GHA	8.7.72	22 Jul
7.85	2.1	Hiroyuki	Oishi	JPN-J	11.5.82	18 Aug
7.84	3.7	Leonard	Cobb	USA	20.1.75	14 Apr
7.84	2.9	Darren	Thompson	GBR	6.11.79	16 Jun
7.83	3.3	Jason	Howard	USA	28.11.79	6 Apr
7.81	3.3	Andrea	Baldi	ITA	2.1.70	2 Jun
7.81	3.3	Josep María	Gener	ESP	4.2.80	1 Jul
7.81A	3.1	Leonardo	Geremias	BRA	31.1.76	15 Jul
7.81	5.0	Fabrizio	Donato	ITA	14.8.76	22 Sep
7.80	2.9	Milton	Little	USA	13.6.81	5 May
7.80	3.6	Santiago	Sánchez	ESP	22.10.80	2 Jun

Best outdoor marks for athletes with best indoors

Mark	Wind	Name	Pos	Meet	Venue	Date
8.40	1.2	Pedroso	1	WCh	Edmonton	11 Aug
8.13	0.8	Davis	*	NCAA	Eugene	31 May
8.10	0.3	Meliz	2	Sule	Tartu	19 Jun
8.06	0.2	Tretyak	5	Neb	Torino	9 Jun
8.05	0.4	Burge	*		Sydney	16 Feb
8.07w	3.1		1		Sydney	16 Feb
8.01	0.1	Prah	1		Wesel	4 Jun
7.95	1.1	Häggström	1		Uppsala	12 Jun
7.94	0.2	Noúsios	3		Pátra	22 Jul
7.92	0.1	Lister	5	GPF	Saint-Denis	6 Jul
8.08w	2.9		2	KansR	Lawrence	20 Apr
7.91	1.2	Koukodímos	1		Thessaloníki	21 Apr
7.90	0.8	Loria	5	NC	Saint-Etienne	30 Jun

Mark	Wind	Name	Date
7.89	1.4	Oleksy	10 May
7.88	1.3	Yavas	19 Aug
7.88	1.4	Rimoldi	26 Aug
7.85	1.1	Montgomery	18 May
7.84	1.6	Herring	19 May
7.80	-0.6	Shchurenko	4 Jun

Exhibition – irregular conditions

Mark	Name		Nat	Born	Pos	Venue	Date
8.03irr-ex	Milko	Campus	ITA	2.4.69	-	Sassari	7 Sep

Low altitude best

Mark	Wind	Name		Nat	Born	Pos	Venue	Date
8.11	-1.3	Stephan	Louw	NAM	26.2.75	1	Port Elizabeth	16 Feb

Drugs Disqualification

Mark	Wind	Name		Nat	Born	Pos	Meet	Venue	Date
8.08	0.9	Sinisa	Ergotic ¶	CRO	14.9.68	1	MedG	Tunis	12 Sep

JUNIORS

See main list for top 5 juniors. 12 performances by 6 men to 7.85. Additional marks and further juniors:

Name	Mark	Wind	Pos	Meet	Venue	Date
Simms	7.98i	-	1		Fairfax	6 Jan
	7.94i	-	3	NCAA	Fayetteville	9 Mar
	7.87	1.1	2	vGBR-j	Stoke-on-Trent	18 Aug
	7.85i	-	1		Boston (R)	4 Mar
Moore	7.93	0.7	1	vUSA-j	Stoke-on-Trent	18 Aug
Chimier	7.85	-1.7	1		Abidjan	26 Apr

Mark	Wind	Name		Nat	Born	Pos	Meet	Venue	Date
7.88	1.8		Zhang Xin	CHN	24.4.83	2		Tianjin	19 May
7.84	-1.0	Imre	Lörincz	HUN	12.3.82	2		Veszprém	6 Jul
7.82i		Ladji	Doucouré	FRA	28.3.83	1		Moskva	14 Feb
7.82	0.1		Cai Peng	CHN	28.3.83	*		Ningbo	28 Apr
7.82	0.0		Chen Daming	CHN	16.5.83	1		Jinan	13 May
7.82	nwi	Fréderic	Miyoupu	CMR	20.11.82	1		Camporosso	3 Jul
		(& 7.77/2.0 in series)							
7.81		Marijo	Bakovic	CRO	11.4.82	1		Rhodos	9 Sep
7.78		Dmitriy	Sapinskiy	RUS	23.10.83	1	NC-23	Cheboksary	14 Jun
7.78	1.2	Cleavon	Dillon	TRI	5.10.82	1	Jr Oly	Norfolk	31 Jul
7.77	2.0	Howard	Jackson	USA	HS	1		Austin	12 May
7.75	1.8		Li Zhiyuan	CHN	24.2.87	4		Tianjin	19 May
7.73	1.5	Hideaki	Shikama	JPN	29.12.83	1		Shizuoka	25 May
7.72	0.1	Thiago	Dias	BRA	2.3.84	1	WY	Debrecen	13 Jul
7.69	0.9		Kuang Li (20)	CHN	13.8.84	6		Tianjan	19 May
best out: 7.73	1.8	Ladji	Doucouré	FRA	28.3.83	1D	EJ	Grosseto	19 Jul

Wind assisted – see main list for top four men

Mark	Wind	Name		Nat	Born	Pos	Meet	Venue	Date
7.85	2.1	Hiroyuki	Oishi	JPN	11.5.82	1		Oita	18 Aug
7.76	2.7	Tony	Allmond	USA	8.10.82	1		Sacramento	19 May
7.72	3.0	Scott	Crowe	AUS	7.10.83	1	NC	Brisbane	25 Mar
7.72	2.7	Jan	Zumer	SLO	9.6.82	2	EJ	Grosseto	20 Jul

TRIPLE JUMP

Mark	Wind	Name		Nat	Born	Pos	Meet	Venue	Date
17.92	0.7	Jonathan	Edwards	GBR	10.5.66	1	WCh	Edmonton	6 Aug

Mark	Wind	Pos	Meet	Venue	Date	1	2	3	4	5	6
17.92						16.84/-1.1	x	17.92	x	p	x
17.66	0.7	1	v2N	Glasgow	1 Jul	x	17.66	p	p	p	p
17.60i		1		Samara	1 Feb	16.89	16.91	x	17.01	17.60	p
17.59	0.8	1	NC	Birmingham	15 Jul	x	17.59	p	p	p	p
17.56	0.5	1		Milano	6 Jun	x	x	17.56	p	p	p
17.46	-0.2	Q	WCh	Edmonton	4 Aug	x	16.51	17.46			

Mark	Wind	Name		Nat	Born	Pos	Meet	Venue	Date	
17.40	0.4					1	DNG	Stockholm	17 Jul	16.79 17.18/0.4 17.24/-0.4 17.40 p x
17.33	0.9					1		Malmö	20 Aug	x 16.60 16.80 17.12/-0.2 p 17.33
17.29	0.5					1	BrGP	London (CP)	22 Jul	17.29 x x p p 17.13/0.9
17.27	0.0					1		Rovereto	29 Aug	16.54 16.95 17.27 p p x
17.26i						2	WI	Lisboa	9 Mar	17.06 17.12 x 17.12 16.79 17.26
17.26	-0.1					1	ECp	Bremen	24 Jun	17.26 x p 17.04/0.64 only
17.26	1.1					1	GWG	Brisbane	4 Sep	x 16.02 x 17.26 p x
17.22	1.2					1		Madrid	7 Jul	x 17.10/0.3p 17.15/1.3p 17.22
17.53w	4.9					1		Bangor	2 Jun	
17.49	1.6	Christian	Olsson	SWE	25.1.80	1		Réthimno	1 Jul	17.49 p 16.60 16.57 p 16.50
17.47	1.2					2	WCh	Edmonton	6 Aug	13.99 17.28/1.7 17.47 p 16.96 p
17.28	0.9					2	DNG	Stockholm	17 Jul	16.95 17.07/0.0 17.28 16.73 p 15.95
17.24	-0.8					1	EU23	Amsterdam	23 Jul	16.62 16.69 16.82 x 17.24 x
17.44	0.9	Igor	Spasovkhodskiy	RUS	1.8.79	3	WCh	Edmonton	6 Aug	16.79w 16.69 16.37 16.89 17.44 16.38
17.40	1.2	Yoel	García	CUB	25.11.73	3	WCh	Edmonton	6 Aug	17.06 17.40 17.06 17.23/0.9 17.22/0.6 17.34/0.9
17.34	1.2	Paolo	Camossi	ITA	6.1.74	1		Bressanone	17 Jun	16.56 16.77 17.34 p p p
17.32i						1	WI	Lisboa	9 Mar	16.97 16.81 16.48 17.32 x 16.87
17.33	1.2	Phillips	Idowu	GBR	30.12.78	1	Veniz	Haniá	4 Jun	16.92/0.4 17.33/1.2 16.81/0.1 p p p
17.23	0.0					1	ECCp	Madrid	26 May	16.54 16.67 17.23 16.80 4 only
17.30	0.6	Michael	Calvo	CUB	26.12.77	1	NC	La Habana	27 May	x 17.16w 17.30 16.74 p p
17.22	1.2					1		La Habana	16 Feb	17.01 16.63 17.22 x 16.93 16.78
17.24A	0.0	Brian	Wellman	BER	8.9.67	1	CAC	C. de Guatemala	21 Jul	17.24 x p p p p
17.22	0.7	Walter	Davis	USA	2.7.79	Q	WCh	Edmonton	4 Aug	17.22 only jump
17.22	1.6	Kenta	Bell	USA	16.3.77	1	WUG	Beijing	31 Aug	17.10 x x 16.16 16.83 17.22
		(30/10)								
17.21	0.6	Larry	Achike	GBR	31.1.75	2	BrGP	London (CP)	22 Jul	
17.20i	-	Andrew	Murphy	AUS	18.12.69	3	WI	Lisboa	9 Mar	
17.19	1.7	Hrístos	Melétoglou	GRE	2.1.72	2	ECp-S	Bremen	24 Jun	
17.17	0.0	LaMark	Carter	USA	23.8.70	1	NC	Eugene	24 Jun	
17.15	1.6	Arnis	Filet	FRA	17.12.77	1	Franc	Ottawa	23 Jul	
17.13i	-	Charles	Friedek	GER	26.8.71	4	WI	Lisboa	9 Mar	
17.13	-0.7	Jadel	Gregório	BRA	16.9.80	1		São Paulo	18 Mar	
17.11	1.4	Marian	Oprea	ROM-J	6.6.82	2	WUG	Beijing	31 Aug	
17.10	1.0	Karl	Taillepierre	FRA	13.8.76	1		Arles	9 Jun	
17.06i	-	Aleksandr	Glavatskiy	BLR	2.5.70	2		Samara	1 Feb	
		(20)								
17.06	-0.9	Alexander	Martínez	CUB	23.8.77	1		Bern	24 Aug	
17.05i	-	Ionut	Punga	ROM	14.10.79	1		Bucuresti	27 Jan	
17.05	1.8	Fabrizio	Donato	ITA	14.8.76	1	MedG	Tunis	11 Sep	
17.04	0.7		Wu Ji	CHN	14.8.78	1	NG	Guangzhou	23 Nov	
17.02	1.7	Konstadínos	Zalaggítis	GRE	13.12.80	1	NC-23	Katerini	23 Jun	
17.00i	-	Igor	Gavrilenko	RUS	26.7.76	1	NC	Moskva	17 Feb	
16.95	1.4	Ivailo	Rusenov	BUL	9.9.79	1		Sofia	27 May	
16.92i	-	Robert	Howard	USA	26.11.75	2	Tyson	Fayetteville	9 Feb	
16.91i	-	Rostislav	Dimitrov	BUL	26.12.74	5	WI	Lisboa	9 Mar	
16.91	0.3	Viktor	Gushchinskiy	RUS	12.8.78	1	NC	Tula	13 Jul	
		(30)								
16.90	0.0	Thomas	Moede	GER	26.7.77	1	NC	Stuttgart	1 Jul	
16.89	0.9	Andrey	Kurennoy	RUS	12.5.72	2		Milano	6 Jun	
16.88	0.3	Johan	Meriluoto	FIN	22.3.74	2		Lahti	26 Aug	
16.86i	-	Jimmy	Gabriel	FRA	19.10.73	1		Liévin	18 Jan	
16.84	2.0	Yoandri	Betanzos	CUB-J	15.2.82	1		La Habana	16 Feb	
16.84		Vladimir	Letnicov	MDA	7.10.81	1		Chisinau	3 Jun	
16.84		Vasiliy	Sokov	UZB	7.4.68	1	Kuts	Moskva	28 Jul	
16.83		Vitaliy	Moskalenko	RUS	30.6.74	2	Kuts	Moskva	28 Jul	
16.81	1.7	Mohamed	Hamimid	FRA	16.11.73	3	NC	Saint-Etienne	1 Jul	
16.80i	-	Allen	Simms	USA-J	26.7.82	1		Blacksburg	19 Jan	
		(40)								
16.80	1.2	Denis	Saurambayev	KAZ	30.6.77	1		Bishkek	17 Jun	
16.80	1.3	Jérôme	Romain	FRA	12.6.71	2		La Roche-sur-Yon	22 Aug	
16.79		Vyacheslav	Taranov	RUS	20.3.75	3	Kuts	Moskva	28 Jul	
16.77i	-	LeVar	Anderson	USA	26.3.77	1		Baton Rouge	27 Jan	

Mark	Wind	Name		Nat	Born	Pos	Meet	Venue	Date
16.75i	-	Raúl	Chapado	ESP	4.5.70	1	NC	Valencia	25 Feb
16.74	0.5	Jacek	Kazmierowski	POL	2.7.74	1		Lublin	10 Jun
16.73i	-	Denis	Kapustin	RUS	5.10.70	5		Samara	1 Feb
16.73	0.8	Vladimir	Kravchenko	UKR	22.12.69	1	NC	Kiev	3 Jul
16.72	1.3	Avi	Tayari	ISR	25.10.73	1		Tel Aviv	23 Jul
16.70	1.1	Sergey	Arzamasov	KAZ	9.4.71	1		Almaty	23 Jun
		(50)							
16.70	0.1	Andrew	Owusu	GHA	8.7.72	2		Madrid	7 Jul
16.69A	-	Quincy	Howe	TRI	.79	1		USAF Academy	24 Feb
16.69i	-	Chris	Hercules	USA	14.5.79	2	NCAA	Fayetteville	10 Mar
16.69A	1.3	Freddy	Nieves	ECU	14.5.71	1	Bol G	Ambato	15 Sep
16.68	0.4	Julio	López	ESP	8.3.72	3	ECCp	Madrid	26 May
16.68	0.3		Lao Jianfeng	CHN	24.5.75	2	NG	Guangzhou	23 Nov
16.67	0.9	Masanari	Watanabe	JPN	10.12.80	1		Yokohama	20 May
16.66i	-	Lenton	Herring	USA	4.12.78	3	NCAA	Fayetteville	10 Mar
16.66	1.9	Messias	Baptista	BRA	24.5.68	*		São Caetano do Sul	22 Apr
16.66	0.1	Samuel	Okantey	GHA	3.11.74	1		Gavá	10 Jun
		(60)							
16.66A	1.4	Alvin	Rentería	COL	4.1.78	2	Bol G	Ambato	15 Sep
16.65	1.4	Ilja	Tumorin	EST	17.5.79	1	NC	Haapsalu	7 Jul
16.64i	-	Igor	Sautkin	RUS	23.2.72	3	NC	Moskva	17 Feb
16.64	0.7	Sébastien	Pincemail	FRA	21.2.79	1		Miramas	13 Jun
16.63A		Remmy	Limo	KEN	25.8.71	1		Nairobi	26 May
16.63		Jirí	Kuntos	CZE	2.10.73	1		Praha	11 Jun
16.62	0.4	Dmitriy	Valyukevich	BLR	31.5.81	4	BrGP	London (CP)	22 Jul
16.60i	-	Nikolay	Raev	BUL	29.1.71	1	NC	Sofia	27 Jan
16.60	1.5	LeJuan	Simon	USA	7.2.81	1	Tex R	Austin	6 Apr
16.59	0.9	Evgeniy	Timofeev (ex RUS)	CAN	22.2.74	1		Toronto	6 Jun
		(70)							
16.59	0.3	Sergey	Izmailov	UKR	1.5.75	2	NC	Kiev	3 Jul
16.58	1.1	Josh	Rollins	USA	7.6.79	1	IC4A	Princeton	20 May
16.58	0.5	Tim	Rusan	USA	25.6.77	1	NCAA II	Edwardsville	24 May
16.56i	-	Sergey	Kochkin	RUS	1.7.70	4	NC	Moskva	17 Feb
16.56	0.0	Djéké	Mambo	BEL	4.3.77	1		Tucson	16 Mar
16.56	0.9		Gu Junjie	CHN-J	5.5.85	1	EAsG	Osaka	24 May
16.56	0.0	Bostjan	Simunic	SLO	28.12.74	1		Dolenjske Toplice	17 Jun
16.55	-0.4	Yoelbi	Quesada	CUB	4.8.73	4	NC	La Habana	27 May
16.54i	-	Dmitriy	Vasilyev	BLR	27.10.76	1		Gomel	2 Jan
16.54i	-	Aleksandr	Aseledchenko	RUS	10.10.73	5	NC	Moskva	17 Feb
		(80)							
16.54A	1.6	Leigner	Aragón	COL	8.3.76	3	Bol G	Ambato	15 Sep
16.53	0.8	Dmitriy	Semenyuk	RUS	12.7.77	2	NC	Tula	13 Jul
16.51	0.3	Andrey	Trots	UKR	17.1.78	1		Kiev	19 May
16.51	0.0	Mohammed	Hamdi Aadh	QAT	4.12.81	1	PArab	Damascus	4 Oct
16.50	-0.2	Greg	Hughes	BAR	18.3.79	1		Knoxville	13 Apr
16.50	0.6	Vasil	Gergov	BUL	1.7.77	2		Sofia	27 May
16.50		Sergey	Bochkov	AZE	20.8.79	1		Moskva	23 Jun
16.50	0.0	Salem M	Al-Ahmadi	KSA	12.9.69	2	PArab	Damascus	4 Oct
16.49	1.2	Salvatore	Morello	ITA	5.9.74	2	NC	Catania	8 Jul
16.48	1.5	Miguel	Pate	USA	13.6.79	2	SEC	Columbia, SC	13 May
		(90)							
16.48	0.4	Yuriy	Opatskiy	UKR	5.11.79	2		Kiev	19 May
16.48	0.8	Konstantin	Pozatsidi	RUS-J	23.1.83	*	NC-j	Kazan	28 Jun
16.48		Yoeni	Pérez	CUB-J	82	1	NC-j	Santiago de Cuba	4 Jul
16.47i	-	Marcus	Thomas	USA	22.3.79	4		Baton Rouge	27 Jan
16.47		Alexis	Radeiro	CUB-J	30.6.82	2	NC-j	Santiago de Cuba	4 Jul
16.46	2.0	Aliecer	Urrutia	CUB	22.9.74	5	NC	La Habana	27 May
16.46		Von	Ware	USA	30.6.75	1		Long Beach	9 Jun
16.46	-0.1	Takanori	Sugibayashi	JPN	14.3.76	1	NC	Tokyo	10 Jun
16.45		Nattaporn	Nomkanha	THA	15.9.71	1		Bangkok	6 May
16.45	-0.7	Marcelo	da Costa	BRA	1.5.81	2		São Paulo	3 Jun
		(100)							
16.45		Adrian	Ghioroaie	ROM	2.9.79	3		Bucuresti	10 Jun

Mark	Wind	Name		Nat	Born	Date
16.43i	-	Hrvoje	Verzl	GER	12.11.70	27 Jan
16.43	0.4		Shang Yapeng	CHN-J	3.1.83	27 Apr
16.43	1.1	Jonathan	Moore	GBR-J	31.5.84	22 Jul
16.43	1.0	Viktor	Yastrebov	UKR-J	13.1.82	22 Jul
16.42i	-	Pavel	Kalinin	RUS	21.8.79	1 Feb
16.42	0.6	Meyram	Beispekov	KAZ	29.4.74	4 Jun
16.42	-0.6		Zou Sixin	CHN	5.8.67	23 Nov
16.41i	-	Javier	Asensio	ESP	4.9.77	25 Feb
16.40i	-	Julian	Golley	GBR	12.9.71	18 Feb
16.40	0.2	Dimítrios	Tsiámis	GRE-J	12.1.82	7 Aug
16.39	1.9	Leevan	Sands	BAH	16.8.81	6 Apr
16.39	-0.2	Andrius	Raizgys	LTU	4.4.69	23 Jun
16.38i		Yevgeniy	Plotnir	RUS	77	21 Feb
16.38		Aleksandr	Sergeyev	RUS-J	29.7.83	28 Jul
16.37	0.0	Takashi	Komatsu	JPN	30.12.67	26 Aug
16.36i		Brandon	Craven	USA	19.12.74	3 Mar

MEN 2001

Mark	Wind	Name		Nat	Born	Pos	Meet	Venue	Date
16.36	1.8	Colomba	Fofana	FRA	11.4.77				20 May
16.36	0.5	Ketill	Hanstveit	NOR	2.11.73				7 Jun
16.36	1.6		Cheng Yanhu	CHN	17.2.78				17 Jun
16.35	1.6	Koji	Muto	JPN	25.9.72				6 May
16.34	0.8		Hu Haiqiang	CHN	28.8.78				14 Jun
16.34A		Sammy	Ngeno	KEN					26 May
16.33	0.8	Yevgeniy	Yamashev	KAZ	25.6.76				4 Jun
16.33	-0.7	David	Girard	CUB-J	26.8.84				15 Jul
16.32i		Greg	Yeldell	USA	14.10.80				9 Feb
16.32	-1.0	Jason	Howard	USA	28.11.79				2 Jun
16.32	-0.5	Emanuele	Sardano	ITA	16.2.79				30 Jun
16.32		Sergey	Khurbatov	BLR	22.5.79				22 Jul
16.31	2.0	Konrad	Katarzynski	POL	16.7.80				2 Jun
16.30i		Daniel	Donovici	ROM	5.3.80				27 Jan
16.30i		Rephel	Martin	USA	23.4.76				24 Feb
16.29i		Kurt	Kraemer	USA					23 Feb
16.29	-1.5	Rudolf	Helpling	GER	23.2.81				19 May
16.29i		Randy	Lewis	GRN	14.10.80				7 Dec
16.28	1.8	Anísio	Souza Silva	BRA	16.6.69				22 Apr
16.28	-0.7	Steven	Shalders	GBR	24.12.81				13 Jul
16.27	0.8		Jia Dianjia	CHN	4.12.77				17 Jun
16.26	0.0	Jacob	McReynolds	AUS	8.12.78				15 May
16.26		Dmitriy	Byzov	RUS	25.1.66				23 Jun
16.25	1.0	Lauri	Leis	EST	7.10.78				30 Aug

(141)

Wind assisted

Mark	Wind	Name		Nat	Born	Pos	Meet	Venue	Date
17.38	2.6	Phillips	Idowu	GBR	30.12.78	2	v2N	Glasgow	1 Jul
					16.69w	17.38w	x	p p	x
17.28	3.5	Andrew	Murphy	AUS	18.12.69	1		Perth	4 Mar
17.13	4.1	Marian	Oprea	ROM-J	6.6.82	1	ECp-1B	Budapest	24 Jun
17.10A	2.2	Robert	Howard	USA	26.11.75	1		El Paso	14 Apr
17.04	2.4	Johan	Meriluoto	FIN	22.3.74	1	NC	Turku	8 Jul
16.93	3.1	Julian	Golley	GBR	12.9.71	1	vFRA	Ashford	11 Aug
16.86	2.7	Yoandri	Betanzos	CUB-J	15.2.82	5	WUG	Beijing	31 Aug
16.84	3.2	LeVar	Anderson	USA	26.3.77	2		Baton Rouge	14 Apr
16.83	3.0	Sébastien	Pincemail	FRA	21.2.79	3		Montauban	17 Jul
16.75	2.1	Samuel	Okantey	GHA	3.11.74	1		Valladolid	13 May
16.74	3.5	Tim	Rusan	USA	25.6.77	5	NC	Eugene	24 Jun
16.70	3.4	Messias	Baptista	BRA	24.5.68	1		São Caetano do Sul	22 Apr
16.70	2.2	Anísio	Souza Silva	BRA	16.6.69	2	NC	Rio de Janeiro	21 Jul
16.69	2.8	Konstantin	Pozatsidi	RUS-J	23.1.83	1	NC-j	Kazan	28 Jun
16.65	3.2	Takanori	Sugibayashi	JPN	14.3.76	2		Mito	6 May
16.64	3.6	Bostjan	Simunic	SLO	28.12.74	1		Celje	10 Jun
16.60		Von	Ware	USA	30.6.75	1		Long Beach	17 Feb
16.54	3.8	Colomba	Fofana	FRA	11.4.77	2		Montreuil-sous-Bois	20 May
16.54	2.4	Mathias	Hujo	GER	15.12.76	1		Jena	17 Jun
16.53	4.4	Marat	Safiullin	RUS	5.4.75	2		Perth	4 Mar
16.47	3.1	Jacob	McReynolds	AUS	8.12.78	2	NC	Brisbane	25 Mar
16.47		Nattaporn	Nomkanha	THA	15.9.71	1		Malacca	29 Jul
16.45		Lamont	Dagan	USA	30.9.77				28 Apr
16.45	2.4	Lauri	Leis	EST	7.10.78				7 Jul
16.42		John	Moffitt	USA	81				27 Apr
16.42	3.8	Mark	Dzradosi	GHA	29.3.78				19 May
16.38	2.9		Wang Yinglei	CHN-J	4.4.83				18 May
16.37	3.2	Takahisa	Yoshida	JPN	17.2.70				6 May
16.35	4.7	Michael	Velter	BEL	21.3.80				19 May
16.33	3.4	Tim	Barnes	AUS	18.1.68				25 Mar
16.32	2.4	Artyom	Kiryukhin	RUS-J	17.9.82				28 Jun
16.29	5.2	Abdul	Rasheed	USA	14.11.79				21 Apr
16.28	4.4	Femi	Akinsanya	GBR	29.11.69				11 Aug
16.28	4.0	Jefferson	Dias Sabino	BRA-J	4.11.82				30 Sep
16.26	3.3	Leonard	Cobb	USA	20.1.75				14 Apr

Unconfirmed

Mark	Wind	Name		Nat	Born	Pos	Meet	Venue	Date
17.16i	-	Vasiliy	Sokov	UZB	7.4.68	1		Tashkent	1 Feb

Best outdoor marks for athletes with best indoors

Mark	Wind	Name	Pos	Meet	Venue	Date
17.07	0.5	Murphy	1		Newcastle, NSW	3 Feb
17.00	0.1	Glavatskiy	2	Veniz	Haniá	4 Jun
16.90	-0.4	Friedek	3		Nürnberg	17 Jun
16.90	0.9	Dimitrov	Q	WCh	Edmonton	4 Aug
16.87	0.7	Punga	Q	EU23	Amsterdam	12 Jul
16.71	1.7	Howard	4	v2N	Glasgow	1 Jul
16.53	-0.4	Hercules	2	NCAA	Eugene	2 Jun
16.52	1.4	Raev	1		Sofia	2 Jun
16.51	-	Vasilyev		NC	Brest	7 Jun
16.49	-1.7	Anderson	2	KansR	Lawrence	21 Apr
16.48	0.5	Aseledchenko	4		Malmö	20 Aug
16.45	0.3	Gabriel	4		Montauban	17 Jul
16.66w	3.2		6	NC	Saint-Etienne	1 Jul
16.42	0.2	Kapustin	6		Nürnberg	17 Jun
16.37	2.0	Simms (J)	2		Princeton	20 May
16.54w	2.7		2	Tex R	Austin	6 Apr
16.34	0.5	Verzi				4 Jun
16.32	1.6	Herring				17 Mar
16.37w	3.7					28 Apr
16.30	0.5	Golley				15 Jul
16.27	0.4	Kalinin				8 Jun
16.41w	2.7	Chapado				11 Sep
16.30w	3.0	Yeldell				14 Apr

Exhibition – irregular conditions

Mark	Wind	Name		Nat	Born	Pos	Meet	Venue	Date
16.50w	ex	Carlos	Calado	POR	5.10.75	1		Maia	1 Jun

Low altitude best

Mark	Wind	Name		Nat	Born	Pos	Meet	Venue	Date
16.81	0.3	Brian	Wellman	BER	8.9.67	6	WCh	Edmonton	6 Aug
16.44	-0.3	Remmy	Limo	KEN	25.8.71	1		Limoges	11 Jul

JUNIORS

See main list for top 7 juniors. 13 performances by 3 men to 16.60. Additional marks and further juniors:

Name	Mark	Wind	Pos	Meet	Venue	Date
Oprea	16.86		1	NC	Bucuresti	10 Jun
	16.78	0.0	1	Balk	Trikala	8 Jul
	16.75	0.4	Q	EJ	Grosseto	21 Jul
	16.72i	-	1	NC	Bucuresti	24 Feb
	16.65	0.1	1	EJ	Grosseto	22 Jul
	16.62i	-	1		Bucuresti	27 Jan
	16.62	1.2	13Q	WCh	Edmonton	6 Aug
Betanzos	16.76	1.7	4		Arles	9 Jun
	16.66	0.8	1		Alcalá de H	30 Jun
	16.64A	0.2	2	CAC	C do Guatamala	21 Jul
	16.69w	3.5	3	NC	La Habana	27 May

Mark	Wind	Name		Nat	Born	Pos	Meet	Venue	Date
16.43	0.4		Shang Yapeng	CHN	3.1.83	1		Ningbo	27 Apr
16.43	1.1	Jonathan	Moore	GBR	31.5.84	2	EJ	Grosseto	22 Jul
16.43	1.0	Viktor	Yastrebov	UKR	13.1.82	3	EJ	Grosseto	22 Jul

Mark	Wind	Name		Nat	Born	Pos	Meet	Venue		Date
16.40	0.2	Dimítrios	Tsiámis	GRE-	12.1.82	1	NC-j	Halkída		7 Aug
16.38		Aleksandr	Sergeyev	RUS	29.7.83	4	Kuts	Moskva		28 Jul
16.33	-0.7	David	Girard	CUB	26.8.84	2	WY	Debrecen		15 Jul
16.17	0.6	Kazuyoshi	Ishikawa	JPN	6.11.82	1		Tokyo		28 Sep
16.16	1.0	Davy	Manga	FRA	6.5.83	4	EJ	Grosseto		22 Jul
16.16	1.1	Andrew	Howe	ITA	12.5.85	1		Ascoli Piceno		27 Jul
16.15	-0.2	Nelson	Évora	CIV	20.4.84	1		Braga		10 Jun
16.14	0.8	Artyom	Kiryukhin	RUS	17.9.82	*	NC-j	Kazan		28 Jun
16.01	1.0		Qin Shenghui	CHN	14.1.83	6	NC	Baoding		17 Jun
15.99	1.8		Wang Yinglei (20)	CHN	4.4.83	1	Asi-J	B S Begawan		22 Jul
Wind assisted – see main lists for top three juniors										
16.38	2.9		Wang Yinglei	CHN	4.4.83	1		Tianjin		18 May
16.32	2.4	Artyom	Kiryukhin	RUS	17.9.82	2	NC-j	Kazan		28 Jun
16.28	4.0	Jefferson	Dias Sabino	BRA	4.11.82	1	NC-j	Londrina		30 Sep
16.20	2.9	Aleksandr	Petrenko	RUS	83	3	NC-j	Kazan		28 Jun

SHOT

Mark		Name		Nat	Born	Pos	Meet	Venue		Date
21.97		Janus	Robberts	RSA	10.3.79	1	NCAA	Eugene		2 Jun
					18.88	21.09	20.26	21.02	21.68	21.97
21.60	1	WAC	Fresno	19 May	21.60	21.01	21.46	21.30	19.94	x
21.47i	1		Norman	1 Dec	x	x	11.93	20.98	x	21.47
21.36i	1		Reno	24 Feb	20.71	21.36	x	20.54	20.73	20.38
21.36i	1	NCAA	Fayetteville	10 Mar	x	x	21.21	20.13	20.72	21.36
21.26	Q	WCh	Edmonton	4 Aug	21.26		only throw			
21.22	1	Drake	Des Moines	28 Apr	19.72	18.23	20.92	rec21.22	x	20.98
21.95		John	Godina	USA	31.5.72	1	GP	Palo Alto		9 Jun
					21.87	21.44	21.79	21.95	21.06	21.50
21.87	1	WCh	Edmonton	4 Aug	21.87	21.80	x	x	x	x
21.64	1		Sherman Oaks	25 Jul	?					
21.60	1	NC	Eugene	22 Jun	21.60	x; 21.16	x	21.20	x	
21.42	1		Sherman Oaks	18 Jul	?					
21.36	1		Irvine	6 May	21.08	20.49	x	x	20.69	21.36
21.36	1		Luzern	27 Jun	x	20.92	21.36	21.16	20.83	20.84
21.35	1	MSR	Walnut	22 Apr	21.15	x	20.88	20.59	21.35	21.06
21.34	1		Salinas	22 May	?					
21.20	1		Los Angeles (Ww)	14 Apr	x	20.28	21.20	20.97	20.64	20.72
21.53		Adam	Nelson	USA	7.7.75	1		Rüdlingen		19 Aug
					21.04	21.29	21.53	3 only		
21.40i	1	NC	Atlanta	3 Mar	19.50	20.82	20.29	x	21.40	x
21.39	1		Calgary	30 Jul	21.29	21.39	21.39	x	p	p
21.24	2	WCh	Edmonton	4 Aug	19.92	20.86	20.19	21.24	x	x
21.04	1		Rüdlingen	19 Aug	20.83	x	20.51	x	21.04	x
21.35		Manuel	Martínez	ESP	7.12.74	1		San Sebastián		18 Aug
					x	20.74	21.35	x	20.60	x
21.29	1	ECCp	Madrid	27 May	20.59	20.30	20.90	21.29	4 only	
21.04	1		Valladolid	13 May	x	x	21.04	x	20.36	x
21.03	1	ECp	Bremen	23 Jun	x	20.21	x	21.03	4 only	
21.03	1	MedG	Tunis	13 Sep	20.28	x	20.04	20.46	21.03	20.48
21.02	1		Salamanca	19 May	21.02	x	x	x	x	20.40
20.97	1	WUG	Beijing	30 Aug	20.97	x	x	20.92	x	x
20.98		Yuriy	Belonog	UKR	9.3.74	1	Odlozil	Praha		18 Jun
20.98		Arsi	Harju	FIN	18.3.74	1		Lapinlahti		22 Jul
					x	19.60	20.80	20.15	20.01	20.98
		(31/^)								
20.94		Andy	Bloom	USA	11.8.73	1		Indianapolis		22 Jul
20.92		Andrey	Mikhnevich	BLR	12.7.76	1		Staiki		13 Jul
20.91i		Pavel	Chumachenko	RUS	5.4.71	1	NC	Moskva		16 Feb
20.91		Dragan	Peric	YUG	8.5.64	4	WCh	Edmonton		4 Aug
		(10)								
20.88		Tepa	Reinikainen	FIN	16.3.76	2		Lapinlahti		22 Ju
20.86		Paolo	Dal Soglio	ITA	29.7.70	1		Cuneo		8 Sep
20.79		Brad	Snyder	CAN	8.1.76	1		Knoxville		14 Apr
20.78		Ville	Tiisanoja	FIN	24.12.75	3		Lapinlahti		22 Jul
20.78		Conny	Karlsson	FIN	30.12.75	7	WCh	Edmonton		4 Aug
20.68i		Gheorghe	Guset	ROM	28.5.68	1		Bucuresti		3 Feb
20.68i		Miroslav	Menc ¶	CZE	16.3.71	1	NC	Praha		18 Feb
20.66		Mikulás	Konopka	SVK	23.1.79	1	GS	Ostrava		31 May
20.58		Milan	Haborák	SVK	11.1.73	1	NC	Nitra		7 Jul
20.56		Jani	Illikainen	FIN	26.1.76	1		Tornio		4 Aug
		(20)								
20.55		Brian	Miller	USA	20.3.72	2	Drake R	Des Moines		28 Apr

Mark	Name		Nat	Born	Pos	Meet	Venue	Date
20.53	Burger	Lambrechts ¶	RSA	3.4.73	1		Potchefstroom	12 Feb
20.53	John	Davis	USA	19.2.77	3	GP	Palo Alto	9 Jun
20.50	Petr	Stehlík	CZE	15.4.77	1		Turnov	20 May
20.47	Zsolt	Bíber	HUN	31.5.76	1		Budapest	27 May
20.43i	Joachim	Olsen	DEN	31.5.77	1		Moscow, Id.	16 Feb
20.43	Kevin	Toth	USA	29.12.67	2		Indianapolis	22 Jul
20.37i	Jim	Roberts	USA	30.12.76	1		Pocatello	3 Feb
20.32	Oliver-Sven	Buder	GER	23.6.66	1		Gotha	16 Jun
20.30	Ralf	Bartels	GER	21.2.78	2		Gotha	16 Jun
	(30)							
20.27i	Timo	Aaltonen	FIN	11.4.69	1	v 2-N	Umeå	24 Feb
20.22	Reese	Hoffa	USA	8.10.77	1		Atlanta	18 May
20.14	Justin	Anlezark	AUS	14.8.77	1		Brisbane	1 Sep
20.13	Jeff	Chakouian	USA-J	20.4.82	2		Atlanta	18 May
20.12	Pavel	Lyzhin	BLR	24.3.81		NC	Brest	7 Jun
20.12	Dmitriy	Goncharuk	BLR	17.7.70	1	ECp-1A	Vaasa	23 Jun
20.08	Roman	Virastyuk	UKR	20.4.68	2	NC	Kiev	1 Jul
19.96i	Jimmy	Nordin	SWE	19.10.79	1		Malmö	20 Jan
19.89	Mika	Halvari	FIN	13.2.70	2		Porvoo	9 Sep
19.84	Stevimir	Ercegovac	CRO	20.1.74	Q	WUG	Beijing	29 Aug
	(40)							
19.83	Szilárd	Kiss	HUN	9.12.75	1		Szombathely	11 Aug
19.80	Jamie	Beyer	USA	29.12.76	8	NC	Eugene	22 Jun
19.77	Karel	Potgieter	RSA	21.9.75	1		Pretoria	7 Jul
19.76	Yves	Niaré	FRA	20.7.77	1		Saint Maur	6 Jun
19.73	Michael	Mertens	GER	27.12.65	3		Gotha	16 Jun
19.72	Tonyo	Sylvester	USA	17.12.67	2		Sacramento	16 Jun
19.71	Andrey	Borodkin	UKR	18.4.78	1	UTA	Arlington	5 May
19.71	Christian	Cantwell	USA	30.9.80	1		Emporia	12 May
19.71	Leszek	Sliwa	POL	20.9.79	1		Warszawa	7 Jun
19.69	Bahadur	Singh	IND	7.5.73	1		Indianapolis	14 Jun
	(50)							
19.67	René	Sack	GER	14.7.76	1		Schapbach	21 Jul
19.65i	Marco	Dodoni	ITA	5.9.72	2		Torino	25 Feb
19.65	Ivan	Emelianov	MDA	19.2.77	1		Chisinau	2 Jun
19.64	Mark	Edwards	GBR	2.12.74	1		Stretford	8 May
19.63	Andrey	Nemchaninov	RUS	27.11.66	2		Kiev	25 May
19.63	Przemyslaw	Zabawski	POL	8.4.75	3		Kiev	25 May
19.62i	Sergio	Mottin	ITA	15.6.76	1		Ancona	27 Jan
19.59	Detlef	Bock	GER	15.8.74	3		Halle	19 May
19.59	Gjøran	Sørli	NOR	3.6.78	1	NC	Drammen	7 Jul
19.57	Ryan	Beckenhauer	USA	7.1.79	1		Fresno	5 May
	(60)							
19.57	Jarkko	Haukijärvi	FIN	10.6.77	1		Vilppula	26 Jun
19.57	Sören	Tallhem	SWE	16.2.64	1		Väddö	1 Sep
19.55i	Marcus	Clavelle	USA	23.6.78	1		Norman	17 Feb
19.53	Borivoje	Stanic	YUG	2.10.74	2		Beograd	16 Jun
19.52	Yuriy	Belov	BLR	20.3.81	3		Staiki	30 Jun
19.48	Sebastian	Wenta	POL	4.5.75	1		Gdansk	2 Jun
19.46i	Alexis	Paumier	CUB	21.1.75	4		Pireás	21 Feb
19.46	Dan	Ames	USA	16.1.81	1		Los Angeles	5 May
19.45i		Wen Jili	CHN	11.7.73	1	v JPN	Beijing	21 Feb
19.44	Andy	Dittmar	GER	5.7.74	4		Gotha	16 Jun
	(70)							
19.44	Yoger	Medina	VEN	5.9.73	1	Bol G	Ambato	15 Sep
19.42	Marco Antonio	Verni	CHI	27.2.76	1		Santiago de Chile	28 Apr
19.42	Váios	Tíggas	GRE	16.10.78	3	MedG	Tunis	13 Sep
19.41	Aleksandr	Salnikov	RUS	27.9.71	1		Dublin	29 Jun
19.41	Jaroslaw	Cichocki	POL-J	28.7.82	1		Skórcz	29 Sep
19.35	Sergiu	Ursu	MDA	26.4.80	2		Bucuresti	26 May
19.34	Shakti	Singh	IND	14.5.62	2		Ludhiana	20 Nov
19.32	Jon	O'Neil	USA	23.3.79	2		Lancaster	19 Apr
19.30	Richard	Harrison	USA	13.5.70	1		Albuquerque	24 Mar
19.30	Yuriy	Parkhomenko	UKR	7.7.73	3	NC	Kiev	1 Jul
	(80)							
19.30	Mark	Proctor	GBR	15.1.63	1	BIG	Bedford	18 Jul
19.29i	Jarred	Rome	USA	21.12.76	3		Pocatello	17 Feb
19.27	Jeremy	Allen	USA	5.9.79	6	MSR	Walnut	22 Apr
19.24i	Kristian	Pettersson	SWE	5.10.71	4	v 2-N	Umeå	24 Feb
19.24	Paolo	Capponi	ITA	25.3.76	2		Pergine Valsugana	20 Jul
19.23		Wang Zhiyong	CHN	3.1.79	1		Shanghai	7 May

Mark	Name		Nat	Born	Pos	Meet	Venue	Date
19.23	Nedzad	Mulabegovic	CRO	4.2.81	1		Zagreb	29 Sep
19.20i	Pavel	Pankúch	SVK	20.2.75	2		Banská Bystrica	20 Jan
19.16	Tomasz	Chrzanowski	POL	12.7.81	Q	EU23	Amsterdam	14 Jul
19.12	Robert	Sadler	USA	26.1.76	3		Lancaster	19 Apr
	(30)							
19.11i	Ivan	Yushkov	RUS	15.1.81	2	NC	Moskva	16 Feb
19.11	Andreas	Vlasny	AUT	12.9.69	1		Ebensee	16 Jun
19.10		Li Wenkui	CHN	31.12.71	2		Jinan	13 May
19.06	Bilal Saad	Mubarak	QAT	18.12.72	1		Doha	30 Mar
19.06	David	Wood	USA	23.6.79	1	Pac-10	Berkeley	19 May
19.05i	Peter	Sack	GER	27.7.79	2		Bad Segeberg	3 Feb
19.03i	Gunnar	Pfingsten	GER	24.3.75	6		Nordhausen	16 Feb
19.03	Scott	Denbo	USA	2.6.78	1		Palo Alto	31 Mar
19.01	Scott	Moser	USA	15.7.79	1		Berkeley	17 Mar
19.00	Stefan	Blomquist	SWE	7.2.65	1		Abilene	10 May
	(100)							
19.00	Lukasz	Wenta	POL	19.12.79	2		Gdansk	2 Jun

Mark	Name		Nat	Born	Date
18.98i	Ryan	Speers	USA	6.12.79	10 Mar
18.97i	Jason	Tunks	CAN	7.5.75	24 Feb
18.97i	Simon	Stewart	USA	28.1.80	3 Mar
18.97	Zlatan	Zmirak	CRO	20.9.73	29 Sep
18.96i	Chris	Brown	USA	8.1.78	24 Feb
18.95	Marius	Vornicu	ROM	14.1.77	12 May
18.94	Chima	Ugwu	NGR	19.7.73	14 Apr
18.94	Alessandro	Andrei	ITA	3.1.59	17 Jun
18.93	Saulius	Kleiza	LTU	2.4.64	7 Jun
18.92i	Rutger	Smith	NED	9.7.81	2 Feb
18.92	Corrado	Fantini	ITA	7.2.67	10 May
18.91		Liu Hao	CHN	28.11.68	28 Apr
18.90i	Mark	Hoxmeier	USA	16.6.79	17 Feb
18.90	Johnny	Rodríguez	COL	11.12.79	15 Sep
18.86	Margus	Tammaru	EST	24.8.71	28 Jun
18.85i	Jason	Hammond	USA	20.5.78	24 Feb
18.80		Tian Yingchun	CHN	29.5.79	15 Jun
18.79	Taras	Rohde	USA		6 May
18.79	Ian	Waltz	USA	15.4.77	13 May
18.77	Carlos	Fandiño	CUB	10.6.69	18 Mar
18.77	Jon	Kalnas	USA	18.4.80	14 Apr
18.77	Russ	Bell	USA	27.2.81	19 May
18.77	Nate	DeSomber	USA		19 May
18.76i	Steve	Manz	USA	19.9.81	1 Mar
18.76	Andráas	Anastasópoulos	GRE	2.4.76	5 May
18.76	Erik	van Vreumingen	NED	15.6.78	17 Aug
18.74	Leif Olve	Dolonen Larsen	NOR	3.4.75	7 Jul
18.73i	Tony	Thompson	USA	2.3.80	7 Dec
18.72	Ahmed Hassan	Gholoum	KUW	31.5.80	2 Oct
18.70	Aaron	Neighbour	AUS	2.12.77	10 Feb
18.67	Efstáthios	Hatzistáthis	GRE	80	26 May
18.66	Jaiveer	Singh	IND	71	23 Jun
18.66	Andreas	Deuschle	GER	11.2.68	21 Jul
18.65i	Michalis	Louca	CYP	23.2.70	18 Feb
18.64	Robert	Häggblom	FIN-J	9.8.82	16 Sep
18.63	Giovanni	Tubini	ITA	9.4.64	10 Jul
18.63	Tuomo	Tihinen	FIN	12.12.77	19 Jul
18.61	Ronny	Jiménez	VEN	15.1.79	19 May
18.58	Navpreet	Singh	IND	15.6.79	2 Jun
18.56	Josef	Rosúlek	CZE	6.2.71	9 Sep
18.55	Marc	Roos	GER	10.8.73	16 Jun
18.52	Rhuben	Williams	USA-J	14.2.82	12 May
18.52	Edhem	Kacevic	BIH	18.5.70	15 Jun
18.51	Dmitriy	Kruchenok	BLR	13.3..79	7 Jun
18.51	Gintautas	Degutis	LTU	20.7.70	4 Jul
18.51	Manuel	Brändeborn	SWE	7.4.73	24 Aug
18.50i	Okechukwu	Eziuka	NGR	78	24 Feb
18.50		Lin Feng	CHN	27.8.79	23 Nov
18.50i	Chris	Adams	USA	.78	7 Dec
18.49		Zhong Fengzhu	CHN	24.7.79	15 Jun
18.48	Giorgio	Venturi	ITA	23.6.66	27 Jun
18.45	Arpad	Sinko	YUG	30.10.77	19 May
18.44	Pavel	Sofyin	RUS	4.9.81	17 May
18.44	Nick	Smathwood	USA	29.8.78	19 May
18.43	Daniel	Jonsson	SWE	11.4.74	10 May
18.43	Antti	Rauhala	FIN	5.7.77	22 Jul
18.42i	Sergey	Lyakhov	RUS	1.3.68	5 Feb
18.42	Marc	Sandmeier	SUI	6.6.73	4 Jun
18.42	Ibrahim	Al Manai	QAT	79	22 Aug
18.41	Scott	Martin	AUS-J	12.10.82	24 May
18.41	Aleksander	Tammert	EST	2.2.73	28 Jun
18.40	Wim	Blondeel	BEL	25.12.73	24 May
18.40	Panayiótis	Baharídis	GRE	31.5.81	23 Jun
18.39i	Anders	Holmström	SWE	23.8.78	17 Feb
18.39	Luciano	Zerbini	ITA	16.2.60	12 May
18.39	Teijo	Kööpikkä	FIN	7.10.80	3 Jun
18.39	Dan	Armentraut	USA	3.2.74	14 Jun
18.38	Ian	Douglas	USA	23.3.79	12 May
18.38	Henrik	Wennberg	SWE	11.3.66	15 Sep
18.37	Lee	Newman	GBR	1.5.73	13 Jun
18.35i	James	Parker	USA	3.12.75	24 Feb
18.34i	Brian	Trainor	USA	14.3.80	24 Feb
18.34	Tomasz	Majewski	POL	30.8.81	17 Jun
18.32	Ioánnis	Vasilópoulos	GRE	16.1.75	25 Jul
18.31	Daniel	Taylor	USA-J	12.5.82	28 Apr
18.31	Hrístos	Sarákoglou	GRE	5.5.79	23 Jun
18.29i	Emeka	Udechuku	GBR	10.7.79	14 Jan
18.29i	Jason	Gervais	CAN	18.1.76	24 Feb
18.29	Krasimir	Alexandrov	BUL	26.5.68	21 Apr
18.27i	Mikhail	Zabruskov	RUS	26.1.74	16 Feb
18.27	Scott	Wiegand	USA	26.9.80	29 Apr
18.27		Liu Yu	CHN	15.2.78	19 May
18.25i	Gábor	Máté	HUN	28.3.79	25 Feb
	(184)				

Best outdoor marks for athletes with best indoors

Mark	Name	Pos	Meet	Venue	Date
20.54	Chumachenko	2	ECp-S	Bremen	23 Jun
20.43	Olsen	2	NCAA	Eugene	2 Jun
20.39	Guset	3		Rüdlingen	19 Aug
19.92	Nordin	1		Ingolstadt	27 May
19.51	Dodoni	2		Biella	22 Sep
19.47	Aaltonen	1		Valkeakoski	16 Aug
19.47	Mottin	3		Biella	22 Sep
19.38	Clavelle	3	Kans R	Lawrence	21 Apr
19.23	Roberts	1		El Paso	31 Mar
19.21	Wen Jili	1		Ningbo	28 Apr
19.11	Pankúch	1	GP II	Melbourne	1 Mar
19.00	Yushkov	1		Novosibirsk	26 May

Mark	Name	Date
18.81	Hoxmeier	12 May
18.66	Paumier	21 Jul
18.63	Tunks	28 Apr
18.60	Speers	21 Apr
18.60	Stewart	19 May
18.56	Pettersson	9 Jun
18.55	P Sack	2 Jul
18.26	C Brown	6 May

Drugs Disqualification

Mark	Name		Nat	Born	Pos	Meet	Venue	Date
20.90	Burger	Lambrechts ¶	RSA	3.4.73	(1)		Port Elizabeth	16 Feb
20.64	Miroslav	Menc ¶	CZE	16.3.71	(2)	GS	Ostrava	31 May

Light Shot

Mark	Name		Nat	Born	Pos	Meet	Venue	Date
21.27	Dragan	Peric	YUG	8.5.64	1		Beograd (25g lt)	26 Sep

Mark	Name		Nat	Born	Pos	Meet	Venue	Date

JUNIORS

See main list for top 2 juniors. 10 performances by 2 men to 19.30. Additional marks and further juniors:

Chakouian	19.92	1	PAm-J	Santa Fe	18 Oct	19.47i	1		Ames	10 Feb
	19.80	5	MSR	Walnut	22 Apr	19.43	1	NC-j	Richmond	16 Jan
	19.59	4	NCAA	Eugene	2 Jun	19.41	2	SEC	Columbia SC	12 May
	19.54i	1		Lexington	7 Dec	19.39i	3	NCAA	Fayetteville	10 Mar

Mark	Name		Nat	Born	Pos	Meet	Venue	Date
18.64	Robert	Häggblom	FIN	9.8.82	5		Perho	16 Sep
18.52	Rhuben	Williams	USA	14.2.82	4	ModR	Modesto	12 May
18.41	Scott	Martin	AUS	12.10.82	3	EAsG	Osaka	24 May
18.31	Daniel	Taylor	USA	12.5.82	1		Cincinnati	28 Apr
18.23	Michal	Hodun	POL	17.2.83	1	EJ	Grosseto	20 Jul
18.18	Krzysztof	Krzywosz	POL	1.10.83	6		Warszawa	7 Jun
18.13		Jia Peng	CHN	12.1.84	7	NG	Guangzhou	23 Nov
18.08	John	Newell	USA	.82	2	vGBR-j	Stoke-on-Trent	18 Aug
18.02	Marco	Fortes	POR	26.9.82	1		Rio Maior	9 May
18.00i	Mihaíl	Stamatóyiannis	GRE	20.5.82	6	Balki-i	Pireás	18 Feb
	17.93				1	NC-j	Halkída	8 Jul
17.96	Edis	Elkasovic	CRO	18.2.83	1		Rijeka	5 Sep
17.91	Ken	Kemeny	USA	16.4.82	2		Iowa City	5 May
17.84		Hui Zhenbao	CHN	10.1.82	9	NG	Guangzhou	23 Nov
17.76i	Dmitriy	Gorshkov	RUS	8.3.82	3		Moskva	20 Jan
17.72	Jim	Nelson	USA	.8.82	1		La Crosse	15 May
17.66	Amit	Tyagi	IND	3.1.83	1	Asi-J	B S Begawan	19 Jul
17.63	Mika	Vasara	FIN	22.10.83	5	EJ	Grosseto	20 Jul
17.61	Kuldeep Singh	Mann (20)	IND	16.10.82	5		Ludhiana	20 Nov
17.60		Wang Song	CHN	3.6.83	2B	NC	Baoding	14 Jun

DISCUS

Mark	Name		Nat	Born	Pos	Meet	Venue	Date
70.99	Virgilijus	Alekna	LTU	13.2.72	1		Stellenbosch	30 Mar
				70.59 66.11 x x 70.99 x				
	69.95 1 WK	Zürich	17 Aug	66.32 65.95 66.17 66.66 69.95 x				
	69.42 1c2	Rüdlingen	19 Aug	69.42 x 68.22 x x 66.72				
	69.40 2 WCh	Edmonton	8 Aug	67.65 x 69.40 x 67.28 x				
	69.34 1	Tartu	19 Jun	67.82 67.40 67.39 67.43 66.17 69.34				
	68.20 1 NC	Kaunas	4 Jul	65.87 66.18 65.52 65.05 68.20 67.67				
	68.00 2 GP	Sevilla	8 Jun	67.04 68.00 66.41 65.26				
	67.52A 1	Pretoria	23 Mar	67.52 66.63 66.60 66.51				
	67.19 1 Pre	Eugene	27 May	66.10 65.34 66.11 64.77 67.19 x				
69.96	Frantz	Kruger	RSA	22.5.75	2		Stellenbosch	30 Mar
				69.67 69.23 69.96 x 67.46 66.96				
	67.84 1 GWG	Brisbane	5 Sep	63.48 67.84 67.07 62.42 66.66 63.44				
	67.73 2c2	Rüdlingen	19 Aug	66.64 67.73 x 65.96 67.55 67.28				
69.72	Lars	Riedel	GER	28.6.67	1	WCh	Edmonton	8 Aug
				65.41 67.10 66.74 69.50* 69.72 68.36				
	68.26 Q WCh	Edmonton	6 Aug	68.26 only throw				
	67.28 1 NC	Stuttgart	1 Jul	64.55 67.03 67.28 66.24 x x				
	67.25 3c2	Rüdlingen	19 Aug	63.36 67.25 x x x x				
	67.25 1	Sondershausen	25 Aug					
69.62	Timo	Tompuri	FIN	9.6.69	1		Helsingborg	8 Jul
69.44	Adam	Setliff	USA	15.12.69	1		La Jolla	21 Jul
	68.94 1	Atascadero	25 Jul	?				
68.09	Róbert	Fazekas	HUN	18.8.75	1	GP II	Sevilla	8 Jun
				x 62.57 68.09 x four only				
	67.89 1	Salon-de-Provence	24 May	x 66.78 67.89 x x 67.89				
	67.68 1	Budapest	1 Jul	64.61 x 66.73 67.68 65.45 63.95				
67.92	Mario	Pestano	ESP	8.4.78	1	NC	Valencia	22 Jul
				65.89 64.67 63.41 63.64 64.95 67.92				
67.70	Jason	Tunks	CAN	7.5.75	1	GP	Palo Alto	9 Jun
				57.93 65.01 67.70 f 62.90 64.47				
67.66	John	Godina	USA	31.5.72	1eA		Salinas	22 May
				x x x 67.66 x x				
67.61	Michael	Möllenbeck	GER	12.12.69	3	WCh	Edmonton	8 Aug
				67.61 x 65.76 66.60 65.30 64.48				
	67.17 2 NC	Stuttgart	1 Jul	56.91 64.63 67.17 x 64.34 x				
67.57	Dmitriy	Shevchenko	RUS	13.5.68	4	WCh	Edmonton	8 Aug
				63.21 x 66.68 67.16 67.57 65.95)				
67.48	Vasiliy	Kaptyukh	BLR	27.6.67	2	WK	Zürich	17 Aug
				63.72 64.63 66.49 67.48 63.80 61.91				
	67.25 1 Klim	Minsk	30 Jun	?				
	(31/12)							

Mark	Name		Nat	Born	Pos	Meet	Venue	Date
67.13	Libor	Malina	CZE	14.6.73	1	NC	Jablonec	1 Jul
67.10	Aleksander	Tammert	EST	2.2.73	1		College Station	14 Apr
66.93	Zoltán	Kövágó	HUN	10.4.79	2		Budapest	1 Jul
66.17	Andy	Bloom	USA	11.8.73	1		La Jolla	31 Mar
65.86	Roland	Varga	HUN	22.10.77	7	WCh	Edmonton	8 Aug
65.53	Jarred	Rome	USA	21.12.76	2eA		Salinas	22 May
65.25	Romas	Ubartas	LTU	26.5.60	1		Vilnius	10 May
65.20	Doug	Reynolds	USA	11.8.75	2		La Jolla	31 Mar
	(20)							
65.04	Michael	Lischka	GER	23.12.73	1		Wiesbaden	13 May
64.97	Leonid	Cherevko	BLR	21.4.74	Q	WUG	Beijing	28 Aug
64.66	Aleksandr	Borichevskiy	RUS	25.6.70	1		Bryansk	3 Jul
64.57	Andreas	Seelig	GER	6.7.70	2	OD	Jena	2 Jun
64.41	Vladimir	Dubrovshchik	BLR	7.1.72	6	GP II	Zagreb	2 Jul
64.40	Diego	Fortuna	ITA	14.2.68	1	MedG	Tunis	12 Sep
64.24	Jo	Van Daele	BEL	6.4.72	1		Halle	19 May
64.00A	Sergey	Lyakhov	RUS	1.3.68	1		C.de Guatemala	21 Apr
63.88	Alexis	Elizalde	CUB	19.9.67	1		La Habana	16 Feb
63.85	David	Martínez	ESP	31.1.67	2	MedG	Tunis	12 Sep
	(30)							
63.80	Yuriy	Seskin	RUS	7.7.66	1		Moskva	23 Jun
63.78	Carl	Brown	USA	11.2.70	2		Indianapolis	23 Jul
63.68	Hannes	Hopley	RSA	26.1.81	2		Parow	28 Dec
63.64	Ionel	Oprea	ROM	12.10.70	3	Franc	Ottawa	22 Jul
63.50	Olgierd	Stanski	POL	4.4.73	1		Leczyca	12 May
63.41	Gábor	Máté	HUN	28.3.79	1		Zalaegerszeg	9 Jun
63.38	Nick	Petrucci	USA	10.11.75	3		Indianapolis	23 Jul
63.32	Aleksandr	Malasevich	BLR	7.4.77			Brest	21 Jul
63.28	Timo	Sinervo	FIN	5.8.75	1		Oulu	4 Aug
63.20	Tolga	Köseoglu	GER	16.11.76	3	MSR	Walnut	22 Apr
	(40)							
63.11	Andrzej	Krawczyk	POL	11.4.76	1		Biala Podlaska	2 Jun
63.03	Robert	Weir	GBR	4.2.61	1		Bedford	21 Jul
63.00	Scott	Moser	USA	15.7.79	4		La Jolla	31 Mar
62.93	Mika	Loikkanen	FIN	20.2.74	1		Hyvinkää	1 Aug
62.91	Marcelo	Pugliese	ARG	2.9.68	1		Buenos Aires	24 Mar
62.84		Li Shaojie	CHN	26.11.75	1	NG	Guangzhou	21 Nov
62.77	Rashid	Al-Dosari	QAT	8.5.81	8	GP II	Doha	18 May
62.74	Igor	Primc	SLO	8.1.66	1	NC	Maribor	8 Jul
62.44	Jean-Claude	Retel	FRA	11.2.68	3		Salon-de-Provence	24 May
62.41	Einar Kristian	Tveitå	NOR	22.2.73	1		Oslo (So)	20 Jul
	(50)							
62.36		Nu Ermaimaiti	CHN-J	8.3.84	2	NG	Guangzhou	21 Nov
62.35	Mikko	Kyyrö	FIN	12.7.80	1		Järvenpää	11 Jun
62.23	Yuriy	Belonog	UKR	9.3.74	1	NC	Kiev	3 Jul
62.08	Jürgen	Schult	GER	11.5.60	3		Wiesbaden	13 May
62.08	Jason	Gervais	CAN	18.1.76	4	Franc	Ottawa	22 Jul
61.98	Kevin	Fitzpatrick	USA	26.9.69	2		La Jolla	21 Jul
61.92	Ian	Winchester	NZL	27.5.73	5eA		Salinas	22 May
61.72	Jouni	Helppikangas	FIN	10.2.71	3		Jalasjärvi	30 Jun
61.68	Perriss	Wilkins	GBR	12.12.69	1		Cudworth	26 Aug
61.59	Frits	Potgieter	RSA	13.3.74	6		Stellenbosch	30 Mar
	(60)							
61.50	Torsten	Schmidt	GER	9.12.74	1		Obersuhl	3 Jun
61.49	Sávvas	Panávoglou	GRE	14.8.74	4	MedG	Tunis	12 Sep
61.46	Mark	Hoxmeier	USA	16.7.79	2	Mod R	Modesto	12 May
61.40	Pertti	Hynni	FIN	14.2.60	2		Eurajoki	3 Jun
61.37	Cameron	Bolles	USA	24.3.76	1eB		Salinas	22 May
61.36	Kristian	Pettersson	SWE	5.10.71	3		Helsingborg	8 Jul
61.29	Glen	Smith	GBR	21.5.72	1	vFRA	Ashford	11 Aug
61.21		Wu Tao	CHN-J	3.10.83	3	NG	Guangzhou	21 Nov
61.16	Zach	Schiebout	USA	19.9.77	2	Big 12	College Station	18 May
61.00	Dan	Ames	USA	16.1.81	2eB		Salinas	22 May
	(70)							
60.97	Ilya	Kostin	RUS	1.4.79	1	NC-w23	Adler	25 Feb
60.96	Casey	Malone	USA	6.4.77	1		Indianapolis	28 Jul
60.87	Mike	van der Bilt	NED	23.10.76	6		Halle	19 May
60.86	Caba	Guljas	YUG	5.2.78	1		Subotica	13 May
60.79	Attila	Horváth	HUN	28.7.67	1		Szombathely	13 Oct
60.75	Cristiano	Andrei	ITA	14.5.73	1		Pietrasanta	4 Mar
60.70	Roberto	Moya	CUB	11.2.65	1		Gijón	7 Jul

Mark	Name		Nat	Born	Pos	Meet	Venue	Date
60.68	Dragan	Mustapic	CRO	23.3.63	2		Gorizia	4 Jul
60.55	Gjøran	Sørli	NOR	3.6.78	1		Bottnaryd	1 Jul
60.48A	Mikaël (80)	Conjungo	CAF	6.5.69	6		Roodepoort	16 Mar
60.47	Gerd	Kanter	EST	6.5.79	2		Tartu	15 Aug
60.41	Abdullah	Al-Shoumari	KSA	10.7.78	1		Szombathely	11 Aug
60.38	Mattias	Borrman	SWE	20.6.72	5	Mod R	Modesto	12 May
60.31	Ian	Waltz	USA	15.4.77	4eB		Salinas	22 May
60.28	Janus	Robberts	RSA	10.3.79	1	UTA	Arlington	5 May
60.28	Janne	Hummastenniemi	FIN	3.10.79	3		Oulu	4 Aug
60.24	Petri	Hakala	FIN	21.2.79	6		Jalasjärvi	30 Jun
60.20	Joachim	Olsen	DEN	31.5.77	1		Long Beach	18 May
60.02	Kiril	Chuprinin	UKR	22.7.75	2	NC	Kiev	3 Jul
59.98	James (90)	Dennis	USA	25.2.76	1		Louisville	7 Apr
59.98	Mattias	Thriene	GER	28.12.71	1		Dormagen	21 Jul
59.97	Emeka	Udechuku	GBR	10.7.79	2		Bedford	21 Jul
59.96	Rutger	Smith	NED	9.7.81	1	EAA	Nice	17 Mar
59.96A	Jason	Young	USA	27.5.81	1		El Paso	14 Apr
59.95	Ercüment	Olgundeniz	TUR	7.7.76	1		Izmir	13 May
59.66	Rolf	Mordhorst	GER	11.5.73	2B		Halle	19 May
59.64	Curry	Dawson	USA	4.8.79	1	NCAA II	Edwardsville	25 May
59.63	Lance	Jauron	USA	23.11.77	5eB		Salinas	22 May
59.61		Zhang Cunbiao	CHN	11.2.69	4	NG	Guangzhou	21 Nov
59.60	Gerhard (100)	Mayer	AUT	20.5.80	1		Schwechat	1 Sep

Mark	Name		Nat	Born	Date
59.54	Stáfanos	Kónstas	GRE	16.5.77	14 Jul
59.53	Jeremy	Allen	USA	5.9.79	1 Jun
59.51	Anthony	Washington	USA	16.1.66	31 Mar
59.50	Heinrich	Seitz	GER	6.4.80	14 Jul
59.48	Khaled Salm.	Al Khalidi	KSA	14.2.65	15 Sep
59.46	Stefano	Lomater	ITA	23.4.74	22 Sep
59.41	Abbas	Samimi	IRN	9.6.77	9 May
59.41	Stéphane	Nativel	FRA	4.4.75	12 Jun
59.39	Szilárd	Kiss	HUN	9.12.75	11 Aug
59.36	Reedus	Thurmond	USA	15.12.79	6 Apr
59.34	Peter	Elvy	AUS	3.6.80	4 Aug
59.32	Christian	Cantwell	USA	30.9.80	7 Apr
59.29	Valeriy	Borisov	BLR	24.2.75	8 Jun
59.23	Michel	Hemmings	CUB	10.9.75	7 Jul
59.14	Loy	Martínez	CUB	3.6.81	16 Feb
59.14	Josh	Ralston	USA	1.9.80	14 Apr
59.13	Niklas	Arrhenius	SWE-J	10.9.82	15 Jul
59.10	Mark	Simmons	USA	14.9.78	10 May
59.05	Paulo	Bernardo	POR	16.8.74	24 Jun
58.96	Dariusz	Slowik	DEN	15.8.77	3 Jul
58.86	Jon	O'Neil	USA	23.3.79	6 May
58.86	Eric	Forshaw	CAN	14.9.68	22 Jul
58.72	Russ	Bell	USA	27.2.81	18 May
58.70	Michal	Hodun	POL-J	17.2.83	19 May
58.66	Chima	Ugwu	NGR	19.7.73	17 Mar
58.53	Henrik	Wennberg	SWE	11.3.66	29 Sep
58.52	Brian	Trainor	USA	14.3.80	22 Apr
58.35	Pieter	van der Kruk	NED	10.2.72	28 Jun
58.34		Xu Yongyi	CHN-J	28.7.84	16 Jun
58.16	Omer	Inan (TUR/)	USA	20.10.81	20 Apr
58.15	Thomas	Rosvold	NOR	21.7.67	31 May
58.10	Martín	Brea	ESP	26.5.71	22 Jul
57.90	Ben	Lindsey	USA	5.10.77	31 Mar
57.90	Drazen	Prskalo	CRO	26.8.67	3 Oct
57.86	Clark	Wilson	USA-J	8.2.82	7 Apr
57.86	Mike	Ransky	CAN	26.10.70	28 Apr
57.82	Ahville	Black	JAM	77	6 Apr
57.80		Yan Xiaoming	CHN	23.3.80	28 Apr
57.80	Spirídon (139)	Arabatzís	GRE	2.6.78	16 May

JUNIORS

See main list for top 2 juniors. 11 performances by 4 men to 58.36. Additional marks and further juniors:

Nu Ermaimati	59.80	2		Tianjin	18 May	58.36	2	NC	Baoding	16 Jun
Wu Tao	60.64	1		Tianjin	18 May	58.74	1	NC	Baoding	16 Jun
	60.14	1	Asi-J	B S Begawan	21 Jul					
Hodun	58.67	1		Lublin	16 Jun	58.49	3		Lublin	10 Jun

Mark	Name		Nat	Born	Pos	Meet	Venue	Date
59.13	Niklas	Arrhenius	SWE	10.9.82	2		Halmstad	15 Jul
58.70	Michal	Hodun	POL	17.2.83	1		Zamosc	19 May
58.34		Xu Yongyi	CHN	28.7.84	3	NC	Baoding	16 Jun
57.86	Clark	Wilson	USA	8.2.82	1		Notre Dame	7 Apr
56.50	Arnost	Holovsky	CZE	10.4.82	1		Praha	17 Jun
55.88		Chang Ming-huang	TPE	7.8.82	2		Osaka	26 May
55.28	Khalid H	Al-Suwaidi	QAT	.84	3	Asi-J	B S Begawan	21 Jul
54.90	Scott	Martin	AUS	12.10.82	3		Canberra	18 Feb
54.77	Kris	Coene	BEL	29.9.83	1	NC	Bruxelles	1 Jul
54.27	Ben	Harradine	AUS	14.10.82	2		Canberra	19 Dec
54.23	Dmitriy	Sivakov	BLR	15.2.83	3	EJ	Grosseto	21 Jul
54.19	Piotr	Malachowski	POL	7.6.83	1		Zielona Góra	19 May
54.10	Oleksiy	Semenov	UKR	27.6.82	1		Odessa	5 May
53.80	Igor	Parshukov	RUS	82	1		Novosibirsk	27 May
53.78		Zhang Yuhao	CHN	16.2.83	12	NG	Guangzhou	21 Nov
53.77	Edis	Elkasovic	CRO	18.2.83	1		Szombathely	10 May
53.66	Marquis	Johnson	USA	29.3.82	1		Orlando	20 Apr
53.62	Daniel	Vanek (20)	SVK	18.1.83	3		Nitra	8 Jul

Symbols/Abbreviations

A made at an altitude of 1000m or higher, Q qualifying round, -J juniors (born 1982 or later)

HAMMER

Mark	Name		Nat	Born	Pos	Meet	Venue	Date	Series
83.47	Koji	Murofushi	JPN	8.10.74	1		Toyota	14 Jul	79.86 82.16 82.26 83.32 p 83.47
	82.94				1	GWG	Brisbane	7 Sep	x 79.17 80.13 80.91 82.94 81.67
	82.92				2	WCh	Edmonton	5 Aug	79.91 82.46 81.95 81.43 82.92 82.61
	82.60				1		Tokyo	7 Apr	79.98 81.75 81.50 81.77 82.60 81.58
	82.59				1		Osaka	12 May	x 78.85 82.03 81.49 82.59 82.28
	82.23				1		Toyota	1 Apr	82.21 81.85 80.93 p 80.30 82.23
	82.08				1		Yokohama	15 Sep	78.23 79.43 81.79 81.07 80.10 82.08
	81.35				1	Oda	Hiroshima	29 Apr	81.35 x 79.32 p p 80.17
83.39	Adrián	Annus	HUN	28.6.73	1		Zalaegerszeg	9 Jun	only best throw measured
	82.81				1		Tatabánya	26 May	82.81 x x x 80.83 x
	82.37				1		Szombathely	5 May	only best throw measured
	81.09				1		Veszprém	7 Jul	only best throw measured
83.38	Szymon	Ziólkowski	POL	1.7.76	1	WCh	Edmonton	5 Aug	81.88 79.69 x 80.32 83.38 80.39
	82.47				1		Clermont-Ferrand	15 Jun	79.89 79.46 80.48 81.56 82.47 80.84
	82.44				1		Rüdlingen	19 Aug	78.02 79.89 81.38 79.50 82.44 80.23
	82.36				1		Rehlingen	4 Jun	78.54 78.50 79.31 80.30 x 82.36
	82.13				1		Roodepoort	16 Mar	79.40 80.33 x 80.58 80.32 82.13
	81.85				Q	WCh	Edmonton	4 Aug	x 81.85 2 throws
	81.82				2		Yokohama	15 Sep	81.82 x 77.74 81.15 78.19 81.77
	81.56				1		Kassel	13 Jun	?
	81.34				1	NC	Bydgoszcz	1 Jul	78.45 x 79.74 80.39 x 81.34
	81.27				1		Poznan	8 Jun	77.84 81.27 x 78.36 81.17 79.86
82.76	Igor	Astapkovich	BLR	4.1.63	1		Staiki	13 Jul	
82.34	Andrey	Skvaruk	UKR	9.3.67	1	NC	Kiev	2 Jul	80.13 x 81.54 79.98 82.34 x
81.76	Tibor	Gécsek	HUN	22.9.64	1		Szombathely	17 May	
	81.68				1	NC	Nyirogyháza	25 Jul	80.34 x 80.30 80.92 81.68 x
	81.21				2		Clermont-Ferrand	15 Jun	73.95 78.04 81.21 80.30 x x
	80.99				1		Szombathely	3 Jul	80.29 80.99 p 80.76 x x
81.36	Balázs	Kiss	HUN	21.3.72	1		Cottbus	18 Jul	78.34 77.57 81.36 75.36 x 77.60
81.26	Vadim	Khersontsev	RUS	8.7.74	1		Bryansk	3 Jul	
80.99	David	Chaussinand	FRA	19.4.73	2		Rüdlingen	19 Aug	x 78.25 79.57 78.86 80.99 79.11
80.88	Nicolas	Figère	FRA	19.5.79	1	EU23	Amsterdam	15 Jul	
	(32/10)								
80.80	Aleksey	Zagornyy	RUS	31.5.78	2		Bryansk	3 Jul	
80.54	Olli-Pekka	Karjalainen	FIN	7.3.80	2	EU23	Amsterdam	15 Jul	
80.50	Nicola	Vizzoni	ITA	4.11.73	1		Formia	14 Jul	
80.38	Aleksandr	Krykun	UKR	1.3.68	2	NC	Kiev	2 Jul	
80.27	Ilya	Konovalov	RUS	4.3.71	3	WCh	Edmonton	5 Aug	
80.09	Vladimir	Maska	CZE	6.2.73	1		Turnov	12 May	
80.07	Sergey	Kirmasov	RUS	25.3.70	1	NC	Tula	14 Jul	
80.03	Vasiliy	Sidorenko	RUS	1.5.61	3	NC	Tula	14 Jul	
79.60	Vladislav	Piskunov	UKR	7.6.78	2		Koncha-Zaspa	28 Apr	
79.52	Aléxandros	Papadimitríou	GRE	18.6.73	1		Trípoli	28 Apr	
	(20)								
79.40	Chris	Harmse	RSA	31.5.73	1		Pretoria	3 Nov	
79.29	Maciej	Palyszko	POL	4.1.78	3		Formia	14 Jul	
79.18	Pavel	Sedlácek	CZE	5.4.68	1	Odlozil	Praha	18 Jun	
79.15	Karsten	Kobs	GER	16.9.71	1		Dortmund	8 Jun	
78.99	Stuart	Rendell	AUS	30.6.72	1		Calgary	30 Jul	
78.73	Ivan	Tikhon	BLR	24.7.76	1	NC	Brest	8 Jun	
78.63	Holger	Klose	GER	5.12.72	2		Rehlingen	4 Jun	
78.58	Miloslav	Konopka	SVK	23.1.79	2	Odlozil	Praha	18 Jun	
78.34	Hrístos	Polihroníou	GRE	31.3.72	3	ECp	Bremen	23 Jun	
77.87	Zsolt	Németh	HUN	9.11.71	1	NC-w	Budapest	3 Mar	
	(30)								
77.66	András	Haklits	CRO	23.9.77	1		Athens, GA	5 May	
77.65	Libor	Charfreitag	SVK	11.9.77	4		Formia	14 Jul	
77.23	Andrey	Vorontsov	BLR	24.7.75			Brest	21 Jul	
77.06	Wojciech	Kondratowicz	POL	18.4.80	1		Siedlce	23 Sep	
76.72	Konstantin	Astapkovich	BLR	23.10.70	1		Minsk	10 May	
76.58	Kazimierz	Boulge	POL	13.2.76	1		Bydgoszcz	6 Sep	

Mark	Name		Nat	Born	Pos	Meet	Venue	Date
76.52	Kevin	McMahon	USA	26.5.72	1	NC	Eugene	21 Jun
76.43	Michael	Jones	GBR	23.7.63	1		Birmingham	2 Jun
76.42	Juan Ignacio	Cerra	ARG	16.10.76	1		Trieste	25 Jul
76.32	Bengt	Johansson	SWE	7.7.73	1		Magglingen	9 Jun
	(40)							
76.14	Vítor	Costa	POR	28.5.74	1		Auxerre	22 Sep
75.90	Raphaël	Piolanti	FRA	14.11.67	5		Rehlingen	4 Jun
75.75	Jan	Bielecki	DEN	20.2.71	1		Bagsværd	20 Jul
75.69	Markus	Esser	GER	3.2.80	1	NC-23	Schweinfurt	28 Jul
75.55	Yuriy	Voronkin	RUS	18.5.79	1	NC-w23	Adler	24 Feb
75.33	Péter	Botfa	HUN	30.6.79	1		Szombathely	19 May
75.33	Loris	Paoluzzi	ITA	14.5.74	5		Milano	6 Jun
75.30	Vadim	Grabovoy	UKR	5.4.73	2		Yalta	11 Feb
74.96	Artyom	Rubanko	UKR	21.3.74	4	NC	Kiev	2 Jul
74.60	Paddy	McGrath	IRL	1.7.71	1		Dedham	16 Jun
	(50)							
74.57	Dmitriy	Shako	BLR	27.5.79	5	EU23	Amsterdam	15 Jul
74.46	Vitaliy	Alisevich	BLR	15.6.67			Staiki	17 Jul
74.40	Marco	Lingua	ITA	4.6.78	1		Roma	3 Jun
74.21	Andrey	Yevgenyev	RUS	9.7.73	5	NC-w	Adler	24 Feb
74.08	Claus	Dethloff	GER	24.9.68	1		Mönchengladbach	27 May
74.02	Samuele	Dazio	SUI	16.1.75	1		Locarno	15 Sep
73.49	Steve	Harnapp	GER	30.7.75	1		Berlin	14 Jul
73.32	James	Parker	USA	3.12.75	2	NCAA	Eugene	31 May
73.30	David	Smith	GBR	2.11.74	1		Rugby	10 Jun
73.28	Roman	Rozna	MDA	25.3.76	1		Chisinau	26 Apr
	(60)							
73.17	Jay	Harvard	USA	14.3.76	2	NC	Eugene	21 Jun
73.09	Krisztián	Pars	HUN-J	18.2.82	2		Tapolca	18 Aug
73.07	Christophe	Epalle	FRA	23.1.69	1		Castres	18 Jul
73.04		Ye Kuigang	CHN	4.1.75	1	NG	Guangzhou	18 Nov
72.93	Patric	Suter	SUI	17.5.77	2		Rüdlingen	19 Aug
72.82	Esref	Apak	TUR-J	3.1.82	1		Izmir	19 Aug
72.80	Igor	Tugay	UKR	22.3.75	6	NC	Kiev	2 Jul
72.79	Cosmin	Sorescu	ROM	11.7.75	1	NC	Bucuresti	10 Jun
72.62	Roman	Linscheid	IRL	29.12.70	1		Madison	12 May
72.60	William	Beauchamp	GBR	9.9.70	2		London (Colindale)	29 Apr
	(70)							
72.40	Marko	Wahlman	FIN	6.4.69	2		Töysä	10 Jun
72.26	Aleksandr	Vashchilo	BLR	30.8.81			Brest	23 Feb
72.25	David	Söderberg	FIN	11.8.79	3		Töysä	10 Jun
72.18	Giovanni	Sanguin	ITA	14.5.69	1		Conegliano Veneto	20 May
72.16		Liu Fuxiang	CHN	24.3.75	1		Jinan	12 May
72.10	Enrico	Sgrulletti	ITA	24.4.65	2		Pietrasanta	4 Mar
71.94	Samu-Petri	Simo	FIN	22.6.78	3	NC	Turku	7 Jul
71.92	Mikko	Dannbäck	FIN	16.3.77	3		Tampere	22 Aug
71.77	Yosmel	Monte	CUB	26.6.77	1	NC	La Habana	31 May
71.71	Moisés	Campeny	ESP	27.5.79	Q	EU23	Amsterdam	14 Jul
	(80)							
71.67	John	McEwen	USA	5.3.74	4	NC	Eugene	21 Jun
71.51	Róbert	Fazekas	HUN	18.8.75	3		Tatabánya	26 May
71.49	Per	Karlsson	SWE	21.4.67	3	vFIN	Göteborg	1 Sep
71.47	Lukás	Melich	CZE	16.9.80	2B		Halle	20 May
71.47	Ralf	Jossa	GER	2.11.66	6		Cottbus	18 Jul
71.46	Norbert	Horváth	HUN	13.6.75	3	NCAA	Eugene	31 May
71.45	Denis	Kulagin	RUS	23.5.80	2	NC-w23	Adler	24 Feb
71.34	Janne	Vartia	FIN	18.3.77	4	NCAA	Eugene	31 May
71.31	Steffen	Reumann	GER	6.3.68	1		Neuberg	27 May
71.28	Samir	Haouam	ALG	20.6.68	1		Alger	19 Jul
	(90)							
71.17	Primoz	Kozmus	SLO	30.9.79	1		Celje	10 Jun
71.04	Sándor	Végh	HUN	10.3.77	3		Tapolca	18 Aug
70.96	Aaron	Fish	AUS	27.2.81	1		Canberra	19 Dec
70.85	Harálabos	Arsoniádis	GRE	19.1.78	1		Alexandroúpoli	21 Apr
70.85	Marco	Felice	ITA	20.10.79	1		Foggia	14 Jun
70.81	Kevin	Mannon	USA	12.8.76	5	NC	Eugene	21 Jun
70.80	Travis	Nutter	USA	9.2.75	6	NC	Eugene	21 Jun
70.65		Bi Zhong	CHN	1.9.68	3		Jinan	12 May
70.62	Krzysztof	Kaliszewski	POL	9.8.72	3		Lublin	10 Jun
70.48	Eric	Albert	FRA	30.7.79	1		Albi	27 Jun
	(100)							

Mark	Name		Nat	Born	Date
70.41	Dorian	Collaku	ALB	2.6.77	30 Jun
70.40	Thomas	Neumann	GER	7.8.71	21 Jul
70.34	Jim	Heizman	USA	25.1.74	21 Jun
70.33	Paul	Head	GBR	1.7.65	14 Jul
70.31	Marco	Quintarelli	ITA	20.6.73	8 Jul
70.19	Nasser	Al-Jarallah	KUW	26.11.73	4 Oct
70.11	Walter	Edletitsch	AUT	9.8.73	16 May
70.05	Nikólaos	Koronákos	GRE	18.11.77	22 Apr
70.05	Pramod	Kumar Tiwari	IND	74	21 Oct
70.03	Aleksey	Korolyov	RUS-J	5.4.82	24 May
70.03	Yamen	Hussein Moneim	EGY	19.6.78	4 Oct
70.00	Andrey	Mezherov	RUS-J	82	24 May
69.81	Aleksandr	Yeroshin	RUS	69	3 Jul
69.78	Adrián	Marzo	ARG	24.1.68	7 Sep
69.76	Ioánnis	Barlís	GRE	26.1.79	22 Apr
69.73	Igor	Kazarovets	BLR	18.5.79	30 Jun
69.69	Aleksey	Yeliseyev	RUS-J	12.3.82	27 Jun
69.65	Benjamin	Boruschewski	GER	23.4.80	8 Jun
69.58	Edi	Marioni	ITA	10.7.76	24 Jun
69.57	Jérôme	Soupe	FRA	4.1.77	1 Jun
69.50	Wataru	Ebihara	JPN	12.12.73	16 Jun
69.49	Yosvany	Suárez	CUB	20.12.72	31 May
69.48	Dylan	Armstrong	CAN	15.1.81	31 May
69.47	Xavier	Dallet	FRA	24.12.79	1 Jun
69.45	Justin	Carvalho	USA	5.4.74	15 Jun
69.45	Vladimir	Bykov	RUS	29.4.70	13 Jul
69.27	Yuriy	Kravchuk	BLR	.81	21 Jul
69.26	Stefan	Paukner	GER	16.8.76	24 May
69.24	Bert	Sorin	USA	5.6.76	21 Jun
69.22	Gianni	Nadalini	ITA	17.5.66	18 Feb
69.17	Aleksandr	Baburkin	RUS	74	6 May
69.08	Alexey	Mukhortov	RUS	13.7.79	15 Jun
69.08	Ilmari	Verho	FIN	10.8.75	15 Jul
69.04	Carey	Ryan	USA	3.10.79	31 May
69.00	Jarkko	Paljakka	FIN	7.2.79	30 Jun
68.86	Frank	van den Dool	NED	14.7.67	17 Jun
68.85	José Manuel	Pérez	ESP	6.5.73	12 May
68.80	Alberto	Sánchez	CUB	3.2.73	26 May
68.80	Iulian	Ocheana	ROM	29.7.80	23 Jun
68.76	Dan	Bourque	USA	4.7.76	12 May
68.66	Alexander	Sporrer	GER	20.1.71	28 Jul
68.58	Ronald	Gram	NED	31.3.74	1 Jul
68.57	Hiroaki	Doi	JPN	2.12.78	30 Sep
68.52	Alessandro	Beschi	ITA	5.8.81	10 May
68.46	József	Horváth	HUN-J	3.4.84	9 Jun
68.36	Jacob	Freeman	USA	5.11.80	19 May
68.24	Grigoriy	Khatantsev	RUS	78	14 Jul
68.22	Roland	Ciofani	FRA	29.9.71	6 May
68.08	Bernard	Reibel	FRA	13.8.67	11 Feb
68.08	Dilshod	Nazarov	TJK-J	6.5.82	22 Jul
68.04	Peter	Kubera	GER	22.6.74	30 Jun
68.02	Valeriy	Svyatokho	BLR	81	17 Feb
	(152)				

Unconfirmed

Mark	Name		Nat	Born	Venue	Date
73.29	Stanislas	Zakharov	RUS	10.4.77	?	2 Jan

JUNIORS

See main list for top 2 juniors. 12 performances by 2 men to 71.40. Additional marks and further juniors:

	Mark	Pos	Meet	Venue	Date	Mark	Pos	Venue	Date
Pars	72.71	1		Szombathley	2 Sep	72.08	1	Budapest	5 May
	72.53	3		Zalaegerszeg	9 Jun	71.68	3	Nitra	25 Aug
	72.15	2	NC	Nyíregyhazá	25 Jul	71.51	2	Szombathley	13 Oct
Apak	72.45	1		Ankara	21 Jun	71.43	1	Mersin	6 Apr
	72.40	1		Izmir	11 Aug				

Mark	Name		Nat	Born	Pos	Meet	Venue	Date
70.03	Aleksey	Korolyov	RUS	5.4.82	1		Krasnodar	24 May
70.00	Andrey	Mezherov	RUS	82	2		Krasnodar	24 May
69.69	Aleksey	Yeliseyev	RUS	12.3.82	1	NC-j	Kazan	27 Jun
68.46	József	Horváth	HUN	3.4.84	5		Zalaegeszeg	9 Jun
68.08	Dilshod	Nazarov	TJK	6.5.82	1	Asi-J	B.S.Begawan	22 Jul
67.50	Aleksandr	Lutsenko	UKR	3.3.82	7	NC	Kiev	2 Jul
66.80	Moh. Nasser	Al-Dashti	KUW	24.8.82	5	WMil	Beirut	3 Jul
66.71		Shen Yi	CHN	15.12.84	4	NC	Baoding	15 Jun
66.36	Jens	Rautenkranz	GER	11.4.82	4	EJ	Grosseto	22 Jul
65.96		Zhang Dapeng	CHN	6.8.83	6		Jinan	12 May
65.51	Oleg	Sinkevich	BLR	16.1.83	2		Schwechat	3 Jun
65.16	Werner	Smit	RSA	14.9.84	1		Bellville	13 Oct
65.04	Fabián	Di Paolo	ARG	25.11.83	1	PAm-J	Santa Fe	19 Oct
64.66	Ali Mohamed	Al-Zinkawi	KUW	27.2.84	4	PArab	Damascus	4 Oct
64.64	Guram	Feroyev	RUS	83	7	NC-23	Cheboksary	15 Jun
64.54	Dário	Manso	POR	1.7.82	5	EJ	Grosseto	22 Jul
64.38	Moh. Faraj	Al-Kaabi	QAT	.84	5	PArab	Damascus	4 Oct
64.12	Frédéric	Pouzy (20)	FRA	18.2.83	1	vGBR-j	Dôle	29 Jul

MEN 2001

JAVELIN

Mark	Pos	Meet	Name / Venue	Nat	Born	Pos	Meet	Venue	Date
92.80			Jan Zelezny	CZE	16.6.66	1	WCh	Edmonton	12 Aug
					81.76	92.80	89.45	x	87.28 x
91.23	1		Poznan	8 Jun	80.91	85.71	70.08	80.71	91.23 x
90.76	Q	WCh	Edmonton	10 Aug	90.76		only throw		
89.84	1	Athl	Lausanne	4 Jul	x	84.38	x	89.35	89.84 89.31
89.47	1		Ostrava	31 May	89.47	x	88.26	x	x x
88.98	1	GPF	Melbourne	9 Sep	x	86.99	85.75	x	88.98 x
88.29	1	ISTAF	Berlin	31 Aug	88.29	x	p	83.12	p p
87.62	2	WK	Zürich	17 Aug	82.39	x	87.62	x	86.36 x
87.52	1	GWG	Brisbane	6 Sep	x	82.85	x	87.52	x x
92.41			Aki Parviainen	FIN	26.10.74	1	ECp-1A	Vaasa	24 Jun
					92.41	87.25	x	x	4 only
91.31	2	WCh	Edmonton	12 Aug	91.31	x	x	x	x x
88.67	1		Pihtipudas	1 Jul	88.67	86.62	88.27	p	p p
88.61	2	GPI	Athína	11 Jun	88.61	80.32	x	p	p p
91.27			Konstadínos Gatsioúdis	GRE	17.12.73	1	ECCp	Madrid	26 May
					91.27	p	p	p	4 only

Mark	Name		Nat	Born	Pos	Meet	Venue	Date			
	89.95	3	WCh	Edmonton	12 Aug	x	88.39	87.54	89.95	x	x
	89.24	1		Tartu	19 Jun	87.91	86.29	89.24	x	p	p
	88.89	1	GPI	Athína	11 Jun	88.89	x	84.75	84.59	p	x
	88.61	1	NC	Athína	16 Jun	88.61	x	83.89	83.70	83.69	82.42
	88.50	1		Kos	20 May	88.50	p	p	p	p	p
	88.33	1	ECp	Bremen	23 Jun	88.33	p	p	p	4 only	
	87.81	Q	WCh	Edmonton	10 Aug	87.81	only throw				
	87.62	1		Pireás	22 Apr	87.62	p	p	p	p	p
	87.49	1	GGala	Roma	29 Jun	87.49	85.26	82.73	p	p	p
90.81	Steve	Backley	GBR	12.2.69	1	BrGP	London (CP)	22 Jul			
						81.54	82.27	81.95	85.07	85.73	90.81
	87.84	2		Ostrava	31 May	87.84	x	81.41	x	85.57	84.90
88.88	Raymond	Hecht	GER	11.11.68	1	WK	Zürich	17 Aug			
						82.46	87.62	80.81	x	88.88	x
	87.82	2		Cuxhaven	21 Jul	79.78	81.94	83.32	87.82	83.06	78.26
88.70	Peter	Blank	GER	10.4.62	1	NC	Stuttgart	30 Jun			
						88.70	p	p	p	p	p
88.42	Sergey	Makarov	RUS	19.3.73	1		Moskva	17 May			
						88.42	87.50	p	x	p	p
87.00	Breaux	Greer	USA	19.10.76	4	WCh	Edmonton	12 Aug			
						87.00	85.61	x	x	x	x
	(30/8)										
86.67	Andrew	Currey	AUS	7.2.71	1		Wollongong	22 Jul			
86.63	Harri	Haatainen	FIN	5.1.78	2	GP II	Gateshead	19 Aug			
	(10)										
86.53	Boris	Henry	GER	14.12.73	Q	WCh	Edmonton	10 Aug			
86.47	Eriks	Rags	LAT	1.6.75	2	BrGP	London	22 Jul			
85.78	Dariusz	Trafas	POL	16.5.72	2	Bisl	Oslo	13 Jul			
85.40	Juha	Laukkanen	FIN	6.1.69	2		Kuortane	17 Jun			
85.21	Björn	Lange	GER	15.6.79	4	GP II	Gateshead	19 Aug			
84.95	Rajmund	Kólko ¶	POL	1.3.71	1	Kuso	Warszawa	17 Jun			
84.88	Mick	Hill	GBR	22.10.64	Q	WCh	Edmonton	10 Aug			
84.30	Pål Arne	Fagernes	NOR	8.6.74	1	Herc	Monaco	20 Jul			
84.21	Matti	Närhi	FIN	17.8.75	1		Eurajoki	3 Jun			
83.87	Andreas	Thorkildsen	NOR-J	1.4.82	1		Fana	7 Jun			
	(20)										
83.67	Harri	Hakkarainen	FIN	16.10.69	4		Kuortane	17 Jun			
83.55	Aleksandr	Ivanov	RUS-J	25.5.82	2	NC	Tula	14 Jul			
83.00	Andreas	Linden	GER	20.2.65	2		Cuxhaven	21 Jul			
82.93	Nick	Nieland	GBR	31.1.72	1		Dublin	29 Jun			
82.77	Emeterio	González	CUB	11.4.73	1	NC	La Habana	26 May			
82.71	Sergey	Voynov	UZB	26.2.77	1		Tashkent	5 May			
82.48	Esko	Mikkola	FIN	14.2.75	5		Kuortane	17 Jun			
82.40	Miroslav	Guzdek	CZE	3.8.75	1		Kladno	12 Sep			
82.20	Sami	Saksio	FIN	28.4.69	4eA		Pihtipudas	1 Jul			
82.02	Isbel	Luaces	CUB	20.7.75	2	NC	La Habana	26 May			
	(30)										
81.98	Gregor	Högler	AUT	27.6.72	1	ECp-2B	Nicosia	24 Jun			
81.86	Voldemars	Lusis	LAT	7.12.74	1		Riga	2 Jun			
81.80		Li Rongxiang	CHN	8.1.72	9	WCh	Edmonton	12 Aug			
81.74	Peter	Esenwein	GER	7.12.67	3	OD	Jena	2 Jun			
81.66	Scott	Russell	CAN	16.1.79	Q	WCh	Edmonton	10 Aug			
81.63	Pekka	Alaräisänen	FIN	27.12.75	5eA		Pihtipudas	1 Jul			
81.59	Marc	Van Mensel	BEL	18.5.71	1		Lebbeke	9 May			
81.35	Kimmo	Kinnunen	FIN	31.3.68	1		Jyväskylä	1 Aug			
81.27A	Brian	Erasmus	RSA	28.2.80	1		Pretoria	21 Apr			
81.27	Ari	Pakarinen	FIN	14.5.69	1		Pyhäselkä	9 Sep			
	(40)										
81.22	Yuriy	Rybin	RUS	5.3.63	5	v2N	Glasgow	1 Jul			
81.07	Adrian	Hatcher	AUS	6.5.70	1		Sydney	16 Feb			
80.91A	Marius	Corbett	RSA	26.9.75	1		Potchefstroom	24 Mar			
80.88	Laurent	Dorique	FRA	10.7.76	1	MedG	Tunis	14 Sep			
80.83	Andrus	Värnik	EST	27.9.77	1		Haapsalu	19 Jul			
80.80	Alberto	Desiderio	ITA	26.3.73	1		Catania	19 May			
80.80	Mark	Roberson	GBR	13.3.67	1	NC	Birmingham	15 Jul			
80.80	Gergely	Horváth	HUN	5.6.75	1	NC	Nyíregyháza	25 Jul			
80.77A	Hardus	Pienaar	RSA	10.8.81	1		Potchefstroom	12 Feb			
80.72		Zhang Lianbiao	CHN	25.1.69	2	NG	Guangzhou	19 Nov			
	(50)										
80.59	Yukifumi	Murakami	JPN	23.12.79	1		Tokyo	30 Sep			
80.54	Vadim	Bavikin	ISR	4.10.70	2	ECp-2B	Nicosia	24 Jun			

Mark	Name		Nat	Born	Pos	Meet	Venue	Date
79.79		Sun Shipeng	CHN	10.3.76	1		Jinan	12 May
79.78	Janis	Liepa	LAT	14.3.81	4		Ventspils	16 Jun
79.48	Tom	Pukstys	USA	28.5.68	1		Lappeenranta	15 Jul
79.22	Teemu	Pasanen	FIN	24.5.77	1		Jarvenpää	10 Jun
79.00	Pavel	Stasyuk	BLR	14.6.77	3		Sopot	25 May
78.97	Joachim	Kiteau	FRA-J	23.6.82	2	NC	Saint-Etienne	1 Jul
78.72	Vladimir	Ovchinnikov	RUS	2.8.70	2	Gugl	Linz	20 Aug
78.65	Stefan	Wenk	GER	13.3.81	7	NC	Stuttgart	30 Jun
	(60)							
78.64	Toru	Ue	JPN	25.6.75	1		Toin	8 Oct
78.54	Mark	Frank	GER	21.6.77	3		Stendal	2 Sep
78.40	Saku	Kuusisto	FIN-J	9.3.82	1		Kuopio	14 Jul
78.33A	David	Parker	GBR	28.2.80	4		Potchefstroom	24 Mar
78.25	Zahid	Mahmood Hussain	PAK	.4.78	1		Lahore	15 Mar
78.19	Terry	McHugh	IRL	22.8.63	1		Locarno	29 Sep
78.15	Walid Abderrazak	Mohamed	EGY	4.4.72	1		El Maadi	28 Feb
78.12	Tomas	Intas	LTU	15.9.81	1	NC	Kaunas	4 Jul
78.11		Chu Ki-young	KOR	4.3.77	1		Taebeak	16 Aug
78.10	Dimítrios	Polymérou	GRE	17.5.74	1		Thessaloníki	27 May
	(70)							
78.03A	Willie	Human	RSA-J	8.3.82	1		Potchefstroom	7 Nov
77.89		Chen Qi	CHN-J	10.3.82	2	NC	Baoding	15 Jun
77.81	Jarkko	Koski-Vähälä	FIN	21.11.78	1eB		Pihtipudas	1 Jul
77.68	Om Prakash	Dudi	IND	77	1		New Delhi	12 Mar
77.66	Pietari	Skyttä	FIN	24.5.76	5		Eurajoki	3 Jun
77.58	Elefthérios	Karasmanákis	GRE	16.8.78	2	MedG	Tunis	14 Sep
77.56	Tomasz	Damszel	POL	25.3.72	2	NC	Bydgoszcz	30 Jun
77.37	Aleksandr	Baranovskiy	RUS	22.10.80	Q	EU23	Amsterdam	15 Jul
77.34	Daniel	Ragnvaldsson	SWE	3.1.76	1	NC	Växjö	25 Aug
77.23	William	Hamlyn-Harris	AUS	14.1.78	2		Canberra	19 Dec
	(80)							
77.07	John	Stiegeler	USA	17.2.80	1	NCAA	Eugene	30 May
77.06	Philippe	Gandrey	FRA	14.3.73	1		Sens	23 Sep
76.98		Park Jae-myong	KOR	15.12.81	2	NG	Chunan	13 Oct
76.74	Jagdish Singh	Bishnoi	IND	20.5.72	1	NC	Chennai	21 Oct
76.68	Felix	Loretz	SUI	13.11.75	1		Meilen	17 Jun
76.68	Vladimir	Sasimovich	BLR	14.9.68	1		Barcelona	17 Jun
76.67	Arunas	Jurksas	LTU	3.5.72	1	ECp-2A	Riga	23 Jun
76.63	Kari	Vinni	FIN-J	19.3.83	2	NC-j	Kannus	11 Aug
76.60	Manuel	Nau	GER	2.7.77	1		Erfurt	6 Jul
76.58	Ainars	Kovals	LAT	21.11.81	1		Riga	26 May
	(90)							
76.52	Kurt	Thompson	TRI	13.12.67	1		Bloomington	12 May
76.52	David	Brisseault	FRA	7.3.69	1		Miramas	13 Jun
76.47	Oliver	Zschunke	GER	29.4.70	1		Schmiden	16 May
76.46		Gao Wenxu	CHN	1.3.73	4	NG	Guangzhou	19 Nov
76.37		Zhang Houxi	CHN	15.1.81	3		Tianjin	18 May
76.36	Luiz Fernandes da	Silva	BRA	2.7.71	1		Manaus	23 Apr
76.32	Vesa	Jäppinen	FIN	9.3.78	7	NC	Turku	8 Jul
76.29	Armin	Kerer	ITA	27.6.72	2		Pietrasanta	3 Mar
76.12	Ari	Weckström	FIN	23.10.67	1		Loviisa	20 Aug
76.12	Edi	Ponos	CRO	10.4.76	3	MedG	Tunis	14 Sep
	(100)							

Mark	Name		Nat	Born	Date
76.09	Jarkko	Kinnunen	FIN	21.4.70	1 Aug
76.04	Nery	Kennedy	PAR	28.5.73	12 May
76.02	Jitsuya	Utoda	JPN	28.1.81	14 Jul
75.90	Oliver	Dziubak	AUS-J	30.3.82	30 Dec
75.89	Mohamed Fazal	Ansari	IND		23 Jun
75.87	Pauli	Piiparinen	FIN	21.8.79	28 Jun
75.87	Gaetan	Siakinou-Schmidt	FRA	6.4.74	11 Aug
75.83	Andis	Anskins	LAT	25.1.79	26 May
75.83	Marcel	Plautz	GER	1.7.80	16 Jun
75.77	Michal	Safár	CZE	14.3.79	10 Jun
75.68		Wang Yongguang	CHN	17.1.80	14 Jun
75.65	Ron	White	USA	16.5.79	7 Apr
75.62	Dominique	Pausé	FRA	11.1.76	3 Mar
75.60	Christian	Fusenig	GER	9.5.78	30 Jun
75.59	Dorel	Greta	ROM	19.4.76	8 Jul
75.57	Vladimir	Chizhov	RUS	5.8.75	4 Jul
75.54	Josh	Johnson	USA	6.4.75	22 Apr
75.38	Mikael	Snällfot	SWE	23.5.80	28 Jul
75.24	József	Belák	HUN	13.8.58	17 May
75.17	Francesco	Pignata	ITA	14.2.78	26 Sep
75.13	Vitoli	Tipotio	FRA	17.7.75	13 Jun
75.12	Cory	Lehman	USA	2.11.77	7 Apr
75.09	Adrian	Markowski	POL	14.10.78	17 Jun
75.03	Ronny	Nilsen	NOR	7.5.71	21 Aug
75.03	Igor	Janik	POL-J	12.1.83	21 Sep
74.89	Tero	Pitkämäki	FIN-J	19.12.82	11 Aug
74.88	Denis	Davydov	RUS-J	82	14 Jul
74.72	Grzegorz	Krasinski	POL	11.1.75	17 Jun
74.72	Heiko	Väät	EST	25.8.75	28 Aug
74.68	Latrell	Frederick	USA	7.9.80	13 May
74.66	Andrew	Hall	AUS-J	28.9.82	4 Mar
74.64	Oscar	Schermer	NED	28.5.75	7 Jul
74.60	Bronislaw	Korda	POL	7.4.79	24 Jun
74.56	Ryan	Cole	USA	3.3.79	28 Apr
74.56	Marko	Hyytiainen	FIN	27.11.66	10 Jun
74.53	Diego	Moraga	CHI	6.10.76	30 Sep
74.47	Bashir	Ahmad	PAK		15 Mar
74.38	Gustavo	Dacal	ESP	30.3.77	13 Jun
74.33	Maher	Ridane	TUN	11.11.71	19 May
74.28	Milos	Steigauf	CZE	5.2.69	8 Sep

Mark	Name		Nat	Born	Date	Mark	Name		Nat	Born	Date
74.23	Tim	Werner	GER	25.9.80	27 May	74.06	Andrew	Martin	AUS	12.5.80	13 Jan
74.22	Brian	Kollar	USA	15.2.80	17 Mar	74.06	Chris	Clever	USA	10.8.78	6 May
74.20	Patrick	Landmesser	CZE	7.1.69	10 Jun	74.06	Trevor	Snyder	CAN-J	2.6.82	18 Oct
74.15	Vladimir	Novácek	CZE	23.6.68	20 May	(147)					

JUNIORS

See main list for top 7 juniors. 14 performances by 2 men to 79.98. Additional marks and further juniors:

	Mark	Pos	Meet	Venue	Date	Mark	Pos	Meet	Venue	Date
Thorkildsen	82.17	6		Kuortane	17 Jun	80.51	2		Karlstad	29 Aug
	82.15	2	ECp-1A	Vaasa	24 Jun	79.98	1	NC	Drammen	8 Jul
Ivanov	83.18	Q	WCh	Edmonton	10 Aug	81.01	1		Krasnodar	22 May
	81.86	4		Rüdlingen	19 Aug	80.56	10	WC	Edmonton	12 Aug
	81.45	4	v2N	Glasgow	1 Jul	80.18	1	EJ	Grosseto	21 Jul
	81.40	1		Rieti	2 Sep	80.00	1		Adler	11 Feb

Mark	Name		Nat	Born	Pos	Meet	Venue	Date
75.90	Oliver	Dziubak	AUS	30.3.82	1		Perth	30 Dec
75.03	Igor	Janik	POL	12.1.83	2		Kolobrzeg	21 Sep
74.89	Tero	Pitkämäki	FIN	19.12.82	3		Kannus	11 Aug
74.88	Denis	Davydov	RUS	82	5	NC	Tula	14 Jul
74.66	Andrew	Hall	AUS	28.9.82	2		Perth	4 Mar
74.06	Trevor	Snyder	CAN	2.6.82	1	PAm-J	Santa Fe	18 Oct
73.61		Cao Jun	CHN	12.11.83	Q	NC	Baoding	14 Jun
73.25	Vadims	Vasilevskis	LAT	5.1.82	1J		Ventspils	16 Jun
73.20	Vladislav	Shkurlatov	RUS	83	3		Cheboksary	14 Jun
73.00	Ciprian	Morutan	ROM	4.1.83	1		Cluj-Napoca	5 May
72.95	Seppo	Hirvonen	FIN	1.11.82	2		Piteå	15 Jul
72.85	Nikolay	Vasiltsov	BLR	82			Staiki	30 Jun
72.49	Moh. Ibrahim	Al-Khalifa (20)	QAT	.82	1		Muscat	14 Mar

PENTATHLON

Mark						Name		Nat	Born	Pos	Venue	Date
3652	6.51	60.71	23.68	45.56	4:36.37	Johannes	Maier	GER	27.2.77	1	Erfurt	4 Jul
3634	6.89	55.22	22.65	42.25	4:44.68	Thorsten	Didio	GER	1.9.76	1	Weil	23 Ju
3566	7.02	55.32	23.0	41.24	4:48.6	Hans Olav	Uldal	NOR	16.12.82	1	Øyestad	15 Se
3564	6.57	58.48	23.50	44.77	4:47.24	Florian	Schönbeck	GER	13.1.74		Regensburg	22 Se
3551	6.52	60.79	22.89	39.57	4:45.38	Atsuhiko	Iida	JPN	8.8.75	1	Tokyo	7 Ap
3527	6.63	60.71	22.57	33.84	4:39.50	Masatoshi	Ishizawa	JPN	13.3.79	2	Tokyo	7 Ap
3499	6.50	53.29	22.62	38.45	4:35.26	Reiner	Hauser	GER	29.1.77		Weil	23 Ju
3484	6.80	61.14	23.16	31.40	4:36.89	Sebastian	Nehring	GER	12.6.78		Erfurt	4 Jul
3481	6.86	51.15	22.57	38.04	4:46.15	Alexander	Freidrich	GER	.80		Euskirchen	9 Se
3470	6.61	51.88	22.92	36.38	4:29.65	Jirí	Ryba	CZE	15.6.76	1	Olomouc	1 Ma

DECATHLON

Mark	Name			Nat	Born	Pos	Meet	Venue			Date
9026	Roman	Sebrle		CZE	26.11.74	1		Götzis			27 May
	10.64/0.0	8.11/1.9	15.33	2.12	47.79	13.92/-0.2	47.92	4.80	70.16	4:21.98	
8902	Tomás	Dvorák		CZE	11.5.72	1	WCh	Edmonton			7 Aug
	10.62/1.5	8.07/0.9	16.57	2.00	47.74	13.80/-0.4	45.51	5.00	68.53	4:35.13	
8815	Erki	Nool		EST	25.6.70	2	WCh	Edmonton			7 Aug
	10.60/1.5	7.63/2.0	14.90	2.03	46.23	14.40/0.0	43.40	5.40	67.01	4:29.58	
8604		Nool				3		Götzis			27 May
	10.73/0.0	7.80/1.8	14.37	1.97	46.89	14.46/-0.6	43.32	5.30	66.94	4:39.11	
8603	Dean	Macey		GBR	12.12.77	3	WCh	Edmonton			7 Aug
	10.72/-0.7	7.59/0.4	15.41	2.15	46.21	14.34/0.0	46.96	4.70	54.61	4:29.05	
8527		Dvorak				3		Götzis			27 May
	10.84/0.0	7.69/0.4	15.83	1.97	48.76	13.99/-0.2	46.74	4.70	66.66	4:33.58	
8514		Dvorak				1	GWG	Brisbane			7 Sep
	10.78/0.8	7.61/0.5	16.16	1.97	48.77	13.98/0.8	47.62	4.70	69.22	4:46.58	
8465	Lev	Lobodin		RUS	1.4.69	4		Götzis			27 May
	10.66/0.0	7.32/0.9	15.93	2.00	48.91	14.22/-0.2	48.53	5.20	54.56	4:35.97	
8420		Nool				2	GWG	Brisbane			7 Sep
	10.73/0.8	7.35/0.2	14.46	1.94	47.44	14.82/0.8	42.56	5.40	68.83	4:42.81	
8408	Aleksandr	Yurkov		UKR	21.7.75	1		Arles			10 Jun
	10.91/-0.6	7.68/1.1	14.70	2.02	49.27	14.65/1.3	47.23	5.25	60.06	4:41.09	
8380(w)		Yurkov				1	ECp-S	Arles			1 Jul
	10.85/0.9	7.62/-2.3	14.60	2.01	49.77	14.48W/6.1	46.08	5.30	58.76	4:37.92	
8371	Attila	Zsivoczky		HUN	29.4.77	4	WCh	Edmonton			7 Aug
	10.97/0.3	6.99/-0.2	14.65	2.18	48.86	15.19/0.6	47.23	4.90	62.43	4:23.23	
8352		Lobodin				5	WCh	Edmonton			7 Aug
	10.74/1.5	7.15/1.1	16.16	2.03	48.78	14.42/-0.4	44.95	5.10	54.68	4:31.77	
8332	Jirí	Ryba		CZE	15.6.76	6	WCh	Edmonton			7 Aug
	11.14/0.3	7.17/-0.2	13.76	2.09	48.76	14.33/0.6	47.40	5.10	56.04	4:20.66	
8324		Yurkov				1		Talence			16 Sep
	11.06/0.0	7.47/-1.0	15.39	1.97	50.29	14.55/1.9	47.89	5.25	59.18	4:34.88	

Mark	Name		Nat	Born	Pos	Meet	Venue			Date
8323	Tom	Pappas	USA	6.9.76	3	GWG	Brisbane			7 Sep
	10.84/0.8	7.24/0.4	15.30	2.18	50.27	14.05/0.8	45.43	4.90	62.19	4:57.10
8307	Stefan	Schmid (10)	GER	6.5.70	7	WCh	Edmonton			7 Aug
	10.87/-0.7	7.43w/2.9	13.55	1.97	47.86	14.57/0.0	43.16	5.10	65.13	4:33.98
8287		Schmid			1		Ratingen			17 Jun
	10.84/0.9	7.75/1.1	14.04	1.98	48.92	14.31/1.0	42.46	4.76	65.49	4:36.20
8280	Laurent	Hernu	FRA	22.8.76	8	WCh	Edmonton			7 Aug
	10.97/0.3	7.31/-0.4	14.43	2.03	49.31	14.01/0.0	43.93	5.10	59.90	4:37.41
8264		Yurkov			9	WCh	Edmonton			7 Aug
	10.93/-0.7	7.37/-0.9	15.15	1.97	49.45	14.41/0.6	48.10	5.00	58.63	4:38.43
8241	Kip	Janvrin	USA	8.7.65	1	NC	Eugene			22 Jun
	10.98/1.1	7.01w/2.9	14.21	1.89	48.41	14.72/1.2	45.59	5.20	60.41	4:14.96
8227		Lobodin			4	GWG	Brisbane			7 Sep
	10.93/0.8	7.26/0.1	15.83	2.03	49.73	14.25/0.8	47.33	5.00	53.61	4:42.19
8220	Phil	McMullen	USA	3.2.75	2	NC	Eugene			22 Jun
	11.37/0.0	7.06w/2.9	15.24	1.98	49.85	14.72/1.2	48.89	5.20	55.23	4:17.04
8218(w)		Zsivoczky			2	ECp-S	Arles			1 Jul
	11.00/0.1	7.05/-1.0	15.03	2.16	48.86	14.81W/5.8	43.73	4.60	61.67	4:29.02
8213	Mário	Anibal	POR	25.3.72	1	ECp-2	Kaunas			1 Jul
	10.96/0.7	7.23/1.2	15.24	2.01	48.49	14.80/-2.2	48.33	4.80	54.55	4:28.28
8213		Hernu			2		Talence			16 Sep
	11.21/1.4	7.24/-1.0	13.86	2.03	49.66	14.27/0.9	46.76	5.15	60.14	4:35.74
8206	Chiel	Warners	NED	2.4.78	1	ECp-1	Ried			1 Jul
	10.65/0.9	7.50/1.2	14.62	1.98	47.93	14.29/1.6	42.75	4.80	57.39	4:43.12
8192	Frank	Busemann	GER	26.2.75	2		Ratingen			17 Jun
	10.90/1.7	7.73/1.3	13.90	2.04	50.62	14.21/1.0	44.37	4.96	51.11	4:27.07
8174		Sebrle			10	WCh	Edmonton			7 Aug
	10.91/1.5	7.67w/2.2	15.43	2.00	48.18	16.97/-0.4	47.41	4.60	65.75	4:31.04
8173		Zsivoczky			5		Götzis			27 May
	11.01/0.0	7.19/1.1	14.60	2.12	48.81	15.43/-0.6	46.73	4.50	60.57	4:21.85
	(30/16)									
8169	Bryan	Clay	USA	3.1.80	3	NC	Eugene			22 Jun
	10.50/1.1	7.54/1.6	13.28	1.98	48.81	14.16/1.2	46.72	4.50	57.96	4:38.93
8169	Michael	Nolan	CAN	22.9.73	11	WCh	Edmonton			7 Aug
	11.29/0.3	6.98/-1.6	15.17	1.97	49.86	14.86/0.6	50.30	4.90	64.57	4:31.44
8153	Benjamin	Jensen	NOR	13.4.75	3		Talence			16 Sep
	10.75/0.0	6.95/1.0	14.49	1.85	48.35	14.03/0.9	43.45	5.15	60.38	4:35.83
8151	Sebastian	Knabe	GER	13.10.78	3		Ratingen			17 Jun
	10.90w/2.8	7.66/1.4	14.86	2.07	48.93	14.25/1.5	43.39	4.76	50.61	4:42.03
	(20)									
8139	Mike	Maczey	GER	28.9.72	1	v USA	Bernhausen			22 Jul
	11.19/0.0	7.45/-1.1	14.43	2.00	50.28	14.42/-0.4	42.88	4.85	64.85	4:34.08
8122	Klaus	Ambrosch	AUT	23.5.73	6		Götzis			27 May
	10.93/0.3	7.39/0.7	14.71	1.94	49.33	14.56/-0.6	39.52	4.80	68.15	4:36.36
8099	Zsolt	Kürtösi	HUN	21.3.71	7		Götzis			27 May
	11.08/0.2	7.16w/2.8	14.77	2.06	49.07	14.30/-0.2	46.61	4.70	59.83	4:49.58
8075	Chad	Smith	USA	9.1.74	4	NC	Eugene			22 Jun
	10.81/0.0	7.25/0.1	14.52	1.89	48.55	14.13w/2.3	46.23	5.00	52.58	4:42.69
8071(w)	Eduard	Hämäläinen	FIN	21.1.69	4	ECp-S	Arles			1 Jul
	11.00/-1.8	6.96/-2.1	15.25	1.98	47.87	14.05W/5.1	45.87	5.00	47.03	4:37.98
8069	Raúl	Duany	CUB	4.1.75	1	WUG	Beijing			31 Aug
	11.06/0.2	7.36/-0.4	13.76	2.10	49.26	14.54/1.2	40.25	4.50	64.23	4:32.95
8065	Dmitriy	Ivanov	RUS	23.3.77	1		Sankt-Peterburg			10 Jun
	10.82/0.0	7.26/0.0	14.81	1.96	49.59?	14.56/0.0	46.66	4.80	55.81	4:39.90
8059(w)	Pierre-Alexandre	Vial	FRA	25.5.75	5	ECp-S	Arles			1 Jul
	10.68/0.9	7.37/-0.1	13.44	1.83	47.75	14.39W/6.7	41.31	4.90	54.71	4:21.68
8049	Stefan	Drews	GER	12.2.79	1	NC-23	Vaterstetten			26 Aug
	10.67/0.5	7.02/1.2	11.74	1.94	47.47	14.11/-0.1	37.99	5.30	53.93	4:23.76
8042	André	Niklaus	GER	30.8.81	1	EU23	Amsterdam			13 Jul
	11.16/0.3	7.33/-0.2	13.84	1.92	48.90	14.57/-1.2	41.82	5.20	53.91	4:23.86
	(30)									
8036	Jörg	Goedicke	GER	25.6.74	2	v USA	Bernhausen			22 Jul
	11.20/0.1	7.64/0.3	14.42	2.00	50.56	14.72/-0.4	41.81	4.95	59.68	4:38.44
8024	Claston	Bernard	JAM	22.3.79	1	SEC	Columbia, SC			11 May
	11.03/-0.3	7.27/1.0	14.20	2.14	48.95	14.78/-1.0	48.24	4.10	57.36	4:36.84
8021		Qi Haifeng	CHN-J	7.8.83	1	NG	Guangzhou			22 Nov
	11.13/0.6	7.38/-0.3	13.29	1.96	49.52	14.67/0.5	47.63	4.70	59.16	4:30.75
8019	Vladimir	Mikhaylenko	UKR	27.8.73	2	WUG	Beijing			31 Aug
	11.02/1.3	7.33/-1.0	13.95w	2.01	48.49	14.68/1.7	41.19	5.00	49.62	4:25.35

Note: (w) - wind-assisted under old IAAF rules, with weind over 4.0m/s in one event, but OK under new rules, as average <2.0

Mark Name Nat Born Pos Meet Venue Date

7993 Adrian Krebs SUI 8.6.77 1 NC Hochdorf 26 Aug
10.84/-0.2 7.22/-0.4 13.84 1.89 48.56 14.37/0.0 45.19 4.60 58.78 4:34.45
7969 Joe Cebulski USA 25.10.76 1 Jonesboro 7 Jun
10.94/2.0 6.85/0.4 14.42 2.10 51.34 14.62 47.58 4.60 59.08 4:39.65
7964 Thomas Tebbich AUT 4.2.75 2 ECp-1 Ried 1 Jul
10.95/1.3 7.18/-0.2 14.28 2.01 48.84 14.90/1.9 41.94 4.70 62.15 4:44.42
7959 Indrek Kaseorg EST 16.12.67 4 ECp-1 Ried 1 Jul
11.31/0.9 7.20/-0.5 14.00 2.01 49.19 14.63/0.6 38.56 4.80 64.43 4:32.72
7950 Jan Podebradsky CZE 1.3.74 6 Talence 16 Sep
11.01/0.0 7.10/1.0 14.64 1.91 48.17 14.56/1.9 40.34 4.75 52.35 4:17.15
7949 Oscar González ESP 8.8.76 4 WUG Beijing 31 Aug
10.88/0.2 7.59/0.0 13.17 2.07 48.58 14.36/1.6 40.09 4.50 45.98 4:22.69
(40)
7944 Jukka Väkeväinen FIN 12.9.78 7 ECp-S Arles 1 Jul
10.96/0.1 7.34/-0.3 13.03 1.95 47.71 14.95w/2.4 39.53 4.70 57.48 4:22.06
7938 Jón Arnar Magnússon ISL 28.7.69 4 Ratingen 17 Jun
11.11/0.9 7.33/0.8 15.17 1.98 49.77 14.47/1.5 41.78 4.86 58.09 4:52.08
7907 Jaakko Ojaniemi FIN 28.8.80 2 EU23 Amsterdam 13 Jul
10.69/0.3 7.54/0.0 15.39 1.95 49.59 14.97/-0.9 37.01 4.50 62.72 4:48.28
7891 Florian Schönbeck GER 13.1.74 11 Götzis 27 May
11.31/0.8 7.35/1.8 14.17 1.88 50.51 15.06/-0.6 44.07 5.10 58.11 4:31.69
7890 Sergey Blonskiy UKR 7.1.73 1 NC Kiev 14 Jun
11.11/-1.7 7.15/-1.3 14.96 1.95 52.70 14.58/0.0 43.73 5.20 58.03 4:45.97
7889 Santiago Lorenzo ARG 4.4.78 1 NCAA Eugene 31 May
11.03w/3.1 7.06w/3.1 13.38 1.91 48.27 15.10/1.9 42.05 4.90 55.91 4:21.84
7884 David Mewes GER 7.10.76 6 Ratingen 17 Jun
11.26w/2.8 7.48/1.3 14.83 1.86 50.22 14.42/1.5 43.58 4.76 55.49 4:33.47
7876 Romain Barras FRA 1.8.80 5 WUG Beijing 31 Aug
11.24/1.3 7.12/0.0 13.53 1.98 49.68 14.33/1.2 40.07 4.60 62.78 4:30.10
7871w Stephen Harris USA 5.12.80 2 NCAA Eugene 31 May
10.75W/4.4 7.62W/4.2 12.28 2.09 49.17 14.47/1.9 37.01 4.40 50.97 4:25.78
7871 William Frullani ITA 21.9.79 3 EU23 Amsterdam 13 Jul
10.65/0.3 7.58/1.4 13.80 2.13 48.78 14.68/-1.2 41.61 4.40 43.89 4:45.42
(50)
7860 Krzysztof Andrzejak POL 10.1.75 2 ECp-2 Kaunas 1 Jul
10.83/1.5 7.26/0.5 14.47 2.13 48.67 15.05/-1.6 39.16 4.80 51.61 4:57.53
7853 Vladimir Shatkovskiy UKR 8.10.75 2 NC Kiev 14 Jun
11.07/-1.7 6.92/0.3 14.23 1.92 49.35 15.08/0.0 47.35 5.00 56.74 4:46.34
7853(w) Stephan Zeyen GER 11.9.78 9 ECp-S Arles 1 Jul
10.95/0.0 7.23/-0.5 12.97 1.92 48.76 13.96W/6.1 39.72 4.80 59.06 4:47.96
7825 Matt McEwen AUS 16.10.71 1 NC Brisbane 24 Mar
10.98/1.0 7.09/-0.6 14.19 2.02 49.54 14.96/-0.5 40.61 4.60 58.26 4:37.84
7822 Dennis Leyckes GER-J 20.4.82 1 Wesel 6 May
10.95w/2.3 7.20/1.8 13.07 1.92 49.83 14.76/1.1 40.51 5.10 50.97 4:26.84
7814 Bevan Hart USA 1.8.77 2 Atlanta 18 May
11.14/0.2 6.96/0.5 13.12 1.96 49.20 15.05/0.0 41.02 5.10 55.72 4:30.22
7812 Nikolay Afanasyev RUS 11.8.65 1 NC Tula 13 Jul
11.16/0.5 7.01/0.2 15.03 1.98 50.75 14.54/-1.2 40.72 4.70 57.93 4:36.46
7805 Paolo Casarsa ITA 2.7.75 2 Desenzano 13 May
11.06/0.7 6.66/-0.3 15.16 1.94 51.38 14.56/-2.5 49.13 4.81 56.11 4:46.93
7799 Peter Sóldos CZE 27.4.73 3 Arles 10 Jun
11.03/0.5 7.22/0.6 15.20 1.90 49.27 14.60/1.6 46.54 4.55 57.73 5:04.01
7794 Ladji Doucouré FRA-J 28.3.83 4 1 NC-j Arles 10 Jun
10.60/-0.6 7.57/1.5 12.74 1.87 46.82 13.77/1.3 36.05 4.45 45.90 4:33.43
(60)
7790w David Lemen USA 13.11.79 3 NCAA Eugene 31 May
11.24W/4.4 7.12w/3.7 14.04 1.97 52.40 15.05/1.9 40.40 5.30 62.56 4:48.12
7789 Aleksandr Shtepa RUS 15.5.79 2 NC Tula 13 Jul
11.06/0.6 6.80/-0.2 15.29 1.98 50.32 14.93/-1.2 45.76 4.40 53.56 4:26.28
7773w Pródromos Korkízoglou GRE 27.2.75 1 MedG Tunis 12 Sep
10.75w/2.7 7.33W/4.2 14.00 1.98 50.64 14.40/0.0 44.88 4.80 54.81 5:16.54
7763 with LJ 7.29/1.6
7762 Gaëtan Blouin FRA 4.1.74 13 ECp-S Arles 1 Jul
10.90/1.3 6.93/-2.3 12.10w 2.01 49.21 14.33w/2.4 39.35 4.80 55.62 4:36.51
7756 Bruno Lambèse FRA 11.4.69 5 NC Arles 10 Jun
10.98/-1.0 7.17/0.2 14.83 1.99 50.33 14.47w/2.2 42.24 4.55 48.19 4:36.40
7755A Maurice Smith JAM 28.9.80 1 CAC C.de Guatemala 21 Jul
10.92/-1.2 6.89/-0.1 14.96 2.03 49.23 14.69w/3.0 48.00 3.90 53.02 4:39.73
7751 Sergey Dudnik UKR 30.3.77 1 Kiev 18 May
11.33/0.6 7.32/0.6 14.81 1.99 51.54 14.99/-0.6 43.47 4.80 59.17 4:54.17

Mark	Name		Nat	Born	Pos	Meet	Venue	Date
7749	Matthias	Spahn	GER	3.1.79	2	NC-23	Vaterstetten	26 Aug
	10.97/0.5 7.33/0.3 14.01		1.85 48.89		14.75/-0.1	43.64 4.30	62.87	4:49.50
7717	Avery	Anderson	USA	16.3.73	5	NC	Eugene	22 Jun
	10.93/1.1 7.08w/3.2 12.17		2.10 50.64		14.32/1.2	42.45 4.70	52.46	4:50.28
7714	Stephen	Moore	USA	13.8.75	6	NC	Eugene	22 Jun
	11.11/0.0 7.15w/2.6 12.42		2.13 49.73		14.60/1.2	40.31 4.60	50.22	4:38.20
(70)								
7703	Trafton	Rodgers	USA	3.2.72	2	Tex R	Austin	5 Apr
	10.82/1.2 7.07/0.6 14.37		2.01 48.82		14.51w/2.3	45.32 4.40	58.58	5:28.30
7699	Thomas	Pöge	GER	6.9.79	5	EU23	Amsterdam	13 Jul
	11.19/1.7 7.07/-1.1 14.99		1.95 51.18		14.76/-1.2	39.87 4.60	58.89	4:38.54
7696	Philip	Ibe	GER	5.5.75	2	NC	Vaterstetten	26 Aug
	11.07/0.5 7.24/0.2 15.38		1.88 52.82		14.84/-0.1	44.81 4.70	62.85	5:01.71
7695	Paul	Terek	USA	20.10.79	1	Big 10	Bloomington	19 May
	11.15/0.9 6.89w/2.2 13.95		1.85 48.91		16.05/-2.3	44.20 5.20	51.94	4:28.79
7686	Sergey	Nikitin	RUS	13.5.73	3	NC	Tula	13 Jul
	11.31/0.5 6.97/-0.5 14.94		2.01 51.31		15.22/-1.9	41.74 4.60	59.19	4:37.99
7683	Lars	Albert	GER-J	9.2.82	2	EJ	Grosseto	20 Jul
	11.46/-2.4 7.38w/3.8 14.41		1.93 51.75		15.09/1.1	43.62 4.80	58.65	4:45.89
7675	Marc	Magrans	ESP	26.9.76	1		Daimiel	5 Aug
	11.00w/3.1 7.38/0.8 12.33		2.00 49.33		14.92/2.0	36.77 4.60	50.12	4:22.33
7665	Janis	Karlivans	LAT-J	2.6.82	8	ECp-1	Ried	1 Jul
	11.31/1.3 7.01/1.9 12.93		2.10 49.70		14.96/1.6	44.86 4.30	58.04	4:46.25
7659	Andre	Röttger	GER	26.3.79	9		Ratingen	17 Jun
	11.20w/2.8 7.20/1.4 13.55		1.98 49.36		15.08/2.0	40.13 3.86	63.52	4:25.74
7649	David	Gómez	ESP	13.2.81	6	EU23	Amsterdam	13 Jul
	11.22/1.7 7.12/-0.1 13.27		1.95 48.89		14.73/-1.2	36.53 4.50	57.06	4:28.14
(80)								
7648	Francisco José	Caro	ESP	23.10.78	2	NC	Baza	10 Jun
	10.87/1.1 7.73/0.2 13.77		1.96 50.80		15.34/-1.1	39.65 4.40	57.86	4:52.38
7648	Daniel	Lukoschek	GER	16.8.79	10		Ratingen	17 Jun
	10.90/1.7 6.91/0.8 13.96		1.95 49.78		16.00/2.0	38.46 4.86	56.44	4:29.80
7639	Indrek	Turi	EST	30.7.81	9	ECp-1	Ried	1 Jul
	11.02/1.3 7.01/1.4 14.17		1.92 49.83		14.70/1.9	37.76 4.50	59.00	4:38.87
7638	Thomas	Walser	AUT	9.2.78	10	ECp-1	Ried	1 Jul
	10.92/1.3 6.92/0.0 15.31		1.98 49.45		15.15/1.2	38.11 4.20	59.78	4:42.25
7633(w)	Harri	Laiho	FIN	1.3.77	14	ECp-S	Arles	1 Jul
	11.07/1.3 6.86/-1.7 14.03		1.95 51.27		14.92W/5.2	39.22 5.00	58.91	4:49.34
7631	Édson	Bindilatti	BRA	13.3.79	1	NC	Rio de Janeiro	21 Jul
	10.95/1.4 7.22/-1.1 11.88		2.05 48.40		14.70/0.0	39.10 4.80	42.70	4:38.20
7625	Jamie	Quarry	GBR	15.11.72	7		Arles	10 Jun
	11.09/-1.0 7.24/0.9 14.25		1.90 49.38		14.52/1.6	39.04 4.55	46.50	4:29.62
7620(w)	Mark	Schumacher	GER	27.6.76	15	ECp-S	Arles	1 Jul
	10.94/1.3 6.31/-0.8 13.81		1.92 47.98		14.49W/5.2	44.14 4.40	52.91	4:35.45
7619	Andy	Giesler	USA	24.2.78	1		Orlando	21 Apr
	11.23/2.0 6.95w/2.5 14.46		1.95 50.45		15.10w/2.6	43.66 4.70	58.20	4:54.53
7613	Luigi	Llanos	PUR	22.8.78	14		Götzis	27 May
	10.89/0.3 6.89/0.6 13.67		1.97 48.67		14.70/-0.4	41.14 4.10	63.93	4:59.38
(90)								
7612	Sascha	Mäder	GER	1.1.80	3	NC-23	Vaterstetten	26 Aug
	11.46/-1.3 7.10/0.5 14.17		1.91 51.37		15.10/-0.1	48.55 4.20	64.35	4:45.69
7610	Sven	Böhm	GER	5.12.78	3		Filderstadt	3 Jun
	11.40/-1.2 7.03/1.1 13.24		2.06 49.07		15.01/0.9	40.30 4.50	48.30	4:25.59
7590	Patrik	Melin	SWE	7.6.71	11	ECp-1	Ried	1 Jul
	11.44/1.3 6.85/1.0 14.48		1.92 51.31		15.18/1.6	46.32 4.40	67.89	4:54.22
7588	Marcos	Moreno	ESP	14.3.73	1		Logroño	18 Aug
	11.20/-0.4 6.96/0.1 13.77		1.97 49.90		15.34/0.0	45.52 4.40	51.16	4:31.64
7585	Yonelvis	Áquila	CUB	1.8.75	1	NC	La Habana	26 May
	11.19/-1.0 6.85/-0.2 13.15		2.00 49.52		14.51/0.0	42.40 4.10	57.92	4:37.43
7576	Michael	Schnallinger	AUT	29.4.80	15		Götzis	27 May
	11.35/0.8 6.93/-0.2 12.98		1.97 50.25		14.83/-0.4	41.30 4.60	61.65	4:47.22
7574	Rick	Wassenaar	NED	17.1.76	12	ECp-1	Ried	1 Jul
	11.31/0.7 7.07/0.0 13.97		1.89 52.29		15.00/1.7	43.19 4.60	58.54	4:33.61
7571		Zhao Lei	CHN	8.7.78	2	NG	Guangzhou	22 Nov
	11.09/0.7 7.66/1.4 14.11		1.96 53.87		15.51/0.5	42.18 4.60	61.31	4:59.56
7567	Dmitriy	Karpov	KAZ	23.7.81	1	EAsG	Osaka	24 May
	11.26/0.3 7.35/1.4 12.69		1.98 48.86		14.47/0.0	37.62 4.50	47.95	4:34.49
7562	Sébastien	Maillard	FRA	2.5.81	7	EU23	Amsterdam	13 Jul
	11.03/0.3 7.01/0.7 12.53w		2.01 49.42		14.95/-0.9	36.64 4.80	44.64	4:23.82
(100)								

MEN 2001

Mark	Name		Nat	Born	Date
7558	Henri	Kokkonen	FIN	11.8.78	10 Jun
7553	Atis	Vaisjuns	LAT-J	27.9.82	1 Jul
7548	Hamdi	Dhouibi	TUN-J	24.1.82	21 Jul
7543	Chen	Chien-Huang	TPE	12.1.75	22 Oct
7537w	Justin	Conkling	USA	9.3.78	31 May
7536	Ivan	Yarkin	KAZ	21.11.74	24 May
7536	Anis	Riahi	TUN	30.5.71	10 Jun
7534	Kristjan	Rahnu	EST	29.8.79	13 May
7533	Xavier	Brunet	ESP	5.2.71	5 Aug
7531w	Knut H.	Sommerfeldt	NOR	13.7.79	17 May
7529	Peter	Hargasser	GER	20.2.78	26 Aug
7527	Takuro	Hirata	JPN	4.7.80	9 Jun
7521	Denis	Zavlyalov	RUS	19.8.79	19 May
7519	Curtis	Pugsley	USA	78	5 Apr
7509	William	Gallardo	CUB	17.1.73	26 May
7507	Eugene	Martineau	NED	14.5.80	13 Jul
7506	Markus	Walser	AUT	15.12.79	27 May
7504	Michael	Cvelbar	USA	12.8.79	18 May
7495	Jimmy	Watts	USA	10.10.76	24 Mar
7488w	William	Pappas	USA	22.2.79	31 May
7483	Michal	Modelski	POL	16.4.75	1 Jul
7480	Cristian	Gasparro	ITA	15.12.74	1 Jul
7480		Du Xiaopeng	CHN	8.1.77	22 Nov
7477	Nikolay	Tishchenko	RUS	77	13 Jul
7477	Enrique	Aguirre	ARG	6.12.79	21 Jul
7473	Lyndon	McDowell	CAN	10.8.77	5 Apr
7473	Patrick	Hassfeld	GER	20.2.80	26 Aug
7470A	Adam	Bork	USA		27 Apr
7470	Marzio	Viti	ITA	10.8.73	23 Sep
7469	Virgil	Spier	NED	8.1.81	13 Jul
7468	Beniamino	Poserina	ITA	6.11.70	23 Sep
7463		Hong Qingyang	CHN-J	4.2.83	22 Nov
7457	Jeff	Sander	USA	13.2.76	26 Apr
7457	Rudy	Bourguignon	FRA	16.7.79	2 Jun
7445	Sven	Simuste	EST	25.8.75	10 Jun
7443	Toru	Yasui	JPN	21.4.76	9 Jun
7438	Stéphane	Bamboux	FRA	28.2.74	24 Jun
7432	Ales	Pastrnák	CZE	9.4.76	1 Jul
7428	Jason	Goff	USA	1.5.80	13 May
7424	Aleksandr	Parkhomenko	BLR	22.3.81	7 Jun
7423	Igor	Kravtsov	BLR	2.4.77	7 Jun
7416	Hitoshi	Maruono	JPN	27.10.71	24 May
7416	Daniel	Weder	SUI	2.2.79	26 Aug
7413	Grant	Dennis	USA		11 May
7410	Pávlos	Kouromihalákis	GRE	16.2.76	27 May
7410	Barry	Thomas	GBR	28.4.72	10 Jun
7404	Nikolay	Averyanov	RUS	80	13 Jul
	(147)				

Best marks with 'legal' wind

8028 Eduard Hämäläinen FIN 21.1.69 9 Götzis 27 May
10.99/0.8 7.11/0.0 15.67 1.91 48.01 14.36/-0.2 46.41 4.90 50.33 4:42.66

7890 Pierre-Alexandre Vial FRA 25.5.75 1 Franc Ottawa 21 Jul
10.71/0.5 7.19/-2.3 13.11 1.83 48.39 14.88/0.3 43.59 5.00 55.95 4:37.11

7804 Stephen Harris USA 5.12.80 1 Knoxville 12 Apr
10.67w/3.5 7.47w/2.5 12.68 2.05 49.27 14.75w/2.1 40.46 4.40 50.48 4:34.78

7785 Stephan Zeyen GER 11.9.78 1 Filderstadt 3 Jun
10.91/-1.2 7.27/0.6 13.07 1.94 48.70 14.23/0.9 34.17 4.80 59.63 4:43.83

7619 David Lemen USA 13.11.79 7 NC Eugene 22 Jun
11.28/0.0 7.32w/2.7 13.80 1.89 52.54 15.08w/2.3 39.54 5.30 59.32 4:56.44

7567 Harri Laiho FIN 1.3.7 2 v3N Tartu 10 Jun
11.16/0.9 7.10/-0.2 13.76 1.91 51.72 15.02/1.4 44.73 4.60 58.77 4:50.96

7474 Conkling 17 May 7473 Schumacher 26 Aug

JUNIORS

See main list for top 5 marks. Additional marks and juniors:

Qi Haifeng 8019 3 WUG Beijing 31 Aug 7694 1 NC Baoding 17 Jun
7566 1 Ningpo 28 Apr

Doucouré 7747 1 EJ Grosseto 20 Jul 11 performances by 7 men over 7500

7553 Atis Vaisjuns LAT 27.9.82 13 ECp-1 Ried 1 Jul
11.27/1.0 7.04/0.4 12.95 2.07 50.02 15.22/0.6 36.90 4.40 62.69 4:45.04

7548 Hamdi Dhouibi TUN 24.1.82 2 Franc Ottawa-Hull 21 Jul
11.02/0.5 7.36/-0.7 11.91 1.86 49.61 14.98/0.3 39.17 4.90 50.13 4:35.66

7463 Hong Qingyang CHN 4.2.83 4 NG Guangzhou 22 Nov
11.11/0.7 7.11/-0.6 13.36 1.90 51.95 14.89/0.1 43.42 4.60 60.98 5:07.60

7377 Nadir El Fassi FRA 23.9.83 1 Arles 28 Oct
10.9/1.6 6.78/1.5 12.96 1.98 50.41 14.89/0.8 32.01 4.50 50.55 4:19.44

7342 Zhao Dening CHN 12.10.83 4 NC Baoding 17 Jun
10.98 7.06 12.72 1.88 49.17 15.50 41.16 4.20 55.55 4:48.40

7337 Ivan Scolfaro da Silva BRA 30.7.82 1 NC-j Londrina 30 Sep
11.46/-0.7 6.90/-1.7 12.39 1.95 49.71 15.03/0.1 38.08 4.30 57.52 4:37.69

7183 Leonid Andreyev UZB 6.11.83 1 Bangkok 6 May

7183 Aleksey Beresnev RUS 82 2 Sankt-Peterburg 10 Jun
11.35/0.0 7.01/0.0 13.92 1.87 52.44 15.14/0.0 38.68 4.40 51.12 4:43.19

7156 Tatu Pussila FIN 25.5.82 1 NC-23 Gävle 5 Aug
11.12/1.7 7.39/-0.2 12.87 1.81 52.75 14.44/1.5 37.40 4.36 66.38 5:41.64

7155 Ludrick Berrenstein NED 11.5.82 5 EJ Grosseto 20 Jul
11.27/-3.2 6.99w/2.4 11.99 1.87 49.54 14.66/1.2 37.93 4.00 48.23 4:33.64

7120 Álvaro Contreras ESP 27.1.82 1 NC-j Granada 1 Jul
11.26/0.0 7.34/0.2 11.55 1.95 49.49 15.82/0.6 33.35 4.20 45.19 4:26.09

7109 Hao Ming CHN 23.1.83 8 NG Guangzhou 22 Nov
11.33/0.7 6.70/0.2 13.38 1.99 52.05 15.86/0.1 37.40 4.50 50.43 4:44.25

7101 David Naef SUI 6.6.82 6 EJ Grosseto 20 Jul
11.59/-2.1 6.95w/2.7 12.83 1.93 50.84 15.66/1.1 37.39 4.30 54.74 4:45.29

7095 Hans Olav Uldal NOR 16.12.82 2 Gävle 5 Aug
11.31/1.7 7.19/1.6 12.37 1.78 52.17 15.62/1.5 41.50 4.06 57.67 4:40.22

7085 Francois Gourmet (20) BEL 28.12.82 7 EJ Grosseto 20 Jul
11.23/-3.2 7.21w/2.6 10.92 1.90 49.73 15.40/0.4 31.13 4.40 49.08 4:31.57

4 X 100 METRES RELAY

Mark	Name	Nat	Born	Pos	Meet	Venue	Date
37.88	USA (HSI) Drummond, B Williams, C.Johnson, Greene			1	TexR	Austin	7 Apr
37.96	USA Grimes, B Williams, Mitchell, Montgomery			1	WCh	Edmonton	12 Aug
38.03	USA Blue Drummond, Williams, C.Johnson, Greene			1	PennR	Philadelphia	28 Apr
38.19	USA Grimes, Carter, Mitchell, C.Johnson			2	BrGP	London (CP)	22 Jul
38.23	BRA Sousa, Ribeiro, A da Silva, C da Silva			1s1	WCh	Edmonton	12 Aug
38.35	USA Drummond, Grimes, Mitchell, J.Johnson			1h2	WCh	Edmonton	11 Aug
38.44	BRA Sousa, Ribeiro, A da Silva, C da Silva			1h1	WCh	Edmonton	11 Aug
38.47	RSA Nagel, du Plessis, Newton, Quinn			2	WCh	Edmonton	12 Aug
38.52	USA Red Trammell, Harden, Brokenburr, Clay			2	PennR	Philadelphia	28 Apr
38.52	GBR Chambers, Devonish, Malcolm, Barbour			3	BrGP	London (CP)	22 Jul
38.54	JPN Matsuda, Suetsugu, Fujimoto, Asahara			2s1	WCh	Edmonton	12 Aug
38.57	JPN (Tokai Uinv) Miyazaki, Suetsugu, Fujimoto, Okusako			1		Tokyo	29 Sep
38.58	TRI Burns, Boldon, Harper, Brown			3	WCh	Edmonton	12 Aug
38.60	TRI Burns, Boldon, Harper, Brown			2h1	WCh	Edmonton	11 Aug
38.60	CIV Meité, Douhou, Sonan, N'Dri			3s1	WCh	Edmonton	12 Aug
38.60	USA Grimes, B Williams, Mitchell, Montgomery			1s2	WCh	Edmonton	12 Aug
38.63	England (GBR) Condon, Campbell, Devonish, Chambers			1		Loughborough	20 May
38.63	RSA Nagel, du Plessis, Newton, Quinn			4s1	WCh	Edmonton	12 Aug
38.67	BRA de Lima, Sousa, de Oliveira, A da Silva			1	SACh	Manaus	19 May
38.67	JPN Matsuda, Suetsugu, Fujimoto, Asahara			2h2	WCh	Edmonton	11 Aug
	(20 performances by teams from 7 nations)						
38.68	JAM Powell, Jarrett, Logan, C Williams			3	PennR	Philadelphia	28 Apr
38.69	ITA Scuderi, Cavallaro, Checcucci, Colombo			1		Milano	6 Jun
38.79	POL Pilarczyk, Chyla, Balcerzak, Urbas			3h1	WCh	Edmonton	11 Aug
	(10)						
38.83	CAN Akinremi, Gilbert, Joseph, Macrozonaris			1h3	WCh	Edmonton	11 Aug
38.83	AUS Shirvington, Di Bella, Brimacombe, Basil			4	WCh	Edmonton	12 Aug
38.89	FRA Calligny, Krantz, Cheval, Patros			6s1	WCh	Edmonton	12 Aug
38.90	CUB César, Pérez, García, Mayola			1		Dortmund	9 Jun
38.99	GER Kosenkow, M.Blume, H.Blume, Goebel			2		Dortmund	9 Jun
38.99	MRI Casquette, Milazar, Augustin, Buckland			3h4	WCh	Edmonton	11 Aug
39.04	KSA Y Saaed, A Mubarak, S Al-Yami, J Al-Saffar			7s1	WCh	Edmonton	12 Aug
39.05	NGR Bamidele, Oriala, Atorudibo, Ermedolu			5s2	WCh	Edmonton	12 Aug
39.13	ISR Golan, Kafri, Yablonka, Porkhomovskiy			4h4	WCh	Edmonton	11 Aug
39.16	BAH Wells, Tynes, Lewis, Demeritte			5h3	WCh	Edmonton	11 Aug
	(20)						
39.18	THA Natenee, Sophanich, Sriharwong, Suwonprateep			1		Almaty	24 Jun
39.22	BEL Bongelo, Ferro, Rans, Wijmeersch			5h2	WCh	Edmonton	11 Aug
39.29	CHN Gong Wei, Chen Haijian, Xu Zizhou, Liu Xiang			2	EAsG	Osaka	26 May
39.29	CMR Moussambani, Bengono, Batangdon, Toukene			5h4	WCh	Edmonton	11 Aug
39.31A	VEN Morillo, Peña, Carabalí, Ollarves			2	CAC	C. de Guatemala	22 Jul
39.44	UKR Reshetnyak, Vasyukov, Dovgal, Rurak			1	ECp1B	Budapest	23 Jun
39.48	NAM Louw, B Botha, Vries, Akwenye			4	WUG	Beijing	1 Sep
39.55	RUS Smirnov, Sergeyev, Bychkov, Ryabov			6	WUG	Beijing	1 Sep
39.56	SWE Hed, Sandin, Engberg, Wahn (U23 team)			1		Ludvika	27 Jun
39.58	ESP Maestra, Nolet, Santos, Berlanga			6	ECp-S	Bremen	23 Jun
	(30)						

39.62	GRE	23 Jun	39.95	HKG	23 Nov	40.16	CYP	23 Jun	40.26A	MEX	I22 Jul	40.39	SIN	17 Jun
39.63A	PUR	22 Jul	40.01A	COL	13 Sep	40.20A	KEN	23 Jun	40.29	NED	23 Jun	40.49	POR	13 Jun
39.64	SUI	9 Jun	40.02	FIN	23 Jun	40.21	CZE	23 Jun	40.30	IND	20 Oct	40.49	INA	15 Sep
39.83	MAS	15 Sep	40.09	BLR	9 Jul	40.22	YUG	23 Jun	40.32	NZL	31 Mar	**Hand Timed**		
39.84	SLO	23 Jun	40.10	IRL	9 Jun	40.22	BEN	23 Jul	40.34	URU	19 May	40.2	GHA	29 Jun
39.86	OMN	4 Oct	40.12	ROM	7 Jul	40.24A	DOM	I22 Jul	40.38	AUT	23 Jun	40.2	GAM	29 Jun
39.93	CRO	23 Jun	40.14	HUN-J	22 Jul	40.24	QAT	4 Oct	40.38	TPE	22 Oct	40.3	VIE	14 May

Best at low altitude: 39.70 VEN 29 Jul

Mixed nation teams (majority from nation shown in brackets)

Mark	Team	Pos	Meet	Venue	Date
37.93	HSI (USA) Drummond, B Williams, Bolden TRI, Greene	1	BrGP	London (CP)	22 Jul
38.58	Texas Christian Un Frater JAM, Spencer, Patton, Collins STK	1	NCAA	Eugene	1 Jun
38.66	Un of Tennessee, USA Lambert GRN, Gatlin, Stamps, Scott	1h1	NCAA	Eugene	30 May

JUNIORS

Mark	Team	Pos	Meet	Venue	Date
39.24	GBR Edgar, Grant, Benjamin, Lewis-Francis	1	EJ	Grosseto	22 Jul
39.76	FRA Bonvard, Pognon, Guillaume, Doucouré	2	EJ	Grosseto	22 Jul
39.90	CAN (Ontario) Whitty, Fraser, Pitter, Wood	1		Calgary	29 Jul
39.95	USA (Houston FB)	1		Luling	11 May
39.96	POL Latkowski, Swierczynski, Koczon, Ptak	3	EJ	Grosseto	22 Jul
40.10	SWE Sebabi, Nossmy, Wissman, Persson	4	EJ	Grosseto	22 Jul
40.11	THA	1	Asi-j	BS Begawan	22 Jul
40.14	HUN K Horváth, Nagy, Agoston, Lórincz	5	EJ	Grosseto	22 Jul

Mark		Name	Pos	Meet	Venue	Date
40.17	BRA	A Oliveira, Campos, Moraes, Pacheco	1	SAm-J	Santa Fe	12 Oct
40.18	JPN	(Osaka HS) Hasegawa, Takagi, Matsubara, Ohara	1		Kumamoto	4 Aug
40.19	TRI	Neptune, Burns, Straker, Brown	1	Carifta	Bridgetown	15 Apr
40.26	ESP	Rodríguez-Fraile, Vidal, García-Borreguero, Lozano	6	EJ	Grosseto	22 Jul
40.34	JAM	Spence, Anderson, Smith, Mullings	2	Carifta	Bridgetown	15 Apr
40.43	GER	Helmke, Malucha, Gatzka, Dylus	3h1	EJ	Grosseto	22 Jul
40.65	BEL	Verncke, Rans, Broothaerts, Beyens	1		Duffel	27 May
40.75	NZL		1		Auckland	31 Mar
40.88A	RSA	(Western Prov.) Roelf, I Abrahams, S Abrahams, Cornelissen	1		Pretoria	21 Apr

4 X 200 METRES RELAY

Mark	Name	Pos	Meet	Venue	Date
1:19.39	USA Blue Drummond, Crawford, B Williams, Greene	1	PennR	Philadelphia	28 Apr
1:19.71	Texas Christian Un Frater JAM, Spencer, Patton, Collins STK	1h	PennR	Philadelphia	27 Apr
1:19.99	Texas Christian Un Frater JAM, Slowly JAM, Patton, Collins STK	1U	PennR	Philadelphia	27 Apr
1:20.42	Octagon (USA) Crawford, Thompson BAR, M Campbell, Griffin	1	TexR	Austin	7 Apr
1:20.44	USA (HSI) C Johnson, Drummond, Williams, Greene	2	TexR	Austin	7 Apr
1:20.63	USA Red Clay, Brew, Brokenburr, Trammell	2	PennR	Philadelphia	28 Apr
1:20.90	Un of Tennessee, USA Lambert GRN, Gatlin, Frye, Scott	1		Knoxville	14 Apr
1:20.98	USA Brunson, Brew, Davis, M Johnson	1		Gdansk	14 Jul
1:21.22	POL Tulin, Balcerzak, Pilarczyk, Urbas	2		Gdansk	14 Jul
1:21.63	JAM Jarrett, Logan, Stewart, Williams	3	PennR	Philadelphia	28 Apr

4 X 400 METRES RELAY

Mark		Name	Pos	Meet	Venue	Date
2:57.54	USA	Byrd 45.9, Pettigrew 43.9, Brew 44.03, Taylor 43.71	1	WCh	Edmonton	12 Aug
2:58.19	BAH	Moncur 45.1, C Brown 44.5, McIntosh 44.42, Munnings 44.13	2	WCh	Edmonton	12 Aug
2:58.39	JAM		3	WCh	Edmonton	12 Aug
		Simpson 45.71, C Williams 44.50, Haughton 43.88, McFarlane 44.30				
2:58.60	USA Red	Byrd 45.4, A Taylor 44.2, J Young 44.8, M Johnson 44.2	1	PennR	Philadelphia	28 Apr
2:59.71	POL		4	WCh	Edmonton	12 Aug
		Wieruszewski 46.0, Haczek 44.1, Dlugosielski 45.10, Rysiukiewicz 44.50				
2:59.78	JAM	McDonald 45.2, Clarke 44.4, McFarlane 45.1, Blackwood 45.1	2	PennR	Philadelphia	28 Apr
3:00.07	USA	Young 45.2, Pierce 44.7, Byrd 44.35, Brew 45.80	1h1	WCh	Edmonton	11 Aug
3:00.31	USA		1		Nassau	9 Jun
3:00.47	BAH		1		Nassau	9 Jun
3:00.52	USA	Byrd 45.7, Brew 44.8, Pettigrew 44.9, M Johnson 45.1	1	GWG	Brisbane	7 Sep
3:00.75	BRA		1h2	WCh	Edmonton	11 Aug
		Cl da Silva 46.3, A dos Santos 45.0, Godoy 44.87, Parrela 44.64				
3:00.83A	JAM	O Taylor, Simpson, Watts, McFarlane	1	CAC	C de Guatemala	22 Jul
3:00.88	BAH	McIntosh 46.3, Moncur 43.9, Oliver 45.58, Munnings 45.08	1h3	WCh	Edmonton	11 Aug
3:00.96	GBR	Hylton 46.1, Thomas 44.9, Benjamin 45.46, Richardson 44.52	2h1	WCh	Edmonton	11 Aug
3:00.97	JAM		2h2	WCh	Edmonton	11 Aug
		Blackwood 46.2, Simpson 44.5, Mario Watts 45.82, McFarlane 44.44				
3:01.09	BRA		5	WCh	Edmonton	12 Aug
		V da Silva 46.8, A dos Santos 44.8, Godoy 44.80, Parrela 44.66				
3:01.26	GBR	Thomas 45.8, Baulch 44.4, Benjamin 45.85, Richardson 45.17	6	WCh	Edmonton	12 Aug
3:01.32	POL		2h3	WCh	Edmonton	11 Aug
		Wieruszewski 46.0, Haczek 44.4, Bocian 45.78, Rysiukiewicz 45.11				
3:01.33	GER	Schultz 44.8, Faller 45.5, Scheer 45.70, Figura 45.33	3h1	WCh	Edmonton	11 Aug
3:01.42	ESP	I Rodríguez 46.0, Canal 44.1, Andrés 45.88, Reina 45.48	4h1	WCh	Edmonton	11 Aug
		(20 performances by teams from 8 nations)				
3:01.65	FRA	Raquil 46.2, Foucan 45.1, Bouche 45.47, Diagana 44.92	3h2	WCh	Edmonton	11 Aug
3:01.70	RSA		3h3	WCh	Edmonton	11 Aug
		la Grange 45.7, J van Oudtschoorn 45.3, Myburgh 45.21, Malherbe 45.51				
		(10)				
3:01.95	RUS		4h2	WCh	Edmonton	11 Aug
		Ignatov 46.6, Mashchenko 44.8, Golovastov 45.17, Semyonov 45.41				
3:02.35	UKR	Kaybash 46.8, Tverdostup 44.8, Rybalka 45.73, Zyukov 45.01	4h3	WCh	Edmonton	11 Aug
3:02.75	JPN	Tabata 46.7, Osakada 44.6, Tamesue 45.99, Muraki 45.49	5h1	WCh	Edmonton	11 Aug
3:03.19	MEX	Cárdenas 45.7, Juanz 45.2, Carbajal 46.68, Toledo 45.60	5h3	WCh	Edmonton	11 Aug
3:03.32	BOT	Basinyi 46.6, Lekote 45.8, Kubisa 45.59, Molefe 45.39	5h2	WCh	Edmonton	11 Aug
3:03.62	CZE	(Dukla Praha) Muzík, Zachoval, Tesarík, K Bláha	2	GS	Ostrava	31 May
3:03.91	SWE	Ahl, Sandin, Wahn, Martinez	4		Bydgoszcz	15 Jun
3:04.00	TRI	Barry, Kirk, Pierre, Taylor	3		Nassau	9 Jun
3:04.22	KSA	Hamdan Al-Bishi, Hamed Al-Bishi, Al-Housaoui, Al-Somaily	6h3	WCh	Edmonton	11 Aug
3:04.26	IRL	Daly, Comyns, McKee, Coman	7h3	WCh	Edmonton	11 Aug
		(20)				
3:04.3A	KEN	(Armed Forces)	1	NC	Nairobi	23 Jun
3:04.51	AUS	Flowers, Pearce, Hill, Williams	4	WUG	Beijing	1 Sep
3:04.82	KUW	Abdulrahman, Al-Shammari, Al-Johar, Al-Harbi	1	WMilG	Beirut	4 Jul
3:04.83	NED	Som, Keus, Hagen, van Balkom	2	ECp1B	Budapest	24 Jun

Mark	Nat	Name	Pos	Meet	Venue	Date
3:04.87	CAN	Niemi, Reed, Ringwald, Louis	7h1	WCh	Edmonton	11 Aug
3:04.88	VEN	Nuñez, Palma, Silvera, Hernández	1		Caracas	29 Jul
3:05.38	ITA	Gini, Galletti, Saraceni, Attene	6	ECp-S	Bremen	24 Jun
3:05.64	GRE	Dimótsios, Goúsis, Ikonomídis, Iakoveakis	7	ECp-S	Bremen	24 Jun
3:06.27	CHN	(Guangdong) Lu Bing, Han Chaoming, Li Zhijun, Xu Zizhou	1	NG	Guangzhou	23 Nov
3:06.47	CRO	Persic, Habun, Peitel, Juricic	1	ECp2B	Nicosia	24 Jun
	(30)					

3:06.5A ZIM 1 Jul | 3:07.59 NGR 30 Jun | 3:08.67 BUL 8 Jul | 3:09.15 POR 24 Jun | **Indoors**
3:06.72 SRI 11 Jul | 3:07.81 THA 15 Sep | 3:09.01 PHI 15 Sep | 3:09.46A DOM 22 Jul | 3:09.76 NGR 10 Mar
3:06.86 MAR 23 Jul | 3:08.31A BAR 22 Jul | 3:09.02 YUG 27 May | 3:09.51 IND 25 Nov
3:07.35 ROM 8 Jul | 3:08.56 BLR 24 Jun | 3:09.10 SLO 24 Jun | 3:09.83 MAS 15 Sep
3:07.50 ALG 14 Sep | 3:08.60 HUN 24 Jun | 3:09.12 LAT 23 Jun | 3:09.88 NOR 24 Jun

JUNIORS

Mark	Nat	Name	Pos	Meet	Venue	Date
3:06.12	POL	Marciniszyn, Matyjaszczyk, Kedzia, Grzegorczyk	1	EJ	Grosseto	22 Jul
3:06.21	GBR	Tobin, Nicholls, Ellis, Benjamin	2	EJ	Grosseto	22 Jul
3:07.47	ESP	Melo, Ruiz, Vera,Artal	3	EJ	Grosseto	22 Jul
3:08.45	BRA	L de Oliveira, Chyaromont, Silveira, Ambrosio	1	SAm-J	Santa Fe	13 Oct
3:08.69	JAM	Williams, Little, Spencer, Anderson	1	Carifta	Bridgetown	16 Apr
3:09.13A	RSA	(Central Gauteng) Roos, Pretorius, Nkosi, Lorenzen	1	NC-j	Pretoria	21 Apr
3:09.16	USA	(Altanta Lightning) Jon.Walker, Jos.Walker, Fortenberry, Burton	1		Sacramento	Jul
3:09.50	TRI	Barry, Straker, Greaves, James	2	Carifta	Bridgetown	16 Apr
3:09.91	VEN	Acevedo, Granados, Luna, Silvera	2	SAm-J	Santa Fe	13 Oct
3:09.94	RUS	Nikishov, Koldin, Lipskiy, Petrov	4	EJ	Grosseto	22 Jul
3:10.01	SWE	Olszowy, Padilla, Nikitin, Wissman	5	EJ	Grosseto	22 Jul
3:10.15	ITA	Giliberto, Sarati, Moraglio, Pavan	6	EJ	Grosseto	22 Jul
3:10.38	FRA	Panel, Boileau, Negre, Delevoye	7	EJ	Grosseto	22 Jul
3:10.69	CZE	Mazanec, Kmínek, Sech, Vrba	8	EJ	Grosseto	22 Jul
3:10.77	JPN	(Tokai Univ Boyo HS) Yoshida, Tanokashira, Fukuhara, Yamaguchi	3		Yokohama	28 Oct
3:11.11	BAR	Louis, Greenidge, Hunte, Nedd	3	Carifta	Bridgetown	16 Apr
3:11.97	BAH	McKinney, Cartwright, Atkins, Cleare	4	Carifta	Bridgetown	16 Apr

4 X 800 METRES RELAY

Mark	Nat	Name	Pos	Meet	Venue	Date
7:18.84	NED	(Atletico '73) Voltman, Liefers, Okken, Som	1		Amstelveen	28 Sep
7:19.39	USA	(Stanford Un) Carroll, Hejny, Hassell, Stember	1	PennR	Philadelphia	28 Apr

4 X 1 MILE RELAY

Mark	Nat	Name	Pos	Meet	Venue	Date
16:15.70	USA	(Stanford Un) Hejny, Sage, Riley, Stember	1	PennR	Philadelphia	28 Apr

SHUTTLE HURDLE (4 X 110MH)

Mark	Name	Pos	Meet	Venue	Date
54.73	USA (Un of Tennessee) Jennings, Gatlin, Stamps, Rush	1	PennR	Philadelphia	27 Apr
54.93	Un of Florida, USA Harris, Brown, Butler, Jones BAR	1		Knoxville	14 Apr
54.99	Un of Tennessee Jennings, Stamps, Gatlin, Rush	2		Knoxville	14 Apr

3000 METRES WALK

Mark	First name	Name	Nat	Born	Pos	Meet	Venue	Date
11:10.20	Andreas	Erm	GER	12.3.76	1		Schmalkalden	30 Sep
11:32.1	Martin	Pupis	SVK	19.10.78	1		Dubica	9 Sep
11:32.3	Radovan	Elko	SVK	4.4.80	2		Dubica	9 Sep

11:44.95 Jamie Costin IRL 1.6.77 17 Nov | 11:47.53 Craig Barrett NZL 16.11.71 17 Nov
11:46.9 Colin Griffin IRL-J 3.8.82 8 Jul

Indoors

Mark	First name	Name	Nat	Born	Pos	Meet	Venue	Date
10:31.42	Andreas	Erm	GER	12.3.76	1		Halle	4 Feb
10:53.97+		Erm			1	in 5km	Dortmund	25 Feb
11:06.74+	Yevgeniy	Shmalyuk	RUS	14.1.76	1	in 5km	Sankt-Peterburg	6 Feb
11:19.27	Robert	Heffernan	IRL	28.2.78	1	AAA	Birmingham	27 Jan
11:34.83	Mike	Trautmann	GER	13.3.74	2		Halle	4 Feb
11:39.1	Kazimir	Verkin	SVK	27.3.72	1		Hlohovec	30 Nov

11:41.8 Matej Tóth SVK-J 10.2.83 30 Nov | 11:44.3 Peter Korcok SVK 12.8.74 30 Nov

5000 METRES WALK

Mark	First name	Name	Nat	Born	Pos	Meet	Venue	Date
18:44.36	Robert	Korzeniowski	POL	30.7.68	1		Bydgoszcz	15 Jun
18:46.11		Korzeniowski			1		Villeneuve d'Ascq	6 May
18:46.96	Ilya	Markov	RUS	19.6.72	1		Biala Podlaska	2 Jun
18:47.10	Jirí	Malysa	CZE	14.8.66	2		Bydgoszcz	15 Jun
18:47.88	Alejandro	López	MEX	9.2.75	1		Xalapa	10 Nov
18:50.14		Korzeniowski			2		Biala Podlaska	2 Jun
18:54.69	Omar	Segura	MEX	24.3.81	2		Xalapa	10 Nov
19:01.92	Rogelio	Sánchez	MEX	26.10.73	3		Xalapa	10 Nov
19:07.62		Korzeniowski			1		Montreuil-sous-Bois	20 May
19:07.90	Robert	Heffernan	IRL	28.2.78	3		Biala Podlaska	2 Jun
19:08.55	Yevgeniy	Misyulya	BLR	13.3.64	3		Bydgoszcz	15 Jun

Mark	Name		Nat	Born	Pos	Meet	Venue	Date
19:11.53	João	Vieira	POR	20.2.76	1		Vila Real St António	3 Jun
19:11.55+	Andreas	Erm	GER	12.3.76	1	in 5k	Stuttgart	29 Jun
19:11.85	Tomasz	Lipiec	POL	10.5.71	4		Bydgoszcz	15 Jun
19:13.58	Cristian	Berdeja	MEX	21.6.81	4		Xalapa	10 Nov
19:17.87	Denis	Langlois	FRA	10.10.68	1		Miramas	13 Jun
19:25.18	Beniamin	Kucinski	POL-J	1.6.82	3		Poznan	15 Sep

Mark	Name		Nat	Born	Date	Mark	Name		Nat	Born	Date
19:33.3	Jesús Angel	García	ESP	17.10.69	10 Jul	19:35.79	Yuki	Yamazaki	JPN-J	16.1.84	23 Sep
19:33.57	Edgar	Hernández	MEX	6.8.77	10 Nov	19:40.0	Yevgeniy	Shmalyuk	RUS	14.1.76	17 May
19:35.3	José Alejandro	Cambil	ESP	26.1.75	10 Jul	19:42.03	Emilio	Toscano	MEX-J	3.7.83	10 Nov
19:35.58	Grzegorz	Sudol	POL	28.8.78	15 Sep	19:42.54	Augusto	Cardoso	POR	13.12.70	9 May

Indoors

Mark	Name		Nat	Born	Pos	Meet	Venue	Date
18:22.25	Andreas	Erm	GER	12.3.76	1	NC	Dortmund	25 Feb
18:42.98	Yevgeniy	Shmalyuk	RUS	14.1.76	1		Sankt-Peterburg	6 Feb
18:55.5		Markov			1		Yekaterinburg	7 Jan
18:58.97		Korzeniowski			1	FRA Ch	Liévin	17 Feb
18:59.1	Vladimir	Andreyev	RUS	7.9.66	2		Yekaterinburg	7 Jan
19:00.12	Ivano	Brugnetti	ITA	1.9.76	1	NC	Torino	24 Feb
19:06.77		Korzeniowski			1	NC	Spala	24 Feb
	(7/6)							
19:19.2	Sergey	Khripunov	RUS	15.9.76	3		Yekaterinburg	7 Jan
19:23.91	Silviu	Casandra	ROM	27.10.75	1	NC	Bucuresti	24 Feb
19:25.61	Giovanni	Perricelli	ITA	25.8.67	2	NC	Torino	24 Feb
19:27.14	Mike	Trautmann	GER	13.3.74	1		Halle	11 Feb
19:29.91	Lorenzo	Civallero	ITA	8.8.75	3	NC	Torino	24 Feb
19:29.96	Tim	Seaman	USA	14.5.72	1	NC	Atlanta	3 Mar
19:31.85	Vitaliy	Shvetsov	RUS	20.2.73	3		Samara	1 Feb

Mark	Name		Nat	Born	Date	Mark	Name		Nat	Born	Date
19:38.1	Dmitriy	Yesipchuk	RUS	17.11.74	7 Jan	19:41.21	Costica	Balan	ROM	25.8.64	24 Feb
19:40.20	Yuriy	Andronov	RUS	6.11.71	1 Feb	19:43.34	Curt	Clausen	USA	9.10.67	3 Mar

10,000 METRES WALK

Mark	Name		Nat	Born	Pos	Meet	Venue	Date
38:44.74	Robert	Korzeniowski	POL	30.7.68	1		Gdansk	14 Jul
38:53.82	Nathan	Deakes	AUS	17.8.77	1		Canberra	18 Feb
38:58.83	Robert	Heffernan	IRL	28.2.78	1	NC	Dublin	21 Jul
39:34.59	Ivano	Brugnetti	ITA	1.9.76	1		Bressanone	16 Jun
39:37.79	Michele	Didoni	ITA	7.3.74	1		Modena	2 Jun
39:56.18	Lorenzo	Civallero	ITA	8.8.75	2		Bressanone	16 Jun
40:01.0	Hatem	Ghoula	TUN	7.6.73	1		Tunis	3 Jun
40:09.74	Akinori	Matsuzaki	JPN	30.12.81	1		Tokyo	30 Sep
40:09.91	Tomasz	Lipiec	POL	10.5.71	1		Warszawa	8 Sep
40:13.28	Elichi	Yoshizawa	JPN	5.9.80	2		Tokyo	30 Sep
	(10/10)							
40:20.6	Yevgeniy	Demkov	RUS-J	3.1.82	1	NC-w	Adler	3 Mar
40:22.70	Giovanni	Perricelli	ITA	25.8.67	2		Bressanone	16 Jun

Mark	Name		Nat	Born	Date	Mark	Name		Nat	Born	Date
40:34.0	Sergey	Lystsov	RUS-J	14.11.82	3 Mar	40:42.9	Andrey	Talaschko	BLR-J	31.5.82	25 May
40:37.57	Alessandro	Gandellini	ITA	30.4.73	2 Jun	40:42.91	Roman	Magdziarczyz	POL	5.7.77	14 Jul
40:41.72	Aleksandar	Rakovic	YUG	13.4.68	26 Jul	40:43.27	Andrey	Makarov	BLR	2.1.71	14 Jul
40:42.00	Andreas	Erm	GER	12.3.76	29 Jun	40:44.46	Aigars	Fadejevs	LAT	27.12.75	14 Jul

Indoors

Mark	Name		Nat	Born	Pos	Meet	Venue	Date
39:22.0	Aleksey	Voyevodin	RUS	9.8.70	1		Penza	28 Dec
40:36.0	Sergey	Melentyev	RUS	5.12.76	1		Novosibirsk	31 Mar
40:38.0	Georgiy	Sergeyev	RUS	27.4.76	2		Novosibirsk	31 Mar

JUNIORS

Mark	Name		Nat	Born	Pos	Meet	Venue	Date
40:20.6	Yevgeniy	Demkov	RUS	3.1.82	1	NC-w	Adler	3 Mar
40:34.0	Sergey	Lystsov	RUS	14.11.82	2	NC-w	Adler	3 Mar
40:42.9	Andrey	Talaschko	BLR	31.5.82	1		Brest	25 May
40:54.08	Beniamin	Kucinski	POL	1.6.82	1		Warszawa	8 Sep
40:56.6	Aleksandr	Strokov	RUS	21.8.82	3	NC-w	Adler	3 Mar
41:11.9	Ivan	Kuznetsov	RUS	11.9.82	4	NC-w	Adler	3 Mar
41:16.66	Takayuki	Tanii	JPN	14.2.83	5		Tokyo	30 Sep
41:51.1	Sergei	Safarov	RUS	26.10.83	2		Ishevsk	8 Sep
41:59.4	Konstantin	Maksimov	RUS	17.6.82	5	NC-w	Adler	3 Mar
	40:53.0 indoors				3		Novosibirsk	31 Mar
42:05.34	Yuki	Yamazaki (10)	JPN	16.1.84	3	NC-j	Matsumoto	30 Jun
42:14.0	Radek	Parizek	CZE	21.4.82	2		Olomouc	29 Apr
42:17.8	Igor	Kazantsev	RUS	18.12.82	4		Ishevsk	8 Sep
42:21.3	Pyotr	Trofimov	RUS	18.12.83	6	NC-w	Adler	3 Mar
42:24.6	Naoki	Ikeya	JPN	7.6.82	2		Tokyo	21 Apr
42:28.70	Rafal	Dys	POL	14.1.82	2		Warszawa	8 Sep
42:29.70	Douglas	Connolly	AUS	30.10.82	1		Sydney	26 Oct
42:35.29	Koji	Takada	JPN	31.12.83	6	NC-j	Matsumoto	30 Jun
42:36.09	Dmitriy	Malinovskiy	BLR	26.1.82	2		Brest	25 May

20 KILOMETRES WALK

Mark	Name		Nat	Born	Pos	Meet	Venue	Date
1:18:05	Dmitriy	Yesipchuk	RUS	17.11.74	1	NC-w	Adler	4 Mar
1:18:06	Viktor	Burayev	RUS-J	23.2.82	2	NC-w	Adler	4 Mar
1:18:12	Artur	Meleshkevich	BLR	11.4.75	1		Brest	10 Mar
1:18:14	Nathan	Deakes	AUS	17.8.77	1		Dublin	16 Jun
1:18:20	Denis	Nizhegorodov	RUS	26.7.80	3	NC-w	Adler	4 Mar
1:19:12	Andrey	Makarov	BLR	2.1.71			Brest	10 Mar
1:19:14	Vladimir	Stankin	RUS	2.1.74	4	NC-w	Adler	4 Mar
1:19:30		Burayev			1	ECp	Dudince	19 May
1:19:32	Andreas	Erm	GER	12.3.76	1	NC	Eisenhüttenstadt	9 Jun
1:19:36	Ilya	Markov	RUS	19.6.72	1		Calella	22 Apr
1:19:45	Ivan	Trotskiy (10)	BLR	27.5.76			Brest	10 Mar
1:19:45	Yevgeniy	Misyulya	BLR	13.3.64	2	ECp	Dudince	19 May
1:19:47	Francisco	Fernández	ESP	5.3.77	2		Calella	22 Apr
1:19:48.1 t		Deakes			1	GWG	Brisbane	4 Sep
1:19:51		Erm			3	ECp	Dudince	19 May
1:19:52.0t	Robert	Korzeniowski	POL	30.7.68	2	GWG	Brisbane	4 Sep
1:19:53	Aigars	Fadejevs	LAT	27.12.75	3		Calella	22 Apr
1:20:02		Fernández			4	ECp	Dudince	19 May
1:20:14	Vladimir	Andreyev	RUS	7.9.66	5	ECp	Dudince	19 May
1:20:21	Jirí	Malysa	CZE	14.8.66	6	ECp	Dudince	19 May
1:20:31	Roman	Rasskazov	RUS	28.4.79	1	WCh	Edmonton	4 Aug
1:20:31		Korzeniowski			1	NC	Rumia	7 Oct
1:20:33		Markov			2	WCh	Edmonton	4 Aug
1:20:35		Rasskazov			1	NC	Cheboksary	16 Jun
1:20:36		Burayev			3	WCh	Edmonton	4 Aug
1:20:42		Nizhegorodov			7	ECp	Dudince	19 May
1:20:45	Aleksey	Kronin	RUS	23.7.70	2	NC	Cheboksary	16 Jun
1:20:47		Malysa			1	NC		21 Apr
1:20:49	Alejandro	López	MEX	9.2.75	2		Eisenhüttenstadt	9 Jun
1:20:49		Li Zewen	CHN	5.12.73	1	NG	Guangzhou	19 Nov
	(30/20)							
1:20:58		Pei Chuang	CHN	5.12.81	2	NG	Guangzhou	19 Nov
1:21:04		Yu Chaohong	CHN	12.12.76	3	NG	Guangzhou	19 Nov
1:21:09	David	Márquez	ESP	13.10.77	5	WCh	Edmonton	4 Aug
1:21:11	Robert	Heffernan	IRL	28.2.78	1		Leamington	21 Apr
1:21:15		He Xiaodong	CHN	14.1.78	2	NC	Dandong	13 Apr
1:21:20	Satoshi	Yanagisawa	JPN	19.1.71	1	NC	Kobe	28 Jan
1:21:20	Cristian	Berdeja	MEX	21.6.81	2		Turku	3 Jun
1:21:24	Daisuke	Ikeshima	JPN	30.1.75	2	NC	Kobe	28 Jan
1:21:33	Stepan	Yudin	RUS	3.4.80	5	NC-w	Adler	4 Mar
1:21:41	Hatem	Ghoula	TUN	7.6.73	3		Eisenhüttenstadt	9 Jun
	(30)							
1:21:42	Alessandro	Gandellini	ITA	30.4.73	5		Calella	22 Apr
1:21:44.2t	Andrey	Stadnichuk	RUS	14.12.73	1		Izhevsk	8 Sep
1:21:51	Juan Manuel	Molina	ESP	15.3.79	10	ECp	Dudince	19 May
1:21:52	Yevgeniy	Yakovlev	RUS	17.6.79	6	NC-w	Adler	4 Mar
1:21:58		Zhu Hongjun	CHN-J	18.8.83	5	NG	Guangzhou	19 Nov
1:22:04		Wu Ping	CHN	2.5.79	4	NC	Dandong	13 Apr
1:22:05		Yang Yongjian	CHN	28.4.73	5	NC	Dandong	13 Apr
1:22:05		Zhou Yongsheng	CHN	15.10.72	6	NC	Dandong	13 Apr
1:22:05		Bai Liansheng	CHN	28.7.78	7	NC	Dandong	13 Apr
1:22:05		Yu Guoping	CHN-J	13.6.86	8	NC	Dandong	13 Apr
	(40)							
1:22:05	Joel	Sánchez	MEX	15.9.67	6	WCh	Edmonton	4 Aug
1:22:06		Li Mingcai	CHN	22.8.71	9	NC	Dandong	13 Apr
1:22:06		Wang Shigang	CHN	22.2.81	10	NC	Dandong	13 Apr
1:22:10	Lorenzo	Civallero	ITA	8.8.75	12	ECp	Dudince	19 May
1:22:10	Gintaras	Andriuskevicius	LTU	6.7.75	1		Prienai	23 Jun
1:22:13	Nikolay	Matyukhin	RUS	13.12.68	8	NC-w	Adler	4 Mar
1:22:15		Wang Yu	CHN	20.1.79	13	NC	Dandong	13 Apr
1:22:16	Anthony	Gillet	FRA	7.2.76	2		Rio Maior	7 Apr
1:22:16	Denis	Langlois	FRA	10.10.68	3		Rio Maior	7 Apr
1:22:17	Andrey	Stepanchuk	BLR	12.6.79			Brest	24 May
	(50)							
1:22:19	Georgiy	Sergeyev	RUS	27.4.76	9	NC-w	Adler	4 Mar
1:22:20		Chang Wei	CHN-J	5.7.83	13	NC	Dandong	13 Apr
1:22:20	Marco	Giungi	ITA	30.10.74	3		Turku	3 Jun
1:22:20	Jefferson	Pérez	ECU	1.7.74	8	WCh	Edmonton	4 Aug

Mark	Name		Nat	Born	Pos	Meet	Venue	Date
1:22:21		Zhang Tianping	CHN-J	11.1.82	14	NC	Dandong	13 Apr
1:22:24	Aivars	Kadaks	LAT	11.2.81	1	NC	Ogre	29 Apr
1:22:25	David	Domínguez	ESP	29.7.80	7		Calella	22 Apr
1:22:25		Shin Il-yong	KOR	17.2.79	1		Kinchun	3 May
1:22:27	Milos	Holusa	CZE	2.5.65	2		Rumburk	21 Apr
1:22:27	Julio	Martínez	GUA	27.9.73	2		Leamington	21 Apr
	(60)							
1:22:29		Bian Aiguo	CHN	10.6.80	15	NC	Dandong	13 Apr
1:22:31		Wang Libo	CHN	28.10.79	17	NC	Dandong	13 Apr
1:22:32		Yu Qiyun	CHN	28.8.80	18	NC	Dandong	13 Apr
1:22:34	Silviu	Casandra	ROM	27.10.75	13	ECp	Dudince	19 May
1:22:35	Sándor	Urbanik	HUN	15.12.64	1		Balassagyarmat	21 Apr
1:22:36		Liu Dashan	CHN	10.5.80	19	NC	Dandong	13 Apr
1:22:38	Vasiliy	Ivanov	RUS	26.12.76	10	NC-w	Adler	4 Mar
1:22:38	Tomasz	Lipiec	POL	10.5.71	2	NC	Rumia	7 Oct
1:22:38.3t	Semyon	Lovkin	RUS	14.7.77	3		Izhevsk	8 Sep
1:22:42A	David	Kimutai	KEN	19.8.69	1	NC	Nairobi	23 Jun
	(70)							
1:22:44	Costica	Balan	ROM	25.8.64	1	Balk C	Paràlio Astros	21 Apr
1:22:49	Andre	Höhne	GER	10.3.78	5	2 NC	Eisenhüttenstadt	9 Jun
1:22:50.3t	Valeriy	Borisov	KAZ	18.9.66	4		Izhevsk	8 Sep
1:22:52	João	Vieira	POR	20.2.76	15	ECp	Dudince	19 May
1:22:55.0t	Aleksey	Voyevodin	RUS	9.8.70	5		Izhevsk	8 Sep
1:22:57	Vitaliy	Shvetsov	RUS	20.2.73	11	NC-w	Adler	4 Mar
1:23:01	Konstantin	Golubtsov	RUS	1.6.73	12	NC-w	Adler	4 Mar
1:23:03	Noé	Hernández	MEX	15.3.78	1	NC	Morelia	8 Jul
1:23:04	Luis	García	GUA	13.9.74	1		Dubnica nad Vahom	14 Apr
1:23:07		Chang Chunhu	CHN-J	1.5.82	20	NC	Dandong	13 Apr
	(80)							
1:23:17		Sui Jianfeng	CHN-J	29.5.84	21	NC	Dandong	13 Apr
1:23:18		Yu Guohui	CHN	30.4.77	7	NG	Guangzhou	19 Nov
1:23:22	Sergey	Korepanov	KAZ	9.5.64	13		Adler	4 Mar
1:23:24	Alfio	Corsaro	ITA	31.10.79	4	EU23	Amsterdam	15 Jul
1:23:25	Toshihito	Fujinohara	JPN	19.9.75	1		Takahata	28 Oct
1:23:28		Kim Dong-young	KOR	6.3.80	1	NG	Chunan	12 Oct
1:23:34	Jesús Ángel	García	ESP	17.10.69	3		La Coruña	9 Jun
1:23:38		Xu Xingde	CHN-J	12.6.84	22	NC	Dandong	13 Apr
1:23:38	Modris	Liepins	LAT	3.8.66	1		Tukums	3 Jun
1:23:44	Miguel Ángel	Rodríguez	MEX	15.1.67	6		Eisenhüttenstadt	9 Jun
	(90)							
1:23:44	Ivan	Azaronok	BLR	17.7.79	6	EU23	Amsterdam	15 Jul
1:23:46	Martin	Pupis	SVK	19.10.78	2		Dubnica nad Vahom	14 Apr
1:23:46	Tim	Berrett	CAN	23.1.65	1	NC	Edmonton	24 Jun
1:23:48	Augusto	Cardoso	POR	13.12.70	3		Dublin	16 Jun
1:23:48	Mario	Flores	MEX	28.2.79	4	NC	Morelia	8 Jul
1:23:53	Claudio	Vargas	MEX	9.12.74	5	NC	Morelia	8 Jul
1:23:58		Lu Ronghua	CHN-J	21.2.83	23	NC	Dandong	13 Apr
1:24:02	Milos	Bátovsky	SVK	26.5.79	7	EU23	Amsterdam	15 Jul
1:24:08	Jorge Luis	Pino	CUB	6.7.69	1		Santa Clara	17 Mar
1:24:08	Vittorino	Mucci	ITA	29.11.74	3		Riccione	22 Apr
	(100)							

Mark	Name		Nat	Born	Date
1:24:14	Edgar	Hernández	MEX	8.6.77	8 Jul
1:24:15	Daugvinas	Zujus	LTU	16.10.75	19 May
1:24:16	Eiichi	Yoshizawa	JPN	5.9.80	15 Apr
1:24:17	Denis	Trautmann	GER	15.8.72	9 Jun
1:24:17	Radovan	Elko	SVK	4.4.80	15 Jul
1:24:18	Elefthéros	Thanópoulos	GRE	22.2.75	21 Apr
1:24:23	Peter	Korcok	SVK	12.8.74	14 Apr
1:24:32	Peter	Barto	SVK	1.5.75	14 Apr
1:24:32	Aleksey	Shelest	UKR	27.3.73	21 Apr
1:24:32.6t	Sabir	Sharuyayev	KAZ	6.7.75	4 Jun
1:24:34	Sergey	Khripunov	RUS	15.9.76	4 Mar
1:24:35		Zhang Desen	CHN-J	27.9.84	13 Apr
1:24:38	Ivano	Brugnetti	ITA	1.9.76	22 Apr
1:24:39	Vladislav	Kutyavin	RUS	1.6.78	4 Mar
1:24:39	Grzegorz	Sudol	POL	28.8.78	16 Jun
1:24:45	Jan	Albrecht	GER	23.7.81	9 Jun
1:24:46	José Antonio	González	ESP	15.6.79	18 Mar
1:24:50	Curt	Clausen	USA	9.10.67	23 Jun
1:24:51	Róbert	Valícek	SVK	10.3.69	22 Apr
1:24:52A	Juan José	Sánchez	MEX	9.12.71	8 Jul
1:24:54.4t	Sergio	Vieira Galdino	BRA	7.5.69	22 Jun
1:24:55	Beniamin	Kucinski	POL-J	1.6.82	7 Oct
	(122)				

Other best track times

Mark	Name		Nat	Born	Pos	Meet	Venue	Date
1:21:09.0	Roman	Rasskazov	RUS	28.4.79	3	GWG	Brisbane	4 Sep
1:21:29.2	Viktor	Burayev	RUS-J	23.2.82	4	GWG	Brisbane	4 Sep
1:22:09.8	Ilya	Markov	RUS	19.6.72	5	GWG	Brisbane	4 Sep
1:22:24.8	Dmitriy	Yesipchuk	RUS	17.11.74	2		Izhevsk	8 Sep
1:22:31.8	Juan Manuel	Molina	ESP	15.3.79	6	GWG	Brisbane	4 Sep
1:23:37.0	Vladimir	Stankin	RUS	2.1.74	6		Izhevsk	8 Sep
1:24:06.0	Aleksey	Kronin	RUS	23.7.70	7		Izhevsk	8 Sep
1:24:08.1	Vladimir	Andreyev	RUS	7.9.66	7	GWG	Brisbane	4 Sep
1:24:08.8	João	Vieira	POR	20.2.76	1	NC	Lisboa	21 Jul

Mark	Name		Nat	Born	Pos	Meet	Venue	Date
	JUNIORS See main list for top 9 juniors. Then:							
1:24:35		Zhang Desen	CHN	27.9.84	24	NC	Dandong	13 Apr
1:24:55	Beniamin	Kucinski	POL	1.6.82	3	NC	Rumia	7 Oct
1:25:10		Zhang Huabing	CHN	1.9.83	26	NC	Dandong	13 Apr
1:25:14		Yang Xiaoliang	CHN	12.6.82	27	NC	Dandong	13 Apr
1:25:14		Guo Chao	CHN	5.2.86	28	NC	Dandong	13 Apr
1:25:16	Konstantin	Maksimov	RUS	17.6.82	16		Adler	4 Mar
1:25:36		Zhang Jiawei	CHN	27.10.86	29	NC	Dandong	13 Apr
1:25:48	Rafal	Dys	POL	14.1.82	4	NC	Rumia	7 Oct
1:25:49		Chang Ming	CHN	4.11.83	30	NC	Dandong	13 Apr
1:25:59	Yuki	Yamazaki	JPN	16.1.84	6		Kobe	28 Jan
1:26:04	(20)	Zhao Qingwei	CHN	17.8.83	33	NC	Dandong	13 Apr

30 KILOMETRES WALK

Mark	Name		Nat	Born	Pos	Meet	Venue	Date
2:06:45	David	Márquez	ESP	13.10.77	1		Prat de Llobregat	18 Feb
2:07:17	Marco	Giungi	ITA	30.10.74	1		Sesto San Giovanni	1 May
2:07:28	Mikel	Odriozola	ESP	25.5.73	2		Prat de Llobregat	18 Feb
2:08:05+	Vladimir	Potemin	RUS	15.1.80	1	in 35k	Adler	4 Mar
2:08:09	Alessandro	Gandellini	ITA	30.4.73	2		Sesto San Giovanni	1 May
2:08:21+	Aleksey	Voyevodin	RUS	9.8.70	2	in 35k	Adler	4 Mar
2:08:21+ t	German	Skurygin ¶	RUS	15.9.63	1	in 35k	Ishevsk	9 Sep
2:08:34+	Yuriy	Andronov	RUS	6.11.71	3	in 35k	Adler	4 Mar
2:08:41	José M	Rodríguez	ESP	7.11.72	3		Prat de Llobregat	18 Feb
2:08:46+	Andrey	Stadnichuk	RUS	14.12.73	4	in 35k	Adler	4 Mar
	(10)							
2:08:47	Jesús Ángel	García	ESP	17.10.69	4		Prat de Llobregat	18 Feb
2:08:49+	Yevgeniy	Shmalyuk	RUS	14.1.76	5	in 35k	Adler	4 Mar
2:08:57	Santiago	Pérez	ESP	15.1.72	5		Prat de Llobregat	18 Feb
2:08:59	Francesco	Galdenzi	ITA	6.12.76	3		Sesto San Giovanni	1 May
2:09:07+	Vladimir	Andreyev	RUS	7.9.66	6	in 35k	Adler	4 Mar
2:10:17+	Andrey	Plotnikov	RUS	12.8.67	7	in 35k	Adler	4 Mar
2:10:26	José David	Domínguez	ESP	29.7.80	6		Prat de Llobregat	18 Feb
2:10:31+	Aleksandr	Arkhipov	RUS	7.8.73	8	in 35k	Adler	4 Mar
2:11:02+	Oleg	Merkulov	RUS	1.8.70	9	in 35k	Adler	4 Mar
2:11:20+	Aleksandr	Yargunkin	RUS	6.1.81	10	in 35k	Adler	4 Mar
	(20)							
2:11:27	Francisco	Pinardo	ESP	15.3.75	7		Prat de Llobregat	18 Feb
2:11:31	José Antonio	González	ESP	15.6.79	8		Prat de Llobregat	18 Feb
2:11:46	Mario	Avellaneda	ESP	12.11.74	9		Prat de Llobregat	18 Feb
2:11:58+ t	Sergey	Yeroshin	RUS	.80	3	in 35k	Ishevsk	9 Sep
2:12:07	Alessandro	Mistretta	ITA	6.3.71	4		Sesto San Giovanni	1 May
2:12:13.0 t	Gintaras	Andriuskevicius	LTU	6.7.75	1	NC	Alytus	15 Sep
2:12:16	Alejandro	Cambil	ESP	26.1.75	10		Prat de Llobregat	18 Feb

Mark	Name		Nat	Born	Date
2:12:42	Giovanni	De Benedictis	ITA	8.1.68	1 May
2:13:06+t	Sergey	Kirdyatskiy	RUS	.80	9 Sep
2:13:15+	Andrey	Pupyshev	RUS	11.11.72	4 Mar
2:13:53	Ivano	Brugnetti	ITA	1.9.76	1 May

35 KILOMETRES WALK

Mark	Name		Nat	Born	Pos	Meet	Venue	Date
2:28:46	Aleksey	Voyevodin	RUS	9.8.70	1	NC-w	Adler	4 Mar
2:29:03	Vladimir	Potemin	RUS	15.1.80	2	NC-w	Adler	4 Mar
2:29:10	Yuriy	Andronov	RUS	6.11.71	3	NC-w	Adler	4 Mar
2:29:31	Vladimir	Andreyev	RUS	7.9.66	4	NC-w	Adler	4 Mar
2:30:29	Andrey	Stadnichuk	RUS	14.12.73	5	NC-w	Adler	4 Mar
2:31:10.5 t	German	Skurygin ¶	RUS	15.9.63	1		Ishevsk	9 Sep
2:31:45	Andrey	Plotnikov	RUS	12.8.67	6	NC-w	Adler	4 Mar
2:31:48	Yevgeniy	Shmalyuk	RUS	14.1.76	7	NC-w	Adler	4 Mar
2:33:23	Oleg	Merkulov	RUS	1.8.70	8	NC-w	Adler	4 Mar
2:33:53	Aleksandr	Arkhipov	RUS	7.8.73	9	NC-w	Adler	4 Mar
	(10)							
2:34:26	Sándor	Urbanik	HUN	15.12.64	1	NC-w	Budapest	3 Mar
2:34:55	Viktor	Ginko	BLR	7.12.65	1		Brest	10 Mar
2:35:13	Aleksandr	Yargunkin	RUS	6.1.81	10	NC-w	Adler	4 Mar
2:35:26+	Aleksandr	Prilipin	RUS	.79	1	in 50k	Cheboksary	17 Jun
2:35:49	Anton	Trotskiy	BLR	2.11.72	2		Brest	10 Mar
2:35:52.3 t	Aleksey	Voyevodin	RUS	9.8.70	3		Ishevsk	9 Sep

Mark	Name		Nat	Born	Date
2:36:05+	Robert	Korzeniowski	POL	30.7.68	11 Aug
2:36:14+	Aigars	Fadejevs	LAT	27.12.75	11 Aug
2:36:23+	Jesús Ángel	García	ESP	17.10.69	11 Aug
2:36:46	Aleksey	Nasibulin	BLR	12.12.75	10 Mar
2:36:52+	Nikolay	Matyukhin	RUS	13.12.68	11 Aug
2:37:16+	Nathan	Deakes	AUS	17.8.77	8 Apr
2:37:18+	Tomasz	Lipiec	POL	10.5.71	8 Apr
2:37:58+	Germán	Sánchez	MEX	31.7.67	17 Jun
2:38:06	Andrey	Pupyshev	RUS	11.11.72	4 Mar
2:38:07+	Marco	Giungi	ITA	30.10.74	11 Aug
2:38:08+	Giovanni	De Benedictis	ITA	8.1.68	11 Aug
2:38:08+	Edgar	Hernández	MEX	8.6.77	11 Aug
2:38:12+	Valentí	Massana	ESP	5.7.70	11 Aug
2:38:28	Aleksey	Novikov	BLR	18.6.75	10 Mar

50 KILOMETRES WALK

Mark	Name		Nat	Born	Pos	Meet	Venue	Date
3:42:08	Robert	Korzeniowski	POL	30.7.68	1	WCh	Edmonton	11 Aug
3:43:07	Jesus Ángel	García	ESP	17.10.69	2	WCh	Edmonton	11 Aug
3:43:43	Nathan	Deakes	AUS	17.8.77	1		Naumburg	8 Apr
3:44:26		García			1	ECp	Dudince	19 May
3:44:28		Wang Yinhang	CHN	15.2.77	1	NG	Guangzhou	23 Nov
3:44:32	Aleksey	Voyevodin	RUS	9.8.70	1	NC	Cheboksary	17 Jun
3:44:50	Germán	Sánchez	MEX	31.7.67	2	RUS Ch	Cheboksary	17 Jun
3:45:22	Mikel	Odriozola	ESP	25.5.73	1	NC	Mollet des Vallés	18 Mar
3:45:46		Yu Guoping	CHN-J	13.6.86	2	NG	Guangzhou	23 Nov
3:45:48	Nikolay	Matyukhin	RUS	13.12.68	2	ECp	Dudince	19 May
3:46:12	Vladimir	Potemin (10)	RUS	15.1.80	3	ECp	Dudince	19 May
3:46:12	Edgar	Hernández	MEX	8.6.77	3	WCh	Edmonton	11 Aug
3:46:20	Aigars	Fadejevs	LAT	27.12.75	4	WCh	Edmonton	11 Aug
3:46:52	Santiago	Pérez	ESP	15.1.72	4	ECp	Dudince	19 May
3:46:53		Potemin			5	WCh	Edmonton	11 Aug
3:47:04		Yu Chaohong	CHN	12.12.76	3	NG	Guangzhou	23 Nov
3:47:09		García			2	NC	Mollet des Vallés	18 Mar
3:47:34		Yu Guohui	CHN	30.4.77	4	NG	Guangzhou	23 Nov
3:48:05	Craig	Barrett	NZL	16.11.71	1		New Plymouth	16 Jun
3:48:06	Denis	Langlois	FRA	10.10.68	5	ECp	Dudince	19 May
3:48:28	Valentí	Massana	ESP	5.7.70	6	WCh	Edmonton	11 Aug
3:48:41	Sándor	Urbanik	HUN	15.12.64	1	NC	Dudince	24 Mar
3:48:51	Tomasz	Lipiec (20)	POL	10.5.71	2		Naumburg	8 Apr
3:48:51		Voyevodin			6	ECp	Dudince	19 May
3:50:20		Wang Yinhang			1	NC	Dandong	15 Apr
3:50:24		Ma Hongye	CHN	16.4.74	5	NG	Guangzhou	23 Nov
3:50:28	Viktor	Ginko	BLR	7.12.65	3		Naumburg	8 Apr
3:50:29	Mario	Avellaneda	ESP	12.11.74	3	NC	Mollet des Vallés	18 Mar
3:50:32	Andrey	Plotnikov	RUS	12.8.67	3	NC	Cheboksary	17 Jun
3:50:46	Curt	Clausen	USA	9.10.67	7	WCh	Edmonton	11 Aug
	(30/25)							
3:51:09	Marco	Giungi	ITA	30.10.74	8	WCh	Edmonton	11 Aug
3:51:22	Modris	Liepins	LAT	3.8.66	4		Naumburg	8 Apr
3:51:36	David	Boulanger	FRA	11.12.74	8	ECp	Dudince	19 May
3:51:38	Mike	Trautmann	GER	13.3.74	1		Dublin	16 Jun
3:51:43		Yang Yongjian	CHN	28.4.73	2	NC	Dandong	15 Apr
	(30)							
3:51:52		Bai Liansheng	CHN	28.7.78	6	NG	Guangzhou	23 Nov
3:51:58	Stefan	Malík	SVK	11.2.66	9	ECp	Dudince	19 May
3:52:16	Denis	Trautmann	GER	15.8.72	10	ECp	Dudince	19 May
3:52:18	René	Piller	FRA	23.4.65	11	ECp	Dudince	19 May
3:52:37		Han Qiang	CHN	28.6.77	7	NG	Guangzhou	23 Nov
3:52:57	Yuriy	Andronov	RUS	6.11.71	12	ECp	Dudince	19 May
3:53:01	Francesco	Galdenzi	ITA	6.12.76	13	ECp	Dudince	19 May
3:53:18	Zoltán	Czukor	HUN	18.12.62	14	ECp	Dudince	19 May
3:53:20		Wang Shengtang	CHN	8.3.77	3	NC	Dandong	15 Apr
3:53:37		Li Mingcai	CHN	22.8.71	8	NG	Guangzhou	23 Nov
	(40)							
3:53:45	Semyon	Lovkin	RUS	14.7.77	4	NC	Cheboksary	17 Jun
3:54:12	Giovanni	De Benedictis	ITA	8.1.68	15	ECp	Dudince	19 May
3:54:24	Matej	Spisiak	SVK	5.4.78	2		Dudince	24 Mar
3:54:31	Francisco	Pinardo	ESP	15.3.75	5		Naumburg	8 Apr
3:54:37	Liam	Murphy	AUS	5.6.79	1	NC	Melbourne	13 May
3:54:44	Fumio	Imamura	JPN	5.11.66	1	NC	Wajima	15 Apr
3:55:00		Wang Shigang	CHN	22.2.81	7	NC	Dandong	15 Apr
3:55:05	Darren	Bown	AUS	30.6.74	2	NC	Melbourne	13 May
3:55:15		Zhang Jiawei	CHN-J	27.10.86	8	NC	Dandong	15 Apr
3:55:21	Aleksandr	Nadezhdin	RUS	22.3.76	5	NC	Cheboksary	17 Jun
	(50)							
3:55:44A	Miguel Ángel	Rodríguez	MEX	15.1.67	1		Ciudad de México	22 Apr
3:55:54	Pedro	Martins	POR	12.1.68	1	NC	Viseu	17 Feb
3:56:14	Jorge	Costa	POR	20.3.61	2	NC	Viseu	17 Feb
3:56:24		Wang Libo	CHN	28.10.79	9	NC	Dandong	15 Apr
3:56:27	Bengt	Bengtsson	SWE	4.9.61	6		Naumburg	8 Apr
3:56:33	Philip	Dunn	USA	12.6.71	14	WCh	Edmonton	11 Aug
3:56:51A	Omar	Zepeda	MEX	8.7.77	4		Ciudad de México	22 Apr
3:56:56	Aleksandar	Rakovic	YUG	13.4.68	18	ECp	Dudince	19 May
3:56:58	Daugvinas	Zujus	LTU	16.10.75	7		Naumburg	8 Apr

Mark	Name		Nat	Born	Pos	Meet	Venue	Date
3:57:28		Guo Chao	CHN-J	5.2.86	10	NC	Dandong	15 Apr
	(60)							
3:57:31	Fredrik	Svensson	SWE	10.9.73	19	ECp	Dudince	19 May
3:57:35	Spirídon	Kastánis	GRE	23.9.64	16	WCh	Edmonton	11 Aug
3:57:49		Zhou Yongsheng	CHN	15.10.72	11	NC	Dandong	15 Apr
3:57:56	Peter	Tichy	SVK	12.3.69	3		Dudince	24 Mar
3:58:17	Aleksey	Shelest	UKR	27.3.73	4		Dudince	24 Mar
3:58:24	Alessandro	Mistretta	ITA	6.3.71	20	ECp	Dudince	19 May
3:58:47	Yoshimi	Hara	JPN	2.3.68	17	WCh	Edmonton	11 Aug
3:58:54		Li Guoqing	CHN	1.10.79	13	NC	Dandong	15 Apr
3:58:54	Milos	Holusa	CZE	2.5.65	18	WCh	Edmonton	11 Aug
3:59:00		Li Yi	CHN	19.1.81	11	NG	Guangzhou	23 Nov
	(70)							
3:59:10	Juan Antonio	Porras	ESP	19.7.72	4	NC	Mollet des Vallés	18 Mar
3:59:25	Duane	Cousins	AUS	13.7.73	3	NC	Melbourne	13 May
3:59.31	Jacob	Sørensen	DEN	27.12.74	3	Por Ch	Viseu	17 Feb
3:59:34	Martin	Pupis	SVK	19.10.78	5		Dudince	24 Mar
3:59:34	Tim	Berrett	CAN	23.1.65	19	WCh	Edmonton	11 Aug
3:59:57		Liu Jun	CHN	28.2.75	15	NC	Dandong	15 Apr
3:59:57	Sergey	Korepanov	KAZ	9.5.64	20	WCh	Edmonton	11 Aug
4:00:00	Denis	Franke	GER	27.11.69	8	NC	Naumburg	8 Apr
4:00:40		Mao Xinyuan	CHN	2.7.71	17	NC	Dandong	15 Apr
4:01:02	Kenji	Katsurayama	JPN	9.9.70	2	NC	Wajima	15 Apr
	(80)							
4:01:18		Zhang Huabing	CHN-J	1.9.83	18	NC	Dandong	15 Apr
4:01:23		Li Xiaoliang	CHN-J	8.2.86	19	NC	Dandong	15 Apr
4:01:23		Pei Chuang	CHN	5.12.81	20	NC	Dandong	15 Apr
4:01:52	Masato	Yoshihara	JPN	14.3.77	3	NC	Wajima	15 Apr
4:01:53	Dominic	McGrath	AUS	4.6.72	4	NC	Melbourne	13 May
4:02:28	Anton	Trotskiy	BLR	2.11.72	2		Podebrady	1 Apr
4:02:42	Jamie	Costin	IRL	1.6.77	2		Christchurch	25 Nov
4:03:10		Mao Xinli	CHN	26.1.81	23	NC	Dandong	15 Apr
4:03:21	Jirí	Malysa	CZE	14.8.66	1		Prerov	2 Sep
4:03:29	Francisco	Martín	ESP	27.5.75	5	NC	Mollet des Vallés	18 Mar
	(90)							
4:03:52		Ke Ping	CHN-J	5.1.85	24	NC	Dandong	15 Apr
4:04:16		Chang Ming	CHN-J	4.11.83	25	NC	Dandong	15 Apr
4:04:23		Zhang Liping	CHN		26	NC	Dandong	15 Apr
4:04:24	Hirofumi	Tadamasa	JPN	29.8.76	1		Takahata	28 Oct
4:04:47		Yang Jianghua	CHN-J	2.7.82	27	NC	Dandong	15 Apr
4:05:01		He Lin	CHN-J	1.3.83	28	NC	Dandong	15 Apr
4:05:07		Xu Xingde	CHN-J	12.6.84	29	NC	Dandong	15 Apr
4:05:27		Cui Xucai	CHN	24.8.76	30	NC	Dandong	15 Apr
4:05:31	Basilio	Labrador	ESP	29.3.67	6		Mollet del Vallés	18 Mar
4:05:45	Ken	Akashi	JPN	6.11.76	4		Wajima	15 Apr
	(100)							

Mark	Name		Nat	Born	Date
4:05:59	Vitaliy	Gordey	BLR	11.7.73	17 Jun
4:06:12		Zhang Tianping	CHN-J	11.1.82	15 Apr
4:06:15	Diego	Cafagna	ITA	9.7.75	18 Mar
4:06:31A	Miguel	Solís	MEX	30.9.70	22 Apr
4:06:41		Liang Zhenggan	CHN-J	27.8.83	15 Apr
4:06:56	Frantisek	Kmenta	CZE	5.10.58	19 May
4:07:14A	Fernando	Guerrero	MEX	6.9.73	28 Oct
4:07:15	Michael	Lohse	GER	6.6.62	19 May
4:07:34		Zhao Qingwei	CHN-J	17.8.83	15 Apr
4:07:42		Dong Jimin	CHN-J	10.10.85	15 Apr
4:07:57	Ugis	Bruvelis	LAT	20.6.71	29 Apr
4:08:10		Li Hongguang	CHN	10.2.80	15 Apr
4:08:16	Sergey	Kerdyapkin	RUS	18.6.80	17 Jun
4:08:20	Alejandro	Cambil	ESP	26.1.75	18 Mar
4:08:35	Ivano	Brugnetti	ITA	1.9.76	18 Mar
4:08:49		Zhang Lizheng	CHN	30.10.81	23 Nov
4:08:51	A	Latangadasu	CHN-J	27.1.84	15 Apr
4:09:27	Steve	Hollier	GBR	27.2.76	24 Mar
4:09:55	Dmitriy	Kiselyov	RUS	18.11.79	17 Jun
	(119)				

Track: 3:55:37.0 Zoltán Czukor HUN 18.12.62 1 Budapest 11 Aug

100 KILOMETRES WALK

Mark	Name		Nat	Born	Pos	Meet	Venue	Date
8:48:28	Modris	Liepins	LAT	3.8.66	1		Scanzorosciate	28 Oct
9:13:27	Viktor	Ginko	BLR	7.12.65	2		Scanzorosciate	28 Oct
9:21:49	René	Piller	FRA	23.4.65	1	NC	Ligny-en-Barrois	14 Oct
9:23:17	Róbert	Tubak	HUN	1.3.79	3		Scanzorosciate	28 Oct
9:26:11	Zoltán	Czukor	HUN	18.12.65	4		Scanzorosciate	28 Oct
9:28:06	Peter	Tichy	SVK	12.3.69	5		Scanzorosciate	28 Oct
9:31:41	Aleksey	Rodionov	RUS	5.3.57	6		Scanzorosciate	28 Oct
9:35:49	Yuriy	Burban	UKR	18.4.80	7		Scanzorosciate	28 Oct
9:36:06	Pascal	Kieffer	FRA	6.5.61	2	NC	Ligny-en-Barrois	14 Oct
9:43:25	Roberto	Defendenti	ITA	30.5.68	8		Scanzorosciate	28 Oct
9:44:49	David	Régy	FRA	1.5.69	3	NC	Ligny-en-Barrois	14 Oct

WORLD LIST TRENDS

Men 10th Bests

	1980	1984	1988	1992	1995	1996	1997	1998	1999	2000
100m	10.14	10.06	10.07	10.07	10.01	**9.98**	10.00	10.00	10.03	10.05
200m	20.34	20.18	20.15	20.20	20.17	20.21	20.27	20.08	**20.03**	20.19
400m	44.83	44.61	44.52	44.81	**44.51**	44.65	44.65	44.59	44.70	44.80
800m	1:43.93	1:44.10	1:44.33	1:44.05	**1:43.66**	1:44.01	1:44.17	1:43.98	1:44.06	1:43.98
1500m	3:34.20	3:34.61	3:33.80	3:33.69	3:33.00	**3:31.52**	3:31.89	3:31.60	3:32.01	**3:31.49**
5000m	13:16.41	3:17.48	13:10.47	13:03.21	12:59.19	13:02.52	13:00.59	12:59.09	**12:58.70**	13:0164
10000m	27:47.00	7:40.36	27:45.46	27:25.82	27:30.37	27:29.44	27:22.54	**27:18.28**	27:23.65	27:25.55
Marathon	2:10:05	2:08:49	2:09:30	2:09:33	2:09:15	2:08:02	2:07:57	**2:07:09**	2:07:47	2:07:52
3000mSt	8:17.27	8:16.04	8:13.65	**8:09.54**	8:12.54	8:10.20	8:10.67	8:10.56	8:10.23	**8:09.23**
110mh	13.45	13.36	13.33	13.27	13.24	13.26	**13.20**	13.21	13.24	13.26
400mh	48.74	48.65	48.60	48.53	48.28	48.39	48.30	**48.22**	48.40	48.40
HJ	2.33	**2.36**	2.34	2.34	2.34	2.32	2.32	2.32	2.34	2.33
PV	5.75	5.80	5.85	5.80	**5.90**	5.85	**5.90**	5.85	5.85	5.85
LJ	8.27	8.31	8.28	8.34	8.34	**8.36**	8.28	8.26	8.33	8.22
TJ	17.34	17.43	17.30	17.30	17.20	17.33	17.24	17.27	17.26	17.22
SP	**21.63**	21.16	20.93	20.57	20.78	20.88	20.79	20.84	21.27	20.88
DT	67.76	67.38	66.64	65.72	66.70	65.76	66.69	66.95	66.93	67.57
HT	80.50	**81.88**	80.46	79.66	79.52	79.14	80.88	80.51	81.36	80.88
JT (Old)	(90.94)	82.70	85.74	85.60	**87.12**	**87.12**	86.92	87.11	86.65	86.63
Decathlon	8491	8387	8237	8286	8462	8380	**8526**	8379	8467	8307
20kmW	1:21:49	1:20:10	1:20:32	1:19:36	1:19:31	**1:19:05**	1:19:43	1:19:55	1:19:18	1:19:45
50kmW	3:48:50	3:46:30	3:50:01	3:45:56	**3:44:19**	3:44:45	3:45:29	3:46:36	3:44:33	3:46:12

Other peaks: TJ 17.48 (1985), DT: 68.20 (1982).

Men 100th Bests

	1984	1988	1992	1995	1996	1997	1998	1999	2000	2001
100m	10.36	10.34	10.32	10.31	10.27	10.27	10.27	10.26	**10.24**	10.26
200m	20.78	20.79	20.78	20.73	**20.66**	20.69	20.67	20.66	20.67	20.74
400m	46.03	45.99	45.98	45.96	45.91	45.96	45.91	45.88	**45.78**	45.90
800m	1:46.97	1:46.91	1:46.95	1:47.0	1:46.82	1:46.96	1:46.87	**1:46.54**	1:46.71	1:47.00
1500m	3:38.89	3:39.46	3:39.11	3:39.94	3:38.66	**3:38.42**	3:39.10	3:39.05	3:38.68	3:38.94
5000m	13:35.10	13:37.20	13:31.44	13:36.12	13:34.29	13:36.06	13:34.34	13:32.94	**13:28.62**	13:30.56
10000m	28:26.10	28:27.28	28:30.42	28:27.6	28:20.9	28:26.71	28:26.4	28:19.07	**28:15.98**	28:27.33
Marathon	2:13:20	2:13:08	2:13:22	2:12:32	2:12:25	2:12:03	2:11:50	2:11:26	**2:11:24**	2:11:18
3000mSt	8:35.35	8:35.24	8:34.43	8:36.0	8:34.91	8:36.07	8:36.24	8:34.04	**8:33.37**	8:35.17
110mh	13.91	13.83	13.78	13.81	**13.72**	13.79	13.80	13.80	13.76	13.78
400mh	50.53	50.52	50.50	50.32	50.17	50.26	50.20	50.10	**50.06**	50.12
HJ	**2.24**	**2.24**	**2.24**	2.23	**2.24**	2.24	2.23	2.22	2.23	2.22
PV	5.41	5.50	5.50	5.50	5.50	5.50	5.50	5.50	**5.55**	5.45
LJ	7.90	7.93	7.93	7.89	**7.94**	7.91	7.90	7.92	7.93	7.89
TJ	16.41	**16.60**	16.59	16.53	16.56	16.46	16.42	16.37	16.48	16.45
SP	**19.48**	19.17	18.79	18.56	18.81	18.73	18.89	18.81	19.05	19.00
DT	**60.96**	60.84	59.80	58.82	59.82	59.60	59.98	59.87	60.16	59.60
HT	**73.08**	72.34	70.70	70.92	70.88	70.76	71.10	70.93	71.28	70.48
JT	(81.52)	76.48	76.40	76.26	76.20	76.18	76.20	75.78	76.06	76.12
Decathlon	7630	**7702**	7567	7633	7701	7649	7607	7592	7634	7562
20kmW	1:25:57	1:24:54	1:24:09	**1:23:39**	1:23:55	1:23:58	1:24:30	1:24:31	1:24:22	1:24:08
50kmW	4:09:40	4:06:34	4:07:33	4:06:01	4:06:31	4:05:42	4:08:00	**4:03:49**	4:04:34	4:05:45

Other peaks: HJ 2.24 (also 1989), JT 77.14 (1991).

The 100th best mark in 2001 was worse than that of 2000 in 19 of the 22 events – the only exceptions being the marathon, javelin and 20km walk. The story is similar for women (see page 524) where the 2001 mark was worse than that of 2000 in 17 of the 20 events, the only exceptions being marathon, shot and 20km walk.

Looking back a decade – the 2001 men's 100th bests were ahead of those of 1991 by 10-1 in the running events, 1-1 in the walks, but 3-5 with one equal in the field events and decathlon. For women it is 8-1 to 2001 in the running events, but 2-3 in the field and heptathlon (unable to compare the javelin with the new-specification now is use, and PV, TJ and HT new events)

There were no new records for 100th best marks for men. but there were two for women – marathon and hammer. There were, however, new records for 10th best marks for men in the 1500m and steeplechase and for women in the 3000m (despite this no longer being a major championship event), marathon, pole vault and 20km walk.

WOMEN'S WORLD LISTS 2001

100 METRES

Mark	Wind	Name		Nat	Born	Pos	Meet	Venue	Date
10.82	-0.3	Zhanna	Pintusevich-Block	UKR	6.7.72	1	WCh	Edmonton	6 Aug
10.84	0.5	Marion	Jones	USA	12.10.75	1	GP	Saint-Denis	6 Jul
10.84	1.1		Jones			1	GWG	Brisbane	4 Sep
10.85	-0.3		Jones			2	WCh	Edmonton	6 Aug
10.86	0.1		Jones			1	VD	Bruxelles	24 Aug
10.91	-0.3	Ekateríni	Thánou	GRE	1.2.75	3	WCh	Edmonton	6 Aug
10.93	0.6		Pintusevich-Block			1rA	GP	Athína	11 Jun
10.93	-0.2		Jones			1h6	WCh	Edmonton	5 Aug
10.94	-0.1		Jones			1	Bisl	Oslo	13 Jul
10.94	-2.3		Pintusevich-Block			1s1	WCh	Edmonton	6 Aug
10.94	-1.0		Jones			1rA	WK	Zürich	17 Aug
10.95	-2.3		Jones			2s1	WCh	Edmonton	6 Aug
10.95	0.1	Chandra	Sturrup	BAH	12.9.71	2	VD	Bruxelles	24 Aug
10.96	0.1		Jones			1	GGala	Roma	29 Jun
10.96	0.5		Pintusevich-Block			2	GP	Saint-Denis	6 Jul
10.96	0.1		Thánou			3	VD	Bruxelles	24 Aug
10.97	0.0		Jones			1q1	WCh	Edmonton	5 Aug
10.97	-1.3		Thánou			1q4	WCh	Edmonton	5 Aug
10.98	0.6	Léonie Myriam	Mani	CMR	21.5.77	2rA	GP	Athína	11 Jun
10.98	0.1	Chryste	Gaines	USA	14.9.70	1	Herc	Monaco	20 Jul
10.99	0.6	Kelli	White	USA	1.4.77	3rA	GP	Athína	11 Jun
10.99	0.5		Sturrup			3	GP	Saint-Denis	6 Jul
10.99	-1.0		Sturrup			2rA	WK	Zürich	17 Aug
10.99	0.1		Pintusevich-Block			4	VD	Bruxelles	24 Aug
11.00	-0.3		Jones			1	BrGP	London (CP)	22 Jul
11.01	1.1		Pintusevich-Block			2	GWG	Brisbane	4 Sep
11.02	-0.1	LaTasha	Jenkins	USA	19.12.77	1		Athens, GA	5 May
11.02	0.6		Thánou			4rA	GP	Athína	11 Jun
11.02	1.2		Pintusevich-Block			1		Réthimno	1 Jul
11.02	-0.3		Sturrup			4	WCh	Edmonton	6 Aug
		(30/8)							
11.04	0.6	Debbie	Ferguson	BAH	16.1.76	5rA	GP	Athína	11 Jun
11.06	1.0	Mercy	Nku	NGR	17.7.76	1rB	Athl	Lausanne	4 Jul
		(10)							
11.06	1.1	Endurance	Ojokolo	NGR	29.9.75	1rB	WK	Zürich	17 Aug
11.09	-0.8	Marina	Kislova	RUS	7.2.78	1	Veniz	Haniá	4 Jun
11.11	0.6	Torri	Edwards	USA	31.1.77	6rA	GP	Athína	11 Jun
11.12	2.0	Natasha	Mayers	VIN	10.3.79	1		Walnut	12 May
11.13	1.2	Veronica	Campbell	JAM-J	16.5.82	1	NSch	Kingston	6 Apr
11.13	0.1	Shakedia	Jones	USA	15.3.79	1		Los Angeles	5 May
11.13	1.5	Liliana	Allen	MEX	24.5.70	1		Rivas	27 Jun
11.14	-0.6	Glory	Alozie (ex NGR)	ESP	30.12.77	1	ECCp	Madrid	26 May
11.14	0.2	Aleen	Bailey	JAM	25.11.80	1	NC	Kingston	22 Jun
11.14	1.0	Manuela	Levorato	ITA	16.3.77	2rB	Athl	Lausanne	4 Jul
		(20)							
11.14	0.9		Li Xuemei	CHN	5.1.77	1	NG	Guangzhou	18 Nov
11.15	0.6	Christine	Arron	FRA	13.9.73	7rA	GP	Athína	11 Jun
11.17	1.6	Muna	Lee	USA	30.10.81	1h2	NCAA	Eugene	31 May
11.17	0.7	Gabi	Rockmeier	GER	29.11.73	1	NCAA	Stuttgart	30 Jun
11.17	1.0	Sevatheda	Fynes	BAH	17.10.74	3rB	Athl	Lausanne	4 Jul
11.18	0.1	Angela	Williams	USA	30.1.80	2		Los Angeles	5 May
11.20		Yuliya	Tabakova	RUS	1.5.80	1	NC-23	Cheboksary	14 Jun
11.21i	-	Merlene	Ottey	JAM	10.5.60	1		Tampere	12 Feb
		11.31A	0.3			2		Pretoria	23 Mar
11.21	0.5	Alenka	Bikar	SLO	7.1.74	1	NC	Maribor	7 Jul
11.22	-0.6	Candace	Young	USA	9.1.79	1		Los Angeles	24 Mar
		(30)							
11.22	0.9		Liu Xiaomei	CHN	11.1.72	2	NG	Guangzhou	18 Nov
11.23	1.2	Melanie	Paschke	GER	29.6.70	1		Sondershausen	24 Aug
11.24	0.6	Sina	Schielke	GER	19.5.81	1h1		Mannheim	16 Jun
11.25	1.7	Mary	Onyali-Omagbemi	NGR	3.2.68	1		Houston	19 May
11.25	1.1	Yekaterina	Leshchova ¶	RUS	21.4.74	1	NC	Tula	12 Jul
11.25	1.6	Nora	Güner	TUR	1.6.77	1	MedG	Tunis	11 Sep
11.26	1.3	Kim	Gevaert	BEL	5.8.78	1	NC	Bruxelles	1 Jul
11.26	1.1	Natalya	Ignatova	RUS	28.12.73	2	NC	Tula	12 Jul

Mark	Wind	Name		Nat	Born	Pos	Meet	Venue	Date
11.26	1.6	Frédérique	Bangué	FRA	31.12.76	1		Castres	18 Jul
11.27	1.0	Beverly	McDonald	JAM	15.2.70	5rB	Athl	Lausanne	4 Jul
		(40)							
11.27	0.5	Makaridja	Sanganoko	CIV	8.5.80	1	Franc	Ottawa	21 Jul
11.28	0.2	Astia	Walker	JAM	4.4.75	2	NCAA	Kingston	22 Jun
11.29	0.3	Lyubov	Perepelova	UZB	26.2.79	1rB	GP	Athína	11 Jun
11.29	1.6	Abiodun	Oyepitan	GBR	30.12.79	2	v2N	Glasgow	1 Jul
11.29	0.3	Anzhela	Kravchenko	UKR	25.1.71	1h2	NC	Kiev	1 Jul
11.29	0.5	Venolyn	Clarke ¶	CAN	11.7.67	2	Franc	Ottawa	21 Jul
11.30	1.2	Natalya	Safronnikova	BLR	28.2.73	2	GP II	Sevilla	8 Jun
11.31	1.2	Lauren	Hewitt	AUS	25.11.78	1	NC	Brisbane	24 Mar
11.31	1.7	Teneeshia	Jones	USA	28.1.79	2		Baton Rouge	14 Apr
11.31	0.0	Monica	Twum	GHA	14.3.78	1	WAC	Fresno	19 May
		(50)							
11.31	1.8	Effrosíni	Patsoú	GRE	5.6.74	1		Kalamáta	2 Jun
11.31	1.1	Katia	Benth	FRA	16.11.75	1h1		Castres	18 Jul
11.32	-0.5	Ionela	Tîrlea	ROM	9.2.76	1	NC	Bucuresti	9 Jun
11.32	-0.4	Rosemar	Coelho Neto	BRA	2.1.77	1		Americana	16 Jun
11.32	1.1	Irina	Khabarova	RUS	18.3.66	3	NC	Tula	12 Jul
11.33	1.7	Angela	Manuel	USA	10.5.75	1	MSR	Walnut	22 Apr
11.33	1.2	Rachelle	Boone	USA	30.6.81	1		Bloomington	12 May
11.33	0.7	Marion	Wagner	GER	1.2.78	4	NC	Stuttgart	30 Jun
11.33	0.0	Elva	Goulbourne	JAM	21.1.80	1		Lappeenranta	15 Jul
11.33	-1.3	Lucimar	de Moura	BRA	22.3.74	1	NC	Rio de Janeiro	19 Jul
		(60)							
11.33	0.0	Johanna	Manninen	FIN	4.4.80	5q1	WCh	Edmonton	5 Aug
11.33	0.0	Supavadee	Khawpeag	THA	17.7.76	1	SEAG	Kuala Lumpur	12 Sep
11.34	0.0	Cydonie	Mothersill	CAY	19.3.78	1		Orlando	21 Apr
11.34	1.8	Marina	Trandenkova	RUS	7.1.67	2		Kalamáta	2 Jun
11.34	0.2	Peta-Gay	Barrett	JAM	2.10.76	3	NC	Kingston	22 Jun
11.34	0.8	Mireille	Donders	SUI	7.7.74	1	NC	Genève	30 Jun
11.34	-0.3	Inger	Miller	USA	12.6.72	3	BrGP	London (CP)	22 Jul
11.35	1.4	Olga	Shishigina	KAZ	23.12.68	1		Almaty	2 Jun
11.35	0.5		Chen Yueqin	CHN	25.2.77	1h4	NC	Chengdu	28 Jun
11.36	1.8	Hideko	Nihei	JPN	2.1.71	1		Kitakami	14 Jul
		(70)							
11.36	0.4	Aïda	Diop	SEN	27.4.70	1		La Chaux-de-Fonds	19 Aug
11.37	-0.4	Joan Uduak	Ekah	NGR	16.12.80	1h2		Torrevieja	14 Apr
11.37	-0.6	Susanthika	Jayasinghe	SRI	17.12.75	1	GP	Osaka	12 May
11.37	0.2	Vida	Nsiah	GHA	13.4.76	1		Abbotsford	25 May
11.37	1.3	Tania	Woods	USA	23.9.80	3h2	NC	Eugene	21 Jun
11.37	1.9	Amanda	Forrester	GBR	29.9.78	1rB		Glasgow	1 Jul
11.37	1.1	Larisa	Kruglova	RUS	27.10.72	4	NC	Tula	12 Jul
11.38		Vida	Anim	GHA-J	7.12.83	1		Lagos	29 Jun
11.39	0.1	Kinshasa	Davis	USA	10.7.79	3		Los Angeles	5 May
11.39	-0.8	Brianna	Glenn	USA	18.4.80	1	Pac-10	Berkeley	20 May
		(80)							
11.39	1.8	Irina	Pukha	UKR	10.1.73	4		Kalamáta	2 Jun
11.39	-1.4	Vírgen	Benavídes	CUB	31.12.74	2		Arles	9 Jun
11.40	1.7	LaQuinta	Manahan	USA	27.1.79	1		Waco	21 Apr
11.40	1.7	Shani	Anderson	GBR	7.8.75	2B2	MSR	Walnut	22 Apr
11.40	0.3	Oksana	Ekk	RUS	26.11.74	3	FBK	Hengelo	4 Jun
11.40	0.5	Hanitriniaina	Rakotondrabe	MAD	1.1.67	3	Franc	Ottawa	21 Jul
11.41	-0.8	Michelle	Collins	USA	12.2.71	4	Veniz	Haniá	4 Jun
11.41	1.6	Katchi	Habel	GER-J	22.10.82	2		Mannheim	16 Jun
11.41	1.1	Odiah	Sidibé	FRA	13.1.70	3	NC	Saint-Etienne	30 Jun
11.41	0.6	Martha	Adusei	CAN	8.6.76	3h7	WCh	Edmonton	5 Aug
		(90)							
11.42A	0.8	Heide	Seyerling	RSA	19.8.76	1		Potchefstroom	12 Feb
11.42	0.9	Tulia	Robinson	JAM	4.2.79	1		Auburn	21 Apr
11.42	-1.4	Joice	Maduaka	GBR	30.9.73	3		Arles	9 Jun
11.42	1.3	Nancy	Callaerts	BEL	11.8.71	2	NC	Bruxelles	1 Jul
11.42	0.4	Kaori	Sakagami	JPN	12.5.74	1		Kanazawa	30 Sep
11.43A	0.3	Dikeledi	Morapane	RSA	12.3.76	3		Pretoria	23 Mar
11.43	1.7	Marcia	Richardson	GBR	10.2.72	2		Fullerton	26 Apr
11.43	1.8	Amber	Cumberbatch	BAR		1		Springfield	5 May
11.43	0.0	Danielle	Carruthers	USA	22.12.79	1h3	Big 10	Bloomington	19 May
11.43	1.6	SaDonna	Thornton	USA	16.8.78	2h2	NCAA	Eugene	31 May
		(100)							
11.43	0.5	Petya	Pendareva	BUL	20.1.71	2	ECp-1B	Budapest	23 Jun
11.43	1.1	Jacqueline	Poelman	NED	5.10.73	4	NA	Heusden	14 Jul

Mark	Wind	Name		Nat	Born	Pos	Meet	Venue	Date
11.43	0.9		Zeng Xiujun	CHN	10.2.79	4	NG	Guangzhou	18 Nov
11.44	1.8	Shavonda	Benjamin	USA-J	16.6.82				8 Apr
11.44	1.0	Sarah	Wilhelmy	GBR	2.2.80				6 May
11.44	0.0	Erica	Whipple	USA-J	4.12.82				26 May
11.44		Lyudmila	Dmitriadi	UZB	24.9.69				16 Jun
11.44	0.2	Birgit	Rockmeier	GER	29.11.73				14 Jul
11.45A	1.9	Alexis	Joyce	USA-J	5.9.83				28 Apr
11.45	1.1		Huang Mei	CHN	15.4.75				6 May
11.45	2.0	LaKeesha	White	USA	29.7.80				18 May
11.45	0.8	Angel	Perkins	USA-J	5.10.84				19 May
11.45	-1.7	Svetlana	Goncharenko	RUS	28.5.71				19 Jun
11.46	1.5	Mercedes	Carnesolta	CUB	13.5.75				23 Mar
11.46	0.8		Qin Wangping	CHN-J	16.6.82				21 Apr
11.46		Heather	Samuel	ANT	6.7.70				5 May
11.46	-0.3	Me'Lisa	Barber	USA	4.10.80				13 May
11.46	1.6	Severina	Cravid	POR	1.7.78				14 Jul
11.46	0.9		Zou Hua	CHN	7.1.79				18 Nov
11.47		Louise	Ayétotché	CIV	3.6.75				5 May
11.47	-0.7	Willisa	Heintz	USA	28.3.81				13 May
11.47	0.2	Yeoryía	Koklóni	GRE	7.5.81				16 Jun
11.48	1.5	Idalia	Hechavarría	CUB	5.6.74				23 Mar
11.48	1.7	Catherine	Murphy	GBR	21.9.75				22 Apr
11.48	1.8	Verneta	Lesforis	LCA	4.5.75				5 May
11.48	2.0	Ssereta	Lafayette	USA	26.6.79				18 May
11.48	2.0	Jimyria	Hicks	USA	10.8.80				18 May
11.48	0.5	Tiffany	Green	USA	5.12.81				19 May
11.48	-0.6	Vukosava	Djapic	YUG	21.1.78				26 May
11.48	1.3	Grit	Breuer	GER	16.2.72				27 May
11.48	0.2	Nadine	Palmer	JAM-J	19.2.83				22 Jun
11.48	1.9	Patricia	Girard	FRA	8.4.68				2 Sep
11.49	-0.5	Kerine	Black	JAM	5.3.77				24 Mar
11.49	-0.3	Ebony	Shotwell	USA-J	27.1.82				12 May
11.49	0.2	Camille	Harper	USA	11.12.79				19 May
11.49	1.8	Aksel	Gürcan	TUR	2.1.73				2 Jun
11.49	1.4	Barbara	Petráhn	HUN	16.9.78				17 Jun
11.49	-0.9		Xiao Lin	CHN	22.2.78				29 Jun
11.49	0.0	Ruth	Grajeda	MEX	31.7.80				6 Jul
11.50	1.4	Caro	Hunt	NZL	10.1.78				18 Feb
11.50	-0.5	Kisha	Jett	USA	11.2.75				24 Mar
11.50	1.1		Ni Xiaoli	CHN-J	29.1.83				6 May
11.50	1.2	Tami	Zachery	USA	27.11.78				5 May
11.50	-0.8	Donica	Merriman	USA	24.1.79				19 May
11.50	1.7	Diane	Allahgreen	GBR	21.2.75				28 May
11.50	0.1	Ioánna	Kafetzí	GRE	30.5.76				6 Jun
11.50	1.1	Natalya	Mikhaylovskaya	RUS	20.11.75				9 Jun
11.50	0.1		Zhu Juanhong	CHN-J	5.12.85				28 Jun
11.50		Chinedu	Odozor	NGR	24.12.77				29 Jun
11.50	1.6	Heidi	Hannula	FIN	26.2.80				7 Jul
11.51	1.4	Sharon	Cripps	AUS	29.6.77				18 Feb
11.51	1.9	Sonia	Williams	ANT	28.5.79				31 Mar
11.51	1.0	Myra	Combs	USA	17.4.79				31 Mar
11.51	1.2	Staneshia	Bell	USA	30.4.78				5 May
11.51	1.5	Marshevet	Hooker	USA-J	25.9.84				12 May
11.51	0.0	Shana	Robinson	USA-J	13.2.82				19 May
11.51	0.8	Roxana	Díaz	CUB	17.5.81				25 May
11.51	1.6	Natalya	Abramenko	BLR	.75				7 Jun
11.51	1.3	LaKeisha	Backus	USA	15.12.76				21 Jun
11.51	-0.9		Wang Man	CHN	9.10.76				29 Jun
11.51	1.2	Delphine	Combe	FRA	6.12.74				30 Jun
11.51	1.3	Tarama	Perry	CAN	20.11.74				13 Jul
11.51	1.1	Thatiana	Ignâcio	BRA-J	2.7.83				25 Aug
11.51	0.9	Muriel	Hurtis	FRA	25.3.79				26 Aug
11.52		Nolle	Graham	JAM	12.9.81				6 Apr
11.52	-0.1	Monique	Tubbs	USA	23.1.81				5 May
11.52	1.8	Cheasa	Gibson	USA					5 May
11.52	1.2	Sylviane	Félix	FRA	31.10.77				25 May
11.52	0.6	Felipa	Palacios	COL	1.12.75				20 Jun
11.52	1.4	Sylvie	Mballa Eloundo	CMR	21.4.77				30 Jun
11.52	0.3	Kathleen	De Caluwe	BEL	22.12.76				21 Jul
11.53	1.7	Tiffany	Greer	USA	8.6.81				22 Apr
11.53	0.1	Oksana	Guskova/Kaydash	UKR	16.6.74				12 May
11.53	0.5	Aleah	Williams	USA	7.1.81				19 May
11.53	1.3	Allyson	Felix	USA-J	18.11.85				25 May
11.53	1.0	Yuliya	Bartsevich	BLR	15.6.79				7 Jun
11.53	1.1	Céline	Thélamon	FRA	1.3.79				30 Jun
11.53	1.4	Annika	Amundin	SWE	9.2.77				16 Aug
11.54	-0.6	Celena	Clarke	JAM	3.1.75				31 Mar
11.54	2.0	Monique	Wright-Cruse	USA	28.10.80				18 May
11.54	0.6	Oksana	Dragun	BLR	19.4.81				7 Jun
11.54	1.4	Viviane	Sildillia	FRA	23.2.74				30 Jun
11.54	0.2	Marguerite	Barcelo	FRA	10.3.78				30 Jun
		(184)							

Wind assisted

Mark	Wind	Name		Nat	Born	Pos	Meet	Venue	Date
10.89	3.5	Chryste	Gaines	USA	14.9.70	1	NC	Eugene	22 Jun
10.93	3.5	Kelli	White	USA	1.4.77	2	NC	Eugene	22 Jun
10.98	3.1	Nora	Güner	TUR	1.6.77	1h1	MedG	Tunis	11 Sep
11.00	4.0	Glory	Alozie	ESP	30.12.77	1		Valencia	8 Jul
11.01	3.4	Natasha	Mayers	VIN	10.3.79	1		Azusa	14 Apr
11.01	3.5	Angela	Williams	USA	30.1.80	3	NC	Eugene	22 Jun
11.09	2.4	Inger	Miller	USA	12.6.72	1h3	NC	Eugene	21 Jun
11.09	3.5	Torri	Edwards	USA	31.1.77	4	NC	Eugene	22 Jun
11.09	3.1	Frédérique	Bangué	FRA	31.12.76	1		Montauban	17 Jul
11.10	2.9	Shakedia	Jones	USA	15.3.79	2	NCAA	Eugene	2 Jun
11.13	3.5	Muna	Lee	USA	30.10.81	1	USTCA	Austin	21 Apr
11.15	3.5	Brianna	Glenn	USA	18.4.80	6	NC	Eugene	22 Jun
11.16	4.7	Alenka	Bikar	SLO	7.1.74	1		Ljubljana	3 Jun
11.17	3.7	Abiodun	Oyepitan	GBR	30.12.79	1	NC-23	Bedford	30 Jun
11.20	4.0	Anzhela	Kravchenko	UKR	25.1.71	2		Valencia	8 Jul
11.23	5.0	Teneeshia	Jones	USA	28.1.79	1h8	Tex R	Austin	6 Apr
11.24	2.5	Sarah	Wilhelmy	GBR	2.2.80	1r2		Arles	9 Jun
11.24	2.1	Katchi	Habel	GER-J	22.10.82	1	EJ	Grosseto	20 Jul
11.25	3.1	Katia	Benth	FRA	16.11.75	2		Montauban	17 Jul
11.26	4.8	Vida	Nsiah	GHA	13.4.76	1h9	Tex R	Austin	6 Apr
11.26	3.5	LaKeesha	White	USA	29.7.80	2	USTCA	Austin	21 Apr
11.26	2.8	Makaridja	Sanganoko	CIV	8.5.80	1		Dakar	22 Apr
11.26	2.8	Natalya	Safronnikova	BLR	28.2.73	2	ECp-S	Bremen	23 Jun
11.27	3.7	Cydonie	Mothersill	CAY	19.3.78	2h1	NCAA	Eugene	31 May
11.28		Betty-Ann	Haywood	JAM	7.10.80	1		Lebanon, Il.	21 Apr
11.28	4.0	Felipa	Palacios	COL	1.12.75	3		Valencia	8 Jul
11.28	3.1	Odiah	Sidibé	FRA	13.1.70	3		Montauban	17 Jul
11.29	2.5	Tania	Woods	USA	23.9.80	1		Sacramento	19 May
11.29	4.0	Joan Uduak	Ekah	NGR	16.12.80	4		Valencia	8 Jul
11.30	4.3	Tiffany	Green	USA	15.12.81	1		Abilene	10 May
11.31	2.4	Aleah	Williams	USA	7.1.81	3	Tex R	Austin	7 Apr
11.31	3.5	SaDonna	Thornton	USA	16.8.78	3	USTCA	Austin	21 Apr

Mark	Wind	Name		Nat	Born	Pos	Meet	Venue	Date
11.31	3.7	Motoka	Arai	JPN	4.7.74	1	NC	Tokyo	9 Jun
11.32	2.9	Rachelle	Boone	USA	30.6.81	1	Big 10	Bloomington	20 May
11.32	3.7	Kaori	Sakagami	JPN	12.5.74	2	NC	Tokyo	9 Jun
11.33A	2.7	Heide	Seyerling	RSA	19.8.76	1		Bloemfontein	2 Feb
11.33	2.8	Ebony	Shotwell	USA-J	27.1.82	1		Gainesville	21 Apr
11.33	2.8	Vírgen	Benavídes	CUB	31.12.74	1	NC	La Habana	25 May
11.34	2.6	Grit	Breuer	GER	16.2.72	1		Blankenburg	27 May
11.34	2.4	Oksana	Ekk	RUS	26.11.74	3		Torino	9 Jun
11.34	4.2	Consuella	Moore	USA	29.8.81	4h1	NC	Eugene	21 Jun
11.36	4.3	Delloreen	Ennis-London	JAM	5.3.75	2		Abilene	10 May
11.36	5.1	LaQuinta	Manahan	USA	27.1.79	1		Arlington	14 May
11.37	2.1	Louise	Ayétotché	CIV	3.6.75	1	Mod R	Modesto	12 May
11.37	4.4	Shalonda	Solomon	USA-J	19.12.85	1h1		Norwalk	19 May
11.37	3.3	Tonya	Carter	USA	22.3.78	1		Atlanta	2 Jun
11.38	4.1	Camille	Harper	USA	11.12.79	1h1	Tex R	Austin	6 Apr
11.38	2.9	Diane	Allahgreen	GBR	21.2.75	2	CAU	Bedford	28 May
11.38	5.6	Joice	Maduaka	GBR	30.9.73	1		Bangor	2 Jun
11.38	3.1	Patricia	Girard	FRA	8.4.68	4		Montauban	17 Jul
11.40	3.4	Chantal	Brunner	NZL	5.11.70	1		Hastings	25 Feb
11.40	4.1	Shana	Robinson	USA-J	13.2.82	2h1	TexR	Austin	6 Apr
11.40	3.7	Nanceen	Perry	USA	19.4.77	1		College Station	14 Apr
11.40	3.4	LaKeisha	Backus	USA	15.12.76	2		Azusa	14 Apr
11.40	2.4	Petya	Pendareva	BUL	20.1.71	4		Torino	9 Jun
11.41	2.7	Aminata	Diouf	SEN	18.2.77	1		Barnako	24 Apr
11.41	2.4	Yeoryía	Koklóni	GRE	7.5.81	1h3	NC	Athína	16 Jun
11.42	3.1	Stephanie	Durst	USA-J	6.1.82	1		Houston	31 Mar
11.42	2.9	Danielle	Carruthers	USA	22.12.79	2	Big 10	Bloomington	20 May
11.42	2.9	Marcia	Richardson	GBR	10.2.72	4	CAU	Bedford	28 May
11.42	>3	Vukosava	Djapic	YUG	21.1.78	1		Beograd	2 Jun

Mark	Wind	Name		Nat	Born	Date
11.43	3.4	Vernicha	James	GBR-J	6.6.84	14 Apr
11.43	0.2	Kiamesha	Otey	USA	28.5.81	12 May
11.44A	3.2	Me'Lisa	Barber	USA	4.10.80	14 Apr
11.44	5.1	Alicia	McIntosh	JAM	19.9.77	14 May
11.45	3.4	Caro	Hunt	NZL	10.1.78	25 Feb
11.45	2.2	Nolle	Graham	JAM	12.9.81	30 Mar
11.45	3.1	LaToya	Johnson	USA	15.12.79	7 Apr
11.45	3.4	Kerine	Black	JAM	5.3.77	12 May
11.45	4.9	Severina	Cravid	POR	1.7.78	21 Jul
11.46	5.1	LaJuana	Lovett	USA-J	7.5.82	14 May
11.46	3.1	Céline	Thélamon	FRA	1.3.79	17 Jul
11.48	3.4	Delilah	Dillard	USA	17.11.78	7 Apr
11.48	2.9	Oluwaseum	Adetiba	NGR	27.5.79	28 Apr
11.48	2.9	Donica	Merriman	USA	24.1.79	20 May
11.49	2.9	Carla	Christian	USA		28 Apr
11.49	2.5	Kátia Regina	Santos	BRA	31.12.67	29 Apr
11.49	5.1	Shontae	Johnson	USA	18.4.80	14 May
11.49	2.9	Lorraine	Dunlop	USA	12.3.79	20 May
11.49	2.9	Benedicta	Ajudua	NGR	10.7.80	14 Jul
11.50	5.1	Sonia	Williams	ANT	28.5.79	6 Apr
11.50	3.5	Monique	Wright-Cruse	USA	28.10.80	21 Apr
11.50	3.3	Beatrice	Utondu	NGR	23.11.69	2 Jun
11.50	2.5	Christine	Bloomfield	GBR	12.2.68	9 Jun
11.50	3.7	Sabrina	Scott	GBR	2.6.79	30 Jun
11.50	2.1	Gwladys	Bélliard	FRA-J	10.11.82	20 Jul
11.51	3.1	Lolo	Jones	USA-J	5.8.82	31 Mar
11.51		Stephanie	Adams	USA-J	.83	20 Apr
11.51	4.4	Ashlee	Brown	USA-J	3.12.85	19 May
11.51	2.4	Angela	Daigle	USA	28.5.76	21 Jun
11.52	6.3	Inger Elisabeth	Tørre	NOR	1.1.79	1 Jul
11.53	3.1	Linda	Ferga	FRA	24.12.76	20 May
11.53	5.6	Sarah	Reilly	IRL	3.7.73	2 Jun
11.53	2.1	Shanta	Ghosh	GER	3.1.75	14 Jul
11.54	2.9	Francesca	Cola	ITA	11.2.73	11 Sep

Hand timing

Mark	Wind	Name		Nat	Born	Pos	Meet	Venue	Date
10.9		Natalya	Safronnikova	BLR	28.2.73	1		Brest	21 Jul
11.1		Svetlana	Goncharenko	RUS	28.5.71	1		Rostov-na-Donu	5 May
11.1	0.8	Vírgen	Benavídes	CUB	31.12.74	1		Alcalá de Henares	30 Jun
11.1	0.6	Beverly	McDonald	JAM	15.2.70	1		Gdansk	14 Jul
11.1		Yuliya	Bartsevich	BLR	15.6.79	2		Brest	21 Jul
11.1		Natalya	Mikhaylovskaya	RUS	20.11.75	1		Irkutsk	27 Jul
11.2	0.2	Yelena	Goncharova	RUS	.80	1		Vladivostok	26 May

Mark	Wind	Name		Nat	Born	Date
11.3A	-3.2	Ilze	Jordaan	RSA	20.9.79	9 Feb
11.3		Wafae	Tayssir	MAR		18 Mar
11.3		Fatma Zohra	Missour	MAR	.77	18 Mar
11.3		Betty-Ann	Haywood	JAM	7.10.80	21 Apr
11.3		Irina	Khabarova	RUS	18.3.66	28 May
11.3		Monika	Gachevska	BUL	31.1.74	9 Jun
11.3		Rosemar	Coelho Neto	BRA	2.1.77	22 Jun
11.3	-0.6	Petya	Pendareva	BUL	20.1.71	14 Jul
11.3w	3.3	SaDonna	Thornton	USA	16.8.78	18 May

Best at low altitude: 11.52 1.0 Joyce 21 Apr

JUNIORS

See main list for top 3 juniors. 11 performances by 7 women to 11.45. Additional marks and further juniors:

	Mark	Wind	Pos	Meet	Venue	Date	Mark	Wind	Pos	Venue	Date
Campbell	11.32	0.0	1	Carifta	Bridgetown	16 Apr	11.42	-1.2	1	Kingston	17 Mar
	11.41	-1.2	1		Kingston	17 Mar					
Habel	11.42	0.0	1	NC-J	Braunschweig	6 Jul					

Mark	Wind	Name		Nat	Born	Pos	Meet	Venue	Date
11.44	1.8	Shavonda	Benjamin	USA	16.6.82	1		Gainesville	8 Apr
11.44	0.0	Erica	Whipple	USA	4.12.82	1		Orlando	26 May
11.45A	1.9	Alexis	Joyce	USA	5.9.83	1		Denver	28 Apr
11.45	0.8	Angel	Perkins	USA	5.10.84	1rB		Norwalk	19 May
11.46	0.8		Qin Wangping	CHN	16.6.82	1		Zhongshan	21 Apr
11.48	0.2	Nadine	Palmer	JAM	19.2.83	5	NC	Kingston	22 Jun
11.49	-0.3	Ebony	Shotwell	USA	27.1.82	3	SEC	Columbia, SC	12 May
11.50	1.1		Ni Xiaoli	CHN	29.1.83	2		Shanghai	6 May

Mark	Wind	Name		Nat	Born	Pos	Meet	Venue	Date
11.50	0.1		Zhu Juanhong	CHN	5.12.85	1h2	NC	Chengdu	28 Jun
11.51	1.5	Marshevet	Hooker	USA	25.9.84	1rB		Austin	12 May
11.51	0.0	Shana	Robinson	USA	13.2.82	2	WAC	Fresno	19 May
11.51	1.1	Thatiana	Ignâcio	BRA	2.7.83	1		São Paulo	25 Aug
11.53	1.3	Allyson	Felix	USA	18.11.85	1		Norwalk	25 May
11.55	1.5	Zenobia	Reed	USA	24.1.84	2		Austin	12 May
11.57	1.3	Shalonda	Solomon	USA	19.12.85	2		Norwalk	25 May
11.58	-1.1	Sanya	Richards	JAM	26.2.85	1		Sacramento	27 Jul
11.60	-0.7	Stephanie	Durst (20)	USA	6.1.82	3		Los Angeles	24 Mar
11.60	0.1		Lao Quqing	CHN	1.6.83	2h2	NC	Chengdu	28 Jun
Wind assisted see main lists for six women – five performances to 11.42w									
11.43	3.4	Vernicha	James	GBR	6.6.84	3r1		Azusa	14 Apr
11.46	5.1	LaJuana	Lovett	USA-J	7.5.82	3		Arlington	14 May
11.50	2.1	Gwladys	Béllard	FRA	10.11.82	2	EJ	Grosseto	20 Jul
11.51	3.1	Lolo	Jones	USA	5.8.82	2rB		Houston	31 Mar
11.51		Stephanie	Adams	USA	.83	1		Brenham	20 Apr
11.51	4.4	Ashlee	Brown	USA	3.12.85	2		Norwalk	19 May
11.55	2.2	Latoya	Phelps	USA	30.6.84	1		Austin	12 May
11.57	2.5	LaShauntea	Moore	USA	31.7.83	1		Dayton	25 May
11.58	2.3	Ashley	Purnell	CAN	.83	1		London, ONT	24 Aug
11.59	2.2	Simone	Facey	JAM	7.5.85	1s3	NSch	Kingston	6 Apr
11.59	2.1	Amelie	Huyghes	FRA	31.5.82	3	EJ	Grosseto	20 Jul

200 METRES

Mark	Wind	Name		Nat	Born	Pos	Meet	Venue	Date
22.23	1.6	Marion	Jones	USA	12.10.75	1h1	NC	Eugene	23 Jun
22.38	0.5	Kelli	White	USA	1.4.77	1	VD	Bruxelles	24 Aug
22.39	1.8	LaTasha	Jenkins	USA	19.12.77	1h2	NC	Eugene	23 Jun
22.39	-0.3	Debbie	Ferguson	BAH	16.1.76	1s3	WCh	Edmonton	9 Aug
22.39	-0.8		Jones			1	WCh	Edmonton	10 Aug
22.40	0.3		Jones			1s1	WCh	Edmonton	9 Aug
22.46	-1.0		Jenkins			1		Bridgetown	19 May
22.52	-1.6		Jones			1	NC	Eugene	24 Jun
22.52	-0.8		Ferguson			2	WCh	Edmonton	10 Aug
22.54A	-0.4	Cydonie	Mothersill	CAY	19.3.78	1	CAC	C. de Guatemala	21 Jul
22.54	1.2		Mothersill			1h5	WCh	Edmonton	8 Aug
22.54	-0.3		White			2s3	WCh	Edmonton	9 Aug
22.54	1.9	Léonie Myriam	Mani	CMR	21.5.77	1	GP II	Rieti	2 Sep
22.56	-0.8		White			2	WCh	Edmonton	10 Aug
22.57	-0.1		Mothersill			1		Orlando	21 Apr
22.57	0.5	Beverly	McDonald	JAM	15.2.70	2	VD	Bruxelles	24 Aug
22.59	1.8	Aleen	Bailey	JAM	25.11.80	1	KansR	Lawrence	21 Apr
22.59	-0.1		Mani			1s2	WCh	Edmonton	9 Aug
22.62	1.0		White			1r2	Nik	Nice	9 Jul
22.63	1.8	Heide	Seyerling	RSA	19.8.76	1	NC	Durban	3 Mar
22.63	1.8	LaTasha	Richardson (10)	USA	23.8.76	2	KansR	Lawrence	21 Apr
22.63	-0.5	Susanthika	Jayasinghe	SRI	17.12.75	1	GP	Osaka	12 May
22.63	0.4	Lorraine	Fenton	JAM	8.9.73	1r2		Kassel	13 Jun
22.63	-0.1		Jenkins			2s2	WCh	Edmonton	9 Aug
22.63	-0.1		Mothersill			3s2	WCh	Edmonton	9 Aug
22.65	0.8		White			1h2	WCh	Edmonton	8 Aug
22.66	1.0	Mercy	Nku	NGR	17.7.76	2r2	Nik	Nice	9 Jul
22.66	1.5		Jenkins			1	NA	Heusden	14 Jul
22.68	1.0	Yuliya	Tabakova	RUS	1.5.80	1	NC-23	Cheboksary	14 Jun
22.68	0.3	Natalya	Safronnikova	BLR	28.2.73	1	ECp-S	Bremen	24 Jun
22.68	-0.1	Gabi	Rockmeier	GER	29.11.73	1	NC	Stuttgart	1 Jul
22.68	0.0		Jenkins			1	GP II	Zagreb	2 Jul
22.68A	0.4		Mothersill			1h1	CAC	C. de Guatemala	21 Jul
22.68	0.3	Juliet	Campbell	JAM	17.3.70	2s1	WCh	Edmonton	9 Aug
22.68			Nku			3	VD	Bruxelles	24 Aug
		(35/17)							
22.70	-1.4	Yekaterina	Leshchova ¶	RUS	21.4.74	1	NC	Tula	14 Jul
22.74	0.3	Zhanna	Pintusevich-Block	UKR	6.7.72	2		Réthimno	1 Jul
22.75	0.0		Li Xuemei	CHN	5.1.77	1	NG	Guangzhou	22 Nov
		(20)							
22.76	0.0	Alenka	Bikar	SLO	7.1.74	1		Ingolstadt	27 May
22.77	1.9	Ionela	Tîrlea	ROM	9.2.76	2	GP II	Rieti	2 Sep
22.78	1.8	Sina	Schielke	GER	19.5.81	1		Mannheim	16 Jun
22.79	0.5	Grit	Breuer	GER	16.2.72	2		Leverkusen	26 Aug
22.80	-0.3	Mary	Onyali-Omagbemi	NGR	3.2.68	3s3	WCh	Edmonton	9 Aug

Mark	Wind	Name		Nat	Born	Pos	Meet	Venue	Date
22.82	-0.3	Inger	Miller	USA	12.6.72	4s3	WCh	Edmonton	9 Aug
22.83	-1.4	Irina	Khabarova	RUS	18.3.66	2	NC	Tula	14 Jul
22.86	-0.7	Svetlana	Goncharenko	RUS	28.5.71	1	Znam	Tula	9 Jun
22.87	-2.4		Liu Xiaomei	CHN	11.1.72	1	EAsG	Osaka	26 May
22.88	0.2	Damayanthi	Dharsha	SRI	13.2.75	1h1	WCh	Edmonton	8 Aug
		(30)							
22.90	1.3	Lauren	Hewitt	AUS	25.11.78	1	NC	Brisbane	25 Mar
22.90	-0.1	Birgit	Rockmeier	GER	29.11.73	2	NC	Stuttgart	1 Jul
22.91	1.2	Natasha	Mayers	VIN	10.3.79	1		Walnut	12 May
22.91	0.8	Aïda	Diop	SEN	27.4.70	3h2	WCh	Edmonton	8 Aug
22.92	0.5	Veronica	Campbell	JAM-J	16.5.82	1	NSch	Kingston	7 Apr
22.92A	0.9	Felipa	Palacios	COL	1.12.75	1	Bol G	Ambato	15 Sep
22.93	1.4	Vernicha	James	GBR-J	6.6.84	1	EJ	Grosseto	21 Jul
22.93	-0.7	Johanna	Manninen	FIN	4.4.80	4h4	WCh	Edmonton	8 Aug
22.94		Lyubov	Perepelova	UZB	26.2.79	1		Kuala Lumpur	13 May
22.94	0.5	Kim	Gevaert	BEL	5.8.78	2	WUG	Beijing	31 Aug
		(40)							
22.97		Vida	Anim	GHA-J	7.12.83	1		Lagos	30 Jun
22.97	1.8	Nadjina	Kaltouma	CHA	16.11.76	1h1	Franc	Ottawa	22 Jul
22.98	-0.4	Kinshasa	Davis	USA	10.7.79	1		Los Angeles	5 May
22.98	-0.4	Manuela	Levorato	ITA	16.3.77	1	NC	Catania	8 Jul
22.99	-0.1	Chandra	Sturrup	BAH	12.9.71	3	GP II	Doha	18 May
22.99	1.3	Merlene	Frazer	JAM	27.12.73	3	NC	Kingston	23 Jun
23.02	-1.0	Sevatheda	Fynes	BAH	17.10.74	2		Bridgetown	19 May
23.02	0.3	Sarah	Reilly	IRL	3.7.73	3h3	WCh	Edmonton	8 Aug
23.03	-1.2	Oksana	Ekk	RUS	26.11.74	1	ECCp	Madrid	27 May
23.04	1.3	Sharon	Cripps	AUS	29.6.77	2	NC	Brisbane	25 Mar
		(50)							
23.04	0.9		Huang Mei	CHN	15.4.75	1	NC	Chengdu	1 Jul
23.05	1.7	Teneeshia	Jones	USA	28.1.79	1		Baton Rouge	14 Apr
23.05	-0.5	Michelle	Collins	USA	12.2.71	4	GP	Osaka	12 May
23.05	0.6	Lucimar	de Moura	BRA	22.3.74	1h1	NC	Rio de Janeiro	21 Jul
23.07	0.0	Angel	Perkins	USA-J	5.10.84	1	WY	Debrecen	15 Jul
23.07	-0.7	Fabé	Dia	FRA	14.2.77	6h4	WCh	Edmonton	8 Aug
23.08	1.9	Mireille	Donders	SUI	7.7.74	1h2		Genève	1 Jul
23.08	-1.4	Olga	Mishchenko	UKR	24.11.71	1		Banská Bystrica	31 Aug
23.09	1.1	Glory	Alozie	ESP	30.12.77	1		La Laguna	14 Jul
23.09	-0.2	Sanya	Richards	JAM-J	26.2.85	1h3		Sacramento	16 Jul
		(60)							
23.10A	0.4	Rosemar	Coelho Neto	BRA	2.1.77	1		Tunja	15 Jul
23.11	0.3	Anneisha	McLaughlin	JAM-J	6.1.86	1	NSch-y	Kingston	7 Apr
23.12	1.3	Nova	Peris	AUS	25.2.71	3	NC	Brisbane	25 Mar
23.12	1.0	Katharine	Merry	GBR	21.9.74	1		Austin	5 May
23.12	-1.4	Mariya	Enkina	RUS	.77	3	NC	Tula	14 Jul
23.13A	1.3	Liliana	Allen	MEX	24.5.70	1		Ciudad de México	1 Apr
23.13	0.4	Muna	Lee	USA	30.10.81	1	SEC	Columbia, SC	13 May
23.13	0.0	LaDonna	Antoine/Watkins	CAN	20.11.74	1	NC	Edmonton	24 Jun
23.14A	1.0	Joice	Maduaka	GBR	30.9.73	1		Pretoria	23 Mar
23.15	0.3	Louise	Ayétotché	CIV	3.6.75	4h3	WCh	Edmonton	8 Aug
		(70)							
23.16	1.1	Monique	Henderson	USA-J	18.2.83	1	MSR	Walnut	21 Apr
23.16	1.8		Yan Jiankui	CHN	19.3.76	1		Shanghai	7 May
23.17	1.9	Barbara	Petráhn	HUN	16.9.78	1		College Station	10 May
23.17	1.6	Tania	Woods	USA	23.9.80	1		Sacramento	19 May
23.17	-0.4	Monika	Gachevska	BUL	30.1.74	1		Sofia	27 May
23.17	1.5	Jacqueline	Poelman	NED	5.10.73	3	NA	Heusden	14 Jul
23.18	1.4	Amber	Robinson	USA	5.6.80	1		Gainesville	21 Apr
23.18	0.4	Demetria	Washington	USA	31.12.79	2	SEC	Columbia, SC	13 May
23.20	1.7	Myra	Combs	USA	17.4.79	2		Baton Rouge	14 Apr
23.21	0.4	Mikele	Barber	USA	4.10.80	3	SEC	Columbia, SC	13 May
		(80)							
23.21	0.0	Donica	Merriman	USA	24.1.79	1h1	Big 10	Bloomington	19 May
23.21	1.8	Torri	Edwards	USA	31.1.77	3h2	NC	Eugene	23 Jun
23.22A	1.0	Dikeledi	Morapane	RSA	12.3.76	2		Pretoria	23 Mar
23.23	1.0	Nanceen	Perry	USA	19.4.77	2=r1		Austin	5 May
23.23	-1.1	Angel	Patterson	USA	6.8.79	1		Nassau	9 Jun
23.23	0.0	Erica	Witter	CAN	10.12.76	1		Kitchener	9 Jun
23.23	0.0	Monique	Hennagan	USA	26.5.76	5	Gugl	Linz	20 Aug
23.24	0.0	Danielle	Carruthers	USA	22.12.79	2h1	Big 10	Bloomington	19 May
23.25	1.8	Ronetta	Smith	JAM	2.5.80	1rB		Baton Rouge	14 Apr
23.25	1.0	Lakeesha	White	USA	29.7.80	4r1		Austin	5 May
		(90)							

Mark	Wind	Name		Nat	Born	Pos	Meet	Venue	Date
23.25	1.8		Chen Yuxiang	CHN	28.2.78	1		Jinan	13 May
23.25	1.2	Shelia	Burrell	USA	15.1.72	1H		Talence	15 Sep
23.26	-0.4	Brianna	Glenn	USA	18.4.80	1	Pac-10	Berkeley	20 May
23.27	1.3	Jimyria	Hicks	USA	10.8.80	2		Norman	14 Apr
23.27	-0.1	Shekera	Weston	USA	1.9.77	2		Orlando	21 Apr
23.27	1.3		Xiao Lin	CHN	22.2.78	1		Ningbo	28 Apr
23.27	0.8	Monica	Twum	GHA	14.3.78	1	WAC	Fresno	19 May
23.27	-1.0	Sarah	Wilhelmy	GBR	2.2.80	3		Bridgetown	19 May
23.27	-0.4	Angela	Williams	USA	30.1.80	2	Pac-10	Berkeley	20 May
23.27	0.5	Natalya (100)	Roshchupkina	RUS	13.1.78	1H		Götzis	27 May
23.27	0.0	Nora	Güner	TUR	1.6.77	6	Gugl	Linz	20 Aug

Mark	Wind	Name		Nat	Born	Date
23.29	-0.4	Shakedia	Jones	USA	15.3.79	5 May
23.29	0.0	Rachelle	Boone	USA	30.6.81	19 May
23.30A	-0.1	Ilze	Jordaan	RSA	20.9.79	21 Apr
23.30	0.0	Nicole	Marahrens	GER	15.3.77	2 Jun
23.30	-0.1	Shanta	Ghosh	GER	3.1.75	1 Jul
23.30	-0.7	Supavadee	Khawpeag	THA	17.7.76	15 Sep
23.31	1.0	Allyson	Felix	USA-J	18.11.85	20 Apr
23.31	1.8	Katchi	Habel	GER-J	22.10.82	16 Jun
23.31	0.9		Chen Yueqin	CHN	25.2.77	1 Jul
23.31	1.2	Sylviane	Félix	FRA	31.10.77	1 Jul
23.31	-1.2	Jenny	Kallur	SWE	16.2.81	2 Sep
23.32	1.3	Francine	Landre	FRA	26.7.70	2 Sep
23.33	0.4	Stephanie	Durst	USA-J	6.1.82	13 May
23.34		Irina	Rosikhina	RUS	11.5.75	18 May
23.35	-0.6	Willisa	Heintz	USA	28.3.81	13 May
23.35	-0.2	Muriel	Hurtis	FRA	25.3.79	22 Aug
23.36	-1.3	Marina	Kislova	RUS	7.2.78	30 Mar
23.36	-0.5	Erica	Whipple	USA-J	4.12.82	12 May
23.36	1.4	Kisha	Jett	USA	11.2.75	2 Jun
23.36	0.0	Ólga	Kaidantzí	GRE	18.7.79	17 Jun
23.36A	-0.4	Vírgen	Benavides	CUB	31.12.74	21 Jul
23.39	1.0	Viktoria	Koviryeva	KAZ	17.12.75	24 Jun
23.39	1.2	Tatyana	Tkalich	UKR	30.5.75	24 Jun
23.39	-0.1	Marion	Wagner	GER	1.2.78	1 Jul
23.39	0.6		Chen Lisuo	CHN	10.4.81	21 Nov
23.40	1.8		Hu Zhenxia	CHN	22.1.76	13 May
23.40	-1.4	Natalya	Mikhaylovskaya	RUS	20.11.75	14 Jul
23.40	-1.4	Melanie	Paschke	GER	29.6.70	21 Jul
23.41		Monique	Hall	USA	9.10.80	28 Apr
23.41	1.4	Kudirat	Akhigbe	NGR	29.12.81	19 May
23.41	0.9		Ni Xiaoli	CHN-J	29.1.83	1 Jul
23.41	0.5	Makaridja	Sanganoko	CIV	8.5.80	23 Jul
23.42	1.8	Camille	Clarke	JAM	3.12.77	21 Apr
23.42	0.9	Christine	Arron	FRA	13.9.73	27 May
23.43A	1.1	Alexis	Joyce	USA-J	5.9.83	28 Apr
23.43	0.4	Me'Lisa	Barber	USA	4.10.80	13 May
23.43	0.5	Venolyn	Clarke ¶	CAN	11.7.67	24 Jun
23.43	1.0	Melinda	Gainsford-Taylor	AUS	1.10.71	9 Jul
23.43	1.2	Shani	Anderson	GBR	7.8.75	15 Jul
23.43	0.0	Endurance	Ojokolo	NGR	29.9.75	29 Aug
23.44	0.3	Foy	Williams	CAN	27.9.73	15 Jul
23.45	-1.3	Nakeya	Crutchfield	USA	16.9.80	5 May
23.45	0.0	Natalya	Sologub ¶	BLR	31.3.75	15 Jun
23.45	0.0	Amy	Spencer	GBR-J	19.9.85	15 Jul
23.46	0.6	Esther	Jones	USA	7.4.69	29 Apr
23.46	0.5	Lami	Oyewumi	CAN	3.11.76	24 Jun
23.46		Chinedu	Odozor	NGR	24.12.77	30 Jun
23.47	0.9	Erika	Suchovská	CZE	27.7.67	4 Jul
23.48	1.4	Kerine	Black	JAM	5.3.77	21 Apr
23.48	0.0	Consuella	Moore	USA	29.8.81	19 May
23.49	1.1	Benedicta	Ajudua	NGR	10.7.80	14 Jul
23.49	0.5	Mary	Onyemuwa	NGR	78	31 Aug
23.50	0.9	Chryste	Gaines	USA	14.9.70	27 May
23.50	-0.4	Ruth	Grajeda	MEX	31.7.80	8 Jul
23.51	2.0	Mercedes	Carnesolta	CUB	13.5.75	24 Mar
23.51	0.0	Ana María	López	CUB-J	28.8.82	26 May
23.52	0.6		Hou Xiufen	CHN	27.1.80	21 Nov
23.52	0.0		Zeng Xiujun	CHN	10.2.79	22 Nov
23.53	0.4	Marina	Trandenkova	RUS	7.1.67	4 Jun
23.53	-1.4	Anke	Feller	GER	26.9.71	21 Jul
23.54	-0.1	Caro	Hunt	NZL	10.1.78	11 Mar
23.54		Shavonda	Benjamin	USA-J	16.6.82	8 Apr
23.54		Ana H.	Peña	CUB-J	1.1.82	6 Jul
23.54	-0.3	Ciara	Sheehy	IRL	12.8.80	14 Jul
23.55	-1.0	Juliett (166)	Brown	JAM	76	19 May

Faulty wind gauge – possibly wind assisted

Mark		Name		Nat	Born	Pos	Meet	Venue	Date
22.92		Shelia	Burrell	USA	15.1.72	1H2	WCh	Edmonton	4 Aug

Indoors

Mark		Name		Nat	Born	Pos	Meet	Venue	Date
22.64		Juliet	Campbell	JAM	17.3.70	1	WI	Lisboa	10 Mar
22.97		Karin	Mayr	AUT	4.6.71	1		Wien	25 Feb
23.04#		Muna	Lee	USA	30.10.81	1h4	SEC	Lexington	24 Feb
23.06		Muriel	Hurtis	FRA	25.3.79	2s3	WI	Lisboa	9 Mar
23.08		Nora	Güner	TUR	1.6.77	2		Wien	12 Feb
23.24		Anastasiya	Kapachinskaya	RUS	21.11.79	1		Moskva	17 Feb

Mark	Name		Nat	Born	Date
23.31	Natalya	Mikhaylovskaya	RUS	20.11.75	17 Feb
23.35	Catherine	Murphy	GBR	21.9.75	28 Jan
23.50	Yulia	Sotnikova	RUS	18.11.70	17 Jan
23.54	Yulia	Nosova	RUS	21.4.78	4 Feb

Wind assisted

Mark	Wind	Name		Nat	Born	Pos	Meet	Venue	Date
22.26	3.3		Jones			1r1	Pre	Eugene	27 May
22.40	2.9		Jenkins			1	GP II	Gresham	3 Jun
22.53	3.8	Muna	Lee	USA	30.10.81	1h1	NCAA	Eugene	30 May
22.71	2.3	Mikele	Barber	USA	4.10.80	1h2	NCAA	Eugene	30 May
22.77	3.1	Oksana	Ekk	RUS	26.11.74	1		Torino	9 Jun
22.79	3.9	Kinshasa	Davis	USA	10.7.79	1h4	NCAA	Eugene	30 May
22.82	3.6	Natasha	Mayers	VIN	10.3.79	1		Azusa	14 Apr
22.83	4.8	Teneeshia	Jones	USA	28.1.79	1h3	SEC	Columbia, SC	11 May
22.84	4.2	Sarah	Wilhelmy	GBR	2.2.80	1		Arles	10 Jun
22.84	2.6	Natalya	Roshchupkina	RUS	13.1.78	1H		Ratingen	16 Jun
22.85	2.5	Angel	Perkins	USA-J	5.10.84	1		Sacramento	2 Jun
22.86	2.6	Nora	Güner	TUR	1.6.77	1	MedG	Tunis	13 Sep
22.87	7.3	Demetria	Washington	USA	31.12.79	1h2	SEC	Columbia, SC	11 May
22.92	2.6	Barbara	Petráhn	HUN	16.9.78	1h2	Big 12	College Station	18 May
22.92	2.1	Brianna	Glenn	USA	18.4.80	1	NCAA	Eugene	2 Jun
22.94	2.7	Myra	Combs	USA	17.4.79	2	USTCA	Austin	21 Apr
22.94	2.5	Rachelle	Boone	USA	30.6.81	1	Big 10	Bloomington	20 May

Mark	Wind	Name		Nat	Born	Pos	Meet	Venue	Date
22.98	2.6	Tiffany	Green	USA	15.12.81	1	Big 12	College Station	19 May
23.00	3.3	Torri	Edwards	USA	31.1.77	4	Pre	Eugene	27 May
23.01	2.2	Chryste	Gaines	USA	14.9.70	2	MSR	Walnut	22 Apr
23.01	2.6	Fabé	Dia	FRA	14.2.77	1		Montauban	17 Jul
23.04	2.7	Joice	Maduaka	GBR	30.9.73	1	BIG	Bedford	18 Jul
23.05	2.7	Stephanie	Durst	USA-J	6.1.82	3	USTCA	Austin	21 Apr
23.06	3.8	Me'Lisa	Barber	USA	4.10.80	2h1	NCAA	Eugene	30 May
23.09	3.9	Shekera	Weston	USA	1.9.77	3h4	NCAA	Eugene	30 May
23.09	2.5	Monique	Henderson	USA-J	18.2.83	1h4		Sacramento	1 Jun
23.09	2.7	Nova	Peris	AUS	25.2.71	2		Bedford	18 Jul
23.10	2.6	Sylviane	Félix	FRA	31.10.77	2		Montauban	17 Jul
23.11	2.2	Angel	Patterson	USA	6.8.79	1h3	Big 12	College Station	18 May
23.11	2.3	Angela	Williams	USA	30.1.80	2h3	NCAA	Eugene	30 May
23.12	2.6	Shani	Anderson	GBR	7.8.75	1		Istanbul	16 Jun
23.13	3.2	Aleah	Williams	USA	7.1.81	1		College Station	14 Apr
23.13	2.6	Jimyria	Hicks	USA	10.8.80	2	Big 12	College Station	19 May
23.14	2.2	Christine	Arron	FRA	13.9.73	3	MSR	Walnut	22 Apr
23.14	2.6	Muriel	Hurtis	FRA	25.3.79	3		Montauban	17 Jul
23.17	2.5	Consuella	Moore	USA	29.8.81	2	Big 10	Bloomington	20 May
23.20	3.8	Monica	Twum	GHA	14.3.78	4h1	NCAA	Eugene	30 May
23.22	2.2	Ssereta	Lafayette	USA	26.6.79	2h3	Big 12	College Station	18 May
23.22	2.1	Shalonda	Solomon	USA-J	19.12.85	1		Norwalk	19 May

Mark	Wind	Name		Nat	Born	Date
23.27	2.5	Allyson	Felix	USA-J	18.11.85	2 Jun
23.28		Monique	Hall	USA	9.10.80	12 May
23.30	7.3	Illia	Miles	USA-J	11.1.82	11 May
23.31	5.6	Peta-Gaye	Barrett	JAM	2.10.76	11 May
23.31	4.8	Shavonda	Benjamin	USA-J	16.6.82	11 May
23.33	2.9	Nolle	Graham	JAM	12.9.81	20 Apr
23.33	2.9	Alison	Culley	USA	1.3.80	20 May
23.35	2.1	Moushami	Robinson	USA	13.4.81	18 May
23.35	3.6	Catherine	Murphy	GBR	21.9.75	17 Jun
23.36	2.3	Caro	Hunt	NZL	10.1.78	24 Feb
23.38	2.7	Camille	Clarke	JAM	3.12.77	5 May
23.38	2.9	Janice	Davis	USA-J	27.10.84	16 Jun
23.40		Aleen	Bailey	JAM	25.11.80	12 May
23.40	2.9	LaShauntea	Moore	USA-J	31.7.83	16 Jun
23.40	2.6	Aksel	Gürcan	TUR	2.1.73	16 Jun
23.42	5.6	Delilah	Dillard	USA	17.11.78	11 May
23.45	4.7	Lana	Jekabsone	LAT	16.10.74	21 Apr
23.45	3.0	Odiah	Sidibé	FRA	13.1.70	1 Jul
23.46	2.6	Oluwaseum	Adetiba	NGR	27.5.79	18 May
23.46	2.9	Stephanie	Smith	USA-J	27.6.85	16 Jun
23.47	2.5	Carly	Knazze	USA	1.3.81	20 May
23.48	2.9	Falilat	Ogunkoya	NGR	12.5.68	3 Jun
23.49	2.7	Cheasa	Gibson	USA		5 May
23.50	2.2	LaKeisha	Backus	USA	15.12.76	22 Apr
23.50	2.6	Anita	Mormand	FRA	20.2.71	13 Sep
23.51		Elva	Goulbourne	JAM	21.1.80	12 May
23.52	4.0	Danielle	Kot	CAN	9.1.79	22 Apr
23.52	2.5	Lorraine	Dunlop	USA	12.3.79	20 May
23.53	3.0	Delphine	Combe	FRA	6.12.74	1 Jul

Low altitude bests

Mark	Wind	Name	Pos	Meet	Venue	Date
22.54	1.2	Mothersill	1h5	WCh	Edmonton	8 Aug
23.18	1.1	Palacios	2		La Laguna	14 Jul
23.25	-1.5	Coelho Neto	2	NC	Rio de Janeiro	22 Jul
23.32	0.2	L Allen				8 Aug
23.42	1.8	Morapane				3 Mar

Hand Timing

Mark	Wind	Name		Nat	Born	Pos	Meet	Venue	Date
22.0		Natalya	Mikhaylovskaya	RUS	20.11.75	1		Irkutsk	28 Jul
22.4		Natalya	Safronnikova	BLR	28.2.73	1		Brest	22 Jul
22.6	-0.4	Anastasiya	Kapachinskaya	RUS	21.11.79	1		Moskva	23 Jun
22.9		Vida	Anim	GHA-J	7.12,83	1		Kumasi	28 May
22.9		Irina	Khabarova	RUS	18.3.66	1		Yekaterinburg	29 May

Mark	Wind	Name		Nat	Born	Date
23.2		Yekaterina	Stankevich	BLR	5.6.77	18 May
23.2		Olga	Khalandyreva	RUS	13.11.81	30 May
23.2	1.7	Shani	Anderson	GBR	7.8.75	25 Aug
23.3	0.5	Danielle	Perpoli	ITA	7.3.68	20 May
23.3	0.2	Yelena	Goncharova	RUS	.80	27 May
23.3		Valma	Bass	SKN	12.3.74	24 Jun

Wind assisted

Mark	Wind	Name		Nat	Born	Pos	Meet	Venue	Date
22.6	3.0	Myra	Combs	USA	17.4.79	1		Baton Rouge	18 May
23.0	3.0	Ronetta	Smith	JAM	2.5.80	2		Baton Rouge	18 May
23.3	3.3	Amy	Spencer	GBR-J	19.9.85	1	NC-j	Bedford	1 Jul

JUNIORS

See main list for top 7 juniors. 14 performances by 9 women to 23.31. Additional marks and further juniors:

Name	Mark	Wind	Pos	Meet	Venue	Date	Mark	Wind	Pos	Meet	Venue	Date
Campbell	22.93	-1.6	1	Carifta	Bridgetown	16 Apr						
James	23.30	1.8	2		Mannheim	16 Jun						
Perkins	23.14	1.1	1		Norwalk	25 May	23.24w	4.6	1	NSch	Exeter	7 Jul
	23.14		1		Walnut	9 Jun	23.19	1.6	2h1	NC	Eugene	23 Jun

Mark	Wind	Name		Nat	Born	Pos	Meet	Venue	Date
23.31	1.0	Allyson	Felix	USA	18.11.85	2	MSR	Walnut	20 Apr
23.31	1.8	Katchi	Habel	GER	22.10.82	3		Mannheim	16 Jun
23.33	0.4	Stephanie	Durst	USA	6.1.82	5	SEC	Columbia, SC	13 May
23.36	-0.5	Erica	Whipple	USA	4.12.82	1		Coral Springs	12 May
23.41	0.9		Ni Xiaoli	CHN	29.1.83	3	NC	Chengdu	1 Jul
23.43A	1.1	Alexis	Joyce	USA	5.9.83	1		Denver	28 Apr
23.45	0.0	Amy	Spencer	GBR	19.9.85	2	WY	Debrecen	15 Jul
23.51	0.0	Ana María	López	CUB	28.8.82	1	NC	La Habana	26 May
23.54		Shavonda	Benjamin	USA	16.6.82	2		Gainesville	8 Apr
23.54		Ana H.	Peña	CUB	1.1.82	2	NC-j	Santiago de Cuba	6 Jul
23.59	1.0	Marshavet	Hooker	USA	25.9.84	1		Austin	12 May
23.59	0.1	Olga	Levenkova	RUS	84	H		Cheboksary	20 Jun
23.59	0.5	LaShauntea	Moore (20)	USA	31.7.83	2		Sacramento	28 Jul

Mark	Wind	Name		Nat	Born	Pos	Meet	Venue	Date

Wind assisted see main lists for four women – six performances to 23.27w

Mark	Wind	Name		Nat	Born	Pos	Meet	Venue	Date
23.27w	2.5	Allyson	Felix	USA	18.11.85	2		Sacramento	2 Jun
23.30w	7.3	Illia	Miles	USA	11.1.82	2h2	SEC	Columbia	11 May
23.31w	4.8	Shavonda	Benjamin	USA	16.6.82	2h3	SEC	Columbia	11 May
23.38w	2.9	Janice	Davis	USA	27.10.84	1	NC-j	Richmond	16 Jun
23.40w	2.9	LaShauntea	Moore	USA	31.7.83	2	NC-j	Richmond	16 Jun
23.46w	2.9	Stephanie	Smith	USA	27.6.85	3	NC-j	Richmond	16 Jun
23.55	4.7	Ashuanta	McCormick	USA	30.1.82	2		Romeoville	21 Apr
23.58	3.7	Thatiana	Ignâcio	BRA	2.7.83	1	NC-I	Londrina	30 Sep
23.59	2.5		Qin Wangping	CHN	16.6.82	2		Zhongshan	22 Apr

300 METRES

Mark	Name		Nat	Born	Pos	Meet	Venue	Date
35.68	Marion	Jones	USA	12.10.75	1	MSR	Walnut	22 Apr
35.92	Ana	Guevara	MEX	4.3.77	1	GPII	Gateshead	19 Aug
36.08	Cydonie	Mothersill	CAY	19.3.78	2	GPII	Gateshead	19 Aug
36.10	Nadjina	Kaltouma	CHA	16.11.76	3	GPII	Gateshead	19 Aug
36.52	Monique	Hennagan	USA	26.5.76	4	GPII	Gateshead	19 Aug
36.58	Manuela	Levorato	ITA	16.3.77	1		Viareggio	22 Aug
36.61	Kelli	White	USA	1.4.77	2	MSR	Walnut	22 Apr
36.70	Olesya	Zykina	RUS	7.10.80	5	GPII	Gateshead	19 Aug
36.76	Birgit	Rockmeier	GER	29.11.73	6	GPII	Gateshead	19 Aug

Mark	Name		Nat	Born	Date
37.02A	Florence	Ekpo-Umoh	GER	27.12.77	30 Jul
37.07	Karen	Shinkins	IRL	15.10.76	15 Aug
37.08	Sinead	Dudgeon	GBR	9.7.76	22 Apr
37.13A	Shanta	Ghosh	GER	3.1.75	30 Jul
37.18	Mireille	Nguimgo	CMR	7.11.76	22 Aug
37.27	Donna	Fraser	GBR	7.11.72	19 Aug
37.30	Sarah	Reilly	IRL	3.7.73	19 Aug
37.42	Danielle	Perpoli	ITA	7.3.68	22 Aug
37.45	Kudirat	Akhigbe	NGR	29.12.81	18 Apr

400 METRES

Mark	Name		Nat	Born	Pos	Meet	Venue	Date
49.59	Katharine	Merry	GBR	21.9.74	1	GP	Athína	11 Jun
49.78	Grit	Breuer	GER	16.2.72	1	NC	Stuttgart	30 Jun
49.86	Ami Mbacké	Thiam	SEN	10.11.76	1	WCh	Edmonton	7 Aug
49.88	Lorraine	Fenton	JAM	8.9.73	2	WCh	Edmonton	7 Aug
49.97	Ana	Guevara	MEX	4.3.77	3	WCh	Edmonton	7 Aug
50.11		Guevara			1		Stellenbosch	30 Mar
50.15	Olesya	Zykina	RUS	7.10.80	1	NC	Tula	13 Jul
50.18A		Guevara			1		Pretoria	23 Mar
50.21		Thiam			1s2	WCh	Edmonton	6 Aug
50.25A		Guevara			1		Roodepoort	16 Mar
50.32		Breuer			1s1	WCh	Edmonton	6 Aug
50.32		Guevara			1	GWG	Brisbane	4 Sep
50.35		Guevara			1		Leverkusen	26 Aug
50.36	Heide	Seyerling	RSA	19.8.76	2	GP	Athína	11 Jun
50.38	Nadjina	Kaltouma	CHA	16.11.76	2s2	WCh	Edmonton	6 Aug
50.44		Merry			1		Milano	6 Jun
50.49		Breuer			1	ECp-S	Bremen	23 Jun
50.49		Breuer			4	WCh	Edmonton	7 Aug
50.50	Falilat	Ogunkoya	NGR	12.5.68	3s2	WCh	Edmonton	6 Aug
50.58		Guevara			1s3	WCh	Edmonton	6 Aug
50.59		Kaltouma			3	GP	Athína	11 Jun
50.59		Zykina			2s1	WCh	Edmonton	6 Aug
50.60		Breuer			1		Nürnberg	17 Jun
50.61		Fenton			2s3	WCh	Edmonton	6 Aug
50.63	Mikele	Barber (10)	USA	4.10.80	1	SEC	Columbia, SC	13 May
50.64A		Seyerling			2		Roodepoort	16 Mar
50.66	Michelle	Collins	USA	12.2.71	1	GP II	Sevilla	8 Jun
50.67		Merry			1	BrGP	London (CP)	22 Jul
50.68		Seyerling			2		Stellenbosch	30 Mar
50.69		Fenton			1	NC	Kingston	23 Jun
	(30/11)							
50.71	Sandie	Richards	JAM	6.11.68	4	GP	Athína	11 Jun
50.71	Mireille	Nguimgo	CMR	7.11.76	3s1	WCh	Edmonton	6 Aug
50.79	LaTasha	Richardson	USA	23.8.76	1	NC	Eugene	23 Jun
50.80	Jearl	Miles-Clark	USA	4.9.66	1r2		Indianapolis	28 Jul
50.81A	Olga	Kotlyarova	RUS	12.4.76	1		Pretoria	23 Mar
50.86	Suziann	Reid	USA	14.1.77	1r1		Indianapolis	28 Jul
50.87	Zulia	Calatayud	CUB	9.11.79	1		Alcalá de Henares	30 Jun
50.97	Anastasiya	Kapachinskaya	RUS	21.11.79	2	NC	Tula	13 Jul
50.98	Monique	Hennagan	USA	26.5.76	5s2	WCh	Edmonton	6 Aug
	(20)							
51.00	Yuliya	Sotnikova	RUS	18.11.70	2	Znam	Tula	9 Jun

Mark		Name		Nat	Born	Pos	Meet	Venue	Date
51.05		Demetria	Washington	USA	31.12.79	1h1	WUG	Beijing	27 Aug
51.10		Daimí	Pernía	CUB	27.12.76	1		Getafe	10 Jul
51.13		Florence	Ekpo-Umoh	GER	27.12.77	2	NC	Stuttgart	30 Jun
51.19		Natalya	Antyukh	RUS	26.6.81	3	Znam	Tula	9 Jun
51.20		Irina	Rosikhina	RUS	11.5.75	3	NC	Tula	13 Jul
51.21		Francine	Landre	FRA	26.7.70	2	ECp-S	Bremen	23 Jun
51.25		Shanta	Ghosh	GER	3.1.75	3	NC	Stuttgart	30 Jun
51.34		Monique	Henderson	USA-J	18.2.83	1		Sacramento	2 Jun
51.35			Bu Fanfang	CHN	10.2.78	1	NG	Guangzhou	18 Nov
		(30)							
51.37		Karen	Shinkins	IRL	15.10.76	3h5	WCh	Edmonton	5 Aug
51.40			Chen Yuxiang	CHN	28.2.78	2	NG	Guangzhou	18 Nov
51.41		Claudia	Marx	GER	16.9.78	4	NC	Stuttgart	30 Jun
51.42		Debbie-Ann	Parris	JAM	24.3.73	1		Baton Rouge	14 Apr
51.47		Anna	Kozak	BLR	22.6.74	1h	NC	Brest	7 Jun
51.47		Otilia	Ruicu	ROM	20.8.78	2		Funchal	30 Jun
51.50		Allison	Beckford	JAM	8.5.79	1h3	NCAA	Eugene	31 May
51.52		Olabisi	Afolabi	NGR	31.10.75	2	GP II	Sevilla	8 Jun
51.55		Anja	Rücker	GER	20.12.72	5	NC	Stuttgart	30 Jun
51.60		Kudirat	Akhigbe	NGR	29.12.81	3	GP II	Sevilla	8 Jun
		(40)							
51.61		Natalya	Sologub ¶	BLR	31.3.75	1	Kuso	Warszawa	17 Jun
51.74	mx	Jana	Pittman	AUS-J	9.11.82	1		Canberra	8 Dec
51.77		Donna	Fraser	GBR	7.11.72	6s3	WCh	Edmonton	6 Aug
51.79		Moushami	Robinson	USA	13.4.81	1h1	NCAA	Eugene	31 May
51.83		Damayanthi	Dharsha	SRI	13.2.75	7s1	WCh	Edmonton	6 Aug
51.84		Catherine	Murphy	GBR	21.9.75	4	GP II	Sevilla	8 Jun
51.85		Barbara	Petráhn	HUN	16.9.78	1	Big 12	College Station	19 May
51.85		Tsvetelina	Kirilova	BUL	14.7.77	1		Sofia	27 May
51.88		Alice	Kun	HUN	7.6.76	1		Gdansk	14 Jul
51.91		Catherine	Scott	JAM	24.8.73	2h1	NC	Kingston	22 Jun
		(50)							
51.92		Ronetta	Smith	JAM	2.5.80	1		Houston	31 Mar
51.92		Grazyna	Prokopek	POL	20.4.77	4h4	WCh	Edmonton	5 Aug
51.93		Doris	Jacob	NGR	16.12.81	1s	NC	Lagos	21 Jul
51.94		Natalya	Shevtsova	RUS	17.12.74	4	NC	Tula	13 Jul
51.96		Aliann	Pompey	GUY	9.3.78	7s3	WCh	Edmonton	6 Aug
51.99		Allison	Curbishley	GBR	3.6.76	5	ECp-S	Bremen	23 Jun
52.02		Samantha	George	CAN	7.8.76	1		Gosier	1 May
52.03		Charmaine	Howell	JAM	13.3.75	3h1	NC	Kingston	22 Jun
52.03		Yudalis	Díaz	CUB	20.9.79	2		Madrid	7 Jul
52.04		Nova	Peris	AUS	25.2.71	5	Herc	Monaco	20 Jul
		(60)							
52.05		Lee	McConnell	GBR	9.10.78	3s2	WUG	Beiing	28 Aug
52.06		Natalya	Khrushchelyova	RUS	20.3.73	5	NC	Tula	13 Jul
52.07		Birgit	Rockmeier	GER	29.11.73	2		Malles	14 Jul
52.10		Jitka	Burianová	CZE	17.1.77	1	ECCp	Madrid	26 May
52.10		Alyona	Petrova	TKM	8.8.79	1		Almaty	24 Jun
52.11		Olga	Mishchenko	UKR	24.11.71	1	NC	Kiev	1 Jul
52.11		Stephanie	Smith	USA-J	27.6.85	1		Sacramento	29 Jul
52.12		Foy	Williams	CAN	27.9.73	1	NC	Edmonton	23 Jun
52.12		Zana	Minina	LTU	11.6.77	3s1	WUG	Beiing	28 Aug
52.13		Danielle	Perpoli	ITA	7.3.68	7	ECp-S	Bremen	23 Jun
		(70)							
52.13		Carmo	Tavares	POR	27.4.74	4		Madrid	7 Jul
52.17		K. Mathews	Beenamol	IND	15.8.75	5h4	WCh	Edmonton	5 Aug
52.18		Angel	Perkins	USA-J	5.10.84	2		Sacramento	2 Jun
52.18		Me'Lisa	Barber	USA	4.10.80	3rB		Indianapolis	28 Jul
52.20		Nicole	Marahrens	GER	15.3.77	2h2	NC	Stuttgart	29 Jun
52.23		Rosemary	Okafor	NGR	22.5.81	3		Port-Harcourt	19 May
52.24			Zhong Shaoting	CHN	30.1.80	3	NG	Guangzhou	18 Nov
52.27		Lesley	Owusu	GBR	21.12.78	1	NC	Birmingham	15 Jul
52.27		Marie-Louise	Bévis	FRA	12.10.72	2		La Chaux-de-Fonds	19 Aug
52.28		LaDonna	Antoine/Watkins	CAN	20.11.74	2		Gosier	1 May
		(80)							
52.28		Julia	Alba	ESP	30.5.72	5		Madrid	7 Jul
52.29		Antonina	Yefremova	UKR	19.7.81	1	EU23	Amsterdam	13 Jul
52.30		Tatyana	Levina	RUS	28.2.77	1		Poznan	8 Jun
52.31		Anneisha	McLaughlin	JAM-J	6.1.86	1		Kingston	17 Mar
52.31		Donna	Howard	USA	28.8.74	1		Atlanta	2 Jun
52.31		Sheryl	Morgan	JAM-J	6.11.83	1		Nassau	9 Jun

Mark	Name		Nat	Born	Pos	Meet	Venue	Date
52.32	Tia	Trent	USA	25.7.79	2h3	NCAA	Eugene	31 May
52.35	Julia	Duporty	CUB	9.2.71	2		Alcalá de Henares	30 Jun
52.37	Gloria	Nwosu	NGR-J	24.12.84	1		Kumasi	28 May
52.38	Hajarat	Yusuf	NGR-J	.82	1		Kaduna	2 Jun
	(90)							
52.39	Svetlana	Bodritskaya	KAZ	7.11.71	2	EAsG	Osaka	24 May
52.40	Liz	Grow	USA	17.10.79	1h2		Piscataway	5 May
52.44	Olga	Maksimova	RUS	9.8.76	4rA	Znam	Tuka	9 Jun
52.44		Zhang Hengyun	CHN	25.10.74	4	NG	Guangzhou	18 Nov
52.44		Yan Jiankui	CHN	19.3.76	5	NG	Guangzhou	18 Nov
52.46	Carolyn	Jackson	USA	6.12.77	4h1	NC	Eugene	22 Jun
52.46	Anita	Mormand	FRA	20.2.71	2h2	NC	Saint-Etienne	30 Jun
52.47	Svetlana	Usovich	BLR	14.10.80	1	NC	Brest	8 Jun
52.48	Marina	Grishakova	RUS	1.7.78	7	NC	Tula	13 Jul
52.49	Chandra	Burns	USA	4.8.75	2		Durham	7 Apr
	(100)							
52.49	Tatyana	Movchan	UKR	19.9.70	2	NC	Kiev	1 Jul

52.50	Natalya	Lavshuk	RUS	1.1.80	22 Jun
52.51	Natalya	Zhuravlyova	UKR	21.4.80	1 Jul
52.54	Claudine	Komgang	CMR	21.2.74	26 Apr
52.56	Kim	Batten	USA	29.3.69	14 Apr
52.56	Anke	Feller	GER	26.9.71	29 Jun
52.56	Nancy	Kette	GER	24.7.77	30 Jun
52.56	Olga	Goncharova	RUS	77	13 Jul
52.57	Irina	Khlyustova	BLR	14.6.78	8 Jun
52.57	Jane	Arnott	NZL	3.1.76	5 Aug
52.61		Gao Lihua	CHN-J	20.7.84	18 Nov
52.62	Surita	Febbraio	RSA	27.12.73	6 Jul
52.63	Michelle	Burgher	JAM	12.3.77	22 Jun
52.64	Hazel-Ann	Regis	GRN	1.2.81	14 Apr
52.64	Hrísa	Goudenoúdi	GRE	28.3.77	11 Jun
52.64	Maria Laura	Almirão	BRA	20.9.77	20 Jul
52.65	Yelena	Rurak	UKR	7.2.72	23 Jun
52.66	Norfalia	Carabalí	ESP	21.1.64	7 Jul
52.67	Rebecca	Wardell	NZL	21.12.77	24 Mar
52.67	Irina	Anashkina	RUS	31.1.72	17 May
52.68	Helen	Frost	GBR	12.3.74	9 Jun
52.68	Aneta	Lemiesz	POL	17.1.81	17 Jun
52.69	Adia	McKinnon	TRI	18.4.81	20 May
52.70	Faith	Rein	USA	7.4.81	31 May
52.70	Christine	Amertil	BAH	18.8.79	22 Jun
52.71		Huang Xiaoxiao	CHN-J	15.2.85	21 Apr
52.72	Onica	Fraser	GUY	25.9.80	20 May
52.72	Omolade	Akinremi	NGR	13.9.74	20 Jul
52.73	Galina	Misiruk	UKR	18.12.70	17 Jun
52.73	Daniela	Georgieva	BUL	22.9.69	7 Jul
52.73A	Norma	Gonzalez	COL-J	11.8.82	13 Sep
52.75	Helen	Thieme	GBR	28.9.81	13 Jul
52.76	Luciana	Mendes	BRA	26.7.71	19 May
52.77	Nakiya	Johnson	USA	12.5.81	5 May
52.77	Saraque	Whittaker	USA-J	10.1.82	19 May
52.80	Clementine	Bewouda	CMR	19.10.78	30 Jun
52.80	Jerrika	Chapple	USA-J	11.9.84	14 Jul
52.81	Shekera	Weston	USA	1.9.77	21 Apr
52.82	Angel	Patterson	USA	6.8.79	5 May
52.83	Mariya	Lisnichenko	RUS	27.12.80	14 Jun
52.84	Ngozi	Nwokocha	NGR-J	28.9.86	3 Jun
52.84	Jacqueline	Poelman	NED	5.10.73	18 Jul
52.86	Tina	Johnson	USA	24.7.78	20 May
52.86A	Tamsyn	Lewis	AUS	20.7.78	26 Jul
52.91	Libania	Grenot	CUB-J	12.7.83	25 May
52.91	Sonia	Brito	AUS	10.6.79	12 Aug
52.94	Svetlana	Badrankova	KAZ	25.3.77	21 Apr
52.94	Tatyana	Firova	RUS-J	10.10.82	20 Jul
52.94		Xiao Hongfan	CHN-J	6.1.83	17 Nov
52.95	Kazue	Kakinuma	JPN	16.6.74	24 May
52.96	Nerelys	Rodríguez	ITA	21.7.78	26 May
52.96	Olga	Fomenko	UKR	3.8.75	1 Jul
52.97	Michelle	Davis	USA	4.9.80	6 May
52.97	Aoutef	Ben Hassine	TUN	5.4.80	19 Jul
52.99	Anita	Edwards	USA	16.4.80	31 Mar
52.99	Stephanie	Graf	AUT	26.4.73	23 Jun
53.01	Lindsay	Lochhead	CAN	7.5.74	19 Jul
53.02	Claudia Rosa	Vargas	DOM		14 Jul
53.02		Zhou Wei	CHN-J	23.1.82	17 Nov
53.07	Brigita	Langerholc	SLO	23.7.76	23 Jun
53.07	Danielle	Kot	CAN	9.1.79	23 Jun
53.08	Catherine	Obilor	NGR-J	17.7.85	28 May
53.08		Xiang Chirong	CHN	20.6.74	17 Nov
53.10	Aleksandra	Pieluzek	POL	4.4.79	17 Jun
53.11	Katerina	Dressler	AUS	21.9.81	1 Mar
53.12	Shontee	Bryant	USA	20.1.78	19 May
53.13	Yana	Manuilova	UKR	9.12.71	17 May
53.14	Brandy	Spencer	USA	7.10.78	28 Apr
53.14	Sasha	Spencer	USA	4.8.79	5 May
53.17	Licretia	Sibley	USA-J	3.8.83	27 Apr
53.17	Monica	Bumbescu	ROM	21.8.77	9 Jun
53.19	Celena	Clarke	JAM	3.1.75	6 May
53.19	Yekaterina	Kulikova	RUS	7.11.68	6 Jun
53.20	Trenace	Elliott	USA-J	21.8.82	19 May
53.22	Yuliya	Nosova	RUS	21.4.78	1 Jul
53.23	Makiko	Yoshida	JPN	16.7.76	15 Sep
53.25	Yvonne	Teichmann	GER	11.4.77	26 May
53.25	Manjeet	Kaur	IND-J	2.4.82	4 Jul
53.26	Anita	Bragger	SUI	6.10.75	1 Jul
53.26	Svetlana	Klyuka	RUS	.78	27 Jul
53.27	Jayna	Smith	USA	8.3.78	20 May
53.27	Malgorzata	Pskit	POL	25.5.76	14 Jul
53.28	Yvonne	Harrison	PUR	2.12.75	10 Jul
53.29	Lisa	Miller	GBR-J	13.1.83	20 Jul
	(184)				

Hand timed

52.6	Yelena	Budnik	BLR	9.5.76	29 May
52.9	Cynthia	Ngozi	NGR-J	28.9.86	3 Jun

Indoors

50.42	Olga	Kotlyarova	RUS	12.4.76	1rA		Moskva	27 Jan
50.53		Merry			1	Euro	Birmingham	18 Feb
51.99	Helena	Fuchsová	CZE	3.6.65	1	NC	Praha	18 Feb
52.15	Lesley	Owusu	GBR	21.12.78	1h1	NCAA	Fayetteville	9 Mar
52.25	Yuliya	Nosova	RUS	21.4.78	4	NC	Moskva	17 Feb
52.40	Yekaterina	Kulikova	RUS	7.11.68	1rB		Moskva	27 Jan
52.47	Sinead	Dudgeon	GBR	9.7.76	2	NC	Birmingham	27 Jan

52.64	Ionela	Tirlea	ROM	9.2.76	4 Mar
52.75	Deon	Hemmings	JAM	9.10.68	21 Feb
52.90	Anna	Tkach	RUS	17.4.75	3 Feb
52.96	Lorraine	Graham	JAM	8.9.73	2 Feb
53.16	Gelena	Bodunova	RUS	76	16 Feb
53.19	Heike	Meissner	GER	29.1.70	9 Feb
53.19	Tasha	Downing	USA	5.7.70	3 Mar
53.19	Peta-Gaye	Gayle	JAM	19.1.79	9 Mar
53.24	Natalya	Sharova	RUS	4.10.72	27 Jan
53.26	Nadja	Petersen	SWE	14.7.78	27 Jan

Low altitude bests

51.07	Kotlyarova	3	Stellenbosch	30 Mar
53.01	Lewis	3	Bedford	18 Jul

Mark	Name		Nat	Born	Pos	Meet	Venue	Date
Drugs Disqualification								
51.43	Natalya	Sologub ¶	BLR	31.3.75	5s1	WCh	Edmonton	6 Aug

JUNIORS

See main list for top 8 juniors. 11 performances by 8 women to 52.39. Additional marks and further juniors:

S Smith 52.19 1 WY Debrecen 15 Jul 52.38 1 NC Richmond 17 Jun
Nwosu 52.39 1 Lagos 7 Jul

Mark	Name		Nat	Born	Pos	Meet	Venue	Date
52.61		Gao Lihua	CHN	20.7.84	6	NG	Guangzhou	18 Nov
52.71		Huang Xiaoxiao	CHN	15.2.85	1		Zhongshan	21 Apr
52.73A	Norma	Gonzalez	COL	11.8.82	1	BolG	Ambato	13 Sep
52.77	Saraque	Whittaker	USA	10.1.82	1rB		Atlanta	19 May
52.80	Jerrika	Chapple	USA	11.9.84	2	WY	Debrecen	14 Jul
52.84	Ngozi	Nwokocha	NGR	28.9.86	3		Kaduna	3 Jun
52.91	Libania	Grenot	CUB	12.7.83	2	NC	La Habana	25 May
52.94	Tatyana	Firova	RUS	10.10.82	1	EJ	Grosseto	20 Jul
52.94		Xiao Hongfan	CHN	6.1.83	2h1	NG	Guangzhou	17 Nov
53.02		Zhou Wei	CHN	23.1.82	3h1	NG	Guangzhou	17 Nov
53.08	Catherine	Obilor	NGR	17.7.85	2		Kumasi	28 May
53.17	Licretia	Sibley (20)	USA	3.8.83	1		Commerce	27 Apr
52.9 hand	Cynthia	Ngozi	NGR	28.9.86	1		Kaduna	3 Jun

600 METRES

Mark	Name		Nat	Born	Pos	Meet	Venue	Date
1:26.35mx	Adrienne	McIvor	IRL	2.9.70	1		Gold Coast	18 Nov
1:27.6+	Maria Lurdes	Mutola	MOZ	27.10.72	1	in 800	Zürich	17 Aug
Indoors								
1:26.72	Anna	Tkach	RUS	17.4.75	1		Moskva	6 Jan
1:27.1+	Maria Lurdes	Mutola	MOZ	27.10.72	1	in 800	Liévin	25 Feb
1:27.2+	Stephanie	Graf	AUT	26.4.73	2	in 800	Liévin	25 Feb

800 METRES

Mark	Name		Nat	Born	Pos	Meet	Venue	Date
1:56.85	Maria Lurdes	Mutola	MOZ	27.10.72	1	WK	Zürich	17 Aug
1:57.11		Mutola			1	Herc	Monaco	20 Jul
1:57.17		Mutola			1	WCh	Edmonton	12 Aug
1:57.20	Stephanie	Graf	AUT	26.4.73	2	WCh	Edmonton	12 Aug
1:57.35	Letitia	Vriesde	SUR	5.10.64	3	WCh	Edmonton	12 Aug
1:57.46		Graf			1	VD	Bruxelles	24 Aug
1:57.59	Svetlana	Cherkasova	RUS	20.5.78	1	NC	Tula	15 Jul
1:57.88	Kelly	Holmes	GBR	19.4.70	2	WK	Zürich	17 Aug
1:57.90		Holmes			2	VD	Bruxelles	24 Aug
1:57.95		Mutola			3	VD	Bruxelles	24 Aug
1:57.97	Natalya	Tsyganova	RUS	7.2.71	2	NC	Tula	15 Jul
1:57.98		Graf			3	WK	Zürich	17 Aug
1:58.02	Irina	Mistyukevich	RUS	17.6.77	3	NC	Tula	15 Jul
1:58.10		Holmes			1	GPII	Gateshead	19 Aug
1:58.20		Graf			1	Bisl	Oslo	13 Jul
1:58.22		Graf			1	BrGP	London (CP)	22 Jul
1:58.34	Faith	Macharia	KEN	9.2.76	2	Herc	Monaco	20 Jul
1:58.39	Diane	Cummins	CAN	19.1.74	1	GP II	Rieti	2 Sep
1:58.44		Graf			1	GGala	Roma	29 Jun
1:58.57		Cummins			1		Padova	26 Aug
1:58.60	Zulia	Calatayud (10)	CUB	9.11.79	3	Herc	Monaco	20 Jul
1:58.62	Ivonne	Teichmann	GER	11.4.77	4	VD	Bruxelles	24 Aug
1:58.70		Mutola			2	Bisl	Oslo	13 Jul
1:58.7	Natalya	Gorelova	RUS	18.4.73	1		Moskva	23 Jun
1:58.71	Jolanda	Ceplak	SLO	12.9.76	1		Nürnberg	17 Jun
1:58.76		Mutola			1	GWG	Brisbane	5 Sep
1:58.77	Olga	Raspopova	RUS	27.12.78	5=?	VD	Bruxelles	24 Aug
1:58.77		Tsyganova			5=?	VD	Bruxelles	24 Aug
1:58.80		Mistyukevich			1	Athl	Lausanne	4 Jul
1:58.84		Tsyganova			2	Athl	Lausanne	4 Jul
	(30/14)							
1:59.07	Regina	Jacobs	USA	28.8.63	4	Athl	Lausanne	4 Jul
1:59.15	Tina	Paulino	MOZ	7.7.73	1	GP II	Gresham	3 Jun
1:59.29	Luciana	Mendes	BRA	26.7.71	6	Athl	Lausanne	4 Jul
1:59.61	Charmaine	Howell	JAM	13.3.75	3	GP II	Gresham	3 Jun
1:59.63	Tsvetelina	Kirilova	BUL	14.7.77	1		Luzern	27 Jun
1:59.66	Anita	Brägger	SUI	6.10.72	7	Athl	Lausanne	4 Jul
	(20)							
1:59.76	Mayte	Martínez	ESP	17.5.76	1	NA	Heusden	14 Jul
1:59.83	Galina	Misiruk	UKR	18.12.70	1	NC	Kiev	2 Jul

Mark	Name		Nat	Born	Pos	Meet	Venue	Date
1:59.86	Brigita	Langerholc	SLO	23.7.76	6	GGala	Roma	29 Jun
1:59.88	Helena	Fuchsová	CZE	3.6.65	8	Herc	Monaco	20 Jul
1:59.95	Natalya	Dukhnova	BLR	16.7.66	3	ECp-S	Bremen	23 Jun
1:59.95	Hazel	Clark	USA	3.10.77	1		Indianapolis	28 Jul
2:00.19	Mardrea	Hyman	JAM	22.12.72	5	GP II	Gresham	3 Jun
2:00.2	Yuliya	Kosenkova	RUS	28.3.73	4		Moskva	23 Jun
2:00.29	Lwiza Msyani	John	TAN	18.5.80	2	GP	Doha	18 May
2:00.38	Jennifer	Toomey	USA	19.12.71	1		Cuxhaven	21 Jul
	(30)							
2:00.4	Olga	Nelyubova	RUS	12.6.64	5		Moskva	23 Jun
2:00.46	Oksana	Zbrozhek	RUS	12.1.78	3	GP II	Rieti	2 Sep
2:00.47	Mina	Aït Hammou	MAR	18.7.78	4		Nürnberg	17 Jun
2:00.65	Tatyana	Rodionova	RUS	27.8.80	1	Kuts	Moskva	28 Jul
2:00.77		Lin Na	CHN	18.1.80	1	NG	Guangzhou	22 Nov
2:00.81A	Agnes	Samaria	NAM	11.8.72	1		Roodepoort	16 Mar
2:00.81	Yelena	Afanasyeva	RUS	1.3.67	1		Stellenbosch	30 Mar
2:00.84	Olga	Komyagina	RUS	10.2.74	1rB	NC	Tula	15 Jul
2:00.86	Tamsyn	Lewis	AUS	20.7.78	7h1	WCh	Edmonton	9 Aug
2:00.91	Svetlana	Badrankova	KAZ	25.3.77	6	GP II	Gresham	3 Jun
	(40)							
2:01.05		Wang Yuanping	CHN	8.12.76	2	NG	Guangzhou	22 Nov
2:01.19	Irina	Prokofyeva	RUS	13.3.72	2h4	NC	Tula	14 Jul
2:01.23	Natalya	Korneyeva	RUS	77	2h2	NC	Tula	14 Jul
2:01.24	Yanelis	Lara	CUB	19.8.78	1		Strasbourg	19 Jun
2:01.27	Irina	Krakoviak	LTU	16.11.77	2	Franc	Ottawa	21 Jul
2:01.27		Wang Yanchun	CHN	4.2.76	3	NG	Guangzhou	22 Nov
2:01.29	Yekaterina	Puzanova	RUS	1.1.79	2h3	NC	Tula	14 Jul
2:01.32	Nicole	Teter	USA	8.11.73	3		Cuxhaven	21 Jul
2:01.33	Nuria	Fernández	ESP	16.8.76	1		San Sebastián	18 Aug
2:01.35	Natalia	Rodríguez	ESP	2.6.79	5	GP II	Sevilla	8 Jun
	(50)							
2:01.5	Natalya	Dedkova (Keiko)	BLR	2.12.79			Staiki	13 Jul
2:01.54A	Grace	Birungi	UGA	10.10.73	2		Roodepoort	16 Mar
2:01.6	Nouria	Mérah-Benida	ALG	19.10.70	1		Alger	17 Jul
2:01.60	Nédia	Semedo	POR	14.11.78	1		Braga	4 Jul
2:01.61	Virginie	Fouquet	FRA	9.9.75	2		Strasbourg	19 Jun
2:01.66	Peggy	Babin	FRA	24.12.76	3	Franc	Ottawa	21 Jul
2:01.68 mx	Adrienne	McIvor	IRL	2.9.70	1		Gold Coast	30 Dec
	2:04.04				1		Brisbane	23 Nov
2:01.7	Larisa	Mikhaylova	RUS	3.1.69	5		Moskva	23 Jun
2:01.75	Yekaterina	Fedotova	RUS	4.11.75	2rB	NC	Tula	15 Jul
2:01.80		Sun Qiuhong	CHN	13.10.78	4	NG	Guangzhou	22 Nov
	(60)							
2:01.81		Zhang Jian	CHN	5.4.76	5	NG	Guangzhou	22 Nov
2:01.83	Miriam	Bravo	ESP	29.9.74	8	GP II	Sevilla	8 Jun
2:01.87	Tanya	Blake	GBR	16.1.71	2	FBK	Hengelo	4 Jun
2:01.88	Sandra	Teixeira	POR	13.3.78	2		Namur	17 Aug
2:01.89	Svetlana	Kanatova ¶	RUS	10.9.70	3h2	NC	Tula	14 Jul
2:01.89	Aoife	Byrne	IRL	26.3.81	3		Namur	17 Aug
2:01.97	Yulia	Gurtovenko	UKR	8.12.80	2	NC	Kiev	2 Jul
2:02.04	Anna	Zagórska	POL	26.7.80	2		Bydgoszcz	15 Jun
2:02.06	Irina	Belova	RUS	27.3.68	1H		Götzis	27 May
2:02.08	Olga	Mikayeva	RUS	22.10.79	1	NC-23	Cheboksary	15 Jun
	(70)							
2:02.11A	Michelle	Ballentine	JAM	31.8.75	2	CAC	C. de Guatemala	22 Jul
2:02.18	Yelena	Buzhenko	UKR	16.11.72	1		Kiev	25 May
2:02.18	Shayne	Culpepper	USA	3.12.73	7	GP II	Gresham	3 Jun
2:02.19	Stella	Jongmans	NED	17.5.71	2	FBK	Hengelo	4 Jun
2:02.19	Yelena	Orlova	RUS	3.2.70	3rB	NC	Tula	15 Jul
2:02.23	Miki	Nishimura	JPN-J	14.4.82	2	GP	Osaka	12 May
2:02.26	Tamara	Volkova	UKR	17.7.79	3	NC	Kiev	2 Jul
2:02.3	Sultana	Aït Hammou	MAR	21.5.80	1		Meknès	9 Jun
	2:02.32				5	Franc	Ottawa	21 Jul
2:02.37		Feng Lei	CHN	8.4.80	4s2	NG	Guangzhou	21 Nov
2:02.43	Mari-Louise	Henning	RSA	19.2.77	3	FBK	Hengelo	4 Jun
	(80)							
2:02.50	Heidi	Jensen	DEN	14.8.66	4	Odlozil	Praha	18 Jun
2:02.55	Dorota	Fiut	POL	10.12.76	3		Cottbus	18 Jul
2:02.55	Anja	Knippel	GER	19.8.74	4		Cuxhaven	21 Jul
2:02.59	Oksana	Ilyushkina	UKR	25.5.74	3		Kiev	25 May
2:02.61	Yelena	Rurak	UKR	7.2.72	3		Istanbul	16 Jun

Mark	Name		Nat	Born	Pos	Meet	Venue	Date
2:02.64	Kathleen	Friedrich	GER	13.7.77	1		Grudziadz	7 Sep
2:02.67	Petra	Sedlaková	CZE	5.10.77	6	ECp-S	Bremen	23 Jun
2:02.68	Natalya	Vasko	BLR	20.5.80	1		Minsk	30 Jun
2:02.68	Sasha	Spencer	USA	4.8.79	5	WUG	Beijing	1 Sep
2:02.74	Sandra	Stals	BEL	5.6.75	1		Nijmegen	24 May
	(90)							
2:02.74	Simona	Ionescu	ROM	24.8.73	2	BalkC	Tríkala	8 Jul
2:02.78	Ester	Goossens	NED	21.2.72	3		Dortmund	9 Jun
2:02.79	Alice	Nwosu	NGR		1	NC	Lagos	22 Jul
2:02.8	Abir	Nakhli	TUN	21.9.81	1		Nantes	23 Aug
2:02.81	Joanne	Fenn	GBR	19.10.74	6	Znam	Tula	9 Jun
2:02.81	Inna	Kravchenko	BLR	23.7.81	2		Minsk	30 Jun
2:02.88		Yang Jinhua	CHN	10.1.79	2s1	NG	Guangzhou	21 Nov
2:02.93	Nahida	Touhami	ALG	10.2.78	5		Istanbul	16 Jun
2:03.02	Daniela	Yordanova	BUL	8.3.76	1		Athína	9 Jun
2:03.02	Simone	Beutelspacher	GER	8.12.74	2	NC	Stuttgart	30 Jun
	(100)							

Mark	Name		Nat	Born	Date
2:03.03	Monika	Gradzki	GER	21.9.79	30 Jun
2:03.05	Kristina	da Fonseca-Wollheim	GER	10.2.72	30 Jun
2:03.05	Natalya	Alekseyeva	UKR	14.7.73	2 Jul
2:03.06	Lucia	Klocová	SVK-J	20.11.83	12 Jun
2:03.06	Adoración	García	ESP	19.7.76	7 Jul
2:03.07	Tatyana	Petlyuk	UKR-J	22.2.82	2 Jul
2:03.08	Zamira	Amirova	UZB	11.6.79	17 Jun
2:03.09A	Lynelle	Coetzee	RSA-J	26.7.85	16 Mar
2:03.10	Mary Jane	Harrelson	USA	17.6.78	1 Jun
2:03.13	Lyudmila	Vasilyeva	RUS	20.10.69	28 Jul
2:03.16	Florencia	Hunt	AHO	14.5.78	9 Jun
2:03.19	Sabrina	Frédon	FRA	24.1.77	6 Jul
2:03.21	Tomoko	Matsushima	JPN	12.11.81	9 Jun
2:03.21	Tatyana	Borisova	KGZ	3.6.76	17 Jun
2:03.27	Delphine	Wagner	FRA	2.1.78	6 Jul
2:03.30	Allison	Curbishley	GBR	3.6.76	22 Jul
2:03.30	Judit	Varga	HUN	16.4.76	29 Aug
2:03.32	Elisabeth	Grousselle	FRA	6.2.73	6 Jun
2:03.33		Sun Xiuying	CHN	20.7.79	21 Nov
2:03.36	Irina	Lishchinskaya	UKR	15.1.76	18 May
2:03.39	Anastasiya	Fesenko	RUS-J	17.6.82	23 May
2:03.39	Svetlana	Suvorova	RUS	78	14 Jul
2:03.39	Elisabetta	Artuso	ITA	25.4.74	2 Sep
2:03.48	Aurélie	Coulaud	FRA	5.5.79	25 May
2:03.49	Kerstin	Werner	GER-J	18.9.82	30 Jun
2:03.49	Georgie	Clarke	AUS-J	17.6.84	17 Aug
2:03.58	Oksana	Meltsayeva	UKR	16.8.75	25 May
2:03.6	Olga	Karkhalyova	BLR	17.12.74	13 Jul
2:03.61	Renata	Hoppová	CZE	11.6.76	1 Jul
2:03.61	Yulia	Kumpan	UKR	19.10.77	2 Jul
2:03.64	Kristin	Roset	NOR	22.10.79	8 Jul
2:03.64	Lidia	Chojecka	POL	25.1.77	29 Jul
2:03.69	Tamieka	Grizzle	USA	14.7.77	24 Jun
2:03.72	Marlene M	da Silva	BRA	30.8.68	29 Apr
2:03.79	Irina	Somesan	ROM	8.12.80	14 Jul
2:03.82		Liu Xiaoping	CHN	4.1.78	21 Nov
2:03.85		Chen Fang	CHN-J	28.10.82	1 Jul
2:03.86A	Marina	Anisimova	RUS	4.3.73	16 Mar
2:03.86	René	Kalmer	RSA	3.11.80	24 May
2:03.9	Lucy	Vaughan	GBR	20.4.69	29 Aug
2:03.95	Jamie	King	USA	19.1.76	7 Jun
2:03.96	Susan	Scott	GBR	26.9.77	13 Jul
2:03.97	Yuliya	Taranova	RUS	15.2.77	9 Jun
2:03.98A	Niusha	Mancilla	BOL	19.1.71	15 Sep
2:04.03	Elena	Iagar	ROM	16.1.75	10 Jun
2:04.04	Jeina	Mitchell	GBR	21.1.75	9 Jun
2:04.06	Bobbie Jo	Munson	USA	28.12.80	12 May
2:04.09	Tatyana	Andrianova	RUS	79	14 Jul
2:04.10		Yan Wei	CHN	4.10.73	21 Nov
2:04.11	Adriana	Muñoz	CUB-J	16.3.82	6 Jul
2:04.13	Malgorzata	Jamróz	POL	16.10.73	15 Jun
2:04.16	Joanna	Buza	POL	15.4.81	6 Jul
2:04.17		Shi Hua	CHN	21.6.81	21 Nov
2:04.18	Aleksandra	Deren	POL	1.2.78	26 Apr
2:04.18	Nadezhda	Vorobyova	RUS	77	14 Jul
2:04.21	Anjolie	Wisse	NED	17.9.76	24 May
2:04.21	Johanna	Risku	FIN	21.2.79	22 Aug
2:04.22	Rikke	Rønholt	DEN	1.1.76	18 Jul
2:04.23	Ieva	Zunda	LAT	20.7.78	27 Apr
2:04.23	Maile	Magnusson	EST	3.7.73	15 Jul
2:04.23	Noah	Beitler	ISR	5.2.80	18 Jul
2:04.24	Claudia	Schultz	GER	29.1.73	30 Jun
2:04.26	Stephanie	Best	USA	16.10.69	3 Jul
2:04.26	Maura	Prendeville	IRL	27.6.75	13 Jul
2:04.26	Linda	Olsson	SWE	21.8.72	29 Aug
2:04.29	Daniele	Struckmeyer	GER	4.10.72	30 Jun
2:04.29		Song Lijuan	CHN	10.1.80	21 Nov
2:04.33	Aliann	Pompey	GUY	9.3.78	15 Jul
2:04.33	C	Latha	IND		21 Nov
2:04.35	Anna	Ndege	TAN-J	5.3.82	18 May
2:04.38	Korene	Hinds	JAM	18.1.76	23 Jun
2:04.38	Yekaterina	Nikishina	RUS	5.8.78	14 Jul
2:04.42	Larisa	Zhao	RUS	4.2.72	17 Jul
2:04.42	Madhuri A	Singh	IND	25.2.71	21 Nov
2:04.45	Suzy	Walsham	AUS	22.11.73	18 Feb
	(175)				

Drugs Disqualification

Mark	Name		Nat	Born	Pos	Meet	Venue	Date
1:57.16	Fabiane	dos Santos ¶	BRA	30.5.76	(2)	Herc	Monaco	20 Jul
1:57.65		dos Santos			(1)	BrGP	London (CP)	22 Jul
1:58.83		dos Santos			(3)	Bisl	Oslo	13 Jul

Indoors

Mark	Name		Nat	Born	Pos	Meet	Venue	Date
1:57.53		Graf			1	Euro	Liévin	25 Feb
1:57.68		Graf			1	Euro	Stockholm	15 Feb
1:58.02		Mutola			2	Euro	Liévin	25 Feb
1:58.05		Mutola			2	Euro	Stockholm	15 Feb
1:58.37	Helena	Fuchsová	CZE	3.6.65	3	Euro	Liévin	25 Feb
1:58.73	Yelena	Afanasyeva	RUS	1.3.67	1	NC	Moskva	17 Feb
1:58.82		Graf			1		Gent	23 Feb
	(7/4)							
1:58.94	Olga	Kuznetsova	RUS	23.10.67	2	NC	Moskva	17 Feb
1:59.86	Hasna	Benhassi	MAR	1.6.78	1	Euro	Birmingham	18 Feb
2:00.01	Ester	Goossens	NED	21.2.72	4	Euro	Stockholm	15 Feb
2:00.75	Heike	Meissner	GER	29.1.70	1		Karlsruhe	27 Jan
2:00.96	Jearl	Miles-Clark	USA	4.9.66	1	NC	Atlanta	3 Mar
2:00.98	Fabiane	dos Santos ¶	BRA	30.5.76	5	Euro	Stockholm	15 Feb
2:02.12	Anca	Safta	ROM	9.1.78	3		Pireás	21 Feb

Mark		Name	Nat	Born	Pos	Meet	Venue	Date
2:03.48	Laetitia	Valdonado	FRA	4.8.77				23 Feb
2:03.50	Marina	Anisimova	RUS	4.3.73				4 Feb
2:03.61	Brigitte	Mühlbacher	AUT	5.12.75				24 Feb
2:04.38	Svetlana	Lipatova	RUS-J	2.12.82				16 Feb
2:04.39	Miesha	Marzell	USA	29.1.75				10 Feb

JUNIORS

Mark		Name	Nat	Born	Pos	Meet	Venue	Date
2:02.23	Miki	Nishimura	JPN	14.4.82	2	GP	Osaka	12 May
	2:03.29 2 NC Tokyo 9 Jun			2:03.43	3	EAsG	Osaka	25 May
2:03.06	Lucia	Klocová	SVK	20.11.83	1	GP II	Bratislava	12 Jun
2:03.07	Tatyana	Petlyuk	UKR	22.2.82	6	NC	Kiev	2 Jul
2:03.09A	Lynelle	Coetzee	RSA	26.7.85	3		Roodepoort	16 Mar
2:03.39	Anastasiya	Fesenko	RUS	17.6.82	1		Krasnodar	23 May
	2:03.53 1 Krasnodar 23 May				10 performances by 7 women to 2:03.53			
2:03.49	Kerstin	Werner	GER	18.9.82	5	NC	Stuttgart	30 Jun
2:03.49	Georgie	Clarke	AUS	17.6.84	2rB	WK	Zürich	17 Aug
2:03.85		Chen Fang	CHN	28.10.82	4	NC	Chengdu	1 Jul
2:04.11	Adriana	Muñoz	CUB	16.3.82	1	NC-j	Santiago de Cuba	6 Jul
2:04.35	Anna	Ndege	TAN	5.3.82	5	GP	Doha	18 May
2:04.70	Alice	Nwosu	NGR	24.12.84	1	Afr-J	Réduit	19 Aug
2:04.77	Irina	Kuzmenko	RUS	82	1	NC-j	Kazan	28 Jun
2:04.97	Zanelle	Grobler	RSA	27.1.83	1	NC	Durban	3 Mar
2:05.05	Rebecca	Lyne	GBR	4.7.82	1		Stretford	31 Jul
2:05.20	Liliana	Barbulescu	ROM	5.2.82	4	NC	Bucuresti	10 Jun
2:05.25		Lan Hongmei	CHN	10.2.84	7s1	NG	Guangzhou	21 Nov
2:05.36	Minna	Nummela	FIN	23.10.82	1		Lohja	4 Jul
2:05.48	Katarzyna	Grzesiak	POL	18.2.82	5	EJ	Grosseto	21 Jul
2:05.50	Cherotich Kipkorir	Ruto	KEN	13.5.86	1	WY	Debrecen	15 Jul
2:05.57	Mieke	Geens (20)	BEL	10.3.82	6	EJ	Grosseto	21 Jul

1000 METRES

Mark		Name	Nat	Born	Pos	Meet	Venue	Date
2:33.53	Maria Lurdes	Mutola	MOZ	27.10.72	1	DNG	Stockholm	17 Jul
2:34.08	Svetlana	Cherkasova	RUS	20.5.78	2	DNG	Stockholm	17 Jul
2:34.25	Natalya	Gorelova	RUS	18.4.73	3	DNG	Stockholm	17 Jul
2:34.77	Olga	Raspopova	RUS	27.12.78	1	Nik	Nice	9 Jul
2:34.82	Irina	Mistyukevich	RUS	17.6.77	2	Nik	Nice	9 Jul
2:34.90	Natalya	Tsyganova	RUS	7.2.71	3	Nik	Nice	9 Jul
2:35.39	Faith	Macharia	KEN	9.2.76	4	Nik	Nice	9 Jul
2:35.74	Tina	Paulino	MOZ	7.7.73	5	Nik	Nice	9 Jul
2:35.89	Letitia	Vriesde	SUR	5.10.64	6	Nik	Nice	9 Jul
2:36.47	Hazel	Clark	USA	3.10.77	7	Nik	Nice	9 Jul
2:38.07	Natalya	Dukhnova	BLR	16.7.66	8	Nik	Nice	9 Jul
2:38.15 mx	Anita	Brägger	SUI	6.10.72	mx		Bern	21 Jul
2:38.21	Jolanda	Ceplak	SLO	12.9.76	9	Nik	Nice	9 Jul
2:38.96	Luciana	Mendes	BRA	26.7.71	10	Nik	Nice	9 Jul
2:39.08	Mardrea	Hyman	JAM	22.12.72				9 Jul
2:39.64	Yelena	Afanasyeva	RUS	1.3.67				17 Jul

Indoors

Mark		Name	Nat	Born	Pos	Meet	Venue	Date
2:41.08Ai	Miesha	Marzell	USA	29.1.75				17 Feb

Drugs Disqualification

Mark		Name	Nat	Born	Pos	Meet	Venue	Date
2:35.95dq	Fabiane	dos Santos ¶	BRA	30.5.76	(7)	Nik	Nice	9 Jul

1500 METRES

Mark		Name	Nat	Born	Pos	Meet	Venue	Date
3:59.35	Violeta	Szekely	ROM	26.3.65	1	Herc	Monaco	20 Jul
3:59.70	Natalya	Gorelova	RUS	18.4.73	2	Herc	Monaco	20 Jul
3:59.75		Szekely			1	VD	Bruxelles	24 Aug
3:59.94		Szekely			1	WK	Zürich	17 Aug
4:00.32	Carla	Sacramento	POR	10.12.71	2	VD	Bruxelles	24 Aug
4:00.38	Suzy	Favor Hamilton	USA	8.8.68	3	Herc	Monaco	20 Jul
4:00.53		Gorelova			2	WK	Zürich	17 Aug
4:00.57	Gabriela	Szabo	ROM	14.11.75	1	WCh	Edmonton	7 Aug
4:00.67		Gorelova			3	VD	Bruxelles	24 Aug
4:00.80		Szekely			1	ISTAF	Berlin	31 Aug
4:00.92		Szekely			1	GGala	Roma	29 Jun
4:00.94		Sacramento			3	WK	Zürich	17 Aug
4:01.26		Sacramento			4	Herc	Monaco	20 Jul
4:01.31		Sacramento			2	ISTAF	Berlin	31 Aug
4:01.45		Szekely			1	Bisl	Oslo	13 Jul
4:01.55		Szekely			1	GP	Saint-Denis	6 Jul
4:01.58		Gorelova			3	ISTAF	Berlin	31 Aug
4:01.68	Daniela	Yordanova	BUL	8.3.76	1		Kalamáta	2 Jun
4:01.70		Szekely			2	WCh	Edmonton	7 Aug
4:01.84		Gorelova			2	GGala	Roma	29 Jun
4:02.03		Gorelova			2	GP	Saint-Denis	6 Jul

Mark	Name		Nat	Born	Pos	Meet	Venue	Date
4:02.16	Yelena	Zadorozhnaya	RUS	3.12.77	1	Znam	Tula	9 Jun
4:02.40		Gorelova			3	WCh	Edmonton	7 Aug
4:02.45	Lyudmila	Vasilyeva	RUS	20.10.69	4	VD	Bruxelles	24 Aug
4:02.64		Favor Hamilton			3	GP	Saint-Denis	6 Jul
4:02.76	Olga	Yegorova	RUS	28.3.72	1	v2N	Glasgow	1 Jul
4:03.10		Favor Hamilton			1	GGala	Roma	29 Jun
4:03.20	Jacinta	Muraguri (10)	KEN	28.5.70	5	Herc	Monaco	20 Jul
4:03.24	Olga	Nelyubova	RUS	12.6.64	4	GGala	Roma	29 Jun
4:03.31	Tatyana	Tomashova	RUS	1.7.75	2	Znam	Tula	9 Jun
	(30/12)							
4:03.51	Lidia	Chojecka	POL	25.1.77	5	VD	Bruxelles	24 Aug
4:03.54	Hayley	Tullett	GBR	17.2.73	6	Herc	Monaco	20 Jul
4:03.87	Olga	Rosseyeva	RUS	1.8.81	1	Kuts	Moskva	27 Jul
4:03.98	Olga	Komyagina	RUS	10.2.74	1		Leverkusen	26 Aug
4:04.20	Yuliya	Kosenkova	RUS	28.3.73	6	VD	Bruxelles	24 Aug
4:04.27	Kathleen	Friedrich	GER	13.7.77	4	ISTAF	Berlin	31 Aug
4:04.43	Sarah	Schwald	USA	2.1.73	7	VD	Bruxelles	24 Aug
4:04.85	Regina	Jacobs	USA	28.8.63	1	GP	Palo Alto	9 Jun
	(20)							
4:05.02	Diane	Cummins	CAN	19.1.74	8	VD	Bruxelles	24 Aug
4:05.10	Naomi	Mugo	KEN	2.1.77	9	VD	Bruxelles	24 Aug
4:05.25	Mardrea	Hyman	JAM	22.12.72	10	VD	Bruxelles	24 Aug
4:05.37	Paula	Radcliffe	GBR	17.12.73	3	v2N	Glasgow	1 Jul
4:05.38	Irina	Lishchinskaya	UKR	15.1.76	1	NC	Kiev	2 Jul
4:05.60	Sabine	Fischer	SUI	29.6.73	7	GGala	Roma	29 Jun
4:06.01	Abebech	Negussie	ETH-J	2.1.83	5	GP	Saint-Denis	6 Jul
4:06.08	Irina	Mikitenko	GER	23.8.72	1		Dortmund	9 Jun
4:06.13	Veerle	Dejaeghere	BEL	1.8.73	8	GGala	Roma	29 Jun
4:06.31	Marla	Runyan	USA	4.1.69	2	GP	Palo Alto	9 Jun
	(30)							
4:06.31	Tatyana	Krivobok	UKR	17.1.72	2	NC	Kiev	2 Jul
4:06.32	Natalia	Rodríguez	ESP	2.6.79	9	GGala	Roma	29 Jun
4:06.34	Sonia	O'Sullivan	IRL	28.11.69	1		Sydney	16 Feb
4:06.34	Andrea	Suldesová	CZE	11.2.75	2		Dortmund	9 Jun
4:06.68	Natalya	Sidorenko	UKR	22.11.80	3	NC	Kiev	2 Jul
4:06.71	Kristina da	Fonseca-Wollheim	GER	10.2.72	8	Herc	Monaco	20 Jul
4:06.91	Süreyya	Ayhan	TUR	6.9.78	1	WUG	Beijing	29 Aug
4:06.92	Marta	Domínguez	ESP	3.11.75	1		Madrid	7 Jul
4:06.96	Nuria	Fernández	ESP	16.8.76	5	Bisl	Oslo	13 Jul
4:07.06		Lin Na	CHN	18.1.80	1	NG	Guangzhou	18 Nov
	(40)							
4:07.14	Hanane	Baala (Sabri)	FRA	8.12.75	8	GP	Saint-Denis	6 Jul
4:07.25	Alesya	Turova	BLR	6.12.79	7	WCh	Edmonton	7 Aug
4:07.31		Liu Xiaoping	CHN	4.1.78	2	NG	Guangzhou	18 Nov
4:07.37	Mary Jayne	Harrelson	USA	17.6.78	1		Montreal (McG)	10 Jul
4:07.44	Birhane	Hirpassa	ETH-J	30.7.83	9	GP	Saint-Denis	6 Jul
4:07.56	Helen	Pattinson	GBR	2.1.74	11	GGala	Roma	29 Jun
4:07.65	Fatiha	Baouf	BEL	15.7.70	11	VD	Bruxelles	24 Aug
4:07.72		Dong Yanmei	CHN	16.2.77	3	NG	Guangzhou	18 Nov
4:08.05		Yan Wei	CHN	4.10.73	4	NG	Guangzhou	18 Nov
4:08.09		Zhang Jinqing	CHN	21.6.77	5	NG	Guangzhou	18 Nov
	(50)							
4:08.11	Genet	Gebregiorgis	ETH	5.1.75	2		Madrid	7 Jul
4:08.12		Sun Qiuhong	CHN	13.10.78	6	NG	Guangzhou	18 Nov
4:08.15	Shayne	Culpepper	USA	3.12.73	4	GP	Palo Alto	9 Jun
4:08.16	Nouria	Mérah-Benida	ALG	19.10.70	4	Nik	Nice	9 Jul
4:08.27	Seloua	Ouaziz	MAR	27.7.74	10	GP	Saint-Denis	6 Jul
4:08.35	Oksana	Meltsayeva	UKR	16.8.75	4	NC	Kiev	2 Jul
4:08.49	Leah	Pells	CAN	9.11.64	4s2	WCh	Edmonton	5 Aug
4:08.84	Cristina	Grosu	ROM	11.11.76	2	WUG	Beijing	29 Aug
4:08.91	Georgie	Clarke	AUS-J	17.6.84	2		Sydney	16 Feb
4:08.94	René	Kalmer	RSA	3.11.80	1	NC	Durban	2 Mar
	(60)							
4:09.04	Svetlana	Kanatova ¶	RUS	10.9.70	2	GP II	Zagreb	2 Jul
4:09.10	Collette	Liss	USA	29.4.73	1		Brunswick	7 Jul
4:09.11	Amy	Rudolph	USA	18.9.73	5	v2N	Glasgow	1 Jul
4:09.25	Elena	Iagar	ROM	16.1.75	2	FBK	Hengelo	4 Jun
4:09.36	Irina	Krakoviak	LTU	16.11.77	3		Nürnberg	17 Jun
4:09.45	Elisa	Rea	ITA	23.3.68	13	GGala	Roma	29 Jun
4:09.46	Nédia	Semedo	POR	14.11.78	1		Funchal	30 Jun

Mark	Name		Nat	Born	Pos	Meet	Venue	Date
4:09.75	Renata	Hoppová	CZE	11.6.76	1		Cottbus	18 Jul
4:09.80	Heidi	Jensen	DEN	14.8.66	2	NA	Heusden	14 Jul
4:09.98	Susan	Muthoni	KEN		4	GP II	Zagreb	2 Jul
	(70)							
4:10.01	Restituta	Joseph	TAN	30.7.71	1		Kassel	13 Jun
4:10.06	Helena	Javornik	SLO	26.3.66	14	GGala	Roma	29 Jun
4:10.13	Freda	Davoren	IRL	16.3.73	3	NA	Heusden	14 Jul
4:10.28	Elva	Dryer	USA	26.9.71	11	GP	Saint-Denis	6 Jul
4:10.33	Fatma	Lanouar	TUN	14.3.78	1	MedG	Tunis	14 Sep
4:10.43		Xing Huina	CHN-J	25.2.84	1h1	NG	Guangzhou	17 Nov
4:10.61		Wang Chunmei	CHN	10.4.76	3h1	NG	Guangzhou	17 Nov
4:10.7mx	Suzy	Walsham	AUS	22.11.73	1		Sydney	9 Mar
	4:12.27				1		Sydney	10 Feb
4:10.80	Aysen	Barak	TUR	9.9.75	1		Istanbul	28 Jul
4:10.83		Shi Hua	CHN	21.6.81	5h1	NG	Guangzhou	17 Nov
	(80)							
4:10.86	Yelena	Burykina	RUS	1.1.73	5h1	NC	Tula	12 Jul
4:10.98	Benita	Willis	AUS	6.5.79	1	Zat	Melbourne	6 Dec
4:11.04	Sinead	Delahunty	IRL	12.2.71	6	Pre	Eugene	27 May
4:11.09		Lan Lixin	CHN	14.2.79	8s2	WCh	Edmonton	5 Aug
4:11.15	Ivonne	Teichmann	GER	11.4.77	8	FBK	Hengelo	4 Jun
4:11.28	Yekaterina	Puzanova	RUS	1.1.79	10	NC	Tula	13 Jul
4:11.31	Hewan	Abeylegesse	TUR-J	11.9.82	2		Istanbul	28 Jul
4:11.53	Ikuko	Tamura	JPN	24.9.78	3		Montreal (McG)	10 Jul
4:11.57	Natalya	Korneyeva	RUS	77	5	Kuts	Moskva	27 Jul
4:11.84	Maria	Lynch	IRL	3.9.78	5	NA	Heusden	14 Jul
	(90)							
4:11.86	Cheri	Kenah	USA	26.12.70	7	Pre	Eugene	27 May
4:11.95	Simona	Ionescu	ROM	24.8.73	2	NC	Bucuresti	9 Jun
4:11.99	Kelly	Caffell	GBR	10.2.79	1		Watford	25 Jul
4:12.03	Ebru	Kavakliogl u	TUR	14.3.70	3	MedG	Tunis	14 Sep
4:12.04	Liliya	Volkova	RUS	13.11.77	4h3	NC	Tula	12 Jul
4:12.08	Kathy	Butler	GBR	22.10.73	8	GP	Palo Alto	9 Jun
4:12.08	Natalya	Pavlovskaya	RUS	.75	11	NC	Tula	13 Jul
4:12.11		Dai Yanyan	CHN	8.1.80	6h1	NG	Guangzhou	17 Nov
4:12.13		Li Jingnan	CHN-J	17.2.83	1	EAsG	Osaka	23 May
4:12.13	Sara	Palmas	ITA	7.7.77	15	GGala	Roma	29 Jun
	(100)							

Mark	Name		Nat	Born	Date
4:12.23	Leah	Malot	KEN	7.6.72	26 Aug
4:12.24	Maria	Cioncan	ROM	19.6.77	30 Jun
4:12.27	Yelena	Orlova	RUS	3.2.70	27 Jul
4:12.28	Anna	Ndege	TAN-J	5.3.82	16 Feb
4:12.28	Anca	Safta	ROM	9.1.78	9 Jun
4:12.28	Lucy	Wangui	KEN-J	24.3.84	14 Jul
4:12.28	Tatyana	Chulakh	RUS-J	2.6.82	27 Jul
4:12.37	Robyn	Meagher	CAN	17.6.67	10 Jul
4:12.42	Melanie	Schultz	GER	27.8.79	26 Aug
4:12.58	Ljiljana	Culibrk	CRO-J	27.10.82	29 Aug
4:12.71	Grete	Koens	NED	26.5.67	10 Aug
4:12.73	Svetlana	Baygulova	RUS	13.7.75	12 Jul
4:12.80	Rasa	Drazdauskaité	LTU	20.3.81	3 Jul
4:12.81	Sylvia	Kühnemund	GER	25.7.74	4 Jun
4:12.96	Lyudmila	Borisova	RUS	8.3.66	12 Jul
4:12.97	Justyna	Bak	POL	1.8.74	14 Jul
4:13.02	Kerry	Smithson	GBR	13.9.76	23 Jun
4:13.08	Janet	Trujillo	USA	7.8.75	27 May
4:13.09		Guo Lingling	CHN-J	18.6.86	18 Nov
4:13.10	Iris	Fuentes-Pila	ESP	10.8.80	14 Jul
4:13.19	Jolanda	Ceplak	SLO	12.9.76	15 Sep
4:13.35	María	Protópappa	GRE	5.5.73	9 Jun
4:13.38	Emma	Ward	GBR-J	2.1.82	7 May
4:13.38	Sabrina	Mockenhaupt	GER	6.12.80	13 Jun
4:13.40	Yuliya	Kumpan	UKR	10.10.77	17 May
4:13.46	Ana Amelia	Menéndez	ESP	17.3.72	29 Jun
4:13.51	Zanelle	Grobler	RSA-J	27.1.83	2 Mar
4:13.60	Malgorzata	Jamróz	POL	16.10.73	14 Jul
4:13.61	Carrie	Tollefson	USA	18.1.77	7 Jul
4:13.68	Sarah	Bull	GBR	4.6.75	23 Jun
4:13.73	Clare	Taylor	USA	7.12.69	9 Jun
4:13.81	María	Tsírba	GRE	28.7.79	9 Jun
4:13.87	Yelena	Buzhenko	UKR	16.11.72	4 Jun
4:13.88	Olesya	Chumakova	RUS	.81	12 Jul
4:13.89	Jenelle	Deatherage	USA	25.9.77	29 Aug
4:13.89	Minori	Hayakari	JPN	29.11.72	15 Sep
4:13.9	Vicky	Pounds	CAN	6.6.70	3 Jul
4:13.97	Lenka	Svanhalová	CZE	11.6.76	30 May
4:14.01	Rachel	Newcombe	GBR	25.2.67	23 Jun
4:14.01	Sonja	Roman	SLO	11.3.79	2 Jul
4:14.12	Fabiana	da Silva	BRA	3.9.78	4 Jun
4:14.12	Sally	Glynn	USA	3.11.78	7 Jul
4:14.14	Jeina	Mitchell	GBR	21.1.75	20 May
4:14.16	Yelena	Gorodnichova	UKR	6.9.70	2 Jul
4:14.24	Letitia	Vriesde	SUR	5.10.64	29 Apr
4:14.40	Agnes	Samaria	NAM	11.8.72	16 Feb
4:14.40	Luminita	Zaituc	GER	9.10.68	13 Jun
4:14.43	Tatyana	Golovchenko	UKR	13.2.80	2 Jul
4:14.44	Alex	Carter	GBR	1.4.80	7 May
4:14.44	Blake	Russell	USA	24.7.75	7 Jul
4:14.46	Ellen	Leggate	GBR	4.2.78	7 May
4:14.48	Riina	Tolonen	FIN-J	4.5.83	22 Jul
4:14.49	Dulce	Rodríguez	MEX	14.8.72	3 Jun
4:14.54	Inês	Monteiro	POR	18.5.80	30 Jun
4:14.63	Minna	Nummela	FIN-J	23.10.82	7 Jul
4:14.63	Anjolie	Wisse	NED	17.9.76	14 Jul
4:14.66	Malindi	Elmore	CAN	13.3.80	29 Aug
4:14.70	Luminita	Gogîrlea	ROM	5.11.71	9 Jun
4:14.70	Brigitte	Mühlbacher	AUT	5.12.75	4 Jul
4:14.70	Anastasia	Starovoytova	BLR-J	4.11.82	22 Jul
4:14.93	Una	English	IRL	14.8.70	22 Jul
4:14.97	Priscilla	Hein	USA	15.7.76	10 Jul
4:14.98	Yekaterina	Dedkova	RUS	8.3.72	27 Jul
4:15.01	Liz	Yelling	GBR	5.12.74	14 Jul
4:15.04	Karolína	Skoúrti	GRE	1.7.68	8 Jul
4:15.05	Tatyana	Borisova	KGZ	3.6.76	16 Jun
4:15.07	Lyudmila	Rogachova	RUS	30.10.66	9 Jun
4:15.13	Courtney	Babcock	CAN	30.6.72	3 Jun
4:15.16		Chen Fang	CHN-J	28.10.82	28 Jun
4:15.17	Liliana	Barbulescu	ROM-J	5.2.82	9 Jun
4:15.24	Letitia	Vriesde	SUR	5.10.64	29 Apr
4:15.25	Hanna	Karlsson	SWE	18.1.79	14 Jul
4:15.26	Nahida	Touhami	ALG	10.2.78	14 Sep
4:15.29	Inna	Poluskina	LAT-J	7.7.84	22 Jul

Mark	Name		Nat	Born	Pos	Meet	Venue	Date
4:15.33	Svetlana	Klimkovich	BLR	.80				9 Jun
4:15.37		Tong Dejing	CHN	4.9.80				17 Nov
(176)								

Indoors

Mark	Name		Nat	Born	Pos	Meet	Venue	Date
4:04.26	Olga	Kuznetsova	RUS	23.10.67	4		Liévin	25 Feb
4:04.48	Hasna	Benhassi	MAR	1.6.78	2		Dortmund	11 Feb
4:05.75	Kutre	Dulecha	ETH	22.8.78	3		Dortmund	11 Feb
4:06.22	Helena	Javornik	SLO	26.3.66	4		Dortmund	11 Feb
4:07.89	Maria	Cioncan	ROM	19.6.77	3		Stockholm	15 Feb
4:08.98	Mariya	Pantyukhova	RUS	14.8.74	4		Stockholm	15 Feb
4:12.27	Getenesh	Wami	ETH	11.12.74	4		Karlsruhe	27 Jan
4:12.99	Judit	Varga	HUN	16.4.76				27 Jan
4:14.19	Lyubov	Kremlyova	RUS	21.12.61				18 Feb
4:14.37	Larisa	Mikhaylova	RUS	3.1.69				18 Feb
4:14.92	Fernanda	Ribeiro	POR	23.6.69				17 Feb

Drugs Disqualification

Mark	Name		Nat	Born	Pos	Meet	Venue	Date
4:08.37	Svetlana	Kanatova ¶	RUS	10.9.70	4	Kuts	Moskva	27 Jul

JUNIORS

See main list for top 6 juniors. 13/10 performances by 4/5 women to 4:11.31. Additional marks and further juniors:

Name	Mark	Pos	Meet	Venue	Date	Mark	Pos	Meet	Venue	Date
Negussie	4:06.85	10	GGala	Roma	29 Jun	4:07.44	1		Nürnberg	17 Jun
	4:06.93	3		Dortmund	9 Jun	4:09.73	1	GP II	Doha	18 May
	4:07.13	1	APM	Hengelo	4 Jun					
Hirpassa	4:09.84	5	APM	Hengelo	4 Jun	4:11.17	2	GP II	Doha	18 May
	4:10.55	3		Kassel	13 Jun					

Mark	Name		Nat	Born	Pos	Meet	Venue	Date
4:12.28	Anna	Ndege	TAN	5.3.82	2		Port Elizabeth	16 Feb
4:12.28	Lucy	Wangui	KEN	24.3.84	1		Aomori	14 Jul
4:12.28	Tatyana	Chulakh	RUS	2.6.82	7	Kuts	Moskva	27 Jul
4:12.58	Ljiljana	Culibrk	CRO	27.10.82	7	WUG	Beijing	29 Aug
4:13.09		Guo Lingling	CHN	18.6.86	9	NG	Guangzhou	18 Nov
4:13.38	Emma	Ward	GBR	2.1.82	1		Glasgow	7 May
4:13.51	Zanelle	Grobler	RSA	27.1.83	2	NC	Durban	2 Mar
4:14.48	Riina	Tolonen	FIN	4.5.83	3	EJ	Grosseto	22 Jul
4:14.63	Minna	Nummela	FIN	23.10.82	1	NC	Turku	7 Jul
4:14.70	Anastasia	Starovoytova	BLR	4.11.82	4	EJ	Grosseto	22 Jul
4:15.16		Chen Fang	CHN	28.10.82	h	NC	Chengdu	28 Jun
4:15.17	Liliana	Barbulescu	ROM	5.2.82	8	NC	Bucuresti	9 Jun
4:15.29	Inna	Poluskina	LAT	7.7.84	5	EJ	Grosseto	22 Jul
4:15.67	Melissa	Rollison (20)	AUS	13.4.83	1		Melbourne	8 Dec
4:15.71	Florence	Kyalo	KEN	12.2.86	2	WY	Debrecen	15 Jul

1 MILE

Mark	Name		Nat	Born	Pos	Meet	Venue	Date
4:30.30	Lyudmila	Vasilyeva	RUS	20.10.69	1		Falmouth	11 Aug
4:31.10	Cheri	Kenah	USA	26.12.70	1		Princeton	12 May
4:33.15	Carrie	Tollefson	USA	18.1.77	2		Princeton	12 May
4:33.8	Fatiha	Baouf	BEL	15.7.70				15 Aug
4:34.02	Sarah	Schwald	USA	2.1.73				28 Apr
4:34.11	Mary Jayne	Harrelson	USA	17.6.78				11 Aug
4:34.17	Vicky	Lynch-Pounds	CAN	6.6.70				11 Aug
4:35.68	Anna	Brzezinska	POL	9.1.71				11 Aug
4:36.90	Jamie	King	USA	19.1.76				12 May

Indoors

Mark	Name		Nat	Born	Pos	Meet	Venue	Date
4:23.19	Gabriela	Szabo	ROM	14.11.75	1	Spark	Stuttgart	4 Feb
4:23.33	Kutre	Dulecha	ETH	22.8.78	2	Spark	Stuttgart	4 Feb
4:24.11	Yelena	Zadorozhnaya	RUS	3.12.77	3	Spark	Stuttgart	4 Feb
4:26.52	Hayley	Tullett	GBR	17.2.73	4	Spark	Stuttgart	4 Feb
4:28.47	Amy	Rudolph	USA	18.9.73	1		New York	20 Jan
4:35.24	Collette	Liss	USA	29.4.73				3 Mar
4:36.32	Miesha	Marzell	USA	29.1.75				3 Mar

2000 METRES

Mark	Name		Nat	Born	Pos	Meet	Venue	Date
5:39.06+	Olga	Komyagina	RUS	10.2.74	1	in 3k	Zürich	17 Aug
5:39.3+	Paula	Radcliffe	GBR	17.12.73	2	in 3k	Zürich	17 Aug
5:39.5+	Gabriela	Szabo	ROM	14.11.75	3	in 3k	Zürich	17 Aug
5:39.7+	Berhane	Adere	ETH	21.7.73	4	in 3k	Zürich	17 Aug
5:39.9+	Getenesh	Wami	ETH	11.12.74	5=	in 3k	Zürich	17 Aug
5:39.9+	Olga	Yegorova	RUS	28.3.72	5=	in 3k	Zürich	17 Aug
5:40.3+	Edith	Masai	KEN	4.4.67	7	in 3k	Zürich	17 Aug
5:40.6+	Irina	Mikitenko	GER	23.8.72	8	in 3k	Zürich	17 Aug
5:41.3+	Asmae	Leghzaoui	MAR	30.8.76	9	in 3k	Zürich	17 Aug
5:42.14	Sugar (10)	Kihana	KEN		1	NA	Heusden	14 Jul
5:42.15	Veerle	Dejaeghere	BEL	1.8.73	2	NA	Heusden	14 Jul
5:42.55	Alesya	Turova	BLR	6.12.79	1	Cezmi	Istanbul	16 Jun
5:42.66	Naomi	Mugo	KEN	2.1.77	3	NA	Heusden	14 Jul
5:42.76	Deean	Drossin	USA	14.2.73	4	NA	Heusden	14 Jul
5:42.77	Daniela	Yordanova	BUL	8.3.76	2	Cezmi	Istanbul	16 Jun
5:43.3+	Tatyana	Tomashova	RUS	1.7.75	4	in 3k	Roma	29 Jun
5:43.4+	Yelena	Zadorozhnaya	RUS	3.12.77	5=	in 3k	Roma	29 Jun

Mark	Name		Nat	Born	Pos	Meet	Venue	Date
5:44.19	Genet	Gebregiorgis	ETH	5.1.75	5	NA	Heusden	14 Jul
5:44.29	Tatyana	Krivobok	UKR	17.1.72	3	Cezmi	Istanbul	16 Jun
5:44.54	Ebru	Kavakliogłu	TUR	14.3.70	4	Cezmi	Istanbul	16 Jun
	(20)							

3000 METRES

Mark	Name		Nat	Born	Pos	Meet	Venue	Date
8:23.26	Olga	Yegorova	RUS	28.3.72	1	WK	Zürich	17 Aug
8:23.75		Yegorova			1	GP	Saint-Denis	6 Jul
8:23.96		Yegorova			1	GGala	Roma	29 Jun
8:24.19	Gabriela	Szabo	ROM	14.11.75	2	WK	Zürich	17 Aug
8:25.40	Yelena	Zadorozhnaya	RUS	3.12.77	2	GGala	Roma	29 Jun
8:25.56	Tatyana	Tomashova	RUS	1.7.75	3	GGala	Roma	29 Jun
8:25.62	Berhane	Adere	ETH	21.7.73	3	WK	Zürich	17 Aug
8:26.44		Szabo			4	GGala	Roma	29 Jun
8:26.79		Zadorozhnaya			2	GP	Saint-Denis	6 Jul
8:26.97	Paula	Radcliffe	GBR	17.12.73	5	GGala	Roma	29 Jun
8:27.02		Tomashova			3	GP	Saint-Denis	6 Jul
8:27.21		Szabo			4	GP	Saint-Denis	6 Jul
8:27.62	Getenesh	Wami	ETH	11.12.74	4	WK	Zürich	17 Aug
8:28.07		Radcliffe			5	WK	Zürich	17 Aug
8:30.09		Yegorova			1	VD	Bruxelles	24 Aug
8:30.56		Tomashova			2	VD	Bruxelles	24 Aug
8:30.59	Daniela	Yordanova	BUL	8.3.76	5	GP	Saint-Denis	6 Jul
8:30.65		Yordanova			6	GGala	Roma	29 Jun
8:31.40		Wami			3	VD	Bruxelles	24 Aug
8:31.45		Adere			4	VD	Bruxelles	24 Aug
8:31.76	Edith	Masai	KEN	4.4.67	6	WK	Zürich	17 Aug
8:31.90		Szabo			5	VD	Bruxelles	24 Aug
8:32.02		Radcliffe			6	VD	Bruxelles	24 Aug
8:32.70	Katalin	Szentgyörgyi (10)	HUN	1.1.79	6	GP	Saint-Denis	6 Jul
8:32.89	Alesya	Turova	BLR	6.12.79	7	GP	Saint-Denis	6 Jul
8:32.89	Irina	Mikitenko	GER	23.8.72	7	WK	Zürich	17 Aug
8:33.87	Asmae	Leghzaoui	MAR	30.8.76	8	GP	Saint-Denis	6 Jul
8:34.79		Masai			1	Herc	Monaco	20 Jul
8:35.26	Ebru	Kavakliogłu	TUR	14.3.70	7	VD	Bruxelles	24 Aug
8:36.33	Marta	Domínguez	ESP	3.11.75	8	VD	Bruxelles	24 Aug
	(30/15)							
8:36.58	Joanne	Pavey	GBR	20.9.73	9	VD	Bruxelles	24 Aug
8:40.97	Kathy	Butler	GBR	22.10.73	10	VD	Bruxelles	24 Aug
8:41.17	Carla	Sacramento	POR	10.12.71	9	GP	Saint-Denis	6 Jul
8:41.74	Rose	Cheruiyot	KEN	21.7.76	9	GGala	Roma	29 Jun
8:42.24	Pamela	Chepchumba	KEN	28.2.78	4	Herc	Monaco	20 Jul
	(20)							
8:42.39	Genet	Gebregiorgis	ETH	5.1.75	10	GGala	Roma	29 Jun
8:42.95	Benita	Willis	AUS	6.5.79	11	GGala	Roma	29 Jun
8:43.51	Sonia	O'Sullivan	IRL	28.11.69	1	GP	Melbourne	1 Mar
8:43.95	Susan	Chepkemei	KEN	25.6.75	5	Herc	Monaco	20 Jul
8:44.00	Yamna	Belkacem	FRA	20.2.74	6	Herc	Monaco	20 Jul
8:44.28	Restituta	Joseph	TAN	30.7.71	7	Herc	Monaco	20 Jul
8:44.52	Tegla	Loroupe	KEN	9.5.73	8	Herc	Monaco	20 Jul
8:44.69	Marla	Runyan	USA	4.1.69	1	Pre	Eugene	27 May
8:45.07	Beatrice	Chepchumba	KEN-J	25.11.83	11	GP	Saint-Denis	6 Jul
8:45.77	Deena	Drossin	USA	14.2.73	9	Herc	Monaco	20 Jul
	(30)							
8:46.09	Elva	Dryer	USA	26.9.71	3	Pre	Eugene	27 May
8:46.90	Leah	Malot	KEN	7.6.72	3	GP II	Sevilla	8 Jun
8:47.01	Ayelech	Worku	ETH	12.6.79	4	GP II	Sevilla	8 Jun
8:50.42	Merima	Denboba	ETH	21.8.74	6	GP II	Sevilla	8 Jun
8:50.81	Olga	Komyagina	RUS	10.2.74	3	GP II	Rieti	2 Sep
8:51.65	Marina	Dubrova	UKR	9.12.78	1		Kiev	25 May
8:51.73	Hayley	Tullett	GBR	17.2.73	7	GP II	Sevilla	8 Jun
8:52.3	Kayoko	Fukushi	JPN-J	25.3.82	1		Takamatsu	13 Oct
8:52.47	Meseret	Defar	ETH-J	19.11.83	1	GP II	Gresham	3 Jun
8:52.95	Tatyana	Khmeleva	RUS	2.4.79	1	Znam	Tula	9 Jun
	(40)							
8:52.98	Lyudmila	Vasilyeva	RUS	20.10.69	2	GP II	Gresham	3 Jun
8:53.35	Liliya	Volkova	RUS	13.11.77	2	Znam	Tula	9 Jun
8:53.38mx	Helena	Javornik	SLO	26.3.66	1		Wolfsburg	28 Jul
	9:05.13				4	ECp-1B	Budapest	24 Jun

Mark	Name		Nat	Born	Pos	Meet	Venue	Date
8:53.42	Hewan	Abeylegesse	TUR-J	11.9.82	1	EJ	Grosseto	21 Jul
8:53.70	Cheri	Kenah	USA	26.12.70	3	GP II	Gresham	3 Jun
8:54.07	Amy	Rudolph	USA	18.9.73	4	GP II	Gresham	3 Jun
8:54.52	Zhor	El Kamch	MAR	15.3.73	9	GP II	Sevilla	8 Jun
8:55.28	Jen	Rhines	USA	1.7.74	5	GP II	Gresham	3 Jun
8:55.51	Collette	Liss	USA	29.4.73	4	Pre	Eugene	27 May
8:55.51	Olga	Rosseyeva	RUS	1.8.81	3	Gugl	Linz	20 Aug
	(50)							
8:55.67	Simona	Staicu	HUN	5.5.71	1		Lisboa (U)	16 Jun
8:55.82	Una	English	IRL	14.8.70	6	GP II	Gresham	3 Jun
8:55.92	Tatyana	Belovol	UKR	7.10.69	2		Kiev	25 May
8:56.58	Mónica	Rosa	POR	5.5.78	10	GP II	Sevilla	8 Jun
8:56.59	Rodica	Moroianu (Nagel)	FRA	18.11.70	4	GP II	Rieti	2 Sep
8:57.3 mx	Liz	Yelling	GBR	5.12.74	1		Watford	25 Jul
8:57.47	Lucy	Wangui	KEN-J	24.3.84	1		Kumamoto	6 Aug
8:57.61	Carrie	Tollefson	USA	18.1.77	7	GP II	Gresham	3 Jun
8:58.89	Iness	Chenonge	KEN-J	1.2.82	3		Lisboa (U)	16 Jun
8:58.90	Breeda	Dennehy-Willis	IRL	3.2.70	1		Dublin	13 Jul
	(60)							
8:58.98mx	Hayley	Yelling	GBR	3.1.74	1		Cardiff	4 Jul
	9:03.5+				2	in 5k	London (CP)	22 Jul
8:59.70	Sabrina	Mockenhaupt	GER	6.12.80	1		Wiesbaden	30 May
8:59.97	Etaferahu	Tarekegne	ETH	20.3.80	14	GGala	Roma	29 Jun

Mark	Name		Nat	Born	Date
9:00.39	Clare	Taylor	USA	7.12.69	27 May
9:00.90	Hrisostomía	Iakóvou	GRE	9.4.71	7 Jul
9:01.16	Jelena	Prokopcuka	LAT	21.9.76	22 Jun
9:01.21	Olivera	Jevtic	YUG	24.7.77	17 Jun
9:01.22	Natalya	Berkut	UKR	30.5.75	25 May
9:01.5 mx	Suzy	Walsham	AUS	22.11.73	19 Jan
9:01.78	Kerryn	McCann	AUS	2.5.67	1 Mar
9:01.92	Susanne	Pumper	AUT	1.9.70	24 Jun
9:02.0	Yelena	Zhilkina	RUS	.73	30 Jun
9:02.34	Dulce	Rodríguez	MEX	14.8.72	29 May
9:02.43	Cristina	Petite	ESP	10.5.72	8 Jun
9:02.45	Lidia	Chojecka	POL	25.1.77	23 Jun
9:02.52	Clarisse	Cruz	POR	9.7.78	16 Jun
9:02.64	Tatyana	Chulakh	RUS-J	2.6.82	21 Jul
9:02.94	Cristina	Casandra	ROM	21.10.77	20 Aug
9:03.03	Annette	Peters	USA	31.5.65	27 May
9:03.26	Bouchra	Chaabi	MAR	22.9.80	29 Jun
9:03.45	Emi	Ikeda	JPN-J	29.8.83	17 Oct
9:03.64	Melissa	Rollison	AUS-J	13.4.83	6 Dec
9:03.71	Helen	Pattinson	GBR	2.1.74	19 Aug
9:03.74	Worknesh	Kidane	ETH	21.11.81	29 Jun
9:03.94	Kristina da Fonseca Wollheim		GER	10.2.72	19 Aug
9:03.97	Veere	Dejaeghere	BEL	1.8.73	23 Jun
9:04.04	Eyerusalem	Kuma	ETH	4.11.81	3 Jun
9:04.26mx	Amanda	Parkinson	GBR	21.7.71	6 Jun
9:04.35	M Luisa	Larraga	ESP	10.12.70	8 Jun
9:04.50	Justyna	Bak	POL	1.8.74	18 Jun
9:04.86	Ejagayehu	Dibaba	ETH-J	21.3.82	3 Jun
9:04.86	Amaia	Piedra	ESP	2.6.72	8 Jun
9:04.91	Cristina	Grosu	ROM	11.11.76	23 Jun
9:04.95	Kim	Fitchen	USA	3.9.68	3 Jun
9:05.30	Fatima	Yvelain	FRA	31.12.69	23 Jun
9:05.32	María	Protópappa	GRE	5.5.73	23 Jun
9:05.88	Ikuko	Tamura	JPN	24.9.78	8 Apr
9:05.94	Hayley	McGregor	AUS	27.5.79	1 Mar
9:06.43	Irene	Limika	KEN	28.8.79	13 Jul
9:06.63	Miwa	Kirihara	JPN-J	3.8.82	29 Sep
	(100)				
9:06.88	Silvia	Weissteiner	ITA	13.7.79	2 Sep
9:06.9	Yoshiko	Ichikawa	JPN	18.4.76	25 May
9:06.95	Analidia	Torre	POR	10.10.76	16 Jun
9:06.95	Elisa	Rea	ITA	23.3.68	23 Jun
9:07.23	Maiko	Yamaguchi	JPN-J	19.5.82	29 Sep
9:07.35	Ulla	Tuimala	FIN-J	27.4.82	21 Jul
9:07.55	Aysen	Barak	TUR	9.9.75	13 May
9:07.57	Akiko	Kawashima	JPN	5.8.77	30 Jun
9:07.59	Elizabeth	Miller	AUS	8.11.63	1 Mar
9:07.86	Jennifer	Crain	USA	12.2.68	27 May

Indoors

Mark	Name		Nat	Born	Pos	Meet	Venue	Date
8:32.88		Szabo			1	Euro	Birmingham	18 Feb
8:41.34		Dong Yanmei	CHN	16.2.77	5	WI	Lisboa	10 Mar
8:42.75	Benita	Willis	AUS	6.5.79	6	WI	Lisboa	10 Mar
8:43.38	Regina	Jacobs	USA	28.8.63	1		Boston	4 Feb
8:44.33	Leah	Malot	KEN	7.6.72	3		Erfurt	2 Feb
8:45.36	Hayley	Tullett	GBR	17.2.73	8	WI	Lisboa	10 Mar
8:46.39	Violeta	Szekely	ROM	26.3.65	2	Euro	Birmingham	18 Feb
8:46.47	Lidia	Chojecka	POL	25.1.77	3	Euro	Birmingham	18 Feb
8:46.56	Werknesh	Kidane	ETH	21.11.81	9	WI	Lisboa	10 Mar
8:48.33	Amy	Rudolph	USA	18.9.73	2		Boston	4 Feb
8:48.57	Helena	Javornik	SLO	26.3.66	5	Euro	Birmingham	18 Feb
8:48.60	Aysen	Barak	TUR	9.9.75	6	Euro	Birmingham	18 Feb
8:49.55	Marina	Bastos	POR	7.7.71	1	NC	Lisboa	4 Mar
8:50.36	Mariya	Pantyukhova	RUS	14.8.74	7	Euro	Birmingham	18 Feb
8:51.68	Sarah	Schwald	USA	2.1.73	3		Boston	4 Feb
8:53.41	Fernanda	Ribeiro	POR	23.6.69	2	NC	Lisboa	4 Mar
8:57.53	Alla	Zhilyayeva	RUS	5.2.69	3	NC	Moskva	16 Feb
8:57.83	Maria	Cioncan	ROM	19.6.77	1		Budapest	3 Feb
8:59.73	Cristina	Petite	ESP	10.5.72	2	NC	Valencia	24 Feb
8:59.99	Elena	Iagar	ROM	16.1.75	1	NC	Bucuresti	24 Feb

Mark	Name		Nat	Born	Date
9:00.88	Cristina	Grosu	ROM	11.11.76	18 Feb
9:00.90	Margarita	Marusova	RUS	25.11.67	16 Feb
9:02.23	Ana	Dias	POR	15.1.74	28 Jan
9:03.96	Patricia	Arribas	ESP	2.10.77	20 Jan
9:04.42	Andrea	Suldesová	CZE	11.2.75	2 Feb
9:05.74	Luminita	Zaituc	GER	9.10.68	24 Feb
9:06.78		Li Ji ¶	CHN	19.9.79	9 Mar
9:07.39	Kristin	Chisum	USA	30.6.72	4 Feb
9:07.94	Jacqueline	Martín	ESP	14.4.74	18 Feb

Mark	Name		Nat	Born	Pos	Meet	Venue	Date

JUNIORS

See main list for top 6 juniors. 12 performances by 7 women to 9:02.8. Additional marks and further juniors:

Abeylegasse 8:59.51 1 Istanbul 29 Jul 9:01.95 1 Izmir 13 May
Wangui 9:00.32 1 Hirosaki 26 May 9:02.74 1 Sendai 18 Jun
Defar 9:01.84 5 Rieto 2 Sep

Mark	Name		Nat	Born	Pos	Meet	Venue	Date
9:02.64	Tatyana	Chulakh	RUS	2.6.82	2	EJ	Grosseto	21 Jul
9:03.45	Emi	Ikeda	JPN	29.8.83	1		Rifu	17 Oct
9:03.64	Melissa	Rollison	AUS	13.4.83	1		Melbourne	6 Dec
9:04.86	Ejagayehu	Dibaba	ETH	21.3.82	9	GP II	Gresham	3 Jun
9:06.63	Miwa	Kirihara	JPN	3.8.82	1rB		Kanazawa	29 Sep
9:07.23	Maiko	Yamaguchi	JPN	19.5.82	2rB		Kanazawa	29 Sep
9:07.35	Ulla	Tuimala	FIN	27.4.82	3	EJ	Grosseto	21 Jul
9:08.49	Krisztina	Papp	HUN	17.12.82	4	EJ	Grosseto	21 Jul
9:09.46	Georgie	Clarke	AUS	17.6.84	2		Melbourne	6 Dec
9:09.95	Sally	Chepyego	KEN	3.10.85	1	WY	Debrecen	14 Jul
9:11.29	Yukari	So	JPN	20.4.84	2		Rifu	17 Oct
9:11.60	Mestawat	Tufa	ETH	86	2	WY	Debrecen	14 Jul
9:11.70	Mika	Okunaga	JPN	27.10.82	3r2		Kanazawa	29 Sep
9:12.45	Satomi	Kijima (20)	JPN	24.10.83	3		Rifu	17 Oct
9:12.70	Fridah	Domongole	KEN	15.1.84	3	WY	Debrecen	14 Jul

5000 METRES

Mark	Name		Nat	Born	Pos	Meet	Venue	Date
14:29.32	Olga	Yegorova	RUS	28.3.72	1	ISTAF	Berlin	31 Aug
14:31.69	Getenesh	Wami	ETH	11.12.74	2	ISTAF	Berlin	31 Aug
14:32.44	Paula	Radcliffe	GBR	17.12.73	3	ISTAF	Berlin	31 Aug
14:39.22	Tatyana	Tomashova	RUS	1.7.75	4	ISTAF	Berlin	31 Aug
14:40.47	Yelena	Zadorozhnaya	RUS	3.12.77	1	ECp-S	Bremen	24 Jun
14:44.21		Radcliffe			1	BrGP	London (CP)	22 Jul
14:45.86	Edith	Masai	KEN	4.4.67	1	DNG	Stockholm	17 Jul
14:46.06		Masai			1	Bisl	Oslo	13 Jul
14:46.92	Gabriela	Szabo	ROM	14.11.75	2	Bisl	Oslo	13 Jul
14:48.97	Rose	Cheruiyot	KEN	21.7.76	3	Bisl	Oslo	13 Jul
14:49.32	Asmae	Leghzaoui	MAR	30.8.76	4	Bisl	Oslo	13 Jul
14:49.84		Radcliffe			2	ECp-S	Bremen	24 Jun
14:51.58		Dong Yanmei (10)	CHN	16.2.77	1	NG	Guangzhou	23 Nov
14:51.67	Berhane	Adere	ETH	21.7.73	1	FBK	Hengelo	4 Jun
14:53.00	Irina	Mikitenko	GER	23.8.72	2	FBK	Hengelo	4 Jun
14:53.82		Mikitenko			2	BrGP	London (CP)	22 Jul
14:54.00	Ayelech	Worku	ETH	12.6.79	3	FBK	Hengelo	4 Jun
14:55.27	Susan	Chepkemei	KEN	25.6.75	5	Bisl	Oslo	13 Jul
14:56.15		Xing Huina	CHN-J	25.2.84	2	NG	Guangzhou	23 Nov
14:56.75	Pamela	Chepchumba	KEN	28.2.78	4	FBK	Hengelo	4 Jun
14:56.95	Leah	Malot	KEN	7.6.72	5	ISTAF	Berlin	31 Aug
14:57.00		Wami			5	FBK	Hengelo	4 Jun
14:58.12	Marta	Domínguez	ESP	3.11.75	2	DNG	Stockholm	17 Jul
14:58.72		Cheruiyot			3	DNG	Stockholm	17 Jul
15:00.56	Joanne	Pavey	GBR	20.9.73	6	ISTAF	Berlin	31 Aug
15:02.62	Ebru	Kavaklioglu (20)	TUR	14.3.70	7	ISTAF	Berlin	31 Aug
15:02.70		Sun Yingjie	CHN	3.10.77	3	NG	Guangzhou	23 Nov
15:03.39		Yegorova			1	WCh	Edmonton	11 Aug
15:03.56	Elva	Dryer	USA	26.9.71	6	Bisl	Oslo	13 Jul
15:04.18	Benita	Willis	AUS	6.5.79	7	Bisl	Oslo	13 Jul
	(30/23)							
15:05.33	Restituta	Joseph	TAN	30.7.71	3	BrGP	London (CP)	22 Jul
15:05.48	Marla	Runyan	USA	4.1.69	4	BrGP	London (CP)	22 Jul
15:06.08	Merima	Denboba	ETH	21.8.74	6	FBK	Hengelo	4 Jun
15:06.35	Fatima	Yvelain	FRA	31.12.69	5	BrGP	London (CP)	22 Jul
15:08.02	Deena	Drossin	USA	14.2.73	5	DNG	Stockholm	17 Jul
15:08.07	Lornah	Kiplagat	KEN	20.3.74	1		Utrecht	22 Jun
15:08.42		Guo Lingling	CHN-J	18.6.86	4	NG	Guangzhou	23 Nov
	(30)							
15:08.65	Meseret	Defar	ETH-J	19.11.83	2	NA	Heusden	14 Jul
15:08.78	Mihaela	Botezan	ROM	21.11.76	3	ECp-S	Bremen	24 Jun
15:09.31	Tegla	Loroupe	KEN	9.5.73	9	ISTAF	Berlin	31 Aug
15:10.23	Kayoko	Fukushi	JPN-J	25.3.82	3	NA	Heusden	14 Jul
15:10.54	Susanne	Pumper	AUT	1.9.70	6	BrGP	London (CP)	22 Jul
15:10.78	Regina	Jacobs	USA	28.8.63	2	NC	Eugene	24 Jun
15:10.83	Amy	Rudolph	USA	18.9.73	4	NA	Heusden	14 Jul
15:11.01	Beatriz	Santiago	ESP	28.10.68	6	NA	Heusden	14 Jul

Mark	Name		Nat	Born	Pos	Meet	Venue	Date
15:12.76	Teresa	Recio	ESP	7.7.63	1		Braga	4 Jul
15:13.26	Jen	Rhines	USA	1.7.74	8	Bisl	Oslo	13 Jul
	(40)							
15:14.62	Kathy	Butler	GBR	22.10.73	1		Madison	12 May
15:14.73	Jelena	Prokopcuka	LAT	21.9.76	9	Bisl	Oslo	13 Jul
15:15.49	Breeda	Dennehy-Willis	IRL	3.2.70	9	FBK	Hengelo	4 Jun
15:15.75		Wei Yanan	CHN	6.12.81	5	NG	Guangzhou	23 Nov
15:17.31	Rodica	Moroianu (Nagel)	FRA	18.11.70	8	BrGP	London (CP)	22 Jul
15:17.43	Gunhild	Halle Haugen	NOR	1.6.72	11	Bisl	Oslo	13 Jul
15:17.95	Yamna	Belkacem	FRA	20.2.74	12	Bisl	Oslo	13 Jul
15:18.05	Irene	Limika	KEN	28.8.79	9	BrGP	London (CP)	22 Jul
15:18.80	Maria	McCambridge	IRL	10.7.75	7	NA	Heusden	14 Jul
15:19.08		Ju Limei	CHN	9.6.78	6	NG	Guangzhou	23 Nov
	(50)							
15:19.12	Una	English	IRL	14.8.70	2	NA	Heusden	14 Jul
15:19.12	Hayley	Yelling	GBR	3.1.74	10	BrGP	London (CP)	22 Jul
15:19.14		Wang Chunmei	CHN	10.4.76	7	NG	Guangzhou	23 Nov
15:19.75	Megumi	Tanaka	JPN	4.9.75	9	DNG	Stockholm	17 Jul
15:20.46	Hrystosomía	Iakóvou	GRE	9.4.71	9	NA	Heusden	14 Jul
15:21.01	Mónica	Rosa	POR	5.5.78	10	DNG	Stockholm	17 Jul
15:21.12	Hewan	Abeylegesse	TUR-J	11.9.82	1	EJ	Grosseto	20 Jul
15:21.95	Natalya	Berkut	UKR	30.5.75	1	ECp-1B	Budapest	23 Jun
15:22.0A	Nancy	Wambui	KEN-J	15.8.83	1		Nairobi	12 May
15:22.06	Marleen	Renders	BEL	24.12.68	10	NA	Heusden	14 Jul
	(60)							
15:22.26	Dulce	Rodríguez	MEX	14.8.72	1		Montreal (McG)	10 Jul
15:22.70	Akiko	Kawashima	JPN	5.8.77	2		Montreal (McG)	10 Jul
15:23.23	Cristina	Petite	ESP	10.5.72	11	NA	Heusden	14 Jul
15:23.45	Helena	Javornik	SLO	26.3.66	13	BrGP	London (CP)	22 Jul
15:23.87	Susie	Power	AUS	26.3.75	5	GWG	Brisbane	4 Sep
15:23.93	Haruko	Okamoto	JPN	19.8.74	10h2	WCh	Edmonton	9 Aug
15:24.71		Dai Yanyan	CHN	8.1.80	8	NG	Guangzhou	23 Nov
15:24.97		Liu Min	CHN-J	29.11.83	9	NG	Guangzhou	23 Nov
15:25.52	Carrie	Tollefson	USA	18.1.77	12	NA	Heusden	14 Jul
15:26.41	Ana	Dias	POR	15.1.74	1	NC	Lisboa (U)	22 Jul
	(70)							
15:26.6	Ikuko	Tamura	JPN	24.9.78	1		Takamatsu	13 Oct
15:26.84	Olivera	Jevtic	YUG	24.7.77	2	ECp-1B	Budapest	23 Jun
15:26.95	Clare	Taylor	USA	7.12.69	5	NC	Eugene	24 Jun
15:28.07	Yelena	Burykina	RUS	1.1.73	1	Kuts	Moskva	27 Jul
15:28.17	Zhor	El Kamch	MAR	15.3.73	10	FBK	Hengelo	4 Jun
15:28.32	Yoshiko	Fujinaga	JPN	15.8.81	3		Rifu	17 Oct
15:28.94	Yasuko	Hashimoto	JPN	12.8.75	4		Yokohama	15 Sep
15:29.02	Naomi	Sakashita	JPN	25.5.75	6	GP	Osaka	12 May
15:29.47	Yuko	Manabe	JPN	8.2.79	2		Brunswick	7 Jul
15:29.55		Wang Xiaoming	CHN-J	3.2.85	10	NG	Guangzhou	23 Nov
	(80)							
15:29.60	Courtney	Babcock	CAN	30.6.72	2		Eugene	12 May
15:29.64	Takako	Kotorida	JPN	2.4.77	2		Hiroshima	29 Apr
15:29.73	Harumi	Hiroyama	JPN	2.9.68	5		Yokohama	15 Sep
15:29.87	Noriko	Takahashi	JPN	9.11.76	6		Yokohama	15 Sep
15:29.96	Werknesh	Kidane	ETH	21.11.81	11h1	WCh	Edmonton	9 Aug
15:29.98	Inês	Monteiro	POR	18.5.80	3	NC	Lisboa (U)	22 Jul
15:30.0A	Margaret	Okayo	KEN	30.5.76	2	NC	Nairobi	23 Jun
15:30.04	Ikumi	Nagayama	JPN	22.6.74	4		Rifu	17 Oct
15:30.15	Yoshiko	Ichikawa	JPN	18.4.76	2		Shizuoka	3 May
15:30.42	Cheri	Kenah	USA	26.12.70	6	NC	Eugene	24 Jun
	(90)							
15:30.63	Alesya	Turova	BLR	6.12.79	11	ISTAF	Berlin	31 Aug
15:30.88	Mari	Ozaki	JPN	16.7.75	5		Rifu	17 Oct
15:32.31	Ejagayehu	Dibaba	ETH-J	21.3.82	7		Yokohama	15 Sep
15:32.59	Olga	Romanova	RUS	23.5.80	2	Kuts	Moskva	27 Jul
15:32.67		Zhang Yang	CHN-J	20.7.83	8h2	NG	Guangzhou	21 Nov
15:33.02	Naomi	Mugo	KEN	2.1.77	6	GWG	Brisbane	4 Sep
15:33.40	Elisa	Rea	ITA	23.3.68	5	ECp	Bremen	24 Jun
15:33.66	Minori	Hayakari	JPN	29.11.72	1		Kobe	14 Oct
15:33.76	Rie	Ueno	JPN	11.6.76	3	NC	Tokyo	9 Jun
15:34.49	Hisae	Yoshimatsu	JPN	13.5.79	3		Hiroshima	29 Apr
	(100)							

Mark		Name	Nat	Born	Date
15:34.54		Zhang Shujing	CHN	13.9.78	21 Nov
15:34.64	Yumiko	Okamoto	JPN	28.3.78	8 Jul
15:34.90	Chiemi	Takahashi	JPN	16.2.76	17 Oct
15:35.13	Yukiko	Akaba	JPN	18.10.79	8 Jul
15:35.54		Wang Hongxia	CHN	13.1.75	29 Apr
15:35.70	Tatyana	Khmeleva	RUS	2.4.79	15 Jun
15:35.83	Olga	Rosseyeva	RUS	1.8.81	15 Jul
15:36.31	Jenny	Crain	USA	12.2.68	12 May
15:36.38	Momoe	Shinta	JPN	28.5.79	14 Oct
15:36.69	Simone	Staicu	HUN	5.5.71	23 Jun
15:36.88	Miwako	Yamanaka	JPN	24.5.78	14 Oct
15:37.12	Kristen	Chisum	USA	30.6.72	10 Jul
15:37.22	Lyudmila	Vasilyeva	RUS	20.10.69	15 Jul
15:38.17	Mami	Kusunoki	JPN	8.9.75	29 Apr
15:38.43	Yoko	Shibui	JPN	14.3.79	12 May
15:38.53	Anastasiya	Zubova	RUS	7.8.79	15 Jun
15:38.75	Yuki	Saito	JPN	25.9.80	30 Sep
15:39.37	Anja	Smolders	BEL	2.6.73	10 Aug
15:39.38	Makiko	Kawashima	JPN	5.8.77	14 Oct
15:39.77	Tina	Connelly	CAN	16.8.70	25 May
15:39.82		Zheng Guixia	CHN	24.6.73	3 May
15:39.88	Kyoko	Katafuchi	JPN	12.3.80	3 May
15:39.96	Tatyana	Belovol	UKR	7.10.69	1 Jul
15:40.46	Haruko	Yamamoto	JPN	31.10.81	29 Apr
15:40.55	Katalin	Szentgyörgy	HUN	1.1.79	14 Jul
15:40.58	Cláudia	Pereira	POR	20.2.76	4 Jul
15:40.65	Miwa	Kirihara	JPN-J	3.8.82	30 Sep
15:40.84	Kaori	Sato	JPN	15.5.80	30 Sep
15:41.09	Svetlana	Nekhorosh	UKR	22.7.73	1 Jul
15:41.13	Anália	Rosa	POR	28.2.76	23 Jun
15:41.39	Luminita	Zaituc	GER	9.10.68	24 Jun
15:41.59	Annette	Peters	USA	31.5.65	12 May
15:41.6	Mika	Okunaga	JPN-J	27.10.82	13 Oct
15:41.77	Kara	Wheeler	USA	9.7.78	24 Jun
15:41.90	Asuka	Kato	JPN	7.3.80	14 Oct
15:42.0	Liliya	Volkova	RUS	13.11.77	29 May
15:42.0	Rie	Matsuoka	JPN	9.3.77	24 Oct
15:42.19	Kazue	Ogoshi	JPN	2.3.81	3 May
15:42.27	Silvia	Sommaggio	ITA	20.11.69	17 Jul
15:42.52		Li Meihua	CHN	26.12.77	22 Apr
15:42.80	Esther	Wanjiru	KEN	27.3.77	9 Jun
15:42.95	Claudia	Stalder	SUI	20.9.72	14 Jul
15:43.0	Kazumi	Matsuo	JPN	16.4.74	24 Oct
15:43.01	Sachie	Ozaki	JPN	12.3.77	14 Oct
15:43.06	Hanan	Fahroun	MAR	26.5.74	14 Jul
15:43.15	Marina	Dubrova	UKR	9.12.78	17 May
15:43.72	Margarita	Tapia	MEX	16.11.76	25 May
15:43.72	Tomoko	Hatori	JPN	28.5.81	14 Oct
15:43.73	Adriana	Fernández	MEX	4.4.71	9 Jun
15:44.11	M Luisa	Larraga	ESP	10.12.70	23 Jun
15:44.51		Li Ji ¶	CHN	19.9.79	26 May
15:44.54	Lenah	Cheruiyot	KEN	73	22 Jun
15:44.86	Nasria	Baghdad Azaidj	ALG	29.10.71	14 Jul
15:45.04	Tereza	Yohannes	ETH-J	82	14 Jul
15:45.04	Lucy	Wangui	KEN-J	24.3.84	15 Jul
15:45.12	Nicole	Jefferson	USA	8.3.76	24 Jun
15:45.15	Eyerusalem	Kuma	ETH	4.11.81	12 May
15:45.63	Iness	Chenonge	KEN-J	1.2.82	14 Jul
15:45.63	Tomoko	Chakushi	JPN	12.8.81	30 Sep
15:45.95	Maria	Protópappa	GRE	5.5.73	17 Jun
15:46.76	Analídia	Torre	POR	10.10.76	4 Jul
15:46.91	Naoko	Sakata	JPN-J	1.5.82	8 Apr
15:46.99	Galina	Aleksandrova	RUS	15.10.76	15 Jul
15:47.44	Takami	Nishiyama	JPN	17.10.80	14 Oct
15:47.6	Yelena	Samokhvalova	RUS	21.11.80	29 May
15:47.78	Namie	Yamamoto	JPN	18.2.80	30 Sep
15:48.0	Samukeliso	Moyo	ZIM	1.1.74	16 Feb
	(167)				

Indoors

Mark		Name	Nat	Born	Pos	Venue	Date
14:49.36i		Wami			1	Dortmund	11 Feb
14:55.99i		Mikitenko			2	Dortmund	11 Feb
15:27.99i	Aysen	Barak	TUR	9.9.75	3	Dortmund	11 Feb

JUNIORS

See main list for top 10 juniors. 12 performances by 7 women to 15:25.0. Additional marks and further juniors:

	Mark	Pos	Meet	Venue	Date	Mark	Pos	Meet	Venue	Date
Defar	15:17.52	7	DNG	Stockholm	17 Jul	15:24.83	1		Palo Alto	9 Jun
Fukushi	15:15.56	1r2		Kanazawa	30 Sep	15:20.08	1	NG	Rifu	17 Oct
Abeylegasse	15:22.89	8h1	WCh	Edmonton	9 Aug					

Mark		Name	Nat	Born	Pos	Meet	Venue	Date
15:40.65	Miwa	Kirihara	JPN	3.8.82	3rA		Kanazawa	30 Sep
15:41.6	Mika	Okunaga	JPN	27.10.82	2r2		Takamatsu	13 Oct
15:45.04	Tereza	Yohannes	ETH	82	1		Maia	14 Jul
15:45.04	Lucy	Wangui	KEN	24.3.84	1		Aomori	15 Jul
15:45.63	Iness	Chenonge	KEN	1.2.82	2		Lisboa	14 Jul
15:46.91	Naoko	Sakata	JPN	1.5.82	4r3		Kumamoto	8 Apr
15:50.89	Hiromi	Fujii	JPN	7.2.83	1rB		Kanazawa	30 Sep
15:52.66	Yasuko	Owatari	JPN	11.12.83	8r3		Kumamoto	8 Apr
15:53.84		Zhang Yuhong	CHN	15.1.83	12	NG	Guangzhou	23 Nov
15:55.26	Mika	Matsumoto (20)	JPN	24.11.84	11r3		Kumamoto	8 Apr

10,000 METRES

Mark		Name	Nat	Born	Pos	Meet	Venue	Date
30:55.80	Paula	Radcliffe	GBR	17.12.73	1	E Chall	Barakaldo	7 Apr
31:16.94	Asmae	Leghzaoui	MAR	30.8.76	1	MedG	Tunis	12 Sep
31:22.76	Natalya	Berkut	UKR	30.5.75	1	NC	Kiev	2 Jul
31:26.34	Susie	Power	AUS	26.3.75	1	Zat	Melbourne	6 Dec
31:29.55	Irina	Mikitenko	GER	23.8.72	2	E Chall	Barakaldo	7 Apr
31:30.6	Lyudmila	Biktasheva	RUS	25.7.74	1	NC	Tula	8 Jul
31:32.70	Berhane	Adere	ETH	21.7.73	1		Villeneuve d'Ascq	17 Jun
31:33.08	Olivera	Jevtic	YUG	24.7.77	2	MedG	Tunis	12 Sep
31:38.08	Ayelech	Worku	ETH	12.6.79	2		Villeneuve d'Ascq	17 Jun
31:38.18	Restituta	Joseph (10)	TAN	30.7.71	3		Villeneuve d'Ascq	17 Jun
31:39.80	Harumi	Hiroyama	JPN	2.9.68	1		Kobe	14 Oct
31:41.32	Takako	Kotorida	JPN	2.4.77	1		Kobe	22 Apr
31:41.74	Leah	Malot	KEN	7.6.72	4		Villeneuve d'Ascq	17 Jun
31:42.05	Kayoko	Fukushi	JPN-J	25.3.82	1rA		Kanazawa	29 Sep
31:43.41	Werknesh	Kidane	ETH	21.11.81	5		Villeneuve d'Ascq	17 Jun
31:43.59		Dong Yanmei	CHN	16.2.77	1	NG	Guangzhou	19 Nov
31:45.06	Mihaela	Botezan	ROM	21.11.76	1	NC	Bucuresti	9 Jun
31:47.82	Yoshiko	Fujinaga	JPN	15.8.81	2		Kobe	22 Apr

Mark	Name		Nat	Born	Pos	Meet	Venue	Date
31:48.19	Derartu	Tulu	ETH	21.3.72	1	GWG	Brisbane	7 Sep
31:48.50	Yumiko	Hara (20)	JPN-J	9.1.82	2		Kobe	14 Oct
31:48.57		Worku			2	GWG	Brisbane	7 Sep
31:48.73	Yoko	Shibui	JPN	14.3.79	3		Kobe	22 Apr
31:48.81		Tulu			1	WCh	Edmonton	7 Aug
31:48.85		Adere			2	WCh	Edmonton	7 Aug
31:49.47		Sun Yingjie	CHN	3.10.77	2	NG	Guangzhou	19 Nov
31:49.98	Getenesh	Wami	ETH	11.12.74	3	WCh	Edmonton	7 Aug
31:50.06		Radcliffe			4	WCh	Edmonton	7 Aug
31:50.36		Power			3	GWG	Brisbane	7 Sep
31:50.39	Haruko	Okamoto	JPN	19.8.74	1	NC	Tokyo	10 Jun
31:50.56	Mari	Ozaki	JPN	16.7.75	2	NC	Tokyo	10 Jun
31:50.97	Tegla	Loroupe	KEN	9.5.73	6		Villeneuve d'Ascq	17 Jun
31:50.97	Yasuyo	Iwamoto	JPN	8.9.76	1rB		Kanazawa	29 Sep
	(32/27)							
31:51.13	Mizuki	Noguchi	JPN	3.7.78	3	NC	Tokyo	10 Jun
31:53.7	Miwako	Yamanaka	JPN	24.5.78	1		Toyonaka	13 Nov
31:53.78		Liu Min	CHN-J	29.11.83	3	NG	Guangzhou	19 Nov
	(30)							
31:54.86		Wei Yanan	CHN	6.12.81	4	NG	Guangzhou	19 Nov
31:56.47		Zheng Guixia	CHN	24.6.73	3rA		Kanazawa	29 Sep
31:56.48	Ikumi	Nagayama	JPN	22.6.74	4	NC	Tokyo	10 Jun
31:56.78	Nami	Kurosawa	JPN	26.12.78	4rA		Kanazawa	29 Sep
31:57.10	Merima	Denboba	ETH	21.8.74	7		Villeneuve d'Ascq	17 Jun
31:57.49	Aster	Bacha	ETH-J	83	8		Villeneuve d'Ascq	17 Jun
31:59.27	Kathy	Butler	GBR	22.10.73	1	MSR	Walnut	20 Apr
31:59.87	Chiemi	Takahashi	JPN	16.2.76	4		Kobe	22 Apr
31:59.91	Naomi	Sakashita	JPN	25.5.75	5		Kobe	22 Apr
32:00.75	Megumi	Tanaka	JPN	4.9.75	5	NC	Tokyo	10 Jun
	(40)							
32:01.23	Kaori	Yoshida	JPN	4.8.81	5rA		Kanazawa	29 Sep
32:01.43	Kiyomi	Ogawa	JPN	15.9.81	6rA		Kanazawa	29 Sep
32:02.16	Makiko	Kawashima	JPN	5.8.77	7rA		Kanazawa	29 Sep
32:02.37	Elana	Meyer	RSA	10.10.66	9		Villeneuve d'Ascq	17 Jun
32:02.96	Jelena	Prokopcuka	LAT	21.9.76	10		Villeneuve d'Ascq	17 Jun
32:03.26	Yukako	Goto	JPN	16.9.73	8rA		Kanazawa	29 Sep
32:04.94	Lyudmila	Petrova	RUS	7.10.68	6	WCh	Edmonton	7 Aug
32:05.14	Deena	Drossin	USA	14.2.73	1	NC	Eugene	23 Jun
32:05.98	Yamna	Belkacem	FRA	20.2.74	11		Villeneuve d'Ascq	17 Jun
32:06.02		Wang Yanrong	CHN	16.10.76	3rB		Kanazawa	29 Sep
	(50)							
32:07.55		Ren Xiujuan	CHN	14.9.74	5	NG	Guangzhou	19 Nov
32:12.01	Kumi	Tanabe	JPN	2.4.81	9rA		Kanazawa	29 Sep
32:12.47	Breeda	Dennehy-Willis	IRL	3.2.70	12		Villeneuve d'Ascq	17 Jun
32:12.74	Yoko	Manabe	JPN	8.2.79	4rB		Kanazawa	29 Sep
32:12.88		Wang Hongxia	CHN	13.1.75	7		Kobe	22 Apr
32:14.14		Ju Limei	CHN	9.6.78	6	NG	Guangzhou	19 Nov
32:14.39	Yasuko	Hashimoto	JPN	12.8.75	10rA		Kanazawa	29 Sep
32:14.64	Kim	Fitchen	USA	3.9.68	2	MSR	Walnut	20 Apr
32:15.42	Yuko	Manabe	JPN	8.2.79	11rA		Kanazawa	29 Sep
32:15.94	Aki	Fujikawa	JPN	14.11.78	13rA		Kanazawa	29 Sep
	(60)							
32:17.64	Kaori	Tanabe	JPN	30.4.75	5rB		Kanazawa	29 Sep
32:18.27	Hiromi	Ominami	JPN	15.11.75	14rA		Kanazawa	29 Sep
32:18.36	Rie	Matsuoka	JPN	9.3.77	15rA		Kanazawa	29 Sep
32:18.75	Iulia	Olteanu	ROM	26.1.67	9	JPN Ch	Tokyo	10 Jun
32:19.14	Carol	Montgomery	CAN	24.8.66	3	MSR	Walnut	20 Apr
32:20.03	Jen	Rhines	USA	1.7.74	2	NC	Eugene	23 Jun
32:20.48	Ana	Dias	POR	15.1.74	13		Villeneuve d'Ascq	17 Jun
32:20.48		Zhang Yang	CHN-J	20.7.83	7	NG	Guangzhou	19 Nov
32:22.25	Mónica	Rosa	POR	5.5.78	3	E Chall	Barakaldo	7 Apr
32:22.74	Kyoko	Katafuchi	JPN	12.3.80	6rB		Kanazawa	29 Sep
	(70)							
32:22.78	Megumi	Kobayashi	JPN	4.8.76	11		Kobe	22 Apr
32:22.82	Noriko	Matsuoka	JPN	2.5.79	12	NC	Tokyo	10 Jun
32:23.00	Mikie	Takanaka	JPN	6.10.80	3		Kobe	14 Oct
32:24.00	Momoe	Shinta	JPN	28.5.79	7rB		Kanazawa	29 Sep
32:24.17	M Luisa	Larraga	ESP	10.12.70	2	NC	Mataró	15 Jul
32:24.20	Ejagayehu	Dibaba	ETH-J	21.3.82	6	GWG	Brisbane	7 Sep
32:24.62	Kazue	Ogoshi	JPN	2.3.81	13	NC	Tokyo	10 Jun

Mark	Name		Nat	Born	Pos	Meet	Venue	Date
32:25.22	Sylvia	Mosqueda	USA	8.4.66	3	NC	Eugene	23 Jun
32:25.3A	Catherine	Ndereba	KEN	21.7.72	1		Nairobi	12 May
32:25.68	Yuri	Kano	JPN	27.10.78	14	NC	Tokyo	10 Jun
	(80)							
32:26.91	Fumi	Murata	JPN	13.3.75	16rA		Kanazawa	29 Sep
32:27.69	Katalin	Szentgyörgyi	HUN	1.1.79	4	E Chall	Barakaldo	7 Apr
32:28.17	Rodica	Moroianu (Nagel)	FRA	18.11.70	14		Villeneuve d'Ascq	17 Jun
32:28.35		Dai Yanyan	CHN	8.1.80	8	NG	Guangzhou	19 Nov
32:29.11	Teresa	Recio	ESP	7.7.63	5	E Chall	Barakaldo	7 Apr
32:29.20	Hewan	Abeylegesse	TUR-J	11.9.82	3	MedG	Tunis	12 Sep
32:29.4	Galina	Aleksandrova	RUS	15.10.76	3	NC	Tula	8 Jul
32:29.54	Takami	Ominami	JPN	15.11.75	13		Kobe	22 Apr
32:29.6	Svetlana	Nekhorosh	UKR	22.7.73	4	RUS Ch	Tula	8 Jul
32:29.79	Ryoko	Kitajima	JPN	12.6.76	8rB		Kanazawa	29 Sep
	(90)							
32:31.46	Hrystosomía	Iakóvou	GRE	9.4.71	16	WCh	Edmonton	7 Aug
32:32.03	Ayano	Kozuka	JPN	27.10.77	9rB		Kanazawa	29 Sep
32:32.52	Tina	Connelly	CAN	16.8.70	5	MSR	Walnut	20 Apr
32:32.62		Zhang Yuhong	CHN-J	15.1.83	9	NG	Guangzhou	19 Nov
32:32.83	Asuka	Maeda	JPN	4.10.78	10rB		Kanazawa	29 Sep
32:33.00		Wang Xiaoming	CHN-J	3.2.85	10	NG	Guangzhou	19 Nov
32:33.69		Li Meihua	CHN	26.12.77	11	NG	Guangzhou	19 Nov
32:33.72	Gunhild	Halle Haugen	NOR	1.6.72	18	WCh	Edmonton	7 Aug
32:35.0	Sachie	Ozaki	JPN	12.3.77	2		Munakata	26 Dec
32:35.90	Luminita	Zaituc	GER	9.10.68	1rA	NC	Kandel	19 May
	(100)							

Mark	Name		Nat	Born	Date
32:36.00	Tomoko	Hatori	JPN	28.5.81	29 Sep
32:36.19		Sun Rong	CHN-J	8.5.85	19 Nov
32:36.6	Lydiya	Grigoryeva	RUS	21.1.74	8 Jul
32:36.87	María	Abel	ESP	23.10.74	7 Apr
32:36.88	Simona	Staicu	HUN	5.5.71	13 May
32:38.02		Li Helan	CHN	2.1.78	19 Nov
32:38.19	Sabrina	Mockenhaupt	GER	6.12.80	19 May
32:40.51	Maura	Viceconte	ITA	3.10.67	7 Apr
32:40.78	Milena	Glusac	USA	18.9.75	20 Apr
32:40.98	Kristen	Chisum	USA	30.6.72	23 Jun
32:41.72	Petra	Wassiluk	GER	27.10.69	19 May
32:42.62		Dong Zhaoxia	CHN	13.11.74	27 Apr
32:42.79	Irene	Limika	KEN	28.8.79	9 Jun
32:43.67	Kerryn	McCann	AUS	2.5.67	7 Sep
32:45.12	Annette	Peters	USA	31.5.65	23 Jun
32:45.84	Risa	Hagiwara	JPN-J	22.11.82	29 Sep
32:46.23	Mio	Kiuchi	JPN	20.11.78	29 Sep
32:47.9	Lidiya	Vasilevskaya	RUS	1.4.73	8 Jul
32:48.76	Courtney	Babcock	CAN	30.6.72	20 Apr
32:48.76	Anikó	Kálovics	HUN	13.5.77	13 May
32:49.6A	Alice	Chelangat	KEN	77	11 May
32:51.07	Melanie	Kraus	GER	24.10.74	19 May
32:53.02	Takami	Nishiyama	JPN	17.10.80	12 May
32:53.54	Lisa	Harvey	CAN	7.2.70	3 Jun
32:53.79	Kelly	Cordell	USA	24.1.70	31 Mar
32:57.00	Zahia	Dahmani	FRA	2.6.72	17 Jun
32:57.34	Blake	Russell	USA	24.7.75	23 Jun
32:57.35	Yukiko	Akaba	JPN	18.10.79	28 Aug
33:00.59		Lu Jingbo	CHN	18.4.73	19 Nov
33:01.29	Zhor	El Kamch	MAR	15.3.73	3 Jul
33:02.7	Mika	Okunaga	JPN-J	27.10.82	26 Dec
33:03.7A	Susan	Chepkemei	KEN	25.6.75	8 Jun
33:05.9	Masayo	Kobayashi	JPN	4.2.80	26 Dec
33:06.71		Li Ji ¶	CHN	19.9.79	23 May
33:07.86	Ritsuko	Sasaki	JPN	30.11.72	29 Sep
33:08.18	Silvia	Sommaggio	ITA	20.11.69	12 Sep
33:10.35	Alesandra	Aguilar	ESP	1.7.78	15 Jul
33:11.60	Inga	Juodeskiene	LTU	21.10.71	7 Aug
33:14.05	Mayumi	Ichikawa	JPN	3.5.76	19 May
33:14.32	Agata	Balsamo	ITA	11.11.70	7 Apr
	(140)				

JUNIORS

See main list for top 9 juniors. 11 performances by 8 women to 32:35.0. Additional marks and further juniors:

Fukushi	32:03.3				1		Mumakata	26 Dec
Hara	31:53.68				2rB		Kanazawa	29 Sep
Bacha	32:25.81				14	WCh	Edmonton	7 Aug
32:36.19		Sun Rong	CHN	8.5.85	12	NG	Guangzhou	19 Nov
32:45.84	Risa	Hagiwara	JPN	22.11.82	11rB		Kanazawa	29 Sep
33:02.7	Mika	Okunaga	JPN	27.10.82	5		Munakata	26 Dec
33:18.10		Shi Hongjuan	CHN	17.2.84	11		Shanghai	6 May
33:23.85	Satoko	Yagi	JPN	15.2.82	7		Nobeoka	12 May
33:26.09		Lu Juan	CHN	16.8.86	14		Shanghai	6 May
33:40.46	Felista	Wambui	KEN	5.8.83	1		Aomori	14 Jul
33:45.36		Chen Fang	CHN	28.10.82	4		Zhongshan	21 Apr
33:46.80		Chung Bok-eun	KOR	20.2.82	3		Chunan	11 Oct
33:46.84		Chang Jin-suk	KOR	10.1.83	4		Chunan	11 Oct
33:52.7A	Alice	Timbilil (20)	KEN	16.6.83	6	NC	Nairobi	22 Jun

10 KILOMETRES ROAD

30:47	Paula	Radcliffe	GBR	17.12.73	1		New York	9 Jun
30:58	Lornah	Kiplagat	KEN	20.3.74	1	Peach	Atlanta	4 Jul
31:02	Catherine	Ndereba	KEN	21.7.72	1		Budapest	14 Oct
31:03	Asmae	Leghzaoui	MAR	30.8.76	1		Marseille	1 May
31:13	Elana	Meyer	RSA	10.10.66	2		Budapest	14 Oct
31:19		L Kiplagat			1		Voorthuizen	25 Jul
31:23		Leghzaoui			1		La Courneuve	1 Apr
31:27	Pamela	Chepchumba	KEN	28.2.78	1		Paderborn	14 Apr

Mark	Name		Nat	Born	Pos	Meet	Venue	Date
31:27	Edith	Masai	KEN	4.4.67	2		Paderborn	14 Apr
31:28	Caroline	Kwambai	KEN	9.9.75	3		Paderborn	14 Apr
31:29	Isabellah	Ochichi	KEN	.79	1		Marseille	8 Apr
31:31	Olivera	Jevtic (10)	YUG	24.7.77	3		Budapest	14 Oct
31:34		Ndereba			1		Cape Elizabeth	4 Aug
31:36		L Kiplagat			2		Cape Elizabeth	4 Aug
31:37		L Kiplagat			1		San Juan	18 Feb
31:39		Meyer			2		San Juan	18 Feb
31:43	Sally	Barsosio	KEN	21.3.78	1		Cleveland	29 Apr
31:43	Esther	Kiplagat	KEN	8.12.66	2	Peach	Atlanta	4 Jul
31:44	Rose	Cheruiyot	KEN	21.7.76	2		La Courneuve	1 Apr
31:46		Ochichi			3		La Courneuve	1 Apr
	(20/13)							
31:49	Megumi	Tanaka	JPN	4.9.75	1		London	22 Jul
31:52	Susan	Chepkemei	KEN	25.6.75	2		Brunssum	8 Apr
31:53	Restituta	Joseph	TAN	30.7.71	2		New York	9 Jun
31:55	Irene	Kwambai	KEN	25.10.78	4		La Courneuve	1 Apr
31:57	Lenah	Cheruiyot	KEN	73	2		Glasgow	20 May
31:59+	Mizuki	Noguchi	JPN	3.7.78	1	in HMar	Bristol	7 Oct
32:00	Yamna	Belkacem	FRA	20.2.74	5		La Courneuve	1 Apr
32:00	Judy	Kiplimo	KEN	.68	1		Den Haag	27 May
32:00	Alina	Gherasim	ROM	10.11.71	4	Peach	Atlanta	4 Jul
32:00+	Berhane	Adere	ETH	21.7.73	6	in HMar	Bristol	7 Oct
Others where superior to 10,000m track bests:								
32:03	Hellen	Kimaiyo-Koskei	KEN	8.9.68	3		San Juan	18 Feb
32:07	Magdaline	Chemjor	KEN	12.11.78	3		Brunssum	8 Apr
32:11	Colleen	de Reuck	USA	13.4.64	1		Boston	8 Oct
32:14	Edna	Kiplagat	KEN		1		Toronto	6 May
32:15A	Jane	Ekimat	KEN	12.6.74	1		Iten	16 Nov
32:17	Constantina	Dita/Tomescu	ROM	23.1.70	5	Peach	Atlanta	4 Jul
32:18	Milena	Glusac	USA	18.9.75	6	Peach	Atlanta	4 Jul
32:18	Melanie	Kraus	GER	24.10.74	1		Bergisch Gladbach	7 Sep
32:19	Lydiya	Grigoryeva	RUS	21.1.74	3		Cleveland	29 Apr
32:20	Sara	Cedillo	MEX	20.9.76	2		Mazatlan	1 Dec
32:21	Sylvia	Mosqueda	USA	8.4.66	1		Redondo Beach	28 Jan
32:23	Nancy	Omwenga	KEN		1		Morlaix	28 Oct
32:24	Jane Jepkoge	Kiptoo	KEN-J	8.8.82	1		s'Hertogenbosch	23 Sep
32:25	Jane	Omoro	KEN	12.9.74	7	Peach	Atlanta	4 Jul
32:26	Florence	Barsosio	KEN	11.8.76	3		New York	9 Jun
32:26	Beáta	Rakonczai	HUN	25.6.77	4	Avon	Budapest	14 Oct
32:27	Simona	Staicu	HUN	5.5.71	5	Avon	Budapest	14 Oct
32:28	Gladys	Asiba	KEN	31.5.77	4		San Juan	18 Feb
32:28+	Lidia	Simon	ROM	4.9.73	2	in HMar	Sapporo	1 Jul
32:29	Kathrin	Wessel	GER	14.8.67	5		Paderborn	14 Apr
32:29	Hawa	Hussein	TAN-J	5.12.82	6		Paderborn	14 Apr
32:29	Natalie	Harvey	AUS	19.1.75	3		Glasgow	20 May
32:30	Petra	Wassiluk	GER	27.10.69	7		Paderborn	14 Apr
32:30	Iness	Chenonge	KEN-J	1.2.82	1		Seveso	25 Apr
32:32	Uta	Pippig	GER	7.9.65	1		Ottawa	12 May
32:33	Jane	Ngotho	KEN	29.11.69	4		New York	9 Jun
32:34	Dulce M	Rodríguez	MEX	14.8.72	4		Mazatlan	1 Dec
32:35	Sonia	O'Sullivan	IRL	28.11.69	5		Glasgow	20 May

Mark	Name		Nat	Born	Date
32:37	Yumiko	Okamoto	JPN	28.3.78	11 Feb
32:37	Christine	Chepkonga	KEN	12.12.80	29 Apr
32:37	Elisabeth	Chemweno	KEN	13.7.78	20 May
32:38	Margaret	Okayo	KEN	30.5.76	16 Apr
32:38	Martha	Komu	KEN-J	23.3.83	12 May
32:40	Emiko	Nakasato	JPN	.78	11 Feb
32:40	Lidiya	Vasilevskaya	RUS	1.4.73	20 May
32:41	Miyuki	Hikita	JPN	1.3.81	11 Feb
32:41	Inês	Monteiro	POR	18.5.80	30 Dec
32:43	Elva	Dryer	USA	26.9.71	3 Nov
32:43+	Joyce	Chepchumba	KEN	6.11.70	1 Apr
32:43	Irma	Heeren	NED	16.4.67	25 Jul
32:44	Eyerusalem	Kuma	ETH	4.11.81	4 Aug
32:44	Noriko	Geji	JPN	31.5.73	11 Feb
32:45	Fatima	Yvelain	FRA	31.12.69	1 May
32:45	Silviya	Skvortsova	RUS	16.11.74	14 Oct
32:47+	Teyeba	Erkesso	ETH-J	82	7 Oct
32:48	Svetlana	Zakharova	RUS	15.9.70	19 May
32:48	Beatrice	Omwanza	KEN	78	14 Sep
32:48	Yelena	Paramonova	RUS	28.6.62	14 Oct
32:49	Luminita	Talpos	ROM	9.10.72	4 Aug
32:49	Satoko	Yagi	JPN-J	15.2.82	11 Feb
32:51	Silvia	Sommaggio	ITA	20.11.69	9 Jun
32:51	Fernanda	Ribeiro	POR	23.6.69	9 Jun
32:51	Faith	Chemutai	KEN	80	4 Jul
32:52	Alla	Zhilyayeva	RUS	5.2.69	1 Apr
32:52	Margaret	Ngotho	KEN		22 Apr
32:53	Cristina	Pomacu	ROM	15.9.73	4 Jul
32:55	Emi	Nakajima	JPN	8.8.80	11 Feb
32:56	Grete	Koens	NED	25.5.67	23 Sep
32:56	Anne Marie	Lauck	USA	7.3.69	3 Nov
32:56	Zakia	Mrisho	TAN		16 Dec
32:57	Sonja	Oberem	GER	24.2.73	4 Mar
32:57	Teresa	Wanjuku	KEN	7.5.74	24 Mar
32:58	Abeba	Tolla	ETH	3.6.77	24 Jun
32:58	Margaret	Kerubo	KEN	15.5.74	30 Dec
32:59	Junko	Oshi	JPN-J	18.8.82	2 Dec

Downhill: Jul 23, Salt Lake City: 1. Nicole Jefferson CAN 32:39

Mark	Name	Nat	Born	Pos Meet	Venue	Date

Downhill: 30 Sep, Pittsburgh: 1. Gladys AsibaKEN 32:10, 2. Naomi Wangui KEN 32:18, 3. Yelena Paramonova RUS 32:22, 4. Jackline Torori KEN 32:42

Uncertain Distance: Pinkafeld 16 Apr: 1. Simona Staicu HUN 5.5.71 31:32, 2. Anikó Kálovics HUN 13.5.77 31:58

32:33	Tausi	Juma	TAN-J	1.6.83	8 Apr
32:43	Dorota	Ustianowska	POL	24.6.70	31 Aug
32:43	Teresa	Yohannes	ETH-J	82	18 Nov
32:45	Larisa	Timkina	MDA	7.12.66	24 Mar
32:58	Griselda	González	ESP	4.12.65	8 Apr

15 KILOMETRES ROAD

Mark	First	Name	Nat	Born	Pos	Meet	Venue	Date
47:44+	Paula	Radcliffe	GBR	17.12.73	1	in HM	Bristol	7 Oct
47:45+	Susan	Chepkemei	KEN	25.6.75	2	in HM	Bristol	7 Oct
47:54+		Chepkemei			1=	in 10M	Zaandam	23 Sep
47:54+	Isabellah	Ochichi	KEN	.79	1=	in 10M	Bristol	7 Oct
48:06	Catherine	Ndereba	KEN	21.7.72	1		Utica	8 Jul
48:11	Elana	Meyer	RSA	10.10.66	2		Utica	8 Jul
48:11+	Mizuki	Noguchi	JPN	3.7.78	3	in HM	Bristol	7 Oct
48:11+	Berhane	Adere	ETH	21.7.73	4	in HM	Bristol	7 Oct
48:17+		Chepkemei			1	in HM	South Shields	16 Sep
48:22+		Meyer			5	in HM	Bristol	7 Oct
48:25	Esther	Kiplagat	KEN	8.12.66	3		Utica	8 Jul
	(11/8)							
48:37	Edith	Masai	KEN	4.4.67	1		Le Puy-en-Velay	1 May
48:40	Rose	Cheruiyot	KEN	21.7.76	1		Nijmegen	11 Nov
48:47+	Jelena	Prokopcuka	LAT	21.9.76	6	in HM	Bristol	7 Oct
48:49+	Miwako	Yamanaka	JPN	24.5.78	1	in HM	Kobe	16 Dec
48:56+	Asmae	Leghzaoui	MAR	30.8.76	8	in HM	Bristol	7 Oct
49:06+	Olivera	Jevtic	YUG	24.7.77	9	in HM	Bristol	7 Oct
49:09	Deena	Drossin	USA	14.2.73	1		Jacksonville	10 Mar
49:10+	Lidia	Simon	ROM	4.9.73	1=	in HM	Sapporo	1 Jul
49:10+	Yasuyo	Iwamoto	JPN	8.9.76	10	in HM	Bristol	7 Oct
49:11	Constantina	Dita/Tomescu	ROM	23.1.70	4		Utica	8 Jul
49:15	Magdaline	Chemjor	KEN	12.11.78	2		Nijmegen	11 Nov
49:20+	Caroline	Kwambai	KEN	9.9.75	11	in HM	Bristol	7 Oct
	(20)							
49:20	Irma	Heeren	NED	16.4.67	3		Nijmegen	11 Nov
49:22	Sylvia	Mosqueda	USA	8.4.66	2		Jacksonville	10 Mar
49:26+	Restituta	Joseph	TAN	30.7.71	12	in HM	Bristol	7 Oct
49:28	Florence	Barsosio	KEN	11.8.76	1		Porto	17 Jun
49:29	Susie	Power	AUS	26.3.75	1		Melbourne	1 Jul
49:31+	Naoko	Takahashi	JPN	6.5.72	1	in Mar	Berlin	30 Sep
49:33	Beáta	Rakonczai	HUN	25.6.77	4		Nijmegen	11 Nov
49:35+	Mihaela	Botezan	ROM	21.11.76	13	in HM	Bristol	7 Oct
49:39	Lenah	Cheruiyot	KEN	73	5		Nijmegen	11 Nov
49:40	Iress	Chenonge	KEN-J	1.2.82	2		Porto	17 Jun
	(30)							
49:42+	Lyudmila	Biktasheva	RUS	25.7.74	14	in HM	Bristol	7 Oct
49:44	Helena	Sampaio	POR	9.10.73	3		Porto	17 Jun
49:45	Simona	Staicu	HUN	5.5.71	6		Nijmegen	11 Nov
49:49	Taussi	Juma	TAN-J	1.6.83	4		Porto	17 Jun
49:50	Silviya	Skvortsova	RUS	16.11.74	1	NC	Sochi	2 Mar
49:54	Zinayida	Semyonova	RUS	19.3.62	2	NC	Sochi	2 Mar
49:54+	Nuta	Olaru	ROM	28.8.70	15	in HM	Bristol	7 Oct
49:54+	Teyeba	Erkesso	ETH-J	82	16	in HM	Bristol	7 Oct
49:55	Gladys	Asiba	KEN	31.5.77	5		Utica	8 Jul
49:55+	Meseret	Kotu	ETH	.81	17	in HM	Bristol	7 Oct
	(40)							
49:55+	Aura	Buia	ROM	16.2.70	18	in HM	Bristol	7 Oct
49:56+	Elfenesh	Alemu	ETH	10.6.75	1=	in Mar	Osaka	28 Jan
49:56+	Yoko	Shibui	JPN	14.3.79	1=	in Mar	Osaka	28 Jan
49:56+	Viktoriya	Klimina	RUS	1.3.76	19	in HM	Bristol	7 Oct
50:00	Firiya	Zhdanova	RUS	29.4.61	3	NC	Sochi	2 Mar
50:02	Petra	Drajzajtlová	CZE	19.1.73	7		Nijmegen	11 Nov
50:03	Galina	Aleksandrova	RUS	15.10.76	4	NC	Sochi	2 Mar
50:04	Irene	Kwambai	KEN	25.10.78	6		Utica	8 Jul
50:05	Jennifer	Rhines	USA	1.7.74	3	NC	Jacksonville	10 Mar
50:07+	Lyubov	Morgunova	RUS	14.1.71	22	in HM	Bristol	7 Oct
	(50)							
50:09+	Pamela	Chepchumba	KEN	28.2.78		in Mar	London	22 Apr
50:09	Cristina	Pomacu	ROM	15.9.73	7		Utica	8 Jul
50:09+	Iulia	Olteanu	ROM	26.1.67	23	in HM	Bristol	7 Oct

Uncertified course: 5 May Breda: 1. Caroline Kwambai 49:18, 2. Hawa Hussein TAN-J 5.12.82 50:00

Mark	Name		Nat	Born	Pos	Meet	Venue	Date

10 MILES ROAD

Mark	Name		Nat	Born	Pos	Meet	Venue	Date
51:23	Susan	Chepkemei	KEN	25.6.75	1		Zaandam	23 Sep
51:46	Isabellah	Ochichi	KEN	.79	2		Zaandam	23 Sep
52:16	Elana	Meyer	RSA	10.10.66	1		Washington DC	8 Apr
52:36	Catherine	Ndereba	KEN	21.7.72	1		Flint	25 Aug
52:36	Restituta	Joseph	TAN	30.7.71	1		Portsmouth	14 Oct
53:15	Lidiya	Grigoryeva	RUS	21.1.74	2		Washington DC	8 Apr
53:15	Lenah	Cheruiyot	KEN	73	3		Zaandam	23 Sep
53:19	Eyerusalem	Kuma	ETH	4.11.81	3		Washington DC	8 Apr
53:34	Milena	Glusac	USA	18.9.75	4		Washington DC	8 Apr
53:35	Jelena	Prokopcuka	LAT	21.9.76	2		Portsmouth	14 Oct
53:39	Mary	Ptikany	KEN	.78	4		Zaandam	23 Sep
53:51	Leah	Malot	KEN	7.6.72	5		Zaandam	23 Sep
53:58	Caroline	Kwambai	KEN	9.9.75	1		Charleroi	18 Mar
54:03	Olga	Kovpotina	RUS	10.1.68	5		Washington DC	8 Apr
54:06	Stine	Larsen	NOR	5.11.75	1		Lelystad	23 Jun
54:21	Nadezhda	Wijenberg	NED	2.4.64	6		Zaandam	23 Sep
54:24	Jane	Ngotho	KEN	29.11.69	2		Flint	25 Aug

20 KILOMETRES ROAD

Best in 20k races:

Mark	Name		Nat	Born	Pos	Meet	Venue	Date
63:54	Lornah	Kiplagat	KEN	20.3.74	1		Alphen aan Rijn	11 Mar
67:00	Caroline	Kwambai	KEN	9.9.75	2		Alphen aan Rijn	11 Mar
67:37	Nadezhda	Wijenberg	NED	2.4.64	3		Alphen aan Rijn	11 Mar
67:48	Milena	Glusac	USA	18.9.75	1	NC	New Haven	3 Sep
68:21	Luminita	Zaituc	GER	9.10.68	4		Alphen aan Rijn	11 Mar
68:25	Christine	Clifton	USA	2.8.72	2	NC	New Haven	3 Sep
68:33	Irma	Heeren	NED	16.4.67	5		Alphen aan Rijn	11 Mar
68:52	Simona	Staicu	HUN	5.5.71	6		Alphen aan Rijn	11 Mar
68:55	Sylvia	Mosqueda	USA	8.4.66	3	NC	New Haven	3 Sep

Distance?: Jan 21, Almeirim: 1. Ruth Kutol KEN 16.5.73 65:51; 2. Fatima Silva POR 67:29; 3. A P Oliveira POR 68:08; 4.Tiziana Alagia ITA 8.3.73 68:12

Leading times in longer races

Mark	Name		Nat	Born	Pos	Meet	Venue	Date
65:02+	Susan	Chepkemei	KEN	25.6.75	1	in HM	South Shields	16 Sep
65:21+	Miwako	Yamanaka	JPN	24.5.78	1	in HM	Kobe	16 Dec
65:55+	Joyce	Chepchumba	KEN	6.11.70	1	in HM	Berlin	1 Apr
66:11+	Naoko	Takahashi	JPN	6.5.72	1	in Mar	Berlin	30 Sep
66:14+	Lidia	Simon	ROM	4.9.73	1=	in HM	Sapporo	1 Jul
66:14+	Mizuki	Noguchi	JPN	3.7.78	1=	in HM	Sapporo	1 Jul
66:41+	Yoko	Shibui	JPN	14.3.79	1=	in Mar	Osaka	28 Jan
66:41+	Restituta	Joseph	TAN	30.7.71	1=	in Mar	Osaka	28 Jan
66:41+	Elfenesh	Alemu	ETH	10.6.75	1=	in Mar	Osaka	28 Jan
66:45+	Catherine	Ndereba	KEN	21.7.72	1	in Mar	Chicago	7 Oct
67:36+	Pamela	Chepchumba	KEN	28.2.78		in Mar	London	22 Apr
68:17+	Constantina	Dita/Tomescu	ROM	23.1.70	1	in Mar	Tokyo	18 Nov
68:18+	Derartu	Tulu	ETH	21.3.72	2	in Mar	Tokyo	18 Nov
68:22+	Tegla	Loroupe	KEN	9.5.73		in Mar	London	22 Apr

HALF MARATHON

Mark	Name		Nat	Born	Pos	Meet	Venue	Date
65:44	Susan	Chepkemei	KEN	25.6.75	1		Lisboa (69m dh)	1 Apr
66:34	Lornah	Kiplagat	KEN	20.3.74	2		Lisboa	1 Apr
66:47	Paula	Radcliffe	GBR	17.12.73	1	WCh	Bristol	7 Oct
67:03	Derartu	Tulu	ETH	21.3.72	3		Lisboa	1 Apr
67:36		Chepkemei			2	WCh	Bristol	7 Oct
67:53	Edith	Masai	KEN	4.4.67	1		Nice	22 Apr
67:54	Catherine	Ndereba	KEN	21.7.72	1		Den Haag	24 Mar
68:16	Tegla	Loroupe	KEN	9.5.73	4		Lisboa	1 Apr
68:17	Berhane	Adere	ETH	21.7.73	3	WCh	Bristol	7 Oct
68:23	Mizuki	Noguchi	JPN	3.7.78	4	WCh	Bristol	7 Oct
68:27		Masai			5		Lisboa	1 Apr
68:28		Noguchi			1		Nagoya	23 Nov
68:30		Ndereba			1		Philadelphia	16 Sep
68:33	Restituta	Joseph (10)	TAN	30.7.71	6		Lisboa	1 Apr
68:38	Isabella	Ochichi	KEN	79	2		Nice	22 Apr
68:40		Chepkemei			1	GNR	South Shields	16 Sep
68:43	Jelena	Prokopcuka	LAT	21.9.76	5	WCh	Bristol	7 Oct
68:45		Noguchi			1		Yamaguchi	11 Mar
68:45	Joyce	Chepchumba	KEN	6.11.70	2	GNR	South Shields	16 Sep
68:50	Elana	Meyer	RSA	10.10.66	7		Lisboa	1 Apr

Mark	Name		Nat	Born	Pos	Meet	Venue	Date
68:51	Margaret	Okayo	KEN	30.5.76	1		Udine	30 Sep
68:54	Miwako	Yamanaka	JPN	24.5.78	1		Kobe	16 Dec
68:55	Yasuko	Hashimoto	JPN	12.8.75	2		Kobe	16 Dec
68:56		Meyer			6	WCh	Bristol	7 Oct
68:58		Zheng Guixia	CHN	24.6.73	2		Yamaguchi	11 Mar
69:01	Fatuma	Roba	ETH	18.12.73	3		Kobe	16 Dec
69:04	Takako	Kotorida (20)	JPN	2.4.77	3		Yamaguchi	11 Mar
69:05		Ochichi			1		Reims	21 Oct
69:15		J Chepchumba			1	G.Scot	Glasgow	19 Aug
69:19		Roba			1		Kyoto	11 Mar
69:19	Maura	Viceconte	ITA	3.10.67	1		Vitry-sur-Seine	22 Apr
	(31/21)							
69:27	Naoko	Sakamoto	JPN	14.11.80	4		Yamaguchi	11 Mar
69:28	Ikumi	Nagayama	JPN	22.6.74	1		Marugame	4 Feb
69:29	Yoshiko	Fujinaga	JPN	15.8.81	4		Kobe	16 Dec
69:34	Mami	Kusunoki	JPN	8.9.75	5		Yamaguchi	11 Mar
69:34	Olivera	Jevtic	YUG	24.7.77	8		Lisboa	1 Apr
69:37	Silviya	Skvortsova	RUS	16.11.74	1		Novosibirsk	15 Sep
69:41	Harumi	Hiroyama	JPN	2.9.68	2		Kyoto	11 Mar
69:43	Leah	Malot	KEN	7.6.72	9		Lisboa	1 Apr
69:45	Caroline	Kwambai	KEN	9.9.75	2		Den Haag	24 Mar
	(30)							
69:45	Hellen	Kimaiyo-Koskei	KEN	8.9.68	10		Lisboa	1 Apr
69:46	Lidia	Simon	ROM	4.9.73	1		Sapporo	1 Jul
69:46	Judy	Kiplimo	KEN	68	1		Uster	23 Sep
69:47	Yukako	Goto	JPN	16.9.73	6		Yamaguchi	11 Mar
69:50+	Naoko	Takahashi	JPN	6.5.72	1	in Mar	Berlin	30 Sep
69:52	Iulia	Olteanu	ROM	26.1.67	3		Kyoto	11 Mar
69:52	Irene	Kwambai	KEN	25.10.78	3		Vitry-sur-Seine	22 Apr
69:55	Irina	Safarova	RUS	19.6.69	2		Novosibirsk	15 Sep
70:05	Alice	Chelangat	KEN	77	4		Vitry-sur-Seine	22 Apr
70:06	Yasuyo	Iwamoto	JPN	8.9.76	9	WCh	Bristol	7 Oct
	(40)							
70:08	Deena	Drossin	USA	14.2.73	1		Virginia Beach	2 Sep
70:09	Nami	Kurosawa	JPN	26.12.78	7		Yamaguchi	11 Mar
70:11	Eri	Yamaguchi	JPN	14.1.73	8		Yamaguchi	11 Mar
70:11	Mihaela	Botezan	ROM	21.11.76	10	WCh	Bristol	7 Oct
70:11	Esther	Wanjiru	ETH	27.3.77	5		Kobe	16 Dec
70:11	Kazue	Ogoshi	JPN	2.3.81	6		Kobe	16 Dec
70:18	Kaori	Yoshida	JPN	4.8.81	1		Chiba	21 Jan
70:21+	Elfenesh	Alemu	ETH	10.6.75	1=	in Mar	Osaka	28 Jan
70:21+	Yoko	Shibui	JPN	14.3.79	1=	in Mar	Osaka	28 Jan
70:24	Aki	Fujikawa	JPN	14.11.78	3		Marugame	4 Feb
	(50)							
70:27	Nuta	Olaru	ROM	28.8.70	11	WCh	Bristol	7 Oct
70:29	Kazumi	Matsuo	JPN	16.4.74	4		Marugame	4 Feb
70:30	Nadezhda	Wijenberg	NED	2.4.64	3		Den Haag	24 Mar
70:30	Anne	Jelagat	KEN	4.6.69	2		Udine	30 Sep
70:31	Lyudmila	Biktasheva	RUS	25.7.74	13	WCh	Bristol	7 Oct
70:32	Magdalene	Chemjor	KEN	12.11.78	5		Vitry-sur-Seine	22 Apr
70:34	Lyubov	Morgunova	RUS	14.1.71	1		Zelenograd	29 Jul
70:35	Iress	Chenonge	KEN-J	1.2.82	1		Aveiro	1 Dec
70:36	Takami	Ominami	JPN	15.11.75	3		Miyazaki	6 Jan
70:36	Petra	Wassiluk	GER	27.10.69	1	NC	Arnstadt	24 Mar
	(60)							
70:36	Lyudmila	Petrova	RUS	7.10.68	2		Virginia Beach	2 Sep
70:37	Christine	Clifton	USA	2.8.72	3		Udine	30 Sep
70:40	Aurica	Buia	ROM	16.2.70	14	WCh	Bristol	7 Oct
70:43	Marleen	Renders	BEL	24.12.68	5	GNR	South Shields	16 Sep
70:46	Viktoriya	Klimina	RUS	1.3.76	16	WCh	Bristol	7 Oct
70:46	Yumiko	Hara	JPN-J	9.1.82	2		Nagoya	23 Nov
70:48	Meseret	Kotu	ETH	81	17	WCh	Bristol	7 Oct
70:51	Ruth	Kutol	KEN	16.5.73	1		Torino	11 Mar
70:58	Kyoko	Katafuchi	JPN	12.3.80	4		Miyazaki	6 Jan
71:03	Tomoe	Oishi	JPN	27.5.76	9		Yamaguchi	11 Mar
	(70)							
71:04	Kaori	Tanabe	JPN	30.4.75	6		Miyazaki	6 Jan
71:04	Luminita	Zaituc	GER	9.10.68	1		Remich	30 Sep
71:05	Yoko	Miyazaki	JPN	29.10.74	7		Miyazaki	6 Jan
71:05	Kayoko	Obata	JPN	18.9.71	8		Miyazaki	6 Jan

Mark	Name		Nat	Born	Pos	Meet	Venue	Date
71:06	Margaret	Kerubo	KEN	15.5.74	2		Reims	21 Oct
71:06	Mikie	Takanaka	JPN	6.10.80	7		Kobe	16 Dec
71:07	Takami	Nishiyama	JPN	17.10.80	5		Marugame	4 Feb
71:07	Stine	Larsen	NOR	5.11.75	1		Göteborg	12 May
71:08	Etsuko	Kuge	JPN	31.1.81	9		Miyazaki	6 Jan
71:09	Yukari	Komatsu	JPN	27.6.74	6		Marugame	4 Feb
	(80)							
71:09	Kathrin	Wessel	GER	14.8.67	2		Berlin	1 Apr
71:12	Junko	Akagi	JPN	3.12.75	8		Kobe	16 Dec
71:13	Sonja	Oberem	GER	24.2.73	2	NC	Arnstadt	24 Mar
71:15	Gladys	Asiba	KEN	31.5.77	2		Philadelphia	16 Sep
71:15	Teyeba	Erkesso	ETH-J	82	20	WCh	Bristol	7 Oct
71:16	Ai	Yamamoto	JPN	6.7.78	7		Marugame	4 Feb
71:18	Chiemi	Takahashi	JPN	16.2.76	2		Sendai	11 Mar
71:20	Tomoko	Kai	JPN	5.11.76	10		Miyazaki	6 Jan
71:20	Asami	Obi	JPN	22.3.76	4		Kyoto	11 Mar
71:21+	Pamela	Chepchumba	KEN	28.2.78	1=		London	22 Apr
	(90)							
71:22	Florence	Barsosio	KEN	11.8.76	1		Paris	4 Mar
71:22	Ryoko	Kitajima	JPN	12.6.76	10		Yamaguchi	11 Mar
71:23	Fumi	Murata	JPN	13.3.75	11		Miyazaki	6 Jan
71:23	Yukiko	Akaba	JPN	18.10.79	3		Sendai	11 Mar
71:25	Lyubov	Denisova	RUS	6.10.71	7	GNR	South Shields	15 Sep
71:26+	Madina	Biktagirova	BLR	20.9.64	4=		London	22 Apr
71:26+	Adriana	Fernández	MEX	4.4.71	4=		London	22 Apr
71:28	Helena	Sampaio	POR	9.10.73	2		Setúbal	6 May
71:29	Tiziana	Alagia	ITA	8.3.73	1		Ostia	25 Feb
71:29	Taussi	Juma	TAN-J	1.6.83	14		Lisboa	1 Apr
	(100)							
71:29	Liz	Yelling	GBR	5.12.74	23	WCh	Bristol	7 Oct

Mark	Name		Nat	Born	Date
71:30	Kazumi	Urata	JPN	1.2.80	11 Mar
71:33	Sakiyo	Kan	JPN	14.5.80	1 Jul
71:33	Yelena	Paramonova	RUS	28.6.62	16 Sep
71:34	Milena	Glusac	USA	18.9.75	7 Oct
71:39	Rodica	Chirita	ROM	28.10.76	9 Sep
71:40	Melanie	Kraus	GER	24.10.74	17 Jun
71:41	Kiyomi	Ogawa	JPN	15.9.81	18 Mar
71:41	Ramilya	Burangulova	RUS	11.7.61	16 Sep
71:43	Yoko	Manabe	JPN	8.2.79	6 Jan
71:44	Hannah	Njeri	KEN	28.11.68	4 Mar
71:44	Rita	Jeptoo	KEN	15.2.81	30 Sep
71:45	Namie	Yamamoto	JPN	18.2.80	11 Mar
71:46	Noriko	Matsuoka	JPN	2.5.79	6 Jan
71:47	Haruko	Yamamoto	JPN	31.10.81	18 Mar
71:49	Nives	Curti	ITA	1.9.69	11 Mar
71:49	Naomi	Sakashita	JPN	25.5.75	5 Aug
71:54	Masayo	Kobayashi	JPN	4.2.80	16 Dec
71:55	Yoshiko	Ichikawa	JPN	18.4.76	1 Jul
71:56	Mimiko	Nakai	JPN	5.10.77	6 Jan
71:56	Dorota	Gruca	POL	5.12.70	1 Apr
71:57	Eva	Sanz	ESP	4.7.73	1 Apr
71:58	Kumi	Tanabe	JPN	2.4.81	25 Feb
72:04+	Bruna	Genovese	ITA	24.9.76	18 Nov
72:05	Emi	Nakajima	JPN	8.8.80	6 Jan
72:06	Malgorzata	Sobanska	POL	25.4.69	1 Apr
72:07	Tomoko	Motohira	JPN	13.2.81	11 Mar
72:07	Hiromi	Watanabe	JPN	24.2.79	11 Mar
72:07	Luminita	Talpos	ROM	9.10.72	2 Dec
72:08	Miyo	Nakano	JPN	17.3.78	6 Jan
72:08	Beáta	Rakonczai	HUN	25.6.77	7 Oct
72:09	Beatrice	Omwanza	KEN	78	22 Apr
72:10		Cui Guomei	CHN	2.7.79	11 Mar
72:10	Miyuki	Hikita	JPN	1.3.81	11 Mar
72:10	Rina	Oishi	JPN	6.4.78	11 Mar
72:10	Esther	Kiplagat	KEN	8.12.66	19 Aug
72:10	Martha	Komu	KEN-J	23.3.83	23 Sep
72:11	Maki	Hirano	JPN	78	11 Mar
72:11	Simona	Staicu	HUN	5.5.71	7 Oct
72:12	Megumi	Kobayashi	JPN	4.8.76	6 Jan
72:12+	Alina	Ivanova	RUS	16.3.69	22 Apr
72:13+	Svetlana	Zakharova	RUS	15.9.70	22 Apr
72:14	Naoko	Tanaka	JPN	23.3.77	11 Mar
72:14	Silvia	Sommaggio	ITA	20.11.69	7 Oct
72:15	Asuka	Maeda	JPN	4.10.78	11 Mar
72:16	Marie	S-Lundberg	SWE	21.10.60	12 May
72:17+	Constantina	Dita/Tomescu	ROM	23.1.70	12 Aug
72:18	Fatima	Silva	POR	6.5.70	11 Nov
72:19	Jackline	Torori	KEN	78	23 Sep
72:23	Ai	Ichimaru	JPN	24.6.77	16 Dec
72:24	Banwella	Mrashani	TAN	14.11.77	30 Sep
72:24	Inês	Monteiro	POR	18.5.80	5 Oct
72:28	Anastasha	Ndereba	KEN	78	5 Oct
72:30	Mayumi	Nagamori	JPN	22.3.68	6 Jan
72:31	Susan	Michelsson	AUS	29.2.72	25 Feb
72:31	Yelena	Burykina	RUS	1.1.73	29 Jul
72:31	Jepkorir	Ayabei	KEN	17.5.79	30 Sep
72:32	Wioletta	Kryza	POL	10.8.68	1 Apr
72:32	Rosaria	Console	ITA	17.12.79	8 Apr
72:33	Rodica	Moroianu (Nagel)	FRA	18.11.70	16 Sep
72:34	Chie	Watanabe	JPN	14.6.80	6 Jan
72:35	Akemi	Maeda	JPN	11.10.78	6 Jan
72:35	Daniela	Ciocan	ROM	75	9 Sep
72:36	Aiko	Nitta	JPN	18.11.75	6 Jan
72:36	Teresa	Wanjiru	KEN	7.5.74	16 Sep
72:38	Yoriko	Oda	JPN	80	6 Jan
72:38	Lidiya	Grigoryeva	RUS	21.1.74	1 Apr
72:39	Jackline	Okemwa	KEN	78	22 Apr
72:40	Lucy	Karimi	KEN	70	22 Apr
72:40	Fatiha	Klilech	MAR	75	22 Apr
72:41	Mami	Yamashita	JPN	16.1.79	6 Jan
72:43	Amanda	Allen	GBR	14.7.68	16 Sep
72:43	Lyudmila	Korchagina	RUS	26.7.71	23 Sep
72:44	Miho	Oba	JPN	3.2.78	6 Jan
72:44	Galina	Aleksandrova	RUS	15.10.76	5 May
72:45	M. Zeferina	Baldaia	BRA	29.8.72	7 Oct
72:46	Lenah	Cheruiyot	KEN	73	7 Oct
72:47	Miwako	Ueki	JPN		6 Jan
72:48	Annemette	Jensen	DEN	11.4.72	1 Apr
72:49	Petra	Drajzajtlová	CZE	19.1.73	14 Apr
72:49	Svetlana	Demidenko	RUS	16.2.76	23 Sep
72:51	Gloria	Marconi	ITA	31.3.68	25 Feb
72:53	Elizabeth	Chemweno	KEN	13.7.78	6 May
72:53	Winfrida	Kwamboka	KEN	4.3.82	16 Sep
72:54	Ornella	Ferrara	ITA	17.4.68	1 Apr
72:56	Fernanda	Ribeiro	POR	23.6.69	6 Jan
72:56	Teresa	Duffy	IRL	6.7.69	1 Apr
72:57	Ichiyo	Naganuma	JPN	5.11.71	6 Jan
72:57+	Kerryn	McCann	AUS	2.5.67	7 Oct
72:58	Liliya	Yadzhak	RUS	.71	15 Sep
72:59	Nancy	Omwenga	KEN		10 Jun
72:59+	Franca	Fiacconi	ITA	4.10.65	28 Jan
72:59+	Rie	Matsuoka	JPN	9.3.77	28 Jan
	(193)				

Mark		Name		Nat	Born	Pos	Meet	Venue	Date
Short Course									
68:36		Simona	Staicu	HUN	5.5.71	1		Nyíregyháza	1 Apr
69:27		Beáta	Rakonczai	HUN	25.6.77	2		Nyíregyháza	1 Apr
71:56		Bruna	Genovese	ITA	24.9.76	1		Napoli	18 Mar

JUNIORS

See main list for top 4 juniors. And then:

Mark	Name		Nat	Born	Pos	Venue	Date
72:10	Martha	Komu	KEN	23.3.83	1	Arusha	23 Sep
73:50	Satoko	Yagi	JPN	15.2.82	7	Sendai	3 Nov
73:52	Winfrida	Kwamboka	KEN		5	Udine	30 Sep

MARATHON

In second column: first character: L = loop course or start and finish within 30%, P = point-to-point or start and finish more than 30% apart, D = point-to-point and downhil over 1/1000
Second character: M mixed marathon (men and women), W women only race or separated start by time

Mark		Name		Nat	Born	Pos	Meet	Venue	Date
2:18:47	LM	Catherine	Ndereba	KEN	21.7.72	1		Chicago	7 Oct
2:19:46	LM	Naoko	Takahashi	JPN	6.5.72	1		Berlin	30 Sep
2:23:11	LW	Yoko	Shibui	JPN	14.3.79	1		Osaka	28 Jan
2:23:37	LM		Liu Min	CHN-J	29.11.83	1		Beijing	14 Oct
2:23:53	DM		Ndereba			1		Boston (139m dh)	16 Apr
2:23:57	LW	Derartu	Tulu	ETH	21.3.72	1		London	22 Apr
2:24:02	LM		Wei Yanan	CHN	6.12.81	2		Beijing	14 Oct
2:24:04	LW	Svetlana	Zakharova	RUS	15.9.70	2		London	22 Apr
2:24:12	LW	Joyce	Chepchumba	KEN	6.11.70	3		London	22 Apr
2:24:15	LW	Lidia	Simon	ROM	4.9.73	4		London	22 Apr
2:24:21	PM	Margaret	Okayo (10)	KEN	30.5.76	1		New York	4 Nov
2:24:22	LM		Ren Xiujuan	CHN	14.9.74	3		Beijing	14 Oct
2:24:29	LW	Elfenesh	Alemu	ETH	10.6.75	5		London	22 Apr
2:24:41	LM		Dai Yanyan	CHN	8.1.80	4		Beijing	14 Oct
2:24:42	LM		Zhang Shujing	CHN	13.9.78	5		Beijing	14 Oct
2:24:54	LM		Alemu			2		Chicago	7 Oct
2:25:05	LDM		Okayo			1		San Diego	3 Jun
2:25:08	LW		Tulu			1		Tokyo	18 Nov
2:25:12	PM	Susan	Chepkemei	KEN	25.6.75	2		New York	4 Nov
2:25:13	PM		Zakharova			3		New York	4 Nov
2:25:18	LW	Nuta	Olaru	ROM	28.8.70	6		London	22 Apr
2:25:29	LW	Irina	Timofeyeva	RUS	5.4.70	2		Tokyo	18 Nov
2:25:34	LW	Alina	Ivanova	RUS	16.3.69	7		London	22 Apr
2:25:35	LW	Bruna	Genovese	ITA	24.9.76	3		Tokyo	18 Nov
2:25:45	LM		Chepkemei			1		Roterdam	22 Apr
2:25:48	LM		Jin Li (20)	CHN-J	29.5.83	6		Beijing	14 Oct
2:25:51	PM		J Chepchumba			4		New York	4 Nov
2:25:56	LM		Zheng Guixia	CHN	24.6.73	7		Beijing	14 Oct
2:26:01	LW	Kazumi	Matsuo	JPN	16.4.74	1		Nagoya	11 Mar
2:26:01	LW		Simon			1	WCh	Edmonton	12 Aug
2:26:01	LM	Luminita	Zaituc	GER	9.10.68	1		Frankfurt am Main	28 Oct
2:26:04	LW	Takami	Ominami	JPN	15.11.75	2		Nagoya	11 Mar
2:26:04	LM	Kerryn	McCann	AUS	2.5.67	3		Chicago	7 Oct
2:26:06	LW	Reiko	Tosa	JPN	11.6.76	2	WCh	Edmonton	12 Aug
2:26:08	LM	Malgorzata	Sobanska	POL	25.4.69	4		Chicago	7 Oct
2:26:10	LW	Tegla	Loroupe	KEN	9.5.73	8		London	22 Apr
2:26:13	LM	Sonja	Oberem	GER	24.2.73	1		Hamburg	22 Apr
2:26:15	PM	Esther (38/30)	Kiplagat	KEN	8.12.66	5		New York	4 Nov
2:26:18	PM	Lyudmila	Petrova	RUS	7.10.68	6		New York	4 Nov
2:26:21	LW	Yukiko	Okamoto	JPN	29.11.74	3		Nagoya	11 Mar
2:26:22	LW	Adriana	Fernández	MEX	4.4.71	9		London	22 Apr
2:26:33	LM	Maura	Viceconte	ITA	3.10.67	1		Praha	20 May
2:26:36	LM	Alice	Chelangat	KEN	77	1		Milano	2 Dec
2:26:39	LW	Constantina	Dita/Tomescu	ROM	23.1.70	4		Tokyo	18 Nov
2:26:49	LW	Franca	Fiacconi	ITA	4.10.65	2		Osaka	28 Jan
2:26:51	LM	Zinayida	Semyonova	RUS	19.3.62	1	Twin C	St Paul	7 Oct
2:26:58	PW	Deena	Drossin	USA	14.2.73	7		New York	4 Nov
2:27:01	LW	Noriko (40)	Geji	JPN	31.5.73	4		Nagoya	11 Mar
2:27:02	LW	Tomoe	Abe	JPN	13.8.71	5		Nagoya	11 Mar
2:27:14	LW	Madina	Biktagirova	RUS	20.9.64	10		London	22 Apr
2:27:16	LW	Ikuyo	Goto	JPN	6.1.69	6		Nagoya	11 Mar
2:27:18	DM	Lyubov	Morgunova	RUS	14.1.71	3		Boston	16 Apr

WOMEN 2001

Mark		Name		Nat	Born	Pos	Meet	Venue	Date
2:27:20	LM	Fatuma	Roba	ETH	18.12.73	2		San Diego	3 Jun
2:27:22	LW	Mayumi	Ichikawa	JPN	3.5.76	7		Nagoya	11 Mar
2:27:37	LM	Olga	Kovpotina	RUS	10.1.68	2	Twin C	St Paul	7 Oct
2:27:44	LW	Ikumi	Nagayama	JPN	22.6.74	8		Nagoya	11 Mar
2:27:50	LW	Rie	Matsuoka	JPN	9.3.77	3		Osaka	28 Jan
2:27:53	LM	Florence	Barsosio	KEN	11.8.76	1		Paris	8 Apr
		(50)							
2:27:54	LM	Tiziana	Alagia	ITA	8.3.73	1		Torino	1 Apr
2:27:54	LM	Ruth	Kutol	KEN	16.5.73	2		Paris	8 Apr
2:27:56	DM	Lornah	Kiplagat	KEN	20.3.74	4		Boston	16 Apr
2:28:00	LM		Lu Jingbo	CHN	18.4.73	8		Beijing	14 Oct
2:28:09	LW	Naomi	Sakashita	JPN	25.5.75	9		Nagoya	11 Mar
2:28:13	LW	Junko	Akagi	JPN	3.12.75	6		Tokyo	18 Nov
2:28:20	LM		Jong Yong-ok	PRK	24.1.81	9		Beijing	14 Oct
2:28:22	LM	Silviya	Skvortsova	RUS	16.11.74	3	Twin C	St Paul	7 Oct
2:28:27	LW	Aki	Fujikawa	JPN	14.11.78	10		Nagoya	11 Mar
2:28:27	LM	Kathrin	Wessel	GER	14.8.67	3		Berlin	30 Sep
		(60)							
2:28:28	LM	Masako	Koide	JPN	3.1.74	2		Rotterdam	22 Apr
2:28:31	LW	Marleen	Renders	BEL	24.12.68	11		London	22 Apr
2:28:40	LW	Shitaye	Gemechu	ETH	80	7	WCh	Edmonton	12 Aug
2:28:41	LW	Valentina	Yegorova	RUS	16.2.64	11		Nagoya	11 Mar
2:28:59	LM	Nives	Curti	ITA	1.9.69	5		Chicago	7 Oct
2:29:01	LW	Harumi	Hiroyama	JPN	2.9.68	12		London	22 Apr
2:29:03	LM		Zhao Shengzhi	CHN	19.11.75	10		Beijing	14 Oct
2:29:16	LM	Alina	Gherasim	ROM	10.11.71	3		Paris	8 Apr
2:29:16	LM		Sun Yingjie	CHN	3.10.77	11		Beijing	14 Oct
2:29:18	LW	Yoshiko	Ichikawa	JPN	18.4.76	8		Tokyo	18 Nov
		(70)							
2:29:19	LW	Tomoko	Kai	JPN	5.11.76	12		Nagoya	11 Mar
2:29:33	LM	Ornella	Ferrara	ITA	17.4.68	3		San Diego	3 Jun
2:29:44	LM		Ham Bong-sil	PRK	8.7.74	2		Pyongyang	15 Apr
2:29:44	LM	Cristina	Pomacu	ROM	15.9.73	1		Beograd	21 Apr
2:29:46	LM	Sara	Ferrari	ITA	30.9.77	2		Torino	1 Apr
2:29:46	LM	María	Abel	ESP	23.10.74	3		Rotterdam	22 Apr
2:29:47	LM	Jane	Salumäe	EST	17.1.68	1		Wien	20 May
2:29:57	LM	Lydia	Vasilevskaya	RUS	1.4.73	4	Twin C	St Paul	7 Oct
2:29:58	LM	Zahia	Dahmani	FRA	2.6.72	4		Paris	8 Apr
2:30:03	PM	Yelena	Paramonova	RUS	28.6.62	8		New York	4 Nov
		(80)							
2:30:11	LM	M Luisa	Larraga	ESP	10.12.70	1		Valencia	4 Feb
2:30:15	LM	Elzbieta	Jarosz	POL	14.8.71	5	Twin C	St Paul	7 Oct
2:30:22	LM		Ju Limei	CHN	9.6.78	12		Beijing	14 Oct
2:30:25	LM	Nadezhda	Wijenberg	NED	2.4.64	4		Rotterdam	22 Apr
2:30:25	LM		Wang Yanrong	CHN	16.10.76	13		Beijing	14 Oct
2:30:28	PM	Tatyana	Pozdnyakova	UKR	4.3.56	1		Providence	8 Oct
2:30:30	LW	Yukari	Komatsu	JPN	27.6.74	13		Nagoya	11 Mar
2:30:35	LM		Tian Mei	CHN	27.11.71	14		Beijing	14 Oct
2:30:39	LM	Masako	Chiba	JPN	18.7.76	1		Sapporo	26 Aug
2:30:42	LM	Maria	Guida	ITA	23.1.66	1		Roma	25 Mar
		(90)							
2:30:46	LM		Jo Bun-hui	PRK	80	3		Pyongyang	15 Apr
2:30:50	LW	Ai	Sugihara	JPN	12.10.75	14		Nagoya	11 Mar
2:30:55	LM	Rosaria	Console	ITA	17.12.79	1		Padova	29 Apr
2:30:56	LM	Eva	Sanz	ESP	4.7.73	5		Rotterdam	22 Apr
2:30:58	LW	Firiya	Zhdanova	RUS	29.4.61	12	WCh	Edmonton	12 Aug
2:31:00	LW	Yuko	Arimori	JPN	17.12.66	10		Tokyo	18 Nov
2:31:01	LM	Claudia	Dreher	GER	2.5.71	1		Lisboa	2 Dec
2:31:02	LM	Irina	Bogachova	KGZ	30.5.61	6	Twin C	St Paul	7 Oct
2:31:05	LM		Li Helan	CHN	2.1.78	2		Jinan	7 Apr
2:31:05	LM	Griselda	González	ESP	4.12.65	6		Rotterdam	22 Apr
		(100)							

Mark		Name		Nat	Born	Date	
2:31:08	LM	Judy	Kiplimo	KEN	68	7	Oct
2:31:13	LM		Sin Myong-ae	PRK	77	15	Apr
2:31:19	LM	Anna	Kosgei	KEN		25	Nov
2:31:28	LM	Marie	Söderström-Lundberg	SWE	21.10.60	9	Jun
2:31:29	LM	Melanie	Kraus	GER	24.10.74	28	0ct
2:31:31	DM	Kaori	Tanabe	JPN	30.4.75	16	Apr
2:31:33	LM		Kwon Eun-ju	KOR	23.10.77	21	Oct
2:31:43	PM	Elana	Meyer	RSA	10.10.66	4	Nov
2:31:45	LM	Dulce M	Rodríguez	MEX	14.8.72	4	Mar
2:31:54	LM	Sandra	Van den Haesevelde	BEL	1.1.71	21	Oct
2:31:58	LW	Junko	Kataoka	JPN	13.6.70	11	Mar
2:31:58	LM	Lena	Gavelin	SWE	26.2.74	28	Oct
2:32:01	LM	Jackline	Jerotich	KEN	23.9.70	20	May
2:32:02	LM	Meseret	Kotu	ETH	81	2	Dec
2:32:09	LM		Yun Sun-sook	KOR	28.5.72	18	Mar
2:32:14	LW	Kayoko	Obata	JPN	18.9.71	28	Jan
2:32:16	LM		Li Yong-sil	PRK		15	Apr
2:32:21	LM	Mary	Ptikany	KEN	78	8	Apr
2:32:26	LM	Florinda	Andreucci	ITA	19.12.69	25	Nov
2:32:41	JM	Gitte	Karlshøj	DEN	14.5.59	14	Oct

Mark		Name		Nat	Born	Date
2:32:45	DM	Albina	Gallyamova	RUS	8.5.64	16 Apr
2:32:53	LM	Marta	Fernández de Castro	ESP	19.8.71	22 Apr
2:32:58	LM	Abeba	Tola	ETH	3.6.77	18 Mar
2:32:59	LM	Petra	Wassiluk	GER	27.10.69	28 Oct
2:33:01	LM	Inga	Juodeskiene	LTU	21.10.71	28 Oct
2:33:03	LW	Hiromi	Ominami	JPN	15.11.75	11 Mar
2:33:08	LM	Irina	Safarova	RUS	19.6.69	4 Aug
2:33:15	LM	Banuelia	Mrashani	TAN	14.11.77	2 Dec
2:33:21	LM	Alla	Zhilyayeva	RUS	5.2.69	27 May
2:33:21	LM	Annemette	Jensen	DEN	11.4.72	28 Oct
2:33:23	LM	Shiki	Terasaki	JPN	27.3.72	30 Sep
2:33:26	LM	Judit	Földing-Nagy	HUN	9.12.65	8 Apr
2:33:38	PM	Patrizia	Ritondo	ITA	18.9.74	14 Oct
2:33:41	LW	Mineko	Yamanouchi	JPN	10.12.72	11 Mar
2:33:51	LM	Tatyana	Titova	RUS	6.8.65	21 Oct
2:33:57	LM	Eri	Kurotaki	JPN	79	4 Feb
2:34:01	LM		Ri Yong-hui	PRK	80	14 Oct
2:34:02	LM	Ichiyo	Naganuma	JPN	5.11.71	7 Oct
2:34:06	LM	Larisa	Timkina	MDA	7.12.66	6 May
2:34:13	LM	Lyubov	Denisova	RUS	6.10.71	11 Nov
2:34:16	LM	Wioletta	Kryza	POL	10.8.68	6 May
2:34:19	LM	Chantal	Dällenbach	FRA	24.10.62	29 Apr
2:34:21	LM		Jong Ok-ran	PRK		15 Apr
2:34:29	LM	Manuela	Zipse	GER	11.5.74	28 Oct
2:34:34	LW	Mio	Kiuchi	JPN	20.11.78	18 Nov
2:34:36	LW	Miwako	Ueki	JPN		11 Mar
2:34:40	LM	Aura	Buia	ROM	16.2.70	28 Apr
2:34:41	LM	Faustina	María	ESP	28.4.71	25 Feb
2:34:43	LM	Hisako	Tanaka	JPN	6.4.75	4 Feb
2:34:43	LM	Beth	Allott	GBR	9.2.77	2 Dec
2:34:44	LM	Zhanna	Malkova	RUS	27.10.67	23 Sep
2:34:46	LW	Fumi	Murata	JPN	13.3.75	11 Mar
2:34:46	LM	Albina	Ivanova	RUS	16.5.77	4 Aug
2:34:46	PM	Milena	Glusac	USA	18.9.75	4 Nov
2:34:55	LM	Dorota	Gruca	POL	5.12.70	7 Oct
2:34:56	LM		Hong Ok-dan	PRK		15 Apr
2:34:57	PM	Monica	Capelli	ITA	15.12.69	28 Oct
2:35:03	LW	Akiyo	Onishi	JPN	3.5.78	28 Jan
2:35:08	LW	Mimiko	Nakai	JPN	5.10.77	11 Mar
2:35:09	LW	Hiroko	Kinuki	JPN	18.7.74	18 Nov
2:35:16	LM	Fatima	Silva	POR	6.5.70	2 Dec
2:35:19	LM	Zivile	Balciunaite	LIT	3.4.79	22 Apr
2:35:27	LW	Teresa	Duffy	IRL	6.7.69	22 Apr
2:35:27	LM	Yelena	Makolova	BLR	5.1.68	14 Oct
2:35:30	LM		Zhao Yanyan	CHN	28.6.80	14 Oct
2:35:31	PM	Colleen	de Reuck	USA	13.4.64	4 Nov
2:35:32	LM	Anfisa	Kosacheva	RUS	1.3.65	27 May
2:35:40	LM	Debbie	Robinson	GBR	31.1.68	29 Oct
2:35:41	LM	Ramilya	Burangulova	RUS	11.7.61	7 Oct
2:35:42	LM	Valentina	Enaki	MDA	15.2.66	25 Nov
2:35:44	LM		Kim Ok-bin	KOR	23.7.81	18 Mar
2:35:44	LM	Leila	Aman	ETH	24.11.77	3 Jun
2:35:48	LM		Oh Mi-ja	KOR	3.7.70	15 Apr
2:35:49	LM	Klara	Kashapova	RUS	29.1.70	23 Sep
2:35:51	LM		Ri Hyon-gyong	PRK		15 Apr
2:35:54	PM	Francesca	Zanusso	ITA	25.10.75	28 Oct
2:35:56	LM		Jang Chol-ok	PRK		15 Apr
2:35:56	LM	Esther	Barmasai	KEN	72	20 May
2:35:57	LW	Masako	Kusakaya	JPN	26.2.72	11 Mar
2:35:57	LM	Kulli	Kaljus	EST	21.1.73	22 Apr
2:35:59	LM	Karina	Szymanska	POL	16.1.75	8 Apr
2:35:59	u	Ari	ichihashi	JPN	22.11.77	2 Dec
2:36:02	LM	Bev	Hartigan	GBR	10.6.67	30 Sep
2:36:06	DM	Yelena	Plastinina	UKR	5.11.63	18 Feb
2:36:17	LW	Kaoru	Yamada	JPN	24.11.75	28 Jan
2:36:23	LM	Vilija	Birbalaite	LTU	11.8.66	22 Apr
2:36:30	LM	Emebet	Abosa	ETH	73	25 Mar
2:36:37	LM	Asami	Obi	JPN	22.3.76	26 Aug
2:36:39	LM		Jong Song-ok	PRK	18.8.74	15 Apr
2:36:42	LM	Margaret	Kagiri	KEN	25.11.68	6 May
2:36:45	DM	Jill	Gaitenby	USA	21.1.67	16 Apr
2:36:46	LM		Xiao Yuegui	CHN	16.1.79	7 Apr
2:36:50	LM	Dione	D'Agostini	BRA	28.2.70	21 Oct
2:36:52	LM	Annelieke	van der Sluijs	NED	10.2.66	2 Dec
2:36:55	LM	Galina	Zhulyeva	UKR	5.3.66	7 Oct
2:36:58	LM	Agata	Balsamo	ITA	11.11.70	29 Apr
2:37:00	LM		Shi Hongjuan	CHN-J	17.12.84	7 Apr
2:37:06	LM	Norah	Maraga	KEN	76	28 Apr
2:37:07	LM	María	Portillo	PER	10.4.72	4 Mar
2:37:07	LM	Alena	Peterková	CZE	13.11.60	20 May
		(200)				

Short Course

Mark		Name		Nat	Born	Date
2:35:39	LM	Lyudmila	Korchagina	RUS	26.7.71	18 Mar

Drugs Disqualification

Mark		Name		Nat	Born	Date
2:35:01	LM	Silvana	Trampuz	AUS	15.9.66	8 Apr

Downhill

Mark		Name		Nat	Born	Pos	Meet	Venue	Date
2:31:20	DM	Akiyo	Onishi	JPN	3.5.78	1		Nagano (219.5m)	15 Apr
2:32:05	DM	Chihiro	Tanaka	JPN	13.11.69	2		Nagano	15 Apr
2:32:51	DM	Natalya	Galushko	BLR	18.9.71	3		Nagano	15 Apr

JUNIORS

Mark		Name	Nat	Born	Pos	Meet	Venue	Date
2:23:37	LM	Liu Min	CHN	29.11.83	1		Beijing	14 Oct
2:25:48	LM	Jin Li	CHN	29.5.83	6		Beijing	14 Oct
2:37:00	LM	Shi Hongjuan	CHN	17.12.84	5		Jinan	7 Apr
2:39:18	LM	Im Kyong-hee	KOR	16.11.82	3		Chunchon	21 Oct
2:42:51	LM	Park Im-suk	KOR	28.8.82	5		Chunchon	21 Oct

100 KILOMETRES

Mark	Name		Nat	Born	Pos	Meet	Venue	Date
7:28:31	Birgit	Lennartz	GER	22.11.65	1	NC	Neuwittenbek	12 May
7:31:12	Elvira	Kolpakova	RUS	30.10.72	1	WC	Cléder	26 Aug
7:31:55	Ricarda	Botzon	GER	4.9.66	1	EC	Winschoten	29 Sep
7:37:02	Marina	Bychkova	RUS	18.12.75	2	EC	Winschoten	29 Sep
7:38:21		Bychkova			2	WC	Cléder	26 Aug
7:39:42	Monica	Casiraghi	ITA	4.4.69	3	WC	Cléder	26 Aug
7:42:36	Karine	Herry	FRA	2.1.68	3	EC	Winschoten	29 Sep
7:43:40	Tanja	Schäfer	GER	25.9.67	4	WC	Cléder	26 Aug
7.46.28		Schäfer			2	NC	Neuwittenbek	12 May
7.49.18	Magali	Maggiolini	FRA	21.5.59	1		Chavagnes	26 May
7.50.58	Akiko	Sekiya	JPN	65	5	WC	Cléder	26 Aug
7.54.27		Herry			6	WC	Cléder	26 Aug
7.54.42	Elke	Hiebl (10)	GER	12.6.64	4	EC	Winschoten	29 Sep
7.56.31		Maggiolini			5	EC	Winschoten	29 Sep
7.58.16	Danielle	Sanderson	GBR	26.10.62	7	WC	Cléder	26 Aug
7:59:42	Nadezhda	Karasyova	RUS	.60	6	EC	Winschoten	29 Sep
8:00:41	Norimi	Sakurai	JPN	.71	1		Yubetsu	24 Jun
8:01:05	Valentina	Shatyayeva	RUS	23.11.62	7	EC	Winschoten	29 Sep
8:02:31		Maggiolini			8	WC	Cléder	26 Aug

Mark	Name		Nat	Born	Pos	Meet	Venue	Date
8:03:15	Murielle (20/15)	Brionne	FRA	9.12.67	8	EC	Winschoten	29 Sep
8:08:59	Yelena	Bikulova	RUS	14.4.64	1		Torhout	22 Jun
8:10:19	Alcira	Portela Lario	POR	8.4.57	9	WC	Cléder	26 Aug
8:10:45	Yekaterina	Malafeyeva	RUS	.67	1		Moscow	22 Apr
8:12:23	Karin	Stump	SUI	.76	1		Biel	15 Jun
8:12:25	Edit (20)	Bérces	HUN	16.5.64	2		Torhout	22 Jun
8:13:23	Sylvie	Beaulieu	FRA	15.6.62	10	WC	Cléder	26 Aug
8:13:57	Anne	Riddle	USA	21.6.66	1	NC	Pittsburgh	21 Mar
8:17:40	Kazuko	Kondo	JPN	.56	12	WC	Cléder	26 Aug
8:17:50	Anke	Drescher	GER	14.12.67	3	NC	Neuwittenbek	12 May
8:18:18	Danielle	Cherniak	USA	24.10.61	13	WC	Cléder	26 Aug
8:19:04	Irina	Reutovich	RUS	21.1.50	2		Moscow	22 Apr
8:21:39	Oksana	Ladyzhina	RUS	21.7.67	14	WC	Cléder	26 Aug
8:24:35	Dominique	Duval	FRA	2.3.54	16	WC	Cléder	26 Aug
8:25:26	Jennifer	Devine Pfeiffer	USA	1.11.71	17	WC	Cléder	26 Aug

24 HOURS

Mark	Name		Nat	Born	Pos	Meet	Venue	Date
235.029 t	Edit	Bérces	HUN	16.5.64	1	IAU	S Gio. Lupatoto	22/23 Sep
226.781 t	Irina	Reutovich	RUS	21.1.50	2	IAU	S Gio. Lupatoto	22/23 Sep
226.634		Reutovich			1	EC	Apeldoorn	25/26 May
223,673		Bérces			1		Köln	13-14 Jul
223.240		Reutovich			1		Wörschach	28-29 Jul
222.650	Irina	Koval	RUS	19.11.58	2	EC	Apeldoorn	25-26 May
222.445 t		Koval			3	IAU	S Gio. Lupatoto	22/23 Sep
221.911 t	Hiroko	Okiyama	JPN	21.4.62	4	IAU	S Gio. Lupatoto	22/23 Sep
221.071 t	Véronique	Jehanno	FRA	27.12.62	5	IAU	S Gio. Lupatoto	22/23 Sep
218.321 t	Rimma	Paltseva	RUS	14.10.48	6	IAU	S Gio. Lupatoto	22/23 Sep
212.692	Helga	Backhaus	GER	19.01.53	3	EC	Apeldoorn	25-26 May
	203.582 t				11	IAU	S Gio. Lupatoto	22/23 Sep
211.375 t	Nadezhda	Tarasova	RUS	7.4.52	7	IAU	S Gio. Lupatoto	22/23 Sep
210.850	Galina	Gordeyeva	RUS	18.4.55	2		Wörschach	28-29 Jul
208.593 t	Colette	Musy	FRA	11.4.59	8	IAU	S Gio. Lupatoto	22/23 Sep
208.176	Julia	Alter	GER	24.2.72	4	EC	Apeldoorn	25-26 May
205.963 t	Christiane	Le Cerf	FRA	12.6.50	9	IAU	S Gio. Lupatoto	22/23 Sep
204.638 t	Lyudmila	Kalinina	RUS	30.8.68	10	IAU	S Gio. Lupatoto	22/23 Sep
203.403 t	Barbara	Szlachetka	POL	17.5.56	12	IAU	S Gio. Lupatoto	22/23 Sep
203.056	Sue Ellen	Trapp	USA	3.3.46	1	NC	Sylvania	15-16 Sep
201.420	Berta	Höfler	AUT		3		Wörschach	28-29 Jul

2000 METRES STEEPLECHASE

Mark	Name		Nat	Born	Pos	Meet	Venue	Date
6:19.00	Irene	Limika	KEN	28.8.79	1		Loughborough	20 May
6:24.28	Cristina	Casandra (Iloc)-	ROM	21.10.77	1		Visby	19 Jun
6:29.66	Lisa	Nye	USA	17.11.68	1		Eugene	26 Jul
6:29.79	Tara	Krzywicki	GBR	9.3.74	2		Loughborough	20 May
6:32.04	Ragnhild	Kvarberg	NOR	23.3.81	1	Nord21	Lillehammer	19 Aug
6:32.23	Melissa	Rollison	AUS-J	13.4.83	1		Brisbane	24 Oct
6:34.89	Catalina	Oprea	ROM-J	11.4.86	1	EJ	Grosseto	22 Jul
6:35.30	Ida	Nilsson	SWE	8.2.81	2		Västerås	3 Jul

Further JUNIORS

Mark	Name		Nat	Born	Pos	Meet	Venue	Date
6:36.06	Gwendoline	Depres	FRA-J	27.11.83	2	EJ	Grosseto	22 Jul
6:36.67	Antje	Hoffmann	GER-J	12.10.82	3	EJ	Grosseto	22 Jul
6:36.84	Anni	Tuimala	FIN-J	27.4.82	2	Nord-J	Lillehammer	19 Aug
6:40.63	Ulla	Tuimala	FIN-J	27.4.82	1		Kannus	10 Aug

3000 METRES STEEPLECHASE

Mark	Name		Nat	Born	Pos	Meet	Venue	Date
9:25.31	Justyna	Bak	POL	1.8.74	1	Nik	Nice	9 Jul
9:30.70	Melissa	Rollison	AUS-J	13.4.83	1	GWG	Brisbane	4 Sep
9:39.51	Irene	Limika	KEN	28.8.79	2	Nik	Nice	9 Jul
9:39.65		Limika			2	GWG	Brisbane	4 Sep
9:41.54	Yekaterina	Volkova	RUS	16.2.78	3	GWG	Brisbane	4 Sep
9:41.94	Elizabeth	Jackson	USA	27.10.77	4	GWG	Brisbane	4 Sep
9:43.36		Jackson			3	Nik	Nice	9 Jul
9:44.36		Bak			1		Poznan	8 Jun
9:44.68	Élodie	Olivarès	FRA	22.5.76	1	MedG	Tunis	11 Sep
9:45.12	Cristina	Casandra (Iloc)	ROM	21.10.77	1	FBK	Hengelo	4 Jun
9:45.92		Casandra			1		Noisy-le-Grand	19 Jun
9:46.53		Olivarès			2		Noisy-le-Grand	19 Jun

Mark	Name		Nat	Born	Pos	Meet	Venue	Date
9:46.56		Casandra			5	GWG	Brisbane	4 Sep
9:48.72		Jackson			1	v2N	Glasgow	1 Jul
9:48.84	Laurence	Duquénoy	FRA	29.9.69	4	Nik	Nice	9 Jul
9:49.41	Lisa	Nye	USA	17.11.68	1	NC	Eugene	23 Jun
9:49.73		Jackson			1	NCAA	Eugene	1 Jun
9:49.94		Jackson			2	NC	Eugene	23 Jun
9:51.88		Casandra			1	NC	Bucuresti	10 Jun
9:52.62		Duquénoy			3		Noisy-le-Grand	19 Jun
9:52.71	Tara	Krzywicki (10)	GBR	9.3.74	2	v2N	Glasgow	1 Jul
9:53.97		Nye			6	GWG	Brisbane	4 Sep
9:54.46		Volkova			1	NC	Tula	12 Jul
9:54.84	Rebecca	Bennion	USA	16.9.80	2	NCAA	Eugene	1 Jun
9:54.99	Melanie	Schulz	GER	27.8.79	1		Malmö	20 Aug
9:55.01		Krzywicki			1	NC	Glasgow	11 Aug
9:55.07	Natalya	Cherepanova	RUS	9.3.67	1	Znam	Tula	8 Jun
9:55.49	Kelly	MacDonald	USA	27.9.78	3	NC	Eugene	23 Jun
9:55.63		Jackson			1		San Diego	19 May
9:55.74		Casandra			5	Nik	Nice	9 Jul
	(30/14)							
9:57.06	Anita	Weyermann	SUI	8.12.77	2	FBK	Hengelo	4 Jun
9:57.06	Luminita	Gogîrlea	ROM	5.11.71	3	FBK	Hengelo	4 Jun
9:59.28	Courtney	Meldrum	USA	31.1.77	4	NCAA	Eugene	1 Jun
9:59.50	Nanette	Evans	USA	18.8.81	5	NCAA	Eugene	1 Jun
9:59.75	Ida	Nilsson	SWE	8.2.81	6	NCAA	Eugene	1 Jun
10:00.36	Alina	Cucerzan	ROM	28.7.74	7	Nik	Nice	9 Jul
	(20)							
10:01.52	Larissa	Kleinmann	GER	10.9.78	1	Penn R	Philadelphia	26 Apr
10:03.01	Rimma	Pushkina	RUS	10.1.74	1	Kuts	Moskva	29 Jul
10:03.02	Sigrid	Vanden Bempt	BEL	10.2.81	1		Oordegem	2 Jun
10:04.14	Kara	Ormond	USA	17.6.77	4	v2N	Glasgow	1 Jul
10:04.49	Susanne	Wigene	NOR	12.2.78	1		Fana	7 Jun
10:04.76	Meriem	Méred	FRA	4.4.76	9	Nik	Nice	9 Jul
10:04.99	Lívia	Tóth	HUN	7.1.80	2	EU23	Amsterdam	13 Jul
10:04.99	Ulla	Tuimala	FIN-J	27.4.82	1	v SWE	Göteborg	2 Sep
10:05.15	Margaret	Kerubo	KEN	15.5.74	1		Reims	5 Jul
10:05.28	Céline	Rajot	FRA	22.3.75	10	Nik	Nice	9 Jul
	(30)							
10:05.38	Katie	Sabino	USA	23.1.79	8	NCAA	Eugene	1 Jun
10:06.48	Varvara	Shestok	UKR	17.12.74	1		Kiev	25 May
10:06.60	Daniela	Petrescu	ROM	13.4.68	11	Nik	Nice	9 Jul
10:07.41	Anni	Tuimala	FIN-J	27.4.82	2	vSWE	Göteborg	2 Sep
10:08.51	Fanny	Pruvost	FRA	21.5.79	4	EU23	Amsterdam	13 Jul
10:08.61	Kerry	Hils	USA	21.3.81	9	NCAA	Eugene	1 Jun
10:08.85	Lisa	Aguilera	USA	30.11.79	1		Palo Alto	31 Mar
10:09.70	Janet	Trujillo	USA	7.8.75	1		Eugene	12 May
10:09.83	Galina	Yegorova	RUS-J	5.8.83	1		Sochi	14 Oct
10:09.96	Johanna	Risku	FIN	21.2.79	5	EU23	Amsterdam	13 Jul
	(40)							
10:10.16	Margaret	Larson	USA	13.9.79	2		San Diego	18 May
10:10.83	Tonya	Dodge	USA	24.5.75	3		Eugene	12 May
10:11.45	Desiree	Owen	USA	22.2.75	8	NC	Eugene	23 Jun
10:11.45	Mariya	Vilisova	RUS	69	4	NC	Tula	12 Jul
10:11.65	Jennifer	Michel	USA		9	NC	Eugene	23 Jun
10:12.24	Molly	De Francesco	USA	17.2.80	10	NC	Eugene	23 Jun
10:12.86	Andrea	Kremer	USA-J	2.7.82	5h1	NCAA	Eugene	30 May
10:13.53	Anzhelika	Averkova	UKR	13.3.69	1	NC	Kiev	2 Jul
10:14.54	Stephanie	De Croock	BEL	3.4.79	1		Beveren	9 Sep
10:15.27	Laura	Turner	USA	7.4.80	5h2	NCAA	Eugene	30 May
	(50)							

Mark	Name		Nat	Born	Date	Mark	Name		Nat	Born	Date
10:15.32	Ragnhild	Kvarberg	NOR	23.3.81	7 Jun	10:17.73	Elena	Mandrila	ROM	1.7.79	10 Jun
10:15.40	Christine	Bardelle	FRA	16.8.74	18 Jul	10:18.3	Susanne	Strunz	GER	22.6.77	18 May
10:15.67	Yamina	Bouchaouante	FRA	31.7.80	29 Jul	10:18.31	Hana	Chaouach	TUN	18.9.81	11 Sep
10:16.21	Carla	Tavarès	FRA	29.6.75	19 Jun	10:18.54	Emily	Mulick	USA	10.10.77	20 Apr
10:16.98	Kristina	Ahlepil	SWE	25.4.78	7 Jun	10:18.67	Malika	Coutant	FRA	19.2.72	9 Jun
10:17.39	Tara	Haynes	USA	6.8.78	18 May	10:19.37	Pierangela	Baronchelli	ITA	8.11.72	24 Jun
10:17.39	Lesley	Higgins	USA	8.10.80	20 Apr		(63)				

Time Trials: Rollison 9:47.30 at Gold Coast 29 Jun, 9:47.86 at Gold Coast 12 Aug

Symbols/Abbreviations

\+ intermediate time in longer race, A made at an altitude of 1000m or higher, H made in a heptathlon, h made in a heat, qf quarter-final, sf semi-final, i indoors, Q qualifying round, r race number, -J juniors (born 1982 or later)

Mark	Wind	Name		Nat	Born	Pos	Meet	Venue	Date

JUNIORS

See main list for top 5 juniors. 8 + 2 TT performances by 5 women to 10:16.00. Additional marks and further juniors:

Yegorova 10:15.43 1 NC-j Kazan 28 Jun

Kremer 10:14.62 10 NCAA Eugene 1 Jun 10:15.77 1 Oxford OH 19 May

Mark	Name		Nat	Born	Pos	Meet	Venue	Date
10:25.2	Susan	Jepketer	KEN	82	1		Trento	30 May
10:25.87	Jen	Hanifan (10)	USA	6.5.82	3		Palo Alto	13 May
10:25.94	Jennifer	Donovan	USA	4.5.82	2		Piscataway	5 May
10:29.5	Victoria	Mitchell	AUS	25.4.82	1		Melbourne	15 Nov
10:33.45	Catalina	Oprea	ROM	11.4.86	hc		Bucuresti	12 May
10:36.00	Marina	Ivanova	RUS	30.6.83	3	Kuts	Moskva	29 Jul
10:36.77	Brianna	Dahm	USA	13.3.82	1		Kalamazoo	5 May
10:38.77	Yuliya	Ignatova	UKR	30.7.83	3		Kiev	25 May
10:39.74	Eszter	Erdélyi	HUN	22.5.82	1		Lincoln, NE	12 May

100 METRES HURDLES

Mark	Wind	Name		Nat	Born	Pos	Meet	Venue	Date
12.42	2.0	Anjanette	Kirkland	USA	24.2.74	1	WCh	Edmonton	11 Aug
12.53	-1.2	Gail	Devers	USA	19.11.66	1	WK	Zürich	17 Aug
12.54	2.0		Devers			2	WCh	Edmonton	10 Aug
12.56	-0.3		Devers			1s2	WCh	Edmonton	10 Aug
12.57	0.9	Delloreen	Ennis-London	JAM	5.3.75	1	GP II	Sevilla	8 Jun
12.58	2.0	Olga	Shishigina	KAZ	23.12.68	3	WCh	Edmonton	11 Aug
12.58	2.0	Svetla	Dimitrova	BUL	27.1.70	4	WCh	Edmonton	11 Aug
12.61	0.3		Devers			1	GWG	Brisbane	4 Sep
12.62	1.3		Ennis-London			1	NC	Kingston	23 Jun
12.63	2.0	Jenny	Adams	USA	8.7.78	5	WCh	Edmonton	11 Aug
12.64	-1.2		Kirkland			2	WK	Zürich	17 Aug
12.65	-0.8		Dimitrova			1s1	WCh	Edmonton	10 Aug
12.67	1.3		Shishigina			1		Almaty	3 Jun
12.67	-0.8		Adams			2s1	WCh	Edmonton	10 Aug
12.67	-0.3	Linda	Ferga	FRA	24.12.76	2s2	WCh	Edmonton	10 Aug
12.68	0.0		Ennis-London			1	Pre	Eugene	27 May
12.68	-0.4		Adams			1rA	Athl	Lausanne	4 Jul
12.69	0.0		Devers			2	Pre	Eugene	27 May
12.69	0.9	Glory	Alozie (ex NGR)	ESP	30.12.77	2	GP II	Sevilla	8 Jun
12.69	-0.6		Kirkland			1h1	WCh	Edmonton	9 Aug
12.70	1.3	Bridgette	Foster	JAM	7.11.74	2	NC	Kingston	23 Jun
12.70	-0.3		Shishigina			1	Herc	Monaco	20 Jul
12.71	0.1	Maurren	Maggi (10)	BRA	25.6.76	1	SACh	Manaus	19 May
12.72	1.0		Adams			1	GP II	Zagreb	2 Jul
12.72	0.8	Svetlana	Laukhova	RUS	1.2.73	1	NC	Tula	13 Jul
12.72	-0.5		Devers			1h2	WCh	Edmonton	9 Aug
12.73	1.1	Perdita	Felicien	CAN	29.8.80	1	Big 10	Bloomington	20 May
12.73	-0.4		Ennis-London			2rA	Athl	Lausanne	4 Jul
12.74	-0.5		Dimitrova			2h2	WCh	Edmonton	9 Aug
12.74	0.3	Susanna	Kallur	SWE	16.2.81	1h3	WCh	Edmonton	9 Aug
		(30/13)							
12.77	-0.3	Dionne	Rose-Henley	JAM	7.11.69	4s2	WCh	Edmonton	10 Aug
12.78	0.5	Eunice	Barber	FRA	17.11.74	1H3	WCh	Edmonton	4 Aug
12.81	1.4	Irina	Korotya	RUS	2.9.75	2	Znam	Tula	8 Jun
12.82	1.1	Donica	Merriman	USA	24.1.79	2	Big 10	Bloomington	20 May
12.82	1.5	Patricia	Girard	FRA	8.4.68	1	MedG	Tunis	12 Sep
12.83	1.3	Vonette	Dixon	JAM	26.11.75	3	NC	Kingston	23 Jun
12.85	0.6	Damu	Cherry	USA	29.11.77	1h1		Atlanta	19 May
		(20)							
12.87	0.9	Yelena	Krasovskaya	UKR	17.8.76	3	GP II	Sevilla	8 Jun
12.89	1.7	Michelle	Freeman	JAM	5.5.69	2		Réthimno	1 Jul
12.91	1.3	Aliuska	López	CUB	29.8.69	1		Sotteville	12 Jul
12.91	-0.8	Nicole	Ramalalanirina	FRA	5.3.72	6s1	WCh	Edmonton	10 Aug
12.92	1.2	Yahumara	Neyra	CUB	18.4.76	1		Salamanca	13 Jul
12.93	1.0	Nadine	Faustin	HAI	14.4.76	2rB	Athl	Lausanne	4 Jul
12.93	1.4		Feng Yun	CHN	23.2.76	1h1	NG	Guangzhou	17 Nov
12.95	1.9	Danielle	Carruthers	USA	22.12.79	1		Bloomington	12 May
12.95	-0.1		Su Yiping	CHN	4.8.79	1	WUG	Beijing	28 Aug
12.96	0.8	Natalya	Shekhodanova	RUS	29.12.71	3	NC	Tula	13 Jul
		(30)							
12.96	0.9	Haydy	Aron	FRA	21.5.73	1h2	MedG	Tunis	12 Sep
12.97	1.6	Lacena	Golding	JAM	20.3.75	1		Fort-de-France	28 Apr
12.98	0.8	Kirsten	Bolm	GER	4.3.75	1	NC	Stuttgart	1 Jul
12.99	-0.1		Liu Jing ¶	CHN	8.8.77	3	NC	Chengdu	30 Jun

Mark	Wind	Name		Nat	Born	Pos	Meet	Venue	Date
13.00	1.7	Nicole	Hoxie	USA	22.7.79	2	Tex R	Austin	7 Apr
13.00	0.7	Melissa	Morrison	USA	9.7.71	1	Penn R	Philadelphia	28 Apr
13.01	1.3	Astia	Walker	JAM	4.4.75	5	NC	Kingston	23 Jun
13.01	0.0	Trecia	Roberts	THA	4.2.71	2		Ludvika	27 Jun
13.02	1.8	Vida	Nsiah	GHA	13.4.76	1h2	Penn R	Philadelphia	27 Apr
13.02	0.5	Gergana	Stoyanova	BUL-J	3.1.82	1h3	NC-j	Sofia	15 Jun
		(40)							
13.02	0.9	Rosa-[illegible]	Rakotozafy	MAD	12.11.77	2h2	Fra Ch	Saint-Etienne	1 Jul
13.02	-0.5	Patricia	Buval	FRA	22.1.76	2	Franc	Ottawa	20 Jul
13.03	1.1	Gillian	Love (Russell)	JAM	28.9.73	1		Coral Gables	14 Apr
13.03	1.4	Irina	Lenskiy	ISR	12.6.71	1		Tel Aviv	15 May
13.03	0.7	Kisha	Jett	USA	11.2.75	1		Atlanta	2 Jun
13.04	1.9	Svetlana	Gnedzilov	ISR	20.7.69	1H		Minsk	6 Jun
13.05	0.4	Anete	Sosnowska	POL	10.5.74	1		Biala Podlaska	6 Jul
13.05	0.5	Shelia	Burrell	USA	15.1.72	2H3	WCh	Edmonton	4 Aug
13.06	0.0	EllaKisha	Williamson	USA	19.3.75	1		Ingolstadt	27 May
13.07	1.9	Kim	Carson	USA	12.3.74	4h3	NC	Eugene	23 Jun
		(50)							
13.08	1.9	Yolanda	McCray	USA	11.9.76	1	Kans R	Lawrence	21 Apr
13.08	0.8	Diane	Allahgreen	GBR	21.2.75	1	BIG	Bedford	18 Jul
13.09	1.7	Christina	Ohaeri	USA	30.3.79	1	Big 12	College Station	19 May
13.09	1.7	Chimika	Carter	USA	17.8.78	2	Big 12	College Station	19 May
13.09	1.9	Daveetta	Shepherd	USA	15.1.79	5h3	NC	Eugene	23 Jun
13.09	0.9	Reïna-Flor	Okori	FRA	2.5.80	3h2	NC	Saint-Etienne	1 Jul
13.09	-0.5	Angela	Whyte	CAN	27.5.80	4	Franc	Ottawa	20 Jul
13.10	-1.1	Surita	Febbraio	RSA	27.12.73	1	NC	Durban	2 Mar
13.10		Mariya	Koroteyeva	RUS	10.11.81	1	NC-23	Cheboksary	14 Jun
13.12	1.5	Jacqui	Munro	AUS	4.10.81	1h2	WUG	Beijing	27 Aug
		(60)							
13.13	0.4	Juliane	Sprenger	GER	22.3.77	1h1	NC	Stuttgart	30 Jun
13.14	-0.2	Toni Ann	D'Oyley	JAM	25.10.81	3		Bridgetown	19 May
13.15	1.9	Jenny	Kallur	SWE	16.2.81	2h3	NCAA	Eugene	31 May
13.16	-0.2	Sharon	Couch	USA	13.9.69	4		Bridgetown	19 May
13.16	1.0	Sonia	Paquette	CAN	7.2.73	1		Sherbrooke	16 Jun
13.17	0.8	Joyce	Bates	USA	16.2.77	1		Baton Rouge	14 Apr
13.17	1.0	Maíla Paula	Machado	BRA	22.1.81	4	GP II	Zagreb	2 Jul
13.17	-0.7	Margaret	Macchiut	ITA	25.7.74	1	NC	Catania	7 Jul
13.18	0.1	Michelle	Perry	USA	1.5.79	1		Los Angeles	5 May
13.18	0.4	Maya	Shemchishina	UKR	6.5.72	2		Kiev	25 May
		(70)							
13.19	-0.5	Yvonne	Kanazawa	JPN	19.11.74	1	GP II	Osaka	12 May
13.19	0.9	Yuliya	Graudyn	RUS	13.11.70	7	GP II	Sevilla	8 Jun
13.20	1.3	Kia	Davis	USA	23.5.76	1		Durham	7 Apr
13.20	-1.2	Anay	Tejeda	CUB-J	3.4.83	2		Salamanca	13 Jul
13.20	0.0	Angela	Atede	NGR	8.2.72	3		San Sebastián	18 Aug
13.22	-0.2	Mame Tacko	Diouf	SEN	17.10.76	1h2	Franc	Ottawa	19 Jul
13.23	1.0	Ashlee	Williams	USA-J	27.3.84	1		Houston	24 Mar
13.23	0.6	Adrianna	Lamalle	FRA-J	27.9.82	1		Tours	31 May
13.23	0.3	Sriyani	Kulawansa	SRI	1.3.70	6h3	WCh	Edmonton	9 Aug
13.24	1.9	Natasha	Neal	USA	22.7.80	3h3	NCAA	Eugene	31 May
		(80)							
13.24	0.8	Melani	Wilkins	GBR	18.1.73	2	NC	Birmingham	15 Jul
13.24	1.6	Keri	Maddox	GBR	4.7.72	1		Bedford	21 Jul
13.25	1.8	Nadine	Hentschke	GER-J	27.1.82	1h2	EJ	Grosseto	20 Jul
13.26	1.5	Hannah	Cooper	LBR	10.6.79	1		Palo Alto	13 May
13.26	0.4	Bisa	Grant	USA	16.7.76	1		Los Angeles	2 Jun
13.26	-2.0	Flóra	Redoúmi	GRE	11.9.76	1	NC	Athína	16 Jun
13.26	0.2	Tessy	Prediger	GER	29.1.79	2		Mannheim	16 Jun
13.26	1.7	Hristiána	Tabáki	GRE	13.1.73	6		Réthimno	1 Jul
13.27	0.4	Felicia	Stone	USA	10.8.77	3	MSR	Walnut	22 Apr
13.27	1.4		Tan Yali	CHN	17.1.77	3		Ningbo	27 Apr
		(90)							
13.27	1.0	Teneeshia	Jones	USA	28.1.79	1h2	SEC	Columbia, SC	12 May
13.28	0.0	Natalya	Sazanovich	BLR	15.8.73	2H		Götzis	26 May
13.29	2.0	Cécile	Michot	FRA	2.6.74	1rB	NC	Saint-Etienne	1 Jul
13.29	1.4		Zhang Yu	CHN	8.4.71	2h1	NG	Guangzhou	17 Nov
13.29	1.1		Xiong Yanling	CHN	5.5.80	1h3	NG	Guangzhou	17 Nov
13.30	-0.4	Nadine	Grouwels	BEL	1.11.73	4		Cuxhaven	21 Jul
13.31	1.5	Lolo	Jones	USA-J	5.8.82	5	TexR	Austin	7 Apr
13.31	1.7	Emily	Waibel	USA	10.2.81	5	Big 12	College Station	19 May
13.31	0.6	Isabel	Abrantes	POR	20.3.73	3		Funchal	30 Jun

Mark	Wind	Name		Nat	Born	Pos	Meet	Venue	Date
13.31A	-0.8	Dainelky (100)	Pérez	CUB	6.1.76	1	CAC	C. de Guatemala	21 Jul
13.31	-0.3	Judith	Vis	NED	21.6.80	1		Namur	17 Aug
13.31	1.4		Zeng Xiaoling	CHN	1.1.80	3h1	NG	Guangzhou	17 Nov
13.31	1.7	Fiona	Cullen	AUS	31.8.79	1		Brisbane (St L)	21 Dec

Mark	Wind	Name		Nat	Born	Date
13.32	1.2	Debbie	Edwards	AUS	25.9.78	25 Mar
13.33	0.2	Alesha	Peel	USA	27.9.78	28 Apr
13.33	0.0	Jacqueline	Madison	USA	14.7.79	19 May
13.33	-1.2	Raquel	Fraguas	ESP	2.3.76	8 Jun
13.33	0.2	Mona	Steigauf	GER	17.1.70	16 Jun
13.33	-0.6		Zeng Yan	CHN	29.6.76	29 Jun
13.34	0.0	Charmaine	Walker	USA	5.5.78	19 May
13.35		Polina	Denisova	RUS	78	19 Jun
13.35	1.9	Monifa	Taylor	USA	3.3.71	23 Jun
13.35	0.9	Natacha	Casy	FRA	26.4.74	1 Jul
13.36	1.1	Olutoyin	Augustus	USA	24.12.79	20 May
13.36	0.6	Sarah	Claxton	GBR	23.9.79	27 May
13.36	0.0	Fanny	Gérance	FRA	4.1.81	28 Jul
13.36	1.1		Pang Meijuan	CHN-J	10.1.82	17 Nov
13.37	2.0	Gi-Gi	Miller	USA	12.1.79	10 May
13.37	0.0	Urska	Beti	SLO	19.6.78	14 Jul
13.38	1.0	Ranysha	LeBlanc	USA-J	1.1.83	24 Mar
13.38	-0.7	Kumiko	Ikeda	JPN	10.1.81	9 Jun
13.38	1.0	Monica	Pellegrinelli	SUI	14.5.65	1 Jul
13.38		Oksana	Samoylenko	UZB	5.12.72	27 Jul
13.39	-0.7	Tomoko	Motegi	JPN	8.8.78	9 Jun
13.39	1.6	Akiko	Morimoto	JPN	17.2.77	24 Jun
13.39	0.6	Virginia	Powell	USA-J	7.9.83	29 Jul
13.40	0.1	Sani	Roseby	USA-J	5.2.82	5 May
13.40	1.1		Deng Xiaocen	CHN	8.7.76	17 Nov
13.41	1.4	Myriam	Tschomba	BEL	14.1.77	19 May
13.41	1.7	Nicole	Denby	USA-J	10.10.82	19 May
13.41	0.0	Sabrina	Previtali	ITA	8.5 75	2 Jun
13.41	0.2	Annette	Thimm	GER	24.11.77	24 Aug
13.42	0.8	Denise	Lewis	GBR	27.8.72	15 Jul
13.43	1.6	Tiffany	Talbert	USA		5 May
13.43	-0.7	Yana	Kasova	BUL	13.8.81	27 May
13.43	-0.7	Ayumi	Fujita	JPN	2.11.77	9 Jun
13.43	0.0		Moh Siew Wei	MAS	30.4.78	13 Sep
13.43	1.4		Xu Jia	CHN	23.9.79	17 Nov
13.44	1.7	Andrea	Blackett	BAR	24.1.76	7 Apr
13.44	0.0	Kyana	Elder	USA	22.4.80	19 May
13.44	1.3	Yelena	Nikitenko	KAZ-J	4.2.82	3 Jun
13.44	1.4	Irina	Belova	RUS	27.3.68	16 Jun
13.45	0.0	Lutisha	Shittu	USA	9.5.79	19 May
13.45	1.8	Joanna	Bujak	FRA	30.8.79	19 Jun
13.46	0.6	Iwona	Konrad	POL	14.9.74	7 Jun
13.46	1.4	Maren	Freisen	GER-J	15.2.82	16 Jun
13.46	0.3	Leshley	Tashlin	CAN	27.5.69	24 Jun
13.46	-0.9	Christy	Akinremi	NGR	29.3.72	4 Jul
13.46	1.2	Julie	Pratt	GBR	20.3.79	15 Jul
13.46	1.5	Princesa	Oliveros	COL	10.8.75	27 Aug
13.46	0.5		Zhu Shuiying	CHN	21.7.77	17 Nov
13.47	0.8	Sayuri	Kawakami	JPN	14.4.79	20 May
13.47	1.1	Daniela	Wöckinger	AUT	9.5.81	26 May
13.47	1.8	DeDee	Nathan	USA	20.4.68	21 Jun
13.47	0.0		Vu Bich Huong	VIE	30.11.69	13 Sep
13.48	1.1	Jerkita	McClorin	USA	16.6.80	24 Mar
13.48	0.5	Agneta	Rosenblad	SWE	8.8.77	14 Apr
13.48	1.1	Camee	Williams	USA	6.9.80	20 May
13.48	1.4	Jennifer	Komoll	GER	17.4.80	24 Jun
13.48		Yevgeniya	Likhuta	BLR	24.3.81	30 Jun
13.48	1.8	Agnieszka	Frankowska	POL-J	9.3.83	20 Jul
13.48	0.1	Corinna	Rehwagen	GER	17.5.81	29 Jul
13.48			Ji Fangqian	CHN-J	18.7.84	8 Aug
13.49	0.3	Rori	Kelly	USA	3.10.78	24 Mar
13.49	1.0	Georgina	Power	AUS-J	4.11.82	25 Mar
13.49	1.9	Aurelia	Trywianska	POL	9.5.76	21 Apr
13.49	1.1		Han Chunping	CHN	14.3.80	17 Nov
13.51	-1.1	Lana	van Heerden	RSA	9.12.68	3 Mar
13.51	1.1	Dalanda	Jackson	USA-J	21.1.82	20 May
13.51		Yuliya	Kondakova	RUS	4.12.81	14 Jun
13.51	-2.6	Rachel	King	GBR	11.5.76	1 Jul
13.52	0.4	Sheena	Johnson	USA-J	1.10.82	14 Apr
13.52	1.6	Marisa	Robinson	USA	16.5.78	5 May
13.52	1.9	Le'Gretta	Smith	USA	13.1.74	12 May
13.52	0.0	Sabine	Braun	GER	19.6.65	26 May
13.52	-0.4	Lucie	Skrobáková	CZE-J	4.1.82	1 Jul
13.52	1.6	Shelley-Ann	Brown	CAN	15.5.80	1 Jul
13.52	0.7	Barbara	Panno	ITA	25.5.75	7 Jul
13.53	-1.5	April	Sams	USA	23.8.79	24 Mar
13.53	0.6	Eva	Miklos	ROM	30.7.78	24 Jun
13.53	1.6	Johanna	Halkoaho	FIN	13.1.77	27 Jun
13.53	0.4	Katja	Keller	GER	9.8.80	30 Jun
13.54		Dawn (183)	Harper	USA-J	14.6.84	19 May

Irregular

Mark	Wind	Name		Nat	Born	Pos	Meet	Venue	Date
12.62	0.2	Patricia	Girard	FRA	8.4.68	1		La Roche-sur-Yon	22 Aug
12.87	0.2	Nicole	Ramalalanirina	FRA	5.3.72	2		La Roche-sur-Yon	22 Aug

Wind assisted

Mark	Wind	Name		Nat	Born	Pos	Meet	Venue	Date
12.61	4.0	Jenny	Adams	USA	8.7.78	1h1	NC	Eugene	23 Jun
12.61	3.5		Dimitrova			1	ECp-1B	Budapest	24 Jun
12.70	2.9	Yahumara	Neyra	CUB	18.4.76	1		Valencia	8 Jul
12.70	2.2		Su Yiping	CHN	4.8.79	1	NG	Guangzhou	18 Nov
12.73	2.6	Donica	Merriman	USA	24.1.79	1	NCAA	Eugene	2 Jun
12.77	2.4	Patricia	Girard	FRA	8.4.68	1h1	MedG	Tunis	12 Sep
12.79	2.6	Danielle	Carruthers	USA	22.12.79	2	NCAA	Eugene	2 Jun
12.82	2.4	Melissa	Morrison	USA	9.7.71	1	MSR	Walnut	22 Apr
12.82	2.6	Angela	Whyte	CAN	27.5.80	3	NCAA	Eugene	2 Jun
12.84	2.6	Nicole	Ramalalanirina	FRA	5.3.72	1		Montauban	17 Jul
12.86	2.2		Feng Yun	CHN	23.2.76	2	NG	Guangzhou	18 Nov
12.89	2.2	Gillian	Love (Russell)	JAM	28.9.73	1	Mod R	Modesto	12 May
12.90	3.0	Adrianna	Lamalle	FRA-J	27.9.82	1		Fort-de-France	28 Apr
12.90	2.3	Trecia	Roberts	THA	4.2.71	1		Västerås	3 Jul
12.91	2.2		Zeng Xiaoling	CHN	1.1.80	3	NG	Guangzhou	18 Nov
12.96	2.2	Bisa	Grant	USA	16.7.76	2	Mod R	Modesto	12 May
12.98	3.0	Kim	Carson	USA	12.3.74	1	DrakeR	Des Moines	28 Apr
12.98	2.1	Diane	Allahgreen	GBR	21.2.75	4	v2N	Glasgow	1 Jul
12.98	2.7	Patricia	Buval	FRA	22.1.76	3h1	NC	Saint-Etienne	1 Jul
13.00	3.5	Gergana	Stoyanova	BUL-J	3.1.82	1h1	EJ	Grosseto	20 Jul
13.02	2.3	Dainelky	Pérez	CUB	6.1.76	2	NC	La Habana	25 May
13.03	5.6	Kia	Davis	USA	23.5.78	1	NCAA II	Edwardsville	26 May
13.03	2.2		Zhang Yu	CHN	8.4.71	4	NG	Guangzhou	18 Nov
13.04	2.8	Chimika	Carter	USA	17.8.78	1h1	Big 12	College Station	18 May
13.05	2.5	Christina	Ohaeri	USA	30.3.79	1	USTCA	Austin	21 Apr
13.07	3.2	Anay	Tejeda	CUB-J	3.4.83	2		Maia	14 Jul

Mark	Wind	Name		Nat	Born	Pos	Meet	Venue	Date
13.08	2.1	Melani	Wilkins	GBR	18.1.73	6	v2N	Glasgow	1 Jul
13.09	2.3	Toni Ann	D'Oyley	JAM	25.10.81	3	Cub Ch	La Habana	25 May
13.11	2.6	Jenny	Kallur	SWE	16.2.81	7	NCAA	Eugene	2 Jun
13.11	4.0	Gi-Gi	Miller	USA	12.1.79	1H	NC	Eugene	21 Jun
13.13	2.3	Yenima	Arencibia	CUB-J	25.12.84	4	NC	La Habana	25 May
13.13	2.2		Pang Meijuan	CHN-J	10.1.82	5	NG	Guangzhou	18 Nov
13.14	2.7	Yuliya	Graudyn	RUS	13.11.70	2		Lisboa (U)	16 Jun
13.14		Mame Tacko	Diouf	SEN	17.10.76	3		Valencia	8 Jul
13.16	2.2		Xiong Yanling	CHN	5.5.80	6	NG	Guangzhou	18 Nov
13.17	3.6	Lolo	Jones	USA-J	5.8.82	1h1	USTCA	Austin	21 Apr
13.17	3.3	Alesha	Peel	USA	27.9.78	2h3	Big 12	College Station	18 May
13.19	2.2	Natasha	Neal	USA	22.7.80	1h3	Pac-10	Berkeley	19 May
13.21	2.8	Jackie	Madison	USA	14.7.79	5h2	NCAA	Eugene	31 May
13.21	3.2	Isabel	Abrantes	POR	20.2.73	3		Maia	14 Jul
13.22	5.1	Akiko	Morimoto	JPN	17.2.77	1		Maebashi	22 Apr
13.23	2.5	Tomoko	Motegi	JPN	8.8.78	1		Kitakami	14 Jul
13.25A	3.2	Rachel	Joy	USA	29.4.78	1		Greeley	14 Apr
13.25	2.8	Hannah	Cooper	LBR	10.6.79	2h2	Big 12	College Station	18 May
13.26	2.2	Felicia	Stone	USA	10.8.77	3	Mod R	Modesto	12 May
13.27	2.9	Kyla	Shoemake	USA	6.6.77	1		Fayetteville	14 Apr
13.28	3.3	Emily	Waibel	USA	10.2.81	3h3	Big 12	College Station	18 May
13.28	2.3	Agneta	Rosenblad	SWE	8.8.77	1h2	Pac-10	Berkeley	19 May
13.28	2.2	Fanny	Gérance	FRA	4.1.81	2		Obernai	29 Jul
13.29	2.1	Denise	Lewis	GBR	27.8.72	7	v2N	Glasgow	1 Jul

Mark	Wind	Name		Nat	Born	Date	Mark	Wind	Name		Nat	Born	Date
13.30	5.1	Ayumi	Fujita	JPN	2.11.77	22 Apr	13.43	2.1	Julie	Pratt	GBR	20.3.79	2 Jun
13.30	4.0	Brandit	Copper	USA	25.8.78	23 Jun	13.44	3.0	Tamika	Higgins-Francis	USA	19.4.71	19 May
13.30	2.1	Lucie	Skrobáková	CZE-J	4.1.82	20 Jul	13.44	6.2	Salla	Käppi	FIN	22.5.80	12 Aug
13.35	3.0	Iwona	Konrad	POL	14.9.74	23 Jun	13.46	3.5	Jerkita	McClorin	USA	16.6.80	28 Apr
13.36	2.2		Zhu Shuying	CHN	21.7.77	18 Nov	13.46	3.5	Daniela	Wöckinger	AUT	9.5.81	24 Jun
13.37	2.1	Agnieszka	Frankowska	POL-J	9.3.83	20 Jul	13.48	3.2	Marteen	Caldwell	USA	24.11.81	14 May
13.39	5.1	Sayuri	Kawakami	JPN	14.4.79	22 Apr	13.49	3.2	Marisa	Robinson	USA	16.5.78	18 May
13.39	2.7	Tiffany	Talbert	USA		10 May	13.50	4.2	April	Sams	USA	23.8.79	6 Apr
13.39	3.4	Lutisha	Shittu	USA	9.5.79	12 May	13.50	3.5	Anzhela	Kinet (Atroshenko)	TUR	14.11.70	24 Jun
13.39	2.8	Nicole	Denby	USA-J	10.10.82	18 May	13.51	3.1	Anna	Pettersson	SWE	3.10.77	4 Aug
13.39	2.9	Lashinda	Demus	USA-J	10.3.83	2 Jun	13.52	2.2	DeeDee	Brown	USA	5.5.78	14 Apr
13.40	2.8	Shelley-Ann	Brown	CAN	15.5.80	18 May	13.53	3.5	Tina	Klein	GER-J	24.4.83	20 Jul
13.43	2.5	Zamyal	Jackson	USA-J	29.5.82	21 Apr	13.54	2.2	Loren	Leaverton	USA	1.2.80	14 Apr

Hand timed

Mark	Wind	Name		Nat	Born	Pos	Meet	Venue	Date
13.0A	-0.5	Princesa	Oliveros	COL	10.8.75	1	BolG	Ambato	13 Sep
13.1	1.2	Olga	Korsunova	RUS	.81				29 May
13.2	1.2	Yana	Kasova	BUL	13.8.81				7 May
12.5w	3.9	Joyce	Bates	USA	16.2.77	1		Baton Rouge	18 May
12.7w	3.9	Lolo	Jones	USA-J	5.8.82	2		Baton Rouge	18 May
13.2w	3.9	Zamyal	Jackson	USA-J	29.5.82	3		Baton Rouge	18 May

JUNIORS

See main list for top 6 juniors. 10 performances by 5 women to 13.29. Additional marks and further juniors:

Stoyanova 13.07 1.6 1 NC-j Sofia 15 Jun | 13.25 -0.7 2 Sofia 27 May

Hentschke 13.25 0.1 1 NC-23 Schweinfurt 29 Jul | 13.29 1.8 1s1 NC-j Braunschweig 7 Jul

13.27 0.8 3 NC Stuttgart 1 Jul

Mark	Wind	Name		Nat	Born	Pos	Meet	Venue	Date
13.36	1.1		Pang Meijuan	CHN	10.1.82	2h3	NG	Guangzhou	17 Nov
13.38	1.0	Ranysha	LeBlanc	USA	1.1.83	2		Houston	24 Mar
13.39	0.6	Virginia	Powell	USA	7.9.83	1		Sacramento	29 Jul
13.40	0.1	Sani	Roseby	USA	5.2.82	3		Los Angeles	5 May
13.41	1.7	Nicole	Denby	USA	10.10.82	7	Big 12	College Station	19 May
13.44	1.3	Yelena	Nikitenko	KAZ	4.2.82	2		Almaty	3 Jun
13.46	1.4	Maren	Freisen	GER	15.2.82	2H		Ratingen	16 Jun
13.48	1.8	Agnieszka	Frankowska	POL	9.3.83	2h2	EJ	Grosseto	20 Jul
13.48			Ji Fangqian	CHN	18.7.84	1		Changde	8 Aug
13.49	1.0	Georgina	Power	AUS	4.11.82	1	NC	Brisbane	25 Mar
13.51	1.1	Dalanda	Jackson	USA	21.1.82	7	Big 10	Bloomington	20 May
13.52	0.4	Sheena	Johnson	USA	1.10.82	1rB		Westwood	14 Apr
13.52	-0.4	Lucie	Skrobáková	CZE	4.1.82	1	NC	Jablonec	1 Jul
13.54		Dawn	Harper	USA	14.6.84	1		Champaign	19 May

Wind assisted see main lists for six women – 10 performances to 13.17w

Lamalle 12.99w2.6 1h3 EJ Grosseto 20 Jul | 13.08w2.1 2 EJ Grosseto 20 Jul

Stoyanova 13.04w2.1 1 EJ Grosseto 20 Jul

Tejeda 13.16w 4 Valencia 8 Jul

Mark	Wind	Name		Nat	Born	Pos	Meet	Venue	Date
13.30	2.1	Lucie	Skrobáková	CZE	4.1.82	3	EJ	Grosseto	20 Jul
13.37	2.1	Agnieszka	Frankowska	POL	9.3.83	5	EJ	Grosseto	20 Jul
13.39	2.8	Nicole	Denby	USA	10.10.82	2h1	Big 12	College Station	18 May
13.39	2.9	Lashinda	Demus	USA	10.3.83	1		Sacramento	2 Jun
13.53	3.5	Tina	Klein	GER	24.4.83	3h1	EJ	Grosseto	20 Jul

Mark	Name		Nat	Born	Pos	Meet	Venue	Date

200 Metres Hurdles

Nantes 23 Aug: (-0.7) 1. Patricia Girard FRA 25.6, 2. Mame Tacko Diouf SEN 26.0, 3. Nicole Ramalalanirina FRA 26.6, 4. Rosa Rakotozafy MAD 26.7, 5. Vivian Dorsile FRA 27.3

300 Metres Hurdles

Mark	Name		Nat	Born	Pos	Meet	Venue	Date
39.73	Kim	Batten	USA	29.3.69	1		Tallahassee	17 Mar
39.98	Lashinda	Demus	USA-J	10.3.83	1		Norwalk	19 May

400 METRES HURDLES

Mark	Name		Nat	Born	Pos	Meet	Venue	Date
53.34	Nezha	Bidouane	MAR	18.9.69	1	WCh	Edmonton	8 Aug
53.81	Daimí	Pernía	CUB	27.12.76	1s1	WCh	Edmonton	6 Aug
53.84	Yuliya	Nosova	RUS	21.4.78	1	ECp-S	Bremen	23 Jun
53.85		Bidouane			2s1	WCh	Edmonton	6 Aug
53.88	Debbie-Ann	Parris	JAM	24.3.73	3s1	WCh	Edmonton	6 Aug
53.89A	Tatyana	Tereshchuk	UKR	11.10.69	1		Roodepoort	16 Mar
53.94		Nosova			1	Znam	Tula	9 Jun
53.96		Bidouane			1	VD	Bruxelles	24 Aug
53.96		Song Yinglan	CHN	14.9.75	1	NG	Guangzhou	22 Nov
53.98		Bidouane			1	WK	Zürich	17 Aug
54.01		Tereshchuk			1	GP	Saint-Denis	6 Jul
54.02		Bidouane			1	Athl	Lausanne	4 Jul
54.03		Nosova			1s2	WCh	Edmonton	6 Aug
54.10A	Surita	Febbraio	RSA	27.12.73	2		Roodepoort	16 Mar
54.12A		Tereshchuk			1		Pretoria	23 Mar
54.15	Tonja	Buford-Bailey	USA	13.12.70	2s2	WCh	Edmonton	6 Aug
54.21		Pernía			1	Herc	Monaco	20 Jul
54.27		Nosova			2	WCh	Edmonton	8 Aug
54.30		Tereshchuk			1	Bisl	Oslo	13 Jul
54.30	Sandra	Glover	USA	30.12.68	2	VD	Bruxelles	24 Aug
54.34		Parris			2	GP	Saint-Denis	6 Jul
54.35		Tereshchuk			2	Athl	Lausanne	4 Jul
54.35		Parris			3	VD	Bruxelles	24 Aug
54.38		Tereshchuk			2	WK	Zürich	17 Aug
54.43		Nosova			1h2	WCh	Edmonton	4 Aug
54.45		Nosova			3	Athl	Lausanne	4 Jul
54.45		Buford-Bailey			3	WK	Zürich	17 Aug
54.47	Deon	Hemmings	JAM	9.10.68	3s2	WCh	Edmonton	6 Aug
54.47		Tereshchuk			1	GWG	Brisbane	5 Sep
54.48		Febbraio			1		Stellenbsoch	23 Mar
54.49A		Febbraio			2		Pretoria	23 Mar
	(31/10)							
54.65	Ionela	Tîrlea	ROM	9.2.76	1	DNG	Stockholm	17 Jul
54.94	Natasha	Danvers	GBR	19.9.77	1	WUG	Beijing	31 Aug
55.03	Heike	Meissner	GER	29.1.70	1	NC	Stuttgart	30 Jun
55.04	Malgorzata	Pskit	POL	25.5.76	1	NC	Bydgoszcz	30 Jun
55.15		Huang Xiaoxiao	CHN-J	15.2.85	2	NG	Guangzhou	22 Nov
55.37	Natalya	Torshina	KAZ	4.10.68	2	Veniz	Haniá	4 Jun
55.44	Maren	Schott	GER	11.2.76	2	NC	Stuttgart	30 Jun
55.46	Brenda	Taylor	USA	9.2.79	2	GP II	Zagreb	2 Jul
55.49mx	Kim	Batten	USA	29.3.69	1mx		Tallahassee	12 May
	55.80				1		Torino	9 Jun
55.49	Sylvanie	Morandais	FRA	14.7.79	7	Herc	Monaco	20 Jul
	(20)							
55.58		Yao Yuehua	CHN	27.8.80	3	NG	Guangzhou	22 Nov
55.61	Anna	Olichwierczuk	POL	10.12.78	2	NC	Bydgoszcz	30 Jun
55.62	Melanie	Walker	JAM-J	1.1.83	1		Bridgetown	19 May
55.63	Yvonne	Harrison	PUR	2.12.75	4h1	WCh	Edmonton	5 Aug
55.68	Andrea	Blackett	BAR	24.1.76	8	Herc	Monaco	20 Jul
55.68	Karlene	Haughton	CAN	18.10.72	6s1	WCh	Edmonton	6 Aug
55.72	Sonia	Brito	AUS	10.6.79	3	WUG	Beijing	31 Aug
55.76	Lashinda	Demus	USA-J	10.3.83	2s1	NC	Eugene	22 Jun
55.83	Monika	Niederstätter	ITA	2.3.74	3h3	WCh	Edmonton	5 Aug
55.86	Stephanie	Kampf	GER	25.4.78	3	NC	Stuttgart	30 Jun
	(30)							
55.87	Michelle	Johnson	USA	12.4.74	1h1	NC	Eugene	21 Jun
55.92A	Peta Gaye	Gayle	JAM	19.1.79	2	CAC	C. de Guatemala	22 Jul
55.93	Jana	Pittman	AUS-J	9.11.82	1		Canberra	15 Dec
55.98	Omolade	Akinremi	NGR	13.9.74	1	NC	Lagos	21 Jul
55.99	Ulrike	Urbansky	GER	6.4.77	1		Mönchengladbach	27 May
56.02	Sheena	Johnson	USA-J	1.10.82	1	Pac-10	Berkeley	20 May

Mark	Name		Nat	Born	Pos	Meet	Venue	Date
56.05	Saidat	Onanuga	NGR	18.6.74	2	MSR	Walnut	22 Apr
56.07	Sinead	Dudgeon	GBR	9.7.76	2h4	WCh	Edmonton	5 Aug
56.09	Angel	Patterson	USA	6.8.79	1	Big 12	College Station	19 May
56.13		Li Yulian	CHN	17.2.79	4	NG	Guangzhou	22 Nov
	(40)							
56.14	TaNisha	Mills	USA	2.11.74	3	GP II	Palo Alto	9 Jun
56.17	Tatyana	Kurochkina	BLR	15.9.67	5	ECp-S	Bremen	23 Jun
56.22	Allison	Beckford	JAM	8.5.79	2	NCAA	Eugene	1 Jun
56.23	Michelle	Perry	USA	1.5.79	1		Los Angeles	5 May
56.24	Lana	Jekabsone	LAT	16.10.74	1	DrakeR	Des Moines	27 Apr
56.26	Natalya	Chulkova	RUS	5.12.77	3	Znam	Tula	9 Jun
56.27	Svetlana	Sagaydak	RUS	70	1		Kiev	25 May
56.28	Mame Tacko	Diouf	SEN	17.10.76	1	WCh	La Chaux-de-Fonds	19 Aug
56.34	Ann	Mercken	BEL	6.5.74	1	NC	Bruxelles	1 Jul
56.40	Catherine	Scott	JAM	24.8.73	3	GP II	Rio de Janeiro	6 May
	(50)							
56.40	Yekaterina	Bakhvalova	RUS	29.10.72	2	NC	Tula	14 Jul
56.49	Cendrino	Razaiarimalala	MAD	8.2.78	2	Fra Ch	Saint-Etienne	1 Jul
56.50	Catherine	Obilor	NGR-J	17.7.85	2	NC	Lagos	21 Jul
56.51	Aleksandra	Pieluzek	POL	4.4.79	2	EU23	Amsterdam	14 Jul
56.52	Perla	dos Santos	BRA-J	29.1.82	1	PAm-j	Santa Fe	20 Oct
56.55	Omotayo	Akinremi	NGR	13.9.74	2		Tempe	14 Apr
56.55	Yevgeniya	Isakova	RUS	78	3	NC	Tula	14 Jul
56.57	Anna	Knoroz	RUS	30.7.70	4	NC	Tula	14 Jul
56.58	Ryan	Tolbert	USA	16.6.76	4	GP	Palo Alto	9 Jun
56.61		Xiao Hongfan	CHN-J	6.1.83	1h3	NG	Guangzhou	21 Nov
	(60)							
56.64	Frances	Santin	USA	27.7.80	1		Fresno	5 May
56.70	Nathalie	Zamboni	SUI	23.12.73	4s2	WUG	Beijing	30 Aug
56.74	Tatyana	Debelaya	UKR	28.1.70	2	NC	Kiev	2 Jul
56.83	Makiko	Yoshida	JPN	16.7.76	1		Kitakami	15 Jul
56.85	Sandra	Farmer-Patrick	USA	18.8.62	3s2	NC	Eugene	22 Jun
56.85	Melinda	Sallins	USA	30.6.73	5	NC	Eugene	23 Jun
56.87	Marjorlein	de Jong	NED	12.6.81	1	NC	Tilburg	7 Jul
56.88	Carmo	Tavares	POR	27.4.74	1h4	WUG	Beijing	30 Aug
56.93A	Kerryn	van Zyl	RSA	5.10.74	3		Roodepoort	16 Mar
56.93	Meta	Macus	SLO	23.3.75	1	NC	Maribor	8 Jul
	(70)							
56.99	Tawa	Babatunde	CAN	19.12.79	3		Atlanta	19 May
57.01		Li Rui	CHN	22.11.79	2		Tianjin	19 May
57.02	Isabel	Rocha Silva	BRA	15.6.79	1	NC	Rio de Janeiro	22 Jul
57.03	Irena	Zauna	LAT	16.3.81	3	EU23	Amsterdam	14 Jul
57.05	Chava	Demart	USA	5.5.79	2	Big 12	College Station	19 May
57.08	Corinne	Tafflet	FRA	8.11.75	1		Nogent-sur-Marne	24 Jun
57.09	Wassanee	Winatho	THA	30.6.80	1	SEAG	Kuala Lumpur	14 Sep
57.16	Natasha	Neal	USA	22.7.80	3		Los Angeles	5 May
57.16		Chen Lin	CHN	22.8.81	3h1	NG	Guangzhou	21 Nov
57.17	Adri	Vlok	RSA	17.6.76	3	NC	Durban	3 Mar
	(80)							
57.18	Keri	Maddox	GBR	4.7.72	7	BrGP	London (CP)	22 Jul
57.18	Nadja	Petersen	SWE	14.7.78	1	Owens	Columbus	6 May
57.19	Raasin	McIntosh	USA-J	29.4.82	3	Big 12	College Station	19 May
57.19	Princesa	Oliveros	COL	10.8.75	4s1	WUG	Beijing	30 Aug
57.21	Vivian	Dorsile	FRA	1.6.67	2h2	NC	Saint-Etienne	30 Jun
57.24	Tanya	Jarrett	JAM	18.9.77	1h1	Tex R	Austin	5 Apr
57.24	Yudalis	Díaz	CUB	20.9.79	2		Alcalá de Henares	30 Jun
57.25	Natalee	Sterling	JAM	26.9.78	1		Atlanta	19 May
57.26A	Yamelis	Ortiz	PUR	26.2.78	3	CAC	C. de Guatemala	22 Jul
57.28	Silvia	Rieger	GER	14.11.70	6		Dortmund	9 Jun
	(90)							
57.31	Tacita	Bass	USA	28.10.79	1	SEC	Columbia, SC	13 May
57.32	Ester	Goossens	NED	21.2.72	2	NC	Tilburg	7 Jul
57.34	Ysanne	Williams	USA	25.9.80	1h3	NC	Eugene	21 Jun
57.34	Androula	Sialou	CYP	27.1.73	1		Larnaca	5 Sep
57.36	Lara	Rocco	ITA	20.12.75	2	NC	Catania	8 Jul
57.43	Nicole	Ireland	USA-J	23.4.82	2	SEC	Columbia, SC	13 May
57.44	Miriam	Hrdlicková	SVK	4.1.76	2	GP II	Bratislava	12 Jun
57.48	Tawana	Watkins	USA-J	27.3.84	1	NSch	Raleigh	16 Jun
57.48		He Linlin	CHN	24.1.80	1h1	NC	Chengdu	30 Jun
57.50	Randi	Smith	USA	14.5.81	2h1	Pac-10	Berkeley	19 May
	(100)							

Mark	Name		Nat	Born	Date
57.54	Erica	Mårtensson	SWE	24.6.79	26 Aug
57.55	Ieva	Zunda	LAT	20.7.78	6 Jul
57.55	Stephanie	Price	AUS	17.7.72	24 Nov
57.58	Eléni	Kaloyírou	GRE	26.9.72	17 Jun
57.59	Tia	Tabb	USA	17.3.80	7 Apr
57.60	Alena	Rücklová	CZE	7.10.81	23 Jun
57.61A	Vanessa	Becker	RSA	15.3.79	27 Jan
57.61	Yekaterina	Bikert	RUS	80	14 Jul
57.62	Marina	Shiyan	RUS	22.1.80	15 Jun
57.63	Cora	Olivero	ARG	28.8.78	28 Jul
57.64		Wang Yamei	CHN	30.9.78	30 Jun
57.66	Angela	Craft	USA	21.4.79	12 May
57.72	Meka	Thompson	USA	10.1.74	25 May
57.73	Tatyana	Sautkina	RUS	16.4.69	14 Jul
57.74	Emanuela	Baggiolini	ITA	10.6.72	8 Jul
57.75	P Uday	Laxmi	IND		24 Nov
57.76	Andria	King	USA	22.6.76	19 May
57.78	Karolina	Tlustochowska	POL	19.9.81	30 Jun
57.78	Zofia	Malachowska	POL-J	14.5.82	21 Jul
57.79	Michelle	Burgher	JAM	12.3.77	21 Apr
57.79	Ana Paula	Pereira	BRA	11.12.78	2 Jun
57.81	Maiteland	Marks	USA	19.9.76	17 Aug
57.82	Luciana	França	BRA	19.5.77	29 Apr
57.82	Anja	Höcke	GER	16.10.74	30 Jun
57.83	Mie	Suzuki	JPN	20.1.74	10 Jun
57.87		Li Shuju	CHN	20.7.81	22 Nov
57.88	Olivia	Abderrhamane	FRA	2.8.79	24 Jun
57.89	Tina	Kron	GER	3.4.81	30 Jun
57.89	Megan	Addy	USA	22.5.78	28 Jul
57.90	Le'Gretta	Smith	USA	13.1.74	26 Apr
57.90	Sachiko	Eguchi	JPN-J	4.8.83	10 Jun
57.91	Tiffany	Ross	USA-J	5.2.83	16 Jun
57.93	Schérazad	Rébihi	FRA	15.9.72	21 Jul
57.93	Patrícia	Lopes	POR-J	3.3.82	21 Jul
57.95	Krissy	Liphardt	CAN	13.4.80	11 May
57.95		Zhai Lin	CHN-J	15.9.83	1 Jul
57.96		Xun Penghua	CHN	15.9.80	21 Nov
58.02	Adrienne	McIvor	IRL	2.9.70	23 Jun
58.03	Hristína	Hantzí-Neag	GRE	26.12.76	17 Jun
58.03	Anja	Neupert	GER	10.10.78	30 Jun
58.03	Isabelle	Gervais	CAN	27.7.77	30 Aug
58.09	Svetlana	Starkova	RUS	5.12.68	14 Jul
58.11A	Dominique	Koster	RSA	3.1.77	27 Jan
58.14		Peng Yinghua	CHN	21.2.79	22 Apr
58.15	Isabelle	Dherbercourt	FRA	15.5.73	24 Jun
58.15	Tracey	Duncan	GBR	16.5.79	11 Aug
58.18	Alyssa	Aiken	USA-J	15.9.82	16 Jun
58.18	Eva	Paniagua	ESP	2.2.74	22 Jul
58.21		Huang Lili	CHN	14.6.81	1 Jul
58.21	Miriam	Alonso	ESP	6.6.70	22 Jul
58.25	Maite	Urcelay	ESP	8.9.72	13 Jun
58.30	Lucie	Sichertová	CZE	14.12.76	1 Jul
58.31	Candida	Coulson	USA	25.4.80	14 Apr
58.31	Lyudmila	Rabchenyuk	UKR-J	14.9.83	2 Jul
58.32	Ilmira	Buynova	RUS	76	13 Jul
58.37	Corinne	Pierre-Joseph	FRA	27.10.66	1 Jul
58.39	Lena	Melin	SWE	22.8.72	16 Aug
58.40	Oksana	Yelyasova	RUS-J	82	14 Jul
58.40		Jia Wanhong	CHN	15.3.81	21 Nov
58.41	Patricia	Hall	JAM-J	16.10.82	7 Apr
58.43	Yelena	Doronina	RUS	81	14 Jul
58.44	Verónica	Quijano	ESA-J	30.1.82	27 May
	(162)				

Hand timed

Mark	Name		Nat	Born	Date
58.4	Irina	Golubets	RUS-J	82	27 May

Low altitude bests

Mark	Name		Nat	Born	Pos	Meet	Venue	Date
54.01	Tatyana	Tereshchuk	UKR	11.10.69	1	GP	Saint-Denis	6 Jul
54.48	Surita	Febbraio	RSA	27.12.73	1		Stellenbosch	30 Mar
56.49	Peta Gaye	Gayle	JAM	19.1.79	3	NC	Kingston	22 Jun
57.12	Kerryn	van Zyl	RSA	5.10.74	2	NC	Durban	3 Mar
58.36	Vanessa	Becker	RSA	15.3.79	4	NC	Durban	3 Mar

JUNIORS

See main list for top 11 juniors. 11 performances by 6 women to 56.50. Additional mark and further juniors:

Name	Mark	Pos	Meet	Venue	Date					
Huang X	55.61	1h1	NG	Guangzhou	21 Nov					
	56.28	1		Tianjin	19 May					
Walker	56.50	4	NC	Kingston	22 Jun					
Johnson	56.23	2	PennR	Philadelphia	26 Apr	56.24	1	NC-j	Richmond	17 Jun

Mark	Name		Nat	Born	Pos	Meet	Venue	Date
57.78	Zofia	Malachowska	POL-J	14.5.82	1	EJ	Grosseto	21 Jul
57.90	Sachiko	Eguchi	JPN-J	4.8.83	3	NC	Tokyo	10 Jun
57.91	Tiffany	Ross	USA-J	5.2.83	2		Raleigh	16 Jun
57.93	Patrícia	Lopes	POR-J	3.3.82	2	EJ	Grosseto	21 Jul
57.95		Zhai Lin	CHN-J	15.9.83	1rB	NC	Chengdu	1 Jul
58.18	Alyssa	Aiken	USA-J	15.9.82	1h2	NC-j	Richmond	16 Jun
58.31	Lyudmila	Rabchenyuk	UKR-J	14.9.83	3	NC	Kiev	2 Jul
58.40	Oksana	Yelyasova	RUS-J	82	3rB	NC	Tula	14 Jul
58.41	Patricia	Hall	JAM-J	16.10.82	2		Kingston	7 Apr

HIGH JUMP

2.04 Venelina Veneva BUL 13.6.74 1 Kalamáta 2 Jun
1.85/2 1.91/1 1.94/1 1.97/3 1.99/1 2.01/2 2.04/1
2.00 1 Sofia 27 May ?
2.00 1 Athína 30 May 1.85/1 1.90/1 1.94/2 1.97/2 2.00/3
2.00 1 GL Saint-Denis 6 Jul 1.80, 1.85, 1.89, 1.93, 1.96/all 1 1.98/2 2.00/2 2.02/xxx
1.98i 1 Budapest 20 Jan 1.75, 1.81, 1.86/1 1.90/2 1.92/1 1.94/2 1.96/1 1.98/3 2.00/xxx
2.03 Inga Babakova UKR 27.6.67 1 Athl Lausanne 4 Jul
1.80/1 1.85/1 1.90/1 1.94/1 1.97/1 2.00/1 2.03/2 2.06/xxx
2.01 1 Wörrstadt 26 May 1.91/1 1.93/1 1.97/1 2.01/1 2.06/xxx
2.00i 2 WI Lisboa 9 Mar 1.80, 1.85, 1.90, 1.93, 1.96, 1.98/all 1 2.00/3 2.02/xxx
2.00 2 Poznan 8 Jun 1.80, 1.85, 1.88, 1.91, 1.94, 1.96, 1.98/1 2.00/2 2.02/xxx
2.00 1 Bisl Oslo 13 Jul 1.80, 1.85, 1.90, 1.93, 1.95, 1.97/all 1 2.00/2 2.04/xxx
2.00 2 WCh Edmonton 12 Aug 1.85/1 1.90/2 1.94/1 1.97/2 2.00/2 2.02/xxx
1.98i 1 Spala 9 Feb 1.80/1 1.85/2 1.88/1 1.91/2 1.94/3 1.96/3 1.98/1 2.00/xxx
2.01 Hestrie Cloete RSA 26.8.78 1 WK Zürich 17 Aug
1.80/1 1.85/1 1.88/1 1.91/1 1.94/1 1.97/1 1.99/2 2.01/1 2.03/xxx
2.00 1 WCh Edmonton 12 Aug 1.85/1 1.90/1 1.94/1 1.97/1 2.00/2 2.02/xxx
2.00 1 GWG Brisbane 6 Sep 1.85/1 1.89/1 1.93/1 1.97/1 2.00/1 2.05/xxx

Mark	Name		Nat	Born	Pos	Meet	Venue	Date	Series
1.99					1	BrGP	London (CP)	22 Jul	1.80/1 1.85/1 1.89/1 1.93/1 1.96/1 1.99/3 2.01/xxx
1.99					2	VD	Bruxelles	24 Aug	1.80, 1.85, 1.88, 1.91/1 1.94/2 1.97/1 1.99/2 2.01/xxx
1.98					1	GPF	Melbourne	9 Sep	1.80/1 1.85/1 1.90/1 1,94/1 1.96/1 1.98/3 2.01/xxx
2.00i	Kajsa	Bergqvist	SWE	12.10.76	1	WI	Lisboa	9 Mar	
									1.80/1 1.85/1 1.90/1 1.93/2 1.96/1 1.98/1 2,00/1 2.02/xxx
2.00					1		Poznan	8 Jun	1.80, 1.85, 1.88, 1.91, 1.94/1 1.96/2 1.98/1 2.00/1 2.02/xxx
1.99i					1	Euro	Stockholm	15 Feb	1.83/1 1.87/1 1.91/1 1.94/1 1.97/1 1.99/2 2.01/xxx
1.99					1	Herc	Monaco	20 Jul	1.80, 1.85, 1.89/1 1.92/2 1.95/1 1.97/1 1.99/2 2.02/xxx
1.98					1	GGala	Roma	29 Jun	1.80/1 1.85/1 1.90/1 1.93/2 1.96/3 1.98/1 2.02/xxx
1.98					1		Båstad	1 Jul	1.80/1 1.88/1 1.91/1 1.94/1 1.96/1 1.98/3 2.02/xxx
1.98					2=	GL	Saint-Denis	6 Jul	1.80/1 1.85/1 1.89/1 1.93/1 1.96/1 1.98/1 2.00/xxx
1.98					1		Malmö	20 Aug	1.85/1 1.90/1 1.93/1 1.96/1 1.98/1 2.02/xxx
2.00	Dóra	Györffy	HUN	23.2.78	1	NC	Nyíregyháza	26 Jul	
									1.79/11.82/1 1.86/1 1.90/1 1.93/1 1.98/1 2.00/2 2.02/x
1.99	Vita	Palamar	UKR	12.10.77	2	WK	Zürich	17 Au	
									1.80/1 1.85/1 1.88/1 1.91/1 1.94/1 1.97/1 1.99/2 2.01/xxx
1.99					1	VD	Bruxelles	24 Aug	1.80, 1.85, 1.88, 1.91/1 1.94/2 1.97/1 1.99/1 2.01/xxx
1.98					2=	GL	Saint-Denis	6 Jul	1.80/1 1.85/1 1.89/1 1.93/1 1.96/1 1.98/1 2.00/xxx
1.98	Amy	Acuff	USA	14.7.75	1	Pre	Eugene	27 May	
									1.80/1 1.85/1 1.89/1 1.92/1 1.95/1 1.98/2 2.01/xxx
1.98	Antonietta	Di Martino	ITA	1.6.78	1	NC	Catania	7 Jul	
									1.73/1 1.78/1 1.80/1 1.82/1 1.84/1 1.86/1 1.88/1 1.92/3 1.95/2 1.98/1 2.02/xxx
	(32/8)								
1.97i	Monica	Iagar	ROM	2.4.73	1		Liévin	25 Feb	
1.96i	Viktoriya	Seryogina	RUS	22.5.73	1		Wien	12 Feb	
	(10)								
1.96i	Yuliya	Lyakhova	RUS	8.7.77	1	NC	Moskva	18 Feb	
1.96	Olga	Kaliturina	RUS	9.3.76	1	Znam	Tula	9 Jun	
1.96	Yekaterina	Aleksandrova	RUS	3.6.77	1		Moskva	23 Jun	
1.96	Miki	Imai	JPN	30.5.75	2		Yokohama	15 Sep	
1.95	Susan	Jones	GBR	8.6.78	1	ECp-S	Bremen	24 Jun	
1.95	Blanka	Vlasic	CRO-J	8.11.83	1	NC	Zagreb	8 Jul	
1.95	Yelena	Yelesina	RUS	4.4.70	2	NC	Tula	15 Jul	
1.95	Yelena	Gulyayeva	RUS	14.8.67	3	NC	Tula	15 Jul	
1.95	Tatyana	Babashkina	RUS	23.11.68	4	NC	Tula	15 Jul	
1.94i	Yelena	Sivushenko	RUS-J	28.2.82	1		Lipetsk	9 Feb	
	(20)								
1.94i	Elena	Herzenberg	GER	24.6.79	1		Siegen	9 Feb	
1.94i	Marta	Mendía	ESP	18.5.75	1	NC	Valencia	25 Feb	
1.94i	Ruth	Beitia	ESP	1.4.79	2	NC	Valencia	25 Feb	
1.94	Viktoria	Styopina	UKR	21.2.76	3		Athína	30 May	
1.94	Irina	Mikhalchenko	UKR	20.1.72	2		Kalamáta	2 Jun	
1.94	Nicole	Forrester	CAN	17.11.76	2	WUG	Beijing	31 Aug	
1.93i	Alina	Astafei	GER	7.6.69	2	NC	Dortmund	24 Feb	
1.93	Oana	Pantelimon	ROM	27.9.72	1	Rom IC	Bucuresti	9 Jun	
1.93	Liga	Klavina	LAT	27.1.80	1H	EU23	Amsterdam	14 Jul	
1.92i	Anna	Chicherova	RUS-J	22.7.82	1		Moskva	27 Jan	
	(30)								
1.92i	Karol	Damon	USA	20.12.69	1		Ames	10 Feb	
1.92	Mária	Melová	SVK	21.10.75	1		Rehlingen	4 Jun	
1.92	Tatyana	Gulyevich	BLR	10.2.71	1	NC	Brest	8 Jun	
1.92	Inna	Gliznutza	MDA	18.4.73	1	ECp-2A	Riga	23 Jun	
1.92	Nele	Zilinskiené	LTU	29.12.69	1	NC	Kaunas	4 Jul	
1.92	Kathryn	Holinski	GER-J	19.7.82	1		Braunschweig	7 Jul	
1.92	Irina	Zhukovskaya	RUS	78	5	NC	Tula	15 Jul	
1.92	Ramona	Pop	ROM-J	5.4.82	1	EJ	Grosseto	22 Jul	
1.92	Candeger	Kilincer	TUR	16.7.80	1		Istanbul	29 Jul	
1.91i	Marina	Kuptsova	RUS	22.12.81	4		Athína	24 Jan	
	(40)								
1.91i	Solange	Witteveen ¶	ARG	6.2.76	4	Euro	Birmingham	18 Feb	
1.91i	Svetlana	Zalevskaya	KAZ	14.6.73	6=		Liévin	25 Feb	
1.91	Tatyana	Nikolayeva-Shchurenko	UKR	26.2.76	4		Kalamáta	2 Jun	
1.91	Anna	Ksok	POL-J	29.9.83	3		Poznan	8 Jun	
1.91	Yoko	Ota	JPN	14.1.75	5		Båstad	1 Jul	
1.91	Wanita	May	CAN	30.1.75	1	Franc	Ottawa	23 Jul	
1.91	Nevena	Lendjel	CRO	18.7.79	3	WUG	Beijing	31 Aug	
1.90A	Marizca	Gertenbach	RSA-J	20.10.82	2		Rustenberg	22 Jan	
1.90i	Anna	Visigalli	ITA	24.2.81	1		Ancona	3 Feb	
1.90	Gwen	Wentland	USA	29.4.72	1		Tempe	24 Mar	
	(50)								

WOMEN 2001

Mark	Name		Nat	Born	Pos	Meet	Venue	Date
1.90	Eleonora	Milusheva	BUL	8.4.73	2		Sofia	27 May
1.90	Tatyana	Efimenko	KGZ	2.1.81	1		Bishkek	17 Jun
1.90	Michelle	Dunkley	GBR	26.1.78	1	Scot	Glasgow (S)	24 Jun
1.90		Jing Xuezhu	CHN	20.4.75	1	NG	Guangzhou	22 Nov
1.90	Petrina	Price	AUS-J	26.4.84	1	NSch	Melbourne	8 Dec
1.89i	Tia	Hellebaut	BEL	16.2.78	5	Euro	Gent	23 Feb
1.89i	Olga	Bolshova	MDA	16.6.68	3	ESP Ch	Valencia	25 Feb
1.89	Eunice	Barber	FRA	17.11.74	1H	MSR	Azusa	19 Apr
1.89	Erin	Aldrich	USA	27.12.77	4	Pre	Eugene	27 May
1.89	María	Hotokourídou	GRE	22.5.77	2	Veniz	Haniá	4 Jun
	(60)							
1.89	Nadezhda	Pekhlivanova	BUL	12.6.79	2	NC	Sofia	9 Jun
1.89	Barbora	Laláková	CZE	2.5.81	3		Tettnang	23 Jun
1.88i	Tatyana	Grigoryeva	RUS	13.5.81	1		Moskva	17 Jan
1.88i	Stefania	Cadamuro	ITA	23.2.79	2		Ancona	3 Feb
1.88i	Sabrina	De Leeuw	BEL	19.8.74	1	FRA Ch	Liévin	17 Feb
1.88	Agni	Charalambous	CYP	2.9.75	1		Halkída	5 May
1.88	Stacy Ann	Grant	USA	18.8.77	2	MSR	Walnut	22 Apr
1.88	Tayibba	Haneef	USA	23.3.79	1		Long Beach	18 May
1.88	Sónia	Carvalho	POR	10.5.77	1		Vila Real St. António	3 Jun
1.88	Olga	Shedova	BLR	6.4.81	2	NC	Brest	8 Jun
	(70)							
1.88	Viktoriya	Slivka	RUS	28.9.80	3	Znam	Tula	9 Jun
1.88	Gaëlle	Niaré	FRA-J	12.3.82	4=	EJ	Grosseto	22 Jul
1.88	Luciane	Dambacher	BRA	10.5.76	1	NC	Rio de Janeiro	21 Jul
1.88	Lea	Cimperman	SLO	25.7.78	1		Trieste	25 Jul
1.88	Yelena	Prokhorova	RUS	16.4.78	1H	WCh	Edmonton	4 Aug
1.88	Juana	Arrendel	DOM	16.6.78	Q	WCh	Edmonton	10 Aug
1.88A	Nicolize	Steyn	RSA	28.5.81	1		Pretoria	3 Nov
1.87i	Sophie	Sagonas	GER	18.9.81	4		Wuppertal	2 Feb
1.87i	Katja	Vainikainen	FIN	30.7.77	1		Umeå	24 Feb
1.87	Thaís	de Andrade	BRA	15.12.69	1		São Caetano do Sul	22 Apr
	(80)							
1.87	Amewu	Mensah	GER	21.3.77	1		Sinn	2 Jun
1.87	Diana	Láznicková	SVK	14.8.74	1	GP II	Bratislava	12 Jun
1.87	Svetlana	Stavskaya	KAZ	10.5.77	2		Almaty	23 Jun
1.87	Hanna	Mikkonen	FIN	15.1.81	1	NC	Turku	7 Jul
1.87	Aileen	Wilson	GBR-J	30.3.84	1	WY	Debrecen	15 Jul
1.87		Lu Jieming	CHN-J	25.1.83	2	NG	Guangzhou	22 Nov
1.87i	Gina	Curtis	USA	2.1.79	1		Ames	7 Dec
1.86i	Birgit	Kähler	GER	14.8.70	1		Düsseldorf	14 Jan
1.86i	Tatyana	Shevchik	BLR	11.6.69	1		Gomel	20 Jan
1.86i	Raffaella	Lamera	ITA-J	13.4.83	1		Caravaggio	21 Jan
	(90)							
1.86i	Daniele	Galeotti	ITA	22.3.77	1		Firenze	24 Jan
1.86i	Angie	Spangler	USA	4.9.68	4	Mill	New York	2 Feb
1.86i	Marina	Korzhova	KAZ-J	13.9.82	11	RUS Ch	Moskva	18 Feb
1.86i	Mary	Varga	USA	1.5.80	1		Mt Pleasant	24 Feb
1.86	Maiko	Iwakiri	JPN	6.5.78	1		Toyota	26 May
1.86	Marisa	Cadienhead	JAM	7.4.76	1		Miami	10 Jun
1.86	Bernadett	Bódi	HUN	14.4.80	1		Budapest	13 Jun
1.86	Sarah	Bettoso	ITA	25.5.80	2	NC	Catania	7 Jul
1.86	Tatyana	Gordeyeva	RUS	3.6.73	1H	NC	Tula	13 Jul
1.86	Alina	Dinu	ROM-J	9.2.82	9	EJ	Grosseto	22 Jul
	(100)							
1.86	Melanie	Skotnik	GER-J	8.11.82	10	EJ	Grosseto	22 Jul
1.86	Katja	Schötz	GER	22.7.81	4	NC-23	Schweinfurt	29 Jul
1.86	Heike	Siener	GER	19.11.80	5	NC-23	Schweinfurt	29 Jul

Mark	Name		Nat	Born	Date
1.85i	Marianne	Mattas	FIN	20.8.79	28 Jan
1.85i	Olga	Fetisova	RUS-J	82	14 Feb
1.85Ai	Darnesha	Griffith	USA	11.6.80	17 Feb
1.85Ai	Jeana	Bingham	USA	22.6.78	17 Feb
1.85i	Andrea	Szoboszlai	ROM	2.6.78	25 Feb
1.85i	Kart	Siilats	EST	7.9.80	9 Mar
1.85	Jane	Jamieson	AUS	23.6.75	11 Mar
1.85	Kerstin	Schlawitz	GER	30.8.70	19 Apr
1.85A	Dianie	Wondergem	RSA-J	2.3.82	21 Apr
1.85	Sonja	Kesselschläger	GER	20.1.78	26 May
1.85	Julia	Farmaka	CYP	20.4.78	2 Jun
1.85	Corinne	Müller	SUI	20.11.75	4 Jun
1.85	Renata	Medgyesová	SVK-J	28.1.83	12 Jun
1.85	Oksana	Zubovskaya	UKR	15.7.81	20 Jun
1.85	Adriana	Maximiuc	ROM	1.10.73	15 Jul
1.85	Deirdre	Ryan	IRL-J	1.6.82	29 Jul
1.85	Carri	Long	USA	23.4.77	29 Aug
1.84i	Anne Gerd	Eieland	NOR-J	28.12.82	4 Feb
1.84i		Zhao Ning	CHN	26.7.81	17 Feb
1.84	Whitney	Evans	CAN	10.4.80	14 Apr
1.84		Li Shan	CHN-J	4.3.83	21 Apr
1.84		Li Rong	CHN-J	14.9.83	28 Apr
1.84	Edith	Montgomery	USA		11 May
1.84		Wang Wei	CHN	19.10.68	12 May
1.84		Xu Kui	CHN	20.1.78	12 May
1.84	Tamika	Toppin	USA	5.6.79	2 Jun
1.84	Miriam	Bielert	GER	17.6.75	3 Jun
1.84	Ágota	Stáhl	HUN	17.12.78	9 Jun

Mark	Name		Nat	Born	Pos	Meet	Venue	Date
1.84	Christelle	Préau	FRA	3.11.81				15 Jun
1.84	Chaunte	Howard	USA-J	12.1.84				15 Jun
1.84	Sheena	Gordon	USA-J	26.9.83				15 Jun
1.84	Lavern	Spencer	LCA-J	23.6.84				27 Jun
1.84	Olga	Kychanova	RUS	14.7.75				28 Jun
1.84	Tatyana	Ivanova	RUS	22.1.76				28 Jun
1.84		Liang Xiuli	CHN	29.9.77				1 Jul
1.84		Li Shizhang	CHN	4.11.76				1 Jul
1.84	Jolanta	Kviatkovskaja	LTU-J	6.2.82				4 Jul
1.84	Julia	Bennett	GBR	26.3.70				4 Aug
1.84	Angelica	Johansson	SWE-J	1.10.83				26 Aug
	(142)							

Best outdoor marks for athletes with best indoors

Mark	Name	Pos	Meet	Venue	Date
2.00	Bergqvist	1		Poznan	8 Jun
1.92	Lyakhova	2		Tettnang	23 Jun
1.92	Chicherova	1		Kazan	27 Jun
1.92	Iagar	9	Herc	Monaco	20 Jul
1.91	Witteveen ¶	1		Santiago de Chile	13 May
1.91	Beitia	1		Prat de Llobregat	30 Jun
1.91	Astafei	1		Cottbus	18 Jul
1.90	Zalevskaya	2	EAsG	Osaka	24 May
1.90	Damon	3	GP	Palo Alto	9 Jun
1.85	Bingham				24 Mar
1.85	Korzhova				2 Jun
1.85	Mattas				24 Jun
1.85	Vainikainen				30 Jun
1.84	Zhao Ning				21 Apr
1.84	Eieland				12 May
1.90	Kuptsova	1	NC-23	Cheboksary	14 Jun
1.90	Seryogina	2		Bryansk	3 Jul
1.88	Mendía	1		Pamplona	16 Jun
1.88	Sivushenko	2	NC-j	Kazan	27 Jun
1.88	Herzenberg	1	NC-23	Schweinfurt	29 Jul
1.87	Hellebaut	1H	ECp-2	Kaunas	1 Jul
1.87	Visigalli	1		Mezzano di Primiero	19 Aug
1.86	Galeotti	1		Rieti	19 May
1.86	Grigoryeva	3	NC-23	Cheboksary	14 Jun
1.86	De Leeuw	2		Brasschaat	15 Aug
1.84	Lamera				30 Jun
1.84	Kähler				23 Sep

Drugs disqualification

Mark	Name		Nat	Born	Pos	Meet	Venue	Date
1.97	Solange	Witteveen ¶	ARG	6.2.76	1	SACh	Manaus	19 May

JUNIORS

See main list for top 15 juniors. 14 performances by 5 women to 1.92. Additional mark and further juniors:

Name	Mark	Pos	Meet	Venue	Date	Mark	Pos	Meet	Venue	Date
Vlasic	1.94	6	WCh	Edmonton	12 Aug	1.93	5	GWG	Brisbane	6 Sep
	1.93	1		Zagreb	2 Jul	1.92	1		Celje	15 Jun
Sivushenko	1.93i	3		Athína	24 Jan	1,92i	2		Moskva	27 Jan
	1.92i	1		Moskva	20 Jan	1.92i	3	NC	Moskva	18 Feb

Mark	Name		Nat	Born	Pos	Meet	Venue	Date
1.85i	Olga	Fetisova	RUS	82	3		Moskva	14 Feb
1.85A	Dianie	Wondergem	RSA	2.3.82	2	NC-23	Pretoria	21 Apr
1.85	Renata	Medgyesová	SVK	28.1.83	2	GP II	Bratislava	12 Jun
1.85	Deirdre	Ryan	IRL	1.6.82	1		Derby	29 Jul
1.84i	by eight juniors							
Best out:	1.85	Korzhova	KAZ	13.9.82	1		Almaty	2 Jun

POLE VAULT

Mark	Name		Nat	Born	Pos	Meet	Venue	Date
4.81	Stacy	Dragila	USA	25.3.71	1	GP	Palo Alto	9 Jun
			4.21/1	4.31/1 4.41/1 4.51/2 4.61/1 4.71/1 4.81/2 4.88/xxx				
	4.75	1 WCh	Edmonton	6 Aug	4.35, 4.45, 4.55, 4.60/1 4.65/2 4.70/1 4.75/1 4.82/xxx			
	4.72	1 GGala	Roma	29 Jun	4.20/1 4.32/1 4.42/1 4.52/1 4.62/1 4.72/1 4.82/xxx			
	4.72	1	Rethimnó	1 Jul	4.27/1 4.37/1 4.47/1 4.57/1 4.62/1 4.72/1 4.82/xxx			
	4.72	1 DNG	Stockholm	17 Jul	4.22/1 4.32/1 4.42/1 4.52/1 4.62/1 4.72/3 4.82/xxx			
	4.72	1 BrGP	London (CP)	22 Jul	4.25/1 4.35/1 4.45/1 4.55/1 4.65/2 4.72/1 4.82/xxx			
	4.70Ai	1	Pocatello	17 Feb	4.21/1 4.36/1 4.46/1 4.56/2 4.66/1 4.70/3 4.80/xxx			
	4.70A	1	Pocatello	27 Apr	4.11/1 4.27/1 4.42/1 4.60/1 4.65/1 4.70/1 4.80/xxx			
	4.67	1 Nik	Nice	9 Jul	4.22, 4.32, 4.42, 4.47, 4.52, 4.57, 4.62, 4.67/all 1 4.77/xxx			
	4.65Ai	1	Pocatello	9 Feb	3.99/1 4.14/3 4.39/1 4.50/1 4.57/1 4.65/2 4.75/xxx			
	4.63i	1	New York	2 Feb	4.10/1 4.20/1 4.30/1 4.40/3 4.50/1 4.63/2			
	4.62	1 NC	Eugene	23 Jun	4.20/1 4.30/1 4.40/1 4.50/1 4.62/1 4.75/xxx			
	4.61	1 Pre	Eugene	27 May	4.11/2 4.21/2 4.31/2 4.41/1 4.51/2 4.61/1 4.71/xxx			
	4.57Ai	1	Pocatello	13 Jan	3.96/1 4.11/1 4.27/1 4.37/2 4.47/3 4.57/1 4.65/xxx			
4.75	Svetlana	Feofanova	RUS	16.7.80	2	WCh	Edmonton	6 Aug
			4.35/14.45/1	4.55/1 4.60/1 4.65/3 4.70/1 4.75/1 4.82/xxx				
	4.70	1 NC	Tula	14 Jul	4.40 4.50 4.65 4.70			
	4.65i	1	Pireás	21 Feb	4.35/2 4.50/1 4.65/3 4.71/xxx			
	4.65	2 BrGP	London (CP)	22 Jul	4.35/1 4.45/1 4.55/1 4.65/3 4.72/xxx			
	4.64i	1	Dortmund	11 Feb	4.30/1 4.45/1 4.60/2 4.64/3			
	4.62	2 Nik	Nice	9 Jul	4.32/3 4.42/1 4.52/2 4.62/1 4.67/xxx			
	4.62	2 DNG	Stockholm	17 Jul	4.32/1 4.42/2 4.52/1 4.62/1 4.72/xxx			
	4.62	1	Thessaloníki	22 Aug	4.30/1 4.42/1 4.52/2 4.57/1 4.62/3 4.76/xxx			
	4.61i	1	Madrid	14 Mar	4.36/1 4.46/3 4.56/1 4.61/1 4.71/xxx			
	4.60	1 ECp	Bremen	23 Jun	4.34/2 4.52/2 4.60/1			
	4.58i	1	Karlsruhe	27 Jan	4.28/1 4.38/1 4.48/1 4.58/1			
	4.57	1 GPI	Athína	11 Jun	4.37/1 4.47/2 4.57/1 4.70/xxx			
4.61	Mary	Sauer	USA	31.10.75	1		Irvine	16 Jun
				4.21/1 4.31/1 4.41/2 4.51/1 4.61/2 4.66/xxx				
4.61	Monika	Pyrek	POL	11.8.80	1	NC	Bydgoszcz	1 Jul
				4.00/1 4.20/1 4.40/3 4.55/2 4.61/2				
	4.57	3 Nik	Nice	9 Jul	4.22/1 4.32/1 4.42/1 4.47/2 4.52/1 4.57/1 4.62/xxx			
	4.57	3 DNG	Stockholm	17 Jul	4.22/1 4.42/1 4.52/2 4.57/2 4.62/xxx			

Mark	Name		Nat	Born	Pos	Meet	Venue	Date
4.60	Kellie	Suttle	USA	9.5.73	1	Mod R	Modesto	12 May
				4.10/2 4.25/1 4.40/2 4.60/2 4.71/xxx				
4.58	1 Drake Des Moines		28 Apr	3.99/2 4.10/1 4.30/1 4.45/1 4.58/2 4.64/xxx				
	(32/5)							
4.56i	Pavla	Hamácková	CZE	20.5.78	1	WI	Lisboa	9 Mar
4.56	Tatiana	Grigorieva	AUS	8.10.75	1		Yokohama	15 Sep
4.55i	Yelena	Belyakova	RUS	7.4.76	2		Pireás	21 Feb
4.55	Annika	Becker	GER	12.11.81	1	NC	Stuttgart	1 Jul
4.52	Anzhela	Balakhonova	UKR	18.12.72	2	GP	Athína	11 Jun
	(10)							
4.52		Gao Shuying	CHN	28.10.79	1	WUG	Beijing	29 Aug
4.51i	Thórey Edda	Elísdottír	ISL	30.6.77	1	NCAA	Fayetteville	10 Mar
4.51	Nicole	Humbert	GER	5.2.72	1		Salamanca	13 Jul
4.50	Alicia	Warlick	USA	11.10.77	1		Houston	24 Mar
4.50	Carolin	Hingst	GER	18.9.80	2	NC	Stuttgart	1 Jul
4.47i	Yelena	Isinbayeva	RUS-J	3.6.82	1		Budapest	10 Feb
4.47	Melissa	Mueller	USA	16.11.72	1	GP II	Zagreb	2 Jul
4.46	Yvonne	Buschbaum	GER	14.7.80	3	ISTAF	Berlin	31 Aug
4.44i	Doris	Auer	AUT	10.5.71	2		Glasgow	18 Mar
4.43	Tania	Koleva	BUL	8.3.72	1		Athína	30 May
	(20)							
4.42	Tracy	O'Hara	USA	20.7.80	1		Irvine	29 Apr
4.42	Martina	Strutz	GER	4.11.81	1		Schwerin	24 Jun
4.41	Krisztina	Molnár	HUN	8.4.76	1		Budapest	13 Jun
4.40	Janine	Whitlock	GBR	11.8.73	1	NC	Birmingham	14 Jul
4.37	Becky	Holliday	USA	12.3.80	1		Spokane	24 May
4.36	Yeoryía	Tsiliggíri	GRE	21.6.72	1	NC	Athína	17 Jun
4.35i	Christine	Adams	GER	28.2.74	3	NC	Dortmund	25 Feb
4.35i	Marie	Poissonnier	FRA	4.5.79	1		Cercy-la-Tour	25 Mar
4.35	Jenny	Dryburgh	NZL	30.8.78	1	Aus Ch	Brisbane	25 Mar
4.35	Monique	de Wilt	NED	21.3.76	1		Kassel	13 Jun
	(30)							
4.35	Sabine	Schulte	GER	29.1.76	2	WUG	Beijing	29 Aug
4.33i	Vanessa	Boslak	FRA-J	11.6.82	5		Liévin	25 Feb
4.31	María Mar	Sánchez	ESP	25.12.79	1	NC	Valencia	22 Jul
4.30i	Nastja	Ryshich	GER	19.9.77	1		Ludwigshafen	20 Jan
4.30	Anastasiya	Ivanova	RUS	3.5.79	2		Kiev	25 May
4.30	Jill	Starkey	USA	7.3.71	1		Atascadero	27 May
4.30	Elmarie	Gerryts	RSA	25.8.72	2		Bydgoszcz	15 Jun
4.30	Katerina	Badurová	CZE-J	18.12.82	1		Kladno	16 Jun
4.30	Alejandra	García	ARG	13.6.73	1		Buenos Aires	3 Nov
4.30	Kym	Howe	AUS	12.6.80	1		Perth	29 Dec
	(40)							
4.27	Shannon	Pierson	USA	30.9.74	1		Berkeley	3 Jun
4.25i	Francesca	Dolcini	ITA	28.12.74	1	NC	Torino	25 Feb
4.25	Agnès	Livebardon	FRA	31.5.80	1		Aix-les-Bains	23 Jun
4.25	Stephanie	McCann	CAN	22.4.77	Q	WCh	Edmonton	4 Aug
4.25	Marie Bagger	Rasmussen	DEN	1.11.72	Q	WCh	Edmonton	4 Aug
4.25	Émilie	Bécot	FRA	20.10.80	1	vGBR	Ashford	11 Aug
4.22	Vala	Flosadóttir	ISL	16.2.78	9	DNG	Stockholm	17 Jul
4.22	Kirsten	Belin	SWE	2.5.81	1	NC	Växjö	25 Aug
4.21	Amy	Linnen	USA-J	15.7.82	1	NC-j	Richmond	17 Jun
4.21	Dana	Cervantes	ESP	18.8.78	2		Salamanca	13 Jul
	(50)							
4.21	Hanna-Mia	Persson	SWE	11.2.78	1		Falkenberg	18 Jul
4.20i	Andrea	Müller	GER	29.6.74	4		Zweibrücken	26 Jan
4.20i	Floé	Kühnert	GER-J	6.3.84	5		Chemnitz	9 Feb
4.20i	Natalya	Kusch	UKR-J	5.3.83	1	NC	Brovary	10 Feb
4.20i	Andrea	Dutoit (Neary)	USA	28.8.78	2=	NCAA	Fayetteville	10 Mar
4.20i	Rhian	Clarke	GBR	19.4.77	4	NCAA	Fayetteville	10 Mar
4.20	Alla	Checheleva	RUS	1.7.81	1		Krasnodar	22 May
4.20	Arianna	Farfaletti-Casali	ITA	22.6.76	2	ECCp	Madrid	27 May
4.20	Jillian	Schwartz	USA	19.9.79	2	NCAA	Eugene	1 Jun
4.20	Anastasiya	Kiryanova	RUS-J	26.7.82	1	NC- j	Kazan	28 Jun
	(60)							
4.20	Aurore	Pignot	FRA	24.12.79	2	NC	Saint-Etienne	30 Jun
4.20	Tatyana	Polnova	RUS	4.12.73	1		Krasnodar	30 Jun
4.20	Zsuzsanna	Szabó	HUN	6.5.73	1		Veszprém	7 Jul
4.20	Thália	Iakovídou	GRE	10.9.72	2	BalkC	Tríkala	7 Jul
4.20	Monika	Götz	GER	15.6.81	2=		Cottbus	18 Jul
4.20	Céline	Poissonnier	FRA	4.5.79	2		Obernai	29 Jul

Mark	Name		Nat	Born	Pos	Meet	Venue	Date
4.20	Rachel	Dacy	AUS	10.11.76	1		Melbourne	4 Aug
4.20	Sárka	Mládková	CZE	30.8.76	3	WUG	Beijing	29 Aug
4.18	Lesa	Kubishta	USA	19.4.78	3		Irvine	6 May
4.17	Stephanie	Maugham	USA	29.9.77	2		Atascadero	29 Apr
	(70)							
4.16	Shayla	Balentine	USA-J	7.8.82	1		Sacramento	2 Jun
4.15Ai	Jacqueline	Honey	CAN	25.6.75	1		Flagstaf	3 Feb
4.15	Julie	Vigourt	FRA	19.10.79	2		Miramas	13 Jun
4.15	Maria Carla	Bresciani	ITA	16.7.73	1	NC	Catania	8 Jul
4.15	Fanni	Juhász	HUN	31.3.81	2	NC	Nyíregyháza	26 Jul
4.13i	April	Steiner	USA	22.4.80	2	Tyson	Fayetteville	9 Feb
4.12i	Yuliya	Lukinskaya	RUS	3.5.76	2		Tsaotun	3 Feb
4.12i	Masumi	Ono	JPN	5.12.75	1		Toyota	20 Mar
4.12	Bridgid	Isworth	AUS	15.10.81	1		Los Angeles	30 Dec
4.11		Sun Yufei	CHN-J	18.4.84	1	Asi-J	B.S. Begawan	21 Jul
	(80)							
4.11		Cai Weiyan	CHN	25.10.73	2	NG	Guangzhou	23 Nov
4.10i	Tünde	Vaszi	HUN	18.4.72	1		Budapest	18 Jan
4.10i	Sereen	Balti	TUN-J	31.10.83	1		Fronton	21 Jan
4.10i	Misty	Ballard	USA	16.11.78	1		Houston	17 Feb
4.10i		Zhang Na	CHN	27.9.80	2	v JPN	Yokohama	21 Feb
4.10i	Katalin	Donáth	HUN	12.11.79	2	NC	Budapest	25 Feb
4.10i	Anja	Wilhelm	GER	5.5.80	8	NC	Dortmund	25 Feb
4.10i	Hanna	Palamaa	FIN	8.9.77	6	NCAA	Fayetteville	10 Mar
4.10i	Sandrine	Toulouse	FRA	14.9.72	3		Cercy-la-Tour	25 Mar
4.10	Michelle	Legatt	USA-J	13.4.82	5	Tex R	Austin	6 Apr
	(90)							
4.10	Niki	Reed	USA	1.4.80	1		Eugene	14 Apr
4.10	Takayo	Kondo	JPN	17.11.75	5	GP	Osaka	12 May
4.10	Erica	Hoernig	USA	19.10.78	6=	Mod R	Modesto	12 May
4.10	Dana	Ellis	CAN	7.12.78	1		Toronto	26 May
4.10	Michaela	Boulová	CZE	2.8.81	3		Praha	2 Jun
4.10	Lyudmila	Vaylenko (Prikhodko)	UKR	18.3.74	3	NC	Kiev	1 Jul
4.10	Anna	Wielgus	POL	27.10.81	2	NC	Bydgoszcz	1 Jul
4.10	Anastasiya	Kuznetsova	RUS	15.3.80	4	NC	Tula	14 Jul
4.10	Teija	Saari	FIN	21.3.78	1		Lappeenranta	15 Jul
4.08	Dímitra	Emmanouíl	GRE-J	13.5.84	4		Athína	30 May
	(100)							

Mark	Name		Nat	Born	Date
4.07i	Naroa	Agirre	ESP	15.5.79	23 Dec
4.06Ai	Paula	Serrano	USA	28.12.76	17 Feb
4.05i	Paula	Fernández	ESP	8.6.78	27 Jan
4.05i	Samantha	Shepherd	USA-J	11.11.83	10 Mar
4.05	Leslie	Dunlap	USA-J	15.2.82	6 Apr
4.05	Heather	Sickler	USA	8.2.80	5 May
4.05	Anna	Tamburini	ITA	6.1.73	30 May
4.05	Katiuska	Pérez	CUB	21.12.75	31 May
4.05	Teja	Melink	SLO	23.3.80	10 Jun
4.05	Evridíki	Prezerákou	GRE	8.3.75	17 Jun
4.05	Linda	Persson	SWE	22.9.81	12 Jul
4.05	Petra	Pechstein	SUI	26.7.71	18 Aug
4.05		Chang Ko-Hsin	TPE	20.6.80	21 Oct
4.05i	Andrea	Wildrick	USA	23.12.79	10 Dec
4.04	Jeannette	Martus	USA	25.1.79	20 May
4.04	Kathleen	Donoghue	USA	29.8.81	20 May
4.03	Maria	Lopez	USA	18.8.79	5 May
4.03	Emily	Tharpe	USA-J	2.9.82	9 May
4.02i	Amandine	Homo	FRA	24.12.80	10 Feb
4.02	Aimee	Crabtree	USA	22.1.78	29 Apr
4.02	Erica	Boren	USA	15.5.80	10 May
4.02A	Vanessa	Ríos	ESP	5.1.80	25 Jul
4.02	Tamara	Diles	USA-J	5.11.82	8 Dec
4.01i	Stacie	Manuel	USA-J	6.12.83	10 Mar
4.01	Ebbie	Metzinger	USA	16.6.79	21 Apr
4.01	Lacy	Janson	USA-J	20.2.83	19 May
4.01	Iréna	Dufour	BEL	1.6.78	15 Aug
4.01		Peng Xiaoming	CHN	15.5.75	23 Nov
4.00i	Mariya	Smirnova	RUS-J	83	4 Jan
4.00	Melina	Hamilton	NZL	15.6.76	6 Jan
4.00i	Vyara	Chavdarova	BUL	19.11.80	3 Feb
4.00i	Cecile	Dupays	FRA	20.2.81	4 Feb
4.00	Rosanna	Ditton	AUS	7.6.79	11 Feb
4.00i	Akane	Eguchi	JPN	20.6.76	12 Feb
4.00i	Hristína	Tsirba	GRE	26.8.77	18 Feb
4.00i	Laura	Hawkins	USA	15.2.79	25 Feb
4.00	Irie	Hill	GBR	16.1.69	10 Mar
4.00i	Suzanne	Krings	USA	10.3.80	10 Mar
4.00i	Shannon	Agee	USA	7.3.79	10 Mar
4.00	Connie	Jerz	USA-J	26.4.82	14 Apr
4.00A	Lucy	Webber	GBR	5.2.72	14 Apr
4.00		Du Na	CHN	7.1.79	21 Apr
4.00	Daniela	Bártová	CZE	6.5.74	18 May
4.00	Annalisa	Meacci	ITA	8.3.76	20 May
4.00	Natalya	Belinskaya	RUS-J	83	22 May
4.00	Ardin	Harrison	CAN	14.3.74	25 May
4.00	Yelena	Reznik	KAZ	20.8.78	3 Jun
4.00	Lucie	Palasová	CZE	26.3.81	10 Jun
4.00	Desy	Margawati	INA	19.12.80	20 Jun
4.00	Alina	Alló	ARG-J	30.5.82	23 Jun
4.00	Francesca	Zanini	ITA-J	4.4.82	29 Jun
4.00	Silke	Spiegelburg	GER-J	17.3.86	14 Jul
4.00	Aleksandra	Kiryashova	RUS-J	21.8.85	14 Jul
4.00	Caroline	Goetghebeur	BEL	2.6.78	20 Jul
4.00	Gaëlle	Delcourt	FRA	31.7.79	21 Jul
4.00	Nadine	Rohr	SUI	29.6.77	24 Jul
3.99i	Molly	Lederman	USA-J	5.6.84	20 Jan
3.98	Meredith	Garner	USA	19.7.80	31 Mar
3.98	Melissa	Astete	USA-J	22.10.83	9 Jun
3.97	Jamie	Kolar	USA-J	19.10.83	28 Mar
3.96i	Megan	Westfall	USA	14.8.80	2 Mar
3.96	Katie	Meyer	USA	19.6.79	18 May
3.96	Michaela	Kohlbauer	AUT-J	28.10.82	7 Jul
3.95i	Amy	Spellmeyer	USA	4.9.79	10 Feb
3.95	Annelie	van Wyk	RSA-J	28.5.84	10 Mar
3.95i	Solenne	Allain	FRA-J	5.3.82	18 Mar
3.95	Tracy	Carrington	USA	12.3.77	29 Apr
3.95	Sabine	Verbeek	NED	25.3.80	12 Jul
3.95	Anna	Olko	POL-J	15.2.84	14 Jul
3.95	Sandra	van der Geer	NED	25.5.72	26 Aug
3.93	Mandy	McLane	USA	9.2.79	24 Mar
3.93	Leila	Ben Youssef	USA	13.11.81	5 May

Mark	Name			Nat	Born	Pos	Meet	Venue	Date

Mark	First	Name	Nat	Born	Date	Mark	First	Name	Nat	Born	Date
3.93	Jennifer	Culp	USA		13 May	3.91i	Andrea	Stürmer	GER	4.4.79	24 Feb
3.92i	Corrie	Drakulich	USA	23.11.81	25 Feb	3.91	Marie	Gerbier	FRA	17.7.78	16 Jun
3.92	Elke	Andries	BEL	4.8.76	19 Aug	3.91	Fabiana	Murer	BRA	16.3.81	16 Jun
3.91i	Merle	Kivimets	EST	21.7.74	11 Feb	(179) and 34 women at 3.90					

Street competition, raised runway, slightly uphill

Mark	Name		Nat	Born	Pos	Meet	Venue	Date
4.62	Melissa	Mueller	USA	16.11.72	1		Clovis	4 Aug

Exhibition

Mark	Name		Nat	Born	Pos	Meet	Venue	Date
4.00	Joanna	Piwowarska	POL-J	4.11.83	5		Sopot	13 Jun

Best outdoor marks for athletes with best indoors

Mark	Name	Pos	Meet	Venue	Date	Mark	Name	Pos	Meet	Venue	Date
4.47	Hamácková	4	GP	Athína	11 Jun	4.20	Kusch	3		Kiev	25 May
4.46	Isinbayeva	2	ISTAF	Berlin	31 Aug	4.12A	Honey	1		El Paso	5 May
4.45	Elísdottír	6	WCh	Edmonton	6 Aug	4.11	Ryshich	7	Pre	Eugene	27 May
4.42	Belyakova	4	GGala	Roma	29 Jun	4.10	Clarke	4	Tex R	Austin	6 Apr
4.40	Auer	2	Gugl	Linz	20 Aug	4.10	Ballard	1		College Station	10 May
4.35	Adams	1		Weissach	8 Jun	4.10	Dolcini	1		Torino	9 Jun
4.30	Boslak	1		Miramas	13 Jun	4.10	Lukinskaya	3		Bydgoszcz	15 Jun
4.25	M Poissonnier	1		Clermont-Ferrand	6 Jun	4.10	Zhang Na	6=	WUG	Beijing	29 Aug
4.20	Dutoit	2	Pac 10	Berkeley	20 May	4.10	Ono	3		Yokohama	15 Sep

Mark	Name	Date	Mark	Name	Date	Mark	Name	Date	Mark	Name	Date
4.07	Steiner	14 Apr	4.03	Wildrick	10 May	4.00	Tsírba	9 Jun	4.00	Eguchi	15 Sep
4.05	Serrano	17 Mar	4.01	Balti	3 Jun	4.00	Toulouse	16 Jun	3.98	Shepard	9 Jun
4.05	Agirre	28 Jul	4.00	F Kühnert	27 May	4.00	Homo	30 Jun	3.95	Agee	17 Mar
4.03	Palamaa	6 May	4.00	Chavdarova	9 Jun	4.00	Wilhelm	1 Jul	3.93	Westfall	13 May
									3.91	Spellmeyer	27 Apr

4.13 exh F Kühnert 2 Recklinghausen 26 May

JUNIORS

See main list for top 12 juniors. 13 performances by 3 women to 4.30. Additional mark and further juniors:

	Mark	Pos	Meet	Venue	Date	Mark	Pos	Meet	Venue	Date
Isinbayeva 2+	4.45i	2	NC	Moskva	16 Feb	4.40	1	EJ	Grosseto	21 Jul
	4.42	2	GGala	Roma	29 Jun	4.35	7	BrGP	London (CP)	22 Jul
	4.40	2		Zagreb	2 Jul	4.30	2	NC	Tula	14 Jul
Boslak 2+	4.32i	1		Grenoble	10 Feb	4.30i	1	NC	Liévin	18 Feb

Mark	Name		Nat	Born	Pos	Meet	Venue	Date
4.05i	Samantha	Shepherd	USA	11.11.83	1		New York	10 Mar
4.05	Leslie	Dunlap	USA	15.2.82	1eB	Tex R	Austin	6 Apr
4.03	Emily	Tharpe	USA	2.9.82	1		Erie	9 May
4.02	Tamara	Diles	USA	5.11.82	1		Long Beach	8 Dec
4.01i	Stacie	Manuel	USA	6.12.83	2		New York	10 Mar
4.01	Lacy	Janson	USA	20.2.83	1		Sarasota	19 May
4.00i	Mariya	Smirnova	RUS	83	2		Sankt Peterburg	4 Jan
4.00	Connie	Jerz	USA	26.4.82	1		Tempe	14 Apr
4.00	Natalya	Belinskaya	RUS	83	1		Krasnodar	22 May
4.00	Alina	Alló	ARG	30.5.82	1		Mar del Plata	23 Jun
4.00	Francesca	Zanini	ITA	4.4.82	1		Milano	29 Jun
4.00	Silke	Spiegelburg	GER	17.3.86	1	WY	Debrecen	14 Jul
4.00	Aleksandra	Kiryashova	RUS	21.8.85	2	WY	Deberecen	14 Jul
Best out:	4.01	Balti	TUN	31.10.83	1		Tunis	3 Jun

LONG JUMP

Mark	Wind	Name		Nat	Born	Pos	Meet	Venue	Date
7.12	0.5	Tatyana	Kotova	RUS	11.12.76	1		Torino	9 Jun

6.81/1.6 6.95/1.2 6.83/2.0 6.90w/5.2 7.12 6.82/0.7

Mark	Wind	Pos	Meet	Venue	Date	1	2	3	4	5	6
7.09	0.8	1	NC	Tula	14 Jul	?					
7.00	1.0	1		Thessaloníki	22 Aug	6.44	6.68	6.79	x	7.00	p
6.98i		2	WI	Lisboa	10 Mar	6.83	6.88	6.88	6.94	6.98	x
6.95	0.3	1		Kalamatá	2 Jun	5.95	6.71	6.57	6.56	6.95	x
6.84	1.2	3	GWG	Brisbane	4 Sep	6.74	4.97	6.73	6.84	6.59	x
6.84i		1		Sindelfingen	4 Mar	6.65	6.50	6.61	6.84	6.51	p
6.82	?	1		Athína	30 May	6.47	4.85	x	6.58	6.70/-0.4	6.82
6.82	0.2	* (2)	WCh	Edmonton	5 Aug	6.60	6.82	6.67	7.01w/3.6	6.81w/3.4	x

Mark	Wind	Name		Nat	Born	Pos	Meet	Venue	Date
7.03i	-	Dawn	Burrell	USA	1.11.73	1	WI	Lisboa	10 Mar

6.67 6.83 6.08 6.69 x 7.03

Mark	Wind	Name		Nat	Born	Pos	Meet	Venue	Date
7.00i	-	Lyudmila	Galkina	RUS	20.1.72	1	NC	Moskva	16 Feb

x 6.63 6.77 6.80 6.80 7.00

Mark	Wind	Pos	Meet	Venue	Date	1	2	3	4	5	6
6.84i		1		Stuttgart	4 Feb	6.64	x	6.84	6.54	6.68	6.78

Mark	Wind	Name		Nat	Born	Pos	Meet	Venue	Date
6.97	1.2	Fiona	May	ITA	12.12.69	*	WCh	Edmonton	7 Aug

6.86w/3.7 6.97/1.2 7.02w/2.6 6.73/1.5 6.97/1.3 6.80w

Mark	Wind	Pos	Meet	Venue	Date	1	2	3	4	5	6
6.92	0.1	2		Thessaloníki	22 Aug	x	6.68	6.65	6.63	6.82/1.1	6.91
6.87i		4	WI	Lisboa	10 Mar	6.87	6.65	6.72	x	6.62	6.52

Mark	Wind	Name		Nat	Born	Pos	Meet	Venue	Date
6.97	0.8	Eunice	Barber	FRA	17.11.74	1	WK	Zürich	17 Aug

6.53 6.59 6.97 6.86 6.80 x

Mark	Wind	Pos	Meet	Venue	Date	1	2	3	4	5	6
6.87	1.4	1		Strasbourg	19 Jun	x	6.79w	6.87	6.78	p	6.70

Mark	Wind	Name		Nat	Born	Pos	Meet	Venue	Date
6.94	1.7	Maurren	Maggi	BRA	25.6.76	1	GWG	Brisbane	7 Sep

6.33w 6.81 6.83w 6.56 6.72 6.94

Mark	Wind	Pos	Meet	Venue	Date	1	2	3	4	5	6
6.87	1.8	*		São Caetano do Sul	21 Apr	6.87	6.98w/2.1		6.80/1.7	6.52	x p

Mark	Wind	Name		Nat	Born	Pos	Meet	Venue		Date
6.87	-0.3	1	Sevilla	8 Jun	6.87	6.76/0.2	x	6.83/0.4	four only	
6.86	0.4	1	Nürnberg	17 Jun	6.66	6.86	6.34	6.59	6.75	x
6.84	-0.4	1	Milano	6 Jun	6.40	6.66	6.55	6.52	6.84	x
6.83	1.6	1 WUG	Beijing	28 Aug	6.49	6.79	p	6.82/1.3	6.72	6.83
6.91	0.3	Niurka	Montalvo	ESP	4.6.68	3		Thessaloníki		22 Aug
					6.59	x	6.64	5.01	6.69	6.91
6.88i		3 WI	Lisboa	10 Mar	6.76	x	6.71	6.85	6.69	6.88
6.82i		1 NC	Valencia	25 Feb	6.40	6.69	6.57	6.63	6.74	6.82
6.88w	2.1	3 WCh	Edmonton	5 Aug	6.73w	x	6.59	6.88w	6.76/1.4	6.54
6.83w	2.4	1	La Laguna	14 Jul	x	6.49	6.78/1.7	6.76w/2.5	6.83w	x
6.91w	3.6	exh	Córdoba	5 May	6.47w	x	6.45w	x	6.74	6.91w
6.88	1.3	Valentina	Gotovska	LAT	3.9.65	2		Torino		9 Jun
					6.52	6.68	6.63	6.62	6.88	6.64
6.84w	3.5	5 WCh	Edmonton	5 Aug	6.84w	6.67/1.5	6.66	x	6.59w	6.23
6.88	2.0	Bronwyn	Thompson	AUS	29.1.78	2	GWG	Brisbane		7 Sep
					6.78	6.52	6.65	4.99	6.88	6.01
6.87	1.2	Erica	Johansson	SWE	5.2.74	1		Fort-de-France		28 Apr
					6.65	x	6.71	6.73	6.81	6.87
6.86	0.4	Elva	Goulbourne	JAM	21.1.80	1		Tucson		3 May
6.86	0.3	Olga	Rublyova	RUS	28.10.74	2	NC	Tula		14 Jul
6.86	1.3	Tünde	Vaszi	HUN	18.4.72	4	WCh	Edmonton		7 Aug
					6.68	x	6.88	6.84/17	x	x
6.82w	2.8	1	Budapest	24 Jun	6.82w	x	x	x	four only	
6.82	1.6	Maho	Hanaoka	JPN	3.8.76	1	NC	Tokyo		10 Jun
					6.82	6.43	6.32	x	x	6.52
		(33/14)								
6.80	2.0	Níki	Xánthou	GRE	11.10.73	1		Kós		20 May
6.79	-1.0	Heike	Drechsler	GER	16.12.64	1	ECp-S	Bremen		24 Jun
6.78		Jackie	Edwards	BAH	14.4.71	1		Palo Alto		31 Mar
6.78	0.8	Kumiko	Ikeda	JPN	10.1.81	2	NC	Tokyo		10 Jun
6.77	1.3		Guan Yingnan	CHN	25.4.77	1		Ningbo		28 Apr
6.74	1.4	Trecia	Smith	JAM	5.11.75	1		Tuscaloosa		24 Mar
		(20)								
6.74	1.3	Anju	George (Markose)	IND	77	1		Trivandrum		4 Jun
6.73	0.9	Yelena	Bobrovskaya	KGZ	11.4.75	1		Almaty		3 Jun
6.71i	-	Inna	Ivleva	RUS	71	2		Moskva		19 Jan
6.71i	-	Tatyana	Lebedeva	RUS	21.7.76	3		Moskva		19 Jan
6.71	-0.3	Yelena	Pershina	KAZ	24.12.63	1		Baden-Baden		8 Jul
6.69i	-	Natalya	Sazanovich	BLR	15.8.73	P	WI	Lisboa		9 Mar
6.69	1.3		Zhong Mei	CHN	7.1.78	1	NC	Chengdu		29 Jun
6.69	0.7	Yevgeniya	Zhdanova	RUS	21.7.66	4	NC	Tula		14 Jul
6.68i	-	Tatyana	Ter-Mesrobyan	RUS	12.5.68	3	NC	Moskva		16 Feb
6.68i	-	Jenny	Adams	USA	8.7.78	1	NCAA	Fayetteville		9 Mar
		(30)								
6.68	0.7	Chantal	Brunner	NZL	5.11.70	1	Aus Ch	Brisbane		25 Mar
6.65i	-	Yelena	Shekhovtsova	UKR	31.5.72	1	NC	Brovary		10 Feb
6.65i	-	Stilianí	Pilátou	GRE	28.3.80	1	Balk C	Pireás		18 Feb
6.65	1.5	Inge	Leiwesmeier	GER	17.5.77	1		Wesel		4 Jun
6.65	0.0	Eva	Miklos	ROM	30.7.78	1	NC	Bucuresti		10 Jun
6.65		Chioma	Ajunwa	NGR	25.12.70	1	NC	Lagos		20 Jul
6.64i	-	Aurélie	Félix	FRA	26.3.79	1	NC	Liévin		18 Feb
6.63	0.5	Nolle	Graham	JAM	12.9.81	1		Princeton		19 May
6.63	0.4	Yelena	Prokhorova	RUS	16.4.78	5	NC	Tula		14 Jul
6.63	0.9	Nicole	Boegman	AUS	5.3.67	1		Lake Buena Vista		22 Jul
		(40)								
6.62	2.0	Grace	Upshaw	USA	22.9.75	2	NC	Eugene		21 Jun
6.61i	-	Irina	Yermolayeva	RUS	14.10.79	4	NC	Moskva		16 Feb
6.61i	-	Yelena	Kashcheyeva	KAZ	17.2.73	1	v 2N	Tianjin		18 Feb
6.61i	-	Concepción	Montaner	ESP	14.1.81	2	NC	Valencia		25 Feb
6.61	0.2		Hu Yaoyao	CHN-J	16.4.83	1		Zhongshan		21 Apr
6.61	1.8		Gu Ying	CHN	26.5.80	1		Tianjin		18 May
6.61		Svetlana	Zaytseva	RUS	14.8.81	1	NC-23	Cheboksary		14 Jun
6.60i	-	Antoinette	Wilks	USA	14.10.80	1		Gainesville		3 Feb
6.60	0.0		Liang Shuyan	CHN	16.9.77	2		Zhongshan		21 Apr
6.59i	-	Elisha	Williams	USA	9.1.79	2	NCAA	Fayetteville		9 Mar
		(50)								
6.59	1.9	Jade	Johnson	GBR	7.6.80	*	vFRA	Ashford		11 Aug
6.58i	-	Anastasiya	Ilyina	RUS-J	16.1.82	1		Lipetsk		9 Feb
6.58		Nadezhda	Bazhenova	RUS	22.9.78	1		Tula		30 May
6.58	1.1	Zita	Ajkler	HUN	9.6.75	3		Pátra		22 Jul
6.57		Phan Thi	Thu Lan	VIE	79	1		Hanoi		13 May

Mark	Wind	Name		Nat	Born	Pos	Meet	Venue	Date
6.57	1.2	Lissette	Cuza	CUB	26.2.75	2	Sule	Tartu	19 Jun
6.56i	-		Wang Lina	CHN-J	28.2.83	2		Tianjin	17 Feb
6.56i	-	Brianna	Glenn	USA	18.4.80	1		Ames	2 Mar
6.56	0.9	Liliana	Zagacka	POL	28.1.77	1		Warszawa	7 Jun
6.55		Yevgeniya	Stavchanskaya	UKR	25.9.81	2		Moskva	22 Jun
		(60)							
6.54i	-	Viviane	Sildillia	FRA	23.2.74	2	NC	Liévin	18 Feb
6.54	0.7	Irina	Melnikova- 2	RUS	14.5.75	1	Znam	Tula	9 Jun
6.53	0.4	Joanna	Halkoaho	FIN	13.1.77	1		Lapinlahti	22 Jul
6.53	-2.1		Zhu Yanyan	CHN	3.12.78	2	NG	Guangzhou	19 Nov
6.52i	-	Natalya	Budarina	RUS	77	1		Moskva	3 Feb
6.52	1.6	Agneta	Rosenblad	SWE	8.8.77	1	Pac-10	Berkeley	19 May
6.51i	-	Alice	Falaiye	CAN	24.12.78	3	NCAA	Fayetteville	9 Mar
6.51		Lucie	Komrsková	CZE	24.10.77	1		Rheinau-Freisett	8 Jul
6.50	2.0	Kerine	Black	JAM	5.3.77	1		Coral Gables	17 Mar
6.50		Nguyen Thi	Bich Van	VIE	21.2.75	2		Hanoi	13 May
		(70)							
6.50	-0.4	Yuliya	Akulenko	UKR	3.6.77	1H		Kiev	18 May
6.50	1.8	Thaimi	O'Reilly	ITA	20.7.76	1		Lorient	26 May
6.50	2.9-	Irina	Belova	RUS	27.3.68	4H		Götzis	27 May
6.50	1.7	Hristína	Athanasíou	GRE	11.1.74	4		Kalamáta	2 Jun
6.50	2.0	Bianca	Kappler	GER	8.8.77	1		Rhede	13 Jul
6.50	0.5	Liga	Klavina	LAT	27.1.80	1H	EU23	Amsterdam	15 Jul
6.49i	-	Sabine	Braun	GER	19.6.65	2	NC	Dortmund	24 Feb
6.49	0.0	Lacena	Golding	JAM	20.3.75	6		Milano	6 Jun
6.48	1.7	Yolanda	Thompson	USA	29.5.81	1		Gainesville	8 Apr
6.48	1.0		Yu Yiqun	CHN	12.1.76	2		Ningbo	28 Apr
		(80)							
6.48		Cristina	Nicolau	ROM	8.8.77	1		Bucuresti	27 May
6.48	1.8	Shana	Williams	USA	7.4.72	*	NC	Eugene	21 Jun
6.47i	-	Lyudmila	Nikitina	RUS	2.3.70	2		Samara	1 Feb
6.47	-2.3	Regla	Cárdenas	CUB	21.1.75	1		La Habana	16 Feb
6.47	0.9	Luciana	Alves dos Santos	BRA	10.2.70	2		Americana	29 Apr
6.47	0.9		Yu Shaohua	CHN-J	4.1.85	1		Shanghai	6 May
6.47		Antonia	Yordanova	BUL	17.8.76	1		Plovdiv	30 Jun
6.46i	-	Nicole	Herschmann	GER	27.10.75	2		Chemnitz	9 Feb
6.46	2.0	Valerie	Williams	USA	12.12.79	1		Tempe	5 May
6.46	0.2	Pamela	Simpson	USA	28.4.77	1		Los Angeles	2 Jun
		(90)							
6.46	1.8	Denise	Lewis	GBR	27.8.72	3	GP II	Sevilla	8 Jun
6.46	-0.4	Natalia	Kilpeläinen	FIN	19.7.70	*		Lapinlahti	22 Jul
6.45i	-	Beatrice	Albert	GER	9.5.70	1		München	10 Feb
6.45i	-	Viktoria	Vershinina	UKR	11.6.71	2	NC	Brovary	10 Feb
6.45i	-	Mirela	Dulgheru	ROM	5.10.66	2	NC	Bucuresti	25 Feb
6.45	0.8	Shermin	Oksuz	AUS-J	24.3.84	1	NC-j	Brisbane	24 Mar
6.45	1.6	Laura	Gatto	ITA	4.3.77	1		Conegliano	19 May
6.45	1.3	Silvia	Favre	ITA	15.8.80	6		Torino	9 Jun
6.45		Ibifuro	Tobin-West	NGR		1		Lagos	29 Jun
6.45	0.4	Shelia	Burrell	USA	15.1.72	3H	WCh	Edmonton	5 Aug
		(100)							

Mark	Wind	Name		Nat	Born	Date
6.44i		Anzhela	Kinet (Atroshchenko)	TUR	14.11.70	25 Jan
6.44i		Tasha	Mahone	USA	5.8.79	24 Feb
6.44	1.1	Sofia	Schulte	GER	8.4.76	13 May
6.43i		Anna	Pyatykh	RUS	4.4.81	6 Jan
6.43	1.7	Sharon	Sutherland	AUS	10.3.77	25 Mar
6.43	0.8	Olga	Salazhenkova	RUS	76	9 Jun
6.43	0.0	Elmira	Bulauitan	PHI	17.10.74	12 Sep
6.43	-1.5	G.Pramila	Ganapathy	IND	8.5.77	19 Oct
6.42	1.2	Célia	Harmenil	FRA	7.9.81	28 Apr
6.42	1.2	Tiffany	Greer	USA	8.6.81	30 May
6.42		Mihaela	Gîndila	ROM	29.10.74	30 Jun
6.41i		Irina	Simagina	RUS-J	25.5.82	14 Feb
6.41i		Maria Chiara	Baccini	ITA	21.7.81	24 Feb
6.41	1.6	Oksana	Udmurtova	RUS-J	.82	28 May
6.41		Esther	Aghatise	NGR		7 Jul
6.40i		Yelena	Ivanova	RUS	16.3.79	4 Jan
6.40	-0.1		Wu Lingmei	CHN	16.2.73	21 Apr
6.40	0.0	Karolina	Binas	POL	9.3.79	2 Jun
6.39i		Keyon	Soley	USA	8.9.79	19 Jan
6.39i		Ola	Sesay	USA	30.5.79	20 Jan
6.39i		Karin	Ertl	GER	23.6.74	20 Jan
6.39i		Sandra	Turpin	POR	5.6.76	17 Feb
6.39		Olga	Yershova	RUS	13.8.76	17 May
6.39	0.4	Katarzyna	Klisowska	POL-J	2.2.83	2 Jun
6.39	0.3	Natalya	Bastrygina	RUS	71	14 Jul
6.38i		Yelena	Shchinova	RUS	80	23 Feb
6.38i		Marta	Godinho	POR	24.6.80	3 Mar
6.38	0.2	Natalya	Sorokina	UKR	24.3.75	9 May
6.38	1.2	Stephanie	Hort	GER	13.2.75	24 May
6.38	1.1	Alena	Vindyuk	RUS	31.7.74	14 Jul
6.37	0.0	Olga	Bolshova	MDA	16.6.68	18 Apr
6.37	0.1	Patience	Itanyi	NGR	2.7.73	13 May
6.37	0.0	Joanna	Olesinska	POL	5.11.74	2 Jun
6.37	0.0		Guo Chunfang	CHN	4.1.79	28 Jun
6.37	1.0	Françoise	Mbango	CMR	14.4.76	21 Jul
6.36i		Svetlana	Sokolova	RUS	9.1.81	19 Jan
6.36i		Enezenaide	Gomes	STP	10.11.79	17 Feb
6.36	1.9	Eri	Yamamoto	JPN	25.9.79	3 May
6.36	2.0	Kirsten	Bolm	GER	4.3.75	18 May
6.35A	0.0	Joanne	Wise	GBR	15.3.71	12 Feb
6.35i			Huang Jianfen	CHN	10.10.78	18 Feb
6.35	-0.4	Martina	Darmovzalová	CZE	12.10.78	2 Jun
6.35		Yudelkis	Fernández	CUB-J	28.2.85	21 Jun
6.35	0.0		Bi Xiaohua	CHN-J	16.1.83	28 Jun
6.35	1.4	Julie	Hollman	GBR	16.2.77	1 Jul
6.35	0.8	Monica	Falchi	ITA	23.2.76	11 Jul

Mark	Wind		Name	Nat	Born	Date
6.35	0.7		Shen Shengfei	CHN	21.1.81	18 Nov
6.34	0.8		Gan Xiaohua	CHN	7.1.79	21 Apr
6.34	-0.6	Maren	Freisen	GER-J	15.2.82	19 May
6.34	1.5	Panayióta	Koutsioumári	GRE	23.3.81	2 Jun
6.34	0.9	Natalya	Safronova	BLR	11.4.74	24 Jun
6.34	0.9	Larisa	Netseporuk	EST	24.12.70	1 Jul
6.34	-1.2		Kim Su-yeon	KOR	2.5.77	11 Oct
6.33i		Elena	Anghelescu	ROM-J	20.6.84	18 Mar
6.33		Chantal	Ouaba	BUR	2.9.75	21 Apr
6.33	0.7		Zhang Nina	CHN	3.3.81	6 May
6.33	1.5	Kathy	Norman	AUS	22.8.80	28 May
6.33	1.8	Ruth	Irving	GBR	20.7.74	2 Jun
6.33	1.5	Olesya	Belyayeva	KAZ	29.6.80	23 Jun
		(159)				

Wind assisted

Mark	Wind		Name	Nat	Born	Pos	Meet	Venue	Date
7.02	2.6	Fiona	May	ITA	12.12.69	1	WCh	Edmonton	7 Aug
6.98	2.1	Maurren	Maggi	BRA	25.6.76	1		São Caetano do Sul	21 Apr
6.90	2.1	Elva	Goulbourne	JAM	21.1.80	1	JUCO	Odessa, TX	11 May
6.82A	7.0	Jackie	Edwards	BAH	14.4.71	1		El Paso	14 Apr
6.75	3.9	Jenny	Adams	USA	8.7.78	1	Mod R	Modesto	12 May
6.72A	2.2	Aurélie	Félix	FRA	26.3.79	1		Font Romeu	22 Jul
6.71	2.6	Nicole	Boegman	AUS	5.3.67	6	GWG	Brisbane	7 Sep
6.70	4.2	Grace	Upshaw	USA	22.9.75	2	Mod R	Modesto	12 May
6.68	2.7	Jade	Johnson	GBR	7.6.80	1	CAU	Bedford	28 May
6.67	2.4	Nolle	Graham	JAM	12.9.81	1		Piscataway	5 May
6.67	2.8	Concepción	Montaner	ESP	14.1.81	1		Valencia	27 Aug
6.66A	3.4	Helena	Guerrero	COL	10.3.76	1	Bol G	Ambato	12 Sep
6.65	3.0	Shermin	Oksuz	AUS-J	24.3.84	2	NC	Brisbane	25 Mar
6.64	2.3	Lucie	Komrsková	CZE	24.10.77	1		Praha	6 Jul
6.63	4.3	Tereza	Marinova	BUL	5.9.77	1		Shizuoka	3 May
6.62	2.5		Guo Chunfang	CHN	4.1.79	2	NC	Chengdu	29 Jun
6.61	4.8	Lacena	Golding	JAM	20.3.75	1		Bridgetown	19 May
6.57	5.6	Chimika	Carter	USA	17.8.78	1	Big 12	College Station	18 May
6.56		Shana	Williams	USA	7.4.72	1	Penn R	Philadelphia	28 Apr
6.54	2.5	Tisha	Parker	USA	18.9.77	1		Baton Rouge	14 Apr
6.53	2.3	Denise	Lewis	GBR	27.8.72	3	v2N	Glasgow	1 Jul
6.52	2.3	Alice	Falaiye	CAN	24.12.78	1	DrakeR	Des Moines	28 Apr
6.51	2.5	Anastasiya	Ilyina	RUS-J	16.1.82	1	NC-J	Kazan	27 Jun
6.50		Mashevet	Hooker	USA-J	25.9.84	1		San Antonio	24 Mar
6.50		Ychlindria	Spears	USA-J	17.7.84	1		Lockhart	20 Apr
6.50	2.4	Natalia	Kilpeläinen	FIN	19.7.70	2		Lapinlahti	22 Jul
6.47A	6.7	Nicole	Gilmore	CAN	24.8.73	2		El Paso	14 Apr
6.46	7.5	Joanne	Wise	GBR	15.3.71	1		Stellenbosch	23 Feb

Mark	Wind		Name	Nat	Born	Date
6.45	3.5	Nayanthi	Chandrasena	SRI	13.1.75	20 Jul
6.44	3.3		Bi Xiaohui	CHN-J	16.1.83	18 May
6.44A	2.7	Jennifer	Arveláez	VEN-J	28.10.82	12 Sep
6.43	4.8	Andrea	Ávila	ARG	4.4.70	21 Apr
6.43	3.1	Meredith	Davis	USA		11 May
6.41	2.6	Chenelle	Marshall	JAM	4.4.78	18 May
6.41	2.8	Jana	Veldáková	SVK	3.6.81	24 Jun
6.40	4.9	Austra	Skujyté	LTU	12.8.79	17 May
6.40	2.2	Olesya	Belyayeva	KAZ	29.6.80	3 Jun
6.40	6.9	Susanna	Rajamäki	FIN	19.9.79	1 Jul
6.39	2.8	Marie-Hélène	Carabin	FRA	7.7.79	16 Jun
6.38	3.3	Ioánna	Kafetzí	GRE	30.5.76	5 May
6.38	2.2	Monica	Falchi	ITA	23.2.76	11 Jul
6.37	2.3	Julie	Hollman	GBR	16.2.77	1 Jul
6.36	2.6	Emma	Cochrane	AUS	5.12.79	1 Mar
6.36	4.9	Simidele	Adeagbo	USA	29.7.81	6 Apr
6.36	2.7	Sharesa	Turner	USA		5 May
6.36	8.5	Sonja	Kesselschläger	GER	20.1.78	1 Jul
6.36	3.2	Ann	Danson	GBR	4.5.71	11 Aug
6.35A	4.3	Charlene	Lawrence	RSA	25.9.79	2 Feb
6.35	5.5	Myra	Combs	USA	17.4.79	6 Apr
6.35	2.4	Precious	Madison	USA	8.6.79	14 Apr
6.34	2.8	Takako	Baba	JPN	23.12.81	22 Apr
6.34	4.8	Sayoko	Sato	JPN	23.10.77	22 Apr
6.33	2.7	Nadia	Smith	NZL	8.5.76	25 Mar
6.33	4.0	Barbara	Szlendaková	CZE	6.8.78	17 May
6.33	3.3	Janel	Hayes	USA	28.10.79	18 May
6.33	5.1	DeDee	Nathan	USA	20.4.68	22 Jun
6.33	2.2	Carolina	Klüft	SWE-J	2.2.83	15 Sep

Best outdoor marks for athletes with best indoors

Mark	Wind	Name	Pos	Meet	Venue	Date
6.70	0.1	Galkina	8	WCh	Edmonton	7 Aug
6.62	-0.1	Shekhovtsova	3		Athína	30 May
6.61A	0.3	Félix	*		Font Romeu	22 Jul
6.59		Yermolayeva	2	NC23	Cheboksary	14 Jun
6.58	1.5	Kashcheyeva	1		Almaty	23 Jun
6.57	0.8	Montaner	1		Castellón	24 Jul
6.56	0.7	Sazanovich	3H		Götzis	27 May
6.52	0.3	Ivleva	2	Znam	Tula	9 Jun
		6.59w 2.6	2		Budapest	1 Jul
6.51	-1.9	Wang Lina	3	NG	Guangzhou	19 Nov
6.48	0.4	Williams	2		Tuscaloosa	24 Mar
		6.58w 6.2	1	TexR	Austin	6 Apr
6.48	w?	Braun	1		Recklinghausen	6 May
6.48	0.8	Glenn	*	NC	Eugene	21 Jun
		6.56w 3.7	1	NCAA	Eugene	30 May
6.48	-2.5	Adams	Q	WCh	Edmonton	5 Aug
6.48	0.7	Pilátou	5	WUG	Beijing	28 Aug
6.46	0.0	Falaiye	1	WAC	Fresno	18 May

Mark	Wind	Name	Date
6.43	1.3	Ilyina	28 Aug
6.36	0.8	Gomes	9 May
6.36	-0.1	Ertl	17 Jun
6.35	0.0	Sildillia	6 May
		6.40w 3.3	1 Jul
6.35	-0.2	Nikitina	14 Jul
6.34	0.0	Huang Jianfen	28 Jun
6.33		Godinho	26 May
		6.37w 2.8	26 May
6.33		Y Ivanova	14 Jun
6.33	-1.3	Ter-Mesrobyan	12 Jul
6.41Aw	2.9	Wilks (dq?)	14 Apr
6.38w	3.3	Mahone	31 Mar

Low altitude bests

Mark	Wind	Name	Pos	Meet	Venue	Date
6.57	1.5	Félix	1	NC	Saint-Etienne	1 Jul
6.34i		Wise	1		Birmingham	3 Feb

JUNIORS

See main list for top 5 juniors. 8 performances by 5 women to 6.43. Additional marks and further juniors:

Name	Mark	Wind	Pos	Meet	Venue	Date	
Hu Yaoyao	6.50i	-	3		Tianjin	17 Feb	
Ilyina 2+	6.43	1.3	6	WUG	Beijing	28 Aug	(her best outdoors)
Spears	6.49w	2.7	1		Austin	11 May	

WOMEN 2001

Mark	Wind	Name		Nat	Born	Pos	Meet	Venue	Date
6.41i		Irina	Simagina	RUS	25.5.82	1		Moskva	14 Feb
6.41	1.6	Oksana	Udmurtova	RUS	.82	1		Yekaterinburg	28 May
6.39	0.4	Katarzyna	Klisowska	POL	2.2.83	1		Zielona Góra	2 Jun
6.35		Yudelkis	Fernández	CUB	28.2.85			La Habana	21 Jun
6.35	0.0		Bi Xiaohua	CHN	16.1.83	Q	NC	Chengdu	28 Jun
6.34	-0.6	Maren	Freisen	GER	15.2.82	3		Garbsen	19 May
6.33i		Elena	Anghelescu	ROM	20.6.84	1		Bucuresti	18 Mar
		6.32	1.5			2	WY	Debrecen	15 Jul
6.32	1.7	Ychlindria	Spears	USA	17.7.84	*		Austiin	11 May
6.32	0.5	Kathrin	Geissler	GER	10.6.85	1		Málaga	25 Jun
6.32	0.3	Alina	Militaru	ROM	10.4.82	2	EJ	Grosseto	22 Jul
6.30i		Viktoriya	Lofytska	UKR	14.3.83	1		Kiev	22 Feb
6.29i		Kristin	Baarck	GER	22.3.82	1	NC-j	Neubrandenburg	18 Feb
6.28i		Anna	Simavonova	RUS	82	3		Lipetsk	9 Feb
6.28	-0.1		Sun Mingming	CHN	23.9.86	8		Zhongshan	21 Apr
6.28	1.6	Angela	Dies (20)	GER	16.3.84	2	NC-y	Braunschweig	7 Jul

Wind assisted – see maion list for five juniors.

Mark	Wind	Name		Nat	Born	Pos	Meet	Venue	Date
6.44	3.3		Bi Xiaohui	CHN	16.1.83	2		Tianjin	18 May
6.44A	2.7	Jennifer	Arveláez	VEN	28.10.82	2	BolG	Ambato	12 Sep
6.33w=	2.2	Carolina	Klüft	SWE	2.2.83	1		Stockholm	15 Sep

TRIPLE JUMP

Mark	Wind	Name		Nat	Born	Pos	Meet	Venue	Date
15.25	-0.8	Tatyana	Lebedeva	RUS	21.7.76	1	WCh	Edmonton	10 Aug
					15.11/-1.1 14.93/1.4 x x x 15.25				
	15.00i	1 NC	Moskva	18 Feb	14.42 14.34 14.39 15.00 p p				
	14.91	0.1 1 GPI	Athína	11 Jun	14.91 14.55/-0.1 14.23 14.86 14.75/-0.6 14.76/0.0				
	14.89i	1	Pireás	21 Feb	14.21 14.51 14.79 14.89 x 14.70				
	14.89	-1.2 1 ECp	Bremen	23 Jun	14.89 x 14.65/ -0.2 x 4 only				
	14.85i	2 WI	Lisboa	11 Mar	14.08 14.29 14.53 x 14.85 14.47				
	14.85i	1	Madrid	14 Mar	14.23 14.58 14.51 14.78 14.85 14.17				
	14.84	0.9 1 NC	Tula	15 Jul	?				
	14.82	-0.4 1 GPII	Bratislava	12 Jun	14.60/0.0 14.82 14.66/-1.5 14.63/-1.6				
	14.81	1.4 1 WUG	Beijing	28 Aug	14.27 x 14.55/1.7 14.81 14.62w/2.2 14.74/1.7				
	14.72	0.7 2 GP	Sevilla	8 Jun	14.40/-0.3 14.62/0.314.72 x				
	14.72	0.3 1 BrGP	London (CP)	22 Jul	14.72 14.49 x x 14.68 x				
	14.69	0.3 *(1) Nik	Nice	9 Jul	14.69/0.3 x x 14.45/0.2 x 14.83w/2.3				
	14.64	1.8 1	Villeneuve d'Ascq	17 Jun	14.64w/3.2 14.64 14.43w 14.41w x 14.54/1.0				
	14.62	2.0 *(1)	Rethimnó	1 Jul	14.58w/3.9 14.87w/2.3 14.33w 14.59w/2.9 x 14.62				
	14.61	0.9 2 GPF	Melbourne	9 Sep	14.61 14.36 14.03 14.17 14.31 14.46				
	14.58	0.0 1 GWG	Brisbane	6 Sep	14.28 14.36 14.58 14.30 x 14.45				
14.91i	-	Tereza	Marinova	BUL	5.9.77	1	WI	Lisboa	11 Mar
					14.91 x x 14.68 x x				
	14.77	0.3 1 GPF	Melbourne	9 Sep	14.77 x 14.62/0.7 14.68/0.6 14.59/1.0 12.54				
	14.74	1.9 1	Mito	6 May	14.58w/2.7 x 14.74 x p x				
	14.73	0.7 1 GP	Sevilla	8 Jun	14.73 14.44/0.4x 14.07				
	14.70	0.6 1 Gugl	Linz	20 Aug	x 14.37 14.39 14.53 14.70 14.56				
	14.58i	2	Pireás	21 Feb	x 14.22 14.56 14.47 x 14.58				
	14.58	-1.3 3 WCh	Edmonton	10Aug	14.36/-0.6 14.58 14.33/-1.8 14.12 14.54/0.0 14.57/-0.4				
14.83i	-	Yelena	Lebedenko	RUS	16.1.71	1		Samara	1 Feb
					14.01 13.92 14.24 14.57 14.83 x				
	14.62i	1	Eaubonne	7 Feb	13.65 14.50 x 14.18 14.62 14.52				
14.72	1.8		Huang Qiuyan	CHN	25.1.80	1	NG	Guangzhou	22 Nov
14.65	1.1	Françoise	Mbango	CMR	14.4.76	1	FRA Ch	Saint-Etienne	30 Jun
					x 14.19 13.92 14.08 13.95 14.65				
	14.64	0.1 Q WCh	Edmonton	8 Aug	14.64 only jump				
	14.60	-0.6 2 WCh	Edmonton	10 Aug	14.26 14.43/-0.6 x 14.23 14.44/-0.5 14.60				
14.62	1.3	Cristina	Nicolau	ROM	9.8.77	1	Franc	Ottawa	22 Jul
					14.38w/2.7 14.49w/3.0 14.62 x x 14.16w/3.5				
14.60		Nadezhda	Bazhenova	RUS	22.9.78	1		Moskva	23 Jun
14.59	0.3	Yelena	Oleynikova	RUS	9.12.76	2	NC	Tula	15 Jul
14.59	1.9	Magdelin	Martínez	ITA	10.2.76	Q	WCh	Edmonton	8 Aug
					14.59 only jump				
		(34/9)							
14.57		Irina	Vasilyeva	RUS	9.4.79	2		Moskva	23 Jun
		(10)							
14.57	1.5	Natalya	Safronova	BLR	11.7.74	2	WUG	Beijing	1 Sep
14.51	1.1	Ashia	Hansen	GBR	5.12.71	Q	WCh	Edmonton	8 Aug
14.38	1.2	Olga	Yershova	RUS	13.8.76	Q	NC	Tula	13 Jul
14.37i	-	Oksana	Rogova	RUS	7.10.78	3		Pireás	21 Feb
14.33	0.8	Yelena	Govorova	UKR	18.9.73	2	GP II	Rieti	2 Sep

Mark	Wind	Name		Nat	Born	Pos	Meet	Venue	Date
14.31i	-	Anja	Valant	SLO	8.9.77	2		Karlsruhe	27 Jan
14.29	-0.4		Ren Ni	CHN	14.5.79	3	NG	Guangzhou	22 Nov
14.28	-0.2	Heli	Koivula	FIN	27.6.75	Q	WCh	Edmonton	8 Aug
14.27	-0.3	Yevgeniya	Zhdanova	RUS	21.7.66	4	NC	Tula	15 Jul
14.26i	-	Olga	Rublyova	RUS	28.10.74	1		Moskva	21 Jan
		(20)							
14.22	0.4	Liliana	Zagacka	POL	28.1.77	1		Biala Podlaska	6 Jul
14.21		Galina	Sharova	RUS	30.1.79	4		Moskva	23 Jun
14.21	1.0	Anna	Pyatykh	RUS	4.4.81	5	NC	Tula	15 Jul
14.19i	-	Tiombé	Hurd	USA	17.8.73	3	WI	Lisboa	11 Mar
14.19	-1.2	Anastasiya	Ilyina	RUS-J	16.1.82	2	Veniz	Haniá	4 Jun
14.19A	1.3	Yuliana	Pérez	USA	21.7.81	1		Albuquerque	8 Jul
14.18i	-	Maria	Dimitrova	BUL	7.8.76	1		Sofia	21 Jan
14.18	0.0	Adelina	Gavrila	ROM	26.11.78	1	BalkC	Tríkala	7 Jul
14.17i	-	Olga	Bolshova	MDA	16.6.68	4	WI	Lisboa	11 Mar
14.16	1.1		Miao Chunqing	CHN	27.2.78	*	NG	Guangzhou	22 Nov
		(30)							
14.15	1.0	Silvia	Biondini	ITA	24.1.76	1	NC	Catania	7 Jul
14.12	0.2	Natalya	Kayukova	RUS	10.12.66	7	NC	Tula	15 Jul
14.12A	0.8	Trecia	Smith	JAM	5.11.75	1	CAC	C. de Guatemala	22 Jul
14.12	0.0		Wu Lingmei	CHN	16.2.73	*	NG	Guangzhou	22 Nov
14.09	1.1	Nicole	Herschmann	GER	27.10.75	1		Mainz	9 Jun
14.06	0.4	Paraskeví	Tsiamíta	GRE	10.3.72	3	GP	Doha	18 May
14.05	2.0		Li Jiahui	CHN	8.8.79	2	NC	Chengdu	1 Jul
14.05		Mabel	Gay	CUB-J	5.5.83	1	NC-j	Santiago de Cuba	7 Jul
14.05	1.3	Camilla	Johansson	SWE	3.11.76	2		Visby	19 Jul
14.04i	-	Lyudmila	Nikitina	RUS	2.3.70	5	NC	Moskva	18 Feb
		(40)							
14.02i	-	Niurka	Montalvo	ESP	4.6.68	4		Madrid	14 Mar
14.02	1.2	Viktoriya	Brigadnaya	TKM	4.8.80	1		Ashkhabad	13 May
14.01i	-	Katja	Umlauft	GER	22.11.74	1		Berlin	28 Jan
14.01	1.1	Barbara	Lah	ITA	24.3.72	1	ECCp	Madrid	27 May
14.01	0.7	Ioánna	Kafetzí	GRE	30.5.76	2		Spárti	25 Jul
14.00	0.8	Keila	Costa	BRA-J	6.2.83	*		São Caetano do Sul	22 Apr
14.00	1.1	Hrisopiyí	Devetzí	GRE	2.1.76	4		Kalamáta	2 Jun
14.00	1.4	Marija	Martinovic	YUG	17.4.79	1		Kragujevac	30 Jun
13.99	1.9	Suzette	Lee	JAM	6.3.75	1		Houston	19 May
13.99	-0.5	Carlota	Castrejana	ESP	25.4.73	3	ECCp	Madrid	27 May
		(50)							
13.96i		Mariana	Solomon	ROM	8.9.80	2		Bucuresti	3 Feb
13.94	0.9		Ren Ruiping	CHN	1.2.76	2		Zhongshan	22 Apr
13.91i	-	Tatyana	Ter-Mesrobyan	RUS	12.5.68	1		Sankt Peterburg	6 Jan
13.90A	1.6	Sheila	Hudson	USA	30.6.67	1		El Paso	14 Apr
13.89i	-	Yelena	Ivanova	RUS	16.3.79	2		Sankt Peterburg	6 Jan
13.88	1.7	Natalia	Kilpeläinen	FIN	19.7.70	3		Visby	19 Jul
13.88		Baya	Rahouli	ALG	27.7.79	4		Viareggio	22 Aug
13.87	1.4		Zhang Hao	CHN	26.2.78	6	NG	Guangzhou	22 Nov
13.87	0.2		Tang Zhimin	CHN	26.6.79	7	NG	Guangzhou	22 Nov
13.85i	-	Yamilé	Aldama	CUB	14.8.72	1	Gre Ch	Pireás	25 Feb
		(60)							
13.84i	-	Dímitra	Márkou	GRE	28.7.80	5		Pireás	21 Feb
13.83i	-	Nicole	Gamble	USA	21.6.77	2		Blacksburg	9 Feb
13.82	1.0	Yelena	Khlusovich	UKR	2.12.69	1		Kiev	19 May
13.82	2.0	Elena	Gilardoni	ITA	20.5.75	*		Torino	9 Jun
13.82	0.5	Maria Costanza	Moroni	ITA	23.3.69	2	NC	Catania	7 Jul
13.81i	-	Federica	Cresci	ITA	13.4.74	2		Firenze	13 Feb
13.81i	-	Mariana	Bogatie	ROM	12.6.81	4	NC	Bucuresti	24 Feb
13.78		Constanta	Stucan #	ROM	12.7.81	3	NC	Bucuresti	10 Jul
13.78	2.0	Wacharee	Ritthiwat	THA	18.10.76	1		Singapore	18 Aug
13.77	1.6	Michelle	Hastick	CAN	16.9.73	1	NC	Edmonton	24 Jun
		(70)							
13.76	1.8	Elena-Alina	Popescu	ROM-J	27.10.85	1	WY	Debrecen	13 Jul
13.75	1.2	Viktoriya	Gurova	RUS-J	22.5.82	1	NC-j	Kazan	28 Jun
13.75	1.1	Andreja	Ribac	SLO	14.1.76	1	NC	Maribor	7 Jul
13.74i	-	Inna	Lasovskaya	RUS	17.12.69	7	NC	Moskva	18 Feb
13.74	1.1	Nicole	Mladenis	AUS	22.9.75	1	NC	Brisbane	24 Mar
13.73	1.7	Dana	Veldáková	SVK	3.6.81	1		Kosice	5 May
13.73	0.0	Luciana	Alves dos Santos	BRA	10.2.70	1		São Caetano do Sul	26 May
13.72	1.2	Zita	Balint	HUN	25.10.71	1		Zalaegerszeg	9 Jun
13.72	1.9	Amy	Zongo	FRA	4.10.80	2	NC	Saint-Etienne	30 Jun

Mark	Wind	Name		Nat	Born	Pos	Meet	Venue	Date
13.71	-0.2	Yusmay	Bicet	CUB-J	8.12.83	1	NC	La Habana	26 May
		(80)							
13.71		Yelena	Shekhovtsova	UKR	31.5.72	1		Kiev	8 Jun
13.71	1.7	Irina	Beskrovnaja	SVK-J	28.12.82	1		St Pölten	24 Jun
13.71	-0.3		Peng Fengmei	CHN	9.7.79	1eB	NC	Chengdu	30/6? 1 Jul
13.71	-0.2		Yan Xueqin	CHN	1.11.73	7	NC	Chengdu	1 Jul
13.71	0.3		Wu Xueli	CHN	5.1.78	9	NG	Guangzhou	22 Nov
13.70		Zhanna	Gureyeva	BLR	10.6.70	2		Brest	7 Jun
13.67	1.5	Shonda	Swift	USA	28.2.74	2		Fort-de-France	28 Apr
13.67	0.4	Olga	Voropinova	RUS	.81	1		Krasnodar	1 Jul
13.66i	-	Concepción	Paredes	ESP	19.7.70	1		Sant Cugat	17 Feb
13.65	1.1	Stéphane	Luzieux	FRA-J	7.7.82	5	EJ	Grosseto	20 Jul
		(90)							
13.64A	1.2	Anna	Tarasova	KAZ	23.3.80	1		El Paso	31 Mar
13.64	0.4	Marina	Ogorodova	RUS	76	10	NC	Tula	15 Jul
13.63	-0.1	Krystyna	Neyzhpapa	UKR	27.3.79	2		Kiev	19 May
13.61	-0.4	Anju	George (Markose)	IND	77	1		Ludhiana	22 Nov
13.60i	-	Yelena	Lysak	RUS	19.10.75	9	NC	Moskva	18 Feb
13.60		Jackie	Edwards	BAH	14.4.71	1		Palo Alto	1 Apr
13.60	1.5	Maurren	Maggi	BRA	25.6.76	2		São Caetano do Sul	22 Apr
13.60	1.9	Gi-Gi	Miller	USA	12.1.79	5	NC	Eugene	23 Jun
13.60	1.0	Renata	Szykulska	POL	17.8.74	2	NC	Bydgoszcz	1 Jul
13.60		Nadezhda	Shestakova	BLR	.77			Staiki	13 Jul
		(100)							

Mark	Wind	Name		Nat	Born	Date
13.59i	-	Oksana	Nechayeva	RUS	74	18 Feb
13.59	-1.0	Maho	Hanaoka	JPN	3.8.76	8 Jun
13.59	0.8	Lene	Espegren	NOR	8.5.71	6 Jul
13.58		Anzhela	Zhalnerchik	BLR	13.8.75	22 Jul
13.58		Natalya	Kostyuchenko	BLR	9.4.77	22 Jul
13.58	1.5	Zita	Ajkler	HUN	9.6.75	1 Sep
13.58A	0.6	Jennifer	Arveláez	VEN-J	28.10.82	14 Sep
13.57	-0.4	Olga Lidia	Cepero	CUB	4.2.75	26 May
13.57	1.3	Yelena	Parfyonova	KAZ	26.1.74	4 Jun
13.57	1.1	Colleen	Gillies-Scott	JAM	18.8.74	22 Jun
13.57	1.9	Sandra	Swennen	BEL	12.2.73	18 Aug
13.56	0.5	Aneta	Sadach	POL	22.4.75	23 Sep
13.55	0.0	Gisele	de Oliveira	BRA	1.8.80	20 Jul
13.54	0.5		Yu Shaohua	CHN-J	4.1.85	22 Nov
13.54	-0.4		Li Xiaoling	CHN	15.8.80	22 Nov
13.53		Livia	Pruteanu	ROM	22.12.81	9 Jun
13.52	1.1	Althea	Williams	CAN	4.1.75	24 Jun
13.52	1.1	Athanasía	Pérra	GRE-J	2.2.83	25 Jul
13.52	1.8	Sari	Kulmala	FIN	25.5.74	28 Jul
13.51		Nkechinyere	Mbaoma	NGR		30 Jun
13.51	0.3	Ilona	Pazola	POL	22.3.69	6 Jul
13.51	0.3	Simona	La Mantia	ITA-J	14.4.83	7 Jul
13.50i		Vanitta	Kinard	USA	26.7.75	10 Feb
13.50	0.7	Olga	Lapina	KAZ	22.6.78	1 Sep
13.49	-0.1	Tanja	König	GER	11.4.70	9 Jun
13.48	1.5	Olga	Saladukha	UKR-J	4.6.83	19 May
13.48		Svetlana	Bolshakova	RUS-J	14.10.84	22 Jun
13.47i		Deanna	Simmons	USA	22.10.78	10 Mar
13.47	0.5	Ychlindria	Spears	USA-J	17.7.84	11 May
13.47	0.8	Yelena	Portugal	RUS-J	82	15 Jul
13.46i		Shakeema	Walker	USA	10.11.76	19 Jan
13.46	-1.4	Martina	Darmovzalová	CZE	12.10.78	2 Jun
13.46A	0.7	Ludmila	Reyes	VEN	22.3.76	14 Sep
13.45i		Elena	Dumitrascu	ROM	14.5.74	24 Feb
13.45	0.5		Wang Xiaoting	CHN	4.3.81	13 May
13.45	1.7	Silvia	Otto	GER	3.1.79	16 Jun
13.45	0.8		Xu Junfang	CHN	10.2.79	1 Jul
13.44i			Zhou Yangxia	CHN-J	10.2.83	17 Feb
13.44	-1.6		Jin Yan	CHN-J	20.4.82	30 Jun
13.43	1.6	Mónica	Falcioni	URU	10.10.68	19 May
13.43	2.0		Lee Kyung-sun	KOR	11.9.77	12 Oct
13.42	0.0	Elisha	Williams ??	USA	9.1.79	28 Apr
13.41i			Zhu Yanyan	CHN	3.12.78	17 Feb
13.41	1.9	Shelly-Ann	Gallimore	JAM	10.3.81	17 Mar
13.41		Yaima	Kindelán	CUB-J	25.9.82	7 Jul
13.40	-0.3	Aleksandra	Stadnyuk	UKR	16.4.80	1 Jul
13.39i		Michelle	Griffith	GBR	6.10.71	11 Feb
13.39	-0.4	Iskra	Petrishka	BUL	3.10.80	27 May
13.39	0.0	Marina	Samborskaya	UKR	6.4.77	1 Jul
13.38	0.1	Henny	Gastel	GER	1.7.79	30 Jun
13.38i	-	Zinayida	Lifintseva	RUS-J	.84	23 Dec
13.37i		Aysegul	Baklaci	TUR	25.12.77	21 Jan
13.37	1.9	Sandrine	Domain	FRA	6.9.71	30 Jun
13.36i			Song Ying	CHN-J	18.1.82	17 Feb
13.36	1.9	Stacey	Bowers	USA	22.8.77	23 Jun
13.36	0.9	Nathalie	Jacques-Gustave	FRA	12.5.76	30 Jun
13.35		Chantal	Ouaba	BUR	2.9.75	27 Jun
13.34i		Yelena	Nazarenko	RUS	80	18 Feb
13.34	1.0	Alina	Dinu	ROM-J	2.9.82	20 Jul
13.34	1.1	Yuliya	Kolesnikova	AZE-J	3.10.82	20 Jul
13.33i		Roselise	Retel	FRA	27.6.73	17 Feb
13.33	-0.1	Kareen	Clarke	JAM	10.4.81	14 Apr
13.32i			Zhao Fan	CHN	1.3.78	17 Feb
13.32	0.5	Tatyana	Bocharova	KAZ-J	22.4.83	1 Sep
13.31	2.0	Zivile	Zebarauskaite	LTU	9.11.79	3 Jul
13.30	-0.4	Dagmar	Urbanková	CZE	8.4.62	1 Jul
13.28	0.2		Pham Thi Thu Lan	VIE	79	28 Apr
13.28	0.1	Oksana	Bufalova	RUS-J	6.10.82	23 May
13.28		Natalya	Mikhan	BLR	19.3.78	7 Jun
13.26	0.6		Wang Kuo-huei	TPE	12.9.78	21 Oct
13.25	2.0	Vanessa	Vlacancich	ITA	23.10.81	1 Jul
13.25	1.0	Barbara	Cannet	FRA	20.5.76	18 Jul
13.25	0.0	Maria Ap.	de Souza	BRA	5.9.71	20 Jul
		(173)				

Wind assisted

Mark	Wind	Name		Nat	Born	Pos	Meet	Venue	Date
14.94	2.4		Lebedeva			1	GP II	Gateshead	19 Aug
					14.57/0.0	x	14.46	14.22	14.94w 14.13
14.89	3.0		Marinova			Q	WCh	Edmonton	8 Aug
					14.89w		only jump		
14.88	3.8	Trecia	Smith	JAM	5.11.75	1	Kans R	Lawrence	21 Apr
14.48	2.2	Yelena	Govorova	UKR	18.9.73	Q	WCh	Edmonton	8 Aug
14.43	2.3		Miao Chunqing	CHN	27.2.78	2	NG	Guangzhou	22 Nov
14.30	2.2	Baya	Rahouli	ALG	27.7.79	1	MedG	Tunis	14 Sep
14.29	2.2	Yuliana	Pérez (Martínez)	USA	21.7.81	4	WUG	Beijing	1 Sep
14.24	3.4	Maria	Dimitrova	BUL	7.8.76	1	ECp-1B	Budapest	23 Jun
14.24	2.3		Wu Lingmei	CHN	16.2.73	4	NG	Guangzhou	22 Nov
14.22	2.2	Anna	Pyatykh	RUS	4.4.81	1		Lapinlahti	22 Jul
14.17	3.3	Camilla	Johansson	SWE	3.11.76	Q	WCh	Edmonton	8 Aug

Mark	Wind	Name		Nat	Born	Pos	Meet	Venue	Date
14.15	2.2	Keila	Costa	BRA-J	6.2.83	1		São Caetano do Sul	22 Apr
14.12	2.4	Hrisopiyí	Devetzí	GRE	2.1.76	3		Réthimno	1 Jul
13.92	5.2	Viktoriya	Gurova	RUS-J	22.5.82	Q	EJ	Grosseto	19 Jul
13.91	2.1	Elena	Gilardoni	ITA	20.5.75	3		Torino	9 Jun
13.87	3.5	Yelena	Parfyonova	KAZ	26.1.74	1		Almaty	24 Jun
13.86	2.6	Lene	Espegren	NOR	8.5.71	1	NC	Drammen	6 Jul
13.82	2.6	Michelle	Hastick	CAN	16.9.73	4	Franc	Ottawa	22 Jul
13.81	3.0	Nicole	Mladenis	AUS	22.9.75	1		Perth	10 Feb
13.81	2.8	Andreja	Ribac	SLO	14.1.76	1		Celje	9 Jun
13.74	3.2	Luciana A.	dos Santos	BRA	10.2.70	1		São Caetano do Sul	7 Apr
13.74	4.8	Stéphane	Luzieux	FRA-J	7.7.82	1	vGBR	Ashford	11 Aug
13.73	3.0	Athanasía	Pérra	GRE-J	2.2.83	2	EJ	Grosseto	20 Jul
13.69	2.5	Zita	Ajkler	HUN	9.6.75	7	WUG	Beijing	1 Sep
13.67	2.9	Alina	Dinu	ROM-J	2.9.82	4	EJ	Grosseto	20 Jul
13.66	2.5	Vanitta	Kinard	USA	26.7.75	1		Emporia	12 May
13.64		Colleen	Gillies-Scott	JAM	18.8.74	3	Penn R	Philadelphia	27 Apr
13.63	3.3	Simona	La Mantia	ITA-J	14.4.83	1		Palermo	2 Jun
13.60	2.8	Althea	Williams	CAN	4.1.75	1	MSR	Walnut	22 Apr
13.60	2.2	Sari	Kulmala	FIN	25.5.74	1		Valkeakoski	15 Aug

Mark	Wind	Name		Nat	Born	Date	Mark	Wind	Name		Nat	Born	Date
13.50	2.5	Dejana	Cachot	SUI	2.11.68	24 Jun	13.32	3.1	Barbara	Cannet	FRA	20.5.76	11 Aug
13.47	3.3	Elena	Dumitrascu	ROM	14.5.74	16 Jun	13.29	2.8	Sara	Brankell	SWE	6.2.81	4 Jun
13.34	3.7	Marie	Åhlander	SWE	15.4.78	18 May	13.26	2.8	Stilianí	Pilátou	GRE	28.3.80	1 Jul

Best outdoor marks for athletes with best indoors

Mark	Wind	Name	Pos	Meet	Venue	Date	Mark	Wind	Name	Pos	Meet	Venue	Date
14.20	0.4	Rogova	2		Kalamáta	2 Jun	14.07		Hurd	1	Penn	Philadelphia	28 Apr
		14.23w 2.1	1	Veniz	Haniá	4 Jun	13.95	1.6	Valant	5	GP	Doha	18 May
14.18	0.0	Dimitrova	1		Dimitrovgrad	18 Jul	13.93	0.5	Umlauft	6	WUG	Beijing	1 Sep
14.17		Lebedenko	2	Kuts	Moskva	28 Jul	13.73		Solomon	4	NC	Bucuresti	9 Jun
14.15	0.5	Bolshova	1		Barcelona	25 Jul	13.62	-2.1	Cresci	1		Lucca	19 May

Mark	Wind	Name	Date	Mark	Wind	Name	Date	Mark	Wind	Name	Date
13.57	0.0	Montalvo	12 May	13.41	1.8	Paredes	21 Jul	13.35	1.5	Márkou	16 Jun
13.54		Bogatie	9 Jun			13.57w 2.9	21 Jul			13.68w 2.1	23 Jun
13.48		Ivanova	15 Jun	13.39		Lasovskaya	23 Jun	13.34	1.3	Zhu Yanyan	22 Apr
13.47	0.5	Kinard	28 Apr	13.38		Dumitrascu	26 May	13.33	0.2	Baklaci	16 Jun
								13.28	0.0	Zhou Yangxia	1 Jul
								13.30w	4.0	Retel	29 Apr

Low altitude bests

Mark	Wind	Name	Pos	Meet	Venue	Date	Mark	Wind	Name	Pos	Meet	Venue	Date
14.11	1.0	Smith	1	NC	Kingston	22 Jun	13.69		Hudson	1		Sacramento	16 Jun
14.10	1.0	Pérez	1	JUCO	Odessa, TX	12 May	13.80w	2.7		1	ModR	Modesto	12 May
13.35	1.6	Arveláez (J)	4	SACh	Manaus	19 May							

Drugs disqualification

Mark	Wind	Name		Nat	Born	Pos	Meet	Venue	Date
13.88	0.7	Constanta	Stucan	ROM	12.7.81	1		Istanbul	28 Jul

JUNIORS

See main list for top 8 juniors. 12 performances by 3 women to 13.98. Additional mark and further juniors:

	Mark	Wind	Pos	Meet	Venue	Date	Mark	Wind	Pos	Meet	Venue	Date
Ilyina	14.18	0.1	4		Athína	11 Jun	14.12	0.8	1	EJ	Grosseto	20 Jul
	14.15		1	NC-j	Kazan	28 Jun	14.03i		5		Samara	1 Feb
	14.13i	-	1		Moskva	14 Feb	14.03i		1		Lipetsk	8 Feb
	14.13	0.2	1		Krasnodar	23 May	13.98	1.0	Q	EJ	Grosseto	19 Jul

Mark	Wind	Name		Nat	Born	Pos	Meet	Venue	Date
13.58A	0.6	Jennifer	Arveláez	VEN	28.10.82	1	Bol G	Ambato	14 Sep
13.54	0.5		Yu Shaohua	CHN	4.1.85	12	NG	Guangzhou	22 Nov
13.52	1.1	Athanasía	Pérra	GRE	2.2.83	4		Spárti	25 Jul
13.51	0.3	Simona	La Mantia	ITA	14.4.83	5	NC	Catania	7 Jul
13.48	1.5	Olga	Saladukha	UKR	4.6.83	3		Kiev	19 May
13.48		Svetlana	Bolshakova	RUS	14.10.84	1		Cheboksary	22 Jun
13.47	0.5	Ychlindria	Spears	USA	17.7.84	1		Austin	11 May
13.47	0.8	Yelena	Portugal	RUS	82	11	NC	Tula	15 Jul
13.44i			Zhou Yangxia	CHN	10.2.83	4		Tianjin	17 Feb
13.44	-1.6		Jin Yan	CHN	20.4.82	Q	NC	Chengdu	30 Jun
13.41		Yaima	Kindelán	CUB	25.9.82	3	NC	Santiago de Cuba	7 Jul
13.38i	-	Zinayida	Lifintseva	RUS	.84	1		Moskva	23 Dec

Wind assisted – see main list for six juniors

SHOT

Mark		Name		Nat	Born	Pos	Meet	Venue		Date
20.79		Larisa	Peleshenko	RUS	29.2.64	1	NC	Tula		13 Jul
					19.69	19.94	19.66	20.00	20.51	20.79
20.12i	1	NC	Moskva	17 Feb	19.20	19.87	x	19.90	19.81	20.12
20.01i	1		Moskva	27 Jan	19.37	19.42	19.34	20.01		
19.84i	1	WI	Lisboa	10 Mar	18.87	19.15	19.52	x	19.51	19.84
19.37	4	WCh	Edmonton	5 Aug	x	19.06	19.37	19.32	19.30	19.15
20.61		Yanina	Korolchik	BLR	26.12.76	1	WCh	Edmonton		5 Aug
					x	19.71	20.61	x	19.21	19.61
20.29	1	GP II	Hengelo	4 Jun	19.25	19.56	19.58	20.29	4 only	
20.10	1	GPII	Bratislava	12 Jun	18.71	20.10	x	19.79	4 only	
19.87	Q	WCh	Edmonton	5 Aug		only throw				

WOMEN 2001

Mark	Name		Nat	Born	Pos	Meet	Venue		Date
20.17	Svetlana	Krivelyova	RUS	13.6.69	2	NC	Tula		13 Jul
19.64i	2	Moskva	27 Jan	18.90	19.00	19.33	19.64		
19.53i	2 NC	Moskva	17 Feb	19.53	19.11	19.09	x	p	p
19.49	2	Doha	18 May	19.49	19.41	x	x	x	18.89
19.87	Astrid	Kumbernuss	GER	5.2.70	1		Calgary		30 Jul
				19.87	x	19.21	19.12	x	p
19.58	1	Cottbus	18 Jul	19.58	x	19.20	x	x	x
19.51	1	Doha	18 May	19.09	19.11	19.51	x	x	p
19.41	1	Halle	19 May	18.89	19.41	18.92	18.94	19.21	19.13
19.86	Nadine	Kleinert-Schmitt	GER	20.10.75	2	WCh	Edmonton		5 Aug
				19.54	18.88	19.45	19.10	x	19.86
19.85	1	Gotha	16 Jun	19.66	19.85	19.69	x	19.60	19.50
19.58	1	Dortmund	9 Jun	19.30	19.58	x	19.18	19.24	19.42
19.35	Q WCh	Edmonton	5 Aug	x	19.35		2 throws		
19.73	Nadezhda	Ostapchuk	BLR	12.10.80	1	EU23	Amsterdam		12 Jul
				x	19.16	x	19.73	x	x
19.71	1	Rüdlingen	19 Aug	18.30	18.79	19.14	19.45	19.71	x
19.69	1 Nik	Nice	9 Jul	18.74	19.37	x	x	19.02	19.69
19.53	2 GP II	Hengelo	4 Jun	18.49	19.13	19.53	x	4 only	
19.62	Viktoriya	Pavlysh	UKR	15.1.69	1	NC	Kiev		1 Jul
				x	18.58	19.62	19.25	x	19.55
19.49i	1	Brovary	23 Dec						
19.47	1 EAA	Nice	17 Mar	19.06	x	19.47	18.39	18.25	18.33
19.41	3 WCh	Edmonton	5 Aug	19.01	19.41	18.80	x	18.98	x
19.37	Irina	Korzhanenko	RUS	16.5.74	3	NC	Tula		13 Jul
19.35	5 WCh	Edmonton	5 Aug	19.35	x	x	18.55	18.63	x
	(31/8)								
19.34	Lyudmila	Sechko	RUS	27.11.74	1		Sankt-Peterburg		27 Jun
19.30	Elisângela	Adriano	BRA	27.7.72	1		Tunja		14 Jul
	(10)								
19.21	Teri	Steer (Tunks)	USA	30.10.75	1	Drake	Des Moines		28 Apr
19.10i	Yumileidi	Cumbá	CUB	11.2.75	1	Balk C	Pireás		18 Feb
19.10	Krystyna	Zabawska	POL	14.1.68	1		Bydgoszcz		15 Jun
18.92		Li Meiju	CHN	23.1.81	1	NG	Guangzhou		21 Nov
18.79		Lee Myung-sun	KOR	12.2.76	2	WUG	Beijing		27 Aug
18.78		Cheng Xiaoyan	CHN	30.11.75	2	NG	Guangzhou		21 Nov
18.73		Song Feina	CHN	25.1.77	3	NG	Guangzhou		21 Nov
18.67	Irina	Khudoroshkina	RUS	13.10.68	1		Moskva		17 May
18.59i	Katarzyna	Zakowicz	POL	12.5.75	6	WI	Lisboa		10 Mar
18.59	Elena	Hila	ROM	20.5.74	1		Istanbul		16 Jun
	(20)								
18.59		Jiang Ping	CHN	10.1.79	Q	NG	Guangzhou		19 Nov
18.57		Zhang Liuhong	CHN	16.1.69	Q	NG	Guangzhou		19 Nov
18.56	Lieja	Koeman	NED	10.3.76	1	NC	Tilburg		7 Jul
18.49		Zhang Xiaoyu	CHN-J	16.3.83	1		Ningbo		28 Apr
18.41		Qian Chunhua	CHN	11.2.79	6	NG	Guangzhou		21 Nov
18.41		Jia Lina	CHN	26.4.80	7	NG	Guangzhou		21 Nov
18.39		Li Meisu	CHN	17.4.59	8	NG	Guangzhou		21 Nov
18.35i	Connie	Price-Smith	USA	3.6.62	1	NC	Atlanta		3 Mar
18.06		Sui Xinmei	CHN	29.1.65	4		Shanghai		6 May
18.05		Zhang Ying	CHN-J	19.3.84	Q	NG	Guangzhou		19 Nov
	(30)								
18.03	Oksana	Zakharchuk	UKR	3.4.80	1		Koncha Zaspa		12 May
18.02	Nadine	Beckel	GER	27.5.77	3		Gotha		16 Jun
18.00	Yelena	Dementiy	UKR	6.3.69	2	NC	Kiev		1 Jul
17.98		Yu Juan	CHN	29.3.75	6eA	NC	Chengdu		1 Jul
17.97	Seilala	Sua	USA	25.2.78	1	NC	Eugene		24 Jun
17.92	Kalliópi	Ouzouni	GRE	8.2.73	1		Athína (K)		29 Jul
17.85	Olga	Ryabinkina	RUS	24.9.76	2		Moskva		17 May
17.83	Vivian	Peters	NGR	4.5.77	1	NC	Lagos		21 Jul
17.82	Corrie	de Bruin	NED	26.10.76	1		Leiden		9 Jun
17.79i	Yuliya	Zaginay	RUS	3.8.63	2		Moskva		19 Jan
	(40)								
17.79	Assunta	Legnante	ITA	14.5.78	4	GP	Rio de Janeiro		6 May
17.77	Christina	Tolson	USA	16.1.78	1	Pac 10	Berkeley		19 May
17.74	Jamine	Moton	USA	14.12.78	1		Clemson		13 May
17.68	Drienke	van Wyk	RSA	13.1.71	1		Johannesburg		10 Feb
17.67		Yang Dehui	CHN-J	28.4.83	11	NG	Guangzhou		21 Nov
17.65	Iolanta	Ulyeva	KAZ	27.7.76	1		Almaty		23 Jun
17.65		Li Fengfeng	CHN	9.1.79	Q	NC	Chengdu		30 Jun
17.59	Lucica	Ciobanu	ROM	10.5.79	2	EU23	Amsterdam		12 Jul

Mark	Name		Nat	Born	Pos	Meet	Venue	Date
17.56i	Alina	Frunza	ROM	17.4.79	1	NC	Bucuresti	24 Feb
17.54		Du Xianhui	CHN	4.1.81	1		Manila	17 May
	(50)							
17.54	Misleydis	González	CUB	19.6.78	2	NC	La Habana	27 May
17.52	Valentina	Fedyushina	AUT	10.2.65	1		Lisboa	29 Apr
17.51		Zhang Zhiying	CHN	19.7.73	4		Zhongshan	21 Apr
17.50i	Laurence	Manfrédi	FRA	20.5.74	1	NC	Liévin	18 Feb
17.42	Martina	de la Puente	ESP	4.4.75	1	NC	Valencia	22 Jul
17.41		Yu Jing	CHN-J	7.3.83	3		Ningbo	28 Apr
17.38	Juttaporn	Krasaeyan	THA	13.2.72	1		Bangkok	5 May
17.38		Zhang Guirong	CHN	78	1		Singapore	26 Aug
17.37	Iríni-Hrisovaládo	Terzóglou	GRE	2.2.79	5		Réthimno	1 Jul
17.35i	Natalya	Lisovskaya	FRA	16.7.62	2	NC	Liévin	18 Feb
	(60)							
17.32		Zhang Juan	CHN-J	8.4.83	13Q	NG	Guangzhou	19 Nov
17.29	Veronica	Abrahamse	RSA	18.3.80	1	NC	Durban	2 Mar
17.26i	Ilona	Beyer	GER	8.1.76	2	NC	Dortmund	25 Feb
17.25	Nataly	Khoroneko	BLR-J	25.5.82	1		Staiki	30 Jun
17.22	Yelena	Ivanenko	BLR	5.5.78	5	ECp-S	Bremen	24 Jun
17.20	Karin	Wurm	GER	6.2.78	4		Gotha	16 Jun
17.17	Kristin	Heaston	USA	23.11.75	3	NC	Eugene	24 Jun
17.16		Gong Jian	CHN	16.1.77	Q	NC	Chengdu	30 Jun
17.13	Anna	Tolokina	RUS	3.10.81	1		Krasnodar	30 Jun
17.08	Valerie	Adams	NZL-J	6.10.84	Q	WY	Debrecen	13 Jul
	(70)							
17.08	Joanne	Duncan	GBR	27.12.66	1		London (WF)	19 Aug
17.07	Rebekah	Green	USA	19.9.80	1	Kans R	Lawrence	20 Apr
17.07	Cristiana	Checchi	ITA	8.7.77	1		Modena	2 Jun
17.06	Kathleen	Kluge	GER	17.11.81	3	EU23	Amsterdam	12 Jul
17.05		Mao Lingyan	CHN	12.2.78	Q	NC	Chengdu	30 Jun
17.03		Tian Xiue	CHN	4.10.71	Q	NC	Chengdu	30 Jun
17.00	Katja	Kròl	GER	5.2.80	1		Obersuhl	3 Jun
17.00i	Oksana	Chibisova	RUS	31.3.77	2		Moskva	22 Dec
16.97	Lyudmila	Starovoytova	BLR	8.4.74			Brest	21 Jul
16.96		Zheng Hui	CHN	18.12.73	Q	NC	Chengdu	30 Jun
	(80)							
16.92	Véra	Pospísilová	CZE	19.11.78	1	NC	Jablonec	30 Jun
16.91i	Linda-Marie	Mårtensson	SWE	22.6.71	1	NC	Bollnäs	3 Feb
16.87i	Aleksandra	Kopaneva	RUS	80	3		Moskva	22 Dec
16.87i	Cleopatra	Borel	TRI		1		Lewisburg	1 Dec
16.84	Chinatsu	Mori	JPN	20.5.80	1		Tokyo	9 Jun
16.83	Maranelle	du Toit	RSA	31.12.78	1		Parow	19 Oct
16.81i	Teresa	Machado	POR	22.7.69	1	v ESP	Espinho	17 Feb
16.77	Cynthia	Ademiluyi	USA	23.1.79	3	NCAA	Eugene	31 May
16.75i	Amber	Crumbo	USA	16.8.78	1		Normal	7 Dec
16.71	Olympia	Menelaou	CYP	29.4.66	1		Limassol	25 Mar
	(90)							
16.71	Irache	Quintanal	ESP	18.9.78	1		Barcelona	23 Jun
16.69	Aline	Schäffel	GER	15.5.80	6		Gotha	16 Jun
16.68i	Anca	Vílceanu-Heltne	ROM	1.1.78	1		Bacau	11 Mar
16.68	Jessica	Cosby	USA-J	31.5.82	1	NC-j	Richmond	17 Jun
16.67	Anna	Romanova	RUS	9.3.68	Q	NC	Tula	13 Jul
16.65	Lisa	Griebel	USA	8.3.79	4	NCAA	Eugene	31 May
16.64	Amber	Knighten	USA	28.6.80	5	NCAA	Eugene	31 May
16.58	Natalya	Sazanovich	BLR	15.8.73			Staiki	30 Jul
16.57	Jenny	Folz	USA	24.12.75	1		Long Beach	9 Jun
16.57	Svetla	Sinirtas	TUR	17.6.64	2		Istanbul	16 Jun
	(100)							

Mark	Name		Nat	Born	Date	Mark	Name		Nat	Born	Date
16.55	Chaniqua	Ross	USA	24.5.80	22 Apr	16.34	Karen	Freberg	USA-J	30.9.82	29 Mar
16.54	Veerle	Blondeel	BEL	14.1.75	1 May	16.34	Sumi	Ichioka	JPN	25.7.79	9 Jun
16.49	Helena	Engman	SWE	16.6.76	27 Jun	16.31	Stephanie	Brown	USA	1.12.79	31 May
16.48	Martina	Greithanner	GER	21.10.74	1 Jul	16.31	Julie	Dunkley	GBR	11.9.79	1 Jul
16.47	Svetlana	Kravchenko	UKR	11.2.80	28 Apr	16.30	Kristin	Marten	GER-J	23.3.83	20 May
16.47	Vera	Yepimashko	BLR	10.7.76	6 Jun	16.28	Heather	Leverington	USA	20.2.79	26 May
16.44i	Éva	Kürti	HUN	21.7.76	24 Feb	16.28	Yoko	Toyonaga	JPN	15.4.77	8 Jul
16.43i	Laura	Gerraughty	USA-J	29.7.83	19 Jan	16.26		Cho Jin-sook	KOR	21.2.77	16 Aug
16.40	Anna	Rauhala	FIN	26.3.75	30 Jun	16.24	L'Orangeril	Crawford	USA	23.12.81	31 May
16.39i	Linda	Nestorsson	SWE	2.12.75	16 Feb	16.23i	Bambi	Carson	USA	10.8.79	2 Mar
16.38	Karolina	Konkolewska	POL	16.8.80	12 May	16.17i	Margarita	Ramos	ESP	26.6.66	4 Feb
16.38	Jill	Camarena	USA-J	2.8.82	19 May	16.17	Austra	Skujyté	LTU	12.8.79	14 Jul
16.37i	Liz	Toman	CAN	17.4.78	24 Feb	16.15	Michelle	Haage	AUS	14.11.74	31 Mar
16.34i	Dana	Lawson	USA	13.7.79	9 Mar	16.11	Olga	Shchukina	UZB	6.4.77	5 May

Mark	Name		Nat	Born	Date
16.10	Lucie	Vrbenská	CZE	12.5.77	30 Jun
16.09	Isabelle	Berthoud	FRA	8.9.78	6 May
16.07i	Bianca	Grosser	GER	14.4.80	21 Jan
16.07	Anja	Burkhardt	GER	13.10.81	2 Jul
16.06i	Aubrey	Schmitt	USA	22.11.77	24 Feb
16.06i	Alexis	McCall	USA-J	10.7.82	24 Feb
16.06i	Ashley	Dorsey	USA	29.1.80	9 Mar
16.06	DeDee	Nathan	USA	20.4.68	14 Apr
16.02i	Leann	Boerema	USA	25.8.80	3 Mar
16.02	Christina	Strovolidou	CYP	10.10.74	29 Apr
16.00	Georgette	Reed	CAN	26.1.67	21 Jul
15.99	Melanie	Pöche	GER-J	21.6.82	27 May
15.96	Luz Dary	Castro	COL	30.5.78	21 Jul
15.94i	Melissa	Gibbons	JAM	18.3.80	27 Jan
15.93	Catarina	Andersson	SWE	17.11.77	25 Aug
15.92i	Jennifer	Brown	USA	1.9.79	17 Feb
15.92i	Lynetta	Keppeler	USA	16.6.78	17 Feb
15.91	Claudia	Villeneuve	FRA-J	23.8.83	18 Mar
15.91	Olga	Ivanova	RUS	79	17 May
15.91	Gaëlle	Eléléara	FRA	14.10.81	9 Jun
15.89		Zhang Changyan	CHN-J	14.2.84	18 May
15.85	Marianne	Berndt	CHI	24.12.78	6 May
15.84	Magnolia	Iglesias	ESP	25.5.79	1 Jul
15.84i	Ruta	Rakskyté	LTU	28.7.80	1 Dec
15.80i	Beth	Obruba	USA	30.4.77	20 Jan
15.80	Amel	Ben Khaled	TUN	6.6.74	3 Oct

(154)

Best outdoor marks for athletes with best indoors

Mark	Name		Nat	Born	Pos	Meet	Venue	Date
19.00	Yumileidi	Cumbá	CUB	11.2.75	1		Salamanca	13 Jul
18.59	Katarzyna	Zakowicz	POL	12.5.75	2	NC	Bydgoszcz	29 Jun
18.22	Connie	Price-Smith	USA	3.6.62	2	Drake	Des Moines	28 Apr
17.72	Yuliya	Zaginay	RUS	3.8.63	1		Bryansk	4 Jul
17.37	Laurence	Manfrédi	FRA	20.5.74	1		Bonneuil-sur-Marne	1 Jun
17.33	Natalya	Lisovskaya	FRA	16.7.62	1	NC	Saint-Etienne	30 Jun
17.13	Ilona	Beyer	GER	8.1.76	1		Reinheim	29 Apr
16.88	Oksana	Chibisova	RUS	31.3.77	2		Rostov-na-Donu	5 May
16.68	Linda-Marie	Mårtensson	SWE	22.6.71	1		Ludvika	27 Jun
16.64	Alina	Frunza	ROM	17.4.79	3		Onesti	19 May

Mark	Name		Nat	Born	Date
16.44	Cleopatra	Borel	TRI		31 May
16.42	Teresa	Machado	POR	22.7.69	22 Jul
16.30	Dana	Lawson	USA	13.7.79	12 May
16.18	Aleksandra	Kopaneva	RUS	80	14 Jun
16.13	Linda	Nestorsson	SWE	2.12.75	14 Apr
16.05	Ashley	Dorsey	USA	29.1.80	7 Apr
16.02	Bianca	Grosser	GER	14.4.80	2 Jun
15.92	Margarita	Ramos	ESP	26.6.66	3 Mar
15.90	Bambi	Carson	USA	10.8.79	21 Apr
15.88	Liz	Toman	CAN	17.4.78	7 Apr
15.80	Éva	Kürti	HUN	21.7.76	9 Jun

JUNIORS

See main list for top 8 juniors. 11 performances by 3 women to 17.60. Additional mark and further juniors:

Name	Mark	Pos	Meet	Venue	Date	Mark	Pos	Meet	Venue	Date
Zhang X	18.32	3		Shanghai	6 May	17.80	9	NG	Guangzhou	21 Nov
	18.04	1	Asi-J	BS Begawan	21 Jul	17.74	4		Jinan	13 May
	17.88	8	NC	Chengdu	1 Jul	17.67	Q	NG	Guangzhou	19 Nov
Zhang Ying	17.60	12	NG	Guangzhou	21 Nov					
Yang Dehui	17.64	7		Jinan	12 May					

Mark	Name		Nat	Born	Pos	Meet	Venue	Date
16.43i	Laura	Gerraughty	USA	29.7.83	1		Durham	19 Jan
16.38	Jill	Camarena	USA	2.8.82	3	Pac10	Berkeley	19 May
16.34	Karen	Freberg	USA	30.9.82	1		Santa Maria	29 Mar
16.30	Kristin	Marten	GER	23.3.83	1		Thum	20 May
16.06i	Alexis	McCall	USA	10.7.82	2	Big 10	West Lafayette	24 Feb
15.99	Melanie	Pöche	GER	21.6.82	1		Kaiserlautern	27 May
15.91	Claudia	Villeneuve	FRA	23.8.83	1		Fort-de-France	18 Mar
15.89		Zhang Changyan	CHN	14.2.84	4		Tianjin	18 May
15.62	Chiara	Rosa	ITA	28.1.83	1		Conegliano Veneto	19 May
15.60	Elizabeth	Podominck	USA	5.12.84	3	NC-j	Richmond	17 Jun
15.59		Qin Na	CHN	.83	1		Changde	10 Aug
15.57i	Lucia	Korceková (20)	SVK	23.7.82	1	NC	Bratislava	24 Feb
15.56	Olga	Olshevskaya	RUS	5.7.82	1		Krasnodar	22 May

DISCUS

Mark	Perf	Pos	Meet	Venue	Date						
68.57		Natalya		Sadova	RUS	15.6.72	1	WCh	Edmonton		11 Aug
						65.24	66.87	66.36	68.57	67.80	67.18
	67.18	2	GPI	Athína	11 Jun	65.85	66.86	65.84	x	66.98	67.18
	66.69	1	Znam	Tula	9 Jun	64.82	66.69	x	x		only four
	65.42	2	Veniz	Haniá	4 Jun	63.86	63.27	65.42	x	x	63.97
	65.37	1		Lisboa (U)	16 Jun	64.88	61.48	64.38	x	65.37	63.79
	64.89	1		Rüdlingen	19 Aug	63.61	62.54	60.26	64.89	63.13	64.25
68.31		Nicoleta		Grasu	ROM	11.9.71	1	GP	Athína		11 Jun
						65.36	64.93	66.56	63.91	67.17	68.31
	67.57	1	NC-w	Bucuresti	4 Mar	64.29	67.57	x	x	x	64.45
	66.71	1	Veniz	Haniá	4 Jun	x	62.31	66.71	64.72	x	x
	66.32	1		Bucuresti	27 May	65.46	64.39	64.87	63.68	x	66.32
	66.24	3	WCh	Edmonton	11 Aug	55.70	65.34	63.74	x	66.24	65.73
	66.18	1		Rüdlingen	18 Aug	62.03	66.18	61.23	p	p	p
	66.02	1		Rethimnó	1 Jul	65.14	x	66.02	64.25	x	64.57
	65.54	1	EAA	Nice	18 Mar	64.97	60.97	63.86	63.25	62.16	65.54
	65.10	1		Snagov	9 May	?					
	64.78	2		Rüdlingen	19 Aug	62.46	64.78	62.33	63.50	63.92	x
	64.54	2		Lisboa (U)	16 Jun	61.83	62.76	x	64.54	53.51	x
	64.53	1	Franc	Ottawa	21 Jul	=61.61	60.05	64.53	x	62.50	62.38

Mark	Name		Nat	Born	Pos	Meet	Venue	Date
67.10	Ellina	Zvereva	BLR	16.11.60	2	WCh	Edmonton	11 Aug
				x 67.10 x 64.70 65.37 x				
66.36	1 GWG	Brisbane	6 Sep	61.16 65.61 x x 66.36 65.86				
65.78	Q WCh	Edmonton	9 Aug	65.78 only throw				
66.65	Irina	Yatchenko	BLR	31.10.65	1		Staiki	13 Jul
65.87A	Franka	Dietzsch	GER	22.1.68	1		Calgary	30 Jul
	not surveyed, but slightly uphill			64.55 63.33 60.35 65.87 63.05 65.87				
65.38	5 WCh	Edmonton	11 Aug	63.62 x 63.12 x 64.60 65.38				
65.64	Seilala	Sua	USA	25.2.78	1		La Jolla	31 Mar
65.11	1	Salinas	22 May	60.65 61.64 x 62.07 x 65.11				
65.52	Anastasía	Kelesídou	GRE	28.11.72	1		Pátra	22 Jul
				x 65.43 64.96 62.65 65.52 59.74				
65.50	4 WCh	Edmonton	11 Aug	61.02 65.50 62.70 63.47 62.37 65.14				
65.50	Vladimíra	Racková	CZE	15.5.67	1		Kladno	28 Jun
65.27	Kristin	Kuehl	USA	30.7.70	1	Mod R	Modesto	12 May
65.12A	Valentina	Ivanova (10)	RUS	1.5.63	1		Pietersburg	27 Jan
				60.02 65.12 59.43 62.76 x 60.12				
64.50	Suzy	Powell	USA	3.9.76	2		Salinas	22 May
	(32/11)							
64.20	Yelena	Antonova	UKR	16.6.72	1	RUS-w	Yalta	11 Feb
63.87	Melina	Robert-Michon	FRA	18.7.79	1		Miramas	13 Jun
63.75	Joanna	Wisniewska	POL	24.5.72	2		Halle	19 May
63.55	Lyudmila	Starovoytova	BLR	8.4.74			Minsk	18 May
63.47	Ekateríni	Vóggoli	GRE	30.10.70	1	NC	Athína	17 Jun
63.43	Viktoriya	Boyko	UKR	20.1.74	1		Kiev	18 May
63.42	Anja	Möllenbeck	GER	18.3.72	1		Obersuhl	3 Jun
63.25	Alison	Lever	AUS	13.10.72	1		Townsville	23 Jun
63.20	Véra	Pospísilová	CZE	19.11.78	1		Kladno	10 Jun
	(20)							
63.18	Stilianí	Tsikoúna	GRE	19.10.72	1		Iráklio	14 Jul
63.01	Teresa	Machado	POR	22.7.69	3		Lisboa (U)	16 Jun
62.95	Aretí	Abatzí	GRE	14.5.74	2		Pátra	22 Jul
62.48	Marzena	Wysocka	POL	17.2.69	1		Wroclaw	27 May
62.35	Natalya	Ampleyeva	RUS	25.9.72	1		Adler	10 Feb
62.34		Song Aimin	CHN	15.3.78	1	NG	Guangzhou	18 Nov
62.21		Ma Shuli	CHN	20.1.78	2	NG	Guangzhou	18 Nov
62.20		Luan Zhili	CHN	6.1.73	3	NG	Guangzhou	18 Nov
62.01	Oksana	Yesipchuk	RUS	13.12.76	1		Moskva	18 May
61.90		Li Qiumei	CHN	20.4.74	Q	WCh	Edmonton	9 Aug
	(30)							
61.81		Xiao Yanling	CHN	27.3.68	4	NG	Guangzhou	18 Nov
61.77		Li Yanfeng	CHN	15.5.79	5	NG	Guangzhou	18 Nov
61.64	Aretha	Hill	USA	14.8.76	3	Mod R	Modesto	12 May
61.54	Beatrice	Faumuiná	NZL	23.10.74	1		Papakura	9 Nov
61.44	Olga	Chernyavskaya	RUS	17.9.63	2		Adler	10 Feb
60.75	Lacramioara	Ionescu	ROM	3.4.79	2		Snagov	9 May
60.40	Agnese	Maffeis	ITA	9.3.65	1		Clusone	22 Jul
60.32	Katja	Schreiber	GER	30.6.78	1	NCAA	Eugene	30 May
60.09		Qin Lei	CHN	16.10.76	6	NG	Guangzhou	18 Nov
60.03	Lyudmila	Rublevskaya	RUS	7.6.77	1		Krasnodar	1 Jul
	(40)							
59.97		Xu Shaoyang	CHN-J	9.2.83	7	NG	Guangzhou	18 Nov
59.89		Liu Yanxia	CHN	3.4.81	8	NG	Guangzhou	18 Nov
59.88	Natalya	Fokina	UKR-J	7.7.82	2		Kiev	18 May
59.76	Tina	McDonald	CAN	12.1.76	1		Toronto	3 May
59.68	Elisângela	Adriano	BRA	27.7.72	1		Americana	16 Jun
59.22	María	Kolétsou	GRE	14.6.77	3	NC	Athína	17 Jun
59.18	Alice	Matejková	ESP	11.1.69	1		Orense	13 Jun
59.18	Anna	Söderberg	SWE	11.6.73	1	vFIN	Göteborg	1 Sep
59.14	Neelam Jaswant	Singh	IND	8.1.71	1		Bangalore	23 Jun
59.10	Shelley	Drew/Newman	GBR	8.8.73	1	vFRA	Ashford	11 Aug
	(50)							
59.06	Olga	Goncharenko	BLR	13.7.81			Brest	21 Jul
58.98		Chang Xinhong	CHN	24.3.74	2		Ningbo	28 Apr
58.98	Philippa	Roles	GBR	1.3.78	1		Loughborough	20 May
58.70	Jacqueline	Goormachtigh	NED	28.2.70	5	MSR	Walnut	22 Apr
58.66	Corrie	de Bruin	NED	26.10.76	1		Arnhem	4 Jul
58.65		Ma Xuejun	CHN-J	26.3.85	9	NG	Guangzhou	18 Nov
58.64	Roberta	Collins	USA	31.7.77	1		Kent	7 Apr
58.60	Adina	Mocanu	ROM	4.3.80	3		Bucuresti	26 May
58.57	Wioletta	Potepa	POL	14.12.80	2	Sidlo	Sopot	25 May

Mark		Name	Nat	Born	Pos	Meet	Venue	Date
58.40	Ilona	Zakharchenko	UKR	16.6.67	1		Kiev	8 Jun
	(60)							
58.35		Cao Qi	CHN	15.1.74	6	NC	Chengdu	29 Jun
58.30	Elizna	Naude	RSA	14.9.78	1		Port Elizabeth	28 Apr
58.25	Ileana	Brîndusoiu	ROM	9.5.79	2	EU23	Amsterdam	15 Jul
58.12	Seema	Antil	IND-J	27.7.83	2		Bangalore	23 Jun
58.01		Tao Hongbo	CHN	20.9.79	3		Tianjin	19 May
57.99	Tiina	Kankanpää	FIN	16.8.76	1		Seinäjoki	19 Jul
57.93	Monique	Nacsa	AUS	26.10.76	1		Sydney	15 May
57.93	Harwant	Kaur	IND	5.7.80	2	NC	Chennai	19 Oct
57.80	Gheorghita	Bosneaga	ROM	15.7.81	4		Snagov	9 May
57.76	Gia	Lewis	USA	1.4.79	1		Champaign	11 May
	(70)							
57.72	Éva	Kürti	HUN	21.7.76	3		Budapest	1 Jul
57.55		Yu Xin	CHN	23.2.77	5		Jinan	13 May
57.20	Rita	Lora	ESP	23.3.73	1		Málaga	28 Jul
57.19	Jana	Tucholke	GER	20.5.81	1		Wiesbaden	13 May
57.16		Chou Ying	CHN-J	26.12.83	Q	NC	Chengdu	28 Jun
57.13	Christy	Thiel	AUS	30.4.74	1		Sydney	24 Feb
56.98	Teri	Tunks	USA	30.10.75	1	Towns	Athens, GA	6 Apr
56.98	Krista	Keir	USA	19.12.79	2		Indianapolis	28 Jul
56.90	Yania	Ferrales	CUB	28.7.77	1		Las Tunas	17 Mar
56.89		Hu Honglian	CHN	20.2.73	4		Ningbo	28 Apr
	(80)							
56.44	Monia	Kari	TUN	14.4.71	3	MedG	Tunis	11 Sep
56.39	Irache	Quintanal	ESP	18.9.78	1		Barcelona	28 Apr
56.38	Lieja	Koeman	NED	10.3.76	6	MSR	Walnut	22 Apr
56.32		Min Chungfeng	CHN	17.3.69	5		Tianjin	19 May
56.22	Liz	Toman	CAN	17.4.78	2	NCAA	Eugene	30 May
56.22	Sugan	Kumari Yadav	IND	77	2		Trivandrum	4 Jun
56.18	Giorgia	Baratella	ITA	8.1.75	1		Brescia	17 Jun
56.15	Luz Dary	Castro	COL	30.5.78	1		Medellín	28 Apr
56.02	Chaniqua	Ross	USA	24.5.80	1		Los Angeles	5 May
56.02		Wang Qiuju	CHN	12.10.75	Q	NC	Chengdu	28 Jun
	(90)							
55.99	Anita	Hietalahti	FIN	17.2.77	2	v SWE	Göteborg	1 Sep
55.94	Vera	Begic	CRO-J	17.3.82	1	ECp-2B	Nicosia	23 Jun
55.87	Ilona	Rutjes	NED	28.5.80	1		Glendale	7 Apr
55.72	Annika	Larsson	SWE	10.7.70	1		Gävle	21 Jul
55.69		Sun Yali	CHN	6.1.78	7		Tianjin	19 May
55.68	Amélie	Perrin	FRA	30.3.80	5		Salon-de-Provence	25 May
55.58		Qiu Qiaoping	CHN	31.1.71	Q	NC	Chengdu	28 Jun
55.56	Diane	Slinden	USA	7.4.80	6		La Jolla	31 Mar
55.56	Deshaya	Williams	USA	8.7.80	3		Indianapolis	23 Jul
55.54	Summer	Pierson	USA	3.9.78	1		Palo Alto	25 Mar
	(100)							

Mark		Name	Nat	Born	Date
55.52	Jamine	Moton	USA	14.12.78	27 Apr
55.51	Katja	Kròl	GER	5.2.80	29 Jul
55.43	Isabelle	Devaluez	FRA	17.3.66	13 Jun
55.40		Sun Tanfeng	CHN-J	26.8.82	19 May
55.36		Wang Pingping	CHN	27.2.79	29 Jul
55.33		Cao Liping	CHN	8.11.78	28 Apr
55.30		Cui Limin	CHN	22.5.79	19 May
55.28	Mayoko	Nakanishi	JPN	17.1.75	23 May
55.27	Veerle	Blondeel	BEL	14.1.75	15 Jul
55.26	Darya	Pishchalnikova	RUS-J	19.7.85	28 Jun
55.18	Yelena	Dementiy	UKR	6.3.69	3 Jul
55.15	Grete	Etholm	NOR	25.1.76	1 Jul
55.09	Agnès	Teppe	FRA	4.5.68	20 Jun
55.08	Ina	Reiber	GER	12.3.80	29 Jul
55.03	Bambi	Carson	USA	10.8.79	30 May
54.93		Gong Yaqin	CHN	20.7.79	28 Jun
54.81	Claire	Smithson	GBR-J	3.8.83	1 Jul
54.80	Debbie	Pickersgill	AUS	23.3.80	14 Dec
54.68	Aubrey	Schmitt	USA	22.11.77	12 May
54.68	Dace	Ruskule	LAT	20.9.81	17 Jun
54.65		Zhang Lulu	CHN-J	4.10.83	19 May
54.60		Luo Xiaorong	CHN-J	4.11.83	18 May
54.57		Jing Xin	CHN-J	9.4.85	18 May
54.51	Yelena	Lebusova	RUS	26.6.81	23 Jun
54.49	Olga	Chernogorova	BLR-J	30.1.82	20 Jul
54.42	Eha	Rünne	EST	25.5.63	28 Aug
54.32	Amalía	Láboura	GRE	16.3.68	27 May
54.30	Katalin	Divós ¶	HUN	11.5.74	3 Mar
54.30	Renata	Gustaityté	LTU	7.4.74	10 May
54.30	Marija	Kurtovic	CRO-J	7.1.82	20 Jul
54.25	Jill	Pedretti	USA	30.9.80	14 Apr
54.16	Yuneidis	Bonne	CUB	7.3.78	16 Feb
54.13	Olga	Olshevskaya	RUS-J	5.7.82	28 Jun
54.12	Mirjam	Burchard	GER	1.2.72	3 Jun
54.06	Yuka	Murofushi	JPN	11.2.77	7 Apr
54.04	Nadine	Beckel	GER	27.5.77	27 May
54.00	Julia	Bremser	GER-J	27.5.82	20 May
53.92	Nicole	Chimko	CAN	31.7.78	4 May
53.88	Hiba Mecilhi	Abou Zaghari	EGY		18 Apr
53.85		Liu Yinpeng	CHN-J	22.2.87?	18 May
53.82		Huang Qun	CHN	12.4.79	28 Apr
53.69	Niina	Kelo	FIN	26.3.80	11 Jun
53.67	Rie	Ikeda	JPN	2.12.78	22 Apr
53.67		Jing Junyan	CHN-J	4.1.83	18 May
	(144)				

JUNIORS

See main list for top 6 juniors. 11 performances by 5 women to 57.00. Additional mark and further juniors:

Xu S	59.69	4	NC	Chengdu	29 Jun	58.03	1	Asi-J	BS Begawan	21 Jul
	57.08	Q	NC	Chengdu	28 Jun					

Mark	Name		Nat	Born	Pos	Meet	Venue	Date	
Fokina	57.39	1	Koncha Zaspa	13 May					
Ma Xuejen	57.09	Q NC	Chengdu	28 Jun					
Antil	57.91	2	Budapest	1 Jul					
55.40		Sun Tanfeng	CHN	26.8.82	9		Tianjin	19 May	
55.26	Darya	Pishchalnikova	RUS	19.7.85	1	NC-j	Kazan	28 Jun	
54.81	Claire	Smithson	GBR	3.8.83	1	NC-j	Bedford	1 Jul	
54.65		Zhang Lulu	CHN	4.10.83	13		Tianjin	19 May	
54.60		Luo Xiaorong	CHN	4.11.83	14		Tianjin	18 May	
54.57		Jing Xin	CHN	9.4.85	15		Tianjin	18 May	
54.49	Olga	Chernogorova	BLR	30.1.82	3	EJ	Grosseto	20 Jul	
54.30	Marija	Kurtovic	CRO	7.1.82	4	EJ	Grosseto	20 Jul	
54.13	Olga	Olshevskaya	RUS	5.7.82	2	NC-j	Kazan	28 Jun	
54.00	Julia	Bremser	GER	27.5.82	3		Halle	20 May	
53.85		Liu Yinpeng	CHN	22.2.87?	16		Tianjin	18 May	
53.67		Jing Junyan	CHN	4.1.83	17		Tianjin	18 May	
53.39	Sabine	Rumpf	GER	18.3.83	1		Wiesbaden	14 Aug	
53.12	Emma	Carpenter (20)	GBR	16.5.82	1		Exeter	1 Sep	

HAMMER

Mark	Name		Nat	Born	Pos	Meet	Venue	Date	
73.62	Olga	Kuzenkova	RUS	4.10.70	1	NC-w	Adler	24 Feb	
				70.60	x	73.20	73.62	p	p
73.40	1 NC	Tula	13 Jul	71.58	71.57	71.59	73.40	70.55	?
71.57	1	Doha	18 May	x	67.75	69.76	71.57	69.48	x
71.30	1 EAA	Nice	17 Mar	70.09	70.78	69.25	70.79	71.30	x
70.99	1	Rüdlingen	18 Aug	x	70.99	68.99	x	x	p
70.79	1	Adler	17 Feb	67.78	69.78	70.79	x	p	p
70.61	2 WCh	Edmonton	7 Aug	70.61	69.94	x	x	x	69.78
70.45	1	Nürnberg	7 Jun	x	67,85	67,54	69.31	x	70.45
70.43	Q WCh	Edmonton	6 Aug	70.43		only throw			
70.14	2 GP	Sevilla	8 Jun	68.50	66.81	70.14	69.87	4 only	
70.12	1	Clermont-Ferrand	15 Jun	68.56	68.96	70.12	70.04	69.03	x
69.98	2 GWG	Brisbane	4 Sep	67.51	69.98	x	x	x	x
69.19	1 GPII	Helsinki	14 Jun	69.19	x	x	66.37	4 only	
69.10	1	Adler	10 Feb	x	69.10	64.48	x	p	p
68.91	1 GPII	Gateshead	19 Aug	68.82	x	68.91	x	x	x
71.71	Kamila	Skolimowska	POL-J	4.11.82	1	GPF	Melbourne	9 Sep	
				67.55	67.36	x	66.75	70.07	71.71
70.31	1 GWG	Brisbane	4 Sep	66.39	70.31	x	x	p	p
70.79	Katalin	Divós ¶	HUN	11.5.74	2	GP	Doha	18 May	
				69.27	x	66.01	70.79	x	65.51
69.11	1	Szombathely	10 May		only best throw measured				
70.65	Yipsi	Moreno	CUB	19.11.80	1	WCh	Edmonton	7 Aug	
				69.55	69.34	70.65	61.45	68.84	66.95
70.41	2	Nürnberg	7 Jun	67.59	x	x	x	69.44	70.41
70.34	1	Rhede	13 Jul	68.24	69.01	70.34	69.31	69.74	x
70.62	Dawn	Ellerbe	USA	3.4.74	1	Penn R	Philadelphia	28 Apr	
				70.62	67.18	68.58	65.52	69.04	67.32
69.08	1 NC	Eugene	22 Jun	65.12	68.91	67.12	69.08	66.69	67.42
70.28	Manuela	Montebrun	FRA	13.11.79	1	GP II	Sevilla	8 Jun	
				70.28	67.63	69.37	x	4 only	
69.80	3 GWG	Brisbane	4 Sep	67.99	67.03	69.55	69.80	67.67	x
69.78	1 WUG	Beijing	30 Aug	67.50	66.45	69.78	68.66	69.25	68.73
70.19	Bronwyn	Eagles	AUS	23.8.80	1		Calgary	30 Jul	
not surveyed		but slightly uphill		66.02	65.07	67.75	68.20	70.19	69.49
69.24	1	Calgary	26 Jul	65.66	65.51	69.24	66.38	64.85	67.39
68.87	3 WCh	Edmonton	7 Aug	67.62	68.87	64.64	63.81	68.17	67.43
69.63	Mia	Strömmer	FIN	26.2.74	1		Potchefstroom	24 Mar	
				69.63	x	x	p	p	p
68.94	Olga	Tsander	BLR	18.5.76	3	GP II	Sevilla	8 Jun	
				65.96	68.94	66.69	x	4 only	
	(32/9)								
68.50	Martina	Danisová (10)	SVK-J	21.3.83	1		Kladno	16 Jun	
68.50	Ester	Balassini	ITA	20.10.77	1		Ancona	15 Jul	
68.15	Lorraine	Shaw	GBR	2.4.68	3	EAA	Nice	17 Mar	
68.09	Kirsten	Münchow	GER	21.1.77	2	ECp-S	Bremen	24 Jun	
68.07	Susanne	Keil	GER	18.5.78	1		Baunatal	23 Jun	
67.98	Agnieszka	Pogroszewska	POL	20.2.77	2		Poznan	8 Jun	
67.97	Lyudmila	Gubkina	BLR	13.8.73	3	WUG	Beijing	30 Aug	
67.46	Lisa	Misipeka	ASA	3.1.75	2		Rüdlingen	18 Aug	
67.00	Irina	Sekachova	UKR	21.7.76	1		Yalta	11 Feb	

Mark	Name		Nat	Born	Pos	Meet	Venue	Date
66.97		Gu Yuan	CHN-J	9.5.82	1	NG	Guangzhou	22 Nov
66.88	Anna	Norgren	USA	19.12.74	1		Knoxville	13 Apr
	(20)							
66.85	Florence	Ezeh	FRA	29.12.77	1	NCAA	Eugene	2 Jun
66.58	Marina	Grin	BLR	23.1.76	1		Staiki	30 Jun
66.49	Ivana	Brkljacic	CRO-J	25.1.83	3	GP II	Zagreb	2 Jul
66.40	Natalya	Kunitskaya	UKR	17.8.72	1		Kiev	17 May
66.31	Sini	Pöyry	FIN	3.2.80	1		Uppsala	12 Jun
66.30		Zhang Wenxiu	CHN-J	11.2.83	1		Jinan	12 May
66.25	Melissa	Price	USA	5.9.79	3	NC	Eugene	22 Jun
66.20	Lucie	Vrbenská	CZE	12.5.77	1		Pardubice	22 Aug
66.16		Zhao Wei	CHN	27.1.79	1		Shanghai	7 May
66.15		Liu Yinghui	CHN	29.6.79	2	NG	Guangzhou	22 Nov
	(30)							
66.12	Jesseca	Cross	USA	10.5.75	3	Penn R	Philadelphia	28 Apr
65.91	Tasha	Williams	NZL	31.7.73	1	NC	Hastings	24 Feb
65.91	Markéta	Hajdu	CZE	9.9.74	1		Praha	2 Jun
65.86	Marina	Rezanova	UKR	28.8.74	1		Kiev	8 Jun
65.83	Evdokía	Tsámoglou	GRE	15.12.78	1		Thessaloníki	27 May
65.81	Alla	Davydova	RUS	21.5.66	2	NC-w	Adler	24 Feb
65.67	Yunaika	Crawford	CUB-J	2.11.82	1	NC-j	Santiago de Cuba	7 Jul
65.54	Christina	Tolson	USA	16.1.78	2	NCAA	Eugene	2 Jun
65.46	Yelena	Matoshko	BLR-J	23.6.82	2		Staiki	30 Jun
65.28	Norbi	Balantén	CUB	24.6.72	1		Las Tunas	16 Mar
	(40)							
65.21		Yang Meiping	CHN-J	23.10.85	1	Asi-J	B.S. Begawan	19 Jul
65.00	Tatyana	Gromada	BLR	30.3.81	1	NC	Brest	8 Jun
64.97	Bianca	Achilles	GER	17.4.81	1		Sythen	29 Apr
64.97	Manuela	Priemer	GER	29.11.78	5		Halle	19 May
64.91	Aldenay	Vasallo	CUB	25.2.77	2		Las Tunas	16 Mar
64.81	Karyne	DiMarco	AUS	14.3.78	4		Calgary	30 Jul
64.53	Cecilia	Nilsson	SWE	22.6.79	1		Halle	20 May
64.43	Masumi	Aya	JPN	1.1.80	1		Rifu	16 Oct
64.37	Maureen	Griffin	USA	6.10.80	4	NC	Eugene	22 Jun
64.32	Tatyana	Konstantinova	RUS	18.11.70	6	GP II	Sevilla	8 Jun
	(50)							
64.29	Julianna	Tudja	HUN	13.10.79	3	NCAA	Eugene	2 Jun
64.24	Cari	Soong	USA	11.7.81	2	MSR	Walnut	22 Apr
64.01	Leslie	Coons	USA	16.7.73	5	NC	Eugene	22 Jun
63.99	Alexándra	Papayeoryíou	GRE	17.12.80	1		Pireás	22 Apr
63.93	Bethany	Hart	USA	10.4.77	1		West Point	12 May
63.90		Li Xiaoxue	CHN	11.1.80	3	NG	Guangzhou	22 Nov
63.89	Margarita	Grechikho	BLR	15.4.81	4		Staiki	30 Jun
63.85	Yelena	Tauryanina	RUS	11.9.80	2		Moskva	18 May
63.75	Grettel	Miller-Tjiroze	JAM	6.6.75	1		Provo	7 Jul
63.64	Vânia	Silva	POR	8.6.80	4	EU23	Amsterdam	13 Jul
	(60)							
63.63		Chen Ying	CHN	4.11.75	4	NC	Chengdu	1 Jul
63.54	Clarissa	Claretti	ITA	7.10.80	2		Trento	30 May
63.51	Merja	Korpela	FIN	15.5.81	5	EU23	Amsterdam	13 Jul
63.42	Andrea	Bunjes	GER	5.2.76	1		Hesel	28 Apr
63.40	Tatyana	Dyomina	BLR	29.9.73	1		Staiki	13 Jul
63.34		Wang Xiaoyu	CHN	25.12.81	4		Jinan	12 May
63.28	Maroua Ahmed	Hussein	EGY	19.6.78	1		Cairo	2 Sep
63.26	Gulya	Khanafeyeva	RUS-J	12.6.82	1		Bryansk	3 Jul
63.16	Angela	Foster	USA	27.12.79	1		Tucson	17 Mar
63.11	Berta	Castells	ESP-J	24.1.84	1		Mataró	4 Jul
	(70)							
63.11	Virginia	Balut	ROM	3.3.81	1		Craiova	9 Sep
62.99	Kaisa	Kiintonen	FIN	18.3.80	1		Helsinki	27 May
62.99	Lyn	Sprules	GBR	11.9.75	1		London (Ha)	16 Jun
62.96	Michelle	Clayton-Boswell	USA	29.10.76	1		Conway, SC	18 May
62.91	Barbara	Németh	HUN	7.11.80	2		Szombathely	28 Apr
62.83	Olga	Klopova	UKR	19.2.80	3	NC	Kiev	2 Jul
62.72	Simone	Mathes	GER	13.3.75	5		Dortmund	9 Jun
62.68	Katie	McCoy	USA	10.4.79	2		Athens, GA	5 May
62.67	Olga	Markevich	BLR	13.10.79	Q?	NC	Brest	7 Jun
62.64	Brooke	Krueger	AUS	9.7.80	4	GP II	Melbourne	1 Mar
	(80)							
62.63	Jennifer	Joyce	CAN	25.9.80	4	Franc	Ottawa	22 Jul

Mark	Name		Nat	Born	Pos	Meet	Venue	Date
62.60	Jenny	Folz	USA	24.12.75	1		Northridge	23 Mar
62.55	Barbara	Sugár	HUN	9.10.77	1		Veszprém	20 Jun
62.52	Veronika	Ushakova	RUS	8.11.77	2		Bryansk	3 Jul
62.43	Nancy	Guillén	ESA	14.10.76	1		San Salvador	9 Jun
62.26	Jennifer	Vail	USA	16.3.78	6	MSR	Walnut	22 Apr
62.22	Irina	Martinenko	UKR	19.10.76	2		Kiev	3 May
62.20	Jukina	Dickerson	USA	7.8.81	1		Gainesville	8 Apr
62.16	Karina	Moya	ARG	28.9.73	1		Santa Fe	9 Jun
62.08	Amber	Campbell	USA	5.6.81	2		Conway, SC	18 May
	(90)							
62.03	Caroline	Wittrin	CAN	10.12.68	1		Edmonton	22 Jun
62.00	Elizabeth	Pidgeon	GBR	27.4.77	1		Varazdin	5 Jul
61.96	Mária	Hajnal	HUN	5.3.79	1		Budapest	19 May
61.93		Cui Xiaohong	CHN	10.2.80	6	NC	Chengdu	1 Jul
61.90	Sónia	Alves	POR	3.6.79	1		Quinta do Anjo	24 Mar
61.90	Monica	Torazzi	ITA	26.2.71	2	NC	Catania	7 Jul
61.80	Cristina	Buzau	ROM	12.4.76	7	ECp-S	Bremen	24 Jun
61.73	Amalia	Láboura	GRE	16.3.68	2		Pireás	22 Apr
61.56	Hardeep	Kaur	IND	.79	1		Ludhiana	21 Nov
61.46	Dolores	Pedrades	ESP	17.1.73	1		Torrevieja	14 Apr
	(100)							

Mark	Name		Nat	Born	Date
61.35	Evaggelía	Dervéni	GRE	2.5.80	29 May
61.20		Wang Dan	CHN-J	82	20 May
60.88	Aya	Suzuki	JPN	18.11.67	10 Jun
60.80	Larisa	Tarasyuk	RUS	14.6.70	5 May
60.78	Jolanta	Borowska	POL	16.1.76	8 Jun
60.64		Wei Xiaoyan	CHN-J	13.3.83	22 Nov
60.54	Betty	Heidler	GER-J	14.10.83	7 Jul
60.35	Zoe	Derham	GBR	24.11.80	10 Jun
60.34	Maria	Smolyachkova	BLR-J	10.2.85	25 May
60.13	Svetlana	Sherina	RUS	29.4.71	17 Feb
60.12	Tara	Loper	USA	12.8.77	19 May
60.04	Caroline	Fournier	MRI	7.5.75	22 Apr
60.04	Olga	Andreyeva	RUS-J	14.3.82	27 Jun
59.92	Amélie	Perrin	FRA	30.3.80	26 May
59.86	Andrea	Kéri	HUN-J	3.7.84	14 Jul
59.83	Anne Laure	Grémillet	FRA	27.9.78	2 Jun
59.81	Elena	Teloni	CYP	12.12.64	29 Jun
59.80	Natalya	Zledennaya	UKR	22.11.77	2 Jul
59.70	Asimína	Mórfi	GRE	4.5.73	22 Apr
59.69		Shang Lina	CHN-J	11.3.83	22 Nov
59.68	Alexandria	Earl-Givan	USA	25.4.70	23 Jul
59.64	Yuka	Murofushi	JPN	11.2.77	7 Apr
59.53	Alessandra	Coaccioli	ITA	11.9.75	19 Jul
59.52	Lívia	Marx	HUN	5.4.80	3 Jul
59.50	Katy	Craig	USA	18.11.80	19 May
59.49	Tina	Schäfer	GER	27.12.77	19 May
59.48	Sandrine	Gardes	FRA	13.10.75	30 May
59.44	Andrea	Thornton	USA	14.12.78	13 May
59.36	Katri	Räsänen	FIN	31.5.80	9 Jun
59.34	Erika	Melián	ARG	8.3.75	9 Jun
59.26	Wendy	Koolhaas	NED	5.1.80	28 Aug
59.24	Oksana	Menkova	BLR-J	28.3.82	21 Jul
59.10	Carol	Stevenson	CAN	15.5.81	19 May
59.08		Huang Chih-Feng	TPE	9.5.77	28 Apr
59.03	Svetlana	Kovalchuk	UKR-J	3.1.84	25 May
59.01	Inna	Sayenko	UKR-J	8.3.82	8 Jun
58.90	Marina	Lapina	RUS	81	14 Jun
58.88		Chen Juanying	CHN	13.7.74	12 May
58.86	Zubeide	Yildiz	TUR	7.9.80	9 Jun
58.81	Josiane	Soares	BRA	21.6.76	19 May
58.80	Renate	Beunder	NED	31.8.70	5 May
58.80	Maureen	Onyeagbako	USA	10.10.78	5 May
58.77	Maree	Ryabovitch	AUS	1.3.80	17 Nov
58.76		Cai Yan	CHN	26.3.80	22 Nov
58.74	Meshel	Trotter	USA	2.9.78	19 May
58.72	Aubrey	Schmitt	USA	22.11.77	2 Jun
58.69	Debby	van der Schilt	NED	24.11.81	19 May
58.66	Serene	Ross	USA	15.10.77	5 Apr
58.60	Simona	Kozmus	SLO	18.3.78	11 Jul
58.48	Nicola	Coffey	IRL	8.9.76	6 May
58.46	Eva	Danielsen	NOR	16.7.81	26 Apr
58.45		Wang Shu-Chuan	TPE	23.12.78	23 May
58.44	Rachelle	Noble	USA	12.6.75	2 Jun
58.40	Silke	Grundmann	GER-J	7.8.82	19 May
58.40	Elmarie	Knoetzen	RSA	18.7.78	3 Jul
58.40	Orsolya	Németh	HUN-J	14.4.86	21 Jul
58.31	Mhairi	Walters	GBR	19.6.81	25 Aug
58.30	Kellie	Hall	AUS	21.1.79	17 Nov
58.28	Malgorzata	Zadura	POL-J	3.10.82	7 Jun
58.26	L'Orangeril	Crawford	USA	23.12.81	26 Apr
58.26	M Eugenia	Villamizar	COL	30.8.70	13 Sep
58.24	Erin	Wibbels	USA	3.7.78	5 Apr
58.22	Jennifer	Allen	USA	29.6.81	21 Apr
58.20	Monika	Královenská	SVK-J	31.12.82	30 Jun
58.18	Brenda	Start	USA	4.5.75	19 May
58.16	Yelena	Kiselyova	RUS	78	17 Feb
58.10	Adrienne	Judie	USA	4.8.79	14 Apr
58.04	Éva	Orbán	HUN-J	29.11.84	7 Jul
57.91	Ainhoa	Cabré	ESP	21.6.79	11 Mar
57.90	Dana	Lawson	USA	13.7.79	29 Apr
57.84	Klára	Chytrá	CZE	1.10.80	18 Jun
57.83	Stilianí	Papadopoúlou	GRE-J	15.3.82	27 May
57.80	Caryn	Poliquin	USA		18 May
57.78	Abbey	Elsberry	USA	5.4.81	28 Apr
57.73	Yuliya	Rozenfeld	RUS-J	5.4.84	22 Jun
57.70	Nicole	Robertson	AUS-J	4.7.82	15 Dec
57.69		Yang Jie	CHN-J	10.12.83	7 May
57.68	Jamine	Moton	USA	14.12.78	26 Apr
57.68	Amy	Palmer	USA	20.4.75	5 May
57.68	Kate	Johnston	USA-J	29.12.83	27 May
57.62	Suzanne	Roberts	GBR	19.12.78	19 Aug
57.61	Emiljana	Ciko	ALB	1.3.78	4 Oct
57.54	Windy	Dean	USA	7.9.76	21 Apr
57.54	Chantel	Goldsberry	USA	3.4.79	9 May
57.54	Ruth	Conlon	CAN	14.6.76	16 Jun
57.53	Adeline	Dupuy	FRA	20.3.77	18 Mar
57.50	Jennifer	Dahlgren	ARG-J	27.8.84	12 Oct
57.49	Betina	Gabler	GER	22.8.71	28 Jul
57.46	Eva	Charfreitagová	SVK	9.9.79	10 Jun
57.42	Anna	Bullock	USA		12 May
57.40	Sarah	Moore	GBR	15.3.73	29 Apr
57.37	Marie	Hilmersson	SWE	14.1.81	12 Aug
57.31	Stéphanie	Falzon	FRA-J	7.1.83	21 Jul
57.30	Natalya	Zolotukhina	UKR-J	4.1.85	28 Apr
57.29	Byrony	Glass	AUS	31.3.77	17 Feb
57.27	Liliya	Razinkova	UKR-J	29.11.85	28 Mar
57.21	Anelis	Molina	CUB	25.8.81	27 May
57.18	Evelyn	Günther	GER	26.1.80	29 Jun
57.17	Eileen	O'Keefe	IRL	31.5.81	21 Apr
57.15	Yelena	Priyma	RUS-J	.83	24 May
57.13	Maria	Airaksinen	FIN	7.1.77	8 Jul
57.12	Nathalie	Thenor	CAN	26.2.81	28 Apr
57.04	Glori	Rozzini	ITA	20.12.80	19 May
57.00	Jessica	Pluth	USA	3.12.81	1 Apr
	(204)				

Annual number of women hammer throwers exceeding 60m: 1989- 2, 1990- 4, 1991- 5, 1992- 3, 1993- 4, 1994- 9, 1995- 14, 1996- 18, 1997- 28, 1998- 57, 1999- 84, 2000- 115, 2001- 113

Mark Name Nat Born Pos Meet Venue Date

JUNIORS

See main list for top 10 juniors. 18 performances by 3 women to 66.60. Additional mark and further juniors:

Skolimowska 68.48 1 Poznan 8 Jun | 67.43 Q WCh Edmonton 6 Aug
2+ 68.12 1 NC Bydgoscz 29 Jun | 67.24 1 Zagreb 2 Jul
68.05 4 WCh Edmonton 7 Aug | 66.97 2 Helsinki 14 Jun
67.95 1 Franc Ottawa 22 Jul | 66.78 2 Gdansk 14 Jul
67.84 1 Kuso Warszawa 17 Jun | 66.64 4 GP Saint-Denis 6 Jul
67.45 1 APM Hengelo 4 Jun
Danisová 67.25 1 NC-j Bans. Bystrica 30 Jun | 66.61 1 Nitra 26 Aug

61.20 Wang Dan CHN 82 1 Manila 20 May
60.64 Wei Xiaoyan CHN 13.3.83 7 NG Guangzhou 22 Nov
60.54 Betty Heidler GER 14.10.83 1 Braunschweig 7 Jul
60.34 Maria Smolyachkova BLR 10.2.85 1 Kiev 25 May
60.04 Olga Andreyeva RUS 14.3.82 1 NC-j Kazan 27 Jun
59.86 Andrea Kéri HUN 3.7.84 1 WY Debrecen 14 Jul
59.69 Shang Lina CHN 11.3.83 9 NG Guangzhou 22 Nov
59.24 Oksana Menkova BLR 28.3.82 5 EJ Grosseto 21 Jul
59.03 Svetlana Kovalchuk UKR 3.1.84 2 Kiev 25 May
59.01 Inna Sayenko (20) UKR 8.3.82 3 Kiev 8 Jun

JAVELIN

71.54 Osleidys Menéndez CUB 14.11.79 1 Réthimno 1 Jul
x 71.54 p p p 63.73
69.82 1 WUG Beijing 29 Aug 65.71 69.82 61.42 66.08 p p
69.53 1 WCh Edmonton 7 Aug 66.56 69.42* 69.53 x 65.63 66.70
68.40 1 Tartu 19 Jun 64.55 68.40 x x p 66.83
66.74 1 GPII Helsinki 14 Jun 64.08 66.74 63.93 63.31 4 only
66.38 2 Madrid 7 Jul 62.49 64.55 66.38 65.41 64.79 64.87
66.14 1 GWG Brisbane 4 Sep 63.32 66.14 63.48 64.12 63.78 p
65.76 1 GP Sevilla 8 Jun 62.26 62.16 62.83 65.76 4 only
65.33 1 Formia 14 Jul 61.19 x 62.98 65.33 x 63.10
65.09 1 Villeneuve d'Ascq 17 Jun 60.71 61.11 64.02 61.74 65.09 x
64.78 2 Santiago de Cuba 16 Mar x 59.11 64.78 x 62.37 62.27
64.39 Q WCh Edmonton 4 Aug 64.39 only throw
64.09 1 NC La Habana 24 May x 59.11 64.09 x x 63.99
66.70 Miréla Manjani GRE 21.12.76 1 NC Athína 16 Jun
62.26 63.85 63.72 66.70 p p
65.78 2 WCh Edmonton 7 Aug 64.69 63.80 x x 65.78 62.68
65.05 1 ECp-1 Vaasa 23 Jun 65.05 64.71 63.07 x 4 only
66.54 Sonia Bisset CUB 1.4.71 1 Madrid 7 Jul
62.32 62.09 63.79 66.54 x 63.06
64.94 3 Tartu 19 Jun 61.04 60.51 61.66 61.55 58.60 64.94
64.69 3 WCh Edmonton 7 Aug 63.14 x 57.77 61.32 64.69 x
64.01 2 Villeneuve d'Ascq 17 Jun x 59.25 59.16 x 64.01 x
66.09 Tatyana Shikolenko RUS 10.5.68 2 Sule Tartu 19 Jun
64.09 62.49 x x 63.71 66.09
64.49 2 GPII Helsinki 14 Jun 60.25 63.56 62.33 64.49 4 only
65.71 Nikola Tomecková CZE 25.6.74 Q WCh Edmonton 4 Aug
x 65.71
65.59 1 Rüdlingen 19 Aug 65.59 58.03 x 63.89 61.90 62.40
64.77 1 ECp Bremen 23 Jun 61.66 62.58 64.77 63.39 4 only
64.70 2 GWG Brisbane 4 Sep 58.73 62.22 63.95 x x 64.70
65.29 Xiomara Rivero CUB 22.11.68 1 Santiago de Cuba 17 Mar
65.29 61.79 64.46 60.30 62.24 x
65.08 Ana Mirela Termure ¶ ROM 13.1.75 1 NC Bucuresti 10 Jun
63.74 59.06 65.08 x p p
64.62 Nikolett Szabó HUN 3.3.80 1 Pátra 22 Jul
64.62 x 59.;01 58.21 x x
64.54 Yekaterina Ivakina RUS 4.12.64 1 ECCp Madrid 27 May
60.79 x 64.54 p 4 only
64.30 Claudia Coslovich ITA 26.4.72 1 Gorizia 6 May
? x 64.30 p p p
(31/10)
63.72 Steffi Nerius GER 1.7.72 1 Regensburg 16 Jun
63.13 Mikaela Ingberg FIN 29.7.74 1 Pihtipudas 1 Jul
63.05 Paula Huhtaniemi FIN 17.2.73 1 v SWE Göteborg 1 Sep
62.90 Aggelikí Tsiolakoúdi GRE 10.5.76 1 Trípoli 28 Apr
62.27 Felicia Tilea-Moldovan ROM 29.9.67 2 GP II Sevilla 8 Jun
61.56 Wei Jianhua CHN 23.3.79 Q WCh Edmonton 4 Aug
61.30 Oksana Velichko BLR 26.3.75 Q NC Brest 7 Jun

Mark	Name		Nat	Born	Pos	Meet	Venue	Date
61.15	Takako	Miyake	JPN	22.7.74	1		Mito	6 May
61.10 mx	Khristina	Georgieva	BUL	3.1.72	1		Plovdiv	30 Jun
60.89	Dörthe	Friedrich	GER	21.6.73	2	NC	Stuttgart	1 Jul
	(20)							
60.75	Monika	Mrówka	POL	6.3.79	1		Biala Podlaska	2 Jun
60.55	Taina	Kolkkala (Uppa)	FIN	24.10.76	3	v SWE	Göteborg	1 Sep
60.26	Laverne	Eve	BAH	16.6.65	1		Atlanta	18 May
60.04	Nadine	Auzeil	FRA	19.8.64	1		Grenoble	27 Oct
60.02	Oksana	Yarygina	RUS	24.12.72	2		Budapest	1 Jul
59.95		Tang Xiaoling	CHN	3.2.77	1	NG	Guangzhou	23 Nov
59.85		Chu Chunxia	CHN	28.1.78	2	NG	Guangzhou	23 Nov
59.82		Liang Lili	CHN-J	16.11.83	3	NG	Guangzhou	23 Nov
59.76		Ha Xiaoyan	CHN	30.1.72	1	NC	Chengdu	30 Jun
59.54	Barbara	Madejczyk	POL	30.9.76	1		Bialogard	29 Sep
	(30)							
59.48	Galina	Kakhova	BLR-J	26.3.82	1	Klim	Staiki	30 Jun
59.43	Marta	Míguez	ESP	3.3.73	1	NC	Valencia	21 Jul
59.14A	Sabina	Moya	COL	27.1.77	1		Cali	12 May
59.11	Evfemija	Storga	SLO	7.10.75	1		Celje	10 Jun
59.10	Claudia	Isaila	ROM	17.7.73	2		Bucuresti	27 May
59.09A	Zuleima	Araméndiz	COL	23.9.75	1		Medellín	21 Jul
58.88	Lada	Chernova	RUS	1.1.70	1		Adler	17 Feb
58.84	Nadezhda	Kobrin	UKR	21.1.72	1		Koncha-Zaspa	28 Apr
58.83	María	Álvarez	CUB	30.8.75	2		La Habana	16 Feb
58.70	Nora Aïda	Bicet	CUB	29.10.77	1		La Habana	9 Feb
	(40)							
58.53	Voisávva	Líka	GRE	70	8		Réthimno	1 Jul
58.48	Oksana	Makarova	RUS	21.7.71	1	Znam	Tula	8 Jun
58.41	Sarah	Walter	FRA	5.5.78	1		Saint-Denis	6 Jul
58.23	Ewa	Rybak	POL	22.12.74	2	NC	Bydgoszcz	30 Jun
58.19	Rita	Ramaunaskaité	LTU	22.2.70	2		Eurajoki	3 Jun
58.18	Valeriya	Zabruskova	RUS	29.7.75	2	Znam	Tula	8 Jun
58.16		Du Beibei	CHN-J	6.1.83	3	NC	Chengdu	30 Jun
58.07		Li Lei	CHN	4.5.74	3		Jinan	13 May
58.05	Alina	Serdyuk	BLR	22.1.75	2		Staiki	30 Jun
57.98	Monika	Aava	EST	19.6.79	5	Sule	Tartu	19 Jun
	(50)							
57.82		Ma Ning	CHN-J	4.11.83	Q	NC	Chengdu	28 Jun
57.78	Mercedes	Chilla	ESP	19.1.80	2	EU23	Amsterdam	12 Jul
57.75		Liu Jingqing	CHN	18.3.74	2		Tianjin	18 May
57.72		Yi Chunmei	CHN-J	15.3.83	5	NC	Chengdu	30 Jun
57.22	Kim	Kreiner	USA	26.7.77	2		Atlanta	18 May
57.17	Harumi	Yamamoto	JPN	8.5.74	2	NC	Tokyo	8 Jun
57.00	Kirsi	Ahonen	FIN	8.4.76	2		Vaasa	15 Jul
56.93		Zhang Li	CHN	19.10.78	7	NG	Guangzhou	23 Nov
56.83	Christina	Obergföll	GER	22.8.81	1		Ettlingen	27 May
56.82	Liliya	Titarenko	UKR	17.2.78	1		Kiev	17 May
	(60)							
56.81	Erica	Wheeler	USA	28.11.67	1		Indianapolis	22 Jul
56.72	Genowefa	Patla	POL	17.10.62	3		Biala Podlaska	2 Jun
56.60		Chang Jung-yeon	KOR	6.4.77	1		Sokcho	19 Apr
56.55	Annika	Petersson	SWE	10.1.79	1		Alingsås	5 Aug
56.45		Xu Xin	CHN-J	30.8.87	8	NG	Guangzhou	23 Nov
56.32	Izabela	Wojczakowska	POL	24.3.74	4	NC	Bydgoszcz	30 Jun
56.30	Tatyana	Lyakhovich	UKR	20.5.79	2		Kiev	17 May
56.20	Aïda	Sellam	TUN	13.9.77	1		Tunis	3 Jun
56.20	Constanta	Iancu	ROM	12.9.76	3	NC	Bucuresti	10 Jun
56.19	Heli	Rantanen	FIN	26.2.70	4		Vaasa	15 Jul
	(70)							
56.08	Yanuris	La Montaña	CUB	29.8.75	6		Santiago de Cuba	17 Mar
56.08		Geng Aihua	CHN-J	29.6.83	9	NG	Guangzhou	23 Nov
55.95	Laura	Radu	ROM	7.12.80	2	NC-w	Bucuresti	4 Mar
55.85	Karen	Martin	GBR	24.11.74	1		Derby	29 Apr
55.85	Yayoi	Shibano	JPN	10.3.75	3	NC	Tokyo	8 Jun
55.78	Jana	Woytowska	GER	7.8.77	2		Rheinau-Freistett	8 Jul
55.68	Tiziana	Rocco	ITA	2.12.78	1		Salerno	30 Jun
55.54	Natalya	Shimchuk	BLR	1.10.81	1		Schwechat	3 Jun
55.40	Goldie	Sayers	GBR-J	16.7.82	2	EJ	Grosseto	22 Jul
55.38	Kazuyo	Komasa	JPN	21.6.79	1		Kumatori	24 Mar
	(80)							

Mark		Name	Nat	Born	Pos	Meet	Venue	Date
55.38		Park Ho-hyun	KOR	21.3.78	2	NG	Chunan	12 Oct
55.17	Natalya	Davydova	RUS	.78	Q	NC	Tula	15 Jul
55.14		Lee Young-sun	KOR	21.2.74	2	NC	Seoul	12 Jun
55.11	Zsuzsanna	Füredi	HUN	26.9.71	1		Budapest	13 Jun
55.05	Anna	Slastina	UKR	4.9.77	4		Kiev	25 May
55.05	Åsa	Lindberg	FIN	12.4.79	1		Pihtipudas	28 Jun
55.02	Isel	López	CUB	11.7.70	4		La Habana	16 Feb
54.98	Zahra	Bani	ITA	31.12.79	2	NC	Catania	8 Jul
54.98	Kathryn	Mitchell	AUS-J	10.7.82	1		Ballarat	7 Dec
54.94	Elisabetta (90)	Marin	ITA	5.11.77	1		Cagliari	12 May
54.92	Stephanie	Hessler	GER-J	16.3.83	1		Halle	19 May
54.89	Dana	Lehmann	GER	1.7.79	4	NC	Stuttgart	1 Jul
54.80	Candy	Mitchell	USA	17.3.77	1		Raleigh	31 Mar
54.80	Buaban	Phamang	THA-J	82?	1	SEAG	Kuala Lumpur	13 Sep
54.72	Jana	Ladewig	GER	16.9.81	5	NC	Stuttgart	1 Jul
54.72	Serene	Ross	USA	15.10.77	3		Indianapolis	22 Jul
54.68	Maria	Yakovenko	RUS-J	6.1.82	1	NC-23	Cheboksary	15 Jun
54.62	Yuko	Kojima	JPN	20.11.73	3		Kobe	22 Apr
54.58	Ann	Crouse	USA	6.4.76	4c1		Indianapolis	22 Jul
54.56	Lyudmila (100)	Gamanyuk	UKR	11.10.77	2		Yalta	11 Feb

Mark		Name	Nat	Born	Date
54.55	Bina	Ramesh	FRA	19.8.79	19 Jun
54.51	Vigdís	Gudjónsdóttir	ISL	27.6.75	24 Jun
54.49	Lindy	Leveaux	SEY	14.11.79	12 May
54.49	Kelly	Morgan	GBR	17.6.80	14 Jul
54.46	Ilze	Gribule	LAT-J	25.1.84	26 May
54.43	Silvia	Cruz	POR	29.12.80	21 Jul
54.34		Zhang Guirong	CHN	78	18 May
54.31	Andrea	Kvetová	CZE-J	27.2.84	12 May
54.27	Andrea	Gránicz	HUN	5.7.79	25 Jul
54.25	Lynda	Blutreich	USA	13.12.71	31 Mar
54.23		Yang Lina	CHN-J	6.3.83	28 Jun
54.18	Stephanie	Ulmer	USA-J	15.10.82	5 May
54.17	Xénia	Frajka	HUN-J	24.1.82	25 Jul
54.14	Beatrice	Mau-Repnak	GER	20.2.71	26 Aug
54.12	Indre	Jakubaityte	LTU	24.10.76	15 Sep
54.06	Inga	Stasiulionyte	LTU	29.6.81	12 Jul
53.88	Rosemary	Hooper	AUS	4.8.78	25 Mar
53.86	Margaret	Simpson	GHA-J	2.8.82	13 May
53.78		Wang Yan	CHN	4.10.75	13 May

Mark		Name	Nat	Born	Date
53.74	Geralyn	Amandoron	PHI	18.10.78	18 May
53.73	Jarmila	Klimesová	CZE	9.2.81	12 Jul
53.71	Marion	Bonaudo	FRA-J	12.9.82	22 Jul
53.67	Cecilia	McIntosh	AUS	21.6.79	31 Mar
53.55	Oksana	Gromova	RUS	23.9.80	15 Jun
53.50		He Huaying	CHN	4.7.80	21 Apr
53.50	Kristina	Klyshevskaya	UKR	17.12.74	13 May
53.44	Barbara	Vontein	GER	7.6.78	19 May
53.42	Inge	Jorgensen	USA	6.10.80	12 May
53.41	Katharina	von Loga	GER	4.9.81	27 May
53.23	Kitty	van Haperen	NED	20.4.76	17 Jun
53.20 ?	Anna	Davydova	RUS	.78	31 May
53.10	Kirsty	Morrison	GBR	28.10.75	18 Apr
53.10	Yelena	Makarova	RUS	21.12.81	15 Jun
53.10	Anne Maheshi	De Silva	SRI	15.11.77	30 Aug
53.09		Song Ruiling	CHN	1.11.66	13 May
53.07	Veronica	Becuzzi	ITA	8.12.71	14 Jul
53.04	Kendra	Wecker	USA-J	16.12.82	23 Apr
53.04	Sarah (138)	Malone	USA	14.9.81	12 May

JUNIORS

See main list for top 12 juniors. 10 performances by 5 women to 57.35. Additional mark and further juniors:

Liang Lili	59.79	1		Jinan	13 May	57.35	2	Zhongshan	21 Apr
	58.45	2	NC	Chengdu	30 Jun				
Du Beibei	58.08	2		Jinan	13 May	57.83	5	NG Guangzhou	23 Nov

Mark		Name	Nat	Born	Pos	Meet	Venue	Date
54.46	Ilze	Gribule	LAT	25.1.84	1		Riga	26 May
54.31	Andrea	Kvetová	CZE	27.2.84	1		Praha	12 May
54.23		Yang Lina	CHN	6.3.83	Q	NC	Chengdu	28 Jun
54.18	Stephanie	Ulmer	USA	15.10.82	1		Ellensburg	5 May
54.17	Xénia	Frajka	HUN	24.1.82	3	NC	Nyíregyháza	25 Jul
53.86	Margaret	Simpson	GHA	2.8.82	1H		Desenzano del Garza	13 May
53.71	Marion	Bonaudo	FRA	12.9.82	3	EJ	Grosseto	22 Jul
53.04	Kendra	Wecker (20)	USA	16.12.82	1		Marysville	23 Apr

HEPTATHLON

Mark		Name	Nat	Born	Pos	Meet	Venue	Date
6736	Eunice	Barber	FRA	17.11.74	1		Götzis	27 May
	13.17/0.0 1.88 12.61 24.23/0.5			6.81/0.2		48.43	2:10.55	
6694	Yelena	Prokhorova	RUS	16.4.78	1	WCh	Edmonton	5 Aug
	13.77/0.5 1.88 13.15 23.73			6.61/1.7		50.73	2:11.53	
6576		Prokhorova			2		Götzis	27 May
	13.74/0.0 1.82 13.16 23.80/0.5			6.59/0.0		44.05	2:05.00	
6551	Natalya	Roshchupkina	RUS	13.1.78	3		Götzis	27 May
	14.06/-1.0 1.82 14.64 23.27/0.5			6.16/0.0		45.65	2:06.67	
6539	Natalya	Sazanovich	BLR	15.8.73	2	WCh	Edmonton	5 Aug
	13.29/0.5 1.76 15.90 23.87			6.50/0.5		46.72	2:20.87	
6528	Irina	Belova	RUS	27.3.68	4		Götzis	27 May
	13.49/0.0 1.76 13.76 23.57/-0.1			6.50/-2.9		39.48	2:02.06	
6472	Shelia	Burrell	USA	15.1.72	3	WCh	Edmonton	5 Aug
	13.05/0.5 1.67 12.87 22.92			6.45/0.4		48.74	2:14.24	
6454		Burrell			1		Talence	16 Sep
	13.06/0.9 1.67 13.24 23.25/1.2			6.45w/2.5		48.31	2:14.09	

Mark		Name	Nat	Born	Pos	Meet	Venue	Date
6433		Roshchupkina			1		Ratingen	17 Jun
	13.81/1.4 1.80 14.96 22.84w/2.6 5.82/-0.2 44.16 2:10.66							
6402		Sazanovich			5		Götzis	27 May
	13.28/0.0 1.73 15.71 24.02/0.5 6.56/0.7 43.27 2:23.03							
6373		Roshchupkina			1	GWG	Brisbane	5 Sep
	13.98/-0.1 1.77 14.35 23.49/0.9 6.16/-0.8 45.25 2:11.93							
6365	Karin	Ertl	GER	23.6.74	2		Ratingen	17 Jun
	13.59/1.4 1.83 14.34 24.45w/2.6 6.36/-0.1 44.16 2:18.19							
6354		Prokhorova			2		Talence	16 Sep
	13.64/0.9 1.85 13.16 24.63/1.2 6.13/1.3 46.88 2:12.12							
6352		Prokhorova			2	GWG	Brisbane	6 Sep
	13.79/-0.1 1.80 12.62 24.65/0.9 6.34/-0.6 49.31 2:11.52							
6323		Sazanovich			3	GWG	Brisbane	7 Sep
	13.44/-0.1 1.80 14.77 24.43/0.9 6.33/0.9 44.97 2:22.85							
6315		Belova			3		Ratingen	17 Jun
	13.44/1.4 1.74 13.62 23.98w/2.6 5.89/0.0 42.52 2:03.01							
6294		Roshchupkina			4	WCh	Edmonton	6 Aug
	14.12/0.5 1.79 14.74 23.41 6.02/1.7 44.04 2:15.56							
6283		Ertl			5	WCh	Edmonton	6 Aug
	13.56/0.5 1.82 13.83 24.91 6.28/1.6 45.89 2:18.54							
6279	Liga	Klavina	LAT	27.1.80	1	EU23	Amsterdam	15 Jul
	14.31/-1.0 1.93 14.82 24.45/0.6 6.50/0.5 39.84 2:26.22							
6275	DeDee	Nathan	USA	20.4.68	4	GWG	Brisbane	5 Sep
	13.50/-0.1 1.74 14.59 24.54/0.9 6.32/-1.2 44.67 2:17.79							
6270w	Svetlana	Sokolova (10)	RUS	9.1.81	1	ECp	Arles	1 Jul
	13.64/0.8 1.72 14.85 23.62w/2.7 6.00W/4.6 42.20 2:12.20							
6263		Shen Shengfei	CHN	21.1.81	1	NG	Guangzhou	18 Nov
	13.96/-0.5 1.81 14.76 25.23/-0.5 6.35/0.7 48.91 2:23.31							
6179		Sokolova			2	EU23	Amsterdam	15 Jul
	13.64/-1.2 1.72 14.43 24.25/0.2 6.01/0.6 43.61 2:14.49							
6174w		Nathan			1	NC	Eugene	22 Jun
	13.47/1.8 1.71 14.24 24.54w/2.1 6.33W/5.1 43.41 2:19.77 legal 6120 LJ 6.16/2.0							
6172	Larisa	Netseporuk	EST	24.12.70	1	ECp-2	Kaunas	1 Jul
	13.94/0.1 1.78 13.76 25.02/1.3 6.34/0.9 46.43 2:20.10							
6159	Svetlana	Kazanina	KAZ	31.10.71	1		Desenzano del Garda	13 May
	14.70/0.3 1.79 12.94 24.80/0.3 6.16w/2.8 47.85 2:09.99							
6152		Ertl			1	NC	Vaterstetten	26 Aug
	13.72/-0.9 1.81 13.28 24.37/1.1 6.30/0.6 45.59 2:26.75							
6150w	Austra	Skujyté	LTU	12.8.79	1	Big 12	College Station	17 May
	14.43w/3.6 1.78 15.28 24.98w/3.1 6.40W/4.9 43.16 2:21.25 legal 6128 LJ 6.33w/3.3							
6146	Alena	Vindyuk	RUS	31.7.79	1	NC	Tula	14 Jul
	13.98/-1.0 1.77 13.06 24.32/0.1 6.38/1.1 40.63 2:14.86							
6136		Ertl			6		Götzis	27 May
	13.77/0.0 1.79 14.04 24.57/-0.1 6.23/0.2 42.52 2:21.87							
	(30/15)							
6130	Yelena	Chernyavskaya	RUS	13.4.78	7		Götzis	27 May
	14.04/-0.4 1.82 12.58 24.85/-0.1 6.18w/2.4 41.12 2:10.37							
6092	Tatyana	Gordeyeva	RUS	3.6.73	2		Krasnodar	19 May
	14.10/0.7 1.85 13.77 25.24/0.1 6.06/1.2 38.14 2:11.48							
6082	Katja	Keller	GER	9.8.80	8		Götzis	27 May
	13.67/-1.0 1.76 12.80 24.45/-0.1 6.27/0.4 38.22 2:13.83							
6070	Jane	Jamieson	AUS	23.6.75	1	NC	Brisbane	24 Mar
	14.05/1.4 1.84 13.17 25.23/0.7 6.20/0.8 45.30 2:22.91							
6064w	Sonja	Kesselschläger	GER	20.1.78	2	ECp	Arles	1 Jul
	13.66/0.0 1.75 13.71 25.23/0.9 6.36W/8.5 40.73 2:19.03							
	(20)							
6062w	Gertrud	Bacher	ITA	28.2.71	4	ECp	Arles	1 Jul
	13.83/0.0 1.69 13.38 24.55w/3.2 6.07W/5.0 43.79 2:12.79							
6056	Maren	Freisen	GER-J	15.2.82	4		Ratingen	17 Jun
	13.46/1.4 1.74 11.93 24.33/1.5 5.95/0.2 47.17 2:17.84							
6052w	Sabine	Krieger	GER	4.9.73	5	ECp	Arles	1 Jul
	13.97/1.6 1.75 13.71 25.15/0.8 6.22W/8.0 41.35 2:14.90							
6030	Svetlana	Parfyonova	RUS	14.7.73	3	NC	Tula	14 Jul
	13.76/-1.0 1.80 12.43 23.95/0.1 6.22/1.6 30.80 2:10.80							
6026w	Michaela	Hejnová	CZE	10.4.80	6	ECp	Arles	1 Jul
	13.85/0.0 1.69 12.64 24.90/1.3 6.12W/6.5 50.00 2:18.99							
6026	Beatrice	Mau-Repnak	GER	20.2.71	2	NC	Vaterstetten	26 Aug
	14.02/-0.9 1.66 13.64 25.20/1.1 5.97/0.2 54.14 2:19.88							
6022	Carolina	Klüft	SWE-J	2.2.83	1	EJ	Grosseto	22 Jul
	14.10/-0.1 1.81 11.76 24.41/0.2 6.15/0.1 43.73 2:18.45							

Mark	Name		Nat	Born	Pos	Meet	Venue	Date
6002	Nicole	Haynes	CAN	18.9.74	11		Götzis	27 May
	14.30/-1.0 1.73 14.91 25.87/0.4 6.01/0.0 47.31 2:18.05							
6002	Tiia	Hautala	FIN	3.4.72	10	WCh	Edmonton	5 Aug
	13.79/0.5 1.79 13.32 25.52 5.94/0.0 45.40 2:18.98							
6001	Yuliya	Akulenko	UKR	3.6.77	1	ECp-1	Ried	1 Jul
	14.43/-0.1 1.72 13.35 25.01/0.5 6.48/1.5 45.18 2:21.83							
	(30)							
5983	Kristina	Porsche	GER	25.2.80	6		Ratingen	17 Jun
	14.07/0.7 1.83 13.40 24.88w/2.5 5.79/0.4 40.53 2:15.64							
5978	Izabella	Oblekowska	POL	18.2.72	8	ECp	Arles	1 Jul
	13.61/0.0 1.72 12.05 24.67w/2.6 6.30w/3.7 43.63 2:21.44							
5946	Lidia	Bashlykova	RUS	10.1.81	4	NC	Tula	14 Jul
	14.51/-1.0 1.80 13.42 24.70/0.1 5.96/1.0 41.50 2:17.50							
5933	Julie	Hollman	GBR	16.2.77	2	ECp-1	Ried	1 Jul
	14.38/0.0 1.78 12.40 24.75/0.4 6.37w/2.3 38.83 2:18.30							
5925	Gi-Gi	Miller	USA	12.1.79	2	NC	Eugene	22 Jun
	13.11w/4.0 1.74 12.49 23.65/2.0 5.98w/3.5 30.55 2:16.24							
5917		Wang Hailan	CHN	6.4.76	1	NC	Chengdu	29 Jun
	13.80/0.1 1.65 12.97 24.65w/3.2 6.15/0.0 42.44 2:17.27							
5912	Taisia	Dobrovitskaya	BLR	8.12.67	1	NC	Staiki	7 Jun
	13.74/1.6 1.67 13.33 24.48/1.1 6.13/1.7 38.84 2:17.32							
5902	Tatyana	Alisevich	BLR	22.1.69	2	NC	Staiki	7 Jun
	13.80/1.6 1.55 14.58 24.49/1.5 5.70/1.4 48.72 2:17.66							
5897	Irina	Tyukhay	RUS	14.1.67	5	NC	Tula	14 Jul
	13.73/-1.0 1.71 14.06 24.93/0.1 5.97/0.8 42.95 2:24.92							
5891		Shi Wei	CHN-J	7.7.83	3	NG	Guangzhou	18 Nov
	13.69/1.1 1.69 13.48 24.52/-0.1 6.10/0.6 41.05 2:24.05							
	(40)							
5887	Marie	Collonvillé	FRA	23.11.73	11	WCh	Edmonton	5 Aug
	13.87/0.5 1.79 11.89 25.59 5.93/-0.1 41.61 2:13.70							
5877	Mandy	Heath	AUS	14.11.80	2	EAsG	Osaka	26 May
	14.76/0.0 1.80 12.63 24.84/0.0 5.97/0.0 44.07 2:19.24							
5870	Urszula	Wlodarczyk	POL	22.12.65	7		Ratingen	17 Jun
	14.00/1.4 1.74 13.89 25.26w/2.6 5.85/0.7 42.98 2:20.97							
5862	Athína	Papasotiríou	GRE	24.5.72	3	ECp-1	Ried	1 Jul
	13.99/0.0 1.66 13.28 25.56/0.4 6.26w/2.2 44.32 2:20.73							
5862	Yuki	Nakata	JPN	10.3.77	1		Mattou	7 Oct
	13.78 1.73 11.10 25.36 6.29 46.23 2:23.42							
5859	Tia	Hellebaut	BEL	16.2.78	2	ECp-2	Kaunas	1 Jul
	14.39/0.1 1.87 12.32 26.00/1.3 5.97/1.0 42.90 2:19.78							
5846	Asimína	Vanakára	GRE	14.7.79	1	NC-23	Lárisa	29 Jul
	14.22/0.9 1.72 11.22 24.26/0.7 6.31 38.00 2:16.01							
5837		Ding Ying	CHN	28.9.76	4	NG	Guangzhou	18 Nov
	13.98/1.1 1.69 14.20 25.63/-0.5 5.98/0.7 44.48 2:23.15							
5836	Margaret	Simpson	GHA-J	2.8.82	4		Arles	10 Jun
	14.09/0.5 1.77 11.48 25.02/0.7 6.00/1.3 53.04 2:33.61							
5835	Lyudmila	Blonskaya	UKR	18.3.75	4	ECp-1	Ried	1 Jul
	14.93/0.0 1.72 13.01 25.85/1.1 6.16/1.3 45.54 2:14.90							
	(50)							
5834	Marina	Bryukhach	UKR	16.1.77	5	ECp-1	Ried	1 Jul
	13.57/0.8 1.78 12.09 25.09/0.4 6.05/1.1 38.03 2:21.73							
5833	Anzhela	Kinet (Atroshchenko)	TUR	14.11.70	1	MedG	Tunis	14 Sep
	14.10/-1.8 1.68 12.61 24.75/0.8 5.87/-0.6 39.94 2:10.95							
5825	G. Pramila	Ganapathy	IND	8.5.77	1		Bangalore	25 Jun
	14.11 1.70 11.64 24.29 6.25 39.25 2:19.02							
5820	Simone	Oberer	SUI	8.4.80	6	ECp-1	Ried	1 Jul
	13.88/0.8 1.78 12.01 25.24/1.0 6.15w/2.4 38.19 2:20.52							
5811		Zhang Nina	CHN	3.3.81	5	NG	Guangzhou	18 Nov
	13.93/1.0 1.72 11.76 25.43/-0.1 6.18/0.4 37.69 2:12.86							
5801w	Salla	Käppi	FIN	22.5.80	12	ECp	Arles	1 Jul
	13.69/0.0 1.72 12.94 25.58/0.8 6.12W/6.4 43.52 2:27.82							
5791h	Vera	Yepimashko	BLR	10.7.76	1		Brest	22 Jul
	13.9 1.72 16.41 25.9 5.85 43.83 2:31.9 = 5793?							
5784	Nicola	Gautier	GBR	21.3.78	8	ECp-1	Ried	1 Jul
	14.05/0.8 1.60 14.64 25.13/1.1 5.53/1.4 49.25 2:21.00							
5781	Katerina	Nekolná	CZE	23.6.75	10		Ratingen	17 Jun
	14.07/0.7 1.65 12.30 24.75w/2.5 6.01/0.8 41.64 2:16.24							
5778	Natalya	Germanyuk	BLR	30.3.75	3	NC	Staiki	7 Jun
	14.34/1.6 1.67 14.43 25.37/1.2 5.84/1.7 42.98 2:19.74							
	(60)							

Mark	Name		Nat	Born	Pos	Meet	Venue	Date
5775	Maria	Richtnér	SWE	5.2.73	9	ECp-1	Ried	1 Jul
	13.98/0.0 1.63 13.16 25.75/1.1			5.91w/2.2		47.16 2:18.88		
5773	Julie	Mézerette	FRA	28.9.79	8	EU23	Amsterdam	15 Jul
	14.48/-1.0 1.81 10.62 25.05/1.5			6.01/0.6		41.40 2:16.52		
5767w	Tracye	Lawyer	USA	28.8.77	4	NC	Eugene	22 Jun
	13.75w/4.0 1.77 14.72 24.64/2.0			5.71W/4.8		37.02 2:31.20		
5759	Michelle	Perry	USA	1.5.79	2	NCAA	Eugene	2 Jun
	13.60/1.2 1.64 11.51 23.99/-2.2			5.84/0.6		37.86 2:14.36		
5755w	Heather	Sterlin	USA	12.4.74	5	NC	Eugene	22 Jun
	13.73/1.8 1.62 11.58 24.35w/2.9			6.20W/4.1		36.00 2:14.76	legal 5702 LJ 6.03w/3.4	
5751	Aja	Frary	USA	1.7.78	3	NCAA	Eugene	2 Jun
	13.88/1.5 1.73 11.32 24.57/-2.2			6.20/1.0		33.54 2:16.94		
5747	María	Peinado	ESP	8.2.77	3	ECp-2	Kaunas	1 Jul
	13.76/0.1 1.69 11.95 24.98/1.3			6.22/1.0		35.55 2:18.44		
5746	Natalya	Pavlikovskaya	RUS	80	4		Krasnodar	19 May
	14.72/0.4 1.73 14.30 25.90/0.1			6.00/1.3		38.28 2:16.48		
5745	Olga	Karas	RUS-J	9.7.82	3	EJ	Grosseto	22 Jul
	14.88/1.7 1.66 13.19 25.00/0.5			6.10/0.3		41.01 2:15.44		
5742	Natalya	Dobrinskaya	UKR-J	29.5.82	1		Kiev	19 May
	14.65/-0.4 1.70 15.11 25.85/-0.6			5.86/0.0		43.23 2:22.88		
	(70)							
5739	Soma	Biswas	IND	16.5.78	1	NC	Chennai	21 Oct
	14.37 1.70 11.44 25.16			6.05		42.95 2:16.50		
5737	Mihaela	Gîndila	ROM	29.10.74	1	NC	Bucuresti	17 Jun
	13.97 1.77 12.85 26.54			6.26		35.90 2.19.85		
5736	Svetlana	Gnezdilov	ISR	20.7.69	4	UKR Ch	Minsk	7 Jun
	13.04/1.9 1.61 12.32 24.25/1.7			5.82/2.0		34.60 2:16.40		
5735	Karin	Ruckstuhl	NED	2.11.80	1		Emmeloord	27 May
	13.98/0.7 1.79 11.22 24.81/0.0			6.21w/4.0		36.23 2:24.45		
5735w	Susanna	Rajamäki	FIN	19.9.79	15	ECp	Arles	1 Jul
	13.82/1.6 1.60 14.05 24.51w/2.6			6.40W/6.9		32.34 2:24.03		
5733	Kim	Schiemenz	USA	13.4.77	6	NC	Eugene	22 Jun
	14.13w/4.0 1.83 12.42 25.07w/2.1			5.50w/3.6		41.88 2:22.88		
5727	Barbara	Szlendaková	CZE	6.8.78	2	Big 12	College Station	17 May
	13.89w/3.6 1.66 11.48 23.84w/3.1			6.33w/4.0		31.80 2:18.79		
5724w	Silvia	Dalla Piana	ITA	3.2.75	16	ECp	Arles	1 Jul
	13.89/1.7 1.78 11.50 25.55/0.8			6.02W/6.5		38.45 2:20.37		
5717	Irina	Butor	BLR	26.2.80	5	NC	Staiki	7 Jun
	14.00/1.9 1.70 11.36 25.30/1.8			5.99/1.9		41.96 2:17.72		
5713	Sayoko	Sato	JPN	23.10.77	1	NC	Tokyo	9 Jun
	14.05/-0.5 1.63 11.17 24.80/0.5			6.22/0.3		40.57 2:17.07		
	(80)							
5710	Patience	Itanyi	NGR	2.7.73	8		Arles	10 Jun
	13.60/-1.2 1.74 10.62 25.22/1.3			6.25/1.5		40.01 2:26.27		
5709	Annika	Meyer	GER	9.6.80	12		Ratingen	17 Jun
	13.89/0.7 1.71 12.46 25.75/1.5			5.87/0.6		39.77 2:17.05		
5702	Kylie	Wheeler	AUS	17.1.80	3	EAsG	Osaka	26 May
	14.12/0.0 1.80 11.44 25.05/0.0			5.94/0.0		33.23 2:15.31		
5700	DeeDee	Brown	USA	5.5.78	2	SEC	Columbia, SC	11 May
	13.69/2.0 1.71 12.46 25.36/0.5			5.79/-1.0		42.14 2:24.01		
5695	Joanna	Grzesiak	POL	15.8.80	2	NC	Siedlce	23 Sep
	13.67w/3.2 1.66 11.92 24.52/0.0			6.10/0.0		30.87 2:14.31		
5694	Regla	Cárdenas	CUB	21.1.75	13		Götzis	27 May
	14.27/-0.4 1.76 13.21 25.97/0.4			6.32/-0.1		36.62 2:26.88		
5687	Kerry	Jury	GBR	19.11.68	10	ECp-1	Ried	1 Jul
	13.71/1.0 1.78 11.42 24.32/0.9			5.66/1.5		33.49 2:17.96		
5687w	Antonietta	Di Martino	ITA	1.6.78	17	ECp	Arles	1 Jul
	14.11/1.9 1.93 10.20 25.71w/3.0			5.33W/5.3		46.64 2:24.21		
5687	Niina	Kelo	FIN	26.3.80	1	NC-23	Huittinen	26 Aug
	14.22/0.3 1.69 14.46 26.23/1.7			5.61/1.0		49.01 2:27.65		
5684	Annu	Montell	FIN	7.5.76	1	v3N	Tartu	10 Jun
	14.02/0.7 1.74 13.12 25.84/1.3			5.84/0.0		43.20 2:27.14		
	(90)							
5677	Ellannee	Richardson	USA	18.3.80	4	NCAA	Eugene	2 Jun
	13.70/1.2 1.61 10.34 24.63/-2.2			5.81/-1.5		43.48 2:13.76		
5675	Ottelien	Olsthoorn	NED	20.6.78	11	ECp-1	Ried	1 Jul
	14.09/0.0 1.66 13.68 24.44/0.4			5.98/2.0		38.80 2:29.11		
5672	Elzbieta	Raczka-Lasota	POL	19.11.70	11		Arles	10 Jun
	14.13/-1.1 1.77 12.18 25.40/0.7			5.75/0.5		42.77 2:25.26		
5671	Hana	Dolezelová	CZE	8.4.79	8		Desenzano del Garda	13 May
	14.65/0.6 1.76 13.40 26.28/-0.2			6.03/1.1		41.72 2:24.09		

WOMEN 2001

Mark	Name		Nat	Born	Pos	Meet	Venue	Date
5670w	Tatyana	Zhevnova	BLR	17.10.77	18	ECp	Arles	1 Jul
	13.93w/2.1 1.72	12.87 25.33/1.3		5.84W/6.9		38.02	2:21.97	legal 5640 LJ 5.74/w3.6
5665	Emilie	Boulleret	FRA	23.5.73	13	NC	Arles	10 Jun
	14.52/-1.8 1.62	12.76 25.37/-0.1		5.68/1.8		48.02	2:17.25	
5664	Karin	Periginelli	ITA	5.2.70	9		Desenzano del Garda	13 May
	14.52/-1.1 1.73	12.95 25.74/0.4		5.50/0.8		44.77	2:17.03	
5664	Sárka	Beránková	CZE	16.4.78	5		Maribor	27 May
	14.42/0.0 1.73	12.71 24.54/1.6		6.05w/2.5		39.30	2:29.64	
5642	Irina	Ilyina	RUS	76	6		Krasnodar	19 May
	14.21/0.6 1.61	12.74 25.33/1.1		5.64/1.1		42.90	2:13.44	
5640	Aryiró	Stratáki	GRE	3.8.75	12	ECp-1	Ried	1 Jul
	14.13/0.0 1.66	12.48 25.10/1.1		6.03/1.7		39.04	2:22.09	
	(100)							

Mark	Name		Nat	Born	Date
5634	Franziska	Lakomy	GER-J	12.2.83	6 May
5631	Tacita	Bass	USA	28.10.79	5 Apr
5628	Jana	Klecková	CZE	19.3.75	27 May
5622	Andrea	Tittmann	GER	1.3.76	26 Aug
5615	Annelie	Schrader	GER	9.12.79	26 Aug
5614w	Christi	Smith	USA	5.11.77	22 Jun
5606w	Enezenaide	Gomes	POR	10.11.79	3 Jun
5603	Magdalena	Szczepanska	POL	25.1.80	10 Jun
5591	Mary	Varga	USA	1.5.80	5 Apr
5590	Elizete Gomes da Silva		BRA	2.5.71	20 Jul
5584	Yvonne	Wisse	NED-J	6.6.82	26 Aug
5583	Ifoma	Jones	USA	4.9.77	22 Jun
5575(w)	Sanna	Saarman	FIN	14.5.81	26 Aug
5570	Clare	Thompson	AUS	28.12.77	24 Mar
5569w	Sophie	Marrot	FRA	13.2.75	1 Jul
5567	Keiko	Kikugawa	JPN	10.10.79	20 May
5567	Deborah	Feltrin	ITA	10.3.76	23 Sep
5556	Rannveig	Kvalvik	NOR	2.10.76	1 Jul
5554	Katherine	Livesey	GBR	15.12.79	17 May
5548	Stefanie	Fuchs	GER	24.7.79	13 May
5547w	Angela	Craft	USA	21.4.79	2 Jun
5546	Whitney	Evans	CAN	10.4.80	13 May
5543	Desi	Hudson	USA	10.3.75	17 May
5542	Frenke	Bolt	NED	8.6.80	15 Jul
5539	Kendra	Reimer	USA	7.4.80	17 May
5534	Julia	Bennett	GBR	26.3.70	1 Jul
5531	Jennifer	Oeser	GER-J	29.11.83	26 Aug
5528	Anna	Snetkova	RUS	80	19 May
5522	Robin	Unger	USA	12.12.72	9 Dec
5517	Yuliya	Ignatkina	RUS-J	82	28 Jun
5514	Christiane	Mendy	FRA-J	25.8.82	22 Jul
5505	Aleksandra	Grineva	RUS	80	19 May
5505	Silke	Bachmann	GER	21.6.79	26 Aug
5502	Kim	Vanderhoek	CAN	30.11.70	23 Jul
5500	Yevgenia	Mazurenko	UKR	26.8.78	1 Jul
5497	Anastasía	Kivelídou	GRE	23.9.79	27 May
5490	Ursula	Neumair	GER-J	21.1.82	26 Aug
5482		Liu Xing	CHN	27.4.70	29 Jun
5481	Kerry	O'Bric	USA	22.9.78	17 May
5480w	Alexandra	Barlet	FRA	17.2.77	1 Jul
5480	Imma	Clopés	ESP	19.1.68	5 Aug
5479	Lucia	Tomaseková	SVK-J	26.10.82	22 Jul
5476	Claudia	Tonn	GER	18.4.81	24 Jun
5474	Claudia	Wälti	SUI-J	16.5.82	13 May
5472		Dan Jiao	CHN-J	6.9.84	18 Nov
5469		Fu Pengcheng	CHN	15.1.80	18 Nov
5463	Eli	Sommerfeldt	NOR	27.7.77	17 May
5456	Jamie	Walker	USA	31.3.81	5 Apr
5456h	Véronique	Boyer	FRA	24.2.72	20 May
5443	Andrea	Pressley	USA	20.6.81	18 May
5439	Gabriela	Kouassi	FRA	18.11.79	2 Jun
5438	Akiko	Hirado	JPN	8.10.80	29 Sep
5436	Jennifer	Higgins	USA	.73	1 May
5436	Maike	Goldkuhle	GER	10.3.80	26 Aug
5436hA	Zorobabelia	Córdoba	COL	28.3.68	15 Sep
5434w	Kathrine	Nielsen	DEN	9.2.77	17 May
5432h	Julie	Tinker	USA	17.9.78	13 May
5431w	Saskia	Meijer	NED	8.2.79	27 May
5430	Beata	Lukaszewska	POL	19.2.80	20 May
5423	Jessica	Zelinka	CAN	3.9.81	5 May
5423	Tine	Veenstra	NED-J	20.3.83	1 Jul
5418	Piia	Peltosaari	FIN	27.2.73	29 Aug
5414A	Maret	Komarova	EST	23.6.81	3 May
5414	Barbora	Spotáková	CZE	30.6.81	27 May
5410	Kelly	Sotherton	GBR	13.11.76	10 Jun
5407	Andrea	Geurtsen	SWE	13.6.79	20 Apr
5400		Qiu Yuqin	CHN-J	5.5.82	18 Nov
53965450?	Anzhela	Laitinen	RUS	71	14 Jul
	(168)				

Best with legal wind

Mark	Name		Nat	Born	Pos	Meet	Venue	Date
6053	Sonja	Kesselschläger	GER	20.1.78	9		Götzis	27 May
	13.88/-1.0 1.85	13.08 25.30/0.4		6.20/0.0		40.09	2:18.53	
6030	Gertrud	Bacher	ITA	28.2.71	10		Götzis	27 May
	13.94/-0.4 1.76	13.35 24.63/-0.1		5.93/0.1		40.92	2:12.40	
6009	Sabine	Krieger	GER	4.9.73	3	NC	Vaterstetten	26 Aug
	14.07/-0.9 1.72	13.75 25.21/1.1		5.96/0.5		44.85	2:13.12	
5958	Michaela	Hejnová	CZE	10.4.80	5	EU23	Amsterdam	15 Jul
	13.83/-1.2 1.66	12.55 24.92/1.5		6.06/0.6		50.35	2:20.11	
5788	Salla	Käppi	FIN	22.5.80	4		Desenzano	13 May
	13.94/-1.1 1.73	12.41 25.86/-0.2		6.08w/2.3		45.11	2:23.75	
5728	Tracye	Lawyer	USA	28.8.77	*	NC	Eugene	22 Jun
	13.75w/4.0 1.77	14.72 24.64/2.0		5.58/1.7		37.02	2:31.20	
5702	Heather	Sterlin	USA	12.4.74	*	NC	Eugene	22 Jun
	13.73/1.8 1.62	11.58 24.35w/2.9		6.03w/3.4		36.00	2:14.76	
5698	Silvia	Dalla Piana	ITA	3.2.75	4		Maribor	27 May
	14.44/0.0 1.76	11.51 25.79/1.6		5.91w/2.1		43.06	2:17.32	
5641	Susanna	Rajamäki	FIN	19.9.79	2	v3N	Tartu	3 Jun
	13.88/0.7 1.62	13.22 24.86/1.3		6.21/-0.4		34.16	2:23.67	

5588 C Smith 5 Apr | 5442 Di Martino 27 May | 5440 Craft 19 May | 5417 Saarman 5 Aug | 5414 Marrot 23 Jul

JUNIORS

See main list for top 6 juniors. 12 performances by 6 women over 5700. Additional marks and further juniors:

Name	Mark	Pos	Meet	Venue	Date	Mark	Pos	Meet	Venue	Date
Freisen	5956	2	EJ	Grosseto	22 Jul	5832	1	NC-j	Vaterstetten	26 Aug
	5909	1		Wesel	5 May					
Klüft	5807	1	ECp-1	Ried	1 Jul					
Simpson	5748	13	WCh	Edmonton	6 Aug					
Karas	5727	1	NC-j	Kazan	28 Jun					

Mark	Name		Nat	Born	Pos	Meet	Venue	Date
5634	Franziska	Lakomy	GER	12.2.83	3		Wesel	6 May
	14.09/1.1 1.56 12.32 25.09/1.0			6.01/1.8		43.20	2:19.11	
5584	Yvonne	Wisse	NED	6.6.82	1	NC-j	Vught	26 Aug
	14.48/1.0 1.81 11.12 24.72/-1.4			5.76/0.4		30.41	2:14.23	
5531	Jennifer	Oeser	GER	29.11.83	2	NC-j	Vaterstetten	26 Aug
	14.53/0.5 1.75 11.11 25.51/-1.1			5.79/0.2		39.92	2:20.64	
5517	Yuliya	Ignatkina	RUS	82	2	NC-j	Kazan	28 Jun
	14.70 1.69 11.08 25.13			6.12		38.83	2:22.77	
5514	Christiane	Mendy	FRA	25.8.82	5	EJ	Grosseto	22 Jul
	14.28/-0.1 1.63 11.07 24.65/0.2			6.02/-0.2		36.00	2:18.91	
5490	Ursula	Neumair	GER	21.1.82	3	NC-j	Vaterstetten	26 Aug
	15.29/-1.4 1.66 12.97 26.18/-1.1			5.84/0.3		44.27	2:19.97	
5479	Lucia	Tomaseková	SVK	26.10.82	7	EJ	Grosseto	22 Jul
	14.33/-0.1 1.72 10.64 25.74/0.5			5.92/-0.3		38.83	2:21.22	
5474	Claudia	Wälti	SUI	16.5.82	13		Desenzano del Garza	13 May
	14.61/0.3 1.67 11.70 25.00/1.3			5.69w/3.3		37.60	2:17.54	
5472		Dan Jiao	CHN	6.9.84	6	NG	Guangzhou	18 Nov
	14.20/1.5 1.60 11.90 25.06/-0.1			5.84/0.6		39.52	2:22.33	
5423	Tine	Veenstra	NED	20.3.83	16	ECp-1	Ried	1 Jul
	14.50/-0.1 1.63 13.22 25.31/0.5			5.41/1.2		46.42	2:31.25	
5400		Qiu Yuqin	CHN	5.5.82	8	NG	Guangzhou	18 Nov
	14.37/1.1 1.75 12.18 26.94/-0.1			5.64/0.6		42.35	2:28.33	
5399	Nadja	Casadei	SWE	3.4.83	17	ECp-1	Ried	1 Jul
	15.21/0.0 1.78 11.49 25.81/0.9			5.43w/2.8		36.41	2:13.66	
5365	Diana	Pickler	USA	9.12.83	1		Sacramento	25 Jul
	14.23/-1.3 1.70 11.02 25.24/0.0			5.63		36.12	2:23.82	
5357Aw	Lauren	Reimer (20)	USA	13.3.83	1		Albuquerque	25 May
	14.54 1.71 12.82 25.74			5.51		37.48	2:27.04	
5349	Laurien	Hoos	NED	18.8.83	20	ECp-1	Ried	1 Jul
	14.73/1.0 1.69 12.89 25.69/0.9			5.44/1.9		44.87	2:34.21	

4 X 100 METRES RELAY

Mark	Nat	Team	Pos	Meet	Venue	Date
41.71	USA	White, Gaines, Miller, Jones	1	WCh	Edmonton	11 Aug
42.32	GER	Paschke, G Rockmeier, B Rockmeier, Wagner	2	WCh	Edmonton	11 Aug
42.39	FRA	Félix, Bangué, Hurtis, Sidibé	3	WCh	Edmonton	11 Aug
42.40	JAM	J Campbell, Frazer, McDonald, A Walker	4	WCh	Edmonton	11 Aug
42.49	FRA	Félix, Bangué, Hurtis, Sidibé	1h2	WCh	Edmonton	11 Aug
42.52	NGR	Ajunwa, Ojokolo, Nku, Onyali-Omagbemi	5	WCh	Edmonton	11 Aug
42.60	GBR	Richardson, Wilhelmy, James, Oyepitan	6	WCh	Edmonton	11 Aug
42.64	USA	Williams, Gaines, Miller, Edwards	2h2	WCh	Edmonton	11 Aug
42.92	GER	Paschke, G Rockmeier, B Rockmeier, Wagner	1h1	WCh	Edmonton	11 Aug
42.93	GER	Paschke, Schielke, G Rockmeier, Wagner	1		Dortmund	9 Jun
42.98	USA	Adams, White, Miller, Gaines	2	GWG	Brisbane	7 Sep
42.99	GER	(LGO Dortmund) Habel, Schielke, B Rockmeier, G Rockmeier	1		Stuttgart	30 Jun
43.02	GER	Paschke, Schielke, B Rockmeier, Wagner	1	ECp-S	Bremen	23 Jun
43.04	NGR	Ajunwa, Ojokolo, Nku, Onyali-Omagbemi	2h1	WCh	Edmonton	11 Aug
43.08	GBR	Richardson, Wilhelmy, James, Oyepitan	3h2	WCh	Edmonton	11 Aug
43.09	JAM	A Walker, Frazer, McDonald, Goulbourne	3h1	WCh	Edmonton	11 Aug
43.12	USA	Blue Edwards, Perry, Miller, Gaines	1	PennR	Philadelphia	28 Apr
43.13	JAM	A Walker, J Campbell, McDonald, Frazer	3	GWG	Brisbane	7 Sep
43.14A	GER	Paschke, G Rockmeier, B Rockmeier, Wagner	1		Calgary	30 Jul
43.15	RUS	Ignatova, Khabarova, Kislova, Ekk	2	ECp-S	Bremen	23 Jun
		(20 performances by teams from 7 nations)				
43.18	CHN	(Sichuan Prov) Zeng Xiujun, Liu Xiaomei, Li Yali, Li Xuemei	1	NG	Guangzhou	23 Nov
43.25	GRE	Koklóni, Patsoú, Kaidantzi, Thánou	7	WCh	Edmonton	11 Aug
43.73	CAN	Clarke, Witter, Benyarku, Adusei	1	Franc	Ottawa	23 Jul
	(10)					
43.89	CIV	Gnahore, Allou, Sanganoko, Ayétoché	2	Franc	Ottawa	23 Jul
43.89	SRI	Jayasinghe, Sooriyaarachchi, De Soysa, Dharsha	5h1	WCh	Edmonton	11 Aug
43.97	SWE	J Kallur, Amundin, S Kallur, Barenfeld	1	v FIN	Göteborg	1 Sep
44.09	ITA	Cola, Graglia, Grillo, Levorato	1		Milano	6 Jun
44.12	MAD	Rahanitraniriana, Ratsimbazafy, Rakotondrabe, Rakotozafy	3	Franc	Ottawa	23 Jul
44.13	BRA	Machado, de Moura, Maggi, Coelho Neto	2	WUG	Beijing	1 Sep
44.18A	COL	M Caicedo, Murillo, Palacios, Brock	1	BolG	Ambato	13 Sep
44.19	BEL	Callaerts, De Caluwé, Ouédraogo, Gevaert	5h2	WCh	Edmonton	11 Aug
44.24	JPN	Sakagami, Arai, Nihei, Shimazaki	2	EAsG	Osaka	26 May
44.33	POL	Pawlak, Sznajder, Rysiukiewicz, Nielacna	1		Gdansk	14 Jul
	(20)					
44.46	SUI	Della Corte, Riesen, N'Koué, Donders	1	ECp2B	Nicosia	23 Jun
44.48	BUL	Pendareva, Gachevska, Mashova, Georgieva	1	ECp1B	Budapest	23 Jun

Mark		Name	Pos	Meet	Venue	Date
44.58	THA	Tawoncharoen, Khawpeag, Klomdee, Roberts	1	SEAG	Kuala Lumpur	15 Sep
44.60	NZL	Brunner, Hunt, Wardell, Arnott	1	vAUS	Auckland	31 Mar
44.60	BLR	Bartsevich, Dragun, Nevmerzhitskaya, Likuta (U23)	1		Minsk	30 Jun
44.63	ESP	(Valencia Terra y Mar) Blay, Alba, Montaner, Alozie	1	NC	Valencia	22 Jul
44.65	UKR	Pukha, Tkalich, Kozemyakina, Guskova	2	ECp1B	Budapest	23 Jun
44.75	FIN	Lax, Hannula, Manninen, Salivaara	5	ECp1A	Vaasa	23 Jun
44.90	AUS	Goon Chew, Munro, Porter. Apps	4	WUG	Beijing	1 Sep
44.92	IRL	Maher, Reilly, O'Rourke, Sheehy	1	ECp2A	Riga	22 Jun
	(30)					

44.98	CUB	27 May	45.30	VIE	15 Sep	45.50	CZE	23 Jun	45.79	AUT	23 Jun	**Best at low altitude**		
45.11	UZB	24 Jun	45.37	BAR-J	15 Apr	45.61	YUG	23 Jun	45.80	PUR	7 Apr	45.43	COL	19 May
45.20	NED	23 Jun	45.39	KAZ	4 Jun	45.62	ROM	7 Jul	45.81	SLO	23 Jun	**Hand Timed**		
45.30	HUN	13 Jun	45.40	TUR	23 Jun	45.63	LTU	23 Jun	45.90	MAS	15 Sep	45.2	VIE	4 Jul
									45.90	RSA	1 Sep	45.8	GHA	29 Jun

Mixed Nation Team

42.95	World	Alozie ESP, Nku NGR, Mani CMR, Pintusevich UKR	1	GWG	Brisbane	7 Sep

JUNIORS

44.16	GER	Hentschke, Kaufmann, Grötzinger, Habel	1	EJ	Grosseto	22 Jul
44.37	FRA	Huyghes, Sellier, Belliard, Lamalla	2	EJ	Grosseto	22 Jul
44.66	GBR	Norville, Caney, Spencer, James	3	EJ	Grosseto	22 Jul
44.89	POL	Wojtczak, Wardowska, Hennig, Flejszar	4	EJ	Grosseto	22 Jul
44.96	JAM	Davidson, Walker, Stewart, Campbell	1	Carifta	Bridgetown	15 Apr
45.09	BRA	A Oliveira, Campos, Moraes, Pacheco	1	SAm-J	Santa Fe	12 Oct
45.28	USA	(Wilson HS)	1		Norwalk	19 May
45.37	BAR	Carter, Williams, Cox, Norville	2	Carifta	Bridgetown	15 Apr
45.40	ITA	Morana, Cattaneo, Avogadri, Scaccabarozzi	5	EJ	Grosseto	22 Jul
45.61	CZE	Subrtová, Smídová, Batlíková, Ficková	1		Praha	18 Jun
45.92	COL	Ibargüen, Murillo, Petty, González	2	SAm-J	Santa Fe	12 Oct
45.95	SUI	Kissling, Barmettler, Stempfel, Koller	6	EJ	Grosseto	22 Jul

4 X 200 METRES RELAY

1:30.23	JAM	McDonald, Frazier, V Campbell, A Walker	1	PennR	Philadelphia	28 Apr
1:30.85	USA Blue		2	PennR	Philadelphia	28 Apr
1:31.24	Louisiana State Univ.	R Smith JAM, Combs, Durst Lee	1U	PennR	Philadelphia	28 Apr
1:33.83	GER	(Olympia Dortmund) B Rockmeier, Habel, G Rockmeier, Möller	1		Leverkusen	26 Aug

4 X 400 METRES RELAY

3:20.65	JAM	Richards 50.9, Scott 50.1, Parris 49.70, Fenton 49.95	1	WCh	Edmonton	12 Aug
3:21.34	USA	(Blue) Hennagan 50.8, Collins 51.4, C-Richardson 49.7, Jones 49.4	1	Penn R	Philadelphia	28 Apr
3:21.97	USA	Washington 50.5, Collins 50.1, Mik. Barber 50.98, Reid 50.39	1h1	WCh	Edmonton	11 Aug
3:21.97	GER	Ekpo-Umoh 51.7, Ghosh 50.0, Marx 50.61, Breuer 49.65	2	WCh	Edmonton	12 Aug
3:23.81	GER	Marx 52.3, Ghosh 50.3, Ekpo-Umoh 51.52, Breuer 49.70	1	ECp-S	Bremen	24 Jun
3:24.58	RUS	Maksimova 52.5, Khrushchelyova 51.0, Nosova 51.19, Antyukh 49.95	2	ECp-S	Bremen	24 Jun
3:24.63	USA	Miles-Clark 51.6, Hennagan 50.5, Collins 51.3, Reid 51.2	1	GWG	Brisbane	7 Sep
3:24.87	JAM	Burgher 52.5, Scott 50.5, Hemmings 51.49, Richards 50.42	2h1	WCh	Edmonton	11 Aug
3:24.87	JAM	Richards, Scott, Parris, Fenton	2	GWG	Brisbane	7 Sep
3:24.92	RUS	Rosikhina 52.6, Nosova 50.6, Kapachinskaya 51.11, Zykina 50.56	3	WCh	Edmonton	12 Aug
3:25.33	JAM	Hemmings 52.0, Scott 51.1, Richards 50.4, Clarke 51.8	2	PennR	Philadelphia	28 Apr
3:25.68	CAN	Williams 51.5, George 51.8, Kot 51.47, Antoine 50.91	3h1	WCh	Edmonton	11 Aug
3:26.23	FRA	Landre 51.7, Babin 51.9, Morandais 51.41, Mormand 51.22	3	ECp-S	Bremen	24 Jun
3:26.81	GER	Ekpo-Umoh 52.3, Ghosh 51.0, Marx 52.59, Breuer 50.88	1h2	WCh	Edmonton	11 Aug
3:26.88	USA	Miles-Clark 50.2, Hennagan 49.7, Collins 49.96, Reid 57.01	4	WCh	Edmonton	12 Aug
3:26.92	FRA	Landre 52.0, Mormand 51.3, Morandais 52.27, Bévis 51.41	4h1	WCh	Edmonton	11 Aug
3:26.94	GBR	McDonnell 52.2, Frost 51.1, Danvers 51.97, Murphy 51.65	5	WCh	Edmonton	12 Aug
3:27.25	GBR	McConnell 52.4, Owusu 51.8, Murphy 51.49, Fraser 51.57	2h2	WCh	Edmonton	11 Aug
3:27.37	POL	Pieluzek 52.7, Prokopek 50.7, Lemiesz 51.97, Pskit 52.01	5h1	WCh	Edmonton	11 Aug
3:27.39	RUS	Shevtsova 52.9, Rosikhina 51.9, Kapachinskaya 51.47, Zykina 51.12	3h2	WCh	Edmonton	11 Aug
	(20 performances by teams from 8 nations)					
3:28.11	CHN	(Shandong) Huang Xiaoxiao, Bu Fanfang, Xiang Chirong, Chen Yuxiang	1	NG	Guangzhou	23 Nov
3:28.17	BLR	Sologub 52.3, Usovich 52.2, Khlystova 52.48, Kozak 51.24	5	ECp-S	Bremen	24 Jun
	(10)					
3:28.68	CUB	Díaz 53.3, Duporty 50.5, Grenot 53.22, Pernía 51.63	6h1	WCh	Edmonton	11 Aug
3:29.04	ROM	Bumbescu 54.0, Ruicu 51.9, Rus 53.04, Tîrlea 50.13	6	ECp-S	Bremen	24 Jun
3:30.03	SEN	Diop 52.4, Diouf 52.0, Fall 54.62, Thiam 51.00	6h2	WCh	Edmonton	11 Aug
3:30.81	PUR	Castro 53.5, Harrison 50.8, Moya 53.34, Ortiz 53.14	7h1	WCh	Edmonton	11 Aug
3:30.94	AUS	Sadler, Brito, Robson, Lewis	5	GWG	Brisbane	7 Sep
3:31.96	ITA	Rodríguez 53.6, Piroddi 53.6, Graglia 52.87, Perpoli 51.88	7	ECp-S	Bremen	24 Jun
3:32.43	BRA	Almirâo, Figueirédo, Teodoro, Mendes	1	SACh	Manaus	20 May
3:33.06	JPN	Sugimori, Kakinuma, Nobuoka, Yoshida	2	EAsG	Osaka	26 May
3:33.06	UKR	Movchan, Rurak, Zhuravlyova, Debelaya	1	ECp1B	Budapest	24 Jun

Mark	Nat	Name	Pos	Meet	Venue	Date
3:33.14	NGR	Om.Akinremi, Ok.Akinremi, C.Akiremi, Ogunkoya 51.7	5	Penn R	Philadelphia	28 Apr
	(20)					
3:33.39	BUL	Gachevska, Kirilova, Mashova, Georgieva	2	ECp1B	Budapest	24 Jun
3:33.53	CMR	Béwouda, Nguimgo, Komgang, Kaboud	4	Franc	Ottawa	23 Jul
3:33.78	ESP	Alba 53.7, Carabalí 52.7, Bravo 53.79, Reyes 53.53	7h2	WCh	Edmonton	11 Aug
3:34.23	HUN	Kun, Dóczi, Bobcsek, Petráhn	3	ECp1B	Budapest	24 Jun
3:36.04	SWE	Dahlgren, Udd, Blomstrand, Petersen	1	v FIN	Göteborg	2 Sep
3:36.32A	COL	Oliveros, Brock, Palacios, González	1	BolG	Ambato	15 Sep
3:36.35	CZE	Zízalová, Sedláková, Rücklová, Dubská	8	ECp-S	Bremen	24 Jun
3:36.48	RSA	(KwaZulu Natal)	1	NC	Durban	3 Mar
3:36.87	NED	Baarssen, Visschers, de Jong, Poelman	4	ECp1B	Budapest	24 Jun
3:37.60	IRL	Shinkins, McIvor, Sheehy, McCarty	2	ECp2A	Riga	23 Jun
	(30)					

3:37.61 GRE 24 Jun
3:37.69 IND 25 Nov
3:37.78 POR 24 Jun
3:38.65 DEN 23 Jun
3:38.65 SLO 24 Jun
3:38.70 THA 15 Sep
3:39.61 SUI 24 Jun
3:39.71 KAZ 5 Jun
3:40.23 FIN 24 Jun
3:41.04 LAT 23 Jun
3:41.05 VIE 4 Jul
3:41.30 LTU 24 Jun
3:41.98 BEL 24 Jun
3:42.07 TUR 29 Jul
3:42.25 TRI-1716 Apr
3:42.60 CYP 24 Jun
3:42.74 YUG 24 Jun
3:43.07 AUT 24 Jun
3:43.7A KEN 23 Jun
3:44.05 SVK 24 Jun
3:44.07 ISR 24 Jun
3:44.30 EST 23 Jun
3:44.38A ECU 15 Sep
3:44.45 BAR-116 Apr
3:44.63 NOR 23 Jun
3:44.74 VEN 20 May

Best at low altitude
3:40.27 COL 20 May

JUNIORS

Mark	Nat	Name	Pos	Meet	Venue	Date
3:29.66	JAM	Stewart, Morgan, Walker, Hall	1	PennR	Philadelphia	28 Apr
3:34.63	GBR	Wall, Hines, James, Miller	1	EJ	Grosseto	22 Jul
3:35.51	USA		1		Sacramento	29 Jul
3:36.20	GER	Müller, Hoffmna, Balkow, Kettenis	2	EJ	Grosseto	22 Jul
3:40.08	RUS	Panteleyeva, Semicheva, Dryakhlova, Firova	1		Kazan	27 Jun
3:41.04	BRA	da Cruz, Fontes, Chagas, dos Santos	1	SAm-J	Santa Fe	13 Oct
3:41.12	ROM	Koroszi, Barbulescu, Manafu, Rus	3	EJ	Grosseto	22 Jul
3:41.65	CHN		1	Asi-J	BS Begawan	22 Jul
3:42.25	TRI	Modeste, Clarke, Prime, Cave	2	Carifta	Bridgetown	16 Apr
3:42.34	IND		2	Asi-J	BS Begawan	22 Jul
3:43.18	ITA	Finesso, Ellecosta, Lunghi, Giannetto	4	EJ	Grosseto	22 Jul
3:44.29	JPN	(Saitamasa Kae HS) Takemoto, Izumi, Kurimoto Anraku	1		Kumamoto	6 Aug
3:44.38A	ECU	Re. Cabezas, Ro. Cabezas, Chalá, Jaramillo	2	BolG	Ambato	15 Sep
3:44.45	BAR	Brathwaite, Bailey, Williams, Holder	3	Carifta	Bridgetown	16 Apr
3:44.77A	RSA	(Gauteng North)	1		Pretoria	21 Apr
3:44.99	FRA	Monthe, Charles, Sigère, Fleurvil	2		Dôle	29 Jul

4 X 800 METRES RELAY

Mark	Team	Pos	Meet	Venue	Date
8:24.25	USA (Un Florida) Ka.Bratton, Kr.Bratton, Allen, Merten	1	PennR	Philadelphia	28 Apr

SHUTTLE HURDLE (4 X 100MH)

Mark	Team	Pos	Meet	Venue	Date
52.85	Un of Illinois J Kallur SWE, Williams USA, S Kallur SWE, Felicien CAN	1	DrakeR	Des Moines	28 Apr

3000 METRES WALK

Mark	First name	Name	Nat	Born	Pos	Meet	Venue	Date
11:57.80	Erica	Alfridi	ITA	22.2.68	1		Milano	6 Jun
11:58.17	Elisabetta	Perrone	ITA	9.7.68	2		Milano	6 Jun
11:59.25	Olimpiada	Ivanova	RUS	5.5.70	3		Milano	6 Jun
12:04.42	Kjersti	Plätzer (Tysse)	NOR	18.1.72	1	NC	Drammen	7 Jul
12:08.30	Susana	Feitor	POR	28.1.75	1		Vila Real St António	3 Jun
	(5/5)							
12:38.43	Elisa	Rigaudo	ITA	17.6.80	4		Milano	6 Jun

12:44.54+ Kathrin Boyde GER 4.12.70 30 Jun
12:46.51 Nora Leksir FRA 13.5.74 24 May
12:47.13 Fatiha Ouali FRA 28.10.74 24 May
12:48.3 Jolanta Dukure LAT 20.9.79 21 Jun

Indoors

Mark	First name	Name	Nat	Born	Pos	Meet	Venue	Date
12:08.63		Plätzer			1	NC	Stange	25 Feb
12:20.62	Gillian	O'Sullivan	IRL	21.8.76	1	NC	Nenagh	4 Feb
12:25.97	Annarita	Sidoti	ITA	25.7.69	1	NC	Torino	24 Feb
12:28.32	Michelle	Rohl	USA	12.11.65	1	NC	Atlanta	3 Mar
12:29.08	Sabine	Zimmer	GER	6.2.81	1	NC	Dortmund	25 Feb
12:33.56	Norica	Cîmpean	ROM	22.3.72	1	NC	Bucuresti	24 Feb
12:35.71	Melanie	Seeger	GER	8.1.77	2	NC	Dortmund	25 Feb
12:37.28	Lisa	Barbieri	ITA	18.5.78	3	NC	Torino	24 Feb

12:45.68 Gisella Orsini ITA 9.12.71 24 Feb
12:46.72 Fatiha Ouali FRA 28.10.74 17 Feb
12:47.97 Andrea Meloni GER 1.10.67 25 Feb

5000 METRES WALK

Mark	First name	Name	Nat	Born	Pos	Meet	Venue	Date
20:37.83	Kjersti	Plätzer (Tysse)	NOR	18.1.72	1	NC	Drammen	7 Jul
20:40.24	Susana	Feitor	POR	28.1.75	1		Rio Maior	9 May
20:46.60	Valentina	Savchuk	UKR	19.1.75	1		Uzhgorod	9 May

Mark	Name		Nat	Born	Pos	Meet	Venue	Date
20:50.13	Gillian	O'Sullivan	IRL	21.8.76	1	NC	Dublin	22 Jul
21:01.23	Erica	Alfridi	ITA	22.2.68	1		Bressanone	16 Jun
21:09.74	Olga	Lukyanchuk	UKR	7.12.76	2		Uzhgorod	9 May
21:11.0	Maya	Sazonova	KAZ	28.5.65	1		Almaty	24 Jun
21:11.46	Nevena	Mineva	BUL	14.6.72	1	NC	Sofia	11 Jun
21:20.76	Melanie	Seeger	GER	8.1.77	1	NC	Dortmund	30 Jun
21:29.66	Annarita	Sidoti	ITA	25.7.69	2		Bressanone	16 Jun
21:35.5	Cristina	Pellino	ITA	21.9.70	1	NC	Catania	8 Jul
21:36.93	Elisa	Rigaudo	ITA	17.6.80	3		Bressanone	16 Jun
21:43.5+	Olimpiada	Ivanova	RUS	5.5.70	1	in 20k	Brisbane	6 Sep
21:43.9	Lisa	Barbieri	ITA	18.5.78	2	NC	Catania	8 Jul
21:46.76	Lyudmila	Yegorova	UKR	4.10.74	3		Uzhgorod	9 May
21:47.11	Takako	Terui	JPN	11.1.78	1		Kanazawa	29 Sep

Mark	Name		Nat	Born	Date
21:51.0	Svetlana	Tolstaya	KAZ	9.8.71	24 Jun
21:51.70	Fatiha	Ouali	FRA	28.10.74	13 Jun
21:52.1	Jolanta	Dukure	LAT	20.9.79	9 Jun
21:53.31		Kim Mi-jung	KOR	10.6.79	18 Apr
22:00.0+	Tatyana	Korotkova	RUS	24.4.80	9 Srp
22:00.1+	Margarita	Nazarova	RUS	1.10.76	9 Srp
22:00.9	Kathrin	Boyde	GER	4.12.70	15 Jul

10 KILOMETRES WALK

Mark	Name		Nat	Born	Pos	Meet	Venue	Date
42:23	Kjersti	Plätzer (Tysse)	NOR	18.1.72	1	NC	Os	5 May
42:34+	Olimpiada	Ivanova	RUS	5.5.70	1	in 20k	Adler	4 Mar
42:39	Susana	Feitor	POR	28.1.75	1		Lanciano	11 Mar
42:54+		Feitor			1	in 20k	Rio Maior	7 Apr
42:55+		Ivanova			1=	ECp	Dudince	19 May
42:55+	Yelena	Nikolayeva	RUS	1.2.66	1=	ECp	Dudince	19 May
42:58+		Feitor			3	ECp	Dudince	19 May
43:02.04t	María	Vasco	ESP	26.12.75	1	NC-w	Valencia	21 Jul
43:07	Elisabetta	Perrone	ITA	9.7.68	1		Sesto San Giovanni	1 May
43:13+	Valentina	Savchuk	UKR	19.1.75	2	in 20k	Adler	4 Mar
43:17+	Tatyana	Gudkova	RUS	23.12.78	3	in 20k	Adler	4 Mar
43:20+	Olga	Lukyanchuk	UKR	7.12.76	4	in 20k	Adler	4 Mar
43:20+	Natalya	Fedoskina (10)	RUS	25.6.80	5	in 20k	Adler	4 Mar
43:20		Gao Hongmiao	CHN	17.3.74	1	WUG	Beijing	29 Aug
43:23	Erica	Alfridi	ITA	22.2.68	2		Sesto San Giovanni	1 May
43:27		Plätzer			1		Hildesheim	25 Aug
43:30		Feitor			1		Montiju	24 Mar
43:32		Plätzer			3		Sesto San Giovanni	1 May
43:33+		Perrone			4=	ECp	Dudince	19 May
43:33+		Alfridi			4=	ECp	Dudince	19 May
43:35+		Vasco			6	ECp	Dudince	19 May
43:39+	Norica (22/13)	Cîmpean	ROM	22.3.72	7	in 20k	Dudince	19 May
43:45+	Tatyana	Sibilyeva	RUS	17.5.80	6	in 20k	Adler	4 Mar
43:47	Lisa	Barbieri	ITA	18.5.78	1		Fiera di Primiero	18 Aug
43:48	Annarita	Sidoti	ITA	25.7.69	4		Sesto San Giovanni	1 May
43:51+	Valentina	Tsybulskaya	BLR	19.2.68	9	in 20k	Dudince	19 May
43:55	Irina	Petrova	RUS-J	26.5.85	1		Gachina	1 Apr
44:01		Wang Liping	CHN	8.7.76	3	WUG	Beijing	29 Aug
44:23+	Maya (20)	Sazonova	KAZ	28.5.65	7	in 20k	Edmonton	9 Aug
44:29		Li Hong	CHN	1.6.79	1	NC	Dandong	15 Apr
44:30	Viktoriya	Mazurko	RUS-J	14.8.85	2		Gachina	1 Apr
44:32+	Larisa	Safronova	RUS	6.1.80	1=	in 20k	Cheboksary	16 Jun
44:32+	Lyudmila	Yefimkina	RUS	22.8.81	1=	in 20k	Cheboksary	16 Jun
44:37		Tang Yinghua	CHN	18.5.73	2	NC	Dandong	15 Apr
44:40+	Gillian	O'Sullivan	IRL	21.8.76	2=		Dublin	16 Jun
44:40+	Jane	Saville	AUS	5.11.74	2=		Dublin	16 Jun
44:41	Cristiana	Pellino	ITA	21.9.70	2		Lanciano	11 Mar
44:41	Gisella	Orsini	ITA	9.12.71	3		Lanciano	11 Mar
44:42+	Svetlana (30)	Tolstaya	KAZ	9.8.71	12	in 20k	Edmonton	9 Aug
44:44+	Tatyana	Korotkova	RUS	24.4.80	7	in 20k	Adler	4 Mar
44:44.1t	Eva	Pérez	ESP	18.7.75	1		Gerona	7 Jul
44:45+	Lyudmila	Dedekina	RUS	5.1.79	8	in 20k	Adler	4 Mar
44:48		Sun Chunfang	CHN	1.3.77	3	NC	Dandong	15 Apr
44:49+	Natalya	Misyulya	BLR	16.4.66	13	ECp	Dudince	19 May
44:49.3t	Tatyana	Kozlova	RUS-J	2.9.83	1		Adler	3 Mar
44:49.56tmx	Kerry	Saxby-Junna	AUS	2.6.61	1		Canberra	18 Feb
44:52+	Michelle	Rohl	USA	12.11.65	1	NC	Eugene	24 Jun

Mark	Name		Nat	Born	Pos	Meet	Venue	Date
44:54+	Melanie	Seeger	GER	8.1.77	14	WCh	Edmonton	9 Aug
44:56		Zang Yan	CHN-J	13.12.83	4	NC	Dandong	15 Apr
	(40)							
44:57		Gao Kelian	CHN-J	15.8.83	5	NC	Dandong	15 Apr
44:58.6t	Fatiha	Ouali	FRA	28.10.74	1		Chalon sur Saône	22 Apr
44:59		Fan Haixia	CHN-J	10.3.82	6	NC	Dandong	15 Apr
44:59		Hou Hongjuan	CHN	5.8.76	7	NC	Dandong	15 Apr
44:59	Anne Haaland	Simonsen	NOR	18.6.80	2	NC	Os	5 May
44:59.77+t	Isilda	Gonçalves	POR	11.11.69	2		Lisboa	22 Jul
45:00+	Guadalupe	Sánchez	MEX	3.1.77	15	in 20k	Edmonton	9 Aug
45:01	Elisa	Rigaudo	ITA	17.6.80	6		Sesto San Giovanni	1 May
45:01+	Jolanta	Dukure	LAT	20.9.79	14	in 20k	Dudince	19 May
45:02+	Natalya	Shiviryova	RUS	31.8.78	9	in 20k	Adler	4 Mar
	(50)							
45:03		Guo Dongmei	CHN-J	5.2.83	8	NC	Dandong	15 Apr
45:09+	Daniela	Cirlan	ROM	18.9.80		in 20k	Dudince	19 May
45:12		Yang Wenjing	CHN	26.9.79	9	NC	Dandong	15 Apr
45:12+	Olga	Polyakova	RUS	23.9.80			Cheboksary	16 Jun
45:14.3+ t	Inês	Henriques	POR	1.5.80	3	NC	Lisboa (U)	21 Jul
45:15+	Elena	Isar	ROM	7.12.71		in 20k	Dudince	19 May
45:18	Rossella	Giordano	ITA	1.12.72	7		Sesto San Giovanni	1 May
45:18+	Margarita	Turova	BLR	28.12.80	1	in 20k	Amsterdam	15 Jul
45:25		Zhang Libo	CHN-J	4.2.82	10	NC	Dandong	15 Apr
45:27	Rocío	Florido	ESP	16.1.76	2		L'Hospitalet	8 Apr
	(60)							
45:29 t?	Yelena	Miroshnichenko	UKR	3.1.77	1		Kiev	18 May
45:31+	Victoria	Palacios	MEX	29.3.77	17	in 20k	Edmonton	9 Aug
45:34		Jiang Qiuyan	CHN-J	5.7.83	11	NC	Dandong	15 Apr
45:37.77	Sofia	Avoila	POR	30.7.76	4	NC	Lisboa	21 Jul
45:40		Jian Xingli	CHN-J	4.12.83	12	NC	Dandong	15 Apr
45:41	Lyudmila	Yegorova	UKR	4.10.74	4		Hildesheim	25 Aug
45:44	Sonata	Milusauskaité	LTU	31.8.73	2		Birstonas	5 May
45:47A	Rosario	Sánchez	MEX	26.10.73	1	CAC	C. de Guatemala	20 Jul
45:49		Kim Mi-jung	KOR	10.6.79	7	WUG	Beijing	29 Aug
45:52		Chen Haiyan	CHN	16.1.81	13	NC	Dandong	15 Apr
	(70)							
45:53		Hu Ming	CHN-J	8.10.84	14	NC	Dandong	15 Apr
45:54	Beatriz	Pascual	ESP-J	9.5.82	3		Calella	22 Apr
45:55	Kathrin	Boyde	GER	4.12.70	5		Hildesheim	25 Aug
45:56.7	Alena	Zenkova	RUS-J	1.1.82	2		Adler	3 Mar
45:57+	Antonina	Petrova	RUS	1.5.77	10	in 20k	Adler	4 Apr

Mark	Name		Nat	Born	Date
46:00		Wu Cuilian	CHN	27.4.81	15 Apr
46:03		Zhang Ruihong	CHN-J	25.12.83	15 Apr
46:04+	Tatyana	Melnikova	RUS	12.9.75	4 Apr
46:08	Andrea	Meloni	GER	1.10.67	5 May
46:08+	Teresa	Linares	ESP	29.4.69	19 May
46:09+	Yevdokiya	Korotkova	RUS	28.2.79	4 Apr
46:10	Sylwia	Korzeniowska	POL	25.4.80	18 Aug
46:11+	Margarita	Nazarova	RUS	1.10.76	16 Jun
46:11.2 t	Hristína	Kokótou	GRE	9.1.72	22 Apr
46:13+	Yelena	Ginko	BLR	30.7.76	19 May
46:14	Veronica	Budileanu	ROM	27.2.76	9 Sep
46:16		Sun Lihua	CHN-J	30.9.83	15 Apr
46:24	Joanna	Baj	POL	31.5.80	16 Jun
46:24+	Nevena	Mineva	BUL	14.6.72	9 Aug
46:25		Song Hongjuan	CHN-J	4.7.84	15 Apr
46:26+	Yelena	Kuznetsova	KAZ	4.8.77	16 Jun
46:29		Zuo Yan	CHN-J	18.8.83	15 Apr
46:29.20	Athanasía	Tsoumeléka	GRE-J	2.1.82	19 Jul
46:31	Marina	Tikhonova	BLR-J	14.12.83	19 May
46:32+	Kaori	Nikaido	JPN	25.7.79	28 Jan
46:32+	Ryoko	Tadamasa	JPN	9.5.76	28 Jan
46:32+	Vera	Zozulya	UKR	31.8.70	19 May
46:35	Olive	Loughane	IRL	14.1.76	5 May
46:37	Maria	Urbanik-Rosza	HUN	12.2.67	6 May
46:38	Mária	Galiková	SVK	21.8.80	26 May
	(100)				
46:40.4 t	Yekaterina	Izmaylova	RUS-J	6.3.83	3 Mar
46:41.0+t	Alexandra	Sorokina	RUS	24.2.79	9 Sep
46:41.0+t	Tatyana	Matyushkina	RUS	22.1.79	9 Sep
46:41.2+t	Anna	Pudovkina	RUS-J	85	9 Sep
46:42+	Athína	Papayiánni	GRE	18.8.80	15 Jul
46:44+	Tatyana	Dotsenko	RUS	24.4.81	4 Apr
46:44.01t	Edina	Füsti	HUN-J	24.6.82	26 Jun
46:48	Debbi	Lawrence	USA	15.10.61	19 Aug
46:49 t	Yelena	Krivokhizha	UKR	10.3.79	13 Oct
46:53		Li Jing	CHN	19.10.81	15 Apr
46:59	Tatiana	Boulanger	FRA	13.7.73	1 Jul

Indoors

Mark	Name		Nat	Born	Date
46:49.4i	Marina	Smyslova	RUS	25.2.66	21 Jan
46:54.2i	Tatyana	Matyushkina	RUS	22.1.79	21 Jan

Best track times

Mark	Name		Nat	Born	Pos	Meet	Venue	Date
43:24.4+	Olimpiada	Ivanova	RUS	5.5.70	1	in 20k	Brisbane	6 Sep
43:52.0	Yelena	Nikolayeva	RUS	1.2.66	1	NC	Alytus	15 Sep
44:38.87 +	Susana	Feitor	POR	28.1.75	1	in 20k	Lisboa	21 Jul
45:05.4+	Elisabetta	Perrone	ITA	9.7.68	1	in 15k	Castelnovo Monti	21 Jul
45:19.5	Maya	Sazonova	KAZ	28.5.65	1		Almaty	4 Jun
45:21.5 +	Annarita	Sidoti	ITA	25.7.69	2	in 15k	Castelnovo Monti	21 Jul
45:54.0 +	Tatyana	Korotkova	RUS	24.4.80	1	in 20k	Izhevsk	9 Sep

Mark	Name		Nat	Born	Date
46:21.0+t	Margarita	Nazarova	RUS	1.10.76	9 Sep
46:23.16	Teresa	Linares	ESP	29.4.69	21 Jul
46:23.7	Rossella	Giordano	ITA	1.12.72	21 Jul
46:24.85	Rocío	Florido	ESP	16.1.76	21 Jul
46:49.81	Beatriz	Pascual	ESP-J	9.5.82	19 Jul

20 KILOMETRES WALK

Mark	Name		Nat	Born	Pos	Meet	Venue	Date
1:24:50	Olimpiada	Ivanova	RUS	5.5.70	1	NC-w	Adler	4 Mar
1:26:22		Wang Yan	CHN	3.5.71	1	NG	Guangzhou	19 Nov
1:26:23		Wang Liping	CHN	8.7.76	2	NG	Guangzhou	19 Nov
1:26:35		Liu Hongyu	CHN	11.1.75	3	NG	Guangzhou	19 Nov
1:26:48		Ivanova			1	ECp	Dudince	19 May
1:26:50	Natalya	Fedoskina	RUS	25.6.80	2	ECp	Dudince	19 May
1:26:53.2 t		Ivanova			1	GWG	Brisbane	6 Sep
1:27:09	Elisabetta	Perrone	ITA	9.7.68	3	ECp	Dudince	19 May
1:27:29	Erica	Alfridi	ITA	22.2.68	4	ECp	Dudince	19 May
1:27:33	Tatyana	Sibilyeva	RUS	17.5.80	2	NC-w	Adler	4 Mar
1:27:35		Fedoskina			3	NC-w	Adler	4 Mar
1:27:48		Ivanova			1	WCh	Edmonton	9 Aug
1:27:49.3 t	Yelena	Nikolayeva	RUS	1.2.66	2	GWG	Brisbane	6 Sep
1:27:55	Susana	Feitor (10)	POR	28.1.75	1		Rio Maior	7 Apr
1:28:06		Feitor			1		Dublin	16 Jun
1:28:20		Nikolayeva			5	ECp	Dudince	19 May
1:28:45		Gao Hongmiao	CHN	17.3.74	1	NC	Dandong	13 Apr
1:28:49	Valentina	Tsybulskaya	BLR	19.2.68	2	WCh	Edmonton	9 Aug
1:28:52		Wang Liping			2	NC	Dandong	13 Apr
1:28:56	Valentina	Savchuk	UKR	19.1.75	4	RUS-w	Adler	4 Mar
1:28:56		Perrone			3	WCh	Edmonton	9 Aug
1:29:08	Olga	Lukyanchuk	UKR	7.12.76	5	RUS-w	Adler	4 Mar
1:29:25	Norica	Cîmpean	ROM	22.3.72	6	ECp	Dudince	19 May
1:29:31	Margarita	Turova	BLR	28.12.80			Brest	10 Mar
1:29:31		Jian Xingli	CHN-J	4.12.83	3	NG	Guangzhou	19 Nov
1:29:36	Maya	Sazonova	KAZ	28.5.65	1		Almaty	31 Mar
1:29:36.4 t		Feitor			1	NC	Lisboa (U)	21 Jul
1:29:39		Liu Hongyu			3	NC	Dandong	13 Apr
1:29:39		Gao Kelian	CHN-J	15.8.83	5	NG	Guangzhou	19 Nov
1:29:43		Li Hong	CHN	1.6.79	4	NC	Dandong	13 Apr
	(30/20)							
1:29:44		Wang Qingqing	CHN-J	7.2.83	6	NG	Guangzhou	19 Nov
1:29:47		Pan Hailian	CHN	21.11.77	7	NG	Guangzhou	19 Nov
1:29:54	Elisa	Rigaudo	ITA	17.6.80	1	EU23	Amsterdam	15 Jul
1:29:55	Kjersti	Plätzer	NOR	18.1.72	1		Eisenhüttenstadt	9 Jun
1:29:57	Gillian	O'Sullivan	IRL	21.8.76	1		Douglas	17 Feb
1:30:00		Xu Aihui	CHN	25.4.78	6	NC	Dandong	13 Apr
1:30:09	María	Vasco	ESP	26.12.75	1		Prat de Llobregat	18 Feb
1:30:12	Tatyana	Gudkova	RUS	23.12.78	6	NC-w	Adler	4 Mar
1:30:13		Jiang Qiuyan	CHN-J	5.7.83	8	NC	Dandong	13 Apr
1:30:31		Guo Dongmei	CHN-J	5.2.83	9	NC	Dandong	13 Apr
	(30)							
1:30:41	Melanie	Seeger	GER	8.1.77	7	WCh	Edmonton	9 Aug
1:30:48		Sun Chunfang	CHN	1.3.77	11	NC	Dandong	13 Apr
1:30:49	Larisa	Safronova	RUS	6.1.80	2	NC	Cheboksary	16 Jun
1:30:51	Tatyana	Korotkova	RUS	24.4.80	7	NC-w	Adler	4 Mar
1:30:52		Jiang Kun	CHN-J	18.5.85	12	NC	Dandong	13 Apr
1:30:56		Han Min	CHN-J	8.7.83	13	NC	Dandong	13 Apr
1:31:12	Antonina	Petrova	RUS	1.5.77	8	NC-w	Adler	4 Mar
1:31:18		Li Jingxue	CHN	10.2.70	14	NC	Dandong	13 Apr
1:31:20	Jane	Saville	AUS	5.11.74	3		Dublin	16 Jun
1:31:21	Natalya	Misyulya	BLR	16.4.66	10	ECp	Dudince	19 May
	(40)							
1:31:28	Lyudmila	Dedekina	RUS	5.1.79	9	NC-w	Adler	4 Mar
1:31:30	Vera	Zozulya	UKR	31.8.70	2		Lutsk	31 Mar
1:31:31	Kathrin	Boyde	GER	4.12.70	1	SUI Ch	Möhlin	9 Sep
1:31:40	Annarita	Sidoti	ITA	25.7.69	8	WCh	Edmonton	9 Aug
1:31:47	Jolanta	Dukure	LAT	20.9.79	1	NC	Ogre	29 Apr
1:31:48		Li Yuxin	CHN	4.12.74	16	NC	Dandong	13 Apr
1:31:49	Svetlana	Tolstaya	KAZ	9.8.71	10	RUS-w	Adler	4 Mar
1:31:55		Hu Guangkun	CHN	4.8.76	17	NC	Dandong	13 Apr
1:32:11		Zuo Yan	CHN-J	18.8.83	18	NC	Dandong	13 Apr
1:32:11	Nevena	Mineva	BUL	14.6.72	1		Nova Zagora	30 Jun
	(50)							
1:32:12	Ana Maria	Groza	ROM	1.6.76	1	BalkC	Paralio Astros	20 Apr
1:32:22.4 t	Eva	Pérez	ESP	18.7.75	3	GWG	Brisbane	6 Sep
1:32:27	Guadalupe	Sánchez	MEX	3.1.77	9	WCh	Edmonton	9 Aug
1:32:36	Cristiana	Pellino	ITA	21.9.70	1		Riccione	22 Apr

Mark	Name		Nat	Born	Pos	Meet	Venue	Date
1:32:36	Elena	Isar	ROM	7.12.71	14	ECp	Dudince	19 May
1:32:45.7 t	Olga	Polyakova	RUS	23.9.80	1	Kuts	Moskva	28 Jul
1:32:47	Sylwia	Korzeniowska	POL	25.4.80	5	EU23	Amsterdam	15 Jul
1:32:49	Michelle	Rohl	USA	12.11.65	1	NC	Eugene	24 Jun
1:32:59		Nie Yulin	CHN	2.9.78	19	NC	Dandong	13 Apr
1:32:59	Gisella	Orsini	ITA	9.12.71	2		Riccione	22 Apr
	(60)							
1:33:02		Ha Mingming	CHN-J	15.4.82	20	NC	Dandong	13 Apr
1:33:04	Fatiha	Ouali	FRA	28.10.74	16	ECp	Dudince	19 May
1:33:04		Tang Yinghua	CHN	18.5.73	13	NG	Guangzhou	19 Nov
1:33:09		Hou Hongjuan	CHN	5.8.76	21	NC	Dandong	13 Apr
1:33:13	Lisa	Barbieri	ITA	18.5.78	3		Riccione	22 Apr
1:33:21	Yelena	Ginko	BLR	30.7.76	17	ECp	Dudince	19 May
1:33:23	Teresa	Vaill	USA	20.11.62	1		Manassas	1 Apr
1:33:27	Teresa	Linares	ESP	29.4.69	18	ECp	Dudince	19 May
1:33:29	Kaori	Nikaido	JPN	25.7.79	1	NC	Kobe	28 Jan
1:33:34	Andrea	Meloni	GER	1.10.67	2	SUI Ch	Möhlin	9 Sep
	(70)							
1:33:37	Athína	Papayiánni	GRE	18.8.80	6	EU23	Amsterdam	15 Jul
1:33:38	Daniela	Cîrlan	ROM	18.9.80	2	BalkC	Paralio Astros	20 Apr
1:33:40.2 t	Kerry	Saxby-Junna	AUS	2.6.61	5	GWG	Brisbane	6 Sep
1:33:52	Victoria	Palacios	MEX	29.3.77	10	WCh	Edmonton	9 Aug
1:33:58.1 t	Sofia	Avoila	POR	30.7.76	2	NC	Lisboa (U)	21 Jul
1:33:59		Liu Shu	CHN	17.6.81	22	NC	Dandong	13 Apr
1:34:02	Oslaidis	Cruz	CUB	12.3.74	1		Santa Clara	17 Mar
1:34:02	Lyudmila	Yegorova	UKR	4.10.74	3		Lutsk	31 Mar
1:34:08	Sonata	Milusauskaite	LTU	31.8.73	1	NC	Prienai	23 Jun
1:34:10	Rocío	Florido	ESP	16.1.76	2		Prat de Llobregat	18 Feb
	(80)							
1:34:10		Zhang Libo	CHN-J	4.2.82	23	NC	Dandong	13 Apr
1:34:10	Takako	Terui	JPN	11.1.78	1		Takahata	28 Oct
1:34:15	Natalya	Shiviryova	RUS	31.8.78	11	NC-w	Adler	4 Mar
1:34:23	Tatyana	Melnikova	RUS	12.9.75	12	NC-w	Adler	4 Mar
1:34:23	Yevdokiya	Korotkova	RUS	28.2.79	13	NC-w	Adler	4 Mar
1:34:25		Hu Ming	CHN-J	8.10.84	24	NC	Dandong	13 Apr
1:34:26	Anne Haaland	Simonsen	NOR	18.6.80	7	EU23	Amsterdam	15 Jul
1:34:29	Yelena	Kuznetsova	KAZ	4.8.77	3		Almaty	31 Mar
1:34:31.2 t	Aleksandra	Sorokina	RUS	24.2.79	2		Izhevsk	9 Sep
1:34:40		Yang Wenjing	CHN	26.9.79	25	NC	Dandong	13 Apr
	(90)							
1:34:44	Lyn	Ventris	AUS	2.10.56	1		Melbourne	16 Dec
1:34:49	Ryoko	Tadamasa	JPN	9.5.76	2	NC	Kobe	28 Jan
1:34:49	Inês	Henriques	POR	1.5.80	10	EU23	Amsterdam	15 Jul
1:34:50	Tatyana	Dotsenko	RUS	24.4.81	14	NC-w	Adler	4 Mar
1:34:51		Li Jing	CHN	19.10.81	26	NC	Dandong	13 Apr
1:34:51	Maria	Rozsa-Urbaník	HUN	12.2.67	3		Eisenhüttenstadt	9 Jun
1:34:54	Olive	Loughnane	IRL	14.1.76	4		Dublin	16 Jun
1:34:56	Joanna	Baj	POL	31.5.80	11	EU23	Amsterdam	15 Jul
1:35:06	Isilda	Gonçalves	POR	11.11.69	2		Setúbal	24 Jun
1:35:14.5 t	Margarita	Nazarova	RUS	1.10.76	3		Izhevsk	9 Sep
	(100)							

Mark	Name		Nat	Born	Date
1:35:22		Kim Mi-jung	KOR	10.6.79	1 May
1:35:25		Sun Lihua	CHN-J	30.9.83	13 Apr
1:35:28.4t	Tatyana	Matyushkina	RUS	22.1.79	9 Sep
1:35:34	Kristina	Saltanovic	LTU	20.2.75	7 Apr
1:35:37		Wu Cuilian	CHN	27.4.81	13 Apr
1:35:50	Geovanna	Irusta	BOL	26.9.75	8 Apr
1:35:51	Vera	Santos	POR	3.12.81	15 Jul
1:35:58	Tiina	Muinonen	FIN	30.9.81	7 Apr
1:35:59		Zhu Qiaomei	CHN	21.11.77	13 Apr
1:36:13	Rossella	Giordano	ITA	1.12.72	24 Jun
1:36:23	Viktoriya	Nikolayeva	RUS	9.5.81	4 Mar
1:36:28	Celia	Marcén	ESP	6.12.73	18 Mar
1:36:35.3t	Irina	Pudovkina	RUS	7.2.80	9 Sep
1:36:37	Amber	Antonia	USA	4.11.79	24 Jun
1:36:47		Chen Haiyan	CHN	16.1.81	13 Apr
1:36:59	Tatiana	Boulanger	FRA	13.7.73	19 May
1:37:02	Yelena	Miroshnichenko	UKR	3.1.77	2 Jul
1:37:06		Zhang Ruihong	CHN-J	25.12.83	13 Apr
1:37:09.0t	Marina	Smyslova	RUS	25.2.66	28 Jul
1:37:10	Jill	Zenner	USA	13.2.75	24 Jun
1:37:19		Ding Mei	CHN-J	3.11.85	13 Apr
1:37:19	Francisca	Martínez	MEX	4.10.66	16 Jun
1:37:37	Rosa María	Mantecón	ESP	28.9.80	9 Jun
1:37:40	Veronica	Budileanu	ROM	27.2.76	20 Jun
1:37:42	Sachiyo	Matsunobu	JPN	26.3.73	28 Jan
1:37:46A	Rosario	Sánchez	MEX	26.10.73	21 Apr
1:37:50	Hristína	Kokótou	GRE	9.1.72	18 Mar
1:37:53A	Mara	Ibáñez	MEX	17.12.74	21 Apr
1:37:57	Outi	Sillanpää	FIN	2.2.76	3 Jun
1:37:57	Debbi	Lawrence	USA	15.10.61	9 Aug
1:37:58	Agnieszka	Olesz	POL	27.8.79	19 May
1:38:00	Svetlana	Kalitka	UKR	28.3.70	31 Mar
1:38:09	Karen	Foan	CAN	11.6.79	9 Aug
1:38:11		Xu Qing	CHN-J	17.4.85	13 Apr
1:38:16	Toshie	Kawatsu	JPN	17.12.81	28 Jan
1:38:18	Yelena	Kuznetsova	RUS	4.8.77	16 Jun
1:38:20		Huang Nana	CHN-J	16.1.83	13 Apr
1:38:27	Mária	Galiková	SVK	21.8.80	9 Jun
1:38:28	Francesca	Balloni	ITA	23.11.81	3 Jun
1:38:29		Lu Yanmei	CHN-J	29.6.85	13 Apr
1:38:38	Heidi	Lindewall	FIN	28.8.79	15 Jul
1:38:52	Joanne	Dow	USA	19.3.64	24 Jun
1:38:56		Ma Fulian	CHN-J	12.1.86	13 Apr
1:38:57	Emanuela	Perilli	ITA	19.5.73	22 Apr

Mark	Name		Nat	Born	Pos	Meet	Venue	Date
1:39:00	Edina	Füsti	HUN-J	24.6.82				8 Apr
1:39:05	Monica	Svensson	SWE	26.12.78				30 Jun
1:39:10	Sara-Jane	Cattermole	GBR	29.1.77				21 Jan
1:39:12A	Teresita	Collado	GUA	20.11.71				21 Apr
1:39:18	Vanessa	Espinoza	ESP	4.2.79				18 Feb
1:39:40	Aya	Kamikawa	JPN	22.1.77				28 Jan
1:39:46	Yekaterina	Dergunova	RUS-J	13.8.82				4 Mar
1:39:47		Wang Meiyan	CHN-J	28.9.82				13 Apr
1:39:50	Christine	Guinaudeau	FRA	20.6.78				23 Sep
1:39:54	Dina	Suleymanova	RUS	26.7.79				4 Mar
1:39:56	Carolina	Jiménez	ESP	2.2.80				9 Jun
1:39:58		An Shiyan	CHN-J	27.5.84				13 Apr
1:39:58	Yelena	Syrovatkaya	UKR-J	15.2.82				2 Jul
	(157)							

Best track times

Mark	Name		Nat	Born	Pos	Meet	Venue	Date
1:33:25.5 t	Valentina	Tsybulskaya	BLR	19.2.68	4	GWG	Brisbane	6 Sep
1:33:31.6 t	Tatyana	Korotkova	RUS	24.4.80	1		Izhevsk	9 Sep
1:34:15.2 t	Larisa	Safronova	RUS	6.1.80	2		Moskva	28 Jul
1:36:41.7 t	Vera	Santos	POR	3.12.81	3	NC	Lisboa (U)	21 Jul
1:38:20.1 t	Yevdokiya	Korotkova	RUS	28.2.79	6		Izhevsk	9 Sep

JUNIORS

See main list for top 11 juniors. 11 performances by 7 women to 1:31:30. Additional marks and further juniors:

Name	Mark	Pos	Meet	Venue	Date
Jian Xingli	1:31:29	15	NC	Dandong	13 Apr
Gao Kelian	1:30:45	10	NC	Dandong	13 Apr
Wang Q	1:30:01	7	NC	Dandong	13 Apr
Jiang Q	1:30:01	11	NG	Guangzhou	19 Nov

Mark	Name		Nat	Born	Pos	Meet	Venue	Date
1:35:25		Sun Lihua	CHN	30.9.83	27	NC	Dandong	13 Apr
1:37:06		Zhang Ruihong	CHN	25.12.83	31	NC	Dandong	13 Apr
1:37:19		Ding Mei	CHN	3.11.85	32	NC	Dandong	13 Apr
1:38:11		Xu Qing	CHN	17.4.85	33	NC	Dandong	13 Apr
1:38:20		Huang Nana	CHN	16.1.83	34	NC	Dandong	13 Apr
1:38:29		Lu Yanmei	CHN	29.6.85	35		Dandong	13 Apr
1:38:56		Ma Fulian	CHN	12.1.86	36	NC	Dandong	13 Apr
1:39:00	Edina	Füsti	HUN	24.6.82	4	NC	Békéscsaba	8 Apr
1:39:46	Yekaterina	Dergunova	RUS	13.8.82	16	NC-w	Adler	4 Mar
1:39:47	(20)	Wang Meiyan	CHN	28.9.82	37	NC	Dandong	13 Apr
1:39:58		An Shiyan	CHN	27.5.84	38	NC	Dandong	13 Apr

50 KILOMETRES WALK

Mark	Name		Nat	Born	Pos	Meet	Venue	Date
4:34:16	Yelena	Ginko	BLR	30.7.76	1		Scanzorosciate	28 Oct
4:34:24	Natalia	Bruniko	ITA	23.2.73	2		Scanzorosciate	28 Oct
4:36:45	Yelena	Krivokhizha	UKR	10.3.79	3		Scanzorosciate	28 Oct
4:44:39	Anita	Liepina	LAT	17.11.67	4		Scanzorosciate	28 Oct
4:49:42	Susan	Armenta	USA	19.9.73	1		Manassas	1 Apr
4:53:41	Monika	Gardini	ITA	3.11.73	5		Scanzorosciate	28 Oct
4:59:21	Monika	Choderová	CZE	15.4.76	6		Scanzorosciate	28 Oct
5:01:31	Silvia	Panseri	ITA	17.9.80	7		Scanzorosciate	28 Oct
5:05:18	Yelena	Mikhaylova	RUS-J	16.1.83	1		Sankt-Peterburg	8 Sep
5:07:02	Kora	Boufflert	FRA	23.4.66	2		Manassas	1 Apr

WORLD LIST TRENDS

Women 10th Bests

	1984	1988	1992	1995	1996	1997	1998	1999	2000	2001
100m	11.10	**10.92**	11.07	11.09	11.03	11.05	10.99	10.98	10.99	11.06
200m	22.36	**22.24**	22.44	22.50	22.27	22.45	22.53	22.31	22.49	22.63
400m	**49.74**	49.90	50.30	50.50	50.32	50.41	50.33	50.34	50.04	50.63
800m	1:57.20	**1:56.91**	1:57.93	1:58.74	1:58.22	1:58.48	1:58.39	1:58.24	1:58.34	1:58.60
1500m	4:00.18	4:01.02	4:01.23	4:04.31	4:02.38	**3:58.07**	4:00.60	4:03.14	4:01.23	4:03.20
3000m	8:37.36	8:37.70	8:42.09	8:43.19	8:43.72	8:45.70	8:44.10	8:34.19	**8:33.85**	**8:32.70**
5000m	15:30.63	15:17.89	15:19.20	14:56.94	14:48.36	14:46.72	15:03.67	14:56.00	**14:45.35**	14:51.58
10000m	32:30.91	31:42.02	31:28.06	31:43.41	31:24.08	31:16.39	31:52.98	31:32.63	**31:03.60**	31:38.18
Marathon	2:29:10	2:28:40	2:27:42	2:28:00	2:27:41	2:26:51	2:26:11	2:25:29	**2:24:33**	**2:24:21**
100mh	12.74	12.73	12.76	12.86	12.69	12.74	**12.67**	12.73	12.70	12.71
400mh	54.93	54.49	54.70	55.01	54.40	54.63	54.49	**54.15**	54.41	54.47
HJ	1.97	1.98	1.96	1.98	1.98	1.97	1.96	**1.99**	1.98	1.96
PV		-	3.70	4.01	4.15	4.20	4.34	4.46	**4.50**	**4.52**
LJ	7.01	**7.07**	6.92	6.90	6.92	6.86	6.91	6.93	6.93	6.87
TJ		13.07	14.07	14.46	14.55	14.58	14.53	**14.70**	14.52	14.57
SP	20.55	20.81	19.78	19.56	19.46	19.19	19.12	19.21	19.32	19.30
DT	68.56	**70.34**	67.08	63.90	64.90	65.86	65.05	64.68	65.41	65.12
HT		-	56.40	60.90	61.84	63.48	64.61	67.24	**69.36**	68.50
JT	66.56	**68.42**	65.02	65.22	66.14	66.52	66.43	63.52*	64.89*	64.30*
Heptathlon		**6540**	6460	6374	6406	6350	6381	6287	6396	6270
10kmW	47:08	44:20	42:50	42:18	42:16	**42:15**	42:49	42:37	43:11	43:20
20kmW								1:28:51	**1:28:06**	**1:27:55**

Other peaks: SP 20.85 (1987). Note 5000m standard event from 1995, 20km walk from 1999.

For Women's 100th bests see page 127.

MEN'S INDEX 2001

Athletes included are those ranked in ther top 100s at standard (World Championships) events (plus shorter lists for 1000m, 1M, 2000m and 3000m). Those with detailed biographical profiles are indicated in first column by:
* in this year's Annual, ^ in a previous year's Annual.

Name		Nat	Born	Ht/Wt	Event	2001 Mark	Pre-2001 Best
* Aaltonen	Timo	FIN	11.4.69	189/123	SP	20.27i, 19.47	20.70- 00
* Abate	Abiyote	ETH	20.11.80	174/56	3000	7:32.38	7:42.58- 00
					5000	13:00.36	13:10.7 - 00
Abdellah	Abdelhaq	MAR	13.8.68	174/57	1500	3:37.66	3:35.42- 96
					2000	5:00.83	5:01.95- 95
					3000	7:48.7	7:47.18- 99
Abdi	Youcef	AUS	7.12.77		1500	3:37.81	3:39.77- 00
Abdirahman	Abdi	USA	1.1.77	178/60	3000	7:47.63	
					5000	13:19.82	13:37.01- 00
					10000	28:01.02	27:46.17- 00
* Abdullah	Khamis Seif	QAT	1.12.76	181/64	3kSt	8:14.38	8:17.56- 00
* Abera	Gezahegne	ETH	23.4.78	168/57	Mar	2:09:25	2:07:54- 99
Abraham	Aléxis	FRA	14.2.76	185/70	1500	3:36.05	3:36.28- 00
Abrahams	Shawn	RSA	4.7.70		800	1:46.49	1:45.03- 00
* Aburaya	Shigeru	JPN	6.2.77	163/51	Mar	2:07:52	2:10:48- 00
* Achike	Larry	GBR	31.1.75	188/75	TJ	17.21	17.30, 17.31w- 00
Achon	Julius	UGA	12.12.76	168/55	1500	3:37.60	3:35.68- 97
Adán	José Carlos	ESP	22.7.67	166/57	10000	28:22.54	27:59.49- 93
Aden	Ibrahim	USA	11.11.72	177/57	1500	3:38.19	3:36.47- 97
* Admassu	Yibeltal	ETH	80	165/52	10000	27:55.24	
Adsuar	Antonio	ESP	4.7.78	178/79	LJ	8.03	7.95, 8.06w- 00
Afanasyev	Nikolay	RUS	11.8.65	187/80	Dec	7812	8090h- 85
Aggoune	Khoudir	ALG	5.1.81		5000	13:22.32	14:01.16- 00
Agoston	Tiberiu	ROM/FRA	25.12.76	185/75	PV	5.61i	5.45i, 5.35- 00
Aïssat	Nicolas	FRA	24.7.80	175/60	800	1:44.98	1:47.82- 00
					1000	2:16.86	2:23.9 - 98
Akashi	Ken	JPN	6.11.76	169/59	50kW	4:05:45	
* Al Bishi	Hamdam Odha	KSA	5.5.81	180/70	400	45.00	44.66- 00
Al-Ahmadi	Salem M	KSA	12.9.69	185/75	TJ	16.50	17.07- 97
Alaräisänen	Pekka	FIN	27.12.75	188/110	JT	81.63	80.26- 00
Al-Asmari	Sa'ad Shaddad	KSA	24.9.68	185/72	3kSt	8:15.01	8:08.26- 97
Al-Bekheet	Khaled	KUW	12.1.76		LJ	7.91	7.75- 98
Al-Bekheet	Said Mansour	QAT			LJ	7.94	7.49- 00
Albert	Eric	FRA	30.7.79	186/108	HT	70.48	70.58- 00
Albert	Lars	GER	9.2.82		Dec	7683	7156- 00
Al-Dosari	Rashid	QAT	8.5.81	198/130	DT	62.77	60.16- 00
* Alekna	Virgilijus	LTU	13.2.72	200/130	DT	70.99	73.88- 00
Aleksejev	Marko	EST	14.2.79	196/78	HJ	2.25i	2.26i, 2.22- 00
Alemayehu	Simeretu	ETH	18.10.70	182/68	Mar	2:07:45	2:08:33- 00
* Alemu	Birhane	ETH	16.7.82	178/63	1500	3:38.75i	3:35.67- 00
Alexander	Niconnor	TRI	4.2.77	178/68	100	10.23w	10.19, 10.0- 00, 10.13w- 99
^ Alisevich	Vitaliy	BLR	15.6.67	186/112	HT	74.46	82.16- 88
* Aliu	Deji	NGR	22.11.75	187/75	100	10.07	10.02- 95, 9.9- 96
					200	20.55	20.43A- 98, 20.43- 99
Allaert	Koen	BEL	29.9.72		10000	28:20.89	28:11.42- 00
					Mar	2:10:45	2:11:19- 00
Allen	Jeremy	USA	5.9.79	185/109	SP	19.27	18.55- 00
Allen	Joe	USA	7.7.78	190/82	LJ	7.94	7.68, 7.89w- 00
Allen	Kris	USA	14.4.79	178/68	110H	13.60, 13.52w	13.76, 13.61w- 00
Allevi	Massimo	ITA	23.11.69	182/75	PV	5.55	5.60- 98
Al-Nubi	Abdulrahman	QAT	17.10.79	190/80	LJ	7.92	8.11- 98
^ Al-Nubi	Mubarak	QAT	30.12.77	185/72	400H	49.36	48.17A- 78
Al-Sabee	Hussein	KSA	14.11.79	186/82	LJ	8.31	8.33- 00
Al-Saffar	Jamal	KSA	24.10.71	175/64	100	10.24, 10.17w?	10.33- 99
Al-Shoumari	Abdullah	KSA	10.7.78		DT	60.41	56.68- 00
* Al-Somaily	Hadi Soua'an	KSA	30.12.76	191/72	400H	47.99	47.53- 00
Álvarez	Alberto	ESP	22.12.75		3kSt	8:22.06	8:37.95- 00
Al-Yami	Salem Mubarak	KSA	9.2.82	175/70	100	10.25, 10.12w?	10.27- 00
Ambrosch	Klaus	AUT	23.5.73	188/88	Dec	8122	8113- 00
Ames	Dan	USA	16.1.81	193/109	SP	19.46	18.40- 00
					DT	61.00	58.53- 00
Amine	Mohammed	MAR	25.5.76	168/53	3000	7:35.35	7:38.97- 98
					5000	13:05.44	13:29.2 - 97
Ammons	Andre	USA	12.11.78	175/73	400	45.89	46.16- 00
Andam	Kenneth	GHA	8.1.76	186/70	100	10.22A, 10.12Aw	10.21, 10.13Aw - 00
					200	20.66A	20.68A- 78, 20.47Aw- 99

	Name		Nat	Born	Ht/Wt	Event	2001 Mark	Pre-2001 Best
	Anderson	Avery	USA	16.3.73	188/84	Dec	7717	7952- 00
	Anderson	LeVar	USA	26.3.77	183/77	TJ	16.77i, 16.84w, 16.49	16.98, 17.00i- 00, 17.12w- 99
	Anderson	Stuart	AUS	19.6.79		110H	13.73	14.11- 00
^	Andji	Alain	FRA	20.11.74	187/89	PV	5.60i, 5.50	5.85- 97
	André	João	POR	28.5.76	181/82	PV	5.51i, 5.45	5.60- 00
	Andrei	Cristiano	ITA	14.5.73	198/115	DT	60.75	63.55- 00
*	Andreyev	Vladimir	RUS	7.9.66	180/68	20kW	1:20:14. 1:24:08.1t	1:18:16- 00
	Andriani	Ottaviano	ITA	4.1.74	171/61	Mar	2:09:07	2:11:42- 99
	Andriuskevicius	Gintaras	LTU	6.7.75	176/60	20kW	1:22:10	1:22:29- 97
	Andronov	Yuriy	RUS	6.11.71	180/68	50kW	3:52:57	3:47:04- 96
	Andrzejak	Krzysztof	POL	10.1.75	192/79	Dec	7860	7508- 00
	Anibal	Mário	POR	25.3.72	187/90	Dec	8213	8136- 00
	Anlezark	Justin	AUS	14.8.77	187/118	SP	20.14	20.35- 00
*	Annus	Adrián	HUN	28.6.73	194/102	HT	83.39	81.73- 99
	Antona	David	ESP	18.11.78	180/73	HJ	2.25i, 2.23	2.22- 00
	Apablaza	Felipe	CHI	19.4.77	184/72	HJ	2.22A	2.21- 99
	Apak	Esref	TUR	3.1.82	185/97	HT	72.82	69.97- 00
	Áquila	Yonelvis	CUB	1.8.75		Dec	7585	7844- 98
	Aracic	Luka	CRO	13.3.81	184/78	LJ	8.12	7.77- 00
	Aragón	Leigner	COL	8.3.76		TJ	16.54A	16.15A- 00
	Aritkulov	Ramil	RUS	78		800	1:46.93	1:48.32- 98
	Armstrong	Aaron	USA	14.10.77	173/70	200	20.58, 20.37w	20.08- 99
	Armstrong	Lawrence	USA	19.3.78	178/77	100	10.15w	10.16, 10.07w- 00
						200	20.62w	20.66, 20.44w- 00
	Armstrong	Sherman	USA	22.9.78	185/75	400H	49.91	48.61- 00
*	Arnold	Dominique	USA	14.9.73	185/76	110H	13.14	13.11- 00
	Arsoniádis	Harálabos	GRE	19.1.78		HT	70.85	70.40- 00
	Arzamasov	Sergey	KAZ	9.4.71	190/75	TJ	16.70	17.27- 95, 17.28w- 93
	Asahara	Nobuharu	JPN	21.6.72	178/72	100	10.02	10.08, 10.04w- 97
	Asami	Kimihiro	JPN	8.11.72	185/78	110H	13.60	13.72- 00
^	Aseledchenko	Aleksandr	RUS	10.10.73	190/76	TJ	16.54i, 16.48	17.29- 97
	Ash	Contrell	USA	21.10.80	173/66	200	20.71	21:8 - 99
	Assmus	Ralf	GER	28.1.77	177/69	1500	3:38.78	3:40.54- 99
						3kSt	8:19.32	8:24.11- 00
*	Astapkovich	Igor	BLR	4.1.63	191/118	HT	82.76	84.62- 92
	Astapkovich	Konstantin	BLR	23.10.70	185/120	HT	76.72	79.08- 99
	Atanasov	Nikolay	BUL	11.12.74	188/72	LJ	8.07	8.20- 00
	Attene	Alessandro	ITA	10.9.77	181/81	200	20.72	20.57- 97
*	Austin	Charles	USA	19.12.67	184/77	HJ	2.31i, 2.30	2.40- 91
	Avellaneda	Mario	ESP	12.11.74	168/58	50kW	3:50:29	3:49:50- 00
*	Averbukh	Alex	ISR	1.10.74	178/76	PV	5.91	5.85- 00
	Awazie	Nduka	NGR	4.4.81	172/74	400	45.65	45.44- 98
	Awere	Mark Anthony	GHA	16.7.71	179/69	LJ	8.02	8.04- 99
	Ayre	Sanjay	JAM	19.6.80	188/75	400	45.58	45.58- 00
	Azaronok	Ivan	BLR	17.7.79	177/65	20kW	1:23:44	1:24:34- 00
*	Baala	Mehdi	FRA	17.8.78	183/65	800	1:46.94	1:46.24- 00
						1000	2:17.80, 2:17.36i	2:15.45- 00
						1500	3:31.97	3:32.05- 00
	Baba	Youssef	MAR	7.8.79	173/55	1500	3:34.21	3:33.92- 00
						1M	3:55.10	3:52.85- 00
						2000	4:58.93i	
*	Backley	Steve	GBR	12.2.69	196/100	JT	90.81	91.46- 92
	Bada	Sunday	NGR	21.6.69	188/79	400	45.83	44.63- 93
	Baday	Ahmed Ibrahim	MAR	12.1.79	182/74	10000	28:09.3	
	Bae Kyung-ho		KOR	16.3.76		HJ	2.24	2.20- 97
	Bagy	Hakim	FRA	31.3.68	175/60	Mar	2:11:06	2:12:49- 00
*	Baha	Faustin	TAN	30.5.82		HMar	61:53	59:38- 00
	Bai Liansheng		CHN	28.7.78	178/65	20kW	1:22:05	1:23:34- 00
						50kW	3:51:52	3:59:08- 00
	Bailey	Donovan	CAN	16.12.67	183/82	100	10.20, 10.11w?	9.84- 96
	Baillie	Chris	GBR	21.4.81	184/72	110H	13.70w	13.84- 00
*	Bakken	Marius	NOR	27.3.78	183/63	3000	7:40.77	7:42.05- 00
						5000	13:09.19	13:11.30- 00
	Balan	Costica	ROM	25.8.64	172/62	20kW	1:22:44	1:21:06- 96
*	Baldini	Stefano	ITA	25.5.71	176/58	10000	28:21.38	27:43.98- 96
						HMar	61:30	60:56- 97, 60:50w- 00
						Mar	2:08:51	2:07:57- 97
	Bamidele	Taiwo	NGR			100	10.21	
	Bamouh	Mustapha	MAR	21.12.72	182/74	10000	28:09.3	
	Bangué	Emmanuel	FRA	21.7.71	180/72	LJ	7.95	8.25- 96, 8.32w- 99

	Name		Nat	Born	Ht/Wt	Event	2001 Mark	Pre-2001 Best
	Baptista	Messias	BRA	24.5.68		TJ	16.66, 16.70w	16.99A- 96, 16.69- 97
	Baranovskiy	Aleksandr	RUS	22.10.80	180/90	JT	77.37	73.87- 99
	Barbour	Jonathan	GBR	3.11.80	184/79	100	10.13w	10.28- 00
*	Barmasai	Bernard	KEN	6.5.74	173/55	3kSt	8:05.00	7:55.72- 97
	Barnaby	Marlon	JAM	26.10.79	179/71	100	10.10w	10.43, 10.23w- 00
	Barras	Romain	FRA	1.8.80	192/80	Dec	7876	7609- 00
	Barré	Franck	FRA	15.7.77	181/67	800	1:46.53	1:48.69- 00
	Barrett	Craig	NZL	16.11.71	183/70	50kW	3:48:05	3:48:14- 99
	Barry	Damion	TRI	3.3.82	188/83	400	45.75	45.86- 00
	Bartels	Ralf	GER	21.2.78	186/116	SP	20.30	19.34- 00
	Barthel	Trond	NOR	11.9.70	190/90	PV	5.45	5.72- 96
	Barus	Benson	KEN	4.7.80		10000	28:09.32A	28:23.01- 00
	Batangdon	Joseph	CMR	29.7.78	180/75	200	20.31	20.31A, 20.3- 99, 20.31- 00
	Bátovsky	Milos	SVK	26.5.79	178/65	20kW	1:24:02	1:26:51- 00
*	Baumann ¶	Dieter	GER	9.2.65	178/64	3000	7:47.29idq	7:30.50- 98
	Bavikin	Vadim	ISR	4.10.70	186/90	JT	80.54	80.48- 00, 81.56R- 91
	Baxter	Jimmy	USA	17.11.81	196/84	HJ	2.23	2.18- 00
	Bay	Abdellah	MAR	.75		10000	28:26.6	
	Bayo	Zebedayio	TAN	20.5.76	178/64	HMar	62:01	60:26- 98
						Mar	2:11:12	2:08:51- 98
	Beauchamp	William	GBR	9.9.70	196/110	HT	72.60	72.63- 99
	Beckenhauer	Ryan	USA	7.1.79	188/129	SP	19.57	
*	Beckford	James	JAM	9.1.75	183/73	LJ	8.41	8.62- 97, 8.68w- 95
	Béhar	Abdellah	FRA	5.7.63	172/58	Mar	2:09:05	2:09:09- 00
*	Bekele	Kenenisa	ETH	13.6.82	160/54	3000	7:30.67	7:46.95- 00
						5000	13:13.33	13:20.57- 00
	Bell	Kenta	USA	16.3.77		LJ	7.90, 8.00w	8.05- 00
						TJ	17.22	17.22- 00
*	Belonog	Yuriy	UKR	9.3.74	200/130	SP	20.98	21.64- 00
						DT	62.23	65.32- 99
	Belov	Aleksey	RUS	76		HJ	2.22i	2.24- 00
	Belov	Yuriy	BLR	20.3.81	183/115	SP	19.52	18.83- 00
	Belz	Christian	SUI	11.9.74	178/63	3kSt	8:22.24	8:24.10- 99
	Bengtsson	Bengt	SWE	4.9.61	176/65	50kW	3:56:27	3:59:27- 99, 3:49:24sc- 00
	Benjamin	Tim	GBR	2.5.82	183/72	200	20.67	20.72, 20.60w- 99
	Benoy	Rich	USA	14.7.68	193/90	110H	13.70w	13.49- 95, 13.3- 99
	Benslimani	Mourad	ALG	19.2.74	178/64	3kSt	8:28.85	8:25.32- 00
	Benzine	Réda	ALG	19.4.71	180/63	3000	7:44.72	7:41.85- 00
						5000	13:27.44	13:20.85- 96
	Berdeja	Cristian	MEX	21.6.81		20kW	1:21:20	1:23:46- 00
	Bergdahl	Kim	FIN	5.3.78	183/66	3kSt	8:35.06	8:35.30- 00
*	Bérioui	Saïd	MAR	3.6.75	178/65	3000	7:48.74, 7:48.65i	7:42.39- 98
						5000	13:24.16	13:15.10- 99
	Bernard	Claston	JAM	22.3.79	193/90	Dec	8024	7806- 00
	Berrabah	Yahya	MAR	13.10.81		LJ	8.12	
	Berradi	Rachid	ITA	29.8.75	176/56	10000	28:25.77	27:54.23- 00
^	Berrett	Tim	CAN	23.1.65	179/66	20kW	1:23:46	1:21:46- 00
						50kW	3:59:34	3:50:23- 93
	Berrian	Tony	USA	12.2.79	183/72	400	45.61	45.83- 99
	Berryhill	Bryan	USA	15.12.77	183/75	800	1:46.03	1:46.98- 99
						1500	3:35.48	3:39.96- 99
						1M	3:54.87	3:56.52- 99
	Bessou	Laïd	ALG	5.2.76	179/62	3kSt	8:19.87	8:10.23- 00
	Betanzos	Yoandri	CUB	15.2.82	179/71	TJ	16.84, 16.86w	16.82- 00
*	Bett	Mark	KEN	22.12.76	180/64	3000	7:36.66	7:44.20- 98
						5000	12:58.72	12:55.63- 00
						10000	27:24.68	27:18.66- 98
	Beumer	Stefan	NED	28.4.81	191/68	800	1:46.71	1:47.23- 00
	Beyer	Jamie	USA	29.12.76	193/113	SP	19.80	19.53i, 19.33- 99
	Bi Zhong		CHN	1.9.68	188/110	HT	70.65	77.04- 89
	Bian Aiguo		CHN	10.6.80	178/65	20kW	1:22:29	1:26:01- 00
	Bíber	Zsolt	HUN	31.5.76	194/104	SP	20.47	19.46- 00
	Bielecki	Jan	DEN	20.2.71	188/103	HT	75.75	76.11- 99
	Bigdeli	Schahriar	GER	26.3.80	182/71	LJ	8.15	8.04, 8.22w- 00
	Bindilatti	Édson	BRA	13.3.79		Dec	7631	7539- 00
^	Birir	Matthew	KEN	5.7.72	172/62	3kSt	8:28.2A	8:08.12- 95
*	Bitok	Paul	KEN	26.6.70	173/58	1500	3:31.96	3:35.82- 98
						3000	7:31.00	7:28.41- 96
						5000	13:00.10	13:04.15- 00
	Bitzi	Ivan	SUI	4.8.75	185/73	110H	13.74	13.61- 99
	Biwott	Paul	KEN	78		HMar	62:08	

Name		Nat	Born	Ht/Wt	Event	2001 Mark	Pre-2001 Best
Biwott	Peter	KEN	22.8.76	182/67	1500	3:34.81	3:35.25- 00
					1M	3:53.16	
* Biwott	Simon	KEN	3.3.70		Mar	2:09:40	2:07:41- 99
Blackwood	Michael	JAM	29.8.76	190/79	400	45.66	44.69- 00
Blaha	Karel	CZE	1.6.75	180/74	400	45.82	45.82- 00
Blanco	José Luis	ESP	3.6.75	175/61	3kSt	8:15.36	8:20.44- 00
* Blank	Peter	GER	10.4.62	195/103	JT	88.70	88.12- 96
Blanton	DaBryan	USA	83?	183/75	200	20.37	21.33, 20.79w- 00
Blom	Rens	NED	1.3.77	178/75	PV	5.70	5.75- 00
Blomquist	Stefan	SWE	7.2.65		SP	19.00	19.04- 00
Blonskiy	Sergey	UKR	7.1.73	187/85	Dec	7890	7706- 95
* Bloom	Andy	USA	11.8.73	185/120	SP	20.94	21.82- 00
					DT	66.17	68.46- 00
Blouin	Gaëtan	FRA	4.1.74	190/85	Dec	7762	7909- 00, 7998w- 98
* Boateng	Kwaku	CAN	30.6.74	193/84	HJ	2.31	2.34- 00
^ Bochkaryov	Pyotr	RUS	3.11.67	186/82	PV	5.60i, 5.50	5.90i- 94, 5.86- 96
Bochkov	Sergey	AZE	20.8.79	185/74	TJ	16.50	16.70- 99
Bock	Detlef	GER	15.8.74	194/114	SP	19.59	20.16- 00
Bogdanov	Dmitriy	RUS	11.4.79	190/77	800	1:46.02	1:45.76- 00
Böhm	Sven	GER	5.12.78		Dec	7610	7534- 99
Boisrond	Mathieu	FRA	8.1.77	175/69	PV	5.50	5.51- 99
Boit	Josphat	KEN	83		5000	13:17.12	13:45.15- 00
* Boit Kipketer	Wilson	KEN	6.10.73	167/52	3kSt	8:01.73	7:59.08- 97
* Boldon	Ato	TRI	30.12.73	176/75	100	9.88	9.86- 98
					200	20.24	19.77- 97
Bolles	Cameron	USA	24.3.76		DT	61.37	58.69- 00
Bongelo	Nathan B.	BEL	2.12.73		100	10.21w	10.33 - 00
Bönisch	Stefan	GER	10.8.77	183/67	400H	50.07	50.42- 98
Bor	Simon	KEN	13.2.69		Mar	2:09:27	2:08:47- 98
* Börgeling	Lars	GER	16.4.79	187/84	PV	5.80i, 5.80	5.80- 99
* Borichevskiy	Aleksandr	RUS	25.6.70	195/120	DT	64.66	65.08- 99
Borisov	Valeriy	KAZ	18.9.66	180/62	20kW	1:22:50.3t	1:19:55- 96
Borodkin	Andrey	UKR	18.4.78	202/122	SP	19.71	19.01- 00
Borrman	Mattias	SWE	20.6.72	184/111	DT	60.38	62.01- 99
Borsumato	Anthony	GBR	13.12.73	185/82	400H	49.30	49.68- 00
* Borzakovskiy	Yuriy	RUS	12.4.81	181/70	800	1:42.47	1:44.33- 00
Bosch	Nadir	FRA	16.5.73	191/68	1500	3:34.35	3:32.06- 99
* Boswell	Mark	CAN	28.7.77	189/77	HJ	2.33	2.35- 99
Botfa	Péter	HUN	30.6.79	187/123	HT	75.33	77.42- 00
Botha	Adriaan	RSA	8.3.77	183/79	400	45.14A, 45.42	45.40A- 99
Botha	Hennie	RSA	20.2.75	180/68	400H	50.06	49.02A, 49.60- 00
^ Botha	Johan	RSA	10.1.74	181/68	800	1:45.80i	1:43.91- 99
Botha	Werner	RSA	31.1.78	186/73	800	1:46.3A	1:44.41- 00
Ould Bouchiba	Merzak	ALG	27.4.75		3kSt	8:26.90	8:27.19- 00
Boukensa	Tarek	ALG	19.11.81		1500	3:36.22	3:41.08- 00
Boulahfane	Kamal	ALG	1.7.76	178/63	1500	3:38.61i	3:33.07- 00
* Boulami	Brahim	MAR	20.4.72	180/64	3kSt	7:55.28	8:02.90- 00
Boulanger	David	FRA	11.12.74	176/64	50kW	3:51:36	3:56:42- 00
Boulge	Kazimierz	POL	13.2.76	195/99	HT	76.58	76.20- 00
Bourgeois	Joël	CAN	25.4.71	175/58	3kSt	8:26.92	8:20.08- 99
Bourifa	Migidio	ITA	31.1.69		Mar	2:11:04	2:10:15- 00
Bourrouag	Tarik	GER	9.7.76	185/74	800	1:46.85	1:45.98- 98
Boussombo	Antoine	GAB	18.5.68	178/69	100	10.18	10.13, 10.02w- 00, 10.0w- 98
Bown	Darren	AUS	30.6.74	178/63	50kW	3:55:05	4:35:13- 97
* Bownes	Shaun	RSA	24.10.70	194/90	110H	13.26	13.39- 99, 13.2A- 98, 13.38w- 00
* Bramlett	Ron	USA	22.10.79	181/68	110H	13.43, 13.39w	13.47- 00
Brannen	Nathan	CAN	8.9.82		800	1:46.60	1:50.35- 00
Braunskill	Kevin	USA	31.3.69	175/70	100	10.25A, 10.23w	10.16- 98, 10.11w- 93
					200	20.39	20.22A- 94, 20.37- 98,20.21w- 91,19.9-90
Brayko	Pyotr	RUS	27.3.77	202/74	HJ	2.29	2.30i- 99, 2.28- 00
Bredwood	Llewellyn	JAM	30.4.76	178/77	100	10.13	10.09, 10.07w- 00
					200	20.47	20.55- 98
Brew	Derrick	USA	28.12.77	185/82	400	44.80	44.29- 99
Brisseault	David	FRA	7.3.69	185/95	JT	76.52	79.85- 00
* Brits	Okkert	RSA	22.8.73	198/84	PV	5.70i, 5.60A	6.03- 95
Broe	Tim	USA	20.6.77	180/66	3000	7:39.45	7:53.26i- 99
					5000	13:24.13	13:43.61- 00
					3kSt	8:14.82	8:21.50- 00
Brokenburr	Kenny	USA	29.10.68	178/79	100	10.13	10.04- 97, 9.90w- 99
Brown	Carl	USA	11.2.70	193/105	DT	63.78	63.35- 00
Brown	Chris	BAH	14.10.79	178/68	400	45.45/45.20?	45.08- 00

	Name		Nat	Born	Ht/Wt	Event	2001 Mark	Pre-2001 Best
	Brown	Darrel	TRI	11.10.84	184/79	100	10.24	10.34- 00
						200	20.41	21.14, 20.76w- 00
	Brown	Shawn	USA	79		HJ	2.25	2.20, 2.21i- 99
	Browne	Pierre	CAN	14.1.80	178/75	100	10.19, 10.17w	10.24, 10.21w- 00
						200	20.57	20.49- 00
	Brunson	Marcus	USA	24.4.78	185/79	100	10.10, 10.06w	10.10- 99
						200	20.37	20.42- 99
*	Bucher	André	SUI	19.10.76	185/75	800	1:42.55	1:42.92- 99
						1000	2:15.63	2:15.66- 99
	Buciarski	Piotr	DEN	22.11.75	183/79	PV	5.61	5.60- 00
	Buckfield	Nick	GBR	5.6.73	187/78	PV	5.75A, 5.60	5.80- 98
*	Buckland	Stéphane	MRI	20.1.77	187/73	100	10.13	10.16- 00, 10.0A- 99
						200	20.15	20.31- 00
*	Buder	Oliver-Sven	GER	23.6.66	200/150	SP	20.32	21.47i- 98, 21.42- 99
	Budzillo	Artur	POL	21.7.79	184/66	110H	13.70	13.98- 00
	Buller	Russ	USA	10.9.78	178/72	PV	5.81	5.80i- 99, 5.71- 00
	Bunce	Alan	NZL	23.8.67	178/66	10000	28:26.80	
*	Bungei	Wilfred	KEN	24.7.80	172/60	800	1:42.96	1:44.23- 00
	Burayev	Viktor	RUS	23.2.82	176/58	20kW	1:18:06, 1:21:29.2t	1:28:18- 99
^	Burge	Peter	AUS	3.7.74	187/80	LJ	8.11i, 8.05, 8.07w	8.30, 8.48w- 00
	Burgess	Paul	AUS	14.8.79	183/78	PV	5.71	5.60- 98
	Burkenya	Danila	RUS	20.7.78	198/84	LJ	8.31	8.12- 00
	Burlachenko	Pavel	RUS	7.4.76	184/80	PV	5.86A, 5.55	5.81- 98
	Burnett	Gabriel	BAR	20.9.75	170/73	110H	13.69	13.62- 00
*	Busemann	Frank	GER	26.2.75	191/80	LJ	8.04	8.07- 96
						Dec	8192	8706- 96
*	Buss	Martin	GER	7.4.76	195/82	HJ	2.36	2.35- 99
*	Byrd	Leonard	USA	17.3.75	178/64	400	44.83	44.88- 96
	Caballero	Francisco Javier	ESP	24.3.72	172/60	Mar	2:10:41	
	Cai Peng		CHN	28.3.83	188/80	LJ	7.92w	8.02- 99
	Caimmi	Daniele	ITA	17.12.72	180/62	5000	13:26.26	13:30.92- 00
						Mar	2:10:26	2:11:29- 99
*	Caines	Daniel	GBR	15.5.79	180/72	400	45.58	45.37- 00
*	Calado	Carlos	POR	5.10.75	186/80	LJ	8.21	8.36- 97
						TJ	16.50w	
	Calligny	Fabrice	FRA	4.11.81	180/74	100	10.26, 10.22w	10.34, 10.19w- 99
	Calvin	Mark	USA	17.11.74		PV	5.47	5.51A- 97
	Calvo	Michael	CUB	26.12.77	182/65	TJ	17.30	17.30- 97
*	Camossi	Paolo	ITA	6.1.74	176/68	TJ	17.34	17.45- 00
	Campbell	Brandon	USA	12.7.80	193/88	HJ	2.25	2.16- 98
*	Campbell	Darren	GBR	12.9.73	185/86	100	10.16	10.04- 98
						200	20.41	20.13- 00
	Campbell	Kendrick	USA	16.12.77	188/79	200	20.62w	20.66A- 00
	Campbell	Michael	JAM	11.9.78	188/79	400	45.65	45.79- 98
*	Campbell	Milton	USA	15.5.76	178/75	400	45.39, 45.3	44.67- 97
	Campeny	Moisés	ESP	27.5.79	186/90	HT	71.71	73.65- 99
	Campus	Milko	ITA	2.4.69	173/65	LJ	8.03irr-ex	8.13, 8.15ex, 8.31Aw- 94
	Canal	David	ESP	7.12.78	183/63	400	45.04	45.20- 98
*	Cankar	Gregor	SLO	25.1.75	180/68	LJ	8.12, 8.19w	8.40- 97
	Cantwell	Christian	USA	30.9.80	198/132	SP	19.71	19.67- 00
	Cao Jing		CHN	31.1.78		110H	13.69w	13.92, 13.83w- 99
	Capponi	Paolo	ITA	25.3.76	181/98	SP	19.24	18.57- 00
	Carabelli	Gianni	ITA	30.5.79	187/69	400H	50.09	49.92- 00
*	Cárdenas	Alejandro	MEX	4.10.74	186/73	400	45.85A	44.31- 99
	Cardoso	Augusto	POR	13.12.70	176/65	20kW	1:23:48	1:22:40- 99
	Caro	Francisco José	ESP	23.10.78	190/80	Dec	7648	7689- 00
^	Carosi	Angelo	ITA	20.1.64	182/66	3kSt	8:29.13	8:14.02- 94
*	Carroll	Mark	IRL	15.1.72	177/66	1500	3:35.09	3:34.91- 00
						1M	3:54.5i	3:50.62- 00
						3000	7:33.52	7:30.36- 99
						5000	13:08.32	13:03.93- 98
*	Carter	James	USA	7.5.78	185/77	400H	48.44	48.04- 00
	Carter	Jonathan	USA	10.5.72	178/73	100	10.24, 10.23w	10.04, 10.00w- 98
*	Carter	LaMark	USA	23.8.70	180/75	TJ	17.17	17.44- 98
	Carter	Marcel	USA	26.3.71	170/66	200	20.62	20.34- 93
	Casandra	Silviu	ROM	27.10.75	183/64	20kW	1:22:34	1:21:35- 00
	Casarsa	Paolo	ITA	2.7.75	192/85	Dec	7805	7586- 00
	Catarino	Paulo	POR	30.9.63	174/55	HMar	62:09	62:13- 99
	Caulfield	Daniel	IRL	16.10.72		800	1:46.80	1:46.65- 00
	Cavallaro	Alessandro	ITA	22.2.80	180/71	200	20.56	20.48- 00, 20.46w- 99
	Cebulski	Joe	USA	25.10.76		Dec	7969	7624w-00

	Name		Nat	Born	Ht/Wt	Event	2001 Mark	Pre-2001 Best
	Cerra	Juan Ignacio	ARG	16.10.76	180/110	HT	76.42	74.32- 00
	César	José Angel	CUB	4.1.78	178/75	100	10.18w	10.36, 10.22w- 00
	Chakouian	Jeff	USA	20.4.82	183/118	SP	20.13	20.08i, 18.89- 00
	Challenger	Ben	GBR	7.3.78	186/75	HJ	2.26	2.30- 99
*	Chambers	Dwain	GBR	5.4.78	180/83	100	9.99, 9.97w?	9.97- 99
						200	20.31	20.68- 99
	Chang Chunhu		CHN	1.5.82		20kW	1:23:07	
	Chang Ming		CHN	4.11.83		50kW	4:04:16	
	Chang Wei		CHN	5.7.83		20kW	1:22:20	1:29:51- 00
	Chapado	Raúl	ESP	4.5.70	194/85	TJ	16.75i	16.83- 97, 16.87i 98
	Charfreitag	Libor	SVK	11.9.77	191/110	HT	77.65	77.22- 00
	Chaussinand	David	FRA	19.4.73	193/105	HT	80.99	79.81- 99
	Chebet	Peter	KEN	74		HMar	60:56	
*	Chebii	Abraham	KEN	23.12.79	172/63	3000	7:40.30	7:45.29- 99
						5000	13:12.53	13:01.9 - 00
						10000	27:04.20	28:01.63- 99
	Chébili	Saïd	FRA	6.5.73	180/66	1500	3:35.64	3:33.66- 99
						2000	4:59.31	4:57.39- 97
	Cheboiboch	Christopher	KEN	3.3.77		HMar	60:45	60:49- 00
	Checcucci	Maurizio	ITA	26.2.74	182/72	100	10.09w	10.32- 00
	Chege	Laban	KEN	10.9.69	172/66	HMar	61:16	60:12sh?- 95, 61:02- 95
	Chehibi	Mouhsin	MAR	28.1.78	182/70	800	1:46.54	1:46.15- 99
	Chékhémani	Abdelkader	FRA	18.7.71	180/70	1500	3:38.46	3:33.10- 96
	Chékhémani	Rachid	FRA	1.10.73	174/62	3000	7:38.57	7:58.53- 99
						5000	13:20.14	13:28.65- 00
	Chelanga	Joshua	KEN	7.4.73		HMar	61:05	61:02- 97
						Mar	2:10:29	
*	Chelule	David	KEN	7.7.77	179/63	10000	28:22.39	27:32.18- 96
	Chelule	Julius	KEN	25.12.78	171/55	3kSt	8:35.17	8:10.41- 99
	Chemlal	Abdellatif	MAR	1.1.82		3kSt	8:32.3	8:33.5- 00
	Chemweno	David	KEN	18.12.81	175/58	1M	3:56.60	
						3kSt	8:30.12	8:31.95- 00
	Chen Haijian		CHN	5.4.80	173/70	100	10.20	10.30- 00
	Chen Qi		CHN	10.3.82		JT	77.89	77.88- 00
	Chen Tien-Wen		TPE	1.6.78	180/70	400H	48.63	49.93- 00
	Chen Yanhao		CHN	2.1.72	183/72	110H	13.37	13.39- 94, 13.26w- 96
	Chenn	Marc	USA	6.3.76	189/77	HJ	2.25iA, 2.22A	2.25A- 00
	Chepkisa	David	KEN	1.1.74	175/62	3kSt	8:16.28	8:23.36- 00
*	Chepkurui	Albert	KEN	4.4.81	170/54	3000	7:48.90	7:43.01- 99
						5000	13:18.71	12:59.90- 00
						10000	28:06.86	
	Chepkwony	Julius	KEN	6.6.69	175/73	400	45.46A	45.15A- 96, 45.75- 95
	Cherevko	Leonid	BLR	21.4.74	198/126	DT	64.97	65.56- 00
	Chernovol	Gennadiy	KAZ	6.6.76	185/71	100	10.23	10.32- 98
						200	20.47	20.70- 98
	Cherono	Abraham	KEN	21.7.80	174/62	3kSt	8:16.57	8:13.22- 00
	Cherono	Joseph	KEN			Mar	2:10:47	
*	Cherono	Stephen	KEN	15.10.82	177/64	1500	3:35.47	3:41.08- 99
						3000	7:46.03	7:48.6+- 00
						3kSt	7:58.66	8:16.27- 00
	Cheruiyot	Fred	KEN	20.9.70	172/62	1500	3:35.31	3:34.48- 99
						1M	3:54.79	3:52.92- 98
	Cheruiyot	Kenneth	KEN	2.8.74	173/53	Mar	2:07:18	2:08:22- 00
	Cheruiyot	Robert	KEN	20.12.74		Mar	2:10:41	
	Cheruiyot	William	KEN	67		Mar	2:08:58	2:08:48- 00
	Cheseret	William	KEN	71		HMar	62:12	
	Cheval ¶	Christophe	FRA	25.2.71	177/72	100	10.21dq	10.21- 98
						200	20.58dq, 20.56wdq	20.41, 20.38w- 98
	Chiba	Yoshihiro	JPN	29.4.79	177/63	400H	48.65	49.35- 00
	Chiesa	Sergio	ITA	7.9.72		Mar	2:10:30	2:15:54- 00
	Chimier	Jonathan	MRI	6.8.82	175/75	LJ	7.89, 8.03w	7.85- 00
	Chipu	Abner	RSA	2.1.72	160/77	HMar	61:50	
	Chirchir	Cornelius	KEN	7.10.83	172/58	800	1:44.98	
						1500	3:34.53	3:35.16- 00
	Chirchir	Robert	KEN	26.11.72	173/60	800	1:46.8A	1:43.33- 98
*	Chirchir	William	KEN	6.2.79	175/55	800	1:44.02	1:43.33- 99
						1500	3:29.29	3:31.02- 00
						1M	3:52.86	3:47.94- 00
*	Chistiakov	Viktor	AUS	9.2.75	202/92	PV	5.80	5.90, 5.95ex- 99
	Chorny	Thomas	USA	23.11.76	183/70	3kSt	8:22.16	8:27.67- 00
	Chouki	Fouad	FRA	1.10.78	183/69	1500	3:33.89	3:36.83- 00

Name		Nat	Born	Ht/Wt	Event	2001 Mark	Pre-2001 Best
Christian	Brendan	USA	11.12.83	170/64	200	20.56, 20.3w	20.78- 00
Chrzanowski	Tomasz	POL	12.7.81	189/119	SP	19.16	19.00- 00
Chu Ki-young		KOR	4.3.77	180/80	JT	78.11	77.96- 98
Chubsa	Andrey	BLR	29.11.82	191/75	HJ	2.31i, 2.25	2.28- 00
Chumachenko	Pavel	RUS	5.4.71	187/128	SP	20.91i, 20.54	20.31i- 99, 20.09- 00
Chumba	Frederick	KEN	24.7.74		Mar	2:10:36	
Chuprinin	Kiril	UKR	22.7.75	197/127	DT	60.02	63.54- 00
Chyla	Lukasz	POL	31.3.81	186/81	100	10.22	10.35- 00
Cichocki	Jaroslaw	POL	28.7.82	190/105	SP	19.41	18.26- 00
Cilliers	Ockert	RSA	21.4.81	186/76	400H	49.40A	50.53A- 00
Ciotti	Giulio	ITA	5.10.76	189/78	HJ	2.27	2.26- 00
Ciotti	Nicola	ITA	5.10.76	188/76	HJ	2.27	2.22- 98
Civallero	Lorenzo	ITA	8.8.75	183/63	20kW	1:22:10	1:22:54- 00
Clarico	Vincent	FRA	8.1.66	184/79	110H	13.55	13.41- 97, 13.3- 98
Clarke	Davian	JAM	30.4.76	178/67	400	44.98	44.87- 96
Claudel	Laurent	FRA	12.3.78	180/68	400H	50.05	50.59- 98
* Clausen	Curt	USA	9.10.67	188/71	50kW	3:50:46	3:48:04- 99
Clavelle	Marcus	USA	23.6.78	203/152	SP	19.55i, 19.38	19.58- 00
Clay	Bryan	USA	3.1.80	180/79	Dec	8169	7373- 00
* Clay	Ramon	USA	29.6.75	186/77	100	10.25	10.29- 00
					200	20.05	20.06, 20.0A- 98, 19.99w- 96
* Clinger	Charles	USA	28.12.76	206/100	HJ	2.35A, 2.32	2.31A, 2.30- 00
Coad	Matthew	NZL	9.8.75	188/81	100	10.23w	10.49- 98, 10.35w- 96
Coertze	Francois	RSA	23.2.79	196/80	400H	50.06A	50.00A- 99
Coetzee	Francois	RSA	30.7.75	185/68	LJ	7.93A, 7.99Aw	7.94A- 98
Coghlan	Peter	IRL	27.3.75	186/81	110H	13.53	13.30- 99
Colenso	Clyde	RSA	11.5.77	188/75	1M	3:54.27i	3:59.19i- 99
Coley	Peter	JAM	21.2.81		400	45.6	46.73- 00
* Collins	Kim	SKN	5.4.76	175/64	100	10.04A, 10.06, 10.00w?, 9.99w	
							10.15, 10.13A, 10.02w- 00
					200	20.20. 20.08w	20.31A, 20.18w- 00, 20.43- 99
Colombo	Andrea	ITA	14.2.74	191/77	200	20.60	20.63- 99
Colquhoun	Leroy	JAM	1.3.80	185/73	400	45.50u	46.58- 98
Coman	Tomas	IRL	10.11.79	188/84	400	45.90	45.84- 00
Compernolle	Tom	BEL	13.11.75	171/53	5000	13:20.13	13:31.34- 00
Condon	Allyn	GBR	24.8.74	176/74	200	20.60i	20.63- 97, 20.53i- 98
Conjungo	Mikaël	CAF	6.5.69	194/100	DT	60.48A	63.78- 94
Conwright	Kaaron	USA	8.8.76	175/73	100	10.20	10.10, 10.05A- 00
Cooper	Jermaine	USA	31.8.80	178/77	110H	13.70, 13.52w	13.95, 13.83w- 00
Copland	Esteban	VEN	12.10.79	179/62	LJ	7.90, 8.18A	7.97- 00
^ Corbett	Marius	RSA	26.9.75	197/122	JT	80.91A	88.75- 98
Corsaro	Alfio	ITA	31.10.79	175/63	20kW	1:23:24	1:24:25- 99
Cortés	Francisco Javier	ESP	25.10.71	173/59	Mar	2:07:48	2:08:30- 00
Costa	Jorge	POR	20.3.61	170/65	50kW	3:56:14	4:13:11- 00
da Costa	Marcelo	BRA	1.5.81	180/72	TJ	16.45	16.11- 00
Costa	Vítor	POR	28.5.74	183/105	HT	76.14	76.34- 00
Costin	Jamie	IRL	1.6.77	179/72	50kW	4:02:42	3:59:02- 00
Cousins	Duane	AUS	13.7.73	178/66	50kW	3:59:25	3:54:38- 95
Couts	Brandon	USA	17.2.79	175/71	200	20.58w	20.48- 00
					400	45.41	44.72- 00
* Crawford	Shawn	USA	14.1.78	181/75	100	10.09	10.16- 00, 10.15w- 98
					200	20.17	20.09- 00
* Crear	Mark	USA	2.10.68	186/79	110H	13.26	12.98- 99
Cremer	Grant	AUS	9.6.78	185/74	800	1:45.75	1:45.21- 99
Crepaldi	Gianni	ITA	19.10.68	182/65	3kSt	8:34.08	8:27.20- 95
Crews	Jerome	GER	20.2.77	188/77	110H	13.51	13.41- 98
^ Croghan	Mark	USA	8.1.68	175/60	3kSt	8:26.14	8:09.76- 93
Cruse	Bobby	USA	20.3.78	183/79	200	20.46, 20.36w	20.39, 19.83w- 99
Csillag	Levente	HUN	22.3.73	190/81	110H	13.77	13.44- 97, 13.3- 00
Cui Xucai		CHN	24.8.76		50kW	4:05:27	3:56:42- 96
Cullum	Dave	USA	26.10.73		3kSt	8:32.52	8:33.34- 00
Culpepper	Alan	USA	15.9.72	185/59	3000	7:47.30	7:47.57- 98
					5000	13:29.66	13:28.64- 97
					10000	27:33.93	27:39.27- 99
Cuñado	Teodoro	ESP	13.2.70	172/60	10000	28:10.79	27:36.90- 00
Currey	Andrew	AUS	7.2.71	184/95	JT	86.67	85.75- 98
Czaja	Jakub	POL	12.9.80	176/64	3kSt	8:23.00	8:34.86- 00
* Czapiewski	Pawel	POL	30.3.78	178/57	800	1:43.22	1:46.07- 00
Czukor	Zoltán	HUN	18.12.62	186/74	50kW	3:53:18, 3:55:37.0t	3:50:02- 95
Daas	Abderrahmane	ALG	8.12.73	170/55	3kSt	8:32.82	8:25.0 - 97
* Dachev	Petar	BUL	15.6.79	181/77	LJ	8.02i	8.30- 00

Name		Nat	Born	Ht/Wt	Event	2001 Mark	Pre-2001 Best
* Dal Soglio	Paolo	ITA	29.7.70	189/115	SP	20.86	21.23- 96
Damszel	Tomasz	POL	25.3.72	188/95	JT	77.56	77.60- 93
Dannbäck	Mikko	FIN	16.3.77	196/115	HT	71.92	74.85- 00
D'Apolito	Giacomo	ITA	23.10.71	184/78	LJ	7.91	7.85- 00
Darouèche	Bakri	FRA	22.8.74	174/77	LJ	7.92w	8.04, 8.11w- 96
* Davis	Calvin	USA	2.4.72	183/79	400H	48.75	47.91- 96
Davis	Devon	CAN	29.12.78		100	10.19w	10.43- 99
Davis	James	USA	19.3.76	185/82	400	45.79i	45.26- 00
^ Davis	Jerome	USA	20.8.77	188/81	400	45.33	44.51- 99
Davis	John	USA	19.2.77	190/104	SP	20.53	20.19- 00
Davis	Lancford	JAM	11.10.78		100	10.23w	10.60- 00
					200	20.60w	20.95- 00
					400	45.87	45.91- 00
* Davis	Walter	USA	2.7.79	188/78	LJ	8.14i, 8.19w, 8.13	8.16- 00
					TJ	17.22	17.07, 17.08w- 00
Dawson	Curry	USA	4.8.79	196/113	DT	59.64	59.21- 00
Dazio	Samuele	SUI	16.1.75	195/102	HT	74.02	71.40- 99
^ de Araújo	Eronilde	BRA	31.12.70	182/78	400H	49.54	48.04- 95
^ De Benedictis	Giovanni	ITA	8.1.68	180/63	50kW	3:54:12	3:49:17- 96
De Paepe	Patrick	BEL	25.2.76		HJ	2.25i	2.20- 00
de Villiers	Ter	RSA	13.7.82	179/75	400H	49.65A, 49.98	50.21- 00
* Deakes	Nathan	AUS	17.8.77	183/66	20kW	1:18:14	1:20:15- 99
					50kW	3:43:43	3:47:29- 00
Decker	Mike	USA	13.6.78	185/84	400	45.89	45.59- 00
Demeritte	Dominic	BAH	22.2.78	180/67	200	20.46	20.53, 20.42w- 00
Demissie	Ashebir	ETH	77		Mar	2:10:45	
Demps	Jasper	USA	22.10.79		110H	13.75	13.97- 00
Denbo	Scott	USA	2.6.78		SP	19.03	18.90- 00
Denis	Frédéric	FRA	3.3.75	172/57	3kSt	8:22.03	8:23.55- 00
Dennis	James	USA	25.2.76		DT	59.98	63.54- 00
Derby	Brian	USA	18.2.81	178/79	400H	49.77	51.63- 00
Derevyagin	Aleksandr	RUS	79		400H	49.82	
Desaulty	Stéphane	FRA	8.1.72	183/68	3kSt	8:16.00	8:22.74- 97
Desiderio	Alberto	ITA	26.3.73	186/85	JT	80.80	77.83- 98
Dethloff	Claus	GER	24.9.68	187/97	HT	74.08	77.68- 94
Devonish	Marlon	GBR	1.6.76	180/72	200	20.29	20.25- 99
Dghoughi	Aïssa	MAR			10000	28.12.6	
Di Bella	Paul	AUS	12.2.77	178/69	100	10.26, 10.21w	10.34- 98, 10.15w- 00
					200	20.66	20.86- 97
Di Pardo	Luciano	ITA	3.2.75	182/66	3kSt	8:32.84	8:17.32- 99
* Diagana	Stéphane	FRA	23.7.69	184/75	400	45.57	45.18- 92
					400H	48.08	47.37- 95
Diallo	Assane	SEN	10.2.75		800	1:46.23	1:45.11- 99
* Díaz	Andrés	ESP	12.7.69	187/71	1500	3:32.66+	3:31.48- 00
					1M	3:48.38	3:51.15- 99
Díaz	Mauricio	CHI	7.8.68	171/59	5000	13:23.68	13:35.78- 00
* Dilworth	Kevin	USA	14.2.74	180/76	LJ	8.30	8.47- 96
Dimitrik	Aleksey	RUS	12.4.84	191/69	HJ	2.23	2.08- 00
* Dimitrov	Rostislav	BUL	26.12.74	182/80	TJ	16.91i, 16.90	17.49- 99
Dittmar	Andy	GER	5.7.74	196/115	SP	19.44	19.72- 97, 20.09i- 00
Djhone	Leslie	FRA	18.3.81	187/68	LJ	7.91, 8.06w	7.92- 99
Dlugosielski	Piotr	POL	4.4.77	176/64	400	45.67	46.28- 00
^ Dodoni	Marco	ITA	5.9.72	197/120	SP	19.65i, 19.51	19.61- 99
Doménech	Yann	FRA	17.3.79	173/61	LJ	8.13, 8.24w	8.05- 98, 8.17w- 00
Domínguez	David	ESP	29.7.80	172/55	20kW	1:22:25	1:22:34- 00
* Donato	Fabrizio	ITA	14.8.76	189/81	TJ	17.05	17.60- 00
Dorique	Laurent	FRA	10.7.76	191/92	JT	80.88	79.93- 00
* Dorival	Dudley	HAI	1.9.75	185/77	110H	13.25	13.30- 98, 13.29w- 99
Doucouré	Ladji	FRA	28.3.83	183/74	110H	13.58	13.75- 00
					Dec	7794	-0-
Douglas	Caimin	AHO	11.5.77	179/80	200	20.48, 20.19w	20.89A- 00, 20.73Aw- 99
Douglas	Matthew	GBR	26.11.76	190/82	400H	49.68	49.26- 00
Douglas	Troy	NED	30.11.62	173/71	100	10.19, 10.109w	10.32- 96, 10.16dq- 99
					200	20.19	20.30- 97
Downin	Andy	USA	12.5.73	178/67	1500	3:36.70	3:38.36- 00
					1M	3:56.25	4:00.89- 97
Drews	Stefan	GER	12.2.79	189/77	PV	5.50i	5.50- 00
					Dec	8049	7812- 00
Driouche	Aziz	MAR	15.11.77	170/58	3kSt	8:25.69	8:32.08- 99
* Drummond	Jon	USA	9.9.68	175/75	100	10.09, 10.04w	9.92- 97
					200	20.44	20.03- 97

	Name		Nat	Born	Ht/Wt	Event	2001 Mark	Pre-2001 Best
	du Plessis	Corne	RSA	20.3.78	190/84	100	10.25	10.56A- 00
						200	20.39A, 20.58	20.58A- 99
	Duany	Raúl	CUB	4.1.75	179/79	Dec	8069	8252- 00
	Dube	Glody	BOT	2.7.78	165/56	800	1:44.59	1:44.70- 00
*	Dubrovshchik	Vladimir	BLR	7.1.72	191/115	DT	64.41	69.28- 00
	Dudi	Om Prakash	IND	77		JT	77.68	76.96- 00
	Dudnik	Sergey	UKR	30.3.77	183/80	Dec	7751	7226- 98
	Duncan	Kurt	JAM	3.6.78		400H	50.05	50.68- 00
	Duncan	Richard	CAN	25.12.73	190/80	LJ	7.91	8.19- 00, 8.23w- 97
	Dunkley	Julien	JAM	20.12.75	186/83	100	10.21	10.47- 00
	Dunn	Philip	USA	12.6.71	175/60	50kW	3:56:33	3:59:53- 99
	Durand	Nicolas	FRA	23.1.79	176/71	PV	5.45	5.30- 00
*	Dvorák	Tomás	CZE	11.5.72	186/88	LJ	8.07	8.03- 00
						Dec	8902	8994- 99
	Dwyer	Pat	AUS	3.11.77	186/80	400	45.61	44.73A, 45.19- 00
	Dymchenko	Sergey	UKR	23.8.67	203/82	HJ	2.32	2.37- 90
	Dzingai	Brian	ZIM	29.4.81	168/64	100	10.19w and 200m 20.50	
	East	Michael	GBR	20.1.78	183/70	1500	3:38.94	3:40.13- 00
*	Ecker	Danny	GER	21.7.77	192/78	PV	6.00i, 5.85	5.93- 98
	Edgar	Tyrone	GBR	29.3.82	182/72	100	10.17w	10.39- 00
	Edorh	Claude	GER	27.2.72	183/82	110H	13.54	13.41- 94
*	Edwards	Jonathan	GBR	10.5.66	182/73	TJ	17.92	18.29, 18.43w- 95
	Edwards	LeShaunte	USA	26.7.79	168/67	100	10.23w	10.23- 99
						200	20.35w	20.45, 20.34w- 00
	Edwards	Mark	GBR	2.12.74	180/115	SP	19.64	19.72- 00
	Efremov	Ilian	BUL	2.8.70	191/84	PV	5.60i	5.70i, 5.70- 98
	Efthimiou	Dino	USA	23.7.79	173/73	PV	5.48i	5.30 -00
	Egbele	Aaron	USA	29.1.79	181/79	100	10.25	10.49A, 10.45Aw- 00
	Ejiogu	Okedikwu Raymond	NGR	76	178/73	100	10.26	10.30, 10.13w- 00
	El Ghazi	Salah	MAR	2.11.75	172/62	1500	3:34.26	3:33.21- 97
						3000	7:33.42	7:38.57- 98
	El Gorche	Abdelhak	MAR	20.7.74		5000	13:29.86	13:36.78- 99
*	El Guerrouj	Hicham	MAR	14.9.74	176/58	1500	3:26.12	3:26.00- 98
						1M	3:44.95	3:43.13- 99
						2000	4:51.17	4:44.79- 99
						3000	7:36.85+i	7:23.09- 99
*	El Himer	Driss	FRA	4.4.74	178/58	3000	7:49+ ?e	
						5000	13:15.10	13:10.99- 00
						HMar	62:08	
						Mar	2:07:02	2:27:08- 97
*	El Mouaziz	Abdelkader	MAR	1.1.69	172/58	Mar	2:07:11	2:07:33- 00
	El Mouaziz	Hamid	MAR	17.2.79		1500	3:38.04	
						2000	4:59.22	
	El Nasri	Yusef	ESP	28.7.79	178/65	3000	7:48.26i	7:39.80- 99
	El Ouardi	Zouhair	MAR	15.2.72		3kSt	8:24.3	8:19.44- 99
	El Wardi	Mohamed Saïd	MAR	19.4.72	178/65	3000	7:41.97	7:34.67- 00
						5000	13:21.88	13:04.46- 00
	Elias	Matthew	GBR	25.4.79	182/68	400H	49.57	50.84- 99
^	Elizalde	Alexis	CUB	19.9.67	192/118	DT	63.88	65.76- 97
	Emedolu	Uchenna	NGR	17.9.76	183/79	100	10.11, 10.06w	10.2, 10.54- 00
						200	20.34	20.69- 00
	Emere ¶	Alene	ETH	5.3.82	183/66	5000	13:26.33dq	13:21.17- 00
						10000	27:29.53dq	27:48.34- 00
	Emilianov	Ivan	MDA	19.2.77	202/130	SP	19.65	19.05, 20.26i- 00
^	Epalle	Christophe	FRA	23.1.69	194/116	HT	73.07	81.79- 00
	Erasmus	Brian	RSA	28.2.80		JT	81.27A	77.16A- 00
	Ercegovac	Stevimir	CRO	20.1.74	185/130	SP	19.84	20.28- 00
	Erese	William	NGR	12.9.73	180/73	110H	13.64	13.53- 95, 13.5- 98
	Ergotic ¶	Sinisa	CRO	14.9.68	179/63	LJ	7.98, 8.09w, 8.08dq	8.06- 96
	Eriksson	Martin	SWE	15.6.71	174/76	PV	5.70	5.80A, 5.72i- 00, 5.70- 97
*	Erm	Andreas	GER	12.3.76	184/70	20kW	1:19:32	1:18:42- 00
	Errebbah	Mostafa	ITA	1.8.71		HMar	62:19	
	Ertzgaard	John	NOR	18.6.77	184/77	100	10.26, 10.25w?, 10.23w	10.27, 10.15w- 99
						200	20.67	20.47- 99
	Esenwein	Peter	GER	7.12.67	188/85	JT	81.74	85.60- 97
	Eshbach	Eric	USA	4.2.81	183/84	PV	5.48i, 5.45	5.55- 00
^	Espinosa	Andrés	MEX	4.2.63	167/55	Mar	2:10:57	2:07:19- 94
^	Essaïd	Mustapha	FRA	20.1.70	180/61	3000	7:38.83	7:30.78- 98
						5000	13:27.38	13:02.15- 98
	Esser	Markus	GER	3.2.80	180/92	HT	75.69	76.66- 00
	Esteso	Pedro A	ESP	13.10.76	181/70	1500	3:37.3	3:37.52- 98

Name		Nat	Born	Ht/Wt	Event	2001 Mark	Pre-2001 Best
* Estévez	Reyes	ESP	2.8.76	187/70	800	1:46.93	1:46.90- 96
					1500	3:32.34	3:30.57- 99
					1M	3:52.68	3:52.61- 97
Eticha	Tesfaye	ETH	16.9.74		Mar	2:10:33	2:12:48- 99
Evans	Kenny	USA	6.4.79	188/74	HJ	2.26i, 2.25	2.31i, 2.30- 00
Evilä	Tommy	FIN	6.4.80	192/82	LJ	8.04, 8.11w	7.69, 7.80w- 00
Éyana	Jérôme	FRA	5.7.77	186/75	100	10.25	10.30- 99
Ezzher	Mohamed	FRA	26.4.60	176/58	Mar	2:10:33	2:11:02- 00
* Ezzine	Ali	MAR	3.9.78	175/57	3kSt	8:10.23	8:03.57- 00
* Fadejevs	Aigars	LAT	27.12.75	175/59	20kW	1:19:53	1:19:36- 97
					50kW	3:46:20	3:43:18- 98
* Fagernes	Pål Arne	NOR	8.6.74	185/103	JT	84.30	86.74- 00
Famiglietti	Anthony	USA	8.11.78	173/57	3kSt	8:21.00	8:25.37- 00
Fang Zetao		CHN	11.2.79		LJ	7.91	7.62- 00
Faouzi	Taoufik	MAR	.73		3kSt	8.34.93	8:33.5- 00
Favaro	Devis	ITA	14.7.72	188/75	110H	13.77	13.87- 00
Faye	Ibou	SEN	13.12.69	190/75	400H	49.77	48.80- 00, 48.30A- 99
* Fazekas	Róbert	HUN	18.8.75	193/105	DT	68.09	66.61- 98
					HT	71.51	75.33- 98
Feiteira	Luís	POR	21.4.73	178/58	1500	3:34.20	3:37.5 - 96
Felice	Marco	ITA	20.10.79	190/105	HT	70.85	68.24- 00
Fenner	Mike	GER	24.4.71	187/88	110H	13.37	13.17- 98, 13.06dt- 95
Fernandes	Nuno	POR	1.4.69	187/84	PV	5.50i	5.66- 96
* Fernández	Francisco	ESP	5.3.77	172/65	20kW	1:19:47	1:18:56- 00
Fernández	Oscar	ESP	23.10.74	165/60	Mar	2:10:33	
Fernández	Raúl	ESP	8.3.78	174/64	LJ	8.11	8.17- 98, 8.18w- 97
Fernández	Ricardo	ESP	7.5.74	165/52	3000	7:49.02	8:00.09- 00
					5000	13:26.68	13:45.67- 00
^ Ferreira Junior	Nelson	BRA	1.1.73	188/82	LJ	8.08w	8.36A, 8.32, 8.41Aw- 96
Ferro	Anthony	BEL	12.12.80	184/76	100	10.26	10.40- 00, 10.37w- 99
					200	20.74	21.06- 00
Fields	Jabari	USA	10.9.81	183/75	100	10.26	
* Figère	Nicolas	FRA	19.5.79	177/91	HT	80.88	79.01- 00
Fika	Makhosonke	RSA	20.1.72	176/59	HMar	61:58	
					Mar	2:10:47	2:10:39- 99
Filet	Arnis	FRA	17.12.77	182/67	TJ	17.15	16.33- 00, 17.01w- 99
Filíndras	Dimítrios	GRE	9.2.73	183/70	LJ	7.94	8.03- 96
Fillion	Daryl	CAN	10.2.73		800	1:46.65	1:47.24- 99
Fish	Aaron	AUS	27.2.81	192/103	HT	70.96	68.67- 00
Fitschen	Jan	GER	2.5.77	175/70	3000	7:48.76i	
Fitzpatrick	Kevin	USA	26.9.69	193/105	DT	61.98	65.28- 97
Flores	Mario	MEX	28.2.79	165/53	20kW	1:23:48	1:21:28- 99
Fofana	Colomba	FRA	11.4.77	186/76	TJ	16.54w	17.00- 00
Fomenko	Pavel	RUS	29.6.76	198/76	HJ	2.25	2.24- 99
Fortuna	Diego	ITA	14.2.68	190/116	DT	64.40	64.69- 00
Foster	Robert	USA	15.5.81	180/82	100	10.21w	10.35- 00
					200	20.70	20.85- 00
Foster	Robert	JAM	12.7.70	190/88	110H	13.71	13.49- 95
Fourth	Jeffery	USA	9.9.79	182/77	100	10.18	10.40- 00
Francique	Alleyne	GRN	7.6.76	188/75	400	44.99	46.46- 99
Frank	Mark	GER	21.6.77	185/90	JT	78.54	77.62- 99
Franke	Denis	GER	27.11.69	183/70	50kW	4:00:00	3:51:27- 99
Frater	Lindel	JAM	13.11.77	170/66	100	10.11	10.07- 00, 9.9w- 98
Frater	Michael	JAM	6.10.82	170/67	100	10.26	10.48- 00
* Fredericks	Frank	NAM	2.10.67	180/73	100	10.06	9.86- 96
					200	20.64	19.68- 96
* Freitag	Jacques	RSA	11.6.82	204/83	HJ	2.31	2.30A, 2.29- 00
* Friedek	Charles	GER	26.8.71	184/76	TJ	17.13i, 16.90	17.59- 97
Frinolli	Giorgio	ITA	12.7.70	184/81	400H	49.04, 48.8	49.17- 00
Frösén	Oskari	FIN	24.1.76	194/85	HJ	2.30	2.30i- 00, 2.27- 98
Frullani	William	ITA	21.9.79	191/88	Dec	7871	7345- 00
Fujimoto	Toshiyuki	JPN	25.6.79	170/72	200	20.56	20.87- 00
Fujinohara	Toshihito	JPN	19.9.75	164/53	20kW	1:23:25	1:22:39- 98
Gabella	Grégory	FRA	22.6.80	190/70	HJ	2.25	2.24- 00
Gabriel	Jimmy	FRA	19.10.73	185/76	TJ	16.86i, 16.45, 16.66w	16.70i- 97, 16.68, 16.80w- 00
Gachara	Daniel	KEN	19.12.72	170/53	1500	3:37.99	3:40.43- 99
					3000	7:45.40	7:38.19- 99
					5000	13:26.46	13:07.27- 98
Galdenzi	Francesco	ITA	6.12.76	174/60	50kW	3:53:01	3:53:01- 00
* Galfione	Jean	FRA	9.6.71	184/82	PV	5.55, 5.60iex	5.98, 6.00i- 99, 6.00ex- 97

Name		Nat	Born	Ht/Wt	Event	2001 Mark	Pre-2001 Best
Gallardo	Sergio	ESP	22.3.79	178/67	800	1:46.65	1:47.62- 00
* Gandellini	Alessandro	ITA	30.4.73	179/68	20kW	1:21:42	1:20:28- 00
Gandrey	Philippe	FRA	14.3.73	175/77	JT	77.06	77.56- 00
Gao Wenxu		CHN	1.3.73	188/82	JT	76.46	78.32, 81.74dq- 97
* García	Alberto	ESP	22.2.71	163/45	1500	3:35.69	3:37.38- 98
					3000	7:36.53	7:38.01- 98
					5000	13:02.54	13:04.64- 98
* García	Anier	CUB	9.3.76	189/85	110H	13.07	13.00- 00
Garcia	Carlos	USA	20.9.76		200	20.4w	
^ García	Javier	ESP	22.7.66	177/71	PV	5.55i, 5.50	5.77i- 92, 5.75- 90
* García	Jesús Ángel	ESP	17.10.69	171/62	20kW	1:23:34	1:24:07- 95
					50kW	3:43:07	3:39:54- 97
García	Luis	GUA	13.9.74	174/62	20kW	1:23:04	1:21:52- 99
García	Roberto	ESP	20.8.75	168/55	3000	7:43.59i	7:43.73- 00
* García	Yoel	CUB	25.11.73	182/83	TJ	17.40	17.62i- 97, 17.47- 95
* Gardener	Jason	GBR	18.9.75	175/70	100	10.23	9.98- 99
Gardner	Neil	JAM	8.12.74	178/72	400H	48.71	48.30- 96
Garenamotse	Gable	BOT	28.2.77	183/75	LJ	7.99, 8.26w	7.97- 99
Garrett	Ken	USA	9.11.76	181/75	400H	49.76	50.25- 00
Gary	Robert	USA	5.4.73	178/68	3kSt	8:27.54	8:19.26- 96
Garzón	Glauder	CUB	13.2.82		400	45.48	47.00- 99
^ Gataullin	Rodion	RUS	23.11.65	189/78	PV	5.70i, 5.65	6.02i, 6.00- 89
* Gatlin	Justin	USA	10.2.82	185/79	100	10.08	10.36- 00
					200	20.29, 1.986w	
					110H	13.78, 13.74w	-0-
* Gatsioúdis	Konstadínos	GRE	17.12.73	189/95	JT	91.27	91.69- 00
Gavélas	Aristotélis	GRE	10.11.78		100	10.14	10.33- 99
Gavrilenko	Igor	RUS	26.7.76	185/78	TJ	17.00i	16.93- 98
Gazol	Javier	ESP	27.10.80	184/70	PV	5.52i, 5.47	5.40- 00
* Gebrselassie	Haile	ETH	18.4.73	164/53	10000	27:54.41	26:22.75- 98
					HMar	60:03	-0-
* Gécsek	Tibor	HUN	22.9.64	184/100	HT	81.76	83.68- 98
Geemi	Richard	KEN	23.8.73	168/55	1500	3:35.07	3:36.00- 00
					3000	7:46.03	
* Gerasimov	Pavel	RUS	29.5.79	193/84	PV	5.81i, 5.50	5.90- 00
Gerding	Thomas	USA	17.12.78	190/82	400	45.38	45.86- 00
Gergov	Vasil	BUL	1.7.77	188/76	TJ	16.50	16.39, 16.53w- 99, 16.65i- 00
Gervais	Jason	CAN	18.1.76	198/134	DT	62.08	64.26A- 00
Geshko	Ivan	UKR	19.8.79	178/65	1500	3:37.10	3:38.48- 00
Getanda	James	KEN	5.7.82	178/66	3000	7:40.69	7:51.37- 00
					5000	13:23.59	13:31.02- 00
Gharib	Jaouad	MAR	22.5.72		3000	7:39.22	
					5000	13:19.69	
					10000	27:29.51	
					HMar	61:36	
Ghioroaie	Adrian	ROM	2.9.79	187/68	TJ	16.45	16.09- 98
Ghirmai	Filmon	GER	25.1.79	182/63	3kSt	8:31.43	8:39.57- 99
Ghoula	Hatem	TUN	7.6.73	180/67	20kW	1:21:41	1:19:02- 97
Giannini	Andrea	ITA	18.12.76	184/70	PV	5.45	5.65- 97
Gibilisco	Giuseppe	ITA	5.1.79	182/71	PV	5.60i, 5.50	5.70- 00
Giesler	Andy	USA	24.2.78	188/91	Dec	7619	7348- 00
Gillet	Anthony	FRA	7.2.76	175/63	20kW	1:22:16	1:21:26- 00
* Ginko	Viktor	BLR	7.12.65	186/77	50kW	3:50:28	3:42:20- 95
Giocondi	Andrea	ITA	17.1.69	180/70	800	1:46.76	1:44.78- 96
* Gitahi	Julius	KEN	29.4.78	168/52	5000	13:11.66	13:01.89- 98
					10000	28:01.60	27:11.17- 98
Githuka	Peter	KEN	14.2.69		Mar	2:09:00	2:08:02- 00
Giungi	Marco	ITA	30.10.74	175/58	20kW	1:22:20	1:20:19- 00
					50kW	3:51:09	3:50:19- 99
Giwa-Agbomeirle	Okoineme	NGR	30.11.78		LJ	7.93	7.53- 98, 7.66w- 00
* Glavatskiy	Aleksandr	BLR	2.5.70	185/72	TJ	17.06i, 17.00	17.53- 98
Glivinskiy	Ruslan	UKR	7.2.75	204/92	HJ	2.23	2.28- 00
* Godina	John	USA	31.5.72	193/129	SP	21.95	22.02- 99
					DT	67.66	69.91- 98
Godoy	Flávio	BRA	13.12.69	185/80	400	45.56	46.24- 00
Goebel	Tim	GER	4.3.82	199/95	100	10.21, 10.18w	10.38- 00
Goedicke	Jörg	GER	25.6.74	192/82	Dec	8036	7882- 99
^ Goffi	Danilo	ITA	3.12.72	173/52	Mar	2:10:35	2:08:33- 98
^ Golley	Julian	GBR	12.9.71	186/80	TJ	16.40i, 16.93w	17.06- 94
Golovastov	Dmitriy	RUS	14.7.71	190/79	400	45.81	45.26- 00
Golubtsov	Konstantin	RUS	1.6.73	172/60	20kW	1:23:01	1:22:10- 99

	Name		Nat	Born	Ht/Wt	Event	2001 Mark	Pre-2001 Best
	Gómez	David	ESP	13.2.81	185/85	Dec	7649	7772- 00
	Goncharuk	Dmitriy	BLR	17.7.70	190/112	SP	20.12	20.33- 95
	Gong Ke		CHN	16.8.79		Mar	2:10:11	2:20:04- 99
*	González	Emeterio	CUB	11.4.73	184/105	JT	82.77	87.12- 00
	González	José María	ESP	3.3.73	177/63	3kSt	8:26.52	8:22.72- 99
	González	Oscar	ESP	8.8.76	193/83	Dec	7949	7706- 00
*	Gorban	Boris	RUS	26.9.78	192/74	400H	48.50	49.09- 00
^	Gorbenko	Gennadiy	UKR	22.9.75	187/72	400H	49.46	48.40- 00
	Gordienko	Aleksey	UKR	9.5.79	184/73	HJ	2.24	2.23i- 00, 2.20- 99
	Gorries	Paul	RSA	28.2.81	184/75	100	10.22Aw	10.45- 00
						200	20.63A, 20.51w	20.62, 20.59A- 00
						400	45.47A	46.8 - 99
	Gorshkov	Vasiliy	RUS	5.2.77		PV	5.75, 5.81ex	5.70- 98
	Goucher	Adam	USA	18.2.75	178/64	1500	3:36.64	3:39.15- 99
						1M	3:55.47	3:54.17- 99
						3000	7:34.96	7:43.31- 99
						5000	13:22.29	13:11.25- 99
	Goumri	Abderrahim	MAR	21.5.76	167/60	3000	7:32.36	7:48.97- 99
						5000	13:03.60	13:20.70- 99
						10000	27:26.01	
						HMar	61:19	
	Grabovoy	Vadim	UKR	5.4.73	190/102	HT	75.30	77.14- 94
	Graffin	Andrew	GBR	20.12.77	179/63	1500	3:35.97	3:36.18- 00
						1M	3:55.42	3:56.13- 00
^	Grant	Dalton	GBR	8.4.66	186/73	HJ	2.26i, 2.23	2.36- 91, 2.37i- 94
	Grant	Dwayne	GBR	17.7.82	183/76	100	10.22w	
						200	20.64, 20.4w	20.88- 00
	Grava	Jean Marc	FRA	2.12.71	186/80	110H	13.67	13.40- 00
	Gray	Paul	GBR	25.5.69	184/79	110H	13.63	13.53- 94
	Gray	Trinity	USA	3.4.78	184/73	800	1:44.54	1:44.91- 00
	Greaves	Damien	GBR	9.9.77	183/85	110H	13.68	13.62- 00
	Green	André	GER	21.4.73	182/65	3kSt	8:28.08	8:20.24- 99
*	Greene	Maurice	USA	23.7.74	176/75	100	9.82	9.79- 99
*	Greer	Breaux	USA	19.10.76	188/102	JT	87.00	82.63- 00
	Gregório	Jadel	BRA	16.9.80		TJ	17.13	16.48- 00
^	Griffin	Rohsaan	USA	21.2.74	175/64	200	20.53w	20.13, 19.96w- 99
	Grimes	Mickey	USA	10.10.76	185/84	100	10.18	10.19A- 99, 10.20, 10.17w- 00
						200	20.61	20.90- 99
	Grzegorzewski	Marcin	POL	5.6.78	173/58	3kSt	8:34.01	8:45.04- 99
	Gu Junjie		CHN	5.5.85	184/60	TJ	16.56	16.89- 00
	Guermoud	Hicham	MAR	79		3kSt	8:25.25	8:32.49- 99
*	Guerni	Djabir Saïd	ALG	29.3.77	187/70	800	1:44.55	1:43.09- 99
	Guerra	Silvio	ECU	18.9.68	158/49	Mar	2:10:07	2:09:49- 97
	Guice	Shaun	USA	11.8.80	180/70	HJ	2.26i, 2.22	2.23i, 2.21- 00
	Gulcz	Pawel	POL	28.1.79	189/82	HJ	2.22	2.25- 00
	Guljas	Caba	YUG	5.2.78	184/95	DT	60.86	59.83- 00
	Guo Chao		CHN	5.2.86	??	50kW	3:57:28	
	Guset	Gheorghe	ROM	28.5.68	185/110	SP	20.68i, 20.39	20.84- 99
	Gushchinskiy	Viktor	RUS	12.8.78	202/84	TJ	16.91	16.78- 97
	Guymon	Brett	USA	9.1.77		400H	49.91A	49.79A- 00
	Guzdek	Miroslav	CZE	3.8.75	191/93	JT	82.40	79.13- 00
	Gwako	John	KEN	4.9.78		HMar	62:15	61:00- 97
*	Haatainen	Harri	FIN	5.1.78	186/85	JT	86.63	86.10- 00
	Habassa	Abdelhadi	MAR	13.1.76		10000	28:05.7	
	Haborák	Milan	SVK	11.1.73	191/106	SP	20.58	20.35- 00
	Hachlaf	Abdelkader	MAR	3.7.78		1500	3:33.59	3:39.28- 00
						2000	4:57.97	
	Hackley	Jimmie	USA	11.9.75		200	20.74i	
	Hadebe	Lucky	RSA	2.1.80	172/59	800	1:46.3A	1:45.73- 99
	Häggström	Peter	SWE	27.1.76	173/70	LJ	8.05i, 7.95	8.07, 8.08w- 00
	Hakala	Petri	FIN	21.2.79	194/95	DT	60.24	62.59- 00
*	Hakkarainen	Harri	FIN	16.10.69	194/110	JT	83.67	87.82- 95
	Haklits	András	CRO	23.9.77	189/103	HT	77.66	77.75- 00
*	Halvari	Mika	FIN	13.2.70	191/135	SP	19.89	21.50- 95, 22.09i- 00
*	Hämäläinen	Eduard	FIN	21.1.69	192/88	Dec	8071(w), 8028	8735- 94
	Hamano	Takeshi	JPN	30.7.74	174/62	10000	28:26.54	28:08.23- 00
	Hamdi Awadh	Mohammed	QAT	4.12.81	189/80	TJ	16.51	16.47- 00
	Hamimid	Mohamed	FRA	16.11.73	184/72	TJ	16.81	16.90, 16.98w- 99
	Hamlyn-Harris	William	AUS	14.1.78		JT	77.23	71.52- 00
*	Hammad	Abderahmane	ALG	27.5.77	189/70	HJ	2.29	2.34- 00
	Han Qiang		CHN	28.6.77		50kW	3:52:37	

	Name		Nat	Born	Ht/Wt	Event	2001 Mark	Pre-2001 Best
	Hanna	Kurt	USA	23.4.75	178/73	PV	5.75	5.65i- 98, 5.62- 97
	Hansen	Jeff	USA	13.10.76	178/75	PV	5.55	5.46A- 99
	Haouam	Samir	ALG	20.6.68	188/103	HT	71.28	70.94- 93
	Hara	Kazushi	JPN	16.11.80	170/56	HMar	61:52	64:33- 00
	Hara	Yoshimi	JPN	2.3.68	170/60	50kW	3:58:47	3:52:26- 00
*	Harden	Tim	USA	27.1.74	178/79	100	10.14	9.92- 99, 9.88w- 98
*	Harju	Arsi	FIN	18.3.74	183/125	SP	20.98	21.39- 00
	Harmse	Chris	RSA	31.5.73	184/118	HT	79.40	78.71- 00
	Harnapp	Steve	GER	30.7.75		HT	73.49	66.54- 94
	Harper	Jacey	TRI	20.5.80	183/77	100	10.21	10.45, 10.2- 99
						200	20.71	21.46, 20.87w- 99
	Harrell	Reggie	USA	28.11.81	190/93	110H	13.73	14.24, 13.94w- 99
	Harris	Micah	USA	30.4.79	190/84	110H	13.73	14.08- 99, 13.96w- 00
	Harris	Otis	USA	30.6.82	185/73	400	45.79A	46.56- 00
	Harris	Rickey	USA	29.9.81	176/70	400	45.22	46.21- 00
						400H	49.65	50.07- 00
	Harris	Stephen	USA	5.12.80	191/82	Dec	7871w, 7804	7651- 00
	Harris	Tora	USA	21.9.78	190/83	HJ	2.27	2.25- 00
*	Harrison	Calvin	USA	20.1.74	186/75	400	44.97	44.64- 00
	Harrison	Richard	USA	13.5.70		SP	19.30	19.68- 00
	Hart	Bevan	USA	1.8.77	180/75	Dec	7814	8002- 00
	Harting	Chad	USA	20.2.72	183/75	PV	5.70i	5.80Ai, 5.80b- 00
	Hartonen	Tommi	FIN	12.5.77	188/85	100	10.21	10.27- 00
						200	20.57	20.47- 00
*	Hartwig	Jeff	USA	25.9.67	190/82	PV	5.90	6.03- 00
	Harvard	Jay	USA	14.3.76	184/109	HT	73.17	70.90- 00
*	Harvey	Tye	USA	25.9.74	186/73	PV	5.93i, 5.80	5.80- 00
	Haschke	Franek	GER	28.3.80	191/72	800	1:46.63	1:49.30- 99
						1500	3:38.56	3:43.09- 99
	Hatcher	Adrian	AUS	6.5.70	182/93	JT	81.07	84.36- 99
*	Hatungimana	Arthémon	BDI	21.1.74	180/64	800	1:43.38	1:43.46- 96
						1000	2:17.34	2:15.48- 95
*	Haughton	Greg	JAM	10.11.73	185/79	400	44.58	44.56- 95
	Haukijärvi	Jarkko	FIN	10.6.77	189/117	SP	19.57	20.31- 00
	He Lin		CHN	1.3.83		50kW	4:05:01	4:22:21- 00
	He Xiaodong		CHN	14.1.78	180/64	20kW	1:21:15	1:22:42- 00
^	Heard	Floyd	USA	24.3.66	178/71	200	20.40	19.88- 00
	Hechavarría	Alianni	CUB	10.10.82		400	45.58	47.06- 00
*	Hecht	Raymond	GER	11.11.68	191/95	JT	88.88	92.60- 95
	Hecini	Adem	ALG	13.12.75	175/66	800	1:44.87	1:44.59- 97
	Heffernan	Robert	IRL	28.2.78	173/55	20kW	1:21:11	1:22:43- 00
	Heinze	Dirk	GER	2.7.76	182/64	800	1:45.95i	1:46.64- 99
	Helppikangas	Jouni	FIN	10.2.71	201/118	DT	61.72	60.84- 98
*	Henry	Boris	GER	14.12.73	193/108	JT	86.53	90.44- 97
	Henwood	John	NZL	30.8.72		10000	27:57.5	28:40.58- 00
*	Herbert	Llewellyn	RSA	21.7.77	185/80	400H	48.52A, 48.77	47.81- 00
	Hercules	Chris	USA	14.5.79	188/86	LJ	7.92	7.80- 99
						TJ	16.69i, 16.53	16.63- 00
	Herman	Billy	USA	3.7.77		3kSt	8:23.94	8:26.02- 00
	Herms	René	GER	17.7.82		800	1:46.81	-0-
*	Hernández	Edgar	MEX	8.6.77	174/57	50kW	3:46:12	3:56:36- 00
*	Hernández	Noé	MEX	15.3.78	175/64	20kW	1:23:03	1:19:03- 00
*	Hernández	Yoel	CUB	12.12.77	184/77	110H	13.30	13.24- 99, 13.20w- 00
	Hernández	Yuniel	CUB	28.3.81	183/76	110H	13.26	13.60, 13.5- 00
*	Hernu	Laurent	FRA	22.8.76	190/85	Dec	8280	8178- 00
	Herring	Aubrey	USA	19.9.78	183/77	110H	13.42, 13.36w	13.49- 00
	Herring	Godfrey	USA	18.5.78	183/68	400	45.35	45.59- 00
	Herring	Lenton	USA	4.12.78	180/73	LJ	7.90i	7.86- 00
						TJ	16.66i	16.29i, 16.56w- 00, 16.03- 99
	Higuero	Juan Carlos	ESP	3.8.78	178/72	800	1:46.84	1:46.42- 00
						1500	3:32.30	3:36.63- 00
	Hill	Clinton	AUS	19.4.80		400	45.54	46.8, 47.02- 00
*	Hill	Mick	GBR	22.10.64	190/98	JT	84.88	86.94- 93
*	Hissou	Salah	MAR	16.1.72	176/62	HMar	61:56	62:20- 94
	Hjartarson	Einar Karl	ISL	28.10.80	190/72	HJ	2.28i, 2.25	2.22- 99
	Hoff	Shadrack	RSA	19.5.73	169/51	5000	13:29.32	13:14.16- 95
						10000	27:48.65	27:43.89- 96
						HMar	62:19	
	Hoffa	Reese	USA	8.10.77	183/115	SP	20.22	19.79- 00
	Hoffman	Dave	USA	22.4.75		HJ	2.30	2.23i- 99, 2.20- 00
	Högler	Gregor	AUT	27.6.72	181/91	JT	81.98	84.03- 99

	Name		Nat	Born	Ht/Wt	Event	2001 Mark	Pre-2001 Best
	Höhne	Andre	GER	10.3.78	184/68	20kW	1:22:49	1:22:05- 00
*	Holm	Stefan	SWE	25.5.76	181/70	HJ	2.34i, 2.33	2.34- 00
	Holmén	Janne	FIN	26.9.77	176/59	10000	28:23.84	28:36.46- 00
	Holusa	Milos	CZE	2.5.65	174/62	20kW	1:22:27	1:21:58- 97
						50kW	3:58:54	3:49:08- 96
^	Hood	Graham	CAN	2.4.72	186/68	1500	3:34.98	3:33.94- 97
						1M	3:54.62	3:51.55- 97
*	Hooker	Ja'Warren	USA	24.9.78	183/77	200	20.57, 20.56i, 20.33w	20.23A, 20.33- 00
						400	45.79	44.78- 00
	Hopley	Hannes	RSA	26.1.81	182/100	DT	63.68	59.51- 00
^	Horváth	Attila	HUN	28.7.67	194/128	DT	60.79	68.58- 94
	Horváth	Gergely	HUN	5.6.75	186/90	JT	80.80	80.53- 98
	Horváth	Norbert	HUN	13.6.75	183/104	HT	71.46	73.75- 99
	Howard	Josephus	USA	14.4.78	180/80	200	20.58, 20.47w	20.53- 97
^	Howard	Robert	USA	26.11.75	178/75	LJ	8.10w	8.40- 97
						TJ	16.92i, 17.10Aw, 16.71	17.19- 96
	Howe	Quincy	TRI	.79		TJ	16.69A	15.88, 16.00Aw- 00
	Hoxmeier	Mark	USA	16.7.79	188/107	DT	61.46	60.32- 00
	Hudec	Leonard	AUT	13.6.73	185/70	110H	13.78	13.67- 00
	Hughes	Greg	BAR	18.3.79		TJ	16.50	16.19, 16.52w- 00
	Hughes	Ray	USA	9.5.75		3kSt	8:25.94	8:33.29- 00
	Huikuri	Toni	FIN	17.9.79	191/77	HJ	2.22	2.28- 00
	Hujo	Mathias	GER	15.12.76		TJ	16.54w	15.98- 00
	Human	Willie	RSA	8.3.82	181/75	JT	78.03A	74.30A- 00
	Hummastenniemi	Janne	FIN	3.10.79	196/107	DT	60.28	59.44- 00
	Hunter	Brian	USA	28.3.79	185/88	PV	5.69	5.60- 00
	Hynni	Pertti	FIN	14.2.60	193/110	DT	61.40	63.25- 98
*	Hysong	Nick	USA	9.12.71	183/77	PV	5.85	5.90- 00
	Iakovákis	Periklís	GRE	24.3.79	184/73	400H	48.87	49.35- 00
	Iannelli	Angelo	ITA	27.7.76	183/61	3kSt	8:29.50	8:22.06- 99
	Ibe	Philip	GER	5.5.75		Dec	7696	8000- 99
	Ichinose	Susumu	JPN	11.7.75	175/57	10000	28:18.19	28:11.43- 00
*	Idowu	Phillips	GBR	30.12.78	192/87	TJ	17.33, 17.38w	17.12- 00
	Ietani	Kazuo	JPN	25.8.75		10000	28:13.83	28:18.10- 00
						HMar	61:30	64:07- 00
	Igarashi	Noriaki	JPN	28.10.72	165/54	Mar	2:09:35	2:09:26- 00
	Ikegaya	Hiroyuki	JPN	29.4.75	175/58	10000	28:12.64	28:07.09- 00
	Ikeshima	Daisuke	JPN	30.1.75	183/68	20kW	1:21:24	1:19:42- 00
	Illikainen	Jani	FIN	26.1.76	196/110	SP	20.56	20.43i- 99, 20.12- 00
	Imamura	Fumio	JPN	5.11.66	178/63	50kW	3:54:44	3:49:38- 98
	Intas	Tomas	LTU	15.9.81	200/108	JT	78.12	77.88- 99
	Irifune	Satoshi	JPN	14.12.75	176/60	5000	13:22.12	13:35.91- 98
						10000	27:53.92	27:58.57- 00
	Ishige	Toyoshi	JPN	16.4.75	168/53	10000	28:24.19	
						HMar	61:44	61:55- 98
	Ishikura	Kazuki	JPN	1.10.80		100	10.17w	10.47- 00
	Ivanov	Aleksandr	RUS	25.5.82	192/88	JT	83.55	77.11- 00
	Ivanov	Dmitriy	RUS	23.3.77	187/77	Dec	8065	7929- 00
	Ivanov	Vasiliy	RUS	26.12.76	174/62	20kW	1:22:38	1:21:56- 98
*	Ivuti	Patrick	KEN	30.6.78	165/52	5000	13:24.48	13:02.68- 00
						HMar	60:42	59:31- 00
	Iwamizu	Yoshitaka	JPN	20.6.79	172/50	10000	28:26.18	28:59.38- 00
						3kSt	8:26.77	8:32.99- 00
	Iwasa	Toshihiro	JPN	18.5.76	172/58	10000	28:24.31	28:06.89- 00
	Izmailov	Sergey	UKR	1.5.75	180/75	TJ	16.59	17.02- 96, 17.09dq- 99
*	Jackson	Colin	GBR	18.2.67	182/75	110H	13.32	12.91- 93, 12.8w- 90
	Jackson	Eddie	USA	19.12.80	187/84	110H	13.70	13.78, 13.75w- 00
	Jahic	Danijal	YUG	1.7.79	191/76	LJ	8.06	8.18, 8.27w- 99
	Jakobsson	Mikael	SWE	9.1.81	193/90	400H	49.94	50.85- 00
	James	Derrick	USA	18.10.76		110H	13.75	14.15, 13.87W- 00
	Janácek	Stepán	CZE	12.6.77	189/79	PV	5.75i, 5.75	5.72- 00
	Jankú	Jan	CZE	10.8.71	197.84	HJ	2.28	2.30i- 96, 2.29- 97
	Jansen	Joeri	BEL	28.5.79	180/62	800	1:44.52	1:46.12- 00
	Janson	Oscar	SWE	22.7.75	192/88	PV	5.62	5.55i, 5.55- 00
*	Januszewski	Pawel	POL	2.1.72	178/68	400H	48.40	48.17- 98
^	Janvrin	Kip	USA	8.7.65	183/84	Dec	8241	8462w, 8345- 96
	Jaoane	Hamid	FRA	3.4.72	180/63	3kSt	8:26.82	8:28.78- 00
	Jäppinen	Vesa	FIN	9.3.78	183/100	JT	76.32	78.91- 98
^	Jarrett	Anthony	GBR	13.8.68	188/80	110H	13.45	13.00- 93
	Jarrett ¶	Patrick	JAM	2.10.77	186/82	100	10.12, 9.89rw, 10.08dq	10.14- 00
	Jauron	Lance	USA	23.11.77	188/109	DT	59.63	55.20- 00

	Name		Nat	Born	Ht/Wt	Event	2001 Mark	Pre-2001 Best
	Jaworski	Dawid	POL	31.1.78	190/74	HJ	2.22	2.22- 79
	Jean-Théodore	Olivier	FRA	13.11.74	183/75	400H	49.21	49.90- 00
	Jedrusinski	Marcin	POL	28.9.81	190/88	200	20.69	20.69- 00
	Jeng	Alhaji	SWE	13.12.81	186/72	PV	5.49	5.40- 00
	Jennings	Gabe	USA	25.1.79	181/70	800	1:46.83	1:46.99- 98
						1500	3:37.56	3:35.21- 00
	Jennings	Michael	USA	80	186/77	400	45.55	46.42- 00
	Jensen	Benjamin	NOR	13.4.75	188/78	Dec	8153	8160- 99
	Jensen	Dennis	DEN	11.9.69		5000	13:26.46	13:25.39- 00
						10000	28:17.50	28:31.75- 00
	Jensen ¶	Jake	USA	29.5.74	190/80	200	20.58	20.61A, 20.41Aw- 00
	Jesus	Luis	POR	19.11.68	170/65	HMar	61:28	61:47- 95
*	Jifar	Habte	ETH	29.1.76	176/53	10000	27:57.23	27:06.45- 99
*	Jifar	Tesfaye	ETH	23.4.76	168/55	HMar	60:04	61:51- 99
						Mar	2:07:43	2:06:49- 99
*	Jiménez	Antonio	ESP	18.2.77	178/61	3kSt	8:11.52	8:20.34- 00
	Jimmerson	Greg	USA	1.2.75		3kSt	8:31.88	8:32.46- 00
	Johansson	Bengt	SWE	7.7.73	190/102	HT	76.32	75.62- 00
*	Johnson	Allen	USA	1.3.71	178/70	110H	13.04	12.92- 96
	Johnson	Brian	USA	25.3.80		LJ	8.01, 8.06w	7.65, 8.04w- 00
*	Johnson	Curtis	USA	24.12.73	180/80	100	10.10, 10.00w	10.07- 00
	Johnson	Dominic	LCA	31.10.75	185/77	PV	5.60	5.65- 98, 5.70A- 00
*	Johnson	Joshua 'J.J'	USA	10.5.76	191/91	100	10.22, 10.10w	10.24, 10.19w- 00
						200	19.88	20.60- 00
*	Johnson	Lawrence	USA	7.5.74	185/86	PV	5.96i, 5.90	5.98- 96
	Johnson	Patrick	AUS	26.9.72	177/73	100	10.25, 10.13w	10.10- 00
						200	20.52	20.54- 97
	Johnson	Tyrone	USA	5.2.81	186/87	LJ	7.94	
	Johnson	Weldon	USA	24.7.73		10000	28:10.14	28:27.8 00
	Jokihaara	Jarno	FIN	2.9.73	176/75	110H	13.75	13.72- 00
	Jolivet	Nicolas	FRA	24.3.77	182/70	PV	5.45i	5.65- 97
	Jones	Michael	GBR	23.7.63	187/119	HT	76.43	75.94- 00
	Jones	Stephen	BAR	25.7.78	184/66	110H	13.64	13.76- 98, 13.66w- 00
	Jordan	Robert	USA	22.6.80	188/77	HJ	2.23	2.24- 99, 2.25i- 00
	Joseph	Jermaine	CAN	25.7.80	178/75	200	20.67Aw	20.81A- 00
	Joseph	Moise	USA	27.12.81	180/67	800	1:46.58	1:50.30- 00
	Jossa	Ralf	GER	2.11.66	189/105	HT	71.47	74.14- 97
	Juan	Jaime	ESP	28.8.77	186/76	400H	49.92	50.08- 00
	Juanz	Oscar	MEX	17.9.73		400H	50.11A	50.60- 98
	Jurksas	Arunas	LTU	3.5.72	198/108	JT	76.67	82.24- 00
	Kabara	Anthony	KEN	9.3.75	182/73	800	1:45.29	1:47.34- 99
	Kabil (Kabiru?)	Samuel	KEN	6.6.83	175/57	10000	28:21.01	
	Kaczocha	Marcin	POL	22.9.77	189/72	HJ	2.22	2.25i- 98, 2.24- 97
	Kadaks	Aivars	LAT	11.2.81	178/63	20kW	1:22:24	1:23:50- 00
	Kagika	Laban	KEN	17.7.78	164/50	10000	28:14.45	27:57.81- 00
						Mar	2:10:24	-0-
	Kagwe	John	KEN	9.1.69		HMar	62:01	61:18- 97
						Mar	2:10:07	2:08:12- 97
	Kaihoko	Yoshiteru	JPN	19.11.71	182/70	HJ	2.23i	2.26- 98
	Kaliszewski	Krzysztof	POL	9.8.72	185/110	HT	70.62	71.97- 00
*	Kalya	William	KEN	4.8.74	171/62	3000	7:48.47	7:31.14- 97
						5000	13:17.00	13:03.08- 95
						10000	27:52.26	27:23.65- 00
	Kamani	Bayano	USA	17.4.80	188/79	400H	48.99	48.43- 00
*	Kamathi	Charles	KEN	18.5.78	165/51	3000	7:47.0+	7:43.50- 00
						5000	13:05.16	13:05.29- 99
						10000	27:22.58	26:51.49- 99
	Kandie	Samson	KEN	20.4.71		Mar	2:10:21	2:08:31- 99
	Kanter	Gerd	EST	6.5.79	196/108	DT	60.47	57.68- 00
	Kanyi	John	KEN	6.9.80	160/50	10000	28:26.04	27:47.44- 00
	Kaouch	Adil	MAR	1.1.79	170/60	1500	3:36.01	3:34.28- 99
						1M	3:53.40	3:51.62- 99
	Kapitonov	Dmitriy	RUS	10.4.68	186/70	Mar	2:11:09	2:09:32- 99
*	Kaptyukh	Vasiliy	BLR	27.6.67	197/120	DT	67.48	67.59- 00
*	Kapustin	Denis	RUS	5.10.70	189/86	TJ	16.73i	17.65- 98, 17.86w- 94
	Kararadev	Angel	BUL	18.4.79		HJ	2.23	2.20- 00
	Karasmanákis	Elefthérios	GRE	16.8.78		JT	77.58	71.58- 00
	Kariuki	David	KEN	23.5.80	164/53	10000	28:22.83	28:16.31- 00
*	Karjalainen	Olli-Pekka	FIN	7.3.80	194/108	HT	80.54	80.55- 00
	Karlivans	Janis	LAT	2.6.82	193/82	Dec	7665	6817- 00
*	Karlsson	Conny	FIN	30.12.75	195/120	SP	20.78	19.48- 97

Name		Nat	Born	Ht/Wt	Event	2001 Mark	Pre-2001 Best
Karlsson	Per	SWE	21.4.67	182/115	HT	71.49	75.78- 00
Karpov	Dmitriy	KAZ	23.7.81	196/80	Dec	7567	7620- 00
Kaseorg	Indrek	EST	16.12.67	194/86	Dec	7959	8179- 98
Kasimili	Simon	KEN	12.12.80		HMar	61:45	61:14- 00
Kastánis	Spirídon	GRE	23.9.64	175/65	50kW	3:57:35	3:54:11- 90
Katsurayama	Kenji	JPN	9.9.70	178/68	50kW	4:01:02	4:06:11- 99
Kaveshnikov	Boris	RUS	30.9.74	180/64	800	1:45.82	1:45.71- 00
Kawabata	Shingo	JPN	15.5.78	175/70	100	10.23	10.11- 00
Kawakita	Naohiro	JPN	10.7.80	180/75	400H	49.70	50.61- 00
Kawamura	Hideaki	JPN	15.9.74	175/67	400H	49.53	48.84- 00
Kawashima	Shinji	JPN	4.6.66	166/53	Mar	2:10:36	2:09:04- 00
Kazmierowski	Jacek	POL	2.7.74	185/76	TJ	16.74	16.59- 98
Ke Ping		CHN	5.1.85	??	50kW	4:03:52	
* Kedéris	Konstadínos	GRE	11.6.73	180/78	100	10.15	10.16- 00
					200	20.03	20.09- 00
Keflezighi	Mebrahtom	USA	5.5.75	169/58	5000	13:23.16	13:11.77- 00
					10000	27:13.98	27:53.63- 00
^ Keino	Martin	KEN	20.6.72	180/67	1500	3:38.40	3:33.00- 96
					2000	5:00.7+	4:53.84- 96
					3000	7:45.21+	7:35.97- 97
Keiring	Eliud	KEN	74		Mar	2:11:11	2:11:19- 99
Kemboi	Ezekiel	KEN	25.5.82	175/62	3kSt	8:23.66	
Kemboi	Moses	KEN			HMar	61:41	
Kemboi	Nicholas	KEN	25.11.83		5000	13:26.36	13:41.5A- 00
Kemei	Philip	KEN	6.6.77		HMar	62:13	
* Kennedy	Bob	USA	18.8.70	183/66	3000	7:40.64	7:30.84- 98
					5000	13:17.51	12:58.21- 96
Kenyon	Mike	USA	26.8.79	178/73	400	45.43	45.78- 00
Kerer	Armin	ITA	27.6.72	178/82	JT	76.29	80.25- 99
Keska	Karl	GBR	7.5.72	183/68	5000	13:24.63	13:23.07- 99
					10000	28:06.29	27:44.09- 00
Keul	Adam	USA	27.1.80	193/88	PV	5.68i, 5.59	5.42- 00
Khaldi	Mohamed	ALG	3.5.75	172/60	1500	3:33.03	3:33.40- 00
					2000	4:58.06	
					3000	7:38.78	
Khanafin	Aleksey	RUS	27.4.81		PV	5.50i	
* Khattabi	Elarbi	MAR	16.5.67	174/61	3kSt	8:09.49	8:09.03- 99
* Khersontsev	Vadim	RUS	8.7.74	192/106	HT	81.26	80.68- 96
Khodanovich	Sergey	BLR	11.6.78	180/74	110H	13.73	13.85- 99
Kholev	Dennis	ISR	21.10.75	182/76	PV	5.65	5.70- 00
Khouya	Rachid	MAR	9.11.79	186/74	800	1:46.99	1:45.38- 99
Kibet	Lukas	KEN	19.6.73		Mar	2:10:18	2:11:16- 00
Kibet	Philemon	KEN	20.11.82		800	1:47.00	
Kibitok	Philip	KEN	23.3.71	170/62	800	1:46.9A	1:43.55- 96
Kibiwott	Stanley	KEN	8.8.69	179/63	3kSt	8:16.62	8:16.04- 99
* Kibowen	John	KEN	21.4.69	175/64	3000	7:31.58	7:29.09- 98
					5000	12:59.97	13:48.5 - 96
Kido	Masaki	JPN	10.12.70	169/55	HMar	61:58	64:46- 00
Kifle	Yonas	ERI	24.3.77	168/55	5000	13:25.07	13:46.82- 99
Kigen	Moses	KEN	22.4.73	182/68	3kSt	8:27.92	8:37.34- 00
Kigen	Kibet	KEN	23.2.75		HMar	62:03	
Kigen	Wilson Kipkemboi	KEN	80		HMar	62:04	
Kikaya	Gary	COD	4.2.78		400	45.58A	46.51A- 00
Kim Dong-young		KOR	6.3.80	174/56	20kW	1:23:28	1:28:46- 99
Kimani	David	KEN	28.2.78	183/66	1500	3:38.74	3:40.58- 00
					3000	7:43.82	
					5000	13:10.29	13:25.37- 00
* Kimani	Joseph	KEN	1.9.72	170/60	HMar	61:57	60:04- 98
Kimeli	Musa	KEN	23.6.68		1500	3:36.87	3:36.07- 99
Kimino	Takahiro	JPN	19.2.73	175/55	HJ	2.22	2.32- 93
Kimondiu	Ben (?21.7.72)	KEN	30.11.77		Mar	2:08:52	-0-
Kimutai	David	KEN	19.8.69	165/57	20kW	1:22:42A	1:20:40A- 96
* Kimutai	Japheth	KEN	20.12.78	173/55	800	1:45.75	1:42.69- 99
					1500	3:37.24i	3:34.14- 00
Kimutai	Julius	KEN			HMar	61:36	
Kimutai	Sylas	KEN	12.10.83		800	1:46.61	1:48.4A- 00
* Kimwetich	Kenneth	KEN	1.1.73	183/73	800	1:44.21	1:43.03- 98
					1000	2:17.35	2:13.56- 99
^ Kinnunen	Kimmo	FIN	31.3.68	187/98	JT	81.35	90.82R- 91, 85.96- 99
Kino	Yukiyoshi	JPN	10.9.80		HMar	62:19	
Kipchoge Rop	Josephat	KEN	68		HMar	62:12	

	Name		Nat	Born	Ht/Wt	Event	2001 Mark	Pre-2001 Best
*	Kipchumba	Robert	KEN	24.2.84	170/62	3000	7:44.36	
						5000	13:19.76	13:46.03- 00
						10000	27:25.55	27:43.14- 00
	Kipkemboi	Laban	KEN	30.12.77	172/66	HMar	61:40	
*	Kipketer	Sammy	KEN	29.9.81	166/52	3000	7:33.62	7:34.58- 99
						5000	12:59.34	12:54.07- 00
*	Kipkosgei	Luke	KEN	27.11.75	176/57	3000	7:32.68	7:27.59- 98
						5000	13:02.25	12:56.50- 00
						10000	27:12.37	27:22.54- 98
*	Kipkurui	Benjamin	KEN	28.12.80	174/57	800	1:44.80	1:44.56- 99
						1500	3:30.67	3:30.73- 00
						1M	3:52.52	3:49.34- 00
	Kiplagat	William	KEN	21.6.72		HMar	60:38	59:51- 00
						Mar	2:09:55	2:06:50- 99
	Kiplimo	Muneria	KEN	28.8.83		5000	13:20.32	
						10000	28:14.10	
	Kiprono	Isaac	KEN	5.9.76		Mar	2:09:59	2:10:09- 00
*	Kiprono	Josephat	KEN	12.12.73	172/52	Mar	2:06:50	2:06:44- 99
	Kiprop	Francis	KEN			5000	13:22.85	
*	Kiprop	Fred	KEN	3.6.74		Mar	2:09:43	2:06:47- 99
	Kipruto	David	KEN	20.11.75		HMar	62:05	62:41- 00
	Kipsang	Salim	KEN	22.12.79	172/52	5000	13:29.8+	13:29.95- 00
						10000	28:06.49	27:32.97- 00
						HMar	62:09	
	Kiptanui	Michael	KEN			3kSt	8:32.5A	
	Kiptoo Singoei	David	KEN	26.6.65	175/68	800	1:45.74	1:43.38- 96
*	Kirmasov	Sergey	RUS	25.3.70	181/115	HT	80.07	82.62- 98
	Kirui	David	KEN	15.12.74	175/71	400	45.77	45.69- 00
	Kirui	David Kiptoo	KEN	29.12.77		Mar	2:09:40	2:17:12- 00
	Kirui	Eliud	KEN	15.8.75		3kSt	8:30.37	8:57.46- 00
	Kirwa	Wilson	FIN	28.12.74	168/57	800	1:46.54	1:44.69- 00
	Kirwa Too	Daniel	KEN	21.11.76		Mar	2:10:38	
						HMar	62:15	
	Kisilu	Bernard	KEN	6.12.74	173/64	800	1:45.39	1:44.76- 95
*	Kiss	Balázs	HUN	21.3.72	192/115	HT	81.36	83.00- 98
	Kiss	Szilárd	HUN	9.12.75	198/106	SP	19.83	20.01- 00
	Kiteau	Joachim	FRA	23.6.82	181/88	JT	78.97	74.37- 00
	Klose	Holger	GER	5.12.72	191/104	HT	78.63	82.22- 98
	Klouchi	Kader	FRA	1.6.69	177/70	LJ	8.12, 8.24w	8.30, 8.33w- 98
*	Klyugin	Sergey	RUS	24.3.74	192/82	HJ	2.31	2.36- 98
	Knabe	Sebastian	GER	13.10.78	184/83	Dec	8151	7812- 00
	Knight	Bryce	USA	4.4.78		800	1:46.60	1:48.02A- 00
	Knight	Derek	USA	11.10.67	180/73	110H	13.47	13.37, 13.35w- 95
	Knoblich	Christian	GER	1.10.76	177/60	3kSt	8:33.71	8:24.52- 99
*	Kobs	Karsten	GER	16.9.71	196/118	HT	79.15	82.78- 99
	Kochkin	Sergey	RUS	1.7.70		TJ	16.56i	17.30- 96
^	Koech	Benson	KEN	10.11.74	178/65	1500	3:34.12	3:32.09- 99
						1M	3:55.45i	
*	Koech	Enock	KEN	4.4.81	178/64	1500	3:31.28	3:40.5A- 00
						1M	3:51.50	
						2000	4:55.92	
	Koech	Jackson	KEN	79		3000	7:47.89	
						5000	13:26.17	
						HMar	61:55	62:11- 00
	Koech	Paul	KEN	10.11.81	170/60	1500	3:38.87	
						3000	7:42.14	7:33.79- 97
						3kSt	8:15.92	
^	Koers	Marko	NED	3.11.72	193/78	800	1:46.22	1:44.01- 97
						1500	3:37.08	3:33.05- 96
	Kogo	Hosea	KEN	11.8.72		10000	28:19.81	28:50.0 - 94
^	Kohutek	Artur	POL	1.5.71	190/78	110H	13.53	13.27- 97
	Kojima	Daisuke	JPN	15.7.76	170/45	HMar	61:46	
	Kokótis	Dimítrios	GRE	12.4.72	190/70	HJ	2.26	2.32- 98
	Kolasa	Adam	POL	2.8.75	191/75	PV	5.75	5.51- 99, 5.65sq- 00
	Kólko ¶	Rajmund	POL	1.3.71	186/83	JT	84.95	82.50- 97
	Kologinczak	Shaun	USA	13.10.79		HJ	2.23i	2.22- 00
	Komar	Ivan	BLR	18.3.70	187/70	800	1:46.86	1:45.44- 97
*	Komen	Daniel	KEN	17.5.76	170/60	3000	7:43.76, 7:43.1i	7:20.67- 96
						5000	13:01.98	12:39.74- 97
	Kondo	Shigekatsu	JPN	17.10.74	167/53	Mar	2:11:14	2:14:15- 99
	Kondratowicz	Wojciech	POL	18.4.80	196/114	HT	77.06	76.59- 00

	Name		Nat	Born	Ht/Wt	Event	2001 Mark	Pre-2001 Best
*	Konopka	Mikulás	SVK	23.1.79	192/105	SP	20.66	19.94- 00
	Konopka	Miloslav	SVK	23.1.79	189/102	HT	78.58	76.12- 00
*	Konovalov	Ilya	RUS	4.3.71	189/103	HT	80.27	81.93- 00
	Korchmyd	Aleksandr	UKR	22.1.82	187/75	PV	5.55i	5.50, 5.60sq- 00
*	Korepanov	Sergey	KAZ	9.5.64	170/61	20kW	1:23:22	1:20:34- 95
						50kW	3:59:57	3:39:22- 99
	Korir	Anthony	KEN	25.10.80		HMar	62:09	61:06- 00
*	Korir	John Cheruiyot	KEN	13.12.81	172/57	5000	13:19.58	13:09.58- 00
						10000	27:49.34A	27:24.75- 00
	Korir	Paul	KEN	15.7.77	180/64	800	1:45.02	1:44.21- 00
^	Korir	Sammy	KEN	12.12.71		Mar	2:08:14	2:08:02- 97
	Korir	Shadrack	KEN	14.12.78	170/54	1500	3:35.16	3:42.34- 99
						1M	3:55.72	
						2000	4:56.62	
	Korkízoglou	Pródromos	GRE	27.2.75	190/84	Dec	7773w	8069- 00
*	Korzeniowski	Robert	POL	30.7.68	168/60	20kW	1:19:52.0t	1:18:22- 00
						50kW	3:42:08	3:41:50- 00
	Kosenkow	Alexander	GER	14.3.77	178/68	200	20.63	21.39- 00
	Köseoglu	Tolga	GER	16.11.76	194/90	DT	63.20	63.94- 00
*	Kosgei	Japhet	KEN	20.12.68	165/52	HMar	61:23	60:01- 99
						Mar	2:09:19	2:07:09- 99
*	Kosgei	John	KEN	13.7.73	184/71	3kSt	8:12.11	8:03.89- 97
	Kosgei	Joseph	KEN	74		5000	13:16.78	
*	Kosgei	Paul	KEN	22.4.78	175/57	5000	13:06.29	13:05.44- 00
						10000	27:51.87A	27:38.22- 00
*	Kosgei	Reuben	KEN	2.8.79	170/55	3kSt	7:57.29	8:03.92- 00
	Koskei	James Kimutai	KEN	23.11.68	172/62	5000	13:17.06	13:04.3 - 00
	Koski-Vähälä	Jarkko	FIN	21.11.78	194/100	JT	77.81	77.95- 00
	Kostin	Ilya	RUS	1.4.79	192/110	DT	60.97	57.65- 00
^	Koukodímos	Konstadínos	GRE	14.9.69	186/80	LJ	7.98i	8.36, 8.40w- 94
	Kovács	Dusán	HUN	31.7.71	188/80	400H	49.74	48.45- 97
*	Kővágó	Zoltán	HUN	10.4.79	204/127	DT	66.93	66.76- 00
	Kovals	Ainars	LAT	21.11.81	192/100	JT	76.58	72.68- 00
	Koykov	Nikolay	BUL	12.10.81		110H	13.5	14.19- 00
	Kozhevnikov	Sergey	RUS	12.5.70	180/64	800	1:46.25	1:46.27- 00
	Kozmus	Primoz	SLO	30.9.79	188/102	HT	71.17	76.84- 00
	Krantz	Frédéric	FRA	13.9.78	176/70	100	10.17	10.26, 10.24w- 00
						200	20.49, 20.41w	20.63- 00, 20.40dq- 99
	Krause	Konstantin	GER	8.10.67	189/79	LJ	7.97	8.27- 97
	Kravchenko	Vladimir	UKR	22.12.69	184/76	TJ	16.73	17.09- 97, 17.29w- 96
	Kravtsov	Aleksandr	RUS	18.3.74		HJ	2.31	2.24- 00
	Krawczyk	Andrzej	POL	11.4.76	195/100	DT	63.11	63.60- 99
	Krebs	Adrian	SUI	8.6.77	184/86	Dec	7993	7758- 00
	Krehmic	Elvir	BIH	27.4.73	198/83	HJ	2.27	2.31- 98
	Krehula	Jirí	CZE	17.7.82	187/78	HJ	2.26	2.20- 00
^	Kreissig	Wolfgang	GER	29.8.70	197/82	HJ	2.31	2.34- 99
	Kristiansson	Patrik	SWE	3.6.77	193/81	PV	5.83	5.77- 98
	Kritzinger	Marthinus	RSA	10.2.82		400H	49.57A	50.63- 00
*	Kronberg	Robert	SWE	15.8.76	182/80	110H	13.35	13.36- 00
	Kronin	Aleksey	RUS	23.7.70	180/69	20kW	1:20:45, 1:24:06.0t	1:20:01- 99
*	Kruger	Frantz	RSA	22.5.75	203/118	DT	69.96	69.75A- 00
	Krummenacker	David	USA	24.5.75	190/79	800	1:45.44	1:44.57- 99
^	Krykun	Aleksandr	UKR	1.3.68	194/125	HT	80.38	80.36- 93
	Krysin	Aleksey	RUS	25.11.76	202/80	HJ	2.28	2.30- 98
	Krzosek	Grzegorz	POL	10.1.76	182/67	800	1:45.97	1:46.33- 00
	Krzywanski #	Marcin	POL	29.8.75	185/74	100	10.23dq	10.23- 98
	Kulagin	Denis	RUS	23.5.80		HT	71.45	69.32- 00
	Kumara	Rohan Pradeep	SRI	10.3.75		400	45.76	45.25- 00
	Kunichika	Tomoaki	JPN	22.7.73	179/60	HMar	62:14	
	Kunkel	Adam	CAN	24.2.81		400H	49.87	52.00- 99
	Kuntos	Jirí	CZE	2.10.73	188/78	TJ	16.63	17.29- 99
	Kuptsov	Dmitriy	RUS	9.11.82		PV	5.55	5.30- 00
^	Kurennoy	Andrey	RUS	12.5.72	185/80	TJ	16.89	17.44- 97
	Kurgat	Eliud	KEN	20.8.73		HMar	61:31	
	Kürtösi	Zsolt	HUN	21.3.71	188/86	Dec	8099	8149- 00
	Kuusisto	Saku	FIN	9.3.82	190/100	JT	78.40	70.40- 98
	Kysela	Martin	CZE	25.3.74	178/66	PV	5.60	5.60- 96, 5.65i- 98, 5.70sq- 00
	Kyyrö	Mikko	FIN	12.7.80	191/106	DT	62.35	59.00- 00
	la Grange	Marcus	RSA	12.12.77	186/75	200	20.60, 20.45w	20.35- 00
						400	45.08A, 45.20	44.99A- 00
	Labidi	Sofiane	TUN	29.9.79	186/69	400	45.40	45.81- 00

Name		Nat	Born	Ht/Wt	Event	2001 Mark	Pre-2001 Best
^ Labrador	Basilio	ESP	29.3.67	168/60	50kW	4:05:31	3:46:46- 93
Lacasse	Florent	FRA	21.1.81	185/65	800	1:46.80	1:47.41- 00
Lachheb	Khalid	FRA	16.1.75	180/72	PV	5.68	5.80- 98
Lachheb	Taoufik	FRA	16.1.75	181/78	PV	5.60	5.72i- 99, 5.65- 00
Lacis	Viktors	LAT	28.11.77	191/79	400H	49.60	-0-
Lacy	Aaron	USA	1.4.71	188/79	400H	50.00	50.33- 96
* Lagat	Bernard	KEN	12.12.74	175/61	1500	3:26.34	3:28.51- 00
					1M	3:47.28	3:49.84- 00
					3000	7:45.52i	7:33.51- 00
					5000	13:30.54	13:23.46- 00
^ Lahssini	El Hassan	FRA	1.1.75	175/62	10000	28:17.12	-0-
Laiho	Harri	FIN	1.3.77	188/85	Dec	7633(w), 7567	7701- 00
Lakhal	Irba	MAR	12.2.75	168/61	3kSt	8:23.29	8:22.09- 95
Lambert	Chris	GBR	6.4.81	186/77	100	10.24	10.31- 99
Lambert	Sean	GRN	16.8.82	170/70	100	10.17, 10.13w	10.60- 98
					200	20.62w	21.35- 00
Lambèse	Bruno	FRA	11.4.69	190/96	Dec	7756	7650- 00
^ Lambrechts ¶	Burger	RSA	3.4.73	200/145	SP	20.53, 20.90dq	20.56- 00
* Lamela	Yago	ESP	24.7.77	178/68	LJ	8.07	8.56i, 8.56- 99
Lamine	Philippe	FRA	4.10.76	183/80	110H	13.76	13.75, 13.66w- 00
Lane	Matt	USA	5.9.77	178/64	3000	7:48.02	7:53.41- 00
					5000	13:25.38	13:27.24- 00
Langat	John	KEN	27.11.74	185/72	3kSt	8:15.17	
Langat	Shadrack	KEN	22.7.78	168/55	1500	3:38.2	3:34.93- 99
Lange	Björn	GER	15.6.79	193/102	JT	85.21	81.49- 00
Langlois	Denis	FRA	10.10.68	172/60	20kW	1:22:16	1:20:35- 97
					50kW	3:48:06	3:47:38- 00
Lao Jianfeng		CHN	24.5.75	183/70	LJ	8.10	8.40- 97
					TJ	16.68	16.91- 00
Lassiter	Seneca	USA	12.3.77	175/60	1000	2:17.79	2:21.48- 99
					1500	3:34.32	3:33.72- 99
					1M	3:54.36, 3:54.21i	3:54.85- 00
Latvala	Mikko	FIN	8.7.80	181/75	PV	5.66	5.40- 00
* Laukkanen	Juha	FIN	6.1.69	186/90	JT	85.40	88.22- 92
Laursen	Jimisola	SWE	13.7.77	184/86	400	45.54	45.68- 00
Lavanne	Cédric	FRA	13.11.80	183/72	110H	13.62	13.91- 00
Lavy	Shane	USA	15.2.76	185/72	HJ	2.22i	2.32i- 00, 2.30- 99
Laynes ¶	Jeff	USA	3.10.70	178/84	100	10.19	10.01- 96, 9.9- 95
					200	20.62dq	20.59- 92
Le Dauphin	Vincent	FRA	28.6.76	190/72	3kSt	8:34.12	8:15.76- 99
* Lebed	Sergey	UKR	15.7.75	180/65	3000	7:43.07	7:37.76- 99
					5000	13:14.51	13:18.18- 99
					HMar	62:09	
Leberer	Ralf	GER	26.10.73	184/78	110H	13.58	13.42- 99, 13.40w- 00
* Lee Bong-ju		KOR	11.10.70	168/56	Mar	2:09:11	2:07:20- 00
Lee Doo-yeon		KOR	9.4.75	180/70	400H	50.08	50.00- 00
^ Lee Jin-taek		KOR	13.4.72	190/72	HJ	2.24	2.34- 97
* Leeper	Nathan	USA	13.6.77	188/82	HJ	2.33i, 2.30	2.35- 00
Lekote	Otukile	BOT	19.10.78	178/64	800	1:44.47	
* Lelei	David	KEN	10.5.71	176/60	800	1:44.96	1:43.97- 00
					1000	2:17.74	2:22.61- 97
Lemen	David	USA	13.11.79	190/82	Dec	7790w, 7619	7532- 00
* Leone	Giacomo	ITA	10.4.71	171/59	Mar	2:07:52	2:08:41- 00
Lesnichiy	Aleksey	BLR	3.2.78	195/69	HJ	2.25	2.22- 96, 2.28i- 99
Letherby	Andrew	AUS	19.9.73		10000	28:25.56	28:37.05- 00
Letnicov	Vladimir	MDA	7.10.81		TJ	16.84	16.07- 00
* Lewis	Brian	USA	5.12.74	170/72	100	10.10	10.00- 97, 9.96w- 00
					200	20.42	20.26, 20.06r- 00
Lewis	Lubert	USA	6.8.78		800	1:46.86	1:46.72- 00
* Lewis-Francis	Mark	GBR	4.9.82	183/88	100	10.12. 9.97w?	10.10- 00
Leyckes	Dennis	GER	20.4.82	183/73	Dec	7822	7897- 00
Li Aiguo		CHN	12.6.79		Mar	2:10:25	2:20:15- 99
Li Dalong		CHN	21.10.80	190/69	LJ	8.22	7.91- 00
Li Guoqing		CHN	1.10.79	165/57	50kW	3:58:54	3:54:56- 00
Li Mingcai		CHN	22.8.71	168/55	20kW	1:22:06	1:19:34- 96
					50kW	3:53:37	3:49:17- 96
Li Rongxiang		CHN	8.1.72	180/80	JT	81.80	84.29- 00
Li Shaojie		CHN	26.11.75	194/100	DT	62.84	65.16- 96
Li Wenkui		CHN	31.12.71		SP	19.10	19.00- 96
Li Xiaoliang		CHN	8.2.86		50kW	4:01:23	
Li Yi		CHN	19.1.81		50kW	3:59:00	4:14:37- 99

Name		Nat	Born	Ht/Wt	Event	2001 Mark	Pre-2001 Best
* Li Zewen		CHN	5.12.73	172/55	20kW	1:20:49	1:18:32- 97
Li Zhuhong		CHN	22.10.83		Mar	2:10:46	-0-
Liang Tong		CHN	30.5.78	186/72	HJ	2.24	2.18- 00
* Lichtenegger	Elmar	AUT	25.5.74	187/83	110H	13.36	13.33- 99
Liefers	Gert-Jan	NED	26.9.78	185/71	1500	3:32.89	3:34.27- 98
					2000	4:56.56	
Liepa	Janis	LAT	14.3.81	193/90	JT	79.78	76.12- 99
Liepins	Modris	LAT	3.8.66	178/68	20kW	1:23:38	1:20:09- 97
					50kW	3:51:22	3:47:48- 98
de Lima	Jessé	BRA	17.2.81	186/85	HJ	2.25	2.21- 99
^ de Lima	Vanderlei	BRA	11.8.69	168/54	Mar	2:10:02	2:08:31- 98
* Limo	Benjamin	KEN	23.8.74	178/65	3000	7:33.10	7:28.67- 99
					5000	12:59.53	12:55.82- 00
* Limo	Felix	KEN	22.8.80	174/58	3000	7:40.67	7:43.50- 00
					5000	13:16.42	13:23.43- 99
					10000	27:26.86	27:04.54- 00
Limo	Remmy	KEN	25.8.71	182/79	LJ	8.00w	7.94- 99, 8.02A- 98
					TJ	16.63A, 16.44	16.89- 98
* Limo	Richard	KEN	18.11.80	167/53	3000	7:32.23	7:34.32- 99
					5000	12:56.72	12:58.15- 99
					10000	27:25.27	
Lincoln	Dan	USA	20.10.80	190/70	3kSt	8:26.91	8:44.43- 00
Linden	Andreas	GER	20.2.65	185/90	JT	83.00	85.42- 95
Lingua	Marco	ITA	4.6.78	179/94	HT	74.40	76.72- 99
Linscheid	Roman	IRL	29.12.70	183/100	HT	72.62	76.25- 99
* Lipiec	Tomasz	POL	10.5.71	185/72	20kW	1:22:38	1:20:48- 00
					50kW	3:48:51	3:40:08- 99
Lischka	Michael	GER	23.12.73	197/135	DT	65.04	63.42- 98
* Lister	Melvin	USA	29.8.77	188/75	LJ	8.10i, 7.92, 8.08w	8.49- 00
* Little	Kevin	USA	3.4.68	183/73	200	20.13	20.10- 99, 19.94w- 95
Liu Dashan		CHN	10.5.80		20kW	1:22:36	
Liu Fuxiang		CHN	24.3.75		HT	72.16	69.63- 00
Liu Jun		CHN	28.2.75	162/55	50kW	3:59:57	3:57:10- 96
* Liu Xiang		CHN	13.7.83	186/74	110H	13.32	13.75- 00
Liu Yang		CHN	16.2.80		100	10.25	10.65- 00
Liu Zhiwen		CHN	17.1.75		LJ	7.91	
Llanos	Luigi	PUR	22.8.78	180/80	Dec	7613	7416- 00
* Lobinger	Tim	GER	3.9.72	193/83	PV	5.80	6.00- 97
* Lobodin	Lev	RUS	1.4.69	188/88	Dec	8465	8571- 98
Loikkanen	Mika	FIN	20.2.74	194/115	DT	62.93	62.24- 99
Lomba	Jimmy	FRA	30.6.78	182/73	800	1:46.16	1:48.29- 00
^ Longo ¶	Andrea	ITA	26.6.75	191/85	800	1:44.55	1:43.74- 00
Looije	Laurens	NED	12.1.73	185/75	PV	5.60	5.71- 98
López	Alejandro	MEX	9.2.75	173/61	20kW	1:20:49	1:17:56- 99
López	Julio	ESP	8.3.72	196/79	TJ	16.68	16.51- 94, 16.76w- 95
Lopuchovsky	Marcel	SVK	2.5.77	196/80	400H	49.92	50.54- 97
Lopuyet	Simon	KEN	24.12.72		HMar	61:23	62:57- 97
					Mar	2:11:04	2:08:19- 97
Lorenzo	Santiago	ARG	4.4.78	191/88	Dec	7889	7649- 00
Loretz	Felix	SUI	13.11.75	181/90	JT	76.68	75.36- 00
Loria	Mickaël	FRA	9.6.73	182/74	LJ	8.10i	8.23A- 98, 7.99- 00
Loskutov	Pavel	EST	2.12.69	178/63	Mar	2:11:09	2:12:37- 99
Louahla	Malik	ALG	19.12.77	174/72	400	45.13	45.55- 00
Loum	Oumar	SEN	31.12.73	184/79	100	10.19	10.19- 94, 10.06Aw- 00
					200	20.43	20.21A, 20.19w -00, 20.42- 94
Louw	Stephan	NAM	26.2.75	187/76	LJ	8.15A, 8.11	8.17A- 99, 7.86- 00
Lovkin	Semyon	RUS	14.7.77	180/67	20kW	1:22:38.3t	1:20:12- 00
					50kW	3:53:45	
Lu Ronghua		CHN	21.2.83		20kW	1:23:58	1:30:50- 00
Luaces	Isbel	CUB	20.7.75	187/97	JT	82.02	83.30- 00
Luis	Yacnier	CUB	24.1.82		400H	50.05	51.47- 00
* Lukashevich	Aleksey	UKR	11.1.77	175/70	LJ	8.20	8.27- 00
Lukoschek	Daniel	GER	16.8.79		Dec	7648	7309- 00
Lunn	Jason	USA	19.9.74	187/71	1500	3:36.5	3:36.74- 00
Lusis	Voldemars	LAT	7.12.74	187/102	JT	81.86	83.08- 00
^ Lyakhov	Sergey	RUS	1.3.68	195/107	DT	64.00A	66.78- 95
Lyolin	Aleksey	BLR	27.11.78	190/74	HJ	2.25i	2.30- 00
Lyzhin	Pavel	BLR	24.3.81	189/110	SP	20.12	19.12- 00
Ma Hongye		CHN	16.4.74	175/62	50kW	3:50:24	3:52:58- 97
* Maase	Kamiel	NED	20.10.71	191/71	5000	13:19.86	13:14.13- 00
					10000	28:02.37	27:34.02- 99

	Name		Nat	Born	Ht/Wt	Event	2001 Mark	Pre-2001 Best
*	Maazouzi	Driss	FRA	15.10.69	180/65	1000	2:17.10	2:15.26- 99
						1500	3:31.54	3:31.51- 99
						2000	4:55.55	4:59.80- 95
*	Macey	Dean	GBR	12.12.77	196/92	Dec	8603	8567- 00
*	Mack	Tim	USA	15.9.72	188/78	PV	5.81	5.81- 00
	Mackie	Ian	GBR	27.2.75	188/82	100	10.19w	10.17- 96, 10.00w- 98
*	Mackowiak	Robert	POL	13.5.70	181/76	400	44.84	45.01- 00
	Macrozonaris	Nicolas	CAN	22.8.80	178/82	100	10.20	10.19, 10.18Aw- 00
	Maczey	Mike	GER	28.9.72	188/81	Dec	8139	8461- 00
	Mäder	Sascha	GER	1.1.80		Dec	7612	7374- 00
	Maeda	Kazuhiro	JPN	19.4.81	166/55	10000	28:16.17	28:48.46- 00
	Maeda	Yusuke	JPN	16.3.78		LJ	8.08w	7.89- 00
	Maffei	Giuseppe	ITA	28.1.74	182/64	3kSt	8:34.66	8:11.85- 99
*	Magnússon	Jón Arnar	ISL	28.7.69	183/87	Dec	7938	8573, 8583w- 98
	Magrans	Marc	ESP	26.9.76	185/80	Dec	7675	7783- 00
	Mahmood Hussain	Zahid	PAK	.4.78		JT	78.25	69.45- 00
	Maillard	Sébastien	FRA	2.5.81	184/81	Dec	7562	7275- 00
*	Maina Munyi	Simon	KEN	18.3.78	177/52	5000	13:15.92	13:10.71- 98
						10000	27:56.82	27:18.74- 99
*	Maiyo	Benjamin	KEN	6.10.78	175/58	3000	7:41.83	7:32.36- 00
						5000	13:05.43	13:02.28- 00
						10000	27:07.55	27:34.38- 98
	Makarov	Andrey	BLR	2.1.71	181/72	20kW	1:19:12	1:18:23- 00
*	Makarov	Sergey	RUS	19.3.73	192/95	JT	88.42	89.93- 99
	Makori	David	KEN	6.11.73	178/63	HMar	61:39	61:40- 00
	Malasevich	Aleksandr	BLR	7.4.77	200/115	DT	63.32	63.78- 99
*	Malcolm	Christian	GBR	3.6.79	174/67	100	10.11, 10.09w?	10.12, 10.10w- 98
						200	20.08	20.19- 00
	Malherbe	Arnaud	RSA	20.11.72	188/69	400	45.12A, 45.30	44.59A- 99, 44.74- 00
	Malík	Stefan	SVK	11.2.66	183/69	50kW	3:51:58	3:48:52- 97
	Malina	Libor	CZE	14.6.73	192/120	DT	67.13	65.08- 98
	Malone	Casey	USA	6.4.77	203/106	DT	60.96	64.47A- 00
	Malyavin	Vladimir	RUS	4.3.73	188/75	LJ	8.22	8.25- 00
	Malysa	Jirí	CZE	14.8.66	180/71	20kW	1:20:21	1:19:18- 00
						50kW	4:03:21	4:22:33- 99
	Mambo	Djéké	BEL	4.3.77	182/76	TJ	16.56	16.62i, 16.41- 00
	Mannon	Kevin	USA	12.8.76	193/118	HT	70.81	71.50- 00
	Manson	Pat	USA	29.11.67	178/75	PV	5.55Ai, 5.55	5.85- 94
	Mao Xinli		CHN	26.1.81		50kW	4:03:10	4:17:02- 00
	Mao Xinyuan		CHN	2.7.71	176/68	50kW	4:00:40	3:48:59- 96
	Maranga	Edwin	KEN	15.8.71	172/63	1M	3:55.80	3:57.5 - 00
	Marciniszyn	Grzegorz	POL	22.5.77	187/82	LJ	8.28	8.04- 97, 8.12w- 98
	Marcoullides	Anninos	CYP	8.2.71	185/79	100	10.23, 10.18w	10.12- 98
						200	20.60	20.43- 98
	Maritim	Julius	KEN	80		HMar	62:16	
*	Markov	Dmitriy	AUS	14.3.75	182/85	PV	6.05	6.00- 98
*	Markov	Ilya	RUS	19.6.72	176/64	20kW	1:19:36, 1:22:09.8t	1:18:30- 97
*	Márquez	David	ESP	13.10.77	170/51	20kW	1:21:09	1:21:44- 00
	Martin	Blair	NZL	25.4.75	174/60	10000	28:27.23	
*	Martín	Eliseo	ESP	5.11.73	173/62	3kSt	8:19.20	8:13.59- 99
	Martín	Francisco	ESP	27.5.75	173/74	50kW	4:03:29	4:00:16- 00
	Martin	Garland	USA	1.3.81	178/70	110H	13.73	13.90- 00
*	Martín	Luis Miguel	ESP	11.1.72	180/69	3kSt	8:08.74	8:09.77- 00
	Martínez	Alexander	CUB	23.8.77		TJ	17.06	16.80- 00
	Martínez	David	ESP	31.1.67	195/105	DT	63.85	65.36- 92, 65.52dq- 97
	Martínez	Joan Lino	CUB	17.1.78	176/69	LJ	8.08, 8.13w	8.19- 98, 8.39ic- 99
	Martínez	José Manuel	ESP	22.10.71	176/65	5000	13:26.94	13:28.60- 00
						10000	27:54.81	27:51.82- 99
	Martínez	Julio	GUA	27.9.73	165/44	20kW	1:22:27	1:17:46- 99
*	Martínez	Manuel	ESP	7.12.74	185/140	SP	21.35	20.79i- 99, 20.55- 00
	Martins	Pedro	POR	12.1.68	163/60	50kW	3:55:54	3:55:55- 00
	Marwa	Francis	KEN	76	178/64	800	1:45.81	1:45.78- 99
	Marwa	Joel	KEN	30.8.74	179/63	800	1:46.0A, 1:46.05	1:44.5A- 98
*	Mashchenko	Ruslan	RUS	11.11.71	193/83	400H	48.88	48.06- 98
	Maska	Vladimir	CZE	6.2.73	190/115	HT	80.09	81.28- 99
*	Massana	Valentí	ESP	5.7.70	165/51	50kW	3:48:28	3:38:43- 94
	Mastrov	Artyom	RUS	12.11.76	175/62	800	1:46.53	1:46.04- 00
	Máté	Gábor	HUN	28.3.79	199/104	DT	63.41	66.91- 00
	Matete	Samuel	ZAM	27.7.68	183/81	400H	49.82	47.10- 91
	Matsuda	Ryo	JPN	26.12.79	176/68	200	20.68, 20.64w	20.75- 99
	Matsumiya	Takayuki	JPN	21.2.80	162/47	10000	28:13.63	28:02.80- 00

Name		Nat	Born	Ht/Wt	Event	2001 Mark	Pre-2001 Best
Matsumoto	Kazuteru	JPN	25.11.83		200	20.71	21.27- 00
Matsunaga	Nobuya	JPN	8.11.74	166/52	HMar	61:33	
Matthews	Todd	USA	28.6.79	193/86	110H	13.60	13.57- 00
^ Matusevich	Konstantin	ISR	25.1.71	202/85	HJ	2.25i	2.36- 00
* Matyukhin	Nikolay	RUS	13.12.68	179/68	20kW	1:22:13	1:19:43- 93
					50kW	3:45:48	3:40:13- 99
Mavuso	Richard	RSA	30.3.78		10000	28:14.23	28:41.31- 00
Mayer	Gerhard	AUT	20.5.80	191/93	DT	59.60	56.64- 00
^ Mayo	Gilmar	COL	30.9.69	190/72	HJ	2.28A, 2.25	2.33- 94
Mayo	Tom	GBR	2.5.77	194/74	1500	3:38.3+/3:38.34	3:41.2- 98
					1M	3:55.57	4:00.02- 98
* Mayock	John	GBR	26.10.70	177/66	1500	3:34.43	3:31.86- 97
					1M	3:54.05	3:50.32- 96
					2000	4:57.09i	4:56.75- 99
					3000	7:44.08i	7:43.31i- 97, 7:47.28- 95
^ Mayola	Freddy	CUB	1.11.77	176/74	100	10.11, 10.08w	10.10- 99, 10.00rw- 00
Mazza	Marco	ITA	25.6.77	168/53	3000	7:47.14	7:58.03- 98
					10000	27:54.25	28:04.71- 00
McCarthy	Kris	AUS	15.10.79	188/75	800	1:46.15	1:45.57- 00
McClintock	Martin	RSA	30.6.75		LJ	7.97	7.84A- 00
McCullough	Edorian	USA	83	175/82	100	10.0w	10.2w- 00
* McDonald	Michael	JAM	17.3.75	183/85	400	44.71	44.64A- 96, 44.65- 97
McEwen	John	USA	5.3.74	190/114	HT	71.67	70.27- 99
McEwen	Matt	AUS	16.10.71		Dec	7825	7684- 97
* McFarlane	Danny	JAM	14.2.72	185/81	400	45.20A, 45.59	44.90- 95
McGhee	Roland	USA	15.10.71	180/70	LJ	8.18	8.51- 95
McGrath	Dominic	AUS	4.6.72	180/70	50kW	4:01:53	3:57:51- 00
McGrath	Paddy	IRL	1.7.71	183/120	HT	74.60	77.49- 99
McHugh	Terry	IRL	22.8.63	191/106	JT	78.19	82.75- 00, 84.54R- 91
McIntosh	Troy	BAH	29.3.73	178/75	400	45.52	44.73A- 96, 44.79- 99
McLean	Bubba	USA	2.9.79	175/73	PV	5.45	
McMahon	Kevin	USA	26.5.72	183/102	HT	76.52	79.26- 99
McMullen	Paul	USA	19.2.72	188/79	800	1:45.71	1:45.96- 95
					1500	3:33.89	3:34.45- 95
					1M	3:54.94	3:55.84i, 3:56.14- 98
McMullen	Phil	USA	3.2.75	188/84	Dec	8220	8097- 00
McReynolds	Jacob	AUS	8.12.78		TJ	16.47w	15.92- 99
Medina	Yoger	VEN	5.9.73	185/108	SP	19.44	20.01- 00
Mehlich	Krzysztof	POL	2.8.74	190/80	110H	13.65	13.40- 96
Meité	Ibrahim	CIV	18.11.76	183/75	100	10.25	10.24- 00, 10.12w- 96, 10.0A- 99
* Mekonnen	Hailu	ETH	4.4.80	172/61	1500	3:38.41i	3:33.14- 00
					3000	7:30.53	7:33.00- 99
					5000	12:58.57	13:10.98- 99
Meleshenko	Yevgeniy	KAZ	19.1.81	183/68	400H	48.46	50.54- 00
Meleshkevich	Artur	BLR	11.4.75	173/69	20kW	1:18:12	1:19:15- 00
Melétoglou	Hrístos	GRE	2.1.72	189/72	TJ	17.19	17.12- 97
Melich	Lukás	CZE	16.9.80	186/105	HT	71.47	69.08- 00
Melin	Patrik	SWE	7.6.71		Dec	7590	7534- 99
* Meliz	Luis	CUB	11.8.79	177/76	LJ	8.11i, 8.10	8.43- 00
^ Menc ¶	Miroslav	CZE	16.3.71	197/130	SP	20.68i, 20.64dq	20.64- 00, 21.19ex/dq- 99
Meriluoto	Johan	FIN	22.3.74	187/73	TJ	16.88, 17.04w	16.95- 00
Mertens	Michael	GER	27.12.65	191/105	SP	19.73	20.24- 98
* Mesnil	Romain	FRA	13.7.77	188/79	PV	5.86i, 5.85	5.93- 99
Metto	Luke	KEN	76		HMar	62:02	61:21- 00
Mewes	David	GER	7.10.76	196/95	Dec	7884	8108- 00
Meystedt	Jay	USA	15.10.77		HJ	2.22	2.15- 00
* Mezgebu	Assefa	ETH	19.6.78	175/55	3000	7:35.98	7:28.45- 98
					5000	13:00.86	12:53.84- 98
					10000	27:22.30	27:18.28- 99
Mikhaylenko	Vladimir	UKR	27.8.73	196/84	Dec	8019	8052- 00
Mikhaylichenko	Yevgeniy	RUS	13.2.79	184/80	PV	5.50i	5.65- 00
Mikhnevich	Andrey	BLR	12.7.76	202/115	SP	20.92	20.52i, 20.30 99
Mikkola	Esko	FIN	14.2.75	183/85	JT	82.48	81.86- 98
* Milazar	Éric	MRI	1.6.75	192/80	400	44.69	44.87- 00
Miles	Derek	USA	28.9.72	188/84	PV	5.82	5.65- 00
Miller	Brian	USA	20.3.72	193/135	SP	20.55	20.43- 97
* Miller	Coby	USA	19.10.76	168/68	200	20.31i	19.96- 00
Miller	Lavar	USA	16.2.77	188/79	HJ	2.24i, 2.23	2.25i, 2.22- 99
^ Mills	Derek	USA	9.7.72	175/68	400	45.62	44.13- 95
Miranda	Montxu	ESP	27.12.76	191/83	PV	5.70i, 5.60	5.81- 00
Mishiro	Naoki	JPN	16.3.77	165/53	10000	28:25.18	27:59.39- 00

	Name		Nat	Born	Ht/Wt	Event	2001 Mark	Pre-2001 Best
	Mishukov	Oleg	RUS	31.8.81	184/72	400	45.79	46.79- 00
*	Misoi	Kipkirui	KEN	23.12.78	177/59	3kSt	8:01.69	8:07.21- 00
	Mistretta	Alessandro	ITA	6.3.71	172/58	50kW	3:58:24	3:51:33- 99
^	Misyulya	Yevgeniy	BLR	13.3.64	178/68	20kW	1:19:45	1:18:18- 96
	Mitchell	Dennis	USA	20.2.66	174/69	100	10.11, 10.07w	9.91- 91, 9.85w- 93
						200	20.45	20.20- 92, 20.09A- 89
	Mitchell	Michael	USA	16.5.81		200	20.68	20.59- 00
	Mitchell	Robert	GBR	14.9.80	190/78	HJ	2.25	2.20- 00
	Mitrofanov	Dmitriy	RUS	76		LJ	8.08	7.57- 99
	Modibo	Ato	TRI	19.6.79	188/75	400	44.87	45.33- 99
	Moede	Thomas	GER	26.7.77	184/77	TJ	16.90	16.32- 99
	Moeketsane	Motsehi	RSA	2.1.70		10000	28:23.60	28:55.14- 99
	Moffitt	John	USA	81		LJ	7.92w	7.43w- 00
	Mofokeng	George	RSA	19.2.79	155/44	HMar	62:05	61:42- 00
	Mogaka	Ronald	KEN	17.4.78		HMar	61:25	
	Mohamed	Walid Abderrazak	EGY	4.4.72		JT	78.15	75.23- 98
	Moiben	James	KEN	20.4.77		Mar	2:10:44	2:10:07- 99
*	Mokganyetsi	Hendrik	RSA	7.9.75	190/76	400	44.70	44.59- 00
^	Molina	Enrique	ESP	25.2.68	175/62	3000	7:44.56	7:32.32- 97
						5000	13:18.20	13:07.34- 97
	Molina	Juan Manuel	ESP	15.3.79	170/52	20kW	1:21:51	1:22:43- 00
						20kW	1:22:31.8	
*	Möllenbeck	Michael	GER	12.12.69	200/120	DT	67.61	67.44- 96
*	Moncur	Avard	BAH	2.11.78	196/82	400	44.45	44.72- 00
	Mononen	Matti	FIN	25.11.83		PV	5.45	5.15- 00
	Monte	Yosmel	CUB	26.6.77	189/100	HT	71.77	71.99- 00
	Monteiro	Edivaldo	POR	28.4.76		400H	49.64	50.26- 00
	Montesinos	Hipólito	ESP	24.5.76	186/79	110H	13.76	13.59- 99
*	Montgomery	Tim	USA	28.1.75	178/69	100	9.84	9.92- 97
	Monye	Jude	NGR	16.11.73	188/79	400	45.54	44.83- 96
	Moore	Jonathan	GBR	31.5.84	180/74	LJ	7.98	7.46- 00
	Moore	Stephen	USA	13.8.75	180/75	Dec	7714	8037- 99
	Morán	Ramiro	ESP	17.5.69	173/63	3kSt	8:27.44	8:17.49- 98
	Mordhorst	Rolf	GER	11.5.73	201/110	DT	59.66	59.13- 98
	Morello	Salvatore	ITA	5.9.74	176/65	TJ	16.49	16.37- 99
	Moreno	Jorge	CUB	25.5.77		400H	50.05A	50.85- 00
	Moreno	Marcos	ESP	14.3.73	193/94	Dec	7588	7790- 00
^	Morgan	Dinsdale	JAM	19.11.72	188/77	400H	49.30	48.13- 98
	Morgan	Nathan	GBR	30.6.78	187/86	LJ	7.97	8.11- 98
*	Mori	Fabrizio	ITA	28.6.69	175/68	400H	47.54	47.72- 99
	Mori	Yuki	JPN	8.3.79	171/51	HMar	61:27	
	Morimasa	Tatsumi	JPN	3.4.76	171/56	HMar	61:38	61:49- 00
^	Morinaga	Masaki	JPN	27.3.72	175/64	LJ	8.06, 8.18w	8.25- 92, 8.34w- 00
	Morishita	Yoshiteru	JPN	26.5.71	180/63	Mar	2:07:59	2:09:36- 99
	Moroney	Nick	AUS	3.8.72	186/72	HJ	2.24	2.25- 00
	Moroz	Gennadiy	BLR	27.5.78	200/77	HJ	2.33	2.28i- 99, 2.25- 98
	Moser	Scott	USA	15.7.79	190/106	SP	19.01	18.57- 99
						DT	63.00	59.78- 00
	Mosili	Mojafela	LES	3.12.78	160/78	400	45.4A	46.5 - 00
^	Mosima	Philip	KEN	2.1.77	168/55	3000	7:39.17	7:35.52- 96
						5000	13:26.50	12:53.72- 96
	Moskalenko	Vitaliy	RUS	30.6.74		TJ	16.83	17.00i, 16.84- 99
^	Motchebon	Nico	GER	13.11.69	186/81	800	1:46.38	1:43.91- 96
	Mottin	Sergio	ITA	15.6.76	186/115	SP	19.62i, 19.47	19.01- 00
*	Mottram	Craig	AUS	18.6.80	188/72	1500	3:35.40	3:38.27- 00
						1M	3:53.06	
						3000	7:41.35	7:51.32- 00
						5000	13:23.94	13:26.20- 00
						10000	28:19.26	
*	Moudrik	Younès	MAR	1.10.77	176/72	LJ	8.23	8.34- 00
	Mourhej	Hani	SYR	20.10.81	183/60	400H	49.40	51.46- 00
*	Mourhit	Mohammed	BEL	10.10.70	164/55	1500	3:38.8	3:36.14- 00
						3000	7:41.03, 7:38.94i	7:26.62- 00
						5000	13:09.63	12:49.71- 00
	Moussaoui	Samir	MAR	15.5.75	178/68	3000	7:45.47	7:53.16- 98
						5000	13:20.71	13:30.45- 99
	Moya	Roberto	CUB	11.2.65	196/120	DT	60.70	65.68- 90
	Mpholo	Simon	RSA	17.8.75		10000	28:08.92	28:37.72- 00
						HMar	61:56	
	Mpror	Sammy	KEN			HMar	62:09	
	Mubarak	Bilal Saad	QAT	18.12.72	189/110	SP	19.06	19.65- 97

Name		Nat	Born	Ht/Wt	Event	2001 Mark	Pre-2001 Best
Mubarak	Mubarak Ata	KSA	17.12.81	175/67	110H	13.72	13.81- 00
Mucci	Vittorino	ITA	29.11.74	183/62	20kW	1:24:08	1:25:05- 99
Mucheru	Leonard	KEN	13.6.78	182/66	1500	3:33.79+	
					1M	3:49.75	3:56.43- 00
					3000	7:35.35	7:41.56- 00
					5000	13:14.94	13:21.14- 00
Mugi	Gordon	KEN	27.11.81	/56	3000	7:45.60	
					5000	13:17.40	13:36.0A- 00
					10000	27:29.09	
Mukae	Tadakatsu	JPN	17.10.76	178/58	HMar	62:14	63:07- 00
Mulabegovic	Nedzad	CRO	4.2.81	189/100	SP	19.23	18.19- 00
* Mulaudzi	Mbulaeni	RSA	8.9.80	171/62	800	1:44.01	1:45.55- 00
Muli	Pius	KEN	15.12.82		3000	7:44.94	7:56.31- 99
					5000	13:24.27	13:21.55- 99
Müller	Wolfram	GER	8.7.81	190/65	800	1:45.14	1:47.17- 00
					1500	3:37.61	3:39.09- 00
					3000	7:45.41	7:52.46- 00
Munji	Titus	KEN	79		HMar	60:27	62:26- 00
Munnings	Timothy	BAH	22.6.66	185/74	400	45.81	45.67- 99
Munuera	Francisco Javier	ESP	7.7.72	180/64	3kSt	8:22.91	8:23.24- 99
Murakami	Yukifumi	JPN	23.12.79	185/80	JT	80.59	78.57- 00
Muraki	Ryuji	JPN	29.12.79	178/66	400	45.88	46.41- 00
* Murofushi	Koji	JPN	8.10.74	187/97	HT	83.47	81.08- 00
* Murphy	Andrew	AUS	18.12.69	185/82	TJ	17.20i, 17.28w, 17.07	17.32- 99
Murphy	Liam	AUS	5.6.79	174/60	50kW	3:54:37	4:14:53- 99
Mustapic	Dragan	CRO	23.3.63	196/110	DT	60.68	64.40- 00
Mutai	Richard	KEN	74		HMar	62:12	62:28- 00
Mutai	Sammy	KEN	20.12.74	180/68	1500	3:34.88+	3:33.44- 99
					1M	3:50.60	3:52.19- 99
Mutanya	Obed	ZAM	10.8.81		5000	13:25.25	
* Mutua	Joseph Mwengi	KEN	10.12.78	170/58	800	1:43.63	1:45.49A- 00
Muzík	Jirí	CZE	1.9.76	181/75	400H	48.53	48.27- 97
Mwangi	Paul	KEN	19.11.73	179/63	1500	3:35.95	3:34.29- 00
					1M	3:55.08	3:54.81- 98
Myburgh	Alwyn	RSA	13.10.80	188/71	400H	48.09	49.07A, 49.11- 00
Nada Saya	John	TAN	8.8.78		HMar	61:58	
					Mar	2:08:57	
Nadezhdin	Aleksandr	RUS	22.3.76	181/72	50kW	3:55:21	
Nagata	Koichiro	JPN	19.12.78	175/59	HMar	61:09	
* Nagel	Morné	RSA	23.3.78	183/77	100	10.15A	10.36A, 10.22Aw- 99
					200	20.59A, 20.5w	20.72A, 20.65Aw- 99
Naito	Masato	JPN	31.7.80	185/70	110H	13.50	13.85- 00
Nakahara	Daisuke	JPN	10.8.74		HMar	62:18	
Nakano	Tsuyoshi	JPN	12.3.73	168/52	HMar	62:12	
Nance	Jon	USA	28.8.77	183/73	PV	5.60	5.55- 97
Nara	Kenji	JPN	26.12.79	175/66	100	10.22	10.42- 99
* Närhi	Matti	FIN	17.8.75	188/100	JT	84.21	88.24- 97
Nau	Manuel	GER	2.7.77	190/90	JT	76.60	83.04- 00
Nazipov	Mukhamet	RUS	10.9.64	178/64	Mar	2:11:14	2:10:35- 00
Ndereva Njeru	Nelson	KEN	14.7.67		Mar	2:10:58	2:10:37- 96
Ndiritu	Julius	KEN	76		5000	13:30.35	
N'Dri	Eric Pacôme	CIV	24.3.78	185/83	100	10.17, 10.11w	10.34- 97, 10.23w- 96
Ndungu	James	KEN	30.4.79	173/56	5000	13:30.32	
					10000	28:05.93	28:02.06- 00
* Nduwimana	Jean-Patrick	BDI	9.5.78	178/61	800	1:42.81	1:44.06- 00
					1000	2:17.34	2:16.98- 00
Neale	Alfred	USA	1.7.81	196/81	HJ	2.23	2.25i, 2.22- 00
Negussie	Hailu	ETH			Mar	2:10:32	
Nejedly	Michael	CZE	1.10.69	188/72	3kSt	8:34.00	8:27.60- 00
* Nelson	Adam	USA	7.7.75	181/115	SP	21.53	22.12- 00
Nelson	Thavius 'T.J'	USA	7.12.77	180/77	110H	13.49	13.72- 97
Nemchaninov	Andrey	RUS	27.11.66	180/105	SP	19.63	20.95i- 88, 20.60- 92
* Németh	Zsolt	HUN	9.11.71	190/110	HT	77.87	81.56- 99
Newman	Terence	USA	4.9.78	178/77	100	10.22	10.48- 00
Newton	Lee-Roy	RSA	19.12.78	180/67	200	20.55w	20.74- 99, 20.71Aw- 98
Ngadi	Salaho	TAN	12.3.79		HMar	61:46	61:53- 00
					Mar	2:10:36	
Ngatho	Zakayo	KEN	18.3.78	165/54	5000	13:09.31	13:21.33- 00
					10000	28:01.11	27:44.01- 00
* Ngeny	Noah	KEN	2.11.78	182/68	800	1:44.85	1:44.49- 00
					1000	2:16.93	2:11.96- 99

Name		Nat	Born	Ht/Wt	Event	2001 Mark	Pre-2001 Best
(Ngeny)					1500	3:31.94	3:28.12- 00
					1M	3:50.29	3:43.40- 99
					2000	4:56.40i	4:50.08- 99
Ngetich	David	KEN	12.5.72		Mar	2:10:19	2:09:24- 99
Ngolepus	Joseph	KEN	75		Mar	2:08:47	2:08:49- 00
Niaré	Yves	FRA	20.7.77	195/100	SP	19.76	19.22- 00
Nichols	Regan	USA	26.7.73	183/79	400H	49.31	48.66- 98
Nicolas	Benoit	FRA	17.4.77	182/70	1500	3:38.84	3:43.65- 00
Nieland	Nick	GBR	31.1.72	193/95	JT	82.93	85.09- 00
Niemi	Shane	CAN	2.6.78	186/80	200	20.61	20.69A- 99, 20.62w- 00
					400	44.86	45.52- 99
Nieto	James	USA	2.11.76	193/79	HJ	2.27	2.30- 99
Nieves	Freddy	ECU	14.5.71		TJ	16.69A	
Niketic	Djordje	YUG	11.3.76	200/75	HJ	2.26i, 2.22	2.26- 98
					HJ	2.22	
Nikitin	Sergey	RUS	13.5.73		Dec	7686	7862- 99, 8012h- 98
Niklaus	André	GER	30.8.81	190/78	Dec	8042	7712- 00
Nishida	Takayuki	JPN	26.4.77	177/56	Mar	2:08:45	2:13:46- 00
Nishikawa	Tetsuo	JPN	14.7.77	165/52	HMar	61:42	62:52- 98
Nizhegorodov	Denis	RUS	26.7.80	180/61	20kW	1:18:20	1:21:47- 00
Njenga	Daniel	KEN	7.5.76	175/60	10000	28:05.43	28:10.50- 99
Nkuna	Isaiah	RSA	5.3.77		800	1:46.93A	1:48.04A- 99
Nolan	James	IRL	27.1.77	183/71	1500	3:36.50	3:36.30- 00
					1M	3:56.50i	
Nolan	Michael	CAN	22.9.73	188/93	Dec	8169	7886- 96, 8009w- 97, 7914A-00
Nomkanha	Nattaporn	THA	15.9.71		TJ	16.45, 16.47w	16.53- 00
* Nool	Erki	EST	25.6.70	184/84	Dec	8815	8742- 00
Nordin	Jimmy	SWE	19.10.79	179/115	SP	19.96i, 19.92	20.07- 00
Norman	Josh	USA	26.7.80	188/60	100	10.17	10.40w- 99
Nossmy	Philip	SWE	6.12.82	187/83	110H	13.65	13.63- 00
Noúsios	Astérios	GRE	25.2.79		LJ	7.98i, 7.94	8.00- 00
Novo	Luis	POR	29.5.70	173/60	Mar	2:10:28	2:10:32- 98
Nowill	Peter	AUS	15.6.79		3kSt	8:33.48	8:53.15- 00
Nsenga	Jonathan	BEL	21.4.73	188/82	110H	13.63	13.25- 98
^ Ntawulikiura	Mathias	RWA	14.7.64	171/60	HMar	62:14	61:41- 00
Nu Ermaimaiti		CHN	8.3.84		DT	62.36	55.31- 00
Nutter	Travis	USA	9.2.75	178/95	HT	70.80	69.34- 98
Nyamu	Julius	KEN	1.12.77	178/66	3kSt	8:07.59	
* Nyariki	Tom	KEN	27.9.71	170/62	3000	7:38.30	7:27.75- 96
					5000	13:03.60	12:55.94- 97
* Obikwelu	Francis	NGR/POR	22.11.78	195/79	100	9.98	9.97- 00
					200	20.33	19.84- 99
Obinata	Hideyuki	JPN	2.12.76	173/65	Mar	2:08:52	2:17:24- 00
Oda	Takenori	JPN	5.12.80	162/46	10000	28:27.33	28:42.70- 00
Odom	Deworski	USA	11.4.77	188/84	110H	13.59w	13.44A,13.38Aw- 00,13.59,13.56w- 99
O'Dowd	Matthew	GBR	15.4.76	174/59	5000	13:30.56	13:37.00- 99
Odriozola	Mikel	ESP	25.5.73	180/62	50kW	3:45:22	3:45:57- 00
Ogata	Tsuyoshi	JPN	11.5.73	165/50	Mar	2:10:06	
Ogawa	Hiroyuki	JPN	17.6.78	169/52	10000	28:24.15	28:29.0 - 99
Ojaniemi	Jaakko	FIN	28.8.80	192/83	Dec	7907	7763- 99
Okantey	Samuel	GHA	3.11.74	183/77	TJ	16.66, 16.75w	16.74- 99
Okeke	Aham	NOR	19.8.69	172/76	100	10.26, 10.15w	?10.26, 10.19dq, 10.10w-dt- 94
Okken	Arnoud	NED	20.4.82	182/65	800	1:45.64	1:48.08- 00
Okworo	George	KEN	12.5.79		5000	13:28.94	13:29.19- 00
Oleksy	Tommy	USA	26.3.81	190/79	LJ	7.89i	7.71, 7.73w- 00
Olgundeniz	Ercüment	TUR	7.7.76		DT	59.95	62.90- 00
* Olijar	Stanislav	LAT	22.3.79	190/80	110H	13.29	13.25- 00
de Oliveira	Raphael R.	BRA	5.2.79	170/68	100	10.23, 10.16w	10.20A- 00, 10.36- 99
Olmedo	Pablo	MEX	8.5.75	175/60	10000	28:17.36	28:13.01- 00
* Olsen	Joachim	DEN	31.5.77	184/120	SP	20.43i, 20.43	20.88- 00
					DT	60.20	58.73- 99
Olsen	Tom Erik	NOR	20.10.74	198/90	PV	5.45i	5.50- 00
Olsson	Bjørn	NOR	10.8.75	200/75	HJ	2.22i	2.23- 96
* Olsson	Christian	SWE	25.1.80	192/73	TJ	17.49	16.97- 00
Omae	Yusuke	JPN	6.4.82	176/68	200	20.29	20.81- 00
Omey	Tom	BEL	24.4.75	182/63	800	1:45.93	1:47.04- 00
Omodiale	Sylvester	NGR	5.9.77	173/68	400H	49.80	49.44- 00
Omoto	Yuki	JPN	29.10.78	172/60	400H	49.95	49.74- 00
O'Neil	Jon	USA	23.3.79		SP	19.32	17.80- 00
Onsare	Wilson	KEN	15.6.76		HMar	61:51	
^ Onyancha	Fred	KEN	25.12.69	170/64	800	1:45.27	1:42.79- 96

Name		Nat	Born	Ht/Wt	Event	2001 Mark	Pre-2001 Best
Opatskiy	Yuriy	UKR	5.11.79	180/75	TJ	16.48	16.17i- 99, 16.04- 98
Openshaw	Mike	GBR	8.4.72	175/66	5000	13:24.44	13:37.97- 00
Oprea	Ionel	ROM	12.10.70	191/120	DT	63.64	62.79- 00
* Oprea	Marian	ROM	6.6.82	190/80	TJ	17.11, 17.13w	16.49- 00
Oriala	Chinedu	NGR	17.12.75	168/69	100	10.25, 10.0	10.41, 10.0- 99
Ornelas	Hélder	POR	6.5.74	176/63	5000	13:23.15	13:18.56- 00
					10000	28:01.94	-0-
Ort	Tomás	CZE	9.9.76	192/71	HJ	2.25	2.21i- 96, 2.20- 97
Osakada	Jun	JPN	2.4.74	177/67	400	45.26	45.05- 00
Osovnikar	Matic	SLO	19.1.80	177/75	100	10.21w	10.34- 00
Ota	Takashi	JPN	27.4.76	175/58	HMar	62:09	62:21- 00
Otsu	Makoto	JPN	3.7.80	164/44	10000	28:20.05	28:50.97- 00
Otto	Björn	GER	16.10.77	188/84	PV	5.51, 5.63ex	5.65, 5.71ex- 00
^ Ottoz	Laurent	ITA	10.4.70	180/69	400H	49.41	48.52- 96
Ouaadi	Mohamed	FRA	1.1.69	172/57	Mar	2:09:26	2:07:55- 99
^ Ovchinnikov	Vladimir	RUS	2.8.70	194/100	JT	78.72	88.00- 95
Owusu	Andrew	GHA	8.7.72	180/75	TJ	16.70	17.23- 98
Pacheco	Yoelmis	CUB	9.6.82	180/74	LJ	7.91	7.95- 00
^ Pakarinen	Ari	FIN	14.5.69	188/100	JT	81.27	85.18- 95
Palma	Jonathan	VEN	8.12.81	179/65	400	45.55A	46.36- 00
Palyszko	Maciej	POL	4.1.78	186/112	HT	79.29	80.25- 00
Panávoglou	Sávvas	GRE	14.8.74		DT	61.49	59.63- 00
Pankúch	Pavel	SVK	20.2.75	193/115	SP	19.20i, 19.11	19.78- 99
Paoluzzi	Loris	ITA	14.5.74	191/110	HT	75.33	80.98- 99
* Papadimitríou	Aléxandros	GRE	18.6.73	183/123	HT	79.52	80.45- 00
* Pappas	Tom	USA	6.9.76	193/93	Dec	8323	8467- 00
Paredes	Benjamín	MEX	7.8.61	162/50	Mar	2:10:58	2:10:40- 94
Parham	Robert	USA	2.6.82	190/82	400	45.5	
Park Jae-myong		KOR	15.12.81	181/88	JT	76.98	75.87- 00
Parker	David	GBR	28.2.80	189/93	JT	78.33A	78.24- 00
Parker	James	USA	3.12.75	180/107	HT	73.32	72.30- 00
Parkhomenko	Yuriy	UKR	7.7.73	194/140	SP	19.30	19.75- 97
Parra	Roberto	ESP	6.4.76	185/66	800	1:46.48i	1:44.97- 96
Parravacini	Tim	AUS	25.4.81	189/83	LJ	7.94	7.65, 7.66w- 00
* Parrela	Sanderlei	BRA	7.10.74	194/77	400	45.11, 45.1	44.29- 99
Pars	Krisztián	HUN	18.2.82		HT	73.09	66.80- 00
^ Partyka	Artur	POL	25.7.69	192/71	HJ	2.24i	2.38- 96
* Parviainen	Aki	FIN	26.10.74	191/96	JT	92.41	93.09- 99
Pasanen	Teemu	FIN	24.5.77	186/98	JT	79.22	78.37- 99
* Pate	Miguel	USA	13.6.79	188/84	LJ	8.20, 8.48w	8.26- 00
					TJ	16.48	15.90, 16.04w- 99
Patterson	Henry	USA	27.5.75	196/86	HJ	2.27i, 2.27	2.32- 99
Patton	Darvis	USA	4.12.77	183/75	100	10.16, 10.14w	10.22A, 10.09w- 00
					200	20.31	20.29- 00
					LJ	8.12	8.04, 8.07w- 00
Pauli	Jacob	USA	15.6.79	191/86	PV	5.68i, 5.65	5.65- 00
Paumier	Alexis	CUB	21.1.75	191/100	SP	19.46i	20.78- 00
Pavlov	Igor	RUS	18.7.79		PV	5.60i	5.70sq, 5.55- 00
Pearce	Paul	AUS	8.1.77	184/77	400	45.87	46.68- 00
* Pechonkin	Yevgeniy	RUS	9.10.73	190/90	110H	13.38	13.38- 96, 13.37w- 00
* Pedroso	Iván	CUB	17.12.72	176/70	LJ	8.43i, 8.40	8.71, 8.96Adw- 95, 8.79w-92
Pei Chuang		CHN	5.12.81		20kW	1:20:58	1:27:04- 00
					50kW	4:01:23	3:56:20- 00
* Peña	Antonio	ESP	26.8.70	175/60	Mar	2:07:34	2:07:47- 00
Pencréach	Gaël	FRA	5.8.77	180/68	3kSt	8:17.98	8:13.16- 99
Pennings	Wilbert	NED	12.2.75	194/81	HJ	2.24i	2.30- 99
* Pérez	Jefferson	ECU	1.7.74	174/59	20kW	1:22:20	1:18:24- 97
Pérez	Lisvany	CUB	24.1.82		HJ	2.22	2.15- 00
Pérez	Santiago	ESP	15.1.72	179/70	50kW	3:46:52	3:45:55- 98
Pérez	Yoeni	CUB	82		TJ	16.48	
Pérez Rionda	Luis	CUB	16.8.69	172/72	100	10.22w	10.18- 97, 10.13w- 00
* Peric	Dragan	YUG	8.5.64	186/107	SP	20.91. 21.27 lt	21.77- 98
Perin	Emerson	BRA	17.3.75	190/78	110H	13.69	13.60- 99
Perrone	Lorenzo	ITA	26.9.81	183/59	1500	3:38.52	3:41.70- 00
Pestano	Mario	ESP	8.4.78	193/105	DT	67.92	61.73- 99
Peterson	Derrick	USA	28.11.77	182/73	800	1:45.49	1:45.18- 00
Petrucci	Nick	USA	10.11.75		DT	63.38	64.74- 00
Pettersson	Kristian	SWE	5.10.71	193/129	SP	19.24i	19.74- 94
					DT	61.36	65.10- 00
* Pettigrew	Antonio	USA	3.11.67	183/76	400	44.99	44.21- 99
Peuf	Pierre-Charles	FRA	27.4.79	187/82	PV	5.52i, 5.50	5.50- 99

	Name		Nat	Born	Ht/Wt	Event	2001 Mark	Pre-2001 Best
	Pfingsten	Gunnar	GER	24.3.75	196/120	SP	19.03i	20.08- 00
	Philipp	Peter	SUI	18.2.72	185/73	1500	3:35.88	3:35.87- 99
	Phillips	Chris	USA	24.7.72	183/77	110H	13.32	13.27- 00
*	Phillips	Dwight	USA	1.10.77	181/82	LJ	8.13, 8.23w	8.21, 8.30w- 00
	Phillips	Matt	USA	28.12.77		PV	5.45	5.45- 00
	Pienaar	Hardus	RSA	10.8.81	190/88	JT	80.77A	78.11- 00
	Pierce	Andrew	USA	8.6.79	196/77	400	44.94	44.87- 00
	Pierre	Simon	TRI	3.12.79	185/83	400	45.62	46.22- 98, 45.9- 99
	Piétris	Dimítrios	GRE	24.10.79	184/79	110H	13.70w	13.86- 00
	Pike	Rob	CAN	8.1.70	180/82	PV	5.50A	5.40- 97
	Piller	René	FRA	23.4.65	168/57	50kW	3:52:18	3:41:28.2t- 94
	Pinardo	Francisco	ESP	15.3.75	179/64	50kW	3:54:31	4:00:28- 99
	Pincemail	Sébastien	FRA	21.2.79	186/84	TJ	16.64, 16.83w	16.69- 00
	Pinnock	Chris	USA	81/82		110H	13.64, 13.54w	14.12, 13.88w- 00
	Pino	Jorge Luis	CUB	6.7.69	174/65	20kW	1:24:08	1:24:15- 96
*	Pinto	António	POR	22.3.66	165/59	HMar	61:16	59:43- 98
						Mar	2:09:36	2:06:36- 00
	Piolanti	Raphaël	FRA	14.11.67	182/103	HT	75.90	79.68- 92
	Pires	João	POR	10.6.79	175/70	800	1:46.34	1:45.59- 00
*	Piskunov	Vladislav	UKR	7.6.78	183/106	HT	79.60	81.56- 00
	Pita	Juan	CUB	29.11.79	177/76	100	10.21w	10.45- 98, 10.39w- 99
	Pizzoli	Emiliano	ITA	29.6.74	192/80	110H	13.68	13.54- 00, 13.5- 99, 13.43r- 98
*	Plawgo	Marek	POL	25.2.81	181/72	400H	48.16	49.23- 00
*	Plotnikov	Andrey	RUS	12.8.67	186/77	50kW	3:50:32	3:40:07- 90
	Pochanis	Konstantinos	CYP	29.7.73	183/73	400H	49.95	49.88- 99
	Podebradsky	Jan	CZE	1.3.74	186/80	Dec	7950	8314- 00
	Pöge	Thomas	GER	6.9.79	190/80	Dec	7699	7753- 00
	Pognon	Ronald	FRA	16.11.82	185/75	200	20.4w	
*	Polihroníou	Hrístos	GRE	31.3.72	186/107	HT	78.34	79.83- 99, 79.95ic- 00
	Polku	Mika	FIN	19.7.75	184/64	HJ	2.25	2.31- 00
	Polymérou	Dimítrios	GRE	17.5.74	188/98	JT	78.10	81.20- 99
	Ponikvar	Mike	CAN	26.12.79		HJ	2.25	2.24- 97, 2.26i- 00
	Ponos	Edi	CRO	10.4.76		JT	76.12	72.24- 96
	Porras	Juan Antonio	ESP	19.7.72	174/65	50kW	3:59:10	4:13:23- 97
	Porter	William	USA	15.4.73	193/87	400H	49.02	48.65- 99
*	Potemin	Vladimir	RUS	15.1.80	177/69	50kW	3:46:12	3:39:21- 00
	Potgieter	Frits	RSA	13.3.74	195/110	DT	61.59	64.16- 97
	Potgieter	Karel	RSA	21.9.75	187/116	SP	19.77	20.29- 00
	Potter	Mitch	USA	16.9.80	182/73	400	45.40	
	Powell	Donovan	JAM	31.10.71	183/84	100	10.21w	10.07, 9.7- 95
^	Powell	Mike	USA	10.11.63	188/77	LJ	8.05, 8.10w	8.95- 91, 8.99Aw- 92
	Power	Michael	AUS	9.5.76	183/70	3000	7:47.84	7:46.22- 00
						5000	13:23.56	13:27.07- 00
	Power	Seamus	IRL	28.11.70		10000	28:18.38	28:23.11- 00
	Pozatsidi	Konstantin	RUS	23.1.83		TJ	16.48, 16.69w	16.00- 00
^	Prah	Kofi Amoah	GER	20.12.74	178/73	LJ	8.13i, 8.01	8.20- 00
	Prezelj	Rozle	SLO	26.9.79	193/73	HJ	2.24	2.23i, 2.20- 00
	Primc	Igor	SLO	8.1.66	183/108	DT	62.74	64.79- 99
	Proctor	Mark	GBR	15.1.63	193/131	SP	19.30	20.85i- 98, 20.40- 99
	Prokopov	Oleg	BLR	8.3.77	190/67	HJ	2.22i	2.28- 99
	Pröll	Martin	AUT	21.3.81	175/58	3kSt	8:28.08	8:46.80- 00
^	Pronin	Vladimir	RUS	27.5.69	180/72	3kSt	8:25.29	8:16.59- 95
	Ptácek	Adam	CZE	8.10.80	178/65	PV	5.62	5.61- 00
	Pugliese	Marcelo	ARG	2.9.68	191/105	DT	62.91	64.20- 97
*	Pukstys	Tom	USA	28.5.68	188/98	JT	79.48	87.12- 97
	Punga	Ionut	ROM	14.10.79	180/66	TJ	17.05i, 16.87	17.04- 99
	Pupis	Martin	SVK	19.10.78	175/60	20kW	1:23:46	1:26:40- 99
						50kW	3:59:34	3:59:13- 00
	Pyrah	Jason	USA	6.4.69	172/64	1M	3:56.33i	3:55.14- 96
	Qi Haifeng		CHN	7.8.83	181/75	Dec	8021	7437- 99
	Qi Zhen		CHN	4.8.76		110H	13.70	13.74- 98
	Quarry	Jamie	GBR	15.11.72	185/88	Dec	7625	7739- 99
*	Quesada	Yoelbi	CUB	4.8.73	181/71	TJ	16.55	17.85- 97, 17.97w- 95
	Quiñónez	Jackson	ECU	12.6.80		110H	13.64A	14.06- 00
	Radeiro	Alexis	CUB	30.6.82		TJ	16.47	
	Radke	Karol	POL	13.1.76	188/69	400H	50.08	50.72- 00
	Radomirovic	Darko	YUG	5.8.77	183/60	1500	3:38.70	3:37.52- 00
	Raev	Nikolay	BUL	29.1.71	184/71	TJ	16.60i, 16.52	17.18- 98, 17.27idq- 93
	Ragnvaldsson	Daniel	SWE	3.1.76		JT	77.34	75.65- 98
*	Rags	Eriks	LAT	1.6.75	183/93	JT	86.47	83.78- 99
	Rai	Sanjay Kumar	IND	1.5.79	178/72	LJ	7.92, 8.02w	8.03- 00

	Name		Nat	Born	Ht/Wt	Event	2001 Mark	Pre-2001 Best
	Raifak	Mustapha	FRA	9.9.75	184/67	HJ	2.24	2.28- 97
	Rakotoarimiandry	Yvon	MAD	5.1.76	180/72	400H	49.53	49.74- 00
	Rakovic	Aleksandar	YUG	13.4.68	183/70	50kW	3:56:56	3:48:01- 99
*	Ramaala	Hendrick	RSA	2.2.72	172/58	10000	27:38.36	27:29.94- 99
						HMar	60:15	59:20- 00
						Mar	2:11:18	2:09:43- 00
	Ramoul	Lyès	FRA	17.4.76	175/65	3kSt	8:25.12	8:27.04- 00
	Ramzy	Bashir	USA	4.5.79	185/86	110H	13.74, 13.58w	13.76, 13.67w- 00
	Randriamihaja	Joseph-Berlioz	MAD	30.11.75	188/75	110H	13.61	13.74, 13.70A- 00
	Rans	Kevin	BEL	19.8.82	180/81	PV	5.60	5.30- 00
	Rantanen	Vesa	FIN	2.12.75	181/65	PV	5.72	5.65- 97
	Raquil	Marc	FRA	2.4.77	191/81	400	44.95	45.31- 00
*	Rasskazov	Roman	RUS	28.4.79	186/64	20kW	1:20:31, 1:21:09.0t	1:17:46- 00
*	Rawlinson	Chris	GBR	19.5.72	185/82	400H	48.27	48.14- 99
	Raymond	Monte	CAN	18.11.73	188/86	400H	49.78	49.64A, 49.80- 99
	Rebenciuc	Sandu	USA	26.5.69		3kSt	8:32.89	8:35.02- 00
	Redko	Sergey	UKR	24.1.73	184/67	3kSt	8:27.51	8:24.35- 99
*	Redolat	José Antonio	ESP	17.2.76	181/66	800	1:46.71	1:45.39- 00
						1500	3:31.21	3:31.48- 00
						1M	3:49.60	
	Reese	Terry	USA	20.6.67	183/79	110H	13.44	13.22- 97
	Reina	Antonio Manuel	ESP	13.6.81	181/58	800	1:46.00	1:47.33- 00
	Reinikainen	Tepa	FIN	16.3.76	198/130	SP	20.88	20.11- 00
	Rendell	Stuart	AUS	30.6.72	187/112	HT	78.99	77.68- 00
	Rentería	Alvin	COL	4.1.78		TJ	16.66A	
	Retel	Jean-Claude	FRA	11.2.68	193/100	DT	62.44	62.26- 00
	Reumann	Steffen	GER	6.3.68		HT	71.31	69.52- 98
	Rey	José Ramón	ESP	3.11.67	167/60	Mar	2:10:49	2:13:12- 98, 2:10:49dh- 97
	Rey	Julio	ESP	13.1.72	168/57	Mar	2:07:46	2:08:33- 98
	Reynolds	Doug	USA	11.8.75	196/124	DT	65.20	66.76- 99
	Rhoden	Christian	GER	27.3.74	192/75	HJ	2.24	2.32- 98
*	Richardson	Mark	GBR	26.7.72	180/74	400	45.14	44.37- 98
*	Riedel	Lars	GER	28.6.67	199/110	DT	69.72	71.50- 97
	Riley	Jonathan	USA	29.12.78		3000	7:48.79i	7:57.05- 99
	Riley	Wenston	USA	24.4.77		110H	13.67	13.76- 00
	Rimoldi	Alessio	ITA	4.7.76	190/73	LJ	7.89i	7.73A- 97, 7.72- 00
*	Ríos	José	ESP	15.3.74	170/50	3000	7:43.36	7:42.51- 00
						5000	13:09.83	13:07.59- 00
						10000	27:38.57	27:22.20- 00
*	Robberts	Janus	RSA	10.3.79	197/117	SP	21.97	20.39- 98
						DT	60.28	61.18- 99
	Roberson	Mark	GBR	13.3.67	193/104	JT	80.80	85.67- 98
	Robert	Rémi	FRA	21.1.76	187/80	LJ	7.96, 8.12w	7.77- 96
	Roberts	Jim	USA	30.12.76	196/107	SP	20.37i, 19.23	20.09- 00
	Robinson	Khadevis	USA	19.7.76	183/74	800	1:45.15	1:45.23- 99
	Robinson	Rohan	AUS	15.11.71	188/79	400H	49.92	48.28- 96
	Rodgers	Trafton	USA	3.2.72	188/84	Dec	7703	8128- 98
	Rodríguez	Iván	ESP	7.4.78	179/64	400H	49.46	49.98- 00
*	Rodríguez	Miguel Ángel	MEX	15.1.67	174/62	20kW	1:23:44	1:20:59- 93
						50kW	3:55:44A	3:42:45- 97
	Rogers	Cedric	USA	18.2.79		LJ	7.95	7.59w- 00
	Rohr	Alain	SUI	25.12.71	182/74	400H	49.19	50.16- 00
	Rollins	Josh	USA	7.6.79		TJ	16.58	15.87- 99
^	Romain	Jérôme	FRA	12.6.71	183/76	TJ	16.80	17.48, 17.59w- 95
	Román	Iván	ESP	22.3.78	185/73	LJ	7.95w	7.77- 00, 7.90w- 99
	Rome	Jarred	USA	21.12.76	196/145	SP	19.29i	19.90- 00
						DT	65.53	64.00- 00
	Romera	José María	ESP	2.9.80	170/62	400H	49.89	52.03- 00
	Romero	Fabrício	BRA	13.5.78	190/72	HJ	2.22	2.26A- 99, 2.25- 00
*	Roncero	Fabián	ESP	19.10.70	171/58	5000	13:22.46	13:28.10- 99
						10000	27:45.17	27:14.44- 98
						HMar	59:52	61:12- 00
						Mar	2:10:08	2:07:23- 99
	Rono	Robert	KEN	11.10.74	180/67	1500	3:31.49	3:45.2A- 00
						1M	3:54.05	
	Rop	Rodgers	KEN	73		HMar	60:57	
						Mar	2:09:51	
	Rose	Guy	USA	6.2.80	188/77	110H	13.56	14.33- 80
	Ross	Duane	USA	5.12.72	183/78	110H	13.54	13.12- 99
	Röthlin	Viktor	SUI	14.10.74	174/58	Mar	2:10:54	2:12:53- 00
	Rotich	Henry	KEN	5.12.81	175/60	800	1:45.25	1:47.24- 00

	Name		Nat	Born	Ht/Wt	Event	2001 Mark	Pre-2001 Best
*	Rotich	Laban	KEN	20.1.69	163/45	1500	3:31.38	3:29.91- 98
						1M	3:52.19	3:47.65- 97
	Rotich	Michael	KEN	78		800	1:45.24	1:48.1A- 00
	Rotich	Willy	KEN	23.3.76	177/58	800	1:46.27	1:46.70- 00
	Röttger	Andre	GER	26.3.79	178/72	Dec	7659	7747- 99
	Routt	Stanford	USA			200	20.74	
	Rovan	Jurij	SLO	23.1.75	187/81	PV	5.45i	5.56i- 00, 5.55- 98
	Rozna	Roman	MDA	25.3.76	190/105	HT	73.28	72.20- 00
	Ruban	Dmitriy	RUS	77		LJ	7.98i	7.48- 97
	Rubanko	Artyom	UKR	21.3.74	192/100	HT	74.96	73.22- 98
	Rubbiani	Matteo	ITA	31.8.78		PV	5.50ex	
	Rufo	Marco Antonio	ESP	9.3.68	178/65	5000	13:25.05	13:32.16- 99
	Ruggiero	Giovanni	ITA	19.1.74	181/60	Mar	2:09:53sh	2:13:31- 99
	Rugut	Philip	KEN	18.5.77	165/50	HMar	61:28	60:05- 99, 60:00w- 00
	Rusan	Tim	USA	25.6.77		TJ	16.58, 16.74w	16.52- 00
	Rusenov	Ivailo	BUL	9.9.79	178/65	TJ	16.95	16.91- 00
	Russell	Scott	CAN	16.1.79	206/130	JT	81.66	78.94- 00
	Rutto	Barnabas	KEN	.77		HMar	62:04	61:33- 00
						Mar	2:11:06	
*	Rutto	Evans	KEN	8.4.78	168/56	3000	7:49.2+	
						5000	13:28.25	13:02.71- 00
						HMar	60:30	
*	Ryba	Jirí	CZE	15.6.76	192/89	Dec	8332	8339- 00
*	Rybakov	Yaroslav	RUS	22.11.80	198/84	HJ	2.33i, 2.33	2.28- 00
	Rybin	Yuriy	RUS	5.3.63	186/97	JT	81.22	86.98- 95
	Rysiukewicz	Piotr	POL	14.7.74	174/65	400	45.55	45.54- 99
	Sack	Peter	GER	27.7.79	192/113	SP	19.05i	18.23- 98
	Sack	René	GER	14.7.76	190/120	SP	19.67	19.19- 00
	Sadler	Robert	USA	26.1.76		SP	19.12	
	Safiullin	Marat	RUS	5.4.75	187/76	TJ	16.53w	16.69- 97, 16.97w- 99
*	Saïdi Sief ¶	Ali	ALG	15.3.78	170/55	1500	3:29.51	3:30.82- 00
						1M	3:48.23	3:51.90- 99
						2000	4:46.88	4:56.43- 99
	Sainah	Mark	KEN	10.11.70		Mar	2:10:41	2:09:00- 00
	Saint-Jean	Fabrice	FRA	21.11.80	190/84	HJ	2.24	2.15- 00
	Sakamoto	Tomokazu	JPN	21.7.76	182/63	HMar	62:08	
	Saksio	Sami	FIN	28.4.69	190/112	JT	82.20	84.26- 97
	Sakurai	Ken-ichi	JPN	26.12.76	179/72	110H	13.69	13.67- 99
	Sales	Louis	USA	29.11.71	185/81	400H	49.51	49.36- 00
	Salnikov	Aleksandr	RUS	27.9.71		SP	19.41	19.52- 99
^	Sambu	Andrew	TAN	5.10.72		Mar	2:10:14	2:10:17- 97
	Sambu	Ezra	KEN	4.9.78	175/70	400	44.47A	
*	Sánchez	Felix	DOM	30.8.77	178/73	400	44.90	46.34- 00
						400H	47.38	48.33- 00
^	Sánchez	Germán	MEX	31.7.67	173/63	50kW	3:44:50	3:48:06- 00
*	Sánchez	Joel	MEX	15.9.67	175/53	20kW	1:22:05	1:19:00- 99
	Sands	Leevan	BAH	16.1.81		LJ	8.00w	7.83- 00
	Sanguin	Giovanni	ITA	14.5.69	180/95	HT	72.18	74.52- 97
	dos Santos	Anderson C	BRA	15.6.75		400H	50.12	49.90- 00
	dos Santos	Anderson J.	BRA	23.4.72	186/75	400	45.47	45.39A, 45.54- 99
	dos Santos	Osmar B.	BRA	20.10.68	175/65	800	1:46.04	1:44.87- 00
	dos Santos	Redelén	BRA	24.4.76		110H	13.67	13.59- 00
	Sarrís	Panayiótis	GRE	14.9.75	181/74	200	20.72	20.65, 20.63w- 99
^	Sasimovich	Vladimir	BLR	14.9.68	178/86	JT	76.68	87.40- 95
	Sato	Atsushi	JPN	8.5.78	170/54	10000	28:13.18	28:25.84- 00
^	Sato	Nobuyuki	JPN	8.8.72	175/57	Mar	2:10:32	2:08:48- 98
	Saurambayev	Denis	KAZ	30.6.77		TJ	16.80	16.37- 00
	Sautkin	Igor	RUS	23.2.72	190/79	TJ	16.64i	17.15- 94
	Sawano	Daichi	JPN	16.9.80	182/60	PV	5.52	5.50- 99
	Scales	Mardy	USA	10.9.81	173/73	200	20.65	21.31- 00
^	Schelbert	Marcel	SUI	26.2.76	191/83	400H	50.03	48.13- 99
	Schiebler	Jeff	CAN	1.6.73	171/55	5000	13:29.15	13:13.96- 98
						10000	27:36.01	27:45.75- 98
	Schiebout	Zach	USA	19.9.77	190/109	DT	61.16	59.84- 00
	Schinz	Frédéric	SUI	25.6.77	192/70	HJ	2.23	2.23i- 00, 2.20- 99
*	Schmid	Stefan	GER	6.5.70	187/85	Dec	8307	8485- 00
	Schmidt	Ralf	GER	1.9.75	179/65	PV	5.50i	5.51i- 99, 5.50- 00
	Schmidt	Torsten	GER	9.12.74	207/105	DT	61.50	62.90- 00
	Schnallinger	Michael	AUT	29.4.80	190/96	Dec	7576	7634- 00
	Schneider	Jan	GER	24.1.76		400H	49.63	49.89- 99
	Schönbeck	Florian	GER	13.1.74	191/80	Dec	7891	8127- 00

Name		Nat	Born	Ht/Wt	Event	2001 Mark	Pre-2001 Best
^ Schult	Jürgen	GER	11.5.60	193/110	DT	62.08	74.08- 86
* Schultz	Ingo	GER	26.7.75	201/96	200	20.71	21.02- 00
					400	44.66	45.79- 00
Schumacher	Mark	GER	27.6.76	194/88	Dec	7620(w)	7661- 98
* Schumann	Nils	GER	20.5.78	192/77	800	1:44.32	1:44.22- 00
Schwabe	Clay	USA	3.7.79	188/79	1500	3:38.53	3:43.42- 00
* Schwarthoff	Florian	GER	7.5.68	201/83	110H	13.53	13.05- 95
Scott	Leonard	USA	19.1.80	181/84	100	10.05	10.26- 00, 9.83w 99
					200	20.34, 20.10w	20.59, 20.55i- 00, 20.08w- 99
Scuderi	Francesco	ITA	4.10.77	171/70	100	10.20	10.19- 00
Sdad	Mustapha	MAR	11.4.70	180/72	400H	48.96	49.05- 97
* Sebrle	Roman	CZE	26.11.74	185/86	110H	13.68w	13.79- 99
					LJ	8.11	8.03- 98
					Dec	9026	8757- 00
Sedlácek	Pavel	CZE	5.4.68	198/111	HT	79.18	79.56- 96
* Seelig	Andreas	GER	6.7.70	200/120	DT	64.57	66.00- 97
Semenyuk	Dmitriy	RUS	12.7.77	180/67	TJ	16.53	16.65- 98
* Sepeng	Hezekiél	RSA	30.6.74	178/64	800	1:43.57	1:42.69- 99
					1000	2:17.26	2:16.47- 00
Sergeyev	Georgiy	RUS	27.4.76	178/69	20kW	1:22:19	1:24:52- 98
Seskin	Yuriy	RUS	7.7.66	196/110	DT	63.80	64.58- 88
* Setliff	Adam	USA	15.12.69	193/125	DT	69.44	68.51- 00
Seto	Tomohiro	JPN	19.10.76	168/53	10000	28:14.08	28:15.63- 00
Settle	Leon	USA	19.10.75	183/73	200	20.59	20.50, 20.17Aw- 00
* Sghyr	Ismaïl	FRA	16.3.72	168/50	1500	3:37.11	3:36.20- 95
					3000	7:38.37	7:30.09- 95
					5000	13:01.64	12:58.83- 00
^ Sgrulletti	Enrico	ITA	24.4.65	182/100	HT	72.10	81.64- 97
* Shabunin	Vyacheslav	RUS	27.9.69	171/56	1500	3:33.01	3:32.28- 00
					1M	3:49.83	3:50.54- 00
					2000	4:57.24	4:57.18- 97
Shako	Dmitriy	BLR	27.5.79	192/92	HT	74.57	75.59- 00
Sharpe	Fred	USA	21.8.78		400H	49.60	50.43- 00
Shatkovskiy	Vladimir	UKR	8.10.75	189/84	Dec	7853	7966- 99
* Shchurenko	Roman	UKR	14.9.76	186/83	LJ	7.97i, 8.00w	8.35- 00
Shears	Adrian	USA	.78		HJ	2.25	
Shelest	Aleksey	UKR	27.3.73	173/64	50kW	3:58:17	3:58:09- 99
* Shevchenko	Dmitriy	RUS	13.5.68	200/140	DT	67.57	67.30- 92, 68.04dq- 95
Shi Dongpeng		CHN	6.1.84		110H	13.43	14.10- 00
Shimazaki	Takayuki	JPN	3.5.69	165/52	Mar	2:11:01	2:12:46- 98
Shimizu	Koji	JPN	17.10.69	176/52	Mar	2:09:28	2:09:00- 99
Shin Il-yong		KOR	17.2.79	173/66	20kW	1:22:25	1:23:00- 99
^ Shirvington	Matt	AUS	25.10.78	184/82	100	10.11	10.03- 98
Shiryayev	Vladislav	RUS	30.10.73	176/72	400H	49.63	49.02- 00
* Shkurlatov	Vitaliy	RUS	25.5.79	182/76	LJ	8.18	8.38i, 8.22- 00
Shtepa	Aleksandr	RUS	15.5.79	197/84	Dec	7789	7436- 99
Shunk	Adam	USA	29.8.79		HJ	2.23	2.22- 00
Shvetsov	Vitaliy	RUS	20.2.73	181/67	20kW	1:22:57	1:21:01- 00
* Sidorenko	Vasiliy	RUS	1.5.61	187/106	HT	80.03	82.54- 92
da Silva	André Domingos	BRA	26.11.72	187/78	100	10.17, 10.10w	10.16, 10.05dt- 97, 10.10w- 95, 10.06A-99
					200	20.36	20.35, 20.17A- 00
Silva	Carlos	POR	8.6.74	174/64	400H	49.07	48.77- 99
* da Silva	Claudinei	BRA	19.11.70	186/86	200	20.58	19.89- 99
Silva	Germán	MEX	9.1.68		HMar	62:18	
da Silva	Luiz Fernandes	BRA	2.7.71	186/87	JT	76.36	79.50A- 00
Silva	Manuel	POR	8.10.78	179/65	3kSt	8:32.22	8:24.60- 00
* Silva	Rui	POR	3.8.77	174/62	800	1:46.60	1:45.29- 00
					1000	2:17.36i	2:16.30- 99
					1500	3:30.36	3:30.88- 99
					1M	3:52.18i	3:50.91- 99
					3000	7:39.52i	7:39.44i- 00, 7:53.87- 99
da Silva	Valdinei	BRA	29.3.72	180/71	400	45.89	45.74- 96
					800	1:46.81	1:45.88- 98
Simms	Allen	USA	26.7.82	178/75	LJ	8.00	7.56- 00
					TJ	16.80i, 16.37, 16.54w	16.11- 00
Simo	Samu-Petri	FIN	22.6.78	194/118	HT	71.94	73.62- 00
Simon	LeJuan	USA	7.2.81		LJ	7.98w	7.35, 7.49w- 00
					TJ	16.60	15.51, 15.57w- 00
Simón	Gabriel	ARG	25.10.74	170/60	100	10.26	10.23A- 99
Simpson	Brandon	JAM	6.9.81	172/75	400	45.46A, 45.68	45.73- 00

	Name		Nat	Born	Ht/Wt	Event	2001 Mark	Pre-2001 Best
	Simunic	Bostjan	SLO	28.12.74	186/73	TJ	16.56, 16.64w	16.13- 98, 16.68w- 00
	Sinervo	Timo	FIN	5.8.75	190/100	DT	63.28	61.62- 00
	Singh	Bahadur	IND	7.5.73	187/95	SP	19.69	20.01- 00
	Singh Bishnoi	Jagdish	IND	20.5.72	182/86	JT	76.74	79.67- 00
	Singh	Shakti	IND	14.5.62	185/100	SP	19.34	20.60- 00
	Sirrákos	Dimítrios	GRE	26.1.74		HJ	2.22	2.24- 00
	Sithole	Petros	RSA	29.3.76		3kSt	8:33.90	8:34.22- 00
*	Skah	Khalid	MAR	29.1.67	170/58	10000	27:51.87	27:14.53- 95
						HMar	61:41	60:24- 98
	Skoog	Henrik	SWE	17.4.79	186/69	3kSt	8:30.32	8:37.60- 00
	Skosana	Enoch	RSA	20.2.74	190/57	10000	28:11.03	27:57.49- 99
*	Skvaruk	Andrey	UKR	9.3.67	186/106	HT	82.34	81.72- 94
	Skyttä	Pietari	FIN	24.5.76	186/95	JT	77.66	83.28- 97
	Slattery	Steve	USA	14.8.80		3kSt	8:26.45	8:35.15- 00
	Sliwa	Leszek	POL	20.9.79	187/110	SP	19.71	19.62- 00
	Slover	Scott	USA	9.7.75	185/79	PV	5.51	5.70- 99
	Slowly	Steve	JAM	18.4.79		200	20.65	20.95- 97, 20.55w- 99
*	Smiryagin	Yevgeniy	RUS	17.5.76	185/77	PV	5.71i, 5.70	5.85- 97
	Smith	Chad	USA	9.1.74	185/82	Dec	8075	8045- 99
	Smith	David	GBR	2.11.74	196/115	HT	73.30	75.10- 96
	Smith	Glen	GBR	21.5.72	190/110	DT	61.29	65.11- 99
	Smith	Maurice	JAM	28.9.80		Dec	7755A	7110- 00
	Smith	Michael	USA	26.4.79	183/75	400H	49.34	49.60- 00
	Smith	Rutger	NED	9.7.81	197/120	DT	59.96	58.74- 00
	Smith	Steven	USA	11.1.71	190/66	HJ	2.27	2.31- 94
	Smith	Willie	NAM	20.9.77	170/64	400H	49.05A	49.47A- 00
*	Snyder	Brad	CAN	8.1.76	196/128	SP	20.79	20.51- 99
	Söderberg	David	FIN	11.8.79	185/105	HT	72.25	68.53- 00
*	Sokolovskiy	Andrey	UKR	16.7.78	196/80	HJ	2.35i, 2.34	2.32- 99
^	Sokov	Vasiliy	UZB	7.4.68	186/73	TJ	16.84, 17.16iu	17.59- 93, 17.73w- 89
	Sóldos	Peter	CZE	27.4.73	189/82	Dec	7799	7834- 96
	Som	Bram	NED	20.2.80	177/62	800	1:43.98	1:44.01- 00
	Songok	Isaac	KEN	25.4.84	170/54	1500	3:35.55	
						1M	3:54.56	
						2000	4:56.86	
	Songok	Yusuf	KEN	79		HMar	61:16	
	Sørensen	Jacob	DEN	27.12.74	186/76	50kW	3:59.31	3:58:09- 00
	Sorescu	Cosmin	ROM	11.7.75	188/95	HT	72.79	71.27- 99
	Sørli	Gjøran	NOR	3.6.78	191/125	SP	19.59	19.24- 00
						DT	60.55	59.20- 00
^	Sotomayor	Javier	CUB	13.10.67	193/80	HJ	2.35	2.45- 93
	Sousa	Cláudio Roberto	BRA	14.10.73	168/68	100	10.20	10.33- 99, 10.24A- 00
						200	20.68	20.77, 20.69w- 98
	de Souza	Hudson	BRA	25.2.77	180/65	1500	3:33.99	3:34.97- 00
						1M	3:53.75	3:53.74- 00
						3000	7:42.55	
	de Souza	Márcio	BRA	24.1.75	180/72	110H	13.50, 13.49w	13.38- 99
	de Souza	Walmes	BRA	14.9.74	192/80	110H	13.69	13.72- 96
	Souza Silva	Anísio	BRA	16.6.69	185/79	TJ	16.70w	17.32- 93
	Spacek	Petr	CZE	23.7.75	183/75	PV	5.50	5.65i- 01, 5.60- 99
	Spahn	Matthias	GER	3.1.79		Dec	7749	7701- 00
*	Spasovkhodskiy	Igor	RUS	1.8.79	191/91	TJ	17.44	16.86- 00
	Spiegelburg	Richard	GER	12.8.77	182/77	PV	5.85	5.65- 99
	Spisiak	Matej	SVK	5.4.78	193/73	50kW	3:54:24	4:09:36- 00
	Sposób	Grzegorz	POL	12.2.76	200/87	HJ	2.30	2.25- 00
	Stadnichuk	Andrey	RUS	14.12.73	176/64	20kW	1:21:44.2t	1:22:03- 98
	Stanic	Borivoje	YUG	2.10.74	198/130	SP	19.53	18.46- 00
	Stankin	Vladimir	RUS	2.1.74	184/71	20kW	1:19:14, 1:23:37/0t	1:20:21- 99
	Stanski	Olgierd	POL	4.4.73	196/98	DT	63.50	64.20- 00
	Stasyuk	Pavel	BLR	14.6.77		JT	79.00	76.43- 00
	Stauffer	Martin	SUI	7.7.75	205/85	HJ	2.24i, 2.23	2.27i- 00, 2.23- 99
	Stehlík	Petr	CZE	15.4.77	185/102	SP	20.50	19.56- 00
	Steinle	Mark	GBR	22.11.74	183/63	Mar	2:10:46	2:11:18- 00
	Stember	Michael	USA	30.1.78	179/66	1500	3:36.9	3:35.11- 00
	Stenzel	Rüdiger	GER	16.4.68	180/65	1500	3:38.87	3:33.60- 97
	Stepanchuk	Andrey	BLR	12.6.79	176/65	20kW	1:22:17	1:27:39- 99
	Stiegeler	John	USA	17.2.80	183/93	JT	77.07	68.64- 00
	Stokes	Stuart	GBR	15.12.76		3kSt	8:33.15	8:33.61- 00
*	Stolle	Michael	GER	17.12.74	192/85	PV	5.85i, 5.85	5.95- 00
*	Strand	Staffan	SWE	18.4.76	188/74	HJ	2.34i, 2.31/2.30	2.32- 00
*	Streete-Thompson	Kareem	CAY	30.3.73	183/84	LJ	8.20	8.63, 8.64w- 94

Name		Nat	Born	Ht/Wt	Event	2001 Mark	Pre-2001 Best
* Stringfellow	Savanté	USA	6.11.78	191/84	200	20.66	20.84w- 00
					LJ	8.38, 8.47w	8.30- 00
^ Strogalyov	Vadim	RUS	9.2.75	184/77	PV	5.60	5.85- 98
Stroh	Johan	RSA	3.8.80		LJ	7.89A	7.76A- 00
Stroubákos	Panayiótis	GRE	8.9.72	187/73	1500	3:38.86	3:36.74- 97
Strutzel	Jess	USA	4.1.78	185/70	800	1:46.03	1:45.81- 99
Stuart	Leigh	AUS	2.1.71		LJ	7.93	7.74, 7.81w- 98
Suárez	Alejandro	MEX	30.11.80		10000	28:17.65	
Suárez	Carlos	ESP	25.9.75	186/68	3kSt	8:33.75	8:27.49- 00
Suetsugu	Shingo	JPN	2.6.80	178/62	200	20.30	20.26- 00
Sugibayashi	Takanori	JPN	14.3.76	185/65	TJ	16.46, 16.65w	17.02- 00
Sui Jianfeng		CHN	29.5.84		20kW	1:23:17	1:31:12- 00
Sulle	Martin Hhaway	TAN	28.12.82		HMar	61:59	61:53- 00
* Sullivan	Kevin	CAN	20.3.74	180/68	1500	3:33.91	3:31.71- 00
					1M	3:51.82	3:50.26- 00
Sun Shipeng		CHN	10.3.76		JT	79.79	77.54- 00
Sundsten	Simon	FIN	27.5.78	186/80	LJ	8.09w	7.73, 7.77w- 99
^ Sunneborn	Mattias	SWE	27.9.70	187/83	LJ	8.03, 8.15w	8.21- 96
* Surin	Bruny	CAN	12.7.67	180/81	100	10.11	9.84- 99
Suter	Patric	SUI	17.5.77	192/100	HT	72.93	72.96- 99
^ Svenøy	Jim	NOR	22.4.72	186/70	3kSt	8:21.66	8:12.05- 97
Svensson	Fredrik	SWE	10.9.73	184/77	50kW	3:57:31	4:01:52- 98
^ Swift	Eugene	USA	14.9.64	183/79	110H	13.61, 13.49w	13.21- 96
Sylvester	Tonyo	USA	17.12.67	188/99	SP	19.72	19.15- 00
Szeglet	Zsolt	HUN	4.5.77	180/73	400	45.43	45.95- 99
Tabata	Kenji	JPN	24.9.74	176/66	400	45.72	45.69- 98
Tadamasa	Hirofumi	JPN	29.8.76	170/58	50kW	4:04:24	4:04:57- 00
Tadili	Achraf	CAN	8.7.80		800	1:45.48	1:47.59- 00
Tagawa	Shigeru	JPN	22.11.75	181/75	LJ	7.97w	8.15- 99
* Tahri	Bouabdellah	FRA	20.12.78	190/65	1500	3:36.5	3:36.53- 99
					2000	4:57.72	5:00.21- 00
					3000	7:42.68i	7:48.98- 97
					3kSt	8:09.23	8:12.24- 99
Taillepierre	Karl	FRA	13.8.76	176/64	TJ	17.10	16.62- 00
Takahashi	Ken-ichi	JPN	16.1.73	172/55	Mar	2:10:51	2:15:27- 98
Takahashi	Naotaka	JPN	28.6.76	179/64	HMar	61:32	61:59- 00
Takaoka	Toshinari	JPN	24.9.70	178/52	10000	27:35.09	27:40.44- 00
					Mar	2:09:41	-0-
Takatsuka	Kazutoshi	JPN	8.8.76		HMar	62:19	
Talel	Wilberforce Kapkeny	KEN	10.1.80		5000	13:25.59	13:13.15- 00
					10000	28:02.30	27:36.48- 00
Tallhem	Sören	SWE	16.2.64	192/110	SP	19.57	20.91, 21.24i- 85
Talotti	Alessandro	ITA	7.10.80	193/73	HJ	2.22	2.25- 00
* Tamesue	Dai	JPN	3.5.78	170/67	400H	47.89	48.47- 00
* Tammert	Aleksander	EST	2.2.73	196/117	DT	67.10	67.41- 00
Tamminga	Chris	NED	30.4.74	172/67	PV	5.75	5.76- 98
Tan Chunhua		CHN	13.3.77	183/76	400H	49.42	49.25- 98
Tanigawa	Satoru	JPN	5.7.72	183/74	110H	13.73	13.55- 99
Tanonaka	Tasuku	JPN	23.9.78	183/73	110H	13.78	13.77- 00
Tapala	Stephen	KEN			HMar	62:11	
Taranov	Vyacheslav	RUS	20.3.75	190/74	TJ	16.79	17.33- 97
* Tarasov	Maksim	RUS	2.12.70	194/80	PV	5.75	6.05- 99
Tarus	Bogdan	ROM	1.8.75	190/77	LJ	8.15	8.30i- 00, 8.29- 96
Tarus	Henry	KEN	6.12.78		Mar	2:10:10	
Tarus	Philip	KEN	11.9.74	170/55	HMar	61:55	60:24- 98
					3kSt	8:28.90	8:29.00- 96
* Taurima	Jai	AUS	26.6.72	188/80	LJ	7.93	8.49- 00
Tayari	Avi	ISR	25.10.73	181/74	TJ	16.72	16.94, 16.95w- 97
Taye	Moges	ETH	12.11.73	167/54	Mar	2:10:08	2:09:21- 98
* Taylor	Angelo	USA	29.12.78	188/77	400	44.68	44.89- 00
					400H	47.95	47.50- 00
Taylor	Orville	JAM	11.5.70		400	45.43	45.37A- 95
Tebbich	Thomas	AUT	4.2.75	186/83	Dec	7964	8039- 99
Teixeira	Mário	POR	20.9.74		3kSt	8:33.53	8:33.2 - 99
* Téllez	Norberto	CUB	22.1.72	186/78	800	1:45.01	1:42.85- 96
Terano	Shin-ichi	JPN	10.7.79	175/65	LJ	7.99	7.84, 8.08w- 00
Terek	Paul	USA	20.10.79	186/83	PV	5.56i	5.26- 98
					Dec	7695	7225- 99
* Tergat	Paul	KEN	17.6.69	183/61	HMar	60:27	59:06- 00, 58:51sc- 96
					Mar	2:08:15	-0-
Tesarík	Stepán	CZE	6.7.78	187/70	400H	49.49A, 48.87	50.93- 98

	Name		Nat	Born	Ht/Wt	Event	2001 Mark	Pre-2001 Best
	Thénault	François	FRA	4.5.72	175/64	PV	5.50i	5.50- 94
	Thilakeratne	Sugath	SRI	30.7.73	170/57	400	45.41	44.61- 98
	Thomas	Dwight	JAM	23.9.80	185/82	100	10.19	10.12- 00
*	Thomas	Eric	USA	1.12.73	190/88	400H	48.53	47.94- 00
*	Thomas	Iwan	GBR	5.1.74	188/80	400	45.70	44.36- 97
	Thomas	Marcus	USA	22.3.79	183/82	TJ	16.47i	16.63- 00
	Thompson	Kurt	TRI	13.12.67	178/80	JT	76.52	78.06- 96
*	Thompson	Obadele	BAR	30.3.76	175/67	100	10.25, 10.03w?	9.87A-98, 9.96- 99, 9.69Aw- 96
	Thorkildsen	Andreas	NOR	1.4.82	188/90	JT	83.87	77.48- 00
^	Thorne-Ladejo	Du'aine	GBR	14.2.71	186/82	400H	49.29	50.09- 00
	Thriene	Mattias	GER	28.12.71		DT	59.98	58.46- 00
*	Thys	Gert	RSA	12.11.71	167/55	10000	28:26.71	
	Tichy	Peter	SVK	12.3.69	177/67	50kW	3:57:56	3:51:22- 96
	Tíggas	Váios	GRE	16.10.78	186/96	SP	19.42	19.47- 99
	Tighazouine	Khalid	MAR	18.6.77	175/68	800	1:45.27	1:45.38- 00
*	Tiisanoja	Ville	FIN	24.12.75	192/119	SP	20.78	20.76- 00
*	Tikhon	Ivan	BLR	24.7.76	185/105	HT	78.73	79.85- 00
^	Tilli	Stefano	ITA	22.8.62	175/78	100	10.26	10.16- 84, 10.06w- 83
	Timofeev	Evgeniy (ex RUS)	CAN	22.2.74		TJ	16.59	17.00- 93
^	Tivontchik	Andrei	GER	13.7.70	184/80	PV	5.72i, 5.50, 5.60ex	5.95- 96
	Tluway	Jumanne	TAN	5.7.80		HMar	62:12	
	Togom	Augustine	KEN			HMar	62:01	
	Tokumoto	Kazuyoshi	JPN	22.6.79	173/59	10000	28:25.59	28:41.8- 99
*	Tola	Girma	ETH	13.10.75	174/57	3000	7:46.60	7:42.98- 99, 7:38.68i- 00
						3000	7:38.48i	
						10000	27:22.84	27:13.48- 99
*	Tola	Tesfaye	ETH	19.10.74	167/60	HMar	60:24	61:37- 97, 59:51w- 00
	Tolossa	Ambesse	ETH	28.8.77	171/53	Mar	2:10:37	2:10:13- 98
	Tomlinson	Chris	GBR	15.9.81	196/75	LJ	8.19w	7.62- 00
	Tompuri	Timo	FIN	9.6.69	189/117	DT	69.62	65.13- 00
	Ton	Svatoslav	CZE	20.10.78	192/75	HJ	2.26	2.27i, 2.25- 97
^	Topic ¶	Dragutin	YUG	12.3.71	197/74	HJ	2.27i, 2.31idq	2.38- 93
	Toroitich	Haron	KEN	78		HMar	60:49	61:39- 00
	Torrieri	Marco	ITA	14.5.78	178/74	100	10.26	10.31, 10.29w- 00
						200	20.38	20.87, 20.82w- 00
*	Toth	Kevin	USA	29.12.67	193/144	SP	20.43	21.78- 97
	Totton	Andre	USA	17.7.80	183/73	100	10.09Aw	10.57, 10.23w- 00
						200	20.51Aw	20.93- 99, 20.74w- 00
^	Touré	Cheikh Tidiane	FRA	25.1.70	195/89	LJ	8.05, 8.17w	8.46- 97
	Touset	Raúl	CUB	14.7.78		HJ	2.22	2.23- 00
*	Trafas	Dariusz	POL	16.5.72	188/87	JT	85.78	87.17- 00
*	Trammell	Terrence	USA	23.11.78	188/84	110H	13.23	13.16- 00
	Trautmann	Denis	GER	15.8.72	182/71	50kW	3:52:16	3:48:05- 99
	Trautmann	Mike	GER	13.3.74	180/72	50kW	3:51:38	3:52:41- 00
	Treacy	Brian	IRL	29.7.71	176/61	1500	3:38.83	3:37.74- 99
	Trentin	Nicola	ITA	20.6.74	178/62	LJ	8.18w	8.00sq, 8.32w- 96, 8.07A- 99, 7.98- 00
	Tretyak	Yevgeniy	RUS	18.7.71	184/75	LJ	8.11i, 8.06	8.29- 94
	Troop	Lee	AUS	22.3.73	176/55	Mar	2:10:04	2:11:21- 99
	Trots	Andrey	UKR	17.1.78	188/78	TJ	16.51	16.73- 00
	Trotskiy	Anton	BLR	2.11.72	176/67	50kW	4:02:28	3:50:04- 96
	Trotskiy	Ivan	BLR	27.5.76	167/50	20kW	1:19:45	1:19:48- 98
	Tsátoumas	Loúis	GRE	12.2.82	183/77	LJ	7.93, 7.98w	7.64- 99
	Tsubota	Tomoo	JPN	16.6.77	174/58	10000	28:05.95	28:29.50- 00
						HMar	61:33	62:42- 98
	Tsvetkov	Mikhayil	RUS	4.5.80	194/73	HJ	2.25i	2.20- 00
	Tucker	Sultan	LBR	24.10.78	181/75	110H	13.69	13.73- 99
	Tugay	Igor	UKR	22.3.75	185/102	HT	72.80	75.74- 00
	Tumorin	Ilja	EST	17.5.79	183/72	TJ	16.65	16.04- 00
*	Tunks	Jason	CAN	7.5.75	197/120	DT	67.70	67.88- 98
	Turi	Indrek	EST	30.7.81	190/84	Dec	7639	7451- 00
	Turki	Lotfi	TUN	6.3.75	190/65	3kSt	8:21.78	8:22.98- 00
	Turnbull	Gareth	IRL	14.5.79	185/77	1500	3:38.28	3:39.08- 00
	Turner	Doug	GBR	2.12.66	188/86	200	20.54	20.43- 96, 20.36w- 97
	Turner	Lewis	USA	77		100	10.23, 10.12w	10.33- 99
	Tuwei	David	KEN	22.2.79	176/56	5000	13:29.90	13:20.83- 00
	Tveitå	Einar Kristian	NOR	22.2.73	185/120	DT	62.41	63.64- 99
	Tverdostup	Andrey	UKR	18.6.77	180/70	400	45.78	46.59- 98
^	Ubartas	Romas	LTU	26.5.60	202/128	DT	65.25	70.06- 88
	Uchida	Takahiro	JPN	9.12.80	188/73	HJ	2.25	2.17- 00
	Uchitomi	Yasunori	JPN	29.10.72	173/64	3kSt	8:29.63	8:26.48- 97
	Udechuku	Emeka	GBR	10.7.79	176/102	DT	59.97	62.07- 00

	Name		Nat	Born	Ht/Wt	Event	2001 Mark	Pre-2001 Best
	Udo-Obong	Enefiok	NGR	22.5.82	185/82	200	20.68	20.80, 20.4- 00
						400	45.5	45.68- 00
	Ue	Toru	JPN	25.6.75	184/90	JT	78.64	78.32- 96
	Unger	Tobias	GER	10.7.79	179/66	200	20.68	20.96- 00
^	Urbanik	Sándor	HUN	15.12.64	173/58	20kW	1:22:35	1:20:41- 97
						50kW	3:48:41	3:52:07- 95
*	Urbas	Marcin	POL	17.9.76	179/75	200	20.41, 20.39w	19.98- 99
	Urrutia	Aliecer	CUB	22.9.74	174/76	TJ	16.46	17.70- 96, 17.83i- 97
	Ursu	Sergiu	MDA	26.4.80	202/127	SP	19.35	18.96- 00
	Usivivu	Boniface	KEN	5.9.74		HMar	62:10	62:14- 99
	Usov	Roman	RUS	4.6.78	176/56	3kSt	8:35.08	8:26.96- 00
	Vaden	Jordan	USA			200	20.65	
	Väkeväinen	Jukka	FIN	12.9.78	182/88	Dec	7944	7393- 00
	Valle	Emilio	CUB	21.4.67	183/74	110H	13.62w	13.18- 96
	Valyukevich	Dmitriy	BLR	31.5.81	186/78	TJ	16.62	16.39- 00
	van Balkom	Patrick	NED	14.9.74	184/80	200	20.36A, 20.57	20.36- 99
	Van Daele	Jo	BEL	6.4.72	191/110	DT	64.24	63.49- 00
	van de Westen	Marcel	NED	1.8.76		110H	13.71	13.95- 00
	van der Bilt	Mike	NED	23.10.76	197/115	DT	60.87	60.88- 98
	Van Mensel	Marc	BEL	18.5.71		JT	81.59	75.18- 00
	van Oudtshoorn	Jopie	RSA	5.2.76	189/80	400	45.67A, 45.68	44.75A, 45.21- 99
	van Wyk	Christie	NAM	12.10.77	171/65	100	9.99w	10.31- 00
						200	20.71, 20.67w	20.50- 00
	van Zyl	Frikkie	RSA	30.7.81		110H	13.67w	
^	Vander-Kuyp	Kyle	AUS	30.5.71	192/82	110H	13.55	13.29- 95, 13.27Aw, 13.2- 94
	Vandewiele	Jürgen	BEL	10.5.74	182/68	1500	3:34.93	3:36.64- 99
	Vanko	Miroslav	SVK	14.2.73	179/70	10000	28:20.50	28:01.84- 98
*	Varga	Roland	HUN	22.10.77	197/102	DT	65.86	65.39- 00
	Vargas	Claudio	MEX	9.12.74		20kW	1:23:53	1:25:18- 00
	Värnik	Andrus	EST	27.9.77	182/93	JT	80.83	82.16- 00
	Vartia	Janne	FIN	18.3.77	192/115	HT	71.34	71.90- 00
	Vasala	Samuli	FIN	29.11.76	181/67	1500	3:38.39	3:41.04- 98
	Vashchilo	Aleksandr	BLR	30.8.81	197/108	HT	72.26	67.28- 00
	Vasilache	Stefan	ROM	9.5.79	190/70	HJ	2.24	2.22i- 00
	Vasilyev	Dmitriy	BLR	27.10.76	190/74	TJ	16.54i, 16.51	16.53- 00, 16.68i- 98
	Veal	Brian	USA	4.1.82	186/68	LJ	7.95Aw	7.45- 00
	Vega	Javier	ESP	10.12.75	186/69	110H	13.74	13.82A- 99, 13.81Aw- 00
	Vega	Teodoro	MEX	14.7.76		10000	28:00.91	
	Végh	Sándor	HUN	10.3.77		HT	71.04	69.57- 99
	Verbist	Gildas	FRA	9.6.79	180/70	PV	5.50	5.50- 99, 5.55i- 00
	Verni	Marco Antonio	CHI	27.2.76	188/114	SP	19.42	18.60- 99
	Vershinin	Leonid	BLR	23.6.77		400H	49.96	50.19- 00
	Veryutin	Aleksandr	BLR	18.11.79	197/79	HJ	2.25	2.21- 98
	Vial	Pierre-Alexandre	FRA	25.5.75	180/75	Dec	8059(w), 7890	8070- 97
	Vicari	Ferdinando	ITA	26.9.73	170/54	1500	3:38.74	3:41.45- 98
^	Viciosa	Isaac	ESP	26.12.69	176/64	1500	3:38.40	3:30.94- 98
						3000	7:46.79	7:29.34- 98
						5000	13:15.94	13:09.63- 98
	Videnov	Zhivko	BUL	23.5.77	193/80	110H	13.43	13.33- 00
	Vieira	João	POR	20.2.76	174/58	20kW	1:22:52, 1:24:08.8t	1:20:59- 97
	Viera	Heber	URU	29.4.79	180/74	100	10.26	10.15A- 99
						200	20.68, 20.67w	20.76- 99
	Villar	Paulo	COL	28.7.78		110H	13.58A	13.98A- 00
	Vincent	Matthew	USA	6.3.81	196/85	HJ	2.25	2.18- 99
	Vinni	Kari	FIN	19.3.83		JT	76.63	67.61- 00
*	Virastyuk	Roman	UKR	20.4.68	189/135	SP	20.08	21.34- 00
*	Vizzoni	Nicola	ITA	4.11.73	194/126	HT	80.50	79.64- 00
	Vlasny	Andreas	AUT	12.9.69	182/96	SP	19.11	19.32- 00
	Vojnovic	Dejan	CRO	23.3.75	183/75	100	10.25	10.40, 10.34w- 99
*	Voronin	Vyacheslav	RUS	5.4.74	190/78	HJ	2.37	2.40- 00
	Voronkin	Yuriy	RUS	18.5.79	184/83	HT	75.55	76.03- 00
	Vorontsov	Andrey	BLR	24.7.75		HT	77.23	76.02- 00
	Voyevodin	Aleksey	RUS	9.8.70	178/65	20kW	1:22:55.0t	1:19:31- 98
						50kW	3:44:32	3:41:33- 97
	Voynov	Sergey	UZB	26.2.77	188/89	JT	82.71	84.80- 00
	Vries	Sherwin	NAM	22.3.80	179/74	200	20.53w	20.88A- 99
	Vroemen	Simon	NED	11.5.69	189/68	3kSt	8:20.67	8:13.45- 00
	Wachira	Nicholas	KEN	19.11.82	181/67	800	1:44.46	1:45.05- 00
	Wachira	Solomon	KEN	5.11.76	170/55	10000	27:57.33	27:57.19- 00
*	Wade	Larry	USA	22.11.74	187/83	110H	13.12	13.01- 99
	Wahlman	Marko	FIN	6.4.69	196/110	HT	72.40	78.70- 95

	Name		Nat	Born	Ht/Wt	Event	2001 Mark	Pre-2001 Best
	Wainaina	James	KEN	16.6.81	170/56	10000	28:03.41	28:01.21- 00
						HMar	61:04	61:26- 00
	Wakae	Masashi	JPN	28.4.80	173/58	400H	49.97	50.40- 00
	Walker	Brad	USA	21.6.81		PV	5.48i	
*	Wallace	Dawane	USA	30.12.76	190/79	110H	13.22	13.22- 00
	Walser	Thomas	AUT	9.2.78	192/77	Dec	7638	7346- 00
	Walters	Chad	USA	19.5.79	180/82	PV	5.45	5.10- 00
	Waltz	Ian	USA	15.4.77	186/122	DT	60.31	64.44- 98
	Wang Cheng		CHN	4.11.80	178/70	LJ	8.08	8.16- 98
	Wang Libo		CHN	28.10.79		20kW	1:22:31	
						50kW	3:56:24	3:59:44- 00
	Wang Shengtang		CHN	8.3.77		50kW	3:53:20	4:09:40- 00
	Wang Shigang		CHN	22.2.81		20kW	1:22:06	1:27:24- 00
						50kW	3:55:00	4:24:15- 00
	Wang Yinhang		CHN	15.2.77	170/54	50kW	3:44:28	3:50:19- 00
	Wang Yonghua		CHN	23.5.81	181/63	Mar	2:10:26	2:18:53- 00
	Wang Yu		CHN	20.1.79		20kW	1:22:15	1:25:34- 99
	Wang Zhiyong		CHN	3.1.79	191/110	SP	19.23	18.57- 00
	Wang Zhouzhou		CHN	20.4.77	190/72	HJ	2.26	2.27- 99
	Ward	Devon	USA	10.11.80	183/79	100	10.26	10.35w, 10.1w- 00
	Ware	Von	USA	30.6.75	175/79	TJ	16.46, 16.60w	16.97, 17.21w- 98
	Warners	Chiel	NED	2.4.78	194/85	Dec	8206	8363- 99
	Warsama	Ahmed Ibrahim	QAT	4.2.66	182/62	5000	13:21.18	13:13.52- 00
*	Washington	Tyree	USA	28.8.76	185/84	400	44.28	44.29- 98
	Wassenaar	Rick	NED	17.1.76	190/91	Dec	7574	7872- 99
	Wassilew	Georgi	GER	16.2.80	183/75	PV	5.50i	5.45- 98
	Watanabe	Daisuke	JPN	29.5.75	185/75	LJ	8.10	8.12- 99, 8.19w- 97
	Watanabe	Masanari	JPN	10.12.80	169/63	TJ	16.67	16.14- 00
	Watanabe	Satoshi	JPN	6.5.80	173/54	HMar	61:35	63:22- 98
	Watkins	Arend	USA	23.5.79	190/86	110H	13.47	13.51- 00
	Watts	Mario	JAM	21.5.75	178/70	400H	49.31A, 49.61	49.08- 00
	Watts	Marvin	JAM	21.5.75	188/71	800	1:46.43	1:46.57- 00
	Waweru	Joseph	KEN	22.6.77		HMar	61:18	60:49- 99
	Weakley	Ian	JAM	24.2.74	180/68	400H	48.80	48.83- 97
	Weatherborne	Haddow	USA?	81		200	20.72	21.45- 99
	Webb	Alan	USA	13.1.83	175/64	1500	3:38.26+	3:47.4 - 00
						1M	3:53.43	4:03.33- 00
	Weckström	Ari	FIN	23.10.67	183/83	JT	76.12	76.24- 93
*	Weidlinger	Günther	AUT	5.4.78	169/53	3000	7:47.86i	7:47.79i- 00
						3kSt	8:23.62	8:10.83- 99
^	Weir	Robert	GBR	4.2.61	191/119	DT	63.03	65.08- 00
*	Wellman	Brian	BER	8.9.67	175/72	TJ	17.24A, 16.81	17.72i, 17.62A, 17.75w- 95
	Wells	Clint	USA	2.5.75	185/68	3kSt	8:25.73	8:23.26- 00
	Wen Jili		CHN	11.7.73	193/148	SP	19.45i, 19.21	19.46- 97
	Wenk	Stefan	GER	13.3.81	192/83	JT	78.65	73.06- 00
	Wenta	Lukasz	POL	19.12.79	196/95	SP	19.00	17.60- 98
	Wenta	Sebastian	POL	4.5.75	201/126	SP	19.48	18.70- 97
	Wesley	DeMario	USA	20.4.80		100	10.09w	10.23, 10.19w- 98
	Westlund	Mike	USA	24.3.80	188/82	PV	5.50	5.47- 00
	Whitby	Ben	GBR	6.1.77	188/69	3kSt	8:32.68	8:41.79- 98
	White	Geno	USA	10.3.78	180/78	200	20.55, 20.50w	20.77, 20.5- 97, 20.52Aw- 00
						400	45.29	45.02- 00
^	Whiteman	Anthony	GBR	13.11.71	189/72	1500	3:34.88	3:32.34- 97
						1M	3:55.16	3:51.90- 98
	Whitmarsh	Zach	CAN	5.4.77	182/72	800	1:46.12	1:45.94- 99
	Wieruszewski	Rafal	POL	24.2.81	181/63	400	45.76	46.26- 00
	Wignall	Maurice	JAM	17.4.76	186/75	110H	13.70	13.66- 99
	Wijmeersch	Erik	BEL	23.1.70	182/79	100	10.23w	10.17- 97, 10.12w- 96
						200	20.60	20.42, 20.35w- 96
	Wilkins	Perriss	GBR	12.12.69	188/112	DT	61.68	66.64- 98
	Willemse	Martin	RSA	23.4.75		400H	48.96	50.13A- 99
*	Williams	Bernard	USA	19.1.78	183/81	100	9.94	9.99- 00
						200	20.01	20.03- 00
*	Williams	Chris	JAM	15.3.72	177/68	100	10.07	10.05, 10.04w- 00
						200	20.11	20.02- 00
	Williams	Gerald	USA	24.2.78	183/79	100	10.16	10.09- 99
	Williams	Ricardo	JAM	29.9.76	183/73	100	10.23	10.23- 00, 10.19w- 98
						200	20.56	20.33- 00
	Williams	Saidric	USA	16.12.81	175/73	100	10.11w	10.45- 00, 10.22w- 99
	Wilson	Robert	USA	19.6.77	184/73	400	45.90	45.35- 99
	Wilson	Ryan	USA	19.12.80		110H	13.69	14.00, 13.79w- 00

	Name		Nat	Born	Ht/Wt	Event	2001 Mark	Pre-2001 Best
	Winchester	Ian	NZL	27.5.73	193/109	DT	61.92	64.26- 00
	Wójcik	Rafal	POL	18.9.72	180/66	3kSt	8:27.07	8:17.09- 00
*	Wolde	Million	ETH	17.3.79	175/59	3000	7:39.59, 7:37.99i	7:32.36- 00
						5000	13:02.17	12:59.39- 98
	Wood	David	USA	23.6.79	188/105	SP	19.06	
	Woodley	Adrian	CAN	25.11.75	180/73	110H	13.65	13.52, 13.50w- 00
	Woodson	Detrion	USA	5.8.78	180/82	100	10.22w	10.33- 99
*	Woody	Joey	USA	22.5.73	188/78	400H	49.03	47.97- 98
	Wooten	Adam	USA	18.3.82	175/73	100	10.23w	10.42, 10.33w- 00
						200	20.59w	21.27, 20.91w- 00
	Wright	Gerald	USA		173/68	100	10.20	
	Wu Ji		CHN	14.8.78		TJ	17.04	16.75- 98
	Wu Ping		CHN	2.5.79	170/50	20kW	1:22:04	1:21:25- 96
	Wu Tao		CHN	3.10.83		DT	61.21	55.88- 00
	Wyatt	Jonathan	NZL	20.12.72	175/63	10000	28:21.4	28:18.07- 95
	Xu Gang		CHN	4.2.79	187/70	PV	5.56i	5.50- 97, 5.52i- 98
	Xu Xingde		CHN	12.6.84		20kW	1:23:38	1:39:59- 00
						50kW	4:05:07	
	Xu Zizhou		CHN	8.1.81	179/64	200	20.60, 20.39w	20.62- 00
						400	45.25	45.55- 00
	Yagoub	Mohamed	SUD	2.9.77	175/64	3000	7:48.65	8:04.68- 00
						5000	13:27.09	
	Yakovlev	Yevgeniy	RUS	17.6.79	176/65	20kW	1:21:52	1:21:58- 00
	Yakushev	Vladimir	RUS	.79		LJ	8.11	7.45- 99
	Yamada	Shinri	JPN	17.6.79	181/65	110H	13.72	13.79- 00
	Yamamura	Takahiko	JPN	13.8.79	176/68	400	45.78	45.03- 00
	Yanagisawa	Satoshi	JPN	19.1.71	170/60	20kW	1:21:20	1:19:29- 00
	Yang Jianghua		CHN	2.7.82		50kW	4:04:47	
	Yang Yongjian		CHN	28.4.73	182/68	20kW	1:22:05	1:25:09- 96
						50kW	3:51:43	3:48:42- 00
*	Yator	Raymond	KEN	7.4.81	172/55	1500	3:38.62+	3:41.20- 00
						1M	3:55.12	
						5000	13:30.02	
						3kSt	8:09.20	8:03.74- 00
	Yavas	Mesut	TUR	14.4.78	185/81	LJ	7.89i, 7.94w	8.09i, 8.08- 00
	Ye Kuigang		CHN	4.1.75	188/96	HT	73.04	73.67- 00
^	Yegorov	Grigoriy	KAZ	12.1.67	184/79	PV	5.70i, 5.55	5.90- 93
	Yeliseyev	Yuriy	RUS	27.5.75	178/65	PV	5.60i	5.70- 96
	Yeremenko	Ruslan	UKR	31.7.78	193/80	PV	5.70	5.40, 5.60sq- 00
	Yesipchuk	Dmitriy	RUS	17.11.74	178/66	20kW	1:18:05, 1:22:24.8t	1:19:22- 97
	Yevgenyev	Andrey	RUS	9.7.73	182/100	HT	74.21	77.92- 97
*	Yiampoy	William	KEN	17.5.74	183/70	800	1:43.00	1:44.23- 00
						1000	2:16.53	2:14.41- 99
						1500	3:34.12	3:37.62- 00
	Yin Hanzhao		CHN	18.2.76	184/75	100	10.25	10.23- 97
	Yokoyama	Manabu	JPN	20.7.74	182/76	PV	5.60	5.70- 00
	York	Jeff	USA	3.9.71	186/77	110H	13.47	13.49- 00
	Yoshida	Yukihiro	JPN	16.7.76	166/53	HMar	61:34	63:16- 98
	Yoshihara	Masato	JPN	14.3.77	169/55	50kW	4:01:52	
	Yoshioka	Yasunori	JPN	19.5.75	181/75	110H	13.74	13.84, 13.82w- 99
	Yoshizawa	Ken	JPN	7.7.78	178/69	400H	49.55	49.11- 00
	Youla	Benjamin	CGO	12.11.75		400	45.74	46.29- 97, 45.9- 98
	Young	Blair	AUS	5.4.71	194/83	400H	49.89	49.20, 49.08A- 00
	Young	Jason	USA	27.5.81	185/107	DT	59.96A	58.80- 00
*	Young	Jerome	USA	14.8.76	181/79	400	45.32	44.09- 98
	Yu Chaohong		CHN	12.12.76	175/63	20kW	1:21:04	1:23:09- 99
						50kW	3:47:04	3:58:44- 00
^	Yu Guohui		CHN	30.4.77	182/70	20kW	1:23:18	1:19:38- 96
						50kW	3:47:34	3:55:20- 00
	Yu Guoping		CHN	13.6.86	170/60	20kW	1:22:05	
						50kW	3:45:46	
	Yu Qiyun		CHN	28.8.80		20kW	1:22:32	1:25:44- 00
*	Yuda	John	TAN	9.6.79		HMar	60:12	61:56- 00
	Yudin	Stepan	RUS	3.4.80	175/61	20kW	1:21:33	1:22:14- 00
	Yurchenko	Denis	UKR	27.1.78	174/74	PV	5.70i, 5.65, 5.71ex	5.72- 00
*	Yurkov	Aleksandr	UKR	21.7.75	183/80	Dec	8408	8574- 00
	Yushkov	Ivan	RUS	15.1.81	185/87	SP	19.11i, 19.00	19.27- 00
	Zabawski	Przemyslaw	POL	8.4.75	201/110	SP	19.63	18.76, 18.80ex- 00
	Zachoval	Radek	CZE	6.7.78	189/78	200	20.67A, 20.10Aw, 20.69i	21.55-98
^	Zadoinov	Vadim	MDA	24.5.69	187/74	400H	49.62	48.61- 90
*	Zagornyy	Aleksey	RUS	31.5.78	199/128	HT	80.80	79.68- 00

	Name		Nat	Born	Ht/Wt	Event	2001 Mark	Pre-2001 Best
*	Zakari	Abdul Aziz	GHA	2.9.76	178/73	100	10.04	10.06- 00
						200	20.27	20.23- 00
	Zakrzewski	Jan	POL	21.12.70	187/73	3kSt	8:22.49	8:24.56- 00
	Zalaggítis	Konstadínos	GRE	13.12.80	185/78	TJ	17.02	17.18, 17.21w- 00
	Zblewski	Leszek	POL	25.12.73	182/76	1500	3:37.83	3:39.07- 00
	Zegeye	Daniel	ETH	13.3.79	180/62	1500	3:38.25	3:36.33- 00
						3000	7:48.46i	
*	Zelezny	Jan	CZE	16.6.66	186/88	JT	92.80	98.48- 96
^	Zellner	Torrance	USA	6.1.70	187/75	400H	49.28	48.18- 96
	Zepeda	Omar	MEX	8.7.77		50kW	3:56:51A	3:54:26- 98
	Zeyen	Stephan	GER	11.9.78		Dec	7853(w), 77.85	7830- 00
	Zhan Donglin		CHN	15.7.70	175/60	Mar	2:10:38	2:14:06- 00
	Zhang Cunbiao		CHN	11.2.69	183/100	DT	59.61	62.42- 96
	Zhang Feng		CHN	9.5.72		110H	13.75w	13.80- 99
	Zhang Houxi		CHN	15.1.81		JT	76.37	76.78- 00
	Zhang Huabing		CHN	1.9.83		50kW	4:01:18	4:17:16- 00
	Zhang Jiawei		CHN	27.10.86		50kW	3:55:15	
	Zhang Lianbiao		CHN	25.1.69	193/110	JT	80.72	83.38- 94
	Zhang Liping		CHN			50kW	4:04:23	
	Zhang Tianping		CHN	11.1.82		20kW	1:22:21	1:26:58- 00
	Zhao Lei		CHN	8.7.78		Dec	7571	7479- 97
	Zhou Can		CHN	20.5.79	184/68	LJ	7.89	8.11- 99
	Zhou Yongsheng		CHN	15.10.72	178/70	20kW	1:22:05	1:20:06- 94
						50kW	3:57:49	3:43:16- 94
	Zhou Zhongge		CHN	15.2.67	189/75	HJ	2.24	2.33- 90
	Zhu Hongjun		CHN	18.8.83		20kW	1:21:58	1:23:34- 00
	Ziani	Kamal	ESP	20.2.72	178/68	Mar	2:10:36	2:10:18- 97
	Zioini	Badredin	FRA	25.3.76	175/53	3kSt	8:24.22	8:26.10- 00
*	Ziólkowski	Szymon	POL	1.7.76	188/104	HT	83.38	81.42- 00
	Zlatnar	Damjan	SLO	16.12.77	187/72	110H	13.66, 13.62w	13.90- 99
	Zschunke	Oliver	GER	29.4.70		JT	76.47	79.02- 96
*	Zsivoczky	Attila	HUN	29.4.77	193/82	Dec	8371	8554- 00
	Zujus	Daugvinas	LTU	16.10.75	182/65	50kW	3:56:58	3:55:10- 98
	Zyukov	Yevgeniy	UKR	31.5.78	182/74	400	45.67	46.15- 00
	Zyuskov	Vladimir	UKR	29.8.81	187/71	LJ	8.13	7.84- 00

WOMEN'S INDEX 2001

Athletes included are those ranked in ther top 100s at standard (World Champs) events (plus shorter lists for 1000m, 1M, 2000m, 3000m and 3000m St). Those with detailed biographical profiles are indicated in first column by: * in this year's Annual, ^ in a previous year's Annual, # old javelin

	Name		Nat	Born	Ht/Wt	Event	2001 Mark	Pre-2001 Best
	Aava	Monika	EST	19.6.79	171/61	JT	57.98	55.63- 99, 55.96#- 96
	Abatzí	Aretí	GRE	14.5.74	183/78	DT	62.95	61.22- 97
	Abe	Tomoe	JPN	13.8.71	149/38	Mar	2:27:02	2:26:09- 94
*	Abel	María	ESP	23.10.74	162/45	Mar	2:29:46	
	Abeylegesse	Hewan	TUR	11.9.82		1500	4:11.31	4:18.7- 00
						3000	8:53.42	9:08.29- 99
						5000	15:21.12	16:06.40- 99
						10000	32:29.20	-0-
	Abrahamse	Veronica	RSA	18.3.80	180/98	SP	17.29	16.82- 00
	Abrantes	Isabel	POR	20.3.73	170/55	100H	13.31, 13.21w	13.14- 00
	Achilles	Bianca	GER	17.4.81	180/128	HT	64.97	68.40- 99
*	Acuff	Amy	USA	14.7.75	188/66	HJ	1.98	2.00-97
*	Adams	Christine	GER	28.2.74	182/72	PV	4.35i, 4.35	4.40i, 4.30 - 00
*	Adams	Jenny	USA	8.7.78	165/55	100H	12.63, 12.61w	12.86- 00
						LJ	6.68i, 6.75w, 6.48	6.64- 00
	Adams	Valerie	NZL	6.10.84	192/110	SP	17.08	15.72- 00
	Ademiluyi	Cynthia	USA	23.1.79	178/95	SP	16.77	16.12- 00
*	Adere	Berhane	ETH	21.7.73	170/48	2000	5:39.7+	
						3000	8:25.62	8:40.14- 97
						5000	14:51.67	14:52.61- 00
						10000	31:32.70	30:51.30- 00
						HMar	68:17	69:28- 00
	Adriano	Elisângela	BRA	27.7.72	180/95	SP	19.30	19.02- 99
						DT	59.68	61.96- 98, 62.23dq- 99
	Adusei	Martha	CAN	8.6.76	165/64	100	11.41	11.29- 00
*	Afanasyeva	Yelena	RUS	1.3.67	164/56	800	2:00.81. 1:58.73i	1:56.61- 97
*	Afolabi	Olabisi	NGR	31.10.75	171/62	400	51.52	50.34A, 50.40- 99
	Aguilera	Lisa	USA	30.11.79		3kSt	10:08.85	

Name		Nat	Born	Ht/Wt	Event	2001 Mark	Pre-2001 Best
Ahonen	Kirsi	FIN	8.4.76	170/78	JT	57.00	59.75- 00
Aït Hammou	Mina	MAR	18.7.78	166/52	800	2:00.47	2:03.16- 00
Aït Hammou	Sultana	MAR	21.5.80	165/49	800	2:02.3/2:02.32	2:07.2- 00
Ajkler	Zita	HUN	9.6.75	170/56	LJ	6.58	6.70- 00
					TJ	13.69w	13.74- 00
* Ajunwa	Chioma	NGR	25.12.70	164/57	LJ	6.65	7.12- 96
Akaba	Yukiko	JPN	18.10.79	156/46	HMar	71:23	73:19- 99
Akagi	Junko	JPN	3.12.75	168/50	HMar	71:12	72:50- 96
					Mar	2:28:13	2:36:03- 99
Akhigbe	Kudirat	NGR	29.12.81	166/52	400	51.60	52.38- 99
Akinremi	Omolade	NGR	13.9.74	158/60	400H	55.98	55.44- 95
Akinremi	Omotayo	NGR	13.9.74	158/60	400H	56.55	56.66- 96, 56.4- 91
Akulenko	Yuliya	UKR	3.6.77	176/64	LJ	6.50	6.48- 97
					Hep	6001	6117- 97
Alagia	Tiziana	ITA	8.3.73	171/54	HMar	71:29	72:45- 00
					Mar	2:27:54	2:32:18- 00
Alba	Julia	ESP	30.5.72	169/57	400	52.28	53.70- 00
Albert	Beatrice	GER	9.5.70		LJ	6.45i	6.34, 6.44w- 00
^ Aldama	Yamilé	CUB	14.8.72	172/65	TJ	13.85i	14.77- 99
Aldrich	Erin	USA	27.12.77	186/62	HJ	1.89	1.97i- 98, 1.95- 00
Aleksandrova	Galina	RUS	15.10.76		10000	32:29.4	33:19.37- 99
Aleksandrova	Yekaterina	RUS	3.6.77	181/57	HJ	1.96	1.96i- 98, 1.94- 96
* Alemu	Elfenesh	ETH	10.6.75	165/51	HMar	70:22+	69:46- 00
					Mar	2:24:29	2:24:47- 00
* Alfridi	Erica	ITA	22.2.68	168/53	20kW	1:27:29	1:28:06- 00
Alisevich	Tatyana	BLR	22.1.69	173/63	Hep	5902	6146- 00
Allahgreen	Diane	GBR	21.2.75	164/63	100	11.38w	11.66, 11.6- 99
					100H	13.08, 12.98w	12.99- 99
^ Allen	Liliana	MEX	24.5.70	170/62	100	11.13	11.09A- 99, 11.10- 92
					200	23.13A	22.72- 94
Alozie	Glory ex NGR)	ESP	30.12.77	165/51	100	11.14, 11.00w	10.90- 99
					200	23.09	22.63w- 99
					100H	12.69	12.44, 12.4w- 98
Álvarez	María	CUB	30.8.75	165/62	JT	58.83	63.02#- 95, 61.57- 00
Alves	Sónia	POR	3.6.79	174/88	HT	61.90	59.92- 00
Ampleyeva	Natalya	RUS	25.9.72		DT	62.35	61.76- 00
Anderson	Shani	GBR	7.8.75	173/63	100	11.40	11.34- 00
					200	23.12w	23.20- 00
de Andrade	Thaís	BRA	15.12.69		HJ	1.87	1.83- 97
Anim	Vida	GHA	7.12.83		100	11.38	11.58- 00
					200	22.97, 22.9	23.32- 00
Antil	Seema	IND	27.7.83	178/79	DT	58.12	57.20- 00
Antoine/Watkins	LaDonna	CAN	20.11.74	164/54	200	23.13	23.23, 22.9- 97, 22.82w- 00
					400	52.28	50.92- 00
* Antonova	Yelena	UKR	16.6.72	182/95	DT	64.20	66.67- 00
* Antyukh	Natalya	RUS	26.6.81	181/68	400	51.19	54.79- 00
Arai	Motoka	JPN	4.7.74	157/50	100	11.31w	11.45- 99
Araméndiz	Zuleima	COL	23.9.75	172/75	JT	59.09A	59.33A- 00, 61.72#- 96
Arencibia	Yenima	CUB	25.12.84		100H	13.13w	14.00, 13.87w- 00
^ Arimori	Yuko	JPN	17.12.66	164/48	Mar	2:31:00	2:26:39- 99
Aron	Haydy	FRA	21.5.73	170/58	100H	12.96	13.08, 12.92w- 00
Arrendel	Juana	DOM	16.6.78	191/60	HJ	1.88	1.90- 98, 1.93dq- 99
* Arron	Christine	FRA	13.9.73	177/64	100	11.15	10.73- 98
					200	23.14w	22.26- 99
Asiba	Gladys	KEN	31.5.77		HMar	71:15	70:05- 00
^ Astafei	Alina	GER	7.6.69	181/59	HJ	1.93i, 1.91	2.04i, 2.01- 95
^ Atede	Angela	NGR	8.2.72	170/66	100H	13.20	12.72- 98, 12.63dt- 97
Athanasíou	Hristína	GRE	11.1.74	165/60	LJ	6.50	6.60- 98
* Auer	Doris	AUT	10.5.71	168/55	PV	4.44i, 4.40	4.40- 00
Auzeil	Nadine	FRA	19.8.64	176/64	JT	60.04	62.16- 00, 64.10#- 96
Avoila	Sofia	POR	30.7.76	160/50	20kW	1:33:58.1	1:36:50- 99
Aya	Masumi	JPN	1.1.80	165/70	HT	64.43	58.87- 00
Ayétotché	Louise	CIV	3.6.75	160/56	100	11.37w	11.35- 00, 11.2A- 99
					200	23.15	22.76- 00
* Ayhan	Süreyya	TUR	6.9.78	163/52	1500	4:06.91	4:03.02- 00
Baala (Sabri)	Hanane	FRA	8.12.75	178/58	1500	4:07.14	4:14.03- 00
* Babakova	Inga	UKR	27.6.67	180/60	HJ	2.03	2.05- 95
^ Babashkina	Tatyana	RUS	23.11.68	175/68	HJ	1.95	2.03- 95
Babatunde	Tawa	CAN	19.12.79	175/60	400H	56.99	57.02- 00
Babcock	Courtney	CAN	30.6.72	163/50	5000	15:29.60	15:34.91- 00

	Name		Nat	Born	Ht/Wt	Event	2001 Mark	Pre-2001 Best
	Babin	Peggy	FRA	24.12.76	165/51	800	2:01.66	2:03.09- 00
	Bacha	Aster	ETH	83		10000	31:57.49	
	Bacher	Gertrud	ITA	28.2.71	180/63	Hep	6062w, 6030	6185- 99
	Backus	LaKeisha	USA	15.12.76	158/52	100	11.40w	11.11- 98
	Badrankova	Svetlana	KAZ	25.3.77	169/49	800	2:00.91	2:05.62- 00
	Badurová	Katerina	CZE	18.12.82	167/50	PV	4.30	4.30- 00
	Bailey	Aleen	JAM	25.11.80	170/	100	11.14	11.37- 98
						200	22.59	23.37- 99, 22.86w- 00
	Baj	Joanna	POL	31.5.80	164/57	20kW	1:34:56	-0-
*	Bak	Justyna	POL	1.8.74	164/48	3kSt	9:25.31	9:57.03- 00
^	Bakhvalova	Yekaterina	RUS	29.10.72	175/61	400H	56.40	54.65- 00
*	Balakhonova	Anzhela	UKR	18.12.72	162/55	PV	4.52	4.56- 00
	Balantén	Norbi	CUB	24.6.72	176/83	HT	65.28	65.20- 00
	Balassini	Ester	ITA	20.10.77	174/79	HT	68.50	66.17- 00
	Balentine	Shayla	USA	7.8.82		PV	4.16	
	Balint	Zita	HUN	25.10.71	178/64	TJ	13.72	14.00- 96
	Ballard	Misty	USA	16.11.78	170/60	PV	4.10i, 4.10	3.81- 00
	Ballentine	Michelle	JAM	31.8.75	178/63	800	2:02.11A	2:03.65- 98
	Balti	Sereen	TUN	31.10.83		PV	4.10i	4.00- 00
	Balut	Virginia	ROM	3.3.81	172/73	HT	63.11	60.23- 00
	Bangué	Frédérique	FRA	31.12.76	179/61	100	11.26, 11.09w	11.16- 98
	Bani	Zahra	ITA	31.12.79	173/71	JT	54.98	54.26- 00
	Baouf	Fatiha	BEL	15.7.70		1500	4:07.65	4:18.27- 99
	Barak	Aysen	TUR	9.9.75	174/59	1500	4:10.80	4:14.13- 97
						3000	8:48.60i	9:07.41- 98
						5000	15:27.99i	15:45.22- 97
	Baratella	Giorgia	ITA	8.1.75	176/82	DT	56.18	54.56- 00
*	Barber	Eunice	FRA	17.11.74	175/68	100H	12.78	12.89- 99
						HJ	1.89	1.93- 99
						LJ	6.97	7.01- 99
						Hep	6736	6861- 99
	Barber	Me'Lisa	USA	4.10.80	160/52	200	23.06w	23.23- 00, 23.16w- 99
						400	52.18	53.93- 00
	Barber	Mikele	USA	4.10.80	159/50	200	23.21, 22.71w	22.98, 22.84w- 00
						400	50.63	50.98- 00
	Barbieri	Lisa	ITA	18.5.78	149/43	20kW	1:33:13	1:35:12- 00
	Barrett	Peta-Gay	JAM	2.10.76		100	11.34	11.55, 11.54w- 98
	Barsosio	Florence	KEN	11.8.76	160/50	HMar	71:22	71:03- 00
						Mar	2:27:53	2:27:00- 00
	Bartsevich	Yuliya	BLR	15.6.79	173/61	100	11.1	11.87- 00
	Bashlykova	Lidia	RUS	10.1.81	179/65	Hep	5946	5979- 00
	Bass	Tacita	USA	28.10.79		400H	57.31	59.42- 00
	Bastos	Marina	POR	7.7.71	165/50	3000	8:49.55i	8:38.13- 99
	Bates	Joyce	USA	16.2.77	163/59	100H	13.17, 12.5w	12.85, 12.79w- 00
*	Batten	Kim	USA	29.3.69	170/57	400H	55.49mx, 55.80	52.61- 95
*	Bazhenova	Nadezhda	RUS	22.9.78	176/63	LJ	6.58	6.51- 00
						TJ	14.60	14.25- 99
	Beckel	Nadine	GER	27.5.77	190/89	SP	18.02	18.02i, 18.01- 00
*	Becker	Annika	GER	12.11.81	170/63	PV	4.55	4.30- 99
	Beckford	Allison	JAM	8.5.79	175/60	400	51.50	53.19- 98
						400H	56.22	56.52- 99
	Bécot	Émilie	FRA	20.10.80	165/58	PV	4.25	4.20- 00
	Beenamol	K. Mathews	IND	15.8.75	161/42	400	52.17	51.21- 00
	Begic	Vera	CRO	17.3.82	169/69	DT	55.94	56.22- 00
	Beitia	Ruth	ESP	1.4.79	178/56	HJ	1.94i, 1.91	1.89- 98
	Belin	Kirsten	SWE	2.5.81	175/59	PV	4.22	3.68- 99
*	Belkacem	Yamna	FRA	20.2.74	164/52	3000	8:44.00	8:38.13- 99
						5000	15:17.95	14:47.79- 00
						10000	32:05.98	0
*	Belova	Irina	RUS	27.3.68	175/63	800	2:02.06	2:02.75- 90
						LJ	6.50	6.82- 92
						Hep	6528	6845- 92
	Belovol	Tatyana	UKR	7.10.69	162/52	3000	8:55.92	8:58.2- 95
*	Belyakova	Yelena	RUS	7.4.76	177/56	PV	4.55i, 4.42	4.50- 00
	Benavídes	Vírgen	CUB	31.12.74	165/56	100	11.39, 11.33w, 11.1	11.14, 11.10w- 99
*	Benhassi	Hasna	MAR	1.6.78	166/55	800	1:59.86i	1:57.45- 99
						1500	4:04.48i	4:05.15- 98
	Bennion	Rebecca	USA	16.9.80		3kSt	9:54.84	
	Benth	Katia	FRA	16.11.75	172/56	100	11.31, 11.25w	11.20- 98
	Beránková	Sárka	CZE	16.4.78	176/69	Hep	5664	6079- 00
*	Bergqvist	Kajsa	SWE	12.10.76	175/59	HJ	2.00i, 2.00	2.01- 00

Name		Nat	Born	Ht/Wt	Event	2001 Mark	Pre-2001 Best
Berkut	Natalya	UKR	30.5.75	172/53	5000	15:21.95	15:38.78- 99
					10000	31:22.76	32:52.19- 00
Beskrovnaja	Irina	SVK	28.12.82	174/66	TJ	13.71	13.56- 00
Bettoso	Sarah	ITA	25.5.80		HJ	1.86	1.82- 97
Beutelspacher	Simone	GER	8.12.74	170/60	800	2:03.02	2:02.44- 99, 2:01.72i- 00
Bévis	Marie-Louise	FRA	12.10.72	170/58	400	52.27	51.79- 96
Beyer	Ilona	GER	8.1.76	184/90	SP	17.26i, 17.13	17.63- 00
Bicet	Nora Aïda	CUB	29.10.77	178/78	JT	58.70	60.67- 00
Bicet	Yusmay	CUB	8.12.83	178/67	TJ	13.71	13.80- 00
* Bidouane	Nezha	MAR	18.9.69	174/60	400H	53.34	52.90- 99
* Bikar	Alenka	SLO	7.1.74	161/53	100	11.21, 11.16w	11.30- 98
					200	22.76	22.79- 99
* Biktagirova	Madina	BLR	20.9.64	158/50	HMar	71:26+	71:34- 91
					Mar	2:27:14	2:24:46- 97
Biktasheva	Lyudmila	RUS	25.7.74	160/48	10000	31:30.6	31:33.58- 00
					HMar	70:31	70:35- 99
Biondini	Silvia	ITA	24.1.76	166/58	TJ	14.15	13.70- 99, 13.71w- 00
Birungi	Grace	UGA	10.10.73	164/48	800	2:01.54A	2:00.97- 00
* Bisset	Sonia	CUB	1.4.71	171/69	JT	66.54	65.87- 00, 68.24#- 97
Biswas	Soma	IND	16.5.78	173/60	Hep	5739	6186- 00
Black	Kerine	JAM	5.3.77		LJ	6.50	6.23, 6.30w- 00
* Blackett	Andrea	BAR	24.1.76	160/54	400H	55.68	53.36- 99
Blake	Tanya	GBR	16.1.71	167/58	800	2:01.87	2:00.10- 98
Blonskaya	Lyudmila	UKR	18.3.75	176/68	Hep	5835	6230- 99
Bobrovskaya	Yelena	KGZ	11.4.75	174/56	LJ	6.73	6.66- 00
Bódi	Bernadett	HUN	14.4.80	174/57	HJ	1.86	1.82- 98
Bodritskaya	Svetlana	KAZ	7.11.71	171/54	400	52.39	52.01- 98
^ Boegman	Nicole	AUS	5.3.67	174/66	LJ	6.63, 6.71w	6.87- 88, 7.12Aw- 95
Bogachova	Irina	KGZ	30.5.61	167/52	Mar	2:31:02	2:26:27- 00
Bogatie	Mariana	ROM	12.6.81	182/55	TJ	13.81i	13.57- 99
Bolm	Kirsten	GER	4.3.75	181/69	100H	12.98	12.92- 00, 12.86Aw- 99
Bolshova	Olga	MDA	16.6.68	174/60	HJ	1.89i	1.97- 93
					TJ	14.17i, 14.15	13.88- 00
Boone	Rachelle	USA	30.6.81	163/59	100	11.33. 11.32w	11.49, 11.38w- 00
					200	22.94w	23.37- 00
Borel	Cleopatra	TRI			SP	16.87i	
Boslak	Vanessa	FRA	11.6.82	169/57	PV	4.33i, 4.30	4.32- 00
Bosneaga	Gheorghita	ROM	15.7.81	184/86	DT	57.80	54.43- 00
* Botezan	Mihaela	ROM	21.11.76	160/46	5000	15:08.78	15:54.86- 99
					10000	31:45.06	34:00.27- 00
					HMar	70:11	70:07- 00
Boulleret	Emilie	FRA	23.5.73	171/57	Hep	5665	5528- 93
Boulová	Michaela	CZE	2.8.81	165/52	PV	4.10	4.20- 00
Boyde	Kathrin	GER	4.12.70	172/62	20kW	1:31:31	1:30:42- 00
Boyko	Viktoriya	UKR	20.1.74	180/84	DT	63.43	61.96- 99
Brägger	Anita	SUI	6.10.72	170/59	800	1:59.66	2:00.23- 99
* Braun	Sabine	GER	19.6.65	174/65	LJ	6.49i, 6.48	6.76, 6.83w- 97
Bravo	Miriam	ESP	29.9.74	163/45	800	2:01.83	2:03.04- 99
Bresciani	Maria Carla	ITA	16.7.73	171/64	PV	4.15	4.20- 00
* Breuer	Grit	GER	16.2.72	166/60	100	11.34w	11.13- 90
					200	22.79	22.45- 91
					400	49.78	49.42- 91
Brigadnaya	Viktoriya	TKM	4.8.80	176/60	TJ	14.02	13.97- 99
Brîndusoiu	Ileana	ROM	9.5.79	174/77	DT	58.25	55.88- 98
Brito	Sonia	AUS	10.6.79	165/52	400H	55.72	57.80- 00
* Brkljacic	Ivana	CRO	25.1.83	170/65	HT	66.49	68.18- 00
Brown	DeeDee	USA	5.5.78	173/60	Hep	5700	5560- 00
Brunner	Chantal	NZL	5.11.70	168/58	100	11.40w	11.64, 11.36w- 99
					LJ	6.68	6.68- 97, 6.77Aw- 00
Bryukhach	Marina	UKR	16.1.77	168/60	Hep	5834	6021- 00
Bu Fanfang		CHN	10.2.78	170.65	400	51.35	51.85- 97
Budarina	Natalya	RUS	77		LJ	6.52i	6.52- 99
* Buford-Bailey	Tonja	USA	13.12.70	175/62	400H	54.15	52.62- 95
Buia	Aurica	ROM	16.2.70	161/52	HMar	70:40	70:43- 95
Bunjes	Andrea	GER	5.2.76	175/80	HT	63.42	60.78- 00
Burianová	Jitka	CZE	17.1.77	174/57	400	52.10	50.85- 00
Burns	Chandra	USA	4.8.75	178/64	400	52.49	51.71- 97
* Burrell	Dawn	USA	1.11.73	174/58	LJ	7.03i	6.98, 6.99w- 00
* Burrell	Shelia	USA	15.1.72	171/64	200	23.25, 22.92w?	23.32A- 99
					100H	13.05	13.22- 98, 13.14w- 00, 13.20A- 99
					LJ	6.45	6.46- 00

	Name		Nat	Born	Ht/Wt	Event	2001 Mark	Pre-2001 Best
	(S Burrell)					Hep	6472	6422- 00
	Burykina	Yelena	RUS	1.1.73		1500	4:10.86	4:11.8- 99
						5000	15:28.07	15:44.65- 00
*	Buschbaum	Yvonne	GER	14.7.80	173/56	PV	4.46	4.45- 00
	Butler	Kathy	GBR	22.10.73	175/55	1500	4:12.08	4:07.68- 97
						3000	8:40.97	8:48.37- 99
						5000	15:14.62	15:10.69- 98
						10000	31:59.27	0-
	Butor	Irina	BLR	26.2.80	167/59	Hep	5717	5494- 98
	Buval	Patricia	FRA	22.1.76	168/57	100H	13.02, 12.98w	13.14- 00
	Buzau	Cristina	ROM	12.4.76	176/76	HT	61.80	62.60- 98
	Buzhenko	Yelena	UKR	16.11.72	170/55	800	2:02.18	1:59.46- 99
	Byrne	Aoife	IRL	26.3.81		800	2:01.89	2:06.07- 00
	Cadamuro	Stefania	ITA	23.2.79	178/58	HJ	1.88i	1.88- 99
	Cadienhead	Marisa	JAM	7.4.76		HJ	1.86	1.79- 00
	Caffell	Kelly	GBR	10.2.79	168/49	1500	4:11.99	4:10.22- 00
^	Cai Weiyan		CHN	25.10.73	169/56	PV	4.11	4.35i- 97, 4.33- 96
*	Calatayud	Zulia	CUB	9.11.79	169/59	400	50.87	51.69- 00
						800	1:58.60	1:58.66- 00
	Callaerts	Nancy	BEL	11.8.71		100	11.42	11.64- 98
	Campbell	Amber	USA	5.6.81		HT	62.08	49.16- 00
*	Campbell	Juliet	JAM	17.3.70	178/62	200	22.68, 22.64i	22.50- 99
*	Campbell	Veronica	JAM	16.5.82	163/61	100	11.13	11.12, 11.1- 00
						200	22.92	22.87- 00
^	Cao Qi		CHN	15.1.74	182/83	DT	58.35	66.08- 93
	Cárdenas	Regla	CUB	21.1.75	186/77	LJ	6.47	6.72- 96
						Hep	5694	6306- 95
	Carruthers	Danielle	USA	22.12.79		100	11.43	
						200	23.24	23.71- 00
						100H	12.95, 12.79w	13.33, 13.10w- 00
^	Carson	Kim	USA	12.3.74	170/56	100H	13.07, 12.98w	12.72- 96, 12.69w- 98
	Carter	Chimika	USA	17.8.78	170/54	100H	13.09, 13.04w	13.37, 13.13w- 99
						LJ	6.57w	6.16, 6.30w- 99
	Carter	Tonya	USA	22.3.78	163/61	100	11.37w	11.30, 11.15w- 00
	Carvalho	Sónia	POR	10.5.77		HJ	1.88	1.84- 00
	Casandra (Iloc)	Cristina	ROM	21.10.77		3kSt	9:45.12	9:40.20- 00
	Castells	Berta	ESP	24.1.84	174/73	HT	63.11	51.04- 00
	Castrejana	Carlota	ESP	25.4.73	188/67	TJ	13.99	14.10- 00
	Castro	Luz Dary	COL	30.5.78		DT	56.15	53.01- 98
*	Ceplak	Jolanda	SLO	12.9.76	168/55	800	1:58.71	2:00.80- 00
	Cervantes	Dana	ESP	18.8.78	166/63	PV	4.21	4.25- 99
	Chang Jung-yeon		KOR	6.4.77		JT	56.60	52.15- 00, 53.84#- 97
	Chang Xinhong		CHN	24.3.74		DT	58.98	61.82- 97
	Charalambous	Agni	CYP	2.9.75	176/57	HJ	1.88	1.82- 96, 1.86dq- 97
	Checchi	Cristiana	ITA	8.7.77	175/69	SP	17.07	15.69- 00
	Checheleva	Alla	RUS	1.7.81	166/54	PV	4.20	4.10- 00
	Chelangat	Alice	KEN	77		HMar	70:05	70:16- 00
						Mar	2:26:36	
	Chemjor	Magdalene	KEN	12.11.78		HMar	70:32	71:49- 00
	Chen Lin		CHN	22.8.81		400H	57.16	57.44- 99
	Chen Ying		CHN	4.11.75	171/85	HT	63.63	62.93- 00
	Chen Yueqin		CHN	25.2.77		100	11.35	11.48- 99
	Chen Yuxiang		CHN	28.2.78	172/65	200	23.25	22.83- 97
						400	51.40	51.15- 97
*	Cheng Xiaoyan		CHN	30.11.75	176/90	SP	18.78	20.02- 94
	Chenonge	Iness	KEN	1.2.82		3000	8:58.89 & HMar 70:35	
	Chepchumba	Beatrice	KEN	25.11.83	155/46	3000	8:45.07	9:08.80- 00
*	Chepchumba	Joyce	KEN	6.11.70	160/52	HMar	68:45	68:18- 00
						Mar	2:24:12	2:23:22- 99
	Chepchumba	Pamela	KEN	28.2.78		3000	8:42.24	
						5000	14:56.75	
						HMar	71:21+	71:03- 00
*	Chepkemei	Susan	KEN	25.6.75	164/48	3000	8:43.95	8:59.45- 98
						5000	14:55.27	15:06.14- 99
						HMar	65:44	69:10- 00
						Mar	2:25:12	2:26:39- 99
	Cherepanova	Natalya	RUS	9.3.67		3kSt	9:55.07	10:11.86- 00
	Cherkasova	Svetlana	RUS	20.5.78	170/52	800	1:57.59	1:59.23- 00
						1000	2:34.08	
	Chernova	Lada	RUS	1.1.70		JT	58.88	56.85- 00, 61.34#- 96
^	Chernyavskaya	Olga	RUS	17.9.63	180/80	DT	61.44	68.38- 92

Name		Nat	Born	Ht/Wt	Event	2001 Mark	Pre-2001 Best
Chernyavskaya	Yelena	RUS	13.4.78	180/63	Hep	6130	6384- 00
Cherry	Damu	USA	29.11.77		100H	12.85	13.26, 13.24w- 00
* Cheruiyot	Rose	KEN	21.7.76	163/48	3000	8:41.74	8:39.34- 96
					5000	14:48.97	14:46.41- 96
^ Chiba	Masako	JPN	18.7.76	155/38	Mar	2:30:39	2:29:00- 99
Chibisova	Oksana	RUS	31.3.77	177/87	SP	17.00i, 16.88	17.21- 00
Chicherova	Anna	RUS	22.7.82	178/53	HJ	1.92i, 1.92	1.90- 00
Chilla	Mercedes	ESP	19.1.80	165/54	JT	57.78	57.91- 00
* Chojecka	Lidia	POL	25.1.77	166/46	1500	4:03.51	3:59.22- 00
					3000	8:46.47i	8:33.35- 00
Chou Ying		CHN	26.12.83		DT	57.16	55.53- 99
Chu Chunxia		CHN	28.1.78	182/60	JT	59.85	59.56- 00, 61.91#- 98
Chulkova	Natalya	RUS	5.12.77	170/56	400H	56.26	55.73- 00
* Cîmpean	Norica	ROM	22.3.72	164/58	20kW	1:29:25	1:27:46- 99
Cimperman	Lea	SLO	25.7.78		HJ	1.88	1.78- 99
Ciobanu	Lucica	ROM	10.5.79	175/80	SP	17.59	18.94- 00
Cioncan	Maria	ROM	19.6.77	167/50	1500	4:07.89i	4:06.20- 00
					3000	8:57.83i	9:05.74- 96
Cirlan	Daniela	ROM	18.9.80	162/45	20kW	1:33:38	1:31:30- 00
Claretti	Clarissa	ITA	7.10.80	170/70	HT	63.54	60.83- 00
* Clark	Hazel	USA	3.10.77	178/55	800	1:59.95	1:58.75- 00
					1000	2:36.47	
Clarke	Georgie	AUS	17.6.84	170/46	1500	4:08.91	4:06.77- 00
Clarke	Rhian	GBR	19.4.77	170/57	PV	4.20i, 4.10	4.15- 00
Clarke ¶	Venolyn	CAN	11.7.67	163/57	100	11.29	11.57- 00
Clayton-Boswell	Michelle	USA	29.10.76		HT	62.96	61.40- 00
Clifton	Christine	USA	2.8.72		HMar	70:37	
Cloete	Hestrie	RSA	26.8.78	185/68	HJ	2.01	2.04- 99
Coelho Neto	Rosemar	BRA	2.1.77		100	11.32	11.48, 11.36w- 00
					200	23.10A, 23.25	23.29, 22.99w- 00
* Collins	Michelle	USA	12.2.71	176/62	100	11.41	11.19- 00
					200	23.05	22.57- 00
					400	50.66	50.11- 00
Collins	Roberta	USA	31.7.77	170/122	DT	58.64	58.32- 00
Collonvillé	Marie	FRA	23.11.73	163/54	Hep	5887	6350- 97
Combs	Myra	USA	17.4.79	170/54	200	23.20, 22.94w, 22.6w	22.73- 98
Connelly	Tina	CAN	16.8.70	165/52	10000	32:32.52	32:21.27- 00
Console	Rosaria	ITA	17.12.79	162/45	Mar	2:30:55	0
Coons	Leslie	USA	16.7.73	175/74	HT	64.01	63.80- 00
Cooper	Hannah	LBR	10.6.79		100H	13.26. 13.25w	13.26- 00
Cosby	Jessica	USA	31.5.82	173/77	SP	16.68	15.33- 00
Coslovich	Claudia	ITA	26.4.72	170/72	JT	64.30	65.30- 00, 65.55#- 98
Costa	Keila	BRA	6.2.83		TJ	14.00, 14.15w	12.98, 13.65w- 00
* Couch	Sharon	USA	13.9.69	170/63	100H	13.16	12.68- 00, 12.65w- 99
Crawford	Yunaika	CUB	2.11.82	165/75	HT	65.67	65.88- 00
Cresci	Federica	ITA	13.4.74	179/65	TJ	13.81i, 13.62	13.69, 13.80w- 99
Cripps	Sharon	AUS	29.6.77	165/56	200	23.04	23.13- 00
Cross	Jesseca	USA	10.5.75	178/88	HT	66.12	66.52- 00
Crouse	Ann	USA	6.4.76	183/84	JT	54.58	57.38- 99
Crumbo	Amber	USA	16.8.78	170/	SP	16.75i	16.18i- 99
Cruz	Oslaidis	CUB	12.3.74	174/55	20kW	1:34:02	1:35:50- 00
Cucerzan	Alina	ROM	28.7.74	160/42	3kSt	10:00.36	10:03.68- 99
Cui Xiaohong		CHN	10.2.80		HT	61.93	61.78- 00
Cullen	Fiona	AUS	31.8.79		100H	13.31	
Culpepper	Shayne	USA	3.12.73	165/55	800	2:02.18	2:02.51- 00
					1500	4:08.15	4:07.99- 00
* Cumbá	Yumileidi	CUB	11.2.75	183/100	SP	19.10i, 19.00	19.48- 00
Cumberbatch	Amber	BAR			100	11.43	
* Cummins	Diane	CAN	19.1.74	165/50	800	1:58.39	2:01.95- 00
					1500	4:05.02	
^ Curbishley	Allison	GBR	3.6.76	167/58	400	51.99	50.71- 98
Curti	Nives	ITA	1.9.69	167/49	Mar	2:28:59	2:38:30- 96
Curtis	Gina	USA	2.1.79		HJ	1.87i	
Cuza	Lissette	CUB	26.2.75	165/55	LJ	6.57	6.99- 00
Dacy	Rachel	AUS	10.11.76	170/62	PV	4.20	4.20- 00
Dahmani	Zahia	FRA	2.6.72	160/49	Mar	2:29:58	2:34:52- 00
Dai Yanyan		CHN	8.1.80	175/55	1500	4:12.11	
					5000	15:24.71	16:21.76- 97
					10000	32:28.35	32:23.45- 00
					Mar	2:24:41	2:41:37- 00
Dalla Piana	Silvia	ITA	3.2.75	173/60	Hep	5724w, 5698	5795- 00

	Name		Nat	Born	Ht/Wt	Event	2001 Mark	Pre-2001 Best
	Dambacher	Luciane	BRA	10.5.76	176/61	HJ	1.88	1.88- 99
	Damon	Karol	USA	20.12.69	178/58	HJ	1.92i, 1.90	1.93- 99
	Danisová	Martina	SVK	21.3.83	176/75	HT	68.50	61.62- 00
*	Danvers	Natasha	GBR	19.9.77	175/58	400H	54.94	54.95- 00
	Davis	Kia	USA	23.5.76		100H	13.20, 13.03w	13.28- 97
	Davis	Kinshasa	USA	10.7.79	178/63	100	11.39	11.59, 11.42w- 00
						200	22.98, 22.79w	22.69- 00
	Davoren	Freda	IRL	16.3.73		1500	4:10.13	4:18.21- 98
*	Davydova	Alla	RUS	21.5.66	167/82	HT	65.81	68.47- 00
	Davydova	Natalya	RUS	.78		JT	55.17	52.04- 00
^	de Bruin	Corrie	NED	26.10.76	180/80	SP	17.82	18.97i, 18.87- 98
						DT	58.66	63.88- 98
	De Francesco	Molly	USA	17.2.80		3kSt	10:12.24	
	de Jong	Marjorlein	NED	12.6.81	184/62	400H	56.87	56.26- 00
	de la Puente	Martina	ESP	4.4.75	180/97	SP	17.42	18.17- 99
	De Leeuw	Sabrina	BEL	19.8.74	182/63	HJ	1.88i, 1.86	1.94i- 94, 1.93- 93
	de Wilt	Monique	NED	21.3.76	170/68	PV	4.35	4.30, 4.35sq- 00
	Debelaya	Tatyana	UKR	28.1.70	174/64	400H	56.74	55.67- 99
	Dedekina	Lyudmila	RUS	5.1.79	165/55	20kW	1:31:28	1:30:52- 99
	Dedkova (Keiko)	Natalya	BLR	2.12.79	162/51	800	2:01.5	2:02.04- 99
	Defar	Meseret	ETH	19.11.83	155/42	3000	8:52.47	8:59.90- 00
						5000	15:08.65	15:08.36- 00
	Dejaeghere	Veerle	BEL	1.8.73	164/52	1500	4:06.13	4:05.77- 00
						2000	5:42.15	
	Delahunty	Sinead	IRL	12.2.71	172/60	1500	4:11.04	4:04.22- 98
	Demart	Chava	USA	5.5.79		400H	57.05	59.06- 98
	Dementiy	Yelena	UKR	6.3.69	180/82	SP	18.00	17.54- 00
	Demus	Lashinda	USA	10.3.83		400H	55.76	57.04- 99
*	Denboba	Merima	ETH	21.8.74	168/48	3000	8:50.42	8:44.21- 99
						5000	15:06.08	15:08.52- 99
						10000	31:57.10	31:32.63- 99
	Denisova	Lyubov	RUS	6.10.71		HMar	71:25	73:49- 99
	Dennehy-Willis	Breeda	IRL	3.2.70	175/53	3000	8:58.90	9:19.5 - 91
						5000	15:15.49	15:12.83- 00
						10000	32:12.47	32:11.30- 00
*	Devers	Gail	USA	19.11.66	160/55	100H	12.53	12.33- 00
	Devetzí	Hrisopiyí	GRE	2.1.76	170/60	TJ	14.00, 14.12w	13.61, 13.66w- 99
	Dharsha	Damayanthi	SRI	13.2.75	168/60	200	22.88	22.48- 98
						400	51.83	51.05- 00
	Di Martino	Antonietta	ITA	1.6.78	169/58	HJ	1.98	1.88- 00
						Hep	5687w	5436- 00
	Dia	Fabé	FRA	14.2.77	173/62	200	23.07, 23.01w	23.02, 22.99w- 99
	Dias	Ana	POR	15.1.74	169/50	5000	15:26.41	15:27.74- 00
						10000	32:20.48	31:39.52- 99
	Díaz	Yudalis	CUB	20.9.79	164/58	400	52.03	51.94- 99
						400H	57.24	
	Dibaba	Ejagayehu	ETH	21.3.82		5000	15:32.31	
						10000	32:24.20	
	Dickerson	Jukina	USA	7.8.81	173/90	HT	62.20	53.94- 00
*	Dietzsch	Franka	GER	22.1.68	183/90	DT	65.87A	69.51- 99
	DiMarco	Karyne	AUS	14.3.78	168/77	HT	64.81	65.38- 00
	Dimitrova	Maria	BUL	7.8.76	170/55	TJ	14.18i, 14.18, 14.24w	14.28- 98
*	Dimitrova	Svetla	BUL	27.1.70	172/59	100H	12.58	12.53, 12.50w- 94, 12.4- 97
	Ding Ying		CHN	28.9.76	178/75	Hep	5837	5992- 94
	Dinu	Alina	ROM	9.2.82		HJ	1.86	1.81- 99
						TJ	13.67w	13.49- 00
	Diop	Aïda	SEN	27.4.70	164/59	100	11.36	11.41A, 11.2 - 99, 11.23Aw- 00
						200	22.91	22.64A, 22.76- 00
	Diouf	Mame Tacko	SEN	17.10.76	169/57	100H	13.22, 13.14w	12.94- 00, 12.8- 99
						400H	56.28	54.75- 99
^	Divós ¶	Katalin	HUN	11.5.74	180/84	HT	70.79	68.98- 00
*	Dixon	Vonette	JAM	26.11.75		100H	12.83	12.90- 00
	Dobrinskaya	Natalya	UKR	29.5.82	180/72	Hep	5742	5322- 00
	Dobrovitskaya	Taisia	BLR	8.12.67	179/62	Hep	5912	6337h- 93
	Dodge	Tonya	USA	24.5.75		3kSt	10:10.83	10:13.83- 00
	Dolcini	Francesca	ITA	28.12.74	162/55	PV	4.25i, 4.10	4.27- 00
	Dolezelová	Hana	CZE	8.4.79	180/59	Hep	5671	5547- 96
*	Domínguez	Marta	ESP	3.11.75	163/52	1500	4:06.92	4:06.08- 00
						3000	8:36.33	8:28.80- 00
						5000	14:58.12	14:59.49- 98
	Donáth	Katalin	HUN	12.11.79	161/50	PV	4.10i	4.30- 00

Name		Nat	Born	Ht/Wt	Event	2001 Mark	Pre-2001 Best
Donders	Mireille	SUI	7.7.74	166/52	100	11.34	11.38- 99
					200	23.08	23.06- 00, 22.96i- 98
* Dong Yanmei		CHN	16.2.77	166/51	1500	4:07.72	3:55.07- 97
					3000	8:41.34i	8:33.07- 00
					5000	14:51.58	14:29.82- 97
					10000	31:43.59	30:38.09- 97
Dorsile	Vivian	FRA	1.6.67	170/60	400H	57.21	58.36- 95
Dotsenko	Tatyana	RUS	24.4.81	171/59	20kW	1:34:50	1:40:41- 99
D'Oyley	Toni Ann	JAM	25.10.81	182/64	100H	13.14, 13.09w	13.29- 00
* Dragila	Stacy	USA	25.3.71	172/62	PV	4.81	4.70- 00
* Drechsler	Heike	GER	16.12.64	180/67	LJ	6.79	7.48- 88, 7.63Aw- 92
Dreher	Claudia	GER	2.5.71	170/53	Mar	2:31:01	2:27:55- 99
Drew	Shelley	GBR	8.8.73	182/81	DT	59.10	60.82- 98
* Drossin	Deean	USA	14.2.73	163/48	3000	8:45.77	8:42.59- 00
					5000	15:08.02	14:51.62- 00
					10000	32:05.14	31:51.05- 00
					HMar	70:08	73:16- 00
					Mar	2:26:58	-0 -
Dryburgh	Jenny	NZL	30.8.78	173/65	PV	4.35	4.10- 00
Dryer	Elva	USA	26.9.71	165/51	1500	4:10.28	4:10.02- 98
					3000	8:46.09	8:58.10- 99
					5000	15:03.56	15:09.19- 00
Du Beibei		CHN	6.1.83		JT	58.16	57.29- 00
du Toit	Maranelle	RSA	31.12.78		SP	16.83	16.87- 00
Du Xianhui		CHN	4.1.81	188/90	SP	17.54	18.23- 99
Dubrova	Marina	UKR	9.12.78	161/50	3000	8:51.65	9:01.9 - 00
Dudgeon	Sinead	GBR	9.7.76	172/56	400	52.47i	52.05- 99
					400H	56.07	55.24- 99
^ Dukhnova	Natalya	BLR	16.7.66	176/60	800	1:59.95	1:57.24- 96
Dukure	Jolanta	LAT	20.9.79	168/52	20kW	1:31:47	1:32:59- 99
* Dulecha	Kutre	ETH	22.8.78	166/48	1500	4:05.75i	3:58.38- 98
					1M	4:23.33i	4:25.73i- 00
^ Dulgheru	Mirela	ROM	5.10.66	175/64	LJ	6.45i	7.14- 92
Duncan	Joanne	GBR	27.12.66	172/82	SP	17.08	16.12- 99
Dunkley	Michelle	GBR	26.1.78	178/62	HJ	1.90	1.93- 00
Duporty	Julia	CUB	9.2.71	171/63	400	52.35	50.61- 94
Duquénoy	Laurence	FRA	29.9.69	160/46	3kSt	9:48.84	9:55.69- 99
Durst	Stephanie	USA	6.1.82		200	23.05w	
Dutoit (Neary	Andrea	USA	28.8.78	178/66	PV	4.20i, 4.20	4.00- 00
Dyomina	Tatyana	BLR	29.9.73		HT	63.40	61.40- 99
* Eagles	Bronwyn	AUS	23.8.80	178/100	HT	70.19	66.55- 00
Edwards	Jackie	BAH	14.4.71	172/64	LJ	6.78, 6.82Aw	6.80- 96, 6.89Aw- 95
					TJ	13.60	13.66- 97
Edwards	Torri	USA	31.1.77	163/52	100	11.11, 11.09w	11.06, 10.92w- 00
					200	23.21, 23.00w	22.65- 00
Efimenko	Tatyana	KGZ	2.1.81	187/70	HJ	1.90	1.95- 99
Ekah	Joan Uduak	NGR	16.12.80	160/55	100	11.37, 11.92w	11.11- 99
Ekk	Oksana	RUS	26.11.74	175/63	100	11.40, 11.34w	11.21- 98, 11.2- 94
					200	23.03, 22.77w	22.69- 00
Ekpo-Umoh	Florence	GER	27.12.77	178/64	400	51.13	51.32- 98
El Kamch	Zhor	MAR	15.3.73	167/52	3000	8:54.52	8:41.96- 00
					5000	15:28.17	15:12.23- 00
* Elísdottír	Thórey Edda	ISL	30.6.77	181/64	PV	4.51i, 4.45	4.37i- 99, 4.30- 00
* Ellerbe	Dawn	USA	3.4.74	186/111	HT	70.62	70.46- 00
Ellis	Dana	CAN	7.12.78		PV	4.10	4.02A- 00
Emmanouií	Dimitra	GRE	13.5.84	171/59	PV	4.08	3.85-00
English	Una	IRL	14.8.70	181/61	3000	8:55.82	8:57.89- 99
					5000	15:19.12	15:26.69- 00
Enkina	Mariya	RUS	.77		200	23.12	
Ennis-London	Delloreen	JAM	5.3.75	180/67	100	11.36w	11.50- 99, 11.43w- 00
					100H	12.57	12.52- 00
Erkesso	Teyeba	ETH	82		HMar	71:15	74:58- 00
* Ertl	Karin	GER	23.6.74	177/65	Hep	6365	6396- 00
Espegren	Lene	NOR	8.5.71	170/53	TJ	13.59, 13.86w	13.83, 13.97w-99
Evans	Nanette	USA	18.8.81	163/48	3kSt	9:59.50	
^ Eve	Laverne	BAH	16.6.65	179/77	JT	60.26	63.73- 00, 64.78#- 89
* Ezeh	Florence	FRA	29.12.77	173/96	HT	66.85	66.12- 99
Falaiye	Alice	CAN	24.12.78		LJ	6.51i, 6.46, 6.52w	6.63A, 6.46- 00
Farfaletti-Casali	Arianna	ITA	22.6.76	158/51	PV	4.20	4.28- 00
^ Farmer-Patrick	Sandra	USA	18.8.62	173/63	400H	56.85	52.79- 93
* Faumuiná	Beatrice	NZL	23.10.74	180/125	DT	61.54	68.52- 97

Name		Nat	Born	Ht/Wt	Event	2001 Mark	Pre-2001 Best
Faustin	Nadine	HAI	14.4.76	160/56	100H	12.93	12.80- 00
* Favor Hamilton	Suzy	USA	8.8.68	160/44	1500	4:00.38	3:57.40- 00
Favre	Silvia	ITA	15.8.80	179/59	LJ	6.45	6.50- 99
Febbraio	Surita	RSA	27.12.73	168/58	100H	13.10	13.35A- 99
					400H	54.10A, 54.48	55.22A, 55.77- 00
* Fedoskina	Natalya	RUS	25.6.80	167/52	20kW	1:26:50	1:27:35- 99
Fedotova	Yekaterina	RUS	4.11.75		800	2:01.75	2:01.68- 00
^ Fedyushina	Valentina	AUT	10.2.65	190/90	SP	17.52	21.08- 88
* Feitor	Susana	POR	28.1.75	160/52	20kW	1:27:55/1:29:36.4t	1:28:19- 00
Felicien	Perdita	CAN	29.8.80	165/57	100H	12.73	12.91- 00
Félix	Aurélie	FRA	26.3.79	180/60	LJ	6.64i, 6.61A, 6,57m 6.72Aw	6.85- 99
Félix	Sylviane	FRA	31.10.77	174/58	200	23.10w	22.56- 97
Feng Lei		CHN	8.4.80		800	2:02.37	2:04.88- 99
Feng Yun		CHN	23.2.76	170/60	100H	12.93, 12.86w	12.85- 99
Fenn	Joanne	GBR	19.10.74	172/55	800	2:02.81	2:04.19- 00
* Fenton	Lorraine	JAM	8.9.73	174/59	200	22.63	22.85- 98
(Graham)					400	49.88	49.58- 00
* Feofanova	Svetlana	RUS	16.7.80	162/52	PV	4.75	4.50- 00
* Ferga	Linda	FRA	24.12.76	169/51	100H	12.67	12.81, 12.77w- 00
* Ferguson	Debbie	BAH	16.1.76	167/59	100	11.04	10.96- 00, 10.91w- 99, 10.9w- 95
					200	22.39	22.19- 99
* Fernández	Adriana	MEX	4.4.71	163/59	HMar	71:26+	74:21- 97
					Mar	2:26:22	2:24:06- 99
Fernández	Nuria	ESP	16.8.76	168/58	800	2:01.33	2:01.38- 00
					1500	4:06.96	4:06.37- 00
Ferrales	Yania	CUB	28.7.77	180/86	DT	56.90	57.40- 00
Ferrara	Ornella	ITA	17.4.68	153/40	Mar	2:29:33	2:28:01- 97
Ferrari	Sara	ITA	30.9.77	157/41	Mar	2:29:46	2:31:48- 00
* Fiacconi	Franca	ITA	4.10.65	173/56	Mar	2:26:49	2:25:17- 98
Fischer	Sabine	SUI	29.6.73	174/58	1500	4:05.60	4:05.14- 00
Fitchen	Kim	USA	3.9.68		10000	32:14.64	32:16.95- 00
Fiut	Dorota	POL	10.12.76	170/54	800	2:02.55	2:00.99- 97
Florido	Rocío	ESP	16.1.76	163/56	20kW	1:34:10	1:35:26- 00
* Flosadóttir	Vala	ISL	16.2.78	181/70	PV	4.22	4.50- 00
Fokina	Natalya	UKR	7.7.82	176/80	DT	59.88	51.44- 00
Folz	Jenny	USA	24.12.75		SP	16.57	17.52- 00
					HT	62.60	64.22- 00
^ Fonseca-Wollheim	Kristina da	GER	10.2.72	180/56	1500	4:06.71	4:01.42- 98
Forrester	Amanda	GBR	29.9.78	165/51	100	11.37	11.55- 00
Forrester	Nicole	CAN	17.11.76	191/73	HJ	1.94	1.93i- 99, 1.91- 98
Foster	Angela	USA	27.12.79	165/79	HT	63.16	57.52- 00
* Foster	Bridgette	JAM	7.11.74	170/62	100H	12.70	12.70- 00
Fouquet	Virginie	FRA	9.9.75	162/48	800	2:01.61	2:01.08- 98, 2:00.20mx- 97
Frary	Aja	USA	1.7.78	170/58	Hep	5751	5596A- 00
* Fraser	Donna	GBR	7.11.72	181/70	400	51.77	49.79- 00
* Frazer	Merlene	JAM	27.12.73	174/62	200	22.99	22.18- 99
* Freeman	Michelle	JAM	5.5.69	170/63	100H	12.89	12.52, 12.40w- 97
Freisen	Maren	GER	15.2.82	173/60	Hep	6056	5909- 99
Friedrich	Dörthe	GER	21.6.73	174/68	JT	60.89	65.25#- 98, 60.30- 99
Friedrich	Kathleen	GER	13.7.77	174/57	800	2:02.64	2:02.52- 98, 2:02.18I- 99
					1500	4:04.27	4:05.94- 00
Frunza	Alina	ROM	17.4.79	182/100	SP	17.56i, 16.64	17.31- 99
* Fuchsová	Helena	CZE	3.6.65	170/58	400	51.99i	50.21- 98
					800	1:59.88, 1:58.37i	1:58.56- 00
Fujikawa	Aki	JPN	14.11.78	158/43	10000	32:15.94	32:14.35- 98
					HMar	70:24	70:22- 98
					Mar	2:28:27	2:27:42- 99
Fujinaga	Yoshiko	JPN	15.8.81	169/50	5000	15:28.32	15:22.68- 99
					10000	31:47.82	31:58.93- 00
					HMar	69:29	
* Fukushi	Kayoko	JPN	25.3.82	161/45	3000	8:52.3	9:14.71- 00
					5000	15:10.23	15:29.70- 00
					10000	31:42.05	
Füredi	Zsuzsanna	HUN	26.9.71	167/60	JT	55.11	54.26- 00. 60.06#- 95
* Fynes	Sevatheda	BAH	17.10.74	165/58	100	11.17	10.91- 99, 10.7w- 95
					200	23.02	22.32- 99
Gachevska	Monika	BUL	30.1.74	176/58	200	23.17	22.93- 98
* Gaines	Chryste	USA	14.9.70	170/57	100	10.98, 10.89w	10.89- 98
					200	23.01w	22.81- 93, 22.53w- 97
Galeotti	Daniele	ITA	22.3.77	183/68	HJ	1.86i, 1.86	1.92- 99
* Galkina	Lyudmila	RUS	20.1.72	172/58	LJ	7.00i, 6.70	7.05- 97, 7.08w- 99

Name		Nat	Born	Ht/Wt	Event	2001 Mark	Pre-2001 Best
Gamanyuk	Lyudmila	UKR	11.10.77	172/69	JT	54.56	56.19- 99
Gamble	Nicole	USA	21.6.77	163/55	TJ	13.83i	14.05i, 14.08w- 99, 13.96- 00
Ganapathy	G. Pramila	IND	8.5.77	167/57	Hep	5825	6105- 00
* Gao Hongmiao		CHN	17.3.74	162/51	20kW	1:28:45	1:30:03- 99
Gao Kelian		CHN	15.8.83		20kW	1:29:39	1:33:38- 00
* Gao Shuying		CHN	28.10.79	180/63	PV	4.52	4.35- 00
^ García	Alejandra	ARG	13.6.73	172/58	PV	4.30	4.42- 00
Gatto	Laura	ITA	4.3.77	170/58	LJ	6.45	6.48- 99
Gautier	Nicola	GBR	21.3.78	165/71	Hep	5784	5760- 99
Gavrila	Adelina	ROM	26.11.78	175/56	TJ	14.18	14.71- 99
Gay	Mabel	CUB	5.5.83	178/67	TJ	14.05	14.02- 00
Gayle	Peta Gaye	JAM	19.1.79		400H	55.92A, 56.49	55.93- 00
Gebregiorgis	Genet	ETH	5.1.75	160/45	1500	4:08.11	4:08.05- 99
					3000	8:42.39	8:49.48- 99
Geji	Noriko	JPN	31.5.73	169/50	Mar	2:27:01	2:27:41- 00
Gemechu	Shitaye	ETH	80		Mar	2:28:40	
Geng Aihua		CHN	29.6.83		JT	56.08	48.90- 99
Genovese	Bruna	ITA	24.9.76	161/50	Mar	2:25:35	2:31:06- 99
George	Anju	IND	77		LJ	6.74	6.59- 00
(Markose)					TJ	13.61	13.27- 99
George	Samantha	CAN	7.8.76	165/57	400	52.02	51.98- 99
Georgieva	Khristina	BUL	3.1.72	176/74	JT	61.10mx	63.32- 00
Gérance	Fanny	FRA	4.1.81	171/61	100H	13.28w	13.21- 00
Germanyuk	Natalya	BLR	30.3.75	174/63	Hep	5778	5796- 97
Gerryts	Elmarie	RSA	25.8.72	170/62	PV	4.30	4.42- 00
Gertenbach	Marizca	RSA	20.10.82	177/65	HJ	1.90A	1.88- 00
Gevaert	Kim	BEL	5.8.78	170/60	100	11.26	11.17- 99
					200	22.94	23.03- 99
Gherasim (Tecuta)	Alina	ROM	10.11.71	166/46	Mar	2:29:16	2:28:17- 00
Ghosh	Shanta	GER	3.1.75	168/53	400	51.25	51.74- 00
Gilardoni	Elena	ITA	20.5.75	171/58	TJ	13.82, 13.91w	13.36- 00
Gillies-Scott	Colleen	JAM	18.8.74	183/64	TJ	13.64w	13.83- 98
Gilmore	Nicole	CAN	24.8.73	179/68	LJ	6.47Aw	6.66- 96
Gîndila	Mihaela	ROM	29.10.74	178/62	Hep	5737	5342- 00
Ginko	Yelena	BLR	30.7.76	165/53	20kW	1:33:21	1:29:47- 00
* Girard	Patricia	FRA	8.4.68	162/48	100	11.38w	11.11- 94
					100H	12.82, 12.62irr, 12.77w	12.59- 96
Glenn	Brianna	USA	18.4.80	168/55	100	11.39, 11.15w	11.33, 11.24w- 00
					200	23.26, 22.92w	23.64, 22.97w- 00
					LJ	6.56i, 6.48, 6.56w	6.65A, 6.47- 00
Gliznutza	Inna	MDA	18.4.73	184/65	HJ	1.92	1.95- 99
* Glover	Sandra	USA	30.12.68	173/59	400H	54.30	53.33- 00
Gnedzilov	Svetlana	ISR	20.7.69	170/58	100H	13.04	13.09- 00
					Hep	5736	5632- 00
Gogîrlea	Luminita	ROM	5.11.71	160/46	3kSt	9:57.06	9:56.99- 00
Golding	Lacena	JAM	20.3.75	168/57	100H	12.97	12.93- 00
					LJ	6.49, 6.61w	6.87- 98
Gonçalves	Isilda	POR	11.11.69	157/48	20kW	1:35:06	1:37:12- 99
Goncharenko	Olga	BLR	13.7.81		DT	59.06	57.06- 00
* Goncharenko	Svetlana	RUS	28.5.71	176/61	100	11.1	11.13- 98
					200	22.86	22.43i, 22.46, 21.9- 98
Goncharova	Yelena	RUS	.80		100	11.2	
Gong Jian		CHN	16.1.77		SP	17.16	17.23- 00
González	Griselda	ESP	4.12.65	172/57	Mar	2:31:05	2:30:32- 97
González	Misleydis	CUB	19.6.78		SP	17.54	17.50- 00
Goormachtigh	Jacqueline	NED	28.2.70	179/85	DT	58.70	63.86- 98
^ Goossens	Ester	NED	21.2.72	175/65	800	2:02.78, 2:00.01i	1:59.24- 98
					400H	57.32	54.62- 98
Gordeyeva	Tatyana	RUS	3.6.73	180/63	HJ	1.86	1.91- 97
					Hep	6092	6336- 00
* Gorelova	Natalya	RUS	18.4.73	173/56	800	1:58.7	1:57.90- 99
					1000	2:34.25	
					1500	3:59.70	4:01.50- 00
Goto	Ikuyo	JPN	6.1.69	160/47	Mar	2:27:16	2:26:37- 96
Goto	Yukako	JPN	16.9.73	160/47	10000	32:03.26	32:54.76- 99
					HMar	69:47	71:06- 00
* Gotovska	Valentina	LAT	3.9.65	176/62	LJ	6.88	6.91- 00
^ Götz	Monika	GER	15.6.81	178/61	PV	4.20	4.31- 98
* Goulbourne	Elva	JAM	21.1.80	170/50	100	11.33	11.30- 01
					LJ	6.86, 6.90w	6.74, 6.79w- 00
* Govorova	Yelena	UKR	18.9.73	175/63	TJ	14.33, 14.48w	14.96- 00, 14.99w- 99

Name		Nat	Born	Ht/Wt	Event	2001 Mark	Pre-2001 Best
* Graf	Stephanie	AUT	26.4.73	170/60	800	1:57.20	1:56.64- 00
Graham	Nolle	JAM	12.9.81	167/59	LJ	6.63, 6.67w	6.53- 00
Grant	Bisa	USA	16.7.76	166/61	100H	13.26, 12.96w	13.04, 12.95w- 00
Grant	Stacy Ann	USA	18.8.77	180/62	HJ	1.88	1.86i, 1.85-98
* Grasu	Nicoleta	ROM	11.9.71	176/88	DT	68.31	68.80- 99
^ Graudyn	Yuliya	RUS	13.11.70	171/60	100H	13.19, 13.14w	12.62, 12.51Aw- 94
Grechikho	Margarita	BLR	15.4.81		HT	63.89	58.28- 00
Green	Rebekah	USA	19.9.80	175/86	SP	17.07	15.37- 99
Green	Tiffany	USA	15.12.81	170/57	100	11.30w	11.62- 00
					200	22.98w	23.78- 00
Griebel	Lisa	USA	8.3.79	172/80	SP	16.65	16.41- 99, 16.46i- 00
Griffin	Maureen	USA	6.10.80	176/88	HT	64.37	63.66- 00
* Grigorieva	Tatiana	AUS	8.10.75	180/65	PV	4.56	4.55- 00
Grigoryeva	Tatyana	RUS	13.5.81		HJ	1.88i, 1.86	1.86- 00
Grin (Savitskaya)	Marina	BLR	23.1.76	182/79	HT	66.58	65.11- 00
Grishakova	Marina	RUS	1.7.78		400	52.48	52.78- 00
Gromada	Tatyana	BLR	30.3.81	172/84	HT	65.00	59.75- 00
Grosu	Cristina	ROM	11.11.76	176/58	1500	4:08.84	4:11.11- 98
Grouwels	Nadine	BEL	1.11.73	170/53	100H	13.30	13.30- 00, 13.13w- 99
Grow	Liz	USA	17.10.79	170/60	400	52.40	53.10- 00
Groza	Ana Maria	ROM	1.6.76	167/53	20kW	1:32:12	1:29:59- 00
Grzesiak	Joanna	POL	15.8.80	173/56	Hep	5695	4942- 00
Gu Ying		CHN	26.5.80		LJ	6.61	6.63- 98
Gu Yuan		CHN	9.5.82		HT	66.97	64.72- 00
Guan Yingnan		CHN	25.4.77	176/60	LJ	6.77	6.95- 00
* Gubkina	Lyudmila	BLR	13.8.73	174/76	HT	67.97	69.92- 00
* Gudkova	Tatyana	RUS	23.12.78	170/60	20kW	1:30:12	1:25:18- 00
Guerrero	Helena	COL	10.3.76		LJ	6.66Aw	6.18A- 97
* Guevara	Ana	MEX	4.3.77	170/60	400	49.97	49.96, 49.70A- 00
^ Guida	Maria	ITA	23.1.66	160/49	Mar	2:30:42	2:25:57- 99
Guillén	Nancy	ESA	14.10.76	168/70	HT	62.43	62.16- 00
* Gulyayeva	Yelena	RUS	14.8.67	182/64	HJ	1.95	2.01- 98
Gulyevich	Tatyana	BLR	10.2.71	187/66	HJ	1.92	1.92- 95
Güner	Nora	TUR	1.6.77	174/59	100	11.25, 10.98w	11.23- 98
					200	23.27, 23.08i, 22.86w	22.72- 96
Guo Chunfang		CHN	4.1.79	174/65	LJ	6.62w	6.82- 00
Guo Dongmei		CHN	5.2.83		20kW	1:30:31	1:35:31- 00
Guo Lingling		CHN	18.6.86		5000	15:08.42	
Gureyeva	Zhanna	BLR	10.6.70	178/54	TJ	13.70	14.35- 97, 14.41w- 95
Gurova	Viktoriya	RUS	22.5.82		TJ	13.75, 13.92w	13.44- 00
Gurtovenko	Yulia	UKR	8.12.80	170/54	800	2:01.97	2:02.18- 00
* Györffy	Dóra	HUN	23.2.78	176/58	HJ	2.00	1.97i, 1.95- 00
Ha Mingming		CHN	15.4.82		20kW	1:33:02	1:36:22- 00
Ha Xiaoyan		CHN	30.1.72	176/73	JT	59.76	59.73- 99, 65.44#- 93
Habel	Katchi	GER	22.10.82	174/65	100	11.41, 11.24w	11.39- 00
Hajdu	Markéta	CZE	9.9.74	178/90	HT	65.91	61.80- 00
Hajnal	Mária	HUN	5.3.79		HT	61.96	55.48- 00
Halkoaho	Joanna	FIN	13.1.77	165/55	LJ	6.53	6.79- 98
Ham Bong-sil		PRK	8.7.74	155/44	Mar	2:29:44	2:27:07- 00
* Hamácková	Pavla	CZE	20.5.78	170/68	PV	4.56i, 4.47	4.45- 00
Han Min		CHN	8.7.83		20kW	1:30:56	1:33:27- 00
Hanaoka	Maho	JPN	3.8.76	171/60	LJ	6.82	6.61- 00
Haneef	Tayibba	USA	23.3.79		HJ	1.88	1.86- 00
* Hansen	Ashia	GBR	5.12.71	170/63	TJ	14.51	15.16i- 98, 15.15- 97
Hara	Yumiko	JPN	9.1.82	163/43	10000	31:48.50	33:13.99- 99
					HMar	70:46	
Harper	Camille	USA	11.12.79	163/50	100	11.38w	11.63, 11.48w- 99
Harrelson	Mary Jayne	USA	17.6.78	170/54	1500	4:07.37	4:08.76- 00
Harrison	Yvonne	PUR	2.12.75	178/64	400H	55.63	55.09- 00
Hart	Bethany	USA	10.4.77	173/68	HT	63.93	63.09- 00
Hashimoto	Yasuko	JPN	12.8.75	162/49	5000	15:28.94	15:37.83- 00
					10000	32:14.39	32:12.56- 00
					HMar	68:55	72:01- 00
Hastick	Michelle	CAN	16.9.73	173/57	TJ	13.77, 13.82w	13.64- 97, 14.13w- 98
Haugen (Halle)	Gunhild	NOR	1.6.72	165/48	5000	15:17.43	15:09.00- 96
					10000	32:33.72	31:47.89- 00
Haughton	Karlene	CAN	18.10.72	165/57	400H	55.68	55.11- 97
^ Hautala	Tiia	FIN	3.4.72	171/66	Hep	6002	6369- 99
Hayakari	Minori	JPN	29.11.72	163/46	5000	15:33.66	15:55.3- 98
Haynes	Nicole	CAN	18.9.74	180/75	Hep	6002	6077- 00
Haywood	Betty-Ann	JAM	7.10.80		100	11.28w	11.59- 00

	Name		Nat	Born	Ht/Wt	Event	2001 Mark	Pre-2001 Best
	He Linlin		CHN	24.1.80		400H	57.48	
	Heaston	Kristin	USA	23.11.75	180/127	SP	17.17	16.95- 98
	Heath	Mandy	AUS	14.11.80		Hep	5877	5370- 00
	Hejnová	Michaela	CZE	10.4.80	167/62	Hep	6026w, 5958	6015- 00
	Hellebaut	Tia	BEL	16.2.78	182/66	HJ	1.89i, 1.87	1.89- 00
						Hep	5859	5646- 00
*	Hemmings	Deon	JAM	9.10.68	176/62	400H	54.47	52.82- 96
	Henderson	Monique	USA	18.2.83	170/54	200	23.16, 23.09w	23.19, 23.16w- 00
						400	51.34	50.74- 00
*	Hennagan	Monique	USA	26.5.76	173/55	200	23.23	23.50- 97
						400	50.98	50.82- 00
	Henning	Mari-Louise	RSA	19.2.77	172/51	800	2:02.43	2:01.64- 98
	Henriques	Inês	POR	1.5.80	156/48	20kW	1:34:49	1:37:12- 99
	Hentschke	Nadine	GER	27.1.82	176/63	100H	13.25	13.33, 13.27w- 00
	Herschmann	Nicole	GER	27.10.75	179/68	LJ	6.46i	6.29- 00
						TJ	14.09	13.91- 00
	Herzenberg	Elena	GER	24.6.79	185/64	HJ	1.94i, 1.88	1.88- 99
	Hessler	Stephanie	GER	16.3.83		JT	54.92	54.00- 00
*	Hewitt	Lauren	AUS	25.11.78	170/60	100	11.31	11.28- 99, 11.18w- 00
						200	22.90	22.52- 00
	Hicks	Jimyria	USA	10.8.80	173/60	200	23.27, 23.13w	23.97- 00
	Hietalahti	Anita	FIN	17.2.77	177/70	DT	55.99	56.25- 00
	Hila	Elena	ROM	20.5.74	180/98	SP	18.59	18.73i, 18.35- 99
	Hill	Aretha	USA	14.8.76	181/98	DT	61.64	65.62- 98
	Hils	Kerry	USA	21.3.81		3kSt	10:08.61	
	Hingst	Carolin	GER	18.9.80	174/60	PV	4.50	4.01- 00
	Hiroyama	Harumi	JPN	2.9.68	160/47	5000	15:29.73	15:03.67- 98
						10000	31:39.80	31:22.72- 97
						HMar	69:41	70:49- 00
						Mar	2:29:01	2:22:56- 00
	Hirpassa	Birhane	ETH	30.7.83		1500	4:07.44	4:10.73- 00
	Hoernig	Erica	USA	19.10.78	175/65	PV	4.10	4.14- 00
	Holinski	Kathryn	GER	19.7.82	178/61	HJ	1.92	1.86i- 00, 1.80- 99
	Holliday	Becky	USA	12.3.80		PV	4.37	3.73- 98
	Hollman	Julie	GBR	16.2.77	180/69	Hep	5933	5816w- 98, 5685- 00
*	Holmes	Kelly	GBR	19.4.70	164/55	800	1:57.88	1:56.21- 95
	Honey	Jacqueline	CAN	25.6.75	175/64	PV	4.15Ai, 4.12A	4.05Ai, 4.00- 00
	Hooker	Mashevet	USA	25.9.84		LJ	6.50w	6.17- 00
	Hoppová	Renata	CZE	11.6.76	171/58	1500	4:09.75	4:14.37- 00
	Hotokourídou	María	GRE	22.5.77		HJ	1.89	1.85- 00
	Hou Hongjuan		CHN	5.8.76		20kW	1:33:09	1:42:41- 00
	Howard	Donna	USA	28.8.74	163/56	400	52.31	52.22- 96
	Howe	Kym	AUS	12.6.80	176/63	PV	4.30	4.20- 00
	Howell	Charmaine	JAM	13.3.75	170/60	400	52.03	51.94- 99
						800	1:59.61	2:00.63- 00
	Hoxie	Nicole	USA	22.7.79		100H	13.00	12.97, 12.83w- 00
	Hrdlicková	Miriam	SVK	4.1.76		400H	57.44	57.26- 00
	Hu Guangkun		CHN	4.8.76		20kW	1:31:55	1:36:56- 96
	Hu Honglian		CHN	20.2.73		DT	56.89	62.22- 97
	Hu Ming		CHN	8.10.84		20kW	1:34:25	1:40:55- 00
	Hu Yaoyao		CHN	16.4.83		LJ	6.61	6.21- 00
	Huang Mei		CHN	15.4.75		200	23.04	23.19- 98
	Huang Qiuyan		CHN	25.1.80		TJ	14.72	14.57- 97
	Huang Xiaoxiao		CHN	15.2.85	171/51	400H	55.15	
	Hudson	Sheila	USA	30.6.67	165/50	TJ	13.90A, 13.69, 13.80w	14.41- 96, 14.66w- 95
	Huhtaniemi	Paula	FIN	17.2.73	168/67	JT	63.05	61.01- 00
*	Humbert	Nicole	GER	5.2.72	168/53	PV	4.51	4.56i- 99, 4.50- 00
	Hurd	Tiombé	USA	17.8.73	178/64	TJ	14.19i, 14.07	14.06i- 00, 14.00- 99
*	Hurtis	Muriel	FRA	25.3.79	180/68	200	23.06i, 23.14w	22.31- 99
	Hussein	Maroua Ahmed	EGY	19.6.78		HT	63.28	58.97- 99
	Hyman	Mardrea	JAM	22.12.72	168/52	800	2:00.19	1:59.71- 98
						1500	4:05.25	4:09.83- 00
*	Iagar	Elena	ROM	16.1.75	173/54	1500	4:09.25	4:04.27- 99
						3000	8:59.99i	
*	Iagar	Monica	ROM	2.4.73	186/68	HJ	1.97i, 1.92	2.03i- 99, 2.02- 98
	Iakovídou	Thália	GRE	10.9.72	171/56	PV	4.20	4.22- 00
	Iakóvou	Hrystosomía	GRE	9.4.71	170/52	5000	15:20.46	15:25.16- 00
						10000	32:31.46	32:34.87- 97
	Iancu	Constanta	ROM	12.9.76	179/82	JT	56.20	56.69- 00
	Ichikawa	Mayumi	JPN	3.5.76	154/40	Mar	2:27:22	2:27:57- 99

Name		Nat	Born	Ht/Wt	Event	2001 Mark	Pre-2001 Best
Ichikawa	Yoshiko	JPN	18.4.76	162/46	5000	15:30.15	15:20.53- 97
					Mar	2:29:18	2:29:29- 98
Ignatova	Natalya	RUS	28.12.73	168/59	100	11.26	11.12, 11.08w- 00, 11.0- 98
Ikeda	Kumiko	JPN	10.1.81	167/55	LJ	6.78	6.43- 00
Ilyina	Anastasiya	RUS	16.1.82	172/57	LJ	6.58i, 6.51w	6.51- 00
					TJ	14.19	14.52- 00
Ilyina	Irina	RUS	76		Hep	5642	5689- 00
Ilyushkina	Oksana	UKR	25.5.74	169/55	800	2:02.59	2:02.20- 99
Imai	Miki	JPN	30.5.75	174/54	HJ	1.96	1.94- 98
* Ingberg	Mikaela	FIN	29.7.74	174/75	JT	63.13	67.32#- 97, 64.03- 00
Ionescu	Lacramioara	ROM	3.4.79	180/85	DT	60.75	60.40- 00
Ionescu	Simona	ROM	24.8.73	170/60	800	2:02.74	2:02.08- 00
					1500	4:11.95	4:09.60- 97
Ireland	Nicole	USA	23.4.82	178/66	400H	57.43	
Isaila	Claudia	ROM	17.7.73	167/62	JT	59.10	66.56#- 94, 57.16- 00
Isakova	Yevgeniya	RUS	78		400H	56.55	60.46- 97
Isar	Elena	ROM	7.12.71	165/54	20kW	1:32:36	1:32:19- 00
* Isinbayeva	Yelena	RUS	3.6.82	174/65	PV	4.47i, 4.46	4.45i, 4.40- 00
Isworth	Bridgid	AUS	15.10.81		PV	4.12	4.25- 00
Itanyi	Patience	NGR	2.7.73	170/57	Hep	5710	5730- 00
^ Ivakina	Yekaterina	RUS	4.12.64	168/67	JT	64.54	65.36#- 93, 64.89- 00
Ivanenko	Yelena	BLR	5.5.78	180/90	SP	17.22	19.13- 99
^ Ivanova	Alina	RUS	16.3.69	163/52	Mar	2:25:34	2:27:42- 00
Ivanova	Anastasiya	RUS	3.5.79		PV	4.30	4.10- 00
* Ivanova	Olimpiada	RUS	5.5.70	168/54	20kW	1:24:50/1:26:53.2t	1:26:08- 00
Ivanova	Valentina	RUS	1.5.63	178/90	DT	65.12A	63.68- 00
Ivanova	Yelena	RUS	16.3.79		TJ	13.89i	13.75- 00
Ivleva	Inna	RUS	71		LJ	6.71i, 6.52, 6.59w	6.44i, 6.43- 00
Iwakiri	Maiko	JPN	6.5.78	171/52	HJ	1.86	1.81- 95
Iwamoto	Yasuyo	JPN	8.9.76	155/50	10000	31:50.97	33:55.28- 98
					HMar	70:06	
Jackson	Carolyn	USA	6.12.77	168/60	400	52.46	52.10- 99
Jackson	Elizabeth	USA	27.10.77	170/59	3kSt	9:41.94	9:57.20- 00
Jacob	Doris	NGR	16.12.81	155/55	400	51.93	51.04- 99
* Jacobs	Regina	USA	28.8.63	168/51	800	1:59.07	1:58.08- 00
					1500	4:04.85	4:00.35- 99
					3000	8:43.38i	8:39.14i- 99. 8:39.56- 98
					5000	15:10.78	14:45.35- 00
James	Vernicha	GBR	6.6.84	175/57	200	22.93	23.59- 00, 23.48w- 99
Jamieson	Jane	AUS	23.6.75	171/58	Hep	6070	6354- 98
Jarosz	Elzbieta	POL	14.8.71	164/50	Mar	2:30:15	2:31:58- 98
Jarrett	Tanya	JAM	18.9.77	169/54	400H	57.24	55.55- 00
Javornik	Helena	SLO	26.3.66	163/50	1500	4:10.06, 4:06.22i	4:06.77- 00
					3000	8:53.38, 8:48.57i	8:50.71- 00
					5000	15:23.45	15:15.40- 99
^ Jayasinghe	Susanthika	SRI	17.12.75	170/62	100	11.37	11.04- 00
					200	22.63	22.28- 00
Jekabsone	Lana	LAT	16.10.74	175/60	400H	56.24	55.46- 96
Jelagat	Anne	KEN	4.6.69		HMar	70:30	
* Jenkins	LaTasha	USA	19.12.77	170/55	100	11.02	11.08- 99
					200	22.39	22.29, 22.22w- 99
Jensen	Heidi	DEN	14.8.66	173/56	800	2:02.50	2:01.12- 99
					1500	4:09.80	4:08.32- 00
Jett	Kisha	USA	11.2.75	168/56	100H	13.03	14.34- 00
* Jevtic	Olivera	YUG	24.7.77	174/52	5000	15:26.84	15:11.25- 00
					10000	31:33.08	31:29.65- 00
					HMar	69:34	70:02- 98
Jia Lina		CHN	26.4.80		SP	18.41	17.87- 00
Jian Xingli		CHN	4.12.83		20kW	1:29:31	
Jiang Kun		CHN	18.5.85	160/52	20kW	1:30:52	
Jiang Ping		CHN	10.1.79		SP	18.59	18.35- 00
Jiang Qiuyan		CHN	5.7.83		20kW	1:30:13	1:33:28- 00
Jin Li		CHN	29.5.83		Mar	2:25:48	- 0-
Jing Xuezhu		CHN	20.4.75		HJ	1.90	1.90- 97
Jo Bun-hui		PRK	80		Mar	2:30:46	2:38:50- 00
Johansson	Camilla	SWE	3.11.76	166/52	TJ	14.05, 14.17w	14.14- 00
* Johansson	Erica	SWE	5.2.74	178/69	LJ	6.87	6.99, 7.07Aw- 00
John	Lwiza Msyani	TAN	18.5.80	156/48	800	2:00.29	1:59.58- 00
Johnson	Jade	GBR	7.6.80	185/72	LJ	6.59, 6.68w	6.58- 00
^ Johnson	Michelle	USA	12.4.74	170/61	400H	55.87	54.15- 99
Johnson	Sheena	USA	1.10.82		400H	56.02	56.82- 00

	Name		Nat	Born	Ht/Wt	Event	2001 Mark	Pre-2001 Best
	Jones	Lolo	USA	5.8.82		100H	13.31, 13.17w, 12.7w	14.04- 00
*	Jones	Marion	USA	12.10.75	178/64	100	10.84	10.65A- 98, 10.70- 99
						200	22.23	21.62A- 98, 21.76- 97
	Jones	Shakedia	USA	15.3.79	163/53	100	11.13, 11.10w	11.11- 98
	Jones	Susan	GBR	8.6.78	179/62	HJ	1.95	1.93- 00
	Jones	Teneeshia	USA	28.1.79	163/54	100	11.31, 11.23w	11.24- 00
						200	23.05, 22.83w	23.14- 00
						100H	13.27	13.46- 99
	Jong Yong-ok		PRK	24.1.81	155/43	Mar	2:28:20	2:31:40- 00
^	Jongmans	Stella	NED	17.5.71	174/59	800	2:02.19	1:58.61- 92
	Joseph	Restituta	TAN	30.7.71	164/56	1500	4:10.01	
						3000	8:44.28	9:03.96- 00
						5000	15:05.33	15:20.59- 99
						10000	31:38.18	31:32.02- 99
						HMar	68:33	67:59- 00
	Joy	Rachel	USA	29.4.78	155/	100H	13.25Aw	13.47- 98, 13.26w- 00
	Joyce	Jennifer	CAN	25.9.80	178/	HT	62.63	62.86- 00
	Ju Limei		CHN	9.6.78		5000	15:19.08	
						10000	32:14.14	33:02.74- 00
						Mar	2:30:22	2:34:33- 00
	Juhász	Fanni	HUN	31.3.81	169/58	PV	4.15	4.11- 99
	Juma	Taussi	TAN	1.6.83		HMar	71:29	
	Jury	Kerry	GBR	19.11.68	178/67	Hep	5687	6005w- 98, 5908- 99
	Kafetzí	Ioánna	GRE	30.5.76		TJ	14.01	13.65- 00
	Kähler	Birgit	GER	14.8.70	182/60	HJ	1.86i	1.94- 91
	Kai	Tomoko	JPN	5.11.76	156/36	HMar	71:20	73:20- 97
						Mar	2:29:19	2:28:13- 98
	Kakhova	Galina	BLR	26.3.82	167/62	JT	59.48	56.52- 00
*	Kaliturina	Olga	RUS	9.3.76	180/57	HJ	1.96	1.96- 97
	Kallur	Jenny	SWE	16.2.81	170/60	100H	13.15, 13.11w	13.18- 00
*	Kallur	Susanna	SWE	16.2.81	170/60	100H	12.74	13.02- 00
	Kalmer	René	RSA	3.11.80	167/55	1500	4:08.94	4:09.56- 98
*	Kaltouma	Nadjina	CHA	16.11.76	171/60	200	22.97	23.10- 97
						400	50.38	51.90- 99
	Kampf	Stephanie	GER	25.4.78		400H	55.86	57.49- 00
	Kanatova ¶	Svetlana	RUS	10.9.70		800	2:01.89	2:02.53- 99
						1500	4:09.04, 4:08.37dq	4:06.19- 00
	Kanazawa	Yvonne	JPN	19.11.74	173/63	100H	13.19	13.00, 12.90Aw- 00
	Kankanpää	Tiina	FIN	16.8.76	178/80	DT	57.99	61.04- 99
	Kano	Yuri	JPN	27.10.78	151/37	10000	32:25.68	32:32.77- 00
	Kapachinskaya	Anastasiya	RUS	21.11.79		200	23.24i, 22.6	23.66- 00
						400	50.97	53.32- 00
	Käppi	Salla	FIN	22.5.80	176/64	Hep	5801w, 5788	5699- 00
	Kappler	Bianca	GER	8.8.77	179/62	LJ	6.50	6.55- 00
	Karas	Olga	RUS	9.7.82	174/66	Hep	5745	5584- 00
	Kari	Monia	TUN	14.4.71	172/72	DT	56.44	61.74- 96
	Kashcheyeva	Yelena	KAZ	17.2.73	175/58	LJ	6.61i, 6.58	6.76- 98
	Katafuchi	Kyoko	JPN	12.3.80	148/39	10000	32:22.74	33:15.19- 00
						HMar	70:58	72:54- 00
	Kaur	Hardeep	IND	.79		HT	61.56	58.95- 00
	Kaur	Harwant	IND	5.7.80		DT	57.93	56.55- 00
*	Kavaklioglu	Ebru	TUR	14.3.70	167/58	1500	4:12.03	4:08.45- 99
						3000	8:35.26	8:38.98- 99
						5000	15:02.62	14:51.69- 00
	Kawashima	Akiko	JPN	5.8.77	157/41	5000	15:22.70	15:23.65- 98
	Kawashima	Makiko	JPN	5.8.77	159/43	10000	32:02.16	32:42.27- 00
	Kayukova	Natalya	RUS	10.12.66	175/66	TJ	14.12	14.51- 99
	Kazanina	Svetlana	KAZ	31.10.71	172/62	Hep	6159	6228- 99
	Keil	Susanne	GER	18.5.78	172/59	HT	68.07	64.50- 98
	Keir	Krista	USA	19.12.79	178/109	DT	56.98	55.44- 97
*	Kelesídou	Anastasía	GRE	28.11.72	192/90	DT	65.52	67.70- 99
	Keller	Katja	GER	9.8.80	175/62	Hep	6082	5598- 99
	Kelo	Niina	FIN	26.3.80	179/67	Hep	5687	5728- 00
	Kenah	Cheri	USA	26.12.70	173/57	1500	4:11.86	4:09.33- 99
						1M	4:31.10	4:30.75- 97
						3000	8:53.70	8:42.68- 99
						5000	15:30.42	15:10.50- 00
	Kerubo	Margaret	KEN	15.5.74		HMar	71:06	71:22- 00
						3kSt	10:05.15	
	Kesselschläger	Sonja	GER	20.1.78	178/66	Hep	6064w, 6053	6039- 00

Name		Nat	Born	Ht/Wt	Event	2001 Mark	Pre-2001 Best
Khabarova	Irina	RUS	18.3.66	170/62	100	11.32	11.32, 11.19w- 00
					200	22.83	22.76- 00
Khanafeyeva	Gulya	RUS	12.6.82		HT	63.26	57.20- 00
Khawpeag	Supavadee	THA	17.7.76		100	11.33	11,65, 11.62w- 98
Khlusovich	Yelena	UKR	2.12.69	186/70	TJ	13.82	14.38- 96
Khmeleva	Tatyana	RUS	2.4.79		3000	8:52.95	9:42.95i- 98
Khoroneko	Nataly	BLR	25.5.82	180/81	SP	17.25	16.58- 00
Khrushchelyova	Natalya	RUS	20.3.73	172/55	400	52.06	51.49- 00
Khudoroshkina	Irina	RUS	13.10.68	182/100	SP	18.67	20.32- 96
* Kidane	Werknesh	ETH	21.11.81	158/42	3000	8:46.56i	8:44.14- 00
					5000	15:29.96	14:47.40- 00
					10000	31:43.41	
Kihana	Sugar	KEN			2000	5:42.14	
Kiintonen	Kaisa	FIN	18.3.80	167/72	HT	62.99	61.50- 00
Kilincer	Candeger	TUR	16.7.80	182/63	HJ	1.92	1.79- 00
Kilpeläinen	Natalia	FIN	19.7.70	168/57	LJ	6.46, 6.50w	6.44- 94
					TJ	13.88	14.10- 94
^ Kimaiyo-Koskei	Hellen	KEN	8.9.68	163/50	HMar	69:45	69:13- 95
Kinard	Vanitta	USA	26.7.75	178/58	TJ	13.66w	13.76- 97, 13.82w- 00
Kinet (Atroshchenko)	Anzhela	TUR	14.11.70	178/65	Hep	5833	6339- 93
^ Kiplagat	Esther	KEN	8.12.66	168/50	Mar	2:26:15	2:30:30- 00
* Kiplagat	Lornah	KEN	20.3.74	161/47	5000	15:08.07	15:06.40- 99
					HMar	66:34	66:56- 00
					Mar	2:27:56	2:22:36- 00
Kiplimo	Judy	KEN	68		HMar	69:46	72:01- 00
Kirilova	Tsvetelina	BUL	14.7.77	173/53	400	51.85	51.63- 99
					800	1:59.63	1:59.77- 98
* Kirkland	Anjanette	USA	24.2.74	172/66	100H	12.42	12.63-00
Kiryanova	Anastasiya	RUS	26.7.82		PV	4.20	3.90- 00
Kislova	Marina	RUS	7.2.78	167/59	100	11.09	11.22- 00
Kitajima	Ryoko	JPN	12.6.76	158/73	10000	32:29.79	33:28.89- 00
					HMar	71:22	72:37- 98
* Klavina	Liga	LAT	27.1.80	180/69	HJ	1.93	1.94- 00
					LJ	6.50	6.33- 00
					Hep	6279	5305- 98
* Kleinert-Schmitt	Nadine	GER	20.10.75	185/93	SP	19.86	19.81- 00
Kleinmann	Larissa	GER	10.9.78		3kSt	10:01.52	-0-
Klimina	Viktoriya	RUS	1.3.76		HMar	70:46	73:43- 99
Klopova	Olga	UKR	19.2.80	172/96	HT	62.83	59.84- 00
Klüft	Carolina	SWE	2.2.83	178/64	Hep	6022	6056- 00
Kluge	Kathleen	GER	17.11.81	170/100	SP	17.06	17.37- 00
Knighten	Amber	USA	28.6.80	180/82	SP	16.64	16.16- 00
Knippel	Anja	GER	19.8.74	166/57	800	2:02.55	-0-
^ Knoroz	Anna	RUS	30.7.70	162/50	400H	56.57	54.11- 94
Kobayashi	Megumi	JPN	4.8.76	156/45	10000	32:22.78	32:27.05- 97
Kobrin	Nadezhda	UKR	21.1.72	165/67	JT	58.84	62.04#- 98, 59.79- 00
Koeman	Lieja	NED	10.3.76	183/95	SP	18.56	18.48- 99
					DT	56.38	58.17- 98
Koide	Masako	JPN	3.1.74	160/49	Mar	2:28:28	2:30:50- 00
* Koivula	Heli	FIN	27.6.75	174/60	TJ	14.28	14.34- 99
Kojima	Yuko	JPN	20.11.73	166/63	JT	54.62	57.79- 99, 58.78#- 95
Kolétsou	María	GRE	14.6.77		DT	59.22	58.72- 99
Koleva	Tania	BUL	8.3.72	178/62	PV	4.43	4.42- 00
* Kolkkala (Uppa)	Taina	FIN	24.10.76	173/75	JT	60.55	66.00#- 95, 64.06- 00
Komasa	Kazuyo	JPN	21.6.79	168/67	JT	55.38	53.67- 00
Komatsu	Yukari	JPN	27.6.74	160/49	HMar	71:09	72:26- 97
					Mar	2:30:30	2:28:48- 98
Komrsková	Lucie	CZE	24.10.77	165/56	LJ	6.51, 6.64w	6.42, 6.55w- 99
Komyagina	Olga	RUS	10.2.74	162/48	800	2:00.84	2:00.64- 99
					1500	4:03.98	4:02.32- 00
					2000	5:39.06+	
					3000	8:50.81	8:42.58- 99
Kondo	Takayo	JPN	17.11.75	160/56	PV	4.10	4.10- 99
* Konstantinova	Tatyana	RUS	18.11.70	178/95	HT	64.32	72.09- 99
Kopaneva	Aleksandra	RUS	80		SP	16.87i	16.86- 00
Korneyeva	Natalya	RUS	77		800	2:01.23	2:07.88- 00
					1500	4:11.57	4:19.45- 00
* Korolchik	Yanina	BLR	26.12.76	187/87	SP	20.61	20.56- 00
Koroteyeva	Mariya	RUS	10.11.81	176/67	100H	13.10	13.36- 00
Korotkova	Tatyana	RUS	24.4.80	166/56	20kW	1:30:51, 1:33:31.6t	1:30:17- 00
Korotkova	Yevdokiya	RUS	28.2.79		20kW	1:34:23	1:39:49- 00

	Name		Nat	Born	Ht/Wt	Event	2001 Mark	Pre-2001 Best
^	Korotya	Irina	RUS	2.9.75	171/64	100H	12.81	12.82, 12.71w- 99
	Korpela	Merja	FIN	15.5.81	170/70	HT	63.51	60.19- 00
	Korsunova	Olga	RUS	.81		100H	13.1	
	Korzeniowska	Sylwia	POL	25.4.80	164/52	20kW	1:32:47	1:34:24- 00
*	Korzhanenko	Irina	RUS	16.5.74	178/85	SP	19.37	21.15i- 99, 20.82- 98
	Korzhova	Marina	KAZ	13.9.82	180/60	HJ	1.86i	1.90- 00
	Kosenkova	Yuliya	RUS	28.3.73	170/58	800	2:00.2	2:00.71- 99
						1500	4:04.20	4:04.28- 00
*	Kotlyarova	Olga	RUS	12.4.76	180/65	400	50.81A, 50.42i, 51.07	49.95- 00
	Kotorida	Takako	JPN	2.4.77	167/49	5000	15:29.64	15:43.60- 99
						10000	31:41.32	32:18.59- 98
						HMar	69:04	70:29- 00
*	Kotova	Tatyana	RUS	11.12.76	182/59	LJ	7.12	7.04, 7.05iu- 00
	Kotu	Meseret	ETH	81		HMar	70:48	76:29- 00
	Kovpotina	Olga	RUS	10.1.68		Mar	2:27:37	2:32:32- 99
	Kozak	Anna	BLR	22.6.74	172/56	400	51.47	50.94- 96
	Kozuka	Ayano	JPN	27.10.77	159/48	10000	32:32.03	32:43.02- 99
	Krakoviak	Irina	LTU	16.11.77	167/53	800	2:01.27	2:01.04- 98
						1500	4:09.36	4:07.99- 00
	Krasaeyan	Juttaporn	THA	13.2.72	175/90	SP	17.38	19.43- 95
	Krasovskaya	Yelena	UKR	17.8.76	176/62	100H	12.87	12.82- 00, 12.8- 97
	Kravchenko	Anzhela	UKR	25.1.71	166/60	100	11.29, 11.20w	11.16- 98, 11.13w- 99
	Kravchenko	Inna	BLR	23.7.81	167/56	800	2:02.81	2:05.43- 99, 2:05.4- 00
	Kreiner	Kim	USA	26.7.77	176/76	JT	57.22	57.06- 00
	Kremer	Andrea	USA	2.7.82		3kSt	10:12.86	
	Krieger	Sabine	GER	4.9.73	180/64	Hep	6052w, 6009	5826- 00
*	Krivelyova	Svetlana	RUS	13.6.69	182/95	SP	20.17	21.06- 92
	Krivobok	Tatyana	UKR	17.1.72	164/52	1500	4:06.31	4:07.57- 99
	Kròl	Katja	GER	5.2.80	185/100	SP	17.00	16.25- 00
	Krueger	Brooke	AUS	9.7.80	180/125	HT	62.64	56.89- 98
	Kruglova	Larisa	RUS	27.10.72	166/63	100	11.37	11.41- 99
	Krzywicki	Tara	GBR	9.3.74	160/52	3kSt	9:52.71	10:08.11- 00
	Ksok	Anna	POL	29.9.83	181/68	HJ	1.91	1.87- 00
	Kubishta	Lesa	USA	19.4.78		PV	4.18	4.37- 00
*	Kuehl	Kristin	USA	30.7.70	183/89	DT	65.27	65.34- 00
	Kuge	Etsuko	JPN	31.1.81	164/50	HMar	71:08	
	Kühnert	Floé	GER	6.3.84		PV	4.20i	4.15- 00
	Kulawansa	Sriyani	SRI	1.3.70	168/57	100H	13.23	12.91- 96
	Kulikova	Yekaterina	RUS	7.11.68	172/59	400	52.40i	51.16- 00
	Kumari Yadav	Sugan	IND	77		DT	56.22	56.72- 00
*	Kumbernuss	Astrid	GER	5.2.70	181/86	SP	19.87	21.22- 95
	Kun	Alice	HUN	7.6.76	169/54	400	51.88	52.00- 00
	Kunitskaya	Natalya	UKR	17.8.72	172/70	HT	66.40	64.86- 00
*	Kuptsova	Marina	RUS	22.12.81	185/68	HJ	1.91i, 1.90	1.96- 00
	Kurochkina	Tatyana	BLR	15.9.67	174/62	400H	56.17	54.39- 88
	Kurosawa	Nami	JPN	26.12.78	161/49	10000	31:56.78	32:57.20- 00
						HMar	70:09	72:51- 00
	Kürti	Éva	HUN	21.7.76	183/82	DT	57.72	55.35- 00
	Kusch	Natalya	UKR	5.3.83	168/56	PV	4.20i, 4.20	4.10i, 4.00- 00
	Kusunoki	Mami	JPN	8.9.75	161/47	HMar	69:34	69:39- 00
	Kutol	Ruth	KEN	16.5.73		HMar	70:51	69:24- 00
						Mar	2:27:54	2:28:16- 00
*	Kuzenkova	Olga	RUS	4.10.70	176/76	HT	73.62	75.68- 00
	Kuznetsova	Anastasiya	RUS	15.3.80		PV	4.10	4.00- 99
	Kuznetsova	Olga	RUS	23.10.67	168/53	800	1:58.94i	1:58.77- 99
						1500	4:04.26i	4:03.18- 00
	Kuznetsova	Yelena	KAZ	4.8.77	164/53	20kW	1:34:29	1:32:23- 00
	Kwambai	Caroline	KEN	9.9.75	148/37	HMar	69:45	71:56- 00
	Kwambai	Irene	KEN	25.10.78		HMar	69:52	71:41- 00
	La Mantia	Simona	ITA	14.4.83	176/64	TJ	13.63w	12.71- 98
	La Montaña	Yanuris	CUB	29.8.75	168/67	JT	56.08	62.57#- 98, 61.24- 00
	Láboura	Amalia	GRE	16.3.68		HT	61.73	62.69- 00
	Ladewig	Jana	GER	16.9.81	169/61	JT	54.72	53.15- 00
	Lafayette	Ssereta	USA	26.6.79	160/	200	23.22w	23.46- 98
	Lah	Barbara	ITA	24.3.72	180/61	TJ	14.01	14.17, 14.18w- 95
	Laláková	Barbora	CZE	2.5.81	176/52	HJ	1.89	1.88- 99
	Lamalle	Adrianna	FRA	27.9.82	170/58	100H	13.23, 12.90w	13.08- 00
	Lamera	Raffaella	ITA	13.4.83	175/56	HJ	1.86i	1.81i- 00, 1.80- 99
*	Lan Lixin		CHN	14.2.79	164/50	1500	4:11.09	3:53.97- 97
	Landre	Francine	FRA	26.7.70	164/50	400	51.21	51.21- 94
*	Langerholc	Brigita	SLO	23.7.76	170/56	800	1:59.86	1:58.51- 00

Name		Nat	Born	Ht/Wt	Event	2001 Mark	Pre-2001 Best
Lanouar	Fatma	TUN	14.3.78	165/52	1500	4:10.33	4:06.91- 00
Lara	Yanelis	CUB	19.8.78	167/56	800	2:01.24	2:01.2- 99
Larraga	M Luisa	ESP	10.12.70	163/48	10000	32:24.17	32:14.99- 99
					Mar	2:30:11	
Larsen	Stine	NOR	5.11.75	157/48	HMar	71:07	70:24- 99
Larson	Margaret	USA	13.9.79		3kSt	10:10.16	
Larsson	Annika	SWE	10.7.70		DT	55.72	57.39- 00
^ Lasovskaya	Inna	RUS	17.12.69	177/67	TJ	13.74i	15.09- 97
Laukhova	Svetlana	RUS	1.2.73	170/62	100H	12.72	12.85- 99
Lawyer	Tracye	USA	28.8.77	178/67	Hep	5767w, 5728	5995w, 5844- 00
Láznicková	Diana	SVK	14.8.74		HJ	1.87	1.83i- 00. 1.81- 99
* Lebedenko	Yelena	RUS	16.1.71	177/63	TJ	14.83i, 14.17	14.74i- 99, 14.41- 98
* Lebedeva	Tatyana	RUS	21.7.76	171/60	LJ	6.71i	6.65- 94
					TJ	15.25	14.94- 99
Lee	Muna	USA	30.10.81	173/50	100	11.17, 11.13w	11.36- 00
					200	23.13, 23.04i, 22.53w	23.83- 00
Lee	Suzette	JAM	6.3.75	181/71	TJ	13.99	14.09- 99, 14.25i- 97
Lee Myung-sun		KOR	12.2.76	168/89	SP	18.79	19.36- 00
Lee Young-sun		KOR	21.2.74	165/65	JT	55.14	63.32#- 92, 57.91- 00
Legatt	Michelle	USA	13.4.82		PV	4.10	3.73- 00
* Leghzaoui	Asmae	MAR	30.8.76	155/40	3000	8:33.87	8:33.85- 00
					5000	14:49.32	14:48.31- 00
					10000	31:16.94	31:59.21- 00
Legnante	Assunta	ITA	14.5.78	183/86	SP	17.79	17.31, 17.84dq- 00
Lehmann	Dana	GER	1.7.79	172/68	JT	54.89	55.42- 99
Leiwesmeier	Inge	GER	17.5.77	183/74	LJ	6.65	6.66- 99
Lendjel	Nevena	CRO	18.7.79	181/62	HJ	1.91	1.91- 99
Lenskiy	Irina	ISR	12.6.71	176/54	100H	13.03	13.05- 00
Leshchova ¶	Yekaterina	RUS	21.4.74	176/68	100	11.25	11.13- 98
					200	22.70	22.47- 97
Lever	Alison	AUS	13.10.72	182/85	DT	63.25	63.73- 00
Levina	Tatyana	RUS	28.2.77	173/60	400	52.30	52.39-00
Levorato	Manuela	ITA	16.3.77	179/65	100	11.14	11.20- 99, 11.16r, 11.13w- 00
					200	22.98	22.60- 99
* Lewis	Denise	GBR	27.8.72	173/64	100H	13.29w	13.13- 00
					LJ	6.46, 6.53w	6.69- 00, 6.77w- 97
Lewis	Gia	USA	1.4.79		DT	57.76	55.52- 00
Lewis	Tamsyn	AUS	20.7.78	168/57	800	2:00.86	1:59.21- 00
Li Fengfeng		CHN	9.1.79		SP	17.65	16.81- 99
Li Helan		CHN	2.1.78		Mar	2:31:05	2:41:21- 00
Li Hong		CHN	1.6.79	158/58	20kW	1:29:43	1:30:35- 99
Li Jiahui		CHN	8.8.79		TJ	14.05	14.23- 97
Li Jing		CHN	19.10.81		20kW	1:34:51	1:46:22- 00
Li Jingnan		CHN	17.2.83		1500	4:12.13	4:04.84- 00
Li Jingxue		CHN	10.2.70	163/57	20kW	1:31:18	1:30:03- 95
Li Lei		CHN	4.5.74	175/74	JT	58.07	66.88#- 98, 57.83- 99
Li Meihua		CHN	26.12.77		10000	32:33.69	-0 -
Li Meiju		CHN	23.1.81	173/85	SP	18.92	17.48- 00
^ Li Meisu		CHN	17.4.59	176/92	SP	18.39	21.76- 88
Li Qiumei		CHN	20.4.74	180/80	DT	61.90	67.50- 94
Li Rui		CHN	22.11.79		400H	57.01	54.93- 97
Li Xiaoxue		CHN	11.1.80		HT	63.90	64.50- 00
^ Li Xuemei		CHN	5.1.77	166/60	100	11.14	10.79- 97
					200	22.75	22.01- 97
Li Yanfeng		CHN	15.5.79	179/76	DT	61.77	63.67- 99
Li Yulian		CHN	17.2.79	166/52	400H	56.13	55.72- 97
Li Yuxin		CHN	4.12.74	163/51	20kW	1:31:48	1:34:02- 00
Liang Lili		CHN	16.11.83	170/75	JT	59.82	61.81#- 98, 60.90- 99
Liang Shuyan		CHN	16.9.77		LJ	6.60	6.70- 00
Líka	Voisávva	GRE	70		JT	58.53	57.61- 00
Limika	Irene	KEN	28.8.79		5000	15:18.05	
					3kSt	9:39.51	
Lin Na		CHN	18.1.80		800	2:00.77	1:58.16- 97
					1500	4:07.06	4:14.47- 00
Linares	Teresa	ESP	29.4.69	157/49	20kW	1:33:27	1:31:55- 00
Lindberg	Åsa	FIN	12.4.79	173/75	JT	55.05	56.36- 00
Linnen	Amy	USA	15.7.82		PV	4.21	3.97- 00
Lishchinskaya	Irina	UKR	15.1.76	163/53	1500	4:05.38	4:18.47- 94
^ Lisovskaya	Natalya	FRA	16.7.62	187/92	SP	17.35i, 17.33	22.63- 87
Liss	Collette	USA	29.4.73		1500	4:09.10	4:11.24- 00
					3000	8:55.51	8:58.47i- 00

	Name		Nat	Born	Ht/Wt	Event	2001 Mark	Pre-2001 Best
*	Liu Hongyu		CHN	11.1.75	164/51	20kW	1:26:35	1:27:30- 95
	Liu Jing ¶		CHN	8.8.77		100H	12.99	12.76- 97
	Liu Jingqing		CHN	18.3.74		JT	57.75	60.30#- 96, 54.87- 00
	Liu Min		CHN	29.11.83		5000	15:24.97	15:58.61- 99
						10000	31:53.78	32:50.92- 00
						Mar	2:23:37	- 0 -
	Liu Shu		CHN	17.6.81		20kW	1:33:59	1:35:43- 00
	Liu Xiaomei		CHN	11.1.72	168/57	100	11.22	10.89- 97
						200	22.87	22.36- 97
	Liu Xiaoping		CHN	4.1.78		1500	4:07.31	4:18.29- 96
	Liu Yanxia		CHN	3.4.81	175/81	DT	59.89	55.94- 99
	Liu Yinghui		CHN	29.6.79	180.70	HT	66.15	65.06- 00
	Livebardon	Agnès	FRA	31.5.80	167/61	PV	4.25	4.07i- 00, 3.90- 99
^	López	Aliuska	CUB	29.8.69	169/53	100H	12.91	12.67- 96
^	López	Isel	CUB	11.7.70	174/76	JT	55.02	66.18#- 90, 61.66- 99
	Lora	Rita	ESP	23.3.73	175/80	DT	57.20	56.92- 98
*	Loroupe	Tegla	KEN	9.5.73	156/48	3000	8:44.52	8:30.95- 00
						5000	15:09.31	14:45.95- 00
						10000	31:50.97	30:32.03- 99
						HMar	68:16	67:12- 96
						Mar	2:26:10	2:20:43- 99
	Loughnane	Olive	IRL	14.1.76	160/49	20kW	1:34:54	1:34:59- 00
^	Love (Russell)	Gillian	JAM	28.9.73	169/57	100H	13.03, 12.89w	12.66- 98
	Lu Jieming		CHN	25.1.83	173/57	HJ	1.87	1.88- 00
	Lu Jingbo		CHN	18.4.73	163/52	Mar	2:28:00	2:30:43- 00
	Luan Zhili		CHN	6.1.73	173/	DT	62.20	64.62- 93
	Lukinskaya	Yuliya	RUS	3.5.76		PV	4.12i, 4.10	4.10- 00
	Lukyanchuk	Olga	UKR	7.12.76	167/59	20kW	1:29:08	1:32:01- 00
	Luzieux	Stéphane	FRA	7.7.82	175/65	TJ	13.65, 13.74w	13.50- 00
*	Lyakhova	Yuliya	RUS	8.7.77	185/60	HJ	1.96i, 1.92	2.00i- 99, 1.99- 97
	Lyakhovich	Tatyana	UKR	20.5.79	171/70	JT	56.30	57.41- 00
	Lynch	Maria	IRL	3.9.78		1500	4:11.84	4:17.68- 00
^	Lysak	Yelena	RUS	19.10.75	175/55	TJ	13.60i	14.32, 14.43w- 94
	Ma Ning		CHN	4.11.83		JT	57.82	52.79- 00
	Ma Shuli		CHN	20.1.78	178/75	DT	62.21	61.23- 98
	Ma Xuejun		CHN	26.3.85	185/90	DT	58.65	52.79- 99
	Macchiut	Margaret	ITA	25.7.74	171/48	100H	13.17	13.21- 99
	MacDonald	Kelly	USA	27.9.78		3kSt	9:55.49	
	Machado	Maíla Paula	BRA	22.1.81	167/62	100H	13.17	13.25- 00
^	Machado	Teresa	POR	22.7.69	170/80	SP	16.81i	17.26i- 98, 17.18- 96
						DT	63.01	65.40- 98
*	Macharia	Faith	KEN	9.2.76	165/55	800	1:58.34	2:01.09- 00
						1000	2:35.39	
	Macus	Meta	SLO	23.3.75	166/58	400H	56.93	56.80- 98
	Maddox	Keri	GBR	4.7.72	172/63	100H	13.24	12.95- 99
						400H	57.18	55.22- 00
	Madejczyk	Barbara	POL	30.9.76	179/78	JT	59.54	55.16#- 98, 55.10- 00
	Madison	Jackie	USA	14.7.79	175/60	100H	13.21w	13.08, 12.93w- 00
	Maduaka	Joice	GBR	30.9.73	172/65	100	11.42, 11.38w	11.24- 99
						200	23.14A, 23.04w	22.83- 99
	Maeda	Asuka	JPN	4.10.78	164/49	10000	32:32.83	33:13.25- 00
	Maffeis	Agnese	ITA	9.3.65	187/84	DT	60.40	63.66- 96
*	Maggi	Maurren	BRA	25.6.76	178/66	100H	12.71	12.86- 99
						LJ	6.94, 6.98w	7.26A- 99, 6.93- 00
						TJ	13.60	
	Makarova	Oksana	RUS	21.7.71	180/80	JT	58.48	68.72#- 96, 64.61- 99
	Maksimova	Olga	RUS	9.8.76	167/58	400	52.44	
*	Malot	Leah	KEN	7.6.72	168/46	3000	8:46.90, 8:44.33i	8:35.74- 99
						5000	14:56.95	14:39.83- 00
						10000	31:41.74	30:57.70- 00
						HMar	69:43	69:46- 00
	Manabe	Yoko	JPN	8.2.79	158/41	10000	32:12.74	33:46.59- 99
	Manabe	Yuko	JPN	8.2.79	158/41	5000	15:29.47	15:30.89- 99
						10000	32:15.42	32:07.58- 00
	Manahan	LaQuinta	USA	27.1.79	160/50	100	11.40, 11.36w	11.46, 11.30w- 00
	Manfrédi	Laurence	FRA	20.5.74	175/92	SP	17.50i, 17.37	18.68, 18.69i- 00
*	Mani	Léonie Myriam	CMR	21.5.77	164/60	100	10.98	11.01- 00
						200	22.54	22.41- 00
*	Manjani	Miréla	GRE	21.12.76	165/60	JT	66.70	67.51- 00
	Manninen	Johanna	FIN	4.4.80	173/60	100	11.33	11.39- 97, 11.33w- 99
						200	22.93	23.00- 99

	Name		Nat	Born	Ht/Wt	Event	2001 Mark	Pre-2001 Best
	Manuel	Angela	USA	10.5.75		100	11.33	11.31- 00
	Mao Lingyan		CHN	12.2.78		SP	17.05	16.92- 00
	Marahrens	Nicole	GER	15.3.77	172/55	400	52.20	52.77- 99
	Marin	Elisabetta	ITA	5.11.77	177/75	JT	54.94	54.94- 00
*	Marinova	Tereza	BUL	5.9.77	173/56	LJ	6.63w	6.46- 00
						TJ	14.91i	15.20- 00
	Markevich	Olga	BLR	13.10.79	174/74	HT	62.67	61.86- 99
	Márkou	Dímitra	GRE	28.7.80	178/58	TJ	13.84i, 13.68w	14.05- 00
	Mårtensson	Linda-Marie	SWE	22.6.71	185/81	SP	16.91i, 16.68	17.52- 99
	Martin	Karen	GBR	24.11.74	174/70	JT	55.85	59.50- 99
	Martinenko	Irina	UKR	19.10.76	174/93	HT	62.22	61.60- 98
*	Martínez	Magdelin	ITA	10.2.76	174/63	TJ	14.59	14.40- 00
	Martínez	Mayte	ESP	17.5.76	168/56	800	1:59.76	1:59.60- 00
	Martinovic	Marija	YUG	17.4.79	176/56	TJ	14.00	14.06- 00
	Marx	Claudia	GER	16.9.78	172/60	400	51.41	52.26- 99, 52.25i- 00
*	Masai	Edith	KEN	4.4.67	168/55	2000	5:40.3+	
						3000	8:31.76	9:42.2A- 00
						5000	14:45.86	
						HMar	67:53	
	Matejková	Alice	ESP	11.1.69	180/74	DT	59.18	62.66- 97
^	Mathes	Simone	GER	13.3.75	173/82	HT	62.72	67.13- 99
	Matoshko	Yelena	BLR	23.6.82		HT	65.46	54.51- 99
*	Matsuo	Kazumi	JPN	16.4.74	165/47	HMar	70:29	71:43- 99
						Mar	2:26:01	2:26:15- 00
	Matsuoka	Noriko	JPN	2.5.79	156/40	10000	32:22.82	31:50.53- 00
	Matsuoka	Rie	JPN	9.3.77	150/40	10000	32:18.36	31:52.50- 00
						Mar	2:27:50	2:35:10- 00
	Maugham	Stephanie	USA	29.9.77		PV	4.17	3.80- 00
	Mau-Repnak	Beatrice	GER	20.2.71	174/56	Hep	6026	6349- 94
*	May	Fiona	ITA	12.12.69	181/60	LJ	6.97, 7.02w	7.11- 98, 7.23Aw- 95
	May	Wanita	CAN	30.1.75	170/61	HJ	1.91	1.92- 93
	Mayers	Natasha	VIN	10.3.79	168/69	100	11.12, 11.01w	11.24- 00
						200	22.91, 22.82w	23.60, 23.57w- 00
	Mayr	Karin	AUT	4.6.71	179/69	200	22.97i	23.39- 00
*	Mbango	Françoise	CMR	14.4.76	172/63	TJ	14.65	14.70A, 14.65- 99
	McCambridge	Maria	IRL	10.7.75		5000	15:18.80	15:18.78- 00
	McCann	Kerryn	AUS	2.5.67	162/48	Mar	2:26:04	2:25:59- 00
	McCann	Stephanie	CAN	22.4.77	173/59	PV	4.25	4.02A- 00
	McConnell	Lee	GBR	9.10.78	178/	400	52.05	53.81- 99
	McCoy	Katie	USA	10.4.79	178/88	HT	62.68	55.79- 00
	McCray	Yolanda	USA	11.9.76	168/60	100H	13.08	12.78, 12.77w- 99
	McDonald	Beverly	JAM	15.2.70	169/59	100	11.27, 11.1	10.99- 98
						200	22.57	22.22- 99
	McDonald	Tina	CAN	12.1.76	176/107	DT	59.76	53.99- 00
	McIntosh	Raasin	USA	29.4.82	170/51	400H	57.19	59.46- 00
	McIvor	Adrienne	IRL	2.9.70	172/59	800	2:01.68	
	McLaughlin	Anneisha	JAM	6.1.86	152/50	200	23.11	24.33w- 00
						400	52.31	53.54- 00
^	Meissner	Heike	GER	29.1.70	172/57	800	2:00.75i	1:59.50- 98
						400H	55.03	54.03- 96
	Meldrum	Courtney	USA	31.1.77	168/54	3kSt	9:59.28	10:04.41- 00
	Melnikova	Tatyana	RUS	12.9.75	170/62	20kW	1:34:23	1:36:57- 99
	Melnikova- 2	Irina	RUS	14.5.75	169/57	LJ	6.54	6.68- 96
	Meloni	Andrea	GER	1.10.67	168/52	20kW	1:33:34	1:38:14- 00
	Melová	Mária	SVK	21.10.75	179/60	HJ	1.92	1.96i- 97, 1.90- 00
	Meltsayeva	Oksana	UKR	16.8.75	175/55	1500	4:08.35	4:10.12- 99
^	Mendes	Luciana	BRA	26.7.71	170/55	800	1:59.29	1:58.27- 94
	Mendía	Marta	ESP	18.5.75	172/58	HJ	1.94i, 1.88	1.93- 00
	Menelaou	Olympia	CYP	29.4.66	180.68	SP	16.71	16.36- 00
*	Menéndez	Osleidys	CUB	14.11.79	178/80	JT	71.54	68.17#- 98, 67.83- 00
	Mensah	Amewu	GER	21.3.77	182/64	HJ	1.87	1.94- 00
*	Mérah-Benida	Nouria	ALG	19.10.70	162/52	800	2:01.6	1:59.49- 99
						1500	4:08.16	3:59.12- 00
	Mercken	Ann	BEL	6.5.74	177/71	400H	56.34	54.95- 96
	Méred	Meriem	FRA	4.4.76	166/48	3kSt	10:04.76	10:07.63- 00
	Merriman	Donica	USA	24.1.79	178/65	200	23.21	23.08, 22.75w- 00
						100H	12.82, 12.73w	12.70- 00
*	Merry	Katharine	GBR	21.9.74	173/63	200	23.12	22.76- 00
						400	49.59	49.72- 00
	Meyer	Annika	GER	9.6.80	171/61	Hep	5709	5979- 00

Name		Nat	Born	Ht/Wt	Event	2001 Mark	Pre-2001 Best
* Meyer	Elana	RSA	10.10.66	158/55	10000	32:02.37	30:52.51- 94
					HMar	68:50	66:44- 99
Mézerette	Julie	FRA	28.9.79	175/59	Hep	5773	5489- 99
Miao Chunqing		CHN	27.2.78	178/66	TJ	14.16, 14.43w	14.31- 99
Michel	Jennifer	USA			3kSt	10:11.65	
Michot	Cécile	FRA	2.6.74	170/57	100H	13.29	13.91, 13.50w- 00
Míguez	Marta	ESP	3.3.73	171/62	JT	59.43	59.02- 00
Mikayeva	Olga	RUS	22.10.79	164/52	800	2:02.08	2:02.34- 00
Mikhalchenko	Irina	UKR	20.1.72	179/60	HJ	1.94	1.98- 00
Mikhaylova	Larisa	RUS	3.1.69	158/50	800	2:01.7	1:57.70- 99
Mikhaylovskaya	Natalya	RUS	20.11.75		100	11.1	11.81- 98
					200	22.0	23.86w- 98
* Mikitenko	Irina	GER	23.8.72	158/49	1500	4:06.08	4:06.68- 99
					2000	5:40.6+	
					3000	8:32.89	8:30.39- 00
					5000	14:53.00	14:42.03- 99
					10000	31:29.55	31:38.68- 99
Mikkonen	Hanna	FIN	15.1.81	170/54	HJ	1.87	1.85- 00
Miklos	Eva	ROM	30.7.78	174/56	LJ	6.65	6.62- 00
* Miles-Clark	Jearl	USA	4.9.66	170/60	400	50.80	49.40- 97
					800	2:00.96i	1:56.40- 99
Miller	Gi-Gi	USA	12.1.79	165/55	100H	13.11w	13.36- 00
					TJ	13.60	13.06- 00
					Hep	5925	5777- 00
Miller	Inger	USA	12.6.72	163/55	100	11.34, 11.09w	10.79- 99
					200	22.82	21.77- 99
Miller-Tjiroze	Grettel	JAM	6.6.75		HT	63.75	61.50- 00
Mills	TaNisha	USA	2.11.74	172/62	400H	56.14	56.45- 99
Milusauskaite	Sonata	LTU	31.8.73	163/53	20kW	1:34:08	1:33:29- 99
Milusheva	Eleonora	BUL	8.4.73	176/59	HJ	1.90	1.95- 00
Min Chungfeng		CHN	17.3.69	174/72	DT	56.32	66.76- 91
Mineva	Nevena	BUL	14.6.72	165/52	20kW	1:32:11	1:35:46- 00
Minina	Zana	LTU	11.6.77	174/58	400	52.12	52.25- 00
Mishchenko	Olga	UKR	24.11.71	180/67	200	23.08	23.62- 96
					400	52.11	52.38, 52.0- 99
* Misipeka	Lisa	ASA	3.1.75	170/84	HT	67.46	67.55- 00
Misiruk	Galina	UKR	18.12.70	168/54	800	1:59.83	2:00.54- 00
* Mistyukevich	Irina	RUS	17.6.77	177/63	800	1:58.02	1:57.49- 00
					1000	2:34.82	
^ Misyulya	Natalya	BLR	16.4.66	162/48	20kW	1:31:21	1:28:24- 00
Mitchell	Candy	USA	17.3.77	175/74	JT	54.80	53.24- 00
Mitchell	Kathryn	AUS	10.7.82		JT	54.98	51.44- 00
Miyake	Takako	JPN	22.7.74	161/61	JT	61.15	59.22#- 96, 57.27- 99
Miyazaki	Yoko	JPN	29.10.74	164/52	HMar	71:05	
Mladenis	Nicole	AUS	22.9.75	170/58	TJ	13.74, 13.81w	13.82- 00
Mládková	Sárka	CZE	30.8.76	173/58	PV	4.20	4.20- 99, 4.26sq- 00
Mocanu	Adina	ROM	4.3.80	181/81	DT	58.60	58.60- 00
Mockenhaupt	Sabrina	GER	6.12.80	155/45	3000	8:59.70	9:10.28- 00
* Möllenbeck	Anja	GER	18.3.72	184/86	DT	63.42	64.63- 98
Molnár	Krisztina	HUN	8.4.76	168/51	PV	4.41	4.30i, 4.22- 00
* Montalvo	Niurka	ESP	4.6.68	172/57	LJ	6.91	7.06- 99
					TJ	14.02i	14.60- 94
Montaner	Concepción	ESP	14.1.81	170/56	LJ	6.61i, .57, 6.67w	6.64, 6.79w- 00
* Montebrun	Manuela	FRA	13.11.79	175/92	HT	70.28	71.18- 00
Monteiro	Inês	POR	18.5.80		5000	15:29.98	15:44.81- 99
Montell	Annu	FIN	7.5.76	173/64	Hep	5684	5931- 00
Montgomery	Carol	CAN	24.8.66	166/52	10000	32:19.14	32:11.79- 00
Moore	Consuella	USA	29.8.81	165/63	100	11.34w	11.57- 00
					200	23.17w	23.96- 00
Morandais	Sylvanie	FRA	14.7.79	162/50	400H	55.49	58.11- 00
Morapane	Dikeledi	RSA	12.3.76		100	11.43A	11.38A, 11.32Aw- 00
					200	23.22A	23.07A- 00
* Moreno	Yipsi	CUB	19.11.80	178/80	HT	70.65	69.36- 00
Morgan	Sheryl	JAM	6.11.83	170/57	400	52.31	53.33- 00
Morgunova	Lyubov	RUS	14.1.71	167/48	HMar	70:34	68:45- 00
					Mar	2:27:18	2:26:33- 00
Mori	Chinatsu	JPN	20.5.80	168/80	SP	16.84	16.43- 00
Morimoto	Akiko	JPN	17.2.77	163/49	100H	13.22w	13.29- 99, 13.14w- 00
Mormand	Anita	FRA	20.2.71	175/60	400	52.46	51.94- 98
Moroianu	Rodica	FRA	18.11.70	170/50	3000	8:56.59	8:53.16- 98
(Nagel)					5000	15:17.31	15:28.14- 98

Name		Nat	Born	Ht/Wt	Event	2001 Mark	Pre-2001 Best
(Moroainu)					10000	32:28.17	
Moroni	Maria Costanza	ITA	23.3.69	178/62	TJ	13.82	14.25- 98
* Morrison	Melissa	USA	9.7.71	163/50	100H	13.00, 12.82w	12.53- 98
Mosqueda	Sylvia	USA	8.4.66	160/48	10000	32:25.22	31:54.03- 96
Motegi	Tomoko	JPN	8.8.78	155/50	100H	13.23w	13.38, 13.27w- 00
* Mothersill	Cydonie	CAY	19.3.78	168/53	100	11.34, 11.27w	11.35- 96, 11.21w- 00
					200	22.54A, 22.54	22.66- 00
Moton	Jamine	USA	14.12.78		SP	17.74	15.32, 15.52i- 00
de Moura	Lucimar	BRA	22.3.74	174/60	100	11.33	11.29, 11.17A- 99
					200	23.05	22.75, 22.75- 99
Movchan	Tatyana	UKR	19.9.70	160/52	400	52.49	51.66- 97
Moya	Karina	ARG	28.9.73	171/76	HT	62.16	61.85- 98
Moya	Sabina	COL	27.1.77	162/70	JT	59.14A	60.10#- 98, 58.81A- 99
Mrówka (Kolodziejska)	Monika	POL	6.3.79	177/74	JT	60.75	55.46- 99
* Mueller	Melissa	USA	16.11.72	178/66	PV	4.47, 4.62st	4.50i- 99, 4.45- 00
* Mugo	Naomi	KEN	2.1.77	163/50	1500	4:05.10	3:58.12- 98
					2000	5:42.66	
					5000	15:33.02	15:25.13- 00
^ Müller	Andrea	GER	29.6.74	167/60	PV	4.20i	4.30- 97, 4.40sq-ex- 95
* Münchow	Kirsten	GER	21.1.77	172/62	HT	68.09	69.28- 00
Munro	Jacqui	AUS	4.10.81	166/57	100H	13.12	13.12, 13.03w- 00
Muraguri	Jacinta	KEN	28.5.70	163/50	1500	4:03.20	4:07.44- 97
Murata	Fumi	JPN	13.3.75	151/40	10000	32:26.91	32:44.14- 00
					HMar	71:23	69:26- 00
Murphy	Catherine	GBR	21.9.75	172/60	400	51.84	52.72- 00
Muthoni	Susan	KEN			1500	4:09.98	
* Mutola	Maria Lurdes	MOZ	27.10.72	162/61	800	1:56.85	1:55.19- 94
					1000	2:33.53	2:29.34- 95
Nacsa	Monique	AUS	26.10.76	177/85	DT	57.93	57.53- 00
Nagayama	Ikumi	JPN	22.6.74	155/42	5000	15:30.04	15:20.48- 98
					10000	31:56.48	31:55.08- 99
					HMar	69:28	69:40- 00
					Mar	2:27:44	
Nakata	Yuki	JPN	10.3.77	167/56	Hep	5862	5513- 99
Nakhli	Abir	TUN	21.9.81	180/52	800	2:02.8	2:03.39- 99
* Nathan	DeDee	USA	20.4.68	180/75	Hep	6275	6577- 99
Naude	Elizna	RSA	14.9.78		DT	58.30	58.51- 00
Nazarova	Margarita	RUS	1.10.76	167/58	20kW	1:35:14.5	1:30:58- 00
* Ndereba	Catherine	KEN	21.7.72		10000	32:25.3A	32:17.58- 00
					HMar	67:54	69:02- 00
					Mar	2:18:47	2:21:33- 00
Neal	Natasha	USA	22.7.80		100H	13.24, 13.19w	13.52- 99, 13.22w- 00
					400H	57.16	56.86- 99
Negussie	Abebech	ETH	2.1.83	155/42	1500	4:06.01	4:06.20- 00
Nekhorosh	Svetlana	UKR	22.7.73	165/51	10000	32:29.6	33:09.00- 99
Nekolná	Katerina	CZE	23.6.75	173/65	Hep	5781	5997- 99
Nelyubova	Olga	RUS	12.6.64	168/58	800	2:00.4	1:59.29- 97
					1500	4:03.24	4:01.42- 98
Németh	Barbara	HUN	7.11.80	169/71	HT	62.91	60.23- 00
* Nerius	Steffi	GER	1.7.72	178/69	JT	63.72	69.42#- 96, 65.76- 00
Netseporuk	Larisa	EST	24.12.70	170/56	Hep	6172	6331- 00
Neyra	Yahumara	CUB	18.4.76	158/50	100H	12.92, 12.70w	13.13- 00, 13.00w- 99
Neyzhpapa	Krystyna	UKR	27.3.79	168/56	TJ	13.63	12.94- 00
Nguimgo	Mireille	CMR	7.11.76	172/56	400	50.71	50.69- 00
Nguyen Thi	Bich Van	VIE	21.2.75	160/54	LJ	6.50	6.32- 98
Niaré	Gaëlle	FRA	12.3.82	182/70	HJ	1.88	1.87i, 1.85- 99
* Nicolau	Cristina	ROM	8.8.77	186/68	LJ	6.48	6.61i- 00, 6.58- 96, 6.69w- 99
					TJ	14.62	14.94i- 00, 14.70- 99
Nie Yulin		CHN	2.9.78	153/50	20kW	1:32:59	1:31:25- 96
Niederstätter	Monika	ITA	2.3.74	169/47	400H	55.83	55.10- 99
Nihei	Hideko	JPN	2.1.71	156/48	100	11.36	11.63- 00, 11.57w- 99
Nikaido	Kaori	JPN	25.7.79	162/51	20kW	1:33:29	1:32:44- 00
Nikitina	Lyudmila	RUS	2.3.70		LJ	6.47i	6.48- 98
					TJ	14.04i	14.33i, 14.14- 99
* Nikolayeva	Yelena	RUS	1.2.66	168/58	20kW	1:27:49.3	1:28:01- 99
Nikolayeva-Shchurenko	Tatyana	UKR	26.2.76	184/63	HJ	1.91	1.93- 99
Nilsson	Cecilia	SWE	22.6.79	177/82	HT	64.53	62.54- 00
Nilsson	Ida	SWE	8.2.81	173/60	3kSt	9:59.75	10:22.92- 00
Nishimura	Miki	JPN	14.4.82	157/45	800	2:02.23	2:04.00- 00
Nishiyama	Takami	JPN	17.10.80	166/49	HMar	71:07	72:18- 00

Name		Nat	Born	Ht/Wt	Event	2001 Mark	Pre-2001 Best
* Nku	Mercy	NGR	17.7.76	170/67	100	11.06	11.03A, 11.09, 10.98w- 99
					200	22.66	22.53- 99
* Noguchi	Mizuki	JPN	3.7.78	150/40	10000	31:51.13	32:05.23- 00
					HMar	68:23	68:30- 99
Norgren	Anna	USA	19.12.74	180/75	HT	66.88	65.88- 00
Nosova	Yuliya	RUS	21.4.78	180/66	400	52.25i	53.42A- 00
(-Pechonkina)					400H	53.84	53.98- 99
Nsiah	Vida	GHA	13.4.76	169/68	100	11.37, 11.26w	11.18- 00
					100H	13.02	13.04- 98
Nwosu	Alice	NGR			800	2:02.79	
Nwosu	Gloria	NGR	24.12.84		400	52.37	54.6 - 00
Nye	Lisa	USA	17.11.68	178/60	3kSt	9:49.41	10:00.63- 00
Obata	Kayoko	JPN	18.9.71	156/46	HMar	71:05	70:47+- 00, 71:56- 99
* Oberem	Sonja	GER	24.2.73	170/50	HMar	71:13	70:13- 96
					Mar	2:26:13	2:27:25- 00
Oberer	Simone	SUI	8.4.80		Hep	5820	5411- 99
Obergföll	Christina	GER	22.8.81	175/71	JT	56.83	54.50- 00
Obi	Asami	JPN	22.3.76	157/43	HMar	71:20	70:04- 00
Obilor	Catherine	NGR	17.7.85		400H	56.50	
Oblekowska	Izabella	POL	18.2.72	172/56	Hep	5978	5919- 99
Ochichi	Isabella	KEN	79		HMar	68:38	70:15- 00
Ogawa	Kiyomi	JPN	15.9.81	157/46	10000	32:01.43	
Ogorodova	Marina	RUS	76		TJ	13.64	13.51- 00
Ogoshi	Kazue	JPN	2.3.81	160/44	10000	32:24.62	31:58.95- 00
					HMar	70:11	71:16- 00
* Ogunkoya	Falilat	NGR	12.5.68	172/66	400	50.50	49.10- 96
Ohaeri	Christina	USA	30.3.79	175/64	100H	13.09, 13.05w	13.13, 13.06w- 00
O'Hara	Tracy	USA	20.7.80	165/55	PV	4.42	4.45- 00
Oishi	Tomoe	JPN	27.5.76	162/49	HMar	71:03	74:24- 97
Ojokolo	Endurance	NGR	29.9.75	178/67	100	11.06	11.08- 98
Okafor	Rosemary	NGR	22.5.81	165/58	400	52.23	51.84- 00
Okamoto	Haruko	JPN	19.8.74	155/40	5000	15:23.93	15:36.57- 00
					10000	31:50.39	32:30.14- 00
Okamoto	Yukiko	JPN	29.11.74	159/45	Mar	2:26:21	2:30:48- 96
* Okayo	Margaret	KEN	30.5.76		5000	15:30.0A	15:48.25- 96
					HMar	68:51	69:03- 00
					Mar	2:24:21	2:26:00- 99
Okori	Reïna-Flor	FRA	2.5.80	167/56	100H	13.09	12.96, 12.91w- 00
Oksuz	Shermin	AUS	24.3.84	169/62	LJ	6.45, 6.65w	6.32- 99, 6.33w- 00
Olaru	Nuta	ROM	28.8.70	161/40	HMar	70:27	69:52- 97
					Mar	2:25:18	2:34:25- 97
* Oleynikova	Yelena	RUS	9.12.76	178/56	TJ	14.59	14.25- 00
Olichwierczuk	Anna	POL	10.12.78	168/56	400H	55.61	55.75- 00
Olivarès	Élodie	FRA	22.5.76	170/55	3kSt	9:44.68	10:09.64- 00
Oliveros	Princesa	COL	10.8.75		100H	13.0A	13.49, 13.3- 99
					400H	57.19	58.27A- 00
Olsthoorn	Ottelien	NED	20.6.78	179/63	Hep	5675	5530- 00
^ Olteanu	Iulia	ROM	26.1.67	166/57	10000	32:18.75	31:26.46- 96
					HMar	69:52	69:15- 94
Ominami	Hiromi	JPN	15.11.75	164/48	10000	32:18.27	31:50.89- 00
Ominami	Takami	JPN	15.11.75	164/48	10000	32:29.54	32:11.64- 00
					HMar	70:36	70:21- 00
					Mar	2:26:04	2:26:58- 00
Onanuga	Saidat	NGR	18.6.74	168/59	400H	56.05	56.10- 97
Ono	Masumi	JPN	5.12.75	161/50	PV	4.12i, 4.10	4.21i- 00, 4.20- 99
Onyali	Mary	NGR	3.2.68	168/54	100	11.25	10.97- 93, 10.7- 96
(-Omagbemi)					200	22.80	22.07- 96
O'Reilly	Thaimi	ITA	20.7.76	174/60	LJ	6.50	6.33- 97
Orlova	Yelena	RUS	3.2.70		800	2:02.19	2:02.03- 99
Ormond	Kara	USA	17.6.77	170/55	3kSt	10:04.14	10:03.09- 00
Orsini	Gisella	ITA	9.12.71	161/49	20kW	1:32:59	1:32:57- 00
Ortiz	Yamelis	PUR	26.2.78	165/51	400H	57.26A	57.91- 97
Ostapchuk	Nadezhda	BLR	12.10.80	180/78	SP	19.73	19.13i, 18.83- 00
O'Sullivan	Gillian	IRL	21.8.76	163/61	20kW	1:29:57	1:31:31- 00
* O'Sullivan	Sonia	IRL	28.11.69	173/53	1500	4:06.34	3:58.85- 95
					3000	8:43.51	8:21.64- 94
Ota	Yoko	JPN	14.1.75	174/51	HJ	1.91	1.94- 99
Otey	Kiamesha	USA	28.5.81		100	11.43	
^ Ottey	Merlene	JAM	10.5.60	173/61	100	11.21i/11.31A	10.74- 96
Ouali	Fatiha	FRA	28.10.74	159/52	20kW	1:33:04	1:32:14- 00
Ouaziz	Seloua	MAR	27.7.74	161/45	1500	4:08.27	4:08.18- 00

Name		Nat	Born	Ht/Wt	Event	2001 Mark	Pre-2001 Best
Ouzouni	Kalliópi	GRE	8.2.73	182/80	SP	17.92	19.03i, 18.63- 00
Owen	Desiree	USA	22.2.75		3kSt	10:11.45	10:18.85- 00
Owusu	Lesley	GBR	21.12.78	168/66	400	52.27, 52.15i	53.02- 00
Oyepitan	Abiodun	GBR	30.12.79	165/53	100	11.29, 11.17w	11.52- 00, 11.45w- 98
Ozaki	Mari	JPN	16.7.75	163/46	5000	15:30.88	15:25.99- 98
					10000	31:50.56	31:58.05- 99
Ozaki	Sachie	JPN	12.3.77	161/47	10000	32:35.0	33:18.82- 96
Palacios	Felipa	COL	1.12.75	168/60	100	11.28w	11.31, 11.15Aw- 97
					200	22.92A, 23.18	
							22.74Aw, 22.7w- 97, 22.8A- 98, 23.05- 99, 22.93A- 96
Palacios	Victoria	MEX	29.3.77		20kW	1:33:52	1:35:36- 99
Palamaa	Hanna	FIN	8.9.77	168/60	PV	4.10i	3.75- 00
Palamar	Vita	UKR	12.10.77	187/64	HJ	1.99	1.98- 00
Palmas	Sara	ITA	7.7.77	160/48	1500	4:12.13	4:12.44- 98
Pan Hailian		CHN	21.11.77	163/51	20kW	1:29:47	1:30:51- 00
Pang Meijuan		CHN	10.1.82		100H	13.13w	
* Pantelimon	Oana	ROM	27.9.72	179/61	HJ	1.93	1.99- 00
^ Pantyukhova	Mariya	RUS	14.8.74	178/62	1500	4:08.98i	4:05.10- 98
					3000	8:50.36i	8:30.18- 99
Papasotiríou	Athína	GRE	24.5.72	174/60	Hep	5862	5801- 99
Papayeoryíou	Alexándra	GRE	17.12.80		HT	63.99	57.67- 00
Papayiánni	Athína	GRE	18.8.80	170/56	20kW	1:33:37	1:33:14- 00
Paquette	Sonia	CAN	7.2.73	173/57	100H	13.16	13.16- 97, 13.11A- 96, 12.96Aw- 00
Paramonova	Yelena	RUS	28.6.62		Mar	2:30:03	2:36:51- 94
Paredes	Concepción	ESP	19.7.70	174/67	TJ	13.66i	14.30- 94
Parfyonova	Svetlana	RUS	14.7.73	175/62	Hep	6030	6187- 00
Parfyonova	Yelena	KAZ	26.1.74		TJ	13.87w	14.20- 00
Park Ho-hyun		KOR	21.3.78		JT	55.38	56.32#- 97, 52.16- 99
Parker	Tisha	USA	18.9.77	173/60	LJ	6.54w	6.63- 00
* Parris	Debbie-Ann	JAM	24.3.73	162/52	400	51.42	51.61- 95
					400H	53.88	53.97- 96
Paschke	Melanie	GER	29.6.70	168/59	100	11.23	11.04- 95, 11.01w- 96
Patla	Genowefa	POL	17.10.62	175/73	JT	56.72	65.96#- 91, 61.50- 00
Patsoú	Effrosíni	GRE	5.6.74	176/57	100	11.31	11.49- 00, 11.39w- 99
Patterson	Angel	USA	6.8.79		200	23.23, 23.11w	23.28, 23.23w- 00
					400H	56.09	55.50- 00
Pattinson	Helen	GBR	2.1.74	170/57	1500	4:07.56	4:04.82- 00
^ Paulino	Tina	MOZ	7.7.73	166/61	800	1:59.15	1:56.62- 93
					1000	2:35.74	
* Pavey	Joanne	GBR	20.9.73	162/51	3000	8:36.58	8:36.70- 00
					5000	15:00.56	14:58.27- 00
Pavlikovskaya	Natalya	RUS	80		Hep	5746	5385- 00
Pavlovskaya	Natalya	RUS	.75		1500	4:12.08	
* Pavlysh	Viktoriya	UKR	15.1.69	174/85	SP	19.62	21.69- 98
Pedrades	Dolores	ESP	17.1.73	168/69	HT	61.46	61.39- 00
Peel	Alesha	USA	27.9.78		100H	13.17w	13.94, 13.65w- 00
Peinado	María	ESP	8.2.77	176/66	Hep	5747	5548- 00
Pekhlivanova	Nadezhda	BUL	12.6.79	182/55	HJ	1.89	1.77- 98
* Peleshenko	Larisa	RUS	29.2.64	187/95	SP	20.79	21.46- 00
Pellino	Cristiana	ITA	21.9.70	164/49	20kW	1:32:36	1:30:42- 00
^ Pells	Leah	CAN	9.11.64	173/55	1500	4:08.49	4:03.56- 96
^ Pendareva	Petya	BUL	20.1.71	163/56	100	11.43, 11.40w	11.12- 98, 11.0- 95, 11.04w- 99
Peng Fengmei		CHN	9.7.79	164/55	TJ	13.71	14.46- 98
Perepelova	Lyubov	UZB	26.2.79	163/53	100	11.29	11.37- 99
					200	22.94	22.72- 00
Pérez	Dainelky	CUB	6.1.76	163/61	100H	13.31A, 13.02w	13.22- 98
Pérez	Eva	ESP	18.7.75	165/52	20kW	1:32:22.4	1:32:03- 00
Pérez (Martínez)	Yuliana	USA	21.7.81	171/70	TJ	14.19A, 14.10, 14.29w	13.78- 99
Periginelli	Karin	ITA	5.2.70	179/63	Hep	5664	6059- 96
Peris	Nova	AUS	25.2.71	170/58	200	23.12, 23.09w	22.74- 99, 22.70Aw- 00
					400	52.04	51.28- 00
Perkins	Angel	USA	5.10.84		200	23.07, 22.85w	23.40- 00
					400	52.18	52.44- 00
* Pernía	Daimí	CUB	27.12.76	175/61	400	51.10	51.13- 00
					400H	53.81	52.89- 99
Perpoli	Danielle	ITA	7.3.68	168/60	400	52.13	52.46- 95
Pérra	Athanasía	GRE	2.2.83		TJ	13.73w	12.73- 00
Perrin	Amélie	FRA	30.3.80	171/85	DT	55.68	54.54- 00
* Perrone	Elisabetta	ITA	9.7.68	168/60	20kW	1:27:09	1:27:42- 00
Perry	Michelle	USA	1.5.79	175/60	100H	13.18	13.15, 13.03w- 00, 12.9w- 99
					400H	56.23	56.50- 00

	Name		Nat	Born	Ht/Wt	Event	2001 Mark	Pre-2001 Best
	(M Perry)					Hep	5759	
*	Perry	Nanceen	USA	19.4.77	175/69	100	11.40w	11.15- 99, 11.10w- 00
						200	23.23	22.38, 22.16w- 00
	Pershina	Yelena	KAZ	24.12.63	175/60	LJ	6.71	6.91- 92
	Persson	Hanna-Mia	SWE	11.2.78	177/62	PV	4.21	3.92- 00
	Peters (-Chukwuemeka)	Vivian	NGR	4.5.77	178/90	SP	17.83	17.93- 00
	Petersen	Nadja	SWE	14.7.78		400H	57.18	57.51- 99
	Petersson	Annika	SWE	10.1.79	176/74	JT	56.55	56.70- 00
	Petite	Cristina	ESP	10.5.72	163/53	3000	8:59.73i	8:59.38- 98, 8:52.85i- 99
						5000	15:23.23	15:32.66- 00
	Petráhn	Barbara	HUN	16.9.78	160/55	200	23.17, 22.92w	23.64, 23.47w- 00
						400	51.85	52.05- 00
	Petrescu	Daniela	ROM	13.4.68	170/52	3kSt	10:06.60	9:54.86- 00
	Petrova	Alyona	TKM	8.8.79	172/60	400	52.10	54.40- 00
	Petrova	Antonina	RUS	1.5.77	162/52	20kW	1:31:12	1:35:56- 98
*	Petrova	Lyudmila	RUS	7.10.68	160/44	10000	32:04.94	31:52.75- 00
						HMar	70:36	69:26- 00
						Mar	2:26:18	2:25:45- 00
	Phamang	Buaban	THA	82?		JT	54.80	
	Pidgeon	Elizabeth	GBR	27.4.77	160/77	HT	62.00	63.61- 00
	Pieluzek	Aleksandra	POL	4.4.79	170/58	400H	56.51	58.07- 00
	Pierson	Shannon	USA	30.9.74	175/55	PV	4.27	4.10- 00
	Pierson	Summer	USA	3.9.78		DT	55.54	60.40- 98
	Pignot	Aurore	FRA	24.12.79	175.63	PV	4.20	4.16i, 4.15- 00, 4.25ex- 99
	Pilátou	Stilianí	GRE	28.3.80	172/56	LJ	6.65i, 6.48	6.50- 00
*	Pintusevich-Block	Zhanna	UKR	6.7.72	164/62	100	10.82	10.85, 10.6- 97
						200	22.74	22.17A, 22.32- 97
*	Pittman	Jana	AUS	9.11.82	181/68	400	51.74 mx	51.76A- 00, 51.80- 99
						400H	55.93	55.20A, 55.63 - 00
*	Plätzer (Tysse)	Kjersti	NOR	18.1.72	176/57	20kW	1:29:55	1:27:53- 00
	Poelman	Jacqueline	NED	5.10.73	171/63	100	11.43	11.27- 94
						200	23.17	23.17- 94
	Pogroszewska	Agnieszka	POL	20.2.77	170/75	HT	67.98	65.26- 00
	Poissonnier	Céline	FRA	4.5.79	160/50	PV	4.20	4.02- 99
	Poissonnier	Marie	FRA	4.5.79	166/58	PV	4.35i, 4.25	4.35- 00
	Polnova (Gubaryova)	Tatyana	RUS	4.12.73	178/54	PV	4.20	4.30i, 4.20- 99
*	Polyakova	Olga	RUS	23.9.80	168/50	20kW	1:32:45.7	1:25:20- 00
^	Pomacu	Cristina	ROM	15.9.73	164/46	Mar	2:29:44	2:30:56- 99
	Pompey	Aliann	GUY	9.3.78	165/55	400	51.96	52.65- 99, 52.21i- 00
	Pop	Ramona	ROM	5.4.82	181/65	HJ	1.92	1.86- 00
	Popescu	Elena-Alina	ROM	27.10.85	172/52	TJ	13.76	-0-
	Porsche	Kristina	GER	25.2.80	190/73	Hep	5983	5474- 00
	Pospísilová	Véra	CZE	19.11.78	178/78	SP	16.92	15.80- 00
						DT	63.20	58.28- 00
	Potepa	Wioletta	POL	14.12.80	186/83	DT	58.57	58.14- 00
	Powell	Suzy	USA	3.9.76	178/73	DT	64.50	65.30- 00
*	Power	Susie	AUS	26.3.75	176/53	5000	15:23.87	15:23.18- 99
						10000	31:26.34	33:00.09- 96
	Pöyry	Sini	FIN	3.2.80	182/90	HT	66.31	65.50- 00
^	Pozdnyakova	Tatyana	UKR	4.3.56	164/59	Mar	2:30:28	2:29:25- 98
	Prediger	Tessy	GER	29.1.79	170/52	100H	13.26	13.25- 99
	Price	Melissa	USA	5.9.79		HT	66.25	64.94- 99
	Price	Petrina	AUS	26.4.84	178/51	HJ	1.90	1.85- 00
^	Price-Smith	Connie	USA	3.6.62	192/95	SP	18.35i, 18.22	19.60- 94
	Priemer	Manuela	GER	29.11.78	178/75	HT	64.97	66.30- 99
*	Prokhorova	Yelena	RUS	16.4.78	171/59	HJ	1.88	1.82- 00
						LJ	6.63	6.72- 00
						Hep	6694	6765- 00
	Prokofyeva	Irina	RUS	13.3.72		800	2:01.19	2:00.77- 99
*	Prokopcuka	Jelena	LAT	21.9.76	168/51	5000	15:14.73	14:47.71- 00
						10000	32:02.96	31:27.86- 00
						HMar	68:43	71:05- 99
	Prokopek	Grazyna	POL	20.4.77	170/51	400	51.92	52.15- 00
	Pruvost	Fanny	FRA	21.5.79	166/49	3kSt	10:08.51	-0-
	Pskit	Malgorzata	POL	25.5.76	172/56	400H	55.04	55.86- 00
	Pukha	Irina	UKR	10.1.73	171/68	100	11.39	11.12- 00
	Pumper	Susanne	AUT	1.9.70	170/50	5000	15:10.54	15:16.32- 00
	Pushkina	Rimma	RUS	10.1.74		3kSt	10:03.01	10:35.62- 00
*	Puzanova	Yekaterina	RUS	1.1.79	168/57	800	2:01.29	2:01.86- 00
						1500	4:11.28	
	Pyatykh	Anna	RUS	4.4.81	175/64	TJ	14.21, 14.22w	14.19- 00

Name		Nat	Born	Ht/Wt	Event	2001 Mark	Pre-2001 Best
* Pyrek	Monika	POL	11.8.80	174/52	PV	4.61	4.40- 00
Qian Chunhua		CHN	11.2.79		SP	18.41	17.59- 00
Qin Lei		CHN	16.10.76		DT	60.09	61.02- 98
Qiu Qiaoping		CHN	31.1.71	181/90	DT	55.58	66.60- 94
Quintanal	Irache	ESP	18.9.78	170/70	SP	16.71	16.76i, 16.25- 00
					DT	56.39	54.67- 99
Racková	Vladimíra	CZE	15.5.67	180/85	DT	65.50	63.92- 93
Raczka-Lasota	Elzbieta	POL	19.11.70	178/63	Hep	5672	6051- 99
* Radcliffe	Paula	GBR	17.12.73	173/54	1500	4:05.37	4:05.81- 98
					2000	5:39.3+	5:39.20- 93
					3000	8:26.97	8:27.40- 99
					5000	14:32.44	14:43.54- 99
					10000	30:55.80	30:26.97- 00
					HMar	66:47	67:07- 00
Radu	Laura	ROM	7.12.80	176/75	JT	55.95	51.59- 00
^ Rahouli	Baya	ALG	27.7.79	176/58	TJ	13.88, 14.30w	14.64A, 14.30- 99, 14.42w- 00
Rajamäki	Susanna	FIN	19.9.79	176/60	Hep	5735w, 5641	6021- 00
Rajot	Céline	FRA	22.3.75	162/50	3kSt	10:05.28	10:04.85- 00
Rakonczai	Beáta	HUN	25.6.77		HMar	69:27sc	73:04- 00
Rakotondrabe	Hanitriniaina	MAD	1.1.67	165/57	100	11.40	11.32- 96
Rakotozafy	Rosa	MAD	12.11.77	165/55	100H	13.02	12.84- 99
* Ramalalanirina	Nicole	FRA	5.3.72	164/57	100H	12.91, 12.87irr, 12.84w	12.76- 00
Ramaunaskaité	Rita	LTU	22.2.70	174/72	JT	58.19	65.46#- 96, 62.69- 00
^ Rantanen	Heli	FIN	26.2.70	174/69	JT	56.19	67.94#- 96, 61.61- 99
Rasmussen	Marie Bagger	DEN	1.11.72	178/65	PV	4.25	4.35- 00
* Raspopova	Olga	RUS	27.12.78	175/56	800	1:58.77	1:56.85- 00
					1000	2:34.77	
Razaiarimalala	Cendrino	MAD	8.2.78		400H	56.49	57.28A- 97
Rea	Elisa	ITA	23.3.68	164/50	1500	4:09.45	4:09.32- 98
					5000	15:33.40	15:26.50- 99
Recio	Teresa	ESP	7.7.63	154/45	5000	15:12.76	15:12.06- 00
					10000	32:29.11	31:43.80- 99
Redoúmi	Flóra	GRE	11.9.76	168/59	100H	13.26	13.50- 99
Reed	Niki	USA	1.4.80	176/	PV	4.10	4.10- 00
Reid	Suziann	USA	14.1.77	168/64	400	50.86	50.74- 99
Reilly	Sarah	IRL	3.7.73	165/56	200	23.02	23.12- 00
Ren Ni		CHN	14.5.79		TJ	14.29	13.71- 00
^ Ren Ruiping		CHN	1.2.76	176/64	TJ	13.94	14.66- 97, 14.83Aw- 95
^ Ren Xiujuan		CHN	14.9.74	160/56	10000	32:07.55	31:13.21- 96
					Mar	2:24:22	2:25:32- 00
* Renders	Marleen	BEL	24.12.68	166/47	5000	15:22.06	15:19.20- 99
					HMar	70:43	69:24- 94
					Mar	2:28:31	2:23:43- 00
Rezanova	Marina	UKR	28.8.74	180/75	HT	65.86	62.22- 94
Rhines	Jen	USA	1.7.74	160/50	3000	8:55.28	8:50.72- 00
					5000	15:13.26	15:19.88- 00
					10000	32:20.03	31:58.34- 00
Ribac	Andreja	SLO	14.1.76		TJ	13.75, 13.81w	13.27, 13.72w- 00
* Ribeiro	Fernanda	POR	23.6.69	161/48	3000	8:53.41i	8:30.66- 99
* Richards	Sandie	JAM	6.11.68	175/67	400	50.71	49.79- 97
Richards	Sanya	JAM	26.2.85		200	23.09	23.57- 00
Richardson	Ellannee	USA	18.3.80	174/61	Hep	5677	5678- 99
* Richardson	LaTasha	USA	23.8.76	168/52	200	22.63	22.49- 00
					400	50.79	49.87- 00
Richardson	Marcia	GBR	10.2.72	178/67	100	11.43	11.35, 11.29w- 00
Richtnér	Maria	SWE	5.2.73	180/63	Hep	5775	5664- 98
^ Rieger	Silvia	GER	14.11.70	175/60	400H	57.28	54.22A- 98, 54.27- 96
Rigaudo	Elisa	ITA	17.6.80	169/56	20kW	1:29:54	1:32:50- 00
Risku	Johanna	FIN	21.2.79	170/55	3kSt	10:09.96	10.22.76- 00
Ritthiwat	Wacharee	THA	18.10.76		TJ	13.78	13.39 - 95
Rivero	Xiomara	CUB	22.11.68	176/78	JT	65.29	67.06#- 95, 62.92- 00
* Roba	Fatuma	ETH	18.12.73	160/48	HMar	69:01	69:43- 97
					Mar	2:27:20	2:23:21- 98
Robert-Michon	Melina	FRA	18.7.79	178/87	DT	63.87	63.19, 63.65dh- 00
Roberts	Trecia	THA	4.2.71	163/59	100H	13.01, 12.90w	12.73A- 98, 12.83- 99
Robinson	Amber	USA	5.6.80	165/56	200	23.18	23.21- 99
Robinson	Moushami	USA	13.4.81		400	51.79	52.37- 00
Robinson	Shana	USA	13.2.82		100	11.40w	11.66- 00
Robinson	Tulia	JAM	4.2.79		100	11.42	11.56- 98
Rocco	Lara	ITA	20.12.75	163/51	400H	57.36	56.43- 98
Rocco	Tiziana	ITA	2.12.78	166/62	JT	55.68	57.27#- 99, 56.88- 00

Name		Nat	Born	Ht/Wt	Event	2001 Mark	Pre-2001 Best
Rocha Silva	Isabel	BRA	15.6.79		400H	57.02	58.34- 00
Rockmeier	Birgit	GER	29.11.73	173/62	200	22.90	23.11- 97, 22.89i- 98
					400	52.07	51.45- 00
Rockmeier	Gabi	GER	29.11.73	176/53	100	11.17	11.36- 99
					200	22.68	23.02- 96
Rodionova	Tatyana	RUS	27.8.80	163/53	800	2:00.65	2:06.59- 00
Rodríguez	Dulce	MEX	14.8.72	157/54	5000	15:22.26	15:27.46- 00
* Rodríguez	Natalia	ESP	2.6.79	164/49	800	2:01.35	2:01.66- 99
					1500	4:06.32	4:04.24- 00
* Rogova	Oksana	RUS	7.10.78	183/60	TJ	14.37i, 14.20, 14.23w	14.59, 14.65w- 99
Rohl	Michelle	USA	12.11.65	150/41	20kW	1:32:49	1:31:51- 00
Roles	Philippa	GBR	1.3.78	180/100	DT	58.98	60.00- 99
* Rollison	Melissa	AUS	13.4.83	166/50	3kSt	9:30.70	10:10.73- 00
^ Romanova	Anna	RUS	9.3.68	182/88	SP	16.67	20.24- 93
Romanova	Olga	RUS	23.5.80		5000	15:32.59	15:37.76- 00
Rosa	Mónica	POR	5.5.78	164/53	3000	8:56.58	9:04.14- 00
					5000	15:21.01	15:34.84- 00
					10000	32:22.25	-0-
* Rose-Henley	Dionne	JAM	7.11.69	169/57	100H	12.77	12.64- 96
Rosenblad	Agneta	SWE	8.8.77	166/58	100H	13.28w	13.61, 13.59w- 00
					LJ	6.52	6.36- 00
* Roshchupkina	Natalya	RUS	13.1.78	182/70	200	23.27, 22.84w	23.47- 00
					Hep	6551	6633- 00
Rosikhina	Irina	RUS	11.5.75	175/65	400	51.20	50.76- 00, 50.5- 98
Ross	Chaniqua	USA	24.5.80	173/80	DT	56.02	54.66- 99
Ross	Serene	USA	15.10.77		JT	54.72	51.54- 99
Rosseyeva	Olga	RUS	1.8.81		1500	4:03.87	4:10.97- 99
					3000	8:55.51	9:07.79- 99
^ Rozsa-Urbaník	Maria	HUN	12.2.67	169/52	20kW	1:34:51	1:31:21- 00
Rublevskaya	Lyudmila	RUS	7.6.77	186/87	DT	60.03	60.04- 99
* Rublyova	Olga	RUS	28.10.74	175/65	LJ	6.86	6.90, 7.01w- 95
					TJ	14.26i	14.45i, 14.21- 00
^ Rücker	Anja	GER	20.12.72	174/58	400	51.55	49.74- 99
Ruckstuhl	Karin	NED	2.11.80		Hep	5735	5329- 99
^ Rudolph	Amy	USA	18.9.73	176/55	1500	4:09.11	4:06.02- 00
					1M	4:28.47i	4:27.66- 99
					3000	8:54.07, 8:48.33i	8:39.86- 00
					5000	15:10.83	14:56.04- 96
Ruicu	Otilia	ROM	20.8.78	172/52	400	51.47	51.50- 99
Runyan	Marla	USA	4.1.69	170/60	1500	4:06.31	4:05.27- 99
					3000	8:44.69	8:56.27i- 00
					5000	15:05.48	15:07.66- 00
Rurak	Yelena	UKR	7.2.72	168/58	800	2:02.61	
Rutjes	Ilona	NED	28.5.80	181/76	DT	55.87	56.12- 99
Ryabinkina	Olga	RUS	24.9.76	186/81	SP	17.85	19.32- 00
Rybak	Ewa	POL	22.12.74	174/67	JT	58.23	63.93#- 98, 60.76- 99
^ Ryshich	Nastja	GER	19.9.77	170/58	PV	4.30i, 4.11	4.50i, 4.44- 99
Saari	Teija	FIN	21.3.78	162/54	PV	4.10	4.05- 98
Sabino	Katie	USA	23.1.79		3kSt	10:05.38	
* Sacramento	Carla	POR	10.12.71	168/53	1500	4:00.32	3:57.71- 98
					3000	8:41.17	8:30.22- 99
* Sadova	Natalya	RUS	15.6.72	180/100	DT	68.57	70.02- 99
Safarova	Irina	RUS	19.6.69		HMar	69:55	70:03- 96
Safronnikova	Natalya	BLR	28.2.73	174/60	100	11.30, 11.26w, 10.9	11.17- 99, 10.9- 98
					200	22.68, 22.4	22.74- 99, 22.3- 98
Safronova	Larisa	RUS	6.1.80	164/52	20kW	1:30:49, 1:34:15.2t	1:30:41- 00
* Safronova	Natalya	BLR	11.7.74	176/60	TJ	14.57	14.65- 00
Safta	Anca	ROM	9.1.78	172/52	800	2:02.12i	2:02.31- 96
Sagaydak	Svetlana	RUS	70		400H	56.27	55.98- 00
Sagonas	Sophie	GER	18.9.81		HJ	1.87i	1.88i- 00, 1.85- 99
Sakagami	Kaori	JPN	12.5.74	159/51	100	11.42, 11.32w	11.42, 11.29w- 00
Sakamoto	Naoko	JPN	14.11.80	160/45	HMar	69:27	
Sakashita	Naomi	JPN	25.5.75	158/42	5000	15:29.02	15:28.99- 00
					10000	31:59.91	31:53.40- 96
					Mar	2:28:09	
Sallins	Melinda	USA	30.6.73	178/64	400H	56.85	56.06- 97
Salumäe	Jane	EST	17.1.68	169/53	Mar	2:29:47	2:27:04- 97
Samaria	Agnes	NAM	11.8.72	166/56	800	2:00.81A	2:03.99- 00
Sampaio	Helena	POR	9.10.73	159/46	HMar	71:28	70:15- 00
* Sánchez	Guadalupe	MEX	3.1.77	169/58	20kW	1:32:27	1:30:49- 00

Name		Nat	Born	Ht/Wt	Event	2001 Mark	Pre-2001 Best
Sánchez	María Mar	ESP	25.12.79	170/60	PV	4.31	4.30- 00
Sanganoko	Makaridja	CIV	8.5.80	160/58	100	11.27, 11.26w	11.71, 11.4- 99
Santiago	Beatriz	ESP	28.10.68	160/50	5000	15:11.01	15:17.14- 00
Santin	Frances	USA	27.7.80	175/57	400H	56.64	56.67- 00
dos Santos ¶	Fabiane	BRA	30.5.76		800	2:00.98i, 1:57.16dq	2:01.70- 00
					1000	2:35.95dq	
dos Santos	Luciana Alves	BRA	10.2.70	160/56	LJ	6.47	6.72- 00, 6.81A- 99
					TJ	13.73, 13.74w	14.01- 00
dos Santos	Perla	BRA	29.1.82	155/49	400H	56.52	57.73- 00
Sanz	Eva	ESP	4.7.73	159/40	Mar	2:30:56	2:37:56- 99
Sato	Sayoko	JPN	23.10.77	169/57	Hep	5713	5637- 00
* Sauer	Mary	USA	31.10.75	164/59	PV	4.61	4.47- 00
Savchuk	Valentina	UKR	19.1.75	157/49	20kW	1:28:56	1:29:06- 00
* Saville	Jane	AUS	5.11.74	164/53	20kW	1:31:20	1:28:56- 00
^ Saxby-Junna	Kerry	AUS	2.6.61	166/59	20kW	1:33:40.2	1:29:36- 00
Sayers	Goldie	GBR	16.7.82	172/67	JT	55.40	54.58- 00
* Sazanovich	Natalya	BLR	15.8.73	179/65	100H	13.28	13.31- 98
					LJ	6.69i, 6.56	6.86- 96
					SP	16.58	15.64- 96
					Hep	6539	6563- 96
Sazonova	Maya	KAZ	28.5.65	166/53	20kW	1:29:36	1:30:18- 00
Schäffel	Aline	GER	15.5.80	178.80	SP	16.69	15.71- 00
Schielke	Sina	GER	19.5.81	167/56	100	11.24	11.39, 11.33w- 99
					200	22.78	23.03- 99
Schiemenz	Kim	USA	13.4.77	178/66	Hep	5733	5602- 00
Schott	Maren	GER	11.2.76		400H	55.44	56.02- 00
Schötz	Katja	GER	22.7.81	183/57	HJ	1.86	1.89- 00
Schreiber	Katja	GER	30.6.78		DT	60.32	55.56- 00
Schulte	Sabine	GER	29.1.76	169/58	PV	4.35	4.30- 00
Schulz	Melanie	GER	27.8.79	166/48	3kSt	9:54.99	
Schwald	Sarah	USA	2.1.73	165/48	1500	4:04.43	4:09.89- 96
					3000	8:51.68i	9:06.30- 95
Schwartz	Jillian	USA	19.9.79		PV	4.20	4.10- 00
Scott	Catherine	JAM	24.8.73	174/61	400	51.91	51.65- 00
					400H	56.40	54.90- 00
* Sechko	Lyudmila	RUS	27.11.74	180/80	SP	19.34	19.51- 00
Sedlaková	Petra	CZE	5.10.77	173/60	800	2:02.67	2:04.20- 99
Seeger	Melanie	GER	8.1.77	166/49	20kW	1:30:41	1:32:10- 00
Sekachova	Irina	UKR	21.7.76	165/72	HT	67.00	69.53- 00
Sellam	Aïda	TUN	13.9.77		JT	56.20	55.90- 00
Semedo	Nédia	POR	14.11.78		800	2:01.60	2:02.52- 00
					1500	4:09.46	4:13.56- 00
Semyonova	Zinayida	RUS	19.3.62	150/43	Mar	2:26:51	2:28:46- 00
Serdyuk	Alina	BLR	22.1.75	175/68	JT	58.05	59.93- 00
Seryogina	Viktoriya	RUS	22.5.73	170/60	HJ	1.96i, 1.90	1.98i, 1.97sq, 1.96- 99
* Seyerling	Heide	RSA	19.8.76	168/55	100	11.42A, 11.33Aw	11.35- 99, 11.1w- 97
					200	22.63	22.87A, 22.59Aw- 00, 22.89- 98
					400	50.36	50.05- 00
Sharova	Galina	RUS	30.1.79	179/59	TJ	14.21	14.01- 99
* Shaw	Lorraine	GBR	2.4.68	170/87	HT	68.15	67.44- 00
Shedova	Olga	BLR	6.4.81	179/57	HJ	1.88	1.90- 00
Shekhodanova	Natalya	RUS	29.12.71	169/55	100H	12.96	12.59- 96
^ Shekhovtsova	Yelena	UKR	31.5.72	178/58	LJ	6.65i, 6.62	6.97- 96
					TJ	13.71	13.77- 97
Shemchishina	Maya	UKR	6.5.72	174/52	100H	13.18	12.88- 00, 12.8- 98
Shen Shengfei		CHN	21.1.81	178/70	Hep	6263	6185- 97
Shepherd	Daveetta	USA	15.1.79	170/57	100H	13.09	13.31- 98, 13.04w- 99
Shestakova	Nadezhda	BLR	.77		TJ	13.60	13.32- 97
Shestok	Varvara	UKR	17.12.74	166/51	3kSt	10:06.48	10:05.12- 00
^ Shevchik	Tatyana	BLR	11.6.69	178/60	HJ	1.86i	2.00- 93
Shevtsova	Natalya	RUS	17.12.74		400	51.94	52.46- 99
Shi Hua		CHN	21.6.81		1500	4:10.83	4:14.02- 00
Shi Wei		CHN	7.7.83		Hep	5891	5304- 00
Shibano	Yayoi	JPN	10.3.75	170/65	JT	55.85	57.07- 99
* Shibui	Yoko	JPN	14.3.79	165/50	10000	31:48.73	31:48.89- 00
					HMar	70:22+	69:31- 00
					Mar	2:23:11	- 0 -
* Shikolenko	Tatyana	RUS	10.5.68	174/65	JT	66.09	67.84#- 98, 67.20- 00
Shimchuk	Natalya	BLR	1.10.81	179/77	JT	55.54	54.26- 00
Shinkins	Karen	IRL	15.10.76	165/53	400	51.37	51.07- 99
Shinta	Momoe	JPN	28.5.79	156/44	10000	32:24.00	

	Name		Nat	Born	Ht/Wt	Event	2001 Mark	Pre-2001 Best
*	Shishigina	Olga	KAZ	23.12.68	162/57	100	11.35	11.13- 00
						100H	12.58	12.44, 12.41w- 95
	Shiviryova	Natalya	RUS	31.8.78	164/54	20kW	1:34:15	1:31:51- 00
	Shoemake	Kyla	USA	6.6.77	175/62	100H	13.27w	13.05- 00
	Shotwell	Ebony	USA	27.1.82		100	11.33w	11.65- 98
	Sialou	Androula	CYP	27.1.73	170/58	400H	57.34	60.08- 95
	Sibilyeva	Tatyana	RUS	17.5.80	164/51	20kW	1:27:33	1:29:53- 98
	Sidibé	Odiah	FRA	13.1.70	176/64	100	11.41, 11.28w	11.23- 95
	Sidorenko	Natalya	UKR	22.11.80	160/49	1500	4:06.68	4:10.14- 00
*	Sidoti	Annarita	ITA	25.7.69	150/42	20kW	1:31:40	1:28:38- 00
	Siener	Heike	GER	19.11.80	182/60	HJ	1.86	1.77- 00
	Sildillia	Viviane	FRA	23.2.74	175/60	LJ	6.54i	6.43, 6.54w- 00
	Silva	Vânia	POR	8.6.80		HT	63.64	62.14- 00
*	Simon	Lidia	ROM	4.9.73	157/44	HMar	69:46	68:34- 00
						Mar	2:24:15	2:22:54- 00
	Simonsen	Anne Haaland	NOR	18.6.80	169/56	20kW	1:34:26	1:34:22- 00
	Simpson	Margaret	GHA	2.8.82		Hep	5836	5543- 00
	Simpson	Pamela	USA	28.4.77	160/55	LJ	6.46	6.69- 00
	Singh	Neelam Jaswant	IND	8.1.71	166/80	DT	59.14	63.02- 00
	Sinirtas	Svetla	TUR	17.6.64	178/96	SP	16.57	20.91- 87
	Sivushenko	Yelena	RUS	28.2.82	179/55	HJ	1.94i, 1.88	1.88- 00
*	Skolimowska	Kamila	POL	4.11.82	180/88	HT	71.71	71.16- 00
	Skotnik	Melanie	GER	8.11.82	182/59	HJ	1.86	1.86- 00
	Skujyté	Austra	LTU	12.8.79	188/75	Hep	6150w	6104- 00
	Skvortsova	Silviya	RUS	16.11.74		HMar	69:37	71:19- 97
						Mar	2:28:22	2:38:52- 00
	Slastina	Anna	UKR	4.9.77	167/53	JT	55.05	53.53- 00, 54.02#- 99
	Slinden	Diane	USA	7.4.80	180/	DT	55.56	53.83- 00
	Slivka	Viktoriya	RUS	28.9.80	178/54	HJ	1.88	1.94- 99
	Smith	Randi	USA	14.5.81		400H	57.50	57.07- 00
	Smith	Ronetta	JAM	2.5.80	170/58	200	23.25, 23.0w	
						400	51.92	53.60- 99
	Smith	Stephanie	USA	27.6.85		400	52.11	52.64- 00
	Smith	Trecia	JAM	5.11.75	185/66	LJ	6.74	6.72, 6.84w- 97
						TJ	14.12A, 14.11, 14.88w	14.22- 97
*	Sobanska	Malgorzata	POL	25.4.69	165/50	Mar	2:26:08	2:27:30- 99
^	Söderberg	Anna	SWE	11.6.73	177/82	DT	59.18	64.54- 99
	Sokolova	Svetlana	RUS	9.1.81	175/55	Hep	6270w	5826h- 98, 5761- 99
	Sologub ¶	Natalya	BLR	31.3.75	176/64	400	51.61, 51.43dq	51.70- 00
	Solomon	Mariana	ROM	8.9.80	172/58	TJ	13.96i, 13.73	13.75- 98
	Solomon	Shalonda	USA	19.12.85		100	11.37w	
						200	23.22w	
	Song Aimin		CHN	15.3.78		DT	62.34	60.50- 99
	Song Feina		CHN	25.1.77	183/95	SP	18.73	18.68- 00
	Song Yinglan		CHN	14.9.75	173/60	400H	53.96	55.58- 97
	Soong	Cari	USA	11.7.81	173/89	HT	64.24	60.22- 00
	Sorokina	Aleksandra	RUS	24.2.79		20kW	1:34:31.2	1:39:33- 00
	Sosnowska	Anete	POL	10.5.74	170/58	100H	13.05	13.14- 97, 13.10w- 96
	Sotnikova	Yuliya	RUS	18.11.70	164/53	400	51.00	50.73- 00
	Spangler	Angie	USA	4.9.68	178/61	HJ	1.86i	1.96i- 92, 1.95- 94
	Spears	Ychlindria	USA	17.7.84	170/54	LJ	6.50w	6.44- 00
	Spencer	Sasha	USA	4.8.79		800	2:02.68	2:03.36- 00
	Sprenger	Juliane	GER	22.3.77	164/52	100H	13.13	13.00- 00
	Sprules	Lyn	GBR	11.9.75	175/95	HT	62.99	63.96- 00
	Staicu	Simona	HUN	5.5.71	163/46	3000	8:55.67	9:06.90- 86
						HMar	68:36sc	70:11- 00
	Stals	Sandra	BEL	5.6.75	170/55	800	2:02.74	1:58.31- 98
	Starkey (Wittenwyler)	Jill	USA	7.3.71	175/56	PV	4.30	4.15- 99
	Starovoytova	Lyudmila	BLR	8.4.74		SP	16.97	16.46- 00
						DT	63.55	62.42- 00
	Stavchanskaya	Yevgeniya	UKR	25.9.81	163/50	LJ	6.55	6.54- 99
	Stavskaya	Svetlana	KAZ	10.5.77	180/60	HJ	1.87	1.87- 00
	Steer (Tunks)	Teri	USA	30.10.75	180/75	SP	19.21	19.04i, 18.80- 99
	Steiner	April	USA	22.4.80		PV	4.13i	3.75- 00
	Sterlin	Heather	USA	12.4.74	166/54	Hep	5755w, 5702	5688- 97
	Sterling	Natalee	JAM	26.9.78		400H	57.25	59.83- 98
	Steyn	Nicolize	RSA	28.5.81	169/58	HJ	1.88A	1.90A- 00
	Stone	Felicia	USA	10.8.77		100H	13.27, 13.26w	13.21- 00
	Storga	Evfemija	SLO	7.10.75	168/68	JT	59.11	61.14- 00
	Stoyanova	Gergana	BUL	3.1.82	170/62	100H	13.02, 13.00w	13.69- 00
	Stratáki	Aryiró	GRE	3.8.75		Hep	5640	5551- 00

	Name		Nat	Born	Ht/Wt	Event	2001 Mark	Pre-2001 Best
	Strömmer	Mia	FIN	26.2.74	171/70	HT	69.63	66.37- 00
	Strutz	Martina	GER	4.11.81	160/53	PV	4.42	4.20- 00
	Stucan #	Constanta	ROM	12.7.81	174/60	TJ	13.78, 13.88dq	13.96- 00
*	Sturrup	Chandra	BAH	12.9.71	163/55	100	10.95	10.86- 00
						200	22.99	22.33- 96
^	Styopina	Viktoria	UKR	21.2.76	175/58	HJ	1.94	1.96- 99
	Su Yiping		CHN	4.8.79	174/58	100H	12.95, 12.70w	12.91- 99
*	Sua	Seilala	USA	25.2.78	188/109	SP	17.97	17.65- 99
						DT	65.64	65.90- 00
	Sugár	Barbara	HUN	9.10.77	178/82	HT	62.55	57.59- 98
	Sugihara	Ai	JPN	12.10.75	163/48	Mar	2:30:50	2:33:08- 98
^	Sui Xinmei		CHN	29.1.65	172/90	SP	18.06	21.66- 90
	Suldesová	Andrea	CZE	11.2.75	164/51	1500	4:06.34	4:06.13- 98
	Sun Chunfang		CHN	1.3.77	171/58	20kW	1:30:48	1:29:45- 00
	Sun Qiuhong		CHN	13.10.78	162/50	800	2:01.80	2:05.44- 00
						1500	4:08.12	4:13.52- 00
	Sun Yali		CHN	6.1.78		DT	55.69	56.64- 97
	Sun Yingjie		CHN	3.10.77	165/50	5000	15:02.70	15:32.14- 99
						10000	31:49.47	32:12.7 - 99
						Mar	2:29:16	2:25:45- 98
	Sun Yufei		CHN	18.4.84		PV	4.11	
*	Suttle	Kellie	USA	9.5.73	170/59	PV	4.60	4.53- 00
	Swift	Shonda	USA	28.2.74	178/67	TJ	13.67	13.82- 97
*	Szabo	Gabriela	ROM	14.11.75	158/43	1500	4:00.57	3:56.97- 98
						1M	4:23.19i	4:19.30- 98
						2000	5:39.5+	5:30.53i- 98, 5:36.88+- 97
						3000	8:24.19	8:24.31- 98
						5000	14:46.92	14:31.48- 98
*	Szabó	Nikolett	HUN	3.3.80	168/65	JT	64.62	65.10#- 98, 61.79- 99
^	Szabó	Zsuzsanna	HUN	6.5.73	176/63	PV	4.20	4.51i, 4.40- 99
*	Szekely	Violeta	ROM	26.3.65	167/52	1500	3:59.35	3:58.29- 00
						3000	8:46.39i	8:47.3 - 98
*	Szentgyörgyi	Katalin	HUN	1.1.79	166/48	3000	8:32.70	8:53.92- 99
						10000	32:27.69	35:56.92- 96
	Szlendaková	Barbara	CZE	6.8.78	178/64	Hep	5727	5488- 00
	Szykulska	Renata	POL	17.8.74	176/60	TJ	13.60	13.34, 13.44w- 00
	Tabáki	Hristiána	GRE	13.1.73	173/59	100H	13.26	13.27- 99
	Tabakova	Yuliya	RUS	1.5.80	168/64	100	11.20	11.40, 11.38w- 00
						200	22.68	
	Tadamasa	Ryoko	JPN	9.5.76	164/46	20kW	1:34:49	1:33:43- 99
	Tafflet	Corinne	FRA	8.11.75	163/48	400H	57.08	57.74- 00
	Takahashi	Chiemi	JPN	16.2.76	159/43	10000	31:59.87	31:27.57- 98
						HMar	71:18	71:35- 96
*	Takahashi	Naoko	JPN	6.5.72	161/52	HMar	69:48+	68:55- 00
						Mar	2:19:46	2:21:47- 98
	Takahashi	Noriko	JPN	9.11.76	163/50	5000	15:29.87	15:42.06- 00
	Takanaka	Mikie	JPN	6.10.80	164/46	10000	32:23.00	
						HMar	71:06	
	Tamura	Ikuko	JPN	24.9.78	155/41	1500	4:11.53	4:16.86- 00
						5000	15:26.6	15:24.9 - 00
	Tan Yali		CHN	17.1.77	175/53	100H	13.27	13.12- 97
	Tanabe	Kaori	JPN	30.4.75	152/39	10000	32:17.64	33:38.02- 00
						HMar	71:04	71:44- 00
	Tanabe	Kumi	JPN	2.4.81	158/41	10000	32:12.01	33:45.83- 00
	Tanaka	Megumi	JPN	4.9.75	160/43	5000	15:19.75	15:17.92- 99
						10000	32:00.75	31:53.35- 98
	Tang Xiaoling		CHN	3.2.77		JT	59.95	54.44- 99
	Tang Yinghua		CHN	18.5.73	164/45	20kW	1:33:04	1:30:36- 00
	Tang Zhimin		CHN	26.6.79		TJ	13.87	13.83- 00
	Tao Hongbo		CHN	20.9.79		DT	58.01	60.83- 99
	Tarasova	Anna	KAZ	23.3.80	176/62	TJ	13.64A	13.85- 98, 14.17A- 00
	Tarekegne	Etaferahu	ETH	20.3.80	165/45	3000	8:59.97	8:53.77- 96
	Tauryanina	Yelena	RUS	11.9.80	185/80	HT	63.85	60.41- 00
	Tavares	Carmo	POR	27.4.74	168/52	400	52.13	51.92- 99
						400H	56.88	57.88- 99
	Taylor	Brenda	USA	9.2.79		400H	55.46	56.64- 00
	Taylor	Clare	USA	7.12.69	171/52	5000	15:26.95	15:30.44- 00
	Teichmann	Ivonne	GER	11.4.77	170/50	800	1:58.62	1:59.20- 00
						1500	4:11.15	4:17.05- 96
	Teixeira	Sandra	POR	13.3.78		800	2:01.88	2:02.86- 00
	Tejeda	Anay	CUB	3.4.83	163/55	100H	13.20, 13.07w	13.38- 00

Name		Nat	Born	Ht/Wt	Event	2001 Mark	Pre-2001 Best
* Tereshchuk	Tatyana	UKR	11.10.69	176/61	400H	53.89A, 54.01	53.40- 98
Ter-Mesrobyan	Tatyana	RUS	12.5.68	180/62	LJ	6.68i	6.94- 98
					TJ	13.91i	13.99i- 98, 13.41- 99
Termure ¶	Ana Mirela	ROM	13.1.75	175/66	JT	65.08	63.29- 00
Terui	Takako	JPN	11.1.78	153/46	20kW	1:34:10	1:37:34- 00
Terzóglou	Iríni-Hrisovaládo	GRE	2.2.79	176/86	SP	17.37	16.88- 00
Teter	Nicole	USA	8.11.73	172/57	800	2:01.32	2:01.59- 00
* Thánou	Ekateríni	GRE	1.2.75	165/56	100	10.91	10.83, 10.77w- 99
* Thiam	Ami Mbacké	SEN	10.11.76	176/60	400	49.86	50.77- 99
Thiel	Christy	AUS	30.4.74		DT	57.13	54.69- 00
Thompson	Bronwyn	AUS	29.1.78	177/68	LJ	6.88	6.56, 6.64w- 00
Thompson	Yolanda	USA	29.5.81	175/60	LJ	6.48	6.17, 6.48w- 00
Thornton	SaDonna	USA	16.8.78	157/48	100	11.43, 11.31w	11.35, 11.30w- 00
Thu Lan	Phan Thi	VIE	79		LJ	6.57	6.27- 00
Tian Mei		CHN	27.11.71	161/50	Mar	2:30:35	2:28:15- 97
Tian Xiue		CHN	4.10.71		SP	17.03	18.51- 93
* Tilea-Moldovan	Felicia	ROM	29.9.67	169/70	JT	62.27	63.12- 00, 69.26#- 96
Timofeyeva	Irina	RUS	5.4.70	156/48	Mar	2:25:29	2:27:46- 99
* Tîrlea	Ionela	ROM	9.2.76	169/54	100	11.32	11.30- 99
					200	22.77	22.35- 99
					400H	54.65	53.25- 99
Titarenko	Liliya	UKR	17.2.78		JT	56.82	55.55- 00
Tobin-West	Ibifuro	NGR			LJ	6.45	6.17- 00
Tolbert	Ryan	USA	16.6.76	174/64	400H	56.58	54.21- 97
Tollefson	Carrie	USA	18.1.77	175/54	3000	8:57.61	9:08.20- 00
					5000	15:25.52	15:51.55, 15:51.39i- 00
Tolokina	Anna	RUS	3.10.81	182/90	SP	17.13	16.12- 00
Tolson	Christina	USA	16.1.78		SP	17.77	17.34- 00
					HT	65.54	63.68- 00
Tolstaya	Svetlana	KAZ	9.8.71	168/52	20kW	1:31:49	1:30:44- 00, 1:29:23sh- 99
Toman	Liz	CAN	17.4.78		DT	56.22	53.44- 00
* Tomashova	Tatyana	RUS	1.7.75	168/58	1500	4:03.31	4:04.80- 00
					3000	8:25.56	8:34.53- 00
					5000	14:39.22	14:53.00- 00
* Tomecková	Nikola	CZE	25.6.74	180/77	JT	65.71	64.50#- 96, 64.19- 00
Tomescu (Dita)	Constantina	ROM	23.1.70	165/48	Mar	2:26:39	2:34:35- 98
Toomey	Jennifer	USA	19.12.71		800	2:00.38	2:03.58- 00
Torazzi	Monica	ITA	26.2.71	174/88	HT	61.90	60.84- 00
^ Torshina	Natalya	KAZ	4.10.68	172/57	400H	55.37	54.50- 00
* Tosa	Reiko	JPN	11.6.76	166/51	Mar	2:26:06	2:24:36- 00
Tóth	Lívia	HUN	7.1.80		3kSt	10:04.99	-0-
Touhami	Nahida	ALG	10.2.78		800	2:02.93	2:03.10- 99
Toulouse	Sandrine	FRA	14.9.72	170/58	PV	4.10i	3.90- 99
^ Trandenkova	Marina	RUS	7.1.67	171/61	100	11.34	11.06- 96, 10.8- 99
Trent	Tia	USA	25.7.79	175/62	400	52.32	53.53- 00
Trujillo	Janet	USA	7.8.75	165/50	3kSt	10:09.70	10:55.57- 97
Tsámoglou	Evdokía	GRE	15.12.78	174/84	HT	65.83	63.20- 00
* Tsander	Olga	BLR	18.5.76	174/83	HT	68.94	69.81- 00
* Tsiamíta	Paraskeví	GRE	10.3.72	171/60	TJ	14.06	15.07- 99
* Tsikoúna	Stilianí	GRE	19.10.72	171/75	DT	63.18	65.13- 00
Tsiliggíri	Yeoryía	GRE	21.6.72	158/46	PV	4.36	4.25i- 99, 4.20- 00
Tsiolakoúdi	Aggelikí	GRE	10.5.76	172/66	JT	62.90	63.32#- 97, 60.26A- 00
* Tsybulskaya	Valentina	BLR	19.2.68	163/54	20kW	1:28:49. 1:33:25.5t	1:29:20- 99
* Tsyganova	Natalya	RUS	7.2.71	162/50	800	1:57.97	1:56.60- 00
					1000	2:34.90	2:32.77- 99
Tucholke	Jana	GER	20.5.81	185/90	DT	57.19	53.97- 00
Tudja	Julianna	HUN	13.10.79	175/77	HT	64.29	61.42- 00
Tuimala	Anni	FIN	27.4.82	160/45	3kSt	10:07.41	-0-
Tuimala	Ulla	FIN	27.4.82	160/45	3kSt	10:04.99	-0-
^ Tullett	Hayley	GBR	17.2.73	166/58	1500	4:03.54	4:01.23- 00
					1M	4:26.52i	4:26.50i- 00
					3000	8:51.73, 8:45.36i	8:45.39- 00
* Tulu	Derartu	ETH	21.3.72	155/45	10000	31:48.19	30:17.49- 00
					HMar	67:03	68:04- 00
					Mar	2:23:57	2:26:09- 00
Tunks	Teri	USA	30.10.75	180/75	DT	56.98	56.60- 98
* Turova	Alesya	BLR	6.12.79	180/64	1500	4:07.25	4:05.99- 00
					2000	5:42.55	
					3000	8:32.89	8:44.81- 00
					5000	15:30.63	15:23.84- 00
Turova	Margarita	BLR	28.12.80	174/55	20kW	1:29:31	

Name		Nat	Born	Ht/Wt	Event	2001 Mark	Pre-2001 Best
Twum	Monica	GHA	14.3.78	159/58	100	11.31	11.35- 00, 11.29w- 99
					200	23.27, 23.20w	23.21- 00
^ Tyukhay	Irina	RUS	14.1.67	171/64	Hep	5897	6604- 95
Ueno	Rie	JPN	11.6.76	163/50	5000	15:33.76	15:28.73- 00
Ulyeva	Iolanta	KAZ	27.7.76	172/85	SP	17.65	17.82- 00
Umlauft	Katja	GER	22.11.74	180/	TJ	14.01i, 13.93	13.80i, 13.72- 99
Upshaw	Grace	USA	22.9.75	173/59	LJ	6.62, 6.70w	6.47A- 00
^ Urbansky	Ulrike	GER	6.4.77	170/52	400H	55.99	54.57- 00
Ushakova	Veronika	RUS	8.11.77	178/82	HT	62.52	63.08- 99
Usovich	Svetlana	BLR	14.10.80		400	52.47	53.68- 00
Vail	Jennifer	USA	16.3.78	173/77	HT	62.26	62.26- 00
Vaill	Teresa	USA	20.11.62	162/48	20kW	1:33:23	1:35:45- 00
Vainikainen	Katja	FIN	30.7.77	177/63	HJ	1.87i	1.86- 97
Valant	Anja	SLO	8.9.77	183/66	TJ	14.31i, 13.95	14.69- 00
van Wyk	Drienke	RSA	13.1.71		SP	17.68	17.38dq- 99, 15.02- 96
van Zyl	Kerryn	RSA	5.10.74		400H	56.93A, 57.12	57.55A- 00
Vanakára	Asimína	GRE	14.7.79	173/55	Hep	5846	5927- 00
Vanden Bempt	Sigrid	BEL	10.2.81		3kSt	10:03.02	10:34.45- 00
Varga	Mary	USA	1.5.80		HJ	1.86i	
Vasallo	Aldenay	CUB	25.2.77	170/73	HT	64.91	63.70- 00
* Vasco	María	ESP	26.12.75	156/47	20kW	1:30:09	1:30:20- 00
Vasilevskaya	Lydia	RUS	1.4.73	163/48	Mar	2:29:57	
Vasilyeva	Irina	RUS	9.4.79	171/57	TJ	14.57	14.14- 00
Vasilyeva	Lyudmila	RUS	20.10.69	170/54	1500	4:02.45	4:05.07- 00
					1M	4:30.30	4:31.62- 00
					3000	8:52.98	9:06.09i, 9:07.74- 92
Vasko	Natalya	BLR	20.5.80	169/56	800	2:02.68	2:03.1 - 00
* Vaszi	Tünde	HUN	18.4.72	172/58	PV	4.10i	4.22i, 4.15- 99
					LJ	6.86	6.82i- 99, 6.77- 98, 8, 6.82Aw- 96
Vaylenko (Prikhodko)	Lyudmila	UKR	18.3.74	169/62	PV	4.10	4.10i, 4.00- 00
Veldáková	Dana	SVK	3.6.81	178/59	TJ	13.73	13.92- 00
Velichko	Oksana	BLR	26.3.75	172/69	JT	61.30	62.06- 00
* Veneva	Venelina	BUL	13.6.74	179/61	HJ	2.04	2.03- 98
Ventris	Lyn	AUS	2.10.56		20kW	1:34:44	
Vershinina	Viktoria	UKR	11.6.71	177/60	LJ	6.45i	6.98sq- 95, 6.92- 96
* Viceconte	Maura	ITA	3.10.67	166/51	HMar	69:19	70:48- 00
					Mar	2:26:33	2:23:47- 00
Vigourt	Julie	FRA	19.10.79	163/53	PV	4.15	4.15- 00
Vílceanu-Heltne	Anca	ROM	1.1.78	175/76	SP	16.68i	17.51- 99
Vilisova	Mariya	RUS	69		3kSt	10:11.45	10:12.07- 00
Vindyuk	Alena	RUS	31.7.79		Hep	6146	5739- 00
Vis	Judith	NED	21.6.80	183/72	100H	13.31	13.36- 99
Visigalli	Anna	ITA	24.2.81	182/62	HJ	1.90i, 1.87	1.83- 00
* Vlasic	Blanka	CRO	8.11.83	191/75	HJ	1.95	1.93- 00
Vlok	Adri	RSA	17.6.76		400H	57.17	57.46A- 99
* Vóggoli	Ekateríni	GRE	30.10.70	175/89	DT	63.47	64.82- 99
Volkova	Liliya	RUS	13.11.77	168/57	1500	4:12.04	4:17.62- 99
					3000	8:53.35	9:37.24- 00
Volkova	Tamara	UKR	17.7.79	166/55	800	2:02.26	2:05.12- 00
Volkova	Yekaterina	RUS	16.2.78		3kSt	9:41.54	9:52.40- 00
Voropinova	Olga	RUS	.81		TJ	13.67	13.42- 00
Vrbenská	Lucie	CZE	12.5.77	180/85	HT	66.20	62.62- 00
* Vriesde	Letitia	SUR	5.10.64	159/55	800	1:57.35	1:56.68- 95
					1000	2:35.89	2:32.25- 91
Wagner	Marion	GER	1.2.78	175/52	100	11.33	11.38- 99
Waibel	Emily	USA	10.2.81	163/57	100H	13.31, 13.28w	13.48- 00
Walker	Astia	JAM	4.4.75	178/59	100	11.28	11.33- 00
					100H	13.01	12.82- 97
Walker	Melanie	JAM	1.1.83	165/53	400H	55.62	56.96- 00
Walsham	Suzy	AUS	22.11.73	163/42	1500	4:10.7mx/4:12.27	4:11.04- 90
Walter	Sarah	FRA	5.5.78	173/64	JT	58.41	59.02- 99
Wambui	Nancy	KEN	15.8.83		5000	15:22.0A	
* Wami	Getenesh	ETH	11.12.74	153/44	2000	5:39.9+	
					3000	8:27.62	8:29.24- 98
					5000	14:31.69	14:30.88- 00
					10000	31:49.98	30:22.48- 00
Wang Chunmei		CHN	10.4.76	165/50	1500	4:10.61	3:59.48- 97
					5000	15:19.14	15:07.16- 98
Wang Hailan		CHN	6.4.76	168/59	Hep	5917	5808- 99
Wang Hongxia		CHN	13.1.75	159/47	10000	32:12.88	33:30.32- 98
Wang Lina		CHN	28.2.83	168/58	LJ	6.56i, 6.51	6.26- 99

	Name		Nat	Born	Ht/Wt	Event	2001 Mark	Pre-2001 Best
*	Wang Liping		CHN	8.7.76	165/48	20kW	1:26:23	1:28:33- 00
	Wang Qingqing		CHN	7.2.83		20kW	1:29:44	1:35:50- 00
	Wang Qiuju		CHN	12.10.75		DT	56.02	60.36- 95
	Wang Xiaoming		CHN	3.2.85		5000	15:29.55	
						10000	32:33.00	32:44.84- 00
	Wang Xiaoyu		CHN	25.12.81		HT	63.34	59.51- 00
*	Wang Yan		CHN	3.5.71	170/52	20kW	1:26:22	1:28:27- 00
	Wang Yanchun		CHN	4.2.76		800	2:01.27	2:03.22- 96
	Wang Yanrong		CHN	16.10.76	155/43	10000	32:06.02	33:05.39- 00
						Mar	2:30:25	2:28:41- 97
	Wang Yuanping		CHN	8.12.76	165/55	800	2:01.05	2:00.63- 00
	Wangui	Lucy	KEN	24.3.84	155/42	3000	8:57.47	
*	Wanjiru	Esther	ETH	27.3.77	162/48	HMar	70:11	66:49- 99
	Warlick	Alicia	USA	11.10.77		PV	4.50	4.35- 00
	Washington	Demetria	USA	31.12.79	178/65	200	23.18, 22.87w	23.43, 23.38w- 00
						400	51.05	51.71- 00
	Wassiluk	Petra	GER	27.10.69	167/51	HMar	70:36	68:13- 97
	Watkins	Tawana	USA	27.3.84		400H	57.48	58.50- 00
	Wei Jianhua		CHN	23.3.79	170/68	JT	61.56	66.64#- 97, 63.92- 00
	Wei Yanan		CHN	6.12.81	160/48	5000	15:15.75	
						10000	31:54.86	32:46.75- 00
						Mar	2:24:02	2:26:34- 00
	Wentland	Gwen	USA	29.4.72	178/64	HJ	1.90	1.96i, 1.94- 95
^	Wessel	Kathrin	GER	14.8.67	172/52	HMar	71:09	70:47- 94
						Mar	2:28:27	2:30:05- 00
	Weston	Shekera	USA	1.9.77		200	23.27, 23.09w	23.23, 22.91w- 99
*	Weyermann	Anita	SUI	8.12.77	162/50	3kSt	9:57.06	-0-
	Wheeler	Erica	USA	28.11.67	172/68	JT	56.81	62.76#- 96, 55.06- 99
	Wheeler	Kylie	AUS	17.1.80	180/59	Hep	5702	5583- 00
*	White	Kelli	USA	1.4.77	163/57	100	10.99, 10.93w	11.19- 00, 10.96w- 99
						200	22.38	22.58- 98, 22.49w- 99
	White	LaKeesha	USA	29.7.80	168/57	100	11.26w	11.36, 11.22w- 00
						200	23.25	23.22- 99, 22.74w- 00
^	Whitlock	Janine	GBR	11.8.73	163/54	PV	4.40	4.35- 00
	Whyte	Angela	CAN	27.5.80	170/60	100H	13.09, 12.82w	13.37A- 00
	Wielgus	Anna	POL	27.10.81	170/60	PV	4.10	4.10- 00
	Wigene	Susanne	NOR	12.2.78		3kSt	10:04.49	10:01.54- 00
	Wijenberg	Nadezhda	NED	2.4.64	165/49	HMar	70:30	68:58- 94
						Mar	2:30:25	2:28:45- 99
	Wilhelm	Anja	GER	5.5.80		PV	4.10i	3.80- 00
	Wilhelmy	Sarah	GBR	2.2.80	175/64	100	11.24w	11.49- 00
						200	23.27, 22.84w	23.23, 23.20w- 98
	Wilkins	Melani	GBR	18.1.73	178/61	100H	13.24, 13.08w	13.17- 00, 13.1- 95
	Wilks	Antoinette	USA	14.10.80	170/55	LJ	6.60i	6.38i, 6.13, 6.44w- 00
	Williams	Aleah	USA	7.1.81		100	11.31w	11.36, 11.25w- 00
	Williams	Aleah	USA	7.1.81		200	23.13w	23.24, 22.81w- 00
*	Williams	Angela	USA	30.1.80	156/52	100	11.18, 11.01w	11.04, 10.96w- 99
						200	23.27, 23.11w	23.02- 98, 22.78w- 00
	Williams	Angela	USA	30.1.80		200	23.11w	
	Williams	Ashlee	USA	27.3.84	170/54	100H	13.23	13.65, 13.39w- 00
	Williams	Deshaya	USA	8.7.80	173/82	DT	55.56	54.46- 99
	Williams	Elisha	USA	9.1.79	183/65	LJ	6.59i, 6.48, 6.58w	6.38- 99
	Williams	Foy	CAN	27.9.73	168/54	400	52.12	51.62A, 52.00- 00
^	Williams	Shana	USA	7.4.72	178/62	LJ	6.48, 6.56w	7.01- 96
	Williams	Tasha	NZL	31.7.73	174/72	HT	65.91	64.60- 00
	Williams	Valerie	USA	12.12.79		LJ	6.46	6.36i- 00, 6.20- 95
	Williams	Ysanne	USA	25.9.80	168/55	400H	57.34	59.97- 99
	Williamson	EllaKisha	USA	19.3.75	160/59	100H	13.06	12.81- 00
	Willis	Benita	AUS	6.5.79	163/53	1500	4:10.98	4:07.05- 00
						3000	8:42.95, 8:42.75i	9:02.19- 00
						5000	15:04.18	15:21.37- 00
	Wilson	Aileen	GBR	30.3.84	181/65	HJ	1.87	1.83- 00
	Winatho	Wassanee	THA	30.6.80		400H	57.09	59.00- 00
	Wise	Joanne	GBR	15.3.71	161/53	LJ	6.46w	6.76- 99
	Wisniewska	Joanna	POL	24.5.72	187/82	DT	63.75	63.97- 99
	Witter	Erica	CAN	10.12.76	180/65	200	23.23	23.29, 23.09Aw- 00
	Witteveen ¶	Solange	ARG	6.2.76	171/60	HJ	1.91i, 1.91, 1.97dq	1.96- 97
	Wittrin	Caroline	CAN	10.12.68	175/84	HT	62.03	63.47- 99
^	Wlodarczyk	Urszula	POL	22.12.65	180/67	Hep	5870	6542- 97
	Wojczakowska	Izabela	POL	24.3.74	180/65	JT	56.32	54.95- 00
	Woods	Tania	USA	23.9.80		100	11.37, 11.29w	11.41- 99
						200	23.17	22.88- 99

Name		Nat	Born	Ht/Wt	Event	2001 Mark	Pre-2001 Best
* Worku	Ayelech	ETH	12.6.79	165/47	3000	8:47.01	8:39.51- 99
					5000	14:54.00	14:41.23- 00
					10000	31:38.08	
Woytowska	Jana	GER	7.8.77		JT	55.78	58.35- 99
Wu Lingmei		CHN	16.2.73	168/60	TJ	14.12, 14.24w	14.39- 98, 14.55w- 99
Wu Xueli		CHN	5.1.78	172/62	TJ	13.71	13.60- 96
Wurm	Karin	GER	6.2.78		SP	17.20	16.34- 00
Wysocka	Marzena	POL	17.2.69	176/80	DT	62.48	63.20- 99
* Xánthou	Níki	GRE	11.10.73	174/56	LJ	6.80	7.03- 97, 7.12Aw- 95
Xiao Hongfan		CHN	6.1.83		400H	56.61	
Xiao Lin		CHN	22.2.78		200	23.27	24.42- 97
Xiao Yanling		CHN	27.3.68	180/92	DT	61.81	71.68- 92
Xing Huina		CHN	25.2.84		1500	4:10.43	
					5000	14:56.15	16:11.09- 00
Xiong Yanling		CHN	5.5.80		100H	13.29, 13.16w	13.37- 00
Xu Aihui		CHN	25.4.78	167/54	20kW	1:30:00	1:32:07- 00
Xu Shaoyang		CHN	9.2.83		DT	59.97	54.90- 00
Xu Xin		CHN	30.8.87		JT	56.45	
Yakovenko	Maria	RUS	6.1.82		JT	54.68	50.65- 00
^ Yamaguchi	Eri	JPN	14.1.73	163/47	HMar	70:11	69:31- 99
Yamamoto	Ai	JPN	6.7.78	158/43	HMar	71:16	74:47- 99
Yamamoto	Harumi	JPN	8.5.74	168/69	JT	57.17	56.80#- 96, 56.33- 99
Yamanaka	Miwako	JPN	24.5.78	163/48	10000	31:53.7	33:09.01- 97
					HMar	68:54	73:14- 00
Yan Jiankui		CHN	19.3.76	160/50	200	23.16	22.85- 98
					400	52.44	
Yan Wei		CHN	4.10.73	164/52	1500	4:08.05	3:58.74- 97
Yan Xueqin		CHN	1.11.73		TJ	13.71	14.00- 97, 14.16Aw- 95
Yang Dehui		CHN	28.4.83		SP	17.67	15.91- 99
Yang Jinhua		CHN	10.1.79		800	2:02.88	2:05.65- 98
Yang Meiping		CHN	23.10.85		HT	65.21	61.44- 00
Yang Wenjing		CHN	26.9.79		20kW	1:34:40	1:34:08- 00
Yao Yuehua		CHN	27.8.80		400H	55.58	57.60- 99
Yarygina	Oksana	RUS	24.12.72	170/65	JT	60.02	64.62#- 94, 58.80- 99
* Yatchenko	Irina	BLR	31.10.65	187/96	DT	66.65	68.94- 92
Yefremova	Antonina	UKR	19.7.81	176/58	400	52.29	51.95- 00
Yegorova	Galina	RUS	5.8.83		3kSt	10:09.83	-0-
Yegorova	Lyudmila	UKR	4.10.74	164/54	20kW	1:34:02	1:32:02- 00
* Yegorova	Olga	RUS	28.3.72	160/48	1500	4:02.76	4:04.75- 00
					2000	5:39.9+	
					3000	8:23.26	8:33.02- 99
					5000	14:29.32	14:42.91- 00
^ Yegorova	Valentina	RUS	16.2.64	156/52	Mar	2:28:41	2:23:33- 94
* Yelesina	Yelena	RUS	4.4.70	182/62	HJ	1.95	2.02- 90
Yelling	Hayley	GBR	3.1.74	157/46	3000	8:58.98	9:02.88mx, 9:11.20- 00
					5000	15:19.12	15:36.27- 00
Yelling	Liz	GBR	5.12.74	174/56	3000	8:57.3mx	9:11.4- 00
					HMar	71:29	72:31- 00
Yepimashko	Vera	BLR	10.7.76		Hep	5791h	
Yermolayeva	Irina	RUS	14.10.79	170/59	LJ	6.61i, 6.59	6.71- 00
Yershova	Olga	RUS	13.8.76		TJ	14.38	14.47- 00
Yesipchuk	Oksana	RUS	13.12.76	183/95	DT	62.01	63.68- 00
Yi Chunmei		CHN	15.3.83		JT	57.72	55.96- 00
Yordanova (Stoyanova)	Antonia	BUL	17.8.76	170/52	LJ	6.47	6.34- 98
Yordanova	Daniela	BUL	8.3.76	165/52	800	2:03.02	2:05.16- 00
					1500	4:01.68	4:03.83- 00
					3000	8:30.59	8:45.26- 00
(Yordanova)							
Yoshida	Kaori	JPN	4.8.81	155/38	10000	32:01.23	
					HMar	70:18	
Yoshida	Makiko	JPN	16.7.76	164/49	400H	56.83	57.92- 00
Yoshimatsu	Hisae	JPN	13.5.79	163/46	5000	15:34.49	15:48.62- 00
Young	Candace	USA	9.1.79	176/	100	11.22	11.49, 11.2- 00, 11.36w- 99
Yu Jing		CHN	7.3.83		SP	17.41	16.75- 00
Yu Juan		CHN	29.3.75	175/88	SP	17.98	19.13- 95
Yu Shaohua		CHN	4.1.85		LJ	6.47	6.34- 99
Yu Xin		CHN	23.2.77	188/90	DT	57.55	63.80- 96
Yu Yiqun		CHN	12.1.76		LJ	6.48	6.74- 97
Yusuf	Hajarat	NGR	.82		400	52.38	
Yvelain	Fatima	FRA	31.12.69	165/52	5000	15:06.35	14:58.18- 99
* Zabawska	Krystyna	POL	14.1.68	183/92	SP	19.10	19.42- 92

Name		Nat	Born	Ht/Wt	Event	2001 Mark	Pre-2001 Best
Zabruskova	Valeriya	RUS	29.7.75		JT	58.18	62.04, 63.87#- 99
* Zadorozhnaya	Yelena	RUS	3.12.77	157/42	1500	4:02.16	4:03.32- 00
					1M	4:24.11i	
					3000	8:25.40	8:51.2- 00
					5000	14:40.47	16:22.3 - 99
Zagacka	Liliana	POL	28.1.77	168/56	LJ	6.56	6.54- 00
					TJ	14.22	13.96- 00
Zaginay	Yuliya	RUS	3.8.63		SP	17.79i, 17.72	19.06- 99
Zagórska	Anna	POL	26.7.80	170/53	800	2:02.04	2:03.76- 00
Zaituc	Luminita	GER	9.10.68	163/47	10000	32:35.90	32:41.03- 97
					HMar	71:04	
					Mar	2:26:01	
Zakharchenko	Ilona	UKR	16.6.67	178/80	DT	58.40	64.80-92
Zakharchuk	Oksana	UKR	3.4.80	180/92	SP	18.03	16.56- 00
* Zakharova	Svetlana	RUS	15.9.70		Mar	2:24:04	2:27:08- 99
Zakowicz	Katarzyna	POL	12.5.75	184/94	SP	18.59i, 18.59	19.28- 00
* Zalevskaya	Svetlana	KAZ	14.6.73	188/63	HJ	1.91i, 1.90	1.98i, 1.97- 96
Zamboni	Nathalie	SUI	23.12.73		400H	56.70	56.89- 00
Zauna	Irena	LAT	16.3.81	179/59	400H	57.03	56.40- 00
Zaytseva	Svetlana	RUS	14.8.81		LJ	6.61	6.44- 00
Zbrozhek	Oksana	RUS	12.1.78	167/49	800	2:00.46	2:04.99- 98
Zeng Xiaoling		CHN	1.1.80		100H	13.31, 12.91w	13.47- 00
Zeng Xiujun		CHN	10.2.79	161/58	100	11.43	11.25- 98
Zhang Guirong		CHN	78		SP	17.38	17.45- 00
Zhang Hao		CHN	26.2.78		TJ	13.87	13.64- 97
Zhang Hengyun		CHN	25.10.74	170.56	400	52.44	51.22- 97
Zhang Jian		CHN	5.4.76	162/50	800	2:01.81	1:58.98- 97
Zhang Jinqing		CHN	21.6.77	168/58	1500	4:08.09	4:04.05- 97
Zhang Juan		CHN	8.4.83		SP	17.32	15.42- 99
Zhang Li		CHN	19.10.78		JT	56.93	60.02- 00
Zhang Libo		CHN	4.2.82		20kW	1:34:10	
^ Zhang Liuhong		CHN	16.1.69	181/86	SP	18.57	20.54- 94
Zhang Na		CHN	27.9.80	178/60	PV	4.10i, 4.10	4.10- 00
Zhang Nina		CHN	3.3.81		Hep	5811	5383- 00
Zhang Shujing		CHN	13.9.78	158/55	Mar	2:24:42	2:27:14- 00
Zhang Wenxiu		CHN	11.2.83		HT	66.30	60.30- 00
Zhang Xiaoyu		CHN	16.3.83		SP	18.49	16.55- 00
Zhang Yang		CHN	20.7.83		5000	15:32.67	15:38.35- 00
					10000	32:20.48	33:29.52- 00
Zhang Ying		CHN	19.3.84		SP	18.05	
Zhang Yu		CHN	8.4.71	180/64	100H	13.29, 13.03w	12.64- 93
Zhang Yuhong		CHN	15.1.83		10000	32:32.62	
Zhang Zhiying		CHN	19.7.73	174/80	SP	17.51	19.77- 93
Zhao Shengzhi		CHN	19.11.75		Mar	2:29:03	2:35:59- 98
Zhao Wei		CHN	27.1.79	185/95	HT	66.16	65.70- 00
Zhdanova (Sultanova)	Firiya	RUS	29.4.61	166/52	Mar	2:30:58	2:30:45- 99
Zhdanova	Yevgeniya	RUS	21.7.66	175/53	LJ	6.69	6.61i, 6.37- 99
					TJ	14.27	
Zheng Guixia		CHN	24.6.73	160/52	10000	31:56.47	32:10.51- 99
					HMar	68:58	69:25- 00
					Mar	2:25:56	2:29:38- 96
Zheng Hui		CHN	18.12.73		SP	16.96	18.73- 92
Zhevnova	Tatyana	BLR	17.10.77	173/60	Hep	5670w	5871- 97
^ Zhilyayeva	Alla	RUS	5.2.69	163/47	3000	8:57.53i	8:58.75- 95
Zhong Mei		CHN	7.1.78	167/63	LJ	6.69	6.76- 97
Zhong Shaoting		CHN	30.1.80		400	52.24	52.21- 99
Zhu Yanyan		CHN	3.12.78		LJ	6.53	6.30- 00
Zhukovskaya	Irina	RUS	78		HJ	1.92	1.88- 00
^ Zilinskiené	Nele	LTU	29.12.69	176/58	HJ	1.92	1.96- 94
Zongo	Amy	FRA	4.10.80	163/49	TJ	13.72	12.97- 99
Zozulya	Vera	UKR	31.8.70	166/56	20kW	1:31:30	1:31:26- 00
Zuo Yan		CHN	18.8.83		20kW	1:32:11	
* Zvereva	Ellina	BLR	16.11.60	186/96	DT	67.10	71.58- 88
* Zykina	Olesya	RUS	7.10.80	170/60	400	50.15	50.36- 00

WORLD INDOOR LISTS 2002 – MEN

(also * some marks made in December 2001

50 METRES

Mark	First name	Surname	Nat	Born	Pos	Meet	Venue	Date
5.62+	Morne	Nagel	RSA	23.3.78	1h1		Liévin	24 Feb
5.66+	Brian	Lewis	USA	5.12.74	2h1		Liévin	24 Feb
5.67+	Gregory	Saddler	USA	29.6.74	2		Liévin	24 Feb

Mark	First name	Surname	Nat	Born	Date
5.69	Nicolas	Macrozonaris	CAN	22.8.80	12 Jan
5.69+	Gennadiy	Chernovol	KAZ	6.6.76	24 Feb

60 METRES

Mark	First name	Surname	Nat	Born	Pos	Meet	Venue	Date
6.48	Tim	Montgomery	USA	28.1.75	1		Dortmund	27 Jan
6.48	Morne	Nagel	RSA	23.3.78	2		Dortmund	27 Jan
6.48A	Marcus	Brunson	USA	24.4.78	1		Flagstaff	9 Feb
6.49	Shawn	Crawford	USA	14.1.78	1	Mill	New York	1 Feb
6.49	Jason	Gardener	GBR	18.9.75	1	EI	Wien	3 Mar
6.53	Mark	Lewis-Francis	GBR	4.9.82	2	NC	Cardiff	3 Feb
6.54	Gregory	Saddler	USA	29.6.74	2		Gent	10 Feb
6.54	Brian	Lewis	USA	5.12.74	1		Chemnitz	22 Feb
6.54	Justin	Gatlin	USA	10.2.82	1	SEC	Fayetteville	24 Feb
6.55	Joshua J.	Johnson	USA	10.5.76	2	Mill	New York	1 Feb
6.55	Leonard	Scott	USA	19.1.80	1h1	NCAA	Fayetteville	8 Mar
6.56	Coby	Miller	USA	19.10.76	3		Gent	10 Feb
6.56	Anatoliy	Dovgal	UKR	29.1.76	1h2		Chemnitz	22 Feb
6.56	Terrence	Trammell	USA	23.11.78	1	NC	New York	2 Mar
6.56	Jason	Smoots	USA	13.7.80	2	NC	New York	2 Mar
6.57	Gennadiy	Chernovol	KAZ	6.6.76	1		Erfurt	1 Feb
6.57	Jon	Drummond	USA	9.9.68	3	NC	New York	2 Mar
6.58	Ibrahim	Meité	CIV	18.11.76	1		Sherbrooke	9 Mar

Mark	First name	Surname	Nat	Born	Date
6.59A	Gerald	Williams	USA	24.2.78	9 Feb
6.59	Frank	Fredericks	NAM	2.10.67	17 Feb
6.59	Marc	Blume	GER	28.12.73	17 Feb
6.60	Nobuharu	Asahara	JPN	21.6.72	17 Feb
6.60	Nicolas	Macrozonaris	CAN	22.8.80	1 Mar
6.60	Mickey	Grimes	USA	10.10.76	2 Mar
6.61A	Dwight	Phillips	USA	1.10.77	9 Feb
6.61	K.	Streete-Thompson	CAY	30.3.73	13 Feb
6.62	Tre	Gardner	USA	25.10.79	26 Jan
6.62	Aristotelís	Gavélas	GRE	10.11.78	26 Jan
6.62	Patrik	Lövgren	SWE	12.10.75	20 Feb
6.62	Freddy	Mayola	CUB	1.11.77	20 Feb
6.62	Terence	Newman	USA	4.9.78	22 Feb
6.62	James	Shelton	USA	11.10.80	2 Mar

200 METRES

Mark	First name	Surname	Nat	Born	Pos	Meet	Venue	Date
20.30	Shawn	Crawford	USA	14.1.78	1		Birmingham	17 Feb
20.42	Justin	Gatlin	USA	10.2.82	1r2	SEC	Fayetteville	24 Feb
20.54	Morne	Nagel	RSA	23.3.78	1rB		Liévin	24 Feb
20.55	Marcin	Urbas	POL	17.9.76	1s1	EI	Wien	1 Mar
20.58	Christian	Malcolm	GBR	3.6.79	2		Birmingham	17 Feb
20.59	Douglas	Turner	GBR	2.12.66	3		Birmingham	17 Feb
20.62	Daniel	Caines	GBR	15.5.79	2s1	EI	Wien	1 Mar
20.68	Robert	Mackowiak	POL	13.5.70	1s2	EI	Wien	1 Mar
20.73	Marquis	Davis	USA	14.8.80	1h1	SEC	Fayetteville	23 Feb
20.75	Marcin	Jedrusinski	POL	28.9.81	2s3	EI	Wien	1 Mar
20.76	Leonard	Scott	USA	19.1.80	1r1	SEC	Fayetteville	24 Feb
20.78	Pierre	Browne	CAN	14.1.80	2r1	SEC	Fayetteville	24 Feb
20.79	Anninos	Marcoullides	CYP	8.2.71	2h5	EI	Wien	1 Mar

Mark	First name	Surname	Nat	Born	Date
20.81	Radek	Zachoval	CZE	6.7.78	1 Mar
20.84	Uchenna	Emedolu	NGR	17.9.76	3 Feb
20.84	Ingo	Schultz	GER	26.7.75	3 Feb
20.85	Johan	Wissman	SWE	2.11.82	9 Mar
20.87	Alessandro	Attene	ITA	10.9.77	1 Mar
20.88	Milton	Campbell	USA	15.5.76	9 Feb

300 METRES

Mark	First name	Surname	Nat	Born	Pos	Meet	Venue	Date
32.95	Shane	Niemi	CAN	2.6.78	1		Montréal	26 Jan
33.02	Ingo	Schultz	GER	26.7.75	1		Chemnitz	22 Feb

400 METRES

Mark	First name	Surname	Nat	Born	Pos	Meet	Venue	Date
45.35	Alleyne	Francique	GRN	7.6.76	1r2	SEC	Fayetteville	24 Feb
45.37	Pete	Coley	JAM	21.2.81	2r2	SEC	Fayetteville	24 Feb
45.39	Marek	Plawgo	POL	25.2.81	1	EI	Wien	3 Mar
45.59	Jimisola	Laursen	SWE	13.7.77	2	EI	Wien	3 Mar
45.93	Gary	Kikaya	COD	4.2.78	3r2	NCAA	Fayetteville	9 Mar
45.94	Ioan	Vieru	ROM	4.1.79	2s2	EI	Wien	2 Mar
46.06	Daniel	Caines	GBR	15.5.79	1		Birmingham	17 Feb
46.19	Sanjay	Ayre	JAM	19.6.80	3r2	SEC	Fayetteville	24 Feb

Mark	First name	Surname	Nat	Born	Date
46.21	David	Canal	ESP	7.12.78	9 Feb
46.21	Shameron	Turner	USA	9.12.77	23 Feb
46.22	Bastian	Swillims	GER	9.12.82	17 Feb
46.28	Otis	Harris	USA	30.6.82	23 Feb
46.28	Piotr	Rysiukiewicz	POL	14.7.74	2 Mar
46.31	Rickey	Harris	USA	29.9.81	8 Mar
46.32	Jirí	Muzík	CZE	1.9.76	2 Mar
46.34	Tomas	Coman	IRL	10.11.79	2 Mar
46.35	Leroy	Colquhoun	JAM	1.3.80	9 Mar
46.39	Cedric	van Branteghem	BEL	13.3.79	1 Mar

Oversized track:

Mark	First	Last	Nat	Born	Pos	Meet	Venue	Date
45.78	Rickey	Harris	USA	29.9.81	1		Notre Dame	2 Mar
45.96	Mitch	Potter	USA	16.9.80	1r1		Ames	1 Mar
46.04A	Mike	Kenyon	USA	26.8.79	1r2		Flagstaff	23 Feb

600 METRES

Mark	First	Last	Nat	Born	Pos	Meet	Venue	Date
1:16.15	Trinity	Gray	USA	3.4.78	1r		New York	18 Jan

800 METRES

Mark	First	Last	Nat	Born	Pos	Meet	Venue	Date
1:44.78	Pawel	Czapiewski	POL	30.3.78	1	EI	Wien	3 Mar
1:44.93	André	Bucher	SUI	19.10.76	2	EI	Wien	3 Mar
1:45.25	Antonio Manuel	Reina	ESP	13.6.81	3	EI	Wien	3 Mar
1:45.54	Wilson	Kipketer	DEN	12.12.70	2		Liévin	24 Feb
1:45.65	Hezekiél	Sepeng	RSA	30.6.74	3		Liévin	24 Feb
1:45.84	Dmitriy	Bogdanov	RUS	11.4.79	4	EI	Wien	3 Mar
1:46.06	Joseph	Mutua	KEN	10.12.78	1		Chemnitz	22 Feb
1:46.12	Trinity	Gray	USA	3.4.78	1		New York	8 Feb
1:46.13	Sergey	Kozhevnikov	RUS	12.5.70	5	EI	Wien	3 Mar
1:46.16	Sylas	Kimutai	KEN-J	12.10.83	2		Chemnitz	22 Feb
1:46.35	Wilfred	Bungei	KEN	24.7.80	3		Chemnitz	22 Feb
1:46.60	Derrick	Peterson	USA	28.11.77	1	NC	New York	2 Mar
1:46.62	Glody	Dube	BOT	2.7.78	7		Liévin	24 Feb
1:46.68	René	Herms	GER	17.7.82	4		Chemnitz	22 Feb
1:46.86	Nils	Schumann	GER	20.5.78	4rA	Spark	Stuttgart	3 Feb
1:46.88	Otukile	Lekote	BOT	19.10.78	1	NCAA	Fayetteville	9 Mar
1:46.92	Florent	Lacasse	FRA	21.1.81	8		Liévin	24 Feb

Mark	First	Last	Nat	Born	Date
1:46.97	Michael	Stember	USA	30.1.78	2 Mar
1:47.06	Nicolas	Aïssat	FRA	24.7.80	3 Feb
1:47.10	David	Lelei	KEN	10.5.71	3 Feb
1:47.24	Yuriy	Borzakovskiy	RUS	12.4.81	6 Feb
1:47.27	Manuel	Olmedo	ESP-J	17.5.83	9 Feb
1:47.33	João	Pires	POR	10.6.79	3 Feb
1:47.41	Marc	Sylvester	USA	21.11.82	9 Mar
1:47.44	David	Fiegen	LUX-J	3.9.84	3 Mar
1:47.48	Arnoud	Okken	NED	20.4.82	17 Feb
1:47.54	Rui	Silva	POR	3.8.77	10 Feb
1:47.55	Bram	Som	NED	20.2.80	10 Feb
1:47.58	Paskar	Owor	UGA	22.12.80	3 Feb

1000 METRES

Mark	First	Last	Nat	Born	Pos	Meet	Venue	Date
2:17.86	David	Krummenacker	USA	24.5.75	1		Boston (R)	27 Jan
2:17.96	Sylas	Kimutai	KEN-J	12.10.83	1		Pireás	20 Feb
2:18.78	Yuriy	Borzakovskiy	RUS	12.4.81	1		Karlsruhe	25 Jan
2:19.05	Laban	Rotich	KEN	20.1.69	2		Boston (R)	27 Jan

Mark	First	Last	Nat	Born	Date
2:19.23	Anthony	Whiteman	GBR	13.11.71	20 Feb
2:19.45	Christian	Neunhauserer	ITA	21.6.78	20 Feb

1500 METRES

Mark	First	Last	Nat	Born	Pos	Meet	Venue	Date
3:35.26	Rui	Silva	POR	3.8.77	1		Liévin	24 Feb
3:35.56	Mehdi	Baala	FRA	17.8.78	2		Liévin	24 Feb
3:36.27	Fouad	Chouki	FRA	1.10.78	3		Liévin	24 Feb
3:36.34	Bouabdellah	Tahri	FRA	20.12.78	2	Spark	Stuttgart	3 Feb
3:36.37	Michael	Too	KEN-J	3.8.83	3	Spark	Stuttgart	3 Feb
3:36.65	Juan Carlos	Higuero	ESP	3.8.78	1		Sevilla	9 Feb
3:37.68	Mohamed	Khaldi	ALG	3.5.75	4		Liévin	24 Feb
3:38.21	Wolfram	Müller	GER	8.7.81	2		Dortmund	27 Jan
3:38.49	José Antonio	Redolat	ESP	17.2.76	2		Karlsruhe	25 Jan
3:38.69	James	Nolan	IRL	27.1.77	3		Dortmund	27 Jan
3:38.90	John	Mayock	GBR	26.10.70	3		Gent	10 Feb
3:38.96	Pawel	Czapiewski	POL	30.3.78	6	Spark	Stuttgart	3 Feb
3:39.00	Vyacheslav	Shabunin	RUS	27.9.69	3		Karlsruhe	25 Jan
3:39.01	Saïd	Chébili	FRA	6.5.73	4		Gent	10 Feb
3:39.54	Hamid	El Mouaziz	MAR	17.2.79	4		Dortmund	27 Jan
3:39.74+	Leonard	Mucheru	KEN	13.6.78	1		New York	19 Jan
3:39.81	Branko	Zorko	CRO	1.7.67	4		Karlsruhe	25 Jan

Mark	First	Last	Nat	Born	Date
3:40.28	Bernard	Lagat	KEN	12.12.74	17 Feb
3:40.32	Abdelkader	Hachlaf	MAR	3.7.78	17 Feb
3:40.52	Michael	East	GBR	20.1.78	1 Mar
3:40.60	Andrey	Zadorozhniy	RUS	3.9.73	1 Mar
3:40.64	Michal	Sneberger	CZE	23.6.78	25 Jan
3:40.71	Ferdinando	Vicari	ITA	26.9.73	25 Jan
3:40.88	Javier	Moro	ESP	16.4.75	9 Feb
3:40.93	Sébastien	Cosson	FRA	15.3.80	24 Feb

1 MILE

Mark	First	Last	Nat	Born	Pos	Meet	Venue	Date
3:55.07	Bernard	Lagat	KEN	12.12.74	1		Lincoln	9 Feb
3:55.54	Leonard	Mucheru	KEN	13.6.78	1		New York	19 Jan
3:55.80	Kevin	Sullivan	CAN	20.3.74	2		Boston (R)	27 Jan
3:57.04	Laban	Rotich	KEN	20.1.69	1	Mill	New York	1 Feb
3:57.11	Bryan	Berryhill	USA	15.12.77	3		Boston (R)	27 Jan
3:57.45	Jason	Lunn	USA	19.9.74	1	NC	New York	1 Mar
3:57.48	Andrew	Graffin	GBR	20.12.77	1		New York (A)	8 Feb
3:57.95	Dirk	Heinze	GER	2.7.76	1		Fayetteville	18 Jan

Mark	First	Last	Nat	Born	Date
3:58.19	Adrian	Blincoe	NZL	4.11.79	9 Feb
3:58.39	Jason	Pyrah	USA	6.4.69	2 Feb
3:58.78	Zach	Whitmarsh	CAN	5.4.77	1 Feb
3:58.81	Tim	Broe	USA	20.6.77	1 Mar
3:58.92	Daniel	Zegeye	ETH	13.3.79	27 Jan
3:58.93#	Eric	Garner	USA	26.1.81	2 Mar

3000 METRES

7:37.13	Alberto	García	ESP	22.2.71	1		Sevilla	9 Feb
7:37.46	Leonard	Mucheru	KEN	13.6.78	1		Boston (R)	27 Jan
7:38.77	Luke	Kipkosgei	KEN	27.11.75	1	Spark	Stuttgart	3 Feb
7:39.23	Tim	Broe	USA	20.6.77	2		Boston (R)	27 Jan
7:39.58	Abderrahim	Goumri	MAR	21.5.76	2r	Spark	Stuttgart	3 Feb
7:40.16	Million	Wolde	ETH	17.3.79	3	Spark	Stuttgart	3 Feb
7:40.54	Abiyote	Abate	ETH	20.11.80	4	Spark	Stuttgart	3 Feb
7:40.68	Dieter	Baumann	GER	9.2.65	5	Spark	Stuttgart	3 Feb
7:40.80	Salah	Hissou	MAR	16.1.72	6	Spark	Stuttgart	3 Feb
7:40.92	Rui	Silva	POR	3.8.77	2		Stockholm	6 Feb
7:41.09	John	Mayock	GBR	26.10.70	3		Stockholm	6 Feb
7:41.41	Bouabdellah	Tahri	FRA	20.12.78	4		Stockholm	6 Feb
7:42.60	Vyacheslav	Shabunin	RUS	27.9.69	5		Stockholm	6 Feb
7:45.28	Mohamed	Khaldi	ALG	3.5.75	2		Pireás	20 Feb
7:45.75	Abdelhak	Abdellah	MAR	13.8.68	6		Stockholm	6 Feb
7:46.13	Mohammed	Amine	MAR	25.5.76	3		Pireás	20 Feb
7:46.49	Antonio	Jiménez	ESP	18.2.77	2	EI	Wien	2 Mar
7:46.84	Jonathon	Riley	USA	29.12.78	3		Boston (R)	27 Jan
7:47.39	Wolfram	Müller	GER	8.7.81	2		Karlsruhe	25 Jan
7:47.50	Adrian	Blincoe	NZL	4.11.79	4		Boston (R)	27 Jan
7:47.90	Markos	Geneti	ETH-J	84	5		Boston (R)	27 Jan
7:47.96	Matthew	Lane	USA	5.9.77	6		Boston (R)	27 Jan

7:48.08	Anthony	Famiglietti	USA	8.11.78	27 Jan	7:50.05	Khoudir	Aggoune	ALG	5.1.81	20 Feb
7:48.08	Jesús	España	ESP	21.8.78	2 Mar	7:50.21	Hailu	Mekonnen	ETH	4.4.80	3 Feb
7:48.09	Paul	Bitok	KEN	26.6.70	20 Feb	7:50.38	Irba	Lakhal	MAR	12.2.75	6 Feb
7:49.57	Martin	Keino	KEN	20.6.72	20 Feb	7:50.87	Isaac	Viciosa	ESP	26.12.69	9 Feb

2 MILES

8:15.60	Salah	Hissou	MAR	16.1.72	1	Birmingham	17 Feb
8:17.06	John	Mayock	GBR	26.10.70	2	Birmingham	17 Feb
8:19.57	Mohammed	Amine	MAR	25.5.76	3	Birmingham	17 Feb
8:22.49	Paul	Bitok	KEN	26.6.70	4	Birmingham	17 Feb

10 000 METRES

27:50.29	Mark	Bett	KEN	22.12.76	1	Gent	10 Feb
27:50.37	Luke	Kipkosgei	KEN	27.11.75	2	Gent	10 Feb
27:52.62	Abderrahim	Goumri	MAR	21.5.76	3	Gent	10 Feb
28:02.09	Jaouad	Gharib	MAR	22.5.72	4	Gent	10 Feb
28:20.31	Paul	Bitok	KEN	26.6.70	5	Gent	10 Feb

50 METRES HURDLES

6.43+	Allen	Johnson	USA	1.3.71	1	Liévin	24 Feb
6.49+	Yevgeniy	Pechonkin	RUS	9.10.73	2	Liévin	24 Feb
6.50+	Dawane	Wallace	USA	30.12.76	1h2	Liévin	24 Feb
6.52+		Liu Xiang	CHN-J	13.7.83	4	Liévin	24 Feb
6.56+	Florian	Schwarthoff	GER	7.5.68	5	Liévin	24 Feb

6.58	Ivan	Bitzi	SUI	4.8.75	27 Jan	6.60+	Arend	Watkins	USA	23.10.79	24 Feb

55 METRES HURDLES

7.03	Ron	Bramlett	USA	22.10.79	1r2	Gainesville	10 Feb
7.14	Dawane	Wallace	USA	30.12.76	1h1	Knoxville	6 Jan

60 METRES HURDLES

7.40	Colin	Jackson	GBR	18.2.67	1	EI	Wien	2 Mar
7.44	Elmar	Lichtenegger	AUT	25.5.74	2	EI	Wien	2 Mar
7.45	Allen	Johnson	USA	1.3.71	1	NC	New York	2 Mar
7.46	Yevgeniy	Pechonkin	RUS	9.10.73	1		Moskva	31 Jan
7.47	Larry	Wade	USA	22.11.74	1		Lincoln	9 Feb
7.49	Arend	Watkins	USA	23.10.79	2		Lincoln	9 Feb
7.49	Stanislav	Olijar	LAT	22.3.79	1		Eaubonne	13 Feb
7.52	Ron	Bramlett	USA	22.10.79	1h2	SEC	Fayetteville	23 Feb
7.54	Mark	Crear	USA	2.10.68	3		Lincoln	9 Feb
7.54	Yuniel	Hernández	CUB	28.3.81	1rB		Pireás	20 Feb
7.55		Liu Xiang	CHN-J	13.7.83	3		Gent	10 Feb
7.56	Yoel	Hernández	CUB	12.12.77	2h1	Spark	Stuttgart	3 Feb
7.56	Florian	Schwarthoff	GER	7.5.68	2s2	EI	Wien	2 Mar
7.57	Mike	Fenner	GER	24.4.71	1	NC	Sindelfingen	16 Feb
7.57	Shaun	Bownes	RSA	24.10.70	2rB		Pireás	20 Feb
7.58	Dawane	Wallace	USA	30.12.76	2h2		Dortmund	27 Jan
7.60	Chris	Pinnock	USA	.81/82	2	NCAA	Fayetteville	8 Mar
7.60	Peter	Coghlan	IRL	27.3.75	2	v4N	Glasgow	9 Mar
7.62	Ivan	Bitzi	SUI	4.8.75	1	NC	Magglingen	17 Feb

7.64	Claude	Edorh	GER	27.2.72	16 Feb
7.65	Jan	Schindzielorz	GER	8.8.78	16 Feb
7.65	Dudley	Dorival	HAI	1.9.75	17 Feb
7.65	Robert	Kronberg	SWE	15.8.76	9 Mar
7.66	Greg	Richardson	USA	27.12.76	8 Feb
7.66	Jerome	Crews	GER	20.2.77	16 Feb
7.68	Ladji	Doucouré	FRA-J	28.3.83	16 Feb
7.68	Marcel	van de Westen	NED	1.8.76	16 Feb
7.69	Jermaine	Cooper	USA	31.8.80	8 Ma
7.71	Krzysztof	Mehlich	POL	2.8.74	9 Feb
7.71A	Tony	Galaviz	USA	23.9.78	9 Feb

HIGH JUMP

2.35	Staffan	Strand	SWE	18.4.76	1		Stockholm	6 Feb
2.33	Mark	Boswell	CAN	28.7.77	1		Liévin	24 Feb
2.32	Stefan	Holm	SWE	25.5.76	2		Lódz	2 Feb
2.32	Pavel	Fomenko	RUS	29.6.76	1	NC	Volgograd	14 Feb
2.32	Nathan	Leeper	USA	13.6.77	1	NC	New York	2 Mar
2.31	Pyotr	Brayko	RUS	27.3.77	1		Arnstadt	26 Jan
2.31	Yaroslav	Rybakov	RUS	22.11.80	2		Arnstadt	26 Jan
2.31	Charles	Clinger	USA	28.12.76	1	Mill	New York	1 Feb
2.31	Wilbert	Pennings	NED	12.2.75	1		Siegen	9 Feb
2.30	Mikhail	Tsvetkov	RUS	4.5.80	1		Moskva	7 Jan
2.30	Andrey	Sokolovskiy	UKR	16.7.78	1		Iraklio	4 Feb
2.30	Gennadiy	Moroz	BLR	27.5.78	2		Brno	6 Feb
2.30	Svatoslav	Ton	CZE	20.10.78	1		Cejkovice	12 Feb
2.30	Nicola	Ciotti	ITA	5.10.76	1	NC	Genova	17 Feb
2.30	Andrea	Bettinelli	ITA	6.10.78	2	NC	Genova	17 Feb
2.28	Tomás	Jankú	CZE	27.12.74	3		Weinheim	23 Jan
2.28	Aleksandr	Veryutin	BLR	18.11.79	2		Wuppertal	1 Feb
2.28	Christian	Olsson	SWE	25.1.80	1		Göteborg	9 Feb
2.28	Andrey	Chubsa	BLR	29.11.82	3		Pireás	20 Feb
2.28	Stefan	Vasilache	ROM	9.5.79	1	Balk	Pireás	23 Feb
2.27	Grzegorz	Sposób	POL	12.2.76	3		Brno	6 Feb
2.27	Jan	Jankú	CZE	10.8.71	2=		Siegen	9 Feb

2.26	Dimítrios	Kokótis	GRE	12.4.72	19 Jan
2.26	Vyacheslav	Voronin	RUS	5.4.74	23 Feb
2.26	David	Furman	USA	5.11.78	2 Mar
2.26	Tora	Harris	USA	21.9.78	8 Mar
2.25	Adam	Shunk	USA	29.8.79	18 Jan
2.25	Shane	Lavy	USA	15.2.76	20 Jan
2.25	Joan	Charmant	FRA	4.6.78	3 Feb
2.25	Ron	Nelson	USA	15.1.80	23 Feb
2.25	Terrance	Woods	USA	18.4.79	9 Mar

POLE VAULT

6.02	Jeff	Hartwig	USA	25.9.67	1		Sindelfingen	10 Mar
5.85	Timothy	Mack	USA	15.9.72	2		Donetsk	24 Feb
5.82	Derek	Miles	USA	28.9.72	1		Vermillion	16 Feb
5.82	Danny	Ecker	GER	21.7.77	1		Dessau	24 Feb
5.81	Nick	Buckfield	GBR	5.6.73	1		Bad Segeberg	8 Feb
5.81A	Tye	Harvey	USA	25.9.74	2		Flagstaff	17 Feb
5.80	Lawrence	Johnson	USA	7.5.74	1		Knoxville	6 Jan
5.80	Tim	Lobinger	GER	3.9.72	1=		Erfurt	1 Feb
5.80	Ruslan	Yeremenko	UKR	31.7.78	1=		Erfurt	1 Feb
5.80	Pavel	Gerasimov	RUS	29.5.79	3		Donetsk	24 Feb
5.75	Patrik	Kristiansson	SWE	3.6.77	2	EI	Wien	2 Mar
5.75	Lars	Börgeling	GER	16.4.79	3	EI	Wien	2 Mar
5.71	Romain	Mesnil	FRA	13.7.77	1		Clermont-Ferrand	8 Feb
5.70	Denis	Yurchenko	UKR	27.1.78	4		Erfurt	1 Feb
5.70	Stepán	Janácek	CZE	12.6.77	2		Praha	14 Feb
5.70	Adam	Kolasa	POL	2.8.75	3		Praha	14 Feb
5.70	Richard	Spiegelburg	GER	12.8.77	1	NC	Sindelfingen	16 Feb
5.70	Vasiliy	Gorshkov	RUS	5.2.77	3		Chemnitz	22 Feb
5.70	Montxu	Miranda	ESP	27.12.76	1		Valencia	23 Feb
5.70	Nick	Hysong	USA	9.12.71	4		Donetsk	24 Feb
5.70	Radion	Gataullin	RUS	23.11.65	5		Donetsk	24 Feb
5.70	Thibaut	Duval	BEL	1.2.79	5	EI	Wien	2 Mar
5.65	Yuriy	Yeliseyev	RUS	27.5.75	1		Moskva	21 Jan
5.65A	Toby	Stevenson	USA	19.11.76	1		Reno	16 Feb
5.65	Piotr	Buciarski	DEN	22.11.75	Q	EI	Wien	1 Mar
5.61	Mikko	Latvala	FIN	8.7.80	1		Kuortane	27 Jan
5.61	Jean	Galfione	FRA	9.6.71	2=		Clermont-Ferrand	8 Feb

5.60	Vadim	Strogalyov	RUS	9.2.75	7 Jan
5.60A	Russ	Buller	USA	10.9.78	11 Jan
5.60A	Chad	Harting	USA	20.2.72	11 Jan
5.60	Yevgeniy	Mikhaylichenko	RUS	13.2.79	21 Jan
5.60	Massimo	Allevi	ITA	23.11.69	1 Feb
5.60	Giuseppe	Gibilisco	ITA	5.1.79	1 Feb
5.60	Christian	Tamminga	NED	30.4.74	1 Feb
5.60	Grigoriy	Yegorov	KAZ	12.1.67	1 Feb
5.60	Laurens	Looije	NED	12.1.73	8 Feb
5.60	Matt	Phillips	USA	28.12.77	9 Feb
5.60	Yevgeniy	Smiryagin	RUS	17.5.76	9 Feb
5.60	Scott	Slover	USA	9.7.75	23 Feb
5.60	Kurt	Hanna	USA	23.4.75	23 Feb
5.55	Aleksandr	Korchmyd	UKR	22.1.82	20Dec*
5.55	Jim	Davis	USA	15.6.78	2 Feb
5.55	Martin	Eriksson	SWE	15.6.71	23 Feb
5.55	Dennis	Kholev	ISR	21.10.75	1 Mar

LONG JUMP

8.59	Miguel	Pate	USA	13.6.79	1	NC	New York	1 Mar
8.33	Roman	Shchurenko	UKR	14.9.76	1	NC	Brovary	16 Feb
8.27	Petar	Dachev	BUL	15.6.79	1	NC	Sofia	10 Feb
8.22	Carlos	Calado	POR	5.10.75	1		Espinho	26 Jan
8.22	Raúl	Fernández	ESP	8.3.78	1	EI	Wien	2 Mar
8.20	Kevin	Dilworth	USA	14.2.74	1		Joplin	12 Jan
8.17	Yago	Lamela	ESP	24.7.77	2	EI	Wien	2 Mar
8.15	Vitaliy	Shkurlatov	RUS	25.5.79	1		Moskva	21 Jan
8.15	Walter	Davis	USA	2.7.79	2	NCAA	Fayetteville	8 Mar
8.12	Savanté	Stringfellow	USA	6.11.78	1		Gent	10 Feb
8.11	Aleksey	Lukashevich	UKR	11.1.77	4	EI	Wien	2 Mar
8.06	James	Beckford	JAM	9.1.75	1		Budapest	9 Feb
8.03	Iván	Pedroso	CUB	17.12.72	2	Spark	Stuttgart	3 Feb
8.03	Sean	Robbins	USA	9.10.72	1		Findlay	8 Feb
8.02	Younès	Moudrik	MAR	1.10.77	1		Erfurt	1 Feb
8.02	Kirill	Sosunov	RUS	1.11.75	1		Volgograd	6 Feb
8.02	Kofi Amoah	Prah	GER	20.12.74	1	NC	Sindelfingen	17 Feb
8.01	Gable	Garenamotse	BOT	28.2.77	1	AAA	Cardiff	3 Feb
8.00	Lenton	Herring	USA	4.12.78	1		Madison	12 Jan
8.00	Vladimir	Zyuskov	UKR	29.8.81	2	NC	Brovary	16 Feb

7.99	Dwight	Phillips	USA	1.10.77	1 Mar		7.94	Kenta	Bell	USA	16.3.77	1 Feb
7.98	Schahriar	Bigdeli	GER	26.3.80	17 Feb		7.94	Joan Lino	Martínez	CUB	17.1.78	16 Feb
7.98	Kader	Klouchi	FRA	1.6.69	1 Mar		7.94	Vaughaligan	Walwyn	IVB	2.12.80	8 Mar
7.95	Gregor	Cankar	SLO	25.1.75	16 Feb		7.93	Vladimir	Malyavin	RUS	4.3.73	7 Jan
							7.93	Erick	Walder	USA	5.11.71	1 Feb

TRIPLE JUMP

17.80	Christian	Olsson	SWE	25.1.80	1		Göteborg	5 Mar
17.35	Jadel	Gregório	BRA	16.9.80	1		Samara	3 Feb
17.29	Marian	Oprea	ROM	6.6.82	1	NC	Bucuresti	16 Feb
17.23	Walter	Davis	USA	2.7.79	1	NCAA	Fayetteville	9 Mar
17.14	Charles	Friedek	GER	26.8.71	2		Pireás	20 Feb
17.13	Alexander	Martínez	CUB	23.8.77	1		Torino	26 Jan
17.05	Aleksandr	Glavatskiy	BLR	2.5.70	3		Pireás	20 Feb
17.03	Fabrizio	Donato	ITA	14.8.76	1	NC	Genova	17 Feb
17.01	Timothy	Rusan	USA	25.6.77	1	NC	New York	2 Mar
17.00	Igor	Spasovkhodskiy	RUS	1.8.79	1	NC	Volgograd	14 Feb
16.99	Aleksandr	Aseledchenko	RUS	18.10.73	2	NC	Volgograd	14 Feb
16.98	Andrey	Trots	UKR	17.1.78	2		Samara	3 Feb
16.97	Viktor	Gushchinskiy	RUS	12.8.78	3		Samara	3 Feb
16.95	Kenta	Bell	USA	16.3.77	2	NC	New York	2 Mar
16.94	Rostislav	Dimitrov	BUL	26.12.74	4		Pireás	20 Feb
16.89	Aleksandr	Sergeyev	RUS-J	.29.7.83	1		Moskva	8 Feb
16.88	Karl	Taillepierre	FRA	13.8.76	1	NC	Liévin	16 Feb
16.87	Brandon	Craven	USA	19.12.74	1		Fayetteville	2 Feb
16.85	LeJuan	Simon	USA	7.2.81	1		Norman	16 Feb
16.80	Sanuel	Okantey	GHA	3.11.74	1		Landover	27 Jan

16.79	Leevan	Sands	BAH	16.8.81	2 Mar		16.72	Thomas	Moede	GER	26.7.77	16 Feb
16.75	Andrey	Kurennoy	RUS	12.5.72	14 Feb		16.70	Ketill	Hanstveit	NOR	2.11.73	19 Jan
16.74	Konstadínos	Zalaggítis	GRE	13.12.80	16 Feb		16.62	Aleksey	Musikhin	RUS	8.11.75	3 Feb
16.73	Sébastien	Pincemail	FRA	21.2.79	16 Feb		16.61	Jérôme	Romain	FRA	12.6.71	9 Feb
16.73	Ionut	Punga	ROM	14.10.79	16 Feb		16.60	Von	Ware	USA	30.6.75	23 Feb

SHOT

21.57	Adam	Nelson	USA	7.7.75	1	NC	New York	1 Mar
21.48	Joachim	Olsen	DEN	31.5.77	1		Moscow, ID	15 Feb
21.47	Janus	Robberts	RSA	10.3.79	1		Norman	1 Dec*
	20.83				1		Reno	23 Feb
21.26	Manuel	Martínez	ESP	7.12.74	1	EI	Wien	2 Mar
21.26	Carl	Myerscough	GBR	21.10.79	1	NCAA	Fayetteville	8 Mar
20.86	Christian	Cantwell	USA	30.9.80	2	NC	New York	1 Mar
20.62	Paolo	Dal Soglio	ITA	29.7.70	1	NC	Genova	17 Feb
20.59	Pavel	Chumachenko	RUS	5.4.71	1	v4N	Glasgow	9 Mar
20.34	Milan	Haborák	SVK	11.1.73	1		Bratislava	19 Jan
20.32	Zsolt	Bíber	HUN	31.5.76	1		Budapest	19 Jan
20.27	Kevin	Toth	USA	29.12.67	1		Kent	11 Jan
20.26	Ville	Tiisanoja	FIN	24.12.75	1		Helsinki	27 Jan
20.26	Gheorghe	Guset	ROM	28.5.68	1	NC	Bucuresti	16 Feb
20.25	Tepa	Reinikainen	FIN	16.3.76	1	NC	Tampere	17 Feb
20.21	Conny	Karlsson	FIN	30.12.75	1		Mustasaari	9 Feb
20.09	Petr	Stehlik	CZE	15.4.77	1		Jablonec	19 Feb

20.02	Leszek	Sliwa	POL	20.9.79	1		Spala	9 Feb
20.02	Andy	Bloom	USA	11.8.73	4	NC	New York	1 Mar
20.01	Daniel	Taylor	USA	12.5.82	1		Columbus	2 Feb
19.98	Jeffrey	Chakouian	USA	20.4.82	1		Lexington	12 Jan
19.94	Timo	Aaltonen	FIN	11.4.69	3		Tampere	4 Feb
19.87	Jimmy	Nordin	SWE	19.10.79	4		Tampere	4 Feb
19.85	Detlef	Bock	GER	15.8.74	1		Sondershausen	2 Feb

19.84	Pavel	Lyzhin	BLR	24.3.81	1 Mar
19.83	Ralf	Bartels	GER	21.2.78	1 Feb
19.83	Bradley	Snyder	CAN	8.1.76	9 Feb
19.81	René	Sack	GER	14.7.76	2 Feb
19.70	Scott	Wiegand	USA	26.9.80	9 Feb
19.67	Jonathan	Kalnas	USA	18.4.80	8 Mar
19.62	Reese	Hoffa	USA	8.10.77	2 Feb
19.61	Mikulás	Konopka ¶	SVK	23.1.79	3 Feb
19.61	Marcus	Clavelle	USA	23.6.78	9 Feb
19.60	Sergio	Mottin	ITA	15.6.76	31 Jan
19.60	Andy	Dittmar	GER	5.7.74	2 Feb
19.60	Rutger	Smith	NED	9.7.81	1 Mar
19.58	David	Wood	USA	23.6.79	8 Mar
19.53	Nedzad	Mulabegovic	CRO	4.2.81	9 Feb

Drugs Diuqualification

20.87	Mikulás	Konopka ¶	SVK	23.1.79	3	EI	Wien	2 Mar

35 LBS WEIGHT

24.72	Scott	Russell	CAN	16.1.79	1		Ames	8 Feb
23.37	Kevin	Mannon	USA	12.8.76	1		Columbus	16 Feb
23.25	John	McEwen	USA	5.3.74	1		Findlay	25 Jan
23.19	Jacob.	Freeman	USA	5.11.80	2	NCAA	Fayetteville	9 Mar
22.58	A.G.	Kruger	USA		1		Ames	25 Jan
22.34	Carey	Ryan	USA	3.10.79	1		Notre Dame	1 Mar
22.16	Daniel	Bourque	USA	4.7.76	3	Mill	New York	1 Feb
22.04	Christian	Cantwell	USA	30.9.80	2		Manhattan	26 Jan
21.96	Gerald	Ingalls	USA	24.9.74	4	Mill	New York	1 Feb

21.84	Salvatore	Gigante	USA	17.7.79	9 Mar
21.72	Russ	Bell	USA	27.2.81	9 Mar
21.64	Panayiótis	Mavragánis	GRE	27.5.79	28 Feb
21.60	Micah	Shanks	USA	2.12.78	8 Feb
21.60	András	Haklits	CRO	23.9.77	23 Feb
21.59	Scott	Moser	USA	15.7.79	22 Feb
21.56	Drew	Loftin	USA		22 Feb
21.54	Derek	Woodske	CAN	22.10.76	2 Feb

HEPTATHLON

6291	Frank	Busemann	GER	26.2.75	1		Tallinn	3 Feb
	(6.96, 7.77, 14.57, 2.10, 7.91, 4.85, 2:40.93)							
6280	Roman	Sebrle	CZE	26.11.74	1	EI	Wien	2 Mar
	(6.97, 7.82, 15.62, 2.11, 7.93, 4.80, 2:47.69)							
6165	Tomás	Dvorák	CZE	11.5.72	2	EI	Wien	2 Mar
	(6.92, 7.55, 16.08, 1.90, 7.84, 5.00, 2:46.31)							
6113	Tom	Pappas	USA	6.9.76	1	NC	Chapel Hill	2 Mar
	(6.93, 7.45, 15.47, 2.04, 7.94, 5.03, 2:55.65)							
6084	Erki	Nool	EST	25.6.70	3	EI	Wien	2 Mar
	(6.91, 7.56, 14.01, 1.96, 8.17, 5.20, 2:45.60)							
6033	Dmitriy	Karpov	KAZ	23.7.81	1		Karaganda	9 Feb
	(7.16, 7.89 14.30, 2.11, 7.96, 4.40, 2:46.89)							
6012	Laurent	Hernu	FRA	22.8.76	1	NC	Eaubonne	10 Feb
	(7.19. 7.30, 14.59, 2.07, 8.15, 4.90, 2:41.86)							
5996	Jón Arnar	Magnússon	ISL	28.7.69	4	EI	Wien	2 Mar
	(7.00, 7.51, 15.53, 1.96, 8.24, 5.00, 2:50.91)							
5957	Attila	Zsivoczky	HUN	29.4.77	5	EI	Wien	2 Mar
	(7.23, 6.99, 14.86, 2.17, 8.51, 4.90, 2:41.04)							
5950	Zsolt	Kürtösi	HUN	21.3.71	6	EI	Wien	2 Mar
	(7.10, 7.33, 15.30, 2.05, 8.10, 4.70, 2:48.99)							

5929 #	Jaakko	Ojaniemi	FIN	28.8.80	10 Mar
5928	Jan	Podìbradsky	CZE	1.3.74	10 Feb
5893	Cristian	Gasparro	ITA	15.12.74	3 Feb
5878	Mike	Maczey	GER	28.9.72	27 Jan
5878	Tomás	Komenda	CZE	24.7.78	10 Feb
5873	Oscar	González	ESP	8.8.76	2 Mar
5869	Stefan	Drews	GER	12.2.79	27 Jan
5844	Nadir	El Fassi	FRA-J	23.9.83	2 Mar
5838	Dmitriy	Ivanov	RUS	23.3.77	3 Feb
5836	Mário	Aníbal	POR	25.3.72	2 Mar
5816	Thomas	Tebbich	AUT	4.2.75	10 Feb
5813	Klaus	Ambrosch	AUT	23.5.73	3 Feb
5806	Sebastian	Chmara	POL	21.11.71	3 Feb
5787	Michal	Modelski	POL	16.4.75	17 Feb

3000 METRES WALK

11:10.02	Robert	Heffernan	IRL	28.2.78	1	NC	Cardiff	2 Feb

5000 METRES WALK

18:49.02	Andreas	Erm	GER	12.3.76	1	NC	Sindelfingen	17 Feb
18:53.09	Robert	Heffernan	IRL	28.2.78	1	NC	Nenagh	17 Feb
19:02.88	Robert	Korzeniowski	POL	30.7.68	1	NC	Spala	16 Feb
19:03.2	Vladimir	Andreyev	RUS	7.9.66	1		Samara	3 Feb
19:08.57	Alessandro	Gandellini	ITA	30.4.73	1	NC	Genova	16 Feb
19:09.7	Yuriy	Andronov	RUS	6.11.71	2		Samara	3 Feb

19:21.21	Giovanni	Perricelli	ITA	25.8.67	16 Feb
19:26.9	Aleksey	Kronin	RUS	23.10.70	3 Feb

WORLD INDOOR LISTS 2002 – WOMEN

60 METRES

7.06	Chioma	Ajunwa	NGR	25.12.70	1h1		Birmingham	17 Feb
7.08	Chandra	Sturrup	BAH	12.9.71	1h2		Birmingham	17 Feb
7.09	Savatheda	Fynes	BAH	17.10.74	2		Birmingham	17 Feb
7.10	Yuliya	Tabakova	RUS	1.5.80	1		Samara	3 Feb
7.13	Zhanna	Pintusevich-Block	UKR	6.7.72	3		Birmingham	17 Feb
7.13	Chryste	Gaines	USA	14.9.70	1	NC	New York	2 Mar
7.13	Angela	Williams	USA	30.1.80	1	NCAA	Fayetteville	9 Mar
7.14	Kelli	White	USA	1.4.77	1		Karlsruhe	25 Jan
7.15	Anzhela	Kravchenko	UKR	25.1.71	2		Karlsruhe	25 Jan
7.16	Karin	Mayr	AUT	4.6.71	3		Erfurt	1 Feb
7.16	Juliet	Campbell	JAM	17.3.70	5		Birmingham	17 Feb
7.16	Kim	Gevaert	BEL	5.8.78	1h2	EI	Wien	2 Mar
7.17	Veronica	Campbell	JAM	15.5.82	1		Lincoln	2 Feb
7.17	Yeoryía	Koklóni	GRE	7.5.81	2h2	EI	Wien	2 Mar
7.18	Natalya	Ignatova	RUS	28.12.73	3		Karlsruhe	25 Jan
7.18	Gail	Devers	USA	19.11.66	2	Mill	New York	1 Feb
7.18A	Natasha	Mayers	VIN	10.3.79	1		Flagstaff	9 Feb
7.18	Marina	Kislova	RUS	7.2.78	2	EI	Wien	3 Mar
7.19A	Candace	Young	USA	8.1.79	2		Flagstaff	9 Feb
7.19	Andrea	Philipp	GER	29.7.71	3		Chemnitz	22 Feb

7.20	Larisa	Kruglova	RUS	27.10.72	12 Feb	7.22	Odiah	Sidibé	FRA	13.1.70	16 Feb
7.20	Melanie	Paschke	GER	29.6.70	17 Feb	7.22	Tahesia	Harrigan	IVB	15.2.82	9 Mar
7.21	Muna	Lee	USA	30.10.81	2 Feb	7.23	Endurance	Ojokolo	NGR	29.9.75	10 Feb
7.22	Virgen	Benavídes	CUB	31.12.74	1 Feb	7.23	Marion	Wagner	GER	1.2.78	3 Mar
7.22	Muriel	Hurtis	FRA	25.3.79	4 Feb	7.24	Petya	Pendareva	BUL	20.1.71	25 Jan

Hand timing

6.9	Yuliya	Tabakova	RUS	1.5.80	1r1		Moskva	29 Jan
6.9	Marina	Kislova	RUS	12.12.78	1		Volgograd	6 Feb

200 METRES

22.51	Muriel	Hurtis	FRA	25.3.79	1rA		Liévin	24 Feb
22.70	Karin	Mayr	AUT	4.6.71	2	EI	Wien	2 Mar
22.76	Juliet	Campbell	JAM	17.3.70	2rA		Liévin	24 Feb
22.82	Muna	Lee	USA	30.10.81	1r2	NCAA	Fayetteville	8 Mar
22.99	Gaby	Rockmeier	GER	29.11.73	1h2	EI	Wien	1 Mar
22.99	Rachelle	Boone	USA	30.6.81	1r1	NCAA	Fayetteville	8 Mar
23.00	Stephanie	Durst	USA	6.1.82	2r2	NCAA	Fayetteville	8 Mar
23.03	Svetlana	Goncharenko	RUS	28.5.71	1		Moskva	22 Jan
23.08	Me'Lisa	Barber	USA	4.10.80	h	SEC	Fayetteville	23 Feb
23.08	Nora	Güner	TUR	1.6.77	4	EI	Wien	2 Mar
23.10	Aleen	Bailey	JAM	25.11.80	3r2	SEC	Fayetteville	24 Feb
23.12	Veronica	Campbell	JAM	15.5.82	1		Lincoln	2 Feb
23.13	Erica	Whipple	USA	4.12.82	3r2	NCAA	Fayetteville	8 Mar
23.17	Kelli	White	USA	1.4.77	1rB		Liévin	24 Feb
23.18	Alenka	Bikar	SLO	7.1.74	2		Wien	3 Feb

23.19	Fabé	Dia	FRA	14.2.77	17 Feb	23.30	Birgit	Rockmeier	GER	29.11.73	25 Jan
23.22	Sanya	Richards	JAM-J	26.2.85	10 Mar	23.32	Michelle	Davis	USA	4.9.80	8 Mar
23.26	Sylviane	Félix	FRA	31.10.77	17 Feb	23.34	Ciara	Sheehy	IRL	12.8.80	1 Mar
23.29	Brianna	Glenn	USA	18.4.80	8 Mar	23.35	Yuliya	Tabakova	RUS	1.5.80	1 Mar
23.30	Sarah	Reilly	IRL	3.7.73	13 Jan	23.35	Amber	Robinson	USA	5.6.80	8 Mar

300 METRES

37.43	Nadjina	Kaltouma	CHA	16.11.76	1r		Edmonton	18 Jan
37.49	Yuliya	Pechonkina	RUS	21.4.78	1r2		Moskva	7 Jan

400 METRES

51.17	Natalya	Antyukh	RUS	26.6.81	1		Birmingham	17 Feb
51.49	Grit	Breuer	GER	16.2.72	1	NC	Sindelfingen	17 Feb
51.58	Karen	Shinkins	IRL	15.10.76	1		Blacksburg	9 Feb
51.66	Christine	Amertil	BAH	18.8.79	2		Blacksburg	9 Feb
51.79	Catherine	Murphy	GBR	21.9.75	2		Birmingham	17 Feb
51.80	Claudia	Marx	GER	16.9.78	2	NC	Sindelfingen	17 Feb
51.81	Kudirat	Akhigbe	NGR	29.12.81	3		Birmingham	17 Feb
52.10	Yuliya	Pechonkina	RUS	21.4.78	1h5	NC	Volgograd	12 Feb
52.10	Nadjina	Kaltouma	CHA	16.11.76	2		Pireás	20 Feb
52.10	Sanya	Richards	JAM-J	26.2.85	1		New York (A)	10 Mar
52.13	Demetria	Washington	USA	31.12.79	1	SEC	Fayetteville	24 Feb
52.16	Allison	Beckford	JAM	8.5.79	1	NCAA	Fayetteville	9 Mar
52.21	Anna	Tkach	RUS	17.4.75	1r5		Moskva	26 Jan
52.21	Jearl	Miles-Clark	USA	4.9.66	1		Lincoln	9 Feb

52.23	Natalya	Ivanova	RUS	25.6.81	4	EI	Wien	3 Mar
52.30	Sandie	Richards	JAM	6.11.68	2rA	Spark	Stuttgart	3 Feb
52.49	Natalya	Lavshuk	RUS	1.1.80	2r5		Moskva	26 Jan
52.57	Lashinda	Demus	USA-J	10.3.83	2	SEC	Fayetteville	24 Feb

52.59	Svetlana Usovich	BLR	14.10.80	1 Mar		52.69	Olesya Zykina	RUS	7.10.80	20 Feb
52.59	Ronetta Smith	JAM	2.5.80	24 Feb		52.73	Liz Grow	USA	17.10.79	8 Mar
52.60	Irina Anashkina	RUS	31.1.72	26 Jan		52.83	Birgit Rockmeier	GER	29.11.73	27 Jan
52.62	Me'Lisa Barber	USA	4.10.80	24 Feb		52.83	Nicole Marahrens	GER	15.3.77	22 Feb
52.66	Suziann Reid	USA	14.1.77	3 Feb		52.86	Grazyna Prokopek	POL	20.4.77	1 Feb
52.68	Moushami Robinson	USA	13.4.81	9 Mar		52.87	Olga Maksimova	RUS	9.8.76	21 Jan

500 METRES

1:10.50	Natalya	Khrushchelyova	RUS	20.3.73	1		Yekaterinburg	7 Jan

600 METRES

1:26.55+	Maria Lurdes	Mutola	MOZ	27.10.72	1	in 800	Liévin	24 Feb
1:26.68+	Jolanda	Ceplak	SLO	12.9.76	1	in 800	Wien	3 Mar
1:26.8+	Stephanie	Graf	AUT	26.4.73	2	in 800	Wien	3 Mar
1:26.84	Svetlana	Cherkasova	RUS	20.5.78	1r2		Moskva	7 Jan
1:26.94	Anna	Tkach	RUS	17.4.75	2r2		Moskva	7 Jan

800 METRES

1:55.82	Jolanda	Ceplak	SLO	12.9.76	1	EI	Wien	3 Mar
1:55.85	Stephanie	Graf	AUT	26.4.73	2	EI	Wien	3 Mar
1:57.48	Maria Lurdes	Mutola	MOZ	27.10.72	3		Gent	10 Feb
1:58.71	Nicole	Teter	USA	8.11.73	1	NC	New York	2 Mar
1:59.09	Jearl	Miles-Clark	USA	4.9.66	1		New York	22 Feb
2:00.78	Mayte	Martínez	ESP	17.5.76	2		Liévin	24 Feb
2:01.42	Yekaterina	Puzanova	RUS	1.1.79	1	NC	Volgograd	13 Feb
2:01.46	Elisabeth	Grousselle	FRA	6.2.73	3	EI	Wien	3 Mar
2:01.62	Ivonne	Teichmann	GER	11.4.77	2		Karlsruhe	25 Jan
2:01.86	Helena	Fuchsová	CZE	3.6.65	3		Liévin	24 Feb
2:01.92	Yuliya	Kosenkova	RUS	28.3.73	2	NC	Volgograd	13 Feb
2:01.96	Svetlana	Cherkasova	RUS	20.5.78	1	Spark	Stuttgart	3 Feb
2:02.35	Sandra	Stals	BEL	5.6.75	2h2	EI	Wien	2 Mar

2:02.43	Judit Varga	HUN	16.4.76	2 Mar		2:03.61	Virginie Fouquet	FRA	9.9.75	10 Feb
2:02.49	Natalya Khrushchelyova	RUS	20.3.73	22 Jan		2:03.69	Irina Prokofyeva	RUS	13.3.72	13 Feb
2:02.86	Esther Desviat	ESP	27.1.82	2 Mar		2:03.74	Elena Iagar	ROM	16.1.75	2 Feb
2:03.08	Sandra Teixeira	POR	13.3.78	2 Feb		2:03.76	Mardrea Hyman	JAM	22.12.72	27 Jan
2:03.35	Jennifer Meadows	GBR	17.4.81	17 Feb		2:03.76	Hayley Tullett	GBR	17.2.73	17 Feb
2:03.38	Peggy Babin	FRA	24.12.76	27 Jan		2:03.81	Adoración García	ESP	19.7.76	23 Feb

1000 METRES

2:42.05	Yekaterina	Puzanova	RUS	1.1.79	1		Moskva	7 Jan
2:42.73	Tatyana	Rodionova	RUS	27.8.80	2		Moskva	7 Jan

1500 METRES

4:05.02+	Carla	Sacramento	POR	10.12.71	1	in 1M	Liévin	24 Feb
4:05.44	Jolanda	Ceplak	SLO	12.9.76	1	v4N	Glasgow	9 Mar
4:05.53	Yekaterina	Puzanova	RUS	1.1.79	2	v4N	Glasgow	9 Mar
4:05.54	Berhane	Adere	ETH	21.7.73	1		Stockholm	6 Feb
4:06.90	Elena	Iagar	ROM	16.1.75	2	EI	Wien	3 Mar
4:07.38+	Olga	Komyagina	RUS	10.2.74	2	in 1M	Liévin	24 Feb
4:07.69	Marta	Domínguez	ESP	3.11.75	1		Sevilla	9 Feb
4:07.69	Alesya	Turova	BLR	6.12.79	3	EI	Wien	3 Mar
4:08.10	Helena	Javornik	SLO	26.3.66	2		Stockholm	6 Feb
4:08.63	Yuliya	Kosenkova	RUS	28.3.73	4	EI	Wien	3 Mar
4:08.80+	Lyudmila	Vasilyeva	RUS	20.10.69	3	in 1M	Liévin	24 Feb
4:08.88	Hayley	Tullett	GBR	17.2.73	3		Pireás	20 Feb
4:09.50	Natalya	Yevdokimova	RUS	17.3.78	4		Pireás	20 Feb
4:10.47	Daniela	Yordanova	BUL	8.3.76	5	EI	Wien	3 Mar

4:12.62	Cristina Grosu	ROM	11.11.76	27 Jan		4:13.68	Zoya Kaznovskaya	UKR	22.9.66	6 Feb
4:13.12	Maria Cioncan	ROM	19.6.77	6 Feb		4:13.81	Iris María Fuentes-Pila	ESP	10.8.80	23 Feb
4:13.21	Sara Palmas	ITA	7.7.77	3 Mar		4:13.93	Adoración García	ESP	19.7.76	9 Feb
4:13.37	Zulema Fuentes-Pila	ESP	25.5.77	23 Feb		4:13.98	Jessica Augusto	POR	8.11.81	2 Feb

1 MILE

4:23.00	Carla	Sacramento	POR	10.12.71	1		Liévin	24 Feb
4:25.62	Olga	Komyagina	RUS	10.2.74	2		Liévin	24 Feb
4:27.39	Lyudmila	Vasilyeva	RUS	20.10.69	3		Liévin	24 Feb
4:29.35	Helena	Javornik	SLO	26.3.66	4		Liévin	24 Feb
4:32.13	Regina	Jacobs	USA	28.8.63	1	NC	New York	2 Mar

4:32.71	Nicole Teter	USA	8.11.73	9 Feb		4:33.88	Alesya Turova	BLR	6.12.79	24 Feb
4:33.57	Sarah Schwald	USA	2.1.73	9 Feb		4:33.88	Mary Jayne Harrelson	USA	17.6.78	2 Mar

2000 METRES

5:39.47	Berhane	Adere	ETH	21.7.73	1		Chemnitz	22 Feb
5:41.61	Yelena	Zadorozhnaya	RUS	3.12.77	1		Yekaterinburg	7 Jan
5:41.62+	Olga	Komyagina	RUS	10.2.74	1	Spark	Stuttgart	3 Feb
5:41.83	Olga	Yegorova	RUS	28.3.72	2		Yekaterinburg	7 Jan
5:42.55	Kathleen	Friedrich	GER	13.7.77	2		Chemnitz	22 Feb
5:44.31	Kristina da Fonseca-Wollheim		GER	10.2.72	3		Chemnitz	22 Feb
5:44.93	Helena	Javornik	SLO	26.3.66	4		Chemnitz	22 Feb

3000 METRES

8:29.15	Berhane	Adere	ETH	21.7.73	1	Spark	Stuttgart	3 Feb
8:36.79	Carla	Sacramento	POR	10.12.71	2		Birmingham	17 Feb
8:45.72	Yelena	Zadorozhnaya	RUS	3.12.77	1	NC	Volgograd	12 Feb
8:46.24	Olga	Yegorova	RUS	28.3.72	2	Spark	Stuttgart	3 Feb
8:46.92	Liliya	Volkova	RUS	13.11.77	2	NC	Volgograd	12 Feb
8:47.49	Helena	Javornik	SLO	26.3.66	4	Spark	Stuttgart	3 Feb
8:52.06	Susanne	Pumper	AUT	1.9.70	5	Spark	Stuttgart	3 Feb
8:53.66	Marta	Domínguez	ESP	3.11.75	1	NC	Sevilla	16 Feb
8:55.22	Maria Cristina	Grosu	ROM	11.11.76	1	Balk	Pireás	23 Feb
8:56.20	Kristina da Fonseca-Wollheim		GER	10.2.72	6	Spark	Stuttgart	3 Feb
8:56.51	Fernanda	Ribeiro	POR	23.6.69	1		Espinho	27 Jan
8:56.82	Oksana	Belyakova	RUS	9.9.75	3	NC	Volgograd	12 Feb
8:56.83	Sabrina	Mockenhaupt	GER	6.12.80	7	Spark	Stuttgart	3 Feb
8:58.18	Amy	Rudolph	USA	18.9.73	1	NC	New York	1 Mar
8:58.32	Cheri	Kenah	USA	26.12.70	2	NC	New York	1 Mar
8:58.52	Ana	Dias	POR	15.1.74	2		Espinho	27 Jan

8:59.35	M. Luisa	Larraga	ESP	10.12.70	16 Feb
8:59.44	Jessica	Augusto	POR	8.11.81	10 Feb
8:59.52	María Cristina	Petite	ESP	10.5.72	16 Feb
8:59.83	Melanie	Schulz	GER	27.8.79	3 Feb
9:00.49	Inês	Monteiro	POR	18.5.80	10 Feb
9:01.49	Carrie	Tollefson	USA	18.1.77	1 Mar
9:02.83	Lyubov	Kremlyova	RUS	21.12.61	22 Jan
9:02.95	Alesya	Turova	BLR	6.12.79	17 Feb
9:03.02	Amaia	Piedra	ESP	2.6.72	16 Feb
9:03.12	Jacqueline	Martín	ESP	14.4.74	16 Feb

2 MILES

9:23.38	Regina	Jacobs	USA	28.8.63	1	Boston (R)	27 Jan
9:34.03	Meseret	Defar	ETH-J	19.11.83	2	Boston (R)	27 Jan
9:35.66	Amy	Rudolph	USA	18.9.73	3	Boston (R)	27 Jan
9:38.06	Cheri	Kenah	USA	26.12.70	4	Boston (R)	27 Jan

50 METRES HURDLES

6.82+	Patricia	Girard	FRA	8.4.68	1h1	Liévin	24 Feb
6.82+	Olga	Shishigina	KAZ	23.12.68	1	Liévin	24 Feb
6.83	Miesha	McKelvy	USA	26.7.76	1	Los Angeles	23 Feb
6.85+	Vonette	Dixon	JAM	26.11.75	3	Liévin	24 Feb
6.87+	Nicole	Ramalalanirina	FRA	5.3.72	4	Liévin	24 Feb
6.90+	Glory	Alozie	ESP	30.12.77	5	Liévin	24 Feb
6.91	Bisa	Grant	USA	16.7.76	2	Los Angeles	23 Feb
6.92+	Lacena	Golding	JAM	20.3.75	3h1	Liévin	24 Feb
6.93+	Aliuska	López	CUB	29.8.69	4h1	Liévin	24 Feb

60 METRES HURDLES

7.84	Glory	Alozie	ESP	30.12.77	1	EI	Wien	2 Mar
7.85	Melissa	Morrison	USA	9.7.71	1		Chemnitz	22 Feb
7.88	Lacena	Golding	JAM	20.3.75	1	Spark	Stuttgart	3 Feb
7.89	Olga	Shishigina	KAZ	23.12.68	1		Liévin	24 Feb
7.89	Kirsten	Bolm	GER	4.3.75	1	v4N	Glasgow	9 Mar
7.90	Perdita	Felicien	CAN	29.8.80	1	NCAA	Fayetteville	8 Mar
7.91	Patricia	Girard	FRA	8.4.68	1h2	EI	Wien	2 Mar
7.92	Vonette	Dixon	JAM	26.11.75	3	Spark	Stuttgart	3 Feb
7.92	Danielle	Carruthers	USA	22.12.79	1		University Park	9 Feb
7.96	Linda	Ferga	FRA	24.12.76	2	EI	Wien	2 Mar
7.96	Miesha	McKelvy	USA	26.7.76	2	NC	New York	2 Mar
7.99	Svetlana	Laukhova	RUS	1.2.73	1		Moskva	22 Jan
7.99	Aliuska	López	CUB	29.8.69	4	Spark	Stuttgart	3 Feb
7.99	Nicole	Ramalalanirina	FRA	5.3.72	3		Liévin	24 Feb
8.00	Susanna	Kallur	SWE	16.2.81	3	NCAA	Fayetteville	8 Mar
8.01	Diane	Allahgreen	GBR	21.2.75	1	NC	Cardiff	3 Feb
8.01	Flóra	Redoúmi	GRE	11.9.76	2h2	EI	Wien	2 Mar
8.02	Bisa	Grant	USA	16.7.76	2h1	NC	New York	2 Mar
8.03	Irina	Lenskiy	ISR	12.6.71	1		Moskva	27 Jan
8.04	Nadine	Hentschke	GER	27.1.82	3h2	EI	Wien	2 Mar
8.04	Damu	Cherry	USA	29.11.77	3	NC	New York	2 Mar
8.05	Kimberly	Carson	USA	12.3.74	1h2		Erfurt	1 Feb

8.05	Yahumara	Neyra	CUB	18.4.76	2		Erfurt	1 Feb
8.05	Lolo	Jones	USA	5.8.82	4	NCAA	Fayetteville	8 Mar
8.06	Kia	Davis	USA	23.5.76	4	NC	New York	2 Mar

8.07	Anay	Tejeda	CUB-J	3.4.83	20 Feb
8.09	Haydy	Aron	FRA	21.5.73	17 Feb
8.10	Yuliya	Shabanova	RUS	.82	20 Jan
8.11	Joyce	Bates	USA	16.2.77	27 Jan
8.12	Mariya	Koroteyeva	RUS	10.11.81	27 Jan
8.13	Juliane	Sprenger	GER	22.3.77	1 Feb
8.13	Nicole	Denby	USA	10.10.82	8 Mar
8.14	Tatyana	Pavliy	RUS	18.5.78	3 Feb
8.15	Jenny	Adams	USA	8.7.78	9 Feb
8.15	Fanny	Gérance	FRA	4.1.81	17 Feb

HIGH JUMP

2.03	Marina	Kuptsova	RUS	22.12.81	1	EI	Wien	2 Mar
2.02	Venelina	Veneva	BUL	13.6.74	1		Lódz	2 Feb
1.97	Yelena	Gulyayeva	RUS	14.8.67	1		Moskva	17 Jan
1.97	Kajsa	Bergqvist	SWE	12.10.76	2		Arnstadt	26 Jan
1.97	Dóra	Györffy	HUN	23.2.78	1	Spark	Stuttgart	3 Feb
1.97	Olga	Kaliturina	RUS	9.3.76	2		Stockholm	6 Feb
1.96	Viktoriya	Seryogina	RUS	22.5.73	1		Yekaterinburg	7 Jan
1.96	Yelena	Sivushenko	RUS	28.2.82	1	NC	Volgograd	13 Feb
1.95	Tisha	Waller	USA	1.12.70	1	Mill	New York	1 Feb
1.94	Yuliya	Lyakhova	RUS	8.7.77	2		Moskva	17 Jan
1.94	Irina	Mikhalchenko	UKR	20.1.72	4		Lódz	2 Feb
1.94	Barbora	Laláková	CZE	2.5.81	1		Siegen	9 Feb
1.94	Oana	Pantelimon	ROM	27.9.72	1	NC	Bucuresti	17 Feb
1.94	Tatiana	Yefimenko	KGZ	2.1.81	1		Moskva	23 Feb
1.94	Anna	Ksok	POL-J	29.9.83	Q	EI	Wien	1 Mar
1.93	Anna	Chicherova	RUS	22.7.82	2		Yekaterinburg	7 Jan
1.93	Elena	Herzenberg	GER	24.6.79	1		Ludwigshafen	13 Jan
1.93	Kathryn	Holinski	GER	19.7.82	1	NC	Sindelfingen	16 Feb
1.92	Amy	Acuff	USA	14.7.75	2	Mill	New York	1 Feb
1.92	Blanka	Vlasic	CRO	8.11.83	1		Eaubonne	13 Feb
1.92	Viktoriya	Slivka	RUS	28.9.80	2		Moskva	23 Feb
1.92	Susan	Jones	GBR	8.6.78	Q	EI	Wien	1 Mar

1.91	Viktoriya	Styopina	UKR	21.2.76	28Dec*
1.90	Mária	Melová	SVK	21.10.75	12 Jan
1.90	Ruth	Beitia	ESP	1.4.79	26 Jan
1.90	Alina	Astafei	GER	7.6.69	26 Jan
1.90	Nicole	Forrester	CAN	17.11.76	27 Jan
1.90	Candeger	Kilincer	TUR	16.7.80	4 Feb
1.90	Marianne	Mattas	FIN	20.8.79	9 Feb
1.90	Inge	Jankú	CZE	1.5.74	12 Feb
1.90	Ramona	Pop	ROM	5.4.82	17 Feb
1.90	Yoko	Ota	JPN	14.1.75	17 Feb
1.90	Marta	Mendía	ESP	18.5.75	23 Feb
1.90	Maresa	Cadienhead	CAN	7.4.76	8 Mar
1.89	Tatyana	Gordeyeva	RUS	3.6.73	27 Jan
1.89	Inna	Gliznutsa	MDA	18.4.73	1 Mar
1.88	Raffaella	Lamera	ITA-J	13.4.83	2 Feb
1.88	Tatyana	Babashkina	RUS	23.11.68	2 Feb

POLE VAULT

4.75	Svetlana	Feofanova	RUS	16.7.80	1	EI	Wien	3 Mar
4.66	Christine	Adams	GER	28.2.74	1		Sindelfingen	10 Mar
4.65	Yvonne	Buschbaum	GER	14.7.80	2	EI	Wien	3 Mar
4.62	Annika	Becker	GER	12.11.81	1		Chemnitz	22 Feb
4.61A	Mary	Sauer	USA	31.10.75	1		Flagstaff	17 Feb
4.60A	Melissa	Mueller	USA	16.11.72	1		Flagstaff	9 Feb
4.60	Monika	Pyrek	POL	11.8.80	3	EI	Wien	3 Mar
4.57A	Stacy	Dragila	USA	25.3.71	1		Pocatello	19 Jan
4.56	Pavla	Hamácková	CZE	20.5.78	3		Liévin	24 Feb
4.55	Yelena	Isinbayeva	RUS	3.6.82	2		Sindelfingen	10 Mar
4.53	Amy	Linnen	USA	15.7.82	1	NCAA	Fayetteville	8 Mar
4.50	Yelena	Belyakova	RUS	7.4.76	2		Pireás	20 Feb
4.45		Gao Shuying	CHN	28.10.79	3=		Sindelfingen	10 Mar
4.44	Monique	de Wilt	NED	21.3.76	2		Birmingham	17 Feb
4.44	Janine	Whitlock	GBR	11.8.73	4		Birmingham	17 Feb
4.38	Lesa	Kubishta	USA	19.4.78	1		Lubbock	26 Jan
4.37	Yeorgyía	Tsiliggíri	GRE	21.6.72	1	Balk	Pireás	23 Feb
4.36	Tracy	O'Hara	USA	2.7.80	1		Seattle	2 Feb
4.35A	Tamara	Diles	USA	5.11.82	1		Reno	11 Jan
4.35	Kirsten	Belin	SWE	2.5.81	Q	EI	Wien	1 Mar
4.35	Sabine	Schulte	GER	29.1.76	10		Sindelfingen	10 Mar
4.30	Martina	Strutz	GER	4.11.81	4		Dortmund	27 Jan
4.30	Francesca	Dolcini	ITA	28.12.74	2		Zweibrücken	1 Feb
4.30	Nastja	Ryshich	GER	19.9.77	3		Zweibrücken	1 Feb
4.30	Tanya	Koleva	BUL	8.3.72	1		Budapest	9 Feb
4.30	Krisztina	Molnár	HUN	8.4.76	2		Praha	14 Feb
4.30	Agnès	Livebardon	FRA	31.5.80	1	NC	Liévin	16 Feb
4.30	Katerina	Badurová	CZE	18.12.82	2	NC	Praha	16 Feb
4.30	Tünde	Vaszi	HUN	18.4.72	1	NC	Budapest	17 Feb
4.30A	Stephanie	McCann	CAN	22.4.77	3		Flagstaff	17 Feb

4.30	Vala	Flosadóttir	ISL	16.2.78	1		Malmö	24 Feb
4.30	Masumi	Ono	JPN	5.12.75	1		Tianjin	3 Mar

4.26	Andrea	Wildrick	USA	23.12.79	8 Feb
4.26	Jillian	Schwartz	USA	19.9.79	1 Mar
4.25	Elizabeth	Metzinger	USA	16.6.79	2 Feb
4.25	Dana	Cervantes	ESP	18.8.78	17 Feb
4.25	Ardin	Harrison-Tudker	CAN	14.3.74	23 Feb
4.23A	Stephanie	Maugham	USA	29.9.77	9 Feb
4.23	Doris	Auer	AUT	10.5.71	10 Feb
4.23	Marie	BaggerRasmussen	DEN	1.11.72	17 Feb
4.22	Anna	Rogowska	POL	21.5.81	14 Feb
4.21	Becky	Holliday	USA	12.3.80	2 Feb
4.21	Niki	Reed	USA	1.4.80	2 Feb
4.21	Floe	Kühnert	GER-J	6.3.84	10 Feb
4.20A	Bridgid	Isworth	AUS	15.10.81	12 Jan
4.20	Naroa	Agirre	ESP	15.5.79	3 Feb
4.20	Sárka	Mládková	CZE	30.8.76	3 Feb
4.20	Tatyana	Polnova	RUS	4.12.73	12 Feb
4.20	Nataliya	Kushch	UKR-J	5.3.83	16 Feb
4.20	Émilie	Bécot	FRA	20.10.80	23 Feb
4.20	Hanna-Mia	Persson	SWE	11.2.78	24 Feb

LONG JUMP

7.01	Tatyana	Kotova	RUS	11.12.76	1		Omsk	17 Jan
6.91	Elva	Goulbourne	JAM	21.1.80	1	SEC	Fayetteville	23 Feb
6.77	Lyudmila	Galkina	RUS	20.1.72	1		Moskva	26 Jan
6.74	Irina	Simagina	RUS	25.5.82	1		Samara	3 Feb
6.74	Níki	Xánthou	GRE	11.10.73	1	EI	Wien	3 Mar
6.74	Olga	Rublyova	RUS	28.10.74	2	EI	Wien	3 Mar
6.73	Concepción	Montaner	ESP	14.1.81	1		Valencia	26 Jan
6.69	Tatyana	Ter-Mesrobyan	RUS	12.5.68	1		Sankt-Peterburg	6 Jan
6.69	Irina	Melnikova	RUS	14.5.75	2		Samara	3 Feb
6.65	Anastasiya	Ilyina	RUS	16.1.82	4		Moskva	21 Jan
6.64	Cristina	Nicolau	ROM	9.8.77	1	NC	Bucuresti	17 Feb
6.62	Stilianí	Pilátou	GRE	28.3.80	2	NC	Pireás	16 Feb
6.60	Yuliya	Akulenko	UKR-J	3.6.77	1	NC	Brovary	16 Feb
6.59	Heike	Drechsler	GER	16.12.64	1	NC	Sindelfingen	16 Feb

6.53	Tereza	Marinova	BUL	5.9.77	9 Feb
6.53	Viorica	Tigau	ROM	12.8.79	17 Feb
6.52	Krysha	Bayley	CAN-J	21.1.84	23 Feb
6.50	Antonia	Yordanova	BUL	17.8.76	16 Feb
6.50	Sofia	Schulte	GER	8.4.76	22 Feb
6.50	Naide	Gomes	POR	10.11.79	1 Mar
6.49	Zita	Ajkler	HUN	9.6.75	16 Feb
6.48	Yelena	Shekhovtsova	UKR	31.5.72	1 Feb
6.48	Aleksandra	Stadnyuk	UKR	16.4.80	16 Feb
6.46	Adina	Anton	ROM-J	6.10.84	17 Feb

TRIPLE JUMP

14.81	Tereza	Marinova	BUL	5.9.77	1	EI	Wien	2 Mar
14.71	Ashia	Hansen	GBR	5.12.71	2	EI	Wien	2 Mar
14.70	Oksana	Rogova	RUS	7.10.78	1		Volgograd	6 Feb
14.65	Nadezhda	Bazhenova	RUS	22.9.78	1		Pireás	20 Feb
14.60	Yelena	Oleynikova	RUS	9.12.76	1		Moskva	7 Jan
14.56	Yelena	Lebedenko	RUS	16.1.71	2		Moskva	7 Jan
14.40		Huang Qiuyan	CHN	25.1.80	1	vJPN	Shanghai	10 Mar
14.38	Irina	Vasilyeva	RUS	9.4.79	2	NC	Volgograd	13 Feb
14.37	Cristina	Nicolau	ROM	9.8.77	1		Bucuresti	2 Feb
14.29	Adelina	Gavrila	ROM	26.11.78	2		Bucuresti	2 Feb
14.26	Marija	Martinovic	YUG	17.4.79	1	Balk	Pireás	23 Feb
14.23	Anastasiya	Ilyina	RUS	16.1.82	4		Liévin	24 Feb
14.13	Yevgeniya	Fadeyeva	RUS	21.7.66	3		Moskva	7 Jan
14.12	Aleksandra	Stadnyuk	UKR	16.4.80	1	NC	Brovary	17 Feb
14.00	Heli	Koivula	FIN	27.6.75	1		Mustasaari	9 Feb
13.94	Hrysopiyí	Devetzí	GRE	2.1.76	1	NC	Pireás	17 Feb

13.93	Anja	Valant	SLO	8.9.77	20 Feb
13.90	Vanitta	Kinard	USA	26.7.75	9 Feb
13.90	Mariana	Solomon	ROM	8.9.80	16 Feb
13.89	Carlota	Castrejana	ESP	25.4.73	16 Feb
13.88	Anna	Pyatykh	RUS	4.4.81	27 Jan
13.85	Viktoriya	Gurova	RUS	22.5.82	30 Jan
13.84	Shelly Ann	Gallimore	JAM	10.3.81	24 Feb
13.81	Dana	Veldáková	SVK	3.6.81	26 Jan
13.81	Natalia	Kilpeläinen	FIN	19.7.70	3 Feb
13.80	Yuliya	Cherkasova	RUS-J	.83	9 Feb

SHOT

20.34	Vita	Pavlysh	UKR	15.1.69	1		Brovary	20 Jan
19.29	Lyudmila	Sechko	RUS	27.11.74	1		Moskva	22 Jan
19.20	Assunta	Legnante	ITA	14.5.78	1	NC	Genova	16 Feb
19.15	Astrid	Kumbernuss	GER	5.2.70	1		Bad Segeberg	8 Feb
18.87	Yumileidi	Cumbá	CUB	11.2.75	1		Pireás	20 Feb
18.81	Nadezhda	Ostapchuk	BLR	12.10.80	2		Pireás	20 Feb
18.53	Lieja	Koeman	NED	10.3.76	3	EI	Wien	2 Mar
18.27	Irina	Khudorozhkina	RUS	13.10.68	2		Moskva	22 Jan
18.26		Li Meiju	CHN	23.1.81	1	vJPN	Tianjin	3 Mar
18.24	Elena	Hila	ROM	20.5.74	1	NC	Bucuresti	16 Feb
18.23	Valentina	Fedyushina	AUT	10.2.65	4	EI	Wien	2 Mar
18.02	Iolanta	Ulyeva	KAZ	27.7.76	2		Tianjin	3 Mar
18.00	Teri	Steer	USA	30.10.75	1	NC	New York	1 Mar
17.67	Katarzyna	Zakowicz	POL	12.5.75	3		Pireás	20 Feb

17.57	Nadine	Beckel	GER	27.5.77	8 Feb
17.55	Anna	Romanova	RUS	9.3.68	13 Feb
17.54	Lucica	Ciobanu	ROM	10.5.79	2 Feb
17.52	Irina	Korzhanenko	RUS	16.5.74	13 Feb
17.50	Cleopatra	Borel	TRI		9 Mar
17.46	Laurence	Manfrédi	FRA	20.5.74	16 Feb
17.46	Vivian	Chukwuemeka	NGR	4.5.75	2 Mar
17.43	Seilala	Sua	USA	25.2.78	1 Mar
17.41	Svetlana	Krivelyova	RUS	13.6.69	20 Feb
17.36	Cristiana	Checchi	ITA	8.7.77	2 Mar
17.26	Jamine	Moton	USA	14.12.78	2 Feb
17.16	Yuliya	Zaginay	RUS	3.8.63	22Dec*
17.16		Zhang Xiaoyu	CHN	16.3.83	2 Mar
17.14	Kathleen	Kluge	GER	17.11.81	13 Jan
17.12	Kristin	Heaston	USA	23.11.75	1 Mar
17.10	Martina	de la Puente	ESP	4.4.75	23 Feb

20 LBS WEIGHT

23.56	Anna	Norgren	USA	19.12.74	1	Mill	New York	1 Feb
23.14	Dawn	Ellerbe	USA	3.4.74	2	Mill	New York	1 Feb
23.05	Candace	Scott	TRI	17.9.80	1	NCAA	Fayetteville	8 Mar
22.50	Jamine	Moton	USA	14.12.78	2	NCAA	Fayetteville	8 Mar
21.86	Jukina	Dickerson	USA	7.8.81	1		Gainesville	10 Feb
21.67	Toyinda	Wilson	USA	13.4.76	3	NC	New York	1 Mar
21.11	Katy	Craig	USA	18.11.80	1	Big10	University Park	24 Feb
21.03	Tara	Loper	USA	12.8.77	3		Bloomington	16 Feb

20.99	Amber	Campbell	USA	5.6.81	1 Mar
20.64	Maureen	Griffin	USA	6.10.80	8 Mar
20.53	Jackie	Jeschelnig	USA	.78	8 Mar
20.35	Ruth	Kura	KEN	7.6.80	8 Feb

PENTATHLON

4622	Yelena	Prokhorova	RUS	16.4.78	1	EI	Wien	1 Mar
	(8.56, 1.78, 13.66, 6.42, 2:13.59)							
4595	Naide	Gomes	POR	10.11.79	2	EI	Wien	1 Mar
	(8.59, 1.81, 14.04, 6.50, 2:21.53)							
4535	Carolina	Klüft	SWE-J	2.2.83	3	EI	Wien	1 Mar
	(8.49, 1.81, 12.71, 6.24, 2:14.95)							
4525	Tatyana	Gordeyeva	RUS	3.6.73	1		Halle	27 Jan
	(8.80, 1.89, 13.24, 6.03, 2:16.02)							
4503	Anzhela	Atroshchenko	TUR	14.10.70	4	EI	Wien	1 Mar
	(8.52, 1.75, 13.28, 6.14, 2:12.04)							
4460	Sonja	Kesselschläger	GER	20.1.78	3		Halle	27 Jan
	(8.47, 1.80, 13.02, 6.15, 2:19.28)							
4439	Austra	Skujyte	LTU	12.8.79	1		Lincoln	22 Feb
	(8.91, 1.76, 15.82, 5.97, 2:19.79)							
4382	Magdalena	Szczepanska	POL	25.1.80	6	EI	Wien	1 Mar
	(8.65, 1.78, 13.23, 5.97, 2:17.21)							
4371	Svetlana	Sokolova	RUS	9.1.81	1	NC	Moskva	4 Feb
	(8.62, 1.73, 14.40, 5.21, 2:18.88)							
4368	Marina	Bryukhach	UKR	16.1.77	1	NC	Brovary	14 Feb
	(8.35, 1.79, 12.70, 6.12, 2:24.92)							
4352	María	Peinado	ESP	8.2.77	2	NC	Sevilla	17 Feb
	(8.39, 1.69, 12.13, 6.19, 2:15.12)							
4319	Larisa	Netseporuk	EST	24.12.70	8	EI	Wien	1 Mar
	(8.72, 1.75, 13.72, 6.17, 2:24.97)							
4309	Jana	Klecková	CZE	19.3.75	1	NC	Praha	10 Feb
	(8.60, 1.80, 11.68, 5.92, 2:16.52)							
4298	Karin	Ruckstuhl	NED	2.11.80	1	v4N	Zaragoza	27 Jan
	(8.64, 1.81, 12.32, 6.07, 2:24.26)							
4252	Tiia	Hautala	FIN	3.4.72	2		Tallinn	3 Feb
	(8.59, 1.78, 12.01, 6.00, 2:22.51)							
4236	Yuliya	Akulenko	UKR	3.6.77	9	EI	Wien	1 Mar
	(8.71, 1.72, 13.12, 6.28, 2:28.31)							

4213		Shen Shengfei	CHN	21.1.81	10 Mar
4212	Michaela	Hejnová	CZE	10.4.80	27 Jan
4207	Yvonne	Wisse	NED	6.6.82	3 Feb
4194	Annika	Meyer	GER	9.6.80	27 Jan
4193	Tia	Hellebaut	BEL	16.2.78	3 Feb
4190	Claudia	Tonn	GER	18.4.81	3 Feb
4188	Kelly	Sotherton	GBR	13.11.76	27 Jan
4177	Francine	Passe-Coutrin	FRA	4.6.81	10 Feb

3000 METRES WALK

12:17.56	Gillian	O'Sullivan	IRL	21.8.76	1	NC	Cardiff	2 Feb
12:28.13	Annarita	Sidoti	ITA	25.7.69	1	NC	Genova	16 Feb
12:34.53	Norica	Cîmpean	ROM	22.3.72	1	NC	Bucuresti	16 Feb
12:35.16	Veronica	Budileanu	ROM	27.2.76	2	NC	Bucuresti	16 Feb
12:37.82	Erica	Alfridi	ITA	22.2.68	2	NC	Genova	16 Feb
12:39.99	Elisabetta	Perrone	ITA	9.7.68	3	NC	Genova	16 Feb
12:40.44	Fatiha	Ouali	FRA	28.10.74	1	NC	Liévin	16 Feb

EUROPEAN INDOOR CHAMPIONSHIPS 2002

At Vienna, Austria 1-3 March

MEN

60 METRES (3)
1. Jason Gardener GBR 6.49*=
2. Mark Lewis-Francis GBR 6.55
3. Anatoliy Dovgal UKR 6.62
4. Bongelomba Bongelo BEL 6.67
5. Francesco Scuderi ITA 6.69
6. Patrik Lövgren SWE 6.70

200 METRES (2)
1. Marcin Urbas POL 20.64
2. Christian Malcolm GBR 20.65
3. Robert Mackowiak POL 20.77
4. Daniel Caines GBR 21.14
5. Radek Zachoval CZE 21.15
6. Marcin Jedrusinski POL 21.78

400 METRES (3)
1. Marek Plawgo POL 45.39*
2. Jimisola Laursen SWE 45.59
3. Ioan Vieru ROM 46.17
4. Piotr Rysiukiewicz POL 46.32
5. Jiri Muzik CZE 46.36
6. Marc Foucan FRA 47.40

800 METRES (3)
1. Pawel Czapiewski POL 1:44.78*
2. Andre Bucher SUI 1:44.93
3. Antonio Reina ESP 1:45.25
4. Dmitriy Bogdanov RUS 1:45.84
5. Sergey Kozhevnikov RUS 1:46.13
6. David Fiegen LUX-J 1:47.44

1500 METRES (2)
1. Rui Silva POR 3:49.93
2. Juan C Higuero ESP 3:50.08
3. Michael East GBR 3:50.52
4. Branko Zorko CRO 3:50.66
5. Michal Sneberger CZE 3:50.70
6. James Nolan IRL 3:50.84

3000 METRES (2)
1. Alberto García ESP 7:43.89*
2. Antonio Jiménez ESP 7:46.49
3. Jesus España ESP 7:48.08
3. John Mayock GBR 7:48.08
5. Michael Buchleitner AUT 7:54.39
6. Mohammed Mourhit BEL 7:59.79

60 METRES HURDLES (2)
1. Colin Jackson GBR 7.40
2. Elmar Lichtenegger AUT 7.44
3. Yevgeniy Pechonkin RUS 7.50
4. Stanislav Olijar LAT 7.51
5. Florian Schwarthoff GER 7.59
6. Robert Kronberg SWE 7.67

HIGH JUMP (3)
1. Staffan Strand SWE 2.34
2. Stefan Holm SWE 2.30
3. Yaroslav Rybakov RUS 2.30
4. Andrey Sokolovskiy UKR 2.27
5. Joan Charmant FRA 2.24
6. Tomás Janku CZE 2.24

POLE VAULT (2)
1. Tim Lobinger GER 5.75
2. Patrik Kristiansson SWE 5.75
3. Lars Börgeling GER 5.75
4. Adam Kolasa POL 5.70
5. Thibaut Duval BEL 5.70
6. Pavel Gerasimov RUS 5.60

LONG JUMP (2)
1. Raúl Fernández ESP 8.22
2. Yago Lamela ESP 8.17
3. Petar Dachev BUL 8.17
4. Aleksey Lukashevich UKR 8.11
5. Kirill Sosunov RUS 8.02
6. Vladimir Zyuskov UKR 7.97

TRIPLE JUMP (3)
1. Christian Olsson SWE 17.54*=
2. Marian Oprea ROM 17.22
3. Aleksandr Glavatskiy BLR 17.05
4. Fabrizio Donato ITA 16.90
5. Rostislav Dimitrov BUL 16.79
6. Aleksandr Sergeyev RUS 16.56

SHOT (2)
1. Manuel Martínez ESP 21.26
2. Joachim Olsen DEN 21.23
3. Mikulás Konopka SVK 20.87
4. Pavel Chumachenko RUS 20.30
5. Ville Tiisanoja FIN 20.19
6. Petr Stehlik CZE 19.86

HEPTATHLON (1/2)
1. Roman Sebrle CZE 6280
2. Tomás Dvorák CZE 6165
3. Erki Nool EST 6084
4. Jon Arnár Magnusson ISL 5996
5. Attila Zsivoczky HUN 5957
6. Zsolt Kürtösi HUN 5950

4 x 400 METRES (3)
1. POL (Plawgo, Rysiukiewicz, Gasiewski, Mackowiak) 3:05.50*
2. FRA (Foucan, Claudel, Lerouge, Diagana) 3:06.42
3. ESP (Meléndez, Canal, S Rodríguez, A Martínez) 3:06.60

WOMEN

60 METRES (3)
1. Kim Gevaert BEL 7.16
2. Marina Kislova RUS 7.18
3. Georgia Kokloni GRE 7.22
4. Karin Mayr AUT 7.22
5. Marion Wagner GER 7.23
6. Larisa Kruglova RUS 7.25

200 METRES (2)
1. Muriel Hurtis FRA 22.52
2. Karin Mayr AUT 22.70
3. Gabi Rockmeier GER 23.05
4. Nora Ivanova-Güner TUR 23.08
5. Sylviane Félix FRA 23.87
6. E Tosheva (Mashova) BUL 23.99

400 METRES (3)
1. Natalya Antyukh RUS 51.65
2. Claudia Marx GER 52.15
3. Karen Shinkins IRL 52.17
4. Natalya Ivanova RUS 52.23
5. Yuliya Pechonkina RUS 52.91
6. Catherine Murphy GBR 52.98

800 METRES (3)
1. Jolanda Ceplak SLO 1:55.82* WR
2. Stephanie Graf AUT 1:55.85
3. Elisabeth Grousselle FRA 2:01.46
4. Mayte Martínez ESP 2:01.50
5. Svetlana Cherkasova RUS 2:02.80
6. Sandra Stals BEL 2:07.33

1500 METRES (3)
1. Yekaterina Puzanova RUS 4:06.30
2. Elena Iagar ROM 4:06.90
3. Alesya Turova BLR 4:07.69
4. Yuliya Kosenkova RUS 4:08.63
5. Daniela Yordanova BUL 4:10.47
6. Olga Komyagina RUS 4:11.97

3000 METRES (3)
1. Marta Domínguez ESP 8:53.87
2. Carla Sacramento POR 8:53.96
3. Yelena Zadorozhnaya RUS 8:58.36
4. Susanne Pumper AUT 8:59.93
5. Liliya Volkova RUS 9:02.48
6. Cristina Grosu ROM 9:02.99

60 METRES HURDLES (2)
1. Glory Alozie ESP 7.84
2. Linda Ferga FRA 7.96
3. Kirsten Bolm GER 7.97
4. Patricia Girard FRA 7.98
5. Nicole Ramalalanirina FRA 8.01
6. Flora Redoúmi GRE 8.02

HIGH JUMP (2)
1. Marina Kuptsova RUS 2.03
2= Kajsa Bergqvist SWE 1.95
2= Dóra Györffy HUN 1.95
4. Kathryn Holinski GER 1.93
5= Susan Jones GBR 1.90
5= Anna Ksok POL 1.90
5= Yelena Sivushenko RUS 1.90

POLE VAULT (3)
1. Svetlana Feofanova RUS 4.75* WR
2. Yvonne Buschbaum GER 4.65
3. Monika Pyrek POL 4.60
4. Annika Becker GER 4.55
5. Christine Adams GER 4.50
6. Pavla Hamácková CZE 4.35

LONG JUMP (3)
1. Niki Xánthou GRE 6.74
2. Olga Rublyova RUS 6.74
3. Lyudmila Galkina RUS 6.68
4. Irina Simagina RUS 6.64
5. Styliani Pilátou GRE 6.57
6. Zita Ajkler HUN 6.48

TRIPLE JUMP (2)
1. Tereza Marinova BUL 14.81
2. Ashia Hansen GBR 14.71
3. Yelena Oleynikova RUS 14.30
4. Nadezhda Bazhenova RUS 14.20
5. Cristina Nicolau ROM 14.11
6. Marija Martinovic YUG 14.00

SHOT (2)
1. Vita Pavlysh UKR 19.76
2. Assunta Legnante ITA 18.60
3. Lieja Koeman NED 18.53
4. Valentina Fedyuschina AUT 18.23
5. Lyudmila Sechko RUS 18.14
6. Elena Hila ROM 17.52

PENTATHLON (1)
1. Yelena Prokhorova RUS 4622
2. Naide Gomes POR 4595
3. Carolina Klüft SWE 4535
4. Anzhela Atroshchenko TUR 4503
5. Sonja Kesselschlager GER 4402
6. Magd. Szczepanska POL 4382

4 x 400 METRES (3)
1. BLR (Stankevich, Khlustava, Kazak, Usovich) 3:32.24*
2. POL (Pacholak, Lemiesz, Zagorska, Prokopek) 3:32.45
3. ITA (Reina, Spuri, Barbarino, Perpoli) 3:36.49

WORLD CROSS-COUNTRY CHAMPIONSHIPS 2002

At Leopradstown Racecourse, Dublin, Ireland 23-24 March

Kenenisa Bekele, who had been second in the short race and the winner of the junior race in 2001, became the first man to win both short and long course titles, and he did so in superb style. Kenya still packed brilliantly to win all three men's titles, including their 17th successive success in the men's 12km, and the junior women's team title. In the last, Viola Kibiwott became the first athlete to successfully defend her women's junior title, and her compatriot Vivain Cheruiyot competed for the fifth time (5th, 2nd, 1st, 4th and 3rd 1998-2002). Ethiopia took both women's team titles and provided the winner of the junior men's race, in which Africans filled the top 19 places. Ethiopia and Kenya took the first two team places in all races, except for the USA taking 2nd in the women's 12km, witth Deena Drossin and the former South African Colleen de Reuck (aged 37) 2nd and 3rd behind Paula Radcliffe, who retained her title. Edith Masai won the 4km race and Sonia O'Sullivan was seventh, just 13 weeks after giving birth to her secind child.

Men's 4.27km (23)
1. Kenenisa Bekele ETH 34:52
2. John Yuda TAN 34:58
3. Wilberforce Talel KEN 35:20
4. Richard Limo KEN 35:26
5. Charles Kamathi KEN 35:29
6. Albert Chepkurui KEN 35:32
7. Abderrahim Goumri MAR 35:43
8. Yonas Kifle ERI 35:47
9. Enock Mitei KEN 35:49
10. Jaouad Gharib MAR 35:57
11. Abdi Abdirahman USA 36:03
12. Assefa Mezegebu ETH 36:06
13. Ismaïl Sghyr FRA 36:07
14. Mebrahtom Keflezighi USA 36:09
15. Mustapha Essaïd FRA 36:10
16. Habte Jifar ETH 36:11
17. Fita Bayissa ETH 36:14
18. Samson Ramadhani TAN 36:16
19. Eduardo Henriques POR 36:20
20. Lemma Alemayehu ETH 36:25

123 finished.

Team	17 completed		
1. KEN	20	6. FRA	117
2. ETH	32	7. GBR	120
3. ESP	57	8. AUS	120
4. MAR	78	9. ITA	123
5. USA	113	10. ALG	129

Men's 12.07km (24)
1. Kenenisa Bekele ETH 12:11
2. Luke Kipkosgei KEN 12:18
3. Hailu Mekonnen ETH 12:20
4. Sammy Kipketer KEN 12:26
5. Craig Mottram AUS 12:27
6. Julius Nyamu KEN 12:30
7. Antonio Jiménez ESP 12:30
8. Joseph Kosgei KEN 12:32
9. Khalid El Amri MAR 12:33
10. Driss Maazouzi FRA 12:34
11. Jorge Torres USA 12:35
12. Mohamed El Wardi MAR 12:35
13. Mohammed Awdl ETH 12:38
14. Isaac Viciosa ESP 12:39
15. Abiyote Abate ETH 12:39
16. Million Wolde ETH 12:40
17. Alberto García ESP 12:41
18. Matthew Lane USA 12:42
19. Luciano Di Pardo ITA 12:42
20. Alejandro Suárez MEX 12:43

132 finished.

Team	20 completed		
1. KEN	18	6. ESP	121
2. ETH	43	7. ERI	141
3. MAR	58	8. TAN	146
4. FRA	71	9. POR	166
5. USA	107	10. GBR	173

Junior men 7.87km (24)
1. Gebre Gebremariam ETH 23:18
2. Abel Cheruiyot KEN 23:19
3. Boniface Kiprop KEN 23:28
4. Thomas Kiplitan KEN 23:33
5. Eliud Kipchoge KEN 23:39
6. Sileshi Sihine ETH 23:42
7. Nicholas Kemboi KEN 23:48
8. Girma Assefa ETH 23:49
9. Abebe Dinkessa ETH 23:50
10. Moses Mosop KEN 23:58
11. Martin Toroitich UGA 24:05
12. Michael Kipyego KEN 24:10

119 finished.

Team	18 completed		
1. KEN	18	6. ZAM	94
2. ETH	24	7. USA	113
3. UGA	37	8. ALG	131
4. JPN	77	9. SUD	143
5. MAR	89	10. RSA	146

Women's 4.27km (24)
1. Edith Masai KEN 13:30
2. Werknesh Kidane ETH 13:36
3. Isabella Ochichi KEN 13:39
4. Benita Johnson AUS 13:42
5. Suzy Favor Hamilton USA 13:47
6. Abebech Negussie ETH 13:53
7. Sonia O'Sullivan IRL 13:55
8. Amina Godana ETH 14:00
9. Rosanna Martin ITA 14:01
10. Anne Keenan-Buckley IRL 14:03
11. Carrie Tollefson USA 14:05
12. Bouchra Chaabi MAR 14:06
13. Nancy Wambui KEN 14:06
14. Olga Romanova RUS 14:06
15. Anna Thompson AUS 14:07
16. Genet Gebregiorgis ETH 14:08
17. Jane Kiptoo KEN 14:11
18. Prisca Jepleting KEN 14:13
19. Rosemary Ryan IRL 14:14
20. Helena Sampaio POR 14:15

107 finished.

Teams	17 completed		
1. ETH	32	6. USA	90
2. KEN	34	7. POR	108
3. IRL	85	8. MAR	133
4. RUS	86	9. ROM	158
5. AUS	86	10. TAN	158

Women's 7.87km (23)
1. Paula Radcliffe GBR 26:55
2. Deena Drossin USA 27:04
3. Colleen de Reuck USA 27:17
4. Miwako Yamanaka JPN 27:19
5. Eyerusalem Kuma ETH 27:19
6. Merima Denboba ETH 27:21
7. Leila Aman ETH 27:25
8. Rose Cheruiyot KEN 27:28
9. Pamela Chepchumba KEN 27:30
10. Teyeba Erkesso ETH 27:32
11. Leah Malot KEN 27:35
12. Jennifer Rhines USA 27:43
13. Ayelech Worku ETH 27:50
14. Jane Omoro KEN 27:52
15. Kayoko Fukushi JPN 27:53
16. Jepkorir Ayabei KEN 27:58
17. Rosanna Martin ITA 27:59
18. Liz Yelling GBR 28:07
19. Helena Sampaio POR 28:08
20. Kathy Butler GBR 28:12

81 finished.

Team	13 completed		
1. ETH	28	6. POR	84
2. USA	38	7. ESP	104
3. KEN	41	8. FRA	121
4. JPN	67	9. ITA	125
5. GBR	69	10. BEL	159

Junior women's 6.07 km (23)
1. Viola Kibiwot KEN 20:13
2. Tirunesh Dibaba ETH 20:14
3. Vivian Cheruiyot KEN 20:22
4. Fridah Domongole KEN 20:23
5. Peninah Chepchumba KEN 20:24
6. Bezunesh Bekele ETH 20:34
7. Mestewat Tufa ETH 20:40
8. Melissa Rollison AUS 20:50
10. Sharon Cherop KEN 20:53
11. Yenealem Ayano ETH 20:59
12. Valentine Koech KEN 21:03

108 finished.

Team	18 completed		
1. KEN	13	6. RUS	106
2. ETH	24	7. FRA	128
3. JPN	63	8. GBR	130
4. AUS	77	9. RSA	139
5. USA	87	10. ERI	144

Kenya first took part in the World Cross-Country Championships when they entered a senior men's team in 1981. Their complete record is:
Men: 1st 1986-2002, 2nd 1985, 3rd 1981, 1983; 4th 1982, 1984
Men short race: 1st 1998-2002
Junior men: 1st 1988-97, 1999-02; 2nd 1985-7, 1998
Women: 1st 1991-3, 1995-6, 98, 2001; 2nd 1997, 99-00; 3rd 1994-5, 2002; 5th 1987, 66th 1988, 12th 1990
Women short race: 2nd 2001-02, 4th 1997-9; Junior women: 1st 1989-91, 1993-7, 2000, 2002; 2nd 1998-9, 2001; 3rd 1992